# The Norton Anthology
# of World Masterpieces

## *FOURTH EDITION*

---

## VOLUME 1

---

# The Norton Anthology of World Masterpieces

## FOURTH EDITION

Maynard Mack, *General Editor*
*Yale University*

Bernard M. W. Knox
*Center for Hellenic Studies*

John C. McGalliard
*The University of Iowa*

P. M. Pasinetti
*University of California, Los Angeles*

Howard E. Hugo
*Late of the University of California, Berkeley*

René Wellek
*Yale University*

Kenneth Douglas
*Late of Yale University*

Sarah Lawall
*University of Massachusetts, Amherst*

WITHDRAWN

### VOLUME 1
Literature of Western Culture through the Renaissance

W·W·NORTON & COMPANY· NEW YORK · LONDON

W. W. Norton & Company, Inc. 500 Fifth Avenue, New York, N.Y. 10110

BOOK DESIGN BY JOHN WOODLOCK

Since this page cannot legibly accommodate all the copyright notices, the following page constitutes an extension of the copyright page.

Library of Congress Cataloging in Publication Data
Main entry under title:
The Norton anthology of world masterpieces.
Fourth ed. edited by M. Mack published in 1973 under
title: World masterpieces.
    Includes indexes.
    CONTENTS: v.   1. Literature of Western culture through
the Renaissance.—v.   2. Literature of Western culture
since the Renaissance.
    1. Literature—Collections.   I. Mack, Maynard,
1909–   II. Mack, Maynard, 1909–   ed.
World masterpieces.
PN6014.M1382   1979   808.8   78-26744

                  5 6 7 8 9 0

ISBN 0-393-95036-0 CLOTH
ISBN 0-393-95045-X PBK.

# Contents

viii · *Contents*

## Masterpieces of the Middle Ages

# Masterpieces of the Renaissance

# Preface to the Fourth Edition

This fourth edition is, we think, the best to date. Notable additions to the selections from the ancient world, the middle ages, the romantic poets, and the moderns combine with the introduction of important new authors and several brilliant new translations to make the volumes now before you an immensely flexible, practical, and attractive instrument for teaching the literature of the western world. (For those who wish to extend their courses to include Eastern literatures, we recommend a companion anthology, *Masterpieces of the Orient*, edited by G. L. Anderson, available from the publisher in 397- and 846-page versions.)

Our representation of the twentieth century has been particularly enriched. In this edition there appear for the first time no fewer than eight major modern writers: Wallace Stevens (eleven poems); Virginia Woolf (a short story); Anna Akhmatova (a lyric sequence); Katherine Anne Porter (a short novel); Bertolt Brecht (a full-length play); Jorge Luis Borges and Vladimir Nabokov (a short story by each); and Richard Wright (the chilling first story from *Uncle Tom's Children*, "Big Boy Leaves Home"). And though the canon of authentic masters is better established for earlier periods, and our additions to these periods have therefore mostly been enlargements of existing selections rather than additions of previously unrepresented writers, there have also been a few of the latter: the anonymous authors of the Anglo-Saxon *Dream of the Rood* and the Middle English *Sir Gawain and the Green Knight*, the latter in the incomparable translation by Marie Borroff, and Emily Dickinson (fifteen poems).

We have also made a handful of substitutions. The replacement of Euripides' *The Trojan Women* by his *Hippolytus* permits interesting crossweavings when Racine's *Phaedra* is reached. Ibsen's *Hedda Gabler*, replacing his *The Wild Duck*, invites some fascinating comparisons not only with Euripides' and Racine's Phaedra but (for those with an eye to representative cultural symbols) with

Emma Bovary, Mother Courage, and the heroine of Katherine Anne Porter's *Pale Horse, Pale Rider*. The long opening chapter of Proust's *Remembrance of Things Past*, which we have substituted for his account of the soirée at the Marquise de Saint-Euverte's, affords a more concise entry into the author's themes and methods while supplying at the same time a psychological wellhead in the evolution of the modern American novel, to be placed beside its other sources in the self-enclosed linguistic game-worlds of Borges and the often almost unmediated transcriptions of raw experience in Wright. The two other substitutions have a similar intent. Mann's *Tonio Kröger* replaces his *Felix Krull* because it comments so poignantly on the deep cleavage between life and art, action and contemplation, which characterizes modern culture generally; and Faulkner's *Old Man* replaces his "Delta Autumn" because it is painted on so much broader a canvas of American life and experience. For the teacher who thrives on experiment and exploration, as most of us do, these exchanges are transparent gains.

To the selections from authors already represented, we have been able to add in this edition substantial new portions of the *Odyssey* and the *Aeneid*, two complete books of Wordsworth's *The Prelude* in the preferred 1805 text, further poems by Shelley (all the Shelley poems in *World Masterpieces* are now given in the definitive text lately edited from the manuscripts by Donald Reiman), Keats, Tennyson (not only additional poems but a selection from *In Memoriam* preserving the shape and progression of the whole), and Whitman.

To make this expansion possible we have been obliged to forgo a scattering of works for which our teacher-users assure us they lack time and inclination. Partly in the same interest, we have returned to first principles, and have excluded from this edition most lyric poetry in translation. We have always held (see the Note on Translation which concludes this volume) that lyric poetry loses too much in translation to warrant extensive treatment in either a survey anthology or a survey course; and the reports from our experiment with a large infusion of such poetry in the third edition confirm us in our original conviction. (By way of compensation, we have increased the quantity and variety of lyric poetry in English.)

Finally, our translations. We have always been vigilant about these, as our long-time users know, and have tried with each successive edition to make improvements. We believe we have succeeded in doing so again. A long consideration of the two great modern verse translations of the *Iliad* has persuaded us to give our vote in this edition to Robert Fitzgerald, whose unmatched *Odyssey* we have already used for several years. With less reluctance but some regret, we have also let go Dryden's elegant rendering of

Lucretius in favor of Rolfe Humphries' version, unquestionably more comfortable for a twentieth-century eye and ear. Allen Mandelbaum's fine *Aeneid*, winner of the National Book Award, has replaced C. Day Lewis's on somewhat similar grounds, and Joseph Sheed's *Confessions* of St. Augustine brings a vernacular lucidity where Elizabethan syntax reigned before. To all our translators new and old, not forgetting Rex Warner for our new *Hippolytus*, Robin Kemball for our version of Akhmatova's *Requiem*, and Ralph Manheim for our *Mother Courage and Her Children*, we offer hearty thanks, and to their publishers as well.

In conclusion, we welcome a new colleague, Professor Sarah Lawall of the Comparative Literature department of the University of Massachusetts, Amherst, to our collegium of editors. The revisions in the current Introduction to the Modern World, and the texts, notes, introductions, and bibliographies for the authors and works newly added are all hers, and we look forward to her further collaboration in editions yet to come. We must, unhappily, at this same time record the grievous losses of Kenneth Douglas by accidental death, and Howard E. Hugo, taken from us prematurely by illness. Kenneth and Howard were among the original seven editors of this anthology, and by their judicious choices they probably brought more recalcitrant students to an appreciation of neoclassic, romantic, and modern world writing than any other anthologists in history. We applaud their work and honor their memory. *Si monumentum requiris, circumspice.*

**The Editors**

# Preface

*World Masterpieces* is an anthology of Western literature, based on principles which we believe to be sound, but which have not always been sufficiently observed, we feel, in the existing anthologies in this field.

We have sought to make the range of readings in this collection unusually wide and varied. Its contents reach in time from Genesis and the *Iliad* to Nabokov and Camus, and the literatures represented include English, Irish, American, Russian, German, Scandinavian, French, Italian, Spanish, Argentine, Latin, Hebrew, and Greek. The literatures of the Far East have been omitted, on the ground that the principal aim of a course in world literature is to bring American students into living contact with their own Western tradition, and that this aim cannot be adequately realized in a single course if they must also be introduced to a very different tradition, one requiring extended treatment to be correctly understood. (We refer those who wish to incorporate Eastern literatures into their courses to a companion anthology, *Masterpieces of the Orient*, edited by G. L. Anderson.) Twentieth-century literature has been represented with particular fullness, because we feel that it is important for students to grasp the continuity of literature.

*World Masterpieces* is predominantly an anthology of imaginative literature. We have not tried to cover the entire history of the West in print, and have avoided filling our pages with philosophy, political theory, theology, historiography, and the like. This principle was adopted not because we disapprove of coming at the history of an epoch by way of literature, but because imaginative literature, in our view, itself best defines the character of its epoch: great monuments of art, we would be inclined to say, furnish the *best* documents for history. They lead us deeper into the meaning of a past age than other modes of writing do, because they convey its unformulated aspirations and intuitions as well as its conscious theorems and ideals; and yet, being timeless, they have also an unmatched appeal to our own age. For this reason, we have admitted into *World Masterpieces* only works which have something important to say to modern readers, and we have made it a point to interpret them with reference not only to their time but to ours. Teacher and student will find here a number of selections which they have not encountered before in a text of this kind.

We are convinced that effective understanding of any author depends upon studying an autonomous and substantial piece of his work: a whole drama, a whole story, at least a whole canto or book of a long poem. Our anthology therefore contains no snippets. Where it has been necessary to represent a long work by extracts, they are large extracts, forming a coherent whole. These considerations have also affected our treatment of lyric poems. Experience leads us to the conclusion that lyric poetry cannot be taught with full success in translation, and that very short poems, in whatever language, are nearly useless in a survey of these dimensions. We have accordingly excluded almost all *short* lyrics, and, with rare exceptions, all lyric poetry in foreign languages. We have preferred to represent the romantic movement, in which the lyric becomes a dominant form, with selections in English from the major English and American poets. This is not a flawless solution to the problem, but it seems to us better than printing many pages of inferior translations.

Since nothing has so deterred students from enjoying the great masterpieces of the classical and modern foreign languages as translations in an English idiom that is no longer alive, we have done our best to use translations which show a feeling for the English language as it is written and spoken today. Thus we offer here, with some pride, Robert Fitzgerald's *Iliad* and *Odyssey*; Louis Mac-Neice's *Agamemnon* and his *Faust*; Rex Warner's *Medea* and *Hippolytus*; Allen Mandelbaum's *Aeneid*; Mark Musa's *Inferno* (with selections from *Purgatorio* and *Paradiso* in Lawrence Binyon's translation); Samuel Putnam's *Don Quixote*; and many other renderings of equal quality.

Our introductions—in consonance with the scheme of the book —emphasize criticism rather than history. While providing all that seems to us necessary in the way of historical background (and supplying biographical summaries in the appendix following each introduction), we aim to give the student primarily a critical and analytical discussion of the works themselves. We try to suggest what these works have to say to us today, and why they should be valued now. In every instance, we seek to go beneath the usual generalizations about periods and philosophies, and to focus on men and books.

Our annotations of the texts are, we believe, exceptionally full and helpful. In a number of cases, these texts are annotated in this anthology for the first time. In one instance, we have been able to supply for a work the best-known notes on it in English, those of C. H. Grandgent to the *Divine Comedy*. Every care has been taken to furnish accurate and generous bibliographies as a guide to further reading.

In sum, we have sought to compile a new anthology, a text new in every sense—new in its emphasis on imaginative literature, on major authors, on wholes and large excerpts, on modern translations, on critical rather than historical treatment of texts, and, pervasively, on the tastes and values of our own time.

The Editors

# The Norton Anthology
# of World Masterpieces

## FOURTH EDITION

---

### VOLUME 1

---

# Masterpieces of the
# Ancient World

### EDITED BY

## BERNARD M. W. KNOX

*Director of the Center for Hellenic Studies*

This section represents, not the ancient world as a whole, but the most significant area and period of ancient man's development. The area is the Mediterranean basin, and the period the twelve hundred years from, roughly, 800 B.C. to A.D. 400. In this place and time ancient man laid the intellectual and religious foundations of the modern Western outlook.

The literature of the ancient world, which, whether or not we are acquainted with it, is still the background of our institutions, attitudes, and thought, was written in three languages —Hebrew, Greek, and Latin. The peoples who spoke these languages created their civilizations independently in place and time, but the development of the Mediterranean area into one economic and political unit brought these civilizations into contact with each other and

produced a fusion of their typical attitudes which is the basis of all subsequent Western thought. This process of independent development, interaction, and final fusion is represented in the arrangement of this section: In the last part of it the three separate lines converge, and they finally meet in the figure of St. Augustine, who had the intellectual honesty and curiosity of the Greek at his best, the social seriousness and sense of order of the Roman, and the Hebrew's feeling of man's inadequacy and God's omnipotent justice.

## PALESTINE

The territory of the Hebrews was of no particular strategic importance, and their record is not that of an imperial people. In their period of independence, from their beginnings as a pastoral tribe to their high point as

1

a kingdom with a splendid capital in Jerusalem, they accomplished little of note in the political or military spheres; their later history was a bitter and unsuccessful struggle for freedom against a series of foreign masters—Babylonian, Greek, and Roman. They left no painting or sculpture behind them, no drama, no epic poetry. What they did leave is a religious literature, probably written down between the eighth and second centuries B.C., which is informed by an attitude different from that of all the peoples surrounding them, a conception of divine power and of the government of the universe so simple that to us, who have inherited it from them, it seems obvious, yet in its time so revolutionary that it made them a nation apart, sometimes laughed at, sometimes feared, but always alien.

THE CREATION—THE FALL

The typical attitudes of the Hebrews appear in the story which they told of the creation of the world and of man. This creation is the work of one God, who is omnipotent and omniscient, and who creates a perfect and harmonious order. The disorder which we see all around us, physical and moral, is not God's creation but Adam's; it is the consequence of man's disobedience. The story not only reconciles the undeniable existence of evil and disorder in the world with the conception of God's infinite justice, it also attributes to man himself an independence of God, free will, which in this case he has used for evil. The Hebrew God is not limited in His power by other deities, who oppose His will (as in the Greek stories of Zeus and his undisciplined family); His power over inanimate nature is infinite; in all the range of His creation there is only one being able to resist Him—man.

Since God is all-powerful, even this resistance on Adam's part is in some mysterious way a manifestation of God's will; how this can be is not explained by the story, and we are left with the mystery that still eludes us, the coexistence of God's prescient power and man's unrestricted free will.

The story of the Fall of Man ends with a situation in which Adam has earned for himself and his descendants a short life of sorrow relieved only by death. It was the achievement of later Hebrew teachers to carry the story on and develop a concept of a God who is as merciful as He is just, who watches tenderly over the destinies of the creatures who have rebelled against Him, and brings about the possibility of atonement and full reconciliation.

Adam's son Cain is the first man to shed human blood, but though God drives him out to be a wanderer on the face of the earth, He does not kill him, and the brand on Cain's forehead, while it marks him as a murderer, also protects his life—no man is to touch him. Later when the descendants of Adam grow so wicked that God is sorry He has created the human race, He decides to destroy it by sending a universal flood. But He spares one man, Noah, with his family, to beget a new human race, on which God pins His hopes. His rainbow in the sky reminds men of His promise that He will never again let loose the waters. But men do not learn their lesson: they start to build a tower high enough to reach to Heaven, and God is afraid that if they succeed they will then recognize no limit to their ambitions. Yet He does not destroy them; He merely frustrates their purpose by depriving them of their common language.

And yet Man must eventually atone for Adam's act; human guilt must be wiped out by sacrifice. The development of this idea was extended over centuries of thought and suffering; it reached its highest expression in the figure of Christ, the Son of God, who as a man pays the full measure due in human suffering and human death. Before this event, the idea of the one who suffers for all was a major theme in Hebrew literature; not only did there emerge slowly a concept of the Hebrews as a chosen nation which suffers for the rest, but individual figures of Hebrew history and imagination embodied this theme in the form of the story of the suffering servant whose suffering brings relief to his fellow men and ultimate glory to himself. This is the idea behind the story of Joseph.

### JOSEPH

Joseph, his father's favorite son, has a sense of his own great destiny, confirmed by his dreams, which represent him as the first of all his race. He is indeed to be the first, but to become so he must also be the last. He is sold into slavery by his brothers; the savior is rejected by those whom he is to save, as the Hebrews were rejected by their neighbors and as they rejected their own prophets.

With the loss of his liberty, Joseph's trials have only begun.

In Egypt after making a new and successful life for himself, he is thrown into prison on a false accusation. He interprets the dream of Pharaoh's butler, who promises, if his interpretation is correct, to secure his release; the butler is restored to freedom and royal favor, but, as is the way of the world, forgets his promise and leaves his comforter in jail. Joseph stays in prison two more years but finally obtains his freedom and becomes Pharaoh's most trusted adviser. When his brothers come from starving Palestine and bow down before him asking for help, he saves them; not only does he give them grain but he also provides a home for his people in Egypt. "I am Joseph your brother, whom ye sold into Egypt," he says to them when he reveals his identity. "God sent me before you to preserve you a posterity in the earth, and to save your lives by a great deliverance."

One of the essential points of this story, and the whole conception of the suffering servant, is the distinction which it emphasizes between an external, secular standard of good and a spiritual, religious standard. In the eyes of the average man, prosperity and righteousness are connected, if not identified; he tends to think of the sufferer as one whose misfortune must be explained as a punishment for his wickedness. This feeling is strong in ancient (especially in Greek) literature, but modern man should not be unduly complacent about his superiority to the ancients in this respect, for the attitude is still with us. It is in fact a basic assumption of the competitive society—the view, seldom expressed but strongly rooted, that the plight of the unfortunate is the result of their own laziness, the wealth of the rich the reward of superior virtue.

The writer of the Joseph story sees in the unfortunate sufferer the savior who is the instrument of God's will; it is because of what he suffers that the sun and the moon and the eleven stars will bow down to Joseph. Yet the story does not emphasize the sufferings of Joseph; he is pictured rather as the man of action who through native ability and divine protection turns the injuries done him into advantages. We are not made to feel the torment in his soul; when he weeps it is because of the memory of what he has suffered and his yearning for his youngest brother, and he is in full control of the situation. And his reward in the things of this world is great. Not only does he reveal himself as the savior of his nation, but he becomes rich and powerful beyond his brothers' dreams, and in a greater kingdom. The spiritual and secular standards are at the end of the story combined; Joseph's suffering is neatly balanced by his worldly reward.

### JOB

Later Hebrew writers developed a sadder and profounder view. The greatest literary masterpiece of the Old Testament, the Book of Job, is also concerned with the inadequacy of worldly standards of happiness and righteousness, but the suffering of Job is so overwhelming and so magnificently expressed, that even with our knowledge of its purpose and its meaning it seems excessive. Joseph suffered slavery, exile, and imprisonment, but turned them all to account; Job loses his family and wealth in a series of calamities, which strike one on the other like hammer blows, and is then plagued with a loathsome disease. Unlike Joseph, he is old; he cannot adapt himself and rise above adverse circumstances, and he no longer wishes to live. Except for one thing. He wishes to understand the reason for his suffering.

For his friends the explanation is simple. With the blindness of men who know no standards other than those of this world, they are sure that Job's misfortune must be the result of some wickedness on his part. But Job is confident in his righteousness; his torture is as much mental as physical; he cannot reconcile the fact of his innocence with the calamities that have come upon him with all the decisive suddenness of the hand of God.

The full explanation is never given to him, but it is given to the reader in the two opening chapters of the book. This prologue to the dramatic section of the work gives us the knowledge which is hidden from the participants in the ensuing dialogue; the writer uses the method characteristic of Greek tragedy—irony, the deeper understanding of the dramatic spoken word which is based on the superior knowledge of the audience. The prologue explains God's motive in allowing Job to suffer. It is an important one: God intends to use Job as a demonstration to His skeptical subordinate, Satan, of the fact that a human being can retain faith in God's justice in the face of the greatest imaginable suffering. This motive, which Job does not know and which is never revealed to him, gives to the dialogue between Job and his friends its suspense and its importance; God has rested His case, that humanity is capable of keeping faith in divine justice, against all appearances to the contrary, on this one man.

The arguments of Job's friends are based on the worldly equation, success = virtue. They attempt to undermine Job's faith, not in God, but in himself. ". . . who ever perished, being innocent?" asks Eliphaz, "or where were the righteous cut off?" Job's misfortune is a proof that he must have sinned; all he has to do is to admit his guilt and ask God for pardon, which he will surely receive. He refuses to accept this easy way out, and we know that he is right. In fact, we know from the prologue that he has been selected for misfortune not because he has sinned, but precisely because of his outstanding virtue. "There is none like him in the earth," God says, "a perfect and an upright man, one that feareth God, and escheweth evil." What Job must do is to persevere not only in his faith in God's justice but also in the conviction of his own innocence. He must believe the illogical, accept a paradox. His friends are offering him an easy way out, one which seems to be the way of humility and submission. But it is a false way. And God finally tells them so. "The Lord said to Eliphaz the Temanite, My wrath is kindled against thee, and against thy

two friends: for ye have not spoken of me the thing that is right, as my servant Job hath."

Job's confidence in his own righteousness is not pride, but intellectual honesty. He sees that the problem is much harder than his friends imagine; to let them persuade him of his own guilt would lighten his mental burden by answering the question which tortures him, but his intelligence will not let him yield. Like Oedipus, he refuses to stop short of the truth; he even uses the same words: "let me alone, that I may speak, and let come on me what will." He finally expresses his understanding and acceptance of the paradox involved in the combination of his suffering with his innocence, but he does so with a human independence and dignity. "Though he slay me, yet will I trust in him: but I will maintain mine own ways before him." He sums up his case with a detailed account of the righteousness of his ways, and it is clear that this account is addressed not only to his three friends but also to God. "My desire is, that the Almighty would answer me," he says. His friends are silenced by the majesty and firmness of his statement, they "ceased to answer Job, because he was righteous in his own eyes," but God is moved to reply.

The magnificent poetry of that reply, the voice out of the whirlwind, still does not give Job the full explanation, God's motive in putting him to the torture. It is a triumphant proclamation of God's power and also of His justice, and it silences Job, who accepts it as a sufficient answer. That God does not reveal the key to the riddle even to the man who has victoriously stood the test and vindicated His faith in humanity is perhaps the most significant point in the poem. It suggests that there is not and never will be an explanation of human suffering that man's intelligence can comprehend. The sufferer must, like Job, cling to his faith in himself and in God; he must accept the inexplicable fact that his own undeserved suffering is the working of God's justice.

### ECCLESIASTES

But there were some whose questions about the justice of God were not satisfied by a voice from the whirlwind. In the book known as Ecclesiastes (which claims it is the work of King Solomon but almost certainly comes from a much later time) the impermanence of all things human, the certainty of death, and the prevalence of injustice on earth produce in the writer a mood which at first sight seems a philosophy of despair: life is short, rewards transient—best to enjoy each moment for what it offers, enjoy one's work for the doing of it, without thought of results. But the book is informed throughout by a profoundly religious spirit; the moral that man "should make his soul enjoy good in his labour" is "from the hand of God" and the somberly magnificent evocation of old age and death, with which the book concludes, opens with the words: "Remember now thy Creator in the days of thy youth . . ."

### THE PROPHETS

In the last days of Israel's in-dependence, before conquerors overran the land and transported the population to captivity in the East (an exile mourned in Psalm 137—"By the rivers of Babylon . . ."), a series of prophets reproved the children of Israel for their transgressions and foretold the wrath to come, the end of the kingdom of Israel, and, beyond that, the overthrow of the neighboring kingdoms. The prophet was a man who believed himself to be the spokesman of God, the messenger of a terrifying vision. The horror of the vision of destruction was often too heavy a load for the human mind, and the disbelief and mockery of his hearers tipped the precarious balance so that what might have been merely a strange urgency came often close to madness. The vision of things to come was expressed in magnificent but disconnected images which to the workaday mind of the man in the street seemed only to confirm the suspicion that the prophet was deranged. Amos, Nahum, Jeremiah, and many another poured out their charged and clotted imagery of catastrophe to an unbelieving people.

But the story of Jonah shows us a prophet who *was* believed. When they heard his message, the people and ruler of Nineveh repented of their sins and made amends to God. They were spared, but Jonah objected and God had to rebuke him; God was more forgiving to sinners than the human prophet to his fellow man.

The prophets were not always messengers of doom; it is in the words of an unnamed prophet (whose writings are included in the Book of Isaiah) that the theme of the one who suffers for others finds its most profound and moving expression. In the earlier versions the sufferer has it all made up to him in the end: Job, like Joseph, has his reward. Job's suffering is greater than Joseph's and it is clear that the writer of the Book of Job shows, alike in the speeches and in the ironic framework of the whole, a profounder understanding of the nature and meaning of suffering than the narrator of the story of Joseph, but like Joseph, Job lives to see the end of his troubles and has his material reward. "The Lord gave Job twice as much as he had before. . . . After this lived Job an hundred and forty years, and saw his sons, and his sons' sons, even four generations."

But in the Song of the Suffering Servant there is no recompense in this life: the suffering ends in death. In this deeper vision there is no reconciliation between the standards of this world and the standards of the higher authority behind the suffering. The one who is to save Israel and the world is not well favored like Joseph: "he hath no form nor comeliness." Nor is he, like Job, "the greatest of all the men of the east"; he is "despised and rejected of men." He suffers for his fellow men: "the Lord hath laid on him the iniquity of us all." His suffering knows no limit but death; he is oppressed and afflicted, imprisoned and executed. "He was cut off out of the land of the living" and "he made his grave with the wicked."

The circumstances described here are familiar from other cultures than the Hebrew; they are found in the primitive ritual of many peoples, and ceremonial relics of them still existed in civilized fifth-century Athens. In certain primitive societies, to rid the group of guilt a scapegoat was chosen, who was declared responsible for the misdeeds of all, and who was then mocked, beaten, driven out of the community, and killed. The scapegoat was hated and despised as the embodiment of the guilt of the whole community; his death was the most ignominious imaginable. The memory of some such primitive ritual is unmistakable in the Hebrew song; but its meaning has been utterly changed. It is precisely in the figure of the hated and suffering scapegoat that the Hebrew prophet sees the savior of mankind—an innocent sufferer, "he had done no violence, neither was any deceit in his mouth"— and he sees this without visible confirmation; there is no recognition by the brothers, no vindication by a voice out of the whirlwind. It is the highest expression of the Hebrew vision at its saddest and most profound, this portrayal of the savior who comes not in pomp and power but in suffering and meekness, who dies rejected and despised, and who atones for human sin and makes "intercession for the transgressors." It implies the complete rejection of all worldly standards, a rejection which is to be made explicit later in the words of Christ, the embodiment of the suffering servant: "No man can serve two masters . . . God and Mammon."

## GREECE

### HOMER

Greek literature begins with two masterpieces, the *Iliad* and the *Odyssey*, which cannot be accurately dated (the conjectural dates range over three centuries), and which are attributed to a poet, Homer, about whom nothing is known except his name. They were probably fixed in something like their present form before the art of writing was in general use in Greece; it is certain that they were intended not for reading but for oral recitation. The earliest stages of their composition date from long before the beginnings of literacy in Greece (the late eighth century B.C.): the poems bear unmistakable traces of oral composition. The oral poet had at his disposal not reading and writing, but a vast and intricate system of metrical formulas—phrases which would fit in at different places in the line—and a repertoire of standard scenes (the arming of the warrior, the battle of two champions) as well as the known outline of the story. Of course he could and did invent new phrases and scenes as he recited—but his base was the immense poetic reserve created by many generations of singers before him. When he told again for his hearers the old story of Akhilleus and his wrath, he was recreating a traditional story which had been recited, with differences, additions, and improvements, by a long line of predecessors: the poem was not, in the modern sense, his creation, still less an expression of his personality.

Consequently there is no trace of his identity to be found in it: the poet remains as hidden behind the action and speech of his characters as if he were a dramatist.

The poems as we have them, however, are unlike most of the oral literature we know from other times and places. The poetic organization of each of the two epics, the subtle interrelationship of the parts which creates their structural and emotional unity, suggests that they owe their present form to the shaping hand of a single poet, the architect who selected from the enormous wealth of the oral tradition and fused what he took with original material to create the two magnificently ordered poems known as the *Iliad* and the *Odyssey*.

Of these two the *Iliad* is perhaps the earlier; it is generally agreed that it is the greater poem. Its subject is war; its characters are men in battle and women whose fate depends on the outcome. The war is fought by the Akhaians* against the Trojans for the recovery of Helen, the wife of the Akhaian chieftain Menelaos; the combatants are heroes who in their chariots engage in individual duels before the supporting lines of infantry and archers. This romantic war aim and the outmoded military technique suggest to the modern reader a comparison with chivalrous engagements between medieval knights

* Like the translator, we transliterate the original Greek names—Akhaians, Menelaos, Akhilleus, and so on; in discussing Virgil's *Aeneid* we use the more familiar Latin forms—Achaeans, Menelaus, Achilles.

—a vision of individual prowess in combat which the nostalgia of our mechanized age contrasts sentimentally with the mass slaughter of modern war. But there is no sentimentality in Homer's description of battle. "Patroclus went up to him and drove a spear into his right jaw; he thus hooked him by the teeth and the spear pulled him over the rim of his car. As one who sits at the end of some jutting rock and draws a strong fish out of the sea with a hook and line —even so with his spear did he pull Thestor all gaping from his chariot; he threw him down on his face and he died while falling." This is meticulously accurate; there is no attempt to suppress the ugliness of Thestor's death. The bare, careful description creates the true nightmare quality of battle, in which men perform monstrous actions with the same matter-of-fact efficiency they display in their normal occupations; and the simile reproduces the grotesque appearance of violent death—the simple spear thrust takes away Thestor's dignity as a human being even before it takes his life. He is gaping, like a fish on the hook.

The simile does something else too. The comparison of Patroklos to an angler emphasizes another aspect of battle, its excitement. Homer's lines here combine two contrary emotions, the human revulsion from the horror of violent death and the human attraction to the excitement of violent action. This passage is typical of the poem as a whole. Everywhere in it we are conscious of these two poles, of war's ugly brutality and its "terrible beauty." The poet accepts violence as a basic factor in human life, and accepts it without sentimentality; for it is equally sentimental to pretend that war is not ugly and to pretend that it does not have its beauty. Three thousand years have not changed the human condition in this respect; we are still both lovers and victims of the will to violence, and as long as we are, Homer will be read as its greatest interpreter.

The *Iliad* describes the events of a few weeks in the ten-year siege of Troy. The particular subject of the poem, as its first line announces, is the anger of Akhilleus, the bravest of the Akhaian chieftains encamped outside the city. Akhilleus is a man who lives by and for violence, who is creative and alive only in violent action. He knows that he will be killed if he stays before Troy, but rather than decay, as he would decay, in peace, he accepts that certainty. His inadequacy for peace is shown by the fact that even in war the violence of his temper makes him a man apart and alone. His anger cuts him off from his commander and his fellow princes; to spite them he withdraws from the fighting, the only context in which his life has any meaning. He is brought back into it at last by the death of his one real friend, Patroklos; the consequences of his wrath and withdrawal fall heavily on the Akhaians, but most heavily on himself.

The great champion of the Trojans, Hektor, fights bravely, but reluctantly; war, for him, is a necessary evil, and he thinks nostalgically of the peaceful past, though he has little hope of peace to come. His pre-eminence in peace is emphasized by the tenderness of his relations with his wife and child and also by his kindness to Helen, the cause of the war which he knows in his heart will bring his city to destruction. We see Hektor always against the background of the patterns of civilized life—the rich city with its temples and palaces, the continuity of the family. Akhilleus' background is the discord of the armed camp on the shore, his loneliness, and his certainty of early death. The duel between these two men is the inevitable crisis of the poem, and just as inevitable is Hektor's defeat and death. For against Akhilleus in his native element of violence nothing can stand.

At the climactic moment of Hektor's death, as everywhere in the poem, Homer's firm control of his material preserves the balance in which our contrary emotions are held; pity for Hektor does not entirely rob us of sympathy for Akhilleus. His brutal words to the dying Hektor and the insults he inflicts on his corpse are the mark of the savage, but we are never allowed to forget that this inflexible hatred is the expression of his love for Patroklos. And the final book of the poem shows us an Akhilleus whose iron heart is moved at last; he is touched by the sight of Hektor's father clasping in suppliance the terrible hands that have killed so many of his sons. He remembers that he has a father, and that he

will never see him again; Akhilleus and Priam, the slayer and the father of the slain, weep together:

Then both were overborne as they remembered:
the old King huddled at Akhilleus' feet
wept, and wept for Hektor, killer of men,
while great Akhilleus wept for his own father
as for Patroklos once again: and sobbing
filled the room.

Akhilleus gives Hektor's body to Priam for honorable burial. His anger has run its full course and been appeased; it has brought death, first to the Akhaians and then to the Trojans, to Patroklos and to Hektor, and so to Akhilleus himself, for his death is fated to come "soon after Hektor's." The violence to which he is dedicated will finally destroy him too.

This tragic action is the center of the poem, but it is surrounded by scenes which remind us that the organized destruction of war, though an integral part of human life, is only a part of it. Except for Akhilleus, whose worship of violence falters only in the final moment of pity for his enemy's father and his own, the yearning for peace and its creative possibilities is never far below the surface. This is most poignantly expressed by the scenes which take place in Troy, especially the farewell between Hektor and Andromakhe; but it is made clear that the Akhaians too are conscious of what they have sacrificed. Early in the poem, when Agamemnon, the Akhaian commander, tests the morale of his troops by suggesting that the war be abandoned, they rush for the ships so eagerly and with such heartfelt relief that their commanders are hard put to it to stop them. These two poles of the human condition, war and peace, with their corresponding aspects of human nature, the destructive and the creative, are implicit in every situation and statement of the poem, and they are put before us, in symbolic form, on the shield which the god Hephaistos makes for Akhilleus. Its emblem is an image of human life as a whole. Here are two cities, one at peace and one at war. In one a marriage is celebrated and a quarrel settled by process of law; the other is besieged by a hostile army and fights for its existence. Scenes of violence—peaceful shepherds slaughtered in an ambush, Death dragging away a corpse by its foot—are balanced by scenes of plowing, harvesting, work in the vineyard and on the pasture, a green on which youths and maidens dance. And around the outermost rim of the shield runs "the might of the Ocean stream," a river which is at once the frontier of the known and the imagined world and the barrier between the quick and the dead. The shield of Akhilleus is the total background for the tragic violence of the central figures; it provides a frame which gives the wrath of Akhilleus and the death of Hektor their just proportion and true significance.

### THE ODYSSEY

The other Homeric epic, the *Odyssey*, is concerned with the peace which followed the war, and in particular with the return of the heroes who survived. Its subject is the long drawn out return of one of the heroes, Odysseus of Ithaka, who had come farther than most (all the way from western Greece) and who was destined to spend ten years wandering in unknown seas before he returned to his rocky kingdom. When Odysseus' wanderings began, Akhilleus had already received, at the hands of Apollo, the death which he had chosen, and which was the only appropriate end for his fatal and magnificent violence. Odysseus chose life, and his outstanding quality is a probing and versatile intelligence, which, combined with long experience, keeps him safe and alive through the trials and dangers of twenty years of war and seafaring. To stay alive he has to do things that Akhilleus would never have done, and use an ingenuity and experience that Akhilleus did not possess; but his life is just as much a struggle. Troy has fallen, but "there is no discharge in the war." The way back is as perilous as the ten-year siege.

The opening lines of the poem state the theme:

Sing in me, Muse, and through me tell the story
of that man skilled in all ways of contending
the wanderer, harried for years on end,
after he plundered the stronghold
on the proud height of Troy.
        He saw the townlands
and learned the minds of many distant men,
and weathered many bitter nights and days
in his deep heart at sea, while he fought only
to save his life. . . .

In this world it is a struggle even to stay alive, and it is a struggle for which Odysseus is naturally endowed. But his objective is not life at any price. Where honor demands, he can be soberly courageous in the face of death (as on Kirke's island, where he goes alone and against his mate's advice to save his sailors), and he can even be led into foolhardiness by his insatiable curiosity (as in the expedition to see the island of the Kyklopes). Much as he clings to life, it must be life with honor; what he is trying to preserve is not just existence but a world-wide reputation. His name has become a byword for successful courage and intelligence, and he must not betray it. When he reveals his identity at the palace of the Phaiakians, he speaks of his fame in an objective manner, as if it were something apart from himself.

I am Laertes' son, Odysseus.
　　　　　　Men hold me
formidable for guile in peace and
　　war:
this fame has gone abroad to the
　　sky's rim.

This is not boasting, but a calm recognition of the qualities and achievements for which he stands, and to which he must be true.

Ironically enough, to be true to his reputation, he is often forced to conceal his name. In the Kyklopes' cave, he calls himself "Nobody," in order to assure his escape, and it is clear how hard he finds this denial of his reputation when, out of the cave and on board ship, he insists on telling Polyphemos his name. Not only does this reassertion of his identity bring himself, his ship, and his crew back within reach of Polyphemos' arm, but it also enables the blinded giant to call down on his enemy the wrath of his father Poseidon, who, from this point on, musters the full might of the sea against Odysseus' return. Warned by the consequences of this boastful revelation of his name, he conceals his identity even from the hospitable Phaiakians, until his emotional reaction to the singer's tale of Troy gives him away. And when he finally returns home, to a palace full of violent suitors for his wife's hand who think that he is dead and who have presumed so far that they will kill him if they now find out that he is alive, he has to become Nobody again; he disguises himself as an old dirty beggar, to flatter and fawn on his enemies for bread in his own house.

The trials of the voyage home are not just physical obstacles to his return, they are also temptations. Odysseus is tempted, time after time, to forget his identity, to secede from the life of struggle and constant vigilance for which his name stands. The lotus flower which makes a man forget home and family is the most obvious form of temptation; it occurs early in the voyage and is easily resisted. But he is offered more attractive bait. Kirke gives him a life of ease and self-indulgence on an enchanted island; his resistance has by this time been lowered, and he stays a full year before his sailors remonstrate with him and remind him of his home. At the

Phaiakian palace where he tells the story of his voyages, he is offered the love of a young princess, Nausikaa, and her hand in marriage by her father Alkinoös —a new life in a richer kingdom than his rocky Ithaka. The Sirens tempt him to live in the memory of the glorious past. "Come here, famous Odysseus," they sing, "great glory of the Akhaians, and hear our song. . . . For we know all that at broad Troy the Argives and the Trojans suffered by the will of the gods." If he had not been bound to the mast, he would have gone to hear and join the dead men whose bones rot on the Sirens' island. Kalypso, the goddess with whom he spent seven years, longing all the time to escape, offers him the greatest temptation of all, immortality. If he will stay as her husband, he will live forever, a life of ease and tranquility, like that of the gods. Odysseus refuses this too; he prefers the human condition, with all its struggle, its disappointments, and its inevitable end. And the end, death, is an ever-present temptation. It is always near him; at the slightest slackening of effort, the smallest failure of intelligence, the first weakness of will, death will bring him release from his trials. But he hangs on tenaciously, and, toward the end of his ordeals, he is sent living to the world of the dead to see for himself what death means. It is dark and comfortless; Homer's land of the dead is the most frightening picture of the afterlife in European literature. Odysseus talks to the dead and any illusion he had about death as repose is shattered when he talks to the shade of Akhilleus and hears him reply.

Let me hear no smooth talk
of death from you, Odysseus, light
    of councils.
Better, I say, to break sod as a farm
    hand
for some poor country man, on iron
    rations,
than lord it over all the exhausted
    dead.

When he hears these words Odysseus does not yet understand their full significance (that he, the living man, will taste the depths of degradation, not as a serf, but as a despised beggar, mocked and manhandled in his own palace), but he is prepared now to face everything that may be necessary, to push on without another look behind.

In this scene Homer brings his two great prototypes face to face, and poses the tragic fury of Akhilleus against the mature intelligence of Odyssues. There can be little doubt where his sympathy lies. Against the dark background of Akhilleus' regret for life lost the figure of Odysseus shines more warmly: a man dedicated to life, accepting its limitations and making full use of its possibilities, a man who is destined to endure to the end and be saved. He finds in the end the home and the peace he fought for, his wife faithful, a son worthy of his name ready to succeed him, and the knowledge that the death which must come at last will be gentle.

Then a seaborne death
soft as this hand of mist will come
    upon you

when you are wearied out with rich
old age,
your country folk in blessed peace
around you.

### THE HOMERIC GODS

The Homeric poems played
in the subsequent development
of Greek civilization the same
role that the Old Testament
writings had played in Palestine:
they became the basis of an education and therefore of a whole
culture. Not only did the great
characters of the epic serve as
models of conduct for later generations of Greeks, but the figures of the Olympian gods retained, in the prayers, poems,
and sculpture of the succeeding
centuries, the shapes and attributes set down by Homer. The
difference between the Greek
and the Hebrew hero, between
Akhilleus and Joseph, for example, is remarkable, but the difference between "the God of
Abraham and of Isaac" and the
Olympians who interfere capri-
ciously in the lives of Hektor
and Akhilleus is an unbridgeable
chasm. The two conceptions of
the power which governs the
universe are irreconcilable; and
in fact the struggle between
them ended, not in synthesis,
but in the complete victory of
the one and the disappearance
of the other. The Greek conception of the nature of the gods
and of their relation to man is so
alien to us that it is difficult for
the modern reader to take it
seriously. The Hebrew basis of
European Christianity has made
it almost impossible for us to
imagine a god who can be feared
and laughed at, blamed and admired, and still sincerely wor-
shiped. Yet all these are proper

attitudes toward the gods on
Olympus; they are all implicit in
Homer's poem.

The Hebrew conception of
God is clearly an expression of
an emphasis on those aspects of
the universe which imply a harmonious order. The elements of
disorder in the universe are, in
the story of Creation, blamed on
man, and in all Hebrew literature the evidences of disorder
are something the writer tries to
reconcile with an *a priori* assumption of an all-powerful, just
God; he never tampers with the
fundamental datum. Just as
clearly, the Greeks conceived
their gods as an expression of
the disorder of the world in
which they lived: the Olympian
gods, like the natural forces of
sea and sky, follow their own
will even to the extreme of conflict with each other, and always
with a sublime disregard for the
human beings who may be affected by the results of their
actions. It is true that they are
all subjects of a single more powerful god, Zeus, but his authority over them is based only on
superior strength; though he cannot be openly resisted, he can
be temporarily deceived (as he
is, in comic circumstances, in
the fourteenth book of the
*Iliad*). And Zeus, although in
virtue of his superior power his
will is finally accomplished in
the matter of Akhilleus' wrath,
knows limits to his power too;
he cannot save the life of his
son, the Lycian hero Sarpedon.
Behind Zeus stands the mysterious power of Fate, to which
even he must bow.

Such gods as these, representing as they do the blind forces

of the universe which man cannot control, are not thought of as connected with morality. Morality is a human creation, and though the gods may approve of it, they are not bound by it. And violent as they are, they cannot feel the ultimate consequence of violence; death is a human fear, just as the courage to face it is a human quality. There is a double standard, one for gods, one for men, and the inevitable consequence is that our real admiration and sympathy is directed not toward the gods but toward the men. With Hektor, and even with Akhilleus at his worst, we can sympathize; but the gods, though they may excite terror or laughter, can never have our sympathy; we could as easily sympathize with the blizzard or the force of gravity. Homer imposed on Greek literature the anthropocentric emphasis which is its distinguishing mark and its great contribution to the Western mind; though the gods are ever-present characters in the incidents of his poem, his true concern, first and last, is with men.

### THE CITY-STATES OF GREECE

The stories told in the Homeric poems are set in the age of the Trojan War, which archaeologists (those, that is, who believe that it happened at all) date to the twelfth century B.C. Though the poems do perhaps preserve some blurred and faded memory of that time (the Mycenaean period, as it has been known since archaeologists uncovered the golden treasures in the royal tombs at Mycenae) there is no doubt that the poems as we have them are the creation of later centuries, the ninth to the seventh, the so-called Dark Age which succeeded the collapse (or destruction) of Mycenaean civilization. This was the time of the final settlement of the Greek peoples, an age of invasion and migration, which saw the foundation and growth of many small independent cities. The geography of the Greek peninsula and its scattered islands encouraged this fragmentation: the Greek cities never lost sight of their common Hellenic heritage but it was not enough to unite them except in the face of unmistakable and overwhelming danger, and even then only partially and for a short time. They differed from each other in custom, political constitution, and even dialect: their relations with each other were those of rivals and fierce competitors.

In these cities, constantly at war with each other in the pursuit of more productive land for growing populations, the kings of Homeric society gave way to aristocratic oligarchies, which maintained a strangle hold on the land and the economy of which it was the base. An important safety valve was colonization; in the eighth and seventh centuries B.C. landless men founded new cities (always near the sea and generally owing little or no allegiance to the home base) all over the Mediterranean coasts—in Spain, southern France (Marseilles, Nice, and Antibes were all Greek cities), in South Italy (Naples), Sicily (Syracuse), North Africa (Cyrene), all along the coast of Asia Minor (Smyrna, Miletus), and even on the Black Sea as far as Russian Crimea.

Many of these new outposts of Greek civilization experienced a faster economic and cultural development than the older cities of the mainland. It was in the cities founded on the Asian coast that the Greeks adapted to their own language the Phoenician system of writing (adding signs for the vowels to create the first efficient alphabet); its first use was probably for commercial records and transactions, but as literacy became a general condition all over the Greek world in the course of the seventh century B.C. treaties and political decrees were inscribed on stone and literary works written on rolls of paper made from the Egyptian papyrus plant.

### ATHENS AND SPARTA

By the beginning of the fifth century B.C. the two most prominent city-states were Athens and Sparta; these two cities led the combined Greek resistance to the Persian invasion of Europe in the years 490 to 479 B.C. The defeat of the solid Persian power by the divided and insignificant Greek cities surprised the world and inspired in Greece, and particularly in Athens, a confidence that knew no bounds.

Athens was at this time a democracy, the first in Western history. It was a direct, not a representative, democracy, for the number of free citizens was small enough to permit the exercise of power by a meeting of the citizens as a body in assembly. Athens' power lay in the fleet with which she had played her decisive part in the struggle against Persia, and with this fleet she rapidly became the leader of a naval alliance which included most of the islands of the Aegean Sea and many Greek cities on the coast of Asia Minor. Sparta, on the other hand, was a totalitarian state, rigidly conservative in government and policy, in which the individual citizen was reared and trained by the state for the state's business, war. The Spartan land army was consequently superior to any other in Greece, and the Spartans controlled, by direct rule or by alliance, the majority of the city-states of the Peloponnese.

These two cities, allies for the war of liberation against Persia, became enemies when the external danger was eliminated. The middle years of the fifth century were disturbed by indecisive hostilities between them and haunted by the probability of full-scale war to come; as the years went by this war came to be accepted as "inevitable" by both sides, and in 431 B.C. it began. It was to end in 404 B.C. with the total defeat of Athens.

Before the beginning of this disastrous war, Athenian democracy provided its citizens with a cultural and political environment which was without precedent in the ancient world. The institutions of Athens encouraged the maximum development of the individual's capacities and at the same time inspired the maximum devotion to the interests of the community. It was a moment in history of delicate and precarious balance between the freedom of the individual and the demands of the state. Its uniqueness was emphasized by the complete lack of balance in Sparta, where the necessities of the state annihilated the individual as a creative and independent being. It was the proud boast of the Athenians that without sacrificing the cultural amenities of civilized life they could yet when called upon surpass in policy and war their adversary, whose citizen body was an army in constant training. The Athenians were, in this respect as in others, a nation of amateurs. "The individual Athenian," said Pericles in the speech which is at once the panegyric of Athenian democracy and its epitaph, "in his own person seems to have the power of adapting himself to the most varied forms of action with the utmost versatility and grace." But the freedom of the individual did not, in Athens' great days, produce anarchy. "While we are . . . unconstrained in our private intercourse," Pericles had observed earlier in his speech, "a spirit of reverence pervades our public acts."

This balance of individual freedom and communal unity was not destined to outlast the century. It went down, with Athens, in the war. The process of disintegration, and the forces behind it, are described and analyzed in the tragic pages of the Athenian historian of the Peloponnesian War, Thucydides. With an apparent dispassionateness which increases the somber effect of his writing, he shows how his countrymen, under the mounting pressure of the long conflict, lost the "spirit of reverence" which Pericles saw as the stabilizing factor in Athenian democracy. They subordinated all considerations to the immediate interest of the city

and surpassed their enemy in the logical ferocity of their actions; they finally fell victims to leaders who carried the process one step further and subordinated all considerations to their own private interest. The most brilliant and dangerous of these new statesmen, Alcibiades, carried his personal freedom to the point of betraying his own city in her critical hour. His career is symptomatic of the decay of the freedom in unity described in Pericles' speech; by the end of the fifth century Athens was divided internally as well as defeated externally. The individual citizen no longer thought of himself and Athens as one and the same; the balance was gone forever.

While it lasted, it provided an atmosphere for the artist which has rarely, if ever, existed since. The dramatic poet, whose play was performed, in competition against two other dramatists for a prize, at a religious festival attended by most of the free citizens, addressed an audience of quick-thinking and keenly critical minds which were yet culturally and politically homogeneous; he spoke to the whole city, at a city festival, and in the city's name. Shakespeare had to please the groundlings as well as the court wits, but the Athenian dramatist speaks with the same emphasis and in the same tone to the entire audience.

#### THE DRAMA

European drama begins in Athens in the fifth century B.C. Its origins are shrouded in obscurity into which the researches of many scholars, especially those who have drawn on comparative anthropology, have brought a certain amount of light, though what has been illuminated is the general nature of the development rather than any particular aspects of it. What no one has explained (and it is perhaps inexplicable) is why the religious dances which are to be found in practically all primitive cultures, gave rise in Greece, and in Greece alone, to what we know as tragedy and comedy.

### TRAGEDY—AESCHYLUS

Tragedy developed from the dance and song of a chorus performing on a circular dancing floor. An actor, whose medium was speech, not song, and who performed outside the circle, was introduced by some unknown innovator (his name was probably Thespis), and as the number of actors was increased to two and then to three, the spoken part of the performance grew in importance. In the *Agamemnon* of Aeschylus, produced in 458 B.C., an equilibrium between the two elements of the performance has been established; the actors, with their speeches, create the dramatic situation and its movement, the plot; the chorus, while contributing to dramatic suspense and illusion, ranges free of the immediate situation in its odes, which extend and amplify the significance of the action.

The *Agamemnon* is the first play of a trilogy; that is, it was followed at its performance by two more plays, the *Choephoroe* and the *Eumenides*, which carried on its story and its theme to a conclusion. The theme of the trilogy is justice; and its story, like that of almost all Greek tragedies, is a legend which was already well-known to the audience which saw the first performance of the play. This particular legend, the story of the house of Atreus, was rich in dramatic potential, for it deals with a series of retributive murders which stained the hands of three generations of a royal family, and it has also a larger, a social and historical significance, of which Aeschylus took full advantage. The legend preserves the memory of an important historical process through which the Greeks had passed, the transition from tribal institutions of justice to communal justice, from a tradition which demanded that a murdered man's next of kin avenge his death, to a system requiring settlement of the private quarrel by the court of law, the typical institution of the city-state which replaced the primitive tribe. When Agamemnon returns victorious from Troy, he is killed by his wife, Clytemnestra, and her lover, Aegisthus, who is Agamemnon's cousin. Clytemnestra kills her husband to avenge her daughter Iphigenia, whom Agamemnon sacrificed to the goddess Artemis when he had to choose between his daughter's life and his ambition to conquer Troy. Aegisthus avenges the crime of a previous generation, the hideous murder of his brothers by Agamemnon's father, Atreus. The killing of Agamemnon is, by the standards of the old system, justice; but it is the nature of this justice that the process can never be arrested, that one act of violence must give rise to another. Agamemnon's murder must be avenged too, as it is in the second play of the trilogy by

Orestes, his son, who kills both Aegisthus and his own mother, Clytemnestra. Orestes has acted justly according to the code of tribal society based on blood relationship, but in doing so he has violated the most sacred blood relationship of all, the bond between mother and son. The old system of justice has produced an insoluble dilemma; it can be surmounted only by the institution of a new system, and this is accomplished in the final play of the trilogy, in which a court of law is set up by the goddess Athene to try the case of Orestes. He is acquitted, but more important than the decision is the nature of the body which makes it. This is the end of an old era and the beginning of a new. The existence of the court is a guarantee that the tragic series of events which drove Orestes to the murder of his mother will never be repeated. The system of communal justice, which allows consideration of circumstance and motive, and which punishes impersonally, has at last replaced the inconclusive anarchy of individual revenge.

But the play is concerned with much more than the history of human institutions, with more even than the general problem of violence between man and man for which the particular instances of the trilogy stand. It is also a religious statement. The whole sequence of events, stretching over many generations, is presented as the working out of the will of Zeus. The tragic action of the *Iliad* was also the expression of the will of Zeus (though it is characteristic of Homer that Achilles was at least equally responsible), but for Aeschylus the will of Zeus means something new. In this trilogy the working out of Zeus's will proceeds intricately through three generations of bloodshed to the creation of a human institution which will prevent any repetition of the cycle of murder that produced it. Agamemnon dies, and Clytemnestra dies in her turn, and Orestes is hounded over land and sea to his trial, but out of all this suffering comes an important advance in human understanding and civilization. The chorus of the *Agamemnon*, celebrating the power of Zeus, tells how he

... setting us on the road
Made this a valid law—
"That men must learn by suffering."

From the suffering comes wisdom, whereas in the *Iliad* nothing at all comes out of the suffering, except the certainty of more. ". . . far from the land of my fathers," says Achilles to Priam, "I sit here in Troy, and bring nothing but sorrow to you and your children"; but his last words to Priam are a reminder that this interval of sympathy is only temporary. After Hector's burial the war will go on as before. This is Zeus's will; Homer does not attempt to explain it. But the Aeschylean trilogy is nothing less than an attempt to justify the ways of God to man; the suffering is shown to us as the fulfillment of a purpose we can understand, a purpose beneficent to man.

The full scope of Zeus's will is apparent only to the audience, which follows the pattern of its execution through the three plays of the trilogy; as in the Book of Job, the characters who act and suffer are in the dark. They claim a knowledge of Zeus's will and boast that their actions are its fulfillment (it is in these terms that Agamemnon speaks of the sack of Troy, and Clytemnestra of Agamemnon's murder), and they are, of course, in one sense, right. But their knowledge is limited; Agamemnon does not realize that Zeus's will includes his death at the hands of Clytemnestra, nor Clytemnestra that it demands her death at the hands of her son. The chorus has, at times, a deeper understanding; in its opening ode it announces the law of Zeus, that men must learn by suffering, and at the end it recognizes the responsibility of Zeus in the death of Agamemnon—"Brought by Zeus, by Zeus, / Cause and worker of all." But the chorus cannot interpret the event in any way it can accept, for it can see no further than the immediate present; its knowledge of Zeus's law is an abstraction which it cannot relate to the terrible fact.

In this murky atmosphere (made all the more terrible by the beacon fire of the opening lines, which brings not light, but deeper darkness), one human being sees clear; she possesses the concrete vision of the future which complements the chorus' abstract knowledge of the law. This is the prophet Cassandra, Priam's daughter, brought from Troy as Agamemnon's share of the spoils. She has been given the power of true prophecy by the god Apollo, but the gift is nullified by the condition that her prophecies will never be be-

lieved. Like the Hebrew prophets, she sees reality—past, present, and future—so clearly that she is cut off from ordinary human beings by the clarity of her vision and the terrible burden of her knowledge; like them she expresses herself in poetic figures, and like them she is rejected by her hearers. To the everyday world, represented by the chorus, she appears to be mad, the fate of prophets in all ages; and it is only as she goes into the palace to the death she foresees that the old men of the chorus begin to accept, fearfully and hesitantly, the truth which she has been telling them.

The great scene in which she mouths her hysterical prophecies at them delays the action for which everything has been prepared—the death of Agamemnon. Before we hear his famous cry off stage, Cassandra presents us with a mysterious vision in which she combines cause, effect, and result: the murders which have led to this terrible moment, the death of Agamemnon (which will not take place until she leaves the stage), and the murders which will follow. We do not see Agamemnon's death—we see much more. The past, present, and future of Clytemnestra's action and Agamemnon's suffering are fused into a timeless unity in Cassandra's great lines, an unearthly unity which is dissolved only when Agamemnon, in the real world of time and space, screams in mortal agony.

The tremendous statement of the trilogy is made in a style which for magnificence and richness of suggestion can be compared only with the style of Shakespeare at the height of his poetic power, the Shakespeare of *King Lear* and *Antony and Cleopatra*. The language of the *Agamemnon* is an oriental carpet of imagery in which combinations of metaphor, which at first seem bombastic in their violence, take their place in the ordered pattern of the poem as a whole. An image, once introduced, recurs, and reappears again, to run its course verbally and visually through the whole length of the trilogy, richer in meaning with each fresh appearance. In the second choral ode, for example, the chorus, welcoming the news of Agamemnon's victory at Troy, sings of the net which Zeus and Night threw over the city, trapping the inhabitants like animals. The net is here an image of Zeus's justice, a retributive justice, since Troy is paying for the crime of taking Helen, and the image identifies Zeus's justice with Agamemnon's action in sacking the city. This image occurs again, with a different emphasis, in the hypocritical speech of welcome which Clytemnestra makes to her husband on his return. She tells how she feared for his safety at Troy, how she trembled at the rumors of his death:

... If Agamemnon
Had had so many wounds as those
    reported ...
Then he would be gashed fuller
    than a net has holes!

This vision of Agamemnon dead she speaks of as her fear, but we know that it represents her deepest desire, and more, the purpose which she is now preparing to execute. When, later, she stands in triumph over her husband's corpse, she uses the same image to describe the robe which she threw over his limbs to blind and baffle him before she stabbed him—"Inextricable like a net for fishes/I cast about him a vicious wealth of raiment" —and this time the image materializes into an object visible on stage. We can see the net, the gashed robe still folded round Agamemnon's body. We shall see it again, for in the second play Orestes, standing over his mother's body as she now stands over his father's, will display the robe before us, with its holes and bloodstains, as a justification for what he has just done. Elsewhere in the *Agamemnon* the chorus compares Cassandra to a wild animal caught in the net, and later Aegisthus exults to see Agamemnon's body lying "in the nets of Justice." For each speaker the image has a different meaning, but not one realizes the terrible sense in which it applies to them all. They are all caught in the net, the system of justice by vengeance which only binds tighter the more its captives struggle to free themselves. Clytemnestra attempts to escape, to arrest the process of the chain of murders and the working out of the will of Zeus. "I am ready to make a contract/With the Evil Genius of the House of Atreus," she says, but Agamemnon's body and the net she threw over him are there on the stage to remind us that her appeal will not be heard; one more generation must act and suffer before the net will vanish, never to be seen again.

THE INTELLECTUAL REVOLUTION OF THE FIFTH CENTURY

Aeschylus belonged to the generation which fought at Marathon; his manhood and his old age were passed in the heroic period of the Persian defeat on Greek soil and the war which Athens fought to liberate her kinsmen in the islands of the Aegean and on the Asiatic coast. Sophocles, his younger contemporary, lived to see an Athens which had advanced in power and prosperity far beyond the city that Aeschylus knew, but it was an Athens in which it became clearer every year that something had gone wrong. The league of free Greek cities against Persia which Athens had led to victory in the Aegean had become an empire, in which Athens taxed and coerced the subject cities that had once been her allies; and inside the city a new and dangerous spirit was abroad. Democratic institutions had created a demand for an education which would prepare men for public life, especially by training them in the art of public speaking. The demand was met by the appearance of the professional teacher, the Sophist, as he was called, who taught, for a handsome fee, not only the techniques of public speaking but also the subjects which gave a man something to talk about —government, ethics, literary criticism, even astronomy. The curriculum of the Sophists, in fact, marks the first appearance in European civilization of the liberal education, just as they themselves were the first professors.

The Sophists were great teachers, but like most teachers they had little or no control over the results of their teaching. Their methods placed an inevitable emphasis on effective presentation of a point of view, to the detriment, and if necessary the exclusion, of anything which might make it less convincing. They produced a generation which had been trained to see both sides of any question and to argue the weaker side as effectively as the stronger, the false as effectively as the true; to argue inferentially from probability in the absence of concrete evidence; to appeal to the audience's sense of its own advantage rather than to accepted moral standards; and to justify individual defiance of general prejudice and even of law by the distinction between "nature" and "convention." These methods dominated the thinking of the Athenians of the last half of the century. The emphasis on the technique of effective presentation of both sides of any case encouraged a relativistic point of view and finally produced a cynical mood which denied the existence of any absolute standards. The canon of probability (which implies an appeal to human reason as the supreme authority) became a critical weapon for an attack on myth and on traditional conceptions of the gods; it had its constructive aspect too, for it is the basis of Thucydides' magnificent guesswork about early Greek history. The appeal to the self-interest of the audience, to expediency, became the method of new political leaders and the fundamental doctrine of a new school of political theory; this theory and its practice, stripped to their terrifying essentials, are set down as an example to future ages in Thucydides' account of the negotiations between Athens and Melos. The distinction between "nature" and "convention" is the source of the doctrine of the superman, who breaks free of the conventional restraints of society and acts according to the law of his own "nature," as Alcibiades did when he betrayed his country in the Peloponnesian War. The new spirit in Athens has magnificent achievements to its credit, but it brought disaster. At its roots was a supreme confidence in the human intelligence and a secular view of man's position in the universe that is best expressed in the statement of Protagoras, the most famous of the Sophists: "Man is the measure of all things."

### TRAGEDY—SOPHOCLES

It was in this atmosphere of critical re-evaluation of accepted standards that Sophocles produced his masterpiece, *Oedipus Tyrannus*, probably performed for the first time in the opening years of the Peloponnesian War, which began in 431 B.C. This tragedy of a man of high principles and probing intelligence who follows the prompting of that intelligence to the final consequence of true self-knowledge, which makes him put out his eyes, was as full of significance for Sophocles' contemporaries as it is for us. Unlike a modern dramatist, Sophocles used for his tragedy a story well known to the audience and as old as their

own history, a legend told by father to son, handed down from generation to generation because of its implicit wealth of meaning, learned in childhood and rooted deep in the consciousness of every member of the community. Such a story the Greeks called a *myth*, and the use of it presented Sophocles, as it did Aeschylus in his trilogy, with material which, apart from its great inherent dramatic potential, already possessed the significance and authority which the modern dramatist must create for himself. It had the authority of history, for the history of ages which leave no records is myth —that is to say, the significant event of the past, stripped of irrelevancies and imaginatively shaped by the oral tradition. It had a religious authority, for the Oedipus story, like the story of the house of Atreus, is concerned with the relation between man and god. Lastly, and this is especially true of the Oedipus myth, it had the power, because of its subject matter, to arouse the irrational hopes and fears which lie deep and secret in the human consciousness.

The use of the familiar myth enabled the dramatist to draw on all its wealth of unformulated meaning, but it did not prevent him from striking a contemporary note. Oedipus, in Sophocles' play, is at one and the same time the mysterious figure of the past who broke the most fundamental human taboos and a typical fifth-century Athenian. His character contains all the virtues for which the Athenians were famous and the vices for which they were notorious. The best commentary on Oedipus' character is the speech which Thucydides put into the mouth of the Corinthian spokesman at Sparta, a hostile but admiring assessment of the Athenian genius. "Athenians . . . [are] equally quick in the conception and in the execution of every new plan . . ."—so Oedipus has already sent to Delphi when the priest advises him to do so, and has already sent for Tiresias when the chorus suggests this course of action. "They are bold beyond their strength; they run risks which prudence would condemn . . ."—as Oedipus risked his life to answer the riddle of the Sphinx and later, in spite of the oracle about his marriage, accepted the hand of the queen. ". . . in the midst of misfortune they are full of hope. . . ."—so Oedipus, when he is told that he is not the son of Polybus and Merope, and Jocasta has already realized whose son he is, claims that he is the "child of Fortune." "When they do not carry out an intention which they have formed, they seem to have sustained a personal bereavement . . ."—so Oedipus, shamed by Jocasta and the chorus into sparing Creon's life, yields sullenly and petulantly.

The Athenian devotion to the city, which received the main emphasis in Pericles' praise of Athens, is strong in Oedipus; his answer to the priest at the beginning of the play shows that he is a conscientious and patriotic ruler. His sudden unreasoning rage is the characteristic fault of Athenian democracy, which in 406 B.C., to give only one instance, condemned and executed the generals who had failed, in the stress of weather and battle, to pick up the drowned bodies of their own men killed in the naval engagement at Arginusae. Oedipus is like the fifth-century Athenian most of all in his confidence in the human intelligence, especially his own. This confidence takes him in the play through the whole cycle of the critical, rationalist movement of the century, from the piety and orthodoxy he displays in the opening scene, through his taunts at oracles when he hears that Polybus is dead, to the despairing courage with which he accepts the consequences when he sees the abyss opening at his feet. "Ah master, do I *have* to speak?" asks the herdsman from whom he is dragging the truth. "You have to," Oedipus replies. "And I *have* to hear." And hear he does. He learns that the oracle he had first fought against and then laughed at has been fulfilled; that every step his intelligence prompted was one step nearer to disaster; that his knowledge was ignorance, his clear vision blindness. Faced with the reality which his determined probing finally reveals, he puts out his eyes.

The relation of Oedipus' character to the development of the action is the basis of the most famous attempt to define the nature of the tragic process, Aristotle's theory that pity and terror are aroused most effectively by the spectacle of a man who is "not eminently good and just, yet whose misfortune is brought about not by vice or depravity, but by some error or frailty. He must be one who is highly renowned and prosperous —a personage like Oedipus. . . ." Other references by Aristotle to this play make it clear that this influential critical canon is based particularly on Sophocles' masterpiece, and the canon has been universally applied to the play. But the great influence (and validity) of the Aristotelian theory should not be allowed to obscure the fact that Sophocles' *Oedipus Tyrannus* is more highly organized and economical than Aristotle implies. The fact that the critics have differed about the nature of Oedipus' error or frailty (his errors are many and his frailties include anger, impiety and self-confidence) is a clue to the real situation. Oedipus falls not through "some vicious mole of nature" or some "particular fault," but because he is the man he is, because of all aspects of his character, good and bad alike; and the development of the action right through to the catastrophe shows us every aspect of his character at work in the process of self-revelation and self-destruction. His first decision in the play, to hear Creon's message from Delphi in public rather than, as Creon suggests, in private, is evidence of his kingly solicitude for his people and his trust in them, but it makes certain the full publication of the truth. His impetuous proclamation of a curse on the murderer of Laius, an unnecessary step prompted by his civic zeal, makes his final situation worse than it need have been. His anger at Tiresias forces a revelation which drives him on to accuse Creon; this in turn provokes Jocasta's revela-

tions. And throughout the play his confidence in the efficacy of his own action, his hopefulness as the situation darkens, and his passion for discovering the truth, guide the steps of the investigation which is to reveal the detective as the criminal. All aspects of his character, good and bad alike, are equally involved; it is no frailty or error that leads him to the terrible truth, but his total personality.

The character of Oedipus as revealed in the play does something more than explain the present action, it also explains his past. In Oedipus' speeches and actions on stage we can see the man who, given the circumstances in which Oedipus was involved, would inevitably do just what Oedipus has done. Each action on stage shows us the mood in which he committed some action in the past; his angry death sentence on Creon reveals the man who killed Laius because of an insult on the highway; his impulsive proclamation of total excommunication for the unknown murderer shows us the man who, without forethought, accepted the hand of Jocasta; his intelligent, persistent search for the truth shows us the brain and the courage which solved the riddle of the Sphinx. The revelation of his character in the play is at once a re-creation of his past and an interpretation of the oracle which predicted his future.

This organization of the material is what makes it possible for us to accept the story as tragedy at all, for it emphasizes Oedipus' independence of the oracle. When we first see Oedipus, he has already committed the actions for which he is to suffer, actions prophesied, before his birth, by Apollo. But the dramatist's emphasis on Oedipus' character suggests that although Apollo has predicted what Oedipus will do, he does not determine it; Oedipus determines his own conduct, by being the man he is. Milton's explanation of a similar situation, Adam's fall and God's foreknowledge of it, may be applied to Oedipus; foreknowledge had no influence on his fault. The relationship between Apollo's prophecy and Oedipus' actions is not that of cause and effect. It is the relationship of two independent entities which are equated.

This correspondence between his character and his fate removes the obstacle to our full acceptance of the play which an external fate governing his action would set up. Nevertheless, we feel that he suffers more than he deserves. He has served as an example of the inadequacy of the human intellect and a warning that there is a power in the universe which humanity cannot control, nor even fully understand, but Oedipus the man still has our sympathy. Sophocles felt this too, and in a later play, his last, the *Oedipus at Colonus*, he dealt with the reward which finally balanced Oedipus' suffering. In *Oedipus Tyrannus* itself there is a foreshadowing of this final development; the last scene shows us a man already beginning to recover from the shock of the catastrophe and reasserting a natural superiority. "I shall go—on this condition," he says to Creon when ordered back into the house, and a few lines later Creon has to say bluntly

to him, "Do not presume that you are still in power." This renewed imperiousness is the first expression of a feeling on his part that he is not entirely guilty, a beginning of the reconstitution of the magnificent man of the opening scenes; it reaches its fulfillment in the final Oedipus play, the *Oedipus at Colonus*, in which he is a titanic figure, confident of his innocence and more masterful than he has ever been.

### ANTIGONE

Oedipus was expelled from Thebes, to wander as a blind beggar, accompanied only by his daughter Antigone. His sons, Eteocles and Polynices, raised no hand to help him and after he died at Athens (where, in death, he became a guardian spirit of the Attic soil), they fought each other for the throne of Thebes. Eteocles expelled his brother, who recruited supporters in Argos; seven champions attacked the seven gates of Thebes. The assault was beaten off; but Polynices and Eteocles killed each other in the battle. The rule of Thebes fell to Creon, the same Creon we have seen in *Oedipus Tyrannus*. His first decision is to forbid burial to the corpse of Polynices, the traitor who brought foreign troops against his own city. Antigone disobeys the decree by scattering dust on the body; captured and brought before Creon, she defies him in the name of the eternal unwritten laws. In the struggle between them it is the king who in the end surrenders; he buries the body of Polynices and orders Antigone's release. But she has already killed herself in her underground prison, thus bringing about the two deaths which crush her enemy, the suicides of his son Haemon and of his wife Eurydice.

Antigone, as a heroine of the resistance to tyrannical power, has deservedly become one of the Western world's great symbolic figures; she is clearly presented, in her famous speech, as a champion of a higher morality against the overriding claims of state necessity, which the Sophist intellectuals of Sophocles' time had begun to formulate in philosophical terms. But Creon, too, is given his due; he is no mere melodramatic tyrant but a ruler whose action stems from political and religious attitudes which were probably shared by many of the audience. Antigone and Creon clash not only as individuals, shaped with all Sophocles' dramatic genius (the ancient anonymous biography of Sophocles says truly that he could "match the moment with the action so as to create a whole character out of half a line or even a single word"), but also as representatives of two irreconcilable social and religious positions.

Antigone's chief loyalty is clearly to the family. She makes no distinction between the brothers though one was a patriot and the other a traitor, and when her sister Ismene refuses to help her defy the state to bury a brother she harshly disowns her. The denial of burial to Polynices strikes directly at her family loyalty, for it was the immemorial privilege and duty of the women of the house to mourn the dead man in unrestrained sorrow, sing his praises,

wash his body, and consign him to the earth. Creon, on the other hand, sees loyalty to the state as the only valid criterion, and in his opening speech expressly repudiates "one whose friend has stronger claims upon him than his country" (the Greek word translated "friend" also means "relative"). This inaugural address of Creon repeats many concepts and even phrases that are to be found in the speeches of the democratic leader Pericles; and in fact, there was an ancient antagonism between the new democratic institutions which stressed the equal rights and obligations of all citizens and the old powerful families which through their wide influence had acted as separate factions in the body politic. The nature of Creon's assertion of state against family, refusal of burial to a corpse, is repellent, but the principle behind it was one most Athenians would have accepted as valid.

These opposing social viewpoints have their corresponding religious sanctions. For Antigone, the gods, especially the gods below, demand equality for all the dead, the common inalienable right of burial. But Creon's gods are the gods who protect the city; how, he asks, could those gods have any feeling for Polynices, a traitor who raised and led a foreign army against the city they protect and which contains their temples? Here again, there must have been many in the audience who saw merit in this argument.

But as the action develops, whatever validity Creon's initial position may have had is destroyed, and by Creon himself.

For like all holders of absolute power, he proceeds, when challenged, to equate loyalty to the community with loyalty to himself—"the city is the King's" he tells his son Haemon. And in the end the prophet Tiresias tells him plainly that Antigone was right—the gods are on her side. He swallows his pride and surrenders, but too late. Antigone's suicide brings him to disaster in that institution, the family, which he subordinated to reasons of state; his son spits in his face before killing himself, and his wife dies cursing him as the murderer of his son.

Creon is punished, but Antigone is dead. "Wisdom we learn at last, when we are old" the chorus sings as the play ends, but the price of wisdom is high: the *Antigone*, like so many of the Shakespearean tragedies, leaves us with a poignant sense of loss.

TRAGEDY—EURIPIDES

Euripides' *Medea*, produced in 431 B.C., the year that brought the beginning of the Peloponnesian War, appeared earlier than the *Oedipus Tyrannus* of Sophocles, but it has a bitterness that is more in keeping with the spirit of a later age. If the *Oedipus* is, in one sense, a warning to a generation which has embarked on an intellectual revolution, the *Medea* is the ironic expression of the disillusion that comes after the shipwreck. In this play we are conscious for the first time of an attitude characteristic of modern literature, the artist's feeling of separation from his audience, the isolation of the poet. "Often previously," says Medea to the king,

Through being considered clever
 I have suffered much....
If you put new ideas before the eyes
 of fools
They'll think you foolish and
 worthless into the bargain;
And if you are thought superior to
 those who have
Some reputation for learning, you
 will become hated.

The common background of audience and poet is disappearing, the old certainties are being undermined, the city divided. Euripides is the first Greek poet to suffer the fate of so many of the great modern writers: rejected by most of his contemporaries, he became universally loved and admired after his death.

The change in atmosphere is clear even in Euripides' choice of subject and central character. He still dramatizes myth, but the myth he chooses is exotic and disturbing, and the protagonist is not a man but a woman. Medea is both woman and foreigner; that is to say, in terms of the audience's prejudice and practice she is a representative of the two free-born groups in Athenian society which had almost no rights at all (though the male foreign resident had more rights than the native woman). The tragic hero is no longer a king, "one who is highly renowned and prosperous—a personage like Oedipus," but a woman, who, because she finds no redress for her wrongs in society, is driven by her passion to violate that society's most sacred laws in a rebellion against its typical representative, Jason, her husband. She is not just a woman and a foreigner; she is also a person of great intellectual power. Compared to her the credulous king and her complacent husband are children, and once her mind is made up, she moves them like pawns to their proper places in her barbaric game. The myth is used for new purposes, to shock the members of the audience, attack their deepest prejudices, and shake them out of their complacent pride in the superiority of Greek masculinity.

But the play is more than a feminist melodrama. Before it is over, our sympathies have come full circle; the contempt with which we regard the Jason of the opening scenes turns to pity as we feel the measure of his loss and the ferocity of Medea's revenge. Medea's passion has carried her too far; the death of Creon and his daughter we might have accepted, but the murder of the children is too much. It was, of course, meant to be. Euripides' theme, like Homer's, is violence, but this is the unspeakable violence of the oppressed, which is greater than the violence of the oppressor and which, because it has been long pent up, cannot be controlled.

In this, as in the other plays, the gods have their place. In the *Agamemnon* the will of Zeus is manifested in every action and implied in every word; in the *Oedipus Tyrannus* the gods bide their time and watch Oedipus fulfill the truth of their prophecy, but in the *Medea*, the divine will, which is revealed at the end, is enigmatic and, far from bringing harmony, concludes the play with a terrifying discord. All through the *Medea* the human beings involved call on the gods; two especially are singled out for attention, Earth and Sun. It is by these two gods that Medea makes Aegeus swear to give her refuge in Athens, the chorus invokes them to prevent Medea's violence against her sons, and Jason wonders how Medea can look upon earth and sun after she has killed her own children. These emphatic appeals clearly raise the question of the attitude of the gods, and the answer to the question is a shock. We are not told what Earth does, but Sun sends the magic chariot on which Medea makes her escape. His reason, too, is stated; it is not any concern for justice, but the fact that Medea is his granddaughter. Euripides is here using the letter of the myth for his own purposes. This jarring detail emphasizes the significance of the whole. The play creates a world in which there is no relation whatsoever between the powers which rule the universe and the fundamental laws of human morality. It dramatizes disorder, not just the disorder of the family of Jason and Medea, but the disorder of the universe as a whole. It is the nightmare in which the dream of the fifth century was to end, the senseless fury and degradation of permanent violence. "Flow backward to your sources, sacred rivers," the chorus sings, "And let the world's great order be reversed."

### HIPPOLYTUS

Three years after the *Medea*, in 428 B.C., Euripides staged the *Hippolytus*; this was one of the rare occasions on which he was awarded the first prize. Like the *Medea* (and unlike *Agamem-*

*non, Antigone,* and *Oedipus*) the play deals with a private, domestic situation: the action and suffering of the characters does not affect the fate of a city. As in *Medea,* the driving force of the plot is love turned to hatred, but this time it is a guilty love, the passion a wife has conceived for her stepson. But no single character (like Medea) dominates the stage from beginning to end. The *Hippolytus* presents the tangled skein of relationships between four principal characters.

In another version of the play staged some years before, Euripides had included a scene in which Phaedra attempted to seduce Hippolytus and was rejected. In the present version the two never meet face to face, and the proposition is made by a go-between, Phaedra's old nurse. The scenes which lead up to this fatal step are masterly in their delineation of human psychology. We are shown how Phaedra's resolve to save her honor and to die in silence is broken down by her nurse's persistence, ending in her distracted, vaguely worded acquiescence in the nurse's thinly disguised intention to approach Hippolytus directly, an action which seals the fate of both principals. Phaedra, in telling of her struggles to overcome her passion, sums up her dilemma (and it is not hers alone) in a dispairing confession of human weakness: "We understand and recognize what things are good / but do not do them. . . ."

Hippolytus' furious, disgusted reaction to the nurse's proposal springs from a deep religious feeling, for his sexual abstinence is motivated by his devotion to the virgin huntress, the goddess Artemis. But his denunciation of women in general goes beyond what the circumstances call for; there is a pathological note in this violent diatribe. For Phaedra who overhears it there is now no recourse but suicide. To protect her honor, however, she must now silence Hippolytus. Her letter to Theseus, which accuses his son of an attempt on her virtue, will effectively counter any accusation he may make, and will also result in his punishment, to which Phaedra, her love now turned to hate, looks forward exultantly.

Hippolytus had been sworn to silence by the nurse before she revealed the secret of Phaedra's love; now, exposed defenseless to his father's anger, he respects his oath—he is, as he says, a man of religious reverence. His only defense is his reputation, but for Theseus the corpse of his wife and her letter accusing Hippolytus are proof enough, and he calls for the sea-god Poseidon to destroy his son.

This is a domestic tragedy, a dark tale of inbred passion and its bloody outcome, but it has also a larger dimension, not political but theological. On the stage throughout, at the door of the stage building which represents the palace of Theseus, stand the statutes of two goddesses, the two who open and close the play. Aphrodite, the divine personification and essence of sexual passion, speaks the prologue; what follows, Phaedra's delirium, her weakening and final numb acquiescence in the nurse's initiative, is the working of Aphrodite in her. And Hippolytus, his body shattered and his life almost at an end, is visited at the play's end by Artemis, Aphrodite's polar opposite, to whom he has dedicated his life. She comes to tell Theseus the truth and clear Hippolytus' honor, but she can bring no comfort to these broken men, father and son, who learn from Artemis that they are the victims, as Phaedra is too, of Aphrodite's terrible revenge. The only consolation Artemis can offer Hippolytus is the announcement that he will be the focus of an Athenian religious cult. Abandoned by the goddess he has served—"Easily now you leave our long companionship"—Hippolytus with his dying breath absolves his father of responsibility, an act of forgiveness of which human beings are capable but the gods are not, a purely human gesture in an inhuman universe.

### COMEDY

By the fifth century both tragedy and comedy were regularly produced at the winter festivals of the god Dionysus in Athens. Comedy, like tragedy, employed a chorus, that is to say, a group of dancers (who also sang) and actors, who wore masks; its tone was burlesque and parodic, though there was often a serious theme emphasized by the crude clowning and the free play of wit. The only comic poet of the fifth century whose work has survived is Aristophanes; in his thirteen extant comedies, produced over the years 425-388 B.C., the institu-

tions and personalities of his time are caricatured and criticized in a brilliant combination of poetry and obscenity, of farce and wit, which has no parallel in European literature. It can be described only in terms of itself, by the adjective "Aristophanic."

### LYSISTRATA

*Lysistrata*, which is outstanding among the Aristophanic comedies in its coherence of structure and underlying seriousness of theme, was first produced in 411 B.C. In 413 the news of the total destruction of the Athenian fleet in Sicily had reached Athens, and though heroic efforts to carry on the war were under way, the confidence in victory with which Athens had begun the war had gone forever. It is a recurring feature of Aristophanic comedy that the comic hero upsets the *status quo*, to produce a series of extraordinary results which are exploited to the full for their comic potential. In this play the Athenian women, who had no political rights, seize the Acropolis and leave the men without women. At the same time similar revolutions take place in all the Greek cities according to a coordinated plan. The men are eventually "starved" into submission and the Spartans come to Athens to end the war.

Aristophanes does not miss a trick in his exploitation of the possibilities for ribald humor inherent in this situation, a female sex-strike against war; Myrrhine's teasing game with her husband Cinesias, for example, is rare fooling and the final appearance of the uncomfortably rigid

Spartan ambassadors and their equally tense Athenian hosts is a visual and verbal climax of astonishing brilliance. But underneath all the fooling real issues are pursued, and they come to the surface with telling effect in the argument between Lysistrata and the magistrate who has been sent to suppress the revolt. Reversing the words of Hector to Andromache, which had become proverbial, Lysistrata claims that "War shall be the concern of Women!"—it is too important a matter to be left to men, for women are its real victims. And when asked what the women will do, she explains that they will treat politics just as they do wool in their household tasks: "when it's confused and snarled . . . draw out a thread here and a thread there . . . we'll unsnarl this war. . . ."

We do not know how the Athenians welcomed the play. All we know is that they were not impressed by its serious undertone; the war continued for seven more exhausting years, until Athens' last fleet was defeated, the city laid open to the enemy, the empire lost.

## SOCRATES

In the last half of the fifth century the whole traditional basis of individual conduct was undermined, gradually at first by the critical approach of the Sophists and their pupils, and then rapidly, as the war accelerated the process of moral disintegration. "In peace and prosperity," says Thucydides, "both states and individuals are actuated by higher motives . . . but war, which takes away the comfortable provision of daily life,

is a hard master, and tends to assimilate men's characters to their conditions." The war brought to Athens the rule of the new politicians, who reckoned only in terms of power, who carried out the massacre of Melos, and many of whom, like Alcibiades and Critias, betrayed their city for their own ends. Community and individual were no longer one, and the individual, cast on his own resources for guidance, found only conflicting attitudes which he could not refer to any absolute standards. The mood of postwar Athens oscillated between a fanatic, unthinking reassertion of traditional values and a weary cynicism which wanted only to be left alone. The only thing common to the two extremes was a distrust of intelligence.

In the disillusioned gloom of the years of defeat the Athenians began to feel more and more exasperation with a voice they had been listening to for many years, the voice of Socrates, a stonemason who for most of his adult life had made it his business to discuss with his fellow citizens the great issues of which the Athenians were now so weary—the nature of justice, of truth, of piety. Unlike the Sophists, he did not lecture nor did he charge a fee; his method was dialectic, the search for truth by a process of questions and answers, and his dedication to his mission had kept him poor. But the initial results of his discussions were often infuriatingly like the results of sophistic teaching. By questions and answers he succeeded in exposing the illogicality of his opponent's position, but Socrates did not often provide a substitute for the erroneous belief he had destroyed. Yet it is clear that he did believe in absolute standards, and what is more, he believed they could be discovered by a process of logical inquiry and supported by logical proof. His ethics rested on an intellectual basis. The resentment against him, which came to a head in 399 B.C., is partly explained by the fact that he satisfied neither extreme of the postwar mood. He questioned the old standards in order to establish new, and he refused to let the Athenians live in peace, for he preached that it was every man's duty to think his way through to the truth. In this last respect he was the prophet of the new age; for him the city and the accepted code were no substitute for the task of self-examination which each individual must set himself and carry through to a conclusion. The characteristic statement of the old Athens was public, in the assembly or the theater; Socrates proclaimed the right and duty of each individual to work out his own salvation and made clear his distrust of public life: "he who will fight for the right . . . must have a private station and not a public one."

Socrates himself wrote nothing; we know what we do about him mainly from the writings of his pupil Plato, a philosophical and literary genius of the first rank. It is very difficult to distinguish between what Socrates actually said and what Plato put into his mouth, but there is general agreement that the *Apology*, which Plato wrote as a representation of what Socrates said at his trial, is the clearest picture we have of the historical Socrates. He is on trial for impiety and "corrupting the youth." He deals with these charges, but he also takes the opportunity to present a defense and explanation of the mission to which his life has been devoted.

The *Apology* is a defiant speech; Socrates rides roughshod over legal forms and seems to neglect no opportunity of outraging his hearers. But this defiance is not stupidity (as he hints himself, he could, if he had wished, have made a speech to please the court), nor is it a deliberate courting of martyrdom. It is the only course possible for him in the circumstances if he is not to betray his life's work, for Socrates knows as well as his accusers that what the Athenians really want is to silence him without having to take his life. What Socrates is making clear is that there is no such easy way out; he will have no part of any compromise that would restrict his freedom of speech or undermine his moral position. The speech is a sample of what the Athenians will have to put up with if they allow him to live; he will continue to be the gadfly which stings the sluggish horse. He will go on persuading them not to be concerned for their persons or their property, but first and chiefly to care about the improvement of the soul. He has spent his life denying the validity of worldly standards, and he will not accept them now.

He was declared guilty, and condemned to death. While in prison awaiting execution, he was approached by a wealthy friend, Crito, who had made arrangements for his escape from Athens. In the dialogue *Crito*, Plato reconstructs the discussion between the two men. Socrates refused to escape, and the arguments put into his mouth in this dialogue show that although he rejected the political life and the unwavering adherence to one political system which it demanded, he still felt himself bound by the laws of the city. Unlike Alcibiades, the typical representative of the sophistic spirit, who betrayed his country when it had found him guilty of a crime, Socrates refused to disobey the laws even when they demanded his own death.

The sentence was duly carried out. And in Plato's account of the execution we can see the calmness and kindness of a man who has led a useful life and who is secure in his faith that, contrary to appearances, "no evil can happen to a good man, either in life or after death."

### THE DIFFUSION OF GREEK CULTURE

The century that followed the death of Socrates saw the exhaustion of the Greek city-states in constant internecine warfare. Politically and economically bankrupt, they fell under the power of the semibarbarous kingdom of Macedon, in the north, whose king, Philip, combined a ferocious energy with a cynicism which enabled him to take full advantage of the corrupt governments of the city-states. Greek liberty ended at the battle of Chaeronea in 338 B.C., and Philip's son Alexander inherited a powerful army and the political control of all Greece. He led his Macedonian and Greek armies against Persia, and in a few brilliant campaigns became master of an empire which extended into Egypt in the south and to the borders of India in the east. He died at Babylon in 323 B.C., and his empire broke up into a number of independent kingdoms ruled by his generals; but the results of his fantastic achievements were more durable than might have been expected. Into the newly conquered territories came thousands of Greeks who wished to escape from the political futility and economic crisis of the homeland. Wherever they went they took with them their language, their culture, and their typical buildings, the gymnasium and the theater. At Alexandria in Egypt, for example, a Greek library was formed to preserve the texts of Greek literature for the scholars who edited them, a school of Greek poetry flourished, Greek mathematicians and geographers made new advances in science. The Middle East became, as far as the cities were concerned, a Greek-speaking area; and when, some two or three centuries later, the first accounts of Christ's life and teaching were written down, they were written in Greek, the language on which the cultural homogeneity of the whole area was based.

## ROME

When Alexander died at Babylon in 323 B.C., the Italian city of Rome, situated on the Tiber in the western coastal plain, was engaged in a struggle for the control of central Italy. Less than a hundred years later

(269 B.C.) Rome, in control of the whole Italian peninsula, was drawn into a hundred-year war against the Phoenician city of Carthage, on the West African coast, from which she emerged mistress of the western Mediterranean. At the end of the first century B.C., in spite of a series of civil wars fought with savage vindictiveness and on a continental scale, Rome was the capital of an empire which stretched from the Straits of Gibraltar to the frontiers of Palestine. This empire gave peace and orderly government to the Mediterranean area for the next two centuries, and for two centuries after that maintained a desperate but losing battle against the invading savage tribes moving in from the north and east. When it finally went down, it left behind it the ideal of the world-state, an ideal which was to be reconstituted as a reality by the medieval church, which ruled from the same center, Rome, and with a spiritual authority as great as the secular authority it replaced.

The achievements of the Romans, not only their conquests but also their success in consolidating the conquests and organizing the conquered, are best understood in the light of the Roman character. Unlike the Greek, the Roman was above all a practical man. He might have no aptitude for pure mathematics, but he could build an aqueduct to last two thousand years; he was not notable as a political theorist, but he organized a complicated yet stable federation which held Italy loyal to him in the presence of invading armies. He was conservative to the core; his strongest authority was *mos maiorum*, the custom of his predecessors; a monument of this conservatism, the great body of Roman law, is one of his greatest contributions to Western civilization. The quality he most admired was *gravitas*, seriousness of attitude and purpose, and his highest words of commendation were "manliness," "industry," "discipline." Pericles, in his funeral speech, praised the Athenian for his adaptability, versatility, and grace; this would have seemed strange praise to a Roman, whose idea of personal and civic virtue was different. "By her ancient custom and her men the Roman state stands," says Ennius the Roman poet, in a line which by its metrical heaviness emphasizes the stability implied in the key word "stands": *moribus antiquis res stat Romana virisque.*

### LATIN LITERATURE— LUCRETIUS AND CICERO

Greek history begins, not with a king, a battle, or the founding of a city, but with an epic poem; the literary achievement preceded the political by many centuries. The Romans, on the other hand, had conquered half the world before they began to write. The stimulus to the creation of Latin literature was the Greek literature which the Romans discovered when, in the second century B.C., they assumed political responsibility for Greece and the Near East. Latin literature began with a translation of the *Odyssey*, made by a Greek prisoner of war, and with the exception of satire, until Latin literature became Christian, the model was always

Greek. The Latin writer (especially the poet) borrowed wholesale from his Greek original, not furtively, but openly and proudly, as a tribute to the master from whom he had learned. But this frank acknowledgment of indebtedness should not blind us to the fact that Latin literature is original, and sometimes profoundly so. Writing in the first century B.C., both Lucretius and Cicero, the one a poet and the other an orator and philosopher, followed Greek models in the works by which they are represented in this volume. Yet the results were not slavish imitations; each made what he borrowed peculiarly his own.

Lucretius' poem *On the Nature of Things* (*De rerum natura*) is a Latin presentation of the philosophical system of Epicurus, a Greek philosopher of the fourth century B.C. Epicurus had reacted to the hopelessness of his age, which saw the breakdown of the Greek city-states, by propounding a philosophy that described the universe as the result of blind combinations of atoms. With Epicurus the philosophy was not completely materialistic, for it allowed the existence of the gods, though it denied them any role in the government of the universe and asserted that they had no interest in human affairs. But in Lucretius' version, especially in his thoroughly materialistic account (in Book V) of the development of human civilization from primitive savagery, the gods play no part; far from creating man or his civilization, the gods are themselves created by humanity out of its dreams and ignorance.

The ethical precepts of Epicurus' philosophy are summed up in his famous admonition to pursue pleasure, which according to his definition, however, consisted in living a virtuous life. It is a philosophy which encourages a withdrawal from public life, and is in this respect a typical product of the political chaos of the fourth century. This is probably one of the reasons why it attracted Lucretius, for he too lived in an age of social conflict which every twenty years or so erupted in revolution and civil war. But it did not attract many Romans; their respect for action and their deep-rooted worship of duty were obstacles too great to be overcome even by Lucretius' great poetic power.

How great that power is can be seen in the conclusion of his third book, in which he draws the moral from his exposition of the atomic basis of phenomena, and proclaims that death is not to be feared. Death is merely not-being, a rearrangement of the atoms of which we are composed, the dead feel neither pleasure nor pain—so runs his argument, and if it were no more complicated than that it would be just a restatement, though admittedly a magnificent one, of an Epicurean commonplace. But as he develops the argument, we can detect beneath the authoritative calm of the teacher the cry of a man in an agony of doubt and fear. As we read Nature's speech to the coward who is afraid to die, we become increasingly aware that no one is more afraid of death than the poet himself. The vehemence and passion of these famous lines is the mark of a man trying to convince himself rather than his audience; the fears of the unenlightened, animal, part of the human being, which in the face of death will abandon everything except the will to live, are too vividly evoked to be stilled by Nature's argument. And the argument itself, that death is no more than the extinction of consciousness, is a frightening one, especially for an Epicurean, who narrows his ethical and intellectual concern to the restricted scope of his individual self, who "cultivates his garden," and who by his withdrawal from society rejects the corporate immortality of family, city, or race. Lucretius believes in the Epicurean system, but on this central point of the fear of death it brings him little comfort. The disturbance in the poet's own soul, expressed in the tension and violence of these great lines, has turned a philosophical sermon into great poetry.

Much more acceptable to the Roman temperament is the vision of a future life of happiness for those who have been outstanding in their service to the state which is the subject of Cicero's "Dream of Scipio." This is the final chapter of his great work *On the Republic* (*De republica*), the myth which concludes the philosophical discussion. The work as a whole is an imitation of Plato's *Republic*, which is also rounded off by a myth, the story told by Er, who returns from the dead and describes to the living the life of the souls, "the just going up the heavenly way to their reward, the unjust going down to the place of punishment." But Cicero's imitation is characteristically Roman. Instead of imagining, as Plato did, the ideal city, Cicero deals with the Roman republic, its birth, growth, and maturity, and his myth shows the same practical, social viewpoint that is the hallmark of Roman philosophy at its best. "But hold fast to this," says Scipio, Cicero's spokesman: "For all those who have guarded, aided, and increased the welfare of their fatherland there is a place reserved in heaven, where they shall dwell in happiness forever." Lucretius' desperate assertion that the individual must live for himself and accept the obliteration of his personality in death is counterpoised by a vision of an eternal heaven for those who devote themselves to the supreme duty, which, for the Roman, is the public duty.

### LATIN LITERATURE—VIRGIL

When Cicero wrote "The Dream of Scipio" the republican form of government which was his larger subject still existed, but its days were numbered. The institutions of the city-state proved inadequate for world government. The civil conflict which had disrupted the republic for more than a hundred years ended finally in the establishment of a powerful executive. Although the Senate, which had been the controlling body of the republic, retained an impressive share of the power, the new arrangement developed inevitably toward autocracy, the rule of the executive, the emperor, as he was called once the system was stabilized. The first of the long line of Roman emperors who gave stable government to the Roman world during the first two centuries A.D. was Octavius, known generally by his title, Augustus. He had made his way cautiously through the intrigues and bloodshed that followed the murder of his uncle Julius Caesar in 44 B.C., until by 31 B.C., he controlled the western half of the empire. In that year he fought a decisive battle with the ruler of the eastern half of the empire, Mark Antony, who was supported by Cleopatra, queen of Egypt. Octavius' victory at Actium united the empire under one authority and ushered in an age of peace and reconstruction. It was in the opening years of the new age that Virgil wrote (and left unfinished at his early death) the great Roman epic, the *Aeneid*.

Like all the Latin poets, Virgil built on the solid foundations of his Greek predecessors. The story of Aeneas, the Trojan prince who came to Italy and whose descendants founded Rome, combines the themes of the *Odyssey* (the wanderer in search of home) and the *Iliad* (the hero in battle). Virgil borrows Homeric turns of phrase, similes, sentiments, whole incidents: his Aeneas, like Achilles, sacrifices prisoners to the shade of a friend and, like Odysseus, descends alive to the world of the dead. But unlike Achilles, Aeneas does not satisfy the great passion of his life, nor, like Odysseus, does he find a home in which to end his days in peace. The personal objectives of both of Homer's heroes are sacrificed by Aeneas for a greater objective. There is something greater than himself. His mission,

imposed on him by the gods, is to found a city, from which, in the fullness of time, will spring the Roman state.

Homer presents us in the *Iliad* with the tragic pattern of the individual will, Achilles' wrath. But Aeneas is more than an individual. He is the prototype of the ideal Roman ruler; his qualities are the devotion to duty and the seriousness of purpose which were to give the Mediterranean world two centuries of ordered government. Aeneas' mission begins in disorder in the burning city of Troy, but he leaves it carrying his father on his shoulders and leading his little son by the hand. This famous picture emphasizes the fact that, unlike Achilles, he is securely set in a continuity of generations, the immortality of the family group, just as his mission to found a city, a home for the gods of Troy whose statues he carries with him, places him in a political and religious continuity. Achilles has no future. When he mentions his father and son, neither of whom he will see again, he emphasizes for us the loneliness of his short career; the brilliance of his life is that of a meteor which burns itself out to darkness. Odysseus has a father, wife, and son, and his heroic efforts are directed toward re-establishing himself in his proper context, that home in which he will be no longer man in a world of magic and terror, but man in an organized and continuous community. But he fights for himself. Aeneas, on the other hand, suffers and fights, not for himself but for the future; his own life is unhappy and his death miserable. Yet he can console himself with the glory of his sons to come, the pageant of Roman achievement which he is shown by his father in the world below and which he carries on his shield. Aeneas' future is Virgil's present; the consolidation of the Roman peace under Augustus is the reward of Aeneas' unhappy life of effort and suffering.

Summarized like this, the *Aeneid* sounds like propaganda, which, in one sense of the word, it is. What saves it from the besetting fault of even the best propaganda—the partial concealment of the truth—is the fact that Virgil maintains an independence of the power which he is celebrating and sees his hero in the round. He knows that the Roman ideal of devotion to duty has another side, the suppression of many aspects of the personality; that the man who wins and uses power must sacrifice much of himself, must live a life which, compared with that of Achilles or Odysseus, is constricted. In Virgil's poem Aeneas betrays the great passion of his life, his love for Dido, queen of Carthage. He does it reluctantly, but nevertheless he leaves her, and the full realization of what he has lost comes to him only when he meets her ghost in the world below. He weeps (as he did not at Carthage) and he pleads, in stronger terms than he did then, the overriding power which forced him to depart: "It was not of my own will, Dido, I left your land." She leaves him without a word, her silence as impervious to pleas and tears as his at Carthage once, and he follows her

weeping as she goes back to join her first love, her husband Sychaeus. He has sacrificed his love to something greater, but this does not insulate him from unhappiness. The limitations upon the dedicated man are emphasized by the contrasting figure of Dido, who follows her own impulse always, even in death. By her death, Virgil tells us expressly, she forestalls fate, breaks loose from the pattern in which Aeneas remains to the bitter end.

The angry reactions which this part of the poem has produced in many critics are the true measure of Virgil's success. Aeneas does act in such a way that he forfeits much of our sympathy, but this is surely exactly what Virgil intended. The Dido episode is not, as many critics have supposed, a flaw in the great design, a case of Virgil's sympathy outrunning his admiration for Aeneas; it is Virgil's emphatic statement of the sacrifice which the Roman ideal of duty demands. Aeneas' sacrifice is so great that few of us could make it ourselves, and none of us can contemplate it in another without a feeling of loss. It is an expression of the famous Virgilian sadness which informs every line of the *Aeneid* and which makes a poem that was in its historical context a command performance into the great epic which has dominated Western literature ever since.

### JESUS OF NAZARETH

In the last years of Augustus' life, in the Roman province of Judea, there was born to Joseph, a carpenter of Nazareth, and his wife, Mary, a son who was at once the final product of an old tradition and the starting point of a new. He was the last of the Hebrew prophets, but his message, unlike theirs, was to spread outside the boundaries of Palestine until it became the religion of the Roman Empire. His life on earth was short; it ended in the agony of crucifixion at about his thirty-third year. This event is a point of intersection of the three main lines of development of the ancient world—Hebrew, Greek, and Latin—for this Hebrew prophet was executed by a Roman governor, and his life and teachings were written down in the Greek language. These documents, which eventually, with some additions, constituted what we now know as the New Testament, circulated in the Greek-speaking half of the Roman Empire and later, in a Latin translation, in the West. They became the sacred texts of a church which, at first persecuted by and then triumphantly associated with Roman imperial power, outlasted the destruction of the empire and ruled over a spiritual kingdom which still exists.

The teaching of Christ was revolutionary not only in terms of Greek and Roman feeling but also in terms of the Hebrew religious tradition. The Hebrew idea of a personal God who is yet not anthropomorphic, who is omnipotent, omniscient, and infinitely just, was now broadened to include an infinite mercy which tempered the justice. Greek and Roman religion was outward and visible, the formal practice of ritual acts in a social context; Christianity was inward and spiritual, the important relationship was that between the individual soul and God. All human beings were on an equal plane in the eyes of their Creator. This idea ran counter to the theory and practice of an institution basic to the economy of the ancient world, slavery. Christ was rejected by his own people, as prophets have always been, and his death on the cross and his resurrection provided his followers and the future converts with an unforgettable symbol of a new dispensation, the son of God in human form suffering to atone for the sins of humanity, the supreme expression of divine mercy. This conception is the basis of the teaching of Paul, the apostle to the gentiles, who in the middle years of the first century A.D. changed Christianity from a Jewish sect to a world-wide movement with flourishing churches all over Asia Minor and Greece, and even in Rome. The burden of his teaching was the frailty and corruption of this life and world, and the certainty of resurrection. "For this corruptible must put on incorruption, and this mortal must put on immortality." To those who had accepted this vision the secular materialism which was the dominant view in the new era of peace and progress guaranteed by the stabilization of Roman rule was no longer tenable.

### LATIN LITERATURE—PETRONIUS

The pragmatic outlook which Christianity was to supplant is to be seen most clearly portrayed in the satiric masterpiece of the Roman aristocrat Petronius. The work which is attributed to him, the *Satyricon*, was probably written during the principate of Nero (A.D. 54-68), a period in which the material benefits and the spiritual weakness of the new order had already become apparent. The *Satyricon* itself has survived only in fragments; we know nothing certain about the scope of the work as a whole, but from the fragments it is clear that this book is the work of a satiric genius, perhaps the most original genius of Latin literature.

"Dinner with Trimalchio," one of the longer fragments, selections from which are included here, shows us a tradesman's world. The narrator, a student of literature, and his cronies may have an aristocratic disdain for the businessmen at whose tables they eat, but they know that Trimalchio and his kind have inherited the earth. Trimalchio began life as a foreign slave, but he is now a multimillionaire. The representative of culture, Agamemnon the teacher, drinks his wine and praises his fatuous remarks; he is content to be the court jester, the butt of Trimalchio's witticisms. Trimalchio knows no god but Mercury, the patron of business operations, but the gold bracelet, a percentage of his income which he has dedicated to Mercury, he wears on his own arm. He identifies himself with the god, and worships himself, the living embodiment of the power of money. The conversation at his table is a sardonic revelation of the temper of a whole civilization. Written in brilliantly humorous and colloquial style it exposes mercilessly a blindness to spiritual values of any kind, a distrust of the intellect, and a ferocious preoccupation with the art of cheating one's neighbor. The point is made more effective by the conscious evocation of the epic tradition throughout the work. The names alone of the teacher, Agamemnon, and his assistant in instruction, Menelaus; the wall paintings which show "the Iliad and the Odyssey and the gladiator's show given by Laenas"; Trimalchio's exhibition of monstrous ignorance of Homer (which nobody dares to correct); the Nestorian tone of Ganymede, who regrets the old days when men were men (he is talking of the time when Safinius forced the bakers to lower the price of bread)—one touch after another reminds us that these figures are the final product of a tradition that began with Achilles and Odysseus.

The satire is witty, but it is nonetheless profound. All of them live for the moment, in material enjoyment, but they know that it cannot last. "Let us remember the living" is their watchword, but they cannot forget the dead. And as the banquet goes on, the thought of death, suppressed beneath the debased Epicureanism of Trimalchio and his associates, emerges slowly to the surface of their consciousness and comes to dominate it completely. The last arrival at the banquet is Habinnas the undertaker, and his coming coincides with the last stage of Trimalchio's drunkenness, the maudlin exhibition of his funeral clothes and the description of his tomb. "I would that I were dead," says the Sibyl in the story Trimalchio tells early in the evening; at its end he himself acts out his own funeral, complete with ointment, robes, wine, and trumpet players. The fact of death, the one fact which the practical materialism of Trimalchio and his circle can neither deny nor assimilate, asserts itself triumphantly as the supreme fact in the emptiness of Trimalchio's mind.

### ST. AUGUSTINE

When Augustine was born in North Africa in A.D. 354, the era of Roman peace was already over. The invading barbarians had pierced the empire's defenses and were increasing their pressure every year. The economic basis of the empire was cracking under the strain of the enormous taxation needed to support the army; the land was exhausted. The empire was Christian, but the Church was split, beset by heresies and organized heretical sects. The empire was about to go down to destruction, and there was every prospect that the Church would go down with it.

Augustine, one of the men responsible for the consolidation of the Church in the West, especially for the systematization of its doctrine and policy, was not converted to Christianity until he had reached middle life. "Late have I loved Thee, O Beauty so ancient and so new," he says in his *Confessions* (A.D. 399), written long after his conversion. The lateness of his conversion and his regret for his wasted youth were among the sources of the energy which drove him to assume the intellectual leadership of the Western Church and to guarantee, by combating heresy on the one hand and laying new ideological foundations for Christianity on the other, the Church's survival through the dark centuries to come. Augustine had been brought up in the literary and philosophical tradition of the classical world, and it is partly because of his assimilation of classical literature and method to Christian training and teaching that the literature of the ancient world survived at all when Roman power collapsed in a welter of bloodshed and destruction which lasted for generations.

In his *Confessions* he set down, for the benefit of others, the story of his early life and his conversion to Christianity. This is, as far as we know, the first authentic ancient autobiography, and that fact itself is a significant expression of the Christian spirit, which proclaims the value of the individual soul and the importance of its relation with God. Throughout the *Confessions* Augustine talks directly to God, in humility, yet conscious that God is concerned for him personally. At the same time he comes to an understanding of his own feelings and development as a human being which marks his *Confessions* as one of the great literary documents of the Western world. His description of his childhood is the only detailed account of the childhood of a great man which antiquity has left us, and his accurate observation and keen perception are informed by the Hebrew and Christian idea of the sense of sin. "So small a boy and so great a sinner"—from the beginning of his narrative to the end Augustine sees man not as the Greek at his most optimistic tended to see him, the center and potential master of the universe, but as a child, wandering in ignorance, capable of reclamation only through the divine mercy which waits eternally for him to turn to it.

In Augustine are combined the intellectual tradition of the ancient world at its best and the religious feeling which was characteristic of the Middle Ages. The transition from the old world to the new can be seen in his pages; his analytical intellect pursues its Odyssey through strange and scattered islands— the mysticism of the Manichees,

the skepticism of the Academic philosophers, the fatalism of the astrologers—until he finds his home in the Church, to which he was to render such great service. His account of his conversion in the garden at Milan records the true moment of transition from the ancient to the medieval world. The innumerable defeats and victories, the burning towns and ravaged farms, the bloodshed, dates, and statistics of the end of an era are all illuminated and ordered by this moment in the history of the human spirit. Here is the point of change itself.

## LIVES, WRITINGS, AND CRITICISM

*Biographical and critical works are listed only if they are available in English.*

### THE BIBLE

Our selections are from the Authorized (King James) version which was published in 1611. In spite of its archaisms and occasional obscurities, it is one of the greatest monuments of English prose, and its influence on all subsequent writers of English is incalculable. For a modern version (which incorporates the findings of modern scholarship and discoveries), see *The New English Bible* (1970).

For background: S. Cook, *An Introduction to the Bible* (1950); *The Cambridge History of the Bible*, edited by R. R. Ackroyd and C. F. Evans, Vol I (1970); R. H. Rowley, *The Growth of the Old Testament* (1950); M. S. Enslin, *Christian Beginnings* (1938); and C. K. Barrett, *The New Testament Background: Selected Documents* (1956).

### GREECE—GENERAL

Sir Alfred Zimmern, *The Greek Commonwealth* (1922; frequently re-issued) is a stimulating account of Greek geography, economy, and political practice. For a good one-volume history see J. B. Bury, *History of Greece*, revised by R. Meiggs (4th edition 1975). See also H. D. F. Kitto, *The Greeks* (1951); C. M. Bowra, *The Greek Experience* (1957); M. I. Finley, *The Ancient Greeks* (1963); and A. Andrewes, *The Greeks* (1967).

### HOMER

LIFE AND WRITINGS. Nothing whatsoever is known about Homer's life. The traditional date for the composition of

the poems is ca. 850 B.C., though the tendency of modern scholarship is to prefer a much later date. On the "Homeric problem," see *The Making of Homeric Verse*, edited by A. Parry (1971); *The Songs of Homer*, G. S. Kirk (1962); *Homer and the Epic*, G. S. Kirk (1965)—a shortened version of *The Songs;* M. I. Finley *The World of Odysseus* (Revised edition 1978); C. M. Bowra, *Homer* (1972).

CRITICISM. *Iliad*. J. P. Shephard, *The Pattern of the Iliad* (1922); C. M. Bowra, *Tradition and Design in the Iliad* (1930); C. H. Whitman, *Homer and the Heroic Tradition* (1958); G. Steiner and R. Fagles, *Homer, A Collection of Critical Essays* (1962); James M. Redfield, *Nature and Culture in the Iliad* (1975); *Essays on the Iliad*, edited by J. Wright (1978); D. L. Page, *History and the Homeric Iliad* (1959). See also Richmond Lattimore's introduction to his translation, *The Iliad of Homer* (1951).

*Odyssey. Essays on the Odyssey*, edited by C. H. Taylor, Jr. (1963); H. W. Clarke, *The Art of the Odyssey* (1967).

### GREEK THEATER

For information about the theater— scenery, machinery, actors, audience, etc. —see A. W. Pickard-Cambridge, *The Theatre of Dionysus* (1946) and *The Dramatic Festivals of Athens*, 2d ed., revised by J. Gould and D. M. Lewis (1968); M. Bieber, *The History of the Greek and Roman Theater*, 2d ed. (1961); T. B. L. Webster, *Greek Thea-*

*tre Production* (1956); and P. Arnott, *Greek Scenic Conventions* (1962). *Illustrations of Greek Drama.* A. D. Trendall and T. B. L. Webster (1971). Critical works on the plays: H. D. F. Kitto, *Greek Tragedy, A Literary Study,* 3d ed. (1961); D. W. Lucas, *The Greek Tragic Poets,* 2d ed. (1959); T. G. Rosenmeyer, *The Masks of Tragedy* (1963); R. Lattimore, *The Poetry of Greek Tragedy* (1958). John Jones, *Aristotle and Greek Tragedy* (1962). *The Greek Tragic Theatre,* H. C. Baldry (1971). *Greek Drama in its Theatrical and Social Context,* P. Walcot (1976).

### AESCHYLUS

LIFE AND WRITINGS. Born in 524? B.C. He fought at Marathon against the Persians in 490 B.C. Among his plays are *The Persians* (472 B.C.); *The Seven against Thebes* (467 B.C.); the *Oresteia* (*Agamemnon, Choephoroe, Eumenides,* 458 B.C.). He died in Sicily in 456 B.C. His other surviving plays are *The Suppliants* and *Prometheus Bound.*

For a translation of the whole trilogy and an excellent introduction see Richmond Lattimore's *Oresteia of Aeschylus* (1953). A more recent translation is by R. Fagles. *Aeschylus. The Oresteia* (1977). Also noteworthy are *Seven Against Thebes,* Anthony Hecht and Helen Bacon and *Suppliants,* Janet Lembke.

CRITICISM. H. Weir Smith, *Aeschylean Tragedy* (1924); Gilbert Murray, *Aeschylus, Creator of Tragedy* (1940); and E. T. Owen, *The Harmony of Aeschylus* (1952). *Aeschylus. A Collection of Critical Essays,* edited by M. H. McCall (1972).

### THUCYDIDES

LIFE AND WRITINGS. The only certain date in his biography is 424 B.C., the year in which he was exiled from Athens because of a failure as general in the north of Greece. He gives an account of his unsuccessful campaign in Book IV, Chapters 103-109, of his *History of the Peloponnesian War,* and mentions his exile in Book V, Chapter 26. He probably returned to Athens after the defeat in 404 B.C., but he did not live long enough to complete his history of the war; his book ends with the events of the year 411 B.C.

A translation by Benjamin Jowett of the complete work is included in *The Greek Historians,* edited by F. R. B. Godolphin, Vol. I (1942). There are also translations by R. Crawley (1876, reprinted 1934) and R. Warner (1954).

CRITICISM. J. H. Finley, Jr., *Thucydides* (1947); and F. E. Adcock, *Thucydides and his History* (1963).

### SOPHOCLES

LIFE AND WRITINGS. Born in 495 B.C. He was victorious over Aeschylus in the dramatic contest in 468 B.C. In 440

B.C. he was appointed one of ten generals for the expedition against Samos. He died in 406 B.C. His plays are *Antigone* (441? B.C.); *Ajax; King Oedipus* (*Oedipus Tyrannus*); *Electra; Trachiniae; Philoctetes* (409 B.C.); *Oedipus at Colonus* (produced after his death, 401 B.C.).

The standard edition in English, by Sir Richard C. Jebb, consists of seven separate volumes (1884-1896), each containing a careful prose translation. More recent translations are to be found in *The Complete Greek Tragedies,* edited by D. Grene and R. Lattimore (1957– ); H. D. F. Kitto, *Sophocles, Three Tragedies* (1962); T. H. Banks, *Three Theban Plays* (1956); B. M. W. Knox, *Oedipus the King* (1959). L. Berkowitz and T. Brunner, *Oedipus Tyrannus* (1970); and S. Berg and D. Clay, *Oedipus the King* (1978).

CRITICISM. C. M. Bowra, *Sophoclean Tragedy* (1944); C. H. Whitman, *Sophocles, A Study in Heroic Humanism* (1951); S. M. Adams, *Sophocles the Playwright* (1957); A. J. A. Waldock, *Sophocles the Dramatist* (1951); B. M. W. Knox, *Oedipus at Thebes* (1957) and *The Heroic Temper* (1964); L. Berkowitz and T. Brunner, *Oedipus Tyrannus* (1970); T. B. L. Webster, *An Introduction to Sophocles* (2nd edition 1969); H. D. F. Kitto, *Sophocles: Dramatist and Philosopher* (1958); G. M. Kirkwood, *A Study of Sophoclean Drama* (1958); V. Ehrenberg, *Sophocles and Pericles* (1954); *Sophocles: A Collection of Critical Essays,* edited by T. Woodward (1966); and G. H. Gellie, *Sophocles: A Reading* (1972).

### EURIPIDES

LIFE AND WRITINGS. Born in 480 B.C. His first dramatic victory was in 441 B.C. Among his plays are *Alcestis,* 438 B.C.; *Medea,* 431 B.C.; *Hippolytus,* 428 B.C.; *Trojan Women,* 415 B.C.; *Orestes,* 408 B.C. Some time after this he left Athens for Macedonia, where he died in 406 B.C. The *Bacchae* and *Iphigenia at Aulis* were produced at Athens after his death. Eighteen of his plays have been preserved. For translations see *The Complete Greek Tragedies* (1957– ) and the versions by P. Vellacott in the Penguin Series. Also R. Warner, *Three Great Plays of Euripides* (1958).

CRITICISM. G. M. A. Grube, *The Drama of Euripides* (1941); D. J. Conacher, *Euripidean Drama* (1967); *Euripides, A Collection of Critical Essays,* edited by E. Segal (1968); B. M. W. Knox, 'The *Medea* of Euripides' and P. E. Easterling "The Infanticide in Euripides *Medea*' both in *Yale Classical Studies* 25 (1977).

### ARISTOPHANES

LIFE AND WRITINGS. Born around 450 B.C. Eleven of his comedies have survived; among the most famous are *The Clouds* (423 B.C.), *The Birds* (414 B.C.), and *The Frogs* (405 B.C.). He died around 385 B.C.

CRITICISM. G. Murray *Aristophanes, A Study* (1933); G. Norwood, *Greek Comedy* (1931) K. Lever, *The Art of Greek Comedy* (1956); C. H. Whitman, *Aristophanes and the Comic Hero* (1964); and K. J. Dover *Aristophanic Comedy* (1972).

### PLATO

LIFE. Born in Athens in 429 or 428 B.C. He was present at the trial of Socrates, his teacher, in 399 B.C. After this he traveled widely, eventually returning to Athens to found his philosophical school, the Academy. He made two visits to Sicily to act as philosophical and political tutor to the younger Dionysius, tyrant of Syracuse, but both of these interventions in practical affairs were unfortunate. He died in 347 B.C.

WRITINGS. The whole of his work is preserved; all of his writings except the last, *The Laws*, are dialogues in which Socrates is the chief speaker. A complete translation is Benjamin Jowett, *The Dialogues of Plato* (1925). The best translation of Plato's most famous work, *The Republic*, is by F. M. Cornford (1945). Translations by Percy Bysshe Shelley of the *Ion* and *Symposium* are to be found in *Five Dialogues of Plato*, Everyman's Library (1952).

CRITICISM. A. E. Taylor, *Plato, The Man and His Work* (1927); G. M. A. Grube, *Plato's Thought* (1935); R. S. Brumbaugh, *Plato for the Modern Age* (1962).

### ARISTOTLE

LIFE. Born at Stagira (Macedonia) in 384 B.C. In 367 B.C. he went to Athens and became a pupil of Plato at the Academy. He left Athens in 347 B.C. (the year Plato died), spent some years in the Greek cities of Asia Minor, and in 342 B.C. went to Macedonia as tutor to the young Alexander, then thirteen years of age. In 335 B.C., when Alexander succeeded to the throne of Macedonia, Aristotle returned to Athens, where he founded a school, the Lyceum. He directed the school, lecturing and writing, until 323 BC.., the year of Alexander's death at Babylon. Aristotle himself died at Chalcis, in Euboea, in the next year.

WRITINGS. His writings cover almost the whole field of human knowledge. Among the subjects he treated are logic, rhetoric, literary criticism, physics, metaphysics, politics, mathematics, meteorology, zoology, and history. For the complete works see the Oxford translation, completed in 1931. For the *Poetics*, see Ingram Bywater, *Aristotle on the Art of Poetry* (1909); and S. H. Butcher, *Aristotle's Theory of Poetry and the Fine Arts* (1907).

CRITICISM. Werner Jaeger, *Aristotle*, (1936); *Aristotle's Poetics*, with an introductory essay by Francis Fergusson (1961); and H. House, *Aristotle's Poetics* (1961).

### ROME—GENERAL

For a good one-volume history of Rome see M. Cary, *History of Rome* (1938): and R. H. Barrow, *The Romans* (1949).

### LUCRETIUS

LIFE AND WRITINGS. Titus Lucretius Carus, born about 99 B.C. He died in 55 B.C., a suicide, according to rumor. His only work is the didactic poem *On the Nature of Things (De rerum natura)*, a philosophical poem in six books The best edition (with prose translation) is by C. Bailey, 3 vol. (1946). For a verse translation of the whole poem see *Lucretius, The Way Things Are*, R. Humphries (1969).

CRITICISM. E. E. Sikes, *Lucretius, Poet and Philosopher* (1936).

### CICERO

LIFE AND WRITINGS. Marcus Tullius Cicero, born in 106 B.C. He studied at Athens, went into law, and soon became prominent in politics. In 70 B.C. he successfully pleaded the case of the Sicilians against Verres, a corrupt governor. In 63 B.C. he attained the highest republican office, the consulate, and during his term put down forcibly an insurrection led by Catiline. Later, a reaction against his policies caused him to retire from Rome; he returned in 55 B.C. When the civil war broke out in 49 B.C., he took sides with Pompey against Julius Caesar: after Pompey's defeat and death he was pardoned and returned to Rome. After Caesar's murder in 44 B.C. Cicero led the opposition against Caesar's lieutenant, Antony, and he was murdered in 43 B.C. at Antony's orders. He has left a great number of speeches, both forensic and political, which have served as models for Western oratory ever since; philosophical works, in which he made available to the Latin-speaking (and medieval) world the achievements of Greek philosophy; works on rhetoric; and a huge collection of private letters, which give a fascinating and uncensored picture of his life and times. Translations of almost all of his works are to be found in the Loeb Classical Library.

BIOGRAPHY AND CRITICISM. D. R. Shackleton Bailey, *Cicero* (1971) and M. Grant, *Cicero: Selected Works* (1960).

### VIRGIL

LIFE AND WRITINGS. Publius Virgilius Maro, born in 79 B.C. in the north of Italy. Very little is known about his life. The earliest work which is certainly his is the *Bucolics*, a collection of poems in the pastoral genre which have had enormous influence. These were followed by the *Georgics*, a didactic poem on farming, in four books, which many critics consider his finest work. The *Aeneid*, the Roman epic, was left unfinished at his early death in 19 B.C. Translations: C. Day Lewis, *The Georgics* (1940) and *The Aeneid* (1952) and A. Mandelbaum, *The Aeneid* (1971).

CRITICISM. W. F. J. Knight, *Roman Vergil* (1944); V. Pöschl, *The Art of Vergil* (1962); B. Otis, *Virgil, A Study in Civilized Poetry* (1963); M. C. J. Putnam, *The Poetry of the Aeneid* (1965); W. A. Camps, *An Introduction to Virgil's Aeneid* (1969); and *Virgil: A Collection of Critical Essays*, edited by Steele Commager (1966).

**PETRONIUS**

LIFE AND WRITINGS. It is not certain that Titus Petronius (Arbiter) was the author of the *Satyricon*, but he is the best candidate. A friend of Nero's, he committed suicide at the imperial order after becoming involved in the Pisonian conspiracy against the emperor in 65 A.D. A brilliant account of Petronius' character and death is given by Tacitus in the eighteenth and nineteenth chapters of Book XVI of the *Annals*.

For another recent translation with a critical introduction, see W. Arrowsmith, *The Satyricon of Petronius* (1959).

**ST. AUGUSTINE**

LIFE AND WRITINGS. Aurelius Augustinus, born in 354 A.D. at Tagaste, in North Africa. He was baptized as a Christian in 387 A.D. and ordained bishop of Hippo, in North Africa, in 395 A.D. When he died there in 430 A.D., the city was besieged by Gothic invaders. Besides the *Confessions* (*Confessiones*, written in 397 A.D.) he wrote *The City of God* (*De civitate dei*, finished in 426 A.D.) and many polemical works against schismatics and heretics. Translations of *The City of God* may be found in Everyman's Library and also in the Loeb Classical Library, which also includes some of his letters. For criticism and biography, see P. Brown, *Augustine of Hippo* (1967).

# The Old Testament*

*Genesis 1–3. [The Creation—The Fall]*

1. In the beginning God created the heaven and the earth. And the earth was without form, and void; and darkness was upon the face of the deep. And the Spirit of God moved upon the face of the waters.

And God said, Let there be light: and there was light. And God saw the light, that it was good· and God divided the light from the darkness. And God called the light Day, and the darkness he called Night. And the evening and the morning were the first day.

And God said, Let there be a firmament in the midst of the waters,[1] and let it divide the waters from the waters. And God made the firmament, and divided the waters which were under the firmament from the waters which were above the firmament: and it was so. And God called the firmament Heaven. And the evening and the morning were the second day.

And God said, Let the waters under the heaven be gathered together unto one place, and let the dry land appear: and it was so. And God called the dry land Earth; and the gathering together of the waters called he Seas: and God saw that it was good And God said, Let the earth bring forth grass, the herb yielding seed, and the fruit tree yielding fruit after his kind, whose seed is in itself, upon the earth: and it was so. And the earth brought forth grass, and herb yielding seed after his kind, and the tree yielding fruit, whose seed was in itself, after his kind: and God saw that it was good. And the evening and the morning were the third day.

And God said, Let there be lights in the firmament of the heaven to divide the day from the night; and let them be for signs, and for seasons, and for days, and years: and let them be for lights in the firmament of the heaven to give light upon the earth: and it was so. And God made two great lights; the greater light to rule the day, and the lesser light to rule the night: he made the stars also. And God set them in the firmament of the heaven to give light upon the earth, and to rule over the day and over the night, and to divide the light from the darkness: and God saw that it was good. And the evening and the morning were the fourth day. And God said, Let the waters bring forth abundantly the moving creature that hath life, and fowl[2] that may fly above the earth in the open firmament of heaven. And God created great whales, and every living creature that moveth,

---

* The text of these selections from the Holy Bible is that of the King James, or Authorized, Version.

1. The firmament is the sky, which seen from below has the appearance of a ceiling: the waters above it are those which come down in the form of rain.

2. winged creatures of all kinds.

which the waters brought forth abundantly, after their kind, and every winged fowl after his kind: and God saw that it was good. And God blessed them, saying, Be fruitful, and multiply, and fill the waters in the seas, and let fowl multiply in the earth. And the evening and the morning were the fifth day.

And God said, Let the earth bring forth the living creature after his kind, cattle, and creeping thing, and beast of the earth after his kind: and it was so. And God made the beast of the earth after his kind, and cattle after their kind, and everything that creepeth upon the earth after his kind: and God saw that it was good.

And God said, Let us make man in our image, after our likeness: and let them have dominion over the fish of the sea, and over the fowl of the air, and over the cattle, and over all the earth, and over every creeping thing that creepeth upon the earth. So God created man in his own image, in the image of God created he him; male and female created he them. And God blessed them, and God said unto them, Be fruitful, and multiply, and replenish the earth, and subdue it: and have dominion over the fish of the sea, and over the fowl of the air, and over every living thing that moveth upon the earth.

And God said, Behold, I have given you every herb bearing seed, which is upon the face of all the earth, and every tree, in the which is the fruit of a tree yielding seed; to you it shall be for meat. And to every beast of the earth, and to every fowl of the air, and to every thing that creepeth upon the earth, wherein there is life, I have given every green herb for meat: and it was so. And God saw every thing that he had made, and, behold, it was very good. And the evening and the morning were the sixth day.

2. Thus the heavens and the earth were finished, and all the host of them. And on the seventh day God ended his work which he had made; and he rested on the seventh day from all his work which he had made. And God blessed the seventh day, and sanctified it: because that in it he had rested from all his work which God created and made.

These are the generations of the heavens and of the earth when they were created,[3] in the day that the Lord God made the earth and the heavens, and every plant of the field before it was in the earth, and every herb of the field before it grew: for the Lord God had not caused it to rain upon the earth, and there was not a man to till the ground. But there went up a mist from the earth, and watered the whole face of the ground. And the Lord God formed

---

3. This is the beginning of a different account of the Creation, which does not agree in all respects with the first.

man of the dust of the ground, and breathed into his nostrils the breath of life; and man became a living soul.

And the Lord God planted a garden eastward in Eden; and there he put the man whom he had formed. And out of the ground made the Lord God to grow every tree that is pleasant to the sight, and good for food; the tree of life also in the midst of the garden, and the tree of knowledge of good and evil. And a river went out of Eden to water the garden; and from thence it was parted, and became into four heads. The name of the first is Pison: that is it which compasseth the whole land of Havilah, where there is gold; and the gold of that land is good: there is bdellium and the onyx stone. And the name of the second river is Gihon: the same is it that compasseth the whole land of Ethiopia. And the name of the third river is Hiddekel: that is it which goeth toward the east of Assyria. And the fourth river is Euphrates. And the Lord God took the man, and put him into the garden of Eden to dress it and to keep it. And the Lord God commanded the man, saying, Of every tree of the garden thou mayest freely eat: but of the tree of the knowledge of good and evil, thou shalt not eat of it: for in the day that thou eatest thereof thou shalt surely die.

And the Lord God said, It is not good that the man should be alone; I will make him an help meet for him. And out of the ground the Lord God formed every beast of the field, and every fowl of the air; and brought them unto Adam to see what he would call them: and whatsoever Adam called every living creature, that was the name thereof. And Adam gave names to all cattle, and to the fowl of the air, and to every beast of the field; but for Adam there was not found an help meet for him. And the Lord God caused a deep sleep to fall upon Adam, and he slept: and he took one of his ribs, and closed up the flesh instead thereof; and the rib, which the Lord God had taken from man, made he a woman, and brought her unto the man. And Adam said, This is now bone of my bones, and flesh of my flesh: she shall be called Woman, because she was taken out of Man. Therefore shall a man leave his father and his mother, and shall cleave unto his wife: and they shall be one flesh. And they were both naked, the man and his wife, and were not ashamed.

3. Now the serpent was more subtil than any beast of the field which the Lord God had made. And he said unto the woman, Yea, hath God said, Ye shall not eat of every tree of the garden? And the woman said unto the serpent, We may eat of the fruit of the trees of the garden: but of the fruit of the tree which is in the midst of the garden, God hath said, Ye shall not eat of it, neither shall ye touch it, lest ye die. And the serpent said unto the woman, Ye shall not surely die: for God doth know that in the day ye eat

thereof, then your eyes shall be opened, and ye shall be as gods, knowing good and evil. And when the woman saw that the tree was good for food, and that it was pleasant to the eyes, and a tree to be desired to make one wise, she took the fruit thereof, and did eat, and gave also unto her husband with her; and he did eat. And the eyes of them both were opened, and they knew that they were naked; and they sewed fig leaves together, and made themselves aprons. And they heard the voice of the Lord God walking in the garden in the cool of the day: and Adam and his wife hid themselves from the presence of the Lord God amongst the trees of the garden. And the Lord God called unto Adam, and said unto him, Where art thou? And he said, I heard thy voice in the garden, and I was afraid, because I was naked; and I hid myself. And he said, Who told thee that thou wast naked? Hast thou eaten of the tree, whereof I commanded thee that thou shouldest not eat? And the man said, The woman whom thou gavest to be with me, she gave me of the tree, and I did eat. And the Lord God said unto the woman, What is this that thou hast done? And the woman said, The serpent beguiled me, and I did eat. And the Lord God said unto the serpent, Because thou hast done this, thou art cursed above all cattle, and above every beast of the field; upon thy belly shalt thou go, and dust shalt thou eat all the days of thy life: and I will put enmity between thee and the woman, and between thy seed and her seed; it shall bruise thy head, and thou shalt bruise his heel. Unto the woman he said, I will greatly multiply thy sorrow and thy conception; in sorrow thou shalt bring forth children; and thy desire shall be to thy husband, and he shall rule over thee. And unto Adam he said, Because thou hast hearkened unto the voice of thy wife, and hast eaten of the tree, of which I commanded thee, saying, Thou shalt not eat of it: cursed is the ground for thy sake; in sorrow shalt thou eat of it all the days of thy life; thorns also and thistles shall it bring forth to thee; and thou shalt eat the herb of the field; in the sweat of thy face shalt thou eat bread, till thou return unto the ground; for out of it wast thou taken: for dust thou art, and unto dust shalt thou return. And Adam called his wife's name Eve; because she was the mother of all living. Unto Adam also and to his wife did the Lord God make coats of skins, and clothed them.

And the Lord God said, Behold, the man is become as one of us, to know good and evil: and now, lest he put forth his hand, and take also of the tree of life, and eat, and live forever: therefore the Lord God sent him forth from the garden of Eden, to till the ground from whence he was taken. So he drove out the man; and he placed at the east of the garden of Eden Cherubims, and a flaming sword which turned every way, to keep the way of the tree of life.

*Genesis 4. [The First Murder]*

4. And Adam knew Eve his wife; and she conceived, and bare Cain, and said, I have gotten a man from the Lord. And she again bare his brother Abel. And Abel was a keeper of sheep, but Cain was a tiller of the ground. And in process of time it came to pass, that Cain brought of the fruit of the ground an offering unto the Lord. And Abel, he also brought of the firstlings of his flock and of the fat thereof. And the Lord had respect unto Abel and to his offering: But unto Cain and to his offering he had not respect. And Cain was very wroth,[1] and his countenance fell. And the Lord said unto Cain, Why art thou wroth? and why is thy countenance fallen? If thou doest well, shalt thou not be accepted? and if thou doest not well, sin lieth at the door. And unto thee shall be his desire, and thou shall rule over him.[2] And Cain talked with Abel his brother: and it came to pass, when they were in the field, that Cain rose up against Abel his brother, and slew him.

And the Lord said unto Cain, Where is Abel thy brother? And he said, I know not: Am I my brother's keeper? And he said, What hast thou done? the voice of thy brother's blood crieth unto me from the ground. And now art thou cursed from the earth, which hath opened her mouth to receive thy brother's blood from thy hand; When thou tillest the ground, it shall not henceforth yield unto thee her strength; a fugitive and a vagabond shalt thou be in the earth. And Cain said unto the Lord, My punishment is greater than I can bear. Behold, thou hast driven me out this day from the face of the earth; and from thy face shall I be hid; and I shall be a fugitive and a vagabond in the earth; and it shall come to pass, that every one that findeth me shall slay me. And the Lord said unto him, Therefore whosoever slayeth Cain, vengeance shall be taken on him sevenfold. And the Lord set a mark upon Cain, lest any finding him should kill him.

1. *wroth:* angry.
2. an obscure sentence. It seems to mean something like: "It (i.e., sin) shall be eager for you, but you must master it."

*Genesis 6–9. [The Flood]*

6. . . . And God saw that the wickedness of man was great in the earth, and that every imagination of the thoughts of his heart was only evil continually. And it repented the Lord that he had made man on the earth, and it grieved him at his heart. And the Lord said, I will destroy man whom I have created from the face of the earth; both man, and beast, and the creeeping thing, and the fowls

of the air; for it repenteth me that I have made them. But Noah found grace in the eyes of the Lord.

These are the generations of Noah: Noah was a just man and perfect in his generations, and Noah walked with God. And Noah begat three sons, Shem, Ham, and Japheth.

The earth also was corrupt before God, and the earth was filled with violence. And God looked upon the earth, and, behold, it was corrupt; for all flesh had corrupted his way upon the earth. And God said unto Noah, The end of all flesh is come before me; for the earth is filled with violence through them; and, behold, I will destroy them with the earth. Make thee an ark of gopher[1] wood; rooms shalt thou make in the ark, and shalt pitch it within and without with pitch. And this is the fashion which thou shalt make it of: The length of the ark shall be three hundred cubits,[2] the breadth of it fifty cubits, and the height of it thirty cubits. A window[3] shalt thou make to the ark, and in a cubit shalt thou finish it above; and the door of the ark shalt thou set in the side thereof; with lower, second, and third stories shalt thou make it. And, behold, I, even I, do bring a flood of waters upon the earth, to destroy all flesh, wherein is the breath of life, from under heaven; and every thing that is in the earth shall die. But with thee will I establish my covenant; and thou shalt come into the ark, thou, and thy sons, and thy wife, and thy sons' wives with thee. And of every living thing of all flesh, two of every sort shalt thou bring into the ark, to keep them alive with thee; they shall be male and female. Of fowls after their kind, and of cattle after their kind, of every creeping thing of the earth after his kind, two of every sort shall come unto thee, to keep them alive. And take thou unto thee of all food that is eaten, and thou shalt gather it to thee; and it shall be for food for thee, and for them. Thus did Noah; according to all that God commanded him, so did he.

7. . . . And Noah was six hundred years old when the flood of waters was upon the earth. And Noah went in, and his sons, and his wife, and his sons' wives with him, into the ark, because of the waters of the flood. Of clean beasts, and of beasts that are not clean,[4] and of fowls, and of everything that creepeth upon the earth, There went in two and two unto Noah into the ark, the male and the female, as God had commanded Noah. And it came to pass after seven days, that the waters of the flood were upon the earth. In the six hundredth year of Noah's life, in the second month, the

---

1. *gopher:* cypress.
2. *cubit:* a Hebrew measure of length, about one and a half feet.
3. *window:* The text is obscure; it may refer to a skylight in the roof.
4. *not clean:* Certain animals were forbidden food to the Hebrews. For a list of them see Leviticus 11.

seventeenth day of the month, the same day were all the fountains of the great deep broken up, and the windows of heaven were opened. And the rain was upon the earth forty days and forty nights. In the selfsame day entered Noah, and Shem, and Ham, and Japheth, the sons of Noah, and Noah's wife, and the three wives of his sons with them, into the ark; They, and every beast after his kind, and all the cattle after their kind, and every creeping thing that creepeth upon the earth after his kind, and every fowl after his kind, every bird of every sort. And they went in unto Noah into the ark, two and two of all flesh, wherein is the breath of life. And they that went in, went in male and female of all flesh, as God had commanded him, and the Lord shut him in. And the flood was forty days upon the earth; and the waters increased, and bare up the ark, and it was lift up above the earth. And the waters prevailed, and were increased greatly upon the earth; and the ark went upon the face of the waters. And the waters prevailed exceedingly upon the earth; and all the high hills, that were under the whole heaven, were covered. Fifteen cubits upward did the waters prevail; and the mountains were covered. And all flesh died that moved upon the earth, both of fowl, and of cattle, and of beast, and of every creeping thing that creepeth upon the earth, and every man: All in whose nostrils was the breath of life, of all that was in the dry land, died. And every living substance was destroyed which was upon the face of the ground, both man, and cattle, and the creeping things, and the fowl of the heaven; and they were destroyed from the earth, and Noah only remained alive, and they that were with him in the ark. And the waters prevailed upon the earth an hundred and fifty days.

8. And God remembered Noah, and every living thing, and all the cattle that was with him in the ark: and God made a wind to pass over the earth, and the waters assuaged; The fountains also of the deep and the windows of heaven were stopped, and the rain from heaven was restrained; And the waters returned from off the earth continually: and after the end of the hundred and fifty days the waters were abated. And the ark rested in the seventh month, on the seventeenth day of the month, upon the mountains of Ararat.[5] And the waters decreased continually until the tenth month: in the tenth month, on the first day of the month, were the tops of the mountains seen.

And it came to pass at the end of forty days, that Noah opened the window of the ark which he had made: And he sent forth a raven, which went forth to and fro, until the waters were dried up

---

5. *Ararat:* a mountain in the eastern part of Asia Minor.

from off the earth. Also he sent forth a dove from him, to see if the waters were abated from off the face of the ground; But the dove found no rest for the sole of her foot, and she returned unto him into the ark, for the waters were on the face of the whole earth: then he put forth his hand, and took her, and pulled her in unto him into the ark. And he stayed yet another seven days; and again he sent forth the dove out of the ark; And the dove came in to him in the evening; and, lo, in her mouth was an olive leaf plucked off: so Noah knew that the waters were abated from off the earth. And he stayed yet other seven days; and sent forth the dove; which returned not again unto him any more.

And it came to pass in the six hundredth and first year, in the first month, the first day of the month, the waters were dried up from off the earth: and Noah removed the covering of the ark, and looked, and, behold, the face of the ground was dry. And in the second month, on the seven and twentieth day of the month, was the earth dried.

And God spake unto Noah, saying, Go forth of the ark, thou, and thy wife, and thy sons, and thy sons' wives with thee. Bring forth with thee every living thing that is with thee, of all flesh, both of fowl, and of cattle, and of every creeping thing that creepeth upon the earth; that they may breed abundantly in the earth, and be fruitful, and multiply upon the earth. And Noah went forth, and his sons, and his wife, and his sons' wives with him: Every beast, every creeping thing, and every fowl, and whatsoever creepeth upon the earth, after their kinds, went forth out of the ark. And Noah builded an altar unto the Lord; and took of every clean beast, and of every clean fowl, and offered burnt offerings on the altar. And the Lord smelled a sweet savour; and the Lord said in his heart, I will not again curse the ground any more for man's sake; for the imagination of man's heart is evil from his youth; neither will I again smite any more every thing living, as I have done. While the earth remaineth, seedtime and harvest, and cold and heat, and summer and winter, and day and night shall not cease.

9. And God blessed Noah and his sons, and said unto them, Be fruitful, and multiply, and replenish the earth. And the fear of you and the dread of you shall be upon every beast of the earth, and upon every fowl of the air, upon all that moveth upon the earth, and upon all the fishes of the sea; into your hand are they delivered. Every moving thing that liveth shall be meat for you; even as the green herb have I given you all things. But flesh with the life thereof, which is the blood thereof, shall ye not eat.[6] And surely

6. This sentence refers to the dietary laws: blood was drained from the slaugh- tered animal.

your blood of your lives will I require; at the hand of every beast will I require it, and at the hand of man; at the hand of every man's brother will I require the life of man. Whoso sheddeth man's blood, by man shall his blood be shed, for in the image of God made he man. And you, be ye fruitful, and multiply; bring forth abundantly in the earth, and multiply therein.

And God spake unto Noah, and to his sons with him, saying, And I, behold, I establish my covenant with you, and with your seed after you; And with every living creature that is with you, of the fowl, of the cattle, and of every beast of the earth with you; from all that go out of the ark, to every beast of the earth. And I will establish my covenant with you; neither shall all flesh be cut off any more by the waters of a flood; neither shall there any more be a flood to destroy the earth. And God said, This is the token of the covenant which I make between me and you and every living creature that is with you, for perpetual generations: I do set my bow in the cloud, and it shall be for a token of a covenant between me and the earth. And it shall come to pass, when I bring a cloud over the earth, that the bow shall be seen in the cloud: And I will remember my covenant, which is between me and you and every living creature of all flesh; and the waters shall no more become a flood to destroy all flesh. And the bow shall be in the cloud; and I will look upon it, that I may remember the everlasting covenant between God and every living creature of all flesh that is upon the earth. And God said unto Noah, This is the token of the covenant, which I have established between me and all flesh that is upon the earth.

## Genesis 11. [*The Origin of Languages*]

11. And the whole earth was of one language, and of one speech. And it came to pass, as they[1] journeyed from the east, that they found a plain in the land of Shinar;[2] and they dwelt there. And they said one to another, Go to, let us make brick, and burn them throughly. And they had brick for stone, and slime[3] had they for mortar. And they said, Go to, let us build us a city and a tower,[4] whose top may reach unto heaven; and let us make us a name, lest we be scattered abroad upon the face of the whole earth. And the Lord came down to see the city and the tower, which the children of men builded. And the Lord said, Behold, the people is one, and they have all one language; and this they begin to do: and now nothing will be restrained from them, which they have imagined to

1. *they:* the human race.
2. *Shinar:* in Mesopotamia.
3. *slime:* bitumen.
4. *tower:* This story is based on the
Babylonian practice of building temples in the form of terraced pyramids (ziggurats).

do. Go to, let us go down, and there confound their language, that they may not understand one another's speech. So the Lord scattered them abroad from thence upon the face of all the earth: and they left off to build the city. Therefore is the name of it called Babel;[5] because the Lord did there confound the language of all the earth: and from thence did the Lord scatter them abroad upon the face of all the earth.

5. *Babel:* Babylon.

### Genesis 37–46. [*The Story of Joseph*]

37. . . . Joseph, being seventeen years old, was feeding the flock with his brethren; and the lad was with the sons of Bilhah, and with the sons of Zilpah, his father's wives: and Joseph brought unto his father[1] their evil report.[2] Now Israel loved Joseph more than all his children, because he was the son of his old age: and he made him a coat of many colours. And when his brethren saw that their father loved him more than all his brethren, they hated him, and could not speak peaceably unto him.

And Joseph dreamed a dream, and he told it his brethren: and they hated him yet the more. And he said unto them, Hear, I pray you, this dream which I have dreamed: for, behold, we were binding sheaves in the field, and, lo, my sheaf arose, and also stood upright; and, behold, your sheaves stood round about, and made obeisance to[3] my sheaf. And his brethren said to him, Shalt thou indeed reign over us? or shalt thou indeed have dominion over us? And they hated him yet the more for his dreams, and for his words.

And he dreamed yet another dream, and told it his brethren, and said, Behold, I have dreamed a dream more; and, behold, the sun and the moon and the eleven stars made obeisance to me. And he told it to his father, and to his brethren: and his father rebuked him, and said unto him, What is this dream that thou hast dreamed? Shall I and thy mother and thy brethren indeed come to bow down ourselves to thee to the earth? And his brethren envied him; but his father observed the saying.

And his brethren went to feed their father's flock in Shechem. And Israel said unto Joseph, Do not thy brethren feed the flock in Shechem? come, and I will send thee unto them. And he said to him, Here am I. And he said to him, Go, I pray thee, see whether it be well with thy brethren, and well with the flocks; and bring me word again. So he sent him out of the vale of Hebron, and he came to Shechem.

1. Israel.
2. Joseph reported their misdeeds.
3. bowed down to.

And a certain man found him, and, behold, he was wandering
in the field: and the man asked him, saying, What seekest thou?
And he said, I seek my brethren: tell me, I pray thee, where they
feed their flocks. And the man said, They are departed hence; for
I heard them say, Let us go to Dothan. And Joseph went after his
brethren, and found them in Dothan. And when they saw him afar
off, even before he came near unto them, they conspired against
him to slay him. And they said one to another, Behold, this dreamer
cometh. Come now therefore, and let us slay him, and cast him
into some pit, and we will say, Some evil beast hath devoured him:
and we shall see what will become of his dreams. And Reuben
heard it, and he delivered him out of their hands; and said, Let
us not kill him. And Reuben said unto them, Shed no blood, but
cast him into this pit that is in the wilderness, and lay no hand upon
him; that he might rid him out of their hands, to deliver him to
his father again.

And it came to pass, when Joseph was come unto his brethren,
that they stripped Joseph out of his coat, his coat of many colours
that was on him; and they took him, and cast him into a pit: and
the pit was empty, there was no water in it. And they sat down to
eat bread: and they lifted up their eyes and looked, and, behold,
a company of Ishmeelites came from Gilead with their camels
bearing spicery and balm and myrrh, going to carry it down to
Egypt. And Judah said unto his brethren, What profit is it if we slay
our brother, and conceal his blood? Come, and let us sell him to the
Ishmeelites, and let not our hand be upon him; for he is our brother
and our flesh. And his brethren were content. Then there passed by
Midianites merchantmen;[4] and they[5] drew and lifted up Joseph
out of the pit, and sold Joseph to the Ishmeelites for twenty pieces
of silver: and they[6] brought Joseph into Egypt.

And Reuben returned unto the pit; and, behold, Joseph was not
in the pit; and he rent his clothes. And he returned unto his brethren, and said, The child is not; and I, whither shall I go? And they
took Joseph's coat, and killed a kid of the goats, and dipped the
coat in the blood; and they sent the coat of many colours, and they
brought it to their father; and said, This have we found: know now
whether it be thy son's coat or no. And he knew it, and said, It
is my son's coat; an evil beast hath devoured him; Joseph is without
doubt rent in pieces. And Jacob[7] rent his clothes, and put sackcloth
upon his loins, and mourned for his son many days. And all his
sons and all his daughters rose up to comfort him; but he refused to

---

4. The confusion in this passage may
be due to the fact that the version we
have is a composite of two different
versions.

5. the brothers.
6. the Ishmeelites.
7. Israel.

be comforted; and he said, For I will go down into the grave unto my son mourning. Thus his father wept for him. . . .

39. And Joseph was brought down to Egypt; and Potiphar, an officer of Pharaoh,[8] captain of the guard, an Egyptian, bought him of the hands of the Ishmeelites, which had brought him down thither. And the Lord was with Joseph, and he was a prosperous man; and he was in the house of his master the Egyptian. And his master saw that the Lord was with him, and that the Lord made all he did to prosper in his hand. And Joseph found grace in his sight, and he served him: and he made him overseer over his house, and all that he had he put into his hand. And it came to pass from the time that he had made him overseer in his house, and over all that he had, that the Lord blessed the Egyptian's house for Joseph's sake; and the blessing of the Lord was upon all that he had in the house, and in the field. And he left all that he had in Joseph's hand; and he knew not ought he had, save the bread which he did eat. And Joseph was a goodly person, and well favoured.[9]

And it came to pass after these things, that his master's wife cast her eyes upon Joseph; and she said, Lie with me. But he refused, and said unto his master's wife, Behold, my master wotteth not what is with me in the house, and he hath committed all that he hath to my hand; there is none greater in this house than I; neither hath he kept back any thing from me but thee, because thou art his wife: how then can I do this great wickedness, and sin against God? And it came to pass, as she spake to Joseph day by day, that he hearkened not unto her, to lie by her, or to be with her. And it came to pass about this time, that Joseph went into the house to do his business; and there was none of the men of the house there within. And she caught him by his garment, saying, Lie with me: and he left his garment in her hand, and fled and got him out. And it came to pass, when she saw that he had left his garment in her hand, and was fled forth, that she called unto the men of her house, and spoke unto them, saying, See, he hath brought in an Hebrew unto us to mock us; he came in unto me to lie with me, and I cried with a loud voice: and it came to pass, when he heard that I lifted up my voice and cried, that he left his garment with me, and fled, and got him out. And she laid up his garment by her, until his lord came home. And she spake unto him according to these words, saying, The Hebrew servant, which thou hast brought unto us, came in unto me to mock me: and it came to pass, as I lifted up my voice and cried, that he left his garment with me, and fled out. And it came to pass, when his master heard the words of his wife, which she

8. the Egyptian king.    9. handsome.

spake unto him, saying, After this manner did thy servant to me; that his wrath was kindled. And Joseph's master took him, and put him into the prison, a place where the king's prisoners were bound: and he was there in the prison.

But the Lord was with Joseph, and showed him mercy, and gave him favour in the sight of the keeper of the prison. And the keeper of the prison committed to Joseph's hand all the prisoners that were in the prison; and whatsoever they did there, he was the doer of it. The keeper of the prison looked not to any thing that was under his[10] hand; because the Lord was with him,[11] and that which he did, the Lord made it to prosper.

40. And it came to pass after these things that the butler of the king of Egypt and his baker had offended their lord the king of Egypt. And Pharaoh was wroth against two of his officers, against the chief of the butlers, and against the chief of the bakers. And he put them in ward in the house of the captain of the guard, into the prison, the place where Joseph was bound. And the captain of the guard charged Joseph with them, and he served them: and they continued a season in ward.

And they dreamed a dream both of them, each man his dream in one night, each man according to the interpretation of his dream, the butler and the baker of the king of Egypt, which were bound in the prison. And Joseph came in unto them in the morning, and looked upon them, and, behold, they were sad. And he asked Pharaoh's officers that were with him in the ward of his lord's house, saying, Wherefore look ye so sadly to day? And they said unto him, We have dreamed a dream, and there is no interpreter of it. And Joseph said unto them, Do not interpretations belong to God? tell me them, I pray you. And the chief butler told his dream to Joseph, and said to him, In my dream, behold, a vine was before me; and in the vine were three branches: and it was as though it budded, and her blossoms shot forth; and the clusters thereof brought forth ripe grapes: and Pharaoh's cup was in my hand: and I took the grapes, and pressed them into Pharaoh's cup, and I gave the cup into Pharaoh's hand. And Joseph said unto him, This is the interpretation of it: the three branches are three days: yet within three days shall Pharaoh lift up thine head, and restore thee unto thy place: and thou shalt deliver Pharaoh's cup into his hand, after the former manner when thou wast his butler. But think on me when it shall be well with thee, and shew kindness, I pray thee, unto me, and make mention of me unto Pharaoh, and bring me out of this house: for indeed I was stolen away out of the land of the Hebrews: and

10. Joseph's.     11. Joseph.

here also have I done nothing that they should put me into the dungeon. When the chief baker saw that the interpretation was good, he said unto Joseph, I also was in my dream, and, behold, I had three white baskets on my head: and in the uppermost basket there was of all manner of bakemeats for Pharaoh; and the birds did eat them out of the basket upon my head. And Joseph answered and said, This is the interpretation thereof: the three baskets are three days: yet within three days shall Pharaoh lift up thy head from off thee, and shall hang thee on a tree; and the birds shall eat thy flesh from off thee.

And it came to pass the third day, which was Pharaoh's birthday, that he made a feast unto all his servants: and he lifted up the head of the chief butler and of the chief baker among his servants. And he restored the chief butler unto his butlership again; and he gave the cup into Pharaoh's hand. But he hanged the chief baker: as Joseph had interpreted to them. Yet did not the chief butler remember Joseph, but forgat him.

41. And it came to pass at the end of two full years, that Pharaoh dreamed: and, behold, he stood by the river. And, behold, there came up out of the river seven well favoured kine[12] and fat-fleshed; and they fed in a meadow. And, behold, seven other kine came up after them out of the river, ill favoured and leanfleshed; and stood by the other kine upon the brink of the river. And the ill favoured and leanfleshed kine did eat up the seven well favoured and fat kine. So Pharaoh awoke. And he slept and dreamed the second time: and, behold, seven ears of corn came up upon one stalk, rank[13] and good. And, behold, seven thin ears and blasted with the east wind sprung up after them. And the seven thin ears devoured the seven rank and full ears. And Pharaoh awoke, and, behold, it was a dream. And it came to pass in the morning that his spirit was troubled; and he sent and called for all the magicians of Egypt, and all the wise men thereof: and Pharaoh told them his dream; but there was none that could interpret them unto Pharaoh.

Then spake the chief butler unto Pharaoh, saying, I do remember my faults this day: Pharaoh was wroth with his servants, and put me in ward in the captain of the guard's house, both me and the chief baker: and we dreamed a dream in one night, I and he; we dreamed each man according to the interpretation of his dream. And there was there with us a young man, an Hebrew, servant to the captain of the guard; and we told him, and he interpreted to us our dreams; to each man according to his dream he did interpret. And it came to pass, as he interpreted to us, so it was; me he restored

12. cattle.                    13. fat.

unto mine office, and him he hanged.

Then Pharaoh sent and called Joseph, and they brought him hastily out of the dungeon: and he shaved himself, and changed his raiment, and came in unto Pharaoh. And Pharaoh said unto Joseph, I have dreamed a dream, and there is none that can interpret it: and I have heard say of thee that thou canst understand a dream to interpret it. And Joseph answered Pharaoh, saying, It is not in me: God shall give Pharaoh an answer of peace. And Pharaoh said unto Joseph, In my dream, behold, I stood upon the bank of the river: and, behold, there came up out of the river seven kine, fatfleshed and well favoured; and they fed in a meadow: and, behold, seven other kine came up after them, poor and very ill favoured and lean-fleshed, such as I never saw in all the land of Egypt for badness: and the lean and the ill favoured kine did eat up the first seven fat kine; and when they had eaten them up, it could not be known that they had eaten them; but they were still ill favoured, as at the beginning. So I awoke. And I saw in my dream, and, behold, seven ears came up in one stalk, full and good: and, behold, seven ears, withered, thin, and blasted with the east wind, sprung up after them: and the thin ears devoured the seven good ears: and I told this unto the magicians; but there was none that could declare it to me.

And Joseph said unto Pharaoh, The dream of Pharaoh is one: God hath shewed Pharaoh what he is about to do. The seven good kine are seven years; and the seven goods ears are seven years: the dream is one. And the seven thin and ill favoured kine that came up after them are seven years; and the seven empty ears blasted with the east wind shall be seven years of famine. This is the thing which I have spoken unto Pharaoh: what God is about to do he sheweth unto Pharaoh. Behold, there come seven years of great plenty throughout all the land of Egypt: and there shall arise after them seven years of famine; and all the plenty shall be forgotten in the land of Egypt; and the famine shall consume the land; and the plenty shall not be known in the land by reason of that famine following; for it shall be very grievous. And for that the dream was doubled unto Pharaoh twice; it is because the thing is established by God, and God will shortly bring it to pass. Now therefore let Pharaoh look out a man discreet and wise, and set him over the land of Egypt. Let Pharaoh do this, and let him appoint officers over the land, and take up the fifth part of the land[14] of Egypt in the seven plenteous years. And let them gather all the food of those good years that come, and lay up corn under the hand of Pharaoh, and let them keep food in the cities. And that food shall be for

14. i.e., of the crop.

store to the land against the seven years of famine, which shall be in the land of Egypt; that the land perish not through the famine.

And the thing was good in the eyes of Pharaoh, and in the eyes of all his servants. And Pharaoh said unto his servants, Can we find such a one as this is, a man in whom the Spirit of God is? And Pharaoh said unto Joseph, Forasmuch as God hath shewed thee all this, there is none so discreet and wise as thou art: thou shalt be over my house, and according unto thy word shall all my people be ruled: only in the throne will I be greater than thou. And Pharaoh said unto Joseph, See, I have set thee over all the land of Egypt. And Pharaoh took off his ring from his hand, and put it upon Joseph's hand, and arrayed him in vestures of fine linen, and put a gold chain about his neck; and he made him to ride in the second chariot which he had; and they cried before him, Bow the knee: and he made him ruler over all the land of Egypt. And Pharaoh said unto Joseph, I am Pharaoh, and without thee shall no man lift his hand or foot in all the land of Egypt. And Pharaoh called Joseph's name Zaphnath-paaneah; and he gave him to wife Asenath the daughter of Poti-pherah priest of On. And Joseph went out over all the land of Egypt.

And Joseph was thirty years old when he stood before Pharaoh king of Egypt. And Joseph went out from the presence of Pharaoh, and went throughout all the land of Egypt. And in the seven plenteous years the earth brought forth by handfuls. And he gathered up all the food of the seven years, which were in the land of Egypt, and laid up the food in the cities: the food of the field, which was round about every city, laid he up in the same. And Joseph gathered corn as the sand of the sea, very much, until he left numbering; for it was without number. And unto Joseph were born two sons before the years of famine came, which Asenath the daughter of Poti-pherah priest of On bare unto him. And Joseph called the name of the first born Manasseh:[15] For God, said he, hath made me forget all my toil, and all my father's house. And the name of the second called he Ephraim:[16] For God hath caused me to be fruitful in the land of my affliction.

And the seven years of plenteousness, that was in the land of Egypt, were ended. And the seven years of dearth[17] began to come, according as Joseph had said: and the dearth was in all lands; but in all the land of Egypt there was bread. And when all the land of Egypt was famished, the people cried to Pharaoh for bread: and Pharaoh said unto all the Egyptians, Go unto Joseph; what he saith to you, do. And the famine was over all the face of the earth. And Joseph opened all the storehouses, and sold unto the Egyptians;

15. meaning "causing to forget."
16. meaning "fruitfulness."
17. scarcity.

and the famine waxed sore in the land of Egypt. And all countries came into Egypt to Joseph for to buy corn; because that the famine was so sore in all lands.

42. Now when Jacob saw that there was corn in Egypt, Jacob said unto his sons, Why do ye look one upon another? And he said, Behold, I have heard that there is corn in Egypt: get you down thither, and buy for us from thence; that we may live, and not die. And Joseph's ten brethren went down to buy corn in Egypt. But Benjamin,[18] Joseph's brother, Jacob sent not with his brethren; for he said, Lest peradventure mischief befall him. And the sons of Israel came to buy corn among those that came: for the famine was in the land of Canaan. And Joseph was the governor over the land, and he it was that sold to all the people of the land: and Joseph's brethren came, and bowed down themselves before him with their faces to the earth. And Joseph saw his brethren, and he knew them, but made himself strange unto them, and spake roughly unto them; and he said unto them, Whence come ye? And they said, From the land of Canaan to buy food. And Joseph knew his brethren, but they knew not him. And Joseph remembered the dreams which he dreamed of them, and said unto them, Ye are spies; to see the nakedness of the land ye are come. And they said unto him, Nay, my lord, but to buy food are thy servants come. We are all one man's sons; we are true men, thy servants are no spies. And he said unto them, Nay, but to see the nakedness of the land ye are come. And they said, Thy servants are twelve brethren, the sons of one man in the land of Canaan; and, behold, the youngest is this day with our father, and one is not. And Joseph said unto them, That is it that I spake unto you, saying, Ye are spies: Hereby ye shall be proved: By the life of Pharaoh ye shall not go forth hence, except your youngest brother come hither. Send one of you, and let him fetch your brother, and ye shall be kept in prison, that your words may be proved, whether there be any truth in you: or else by the life of Pharaoh surely ye are spies. And he put them all together into ward three days. And Joseph said unto them the third day, This do, and live; for I fear God: if ye be true men, let one of your brethren be bound in the house of your prison: go ye, carry corn for the famine of your houses: but bring your youngest brother unto me; so shall your words be verified, and ye shall not die. And they did so.

And they said one to another, We are verily guilty concerning our brother, in that we saw the anguish of his soul, when he besought us, and we would not hear; therefore is this distress come

18. more closely related than the other ten since he is the son of the same mother.

upon us. And Reuben answered them, saying, Spake I not unto you, saying, Do not sin against the child; and ye would not hear? therefore, behold, also his blood is required. And they knew not that Joseph understood them; for he spake unto them by an interpreter. And he turned himself about from them, and wept; and returned to them again, and communed with them, and took from them Simeon, and bound him before their eyes.

Then Joseph commanded to fill their sacks with corn, and to restore every man's money into his sack, and to give them provision for the way: and thus did he unto them. And they laded their asses with the corn, and departed thence. And as one of them opened his sack to give his ass provender in the inn, he espied his money; for, behold, it was in his sack's mouth. And he said unto his brethren, My money is restored; and, lo, it is even in my sack: and their heart failed them, and they were afraid, saying one to another, What is this that God hath done unto us?

And they came unto Jacob their father unto the land of Canaan, and told him all that befell unto them; saying, The man, who is lord of the land, spake roughly to us, and took us for spies of the country. And we said unto him, We are true men; we are no spies: we be twelve brethren, sons of our father; one is not, and the youngest is this day with our father in the land of Canaan. And the man, the lord of the country, said unto us, Hereby shall I know that ye are true men; leave one of your brethren here with me, and take food for the famine of your households, and be gone: and bring your youngest brother unto me: then shall I know that ye are no spies, but that ye are true men: so will I deliver you your brother, and ye shall traffick in the land.

And it came to pass as they emptied their sacks, that, behold, every man's bundle of money was in his sack: and when both they and their father saw the bundles of money, they were afraid. And Jacob their father said unto them, Me have ye bereaved of my children: Joseph is not, and Simeon is not, and ye will take Benjamin away: all these things are against me.

And Reuben spake unto his father, saying, Slay my two sons, if I bring him not to thee: deliver him into my hand, and I will bring him to thee again. And he said, My son shall not go down with you; for his brother is dead, and he is left alone: if mischief befall him by the way in the which ye go, then shall ye bring down my gray hairs with sorrow to the grave.

43. And the famine was sore in the land. And it came to pass, when they had eaten up the corn which they had brought out of Egypt, their father said unto them, Go again, buy us a little food. And Judah spake unto him, saying, The man did solemnly protest

unto us, saying, Ye shall not see my face, except your brother be with you. If thou wilt send our brother with us, we will go down and buy thee food: but if thou wilt not send him, we will not go down: for the man said unto us, Ye shall not see my face, except your brother be with you. And Israel said, Wherefore dealt ye so ill with me, as to tell the man whether ye had yet a brother? And they said, The man asked us straitly[19] of our state, and of our kindred, saying, Is your father yet alive? have ye another brother? and we told him according to the tenor of these words: could we certainly know that he would say, Bring your brother down? And Judah said unto Israel his father, Send the lad with me, and we will arise and go; that we may live, and not die, both we, and thou, and also our little ones. I will be surety for him; of my hand shalt thou require him: if I bring him not unto thee, and set him before thee, then let me bear the blame for ever: for except we had lingered, surely now we had returned this second time. And their father Israel said unto them, If it must be so now, do this; take of the best fruits in the land in your vessels, and carry down the man a present, a little balm, and a little honey, spices, and myrrh, nuts, and almonds: and take double money in your hand; and the money that was brought again in the mouth of your sacks, carry it again in your hand; peradventure it was an oversight: take also your brother, and arise, go again unto the man: and God Almighty give you mercy before the man, that he may send away your other brother, and Benjamin. If I be bereaved of my children, I am bereaved.

And the men took that present, and they took double money in their hand, and Benjamin; and rose up, and went down to Egypt, and stood before Joseph. And when Joseph saw Benjamin with them, he said to the ruler of his house, Bring these men home, and slay,[20] and make ready; for these men shall dine with me at noon. And the man did as Joseph bade; and the man brought the men into Joseph's house. And the men were afraid, because they were brought into Joseph's house; and they said, Because of the money that was returned in our sacks at the first time are we brought in; that he may seek occasion against us, and fall upon us, and take us for bondmen,[21] and our asses. And they came near to the steward of Joseph's house, and they communed with him at the door of the house, and said, O sir, we came indeed down at the first time to buy food; and it came to pass, when we came to the inn, that we opened our sacks, and, behold, every man's money was in the mouth of his sack, our money in full weight: and we have brought it again in our hand. And other money have we brought down in our hands to buy food: we cannot tell who put our money in our sacks. And

---

19. strictly, precisely.
20. kill an animal for meat.
21. slaves.

he said, Peace be to you, fear not: your God, and the God of your father, hath given you treasure in your sacks: I had your money. And he brought Simeon out unto them. And the man brought the men into Joseph's house, and gave them water, and they washed their feet; and he gave their asses provender. And they made ready the present against Joseph came at noon: for they heard that they should eat bread there.

And when Joseph came home, they brought him the present which was in their hand into the house, and bowed themselves to him to the earth. And he asked them of their welfare, and said, Is your father well, the old man of whom ye spoke? Is he yet alive? And they answered, Thy servant our father is in good health, he is yet alive. And they bowed down their heads, and made obeisance. And he lifted up his eyes, and saw his brother Benjamin, his mother's son, and said, Is this your younger brother, of whom ye spoke unto me? And he said, God be gracious unto thee, my son. And Joseph made haste; for his bowels did yearn upon his brother: and he sought where to weep; and he entered into his chamber, and wept there. And he washed his face, and went out, and refrained himself and said, Set on bread. And they set on for him by himself, and for them by themselves, and for the Egyptians, which did eat with him, by themselves: because the Egyptians might not eat bread with the Hebrews; for that is an abomination unto the Egyptians. And they sat before him, the firstborn according to his birthright, and the youngest according to his youth: and the men marvelled one at another. And he took and sent messes[22] unto them from before him: but Benjamin's mess was five times so much as any of theirs. And they drank, and were merry with him.

44. And he commanded the steward of his house, saying, Fill the men's sacks with food, as much as they can carry, and put every man's money in his sack's mouth. And put my cup, the silver cup, in the sack's mouth of the youngest, and his corn money. And he did according to the word that Joseph had spoken. As soon as the morning was light, the men were sent away, they and their asses. And when they were gone out of the city, and not yet far off, Joseph said unto his steward, Up, follow after the men; and when thou dost overtake them, say unto them, Wherefore have ye rewarded evil for good? Is not this it in which my lord drinketh, and whereby indeed he divineth?[23] ye have done evil in so doing.

And he overtook them, and he spake unto them these same words.

22. portions.
23. Joseph's servant is to claim that this is the cup Joseph uses for clairvoyance; the diviner stared into a cup of water and foretold the future.

And they said unto him, Wherefore saith my lord these words? God
forbid that thy servants should do according to this thing: behold,
the money, which we found in our sacks' mouths, we brought again
unto thee out of the land of Canaan: how then should we steal out
of thy lord's house silver or gold? With whomsoever of thy servants
it be found, both let him die, and we also will be my lord's bondmen. And he said, Now also let it be according unto your words:
he with whom it is found shall be my servant; and ye shall be
blameless. Then they speedily took down every man his sack to the
ground, and opened every man his sack. And he searched, and
began at the eldest, and left at the youngest: and the cup was found
in Benjamin's sack. Then they rent their clothes, and laded every
man his ass, and returned to the city.

And Judah and his brethren came to Joseph's house; for he was
yet there: and they fell before him on the ground. And Joseph said
unto them, What deed is this that ye have done? wot ye not that
such a man as I can certainly divine? And Judah said, What shall
we say unto my lord? what shall we speak? or how shall we clear
ourselves? God hath found out the iniquity of thy servants: behold,
we are my lord's servants, both we, and he also with whom the cup
is found. And he said, God forbid that I should do so: but the man
in whose hand the cup is found, he shall be my servant; and as for
you, get you up in peace unto your father.

Then Judah came near unto him, and said, Oh my lord, let thy
servant, I pray thee, speak a word in my lord's ears, and let not
thine anger burn against thy servant: for thou art even as Pharaoh.
My lord asked his servants, saying, Have ye a father, or a brother?
And we said unto my lord, We have a father, an old man, and a
child of his old age, a little one; and his brother is dead, and he
alone is left of his mother, and his father loveth him. And thou
saidst unto thy servants, Bring him down unto me, that I may set
mine eyes upon him. And we said unto my lord, The lad cannot
leave his father: for if he should leave his father, his father would
die. And thou saidst unto thy servants, Except your youngest
brother come down with you, ye shall see my face no more. And it
came to pass when we came up unto thy servant my father, we
told him the words of my lord. And our father said, Go again, and
buy us a little food. And we said, We cannot go down: if our
youngest brother be with us, then will we go down: for we may not
see the man's face, except our youngest brother be with us. And
thy servant my father said unto us, Ye know that my wife bare me
two sons; and the one went out from me, and I said, Surely he is
torn in pieces; and I saw him not since: and if ye take this also from
me, and mischief befall him, ye shall bring down my gray hairs with

sorrow to the grave. Now therefore when I come to thy servant my
father, and the lad be not with us; seeing that his life is bound up
in the lad's life; it shall come to pass, when he seeth that the lad is
not with us, that he will die: and thy servants[24] shall bring down the
gray hairs of thy servant our father with sorrow to the grave. For
thy servant[25] became surety for the lad unto my father, saying, If
I bring him not unto thee, then I shall bear the blame to my father
for ever. Now therefore, I pray thee, let thy servant[26] abide instead
of the lad a bondman to my lord; and let the lad go up with his
brethren. For how shall I go up to my father, and the lad be not
with me? lest peradventure I see the evil that shall come on my
father.

45. Then Joseph could not refrain himself before all them that
stood by him; and he cried, Cause every man to go out from me.
And there stood no man with him, while Joseph made himself
known unto his brethren. And he wept aloud: and the Egyptians
and the house of Pharaoh heard. And Joseph said unto his brethren,
I am Joseph; doth my father yet live? And his brethren could not
answer him; for they were troubled at his presence. And Joseph said
unto his brethren, Come near to me, I pray you. And they came
near. And he said, I am Joseph your brother, whom ye sold into
Egypt. Now therefore be not grieved, nor angry with yourselves,
that ye sold me hither: for God did send me before you to preserve
life. For these two years hath the famine been in the land: and yet
there are five years, in the which there shall neither be earing nor
harvest. And God sent me before you to preserve you a posterity
in the earth, and to save your lives by a great deliverance. So now
it was not you that sent me hither, but God: and he hath made
me a father to Pharaoh, and lord of all his house, and a ruler throughout all the land of Egypt. Haste ye, and go up to my father, and
say unto him, Thus saith thy son Joseph, God hath made me lord
of all Egypt: come down unto me, tarry not: and thou shalt dwell in
the land of Goshen, and thou shalt be near unto me, thou, and thy
children, and thy children's children, and thy flocks, and thy herds,
and all thou hast: and there will I nourish thee; for yet there are
five years of famine; lest thou, and thy household, and all that thou
hast, come to poverty. And, behold, your eyes see, and the eyes of
my brother Benjamin, that it is my mouth that speaketh unto you.
And ye shall tell my father of all my glory in Egypt, and of all that
ye have seen; and ye shall haste and bring down my father hither.
And he fell upon his brother Benjamin's neck, and wept; and Ben-

24. we.
25. I.
26. me.

jamin wept upon his neck. Moreover he kissed all his brethren, and wept upon them: and after that his brethren talked with him.

And the fame thereof was heard in Pharaoh's house, saying, Joseph's brethren are come: and it pleased Pharaoh well, and his servants. And Pharaoh said unto Joseph, Say unto thy brethren, This do ye; lade[27] your beasts, and go, get you unto the land of Canaan; and take your father and your households, and come unto me: and I will give you the good of the land of Egypt, and ye shall eat the fat of the land. Now thou art commanded, this do ye; take you wagons out of the land of Egypt for your little ones, and for your wives, and bring your father, and come. Also regard not your stuff; for the good of all the land of Egypt is yours. And the children of Israel did so: and Joseph gave them wagons, according to the commandment of Pharaoh, and gave them provision for the way. To all of them he gave each man changes of raiment; but to Benjamin he gave three hundred pieces of silver, and five changes of raiment. And to his father he sent after this manner; ten asses laden with the good things of Egypt, and ten she-asses laden with corn and bread and meat for his father by the way. So he sent his brethren away, and they departed: and he said unto them, See that ye fall not out by the way.

And they went up out of Egypt, and came into the land of Canaan unto Jacob their father, and told him, saying, Joseph is yet alive, and he is governor over all the land of Egypt. And Jacob's heart fainted, for he believed them not. And they told him all the words of Joseph, which he had said unto them: and when he saw the wagons which Joseph had sent to carry him, the spirit of Jacob their father revived. And Israel said, It is enough; Joseph my son is yet alive: I will go and see him before I die.

46. And Israel took his journey with all that he had, and came to Beer-sheba, and offered sacrifices unto the God of his father Isaac. And God spake unto Israel in the visions of the night, and said, Jacob, Jacob. And he said, Here am I. And he said, I am God, the God of thy father: fear not to go down into Egypt; for I will there make of thee a great nation: I will go down with thee into Egypt; and I will also surely bring thee up again: and Joseph shall put his hand upon thine eyes. And Jacob rose up from Beer-sheba: and the sons of Israel carried Jacob their father, and their little ones, and their wives, in the wagons which Pharaoh had sent to carry him. And they took their cattle, and their goods, which they had gotten in the land of Canaan, and came into Egypt, Jacob, and all his seed with him: his sons, and his sons' sons with him, his

27. load.

daughters, and his sons' daughters, and all his seed brought he with him into Egypt.

## Job*

1. There was a man in the land of Uz whose name was Job, and that man was perfect and upright, and one that feared God, and eschewed[1] evil. And there were born unto him seven sons and three daughters. His substance also was seven thousand sheep, and three thousand camels, and five hundred yoke of oxen, and five hundred she asses, and a very great household; so that this man was the greatest of all the men of the east. And his sons went and feasted in their houses, every one his day;[2] and sent and called for their three sisters to eat and to drink with them. And it was so, when the days of their feasting were gone about, that Job sent and sanctified them,[3] and rose up early in the morning, and offered burnt offerings according to the number of them all: for Job said, It may be that my sons have sinned, and cursed God in their hearts. Thus did Job continually.

Now there was a day when the sons of God came to present themselves before the Lord, and Satan[4] came also among them. And the Lord said unto Satan, Whence comest thou? Then Satan answered the Lord, and said, From going to and fro in the earth, and from walking up and down in it. And the Lord said unto Satan, Hast thou considered my servant Job, that there is none like him in the earth, a perfect and an upright man, one that feareth God, and echeweth evil? Then Satan answered the Lord, and said, Doth Job fear God for nought? Hast not thou made an hedge about him, and about his house, and about all that he hath on every side? thou hast blessed the work of his hands, and his substance is increased in the land. But put forth thine hand now, and touch all that he hath, and he will curse thee to thy face. And the Lord said unto Satan, Behold, all that he hath is in thy power; only upon himself put not forth thine hand. So Satan went forth from the presence of the Lord.

And there was a day when his sons and his daughters were eating and drinking wine in their eldest brother's house: and there came a messenger unto Job, and said, The oxen were plowing, and the asses feeding beside them: and the Sabeans fell upon them, and took them away; yea, they have slain the servants with the edge of the sword; and I only am escaped alone to tell thee. While he was yet speaking, there came also another, and said, The fire of God is fallen from heaven, and hath burned up the sheep, and the servants,

---

* Chapters 1–14, 29–31, 38–42.
1. avoided.
2. in rotation at each son's house.
3. by ritual purification.
4. His name means "the accuser," "the opposer."

and consumed them; and I only am escaped alone to tell thee. While he was yet speaking, there came also another, and said, The Chaldeans made out three bands,[5] and fell upon the camels, and have carried them away, yea, and slain the servants with the edge of the sword; and I only am escaped alone to tell thee. While he was yet speaking, there came also another, and said, Thy sons and thy daughters were eating and drinking wine in their eldest brother's house: and, behold, there came a great wind from the wilderness, and smote the four corners of the house, and it fell upon the young men, and they are dead; and I only am escaped alone to tell thee.

Then Job arose and rent[6] his mantle,[7] and shaved his head, and fell down upon the ground, and worshipped, and said, Naked came I out of my mother's womb, and naked shall I return thither: the Lord gave, and the Lord hath taken away; blessed be the name of the Lord. In all this Job sinned not, nor charged God foolishly.

2. Again there was a day when the sons of God came to present themselves before the Lord, and Satan came also among them to present himself before the Lord. And the Lord said unto Satan, From whence comest thou? And Satan answered the Lord, and said, From going to and fro in the earth, and from walking up and down in it. And the Lord said unto Satan, Hast thou considered my servant Job, that there is none like him in the earth, a perfect and an upright man, one that feareth God, and escheweth evil? and still he holdeth fast his integrity, although thou movedst me against him, to destroy him without cause. And Satan answered the Lord, and said, Skin for skin, yea, all that a man hath will he give for his life. But put forth thine hand now, and touch his bone and his flesh, and he will curse thee to thy face. And the Lord said unto Satan, Behold, he is in thine hand; but save his life.

So went Satan forth from the presence of the Lord, and smote Job with sore boils from the sole of his foot unto his crown. And he took him a potsherd to scrape himself withal;[8] and he sat down among the ashes.

Then said his wife unto him, Dost thou still retain thine integrity? curse God, and die. But he said unto her, Thou speakest as one of the foolish women speaketh. What? shall we receive good at the hand of God, and shall we not receive evil? In all this did not Job sin with his lips.

Now when Job's three friends heard of all this evil that was come upon him, they came every one from his own place; Eliphaz the Temanite, and Bildad the Shuhite, and Zophar the Naamathite:

5. split up into three groups.
6. tore.
7. cloak.
8. with.

for they had made an appointment together to come to mourn with him and to comfort him. And when they lifted up their eyes afar off, and knew him not, they lifted up their voice, and wept; and they rent every one his mantle, and sprinkled dust upon their heads toward heaven. So they sat down with him upon the ground seven days and seven nights, and none spake a word unto him: for they saw that his grief was very great.

3. After this opened Job his mouth, and cursed his day. And Job spake, and said, Let the day perish wherein I was born, and the night in which it was said, There is a man child conceived. Let that day be darkness; let not God regard it from above, neither let the light shine upon it. Let darkness and the shadow of death stain it; let a cloud dwell upon it; let the blackness of the day terrify it. As for that night, let darkness seize upon it; let it not be joined unto the days of the year, let it not come into the number of the months. Lo, let that night be solitary, let no joyful voice come therein. Let them curse it that curse the day,[9] who are ready to raise up their mourning. Let the stars of the twilight thereof be dark; let it look for light, but have none; neither let it see the dawning of the day: because it shut not up the doors of my mother's womb, nor hid sorrow from mine eyes. Why died I not from the womb? Why did I not give up the ghost when I came out of the belly? Why did the knees prevent[10] me? or why the breasts that I should suck? For now should I have lain still and been quiet, I should have slept: then had I been at rest, with kings and counsellors of the earth, which built desolate places for themselves; or with princes that had gold, who filled their houses with silver: or as an hidden untimely birth I had not been; as infants which never saw light. There the wicked cease from troubling; and there the weary be at rest. There the prisoners rest together; they hear not the voice of the oppressor. The small and great are there; and the servant is free from his master. Wherefore is light given to him that is in misery, and life unto the bitter in soul; which long for death, but it cometh not; and dig for it more than for hid treasures; which rejoice exceedingly, and are glad, when they can find the grave? Why is light given to a man whose way is hid, and whom God hath hedged in? For my sighing cometh before I eat, and my roarings are poured out like the waters. For the thing which I greatly feared is come upon me, and that which I was afraid of is come unto me. I was not in safety, neither had I rest, neither was I quiet;[11] yet trouble came.

9. sorcerers, magicians. A more literal translation of the next clause would read, "who are ready to rouse up leviathan." Leviathan was a dragon that was thought to produce darkness.
10. receive.
11. For *was*, *had*, and *was*, read, "am," "have," and "am."

4. Then Eliphaz the Temanite answered and said, If we assay to commune with thee, wilt thou be grieved? But who can withhold himself from speaking? Behold, thou hast instructed many, and thou hast strengthened the weak hands. Thy words have upholden him that was falling, and thou hast strengthened the feeble knees. But now it is come upon thee, and thou faintest; it toucheth thee, and thou art troubled. Is not this thy fear, thy confidence, thy hope, and the uprightness of thy ways?[12] Remember, I pray thee, who ever perished, being innocent? or where were the righteous cut off? Even as I have seen, they that plow iniquity, and sow wickedness, reap the same. By the blast of God they perish, and by the breath of his nostrils are they consumed. The roaring of the lion, and the voice of the fierce lion, and the teeth of the young lions, are broken. The old lion perisheth for lack of prey, and the stout lion's whelps are scattered abroad. Now a thing was secretly brought to me, and mine ear received a little[13] thereof. In thoughts from the visions of the night, when deep sleep falleth on men, fear came upon me, and trembling, which made all my bones to shake. Then a spirit passed before my face; the hair of my flesh stood up: It stood still, but I could not discern the form thereof: an image was before mine eyes, there was silence, and I heard a voice, saying, Shall mortal man be more just than God? Shall a man be more pure than his maker? Behold, he put no trust in his servants; and his angels he charged with folly: How much less[14] in them that dwell in houses of clay, whose foundation is in the dust, which are crushed before the moth? They are destroyed from morning to evening: they perish for ever without any regarding it. Doth not their excellency which is in them go away? They die, even without wisdom.

5. Call now, if there be any that will answer thee; and to which of the saints wilt thou turn? For wrath killeth the foolish man, and envy slayeth the silly one. I have seen the foolish taking root: but suddenly I cursed his habitation. His children are far from safety, and they are crushed in the gate, neither is there any to deliver them. Whose harvest the hungry eateth up, and taketh it even out of the thorns,[15] and the robber swalloweth up their substance. Although affliction cometh not forth of the dust, neither doth trouble spring out of the ground; yet man is born unto trouble, as the sparks fly upward. I would seek unto God, and unto God would I commit my cause: which doeth great things and unsearchable; marvellous things without number: who giveth rain upon the earth, and

12. A more literal translation of this sentence would read, "Is not thy fear of God thy confidence, and thy hope the uprightness of thy ways?"

13. a whisper.
14. how much less does he trust.
15. perhaps a hedge of thorn.

sendeth waters upon the fields: to set up on high those that be low; that those which mourn may be exalted to safety. He disappointeth the devices of the crafty, so that their hands cannot perform their enterprise. He taketh the wise in their own craftiness: and the counsel of the froward is carried headlong. They meet with darkness in the daytime, and grope in the noonday as in the night. But he saveth the poor from the sword, from their mouth, and from the hand of the mighty. So the poor hath hope, and iniquity stoppeth her mouth. Behold, happy is the man whom God correcteth: therefore despise not thou the chastening of the Almighty: for he maketh sore, and bindeth up: he woundeth, and his hands make whole. He shall deliver thee in six troubles: yea, in seven there shall no evil touch thee. In famine he shall redeem thee from death: and in war from the power of the sword. Thou shalt be hid from the scourge of the tongue: neither shalt thou be afraid of destruction when it cometh. At destruction and famine thou shalt laugh: neither shalt thou be afraid of the beasts of the earth. For thou shalt be in league with the stones of the field: and the beasts of the field shall be at peace with thee. And thou shalt know that thy tabernacle[16] shall be in peace; and thou shalt visit thy habitation, and shalt not sin. Thou shalt know also that thy seed shall be great, and thine offspring as the grass of the earth. Thou shalt come to thy grave in a full age, like as a shock of corn cometh in in his season. Lo this, we have searched it, so it is; hear it, and know thou it for thy good.

6. But Job answered and said, Oh that my grief were thoroughly weighed, and my calamity laid in the balances together! For now it would be heavier than the sand of the sea: therefore my words are swallowed up.[17] For the arrows of the Almighty are within me, the poison whereof drinketh up my spirit: the terrors of God do set themselves in array against me. Doth the wild ass bray when he hath grass? or loweth the ox over his fodder?[18] Can that which is unsavoury be eaten without salt? or is there any taste in the white of an egg? The things that my soul refused to touch are as my sorrowful meat.[19] Oh that I might have my request; and that God would grant me the thing that I long for! Even that it would please God to destroy me; that he would let loose his hand, and cut me off! Then should I yet have comfort; yea, I would harden myself in

---

16. tent.

17. A more literal translation of this clause would read, "therefore have my words been rash." Job recognizes the exaggeration of his first outburst.

18. Animals do not complain without reason; therefore when a rational man complains, he must have some justification for it.

19. more literally, "My soul refuseth to touch them, they are as loathsome meat to me." He is referring to the statements of his friends.

sorrow: let him not spare; for I have not concealed[20] the words of the Holy One. What is my strength, that I should hope? and what is mine end, that I should prolong my life? Is my strength the strength of stones? or is my flesh of brass? Is not my help in me? and is wisdom driven quite from me?[21] To him that is afflicted pity should be shewed from his friend; but he forsaketh the fear of the Almighty. My brethren have dealt deceitfully as a brook, and as the stream of brooks they pass away; which are blackish by reason of the ice, and wherein the snow is hid: what time they wax warm, they vanish: when it is hot, they are consumed out of their place. The paths of their way are turned aside; they go to nothing, and perish. The troops of Tema looked, the companies of Sheba waited for them. They were confounded because they had hoped;[22] they came thither, and were ashamed. For now ye are nothing; ye see my casting down, and are afraid. Did I say, Bring unto me? or, Give a reward for me of your substance? or, Deliver me from the enemy's hand? or, Redeem me from the hand of the mighty? Teach me, and I will hold my tongue: and cause me to understand wherein I have erred. How forcible are right words! But what doth your arguing reprove? Do ye imagine to reprove words, and the speeches of one that is desperate, which are as wind? Yea, ye overwhelm the fatherless, and ye dig a pit for your friend. Now therefore be content, look upon me; for it is evident unto you if I lie. Return, I pray you, let it not be iniquity;[23] yea, return again, my righteousness is in it.[24] Is there iniquity in my tongue? Cannot my taste discern perverse things?

7. Is there not an appointed time to man upon earth? Are not his days also like the days of an hireling? As a servant earnestly desireth the shadow,[25] and as an hireling looketh for the reward of his work: so am I made to possess months of vanity, and wearisome nights are appointed to me. When I lie down, I say, When shall I arise, and the night be gone? and I am full of tossings to and fro unto the dawning of the day. My flesh is clothed with worms and clods of dust; my skin is broken, and become loathsome. My days are swifter than a weaver's shuttle, and are spent without hope. O remember that my life is wind: mine eye shall no more see good. The eye of him that hath seen me shall see me no more: thine eyes are upon me, and I am not. As the cloud is consumed and vanisheth away: so he that goeth down to the grave shall come up no more.

20. more literally, "denied."
21. more literally, "Is not my help within me gone, and is not wisdom driven quite away from me?"
22. The caravans reached the springs they had counted on and found them dry.
23. let there be no injustice.
24. my cause is righteous.
25. evening, the end of the working day.

He shall return no more to his house, neither shall his place know him any more. Therefore I will not refrain my mouth; I will speak in the anguish of my spirit; I will complain in the bitterness of my soul. Am I a sea, or a whale, that thou settest a watch over me?[26] When I say, My bed shall comfort me, my couch shall ease my complaint; then thou scarest me with dreams, and terrifiest me through visions: so that my soul chooseth strangling, and death rather than my life. I loathe it; I would not live alway: let me alone; for my days are vanity. What is man, that thou shouldest magnify him? and that thou shouldest set thine heart upon him? and that thou shouldest visit him every morning, and try him every moment? How long wilt thou not depart from me, nor let me alone till I swallow down my spittle?[27] I have sinned; what shall I do unto thee, O thou preserver[28] of men? Why hast thou set me as a mark[29] against thee, so that I am a burden to myself? And why dost thou not pardon my transgression, and take away mine iniquity? For now shall I sleep in the dust; and thou shalt seek me in the morning, but I shall not be.

8. Then answered Bildad the Shuhite, and said, How long wilt thou speak these things? and how long shall the words of thy mouth be like a strong wind? Doth God pervert judgment? or doth the Almighty pervert justice? If thy children have sinned against him, and he have cast them away for their transgression; if thou wouldest seek unto God betimes,[30] and make thy supplication to the Almighty; if thou wert pure and upright; surely now he would awake for thee, and make the habitation of thy righteousness prosperous. Though thy beginning was small, yet thy latter end should greatly increase. For enquire, I pray thee, of the former age, and prepare thy self to the search of their fathers: (For we are but of yesterday, and know nothing, because our days upon earth are a shadow:) shall not they teach thee, and tell thee, and utter words out of their heart? Can the rush[31] grow up without mire? Can the flag grow without water? Whilst it is yet in his greenness, and not cut down, it withereth before any other herb. So are the paths of all that forget God; and the hypocrite's hope shall perish: whose hope shall be cut off, and whose trust shall be a spider's web. He shall lean upon his house, but it shall not stand: he shall hold it fast, but it shall not endure. He is green before the sun, and his branch shooteth

---

26. Job, now addressing God directly, compares his situation with that of the sea monster whom a god fought against in the Babylonian myth. He reproves God for exerting His power against anything as small as himself.

27. even for a moment.

28. A more literal translation would read, "watcher."

29. target.

30. early.

31. the papyrus, which grows rapidly when the Nile is high, but withers at once when the waters go down.

forth in his garden. His roots are wrapped about the heap, and seeth the place of stones. If he destroy him from his place, then it shall deny him, saying, I have not seen thee. Behold, this is the joy of his way, and out of the earth shall others grow. Behold, God will not cast away a perfect man, neither will he help the evil doers: till he fill thy mouth with laughing, and thy lips with rejoicing. They that hate thee shall be clothed with shame; and the dwelling place of the wicked shall come to nought.

9. Then Job answered and said, I know it is so of a truth: but how should man be just with God? If he will contend with him, he cannot answer him one of a thousand.[32] He is wise in heart, and mighty in strength: who hath hardened himself against him, and hath prospered? Which removeth the mountains, and they know not: which overturneth them in his anger. Which shaketh the earth out of her place, and the pillars thereof tremble. Which commandeth the sun, and it riseth not; and sealeth up the stars. Which alone spreadeth out the heavens, and treadeth upon the waves of the sea. Which maketh Arcturus, Orion, and Pleiades, and the chambers of the south. Which doeth great things past finding out; yea, and wonders without number. Lo, he goeth by me, and I see him not: he passeth on also, but I perceive him not. Behold, he taketh away, who can hinder him? Who will say unto him, What doest thou? If[33] God will not withdraw his anger, the proud helpers do stoop under him. How much less shall I answer him, and choose out my words to reason with him? Whom, though I were righteous, yet would I not answer, but I would make supplication to my judge. If I had called, and he had answered me; yet would I not believe that he had hearkened unto my voice. For he breaketh me with a tempest, and multiplieth my wounds without cause. He will not suffer me to take my breath, but filleth me with bitterness. If I speak of strength, lo, he is strong: and if of judgment, who shall set me a time to plead? If I justify myself, mine own mouth shall condemn me: if I say, I am perfect, it shall also prove me perverse. Though I were perfect, yet would I not know my soul: I would despise my life.[34] This is one thing, therefore I said it, He destroyeth the perfect and the wicked. If the scourge slay suddenly, he will laugh at the trial of the innocent. The earth is given into the hand of the wicked: he covereth the faces of the judges thereof; if not,[35] where, and who is he? Now my days are swifter than a post:[36] they flee away, they see no good. They are passed away as the swift ships:

---

32. one of a thousand questions.
33. In a more literal translation, *If* would be omitted.
34. In a more literal translation this sentence would read, "I am perfect, I regard not myself. I despise my life."
35. if not he.
36. courier.

as the eagle that hasteth to the prey. If I say, I will forget my complaint, I will leave off my heaviness, and comfort myself: I am afraid of all my sorrows, I know that thou wilt not hold me innocent. If I be wicked, why then labour I in vain? If I wash myself with snow water, and make my hands never so clean; yet shalt thou plunge me in the ditch, and mine own clothes abhor me.[37] For he is not a man, as I am, that I should answer him, and we should come together in judgment. Neither is there any daysman[38] betwixt us, that might lay his hand upon us both. Let him take his rod away from me, and let not his fear terrify me: then would I speak, and not fear him; but it is not so with me.

10. My soul is weary of my life; I will leave[39] my complaint upon[40] myself; I will speak in the bitterness of my soul. I will say unto God, Do not condemn me; shew me wherefore thou contendest with me. Is it good unto thee that thou shouldest oppress, that thou shouldest despise the work of thine hands, and shine upon the counsel of the wicked? Hast thou eyes of flesh? or seest thou as man seeth?[41] Are thy days as the days of man? Are thy years as man's days,[42] that thou enquirest after mine iniquity, and searchest after my sin? Thou knowest that I am not wicked; and there is none that can deliver out of thine hand. Thine hands have made me and fashioned me together round about; yet thou dost destroy me. Remember, I beseech thee, that thou hast made me as the clay; and wilt thou bring me into dust again? Hast thou not poured me out as milk and curdled me like cheese? Thou hast clothed me with skin and flesh, and hast fenced me with bones and sinews. Thou hast granted me life and favour, and thy visitation hath preserved my spirit. And these things hast thou hid in thine heart: I know that this is with thee.[43] If I sin, then thou markest me, and thou wilt not acquit me from mine iniquity. If I be wicked, woe unto me; and if I be righteous, yet will I not lift up my head. I am full of confusion; therefore see thou mine affliction; for it increaseth. Thou huntest me as a fierce lion: and again thou shewest thyself marvellous upon me. Thou renewest thy witnesses[44] against me, and increasest thine indignation upon me; changes and war are against me. Wherefore then hast thou brought me forth out of the womb? Oh that I had given up the ghost, and no eye had seen me! I should have been as though I had not been; I should

---

37. shall abhor me.
38. arbitrator.
39. give free course to.
40. on behalf of.
41. Are you capable of mistakes, of seeing as a man sees?
42. Is your time, like man's, short,
so that you have to judge hastily?
43. The meaning is, "My destruction (*this*) is your purpose." Job accuses God of planning his destruction while showing favor to him.
.4. his afflictions, which prove (to his friends) his guilt.

have been carried from the womb to the grave. Are not my days few? Cease then, and let me alone, that I may take comfort a little, before I go whence I shall not return, even to the land of darkness and the shadow of death: a land of darkness, as darkness itself; and of the shadow of death, without any order, and where the light is as darkness.

11. Then answered Zophar the Naamathite, and said, Should not the multitude of words be answered? And should a man full of talk be justified? Should thy lies make men hold their peace? And when thou mockest, shall no man make thee ashamed? For thou hast said, My doctrine is pure, and I am clean in thine eyes. But oh that God would speak, and open his lips against thee; and that he would shew thee the secrets of wisdom, that they are double to that which is![45] Know therefore that God exacteth of thee less than thine iniquity deserveth. Canst thou by searching find out God? Canst thou find out the Almighty unto perfection? It is as high as heaven; what canst thou do? Deeper than hell; what canst thou know? The measure thereof is longer than the earth, and broader than the sea. If he cut off, and shut up, or gather together,[46] then who can hinder him? For he knoweth vain men: he seeth wickedness also; will he not then consider it? For vain man would be wise, though man be born like a wild ass's colt. If thou prepare thine heart, and stretch out thine hands toward him; if iniquity be in thine hand, put it far away, and let not wickedness dwell in thy tabernacles. For then shalt thou lift up thy face without spot; yea, thou shalt be stedfast, and shalt not fear: because thou shalt forget thy misery, and remember it as waters that pass away: and thine age shall be clearer than the noonday; thou shalt shine forth, thou shalt be as the morning. And thou shalt be secure, because there is hope; yea, thou shalt dig[47] about thee, and thou shalt take thy rest in safety. Also thou shalt lie down, and none shall make thee afraid; yea, many shall make suit unto thee. But the eyes of the wicked shall fail, and they shall not escape, and their hope shall be as the giving up of the ghost.

12. And Job answered and said, No doubt but ye are the people, and wisdom shall die with you. But I have understanding as well as you; I am not inferior to you: yea, who knoweth not such things as these? I am as one mocked of his neighbour, who calleth upon God, and he answered him: the just upright man is laughed to scorn. He that is ready to slip with his feet is as a lamp despised in the

---

45. *double to that which is:* obscure in the original, usually taken to mean simply "manifold," "various."

46. for judgment.

47. search. The master inspects his property before retiring.

thought of him that is at ease. The tabernacles of robbers prosper, and they that provoke God are secure; into whose hand God bringeth abundantly. But ask now the beasts, and they shall teach thee; and the fowls of the air, and they shall tell thee: or speak to the earth, and it shall teach thee: and the fishes of the sea shall declare unto thee. Who knoweth not in all these that the hand of the Lord hath wrought this? In whose hand is the soul of every living thing, and the breath of all mankind. Doth not the ear try words? and the mouth taste his meat? With the ancient is wisdom; and in length of days understanding. With him is wisdom and strength, he hath counsel and understanding. Behold, he breaketh down, and it cannot be built again: he shutteth up a man, and there can be no opening. Behold, he withholdeth the waters, and they dry up: also he sendeth them out, and they overturn the earth. With him is strength and wisdom: the deceived and the deceiver are his. He leadeth counsellors away spoiled, and maketh the judges fools. He looseth the bond of kings, and girdeth their loins with a girdle. He leadeth princes away spoiled, and overthroweth the mighty. He removeth away the speech of the trusty, and taketh away the understanding of the aged. He poureth contempt upon princes, and weakeneth the strength of the mighty. He discovereth deep things out of darkness, and bringeth out to light the shadow of death. He increaseth the nations, and destroyeth them: he enlargeth the nations, and straiteneth[48] them again. He taketh away the heart of the chief of the people of the earth, and causeth them to wander in a wilderness where there is no way. They grope in the dark without light, and he maketh them to stagger like a drunken man.

13. Lo, mine eye hath seen all this, mine ear hath heard and understood it. What ye know, the same do I know also: I am not inferior unto you. Surely I would speak to the Almighty, and I desire to reason with God. But ye are forgers of lies, ye are all physicians of no value. O that ye would altogether hold your peace! and it should be your wisdom. Hear now my reasoning, and hearken to the pleadings of my lips. Will ye speak wickedly for God? and talk deceitfully for him? Will ye accept[49] his person? Will ye contend for God? Is it good that he should search you out? or as one man mocketh another, do ye so mock him? He will surely reprove you, if ye do secretly accept persons.[50] Shall not his excellency make you afraid? and his dread fall upon you? Your remembrances[51] are like unto ashes, your bodies to bodies of clay. Hold your peace, let me alone, that I may speak, and let come on me what will. Where-

48. contracts their boundaries.
49. respect.
50. This phrase seems to mean some-

thing like, "back the winning side for personal reasons."
51. memorable sayings.

fore do I take my flesh in my teeth,[52] and put my life in mine hand? Though he slay me, yet will I trust in him: but I will maintain mine own ways before him. He also shall be my salvation: for an hypocrite shall not come before him. Hear diligently my speech, and my declaration with your ears. Behold now, I have ordered my cause; I know that I shall be justified. Who is he that will plead with me?[53] for now, if I hold my tongue, I shall give up the ghost.[54] Only do not two things unto me: then will I not hide myself from thee.[55] Withdraw thine hand far from me: and let not thy dread make me afraid. Then call thou, and I will answer: or let me speak, and answer thou me. How many are mine iniquities and sins? Make me to know my transgression and my sin. Wherefore hidest thou thy face, and holdest me for thine enemy? Wilt thou break a leaf driven to and fro? and wilt thou pursue the dry stubble? For thou writest bitter things against me, and makest me to possess[56] the iniquities of my youth. Thou puttest my feet also in the stocks, and lookest narrowly unto all my paths; thou settest a print upon[57] the heels of my feet. And he,[58] as a rotten thing, consumeth, as a garment that is moth eaten.

14. Man that is born of a woman is of few days, and full of trouble. He cometh forth like a flower, and is cut down: he fleeth also as a shadow, and continueth not. And dost thou open thine eyes upon such an one, and bringest me into judgment with thee? Who can bring a clean thing out of an unclean? not one. Seeing his days are determined, the number of his months are with thee, thou hast appointed his bounds that he cannot pass; turn from him, that he may rest, till he shall accomplish, as an hireling, his day. For there is hope of a tree, if it be cut down, that it will sprout again, and that the tender branch thereof will not cease. Though the root thereof wax old in the earth, and the stock thereof die in the ground; yet through the scent of water it will bud, and bring forth boughs like a plant. But man dieth, and wasteth away: yea, man giveth up the ghost, and where is he? As the waters fail from the sea, and the flood decayeth and drieth up: so man lieth down, and riseth not: till the heavens be no more, they shall not awake, nor be raised out of their sleep. O that thou wouldest hide me in the grave, that thou wouldest keep me secret, until thy wrath be past, that thou wouldest appoint me a set time, and remember me! If a man die, shall he live again? All the days of my appointed time will

52. like a wild beast at bay, defending its life with its teeth.
53. accuse me.
54. In a more literal translation this would read, "If anyone does accuse me I shall hold my tongue and die."
55. He now addresses himself directly to God.
56. inherit.
57. drawest a line about.
58. the prisoner in the stocks, Job.

I wait, till my change[59] come. Thou shalt call, and I will answer thee: thou wilt have a desire to[60] the work of thine hands. For now thou numberest my steps: dost thou not watch over my sin? My transgression is sealed up in a bag, and thou sewest up mine iniquity. And surely the mountain falling cometh to nought, and the rock is removed out of his place. The waters wear the stones: thou washest away the things which grow out of the dust of the earth; and thou destroyest the hope of man. Thou prevailest for ever against him, and he passeth. thou changest his countenance, and sendest him away. His sons come to honour, and he knoweth it not; and they are brought low, but he perceiveth it not of them. But his flesh upon him shall have pain, and his soul within him shall mourn.

29. Moreover Job continued his parable, and said, Oh that I were as in months past, as in the days when God preserved me; when his candle shined upon my head, and when by his light I walked through darkness; as I was in the days of my youth, when the secret of God was upon my tabernacle; when the Almighty was yet with me, when my children were about me; when I washed my steps with butter and the rock poured me out rivers of oil; when I went out to the gate[61] through the city, when I prepared my seat in the street! The young men saw me, and hid themselves: and the aged arose, and stood up. The princes refrained talking, and laid their hand on their mouth. The nobles held their peace, and their tongue cleaved to the roof of their mouth. When the ear heard me, then it blessed me; and when the eye saw me, it gave witness to me: because I delivered the poor that cried, and the fatherless, and him that had none to help him. The blessing of him that was ready to perish came upon me: and I caused the widow's heart to sing for joy. I put on righteousness, and it clothed me: my judgment was as a robe and a diadem. I was eyes to the blind, and feet was I to the lame. I was a father to the poor: and the cause which I knew not I searched out. And I brake the jaws of the wicked, and plucked the spoil out of his teeth. Then I said, I shall die in my nest, and I shall multiply my days as the sand. My root was spread out by the waters, and the dew lay all night upon my branch. My glory was fresh in me, and my bow was renewed in my hand. Unto me men gave ear, and waited, and kept silence at my counsel. After my words they spake not again; and my speech dropped upon them. And they waited for me as for the rain; and they opened their mouth wide as for the latter rain. If I laughed on them, they believed it not;[62]

59. release.
60. for.
61. The town meeting place and law court was just inside the gate.

62. obscure in the original; perhaps, "I smiled on them and they were confident."

and the light of my countenance they cast not down. I chose out
their way, and sat chief, and dwelt as a king in the army, as one
that comforteth the mourners.

30. But now they that are younger than I have me in derision,
whose fathers I would have disdained to have set with the dogs of
my flock. Yea, whereto might the strength of their hands profit me,[63]
in whom old age was perished? For want and famine they were
solitary; fleeing into the wilderness in former time desolate and
waste. Who cut up mallows by the bushes, and juniper roots for
their meat. They were driven forth from among men, (they cried
after them as after a thief;) to dwell in the cliffs of the valleys, in
caves of the earth, and in the rocks. Among the bushes they brayed;
under the nettles they were gathered together. They were children
of fools, yea, children of base men: they were viler than the earth.
And now am I their song, yea, I am their byword. They abhor me,
they flee far from me, and spare not to spit in my face. Because he
hath loosed my cord, and afflicted me, they have also let loose the
bridle before me. Upon my right hand rise the youth; they push
away my feet, and they raise up against me the ways of their destruction. They mar my path, they set forward my calamity, they
have no helper.[64] They came upon me as a wide breaking in of
waters: in the desolation they rolled themselves upon me. Terrors
are turned upon me: they pursue my soul as the wind: and my
welfare passeth away as a cloud. And now my soul is poured out
upon[65] me; the days of affliction have taken hold upon me. My
bones are pierced in me in the night season: and my sinews take
no rest. By the great force of my disease is my garment changed: it
bindeth me about as the collar of my coat. He hath cast me into
the mire, and I am become like dust and ashes. I cry unto thee,
and thou dost not hear me: I stand up, and thou regardest me not.
Thou art become cruel to me: with thy strong hand thou opposest
thyself against me. Thou liftest me up to the wind; thou causest
me to ride upon it, and dissolvest my substance. For I know that
thou wilt bring me to death, and to the house appointed for all living. Howbeit he will not stretch out his hand to the grave, though
they cry in his destruction.[66] Did not I weep for him that was in
trouble? Was not my soul grieved for the poor? When I looked for
good, then evil came unto me: and when I waited for light, there
came darkness. My bowels boiled, and rested not: the days of affliction prevented me.[67] I went mourning without the sun: I stood up,

63. They were too old to work.
64. *they have no helper:* The text
is uncertain at this point.
65. within.

66. This sentence is unintelligible in
the original.
67. came upon me.

and I cried in the congregation. I am a brother to dragons, and a companion to owls. My skin is black upon me, and my bones are burned with heat. My harp also is turned to mourning, and my organ[68] into the voice of them that weep.

31. I made a covenant with mine eyes; why then should I think upon a maid? For what portion of God is there from above? and what inheritance of the Almighty from on high? Is not destruction to the wicked? and a strange punishment to the workers of iniquity? Doth not he see my ways, and count all my steps? If I have walked with vanity, or if my foot hath hasted to deceit; let me be weighed in an even balance, that God may know mine integrity. If my step hath turned out of the way, and mine heart walked after mine eyes, and if any blot hath cleaved to mine hands; then let me sow, and let another eat; yea, let my offspring be rooted out. If mine heart have been deceived by a woman, or if I have laid wait at my neighbour's door; then let my wife grind unto another, and let others bow down upon her. For this is an heinous crime; yea, it is an iniquity to be punished by the judges. For it is a fire that consumeth to destruction, and would root out all mine increase.

If I did despise the cause of my manservant or of my maid-servant, when they contended with me; what then shall I do when God riseth up? and when he visiteth, what shall I answer him? Did not he that made me in the womb make him? and did not one fashion us in the womb? If I have withheld the poor from their desire, or have caused the eyes of the widow to fail; or have eaten my morsel myself alone, and the fatherless hath not eaten thereof; (For from my youth he was brought up with me, as with a father, and I have guided her from my mother's womb;) if I have seen any perish for want of clothing, or any poor without covering; if his loins have not blessed me, and if he were not warmed with the fleece of my sheep; if I have lifted up my hand against the father-less, when I saw my help in the gate:[69] then let mine arm fall from my shoulder blade, and mine arm be broken from the bone. For destruction from God was a terror to me, and by reason of his highness I could not endure. If I have made gold my hope, or have said to the fine gold, Thou art my confidence; if I rejoiced because my wealth was great, and because mine hand had gotten much; if I beheld the sun when it shined, or the moon walking in bright-ness; and my heart hath been secretly enticed, or my mouth hath kissed my hand:[70] this also were an iniquity to be punished by the judge: for I should have denied the God that is above.

68. pipe.
69. The gate is the court; the clause means, "when I had influence in the court."

70. *my heart . . . my hand:* idol-atrous acts of worship of the sun and moon.

If I rejoiced at the destruction of him that hated me, or lifted up myself when evil found him: neither have I suffered my mouth to sin by wishing a curse to his soul. If the men of my tabernacle said not, Oh that we had of his flesh! We cannot be satisfied.[71] The stranger did not lodge in the street: but I opened my doors to the traveller. If I covered my transgressions as Adam, by hiding mine iniquity in my bosom: did I fear a great multitude, or did the contempt of families terrify me, that I kept silence, and went not out of the door? Oh that one would hear me! Behold, my desire is, that the Almighty would answer me, and that mine adversary had written a book. Surely I would take it upon my shoulder, and bind it as a crown to me. I would declare unto him the number of my steps; as a prince would I go near unto him. If my land cry against me, or that the furrows likewise thereof complain; if I have eaten the fruits thereof without money, or have caused the owners thereof to lose their life: let thistles grow instead of wheat, and cockle instead of barley. The words of Job are ended.

. . .

38. Then the Lord answered Job out of the whirlwind, and said, Who is this that darkeneth counsel by words without knowledge? Gird up now thy loins like a man; for I will demand of thee, and answer thou me. Where wast thou when I laid the foundations of the earth? Declare, if thou hast understanding. Who hath laid the measures thereof, if thou knowest? or who hath stretched the line upon it? Whereupon are the foundations thereof fastened? or who laid the corner stone thereof; when the morning stars sang together, and all the sons of God shouted for joy? Or who shut up the sea with doors, when it brake forth, as if it had issued out of the womb? When I made the cloud the garment thereof, and thick darkness a swaddlingband for it, and brake up for it my decreed place,[72] and set bars and doors, and said, Hitherto shalt thou come, but no further: and here shall thy proud waves be stayed? Hast thou commanded the morning since thy days; and caused the dayspring[73] to know his place; that it might take hold of the ends of the earth, that the wicked might be shaken out of it? It is turned as clay to the seal;[74] and they[75] stand as a garment. And from the wicked their light is withholden, and the high arm shall be broken. Hast thou entered into the springs of the sea? or hast thou walked in the search of the depth? Have the gates of death been opened unto

71. Translated literally, the statement of the men of the tabernacle should probably read, "Who can find one that hath not been satisfied with his flesh?" i.e., with meat from his flocks.

72. the broken coastline.
73. dawn.
74. A more literal translation would read, "changed as clay under the seal."
75. all things. God is describing the moment of the creation of the universe.

thee? or hast thou seen the doors of the shadow of death? Hast thou perceived the breadth of the earth? Declare if thou knowest it all. Where is the way where light dwelleth? And as for darkness, where is the place thereof, that thou shouldest take it to the bound thereof, and that thou shouldest know the paths to the house thereof? Knowest thou it, because thou wast then born? or because the number of thy days is great? Hast thou entered into the treasures of the snow? or hast thou seen the treasures of the hail, which I have reserved against the time of trouble, against the day of battle and war? By what way is the light parted, which scattereth the east wind upon the earth?[76] Who hath divided a watercourse for the overflowing of waters, or a way for the lightning of thunder; to cause it to rain on the earth, where no man is; on the wilderness, wherein there is no man; to satisfy the desolate and waste ground; and to cause the bud of the tender herb to spring forth? Hath the rain a father? or who hath begotten the drops of dew? Out of whose womb came the ice? And the hoary frost of heaven, who hath gendered it? The waters are hid as with a stone, and the face of the deep is frozen. Canst thou bind the sweet influences of Pleiades, or loose the bands of Orion? Canst thou bring forth Mazzaroth[77] in his season? or canst thou guide Arcturus with his sons? Knowest thou the ordinances of heaven? Canst thou set the dominion thereof in the earth? Canst thou lift up thy voice to the clouds, that abundance of waters may cover thee? Canst thou send lightnings, that they may go, and say unto thee, Here we are? Who hath put wisdom in the inward parts? or who hath given understanding to the heart? Who can number the clouds in wisdom? or who can stay the bottles of heaven, when the dust groweth into hardness, and the clods cleave fast together? Wilt thou hunt the prey for the lion? or fill the appetite of the young lion, when they couch in their dens, and abide in the covert to lie in wait? Who provideth for the raven his food? when his young ones cry unto God, they[78] wander for lack of meat.

39. Knowest thou the time when the wild goats of the rock bring forth? or canst thou mark when the hinds do calve? Canst thou number the months that they fulfil? or knowest thou the time when they bring forth? They bow themselves, they bring forth their young ones, they cast out their sorrows. Their young ones are in good liking, they grow up with corn; they go forth, and return not unto them. Who hath sent out the wild ass free? or who hath loosed the bands of the wild ass? Whose house I have made the wilderness, and the barren land his dwellings. He scorneth the

76. more literally, "and the east wind scattered upon the earth."

77. meaning disputed; it may be a name for the signs of the zodiac, or for some particular constellation.

78. more literally, "and."

multitude of the city, neither regardeth he the crying of the driver. The range of the mountains is his pasture, and he searcheth after every green thing. Will the unicorn[79] be willing to serve thee, or abide by thy crib? Canst thou bind the unicorn with his band in the furrow? or will he harrow the valleys after thee? Wilt thou trust him, because his strength is great? or wilt thou leave thy labour to him? Wilt thou believe him, that he will bring home thy seed, and gather it into thy barn? Gavest thou the goodly wings unto the peacocks? or wings and feathers unto the ostrich? Which leaveth her eggs in the earth, and warmeth them in dust, and forgetteth that the foot may crush them, or that the wild beast may break them. She is hardened against her young ones, as though they were not her's: her labour is in vain without fear;[80] because God hath deprived her of wisdom, neither hath he imparted to her understanding. What time she lifteth up herself on high, she scorneth the horse and his rider. Hast thou given the horse strength? Hast thou clothed his neck with thunder? Canst thou make him afraid as a grasshopper? The glory of his nostrils is terrible. He paweth in the valley, and rejoiceth in his strength: he goeth on to meet the armed men. He mocketh at fear, and is not affrighted; neither turneth he back from the sword. The quiver rattleth against him, the glittering spear and the shield. He swalloweth the ground with fierceness and rage: neither believeth he that it is the sound of the trumpet. He saith among the trumpets, Ha, ha; and he smelleth the battle afar off, the thunder of the captains, and the shouting. Doth the hawk fly by thy wisdom, and stretch her wings toward the south? Doth the eagle mount up at thy command, and make her nest on high? She dwelleth and abideth on the rock, upon the crag of the rock, and the strong place. From thence she seeketh the prey, and her eyes behold afar off. Her young ones also suck up blood: and where the slain are, there is she.

40. Moreover the Lord answered Job, and said, Shall he that contendeth with the Almighty instruct him? He that reproveth God, let him answer it.

Then Job answered the Lord, and said, Behold, I am vile; what shall I answer thee? I will lay mine hand upon my mouth. Once have I spoken; but I will not answer: yea, twice; but I will proceed no further.

Then answered the Lord unto Job out of the whirlwind, and said, Gird up thy loins now like a man: I will demand of thee, and declare thou unto me. Wilt thou also disannul my judgment? Wilt thou condemn me, that thou mayest be righteous? Hast thou an

---

79. a mythical beast with one horn in the center of his forehead. The Hebrew is less imaginative; it says, "wild ox."

80. though her labor is in vain, she is without fear.

arm like God? or canst thou thunder with a voice like him? Deck thyself now with majesty and excellency; and array thyself with glory and beauty. Cast abroad the rage of thy wrath: and behold every one that is proud, and abase him. Look on every one that is proud, and bring him low; and tread down the wicked in their place. Hide them in the dust together; and bind their faces in secret. Then will I also confess unto thee that thine own right hand can save thee.

Behold now behemoth,[81] which I made with thee; he eateth grass as an ox. Lo now, his strength is in his loins, and his force is in the navel of his belly. He moveth his tail like a cedar: the sinews of his stone[82] are wrapped together. His bones are as strong pieces of brass; his bones are like bars of iron. He is the chief of the ways of God: he that made him can make his sword to approach unto him. Surely the mountains bring him forth food, where all the beasts of the field play. He lieth under the shady trees, in the covert of the reed, and fens. The shady trees cover him with their shadow; the willows of the brook compass him about. Behold, he drinketh up a river, and hasteth not: he trusteth that he can draw up Jordan into his mouth. He taketh it with his eyes:[83] his nose pierceth through snares.

41. Canst thou draw out leviathan[84] with an hook?[85] or his tongue with a cord which thou lettest down? Canst thou put an hook into his nose? or bore his jaw through with a thorn? Will he make many supplications unto thee? will he speak soft words unto thee? Will he make a covenant with thee? wilt thou take him for a servant for ever? Wilt thou play with him as with a bird? or wilt thou bind him for thy maidens? Shall the companions make a banquet of him? Shall they part him among the merchants? Canst thou fill his skin with barbed irons? or his head with fish spears? Lay thine hand upon him, remember the battle, do no more. Behold, the hope of him is in vain: shall not one be cast down even at the sight of him? None is so fierce that dare stir him up: who then is able to stand before me? Who hath prevented[86] me, that I should repay him? Whatsoever is under the whole heaven is mine. I will not conceal his parts, nor his power, nor his comely proportion. Who can discover[87] the face of his garment?[88] or who can come to him with his double bridle? Who can open the doors of his face? His teeth are terrible round about. His scales are his pride, shut up together as with a close seal. One is so near to another, that

---

81. generally identified with the hippopotamus.
82. A more literal translation would read, "thighs."
83. obscure in the original; probably, "None can attack him in the eyes."
84. here probably the crocodile.
85. The Greek historian Herodotus tells how the Egyptians captured the crocodile with a hook.
86. given anything to me first.
87. strip off.
88. his scales.

no air can come between them. They are joined one to another, they stick together, that they cannot be sundered. By his neesings[89] a light doth shine, and his eyes are like the eyelids of the morning. Out of his mouth go burning lamps, and sparks of fire leap out. Out of his nostrils goeth smoke, as out of a seething pot or caldron. His breath kindleth coals, and a flame goeth out of his mouth. In his neck remaineth strength, and sorrow is turned into joy before him. The flakes of his flesh are joined together: they are firm in themselves; they cannot be moved. His heart is as firm as a stone; yea, as hard as a piece of the nether millstone. When he raiseth up himself, the mighty are afraid: by reason of breakings they purify themselves.[90] The sword of him that layeth at him cannot hold: the spear, the dart, nor the habergeon. He esteemeth iron as straw, and brass as rotten wood. The arrow cannot make him flee: slingstones are turned with him into stubble. Darts are counted as stubble: he laugheth at the shaking of a spear. Sharp stones are under him: he spreadeth sharp pointed things upon the mire. He maketh the deep to boil like a pot: he maketh the sea like a pot of ointment. He maketh a path to shine after him; one would think the deep to be hoary.[91] Upon earth there is not his like, who is made without fear. He beholdeth all high things: he is a king over all the children of pride.

42. Then Job answered the Lord, and said, I know that thou canst do every thing, and that no thought can be withholden from thee. Who is he that hideth counsel without knowledge? Therefore have I uttered that I understood not; things too wonderful for me, which I knew not. Hear, I beseech thee, and I will speak: I will demand of thee, and declare thou unto me. I have heard of thee by the hearing of the ear: but now mine eye seeth thee. Wherefore I abhor myself, and repent in dust and ashes.

And it was so, that after the Lord had spoken these words unto Job, the Lord said to Eliphaz the Temanite, My wrath is kindled against thee, and against thy two friends: for ye have not spoken of me the thing that is right, as my servant Job hath. Therefore take unto you now seven bullocks and seven rams, and go to my servant Job, and offer up for yourselves a burnt offering; and my servant Job shall pray for you: for him will I accept: lest I deal with you after your folly, in that ye have not spoken of me the thing which is right, like my servant Job. So Eliphaz the Temanite and Bildad the Shuhite and Zophar the Naamathite went, and did according as the Lord commanded them: the Lord also accepted Job. And

89. his breath (compare, "sneeze"). The vapor exhaled by the crocodile appears luminous in the sunlight.

90. a corrupt text. The clause probably should read, "in consternation they are beside themselves."

91. white (with foam).

the Lord turned the captivity[92] of Job, when he prayed for his friends: also the Lord gave Job twice as much as he had before. Then came there unto him all his brethren, and all his sisters, and all they that had been of his acquaintance before, and did eat bread with him in his house: and they bemoaned him, and comforted him over all the evil that the Lord had brought upon him: every man also gave him a piece of money, and every one an earring of gold. So the Lord blessed the latter end of Job more than his beginning: for he had fourteen thousand sheep, and six thousand camels, and a thousand yoke of oxen, and a thousand she asses. He had also seven sons and three daughters. And he called the name of the first, Jemima; and the name of the second, Kezia; and the name of the third, Kerenhappuch. And in all the land were no women found so fair as the daughters of Job: and their father gave them inheritance among their brethren. After this lived Job an hundred and forty years, and saw his sons, and his sons' sons, even four generations. So Job died, being old and full of days.

92. **changed the fortune.**

## Ecclesiastes
### or, The Preacher*

1. . . . Vanity of vanities, saith the Preacher, vanity of vanities; all is vanity.[1] What profit hath a man of all his labour which he taketh under the sun? One generation passeth away, and another generation cometh: but the earth abideth for ever. The sun also ariseth, and the sun goeth down and hasteth to his place where he arose. The wind goeth toward the south, and turneth about unto the north; it whirleth about continually, and the wind returneth again according to his circuits. All the rivers run into the sea; yet the sea is not full; unto the place from whence the rivers come, thither they return again. All things are full of labour; man cannot utter it; the eye is not satisfied with seeing, nor the ear filled with hearing. The thing that hath been, it is that which shall be; and that which is done is that which shall be done: and there is no new thing under the sun. Is there any thing whereof it may be said, See, this is new? it hath been already of old time, which was before us. There is no remembrance of former things; neither shall there be any remembrance of things that are to come with those that shall come after.

I the Preacher was king over Israel in Jerusalem. And I gave my heart to seek and search out by wisdom concerning all things that are done under heaven: this sore travail hath God given to the sons of man to be exercised therewith. I have seen all the works that are done under the sun; and, behold, all is vanity and vexation of spirit. That which is crooked cannot be made straight: and that which is

* Selections (1:2–18; 2:1–24; 3; 9:2–   1. *vanity:* emptiness.
12; 11; 12:1–8).

wanting cannot be numbered. I communed with mine own heart, saying, Lo, I am come to great estate, and have gotten more wisdom than all they that have been before me in Jerusalem: yea, my heart had great experience of wisdom and knowledge. And I gave my heart to know wisdom, and to know madness and folly: I perceived that this also is vexation of spirit. For in much wisdom is much grief: and he that increaseth knowledge increaseth sorrow.

2. I said in mine heart, Go to now, I will prove thee with mirth,[2] therefore enjoy pleasure: and, behold, this also is vanity. I said of laughter, It is mad: and of mirth, What doeth it? I sought in mine heart to give myself unto wine, yet acquainting mine heart with wisdom; and to lay hold on folly, till I might see what was that good for the sons of men, which they should do under the heaven all the days of their life. I made me great works; I builded me houses; I planted me vineyards: I made me gardens and orchards, and I planted trees in them of all kinds of fruits: I made me pools of water, to water therewith the wood that bringeth forth trees; I got me servants[3] and maidens, and had servants born in my house; also I had great possessions of great and small cattle above all that were in Jerusalem before me: I gathered me also silver and gold, and the peculiar treasure of kings and of the provinces: I gat me men singers and women singers, and the delights of the sons of men, as musical instruments, and that of all sorts. So I was great, and increased more than all that were before me in Jerusalem: also my wisdom remained with me. And whatsoever mine eyes desired I kept not from them, I withheld not my heart from any joy; for my heart rejoiced in all my labour: and this was my portion of all my labour. Then I looked on all the works that my hands had wrought, and on the labour that I had laboured to do: and, behold, all was vanity and vexation of spirit, and there was no profit under the sun. And I turned myself to behold wisdom, and madness, and folly: for what can the man do that cometh after the king? even that which hath been already done. Then I saw that wisdom excelleth folly, as far as light excelleth darkness. The wise man's eyes are in his head; but the fool walketh in darkness: and I myself perceived also that one event happeneth to them all. Then said I in my heart, As it happeneth to the fool, so it happeneth even to me; and why was I then more wise? Then I said in my heart, that this also is vanity. For there is no remembrance of the wise more than of the fool for ever; seeing that which now is in the days to come shall all be forgotten. And how dieth the wise man? as the fool. Therefore I hated life; because the work that is wrought under the sun is grievous unto me: for all is vanity and vexation of spirit.

2. *prove thee with mirth:* i.e., I will try pleasure.    3. *servants:* slaves.

Yea, I hated all my labour which I had taken under the sun: because I should leave it unto the man that shall be after me. And who knoweth whether he shall be a wise man or a fool? yet shall he have rule over all my labour wherein I have laboured, and wherein I have shewed myself wise under the sun. This is also vanity. Therefore I went about to cause my heart to despair of all the labour which I took under the sun. For there is a man whose labour is in wisdom, and in knowledge, and in equity; yet to a man that hath not laboured therein shall he leave it for his portion. This also is vanity and a great evil. For what hath man of all his labour, and of the vexation of his heart, wherein he hath laboured under the sun? For all his days are sorrows, and his travail grief; yea, his heart taketh not rest in the night. This is also vanity.

There is nothing better for a man, than that he should eat and drink, and that he should make his soul enjoy good in his labour. This also I saw, that it was from the hand of God.

3. To every thing there is a season, and a time to every purpose under the heaven: A time to be born, and a time to die; a time to plant, and a time to pluck up that which is planted; A time to kill, and a time to heal; a time to break down, and a time to build up; A time to weep, and a time to laugh; a time to mourn, and a time to dance; A time to cast away stones, and a time to gather stones together; a time to embrace, and a time to refrain from embracing; A time to get, and a time to lose; a time to keep, and a time to cast away; A time to rend, and a time to sew; a time to keep silence, and a time to speak; A time to love, and a time to hate; a time of war, and a time of peace. What profit hath he that worketh in that wherein he laboureth? I have seen the travail,[4] which God hath given to the sons of men to be exercised in it. He hath made every thing beautiful in his time; also he hath set the world in their heart, so that no man can find out the work that God maketh from the beginning to the end. I know that there is no good in them, but for a man to rejoice, and to do good in his life. And also that every man should eat and drink, and enjoy the good of all his labour, it is the gift of God. I know that, whatsoever God doeth, it shall be for ever: nothing can be put to it, nor any thing taken from it; and God doeth it, that men should fear before him. That which hath been is now; and that which is to be hath already been; and God requireth[5] that which is past.

And moreover I saw under the sun the place of judgment, that wickedness was there; and the place of righteousness, that iniquity was there. I said in mine heart, God shall judge the righteous and the wicked: for there is a time there for every purpose and for every work. I said in mine heart concerning the estate of the sons of men,

---

4. *travail:* labor.　　　　5. *requireth:* calls back.

that God might manifest[6] them and that they might see that they themselves are beasts. For that which befalleth the sons of men befalleth beasts; even one thing befalleth them; as the one dieth, so dieth the other; yea, they have all one breath; so that a man hath no preeminence above a beast: for all is vanity. All go unto one place; all are of the dust, and all turn to dust again. Who knoweth the spirit of man that goeth upward, and the spirit of the beast that goeth downward to the earth?[7] Wherefore I perceive that there is nothing better, than that a man should rejoice in his own works; for that is his portion; for who shall bring him to see what shall be after him?

9. . . . All things come alike to all: there is one event to the righteous and to the wicked; to the good and to the clean, and to the unclean; to him that sacrificeth, and to him that sacrificeth not; as is the good, so is the sinner; and he that sweareth, as he that feareth[8] an oath. This is an evil among all things that are done under the sun, that there is one event unto all: yea, also the heart of the sons of men is full of evil, and madness is in their heart while they live, and after that they go to the dead.

For to him that is joined to all the living there is hope: for a living dog is better than a dead lion. For the living know that they shall die: but the dead know not any thing, neither have they any more a reward; for the memory of them is forgotten. Also their love, and their hatred, and their envy, is now perished; neither have they any more a portion for ever in any thing that is done under the sun.

Go thy way, eat thy bread with joy, and drink thy wine with a merry heart; for God now accepteth thy works. Let thy garments be always white; and let thy head lack no ointment. Live joyfully with the wife whom thou lovest all the days of the life of thy vanity, which he hath given thee under the sun, all the days of thy vanity; for that is thy portion in this life, and in thy labour which thou takest under the sun. Whatsoever thy hand findeth to do, do it with thy might; for there is no work, nor device, nor knowledge, nor wisdom, in the grave, whither thou goest.

I returned, and saw under the sun, that the race is not to the swift, nor the battle to the strong, neither yet bread to the wise, nor yet riches to men of understanding, nor yet favour to men of skill; but time and chance happeneth to them all. For man also knoweth not his time: as the fishes that are taken in an evil net, and as the birds that are caught in the snare; so are the sons of men snared in an evil time, when it falleth suddenly upon them.

---

6. *manifest:* make clear.
7. Who knows whether the spirit of man goes upward or whether . . . ?

8. *feareth:* dares not take the oath (that he is innocent).

11. Cast thy bread upon the waters: for thou shalt find it after many days. Give a portion to seven, and also to eight; for thou knowest not what evil shall be upon the earth. If the clouds be full of rain, they empty themselves upon the earth: and if the tree fall toward the south, or toward the north, in the place where the tree falleth, there shall it be. He that observeth the wind shall not sow; and he that regardeth the clouds shall not reap. As thou knowest not what is the way of the spirit, nor how the bones do grow in the womb of her that is with child: even so thou knowest not the works of God who maketh all. In the morning sow thy seed, and in the evening withhold not thine hand: for thou knowest not whether shall prosper, either this or that, or whether they both shall be alike good.

Truly the light is sweet, and a pleasant thing it is for the eyes to behold the sun: But if a man live many years, and rejoice in them all; yet let him remember the days of darkness; for they shall be many. All that cometh is vanity.

Rejoice, O young man, in thy youth; and let thy heart cheer thee in the days of thy youth, and walk in the ways of thine heart, and in the sight of thine eyes: but know thou, that for all these things God will bring thee into judgment. Therefore remove sorrow from thy heart, and put away evil from thy flesh, for childhood and youth are vanity.

12. Remember now thy Creator in the days of thy youth, while the evil days come not, nor the years draw nigh, when thou shalt say, I have no pleasure in them; While the sun, or the light, or the moon, or the stars, be not darkened, nor the clouds return after the rain: In the day when the keepers of the house shall tremble, and the strong men shall bow themselves, and the grinders[9] cease because they are few, and those that look out of the windows be darkened, And the doors shall be shut in the streets, when the sound of the grinding is low, and he shall rise up at the voice of the bird, and all the daughters of musick shall be brought low; Also when they shall be afraid of that which is high, and fears shall be in the way, and the almond tree shall flourish, and the grasshopper shall be a burden, and desire shall fail: because man goeth to his long home, and the mourners go about the streets: Or ever the silver cord be loosed, or the golden bowl be broken, or the pitcher be broken at the fountain, or the wheel broken at the cistern. Then shall the dust return to the earth as it was: and the spirit shall return unto God who gave it.

Vanity of vanities, saith the preacher; all is vanity.

---

9. *grinders:* the servants grinding the wheat at the mill.

## Psalm 8

1. O Lord our Lord, how excellent is thy name in all the earth! who hast set thy glory above the heavens.

2. Out of the mouth of babes and sucklings hast thou ordained strength because of thine enemies, that thou mightest still the enemy and the avenger.

3. When I consider thy heavens, the work of thy fingers, the moon and the stars, which thou hast ordained;

4. What is man, that thou art mindful of him? and the son of man, that thou visitest him?

5. For thou hast made him a little lower than the angels, and hast crowned him with glory and honour.

6. Thou madest him to have dominion over the works of thy hands; thou hast put all things under his feet:

7. All sheep and oxen, yea, and the beasts of the field;

8. The fowl of the air, and the fish of the sea, and whatsoever passeth through the paths of the seas.

9. O Lord our Lord, how excellent is thy name in all the earth!

## Psalm 19

1. The heavens declare the glory of God; and the firmament sheweth his handywork.

2. Day unto day uttereth speech, and night unto night sheweth knowledge.

3. There is no speech nor language, where their voice is not heard.

4. Their line is gone out through all the earth, and their words to the end of the world. In them hath he set a tabernacle for the sun,

5. Which is as a bridegroom coming out of his chamber, and rejoiceth as a strong man to run a race.

6. His going forth is from the end of the heaven, and his circuit unto the ends of it: and there is nothing hid from the heat thereof.

7. The law of the Lord is perfect, converting the soul: the testimony of the Lord is sure, making wise the simple.

8. The statutes of the Lord are right. rejoicing the heart: the commandment of the Lord is pure, enlightening the eyes.

9. The fear of the Lord is clean, enduring for ever: the judgments of the Lord are true and righteous altogether.

10. More to be desired are they than gold, yea, than much fine gold: sweeter also than honey and the honeycomb.

11. Moreover by them is thy servant warned: and in keeping of them there is great reward.

12. Who can understand his errors? cleanse thou me from secret faults.

13. Keep back thy servant also from presumptuous sins; let them not have dominion over me: then shall I be upright, and I shall be innocent from the great transgression.

14. Let the words of my mouth, and the meditation of my heart, be acceptable in thy sight, O Lord, my strength, and my redeemer.

## Psalm 23

1. The Lord is my shepherd; I shall not want.

2. He maketh me to lie down in green pastures: he leadeth me beside the still waters.

3. He restoreth my soul: he leadeth me in the paths of righteousness for his name's sake.

4. Yea, though I walk through the valley of the shadow of death, I will fear no evil: for thou art with me; thy rod and thy staff they comfort me.

5. Thou preparest a table before me in the presence of mine enemies: thou anointest my head with oil; my cup runneth over.

6. Surely goodness and mercy shall follow me all the days of my life: and I will dwell in the house of the Lord for ever.

## Psalm 104

1. Bless the Lord, O my soul. O Lord my God, thou art very great; thou art clothed with honour and majesty.

2. Who coverest thyself with light as with a garment: who stretchest out the heavens like a curtain:

3. Who layeth the beams of his chambers in the waters: who maketh the clouds his chariot: who walketh upon the wings of the wind:

4. Who maketh his angels spirits; his ministers a flaming fire:

5. Who laid the foundations of the earth, that it should not be removed for ever.

6. Thou coveredst it with the deep as with a garment: the waters stood above the mountains.

7. At thy rebuke they fled; at the voice of thy thunder they hasted away.

8. They go up by the mountains; they go down by the valleys unto the place which thou hast founded for them.

9. Thou hast set a bound that they may not pass over; that they turn not again to cover the earth.

10. He sendeth the springs into the valleys, which run among the hills.

11. They give drink to every beast of the field: the wild asses quench their thirst.

12. By them shall the fowls of the heaven have their habitation, which sing among the branches.

13. He watereth the hills from his chambers: the earth is satisfied with the fruit of thy works.

14. He causeth the grass to grow for the cattle, and herb for the service of man: that he may bring forth food out of the earth;

15. And wine that maketh glad the heart of man, and oil to make his face to shine, and bread which strengtheneth man's heart.

16. The trees of the Lord are full of sap; the cedars of Lebanon, which he hath planted;

17. Where the birds make their nests: as for the stork, the fir trees are her house.

18. The high hills are a refuge for the wild goats; and the rocks for the conies.

19. He appointed the moon for seasons: the sun knoweth his going down.

20. Thou makest darkness, and it is night: wherein all the beasts of the forest do creep forth.

21. The young lions roar after their prey, and seek their meat from God.

22. The sun ariseth, they gather themselves together, and lay them down in their dens.

23. Man goeth forth unto his work and to his labour until the evening.

24. O Lord, how manifold are thy works! in wisdom hast thou made them all: the earth is full of thy riches.

25. So is this great and wide sea, wherein are things creeping innumerable, both small and great beasts.

26. There go the ships: there is that leviathan, whom thou hast made to play therein.

27. These wait all upon thee; that thou mayest give them their meat in due season.

28. That thou givest them they gather: thou openest thine hand, they are filled with good.

29. Thou hidest thy face, they are troubled: thou takest away their breath, they die, and return to their dust.

30. Thou sendest forth thy spirit, they are created: and thou renewest the face of the earth.

31. The glory of the Lord shall endure for ever: the Lord shall rejoice in his works.

32. He looketh on the earth, and it trembleth: he toucheth the hills, and they smoke.

33. I will sing unto the Lord as long as I live: I will sing praise to my God while I have my being.

34. My meditation of him shall be sweet: I will be glad in the Lord.

35. Let the sinners be consumed out of the earth, and let the wicked be no more. Bless thou the Lord, O my soul. Praise ye the Lord.

## Psalm 137

1. By the rivers of Babylon,[1] there we sat down, yea, we wept, when we remembered Zion.

2. We hanged our harps upon the willows in the midst thereof.

3. For there they that carried us away captive required of us a song; and they that wasted us required of us mirth, saying, Sing us one of the songs of Zion.

4. How shall we sing the Lord's song in a strange land?

5. If I forget thee, O Jerusalem, let my right hand forget her cunning.

6. If I do not remember thee, let my tongue cleave to the roof of my mouth; if I prefer not Jerusalem above my chief joy.

7. Remember, O Lord, the children of Edom[2] in the day of Jerusalem; who said, Rase it, rase it, even to the foundation thereof.

8. O daughter of Babylon, who art to be destroyed; happy shall he be, that rewardeth thee as thou hast served us.

9. Happy shall he be, that taketh and dasheth thy little ones against the stones.

1. on the river Euphrates. Jerusalem was captured and sacked by the Babylonians in 586 B.C. The Jews were taken away into captivity in Babylon.
2. The Edomites helped the Babylonians to capture Jerusalem.

## Jonah

1. Now the word of the Lord came unto Jonah the son of Amittai, saying, Arise, go to Nineveh,[1] that great city, and cry against it; for their wickedness is come up before me. But Jonah rose up to flee unto Tarshish[2] from the presence of the Lord, and went down to Joppa;[3] and he found a ship going to Tarshish: so he paid the fare thereof, and went down into it, to go with them unto Tarshish from the presence of the Lord. But the Lord sent out a great wind into the sea, and there was a mighty tempest in the sea, so that the ship was like to be broken. Then the mariners were afraid, and cried every man unto his god, and cast forth the wares that were in the ship into the sea, to lighten it of them. But Jonah was gone down into the sides of the ship; and he lay, and was fast asleep. So the shipmaster came to him, and said unto him, What meanest thou, O sleeper? arise, call upon thy God, if so be that God will think upon us, that we perish not. And they said every one to his fellow, Come, and let us cast lots, that we may know for whose cause this

1. *Nineveh:* on the river Tigris, the capital city of the Assyrians.
2. *Tarshish:* probably Tartessus, in Spain. Jonah intends to go west (instead of east to Nineveh) and as far away as he can.
3. *Joppa:* seaport on the coast of Palestine.

evil is upon us. So they cast lots, and the lot fell upon Jonah. Then said they unto him, Tell us, we pray thee, for whose cause this evil is upon us; What is thine occupation? and whence comest thou? what is thy country? and of what people art thou? And he said unto them, I am an Hebrew; and I fear the Lord, the God of heaven, which hath made the sea and the dry land. Then were the men exceedingly afraid, and said unto him, Why hast thou done this? For the men knew that he fled from the presence of the Lord, because he had told them. Then said they unto him, What shall we do unto thee, that the sea may be calm unto us? for the sea wrought, and was tempestuous. And he said unto them, Take me up, and cast me forth into the sea; so shall the sea be calm unto you: for I know that for my sake this great tempest is upon you. Nevertheless the men rowed hard to bring it to the land; but they could not: for the sea wrought, and was tempestuous against them. Wherefore they cried unto the Lord, and said, We beseech thee, O Lord, we beseech thee, let us not perish for this man's life, and lay not upon us innocent blood: for thou, O Lord, hast done as it pleased thee. So they took up Jonah, and cast him forth into the sea: and the sea ceased from her raging. Then the men feared the Lord exceedingly, and offered a sacrifice unto the Lord, and made vows.

Now the Lord had prepared a great fish to swallow up Jonah. And Jonah was in the belly of the fish three days and three nights.

2. Then Jonah prayed unto the Lord his God out of the fish's belly, And said, I cried by reason of mine affliction unto the Lord, and he heard me; out of the belly of hell cried I, and thou heardest my voice. For thou hadst cast me into the deep, in the midst of the seas; and the floods compassed me about; all thy billows and thy waves passed over me. Then I said, I am cast out of thy sight; yet I will look again toward thy holy temple. The waters compassed me about, even to the soul: the depth closed me round about, the weeds were wrapped about my head. I went down to the bottoms of the mountains; the earth with her bars was about me for ever: yet hast thou brought up my life from corruption, O Lord my God. When my soul fainted within me I remembered the Lord: and my prayer came in unto thee, into thine holy temple. They that observe lying vanities forsake their own mercy.[4] But I will sacrifice unto thee with the voice of thanksgiving; I will pay that that I have vowed. Salvation is of the Lord. And the Lord spake unto the fish, and it vomited out Jonah upon the dry land.

4. The general sense is: "those that worship false gods forfeit their claim to mercy."

3. And the word of the Lord came unto Jonah the second time, saying, Arise, go unto Nineveh, that great city, and preach unto it the preaching that I bid thee. So Jonah arose, and went unto Nineveh, according to the word of the Lord. Now Nineveh was an exceeding great city of three days' journey. And Jonah began to enter into the city a day's journey, and he cried, and said. Yet forty days, and Nineveh shall be overthrown.

So the people of Nineveh believed God, and proclaimed a fast, and put on sackcloth, from the greatest of them even to the least of them. For word came unto the king of Nineveh, and he arose from his throne, and he laid his robe from him, and covered him with sackcloth, and sat in ashes. And he caused it to be proclaimed and published through Nineveh by the decree of the king and his nobles, saying, Let neither man nor beast, herd nor flock, taste any thing: let them not feed, nor drink water: But let man and beast be covered with sackcloth, and cry mightily unto God: yea, let them turn every one from his evil way, and from the violence that is in their hands. Who can tell if God will turn and repent, and turn away from his fierce anger, that we perish not?

And God saw their works, that they turned from their evil way; and God repented of the evil, that he had said that he would do unto them; and he did it not.

4. But it displeased Jonah exceedingly, and he was very angry. And he prayed unto the Lord, and said, I pray thee, O Lord, was not this my saying, when I was yet in my country? Therefore I fled before unto Tarshish: for I knew that thou art a gracious God, and merciful, slow to anger, and of great kindness, and repentest thee of the evil.[5] Therefore now, O Lord, take, I beseech thee, my life from me; for it is better for me to die than to live. Then said the Lord, Doest thou well to be angry? So Jonah went out of the city, and sat on the east side of the city, and there made him a booth,[6] and sat under it in the shadow, till he might see what would become of the city. And the Lord God prepared a gourd,[7] and made it to come up over Jonah, that it might be a shadow over his head, to deliver him from his grief. So Jonah was exceeding glad of the gourd. But God prepared a worm when the morning rose the next day, and it smote the gourd that it withered. And it came to pass, when the sun did arise, that God prepared a vehement east wind; and the sun beat upon the head of Jonah, that he fainted, and wished in himself to die, and said, It is better for me to die than to live. And God said to Jonah, Doest thou well to be angry for the gourd? And he said, I do well to be angry, even unto death.

---

5. *a gracious God . . . evil:* Jonah is quoting Scripture ( Exodus 34:6).

6. *booth:* a tent shelter.

7. *gourd:* some kind of climbing plant.

Then said the Lord, Thou hast had pity on the gourd, for the which thou hast not laboured, neither madest it grow; which came up in a night, and perished in a night: And should not I spare Nineveh,. that great city, wherein are more than sixscore thousand persons that cannot discern between their right hand and their left hand;[8] and also much cattle?

8. i.e., children.

## *Isaiah 52–53. [The Song of the Suffering Servant]*

**52:13.** Behold, my servant shall deal prudently, he shall be exalted and extolled, and be very high.

14. As many were astonied at thee; his visage was so marred more than any man, and his form more than the sons of men:

15. So shall he sprinkle many nations; the kings shall shut their mouths at him: for that which had not been told them shall they see; and that which they had not heard shall they consider.

**53:1.** Who hath believed our report? and to whom is the arm of the Lord revealed?

2. For he shall grow up before him as a tender plant, and as a root out of a dry ground: he hath no form nor comeliness; and when we shall see him, there is no beauty that we should desire him.

3. He is despised and rejected of men; a man of sorrows, and acquainted with grief: and we hid as it were our faces from him; he was despised, and we esteemed him not.

4. Surely he hath borne our griefs, and carried our sorrows: yet we did esteem him stricken, smitten of God, and afflicted.

5. But he was wounded for our transgressions, he was bruised for our iniquities: the chastisement of our peace was upon him; and with his stripes we are healed.

6. All we like sheep have gone astray; we have turned every one to his own way; and the Lord hath laid on him the iniquity of us all.

7. He was oppressed, and he was afflicted, yet he opened not his mouth: he is brought as a lamb to the slaughter, and as a sheep before her shearers is dumb, so he openeth not his mouth.

8. He was taken from prison and from judgment: and who shall declare his generation? for he was cut off out of the land of the living: for the transgression of my people was he stricken.

9. And he made his grave with the wicked, and with the rich[1] in his death; because he had done no violence, neither was any deceit in his mouth.

1. Some editors emend the Hebrew to give the meaning, "evildoers."

10. Yet it pleased the Lord to bruise him; he hath put him to grief: when thou shalt make his soul an offering for sin, he shall see his seed, he shall prolong his days, and the pleasure of the Lord shall prosper in his hand.

11. He shall see the travail of his soul, and shall be satisfied: by his knowledge shall my righteous servant justify many; for he shall bear their iniquities.

12. Therefore will I divide him a portion with the great, and he shall divide the spoil with the strong; because he hath poured out his soul unto death: and he was numbered with the transgressors; and he bare the sin of many, and made intercession for the transgressors.

# HOMER
# The Iliad *

## Book I

### [The Quarrel of Akhilleus and Agamemnon]

Anger be now your song, immortal one,
Akhilleus' anger, doomed and ruinous,
that caused the Akhaians loss on bitter loss
and crowded brave souls into the undergloom,
leaving so many dead men—carrion      5
for dogs and birds, and the will of Zeus was done.
Begin it when the two men first contending
broke with one another—

                    the Lord Marshal
Agamémnon, Atreus' son, and Prince Akhilleus.

Among the gods, who brought this quarrel on?     10
The son of Zeus by Lêto. Agamémnon
angered him, so he made a burning wind

---

* Abridged; translated by Robert Fitzgerald.

1. *immortal one*: The Muse, inspiration for epic poetry.

2. *Akhilleus*: The translator has transliterated from the Greek rather than use familiar Latinized forms: Akhilleus for Achilles, Akhaians for Achaeans, and so on. In some cases the stress is marked: Agamémnon, for example, is pronounced with the stress on *mém*, Ténedos with stress on *Tén*. The sign over the *e* in Lêto indicates a long vowel—*Leeto;* so Khrysês is pronounced *Kriseez* and

Athêna *Atheena*. The dieresis (¨) indicates that two adjacent vowels are pronounced distinctly: Danääns is *Danayans*, Laërtês is *Layertees*, Eëtiôn is *Ee-yeh-ti-own*.

3. *Akhaians*: Greeks. *Lêto*: A goddess loved by Zeus.

9. *Atreus*: See the title note to Aeschylus, *Agamemnon*, p. 299.

6. *Zeus*: King of the gods.

11. *son of Zeus*: Apollo, god of prophecy, medicine, music, and archery. The strongest protector of the Trojans.

of plague rise in the army: rank and file
sickened and died for the ill their chief had done
in despising a man of prayer.                                    15
This priest, Khrysês, had come down to the ships
with gifts, no end of ransom for his daughter;
on a golden staff he carried the god's white bands
and sued for grace from the men of all Akhaia,
the two Atreidai most of all:

                                              "O captains  20

Meneláos and Agamémnon, and you other
Akhaians under arms!
The gods who hold Olympos, may they grant you
plunder of Priam's town and a fair wind home,
but let me have my daughter back for ransom       25
as you revere Apollo, son of Zeus!"

Then all the soldiers murmured their assent:

"Behave well to the priest. And take the ransom!"

But Agamémnon would not. It went against his desire,
and brutally he ordered the man away:             30

"Let me not find you here by the long ships
loitering this time or returning later,
old man; if I do,
the staff and ribbons of the god will fail you.
Give up the girl? I swear she will grow old       35
at home in Argos, far from her own country,
working my loom and visiting my bed.
Leave me in peace and go, while you can, in safety."

So harsh he was, the old man feared and obeyed him,
in silence trailing away                          40
by the shore of the tumbling clamorous whispering sea,
and he prayed and prayed again, as he withdrew,
to the god whom silken-braided Lêto bore:

"O hear me, master of the silver bow,
protector of Tenedos and the holy towns,          45

16. *Khrysês*: His daughter is called
Khrysêis and the place where he lives,
Khrysê.
18. *white bands*: Of wool. Attached to
a branch they marked the bearer as a
suppliant, usually to a god, here to the
Atreidai.

20. *Atreidai*: Sons of Atreus, i.e.,
Agamémnon and Meneláos.
24. *Priam's town*: Priam was then
King of Troy.
45. *Ténedos*: An island off the Trojan
coast.

Apollo, Sminthian, if to your liking
ever in any grove I roofed a shrine
or burnt thighbones in fat upon your altar—
bullock or goat flesh—let my wish come true:
your arrows on the Danáäns for my tears!"                    50

Now when he heard this prayer, Phoibos Apollo
walked with storm in his heart from Olympos' crest,
quiver and bow at his back, and the bundled arrows
clanged on the sky behind as he rocked in his anger,
descending like night itself. Apart from the ships        55
he halted and let fly, and the bowstring slammed
as the silver bow sprang, rolling in thunder away.
Pack animals were his target first, and dogs,
but soldiers, too, soon felt transfixing pain
from his hard shots, and pyres burned night and day.      60
Nine days the arrows of the god came down
broadside upon the army. On the tenth,
Akhilleus called all ranks to assembly. Hêra,
whose arms are white as ivory, moved him to it,
as she took pity on Danáäns dying.                         65
All being mustered, all in place and quiet,
Akhilleus, fast in battle as a lion,
rose and said:

                              "Agamémnon, now I take it,
the siege is broken, we are going to sail,
and even so may not leave death behind:                    70
if war spares anyone, disease will take him . . .
We might, though, ask some priest or some diviner,
even some fellow good at dreams—for dreams
come down from Zeus as well—
why all this anger of the god Apollo?                       75

Has he some quarrel with us for a failure
in vows or hekatombs? Would mutton burned
or smoking goat flesh make him lift the plague?"

46. *Sminthian:* A cult-title of Apollo; it probably refers to his role as the destroyer of field-mice (Greek *sminthos,* mouse).
50. *Danáäns:* Another name for the Greek army, equivalent to Akhaians, Argives.
52. *Olympos:* The mountain in northern Greece which was thought of as the home of the gods.
63. *Hêra:* Wife and sister of Zeus, patron goddess of marriage and of the Greek city of Argos. She was bitterly hostile to the Trojans.
77. *hekatombs:* Strictly, the word denotes a sacrifice of one hundred animals, but it is often used to describe smaller offerings.

Putting the question, down he sat. And Kalkhas,
Kalkhas Thestórides, came forward, wisest                          80
by far of all who scanned the flight of birds,
He knew what was, what had been, what would be,
Kalkhas, who brought Akhaia's ships to Ilion
by the diviner's gift Apollo gave him.
Now for their benefit he said:

                                        "Akhilleus,  85

dear to Zeus, it is on me you call
to tell you why the Archer God is angry.
Well, I can tell you. Are you listening? Swear
by heaven that you will back me and defend me,
because I fear my answer will enrage                              90
a man with power in Argos, one whose word
Akhaian troops obey.

                    A great man in his rage is formidable
for underlings: though he may keep it down,
he cherishes the burning in his belly
until a reckoning day. Think well                                95
if you will save me."

Said Akhilleus:

                                          "Courage.

Tell what you know, what you have light to know.
I swear by Apollo, the lord god to whom
you pray when you uncover truth,                                 100
never while I draw breath, while I have eyes to see,
shall any man upon this beachhead dare
lay hands on you—not one of all the army,
not Agamémnon, if it is he you mean,
though he is first in rank of all Akhaians."                     105

The diviner then took heart and said:

                                         "No failure

in hekatombs or vows is held against us.
It is the man of prayer whom Agamémnon
treated with contempt: he kept his daughter,
spurned his gifts: for that man's sake the Archer                110
visited grief upon us and will again.
Relieve the Danáäns of this plague he will not
until the girl who turns the eyes of men
shall be restored to her own father—freely,

80. *Thestórides*: Son of Thestor.          83. *Ilion*: Troy.

with no demand for ransom—and until 115
we offer up a hekatomb at Khrysê.
Then only can we calm him and persuade him."

He finished and sat down. The son of Atreus,
ruler of the great plain, Agamémnon,
rose, furious. Round his heart resentment 120
welled, and his eyes shone out like licking fire.
Then, with a long and boding look at Kalkhas,
he growled at him:

                        "You visionary of hell,
never have I had fair play in your forecasts.
Calamity is all you care about, or see, 125
no happy portents; and you bring to pass
nothing agreeable. Here you stand again
before the army, giving it out as oracle
the Archer made them suffer because of me,
because I would not take the gifts 130
and let the girl Khrysêis go; I'd have her
mine, at home. Yes, if you like, I rate her
higher than Klytaimnestra, my own wife!
She loses nothing by compariosn
in beauty or womanhood, in mind or skill. 135

For all of that, I am willing now to yield her
if it is best; I want the army saved
and not destroyed. You must prepare, however,
a prize of honor for me, and at once,
that I may not be left without my portion— 140
I, of all Argives. It is not fitting so.
While every man of you looks on, my girl
goes elsewhere."

Prince Akhilleus answered him:

"Lord Marshal, most insatiate of men, 145
how can the army make you a new gift?
Where is our store of booty? Can you see it?
Everything plundered from the towns has been
distributed, should troops turn all that in?
Just let the girl go, in the god's name, now; 150
we'll make it up to you, twice over, three
times over, on that day Zeus gives us leave
to plunder Troy behind her rings of stone."

---

128. *as oracle*: I.e., as if it were a pronouncement by a god.

Agamémnon answered:

"Not that way

will I be gulled, brave as you are, Akhilleus.                                     155
Take me in, would you? Try to get around me?
What do you really ask? That you may keep
your own winnings, I am to give up mine
and sit here wanting her? Oh, no:
the army will award a prize to me                                                    160
and make sure that it measures up, or if
they do not, I will take a girl myself,
your own, or Aías', or Odysseus' prize!
Take her, yes, to keep. The man I visit
may choke with rage; well, let him.                                                165
But this, I say, we can decide on later.

Look to it now, we launch on the great sea
a well-found ship, and get her manned with oarsmen,
load her with sacrificial beasts and put aboard
Khryséis in her loveliness. My deputy,                                             170
Aías, Idómeneus, or Prince Odysseus,
or you, Akhilleus, fearsome as you are,
will make the hekatomb and quiet the Archer."

Akhilleus frowned and looked at him, then said:

"You thick-skinned, shameless, greedy fool!                                        175
Can any Akhaian care for you, or obey you,
after this on marches or in battle?
As for myself, when I came here to fight,
I had no quarrel with Troy or Trojan spearmen:
they never stole my cattle or my horses,                                           180
never in the black farmland of Phthía
ravaged my crops. How many miles there are
of shadowy mountains, foaming seas, between!
No, no, we joined for you, you insolent boor,
to please you, fighting for your brother's sake                                    185
and yours, to get revenge upon the Trojans.
You overlook this, dogface, or don't care,
and now in the end you threaten to take my girl,
a prize I sweated for, and soldiers gave me!

Never have I had plunder like your own                                             190
from any Trojan stronghold battered down

163. *Aías*: (Ajax) the bravest of the        171. *Idómeneus*: A prince from Crete.
Greeks after Akhilleus. *Odysseus*: The       181. *Phthía*: Akhilleus' home in north-
most subtle and crafty of the Greeks.         ern Greece.

by the Akhaians. I have seen more action
hand to hand in those assaults than you have,
but when the time for sharing comes, the greater
share is always yours. Worn out with battle          195
I carry off some trifle to my ships.
Well, this time I make sail for home.
Better to take now to my ships. Why linger,
cheated of winnings, to make wealth for you?"

To this the high commander made reply:          200

"Desért, if that's the way the wind blows. Will I
beg you to stay on my account? I will not.
Others will honor me, and Zeus who views
the wide world most of all.

                                    No officer
is hateful to my sight as you are, none          205
given like you to faction, as to battle—
rugged you are, I grant, by some god's favor.
Sail, then, in your ships, and lord it over
your own battalion of Myrmidons. I do not
give a curse for you, or for your anger.          210
But here is warning for you:

                                    Khrysêis

being required of me by Phoibos Apollo,
she will be sent back in a ship of mine,
manned by my people. That done, I myself
will call for Brisêis at your hut, and take her,          215
flower of young girls that she is, your prize,
to show you here and now who is the stronger
and make the next man sick at heart—if any
think of claiming equal place with me."

A pain like grief weighed on the son of Pêleus,          220
and in his shaggy chest this way and that
the passion of his heart ran: should he draw
longsword from hip, stand off the rest, and kill
in single combat the great son of Atreus,
or hold his rage in check and give it time?          225
And as this tumult swayed him, as he slid

209. *Myrmidons*: Akhilleus' troops, disciplined and merciless in battle.
220. *son of Pêleus*: Akhilleus. His father Peleus, now an old man, had been married in his youth to the sea-goddess Thetis, Akhilleus' mother, who has now returned to the sea and lives there with her old father Nereus.

the big blade slowly from the sheath, Athêna
came to him from the sky. The white-armed goddess,
Hêra, sent her, being fond of both,
concerned for both men. And Athêna, stepping                    230
up behind him, visible to no one
except Akhilleus, gripped his red-gold hair.

Startled, he made a half turn, and he knew her
upon the instant for Athêna: terribly
her gray eyes blazed at him. And speaking softly               235
but rapidly aside to her he said:

"What now, O daughter of the god of heaven
who bears the stormcloud, why are you here? To see
the wolfishness of Agamémnon?
Well, I give you my word: this time, and soon,                 240
he pays for his behavior with his blood."

The gray-eyed goddess Athêna said to him:

"It was to check this killing rage I came
from heaven, if you will listen. Hêra sent me,
being fond of both of you, concerned for both.                 245
Enough: break off this combat, stay your hand
upon the sword hilt. Let him have a lashing
with words, instead: tell him how things will be.
Here is my promise, and it will be kept:
winnings three times as rich, in due season,                   250
you shall have in requital for his arrogance.
But hold your hand. Obey."

                                    The great runner,
Akhilleus, answered:

                        "Nothing for it, goddess,
but when you two immortals speak, a man
complies, though his heart burst. Just as well.                255
Honor the gods' will, they may honor ours."

On this he stayed his massive hand
upon the silver pommel, and the blade
of his great weapon slid back in the scabbard.

227. *Athêna*: The daughter of Zeus, patron of human ingenuity and resourcefulness, whether exemplified by handicrafts such as spinning or by skill in human relations, such as that possessed by her favorite among the Greeks, Odysseus. Like Hêra, she was implacably hostile to the Trojans, and for the same reason: the Trojan prince Paris had judged Aphrodite, goddess of love, to be more beautiful than Hêra and Athêna.

The man had done her bidding. Off to Olympos,                          260
gaining the air, she went to join the rest,
the powers of heaven in the home of Zeus.

But now the son of Pêleus turned on Agamémnon
and lashed out at him, letting his anger ride
in execration:

                                                "Sack of wine,     265
you with your cur's eyes and your antelope heart!
You've never had the kidney to buckle on
armor among the troops, or make a sortie
with picked men—oh, no; that way death might lie.
Safer, by god, in the middle of the army—                              270
is it not?—to commandeer the prize
of any man who stands up to you! Leech!
Commander of trash! If not, I swear,
you never could abuse one soldier more!

But here is what I say: my oath upon it                                 275
by this great staff: look: leaf or shoot
it cannot sprout again, once lopped away
from the log it left behind in the timbered hills;
it cannot flower, peeled of bark and leaves;
instead, Akhaian officers in council                                   280
take it in hand by turns, when they observe
by the will of Zeus due order in debate:
let this be what I swear by then: I swear
a day will come when every Akhaian soldier
will groan to have Akhilleus back. That day                            285
you shall no more prevail on me than this
dry wood shall flourish—driven though you are,
and though a thousand men perish before
the killer, Hektor. You will eat your heart out,
raging with remorse for this dishonor                                  290
done by you to the bravest of Akhaians."

He hurled the staff, studded with golden nails,
before him on the ground. Then down he sat,
and fury filled Agamémnon, looking across at him.
But for the sake of both men Nestor arose,                             295
the Pylians' orator, eloquent and clear;

---

268. *Sortie*: Sudden emergence of attacking troops from a defensive position.
289. *Hektor*: Son of King Priam, the
foremost warrior on the Trojan side.

295. *Nestor*: The aged King of Pylos,
on the western coast of mainland
Greece.

argument sweeter than honey rolled from his tongue.
By now he had outlived two generations
of mortal men, his own and the one after,
in Pylos land, and still ruled in the third.                    300
In kind reproof he said:

                            "A black day, this.

Bitter distress comes this way to Akhaia.
How happy Priam and Priam's sons would be,
and all the Trojans—wild with joy—if they
got wind of all these fighting words between you,           305
foremost in council as you are, foremost
in battle. Give me your attention. Both
are younger men than I, and in my time
men who were even greater have I known
and none of them disdained me. Men like those          310
I have not seen again, nor shall: Peiríthoös,
the Lord Marshal Dryas, Kaineus, Exádios,
Polyphêmos, Theseus—Aigeus' son,
a man like the immortal gods. I speak
of champions among men of earth, who fought           315
with champions, with wild things of the mountains,
great centaurs whom they broke and overpowered.
Among these men I say I had my place
when I sailed out of Pylos, my far country,
because they called for me. I fought                          320
for my own hand among them. Not one man
alive now upon earth could stand against them.
And I repeat: they listened to my reasoning,
took my advice. Well, then, you take it too.
It is far better so.

                             Lord Agamémnon,      325
do not deprive him of the girl, renounce her.
The army had allotted her to him.
Akhilleus, for your part, do not defy
your King and Captain. No one vies in honor
with him who holds authority from Zeus.                    330
You have more prowess, for a goddess bore you;
his power over men surpasses yours.

But, Agamémnon, let your anger cool.
I beg you to relent, knowing Akhilleus

---

311. *Peiríthoös . . . Theseus*: Names
of heroes of an older generation. The
most important is Theseus, King of Athens (who plays a role in Euripides' Hippolytus; see p. 449).
    317. *centaurs*: Mythical creatures, half
man, half horse, noted for their ferocity.

a sea wall for Akhaians in the black waves of war."                    335

Lord Agamémnon answered:

                                              "All you say
is fairly said, sir, but this man's ambition,
remember, is to lead, to lord it over
everyone, hold power over everyone,
give orders to the rest of us! Well, one                                340
will never take his orders! If the gods
who live forever made a spearman of him,
have they put insults on his lips as well?"

Akhilleus interrupted:

                                            "What a poltroon,
how lily-livered I should be called, if I                               345
knuckled under to all you do or say!
Give your commands to someone else, not me!
And one more thing I have to tell you: think it
over: this time, for the girl, I will not
wrangle in arms with you or anyone,                                     350
though I am robbed of what was given me;
but as for any other thing I have
alongside my black ship, you shall not take it
against my will. Try it. Hear this, everyone:
that instant your hot blood blackens my spear!"                        355

They quarreled in this way, face to face, and then
broke off the assembly by the ships. Akhilleus
made his way to his squadron and his quarters,
Patróklos by his side, with his companions.

Agamémnon proceeded to launch a ship,                                   360
assigned her twenty oarsmen, loaded beasts
for sacrifice to the god, then set aboard
Khryséis in her loveliness. The versatile
Odysseus took the deck, and, all oars manned,
they pulled out on the drenching ways of sea.                          365
The troops meanwhile were ordered to police camp
and did so, throwing refuse in the water;
then to Apollo by the barren surf
they carried out full-tally hekatombs,
and the savor curled in crooked smoke toward heaven.                    370

___

359. *Patróklos*: Akhilleus' closest friend.

That was the day's work in the army.

Agamémnon

had kept his threat in mind, and now he acted,
calling Eurýbatês and Talthýbios,
his aides and criers:

"Go along," he said, 375

"both of you, to the quarters of Akhilleus
and take his charming Brisêis by the hand
to bring to me. And if he balks at giving her
I shall be there myself with men-at-arms
in force to take her—all the more gall for him."

So, ominously, he sent them on their way, 380
and they who had no stomach for it went
along the waste sea shingle toward the ships
and shelters of the Myrmidons. Not far
from his black ship and hut they found the prince
in the open, seated. And seeing these two come 385
was cheerless to Akhilleus. Shamefast, pale
with fear of him, they stood without a word;
but he knew what they felt and called out:

"Peace to you,

criers and couriers of Zeus and men!
Come forward. Not one thing have I against you: 390
Agamémnon is the man who sent you
for Brisêis. Here then, my lord Patróklos,
bring out the girl and give her to these men.
And let them both bear witness before the gods
who live in bliss, as before men who die, 395
including this harsh king, if ever hereafter
a need for me arises to keep the rest
from black defeat and ruin.

Lost in folly,

the man cannot think back or think ahead
how to come through a battle by the ships." 400

Patróklos did the bidding of his friend,
led from the hut Brisêis in her beauty
and gave her to them. Back along the ships
they took their way, and the girl went, loath to go.

Leaving his friends in haste, Akhilleus wept, 405
and sat apart by the gray wave, scanning the endless sea.

374. *criers*: Heralds.

Often he spread his hands in prayer to his mother:

"As my life came from you, though it is brief,
honor at least from Zeus who storms in heaven
I call my due. He gives me precious little.                    410
See how the lord of the great plains, Agamémnon,
humiliated me! He has my prize,
by his own whim, for himself."

                                       Eyes wet with tears,
he spoke, and her ladyship his mother heard him
in green deeps where she lolled near her old father.          415
Gliding she rose and broke like mist from the inshore
gray sea face, to sit down softly before him,
her son in tears; and fondling him she said:

"Child, why do you weep? What grief is this?
Out with it, tell me, both of us should know."                420
Akhilleus, fast in battle as a lion,
groaned and said:

                               "Why tell you what you know?
We sailed out raiding, and we took by storm
that ancient town of Eëtíôn called Thêbê
plundered the place, brought slaves and spoils away.          425
At the division, later,
they chose a young girl, Khryséis, for the king.
Then Khrysês, priest of the Archer God, Apollo,
came to the beachhead we Akhaians hold,
bringing no end of ransom for his daughter;                   430
he had the god's white bands on a golden staff
and sued for grace from the army of Akhaia,
mostly the two Atreidai, corps commanders.
All of our soldiers murmured in assent:
'Behave well to the priest. And take the ransom!'             435
But Agamémnon would not. It went against his desire,
and brutally he ordered the man away.
So the old man withdrew in grief and anger.
Apollo cared for him: he heard his prayer
and let black bolts of plague fly on the Argives.             440

One by one our men came down with it
and died hard as the god's shots raked the army

---

424. *Eëtíôn*: King of the Kilikians,    Andrómakhê. Thêbê was the Kilikian
and    father    of    Hektor's    wife    capital city.

broadside. But our priest divined the cause
and told us what the god meant by the plague.

I said, 'Appease the god!' but Agamémnon                             445
could not contain his rage; he threatened me,
and what he threatened is now done—
one girl the Akhaians are embarking now
for Khrysê beach with gifts for Lord Apollo;
the other, just now, from my hut—the criers                          450
came and took her, Briseus' girl, my prize,
given by the army.

                         If you can, stand by me:

go to Olympos, pray to Zeus, if ever
by word or deed you served him—
and so you did, I often heard you tell it                            455
in Father's house: that time when you alone
of all the gods shielded the son of Krónos
from peril and disgrace—when other gods,
Pallas Athêna, Hêra, and Poseidon,
wished him in irons, wished to keep him bound,                       460
you had the will to free him of that bondage,
and called up to Olympos in all haste
Aigaion, whom the gods called Briareus,
the giant with a hundred arms, more powerful
than the sea-god, his father. Down he sat                            465
by the son of Krónos, glorying in that place.
For fear of him the blissful gods forbore
to manacle Zeus.

                      Remind him of these things,
cling to his knees and tell him your good pleasure
if he will take the Trojan side                                      470
and roll the Akhaians back to the water's edge,
back on the ships with slaughter! All the troops
may savor what their king has won for them,
and he may know his madness, what he lost
when he dishonored me, peerless among Akhaians."                     475

Her eyes filled, and a tear fell as she answered;

"Alas, my child, why did I rear you, doomed
the day I bore you? Ah, could you only be
serene upon this beachhead through the siege,

---

457. *son of Krónos*: Zeus.
459. *Pallas*: A title of Athena. *Posei-*
*don*: Brother of Zeus, god of the earthquake and the sea.

your life runs out so soon.                                                  480
Oh early death! Oh broken heart! No destiny
so cruel! And I bore you to this evil!

But what you wish I will propose
To Zeus, lord of the lightning, going up
myself into the snow-glare of Olympos                                        485
with hope for his consent.

                                                           Be quiet now

beside the long ships, keep your anger bright
against the army, quit the war.

                                                            Last night

Zeus made a journey to the shore of Ocean,
to feast among the Sunburned, and the gods                                   490
accompanied him. In twelve days he will come
back to Olympos. Then I shall be there
to cross his bronze doorsill and take his knees.
I trust I'll move him.''

                                                        Thetis left her son
still burning for the softly belted girl                                     495
whom they had wrested from him.

                                                      Meanwhile Odysseus
with his shipload of offerings came to Khrysê.
Entering the deep harbor there
they furled the sails and stowed them, and unbent
forestays to ease the mast down quickly aft                                  500
into its rest, then rowed her to a mooring.
Bow-stones were dropped, and they tied up astern,
and all stepped out into the wash and ebb,
then disembarked their cattle for the Archer,
and Khrysêis from the deepsea ship. Odysseus,                                505
the great tactician, led her to the altar,
putting her in her father's hands, and said:

"Khrysês, as Agamémnon's emissary
I bring your child to you, and for Apollo
a hekatomb in the Danääns' name.                                             510

---

**489.** *Ocean*: The river which was thought of as encircling the world. The *Sunburned* (the literal meaning of the Greek name Ethiopians) were supposed to live at the end of the world.

**495.** *softly belted*: Homeric formulaic epithet for beautiful women.

**499–502.** *unbent forestays . . . astern*: Untied the lines from the bow to the top of the mast that hold it upright, so as to "unstep" the mast and lay it on deck. A bow-stone is a primitive anchor made of a stone attached to a rope; the ships were anchored forward and tied up astern with heavy lines or "hawsers" to the moorings.

We trust in this way to appease your lord,
who sent down pain and sorrow on the Argives."

So he delivered her, and the priest received her,
the child so dear to him, in joy. Then hastening
to give the god his hekatomb, they led                              515
bullocks to crowd around the compact altar,
rinsed their hands and delved in barley baskets,
as open-armed to heaven Khrysês prayed:

"Oh hear me, master of the silver bow,
protector of Ténedos and the holy towns,                           520
if while I prayed you listened once before
and honored me, and punished the Akhaians,
now let my wish come true again. But turn
your plague away this time from the Danääns."

And this petition, too, Apollo heard.                              525
When prayers were said and grains of barley strewn,
they held the bullocks for the knife, and flayed them,
cutting out joints and wrapping these in fat,
two layers, folded, with raw strips of flesh,
for the old man to burn on cloven faggots,                         530
wetting it all with wine.

                                    Around him stood
young men with five-tined forks in hand, and when
the vitals had been tasted, joints consumed,
they sliced the chines and quarters for the spits,
roasted them evenly and drew them off.                             535
Their meal being now prepared and all work done,
they feasted to their hearts' content and made
desire for meat and drink recede again,
then young men filled their winebowls to the brim,
ladling drops for the god in every cup.                            540
Propitiatory songs rose clear and strong
until day's end, to praise the god, Apollo,
as One Who Keeps the Plague Afar; and listening
the god took joy.

                              After the sun went down
and darkness came, at last Odysseus' men                           545
lay down to rest under the stern hawsers.

When Dawn spread out her finger tips of rose
they put to sea for the main camp of Akhaians,

534. *chine*: Part of an animal's back. *quarters*: Shoulders and thighs.

and the Archer God sent them a following wind.
Stepping the mast they shook their canvas out,                550
and wind caught, bellying the sail. A foaming
dark blue wave sang backward from the bow
as the running ship made way against the sea,
until they came offshore of the encampment.
Here they put in and hauled the black ship high,             555
far up the sand, braced her with shoring timbers,
and then disbanded, each to his own hut.


Meanwhile unstirring and with smoldering heart,
the godlike athlete, son of Pêleus, Prince
Akhilleus waited by his racing ships.                        560
He would not enter the assembly
of emulous men, nor ever go to war,
but felt his valor staling in his breast
with idleness, and missed the cries of battle.


Now when in fact twelve days had passed, the gods            565
who live forever turned back to Olympos,
with Zeus in power supreme among them.

                                                   Thetis

had kept in mind her mission for her son,
and rising like a dawn mist from the sea
into a cloud she soared aloft in heaven                      570
to high Olympos. Zeus with massive brows
she found apart, on the chief crest enthroned,
and slapping down before him, her left hand
placed on his knees and her right hand held up
to cup his chin, she made her plea to him:                   575

"O Father Zeus, if ever amid immortals
by word or deed I served you, grant my wish
and see to my son's honor! Doom for him
of all men came on quickest.

                               Now Lord Marshal

Agamémnon has been highhanded with him,                      580
has commandeered and holds his prize of war.
But you can make him pay for this, profound
mind of Olympos!

---

556. *shoring timbers*: Beams that hold the ship upright on dry land.
574. *on his knees*: This passage describes the position assumed by the sup- pliant who, by this physical pressure emphasized the urgency of the request. Zeus himself was above all other gods the protector of suppliants.

Lend the Trojans power,

until the Akhaians recompense my son
and heap new honor upon him!"

When she finished, 585

the gatherer of cloud said never a word
but sat unmoving for a long time, silent.
Thetis clung to his knees, then spoke again:

"Give your infallible word, and bow your head,
or else reject me. Can you be afraid 590
to let me see how low in your esteem
I am of all the gods?"

Greatly perturbed,

Lord Zeus who masses cloud said:

"Here is trouble.

You drive me into open war with Hêra
sooner or later: 595
she will be at me, scolding all day long.
Even as matters stand she never rests
from badgering me before the gods: I take
the Trojan side in battle, so she says.

Go home before you are seen. But you can trust me 600
to put my mind on this; I shall ararange it.
Here let me bow my head, then be content
to see me bound by that most solemn act
before the gods. My word is not revocable
not ineffectual, once I nod upon it." 605

He bent his ponderous black brows down, and locks
ambrosial of his immortal head
swung over them, as all Olympos trembled.
After this pact they parted: misty Thetis
from glittering Olympos leapt away 610
into the deep sea; Zeus to his hall retired.
There all the gods rose from their seats in deference
before their father; not one dared
face him unmoved, but all stood up before him,
and thus he took his throne.

But Hêra knew 615

he had new interests; she had seen
the goddess Thetis, silvery-footed daughter

607. *ambrosial*: Divine, from *ambrosia*, the food of the gods.

of the Old One of the sea, conferring with him,
and, nagging, she inquired of Zeus Kroníon:

"Who is it this time, schemer? Who has your ear?          620
How fond you are of secret plans, of taking
decisions privately! You could not bring yourself,
could you, to favor me with any word
of your new plot?"

                            The father of gods and men
said in reply:

                            "Hêra, all my provisions   625
you must not itch to know.
You'll find them rigorous, consort though you are.
In all appropriate matters no one else,
no god or man, shall be advised before you.
But when I choose to think alone,                        630
don't harry me about it with your questions."

The Lady Hêra answered, with wide eyes:

"Majesty, what a thing to say. I have not
'harried' you before with questions, surely;
you are quite free to tell what you will tell.           635
This time I dreadfully fear—I have a feeling—
Thetis, the silvery-footed daughter
of the Old One of the sea, led you astray.
Just now at daybreak, anyway, she came
to sit with you and take your knees; my guess is         640
you bowed your head for her in solemn pact
that you will see to the honor of Akhilleus—
that is, to Akhaian carnage near the ships."

Now Zeus the gatherer of cloud said:

                                 "Marvelous,
you and your guesses; you are near it, too.             645
But there is not one thing that you can do about it,
only estrange yourself still more from me—
all the more gall for you. If what you say
is true, you may be sure it pleases me.
And now you must sit down, be still, obey me,           650
or else not all the gods upon Olympos
can help in the least when I approach your chair

619. *Kroníon*: Son of Kronos.

to lay my inexorable hands upon you."
At this the wide-eyed Lady Hêra feared him,
and sat quite still, and bent her will to his.                     655
Up through the hall of Zeus now all the lords
of heaven were sullen and looked askance, Hêphaistos,
master artificer, broke the silence,
doing a kindness to the snowy-armed
lady, his mother Hêra.

He began:  660

"Ah, what a miserable day, if you two
raise your voices over mortal creatures!
More than enough already! Must you bring
your noisy bickering among the gods?
What pleasure can we take in a fine dinner             665
when baser matters gain the upper hand?
To Mother my advice is—what she knows—
better make up to Father, or he'll start
his thundering and shake our feast to bits.
You know how he can shock us if he cares to—          670
out of our seats with lightning bolts!
Supreme power is his. Oh, soothe him, please,
take a soft tone, get back in his good graces.
Then He'll be benign to us again."
He lurched up as he spoke, and held a winecup         675
out to her, a double-handed one,
and said:

"Dear Mother, patience, hold your tongue,
no matter how upset you are. I would not
see you battered, dearest.

It would hurt me,
and yet I could not help you, not a bit.               680
The Olympian is difficult to oppose.
One other time I took your part he caught me
around one foot and flung me
into the sky from our tremendous terrace.
I soared all day! Just as the sun dropped down        685
I dropped down, too, on Lemnos—nearly dead.
The island people nursed a fallen god."

He made her smile—and the goddess, white-armed Hêra,
smiling took the winecup from his hand.

657. *Hêphaistos*: Patron god of craftsmen, especially workers in metal, and of
fire.

675. *lurched*: Hephaistos was lame.
686. *Lemnos*: An island in the Aegean
sea.

Then, dipping from the winebowl, round he went                    690
from left to right, serving the other gods
nectar of sweet delight.

                  And quenchless laughter
broke out among the blissful gods
to see Hêphaistos wheezing down the hall.
So all day long until the sun went down                           695
they spent in feasting, and the measured feast
matched well their hearts' desire
So did the flawless harp held by Apollo
and heavenly songs in choiring antiphon
that all the Muses sang.

                 And when the shining   700
sun of day sank in the west, they turned
homeward each one to rest, each to that home
the bandy-legged wondrous artisan
Hêphaistos fashioned for them with his craft.
The lord of storm and lightning, Zeus, retired                    705
and shut his eyes where sweet sleep ever came to him,
and at his side lay Hêra, Goddess of the Golden Chair.

[The Greeks, in spite of Akhilleus' withdrawal, continued to
fight. They did not suffer immoderately from Akhilleus' absence; on
the contrary, they pressed the Trojans so hard that Hektor, the
Trojan leader, after rallying his men, returned to the city to urge
the Trojans to offer special prayers and sacrifices to the gods.]

## Book VI

### [*The Meeting of Hektor and Andrómakhē*]

Now, when Hektor reached the Skaian Gates                         281
daughters and wives of Trojans rushed to greet him
with questions about friends, sons, husbands, brothers.
"Pray to the gods!" he said to each in turn,
as grief awaited many. He walked on                               285
and into Priam's palace, fair and still,
made all of ashlar, with bright colonnades.
Inside were fifty rooms of polished stone
one by another, where the sons of Priam
slept beside their wives; apart from these                        290

---

692. *nectar*: The drink of gods.
700. *Muses*: The nine Muses were goddesses of the arts, and the source of artistic inspiration.

281. *Skaian Gates*: One of the principal entrances to Troy.
287. *ashlar*: Squared stone.

across an inner court were twelve rooms more
all in one line, of polished stone, where slept
the sons-in-law of Priam and their wives.
Approaching these, he met his gentle mother
going in with Laódikê, most beautiful                                    295
of all her daughters. Both hands clasping his,
she looked at him and said:

                                  "Why have you come
from battle, child? Those fiends, the Akhaians, fighting
around the town, have worn you out; you come
to climb our Rock and lift your palms to Zeus!                           300
Wait, and I'll serve you honeyed wine.
First you may offer up a drop to Zeus,
to the immortal gods, then slake your thirst.
Wine will restore a man when he is weary
as you are, fighting to defend your own."                                305

Hektor answered her, his helmet flashing:

"No, my dear mother, ladle me no wine;
You'd make my nerve go slack: I'd lose my edge.
May I tip wine to Zeus with hands unwashed?
I fear to—a bespattered man, and bloody,                                 310
may not address the lord of gloomy cloud.
No, it is you I wish would bring together
our older women, with offerings, and go visit
the temple of Athêna, Hope of Soldiers.
Pick out a robe, most lovely and luxurious,                              315
most to your liking in the women's hall;
place it upon Athêna's knees; assure her
a sacrifice of heifers, twelve young ones
ungoaded ever in their lives, if in her mercy
relenting toward our town, our wives and children,                       320
she keeps Diomêdês out of holy Troy.
He is a wild beast now in combat and pursuit.
Make your way to her shrine, visit Athêna,
Hope of Soldiers.

                                    As for me, I go
for Paris to arouse him, if he listens.                                  325
If only earth would swallow him here and now!"

294. *his gentle mother*: Hékabê (Hecuba).
300. *our Rock*: The hill on which
Troy was built.
317. *on Athêna's knees*: On the knees
of the cult-statue.

321. *Diomêdês*: A Greek prince who
has led the assault on Troy in the absence of Akhilleus.
325. *Paris*: Hector's brother. His se-
duction and abduction of Helen, the wife
of Meneláos, is the cause of the war.

What an affliction the Olympian
brought up for us in him—a curse for Priam
and Priam's children! Could I see that man
dwindle into Death's night, I'd feel my soul          330
relieved of its distress!"

So Hektor spoke, and she walked slowly on
into the mégaron. She called her maids,
who then assembled women from the city.
But Hékabê went down to the low chamber            335
fragrant with cedar, where her robes were kept,
embroidered work by women of Sidonia
Aléxandros had brought, that time he sailed
and ravished Helen, princess, pearl of kings.
Hékabê lifted out her loveliest robe,               340
most ample, most luxurious in brocade,
and glittering like starlight under all.
This offering she carried to Athêna
with a long line of women in her train.
On the Akrópolis, Athêna's shrine                   345
was opened for them by Theanô, stately
daughter of Kisseus, wife to Antênor,
and chosen priestess of Athêna. Now
all crying loud stretched out their arms in prayer,
while Theanô with grace took up the robe           350
to place it on fair-haired Athêna's knees.
She made petition then to Zeus's daughter:

                                              "Lady,
excellent goddess, towering friend of Troy,
smash Diomêdês' lance-haft! Throw him hard
below the Skaian Gates, before our eyes!            355
Upon this altar we'll make offering
of twelve young heifers never scarred!
Only show mercy to our town,
mercy to Trojan men, their wives and children."

These were Theanô's prayers, her vain prayers.      360
Pallas Athêna turned away her head.

During the supplication at the shrine,
Hektor approached the beautiful house Aléxandros
himself had made, with men who in that time

---

333. *mégaron*: The great hall of the palace.
337. *Sidonia*: A Phoenician city on the coast of what is now Lebanon.
338. *Aléxandros*: Another name of Paris.
345. *Akrópolis*: The high place of the city.
347. *Antênor*: Advisor to Priam.

were master-builders in the land of Troy.                                365
Bedchamber, hall, and court, in the upper town,
they built for him near Priam's hall and Hektor's.
Now Hektor dear to Zeus went in, his hand
gripping a spear eleven forearms long,
whose bronze head shone before him in the air               370
as shone, around the neck, a golden ring.
He found his brother in the bedchamber
handling a magnificent cuirass and shield
and pulling at his bent-horn bow, while Helen
among her household women sat nearby,                         375
directing needlecraft and splendid weaving.
At sight of him, to shame him, Hektor said:

"Unquiet soul, why be aggrieved in private?
Our troops are dying out there where they fight
around our city, under our high walls.                           380
The hue and cry of war, because of you,
comes in like surf upon this town.
You'd be at odds with any other man
you might see quitting your accursèd war.
Up; into action, before torches thrown                           385
make the town flare!"

                  And shining like a god
Aléxandros replied:

                      "Ah, Hektor,
this call to order is no more than just.
So let me tell you something: hear me out.
No pettishness, resentment toward the Trojans,          390
kept me in this bedchamber so long,
but rather my desire, on being routed,
to taste grief to the full.

                    In her sweet way
my lady rouses me to fight again—
and I myself consider it better so.                               395
Victory falls to one man, then another.
Wait, while I put on the wargod's gear,
or else go back; I'll follow, sure to find you."

For answer, Hektor in his shining helm
said not a word, but in low tones                                 400
enticing Helen murmured:

373. *cuirass*: Armor protecting the torso.
378. *aggrieved*: Paris (like Akhilleus) was sulking, away from the fighting. He had been worsted in a duel with Meneláos, but Aphrodite, the love-goddess, had saved him from death at Meneláos' hands and brought him to his house in Troy.

"Brother dear—
dear to a whore, a nightmare of a woman!
That day my mother gave me to the world
I wish a hurricane blast had torn me away
to wild mountains, or into tumbling sea                    405
to be washed under by a breaking wave,
before these evil days could come—or, granted
terrible years were in the gods' design,
I wish I had had a good man for a lover
who knew the sharp tongues and just rage of men.          410
This one—his heart's unsound, and always will be,
and he will win what he deserves. Come here
and rest upon this couch with me, dear brother.
You are the one afflicted most
by harlotry in me and by his madness,                     415
our portion, all of misery, given by Zeus
that we may live in song for men to come."

Great Hektor shook his head, his helmet flashing,
and said:

                              "No, Helen, offer me no rest;
I know you are fond of me. I cannot rest.                  420
Time presses, and I grow impatient now
to lend a hand to Trojans in the field
who feel a gap when I am gone. Your part
can be to urge him—let him feel the urgency
to join me in the city. He has time:                      425
I must go home to visit my own people,
my own dear wife and my small son. Who knows
if I shall be reprieved again to see them,
or beaten down under Akhaian blows
as the immortals will."

                              He turned away            430
and quickly entered his own hall, but found
Princess Andrómakhê was not at home.
With one nursemaid and her small child, she stood
upon the tower of Ilion, in tears,
bemoaning what she saw.

                              Now Hektor halted       435
upon his threshold, calling to the maids:

"Tell me at once, and clearly, please,
my lady Andrómakhê, where has she gone?

416. *portion*: Destiny.

To see my sisters, or my brothers' wives?
Or to Athêna's temple? Ladies of Troy                    440
are there to make petition to the goddess."

The busy mistress of the larder answered:

"Hektor, to put it clearly as you ask,
she did not go to see your sisters, nor
your brothers' wives, nor to Athêna's shrine             445
where others are petitioning the goddess.
Up to the great square tower of Ilion
she took her way, because she heard our men
were spent in battle by Akhaian power.
In haste, like a madwoman, to the wall                   450
she went, and Nurse went too, carrying the child."

At this word Hektor whirled and left his hall,
taking the same path he had come by,
along byways, walled lanes, all through the town
until he reached the Skaian Gates, whereby              455
before long he would issue on the field.
There his warmhearted lady
came to meet him, running: Andrómakhê,
whose father, Eëtíôn, once had ruled
the land under Mount Plakos, dark with forest,          460
at Thêbê under Plakos—lord and king
of the Kilikians. Hektor was her lord now,
head to foot in bronze; and now she joined him.
Behind her came her maid, who held the child
against her breast, a rosy baby still,                   465
Hektoridês, the world's delight, as fresh
as a pure shining star. Skamándrios
his father named him; other men would say
Astýanax, "Lord of the Lower Town,"
as Hektor singlehanded guarded Troy.                    470
How brilliantly the warrior smiled, in silence,
his eyes upon the child! Andrómakhê
rested against him, shook away a tear,
and pressed his hand in both her own, to say:

"Oh, my wild one, your bravery will be                  475
your own undoing! No pity for our child,
poor little one, or me in my sad lot—
soon to be deprived of you! soon, soon

---

466. *Hektoridês*: Son of Hektor.
467. *Skamándrios*: A name formed
from that of the Trojan river Skaman-
dros.

Akhaians as one man will set upon you
and cut you down! Better for me, without you,                    480
to take cold earth for mantle. No more comfort,
no other warmth, after you meet your doom,
but heartbreak only. Father, is dead, and Mother.
My father great Akhilleus killed when he
besieged and plundered Thêbê, our high town,                    485
citadel of Kilikians. He killed him,
but, reverent at least in this, did not
despoil him. Body, gear, and weapons forged
so handsomely, he burned, and heaped a barrow
over the ashes. Elms were planted round                         490
by mountain-nymphs of him who bears the stormcloud.
Then seven brothers that I had at home
in one day entered Death's dark place. Akhilleus,
prince and powerful runner, killed all seven
amid their shambling cattle and silvery sheep.                  495
Mother, who had been queen of wooded Plakos,
he brought with other winnings home, and freed her,
taking no end of ransom. Artemis
the Huntress shot her in her father's house.
Father and mother—I have none but you,                          500
nor brother, Hektor; lover none but you!
Be merciful! Stay here upon the tower!
Do not bereave your child and widow me!
Draw up your troops by the wild figtree; that way,
the city lies most open, men most easily                        505
could swarm the wall where it is low:
three times, at least, their best men tried it there
in company of the two called Aías, with
Idómeneus, the Atreidai, Diomêdês—
whether someone who had it from oracles                         510
had told them, or their own hearts urged them on."

Great Hektor in his shimmering helmet answered:

"Lady, these many things beset my mind
no less than yours. But I should die of shame
before our Trojan men and noblewomen                            515
if like a coward I avoided battle,
nor am I moved to. Long ago I learned
how to be brave, how to go forward always
and to contend for honor, Father's and mine.

498. *Artemis*: Virgin goddess of the
hunt, also dispenser of natural death to
women.
508. *two called Aías*: Aías (Ajax) son

of Telamon, bravest of the Greeks after
Akhilleus, and Aías son of Oileus,
known as Aías the Lesser.

Honor—for in my heart and soul I know          520
a day will come when ancient Ilion falls,
when Priam and the folk of Priam perish.
Not by the Trojans' anguish on that day
am I so overborne in mind—the pain
of Hékabê herself, or Priam king,          525
or of my brothers, many and valorous,
who will have fallen in dust before our enemies—
as by your own grief, when some armed Akhaian
takes you in tears, your free life stripped away.
Before another woman's loom in Argos          530
it may be you will pass, or at Messêis
or Hypereiê fountain, carrying water,
against your will—iron constraint upon you.
And seeing you in tears, a man may say:
'There is the wife of Hektor, who fought best          535
of Trojan horsemen when they fought at Troy.'
So he may say—and you will ache again
for one man who could keep you out of bondage.
Let me be hidden dark down in my grave
before I hear your cry or know you captive!"          540

As he said this, Hektor held out his arms
to take his baby. But the child squirmed round
on the nurse's bosom and began to wail,
terrified by his father's great war helm—
the flashing bronze, the crest with horsehair plume          545
tossed like a living thing at every nod.
His father began laughing, and his mother
laughed as well. Then from his handsome head
Hektor lifted off his helm and bent
to place it, bright with sunlight, on the ground.          550
When he had kissed his child and swung him high
to dandle him, he said this prayer:

                                                        "O Zeus

and all immortals, may this child, my son,
become like me a prince among the Trojans.
Let him be strong and brave and rule in power          555
at Ilion; then someday men will say
'This fellow is far better than his father!'
seeing him home from war, and in his arms
the bloodstained gear of some tall warrior slain—
making his mother proud."

531–532. *Messêis or Hypereiê*: The one in central, the other in northern Greece.

554. *a prince among the Trojans*: When Troy fell, the child was put to death by the Greeks.

After this prayer, 560
into his dear wife's arms he gave his baby,
whom on her fragrant breast
she held and cherished, laughing through her tears.
Hektor pitied her now. Caressing her,
he said:

                      "Unquiet soul, do not be too distressed 565
by thoughts of me. You know no man dispatches me
into the undergloom against my fate;
no mortal, either, can escape his fate,
coward or brave man, once he comes to be.
Go home, attend to your own handiwork 570
at loom and spindle, and command the maids
to busy themselves, too. As for the war,
that is for men, all who were born at Ilion,
to put their minds on—most of all for me."

He stooped now to recover his plumed helm 575
as she, his dear wife, drew away, her head
turned and her eyes upon him, brimming tears.
She made her way in haste then to the ordered
house of Hektor and rejoined her maids,
moving them all to weep at sight of her. 580
In Hektor's home they mourned him, living still
but not, they feared, again to leave the war
or be delivered from Akhaian fury.

Paris in the meantime had not lingered:
after he buckled his bright war-gear on 585
he ran through Troy, sure-footed with long strides.
Think how a stallion fed on clover and barley,
mettlesome, thundering in a stall, may snap
his picket rope and canter down a field
to bathe as he would daily in the river— 590
glorying in freedom! Head held high
with mane over his shoulders flying,
his dazzling work of finely jointed knees
takes him around the pasture haunts of horses.
That was the way the son of Priam, Paris, 595
ran from the height of Pergamos, his gear
ablaze like the great sun,
and laughed aloud. He sprinted on, and quickly

---

571. *at loom and spindle*: That is,     596. *Pergamos*: The citadel of Troy.
weaving and spinning.

met his brother, who was slow to leave
the place where he had discoursed with his lady.  600
Aléxandros was first to speak:

"Dear fellow,"

he said, "have I delayed you, kept you waiting?
Have I not come at the right time, as you asked?"

And Hektor in his shimmering helm replied:

"My strange brother! No man with justice in him  605
would underrate your handiwork in battle;
you have a powerful arm. But you give way
too easily, and lose interest, lose your will.
My heart aches in me when I hear our men,
who have such toil of battle on your account,  610
talk of you with contempt. Well, come along.
Someday we'll make amends for that, if ever
we drive the Akhaians from the land of Troy—
if ever Zeus permit us, in our hall,
to set before the gods of heaven, undying  615
and ever young, our winebowl of deliverance."

[The Trojans rallied successfully and went over to the offensive.
They drove the Greeks back to the light fortifications they had built
around their beached ships. The Trojans lit their watchfires on the
plain, ready to deliver the attack in the morning.]

## Book VIII

### [*The Eve of Battle*]

They led from under the yokes their sweating teams,  718
tethering each beside his chariot,
then brought down from the city beeves and sheep
in all haste—brought down wine and bread as well
out of their halls. They piled up firewood
and carried out full-tally hekatombs
to the immortals. Off the plain, the wind
bore smoke and savor of roasts into the sky.  725
Then on the perilous open ground of war,
in brave expectancy, they lay all night
while many campfires burned. As when in heaven
principal stars shine out around the moon

---

615–616. *to set . . . of deliverance:*    thanks for the end of the siege.
I.e., to make sacrifices to the gods in    720. *beeves:* Cattle.

when the night sky is limpid, with no wind,                    730
and all the lookout points, headlands, and mountain
clearings are distinctly seen, as though
pure space had broken through, downward from heaven,
and all the stars are out, and in his heart
the shepherd sings: just so from ships to river               735
shone before Ilion the Trojan fires.
There were a thousand burning in the plain,
and round each one lay fifty men in firelight.
Horses champed white barley, near the chariots,
waiting for Dawn to mount her lovely chair.                   740

## Book IX

### [*The Embassy to Akhilleus*]

So Trojans kept their watch that night.

                                                    To seaward
Panic that attends blood-chilling Rout
now ruled the Akhaians. All their finest men
were shaken by this fear, in bitter throes,
as when a shifting gale                                         5
blows up over the cold fish-breeding sea,
north wind and west wind wailing out of Thrace
in squall on squall, and dark waves crest, and shoreward
masses of weed are cast up by the surf:
so were Akhaian hearts torn in their breasts.                 10

By that great gloom hard hit, the son of Atreus
made his way amid his criers and told them
to bid each man in person to assembly
but not to raise a general cry. He led them,
making the rounds himself, and soon the soldiers            15
grimly took their places. Then he rose,
with slow tears trickling, as from a hidden spring
dark water runs down, staining a rock wall;
and groaning heavily he addressed the Argives:

"Friends, leaders of Argives, all my captains,               20
Zeus Kronidês entangled me in folly
to my undoing. Wayward god, he promised
solemnly that I should not sail away
before I stormed the inner town of Troy.
Crookedness and duplicity, I see now!                        25

---

7. *Thrace*: Region northwest of Troy.      21. *Kronidês*: Son of Krónos.

He calls me to return to Argos beaten
after these many losses. That must be
his will and his good pleasure, who knows why?
Many a great town's height has he destroyed
and will destroy, being supreme in power.                    30
Enough. Now let us act on what I say:
Board ship for our own fatherland! Retreat!
We cannot hope any longer to take Troy!"

At this a stillness overcame them all,
the Akhaian soldiers. Long they sat in silence,            35
hearing their own hearts beat. Then Diomêdês
rose at last to speak. He said:

                                            "My lord,

I must contend with you for letting go,
for losing balance. I may do so here
in assembly lawfully. Spare me your anger.                  40
Before this you have held me up to scorn
for lack of fighting spirit; old and young,
everyone knows the truth of that. In your case,
the son of crooked-minded Krónos gave you
one gift and not both: a staff of kingship                   45
honored by all men, but no staying power—
the greatest gift of all.
What has come over you, to make you think
the Akhaians weak and craven as you say?
If you are in a passion to sail home,                       50
sail on: the way is clear, the many ships
that made the voyage from Mykênê with you
stand near the sea's edge. Others here will stay
until we plunder Troy! Or if they, too,
would like to, let them sail for their own country!          55
Sthénelos and I will fight alone
until we see the destined end of Ilion.
We came here under god."

                                        When Diomêdês

finished, a cry went up from all Akhaians                   60
in wonder at his words. Then Nestor stood
and spoke among them:

---

41. *held me up to scorn*: This happened during Agamémnon's review of
the troops before joining battle, a battle
in which Diomedes distinguished himself.
52. *Mykênê*: (Mycenae) a city near

Argos.
56. *Sthénelos*: The companion of
Diomêdês.
61. *Son of Tydeus*: Diomêdês.

"Son of Tydeus, formidable
above the rest in war, in council, too,
you have more weight than others of your age.
No one will cry down what you say, no true
Akhaian will, or contradict you. Still,                              65
you did not push on to the end.
I know you are young; in years you might well be
my last-born son, and yet for all of that
you kept your head and said what needed saying
before the Argive captains. My own part,                           70
as I am older, is to drive it home.
No one will show contempt for what I say,
surely not Agamémnon, our commander.
Alien to clan and custom and hearth fire
is he who longs for war—heartbreaking war—                         75
with his own people.

                                        Let us yield to darkness
and make our evening meal. But let the sentries
take their rest on watch outside the rampart
near the moat; those are my orders for them.
Afterward, you direct us, Agamémnon,                               80
by right of royal power. Provide a feast
for older men, your counselors. That is duty
and no difficulty: your huts are full of wine
brought over daily in our ships from Thrace
across the wide sea, and all provender                             85
for guests is yours, as you are high commander.
Your counselors being met, pay heed to him
who counsels best. The army of Akhaia
bitterly needs a well-found plan of action.
The enemy is upon us, near the ships,                              90
burning his thousand fires. What Akhaian
could be highhearted in that glare? This night
will see the army saved or brought to ruin."

They heeded him and did his will. Well-armed,
the sentries left to take their posts, one company                 95
formed around Thrasymêdês, Nestor's son,
another mustered by Askálaphos
and Iálmenos, others commanded by
Meríonês, Aphareus, Déípyros,
and Kreion's son, the princely Lykomêdês.                          100
Seven lieutenants, each with a hundred men,

79. _the moat:_ The Greeks, driven back on their ships, have fortified their position with rampart and moat; they are, in effect, besieged. Zeus' promise to Thetis is being fulfilled.

carrying long spears, issued from the camp
for outposts chosen between ditch and rampart.
Campfires were kindled, and they took their meal.

The son of Atreus led the elder men                    105
together to his hut, where he served dinner,
and each man's hand went out upon the meal.
When they had driven hunger and thirst away,
Old Nestor opened their deliberations—
Nestor, whose counsel had seemed best before,          110
point by point weaving his argument:

"Lord Marshal of the army, Agamémnon,
as I shall end with you, so I begin,
since you hold power over a great army
and are responsible for it: the Lord Zeus              115
put in your keeping staff and precedent
that you might gather counsel for your men.
You should be first in discourse, but attentive
to what another may propose, to act on it
if he speak out for the good of all. Whatever         120
he may initiate, action is yours.
On this rule, let me speak as I think best.
A better view than mine no man can have,
the same view that I've held these many days
since that occasion when, my lord, for all            125
Akhilleus' rage, you took the girl Briséis
out of his lodge—but not with our consent.
Far from it; I for one had begged you not to.
Just the same, you gave way to your pride,
and you dishonored a great prince,                     130
a hero to whom the gods themselves do honor.
Taking his prize, you kept her and still do.
But even so, and even now, we may
contrive some way of making peace with him
by friendly gifts, and by affectionate words."        135

Then Agamémnon, the Lord Marshal, answered:

"Sir, there is nothing false in your account
of my blind errors. I committed them;
I will not now deny it. Troops of soldiers
are worth no more than one man cherished by Zeus      140
as he has cherished this man and avenged him,
overpowering the army of Akhaians.
I lost my head, I yielded to black anger,

but now I would retract it and appease him
with all munificence. Here before everyone                    145
I may enumerate the gifts I'll give.
Seven new tripods and ten bars of gold,
then twenty shining caldrons, and twelve horses,
thoroughbreds, who by their wind and legs
have won me prizes: any man who owned                          150
what these have brought me could not lack resources,
could not be pinched for precious gold—so many
prizes have these horses carried home.
Then I shall give him seven women, deft
in household handicraft—women of Lesbos                        155
I chose when he himself took Lesbos town,
as they outshone all womankind in beauty.
These I shall give him, and one more, whom I
took away from him then: Briseus' daughter.
Concerning her, I add my solemn oath                           160
I never went to bed or coupled with her,
as custom is with men and women.
These will be his at once. If the immortals
grant us the plundering of Priam's town,
let him come forward when the spoils are shared               165
and load his ship with bars of gold and bronze.
Then he may choose among the Trojan women
twenty that are most lovely, after Helen.
If we return to Argos of Akhaia,
flowing with good things of the earth, he'll be               170
my own adopted son, dear as Orestês,
born long ago and reared in bounteous peace.
I have three daughters now at home, Khrysóthemis,
Laódikê, and Iphiánassa.
He may take whom he will to be his bride                      175
and pay no bridal gift, leading her home
to Pêleus' hall. But I shall add a dowry
such as no man has given to his daughter.
Seven flourishing strongholds I'll give him:
Kardamylê and Enopê and Hirê                                  180

147. *tripods*: Here, a three footed kettle. Such metal equipment was rare and
highly valued.

155. *Lesbos*: A large island off the
coast of Asia Minor.

169. *Argos*: Greece.

173–174. *Khrysóthemis, Laódikê, and
Iphiánassa*:  Homer's  picture  of
Agamémnon's family is different from
that of the later tragic poets. It is possible (but by no means certain) that

Iphiánassa is a different form of the
name Iphigenia but in that case Homer
does not know the story of the sacrifice
of Iphigenia at Aulis (though he mentions the gathering of the ships there in
Book II). Khrysóthemis appears in
Sophocles' play *Electra*, but Electra herself, who appears in all the Orestes tragedies, is not mentioned in Homer.
Laódikê appears only here.

in the wild grassland; holy Phêrai too,
and the deep meadowland of Ántheia,
Aipeia and the vineyard slope of Pêdasos,
all lying near the sea in the far west
of sandy Pylos. In these lands are men                          185
who own great flocks and herds; now as his liegemen,
they will pay tithes and sumptuous honor to him,
prospering as they carry out his plans.
These are the gifts I shall arrange if he
desists from anger. Let him be subdued!                         190
Lord Death indeed is deaf to appeal, implacable;
of all gods therefore he is most abhorrent
to mortal men. So let Akhilleus bow to me,
considering that I hold higher rank
and claim the precedence of age."


To this                                                         195

Lord Nestor of Gerênia replied:

"Lord Marshal of the army, Agamémnon,
this time the gifts you offer Lord Akhilleus
are not to be despised. Come, we'll dispatch
our chosen emissaries to his quarters                           200
as quickly as possible. Those men whom I
may designate, let them perform the mission.
Phoinix, dear to Zeus, may lead the way.
Let Aías follow him, and Prince Odysseus.
The criers, Hódios and Eurýbatês,                               205
may go as escorts. Bowls for their hands here!
Tell them to keep silence, while we pray
that Zeus the son of Krónos will be merciful."


Nestor's proposal fell on willing ears,
and criers came at once to tip our water                        210
over their hands, while young men filled the winebowls
and dipped a measure into every cup.
They spilt their offerings and drank their fill,
then briskly left the hut of Agamémnon.
Nestor accompanied them with final words                        215
and sage looks, especially for Odysseus,
as to the effort they should make to bring
the son of Pêleus round.

196. *Gerênia*: The city in southwestern
Greece where Nestor was brought up.
203. *Phoinix*: Especially appropriate
for this mission, since he was tutor to
the young Akhilleus.

Following Phoinix,
Aías and Odysseus walked together
beside the tumbling clamorous whispering sea,                    220
praying hard to the girdler of the islands
that they might easily sway their great friend's heart.
Amid the ships and huts of the Myrmidons
they found him, taking joy in a sweet harp
of rich and delicate make—the crossbar set                      225
to hold the strings being silver. He had won it
when he destroyed the city of Eëtíôn,
and plucking it he took his joy: he sang
old tales of heroes, while across the room
alone and silent sat Patróklos, waiting                          230
until Akhilleus should be done with song.
Phoinix had come in unremarked, but when
the two new visitors, Odysseus leading,
entered and stood before him, then Akhilleus
rose in wonderment, and left his chair,                          235
his harp still in his hand. So did Patróklos
rise at sight of the two men. Akhilleus
made both welcome with a gesture, saying:

"Peace! My two great friends, I greet your coming.
How I have needed it! Even in my anger,                         240
of all Akhaians, you are closest to me."

And Prince Akhilleus led them in. He seated them
on easy chairs with purple coverlets,
and to Patróklos who stood near he said:

"Put out an ampler winebowl, use more wine                      245
for stronger drink, and place a cup for each.
Here are my dearest friends beneath my roof."

Patróklos did as his companion bade him.
Meanwhile the host set down a carving block
within the fire's rays; a chine of mutton                       250
and a fat chine of goat he placed upon it,
as well as savory pork chine. Automédôn
steadied the meat for him, Akhilleus carved,
then sliced it well and forked it on the spits.
Meanwhile Patróklos, like a god in firelight,                   255
made the hearth blaze up. When the leaping flame
had ebbed and died away, he raked the coals

221. *girdler of the islands*: Poseidon.     leus' chariot.
252. *Automédôn*: The driver of Akhil-

and in the glow extended spits of meat,
lifting these at times from the firestones
to season with pure salt. When all was done          260
and the roast meat apportioned into platters,
loaves of bread were passed round by Patróklos
in fine baskets. Akhilleus served the meat.
He took his place then opposite Odysseus,
back to the other wall, and told                     265
Patróklos to make offering to the gods.
This he did with meat tossed in the fire,
then each man's hand went out upon the meal.
When they had put their hunger and thirst away,
Aías nodded silently to Phoinix,                     270
but Prince Odysseus caught the nod. He filled
a cup of wine and lifted it to Akhilleus,
saying:

        "Health, Akhilleus. We've no lack
of generous feasts this evening—in the lodge
of Agamémnon first, and now with you,                275
good fare and plentiful each time.
It is not feasting that concerns us now,
however, but a ruinous defeat.
Before our very eyes we see it coming
and are afraid. By a blade's turn, our good ships    280
are saved or lost, unless you arm your valor.
Trojans and allies are encamped tonight
in pride before our ramparts, at our sterns,
and through their army burn a thousand fires.
These men are sure they cannot now be stopped        285
but will get through to our good ships. Lord Zeus
flashes and thunders for them on the right,
and Hektor in his ecstasy of power
is mad for battle, confident in Zeus,
deferring to neither men nor gods. Pure frenzy       290
fills him, and he prays for the bright dawn
when he will shear our stern-post beaks away
and fire all our ships, while in the shipways
amid that holocaust he carries death
among our men, driven out by smoke. All this         295
I gravely fear; I fear the gods will make
good his threatenings, and our fate will be

---

292. *stern-post beaks*: The stern of the
Homeric ship ended in an upward
projection, handy for dragging it up on
the beach. Hektor will "shear them

away" to display them as trophies in
Troy.
293. *shipways*: Where the ships have
been beached.

to die here, far from the pastureland of Argos.
Rouse yourself, if even at this hour
you'll pitch in for the Akhaians and deliver them          300
from Trojan havoc. In the years to come
this day will be remembered pain for you
if you do not. No remedy, no remedy
will come to hand, once the great ill is done.
While there is time, think how to keep this evil          305
day from the Danääns!

                                         **My dear lad,**

how rightly in your case your father, Pêleus,
put it in his farewell, sending you out
from Phthía to make ship with Agamémnon!
'Now as to fighting power, child,' he said,          310
'if Hêra and Athêna wish, they'll give it.
Control your passion, though, and your proud heart,
for gentle courtesy is a better thing.
Break off insidious quarrels, and young and old,
the Argives will respect you for it more.'          315
That was your old father's admonition:
you have forgotten. Still, even now, abandon
heart-wounding anger. If you will relent,
Agamémnon will match this change of heart
with gifts. Now listen and let me list for you          320
what just now in his quarters he proposed:
seven new tripods, and ten bars of gold,
then twenty shining caldrons, and twelve horses,
thoroughbreds, that by their wind and legs
have won him prizes: any man who owned          325
what these have brought him would not lack resources,
could not be pinched for precious gold—so many
prizes have these horses carried home.
Then he will give you seven women, deft
in household handicraft: women of Lesbos          330
chosen when you yourself took Lesbos town,
as they outshone all womankind in beauty.
These he will give you, and one more, whom he
took away from you then: Briseus' daughter,
concerning whom he adds a solemn oath          335
never to have gone to bed or coupled with her,
as custom is, my lord, with men and women.
These are all yours at once. If the immortals
grant us the pillaging of Priam's town,
you may come forward when the spoils are shared          340
and load your ship with bars of gold and bronze.

Then you may choose among the Trojan women
twenty that are most lovely, after Helen.
And then, if we reach Argos of Akhaia,
flowing with good things of the earth, you'll be           345
his own adopted son, dear as Orestês,
born long ago and reared in bounteous peace.
He has three daughters now at home, Khrysóthemis,
Laódikê, and Iphiánassa.
You may take whom you will to be your bride                 350
and pay no gift when you conduct her home
to your ancestral hall. He'll add a dowry
such as no man has given to his daughter.
Seven flourishing strongholds he'll give to you:
Kardamylé and Enopé and Hirê                                355
in the wild grassland; holy Phêrai too,
and the deep meadowland of Ántheia,
Aipeia and the vineyard slope of Pêdasos,
all lying near the sea in the far west
of sandy Pylos. In these lands are men                      360
who own great flocks and herds; now as your liegemen,
they will pay tithes and sumptuous honor to you,
prospering as they carry out your plans.
These are the gifts he will arrange if you
desist from anger.

                              Even if you abhor 365
the son of Atreus all the more bitterly,
with all his gifts, take pity on the rest,
all the old army, worn to rags in battle.
These will honor you as gods are honored!
And ah, for these, what glory you may win!                  370
Think: Hektor is your man this time: being crazed
with ruinous pride, believing there's no fighter
equal to him among those that our ships
brought here by sea, he'll put himself in range!"

Akhilleus the great runner answered him:                    375

"Son of Laërtês and the gods of old,
Odysseus, master soldier and mariner,
I owe you a straight answer, as to how
I see this thing, and how it is to end.
No need to sit with me like mourning doves                  380
making your gentle noise by turns. I hate
as I hate Hell's own gate that man who hides
one thought within him while he speaks another.

What I shall say is what I see and think.
Give in to Agamémnon? I think not,                              385
neither to him nor to the rest. I had
small thanks for fighting, fighting without truce
against hard enemies here. The portion's equal
whether a man hangs back or fights his best;
the same respect, or lack of it, is given                       390
brave man and coward. One who's active dies
like the do-nothing. What least thing have I
to show for it, for harsh days undergone
and my life gambled, all these years of war?
A bird will give her fledglings every scrap                     395
she comes by, and go hungry, foraging.
That is the case with me.
Many a sleepless night I've spent afield
and many a day in bloodshed, hand to hand
in battle for the wives of other men.                           400
In sea raids I plundered a dozen towns,
eleven in expeditions overland
through Trojan country, and the treasure taken
out of them all, great heaps of handsome things,
I carried back each time to Agamémnon.                          405
He sat tight on the beachhead, and shared out
a little treasure; most of it he kept.
He gave prizes of war to his officers;
the rest have theirs, not I; from me alone
of all Akhaians, he pre-empted her.                             410
He holds my bride, dear to my heart. Aye, let him
sleep with her and enjoy her!

                                           Why must Argives
fight the Trojans? Why did he raise an army
and lead it here? For Helen, was it not?
Are the Atreidai of all mortal men                              415
the only ones who love their wives? I think not.
Every sane decent fellow loves his own
and cares for her, as in my heart I loved
Brisêis, though I won her by the spear.
Now, as he took my prize out of my hands,                       420
tricked and defrauded me, he need not tempt me;
I know him, and he cannot change my mind.
Let him take thought, Odysseus, with you
and others how the ships may be defended
against incendiary attack. By god,                              425
he has achieved imposing work without me,
a rampart piled up overnight, a ditch

running beyond it, broad and deep,
with stakes implanted in it! All no use!
He cannot hold against the killer's charge. 430
As long as I was in the battle, Hektor
never cared for a fight far from the walls;
his limit was the oak tree by the gate.
When I was alone one day he waited there,
but barely got away when I went after him. 435
Now it is I who do not care to fight.
Tomorrow at dawn when I have made offering
to Zeus and all the gods, and hauled my ships
for loading in the shallows, if you like
and if it interests you, look out and see 440
my ships on Hellê's waters in the offing,
oarsmen in line making the sea-foam scud!
And if the great Earthshaker gives a breeze,
the third day out I'll make it home to Phthía.
Rich possessions are there I left behind 445
when I was mad enough to come here; now
I take home gold and ruddy bronze, and women
belted luxuriously, and hoary iron,
all that came to me here. As for my prize,
he who gave her took her outrageously back. 450
Well, you can tell him all this to his face,
and let the other Akhaians burn
if he in his thick hide of shamelessness
picks out another man to cheat. He would not
look me in the eye, dog that he is! 455
I will not share one word of counsel with him,
nor will I act with him; he robbed me blind,
broke faith with me: he gets no second chance
to play me for a fool. Once is enough.
To hell with him, Zeus took his brains away! 460
His gifts I abominate, and I would give
not one dry shuck for him. I would not change,
not if he multiplied his gifts by ten,
by twenty times what he has now, and more,
no matter where they came from: if he gave 465
what enters through Orkhómenos' town gate
or Thebes of Egypt, where the treasures lie—
that city where through each of a hundred gates
two hundred men drive out in chariots.

441. *Hellê's waters*: The Hellespont.
443. *Earthshaker*: Poseidon.
466. *Orkhómenos*: Great city north of Athens.
467. *Thebes of Egypt*: The splendid ancient capital of Upper Egypt.

Not if his gifts outnumbered the sea sands 470
or all the dust grains in the world could Agamémnon
ever appease me—not till he pays me back
full measure, pain for pain, dishonor for dishonor.
The daughter of Agamémnon, son of Atreus,
I will not take in marriage. Let her be 475
as beautiful as pale-gold Aphrodítê,
skilled as Athêna of the sea-gray eyes,
I will not have her, at any price. No, let him
find someone else, an eligible Akhaian,
kinglier than I.

                              Now if the gods 480
preserve me and I make it home, my father
Pêleus will select a bride for me.
In Hellas and in Phthía there are many
daughters of strong men who defend the towns.
I'll take the one I wish to be my wife. 485
There in my manhood I have longed, indeed,
to marry someone of congenial mind
and take my ease, enjoying the great estate
my father had acquired.

                                 Now I think
no riches can compare with being alive, 490
not even those they say this well-built Ilion
stored up in peace before the Akhaians came.
Neither could all the Archer's shrine contains
at rocky Pytho, in the crypt of stone.
A man may come by cattle and sheep in raids; 495
tripods he buys, and tawny-headed horses;
but his life's breath cannot be hunted back
or be recaptured once it pass his lips.
My mother, Thetis of the silvery feet,
tells me of two possible destinies 500
carrying me toward death: two ways:
if on the one hand I remain to fight
around Troy town, I lose all hope of home
but gain unfading glory; on the other,
if I sail back to my own land my glory 505
fails—but a long life lies ahead for me.
To all the rest of you I say: 'Sail home:
you will not now see Ilion's last hour,'
for Zeus who views the wide world held his sheltering
hand over that city, and her troops 510
have taken heart.

    494. *Pytho:* Apollo's shrine at Delphi.     to the god by his worshippers.
The treasure consisted of offerings made

Return, then, emissaries,
deliver my answer to the Akhaian peers—
it is the senior officer's privilege—
and let them plan some other way, and better,
to save their ships and save the Akhaian army.          515
This one cannot be put into effect—
their scheme this evening—while my anger holds.
Phoinix may stay and lodge the night with us,
then take ship and sail homeward at my side
tomorrow, if he wills. I'll not constrain him."          520

After Akhilleus finished, all were silent,
awed, for he spoke with power.
Then the old master-charioteer, Lord Phoinix,
answered at last, and let his tears come shining,
fearing for the Akhaian ships:

"Akhilleus,          525
if it is true you set your heart on home
and will not stir a finger to save the ships
from being engulfed by fire—all for this rage
that has swept over you—how, child, could I
be sundered from you, left behind alone?          530
For your sake the old master-charioteer,
Pêleus, made provision that I should come,
that day he gave you godspeed out of Phthía
to go with Agamémnon. Still a boy,
you knew nothing of war that levels men          535
to the same testing, nothing of assembly
where men become illustrious. That is why
he sent me, to instruct you in these matters,
to be a man of eloquence and action.
After all that, dear child, I should not wish          540
to be left here apart from you—not even
if god himself should undertake to smooth
my wrinkled age and make me fresh and young,
as when for the first time I left the land
of lovely women, Hellas. I went north          545
to avoid a feud with Father, Amyntor
Orménidês. His anger against me rose
over a fair-haired slave girl whom he fancied,
without respect for his own wife, my mother.
Mother embraced my knees and begged that I          550
make love to this girl, so that afterward
she might be cold to the aging man. I did it.
My father guessed the truth at once, and cursed me,

praying the ghostly Furies that no son
of mine should ever rest upon his knees:                               555
a curse fulfilled by the immortals—Lord
Zeus of undergloom and cold Perséphoně.
I planned to put a sword in him, and would have,
had not some god unstrung my rage, reminding me
of country gossip and the frowns of men;                               560
I shrank from being called a parricide
among the Akhaians. But from that time on
I felt no tie with home, no love for lingering
under the rooftree of a raging father.
Our household and our neighbors, it is true,                           565
urged me to stay. They made a handsome feast
of shambling cattle butchered, and fat sheep;
young porkers by the litter, crisp with fat,
were singed and spitted in Hêphaistos' fire,
rivers of wine drunk from the old man's store.                        570
Nine times they spent the night and slept beside me,
taking the watch by turns, leaving a fire
to flicker under the entrance colonnade,
and one more in the court outside my room.
But when the tenth night came, starless and black,                    575
I cracked the tight bolt on my chamber door,
pushed out, and scaled the courtyard wall, unseen
by household men on watch or women slaves.
Then I escaped from that place, made my way
through Hellas where the dancing floors are wide,                     580
until I came to Phthía's fertile plain,
mother of flocks, and Pêleus the king.
He gave me welcome, treated me with love,
as a father would an only son, his heir
to rich possessions. And he made me rich,                             585
appointing me great numbers of retainers
on the frontier of Phthía, where I lived
as lord of Dolopês. Now, it was I
who formed your manhood, handsome as a god's,
Akhilleus: I who loved you from the heart;                            590
for never in another's company
would you attend a feast or dine in hall—
never, unless I took you on my knees
and cut your meat, and held your cup of wine.
Many a time you wet my shirt, hiccuping                               595
wine-bubbles in distress, when you were small.

---

554. *Furies*: Avenging spirits, particularly concerned with crimes committed
by kinsmen against kinsmen.

557. *Zeus of undergloom*: The god
Hades. *Persephone*: His wife.

Patient and laborious as a nurse
I had to be for you, bearing in mind
that never would the gods bring into being
any son of mine. Godlike Akhilleus,                           600
you were the manchild that I made my own
to save me someday, so I thought, from misery.
Quell your anger, Akhilleus! You must not
be pitiless! The gods themselves relent,
and are they not still greater in bravery,                    605
in honor and in strength? Burnt offerings,
courteous prayer, libation, smoke of sacrifice,
with all of these, men can placate the gods
when someone oversteps and errs. The truth is,
prayers are daughters of almighty Zeus—                       610
one may imagine them lame, wrinkled things
with eyes cast down, that toil to follow after
passionate Folly. Folly is strong and swift,
outrunning all the prayers, and everywhere
arriving first to injure mortal men;                          615
still they come healing after. If a man
reveres the daughters of Zeus when they come near,
he is rewarded, and his prayers are heard;
but if he spurns them and dismisses them,
they make their way to Zeus again and ask                     620
that Folly dog that man till suffering
has taken arrogance out of him.

                                  Relent,

be courteous to the daughters of Zeus, you too,
as courtesy sways others, and the best.
If Agamémnon had no gifts for you,                            625
named none to follow, but inveighed against you
still in fury, then I could never say,
'Discard your anger and defend the Argives—'
never, no matter how they craved your help.
But this is not so: he will give many things                 630
at once; he promised others; he has sent
his noblest men to intercede with you,
the flower of the army, and your friends,
dearest among the Argives. Will you turn
their words, their coming, into humiliation?                  635
Until this moment, no one took it ill
that you should suffer anger; we learned this
from the old stories of how towering wrath
could overcome great men; but they were still
amenable to gifts and to persuasion.                          640
Here is an instance I myself remember

not from our own time but in ancient days:
I'll tell it to you all, for all are friends.
The Kourêtês were fighting a warlike race,
Aitolians, around the walls of Kálydôn,                                645
with slaughter on both sides: Aitolians
defending their beloved Kálydôn
while the Kourêtês longed to sack the town.
The truth is, Artemis of the Golden Chair
had brought the scourge of war on the Aitolians;                      650
she had been angered because Oineus made
no harvest offering from his vineyard slope.
While other gods enjoyed his hekatombs
he made her none, either forgetful of it
or careless—a great error, either way.                                655
In her anger, the Mistress of Long Arrows
roused against him a boar with gleaming tusks
out of his wild grass bed, a monstrous thing
that ravaged the man's vineyard many times
and felled entire orchards, roots,                                    660
blooms, apples and all. Now this great boar
Meléagros, the son of Oineus, killed
by gathering men and hounds from far and near.
So huge the boar was, no small band could master him,
and he brought many to the dolorous pyre.                             665
Around the dead beast Artemis set on
a clash with battlecries between Kourêtês
and proud Aitolians over the boar's head
and shaggy hide. As long, then, as Meléagros,
backed by the wargod, fought, the Kourêtês                            670
had the worst of it for all their numbers
and could not hold a line outside the walls.
But then a day came when Meléagros
was stung by venomous anger that infects
the coolest thinker's heart: swollen with rage                        675
at his own mother, Althaiê, he languished
in idleness at home beside his lady,
Kleopátrê.

645. *Kálydôn*: A city in northwest
Greece.
651. *Oineus*: King of the Aitolians.
665. *dolorous pyre*: I.e., to their
deaths. Cremation was the normal funeral custom.
675–676. *rage/at his own mother*: Explained below. She had prayed for his
death because he killed her brother in
the fighting.
678. *Kleopátrê*: (Cleopatra). This
short digression (to line 686) tells, in
highly allusive fashion, the story of

Kleopátrê's mother Marpessê, daughter
of Euênos. The famous archer Idês carried her off and married her. But the
god Apollo, who had also been her
suitor, overtook Idês and seized
Marpessê. Idês defied Apollo to combat,
but Zeus decided that the choice should
be Marpessê's and she chose Idês. They
gave their daughter Kleopátrê the nickname Alkýonê, the name of the sea-bird
that was supposed to mourn for its
mate, as Marpessê, carried off by
Apollo, mourned for Idês.

This lovely girl was born
to Marpessê of ravishing pale ankles,
Euênos' child, and Idês, who had been                    680
most powerful of men on earth. He drew
the bow against the Lord Phoibos Apollo
over his love, Marpessê, whom her father
and gentle mother called Alkýonê,
since for her sake her mother gave that seabird's        685
forlorn cry when Apollo ravished her.
With Kleopátrê lay Meléagros,
nursing the bitterness his mother stirred,
when in her anguish over a brother slain
she cursed her son. She called upon the gods,            690
beating the grassy earth with both her hands
as she pitched forward on her knees, with cries
to the Lord of Undergloom and cold Perséphonê,
while tears wetted her veils—in her entreaty
that death come to her son. Inexorable                    695
in Érebos a vampire Fury listened.
Soon, then, about the gates of the Aitolians
tumult and din of war grew loud; their towers
rang with blows. And now the elder men
implored Meléagros to leave his room,                    700
and sent the high priests of the gods, imploring him
to help defend the town. They promised him
a large reward: in the green countryside
of Kálydôn, wherever it was richest,
there he might choose a beautiful garden plot            705
of fifty acres, half in vineyard, half
in virgin prairie for the plow to cut.
Oineus, master of horsemen, came with prayers
upon the doorsill of the chamber, often
rattling the locked doors, pleading with his son.        710
His sisters, too, and then his gentle mother
pleaded with him. Only the more fiercely
he turned away. His oldest friends, his dearest,
not even they could move him—not until
his room was shaken by a hail of stones                  715
as Kourêtês began to scale the walls
and fire the city.

                                    Then at last his lady
in her soft-belted gown besought him weeping,
speaking of all the ills that come to men
whose town is taken: soldiers put to the sword;         720

---

696. *Érebos*: The lower depths of the underworld.

the city razed by fire; alien hands
carrying off the children and the women.
Hearing these fearful things, his heart was stirred
to action: he put on his shining gear
and fought off ruin from the Aitolians.                               725
Mercy prevailed in him. His folk no longer
cared to award him gifts and luxuries,
yet even so he saved that terrible day.
Oh, do not let your mind go so astray!
Let no malignant spirit                                              730
turn you that way, dear son! It will be worse
to fight for ships already set afire!
Value the gifts; rejoin the war; Akhaians
afterward will give you a god's honor.
If you reject the gifts and then, later,                             735
enter the deadly fight, you will not be
accorded the same honor, even though
you turn the tide of war!"

                              But the great runner
Akhilleus answered:

                              "Old uncle Phoinix, bless you,
that is an honor I can live without.                                 740
Honored I think I am by Zeus's justice,
justice that will sustain me by the ships
as long as breath is in me and I can stand.
Here is another point: ponder it well:
best not confuse my heart with lamentation                           745
for Agamémnon, whom you must not honor;
you would be hateful to me, dear as you are.
Loyalty should array you at my side
in giving pain to him who gives me pain.
Rule with me equally, share half my honor,                           750
but do not ask my help for Agamémnon.
My answer will be reported by these two.
Lodge here in a soft bed, and at first light
we can decide whether to sail or stay."

He knit his brows and nodded to Patróklos                            755
to pile up rugs for Phoinix' bed—a sign
for the others to be quick about departing.
Aías, however, noble son of Télamôn
made the last appeal. He said:

"Odysseus,
master soldier and mariner, let us go.                                    760
I do not see the end of this affair
achieved by this night's visit. Nothing for it
but to report our talk for what it's worth
to the Danáäns, who sit waiting there.
Akhilleus hardened his great heart against us,                            765
wayward and savage as he is, unmoved
by the affections of his friends who made him
honored above all others on the beachhead.
There is no pity in him. A normal man
will take the penalty for a brother slain                                 770
or a dead son. By paying much, the one
who did the deed may stay unharmed at home.
Fury and pride in the bereaved are curbed
when he accepts the penalty. Not you.
Cruel and unappeasable rage the gods                                      775
put in you for one girl alone. We offer
seven beauties, and much more besides!
Be gentler, and respect your own rooftree
whereunder we are guests who speak for all
Danáäns as a body. Our desire                                             780
is to be closest to you of them all."

Akhilleus the great runner answered him:

"Scion of Télamôn and gods of old,
Aías, lord of fighting men, you seemèd
to echo my own mind in what you said!                                     785
And yet my heart grows large and hot with fury
remembering that affair: as though I were
some riffraff or camp follower, he taunted me
before them all!
                        Go back, report the news:
I will not think of carnage or of war                                     790
until Prince Hektor, son of Priam, reaches
Myrmidon huts and ships in his attack,
slashing through Argives, burning down their ships.
Around my hut, my black ship, I foresee
for all his fury, Hektor will break off combat."                         795

That was his answer. Each of the emissaries
took up a double-handed cup and poured
libation by the shipways. Then Odysseus
led the way on their return. Patróklos

commanded his retainers and the maids                                    800
to make at once a deep-piled bed for Phoinix.
Obediently they did so, spreading out
fleeces and coverlet and a linen sheet,
and down the old man lay, awaiting Dawn.
Akhilleus slept in the well-built hut's recess,                          805
and with him lay a woman he had brought
from Lesbos, Phorbas' daughter, Dioméde.
Patróklos went to bed at the other end,
and with him, too, a woman lay—soft-belted
Iphis, who had been given to him by Akhilleus                            810
when he took Skyros, ringed by cliff, the mountain
fastness of Enyéus.

                                            Now the emissaries

arrived at Agamémnon's lodge. With cups
of gold held up, and rising to their feet
on every side, the Akhaians greeted them,                                815
curious for the news. Lord Agamémnon
put the question first:

                                            "Come, tell me, sir,

Odysseus, glory of Akhaia—will Akhilleus
fight off ravenous fire from the ships
or does he still refuse, does anger still                                820
hold sway in his great heart?"

                                            That patient man,

the Prince Odysseus, made reply:

                                            "Excellency,

Lord Marshal of the army, son of Atreus,
the man has no desire to quench his rage.
On the contrary, he is more than ever                                    825
full of anger, spurns you and your gifts,
calls on you to work out your own defense
to save the ships and the Akhaian army.
As for himself, he threatens at daybreak
to drag his well-found ships into the surf,                              830
and says he would advise the rest as well
to sail for home. 'You shall not see,' he says,
'the last hour that awaits tall Ilion,
for Zeus who views the wide world held his sheltering
hand over the city, and her troops                                       835
have taken heart.' That was Akhilleus' answer.
Those who were with me can confirm all this,
Aías can, and the two clearheaded criers.

830. *well-found*: Solidly built.

As to old Phoinix, he is sleeping there
by invitation, so that he may sail                                    840
to his own country, homeward with Akhilleus,
tomorrow, if he wills, without constraint."

When he had finished everyone was still,
sitting in silence and in perturbation
for a long time. At last brave Diomêdês,                              845
lord of the warcry, said:

                                                       "Excellency,
Lord Marshal of the army, Agamémnon,
you never should have pled with him, or given
so many gifts to him. At the best of times
he is a proud man; now you have pushed him far                       850
deeper into his vanity and pride.
By god, let us have done with him—
whether he goes or stays! He'll fight again
when the time comes, whenever his blood is up
or the god rouses him. As for ourselves,                             855
let everyone now do as I advise
and go to rest. Your hearts have been refreshed
with bread and wine, the pith and nerve of men.
When the fair Dawn with finger tips of rose
makes heaven bright, deploy your men and horses                      860
before the ships at once, and cheer them on,
and take your place, yourself, in the front line
to join the battle."

                                          All gave their assent
in admiration of Diomêdês,
breaker of horses. When they had spilt their wine                    865
they all dispersed, each man to his own hut,
and lying down they took the gift of sleep.


[After Akhilleus' refusal, the situation of the Greeks worsened
rapidly. Agamémnon, Diomêdês, and Odysseus were all wounded.
The Trojans breached the stockade and fought beside the ships.
Patróklos tried to bring Akhilleus to the aid of the Greeks, but the
most he could obtain was permission for himself to fight, clad in
Akhilleus' armor, at the head of the Myrmidons. He turned the tide
of battle and drove the Trojans back to their walls, only to fall himself through the direct intervention of Apollo. Hektor stripped
Akhilleus' armor from the body. A fierce fight for the body itself
ended in partial success for the Greeks; they took Patróklos' body
but had to retreat to their camp, with the Trojans at their heels.]

## Book XVIII

### [*The Arming of Akhilleus*]

While they were still in combat, fighting seaward
raggedly as fire, Antílokhos
ran far ahead with tidings for Akhilleus.
In shelter of the curled, high prows he found him
envisioning what had come to pass,                           5
in gloom and anger saying to himself:

"Ai! why are they turning tail once more,
unmanned, outfought, and driven from the field
back on the beach and ships? I pray the gods
this may not be the last twist of the knife!                 10
My mother warned me once that, while I lived,
the most admirable of Myrmidons
would quit the sunlight under Trojan blows.
It could indeed be so. He has gone down,
my dear and wayward friend!                                  15
Push their deadly fire away, I told him,
then return! You must not fight with Hektor!"

And while he called it all to mind,
the son of gallant Nestor came up weeping
to give his cruel news:

                      "Here's desolation,    20
son of Pêleus, the worst news for you—
would god it had not happened!—Lord Patróklos
fell, and they are fighting over his body,
stripped of armor. Hektor has your gear."

A black stormcloud of pain shrouded Akhilleus.            25
On his bowed head he scattered dust and ash
in handfuls and befouled his beautiful face,
letting black ash sift on his fragrant khiton.
Then in the dust he stretched his giant length
and tore his hair with both hands.

                            From the hut    30
the women who had been spoils of war to him
and to Patróklos flocked in haste around him,
crying loud in grief. All beat their breasts,
and trembling came upon their knees.

                                Antílokhos
wept where he stood, bending to hold the hero's            35

---

2. *Antílokhos*: A son of Nestor.        28. *khiton*: Tunic.

hands when groaning shook his heart: he feared
the man might use sharp iron to slash his throat.
And now Akhilleus gave a dreadful cry.

Her ladyship

his mother heard him, in the depths offshore
lolling near her ancient father. Nymphs                          40
were gathered round her: all Nêrêïdês
who haunted the green chambers of the sea.
Glaukê, Thaleia, and Kymodokê,
Nesaiê, Speiô, Thoê, Haliê
with her wide eyes; Kymothoê, Aktaiê,                            45
Limnôreia, Melitê and Iaira,
Amphitoê, Agauê, Dôtô, Prôtô,
Pherousa, Dynaménê, Dexaménê,
Amphinomê, Kallianeira, Dôris,
Panopê, and storied Galateia,                                   50
Nêmertês and Apseudês, Kallianassa,
Klyméne, Ianeira, Ianassa,
Maira, Oreithyia, Amathyia,
and other Nêrêïdês of the deep sea,
filling her glimmering silvery cave. All these                  55
now beat their breasts as Thetis cried in sorrow:

"Sisters, daughters of Nêreus, hear and know
how sore my heart is! Now my life is pain
· for my great son's dark destiny! I bore
a child flawless and strong beyond all men.                     60
He flourished like a green shoot, and I brought him
to manhood like a blossoming orchard tree,
only to send him in the ships to Ilion
to war with Trojans. Now I shall never see him
entering Pêleus' hall, his home, again.                         65
But even while he lives, beholding sunlight,
suffering is his lot. I have no power
to help him, though I go to him. Even so,
I'll visit my dear child and learn what sorrow
came to him while he held aloof from war."                      70

On this she left the cave, and all in tears
her company swam aloft with her. Around them
a billow broke and foamed on the open sea.
As they made land at the fertile plain of Troy,
they went up one by one in line to where,                       75
in close order, Myrmidon ships were beached
to right and left of Akhilleus. Bending near

41. *Nêrêïdês*: Literally, daughters of Nêreus; sea-nymphs.

her groaning son, the gentle goddess wailed
and took his head between her hands in pity,
saying softly:

                "Child, why are you weeping?   80
What great sorrow came to you? Speak out,
do not conceal it. Zeus
did all you asked: Akhaian troops,
for want of you, were all forced back again
upon the ship sterns, taking heavy losses         85
none of them could wish."

                           The great runner
groaned and answered:

                     "Mother, yes, the master
of high Olympos brought it all about,
but how have I benefited? My greatest friend
is gone: Patróklos, comrade in arms, whom I      90
held dear above all others—dear as myself—
now gone, lost; Hektor cut him down, despoiled him
of my own arms, massive and fine, a wonder
in all men's eyes. The gods gave them to Pêleus
that day they put you in a mortal's bed—        95
how I wish the immortals of the sea
had been your only consorts! How I wish
Pêleus had taken a mortal queen! Sorrow
immeasurable is in store for you as well,
when your own child is lost: never again       100
on his homecoming day will you embrace him!
I must reject this life, my heart tells me,
reject the world of men,
if Hektor does not feel my battering spear
tear the life out of him, making him pay       105
in his own blood for the slaughter of Patróklos!"

Letting a tear fall, Thetis said:

                        "You'll be
swift to meet your end, child, as you say:
your doom comes close on the heels of Hektor's own."

Akhilleus the great runner ground his teeth      110
and said:

                  "May it come quickly. As things were,
I could not help my friend in his extremity.
Far from his home he died; he needed me

to shield him or to parry the death stroke.
For me there's no return to my own country. 115
Not the slightest gleam of hope did I
afford Patróklos or the other men
whom Hektor overpowered. Here I sat,
my weight a useless burden to the earth,
and I am one who has no peer in war 120
among Akhaian captains—

though in council

there are wiser. Ai! let strife and rancor
perish from the lives of gods and men,
with anger that envenoms even the wise
and is far sweeter than slow-dripping honey, 125
clouding the hearts of men like smoke: just so
the marshal of the army, Agamémnon,
moved me to anger. But we'll let that go,
though I'm still sore at heart; it is all past,
and I have quelled my passion as I must. 130

Now I must go to look for the destroyer
of my great friend. I shall confront the dark
drear spirit of death at any hour Zeus
and the other gods may wish to make an end.
Not even Hêraklês escaped that terror 135
though cherished by the Lord Zeus. Destiny
and Hêra's bitter anger mastered him.
Likewise with me, if destiny like his
awaits me, I shall rest when I have fallen!
Now, though, may I win my perfect glory 140
and make some wife of Troy break down,
or some deep-breasted Dardan woman sob
and wipe tears from her soft cheeks. They'll know then
how long they had been spared the deaths of men,
while I abstained from war! 145
Do not attempt to keep me from the fight,
though you love me; you cannot make me listen."

Thetis, goddess of the silvery feet,
answered:

"Yes, of course, child: very true.
You do no wrong to fight for tired soldiers 150
and keep them from defeat. But still, your gear,

135. *Hêraklês*: Or Hercules, son of
Zeus by a mortal woman. Pursued by
the jealousy of Hêra, he was forced to
undertake twelve great labors and finally
died in agony from the effects of a poisoned garment.
142. *Dardan*: Another name for the
Trojans, from Dárdanos, son of Zeus
and ancestor of the Trojan kings.

all shining bronze, remains in Trojan hands.
Hektor himself is armed with it in pride!—
Not that he'll glory in it long, I know,
for violent death is near him.

                             Patience, then. 155

Better not plunge into the moil of Arês
until you see me here once more. At dawn,
at sunrise, I shall come
with splendid arms for you from Lord Hêphaistos."

She rose at this and, turning from her son, 160
told her sister Nêrêïdês:

                                  "Go down

into the cool broad body of the sea
to the sea's Ancient; visit Father's hall,
and make all known to him. Meanwhile, I'll visit
Olympos' great height and the lord of crafts, 165
Hêphaistos, hoping he will give me
new and shining armor for my son."

At this they vanished in the offshore swell,
and to Olympos Thetis the silvery-footed
went once more, to fetch for her dear son 170
new-forged and finer arms.

                           Meanwhile, Akhaians,
wildly crying, pressed by deadly Hektor,
reached the ships, beached above Hellê's water.
None had been able to pull Patróklos clear
of spear- and swordplay: troops and chariots 175
and Hektor, son of Priam, strong as fire,
once more gained upon the body. Hektor
three times had the feet within his grasp
and strove to wrest Patróklos backward, shouting
to all the Trojans—but three times the pair 180
named Aías in their valor shook him off.
Still he pushed on, sure of his own power,
sometimes lunging through the battle-din,
or holding fast with a great shout: not one step
would he give way. As from a fresh carcass 185
herdsmen in the wilds cannot dislodge
a tawny lion, famished: so those two
with fearsome crests could not affright the son

---

156. *Arês*: God of war.

of Priam or repel him from the body.
He might have won it, might have won unending 190
glory, but Iris running on the wind
came from Olympos to the son of Pêleus,
bidding him gird for battle. All unknown
to Zeus and the other gods she came, for Hêra
sent her down. And at his side she said: 195

"Up with you, Pêleidês, who strike cold fear
into men's blood! Protect your friend Patróklos,
for whom, beyond the ships, desperate combat
rages now. They are killing one another
on both sides: the Akhaians to defend him, 200
Trojans fighting for that prize
to drag to windy Ilion. And Hektor
burns to take it more than anyone—
to sever and impale Patróklos' head
on Trojan battlements. Lie here no longer. 205
It would be shameful if wild dogs of Troy
made him their plaything! If that body suffers
mutilation, you will be infamous!"

Prince Akhilleus answered:

"Iris of heaven,
what immortal sent you to tell me this?" 210

And she who runs upon the wind replied:

"Hêra, illustrious wife of Zeus,
but he on his high throne knows nothing of it.
Neither does any one of the gods undying
who haunt Olympos of eternal snows." 215

Akhilleus asked:

"And now how shall I go
into the fighting? Those men have my gear.
My dear mother allows me no rearming
until I see her again here.
She promises fine arms from Lord Hêphaistos. 220
I don't know whose armor I can wear,
unless I take Aías' big shield.
But I feel sure he's in the thick of it,
contending with his spear over Patróklos."

191. *Iris:* A messenger of the gods.   192. *Pêleidês:* Son of Pêleus.

Then she who runs upon the wind replied:                                           225

"We know they have your arms, and know it well.
Just as you are, then, stand at the moat; let Trojans
take that in; they will be so dismayed
they may break off the battle, and Akhaians
in their fatigue may win a breathing spell,                                        230
however brief, a respite from the war."

                                                                        At this,

Iris left him, running downwind. Akhilleus,
whom Zeus loved, now rose. Around his shoulders
Athêna hung her shield, like a thunderhead
with trailing fringe. Goddess of goddesses,                                        235
she bound his head with golden cloud, and made
his very body blaze with fiery light.
Imagine how the pyre of a burning town
will tower to heaven and be seen for miles
from the island under attack, while all day long                                   240
outside their town, in brutal combat, pikemen
suffer the wargod's winnowing; at sundown
flare on flare is lit, the signal fires
shoot up for other islanders to see,
that some relieving force in ships may come:                                       245
just so the baleful radiance from Akhilleus
lit the sky. Moving from parapet
to moat, without a nod for the Akhaians,
keeping clear, in deference to his mother,
he halted and gave tongue. Not far from him                                        250
Athêna shrieked. The great sound shocked the Trojans
into tumult, as a trumpet blown
by a savage foe shocks an encircled town,
so harsh and clarion was Akhilleus' cry.
The hearts of men quailed, hearing that brazen voice.                              255
Teams, foreknowing danger, turned their cars
and charioteers blanched, seeing unearthly fire,
kindled by the gray-eyed goddess Athêna,
brilliant over Akhilleus. Three great cries
he gave above the moat. Three times they shuddered,                                260
whirling backward, Trojans and allies,
and twelve good men took mortal hurt
from cars and weapons in the rank behind.
Now the Akhaians leapt at the chance
to bear Patróklos' body out of range.                                              265

---

241. *pikemen*: Soldiers armed with     256. *teams*: Of horses. *cars*: Chariots.
long spears.

They placed it on his bed,
and old companions there with brimming eyes
surrounded him. Into their midst Akhilleus
came then, and he wept hot tears to see
his faithful friend, torn by the sharp spearhead,                    270
lying cold upon his cot. Alas,
the man he sent to war with team and chariot
he could not welcome back alive.

                                                  Her majesty,
wide-eyed Hêra, made the reluctant sun,
unwearied still, sink in the streams of Ocean.                       275
Down he dropped, and the Akhaian soldiers
broke off combat, resting from the war.
The Trojans, too, retired. Unharnessing
teams from war-cars, before making supper,
they came together on the assembly ground,                           280
every man on his feet; not one could sit,
each being still in a tremor—for Akhilleus,
absent so long, had once again appeared.
Clearheaded Poulýdamas, son of Pánthoös,
spoke up first, as he alone could see                                285
what lay ahead and all that lay behind.
He and Hektor were companions-in-arms,
born, as it happened, on the same night; but one
excelled in handling weapons, one with words.
Now for the good of all he spoke among them:                        290

"Think well of our alternatives, my friends.
What I say is, retire upon the town,
instead of camping on the field till dawn
here by the ships. We are a long way
from our stone wall. As long as that man raged                      295
at royal Agamémnon, we could fight
the Akhaians with advantage. I was happy
to spend last night so near the beach and think
of capturing ships today. Now, though, I fear
the son of Pêleus to my very marrow!                                 300
There are no bounds to the passion of that man.
He will not be contained by the flat ground
where Trojans and Akhaians share between them
raging war: he will strive on to fight
to win our town, our women. Back to Troy!                            305
Believe me, this is what we face!
Now, starry night has made Akhilleus pause,
but when day comes, when he sorties in arms
to find us lingering here, there will be men

who learn too well what he is made of. Aye,                     310
I daresay those who get away will reach
walled Ilion thankfully, but dogs and kites
of Troy will feed on many. May that story
never reach my ears! If we can follow
my battle plan, though galled by it, tonight           315
we'll husband strength, at rest in the market place.
Towers, high gates, great doors of fitted planking,
bolted tight, will keep the town secure.
Early tomorrow we shall arm ourselves
and man the walls. Worse luck then for Akhilleus,       320
if he comes looking for a head-on fight
on the field around the wall! He can do nothing
but trot back, after all, to the encampment,
his proud team in a lather from their run,
from scouring every quarter below the town.              325
Rage as he will, he cannot force an entrance,
cannot take all Troy by storm. Wild dogs
will eat him first!"

                           Under his shimmering helmet
Hektor glared at the speaker. Then he said:

"Poulýdamas, what you propose no longer              330
serves my turn.. To go on the defensive
inside the town again? Is anyone
not sick of being huddled in those towers?
In past days men told tales of Priam's city,
rich in gold and rich in bronze, but now              335
those beautiful treasures of our home are lost.
Many have gone for sale to Phrygia
and fair Mễïoniễ, since Lord Zeus
grew hostile toward us.

                          Now when the son of Krónos
Crooked Wit has given me a chance                     340
of winning glory, pinning the Akhaians
back on the sea—now is no time to publish
notions like these to troops, you fool! No Trojan
goes along with you, I will not have it!
Come, let each man act as I propose.                  345
Take your evening meal by companies;
remember sentries; keep good watch; and any
Trojan tired of his wealth, who wants
to lose everything, let him turn it over

312. *kites*: Scavenger hawks.     ferring to his devious and mysterious
340. *Crooked Wit*: A title of Zeus, re-  ways.

to the army stores to be consumed in common! 350
Better our men enjoy it than Akhaians.
At first light we shall buckle armor on
and bring the ships under attack. Suppose
the man who stood astern there was indeed
Akhilleus, then worse luck for him, 355
if he will have it so. Shall I retreat
from him, from clash of combat? No, I will not.
Here I'll stand, though he should win; I might
just win, myself: the battle-god's impartial,
dealing death to the death-dealing man." 360

This was Hektor's speech. The Trojans roared
approval of it—fools, for Pallas Athêna
took away their wits. They all applauded
Hektor's poor tactics, but Poulýdamas
with his good judgment got not one assent. 365
They took their evening meal now, through the army,
while all night long Akhaians mourned Patróklos.

Akhilleus led them in their lamentation,
laying those hands deadly to enemies
upon the breast of his old friend, with groans 370
at every breath, bereft as a lioness
whose whelps a hunter seized out of a thicket;
late in returning, she will grieve, and roam
through many meandering valleys on his track
in hope of finding him; heart-stinging anger 375
carries her away. Now with a groan
he cried out to the Myrmidons:

                                 "Ah, god,
what empty prophecy I made that day
to cheer Menoitios in his mégaron!
I promised him his honored son, brought back 380
to Opoeis, as pillager of Ilion
bearing his share of spoils.
But Zeus will not fulfill what men design,
not all of it. Both he and I were destined
to stain the same earth dark red here at Troy. 385
No going home for me; no welcome there
from Pêleus, master of horse, or from my mother,
Thetis. Here the earth will hold me under.
Therefore, as I must follow you into the grave,

---

379. *Menoitios*: Father of Patróklos.    ern coast of the Greek mainland, home
381. *Opoeis*: Ancient city on the east-    of Menoitios.

I will not give you burial, Patróklos, 390
until I carry back the gear and head
of him who killed you, noble friend.
Before your funeral pyre I'll cut the throats
of twelve resplendent children of the Trojans—
that is my murdering fury at your death. 395
But while you lie here by the swanlike ships,
night and day, close by, deep-breasted women
of Troy, and Dardan women, must lament
and weep hot tears, all those whom we acquired
by labor in assault, by the long spear, 400
pillaging the fat market towns of men."

With this Akhilleus called the company
to place over the campfire a big tripod
and bathe Patróklos of his clotted blood.
Setting tripod and caldron on the blaze 405
they poured it full, and fed the fire beneath,
and flames licked round the belly of the vessel
until the water warmed and bubbled up
in the bright bronze. They bathed him then, and took
sweet oil for his anointing, laying nard 410
in the open wounds; and on his bed they placed him,
covering him with fine linen, head to foot,
and a white shroud over it.

So all that night

beside Akhilleus the great runner,
the Myrmidons held mourning for Patróklos. 415
Now Zeus observed to Hêra, wife and sister:
"You had your way, my lady, after all,
my wide-eyed one! You brought him to his feet,
the great runner! One would say the Akhaian
gentlemen were progeny of yours." 420

And Hêra with wide eyes replied:

"Dread majesty,

Lord Zeus, why do you take this tone? May not
an ordinary mortal have his way,
though death awaits him, and his mind is dim?
Would anyone suppose that I, who rank 425
in two respects highest of goddesses—
by birth and by my station, queen to thee,
lord of all gods—that I should not devise
ill fortune for the Trojans whom I loathe?"

410. *nard*: An ointment.

So ran their brief exchange. Meanwhile          430
the silvery-footed Thetis reached Hêphaistos'
lodging, indestructible and starry,
framed in bronze by the bandy-legged god.
She found him sweating, as from side to side
he plied his bellows; on his forge were twenty          435
tripods to be finished, then to stand
around his mégaron. And he wrought wheels
of gold for the base of each, that each might roll
as of itself into the gods' assembly,
then roll home, a marvel to the eyes.          440
The caldrons were all shaped but had no handles.
These he applied now, hammering rivets in;
and as he toiled surehandedly at this,
Thetis arrived.

                    Grace in her shining veil
just going out encountered her—that Grace          445
the bowlegged god had taken to wife. She greeted
Thetis with a warm handclasp and said:

"My lady Thetis, gracious goddess, what
has brought you here? You almost never honor us!
Please come in, and let me give you welcome."          450

Loveliest of goddesses, she led the way
to seat her guest on a silver-studded chair,
elaborately fashioned, with a footrest.
Then she called to Hêphaistos:

                        "Come and see!
Thetis is here, in need of something from you!"          455

To this the Great Gamelegs replied:

"Ah, then we have a visitor I honor.
She was my savior, after the long fall
and fractures that I had to bear, when Mother,
bitch that she is, wanted to hide her cripple.          460
That would have been a dangerous time, had not
Thetis and Eurýnomê taken me in—
Eurýnomê, daughter of the tidal Ocean.
Nine years I stayed, and fashioned works of art,
brooches and spiral bracelets, necklaces,          465
in their smooth cave, round which the stream of Ocean
flows with a foaming roar: and no one else
knew of it, gods or mortals. Only Thetis

---

444. *Grace*: In the *Odyssey*, Hêphaistos is married to Aphrodite.

knew, and Eurýnomê, the two who saved me.
Now she has come to us. Well, what I owe          470
for life to her ladyship in her soft braids
I must repay. Serve her our choicest fare
while I put up my bellows and my tools."

At this he left the anvil block, and hobbled
with monstrous bulk on skinny legs to take          475
his bellows from the fire. Then all the tools
he had been toiling with he stowed
in a silver chest.

             That done, he sponged himself,
his face, both arms, bull-neck and hairy chest,
put on a tunic, took a weighty staff,          480
and limped out of his workshop. Round their lord
came fluttering maids of gold, like living girls:
intelligences, voices, power of motion
these maids have, and skills learnt from immortals.
Now they came rustling to support their lord,          485
and he moved on toward Thetis, where she sat
upon the silvery chair. He took her hand
and warmly said:

                   "My Lady Thetis, gracious
goddess, why have you come? You almost never honor us.
Tell me the favor that you have in mind,          490
for I desire to do it if I can,
and if it is a thing that one may do."

Thetis answered, tear on cheek:

                           "Hêphaistos,
who among all Olympian goddesses
endured anxiety and pain like mine?          495
Zeus chose me, from all of them, for this!
Of sea-nymphs I alone was given in thrall
to a mortal warrior, Pêleus Aiákidês,
and I endured a mortal warrior's bed
many a time, without desire. Now Pêleus          500
lies far gone in age in his great hall,
and I have other pain. Our son, bestowed
on me and nursed by me, became a hero
unsurpassed. He grew like a green shoot;
I cherished him like a flowering orchard tree,          505
only to send him in the ships to Ilion
to war with Trojans. Now I shall never see him
entering Pêleus' hall, his home, again.

But even while he lives, beholding sunlight,
suffering is his lot. I have no power                                     510
to help him, though I go to him. A girl,
his prize from the Akhaians, Agamémnon
took out of his hands to make his own,
and ah, he pined with burning heart! The Trojans
rolled the Akhaians back on the ship sterns,                              515
and left them no escape. Then Argive officers
begged my son's help, offering every gift,
but he would not defend them from disaster.
Arming Patróklos in his own war-gear,
he sent him with his people into battle.                                 520
All day long, around the Skaian Gates,
they fought, and would have won the city, too,
had not Apollo, seeing the brave son
of Menoitios wreaking havoc on the Trojans,
killed him in action, and then given Hektor                              525
the honor of that deed.

On this account
I am here to beg you: if you will, provide
for my doomed son a shield and crested helm,
good legging-greaves, fitted with ankle clasps,
a cuirass, too. His own armor was lost                                    530
when his great friend went down before the Trojans.
Now my son lies prone on the hard ground in grief."

The illustrious lame god replied:

"Take heart.
No trouble about the arms. I only wish
that I could hide him from the power of death                            535
in his black hour—wish I were sure of that
as of the splendid gear he'll get, a wonder
to any one of the many men there are!"

He left her there, returning to his bellows,
training them on the fire, crying, "To work!"                            540
In crucibles the twenty bellows breathed
every degree of fiery air: to serve him
a great blast when he labored might and main,
or a faint puff, according to his wish
and what the work demanded.

Durable   545
fine bronze and tin he threw into the blaze
with silver and with honorable gold,
then mounted a big anvil in his block

and in his right hand took a powerful hammer,
managing with his tongs in his left hand.                          550

His first job was a shield, a broad one, thick,
well-fashioned everywhere. A shining rim
he gave it, triple-ply, and hung from this
a silver shoulder strap. Five welded layers
composed the body of the shield. The maker                         555
used all his art adorning this expanse.
He pictured on it earth, heaven, and sea,
unwearied sun, moon waxing, all the stars
that heaven bears for garland: Plêïadês,
Hyadês, Oríôn in his might,                                        560
the Great Bear, too, that some have called the Wain,
pivoting there, attentive to Oríôn,
and unbathed ever in the Ocean stream.

He pictured, then, two cities, noble scenes:
weddings in one, and wedding feasts, and brides                    565
led out through town by torchlight from their chambers
amid chorales, amid the young men turning
round and round in dances; flutes and harps
among them, keeping up a tune, and women
coming outdoors to stare as they went by.                          570
A crowd, then, in a market place, and there
two men at odds over satisfaction owed
for a murder done: one claimed that all was paid,
and publicly declared it; his opponent
turned the reparation down, and both                               575
demanded a verdict from an arbiter,
as people clamored in support of each,
and criers restrained the crowd. The town elders
sat in a ring, on chairs of polished stone,
the staves of clarion criers in their hands,                       580
with which they sprang up, each to speak in turn,
and in the middle were two golden measures
to be awarded him whose argument
would be the most straightforward.

                                        Wartime then;
around the other city were emplaced                                585
two columns of besiegers, bright in arms,
as yet divided on which plan they liked:

---

559–561. *Plêïadês . . . Wain*: Constellations. *Oríôn*: Giant hunter of Greek
myth. *Great Bear*: Also known as the
*Wain* (wagon or chariot) and the Big
Dipper, it never descends below the horizon.

whether to sack the town, or treat for half
of all the treasure stored in the citadel.
The townsmen would not bow to either: secretly          590
they armed to break the siege-line. Women and children
stationed on the walls kept watch, with men
whom age disabled. All the rest filed out,
as Arês led the way, and Pallas Athêna,
figured in gold, with golden trappings, both          595
magnificent in arms, as the gods are,
in high relief, while men were small beside them.
When these had come to a likely place for ambush,
a river with a watering place for flocks,
they there disposed themselves, compact in bronze.          600
Two lookouts at a distance from the troops
took their posts, awaiting sight of sheep
and shambling cattle. Both now came in view,
trailed by two herdsmen playing pipes, no hidden
danger in their minds. The ambush party          605
took them by surprise in a sudden rush;
swiftly they cut off herds and beautiful flocks
of silvery gray sheep, then killed the herdsmen.
When the besiegers from their parleying ground
heard sounds of cattle in stampede, they mounted          610
behind mettlesome teams, following the sound,
and came up quickly. Battle lines were drawn,
and on the riverbanks the fight began
as each side rifled javelins at the other.
Here then Strife and Uproar joined the fray,          615
and ghastly Fate, that kept a man with wounds
alive, and one unwounded, and another
dragged by the heels through battle-din in death.
This figure wore a mantle dyed with blood,
and all the figures clashed and fought          620
like living men, and pulled their dead away.

Upon the shield, soft terrain, freshly plowed,
he pictured: a broad field, and many plowmen
here and there upon it. Some were turning
ox teams at the plowland's edge, and there          625
as one arrived and turned, a man came forward
putting a cup of sweet wine in his hands.
They made their turns-around, then up the furrows
drove again, eager to reach the deep field's
limit; and the earth looked black behind them,          630

as though turned up by plows. But it was gold,
all gold—a wonder of the artist's craft.

He put there, too, a king's field. Harvest hands
were swinging whetted scythes to mow the grain,
and stalks were falling along the swath                      635
while binders girded others up in sheaves
with bands of straw—three binders, and behind them
children came as gleaners, proffering
their eager armfuls. And amid them all
the king stood quietly with staff in hand,                   640
happy at heart, upon a new-mown swath.
To one side, under an oak tree his attendants
worked at a harvest banquet. They had killed
a great ox, and were dressing it; their wives
made supper for the hands, with barley strewn.               645

A vineyard then he pictured, weighted down
with grapes: this all in gold; and yet the clusters
hung dark purple, while the spreading vines
were propped on silver vine-poles. Blue enamel
he made the enclosing ditch, and tin the fence,              650
and one path only led into the vineyard
on which the loaded vintagers took their way
at vintage time. Lighthearted boys and girls
were harvesting the grapes in woven baskets,
while on a resonant harp a boy among them                    655
played a tune of longing, singing low
with delicate voice a summer dirge. The others,
breaking out in song for the joy of it,
kept time together as they skipped along.

The artisan made next a herd of longhorns,                   660
fashioned in gold and tin: away they shambled,
lowing, from byre to pasture by a stream
that sang in ripples, and by reeds a-sway.
Four cowherds all of gold were plodding after
with nine lithe dogs beside them.
                               On the assault,               665
in two tremendous bounds, a pair of lions
caught in the van a bellowing bull, and off
they dragged him, followed by the dogs and men.
Rending the belly of the bull, the two

662. *byre*: Stable.

gulped down his blood and guts, even as the herdsmen 670
tried to set on their hunting dogs, but failed:
no trading bites with lions for those dogs,
who halted close up, barking, then ran back.

And on the shield the great bowlegged god
designed a pasture in a lovely valley, 675
wide, with silvery sheep, and huts and sheds
and sheepfolds there.

                  A dancing floor as well
he fashioned, like that one in royal Knossos
Daidalos made for the Princess Ariadnê.
Here young men and the most desired young girls 680
were dancing, linked, touching each other's wrists,
the girls in linen, in soft gowns, the men
in well-knit khitons given a gloss with oil;
the girls wore garlands, and the men had daggers
golden-hilted, hung on silver lanyards. 685
Trained and adept, they circled there with ease
the way a potter sitting at his wheel
will give it a practice twirl between his palms
to see it run; or else, again, in lines
as though in ranks, they moved on one another: 690
magical dancing! All around, a crowd
stood spellbound as two tumblers led the beat
with spins and handsprings through the company.

Then, running round the shield-rim, triple-ply,
he pictured all the might of the Ocean stream. 695

Besides the densely plated shield, he made
a cuirass, brighter far than fire light,
a massive helmet, measured for his temples,
handsomely figured, with a crest of gold;
then greaves of pliant tin.

              Now when the crippled god 700
had done his work, he picked up all the arms
and laid them down before Akhilleus' mother,
and swift as a hawk from snowy Olympos' height
she bore the brilliant gear made by Hêphaistos.

---

678. *Knossos*: In Crete, the site of the great palace excavated by Evans and known as "The palace of Minos."

679. *Daidalos*: The "fabulous artificer" who built the labyrinth for King Minos. *Ariadnê*: Daughter of Minos.

## Book XIX

### [*Akhilleus Prepares for Battle*]

Dawn in her yellow robe rose in the east
out of the flowing Ocean, bearing light
for deathless gods and mortal men. And Thetis
brought to the beach her gifts from the god of fire.
She found her dear son lying beside Patróklos,     5
wailing, while his men stood by
in tears around him. Now amid that throng
the lovely goddess bent to touch his shoulder
and said to him:

         "Ah, child, let him lie dead,
for all our grief and pain, we must allow it;     10
he fell by the gods' will.
But you, now—take the war-gear from Hêphaistos.
No man ever bore upon his shoulders
gear so magnificent."

         And she laid the armor
down before Akhilleus, clanging loud     15
in all its various glory. Myrmidons
began to tremble at the sound, and dared not
look straight at the armor; their knees shook.
But anger entered Akhilleus as he gazed,
his eyes grown wide and bright as blazing fire,     20
with fierce joy as he handled the god's gifts.
After appraising them in his delight
he spoke out to his mother swiftly:

         "Mother,
these the god gave are miraculous arms,
handiwork of immortals, plainly—far     25
beyond the craft of men. By heaven, I'll wear them!
Only, I feel the dread that while I fight
black carrion flies may settle on Patróklos'
wounds, where the spearheads marked him, and I fear
they may breed maggots to defile the corpse,     30
now life is torn from it. His flesh may rot."

But silvery-footed Thetis answered:

         "Child,
you must not let that prey on you. I'll find
a way to shield him from the black fly hordes

that eat the bodies of men killed in battle.                    35
Though he should lie unburied a long year,
his flesh will be intact and firm. Now, though,
for your part, call the Akhaians to assembly.
Tell them your anger against Agamémnon
is over and done with!                                          40
After that, at once
put on your gear, prepare your heart, for war!"

Her promise gave her son wholehearted valor.
Then, turning to Patróklos, she instilled
red nectar and ambrosia in his nostrils                         45
to keep his body whole.

                              And Prince Akhilleus

passed along the surf-line with a shout
that split the air and roused men of Akhaia,
even those who, up to now, had stayed
amid the massed ships—navigators, helmsmen,                     50
men in charge of rations and ship stores.
Aye, even these now headed for assembly,
since he who for so long had shunned the battle,
Akhilleus, now appeared upon the field.
Resolute Diomêdês and Odysseus,                                 55
familiars of the wargod, limped along,
leaning on spears, for both had painful wounds.
They made their way to the forefront and sat down,
and last behind them entered the Lord Marshal
Agamémnon, favoring his wound: he too                           60
had taken a slash, from Antênor's son, Koôn.
When everyone had crowded in, Akhilleus,
the great battlefield runner, rose and said:

"Agamémnon, was it better for us
in any way, when we were sore at heart,                         65
to waste ourselves in strife over a girl?
If only Artemis had shot her down
among the ships on the day I made her mine,
after I took Lyrnessos!
Fewer Akhaians would have died hard                             70
at enemy hands, while I abstained in anger—
Hektor's gain, the Trojans' gain. Akhaians
years hence will remember our high words,
mine and yours. But now we can forget them,
and, as we must, forego our passion. Aye,                       75
by heaven, I drop my anger now!

No need to smolder in my heart forever! Come,
send your long-haired Akhaians into combat,
and let me see how Trojans will hold out,
if camping near the beachhead's their desire!                    80
I rather thank some will be glad to rest,
provided they get home, away from danger,
out of my spear's range!"

                              These were his words,
and all the Akhaians gave a roar of joy
to hear the prince abjure his rage.                              85
Lord Marshal Agamémnon then addressed them,
standing up, not in the midst of them,
but where he had been sitting:

                                "Friends, fighters,
Danáäns, companions of Arês: it is fair
to listen to a man when he has risen                             90
and not to interrupt him. That's vexation
to any speaker, able though he may be.
In a great hubbub how can any man
attend or speak? A fine voice will be muffled.
While I open my mind to the son of Pêleus,                       95
Argives, attention! Each man weigh my words!
The Akhaians often brought this up against me,
and chided me. But I am not to blame.
Zeus and Fate and a nightmare Fury are,
for putting savage Folly in my mind                              100
in the assembly that day, when I wrested
Akhilleus' prize of war from him. In truth,
what could I do? Divine will shapes these things.
Ruinous Folly, eldest daughter of Zeus,
beguiles us all. Her feet are soft, from walking                 105
not on earth but over the heads of men
to do them hurt. She traps one man or another.
Once indeed she deluded Zeus, most noble
of gods and men, they say. But feminine
Hêra with her underhanded ways                                   110
tricked him, the day Alkmênê, in high Thebes,
was to have given birth to Hêraklês.
Then glorying Zeus remarked to all the gods;
'Hear me, all gods and goddesses, I'll tell you
of something my heart dwells upon. This day                      115
the childbirth goddess, Eileithyía, brings

111. *Alkmênê*: Mortal woman who,    Thebes, was pregnant by Zeus.
though married to Amphitryon, King of

into the light a man who will command
all those around him, being of the race of men
who come of my own blood!' But in her guile
the Lady Hêra said: 'You may be wrong,                                 120
unable to seal your word with truth hereafter.
Come, Olympian, swear me a great oath
he will indeed be lord of all his neighbors,
the child of your own stock in the race of men
who drops between a woman's legs today!'                              125
Zeus failed to see her crookedness: he swore
a mighty oath, and mightily went astray,
for flashing downward from Olympos crest
Hêra visited Argos of Akhaia,
aware that the strong wife of Perseus' son,                           130
Sthénelos, was big with child,
just entering her seventh month. But Hêra
brought this child into the world's daylight
beforehand by two months, and checked Alkmênê's
labor, to delay the birth of hers.                                    135
To Zeus the son of Krónos then she said:
'Zeus of the bright bolt, father, let me add
a new event to your deliberations.
Even now a superior man is born
to be a lord of Argives: Eurýstheus,                                  140
a son of Sthénelos, the son of Perseus,
of your own stock. And it is not unfitting
for him to rule the Argives.' This report
sharply wounded the deep heart of Zeus.
He picked up Folly by her shining braids                              145
in sudden anger—swearing a great oath
that never to starred heaven or Olympos
Folly, who tricks us all, should come again.
With this he whirled her with one hand and flung her
out of the sky. So to men's earth she came,                          150
but ever thereafter made Zeus groan to see
his dear son toil at labors for Eurýstheus.

So, too, with me: when in his shimmering helm
great Hektor slaughtered Argives near the ships,
could I ignore my folly, my delusion?                                 155
Zeus had stolen my wits, my act was blind.
But now I wish to make amends, to give
all possible satisfaction. Rouse for war,

130. *Perseus*: A son of Zeus.
140. *Eurýstheus*: Became King of
Argos and taskmaster of Hêraklês, who
had to perform the twelve labors for
him.

send in your troops! I here repeat my offer
of all that Odysseus promised yesterday!                    160
Stay if you will, though the wargod presses you.
Men in my service will unload the gifts
from my own ship, that you may see how richly
I reward you!"

Akhilleus answered:

"Excellency,   165

Lord Marshal Agamémnon, make the gifts
if you are keen to—gifts are due; or keep them.
It is for you to say. Let us recover
joy of battle soon, that's all!
No need to dither here and lose our time,                   170
our great work still undone. When each man sees
Akhilleus in a charge, crumpling the ranks
of Trojans with his bronze-shod spear, let each
remember that is the way to fight his man!"

Replied Odysseus, the shrewd field commander:               175

"Brave as you are, and like a god in looks,
Akhilleus, do not send Akhaian soldiers
into the fight unfed! Today's mêlée
will not be brief, when rank meets rank, and heaven
breathes fighting spirit into both contenders.              180
No, tell all troops who are near the ships to take
roast meat and wine, for heart and staying power.
No soldier can fight hand to hand, in hunger,
all day long until the sun goes down!
Though in his heart he yearns for war, his legs             185
go slack before he knows it: thirst and famine
search him out, and his knees fail as he moves.
But that man stayed with victualing and wine
can fight his enemies all day: his heart
is bold and happy in his chest, his legs                    190
hold out until both sides break off the battle!
Come, then, dismiss the ranks to make their breakfast.
Let the Lord Marshal Agamémnon
bring his gifts to the assembly ground
where all may see them; may your heart be warmed.           195
Then let him swear to you, before the Argives,
never to have made love to her, my lord,

197. *her*: Brisêis.

as men and women by their nature do.
So may your heart be peaceable toward him!
And let him sate your hunger with rich fare                           200
in his own shelter, that you may lack nothing
due you in justice. Afterward, Agamémnon,
you'll be more just to others, too. There is
no fault in a king's wish to conciliate
a man with whom he has been quick to anger!"                          205

And the Lord Marshal Agamémnon answered:

"Glad I am to hear you, son of Laërtês,
finding the right word at the right time
for all these matters. And the oath you speak of
I'll take willingly, with all my heart,                               210
and will not, before heaven, be forsworn.
Now let Akhilleus wait here, though the wargod
tug his arm; and all the rest of you
wait here assembled till the gifts have come
down from our quarters, and our peace is made.                        215
For you, Odysseus, here is my command:
choose the finest young peers of all Akhaia
to fetch out of my ship those gifts we pledged
Akhilleus yesterday; and bring the women.
Let Talthýbios prepare for sacrifice,                                 220
in the army's name, a boar to Zeus and Hêlios."

Replied Akhilleus:

                              "Excellency, Lord Marshal,
another time were better for these ceremonies,
some interval in the war, and when I feel
less passion in me. Look, those men lie dead                         225
whom Hektor killed when Zeus allowed him glory,
and yet you two propose a meal! By god,
I'd send our soldiers into action now
unfed and hungry. Have a feast, I'd say,
at sundown, when our shame has been avenged!                         230
Before that, for my part, I will not swallow
food or drink—my dear friend being dead,
lying before my eyes, bled white by spear-cuts,
feet turned to his hut's door, his friends in mourning
around him. Your concerns are none of mine.                          235

211. *be forsworn*: Swear falsely.     221. *Hêlios*: The sun god.
220. *Talthýbios*: Agamémnon's herald.

Slaughter and blood are what I crave, and groans
of anguished men!"

                                    But the shrewd field commander
Odysseus answered:

                                    "Akhilleus, flower and pride
of the Akhaians, you are more powerful
than I am—and a better spearman, too—                    240
only in sizing matters up I'd say
I'm just as far beyond you, being older,
knowing more of the world. So bear with me.
Men quickly reach satiety with battle
in which the reaping bronze will bring to earth          245
big harvests, but a scanty yield, when Zeus,
war's overseer for mankind, tips the scales.
How can a fasting belly mourn our dead?
So many die, so often, every day,
when would soldiers come to an end of fasting?          250
No, we must dispose of him who dies
and keep hard hearts, and weep that day alone.
And those whom the foul war has left unhurt
will do well to remember food and drink,
so that we may again close with our enemies,            255
our dangerous enemies, and be tough soldiers,
hardened in mail of bronze. Let no one, now,
be held back waiting for another summons:
here is your summons! Woe to the man who lingers
beside the Argive ships! No, all together,              260
let us take up the fight against the Trojans!"

He took as escort sons of illustrious Nestor:
Phyleus' son Mégês, Thoas, and Meríonês,
and the son of Kreion, Lykomêdês, and
Melánippos, to Agamémnon's quarters.                    265
No sooner was the work assigned than done:
they brought the seven tripods Agamémnon
promised Akhilleus, and the twenty caldrons
shining, and the horses, a full dozen;
then they conducted seven women, skilled               270
in housecraft, with Brisêis in her beauty.
Odysseus weighed ten bars of purest gold
and turned back, followed by his young Akhaians,
bearing the gifts to place in mid-assembly.
Now Agamémnon rose. Talthýbios                          275
the crier, with his wondrous voice, stood near him,

holding the boar. The son of Atreus drew
the sheath knife that he carried, hung
beside the big sheath of his sword, and cut
first bristles from the boar. Arms wide to heaven                    280
he prayed to Zeus, as all the troops kept still,
all sitting in due order in their places,
hearing their king. In prayer he raised his eyes
to the broad sky and said:

                          "May Zeus, all-highest
and first of gods, be witness first, then Earth                    285
and Hêlios and the Furies underground
who punish men for having broken oaths,
I never laid a hand on your Brisêis,
proposing bed or any other pleasure;
in my quarters the girl has been untouched.                    290
If one word that I swear is false,
may the gods plague me for a perjured liar!"

He slit the boar's throat with his blade of bronze.
Then Talthýbios, wheeling, flung the victim
into the offshore water, bait for fish.                    295
Akhilleus rose amid the Argive warriors,
saying:

                        "Father Zeus, you send mankind
prodigious follies. Never otherwise
had Agamémnon stung me through and through;
never would he have been so empty-headed                    300
as to defy my will and take the girl!
No, for some reason Zeus had death at heart
for the Akhaians, and for many.

                                          Well:
go to your meat, then we'll resume the fighting."

Thus he dismissed the assembly. All the men                    305
were quick to scatter, each to his own ship.
As for the gifts, the Myrmidons took over
and bore them all to Akhilleus' ship, to stow
within his shelter. There they left the women
and drove the horses to the herd.

                                 The girl     310
Brisêis, in her grace like Aphrodítê,
on entering saw Patróklos lying dead
of spear wounds, and she sank down to embrace him
with a sharp sobbing cry, lifting her hands

to tear her breast, soft throat, and lovely face,    315
this girl, shaped like the goddesses of heaven.
Weeping, she said:

                                    "Patróklos, very dear,
most dear to me, cursed as I am, you were
alive still when I left you, left this place!
Now I come back to find you dead, my captain!    320
Evil follows evil so, for me.
The husband to whom father and mother gave me
I saw brought down by spears before our town,
with my three brothers, whom my mother bore.
Dear brothers, all three met their day of wrath.    325
But when Akhilleus killed my lord, and sacked
the city of royal Mynês, not a tear
would you permit me: no, you undertook
to see me married to the Prince Akhilleus,
conveyed by ship to Phthía, given a wedding    330
among the Myrmidons. Now must I mourn
your death forever, who were ever gentle."

She wailed again, and women sobbed about her,
first for Patróklos, then for each one's grief.
Meanwhile Akhaian counselors were gathered    335
begging Akhilleus to take food. He spurned it,
groaning:

                     "No, I pray you, my dear friends,
if anyone will listen!—do not nag me
to glut and dull my heart with food and drink!
A burning pain is in me. I'll hold out    340
till sundown without food. I say I'll bear it."

With this he sent the peers away, except
the two Atreidai and the great Odysseus,
Nestor, Idómeneus, and old Lord Phoinix.
These would have comforted him, but none    345
could quiet or comfort him until he entered
the bloody jaws of war. Now pierced by memory,
he sighed and sighed again, and said:

                                   "Ah, once
you, too, poor fated friend, and best of friends,
would set a savory meal deftly before us    350
in our field shelter, when the Akhaians wished
no time lost between onsets against Trojans.

Now there you lie, broken in battle. Ah,
lacking you, my heart will fast this day
from meat and drink as well. No greater ill        355
could come to me, not news of Father's death—
my father, weeping soft tears now in Phthía
for want of that son in a distant land
who wars on Troy for Helen's sake—that woman
who makes the blood run cold. No greater ill,      360
even should my son die, who is being reared
on Skyros, Neoptólemos, if indeed
he's living still. My heart's desire has been
that I alone should perish far from Argos
here at Troy; that you should sail to Phthía,      365
taking my son aboard your swift black ship
at Skyros, to introduce him to his heritage,
my wide lands, my servants, my great hall.
In this late year Pêleus may well be dead
and buried, or have few days yet to live,          370
beset by racking age, always awaiting
dire news of me, of my own death."

As he said this he wept. The counselors groaned,
remembering each what he had left at home;
and seeing them sorrow, Zeus took pity on them,    375
saying quickly to Athêna:

                                 "Daughter,
you seem to have left your fighting man alone.
Should one suppose you care no more for Akhilleus?
There he sits, before the curving prows,
and grieves for his dear friend. The other soldiers  380
flock to meat; he thirsts and hungers. Come,
infuse in him sweet nectar and ambrosia,
that an empty belly may not weaken him."

He urged Athêna to her own desire,
and like a gliding sea hawk, shrilling high,        385
she soared from heaven through the upper air,
while the Akhaians armed throughout the ranks.
Nectar and ambrosia she instilled
within Akhilleus, that his knees be not
assailed by hollow famine; then she withdrew       390
to her mighty father's house. Meanwhile the troops
were pouring from the shipways to the field.

367. *Skyros*: An island in the North Aegean.

As when cold snowflakes fly from Zeus in heaven,
thick and fast under the blowing north wind,
just so, that multitude of gleaming helms                        395
and bossed shields issued from the ships, with plated
cuirasses and ashwood spears. Reflected
glintings flashed to heaven, as the plain
in all directions shone with glare of bronze
and shook with trampling feet of men. Among them              400
Prince Akhilleus armed. One heard his teeth
grind hard together, and his eyes blazed out
like licking fire, for unbearable pain
had fixed upon his heart. Raging at Trojans,
he buckled on the arms Hêphaistos forged.                        405
The beautiful greaves, fitted with silver anklets,
first he put upon his legs, and next
the cuirass on his ribs; then over his shoulder
he slung the sword of bronze with silver scabbard;
finally he took up the massive shield                            410
whence came a radiance like the round full moon.
As when at sea to men on shipboard comes
the shining of a campfire on a mountain
in a lone sheepfold, while the gusts of nightwind
take them, loath to go, far from their friends                  415
over the teeming sea: just so
Akhilleus' finely modeled shield sent light
into the heavens. Lifting his great helm
he placed it on his brows, and like a star
the helm shone with its horsetail blowing free,                 420
all golden, that Hêphaistos had set in
upon the crest. Akhilleus tried his armor,
shrugging and flexing, making sure it fitted,
sure that his gleaming legs had play. Indeed
the gear sat on him light as wings: it buoyed him!              425
Now from a spear-case he withdrew a spear—
his father's—weighty, long, and tough. No other
Akhaian had the strength to handle it,
this great Pêlian shaft
of ashwood, given his father by the centaur                     430
Kheirôn from the crest of Pêlion
to be the death of heroes.

                                                    Automédôn
and Álkimos with swift hands yoked his team,
making firm the collars on the horses,

431. *Kheirôn*: A centaur famous as a      mountain in central Greece.
wise teacher. *Pêlion*: A heavily wooded

placing the bits between their teeth, and pulling                435
reins to the war-car. Automédôn then
took in hand the shining whip and mounted
the chariot, and at his back Akhilleus
mounted in full armor, shining bright
as the blinding Lord of Noon. In a clarion voice                440
he shouted to the horses of his father:

"Xánthos and Balíos! Known to the world
as foals of great Podargê! In this charge
care for your driver in another way!
Pull him back, I mean, to the Danáäns,                          445
back to the main body of the army,
once we are through with battle; this time,
no leaving him there dead, like Lord Patróklos!"

To this, from under the yoke, the nimble Xánthos
answered, and hung his head, so that his mane                    450
dropped forward from the yokepad to the ground—
Hêra whose arms are white as ivory
gave him a voice to say:

                     "Yes, we shall save you,
this time, too, Akhilleus in your strength!
And yet the day of your destruction comes,                      455
and it is nearer. We are not the cause,
but rather a great god is, and mighty Fate.
Nor was it by our sloth or sluggishness
the Trojans stripped Patróklos of his armor.
No, the magnificent god that Lêto bore                          460
killed him in action and gave Hektor glory.
We might run swiftly as the west wind blows,
most rapid of all winds, they say; but still
it is your destiny to be brought low
by force, a god's force and a man's!"

                                  On this,  465
the Furies put a stop to Xánthos' voice;
In anger and gloom Akhilleus said to him:

"Xánthos, why prophesy my death? No need.
What is in store for me I know, know well:
to die here, far away from my dear father,                      470

---

465. *a god's force and a man's*: Akhilleus will eventually fall by the hand of Paris but through the intervention of Apollo.

466. *Furies*: One of the functions of these goddesses was to ensure that all the creatures of the universe observed their proper limits.

my mother, too. No matter. All that matters
is that I shall not call a halt today
till I have made the Trojans sick of war!"

And with a shout he drove his team
of trim-hooved horses into the front line.                           475

[Akhilleus' return to the fighting brought terror to the Trojans,
and turned the battle into a rout in which Akhilleus killed every
Trojan that crossed his path. As he pursued Agénor, Apollo tricked
him by rescuing his intended victim (he spirited him away in a
mist) and assumed Agénor's shape to lead Akhilleus away from the
walls of Troy. The Trojans took refuge in the city, all except
Hektor.]

### Book XXII

#### [*The Death of Hektor*]

Once in the town, those who had fled like deer
wiped off their sweat and drank their thirst away,
leaning against the cool stone of the ramparts.
Meanwhile Akhaians with bright shields aslant
came up the plain and nearer. As for Hektor,                          5
fatal destiny pinned him where he stood
before the Skaian Gates, outside the city.

Now Akhilleus heard Apollo calling
back to him:

                              "Why run so hard, Akhilleus,
mortal as you are, after a god?                                       10
Can you not comprehend it? I am immortal.
You are so hot to catch me, you no longer
think of finishing off the men you routed.
They are all in the town by now, packed in
while you were being diverted here. And yet                           15
you cannot kill me; I am no man's quarry."

Akhilleus bit his lip and said:

"Archer of heaven, deadliest
of immortal gods, you put me off the track,
turning me from the wall this way. A hundred                          20
might have sunk their teeth into the dust
before one man took cover in Ilion!
You saved my enemies with ease and stole

my glory, having no punishment to fear.
I'd take it out of you, if I had the power." 25

Then toward the town with might and main he ran,
magnificent, like a racing chariot horse
that holds its form at full stretch on the plain.
So light-footed Akhilleus held the pace.
And aging Priam was the first to see him 30
sparkling on the plain, bright as that star
in autumn rising, whose unclouded rays
shine out amid a throng of stars at dusk—
the one they call Oríôn's dog, most brilliant,
yes, but baleful as a sign: it brings 35
great fever to frail men. So pure and bright
the bronze gear blazed upon him as he ran.
The old man gave a cry. With both his hands
thrown up on high he struck his head, then shouted,
groaning, appealing to his dear son. Unmoved, 40
Lord Hektor stood in the gateway, resolute
to fight Akhilleus.

Stretching out his hands,

old Priam said, imploring him:

"No, Hektor!

Cut off as you are, alone, dear son,
don't try to hold your ground against this man, 45
or soon you'll meet the shock of doom, borne down
by the son of Pêleus. He is more powerful
by far than you, and pitiless. Ah, were he
but dear to the gods as he is dear to me!
Wild dogs and kites would eat him where he lay 50
within the hour, and ease me of my torment.
Many tall sons he killed, bereaving me,
or sold them to far islands. Even now
I cannot see two sons of mine, Lykáôn
and Polydôros, among the Trojans massed 55
inside the town. A queen, Laóthoê,
conceived and bore them. If they are alive
amid the Akhaian host, I'll ransom them
with bronze and gold: both I have, piled at home,
rich treasures that old Altês, the renowned, 60
gave for his daughter's dowry. If they died,

34. *Oríôn's dog*: The constellation *Canis Major*. The star (31) is Sirius, the "dog star."
54. *Lykáôn and Polydôros*: Both already killed by Akhilleus in the fighting outside the city.
56. *Laóthoê*: Priam, in oriental style, has more than one wife.
60. *Altês*: Laóthoê's father.

if they went under to the homes of Death,
sorrow has come to me and to their mother.
But to our townsmen all this pain is brief,
unless you too go down before Akhilleus.                    65
Come inside the wall, child; here you may
fight on to save our Trojan men and women.
Do not resign the glory to Akhilleus,
losing your own dear life! Take pity, too,
on me and my hard fate, while I live still.                 70
Upon the threshold of my age, in misery,
the son of Krónos will destroy my life
after the evil days I shall have seen—
my sons brought down, my daughters dragged away,
bedchambers ravaged, and small children hurled             75
to earth in the atrocity of war,
as my sons' wives are taken by Akhaians'
ruinous hands. And at the end, I too—
when someone with a sword-cut or a spear
has had my life—I shall be torn apart                       80
on my own doorstep by the hounds
I trained as watchdogs, fed from my own table.
These will lap my blood with ravenous hearts
and lie in the entranceway.

                                        Everything done
to a young man killed in war becomes his glory,             85
once he is riven by the whetted bronze:
dead though he be, it is all fair, whatever
happens then. But when an old man falls,
and dogs disfigure his gray head and cheek
and genitals, that is most harrowing                        90
of all that men in their hard lives endure."

The old man wrenched at his gray hair and pulled out
hanks of it in both his hands, but moved
Lord Hektor not at all. The young man's mother
wailed from the tower across, above the portal,            95
streaming tears, and loosening her robe
with one hand, held her breast out in the other,
saying:

                    "Hektor, my child, be moved by this,
and pity me, if ever I unbound
a quieting breast for you. Think of these things,          100
dear child, defend yourself against the killer
this side of the wall, not hand to hand.

He has no pity. If he brings you down,
I shall no longer be allowed to mourn you
laid out on your bed, dear branch in flower,    105
born of me! And neither will your lady,
so endowed with gifts. Far from us both,
dogs will devour you by the Argive ships.' "


With tears and cries the two implored their son,
and made their prayers again, but could not shake him.    110
Hektor stood firm, as huge Akhilleus neared.
The way a serpent, fed on poisonous herbs,
coiled at his lair upon a mountainside,
with all his length of hate awaits a man
and eyes him evilly: so Hektor, grim    115
and narrow-eyed, refused to yield. He leaned
his brilliant shield against a spur of wall
and in his brave heart bitterly reflected:
"Here I am badly caught. If I take cover,
slipping inside the gate and wall, the first    120
to accuse me for it will be Poulýdamas,
he who told me I should lead the Trojans
back to the city on the cursed night
Akhilleus joined the battle. No, I would not,
would not, wiser though it woud have been.    125
Now troops have perished for my foolish pride,
I am ashamed to face townsmen and women.
Someone inferior to me may say:
'He kept his pride and lost his men, this Hektor!'
So it will go. Better, when that time comes,    130
that I appear as he who killed Akhilleus
man to man, or else that I went down
before him honorably for the city's sake.
Suppose, though, that I lay my shield and helm
aside, and prop my spear against the wall,    135
and go to meet the noble Prince Akhilleus,
promising Helen, promising with her
all treasures that Aléxandros brought home
by ship to Troy—the first cause of our quarrel—
that he may give these things to the Atreidai?    140
Then I might add, apart from these, a portion
of all the secret wealth the city owns.
Yes, later I might take our counselors' oath
to hide no stores, but share and share alike
to halve all wealth our lovely city holds,    145

all that is here within the walls. Ah, no,
why even put the question to myself?
I must not go before him and receive
no quarter, no respect! Aye, then and there
he'll kill me, unprotected as I am,                                      150
my gear laid by, defenseless as a woman.
No chance, now, for charms from oak or stone
in parley with him—charms a girl and boy
might use when they enchant each other talking!
Better we duel, now at once, and see                                   155
to whom the Olympian awards the glory."

These were his shifts of mood. Now close at hand
Akhilleus like the implacable god of war
came on with blowing crest, hefting the dreaded
beam of Pêlian ash on his right shoulder.                               160
Bronze light played around him, like the glare
of a great fire or the great sun rising,
and Hektor, as he watched, began to tremble.
Then he could hold his ground no more. He ran,
leaving the gate behind him, with Akhilleus                             165
hard on his heels, sure of his own speed.
When that most lightning-like of birds, a hawk
bred on a mountain, swoops upon a dove,
the quarry dips in terror, but the hunter,
screaming, dips behind and gains upon it,                               170
passionate for prey. Just so, Akhilleus
murderously cleft the air, as Hektor
ran with flashing knees along the wall.
They passed the lookout point, the wild figtree
with wind in all its leaves, then veered away                          175
along the curving wagon road, and came
to where the double fountains well, the source
of eddying Skamánder. One hot spring
flows out, and from the water fumes arise
as though from fire burning; but the other                             180
even in summer gushes chill as hail
or snow or crystal ice frozen on water.
Near these fountains are wide washing pools
of smooth-laid stone, where Trojan wives and daughters
laundered their smooth linen in the days                               185
of peace before the Akhaians came. Past these
the two men ran, pursuer and pursued,
and he who fled was noble, he behind

152. *charms*: I.e., charming talk.

a greater man by far. They ran full speed,
and not for bull's hide or a ritual beast 190
or any prize that men compete for: no,
but for the life of Hektor, tamer of horses.
Just as when chariot-teams around a course
go wheeling swiftly, for the prize is great,
a tripod or a woman, in the games 195
held for a dead man, so three times these two
at full speed made their course round Priam's town,
as all the gods looked on. And now the father
of gods and men turned to the rest and said:

"How sad that this beloved man is hunted 200
around the wall before my eyes! My heart
is touched for Hektor; he has burned thigh flesh
of oxen for me often, high on Ida,
at other times on the high point of Troy.
Now Prince Akhilleus with devouring stride 205
is pressing him around the town of Priam.
Come, gods, put your minds on it, consider
whether we may deliver him from death
or see him, noble as he is, brought down
by Pêleus' son, Akhilleus."

                              Gray-eyed Athêna 210
said to him:

                         "Father of the blinding bolt,
the dark stormcloud, what words are these? The man
is mortal, and his doom fixed, long ago.
Would you release him from his painful death?
Then do so, but not all of us will praise you." 215

Zeus who gathers cloud replied:

                                    "Take heart,
my dear and honored child. I am not bent
on my suggestion, and I would indulge you.
Act as your thought inclines, refrain no longer."

So he encouraged her in her desire, 220
and down she swept from ridges of Olympos.
Great Akhilleus, hard on Hektor's heels,
kept after him, the way a hound will harry
a deer's fawn he has startled from its bed
to chase through gorge and open glade, and when 225

203. *Ida:* The great mountain range near Troy.

the quarry goes to earth under a bush
he holds the scent and quarters till he finds it;
so with Hektor: he could not shake off
the great runner, Akhilleus. Every time
he tried to sprint hard for the Dardan gates          230
under the towers, hoping men could help him,
sending missiles down, Akhilleus loomed
to cut him off and turn him toward the plain,
as he himself ran always near the city.
As in a dream a man chasing another                   235
cannot catch him, nor can he in flight
escape from his pursuer, so Akhilleus
could not by his swiftness overtake him,
nor could Hektor pull away. How could he
run so long from death, had not Apollo               240
for the last time, the very last, come near
to give him stamina and speed?

                                        Akhilleus

shook his head at the rest of the Akhaians,
allowing none to shoot or cast at Hektor—
none to forestall him, and to win the honor.          245
But when, for the fourth time, they reached the springs,
the Father poised his golden scales.

                                        He placed

two shapes of death, death prone and cold, upon them,
one of Akhilleus, one of the horseman, Hektor,
and held the midpoint, pulling upward. Down           250
sank Hektor's fatal day, the pan went down
toward undergloom, and Phoibos Apollo left him.
Then came Athêna, gray-eyed, to the son
of Pêleus, falling in with him, and near him,
saying swiftly:

                        "Now at last I think     255
the two of us, Akhilleus loved by Zeus,
shall bring Akhaians triumph at the ships
by killing Hektor—unappeased
though he was ever in his thirst for war.
There is no way he may escape us now,                 260
not though Apollo, lord of distances,
should suffer all indignity for him
before his father Zeus who bears the stormcloud,
rolling back and forth and begging for him.
Now you can halt and take your breath, while I        265
persuade him into combat face to face."

227. *quarters*: Criss-crosses.        meaning of this title of Apollo is "who
261. *lord of distances*: The literal   works from far off."

These were Athêna's orders. He complied,
relieved. and leaning hard upon the spearshaft
armed with its head of bronze. She left him there
and overtook Lord Hektor—but she seemed                    270
Dêíphobos in form and resonant voice,
appearing at his shoulder, saying swiftly:

"Ai! Dear brother, how he runs, Akhilleus,
harrying you around the town of Priam!
Come, we'll stand and take him on."

                                                To this,   275

great Hektor in his shimmering helm replied:

"Dêíphobos, you were the closest to me
in the old days, of all my brothers, sons
of Hékabê and Priam. Now I can say
I honor you still more                                      280
because you dared this foray for my sake,
seeing me run. The rest stay under cover."

Again the gray-eyed goddess Athêna spoke:

"Dear brother, how your father and gentle mother
begged and begged me to remain! So did                     285
the soldiers round me, all undone by fear.
But in my heart I ached for you.
Now let us fight him, and fight hard.
No holding back. We'll see if this Akhilleus
conquers both, to take our armor seaward,                  290
or if he can be brought down by your spear."

This way, by guile, Athêna led him on.
And when at last the two men faced each other,
Hektor was the first to speak. He said:

"I will no longer fear you as before,                      295
son of Pêleus, though I ran from you
round Priam's town three times and could not face you.
Now my soul would have me stand and fight,
whether I kill you or am killed. So come,
we'll summon gods here as our witnesses,                   300
none higher, arbiters of a pact: I swear
that, terrible as you are,
I'll not insult your corpse should Zeus allow me
victory in the end, your life as prize.

271. *Dêíphobos*: A brother of Hektor.

Once I have your gear, I'll give your body          305
back to Akhaians. Grant me. too, this grace."

But swift Akhilleus frowned at him and said:

"Hektor, I'll have no talk of pacts with you,
forever unforgiven as you are.
As between men and lions there are none,          310
no concord between wolves and sheep, but all
hold one another hateful through and through,
so there can be no courtesy between us,
no sworn truce, till one of us is down
and glutting with his blood the wargod Arês.          315
Summon up what skills you have. By god,
you'd better be a spearman and a fighter!
Now there is no way out. Pallas Athêna
will have the upper hand of you. The weapon
belongs to me. You'll pay the reckoning          320
in full for all the pain my men have borne,
who met death by your spear."

                              He twirled and cast
his shaft with its long shadow. Splendid Hektor,
keeping his eye upon the point, eluded it
by ducking at the instant of the cast,          325
so shaft and bronze shank passed him overhead
and punched into the earth. But unperceived
by Hektor, Pallas Athêna plucked it out
and gave it back to Akhilleus. Hektor said:

"A clean miss. Godlike as you are,          330
you have not yet known doom for me from Zeus.
You thought you had, by heaven. Then you turned
into a word-thrower, hoping to make me lose
my fighting heart and head in fear of you.
You cannot plant your spear between my shoulders          335
while I am running. If you have the gift,
just put it through my chest as I come forward.
Now it's for you to dodge my own. Would god
you'd give the whole shaft lodging in your body!
War for the Trojans would be eased          340
if you were blotted out, bane that you are."

With this he twirled his long spearshaft and cast it,
hitting his enemy mid-shield, but off
and away the spear rebounded. Furious

that he had lost it, made his throw for nothing,    345
Hektor stood bemused. He had no other.
Then he gave a great shout to Dêíphobos
to ask for a long spear. But there was no one
near him, not a soul. Now in his heart
the Trojan realized the truth and said:    350

"This is the end. The gods are calling deathward.
I had thought
a good soldier, Dêíphobos, was with me.
He is inside the walls. Athêna tricked me.
Death is near, and black, not at a distance,    355
not to be evaded. Long ago
this hour must have been to Zeus's liking
and to the liking of his archer son.
They have been well disposed before, but now
the apppointed time's upon me. Still, I would not    360
die without delivering a stroke,
or die ingloriously, but in some action
memorable to men in days to come."

With this he drew the whetted blade that hung
upon his left flank, ponderous and long,    365
collecting all his might the way an eagle
narrows himself to dive through shady cloud
and strike a lamb or cowering hare: so Hektor
lanced ahead and swung his whetted blade.
Akhilleus with wild fury in his heart    370
pulled in upon his chest his beautiful shield—
his helmet with four burnished metal ridges
nodding above it, and the golden crest
Hêphaistos locked there tossing in the wind.
Conspicuous as the evening star that comes,    375
amid the first in heaven, at fall of night,
and stands most lovely in the west, so shone
in sunlight the fine-pointed spear
Akhilleus poised in his right hand, with deadly
aim at Hektor, at the skin where most    380
it lay exposed. But nearly all was covered
by the bronze gear he took from slain Patróklos,
showing only, where his collarbones
divided neck and shoulders, the bare throat
where the destruction of a life is quickest.    385
Here, then, as the Trojan charged, Akhilleus
drove his point straight through the tender neck,
but did not cut the windpipe, leaving Hektor

able to speak and to respond. He fell
aside into the dust. And Prince Akhilleus
now exulted:                                                                    390

                              "Hektor, had you thought
that you could kill Patróklos and be safe?
Nothing to dread from me; I was not there.
All childishness. Though distant then, Patróklos'
comrade in arms was greater far than he—                                       395
and it is I who had been left behind
that day beside the deepsea ships who now
have made your knees give way. The dogs and kites
will rip your body. His will lie in honor
when the Akhaians give him funeral."                                           400

Hektor, barely whispering, replied:

"I beg you by your soul and by your parents,
do not let the dogs feed on me
in your encampment by the ships. Accept
the bronze and gold my father will provide                                     405
as gifts, my father and her ladyship
my mother. Let them have my body back,
so that our men and women may accord me
decency of fire when I am dead."

Akhilleus the great runner scowled and said:                                   410

"Beg me no beggary by soul or parents,
whining dog! Would god my passion drove me
to slaughter you and eat you raw, you've caused
such agony to me! No man exists
who could defend you from the carrion pack—                                    415
not if they spread for me ten times your ransom,
twenty times, and promise more as well;
aye, not if Priam, son of Dárdanos,
tells them to buy you for your weight in gold!
You'll have no bed of death, nor will you be                                   420
laid out and mourned by her who gave you birth.
Dogs and birds will have you, every scrap."

Then at the point of death Lord Hektor said:

"I see you now for what you are. No chance
to win you over. Iron in your breast                                           425
your heart is. Think a bit, though: this may be
a thing the gods in anger hold against you

on that day when Paris and Apollo
destroy you at the Gates, great as you are."

Even as he spoke, the end came, and death hid him;     430
spirit from body fluttered to undergloom,
bewailing fate that made him leave his youth
and manhood in the world. And as he died
Akhilleus spoke again. He said:

"Die, make an end. I shall accept my own     435
whenever Zeus and the other gods desire."

At this he pulled his spearhead from the body,
laying it aside, and stripped
the bloodstained shield and cuirass from his shoulders.
Other Akhaians hastened round to see     440
Hektor's fine body and his comely face,
and no one came who did not stab the body.
Glancing at one another they would say:

"Now Hektor has turned vulnerable, softer
than when he put the torches to the ships!"     445

And he who said this would inflict a wound.
When the great master of pursuit, Akhilleus,
had the body stripped, he stood among them,
saying swiftly:

                "Friends, my lords and captains
of Argives, now that the gods at last have let me     450
bring to earth this man who wrought
havoc among us—more than all the rest—
come, we'll offer battle around the city,
to learn the intentions of the Trojans now.
Will they give up their strongpoint at this loss?     455
Can they fight on, though Hektor's dead?

                         But wait:

why do I ponder, why take up these questions?
Down by the ships Patróklos' body lies
unwept, unburied. I shall not forget him
while I can keep my feet among the living.     460
If in the dead world they forget the dead,
I say there, too, I shall remember him,
my friend. Men of Akhaia, lift a song!
Down to the ships we go, and take this body,

---

429. *the Gates*: The Skaian Gates of Troy.

our glory. We have beaten Hektor down,                                    465
to whom as to a god the Trojans prayed."

Indeed, he had in mind for Hektor's body
outrage and shame. Behind both feet he pierced
the tendons, heel to ankle. Rawhide cords
he drew through both and lashed them to his chariot,                      470
letting the man's head trail. Stepping aboard,
bearing the great trophy of the arms,
he shook the reins, and whipped the team ahead
into a willing run. A dustcloud rose
above the furrowing body; the dark tresses                                475
flowed behind, and the head so princely once
lay back in dust. Zeus gave him to his enemies
to be defiled in his own fatherland.
So his whole head was blackened. Looking down,
his mother tore her braids, threw off her veil,                           480
and wailed, heartbroken to behold her son.
Piteously his father groaned, and round him
lamentation spread throughout the town,
most like the clamor to be heard if Ilion's
towers, top to bottom, seethed in flames.                                 485
They barely stayed the old man, mad with grief,
from passing through the gates. Then in the mire
he rolled, and begged them all, each man by name:

"Relent, friends. It is hard; but let me go
out of the city to the Akhaian ships.                                     490
I'll make my plea to that demonic heart.
He may feel shame before his peers, or pity
my old age. His father, too, is old,
Pêleus, who brought him up to be a scourge
to Trojans, cruel to all, but most to me,                                 495
so many of my sons in flower of youth
he cut away. And, though I grieve, I cannot
mourn them all as much as I do one,
for whom my grief will take me to the grave—
and that is Hektor. Why could he not have died                           500
where I might hold him? In our weeping, then,
his mother, now so destitute, and I
might have had surfeit and relief of tears."

These were the words of Priam as he wept,
and all his people groaned. Then in her turn.                             505
Hékabê led the women in lamentation:

"Child, I am lost now. Can I bear my life
after the death of suffering your death?
You were my pride in all my nights and days,
pride of the city, pillar to the Trojans                                510
and Trojan women. Everyone looked to you
as though you were a god, and rightly so.
You were their greatest glory while you lived.
Now your doom and death have come upon you."

These were her mournful words. But Hektor's lady          515
still knew nothing; no one came to tell her
of Hektor's stand outside the gates. She wove
upon her loom, deep in the lofty house,
a double purple web with rose design.
Calling her maids in waiting,                                          520
she ordered a big caldron on a tripod
set on the hearthfire. to provide a bath
for Hektor when he came home from the fight.
Poor wife, how far removed from baths he was
she could not know, as at Akhilleus' hands                      525
Athêna brought him down.

                                  Then from the tower

she heard a wailing and a distant moan.
Her knees shook, and she let her shuttle fall,
and called out to her maids again:

                                        "Come here.
Two must follow me, to see this action.                          530
I heard my husband's queenly mother cry.
I feel my heart rise, throbbing in my throat.
My knees are like stone under me. Some blow
is coming home to Priam's sons and daughters.
Ah, could it never reach my ears! I die                            535
of dread that Akhilleus may have cut off Hektor,
blocked my bold husband from the city wall,
to drive him down the plain alone! By now
he may have ended Hektor's deathly pride.
He never kept his place amid the chariots                       540
but drove ahead. He would not be outdone
by anyone in courage."

                                     Saying this, she ran

like a madwoman through the mégaron,
her heart convulsed. Her maids kept at her side.
On reaching the great tower and the soldiers,               545

Andrómakhê stood gazing from the wall
and saw him being dragged before the city.
Chariot horses at a brutal gallop
pulled the torn body toward the decked ships.
Blackness of night covered her eyes; she fell          550
backward swooning, sighing out her life,
and let her shining headdress fall, her hood
and diadem. her plaited band and veil
that Aphrodítê once had given her,
on that day when, from Eëtíôn's house,                  555
for a thousand bridal gifts, Lord Hektor led her.
Now, at her side, kinswomen of her lord
supported her among them, dazed and faint
to the point of death. But when she breathed again
and her stunned heart recovered, in a burst            560
of sobbing she called out among the women:

"Hektor! Here is my desolation. Both
had this in store from birth—from yours in Troy
in Priam's palace, mine by wooded Plakos
at Thêbê in the home of Eëtíôn,                          565
my father, who took care of me in childhood,
a man cursed by fate, a fated daughter.
How I could wish I never had been born!
Now under earth's roof to the house of Death
you go your way and leave me here, bereft,             570
lonely, in anguish without end. The child
we wretches had is still in infancy;
you cannot be a pillar to him, Hektor,
now you are dead, nor he to you. And should
this boy escape the misery of the war,                 575
there will be toil and sorrow for him later,
as when strangers move his boundary stones.
The day that orphans him will leave him lonely,
downcast in everything, cheeks wet with tears,
in hunger going to his father's friends                580
to tug at one man's cloak, another's khiton.
Some will be kindly: one may lift a cup
to wet his lips at least, though not his throat;
but from the board some child with living parents
gives him a push, a slap, with biting words:           585
'Outside, you there! Your father is not with us
here at our feast!' And the boy Astýanax
will run to his forlorn mother. Once he fed

---

577. *move his boundary stones*: I.e., confiscate his land.

on marrow only and the fat of lamb,
high on his father's knees. And when sleep came                    590
to end his play, he slept in a nurse's arms,
brimful of happiness, in a soft bed.
But now he'll know sad days and many of them,
missing his father. 'Lord of the lower town'
the Trojans call him. They know, you alone,                        595
Lord Hektor, kept their gates and their long walls.
Beside the beaked ships now, far from your kin,
the blowflies' maggots in a swarm will eat you
naked, after the dogs have had their fill.
Ah, there are folded garments in your chambers,                    600
delicate and fine, of women's weaving.
These, by heaven, I'll burn to the last thread
in blazing fire! They are no good to you,
they cannot cover you in death. So let them
go, let them be burnt as an offering                               605
from Trojans and their women in your honor."

Thus she mourned. and the women wailed in answer.

[Akhilleus buried Patróklos, and the Greeks celebrated the dead
hero's fame with athletic games, for which Akhilleus gave the
prizes.]

## Book XXIV

### [Akhilleus and Priam]

The funeral games were over. Men dispersed
and turned their thoughts to supper in their quarters,
then to the boon of slumber. But Akhilleus
thought of his friend, and sleep that quiets all things
would not take hold of him. He tossed and turned                     5
remembering with pain Patróklos' courage,
his buoyant heart; how in his company
he fought out many a rough day full of danger,
cutting through ranks in war and the bitter sea.
With memory his eyes grew wet. He lay                                10
on his right side, then on his back. and then
face downward—but at last he rose, to wander
distractedly along the line of surf.
This for eleven nights. The first dawn, brightening
sea and shore, became familiar to him,                              15
as at that hour he yoked his team, with Hektor
tied behind, to drag him out, three times

around Patróklos' tomb. By day he rested
in his own hut, abandoning Hektor's body
to lie full-length in dust—though Lord Apollo,                    20
pitying the man, even in death,
kept his flesh free of disfigurement.
He wrapped him in his great shield's flap of gold
to save him from laceration. But Akhilleus
in rage visited indignity on Hektor                              25
day after day, and, looking on,
the blessed gods were moved. Day after day
they urged the Wayfinder to steal the body—
a thought agreeable to all but Hêra,
Poseidon, and the gray-eyed one, Athêna.                         30
These opposed it, and held out, since Ilion
and Priam and his people had incurred
their hatred first, the day Aléxandros
made his mad choice and piqued two goddesses,
visitors in his sheepfold: he praised                            35
a third, who offered ruinous lust.
Now when Dawn grew bright for the twelfth day,
Phoibos Apollo spoke among the gods:

"How heartless and how malevolent you are!
Did Hektor never make burnt offering                             40
of bulls' thighbones to you, and unflawed goats?
Even in death you would not stir to save him
for his dear wife to see, and for his mother,
his child, his father, Priam, and his men:
they'd burn the corpse at once and give him burial.              45
Murderous Akhilleus has your willing help—
a man who shows no decency, implacable.
barbarous in his ways as a wild lion
whose power and intrepid heart
sway him to raid the flocks of men for meat.                     50
The man has lost all mercy;
he has no shame—that gift that hinders mortals
but helps them, too. A sane one may endure
an even dearer loss: a blood brother,
a son; and yet, by heaven, having grieved                        55
and passed through mourning, he will let it go.
The fates have given patient hearts to men.
Not this one: first he took Prince Hektor's life
and now he drags the body, lashed to his car,

---

28. *the Wayfinder*: Hermês, messenger
of the gods.
34. *his mad choice*: The judgment of
Paris. He was asked to judge which goddess was most beautiful: Hêra, Athêna
and Aphroditê all offered him bribes,
but Aphroditê offered him the love of
Helen, and he therefore chose her.

around the barrow of his friend, performing    60
something neither nobler in report
nor better in itself. Let him take care,
or, brave as he is, we gods will turn against him,
seeing him outrage the insensate earth!"

Hêra whose arms are white as ivory    65
grew angry at Apollo. She retorted:

"Lord of the silver bow, your words would be
acceptable if one had a mind to honor
Hektor and Akhilleus equally.
But Hektor suckled at a woman's breast,    70
Akhilleus is the first-born of a goddess—
one I nursed myself. I reared her, gave her
to Pêleus, a strong man whom the gods loved.
All of you were present at their wedding—
you too—friend of the base, forever slippery!—    75
came with your harp and dined there!"

                                        Zeus the stormking
answered her:


                                    "Hêra, don't lose your temper
altogether. Clearly the same high honor
cannot be due both men. And yet Lord Hektor,
of all the mortal men in Ilion,    80
was dearest to the gods, or was to me.
He never failed in the right gift; my altar
never lacked a feast
of wine poured out and smoke of sacrifice—
the share assigned as ours. We shall renounce    85
the theft of Hektor's body; there is no way;
there would be no eluding Akhilleus' eye,
as night and day his mother comes to him.
Will one of you now call her to my presence?
I have a solemn message to impart:    90
Akhilleus is to take fine gifts from Priam,
and in return give back Prince Hektor's body."

At this, Iris who runs on the rainy wind
with word from Zeus departed. Midway between
Samos and rocky Imbros, down she plunged    95
into the dark gray sea, and the brimming tide

---

60. *barrow*: Grave-mound.                in the Aegean, off the coast of Asia
95. *Samos . . . Imbros*: Two islands     Minor.

roared over her as she sank into the depth—
as rapidly as a leaden sinker, fixed
on a lure of wild bull's horn, that glimmers down
with a fatal hook among the ravening fish.                    100
Soon Iris came on Thetis in a cave,
surrounded by a company of Nereids
lolling there, while she bewailed the fate
of her magnificent son, now soon to perish
on Troy's rich earth, far from his fatherland.                105
Halting before her, Iris said:

                                        "Come, Thetis,
Zeus of eternal forethought summons you."

Silvery-footed Thetis answered:

                                        "Why?

Why does the great one call me to him now,
when I am shy of mingling with immortals,                     110
being so heavyhearted? But I'll go.
Whatever he may say will have its weight."

That loveliest of goddesses now put on
a veil so black no garment could be blacker,
and swam where windswift Iris led. Before them             115
on either hand the ground swell fell away.
They rose to a beach, then soared into the sky
and found the viewer of the wide world, Zeus,
with all the blissful gods who live forever
around him seated. Athêna yielded place,                      120
and Thetis sat down by her father, Zeus,
while Hêra handed her a cup of gold
and spoke a comforting word. When she had drunk,
Thetis held out the cup again to Hêra.
The father of gods and men began:

                                        "You've come     125

to Olympos, Thetis, though your mind is troubled
and insatiable pain preys on your heart.
I know, I too. But let me, even so,
explain why I have called you here. Nine days
of quarreling we've had among the gods                        130
concerning Hektor's body and Akhilleus.
They wish the Wayfinder to make off with it.
I, however, accord Akhilleus honor
as I now tell you—in respect for you

whose love I hope to keep hereafter. Go, now,                    135
down to the army, tell this to your son:
the gods are sullen toward him, and I, too,
more than the rest, am angered at his madness,
holding the body by the beaked ships
and not releasing it. In fear of me                              140
let him relent and give back Hektor's body!
At the same time I'll send Iris to Priam,
directing him to go down to the beachhead
and ransom his dear son. He must bring gifts
to melt Akhilleus' rage."

                                                  Thetis obeyed,   145

leaving Olympos' ridge and flashing down
to her son's hut. She found him groaning there,
inconsolable, while men-at-arms
went to and fro, making their breakfast ready—
having just put to the knife a fleecy sheep.                     150
His gentle mother sat down at his side,
caressed him, and said tenderly:

                                                   "My child,

will you forever feed on your own heart
in grief and pain, and take no thought of sleep
or sustenance? It would be comforting                           155
to make love with a woman. No long time
will you live on for me: Death even now
stands near you, appointed and all-powerful.
But be alert and listen: I am a messenger
from Zeus, who tells me the gods are sullen toward you           160
and he himself most angered at your madness,
holding the body by the beaked ships
and not releasing it. Give Hektor back.
Take ransom for the body."

                                                  Said Akhilleus:

"Let it be so. Let someone bring the ransom                      165
and take the dead away, if the Olympian
commands this in his wisdom."

                                            So, that morning,

in camp, amid the ships, mother and son
conversed together, and their talk was long.
Lord Zeus meanwhile sent Iris to Ilion.                          170

"Off with you, lightfoot, leave Olympos, take
my message to the majesty of Priam
at Ilion. He is to journey down
and ransom his dear son upon the beachhead.
He shall take gifts to melt Akhilleus' rage,                    175
and let him go alone, no soldier with him,
only some crier, some old man, to drive
his wagon team and guide the nimble wagon,
and afterward to carry home the body
of him that Prince Akhilleus overcame.                          180
Let him not think of death, or suffer dread,
as I'll provide him with a wondrous guide,
the Wayfinder, to bring him across the lines
into the very presence of Akhilleus.
And he, when he sees Priam within his hut,                      185
will neither take his life nor let another
enemy come near. He is no madman,
no blind brute, nor one to flout the gods,
but dutiful toward men who beg his mercy."

Then Iris at his bidding ran                                    190
on the rainy winds to bear the word of Zeus,
until she came to Priam's house and heard
voices in lamentation. In the court
she found the princes huddled around their father,
faces and clothing wet with tears. The old man,                195
fiercely wrapped and hooded in his mantle,
sat like a figure graven—caked in filth
his own hands had swept over head and neck
when he lay rolling on the ground. Indoors
his daughters and his sons' wives were weeping,                200
remembering how many and how brave
the young men were who had gone down to death
before the Argive spearmen.
                                            Zeus's courier,
appearing now to Priam's eyes alone,
alighted whispering, so the old man trembled:                  205

"Priam, heir of Dárdanos, take heart,
and have no fear of me; I bode no evil,
but bring you friendly word from Zeus,
who is distressed for you and pities you
though distant far upon Olympos. He                             210
commands that you shall ransom the Prince Hektor,
taking fine gifts to melt Akhilleus' rage.

And go alone; no soldier may go with you,
only some crier, some old man, to drive
your wagon team and guide the nimble wagon,                215
and afterward to carry home the body
of him that Prince Akhilleus overcame.
Put away thoughts of death, shake off your dread,
for you shall have a wondrous guide,
the Wayfinder, to bring you across the lines               220
into the very presence of Akhilleus.
He, for his part, seeing you in his quarters,
will neither take your life nor let another
enemy come near. He is no madman,
no blind brute, nor one to flout the gods,                 225
but dutiful toward men who beg his mercy."

Iris left him, swift as a veering wind.
Then Priam spoke, telling the men to rig
a four-wheeled wagon with a wicker box,
while he withdrew to his chamber roofed in cedar,          230
high and fragrant, rich in precious things.
He called to Hékabê, his lady:

                                                "Princess,

word from Olympian Zeus has come to me
to go down to the ships of the Akhaians
and ransom our dead son. I am to take                      235
gifts that will melt Akhilleus' anger. Tell me
how this appears to you, tell me your mind,
for I am torn with longing, now, to pass
inside the great encampment by the ships."

The woman's voice broke as she answered:                   240

                                                "Sorrow,

sorrow. Where is the wisdom now that made you
famous in the old days, near and far?
How can you ever face the Akhaian ships
or wish to go alone before those eyes,
the eyes of one who stripped your sons in battle,          245
how many, and how brave? Iron must be
the heart within you. If he sees you, takes you,
savage and wayward as the man is,
he'll have no mercy and no shame. Better
that we should mourn together in our hall.                 250
Almighty fate spun this thing for our son

the day I bore him: destined him to feed
the wild dogs after death, being far from us
when he went down before the stronger man.
*I could devour the vitals of that man,*                    255
*leeching into his living flesh!* He'd know
pain then—pain like mine for my dead son.
It was no coward the Akhaian killed;
he stood and fought for the sweet wives of Troy,
with no more thought of flight or taking cover."          260

In majesty old Priam said:

                                                      "My heart

is fixed on going. Do not hold me back,
and do not make yourself a raven crying
calamity at home. You will not move me.
If any man on earth had urged this on me—                 265
reader of altar smoke, prophet or priest—
we'd say it was a lie, and hold aloof.
But no: with my own ears I heard the voice,
I saw the god before me. Go I shall,
and no more words. If I must die alongside                 270
the ships of the Akhaians in their bronze,
I die gladly. May I but hold my son
and spend my grief; then let Akhilleus kill me."

Throwing open the lids of treasure boxes
he picked out twelve great robes of state, and twelve     275
light cloaks for men, and rugs, an equal number,
and just as many capes of snowy linen,
adding a dozen khitons to the lot;
then set in order ten pure bars of gold,
a pair of shining tripods, four great caldrons,           280
and finally one splendid cup, a gift
Thracians had made him on an embassy.
He would not keep this, either—as he cared
for nothing now but ransoming his son.

And now, from the colonnade,                               285
he made his Trojan people keep their distance,
berating and abusing them:

                                                        "Away,

you craven fools and rubbish! In your own homes
have you no one to mourn, that you crowd here,
to make more trouble for me? Is this a show,                290

that Zeus has crushed me, that he took the life
of my most noble son? You'll soon know what it means,
as you become child's play for the Akhaians
to kill in battle, now that Hektor's gone.
As for myself, before I see my city                              295
taken and ravaged, let me go down blind
to Death's cold kingdom!"

                                                         **Staff in hand,**
he herded them, until they turned away
and left the furious old man. He lashed out
now at his sons, at Hélenos and Paris,                           300
Agathôn, Pammôn, Antíphonos,
Polítês, Dêíphobos, Hippóthoös,
and Dios—to these nine the old man cried:

"Bestir yourselves, you misbegotten whelps,
shame of my house! Would god you had been killed              305
instead of Hektor at the line of ships.
How curst I am in everything! I fathered
first-rate men, in our great Troy; but now
I swear not one is left: Mêstôr, Trôïlos,
laughing amid the war-cars; and then Hektor—                   310
a god to soldiers, and a god among them,
seeming not a man's child, but a god's.
Arês killed them. These poltroons are left,
hollow men, dancers, heroes of the dance,
light-fingered pillagers of lambs and kids                     315
from the town pens!

                                    **Now will you get a wagon**
ready for me, and quickly? Load these gifts
aboard it, so that we can take the road."

Dreading the rough edge of their father's tongue,
they lifted out a cart, a cargo wagon,                          320
neat and maneuverable, and newly made,
and fixed upon it a wicker box; then took
a mule yoke from a peg, a yoke of boxwood
knobbed in front, with rings to hold the reins.
They brought out, too, the band nine forearms long             325
called the yoke-fastener, and placed the yoke
forward at the shank of the polished pole,
shoving the yoke-pin firmly in. They looped
three turns of the yoke-fastener round the knob
and wound it over and over down the pole,                       330

tucking the tab end under. Next, the ransom:
bearing the weight of gifts for Hektor's person
out of the inner room, they piled them up
on the polished wagon. It was time to yoke
the mule-team, strong in harness, with hard hooves,           335
a team the Mysians had given Priam.
Then for the king's own chariot they harnessed
a team of horses of the line of Trôs,
reared by the old king in his royal stable.
So the impatient king and his sage crier                      340
had their animals yoked in the palace yard
when Hékabê in her agitation joined them,
carrying in her right hand a golden cup
of honeyed wine, with which, before they left,
they might make offering. At the horses' heads                345
she stood to tell them:

                                        "Here, tip wine to Zeus,
the father of gods. Pray for a safe return
from the enemy army, seeing your heart is set
on venturing to the camp against my will.
Pray in the second place to Zeus the stormking,              350
gloomy over Ida, who looks down
on all Troy country. Beg for an omen-bird,
the courier dearest of all birds to Zeus
and sovereign in power of flight,
that he appear upon our right in heaven.                      355
When you have seen him with your own eyes, then,
under that sign, you may approach the ships.
If Zeus who views the wide world will not give you
vision of his bird, then I at least
cannot bid godspeed to your journey,                          360
bent on it though you are."

                                                    In majesty
Priam replied:

                                        "My lady, in this matter
I am disposed to trust you and agree.
It is an excellent thing and salutary
to lift our hands to Zeus, invoking mercy."                   365

The old king motioned to his housekeeper,
who stood nearby with a basin and a jug,

---

336. *Mysians*: A people of central   Kings.
Asia Minor.                            353. *dearest of all birds to Zeus*: The
338. *Trôs*: Ancestor of the Trojan    eagle.

to pour clear water on his hands. He washed them,
took the cup his lady held, and prayed
while standing there, midway in the walled court. 370
Then he tipped out the wine, looking toward heaven,
saying:

                    "Zeus, our Father, reigning from Ida,
god of glory and power, grant I come
to Akhilleus' door as one to be received
with kindliness and mercy. And dispatch 375
your courier bird, the nearest to your heart
of all birds, and the first in power of flight.
Let him appear upon our right in heaven
that I may see him with my own eyes
and under that sign journey to the ships." 380

Zeus all-foreseeing listened to this prayer
and put an eagle, king
of winged creatures, instantly in flight:
a swamp eagle, a hunter, one they call
the duskwing. Wide as a doorway in a chamber 385
spacious and high, built for a man of wealth,
a door with long bars fitted well, so wide
spread out each pinion. The great bird appeared
winging through the town on their right hand,
and all their hearts lifted with joy to see him. 390
In haste the old king boarded his bright car
and clattered out of the echoing colonnade.
Ahead, the mule-team drew the four-wheeled wagon,
driven by Idaíos, and behind
the chariot rolled, with horses that the old man 395
whipped into a fast trot through the town.
Family and friends all followed weeping
as though for Priam's last and deathward ride.
Into the lower town they passed, and reached
the plain of Troy. Here those who followed after 400
turned back, sons and sons-in-law. And Zeus
who views the wide world saw the car and wagon
brave the plain. He felt a pang for Priam
and quickly said to Hermês, his own son:

"Hermês, as you go most happily 405
of all the gods with mortals, and give heed
to whom you will, be on your way this time
as guide for Priam to the deepsea ships.
Guide him so that not one of the Danáäns
may know or see him till he reach Akhilleus." 410

Argeiphontês the Wayfinder obeyed.
He bent to tie his beautiful sandals on,
ambrosial, golden, that carry him over water
and over endless land on a puff of wind,
and took the wand with which he charms asleep—                415
or, when he wills, awake—the eyes of men.
So, wand in hand, the strong god glittering
paced into the air. Quick as a thought
he came to Hellê's waters and to Troy,
appearing as a boy whose lip was downy                          420
in the first bloom of manhood, a young prince,
all graciousness.

                      After the travelers
drove past the mound of Ilos, at the ford
they let the mules and horses pause to drink
the running stream. Now darkness had come on               425
when, looking round, the crier
saw Hermês near at hand. He said to Priam:

"You must think hard and fast, your grace;
there is new danger; we need care and prudence.
I see a man-at-arms there—ready, I think,                       430
to prey on us. Come, shall we whip the team
and make a run for it? Or take his knees
and beg for mercy?"

                    Now the old man's mind
gave way to confusion and to terror.
On his gnarled arms and legs the hair stood up,            435
and he stared, breathless. But the affable god
came over and took his hand and asked:

                       "Old father,
where do you journey, with your cart and car,
while others rest, below the evening star?
Do you not fear the Akhaians where they lie                    440
encamped, hard, hostile outlanders, nearby?
Should someone see you, bearing stores like these
by night, how would you deal with enemies?
You are not young, your escort's ancient, too.
Could you beat off an attacker, either of you?"            445

411. *Argeiphontês*: A title of Hermês,
of unknown meaning.
   423. *mound of Ilos*: The tomb of
Priam's grandfather, a landmark on the
Trojan plain.

426. *the crier*: Idaîos, Priam's *herald*.
438–559. The translator has used
rhymed couplets for Hermês' speeches;
in the original Greek Hermês speaks just
like everyone else, in unrhymed lines.

I'll do no hurt to you but defend you here.
You remind me of my father, whom I hold dear."

Old Priam answered him:

                                        "Indeed, dear boy,
the case is as you say. And yet some god
stretched out his hand above me, he who sent          450
before me here—and just at the right time—
a traveler like yourself, well-made, well-spoken,
clearheaded, too. You come of some good family."

The Wayfinder rejoined:

                                "You speak with courtesy,
dear sir. But on this point enlighten me:              455
are you removing treasure here amassed
for safety abroad, until the war is past?
Or can you be abandoning Ilion
in fear, after he perished, that great one
who never shirked a battle, your own princely son?"    460

Old Priam replied:

                        "My brave young friend, who are you?
Born of whom? How nobly you acknowledge
the dreadful end of my unfortunate son."

To this the Wayfinder replied:

                                             "Dear sir,
you question me about him? Never surmise               465
I have not seen him with my very eyes,
and often, on the field. I saw him chase
Argives with carnage to their own shipways,
while we stood wondering, forbidden war
by the great anger that Akhilleus bore                 470
Lord Agamémnon. I am of that company
Akhilleus led. His own ship carried me
as one of the Myrmidons. My father is old,
as you are, and his name's Polyktôr; gold
and other wealth he owns;                              475
and I am seventh and last of all his sons.
When I cast lots among them, my lot fell
to join the siege against Troy citadel.
Tonight I've left the camp to scout this way

where, circling Troy, we'll fight at break of day;        480
our men are tired of waiting and will not stand
for any postponement by the high command."

Responded royal Priam:

                                     "If you belong
to the company of Akhilleus, son of Pêleus,
tell me this, and tell me the whole truth:        485
is my son even now beside the ships?
Or has Akhilleus by this time dismembered him
and thrown him to the wild dogs?"

                                   The Wayfinder
made reply again:

                                     "Dear sir,
no dogs or birds have yet devoured your son.        490
Beside Akhilleus' ship, out of the sun,
he lies in a place of shelter. Now twelve days
the man has lain there, yet no part decays,
nor have the blowfly's maggots, that devour
dead men in war, fed on him to this hour.        495
True that around his dear friend's barrow tomb
Akhilleus drags him when dawn-shadows come,
driving pitilessly; but he mars him not.
You might yourself be witness, on the spot,
how fresh with dew he lies, washed of his gore,        500
unstained, for the deep gashes that he bore
have all closed up—and many thrust their bronze
into his body. The blest immortal ones
favor your prince, and care for every limb
even in death, as they so cherished him."        505

The old king's heart exulted, and he said:

"Child, it was well to honor the immortals.
He never forgot, at home in Ilion—
ah, did my son exist? was he a dream?—
the gods who own Olympos. They in turn        510
were mindful of him when he met his end.
Here is a goblet as a gift from me.
Protect me, give me escort, if the gods
attend us, till I reach Akhilleus' hut."

And in response Hermês the Wayfinder        515
said:

"You are putting a young man to the test,
dear sir, but I may not, as you request,
accept a gift behind Akhilleus' back.
Fearing, honoring him, I could not lack
discretion to that point. The consequence, too,                    520
could be unwelcome. As for escorting you,
even to Argos' famous land I'd ride
a deck with you, or journey at your side.
No cutthroat ever will disdain your guide."

With this, Hermês who lights the way for mortals                    525
leapt into the driver's place. He caught up
reins and whip, and breathed a second wind
into the mule-team and the team of horses.
Onward they ran toward parapet and ships,
and pulled up to the moat.

           Now night had fallen,    530
bringing the sentries to their supper fire,
but the glimmering god Hermês, the Wayfinder,
showered a mist of slumber on them all.
As quick as thought, he had the gates unbarred
and open to let the wagon enter, bearing                            535
the old king and the ransom.

           Going seaward
they came to the lofty quarters of Akhilleus,
a lodge the Myrmidons built for their lord
of pine trees cut and trimmed, and shaggy thatch
from mowings in deep meadows. Posts were driven                     540
round the wide courtyard in a palisade,
whose gate one crossbar held, one beam of pine.
It took three men to slam this home, and three
to draw the bolt again—but great Akhilleus
worked his entryway alone with ease.                                545
And now Hermês, who lights the way for mortals,
opened for Priam, took him safely in
with all his rich gifts for the son of Pêleus.
Then the god dropped the reins, and stepping down
he said:                                                            550

        "I am no mortal wagoner,
but Hermês, sir. My father sent me here
to be your guide amid the Akhaian men.
Now that is done, I'm off to heaven again
and will not visit Akhilleus. That would be
to compromise an immortal's dignity—                                555
to be received with guests of mortal station.

Go take his knees, and make your supplication:
invoke his father, his mother, and his child;
pray that his heart be touched, that he be reconciled."

Now Hermês turned, departing for Olympos,                    560
and Priam vaulted down. He left Idaíos
to hold the teams in check, while he went forward
into the lodge. He found Akhilleus, dear
to Zeus, there in his chair, with officers
at ease across the room. Only Automédôn                      565
and Alkimos were busy near Akhilleus,
for he had just now made an end of dinner,
eating and drinking, and the laden boards
lay near him still upon the trestles.

                                        Priam,
the great king of Troy, passed by the others,               570
knelt down, took in his arms Akhilleus' knees,
and kissed the hands of wrath that killed his sons.

When, taken with mad Folly in his own land,
a man does murder and in exile finds
refuge in some rich house, then all who see him              575
stand in awe.
So these men stood.

                                         Akhilleus
gazed in wonder at the splendid king,
and his companions marveled too, all silent,
with glances to and fro. Now Priam prayed                    580
to the man before him:

                        "Remember your own father,
Akhilleus, in your godlike youth: his years
like mine are many, and he stands upon
the fearful doorstep of old age. He, too,
is hard pressed, it may be, by those around him,             585
there being no one able to defend him
from bane of war and ruin. Ah, but he
may nonetheless hear news of you alive,
and so with glad heart hope through all his days
for sight of his dear son, come back from Troy,             590
while I have deathly fortune.

                                  Noble sons
I fathered here, but scarce one man is left me.
Fifty I had when the Akhaians came,
nineteen out of a single belly, others

born of attendant women. Most are gone.                              595
Raging Arês cut their knees from under them.
And he who stood alone among them all,
their champion, and Troy's, ten days ago
you killed him, fighting for his land, my prince,
Hektor.

      It is for him that I have come  600
among these ships, to beg him back from you,
and I bring ransom without stint.

            Akhilleus,
be reverent toward the great gods! And take
pity on me, remember your own father.
Think me more pitiful by far, since I                              605
have brought myself to do what no man else
has done before—to lift to my lips the hand
of one who killed my son."

         Now in Akhilleus
the evocation of his father stirred
new longing, and an ache of grief. He lifted                      610
the old man's hand and gently put him by.
Then both were overborne as they remembered:
the old king huddled at Akhilleus' feet
wept, and wept for Hektor, killer of men,
while great Akhilleus wept for his own father                     615
as for Patróklos once again; and sobbing
filled the room.

       But when Akhilleus' heart
had known the luxury of tears, and pain
within his breast and bones had passed away,
he stood then, raised the old king up, in pity                    620
for his gray head and graybeard cheek, and spoke
in a warm rush of words:

           "Ah, sad and old!
Trouble and pain you've borne, and bear, aplenty.
Only a great will could have brought you here
among the Akhaian ships, and here alone                           625
before the eyes of one who stripped your sons,
your many sons, in battle. Iron must be
the heart within you. Come, then, and sit down.
We'll probe our wounds no more but let them rest,
though grief lies heavy on us. Tears heal nothing,                630

---

611. *put him by*: Moved him away.

drying so stiff and cold. This is the way
the gods ordained the destiny of men,
to bear such burdens in our lives, while they
feel no affliction. At the door of Zeus
are those two urns of good and evil gifts                     635
that he may choose for us; and one for whom
the lightning's joyous king dips in both urns
will have by turns bad luck and good. But one
to whom he sends all evil—that man goes
contemptible by the will of Zeus; ravenous                   640
hunger drives him over the wondrous earth,
unresting, without honor from gods or men.
Mixed fortune came to Pêleus. Shining gifts
at the gods' hands he had from birth: felicity,
wealth overflowing, rule of the Myrmidons,                   645
a bride immortal at his mortal side.
But then Zeus gave afflictions too—no family
of powerful sons grew up for him at home,
but one child, of all seasons and of none.
Can I stand by him in his age? Far from my country          650
I sit at Troy to grieve you and your children.
You, too, sir, in time past were fortunate,
we hear men say. From Makar's isle of Lesbos
northward, and south of Phrygia and the Straits,
no one had wealth like yours, or sons like yours.           655
Then gods out of the sky sent you this bitterness:
the years of siege, the battles and the losses.
Endure it, then. And do not mourn forever
for your dead son. There is no remedy.
You will not make him stand again. Rather                    660
await some new misfortune to be suffered."

The old king in his majesty replied:

"Never give me a chair, my lord, while Hektor
lies in your camp uncared for. Yield him to me
now. Allow me sight of him. Accept                           665
the many gifts I bring. May they reward you,
and may you see your home again.
You spared my life at once and let me live."

Akhilleus, the great runner, frowned and eyed him
under his brows:                                             670

---

653–654. *Makar's isle* . . . *Straits:*
Makar is the legendary first king of Lesbos, a large and fertile island off the
coast of Asia Minor. *The Straits* refers
to the Hellespont. The whole phrase
means that Priam was the richest king in
the whole of northwest Asia Minor.

"Do not vex me, sir," he said.
"I have intended, in my own good time,
to yield up Hektor to you. She who bore me,
the daughter of the Ancient of the sea,
has come with word to me from Zeus. I know
in your case, too—though you say nothing, Priam—          675
that some god guided you to the shipways here.
No strong man in his best days could make entry
into this camp. How could he pass the guard,
or force our gateway?

Therefore, *let me be.*          680
Sting my sore heart again, and even here,
under my own roof, suppliant though you are,
I may not spare you, sir, but trample on
the express command of Zeus!"

When he heard this,
the old man feared him and obeyed with silence.
Now like a lion at one bound Akhilleus          685
left the room. Close at his back the officers
Automédôn and Álkimos went out—
comrades in arms whom he esteemed the most
after the dead Patróklos. They unharnessed
mules and horses, led the old king's crier          690
to a low bench and sat him down.
Then from the polished wagon
they took the piled-up price of Hektor's body.
One khiton and two capes they left aside
as dress and shrouding for the homeward journey.          695
Then, calling to the women slaves, Akhilleus
ordered the body bathed and rubbed with oil—
but lifted, too, and placed apart, where Priam
could not see his son—for seeing Hektor
he might in his great pain give way to rage,          700
and fury then might rise up in Akhilleus
to slay the old king, flouting Zeus's word.
So after bathing and anointing Hektor
they drew the shirt and beautiful shrouding over him.
Then with his own hands lifting him, Akhilleus          705
laid him upon a couch, and with his two
companions aiding, placed him in the wagon.
Now a bitter groan burst from Akhilleus,
who stood and prayed to his own dead friend:

"Patróklos,
do not be angry with me, if somehow          710
even in the world of Death you learn of this—

that I released Prince Hektor to his father.
The gifts he gave were not unworthy. Aye,
and you shall have your share, this time as well."

The Prince Akhilleus turned back to his quarters.    715
He took again the splendid chair that stood
against the farther wall, then looked at Priam
and made his declaration:

                                        "As you wished, sir,
the body of your son is now set free.
He lies in state. At the first sight of Dawn             720
you shall take charge of him yourself and see him.
Now let us think of supper. We are told
that even Niobê in her extremity
took thought for bread—though all her brood had perished,
her six young girls and six tall sons. Apollo,         725
making his silver longbow whip and sing,
shot the lads down, and Artemis with raining
arrows killed the daughters—all this after
Niobê had compared herself with Lêto,
the smooth-cheeked goddess.
                                  She has borne two children, 730
Niobê said, How many have I borne!
But soon those two destroyed the twelve.
                                              Besides,
nine days the dead lay stark, no one could bury them,
for Zeus had turned all folk of theirs to stone.
The gods made graves for them on the tenth day,        735
and then at last, being weak and spent with weeping,
Niobê thought of food. Among the rocks
of Sipylos' lonely mountainside, where nymphs
who race Akhelôïos river go to rest,
she, too, long turned to stone, somewhere broods on      740
the gall immortal gods gave her to drink.

Like her we'll think of supper, noble sir.
Weep for your son again when you have borne him
back to Troy; there he'll be mourned indeed."

In one swift movement now Akhilleus caught             745
and slaughtered a white lamb. His officers

723. *Niobê*: Wife of Amphion, one of the two founders of the great Greek city of Thebes.
738. *Sipylos*: A mountain in Asia Minor. The legend is thought to have had its origin in a rock face which re-sembled a weeping woman, like Niobê, who wept inconsolably for the loss of her children.
739. *Akhelôïos river*: The river near Mount Sipylos in Asia Minor.

flayed it, skillful in their butchering
to dress the flesh; they cut bits for the skewers,
roasted, and drew them off, done to a turn.
Automédôn dealt loaves into the baskets                    750
on the great board; Akhilleus served the meat.
Then all their hands went out upon the supper.
When thirst and appetite were turned away,
Priam, the heir of Dárdanos, gazed long
in wonder at Akhilleus' form and scale—                     755
so like the gods in aspect. And Akhilleus
in his turn gazed in wonder upon Priam,
royal in visage as in speech. Both men
in contemplation found rest for their eyes,
till the old hero, Priam, broke the silence:                760

"Make a bed ready for me, son of Thetis,
and let us know the luxury of sleep.
From that hour when my son died at your hands
till now, my eyelids have not closed in slumber
over my eyes, but groaning where I sat                      765
I tasted pain and grief a thousandfold,
or lay down rolling in my courtyard mire.
Here for the first time I have swallowed bread
and made myself drink wine.
                            Before, I could not."

Akhilleus ordered men and servingwomen                      770
to make a bed outside, in the covered forecourt,
with purple rugs piled up and sheets outspread
and coverings of fleeces laid on top.
The girls went out with torches in their hands
and soon deftly made up a double bed.                       775
Then Akhilleus, defiant of Agamémnon,
told his guest:

                            "Dear venerable sir,
you'll sleep outside tonight, in case an Akhaian
officer turns up, one of those men
who are forever taking counsel with me—                     780
as well they may. If one should see you here
as the dark night runs on, he would report it
to the Lord Marshal Agamémnon. Then
return of the body would only be delayed.
Now tell me this, and give me a straight answer:            785
How many days do you require
for the funeral of Prince Hektor?—I should know
how long to wait, and hold the Akhaian army."

Old Priam in his majesty replied:

"If you would have me carry out the burial,        790
Akhilleus, here is the way to do me grace.
As we are penned in the town, but must bring wood
from the distant hills, the Trojans are afraid.
We should have mourning for nine days in hall,
then on the tenth conduct his funeral        795
and feast the troops and commons;
on the eleventh we should make his tomb,
and on the twelfth give battle, if we must."

Akhilleus said:

                              "As you command, old Priam,
the thing is done. I shall suspend the war        800
for those eleven days that you require."

He took the old man's right hand by the wrist
and held it, to allay his fear.

                                        Now crier

and king with hearts brimful retired to rest
in the sheltered forecourt, while Akhilleus slept        805
deep in his palisaded lodge. Beside him,
lovely in her youth, Brisêis lay.
And other gods and soldiers all night long,
by slumber quieted, slept on. But slumber
would not come to Hermês the Good Companion,        810
as he considered how to ease the way
for Priam from the camp, to send him through
unseen by the formidable gatekeepers.
Then Hermês came to Priam's pillow, saying:

"Sir, no thought of danger shakes your rest,        815
as you sleep on, being great Akhilleus' guest,
amid men fierce as hunters in a ring.
You triumphed in a costly ransoming,
but three times costlier your own would be
to your surviving sons—a monarch's fee—        820
if this should come to Agamémnon's ear
and all the Akhaian host should learn that you are here."

The old king started up in fright, and woke
his herald. Hermês yoked the mules and horses,
took the reins, then inland like the wind        825
he drove through all the encampment, seen by no one.

When they reached Xánthos, eddying and running
god-begotten river, at the ford,
Hermês departed for Olympos. Dawn
spread out her yellow robe on all the earth,                    830
as they drove on toward Troy, with groans and sighs,
and the mule-team pulled the wagon and the body.
And no one saw them, not a man or woman,
before Kassandra. Tall as the pale-gold
goddess Aphrodítê, she had climbed                             835
the citadel of Pergamos at dawn.
Now looking down she saw her father come
in his war-car, and saw the crier there,
and saw Lord Hektor on his bed of death
upon the mulecart. The girl wailed and cried                   840
to all the city:

                         "Oh, look down, look down,
go to your windows, men of Troy, and women,
see Lord Hektor now! Remember joy
at seeing him return alive from battle,
exalting all our city and our land!"                           845

Now, at the sight of Hektor, all gave way
to loss and longing, and all crowded down
to meet the escort and body near the gates,
till no one in the town was left at home.
There Hektor's lady and his gentle mother                      850
tore their hair for him, flinging themselves
upon the wagon to embrace his person
while the crowd groaned. All that long day
until the sun went down they might have mourned
in tears before the gateway. But old Priam                     855
spoke to them from his chariot:

                                        "Make way,
let the mules pass. You'll have your fill of weeping
later, when I've brought the body home."

They parted then, and made way for the wagon,
allowing Priam to reach the famous hall.                       860
They laid the body of Hektor in his bed,
and brought in minstrels, men to lead the dirge.
While these wailed out, the women answered, moaning.
Andrómakhê of the ivory-white arms
held in her lap between her hands                              865
the head of Hektor who had killed so many.

Now she lamented:

"You've been torn from life,
my husband, in young manhood, and you leave me
empty in our hall. The boy's a child
whom you and I, poor souls, conceived; I doubt          870
he'll come to manhood. Long before, great Troy
will go down plundered, citadel and all,
now that you are lost, who guarded it
and kept it, and preserved its wives and children.
They will be shipped off in the murmuring hulls         875
one day, and I along with all the rest.
You, my little one, either you come with me
to do some grinding labor, some base toil
for a harsh master, or an Akhaian soldier
will grip you by the arm and hurl you down               880
from a tower here to a miserable death—
out of his anger for a brother, a father,
or even a son that Hektor killed. Akhaians
in hundreds mouthed black dust under his blows.
He was no moderate man in war, your father,             885
and that is why they mourn him through the city.
Hektor, you gave your parents grief and pain
but left me loneliest, and heartbroken.
You could not open your strong arms to me
from your deathbed, or say a thoughtful word,            890
for me to cherish all my life long
as I weep for you night and day."

                                        Her voice broke,
and a wail came from the women. Hékabê
lifted her lamenting voice among them:

"Hektor, dearest of sons to me, in life                   895
you had the favor of the immortal gods,
and they have cared for you in death as well.
Akhilleus captured other sons of mine
in other years, and sold them overseas
to Samos, Imbros, and the smoky island,                  900
Lemnos. That was not his way with you.
After he took your life, cutting you down
with his sharp-bladed spear, he trussed and dragged you
many times round the barrow of his friend,
Patróklos, whom you killed—though not by this            905
could that friend live again. But now I find you
fresh as pale dew, seeming newly dead,

like one to whom Apollo of the silver bow
had given easy death with his mild arrows."

Hékabê sobbed again, and the wails redoubled.                    910
Then it was Helen's turn to make lament:

"Dear Hektor, dearest brother to me by far!
My husband is Aléxandros,
who brought me here to Troy—God, that I might
have died sooner! This is the twentieth year            915
since I left home, and left my fatherland.
But never did I have an evil word
or gesture from you. No—and when some other
brother-in-law or sister would revile me,
or if my mother-in-law spoke to me bitterly—            920
but Priam never did, being as mild
as my own father—you would bring her round
with your kind heart and gentle speech. Therefore
I weep for you and for myself as well,
given this fate, this grief. In all wide Troy            925
no one is left who will befriend me, none;
they all shudder at me."

                                          Helen wept,
and a moan came from the people, hearing her.
Then Priam, the old king, commanded them:

"Trojans, bring firewood to the edge of town.            930
No need to fear an ambush of the Argives.
When he dismissed me from the camp, Akhilleus
told me clearly they will not harass us,
not until dawn comes for the twelfth day."

Then yoking mules and oxen to their wagons            935
the people thronged before the city gates.
Nine days they labored, bringing countless loads
of firewood to the town. When Dawn that lights
the world of mortals came for the tenth day,
they carried greathearted Hektor out at last,            940
and all in tears placed his dead body high
upon its pyre, then cast a torch below.
When the young Dawn with finger tips of rose
made heaven bright, the Trojan people massed
about Prince Hektor's ritual fire.                        945
All being gathered and assembled, first
they quenched the smoking pyre with tawny wine

wherever flames had licked their way, then friends
and brothers picked his white bones from the char
in sorrow, while the tears rolled down their cheeks.                950
In a golden urn they put the bones,
shrouding the urn with veiling of soft purple.
Then in a grave dug deep they placed it
and heaped it with great stones. The men were quick
to raise the death-mound, while in every quarter              955
lookouts were posted to ensure against
an Akhaian surprise attack. When they had finished
raising the barrow, they returned to Ilion,
where all sat down to banquet in his honor
in the hall of Priam king. So they performed                 960
the funeral rites of Hektor, tamer of horses.


# The Odyssey*

[Ten years after the fall of Troy, Odysseus, king of Ithaca, on
the west coast of Greece, has still not returned home to his wife
Penélopê and his son Telémakhos. He is stranded on Ogýgia, the
far-off island of trhe nymph Kalypso, where he was cast up, sole survivor of his fleet, seven years before, after many adventures in
unknown seas. But in the tenth year the gods contrive his homecoming. Kalypso releases him, and on a raft he makes his way
toward his home, only to be cast up, naked and battered, on the
shore of Phaiákia, home of rich merchant princes.]


## Book VI

Far gone in weariness, in oblivion,
the noble and enduring man slept on;
but Athena in the night went down the land
of the Phaiákians, entering their city.
In days gone by, these men held Hypereia,                     5
a country of wide dancing grounds, but near them
were overbearing Kyklopês, whose power
could not be turned from pillage. So the Phaiákians
migrated thence under Nausíthoös

---

* An extract: five books of the twenty-four. From The Odyssey, translated by
Robert Fitzgerald.

4. Phaiákians: See p. 102, note 2 on
pronunciation.

5. Hypereia: The geography is almost
certainly imaginary, though later Greeks
identified the final home of the

Phaiákians, Skhería (line 11), with
Corcyra (modern Corfu).

7. Kyklopês: A tribe of one-eyed
monsters: Odysseus meets one in Book
IX.

9. Nausíthoös: Son of Poseidon, god of
the sea and of earthquakes, and father
of King Alkínoös.

to settle a New World across the sea,      10
Skhería Island. That first captain walled
their promontory, built their homes and shrines,
and parcelled out the black land for the plow.
But he had gone down long ago to Death.
Alkínoös ruled, and Heaven gave him wisdom,      15
so on this night the goddess, gray-eyed Athena,
entered the palace of Alkínoös
to make sure of Odysseus' voyage home.
She took her way to a painted bedchamber
where a young girl lay fast asleep—so fine      20
in mould and feature that she seemed a goddess—
the daughter of Alkínoös, Nausikaa.
On either side, as Graces might have slept,
her maids were sleeping. The bright doors were shut,
but like a sudden stir of wind, Athena      25
moved to the bedside of the girl, and grew
visible as the shipman Dymas' daughter,
a girl the princess' age, and her dear friend.
In this form gray-eyed Athena said to her:

"How so remiss, and yet thy mother's daughter?      30
leaving thy clothes uncared for, Nausikaa,
when soon thou must have store of marriage linen,
and put thy minstrelsy in wedding dress!
Beauty, in these, will make the folk admire,
and bring thy father and gentle mother joy.      35
Let us go washing in the shine of morning!
Beside thee will I drub, so wedding chests
will brim by evening. Maidenhood must end!
Have not the noblest born Phaiákians
paid court to thee, whose birth none can excel?      40
Go beg thy sovereign father, even at dawn,
to have the mule cart and the mules brought round
to take thy body-linen, gowns and mantles.
Thou shouldst ride, for it becomes thee more,
the washing pools are found so far from home."      45

On this word she departed, gray-eyed Athena,
to where the gods have their eternal dwelling—
as men say— in the fastness of Olympos.
Never a tremor of wind, or a splash of rain,
no errant snowflake comes to stain that heaven,      50
so calm, so vaporless, the world of light.

25. *Athena*: See note to *Iliad*, I, 227, p. 109. She shows Odysseus particular signs of her favor throughout the *Odyssey*.

Here, where the gay gods live their days of pleasure,
the gray-eyed one withdrew, leaving the princess.

And now Dawn took her own fair throne, awaking
the girl in the sweet gown, still charmed by dream.        55
Down through the rooms she went to tell her parents,
whom she found still at home: her mother seated
near the great hearth among her maids—and twirling
out of her distaff yarn dyed like the sea—;
her father at the door, bound for a council              60
of princes on petition of the gentry.
She went up close to him and softly said:

"My dear Papà, could you not send the mule cart
around for me—the gig with pretty wheels?
I must take all our things and get them washed           65
at the river pools; our linen is all soiled.
And you should wear fresh clothing, going to council
with counselors and first men of the realm.
Remember your five sons at home: though two
are married, we have still three bachelor sprigs;        70
they will have none but laundered clothes each time
they go to the dancing. See what I must think of!"

She had no word to say of her own wedding,
though her keen father saw her blush. Said he:

"No mules would I deny you, child, nor anything.         75
Go along, now; the grooms will bring your gig
with pretty wheels and the cargo box upon it."

He spoke to the stableman, who soon brought round
the cart, low-wheeled and nimble;
harnessed the mules, and backed them in the traces.      80
Meanwhile the girl fetched all her soiled apparel
to bundle in the polished wagon box.
Her mother, for their luncheon, packed a hamper
with picnic fare, and filled a skin of wine,
and, when the princess had been handed up,               85
gave her a golden bottle of olive oil
for softening girls' bodies, after bathing.
Nausikaa took the reins and raised her whip,
lashing the mules. What jingling! What a clatter!
But off they went in a ground-covering trot,             90
with princess, maids, and laundry drawn behind.

59. *distaff*: Staff holding wool or plant fibers to be spun.

By the lower river where the wagon came
were washing pools, with water all year flowing
in limpid spillways that no grime withstood.
The girls unhitched the mules, and sent them down          95
along the eddying stream to crop sweet grass.
Then sliding out the cart's tail board, they took
armloads of clothing to the dusky water,
and trod them in the pits, making a race of it.
All being drubbed, all blemish rinsed away,          100
they spread them, piece by piece, along the beach
whose pebbles had been laundered by the sea;
then took a dip themselves, and, all anointed
with golden oil, ate lunch beside the river
while the bright burning sun dried out their linen.          105
Princess and maids delighted in that feast;
then, putting off their veils,
they ran and passed a ball to a rhythmic beat,
Nausikaa flashing first with her white arms.

So Artemis goes flying after her arrows flown          110
down some tremendous valley-side—

Taÿgetos, Erymanthos—
chasing the mountain goats or ghosting deer,
with nymphs of the wild places flanking her;
and Lêto's heart delights to see them running,
for, taller by a head than nymphs can be,          115
the goddess shows more stately, all being beautiful.
So one could tell the princess from the maids.

Soon it was time, she knew, for riding homeward—
mules to be harnessed, linen folded smooth—
but the gray-eyed goddess Athena made her tarry,          120
so that Odysseus might behold her beauty
and win her guidance to the town.

It happened

when the king's daughter threw her ball off line
and missed, and put it in the whirling stream,—
at which they all gave such a shout, Odysseus          125
awoke and sat up, saying to himself:

"Now, by my life, mankind again! But who?
Savages, are they, strangers to courtesy?

---

101. *along the beach*: They did not
have to worry about the tide, as there is
almost no tide in the Mediterranean.
110. *Artemis*: Virgin goddess of the
hunt, and of women's natural deaths.

111. *Taÿgetos*: Mountain range near
Sparta. *Erymanthos*: Mountain in Arcadia.
114. *Lêto*: Lover of Zeus, to whom
she bore Artemis and Apollo.

Or gentle folk, who know and fear the gods?
That was a lusty cry of tall young girls—                          130
most like the cry of nymphs, who haunt the peaks,
and springs of brooks, and inland grassy places.
Or am I amid people of human speech?
Up again, man; and let me see for myself."

He pushed aside the bushes, breaking off                           135
with his great hand a single branch of olive,
whose leaves might shield him in his nakedness;
so came out rustling, like a mountain lion,
rain-drenched, wind-buffeted, but in his might at ease,
with burning eyes—who prowls among the herds                      140
or flocks, or after game, his hungry belly
taking him near stout homesteads for his prey.
Odysseus had this look, in his rough skin
advancing on the girls with pretty braids;
and he was driven on by hunger, too.                              145
Streaked with brine, and swollen, he terrified them,
so that they fled, this way and that. Only
Alkínoös' daughter stood her ground, being given
a bold heart by Athena, and steady knees.

She faced him, waiting. And Odysseus came,                        150
debating inwardly what he should do:
embrace this beauty's knees in supplication?
or stand apart, and, using honeyed speech,
inquire the way to town, and beg some clothing?
In his swift reckoning, he thought it best                       155
to trust in words to please her—and keep away;
he might anger the girl, touching her knees.
So he began, and let the soft words fall:

"Mistress: please: are you divine, or mortal?
If one of those who dwell in the wide heaven,                     160
you are most near to Artemis, I should say—
great Zeus's daughter—in your grace and presence.
If you are one of earth's inhabitants,
how blest your father, and your gentle mother,
blest all your kin. I know what happiness                        165
must send the warm tears to their eyes, each time
they see their wondrous child go to the dancing!
But one man's destiny is more than blest—
he who prevails, and takes you as his bride.
Never have I laid eyes on equal beauty                           170
in man or woman. I am hushed indeed.

So fair, one time, I thought a young palm tree
at Delos near the altar of Apollo—
I had troops under me when I was there
on the sea route that later brought me grief—                    175
but that slim palm tree filled my heart with wonder:
never came shoot from earth so beautiful.
So now, my lady, I stand in awe so great
I cannot take your knees. And yet my case is desperate:
twenty days, yesterday, in the winedark sea,                     180
on the ever-lunging swell, under gale winds,
getting away from the Island of Ogýgia.
And now the terror of Storm has left me stranded
upon this shore—with more blows yet to suffer,
I must believe, before the gods relent.                          185
Mistress, do me a kindness!
After much weary toil, I come to you,
and you are the first soul I have seen—I know
no others here. Direct me to the town,
give me a rag that I can throw around me,                        190
some cloth or wrapping that you brought along.
And may the gods accomplish your desire:
a home, a husband, and harmonious
converse with him—the best thing in the world
being a strong house held in serenity                           195
where man and wife agree. Woe to their enemies,
joy to their friends! But all this they know best."

Then she of the white arms, Nausikaa, replied:

"Stranger, there is no quirk or evil in you
that I can see. You know Zeus metes out fortune                  200
to good and bad men as it pleases him.
Hardship he sent to you, and you must bear it.
But now that you have taken refuge here
you shall not lack for clothing, or any other
comfort due to a poor man in distress.                          205
The town lies this way, and the men are called
Phaiákians, who own the land and city.
I am daughter to the Prince Alkinoös,
by whom the power of our people stands."

Turning, she called out to her maids-in-waiting:                210

"Stay with me! Does the sight of a man scare you?
Or do you take this one for an enemy?

173. *Delos*: The sacred island of Apollo, in the Cyclades.

Why, there's no fool so brash, and never will be,
as to bring war or pillage to this coast,
for we are dear to the immortal gods,                    215
living here, in the sea that rolls forever,
distant from other lands and other men.
No: this man is a castaway, poor fellow;
we must take care of him. Strangers and beggars
come from Zeus: a small gift, then, is friendly.         220
Give our new guest some food and drink, and take him
into the river, out of the wind, to bathe."

They stood up now, and called to one another
to go on back. Quite soon they led Odysseus
under the river bank, as they were bidden;               225
and there laid out a tunic, and a cloak,
and gave him olive oil in the golden flask.
"Here," they said, "go bathe in the flowing water."
But heard now from that kingly man, Odysseus:

"Maids," he said, "keep away a little; let me            230
wash the brine from my own back, and rub on
plenty of oil. It is long since my anointing.
I take no bath, however, where you see me—
naked before young girls with pretty braids."

They left him, then, and went to tell the princess.      235
And now Odysseus, dousing in the river,
scrubbed the coat of brine from back and shoulders
and rinsed the clot of sea-spume from his hair;
got himself all rubbed down, from head to foot,
then he put on the clothes the princess gave him.        240
Athena lent a hand, making him seem
taller, and massive too, with crisping hair
in curls like petals of wild hyacinth,
but all red-golden. Think of gold infused
on silver by a craftsman, whose fine art                 245
Hephaistos taught him, or Athena: one
whose work moves to delight: just so she lavished
beauty over Odysseus' head and shoulders.
Then he went down to sit on the sea beach
in his new splendor. There the girl regarded him,        250
and after a time she said to the maids beside her:

"My gentlewomen, I have a thing to tell you.
The Olympian gods cannot be all averse

246. *Hephaistos*: Patron god of craftsmen, especially workers in metal.

to this man's coming here among our islanders.                              255
Uncouth he seemed, I thought so, too, before;
but now he looks like one of heaven's people.
I wish my husband could be fine as he
and glad to stay forever on Skhería!

But have you given refreshment to our guest?"

At this the maids, all gravely listening, hastened              260
to set out bread and wine before Odysseus,
and ah! how ravenously that patient man
took food and drink, his long fast at an end.

The princess Nausikaa now turned aside
to fold her linens; in the pretty cart                                    265
she stowed them, put the mule team under harness,
mounted the driver's seat, and then looked down
to say with cheerful prompting to Odysseus:

"Up with you now, friend; back to town we go;
and I shall send you in before my father                            270
who is wondrous wise; there in our house with him
you'll meet the noblest of the Phaiákians.
You have good sense, I think; here's how to do it:
while we go through the countryside and farmland
stay with my maids, behind the wagon, walking                275
briskly enough to follow where I lead.
But near the town—well, there's a wall with towers
around the Isle, and beautiful ship basins
right and left of the causeway of approach;
seagoing craft are beached beside the road                          280
each on its launching ways. The agora,
with fieldstone benches bedded in the earth,
lies either side Poseidon's shrine—for there
men are at work on pitch-black hulls and rigging,
cables and sails, and tapering of oars.                                285
The archer's craft is not for the Phaiákians,
but ship designing, modes of oaring cutters
in which they love to cross the foaming sea.
From these fellows I will have no salty talk,
no gossip later. Plenty are insolent.                                   290
And some seadog might say, after we passed:
'Who is this handsome stranger trailing Nausikaa?

281. *agora:* Place of assembly.            types of sharp-prowed ships.
287. *modes of . . . cutters:* That is,

Where did she find him? Will he be her husband?
Or is she being hospitable to some rover
come off his ship from lands across the sea—                    295
there being no lands nearer. A god, maybe?
a god from heaven, the answer to her prayer,
descending now—to make her his forever?
Better, if she's roamed and found a husband
somewhere else: none of our own will suit her,                  300
though many come to court her, and those the best.'
This is the way they might make light of me.
And I myself should hold it shame
for any girl to flout her own dear parents,
taking up with a man, before her marriage.                      305

Note well, now, what I say, friend, and your chances
are excellent for safe conduct from my father.
You'll find black poplars in a roadside park
around a meadow and fountain—all Athena's—
but Father has a garden on the place—                           310
this within earshot of the city wall.
Go in there and sit down, giving us time
to pass through town and reach my father's house.
And when you can imagine we're at home,
than take the road into the city, asking                        315
directions to the palace of Alkínoös.
You'll find it easily: any small boy
can take you there; no family has a mansion
half so grand as he does, being king.
As soon as you are safe inside, cross over                      320
and go straight through into the mégaron
to find my mother. She'll be there in firelight
before a column, with her maids in shadow,
spinning a wool dyed richly as the sea.
My father's great chair faces the fire, too;                    325
there like a god he sits and takes his wine.
Go past him; cast yourself before my mother,
embrace her knees—and you may wake up soon
at home rejoicing, though your home be far.
On Mother's feeling much depends; if she                        330
looks on you kindly, you shall see your friends
under your own roof in your father's country."

At this she raised her glistening whip, lashing
the team into a run; they left the river
cantering beautifully, then trotted smartly.                    335

321. *mégaron*: Great hall of the palace.

But then she reined them in, and spared the whip,
so that her maids could follow with Odysseus.
The sun was going down when they went by
Athena's grove. Here, then, Odysseus rested,
and lifted up his prayer to Zeus's daughter:                340

"Hear me, unwearied child of royal Zeus!
O listen to me now—thou so aloof
while the Earthshaker wrecked and battered me.
May I find love and mercy among these people."

He prayed for that, and Pallas Athena heard him—           345
although in deference to her father's brother
she would not show her true form to Odysseus,
at whom Poseidon smoldered on
until the kingly man came home to his own shore.

[Odysseus follows Nausikaa's instructions and is received as a
guest in the palace by her mother Arêtê and her father Alkínoös,
who promises to help him return home.]

## *Book VIII*

Under the opening fingers of the dawn
Alkínoös, the sacred prince, arose,
and then arose Odysseus, raider of cities.
As the king willed, they went down by the shipways
to the assembly ground of the Phaiakians.                   5
Side by side the two men took their ease there
on smooth stone benches. Meanwhile Pallas Athena
roamed through the byways of the town, contriving
Odysseus' voyage home—in voice and feature
the crier of the king Alkínoös                              10
who stopped and passed the word to every man:

"Phaiákian lords and counselors, this way!
Come to assembly; learn about the stranger,
the new guest at the palace of Alkínoös—
a man the sea drove, but a comely man;                      15
the gods' own light is on him."

                                        She aroused them,
and soon the assembly ground and seats were filled
with curious men, a throng who peered and saw

343. *Earthshaker*: Odysseus has mortally offended Poseidon by blinding his
son, the Kyklops, Polyphêmos. The god
has pursued Odysseus with suffering on
the element he controls, the sea.
    345. *Pallas*: A title of Athena, of un-
certain meaning.
    10. *crier*: Herald.

the master mind of war, Laërtês' son.
Athena now poured out her grace upon him,                           20
head and shoulders, height and mass—a splendor
awesome to the eyes of the Phaiákians;
she put him in a fettle to win the day,
mastering every trial they set to test him.
When all the crowd sat marshalled, quieted,                         25
Alkínoös addressed the full assembly:

"Hear me, lords and captains of the Phaiákians!
Hear what my heart would have me say!
Our guest and new friend—nameless to me still—
comes to my house after long wandering                              30
in Dawn lands, or among the Sunset races.
Now he appeals to me for conveyance home.
As in the past, therefore, let us provide
passage, and quickly, for no guest of mine
languishes here for lack of it. Look to it:                         35
get a black ship afloat on the noble sea,
and pick our fastest sailer; draft a crew
of two and fifty from our younger townsmen—
men who have made their names at sea. Loop oars
well to your tholepins, lads, then leave the ship,                  40
come to our house, fall to, and take your supper:
we'll furnish out a feast for every crewman.
These are your orders. As for my older peers
and princes of the realm, let them foregather
in festival for our friend in my great hall;                        45
and let no man refuse. Call in our minstrel,
Demódokos, whom God made lord of song,
heart-easing, sing upon what theme he will."

He turned, led the procession, and those princes
followed, while his herald sought the minstrel.                     50
Young oarsmen from the assembly chose a crew
of two and fifty, as the king commanded,
and these filed off along the waterside
to where the ship lay, poised above open water.
They hauled the black hull down to ride the sea,                    55
rigging a mast and spar in the black ship,
with oars at trail from corded rawhide, all
seamanly; then tried the white sail, hoisting,
and moored her off the beach. Then going ashore

---

19. *Laërtês*: The old king of Ithaka.          56. *spar*: Crosspiece at the top of the
40. *Tholepins*: Pegs serving as oar-           mast, to which the sail is fastened.
locks.

the crew went up to the great house of Alkínoös.                    60
Here the enclosures, entrance ways, and rooms
were filled with men, young men and old, for whom
Alkínoös had put twelve sheep to sacrifice,
eight tuskers and a pair of shambling oxen.
These, now, they flayed and dressed to make their banquet.          65
The crier soon came, leading that man of song
whom the Muse cherished; by her gift he knew
the good of life, and evil—
for she who lent him sweetness made him blind.
Pontónoös fixed a studded chair for him                             70
hard by a pillar amid the banqueters,
hanging the taut harp from a peg above him,
and guided up his hands upon the strings;
placed a bread basket at his side, and poured
wine in a cup, that he might drink his fill.                        75
Now each man's hand went out upon the banquet.

In time, when hunger and thirst were turned away,
the Muse brought to the minstrel's mind a song
of heroes whose great fame rang under heaven:
the clash between Odysseus and Akhilleus,                           80
how one time they contended at the godfeast
raging, and the marshal, Agamémnon,
felt inward joy over his captains' quarrel;
for such had been foretold him by Apollo
at Pytho—hallowed height—when the Akhaian                          85
crossed that portal of rock to ask a sign—
in the old days when grim war lay ahead
for Trojans and Danaans, by God's will.
So ran the tale the minstrel sang. Odysseus
with massive hand drew his rich mantle down                        90
over his brow, cloaking his face with it,
to make the Phaiákians miss the secret tears
that started to his eyes. How skillfully
he dried them when the song came to a pause!
thew back his mantle, spilt his gout of wine!                       95
But soon the minstrel plucked his note once more

64. *tuskers*: Boars.
67. *Muse*: Goddess of the arts, source
of artistic inspiration.
70. *Pontónoös*: The herald of Alkínoös.
80. *clash*: This is the only reference to
a quarrel between Odysseus and Akhilleus. This story was perhaps told in
some epic poem now lost.
81. *godfeast*: A religious festival.

85. *Pytho*: Apollo's prophetic shrine
at Delphi. It seems to be implied that
Apollo had foretold the fall of Troy after
such a quarrel, hence Agamémnon's "inward joy." *the Akhaian*: The Greek;
here, Agamémnon.
88. *Danaans*: Greeks.
95. *spilt . . . wine*: As an offering to
the gods.

to please the Phaiákian lords, who loved the song;
then in his cloak Odysseus wept again.
His tears flowed in the mantle unperceived:
only Alkínoös, at his elbow, saw them,                                    100
and caught the low groan in the man's breathing.
At once he spoke to all the seafolk round him:

"Hear me, lords and captains of the Phaiákians.
Our meat is shared, our hearts are full of pleasure
from the clear harp tone that accords with feasting;            105
now for the field and track; we shall have trials
in the pentathlon. Let our guest go home
and tell his friends what champions we are
at boxing, wrestling, broadjump and foot racing."

On this he led the way and all went after.                            110
The crier unslung and pegged the shining harp
and, taking Demódokos's hand,
led him along with all the rest—Phaiákian
peers, gay amateurs of the great games.
They gained the common, where a crowd was forming,     115
and many a young athlete now came forward
with seaside names like Tipmast, Tiderace, Sparwood,
Hullman, Sternman, Beacher and Pullerman,
Bluewater, Shearwater, Runningwake, Boardalee,
Seabelt, son of Grandfleet Shipwrightson;                          120
Seareach stepped up, son of the Launching Master,
rugged as Arês, bane of men; his build
excelled all but the Prince Laódamas;
and Laódamas made entry with his brothers,
Halios and Klytóneus, sons of the king.                              125
The runners, first, must have their quarter mile.
All lined up tense; then Go! and down the track
they raised the dust in a flying bunch, strung out
longer and longer behind Prince Klytóneus.
By just so far as a mule team, breaking ground,                 130
will distance oxen, he left all behind
and came up to the crowd, an easy winner.
Then they made room for wrestling—grinding bouts
that Seareach won, pinning the strongest men;
then the broadjump; first place went to Seabelt;              135
Sparwood gave the discus the mightiest fling,

107. *pentathlon*: Literally, 'five-contests'. At the great games, the event
consisted of competition in long-jump,
footrace, discus-throw, javelin-throw, and
wrestling.
111. *crier*: Herald.
122. *Arês*: God of war.

and Prince Laódamas outboxed them all.
Now it was he, the son of Alkínoös,
who said when they had run through these diversions:

"Look here friends, we ought to ask the stranger          140
if he competes in something. He's no cripple;
look at his leg muscles and his forearms.
Neck like a bollard; strong as a bull, he seems;
and not old, though he may have gone stale under
the rough times he had. Nothing like the sea          145
for wearing out the toughest man alive."

Then Seareach took him up at once, and said:

"Laódamas, you're right, by all powers.
Go up to him, yourself, and put the question."

At this, Alkínoös' tall son advanced          150
to the center ground, and there addressed Odysseus:

"Friend, Excellency, come join our competition,
if you are practiced, as you seem to be.
While a man lives he wins no greater honor
than footwork and the skill of hands can bring him.          155
Enter our games, then; ease your heart of trouble.
Your journey home is not far off, remember;
the ship is launched, the crew all primed for sea."

Odysseus, canniest of men, replied:

"Laódamas, why do you young chaps challenge me?          160
I have more on my mind than track and field—
hard days, and many, have I seen, and suffered.
I sit here at your field meet, yes; but only
as one who begs your king to send him home."

Now Seareach put his words in, and contentiously:          165

"The reason being, as I see it, friend,
you never learned a sport, and have no skill
in any of the contests of fighting men.
You must have been the skipper of some tramp
that crawled from one port to the next, jam full          170
of chaffering hands: a tallier of cargoes,
itching for gold—not, by your looks, an athlete."

143. *bollard*: Massive post on a dock, to which a large ship may be made fast.

Odysseus frowned, and eyed him coldly, saying:

"That was uncalled for, friend, you talk like a fool.
The gods deal out no gift, this one or any—                        175
birth, brains, or speech—to every man alike.
In looks a man may be a shade, a specter,
and yet be master of speech so crowned with beauty
that people gaze at him with pleasure. Courteous,
sure of himself, he can command assemblies,                       180
and when he comes to town, the crowds gather.
A handsome man, contrariwise, may lack
grace and good sense in everything he says.
You now, for instance, with your fine physique—
a god's, indeed—you have an empty noddle.                         185
I find my heart inside my ribs aroused
by your impertinence. I am no stranger
to contests, as you fancy. I rated well
when I could count on youth and my two hands.
Now pain has cramped me, and my years of combat                   190
hacking through ranks in war, and the bitter sea.
Aye. Even so I'll give your games a trial.
You spoke heart-wounding words. You shall be answered."

He leapt out, cloaked as he was, and picked a discus,
a rounded stone, more ponderous than those                        195
already used by the Phaiákian throwers,
and, whirling, let it fly from his great hand
with a low hum. The crowd went flat on the ground—
all those oar-pulling, seafaring Phaiákians—
under the rushing noise. The spinning disk                        200
soared out, light as a bird, beyond all others.
Disguised now as a Phaiákian, Athena
staked it and called out:

                                        "Even a blind man,
friend, could judge this, finding with his fingers
one discus, quite alone, beyond the cluster.                       205
Congratulations; this event is yours;
not a man here can beat you or come near you."

That was a cheering hail, Odysseus thought,
seeing one friend there on the emulous field,
so, in relief, he turned among the Phaiákians                      210
and said:

                                "Now come alongside that one, lads.
The next I'll send as far, I think, or farther.

Anyone else on edge for competition
try me now. By heaven, you angered me.
Racing, wrestling, boxing—I bar nothing          215
with any man except Laódamas,
for he's my host. Who quarrels with his host?
Only a madman—or no man at all—
would challenge his protector among strangers,
cutting the ground away under his feet.          220
Here are no others I will not engage,
none but I hope to know what he is made of.
Inept at combat, am I? Not entirely.
Give me a smooth bow; I can handle it,
and I might well be first to hit my man          225
amid a swarm of enemies, though archers
in company around me drew together.
Philoktêtês alone, at Troy, when we
Akhaians took the bow, used to outshoot me.
Of men who now eat bread upon the earth          230
I hold myself the best hand with a bow—
conceding mastery to the men of old,
Heraklês, or Eurýtos of Oikhalía,
heroes who vied with gods in bowmanship.
Eurýtos came to grief, it's true; old age          235
never crept over him in his long hall;
Apollo took his challenge ill, and killed him.
What then, the spear? I'll plant it like an arrow.
Only in sprinting, I'm afraid, I may
be passed by someone. Roll of the sea waves          240
wearied me, and the victuals in my ship
ran low; my legs are flabby."

                                    When he finished,
the rest were silent, but Alkínoös answered:

"Friend, we take your challenge in good part,
for this man angered and affronted you          245
here at our peaceful games. You'd have us note
the prowess that is in you, and so clearly,
no man of sense would ever cry it down!
Come, turn your mind, now, on a thing to tell
among your peers when you are home again,          250
dining in hall, beside your wife and children:
I mean our prowess, as you may remember it,
for we, too, have our skills, given by Zeus,
and practiced from our father's time to this—

228. *Philoktêtês*: A famous archer,     of Heraklês.
who had inherited the bow and arrows

not in the boxing ring nor the palestra                                    255
conspicuous, but in racing, land or sea;
and all our days we set great store by feasting,
harpers, and the grace of dancing choirs,
changes of dress, warm baths, and downy beds.
O master dancers of the Phaiákians!                                        260
Perform now: let our guest on his return
tell his companions we excel the world
in dance and song, as in our ships and running.
Someone go find the gittern harp in hall
and bring it quickly to Demódokos!"                                        265

At the serene king's word, a squire ran
to bring the polished harp out of the palace,
and place was given to nine referees—
peers of the realm, masters of ceremony—
who cleared a space and smoothed a dancing floor.                          270
The squire brought down, and gave Demódokos,
the clear-toned harp; and centering on the minstrel
magical young dancers formed a circle
with a light beat, and stamp of feet. Beholding,
Odysseus marvelled at the flashing ring.                                   275

Now to his harp the blinded minstrel sang
of Arês' dalliance with Aphroditê:
how hidden in Hephaistos' house they played
at love together, and the gifts of Arês,
dishonoring Hephaistos' bed—and how                                        280
the word that wounds the heart came to the master
from Hêlios, who had seen the two embrace;
and when he learned it, Lord Hephaistos went
with baleful calculation to his forge.
There mightily he armed his anvil block                                    285
and hammered out a chain, whose tempered links
could not be sprung or bent; he meant that they should hold.
Those shackles fashioned, hot in wrath Hephaistos
climbed to the bower and the bed of love,
pooled all his net of chain around the bed posts                           290
and swung it from the rafters overhead—
light as a cobweb even gods in bliss
could not perceive, so wonderful his cunning.
Seeing his bed now made a snare, he feigned

255. *palestra*: Wrestling-ground.
264. *gittern*: Shaped like a guitar.
278. *Hephaistos' house*: Aphroditê was
married to Hephaistos (though in *Iliad*

Book XVIII he is married to Grace).
282. *Hêlios*: The sun, who on his
daily journey across the sky sees everything.

a journey to the trim stronghold of Lemnos,          295
the dearest of earth's towns to him. And Arês?
Ah, golden Arês' watch had its reward
when he,beheld the great smith leaving home.
How promptly to the famous door he came,
intent on pleasure with sweet Kythereia!          300
She, who had left her father's side but now,
sat in her chamber when her lover entered;
and tenderly he pressed her hand and said:

"Come and lie down, my darling, and be happy!
Hephaistos is no longer here, but gone          305
to see his grunting Sintian friends on Lemnos."

As she, too, thought repose would be most welcome,
the pair went in to bed—into a shower
of clever chains, the netting of Hephaistos.
So trussed, they could not move apart, nor rise,          310
at last they knew there could be no escape,
they were to see the glorious cripple now—
for Hêlios had spied for him, and told him;
so he turned back, this side of Lemnos Isle,
sick at heart, making his way homeward.          315
Now in the doorway of the room he stood
while deadly rage took hold of him; his voice,
hoarse and terrible, reached all the gods:

"O Father Zeus, O gods in bliss forever,
here is indecorous entertainment for you,          320
Aphroditê, Zeus's daughter,
caught in the act, cheating me, her cripple,
with Arês—devastating Arês.
Cleanlimbed beauty is her joy, not these
bandylegs I came into the world with:          325
no one to blame but the two gods who bred me!
Come see this pair entwining here
in my own bed! How hot it makes me burn!
I think they may not care to lie much longer,
pressing on one another, passionate lovers;          330
they'll have enough of bed together soon.
And yet the chain that bagged them holds them down

---

295. *Lemnos*: An island in the Aegean sea. As to why it was "dearest" to him, see *Iliad*, I, 686–688.

300. *Kythereia*: Aphroditê, goddess of love, daughter of Zeus, king of the gods. She was born from the sea near Kythera, a large island off the southeast coast of Greece.

301. *her father*: Zeus.

306. *Sintian*: The Sintians preceded the Greeks as inhabitants of Lemnos.

326. *two gods that bred me*: Zeus and Hêra; she was his wife and sister, and the goddess of marriage.

till Father sends me back my wedding gifts—
all that I poured out for his damned pigeon,
so lovely, and so wanton."

                                           **All the others** 335
were crowding in, now, to the brazen house—
Poseidon who embraces earth, and Hermês
the runner, and Apollo, lord of Distance.
The goddesses stayed home for shame; but these
munificences ranged there in the doorway,                 340
and irrepressible among them all
arose the laughter of the happy gods.
Gazing hard at Hephaistos' handiwork
the gods in turn remarked among themselves:

"No dash in adultery now."

                             "The tortoise tags the hare— 345
Hephaistos catches Arês—and Arês outran the wind."

"The lame god's craft has pinned him. Now shall he
pay what is due from gods taken in cuckoldry."

They made these improving remarks to one another,
but Apollo leaned aside to say to Hermês:                 350

"Son of Zeus, beneficient Wayfinder,
would you accept a coverlet of chain, if only
you lay by Aphroditê's golden side?"

To this the Wayfinder replied, shining:

"Would I not, though, Apollo of distances!             355
Wrap me in chains three times the weight of these,
come goddesses and gods to see the fun;
only let me lie beside the pale-golden one!"

The gods gave way again to peals of laughter,
all but Poseidon, and he never smiled,                 360
bur urged Hephaistos to unpinion Arês,
saying emphatically, in a loud voice:

                                        "Free him;
you will be paid, I swear; ask what you will;
he pays up every jot the gods decree."

---

337. *Hermes*: The gods' messenger.
338. *Apollo, lord of Distance*: God of
prophecy, music, medicine, and archery.     The epithet is also translated, "one who
works from afar."

To this the Great Gamelegs replied:

"Poseidon, 365
lord of the earth-surrounding sea, I should not
swear to a scoundrel's honor. What have I
as surety from you, if Arês leaves me
empty-handed, with my empty chain?"

The Earth-shaker for answer urged again: 370

"Hephaistos, let us grant he goes, and leaves
the fine unpaid; I swear, then, I shall pay it."

Then said the Great Gamelegs at last:

"No more;
you offer terms I cannot well refuse."

And down the strong god bent to set them free, 375
till disencumbered of their bond, the chain,
the lovers leapt away—he into Thrace,
while Aphroditê, laughter's darling, fled
to Kypros Isle and Paphos, to her meadow
and altar dim with incense. There the Graces 380
bathed and anointed her with golden oil—
a bloom that clings upon immortal flesh alone—
and let her folds of mantle fall in glory.

So ran the song the minstrel sang.

Odysseus,
listening, found sweet pleasure in the tale, 385
among the Phaiákian mariners and oarsmen.
And next Alkínoös called upon his sons,
Halios and Laódamas, to show
the dance no one could do as well as they—
handling a purple ball carven by Pólybos. 390
One made it shoot up under the shadowing clouds
as he leaned backward; bounding high in air
the other cut its flight far off the ground—
and neither missed a step as the ball soared.
The next turn was to keep it low, and shuttling 395
hard between them, while the ring of boys
gave them a steady stamping beat.

365. *Gamelegs*: Hephaistos was lame.    Aphroditê.
379. *Kypros*: Cyprus. Paphos was its    380. *Graces*: Goddesses of beauty and
principal city, famous for its temple to    refinement.

Odysseus now addressed Alkínoös:

"O majesty, model of all your folk,
your promise was to show me peerless dancers;   400
here is the promise kept. I am all wonder."

At this Alkínoös in his might rejoicing
said to the seafarers of Phaiákia:

"Attend me now, Phaiákian lords and captains:
our guest appears a clear-eyed man and wise.   405
Come, let him feel our bounty as he should.
Here are twelve princes of the kingdom—lords
paramount, and I who make thirteen;
let each one bring a laundered cloak and tunic,
and add one bar of honorable gold.   410
Heap all our gifts together; load his arms;
let him go joyous to our evening feast!
As for Seareach—why, man to man
he'll make amends, and handsomely; he blundered."

Now all as one acclaimed the king's good pleasure,   415
and each one sent a squire to bring his gifts.
Meanwhile Seareach found speech again, saying:

"My lord and model of us all, Alkínoös,
as you require of me, in satisfaction,
this broadsword of clear bronze goes to our guest.   420
Its hilt is silver, and the ringed sheath
of new-sawn ivory—a costly weapon."

He turned to give the broadsword to Odysseus,
facing him, saying blithely:

                                        "Sir, my best
wishes, my respects; if I offended,   425
I hope the seawinds blow it out of mind.
God send you see your lady and your homeland
soon again, after the pain of exile."

Odysseus, the great tactician, answered:

"My hand, friend; may the gods award you fortune.   430
I hope no pressing need comes on you ever
for this fine blade you give me in amends."

He slung it, glinting silver, from his shoulder,
as the light shone from sundown. Messengers

were bearing gifts and treasure to the palace,                    435
where the king's sons received them all, and made
a glittering pile at their grave mother's side;
then, as Alkínoös took his throne of power,
each went to his own high-backed chair in turn,
and said Alkínoös to Arêtê:                                        440

"Lady, bring here a chest, the finest one;
a clean cloak and tunic; stow these things;
and warm a cauldron for him. Let him bathe,
when he has seen the gifts of the Phaiákians,
and so dine happily to a running song.                            445
My own wine-cup of gold intaglio
I'll give him, too; through all the days to come,
tipping his wine to Zeus or other gods
in his great hall, he shall remember me."

Then said Arêtê to her maids:

                              "The tripod:                        450
stand the great tripod legs about the fire."

They swung the cauldron on the fire's heart,
poured water in, and fed the blaze beneath
until the basin simmered, cupped in flame.
The queen set out a rich chest from her chamber                   455
and folded in the gifts—clothing and gold
given Odysseus by the Phaiákians;
then she put in the royal cloak and tunic,
briskly saying to her guest:

                              "Now here, sir,
look to the lid yourself, and tie it down                         460
against light fingers, if there be any,
on the black ship tonight while you are sleeping."

Noble Odysseus, expert in adversity,
battened the lid down with a lightning knot
learned, once, long ago, from the Lady Kirkê.                     465
And soon a call came from the Bathing Mistress
who led him to a hip-bath, warm and clear—
a happy sight, and rare in his immersions
after he left Kalypso's home—where, surely,
the luxuries of a god were ever his.                              470

446. *intaglio*: With designs cut into it
in inverse relief.
465. *Kirkê*: (Circe) a sorceress who
kept Odysseus on her island for several
months.
470. *luxuries of a god*: Kalypso was
immortal, and did indeed entertain Odysseus royally.

When the bath maids had washed him, rubbed him down,
put a fresh tunic and a cloak around him,
he left the bathing place to join the men
at wine in hall.

                            The princess Nausikaa,
exquisite figure, as of heaven's shaping,           475
waited beside a pillar as he passed
and said swiftly, with wonder in her look:

"Fare well, stranger; in your land remember me
who met and saved you. It is worth your thought."

The man of all occasions now met this:         480

"Daughter of great Alkínoös, Nausikaa,
may Zeus the lord of thunder, Hera's consort,
grant me daybreak again in my own country!
But there and all my days until I die
may I invoke you as I would a goddess,         485
princess, to whom I owe my life."

                                  He left her
and went to take his place beside the king.

Now when the roasts were cut, the winebowls full,
a herald led the minstrel down the room
amid the deference of the crowd, and paused      490
to seat him near a pillar in the center—
whereupon that resourceful man, Odysseus,
carved out a quarter from his chine of pork,
crisp with fat, and called the blind man's guide:

"Herald! here, take this to Demódokos:        495
let him feast and be merry, with my compliments.
All men owe honor to the poets—honor
and awe, for they are dearest to the Muse
who puts upon their lips the ways of life."

Gentle Demódokos took the proffered gift       500
and inwardly rejoiced. When all were served,
every man's hand went out upon the banquet,
repelling hunger and thirst, until at length
Odysseus spoke again to the blind minstrel:

"Demódokos, accept my utmost praise.         505
The Muse, daughter of Zeus in radiance,

493. *chine*: Back.

or else Apollo gave you skill to shape
with such great style your songs of the Akhaians—
their hard lot, how they fought and suffered war.
You shared it, one would say, or heard it all.                    510
Now shift your theme, and sing that wooden horse
Epeios built, inspired by Athena—
the ambuscade Odysseus filled with fighters
and sent to take the inner town of Troy.
Sing only this for me, sing me this well,                         515
and I shall say at once before the world
the grace of heaven has given us a song."

The minstrel stirred, murmuring to the god, and soon
clear words and notes came one by one, a vision
of the Akhaians in their graceful ships                          520
drawing away from shore: the torches flung
and shelters flaring: Argive soldiers crouched
in the close dark around Odysseus: and
the horse, tall on the assembly ground of Troy.
For when the Trojans pulled it in, themselves,                   525
up to the citadel, they sat nearby
with long-drawn-out and hapless argument—
favoring, in the end, one course of three:
either to stave the vault with brazen axes,
or haul it to a cliff and pitch it down,                         530
or else to save it for the gods, a votive glory—
the plan that could not but prevail.
For Troy must perish, as ordained, that day
she harbored the great horse of timber; hidden
the flower of Akhaia lay, and bore                               535
slaughter and death upon the men of Troy.
He sang, then, of the town sacked by Akhaians
pouring down from the horse's hollow cave,
this way and that way raping the steep city,
and how Odysseus came like Arês to                               540
the door of Deïphobos, with Meneláos,
and braved the desperate fight there—
conquering once more by Athena's power.

The splendid minstrel sang it.

                                     **And Odysseus**
let the bright molten tears run down his cheeks,                 545
weeping the way a wife mourns for her lord
on the lost field where he has gone down fighting

---

511. The story of the wooden horse
and the fall of Troy is told in *The
Aeneid*, II, p. 589.

531. *votive*: As an offering in thanks
for Troy's deliverance.

the day of wrath that came upon his children.
At sight of the man panting and dying there,
she slips down to enfold him, crying out;                      550
then feels the spears, prodding her back and shoulders,
and goes bound into slavery and grief.
Piteous weeping wears away her cheeks:
but no more piteous than Odysseus' tears,
cloaked as they were, now, from the company.                   555
Only Alkínoös, at his elbow, knew—
hearing the low sob in the man's breathing—
and when he knew, he spoke:

"Hear me, lords and captains of Phaiákia!
And let Demódokos touch his harp no more.                       560
His theme has not been pleasing to all here.
During the feast, since our fine poet sang,
our guest has never left off weeping. Grief
seems fixed upon his heart. Break off the song!
Let everyone be easy, host and guest;                           565
there's more decorum in a smiling banquet!
We had prepared here, on our friend's behalf,
safe conduct in a ship, and gifts to cheer him,
holding that any man with a grain of wit
will treat a decent suppliant like a brother.                   570
Now by the same rule, friend, you must not be
secretive any longer! Come, in fairness,
tell me the name you bore in that far country;
how were you known to family, and neighbors?
No man is nameless—no man, good or bad,                         575
but gets a name in his first infancy,
none being born, unless a mother bears him!
Tell me your native land, your coast and city—
sailing directions for the ships, you know—
for those Phaiákian ships of ours                               580
that have no steersman, and no steering oar,
divining the crew's wishes, as they do,
and knowing, as they do, the ports of call
about the world. Hidden in mist or cloud
they scud the open sea, with never a thought                    585
of being in distress or going down.
There is, however, something I once heard
Nausíthoös, my father, say: Poseidon
holds it against us that our deep sea ships
are sure conveyance for all passengers.                         590
My father said, some day one of our cutters

591–594. This prophecy is fulfilled. Poseidon, angry at the Phaiákians for taking Odysseus back to his home on Ithaka, turns the Phaiákian ship to stone
as it returns, and throws a range of hills
around the city.

homeward bound over the cloudy sea
would be wrecked by the god, and a range of hills
thrown round our city. So, in his age, he said,
and let it be, or not, as the god please.                       595
But come, now, put it for me clearly, tell me
the sea ways that you wandered, and the shores
you touched; the cities, and the men therein,
uncivilized, if such there were, and hostile,
and those godfearing who had kindly manners.                    600
Tell me why you should grieve so terribly
over the Argives and the fall of Troy.
That was all gods' work, weaving ruin there
so it should make a song for men to come!
Some kin of yours, then, died at Ilion,                         605
some first rate man, by marriage near to you,
next your own blood most dear?
Or some companion of congenial mind
and valor? True it is, a wise friend
can take a brother's place in our affection."                   610

## Book IX

Now this was the reply Odysseus made:
"Alkínoös, king and admiration of men,
how beautiful this is, to hear a minstrel
gifted as yours: a god he might be, singing!
There is no boon in life more sweet, I say,                     5
than when a summer joy holds all the realm,
and banqueters sit listening to a harper
in a great hall, by rows of tables heaped
with bread and roast meat, while a steward goes
to dip up wine and brim your cups again.                        10
Here is the flower of life, it seems to me!
But now you wish to know my cause for sorrow—
and thereby give me cause for more.
                                          What shall I
say first? What shall I keep until the end?
The gods have tried me in a thousand ways.                      15
But first my name: let that be known to you,
and if I pull away from pitiless death,
friendship will bind us, though my land lies far.

I am Laërtês' son, Odysseus.
                                  Men hold me
formidable for guile in peace and war:                          20
this fame has gone abroad to the sky's rim.
My home is on the peaked sea-mark of Ithaka

under Mount Neion's wind-blown robe of leaves,
in sight of other islands—Doulíkhion,
Samê, wooded Zakynthos—Ithaka 25
being most lofty in that coastal sea,
and northwest, while the rest lie east and south.
A rocky isle, but good for a boy's training;
I shall not see on earth a place more dear,
though I have been detained long by Kalypso, 30
loveliest among goddesses, who held me
in her smooth caves, to be her heart's delight,
as Kirkê of Aiaia, the enchantress,
desired me, and detained me in her hall.
But in my heart I never gave consent. 35
Where shall a man find sweetness to surpass
his own home and his parents? In far lands
he shall not, though he find a house of gold.

What of my sailing, then, from Troy?
                           What of those years
of rough adventure, weathered under Zeus? 40
The wind that carried west from Ilion
brought me to Ísmaros, on the far shore,
a strongpoint on the coast of the Kikonês.
I stormed that place and killed the men who fought.
Plunder we took, and we enslaved the women, 45
to make division, equal shares to all—
but on the spot I told them: 'Back, and quickly!
Out to sea again!' My men were mutinous,
fools, on stores of wine. Sheep after sheep
they butchered by the surf, and shambling cattle, 50
feasting,—while fugitives went inland, running
to call to arms the main force of Kikonês.
This was an army, trained to fight on horseback
or, where the ground required, on foot. They came
with dawn over that terrain like the leaves 55
and blades of spring. So doom appeared to us,
dark word of Zeus for us, our evil days.
My men stood up and made a fight of it—
backed on the ships, with lances kept in play,
from bright morning through the blaze of noon 60
holding our beach, although so far outnumbered;
but when the sun passed toward unyoking time,
then the Akhaians, one by one, gave way.
Six benches were left empty in every ship

43. *Kikonês:* **allies of the Trojans,**
**but Odysseus does not even mention.**
this fact to excuse his piratical raid; he
did not think any excuse was needed.

that evening when we pulled away from death.    65
And this new grief we bore with us to sea:
our precious lives we had, but not our friends.
No ship made sail next day until some shipmate
had raised a cry, three times, for each poor ghost
unfleshed by the Kikonês on that field.    70

Now Zeus the lord of cloud roused in the north
a storm against the ships, and driving veils
of squall moved down like night on land and sea.
The bows went plunging at the gust; sails
cracked and lashed out strips in the big wind.    75
We saw death in that fury, dropped the yards,
unshipped the oars, and pulled for the nearest lee:
then two long days and nights we lay offshore
worn out and sick at heart, tasting our grief,
until a third Dawn came with ringlets shining.    80
Then we put up our masts, hauled sail, and rested,
letting the steersmen and the breeze take over.

I might have made it safely home, that time,
but as I came round Malea the current
took me out to sea, and from the north    85
a fresh gale drove me on, past Kythera.
Nine days I drifted on the teeming sea
before dangerous high winds. Upon the tenth
we came to the coastline of the Lotos Eaters,
who live upon that flower. We landed there    90
to take on water. All ships' companies
mustered alongside for the mid-day meal.
Then I sent out two picked men and a runner
to learn what race of men that land sustained.
They fell in, soon enough, with Lotos Eaters,    95
who showed no will to do us harm, only
offering the sweet Lotos to our friends—
but those who ate this honeyed plant, the Lotos,
never cared to report, nor to return:
they longed to stay forever, browsing on    100
that native bloom, forgetful of their homeland.
I drove them, all three wailing, to the ships,

---

76–77. *Dropped the yards*: Took in
the sail. *unshipped the oars*: I.e. got
ready to row. *lee*: Shore offering shelter
from the wind.

84. *Malea*: the southeastern tip of the
Peloponnese peninsula of Greece.

89. *Lotos Eaters*: It is generally
thought that this story contains some
memory of early Greek contact with
North Africa; the north wind Odysseus
describes would have taken him to the
area of Cyrenaica, modern Libya. Modern identifications of the lotos range
from dates to hashish.

tied them down under their rowing benches,
and called the rest: 'All hands aboard;
come, clear the beach and no one taste                    105
the Lotos, or you lose your hope of home.'
Filing in to their places by the rowlocks
my oarsmen dipped their long oars in the surf,
and we moved out again on our sea faring.

In the next land we found were Kyklopês,                  110
giants, louts, without a law to bless them.
In ignorance leaving the fruitage of the earth in mystery
to the immortal gods, they neither plow
nor sow by hand, nor till the ground, though grain—
wild wheat and barley—grows untended, and            115
wine-grapes, in clusters, ripen in heaven's rain.
Kyklopês have no muster and no meeting,
no consultation or old tribal ways,
but each one dwells in his own mountain cave
dealing out rough justice to wife and child,              120
indifferent to what the others do.
                              Well, then:
across the wide bay from the mainland
there lies a desert island, not far out,
but still not close inshore. Wild goats in hundreds
breed there; and no human being comes                    125
upon the isle to startle them—no hunter
of all who ever tracked with hounds through forests
or had rough going over mountain trails.
The isle, unplanted and untilled, a wilderness,
pastures goats alone. And this is why:                    130
good ships like ours with cheekpaint at the bows
are far beyond the Kyklopês. No shipwright
toils among them, shaping and building up
symmetrical trim hulls to cross the sea
and visit all the seaboard towns, as men do              135
who go and come in commerce over water.
This isle—seagoing folk would have annexed it
and built their homesteads on it: all good land,
fertile for every crop in season: lush
well-watered meads along the shore, vines in profusion,  140
prairie, clear for the plow, where grain would grow
chin high by harvest time, and rich sub-soil.
The island cove is landlocked, so you need

110. *next land:* According to ancient
tradition the Kyklopes lived in Sicily.
131. *cheekpaint:* On a Greek ship an
emblem (often shown as a huge eye on
vase-paintings) was painted on the bows.

no hawsers out astern, bow-stones or mooring:
run in and ride there till the day your crews                    145
chafe to be under sail, and a fair wind blows.
You'll find good water flowing from a cavern
through dusky poplars into the upper bay.
Here we made harbor. Some god guided us
that night, for we could barely see our bows                     150
in the dense fog around us, and no moonlight
filtered through the overcast. No look-out,
nobody saw the island dead ahead,
nor even the great landward rolling billow
that took us in: we found ourselves in shallows,                 155
keels grazing shore: so furled our sails
and disembarked where the low ripples broke.
There on the beach we lay, and slept till morning.

When Dawn spread out her finger tips of rose
we turned out marvelling, to tour the isle,                      160
while Zeus's shy nymph daughters flushed wild goats
down from the heights—a breakfast for my men.
We ran to fetch our hunting bows and long-shanked
lances from the ships, and in three companies
we took our shots. Heaven gave us game a-plenty:                 165
for every one of twelve ships in my squadron
nine goats fell to be shared; my lot was ten.
So there all day, until the sun went down,
we made our feast on meat galore, and wine—
wine from the ship, for our supply held out,                     170
so many jars were filled at Ismaros
from stores of the Kikonês that we plundered.
We gazed, too, at Kyklopês Land, so near,
we saw their smoke, heard bleating from their flocks.
But after sundown, in the gathering dusk,                        175
we slept again above the wash of ripples.

When the young Dawn with finger tips of rose
came in the east, I called my men together
and made a speech to them:
                    'Old shipmates, friends,
the rest of you stand by; I'll make the crossing                 180
in my own ship, with my own company,
and find out what the mainland natives are—
for they may be wild savages, and lawless,
or hospitable and god fearing men.'

<hr>

144. *bow-stones:* a primitive anchor made of a stone attached to a rope.
145. *hawsers . . . mooring:* cf. *Iliad*, I, 501–502 and note, p. 111.
161. *nymph daughters:* Mountain nymphs.

At this I went aboard, and gave the word                185
to cast off by the stern. My oarsmen followed,
filing in to their benches by the rowlocks,
and all in line dipped oars in the grey sea.

As we rowed on, and nearer to the mainland,
at one end of the bay, we saw a cavern                  190
yawning above the water, screened with laurel,
and many rams and goats about the place
inside a sheepfold—made from slabs of stone
earthfast between tall trunks of pine and rugged
towering oak trees.
           A prodigious man                  195
slept in this cave alone, and took his flocks
to graze afield—remote from all companions,
knowing none but savage ways, a brute
so huge, he seemed no man at all of those
who eat good wheaten bread; but he seemed rather        200
a shaggy mountain reared in solitude.
We beached there, and I told the crew
to stand by and keep watch over the ship;
as for myself I took my twelve best fighters
and went ahead. I had a goatskin full                   205
of that sweet liquor that Euanthês' son,
Maron, had given me. He kept Apollo's
holy grove at Ísmaros; for kindness
we showed him there, and showed his wife and child,
he gave me seven shining golden talents                 210
perfectly formed, a solid silver winebowl,
and then this liquor—twelve two-handled jars
of brandy, pure and fiery. Not a slave
in Maron's household knew this drink; only
he, his wife and the storeroom mistress knew;           215
and they would put one cupful—ruby-colored,
honey-smooth—in twenty more of water,
but still the sweet scent hovered like a fume
over the winebowl. No man turned away
when cups of this came round.
           A wineskin full              220
I brought along, and victuals in a bag.
for in my bones I knew some towering brute
would be upon us soon—all outward power,
a wild man, ignorant of civility.

186. *cast off*: Release the mooring.    was a standard weight.
210. *talents*: Ingots of gold; the talent

We climbed, then, briskly to the cave. But Kyklops  225
had gone afield, to pasture his fat sheep,
so we looked round at everything inside:
a drying rack that sagged with cheeses, pens
crowded with lambs and kids, each in its class:
firstlings apart from middlings, and the 'dewdrops,'  230
or newborn lambkins, penned apart from both.
And vessels full of whey were brimming there—
bowls of earthenware and pails for milking.
My men came pressing round me, pleading:

                      'Why not  235
take these cheeses, get them stowed, come back,
throw open all the pens, and make a run for it?
We'll drive the kids and lambs aboard. We say
put out again on good salt water!'

                           Ah,
how sound that was! Yet I refused, I wished  240
to see the caveman, what he had to offer—
no pretty sight, it turned out, for my friends.
We lit a fire, burnt an offering,
and took some cheese to eat; then sat in silence
around the embers, waiting. When he came  245
he had a load of dry boughs on his shoulder
to stoke his fire at suppertime. He dumped it
with a great crash into that hollow cave,
and we all scattered fast to the far wall.
Then over the broad cavern floor he ushered  250
the ewes he meant to milk. He left his rams
and he-goats in the yard outside, and swung
high overhead a slab of solid rock
to close the cave. Two dozen four-wheeled wagons,
with heaving wagon teams, could not have stirred  255
the tonnage of that rock from where he wedged it
over the doorsill. Next he took his seat
and milked his bleating ewes. A practiced job
he made of it, giving each ewe her suckling:
thickened his milk, then, into curds and whey,  260
sieved out the curds to drip in withy baskets,
and poured the whey to stand in bowls
cooling until he drank it for his supper.
When all these chores were done, he poked the fire,
heaping on brushwood. In the glare he saw us.  265

'Strangers,' he said, 'who are you? And where from?

261. *withy*: Willow.

What brings you here by sea ways—a fair traffic?
Or are you wandering rogues, who cast your lives
like dice, and ravage other folk by sea?'

We felt a pressure on our hearts, in dread                          270
of that deep rumble and that mighty man.
But all the same I spoke up in reply:
'We are from Troy, Akhaians, blown off course
by shifting gales on the Great South Sea;
homeward bound, but taking routes and ways                        275
uncommon; so the will of Zeus would have it.
We served under Agamémnon, son of Atreus—
the whole world knows what city
he laid waste, what armies he destroyed.
It was our luck to come here; here we stand,                      280
beholden for your help, or any gifts
you give—as custom is to honor strangers.
We would entreat you, great Sir, have a care
for the gods' courtesy; Zeus will avenge
the unoffending guest.'
           He answered this                          285
from his brute chest, unmoved:
                   'You are a ninny,
or else you come from the other end of nowhere,
telling me, mind the gods! We Kyklopês
care not a whistle for your thundering Zeus
or all the gods in bliss; we have more force by far.            290
I would not let you go for fear of Zeus—
you or your friends—unless I had a whim to.
Tell me, where was it, now, you left your ship—
around the point, or down the shore, I wonder?'

He thought he'd find out, but I saw through this,               295
and answered with a ready lie:
                 'My ship?
Poseidon Lord, who sets the earth a-tremble,
broke it up on the rocks at your land's end.
A wind from seaward served him, drove us there.
We are survivors, these good men and I.'                        300

Neither reply nor pity came from him,
but in one stride he clutched at my companions
and caught two in his hands like squirming puppies
to beat their brains out, spattering the floor.
Then he dismembered them and made his meal,                     305
gaping and crunching like a mountain lion—

everything: innards, flesh, and marrow bones.
We cried aloud, lifting our hands to Zeus,
powerless, looking on at this, appalled;
but Kyklops went on filling up his belly          310
with manflesh and great gulps of whey,
then lay down like a mast among his sheep.
My heart beat high now at the chance of action,
and drawing the sharp sword from my hip I went
along his flank to stab him where the midriff     315
holds the liver. I had touched the spot
when sudden fear stayed me: if I killed him
we perished there as well, for we could never
move his ponderous doorway slab aside.
So we were left to groan and wait for morning.     320

When the young Dawn with finger tips of rose
lit up the world, the Kyklops built a fire
and milked his handsome ewes, all in due order,
putting the sucklings to the mothers. Then,
his chores being all dispatched, he caught         325
another brace of men to make his breakfast,
and whisked away his great door slab
to let his sheep go through—but he, behind,
reset the stone as one would cap a quiver.
There was a din of whistling as the Kyklops        330
rounded his flock to higher ground, then stillness.
And now I pondered how to hurt him worst,
if but Athena granted what I prayed for.

Here are the means I thought would serve my turn:
a club, or staff, lay there along the fold—        335
an olive tree, felled green and left to season
for Kyklops' hand. And it was like a mast
a lugger of twenty oars, broad in the beam—
a deep-sea-going craft—might carry:
so long, so big around, it seemed. Now I           340
chopped out a six foot section of this pole
and set it down before my men, who scraped it;
and when they had it smooth, I hewed again
to make a stake with pointed end. I held this
in the fire's heart and turned it, toughening it,  345
then hid it, well back in the cavern, under
one of the dung piles in profusion there.
Now came the time to toss for it: who ventured
along with me? whose hand could bear to thrust
and grind that spike in Kyklops' eye, when mild    350

sleep had mastered him? As luck would have it,
the men I would have chosen, won the toss—
four strong men, and I made five as captain.

At evening came the shepherd with his flock,
his woolly flock. The rams as well, this time,                      355
entered the cave: by some sheep-herding whim—
or a god's bidding—none were left outside.
He hefted his great boulder into place
and sat him down to milk the bleating ewes
in proper order, put the lambs to suck,                             360
and swiftly ran through all his evening chores.
Then he caught two more men and feasted on them.
My moment was at hand, and I went forward
holding an ivy bowl of my dark drink,
looking up, saying:
                'Kyklops, try some wine.                    365
Here's liquor to wash down your scraps of men.
Taste it, and see the kind of drink we carried
under our planks. I meant it for an offering
if you would help us home. But you are mad,
unbearable, a bloody monster! After this,                          370
will any other traveller come to see you?'

He seized and drained the bowl, and it went down
so fiery and smooth he called for more:
'Give me another, thank you kindly. Tell me,
how are you called? I'll make a gift will please you.              375
Even Kyklopês know the wine-grapes grow
out of grassland and loam in heaven's rain,
but here's a bit of nectar and ambrosia!'

Three bowls I brought him and he poured them down.
I saw the fuddle and flush come over him,                          380
then I sang out in cordial tones:
                'Kyklops,
you ask my honorable name? Remember
the gift you promised me, and I shall tell you.
My name is Nohbdy: mother, father, and friends,
everyone calls me Nohbdy.'

                And he said:                                385
'Nohbdy's my meat, then, after I eat his friends.

378. *nectar and ambrosia*: The drink and food of the gods.

Others come first. There's a noble gift, now.'

Even as he spoke, he reeled and tumbled backward,
his great head lolling to one side; and sleep
took him like any creature. Drunk, hiccuping,               390
he dribbled streams of liquor and bits of men.

Now, by the gods, I drove my big hand spike
deep in the embers, charring it again,
and cheered my men along with battle talk
to keep their courage up: no quitting now.                  395
The pike of olive, green though it had been,
reddened and glowed as if about to catch.
I drew it from the coals and my four fellows
gave me a hand, lugging it near the Kyklops
as more than natural force nerved them; straight            400
forward they sprinted, lifted it, and rammed it
deep in his crater eye, and I leaned on it
turning it as a shipwright turns a drill
in planking, having men below to swing
the two-handled strap that spins it in the groove.          405
So with our brand we bored that great eye socket
while blood ran out around the red hot bar.
Eyelid and lash were seared; the pierced ball
hissed broiling, and the roots popped.

                         In a smithy
one sees a white-hot axehead or an adze                     410
plunged and wrung in a cold tub, screeching steam—
the way they make soft iron hale and hard—:
just so that eyeball hissed around the spike.
The Kyklops bellowed and the rock roared round him,
and we fell back in fear. Clawing his face                  415
he tugged the bloody spike out of his eye,
threw it away, and his wild hands went groping;
then he set up a howl for Kyklopês
who lived in caves on windy peaks nearby.
Some heard him; and they came by divers ways               420
to clump around outside and call:
                                   'What ails you,
Polyphêmos? Why do you cry so sore
in the starry night? You will not let us sleep.
Sure no man's driving off your flock? No man
has tricked you, ruined you?'

Out of the cave                                          425
the mammoth Polyphêmos roared in answer:
'Nohbdy, Nohbdy's tricked me, Nohbdy's ruined me!'

To this rough shout they made a sage reply;
'Ah well, if nobody has played you foul
there in your lonely bed, we are no use in pain           430
given by great Zeus. Let it be your father,
Poseidon Lord, to whom you pray.'
                              So saying
they trailed away. And I was filled with laughter
to see how like a charm the name deceived them.
Now Kyklops, wheezing as the pain came on him,           435
fumbled to wrench away the great doorstone
and squatted in the breach with arms thrown wide
for any silly beast or man who bolted—
hoping somehow I might be such a fool.
But I kept thinking how to win the game:                 440
death sat there huge; how could we slip away?
I drew on all my wits, and ran through tactics,
reasoning as a man will for dear life,
until a trick came—and it pleased me well.
The Kyklops' rams were handsome, fat, with heavy         445
fleeces, a dark violet.

                    Three abreast
I tied them silently together, twining
cords of willow from the ogre's bed;
then slung a man under each middle one
to ride there safely, shielded left and right.
So three sheep could convey each man. I took            450
the woolliest ram, the choicest of the flock,
and hung myself under his kinky belly,
pulled up tight, with fingers twisted deep
in sheepskin ringlets for an iron grip.                  455
So, breathing hard, we waited until morning.

When Dawn spread out her finger tips of rose
the rams began to stir, moving for pasture,
and peals of bleating echoed round the pens
where dams with udders full called for a milking.        460
Blinded, and sick with pain from his head wound,
the master stroked each ram, then let it pass,
but my men riding on the pectoral fleece
the giant's blind hands blundering never found.
Last of them all my ram, the leader, came,               465

weighted by wool and me with my meditations.
The Kyklops patted him, and then he said:
'Sweet cousin ram, why lag behind the rest
in the night cave? You never linger so,
but graze before them all, and go afar          470
to crop sweet grass, and take your stately way
leading along the streams, until at evening
you run to be the first one in the fold.
Why, now, so far behind? Can you be grieving
over your Master's eye? That carrion rogue      475
and his accurst companions burnt it out
when he had conquered all my wits with wine.
Nohbdy will not get out alive, I swear.
Oh, had you brain and voice to tell
where he may be now, dodging all my fury!       480
Bashed by this hand and bashed on this rock wall
his brains would strew the floor, and I should have
rest from the outrage Nohbdy worked upon me.'
He sent us into the open, then. Close by,
I dropped and rolled clear of the ram's belly,  485
going this way and that to untie the men.
With many glances back, we rounded up
his fat, stiff-legged sheep to take aboard,
and drove them down to where the good ship lay.
We saw, as we came near, our fellows' faces     490
shining; then we saw them turn to grief
tallying those who had not fled from death.
I hushed them, jerking head and eyebrows up,
and in a low voice told them: 'Load this herd;
move fast, and put the ship's head toward the breakers.'  495
They all pitched in at loading, then embarked
and struck their oars into the sea. Far out,
as far off shore as shouted words would carry,
I sent a few back to the adversary:
'O Kyklops! Would you feast on my companions?   500
Puny, am I, in a Caveman's hands?
How do you like the beating that we gave you,
you damned cannibal? Eater of guests
under your roof! Zeus and the gods have paid you!'

The blind thing in his doubled fury broke       505
a hilltop in his hands and heaved it after us.
Ahead of our black prow it struck and sank
whelmed in a spuming geyser, a giant wave
that washed the ship stern foremost back to shore.

I got the longest boathook out and stood 510
fending us off, with furious nods to all
to put their backs into a racing stroke—
row, row, or perish. So the long oars bent
kicking the foam sternward, making head
until we drew away, and twice as far. 515
Now when I cupped my hands I heard the crew
in low voices protesting:

              'Godsake, Captain!
Why bait the beast again? Let him alone!'
'That tidal wave he made on the first throw
all but beached us.'

                'All but stove us in!' 520

'Give him our bearing with your trumpeting,
he'll get the range and lob a boulder.'

                    'Aye
He'll smash our timbers and our heads together!'

I would not heed them in my glorying spirit,
but let my anger flare and yelled:

                'Kyklops, 525
if ever mortal man inquire
how you were put to shame and blinded, tell him
Odysseus, raider of cities, took your eye:
Laërtês' son, whose home's on Ithaka!'

At this he gave a mighty sob and rumbled: 530
'Now comes the weird upon me, spoken of old.
A wizard, grand and wondrous, lived here—Télemos,
a son of Eurymos; great length of days
he had in wizardry among the Kyklopês,
and these things he foretold for time to come: 535
my great eye lost, and at Odysseus' hands.
Always I had in mind some giant, armed
in giant force, would come against me here.
But this, but you—small, pitiful and twiggy—
you put me down with wine, you blinded me. 540
Come back, Odysseus, and I'll treat you well,
praying the god of earthquake to befriend you—
his son I am, for he by his avowal
fathered me, and, if he will, he may

520. *stove us in*: Smashed the hull of the ship.

heal me of this black wound—he and no other     545
of all the happy gods or mortal men.'

Few words I shouted in reply to him:
'If I could take your life I would and take
your time away, and hurl you down to hell!
The god of earthquake could not heal you there!'    550

At this he stretched his hands out in his darkness
toward the sky of stars, and prayed Poseidon:
'O hear me, lord, blue girdler of the islands,
if I am thine indeed, and thou art father:
grant that Odysseus, raider of cities, never    555
see his home: Laërtês' son, I mean,
who kept his hall on Ithaka. Should destiny
intend that he shall see his roof again
among his family in his father land,
far be that day, and dark the years between.    560
Let him lose all companions, and return
under strange sail to bitter days at home.'

In these words he prayed, and the god heard him.
Now he laid hands upon a bigger stone
and wheeled around, titanic for the cast,    565
to let it fly in the black-prowed vessel's track.
But it fell short, just aft the steering oar,
and whelming seas rose giant above the stone
to bear us onward toward the island.
                         There
as we ran in we saw the squadron waiting,    570
the trim ships drawn up side by side, and all
our troubled friends who waited, looking seaward.
We beached her, grinding keel in the soft sand,
and waded in, ourselves, on the sandy beach.
Then we unloaded all the Kyklops' flock    575
to make division, share and share alike,
only my fighters voted that my ram,
the prize of all, should go to me. I slew him
by the sea side and burnt his long thighbones
to Zeus beyond the stormcloud, Kronos' son,    580
who rules the world. But Zeus disdained my offering;
destruction for my ships he had in store
and death for those who sailed them, my companions.
Now all day long until the sun went down
we made our feast on mutton and sweet wine,    585

till after sunset in the gathering dark
we went to sleep above the wash of ripples.

When the young Dawn with finger tips of rose
touched the world, I roused the men, gave orders
to man the ships, cast off the mooring lines;                    590
and filing in to sit beside the rowlocks
oarsmen in line dipped oars in the grey sea.
So we moved out, sad in the vast offing,
having our precious lives, but not our friends.

## Book X

We made our landfall on Aiolia Island,
domain of Aiolos Hippotadês,
the wind king, dear to the gods who never die—
an isle adrift upon the sea, ringed round
with brazen ramparts on a sheer cliffside.                        5
Twelve children had old Aiolos at home—
six daughters and six lusty sons—and he
gave girls to boys to be their gentle brides;
now those lords, in their parents' company,
sup every day in hall—a royal feast                               10
with fumes of sacrifice and winds that pipe
'round hollow courts; and all the night they sleep
on beds of filigree beside their ladies.
Here we put in, lodged in the town and palace,
while Aiolos played host to me. He kept me                        15
one full month to hear the tale of Troy,
the ships and the return of the Akhaians,
all which I told him point by point in order.
When in return I asked his leave to sail
and asked provisioning, he stinted nothing,                       20
adding a bull's hide sewn from neck to tail
into a mighty bag, bottling storm winds;
for Zeus had long ago made Aiolos
warden of winds, to rouse or calm at will.
He wedged this bag under my afterdeck,                            25
lashing the neck with shining silver wire
so not a breath got through; only the west wind
he lofted for me in a quartering breeze

---

1. *Aiolia*: A moving island, the home
of the king of the winds (whose name
in Greek means "shifting, changeable").
It has been located by modern geographers in the Lipari Islands of the Sicilian
coast. The great ancient geographer Era-
tosthenes was not so confident. He once
said that we would know exactly where

Odysseus wandered after we had traced
the leatherworker who made the bag in
which the winds were contained.
2. *Hippotadês*: Son of Hippotas,
"horseman."
28. *quartering breeze*: A breeze blowing diagonally from the rear of the boat,
highly favorable for sailing.

to take my squadron spanking home.
No luck:
the fair wind failed us when our prudence failed.          30

Nine days and nights we sailed without event,
till on the tenth we raised our land. We neared it,
and saw men building fires along the shore;
but now, being weary to the bone, I fell
into deep slumber; I had worked the sheet          35
nine days alone, and given it to no one,
wishing to spill no wind on the homeward run.
But while I slept, the crew began to parley:
silver and gold, they guessed, were in that bag
bestowed on me by Aiolos' great heart;          40
and one would glance at his benchmate and say:
'It never fails. He's welcome everywhere:
hail to the captain when he goes ashore!
He brought along so many presents, plunder
out of Troy, that's it. How about ourselves—          45
his shipmates all the way? Nigh home we are
with empty hands. And who has gifts from Aiolos?
He has. I say we ought to crack that bag,
there's gold and silver, plenty, in that bag!'

Temptation had its way with my companions,          50
and they untied the bag.
Then every wind
roared into hurricane; the ships went pitching
west with many cries; our land was lost.
Roused up, despairing in that gloom, I thought:
"Should I go overside for a quick finish          55
or clench my teeth and stay among the living?'
Down in the bilge I lay, pulling my sea cloak
over my head, while the rough gale blew the ships
and rueful crews clear back to Aiolia.

We put ashore for water; then all hands          60
gathered alongside for a mid-day meal.
When we had taken bread and drink, I picked
one soldier, and one herald, to go with me
and called again on Aiolos. I found him
at meat with his young princes and his lady,          65
but there beside the pillars, in his portico,
we sat down silent at the open door.
The sight amazed them, and they all exclaimed:

35. *the sheet*: The line which keeps   of the wind.
the sail trimmed to take best advantage

'Why back again, Odysseus?'
                                        'What sea fiend
rose in your path?'
                            'Did we not launch you well                70
for home, or for whatever land you chose?'

Out of my melancholy I replied:
'Mischief aboard and nodding at the tiller—
a damned drowse—did for me. Make good my loss,
dear friends! You have the power!'
                                Gently I pleaded,               75
but they turned cold and still. Said Father Aiolos:
'Take yourself out of this island, creeping thing—
no law, no wisdom, lays it on me now
to help a man the blessed gods detest—
out! Your voyage here was cursed by heaven!'                    80

He drove me from the place, groan as I would,
and comfortless we went again to sea,
days of it, till the men flagged at the oars—
no breeze, no help in sight, by our own folly—
six indistinguishable nights and days                          85
before we raised the Laistrygonian height
and far stronghold of Lamos. In that land
the daybreak follows dusk, and so the shepherd
homing calls to the cowherd setting out;
and he who never slept could earn two wages,                   90
tending oxen, pasturing silvery flocks,
where the low night path of the sun is near
the sun's path by day. Here, then, we found
a curious bay with mountain walls of stone
to left and right, and reaching far inland,—                   95
a narrow entrance opening from the sea
where cliffs converged as though to touch and close.
All of my squadron sheltered here, inside
the cavern of this bay.
                            Black prow by prow
those hulls were made fast in a limpid calm                    100
without a ripple, stillness all around them.
My own black ship I chose to moor alone
on the sea side, using a rock for bollard;
and climbed a rocky point to get my bearings.
No farms, no cultivated land appeared,                         105
but puffs of smoke rose in the wilderness;

---

93. *sun's path by day*: Generally   the short summer nights of the far
thought to be a confused reference to   north.

so I sent out two picked men and a herald
to learn what race of men this land sustained.

My party found a track—a wagon road
for bringing wood down from the heights to town;  110
and near the settlement they met a daughter
of Antiphatês the Laistrygon—a stalwart
young girl taking her pail to Artakía,
the fountain where these people go for water.
My fellows hailed her, put their questions to her:  115
who might the king be? ruling over whom?
She waved her hand, showing her father's lodge,
so they approached it. In its gloom they saw
a woman like a mountain crag, the queen—
and loathed the sight of her. But she, for greeting,  120
called from the meeting ground her lord and master,
Antiphatês, who came to drink their blood.
He seized one man and tore him on the spot,
making a meal of him; the other two
leaped out of doors and ran to join the ships.  125
Behind, he raised the whole tribe howling, countless
Laistrygonês—and more than men they seemed,
gigantic when they gathered on the sky line
to shoot great boulders down from slings; and hell's own
crashing rose, and crying from the ships,  130
as planks and men were smashed to bits—poor gobbets
the wildmen speared like fish and bore away.
But long before it ended in the anchorage—
havoc and slaughter—I had drawn my sword
and cut my own ship's cable. 'Men,' I shouted,  135
'man the oars and pull till your hearts break
if you would put this butchery behind!'
The oarsmen rent the sea in mortal fear
and my ship spurted out of range, far out
from that deep canyon where the rest were lost.  140
So we fared onward, and death fell behind,
and we took breath to grieve for our companions.

Our next landfall was on Aiaia, island
of Kirkê, dire beauty and divine,
sister of baleful Aiêtês, like him  145
fathered by Hêlios the light of mortals
on Persê, child of the Ocean stream.
                                        We came

---

113. *Antiphatês*: The king.
145. *Aiêtês*: Father of Medea, heroine
of Euripides' play (p. 415).

147. *Ocean*: The river which was
thought of as encircling the world.

washed in our silent ship upon her shore,
and found a cove, a haven for the ship—
some god, invisible, conned us in. We landed,                    150
to lie down in that place two days and nights,
worn out and sick at heart, tasting our grief
But when Dawn set another day a-shining
I took my spear and broadsword, and I climbed
a rocky point above the ship, for sight                         155
or sound of human labor. Gazing out
from that high place over a land of thicket,
oaks and wide watercourses, I could see
a smoke wisp from the woodland hall of Kirkê.
So I took counsel with myself: should I                         160
go inland scouting out that reddish smoke?
No: better not, I thought, but first return
to waterside and ship, and give the men
breakfast before I sent them to explore.
Now as I went down quite alone, and came                        165
a bowshot from the ship, some god's compassion
set a big buck in motion to cross my path—
a stag with noble antlers, pacing down
from pasture in the woods to the riverside,
as long thirst and the power of sun constrained him.            170
He started from the bush and wheeled: I hit him
square in the spine midway along his back
and the bronze point broke through it. In the dust
he fell and whinnied as life bled away.
I set one foot against him, pulling hard                        175
to wrench my weapon from the wound, then left it,
butt-end on the ground. I plucked some withies
and twined a double strand into a rope—
enough to tie the hocks of my huge trophy;
then pickaback I lugged him to the ship,                        180
leaning on my long spearshaft; I could not
haul that mighty carcass on one shoulder.
Beside the ship I let him drop, and spoke
gently and low to each man standing near:
'Come, friends, though hard beset, we'll not go down            185
into the House of Death before our time.
As long as food and drink remain aboard
let us rely on it, not die of hunger.'

At this those faces, cloaked in desolation
upon the waste sea beach, were bared;                           190
their eyes turned toward me and the mighty trophy,

150. *conned*: Piloted.

lighting, foreseeing pleasure, one by one.
So hands were washed to take what heaven sent us.
And all that day until the sun went down
we had our fill of venison and wine,                                    195
till after sunset in the gathering dusk
we slept at last above the line of breakers.
When the young Dawn with finger tips of rose
made heaven bright, I called them round and said:
'Shipmates, companions in disastrous time,                              200
O my dear friends, where Dawn lies, and the West,
and where the great Sun, light of men, may go
under the earth by night, and where he rises—
of these things we know nothing. Do we know
any least thing to serve us now? I wonder.                              205
All that I saw when I went up the rock
was one more island in the boundless main,
a low landscape, covered with woods and scrub,
and puffs of smoke ascending in mid-forest.'

They were all silent, but their hearts contracted,                      210
remembering Antiphatês the Laistrygon
and that prodigious cannibal, the Kyklops.
They cried out, and the salt tears wet their eyes.
But seeing our time for action lost in weeping,
I mustered those Akhaians under arms,                                    215
counting them off in two platoons, myself
and my godlike Eurýlokhos commanding.
We shook lots in a soldier's dogskin cap
and his came bounding out—valiant Eurýlokhos!—
So off he went, with twenty-two companions                              220
weeping, as mine wept, too, who stayed behind.

In the wild wood they found an open glade,
around a smooth stone house—the hall of Kirkê—
and wolves and mountain lions lay there, mild
in her soft spell, fed on her drug of evil.                             225
None would attack—oh, it was strange, I tell you—
but switching their long tails they faced our men
like hounds, who look up when their master comes
with tidbits for them—as he will—from table.
Humbly those wolves and lions with mighty paws                          230
fawned on our men—who met their yellow eyes

---

201. *where Dawn lies, etc.*: In view of the immediately preceding lines, this can hardly be taken literally. It is possibly a sailor's metaphorical way of saying, "we don't know where we are."

217. *Eurýlokhos*: Odysseus' second in command.

and feared them.

In the entrance way they stayed
to listen there: inside her quiet house
they heard the goddess Kirkê.

Low she sang
in her beguiling voice, while on her loom          235
she wove ambrosial fabric sheer and bright,
by that craft known to the goddesses of heaven.
No one would speak, until Politês—most
faithful and likable of my officers, said:
'Dear friends, no need for stealth: here's a young weaver          240
singing a pretty song to set the air
a-tingle on these lawns and paven courts.
Goddess she is, or lady. Shall we greet her?'

So reassured, they all cried out together,
and she came swiftly to the shining doors          245
to call them in. All but Eurýlokhos—
who feared a snare—the innocents went after her.
On thrones she seated them, and lounging chairs,
while she prepared a meal of cheese and barley
and amber honey mixed with Pramnian wine,          250
adding her own vile pinch, to make them lose
desire or thought of our dear father land.
Scarce had they drunk when she flew after them
with her long stick and shut them in a pigsty—
bodies, voices, heads, and bristles, all          255
swinish now, though minds were still unchanged.
So, squealing, in they went. And Kirkê tossed them
acorns, mast, and cornel berries—fodder
for hogs who rut and slumber on the earth.

Down to the ship Eurýlokhos came running          260
to cry alarm, foul magic doomed his men!
But working with dry lips to speak a word
he could not, being so shaken; blinding tears
welled in his eyes; foreboding filled his heart.
When we were frantic questioning him, at last          265
we heard the tale: our friends were gone. Said he:
'We went up through the oak scrub where you sent us,
Odysseus, glory of commanders,
until we found a palace in a glade,
a marble house on open ground, and someone          270
singing before her loom a chill, sweet song—

236. *ambrosial*: Divine, from *ambro-*
*sia*, the food of the gods.
250. *Pramnian wine*: Evidently a very
strong wine. (We don't know where
Pramnos was.)
258. *mast*: Nuts.

goddess or girl, we could not tell. They hailed her,
and then she stepped through shining doors and said,
"Come, come in!" Like sheep they followed her,
but I saw cruel deceit, and stayed behind.                     275
Then all our fellows vanished. Not a sound,
and nothing stirred, although I watched for hours.'

When I heard this I slung my silver-hilted
broadsword on, and shouldered my long bow,
and said, 'Come, take me back the way you came.'               280
But he put both his hands around my knees
in desperate woe, and said in supplication:
'Not back there, O my lord! Oh, leave me here!
You, even you, cannot return, I know it,
I know you cannot bring away our shipmates;                    285
better make sail with these men, quickly too,
and save ourselves from horror while we may.'

But I replied:
              'By heaven, Eurýlokhos,
rest here then; take food and wine;
stay in the black hull's shelter. Let me go,                   290
as I see nothing for it but to go.'

I turned and left him, left the shore and ship,
and went up through the woodland hushed and shady
to find the subtle witch in her long hall.
But Hermês met me, with his golden wand,                       295
barring the way—a boy whose lip was downy
in the first bloom of manhood, so he seemed.
He took my hand and spoke as though he knew me:
    'Why take the inland path alone,
    poor seafarer, by hill and dale                            300
    upon this island all unknown?
    Your friends are locked in Kirkê's pale;
    all are become like swine to see;
    and if you go to set them free
    you go to stay, and never more make sail                   305
    for your old home upon Thaki.
    But I can tell you what to do
    to come unchanged from Kirkê's power
    and disenthrall your fighting crew:

---

298ff. The four rhymed stanzas which    no rhyme.
follow are a translator's license; in the    302. *pale*: Pen.
original there is no change of meter and    306. *Thaki*: Ithaka.

take with you to her bower                                                310
as amulet, this plant I know—
it will defeat her horrid show,
so pure and potent is the flower;
no mortal herb was ever so.

Your cup with numbing drops of night                                     315
and evil, stilled of all remorse,
she will infuse to charm your sight;
but this great herb with holy force
will keep your mind and senses clear:
when she turns cruel, coming near                                        320
with her long stick to whip you out of doors,
then let your cutting blade appear,

Let instant death upon it shine,
and she will cower and yield her bed—
a pleasure you must not decline,                                         325
so may her lust and fear bestead
you and your friends, and break her spell;
but make her swear by heaven and hell
no witches' tricks, or else, your harness shed,
you'll be unmanned by her as well.'                                      330

He bent down glittering for the magic plant
and pulled it up, black root and milky flower—
a *molü* in the language of the gods—
fatigue and pain for mortals to uproot;
but gods do this, and everything, with ease.                            335

Then toward Olympos through the island trees
Hermês departed, and I sought out Kirkê,
my heart high with excitement, beating hard.
Before her mansion in the porch I stood
to call her, all being still. Quick as a cat                            340
she opened her bright doors and sighed a welcome;
then I strode after her with heavy heart
down the long hall, and took the chair she gave me,
silver-studded, intricately carved,
made with a low footrest. The lady Kirkê                                345
mixed me a golden cup of honeyed wine,
adding in mischief her unholy drug.
I drank, and the drink failed. But she came forward
aiming a stroke with her long stick, and whispered:

326. *bestead*: Help.

'Down in the sty and snore among the rest!'                                        350

Without a word, I drew my sharpened sword
and in one bound held it against her throat.
She cried out, then slid under to take my knees,
catching her breath to say, in her distress:
'What champion, of what country, can you be?                                        355
Where are your kinsmen and your city?
Are you not sluggish with my wine? Ah, wonder!
Never a mortal man that drank this cup
but when it passed his lips he had succumbed.
Hale must your heart be and your tempered will.                                     360
Odysseus then you are, O great contender,
of whom the glittering god with golden wand
spoke to me ever, and foretold
the black swift ship would carry you from Troy.
Put up your weapon in the sheath. We two                                            365
shall mingle and make love upon our bed.
So mutual trust may come of play and love.'

To this I said:
                  'Kirkê, am I a boy,
that you should make me soft and doting now?
Here in this house you turned my men to swine;                                      370
now it is I myself you hold, enticing
into your chamber, to your dangerous bed,
to take my manhood when you have me stripped.
I mount no bed of love with you upon it.
Or swear me first a great oath, if I do,                                            375
you'll work no more enchantment to my harm.'
She swore at once, outright, as I demanded,
and after she had sworn, and bound herself,
I entered Kirkê's flawless bed of love.

Presently in the hall her maids were busy,                                          380
the nymphs who waited upon Kirkê: four,
whose cradles were in fountains, under boughs,
or in the glassy seaward-gliding streams.
One came with richly colored rugs to throw
on seat and chairback, over linen covers;                                           385
a second pulled the tables out, all silver,
and loaded them with baskets all of gold;
a third mixed wine as tawny-mild as honey
in a bright bowl, and set out golden cups.

362. *god with the golden wand*: Hermês.

The fourth came bearing water, and lit a blaze       390
under a cauldron. By and by it bubbled,
and when the dazzling brazen vessel seethed
she filled a bathtub to my waist, and bathed me,
pouring a soothing blend on head and shoulders,
warming the soreness of my joints away.       395
When she had done, and smoothed me with sweet oil,
she put a tunic and a cloak around me
and took me to a silver-studded chair
with footrest, all elaborately carven.
Now came a maid to tip a golden jug       400
of water into a silver finger bowl,
and draw a polished table to my side.
The larder mistress brought her tray of loaves
with many savory slices, and she gave
the best, to tempt me. But no pleasure came;       405
I huddled with my mind elsewhere, oppressed.

Kirkê regarded me, as there I sat
disconsolate, and never touched a crust.
Then she stood over me and chided me:
'Why sit at table mute, Odysseus?       410
Are you mistrustful of my bread and drink?
Can it be treachery that you fear again,
after the gods' great oath I swore for you?'
I turned to her at once, and said:

                      'Kirkê,
where is the captain who could bear to touch       415
this banquet, in my place? A decent man
would see his company before him first.
Put heart in me to eat and drink—you may,
by freeing my companions. I must see them.'

But Kirkê had already turned away.       420
Her long staff in her hand, she left the hall
and opened up the sty. I saw her enter,
driving those men turned swine to stand before me.
She stroked them, each in turn, with some new chrism;
and then, behold! their bristles fell away,       425
the coarse pelt grown upon them by her drug
melted away, and they were men again,
younger, more handsome, taller than before.
Their eyes upon me, each one took my hands,
and wild regret and longing pierced them through,       430
so the room rang with sobs, and even Kirkê

424. *chrism*: Ointment.

pitied that transformation. Exquisite
the goddess looked as she stood near me, saying:
'Son of Laërtês and the gods of old,
Odysseus, master mariner and soldier,                                    435
go to the sea beach and sea-breasting ship;
drag it ashore, full length upon the land;
stow gear and stores in rock-holes under cover;
return; be quick; bring all your dear companions.'

Now, being a man, I could not help consenting.                           440
So I went down to the sea beach and the ship,
where I found all my other men on board,
weeping, in despair along the benches.
Sometimes in farmyards when the cows return
well fed from pasture to the barn, one sees                               445
the pens give way before the calves in tumult,
breaking through to cluster about their mothers,
bumping together, bawling. Just that way
my crew poured round me when they saw me come—
their faces wet with tears as if they saw                                450
their homeland, and the crags of Ithaka,
even the very town where they were born.
And weeping still they all cried out in greeting:
'Prince, what joy this is, your safe return!
Now Ithaka seems here, and we in Ithaka!                                 455
But tell us now, what death befell our friends?'

And, speaking gently, I replied:
'First we must get the ship high on the shingle,
and stow our gear and stores in clefts of rock
for cover. Then come follow me, to see                                    460
your shipmates in the magic house of Kirkê
eating and drinking, endlessly regaled.'

They turned back, as commanded, to this work;
only one lagged, and tried to hold the others;
Eurýlokhos it was, who blurted out:                                       465
'Where now, poor remnants? is it devil's work
you long for? Will you go to Kirkê's hall?
Swine, wolves, and lions she will make us all,
beasts of her courtyard, bound by her enchantment.
Remember those the Kyklops held, remember                                 470
shipmates who made that visit with Odysseus!
The daring man! They died for his foolishness!'

When I heard this I had a mind to draw
the blade that swung against my side and chop him,
bowling his head upon the ground—kinsman                          475
or no kinsman, close to me though he was.
But others came between, saying, to stop me,
'Prince, we can leave him, if you say the word;
let him stay here on guard. As for ourselves,
show us the way to Kirkê's magic hall.'                          480

So all turned inland, leaving shore and ship,
and Eurýlokhos—he, too, came on behind,
fearing the rough edge of my tongue. Meanwhile
at Kirkê's hands the rest were gently bathed,
anointed with sweet oil, and dressed afresh                      485
in tunics and new cloaks with fleecy linings.
We found them all at supper when we came.
But greeting their old friends once more, the crew
could not hold back their tears; and now again
the rooms rang with sobs. Then Kirkê, loveliest                  490
of all immortals, came to counsel me:
'Son of Laërtês and the gods of old.
Odysseus, master mariner and soldier,
enough of weeping fits. I know—I, too—
what you endured upon the inhuman sea,                           495
what odds you met on land from hostile men.
Remain with me, and share my meat and wine;
restore behind your ribs those gallant hearts
that served you in the old days, when you sailed
from stony Ithaka. Now parched and spent,                        500
your cruel wandering is all you think of,
never of joy, after so many blows.'

As we were men we could not help consenting.
So day by day we lingered, feasting long
on roasts and wine, until a year grew fat.                       505
But when the passing months and wheeling seasons
brought the long summery days, the pause of summer,
my shipmates one day summoned me and said:
'Captain, shake off this trance, and think of home—
if home indeed awaits us,
                                  if we shall ever see           510
your own well-timbered hall on Ithaka.'

They made me feel a pang, and I agreed.
That day, and all day long, from dawn to sundown,

475. *kinsman*: Eurýlokhos was related to Odysseus by marriage.

we feasted on roast meat and ruddy wine,
and after sunset when the dusk came on          515
my men slept in the shadowy hall, but I
went through the dark to Kirkê's flawless bed
and took the goddess' knees in supplication,
urging, as she bent to hear:
                    'O Kirkê,
now you must keep your promise; it is time.     520
Help me make sail for home. Day after day
my longing quickens, and my company
give me no peace, but wear my heart away
pleading when you are not at hand to hear.'

The loveliest of goddesses replied:             525
'Son of Laërtês and the gods of old,
Odysseus, master mariner and soldier,
you shall not stay here longer against your will;
but home you may not go
unless you take a strange way round and come    530
to the cold homes of Death and pale Perséphonê.
You shall hear prophecy from the rapt shade
of blind Teirêsias of Thebes, forever
charged with reason even among the dead;
to him alone, of all the flitting ghosts,       535
Perséphonê has given a mind undarkened.'

At this I felt a weight like stone within me,
and, moaning, pressed my length against the bed,
with no desire to see the daylight more.
But when I had wept and tossed and had my fill  540
of this despair, at last I answered her:
'Kirkê, who pilots me upon this journey?
No man has ever sailed to the land of Death.'

That loveliest of goddesses replied:
'Son of Laërtês and the gods of old,            545
Odysseus, master of land ways and sea ways,
feel no dismay because you lack a pilot;
only set up your mast and haul your canvas
to the fresh blowing North; sit down and steer,
and hold that wind, even to the bourne of Ocean,  550
Perséphonê's deserted strand and grove,

---

531. *Perséphonê*: Queen of the underworld.
533. *Teirêsias*: The famous seer; cf.

Sophocles, *Oedipus Tyrannus*, p. 349.
550. *bourne*: Frontier.

dusky with poplars and the drooping willow.
Run through the tide-rip, bring your ship to shore,
land there, and find the crumbling homes of Death.
Here, toward the Sorrowing Water, run the streams                     555
of Wailing, out of Styx, and quenchless Burning—
torrents that join in thunder at the Rock.
Here then, great soldier, setting foot obey me:
dig a well shaft a forearm square; pour out
libations round it to the unnumbered dead:                           560
sweet milk and honey, then sweet wine, and last
clear water, scattering handfulls of white barley.
Pray now, with all your heart, to the faint dead;
swear you will sacrifice your finest heifer,
at home in Ithaka, and burn for them                                 565
her tenderest parts in sacrifice; and vow
to the lord Teirêsias, apart from all,
a black lamb, handsomest of all your flock—
thus to appease the nations of the dead.
Then slash a black ewe's throat, and a black ram,                    570
facing the gloom of Erebos; but turn
your head away toward Ocean. You shall see, now
souls of the buried dead in shadowy hosts,
and now you must call out to your companions
to flay those sheep the bronze knife has cut down,                   575
for offerings, burnt flesh to those below,
to sovereign Death and pale Perséphonê.
Meanwhile draw sword from hip, crouch down, ward off
the surging phantoms from the bloody pit
until you know the presence of Teirêsias.                            580
He will come soon, great captain; be it he
who gives you course and distance for your sailing
homeward across the cold fish-breeding sea.'

As the goddess ended, Dawn came stitched in gold.
Now Kirkê dressed me in my shirt and cloak,                          585
put on a gown of subtle tissue, silvery,
then wound a golden belt about her waist
and veiled her head in linen,
while I went through the hall to rouse my crew.
I bent above each one, and gently said:                              590
'Wake from your sleep; no more sweet slumber. Come,
we sail: the Lady Kirkê so ordains it.'

---

555–556. *Sorrowing Water . . . Burning*: Translations of the Greek names for
the rivers of the underworld: Acheron,
Cocytus, and Pyriphlegethon. *Styx* means
"hateful river."

577. *Erebos*: The darkest region of
the underworld, usually imagined as
below the underworld itself but here to
the west.

They were soon up, and ready at that word;
but I was not to take my men unharmed
from this place, even from this. Among them all          595
the youngest was Elpênor—
no mainstay in a fight nor very clever—
and this one, having climbed on Kirkê's roof
to taste the cool night, fell asleep with wine.
Waked by our morning voices, and the tramp          600
of men below, he started up, but missed
his footing on the long steep backward ladder
and fell that height headlong. The blow smashed
the nape cord, and his ghost fled to the dark.
But I was outside, walking with the rest,          605
saying:
            'Homeward you think we must be sailing
to our own land; no, elsewhere is the voyage
Kirkê has laid upon me. We must go
to the cold homes of Death and pale Perséphonê          610
to hear Teirêsias tell of time to come.'

They felt so stricken, upon hearing this,
they sat down wailing loud, and tore their hair.
But nothing came of giving way to grief.
Down to the shore and ship at last we went,
bowed with anguish, cheeks all wet with tears,          615
to find that Kirkê had been there before us
and tied nearby a black ewe and a ram:
she had gone by like air.
For who could see the passage of a goddess
unless she wished his mortal eyes aware?          620

## Book XI

We bore down on the ship at the sea's edge
and launched her on the salt immortal sea,
stepping our mast and spar in the black ship;
embarked the ram and ewe and went aboard
in tears, with bitter and sore dread upon us.          5
But now a breeze came up for us astern—
a canvas-bellying landbreeze, hale shipmate
sent by the singing nymph with sun-bright hair;
so we made fast the braces, took our thwarts,
and let the wind and steersman work the ship          10

---

598. *roof*: A flat roof, and the coolest place to sleep.
3. *stepping*: Putting up.

9. *braces*: Lines running to the top of the mast to keep it upright. *thwarts*: Seats.

with full sail spread all day above our coursing,
till the sun dipped, and all the ways grew dark
upon the fathomless unresting sea.

                                    By night
our ship ran onward toward the Ocean's bourne,
the realm and region of the Men of Winter,                    15
hidden in mist and cloud. Never the flaming
eye of Hêlios lights on those men
at morning, when he climbs the sky of stars,
nor in descending earthward out of heaven;
ruinous night being rove over those wretches.                 20
We made the land, put ram and ewe ashore,
and took our way along the Ocean stream
to find the place foretold for us by Kirkê.
There Perimêdês and Eurýlokhos
pinioned the sacred beasts. With my drawn blade               25
I spaded up the votive pit, and poured
libations round it to the unnumbered dead:
sweet milk and honey, then sweet wine, and last
clear water; and I scattered barley down.
Then I addressed the blurred and breathless dead,             30
vowing to slaughter my best heifer for them
before she calved, at home in Ithaka,
and burn the choice bits on the altar fire;
as for Teirêsias, I swore to sacrifice
a black lamb, handsomest of all our flock.                    35
Thus to assuage the nations of the dead
I pledged these rites, then slashed the lamb and ewe,
letting their black blood stream into the wellpit.
Now the souls gathered, stirring out of Erebos,
brides and young men, and men grown old in pain,              40
and tender girls whose hearts were new to grief;
many were there, too, torn by brazen lanceheads,
battle-slain, bearing still their bloody gear.
From every side they came and sought the pit
with rustling cries; and I grew sick with fear.               45
But presently I gave command to my officers
to flay those sheep the bronze cut down, and make
burnt offerings of flesh to the gods below—
to sovereign Death, to pale Perséphonê.
Meanwhile I crouched with my drawn sword to keep              50
the surging phantoms from the bloody pit
till I should know the presence of Teirêsias.

---

15. *Men of Winter:* Although Homer usually places Hades below the earth, here he puts it across a great expanse of sea, apparently in the far north.

One shade came first—Elpênor, of our company,
who lay unburied still on the wide earth
as we had left him—dead in Kirkê's hall,                            55
untouched, unmourned, when other cares compelled us.
Now when I saw him there I wept for pity
and called out to him:

                     'How is this, Elpênor,
how could you journey to the western gloom
swifter afoot than I in the black lugger?'                          60

He sighed, and answered:

                   'Son of great Laërtês,
Odysseus, master mariner and soldier,
bad luck shadowed me, and no kindly power;
ignoble death I drank with so much wine.
I slept on Kirkê's roof, then could not see                         65
the long steep backward ladder, coming down,
and fell that height. My neck bone, buckled under,
snapped, and my spirit found this well of dark.
Now hear the grace I pray for, in the name
of those back in the world, not here—your wife                     70
and father, he who gave you bread in childhood,
and your own child, your only son, Telémakhos,
long ago left at home.

                     When you make sail
and put these lodgings of dim Death behind,
you will moor ship, I know, upon Aiaia Island;                     75
there, O my lord, remember me, I pray,
do not abandon me unwept, unburied,
to tempt the gods' wrath, while you sail for home;
but fire my corpse, and all the gear I had,
and build a cairn for me above the breakers—                       80
an unknown sailor's mark for men to come
Heap up the mound there and implant upon it
the oar I pulled in life with my companions.'

He ceased, and I replied:

                     'Unhappy spirit,
I promise you the barrow and the burial.'                          85

So we conversed, and grimly, at a distance,
with my long sword between, guarding the blood,
while the faint image of the lad spoke on.
Now came the soul of Antikleía, dead,
my mother, daughter of Autólykos,                                  90
dead now, though living still when I took ship

60. *lugger*: Small sailing boat.          built as a memorial.
80. *cairn*: Rounded heap of stones,

for holy Troy. Seeing this ghost I grieved,
but held her off, through pang on pang of tears,
till I should know the presence of Teirêsias.
Soon from the dark that prince of Thebes came forward    95
bearing a golden staff; and he addressed me:
'Son of Laërtês and the gods of old,
Odysseus, master of land ways and sea ways,
why leave the blazing sun, O man of woe,
to see the cold dead and the joyless region?    100
Stand clear, put up your sword;
let me but taste of blood, I shall speak true.'

At this I stepped aside, and in the scabbard
let my long sword ring home to the pommel silver,
as he bent down to the sombre blood. Then spoke    105
the prince of those with gift of speech:

              'Great captain,
a fair wind and the honey lights of home
are all you seek. But anguish lies ahead;
the god who thunders on the land prepares it,
not to be shaken from your track, implacable,    110
in rancor for the son whose eye you blinded.
One narrow strait may take you through his blows:
denial of yourself, restraint of shipmates.
When you make landfall on Thrinakia first
and quit the violet sea, dark on the land    115
you'll find the grazing herds of Hêlios
by whom all things are seen, all speech is known.
Avoid those kine, hold fast to your intent,
and hard seafaring brings you all to Ithaka.
But if you raid the beeves, I see destruction    120
for ship and crew. Though you survive alone,
bereft of all companions, lost for years,
under strange sail shall you come home, to find
your own house filled with trouble: insolent men
eating your livestock as they court your lady.    125
Aye, you shall make those men atone in blood!

114ff.: Teirêsias here predicts the future of Odysseus. Like many Greek
prophecies, it contains alternatives. The
second (l. 120ff.) is what happens. In
Book XII (not in our selection) Odysseus and his crew land on Thrinakia
(Sicily), and while Odysseus goes off to
explore, his crew kill and eat the cattle
of the Sun-god Hêlios. As a result the
ship is wrecked when they put to sea
again. Odysseus is the only survivor and
is cast up on the island of Kalypso,
where he is detained for seven years before he makes his way to the land of
the Phaiákians. From there he reaches
Ithaka and after great trials kills the
suitors who besiege his wife and waste
his wealth. The journey inland to find a
people who have never seen the sea (and
so mistake an oar for a winnowing-fan
—1. 136) does not take place within the
*Odyssey* itself.

But after you have dealt out death—in open
combat or by stealth—to all the suitors,
go overland on foot, and take an oar,
until one day you come where men have lived                    130
with meat unsalted, never known the sea,
nor seen seagoing ships, with crimson bows
and oars that fledge light hulls for dipping flight.
The spot will soon be plain to you, and I
can tell you how: some passerby will say,                      135
"What winnowing fan is that upon your shoulder?"
Halt, and implant your smooth oar in the turf
and make fair sacrifice to Lord Poseidon:
a ram, a bull, a great buck boar; turn back,
and carry out pure hekatombs at home                           140
to all wide heaven's lords, the undying gods,
to each in order. Then a seaborne death
soft as this hand of mist will come upon you
when you are wearied out with rich old age,
your country folk in blessed peace around you.                 145
And all this shall be just as I foretell.'

When he had done, I said at once,

                      'Teirêsias,
my life runs on then as the gods have spun it.
But come, now, tell me this; make this thing clear:
I see my mother's ghost among the dead                          150
sitting in silence near the blood. Not once
has she glanced this way toward her son, nor spoken.
Tell me, my lord,
may she in some way come to know my presence?'

To this he answered:

                       'I shall make it clear                   155
in a few words and simply. Any dead man
whom you allow to enter where the blood is
will speak to you, and speak the truth; but those
deprived will grow remote again and fade.'
When he had prophesied, Teirêsias' shade                        160
retired lordly to the halls of Death;
but I stood fast until my mother stirred,
moving to sip the black blood; then she knew me
and called out sorrowfully to me:

                            'Child,
how could you cross alive into this gloom                       165

140. *hekatombs*: Sacrifices of a hundred head of cattle.

at the world's end?—No sight for living eyes;
great currents run between, desolate waters,
the Ocean first, where no man goes a journey
without ship's timber under him.
                                    Say, now,
is it from Troy, still wandering, after years,                    170
that you come here with ship and company?
Have you not gone at all to Ithaka?
Have you not seen your lady in your hall?'

She put these questions, and I answered her:
'Mother, I came here, driven to the land of death               175
in want of prophecy from Teirêsias' shade;
nor have I yet coasted Akhaia's hills
nor touched my own land, but have had hard roving
since first I joined Lord Agamémnon's host
by sea for Ilion, the wild horse country,                       180
to fight the men of Troy.
But come now, tell me this, and tell me clearly,
what was the bane that pinned you down in Death?
Some ravaging long illness, or mild arrows
a-flying down one day from Artemis?                             185
Tell me of Father, tell me of the son
I left behind me; have they still my place,
my honors, or have other men assumed them?
Do they not say that I shall come no more?
And tell me of my wife: how runs her thought,                  190
still with her child, still keeping our domains,
or bride again to the best of the Akhaians?'

To this my noble mother quickly answered:
'Still with her child indeed she is, poor heart,
still in your palace hall. Forlorn her nights                   195
and days go by, her life used up in weeping.
But no man takes your honored place. Telémakhos
has care of all your garden plots and fields,
and holds the public honor of a magistrate,
feasting and being feasted. But your father                     200
is country bound and comes to town no more.
He owns no bedding, rugs, or fleecy mantles,
but lies down, winter nights, among the slaves,
rolled in old cloaks for cover, near the embers
Or when the heat comes at the end of summer,                   205
the fallen leaves, all round his vineyard plot,

---

184–185. *arrows . . . from Artemis*:   death for women.
A formula for mysterious but painless

heaped into windrows, make his lowly bed.
He lies now even so, with aching heart,
and longs for your return, while age comes on him.
So I, too, pined away, so doom befell me,                          210
not that the keen-eyed huntress with her shafts
had marked me down and shot to kill me; not
that illness overtook me—no true illness
wasting the body to undo the spirit;
only my loneliness for you, Odysseus,                              215
for your kind heart and counsel, gentle Odysseus,
took my own life away.'

              I bit my lip,
rising perplexed, with longing to embrace her,
and tried three times, putting my arms around her,
but she went sifting through my hands, impalpable                  220
as shadows are, and wavering like a dream.
Now this embittered all the pain I bore,
and I cried in the darkness:

                      'O my mother,
will you not stay, be still, here in my arms,
may we not, in this place of Death, as well,                       225
hold one another, touch with love, and taste
salt tears' relief, the twinge of welling tears?
Or is this all hallucination, sent
against me by the iron queen, Perséphonê,
to make me groan again?'

                  My noble mother                         230
answered quickly:

                'O my child—alas,
most sorely tried of men—great Zeus's daughter,
Perséphonê, knits no illusion for you.
All mortals meet this judgment when they die.
No flesh and bone are here, none bound by sinew,                   235
since the bright-hearted pyre consumed them down—
the white bones long exanimate—to ash;
dreamlike the soul flies, insubstantial.
You must crave sunlight soon.

                   Note all things strange
seen here, to tell your lady in after days.'                       240

So went our talk; then other shadows came,
ladies in company, sent by Perséphonê—
consorts or daughters of illustrious men—

237. *exanimate*: Lifeless.

crowding about the black blood.
                I took thought
how best to separate and question them,          245
and saw no help for it, but drew once more
the long bright edge of broadsword from my hip,
that none should sip the blood in company
but one by one, in order; so it fell
that each declared her lineage and name.          250

Here was great loveliness of ghosts! I saw
before them all, that princess of great ladies,
Tyro, Salmoneus' daughter, as she told me,
and queen to Krêtheus, a son of Aiolos.
She had gone daft for the river Enipeus,          255
most graceful of all running streams, and ranged
all day by Enipeus' limpid side,
whose form the foaming girdler of the islands,
the god who makes earth tremble, took and so
lay down with her where he went flooding seaward,          260
their bower a purple billow, arching round
to hide them in a sea-vale, god and lady.
Now when his pleasure was complete, the god
spoke to her softly, holding fast her hand:
'Dear mortal, go in joy! At the turn of seasons,          265
winter to summer, you shall bear me sons;
no lovemaking of gods can be in vain.
Nurse our sweet children tenderly, and rear them.
Home with you now, and hold your tongue, and tell
no one your lover's name—though I am yours,          270
Poseidon, lord of surf that makes earth tremble.'

He plunged away into the deep sea swell,
and she grew big with Pelias and Neleus,
powerful vassals, in their time, of Zeus.
Pelias lived on broad Iolkos seaboard          275
rich in flocks, and Neleus at Pylos.
As for the sons borne by that queen of women
to Krêtheus, their names were Aison, Pherês,
and Amytháon, expert charioteer.
Next after her I saw Antiopê,          280

---

251. *loveliness of ghosts:* There follows a "catalogue of women," a list of
famous and beautiful women of former
times.
253. *Tyro:* A queen of Thessaly.
255. *Enipeus:* A river of Thessaly.
Tyro had fallen in love with the river-
god; Poseidon, the "god who makes

earth tremble," assumed his shape.
273. *Neleus:* Father of Nestor of
Pylos. *Pelias:* King of Iolcus, who sent
Jason on the quest for the golden fleece.
278. *Aison:* Father of Jason. *Pherês:*
King of Thessaly, father of Admetus.
279. *Amytháon:* Father of Melampos.
(See line 319 and note.)

daughter of Ásopos. She too could boast
a god for lover, having lain with Zeus
and borne two sons to him: Amphion and
Zêthos, who founded Thebes, the upper city,
and built the ancient citadel. They sheltered                          285
no life upon that plain, for all their power,
without a fortress wall.
             And next I saw
Amphitrion's true wife, Alkmênê, mother,
as all men know, of lionish Heraklês,
conceived when she lay close in Zeus's arms;                          290
and Megarê, high-hearted Kreon's daughter,
wife of Amphitrion's unwearying son.

I saw the mother of Oidipous, Epikastê,
whose great unwitting deed it was
to marry her own son. He took that prize                              295
from a slain father; presently the gods
brought all to light that made the famous story.
But by their fearsome wills he kept his throne
in dearest Thebes, all through his evil days,
while she descended to the place of Death,                            300
god of the locked and iron door. Steep down
from a high rafter, throttled in her noose,
she swung, carried away by pain, and left him
endless agony from a mother's Furies.

And I saw Khloris, that most lovely lady,                             305
whom for her beauty in the olden time
Neleus wooed with countless gifts, and married.
She was the youngest daughter of Amphion,
son of Iasos. In those days he held
power at Orkhómenos, over the Minyai.                                 310
At Pylos then as queen she bore her children—
Nestor, Khromios, Periklýmenos,
and Pêro, too, who turned the heads of men
with her magnificence. A host of princes
from nearby lands came courting her; but Neleus                       315
would hear of no one, not unless the suitor
could drive the steers of giant Iphiklos
from Phylakê—longhorns, broad in the brow,

---

281. *Asopos*: A river in Boeotia, the
territory of Thebes.

291. *Kreon*: Not the same Kreon who
appears in Sophocles' *Oedipus Tyrannus*
and *Antigone*.

292. *unwearying son*: Herakles.

293. *Epikastê*: Usually known as Jocasta.

309. *he*: Amphion (not the same Amphion who founded Thebes, 1. 284).

310. *Orkhómenos*: One of the two
great cities of Boeotia, the region north
of Athens; Thebes was the other. *Minyai*: The original inhabitants of Boeotia.

317. *Iphiklos*: Brother of Herakles.

318. *Phylakê*: In Thessaly, northern
Greece.

so fierce that one man only, a diviner,
offered to round them up. But bitter fate                      320
saw him bound hand and foot by savage herdsmen.

Then days and months grew full and waned, the year
went wheeling round, the seasons came again,
before at last the power of Iphiklos,
relenting, freed the prisoner, who foretold                    325
all things to him. So Zeus's will was done.

And I saw Lêda, wife of Tyndareus,
upon whom Tyndareus had sired twins
indomitable: Kastor, tamer of horses,
and Polydeukês, best in the boxing ring.                       330
Those two live still, though life-creating earth
embraces them: even in the underworld
honored as gods by Zeus, each day in turn
one comes alive, the other dies again.

Then after Lêda to my vision came                              335
the wife of Aloeus, Iphimedeia,
proud that she once had held the flowing sea
and borne him sons, thunderers for a day,
the world-renowned Otos and Ephialtês.
Never were men on such a scale                                 340
bred on the plowlands and the grainlands, never
so magnificent any, after Orion.
At nine years old they towered nine fathoms tall,
nine cubits in the shoulders, and they promised
furor upon Olympos, heaven broken by battle cries,            345
the day they met the gods in arms.
                                    With Ossa's
mountain peak they meant to crown Olympos
and over Ossa Pelion's forest pile
for footholds up the sky. As giants grown
they might have done it, but the bright son of Zeus            350
by Lêto of the smooth braid shot them down
while they were boys unbearded; no dark curls
clustered yet from temples to the chin.

319. *a diviner*: Named Melampos.

327. *Lêda*: She bore Helen to Zeus;
to her husband Tyndareus, she bore twin
sons, Kastor and Polydeuces, and
Klytaimnéstra, who was to be the wife
of Agamémnon.

333. *each day in turn*: They shared,
as it were, one immortality between
them.

337. *flowing sea*: Poseidon.

342. *Orion*: The hunter who was, ac-

cording to later legend, transformed into
the constellation which still bears his
name; in Homer he is in the underworld
after his death (see l. 643*ff*.).

343. *nine fathoms*: 54 feet.

344. *nine cubits*: 14 feet or more.

346-347. *Ossa's mountain peak*: Ossa
and Pelion are mountains near Olympus
in Thessaly.

350. *son of Zeus*: Apollo.

Then I saw Phaidra, Prokris; and Ariadnê,
daughter of Minos, the grim king. Theseus took her     355
aboard with him from Krete for the terraced land
of ancient Athens; but he had no joy of her.
Artemis killed her on the Isle of Dia
at a word from Dionysos.
                              Maira, then,
and Klymênê, and that detested queen,                   360
Erífhylê, who betrayed her lord for gold . . .
but how name all the women I beheld there,
daughters and wives of kings? The starry night
wanes long before I close.
                              Here, or aboard ship,
amid the crew, the hour for sleep has come.            365
Our sailing is the gods' affair and yours."

Then he fell silent. Down the shadowy hall
the enchanted banqueters were still. Only
the queen with ivory pale arms, Arêtê, spoke,
saying to all the silent men:
                              "Phaiákians,                 370
how does he stand, now, in your eyes, this captain,
the look and bulk of him, the inward poise?
He is my guest, but each one shares that honor.
Be in no haste to send him on his way
or scant your bounty in his need. Remember             375
how rich, by heaven's will, your possessions are."

Then Ekhenêos, the old soldier, eldest
of all Phaiákians, added his word:
"Friends, here was nothing but our own thought spoken,
the mark hit square. Our duties to her majesty.        380
For what is to be said and done,
we wait upon Alkínoös' command."

At this the king's voice rang:

---

354. *Phaidra*: The Cretan wife of Theseus of Athens, who fell in love with her stepson Hippolytus. *Prokris:* the unfaithful wife of Cephalus, king of Athens. *Ariadnê:* sister of Phaidra; she helped Theseus slay the Minotaur on Crete and escaped with him, only to die on the island of Dia.

355. *Minos*: King of Crete, father of Phaidra and Ariadnê.

359. *Dionysus*: God of the vine and all green growing things. We have no other account of this version of the episode to explain why Dionysus wanted Ariadnê killed; the prevalent version of the story in later times is that Dionysus carried Ariadnê off to be his bride. *Maira*: A nymph of Artemis who broke her vow of chastity and was killed by the goddess.

360. *Klymênê*: Some story must have been attached to this name, but we do not know what it was.

361. *Eríphylê*: Bribed with a golden necklace by Polynices, son of Oedipus, she persuaded her husband Amphiaraus to take part in the attack on Thebes, where he was killed.

"I so command—
as sure as it is I who, while I live,
rule the sea rovers of Phaiákia. Our friend          385
longs to put out for home, but let him be
content to rest here one more day, until
I see all gifts bestowed. And every man
will take thought for his launching and his voyage,
I most of all, for I am master here."          390

Odysseus, the great tactician, answered:
"Alkínoös, king and admiration of men,
even a year's delay, if you should urge it,
in loading gifts and furnishing for sea—
I too could wish it; better far that I          395
return with some largesse of wealth about me—
I shall be thought more worthy of love and courtesy
by every man who greets me home in Ithaka."
The king said:
          "As to that, one word, Odysseus:
from all we see, we take you for no swindler—          400
though the dark earth be patient of so many,
scattered everywhere, baiting their traps with lies
of old times and of places no one knows.
You speak with art, but your intent is honest.
The Argive troubles, and your own troubles,          405
you told as a poet would, a man who knows the world.
But now come tell me this: among the dead
did you meet any of your peers, companions
who sailed with you and met their doom at Troy?
Here's a long night—an endless night—before us,          410
and no time yet for sleep, not in this hall.
Recall the past deeds and the strange adventures.
I could stay up until the sacred Dawn
as long as you might wish to tell your story."

Odysseus the great tactician answered:          415
"Alkínoös, king and admiration of men,
there is a time for story telling; there is
also a time for sleep. But even so,
if, indeed, listening be still your pleasure,
I must not grudge my part. Other and sadder          420
tales there are to tell, of my companions,
of some who came through all the Trojan spears,
clangor and groan of war,
only to find a brutal death at home—

---

396. *wealth about me*: He lost at sea all the loot he took at Troy and Ismaros.

and a bad wife behind it.
After Perséphoné, 425
icy and pale, dispersed the shades of women,
the soul of Agamémnon, son of Atreus,
came before me, sombre in the gloom,
and others gathered round, all who were with him
when death and doom struck in Aegisthos' hall. 430
Sipping the black blood, the tall shade perceived me,
and cried out sharply, breaking into tears;
then tried to stretch his hands toward me, but could not,
being bereft of all the reach and power
he once felt in the great torque of his arms. 435
Gazing at him, and stirred, I wept for pity,
and spoke across to him:
'O son of Atreus,
illustrious Lord Marshal, Agamémnon,
what was the doom that brought you low in death?
Were you at sea, aboard ship, and Poseidon 440
blew up a wicked squall to send you under,
or were you cattle-raiding on the mainland
or in a fight for some strongpoint, or women,
when the foe hit you to your mortal hurt?'

But he replied at once:
'Son of Laërtês, 445
Odysseus, master of land ways and sea ways,
neither did I go down with some good ship
in any gale Poseidon blew, nor die
upon the mainland, hurt by foes in battle.
It was Aigísthos who designed my death, 450
he and my heartless wife, and killed me, after
feeding me, like an ox felled at the trough.
That was my miserable end—and with me
my fellows butchered, like so many swine
killed for some troop, or feast, or wedding banquet 455
in a great landholder's household. In your day
you have seen men, and hundreds, die in war,
in the bloody press, or downed in single combat,
but these were murders you would catch your breath at:
think of us fallen, all our throats cut, winebowl 460
brimming, tables laden on every side,
while blood ran smoking over the whole floor.
In my extremity I heard Kassandra,

430. *Aigísthos:* Cousin of Agamémnon, who remained at home while Agamémnon went to Troy, seduced his wife Klytaim-néstra, and helped her murder her husband when he returned.

437. *Atreus:* See note to Aeschylus, *Agamemnon*, p. 299.
463. *Kassandra:* She was part of Agamemnon's share of the booty at Troy.

Priam's daughter, piteously crying
as the traitress Klytaimnéstra made to kill her                        465
along with me. I heaved up from the ground
and got my hands around the blade, but she
eluded me, that whore. Nor would she close
my two eyes as my soul swam to the underworld
or shut my lips. There is no being more fell,                         470
more bestial than a wife in such an action,
and what an action that one planned!
The murder of her husband and her lord.
Great god, I thought my children and my slaves
at least would give me welcome. But that woman,                       475
plotting a thing so low, defiled herself
and all her sex, all women yet to come,
even those few who may be virtuous,'
He paused then, and I answered:

                        'Foul and dreadful.
That was the way that Zeus who views the wide world                   480
vented his hatred on the sons of Atreus—
intrigues of women, even from the start.

                             Myriads
died by Helen's fault, and Klytaimnéstra
plotted against you half the world away.'

And he at once said:
                    'Let it be a warning                           485
even to you. Indulge a woman never,
and never tell her all you know. Some things
a man may tell, some he should cover up.
Not that I see a risk for you, Odysseus,
of death at your wife's hands. She is too wise,                       490
too clear-eyed, sees alternatives too well,
Penélopê, Ikários' daughter—
that young bride whom we left behind—think of it!—
when we sailed off to war. The baby boy
still cradled at her breast—now he must be                            495
a grown man, and a lucky one. By heaven,
you'll see him yet, and he'll embrace his father
with old fashioned respect, and rightly.

                          My own
lady never let me glut my eyes
on my own son, but bled me to death first.                            500
One thing I will advise, on second thought;
stow it away and ponder it.

---

468–469. *close my two eyes*: I.e., give
me a proper burial.

500. *own son*: Orestés.

Land your ship
in secret on your island; give no warning.
The day of faithful wives is gone forever.

But tell me, have you any word at all                        505
about my son's life? Gone to Orkhómenos
or sandy Pylos, can he be? Or waiting
with Meneláos in the plain of Sparta?
Death on earth has not yet taken Orestés.'

But I could only answer:

'Son of Atreus,                        510
why do you ask these questions of me? Neither
news of home have I, nor news of him,
alive or dead. And empty words are evil.'

So we exchanged our speech, in bitterness,
weighed down by grief, and tears welled in our eyes,         515
when there appeared the spirit of Akhilleus,
son of Peleus; then Patróklos' shade,
and then Antílokhos, and then Aias,
first among all the Danaans in strength
and bodily beauty, next to prince Akhilleus.                 520
Now that great runner, grandson of Aíakhos,
recognized me and called across to me:
'Son of Laërtês and the gods of old,
Odysseus, master mariner and soldier,
old knife, what next? What greater feat remains             525
for you to put your mind on, after this?
How did you find your way down to the dark
where these dimwitted dead are camped forever,
the after images of used-up men?'

I answered:

'Akhilleus, Peleus' son, strongest of all                    530
among the Akhaians, I had need of foresight
such as Teirêsias alone could give
to help me, homeward bound for the crags of Ithaka.
I have not yet coasted Akhaia, not yet
touched my land; my life is all adversity.                   535
But was there ever a man more blest by fortune
than you, Akhilleus? Can there ever be?
We ranked you with immortals in your lifetime,
we Argives did, and here your power is royal

506. *Pylos*: City on the west coast of Greece, the home of Nestor. The young Orestés had been sent away to the north while Agamémnon was at Troy; he eventually returned home to avenge his father, killing Aigísthos and Klytaimnéstra.

518. *Antílokhos*: Son of Nestor.
519. *Argives*: Greeks. (Likewise *Danaans* means "Greeks.")
521. *grandson of Aíakhos*: Akhilleus.
534. *coasted Akhaia*: Reached the coast of Greece.

among the dead men's shades. Think, then, Akhilleus:  540
you need not be so pained by death.'

To this
he answered swiftly:

'Let me hear no smooth talk
of death from you, Odysseus, light of councils.
Better, I say, to break sod as a farm hand
for some poor country man, on iron rations,  545
than lord it over all the exhausted dead.
Tell me, what news of the prince my son: did he
come after me to make a name in battle
or could it be he did not? Do you know
if rank and honor still belong to Peleus  550
in the towns of the Myrmidons? Or now, may be,
Hellas and Phthia spurn him, seeing old age
fetters him, hand and foot. I cannot help him
under the sun's rays, cannot be that man
I was on Troy's wide seaboard, in those days  555
when I made bastion for the Argives
and put an army's best men in the dust.
Were I but whole again, could I go now
to my father's house, one hour would do to make
my passion and my hands no man could hold  560
hateful to any who shoulder him aside.'

Now when he paused I answered:

'Of all that—
of Peleus' life, that is—I know nothing;
but happily I can tell you the whole story
of Neoptólemos, as you require.  565
In my own ship I brought him out from Skyros
to join the Akhaians under arms.

And I can tell you,
in every council before Troy thereafter
your son spoke first and always to the point;
no one but Nestor and I could out-debate him.  570
And when we formed against the Trojan line
he never hung back in the mass, but ranged
far forward of his troops—no man could touch him
for gallantry. Aye, scores went down before him

---

547. *my son*: Neoptólemos (the name means "new war").
Troy would fall only to the son of Akhilleus, who was living on the rocky island of Skyros.
550. *Peleus*: Father of Akhilleus.
551. *Myrmidons*: The people from whom Akhilleus' army was drawn.
552. *Hellas*: Northeastern Greece. *Phthia*: The home of Peleus and Akhilleus. *Hellas*: Later used to mean the whole of Greece, in Homer it describes the area of Thessaly from which Akhilleus came.
566. *brought him out from Skyros*: The Greeks were told by a prophet that Troy would fall only to the son of Akhilleus, who was living on the rocky island of Skyros.

in hard fights man to man. I shall not tell      575
all about each, or name them all—the long
roster of enemies he put out of action,
taking the shock of charges on the Argives.
But what a champion his lance ran through
in Eurýpulos the son of Télephos! Keteians      580
in throngs around that captain also died—
all because Priam's gifts had won his mother
to send the lad to battle; and I thought
Memnon alone in splendor ever outshone him.

But one fact more: while our picked Argive crew      585
still rode that hollow horse Epeios built,
and when the whole thing lay with me, to open
the trapdoor of the ambuscade or not,
at that point our Danaan lords and soldiers
wiped their eyes, and their knees began to quake,      590
all but Neoptólemos. I never saw
his tanned cheek change color or his hand
brush one tear away. Rather he prayed me,
hand on hilt, to sortie, and he gripped
his tough spear, bent on havoc for the Trojans.      595
And when we had pierced and sacked Priam's tall city
he loaded his choice plunder and embarked
with no scar on him; not a spear had grazed him
nor the sword's edge in close work—common wounds
one gets in war. Arês in his mad fits      600
knows no favorites.'

But I said no more,
for he had gone off striding the field of asphodel,
the ghost of our great runner, Akhilleus Aiákidês,
glorying in what I told him of his son.

Now other souls of mournful dead stood by,      605
each with his troubled questioning, but one
remained alone, apart: the son of Télamon,
Aías, it was—the great shade burning still
because I had won favor on the beachhead
in rivalry over Akhilleus' arms.      610
The Lady Thetis, mother of Akhilleus,

---

580. *Eurýpulos*: He came to the aid of the Trojans with a fresh army. *Télephos*: King of Mysia, a land of central Asia Minor.

584. *Memnon*: Leader of the Ethiopian allies of Troy, killed by Akhilleus. (Not related to Agamémnon.)

603. *Aiákidês*: Akhilleus was the grandson of Aiakos, a son of Zeus.

610. *Akhilleus' arms*: After Akhilleus was killed by the Trojan Paris, his mother Thetis offered them as a prize to the Greek who had done most harm to the Trojans. They were awarded to Odysseus. Aias, after an attempt to kill Odysseus and the two kings, Meneláos and Agamémnon, committed suicide.

laid out for us the dead man's battle gear,
and Trojan children, with Athena,
named the Danaan fittest to own them. Would
god I had not borne the palm that day!                      615
For earth took Aías then to hold forever,
the handsomest and, in all feats of war,
noblest of the Danaans after Akhilleus.
Gently therefore I called across to him:
'Aías, dear son of royal Télamon,                           620
you would not then forget, even in death,
your fury with me over those accurst
calamitous arms?—and so they were, a bane
sent by the gods upon the Argive host.
For when you died by your own hand we lost                  625
a tower, formidable in war. All we Akhaians
mourn you forever, as we do Akhilleus;
and no one bears the blame but Zeus.
He fixed that doom for you because he frowned
on the whole expedition of our spearmen.                    630
My lord, come nearer, listen to our story!
Conquer your indignation and your pride.'

But he gave no reply, and turned away,
following other ghosts toward Erebos.
Who knows if in that darkness he might still                635
have spoken, and I answered?
                           But my heart
longed, after this, to see the dead elsewhere.
And now there came before my eyes Minos,
the son of Zeus, enthroned, holding a golden staff,
dealing out justice among ghostly pleaders                  640
arrayed about the broad doorways of Death.

And then I glimpsed Orion, the huge hunter,
gripping his club, studded with bronze, unbreakable,
with wild beasts he had overpowered in life
on lonely mountainsides, now brought to bay                 645
on fields of asphodel.
                     And I saw Títyos,
the son of Gaia, lying
abandoned over nine square rods of plain.
Vultures, hunched above him, left and right,
rifling his belly, stabbed into the liver,                  650
and he could never push them off.
                               This hulk
had once committed rape of Zeus's mistress,

Léto, in her glory, when she crossed
the open grass of Panopeus toward Pytho.

Then I saw Tántalos put to the torture:          655
in a cool pond he stood, lapped round by water
clear to the chin, and being athirst he burned
to slake his dry weasand with drink, though drink
he would not ever again. For when the old man
put his lips down to the sheet of water          660
it vanished round his feet, gulped underground,
and black mud baked there in a wind from hell.
Boughs, too, drooped low above him, big with fruit,
pear trees, pomegranates, brilliant apples,
luscious figs, and olives ripe and dark;          665
but if he stretched his hand for one, the wind
under the dark sky tossed the bough beyond him.

Then Sísyphos in torment I beheld
being roustabout to a tremendous boulder.
Leaning with both arms braced and legs driving,          670
he heaved it toward a height, and almost over,
but then a Power spun him round and sent
the cruel boulder bounding again to the plain.
Whereon the man bent down again to toil,
dripping sweat, and the dust rose overhead.          675
Next I saw manifest the power of Heraklês—
a phantom, this, for he himself has gone
feasting amid the gods, reclining soft
with Hêbê of the ravishing pale ankles,
daughter of Zeus and Hêra, shod in gold.          680
But, in my vision, all the dead around him
cried like affrighted birds; like Night itself
he loomed with naked bow and nocked arrow
and glances terrible as continual archery.
My hackles rose at the gold swordbelt he wore          685
sweeping across him: gorgeous intaglio
of savage bears, boars, lions with wildfire eyes,
swordfights, battle, slaughter, and sudden death—
the smith who had that belt in him, I hope
he never made, and never will make, another.          690

---

654. *Pytho*: Shrine of Apollo's oracle
on Delphi.
655. *Tántalos*: King of Lydia. He was
the confidant of the gods and ate at
their table, but he betrayed their secrets.
658. *weasand*: Throat.

668. *Sísyphos*: King of Corinth, the
archetype of the liar and trickster. We
do not know what misdeed he is being
punished for in this passage.
679. *Hêbê*: Divine personification of
youth.

The eyes of the vast figure rested on me,
and of a sudden he said in kindly tones:
'Son of Laërtês and the gods of old,
Odysseus, master mariner and soldier,
under a cloud, you too? Destined to grinding          695
labors like my own in the sunny world?
Son of Kroníon Zeus or not, how many
days I sweated out, being bound in servitude
to a man far worse than I, a rough master!
He made me hunt this place one time              700
to get the watchdog of the dead: no more
perilous task, he thought, could be; but I
brought back that beast, up from the underworld
Hermês and grey-eyed Athena showed the way.'

And Heraklês, down the vistas of the dead,        705
faded from sight; but I stood fast, awaiting
other great souls who perished in times past.
I should have met, then, god-begotten Theseus
and Peirithoös, whom both I longed to see,
but first came shades in thousands, rustling        710
in a pandemonium of whispers, blown together,
and the horror took me that Perséphonê
had brought from darker hell some saurian death's head.
I whirled then, made for the ship, shouted to crewmen
to get aboard and cast off the stern hawsers,        715
an order soon obeyed. They took their thwarts,
and the ship went leaping toward the stream of Ocean
first under oars, then with a following wind.

699. **rough master**: Heraklês, son of
Zeus, was made subject to the orders of
Eurýstheus of Argos who ordered him
to perform the twelve famous labors.
One of them was to bring back from
Hades the dog which guarded the gate.

708. *Theseus*: After his adventures in
Crete, he went with his friend Peirithoös
to Hades to kidnap Perséphonê; the
venture failed, and the two heroes, imprisoned in Hades, were rescued by
Heraklês.

# AESCHYLUS

## (524?–456 B.C.)

## Agamemnon*

[The myth on which this play is based is the story of a family which suffered through many generations from a series of acts of vengeance to which there was no foreseeable end as long as private vengeance was a recognized system of justice. Pelops, son of Tantalus, had two sons, Atreus and Thyestes, who quarreled when Thyestes seduced Atreus' wife. Atreus revenged himself by killing the children of Thyestes and serving their flesh to their father at a feast. One son of Thyestes, Aegisthus, escaped the slaughter, and lived to avenge his father. The sons of Atreus, Agamemnon and Menelaus, were kings of Argos and Sparta respectively. Menelaus' wife was Helen, whose abduction caused the Trojan War. Agamemnon, leader of the Greek army, sacrificed his daughter Iphigenia to ensure the departure of the fleet when it lay wind-bound at the port of Aulis. His wife, Clytemnestra, committed adultery with Aegisthus while Agamemnon was away at Troy, and when her husband returned, with Aegisthus' aid, she murdered him. He was avenged seven years later by his son Orestes, who killed Aegisthus and Clytemnestra. (This action is the subject of the second play of the Aeschylean trilogy, the *Choephoroe*.) The *Agamemnon* begins with the moment when the news of the fall of Troy reaches Argos. The play was first produced in the open-air theater of Dionysus at Athens.]

### Characters

| | |
|---|---|
| WATCHMAN | HERALD |
| CHORUS OF OLD MEN | AGAMEMNON |
| OF THE CITY | CASSANDRA |
| CLYTEMNESTRA | AEGISTHUS |

SCENE—A *space in front of the palace of Agamemnon in Argos. Night. A* WATCHMAN *on the roof of the palace.*

WATCHMAN. The gods it is I ask to release me from this watch
A year's length now, spending my nights like a dog,
Watching on my elbow on the roof of the sons of Atreus
So that I have come to know the assembly of the nightly stars

---

* First produced in the spring of 458 B.C. Our text is a translation by Louis MacNeice, published as *The Agamemnon of Aeschylus*, Harcourt, Brace and Company, New York, 1936.
2. *like a dog:* explained by the following words, "Watching on my elbow"; head on arms like a reclining dog.
3. *sons of Atreus:* Agamemnon and Menelaus.

Those which bring storm and those which bring summer to
men,                                                                          5
The shining Masters riveted in the sky—
I know the decline and rising of those stars.
And now I am waiting for the sign of the beacon,
The flame of fire that will carry the report from Troy,
News of her taking. Which task has been assigned me        10
By a woman of sanguine heart but a man's mind.
Yet when I take my restless rest in the soaking dew,
My night not visited with dreams—
For fear stands by me in the place of sleep
That I cannot firmly close my eyes in sleep—                     15
Whenever I think to sing or hum to myself
As an antidote to sleep, then every time I groan
And fall to weeping for the fortunes of this house
Where not as before are things well ordered now.
But now may a good chance fall, escape from pain,           20
The good news visible in the midnight fire.

> [*Pause. A light appears, gradually increasing, the light of
> the beacon.*]

Ha! I salute you, torch of the night whose light
Is like the day, an earnest of many dances
In the city of Argos, celebration of Peace.
I call to Agamemnon's wife; quickly to rise                        25
Out of her bed and in the house to raise
Clamour of joy in answer to this torch
For the city of Troy is taken—
Such is the evident message of the beckoning flame.
And I myself will dance my solo first                                   30
For I shall count my master's fortune mine
Now that this beacon has thrown me a lucky throw.
And may it be when he comes, the master of this house,
That I grasp his hand in my hand.
As to the rest, I am silent. A great ox, as they say,          35
Stands on my tongue. The house itself, if it took voice,
Could tell the case most clearly. But I will only speak
To those who know. For the others I remember nothing.

> [*Enter* CHORUS OF OLD MEN. *During the following chorus
> the day begins to dawn.*]

CHORUS. The tenth year it is since Priam's high
Adversary, Menelaus the king                                           40

---

8. *beacon:* Clytemnestra had arranged to be informed of the fall of
Troy by a chain of signal fires stretching from Troy across the islands of
the Aegean Sea to Argos.
11. *woman . . . mind:* Clytemnestra.

27. *Clamour of joy:* the triumphant
cry with which the women of a city
greeted the news of victory.
40. *Adversary. Menelaus:* Priam's
son Paris carried off Menelaus' wife
Helen.

And Agamemnon, the double-throned and sceptred
Yoke of the sons of Atreus
Ruling in fee from God,
From this land gathered an Argive army
On a mission of war a thousand ships,                              45
Their hearts howling in boundless bloodlust
In eagles' fashion who in lonely
Grief for nestlings above their homes hang
Turning in cycles
Beating the air with the oars of their wings,                      50
    Now to no purpose
    Their love and task of attention.

But above there is One,
Maybe Pan, maybe Zeus or Apollo,
Who hears the harsh cries of the birds                             55
Guests in his kingdom,
Wherefore, though late, in requital
He sends the Avenger.
Thus Zeus our master
Guardian of guest and of host                                      60
Sent against Paris the sons of Atreus
For a woman of many men
Many the dog-tired wrestlings
Limbs and knees in the dust pressed—
    For both the Greeks and Trojans                                65
    An overture of breaking spears.

Things are where they are, will finish
In the manner fated and neither
Fire beneath nor oil above can soothe
The stubborn anger of the unburnt offering.                       70
As for us, our bodies are bankrupt,
The expedition left us behind
And we wait supporting on sticks
Our strength—the strength of a child;

54. *Pan:* a god particularly associated with the forest and all forms of wild life.

56. *guests in his kingdom:* since they live in the sky, his domain.

58. *Avenger:* a Fury. The Furies avenged those who could not avenge themselves. So, later in the trilogy, they come to demand retribution for the murder of Clytemnestra, who has left no avenger behind her.

60. *Guardian of guest and of host:* Zeus himself punished violations of the code of hospitality. In this case he punishes the abduction of Helen by Paris, who was a guest in the house of Menelaus.

73 ff. *And we wait . . .* : The general sense of the passage is that only two classes of the male population are left in Argos, those who are too young to fight and those who, like the chorus, are too old. The emphasis on the age and weakness of the members of the chorus prepares the audience for their complete failure of nerve at the moment of Agamemnon's murder.

For the marrow that leaps in a boy's body 75
Is no better than that of the old
For the War God is not in his body;
While the man who is very old
And his leaf withering away
Goes on the three-foot way 80
No better than a boy, and wanders
A dream in the middle of the day.

But you, daughter of Tyndareus,
Queen Clytemnestra,
What is the news, what is the truth, what have you learnt, 85
On the strength of whose word have you thus
Sent orders for sacrifice round?
All the gods, the gods of the town,
Of the worlds of Below and Above,
By the door, in the square, 90
Have their altars ablaze with your gifts,
From here, from there, all sides, all corners,
Sky-high leap the flame-jets fed
By gentle and undeceiving
Persuasion of sacred unguent, 95
Oil from the royal stores.
Of these things tell
That which you can, that which you may,
Be healer of this our trouble
Which at times torments with evil 100
Though at times by propitiations
A shining hope repels
The insatiable thought upon grief
Which is eating away our hearts.

Of the omen which powerfully speeded 105
That voyage of strong men, by God's grace even I
Can tell, my age can still
Be galvanized to breathe the strength of song,
To tell how the kings of all the youth of Greece
Two-throned but one in mind 110
Were launched with pike and punitive hand
Against the Trojan shore by angry birds.

80. *three-foot:* **two feet and a stick.**
82. **Enter Clytemnestra.**
104. Clytemnestra leaves the stage without giving them an answer.
105. *omen:* The chorus proceeds to describe the omen which accompanied the departure of the army for Troy ten years before. Two eagles seized and tore a pregnant hare; this was interpreted by the prophet Calchas as meaning that the two kings would destroy the city of Troy, thus killing not only the living Trojans but the Trojan generations yet unborn.

Kings of the birds to our kings came,
One with a white rump, the other black,
Appearing near the palace on the spear-arm side .      115
Where all could see them,
Tearing a pregnant hare with the unborn young
Foiled of their courses.

    Cry, cry upon Death; but may the good prevail

But the diligent prophet of the army seeing the sons      120
Of Atreus twin in temper knew
That the hare-killing birds were the two
Generals, explained it thus—
"In time this expedition sacks the town
Of Troy before whose towers      125
By Fate's force the public
Wealth will be wasted.
Only let not some spite from the gods benight the bulky
    battalions,
The bridle of Troy, nor strike them untimely;
For the goddess feels pity, is angry      130
With the winged dogs of her father
Who killed the cowering hare with her unborn young;
Artemis hates the eagles' feast."

    Cry, cry upon Death; but may the good prevail.

"But though you are so kind, goddess,      135
To the little cubs of lions
And to all the sucking young of roving beasts
In whom your heart delights,
Fulfil us the signs of these things,
The signs which are good but open to blame,      140
And I call on Apollo the Healer
That his sister raise not against the Greeks
Unremitting gales to baulk their ships,
Hurrying on another kind of sacrifice, with no feasting,

113. *Kings of the birds:* eagles.
115. *spear-arm side:* the right.
120. *prophet:* Calchas.
130. *goddess:* Artemis, a virgin goddess, patron of hunting and the protectress of wild life. She is angry that the eagles have destroyed a pregnant animal. The prophet fears that she may turn her wrath against the kings whom the eagles represent.
135. *goddess:* Calchas addresses a prayer to Artemis.
143. *Unremitting gales:* He foresees the future. Artemis will send unfavorable winds to prevent the sailing of the Greek expedition from Aulis, the port of embarkation. She will demand the sacrifice of Agamemnon's daughter Iphigenia as the price of the fleet's release.
144. *with no feasting:* At an ordinary sacrifice the celebrants gave the gods their due portion and then feasted on the animal's flesh. The word "sacrifice" comes to have the connotation of "feast." There will be no feast at this sacrifice, since the victim will be a human being. The ominous phrase reminds us of a feast of human flesh which has already taken place, Thyestes' feasting on his children.

Barbarous building of hates and disloyalties                     145
Grown on the family. For anger grimly returns
Cunningly haunting the house, avenging the death of a child,
    never forgetting its due."

So cried the prophet—evil and good together,
Fate that the birds foretold to the king's house.
In tune with this                                                150
    Cry, cry upon Death; but may the good prevail.

Zeus, whoever He is, if this
Be a name acceptable,
By this name I will call him.
There is no one comparable                                       155
When I reckon all of the case
Excepting Zeus, if ever I am to jettison
The barren care which clogs my heart.
Not He who formerly was great
With brawling pride and mad for broils                           160
Will even be said to have been.
And He who was next has met
His match and is seen no more,
But Zeus is the name to cry in your triumph-song
And win the prize for wisdom.                                    165

Who setting us on the road
Made this a valid law—
    "That men must learn by suffering."
Drop by drop in sleep upon the heart
Falls the laborious memory of pain,                              170
Against one's will comes wisdom;
The grace of the gods is forced on us
    Throned inviolably.

So at that time the elder
Chief of the Greek ships                                         175
Would not blame any prophet
Nor face the flail of fortune;

---

147. *avenging the death of a child:*
This prophecy is fulfilled in this play,
by the murder of **Agamemnon**.

159. *He who formerly was great:*
Uranus, father of Cronos, grandfather
of Zeus, the first lord of heaven. This
whole passage refers to a primitive
legend which told how Uranus was
violently supplanted by his son Cronos,
who was in his turn overthrown by his
son Zeus. This legend is made to bear
new meaning by Aeschylus, for he suggests that it is not a meaningless series
of acts of violence, but a progression to
the rule of Zeus, who stands for order
and justice. Thus the law of human life
which Zeus proclaims and administers,
that wisdom comes through suffering,
has its counterpart in the history of the
establishment of the divine rule.

162. *He who was next:* Cronos.

174–175. *elder chief:* Agamemnon.

For unable to sail, the people
Of Greece were heavy with famine,
Waiting in Aulis where the tides                              180
Flow back, opposite Chalcis.

But the winds that blew from the Strymon,
Bringing delay, hunger, evil harbourage,
Crazing men, rotting ships and cables,
By drawing out the time                                      185
Were shredding into nothing the flower of Argos,
When the prophet screamed a new
Cure for that bitter tempest
And heavier still for the chiefs,
Pleading the anger of Artemis so that the sons of Atreus      190
Beat the ground with their sceptres and shed tears.
Then the elder king found voice and answered:
"Heavy is my fate, not obeying,
And heavy it is if I kill my child, the delight of my house,
And with a virgin's blood upon the altar                      195
Make foul her father's hands.
Either alternative is evil.
How can I betray the fleet
And fail the allied army?
It is right they should passionately cry for the winds to be
    lulled                                                    200
By the blood of a girl. So be it. May it be well."

But when he had put on the halter of Necessity
Breathing in his heart a veering wind of evil
Unsanctioned, unholy, from that moment forward
He changed his counsel, would stop at nothing.                205
For the heart of man is hardened by infatuation,
A faulty adviser, the first link of sorrow.
Whatever the cause, he brought himself to slay
His daughter, an offering to promote the voyage
To a war for a runaway wife.                                  210

Her prayers and her cries of father,
Her life of a maiden,
Counted for nothing with those militarists;
But her father, having duly prayed, told the attendants

180–181. *Aulis . . . Chalcis:* the unruly water of the narrows between Aulis
on the mainland and Chalcis on the
island of Euboea.
182. *Strymon:* a river in Thrace;

the winds blew from the north.
190. *anger of Artemis:* The prophet
announces Artemis' demand for the sacrifice of Iphigenia.

To lift her, like a goat, above the altar                          215
With her robes falling about her,
To lift her boldly, her spirit fainting,
And hold back with a gag upon her lovely mouth
By the dumb force of a bridle
The cry which would curse the house.                               220
Then dropping on the ground her saffron dress,
Glancing at each of her appointed
Sacrificers a shaft of pity,
Plain as in a picture she wished
To speak to them by name, for often                                225
At her father's table where men feasted
She had sung in celebration for her father
With a pure voice, affectionately, virginally,
The hymn for happiness at the third libation.
The sequel to this I saw not and tell not                          230
But the crafts of Calchas gained their object.
To learn by suffering is the equation of Justice; the Future
Is known when it comes, let it go till then.
To know in advance is to sorrow in advance.
The facts will appear with the shining of the dawn.               235
    [*Enter* CLYTEMNESTRA.]
But may good, at the least, follow after
As the queen here wishes, who stands
Nearest the throne, the only
    Defence of the land of Argos.
LEADER OF THE CHORUS. I have come, Clytemnestra, reverencing
    your authority.                                                240
For it is right to honour our master's wife
When the man's own throne is empty.
But you, if you have heard good news for certain, or if
You sacrifice on the strength of flattering hopes,
I would gladly hear. Though I cannot cavil at silence.             245
CLYTEMNESTRA. Bearing good news, as the proverb says, may Dawn
Spring from her mother Night.
You will hear something now that was beyond your hopes.
The men of Argos have taken Priam's city.
LEAD. What! I cannot believe it. It escapes me.                    250
CLYT. Troy in the hands of the Greeks. Do I speak plain?
LEAD. Joy creeps over me, calling out my tears.
CLYT. Yes. Your eyes proclaim your loyalty.
LEAD. But what are your grounds? Have you a proof of it?

---

229. *at the third libation:* At the
banquet three libations (offerings of
wine) were poured, the third and last
to Zeus the Savior. The last libation
was accompanied by a hymn of praise.

CLYT. There is proof indeed—unless God has cheated us.    255

LEAD. Perhaps you believe the inveigling shapes of dreams?

CLYT. I would not be credited with a dozing brain!

LEAD. Or are you puffed up by Rumour, the wingless flyer?

CLYT. You mock my common sense as if I were a child.

LEAD. But at what time was the city given to sack?    260

CLYT. In this very night that gave birth to this day.

LEAD. What messenger could come so fast?

CLYT. Hephaestus, launching a fine flame from Ida,
Beacon forwarding beacon, despatch-riders of fire,
Ida relayed to Hermes' cliff in Lemnos    265
And the great glow from the island was taken over third
By the height of Athos that belongs to Zeus,
And towering then to straddle over the sea
The might of the running torch joyfully tossed
The gold gleam forward like another sun,    270
Herald of light to the heights of Mount Macistus,
And he without delay, nor carelessly by sleep
Encumbered, did not shirk his intermediary role,
His farflung ray reached the Euripus' tides
And told Messapion's watchers, who in turn    275
Sent on the message further
Setting a stack of dried-up heather on fire.
And the strapping flame, not yet enfeebled, leapt

263. *Hephaestus:* i.e., fire. Hephaestus was the god of fire and of the crafts dependent upon fire.

263 ff. *Ida:* the mountain range near Troy. The names which follow in this speech designate the places where beacon fires flashed the message of Troy's fall to Argos. The chain extends from Ida to Hermes' cliff on the island of Lemnos (off the coast of Asia Minor), to Mount Athos (which is situated on a rocky peninsula in north Greece), to Mount Macistus on the island of Euboea (off the coast of central Greece), to Messapion, a mountain of the mainland, to Cithaeron, a mountain near Thebes, across Lake Gorgopis to Mount Aegiplanctus on the Isthmus of Corinth, across the sea (the Saronic Gulf) to Mount Arachnaeus in Argive territory. This fire is the one seen by the watchman at the beginning of the play. The speech has often been criticized as discursive, but it has great poetic importance. The image of the light which will dispel the darkness, first introduced by the watchman, is one of the dominant images of the trilogy, and is here developed by Clytemnestra with magnificent ambiguous effect. For the watchman the light means the safe return of Agamemnon and the restoration of order in the house; for Clytemnestra it means the return of Agamemnon to his death at her hands. Each swift jump of the racing light is one step nearer home and death for Agamemnon. The light the watchman longs for brings only greater darkness, but eventually it brings darkness for Clytemnestra too. The final emergence of the true light comes in the glare of the torchlight procession which ends the last play of the trilogy, a procession which symbolizes perfect reconciliation on both the human and the divine levels, and the working out of the will of Zeus in the substitution of justice for vengeance. The conception of the beacons as a chain of descendants (compare, "Issue and image of the fire on Ida," l. 293), is also important; the fire at Argos which announces Agamemnon's imminent death is a direct descendant of the fire on Ida which announces the sack of Troy and Agamemnon's sacrilegious conduct there. The metaphor thus reminds us of the sequence of crimes from generation to generation which is the history of the house of Pelops.

Over the plain of Asopus like a blazing moon
And woke on the crags of Cithaeron                                    280
Another relay in the chain of fire.
The light that was sent from far was not declined
By the look-out men, who raised a fiercer yet,
A light which jumped the water of Gorgopis
And to Mount Aegiplanctus duly come                                   285
Urged the reveille of the punctual fire.
So then they kindle it squanderingly and launch
A beard of flame big enough to pass
The headland that looks down upon the Saronic gulf,
Blazing and bounding till it reached at length                       290
The Arachnaean steep, our neighbouring heights;
And leaps in the latter end on the roof of the sons of Atreus
Issue and image of the fire on Ida.
Such was the assignment of my torch-racers,
The task of each fulfilled by his successor,                         295
And victor is he who ran both first and last.
Such is the proof I offer you, the sign
My husband sent me out of Troy.
LEAD. To the gods, queen, I shall give thanks presently.
But I would like to hear this story further,                         300
To wonder at it in detail from your lips.
CLYT. The Greeks hold Troy upon this day.
The cries in the town I fancy do not mingle.
Pour oil and vinegar into the same jar,
You would say they stand apart unlovingly;                           305
Of those who are captured and those who have conquered
Distinct are the sounds of their diverse fortunes,
For *these* having flung themselves about the bodies
Of husbands and brothers, or sons upon the bodies
Of aged fathers from a throat no longer                              310
Free, lament the fate of their most loved.
But *those* a night's marauding after battle
Sets hungry to what breakfast the town offers
Not billeted duly in any barracks order
But as each man has drawn his lot of luck.                           315
So in the captive homes of Troy already
They take their lodging, free of the frosts
And dews of the open. Like happy men
They will sleep all night without sentry.
But if they respect duly the city's gods,                            320

---

296. *he who ran both first and last.*
The chain of beacons is compared to
a relay race in which the runners carry
torches: the last runner (who runs the
final lap) comes in first to win.

Those of the captured land and the sanctuaries of the gods,
They need not, having conquered, fear reconquest.
But let no lust fall first upon the troops
To plunder what is not right, subdued by gain,
For they must still, in order to come home safe,                    325
Get round the second lap of the doubled course.
So if they return without offence to the gods
The grievance of the slain may learn at last
A friendly talk—unless some fresh wrong falls.
Such are the thoughts you hear from me, a woman.          330
But may the good prevail for all to see.
We have much good. I only ask to enjoy it.
LEAD. Woman, you speak with sense like a prudent man.
I, who have heard your valid proofs, prepare
To give the glory to God.                                          335
Fair recompense is brought us for our troubles.

[CLYTEMNESTRA *goes back into the palace.*]

CHOR. O Zeus our king and Night our friend
Donor of glories,
Night who cast on the towers of Troy
A close-clinging net so that neither the grown          340
Nor any of the children can pass
The enslaving and huge
Trap of all-taking destruction.
Great Zeus, guardian of host and guest,
I honour who has done his work and taken            345
A leisured aim at Paris so that neither
Too short nor yet over the stars
    He might shoot to no purpose.

From Zeus is the blow they can tell of,
This at least can be established,                                350
They have fared according to his ruling. For some
Deny that the gods deign to consider those among men
Who trample on the grace of inviolate things;
It is the impious man says this,
For Ruin is revealed the child                                  355
Of not to be attempted actions
When men are puffed up unduly
And their houses are stuffed with riches.

---

323. *But let no lust fall:* The audience was familiar with the traditional
account, according to which Agamemnon and his army failed signally to
respect the gods and temples of Troy.
337. *Night:* Troy fell to a night
attack.

353. *Who trample . . . things:* The
language throughout this passage is
significantly general. The chorus refers
to Paris, but everything it says is
equally applicable to Agamemnon, who
sacrificed his daughter for his ambitions.

Measure is the best. Let danger be distant,
This should suffice a man                                    360
With a proper part of wisdom.
   For a man has no protection
   Against the drunkenness of riches
   Once he has spurned from his sight
   The high altar of Justice.                               365

Sombre Persuasion compels him,
Intolerable child of calculating Doom;
All cure is vain, there is no glozing it over
But the mischief shines forth with a deadly light
And like bad coinage                                         370
By rubbings and frictions
He stands discoloured and black
Under the test—like a boy
Who chases a winged bird.
He has branded his city for ever.                            375
His prayers are heard by no god.
Who makes such things his practice
The gods destroy him.
   This way came Paris
   To the house of the sons of Atreus                        380
   And outraged the table of friendship
   Stealing the wife of his host.

Leaving to her countrymen clanging of
Shields and spears and
Launching of warships                                        385
And bringing instead of a dowry destruction to Troy
Lightly she was gone through the gates daring
Things undared. Many the groans
Of the palace spokesmen on this theme—
"O the house, the house, and its princes,                    390
O the bed and the imprint of her limbs;
One can see him crouching in silence
Dishonoured and unreviling."
Through desire for her who is overseas, a ghost
Will seem to rule the household.                             395
   And now her husband hates
   The grace of shapely statues;
   In the emptiness of their eyes
   All their appeal is departed.

359. *Measure:* the mean, moderation.   proverbial expression describing a per-
373–374. *like a boy . . . bird:* a       son of insane ambitions.

But appearing in dreams persuasive                                                400
Images come bringing a joy that is vain,
Vain for when in fancy he looks to touch her—
Slipping through his hands the vision
Rapidly is gone
Following on wings the walks of sleep.                                            405
Such are his griefs in his house on his hearth,
Such as these and worse than these,
But everywhere through the land of Greece which men have left
Are mourning women with enduring hearts
To be seen in all houses; many                                                    410
Are the thoughts which stab their hearts;
    For those they sent to war
    They know, but in place of men
    That which comes home to them
    Is merely an urn and ashes.                                                   415

But the money-changer War, changer of bodies,
Holding his balance in the battle
Home from Troy refined by fire
Sends back to friends the dust
That is heavy with tears, stowing                                                 420
A man's worth of ashes
In an easily handled jar.
And they wail speaking well of the men how that one
Was expert in battle, and one fell well in the carnage—
But for another man's wife.                                                       425
Muffled and muttered words;
And resentful grief creeps up against the sons
Of Atreus and their cause.
    But others there by the wall
    Entombed in Trojan ground                                                     430
    Lie, handsome of limb,
    Holding and hidden in enemy soil.

Heavy is the murmur of an angry people
Performing the purpose of a public curse;
There is something cowled in the night                                            435
That I anxiously wait to hear.
For the gods are not blind to the
Murderers of many and the black
Furies in time
When a man prospers in sin                                                        440
By erosion of life reduce him to darkness,

---

406. *his:* Menelaus'.                     417. *balance:* scales.

Who, once among the lost, can no more
Be helped. Over-great glory
Is a sore burden. The high peak
Is blasted by the eyes of Zeus.                                          445
    I prefer an unenvied fortune,
    Not to be a sacker of cities
    Nor to find myself living at another's
    Ruling, myself a captive.

AN OLD MAN. From the good news' beacon a swift                           450
Rumour is gone through the town.
    Who knows if it be true
    Or some deceit of the gods?

ANOTHER OLD MAN. Who is so childish or broken in wit
To kindle his heart at a new-fangled message of flame                   455
And then be downcast
    At a change of report?

ANOTHER OLD MAN. It fits the temper of a woman.
To give her assent to a story before it is proved.

ANOTHER OLD MAN. The over-credulous passion of women
    expands                                          460
In swift conflagration but swiftly declining is gone
The news that a woman announced.

LEAD. Soon we shall know about the illuminant torches,
The beacons and the fiery relays,
Whether they were true or whether like dreams                           465
That pleasant light came here and hoaxed our wits.
Look: I see, coming from the beach, a herald
Shadowed with olive shoots; the dust upon him,
Mud's thirsty sister and colleague, is my witness
That he will not give dumb news nor news by lighting                    470
A flame of fire with the smoke of mountain timber;
In words he will either corroborate our joy—
But the opposite version I reject with horror.
To the good appeared so far may good be added.

ANOTHER SPEAKER. Whoever makes other prayers for this our
    city,                                            475
May he reap himself the fruits of his wicked heart.

[*Enter the* HERALD, *who kisses the ground before speaking.*]

HERALD. Earth of my fathers, O the earth of Argos,
In the light of the tenth year I reach you thus
After many shattered hopes achieving one,
For never did I dare to think that here in Argive land                  480
I should win a grave in the dearest soil of home;

---

468. *Shadowed with olive shoots:* wearing a wreath of olive.

But now hail, land, and hail, light of the sun.
And Zeus high above the country and the Pythian king—
May he no longer shoot his arrows at us
(Implacable long enough beside Scamander)                    485
But now be saviour to us and be healer,
King Apollo. And all the Assembly's gods
I call upon, and him my patron, Hermes,
The dear herald whom all heralds adore,
And the Heroes who sped our voyage, again with favour        490
Take back the army that has escaped the spear.
O cherished dwelling, palace of royalty,
O august thrones and gods facing the sun,
If ever before, now with your bright eyes
Gladly receive your king after much time,                    495
Who comes bringing light to you in the night time,
And to all these as well—King Agamemnon.
Give him a good welcome as he deserves,
Who with the axe of judgment-awarding God
Has smashed Troy and levelled the Trojan land;               500
The altars are destroyed, the seats of the gods,
And the seed of all the land is perished from it.
Having cast this halter round the neck of Troy
The King, the elder son of Atreus, a blessed man,
Comes, the most worthy to have honour of all                 505
Men that are now. Paris nor his guilty city
Can boast that the crime was greater than the atonement.
Convicted in a suit for rape and robbery
He has lost his stolen goods and with consummate ruin
Mowed down the whole country and his father's house.         510
The sons of Priam have paid their account with interest.

LEAD. Hail and be glad, herald of the Greek army.
HER. Yes. Glad indeed! So glad that at the gods' demand
　　　I should no longer hesitate to die.
LEAD. Were you so harrowed by desire for home?               515
HER. Yes. The tears come to my eyes for joy.
LEAD. Sweet then is the fever which afflicts you.
HER. What do you mean? Let me learn your drift.
LEAD. Longing for those whose love came back in echo.
HER. Meaning the land was homesick for the army?            520
LEAD. Yes. I would often groan from a darkened heart.
HER. This sullen hatred—how did it fasten on you?

---

483. *Pythian king:* Apollo.
484. *arrows:* Compare the opening
scenes of the *Iliad*, Book 1.

488. *Hermes:* As the messenger of
Zeus, he was the patron deity of heralds.

LEAD. I cannot say. Silence is my stock prescription.

HER. What? In your masters' absence were there some you feared?

LEAD. Yes. In your phrase, death would now be a gratification.  525

HER. Yes, for success is ours. These things have taken time.
Some of them we could say have fallen well,
While some we blame. Yet who except the gods
Is free from pain the whole duration of life?
If I were to tell of our labours, our hard lodging,  530
The sleeping on crowded decks, the scanty blankets,
Tossing and groaning, rations that never reached us—
And the land too gave matter for more disgust.
For our beds lay under the enemy's walls.
Continuous drizzle from the sky, dews from the marshes,  535
Rotting our clothes, filling our hair with lice.
And if one were to tell of the bird-destroying winter
Intolerable from the snows of Ida
Or of the heat when the sea slackens at noon
Waveless and dozing in a depressed calm—  540
But why make these complaints? The weariness is over;
Over indeed for some who never again
Need even trouble to rise.
Why make a computation of the lost?
Why need the living sorrow for the spites of fortune?  545
I wish to say a long goodbye to disasters.
For us, the remnant of the troops of Argos,
The advantage remains, the pain can not outweigh it;
So we can make our boast to this sun's light,
Flying on words above the land and sea:  550
"Having taken Troy the Argive expedition
Has nailed up throughout Greece in every temple
These spoils, these ancient trophies."
Those who hear such things must praise the city
And the generals. And the grace of God be honoured  555
Which brought these things about. You have the whole story.

LEAD. I confess myself convinced by your report.
Old men are always young enough to learn.

[Enter CLYTEMNESTRA from the palace.]

This news belongs by right first to the house
And Clytemnestra—though I am enriched also.  560

CLYT. Long before this I shouted at joy's command
At the coming of the first night-messenger of fire
Announcing the taking and capsizing of Troy.

523. *Silence:* Throughout this dialogue the chorus has been nerving itself to warn the herald that there is danger for Agamemnon at home; at this point its nerve fails, and it abandons the attempt.

And people reproached me saying, "Do mere beacons
Persuade you to think that Troy is already down?     565
Indeed a woman's heart is easily exalted."
Such comments made me seem to be wandering but yet
I began my sacrifices and in the women's fashion
Throughout the town they raised triumphant cries
And in the gods' enclosures                          570
Lulling the fragrant, incense-eating flame.
And now what need is there for you to tell me more?
From the King himself I shall learn the whole story.
But how the best to welcome my honoured lord
I shall take pains when he comes back—For what       575
Is a kinder light for a woman to see than this,
To open the gates to her man come back from war
When God has saved him? Tell this to my husband,
To come with all speed, the city's darling;
May he returning find a wife as loyal                580
As when he left her, watchdog of the house,
Good to *him* but fierce to the ill-intentioned,
And in all other things as ever, having destroyed
No seal or pledge at all in the length of time.
I know no pleasure with another man, no scandal,     585
More than I know how to dye metal red.
Such is my boast, bearing a load of truth,
A boast that need not disgrace a noble wife.     [*Exit.*]

LEAD. Thus has she spoken; if you take her meaning,
Only a specious tale to shrewd interpreters.         590
But do you, herald, tell me; I ask after Menelaus
Whether he will, returning safe preserved,
Come back with you, our land's loved master.

HER. I am not able to speak the lovely falsehood
To profit you, my friends, for any stretch of time.  595

LEAD. But if only the true tidings could be also good!
It is hard to hide a division of good and true.

HER. The prince is vanished out of the Greek fleet,
Himself and ship. I speak no lie.

LEAD. Did he put forth first in the sight of all from Troy,  600
Or a storm that troubled all sweep him apart?

HER. You have hit the target like a master archer,
Told succinctly a long tale of sorrow.

---

569. *triumphant cries:* the women's victory cry mentioned by the watchman.

591. *Menelaus:* The relevance of this question and the following speeches lies in the fact that Menelaus' absence makes Agamemnon's murder easier (his presence might have made it im- possible), and in the fact that Menelaus is bringing Helen home; the choral ode which follows shows how much the chorus is obsessed with Helen's guilt—so much that it fails to recognize the true responsibility for the war and the imminence of disaster.

LEAD. Did the rumours current among the remaining ships
 Represent him as alive or dead?       605
HER. No one knows so as to tell for sure
 Except the sun who nurses the breeds of earth.
LEAD. Tell me how the storm came on the host of ships
 Through the divine anger, and how it ended.
HER. Day of good news should not be fouled by tongue    610
 That tells ill news. To each god his season.
 When, despair in his face, a messenger brings to a town
 The hated news of a fallen army—
 One general wound to the city and many men
 Outcast, outcursed, from many homes      615
 By the double whip which War is fond of,
 Doom with a bloody spear in either hand,
 One carrying such a pack of grief could well
 Recite this hymn of the Furies at your asking.
 But when our cause is saved and a messenger of good    620
 Comes to a city glad with festivity,
 How am I to mix good news with bad, recounting
 The storm that meant God's anger on the Greeks?
 For they swore together, those inveterate enemies,
 Fire and sea, and proved their alliance, destroying    625
 The unhappy troops of Argos.
 In night arose ill-waved evil,
 Ships on each other the blasts from Thrace
 Crashed colliding, which butting with horns in the violence
 Of big wind and rattle of rain were gone      630
 To nothing, whirled all ways by a wicked shepherd.
 But when there came up the shining light of the sun
 We saw the Aegean sea flowering with corpses
 Of Greek men and their ships' wreckage.
 But for us, our ship was not damaged,      635
 Whether someone snatched it away or begged it off,
 Some god, not a man, handling the tiller;
 And Saving Fortune was willing to sit upon our ship
 So that neither at anchor we took the tilt of waves
 Nor ran to splinters on the crag-bound coast.     640
 But then having thus escaped death on the sea,
 In the white day, not trusting our fortune,
 We pastured this new trouble upon our thoughts,
 The fleet being battered, the sailors weary,
 And now if any of *them* still draw breath,     645
 They are thinking no doubt of us as being lost
 And we are thinking of them as being lost.

625. *Fire:* lightning.

May the best happen. As for Menelaus
The first guess and most likely is a disaster.
But still—if any ray of sun detects him                650
Alive, with living eyes, by the plan of Zeus
Not yet resolved to annul the race completely,
There is some hope then that he will return home.
So much you have heard. Know that it is the truth.     [*Exit.*]

CHOR. Who was it named her thus                        655
In all ways appositely
Unless it was Someone whom we do not see,
Fore-knowing fate
And plying an accurate tongue?
Helen, bride of spears and conflict's                  660
Focus, who as was befitting
Proved a hell to ships and men,
Hell to her country, sailing
Away from delicately-sumptuous curtains,
Away on the wind of a giant Zephyr,                    665
And shielded hunters mustered many
On the vanished track of the oars,
Oars beached on the leafy
Banks of a Trojan river
For the sake of a bloody war.                          670

But on Troy was thrust a marring marriage
By the Wrath that working to an end exacts
In time a price from guests
Who dishonoured their host
And dishonoured Zeus of the Hearth,                    675
From those noisy celebrants
Of the wedding hymn which fell
To the brothers of Paris
To sing upon that day.
But learning this, unlearning that,                    680
Priam's ancestral city now
Continually mourns, reviling
Paris the fatal bridegroom.
The city has had much sorrow,
Much desolation in life,                               685
From the pitiful loss of her people.

So in his house a man might rear
A lion's cub caught from the dam
In need of suckling,

---

656. *appositely:* Helen's name contains a Greek root (*hele-*) which means "to destroy."

675. *Zeus of the Hearth:* Zeus in his capacity as protector of host and guest.

In the prelude of its life 690
Mild, gentle with children,
For old men a playmate,
Often held in the arms
Like a new-born child,
Wheedling the hand, 695
Fawning at belly's bidding.

But matured by time he showed
The temper of his stock and payed
Thanks for his fostering
With disaster of slaughter of sheep 700
Making an unbidden banquet
And now the house is a shambles,
Irremediable grief to its people,
Calamitous carnage;
For the pet they had fostered was sent 705
By God as a priest of Ruin.

So I would say there came
To the city of Troy
A notion of windless calm,
Delicate adornment of riches,
Soft shooting of the eyes and flower 710
Of desire that stings the fancy.
But swerving aside she achieved
A bitter end to her marriage,
Ill guest and ill companion,
Hurled upon Priam's sons, convoyed 715
By Zeus, patron of guest and host,
Dark angel dowered with tears.

Long current among men an old saying
Runs that a man's prosperity
When grown to greatness 720
Comes to birth, does not die childless—
His good luck breeds for his house
Distress that shall not be appeased.
I only, apart from the others, 725
Hold that the unrighteous action
Breeds true to its kind,

---

719–724. *Long current . . . appeased:*
These lines state the traditional Greek
view that immoderate good fortune (or
excellence of any kind beyond the average) is itself the cause of disaster. In
the lines which follow, the chorus rejects this view and states that only an
act of evil produces evil consequences.
It later admits by implication (ll. 739
ff.) that those who are less prosperous
are less likely to commit such an act.

Leaves its own children behind it.
But the lot of a righteous house
Is a fair offspring always.                                    730

Ancient self-glory is accustomed
To bear to light in the evil sort of men
A new self-glory and madness,
Which sometime or sometime finds
The appointed hour for its birth,                              735
And born therewith is the Spirit, intractable, unholy, irresistible,
The reckless lust that brings black Doom upon the house,
A child that is like its parents.

But Honest Dealing is clear
Shining in smoky homes,                                        740
Honours the god-fearing life.
Mansions gilded by filth of hands she leaves,
Turns her eyes elsewhere, visits the innocent house,
Not respecting the power
Of wealth mis-stamped with approval,                           745
But guides all to the goal.
        [*Enter* AGAMEMNON *and* CASSANDRA *on chariots.*]
CHOR. Come then my King, stormer of Troy,
    Offspring of Atreus,
    How shall I hail you, how give you honour
    Neither overshooting nor falling short                     750
        Of the measure of homage?
    There are many who honour appearance too much
    Passing the bounds that are right.
    To condole with the unfortunate man
    Each one is ready but the bite of the grief                755
        Never goes through to the heart.
    And they join in rejoicing, affecting to share it,
    Forcing their face to a smile.
    But he who is shrewd to shepherd his sheep
    Will fail not to notice the eyes of a man                  760
    Which seem to be loyal but lie,
        Fawning with watery friendship.
    Even you, in my thought, when you marshalled the troops
    For Helen's sake, I will not hide it,
    Made a harsh and ugly picture,                             765
    Holding badly the tiller of reason,
    Paying with the death of men

---

740. *smoky homes:* i.e., poor homes.
752. *There are many* . . . : The
chorus is trying to warn Agamemnon,
and goes much further than it did in its
dialogue with the herald.

Ransom for a willing whore.
But now, not unfriendly, not superficially,
I offer my service, well-doers' welcome.                            770
In time you will learn by inquiry
Who has done rightly, who transgressed
In the work of watching the city.
AGAMEMNON. First to Argos and the country's gods
My fitting salutations, who have aided me                           775
To return and in the justice which I exacted
From Priam's city. Hearing the unspoken case
The gods unanimously had cast their vote
Into the bloody urn for the massacre of Troy;
But to the opposite urn                                             780
Hope came, dangled her hand, but did no more.
Smoke marks even now the city's capture.
Whirlwinds of doom are alive, the dying ashes
Spread on the air the fat savour of wealth.
For these things we must pay some memorable return                  785
To Heaven, having exacted enormous vengeance
For wife-rape; for a woman
The Argive monster ground a city to powder,
Sprung from a wooden horse, shield-wielding folk,
Launching a leap at the setting of the Pleiads,                    790
Jumping the ramparts, a ravening lion,
Lapped its fill of the kingly blood.
To the gods I have drawn out this overture
But as for your concerns, I bear them in my mind
And say the same, you have me in agreement.                         795
To few of men does it belong by nature
To congratulate their friends unenviously,
For a sullen poison fastens on the heart,
Doubling the pain of a man with this disease;
He feels the weight of his own griefs and when                     800
He sees another's prosperity he groans.
I speak with knowledge, being well acquainted
With the mirror of comradeship—ghost of a shadow
Were those who seemed to be so loyal to me.
Only Odysseus, who sailed against his will,                        805
Proved, when yoked with me, a ready tracehorse;

779. *bloody urn:* The Greeks voted with pebbles, which were put into different urns and then counted.
789. *wooden horse:* The stratagem with which the Greeks captured the city.
790. *at the setting of the Pleiads:* late in the fall.

805. *Odysseus:* Feigning madness in order to escape going to Troy, he was tricked into demonstrating his sanity. The remark shows that the truth is far from Agamemnon's mind; he has no thought that his danger comes from a woman

I speak of him not knowing if he is alive.
But for what concerns the city and the gods
Appointing public debates in full assembly
We shall consult. That which is well already 810
We shall take steps to ensure it remain well.
But where there is need of medical remedies,
By applying benevolent cautery or surgery
We shall try to deflect the dangers of disease.
But now, entering the halls where stands my hearth, 815
First I shall make salutation to the gods
Who sent me a far journey and have brought me back.
And may my victory not leave my side.

> [*Enter* CLYTEMNESTRA, *followed by women slaves carrying purple tapestries.*]

CLYT. Men of the city, you the aged of Argos,
I shall feel no shame to describe to you my love 820
Towards my husband. Shyness in all of us
Wears thin with time. Here are the facts first hand.
I will tell you of my own unbearable life
I led so long as this man was at Troy.
For first that the woman separate from her man 825
Should sit alone at home is extreme cruelty,
Hearing so many malignant rumours—First
Comes one, and another comes after, bad news to worse,
Clamour of grief to the house. If Agamemnon
Had had so many wounds as those reported 830
Which poured home through the pipes of hearsay, then—
Then he would be gashed fuller than a net has holes!
And if only he had died . . . as often as rumour told us,
He would be like the giant in the legend,
Three-bodied. Dying once for every body, 835
He should have by now three blankets of earth above him—
All that above him; I care not how deep the mattress under!
Such are the malignant rumours thanks to which
They have often seized me against my will and undone
The loop of a rope from my neck. 840
And this is why our son is not standing here,
The guarantee of your pledges and mine,
As he should be, Orestes. Do not wonder;
He is being brought up by a friendly ally and host,

---

820–821. *love towards my husband*
The Greek is ambiguous, and may mean
also "love for men."
821. *Shyness:* The word also means
"modesty," "virtue." Almost every

statement in this speech has a double
meaning.
834. *giant:* Geryon, a fabulous giant
with three heads and six arms.

Strophius the Phocian, who warned me in advance 845
Of dubious troubles, both your risks at Troy
And the anarchy of shouting mobs that might
Overturn policy, for it is born in men
To kick the man who is down.
This is not a disingenuous excuse. 850
For me the outrushing wells of weeping are dried up,
There is no drop left in them.
My eyes are sore from sitting late at nights
Weeping for you and for the baffled beacons,
Never lit up. And, when I slept, in dreams 855
I have been waked by the thin whizz of a buzzing
Gnat, seeing more horrors fasten on you
Than could take place in the mere time of my dream.
Having endured all this, now, with unsorrowed heart
I would hail this man as the watchdog of the farm, 860
Forestay that saves the ship, pillar that props
The lofty roof, appearance of an only son
To a father or of land to sailors past their hope,
The loveliest day to see after the storm,
Gush of well-water for the thirsty traveller. 865
Such are the metaphors I think befit him,
But envy be absent. Many misfortunes already
We have endured. But now, dear head, come down
Out of that car, not placing upon the ground
Your foot, O King, the foot that trampled Troy. 870
Why are you waiting, slaves, to whom the task is assigned
To spread the pavement of his path with tapestries?
At once, at once let his way be strewn with purple
That Justice lead him toward his unexpected home.
The rest a mind, not overcome by sleep 875
Will arrange rightly, with God's help, as destined.
AGAM. Daughter of Leda, guardian of my house,
You have spoken in proportion to my absence.
You have drawn your speech out long. Duly to praise me,
That is a duty to be performed by others. 880
And further—do not by women's methods make me
Effeminate nor in barbarian fashion

845. *Phocian:* Phocis is in central
Greece. Orestes grew up there in exile
and later returned to avenge his father.
872. *tapestries:* To walk on these
tapestries, wall hangings dyed with the
expensive purple (crimson), would be
an act of extravagant pride. Pride is
the keynote of Agamemnon's character,
and it suits Clytemnestra's sense of
fitness that he should go into his death

in godlike state, treading a way "strewn
with purple," the color of blood.
877. *Daughter of Leda:* Clytemnestra and Helen are both daughters of
Leda.
882. *barbarian:* foreign, especially
Asiatic. Aeschylus is thinking of the
pomp and servility of the contemporary
Persian court.

Gape ground-grovelling acclamations at me
Nor strewing my path with cloths make it invidious.
It is the gods should be honoured in this way. 885
But being mortal to tread embroidered beauty
For me is no way without fear.
I tell you to honour me as a man, not god.
Footcloths are very well—Embroidered stuffs
Are stuff for gossip. And not to think unwisely 890
Is the greatest gift of God. Call happy only him
Who has ended his life in sweet prosperity.
I have spoken. This thing I could not do with confidence.

CLYT. Tell me now, according to your judgment.

AGAM. I tell you you shall not override my judgment. 895

CLYT. Supposing you had feared something . . .
Could you have vowed to God to do this thing?

AGAM. Yes. If an expert had prescribed that vow.

CLYT. And how would Priam have acted in your place?

AGAM. He would have trod the cloths, I think, for certain. 900

CLYT. Then do not flinch before the blame of men.

AGAM. The voice of the multitude is very strong.

CLYT. But the man none envy is not enviable.

AGAM. It is not a woman's part to love disputing.

CLYT. But it is a conqueror's part to yield upon occasion. 905

AGAM. You think such victory worth fighting for?

CLYT. Give way. Consent to let me have the mastery.

AGAM. Well, if such is your wish, let someone quickly loose
My vassal sandals, underlings of my feet,
And stepping on these sea-purples may no god 910
Shoot me from far with the envy of his eye.
Great shame it is to ruin my house and spoil
The wealth of costly weavings with my feet.
But of this matter enough. This stranger woman here
Take in with kindness. The man who is a gentle master 915
God looks on from far off complacently.
For no one of his will bears the slave's yoke.
This woman, of many riches being the chosen
Flower, gift of the soldiers, has come with me.
But since I have been prevailed on by your words 920
I will go to my palace home, treading on purples.

[*He dismounts from the chariot and begins to walk up the*

---

898. *expert:* a priest, or prophet; Calchas for instance.

910. *sea-purples:* The dye was made from shellfish.

914. *stranger woman:* Cassandra, daughter of Priam, Agamemnon's share of the human booty of the sack of Troy. She was loved by Apollo and by him given the gift of prophecy; but when she refused her love to the god he added to his gift the proviso that her prophecies, though true, should never be believed until it was too late.

*tapestried path. During the following speech he enters the palace.*]

CLYT. There is the sea and who shall drain it dry? It breeds
  Its wealth in silver of plenty of purple gushing
  And ever-renewed, the dyeings of our garments.
  The house has its store of these by God's grace, King.     925
  This house is ignorant of poverty
  And I would have vowed a pavement of many garments
  Had the palace oracle enjoined that vow
  Thereby to contrive a ransom for his life.
  For while there is root, foliage comes to the house     930
  Spreading a tent of shade against the Dog Star.
  So now that you have reached your hearth and home
  You prove a miracle—advent of warmth in winter;
  And further this—even in the time of heat
  When God is fermenting wine from the bitter grape,     935
  Even then it is cool in the house if only
  Its master walk at home, a grown man, ripe.
  O Zeus the Ripener, ripen these my prayers;
  Your part it is to make the ripe fruit fall.
    [*She enters the palace.*]
CHOR. Why, why at the doors     940
  Of my fore-seeing heart
  Does this terror keep beating its wings?
  And my song play the prophet
  Unbidden, unhired—
  Which I cannot spit out     945
  Like the enigmas of dreams
  Nor plausible confidence
  Sit on the throne of my mind?
  It is long time since
  The cables let down from the stern     950
  Were chafed by the sand when the seafaring army started for
      Troy.

  And I learn with my eyes
  And witness myself their return;
  But the hymn without lyre goes up,
  The dirge of the Avenging Fiend,     955
  In the depths of my self-taught heart
  Which has lost its dear
  Possession of the strength of hope.
  But my guts and my heart
  Are not idle which seethe with the waves     960
  Of trouble nearing its hour.

But I pray that these thoughts
May fall out not as I think
   And not be fulfilled in the end.

Truly when health grows much          965
It respects not limit; for disease,
Its neighbour in the next door room,
Presses upon it.
A man's life, crowding sail,
Strikes on the blind reef:          970
But if caution in advance
Jettison part of the cargo
With the derrick of due proportion,
The whole house does not sink,
Though crammed with a weight of woe    975
The hull does not go under.
The abundant bounty of God
And his gifts from the year's furrows
Drive the famine back.

But when upon the ground there has fallen once  980
The black blood of a man's death,
Who shall summon it back by incantations?
Even Asclepius who had the art
To fetch the dead to life, even to him
Zeus put a provident end.         985
But, if of the heaven-sent fates
One did not check the other,
Cancel the other's advantage,
My heart would outrun my tongue
In pouring out these fears.        990
But now it mutters in the dark,
Embittered, no way of hoping
To unravel a scheme in time
   From a burning mind.

[CLYTEMNESTRA *appears in the door of the palace.*]

CLYT. Go in too, you; I speak to you, Cassandra,  995
Since God in his clemency has put you in this house
To share our holy water, standing with many slaves
Beside the altar that protects the house,

971–979. *But if caution . . . back:*
These lines refer to a traditional Greek
belief that the fortunate man could
avert the envy of heaven by deliberately getting rid of some precious possession.
983. *Asclepius:* the great physician,
who was so skillful that he finally succeeded in restoring a dead man to life.
Zeus struck him with a thunderbolt for
going too far.
997. *holy water:* used in the sacrifice
in honor of Agamemnon's return which
is about to take place inside the house.

Step down from the car there, do not be overproud.
Heracles himself they say was once                                    1000
Sold, and endured to eat the bread of slavery.
But should such a chance inexorably fall,
There is much advantage in masters who have long been rich.
Those who have reaped a crop they never expected
Are in all things hard on their slaves and overstep the line.    1005
From us you will have the treatment of tradition.

LEAD. You, it is you she has addressed, and clearly.
Caught as you are in these predestined toils
Obey her if you can. But should you disobey . . .

CLYT. If she has more than the gibberish of the swallow,         1010
An unintelligible barbaric speech,
I hope to read her mind, persuade her reason.

LEAD. As things now stand for you, she says the best.
Obey her; leave that car and follow her.

CLYT. I have no leisure to waste out here, outside the door.   1015
Before the hearth in the middle of my house
The victims stand already, wait the knife.
You, if you will obey me, waste no time.
But if you cannot understand my language—

    [TO CHORUS LEADER]

You make it plain to her with the brute and voiceless hand.   1020

LEAD. The stranger seems to need a clear interpreter.
She bears herself like a wild beast newly captured.

CLYT. The fact is she is mad, she listens to evil thoughts,
Who has come here leaving a city newly captured
Without experience how to bear the bridle                          1025
So as not to waste her strength in foam and blood.
I will not spend more words to be ignored.

    [She re-enters the palace.]

CHOR. But I, for I pity her, will not be angry.
Obey, unhappy woman. Leave this car.
Yield to your fate. Put on the untried yoke.                        1030

CASSANDRA. Apollo! Apollo!

CHOR. Why do you cry like this upon Apollo?
He is not the kind of god that calls for dirges.

CASS. Apollo! Apollo!

CHOR. Once more her funereal cries invoke the god               1035
Who has no place at the scene of lamentation.

CASS. Apollo! Apollo!

---

1000. *Heracles:* The Greek hero,
famous for his twelve labors which
rid the earth of monsters, was at one
time forced to be slave to Omphale, an
Eastern queen.

1010. *gibberish of the swallow:* The
comparison of foreign speech to the
twittering of the swallow was a Greek
commonplace.

God of the Ways! My destroyer!
Destroyed again—and this time utterly!

CHOR. She seems about to predict her own misfortunes.    1040
The gift of the god endures, even in a slave's mind.

CASS. Apollo! Apollo!
God of the Ways! My destroyer!
Where? To what house, Where, where have you brought me?

CHOR. To the house of the sons of Atreus. If you do not know
    it,    1045
I will tell you so. You will not find it false.

CASS. No, no, but to a god-hated, but to an accomplice
In much kin-killing, murdering nooses,
Man-shambles, a floor asperged with blood.

CHOR. The stranger seems like a hound with a keen scent,    1050
Is picking up a trail that leads to murder.

CASS. Clues! I have clues! Look! They are these.
These wailing, these children, butchery of children;
Roasted flesh, a father sitting to dinner.

CHOR. Of your prophetic fame we have heard before    1055
But in this matter prophets are not required.

CASS. What is she doing? What is she planning?
What is this new great sorrow?
Great crime . . . within here . . . planning
Unendurable to his folk, impossible    1060
Ever to be cured. For help
   Stands far distant.

CHOR. This reference I cannot catch. But the children
I recognized; that refrain is hackneyed.

CASS. Damned, damned, bringing this work to completion—    1065
Your husband who shared your bed
To bathe him, to cleanse him, and then—
How shall I tell of the end?
Soon, very soon, it will fall.
   The end comes hand over hand    1070
   Grasping in greed.

CHOR. Not yet do I understand. After her former riddles
Now I am baffled by these dim pronouncements.

CASS. Ah God, the vision! God, God, the vision!

---

1038. *God of the Ways:* A statue of
Apollo was often placed outside the
house overlooking the street. (Perhaps
there was one on stage in this scene.)
*destroyer:* The Greek word is *apollon,*
a pun on the god's name.

1044. *brought:* another pun on the
god's name; the word translated
"brought" echoes, in the Greek, the

word translated "God of the ways."

1049. *asperged with blood:* She sees
Agamemnon murdered in his bath.

1054. *a father sitting to dinner:*
Thyestes at his feast.

1057. *she:* Clytemnestra.

1061–1062. *help stands far distant:*
a reference to Menelaus (distant in
space) and Orestes (distant in time).

A net, is it? Net of Hell!
But herself is the net; shared bed; shares murder.                    1075
O let the pack ever-hungering after the family
Howl for the unholy ritual, howl for the victim.

CHOR. What black Spirit is this you call upon the house—
To raise aloft her cries? Your speech does not lighten me.        1080
Into my heart runs back the blood
Yellow as when for men by the spear fallen
The blood ebbs out with the rays of the setting life
 And death strides quickly.

CASS. Quick! Be on your guard! The bull—                             1085
Keep him clear of the cow.
Caught with a trick, the black horn's point,
She strikes. He falls; lies in the water.
Murder; a trick in a bath. I tell what I see.

CHOR. I would not claim to be expert in oracles                       1090
But these, as I deduce, portend disaster.
Do men ever get a good answer from oracles?
No. It is only through disaster
That their garrulous craft brings home
The meaning of the prophet's panic.                                  1095

CASS. And for me also, for me, chance ill-destined!
My own now I lament, pour into the cup my own.
Where is this you have brought me in my misery?
Unless to die as well. What else is meant?

CHOR. You are mad, mad, carried away by the god,                     1100
Raising the dirge, the tuneless
Tune, for yourself. Like the tawny
Unsatisfied singer from her luckless heart
Lamenting "Itys, Itys," the nightingale
Lamenting a life luxuriant with grief.                               1105

CASS. Oh the lot of the songful nightingale!
The gods enclosed her in a winged body,
Gave her a sweet and tearless passing.
But for me remains the two-edged cutting blade.

CHOR. From whence these rushing and God-inflicted                    1110
Profitless pains?
Why shape with your sinister crying
The piercing hymn—fear-piercing?
How can you know the evil-worded landmarks

---

1077. *pack ever-hungering:* the Furies.

1102–1103. *tawny unsatisfied singer:* the nightingale. Philomela was raped by Tereus, the husband of her sister Procne. The two sisters avenged them-

selves by killing Tereus' son Itys, and serving up his flesh to Tereus to eat. Philomela was changed into a nightingale, mourning for Itys (the name is an imitation of the sound of the nightingale's song).

On the prophetic path?                                    1115

CASS. Oh the wedding, the wedding of Paris—death to his people!
O river Scamander, water drunk by my fathers!
When I was young, alas, upon your beaches
I was brought up and cared for.
But now it is the River of Wailing and the banks of Hell   1120
That shall hear my prophecy soon.

CHOR. What is this clear speech, too clear?
A child can understand it.
I am bitten with fangs that draw blood
By the misery of your cries,                               1125
Cries harrowing the heart.

CASS. O trouble on trouble of a city lost, lost utterly!
My father's sacrifices before the towers,
Much killing of cattle and sheep,
No cure—availed not at all                                 1130
To prevent the coming of what came to Troy,
And I, my brain on fire, shall soon enter the trap.

CHOR. This speech accords with the former.
What god, malicious, over-heavy, persistently pressing,
Drives you to chant of these lamentable                    1135
Griefs with death their burden?
But I cannot see the end.

[CASSANDRA *now steps down from the car.*]

CASS. The oracle now no longer from behind veils
Will be peeping forth like a newly-wedded bride;
But I can feel it like a fresh wind swoop                  1140
And rush in the face of the dawn and, wave-like, wash
Against the sun a vastly greater grief
Than this one. I shall speak no more conundrums.
And bear me witness, pacing me, that I
Am trailing on the scent of ancient wrongs.                1145
For this house here a choir never deserts,
Chanting together ill. For they mean ill,
And to puff up their arrogance they have drunk
Men's blood, this band of revellers that haunts the house,
Hard to be rid of, fiends that attend the family.          1150
Established in its rooms they hymn their hymn
Of that original sin, abhor in turn
The adultery that proved a brother's ruin.
A miss? Or do my arrows hit the mark?
Or am I a quack prophet who knocks at doors, a babbler?     1155
Give me your oath, confess I have the facts,

1153. *adultery:* Thyestes seduced ginning of strife between the brothers.
the wife of Atreus. This was the be-

The ancient history of this house's crimes.

LEAD. And how could an oath's assurance, however finely assured,
  Turn out a remedy? I wonder, though, that you
  Being brought up overseas, of another tongue,       1160
  Should hit on the whole tale as if you had been standing by.

CASS. Apollo the prophet set me to prophesy.

LEAD. Was he, although a god, struck by desire?

CASS. Till now I was ashamed to tell the story.

LEAD. Yes. Good fortune keeps us all fastidious.       1165

CASS. He wrestled hard upon me, panting love.

LEAD. And did you come, as they do, to child-getting?

CASS. No. I agreed to him. And I cheated him.

LEAD. Were you already possessed by the mystic art?

CASS. Already I was telling the townsmen all their future
    suffering.       1170

LEAD. Then how did you escape the doom of Apollo's anger?

CASS. I did not escape. No one ever believed me.

LEAD. Yet to us your words seem worthy of belief.

CASS. Oh misery, misery!

Again comes on me the terrible labour of true       1175
Prophecy, dizzying prelude; distracts . . .
Do you see these who sit before the house,
Children, like the shapes of dreams?
Children who seem to have been killed by their kinsfolk,
Filling their hands with meat, flesh of themselves,       1180
Guts and entrails, handfuls of lament—
Clear what they hold—the same their father tasted.
For this I declare someone is plotting vengeance—
A lion? Lion but coward, that lurks in bed,
Good watchdog truly against the lord's return—       1185
My lord, for I must bear the yoke of serfdom.
Leader of the ships, overturner of Troy,
He does not know what plots the accursed hound
With the licking tongue and the pricked-up ear will plan
In the manner of a lurking doom, in an evil hour.       1190
A daring criminal! Female murders male.
What monster could provide her with a title?
An amphisbaena or hag of the sea who dwells
In rocks to ruin sailors—
A raving mother of death who breathes against her folk       1195
War to the finish. Listen to her shout of triumph,
Who shirks no horrors, like men in a rout of battle.

1184. *Lion but coward:* Aegisthus.
1188. *hound:* Clytemnestra.
1193. *amphisbaena:* a fabulous serpent with a head at either end; the
word means literally "going in both
directions."

And yet she poses as glad at their return.
If you distrust my words, what does it matter?
That which will come will come. You too will soon stand
    here                                       1200
And admit with pity that I spoke too truly.
LEAD. Thyestes' dinner of his children's meat
I understood and shuddered, and fear grips me
To hear the truth, not framed in parables.
But hearing the rest I am thrown out of my course.     1205
CASS. It is Agamemnon's death I tell you you shall witness.
LEAD. Stop! Provoke no evil. Quiet your mouth!
CASS. The god who gives me words is here no healer.
LEAD. Not if this shall be so. But may some chance avert it.
CASS. You are praying. But others are busy with murder.     1210
LEAD. What man is he promotes this terrible thing?
CASS. Indeed you have missed my drift by a wide margin!
LEAD. But I do not understand the assassin's method.
CASS. And yet too well I know the speech of Greece!
LEAD. So does Delphi but the replies are hard.     1215
CASS. Ah what a fire it is! It comes upon me.
   Apollo, Wolf-Destroyer, pity, pity . . .
It is the two-foot lioness who beds
Beside a wolf, the noble lion away,
It is she will kill me. Brewing a poisoned cup     1220
She will mix my punishment too in the angry draught
And boasts, sharpening the dagger for her husband,
To pay back murder, for my bringing here.
Why then do I wear these mockeries of myself,
The wand and the prophet's garland round my neck?     1225
My hour is coming—but you shall perish first.
Destruction! Scattered thus you give me my revenge;
Go and enrich some other woman with ruin.
See: Apollo himself is stripping me
Of my prophetic gear, who has looked on     1230
When in this dress I have been a laughing-stock
To friends and foes alike, and to no purpose;
They called me crazy, like a fortune-teller,
A poor starved beggar-woman—and I bore it.
And now the prophet undoing his prophetess     1235
Has brought me to this final darkness.
Instead of my father's altar the executioner's block
Waits me the victim, red with my hot blood.

---

1208. *healer:* one of Apollo's titles.
1212. *missed my drift:* in speaking
of a man instead of a woman.

1215. *Delphi:* The replies of the Delphic oracle were celebrated for their
obscurity and ambiguity.

But the gods will not ignore me as I die.
One will come after to avenge my death,                           1240
A matricide, a murdered father's champion.
Exile and tramp and outlaw he will come back
To gable the family house of fatal crime;
His father's outstretched corpse shall lead him home.
Why need I then lament so pitifully?                              1245
For now that I have seen the town of Troy
Treated as she was treated, while her captors
Come to their reckoning thus by the gods' verdict,
I will go in and have the courage to die.
Look, these gates are the gates of Death. I greet them.          1250
And I pray that I may meet a deft and mortal stroke
So that without a struggle I may close
My eyes and my blood ebb in easy death.

LEAD. Oh woman very unhappy and very wise,
Your speech was long. But if in sober truth                      1255
You know your fate, why like an ox that the gods
Drive, do you walk so bravely to the altar?

CASS. There is no escape, strangers. No; not by postponement.

LEAD. But the last moment has the privilege of hope.

CASS. The day is here. Little should I gain by flight.           1260

LEAD. This patience of yours comes from a brave soul.

CASS. A happy man is never paid that compliment.

LEAD. But to die with credit graces a mortal man.

CASS. Oh my father! You and your noble sons!

    [*She approaches the door, then suddenly recoils.*]

LEAD. What is it? What is the fear that drives you back?         1265

CASS. Faugh.

LEAD. Why faugh? Or is this some hallucination?

CASS. These walls breathe out a death that drips with blood.

LEAD. Not so. It is only the smell of the sacrifice.

CASS. It is like a breath out of a charnel-house.                1270

LEAD. You think our palace burns odd incense then!

CASS. But I will go to lament among the dead
My lot and Agamemnon's. Enough of life!
Strangers,
I am not afraid like a bird afraid of a bush                     1275
But witness you my words after my death
When a woman dies in return for me a woman
And a man falls for a man with a wicked wife.
I ask this service, being about to die.

LEAD. Alas, I pity you for the death you have foretold.          1280

---

1240 ff., *one will come after* . . . : These lines refer to Orestes.

CASS. One more speech I have; I do not wish to raise
    The dirge for my own self. But to the sun I pray
    In face of his last light that my avengers
    May make my murderers pay for this my death,
    Death of a woman slave, an easy victim.                    1285
    [*She enters the palace.*]

LEAD. Ah the fortunes of men! When they go well
    A shadow sketch would match them, and in ill-fortune
    The dab of a wet sponge destroys the drawing.
    It is not myself but the life of man I pity.

CHOR. Prosperity in all men cries                             1290
    For more prosperity. Even the owner
    Of the finger-pointed-at palace never shuts
    His door against her, saying "Come no more."
    So to our king the blessed gods had granted
    To take the town of Priam, and heaven-favoured            1295
    He reaches home. But now if for former bloodshed
        He must pay blood
    And dying for the dead shall cause
        Other deaths in atonement
    What man could boast he was born                          1300
        Secure, who heard this story?

AGAM. [*Within*] Oh! I am struck a mortal blow—within!

LEAD. Silence! Listen. Who calls out, wounded with a mortal stroke?

AGAM. Again—the second blow—I am struck again.

LEAD. You heard the king cry out. I think the deed is done.  1305
    Let us see if we can concert some sound proposal.

2ND OLD MAN. Well, I will tell you my opinion—
    Raise an alarm, summon the folk to the palace.

3RD OLD MAN. I say burst in with all speed possible,
    Convict them of the deed while still the sword is wet.    1310

4TH OLD MAN. And I am partner to some such suggestion.
    I am for taking some course. No time to dawdle.

5TH OLD MAN. The case is plain. This is but the beginning.
    They are going to set up dictatorship in the state.

6TH OLD MAN. We are wasting time. The assassins tread to
        earth                                                 1315
    The decencies of delay and give their hands no sleep.

7TH OLD MAN. I do not know what plan I could hit on to pro-
        pose.
    The man who acts is in the position to plan.

8TH OLD MAN. So I think, too, for I am at a loss
    To raise the dead man up again with words.                1320

9TH OLD MAN. Then to stretch out our life shall we yield thus

To the rule of these profaners of the house?

10TH OLD MAN. It is not to be endured. To die is better.
Death is more comfortable than tyranny.

11TH OLD MAN. And are we on the evidence of groans          1325
Going to give oracle that the prince is dead?

12TH OLD MAN. We must know the facts for sure and *then* be
angry.
Guesswork is not the same as certain knowledge.

LEAD. Then all of you back me and approve this plan—
To ascertain how it is with Agamemnon          1330
[*The doors of the palace open, revealing the bodies of*
AGAMEMNON *and* CASSANDRA. CLYTEMNESTRA *stands above
them.*]

CLYT. Much having been said before to fit the moment,
To say the opposite now will not outface me.
How else could one serving hate upon the hated,
Thought to be friends, hang high the nets of doom
To preclude all leaping out?          1335
For me I have long been training for this match,
I tried a fall and won—a victory overdue.
I stand here where I struck, above my victims;
So I contrived it—this I will not deny—
That he could neither fly nor ward off death;          1340
Inextricable like a net for fishes
I cast about him a vicious wealth of raiment
And struck him twice and with two groans he loosed
His limbs beneath him, and upon him fallen
I deal him the third blow to the God beneath the earth,          1345
To the safe keeper of the dead a votive gift,
And with that he spits his life out where he lies
And smartly spouting blood he sprays me with
The sombre drizzle of bloody dew and I
Rejoice no less than in God's gift of rain          1350
The crops are glad when the ear of corn gives birth.
These things being so, you, elders of Argos,
Rejoice if rejoice you will. Mine is the glory.
And if I could pay this corpse his due libation
I should be right to pour it and more than right;          1355
With so many horrors this man mixed and filled
The bowl—and, coming home, has drained the draught himself.

LEAD. Your speech astonishes us. This brazen boast
Above the man who was your king and husband!

CLYT. You challenge me as a woman without foresight          1360

1345. *third blow to the God beneath the earth:* like the third libation to Zeus
above.

But I with unflinching heart to you who know
Speak. And you, whether you will praise or blame,
It makes no matter. Here lies Agamemnon,
My husband, dead, the work of this right hand,
An honest workman. There you have the facts.                    1365

CHOR. Woman, what poisoned
Herb of the earth have you tasted
Or potion of the flowing sea
To undertake this killing and the people's curses?
You threw down, you cut off—The people will cast you out,   1370
Black abomination to the town.

CLYT. Now your verdict—in my case—is exile
And to have the people's hatred, the public curses,
Though then in no way you opposed this man
Who carelessly, as if it were a head of sheep               1375
Out of the abundance of his fleecy flocks,
Sacrificed his own daughter, to me the dearest
Fruit of travail, charm for the Thracian winds.
He was the one to have banished from this land,
Pay off the pollution. But when you hear what I             1380
Have done, you judge severely. But I warn you—
Threaten me on the understanding that I am ready
For two alternatives—Win by force the right
To rule me, but, if God brings about the contrary,
Late in time you will have to learn self-discipline.       1385

CHOR. You are high in the thoughts,
You speak extravagant things,
After the soiling murder your crazy heart
Fancies your forehead with a smear of blood.
Unhonoured, unfriended, you must                            1390
Pay for a blow with a blow.

CLYT. Listen then to this—the sanction of my oaths:
By the Justice totting up my child's atonement,
By the Avenging Doom and Fiend to whom I killed this man,
For me hope walks not in the rooms of fear                  1395
So long as my fire is lit upon my hearth
By Aegisthus, loyal to me as he was before.
The man who outraged me lies here,
The darling of each courtesan at Troy,
And here with him is the prisoner clairvoyant,              1400
The fortune-teller that he took to bed,
Who shares his bed as once his bench on shipboard,
A loyal mistress. Both have their deserts.
*He* lies so; and she who like a swan
Sang her last dying lament                                   1405

Lies his lover, and the sight contributes
An appetiser to my own bed's pleasure.
CHOR. Ah would some quick death come not overpainful,
Not overlong on the sickbed,
Establishing in us the ever-                               1410
Lasting unending sleep now that our guardian
Has fallen, the kindest of men,
Who suffering much for a woman
By a woman has lost his life.
 O Helen, insane, being one                            1415
 One to have destroyed so many
 And many souls under Troy,
 Now is your work complete, blossomed not for oblivion,
 Unfading stain of blood. Here now, if in any home,
 Is Discord, here is a man's deep-rooted ruin.          1420
CLYT. Do not pray for the portion of death
Weighed down by these things, do not turn
Your anger on Helen as destroyer of men,
One woman destroyer of many
Lives of Greek men,                                        1425
 A hurt that cannot be healed.
CHOR. O Evil Spirit, falling on the family,
On the two sons of Atreus and using
Two sisters in heart as your tools,
A power that bites to the heart—                           1430
See on the body
Perched like a raven he gloats
Harshly croaking his hymn.
CLYT. Ah, now you have amended your lips' opinion,
Calling upon this family's three times gorged             1435
Genius—demon who breeds
Blood-hankering lust in the belly:
Before the old sore heals, new pus collects.
CHOR. It is a great spirit—great—
You tell of, harsh in anger,                               1440
A ghastly tale, alas,
Of unsatisfied disaster
Brought by Zeus, by Zeus,
Cause and worker of all.
For without Zeus what comes to pass among us?             1445
Which of these things is outside Providence?
 O my king, my king,
 How shall I pay you in tears,
 Speak my affection in words?
 You lie in that spider's web,                         1450
 In a desecrating death breathe out your life,

Lie ignominiously
Defeated by a crooked death
And the two-edged cleaver's stroke.

CLYT. You say this is *my* work—mine? 1455
Do not cozen yourself that I am Agamemnon's wife.
Masquerading as the wife
Of the corpse there the old sharp-witted Genius
Of Atreus who gave the cruel banquet
Has paid with a grown man's life 1460
The due for children dead.

CHOR. That you are not guilty of
This murder who will attest?
No, but you may have been abetted
By some ancestral Spirit of Revenge. 1465
Wading a millrace of the family's blood
The black Manslayer forces a forward path
To make the requital at last
For the eaten children, the blood-clot cold with time.
O my king, my king, 1470
How shall I pay you in tears,
Speak my affection in words?
You lie in that spider's web,
In a desecrating death breathe out your life,
Lie ignominiously 1475
Defeated by a crooked death
And the two-edged cleaver's stroke.

CLYT. Did he not, too, contrive a crooked
Horror for the house? My child by him,
Shoot that I raised, much-wept-for Iphigencia, 1480
He treated her like this;
So suffering like this he need not make
Any great brag in Hell having paid with death
Dealt by the sword for work of his own beginning.

CHOR. I am at a loss for thought, I lack 1485
All nimble counsel as to where
To turn when the house is falling.
I fear the house-collapsing crashing
Blizzard of blood—of which these drops are earnest.
Now is Destiny sharpening her justice 1490
On other whetstones for a new infliction.
O earth, earth, if only you had received me
Before I saw this man lie here as if in bed
In a bath lined with silver.
Who will bury him? Who will keen him? 1495

1495. *keen:* mourn for.

Will you, having killed your own husband,
Dare now to lament him
And after great wickedness make
Unamending amends to his ghost?
And who above this godlike hero's grave                1500
Pouring praises and tears
Will grieve with a genuine heart?

CLYT. It is not your business to attend to that.
By my hand he fell low, lies low and dead,
And I shall bury him low down in the earth,            1505
And his household need not weep him
For Iphigeneia his daughter
Tenderly, as is right,
Will meet her father at the rapid ferry of sorrows,
Put her arms round him and kiss him!                   1510

CHOR. Reproach answers reproach,
It is hard to decide,
The catcher is caught, the killer pays for his kill.
But the law abides while Zeus abides enthroned
That the wrongdoer suffers. That is established.       1515
Who could expel from the house the seed of the Curse?
The race is soldered in sockets of Doom and Vengeance.

CLYT. In this you say what is right and the will of God.
But for my part I am ready to make a contract
With the Evil Genius of the House of Atreus           1520
To accept what has been till now, hard though it is,
But that for the future he shall leave this house
And wear away some other stock with deaths
Imposed among themselves. Of my possessions
A small part will suffice if only I                    1525
Can rid these walls of the mad exchange of murder.

[*Enter* AEGISTHUS, *followed by soldiers.*]

AEGISTHUS. O welcome light of a justice-dealing day!
From now on I will say that the gods, avenging men,
Look down from above on the crimes of earth,
Seeing as I do in woven robes of the Furies            1530
This man lying here—a sight to warm my heart—
Paying for the crooked violence of his father.
For his father Atreus, when he ruled the country,
Because his power was challenged, hounded out
From state and home his own brother Thyestes.          1535
My father—let me be plain—was this Thyestes,
Who later came back home a suppliant,
There, miserable, found so much asylum
As not to die on the spot, stain the ancestral floor.

But to show his hospitality godless Atreus                    1540
Gave him an eager if not a loving welcome,
Pretending a day of feasting and rich meats
Served my father with his children's flesh.
The hands and feet, fingers and toes, he hid
At the bottom of the dish. My father sitting apart           1545
Took unknowing the unrecognizable portion
And ate of a dish that has proved, as you see, expensive.
But when he knew he had eaten worse than poison
He fell back groaning, vomiting their flesh,
And invoking a hopeless doom on the sons of Pelops           1550
Kicked over the table to confirm his curse—
So may the whole race perish!
Result of this—you see this man lie here.
I stitched this murder together; it was my title.
Me the third son he left, an unweaned infant,                1555
To share the bitterness of my father's exile.
But I grew up and Justice brought me back,
I grappled this man while still beyond his door,
Having pieced together the programme of his ruin.
So now would even death be beautiful to me                   1560
Having seen Agamemnon in the nets of Justice.
LEAD. Aegisthus. I cannot respect brutality in distress.
You claim that you deliberately killed this prince
And that you alone planned this pitiful murder.
Be sure that in your turn your head shall not escape         1565
The people's volleyed curses mixed with stones.
AEG. Do you speak so who sit at the lower oar
While those on the upper bench control the ship?
Old as you are, you will find it is a heavy load
To go to school when old to learn the lesson of tact.        1570
For old age, too, gaol and hunger are fine
Instructors in wisdom, second-sighted doctors.
You have eyes. Cannot you see?
Do not kick against the pricks. The blow will hurt you.
LEAD. You woman waiting in the house for those who return from
    battle                                                   1575
While you seduce their wives! Was it you devised
The death of a master of armies?
AEG. And these words, too, prepare the way for tears.
Contrast your voice with the voice of Orpheus: he
Led all things after him bewitched with joy, but you         1580
Having stung me with your silly yelps shall be

1550. *Pelops:* the founder of the line.

Led off yourself, to prove more mild when mastered.

LEAD. Indeed! So you are now to be king of Argos,
You who, when you had plotted the king's death,
Did not even dare to do that thing yourself!                    1585

AEG. No. For the trick of it was clearly woman's work.
I was suspect, an enemy of old.
But now I shall try with Agamemnon's wealth
To rule the people. Any who is disobedient
I will harness in a heavy yoke, no tracehorse work for him      1590
Like barley-fed colt, but hateful hunger lodging
Beside him in the dark will see his temper soften.

LEAD. Why with your cowardly soul did you yourself
Not strike this man but left that work to a woman
Whose presence pollutes our country and its gods?              1595
But Orestes—does he somewhere see the light
That he may come back here by favour of fortune
And kill this pair and prove the final victor?

AEG. [*Summoning his guards*] Well, if such is your design in deeds
and words, you will quickly learn—
Here my friends, here my guards, there is work for you at
hand.                                                          1600

LEAD. Come then, hands on hilts, be each and all of us prepared.
[*The old men and the guards threaten each other.*]

AEG. Very well! I too am ready to meet death with sword in hand.

LEAD. We are glad you speak of dying. We accept your words for
luck.

CLYT. No, my dearest, do not so. Add no more to the train of wrong.
To reap these many present wrongs is harvest enough of
misery.                                                       1605
Enough of misery. Start no more. Our hands are red.
But do you, and you old men, go home and yield to fate in time,
In time before you suffer. We have acted as we had to act.
If only our afflictions now could prove enough, we should agree—
We who have been so hardly mauled in the heavy claws of the
evil god.                                                     1610
So stands my word, a woman's, if any man thinks fit to hear.

AEG. But to think that these should thus pluck the blooms of an
idle tongue
And should throw out words like these, giving the evil god his
chance,
And should miss the path of prudence and insult their master so!

LEAD. It is not the Argive way to fawn upon a cowardly man.     1615

AEG. Perhaps. But I in later days will take further steps with you.

---

1590. *tracehorse:* an extra horse, outside the yoke, which does less work than
the others.

LEAD. Not if the god who rules the family guides Orestes to his home.
AEG. Yes. I know that men in exile feed themselves on barren hopes.
LEAD. Go on, grow fat defiling justice . . . while you have your hour.
AEG. Do not think you will not pay me a price for your     1620
    stupidity.
LEAD. Boast on in your self-assurance, like a cock beside his hen.
CLYT. Pay no heed, Aegisthus, to these futile barkings. You and I,
Masters of this house, from now shall order all things well.
    [*They enter the palace.*]

# THUCYDIDES

## History of the Peloponnesian War*

[*Athenian Democracy—The Athenians from the
Enemy's Point of View*] †

[This is an extract from a speech made by the representatives of
Corinth, a city bitterly hostile to Athens, at a congress of Spartan
allies meeting at Sparta in 432 B.C. to discuss the question of peace
or war with Athens. The Spartans were hesitant, and in this speech
the Corinthian ambassadors urge them to take a firm stand.]

You have never considered what manner of men are these Athenians with whom you will have to fight, and how utterly unlike
yourselves. They are revolutionary, equally quick in the conception
and in the execution of every new plan; while you are conservative
—careful only to keep what you have, originating nothing, and not
acting even when action is most necessary. They are bold beyond
their strength; they run risks which prudence would condemn; and
in the midst of misfortune they are full of hope. Whereas it is your
nature, though strong, to act feebly; when your plans are most
prudent, to distrust them; and when calamities come upon you, to
think that you will never be delivered from them. They are impetuous, and you are dilatory; they are always abroad, and you are always
at home. For they hope to gain something by leaving their homes;
but you are afraid that any new enterprise may imperil what you
have already. When conquerors, they pursue their victory to the
utmost; when defeated, they fall back the least. Their bodies they

---

* Translated by Benjamin Jowett.     † From Book I, Chapter 70.

devote to their country as though they belonged to other men; their true self is their mind, which is most truly their own when employed in her service. When they do not carry out an intention which they have formed, they seem to have sustained a personal bereavement; when an enterprise succeeds, they have gained a mere instalment of what is to come; but if they fail, they at once conceive new hopes and so fill up the void. With them alone to hope is to have, for they lose not a moment in the execution of an idea. This is the life-long task, full of danger and toil, which they are always imposing upon themselves. None enjoy their good things less, because they are always seeking for more. To do their duty is their only holiday, and they deem the quiet of inaction to be as disagreeable as the most tiresome business. If a man should say of them, in a word, that they were born neither to have peace themselves nor to allow peace to other men, he would simply speak the truth.

### [Athenian Democracy—The Athenians, a Self-Portrait]*

During the same winter,[1] in accordance with an old national custom, the funeral of those who first fell in this war was celebrated by the Athenians at the public charge. The ceremony is as follows: Three days before the celebration they erect a tent in which the bones of the dead are laid out, and every one brings to his own dead any offering which he pleases. At the time of the funeral the bones are placed in chests of cypress wood, which are conveyed on hearses; there is one chest for each tribe.[2] They also carry a single empty litter decked with a pall for all whose bodies are missing, and cannot be recovered after the battle. The procession is accompanied by any one who chooses, whether citizen or stranger, and the female relatives of the deceased are present at the place of interment and make lamentation. The public sepulchre is situated in the most beautiful spot outside the walls; there they always bury those who fall in war; only after the battle of Marathon[3] the dead, in recognition of their pre-eminent valor, were interred on the field. When the remains have been laid in the earth, some man of known ability and high reputation, chosen by the city, delivers a suitable oration over them; after which the people depart. Such is the manner of interment; and the ceremony was repeated from time to time throughout the war. Over those who were the first buried Pericles[4] was chosen to speak. At the fitting moment he advanced from the sepulchre to a

---

*. From Book II, Chapters 34–46.
1. 431–430 B.C.
2. The Athenian citizen body was organized in ten tribes.
3. on the coast of Attica. In this battle (490 B.C.) the Athenians, alone except for a small contingent from the neighboring city of Plataea, defeated a Persian expeditionary force.
4. the statesman who guided the policies of the Athenian democracy during its greatest years. He died in the next year, 430 B.C.

lofty stage, which had been erected in order that he might be heard as far as possible by the multitude, and spoke as follows:

"Most of those who have spoken here before me have commended the lawgiver who added this oration to our other funeral customs; it seemed to them a worthy thing that such an honor should be given at their burial to the dead who have fallen on the field of battle. But I should have preferred that, when men's deeds have been brave, they should be honored in deed only, and with such an honor as this public funeral, which you are now witnessing. Then the reputation of many would not have been imperilled on the eloquence or want of eloquence of one, and their virtues believed or not as he spoke well or ill. For it is difficult to say neither too little nor too much; and even moderation is apt not to give the impression of truthfulness. The friend of the dead who knows the facts is likely to think that the words of the speaker fall short of his knowledge and of his wishes; another who is not so well informed, when he hears of anything which surpasses his own powers, will be envious and will suspect exaggeration. Mankind are tolerant of the praises of others so long as each hearer thinks that he can do as well or nearly as well himself, but, when the speaker rises above him, jealousy is aroused and he begins to be incredulous. However, since our ancestors have set the seal of their approval upon the practice, I must obey, and to the utmost of my power shall endeavor to satisfy the wishes and beliefs of all who hear me.

"I will speak first of our ancestors, for it is right and becoming that now, when we are lamenting the dead, a tribute should be paid to their memory. There has never been a time when they did not inhabit this land,[5] which by their valor they have handed down from generation to generation, and we have received from them a free state. But if they were worthy of praise, still more were our fathers, who added to their inheritance, and after many a struggle transmitted to us their sons this great empire.[6] And we ourselves assembled here to-day, who are still most of us in the vigor of life, have chiefly done the work of improvement, and have richly endowed our city with all things, so that she is sufficient for herself both in peace and war. Of the military exploits by which our various possessions were acquired, or of the energy with which we or our fathers drove back the tide of war, Hellenic or Barbarian,[7] I will not speak; for the tale would be long and is familiar to you. But

5. The Athenians boasted uninterrupted descent from the first inhabitants of the land.

6. After the defeat of the Persian invaders in 479 B.C. the Athenians organized a league of the Greek cities on the islands and the Asiatic mainland for defense against any renewed Persian attack; as the years went by this league was transformed from a league dominated by the Athenians into an empire which they ruled.

7. *Hellenic or Barbarian:* Greek or Persian.

before I praise the dead, I should like to point out by what principles of action we rose to power, and under what institutions and through what manner of life our empire became great. For I conceive that such thoughts are not unsuited to the occasion,[8] and that this numerous assembly of citizens and strangers may profitably listen to them.

"Our form of government does not enter into rivalry with the institutions of others. We do not copy our neighbors, but are an example to them. It is true that we are called a democracy, for the administration is in the hands of the many and not of the few.[9] But while the law secures equal justice to all alike in their private disputes, the claim of excellence is also recognized; and when a citizen is in any way distinguished, he is preferred to the public service, not as a matter of privilege, but as the reward of merit. Neither is poverty a bar, but a man may benefit his country whatever be the obscurity of his condition. There is no exclusiveness in our public life, and in our private intercourse we are not suspicious of one another, nor angry with our neighbor if he does what he likes; we do not put on sour looks at him which, though harmless, are not pleasant. While we are thus unconstrained in our private intercourse, a spirit of reverence pervades our public acts; we are prevented from doing wrong by respect for authority and for the laws, having an especial regard to those which are ordained for the protection of the injured as well as to those unwritten laws which bring upon the transgressor of them the reprobation of the general sentiment.

"And we have not forgotten to provide for our weary spirits many relaxations from toil; we have regular games and sacrifices throughout the year; at home the style of our life is refined; and the delight which we daily feel in all these things helps to banish melancholy. Because of the greatness of our city the fruits of the whole earth flow in upon us; so that we enjoy the goods of other countries as freely as of our own.

"Then, again, our military training is in many respects superior to that of our adversaries. Our city is thrown open to the world, and we never expel a foreigner or prevent him from seeing or learning anything of which the secret if revealed to an enemy might profit

8. Thucydides tells his readers (Book I, Chapter 22) how he composed this and other speeches: "As to the speeches . . . it was hard for me, and for others who reported them to me, to recollect the exact words. I have therefore put into the mouth of each speaker the sentiments proper to the occasion, expressed as I thought he would be likely to express them, while at the same time I endeavoured, as nearly as I could, to give the general purport of what was actually said."

9. The word "democracy" is composed of the two Greek words *demos* and *kratos*, which mean "people" and "power" respectively.

him.[10] We rely not upon management or trickery, but upon our own hearts and hands. And in the matter of education, whereas they from early youth are always undergoing laborious exercises which are to make them brave, we live at ease, and yet are equally ready to face the perils which they face. And here is the proof. The Lacedaemonians[11] come into Attica not by themselves, but with their whole confederacy following; we go alone into a neighbor's country; and although our opponents are fighting for their homes and we on a foreign soil, we have seldom any difficulty in overcoming them. Our enemies have never yet felt our united strength; the care of a navy divides our attention, and on land we are obliged to send our own citizens everywhere. But they, if they meet and defeat a part of our army, are as proud as if they had routed us all, and when defeated they pretend to have been vanquished by us all.

"If then we prefer to meet danger with a light heart but without laborious training, and with a courage which is gained by habit and not enforced by law, are we not greatly the gainers? Since we do not anticipate the pain, although, when the hour comes, we can be as brave as those who never allow themselves to rest; and thus too our city is equally admirable in peace and in war. For we are lovers of the beautiful, yet simple in our tastes, and we cultivate the mind without loss of manliness. Wealth we employ, not for talk and ostentation, but when there is a real use for it. To avow poverty with us is no disgrace: the true disgrace is in doing nothing to avoid it. An Athenian citizen does not neglect the state because he takes care of his own household; and even those of us who are engaged in business have a very fair idea of politics. We alone regard a man who takes no interest in public affairs, not as a harmless, but as a useless character; and if few of us are originators, we are all sound judges of a policy. The great impediment to action is, in our opinion, not discussion, but the want of that knowledge which is gained by discussion preparatory to action. For we have a peculiar power of thinking before we act and of acting too, whereas other men are courageous from ignorance but hesitate upon reflection. And they are surely to be esteemed the bravest spirits who, having the clearest sense both of the pains and pleasures of life, do not on that account shrink from danger. In doing good, again, we are unlike others; we make our friends by conferring, not by receiving favors. Now he who confers a favor is the firmer friend, because he would fain by kindness keep alive the memory of an obligation; but the recipient is colder in his feelings, because he knows that in requiting

10. in contrast to Sparta, where foreigners were admitted only on state business and then kept under surveillance. The next sentence contrasts the Athenian system of education with the Spartan.

11. Spartans.

another's generosity he will not be winning gratitude, but only paying a debt. We alone do good to our neighbors not upon a calculation of interest, but in the confidence of freedom and in a frank and fearless spirit. To sum up: I say that Athens is the school of Hellas, and that the individual Athenian in his own person seems to have the power of adapting himself to the most varied forms of action with the utmost versatility and grace. This is no passing and idle word, but truth and fact; and the assertion is verified by the position to which these qualities have raised the state. For in the hour of trial Athens alone among her contemporaries is superior to the report of her. No enemy who comes against her is indignant at the reverses which he sustains at the hands of such a city; no subject complains that his masters are unworthy of him. And we shall assuredly not be without witnesses; there are mighty monuments of our power which will make us the wonder of this and of succeeding ages;[12] we shall not need the praises of Homer or of any other panegyrist whose poetry may please for the moment, although his representation of the facts will not bear the light of day. For we have compelled every land and every sea to open a path for our valor, and have everywhere planted eternal memorials of our friendship and of our enmity. Such is the city for whose sake these men nobly fought and died; they could not bear the thought that she might be taken from them; and every one of us who survive should gladly toil on her behalf.

"I have dwelt upon the greatness of Athens because I want to show you that we are contending for a higher prize than those who enjoy none of these privileges, and to establish by manifest proof the merit of these men whom I am now commemorating. Their loftiest praise has been already spoken. For in magnifying the city I have magnified them, and men like them whose virtues made her glorious. And of how few Hellenes can it be said as of them, that their deeds when weighed in the balance have been found equal to their fame! Methinks that a death such as theirs has been given the true measure of a man's worth; it may be the first revelation of his virtues, but is at any rate their final seal. For even those who come short in other ways may justly plead the valor with which they have fought for their country; they have blotted out the evil with the good, and have benefited the state more by their public services than they have injured her by their private actions. None of these men were enervated by wealth or hesitated to resign the pleasures of life; none of them put off the evil day in the hope, natural to poverty, that a man, though poor, may one day become rich. But, deeming that the punishment of their enemies was sweeter than

12. The ruins of the fifth-century buildings on the Acropolis of Athens are still the wonder of the world.

any of these things, and that they could fall in no nobler cause, they determined at the hazard of their lives to be honorably avenged, and to leave the rest. They resigned to hope their unknown chance of happiness; but in the face of death they resolved to rely upon themselves alone. And when the moment came they were minded to resist and suffer, rather than to fly and save their lives; they ran away from the word of dishonor, but on the battle-field their feet stood fast, and in an instant, at the height of their fortune, they passed away from the scene, not of their fear, but of their glory.

"Such was the end of these men; they were worthy of Athens, and the living need not desire to have a more heroic spirit, although they may pray for a less fatal issue. The value of such a spirit is not to be expressed in words. Any one can discourse to you for ever about the advantages of a brave defence which you know already. But instead of listening to him I would have you day by day fix your eyes upon the greatness of Athens, until you become filled with the love of her; and when you are impressed by the spectacle of her glory, reflect that this empire has been acquired by men who knew their duty and had the courage to do it, who in the hour of conflict had the fear of dishonor always present to them, and who, if ever they failed in an enterprise, would not allow their virtues to be lost to their country, but freely gave their lives to her as the fairest offering which they could present at her feast. The sacrifice which they collectively made was individually repaid to them; for they received again each one for himself a praise which grows not old, and the noblest of all sepulchres—I speak not of that in which their remains are laid, but of that in which their glory survives, and is proclaimed always and on every fitting occasion both in word and deed. For the whole earth is the sepulchre of famous men; not only are they commemorated by columns and inscriptions in their own country, but in foreign lands there dwells also an unwritten memorial of them, graven not on stone but in the hearts of men. Make them your examples, and, esteeming courage to be freedom and freedom to be happiness, do not weigh too nicely the perils of war. The unfortunate who has no hope of a change for the better has less reason to throw away his life than the prosperous who, if he survive, is always liable to a change for the worse, and to whom any accidental fall makes the most serious difference. To a man of spirit, cowardice and disaster coming together are far more bitter than death, striking him unperceived at a time when he is full of courage and animated by the general hope.

"Wherefore I do not now commiserate the parents of the dead who stand here; I would rather comfort them. You know that your life has been passed amid manifold vicissitudes; and that they may be deemed fortunate who have gained most honor, whether an honorable death like theirs, or an honorable sorrow like yours, and whose days have been so ordered that the term of their happiness is likewise the term of their life. I know how hard it is to make you feel this, when the good fortune of others will too often remind you of the gladness which once lightened your hearts. And sorrow is felt at the want of those blessings, not which a man never knew, but which were a part of his life before they were taken from him. Some of you are of an age at which they may hope to have other children, and they ought to bear their sorrow better; not only will the children who may hereafter be born make them forget their own lost ones, but the city will be doubly a gainer. She will not be left desolate, and she will be safer. For a man's counsel cannot have equal weight or worth, when he alone has no children to risk in the general danger. To those of you who have passed their prime, I say: 'Congratulate yourselves that you have been happy during the greater part of your days; remember that your life of sorrow will not last long, and be comforted by the glory of those who are gone. For the love of honor alone is ever young, and not riches, as some say, but honor is the delight of men when they are old and useless.'

"To you who are the sons and brothers of the departed, I see that the struggle to emulate them will be an arduous one. For all men praise the dead, and, however pre-eminent your virtue may be, hardly will you be thought, I do not say to equal, but even to approach them. The living have their rivals and detractors, but when a man is out of the way, the honor and good-will which he receives is unalloyed. And, if I am to speak of womanly virtues to those of you who will henceforth be widows, let me sum them up in one short admonition: To a woman not to show more weakness than is natural to her sex is a great glory, and not to be talked about for good or for evil among men.

"I have paid the required tribute, in obedience to the law, making use of such fitting words as I had. The tribute of deeds has been paid in part; for the dead have been honorably interred, and it remains only that their children should be maintained at the public charge until they are grown up; this is the solid prize with which, as with a garland, Athens crowns her sons living and dead, after a struggle like theirs. For where the rewards of virtue are greatest, there the noblest citizens are enlisted in the service of the state. And now, when you have duly lamented, every one of his own dead, you may depart."

# SOPHOCLES
## (495?–406 B.C.)

## Oedipus Tyrannus*

### Characters

OEDIPUS, RULER OF THEBES
JOCASTA, WIFE OF OEDIPUS
CREON, BROTHER OF JOCASTA
TEIRESIAS, A BLIND PROPHET
A PRIEST
MESSENGER 1

MESSENGER 2
A SHEPHERD
AN ATTENDANT
ANTIGONE ⎱ DAUGHTERS OF OEDIPUS
ISMENE ⎰ AND JOCASTA
CHORUS OF THEBAN ELDERS

SCENE.—*In front of the doors of the palace of Oedipus at Thebes.
A crowd of citizens sits at an altar in supplication. Among them is
an old man, the* PRIEST *of Zeus.*

[*Enter, through the doors,* OEDIPUS.]

OEDIPUS: What is it, children, sons of the ancient house of
Cadmus?[1] Why do you sit as suppliants crowned with laurel
branches? What is the meaning of the incense which fills the
city? The pleas to end pain? The cries of sorrow? I chose not to
hear it from my messengers, but came myself—I came, Oedipus,
Oedipus, whose name is known to all. You, old one—age gives
you the right to speak for all of them—you tell me why they sit
before my altar. Has something frightened you? What brings you
here? Some need? Some want? I'll help you all I can. I would be
cruel did I not greet you with compassion when you are gathered
here before me.

PRIEST: My Lord and King, we represent the young and old; some
are priests and some the best of Theban youth. And I—I am a
priest of Zeus. There are many more who carry laurel boughs[2]
like these—in the market-places, at the twin altars of Pallas,[3] by
the sacred ashes of Ismenus' oracle.[4] You see yourself how torn
our city is, how she craves relief from the waves of death which
now crash over her. Death is everywhere—in the harvests of the
land, in the flocks that roam the pastures, in the unborn children

* Translated by Luci Berkowitz and
Theodore F. Brunner. Copyright © 1970
by W. W. Norton & Company, Inc. The
date of the play's first production is unknown but is usually taken to be 430 B.C.
or a few years later.

1. *Cadmus:* founder of Thebes and its
first king.

2. *laurel boughs:* the suppliant carried

a branch, which he laid on the altar and
left there until his request was granted.
At the end of this scene, Oedipus tells the
suppliants to take their branches away.

3. *Pallas:* Athena.

4. *Ismenus' oracle:* in a temple of
Apollo near the river Ismenus, where
burnt offerings were made and prophecies given.

of our mothers' wombs. A fiery plague is ravaging the city, festering, spreading its pestilence, wasting the house of Cadmus, filling the house of Hades with screams of pain and of fear. This is the reason why we come to you, these children and I. No, we do not think you a god. But we deem you a mortal set apart to face life's common issues and the trials which the gods dispense to men. It was you who once before came to Thebes and freed us from the spell that hypnotized our lives.[5] You did this, and yet you knew no more than we—less even. You had no help from us. God aided you. Yes, you restored our life. And now a second time, great Oedipus, we turn to you for help. Find some relief for us, whether with god or man to guide your way. You helped us then. Yes. And we believe that you will help us now. O Lord, revive our city; restore her life. Think of your fame, your own repute. The people know you saved us from our past despair. Let no one say you raised us up to let us fall. Save us and keep us safe. You found good omens once to aid you and brought us fortune then. Find them again. If you will rule this land as king and lord, rule over men and not a wall encircling emptiness. No city wall, no ship can justify its claim to strength if it is stripped of men who give it life.

OEDIPUS: O my children, I know well the pain you suffer and understand what brings you here. You suffer—and yet not one among you suffers more than I. Each of you grieves for himself alone, while my heart must bear the strain of sorrow for all—myself and you and all our city's people. No, I am not blind to it. I have wept and in my weeping set my thoughts on countless paths, searching for an answer. I have sent my own wife's brother Creon, son of Menoeceus, to Apollo's Pythian shrine[6] to learn what I might say or do to ease our city's suffering. I am concerned that he is not yet here—he left many days ago. But this promise: whenever he returns, whatever news he brings, whatever course the god reveals—*that* is the course that I shall take.

PRIEST: Well spoken. Look! They are giving signs that Creon is returning.

OEDIPUS: O God! If only he brings news as welcome as his smiling face.

PRIEST: I think he does. His head is crowned with laurel leaves.

OEDIPUS: We shall know soon enough. There. My Lord Creon, what word do you bring from the god?

[*Enter* CREON.]

CREON: Good news. I tell you this: if all goes well, our troubles will be past.

OEDIPUS: But what was the oracle? Right now I'm swaying between hope and fear.

---

5. *spell:* the Sphinx, a winged female monster which terrorized the city of Thebes until her riddle was finally answered by Oedipus. The riddle was: "What is it that walks on four feet and two feet and three feet and has only one voice; when it walks on most feet, it is weakest?" Oedipus' answer was Man. (He has four feet as a child crawling on all fours, and three feet in old age when he walks with the aid of a stick.)

6. *Pythian shrine:* the oracle of Apollo at Delphi.

CREON: If you want to hear it in the presence of these people, I shall tell you. If not, let's go inside.

OEDIPUS: Say it before all of us. I sorrow more for them than for myself.

CREON: Then I shall tell you exactly what the god Apollo answered. These are his words: Pollution. A hidden sore is festering in our land. We are to stop its growth before it is too late.

OEDIPUS: Pollution? How are we to save ourselves?

CREON: Blood for blood. To save ourselves we are to banish a man or pay for blood with blood. It is a murder which has led to this despair.

OEDIPUS: Murder? Whose? Did the god say whose . . . ?

CREON: My Lord, before you came to rule our city, we had a king. His name was Laius . . .

OEDIPUS: I know, although I never saw him.

CREON: He was murdered. And the god's command is clear: we must find the assassin and destroy him.

OEDIPUS: But where? Where is he to be found? How can we find the traces of a crime committed long ago?

CREON: He lives among us. If we seek, we will find; what we do not seek cannot be found.

OEDIPUS: Where was it that Laius met his death? At home? The country? In some foreign land?

CREON: One day he left and told us he would go to Delphi. That was the last we saw of him.

OEDIPUS: And there was no one who could tell what happened? No one who traveled with him? Did no one see? Is there no evidence?

CREON: All perished. All—except one who ran in panic from the scene and could not tell us anything for certain, except . . .

OEDIPUS: Except? What? What was it? One clue might lead to many. We have to grasp the smallest shred of hope.

CREON: He said that robbers—many of them—fell upon Laius and his men and murdered them.

OEDIPUS: Robbers? Who committed *murder*? Why? Unless they were paid assassins?

CREON: We considered that. But the king was dead and we were plagued with trouble. No one came forth as an avenger.

OEDIPUS: Trouble? What could have kept you from investigating the death of your king?

CREON: The Sphinx. The Sphinx was confounding us with her riddles, forcing us to abandon our search for the unknown and to tend to what was then before us.

OEDIPUS: Then I—I shall begin again. I shall not cease until I bring the truth to light. Apollo has shown, and you have shown, the duty which we owe the dead. You have my gratitude. You will find me a firm ally, and together we shall exact vengeance for our land and for the god. I shall not rest till I dispel this defilement—not just for another man's sake, but for my own as well. For whoever the assassin—he might turn his hand against me too. Yes, I shall be serving Laius and myself. Now go, my chil-

dren. Leave the steps of my altar. Go. Take away your laurel
branches. Go to the people of Cadmus. Summon them.[7] Tell
them that I, their king, will leave nothing untried. And with the
help of God, we shall find success—or ruin.

    [*Exit* OEDIPUS.]

PRIEST: Come, children. We have learned what we came to learn.
    Come, Apollo, come yourself, who sent these oracles!
    Come as our savior! Come! Deliver us from this plague!

CHORUS:

O prophecy of Zeus,[8] sweet is the sound of your words
as they come to our glorious city of Thebes
from Apollo's glittering shrine.
Yet I quake and I dread and I tremble at those words.
Io, Delian Lord![9]

What will you bring to pass? Disaster unknown,
or familiar to us, as the ever recurring seasons?
Tell me, O oracle,
heavenly daughter of blessèd hope.

Foremost I call on you, daughter of Zeus,
Athena, goddess supreme;
and on Artemis,[10] shielding the world,
shielding this land from her circular shrine
graced with renown.
And on you I call, Phoebus,[11] Lord of the unerring bow.

Come to my aid, you averters of doom!
Come to my aid if ever you came!
Come to my aid as once you did, when you quenched
the fires of doom that fell on our soil!
Hear me, and come to my aid!

Boundless the pain, boundless the grief I bear;
sickness pervades this land,
affliction without reprieve.
Barren the soil, barren of fruit;
children are born no longer to light;
all of us flutter in agony
winging our way into darkness and death.

Countless the number of dead in the land;
corpses of children cover the plain,
children dying before they have lived,
no one to pity them,
reeking, and spreading diseases and death.

Moaning and wailing our wives,

7. *Summon them:* The people of Thebes
are represented by the chorus, which
comes into the orchestra at the end of
the scene.

8. *Zeus:* Apollo was his son, and spoke
for him.

9. *Delian:* Apollo was born on the sacred island of Delos.

10. *Artemis:* sister of Apollo.

11. *Phoebus:* Apollo.

moaning and wailing our mothers
stream to the altars this way and that,
scream to the air with helpless cries.
Hear us, golden daughter of Zeus,
hear us! Send us release!

Ares[12] now rages in our midst
brandishing in his hands
the firebrands of disease,
raving, consuming, rousing the screams of death.
Hear us, O goddess!
Help us, and still his rage!
Turn back his assault!
Help us! Banish him from our land!
Drive him into the angry sea,
to the wave-swept border of Thrace!

We who escape him tonight
will be struck down at dawn.
Help us, O father Zeus,
Lord of the thunderbolt,
crush him! Destroy him!
Burn him with fires of lightning!

Help us, Apollo, Lycean[13] Lord!
Stand at our side with your golden bow!
Artemis, help us!
Come from the Lycian[14] hills!
Come with your torches aflame!
Dionysus,[15] protector, come to our aid,
come with your revelers' band!
Burn with your torch the god
hated among the gods!

    [*Enter* OEDIPUS.]

OEDIPUS: I have heard your prayers and answer with relief and help, if you will heed my words and tend the sickness with the cure it cries for. My words are uttered as a stranger to the act, a stranger to its tale. I cannot trace its path alone, without a sign. As a citizen newer to Thebes than you, I make this proclamation: If one among you knows who murdered Laius, the son of Labdacus, let him tell us now. If he fears for his life, let him confess and know a milder penalty. He will be banished from this land. Nothing more. Or if you know the assassin to be an alien, do not protect him with your silence. You will be rewarded. But if in fear you protect yourself or any other man and keep your silence, then hear what I say now: Whoever he is, this assassin

---

12. *Ares:* god of war and destruction. He was thought to be at home among the savages of Thrace, to the northeast of Greece proper.

13. *Lycean:* an epithet of Apollo, suggestive of his connection with light (like Phoebus = shining) and also of his role

as protector of the flocks against wolves.

14. *Lycian:* from Lycia, in southern Turkey. The connection of this region with Artemis is not clear.

15. *Dionysus:* son of Zeus, god of the forest and the vine.

must be denied entrance to your homes. Any man where I rule is forbidden to receive him or speak to him or share with him his prayers and sacrifice or offer him the holy rites of purification. I command you to drive this hideous curse out of your homes; I command you to obey the will of Pythian Apollo. I will serve the god and the dead. On the assassin or assassins, I call down the most vile damnation—for this vicious act, may the brand of shame be theirs to wear forever. And if I knowingly harbor their guilt within my own walls, I shall not exempt myself from the curse that I have called upon them. It is for me, for God, and for this city that staggers toward ruin that you must fulfill these injunctions. Even if Heaven gave you no sign, you had the sacred duty to insure that this act did not go unexamined, unavenged! It was the assassination of a noble man—your king! Now that I hold the powers that he once held, his bed, his wife—had fate been unopposed, his children would have bound us closer yet— and now on him has this disaster fallen. I will avenge him as I would avenge my own father. I will leave nothing untried to expose the murderer of Laius, the son of Labdacus, heir to the house of Cadmus and Agenor.[16] On those who deny me obedience, I utter this curse: May the gods visit them with barrenness in their harvests, barrenness in their women, barrenness in their fate. Worse still—may they be haunted and tormented and never know the peace that comes with death. But for you, my people, in sympathy with me—I pray that Justice and all the gods attend you forever.

CHORUS: You have made me swear an oath, my Lord, and under oath I speak. I did not kill the king and cannot name the man who did. The question was Apollo's. He could name the man you seek.

OEDIPUS: I know. And yet no mortal can compel a god to speak.

CHORUS: The next-best thing, it seems to me . . .

OEDIPUS: Tell me. Tell me all your thoughts. We must consider everything.

CHORUS: There is one man, second only to Apollo, who can see the truth, who can clearly help us in our search—Teiresias.[17]

OEDIPUS: I thought of this. On Creon's advice, I sent for him. Twice. He should be here.

CHORUS: There were some rumors once, but no one hears them now.

OEDIPUS: What rumors? I want to look at every tale that is told.

CHORUS: They said that travelers murdered Laius.

OEDIPUS: I have heard that too. And yet there's no one to be found who saw the murderer in the act.

CHORUS: He will come forth himself, once he has heard your curse, if he knows what it means to be afraid.

OEDIPUS: Why? Why should a man now fear words if then he did not fear to kill?

16. *Agenor:* king of Phoenicia, father of Cadmus.
17. *Teiresias:* the blind prophet of Thebes (the same one whose ghost Odysseus goes to consult in Hades, p. 242).

CHORUS: But there is one man who can point him out—the man in whom the truth resides, the god-inspired prophet. And there— they are bringing him now.

[*Enter* TEIRESIAS, *guided by a servant.*]

OEDIPUS: Teiresias, all things are known to you—the secrets of heaven and earth, the sacred and profane. Though you are blind, you surely see the plague that rakes our city. My Lord Teiresias, we turn to you as our only hope. My messengers may have told you—we have sent to Apollo and he has answered us. We must find Laius' murderers and deal with them. Or drive them out. Then—only then will we find release from our suffering. I ask you not to spare your gifts of prophecy. Look to the voices of prophetic birds or the answers written in the flames. Spare nothing. Save all of us—yourself, your city, your king, and all that is touched by this deathly pollution. We turn to you. My Lord, it is man's most noble role to help his fellow man the best his talents will allow.

TEIRESIAS: O God! How horrible wisdom is! How horrible when it does not help the wise! How could I have forgotten? I should not have come.

OEDIPUS: Why? What's wrong?

TEIRESIAS: Let me go. It will be better if you bear your own distress and I bear mine. It will be better this way.

OEDIPUS: This city gave you life and yet you refuse her an answer! You speak as if you were her enemy.

TEIRESIAS: No! No! It is because I see the danger in your words. And mine would add still more.

OEDIPUS: For God's sake, if you know, don't turn away from us! We are pleading. We are begging you.

TEIRESIAS: Because you are blind! No! I shall not reveal my secrets. I shall not reveal yours.

OEDIPUS: What? You know, and yet you refuse to speak? Would you betray us and watch our city fall helplessly to her death?

TEIRESIAS: I will not cause you further grief. I will not grieve myself. Stop asking me to tell; I will tell you nothing.

OEDIPUS: You will not tell? You monster! You could stir the stones of earth to a burning rage! You will never tell? What will it take?

TEIRESIAS: Know yourself, Oedipus. You denounce me, but you do not yet know yourself.

OEDIPUS: Yes! You disgrace your city. And then you expect us to control our rage!

TEIRESIAS: It does not matter if I speak; the future has already been determined.

OEDIPUS: And if it has, then it is for you to tell me, *prophet!*

TEIRESIAS: I shall say no more. Rage, if you wish.

OEDIPUS: I *am* enraged. And now I will tell you what I think. I think this was *your* doing. *You* plotted the crime, *you* saw it carried out. It was *your* doing. All but the actual killing. And had you not been blind, you would have done *that*, too!

TEIRESIAS: Do you believe what you have said? Then accept your own decree! From this day on, deny yourself the right to speak to anyone. You, Oedipus, are the desecrator, the polluter of this land!

OEDIPUS: You traitor! Do you think that you can get away with this?

TEIRESIAS: The truth is my protection.

OEDIPUS: Who taught you this? It did not come from prophecy!

TEIRESIAS: *You* taught me. *You* drove me, *you* forced me to say it against my will.

OEDIPUS: Say it again. I want to make sure that I understand you.

TEIRESIAS: Understand me? Or are you trying to provoke me?

OEDIPUS: No, I want to be sure, I want to know. Say it again.

TEIRESIAS: I say that you, Oedipus Tyrannus, are the murderer you seek.

OEDIPUS: So! A second time! Now twice you will regret what you have said!

TEIRESIAS: Shall I tell you more? Shall I fan your flames of anger?

OEDIPUS: Yes. Tell me more. Tell me more—whatever suits you. It will be in vain.

TEIRESIAS: I say you live in shame with the woman you love, blind to your own calamity.

OEDIPUS: Do you think you can speak like this forever?

TEIRESIAS: I do, if there is any strength in truth.

OEDIPUS: There is—for everyone but you. You—you cripple! Your ears are deaf, your eyes are blind, your mind—your *mind* is crippled!

TEIRESIAS: You fool! You slander me when one day you will hear the same . . .

OEDIPUS: You live in night, Teiresias, in night that never turns to day. And so, you cannot hurt me—or any man who sees the light.

TEIRESIAS: No—it is not I who will cause your fall. That is Apollo's office—and he will discharge it.

OEDIPUS: Was this *your* trick—or Creon's?

TEIRESIAS: No, not Creon's. No, Oedipus. You are destroying yourself!

OEDIPUS: Ah, wealth and sovereignty and skill surpassing skill in life's contentions, why must envy always attend them? This city *gave* me power; I did not ask for it. And Creon, my friend, my trusted friend, would plot to overthrow me—with this charlatan, this impostor, who auctions off his magic wares! His eyes see profit clearly, but they are blind in prophecy. Tell me, Teiresias, what makes you a prophet? Where were you when the monster was here weaving her spells and taunts? What words of relief did Thebes hear from you? Her riddle would stagger the simple mind; it demanded the mind of a seer. Yet, put to the test, all your birds and god-craft proved useless; you had no answer. Then I came—ignorant Oedipus—I came and smothered her, using only my wit. There were no birds to tell me what to do. I am the man you would overthrow so you can stand near Creon's throne. You will regret—you and your conspirator—you will regret your attempt to purify this land. If you were not an old man, I would make you suffer the pain which you deserve for your audacity.

CHORUS: Both of you, my Lord, have spoken in bitter rage. No more—not when we must direct our every thought to obey the god's command

TEIRESIAS: Though you are king, the right to speak does not belong to you alone. It is *my* right as well and I shall claim it. I am not your servant and Creon is not my patron. I serve only Loxian[18] Apollo. And I tell you this, since you mock my blindness. You have eyes, Oedipus, and do not see your own destruction. You have eyes and do not see what lives with you. Do you know whose son you are? I say that you have sinned and do not know it; you have sinned against your own—the living and the dead. A double scourge, your mother's and your father's curse, will drive you from this land. Then darkness will shroud those eyes that now can see the light. Cithæron,[19]—the whole earth will resound with your mournful cries when you discover the meaning of the wedding-song that brought you to this place you falsely thought a haven. More sorrow still awaits you—more than you can know—to show you what you are and what your children are. Damn Creon, if you will; damn the words I say. No man on earth will ever know the doom that waits for you.

OEDIPUS: How much of this am I to bear? Leave! Now! Leave my house!

TEIRESIAS: I would not be here had you not sent for me.

OEDIPUS: I never would have sent for you had I known the madness I would hear.

TEIRESIAS: To you, I am mad; but not to your parents . . .

OEDIPUS: Wait! My parents? Who are my parents?

TEIRESIAS: This day shall bring you birth *and* death.

OEDIPUS: Why must you persist with riddles?

TEIRESIAS: Are you not the best of men when it comes to riddles?

OEDIPUS: You mock the very skill that proves me great.

TEIRESIAS: A great misfortune—which will destroy you.

OEDIPUS: I don't care. If I have saved this land, I do not care.

TEIRESIAS: Then I shall go. [*To his servant.*] Come, take me home.

OEDIPUS: Yes, go home. You won't be missed.

TEIRESIAS: I will go when I've said all that I came to say. I am not afraid of you. You cannot hurt me. And I tell you this: The man you seek—the man whose death or banishment you ordered, the man who murdered Laius—that man is here, passing as an alien, living in our midst. Soon it will be known to all of you—he is a native Theban. And he will find no joy in that discovery. His eyes now see, but soon they will be blind: rich now, but soon a beggar. Holding a scepter now, but soon a cane, he will grope for the earth beneath him—in a foreign land. Both brother and father to the children that he loves. Both son and husband to the woman who bore him. Both heir and spoiler of his father's bed

18. *Loxian:* an epithet of Apollo which means "crooked, ambiguous."

19. *Cithaeron:* the mountain range near Thebes.

and the one who took his life. Go, think of this. And if you find
the words I speak are lies, *then* say that I am blind.

[*Exeunt* OEDIPUS, TEIRESIAS.]

CHORUS:
Who is he? Who is the man?
Who is the man whom the voice of the Delphian shrine
denounced as the killer, the murderer,
the man who committed the terrible crime?
Where is he? Where is he now?
Let him run, let him flee!
Let him rush with the speed of the wind on his flight!
For with fire and lightning the god will attack,
and relentlessly fate will pursue him and haunt him
and drive him to doom.

Do you hear? Do you hear the command of the god?
From Parnassus[20] he orders the hunt.
In vain will the murderer hide,
in vain will he run,
in vain will he lurk in the forests and caves
like an animal roaming the desolate hills.
Let him flee to the edge of the world:
On his heels he will find
the command of the god!

Confusion and fear
have been spread by the prophet's words.
For I cannot affirm, yet I cannot refute
what he spoke. And I'm lost, I am lost—
What am I to believe?
Now foreboding is gripping my heart.
Was there ever a strife between Laius and Polybus'[21] house?
Can I test? Can I prove?
Can I ever believe that the name of my king
has been soiled by a murder unknown?

It is Zeus and Apollo who know,
who can see the affairs of men.
But the seer and I,
we are mortal, and blind.
Who is right? Who can judge?
We are mortal, our wisdom assigned in degrees.
Does the seer know? Do I?
No, I will not believe in the prophet's charge
till the charge has been proved to my mind.
For I saw how the king
in the test with the Sphinx
proved his wisdom and worth
when he saved this city from doom.

---

20. *Parnassus:* mountain above Delphi.
21. *Polybus:* king of Corinth and, so
far as anyone yet knows, the father of
Oedipus.

No! I can *never* condemn the king!
 [*Enter* CREON.]

CREON: My fellow-citizens, anger has impelled me to come because
 I have heard the accusation which Oedipus has brought against
 me—and I will not tolerate it. If he thinks that I—in the midst
 of this torment—I have thought to harm him in any way, I will
 not spend the rest of my life branded by his charge. Doesn't he
 see the implications of such slander? To you, to my friends, to
 my city—I would be a traitor!

CHORUS: He spoke in anger—without thinking.

CREON: Yes—and who was it who said that the prophet lied on my
 advice?

CHORUS: It was said, but I don't know how it was meant.

CREON: And was this a charge leveled by one whose eyes were
 clear? Whose head was clear?

CHORUS: I don't know. I do not judge my master's actions. But
 here he comes.
 [*Enter* OEDIPUS.]

OEDIPUS: Why have you come, Creon? Do you have the audacity
 to show your face in my presence? Assassin! And now you would
 steal my throne! What drove you to this plot? Did you see cowardice in me? Stupidity? Did you imagine that I would not see
 your treachery? Did you expect that I wouldn't act to stop you?
 You fool! Your plot was mad! You go after a throne without
 money, without friends! How do you think thrones are won?

CREON: You listen to me! And when you have heard me out, when
 you have heard the truth, *then* judge for yourself.

OEDIPUS: Ah yes, your oratory! I can learn nothing from that. This
 is what I have learned—you are my enemy!

CREON: Just let me say . . .

OEDIPUS: Say one thing—say that you are not a traitor.

CREON: If you think that senseless stubbornness is a precious gift,
 you are a fool.

OEDIPUS: If you think that you can threaten the house of Cadmus
 —your own house—and not pay for it, you are mad.

CREON: I grant you that. But tell me: just what is this terrible
 thing you say I have done to you?

OEDIPUS: Did you or did you not tell me to send for that—that—
 prophet?

CREON: I did. And I would again.

OEDIPUS: Then, how long since Laius . . . ?

CREON: What? I do not follow . . .

OEDIPUS: . . . Disappeared?

CREON: A long time ago.

OEDIPUS: Your Teiresias—was he—was he a prophet then?

CREON: Yes—and just as honored and just as wise.

OEDIPUS: Did he ever mention me—then?

CREON: Not in my presence.

OEDIPUS: But didn't you investigate the murder?

CREON: Of course we did—

OEDIPUS: And why didn't the prophet say anything *then*?

CREON: I do not know. It's not for me to try to understand.

OEDIPUS: You know this much which you will try to tell me . . .

CREON: What is it? I will tell you if I can.

OEDIPUS: Just this: Had he not acted under your instructions, he would not have named *me* killer of Laius.

CREON: If this is what he said, you ought to know. You heard him. But now I claim the right to question you, as you have me.

OEDIPUS: Ask what you wish. I am not the murderer.

CREON: Then answer me. Did you marry my sister?

OEDIPUS: Of course I did.

CREON: And do you rule on equal terms with her?

OEDIPUS: She has all that she wants from me.

CREON: And am I not the third and equal partner?

OEDIPUS: You are—and that is where you have proved yourself a traitor.

CREON: Not true. Consider rationally, as I have done. First ask yourself—would any man prefer a life of fear to one in which the self-same rank, the self-same rights are guaranteed untroubled peace? I have no wish to be a king when I can act as one without a throne. And any man would feel the same, if he were wise. I share with you a king's prerogatives, yet you alone must face the danger lurking around the throne. If *I* were king, I would have to act in many ways against my pleasure. What added benefit could kingship hold when I have rank and rule without the threat of pain? I am not deluded—no, I would not look for honors beyond the ones which profit me. I have the favor of every man; each greets me first when he would hope to have *your* favor. Why should I exchange this for a throne? Only a fool would. No, I am not a traitor nor would I aid an act of treason. You want proof? Go to Delphi; ask if I have brought you the truth. Then, if you find me guilty of conspiracy with the prophet, command my death. I will face that. But do not condemn me without proof. You are wrong to judge the guilty innocent, the innocent guilty —without proof. Casting off a true friend is like casting off your greatest prize—your life. You will know in time that this is true. Time alone reveals the just; a single day condemns the guilty.

CHORUS: He is right, my Lord. Respect his words. A man who plans in haste will gamble the result.

OEDIPUS: This is a plot conceived in rashness. It must be met with quick response. I cannot sit and wait until the plot succeeds.

CREON: What will you do then? Do you intend to banish me?

OEDIPUS: No. No, not banish you. I want to see you *dead*—to make you an example for all aspiring to my throne.

CREON: Then you won't do as I suggest? You won't believe me?

OEDIPUS: You have not shown that you deserve belief.

CREON: No, because I see that you are mad.

OEDIPUS: In my own eyes, I am sane.

CREON: You should be sane in mine as well.

OEDIPUS: No. You are a traitor!

CREON: And what if you are wrong?

OEDIPUS: Still—I will rule.

CREON: Not when you rule treacherously.

OEDIPUS: O Thebes! My city! Listen to him!

CREON: *My* city too!

CHORUS: My Lords, no more. Here comes Jocasta. Perhaps the queen can end this bitter clash.

[*Enter* JOCASTA.]

JOCASTA: Why do you behave like senseless fools and quarrel without reason? Are you not ashamed to add trouble of your own when your city is sick and dying? Go, Creon. Go and leave us alone. Forget those petty grievances which you exaggerate. How important can they be?

CREON: This important, sister: Oedipus, your husband, in his insanity, has threatened me with banishment or death.

OEDIPUS: Yes, for I have realized his plot—a plot against my person.

CREON: May the gods haunt me forever, if that is true—if I am guilty of that charge.

JOCASTA: In the name of God, believe him, Oedipus! Believe him for the sake of his oath, for my own sake, and for theirs!

CHORUS: Listen to her, my Lord. I beg you to consider and comply.

OEDIPUS: What would you have me do?

CHORUS: Respect the oath that Creon gave you. Respect his past integrity.

OEDIPUS: Do you know what you are asking?

CHORUS: Yes, I know.

OEDIPUS: Then, tell me what you mean.

CHORUS: I mean that you are wrong to charge a friend who has invoked a curse upon his head. You are wrong to slander without proof and be the cause for his dishonor.

OEDIPUS: Then you must know that when you ask for this, you ask for banishment or doom—for *me*.

CHORUS:
O God, no!
O Helios, [22] no!
May Heaven and Earth exact my doom
if that is what I thought!
When our city is torn by sickness
and my heart is torn with pain—
do not compound the troubles
that beset us!

OEDIPUS: Then, let him go, although it surely means my death—or banishment with dishonor. *Your* words—not his—have touched my heart. But Creon—wherever he may be—I will hate him.

CREON: You are hard when you should yield, cruel when you should pity. Such natures deserve the pain they bear.

OEDIPUS: Just go—and leave me in peace.

22. *Helios:* the sun. He is appealed to as a witness to oaths since, in his daily passage over the earth, he sees everything that happens.

CREON: I will go—my guilt pronounced by you alone. Behold my judge and jury—Oedipus Tyrannus!
> [*Exit* CREON.]

CHORUS: My queen, persuade your husband to rest awhile.

JOCASTA: I will—when I have learned the truth.

CHORUS: Blind suspicion has consumed the king. And Creon's passions flared beneath the sting of unjust accusations.

JOCASTA: Are *both* at fault?

CHORUS: Yes, both of them.

JOCASTA: But what is the reason for their rage?

CHORUS: Don't ask again. Our city is weary enough from suffering. Enough. Let the matter rest where it now stands.

OEDIPUS: Do you see what you have done? Do you see where you have come—with your good intentions, your noble efforts to dull the sharpness of my anger?

CHORUS:
My Lord, I have said before
and now I say again:
I would be mad,
a reckless fool
to turn away my king,
who saved us from a sea of troubles
and set us on a fairer course,
and who will lead us once again
to peace, a haven from our pain.

JOCASTA: In the name of Heaven, my Lord, tell me the reason for your bitterness.

OEDIPUS: I will—because you mean more to me than anyone. The reason is Creon and his plot against my throne.

JOCASTA: But can you *prove* a plot?

OEDIPUS: He says that I—Oedipus—bear the guilt of Laius' death.

JOCASTA: How does he justify this charge?

OEDIPUS: He does not stain his own lips by saying it. No. He uses that false prophet to speak for him.

JOCASTA: Then, you can exonerate yourself because no mortal has the power of divination. And I can prove it. An oracle came to Laius once from the Pythian priests—I'll not say from Apollo himself—that he would die at the hands of his own child, his child and mine. Yet the story which *we* heard was that robbers murdered Laius in a place where three roads meet. As for the child —when he was three days old, Laius drove pins into his ankles and handed him to someone to cast upon a deserted mountain path—to die. And so, Apollo's prophecy was unfulfilled—the child did not kill his father. And Laius' fears were unfulfilled—he did not die by the hand of his child. Yet, these had been the prophecies. You need not give them any credence. For the god will reveal what he wants.

OEDIPUS: Jocasta—my heart is troubled at your words. Suddenly, my thoughts are wandering, disturbed . . .

JOCASTA: What is it? What makes you so frightened?

OEDIPUS: Your statement—that Laius was murdered in a place where three roads meet. Isn't that what you said?

JOCASTA: Yes. That was the story then; that is the story now.

OEDIPUS: Where is this place where three roads meet?

JOCASTA: In the land called Phocis where the roads from Delphi and from Daulia converge.

OEDIPUS: How long a time has passed since then?

JOCASTA: We heard it shortly before you came.

OEDIPUS: O God, what have you planned for me?

JOCASTA: What is it, Oedipus? What frightens you?

OEDIPUS: Do not ask me. Do not ask. Just tell me—what was Laius like? How old was he?

JOCASTA: He was tall and his hair was lightly cast with silver tones, the contour of his body much like yours.

OEDIPUS: O God! Am I cursed and cannot see it?

JOCASTA: What is it, Oedipus? You frighten me.

OEDIPUS: It cannot be—that the prophet sees! Tell me one more thing.

JOCASTA: You frighten me, my Lord, but I will try to tell you what I know.

OEDIPUS: Who traveled with the king? Was he alone? Was there a guide? An escort? A few? Many?

JOCASTA: There were five—one of them a herald—and a carriage in which Laius rode.

OEDIPUS: O God! O God! I see it all now! Jocasta, who told you this?

JOCASTA: A servant—the only one who returned alive.

OEDIPUS: Is he here now? In our house?

JOCASTA: No. When he came back and saw you ruling where once his master was, he pleaded with me—begged me—to send him to the fields to tend the flocks, far from the city. And so I did. He was a good servant and I would have granted him more than that, if he had asked.

OEDIPUS: Could we arrange to have him here—now?

JOCASTA: Yes, but what do you want with him?

OEDIPUS: I am afraid, Jocasta. I have said too much and now I have to see him.

JOCASTA: Then he shall be brought. But I, too, must know the cause of your distress. I have the right to know.

OEDIPUS: Yes, you have that right. And I must tell you—now. You, more than anyone, will have to know what I am going through. My father was Polybus of Corinth, my mother a Dorian—Merope. I was held in high regard in Corinth until—until something strange occurred—something uncanny and strange, although I might have given it too much concern. There was a man dining with us one day who had had far too much wine and shouted at me—half-drunk and shouting that I was not rightly called my father's son. I could barely endure the rest of that day and on the next I went to my parents and questioned them. They were enraged at the remark. I felt relieved at their response. But still, this—this thing—kept gnawing at my heart. And it was spread about in vulgar whispers. And then, without my parents' knowledge, I went to Delphi, but Apollo did not say what I had gone to hear. Instead, he answered questions I had not asked and told of horror and misery beyond belief—how I would know my mother's bed and bring to the world a race of children too terrible for men to see and cause the death of my own father. I trembled at those words and fled from Corinth—as far as I could—to where no star could ever guide me back, where I could never see that infamous prophecy fulfilled. And as I traveled, I came to that place where you say the king was murdered. This is the truth, Jocasta—I was in that place where the three roads meet. There was a herald leading a carriage drawn by horses and a man riding in the carriage—just as you described. The man in front, and the old one, ordered me out of the path. I refused. The driver pushed. In anger, I struck him. The old man saw it, reached for his lash and waited till I had passed. Then he struck me on the head. But he paid—oh yes, he paid. He lost his balance and fell from the carriage and as he lay there helpless—on his back—I killed him. I killed them all. But if this stranger had any tie with Laius—O God—who could be more hated in the eyes of Heaven and Earth? I am the one whom strangers and citizens are forbidden to receive! I am the one to whom all are forbidden to speak! I am the one who must be driven out! I am the one for whom my curse was meant! I have touched his bed with the very hands that killed him! O God! The sin! The horror! I am to be banished, never to see my people, never to walk in my fatherland. Or else I must take my mother for a bride and kill my father Polybus, who gave me life and cared for me. What cruel god has sent this torture? Hear me, you gods, you holy gods—I will never see that day! I will die before I ever see the stain of this abominable act!

CHORUS: Your words frighten us, my Lord. But you must have hope until you hear the story from the man who saw.

OEDIPUS: Yes—hope. My only hope is waiting for this shepherd.

JOCASTA: Why? What do you hope to find with him?

OEDIPUS: This—if his story agrees with what you say, then I am safe.

JOCASTA: What did I say that makes you sure of this?

OEDIPUS: You said he told of *robbers*—that *robbers* killed the king. If he still says *robbers*, then I am not the guilty one—because no man can talk of many when he means a single one. But if he names a *single* traveler, there will be no doubt—the guilt is mine.

JOCASTA: You can be sure that this was what he said—and he cannot deny it. The whole city heard him—not I alone. But even if he alters what he said before, he cannot prove that Laius met his death as it was prophesied. For Apollo said that he would die at the hand of a child—of mine. And as it happens, the child is dead. So prophecy is worthless. I wouldn't dignify it with a moment's thought.

OEDIPUS: You are right. But still—send someone for the shepherd. Now.

JOCASTA: I shall—immediately. I shall do what you ask. But now —let us go inside.

      [*Exeunt* OEDIPUS, JOCASTA.]

CHORUS:
I pray, may destiny permit
that honestly I live my life
in word and deed.
That I obey the laws
the heavens have begotten
and prescribed.
Those laws created by Olympus,[23]
laws pure, immortal,
forever lasting, essence of the god
who lives in them.
On arrogance and pride
a tyrant feeds.
The goad of insolence,
of senseless overbearing, blind conceit,
of seeking things unseasonable,
unreasonable,
will prick a man to climb to heights
where he must lose his footing
and tumble to his doom.
Ambition must be used
to benefit the state;
else it is wrong, and God
must strike it from this earth.
Forever, God, I pray,
may you stand at my side!

A man who goes through life
with insolence in word and deed,
who lacks respect for law and right,
and scorns the shrines and temples of the gods,
may he find evil fate and doom
as his reward for wantonness,
for seeking ill-begotten gains
and reaching after sacred things
with sacrilegious hands.
No! Surely no such man
escapes the wrath, the vengeance of the god!
For if he did, if he could find reward
in actions which are wrong,

23. *Olympus:* the highest mountain on the Greek peninsula, considered by the Greeks to be the home of the gods.

why should I trouble to acclaim,
to honor you, God, in my song?

No longer shall my feet
take me to Delphi's sacred shrine;
no longer shall they Abae or Olympia's altars[24] seek
unless the oracles are shown to tell the truth
to mortals without fail!
Where are you, Zeus, all-powerful, all-ruling?
You must be told,
you must know in your all-pervading power:
Apollo's oracles now fall into dishonor,
and what the god has spoken about Laius
finds disregard.
Could God be dead?
    [*Enter* JOCASTA.]

JOCASTA: My Lords, I want to lay these laurel wreaths and incense offerings at the shrines of Thebes—for Oedipus is torturing himself, tearing his heart with grief. His vision to weigh the present against the past is blurred by fear and terror. He devours every word of dread, drinks in every thought of pain, destruction, death. And I no longer have the power to ease his suffering. Now I turn to you, Apollo, since you are nearest, with prayer and suppliant offerings. Find some way to free us, end our agony! O God of Light, release us! You see the fear that grips us—like sailors who watch their captain paralyzed by some unknown terror on the seas.
    [*Enter* MESSENGER 1.]

MESSENGER 1: Strangers, would you direct me to the house of Oedipus? Or if you know where I might find the king himself, please tell me.

CHORUS: This is his house, stranger. He is inside. But this is the queen—his wife, and mother of his children.

MESSENGER 1: Then, blessings on the house of Oedipus—his house, his children, and his wife.

JOCASTA: Blessings on you as well, stranger. Your words are kind. But why have you come? What is it?

MESSENGER 1: Good news, my lady—for your husband and your house.

JOCASTA: What news? Where do you come from?

MESSENGER 1: From Corinth, my lady. My news will surely bring you joy—but sorrow, too.

JOCASTA: What? How can that be?

MESSENGER 1: Your husband now is ruler of the Isthmus![25]

JOCASTA: Do you mean that Polybus of Corinth has been deposed?

MESSENGER 1: Deposed by death, my lady. He has passed away.

JOCASTA: What! Polybus dead?

---

24. *Abae, Olympia:* Abae was a city in central Greece and Olympia a site in the western Peloponnese, where there were important oracles of Apollo and Zeus, respectively.

25. *Isthmus:* Corinth owed its importance to its situation on the narrow neck of land separating the Gulf of Corinth and the westward route from the Saronic gulf to the south.

MESSENGER 1.: I swear on my life that this is true.

JOCASTA: [*to a servant*]: Go! Quickly! Tell your master. [*To the heavens.*] You prophecies—you divinely-uttered prophecies! Where do you stand now? The man that Oedipus feared, the man he dared not face lest he should be his killer—that man is dead! Time claimed his life—not Oedipus!

[*Enter* OEDIPUS.]

OEDIPUS: Why, Jocasta? Why have you sent for me again?

JOCASTA: I want you to listen to this man. Listen to him and judge for yourself the worth of those holy prophecies.

OEDIPUS: Who is he? What news could he have for me?

JOCASTA: He comes from Corinth with the news that—that Polybus—is dead.

OEDIPUS: What! Tell me.

MESSENGER 1: If you must know this first, then I shall tell you—plainly. Polybus has died.

OEDIPUS: How? An act of treason? Sickness? How?

MESSENGER 1: My Lord, only a slight shift in the scales is required to bring the agèd to their rest.

OEDIPUS: Then it was sickness. Poor old man.

MESSENGER 1: Sickness—yes. And the weight of years.

OEDIPUS: Oh, Jocasta! Why? Why should we even look to oracles, the prophetic words delivered at their shrines or the birds that scream above us? They led me to believe that I would kill my father. But he is dead and in his grave, while I stand here—never having touched a weapon. Unless he died of longing for his son. If that is so, then I *was* the instrument of his death. And those oracles! Where are they now? Polybus has taken them to his grave. What worth have they now?

JOCASTA: Have I not been saying this all along?

OEDIPUS: Yes, you have. But I was misled by fear.

JOCASTA: Now you will no longer have to think of it.

OEDIPUS: But—my mother's bed. I still have *that* to fear.

JOCASTA: No. No, mortals have no need to fear when chance reigns supreme. The knowledge of the future is denied to us. It is better to live as you will, live as you can. You need not fear a union with your mother. Men often, in their dreams, approach their mothers' beds, lie with them, possess them. But the man who sees that this is meaningless can live without the threat of fear.

OEDIPUS: You would be right, Jocasta, if my mother were not alive. But she *is* alive. And no matter what you say, I have reason to fear.

JOCASTA: At least your father's death has brought some comfort.

OEDIPUS: Yes—some comfort. But my fear is of *her*—as long as she lives.

MESSENGER 1: Who is *she*? The woman you fear?

OEDIPUS: Queen Merope, old man, the wife of Polybus.

MESSENGER 1: But why does *she* instill fear in you?

OEDIPUS: There was an oracle—a dreadful oracle sent by the gods.

MESSENGER 1: Can you tell me—a stranger—what it is?

OEDIPUS: Yes, it is all right to tell. Once Loxian Apollo said that I would take my mother for my bride and murder my father with my own hands. This is the reason that I left Corinth long ago. Fortunately. And yet, I have often longed to see my parents.

MESSENGER 1: Is this the fear that drove you away from Corinth?

OEDIPUS: Yes. I did not want to kill my father.

MESSENGER 1: But I can free you from this fear, my Lord. My purpose for coming was a good one.

OEDIPUS: And I shall see that you receive a fitting reward.

MESSENGER 1: Yes—that's why I came. To fare well myself by your returning home.

OEDIPUS: Home? To Corinth? To my parents? Never.

MESSENGER 1: My son, you do not realize what you are doing.

OEDIPUS: What do you mean, old man? For God's sake, tell me what you mean.

MESSENGER 1: I mean—the reasons why you dread returning home.

OEDIPUS: I dread Apollo's prophecy—and its fulfillment.

MESSENGER 1: You mean the curse—the stain they say lies with your parents?

OEDIPUS: Yes, old man. That is the fear that lives with me.

MESSENGER 1: Then you must realize that this fear is groundless.

OEDIPUS: How can that be—if I am their son?

MESSENGER 1: Because Polybus was no relative of yours.

OEDIPUS: What are you saying! Polybus was *not* my father?

MESSENGER 1: No more than I.

OEDIPUS: No more than you? But you are nothing to me.

MESSENGER 1: He was not your father any more than I.

OEDIPUS: Then why did he call me his son?

MESSENGER 1: You were a gift to him—from me.

OEDIPUS: A gift? From you? And yet he loved me as his son?

MESSENGER 1: Yes, my Lord. He had been childless.

OEDIPUS: And when you gave me to him—had you bought me? Or found me?

MESSENGER 1: I found you—in the hills of Cithaeron.

OEDIPUS: What were you doing there?

MESSENGER 1: Tending sheep along the mountain side.

OEDIPUS: Then you were a—hired shepherd?

MESSENGER 1: Yes, my son—a hired shepherd who saved you at that time.

OEDIPUS: Saved me? Was I in pain when you found me? Was I in trouble?

MESSENGER 1: Yes, your ankles are the proof of that.

OEDIPUS: Ah, you mean this old trouble. What has that to do with it?

MESSENGER 1: When I found you, your ankles were pierced with rivets. And I freed you.

OEDIPUS: Yes, I have had this horrible stigma since infancy.

MESSENGER 1: And so it was the swelling in your ankles that caused your name: Oedipus—"Clubfoot."

OEDIPUS: Oh! Who did this to me? My father? Or my mother?

MESSENGER 1: I don't know. You will have to ask the man who handed you to me.

OEDIPUS: You mean—*you* did not find me? It was someone else?

MESSENGER 1: Another shepherd.

OEDIPUS: Who? Do you remember who he was?

MESSENGER 1: I think—he was of the house of Laius.

OEDIPUS: The king who ruled this city?

MESSENGER 1: Yes. He was a shepherd in the service of the king.

OEDIPUS: Is he still alive? Can I see him?

MESSENGER 1: [*addressing the* CHORUS]: You—you people here—could answer that.

OEDIPUS: Do any of you know this shepherd? Have you seen him in the fields? Here in Thebes? Tell me now! Now is the time to unravel this mystery—once and for all.

CHORUS: I think it is the shepherd you asked to see before. But the queen will know.

OEDIPUS: Jocasta, is that the man he means? Is it the shepherd we have sent for? Is *he* the one?

JOCASTA: Why? What difference does it make? Don't think about it. Pay no attention to what he said. It makes no difference.

OEDIPUS: No difference? When I must have every clue to untangle the line of mystery surrounding my birth?

JOCASTA: In the name of God, if you care at all for your own life, you must not go on with this. I cannot bear it any longer.

OEDIPUS: Do not worry, Jocasta. Even if I am a slave—a third-generation slave, it is no stain on your nobility.

JOCASTA: Oedipus! I beg you—don't do this!

OEDIPUS: I can't grant you that. I cannot leave the truth unknown.

JOCASTA: It is for *your* sake that I beg you to stop. For your own good.

OEDIPUS: My own good has brought me pain too long.

JOCASTA: God help you! May you never know what you are!

OEDIPUS: Go, someone, and bring the shepherd to me. Leave the queen to exult in her noble birth.

JOCASTA: God help you! This is all that I can say to you—now or ever.

[*Exit* JOCASTA.]

CHORUS: Why has the queen left like this—grief-stricken and tortured with pain? My Lord, I fear—I fear that from her silence some horror will burst forth.

OEDIPUS: Let it explode! I will still want to uncover the secret of my birth—no matter how horrible. She—she is a woman with a woman's pride—and she feels shame for my humble birth. But I am the child of Fortune—beneficent Fortune—and I shall not be shamed! She is my mother. My sisters are the months and they have seen me rise and fall. This is my family. I will never deny my birth—and I will learn its secret!

[*Exit* OEDIPUS.]

CHORUS:
Ah Cithaeron,
if in my judgment I am right,
if I interpret what I hear correctly,
then—by Olympus' boundless majesty!—

tomorrow's full moon will not pass
before, Cithaeron, you will find
that Oedipus will honor you
as mother and as nurse!
That we will praise you in our song,
benevolent and friendly to our king.
Apollo, our Lord, may you find joy in this!

Who bore you, Oedipus? A nymph?
Did Pan[26] beget you in the hills?
Were you begotten by Apollo?
Perhaps so, for he likes the mountain glens.
Could Hermes[27] be your father?
Or Dionysus? Could it be
that he received you as a gift
high in the mountains from a nymph
with whom he lay?

[*Enter* OEDIPUS.]

OEDIPUS: My Lords, I have never met him, but could that be the
shepherd we have been waiting for? He seems to be of the same
age as the stranger from Corinth. And I can see now—those are
my servants who are bringing him here. But, perhaps you know
—if you have seen him before. Is he the shepherd?

[*Enter* SHEPHERD.]

CHORUS: Yes. I recognize him. He was a shepherd in the service of
Laius—as loyal as any man could be.

OEDIPUS: Corinthian, I ask you—is this the man you mean?

MESSENGER 1: Yes, my Lord. This is the man.

OEDIPUS: And you, old man, look at me and answer what I ask.
Were you in the service of Laius?

SHEPHERD: I was. But not bought. I was reared in his house.

OEDIPUS: What occupation? What way of life?

SHEPHERD: Tending flocks—for most of my life.

OEDIPUS: And where did you tend those flocks?

SHEPHERD: Sometimes Cithaeron, sometimes the neighboring
places.

OEDIPUS: Have you ever seen this man before?

SHEPHERD: What man do you mean? Doing what?

OEDIPUS: This man. Have you ever met him before?

SHEPHERD: Not that I recall, my Lord.

MESSENGER 1: No wonder, my Lord. But I shall help him to recall.
I am sure that he'll remember the time we spent on Cithaeron—
he with his two flocks and I with one. Six months—spring to
autumn—every year—for three years. In the winter I would drive
my flocks to my fold in Corinth, and he to the fold of Laius.
Isn't that right, sir?

SHEPHERD: That is what happened. But it was a long time ago.

MESSENGER 1: Then tell me this. Do you remember a child you
gave me to bring up as my own?

---

26. *Pan:* a woodland god; patron of
shepherds and flocks.

27. *Hermes:* son of Zeus and Maia; god
of flocks and shepherds.

SHEPHERD: What are you saying? Why are you asking me this?

MESSENGER 1: This, my friend, this—is that child.

SHEPHERD: Damn you! Will you keep your mouth shut!

OEDIPUS: Save your reproaches, old man. It is you who deserve them—your words deserve them.

SHEPHERD: But master—how have I offended?

OEDIPUS: By refusing to answer his question about the child.

SHEPHERD: He doesn't know what he's saying. He's crazy.

OEDIPUS: If you don't answer of your own accord, we'll make you talk.

SHEPHERD: No! My Lord, please! Don't hurt an old man.

OEDIPUS [*to the* CHORUS]: One of you—twist his hands behind his back!

SHEPHERD: Why? Why? What do you want to know?

OEDIPUS: Did you or did you not give him that child?

SHEPHERD: I did. I gave it to him—and I wish that I had died that day.

OEDIPUS: You tell the truth, or you'll have your wish now.

SHEPHERD: If I tell, it will be worse.

OEDIPUS: Still he puts it off!

SHEPHERD: I said that I gave him the child!

OEDIPUS: Where did you get it? Your house? Someone else's? Where?

SHEPHERD: Not mine. Someone else's.

OEDIPUS: Whose? One of the citizens'? Whose house?

SHEPHERD: O God, master! Don't ask me any more.

OEDIPUS: This is the last time that I ask you.

SHEPHERD: It was a child—of the house of Laius.

OEDIPUS: A slave? Or of his own line?

SHEPHERD: Ah master, do I *have* to speak?

OEDIPUS: You have to. And I *have* to hear.

SHEPHERD: They said—it was his child. But the queen could tell you best.

OEDIPUS: Why? Did *she* give you the child?

SHEPHERD: Yes, my Lord.

OEDIPUS: Why?

SHEPHERD: To—kill!

OEDIPUS: Her own child!

SHEPHERD: Yes. Because she was terrified of some dreadful prophecy.

OEDIPUS: What prophecy?

SHEPHERD: The child would kill his father.

OEDIPUS: Then why did you give him to this man?

SHEPHERD: I felt sorry for him, master. And I thought that he would take him to his own home. But he saved him from his suffering—for worse suffering yet. My Lord, if you are the man he says you are—O God—you were born to suffering!

OEDIPUS: O God! O no! I see it now! All clear! O Light! I will never look on you again! Sin! Sin in my birth! Sin in my marriage! Sin in blood!

[*Exit* OEDIPUS.]

CHORUS:
O generations of men, you are nothing!
You are nothing!
And I count you as not having lived at all!
Was there ever a man,
was there ever a man on this earth
who could say he was happy,
who knew happiness, true happiness,
not an image, a dream,
an illusion, a vision, which would disappear?
Your example, Oedipus,
your example, your fate, your disaster,
show that none of us mortals
ever knew, ever felt what happiness truly is.

Here is Oedipus,
fortune and fame and bliss
leading him by the hand,
prodding him on to heights
mortals had never attained.
Zeus, it was he who removed
the scourge of the riddling maid,
of the sharp-clawed, murderous Sphinx!
He restored me to life from the brink
of disaster, of doom and of death.
It was he who was honored and hailed,
who was crowned and acclaimed as our king.

Here is Oedipus:
Anyone on this earth
struck by a harder blow,
stung by a fate more perverse?
Wretched Oedipus!
Father and son alike,
pleasures you took from where
once you were given life.
Furrows your father ploughed
bore you in silence. How, how, oh how could it be?

Time found you out,
all-seeing, irrepressible time.
Time sits in judgment on
the union that never could be;
judges you, father and son,
begot and begetter alike.
Would that I never had
laid eyes on Laius' child!
Now I wail and I weep,
and my lips are drenched in lament.
It was you, who offered me life;
it is you, who now bring me death.

[*Enter* MESSENGER 2.]

MESSENGER 2: O you most honored citizens of Thebes, you will mourn for the things you will hear, you will mourn for the things you will see, you will ache from the burden of sorrow—if you are true sons of the house of Labdacus, if you care, if you feel. The waters of Ister and Phasis[28] can never cleanse this house of the horrors hidden within it and soon to be revealed—horrors willfully done! Worst of the sorrows we know are those that are willfully done!

CHORUS: We have mourned enough for sorrows we have known. What more is there that you can add?

MESSENGER 2: One more and only one—Jocasta, the queen, is dead.

CHORUS: O God—no! How?

MESSENGER 2: By her own hand. But the most dreadful pain you have not seen. You have not seen the worst. I have seen it and I shall tell you what I can of her terrible suffering. She ran in frenzied despair through the palace halls and rushed straight to her bridal bed—her fingers clutching and tearing at her hair. Then, inside the bedroom, she flung the doors closed and cried out to Laius, long since dead. She cried out to him, remembering the son that she had borne long ago, the son who killed his father, the son who left her to bear a dread curse—the children of her own son! She wept pitifully for that bridal bed which she had twice defiled—husband born of husband, child born of child. I didn't see what happened then. I didn't see her die. At that moment the king rushed in and shrieked in horror. All eyes turned to him as he paced in frantic passion and confusion. He sprang at each of us and begged to have a sword. He begged to know where he could find the wife that was no wife to him, the woman who had been mother to him and to his children. Some power beyond the scope of man held him in its sway and guided him to her. It was none of us. Then—as if someone had beckoned to him and bade him follow—he screamed in terror and threw himself against the doors that she had locked. His body's weight and force shattered the bolts and thrust them from their sockets and he rushed into the room. There we saw the queen hanging from a noose of twisted cords. And when the king saw her, he cried out and moaned in deep, sorrowful misery. Then he untied the rope that hung about her neck and laid her body on the ground. But what happened then was even worse. Her gold brooches, her pins—he tore them from her gown and plunged them into his eyes again and again and again and screamed, "No longer shall you see the suffering you have known and caused! You saw what was forbidden to be seen, yet failed to recognize those whom you longed to see! Now you shall see only darkness!" And as he cried out in such desperate misery, he struck his eyes over and over—until a

28. *Ister and Phasis:* the Danube and   large.
a river flowing into the Black Sea, both

shower of blood and tears splattered down his beard, like a torrent of crimson rain and hail. And now suffering is mingled with pain for man and wife for the sins that both have done. Not one alone. Once—long ago—this house was happy—and rightly so. But now—today—sorrow, destruction, death, shame—all torments that have a name—all, all are theirs to endure.

CHORUS: But the king—does he have any relief from his suffering now?

MESSENGER 2: He calls for someone to unlock the gates and reveal to Thebes his father's killer, his mother's—I can't say it. I cannot say this unholy word. He cries out that he will banish himself from the land to free this house of the curse that he has uttered. But he is weak, drained. There is no one to guide his way. The pain is more than he can bear. You will see for yourselves. The palace gates are opening. You will see a sight so hideous that even his most bitter enemy would pity him.

[*Enter* OEDIPUS.]

CHORUS:
Ah!
Dread horror for men to see!
Most dreadful of all that I have seen!
Ah!
Wretched one,
what madness has possessed you?
What demon has descended upon you
and bound you to this dire fate?
Ah!
Wretched one,
I cannot bear to look at you.
I want to ask you more
and learn still more
and understand—
but I shudder at the sight of you!

OEDIPUS: Ah! Ah! Where has this misery brought me? Is this my own voice I hear—carried on the wings of the air? O Fate! What have you done to me?

CHORUS: Terrible! Too terrible to hear! Too terrible to see!

OEDIPUS: O cloud of darkness! Cruel! Driven by the winds of fate! Assaulting me! With no defense to hold you back! O God! The pain! The pain! My flesh aches from its wounds! My soul aches from the memory of its horrors!

CHORUS: Body and soul—each suffers and mourns.

OEDIPUS: Ah! You still remain with me—a constant friend. You still remain to care for me—a blind man now. Now there is darkness and I cannot see your face. But I can hear your voice and I know that you are near.

CHORUS: O my Lord, how could you have done this? How could you blind yourself? What demon drove you?

OEDIPUS: Apollo! It was Apollo! *He* brought this pain, this suffering to me. But it was my own hand that struck the blow. Not his. O God! Why should I have sight when all that I would see is ugliness?

CHORUS: It is as you say.

OEDIPUS: What is there for me to see and love? What sight would give me joy? What sound? Take me away! Take me out of this land! I am cursed! Doomed! I am the man most hated by the gods!

CHORUS: You have suffered equally for your fortune and for your disaster. I wish that you had never come to Thebes.

OEDIPUS: Damn the man who set me free! Who loosed the fetters from my feet and let me live! I will never forgive him. If he had let me die, I would never have become the cause—the grief . . .

CHORUS: I wish that it had been this way.

OEDIPUS: If it had been, I would not have come to this—killer of my father, bridegroom of the woman who gave me birth, despised by the gods, child of shame, father and brother to my children. Is there any horror worse than these—any horror that has not fallen upon Oedipus?

CHORUS: My Lord, I cannot condone what you have done. You would have been better dead than alive and blind.

OEDIPUS: I did what I had to. You know I did. No more advice. Could these eyes have looked upon my father in the house of Hades? Could these eyes have faced my mother in her agony? I sinned against them both—a sin no suicide could purge. Could I have joy at the sight of my children—born as they were born? With these eyes? Never! Could I look upon the city of Thebes? The turrets that grace her walls? The sacred statues of her gods? Never! Damned! I—the noblest of the sons of Thebes—I have damned myself. It was I who commanded that Thebes must cast out the one who is guilty, unholy, cursed by the heavenly gods. *I* was the curse of Thebes! Could these eyes look upon the people? Never! And if I could raise a wall to channel the fountain of my hearing, I would spare nothing to build a prison for this defiled body where sight and sound would never penetrate. Then only would I have peace—where grief could not reach my mind. O Cithaeron! Why did you receive me? Why did you not let me die then? Why did you let me live to show the world how I was born? O Polybus! O Corinth! My home that was no home! You raised me, thinking I was fair and never knowing the evil that festered beneath. Now—now see the evil from which I was born, the evil I have become. O God! The three roads! The hidden glen! The thickets! The pathway where three roads meet! The blood you drank from my hands—do you not know—it was the blood of my father! Do you remember? Do you remember what I did then and what I did for Thebes? Wedding-rites! You gave me birth and gave my children birth! Born of the same womb that bore my children! Father! Brother! Child! Incestuous sin! Bride! Wife! Mother! All of one union! All the most heinous sins that man can know! The most horrible shame—I can no longer speak of it. For the love of God, hide me somewhere. Hide me away from this land! Kill me! Cast me into the sea where you will never have to look at me again! I beg you—touch me—in my misery. Touch me. Do not be afraid. My sins are mine alone to bear and touch no other man.

[*Enter* CREON.]

CHORUS: My Lord, Creon is here to act or counsel in what you ask. In your stead—he is now our sole protector.

OEDIPUS: What can I say to him? How can I ask for his trust? I have wronged him. I know that now.

CREON: I have not come to mock you, Oedipus, nor to reproach you for the past. But you—if you have no respect for men, at least respect the lord of the sun whose fires give life to men. Hide your naked guilt from his sight. No earth or sacred rain or light can endure its presence. [*To a servant.*] Take him inside. It is impious for any but his own family to see and hear his suffering.

OEDIPUS: I ask you in the name of God to grant one favor. You have been kinder to me than I deserved. But one favor. I ask it for you—not for myself?

CREON: What do you ask of me?

OEDIPUS: Cast me out of this land. Cast me out to where no man can see me. Cast me out now.

CREON: I would have done so, you can be sure. But I must wait and do the will of the god.

OEDIPUS: He has signified his will—with clarity. Destroy the parricide! Destroy the unholy one! Destroy Oedipus!

CREON: That was the god's command, I know. But now—with what has happened—I think it better to wait and learn what we must do.

OEDIPUS: You mean that you would ask for guidance for a man so sorrowful as I?

CREON: Surely, you are ready to put your trust in the god—now.

OEDIPUS: Yes, I am ready now. But I ask this of you. Inside—she is lying inside—give her whatever funeral rites you wish. You will do the right thing for her. She is your sister. But for me—do not condemn this city—my father's city—to suffer any longer from my presence as long as I live. Let me go and live upon Cithaeron —O Cithaeron, your name is ever linked with mine! Where my parents chose a grave for me. Where they would have had me die. Where I shall die in answer to their wish. And yet, I know, neither sickness nor anything else will ever bring me death. For I would not have been saved from death that once. No—I was saved for a more dreadful fate. Let it be. Creon, do not worry about my sons. They are boys and will have all they need, no matter where they go. But my daughters—poor creatures! They never ate a single meal without their father. We shared everything together. Creon, take care of them. Creon, let me touch them one last time. And let me weep—one last time. Please, my Lord, please, allow it—you're generous, you're kind. If I could only touch them and feel that they are with me—as I used to— when I could see them. [*Enter* ANTIGONE *and* ISMENE.] What is that crying? Is it my daughters? Has Creon taken pity on me? Has he sent my daughters to me? Are they here?

CREON: Yes, Oedipus, they are here. I had them brought to you. I know how much you love them, how much you have always loved them.

OEDIPUS: Bless you for this, Creon. Heaven bless you and grant you greater kindness than it has granted me. Ah, children, where are you? Come—come, touch my hands, the hands of your father, the hands of your brother, the hands that blinded these eyes which once were bright—these eyes—your father's eyes which neither saw nor knew what he had done when he became your father. I weep for you, my children. I cannot see you now. But when I think of the bitterness that waits for you in life, what you will have to suffer—the festivals, the holidays—the sadness you will know when you should share in gaiety! And when you are old enough to marry—who will there be, who will be the man strong enough to bear the slander that will haunt you—because you are *my* children? What disgrace will you not know? Your father killed his father. And lay with the woman that bore him and his children. These are the taunts that will follow you. And what man will marry you? No man, my children. You will spend your lives unwed—without children of your own—barren and wasted. Ah, Creon, you are the only father left to them. We—their parents—are lost. We gave them life. And we are lost to them. Take care of them. See that they do not wander poor and lonely. Do not let them suffer for what I have done. Pity them. They are so young. So lost. They have no one but you. Take my hand and promise me. And oh, my children, if you were older, I could make you understand. But now, make this your prayer—to find some place where you can live and have a better life than what your father knew.

CREON: Enough, my Lord. Go inside now.

OEDIPUS: Yes. I do not want to, but I will go.

CREON: All things have their time and their place.

OEDIPUS: I shall go—on this condition.

CREON: What condition? I am listening.

OEDIPUS: That you will send me away.

CREON: That is the god's decision, not mine.

OEDIPUS: The gods will not care where I go.

CREON: Then you shall have your wish.

OEDIPUS: Then—you consent?

CREON: It has nothing to do with my consent.

OEDIPUS: Let me go away from here.

CREON: Go then—but leave the children.

OEDIPUS: No! Do not take them away from me!

CREON: Do not presume that you are still in power. Your power has not survived with you.

CHORUS:
There goes Oedipus—
he was the man who was able
to answer the riddle proposed by the Sphinx.
Mighty Oedipus—
he was an object of envy
to all for his fortune and fame.

There goes Oedipus—
now he is drowning in waves of dread and despair.
Look at Oedipus—
proof that none of us mortals
can truly be thought of as happy
until he is granted deliverance from life,
until he is dead
and must suffer no more.

# Antigone*

## Characters

ANTIGONE, *daughter of Oedipus*    HAEMON, *their son*
ISMENE, *her sister*    TIRESIAS, *a blind prophet*
CREON, *king of Thebes*    GUARD
EURYDICE, *his wife*    MESSENGER

The CHORUS represents the ELDERS OF THEBES.

SCENE:—*Courtyard of the royal palace at Thebes. Daybreak.*

[*Enter* ANTIGONE *and* ISMENE.]

ANTIGONE. Dear sister! Dear Ismene! How many evils
Our father, Oedipus, bequeathed to us!
And is there one of them—do you know of one
That Zeus has not showered down upon our heads?
I have seen pain, dishonor, shame, and ruin,     5
I have seen them all, in what we have endured.
And now comes this new edict by the King
Proclaimed throughout the city. Have you heard?
Do you not know, even yet, our friends are threatened?
They are to meet the fate of enemies.     10

ISMENE. Our friends, Antigone? No, I have heard
Nothing about them either good or bad.
I have no news except that we two sisters
Lost our two brothers when they killed each other.
I know the Argive army fled last night,     15
But what that means, or whether it makes my life
Harder or easier, I cannot tell.

ANTIGONE. This I was sure of. So I brought you here
Beyond the palace gates to talk alone.     19

ISMENE. What is the matter? I know you are deeply troubled.

ANTIGONE. Yes, for our brothers' fate. Creon has given
An honored burial to one, to the other
Only unburied shame. Eteocles
Is laid in the earth with all the rites observed

* From *Three Theban Plays*, translated by T. H. Banks. Copyright © 1956 by Theodore Howard Banks. Reprinted by permission of Oxford University Press, Inc. First produced in 441 B.C.

That give him his due honor with the dead.  [25]
But the decree concerning Polyneices
Published through Thebes is that his wretched body
Shall lie unmourned, unwept, unsepulchered.
Sweet will he seem to the vultures when they find him,
A welcome feast that they are eager for.  [30]
This is the edict the good Creon uttered
For your observance and for mine—yes, mine.
He is coming here himself to make it plain
To those who have not heard. Nor does he think it
Of little consequence, because whoever  [35]
Does not obey is doomed to death by stoning.
Now you can show you are worthy of your birth,
Or bring disgrace upon a noble house.

ISMENE. What can I do, Antigone? As things are,
What can I do that would be of any help?  [40]

ANTIGONE. You can decide if you will share my task.

ISMENE. What do you mean? What are you planning to do?

ANTIGONE. I intend to give him burial. Will you help?

ISMENE. To give him burial! Against the law?

ANTIGONE. He is our brother. I will do my duty.  [45]
Yours too, perhaps. I never will be false.

ISMENE. Creon forbids it! You are too rash, too headstrong.

ANTIGONE. He has no right to keep me from my own.

ISMENE. Antigone! Think! Think how our father perished
In scorn and hatred when his sins, that he  [50]
Himself discovered, drove him to strike blind
His eyes by his own hand. Think how his mother,
His wife—both names were hers—ended her life
Shamefully hanging in a twisted noose.
Think of that dreadful day when our two brothers,  [55]
Our wretched brothers, fought and fell together,
Each slayer and each slain. And now we too,
Left all alone, think how in turn we perish,
If, in defiance of the law, we brave
The power of the commandment of a king.  [60]
O think Antigone! We who are women
Should not contend with men; we who are weak
Are ruled by the stronger, so that we must obey
In this and in matters that are yet more bitter.
And so I pray the dead to pardon me  [65]
If I obey our rulers, since I must.
To be too bold in what we do is madness.

ANTIGONE. I will not urge you. And I would not thank you
For any help that you might care to give me.
Do what you please, but I will bury him,  [70]
And if I die for that, I shall be happy.

Loved, I shall rest beside the one I loved.
My crime is innocence, for I owe the dead
Longer allegiance than I owe the living.
With the dead I lie forever. Live, if you choose,          75
Dishonoring the laws the gods have hallowed.
ISMENE. No, I dishonor nothing. But to challenge
Authority—I have not strength enough.
ANTIGONE. Then make that your excuse. I will go heap
The earth above the brother that I love.                   80
ISMENE. O Sister, Sister! How I fear for you!
ANTIGONE. No, not for me. Set your own life in order.
ISMENE. Well then, at least, tell no one of your plan.
Keep it close hidden, as I too will keep it.
ANTIGONE. Oh! Publish it! Proclaim it to the world!       85
Then I will hate you less than for your silence.
ISMENE. Your heart is hot for deeds that chill the blood.
ANTIGONE. I know that I give pleasure where I should.
ISMENE. Yes, if you can, but you will try in vain.
ANTIGONE. When my strength fails, then I shall try no longer.  90
ISMENE. A hopeless task should never be attempted.
ANTIGONE. Your words have won their just reward: my hatred
And the long-lasting hatred of the dead.
But leave me and the folly that is mine
To undergo the worst that can befall me.                   95
I shall not suffer an ignoble death.
ISMENE. Go then, Antigone, if you must go.
And yet remember, though your act is foolish,
That those who love you do so with all their hearts.
    [*Exeunt* ANTIGONE *and* ISMENE. *Enter* CHORUS.]
CHORUS.
Sunbeam, eye of the golden day, on Thebes the seven-gated,    100
    On Dircé's streams you have dawned at last, O fairest of light.
Dawned on our foes, who had come enflamed by the quarrel
        of Polynices,
    Shone on their glittering arms, made swifter their headlong
        flight.
From Argos they came with their white shields flashing,
    Their helmets, crested with horsehair, agleam:           105
An army that flew like a snow-white eagle
    Across our borders with shrilling scream.
Above our roofs it soared, at our gates with greedy jaws it was
        gaping;
    But before their spears tasted our blood, and before our
        circle of towers

---

101 *ff.* The chorus of old men celebrates the victory won over the Argive
forces and Polynices. Dircé is a river
of the Theban plain.

110. *Theban dragon:* According to
legend, the Thebans sprang from the
dragon's teeth sown by Cadmus.

Felt the flame of their torches, they turned to flight. The foes
   of the Theban dragon        110
Found the surge and clamor of battle too fierce for their
   feebler powers.
   For Zeus, who abhors a proud tongue's boasting,
      Seeing their river of armor flow
   Clashing and golden, struck with his lightning
      To silence the shout of our foremost foe.     115

He crashed to the earth with his torch, who had scaled the top
   of our ramparts.
   Raging in frenzy against us, breathing tempestuous hate,
Raging and threatening in vain. And mighty Ares, our ally,
   Dealing havoc around him, apportioned to other foemen their
   fate.
   For at seven portals, their seven leaders,     120
      Down to the earth their bronze arms threw
   In tribute to Zeus, the lord of the battle;
      Save the fated brothers, the wretched two,
   Who went to their common doom together,
      Each wielding a spear that the other slew.     125

Now glorious Victory smiles upon jubilant Thebes rich in
   chariots.
   Let us give free rein to our joy, forgetting our late-felt war;
Let us visit in night-long chorus the temples of all the immortals,
   With Bacchus, who shakes the land in the dances, going
   before.
   But behold! The son of Menoeceus approaches,    130
      Creon, the new-crowned King of the land,
   Made King by new fortunes the gods have allotted.
      What step has he pondered? What has he planned
   To lay before us, his council of elders,
      Who have gathered together at his command?    135

[*Enter* CREON.]

CREON. Elders of Thebes, our city has been tossed
  By a tempestuous ocean, but the gods
  Have steadied it once more and made it safe.
  You, out of all the citizens, I have summoned,
  Because I knew that you once reverenced     140
  The sovereignty of Laius, and that later,
  When Oedipus was King and when he perished,
  Your steadfast loyalty upheld his children.
  And now his sons have fallen, each one stained
  By his brother's blood, killed by his brother's hand,    145

---

116. *He crashed . . .:* Capaneus, the    118. *Ares:* god of war and a patron
most violent of the Seven against Thebes.   deity of Thebes.

So that the sovereignty devolves on me,
Since I by birth am nearest to the dead.
Certainly no man can be fully known,
Known in his soul, his will, his intellect,
Until he is tested and has proved himself                          150
In statesmanship. Because a city's ruler,
Instead of following the wisest counsel,
May through some fear keep silent. Such a man
I think contemptible. And one whose friend
Has stronger claims upon him than his country,                     155
Him I consider worthless. As for me,
I swear by Zeus, forever all-beholding,
That I would not keep silence, if I saw
Ruin instead of safety drawing near us;
Nor would I think an enemy of the state                            160
Could be my friend. For I remember this:
Our country bears us all securely onward,
And only while it sails a steady course
Is friendship possible. Such are the laws
By which I guard the greatness of the city.                        165
And kindred to them is the proclamation
That I have made to all the citizens
Concerning the two sons of Oedipus:
Eteocles, who has fallen in our defence,
Bravest of warriors, shall be entombed                             170
With every honor, every offering given
That may accompany the noble dead
Down to their rest. But as for Polyneices,
He came from exile eager to consume
The city of his fathers with his fire                              175
And all the temples of his father's gods,
Eager to drink deep of his kindred's blood,
Eager to drag us off to slavery.
To this man, therefore, nothing shall be given.
None shall lament him, none shall do him honor.                    180
He shall be left without a grave, his corpse
Devoured by birds and dogs, a loathsome sight.
Such is my will. For never shall the wicked
Be given more approval than the just,
If I have power to stop it. But whoever                            185
Feels in his heart affection for his city
Shall be rewarded both in life and death.
CHORUS. Creon, son of Menoeceus, it has pleased you
So to pass judgment on our friend and foe.
And you may give commands to all of us,                            190
The living and the dead. Your will is law.
CREON. Then see that this command is carried out.

CHORUS. Sir, lay that burden on some younger man.
CREON. Sentries have been assigned to guard the body.
CHORUS. Then what additional duty would you give us?    195
CREON. Never to countenance the disobedient.
CHORUS. Who is so stupid as to long for death?
CREON. Death is indeed the punishment. Yet men
    Have often been destroyed by hope of gain.

     [*Enter* GUARD.]
GUARD. My Lord, I cannot say that I have hurried,    200
    Or that my running has made me lose my breath.
    I often stopped to think, and turned to go back.
    I stood there talking to myself: 'You fool,'
    I said, 'Why do you go to certain death?'
    And then: 'You idiot, are you still delaying?    205
    If someone else tells Creon, you will suffer.'
    I changed my mind this way, getting here slowly,
    Making a short road long. But still, at last,
    I did decide to come. And though my story
    Is nothing much to tell, yet I will tell it.    210
    One thing I know. I must endure my fate,
    But nothing more than that can happen to me.
CREON. What is the matter? What is troubling you?
GUARD. Please let me tell you first about myself.
    I did not do it. I did not see who did.    215
    It is not right for me to be punished for it.
CREON. You take good care not to expose yourself.
    Your news must certainly be something strange.
GUARD. Yes, it is strange—dreadful. I cannot speak.
CREON. Oh, tell it, will you? Tell it and go away!    220
GUARD. Well, it is this. Someone has buried the body,
    Just now, and gone—has sprinkled it with dust
    And given it other honors it should have.
CREON. What are you saying? Who has dared to do it?
GUARD. I cannot tell. Nothing was to be seen:    225
    No mark of pickaxe, no spot where a spade
    Had turned the earth. The ground was hard and dry,
    Unbroken—not a trace of any wheels—
    No sign to show who did it. When the sentry
    On the first watch discovered it and told us,    230
    We were struck dumb with fright. For he was hidden
    Not by a tomb but a light coat of dust,
    As if a pious hand had scattered it.
    There were no tracks of any animal,
    A dog or wild beast that had come to tear him.    235
    We all began to quarrel, and since no one
    Was there to stop us, nearly came to blows.

Everyone was accused, and everyone
Denied his guilt. We could discover nothing.
We were quite willing to handle red-hot iron,          240
To walk through fire, to swear by all the gods
That we were innocent of the deed itself,
And innocent of taking any part
In planning it or doing it. At last
One of us spoke. We trembled and hung our heads,          245
For he was right; we could not argue with him,
Yet his advice was bound to cause us trouble.
He told us all this had to be reported,
Not kept a secret. We all agreed to that.
We drew lots for it, and I had no luck.          250
I won the prize and was condemned to come.
So here I stand, unwilling, because I know
The bringer of bad news is never welcome.
CHORUS. Sir, as he spoke, I have been wondering.
Can this be, possibly, the work of gods?          255
CREON. Be silent! Before you madden me! You are old.
Would you be senseless also? What you say
Is unendurable. You say the gods
Cared for this corpse. Then was it for reward,
Mighty to match his mighty services,          260
That the gods covered him? He who came to burn
Their pillared temples and their votive offerings,
Ravage their land, and trample down the state.
Or is it your opinion that the gods
Honor the wicked? Inconceivable!          265
However, from the first, some citizens
Who found it difficult to endure this edict,
Muttered against me, shaking their heads in secret,
Instead of bowing down beneath the yoke,
Obedient and contented with my rule.          270
These are the men who are responsible,
For I am certain they have bribed the guards
To bury him. Nothing is worse than money.
Money lays waste to cities, banishes
Men from their homes, indoctrinates the heart,          275
Perverting honesty to works of shame,
Showing men how to practice villainy,
Subduing them to every godless deed.
But all those men who got their pay for this
Need have no doubt their turn to pay will come.          280
[*To the* GUARD] Now, you. As I still honor Zeus the King,
I tell you, and I swear it solemnly,
Either you find the man who did this thing,

The very man, and bring him here to me,
Or you will not just die. Before you die,                    285
You will be tortured until you have explained
This outrage; so that later when you steal
You will know better where to look for money
And not expect to find it everywhere.
Ill-gotten wealth brings ruin and not safety.               290
GUARD. Sir, may I speak? Or shall I merely go?
CREON. You can say nothing that is not offensive.
GUARD. Do I offend your hearing or your heart?
CREON. Is it your business to define the spot?
GUARD. The criminal hurts your heart, and I your ears.      295
CREON. Still talking? Why, you must have been born talking!
GUARD. Perhaps. But I am not the guilty man.
CREON. You are. And what is more you sold yourself.
GUARD. You have judged me, sir, and have misjudged me, too.
CREON. Be clever about judging if you care to.              300
But you will say that treachery leads to sorrow
Unless you find the man and show him to me.
        [*Exit* CREON.]

GUARD. Finding him is the best thing that could happen.
Fate will decide. But however that may be,
You never are going to see me here again.                    305
I have escaped! I could not have hoped for that.
I owe the gods my thanks for guarding me.
        [*Exit* GUARD.]

CHORUS.
Many the marvelous things; but none that can be
    More of a marvel than man! This being that braves       309
With the south wind of winter the whitened streaks of the sea,
    Threading his way through the troughs of engulfing waves.
And the earth most ancient, the eldest of all the gods,
    Earth, undecaying, unwearied, he wears away with his toil;
Forward and back with his plowshare, year after year, he plods,
    With his horses turning the soil.                        315

Man in devising excels. The birds of the air,
    That light-minded race, he entangles fast in his toils.
Wild creatures he catches, casting about them his snare,
    And the salt-sea brood he nets in his woven coils.
The tireless bull he has tamed, and the beast whose lair    320
    Is hidden deep in the wilds, who roams in the wooded hills.
He has fitted a yoke that the neck of the shaggy-maned horse will
        bear;
    He is master of all through his skills.

He has taught himself speech, and wind-like thought, and the lore
   Of ruling a town. He has fled the arrows of rain,    325
The searching arrows of frost he need fear no more,
   That under a starry sky are endured with pain.
Provision for all he has made—unprovided for naught,
   Save death itself, that in days to come will take shape.
From obscure and deep-seated disease he has subtly wrought  330
   A way of escape.

Resourceful and skilled, with an inconceivable art,
   He follows his course to a good or an evil end.
When he holds the canons of justice high in his heart
   And has sworn to the gods the laws of the land to defend,  335
Proud stands his city; without a city is he
   Who with ugliness, rashness, or evil dishonors the day.
Let me shun his thoughts. Let him share no hearthstone with me,
   Who acts in this way!

CHORUS. Look there! Look there! What portent can this be?  340
   Antigone! I know her, it is she!
   Daughter of Oedipus a prisoner brought?
   You defied Creon? You in folly caught?

      [*Enter* GUARD *with* ANTIGONE.]
GUARD. She did it. Here she is. We caught this girl  345
   As she was burying him. Where is the King?
CHORUS. Leaving the palace there, just as we need him.

      [*Enter* CREON.]
CREON. Why do you need my presence? What has happened?
GUARD. My Lord, no one should take a solemn oath
   Not to do something, for his second thoughts
   Make him a liar. I vowed not to hurry back.  350
   I had been battered by your storm of threats.
   But when a joy comes that exceeds our hopes,
   No other happiness can equal it.
   So I have broken my vow. I have returned,
   Bringing this girl along. She was discovered  355
   Busy with all the rites of burial.
   There was no casting lots, no, not this time!
   Such luck as this was mine and no one else's.
   Now sir, take her yourself, examine her,
   Convict her, do what you like. But as for me,  360
   I have the right to a complete acquittal.
CREON. This is the girl you caught? How? Where was she?
GUARD. Burying the dead man, just as I have told you.

CREON. Do you mean that? Or have you lost your mind?
GUARD. Your order was that he should not be buried. 365
I saw her bury him. Is that all clear?
CREON. How was she seen? You caught her in the act?
GUARD. This was what happened. When we had gotten back,
With your threats following us, we swept away
The dust that covered him. We left him bare, 370
A rotting corpse. And then we sat to windward,
Up on the hillside, to avoid the stench.
All of us were alert, and kept awake
Threatening each other. No one could get careless.
So the time passed, until the blazing sun 375
Stood at the zenith, and the heat was burning.
Then suddenly the wind came in a blast,
Lifting a cloud of dust up from the earth,
Troubling the sky and choking the whole plain,
Stripping off all the foliage of the woods, 380
Filling the breadth of heaven. We closed our eyes
And bore the affliction that the gods had sent us.
When it had finally stopped, we saw this girl.
She wailed aloud with a sharp, bitter cry,
The cry a bird gives seeing its empty nest 385
Robbed of its brood. And she too, when she saw
The naked body, was loud in her lament
And cursed the men who had uncovered him.
Quickly she sprinkled him with dust, and then
Lifting a pitcher, poured out three libations 390
To do him honor. When we ran and caught her,
She was unterrified. When we accused her
Both of her earlier and her present act,
She made no effort to deny the charges.
I am part glad, part sorry. It is good 395
To find that you yourself have gotten clear,
But to bring trouble on your friends is hard.
However, nothing counts except my safety.
CREON. [*To* ANTIGONE] You there. You, looking at the ground. Tell
me.
Do you admit this or deny it? Which? 400
ANTIGONE. Yes, I admit it. I do not deny it.
CREON. [*To* GUARD] Go. You are free. The charge is dropped.
[*Exit* GUARD.]
Now you,
Answer this question. Make your answer brief.
You knew there was a law forbidding this?
ANTIGONE. Of course I knew it. Why not? It was public. 405
CREON. And you have dared to disobey the law?

ANTIGONE. Yes. For this law was not proclaimed by Zeus,
Or by the gods who rule the world below.
I do not think your edicts have such power
That they can override the laws of heaven,                    410
Unwritten and unfailing, laws whose life
Belongs not to today or yesterday
But to time everlasting; and no man
Knows the first moment that they had their being.
If I transgressed these laws because I feared             415
The arrogance of man, how to the gods
Could I make satisfaction? Well I know,
Being a mortal, that I have to die,
Even without your proclamations. Yet
If I must die before my time is come,                          420
That is a blessing. Because to one who lives,
As I live, in the midst of sorrows, death
Is of necessity desirable.
For me, to face death is a trifling pain
That does not trouble me. But to have left         425
The body of my brother, my own brother,
Lying unburied would be bitter grief.
And if these acts of mine seem foolish to you,
Perhaps a fool accuses me of folly.
CHORUS. The violent daughter of a violent father,             430
She cannot bend before a storm of evils.
CREON. [To ANTIGONE] Stubborn? Self-willed? People like that, I tell
   you,
Are the first to come to grief. The hardest iron,
Baked in the fire, most quickly flies to pieces.
An unruly horse is taught obedience                        435
By a touch of the curb. How can you be so proud?
You, a mere slave? [To CHORUS] She was well schooled already
In insolence, when she defied the law.
And now look at her! Boasting, insolent,
Exulting in what she did. And if she triumphs
And goes unpunished, I am no man—she is.                    440
If she were more than niece, if she were closer
Than anyone who worships at my altar,
She would not even then escape her doom,
A dreadful death. Nor would her sister. Yes,
Her sister had a share in burying him.                    445
[To ATTENDANT] Go bring her here. I have just seen her, raving,
Beside herself. Even before they act,
Traitors who plot their treason in the dark
Betray themselves like that. Detestable!

[*To* ANTIGONE] But hateful also is an evil-doer 450
Who, caught red-handed, glorifies the crime.
ANTIGONE. Now you have caught me, will you do more than kill me?
CREON. No, only that. With that I am satisfied.
ANTIGONE. Then why do you delay? You have said nothing
I do not hate. I pray you never will. 455
And you hate what I say. Yet how could I
Have won more splendid honor than by giving
Due burial to my brother? All men here
Would grant me their approval, if their lips
Were not sealed up in fear. But you, a king, 460
Blessed by good fortune in much else besides,
Can speak and act with perfect liberty.
CREON. All of these Thebans disagree with you.
ANTIGONE. No. They agree, but they control their tongues.
CREON. You feel no shame in acting without their help? 465
ANTIGONE. I feel no shame in honoring a brother.
CREON. Another brother died who fought against him.
ANTIGONE. Two brothers. The two sons of the same parents.
CREON. Honor to one is outrage to the other.
ANTIGONE. Eteocles will not feel himself dishonored. 470
CREON. What! When his rites are offered to a traitor?
ANTIGONE. It was his brother, not his slave, who died.
CREON. One who attacked the land that he defended.
ANTIGONE. The gods still wish those rites to be performed.
CREON. Are the just pleased with the unjust as their equals? 475
ANTIGONE. That may be virtuous in the world below.
CREON. No. Even there a foe is never a friend.
ANTIGONE. I am not made for hatred but for love.
CREON. Then go down to the dead. If you must love,
Love them. While I yet live, no woman rules me. 480
CHORUS. Look there. Ismene, weeping as sisters weep.
The shadow of a cloud of grief lies deep
On her face, darkly flushed; and in her pain
Her tears are falling like a flood of rain.

[*Enter* ISMENE *and* ATTENDANTS.]
CREON. You viper! Lying hidden in my house, 485
Sucking my blood in secret, while I reared,
Unknowingly, two subverters of my throne.
Do you confess that you have taken part
In this man's burial, or deny it? Speak.
ISMENE. If she will recognize my right to say so, 490
I shared the action and I share the blame.
ANTIGONE. No. That would not be just. I never let you

Take any part in what you disapproved of.

ISMENE. In your calamity, I am not ashamed
To stand beside you, beaten by this tempest.                    495

ANTIGONE. The dead are witnesses of what I did,
To love in words alone is not enough.

ISMENE. Do not reject me, Sister! Let me die
Beside you, and do honor to the dead.

ANTIGONE. No. You will neither share my death nor claim         500
What I have done. My death will be sufficient.

ISMENE. What happiness can I have when you are gone?

ANTIGONE. Ask Creon that. He is the one you value.

ISMENE. Do you gain anything by taunting me?

ANTIGONE. Ah, no! By taunting you, I hurt myself.              505

ISMENE. How can I help you? Tell me what I can do.

ANTIGONE. Protect yourself. I do not grudge your safety.

ISMENE. Antigone! Shall I not share your fate?

ANTIGONE. We both have made our choices: life, and death.

ISMENE. At least I tried to stop you. I protested.            510

ANTIGONE. Some have approved your way; and others, mine.

ISMENE. Yet now I share your guilt. I too am ruined.

ANTIGONE. Take courage. Live your life. But I long since
Gave myself up to death to help the dead.

CREON. One of them has just lost her senses now.              515
The other has been foolish all her life.

ISMENE. We cannot always use our reason clearly.
Suffering confuses us and clouds our minds.

CREON. It clouds your mind. You join in her wrong-doing.

ISMENE. How is life possible without my sister?               520

CREON. Your sister? You have no sister. She is dead.

ISMENE. Then you will kill the wife your son has chosen?

CREON. Yes. There are other fields that he can plow.

ISMENE. He will not find such an enduring love.

CREON. A wicked woman for my son? No, never!                  525

ANTIGONE. O Haemon, Haemon! How your father wrongs you!

CREON. You and your marriage! Let me hear no more!

CHORUS. You are unyielding? You will take her from him?

CREON. Death will act for me. Death will stop the marriage.

CHORUS. It seems, then, you have sentenced her to death.      530

CREON. Yes. And my sentence you yourselves accepted.
Take them inside. From now on, they are women,
And have no liberty. For even the bold
Seek an escape when they see death approaching.

[*Exeunt* ANTIGONE, ISMENE, *and* ATTENDANTS.]

CHORUS.
Blessèd the life that has no evil known,                      535
For the gods, striking, strike down a whole race—

Doomed parent and doomed child both overthrown.
As when the fierce breath of the winds of Thrace
  Across the darkness of the sea has blown
A rushing surge; black sand from deep below     540
  Comes boiling up; wind-beaten headlands moan,
Fronting the full shock of the billow's blow.


The race of Oedipus, from days of old,
To long dead sorrows add new sorrows' weight.
  Some god has sent them sufferings manifold.     545
None may release another, for their fate
  Through generations loosens not its hold.
Now is their last root cut, their last light fled,
  Because of frenzy's curse, words overbold,
And dust, the gods' due, on the bloodstained dead.     550


O Zeus, what human sin restricts thy might?
Thou art unsnared by all-ensnaring sleep
  Or tireless months. Unaging thou dost keep
Thy court in splendor of Olympian light.
  And as this law was true when time began,     555
Tomorrow and forever it shall be:
  Naught beyond measure in the life of man
      From fate goes free.


For hope, wide-ranging, that brings good to some,
  To many is a false lure of desire     560
    Light-minded, giddy; and until the fire
Scorches their feet, they know not what will come.
  Wise is the famous adage: that to one
Whom the gods madden, evil, soon or late,
  Seems good; then can he but a moment shun     565
      The stroke of fate.


But Haemon comes, of your two sons the last.
Is his heart heavy for the sentence passed
  Upon Antigone, his promised bride,
And for his hope of marriage now denied?     570

[*Enter* HAEMON.]
CREON. We soon shall know better than seers could tell us.
  My son, Antigone is condemned to death.
  Nothing can change my sentence. Have you learned
  Her fate and come here in a storm of anger,
  Or do you love me and support my acts?     575
HAEMON. Father, I am your son. Your greater knowledge

Will trace the pathway that I mean to follow.
My marriage cannot be of more importance
Than to be guided always by your wisdom.
CREON. Yes, Haemon, this should be the law you live by!          580
In all things to obey your father's will.
Men pray for children round them in their homes
Only to see them dutiful and quick
With hatred to requite their father's foe,
With honor to repay their father's friend.          585
But what is there to say of one whose children
Prove to be valueless? That he has fathered
Grief for himself and laughter for his foes.
Then, Haemon, do not, at the lure of pleasure,
Unseat your reason for a woman's sake.          590
This comfort soon grows cold in your embrace:
A wicked wife to share your bed and home.
Is there a deeper wound than to find worthless
The one you love? Turn from this girl with loathing,
As from an enemy, and let her go          595
To get a husband in the world below.
For I have found her openly rebellious,
Her only out of all the city. Therefore,
I will not break the oath that I have sworn.
I will have her killed. Vainly she will invoke          600
The bond of kindred blood the gods make sacred.
If I permit disloyalty to breed
In my own house, I nurture it in strangers.
He who is righteous with his kin is righteous
In the state also. Therefore, I cannot pardon          605
One who does violence to the laws or thinks
To dictate to his rulers; for whoever
May be the man appointed by the city,
That man must be obeyed in everything,
Little or great, just or unjust. And surely          610
He who was thus obedient would be found
As good a ruler as he was a subject;
And in a storm of spears he would stand fast
With loyal courage at his comrade's side.
But disobedience is the worst of evils.          615
For it is this that ruins cities; this
Makes our homes desolate; armies of allies
Through this break up in rout. But most men find
Their happiness and safety in obedience.
Therefore we must support the law, and never          620
Be beaten by a woman. It is better
To fall by a man's hand, if we must fall,

Than to be known as weaker than a girl.
CHORUS. We may in our old age have lost our judgment,
And yet to us you seem to have spoken wisely.                    625
HAEMON. The gods have given men the gift of reason,
Greatest of all things that we call our own.
I have no skill, nor do I wish to have it,
To show where you have spoken wrongly. Yet
Some other's thought, beside your own, might prove            630
To be of value. Therefore it is my duty,
My natural duty as your son, to notice,
On your behalf, all that men say, or do,
Or find to blame. For your frown frightens them,
So that the citizen dares not say a word                       635
That would offend you. I can hear, however,
Murmurs in darkness and laments for her.
They say: "No woman ever less deserved
Her doom, no woman ever was to die
So shamefully for deeds so glorious.                           640
For when her brother fell in bloody battle,
She would not let his body lie unburied
To be devoured by carrion dogs or birds.
Does such a woman not deserve reward,
Reward of golden honor?" This I hear,                          645
A rumor spread in secrecy and darkness.
Father, I prize nothing in life so highly
As your well-being. How can children have
A nobler honor than their father's fame
Or father than his son's? Then do not think                    650
Your mood must never alter; do not feel
Your word, and yours alone, must be correct.
For if a man believes that he is right
And only he, that no one equals him
In what he says or thinks, he will be found                    655
Empty when searched and tested. Because a man
Even if he be wise, feels no disgrace
In learning many things, in taking care
Not to be over-rigid. You have seen
Trees on the margin of a stream in winter:                     660
Those yielding to the flood save every twig,
And those resisting perish root and branch.
So, too, the mariner who never slackens
His taut sheet overturns his craft and spends
Keel uppermost the last part of his voyage.                    665
Let your resentment die. Let yourself change.
For I believe—if I, a younger man,
May have a sound opinion—it is best

That men by nature should be wise in all things.
But most men find they cannot reach that goal;                    670
And when this happens, it is also good
To learn to listen to wise counselors.
CHORUS. Sir, when his words are timely, you should heed them.
And Haemon, you should profit by his words.
Each one of you has spoken reasonably.                            675
CREON. Are men as old as I am to be taught
How to behave by men as young as he?
HAEMON: Not to do wrong. If I am young, ignore
My youth. Consider only what I do.
CREON. Have you done well in honoring the rebellious?            680
HAEMON. Those who do wrong should not command respect.
CREON. Then that disease has not infected her?
HAEMON. All of our city with one voice denies it.
CREON. Does Thebes give orders for the way I rule?
HAEMON. How young you are! How young in saying that!             685
CREON. Am I to govern by another's judgment?
HAEMON. A city that is one man's is no city.
CREON. A city is the king's. That much is sure.
HAEMON. You would rule well in a deserted country.
CREON. This boy defends a woman, it appears.                     690
HAEMON. If you are one. I am concerned for you.
CREON. To quarrel with your father does not shame you?
HAEMON. Not when I see you failing to do justice.
CREON. Am I unjust when I respect my crown?
HAEMON. Respect it! When you trample down religion?              695
CREON. Infamous! Giving first place to a woman!
HAEMON. But never to anything that would disgrace me.
CREON. Each word you utter is a plea for her.
HAEMON. For you, too, and for me, and for the gods.
CREON. You shall not marry her this side of death.               700
HAEMON. Then if she dies, she does not die alone.
CREON. What! Has it come to this? You threaten me?
HAEMON. No. But I tell you your decree is useless.
CREON. You will repent this. You! Teaching me wisdom!
HAEMON. I will not call you mad. You are my father.              705
CREON. You woman's slave! Your talk will not persuade me.
HEAMON. Then what you want is to make all the speeches.
CREON. So. Now by all the gods in heaven above us,
One thing is certain: you are going to pay
For taunting and insulting me. [To ATTENDANTS] Bring out         710
That hated object. Let her die this moment,
Here, at her bridegroom's feet, before his eyes.
HAEMON. No, you are wrong. Not at my feet. And never

Will you set eyes upon my face again. 714
Rage, rave, with anyone who can bear to listen. [*Exit* HAEMON.]
CHORUS. Sir, he is gone; his anger gives him speed.
Young men are bitter in their agony.
CREON. Let him imagine more than man can do,
Or let him do more. Never shall he save
These two girls; they are going to their doom. 720
CHORUS. Do you intend to put them both to death?
CREON. That was well said. No, not the innocent.
CHORUS. And the other? In what way is she to die?
CREON. Along a desolate pathway I will lead her,
And shut her, living, in a rocky vault 725
With no more food than will appease the gods,
So that the city may not be defiled.
Hades, who is the only god she worships,
May hear her prayers, and rescue her from death.
Otherwise she will learn at last, though late, 730
That to revere the dead is useless toil. [*Exit* CREON.]
CHORUS.

None may withstand you, O love unconquered,
　　Seizing the wealth of man as your prey,
In the cheek of a maiden keeping your vigil,
　　Till night has faded again to day. 735
You roam the wilds to men's farthest dwellings,
　　You haunt the boundless face of the sea.
No god may escape you, no short-lived mortal
　　From the madness that love inflicts may flee.

You twist our minds until ruin follows. 740
　　The just to unrighteous ways you turn.
You have goaded kinsman to strive with kinsman
　　Till the fires of bitter hatred burn.
In the eyes of a bride you shine triumphant;
　　Beside the eternal laws your throne 745
Eternal stands, for great Aphrodite,
　　Resistless, works her will on her own.

But now I too am moved. I cannot keep
　　Within the bounds of loyalty. I weep
When I behold Antigone, the bride, 750
　　Near the room where all at last abide.

---

726-727. *With no more food . . . defiled:* This passage is obscure; the penalty proposed by Creon seems to be imprisonment in a tomb with a certain ration of food. Since Antigone would die of starvation but not actually by anyone's hand, Creon seems to think that the city will not be "defiled," *i.e.* incur blood-guilt.

[*Enter* ANTIGONE, *guarded.*]

ANTIGONE.

See me, my countrymen! See with what pain
I tread the path I shall not tread again,
Looking my last upon the light of day
That shines for me no more.                                        755
Hades, who gives his sleep to all, me, living, leads away
To Acheron's dark shore.
Not mine the hymeneal chant, not mine the bridal song,
For I, a bride, to Acheron belong.

CHORUS.

Glorious, therefore, and with praise you tread                    760
The pathway to the deep gulf of the dead.
You have not felt the force of fate's decrees,
Struck down by violence, wasted by disease;
But of your own free will you choose to go,
Alone of mortals, to the world below.                             765

ANTIGONE.

I know how sad a death she suffered, she
Who was our guest here, Phrygian Niobe.
Stone spread upon her, close as ivy grows,
And locked her in its chains.
Now on her wasted form, men say, fall ceaselessly the snows,      770
Fall ceaselessly the rains;
While from her grieving eyes drop tears, tears that her bosom
steep.
And like hers, my fate lulls me now to sleep.

CHORUS.

She was a goddess of the gods' great race;
Mortals are we and mortal lineage trace.                          775
But for a woman the renown is great
In life and death to share a godlike fate.

ANTIGONE.

By our fathers' gods, I am mocked! I am mocked! Ah! why,
You men of wealth, do you taunt me before I die?                  780
O sacred grove of the city! O waters that flow
From the spring of Dircé! Be witness; to you I cry.
What manner of woman I am you know
And by what laws, unloved, unlamented, I go
To my rocky prison, to my unnatural tomb.                         785
Alas, how ill-bestead!

767. *Niobe:* a Phrygian princess married to Amphion, king of Thebes. She boasted that she had borne more children than Leto, mother of Apollo and Artemis; these two killed her children. She returned to Phrygia where she was turned into a rock on Mount Sipylus; the melting of the snow on the mountain caused 'tears' to flow down the rock formation which resembled a woman's face.

No fellowship have I; no others can share my doom,
Neither mortals nor corpses, neither the quick nor the dead.

CHORUS.
You have rushed forward with audacious feet
And dashed yourself against the law's high seat.                    790
That was a grievous fall, my child, and yet
In this ordeal you pay your father's debt.

ANTIGONE.
You have touched on the heaviest grief that my heart can hold:
Grief for my father, sorrow that never grows old
For our famous house and its doom that the fates have spun.    795
My mother's bed! Ah! How can its horrors be told?
My mother who yielded her love to one
Who was at once my father and her son.
Born of such parents, with them henceforth I abide,
Wretched, accursed, unwed.                                                    800
And you, Polyneices, you found an ill-fated bride,
And I, the living, am ruined by you, the dead.

CHORUS.
A pious action may of praise be sure,
But he who rules a land cannot endure
An act of disobedience to his rule.                                       805
Your own self-will you have not learned to school.

ANTIGONE.
Unwept, unfriended, without marriage song,
Forth on my road I miserable am led;
I may not linger. Not for long
Shall I, most wretched, see the holy sun.                             810
My fate no friend bewails, not one;
For me no tear is shed.

[*Enter* CREON.]
CREON. Do you not know that singing and lamentation
Would rise incessantly as death approached,
If they could be of service? Lead her away!                        815
Obey my orders. Shut her in her grave
And leave her there, alone. Then she can take
Her choice of living in that home, or dying.
I am not stained by the guilt of this girl's blood,
But she shall see the light of day no longer.                        820

ANTIGONE. O tomb! O cavern! Everlasting prison!
O bridal-chamber! To you I make my way
To join my kindred, all those who have died
And have been greeted by Persephone.

824. *Persephone:* the queen of the underworld.

The last and far most miserable of all,                                825
I seek them now, before I have lived my life.
Yet high are the hopes I cherish that my coming
Will be most welcome to my father; welcome,
Mother, to you; and welcome to you, Brother.
For when you died I ministered to you all,                             830
With my own hands washed you and dressed your bodies,
And poured libations at your graves. And now,
Because I have given to you, too, Polyneices,
Such honors as I could, I am brought to this.
And yet all wise men will approve my act.                             835
Not for my children, had I been a mother,
Not for a husband, for his moldering body,
Would I have set myself against the city
As I have done. And the law sanctions me.
Losing a husband, I might find another.                               840
I could have other children. But my parents
Are hidden from me in the underworld,
So that no brother's life can bud and bloom
Ever again. And therefore, Polyneices,
I paid you special honor. And for this                                845
Creon has held me guilty of evil-doing,
And leads me captive for my too great boldness.
No bridal bed is mine, no bridal song,
No share in the joys of marriage, and no share
In nursing children and in tending them.                              850
But thus afflicted, destitute of friends,
Living, I go down to the vaults of death.
What is the law of heaven that I have broken?
Why should I any longer look to the gods,
Ill-fated as I am? Whose aid should I invoke,                         855
When I for piety am called impious?
If this pleases the gods, then I shall learn
That sin brought death upon me. But if the sin
Lies in my judges, I could wish for them
No harsher fate than they have decreed for me.                        860
CHORUS. Still the storm rages; still the same gusts blow,
   Troubling her spirit with their savage breath.
CREON. Yes. And her guards will pay for being slow.
ANTIGONE. Ah! With those words I have drawn close to death.
CREON. You cannot hope that you will now be freed                     865
   From the fulfillment of the doom decreed.
ANTIGONE.
     O Thebes, O land of my fathers, O city!
   O gods who begot and guarded my house from of old!
     They seize me, they snatch me away!

Now, now! They show no pity. ⁸⁷⁰
They give no second's delay.
You elders, you leaders of Thebes, behold me, behold!
The last of the house of your kings, the last
See what I suffer. See the doom
That is come upon me, and see from whom, ⁸⁷⁵
Because to the laws of heaven I held fast.

[*Exeunt* ANTIGONE *and* GUARDS.]

CHORUS.

This likewise Danaë endured:
The light of heaven she changed for a home brass-bound,
In a tomb-like chamber close immured.
And yet, O my child, her race was with honor crowned, ⁸⁸⁰
And she guarded the seed of Zeus gold-showered.
But naught from the terrible power of fate is free.
Neither war, nor city walls high-towered,
Nor wealth, nor black ships beaten by the sea.

He too bowed down beneath his doom, ⁸⁸⁵
The son of Dryas, swift-angered Edonian king,
Shut fast in a rocky prison's gloom.
How he roused the god with his mad tongue's mocking sting,
As his frenzy faded, he came to know;
For he sought to make the god-filled maenads mute, ⁸⁹⁰
To quench the Bacchic torches' glow,
And angered the Muses, lovers of the flute.

By the double sea and the dark rocks steely blue
The beach of Bosporus lies and the savage shore
Of Thracian Salmydessus. There the bride ⁸⁹⁵
Of Phineus, whose fierce heart no mercy knew,
Dealt his two sons a blow that for vengeance cried;
Ares beheld her hand, all stained with gore,
Grasping the pointed shuttle that pierced through
Their eyes that saw no more. ⁹⁰⁰

877. *Danaë:* daughter of Acrisius, king of Argos. It was prophesied that he would be killed by his daughter's son; so he shut her up in a bronze tower. But Zeus came to her in the form of a golden rainshower and she bore a son, Perseus, who did in the end kill his grandfather.

886. *son of Dryas:* Lycurgus, the Thracian (Edonian) king. He opposed the introduction of Dionysiac religion into his kingdom and was imprisoned by the god.

893*ff. By the double sea . . . :* The whole story is difficult to follow and its application to the case of Antigone obscure. Cleopatra, the daughter of the Athenian princess Orithyia, whom Boreas, the North Wind, carried off to his home in Thrace (*cf. l.* 902*ff.*), was married to Phineus, the Thracian king, and bore him two sons. He tired of her, abandoned her, and married Eidothea, "the bride of Phineus" (ll. 895-896). Eidothea put out the eyes of the two sons of Cleopatra. Ares, the god of war, associated with Thrace, watched the savage act.

In misery pining, their lot they lamented aloud,
  So is of a mother whose fortune in marriage was ill.
From the ancient line of Erechtheus her blood she traced;
  Nurtured in caves far-distant and nursed in cloud,
Daughter of Boreas, daughter of gods, she raced          905
  Swift as a steed on the slope of the soaring hill.
And yet, O child, O child, she also bowed
  To the long-lived fates' harsh will.

[*Enter* TIRESIAS *and* BOY.]

TIRESIAS. Elders of Thebes, we have come to you with one
  Finding for both the pathway that we followed,          910
  For in this fashion must the blind be guided.
CREON. What tidings, old Tiresias, are you bringing?
TIRESIAS. I will inform you, I the seer. Give heed.
CREON. To ignore your counsel has not been my custom.
TIRESIAS. Therefore you kept Thebes on a steady course.   915
CREON. I can bear witness to the help you gave.
TIRESIAS. Mark this. You stand upon the brink of ruin.
CREON. What terrible words are those? What do you mean?
TIRESIAS. My meaning is made manifest by my art
  And my art's omens. As I took my station                920
  Upon my ancient seat of augury,
  Where round me birds of every sort come flocking,
  I could no longer understand their language.
  It was drowned out in a strange, savage clamor,
  Shrill, evil, frenzied, inarticulate.                   925
  The whirr of wings told me their murderous talons
  Tore at each other. Filled with dread, I then
  Made trial of burnt sacrifice. The altar
  Was fully kindled, but no clear, bright flame
  Leaped from the offering; only fatty moisture           930
  Oozed from the flesh and trickled on the embers,
  Smoking and sputtering. The bladder burst,
  And scattered in the air. The folds of fat
  Wrapping the thigh-bones melted and left them bare.
  Such was the failure of the sacrifice,                  935
  That did not yield the sign that I was seeking.
  I learned these things from this boy's observation;
  He is my guide as I am guide to others.
  Your edict brings this suffering to the city,
  For every hearth of ours has been defiled               940
  And every altar. There the birds and dogs
  Have brought their carrion, torn from the corpse
  Of ill-starred Polyneices. Hence, the gods
  Refuse our prayers, refuse our sacrifice,
  Refuse the flame of our burnt-offerings.                945

No birds cry clearly and auspiciously,
For they are glutted with a slain man's blood.
Therefore, my son, consider what has happened.
All men are liable to grievous error;
But he who, having erred, does not remain          950
Inflexible, but rather makes amends
For ill, is not unwise or unrewarded.
Stubborn self-will incurs the charge of folly.
Give to the fallen the honors he deserves
And do not stab him. Are you being brave          955
When you inflict new death upon the dead?
Your good I think of; for your good I speak,
And a wise counselor is sweet to hear
When the advice he offers proves of value.

CREON. Old man, all of you shoot your arrows at me          960
Like archers at a target. You have used
Even the art of prophecy in your plotting.
Long have the tribe of prophets traded in me,
Like a ship's cargo. Drive whatever bargain
May please you, buy, sell, heap up for yourself          965
Silver of Sardis, gold of India. Yet
I tell you this: that man shall not be buried,
Not though the eagles of Zeus himself should bear
The carrion morsels to their master's throne.
Not even from the dread of such pollution          970
Will I permit his burial, since I know
There is no mortal can defile the gods.
But even the wisest men disastrously
May fall, Tiresias, when for money's sake
They utter shameful words with specious wisdom.          975

TIRESIAS. Ah! Do men understand, or even consider—
CREON. Consider what? Doubtless some platitude!
TIRESIAS. How precious beyond any wealth is prudence.
CREON. How full of evil is the lack of prudence.
TIRESIAS. Yet you are sick, sick with that same disease.          980
CREON. I will not in reply revile a prophet.
TIRESIAS. You do. You say my prophecy is false.
CREON. Well, all the race of seers are mercenary.
TIRESIAS. And love of base wealth marks the breed of tyrants.
CREON. Are you aware that you address your King?          985
TIRESIAS. I made you King by helping you save Thebes.
CREON. Wise in your art and vicious in your acts.
TIRESIAS. Do not enrage me. I should keep my secret.
CREON. Reveal it. Speak. But do not look for profit.
TIRESIAS. You too will find no profit in my words.          990
CREON. How can you earn your pay? I will not change.
TIRESIAS. Then know this. Yes, be very sure of it.

Only a few more times will you behold
The swift course of the chariot of the sun
Before you give as payment for the dead                    995
Your own dead flesh and blood. For you have thrust
A living soul to darkness, in a tomb
Imprisoned without pity. And a corpse,
Belonging to the gods below you keep
Unpurified, unburied, unrevered.                           1000
The dead are no concern either of yours
Or of the gods above, yet you offend them.
So the avengers, the destroyers, Furies
Of Hades and the gods, lurking in ambush,
Wait to inflict your sins upon your head.                  1005
Do you still think my tongue is lined with silver?
A time will come, and will not linger coming,
That will awaken in your house the wailing
Of men and women. Hatred shakes the cities,
Hatred of you. Their sons are mangled corpses,            1010
Hallowed with funeral rites by dogs or beasts
Or birds who bear the all-polluting stench
To every city having hearth or altar.
You goaded me, and therefore like an archer
I shoot my angry arrows at your heart,                     1015
Sure arrows; you shall not escape their sting.
Boy, lead me home. Let him expend his rage
On younger men, and let him learn to speak
With a more temperate tongue, and school his heart
To feelings finer than his present mood.                   1020
　　　[*Exeunt* TIRESIAS *and* BOY.]
CHORUS. Sir, he is gone, with fearful prophecies.
　　And from the time that these dark hairs have whitened,
　　I have known this: never has he foretold
　　Anything that proved false concerning Thebes.
CREON. I also know it well, and it dismays me.              1025
　　To yield is bitter. But to resist, and bring
　　A curse upon my pride is no less bitter.
CHORUS. Son of Menoeceus, listen. You must listen.
CREON. What should I do? Tell me, I will obey.
CHORUS. Go. Free the girl. Release her from the cavern,    1030
　　And build a tomb for the man you would not bury.
CREON. So that is your advice—that I should yield?
CHORUS. Sir, you should not delay. The gods are swift
　　In cutting short man's folly with their curse.
CREON. How hard it is to change! Yet I obey.               1035
　　I will give up what I had set my heart on.

1009. *Hatred shakes the cities:* Creon
had exposed the corpses of all seven
champions, not only Polynices.

No one can stand against the blows of fate.
CHORUS. Go. Go yourself. These things are not for others.
CREON. I will go this moment. Guards there! All of you!
    Take up your axes. Quick! Quick! Over there.       1040
    I imprisoned her myself, and I myself
    Will set her free. And yet my mind misgives me.
    Never to break the ancient law is best.       [*Exit* CREON.]
CHORUS.
       Thou art known by many a name.
       O Bacchus! To thee we call.       1045
       Cadmean Semele's glory and pride,
    Begotten of Zeus, whose terrible lightnings flame,
         Whose thunders appall.
Bacchus, thou dost for us all in thy love provide.
       Over Icaria thou dost reign,       1050
       And where the worshippers journey slow
       To the rites of Eleusis, where mountains shield
The multitudes crossing Demeter's welcoming plain.
Thou makest this mother-city of maenads thine own,
       A city beside the rippling flow       1055
Of the gentle river, beside the murderous field
       Where the teeth of the dragon were sown.

       In the torches' wind-blown flare
       Thou art seen, in their flicker and smoke.
       Where the two-fold peaks of Parnassus gleam,       1060
Corycian nymphs, as they move through the ruddy glare,
         Thee, Bacchus, invoke.
They move in their dance beside the Castalian stream.
       O Bacchus, guardian divine!
       Down from the slopes of Nysa's hills       1065
       Where a mantle of ivy covers the ground,
From headlands rich with the purple grape and the vine,
Thou comest to us, thou comest. O be not long!
       Thy triumph the echoing city fills.
The streets are loud with thy praises; the highways resound,       1070
       Resound with immortal song.

---

1044ff. *Thou art known . . . :* a hymn to the god Dionysus (Bacchus), whose mother was a Theban princess, Semele. When she was pregnant by her lover Zeus, she asked the god to appear to her in his own shape; he did, and she was blasted with the fire of his lightning.

1050. *Icaria:* the place where Dionysus was welcomed to Attica.

1052. *Eleusis:* on the coast near Athens, the site of the great mystery religion which had as its cult-deities Demet-ter and her daughter Persephone.

1060. *Parnassus:* the great mountain above Delphi, where Dionysus was worshipped as well as Apollo.

1061. *Corycian nymphs:* named from the Corycian cave on the heights above Delphi.

1063. *Castalian stream:* the spring at Delphi.

1065. *Nysa:* on the island of Euboea, opposite the Boeotian (Theban) coast.

Thou honorest highly our Theban city,
    Thou, and thy mother by lightning slain.
Our people sicken. O Bacchus have pity!
    Across the strait with its moaning wave,         1075
Down from Parnassus, come thou again!
    Come with thy healing feet, and save!

O thou who leadest the stars in chorus,
    Jubilant stars with their breath of fire,
Offspring of Zeus, appear before us!         1080
    Lord of the tumult of night, appear!
With the frenzied dance of thy maenad choir,
    Bacchus, thou giver of good, draw near!

      [*Enter* MESSENGER.]
MESSENGER. You of the house of Cadmus and Amphíon,
    No man's estate can ever be established         1085
Firmly enough to warrant praise or blame.
Fortune, from day to day, exalts the lucky
And humbles the unlucky. No one knows
Whether his present lot can long endure.
For Creon once was blest, as I count blessings;     1090
He had saved this land of Cadmus from its foes;
He was the sovereign and ruled alone,
The noble father of a royal house.
And now, all has been lost. Because a man
Who has forfeited his joy is not alive,         1095
He is a living corpse. Heap, if you will,
Your house with riches; live in regal pomp.
Yet if your life is unhappy, all these things
Are worth not even the shadow of a vapor
Put in the balance against joy alone.         1100
CHORUS. What new disaster has the King's house suffered?
MESSENGER. Death. And the guilt of death lies on the living.
CHORUS. The guilt of death! Who has been killed? Who killed him?
MESSENGER. Haemon is killed, and by no stranger's hand.
CHORUS. He killed himself? Or did his father kill him?     1105
MESSENGER. He killed himself, enraged by his murderous father.
CHORUS. Tiresias! Now your prophecy is fulfilled.
MESSENGER. Consider, therefore, what remains to do.
CHORUS. There is the Queen, wretched Eurydice.
    Perhaps mere chance has brought her from the palace;     1110
    Perhaps she has learned the news about her son.
      [*Enter* EURYDICE.]
EURYDICE. Thebans, I heard you talking here together
    When I was on my way to greet the goddess,

Pallas Athene, and to pray to her.
Just as I loosed the fastening of the door,                    1115
The words that told of my calamity
Struck heavily upon my ear. In terror
I fell back fainting in my women's arms.
But now, repeat your story. I shall hear it
As one who is not ignorant of grief.                           1120
MESSENGER. My Lady, I will bear witness to what I saw,
And will omit no syllable of the truth.
Why should I comfort you with words that later
Would prove deceitful? Truth is always best.
Across the plain I guided my Lord Creon                        1125
To where unpitied Polyneices lay,
A corpse mangled by dogs. Then we besought
Hecate, goddess of the roads, and Pluto
To moderate their wrath, and to show mercy.
We washed the dead with ceremonial water.                      1130
Gathering the scattered fragments that remained,
With fresh-cut boughs we burned them. We heaped up
A mound of native earth above his ashes.
Then we approached the cavern of Death's bride,
The rock-floored marriage-chamber. While as yet                1135
We were far distant, someone heard the sound
Of loud lament in that unhallowed place,
And came to tell our master. As the King
Drew near, there floated through the air a voice,
Faint, indistinct, that uttered a bitter cry.                  1140
The King burst out in anguish: 'Can it be
That I, in my misery, have become a prophet?
Will this be the saddest road I ever trod?
My son's voice greets me. Quickly, slaves! Go quickly!
When you have reached the sepulcher, get through               1145
The opening where the stones are wrenched away,
Get to the mouth of the burial chamber. Look,
See if I know his voice—Haemon's, my son's—
Or if I am deluded by the gods.'
We followed our despairing master's bidding                    1150
And in the farthest recess of the tomb
We found Antigone, hanging, with her veil
Noosed round her neck. And with her we found Haemon,
His arms flung round her waist, grieving aloud
For his bride lost in death, his ruined marriage,              1155
His father's deeds. But when his father saw him,
Creon cried piteously and going in,
Called to him brokenly: "My son, my son,

1128. *Hecate . . . and Pluto:* divinities of the underworld.

What have you done? What are you thinking of?
What dreadful thing has driven you out of your mind?        1160
Son, come away. I beg you. I beseech you."
But Haemon glared at him with furious eyes
Instead of answering, spat in his face,
And drew his sword. His father turned to fly
So that he missed his aim. Immediately,        1165
In bitter self-reproach, the wretched boy
Leaned hard against his sword, and drove it deep
Into his side. Then while his life yet lingered,
With failing strength he drew Antigone close;
And as he lay there gasping heavily,        1170
Over her white cheek his blood ebbed away.
The dead lie clasped together. He is wedded,
Not in this world but in the house of Death.
He has borne witness that of all the evils        1174
Afflicting man, the worst is lack of wisdom.        [*Exit* EURYDICE.]
CHORUS. What does that mean? Who can interpret it?
The Queen has gone without a single word.
MESSENGER. It startles me. And yet I hope it means
That hearing these dreadful things about her son,
She will not let herself show grief in public        1180
But will lament in private with her women.
Schooled in discretion, she will do no wrong.
CHORUS. How can we tell? Surely too great a silence
Is no less ominous than too loud lament.
MESSENGER. Then I will enter. Perhaps she is concealing        1185
Some secret purpose in her passionate heart.
I will find out, for you are right in saying
Too great a silence may be ominous.
        [*Exit* MESSENGER. *Enter* CREON *with* ATTENDANTS, *carrying*
        *the body of* HAEMON *on a bier.*]
CHORUS. Thebans, look there! The King himself draws near,
Bearing a load whose tale is all too clear.        1190
This is a work—if we dare speak our thought—
That not another's but his own hands wrought.
CREON.
        O, how may my sin be told?
The stubborn, death-fraught sin of a darkened brain!
        Behold us here, behold        1195
Father and son, the slayer and the slain!
        Pain, only pain
Has come of my design.
        Fate struck too soon; too soon your spirit fled.
        My son, my young son, you are lying dead        1200
Not for your folly, but for mine, for mine.
CHORUS. Sir, you have come to learn the right too late.

CREON.
>My lesson has been bitter and complete.
>Some god has struck me down with crushing weight,
>Filling my heart with cruelty and hate,               1205
>>Trampling my happiness beneath his feet.
>>>Grief, bitter grief, is man's fate.

[*Enter* MESSENGER.]

MESSENGER. [*Indicating* HAEMON] Your load is heavy, Sir, but there
>is more.
>That is the burden you are bearing now.
>Soon you must bear new woe within your house.        1210
CREON. And what worse misery can follow this?
MESSENGER. Your wife is dead, a mother like her son.
>Poor woman, by her own hand she has died.
CREON.
>>By her own hand she died.
>Death, spare me! Can you never have your fill?       1215
>>Never be satisfied?
>Herald of evil, messenger of ill,
>>Your harsh words kill,
>They smite me now anew.
>>My wife is dead—You tell me my wife is dead.        1220
>Death after death is heaped upon my head.
>Speak to me, boy. Is what you tell me true?
MESSENGER. It is no longer hidden. Sir, look there.
>>[*The body of* EURYDICE *is disclosed through the palace doors.*]
CREON.
>>Another horror that makes blind mine eyes!
>What further agony has fate in store?                1225
>My dead son's body in my arms I bore,
>>And now beside him his dead mother lies.
>>>I can endure no more.
MESSENGER. There at the altar with a keen-edged knife
>She stabbed herself; and as her eyes were darkened,  1230
>She wailed the death of Megareus, her son,
>Who earlier had met a noble fate;
>She wailed for Haemon; then, with her last breath,
>You, as the slayer of your sons, she cursed.
CREON.
>>I am shaken with terror, with terror past belief.   1235
>Is there none here to end my anguish? None?
>>No sword to pierce me? Broken with my grief,
>So steeped in agony that we are one.
MESSENGER. Sir, as she died, she burdened you with guilt,
>Charging you with the death of both your sons.       1240

1231. *Megareus:* killed during the siege of the city.

CREON. And by what act of violence did she die?

MESSENGER. Hearing the shrill lament for Haemon's fate,
Deep in her heart she drove the bright blade home.

CREON. [*To* HAEMON]
I am your slayer, I alone.
I am guilty, only I.                                                    1245
I, and none other, must atone.
Lead me away. The truth I own.
Nothing is left, except to die.

CHORUS. If anything can be good, those words are good.
For when calamity has come upon us,                                    1250
The thing that is the briefest is the best.

CREON.
Draw near me, death! O longed for death, draw near!
Most welcome destiny, make no delay.
To tell me my last hour, my last breath, is here.
I have no wish to see another day.                                     1255

CHORUS. Such things are yet to come. We are concerned
With doing what must needs be done today.
The future rests in other hands than ours.

CREON. That is my whole desire. That is my prayer.

CHORUS. No. Do not pray. Men must accept their doom.                   1260

CREON.
My life's work there before me lies.
My folly slew my wife, my son.
I know not where to turn mine eyes.
All my misdeeds before me rise.                                        1264
Lead me away, brought low, undone.            [*Exit* CREON.]

CHORUS.
The crown of happiness is to be wise.
Honor the gods, and the gods' edicts prize.
They strike down boastful men and men grown bold.
Wisdom we learn at last, when we are old.                             1269

# THUCYDIDES

## History of the Peloponnesian War*

### *The Melian Dialogue†*

[The war between Athens and Sparta which began in 431 B.C.
came to a temporary stop in 421. The uneasy truce which ensued
was only a breathing space in which both sides prepared for the

---

* Translated by Benjamin Jowett.          † From Book V, Chapters 84-116.

renewal of the war and the decisive struggle. The spirit of Athenian democracy had changed during the hard years of the war; Pericles was dead and his place had been taken by younger and less scrupulous politicians. Thucydides describes the Athenian attack on the small island of Melos, in 416 B.C., an incident which, in Thucydides' hands, is made to reveal the depths of cynicism of the new Athenian policies.]

. . . The Athenians next made an expedition against the island of Melos[1] with thirty ships of their own, six Chian, and two Lesbian,[2] twelve hundred hoplites[3] and three hundred archers besides twenty mounted archers of their own, and about fifteen hundred hoplites furnished by their allies in the islands. The Melians are colonists of the Lacedaemonians who would not submit to Athens like the other islanders. At first they were neutral and took no part. But when the Athenians tried to coerce them by ravaging their lands they were driven into open hostilities. The generals, Cleomedes the son of Lycomedes and Tisias the son of Tisimachus, encamped with the Athenian forces on the island. But before they did the country any harm they sent envoys to negotiate with the Melians. Instead of bringing these envoys before the people, the Melians desired them to explain their errand to the magistrates and to the chief men.[4] They spoke as follows:—

"Since we are not allowed to speak to the people, lest, forsooth, they should be deceived by seductive and unanswerable arguments which they would hear set forth in a single uninterrupted oration (for we are perfectly aware that this is what you mean in bringing us before a select few), you who are sitting here may as well make assurance yet surer. Let us have no set speeches at all, but do you reply to each several statement of which you disapprove, and criticise it at once. Say first of all how you like this mode of proceeding."

The Melian representatives answered:—"The quiet interchange of explanations is a reasonable thing, and we do not object to that. But your warlike movements, which are present not only to our fears but to our eyes, seem to belie your words. We see that, although you may reason with us, you mean to be our judges; and that at the end of the discussion, if the justice of our cause prevail and we therefore refuse to yield, we may expect war; if we are convinced by you, slavery."

ATHENIANS. Nay, but if you are only going to argue from fancies about the future, or if you meet us with any other purpose than

---

1. a barren, unimportant island in the Aegean Sea, off the east coast of the Peloponnese.

2. Chios and Lesbos are two large islands off the coast of Asia Minor,

which were at this time subject to Athens.

3. heavy infantry.

4. Melos was governed by an oligarchy.

that of looking your circumstances in the face and saving your city, we have done; but if this is your intention we will proceed.

MELIANS. It is an excusable and natural thing that men in our position should have much to say and should indulge in many fancies. But we admit that this conference has met to consider the question of our preservation; and therefore let the argument proceed in the manner which you propose.

ATH. Well, then, we Athenians will use no fine words; we will not go out of our way to prove at length that we have a right to rule, because we overthrew the Persians;[5] or that we attack you now because we are suffering any injury at your hands. We should not convince you if we did; nor must you expect to convince us by arguing that, although a colony of the Lacedaemonians, you have taken no part in their expeditions, or that you have never done us any wrong. But you and we should say what we really think, and aim only at what is possible, for we both alike know that into the discussion of human affairs the question of justice only enters where the pressure of necessity is equal, and that the powerful exact what they can, and the weak grant what they must.

MEL. Well, then, since you set aside justice and invite us to speak of expediency, in our judgment it is certainly expedient that you should respect a principle which is for the common good; and that to every man when in peril a reasonable claim should be accounted a claim of right, and any plea which he is disposed to urge, even if failing of the point a little, should help his cause. Your interest in this principle is quite as great as ours, inasmuch as you, if you fall, will incur the heaviest vengeance, and will be the most terrible example to mankind.

ATH. The fall of our empire, if it should fall, is not an event to which we look forward with dismay; for ruling states such as Lacedaemon are not cruel to their vanquished enemies.[6] And we are fighting not so much against the Lacedaemonians as against our own subjects who may some day rise up and overcome their former masters. But this is a danger which you may leave to us. And we will now endeavor to show that we have come in the interests of our empire, and that in what we are about to say we are only seeking the preservation of your city. For we want to make you ours with the least trouble to ourselves, and it is for the interests of us both that you should not be destroyed.

MEL. It may be your interest to be our masters, but how can it be ours to be your slaves?

---

5. during the Persian invasion of 480–479 B.C. and during the subsequent offensives against the Persians, which were led by Athens as the most important power in the Delian League.

6. This cynical prophecy turned out to be correct, for after their victory in 404 B.C. the Spartans treated Athens with comparative mildness.

ATH. To you the gain will be that by submission you will avert the worst; and we shall be all the richer for your preservation.

MEL. But must we be your enemies? Will you not receive us as friends if we are neutral and remain at peace with you?

ATH. No, your enmity is not half so mischievous to us as your friendship; for the one is in the eyes of our subjects an argument of our power, the other of our weakness.

MEL. But are your subjects really unable to distinguish between states in which you have no concern, and those which are chiefly your own colonies, and in some cases have revolted and been subdued by you?

ATH. Why, they do not doubt that both of them have a good deal to say for themselves on the score of justice, but they think that states like yours are left free because they are able to defend themselves, and that we do not attack them because we dare not. So that your subjection will give us an increase of security, as well as an extension of empire. For we are masters of the sea, and you who are islanders, and insignificant islanders too, must not be allowed to escape us.

MEL. But do you not recognize another danger? For once more, since you drive us from the plea of justice and press upon us your doctrine of expediency, we must show you what is for our interest, and, if it be for yours also, may hope to convince you:—Will you not be making enemies of all who are now neutrals? When they see how you are treating us they will expect you some day to turn against them; and if so, are you not strengthening the enemies whom you already have, and bringing upon you others who, if they could help, would never dream of being your enemies at all?

ATH. We do not consider our really dangerous enemies to be any of the peoples inhabiting the mainland who, secure in their freedom, may defer indefinitely any measures of precaution which they take against us, but islanders who, like you, happen to be under no control, and all who may be already irritated by the necessity of submission to our empire—these are our real enemies, for they are the most reckless and most likely to bring themselves as well as us into a danger which they cannot but foresee.

MEL. Surely then, if you and your subjects will brave all this risk, you to preserve your empire and they to be quit of it, how base and cowardly it would be in us, who retain our freedom, not to do and suffer anything rather than be your slaves.

ATH. Not so, if you calmly reflect: for you are not fighting against equals to whom you cannot yield without disgrace, but you are taking counsel whether or no you shall resist an overwhelming force. The question is not one of honor but of prudence.

MEL. But we know that the fortune of war is sometimes impartial, and not always on the side of numbers. If we yield now all is over; but if we fight there is yet a hope that we may stand upright.

ATH. Hope is a good comforter in the hour of danger, and when men have something else to depend upon, although hurtful, she is not ruinous. But when her spendthrift nature has induced them to stake their all, they see her as she is in the moment of their fall, and not till then. While the knowledge of her might enable them to be ware of her, she never fails. You are weak and a single turn of the scale might be your ruin. Do not you be thus deluded; avoid the error of which so many are guilty, who, although they might still be saved if they would take the natural means, when visible grounds of confidence forsake them, have recourse to the invisible, to prophecies and oracles and the like, which ruin men by the hopes which they inspire in them.

MEL. We know only too well how hard the struggle must be against your power, and against fortune, if she does not mean to be impartial. Nevertheless we do not despair of fortune; for we hope to stand as high as you in the favor of heaven, because we are righteous, and you against whom we contend are unrighteous; and we are satisfied that our deficiency in power will be compensated by the aid of our allies the Lacedaemonians; they cannot refuse to help us, if only because we are their kinsmen, and for the sake of their own honor. And therefore our confidence is not so utterly blind as you suppose.

ATH. As for the Gods, we expect to have quite as much of their favor as you: for we are not doing or claiming anything which goes beyond common opinion about divine or men's desires about human things. For of the Gods we believe, and of men we know, that by a law of their nature wherever they can rule they will. This law was not made by us, and we are not the first who have acted upon it; we did but inherit it, and shall bequeath it to all time, and we know that you and all mankind, if you were as strong as we are, would do as we do. So much for the Gods; we have told you why we expect to stand as high in their good opinion as you. And then as to the Lacedaemonians—when you imagine that out of very shame they will assist you, we admire the simplicity of your idea, but we do not envy you the folly of it. The Lacedaemonians are exceedingly virtuous among themselves, and according to their national standard of morality. But in respect of their dealings with others, although many things might be said, a word is enough to describe them—of all men whom we know they are the most notorious for identifying what is pleasant with what is honorable, and what is expedient with what is just. But how inconsistent is such a character with your present blind hope of deliverance!

MEL. That is the very reason why we trust them; they will look to their interest, and therefore will not be willing to betray the Melians, who are their own colonists, lest they should be distrusted by their friends in Hellas[7] and play into the hands of their enemies.

ATH. But do you not see that the path of expediency is safe, whereas justice and honor involve danger in practice, and such dangers the Lacedaemonians seldom care to face?

MEL. On the other hand, we think that whatever perils there may be, they will be ready to face them for our sakes, and will consider danger less dangerous where we are concerned. For if they need our aid we are close at hand, and they can better trust our loyal feeling because we are their kinsmen.

ATH. Yes, but what encourages men who are invited to join in a conflict is clearly not the good-will of those who summon them to their side, but a decided superiority in real power. To this no men look more keenly than the Lacedaemonians; so little confidence have they in their own resources that they only attack their neighbors when they have numerous allies, and therefore they are not likely to find their way by themselves to an island, when we are masters of the sea.

MEL. But they may send their allies: the Cretan sea[8] is a large place; and the masters of the sea will have more difficulty in overtaking vessels which want to escape than the pursued in escaping. If the attempt should fail they may invade Attica itself, and find their way to allies of yours whom Brasidas[9] did not reach; and then you will have to fight, not for the conquest of a land in which you have no concern, but nearer home, for the preservation of your confederacy and of your own territory.

ATH. Help may come from Lacedaemon to you as it has come to others, and should you ever have actual experience of it, then you will know that never once have the Athenians retired from a siege through fear of a foe elsewhere. You told us that the safety of your city would be your first care, but we remark that, in this long discussion, not a word has been uttered by you which would give a reasonable man expectation of deliverance. Your strongest grounds are hopes deferred, and what power you have is not to be compared with that which is already arrayed against you. Unless after we have withdrawn you mean to come, as even now you may, to a wiser conclusion, you are showing a great want of sense. For surely you cannot dream of flying to that false sense of honor which has been the ruin of so many when danger and dishonor were staring them in the face. Many men with their eyes still open to the conse-

7. Greece.
8. Melos lies some seventy miles north of Crete.
9. a Spartan commander who had stirred up a great deal of trouble among the Athenian subjects in the north of Greece earlier in the war.

quences have found the word honor too much for them, and have suffered a mere name to lure them on, until it has drawn upon them real and irretrievable calamities; through their own folly they have incurred a worse dishonor than fortune would have inflicted upon them. If you are wise you will not run this risk; you ought to see that there can be no disgrace in yielding to a great city which invites you to become her ally on reasonable terms, keeping your own land, and merely paying tribute; and that you will certainly gain no honor if, having to choose between two alternatives, safety and war, you obstinately prefer the worse. To maintain our rights against equals, to be politic with superiors, and to be moderate towards inferiors is the path of safety. Reflect once more when we have withdrawn, and say to yourselves over and over again that you are deliberating about your one and only country, which may be saved or may be destroyed by a single decision.

The Athenians left the conference: the Melians, after consulting among themselves, resolved to persevere in their refusal, and made answer as follows:—"Men of Athens, our resolution is unchanged; and we will not in a moment surrender that liberty which our city, founded seven hundred years ago, still enjoys; we will trust to the good-fortune which by the favor of the Gods has hitherto preserved us, and for human help to the Lacedaemonians, and endeavor to save ourselves. We are ready however to be your friends, and the enemies neither of you nor of the Lacedaemonians, and we ask you to leave our country when you have made such a peace as may appear to be in the interest of both parties."

Such was the answer of the Melians; the Athenians, as they quitted the conference, spoke as follows:—"Well, we must say, judging from the decision at which you have arrived, that you are the only men who deem the future to be more certain than the present, and regard things unseen as already realized in your fond anticipation, and that the more you cast yourselves upon the Lacedaemonians and fortune, and hope, and trust them, the more complete will be your ruin."

The Athenian envoys returned to the army; and the generals, when they found that the Melians would not yield, immediately commenced hostilities. They surrounded the town of Melos with a wall, dividing the work among the several contingents. They then left troops of their own and of the allies to keep guard both by land and by sea, and retired with the greater part of their army; the remainder carried on the blockade.

. . . The Melians took that part of the Athenian wall which looked towards the agora[10] by a night assault, killed a few men, and brought in as much corn and other necessaries as they could; they

10. market place.

then retreated and remained inactive. After this the Athenians set
a better watch. So the summer ended.

In the following winter . . . the Melians took another part of
the Athenian wall; for the fortifications were insufficiently guarded.
Whereupon the Athenians sent fresh troops, under the command
of Philocrates the son of Demeas. The place was now closely invested, and there was treachery among the citizens themselves. So
the Melians were induced to surrender at discretion. The Athenians
thereupon put to death all who were of military age, and made
slaves of the women and children. They then colonized the island,
sending thither five hundred settlers of their own.

# EURIPIDES
## (480–406 B.C.)
## Medea *

### Characters

MEDEA, *princess of Colchis and*
*wife of Jason*
JASON, *son of Aeson, king of*
*Iolcos*
TWO CHILDREN *of Medea and*
*Jason*

KREON, *king of Corinth*
AIGEUS, *king of Athens*
NURSE *to Medea*
TUTOR *to Medea's children*
MESSENGER
CHORUS OF CORINTHIAN WOMEN

SCENE—*In front of Medea's house in Corinth. Enter from the
house Medea's* NURSE.

NURSE. How I wish the Argo never had reached the land
   Of Colchis, skimming through the blue Symplegades,
   Nor ever had fallen in the glades of Pelion
   The smitten fir-tree to furnish oars for the hands
   Of heroes who in Pelias's name attempted
   The Golden Fleece! For then my mistress Medea                    5
   Would not have sailed for the towers of the land of Iolcos,
   Her heart on fire with passionate love for Jason;
   Nor would she have persuaded the daughters of Pelias

* Produced in 431 B.C. Our text is a
translation by Rex Warner, from *The
Medea of Euripides*, John Lane The
Bodley Head, Ltd., London, 1944.

1. *Argo:* the ship in which Jason and
his companions sailed on the quest for
the Golden Fleece.

2. *Symplegades:* clashing rocks,
which crushed ships endeavoring to
pass between them. They were supposed
to be located at the Hellespont, the
passage between the Mediterranean and
the Black Sea.

3. *Pelion:* a mountain in the north of
Greece near Iolcos, the place from
which Jason sailed.

5. *Pelias:* He seized the kingdom of
Iolcos, expelling Aeson, Jason's father.
When Jason came to claim his rights,
Pelias sent him to get the Golden
Fleece.

To kill their father, and now be living here 10
In Corinth with her husband and children. She gave
Pleasure to the people of her land of exile,
And she herself helped Jason in every way.
This is indeed the greatest salvation of all,—
For the wife not to stand apart from the husband. 15
But now there's hatred everywhere. Love is diseased.
For, deserting his own children and my mistress,
Jason has taken a royal wife to his bed,
The daughter of the ruler of this land, Kreon.
And poor Medea is slighted, and cries aloud on the 20
Vows they made to each other, the right hands clasped
In eternal promise. She calls upon the gods to witness
What sort of return Jason has made to her love.
She lies without food and gives herself up to suffering,
Wasting away every moment of the day in tears. 25
So it has gone since she knew herself slighted by him.
Not stirring an eye, not moving her face from the ground,
No more than either a rock or surging sea water
She listens when she is given friendly advice.
Except that sometimes she twists back her white neck and 30
Moans to herself, calling out on her father's name,
And her land, and her home betrayed when she came away with
A man who now is determined to dishonour her.
Poor creature, she has discovered by her sufferings
What it means to one not to have lost one's own country. 35
She has turned from the children and does not like to see them.
I am afraid she may think of some dreadful thing,
For her heart is violent. She will never put up with
The treatment she is getting. I know and fear her
Lest she may sharpen a sword and thrust to the heart, 40
Stealing into the palace where the bed is made,
Or even kill the king and the new-wedded groom,
And thus bring a greater misfortune on herself.
She's a strange woman. I know it won't be easy
To make an enemy of her and come off best. 45
But here the children come. They have finished playing.
They have no thought at all of their mother's trouble.

---

10. *kill . . . father:* After Jason returned to Iolcos with the Fleece and Medea, Pelias' daughters were persuaded by Medea, who had a reputation as a sorceress, to cut Pelias up and boil the pieces, in order to restore him to youth. The experiment was, of course, unsuccessful, but the son of Pelias expelled Jason and Medea from the kingdom, and they took refuge in Corinth.

11. *Corinth:* on the isthmus between the Peloponnese and Attica. In Euripides' time it was a wealthy trading city, a commercial rival of Athens.

19. *Kreon:* Creon.

32. *home betrayed:* Medea, daughter of the king of Colchis, fell in love with Jason and helped him to take the Golden Fleece away from her own country.

Indeed it is not usual for the young to grieve.

[*Enter from the right the slave who is the* TUTOR *to* **Medea's**
*two small children. The* CHILDREN *follow him.*]

TUTOR. You old retainer of my mistress's household,
Why are you standing here all alone in front of the                50
Gates and moaning to yourself over your misfortune?
Medea could not wish you to leave her alone.

NURSE. Old man, and guardian of the children of Jason,
If one is a good servant, it's a terrible thing
When one's master's luck is out; it goes to one's heart.          55
So I myself have got into such a state of grief
That a longing stole over me to come outside here
And tell the earth and air of my mistress's sorrows.

TUTOR. Has the poor lady not yet given up her crying?

NURSE. Given up? She's at the start, not half-way through her
tears.                                                             60

TUTOR. Poor fool,—if I may call my mistress such a name,—
How ignorant she is of trouble more to come.

NURSE. What do you mean, old man? You needn't fear to speak.

TUTOR. Nothing. I take back the words which I used just now.

NURSE. Don't, by your beard, hide this from me, your fellow-
servant.                                                           65
If need be, I'll keep quiet about what you tell me.

TUTOR. I heard a person saying, while I myself seemed
Not to be paying attention, when I was at the place
Where the old draught-players sit, by the holy fountain,
That Kreon, ruler of the land, intends to drive                   70
These children and their mother in exile from Corinth.
But whether what he said is really true or not
I do not know. I pray that it may not be true.

NURSE. And will Jason put up with it that his children
Should suffer so, though he's no friend to their mother?          75

TUTOR. Old ties give place to new ones. As for Jason, he
No longer has a feeling for this house of ours.

NURSE. It's black indeed for us, when we add new to old
Sorrows before even the present sky has cleared.

TUTOR. But you be silent, and keep all this to yourself.          80
It is not the right time to tell our mistress of it.

NURSE. Do you hear, children, what a father he is to you?
I wish he were dead,—but no, he is still my master.
Yet certainly he has proved unkind to his dear ones.

TUTOR. What's strange in that? Have you only just discovered      85
That everyone loves himself more than his neighbour?
Some have good reason, others get something out of it.

69. *draught-players:* checker-players.

So Jason neglects his children for the new bride.

NURSE. Go indoors, children. That will be the best thing.
And you, keep them to themselves as much as possible.    90
Don't bring them near their mother in her angry mood.
For I've seen her already blazing her eyes at them
As though she meant some mischief and I am sure that
She'll not stop raging until she has struck at someone.
May it be an enemy and not a friend she hurts!    95
   [MEDEA *is heard inside the house.*]

MEDEA. Ah, wretch! Ah, lost in my sufferings,
I wish, I wish I might die.

NURSE. What did I say, dear children? Your mother
Frets her heart and frets it to anger.
Run away quickly into the house,    100
And keep well out of her sight.
Don't go anywhere near, but be careful
Of the wildness and bitter nature
Of that proud mind.
Go now! Run quickly indoors.    105
It is clear that she soon will put lightning
In that cloud of her cries that is rising
With a passion increasing. Oh, what will she do,
Proud-hearted and not to be checked on her course,
A soul bitten into with wrong?    110
   [*The* TUTOR *takes the children into the house.*]

MEDEA. Ah I have suffered
What should be wept for bitterly. I hate you,
Children of a hateful mother. I curse you
And your father. Let the whole house crash.

NURSE. Ah, I pity you, you poor creature.    115
How can your children share in their father's
Wickedness? Why do you hate them? Oh children,
How much I fear that something may happen!
Great people's tempers are terrible, always
Having their own way, seldom checked,    120
Dangerous they shift from mood to mood.
How much better to have been accustomed
To live on equal terms with one's neighbours.
I would like to be safe and grow old in a
Humble way. What is moderate sounds best,    125
Also in practice *is* best for everyone.
Greatness brings no profit to people.
God indeed, when in anger, brings
Greater ruin to great men's houses.

[*Enter, on the right, a* CHORUS OF CORINTHIAN WOMEN.
*They have come to enquire about* MEDEA *and to attempt to
console her.*]

CHORUS. I heard the voice, I heard the cry                    130
  Of Colchis' wretched daughter.
  Tell me, mother, is she not yet
  At rest? Within the double gates
  Of the court I heard her cry. I am sorry
  For the sorrow of this home. O, say, what has happened?    135
NURSE. There is no home. It's over and done with.
  Her husband holds fast to his royal wedding,
  While she, my mistress, cries out her eyes
  There in her room, and takes no warmth from
  Any word of any friend.                                    140
MEDEA. Oh, I wish
  That lightning from heaven would split my head open.
  Oh, what use have I now for life?
  I would find my release in death
  And leave hateful existence behind me.                      145
CHOR. O God and Earth and Heaven!
  Did you hear what a cry was that
  Which the sad wife sings?
  Poor foolish one, why should you long
  For that appalling rest?                                    150
  The final end of death comes fast.
  No need to pray for that.
  Suppose your man gives honour
  To another woman's bed.
  It often happens. Don't be hurt.                            155
  God will be your friend in this.
  You must not waste away
  Grieving too much for him who shared your bed.
MEDEA. Great Themis, lady Artemis, behold
  The things I suffer, though I made him promise,              160
  My hateful husband. I pray that I may see him,
  Him and his bride and all their palace shattered
  For the wrong they dare to do me without cause.
  Oh, my father! Oh, my country! In what dishonour
  I left you, killing my own brother for it.                  165
NURSE. Do you hear what she says, and how she cries
  On Themis, the goddess of Promises, and on Zeus,
  Whom we believe to be the Keeper of Oaths?

---

159. *Themis:* justice. *Artemis:* the
protector of women in pain and distress.

165. *my own brother:* Medea killed
him to delay the pursuit when she
escaped with Jason.

Of this I am sure, that no small thing
Will appease my mistress's anger. 170
CHOR. Will she come into our presence?
Will she listen when we are speaking
To the words we say?
I wish she might relax her rage
And temper of her heart. 175
My willingness to help will never
Be wanting to my friends.
But go inside and bring her
Out of the house to us,
And speak kindly to her: hurry, 180
Before she wrongs her own.
This passion of hers moves to something great.
NURSE. I will, but I doubt if I'll manage
To win my mistress over.
But still I'll attempt it to please you. 185
Such a look she will flash on her servants
If any comes near with a message,
Like a lioness guarding her cubs.
It is right, I think, to consider
Both stupid and lacking in foresight 190
Those poets of old who wrote songs
For revels and dinners and banquets,
Pleasant sounds for men living at ease;
But none of them all has discovered
How to put an end with their singing 195
Or musical instruments grief,
Bitter grief, from which death and disaster
Cheat the hopes of a house. Yet how good
If music could cure men of this! But why raise
To no purpose the voice at a banquet? For *there* is 200
Already abundance of pleasure for men
With a joy of its own.
[*The* NURSE *goes into the house.*]
CHOR. I heard a shriek that is laden with sorrow.
Shrilling out her hard grief she cries out
Upon him who betrayed both her bed and her marriage. 205
Wronged, she calls on the gods,
On the justice of Zeus, the oath sworn,
Which brought her away
To the opposite shore of the Greeks
Through the gloomy salt straits to the gateway 210
Of the salty unlimited sea.
[MEDEA, *attended by servants, comes out of the house.*]

MEDEA. Women of Corinth, I have come outside to you
  Lest you should be indignant with me; for I know
  That many people are overproud, some when alone,
  And others when in company. And those who live    215
  Quietly, as I do, get a bad reputation.
  For a just judgement is not evident in the eyes
  When a man at first sight hates another, before
  Learning his character, being in no way injured;
  And a foreigner especially must adapt himself.    220
  I'd not approve of even a fellow-countryman
  Who by pride and want of manners offends his neighbours.
  But on me this thing has fallen so unexpectedly,
  It has broken my heart. I am finished. I let go
  All my life's joy. My friends, I only want to die.    225
  It was everything to me to think well of one man,
  And he, my own husband, has turned out wholly vile.
  Of all things which are living and can form a judgement
  We women are the most unfortunate creatures.
  Firstly, with an excess of wealth it is required    230
  For us to buy a husband and take for our bodies
  A master; for not to take one is even worse.
  And now the question is serious whether we take
  A good or bad one; for there is no easy escape
  For a woman, nor can she say no to her marriage.    235
  She arrives among new modes of behaviour and manners,
  And needs prophetic power, unless she has learnt at home,
  How best to manage him who shares the bed with her.
  And if we work out all this well and carefully,
  And the husband lives with us and lightly bears his yoke,    240
  Then life is enviable. If not, I'd rather die.
  A man, when he's tired of the company in his home,
  Goes out of the house and puts an end to his boredom
  And turns to a friend or companion of his own age.
  But we are forced to keep our eyes on one alone.    245
  What they say of us is that we have a peaceful time
  Living at home, while they do the fighting in war.
  How wrong they are! I would very much rather stand
  Three times in the front of battle than bear one child.
  Yet what applies to me does not apply to you.    250
  You have a country. Your family home is here.
  You enjoy life and the company of your friends.

220. *a foreigner . . . himself:* Foreign residents were encouraged to come to Athens, but were rarely admitted to the rights of full citizenship, which was a jealously guarded privilege.

229. *women:* Athenian rights and institutions were made for men; the women had few privileges and almost no legal rights. The following two lines refer to the dowry which had to be provided for the bride.

But I am deserted, a refugee, thought nothing of
By my husband,—something he won in a foreign land.
I have no mother or brother, nor any relation                    255
With whom I can take refuge in this sea of woe.
This much then is the service I would beg from you:
If I can find the means or devise any scheme
To pay my husband back for what he has done to me,—
Him and his father-in-law and the girl who married him,—    260
Just to keep silent. For in other ways a woman
Is full of fear, defenceless, dreads the sight of cold
Steel; but, when once she is wronged in the matter of love,
No other soul can hold so many thoughts of blood.
CHOR. This I will promise. You are in the right, Medea,          265
In paying your husband back. I am not surprised at you
For being sad.
     But look! I see our king Kreon
Approaching. He will tell us of some new plan.
  [*Enter, from the right,* KREON, *with attendants.*]
KREON. You, with that angry look, so set against your husband,
Medea, I order you to leave my territories                        270
An exile, and take along with you your two children,
And not to waste time doing it. It is my decree,
And I will see it done. I will not return home
Until you are cast from the boundaries of my land.
MEDEA. Oh, this is the end for me. I am utterly lost.           275
Now I am in the full force of the storm of hate
And have no harbour from ruin to reach easily.
Yet still, in spite of it all, I'll ask the question:
What is your reason, Kreon, for banishing me?
KREON. I am afraid of you,—why should I dissemble it?—      280
Afraid that you may injure my daughter mortally.
Many things accumulate to support my feeling.
You are a clever woman, versed in evil arts,
And are angry at having lost your husband's love.
I hear that you are threatening, so they tell me,               285
To do something against my daughter and Jason
And me, too. I shall take my precautions first.
I tell you, I prefer to earn your hatred now
Than to be soft-hearted and afterwards regret it.
MEDEA. This is not the first time, Kreon. Often previously       290
Through being considered clever I have suffered much.
A person of sense ought never to have his children
Brought up to be more clever than the average.
For, apart from cleverness bringing them no profit,
It will make them objects of envy and ill-will.                  295

If you put new ideas before the eyes of fools
They'll think you foolish and worthless into the bargain;
And if you are thought superior to those who have
Some reputation for learning, you will become hated.
I have some knowledge myself of how this happens;     300
For being clever, I find that some will envy me,
Others object to me. Yet all my cleverness
Is not so much.
            Well, then, are you frightened, Kreon,
That I should harm you? There is no need. It is not
My way to transgress the authority of a king.     305
How have you injured me? You gave your daughter away
To the man you wanted. O, certainly I hate
My husband, but you, I think, have acted wisely;
Nor do I grudge it you that your affairs go well.
May the marriage be a lucky one! Only let me     310
Live in this land. For even though I have been wronged,
I will not raise my voice, but submit to my betters.
KREON. What you say sounds gentle enough. Still in my heart
I greatly dread that you are plotting some evil,
And therefore I trust you even less than before.     315
A sharp-tempered woman, or for that matter a man,
Is easier to deal with than the clever type
Who holds her tongue. No. You must go. No need for more
Speeches. The thing is fixed. By no manner of means
Shall you, an enemy of mine, stay in my country.     320
MEDEA. I beg you. By your knees, by your new-wedded girl.
KREON. Your words are wasted. You will never persuade me.
MEDEA. Will you drive me out, and give no heed to my prayers?
KREON. I will, for I love my family more than you.
MEDEA. O my country! How bitterly now I remember you!     325
KREON. I love my country too,—next after my children.
MEDEA. O what an evil to men is passionate love!
KREON. That would depend on the luck that goes along with it.
MEDEA. O God, do not forget who is the cause of this!
KREON. Go. It is no use. Spare me the pain of forcing you.     330
MEDEA. I'm spared no pain. I lack no pain to be spared me.
KREON. Then you'll be removed by force by one of my men.
MEDEA. No, Kreon, not that! But do listen, I beg you.
KREON. Woman, you seem to want to create a disturbance.
MEDEA. I *will* go into exile. *This* is not what I beg for.     335
KREON. Why then this violence and clinging to my hand?
MEDEA. Allow me to remain here just for this one day,
So I may consider where to live in my exile,
And look for support for my children, since their father

Chooses to make no kind of provision for them.    340
Have pity on them! You have children of your own.
It is natural for you to look kindly on them.
For myself I do not mind if I go into exile.
It is the children being in trouble that I mind.
KREON. There is nothing tyrannical about my nature,    345
And by showing mercy I have often been the loser.
Even now I know that I am making a mistake.
All the same you shall have your will. But this I tell you,
That if the light of heaven tomorrow shall see you,
You and your children in the confines of my land,    350
You die. This word I have spoken is firmly fixed.
But now, if you must stay, stay for this day alone.
For in it you can do none of the things I fear.
   [*Exit* KREON *with his attendants.*]
CHOR. Oh, unfortunate one! Oh, cruel!
Where will you turn? Who will help you?    355
What house or what land to preserve you
From ill can you find?
Medea, a god has thrown suffering
Upon you in waves of despair.
MEDEA. Things have gone badly every way. No doubt of that    360
But not these things this far, and don't imagine so.
There are still trials to come for the new-wedded pair,
And for their relations pain that will mean something.
Do you think that I would ever have fawned on that man
Unless I had some end to gain or profit in it?    365
I would not even have spoken or touched him with my hands.
But he has got to such a pitch of foolishness
That, though he could have made nothing of all my plans
By exiling me, he has given me this one day
To stay here, and in this I will make dead bodies    370
Of three of my enemies,—father, the girl and my husband.
I have many ways of death which I might suit to them,
And do not know, friends, which one to take in hand;
Whether to set fire underneath their bridal mansion,
Or sharpen a sword and thrust it to the heart,    375
Stealing into the palace where the bed is made.
There is just one obstacle to this. If I am caught
Breaking into the house and scheming against it,
I shall die, and give my enemies cause for laughter.
It is best to go by the straight road, the one in which    380
I am most skilled, and make away with them by poison.
So be it then.

And now suppose them dead. What town will receive me?
What friend will offer me a refuge in his land,
Or the guarantee of his house and save my own life? 385
There is none. So I must wait a little time yet,
And if some sure defence should then appear for me,
In craft and silence I will set about this murder.
But if my fate should drive me on without help,
Even though death is certain, I will take the sword 390
Myself and kill, and steadfastly advance to crime.
It shall not be,—I swear it by her, my mistress,
Whom most I honour and have chosen as partner,
Hecate, who dwells in the recesses of my hearth,—
That any man shall be glad to have injured me. 395
Bitter I will make their marriage for them and mournful,
Bitter the alliance and the driving me out of the land.
Ah, come, Medea, in your plotting and scheming
Leave nothing untried of all those things which you know.
Go forward to the dreadful act. The test has come 400
For resolution. You see how you are treated. Never
Shall you be mocked by Jason's Corinthian wedding,
Whose father was noble, whose grandfather Helios.
You have the skill. What is more, you were born a woman,
And women, though most helpless in doing good deeds, 405
Are of every evil the cleverest of contrivers.

CHOR. Flow backward to your sources, sacred rivers,
And let the world's great order be reversed.
It is the thoughts of *men* that are deceitful,
*Their* pledges that are loose. 410
Story shall now turn my condition to a fair one,
Women are paid their due.
No more shall evil-sounding fame be theirs.

Cease now, you muses of the ancient singers,
To tell the tale of my unfaithfulness; 415
For not on us did Phoebus, lord of music,
Bestow the lyre's divine
Power, for otherwise I should have sung an answer
To the other sex. Long time
Has much to tell of us, and much of them. 420

You sailed away from your father's home,
With a heart on fire you passed

394. *Hecate:* the patron of witch-craft, sometimes identified with Artemis. Medea has a statue and shrine of Hecate in the house.

403. *Helios:* the sun, father of Medea's father, Aeëtes.
416. *Phoebus:* Apollo.

The double rocks of the sea.
And now in a foreign country
You have lost your rest in a widowed bed,                    425
And are driven forth, a refugee
In dishonour from the land.

Good faith has gone, and no more remains
In great Greece a sense of shame.
It has flown away to the sky.                                430
No father's house for a haven
Is at hand for you now, and another queen
Of your bed has dispossessed you and
Is mistress of your home.
        [*Enter* JASON, *with attendants.*]
JASON. This is not the first occasion that I have noticed     435
How hopeless it is to deal with a stubborn temper.
For, with reasonable submission to our ruler's will,
You might have lived in this land and kept your home.
As it is you are going to be exiled for your loose speaking.
Not that I mind myself. You are free to continue             440
Telling everyone that Jason is a worthless man.
But as to your talk about the king, consider
Yourself most lucky that exile is your punishment.
I, for my part, have always tried to calm down
The anger of the king, and wished you to remain.             445
But you will not give up your folly, continually
Speaking ill of him, and so you are going to be banished.
All the same, and in spite of your conduct, I'll not desert
My friends, but have come to make some provision for you,
So that you and the children may not be penniless            450
Or in need of anything in exile. Certainly
Exile brings many troubles with it. And even
If you hate me, I cannot think badly of you.
MEDEA. O coward in every way,—that is what I call you,
With bitterest reproach for your lack of manliness,          455
You have come, you, my worst enemy, have come to me!
It is not an example of over-confidence
Or of boldness thus to look your friends in the face,
Friends you have injured,—no, it is the worst of all
Human diseases, shamelessness. But you did well              460
To come, for I can speak ill of you and lighten
My heart, and you will suffer while you are listening.
And first I will begin from what happened first.
I saved your life, and every Greek knows I saved it,
Who was a ship-mate of yours aboard the Argo,                465

When you were sent to control the bulls that breathed fire
And yoke them, and when you would sow that deadly field.
Also that snake, who encircled with his many folds
The Golden Fleece and guarded it and never slept,
I killed, and so gave you the safety of the light. 470
And I myself betrayed my father and my home,
And came with you to Pelias' land of Iolcos.
And then, showing more willingness to help than wisdom,
I killed him, Pelias, with a most dreadful death
At his own daughters' hands, and took away your fear. 475
This is how I behaved to you, you wretched man,
And you forsook me, took another bride to bed
Though you had children; for, if that had not been,
You would have had an excuse for another wedding.
Faith in your word has gone. Indeed I cannot tell 480
Whether you think the gods whose names you swore by then
Have ceased to rule and that new standards are set up,
Since you must know you have broken your word to me.
O my right hand, and the knees which you often clasped
In supplication, how senselessly I am treated 485
By this bad man, and how my hopes have missed their mark!
Come, I will share my thoughts as though you were a friend,—
You! Can I think that you would ever treat me well?
But I will do it, and these questions will make you
Appear the baser. Where am I to go? To my father's? 490
Him I betrayed and his land when I came with you.
To Pelias' wretched daughters? What a fine welcome
They would prepare for me who murdered their father!
For this is my position,—hated by my friends
At home, I have, in kindness to you, made enemies 495
Of others whom there was no need to have injured.
And how happy among Greek women you have made me
On your side for all this! A distinguished husband
I have,—for breaking promises. When in misery
I am cast out of the land and go into exile, 500
Quite without friends and all alone with my children,
That will be a fine shame for the new-wedded groom,
For his children to wander as beggars and she who saved him.
O God, you have given to mortals a sure method
Of telling the gold that is pure from the counterfeit; 505
Why is there no mark engraved upon men's bodies,

---

466. *bulls . . . fire:* This and the
following lines refer to ordeals through
which Jason had to pass to win the
Fleece, and in which Medea helped
him. He had to yoke a team of fire-
breathing bulls, then sow a field which
immediately sprouted armed warriors,
then deal with the snake which guarded
the Fleece.

By which we could know the true ones from the false ones?
CHOR. It is a strange form of anger, difficult to cure
    When two friends turn upon each other in hatred.
JASON. As for me, it seems I must be no bad speaker.                      510
    But, like a man who has a good grip of the tiller,
    Reef up his sail, and so run away from under
    This mouthing tempest, woman, of your bitter tongue.
    Since you insist on building up your kindness to me,
    My view is that Cypris was alone responsible                         515
    Of men and gods for the preserving of my life.
    You are clever enough,—but really I need not enter
    Into the story of how it was love's inescapable
    Power that compelled you to keep my person safe.
    On this I will not go into too much detail.                          520
    In so far as you helped me, you did well enough.
    But on this question of saving me, I can prove
    You have certainly got from me more than you gave.
    Firstly, instead of living among barbarians,
    You inhabit a Greek land and understand our ways,                    525
    How to live by law instead of the sweet will of force.
    And all the Greeks considered you a clever woman.
    You were honoured for it; while, if you were living at
    The ends of the earth, nobody would have heard of you.
    For my part, rather than stores of gold in my house                  530
    Or power to sing even sweeter songs than Orpheus,
    I'd choose the fate that made me a distinguished man.
    There is my reply to your story of my labours.
    Remember it was you who started the argument.
    Next for your attack on my wedding with the princess:                535
    Here I will prove that, first, it was a clever move,
    Secondly, a wise one, and, finally, that I made it
    In your best interests and the children's. Please keep calm.
    When I arrived here from the land of Iolcos,
    Involved, as I was, in every kind of difficulty,                     540
    What luckier chance could I have come across than this,
    An exile to marry the daughter of the king?
    It was not,—the point that seems to upset you—that I
    Grew tired of your bed and felt the need of a new bride;
    Nor with any wish to outdo your number of children.                  545
    We have enough already. I am quite content.
    But,—this was the main reason—that we might live well,
    And not be short of anything. I know that all
    A man's friends leave him stone-cold if he becomes poor.
    Also that I might bring my children up worthily                      550

515. *Cypris:* Aphrodite, goddess of love.

Of my position, and, by producing more of them
To be brothers of yours, we would draw the families
Together and all be happy. You need no children.
And it pays me to do good to those I have now
By having others. Do you think this a bad plan?                555
You wouldn't if the love question hadn't upset you.
But you women have got into such a state of mind
That, if your life at night is good, you think you have
Everything; but, if in that quarter things go wrong,
You will consider your best and truest interests             560
Most hateful. It would have been better far for men
To have got their children in some other way, and women
Not to have existed. Then life would have been good.
CHOR. Jason, though you have made this speech of yours look well,
Still I think, even though others do not agree,              565
You have betrayed your wife and are acting badly.
MEDEA. Surely in many ways I hold different views
From others, for I think that the plausible speaker
Who is a villain deserves the greatest punishment.
Confident in his tongue's power to adorn evil,              570
He stops at nothing. Yet he is not really wise.
As in your case. There is no need to put on the airs
Of a clever speaker, for one word will lay you flat.
If you were not a coward, you would not have married
Behind my back, but discussed it with me first.            575
JASON. And you, no doubt, would have furthered the proposal,
If I had told you of it, you who even now
Are incapable of controlling your bitter temper.
MEDEA. It was not that. No, you thought it was not respectable
As you got on in years to have a foreign wife.             580
JASON. Make sure of this: it was not because of a woman
I made the royal alliance in which I now live,
But, as I said before, I wished to preserve you
And breed a royal progeny to be brothers
To the children I have now, a sure defence to us.          585
MEDEA. Let me have no happy fortune that brings pain with it,
Or prosperity which is upsetting to the mind!
JASON. Change your ideas of what you want, and show more
     sense.
Do not consider painful what is good for you,
Nor, when you are lucky, think yourself unfortunate.       590
MEDEA. You can insult me. You have somewhere to turn to.
But I shall go from this land into exile, friendless.
JASON. It was what you chose yourself. Don't blame others for it.
MEDEA. And how did I choose it? Did I betray my husband?

JASON. You called down wicked curses on the king's family.     595
MEDEA. A curse, that is what I am become to your house too.
JASON. I do not propose to go into all the rest of it;
   But, if you wish for the children or for yourself
   In exile to have some of my money to help you,
   Say so, for I am prepared to give with open hand,     600
   Or to provide you with introductions to my friends
   Who will treat you well. You are a fool if you do not
   Accept this. Cease your anger and you will profit.
MEDEA. I shall never accept the favours of friends of yours,
   Nor take a thing from you, so you need not offer it.     605
   There is no benefit in the gifts of a bad man.
JASON. Then, in any case, I call the gods to witness that
   I wish to help you and the children in every way,
   But you refuse what is good for you. Obstinately
   You push away your friends. You are sure to suffer for it.     610
MEDEA. Go! No doubt you hanker for your virginal bride,
   And are guilty of lingering too long out of her house.
   Enjoy your wedding. But perhaps,—with the help of God—
   You will make the kind of marriage that you will regret.
     [JASON *goes out with his attendants.*]
CHOR. When love is in excess     615
   It brings a man no honour
   Nor any worthiness.
   But if in moderation Cypris comes,
   There is no other power at all so gracious.
   O goddess, never on me let loose the unerring     620
   Shaft of your bow in the poison of desire.

   Let my heart be wise.
   It is the gods' best gift.
   On me let mighty Cypris
   Inflict no wordy wars or restless anger     625
   To urge my passion to a different love.
   But with discernment may she guide women's weddings,
   Honouring most what is peaceful in the bed.

   O country and home,
   Never, never may I be without you,     630
   Living the hopeless life,
   Hard to pass through and painful,
   Most pitiable of all.
   Let death first lay me low and death
   Free me from this daylight.     635
   There is no sorrow above
   The loss of a native land.

I have seen it myself,
Do not tell of a secondhand story.
Neither city nor friend                                          640
Pitied you when you suffered
The worst of sufferings.
O let him die ungraced whose heart
Will not reward his friends,
Who cannot open an honest mind                                   645
No friend will he be of mine.

[*Enter* AIGEUS, *king of Athens, an old friend of* MEDEA.]

AIGEUS. Medea, greeting! This is the best introduction
Of which men know for conversation between friends.
MEDEA. Greeting to you too, Aigeus, son of King Pandion,
Where have you come from to visit this country's soil?          650
AIGEUS. I have just left the ancient oracle of Phoebus.
MEDEA. And why did you go to earth's prophetic centre?
AIGEUS. I went to inquire how children might be born to me.
MEDEA. Is it so? Your life still up to this point childless?
AIGEUS. Yes. By the fate of some power we have no children.     655
MEDEA. Have you a wife, or is there none to share your bed?
AIGEUS. There is. Yes, I am joined to my wife in marriage.
MEDEA. And what did Phoebus say to you about children?
AIGEUS. Words too wise for a mere man to guess their meaning.
MEDEA. Is it proper for me to be told the God's reply?          660
AIGEUS. It is. For sure what is needed is cleverness.
MEDEA. Then what was his message? Tell me, if I may hear.
AIGEUS. I am not to loosen the hanging foot of the wine-skin . . .
MEDEA. Until you have done something, or reached some country?
AIGEUS. Until I return again to my hearth and house.            665
MEDEA. And for what purpose have you journeyed to this land?
AIGEUS. There is a man called Pittheus, king of Troezen.
MEDEA. A son of Pelops, they say, a most righteous man.
AIGEUS. With him I wish to discuss the reply of the god.
MEDEA. Yes. He is wise and experienced in such matters.         670
AIGEUS. And to me also the dearest of all my spear-friends.
MEDEA. Well, I hope you have good luck, and achieve your will.
AIGEUS. But why this downcast eye of yours, and this pale cheek?
MEDEA. O Aigeus, my husband has been the worst of all to me.
AIGEUS. What do you mean? Say clearly what has caused this
    grief.                                                      675
MEDEA. Jason wrongs me, though I have never injured him.

647. *Aigeus:* Aegeus.
663. *not to loosen . . . wine-skin:*
This cryptic phrase probably means
"not to have intercourse."

667. *Pittheus:* Aigeus' father-in-law.
*Troezen:* in the Peloponnese. Corinth
was on the way from Delphi to Troezen.
671. *spear-friends:* allies in war,
companions in fighting.

AIGEUS. What has he done? Tell me about it in clearer words.
MEDEA. He has taken a wife to his house, supplanting me.
AIGEUS. Surely he would not dare to do a thing like that.
MEDEA. Be sure he has. Once dear, I now am slighted by him. 680
AIGEUS. Did he fall in love? Or is he tired of your love?
MEDEA. He was greatly in love, this traitor to his friends.
AIGEUS. Then let him go, if, as you say, he is so bad.
MEDEA. A passionate love,—for an alliance with the king.
AIGEUS. And who gave him his wife? Tell me the rest of it. 685
MEDEA. It was Kreon, he who rules this land of Corinth.
AIGEUS. Indeed, Medea, your grief was understandable.
MEDEA. I am ruined. And there is more to come: I am banished.
AIGEUS. Banished? By whom? Here you tell me of a new wrong.
MEDEA. Kreon drives me an exile from the land of Corinth. 690
AIGEUS. Does Jason consent? I cannot approve of this.
MEDEA. He pretends not to, but he will put up with it.

Ah, Aigeus, I beg and beseech you, by your beard
And by your knees I am making myself your suppliant,
Have pity on me, have pity on your poor friend, 695
And do not let me go into exile desolate,
But receive me in your land and at your very hearth.
So may your love, with God's help, lead to the bearing
Of children, and so may you yourself die happy.
You do not know what a chance you have come on here. 700
I will end your childlessness, and I will make you able
To beget children. The drugs I know can do this.
AIGEUS. For many reasons, woman, I am anxious to do
This favour for you. First, for the sake of the gods,
And then for the birth of children which you promise, 705
For in that respect I am entirely at my wits' end.
But this is my position: if you reach my land,
I, being in my rights, will try to befriend you.
But this much I must warn you of beforehand:
I shall not agree to take you out of this country; 710
But if you by yourself can reach my house, then you
Shall stay there safely. To none will I give you up.
But from this land you must make your escape yourself,
For I do not wish to incur blame from my friends.
MEDEA. It shall be so. But, if I might have a pledge from you 715
For this, then I would have from you all I desire.
AIGEUS. Do you not trust me? What is it rankles with you?
MEDEA. I trust you, yes. But the house of Pelias hates me,
And so does Kreon. If you are bound by this oath,
When they try to drag me from your land, you will not 720
Abandon me; but if our pact is only words,

With no oath to the gods, you will be lightly armed,
Unable to resist their summons. I am weak,
While they have wealth to help them and a royal house.
AIGEUS. You show much foresight for such negotiations.     725
Well, if you will have it so, I will not refuse.
For, both on my side this will be the safest way
To have some excuse to put forward to your enemies,
And for you it is more certain. You may name the gods.
MEDEA. Swear by the plain of Earth, and Helios, father     730
Of my father, and name together all the gods. . . .
AIGEUS. That I will act or not act in what way? Speak.
MEDEA. That you yourself will never cast me from your land,
Nor, if any of my enemies should demand me,
Will you, in your life, willingly hand me over.     735
AIGEUS. I swear by the Earth, by the holy light of Helios,
By all the gods, I will abide by this you say.
MEDEA. Enough. And, if you fail, what shall happen to you?
AIGEUS. What comes to those who have no regard for heaven.
MEDEA. Go on your way. Farewell. For I am satisfied,     740
And I will reach your city as soon as I can,
Having done the deed I have to do and gained my end.
          [AIGEUS *goes out.*]
CHOR. May Hermes, god of travellers,
Escort you, Aigeus, to your home!
And may you have the things you wish     745
So eagerly; for you
Appear to me to be a generous man.
MEDEA. God, and God's daughter, justice, and light of Helios!
Now, friends, has come the time of my triumph over
My enemies, and now my foot is on the road.     750
Now I am confident they will pay the penalty.
For this man, Aigeus, has been like a harbour to me
In all my plans just where I was most distressed.
To him I can fasten the cable of my safety
When I have reached the town and fortress of Pallas.     755
And now I shall tell to you the whole of my plan.
Listen to these words that are not spoken idly.
I shall send one of my servants to find Jason
And request him to come once more into my sight.
And when he comes, the words I'll say will be soft ones.     760
I'll say that I agree with him, that I approve
The royal wedding he has made, betraying me.
I'll say it was profitable, an excellent idea.
But I shall beg that my children may remain here:

755. *town* . . . *Pallas:* Athens, city of Pallas Athene.

Not that I would leave in a country that hates me          765
Children of mine to feel their enemies' insults,
But that by a trick I may kill the king's daughter.
For I will send the children with gifts in their hands
To carry to the bride, so as not to be banished,—
A finely woven dress and a golden diadem.                 770
And if she takes them and wears them upon her skin
She and all who touch the girl will die in agony;
Such poison will I lay upon the gifts I send.
But there, however, I must leave that account paid.
I weep to think of what a deed I have to do               775
Next after that; for I shall kill my own children.
My children, there is none who can give them safety.
And when I have ruined the whole of Jason's house,
I shall leave the land and flee from the murder of my
Dear children, and I shall have done a dreadful deed.     780
For it is not bearable to be mocked by enemies.
So it must happen. What profit have I in life?
I have no land, no home, no refuge from my pain.
My mistake was made the time I left behind me
My father's house, and trusted the words of a Greek,      785
Who, with heaven's help, will pay me the price for that.
For those children he had from me he will never
See alive again, nor will he on his new bride
Beget another child, for she is to be forced
To die a most terrible death by these my poisons.         790
Let no one think me a weak one, feeble-spirited,
A stay-at-home, but rather just the opposite,
One who can hurt my enemies and help my friends;
For the lives of such persons are most remembered.
CHOR. Since you have shared the knowledge of your plan with us,  795
I both wish to help you and support the normal
Ways of mankind, and tell you not to do this thing.
MEDEA. I can do no other thing. It is understandable
For you to speak thus. You have not suffered as I have.
CHOR. But can you have the heart to kill your flesh and blood?   800
MEDEA. Yes, for this is the best way to wound my husband.
CHOR. And you too. Of women you will be most unhappy.
MEDEA. So it must be. No compromise is possible.
    [*She turns to the* NURSE.]
Go, you, at once, and tell Jason to come to me.
You I employ on all affairs of greatest trust.           805
Say nothing of these decisions which I have made,
If you love your mistress, if you were born a woman.
CHOR. From of old the children of Erechtheus are

808. *Erechtheus:* an early king of Athens, a son of Hephaestus.

Splendid, the sons of blessed gods. They dwell
In Athens' holy and unconquered land,                          810
Where famous Wisdom feeds them and they pass gaily
Always through that most brilliant air where once, they say,
That golden Harmony gave birth to the nine
Pure Muses of Pieria.

And beside the sweet flow of Cephisos' stream,                 815
Where Cypris sailed, they say, to draw the water,
And mild soft breezes breathed along her path,
And on her hair were flung the sweet-smelling garlands
Of flowers of roses by the Lovers, the companions
Of Wisdom, her escort, the helpers of men                      820
In every kind of excellence.

How then can these holy rivers
Or this holy land love you,
Or the city find you a home,
You, who will kill your children,                              825
You, not pure with the rest?
O think of the blow at your children
And think of the blood that you shed.
O, over and over I beg you,
By your knees I beg you do not                                 830
Be the murderess of your babes!

O where will you find the courage
Or the skill of hand and heart,
When you set yourself to attempt
A deed so dreadful to do?                                       835
How, when you look upon them,
Can you tearlessly hold the decision
For murder? You will not be able,
When your children fall down and implore you,
You will not be able to dip                                    840
Steadfast your hand in their blood.

    [*Enter* JASON *with attendants.*]

JASON. I have come at your request. Indeed, although you are
    Bitter against me, this you shall have: I will listen
    To what new thing you want, woman, to get from me.

---

810. *unconquered:* It was the Athenians' boast that their descent from the original settlers was uninterrupted by any invasion. There is a topical reference here, for the play was produced in 431 B.C., in a time of imminent war.

809–814. *They dwell . . . Pieria:* The sentence means that the fortunate balance ("Harmony") of the elements and the genius of the people produced the cultivation of the arts ("the nine pure Muses"). Pieria was a fountain in Boeotia where the Muses were supposed to live.

815. *Cephisos:* an Athenian river. Cypris, mentioned in the next line, is the goddess of love and therefore of the principle of fertility.

MEDEA. Jason, I beg you to be forgiving towards me                    845
For what I said. It is natural for you to bear with
My temper, since we have had much love together.
I have talked with myself about this and I have
Reproached myself. 'Fool' I said, 'why am I so mad?
Why am I set against those who have planned wisely?        850
Why make myself an enemy of the authorities
And of my husband, who does the best thing for me
By marrying royalty and having children who
Will be as brothers to my own? What is wrong with me?
Let me give up anger, for the gods are kind to me.           855
Have I not children, and do I not know that we
In exile from our country must be short of friends?'
When I considered this I saw that I had shown
Great lack of sense, and that my anger was foolish.
Now I agree with you. I think that you are wise              860
In having this other wife as well as me, and I
Was mad. I should have helped you in these plans of yours,
Have joined in the wedding, stood by the marriage bed,
Have taken pleasure in attendance on your bride.
But we women are what we are,—perhaps a little              865
Worthless; and you men must not be like us in this,
Nor be foolish in return when we are foolish.
Now I give in, and admit that then I was wrong.
I have come to a better understanding now.
  [*She turns towards the house.*]
Children, come here, my children, come outdoors to us!       870
Welcome your father with me, and say goodbye to him,
And with your mother, who just now was his enemy,
Join again in making friends with him who loves us.
  [*Enter the* CHILDREN, *attended by the* TUTOR.]
We have made peace, and all our anger is over.
Take hold of his right hand,—O God, I am thinking            875
Of something which may happen in the secret future.
O children, will you just so, after a long life,
Hold out your loving arms at the grave? O children,
How ready to cry I am, how full of foreboding!
I am ending at last this quarrel with your father,           880
And, look, my soft eyes have suddenly filled with tears.
CHOR. And the pale tears have started also in my eyes.
  O may the trouble not grow worse than now it is!
JASON. I approve of what you say. And I cannot blame you
  Even for what you said before. It is natural               885
  For a woman to be wild with her husband when he
  Goes in for secret love. But now your mind has turned

To better reasoning. In the end you have come to
The right decision, like the clever woman you are.
And of you, children, your father is taking care.                890
He has made, with God's help, ample provision for you.
For I think that a time will come when you will be
The leading people in Corinth with your brothers.
You must grow up. As to the future, your father
And those of the gods who love him will deal with that.        895
I want to see you, when you have become young men,
Healthy and strong, better men than my enemies.
Medea, why are your eyes all wet with pale tears?
Why is your cheek so white and turned away from me?
Are not these words of mine pleasing for you to hear?          900

MEDEA. It is nothing. I was thinking about these children.

JASON. You must be cheerful. I shall look after them well.

MEDEA. I will be. It is not that I distrust your words,
But a woman is a frail thing, prone to crying.

JASON. But why then should you grieve so much for these
children?                                                      905

MEDEA. I am their mother. When you prayed that they might
live
I felt unhappy to think that these things will be.
But come, I have said something of the things I meant
To say to you, and now I will tell you the rest.
Since it is the king's will to banish me from here,—          910
And for me too I know that this is the best thing,
Not to be in your way by living here or in
The king's way, since they think me ill-disposed to them,—
I then am going into exile from this land;
But do you, so that you may have the care of them,            915
Beg Kreon that the children may not be banished.

JASON. I doubt if I'll succeed, but still I'll attempt it.

MEDEA. Then you must tell your wife to beg from her father
That the children may be reprieved from banishment.

JASON. I will, and with her I shall certainly succeed.        920

MEDEA. If she is like the rest of us women, you will.
And I too will take a hand with you in this business,
For I will send her some gifts which are far fairer,
I am sure of it, than those which now are in fashion,
A finely-woven dress and a golden diadem,                      925
And the children shall present them. Quick, let one of you
Servants bring here to me that beautiful dress.

[*One of her attendants goes into the house.*]

She will be happy not in one way, but in a hundred,
Having so fine a man as you to share her bed,

And with this beautiful dress which Helios of old,　930
My father's father, bestowed on his descendants.
　　[*Enter attendant carrying the poisoned dress and diadem.*]
There, children, take these wedding presents in your hands.
Take them to the royal princess, the happy bride,
And give them to her. She will not think little of them.
JASON. No, don't be foolish, and empty your hands of these.　935
Do you think the palace is short of dresses to wear?
Do you think there is no gold there? Keep them, don't give them
Away. If my wife considers me of any value,
She will think more of me than money, I am sure of it.
MEDEA. No, let me have my way. They say the gods themselves　940
Are moved by gifts, and gold does more with men than words.
Hers is the luck, her fortune that which god blesses;
She is young and a princess; but for my children's reprieve
I would give my very life, and not gold only.
Go children, go together to that rich palace,　945
Be suppliants to the new wife of your father,
My lady, beg her not to let you be banished.
And give her the dress,—for this is of great importance,
That she should take the gift into her hand from yours.
Go, quick as you can. And bring your mother good news　950
By your success of those things which she longs to gain.
　　[JASON *goes out with his attendants, followed by the* TUTOR
　　*and the* CHILDREN *carrying the poisoned gifts.*]
CHOR. Now there is no hope left for the children's lives.
Now there is none. They are walking already to murder.
The bride, poor bride, will accept the curse of the gold,
Will accept the bright diadem.　955
Around her yellow hair she will set that dress
Of death with her own hands.
The grace and the perfume and glow of the golden robe
Will charm her to put them upon her and wear the wreath,
And now her wedding will be with the dead below,　960
Into such a trap she will fall,
Poor thing, into such a fate of death and never
Escape from under that curse.

You too, O wretched bridegroom, making your match with kings,
You do not see that you bring　965
Destruction on your children and on her,
Your wife, a fearful death.
Poor soul, what a fall is yours!

In your grief too I weep, mother of little children,
You who will murder your own,　970

In vengeance for the loss of married love
Which Jason has betrayed
As he lives with another wife.

[*Enter the* TUTOR *with the* CHILDREN.]

TUTOR. Mistress, I tell you that these children are reprieved,
And the royal bride has been pleased to take in her hands     975
Your gifts. In that quarter the children are secure.
But come,
Why do you stand confused when you are fortunate?
Why have you turned round with your cheek away from me?
Are not these words of mine pleasing for you to hear?     980

MEDEA. Oh! I am lost!

TUTOR. That word is not in harmony with my tidings.

MEDEA. I am lost, I am lost!

TUTOR.                         Am I in ignorance telling you
Of some disaster, and not the good news I thought?

MEDEA. You have told what you have told. I do not blame you.     985

TUTOR. Why then this downcast eye, and this weeping of tears?

MEDEA. Oh, I am forced to weep, old man. The gods and I,
I in a kind of madness have contrived all this.

TUTOR. Courage! You too will be brought home by your children.

MEDEA. Ah, before that happens I shall bring others home.     990

TUTOR. Others before you have been parted from their children.
Mortals must bear in resignation their ill luck.

MEDEA. That is what I shall do. But go inside the house,
And do for the children your usual daily work.

[*The* TUTOR *goes into the house.* MEDEA *turns to her*
CHILDREN.]

O children, O my children, you have a city,     995
You have a home, and you can leave me behind you,
And without your mother you may live there for ever.
But I am going in exile to another land
Before I have seen you happy and taken pleasure in you,
Before I have dressed your brides and made your marriage beds
And held up the torch at the ceremony of wedding.     1001
Oh, what a wretch I am in this my self-willed thought!
What was the purpose, children, for which I reared you?
For all my travail and wearing myself away?
They were sterile, those pains I had in the bearing of you.     1005
O surely once the hopes in you I had, poor me,
Were high ones: you would look after me in old age,
And when I died would deck me well with your own hands;
A thing which all would have done. O but now it is gone,
That lovely thought. For, once I am left without you,     1010
Sad will be the life I'll lead and sorrowful for me.

And you will never see your mother again with
Your dear eyes, gone to another mode of living.
Why, children, do you look upon me with your eyes?
Why do you smile so sweetly that last smile of all?                1015
Oh, Oh, what can I do? My spirit has gone from me,
Friends, when I saw that bright look in the children's eyes.
I cannot bear to do it. I renounce my plans
I had before. I'll take my children away from
This land. Why should I hurt their father with the pain          1020
They feel, and suffer twice as much of pain myself?
No, no, I will not do it. I renounce my plans.
Ah, what is wrong with me? Do I want to let go
My enemies unhurt and be laughed at for it?
I must face this thing. Oh, but what a weak woman                1025
Even to admit to my mind these soft arguments.
Children, go into the house. And he whom law forbids
To stand in attendance at my sacrifices,
Let him see to it. I shall not mar my handiwork.
Oh! Oh!                                                          1030
Do not, O my heart, you must not do these things!
Poor heart, let them go, have pity upon the children.
If they live with you in Athens they will cheer you.
No! By Hell's avenging furies it shall not be,—
This shall never be, that I should suffer my children           1035
To be the prey of my enemies' insolence.
Every way is it fixed. The bride will not escape.
No, the diadem is now upon her head, and she,
The royal princess, is dying in the dress, I know it.
But,—for it is the most dreadful of roads for me                1040
To tread, and them I shall send on a more dreadful still—
I wish to speak to the children.
　　　　[*She calls the* CHILDREN *to her.*]
　　　　　　　　　　　　　　Come, children, give
Me your hands, give your mother your hands to kiss them.
O the dear hands, and O how dear are these lips to me,          1045
And the generous eyes and the bearing of my children!
I wish you happiness, but not here in this world.
What is here your father took. O how good to hold you!
How delicate the skin, how sweet the breath of children!
Go, go! I am no longer able, no longer                          1050
To look upon you. I am overcome by sorrow.
　　　　[*The* CHILDREN *go into the house.*]
I know indeed what evil I intend to do,
But stronger than all my afterthoughts is my fury,
Fury that brings upon mortals the greatest evils.

[*She goes out to the right, towards the royal palace.*]

CHOR. Often before                                                    1055
  I have gone through more subtle reasons,
  And have come upon questionings greater
  Than a woman should strive to search out.
  But we too have a goddess to help us
  And accompany us into wisdom.                                 1060
  Not all of us. Still you will find
  Among many women a few,
  And our sex is not without learning.
  This I say, that those who have never
  Had children, who know nothing of it,                          1065
  In happiness have the advantage
  Over those who are parents.
  The childless, who never discover
  Whether children turn out as a good thing
  Or as something to cause pain, are spared                      1070
  Many troubles in lacking this knowledge.
  And those who have in their homes
  The sweet presence of children, I see that their lives
  Are all wasted away by their worries.
  First they must think how to bring them up well and            1075
  How to leave them something to live on.
  And then after this whether all their toil
  Is for those who will turn out good or bad,
  Is still an unanswered question.
  And of one more trouble, the last of all,                      1080
  That is common to mortals I tell.
  For suppose you have found them enough for their living,
  Suppose that the children have grown into youth
  And have turned out good, still, if God so wills it,
  Death will away with your children's bodies,                   1085
  And carry them off into Hades.
  What is our profit, then, that for the sake of
  Children the gods should pile upon mortals
  After all else
  This most terrible grief of all?                               1090
    [*Enter* MEDEA, *from the spectators' right.*]
MEDEA. Friends, I can tell you that for long I have waited
  For the event. I stare towards the place from where
  The news will come. And now, see one of Jason's servants
  Is on his way here, and that laboured breath of his
  Shows he has tidings for us, and evil tidings.                  1095
    [*Enter, also from the right, the* MESSENGER.]
MESSENGER. Medea, you who have done such a dreadful thing,

So outrageous, run for your life, take what you can,
A ship to bear you hence or chariot on land.

MEDEA. And what is the reason deserves such flight as this?

MESS. She is dead, only just now, the royal princess,                    1100
And Kreon dead too, her father, by your poisons.

MEDEA. The finest words you have spoken. Now and hereafter
I shall count you among my benefactors and friends.

MESS. What! Are you right in the mind? Are you not mad,
Woman? The house of the king is outraged by you.                        1105
Do you enjoy it? Not afraid of such doings?

MEDEA. To what you say I on my side have something too
To say in answer. Do not be in a hurry, friend,
But speak. How did they die? You will delight me twice
As much again if you say they died in agony.                           1110

MESS. When those two children, born of you, had entered in,
Their father with them, and passed into the bride's house,
We were pleased, we slaves who were distressed by your wrongs.
All through the house we were talking of but one thing,
How you and your husband had made up your quarrel.                     1115
Some kissed the children's hands and some their yellow hair,
And I myself was so full of my joy that I
Followed the children into the women's quarters.
Our mistress, whom we honour now instead of you,
Before she noticed that your two children were there,                  1120
Was keeping her eye fixed eagerly on Jason.
Afterwards however she covered up her eyes,
Her cheek paled and she turned herself away from him,
So disgusted was she at the children's coming there.
But your husband tried to end the girl's bad temper,                   1125
And said 'You must not look unkindly on your friends.
Cease to be angry. Turn your head to me again.
Have as your friends the same ones as your husband has.
And take these gifts, and beg your father to reprieve
These children from their exile. Do it for my sake.'                   1130
She, when she saw the dress, could not restrain herself.
She agreed with all her husband said, and before
He and the children had gone far from the palace,
She took the gorgeous robe and dressed herself in it,
And put the golden crown around her curly locks,                       1135
And arranged the set of the hair in a shining mirror,
And smiled at the lifeless image of herself in it.
Then she rose from her chair and walked about the room,
With her gleaming feet stepping most soft and delicate,
All overjoyed with the present. Often and often                       1140
She would stretch her foot out straight and look along it.

But after that it was a fearful thing to see.
The colour of her face changed, and she staggered back,
She ran, and her legs trembled, and she only just
Managed to reach a chair without falling flat down.      1145
An aged woman servant who, I take it, thought
This was some seizure of Pan or another god,
Cried out 'God bless us,' but that was before she saw
The white foam breaking through her lips and her rolling
The pupils of her eyes and her face all bloodless.      1150
Then she raised a different cry from that 'God bless us,'
A huge shriek, and the women ran, one to the king,
One to the newly wedded husband to tell him
What had happened to his bride; and with frequent sound
The whole of the palace rang as they went running.      1155
One walking quickly round the course of a race-track
Would now have turned the bend and be close to the goal,
When she, poor girl, opened her shut and speechless eye,
And with a terrible groan she came to herself.
For a two-fold pain was moving up against her.      1160
The wreath of gold that was resting around her head
Let forth a fearful stream of all-devouring fire,
And the finely-woven dress your children gave to her,
Was fastening on the unhappy girl's fine flesh.
She leapt up from the chair, and all on fire she ran,      1165
Shaking her hair now this way and now that, trying
To hurl the diadem away; but fixedly
The gold preserved its grip, and, when she shook her hair,
Then more and twice as fiercely the fire blazed out.
Till, beaten by her fate, she fell down to the ground,      1170
Hard to be recognised except by a parent.
Neither the setting of her eyes was plain to see,
Nor the shapeliness of her face. From the top of
Her head there oozed out blood and fire mixed together.
Like the drops on pine-bark, so the flesh from her bones      1175
Dropped away, torn by the hidden fang of the poison.
It was a fearful sight; and terror held us all
From touching the corpse. We had learned from what had
    happened.
But her wretched father, knowing nothing of the event,
Came suddenly to the house, and fell upon the corpse,      1180
And at once cried out and folded his arms about her,
And kissed her and spoke to her, saying 'O my poor child,

---

1147. *Pan:* As the god of wild
nature he was supposed to be the
source of the sudden, apparently
causeless terror which solitude in wild
surroundings may produce, and thence
of all kinds of sudden madness. (Compare our word "panic".)

What heavenly power has so shamefully destroyed you?
And who has set me here like an ancient sepulchre,
Deprived of you? O let me die with you, my child!'
And when he had made an end of his wailing and crying,                    1185
Then the old man wished to raise himself to his feet;
But, as the ivy clings to the twigs of the laurel,
So he stuck to the fine dress, and he struggled fearfully.
For he was trying to lift himself to his knee,                             1190
And she was pulling him down, and when he tugged hard
He would be ripping his aged flesh from his bones.
At last his life was quenched and the unhappy man
Gave up the ghost, no longer could hold up his head.
There they lie close, the daughter and the old father,                     1195
Dead bodies, an event he prayed for in his tears.
As for your interests, I will say nothing of them,
For you will find your own escape from punishment.
Our human life I think and have thought a shadow,
And I do not fear to say that those who are held                           1200
Wise amongst men and who search the reasons of things
Are those who bring the most sorrow on themselves.
For of mortals there is no one who is happy.
If wealth flows in upon one, one may be perhaps
Luckier than one's neighbour, but still not happy.                         1205
    [*Exit.*]

CHOR. Heaven, it seems, on this day has fastened many
Evils on Jason, and Jason has deserved them.
Poor girl, the daughter of Kreon, how I pity you
And your misfortunes, you who have gone quite away
To the house of Hades because of marrying Jason.                           1210

MEDEA. Women, my task is fixed: as quickly as I may
To kill my children, and start away from this land,
And not, by wasting time, to suffer my children
To be slain by another hand less kindly to them.
Force every way will have it they must die, and since                      1215
This must be so, then I, their mother, shall kill them.
O arm yourself in steel, my heart! Do not hang back
From doing this fearful and necessary wrong.
O come, my hand, poor wretched hand, and take the sword,
Take it, step forward to this bitter starting point,                       1220
And do not be a coward, do not think of them,
How sweet they are, and how you are their mother. Just for
This one short day be forgetful of your children,
Afterwards weep; for even though you will kill them,
They were very dear,—O, I am an unhappy woman!                             1225
    [*With a cry she rushes into the house.*]

CHOR. O Earth, and the far shining
  Ray of the sun, look down, look down upon
  This poor lost woman, look, before she raises
  The hand of murder against her flesh and blood.
  Yours was the golden birth from which       1230
  She sprang, and now I fear divine
  Blood may be shed by men.
  O heavenly light, hold back her hand,
  Check her, and drive from out the house
  The bloody Fury raised by fiends of Hell.     1235

  Vain waste, your care of children;
  Was it in vain you bore the babes you loved,
  After you passed the inhospitable strait
  Between the dark blue rocks, Symplegades?
  O wretched one, how has it come,      1240
  This heavy anger on your heart,
  This cruel bloody mind?
  For God from mortals asks a stern
  Price for the stain of kindred blood
  In like disaster falling on their homes.     1245
    [A *cry from one of the* CHILDREN *is heard*.]
CHOR. Do you hear the cry, do you hear the children's cry?
  O you hard heart, O woman fated for evil!
ONE OF THE CHILDREN. [*From within*] What can I do and how
  escape my mother's hands?
ANOTHER CHILD. [*From within*] O my dear brother, I cannot tell.
  We are lost.
CHOR. Shall I enter the house? O surely I should     1250
  Defend the children from murder.
A CHILD. [*From within*] O help us, in God's name, for now we need
  your help.
  Now, now we are close to it. We are trapped by the sword.
CHOR. O your heart must have been made of rock or steel,
  You who can kill     1255
  With your own hand the fruit of your own womb.
  Of one alone I have heard, one woman alone
  Of those of old who laid her hands on her children,
  Ino, sent mad by heaven when the wife of Zeus
  Drove her out from her home and made her wander;    1260
  And because of the wicked shedding of blood
  Of her own children she threw
  Herself, poor wretch, into the sea and stepped away
  Over the sea-cliff to die with her two children.
  What horror more can be? O women's love,    1265

So full of trouble,
How many evils have you caused already!
[*Enter* JASON, *with attendants.*]
JASON. You women, standing close in front of this dwelling,
Is she, Medea, she who did this dreadful deed,
Still in the house, or has she run away in flight?                    1270
For she will have to hide herself beneath the earth,
Or raise herself on wings into the height of air,
If she wishes to escape the royal vengeance.
Does she imagine that, having killed our rulers,
She will herself escape uninjured from this house?                    1275
But I am thinking not so much of her as for
The children,—her the king's friends will make to suffer
For what she did. So I have come to save the lives
Of my boys, in case the royal house should harm them
While taking vengeance for their mother's wicked deed.               1280
CHOR. O Jason, if you but knew how deeply you are
Involved in sorrow, you would not have spoken so.
JASON. What is it? That she is planning to kill me also?
CHOR. Your children are dead, and by their own mother's hand.
JASON. What! This is it? O woman, you have destroyed me.             1285
CHOR. You must make up your mind your children are no more.
JASON. Where did she kill them? Was it here or in the house?
CHOR. Open the gates and there you will see them murdered.
JASON. Quick as you can unlock the doors, men, and undo
The fastenings and let me see this double evil,                       1290
My children dead and her,—O her I will repay.
        [*His attendants rush to the door.* MEDEA *appears above the*
        *house in a chariot drawn by dragons. She has the dead bodies*
        *of the children with her.*]
MEDEA. Why do you batter these gates and try to unbar them,
Seeking the corpses and for me who did the deed?
You may cease your trouble, and, if you have need of me,
Speak, if you wish. You will never touch me with your hand,          1295
Such a chariot has Helios, my father's father,
Given me to defend me from my enemies.
JASON. You hateful thing, you woman most utterly loathed
By the gods and me and by all the race of mankind,
You who have had the heart to raise a sword against                   1300
Your children, you, their mother, and left me childless,—
You have done this, and do you still look at the sun
And at the earth, after these most fearful doings?
I wish you dead. Now I see it plain, though at that time
I did not, when I took you from your foreign home                     1305
And brought you to a Greek house, you, an evil thing,

A traitress to your father and your native land.
The gods hurled the avenging curse of yours on me.
For your own brother you slew at your own hearthside,
And then came aboard that beautiful ship, the Argo.          1310
And that was your beginning. When you were married
To me, your husband, and had borne children to me,
For the sake of pleasure in the bed you killed them.
There is no Greek woman who would have dared such deeds,
Out of all those whom I passed over and chose you           1315
To marry instead, a bitter destructive match,
A monster not a woman, having a nature
Wilder than that of Scylla in the Tuscan sea.
Ah! no, not if I had ten thousand words of shame
Could I sting you. You are naturally so brazen.             1320
Go, worker in evil, stained with your children's blood.
For me remains to cry aloud upon my fate,
Who will get no pleasure from my newly-wedded love,
And the boys whom I begot and brought up, never
Shall I speak to them alive. Oh, my life is over!           1325

MEDEA. Long would be the answer which I might have made to
These words of yours, if Zeus the father did not know
How I have treated you and what you did to me.
No, it was not to be that you should scorn my love,
And pleasantly live your life through, laughing at me;      1330
Nor would the princess, nor he who offered the match,
Kreon, drive me away without paying for it.
So now you may call me a monster, if you wish,
O Scylla housed in the caves of the Tuscan sea
I too, as I had to, have taken hold of your heart.          1335

JASON. You feel the pain yourself. You share in my sorrow.

MEDEA. Yes, and my grief is gain when you cannot mock it.

JASON. O children, what a wicked mother she was to you!

MEDEA. They died from a disease they caught from their father.

JASON. I tell you it was not my hand that destroyed them.    1340

MEDEA. But it was your insolence, and your virgin wedding.

JASON. And just for the sake of that you chose to kill them.

MEDEA. Is love so small a pain, do you think, for a woman?

JASON. For a wise one, certainly. But you are wholly evil.

MEDEA. The children are dead. I say this to make you suffer.  1345

JASON. The children, I think, will bring down curses on you.

MEDEA. The gods know who was the author of this sorrow.

JASON. Yes, the gods know indeed, they know your loathsome heart.

MEDEA. Hate me. But I tire of your barking bitterness.

1318. *Scylla:* a monster located in
the straits between Italy and Sicily,
who snatched sailors off passing ships
and devoured them.

JASON. And I of yours. It is easier to leave you.                            1350
MEDEA. How then? What shall I do? I long to leave you too.
JASON. Give me the bodies to bury and to mourn them.
MEDEA. No, that I will not. I will bury them myself,
  Bearing them to Hera's temple on the promontory;
  So that no enemy may evilly treat them                                     1355
  By tearing up their grave. In this land of Corinth
  I shall establish a holy feast and sacrifice
  Each year for ever to atone for the blood guilt.
  And I myself go to the land of Erechtheus
  To dwell in Aigeus' house, the son of Pandion.                            1360
  While you, as is right, will die without distinction,
  Struck on the head by a piece of the Argo's timber,
  And you will have seen the bitter end of my love.
JASON. May a Fury for the children's sake destroy you,
  And justice, requitor of blood.                                           1365
MEDEA. What heavenly power lends an ear
  To a breaker of oaths, a deceiver?
JASON. O, I hate you, murderess of children.
MEDEA. Go to your palace. Bury your bride.
JASON. I go, with two children to mourn for.                                1370
MEDEA. Not yet do you feel it. Wait for the future.
JASON. Oh, children I loved!
MEDEA.                              I loved them, you did not.
JASON. You loved them, and killed them.
MEDEA.                                       To make you feel
  pain.                                                                      1375
JASON. Oh, wretch that I am, how I long
  To kiss the dear lips of my children!
MEDEA. Now you would speak to them, now you would kiss them.
  Then you rejected them.
JASON.                          Let me, I beg you,                          1380
  Touch my boys' delicate flesh.
MEDEA. I will not. Your words are all wasted.
JASON. O God, do you hear it, this persecution,
  These my sufferings from this hateful
  Woman, this monster, murderess of children?                               1385
  Still what I can do that I will do:
  I will lament and cry upon heaven,
  Calling the gods to bear me witness
  How you have killed my boys and prevent me from
  Touching their bodies or giving them burial.                              1390
  I wish I had never begot them to see them

1357. *feast and sacrifice:* Some such ceremony was still performed at Corinth in
Euripides' time.

Afterwards slaughtered by you.
CHOR. Zeus in Olympus is the overseer
  Of many doings. Many things the gods
  Achieve beyond our judgment. What we thought          1395
  Is not confirmed and what we thought not god
  Contrives. And so it happens in this story.


# Hippolytus*

## Characters

APHRODITE, *goddess of love*
ARTEMIS, *virgin goddess of the hunt*
THESEUS, *king of Athens*
PHAEDRA, *his wife*
HIPPOLYTUS, *son of Theseus and the Amazon Hippolyta*
ATTENDANT, *servant of Hippolytus*
NURSE, *old woman who cared for Phaedra as a child*
MESSENGER


*The scene is in Troezen, in front of the palace of King Theseus.†
By the gates are two statues, one of Aphrodite and one of Artemis.
The goddess Aphrodite speaks.*

APHRODITE.  Strong am I among mortals, not without a name,
  the goddess Cypris, who in heaven too is known.
  And of those who live and look upon the light of the sun
  from Pontus to the boundaries that Atlas set,
  I give honor to the ones who reverence my power,          5
  and those whose thoughts of me are arrogant I crush.
  You will find this holds even among the gods above:
  they too are pleased when they receive the praise of men.
  And I will show at once that what I say is true.
  The son of Theseus from the Amazon his wife,          10
  Hippolytus, brought up by Pittheus, that saintly man,

---

\* Translated by Rex Warner.
† *Troezen:* City on the Peloponnese
across the Saronic Gulf from Athens.
Hippolytus has been sent here to be
brought up by King Pittheus, and also as
an illegitimate son to be removed far from
Theseus' new wife. However, as Aphrodite explains below, Theseus and Phaedra
are now also living in Troezen.
  2. *Cypris:* So named because Cypris
was the chief center of her cult.
  4. *Pontus:* The Black Sea. *boundaries:*

The Strait of Gibraltar. The whole line
means "from the Black Sea to the Atlantic," in effect the world as the Greeks
knew it. *Atlas:* Giant condemned to
hold up the sky. He was stationed near
the Strait of Gibraltar, where the Atlas
Mountains stand on the African side.
  10. *the Amazon his wife:* Hippolyta,
queen of the Amazon race of warrior
women, conquered by Theseus and made
his mistress (though, despite what
Aphrodite says, evidently not his wife).

alone of all the people in this land, Troezen,
considers me the least important of the gods,
spurns love making and will not join in an embrace.
Instead he worships Phoebus' sister, Artemis,                    15
the child of Zeus, and thinks her greatest of the gods,
and always with the virgin goddess in green woods
he clears the land of beasts with his swift hunting dogs,
in mightier company than that of human kind.
All this I do not grudge him. Why indeed should I?               20
But for sinning against me, upon this very day
I shall take vengeance on Hippolytus. The work
is begun already; there is not much left to do.
For once he came to Athens from the house of Pittheus
to see and to receive the holy mysteries,                        25
and then his father's noble and respected wife,
Phaedra, first saw him, and she found her heart in the grip
of savage passion. This was as I planned it for her.
And before she came into this land of Troezen,
she built upon the rock of Pallas, looking out                   30
over this land, a temple to me, the Cyprian.
Her love was absent, but it was for him she made
the temple and afterwards she called it by his name.
And now that Theseus, fleeing from the stain of blood
of Pallas' murdered sons, has taken on himself                   35
one year of foreign exile and has left the land
of Cecrops and has sailed to this land with his wife,
now she, poor woman, wastes away in agony,
and, driven from her senses by the stings of love,
suffers in silence. No one with her knows her pain.             40
But this is not the way this love of hers must end.
I shall let Theseus know of it. All will come out.
Then this young man, my enemy, will be destroyed
by the curses of his father; for the lord of the sea,
Poseidon, gave to Theseus as an honored right                    45
that he should pray three times and have his prayer fulfilled.
As for the women, Phaedra, she shall keep her name,
but none the less shall die. I shall not think her pain
of enough importance to prevent my enemies

---

25. *mysteries*: Sacred rites of the initiates of the cult of Demeter, goddess of agriculture and fertility of the land. The center of the cult was Eleusis, located between Troezen and Athens.

30. *Pallas*: Alternate name of Athena, the patron goddess of Athens; her *rock* is the Acropolis, the hill on which the gods' temples stood.

35. *Pallas' murdered sons*: This Pallas is not Athena but Thesus' uncle, whose sons Theseus killed in a war over territorial claims.

37. *land of Cecrops*: Athens. Cecrops was an early Attic king.

45. *Poseidon*: God of the sea and of earthquakes, and father of Theseus. Like many of the heroes, Theseus had both a divine and a human father.

from suffering the punishment that I think fit. 50
But now I see the son of Theseus coming here,
Hippolytus, fresh from his hunting exercise.
I therefore shall be gone. Behind him comes a great
and merry band of hunters, singing to Artemis,
hymning the goddess's praise. He does not know the gates 55
of Hell are open and this day he sees his last.

[*Aphrodite goes out. Hippolytus, carrying a garland in his
hand, enters followed by his attendants.*]

HIPPOLYTUS. Sing, as you follow me, sing of her
heavenly daughter of Zeus,
Artemis, in whose care we are.

ATTENDANTS. [*Singing*] Most holy lady, we worship you, 60
child of the Highest.
We worship you, Lady Artemis,
Leto and Zeus's daughter.
You most beautiful far among
maidens, you who in heaven dwell 65
in the space of your father's court,
in the golden palace of Zeus,
hear us, most beautiful
maid among maidens in heaven, most
beautiful, Artemis. 70

[*Hippolytus advances to the statue of Artemis in front of
the palace.*]

HIPPOLYTUS. For you, my lady, I have made and bring to you
this wreath of twined flowers from a virgin meadow,
a place where never shepherd thought to feed his flocks
nor ever came the stroke of iron. Instead the bees
cross and recross this virgin meadow in the spring. 75
And native Shame waters the ground with river dew,
and from his garden only those may pluck the flowers
who were elect from birth by a wise purity
in all things, and never had to learn it. Evil men
have no right there. And so, dear lady, take from this 80
reverent hand a binding for your golden hair.
For I alone of men am so distinguished as to be
constantly with you and to speak and hear your words.
I hear the voice, but I have never seen your face.
O, let me end my life as I have started it! 85

[*One of his attendants approaches him.*]

63. *Zeus*: King of the gods. Leto was a goddess loved by Zeus, mother of Artemis and Apollo.
76. *Shame*: The Greek word covers a wider spectrum of feelings than any one English word. It is a feeling of reverence —for other men, for gods, or for nature. Here it is the spirit which tends the meadow, like a gardener.

ATTENDANT. Sir, for "master" is a word I use for gods—
    if I gave good advice, would you receive it from me?
HIPPOLYTUS. Of course I would. It would be stupid not to do so.
ATTENDANT. Do you know of a rule that is general among men?
HIPPOLYTUS. What rule? What is it you are telling me about?    90
ATTENDANT. People hate pride and an exclusive attitude.
HIPPOLYTUS. Quite right. An arrogant person is always hated.
ATTENDANT. And people are grateful when you talk to them kindly.
HIPPOLYTUS. Certainly. It does much good, and costs little trouble.
ATTENDANT. And do you think that the same thing is true
    of gods?    95
HIPPOLYTUS. Yes, since we mortals live by the same rules as they.
ATTENDANT. Then why do you not say a word to a great goddess?
HIPPOLYTUS. Which one? Be careful that you name what can be
    named.
ATTENDANT. The one that stands there. The Cyprian at your gates.
HIPPOLYTUS. Since I live cleanly, I greet her from a distance.    100
ATTENDANT. Yet she is great and proud and known among all men.
HIPPOLYTUS. I do not care for gods men worship in the night.
ATTENDANT. Still you must recognize the honors due to gods.
HIPPOLYTUS. Both among gods and men there are different tastes.
ATTENDANT. Then I wish you happiness, and the sense you ought to
    have.    105
HIPPOLYTUS. [*Turning away from him*] Come on, my friends,
    and go inside the house and see
the banquet is prepared. After a day of hunting
a well-spread table does one good. Let someone rub
the horses down. When I have had enough to eat,
I shall yoke and drive them out today for exercise.    110
As for your Cyprian goddess—may she be in luck.
    [*He goes into the palace. The Attendant remains behind
    and bows before the statue of Aphrodite.*]
ATTENDANT. But I (and here I shall not imitate young men)
think in a way a slave should think before he speaks.
Let me address my prayers to your holy image,
goddess of Cyprus. You should have some pity on    115
one who, because of his youth, with violent feelings
speaks nonsense of you. You should pretend not to hear.
Gods should be wiser and more moderate than men.
    [*He follows the others into the palace. Enter the Chorus of
    Women of Troezen.*]
CHORUS. There is a rock that wells with Ocean's water

---

98. *name what can be named*: Hippolytus does not even want to hear Aphrodite's name.
119. *Ocean's water*: Not sea-water.

Ocean was the river encircling the earth
from which all fresh-water rivers and
springs were believed to flow.

and from its steeps lets fall a flowing stream 120
where pitchers dip, and there
one that I knew was plunging
red robes in the river dew,
spreading the robes to dry on the slab of a hot
rock in the sun, and she 125
told me first of the queen.

How she is wasting on a bed of sickness
inside her house, and hides her golden head
in the shade of a silken veil;
and now for the third day she 130
refrains with her lovely lips
from the touch of the grains of Demeter, and secretly
suffering, longs to draw in
to the pitiful harbor of death.

Are you astray, my lady, 135
possessed by a god—by Pan
or Hecate or the terrible
Corybantes, or Mountain Mother?
Or are you wasted away for a sin incurred
by failing, unsanctified, to sacrifice 140
to the goddess of beasts, Dictynna?
For she is able to range through the waves
over the ocean to land
on the salt and eddying waters.

Is it your husband, the noble 145
king of Erechtheus' sons?
Is he folded in secret love
away from your bed in the house?
Or has some mariner sailed from the port of Crete
to this most kindly harbor for sailing men 150
and brought to our queen a message?
And is it in grief for what she has learnt
of suffering there in her home
that she lies heartsick in her bed?

In women's difficult unstable natures 155
a pitiful helplessness often dwells
springing from pangs in the womb and unbalanced thought.

---

136. *Pan*: A god of the wild country who might induce madness.

137. *Hecate*: A name of Artemis as witch, who as goddess of the moon might also be the source of lunacy, especially in women.

138. *Corybantes*: Priests of Cybele, the *Mountain Mother*; their frenzied dancing had a hypnotic effect.

141. *Dictynna*: Artemis.

146. *Erechtheus' sons*: Athenians. Erechtheus was a legendary early king of Athens.

149. *Crete*: Phaedra's home. She is the daughter of King Minos and Pasiphae (line 328 and note).

Such an impulse of pain
through my loins also has darted, but then I cried
to heavenly Artemis, giver of gentle birth,                    160
goddess guarding the bow, and she for ever
is honored and blessed by me as she goes with the gods.

> [*Enter Phaedra and her old Nurse. Phaedra lies down on a
> couch.*]

But here at the door is the aged nurse
bringing her mistress out of the palace.
The lowering cloud on her brows is darker.                     165
What can it be? I long to discover
what can have happened
so to alter the form of the queen.

NURSE. How people suffer! How hateful is illness!
What shall I do for you? What leave undone?                    170
Here is the light for you, here is the bright sky.
Here is your sickbed ready for you
outside your doors.
What you wanted was always to come here,
though soon you will hurry back to your bedroom,               175
soon disappointed. Nothing can please you.
Discontented with what you have, you
think what you don't have is better.
I would rather be ill than look after an illness.
Illness is simple, but nursing an illness brings               180
grief to the heart and work for the hands.
The life of men is nothing but evil,
nor is there any respite from suffering.
Yet if there is a state better than living,
darkness surrounds it and hides it in clouds.                  185
So we show ourselves lovesick indeed
for this something that glitters on earth,
having no knowledge of different living
and no revelation of what is beneath,
since there's no direction in idle legends.                    190

PHAEDRA. Lift me upright, give support to my head.
Dear women, the bonds of my limbs are unloosed.
Take hold of my hands and my delicate arms.
Heavy to wear is the veil on my head.
Take it, and let my hair loose on my shoulders.                195

NURSE. Be patient, my child, and do not so fiercely
toss to and fro.
If you keep quiet and are brave in your spirit,
you will find your illness more easy to bear.
It is fated for mortals to suffer.                             200

PHAEDRA. Alas! how I wish I could draw from a dewy
    fountain a draft of the shining waters,
    and take my rest in a leafy meadow,
    lying beneath the shade of the poplars.

NURSE. O my child, what is this you are saying?        205
    Really, you must not before all these people
    speak and let loose such words ridden by madness.

PHAEDRA. Away to the mountains! I will go to the wild wood,
    under the pines, where the hounds are hunting,
    and pressing their chase on the dappled deer.       210
    O, let me do it! I long to be shouting
    out to the hounds, and to poise by my yellow
    hair the Thessalian javelin, and carry
    the bladed lance in my hand.

NURSE. My child, why ever should such things upset you?    215
    Why should you take such an interest in hunting?
    Why should you long for a draft from a fountain?
    Here, close by your towers, is a dewy slope,
    and from here we can fetch you some water.

PHAEDRA. Artemis, queen of sea-girt Limne,        220
    queen of the race-course that echoes with hoof-beats,
    O how I long to be there in your lowlands,
    breaking in the Venetian horses!

NURSE. What are these words that you fling out in madness?
    Only just now you were off to the mountains,       225
    led by a longing for hunting, and now you
    yearn for horses on sandy plains
    away from the sea. It would take some divining
    to find, my child, which one of the gods
    holds the reins of your spirit, and drives it astray.   230

PHAEDRA. What can I have done to make me unhappy?
    And whither so driven aside from my right mind?
    I am mad, I have fallen through spite of some god,
    O, poor wretch that I am.
    Cover my face again, dear mother.       235
    I feel dread at the words I have spoken.
    Cover it up. Tears start in my eyes,
    and shame has come over my face.
    To come to my senses again is an agony;

---

207. *madness*: In fifth-century Athens women of the upper classes were rarely seen outside their own homes: in such a social context Phaedra's wish to run on the mountains would indeed seem strange.

213. *Thessalian javelin*: This light hunting spear was a product of Thessaly, north central Greece.

220. *Limne*: The coastal lagoon of Troezen. Hippolytus raced his horses there; like all the places Phaedra mentions, it is a covert reference to her love.

223. *Venetian*: The city of Venice had not yet been founded, but the district was known by this name and its horses were famous.

yet this madness is evil. The best thing of all 240
is to die, and not know what I'm doing.
NURSE. There, I've covered your face. But, O when will my body
be shrouded in death?
Much I have learned by living a long time.
Mortals, I know, should join with each other
in loving feelings that are not excessive, 245
just on the surface, not touching the quick of the soul.
Light should the heart's affections lie on us,
quick to cast off and quick to pull tighter.
This is a heavy weight, that one soul 250
should suffer itself for two souls,
just as I for my mistress grieve too greatly.
In life, they say, one finds more failure
than delight in this unswerving
heart's devotion, which conflicts with health. 255
"Nothing in excess" is better
far than counsels of perfection.
Wise men will agree with me.
CHORUS. You aged woman, trusted nurse to this our queen.
We see the unhappy sufferings that Phaedra feels, 260
but what the illness is is still unknown to us.
From you we wish to hear and be informed of it.
NURSE. I have asked and do not know. She does not wish to speak.
CHORUS. Nor what was the beginning of these pains of hers?
NURSE. Just the same thing. On all of this she is silent. 265
CHORUS. How weak she is, and how her body wastes away!
NURSE. No wonder, since for three days she has touched no food.
CHORUS. Is it some curse of god or that she aims to die?
NURSE. She wants to die, and starves to make an end of life.
CHORUS. It is a strange thing if her husband bears this calmly. 270
NURSE. She hides her pains from him and says she is not ill.
CHORUS. But when he sees her face, does he not see she is?
NURSE. No. Just now he happens to be away from home.
CHORUS. Can you not try and force some way of finding out
what is her illness and what distraction of her mind? 275
NURSE. I have tried everything and met with no success.
But even now I'll not relax my efforts for her,
so that you too, being here, may bear me witness
how true I am to a mistress in her misfortune.
[*She turns to Phaedra.*]
Come, my dear child, and let us both forget those words 280
we spoke before. You must behave with more kindness,
relax that angry frown and change your way of mind;
and I, if in any way I failed to understand,

will let that be, and turn to other better words.
Now, if your illness is the kind that one keeps private,                  285
here are these women ready to assist you in it.
But if your suffering can be disclosed to men,
speak, so that we can let the doctors know of it.
Now, come! Why don't you speak? You ought to tell me, child.
If what I say is not right, point it out to me;                          290
otherwise you should agree with my well-meant advice.
Say something, do. Or look at me.—Poor wretch I am!
Women, it does no good, the trouble that we take.
We are still as far away as ever. The last time
words could not soften her, and now she will not hear.                    295

    [*She turns to Phaedra again.*]
Yet listen to this. Now, if you like, be more self-willed
than is the sea itself. Dying, you will betray
your children, leaving them without their share in all
their father's wealth. Yes, she, the Amazon huntress,
the royal lady, bore a master for your sons,                              300
a bastard aiming at full rights. You know him well.
Hippolytus.

PHAEDRA.        Alas!

NURSE.        What! This point touches you?

PHAEDRA. Mother, you have destroyed me. Please, I beg of you,
  never again make mention of this man to me.

NURSE. You see? Your mind is sound, and yet in spite of that            305
  you will not help your children and preserve your life.

PHAEDRA. I love my children. Other evils storm my heart.

NURSE. Are your hands pure, my child, from stain of shedding
    blood?

PHAEDRA. My hands are pure: it is my mind that has the stain.

NURSE. Some enemy brings pain on you by magic means.                    310

PHAEDRA. Against his will and mine a friend is killing me.

NURSE. Is it Theseus who has done some injury to you?

PHAEDRA. Let me be never found to have done him a wrong!

NURSE. What is this fearful thing that drives you on to death?

PHAEDRA. Leave me to sin. It is not against you I sin.                  315

NURSE. I'll never leave you. It is your fault if I fail.

    [*She throws herself on her knees in front of Phaedra.*]

PHAEDRA. What are you doing, clinging to my hands and forcing
    me?

NURSE. Yes, and I clasp your knees and will not let you go.

PHAEDRA. Poor thing, my words are bad for you to hear, yes, bad.

---

300. *your sons*: Phaedra's sons by
Theseus were Demophon and Acamas.
Demophon succeeded his father on the
throne.
    305. *Mother*: Term of familiarity, not
to be taken literally.

NURSE. Could anything be worse for me than to lose you?     320
PHAEDRA. You will be lost. And yet to me this thing gives fame.
NURSE. Yet you hide something good, in spite of all my prayers?
PHAEDRA. Yes, since the glory that I plan proceeds from shame.
NURSE. Then you will be more honored still by telling it.
PHAEDRA. Leave me, I beg you, and let go of my right hand.     325
NURSE. Never! You will not give me what you ought to give.
PHAEDRA. I will. For I respect your rights in pleading so.
NURSE. Then I'll be silent. Now it is for you to speak.
PHAEDRA. O my mother, what a love, poor thing, you fell into!
NURSE. Is what you mean, my child, her passion for the bull?     330
PHAEDRA. You too, my wretched sister, Dionysus' wife.
NURSE. What is it, child? You speak ill of your family.
PHAEDRA. And I, the third unhappy one, I too destroyed!
NURSE. I am indeed bewildered. Where will these words end?
PHAEDRA. Where I became unhappy, a long time ago.     335
NURSE. But still I know no more of what I wish to hear.
PHAEDRA. Ah! I wish that you could say the words I have to say.
NURSE. I am no prophetess to make the dark things clear.
PHAEDRA. What do they mean when they say people are in love?
NURSE. Something most sweet, my child, and also painful too.     340
PHAEDRA. I must be one who feels the painfulness of it.
NURSE. What's this you say? You are in love, my child?
  With whom?
PHAEDRA. There is a man I know, the son of the Amazon . . .
NURSE. Hippolytus?     345
PHAEDRA. You heard it from your lips, not mine.
NURSE. Ah, child, what can you mean? O, you have ruined me.
  Women, this is not to be borne, and I will not
  bear to live more. Ill day, ill light it is I see.
  I shall throw and cast away my body, leave my life     350
  and die. I say farewell, since I no longer am.
  Against their will, perhaps, but all the same, the wise
  and chaste love evil. Cypris, then, is not divine,
  but must be something else more mighty than a god
  to have destroyed my mistress, me, and all our house.     355
CHORUS. Oh, did you hear her? Oh, did you listen
  to things unutterable, to the queen
  as she told her woes?

---

321. *fame*: She means that keeping her secret is an honorable act, yet the words show (since fame and honor are public matters that she is thinking of confessing to the nurse.

329. *mother*: Pasiphae, wife of Minos of Crete. She was impregnated by a bull and gave birth to a monster, the Mino-taur.

331. *sister*: Ariadne. She helped Theseus find his way out of the labyrinth after he killed the Minotaur and left Crete with him. But he abandoned her on the island of Naxos and Dionysus became her lover.

O let me die, dear lady, before
I come to a mind like yours! Oh alas!                           360
O poor wretch in your pains!
O troubles in which men live!
You are destroyed, you have brought bad things to the light.
What waits for you now through this long day?
Some new evil will fall on this house.                         365
No longer doubtful the destination
of Cypris' will, O unhappy daughter of Crete.

PHAEDRA.  You women of Troezen, you who live here upon
this verge and entrance to the country of Pelops,
before now idly in the watches of the night                    370
I have considered how the life of man is spoilt.
And to my mind it is not through a lack of wit
that men go wrong, since, as for being sensible,
many are that. But this is how I look at it:
we understand and recognize what things are good,              375
but do not do them, some because of laziness,
others by choosing pleasure of some kind instead
of honor. There are many pleasures in our life,—
long conversations, being idle (a delightful fault),
and shame. There are two kinds of shame,—the one not bad      380
the other a weight on houses. If they were marked out
clearly, the two would not be spelt in the same way.
Now, since it happens that I think as I have said,
the medicine does not exist by which I was
likely to change and fall back from this view of mine.        385
Now to you too I shall describe my way of thought.
When passion wounded me, I tried to find the way
by which I could bear it with most honor. I began
in this way,—to keep silent and conceal my pain.
There is no trusting in the tongue, which well enough          390
knows how to criticize the thoughts of other men,
yet on its own self oftenest brings suffering.
And then my second resolution was to bear
my folly nobly and by reason conquer it.
And, as a third resource, since by these means I failed       395
to subdue Cypris, I made up my mind to die;
and this (no one will question it) is the best plan.
For I would never wish my good deeds to be hid,
nor to have people watching me when I do ill.
The deed, I knew, was shameful and my own disease;            400

---

369. *country of Pelops*: The Peloponnese, main peninsula of Greece,
named for the early Greek king Pelops.
Troezen is on its northeastern shore.

380. *two kinds of shame*: The kind
which prevents one from doing wrong,
and the shame felt after it is done.

clearly I knew as well that I was a woman,
something that's loathed by all. My curses on the wife
who first began, by taking lovers, to bring shame
upon the marriage bed! It was from noble houses
this evil started to descend on womankind.                           405
When what is shameful is condoned by noble people,
then certainly the lower class will think it good.
And then I hate the women who in words are chaste,
while hiding secretly their bold dishonest deeds.
O sea-born lady Cypris, how can these ones ever                      410
look in the faces of their husbands and not fear
and tremble lest the darkness that has covered them
and rooms within their houses might not cry aloud?
This is the thing, my friends, that drives me to my death:
lest I be found to have brought shame on my husband                  415
and on the children whom I bore. I want them free
to live and free to speak and prosperous to dwell
in glorious Athens, famous for their mother's sake.
Consciousness of a father's or a mother's sins
enslaves a man, however stout his heart may be.                      420
And this alone, they say, to those who have it, can
be matched with life itself,—a good and upright mind.
Time, at some moment, must bring evil men to light,
holding to them, as to the face of some young girl,
a mirror up. May I be never seen with them!                          425
CHORUS. Ah, how what's wise and chaste is honored everywhere,
and among men it bears the fruit of good report!
NURSE. My mistress, as you saw, just now the news of your
predicament filled me with sudden dreadful fear.
But now I think that I was silly. Among men                          430
one's second thoughts are in a way the wiser ones.
To you nothing outrageous or unheard-of has
happened. It is the goddess' anger strikes at you.
You are in love. What's strange in that? Most people are.
And then because of love will you destroy your life?                 435
There'll be no point in loving those who are close to us
now or in future, if one has to die for it.
Cypris is irresistible when in full force,
but gently visits those whose spirits yield to her;
and when she finds a man who's proud and arrogant,                   440
of course she seizes him and makes a mock of him.
She ranges through the air, and in the surge of sea
there Cypris is, and everything proceeds from her.
And she it is who plants in us and gives desire
from which all we inhabitants of earth are born.                     445

Indeed those people who possess the books of old
writers and are themselves great readers of their works
know how Zeus once desired to have the joys of love
with Semele, and know how once fair-shining Dawn
snatched up to heaven Cephalus to join the gods,                   450
and all this out of passion; and yet, all the same,
they dwell in heaven, do not shun the paths of gods,
and are, I think, quite pleased to yield to what has passed.
Will you object? Your father then should have made you
on special terms, or else controlled by other gods,               455
if you will not consent to follow these known laws.
How many men, and wise ones, are there, do you think,
who see their beds defiled, and pretend not to see?
How many fathers who assist their erring sons
in finding love affairs? Amongst the wise this is               460
a general rule,—to hide what is not fair to see.
Nor should men try to be too strict about their lives.
They cannot even make the roofs, with which their homes
are covered, absolutely right. And you, fallen
to such a state, how can you hope to swim out clear?            465
No, if the good in you is greater than the bad,
you, being only human, will do very well.
So, please, my dear child, give up these bad thoughts of yours.
Give up your arrogance, for it is nothing else
but arrogance to wish to have more strength than gods.         470
Love, and be bold. It is a god that willed all this.
You may be ill, but find a way to come out well.
Charms do exist and words that soothe and sway the mind.
We shall discover medicine for this ill of yours.
Indeed it's true that men would still be looking for it,       475
unless it was we women could find out the way.

CHORUS. Phaedra, she tells you things that are more useful to you
in your present distress. Yet I think *you* are right.
And you will find this view of mine more hard to bear
than are her words, more painful too to listen to.             480

PHAEDRA. This is the thing that ruins the well-ordered towns
and homes of men,—words spoken too persuasively.
For people should not say what charms the listener's ear
but what will bring to those who hear it good report.

NURSE. Why this grand language? What you need is not fine
     words                                                      485
but to find out as fast as possible about

---

449. *Semele*: Theban princess, the
mother, by Zeus, of Dionysus (Bacchus).
450. *Cephalus*: The young man carried

off by the dawn goddess, also sometimes
called Tithonus (as in Virgil, *The Aeneid*,
IV, 806 p. 631).

the man, and us to tell him the straight story of you.
For if it was not that your life was in this state
of peril, if you were a woman more controlled,
I never would, because of love and your delights,                    490
have urged you on so far; but now the struggle is
to save your life, and I cannot be blamed for this.

PHAEDRA. What awful things you say! Will you please keep your
    mouth
shut, and never again speak such disgraceful words.

NURSE. Disgraceful, yes, but better for you than your fine          495
words, and a better deed if I can save your life
than save your name, to glory in which name you'd die.

PHAEDRA. Please, not to me, I beg you (you speak well, but foully)
go any further now. My heart is well prepared
by love, and, if you speak so well of shameful things,              500
I shall be swept away by what I fly from now.

NURSE. If this is what you think, you ought not to have sinned.
You have. Then listen to me, for the next best thing
is to give way. I have at home some soothing drafts
for love,—the thought has only just occurred to me,—              505
and these, without dishonor, doing no harm to your wits,
will free you from your sickness, if you will be brave.
But I must have something from him whom you desire,
some mark, either a lock of hair or piece of clothing,
so from the two of you to make consentment one.                     510

PHAEDRA. Is this a drug to drink or ointment to put on?

NURSE. I do not know. Be happy and never mind, my child.

PHAEDRA. I am afraid that you may be too clever in all this.

NURSE. Be sure you would fear everything. What do you fear?

PHAEDRA. That you might tell some word of this to Theseus' son. 515

NURSE. Leave me alone, my child. I shall arrange things well.

[She turns to go into the palace but first addresses the
    statue of Aphrodite.]

Only be you my helper, lady of the sea,
Cypris! As for what else I have within my mind
it will be enough to tell it to our friends indoors.

[She goes into the palace.]

CHORUS. Love, O Love, you that make well to the eyes                520
drops of desire, you that bring sweet delight
into the hearts that you with your force invade,
never to me appear in catastrophe,

---

504. *soothing drafts*: Love charms and potions were well known in the ancient world. Usually, however, their purpose was to arouse love, not, as here, to control it. In fact, the Nurse is prevaricat-ing: she intends to tell Hippolytus of Phaedra's love and try to win him over.

517. *lady of the sea*: Aphrodite was born from the sea.

never in discord come!
Since there exists no bolt of the fire and no            525
weightier bolt of the stars than that
arrow of Aphrodite hurled
out of the hands of Love,
Love, the child of the Highest.

Useless it is that still by Alpheus' stream,            530
Useless it is by Phoebus's Pythian shrines
for the land of Hellas to sacrifice more and more
blood of oxen, when we neglect to give
the honor that's due to Love,
Love, the ruler of men, he who keeps the keys            535
of Aphrodite's pleasantest dwelling-place,
he who ravages on his way,
bringing to mortals all
catastrophes at his coming.

The girl in Oichalia,            540
a maiden unyoked to love,
unmarried as yet and husbandless, Cypris took
and loosed her from home in ships,
and, a fugitive thing, like a nymph or Bacchante, she gave her,
with blood and with fire            545
and murder for wedding hymns,
to Alcmene's child.
Poor wretch she was in her marriage!

O holy fortress of Thebes,
O fountain of Dirce, you            550
well could witness the force of Cypris' coming.
For with thunder and lightning flash
she brought to her bed the mother of Bacchus, the Zeusborn,
and gave her a wedding
with death for a fate. She breathes            555
in terror on all
and flies on her way like a bee.

[*Phaedra goes to the door of the palace and listens.*]

530. *Alpheus*: The river of Olympia, site of the great temple of Zeus and of the Olympic games.
531. *Phoebus' Pythian shrines*: The temple of Apollo at Delphi.
532. *Hellas*: Greece.
540. *girl in Oichalia*: Iole, daughter of King Eurytus. To win her, Heracles sacked the city and killed her father and brother.

544. *Bacchante*: Ecstatic worshipper of Bacchus (Dionysus).
546. *Alcmene*: Mother of Heracles.
550. *Dirce*: The spring at Thebes.
553. *mother of Bacchus*: Semele. Pregnant by Zeus, who was invisible when he visited her, she asked to see him in his divine shape. She had her wish, but was blasted to ashes by his lightening.

PHAEDRA. Be silent, women! O now, I am really ruined!

CHORUS. What is it, Phaedra, frightens you inside your house?

PHAEDRA. Be quiet. Let me hear the voice of those inside.　　560

CHORUS. I will. Though this beginning seems to me not good.

PHAEDRA. Oh! Oh! alas! alas!
　O wretched thing I am in these my sufferings!

CHORUS. What are the words you speak? What is the tale you tell?
　Say what speech it is, my lady, that frightens you so,　　565
　tearing into your heart.

PHAEDRA. O I am lost! Just stand beside these gates, and there
　listen to all the uproar falling on the house.

CHORUS. You are there by the door. You it is who must tell
　of the words that come from within.　　570
　Tell me what can it be, what evil is here.

PHAEDRA. He shouts aloud, the son of the huntress Amazon,
　Hippolytus, and to my nurse says dreadful things.

CHORUS. Yes, I can hear the voice; yet cannot clearly tell
　whence came the cry to you,　　575
　came to you through the gates.

PHAEDRA. O listen, clearly now he calls her "procuress
　of evil and betrayer of her master's bed."

CHORUS. O, I weep for your pain. Lady, you are betrayed.
　How can I find you help?　　580
　Secret things are revealed, and you are lost . . .

PHAEDRA. Alas! Alas!

CHORUS. By your friends betrayed.

PHAEDRA. She has destroyed me, telling him of my distress,
　kindly, not nobly, seeking to relieve my pain.　　585

CHORUS. What now? What will you do, caught so much in a trap?

PHAEDRA. I do not know, except for one thing,—that quick death
　remains the only cure for all my present pain.

　　[*Phaedra retires. Hippolytus, with the Nurse following him,
　　comes in.*]

HIPPOLYTUS. O mother Earth and you unfoldings of the sun,
　I have heard the unspeakable sound of most foul words.　　590

NURSE. Be silent, child, lest someone notice your cries.

HIPPOLYTUS. I have heard dreadful things. How can I hold my
　tongue?

NURSE. I beg you, by this right hand of yours, and this strong arm.

HIPPOLYTUS. Take your hands off me! Do not dare to touch my
　clothes.

NURSE. I implore you by your knees. Do not be my ruin.　　595

HIPPOLYTUS. How can I, if, as you pretend, your words were good?

NURSE. O child, this story is not fit for all to hear.

HIPPOLYTUS. More hearers the more honor, when the news is good.

NURSE. O child, you must respect the oath you swore to me.
HIPPOLYTUS. It was my tongue that swore: my mind has made no
    oath.                                  600
NURSE. O child, what will you do? Will you destroy your friends?
HIPPOLYTUS. Your words revolt me. No bad person is my friend.
NURSE. Have pity! It is natural, my child, to make mistakes.
HIPPOLYTUS. O Zeus, why did you house them in the light of day,
women, man's evil, a false glittering counterfeit?       605
For if you wished to propagate the race of men,
this should not have been brought about by women's means.
Instead men should have offered in exchange their wealth
within your temples,—gold or silver or a weight
of bronze,—and bought their children for the price they paid,  610
each at its proper value. And then they could live
in free and easy homes and have no need of wives.
This makes it clear how great an evil a woman is:
the father who breeds and educates one pays a dowry too
that she may live elsewhere and he be free from pain.    615
And then the man who takes this curse inside his house
delights in adding fine adornments to her shape,
worthless itself, spends time in finding dresses for her,
the fool, and wastes away the substance of his house.
He's in a cleft stick; for, if he can marry well        620
and likes his new relations, then his wife will be
a bitter thing; and, if his wife is good, he'll find
worthless relations, bad and good luck counterpoised.
Easiest for him who has settled in his home a wife
whose mind's a total blank, a simple useless thing.    625
I hate a clever woman, and in my house never would
have one with more ideas than women ought to have.
For Cypris inculcates more often evil ways
among the clever ones, whereas the helpless kind
are barred from loose behavior by their lack of wit.    630
No servant ever should have access to a wife:
their company should be some biting speechless beast,
so that they could not even speak to anyone,
nor get an answer back from those whom they address.
But as it is wives who are bad make their bad plots    635
at home, and then their servants carry them outside.
Like you, you miserable wretch, who came to me
to make arrangements for my father's sacred bed.
With running water I shall wash my ears and wipe
away your words. How could I ever be so base,    640
I, who, just hearing you, must think myself unclean?

620. *cleft stick*: Dilemma.

Be sure what saves you, woman, is my sense of right.
If, carelessly, I had not bound myself by oaths,
for sure I should have told my father of all this.
And now, so long as Theseus is away from home,                    645
I shall be absent too, and keep a silent tongue;
and then, returning with my father, I shall watch
how you will meet his eye, you and your mistress too.
Yes, I shall know, having tasted of your shamelessness.
I would destroy you all,—never shall have enough               650
of hating women, though they say that I'm always
saying the same thing. Women too are always bad.
Either let someone teach them to be self-controlled
or else allow me still to tread them under foot.

> [*Hippolytus goes out. Phaedra comes forward.*]

PHAEDRA. O sad they are, unlucky,                                 655
the fates that women have!
Now that our hopes are betrayed, what art
what words can we find to loose the knot of his speech?
The verdict is given. O earth, and light!
Where can I go to escape my fate?                                660
How, dear friends, can I hide my pain?
Which of the gods would succor me now? What man
can appear to stand beside me as fellow worker
in evil deeds? O no, my life's disaster
stays with me still and cannot be escaped.                      665
I am the most unlucky one of women.

CHORUS. Alas! it is all over. They miscarried, those
arts of your servant, lady. Things are bad indeed.

PHAEDRA. [*To the Nurse*] You wicked woman, you destroyer of
    your friends,
what have you done to me? I pray my parent Zeus               670
may blot you out entirely with a blow of fire!
Did I not tell you, seeing in advance your mind,
to make no mention of what now has brought me shame?
But you had no restraint, and now no longer can I die
with a good name. I greatly need some new device.            675
Hippolytus, with anger sharpening his mind,
will speak against me, tell his father of your sins,
and tell the aged Pittheus of my sufferings,
and fill the whole land with the shameful story of it.
My curse on you, and on all those who are so keen            680
to help friends in dishonest ways against their will!

NURSE. You, lady, can reproach me for the wrong I did;
the hurt you feel is stronger than your power to judge.
Yet I too can reply to this, if you will hear.

670. *parent*: Her father Minos was a son of Zeus.

I brought you up and seek your good. I tried to find       685
medicine for your disease, and found not what I wished.
Had I been lucky, I should have been thought most wise
since brains are measured by the way events fall out.

PHAEDRA. Is this your sense of right and proper speech to me,—
to wound me first, and then admit as much in words?       690

NURSE. Our speeches are too long. I have been indiscreet.
Yet from all this, my child, there is a safe way out.

PHAEDRA. Stop talking. You have given me before advice
that was dishonest, and your action too was bad.
So now begone out of my sight, think of yourself;       695
and I shall act with honor in my own affairs.
And now I ask you, noble daughters of Troezen,
to listen to my prayers and grant me this request,—
to hide in silence all that you have heard of here.

CHORUS. I swear by mighty Artemis, the child of Zeus,       700
not ever to bring any of your woes to light.

PHAEDRA. You have spoken fairly. Now, searching my mind, I find
one way and one alone to meet my present pass,
so as to leave my children honor in their lives
and help myself in what has happened to me now.       705
For I shall never put my Cretan home to shame
or, after these disgraceful doings, come within
the sight of Theseus, just to save one single life.

CHORUS. What evil without cure do you intend to do?

PHAEDRA. To die; but how to die is what I now shall plan.       710

CHORUS. O do not say such words!

PHAEDRA. You must give good advice.
In parting from my life upon this very day
I shall give joy to Cypris who is destroying me.
Bitter has been the love which brings me my defeat,       715
yet I, in death, shall prove at least an evil thing
to another, so that he may learn not to be proud
in my misfortune. He will have a share with me
in this complaint of mine, and so learn modest ways.

[*Phaedra goes into the palace.*]

CHORUS. O I would be in aerial hiding-places,       720
that a god might set me there in the flying flocks,
myself a bird on the wing!
I would be borne on high
to the waves of the sea on the Adriatic shore,
to Eridanus' waters, where       725

725. *Eridanus*: The river Po. Phaethon, son of Helios, the sun, begged permission to drive his father's chariot
across the sky. He crashed near the river
Eridanus: his sisters, the *Heliades*
(daughters of Helios), wept for him and
were turned into poplar trees on the
river bank; their tears turned to amber
as they fell into the water. The legend
reflects the fact that amber came from
the Baltic into Greece via the area
around the mouth of the Po.

into the dark-blue stream,
pitying Phaethon, the luckless Heliades
melt in their bright and amber-shining tears.

Or might I make my way to the apple gardens
of the singing Hesperides, where the dark sea's lord          730
ends the journeys of ships!
There he dwells in the terrible
verge of heaven that Atlas holds with his arms,
and ambrosial fountains flow
from the resting places of Zeus,                              735
from his palace halls where life-giving holy earth
still for the gods increases their happiness.

White-winged vessel from Crete
that, through the salt of the wave and the beat of the sea
bore my mistress away from her happy home                     740
with a prize of unfortunate love!
Surely ill-starred both ways, or at least from Crete,
to famous Athens it winged its way,
and there on Munychian shores
they tied the ends of their twisted ropes                     745
and set their feet on the land.

For that Aphrodite broke
her heart with the terrible sickness of passion impure.
Now, since she is overladen with hard events,
she will tie to her bridal roof                               750
the hanging noose of a rope, and fit it tight
to the white of her neck, being filled with shame
at the face of the hateful goddess.
First she will choose good fame and to rid
her heart of the pains of love.                               755
  [*A Servant is heard crying out inside the palace.*]
SERVANT. Oh! Oh!
  Come here and help, all you that are about the house!
  Our mistress and the wife of Theseus is hanged.
CHORUS. Alas! Alas! It is all over, now no more

730. *Hesperides*: Nymphs who guarded
the golden apples of eternal youth in a
garden at the Western end of the Mediterranean, from which the sea-god Nereus
forbade passage of ships into the Atlantic. (Greek ships did of course occasionally pass through the strait of
Gibraltar, but did not venture far beyond.)

736. *ambrosial*: Divine, from *ambrosia*, the food of the gods.
737. *resting places of Zeus*: It was in
this Western garden that the marriage of
Zeus and Hera was consummated. The
golden apple tree was a wedding gift
from Earth.
744. *Munychia*: The old harbor of
Athens.

the royal lady lives, hanged in the swinging noose.

SERVANT. Be quick! Let someone bring a knife with double edge    760
with which we can unloose the knot about her neck.

CHORUS. What should we do, my friends? Do you think, we should
  go
inside and loose our lady from the choking rope?

SEMI-CHORUS. Why should we? Are there not young men as servants there?
By being over-zealous we may risk our lives.                      765

SERVANT. Set the limbs straight, and so lay out this wretched body.
Sad for my master is this housekeeping of hers.

CHORUS. Now she is dead, I hear it, this unhappy woman.
Already they lay out her body as a corpse.

> [*Enter Theseus with his attendants. Since he has been on
> some religious journey, he is wearing a garland on his
> head.*]

THESEUS. Do you know, women, what this uproar means
  indoors?                                                        770
A noise of wailing from my servants reached my ears.
Strange that they do not think it right to unbar the gates
and kindly greet me back from my religious way.
Surely no ill has happened to aged Pittheus?
He is already far advanced in life, yet still,                    775
were he to leave us, it would be a grief to me.

CHORUS. Theseus, this is a thing that does not touch the old.
It is the death of youth that will bring pain to you.

THESEUS. Alas! Not that my children's life is stolen away?

CHORUS. They live. Their mother,—sad, most sad for you—
  is dead.                                                        780

THESEUS. What do you say? My wife dead? How then did she die?

CHORUS. She fastened up a running noose to hang herself.

THESEUS. Had grief frozen her blood, or did some evil come to her?

CHORUS. So much I know, no more. I too have only just,
  Theseus, approached your house in mourning for your loss.       785

THESEUS. Ah, why then have I set this crown of woven leaves
upon my head, unlucky in my holy voyage?
Come, men, undo the bolts that bar the double doors!
Loosen the chains, that I may see this bitter sight
of my dead wife who, by her death, has destroyed me.             790

> [*The doors are opened and the body of Phaedra is discov-
> ered.*]

CHORUS. Oh, alas, poor lady, your pitiful fate!
You have suffered and done
a deed that can utterly ruin this house.

O reckless your doing, this violent death
in the sinful event, overthrown,                                         795
O pitiful, by your own hand!
Which god, my poor lady, has taken the light from your life?
THESEUS. O I weep for my pain! O my city, this is
the worst of the things I have suffered. O fate,
how heavy have you fallen on me and my house,                            800
a spreading stain unknown from some avenging power,
or rather a murderer's blow taking the life from my life.
And an ocean of evil, poor wretch, is in front of my eyes
so great that I can never more swim clear of it
nor cross beyond the wave of this catastrophe.                          805
Alas! my wife, what word can I find,
how can I name your burden of fate?
For like a bird you slipped out of the hand away
from me and leaped a sheer leap to the house of death.
O how pitiful is this suffering! O, alas!                               810
Out of the past somewhere I am reaping the fate
sent by a god for the sins
of someone who lived of old.
CHORUS. My lord, these evils have not come to you alone.
You have lost a worthy wife, and so have many more.                     815
THESEUS. Below the earth, in the cloud that's below the earth
I wish to dwell in the dark, I wish to die,
now separated from your dear companionship;
for, perishing, you have destroyed more than yourself.
O, what news can I hear? Whence, poor wife, did it come,                820
the fate of death to your heart?
Can someone tell me what was done? Or does my royal house
uselessly shelter numbers of my serving men?
O, my heart aches for you!
O I pity the grief I have seen in my home.                              825
It is not to be borne and not to be told. I am lost.
My home is empty and my children motherless.
You have left me, left me behind,
dearest of women and best that the ray of the sun
sees, or the star-faced moon in the night.                              830
CHORUS. Alas, unhappy, the pain that fills the house!
Streaming with tears my eyes
melt for your fate. And for long
I tremble at the woe that will come next.
THESEUS. Ha!                                                            835
What can this mean, this letter that is hanging down
from her dear hand? Has she some news she wants to tell?
Surely she has written down, poor thing, her will about

the children and my love, and made me some request.
Poor creature, be at rest! No woman in the world                840
will enter Theseus' bed or come within his house.
And now the prints of that gold signet ring she had,
she who no longer lives,—these seem to touch my heart.
Come, let me break the fastenings about the seals
and see what thing it is this letter wants to say.             845

CHORUS. Alas! Alas! Here now a god brings on
evil news in its turn. To me no fate
of life deserves to be lived after this that is done.
For I speak of our master's home, alas, alas,
as being destroyed, as being a thing of the past.             850
O god, if such there be, do not betray this house
but listen to my prayer; for, like a prophetess,
from omens I can see the evil on its way.

THESEUS. O what a fearful wrong upon the top of wrong!
Unspeakable, insufferable, O alas!                            855

CHORUS. What is it? Speak if I may share the news at all.

THESEUS. This letter cries and cries what cannot be forgot.
Where can I leave my weight of woe? O, I am lost indeed,
utterly lost! What a speaking strain
in her writing I saw! Ah me!                                  860

CHORUS. Alas, the word you speak leads on the way to pain.

THESEUS. I can keep it no longer behind the gates of my lips,
this evil so deadly, so hard to be mended.
Oh, my city!
Hippolytus has dared to violate my bed                        865
by force and shown contempt for Zeus's holy eye.
O now Poseidon, father, you who promised me
the power to curse three times, with one of these do you
destroy my son, and let him not survive this day.
Do this, if you indeed gave me the power to curse.            870

CHORUS. My lord, recall that curse, I beg you, back again.
Soon you will see that you were wrong. O listen to me!

THESEUS. It is impossible. And also I shall drive
him from this land. By one or other fate he will
be crushed. Either Poseidon, honoring my curse,             875
will end his life and send him to the gates of Hell,
or else, in exile from this land and wandering
abroad, he will live through a hard and bitter life.

[*Enter Hippolytus with his attendants.*]

CHORUS. Look, here Hippolytus, your son, has come himself
at the right time. Relax your cruel anger, lord               880
Theseus, and make the best decision for your house.

HIPPOLYTUS. I heard your cry, my father, and have come to you

with all speed. Yet I do not know what thing it is
for which you grieve. This I would like to learn from you.
O, what is this? My father, now I see your wife                    885
lying dead there. This is a thing to wonder at.
She whom only just now I parted from, she who
not long ago was looking on the light of day!
What happened to her? In what way was she destroyed?
Father, it is from you I wish to learn of this.                    890
You do not speak? Yet silence does no good in pain;
for, when the heart desires to hear of everything,
it must in trouble also be inquisitive.
Then, father, surely it cannot be right to hide
your misery from friends and even more than friends.             895

THESEUS. O how men uselessly and often go astray!
Why give instruction in the many countless arts,
use all devices, make inventions of all kinds,
while one thing is not known and never studied yet—
to teach intelligence to those who have no sense?                 900

HIPPOLYTUS. Some clever expert you must mean, who has the
            power
to force wisdom those who are deprived of it.
But, father, this is not the time for sophistry.
I fear your sufferings must have deranged your speech.

THESEUS. Alas! there should have been for men some certain sign  905
to mark their friends, some way of reading in their minds
which one is true and which one not a friend at all;
everyone should have had two different tones of voice,
one for his plain just dealings, one for all the rest.
Then words from false minds could have been compared and
            judged                                                910
by what was true, and I should not have been deceived.

HIPPOLYTUS. No, surely none of my friends has spoken ill of me
into your ear? And, innocent, am I diseased?
Sir, I am all amazed, and what amazes me
is your strange words that seem to leave the path of sense.      915

THESEUS. O mind of man! To what lengths will it not proceed?
Where will a bound be set to reckless arrogance?
For if in every generation this swells up,
if the younger comes to an excess of shame beyond
the former generation, then the gods will have                   920
to add another world to this one, which will hold
the evil men who are by nature all depraved.
Look at this young man here, who, though he is my son,
has brought pollution to my bed, and without doubt
is proved the greatest villain by this woman's death.            925

And now, since any way your presence stains the air,
turn your head here, and let your father see your face.
So you are he who, as a man marked out, consorts
with gods? You are the chaste one, all untouched by sin?
I certainly will not believe your boasting words                930
or be a fool to credit gods with ignorance.
Now boast away, try to impose on people with
your meatless meals, take Orpheus for your lord and join
the revel, worshipping the smoke of countless books.
You are found out. And people of your sort I bid             935
all men avoid. You are of those who seek their prey
by pompous language while you scheme your shameful deeds.
She's dead. And do you think that this will make you safe?
No, you mean creature. This is where you are most caught.
For where will you find oaths, where words to be more strong  940
for your acquittal than this argument of her?
You will pretend she hated you, and say bastards
and true-born children are by nature enemies.
That would suggest she bargained badly with her life,
through hating you to throw away what she loved best.        945
Or will you say that folly does not go with men
but is a part of woman's nature? I know well
young men no more reliable than women are
when Cypris brings confusion to their youthful hearts,
although they have advantages by being men.                 950
But why should I thus meet you in a strife of words,
When this dead body here is surest evidence?
Go! Leave this land, an exile, quick as you can do,
and neither enter god-built Athens nor the bounds
of any country over which my spear holds sway.              955
I have suffered from you, and if I am worsted by you,
then Sinis of the Isthmus can deny the fact
I ever killed him, say it was an empty boast,
and Sciron's rocks that fall into the sea can say

932. *impose on*: Deceive.
933. *Orpheus*: The followers of Orpheus, a legendary musician, were members of an ascetic sect which practised vegetarianism, carried out frequent purificatory rituals, and appealed to the authority of sacred books (supposed to be written by Orpheus). Hippolytus is not of course an Orphic (as a hunter, for example, he is not likely to have been a vegetarian) but he is a sexual ascetic, or rather, his father now believes, a hypocrite who merely claimed to be one. Since most Greeks regarded Orphic cultists as imposters, Euripides has Theseus employ against his son the vocabulary of abuse normally reserved for the Orphic priests and devotees.
957. *Sinis*: A famous brigand killed by Theseus when he was a young hero. Sinis used to ask travelers to help him bend a pine tree top down to the ground: he would then let go, and the victim would be catapulted to his death.
959. *Sciron*: Another monster killed by the young Theseus. Sciron would make travelers on the cliff-road to Athens wash his feet: he would then kick them over the cliff-top to their deaths. The cliff, or promontory, is mentioned below in the messenger's speech (line 1145).

I am not heavy on the doers of bad deeds. 960
CHORUS. How can I say that anyone at all of men
   is happy? What was first is overturned again.
HIPPOLYTUS. Father, the rage and tension in your heart make me
   afraid. As for the charge, there are good arguments,
   yet, when examined, then it is not fair at all. 965
   I have no skill at making speeches to a crowd
   and am wiser with a few who are my own equals.
   This too is natural. Those who among the wise
   are fools show more intelligence in speaking to
   a crowd. Yet, all the same, since I am in this pass, 970
   I am bound to loose my tongue. And I shall start my speech
   from where you first attacked me surreptitiously,
   thinking to injure me and give me no reply.
   You see this light and earth. In them there is not one,
   deny it as you may, who is more pure than I. 975
   For, first, I know how to give reverence to the gods
   and to have friends who will not try to injure me,
   whose sense of shame prevents them asking what is bad
   or aiding their associates in wicked deeds.
   I, father, do not mock at those with whom I live, 980
   but, near or far, am still a friend in the same way.
   One thing has never touched me,—what you think my guilt.
   This body to this moment is unstained by love.
   I do not know the action, except what I hear
   in talk or see in pictures, and I have no wish 985
   to know about such things. I have a virgin soul.
   Perhaps my purity does not convince your mind.
   Then you must show in what way I became corrupt.
   Was it this woman's body was more beautiful
   than that of all the rest? Or did I hope to make 990
   your house my own by taking on an heiress' bed?
   Could I be such a fool, so quite outside my mind?
   Or do wise-minded men enjoy the sweets of power?
   They do not. For, when power is absolute, it will
   always corrupt the minds of men who feel its charm. 995
   For me, I'd choose to win in the Hellenic games
   first prize, and in my city be the second man,
   and so live happy always with my noble friends.
   This means an active life with no danger attached,
   and gives more pleasure than life of supreme power. 1000
      One thing in my defence I have not said. The rest
   you know. But, if I had a witness like myself,

996. *Hellenic games*: The great ath-    were those held at Olympia.
letic games, the most famous of which

and if this woman saw the light when I was tried,
then, looking at the evidence, you would have seen
which was the guilty. Now, I swear to you by Zeus,                     1005
guardian of oaths, by earth's floor, that I never touched
your wife, nor could have wished to, nor conceived the thought.
And may I die inglorious, without a name,
without a house or city, exiled and wandering,
and, after death, let neither sea nor land receive                    1010
my body, if in truth I am a wicked man.
And, if it was from terror that she threw away
her life, I do not know. More than this I must not say.
She has controlled herself, though lacking in the power;
I have the power, but have made bitter use of it.                     1015
CHORUS. You have said enough to turn away the charge from you,
swearing an oath, no small conviction, to the gods.
THESEUS. Is he some wizard or enchanter who believes
that by his even temper he can get his way
over my spirit, after having wronged his sire?                        1020
HIPPOLYTUS. This too in you, my father, fills me with surprise.
If I had been your father and you been my son,
I should have killed you, not punished you with exile,
if you had dared to lay your hands upon my wife.
THESEUS. That is just like you. No, you shall not die like this,     1025
according to the law you frame to suit yourself.
For a quick death is easiest for wicked men.
But, wandering in exile from your father's land,
abroad you will live through a hard and bitter life.
For this is the correct reward for wicked men.                        1030
HIPPOLYTUS. Alas! What will you do? Will you not wait for time
to inform against me? Will you drive me from the land?
THESEUS. Yes, and beyond the sea and bounds that Atlas made,
if I might do it, so I hate the sight of you.
HIPPOLYTUS. Will you not test the truth by oaths or guarantees       1035
or words of seers, but banish me without a trial?
THESEUS. This letter here, with no prophetic stamp on it,
is evidence enough against you. As for birds
that flit above my head, I take no stock of that.
HIPPOLYTUS. O gods, why then can I not loose my lips,                1040
I who by you am ruined, you whom I revere?
I cannot. Even then I'd fail to move the minds
I should move, and would vainly break the oath I swore.
THESEUS. Oh, these grand airs of yours will drive me to my grave!
Will you not go, and leave at once your father's house?              1045

---

1038. *birds*: Prophets interpreted the flight of birds to foretell the future.

HIPPOLYTUS. O where then can I turn, poor wretch? Which of my
    friends
will take me to his house, exiled on such a charge?

THESEUS. One who enjoys receiving guests who will defile
other men's wives and take their share in deeds of shame.

HIPPOLYTUS. Ah! This goes to my heart and brings me near to
    tears,           1050
that I should look so bad and you should think me so.

THESEUS. The time to groan and feel the future was the time
you dared commit an outrage on your father's wife.

HIPPOLYTUS. O palace, how I wish that you would cry aloud
for me, and witness whether I am really bad!     1055

THESEUS. You wisely look for witnesses that have no voice.
    [*He points to the dead body.*]
This fact that does not speak proclaims your wickedness.

HIPPOLYTUS. Alas!
I wish that I could stand in front of my own self
and see my face. I would have wept for what I feel.     1060

THESEUS. Yes, you are much more trained in worshipping yourself
than in honoring your father with an honest mind.

HIPPOLYTUS. O my poor mother, bitter was your birth of me!
Let bastards never be among the friends I have!

THESEUS. Drag him out, slaves! Do you not hear? For long     1065
I have been ordering this man to leave my land.

HIPPOLYTUS. The first of them who touches me will suffer for it.
Thrust me away yourself, if this is what you will.

THESEUS. That is what I shall do, if you will not obey.
No trace of pity for your exile touches me.     1070
    [*Exit Theseus.*]

HIPPOLYTUS. Then it is fixed, it seems. O, what a wretch I am!
I know the truth, but do not know how I can speak.
O child of Leto, dearest to me of the gods,
who rested with me, hunted with me, must I leave
great Athens as an exile? O farewell, you land     1075
and city of Erechtheus! O, Troezenian plains,
what happiness you gave me as I grew up here!
Farewell! I see you for the last time as I speak.
Now come, my friends and young companions of this land,
speak to me now and see me on my way abroad.     1080
Never will you behold a man more pure than I,
even although my father does not think it so.
    [*Exit Hippolytus with his friends and attendants.*]

CHORUS. Greatly indeed it will ease me of grief, when it comes to
    my mind,
the thought of the gods.
Yet, though guessing in hope at their wisdom,     1085

I am downcast again when I look at the fortunes and actions of
    mortals,
for they alter, now here and now there;
man's life has no fixed station
but is mutable always.

I wish when I make my prayers this fate from the gods might be
    mine—                                  1090
to have wealth for my lot
and a heart unacquainted with grief.
And the thoughts in my mind should not be too subtle, nor
    counterfeit either;
but, easily willing to alter
my ways as the morrow comes,                        1095
I should always be happy.

No more can I look with a mind undisturbed upon things unex-
    pected,
now the brightest of stars
of Hellas, of Athens,—we saw it—
is sent by the rage of his father                      1100
to foreign countries abroad.
O sands of the shores of my city,
O glades in the mountains where he
slew wild beasts with his swift-footed hounds,
and holy Dictynna was with him!                      1105

No more will you stand in the chariot drawn by Venetian fillies
on the Limnean track,
holding in with your foot the wild horses.
And the sleepless strain of the lyre
will cease in your father's house.                      1110
Unwreathed in the green of the forest
are the coverts of Leto's child.
In your exile the contest is ended
of maidens who vied for your love.

O for your misfortune I shall pass                      1115
in tears my ill-fated fate.
Useless, poor mother, was your birth of him.
My anger falls on the gods.
Alas, you band of the Graces,
why have you sent him away                      1120
from this house, from his native land,

1119. *Graces*: The Graces, goddesses whose province is art and beauty, should have protected Hippolytus, instead of letting him go.

he, quite without guilt in this evil?

[A *Messenger, one of Hippolytus' attendants approaches.*]

CHORUS. But now I see one of Hippolytus' men.
He comes up to the house in haste with a wild look.

MESSENGER. Women, which is the way for me to go to find    1125
Theseus, this country's king? If you know where he is,
then tell me of it. Is he now inside the house?

CHORUS. I see him there coming himself outside the house.

MESSENGER. Theseus, I bring you tidings that will make you think,
you and your citizens that live in Athens' town    1130
and in the boundaries of this Troezenian land.

THESEUS. What is it? Can it be that some fresh blow of fate
has come upon these twin and neighboring towns of mine?

MESSENGER. Let me speak plain. Hippolytus no more exists.
He sees the light, but life is hanging by a thread.    1135

THESEUS. Who killed him? Was it one who hated him because
his wife, like mine, was violated and defiled?

MESSENGER. It was the chariot he drove that caused his death;
that, and the curses from your mouth which you called down
from the sea's governor, your father, on your son.    1140

THESEUS. Gods! O Poseidon, so in very truth you were
my father, since you heard the prayer I made to you!
How did he die? Tell me. What was the way in which the trap
of Justice closed on him who shamed me so?

MESSENGER. We were beside the promontory where the waves    1145
beat on the shore, and combing down the horses' manes,
weeping, because a messenger had come to say
that now no longer must Hippolytus set foot
within this land, condemned by you to sad exile.
And then he came himself with the same strain of tears    1150
to us upon the shore, and at his heels there came
with him a countless band of friends of his own age.
For long he did not cease lamenting. Then he said:
"Why do I rave? My father's words must be obeyed.
Prepare my yoke of horses for the chariot,    1155
attendants. In this city I have no more right."
And then each one of us pressed onward with the work,
and, quicker than it takes to tell, we had the mares
standing all ready harnessed in our master's sight.
Then from the chariot rail he snatches up the reins,    1160
plants his feet firmly in the sockets on the floor,
and, stretching out his hands, he first addressed the gods:
"O Zeus, if I am sinful, let me cease to live,
and let my father know that he is wronging me
either when I am dead or while I see the light."    1165
And straight away he took into his hands the goad

and laid it on the horses, while we men ran on
close to the chariot's reins in escort to our lord,
on the straight road to Argos and Epidaurus.
Now, when we reached the open country just beyond    1170
the frontier of this land, there is a stretch of shore
that lies already facing the Saronic gulf.
Here from the ground a roar like Zeus' thunderclap
came sounding heavy round us, terrible to hear.
The horses raised their heads and pricked their ears right up   1175
into the air, and on us fell a lively fear,
wondering what the sound could be. And when we looked
along the foaming shores, we saw a monstrous wave
towering up to the sky, so big it took away
the view of Sciron's promontory from my eyes.    1180
It hid the Isthmus and Asclepius' rock.
Next, swelling up and surging onward, with, all round,
a mass of foam, and with the roaring of the sea,
it neared the shore where stood the four-horse chariot.
And, in the very surge and breaking of the flood,    1185
the wave threw up a bull, a fierce and monstrous thing,
and with his bellowing the land was wholly filled,
and fearful re-echoed. As for us who saw
the sight, it seemed too much for eyes to look upon.
Immediately a dreadful panic seized the steeds.    1190
My master, with his long experience of how
horses behave, gripped tightly in his hands the reins
and pulled upon them, like a boatman pulls his oar,
knotting the straps behind him and leaning back on them.
But the horses, taking in their teeth the fiery bits,    1195
carried him on by force and took no care at all
either of master hand or of the knotted reins
or of the welded chariot, and, if he steered their course,
as with a tiller, to the smoother bits of ground,
then in their faces there appeared, to turn them back,    1200
the bull, and drove the four-horse team all mad with fear.
And, if they rushed with maddened minds upon the rocks,
he silently drew near the chariot, and ran
alongside, till, forcing the wheel against a stone,
he overthrew the car and hurled the driver out.    1205
Then all was huddled in a mass. The naves of wheels
and axle pins together flew into the air.
Hippolytus himself, entangled in the reins,
tied in inextricable bonds, was dragged along,
his dear head dashed upon the rocks, his flesh all torn,    1210

1169. *Argos . . . Epidaurus*: Cities    of Epidaurus, where there was a famous
west of Troezen.                             shrine of the healing god Asclepius.
1181. *Asclepius' rock*: The acropolis

and crying out words terrible for us to hear.
"O stop, you horses that were fed within my stalls!
Do not wipe out my life! Alas, my father's curse!
Will no one come to me and save a noble man?"
And many of us longed to do so, but we were                    1215
left far behind. Yet in the end he was set free
somehow or other from the bonds of these fine reins,
and fell down with a little life left in him still.
The horses and that awful monster of a bull
had disappeared somewhere along the rocky ground.              1220
My lord, I am a slave within your house, and yet
this is a thing that I shall never be induced
to think,—that your son really was a wicked man:
no, not if all the race of women hung themselves,
or if all Ida's pines were filled with written words,          1225
I'd not believe it, since I know that he is good.

CHORUS. Now the disaster of fresh evil is fulfilled.
From fate and from necessity there's no escape.

THESEUS. In hatred for the man who met this fate I was
pleased with your news. But now I feel a reverent awe          1230
both towards the gods and him, since he was born of me;
and by these evils I am neither pleased nor grieved.

MESSENGER. What are we now to do to please you? Shall we bring
this suffering creature here, or what are we to do?
Think carefully. And my advice to you would be                 1235
not to be cruel to your own son in his pain.

THESEUS. Bring him to me, that I may see before my eyes
him who denied that he had made my bed his own,
that I by words and acts of gods may prove him wrong.

CHORUS. The unbending minds of gods and men,                   1240
Cypris, are prisoners to you,
and with you goes on wheeling swiftest wing
the gleaming feathered god.
He flies above the earth, above
the salt resounding sea.                                       1245
Love brings enchantment when in shine of gold
and winged he comes upon the maddened heart.
He charms the tribes of mountain beasts,
beasts of the sea and all that earth supplies,
all creatures brightened by the seeing sun;                    1250
men too, and, Cypris, you alone
rule over all with sovereign power.
        [*The goddess Artemis appears.*]

---

1225. *Ida's pines*: Ida is the great
mountain range near Troy. Pine-wood
tablets, covered with wax, were used as
writing materials.

1243. *feathered god*: Eros (Love),
whose arrows created love in humans
and gods.

ARTEMIS. You I address and bid you to listen,
   great son of Aigeus!
   The daughter of Leto, I, Artemis, speak to you.      1255
   Why are you foolishly pleased with this, Theseus,
   you who have wickedly murdered your son,
   led to believe by your wife's false words
   uncertain things? You have gained certain ruin.
   How you would wish in the depths of the earth      1260
   to hide your body in shame, or, changing
   your life to the air, be a bird and keep far
   away from this pain!
   Since among good men there is certainly
   no lot in life for you.      1265
   Hear, Theseus, now the state of ill in which you are.
   Be sure I do not gain from it and I shall cause you pain.
   But for this reason I have come, to make you see
   how your son's heart was pure, that he may die with fame,
   and make you see the savage passion of your wife      1270
   or, in a way, the nobleness; for she was pricked
   by sting of that most hateful of the gods to us
   who love a virgin life, and she desired your son.
   She tried by resolution to beat Cypris down,
   and then was lost, unwilling, by her nurse's craft,      1275
   who under oath informed your son of her disease.
   And he, just as was right, neither was influenced
   by what she said, nor, when by you he was maligned,
   would break his pledged word, since his nature fears the gods.
   But she, your wife, in fear lest she might be found out,      1280
   Wrote a false story down and by this trick of hers
   destroyed your son, yet all the same persuaded you.
THESEUS. Alas!
ARTEMIS. Does the tale, Theseus, bite your heart? Yet quietly wait
   and hear what follows, that you may lament still more.      1285
   You know you have three certain curses from your sire,
   and one of them, you wicked man, you have misused
   against your son. It might have been against a foe.
   Your father, the sea's king, with honorable mind,
   gave what he had to give since he had promised it.      1290
   But both to him and me your wickedness is clear.
   You did not wait for guarantees or words of seers,
   made no examination, nor by course of time
   allowed enquiry, but, more quickly than you ought,
   you laid the curse upon your son and took his life.      1295
THESEUS. O lady, I am lost.
ARTEMIS. Your deed is dreadful. Yet

1254. *son of Aigeus*: Theseus.

Still there may be forgiveness here even for you.
It was the will of Cypris that these things should be,
to sate her rage. There is this rule among the gods,— 1300
that none of us will check another god's desire
when it is shown. Instead we always stand aside.
Be sure that if I did not fear the power of Zeus
I never would have sunk to such a depth of shame
as to allow the death of him who is to me 1305
dearest of men. As for your sin, first the fact
of ignorance frees you from guilt of evil thought.
And then your wife, who now is dead, poured out her words
of evidence so much that they persuaded you.
And on you chiefly now has broken all this ill, 1310
but I too feel the pain. The gods do not rejoice
when good men die. As for the wicked, we destroy
them, and their houses and the children that they have.

      [*Hippolytus is carried in by his attendants.*]

CHORUS. See! Here the wretched sufferer comes.
  His youthful flesh and golden hair 1315
have lost their beauty. O what pain,
what double grief has fallen on these halls
and swooped on them from heaven!

HIPPOLYTUS. Alas! Alas!
  I in my misery all disfigured 1320
by unjust curse of an unjust father,
I am destroyed. Alas! Alas!
Through my head goes a darting anguish,
spasms leap within my brain.
Stop! Let me rest my weary body. 1325
Hateful my clariot, hateful my horses
fed from my hand!
You have slain and destroyed me.
O, my servants, gently, I beg you
touch my bruised flesh with your hands! 1330
Who is it standing there at my right side?
Lift me up carefully, raise me together,
me the unfortunate, me the cursed one
by fault of my father. O Zeus, do you see it?
I who was holy, I who was reverent, 1335
I who surpassed all men in my purity,
am going to certain death under ground,
losing my life. O useless the efforts
I made out of kindness
in service to men! 1340
Oh! Oh!
It is the pain, the pain coming over me.

Leave me to suffer!
O let Death, the Healer, come for me!
O you are killing me, doubling my pain.                                    1345
How I long for a two-edged spear blade
to cut through my body
and bring my life to its rest!
O sad the curse my father laid upon me.
It is the sin of bloody ancestors,                                         1350
of forefathers in ancient times, that comes
down from the past on me and will not stay.
Yet why on me all guiltless of these sins?
Alas, what should I say?
How can I free my life from this                                           1355
insufferable pain?
O let the black of death and night of fate
lull me, unhappy, to my sleep!
ARTEMIS. Poor youth, how you are yoked together with your pain!
    It was the goodness of your heart destroyed your life.                 1360
HIPPOLYTUS. Ha!
O heavenly breath of fragrance! Even in my pains
I feel your presence, and my body grows more light.
Is Artemis, the goddess, present in this place?
ARTEMIS. Poor youth, she is, and loves you more than all
    the gods.                                                              1365
HIPPOLYTUS. You see me, lady, and my state, my wretched state?
ARTEMIS. I see you, but my eyes are not allowed to weep.
HIPPOLYTUS. No more the huntsman for you and the serving
    man . . .
ARTEMIS. No more. Yet in your dying you are dear to me.
HIPPOLYTUS. No more to guard your statues or to drive your
    steeds                                                                 1370
ARTEMIS. No. It was cruel Cypris wished these things to be.
HIPPOLYTUS. Alas! I recognize the god who took my life.
ARTEMIS. Jealous of honor, angry at your living pure.
HIPPOLYTUS. Alone, I see, she has destroyed all three of us.
ARTEMIS. Yes. You, your father, and his wife, the third of you.          1375
HIPPOLYTUS. Then I must weep too for my father's sufferings.
ARTEMIS. It was the counsel of a god deceived his mind.
HIPPOLYTUS. Unhappy father in this suffering of yours!
THESEUS. My son. I am destroyed and have no joy in life.
HIPPOLYTUS. More than myself, I grieve for you and your
    mistake.                                                               1380
THESEUS. I wish that I, my child, could die instead of you.
HIPPOLYTUS. Bitter the gifts your sire, Poseidon, gave to you.
THESEUS. I wish that it had never mounted to my lips.
HIPPOLYTUS. Why so? You would have killed me, angry as you were.

THESEUS. Yes, for the gods had cheated me of my good sense.  1385
HIPPOLYTUS. Alas!
   I wish the race of men had power to curse the gods.
ARTEMIS. Be satisfied. For no, not in the dark of earth
   shall I allow, at Cypris' pleasure, rage to light
   upon your body unavenged; and this because  1390
   of your godfearingness and of your noble mind.
   For I shall take from her with my own hand the one
   of mortals whom above all others she loves best,
   and so with my unerring bow become avenged.
   And now on you, unhappy one, for all your pains  1395
   I shall bestow the greatest honors in this land
   of Troezen. For unmarried girls, before they wed,
   shall cut their hair to do you honor. You will have
   for ages long the harvest of their mourning tears.
   And always among maidens there will be desire  1400
   to make their songs of you. It will not pass away
   or nameless sink to silence, Phaedra's love for you.
   And you, O child of aged Aigeus, I bid take
   your son up in your arms and give him your embrace.
   It was against your will you slew him, and it is  1405
   natural for men to err when gods point out the way.
   And you, Hippolytus, I counsel not to hate
   your father, for you know the fate by which you died.
   Farewell! For I am not allowed to see the dead,
   or stain my eye with the last gasps of dying men,  1410
   and you I see already near that evil thing.
HIPPOLYTUS. O farewell, blessed maiden, go upon your way.
   Easily now you leave our long companionship.
   I end my quarrel with my father, as you bid,
   and as in old times also I obeyed your words.  1415
      [*Artemis goes out.*]
   Ah! Ah! Already darkness settles on my eyes.
   Take hold of me, my father. Keep my body straight.
THESEUS. My son, what are you doing to me in my pain?
HIPPOLYTUS. Now I am dying. Now I see the gates of Hell.
THESEUS. O will you leave me here with heart unpurified?  1420
HIPPOLYTUS. I will not, since I free you from the stain of blood.
THESEUS. What? You will set me free from guilt of shedding blood?
HIPPOLYTUS. I call the archer Artemis to witness it.
THESEUS. Dear son, how noble to your father's eyes you are.
HIPPOLYTUS. Pray that your true-born children may be like
   to me.  1425

---

1392–1393. Artemis must be referring to her part in the death of Adonis, Aphrodite's human love.
1397–1398. *unmarried girls*: This was, in fact, a religious ceremony in Athens. As in the end of the *Medea*, the tragedy celebrates the mythical basis of a cult.

THESEUS. I weep for your good heart, your true and upright mind.

HIPPOLYTUS. Farewell to you too, father! O, a long farewell!

THESEUS. O my son, do not leave me! Summon up your strength.

HIPPOLYTUS. My strength is done and finished, father, and I die.
　　Now quickly with my garments hide away my face.　　　　　　1430
　　　　[*Hippolytus dies.*]

THESEUS. O famous bounds of Athens and of Pallas' land,
　　How great a man is this that you will lose! Alas!
　　How often, Cypris, shall I think of your ill deeds!

CHORUS. This is a grief that is common to all of us.
　　and came unexpected.　　　　　　　　　　　　　　　　　　1435
　　Many the tears that now will be falling,
　　since for great men mourning voices
　　still last longer.


# ARISTOPHANES

## (448?–380? B.C.)

## Lysistrata*

### *Characters in the Play*†

LYSISTRATA ⎫
CALONICE　⎬ *Athenian women*
MYRRHINE　⎭

LAMPITO, *a Spartan woman*

LEADER *of the Chorus of Old Men*

CHORUS *of Old Men*

LEADER *of the Chorus of Old Women*

CHORUS *of Old Women*

ATHENIAN MAGISTRATE

THREE ATHENIAN WOMEN

CINESIAS, *an Athenian, husband of Myrrhine*

SPARTAN HERALD

SPARTAN AMBASSADORS

ATHENIAN AMBASSADORS

TWO ATHENIAN CITIZENS

CHORUS *of Athenians*

CHORUS *of Spartans*

* From *Greek Literature in Translation* by W. J. Oates and C. T. Murphy. Translation by Charles T. Murphy. Longmans, Green & Co., Inc., 1944. Used by permission of David McKay Company, Inc.

† As is usual in ancient comedy, the leading characters have significant names. *Lysistrata* is "She who disbands the armies"; *Myrrhine's* name is chosen to suggest *myrton*, a Greek word meaning *pudenda muliebria*; *Lampito* is a celebrated Spartan name; *Cinesias*, although a real name in Athens, is chosen to suggest a Greek verb *kinein, to move*, then *to make love, to have intercourse*, and the name of his deme, *Paionidai*, suggests the verb *paiein*, which has about the same significance.

SCENE: *In Athens, beneath the Acropolis. In the center of the stage is the Propylaea, or gate-way to the Acropolis; to one side is a small grotto, sacred to Pan. The Orchestra represents a slope leading up to the gate-way.*

*It is early in the morning.* LYSISTRATA *is pacing impatiently up and down.*

LYSISTRATA. If they'd been summoned to worship the God of Wine, or Pan, or to visit the Queen of Love, why, you couldn't have pushed your way through the streets for all the timbrels.[1] But now there's not a single woman here—except my neighbour; here she comes.

[*Enter* CALONICE.]

Good day to you, Calonice.

CALONICE. And to you, Lysistrata. [*Noticing* LYSISTRATA'S *impatient air*] But what ails you? Don't scowl, my dear; it's not becoming to you to knit your brows like that.

LYSISTRATA. [*Sadly*] Ah, Calonice, my heart aches; I'm so annoyed at us women. For among men we have a reputation for sly trickery—

CALONICE. And rightly too, on my word!

LYSISTRATA. —but when they were told to meet here to consider a matter of no small importance, they lie abed and don't come.

CALONICE. Oh, they'll come all right, my dear. It's not easy for a woman to get out, you know. One is working on her husband, another is getting up the maid, another has to put the baby to bed, or wash and feed it.

LYSISTRATA. But after all, there are other matters more important than all that.

CALONICE. My dear Lysistrata, just what is this matter you've summoned us women to consider? What's up? Something big?

LYSISTRATA. Very big.

CALONICE. [*Interested*] Is it stout, too?

LYSISTRATA. [*Smiling*] Yes indeed—both big and stout.

CALONICE. What? And the women still haven't come?

LYSISTRATA. It's not what you suppose; they'd have come soon enough for *that*. But I've worked up something, and for many a sleepless night I've turned it this way and that.

CALONICE. [*In mock disappointment*] Oh, I guess it's pretty fine and slender, if you've turned it this way and that.

LYSISTRATA. So fine that the safety of the whole of Greece lies in us women.

CALONICE. In us women? It depends on a very slender reed then.

LYSISTRATA. Our country's fortunes are in our hands; and whether the Spartans shall perish—

CALONICE. Good! Let them perish, by all means.

---

1. *timbrels:* These instruments were used in most orgiastic cults, especially in the worship of Dionysus, the "God of Wine."

LYSISTRATA. —and the Boeotians shall be completely annihilated.

CALONICE. Not completely! Please spare the eels.[2]

LYSISTRATA. As for Athens, I won't use any such unpleasant words. But you understand what I mean. But if the women will meet here—the Spartans, the Boeotians, and we Athenians—then all together we will save Greece.

CALONICE. But what could women do that's clever or distinguished? We just sit around all dolled up in silk robes, looking pretty in our sheer gowns and evening slippers.

LYSISTRATA. These are just the things I hope will save us: these silk robes, perfumes, evening slippers, rouge, and our chiffon blouses.

CALONICE. How so?

LYSISTRATA. So never a man alive will lift a spear against the foe—

CALONICE. I'll get a silk gown at once.

LYSISTRATA. —or take up his shield—

CALONICE. I'll put on my sheerest gown!

LYSISTRATA. —or sword.

CALONICE. I'll buy a pair of evening slippers.

LYSISTRATA. Well then, shouldn't the women have come?

CALONICE. Come? Why, they should have *flown* here.

LYSISTRATA. Well, my dear, just watch: they'll act in true Athenian fashion—everything too late! And now there's not a woman here from the shore or from Salamis.[3]

CALONICE. They're coming. I'm sure; at daybreak they were laying —to their oars to cross the straits.

LYSISTRATA. And those I expected would be the first to come—the women of Acharnae[4]—they haven't arrived.

CALONICE. Yet the wife of Theagenes[5] means to come: she consulted Hecate about it. [*Seeing a group of women approaching*] But look! Here come a few. And there are some more over here. Hurrah! Where do they come from?

LYSISTRATA. From Anagyra.[6]

CALONICE. Yes indeed! We've raised up quite a stink from Anagyra anyway.

[*Enter* MYRRHINE *in haste, followed by several other women.*]

MYRRHINE. [*Breathlessly*] Have we come in time, Lysistrata? What do you say? Why so quiet?

LYSISTRATA. I can't say much for you, Myrrhine, coming at this hour on such important business.

---

2. Eels were a favorite Athenian delicacy from the Boeotian lakes; eels were then very rare in Athens because of the war.

3. just across the bay from Piraeus, the port of Athens.

4. a large village a few miles northwest of Athens.

5. was a very superstitious Athenian (perhaps he was sitting in the audience) who never went out without consulting the shrine of Hecate at his doorstep.

6. a district south of Athens. It was also the name of a bad-smelling shrub and the phrase "to stir up the anagyra" was proverbially used to describe people who brought trouble on themselves by interfering.

MYRRHINE. Why, I had trouble finding my girdle in the dark. But if it's so important, we're here now; tell us.

LYSISTRATA. No. Let's wait a little for the women from Boeotia and the Peloponnesus.

MYRRHINE. That's a much better suggestion. Look! Here comes Lampito now.

[*Enter* LAMPITO *with two other women.*]

LYSISTRATA. Greetings, my dear Spartan friend. How pretty you look, my dear. What a smooth complexion and well-developed figure! You could throttle an ox.

LAMPITO. Faith, yes, I think I could. I take exercises and kick my heels against my bum. [*She demonstrates with a few steps of the Spartan "bottom-kicking" dance.*]

LYSISTRATA. And what splendid breasts you have.

LAMPITO. La! You handle me like a prize steer.

LYSISTRATA. And who is this young lady with you?

LAMPITO. Faith, she's an Ambassadress from Boeotia.

LYSISTRATA. Oh yes, a Boeotian, and blooming like a garden too.

CALONICE. [*Lifting up her skirt*] My word! How neatly her garden's weeded!

LYSISTRATA. And who is the other girl?

LAMPITO. Oh, she's a Corinthian swell.

MYRRHINE. [*After a rapid examination*] Yes indeed. She swells very nicely [*Pointing*] here and here.

LAMPITO. Who has gathered together this company of women?

LYSISTRATA. I have.

LAMPITO. Speak up, then. What do you want?

MYRRHINE. Yes, my dear, tell us what this important matter is.

LYSISTRATA. Very well, I'll tell you. But before I speak, let me ask you a little question.

MYRRHINE. Anything you like.

LYSISTRATA. [*Earnestly*] Tell me: don't you yearn for the fathers of your children, who are away at the wars? I know you all have husbands abroad.

CALONICE. Why, yes; mercy me! my husband's been away for five months in Thrace keeping guard on—Eucrates.[7]

MYRRHINE. And mine for seven whole months in Pylus.[8]

LAMPITO. And mine, as soon as ever he returns from the fray, readjusts his shield and flies out of the house again.

LYSISTRATA. And as for lovers, there's not even a ghost of one left. Since the Milesians revolted from us,[9] I've not even seen an eight-inch dingus to be a leather consolation for us widows. Are you willing, if I can find a way, to help me end the war?

7. *Eucrates:* We have no details on this campaign in Thrace.
8. *Pylus:* a point on the west coast of the Peloponnese held by an Athenian garrison.
9. The city of Miletus, an Athenian ally ever since the Persian war, had deserted the Athenian cause in the previous year. The objects Lysistrata speaks of were supposed to be manufactured there.

MYRRHINE. Goodness, yes! I'd do it, even if I had to pawn my dress and—get drunk on the spot!

CALONICE. And I, even if I had to let myself be split in two like a flounder.

LAMPITO. I'd climb up Mt. Taygetus[10] if I could catch a glimpse of peace.

LYSISTRATA. I'll tell you, then, in plain and simple words. My friends, if we are going to force our men to make peace, we must do without—

MYRRHINE. Without what? Tell us.

LYSISTRATA. Will you do it?

MYRRHINE. We'll do it, if it kills us.

LYSISTRATA. Well, then we must do without sex altogether. [*General consternation*] Why do you turn away? Where go you? Why turn so pale? Why those tears? Will you do it or not? What means this hesitation?

MYRRHINE. I won't do it! Let the war go on.

CALONICE. Nor I! Let the war go on.

LYSISTRATA. So, my little flounder? Didn't you say just now you'd split yourself in half?

CALONICE. Anything else you like. I'm willing, even if I have to walk through fire. Anything rather than sex. There's nothing like it, my dear.

LYSISTRATA. [*To* MYRRHINE] What about you?

MYRRHINE. [*Sullenly*] I'm willing to walk through fire, too.

LYSISTRATA. Oh vile and cursed breed! No wonder they make tragedies about us: we're naught but "love-affairs and bassinets."[11] But you, my dear Spartan friend, if you alone are with me, our enterprise might yet succeed. Will you vote with me?

LAMPITO. 'Tis cruel hard, by my faith, for a woman to sleep alone without her nooky; but for all that, we certainly do need peace.

LYSISTRATA. O my dearest friend! You're the only real woman here.

CALONICE. [*Wavering*] Well, if we do refrain from—[*Shuddering*] what you say (God forbid!), would that bring peace?

LYSISTRATA. My goodness, yes! If we sit at home all rouged and powdered, dressed in our sheerest gowns, and neatly depilated, our men will get excited and want to take us; but if you don't come to them and keep away, they'll soon make a truce.

LAMPITO. Aye; Menelaus caught sight of Helen's naked breast and dropped his sword, they say.

CALONICE. What if the men give us up?

LYSISTRATA. "Flay a skinned dog,"[12] as Pherecrates says.

10. The mountain which towers over Sparta.

11. In the *Tyro* of Sophocles, which had recently been produced, the heroine, who had borne twin sons to the god Poseidon, left them exposed in a bassinet.

12. a proverb for useless activity Pherecrates: a fifth-century comic poet.

CALONICE. Rubbish! These make-shifts are no good. But suppose they grab us and drag us into the bedroom?

LYSISTRATA. Hold on to the door.

CALONICE. And if they beat us?

LYSISTRATA. Give in with a bad grace. There's no pleasure in it for them when they have to use violence. And you must torment them in every possible way. They'll give up soon enough; a man gets no joy if he doesn't get along with his wife.

MYRRHINE. If this is your opinion, we agree.

LAMPITO. As for our own men, we can persuade them to make a just and fair peace; but what about the Athenian rabble? Who will persuade them not to start any more monkey-shines?

LYSISTRATA. Don't worry. We guarantee to convince them.

LAMPITO. Not while their ships are rigged so well and they have that mighty treasure in the temple of Athene.

LYSISTRATA. We've taken good care for that too: we shall seize the Acropolis today. The older women have orders to do this, and while we are making our arrangements, they are to pretend to make a sacrifice and occupy the Acropolis.

LAMPITO. All will be well then. That's a very fine idea.

LYSISTRATA. Let's ratify this, Lampito, with the most solemn oath.

LAMPITO. Tell us what oath we shall swear.

LYSISTRATA. Well said. Where's our Policewoman? [*To a Scythian slave*] What are you gaping at? Set a shield upside-down here in front of me, and give me the sacred meats.

CALONICE. Lysistrata, what sort of an oath are we to take?

LYSISTRATA. What oath? I'm going to slaughter a sheep over the shield, as they do in Aeschylus.[13]

CALONICE. Don't, Lysistrata! No oaths about peace over a shield.

LYSISTRATA. What shall the oath be, then?

CALONICE. How about getting a white horse somewhere and cutting out its entrails for the sacrifice?

LYSISTRATA. White horse indeed!

CALONICE. Well then, how shall we swear?

MYRRHINE. I'll tell you: let's place a large black bowl upside-down and then slaughter—a flask of Thasian wine.[14] And then let's swear—not to pour in a single drop of water.

LAMPITO. Lord! How I like that oath!

LYSISTRATA. Someone bring out a bowl and a flask.

[*A slave brings the utensils for the sacrifice.*]

CALONICE. Look, my friends! What a big jar! Here's a cup that

13. In Aeschylus' *Seven against Thebes*, the enemy champions are described as swearing loyalty to each other and slaughtering a bull so that the blood flowed into the hollow of a shield.

14. strong wine from the island of Thasos in the northern Aegean. In Athens the wife was in charge of the household supplies and it is a frequent Aristophanic joke to present her as addicted to the bottle.

'twould give me joy to handle. [*She picks up the bowl.*]

LYSISTRATA. Set it down and put your hands on our victim. [As CALONICE *places her hands on the flask*] O Lady of Persuasion and dear Loving Cup, graciously vouchsafe to receive this sacrifice from us women. [*She pours the wine into the bowl.*]

CALONICE. The blood has a good colour and spurts out nicely.

LAMPITO. Faith, it has a pleasant smell, too.

MYRRHINE. Oh, let me be the first to swear, ladies![15]

CALONICE. No, by our Lady! Not unless you're allotted the first turn.

LYSISTRATA. Place all your hands on the cup, and one of you repeat on behalf of all what I say. Then all will swear and ratify the oath. *I will suffer no man, be he husband or lover,*

CALONICE. *I will suffer no man, be he husband or lover,*

LYSISTRATA. *To approach me all hot and horny.* [As CALONICE *hesitates*] Say it!

CALONICE. [*Slowly and painfully*] *To approach me all hot and horny.* O Lysistrata, I feel so weak in the knees!

LYSISTRATA. *I will remain at home unmated,*

CALONICE. *I will remain at home unmated,*

LYSISTRATA. *Wearing my sheerest gown and carefully adorned,*

CALONICE. *Wearing my sheerest gown and carefully adorned,*

LYSISTRATA. *That my husband may burn with desire for me.*

CALONICE. *That my husband may burn with desire for me.*

LYSISTRATA. *And if he takes me by force against my will,*

CALONICE. *And if he takes me by force against my will,*

LYSISTRATA. *I shall do it badly and keep from moving.*

CALONICE. *I shall do it badly and keep from moving.*

LYSISTRATA. *I will not stretch my slippers toward the ceiling,*

CALONICE. *I will not stretch my slippers toward the ceiling,*

LYSISTRATA. *Nor will I take the posture of the lioness on the knife-handle.*

CALONICE. *Nor will I take the posture of the lioness on the knife-handle.*

LYSISTRATA. *If I keep this oath, may I be permitted to drink from this cup,*

CALONICE. *If I keep this oath, may I be permitted to drink from this cup,*

LYSISTRATA. *But if I break it, may the cup be filled with water.*

CALONICE. *But if I break it, may the cup be filled with water.*

LYSISTRATA. Do you all swear to this?

ALL. I do, so help me!

LYSISTRATA. Come then, I'll just consummate this offering. [*She takes a long drink from the cup.*]

CALONICE. [*Snatching the cup away*] Shares, my dear! Let's drink to our continued friendship.

---

15. *first to swear:* and so the first to drink.

[*A shout is heard from off-stage.*]

LAMPITO. What's that shouting?

LYSISTRATA. That's what I was telling you: the women have just seized the Acropolis. Now, Lampito, go home and arrange matters in Sparta; and leave these two ladies here as hostages. We'll enter the Acropolis to join our friends and help them lock the gates.

CALONICE. Don't you suppose the men will come to attack us?

LYSISTRATA. Don't worry about them. Neither threats nor fire will suffice to open the gates, except on the terms we've stated.

CALONICE. I should say not! Else we'd belie our reputation as unmanageable pests.

[LAMPITO *leaves the stage. The other women retire and enter the Acropolis through the Propylaea.*]

[*Enter the* CHORUS OF OLD MEN, *carrying fire-pots and a load of heavy sticks.*]

LEADER OF MEN. Onward, Draces, step by step, though your shoulder's aching.

Cursèd logs of olive-wood, what a load you're making!

FIRST SEMI-CHORUS OF OLD MEN. [*Singing*]
Aye, many surprises await a man who lives to a ripe old age;
For who could suppose, Strymodorus my lad, that the women we've nourished (alas!),
Who sat at home to vex our days,
Would seize the holy image here
And occupy this sacred shrine,
With bolts and bars, with fell design,
To lock the Propylaea?

LEADER OF MEN. Come with speed, Philourgus, come! to the temple hast'ning.

There we'll heap these logs about in a circle round them,
And whoever has conspired, raising this rebellion,
Shall be roasted, scorched, and burnt, all without exception,
Doomed by one unanimous vote—but first the wife of Lycon.[16]

SECOND SEMI-CHORUS. [*Singing*]
No, no! by Demeter, while I'm alive, no woman shall mock at me.
Not even the Spartan Cleomenes,[17] our citadel first to seize,
Got off unscathed; for all his pride
And haughty Spartan arrogance,
He left his arms and sneaked away,

16. The ancient commentaries tell us that she was called Rhodia and was not too careful about her reputation.

17. *Cleomenes:* In 508 B.C., the Athenians expelled the tyrant Hippias and were about to install a democratic regime under the leadership of Cleisthenes when the oligarchic party appealed to Sparta for help. The Spartan king Cleomenes invaded Attica, seized the city, and began a purge of the democrats. A popular uprising, however, forced him into the Acropolis, where he was besieged; after two days he was allowed to withdraw with his troops and Cleisthenes began the reforms which established the democracy.

Stripped to his shirt, unkempt, unshav'd,
   With six years' filth still on him.
LEADER OF MEN. I besieged that hero bold, sleeping at my
      station,
   Marshalled at these holy gates sixteen deep against him.
   Shall I not these cursèd pests punish for their daring,
   Burning these Euripides-and-God-detested women?[18]
   Aye! or else may Marathon overturn my trophy.[19]
FIRST SEMI-CHORUS. [*Singing*]
      There remains of my road
      Just this brow of the hill;
      There I speed on my way.
   Drag the logs up the hill, though we've got no ass to help.
      (God! my shoulder's bruised and sore!)
      Onward still must we go
      Blow the fire! Don't let it go out
      Now we're near the end of our road.
ALL. [*Blowing on the fire-pots*]
   Whew! Whew! Drat the smoke!
SECOND SEMI-CHORUS. [*Singing*]
      Lord, what smoke rushing forth
      From the pot, like a dog
      Running mad, bites my eyes!
   This must be Lemnos-fire.[20] What a sharp and stinging smoke!
      Rushing onward to the shrine
      Aid the gods. Once for all
      Show your mettle, Laches my boy!
      To the rescue hastening all!
ALL. [*Blowing on the fire-pots*] Whew! Whew! Drat the smoke!
      [*The chorus has now reached the edge of the Orchestra
      nearest the stage, in front of the Propylaea. They begin laying
      their logs and fire-pots on the ground.*]
LEADER OF MEN. Thank heaven, this fire is still alive. Now let's
   first put down these logs here and place our torches in the pots
   to catch; then let's make a rush for the gates with a battering-
   ram. If the women don't unbar the gate at our summons, we'll
   have to smoke them out.
      Let me put down my load. Ouch! That hurts! [*To the
   audience*] Would any of the generals in Samos[21] like to lend a
   hand with this log? [*Throwing down a log*] Well, *that* won't break

18. Euripides is always presented in
Aristophanic comedy as a misogynist
and hence hated by women in return.
There does not seem to be any foundation for Aristophanes' view, though
Euripides' realistic (if sympathetic) presentation of women may possibly have
enraged Athenian society ladies.
19. If the chorus really fought at
Marathon, they are very old men. The
trophy was on a high mound which
covered the Athenian dead and is still in
place.
20. *Lemnos:* a volcanic island in the
Aegean.
21. at this time, the headquarters of
the Athenian fleet.

my back any more, at any rate. [*Turning to his fire-pot*] Your job, my little pot, is to keep those coals alive and furnish me shortly with a red-hot torch.

O mistress Victory, be my ally and grant me to rout these audacious women in the Acropolis.

[*While the men are busy with their logs and fires, the* CHORUS OF OLD WOMEN *enters, carrying pitchers of water.*]

LEADER OF WOMEN. What's this I see? Smoke and flames? Is that a fire ablazing?

Let's rush upon them. Hurry up! They'll find us women ready.

FIRST SEMI-CHORUS OF OLD WOMEN. [*Singing*]
> With wingèd foot onward I fly,
> Ere the flames consume Neodice;
> Lest Critylla be overwhelmed
> By a lawless, accurst herd of old men.
> I shudder with fear. Am I too late to aid them?
> At break of the day filled we our jars with water
> Fresh from the spring, pushing our way straight through the
> crowds. Oh, what a din!
> Mid crockery crashing, jostled by slave-girls,
> Sped we to save them, aiding our neighbours,
> Bearing this water to put out the flames.

SECOND SEMI-CHORUS OF OLD WOMEN. [*Singing*]
> Such news I've heard: doddering fools
> Come with logs, like furnace-attendants,
> Loaded down with three hundred pounds,
> Breathing many a vain, blustering threat,
> That all these abhorred sluts will be burnt to charcoal.
> O goddess, I pray never may they be kindled;
> Grant them to save Greece and our men; madness and war help
> them to end.
> With this as our purpose, golden-plumed Maiden,
> Guardian of Athens, seized we thy precinct.
> Be my ally, Warrior-maiden,
> 'Gainst these old men, bearing water with me.

[*The women have now reached their position in the Orchestra, and their* LEADER *advances toward the* LEADER OF THE MEN.*]

LEADER OF WOMEN. Hold on there! What's this, you utter scoundrels? No decent, God-fearing citizens would act like this.

LEADER OF MEN. Oho! Here's something unexpected: a swarm of women have come out to attack us.

LEADER OF WOMEN. What, do we frighten you? Surely you don't think we're too many for you. And yet there are ten thousand times more of us whom you haven't even seen.

LEADER OF MEN. What say, Phaedria?[22] Shall we let these women wag their tongues? Shan't we take our sticks and break them over their backs?

LEADER OF WOMEN. Let's set our pitchers on the ground; then if anyone lays a hand on us, they won't get in our way.

LEADER OF MEN. By God! If someone gave them two or three smacks on the jaw, like Bupalus,[23] they wouldn't talk so much!

LEADER OF WOMEN. Go on, hit me, somebody! Here's my jaw! But no other bitch will bite a piece out of you before me.

LEADER OF MEN. Silence! or I'll knock out your—senility!

LEADER OF WOMEN. Just lay one finger on Stratyllis, I dare you!

LEADER OF MEN. Suppose I dust you off with this fist? What will you do?

LEADER OF WOMEN. I'll tear the living guts out of you with my teeth.

LEADER OF MEN. No poet is more clever than Euripides: "There is no beast so shameless as a woman."

LEADER OF WOMEN. Let's pick up our jars of water, Rhodippe.

LEADER OF MEN. Why have you come here with water, you detestable slut?

LEADER OF WOMEN. And why have you come with fire, you funeral vault? To cremate yourself?

LEADER OF MEN. To light a fire and singe your friends.

LEADER OF WOMEN. And I've brought water to put out your fire.

LEADER OF MEN. What? You'll put out my fire?

LEADER OF WOMEN. Just try and see!

LEADER OF MEN. I wonder: shall I scorch you with this torch of mine?

LEADER OF WOMEN. If you've got any soap, I'll give you a bath.

LEADER OF MEN. Give *me* a bath, you stinking hag?

LEADER OF WOMEN. Yes—a bridal bath!

LEADER OF MEN. Just listen to her! What crust!

LEADER OF WOMEN. Well, I'm a free citizen.

LEADER OF MEN. I'll put an end to your bawling. [*The men pick up their torches.*]

LEADER OF WOMEN. You'll never do jury-duty[24] again. [*The women pick up their pitchers.*]

LEADER OF MEN. Singe her hair for her!

LEADER OF WOMEN. Do your duty, water! [*The women empty their pitchers on the men.*]

LEADER OF MEN. Ow! Ow! For heaven's sake!

---

22. a man's name; the remark is addressed to another member of the male chorus.

23. a sixth-century sculptor, the target of the poet Hipponax's satirical attacks.

24. paid attendance at the courts, the usual source of income for older Athenians.

LEADER OF WOMEN. Is it too hot?

LEADER OF MEN. What do you mean "hot"? Stop! What are you doing?

LEADER OF WOMEN. I'm watering you, so you'll be fresh and green.

LEADER OF MEN. But I'm all withered up with shaking.

LEADER OF WOMEN. Well, you've got a fire; why don't you dry yourself?

[*Enter an Athenian* MAGISTRATE, *accompanied by four Scythian policemen.*[25]]

MAGISTRATE. Have these wanton women flared up again with their timbrels and their continual worship of Sabazius?[26] Is this another Adonis-dirge[27] upon the roof-tops—which we heard not long ago in the Assembly? That confounded Demostratus was urging us to sail to Sicily, and the whirling women shouted, "Woe for Adonis!" And then Demostratus said we'd best enroll the infantry from Zacynthus, and a tipsy woman on the roof shrieked, "Beat your breasts for Adonis!" And that vile and filthy lunatic forced his measure through. Such license do our women take.

LEADER OF MEN. What if you heard of the insolence of these women here? Besides their other violent acts, they threw water all over us, and we have to shake out our clothes just as if we'd leaked in them.

MAGISTRATE. And rightly, too, by God! For we ourselves lead the women astray and teach them to play the wanton; from these roots such notions blossom forth. A man goes into the jeweler's shop and says, "About that necklace you made for my wife, goldsmith: last night, while she was dancing, the fastening-bolt slipped out of the hole. I have to sail over to Salamis today; if you're free, do come around tonight and fit in a new bolt for her." Another goes to the shoe-maker, a strapping young fellow with manly parts, and says, "See here, cobbler, the sandal-strap chafes my wife's little—toe; it's so tender. Come around during the siesta and stretch it a little, so she'll be more comfortable." Now we see the results of such treatment: here I'm a special Councillor and need money to procure oars for the galleys; and I'm locked out of the Treasury by these women.

---

25. the regular police of Athens. They carried bows and arrows.

26. The cult of the oriental deity Sabazius had been recently introduced in Athens. It was considered somewhat disorderly and immoral by religious conservatives.

27. the lament of the women for Adonis (Tammuz), another oriental cult. When the great expedition to Sicily set sail, the women were mourning the death of Adonis—a bad omen which proved all too true. Demostratus was one of the supporters of the expedition (the most prominent was Alcibiades) and he proposed to enroll heavy armed infantry from the island of Zacynthus, off the west coast of Greece, on the way to Sicily.

But this is no time to stand around. Bring up crow-bars there! I'll put an end to their insolence. [*To one of the policemen*] What are you gaping at, you wretch? What are you staring at? Got an eye out for a tavern, eh? Set your crow-bars here to the gates and force them open. [*Retiring to safe distance*] I'll help from over here.

[*The gates are thrown open and* LYSISTRATA *comes out followed by several other women.*]

LYSISTRATA. Don't force the gates; I'm coming out of my own accord. We don't need crow-bars here; what we need is good sound common-sense.

MAGISTRATE. Is that so, you strumpet? Where's my policeman? Officer, arrest her and tie her arms behind her back.

LYSISTRATA. By Artemis, if he lays a finger on me, he'll pay for it, even if he is a public servant.

[*The policeman retires in terror.*]

MAGISTRATE. You there, are you afraid? Seize her round the waist —and you, too. Tie her up, both of you!

FIRST WOMAN. [*As the second policeman approaches* LYSISTRATA] By Pandrosus,[28] if you but touch her with your hand, I'll kick the stuffings out of you.

[*The second policeman retires in terror.*]

MAGISTRATE. Just listen to that: "kick the stuffings out." Where's another policeman? Tie *her* up first, for her chatter.

SECOND WOMAN. By the Goddess of the Light, if you lay the tip of your finger on her, you'll soon need a doctor.

[*The third policeman retires in terror.*]

MAGISTRATE. What's this? Where's my policeman? Seize *her* too. I'll soon stop your sallies.

THIRD WOMAN. By the Goddess of Tauros,[29] if you go near her, I'll tear out your hair until it shrieks with pain.

[*The fourth policeman retires in terror.*]

MAGISTRATE. Oh, damn it all! I've run out of policemen. But women must never defeat us. Officers, let's charge them all together. Close up your ranks!

[*The policemen rally for a mass attack.*]

LYSISTRATA. By heaven, you'll soon find out that we have four companies of warrior-women, all fully equipped within!

MAGISTRATE. [*Advancing*] Twist their arms off, men!

LYSISTRATA. [*Shouting*] To the rescue, my valiant women!
O sellers-of-barley-green-stuffs-and-eggs,
O sellers-of-garlic, ye keepers-of-taverns, and vendors-of-bread,
Grapple! Smite! Smash!
Won't you heap filth on them? Give them a tongue-lashing!

[*The women beat off the policemen.*]

28. a mythical Athenian princess.       29. Artemis.

Halt! Withdraw! No looting on the field.

MAGISTRATE. Damn it! My police-force has put up a very poor show.

LYSISTRATA. What did you expect? Did you think you were attacking
slaves? Didn't you know that women are filled with passion?

MAGISTRATE. Aye, passion enough—for a good strong drink!

LEADER OF MEN. O chief and leader of this land, why spend your
words in vain?

Don't argue with these shameless beasts. You know not how we've
fared:

A soapless bath they've given us; our clothes are soundly soaked.

LEADER OF WOMEN. Poor fool! You never should attack or strike a
peaceful girl.

But if you do, your eyes must swell. For I am quite content

To sit unmoved, like modest maids, in peace and cause no pain;

But let a man stir up my hive, he'll find me like a wasp.

CHORUS OF MEN. [*Singing*]
O God, whatever shall we do with creatures like Womankind?
This can't be endured by any man alive. Question them!
Let us try to find out what this means.
To what end have they seized on this shrine,
This steep and rugged, high and holy,
Undefiled Acropolis?

LEADER OF MEN. Come, put your questions; don't give in, and probe
her every statement.

For base and shameful it would be to leave this plot untested.

MAGISTRATE. Well then, first of all I wish to ask her this: for what
purpose have you barred us from the Acropolis?

LYSISTRATA. To keep the treasure safe, so you won't make war on
account of it.

MAGISTRATE. What? Do we make war on account of the treasure?

LYSISTRATA. Yes, and you cause all our other troubles for it, too.
Peisander[30] and those greedy office-seekers keep things stirred up so
they can find occasions to steal. Now let them do what they like:
they'll never again make off with any of this money.

MAGISTRATE. What will you do?

LYSISTRATA. What a question! We'll administer it ourselves.

MAGISTRATE. *You* will administer the treasure?

LYSISTRATA. What's so strange in that? Don't we administer the
household money for you?

MAGISTRATE. That's different.

LYSISTRATA. How is it different?

MAGISTRATE. We've got to make war with this money.

LYSISTRATA. But that's the very first thing: you mustn't make war.

30. a leader of the war party.

MAGISTRATE. How else can we be saved?

LYSISTRATA. We'll save you.

MAGISTRATE. *You?*

LYSISTRATA. Yes, we!

MAGISTRATE. God forbid!

LYSISTRATA. We'll save you, whether you want it or not.

MAGISTRATE. Oh! This is terrible!

LYSISTRATA. You don't like it, but we're going to do it none the less.

MAGISTRATE. Good God! it's illegal!

LYSISTRATA. We *will* save you, my little man!

MAGISTRATE. Suppose I don't want you to?

LYSISTRATA. That's all the more reason.

MAGISTRATE. What business have you with war and peace?

LYSISTRATA. I'll explain.

MAGISTRATE. [*Shaking his fist*] Speak up, or you'll smart for it.

LYSISTRATA. Just listen, and try to keep your hands still.

MAGISTRATE. I can't. I'm so mad I can't stop them.

FIRST WOMAN. Then you'll be the one to smart for it.

MAGISTRATE. Croak to yourself, old hag! [*To* LYSISTRATA] Now then, speak up.

LYSISTRATA. Very well. Formerly we endured the war for a good long time with our usual restraint, no matter what you men did. You wouldn't let us say "boo," although nothing you did suited us. But we watched you well, and though we stayed at home we'd often hear of some terribly stupid measure you'd proposed. Then, though grieving at heart, we'd smile sweetly and say, "What was passed in the Assembly today about writing on the treaty-stone?"[31] "What's that to you?" my husband would say. "Hold your tongue!" And I held my tongue.

FIRST WOMAN. But I wouldn't have—not I!

MAGISTRATE. You'd have been soundly smacked, if you hadn't kept still.

LYSISTRATA. So I kept still at home. Then we'd hear of some plan still worse than the first; we'd say, "Husband, how could you pass such a stupid proposal?" He'd scowl at me and say, "If you don't mind your spinning, your head will be sore for weeks. *War shall be the concern of Men.*"[32]

MAGISTRATE. And he was right, upon my word!

LYSISTRATA. Why right, you confounded fool, when your proposals were so stupid and we weren't allowed to make suggestions?

"There's not a *man* left in the country," says one. "No, not one," says another. Therefore all we women have decided in council to make a common effort to save Greece. How long should

---

31. The text of a treaty was inscribed on a stone which was set up in a public place.

32. *War shall be the concern of Men:* Hector to Andromache, *Iliad* VI, 492.

we have waited? Now, if you're willing to listen to our excellent proposals and keep silence for us in your turn, we still may save you.

MAGISTRATE. We men keep silence for you? That's terrible; I won't endure it!

LYSISTRATA. Silence!

MAGISTRATE. Silence for *you*, you wench, when you're wearing a snood? I'd rather die!

LYSISTRATA. Well, if that's all that bothers you—here! take my snood and tie it round your head. [*During the following words the women dress up the* MAGISTRATE *in women's garments.*] And *now* keep quiet! Here, take this spinning-basket, too, and card your wool with robes tucked up, munching on beans. *War shall be the concern of Women!*

LEADER OF WOMEN. Arise and leave your pitchers, girls; no time is this to falter.

We too must aid our loyal friends; our turn has come for action.

CHORUS OF WOMEN. [*Singing*]

I'll never tire of aiding them with song and dance; never may Faintness keep my legs from moving to and fro endlessly.

    For I yearn to do all for my friends;

      They have charm, they have wit, they have grace,

        With courage, brains, and best of virtues—

          Patriotic sapience.

LEADER OF WOMEN. Come, child of manliest ancient dames, off-spring of stinging nettles,

Advance with rage unsoftened; for fair breezes speed you onward.

LYSISTRATA. If only sweet Eros and the Cyprian Queen of Love shed charm over our breasts and limbs and inspire our men with amorous longing and priapic spasms, I think we may soon be called Peacemakers among the Greeks.

MAGISTRATE. What will you do?

LYSISTRATA. First of all, we'll stop those fellows who run madly about the Marketplace in arms.

FIRST WOMAN. Indeed we shall, by the Queen of Paphos.[33]

LYSISTRATA. For now they roam about the market, amid the pots and greenstuffs, armed to the teeth like Corybantes.[34]

MAGISTRATE. That's what manly fellows ought to do!

LYSISTRATA. But it's so silly: a chap with a Gorgon-emblazoned shield buying pickled herring.

FIRST WOMAN. Why, just the other day I saw one of those long-haired dandies who command our cavalry ride up on horseback and pour into his bronze helmet the egg-broth he'd bought from an

33. Aphrodite.         34. the armed priests of the goddess Cybele.

old dame. And there was a Thracian slinger too, shaking his lance like Tereus[35]; he'd scared the life out of the poor fig-peddler and was gulping down all her ripest fruit.

MAGISTRATE. How can you stop all the confusion in the various states and bring them together?

LYSISTRATA. Very easily.

MAGISTRATE. Tell me how.

LYSISTRATA. Just like a ball of wool, when it's confused and snarled: we take it thus, and draw out a thread here and a thread there with our spindles; thus we'll unsnarl this war, if no one prevents us, and draw together the various states with embassies here and embassies there.

MAGISTRATE. Do you suppose you can stop this dreadful business with balls of wool and spindles, you nit-wits?

LYSISTRATA. Why, if *you* had any wits, you'd manage all affairs of state like our wool-working.

MAGISTRATE. How so?

LYSISTRATA. First you ought to treat the city as we do when we wash the dirt out of a fleece: stretch it out and pluck and thrash out of the city all those prickly scoundrels; aye, and card out those who conspire and stick together to gain office, pulling off their heads. Then card the wool, all of it, into one fair basket of good-will, mingling in the aliens residing here, any loyal foreigners, and anyone who's in debt to the Treasury; and consider that all our colonies lie scattered round about like remnants; from all of these collect the wool and gather it together here, wind up a great ball, and then weave a good stout cloak for the democracy.

MAGISTRATE. Dreadful! Talking about thrashing and winding balls of wool, when you haven't the slightest share in the war!

LYSISTRATA. Why, you dirty scoundrel, we bear more than twice as much as you. First, we bear children and send off our sons as soldiers.

MAGISTRATE. Hush! Let bygones be bygones!

LYSISTRATA. Then, when we ought to be happy and enjoy our youth, we sleep alone because of your expeditions abroad. But never mind us married women: I grieve most for the maids who grow old at home unwed.

MAGISTRATE. Don't men grow old, too?

LYSISTRATA. For heaven's sake! That's not the same thing. When a man comes home, no matter how grey he is, he soon finds a girl to marry. But woman's bloom is short and fleeting; if she doesn't grasp her chance, no man is willing to marry her and she sits at home a prey to every fortune-teller.

MAGISTRATE. [*Coarsely*] But if a man can still get it up—

35. a mythical king of Thrace. Thracian mercenaries had served in the Athenian ranks during the war.

LYSISTRATA. See here, you: what's the matter? Aren't you dead yet? There's plenty of room for you. Buy yourself a shroud and I'll bake you a honey-cake.[36] [*Handing him a copper coin for his passage across the Styx*] Here's your fare! Now get yourself a wreath. [*During the following dialogue the women dress up the* MAGISTRATE *as a corpse.*]

FIRST WOMAN. Here, take these fillets.

SECOND WOMAN. Here, take this wreath.

LYSISTRATA. What do you want? What's lacking? Get moving; off to the ferry! Charon is calling you; don't keep him from sailing.

MAGISTRATE. Am I to endure these insults? By God! I'm going straight to the magistrates to show them how I've been treated.

LYSISTRATA. Are you grumbling that you haven't been properly laid out? Well, the day after tomorrow we'll send around all the usual offerings early in the morning.

[*The* MAGISTRATE *goes out still wearing his funeral decorations.* LYSISTRATA *and the women retire into the Acropolis.*]

LEADER OF MEN. Wake, ye sons of freedom, wake! 'Tis no time for sleeping. Up and at them, like a man! Let us strip for action.

[*The* CHORUS OF MEN *remove their outer cloaks.*]

CHORUS OF MEN. [*Singing*]
Surely there is something here greater than meets the eye;
For without a doubt I smell Hippias'[37] tyranny.
Dreadful fear assails me lest certain bands of Spartan men,
Meeting here with Cleisthenes,[38] have inspired through treachery
All these god-detested women secretly to seize
Athens' treasure in the temple, and to stop that pay
  Whence I live at my ease.

LEADER OF MEN. Now isn't it terrible for them to advise the state and chatter about shields, being mere women?

And they think to reconcile us with the Spartans—men who hold nothing sacred any more than hungry wolves. Surely this is a web of deceit, my friends, to conceal an attempt at tyranny. But they'll never lord it over me; I'll be on my guard and from now on,
  "The blade I bear    A myrtle spray shall wear."
I'll occupy the market under arms and stand next to Aristogeiton.[39]
  Thus I'll stand beside him. [*He strikes the pose of the famous*

---

36. The dead were provided with a honey cake to throw to Cerberus, the three-headed dog which guarded the entry to the underworld. The copper coin was to pay the fare required by Charon, the ferryman over the river Styx.

37. the last tyrant of Athens, driven out in 510 B.C.

38. not the great reformer who set up the democracy, but a contemporary of Aristophanes, notorious for his effeminacy (and therefore suspect as a fellow-conspirator of the women).

39. one of the two heroes of the democracy who assassinated Hipparchus, the brother of the tyrant Hippias. A drinking song which was frequently heard at Athenian banquets ran: "In a branch of myrtle, I'll hide my sword, like Harmodius and Aristogeiton, who killed the tyrant, and made Athens free."

*statue of the tyrannicides, with one arm raised.*] And here's my
chance to take this accurst old hag and—[*Striking the* LEADER OF
WOMEN] smack her on the jaw!

LEADER OF WOMEN. You'll go home in such a state your Ma won't
        recognize you!
    Ladies all, upon the ground let us place these garments.
        [*The* CHORUS OF WOMEN *remove their outer garments.*]
CHORUS OF WOMEN. [*Singing*]
    Citizens of Athens, hear useful words for the state.
    Rightly; for it nurtured me in my youth royally.
    As a child of seven years carried I the sacred box;[40]
    Then I was a Miller-maid, grinding at Athene's shrine;
    Next I wore the saffron robe and played Brauronia's Bear;
    And I walked as Basket-bearer, wearing chains of figs,
        As a sweet maiden fair.
LEADER OF WOMEN. Therefore, am I not bound to give good advice
to the city?
    Don't take it ill that I was born a woman, if I contribute some-
thing better than our present troubles. I pay my share; for I contribute MEN. But you miserable old fools contribute nothing, and
after squandering our ancestral treasure, the fruit of the Persian
Wars, you make no contribution in return. And now, all on account of you, we're facing ruin.
    What, muttering, are you? If you annoy me, I'll take this hard,
rough slipper and—[*Striking the* LEADER OF MEN] smack you on
the jaw!

CHORUS OF MEN. [*Singing*]
    This is outright insolence! Things go from bad to worse.
    If you're men with any guts, prepare to meet the foe.
    Let us strip our tunics off! We need the smell of male
    Vigour. And we cannot fight all swaddled up in clothes.
        [*They strip off their tunics.*]
    Come then, my comrades, on to the battle, ye who once to
        Leipsydrion[41] came;
    Then ye were MEN. Now call back your youthful vigour.
        With light, wingèd footstep advance,
        Shaking old age from your frame.
LEADER OF MEN. If any of us give these wenches the slightest hold,

40. This and the next four lines describe the religious duties of a well-born
Athenian girl. The sacred box contained
religious objects connected with the worship of Athena in the Erechtheum. The
miller-maids ground flour for sacred
cakes. At Brauron in Attica, young girls
who represented themselves as bears (the
saffron robe was a substitute for a more
primitive bearskin) worshipped Artemis.
In the Panathenaic procession certain
selected girls carried baskets on their
heads.
    41. the base of the aristocratic family
of the Almaeonidae (the family of Pericles) in their first attempt to overthrow
Hippias.

they'll stop at nothing: such is their cunning.

They will even build ships and sail against us, like Artemisia.[42]
Or if they turn to mounting, I count our Knights as done for: a
woman's such a tricky jockey when she gets astraddle, with a good
firm seat for trotting. Just look at those Amazons that Micon[43]
painted, fighting on horseback against men!

But we must throw them all in the pillory—[*Seizing and choking the* LEADER OF WOMEN] grabbing hold of yonder neck!

CHORUS OF WOMEN. [*Singing*]
'Ware my anger! Like a boar 'twill rush upon you men.
Soon you'll bawl aloud for help, you'll be so soundly trimmed!
Come, my friends, let's strip with speed, and lay aside these
    robes;
Catch the scent of women's rage. Attack with tooth and nail!

    [*They strip off their tunics.*]
Now then, come near me, you miserable man! you'll never eat
    garlic or black beans again.
And if you utter a single hard word, in rage I will "nurse" you
    as once
    The beetle[44] requited her foe.

LEADER OF WOMEN. For you don't worry me; no, not so long as
my Lampito lives and our Theban friend, the noble Ismenia.

You can't do anything, not even if you pass a dozen—decrees!
You miserable fool, all our neighbours hate you. Why, just the
other day when I was holding a festival for Hecate, I invited as
playmate from our neighbours the Boeotians a charming, well-
bred Copaic—eel. But they refused to send me one on account of
your decrees.

And you'll never stop passing decrees until I grab your foot
and—[*Tripping up the* LEADER OF MEN] toss you down and break
your neck!

    [*Here an interval of five days is supposed to elapse.*
    LYSISTRATA *comes out from the Acropolis*]

LEADER OF WOMEN. [*Dramatically*] Empress[45] of this great emprise
    and undertaking,
Why come you forth, I pray, with frowning brow?

LYSISTRATA. Ah, these cursèd women! Their deeds and female
notions make me pace up and down in utter despair.

LEADER OF WOMEN. Ah, what sayest thou?

LYSISTRATA. The truth, alas! the truth.

42. queen of Halicarnassus in Asia
Minor. She played a prominent part in
Xerxes' invasion of Greece and her
ships fought at Salamis.

43. a painter who had lately decorated
several public buildings with frescos.
The battles of the Greeks and Amazons
were favorite subjects of sculptors and
painters all through the fifth century.

44. In a fable of Aesop the beetle re-
venges itself on the eagle by breaking its
eggs.

45. The tone of the following passage
is mock-tragic.

LEADER OF WOMEN. What dreadful tale hast thou to tell thy friends?

LYSISTRATA. 'Tis shame to speak, and not to speak is hard.

LEADER OF WOMEN. Hide not from me whatever woes we suffer.

LYSISTRATA. Well then, to put it briefly, we want—laying!

LEADER OF WOMEN. O Zeus, Zeus!

LYSISTRATA. Why call on Zeus? That's the way things are. I can no longer keep them away from the men, and they're all deserting. I caught one wriggling through a hole near the grotto of Pan, another sliding down a rope, another deserting her post; and yesterday I found one getting on a sparrow's back to fly off to Orsilochus,[46] and had to pull her back by the hair. They're digging up all sorts of excuses to get home. Look, here comes one of them now. [*A woman comes hastily out of the Acropolis.*] Here you! Where are you off to in such a hurry?

FIRST WOMAN. I want to go home. My very best wool is being devoured by moths.

LYSISTRATA. Moths? Nonsense! Go back inside.

FIRST WOMAN. I'll come right back; I swear it. I just want to lay it out on the bed.

LYSISTRATA. Well, you won't lay it out, and you won't go home, either.

FIRST WOMAN. Shall I let my wool be ruined?

LYSISTRATA. If necessary, yes. [*Another woman comes out.*]

SECOND WOMAN. Oh dear! Oh dear! My precious flax! I left it at home all unpeeled.

LYSISTRATA. Here's another one, going home for her "flax." Come back here!

SECOND WOMAN. But I just want to work it up a little and then I'll be right back.

LYSISTRATA. No indeed! If you start this, all the other women will want to do the same. [*A third woman comes out.*]

THIRD WOMAN. O Eilithyia, gooddess of travail, stop my labour till I come to a lawful spot![47]

LYSISTRATA. What's this nonsense?

THIRD WOMAN. I'm going to have a baby—right now!

LYSISTRATA. But you weren't even even pregnant yesterday.

THIRD WOMAN. Well, I am today. O Lysistrata, do send me home to see a midwife, right away.

LYSISTRATA. What are you talking about? [*Putting her hand on her stomach*] What's this hard lump here?

THIRD WOMAN. A little boy.

LYSISTRATA. My goodness, what have you got there? It seems hollow; I'll just find out. [*Pulling aside her robe*] Why, you silly goose,

---

46. the sparrow, Aphrodite's bird, pulled her chariot. *Orsilochus* ran a house of ill-fame.

47. *lawful spot:* The Acropolis was holy ground, and would be polluted by either birth or death.

you've got Athene's sacred helmet there. And you said you were having a baby!

THIRD WOMAN. Well, I *am* having one, I swear!

LYSISTRATA. Then what's this helmet for?

THIRD WOMAN. If the baby starts coming while I'm still in the Acropolis, I'll creep into this like a pigeon and give birth to it there.

LYSISTRATA. Stuff and nonsense! It's plain enough what you're up to. You just wait here for the christening of this—helmet.

THIRD WOMAN. But I can't sleep in the Acropolis since I saw the sacred snake.[48]

FIRST WOMAN. And I'm dying for lack of sleep: the hooting of the owls[49] keeps me awake.

LYSISTRATA. Enough of these shams, you wretched creatures. You want your husbands, I suppose. Well, don't you think they want us? I'm sure they're spending miserable nights. Hold out, my friends, and endure for just a little while. There's an oracle that we shall conquer, if we don't split up. [*Producing a roll of paper*] Here it is.

FIRST WOMAN. Tell us what it says.

LYSISTRATA. Listen.

"When in the length of time the Swallows shall gather together, Fleeing the Hoopoe's amorous flight and the Cockatoo shunning, Then shall your woes be ended and Zeus who thunders in heaven Set what's below on top—"

FIRST WOMAN. What? Are we going to be on top?

LYSISTRATA. "But if the Swallows rebel and flutter away from the temple,
Never a bird in the world shall seem more wanton and worthless."

FIRST WOMAN. That's clear enough, upon my word!

LYSISTRATA. By all that's holy, let's not give up the struggle now. Let's go back inside. It would be a shame, my dear friends, to disobey the oracle.

[*The women all retire to the Acropolis again.*]

CHORUS OF MEN. [*Singing*]
I have a tale to tell,
Which I know full well.
It was told me
In the nursery.

Once there was a likely lad,

---

48. A snake was kept in the Erechtheum.

49. the sacred bird of Athene.

Melanion they name him;
The thought of marriage made him mad,
For which I cannot blame him.[50]

So off he went to mountains fair;
(No women to upbraid him!)
A mighty hunter of the hare,
He had a dog to aid him.

He never came back home to see
Detested women's faces.
He showed a shrewd mentality.
With him I'd fain change places!

ONE OF THE MEN. [*To one of the women*] Come here, old dame.
give me a kiss.
WOMAN. You'll ne'er eat garlic, if you dare!
MAN. I want to kick you—just like this!
WOMAN. Oh, there's a leg with bushy hair!
MAN. Myronides and Phormio[51]
  Were hairy—and they thrashed the foe.

CHORUS OF WOMEN. [*Singing*]
I have another tale,
With which to assail
Your contention
'Bout Melanion.

Once upon a time a man
Named Timon[52] left our city,
To live in some deserted land.
(We thought him rather witty.)

He dwelt alone amidst the thorn;
In solitude he brooded.
From some grim Fury he was born:
Such hatred he exuded.

He cursed you men, as scoundrels through
And through, till life he ended.
He couldn't stand the sight of you!
But women he befriended.

50. The chorus of men here recasts a well-known myth for its own purposes. In the myth it was Atalanta who avoided marriage, challenging her suitors to a foot race which she always won; Melanion threw a golden apple in front of her; when she stopped to pick it up, she lost the race to him.

51. successful Athenian generals.

52. the famous misanthrope, the subject of Shakespeare's play. There is no evidence that he "befriended" women his hatred seems to have been directed at the whole human race.

WOMAN. [*To one of the men*] I'll smash your face in, if you like.

MAN. Oh no, please don't! You frighten me.

WOMAN. I'll lift my foot—and thus I'll strike.

MAN. Aha! Look there! What's that I see?

WOMAN. Whate'er you see, you cannot say
    That I'm not neatly trimmed today.

    [LYSISTRATA *appears on the wall of the Acropolis.*]

LYSISTRATA. Hello! Hello! Girls, come here quick!

    [*Several women appear beside her.*]

WOMAN. What is it? Why are you calling?

LYSISTRATA. I see a man coming: he's in a dreadful state. He's mad with passion. O Queen of Cyprus, Cythera, and Paphos, just keep on this way!

WOMAN. Where is the fellow?

LYSISTRATA. There, beside the shrine of Demeter.

WOMAN. Oh yes, so he is. Who is he?

LYSISTRATA. Let's see. Do any of you know him?

MYRRHINE. Yes indeed. That's my husband, Cinesias.

LYSISTRATA. It's up to you, now: roast him, rack him, fool him, love him—and leave him! Do everything, except what our oath forbids.

MYRRHINE. Don't worry; I'll do it.

LYSISTRATA. I'll stay here to tease him and warm him up a bit. Off with you.

    [*The other women retire from the wall. Enter* CINESIAS *followed by a slave carrying a baby.* CINESIAS *is obviously in great pain and distress.*]

CINESIAS. [*Groaning*] Oh-h! Oh-h-h! This is killing me! O God, what tortures I'm suffering!

LYSISTRATA. [*From the wall*] Who's that within our lines?

CINESIAS. Me.

LYSISTRATA. A *man*?

CINESIAS. [*Pointing*] A *man*, indeed!

LYSISTRATA. Well, go away!

CINESIAS. Who are you to send me away?

LYSISTRATA. The captain of the guard.

CINESIAS. Oh, for heaven's sake, call out Myrrhine for me.

LYSISTRATA. Call Myrrhine? Nonsense! Who are you?

CINESIAS. Her husband, Cinesias of Paionidai.

LYSISTRATA. [*Appearing much impressed*] Oh, greetings, friend. Your name is not without honour here among us. Your wife is always talking about you, and whenever she takes an egg or an apple, she says, "Here's to my dear Cinesias!"

CINESIAS. [*Quivering with excitement*] Oh, ye gods in heaven!

LYSISTRATA. Indeed she does! And whenever our conversations turn to men, your wife immediately says, "All others are mere rubbish compared with Cinesias."

CINESIAS. [*Groaning*] Oh! Do call her for me.

LYSISTRATA. Why should I? What will you give me?

CINESIAS. Whatever you want. All I have is yours—and you see what I've got.

LYSISTRATA. Well then, I'll go down and call her. [*She descends.*]

CINESIAS. And hurry up! I've had no joy of life ever since she left home. When I go in the house, I feel awful: everything seems so empty and I can't enjoy my dinner. I'm in such a state all the time!

MYRRHINE. [*From behind the wall*] I *do* love him so. But he won't let me love him. No, no! Don't ask me to see him!

CINESIAS. O my darling, O Myrrhine honey, why do you do this to me? [MYRRHINE *appears on the wall.*] Come down here!

MYRRHINE. No, I won't come down.

CINESIAS. Won't you come, Myrrhine, when *I* call you?

MYRRHINE. No; you don't want me.

CINESIAS. *Don't want you?* I'm in agony!

MYRRHINE. I'm going now.

CINESIAS. Please don't! At least, listen to your baby. [*To the baby*] Here you, call your mamma! [*Pinching the baby*]

BABY. Ma-ma! Ma-ma! Ma-ma!

CINESIAS. [*To* MYRRHINE] What's the matter with you? Have you no pity for your child, who hasn't been washed or fed for five whole days?

MYRRHINE. Oh, poor child; your father pays no attention to you.

CINESIAS. Come down then, you heartless wretch, for the baby's sake.

MYRRHINE. Oh, what it is to be a mother! I've got to come down, I suppose. [*She leaves the wall and shortly reappears at the gate.*]

CINESIAS. [*To himself*] She seems much younger, and she has such a sweet look about her. Oh, the way she teases me! And her pretty, provoking ways make me burn with longing

MYRRHINE. [*Coming out of the gate and taking the baby*]. O my sweet little angel. Naughty papa! Here, let Mummy kiss you, Mamma's little sweetheart! [*She fondles the baby lovingly.*]

CINESIAS. [*In despair*] You heartless creature, why do you do this? Why follow these other women and make both of us suffer so? [*He tries to embrace her.*]

MYRRHINE. Don't touch me!

CINESIAS. You're letting all our things at home go to wrack and ruin.

MYRRHINE. I don't care.

CINESIAS. You don't care that your wool is being plucked to pieces by the chickens?

MYRRHINE. Not in the least.

CINESIAS. And you haven't celebrated the rites of Aphrodite for ever so long. Won't you come home?

MYRRHINE. Not on your life, unless you men make a truce and stop the war.

CINESIAS. Well then, if that pleases you, we'll do it.

MYRRHINE. Well then, if that pleases *you*, I'll come home—afterwards! Right now I'm on oath not to.

CINESIAS. Then just lie down here with me for a moment.

MYRRHINE. No—[*In a teasing voice*] and yet, I won't say I don't love you.

CINESIAS. You love me? Oh, do lie down here, Myrrhine dear!

MYRRHINE. What, you silly fool! in front of the baby?

CINESIAS. [*Hastily thrusting the baby at the slave*] Of course not. •Here—home! Take him Manes! [*The slave goes off with the baby.*] See, the baby's out of the way. Now won't you lie down?

MYRRHINE. But where, my dear?

CINESIAS. Where? The grotto of Pan's a lovely spot.

MYRRHINE. How could I purify myself before returning to the shrine?

CINESIAS. Easily: just wash here in the Clepsydra.[53]

MYRRHINE. And then, shall I go back on my oath?

CINESIAS. On my head be it! Don't worry about the oath.

MYRRHINE. All right, then. Just let me bring out a bed.

CINESIAS. No, don't. The ground's all right.

MYRRHINE. Heavens, no! Bad as you are, I won't let you lie on the bare ground. [*She goes into the Acropolis.*]

CINESIAS. Why, she really loves me; it's plain to see.

MYRRHINE. [*Returning with a bed*] There! Now hurry up and lie down. I'll just slip off this dress. But—let's see: oh yes, I must fetch a mattress.

CINESIAS. Nonsense! No mattress for me.

MYRRHINE. Yes indeed! It's not nice on the bare springs.

CINESIAS. Give me a kiss.

MYRRHINE. [*Giving him a hasty kiss*] There! [*She goes.*]

CINESIAS. [*In mingled distress and delight*] Oh-h! Hurry back!

MYRRHINE. [*Returning with a mattress*] Here's the mattress; lie down on it. I'm taking my things off now—but—let's see: you have no pillow.

CINESIAS. I don't *want* a pillow!

MYRRHINE. But I do. [*She goes.*]

CINESIAS. Cheated again, just like Heracles and his dinner![54]

MYRRHINE. [*Returning with a pillow*] Here, lift your head. [*To her-*

53. a spring on the Acropolis.
54. The point of this proverb seems to be that the hero is such a glutton that his hosts are never quick enough with their entertainment.

*self, wondering how else to tease him*] Is that all?

CINESIAS. Surely that's all! Do come here, precious!

MYRRHINE. I'm taking off my girdle. But remember: don't go back on your promise about the truce.

CINESIAS. Hope to die, if I do.

MYRRHINE. You don't have a blanket.

CINESIAS. [*Shouting in exasperation*] I don't want one! I WANT TO—

MYRRHINE. Sh-h! There, there, I'll be back in a minute. [*She goes.*]

CINESIAS. She'll be the death of me with these bed-clothes.

MYRRHINE. [*Returning with a blanket*] Here, get up.

CINESIAS. I've got *this* up!

MYRRHINE. Would you like some perfume?

CINESIAS. Good heavens, no! I won't have it!

MYRRHINE. Yes, you shall, whether you want it or not. [*She goes.*]

CINESIAS. O lord! Confound all perfumes anyway!

MYRRHINE. [*Returning with a flask*] Stretch out your hand and put some on.

CINESIAS. [*Suspiciously*] By God, I don't much like this perfume. It smells of shilly-shallying, and has no scent of the marriage-bed.

MYRRHINE. Oh dear! This is Rhodian perfume I've brought.

CINESIAS. It's quite all right dear. Never mind.

MYRRHINE. Don't be silly! [*She goes out with the flask.*]

CINESIAS. Damm the man who first concocted perfumes!

MYRRHINE. [*Returning with another flask*] Here, try this flask.

CINESIAS. I've got another one all ready for you. Come, you wretch, lie down and stop bringing me things.

MYRRHINE. All right; I'm taking off my shoes. But, my dear, see that you vote for peace.

CINESIAS. [*Absently*] I'll consider it. [MYRRHINE *runs away to the Acropolis.*] I'm ruined! The wretch has skinned me and run away! [*Chanting, in tragic style*] Alas! Alas! Deceived, deserted by this fairest of women, whom shall I—lay? Ah, my poor little child, how shall I nurture thee? Where's Cynalopex?[55] I needs must hire a nurse!

LEADER OF MEN. [*Chanting*] Ah, wretched man, in dreadful wise beguiled, bewrayed, thy soul is sore distressed. I pity thee, alas! alas! What soul, what loins, what liver could stand this strain? How firm and unyielding he stands, with naught to aid him of a morning.

CINESIAS. O lord! O Zeus! What tortures I endure!

LEADER OF MEN. This is the way she's treated you, that vile and cursèd wanton.

LEADER OF WOMEN. Nay, not vile and cursèd, but sweet and dear.

LEADER OF MEN. Sweet, you say? Nay, hateful, hateful!

55. a local brothel-keeper.

CINESIAS. Hateful indeed! O Zeus, Zeus!
Seize her and snatch her away,
Like a handful of dust, in a mighty,
Fiery tempest! Whirl her aloft, then let her drop
Down to the earth, with a crash, as she falls—
On the point of this waiting
Thingummybob! [*He goes out.*]

    [*Enter a Spartan* HERALD, *in an obvious state of excitement, which he is doing his best to conceal.*]

HERALD. Where can I find the Senate or the Prytanes?[56] I've got an important message.

    [*The Athenian* MAGISTRATE *enters.*]

MAGISTRATE. Say there, are you a man or Priapus?[57]

HERALD. [*In annoyance*] I'm a herald, you lout! I've come from Sparta about the truce.

MAGISTRATE. Is that a spear you've got under your cloak?

HERALD. No, of course not!

MAGISTRATE. Why do you twist and turn so? Why hold your cloak in front of you? Did you rupture yourself on the trip?

HERALD. By gum, the fellow's an old fool.

MAGISTRATE. [*Pointing*] Why, you dirty rascal, you're all excited.

HERALD. Not at all. Stop this tom-foolery.

MAGISTRATE. Well, what's that I see?

HERALD. A Spartan message-staff.[58]

MAGISTRATE. Oh, certainly! That's just the kind of message-staff I've got. But tell me the honest truth: How are things going in Sparta?

HERALD. All the land of Sparta is up in arms—and our allies are up, too. We need Pellene.[59]

MAGISTRATE. What brought this trouble on you? A sudden Panic?

HERALD. No, Lampito started it and then all the other women in Sparta with one accord chased their husbands out of their beds.

MAGISTRATE. How do you feel?

HERALD. Terrible. We walk around the city bent over like men lighting matches in a wind. For our women won't let us touch them until we all agree and make peace throughout Greece.

MAGISTRATE. This is a general conspiracy of the women; I see it now. Well, hurry back and tell the Spartans to send ambassadors here with full powers to arrange a truce. And I'll go tell the Council to choose ambassadors from here; I've got a little something here that

---

56. *Prytanes:* the permanent committee of the Council (Senate).

57. a god whose grossly phallic statue was set to guard orchards and gardens.

58. an encoding device. The papyrus was wrapped round the staff on a spiral

and the message could be read only when the papyrus was wound round an exactly similar staff.

59. a city held by the Athenians and claimed by the Spartans; also the name of a famous Athenian prostitute.

will soon persuade them!

HERALD. I'll fly there; for you've made an excellent suggestion.

[*The* HERALD *and the* MAGISTRATE *depart on opposite sides of the stage.*]

LEADER OF MEN. No beast or fire is harder than womankind to tame.
Nor is the spotted leopard so devoid of shame.

LEADER OF WOMEN. Knowing this, you dare provoke us to attack?
I'd be your steady friend, if you'd but take us back.

LEADER OF MEN. I'll never cease my hatred keen of womankind.

LEADER OF WOMEN. Just as you will. But now just let me help you
find
That cloak you threw aside. You look so silly there
Without your clothes. Here, put it on and don't go bare.

LEADER OF MEN. That's very kind, and shows you're not entirely
bad.
But I threw off my things when I was good and mad.

LEADER OF WOMEN. At last you seem a man, and won't be mocked,
my lad.
If you'd been nice to me, I'd take this little gnat
That's in your eye and pluck it out for you, like that.

LEADER OF MEN. So that's what's bothered me and bit my eye so
long!
Please dig it out for me. I own that I've been wrong.

LEADER OF WOMEN. I'll do so, though you've been a most ill-natured
brat.
Ye gods! See here! A huge and monstrous little gnat!

LEADER OF MEN. Oh, how that helps! For it was digging wells in me.
And now it's out, my tears can roll down hard and free.

LEADER OF WOMEN. Here, let me wipe them off, although you're such
a knave
And kiss me.

LEADER OF MEN. No!

LEADER OF WOMEN. Whate'er you say, a kiss I'll have. [*She kisses
him.*]

LEADER OF MEN. Oh, confound these women! They've a coaxing
way about them.
He was wise and never spoke a truer word, who said,
"We can't live with women, but we cannot live without them."
Now I'll make a truce with you. We'll fight no more: instead,
I will not injure you if you do me no wrong.
And now let's join our ranks and then begin a song.

COMBINED CHORUS. [*Singing*]
Athenians, we're not prepared,
To say a single ugly word

About our fellow-citizens.
Quite the contrary: we desire but to say and to do
Naught but good. Quite enough are the ills now on hand.

Men and women, be advised:
    If anyone requires
Money—minae two or three—
    We've got what he desires.

My purse is yours, on easy terms:
    When Peace shall reappear,
Whate'er you've borrowed will be due.
    So speak up without fear.

You needn't pay me back, you see,
If you can get a cent from me!

We're about to entertain
    Some foreign gentlemen;
We've soup and tender, fresh-killed pork.
    Come round to dine at ten.

Come early; wash and dress with care,
    And bring the children, too.
Then step right in, no "by your leave."
    We'll be expecting you.

Walk in as if you owned the place.
You'll find the door—shut in your face!

[*Enter a group of Spartan Ambassadors; they are in the same
desperate condition as the Herald in the previous scene.*]

LEADER OF CHORUS. Here come the envoys from Sparta, sprouting
long beards and looking for all the world as if they were carrying
pig-pens in front of them.
    Greetings, gentlemen of Sparta. Tell me, in what state have you
come?
SPARTAN. Why waste words? You can plainly see what state
we're come in!
LEADER OF CHORUS. Wow! You're in a pretty high-strung condition,
and it seems to be getting worse.
SPARTAN. It's indescribable. Won't someone please arrange a peace
for us—in any way you like.
LEADER OF CHORUS. Here come our own, native ambassadors, crouch-

ing like wrestlers and holding their clothes in front of them; this
seems an athletic kind of malady.

[*Enter several Athenian Ambassadors.*]

ATHENIAN. Can anyone tell us where Lysistrata is? You see our condition.

LEADER OF CHORUS. Here's another case of the same complaint. Tell
me, are the attacks worse in the morning?

ATHENIAN. No, we're always afflicted this way. If someone doesn't
soon arrange this truce, you'd better not let me get my hands on—
Cleisthenes!

LEADER OF CHORUS. If you're smart, you'll arrange your cloaks so none
of the fellows who smashed the Hermae[60] can see you.

SPARTAN. Right you are; a very good suggestion.

ATHENIAN. Greetings, Spartan. We've suffered dreadful things.

SPARTAN. My dear fellow, we'd have suffered still worse if one of those
fellows had seen us in this condition.

ATHENIAN. Well, gentlemen, we must get down to business. What's
your errand here?

SPARTAN. We're ambassadors about peace.

ATHENIAN. Excellent; so are we. Only Lysistrata can arrange things
for us; shall we summon her?

SPARTAN. Aye, and Lysistratus too, if you like.

LEADER OF CHORUS. No need to summon her, it seems. She's coming
out of her own accord.

[*Enter* LYSISTRATA *accompanied by a statue of a nude female
figure, which represents Reconciliation.*]

Hail, noblest of women; now must thou be
A judge shrewd and subtle, mild and severe,
Be sweet yet majestic: all manners employ.
The leaders of Hellas, caught by thy love-charms
Have come to thy judgment, their charges submitting.

LYSISTRATA. This is no difficult task, if one catch them still in amorous passion, before they've resorted to each other. But I'll soon
find out. Where's Reconciliation? Go, first bring the Spartans
here, and don't seize them rudely and violently, as our tactless
husbands used to do, but as befits a woman, like an old, familiar
friend; if they won't give you their hands, take them however you
can. Then go fetch these Athenians here, taking hold of whatever
they offer you. Now then, men of Sparta, stand here beside me,
and you Athenians on the other side, and listen to my words.

60. small statues of the god Hermes
equipped with *phalloi*, which stood at the
door of most Athenian houses. Just before the great expedition left for Sicily,
rioters (probably oligarchic conspirators
opposed to the expedition) smashed
many of these statues.

I am a woman, it is true, but I have a mind; I'm not badly off in native wit, and by listening to my father and my elders, I've had a decent schooling.

Now I intend to give you a scolding which you both deserve. With one common font you worship at the same altars, just like brothers, at Olympia, at Thermopylae, at Delphi—how many more might I name, if time permitted;—and the Barbarians stand by waiting with their armies; yet you are destroying the men and towns of Greece.

ATHENIAN. Oh, this tension is killing me!

LYSISTRATA. And now, men of Sparta,—to turn to you—don't you remember how the Spartan Pericleidas came here once as a suppliant, and sitting at our altar, all pale with fear in his crimson cloak, begged us for an army?[61] For all Messene had attacked you and the god sent an earthquake too? Then Cimon went forth with four thousand hoplites and saved all Lacedaemon. Such was the aid you received from Athens, and now you lay waste the country which once treated you so well.

ATHENIAN. [*Hotly*] They're in the wrong, Lysistrata, upon my word, they are!

SPARTAN. [*Absently, looking at the statue of Reconciliation*] We're in the wrong. What hips! How lovely they are!

LYSISTRATA. Don't think I'm going to let you Athenians off. Don't you remember how the Spartans came in arms when you were wearing the rough, sheepskin cloak of slaves and slew the host of Thessalians, the comrades and allies of Hippias?[62] Fighting with you on that day, alone of all the Greeks, they set you free and instead of a sheepskin gave your folk a handsome robe to wear.

SPARTAN. [*Looking at* LYSISTRATA] I've never seen a more distinguished woman.

ATHENIAN. [*Looking at Reconciliation*] I've never seen a more voluptuous body!

LYSISTRATA. Why then, with these many noble deeds to think of, do you fight each other? Why don't you stop this villainy? Why not make peace? Tell me, what prevents it?

SPARTAN. [*Waving vaguely at Reconciliation*] We're willing, if you're willing to give up your position on yonder flank.

LYSISTRATA. What position, my good man?

SPARTAN. Pylus; we've been panting for it for ever so long.

ATHENIAN. No, by God! You shan't have it!

LYSISTRATA. Let them have it, my friend.

---

61. After a disastrous earthquake the Spartans were in great danger as a result of a rebellion of their serfs, the Helots. The Athenians under Cimon sent a large force of soldiers to help them (464 B.C.).

62. Hippias the tyrant had allowed exiled democrats to return to Attica but they had to stay outside the city and wear sheepskins so that they could readily be identified. With the help of Spartan soldiers the exiles and the people of Attica finally defeated the Thessalian troops of Hippias.

ATHENIAN. Then, what shall we have to rouse things up?

LYSISTRATA. Ask for another place in exchange.

ATHENIAN. Well, let's see: first of all [*Pointing to various parts of Reconçiliation's anatomy*] give us Echinus[63] here, this Maliac Inlet in back there, and these two Megarian legs.

SPARTAN. No, by heavens! You can't have *everything*, you crazy fool!

LYSISTRATA. Let it go. Don't fight over a pair of legs.

ATHENIAN. [*Taking off his cloak*] I think I'll strip and do a little planting now.

SPARTAN. [*Following suit*] And I'll just do a little fertilizing, by gosh!

LYSISTRATA. Wait until the truce is concluded. Now if you've decided on this course, hold a conference and discuss the matter with your allies.

ATHENIAN. Allies? Don't be ridiculous! They're in the same state we are. Won't all our allies want the same thing we do—to jump in bed with their women?

SPARTAN. Ours will, I know.

ATHENIAN. Especially the Carystians,[64] by God!

LYSISTRATA. Very well. Now purify yourselves, that your wives may feast and entertain you in the Acropolis; we've provisions by the basketful. Exchange your oaths and pledges there, and then each of you may take his wife and go home.

ATHENIAN. Let's go at once.

SPARTAN. Come on, where you will.

ATHENIAN. For God's sake, let's hurry!

[*They all go into the Acropolis.*]

CHORUS. [*Singing.*]

> Whate'er I have of coverlets
>    And robes of varied hue
> And golden trinkets,—without stint
>    I offer them to you.

> Take what you will and bear it home,
>    Your children to delight,
> Or if your girl's a Basket-maid;
>    Just choose whate'er's in sight.

> There's naught within so well secured
>    You cannot break the seal
> And bear it off; just help yourselves;
>    No hesitation feel.

63. Like Pylus (on the "flank" of the Peloponnese), these names are all double-barrelled references to territories in dispute in the war and salient portions of the anatomy of Reconciliation.

64. The people of Carystus on the island of Euboea were supposed to be of pre-Hellenic stock and therefore primitive and savage.

But you'll see nothing, though you try,
Unless you've sharper eyes than I!

If anyone needs bread to feed
    A growing family,
I've lots of wheat and full-grown loaves;
    So just apply to me.

Let every poor man who desires
    Come round and bring a sack
To fetch the grain; my slave is there
    To load it on his back.

But don't come near my door, I say.
Beware the dog, and stay away!

[*An* ATHENIAN *enters carrying a torch; he knocks at the gate.*]

ATHENIAN. Open the door! [*To the* CHORUS, *which is clustered around the gate*] Make way, won't you! What are you hanging around for? Want me to singe you with this torch? [*To himself*] No; it's a stale trick, I won't do it! [*To the audience*] Still, if I've got to do it to please *you*, I suppose I'll have to take the trouble.

[*A* SECOND ATHENIAN *comes out of the gate.*]

SECOND ATHENIAN. And I'll help you.

FIRST ATHENIAN. [*Waving his torch at the* CHORUS] Get out! Go bawl your heads off! Move on there, so the Spartans can leave in peace when the banquet's over.

[*They brandish their torches until the* CHORUS *leaves the Orchestra.*]

SECOND ATHENIAN. I've never seen such a pleasant banquet: the Spartans are charming fellows, indeed they are! And we Athenians are very witty in our cups.

FIRST ATHENIAN. Naturally: for when we're sober we're never at our best. If the Athenians would listen to me, we'd always get a little tipsy on our embassies. As things are now, we go to Sparta when we're sober and look around to stir up trouble. And then we don't hear what they say—and as for what they *don't* say, we have all sorts of suspicions. And then we bring back varying reports about the mission. But this time everything is pleasant; even if a man should sing the Telamon-song when he ought to sing "Cleitagoras,"[65] we'd praise him and swear it was excellent.

[*The two* CHORUSES *return, as a* CHORUS OF ATHENIANS *and a* CHORUS OF SPARTANS.]

65. At an Athenian banquet each guest in turn, when the time came to sing, was supposed to cap the singer before him by choosing an appropriate drinking song.

Here they come back again. Go to the devil, you scoundrels!

SECOND ATHENIAN. Get out, I say! They're coming out from the feast.

[*Enter the Spartan and Athenian envoys, followed by* LYSIS-
TRATA *and all the women.*]

SPARTAN. [*To one of his fellow-envoys*] My good fellow, take up your pipes; I want to do a fancy two-step and sing a jolly song for the Athenians.

ATHENIAN. Yes, do take your pipes, by all means. I'd love to see you dance.

SPARTAN. [*Singing and dancing with the* CHORUS OF SPARTANS]

> These youths inspire
> To song and dance, O Memory;
> Stir up my Muse, to tell how we
> And Athens' men, in our galleys clashing
> At Artemisium,[66] 'gainst foemen dashing
> In godlike ire,
> Conquered the Persian and set Greece free.

> Leonidas
> Led on his valiant warriors
> Whetting their teeth like angry boars.
> Abundant foam on their lips was flow'ring,
> A stream of sweat from their limbs was show'ring.
> The Persian was
> Numberless as the sand on the shores.

> O Huntress[67] who slayest the beasts in the glade,
> O Virgin divine, hither come to our truce,
> Unite us in bonds which all time will not loose.
> Grant us to find in this treaty, we pray,
> An unfailing source of true friendship today,
> And all of our days, helping us to refrain
> From weaseling tricks which bring war in their train.
> Then hither, come hither! O huntress maid.

LYSISTRATA. Come then, since all is fairly done, men of Sparta, lead away your wives, and you, Athenians, take yours. Let every man stand beside his wife, and every wife beside her man, and then, to celebrate our fortune, let's dance. And in the future, let's take care to avoid these misunderstandings.

CHORUS OF ATHENIANS. [*Singing and dancing*]

> Lead on the dances, your graces revealing.
> Call Artemis hither, call Artemis' twin,

66. the indecisive naval battle which took place off the coast while Leonidas held the pass at Thermopylae.
67. Artemis.

Leader of dances, Apollo the Healing.
Kindly God—hither! let's summon him in!

Nysian Bacchus call,
Who with his Maenads, his eyes flashing fire,
Dances, and last of all
Zeus of the thunderbolt flaming, the Sire.
And Hera in majesty,
Queen of prosperity.

Come, ye Powers who dwell above
Unforgetting, our witnesses be
Of Peace with bonds of harmonious love—
The Peace which Cypris has wrought for me.
Alleluia! Io Paean!
Leap in joy—hurrah! hurrah!
'Tis victory—hurrah! hurrah!
Euoi! Euoi! Euai! Euai!

LYSISTRATA. [*To the Spartans*] Come now, sing a new song to cap ours.
CHORUS OF SPARTANS. [*Singing and dancing*]
Leaving Taygetus fair and renown'd,
Muse of Laconia,[68] hither come:
Amyclae's god[69] in hymns resound,
Athene of the Brazen Home,[70]
And Castor and Pollux, Tyndareus' sons,
Who sport where Eurotas[71] murmuring runs.

On with the dance! Heia! Ho!
All leaping along,
Mantles a-swinging as we go!
Of Sparta our song.
There the holy chorus ever gladdens,
There the beat of stamping feet,
As our winsome fillies, lovely maidens,
Dance, beside Eurotas' banks a-skipping,—
Nimbly go to and fro
Hast'ning, leaping feet in measures tripping,
Like the Bacchae's revels, hair a-streaming.
Leda's child, divine and mild,
Leads the holy dance, her fair face beaming.
On with the dance! as your hand
Presses the hair
Streaming away unconfined.

68. the Spartan region.
69. *Amyclae*: part of Sparta.
70. the bronze-plated temple of Athena in Sparta.
71. the river of Sparta.

Leap in the air
Light as the deer; footsteps resound
Aiding our dance, beating the ground.
Praise Athene, Maid divine, unrivalled in her might,
Dweller in the Brazen Home, unconquered in the fight.
[*All go out singing and dancing.*]

# PLATO

## (429?–347 B.C.)

## The Apology of Socrates*

How you, O Athenians, have been affected by my accusers, I
cannot tell; but I know that they almost made me forget who I
was—so persuasively did they speak; and yet they have hardly
uttered a word of truth. But of the many falsehoods told by them,
there was one which quite amazed me;—I mean when they said
that you should be upon your guard and not allow yourselves to be
deceived by the force of my eloquence. To say this, when they were
certain to be detected as soon as I opened my lips and proved myself
to be anything but a great speaker, did indeed appear to me most
shameless—unless by the force of eloquence they mean the force
of truth; for if such is their meaning, I admit that I am eloquent.
But in how different a way from theirs! Well, as I was saying, they
have scarcely spoken the truth at all; but from me you shall hear
the whole truth: not, however, delivered after their manner in a
set oration duly ornamented with words and phrases. No, by heaven!
but I shall use the words and arguments which occur to me at the
moment; for I am confident in the justice of my cause: at my time
of life I ought not to be appearing before you, O men of Athens,
in the character of a juvenile orator—let no one expect it of me.
And I must beg of you to grant me a favour:—If I defend myself in
my accustomed manner, and you hear me using the words which
I have been in the habit of using in the agora,[1] at the tables of
the money-changers, or anywhere else, I would ask you not to be
surprised, and not to interrupt me on this account. For I am more
than seventy years of age, and appearing now for the first time in
a court of law, I am quite a stranger to the language of the place;
and therefore I would have you regard me as if I were really a
stranger, whom you would excuse if he spoke in his native tongue,
and after the fashion of his country:—Am I making an unfair
request of you? Never mind the manner, which may or may not be

---

* Translated by Benjamin Jowett.    1. the market place.
"Apology" means "defense."

good; but think only of the truth of my words, and give heed to that: let the speaker speak truly and the judge decide justly.

And first, I have to reply to the older charges[2] and to my first accusers, and then I will go on to the later ones. For of old I have had many accusers, who have accused me falsely to you during many years; and I am more afraid of them than of Anytus and his associates, who are dangerous, too, in their own way. But far more dangerous are the others, who began when you were children, and took possession of your minds with their falsehoods, telling of one Socrates, a wise man, who speculated about the heaven above, and searched into the earth beneath, and made the worse appear the better cause.[3] The disseminators of this tale are the accusers whom I dread; for their hearers are apt to fancy that such enquirers do not believe in the existence of the gods. And they are many, and their charges against me are of ancient date, and they were made by them in the days when you were more impressible than you are now—in childhood, or it may have been in youth—and the cause when heard went by default, for there was none to answer. And hardest of all, I do not know and cannot tell the names of my accusers; unless in the chance case of a Comic poet.[4] All who from envy and malice have persuaded you—some of them having first convinced themselves—all this class of men are most difficult to deal with; for I cannot have them up here, and cross-examine them, and therefore I must simply fight with shadows in my own defence, and argue when there is no one who answers. I will ask you then to assume with me, as I was saying, that my opponents are of two kinds; one recent, the other ancient: and I hope that you will see the propriety[5] of my answering the latter first, for these accusations you heard long before the others, and much oftener.

Well, then, I must make my defence, and endeavor to clear away in a short time, a slander which has lasted a long time. May I succeed, if to succeed be for my good and yours, or likely to avail me in my cause! The task is not an easy one; I quite understand the

2. Socrates had been the object of much criticism and satire for many years before the trial. He here disregards legal forms and announces that he will deal first with the prejudices that lie behind the formal charge that has been brought against him.

3. He was accused by some of his enemies of being a materialist philosopher who speculated about the physical nature of the universe, and by others of being one of the Sophists, professional teachers of rhetoric and other subjects, many of whom taught methods which were more effective than honest. (See footnotes 7 and 29, on Protagoras and Anaxagoras.)

4. He is referring to the poet Aristophanes, whose play *The Clouds* (produced in 423 B.C.) is a broad satire on Socrates and his associates, and a good example of the prejudice Socrates is dealing with, for it presents him propounding fantastic theories about matter and religion, and teaching students how to avoid payment of debts.

5. He says this with his tongue in his cheek, for he is actually paying no attention to legal propriety. This becomes clearer below, where he goes so far as to paraphrase the actual terms of the indictment and put into the mouths of his accusers the prejudice he claims is the basis of their action.

nature of it. And so leaving the event with God, in obedience to the law I will now make my defence.

I will begin at the beginning, and ask what is the accusation which has given rise to the slander of me, and in fact has encouraged Meletus to prefer this charge against me. Well, what do the slanderers say? They shall be my prosecutors, and I will sum up their words in an affidavit: 'Socrates is an evil-doer, and a curious person, who searches into things under the earth and in heaven, and he makes the worse appear the better cause; and he teaches the aforesaid doctrines to others.' Such is the nature of the accusation: it is just what you have yourselves seen in the comedy of Aristophanes, who has introduced a man whom he calls Socrates, going about and saying that he walks in air,[6] and talking a deal of nonsense concerning matters of which I do not pretend to know either much or little—not that I mean to speak disparagingly of any one who is a student of natural philosophy. I should be very sorry if Meletus could bring so grave a charge against me. But the simple truth is, O Athenians, that I have nothing to do with physical speculations. Very many of those here present are witnesses to the truth of this, and to them I appeal. Speak then, you who have heard me, and tell your neighbours whether any of you have ever known me hold forth in few words or in many upon such matters. . . . You hear their answer. And from what they say of this part of the charge you will be able to judge of the truth of the rest.

As little foundation is there for the report that I am a teacher, and take money;[7] this accusation has no more truth in it than the other. Although, if a man were really able to instruct mankind, to receive money for giving instruction would, in my opinion, be an honour to him. There is Gorgias[8] of Leontium, and Prodicus[9] of Ceos, and Hippias[10] of Elis, who go the round of the cities, and are able to persuade the young men to leave their own citizens by whom they might be taught for nothing, and come to them whom they not only pay, but are thankful if they may be allowed to pay them. There is at this time a Parian[11] philosopher residing in

---

6. In the comedy of Aristophanes Socrates first appears suspended in a basket, and when asked what he is doing replies, "I walk in air and contemplate the sun." He explains that only by suspending his intelligence can he investigate celestial matters.

7. Unlike Socrates, who beggared himself in the quest for truth, the professional teachers made great fortunes. The wealth of Protagoras, the first of the Sophists who demanded fees, was proverbial.

8. from Leontium in Sicily; he was famous as the originator of an antithetical, ornate prose style which had great influence.

9. from Ceos, an island in the Aegean; he taught rhetoric and was well-known for his pioneering grammatical studies.

10. from Elis, in the Peloponnese; he claimed to be able to teach any and all subjects, including handicrafts.

11. from Paros, a small island in the Aegean.

Athens, of whom I have heard; and I came to hear of him in this way:—I came across a man who has spent a world of money on the Sophists, Callias, the son of Hipponicus, and knowing that he had sons, I asked him: 'Callias,' I said, 'if your two sons were foals or calves, there would be no difficulty in finding some one to put over them; we should hire a trainer of horses, or a farmer probably, who would improve and perfect them in their own proper virtue and excellence; but as they are human beings, whom are you thinking of placing over them? Is there any one who understands human and political virtue? You must have thought about the matter, for you have sons; is there any one?' 'There is,' he said. 'Who is he?' said I; 'and of what country? and what does he charge?' 'Evenus the Parian,' he replied; 'he is the man, and his charge is five minae.'[12] Happy is Evenus, I said to myself; if he really has this wisdom, and teaches at such a moderate charge. Had I the same, I should have been very proud and conceited; but the truth is that I have no knowledge of the kind.

I dare say, Athenians, that some one among you will reply, 'Yes, Socrates, but what is the origin of these accusations which are brought against you; there must have been something strange which you have been doing? All these rumours and this talk about you would never have arisen if you had been like other men: tell us, then, what is the cause of them, for we should be sorry to judge hastily of you.' Now I regard this as a fair challenge, and I will endeavour to explain to you the reason why I am called wise and have such an evil fame. Please to attend then. And although some of you may think that I am joking, I declare that I will tell you the entire truth. Men of Athens, this reputation of mine has come of a certain sort of wisdom which I possess. If you ask me what kind of wisdom, I reply, wisdom such as may perhaps be attained by man, for to that extent I am inclined to believe that I am wise; whereas the persons of whom I was speaking have a superhuman wisdom, which I may fail to describe, because I have it not myself; and he who says that I have, speaks falsely, and is taking away my character. And here, O men of Athens, I must beg you not to interrupt me, even if I seem to say something extravagant. For the word which I will speak is not mine. I will refer you to a witness who is worthy of credit; that witness shall be the God of Delphi[13]—he will tell you about my wisdom, if I have any, and of what sort it is. You must have known Chaerephon;[14] he was early a friend of mine, and also a friend of yours, for he shared in the recent exile of the people,[15] and returned with you. Well, Chaerephon, as you

---

12. a relatively moderate sum; Protagoras is said to have charged a hundred minae for a course of instruction.
13. the oracle of Apollo at Delphi.

14. one of Socrates' closest associates; he appears in Aristophanes' comedy.
15. Chaerephon was an enthusiastic

know, was very impetuous in all his doings, and he went to Delphi
and boldly asked the oracle to tell him whether—as I was saying,
I must beg you not to interrupt—he asked the oracle to tell him
whether any one was wiser than I was, and the Pythian prophetess
answered, that there was no man wiser. Chaerephon is dead himself;
but his brother, who is in court, will confirm the truth of what I
am saying.

Why do I mention this? Because I am going to explain to you
why I have such an evil name. When I heard the answer, I said to
myself, What can the god mean? and what is the interpretation of
his riddle? for I know that I have no wisdom, small or great. What
then can he mean when he says that I am the wisest of men? And
yet he is a god, and cannot lie; that would be against his nature.
After long consideration, I thought of a method of trying the question. I reflected that if I could only find a man wiser than myself,
then I might go to the god with a refutation in my hand. I should
say to him, 'Here is a man who is wiser than I am; but you said
that I was the wisest.' Accordingly I went to one who had the
reputation of wisdom, and observed him—his name I need not
mention; he was a politician whom I selected for examination—and
the result was as follows: When I began to talk with him, I could
not help thinking that he was not really wise, although he was
thought wise by many, and still wiser by himself; and thereupon I
tried to explain to him that he thought himself wise, but was not
really wise; and the consequence was that he hated me, and his
enmity was shared by several who were present and heard me. So
I left him, saying to myself, as I went away: Well, although I do
not suppose that either of us knows anything really beautiful and
good, I am better off than he is,—for he knows nothing, and thinks
that he knows; I neither know nor think that I know. In this latter
particular, then, I seem to have slightly the advantage of him. Then
I went to another who had still higher pretensions to wisdom, and
my conclusion was exactly the same. Whereupon I made another
enemy of him, and of many others besides him.

Then I went to one man after another, being not unconscious
of the enmity which I provoked, and I lamented and feared this:
But necessity was laid upon me,—the word of God, I thought,
ought to be considered first. And I said to myself, Go I must to all
who appear to know, and find out the meaning of the oracle. And
I swear to you, Athenians, by the dog I swear![16]—for I must tell
you the truth—the result of my mission was just this: I found that

enough partisan of the democratic
regime to have to go into exile in 404
B.C. when the Thirty Tyrants carried
on an oligarchic reign of terror. The
phrase "the recent exile of the people"
refers to the exile into which all known
champions of democracy were forced
until the democracy was restored.

16. a euphemistic oath (compare,
"by George").

the men most in repute were all but the most foolish; and that others less esteemed were really wiser and better. I will tell you the tale of my wanderings and of the 'Herculean' labours, as I may call them, which I endured only to find at last the oracle irrefutable. After the politicians, I went to the poets; tragic, dithyrambic,[17] and all sorts. And there, I said to myself, you will be instantly detected; now you will find out that you are more ignorant than they are. Accordingly, I took them some of the most elaborate passages in their own writings, and asked what was the meaning of them— thinking that they would teach me something. Will you believe me? I am almost ashamed to confess the truth, but I must say that there is hardly a person present who would not have talked better about their poetry than they did themselves. Then I knew that not by wisdom do poets write poetry, but by a sort of genius and inspiration; they are like diviners or soothsayers who also say many fine things, but do not understand the meaning of them.[18] The poets appeared to me to be much in the same case; and I further observed that upon the strength of their poetry they believed themselves to be the wisest of men in other things in which they were not wise. So I departed, conceiving myself to be superior to them for the same reason that I was superior to the politicians.

At last I went to the artisans, for I was conscious that I knew nothing at all, as I may say, and I was sure that they knew many fine things; and here I was not mistaken, for they did know many things of which I was ignorant, and in this they certainly were wiser than I was. But I observed that even the good artisans fell into the same error as the poets;—because they were good workmen they thought that they also knew all sorts of high matters, and this defect in them overshadowed their wisdom; and therefore I asked myself on behalf of the oracle, whether I would like to be as I was, neither having their knowledge nor their ignorance, or like them in both; and I made answer to myself and to the oracle that I was better off as I was.

This inquisition has led to my having many enemies of the worst and most dangerous kind, and has given occasion also to many calumnies. And I am called wise, for my hearers always imagine that I myself possess the wisdom which I find wanting in others: but the truth is, O men of Athens, that God only is wise; and by his answer he intends to show that the wisdom of men is worth little or nothing; he is not speaking of Socrates, he is only using my name by way of illustration, as if he said, He, O men, is the wisest, who, like Socrates, knows that his wisdom is in truth worth

---

17. The dithyramb was a short performance by a chorus, produced, like tragedy, at state expense and at a public festival.

18. For a fuller exposition of this famous theory of poetic inspiration see Plato's *Ion*.

nothing. And so I go about the world, obedient to the god, and search and make enquiry into the wisdom of any one, whether citizen or stranger, who appears to be wise; and if he is not wise, then in vindication of the oracle I show him that he is not wise; and my occupation quite absorbs me, and I have no time to give either to any public matter of interest or to any concern of my own, but I am in utter poverty by reason of my devotion to the god.

There is another thing:—young men of the richer classes, who have not much to do, come about me of their own accord; they like to hear the pretenders examined, and they often imitate me, and proceed to examine others; there are plenty of persons, as they quickly discover, who think that they know something, but really know little or nothing; and then those who are examined by them instead of being angry with themselves are angry with me: This confounded Socrates, they say; this villainous misleader of youth! —and then if somebody asks them, Why, what evil does he practice or teach? they do not know, and cannot tell; but in order that they may not appear to be at a loss, they repeat the ready-made charges which are used against all philosophers about teaching things up in the clouds and under the earth, and having no gods, and making the worse appear the better cause; for they do not like to confess that their pretence of knowledge has been detected—which is the truth; and as they are numerous and ambitious and energetic, and are drawn up in battle array and have persuasive tongues, they have filled your ears with their loud and inveterate calumnies. And this is the reason why my three accusers, Meletus and Anytus and Lycon, have set upon me; Meletus, who has a quarrel with me on behalf of the poets; Anytus, on behalf of the craftsmen and politicians; Lycon,[19] on behalf of the rhetoricians: and as I said at the beginning, I cannot expect to get rid of such a mass of calumny all in a moment. And this, O men of Athens, is the truth and the whole truth; I have concealed nothing, I have dissembled nothing. And yet, I know that my plainness of speech makes them hate me, and what is their hatred but a proof that I am speaking the truth?— Hence has arisen the prejudice against me; and this is the reason of it, as you will find out either in this or in any future enquiry.

I have said enough in my defence against the first class of my accusers; I turn to the second class. They are headed by Meletus, that good man and true lover of his country, as he calls himself. Against these, too, I must try to make a defence:—Let their affidavit be read: it contains something of this kind: It says that Socrates is a doer of evil, who corrupts the youth; and who does not believe in the gods of the state, but has other new divinities[20] of his own.

19. the three accusers. Anytus was a prominent politician; the connection of Meletus with poetry and of Lycon with rhetoric is known only from this passage.

20. The precise meaning of the

Such is the charge; and now let us examine the particular counts. He says that I am a doer of evil, and corrupt the youth; but I say, O men of Athens, that Meletus is a doer of evil, in that he pretends to be in earnest when he is only in jest, and is so eager to bring men to trial from a pretended zeal and interest about matters in which he really never had the smallest interest. And the truth of this I will endeavour to prove to you.

Come hither, Meletus, and let me ask a question[21] of you. You think a great deal about the improvement of youth?

Yes, I do.

Tell the judges, then, who is their improver; for you must know, as you have taken the pains to discover their corrupter, and are citing and accusing me before them. Speak, then, and tell the judges who their improver is.—Observe, Meletus, that you are silent, and have nothing to say. But is not this rather disgraceful, and a very considerable proof of what I was saying, that you have no interest in the matter? Speak up, friend, and tell us who their improver is.

The laws.

But that, my good sir, is not my meaning. I want to know who the person is, who, in the first place, knows the laws.

The judges,[22] Socrates, who are present in court.

What, do you mean to say, Meletus, that they are able to instruct and improve youth?

Certainly they are.

What, all of them, or some only and not others?

All of them.

By the goddess Here,[23] that is good news! There are plenty of improvers, then. And what do you say of the audience,—do they improve them?

Yes, they do.

And the senators?[24]

_____

charge is not clear. As this translation indicates, the Greek words may mean "new divinities," with a reference to Socrates' famous inner voice, which from time to time warned him against action on which he had decided. Or the words may mean "practicing strange rites," though this charge is difficult to understand. In any case, the importance of the phrase is that it implies religious belief of some sort and can later be used against Meletus when he loses his head and accuses Socrates of atheism.

21. Socrates avails himself of his right to interrogate the accuser. He is, of course, a master in this type of examination, for he has spent his life in the practice of puncturing inflated pretensions and exposing logical contradictions in the arguments of his adversaries. He is here fulfilling his

earlier promise to defend himself in the manner to which he has been accustomed and use the words which he has been in the habit of using in the agora (p. 521).

22. the jury. There was no judge in the Athenian law court. The Athenian jury was large; in this trial it probably consisted of five hundred citizens. In the following questions Socrates forces Meletus to extend the capacity to improve the youth to successively greater numbers, until it appears that the entire citizen body is a good influence and Socrates the only bad one. Meletus is caught in the trap of his own demagogic appeal.

23. Hera.

24. the members of the standing council of the assembly, five hundred in number.

Yes, the senators improve them.

But perhaps the members of the assembly[25] corrupt them?—or do they too improve them?

They improve them.

Then every Athenian improves and elevates them; all with the exception of myself; and I alone am their corrupter? Is that what you affirm?

That is what I stoutly affirm.

I am very unfortunate if you are right. But suppose I ask you a question: How about horses?[26] Does one man do them harm and all the world good? Is not the exact opposite the truth? One man is able to do them good, or at least not many;—the trainer of horses, that is to say, does them good, and others who have to do with them rather injure them? Is not that true, Meletus, of horses, or any other animals? Most assuredly it is; whether you and Anytus say yes or no. Happy indeed would be the condition of youth if they had one corrupter only, and all the rest of the world were their improvers. But you, Meletus, have sufficiently shown that you never had a thought about the young: your carelessness is seen in your not caring about the very things which you bring against me.

And now, Meletus, I will ask you another question—by Zeus I will: Which is better, to live among bad citizens, or among good ones? Answer, friend, I say; the question is one which may be easily answered. Do not the good do their neighbours good, and the bad do them evil?

Certainly.

And is there any one who would rather be injured than benefited by those who live with him? Answer, my good friend, the law requires you to answer—does any one like to be injured?

Certainly not.

And when you accuse me of corrupting and deteriorating the youth, do you allege that I corrupt them intentionally or unintentionally?

Intentionally, I say.

But you have just admitted that the good do their neighbours good, and evil do them evil. Now, is that a truth which your superior wisdom has recognized thus early in life, and am I, at my age, in such darkness and ignorance as not to know that if a man with whom I have to live is corrupted by me, I am very likely to be harmed by him; and yet I corrupt him, and intentionally, too—so you say, although neither I nor any other human being is ever likely to be convinced by you. But either I do not corrupt them, or I

---

25. the sovereign body in the Athenian constitution, theoretically an assembly of the whole citizen body.

26. This simple analogy is typical of the Socratic method; he is still defending himself in his accustomed manner.

corrupt them unintentionally; and on either view of the case you lie. If my offence is unintentional, the law has no cognizance of unintentional offences: you ought to have taken me privately, and warned and admonished me; for if I had been better advised, I should have left off doing what I only did unintentionally—no doubt I should; but you would have nothing to say to me and refused to teach me. And now you bring me up in this court, which is not a place of instruction, but of punishment.

It will be very clear to you, Athenians, as I was saying, that Meletus has no care at all, great or small, about the matter. But still I should like to know, Meletus, in what I am affirmed to corrupt the young. I suppose you mean, as I infer from your indictment, that I teach them not to acknowledge the gods which the state acknowledges, but some other new divinities or spiritual agencies in their stead. These are the lessons by which I corrupt the youth, as you say.

Yes, that I say emphatically.

Then, by the gods, Meletus, of whom we are speaking, tell me and the court, in somewhat plainer terms, what you mean! for I do not as yet understand whether you affirm that I teach other men to acknowledge some gods, and therefore that I do believe in gods, and am not an entire atheist—this you do not lay to my charge,— but only you say that they are not the same gods which the city recognizes—the charge is that they are different gods. Or, do you mean that I am an atheist simply, and a teacher of atheism?

I mean the latter—that you are a complete atheist.[27]

What an extraordinary statement! Why do you think so, Meletus? Do you mean that I do not believe in the godhead of the sun or moon, like other men?

I assure you, judges, that he does not: for he says that the sun is stone, and the moon earth.[28]

Friend Meletus, you think that you are accusing Anaxagoras: and you have but a bad opinion of the judges, if you fancy them illiterate to such a degree as not to know that these doctrines are found in the books of Anaxagoras[29] the Clazomenian, which are full of them. And so, forsooth, the youth are said to be taught them by Socrates, when there are not unfrequently exhibitions of them at the theatre[30] (price of admission one drachma at the most); and

---

27. Meletus jumps at the most damaging charge, and falls into the trap.
28. Meletus falls back on the old prejudices which Socrates claims are the real indictment against him.
29. a fifth-century philosopher from Clazomenae in Asia Minor. He was an intimate friend of Pericles, but this did not save him from indictment for impiety. He was condemned, and forced to leave Athens. He is famous for his doctrine that matter was set in motion and ordered by Intelligence (Nous), which, however, did not create it. He also declared that the sun was a mass of red-hot metal larger than the Peloponnese, and that there were hills and ravines on the moon.
30. I.e., the doctrines of Anaxagoras are reflected in the works of the tragic

they might pay their money, and laugh at Socrates if he pretends to father these extraordinary views. And so, Meletus, you really think that I do not believe in any god?

I swear by Zeus that you believe absolutely in none at all.

Nobody will believe you, Meletus, and I am pretty sure that you do not believe yourself. I cannot help thinking, men of Athens, that Meletus is reckless and impudent, and that he has written this indictment in a spirit of mere wantonness and youthful bravado. Has he not compounded a riddle, thinking to try me? He said to himself:—I shall see whether the wise Socrates will discover my facetious contradiction, or whether I shall be able to deceive him and the rest of them. For he certainly does appear to me to contradict himself in the indictment as much as if he said that Socrates is guilty of not believing in the gods, and yet of believing in them— but this is not like a person who is in earnest.

I should like you, O men of Athens, to join me in examining what I conceive to be his inconsistency; and do you, Meletus, answer. And I must remind the audience of my request that they would not make a disturbance[31] if I speak in my accustomed manner:

Did ever man, Meletus, believe in the existence of human things, and not of human beings? . . . I wish, men of Athens, that he would answer, and not be always trying to get up an interruption. Did ever any man believe in horsemanship, and not in horses? or in flute-playing, and not in flute-players? No, my friend; I will answer to you and to the court, as you refuse to answer for yourself. There is no man who ever did. But now please to answer the next question: Can a man believe in spiritual and divine agencies, and not in spirits or demigods?

He cannot.

How lucky I am to have extracted that answer, by the assistance of the court! But then you swear in the indictment that I teach and believe in divine or spiritual agencies (new or old, no matter for that); at any rate, I believe in spiritual agencies,—so you say and swear in the affidavit; and yet if I believe in divine beings, how can I help believing in spirits or demigods;—must I not? To be sure I must; and therefore I may assume that your silence gives consent. Now what are spirits or demigods? are they not either gods or the sons of gods?

Certainly they are.

But this is what I call the facetious riddle invented by you: the

poets; or the words may mean simply that Anaxagoras' book was on sale at the theater.

31. The disturbance is presumably due to the frustration of the enemies of Socrates, who see him assuming complete control of the proceedings and turning them into a street-corner argument of the type in which he is invincible.

demigods or spirits are gods, and you say first that I do not believe in gods, and then again that I do believe in gods; that is, if I believe in demigods. For if the demigods are the illegitimate sons of gods, whether by the nymphs or by any other mothers, of whom they are said to be the sons—what human being will ever believe that there are no gods if they are the sons of gods? You might as well affirm the existence of mules, and deny that of horses and asses. Such nonsense, Meletus, could only have been intended by you to make trial of me. You have put this into the indictment because you had nothing real of which to accuse me. But no one who has a particle of understanding will ever be convinced by you that the same men can believe in divine and superhuman things, and yet not believe that there are gods and demigods and heroes.

I have said enough in answer to the charge of Meletus: any elaborate defence is unnecessary; but I know only too well how many are the enmities which I have incurred, and this is what will be my destruction if I am destroyed;—not Meletus, nor yet Anytus, but the envy and detraction of the world, which has been the death of many good men, and will probably be the death of many more; there is no danger of my being the last of them.

Some one will say: And are you not ashamed, Socrates, of a course of life which is likely to bring you to an untimely end? To him I may fairly answer: There you are mistaken; a man who is good for anything ought not to calculate the chance of living or dying; he ought only to consider whether in doing anything he is doing right or wrong—acting the part of a good man or of a bad. Whereas, upon your view, the heroes who fell at Troy were not good for much, and the son of Thetis[32] above all, who altogether despised danger in comparison with disgrace; and when he was so eager to slay Hector, his goddess mother said to him, that if he avenged his companion Patroclus, and slew Hector, he would die himself—'Fate,' she said, in these or the like words, 'waits for you next after Hector;' he, receiving this warning, utterly despised danger and death, and instead of fearing them, feared rather to live in dishonour, and not to avenge his friend. 'Let me die forthwith,' he replies, 'and be avenged of my enemy, rather than abide here by the beaked ships, a laughing-stock and a burden of the earth.' Had Achilles any thought of death and danger? For wherever a man's place is, whether the place which he has chosen or that in which he has been placed by a commander, there he ought to remain in hour of danger; he should not think of death or of anything but of disgrace. And this, O men of Athens, is a true saying.

Strange, indeed, would be my conduct, O men of Athens, if I who, when I was ordered by the generals whom you chose to com-

32. Achilles. See the *Iliad*, Book XVIII, ll. 94 ff.

mand me at Potidaea and Amphipolis and Delium,[33] remained where they placed me, like any other man, facing death—if now, when, as I conceive and imagine, God orders me to fulfil the philosopher's mission of searching into myself and other men, I were to desert my post through fear of death, or any other fear; that would indeed be strange, and I might justly be arraigned in court for denying the existence of the gods, if I disobeyed the oracle because I was afraid of death, fancying that I was wise when I was not wise. For the fear of death is indeed the pretence of wisdom, and not real wisdom, being a pretence of knowing the unknown; and no one knows whether death, which men in their fear apprehend to be the greatest evil, may not be the greatest good. Is not this ignorance of a disgraceful sort, the ignorance which is the conceit that man knows what he does not know? And in this respect only I believe myself to differ from men in general, and may perhaps claim to be wiser than they are:—that whereas I know but little of the world below,[34] I do not suppose that I know: but I do know that injustice and disobedience to a better, whether God or man, is evil and dishonourable, and I will never fear or avoid a possible good rather than a certain evil. And therefore if you let me go now, and are not convinced by Anytus, who said that since I had been prosecuted I must be put to death (or if not that I ought never to have been prosecuted at all); and that if I escape now, your sons will all be utterly ruined by listening to my words—if you say to me, Socrates, this time we will not mind Anytus, and you shall be let off, but upon one condition, that you are not to enquire and speculate in this way any more, and that if you are caught doing so again you shall die:—if this was the condition on which you let me go, I should reply: Men of Athens, I honour and love you; but I shall obey God rather than you, and while I have life and strength I shall never cease from the practice and teaching of philosophy, exhorting any one whom I meet and saying to him after my manner: You, my friend,—a citizen of the great and mighty and wise city of Athens,—are you not ashamed of heaping up the greatest amount of money and honour and reputation, and caring so little about wisdom and truth and the greatest improvement of the soul, which you never regard or heed at all? And if the person with whom I am arguing, says: Yes, but I do care; then I do not leave him or let him go at once; but I proceed to interrogate and examine and cross-examine him, and if I think that he has no virtue in him, but only

33. three of the battles in the Peloponnesian War in which Socrates had fought as an infantryman. The battle at Potidaea (in northern Greece) occurred in 432 B.C. (For a fuller account of Socrates' conduct there see Plato's *Symposium*.) The date of the battle at Amphipolis (in northern Greece) is uncertain. The battle at Delium (in central Greece) took place in 424 B.C.

34. the next world. The dead were supposed to carry on a sort of existence below the earth.

says that he has, I reproach him with undervaluing the greater, and overvaluing the less. And I shall repeat the same words to every one whom I meet, young and old, citizen and alien, but especially to the citizens, inasmuch as they are my brethren. For know that this is the command of God; and I believe that no greater good has ever happened in the state than my service to the God. For I do nothing but go about persuading you all, old and young alike, not to take thought for your persons or your properties, but first and chiefly to care about the greatest improvement of the soul. I tell you that virtue is not given by money, but that from virtue comes money and every other good of man, public as well as private. This is my teaching, and if this is the doctrine which corrupts the youth, I am a mischievous person. But if any one says that this is not my teaching, he is speaking an untruth. Wherefore, O men of Athens, I say to you, do as Anytus bids or not as Anytus bids, and either acquit me or not; but whichever you do, understand that I shall never alter my ways, not even if I have to die many times.

Men of Athens, do not interrupt,[35] but hear me; there was an understanding between us that you should hear me to the end: I have something more to say, at which you may be inclined to cry out; but I believe that to hear me will be good for you, and therefore I beg that you will not cry out. I would have you know, that if you kill such an one as I am, you will injure yourselves more than you will injure me. Nothing will injure me, not Meletus nor yet Anytus—they cannot, for a bad man is not permitted to injure a better than himself. I do not deny that Anytus may, perhaps, kill him, or drive him into exile, or deprive him of civil rights; and he may imagine, and others may imagine, that he is inflicting a great injury upon him: but there I do not agree. For the evil of doing as he is doing—the evil of unjustly taking away the life of another—is greater far.

And now, Athenians, I am not going to argue for my own sake, as you may think, but for yours, that you may not sin against the God by condemning me, who am his gift to you. For if you kill me you will not easily find a successor to me, who, if I may use such a ludicrous figure of speech, am a sort of gadfly, given to the state by God; and the state is a great and noble steed who is tardy in his motions owing to his very size, and requires to be stirred into life. I am that gadfly which God has attached to the state, and all day long and in all places am always fastening upon you, arousing and persuading and reproaching you. You will not easily find another like me, and therefore I would advise you to spare me. I dare say that you may feel out of temper (like a person who is suddenly

35. The disturbance this time is presumably more general, for Socrates is defying the court and the people.

awakened from sleep), and you think that you might easily strike me dead as Anytus advises, and then you would sleep on for the remainder of your lives, unless God in his care of you sent you another gadfly. When I say that I am given to you by God, the proof of my mission is this:—if I had been like other men, I should not have neglected all my own concerns or patiently seen the neglect of them during all these years, and have been doing yours, coming to you individually like a father or elder brother, exhorting you to regard virtue; such conduct, I say, would be unlike human nature. If I had gained anything, or if my exhortations had been paid, there would have been some sense in my doing so; but now, as you will perceive, not even the impudence of my accusers dares to say that I have ever exacted or sought pay of any one; of that they have no witness. And I have a sufficient witness to the truth of what I say— my poverty.

Some one may wonder why I go about in private giving advice and busying myself with the concerns of others, but do not venture to come forward in public and advise the state. I will tell you why. You have heard me speak at sundry times and in divers places of an oracle or sign which comes to me, and is the divinity which Meletus ridicules in the indictment. This sign, which is a kind of voice, first began to come to me when I was a child; it always forbids but never commands me to do anything which I am going to do. This is what deters me from being a politician. And rightly, as I think. For I am certain, O men of Athens, that if I had engaged in politics, I should have perished long ago, and done no good either to you or to myself. And do not be offended at my telling you the truth: for the truth is, that no man who goes to war with you or any other multitude, honestly striving against the many lawless and unrighteous deeds which are done in a state, will save his life; he who will fight for the right, if he would live even for a brief space, must have a private station and not a public one.

I can give you convincing evidence of what I say, not words only, but what you value far more—actions. Let me relate to you a passage of my own life which will prove to you that I should never have yielded to injustice from any fear of death, and that 'as I should have refused to yield' I must have died at once. I will tell you a tale of the courts, not very interesting perhaps, but nevertheless true. The only office of state which I ever held, O men of Athens, was that of senator:[36] the tribe Antiochis,[37] which is my tribe, had the

---

36. The Council of the Five Hundred consisted of fifty members of each of the ten tribes into which the population was divided. Each tribal delegation acted as a standing committee of the whole body for a part of the year. The members of this standing committee were called Prytanes. In acting as a member of the council Socrates was not "engaging in politics" but simply fulfilling his duty as a citizen when called upon.

37. Socrates' tribe, like the other nine, was named after a mythical hero, in this case Antiochus.

presidency at the trial of the generals who had not taken up the bodies of the slain after the battle of Arginusae;[38] and you proposed to try them in a body, contrary to law, as you all thought afterwards; but at the time I was the only one of the Prytanes who was opposed to the illegality, and I gave my vote against you; and when the orators threatened to impeach and arrest me, and you called and shouted, I made up my mind that I would run the risk, having law and justice with me, rather than take part in your injustice because I feared imprisonment and death. This happened in the days of the democracy.[39] But when the oligarchy of the Thirty[40] was in power, they sent for me and four others into the rotunda,[41] and bade us bring Leon the Salaminian from Salamis,[42] as they wanted to put him to death. This was a specimen of the sort of commands which they were always giving with the view of implicating as many as possible in their crimes; and then I showed, not in word only but in deed, that, if I may be allowed to use such an expression, I cared not a straw for death, and that my great and only care was lest I should do an unrighteous or unholy thing. For the strong arm of that oppressive power did not frighten me into doing wrong; and when we came out of the rotunda the other four went to Salamis and fetched Leon, but I went quietly home. For which I might have lost my life, had not the power of the Thirty shortly afterwards come to an end. And many will witness to my words.

Now do you really imagine that I could have survived all these years, if I had led a public life, supposing that like a good man I had always maintained the right and had made justice, as I ought, the first thing? No indeed, men of Athens, neither I nor any other man. But I have been always the same in all my actions, public as well as private, and never have I yielded any base compliance to those who are slanderously termed my disciples, or to any other. Not that I have any regular disciples. But if any one likes to come and hear me while I am pursuing my mission, whether he be young or old, he is not excluded. Nor do I converse only with those who pay; but any one, whether he be rich or poor, may ask and answer me and listen

38. an Athenian naval victory over Sparta, in 406 B.C. The Athenian commanders failed to pick up the bodies of a large number of Athenians whose ships had been destroyed. Whether they were prevented from doing so by the wind or simply neglected this duty in the excitement of victory is not known; in any case, the Athenian population suspected the worst and put all ten generals on trial, not in a court of law but before the assembly. The generals were tried not individually, but in a group, and condemned to death. The six who had returned to Athens were executed, among them a son of Pericles.

39. Socrates gives two instances of his political actions, one under the democracy and one under the Thirty Tyrants. In both cases, he was in opposition to the government.

40. In 404 B.C., with Spartan backing, the Thirty Tyrants (as they were known to their enemies) ruled for eight months over a defeated Athens. Prominent among them was Critias, who had been one of the rich young men who listened eagerly to Socrates.

41. the circular building in which the Prytanes held their meetings.

42. Athenian territory, an island off Piraeus, the port of Athens.

to my words; and whether he turns out to be a bad man or a good one, neither result can be justly imputed to me; for I never taught or professed to teach him anything. And if any one says that he has ever learned or heard anything from me in private which all the world has not heard, let me tell you that he is lying.

But I shall be asked, Why do people delight in continually conversing with you? I have told you already, Athenians, the whole truth about this matter: they like to hear the cross-examination of the pretenders to wisdom; there is amusement in it. Now this duty of cross-examining other men has been imposed upon me by God; and has been signified to me by oracles, visions, and in every way in which the will of divine power was ever intimated to any one. This is true, O Athenians; or, if not true, would be soon refuted. If I am or have been corrupting the youth, those of them who are now grown up and become sensible that I gave them bad advice in the days of their youth should come forward as accusers, and take their revenge; or if they do not like to come themselves, some of their relatives, fathers, brothers, or other kinsmen, should say what evil their families have suffered at my hands. Now is their time. Many of them I see in the court. There is Crito,[43] who is of the same age and of the same deme[44] with myself, and there is Critobulus his son, whom I also see. Then again there is Lysanias of Sphettus, who is the father of Aeschines—he is present; and also there is Antiphon of Cephisus, who is the father of Epigenes; and there are the brothers of several who have associated with me. There is Nicostratus the son of Theosdotides, and the brother of Theodotus (now Theodotus himself is dead, and therefore he, at any rate, will not seek to stop him); and there is Paralus the son of Demodocus, who had a brother Theages; and Adeimantus the son of Ariston, whose brother Plato[45] is present; and Acantodorus, who is the brother of Apollodorus, whom I also see. I might mention a great many others, some of whom Meletus should have produced as witnesses in the course of his speech; and let him still produce them, if he has forgotten—I will make way for him. And let him say, if he has any testimony of the sort which he can produce. Nay, Athenians, the very opposite is the truth. For all these are ready to witness on behalf of the corrupter, of the injurer of their kindred, as Meletus and Anytus call me; not the corrupted youth only—there might have been a motive for that—but their uncorrupted elder relatives. Why should they too support me with their testimony? Why, indeed, except for the sake of truth and justice, and because they know that I am speaking the truth, and that Meletus is a liar.

Well, Athenians, this and the like of this is all the defence which

---

43. a friend of Socrates who later tried to persuade him to escape from prison.

44. precinct; the local unit of Athenian administration.

45. the writer of the *Apology*.

I have to offer. Yet a word more. Perhaps there may be some one who is offended at me, when he calls to mind how he himself on a similar, or even a less serious occasion, prayed and entreated the judges with many tears, and how he produced his children in court, which was a moving spectacle, together with a host of relations and friends;[46] whereas I, who am probably in danger of my life, will do none of these things. The contrast may occur to his mind, and he may be set against me, and vote in anger because he is displeased at me on this account. Now if there be such a person among you,— mind, I do not say that there is,—to him I may fairly reply: My friend, I am a man, and like other men, a creature of flesh and blood, and not 'of wood or stone,' as Homer says;[47] and I have a family, yes, and sons, O Athenians, three in number, one almost a man, and two others who are still young; and yet I will not bring any of them hither in order to petition you for an acquittal. And why not? Not from any self-assertion or want of respect for you. Whether I am or am not afraid of death is another question, of which I will not now speak. But, having regard to public opinion, I feel that such conduct would be discreditable to myself, and to you, and to the whole state. One who has reached my years, and who has a name for wisdom, ought not to demean himself. Whether this opinion of me be deserved or not, at any rate the world has decided that Socrates is in some way superior to other men. And if those among you who are said to be superior in wisdom and courage, and any other virtue, demean themselves in this way, how shameful is their conduct! I have seen men of reputation, when they have been condemned, behaving in the strangest manner: they seemed to fancy that they were going to suffer something dreadful if they died, and that they could be immortal if you only allowed them to live; and I think that such are a dishonour to the state, and that any stranger coming in would have said of them that the most eminent men of Athens, to whom the Athenians themselves give honour and command, are no better than women. And I say that these things ought not to be done by those of us who have a reputation; and if they are done, you ought not to permit them; you ought rather to show that you are far more disposed to condemn the man who gets up a doleful scene and makes the city ridiculous, than him who holds his peace.

But, setting aside the question of public opinion, there seems to be something wrong in asking a favour of a judge, and thus procuring an acquittal, instead of informing and convincing him. For his

46. The accepted ending of the speech for the defense was an unrestrained appeal to the pity of the jury. Socrates' refusal to make it is another shock for the prejudices of the audience.

47. In the Odyssey, Book XIX, ll.

162–163, Penelope says to her husband Odysseus (who is disguised as a beggar), "Tell me of your family and where you come from. For you did not spring from an oak or a rock, as the old saying goes."

duty is, not to make a present of justice, but to give judgment; and he has sworn that he will judge according to the laws, and not according to his own good pleasure; and we ought not to encourage you, nor should you allow yourself to be encouraged, in this habit of perjury—there can be no piety in that. Do not then require me to do what I consider dishonourable and impious and wrong, especially now, when I am being tried for impiety on the indictment of Meletus. For if, O men of Athens, by force of persuasion and entreaty I could overpower your oaths, then I should be teaching you to believe that there are no gods, and in defending should simply convict myself of the charge of not believing in them. But that is not so—far otherwise. For I do believe that there are gods, and in a sense higher than that in which any of my accusers believe in them. And to you and to God I commit my cause, to be determined by you as is best for you and me.[48]

There are many reasons why I am not grieved, O men of Athens, at the vote of condemnation. I expected it, and am only surprised that the votes are so nearly equal; for I had thought that the majority against me would have been far larger; but now, had thirty votes gone over to the other side, I should have been acquitted. And I may say, I think, that I have escaped Meletus. I may say more; for without the assistance of Anytus and Lycon, any one may see that he would not have had a fifth part of the votes,[49] as the law requires, in which case he would have incurred a fine of a thousand drachmae.

And so he proposes death as the penalty. And what shall I propose on my part, O men of Athens? Clearly that which is my due. And what is my due? What return shall be made to the man who has never had the wit to be idle during his whole life; but has been careless of what the many care for—wealth, and family interests, and military offices, and speaking in the assembly, and magistracies, and plots, and parties. Reflecting that I was really too honest a man to be a politician and live, I did not go where I could do no good to you or to myself; but where I could do the greatest good privately to every one of you, thither I went, and sought to persuade every man among you that he must look to himself, and seek virtue and wisdom before he looks to his private interests, and look to the state before he looks to the interests of the state; and that this

48. The jury reaches a verdict of guilty. It appears from what Socrates says later that the jury was split, 280 for this verdict and 220 against it. The penalty is to be settled by the jury's choice between the penalty proposed by the prosecution and that offered by the defense. The jury itself cannot propose a penalty. Meletus demands death. Socrates must propose the lightest sentence he thinks he can get away with, but one heavy enough to satisfy the majority of the jury who voted him guilty. The prosecution probably expects him to propose exile from Athens, but Socrates surprises them.

49. Socrates jokingly divides the votes against him into three parts, one for each of his three accusers, and points out that Meletus' votes fall below the minimum necessary to justify the trial.

should be the order which he observes in all his actions. What shall be done to such an one? Doubtless some good thing, O men of Athens, if he has his reward; and the good should be of a kind suitable to him. What would be a reward suitable to a poor man who is your benefactor, and who desires leisure that he may instruct you? There can be no reward so fitting as maintenance in the Prytaneum,[50] O men of Athens, a reward which he deserves far more than the citizen who has won the prize at Olympia in the horse or chariot race, whether the chariots were drawn by two horses or by many. For I am in want, and he has enough; and he only gives you the appearance of happiness, and I give you the reality. And if I am to estimate the penalty fairly, I should say that maintenance in the Prytaneum is the just return.

Perhaps you think that I am braving you in what I am saying now, as in what I said before about the tears and prayers. But this is not so. I speak rather because I am convinced that I never intentionally wronged any one, although I cannot convince you—the time has been too short; if there were a law at Athens, as there is in other cities, that a capital cause should not be decided in one day,[51] then I believe that I should have convinced you. But I cannot in a moment refute great slander; and, as I am convinced that I never wronged another, I will assuredly not wrong myself. I will not say of myself that I deserve any evil, or propose any penalty. Why should I? Because I am afraid of the penalty of death which Meletus proposes? When I do not know whether death is a good or an evil, why should I propose a penalty which would certainly be an evil? Shall I say imprisonment? And why should I live in prison, and be the slave of the magistrates of the year—of the Eleven?[52] Or shall the penalty be a fine, and imprisonment until the fine is paid? There is the same objection. I should have to lie in prison, for money I have none, and cannot pay. And if I say exile (and this may possibly be the penalty which you will affix), I must indeed be blinded by the love of life, if I am so irrational as to expect that when you, who are my own citizens, cannot endure my discourses and words, and have found them so grievous and odious that you will have no more of them, others are likely to endure me. No indeed, men of Athens, that is not very likely. And what a life should I lead, at my age, wandering from city to city, ever changing my place of exile, and always being driven out! For I am quite sure that wherever I go, there, as here, the young men will flock to me; and if I drive them away, their elders will drive me out at their request; and if I

---

50. the place in which the Prytanes, as representatives of the city, entertained distinguished visitors and winners at the athletic contests at Olympia.

51. There was such a law in Sparta.

52. a committee which had charge of prisons and of public executions.

let them come, their fathers and friends will drive me out for their sakes.

Some one will say: Yes, Socrates, but cannot you hold your tongue, and then you may go into a foreign city, and no one will interfere with you? Now I have great difficulty in making you understand my answer to this. For if I tell you that to do as you say would be a disobedience to the God, and therefore that I cannot hold my tongue, you will not believe that I am serious; and if I say again that daily to discourse about virtue, and of those other things about which you hear me examining myself and others, is the greatest good of man, and that the unexamined life is not worth living, you are still less likely to believe me. Yet I say what is true, although a thing of which it is hard for me to persuade you. Also, I have never been accustomed to think that I deserve to suffer any harm. Had I money I might have estimated the offence at what I was able to pay, and not have been much the worse. But I have none, and therefore I must ask you to proportion the fine to my means. Well, perhaps I could afford a mina,[53] and therefore I propose that penalty: Plato, Crito, Critobulus, and Appollodorus, my friends here, bid me say thirty minae, and they will be the sureties. Let thirty minae be the penalty; for which sum they will be ample security to you.[54]

Not much time will be gained, O Athenians, in return for the evil name which you will get from the detractors of the city, who will say that you killed Socrates, a wise man; for they will call me wise, even although I am not wise, when they want to reproach you. If you had waited a little while, your desire would have been fulfilled in the course of nature. For I am far advanced in years, as you may perceive, and not far from death. I am speaking now not to all of you, but only to those who have condemned me to death. And I have another thing to say to them: You think that I was convicted because I had no words of the sort which would have procured my acquittal—I mean, if I had thought fit to leave nothing undone or unsaid. Not so; the deficiency which led to my conviction was not of words—certainly not. But I had not the boldness or impudence or inclination to address you as you would have liked me to do, weeping and wailing and lamenting, and saying and doing many things which you have been accustomed to hear from others, and

53. It is almost impossible to express the value of ancient money in modern terms. A mina was a considerable sum; in Aristotle's time (fourth century B.C.) one mina was recognized as a fair ransom for a prisoner of war.

54. The jury decides for death (according to a much later source, the vote this time was 300 to 200). The decision is not surprising in view of Socrates' intransigence. Socrates now makes a final statement to the court.

which, as I maintain, are unworthy of me. I thought at the time that I ought not to do anything common or mean when in danger: nor do I now repent of the style of my defence; I would rather die having spoken after my manner, than speak in your manner and live. For neither in war nor yet at law ought I or any man to use every way of escaping death. Often in battle there can be no doubt that if a man will throw away his arms, and fall on his knees before his pursuers, he may escape death; and in other dangers there are other ways of escaping death, if a man is willing to say and do anything. The difficulty, my friends, is not to avoid death, but to avoid unrighteousness; for that runs faster than death. I am old and move slowly, and the slower runner has overtaken me, and my accusers are keen and quick, and the faster runner, who is unrighteousness, has overtaken them. And now I depart hence condemned by you to suffer the penalty of death,—they too go their ways condemned by the truth to suffer the penalty of villainy and wrong; and I must abide by my award—let them abide by theirs. I suppose that these things may be regarded as fated,—and I think that they are well.

And now, O men who have condemned me, I would fain prophesy to you; for I am about to die, and in the hour of death men are gifted with prophetic power.[55] And I prophesy to you who are my murderers, that immediately after my departure punishment far heavier than you have inflicted on me will surely await you. Me you have killed because you wanted to escape the accuser, and not to give an account of your lives. But that will not be as you suppose: far otherwise. For I say that there will be more accusers of you than there are now;[56] accusers whom hitherto I have restrained: and as they are younger they will be more inconsiderate with you, and you will be more offended at them. If you think that by killing men you can prevent some one from censuring your evil lives, you are mistaken; that is not a way of escape which is either possible or honourable; the easiest and the noblest way is not to be disabling others, but to be improving yourselves. This is the prophecy which I utter before my departure to the judges who have condemned me.

Friends, who would have acquitted me, I would like also to talk with you about the thing which has come to pass, while the magistrates are busy, and before I go to the place at which I must die. Stay then a little, for we may as well talk with one another while there is time. You are my friends, and I should like to show you

---

55. as the dying Hector foretells the death of Achilles; see the *Iliad*, Book XXII, ll. 355–360.

56. Socrates' prophecy was fulfilled, for all of the many different philo-sophical schools of the early fourth century claimed descent from Socrates and developed one or another aspect of his teachings.

the meaning of this event which has happened to me. O my judges
—for you I may truly call judges—I should like to tell you of a
wonderful circumstance. Hitherto the divine faculty of which the
internal oracle is the source has constantly been in the habit of
opposing me even about trifles, if I was going to make a slip or
error in any matter; and now as you see there has come upon me
that which may be thought, and is generally believed to be, the
last and worst evil. But the oracle made no sign of opposition,
either when I was leaving my house in the morning, or when I was
on my way to the court, or while I was speaking, at anything which
I was going to say; and yet I have often been stopped in the middle
of a speech, but now in nothing I either said or did touching the
matter in hand has the oracle opposed me. What do I take to be
the explanation of this silence? I will tell you. It is an intimation
that what has happened to me is a good, and that those of us who
think that death is an evil are in error. For the customary sign
would surely have opposed me had I been going to evil and not
to good.

Let us reflect in another way, and we shall see that there is great
reason to hope that death is a good; for one of two things—either
death is a state of nothingness and utter unconsciousness, or, as
men say, there is a change and migration of the soul from this
world to another. Now if you suppose that there is no consciousness,
but a sleep like the sleep of him who is undisturbed even by dreams,
death will be an unspeakable gain. For if a person were to select
the night in which his sleep was undisturbed even by dreams, and
were to compare with this the other days and nights of his life, and
then were to tell us how many days and nights he had passed in
the course of his life better and more pleasantly than this one, I
think that any man, I will not say a private man, but even the great
king will not find many such days or nights, when compared with
the others. Now if death be of such a nature, I say that to die is gain;
for eternity is then only a single night. But if death is the journey
to another place, and there, as men say, all the dead abide, what
good, O my friends and judges, can be greater than this? If indeed
when the pilgrim arrives in the world below, he is delivered from
the professors of justice in this world, and finds the true judges who
are said to give judgment there, Minos and Rhadamanthus and
Aeacus and Triptolemus,[57] and other sons of God who were
righteous in their own life, that pilgrimage will be worth making.
What would not a man give if he might converse with Orpheus and

---

57. Minos appears as a judge of the
dead in Homer's *Odyssey*, Book XI;
Rhadamanthus and Aeacus, like Minos,
were models of just judges in life and
after death; Triptolemus, the mythical
inventor of agriculture, is associated
with judgment in the next world only
in this passage. The first three are sons
of Zeus.

Musaeus[58] and Hesiod[59] and Homer? Nay, if this be true, let me die again and again. I myself, too, shall have a wonderful interest in there meeting and conversing with Palamedes, and Ajax[60] the son of Telamon, and any other ancient hero who has suffered death through an unjust judgment; and there will be no small pleasure, as I think, in comparing my own sufferings with theirs. Above all, I shall then be able to continue my search into true and false knowledge; as in this world, so also in the next and I shall find out who is wise, and who pretends to be wise, and is not. What would not a man give, O judges, to be able to examine the leader of the great Trojan expedition; or Odysseus or Sisyphus,[61] or numberless others, men and women too! What infinite delight would there be in conversing with them and asking them questions! In another world they do not put a man to death for asking questions: assuredly not. For besides being happier than we are, they will be immortal, if what is said is true.

Wherefore, O judges, be of good cheer about death, and know of a certainty, that no evil can happen to a good man, either in life or after death. He and his are not neglected by the gods; nor has my own approaching end happened by mere chance. But I see clearly that the time had arrived when it was better for me to die and be released from trouble; wherefore the oracle gave no sign. For which reason, also, I am not angry with my condemners, or with my accusers; they have done me no harm, although they did not mean to do me any good; and for this I may gently blame them.

Still I have a favour to ask of them. When my sons are grown up, I would ask you, O my friends, to punish them; and I would have you trouble them, as I have troubled you, if they seem to care about riches, or anything more than about virtue; or if they pretend to be something when they are really nothing,—then reprove them, as I have reproved you, for not caring about that for which they ought to care, and thinking that they are something when they are really nothing. And if you do this, both I and my sons will have received justice at your hands.

The hour of departure has arrived, and we go our ways—I to die, and you to live. Which is better God only knows.

58. legendary poets and religious teachers.

59. early Greek poet (eighth century B.C.?) who wrote *The Works and Days*, a didactic poem containing precepts for the farmer.

60. both victims of unjust trials. Palamedes, one of the Greek chieftains at Troy, was unjustly executed for treason on the false evidence of his enemy Odysseus, and Ajax committed suicide after the arms of the dead Achilles were adjudged to his enemy Odysseus as the bravest warrior on the Greek side.

61. Odysseus was the most cunning of the Greek chieftains at Troy, the hero of Homer's *Odyssey;* Sisyphus, was famous for his unscrupulousness and cunning. Each is presumably an example of the man who "pretends to be wise, and is not."

# Crito*

## Persons of the Dialogue

SOCRATES    CRITO

### SCENE—*The prison of Socrates.*

SOCRATES. Why have you come at this hour, Crito?[1] It must be quite early?

CRITO. Yes, certainly.

SOC. What is the exact time?

CR. The dawn is breaking.

SOC. I wonder that the keeper of the prison would let you in.

CR. He knows me, because I often come, Socrates; moreover, I have done him a kindness.

SOC. And are you only just arrived?

CR. No, I came some time ago.

SOC. Then why did you sit and say nothing, instead of at once awakening me?

CR. I should not have liked myself, Socrates, to be in such great trouble and unrest as you are—indeed I should not: I have been watching with amazement your peaceful slumbers; and for that reason I did not awake you, because I wished to minimize the pain. I have always thought you to be of a happy disposition; but never did I see anything like the easy, tranquil manner in which you bear this calamity.

SOC. Why, Crito, when a man has reached my age[2] he ought not to be repining at the approach of death.

CR. And yet other old men find themselves in similar misfortunes, and age does not prevent them from repining.

SOC. That is true. But you have not told me why you come at this early hour.

CR. I come to bring you a message which is sad and painful; not, as I believe, to yourself, but to all of us who are your friends, and saddest of all to me.

SOC. What? Has the ship come from Delos,[3] on the arrival of which I am to die?

CR. No, the ship has not actually arrived, but she will probably be here to-day, as persons who have come from Sunium tell me that they left her there; and therefore to-morrow, Socrates, will be the last day of your life.

SOC. Very well, Crito; if such is the will of God, I am willing; but my belief is that there will be a delay of a day.

* Translated by Benjamin Jowett.

1. an Athenian of ample means, the same age as Socrates, who offered to stand surety for him at his trial.

2. Socrates was seventy years old.

3. Socrates' execution had been delayed by an annual religious ceremony. A ship had been dispatched to the island of Delos (a center of the worship of Apollo) and until it returned no public execution could take place.

CR. Why do you think so?

SOC. I will tell you. I am to die on the day after the arrival of the ship.

CR. Yes; that is what the authorities say.

SOC. But I do not think that the ship will be here until to-morrow; this I infer from a vision which I had last night, or rather only just now, when you fortunately allowed me to sleep.

CR. And what was the nature of the vision?

SOC. There appeared to me the likeness of a woman, fair and comely, clothed in bright raiment, who called to me and said: O Socrates, The third day hence to fertile Phthia shalt thou go.[4]

CR. What a singular dream, Socrates!

SOC. There can be no doubt about the meaning, Crito, I think.

CR. Yes; the meaning is only too clear. But, oh! my beloved Socrates, let me entreat you once more to take my advice and escape. For if you die I shall not only lose a friend who can never be replaced, but there is another evil: people who do not know you and me will believe that I might have saved you if I had been willing to give money,[5] but that I did not care. Now, can there be a worse disgrace than this—that I should be thought to value money more than the life of a friend? For the many will not be persuaded that I wanted you to escape, and that you refused.

SOC. But why, my dear Crito, should we care about the opinion of the many? Good men, and they are the only persons who are worth considering, will think of these things truly as they occurred.

CR. But you see, Socrates, that the opinion of the many must be regarded, for what is now happening shows that they can do the greatest evil to any one who has lost their good opinion.

SOC. I only wish it were so, Crito; and that the many could do the greatest evil; for then they would also be able to do the greatest good—and what a fine thing this would be! But in reality they can do neither; for they cannot make a man either wise or foolish; and whatever they do is the result of chance.

CR. Well, I will not dispute with you; but please tell me, Socrates, whether you are not acting out of regard to me and your other friends: are you not afraid that if you escape from prison we may get into trouble with the informers[6] for having stolen you away, and lose either the whole or a great part of our property; or that even a worse evil may happen to us? Now, if you fear on our account, be at ease; for in order to save you, we ought surely to run this, or even a greater risk; be persuaded, then, and do as I say.

---

4. Socrates adapts the words of Achilles, who, threatening to leave Troy, declares that "on the third day thereafter we might raise generous Phthia." (*Iliad*, Book IX, l. 363.)

5. to bribe the jailers and "fix" the politicians, as he explains below.

6. private citizens who made a living by detecting and prosecuting breaches of the laws.

soc. Yes, Crito, that is one fear which you mention, but by no means the only one.

cr. Fear not—there are persons who are willing to get you out of prison at no great cost; and as for the informers, they are far from being exorbitant in their demands—a little money will satisfy them. My means, which are certainly ample, are at your service, and if you have a scruple about spending all mine, here are strangers[7] who will give you the use of theirs; and one of them, Simmias the Theban, has brought a large sum of money for this very purpose; and Cebes and many others are prepared to spend their money in helping you to escape. I say, therefore, do not hesitate on our account, and do not say, as you did in the court,[8] that you will have a difficulty in knowing what to do with yourself anywhere else. For men will love you in other places to which you may go, and not in Athens only; there are friends of mine in Thessaly,[9] if you like to go to them, who will value and protect you, and no Thessalian will give you any trouble. Nor can I think that you are at all justified, Socrates, in betraying your own life when you might be saved; in acting thus you are playing into the hands of your enemies, who are hurrying on your destruction. And further I should say that you are deserting your own children; for you might bring them up and educate them; instead of which you go away and leave them, and they will have to take their chance; and if they do not meet with the usual fate of orphans, there will be small thanks to you. No man should bring children into the world who is unwilling to persevere to the end in their nurture and education. But you appear to be choosing the easier part, not the better and manlier, which would have been more becoming in one who professes to care for virtue in all his actions, like yourself. And indeed, I am ashamed not only of you, but of us who are your friends, when I reflect that the whole business will be attributed entirely to our want of courage. The trial need never have come on,[10] or might have been managed differently; and this last act, or crowning folly, will seem to have occurred through our negligence and cowardice, who might have saved you, if we had been good for anything; and you might have saved yourself, for there was no difficulty at all. See now, Socrates, how sad and discreditable are the consequences, both to us and you. Make up your mind then, or rather have your mind already made up, for the time of deliberation is over, and there is only one thing to be done, which must be done this very night, and if we delay at all will be no longer practicable or possible; I beseech you therefore, Socrates, be persuaded by me, and do as I say.

7. foreigners. Simmias and Cebes both came from Thebes.
8. See pp. 540–41.
9. in the north; an uncivilized part of Greece.
10. Crito probably means that Socrates could have left Athens as soon as proceedings were started.

soc. Dear Crito, your zeal is invaluable, if a right one; but if wrong, the greater the zeal the greater the danger; and therefore we ought to consider whether I shall or shall not do as you say. For I am and always have been one of those natures who must be guided by reason, whatever the reason may be which upon reflection appears to me to be the best; and now that this chance has befallen me, I cannot repudiate my own words: the principles which I have hitherto honoured and revered I still honour, and unless we can at once find other and better principles, I am certain not to agree with you; no, not even if the power of the multitude could inflict many more imprisonments, confiscations, deaths, frightening us like children with hobgoblin terrors. What will be the fairest way of considering the question? Shall I return to your old argument about the opinions of men?—we are saying that some of them are to be regarded, and others not. Now were we right in maintaining this before I was condemned? And has the argument which was once good now proved to be talk for the sake of talking—mere childish nonsense? That is what I want to consider with your help, Crito:—whether, under my present circumstances, the argument appears to be in any way different or not; and is to be allowed by me or disallowed. That argument, which, as I believe, is maintained by many persons of authority, was to the effect, as I was saying, that the opinions of some men are to be regarded, and of other men not to be regarded. Now you, Crito, are not going to die to-morrow—at least, there is no human probability of this—and therefore you are disinterested and not liable to be deceived by the circumstances in which you are placed. Tell me then, whether I am right in saying that some opinions, and the opinions of some men only, are to be valued, and that other opinions, and the opinions of other men, are not to be valued. I ask you whether I was right in maintaining this?

cr. Certainly.

soc. The good are to be regarded, and not the bad?

cr. Yes.

soc. And the opinions of the wise are good, and the opinions of the unwise are evil?

cr. Certainly.

soc. And what was said about another matter? Is the pupil who devotes himself to the practice of gymnastics supposed to attend to the praise and blame and opinion of every man, or of one man only—his physician or trainer, whoever he may be?

cr. Of one man only.

soc. And he ought to fear the censure and welcome the praise of that one only, and not of the many?

cr. Clearly so.

soc. And he ought to act and train, and eat and drink in the way which seems good to his single master who has understanding, rather than according to the opinion of all other men put together?

CR. True.

SOC. And if he disobeys and disregards the opinion and approval of the one, and regards the opinion of the many who have no understanding, will he not suffer evil?

CR. Certainly he will.

SOC. And what will the evil be, whither tending and what affecting, in the disobedient person?

CR. Clearly, affecting the body; that is what is destroyed by the evil.

SOC. Very good; and is not this true, Crito, of other things which we need not separately enumerate? In questions of just and unjust, fair and foul, good and evil, which are the subjects of our present consultation, ought we to follow the opinion of the many and to fear them; or the opinion of the one man who has understanding? ought we not to fear and reverence him more than all the rest of the world: and if we desert him shall we not destroy and injure that principle in us which may be assumed to be improved by justice and deteriorated by injustice;—there is such a principle?

CR. Certainly there is, Socrates.

SOC. Take a parallel instance:—if, acting under the advice of those who have no understanding, we destroy that which is improved by health and is deteriorated by disease, would life be worth having? And that which has been destroyed is—the body?

CR. Yes.

SOC. Could we live, having an evil and corrupted body?

CR. Certainly not.

SOC. And will life be worth having, if that higher part of man be destroyed, which is improved by justice and depraved by injustice? Do we suppose that principle, whatever it may be in man, which has to do with justice and injustice, to be inferior to the body?

CR. Certainly not.

SOC. More honourable than the body?

CR. Far more.

SOC. Then, my friend, we must not regard what the many say of us: but what he, the one man who has understanding of just and unjust, will say, and what the truth will say. And therefore you begin in error when you advise that we should regard the opinion of the many about just and unjust, good and evil, honourable and dishonourable,—'Well,' some one will say, 'but the many can kill us.'

CR. Yes, Socrates; that will clearly be the answer.

SOC. And it is true: but still I find with surprise that the old argument is unshaken as ever. And I should like to know whether I may say the same of another proposition—that not life, but a good life, is to be chiefly valued?

CR. Yes, that also remains unshaken.

SOC. And a good life is equivalent to a just and honourable one— that holds also?

CR. Yes, it does.

SOC. From these premises I proceed to argue the question whether I ought or ought not to try and escape without the consent of the Athenians: and if I am clearly right in escaping, then I will make the attempt; but if not, I will abstain. The other considerations which you mention, of money and loss of character and the duty of educating one's children, are, I fear, only the doctrines of the multitude, who would be as ready to restore people to life, if they were able, as they are to put them to death—and with as little reason. But now, since the argument has thus far prevailed, the only question which remains to be considered is, whether we shall do rightly either in escaping or in suffering others to aid in our escape and paying them in money and thanks, or whether in reality we shall not do rightly; and if the latter, then death or any other calamity which may ensue on my remaining here must not be allowed to enter into the calculation.

CR. I think that you are right, Socrates; how then shall we proceed?

SOC. Let us consider the matter together, and do you either refute me if you can, and I will be convinced; or else cease, my dear friend, from repeating to me that I ought to escape against the wishes of the Athenians: for I highly value your attempts to persuade me to do so, but I may not be persuaded against my own better judgment. And now please to consider my first position, and try how you can best answer me.

CR. I will.

SOC. Are we to say that we are never intentionally to do wrong, or that in one way we ought and in another we ought not to do wrong, or is doing wrong always evil and dishonourable, as I was just now saying, and as has been already acknowledged by us? Are all our former admissions which were made within a few days to be thrown away? And have we, at our age, been earnestly discoursing with one another all our life long only to discover that we are no better than children? Or, in spite of the opinion of the many, and in spite of consequences whether better or worse, shall we insist on the truth of what was then said, that injustice is always an evil and dishonour to him who acts unjustly? Shall we say so or not?

CR. Yes.

SOC. Then we must do no wrong?

CR. Certainly not.

soc. Nor when injured injure in return, as the many imagine; for we must injure no one at all?

cr. Clearly not.

soc. Again, Crito, may we do evil?

cr. Surely not, Socrates.

soc. And what of doing evil in return for evil, which is the morality of the many—is that just or not?

cr. Not just.

soc. For doing evil to another is the same as injuring him?

cr. Very true.

soc. Then we ought not to retaliate or render evil for evil to any one, whatever evil we may have suffered from him. But I would have you consider, Crito, whether you really mean what you are saying. For this opinion has never been held, and never will be held, by any considerable number of persons; and those who are agreed and those who are not agreed upon this point have no common ground, and can only despise one another when they see how widely they differ. Tell me, then, whether you agree with and assent to my first principle, that neither injury nor retaliation nor warding off evil by evil is ever right. And shall that be the premiss of our argument? Or do you decline and dissent from this? For so I have ever thought, and continue to think; but, if you are of another opinion, let me hear what you have to say. If, however, you remain of the same mind as formerly, I will proceed to the next step.

cr. You may proceed, for I have not changed my mind.

soc. Then I will go on to the next point, which may be put in the form of a question:—Ought a man to do what he admits to be right, or ought he to betray the right?

cr. He ought to do what he thinks right.

soc. But if this is true, what is the application? In leaving the prison against the will of the Athenians, do I wrong any? or rather do I not wrong those whom I ought least to wrong? Do I not desert the principles which were acknowledged by us to be just—what do you say?

cr. I cannot tell, Socrates; for I do not know.

soc. Then consider the matter in this way:—Imagine that I am about to play truant (you may call the proceeding by any name which you like), and the laws and the government come and interrogate me: 'Tell us, Socrates,' they say, 'what are you about? are you not going by an act of yours to overturn us—the laws, and the whole state, as far as in you lies? Do you imagine that a state can subsist and not be overthrown, in which the decisions of law have no power, but are set aside and trampled upon by individuals?' What will be our answer, Crito, to these and the like words? Any one, and especially a rhetorician, will have a good deal to say on behalf of the law which requires a sentence to be carried out. He will argue that this law should not be set aside; and shall we reply, 'Yes; but the state has injured us and given an unjust sentence.' Suppose I say that?

CR. Very good, Socrates.

SOC. 'And was that our agreement with you?' the law would answer; 'or were you to abide by the sentence of the state?' And if I were to express my astonishment at their words, the law would probably add: 'Answer, Socrates, instead of opening your eyes—you are in the habit of asking and answering questions. Tell us,—What complaint have you to make against us which justifies you in attempting to destroy us and the state? In the first place did we not bring you into existence? Your father married your mother by our aid and begat you. Say whether you have any objection to urge against those of us who regulate marriage?' None, I should reply. 'Or against those of us who after birth regulate the nurture and education of children, in which you also were trained? Were not the laws, which have the charge of education, right in commanding your father to train you in music[11] and gymnastic?' Right, I should reply. 'Well then, since you were brought into the world and nurtured and educated by us, can you deny in the first place that you are our child and slave, as your fathers were before you? And if this is true you are not on equal terms with us; nor can you think that you have a right to do to us what we are doing to you. Would you have any right to strike or revile or do any other evil to your father or your master, if you had one, because you have been struck or reviled by him, or received some other evil at his hands?—you would not say this? And because we think right to destroy you, do you think that you have any right to destroy us in return, and your country as far as in you lies? Will you, O professor of true virtue, pretend that you are justified in this? Has a philosopher like you failed to discover that our country is more to be valued and higher and holier far than mother or father or any ancestor, and more to be regarded in the eyes of the gods and of men of understanding? also to be soothed, and gently and reverently entreated when angry, even more than a father, and either to be persuaded, or if not persuaded, to be obeyed? And when we are punished by her, whether with imprisonment or stripes, the punishment is to be endured in silence; and if she leads us to wounds or death in battle, thither we follow as is right; neither may any one yield or retreat or leave his rank, but whether in battle or in a court of law, or in any other place, he must do what his city and his country order him; or he must change their view of what is just: and if he may do no violence to his father or mother, much less may he do violence to his

---

11. The Greek term includes literature as well as music.

country.' What answer shall we make to this, Crito? Do the laws speak truly, or do they not?

CR. I think that they do.

SOC. Then the laws will say, 'Consider, Socrates, if we are speaking truly that in your present attempt you are going to do us an injury. For, having brought you into the world, and nurtured and educated you, and given you and every other citizen a share in every good which we had to give, we further proclaim to any Athenian by the liberty which we allow him, that if he does not like us when he has become of age and has seen the ways of the city, and made our acquaintance, he may go where he pleases and take his goods with him. None of us laws will forbid him or interfere with him. Any one who does not like us and the city, and who wants to emigrate to a colony or to any other city, may go where he likes, retaining his property. But he who has experience of the manner in which we order justice and administer the state, and still remains, has entered into an implied contract that he will do as we command him. And he who disobeys us is, as we maintain, thrice wrong; first, because in disobeying us he is disobeying his parents; secondly, because we are the authors of his education; thirdly, because he has made an agreement with us that he will duly obey our commands; and he neither obeys them nor convinces us that our commands are unjust; and we do not rudely impose them, but give him the alternative of obeying or convincing us;—that is what we offer, and he does neither.

'These are the sort of accusations to which, as we were saying, you, Socrates, will be exposed if you accomplish your intentions; you, above all other Athenians.' Suppose now I ask, why I rather than anybody else? they will justly retort upon me that I above all other men have acknowledged the agreement. 'There is clear proof,' they will say, 'Socrates, that we and the city were not displeasing to you. Of all Athenians you have been the most constant resident in the city, which, as you never leave, you may be supposed to love. For you never went out of the city either to see the games, except once when you went to the Isthmus,[12] or to any other place unless when you were on military service; nor did you travel as other men do. Nor had you any curiosity to know other states or their laws: your affections did not go beyond us and our state; we were your special favourites, and you acquiesced in our government of you; and here in this city you begat your children, which is a proof of your satisfaction. Moreover, you might in the course of the trial, if you had liked, have fixed the penalty at banishment; the state which refuses to let you go now would have let you go then. But you pretended that you preferred death to exile, and that you were not

12. Nothing is known of this journey.

unwilling to die. And now you have forgotten these fine sentiments, and pay no respect to us the laws, of whom you are the destroyer; and are doing what only a miserable slave would do, running away and turning your back upon the compacts and agreements which you made as a citizen. And first of all answer this very question: Are we right in saying that you agreed to be governed according to us in deed, and not in word only? Is that true or not?' How shall we answer, Crito? Must we not assent?

CR. We cannot help it, Socrates.

SOC. Then will they not say: 'You, Socrates, are breaking the covenants and agreements which you made with us at your leisure, not in any haste or under any compulsion or deception, but after you have had seventy years to think of them, during which time you were at liberty to leave the city, if we were not to your mind, or if our covenants appeared to you to be unfair. You had your choice, and might have gone either to Lacedaemon or Crete, both which states are often praised by you for their good government, or to some other Hellenic or foreign state. Whereas you, above all other Athenians, seemed to be so fond of the state, or, in other words, of us her laws (and who would care about a state which has no laws?), that you never stirred out of her; the halt, the blind, the maimed were not more stationary in her than you were. And now you run away and forsake your agreements. Not so, Socrates, if you will take our advice; do not make yourself ridiculous by escaping out of the city.

'For just consider, if you transgress and err in this sort of way, what good will you do either to yourself or to your friends? That your friends will be driven into exile and deprived of citizenship, or will lose their property, is tolerably certain; and you yourself, if you fly to one of the neighboring cities, as, for example, Thebes or Megara, both of which are well governed, will come to them as an enemy, Socrates, and their government will be against you, and all patriotic citizens will cast an evil eye upon you as a subverter of the laws, and you will confirm in the minds of the judges the justice of their own condemnation of you. For he who is a corrupter of the laws is more than likely to be a corrupter of the young and foolish portion of mankind. Will you then flee from well-ordered cities and virtuous men? and is existence worth having on these terms? Or will you go to them without shame, and talk to them, Socrates? And what will you say to them? What you say here about virtue and justice and institutions and laws being the best things among men? Would that be decent of you? Surely not. But if you go away from well-governed states to Crito's friends in Thessaly, where there is great disorder and licence, they will be charmed to hear the tale of your escape from prison, set off with ludicrous particulars of the manner in which you were wrapped in a goatskin or some other disguise, and metamorphosed as the manner is of runaways; but will there be no one to remind you that in your old age you were not ashamed to violate the most sacred laws from a miserable desire of a little more life? Perhaps not, if you keep them in a good temper; but if they are out of temper you will hear many degrading things; you will live, but how?—as the flatterer of all men, and the servant of all men; and doing what?—eating and drinking in Thessaly, having gone abroad in order that you may get a dinner. And where will be your fine sentiments about justice and virtue? Say that you wish to live for the sake of your children —you want to bring them up and educate them—will you take them into Thessaly and deprive them of Athenian citizenship? Is this the benefit which you will confer upon them? Or are you under the impression that they will be better cared for and educated here if you are still alive, although absent from them; for your friends will take care of them? Do you fancy that if you are an inhabitant of Thessaly they will take care of them, and if you are an inhabitant of the other world that they will not take care of them? Nay; but if they who call themselves friends are good for anything, they will—to be sure they will.

'Listen, then, Socrates, to us who have brought you up. Think not of life and children first, and of justice afterwards, but of justice first, that you may be justified before the princes of the world below.[13] For neither will you nor any that belong to you be happier or holier or juster in this life, or happier in another, if you do as Crito bids. Now you depart in innocence, a sufferer and not a doer of evil; a victim, not of the laws but of men. But if you go forth, returning evil for evil, and injury for injury, breaking the covenants and agreements which you have made with us, and wronging those whom you ought least of all to wrong, that is to say, yourself, your friends, your country, and us, we shall be angry with you while you live, and our brethren, the laws of the world below, will receive you as an enemy; for they will know that you have done your best to destroy us. Listen, then, to us and not to Crito.'

This, dear Crito, is the voice which I seem to hear murmuring in my ears, like the sound of the flute in the ears of the mystic;[14] that voice, I say, is humming in my ears, and prevents me from hearing any other. And I know that anything more which you may say will be vain. Yet speak, if you have anything to say.

CR. I have nothing to say, Socrates.

SOC. Leave me then, Crito, to fulfil the will of God, and to follow whither he leads.

---

13. the judges of the dead.
14. like the worshipers at the mysteries, who seem to hear the flutes still playing, after they have stopped.

# Phaedo*

## [The Death of Socrates]

[The narrator, Phaedo, who was present at the execution of Socrates, gives his friend Echecrates an account of Socrates' last hours. Many of his friends were with him on that day, among them Crito and two Theban philosophers, Simmias and Cebes. These two engaged him in an argument about the immortality of the soul, which Socrates succeeded in proving to their satisfaction. He concluded with an account of the next world, describing the place of reward for the virtuous and of punishment for the wicked. The opening words of the following selection are his conclusion of the argument.]

A man of sense ought not to say, nor will I be very confident, that the description which I have given of the soul and her mansions is exactly true. But I do say that, inasmuch as the soul is shown to be immortal, he may venture to think, not improperly or unworthily, that something of the kind is true. The venture is a glorious one, and he ought to comfort himself with words like these, which is the reason why I lengthen out the tale. Wherefore, I say, let a man be of good cheer about his soul, who having cast away the pleasures and ornaments of the body as alien to him and working harm rather than good, has sought after the pleasures of knowledge; and has arrayed the soul, not in some foreign attire, but in her own proper jewels, temperance, and justice, and courage, and nobility, and truth—in these adorned she is ready to go on her journey to the world below, when her hour comes. You, Simmias and Cebes, and all other men, will depart at some time or other. Me already, as a tragic poet would say, the voice of fate calls. Soon I must drink the poison;[1] and I think that I had better repair to the bath first, in order that the women may not have the trouble of washing my body after I am dead.

When he had done speaking, Crito said: And have you any commands for us, Socrates—anything to say about your children, or any other matter in which we can serve you?

Nothing particular, Crito, he replied: only, as I have always told you, take care of yourselves; that is a service which you may be ever rendering to me and mine and to all of us, whether you promise to do so or not. But if you have no thought for yourselves, and care not to walk according to the rule which I have prescribed for you,

---

* Translated by Benjamin Jowett.
1. hemlock. This was the regular method of execution at Athens. The action of the poison is described below.

not now for the first time, however much you may profess or promise at the moment, it will be of no avail.

We will do our best, said Crito: And in what way shall we bury you?

In any way that you like; but you must get hold of me, and take care that I do not run away from you. Then he turned to us, and added with a smile:—I cannot make Crito believe that I am the same Socrates who have been talking and conducting the argument; he fancies that I am the other Socrates whom he will soon see, a dead body—and he asks, How shall he bury me? And though I have spoken many words in the endeavour to show that when I have drunk the poison I shall leave you and go to the joys of the blessed, —these words of mine, with which I was comforting you and myself, have had, as I perceive, no effect upon Crito. And therefore I want you to be surety for me to him now, as at the trial he was surety to the judges for me: but let the promise be of another sort; for he was surety for me to the judges that I would remain, and you must be my surety to him that I shall not remain, but go away and depart; and then he will suffer less at my death, and not be grieved when he sees my body being burned or buried. I would not have him sorrow at my hard lot, or say at the burial, Thus we lay out Socrates, or, Thus we follow him to the grave or bury him; for false words are not only evil in themselves, but they inflict the soul with evil. Be of good cheer then, my dear Crito, and say that you are burying my body only, and do with that whatever is usual, and what you think best.

When he had spoken these words, he arose and went into a chamber to bathe; Crito followed him and told us to wait. So we remained behind, talking and thinking of the subject of discourse, and also of the greatness of our sorrow; he was like a father of whom we were being bereaved, and we were about to pass the rest of our lives as orphans. When he had taken the bath his children were brought to him (he had two young sons and an elder one); and the women of his family also came, and he talked to them and gave them a few directions in the presence of Crito; then he dismissed them and returned to us.

Now the hour of sunset was near, for a good deal of time had passed while he was within. When he came out, he sat down with us again after his bath, but not much was said. Soon the jailer, who was the servant of the Eleven, entered and stood by him, saying:— To you, Socrates, whom I know to be the noblest and gentlest and best of all who ever came to this place, I will not impute the angry feeling of other men, who rage and swear at me, when, in obedience to the authorities, I bid them drink the poison—indeed, I am sure that you will not be angry with me; for others, as you are aware, and not I, are to blame. And so fare you well, and try to bear lightly what must needs be—you know my errand. Then bursting into tears he turned away and went out.

Socrates looked at him and said: I return your good wishes, and will do as you bid. Then turning to us, he said, How charming the man is: since I have been in prison he has always been coming to see me, and at times he would talk to me, and was as good to me as could be, and now see how generously he sorrows on my account. We must do as he says, Crito; and therefore let the cup be brought, if the poison is prepared: if not, let the attendant prepare some.

Yet, said Crito, the sun is still upon the hill-tops, and I know that many a one has taken the draught late, and after the announcement has been made to him, he has eaten and drunk, and enjoyed the society of his beloved: do not hurry—there is time enough.

Socrates said: Yes, Crito, and they of whom you speak are right in so acting, for they think that they will be gainers by the delay; but I am right in not following their example, for I do not think that I should gain anything by drinking the poison a little later; I should only be ridiculous in my own eyes for sparing and saving a life which is already forfeit. Please then to do as I say, and not to refuse me.

Crito made a sign to the servant, who was standing by; and he went out, and having been absent for some time, returned with the jailer carrying the cup of poison. Socrates said: You, my good friend, who are experienced in these matters, shall give me directions how I am to proceed. The man answered: You have only to walk about until your legs are heavy, and then to lie down, and the poison will act. At the same time he handed the cup to Socrates, who in the easiest and gentlest manner, without the least fear or change of colour or feature, looking at the man with all his eyes, Echecrates, as his manner was,[2] took the cup and said: What do you say about making a libation[3] out of this cup to any god? May I, or not? The man answered: We only prepare, Socrates, just so much as we deem enough. I understand, he said: but I may and must ask the gods to prosper my journey from this to the other world—even so—and so be it according to my prayer. Then raising the cup to his lips, quite readily and cheerfully he drank off the poison. And hitherto most of us had been able to control our sorrow; but now when we saw him drinking, and saw too that he had finished the draught, we could no longer forbear, and in spite of myself my own tears were flowing fast; so that I covered my face and wept, not for him, but at the thought of my own calamity in having to part from such a friend.

2. Socrates was famous for his pro-
jecting eyes and his intent stare.

3. He asks if he may pour a little of it out in honor of the gods, as if it were wine.

Nor was I the first; for Crito, when he found himself unable to restrain his tears, had got up, and I followed; and at that moment, Apollodorus, who had been weeping all the time, broke out in a loud and passionate cry which made cowards of us all. Socrates alone retained his calmness: What is this strange outcry? he said. I sent away the women mainly in order that they might not misbehave in this way, for I have been told that a man should die in peace. Be quiet then, and have patience. When we heard his words we were ashamed, and refrained our tears; and he walked about until, as he said, his legs began to fail, and then he lay on his back, according to directions, and the man who gave him the poison now and then looked at his feet and legs; and after a while he pressed his foot hard, and asked him if he could feel; and he said, No; and then his leg, and so upwards and upwards, and showed us that he was cold and stiff. And he felt them himself, and said: When the poison reaches the heart, that will be the end. He was beginning to grow cold about the groin, when he uncovered his face, for he had covered himself up, and said—they were his last words—he said: Crito, I owe a cock to Asclepius;[4] will you remember to pay the debt? The debt shall be paid, said Crito; is there anything else? There was no answer to this question; but in a minute or two a movement was heard, and the attendants uncovered him; his eyes were set, and Crito closed his eyes and mouth.

Such was the end, Echecrates, of our friend; concerning whom I may truly say, that of all men of his time whom I have known, he was the wisest and justest and best.

4. *a cock to Asclepius:* a sacrifice to the god of healing, perhaps as a thank offering for the painlessness of his death.

# ARISTOTLE
## (384–322 B.C.)
## Poetics*

. . . Tragedy, then, is an imitation of an action that is serious, complete, and of a certain magnitude; in language embellished with each kind of artistic ornament, the several kinds being found in separate parts of the play; in the form of action, not of narrative; through pity and fear effecting the proper purgation[1] of these emo-

* Selected passages. Our text is the translation by S. H. Butcher, published by the Oxford University Press.

1. The Greek word is *katharsis*. This is probably the most disputed passage in European literary criticism. There are two main schools of interpretation; they differ in their understanding of the metaphor implied in the word *katharsis*.

Some critics take the word to mean "purification," implying a metaphor from the religious process of purification from guilt; the passions are "purified" by the tragic performance since the excitement of these passions by the performance weakens them and reduces them to just proportions in the individual. (This theory was supported by

tions. By 'language embellished,' I mean language into which rhythm, 'harmony,' and song enter. By 'the several kinds in separate parts,' I mean, that some parts are rendered through the medium of verse alone, others again with the aid of song.

Now as tragic imitation implies persons acting, it necessarily follows, in the first place, that Scenic equipment will be a part of Tragedy. Next, Song and Diction, for these are the means of imitation. By 'Diction' I mean the mere metrical arrangement of the words: as for 'Song,' it is a term whose full sense is well understood.

Again, Tragedy is the imitation of an action; and an action implies personal agents, who necessarily possess certain qualities both of character and thought. It is these that determine the qualities of actions themselves; these—thought and character—are the two natural causes from which actions spring: on these causes, again, all success or failure depends. Hence, the Plot is the imitation of the action—for by plot I here mean the arrangement of the incidents. By Character I mean that in virtue of which we ascribe certain qualities to the agents. By Thought, that whereby a statement is proved, or a general truth expressed. Every Tragedy, therefore, must have six parts, which parts determine its quality—namely, Plot, Character, Diction, Thought, Scenery, Song. Two of the parts constitute the means of imitation, one the manner, and three the objects of imitation. And these complete the list. These elements have been employed, we may say, by almost all poets; in fact, every play contains Scenic accessories as well as Character, Plot, Diction, Song, and Thought.

But most important of all is the structure of the incidents. For Tragedy is an imitation, not of men, but of an action and of life—of happiness and misery; and happiness and misery consist in action, the end of human life being a mode of action, not a quality. Now the characters of men determine their qualities, but it is by their actions that they are happy or the reverse. Dramatic action, therefore, is not with a view to the representation of character: character comes in as subsidiary to the action. Hence the incidents and the plot are the end of a tragedy; and the end[2] is the chief thing of all. Again, without action there cannot be a tragedy; there may be without character. . . .

These principles being established, let us now discuss the proper structure of the Plot, since this is the first, and also the most important part of Tragedy.

---

the German critic Lessing.) Others take the metaphor to be medical, reading the word as "purging" and interpreting the phrase to mean that the tragic performance excites the emotions only to allay them, thus ridding the spectator of the disquieting emotions from which he suffers in everyday life; tragedy thus has a therapeutic effect.

2. purpose.

Now, according to our definition, Tragedy is an imitation of an action, that is complete, and whole, and of a certain magnitude; for there may be a whole that is wanting in magnitude. A whole is that which has beginning, middle, and end. A beginning is that which does not itself follow anything by causal necessity, but after which something naturally is or comes to be. An end, on the contrary, is that which itself naturally follows some other thing, either by necessity, or in the regular course of events, but has nothing following it. A middle is that which follows something as some other thing follows it. A well constructed plot, therefore, must neither begin nor end at haphazard, but conform to the type here described. . . .

Unity of plot does not, as some persons think, consist in the unity of the hero. For infinitely various are the incidents in one man's life, which cannot be reduced to unity; and so, too, there are many actions of one man out of which we cannot make one action. Hence the error, as it appears, of all poets who have composed a Heracleid, a Theseid, or other poems of the kind. They imagine that as Heracles was one man, the story of Heracles ought also to be a unity. . . .

It is, moreover, evident from what has been said, that it is not the function of the poet to relate what has happened, but what may happen—what is possible according to the law of probability or necessity. The poet and the historian differ not by writing in verse or in prose. The work of Herodotus[3] might be put into verse, and it would still be a species of history, with metre no less than without it. The true difference is that one relates what has happened, the other what may happen. Poetry, therefore, is a more philosophical and a higher thing than history: for poetry tends to express the universal, history the particular. The universal tells us how a person of given character will on occasion speak or act, according to the law of probability or necessity; and it is this universality at which Poetry aims in giving expressive names to the characters. The particular is—for example—what Alcibiades did or suffered. . . .

Of all plots and actions the episodic are the worst. I call a plot episodic in which the episodes or acts succeed one another without probable or necessary sequence. Bad poets compose such pieces by their own fault, good poets, to please the players; for, as they write for competing rivals, they draw out the plot beyond its capacity, and are often forced to break the natural continuity. . . .

Plots are either simple or complicated; for such too, in their very nature, are the actions of which the plots are an imitation. An action which is one and continuous in the sense above defined,

3. the fifth-century historian of the Persian wars.

I call Simple, when the turning point is reached without Reversal of Fortune or Recognition:[4] Complicated, when it is reached with Reversal of Fortune, or Recognition, or both. These last should arise from the internal structure of the plot, so that what follows should be the necessary or probable result of the preceding action. It makes all the difference whether one event is the consequence of another, or merely subsequent to it.

A reversal of fortune is, as we have said, a change by which a train of action produces the opposite of the effect intended; and that, according to our rule of probability or necessity. Thus in the *Oedipus*, the messenger,[5] hoping to cheer Oedipus, and to free him from his alarms about his mother, reveals his[6] origin, and so produces the opposite effect. . . .

A Recognition, as the name indicates, is a change from ignorance to knowledge, producing love or hate between the persons destined by the poet for good or bad fortune. The best form of recognition is coincident with a reversal of fortune, as in the *Oedipus*. . . .

As the sequel to what has already been said, we must proceed to consider what the poet should aim at, and what he should avoid, in constructing his plots; and by what means Tragedy may best fulfil its function.

A perfect tragedy should, as we have seen, be arranged not on the simple but on the complex plan. It should, moreover, imitate actions which excite pity and fear, this being the distinctive mark of tragic imitation. It follows plainly, in the first place, that the change of fortune presented must not be the spectacle of a perfectly good man brought from prosperity to adversity: for this moves neither pity nor fear; it simply shocks us. Nor, again, that of a bad man passing from adversity to prosperity: for nothing can be more alien to the spirit of Tragedy; it possesses no single tragic quality; it neither satisfies the moral sense, nor calls forth pity or fear. Nor, again, should the downfall of the utter villain be exhibited. A plot of this kind would, doubtless, satisfy the moral sense, but it would inspire neither pity nor fear; for pity is aroused by unmerited misfortune, fear by the misfortune of a man like ourselves. Such an event, therefore, will be neither pitiful nor terrible. There remains, then, the character between these two extremes—that of a man who is not eminently good and just, yet whose misfortune is brought about not by vice or depravity, but by some error or frailty. He must be one who is highly renowned and prosperous—a personage like Oedipus, Thyestes, or other illustrious men of such families.

4. defined in the following paragraph.  6. Oedipus'.
5. Messenger 1.

A well constructed plot should, therefore, be single, rather than double as some maintain. The change of fortune should be not from bad to good, but, reversely, from good to bad. It should come about as the result not of vice, but of some great error or frailty, in a character either such as we have described, or better rather than worse. The practice of the stage bears out our view. At first the poets recounted any legends that came in their way. Now, tragedies are founded on the story of a few houses—on the fortunes of Alcmaeon, Oedipus, Orestes, Meleager, Thyestes, Telephus, and those others who have done or suffered something terrible. A tragedy, then, to be perfect according to the rules of art should be of this construction. Hence they are in error who censure Euripides just because he follows this principle in his plays, many of which end unhappily. It is, as we have said, the right ending. The best proof is that on the stage and in dramatic competition, such plays, if they are well represented, are most tragic in their effect; and Euripides, faulty as he is in the general management of his subject, yet is felt to be the most tragic of poets. . . .

As in the structure of the plot, so too in the portraiture of character, the poet should always aim either at the necessary or the probable. Thus a person of a given character should speak or act in a given way, by the rule either of necessity or of probability; just as this event should follow that by necessary or probable sequence. It is therefore evident that the unravelling of the plot, no less than the complication, must be brought about by the plot itself, and not by Machinery[7]—as in the *Medea*, or in the Return of the Greeks[8] in the *Iliad*. Machinery should be employed only for events external to the drama—either such as are previous to it and outside the sphere of human knowledge, or subsequent to it and which need to be foretold and announced; for to the gods we ascribe the power of seeing all things. Within the action there must be nothing irrational. If the irrational cannot be excluded, it should be outside the scope of the tragedy. Such is the irrational element in the *Oedipus* of Sophocles. . . .

The Chorus too should be regarded as one of the actors; it should be an integral part of the whole, and share in the action, in the manner not of Euripides but of Sophocles. As for the later poets, their choral songs pertain as little to the subject of the piece as to that of any other tragedy. They are, therefore, sung as mere inter-

7. literally the machine which was employed in the theater to show the gods flying in space. It has come to mean any implausible way of solving the complications of the plot. Medea escapes from Corinth "on the machine" in her magic chariot.

8. Aristotle refers to an incident in the second book of the *Iliad;* an attempt of the Greek rank and file to return home and abandon the siege is arrested by the intervention of Athene. (If it were a drama she would appear "on the machine.")

ludes—a practice first begun by Agathon. Yet what difference is there between introducing such choral interludes, and transferring a speech, or even a whole act, from one play to another? . . .

# LUCRETIUS
## (99?–55 B.C.)
## On the Nature of Things (De rerum natura)

### Book III. [Against the Fear of Death]*

Death 830

Is nothing to us, has no relevance
To our condition, seeing that the mind
Is mortal. Just as, long ago, we felt
Not the least touch of trouble when the wars
Were raging all around the shaken earth 835
And from all sides the Carthaginian hordes
Poured forth to battle, and no man ever knew
Whose subject he would be in life or death,
Which doom, by land or sea, would strike him down,
So, when we cease to be, and body and soul, 840
Which joined to make us one, have gone their ways,
Their separate ways, nothing at all can shake
Our feelings, not if earth were mixed with sea
Or sea with sky. Perhaps the mind or spirit,
After its separation from our body, 845
Has some sensation; what is that to us?
Nothing at all, for what we knew of being,
Essence, identity, oneness, was derived
From body's union with spirit, so, if time,
After our death, should some day reunite 850
All of our present particles, bring them back
To where they now reside, give us once more
The light of life, this still would have no meaning
For us, with our self-recollection gone.
As we are now, we lack all memory 855
Of what we were before, suffer no wound
From those old days. Look back on all that space

---

* Translated by Rolfe Humphries.
836. *Carthaginian hordes*: In the Second Punic War (218–201 B.C.) between Rome and the north African city of Carthage. In this decisive struggle for the domination of the western Mediterranean, the Carthaginian general Hannibal invaded Italy and came close to taking Rome. Lucretius is writing some hundred and fifty years after these events.

Of time's immensity, consider well
What infinite combinations there have been
In matter's ways and groupings. How easy, then,      860
For human beings to believe we are
Compounded of the very selfsame motes,
Arranged exactly in the selfsame ways
As once we were, our long-ago, our now
Being identical. And yet we keep      865
No memory of that once-upon-a-time,
Nor can we call it back; somewhere between
A break occurred, and all our atoms went
Wandering here and there and far away
From our sensations. If there lies ahead      870
Tough luck for any man, he must be there,
Himself, to feel its evil, but since death
Removes this chance, and by injunction stops
All rioting of woes against our state,
We may be reassured that in our death      875
We have no cause for fear, we cannot be
Wretched in nonexistence. Death alone
Has immortality, and takes away
Our mortal life. It does not matter a bit
If we once lived before.

               So, seeing a man      880
Feel sorry for himself, that after death
He'll be a rotting corpse, laid in a tomb,
Succumb to fire, or predatory beasts,
You'll know he's insincere, just making noise,
With rancor in his heart, though he believes,      885
Or tries to make us think so, that death ends all.
And yet, I'd guess, he contradicts himself,
He does not really see himself as gone,
As utter nothingness, but does his best—
Not really understanding what he's doing—      890
To have himself survive, for, in his life,
He will project a future, a dark day
When beast or bird will lacerate his corpse.
So he feels sorry for himself; he fails
To make the real distinction that exists      895
Between his castoff body, and the man
Who stands beside it grieving, and imputes
Some of his sentimental feelings to it.
Resenting mortal fate, he cannot see
That in true death he'll not survive himself      900

To stand there as a mourner, stunned by grief
That he is burned or mangled. If in death
It's certainly no pleasure to be mauled
By beak of bird or fang of beast, I'd guess
It's no voluptuous revel to be laid                    905
Over the flames, or packed in honey and ice,
Stiff on the surface of a marble slab,
Or buried under a great mound of earth.

And men behave the same way at a banquet,
Holding the cups or garlanding the brows,              910
And sighing from the heart, "Ah, life is short
For puny little men, and when it goes
We cannot call it back," as if they thought
The main thing wrong, after their death, will be
That they are very thirsty, or may have               915
A passionate appetite for who knows what.
"No longer will you happily come home
To a devoted wife, or children dear
Running for your first kisses, while your heart
Is filled with sweet unspoken gratitude.              920
You will no longer dwell in happy state,
Their sword and shield. Poor wretch," men tell themselves,
"One fatal day has stolen all your gains."
But they don't add, "And all your covetings."
If they could see this clearly, follow it             925
With proper reasoning, their minds would be
Free of great agony and fear, "As now
You lie asleep in death, forevermore
You will be quit of any sickening pain,
While we, who stood beside your funeral pyre,         930
Have, with no consolation, mourned your death
In sorrow time will never heal." Well, then,
Ask of your dead what bitterness he finds
In sleep and quiet; why should anyone
Wear himself out in everlasting grief?                935
No man, when body and soul are lost in sleep,
Finds himself missing, or conducts a search
For his identity; for all we know,
For all we care, that sleep might last forever
And we would never list ourselves as missing.         940

906. *honey*: Used in an expensive type
of embalming.
936–947: The only difference between
sleep and death is that in sleep the
atoms of which we are composed are
still in ordered motion and combination,
while in death they are scattered; in
both states we are equally unconscious.

Yet, all this while, our motes, our atoms, wander
Not far from sense-producing shift and stir,
And suddenly we come to wakefulness.
So we must think of death as being nothing,
As less than sleep, or less than nothing, even,               945
Since our array of matter never stirs
To reassemble, once the chill of death
Has taken over.

       Hark! The voice of Nature
Is scolding us: "What ails you, little man,
Why this excess of self-indulgent grief,                      950
This sickliness? Why weep and groan at death?
If you have any sense of gratitude
For a good life, if you can't claim her gifts
Were dealt you in some kind of riddled jar
So full of cracks and holes they leaked away                  955
Before you touched them, why not take your leave
As men go from a banquet, fed to the full
On life's good feast, come home, and lie at ease,
Free from anxiety? Alas, poor fool,
If, on the other hand, all of your joys                       960
Are gone, and life is only wretchedness,
Why try to add more to it? Why not make
A decent end? There's nothing, it would seem,
My powers can contrive for your delight.
The same old story, always. If the years                      965
Don't wear your body, don't corrode your limbs
With lassitude, if you keep living on
For centuries, if you never die at all,
What's in it for you but the same old story
Always, and always? " How could we reply                      970
To this, except to say that Nature's case
Is argued to perfection? Now suppose
Some older man, a senior citizen,
Were plaintiff, wretcheder than he ought to be,
Lamenting death, would Nature not be right                    975
To cry him down, with even sharper voice,
"Why, you old scoundrel, take those tears of yours
Somewhere away from here, cut out the whining.
You have had everything from life, and now
You find you're going to pieces. You desire,                  980
Always, what isn't there; what is, you scorn,
So life has slipped away from you, incomplete,

Unsatisfactory, and here comes death,
An unexpected summoner, to stand
Beside you, long before you want to leave,          985
Long, long, before you think you've had enough.
Let it all go, act as becomes your age,
Be a great man, composed; give in; you must."
Such a rebuke from Nature would be right,
For the old order yields before the new,           990
All things require refashioning from others.
No man goes down to Hell's black pit; we need
Matter for generations yet to come,
Who, in their turn, will follow you, as men
Have died before you and will die hereafter.       995
So one thing never ceases to arise
Out of another; life's a gift to no man
Only a loan to him. Look back at time—
How meaningless, how unreal!—before our birth.
In this way Nature holds before our eyes           1000
The mirror of our future after death.
Is this so grim, so gloomy? Is it not
A rest more free from care than any sleep?

Now all those things which people say exist
In Hell, are really present in our lives.           1005
The story says that Tantalus, the wretch,
Frozen in terror, fears the massive rock
Balanced in air above him. It's not true.
What happens is that in our lives the fear,
The silly, vain, ridiculous fear of gods,           1010
Causes our panic dread of accident.
No vultures feed on Tityos, who lies
Sprawled out for them in Hell; they could not find
In infinite eternities of time
What they are searching for in that great bulk,     1015
Nine acres wide, or ninety, or the spread
Of all the globe. No man can ever bear
Eternal pain, nor can his body give
Food to the birds forever. We do have
A Tityos in ourselves, and lie, in love,            1020
Torn and consumed by our anxieties,
Our fickle passions. Sisyphus, too, is here

1006. *Tantalus*: A different version of
Tantalus' punishment from that given in
the *Odyssey* (XI, 655–667 and note, p.
297).

1012. *Tityos*: See *Odyssey*, XI, 647–
645.
1022. *Sisyphus*: See *Odyssey*, XI,
668–675 and note, p. 297.

In our own lives; we see him as the man
Bent upon power and office, who comes back
Gloomy and beaten after every vote.                    1025
To seek for power, such an empty thing,
And never gain it, suffering all the while,
This is to shove uphill the stubborn rock
Which over and over comes bouncing down again
To the flat levels where it started from.               1030
Or take another instance: when we feed
A mind whose nature seems unsatisfied,
Never content, with all the blessings given
Through season after season, with all the charms
And graces of life's harvest, this, I'd say,           1035
Is to be like those young and lovely girls,
The Danaids, trying in vain to fill
Their leaky jars with water. Cerberus,
The Furies, and the dark, and the grim jaws
Of Tartarus, belching blasts of heat—all these         1040
Do not exist at all, and never could.
But here on earth we do fear punishment
For wickedness, and in proportion dread
Our dreadful deeds, imagining all too well
Being cast down from the Tarpeian Rock,                1045
Jail, flogging, hangmen, brands, the rack, the knout;
And even though these never touch us, still
The guilty mind is its own torturer
With lash and rowel, can see no end at all
To suffering and punishment, and fears                 1050
These will be more than doubled after death.
Hell does exist on earth—in the life of fools.

You well might think of saying to yourself:
"Even good Ancus closed his eyes on the light—
A better man than you will ever be,                    1055
You reprobate—and many lords and kings
Rulers of mighty nations, all have died.
Even that monarch, who once paved the way

1037. *Danaids*: The fifty daughters of
Danaus, who murdered their husbands.
They were condemned to carry water in
a sieve.
1038. *Cerberus*: The dog which
guarded the gates of hell.
1039. *the Furies*: Female spirits of revenge, also said to inflict tortures on the
spirits of the dead (such as Sisyphus and
Tantalus).

1040. *Tartarus*: The place of punishment for the wicked in the lower world.
1045. *Tarpeian rock*: A cliff at Rome
from which traitors were hurled.
1046. *knout*: Whip.
1049. *rowel*: Spiked wheel, as on a
spur.
1054. *Ancus*: The fourth of the legendary kings of Rome.

Making the sea a highway for his legions
Where foot and horse alike could march dry-shod          1060
While the deep foamed and thundered at the outrage,
Even he, great Xerxes, died and left the light,
And Scipio, the thunderbolt of war,
Terror of Carthage, gave his bones to earth
As does the meanest lackey. Add to these                 1065
Philosophers and artists, all the throng
Blessed by the Muses; Homer's majesty
Lies low in the same sleep as all the rest.
Democritus, warned by a ripe old age
That, with his memory, his powers of mind                1070
Were also failing, gave himself to death;
And Epicurus perished, that great man
Whose genius towered over all the rest,
Making their starry talents fade and die
In his great sunlight. Who are you, forsooth,            1075
To hesitate, resent, protest your death?
Your life is death already, though you live
And though you see, except that half your time
You waste in sleep, and the other half you snore
With eyes wide open, forever seeing dreams,              1080
Forever in panic, forever lacking wit
To find out what the trouble is, depressed,
Or drunk, or drifting aimlessly around."

Men seem to feel some burden on their souls,
Some heavy weariness; could they but know                1085
Its origin, its cause, they'd never live
The way we see most of them do, each one
Ignorant of what he wants, except a change,
Some other place to lay his burden down.
One leaves his house to take a stroll outdoors           1090
Because the household's such a deadly bore,
And then comes back, in six or seven minutes—
The street is every bit as bad. Now what?
He has his horses hitched up for him, drives,
Like a man going to a fire, full-speed,                  1095

---

1059. *highway*: The reference is to the bridge over the Hellespont built by Xerxes, king of Persia, for his invasion of Greece in 480 B.C.

1063. *Scipio*: The Roman general who defeated Hannibal at Zama in 202 B.C.

1069. *Democritus*: A Greek philosopher; one of the pioneers of the atomic theory on which the doctrines of Epicu-

rus (and Lucretius) were based. According to tradition he starved himself to death when he was over ninety years old.

1072. *Epicurus*: Greek philosopher (342–270 B.C.) whose philosophy is presented in Lucretius' poem.

1075. *forsooth*: Indeed.

Off to his country-place, and when he gets there
Is scarcely on the driveway, when he yawns,
Falls heavily asleep, oblivious
To everything, or promptly turns around,
Whips back to town again. So each man flees     1100
Himself, or tries to, but of course that pest
Clings to him all the more ungraciously.
He hates himself because he does not know
The reason for his sickness; if he did,
He would leave all this foolishness behind,     1105
Devote his study to the way things are,
The problem being his lot, not for an hour,
But for all time, the state in which all men
Must dwell forever and ever after death.

Finally, what's this wanton lust for life     1110
To make us tremble in dangers and in doubt?
All men must die, and no man can escape.
We turn and turn in the same atmosphere
In which no new delight is ever shaped
To grace our living; what we do not have     1115
Seems better than everything else in all the world
But should we get it, we want something else.
Our gaping thirst for life is never quenched.
We have to know what luck next year will bring,
What accident, what end. But life, prolonged,     1120
Subtracts not even one second from the term
Of death's continuance. We lack the strength
To abbreviate that eternity. Suppose
You could contrive to live for centuries,
As many as you will. Death, even so,     1125
Will still be waiting for you; he who died
Early this morning has as many years
Interminably before him, as the man,
His predecessor, has, who perished months
Or years, or even centuries ago.     1130

1106. *the way things are*: The translator's rendering of the poem's title.

# CICERO

## (106–43 B.C.)

## On the Republic (De republica)*

### The Dream of Scipio

On landing in Africa [1]—I had gone there, as you both know, as a military tribune[2] in the Fourth Legion for the consul Manius Manilius[3]—there was nothing that I wanted so much as to meet King Masinissa,[4] who for the best of reasons[5] was a great friend of our family. When I came to his house the old man burst into tears as he embraced me and then lifting his eyes to heaven cried: "Thanks give I to thee, O Sun supreme, and to you, ye other dwellers in the skies, that before I take my leave of this life I see in my kingdom and under my own roof P. Cornelius Scipio whose very name refreshes me; for never from my heart has faded the memory of that great and unconquerable hero!"[6] Then, we spent the whole day in conversing together—I asking him about his kingdom and he questioning me in turn about our country.

And later, after we had dined amidst regal state we prolonged our talk until far into the night. The old man would talk about nothing except of Africanus and remembered not only all that he had done but all as well that he had said. Then, when we had parted to take our rest a sleep much deeper than was usual fell upon me, for I was weary from my journey and had stayed awake until very late. And then—(I suppose it was a result of what we had been talking about; for it happens often that the things that we have been thinking and speaking of bring about something in our sleep. So Ennius[7] relates in his dream about Homer, of whom in hours of wakefulness he used so often to think and speak)— Africanus stood there before me, in figure familiar to me from his bust[8] rather than from life. I shuddered with dread as I recognized

---

* Written from 54 B.C. on; published before 51 B.C. Our selection is the principal surviving fragment of this work. This translation by H. A. Rice is here first published.

1. The speaker is Publius Cornelius Scipio Africanus the Younger, the Roman general who led the legions to victory in the Third Punic War (149–146 B.C.), which resulted in the final subjugation of Rome's rival in the West, Carthage. He is supposed to be speaking at a conversation which took place twenty years later; he tells the story of what happened to him in the first year of the war which made his name, when he was an undistinguished junior officer.

2. officer on the staff of a legion.

3. The consuls were the two chief magistrates at home, and commanders of the armies in the field. Scipio was later to replace Manius Manilius as commander.

4. king of Numidia; he became a trusted ally of the Romans in the Second Punic War (218–201 B.C.). He was a close friend of the first Scipio Africanus, who had adopted as his grandson the Scipio who tells this story.

5. among others because the elder Scipio had enlarged his dominions.

6. the elder Scipio.

7. Roman epic poet (239–169 B.C.) who began his epic of Roman history with an account of Homer's appearance to him in a dream.

8. The Roman aristocrat displayed

him but he said, "Be calm, Scipio, and have no fear, but fail not to remember the things that I shall tell.

"Do you see that city[9] which by me was forced to kneel before the Roman people and is now renewing battle as of old and will not rest in peace?" And from a place high up above, studded with stars and blazing with light, he pointed to Carthage far below. "To the siege of that city you are now marching, a soldier almost in the ranks. Two years from now you will destroy it as consul in command, and will win thereby a surname which hitherto you have held as a legacy from me.[10] And then, after you have blotted out Carthage, celebrated your triumph and become censor[11] and gone as legate[12] to Egypt, Syria, Asia and Greece, you will be chosen, while absent,[13] consul for the second time, complete a mighty war and destroy Numantia.[14] But just when you have been driven in triumph up to the Capitol, you will find the state in turmoil through the schemings of a grandson of mine.[15]

"It is here, Africanus, that you must needs show to our country the lustre of your genius, your capacity and your wisdom. But at that hour, I foresee, the path of your destiny divides. For when the years of your life have completed seven times eight circlings of the sun and those two numbers, each for a different reason, held to be perfect,[16] have fulfilled the sum allotted for you in the revolving ordained by fate, then the whole state will turn to you alone and to the name you bear. To you will turn the eyes of the senate, of all good citizens, allies and Latins, and you will be the man on whom alone the salvation of the state will depend. In a word, it will be your duty to bring back order in the state as dictator[17]— if only you escape the impious hands of your own kinsmen."[18] A cry burst from Laelius at this and deep groans from the others,[19] but Scipio, gently smiling, continued, "Hush, I beg of you! Do not rouse me from my sleep. Listen a while and hear the rest."

the busts of his ancestors in his house.

9. Carthage.

10. Hitherto he has been called Africanus in virtue of his adoption by the elder Scipio; after the capture of Carthage he will deserve the name by his own deeds.

11. the magistrate in charge of the senatorial rolls, who passed judgment on the senators' moral and financial fitness to continue in office.

12. ambassador.

13. He would be elected to the office without campaigning for it.

14. in Spain; it was destroyed in 133 B.C.

15. the agrarian reformer Tiberius Gracchus, son of Africanus' daughter Cornelia. His land law (enacted in 133 B.C.) restricted the holdings of the wealthy families and provided for the resettlement of small landholders. His

law marked the beginning of the century of internal struggle which was to end in the establishment of authoritarian power at Rome. Scipio is here made to speak of him from a conservative standpoint, which is in character, and was Cicero's own standpoint too.

16. Both these numbers were regarded as especially important in various mystical and philosophical systems. Scipio is fifty-six years old at the imagined time of the dialogue.

17. a temporary constitutional office; in times of crisis the Senate appointed a dictator for a specific term.

18. Scipio died in 129 B.C. while trying to bring about a compromise between the two parties; there was a rumor that his death was the work of the partisans of Gracchus.

19. the audience to whom Scipio is talking.

"But hold fast to this, Africanus, that you may be more eager to defend the state: For all those who have guarded, aided, and increased the welfare of their fatherland there is a place reserved in heaven, where they shall dwell in happiness forever. For to that all-ruling God whose power is over all that is there is nothing that is done on earth more acceptable than those meetings for conference of men joined together by the bond of law which are called states. Those who guide and preserve these have come from this heaven and to it they return."

At this, though I was filled with fear more at the thought of treachery from my own kin than by dread of death, I asked whether he and my father Paulus[20] and the others whom we deem to be dead were really living. "In all truth," said he, "they live, for they have made their escape from the fetters of the body as though out of a prison: it is that life of yours—you call it life—that is really death. Do you not see yonder your father Paulus coming to greet you?" When I saw him, I wept a flood of tears, but he embracing and kissing me bade me not to weep.

As soon as I could overcome my weeping and was able to speak I cried, "Tell me, best and most saintly of fathers, since here is life, as I hear Africanus say, why should I linger longer on earth? Why should I not make haste to join you here?" "That may not be," he replied, "for until that God, whose dominion is all that you can see, shall free you from the prison-house of the body, there can be for you no entrance here. For to men life has been given for this purpose, that they shall be care-takers of that sphere called the earth, which you see in the centre of this abode of the divine, and to them a soul has been given out of those never-dying fires which you call planets and stars, which, perfect in their form as spheres, are informed by souls divine and, in their orbits ordained, complete their courses with a motion marvellous in its swiftness. Therefore you, O Publius, and all good men must keep that soul in the guardianship of the body and must not seek to set forth from the life of men save at the bidding of him by whom it was entrusted to you, lest you be found to have fled from the trust imposed upon man by God.

"Rather do you, O Scipio, do as your grandfather here and as I who begat you have done: cherish righteousness and that loyalty, so greatly due to parents and kinsmen but most of all to one's fatherland. That is the life that is the road to the sky overhead and to this gathering of those whose life on earth has been lived. There are they who, lightened of the body's burden, now dwell in that place which you see yonder (it was a circle of light shining out with a radiant glory among the other fires) which you of earth call by a term learned from the Greeks, the Milky Way."

---

20. Scipio's father won a decisive victory at Pydna, in Greece, in 168 B.C.

To me, as I surveyed from that point all that I could see, wondrous and glorious was the sight. There were those stars that we never see from the earth, all larger than we have ever imagined, of these the smallest was one farthest from heaven[21] and nearest to the earth, shining with a reflected light. Much larger than the earth were these starry spheres: to me the earth seemed so small in comparison that I felt ashamed of our empire which includes but a single point on its surface.

As I gazed more and more intently upon the earth, Africanus said, "Tell me, how long will your mind devote itself to the earth below? Do you not see into what lofty heights you have come? Before you are the nine circles or rather spheres which bind together all that is. Of these the outermost is that of the heavens, enclosing all the rest—the God supreme guarding and embracing all the other spheres; within it are included the stars in their courses, revolving without ceasing. Beneath it are the seven other spheres whirling in their course opposite to that of the heaven. Of these one is that which among men is called Saturn. Next comes that radiance so helpful and healthful to mankind that men call Jupiter. Beneath this, red and fearful to mankind, is the star that you call Mars. Next below, almost midway between heaven and earth, is the sun, the leader, chief and ruler of the other lights, the soul of the universe and its controlling power, of such greatness of size that he fills all things and floods them with his light. In his train as companions are the orbits of Venus and Mercury, and in the lowest of the spheres the moon revolves, lighted by the rays of the sun. But below this there is nothing that is not impermanent and doomed to die save only the souls bestowed by nature's gift on the race of men, while above all things are imperishable. For that central sphere the earth, which is the ninth, is motionless and of all things the lowest, and toward it all bodies tend because of their weight."

As I gazed with awe at these marvellous things I said as soon as I could recover from my amazement, "But what is that wondrous sound, so loud and sweet, that fills my ears?"

"That," said he, "is that harmony of the spheres, produced by the sweep of their onward motion, with the intervals between them unequal but composed, by the blending of notes high with low in exact proportion, to produce various harmonies. For not in silence can such mighty motions speed on their way, and it is nature's will that the lowest spheres sound forth in heaviest tones and those above in highest. So that this uppermost sphere of the heavens bearing the stars, since it revolves at greater speed, moves apace with notes of highest pitch, while that one of the moon, the lowest, gives out the lowest tones; for the earth, ninth of the spheres, re-

---

21. the moon.

mains without motion in its fixed place in the centre of the universe. But the other eight spheres, two of which move at the same rate,[22] send out seven different sounds,—that number which is the key of almost everything. It is this harmony that inspired men have reproduced both on strings and in songs and thus have won a return to this place, as have those others who during their life on earth have devoted outstanding gifts to the pursuit of things divine. To this music our human ears, though filled with it, have become deaf—for there is no duller sense in man than that of hearing. So it is that where the Nile falls headlong from those lofty mountains at the place called the Cataracts, the race of men that lives nearby has, because of the loudness of the sound, lost its power of hearing. So this sound so glorious, made by the revolving at the highest speed of the whole universe, cannot be heard by human ears, just as you cannot look directly at the sun, since your sight is blinded by its radiance."

Though I marvelled at these things, I yet kept turning my eyes again and again back to the earth.

Then Africanus continued: "You are still, I see, fixing your eyes upon the abode and the home of men. If it seems a small thing, as it is, to you, keep rather your eyes upon these things of the heavens, scorning those of mankind. For what glory can you gain from what men say, what fame worth striving for? The earth, as you can see, is inhabited in but scattered parts and these small, while between those spots, as it were, where men dwell, stretch vast desert places. Those who inhabit the earth are from each other so widely apart that no word can spread from one group to another, for some live in parts slantwise,[23] others crosswise,[24] and some even opposite[25] to you; from these surely there is no glory that you can hope to have.

"You can see besides, that the earth is girdled and encircled by zones of a sort, of which the two that are farthest apart, supported by the opposite poles of the sky, are both held fast in bonds of ice, while that middle and widest one is scorched by the blazing heat of the sun. Two of the zones are fit for habitation; of these the southern, where men dwell whose footprints press against yours, has no concern for you; while if you consider this northern one inhabited by you, see how small a part of it belongs to you. For that whole stretch of earth which you hold, narrow from north to south and wider from east to west, is in fact only a small island surrounded by that sea which you call the Atlantic, the Great Sea, or the Ocean. See how small it is, in spite of its lordly name. Do you suppose that your name or that of anyone of our people has ever passed from

22. Mercury and Venus.

23. in the opposite (southern) temperate zone of the same hemisphere.

24. in the same (northern) temperate zone of the opposite hemisphere.

25. in the opposite temperate zone of the opposite hemisphere.

those lands that are cultivated and known to us and scaled the Caucasus which you see there, or crossed beyond the Ganges? Who among those who dwell in those remote lands of the rising or the setting sun, or of the farthest north or south will ever hear your name? With these left out you see, surely, within what narrow limits the fame for which you long can spread. And how long will even those who now speak about you continue to do so?

"Why, even if generations yet to be should want to pass on to those yet unborn the praises of anyone of us received from their fathers, still, because of the floods and conflagrations that are bound at certain intervals to happen on the earth, we could not count upon a long-lasting fame among men, much less an endless one. Yet how much does it concern you to be spoken of by those who come after you when you have never been mentioned by those who have lived before you?

"Indeed they were not fewer than the men of now and surely were better; especially since not one of those by whom our names can now be heard will, after a year has passed, have any memory of it. For men generally reckon a year by the circling of only one of the stars, that is, the sun: but when all the stars have come back to the point where they started and have, at long intervals, restored the same arrangement of the whole heavens, then comes about that which can truly be called a completed year.[26] How many generations of men are included in such a year I would not venture to say. For as the sun seemed to men to fail of its light and to be eclipsed at the hour when the soul of Romulus[27] made its way to these shining heights, so when the sun shall again be eclipsed at the same point and the same hour, then, since all the planets and stars will have returned to their starting point you can be assured that such a year has been completed. But you may be sure that one twentieth[28] of such a year has not yet passed.

"If, therefore, you despair of a return to this place where all belongs to great and noble men, of what worth, I ask you, is that fame of yours among men? It can hardly extend to the smallest part of a single year. So if you will but fix your gaze on things on high and on this eternal home and dwelling-place, you will cease to listen to the talking of the common herd, nor will you longer put your trust in the rewards that men can bestow for what you have done; let rather the charm of virtue itself lead you on to the only true glory; whatever men may say of you leave to them; they will say it anyway, and all that they have to say will be confined within those narrow limits which you see: all that they say about any man has not been

26. reckoned by ancient authorities at from twelve thousand to fifteen thousand years.

27. the traditional founder of the city of Rome; the legendary date of his death is 716 B.C.

28. from the death of Romulus to the supposed time of Scipio's dream is 567 years.

for long, for it dies with them and is blotted out by the forgetful-ness of those who come after them." As he said this, "If it is true, Africanus," said I, "that for those who have well served their coun-try there lies open a path to heaven here, then, though from my boyhood I have tried to follow in the footsteps of my father and of you and to be worthy of your fame, now indeed with such a reward before my eyes I shall strive with even greater zeal." "Strive on," said he, "and be assured that you are not, though your body is, born but to die; for that form which your body shows is not your true self: the spirit within each man is the man himself—not the bodily form to which one can point. Know then that you are divine, for that is divine which throbs with life, feels, remembers, foresees, which rules, controls, and makes to move the body over which it has been placed in charge; as over this universe rules that supreme God; so this mortal body is made to move by a deathless soul within.

"For that which is ever in motion is eternal, but that which sets in motion something else but is itself moved by a force outside it, must needs, when the cause of its motion ends, cease to live. Only that therefore which gives itself motion ceases not to move, since it never abandons itself: more than that, it is for all other things that move, the first cause and beginning of their motion. Of a first cause there is of course no beginning, for it is from this first cause that all things begin, while it can never take its beginning from anything else; for it would not be a first cause if it found its begin-ning outside itself. Moreover because it never had a beginning it will never have an end. For if a first cause were destroyed it could never be born again from anything else, nor could it create another thing from itself, since only from a first cause must everything begin to be. So it follows that motion must begin from that which is self-moving: this can neither be born nor die: otherwise all heaven above would fall and all nature cease to be since they are endowed with no power from which they can receive a beginning of motion.

"Since then that which is self-moving is everlasting, who would dare deny that this is the essential nature given to living spirits? For everything that is set in motion by an outside force is without a spirit within it, but that which is animated by spirit is moved by its own power within, for this is the essential property and power of spirit,—which, since it is the only thing among all things that moves itself, cannot have had a beginning nor can it ever have an end. Devote this, then, to the highest tasks! Of these surely the noblest are those on behalf of one's fatherland: a spirit dedicated and devoted to these will swiftly wing its way to this, its own abode and home. And more swiftly will it speed here if, while still prisoned in the body, it soars above it and fixing its gaze on things beyond, it

rids itself as much as is in its power from the body. The souls of
those, however, who have surrendered to the pleasures of the body
as slaves to them and who at the bidding of desires of the body
have transgressed the laws of gods and men, when they have left
their bodies, flit about the earth below, and do not return to this
place until after they have, through many ages, suffered retribution."
He left me then, and I awoke from my sleep.

# VIRGIL
## (70–19 B.C.)
## The Aeneid*

### Book I

I sing of arms and of a man: his fate
had made him fugitive; he was the first
to journey from the coasts of Troy as far
as Italy and the Lavinian shores.
Across the lands and waters he was battered          5
beneath the violence of High Ones, for
the savage Juno's unforgetting anger;
and many sufferings were his in war—
until he brought a city into being
and carried in his gods to Latium;                   10
from this have come the Latin race, the lords
of Alba, and the ramparts of high Rome.

Tell me the reason, Muse: what was the wound
to her divinity, so hurting her
that she, the queen of gods, compelled a man         15
remarkable for goodness to endure

---

* Abridged. Left unfinished when the
poet died in 19 B.C. Translated by Allen
Mandelbaum.
1. *a man*: Aeneas, one of the Trojan
champions in the fight for Troy, son of
Aphrodite (Venus) and Anchises, a
member of the royal house of Troy.
Aeneas survived the fall of the city and
set off in search of another home. After
years of wandering he settled in Italy,
and from his line sprang, in the fullness
of time, the founders of Rome.
4. *Lavinian shores*: The west coast of
Italy in the vicinity of Rome, named
after the nearby city of Lavinium. Lavi-

nia is the name of the Italian princess
whom Aeneas is eventually to marry.
7. *Juno*: The Latin equivalent of
Hera, wife of the ruler of the gods,
Zeus. As in the *Iliad,* she is a bitter
enemy of the Trojans.
10. *Latium*: The coastal plain on
which Rome is situated.
12. *Alba*: The city of Alba Longa was
to be founded by Aeneas' son Ascanius,
and from it were to come Romulus and
Remus, the builders of Rome.
13. *Muse*: Goddess of epic poetry,
and the source of poetic inspiration.

so many crises, meet so many trials?
Can such resentment hold the minds of gods?


There was an ancient city they called Carthage—
a colony of refugees from Tyre—                                    20
a city facing Italy, but far
away from Tiber's mouth: extremely rich
and, when it came to waging war, most fierce.
This land was Juno's favorite—it is said—
more dear than her own Samos; here she kept            25
her chariot and armor; even then
the goddess had this hope and tender plan;
for Carthage to become the capital
of nations, if the Fates would just consent.
But she had heard that, from the blood of Troy,        30
a race had come that some day would destroy
the citadels of Tyre; from it, a people
would spring, wide-ruling kings, men proud in battle
and destined to annihilate her Libya.
The Fates had so decreed. And Saturn's daughter—       35
in fear of this, remembering the old war
that she had long since carried on at Troy
for her beloved Argos (and, indeed,
the causes of her bitterness, her sharp
and savage hurt, had not yet left her spirit;          40
for deep within her mind lie stored the judgment
of Paris and the wrong done to her scorned
beauty, the breed she hated, and the honors
that had been given ravished Ganymede)—
was angered even more; for this, she kept              45
far off from Latium the Trojan remnant
left by the Greeks and pitiless Achilles.
For long years they were cast across all waters,

---

*19. Carthage*: Founded in North Africa by the Phoenicians who came from Tyre and Sidon in Palestine. It was their chief colony in the western Mediterranean. In the third and second centuries B.C. Carthage fought a series of bitter wars against Rome for the domination of the area. Carthage was captured and destroyed by the Romans in 146 B.C.
*22. Tiber*: The river which flows through Rome.
*24. Samos*: Greek island in the Aegean, famous as a center for the worship of Hera (Juno).
*29. Fates*: Goddesses who controlled human destinies and the powers of the gods.
*34. Libya*: Africa (i.e., Carthage).
*35. Saturn's daughter*: Juno. Saturn (Greek Kronos) was the father of Jupiter and Juno.
*38. Argos*: Greece.
*41. judgment of Paris*: Paris, son to King Priam of Troy, was chosen to judge which was the most beautiful goddess—Hera, Aphrodite, or Athene. All three attempted to bribe him, but Aphrodite's promise, the love of Helen, prevailed, and he awarded her the prize.
*44. Ganymede*: A beautiful Trojan boy taken up into heaven by Jupiter (or Zeus) to be his favorite.

fate-driven, wandering from sea to sea.
It was so hard to found the race of Rome.                    50

\*   \*   \*

## [Aeneas Arrives in Carthage]

[The story opens with a storm, provoked by Juno's agency,
which scatters Aeneas' fleet off Sicily and separates him from his
companions. He lands on the African coast near Carthage. Setting
out with his friend Achates to explore the country, he meets his
mother, Venus (Aphrodite), who tells him that the rest of his ships
are safe and directs him to the city just founded by Dido, the queen
of Carthage. Venus surrounds Aeneas and Achates with a cloud so
that they can see without being seen.]

Meanwhile Aeneas and the true Achates                        595
press forward on their path. They climb a hill
that overhangs the city, looking down
upon the facing towers. Aeneas marvels
at the enormous buildings, once mere huts,
and at the gates and tumult and paved streets.               600
The eager men of Tyre work steadily;
some build the city walls or citadel—
they roll up stones by hand; and some select
the place for a new dwelling, marking out
its limits with a furrow; some make laws,                    605
establish judges and a sacred senate;
some excavate a harbor; others lay
the deep foundations for a theater,
hewing tremendous pillars from the rocks,
high decorations for the stage to come.                      610
Just as the bees in early summer, busy
beneath the sunlight through the flowered meadows,
when some lead on their full-grown young and others
press out the flowing honey, pack the cells
with sweet nectar, or gather in the burdens                  615
of those returning; some, in columns, drive
the drones, a lazy herd, out of the hives;
the work is fervent, and the fragrant honey
is sweet with thyme. "How fortunate are those
whose walls already rise!" Aeneas cries                      620
while gazing at the rooftops of the city.
Then, sheltered by a mist, astoundingly,
he enters in among the crowd, mingling
together with the Tyrians. No one sees him.

624. *Tyrians*: Phoenicians, Carthaginians.

Just at the center of the city stood                               625
a thickly shaded wood; this was the place
where, when they landed, the Phoenicians first—
hurled there by whirlwind and by wave—dug up,
an omen that Queen Juno had pointed out:
the head of a fierce stallion. This had meant                      630
the nation's easy wealth and fame in war
throughout the ages. Here Sidonian Dido
was building a stupendous shrine for Juno,
enriched with gifts and with the goddess' statue,
where flights of steps led up to brazen thresholds;                635
the architraves were set on posts of brass;
the grating hinges of the doors were brass.
Within this grove, the sights—so strange to him—
have, for the first time, stilled Aeneas' fear;
here he first dared to hope he had found shelter,                  640
to trust more surely in his shattered fortunes.
For while he waited for the queen, he studied
everything in that huge sanctuary,
marveling at a city rich enough
for such a temple, at the handiwork                                 645
of rival artists, at their skillful tasks.
He sees the wars of Troy set out in order:
the battles famous now through all the world,
the sons of Atreus and of Priam, and
Achilles, savage enemy to both.                                    650
He halted. As he wept, he cried: "Achates,
where on this earth is there a land, a place
that does not know our sorrows? Look! There is Priam!
Here, too, the honorable finds its due
and there are tears for passing things; here, too,                 655
things mortal touch the mind. Forget your fears;
this fame will bring you some deliverance."
He speaks. With many tears and sighs he feeds
his soul on what is nothing but a picture.


He watched the warriors circling Pergamus:                         660
here routed Greeks were chased by Trojan fighters
and here the Phrygian troops pursued by plumed
Achilles in his chariot. Nearby,
sobbing, he recognized the snow-white canvas

---

636. *architraves*: That part of the roof
bearing directly on the tops of columns.
649. *sons of Atreus*: Agamemnon and
Menelaus. *of Priam*: Many, among them
Hector.
660. *Pergamus*: The citadel of Troy.

tents of King Rhesus—with his men betrayed, 665
while still in their first sleep, and then laid waste,
with many dead, by bloody Diomedes,
who carried off their fiery war horses
before they had a chance to taste the pastures
of Troy, or drink the waters of the Xanthus. 670

Elsewhere young Troilus, the unhappy boy—
he is matched unequally against Achilles—
runs off, his weapons lost. He is fallen flat;
his horses drag him on as he still clings
fast to his empty chariot, clasping 675
the reins. His neck, his hair trail on the ground,
and his inverted spear inscribes the dust.
Meanwhile the Trojan women near the temple
of Pallas, the unkindly; hair disheveled,
sad, beating at their breasts, as suppliants, 680
they bear the robe of offering. The goddess
averts her face, her eyes fast to the ground.

Three times Achilles had dragged Hector round
the walls of Troy, selling his lifeless body
for gold. And then, indeed, Aeneas groans 685
within the great pit of his chest, deeply;
for he can see the spoils, the chariot,
the very body of his friend, and Priam
pleading for Hector with defenseless hands.
He also recognized himself in combat 690
with the Achaean chiefs, then saw the Eastern
battalions and the weapons of black Memnon.
Penthesilea in her fury leads
the ranks of crescent-shielded Amazons.
She flashes through her thousands; underneath 695
her naked breast, a golden girdle; soldier-
virgin and queen, daring to war with men.

But while the Dardan watched these scenes in wonder,
while he was fastened in a stare, astonished,

---

665. *Rhesus*: King of Thrace, who
came to the help of Troy just before the
end of the war. An oracle proclaimed
that if his horses ate Trojan grass and
drank the water of the river Xanthus,
Troy would not fall. Odysseus and
Diomedes went into the Trojan lines at
night, killed the king, and stole the
horses.
671. *Troilus*: A son of Priam.

679. *Pallas*: Athena (Minerva), goddess hostile to the Trojans.
692. *Memnon*: King of the Aethiopi-
ans, who fought on the Trojan side.
693. *Penthesilea*: Queen of the Amazons, killed by Achilles.
696. *girdle*: Belt.
698. *Dardan*: Trojan, after the ancestor of the Trojan kings, Dardanus.

the lovely-bodied Dido neared the temple,  700
a crowding company of youths around her.
And just as, on the banks of the Eurotas
or though the heights of Cynthus, when Diana
incites her dancers, and her followers,
a thousand mountain-nymphs, press in behind her,  705
she wears a quiver slung across her shoulder;
and as she makes her way, she towers over
all other goddesses; gladness excites
Latona's silent breast: even so, Dido;
so, in her joy, she moved among the throng  710
as she urged on the work of her coming kingdom.

And then below the temple's central dome—
facing the doorway of the goddess, guarded
by arms—she took her place on a high throne.
Dido was dealing judgments to her people  715
and giving laws, apportioning the work
of each with fairness or by drawing lots;
when suddenly Aeneas sees, as they
press forward through that mighty multitude,
Sergestus, Antheus, and the brave Cloanthus,  720
and other Trojans whom the black whirlwind
had scattered on the waters, driven far
to other coasts. Aeneas is astounded;
both joy and fear have overcome Achates.
They burned to join right hands with their companions,  725
but this strange happening confuses them.
They stay in hiding, screened by folds of fog,
and wait to see what fortune found their friends,
on what beach they have left the fleet, and why
they come; for these were men who had been chosen  730
from all the ships to ask for grace, who now
made for the temple door with loud outcries.

When they had entered and received their leave
to speak in Dido's presence, then the eldest,
Ilioneus, calmly began: "O Queen,  735
whom Jupiter has granted this: to bring
to being a new city, curbing haughty
nations by justice—we, unhappy Trojans,

702. *Eurotas*: A river near Sparta where Artemis (Diana) was worshipped. *Cynthian*: Cynthus is a mountain on the island of Delos, Diana's birthplace.
709. *Latona*: (Leto), mother of Diana.
720. *Antheus . . . Cloanthus*: Aeneas' captains from whom he had been parted by the storm.

men carried by the winds across all seas,
beg you to keep the terror of fire from                    740
our fleet, to spare a pious race, to look
on us with kindliness. We do not come
to devastate your homes and with the sword
to loot the household gods of Libya or
to drive down stolen booty toward the beaches            745
That violence is not within our minds;
such arrogance is not for the defeated.
There is a place the Greeks have named Hesperia,
an ancient land with strong arms and fat soil.
Its colonists were the Oenotrians.                        750
Now rumor runs that their descendants call
that nation 'Italy,' after their leader.
Our prows were pointed there when suddenly,
rising upon the surge, stormy Orion
drove us against blind shoals; and insolent              755
south winds then scattered us, undone by brine,
across the crushing sea, the pathless rocks
A few of us have drifted to your shores.
What kind of men are these? Or is your country
so barbarous that it permits this custom?                 760
We are denied the shelter of the beach;
they goad us into war; they will not let us
set foot upon the border of their land.
If you despise the human race and mortal
weapons, then still consider that the gods               765
remember right and wrong. We had a king,
Aeneas, none more just, no one more pious,
no man his better in the arts of war.
If fate has saved this man, if he still feeds
upon the upper air, if he is not                          770
laid low to rest among the cruel Shades,
then we are not afraid and you will not
repent if you compete with him in kindness.
Within Sicilian territory, too,
are fields and cities and the famed Acestes,             775
born of the blood of Troy. Let us haul up
our fleet, smashed by the winds, along your beaches
and fit out timber from your forests, trim
our oars; and if we find our king and comrades

---

748. *Hesperia*: Italy, literally, "the western country."
750. *Oenotrians*: The original inhabitants of Italy.
752. *leader*: Italus.
754. *Orion*: The setting of this constellation in November signalled the onset of stormy weather at sea.
771. *Shades*: Spirits of the dead.
775. *Acestes*: A Sicilian king; his mother was a Trojan, and he had offered Aeneas a home in his dominions.

and are allowed to turn toward Italy                      780
and Latium, then let us sail out gladly.
But if our shelter there has been denied us,
and you, the finest father of the Trojans,
were swallowed by the sea of Libya, and
no hope is left us now for Iülus, then                    785
at least let us seek out again the straits
of Sicily, the land from which we sailed.
There houses wait for us, and King Acestes."
So spoke Ilioneus. The others sons
of Dardanus approved his words with shouts.               790

Then Dido softly, briefly answers him:
"O Teucrians, enough of fear, cast out
your cares. My kingdom is new; hard circumstances
have forced me to such measures for our safety,
to post guards far and wide along our boundaries.         795
But who is ignorant of Aeneas' men?
Who has not heard of Troy, its acts and heroes,
the flames of that tremendous war? We Tyrians
do not have minds so dull, and we are not
beyond the circuit of the sun's yoked horses.             800
Whatever you may choose—Hesperia and
the fields of Saturn, or the land of Eryx
and King Acestes—I shall send you safe
with escort, I shall help you with my wealth.
And should you want to settle in this kingdom             805
on equal terms with me, then all the city
I am building now is yours. Draw up your ships.
I shall allow no difference between
the Tyrian and the Trojan. Would your king,
Aeneas, too, were present, driven here                    810
by that same south wind. I, in fact, shall send
my trusted riders out along the shores,
to comb the farthest coast of Libya and
to see if, cast out of the waters, he
is wandering through the forests or the cities."          815

The words of Dido stir the brave Achates
and father Aeneas; long since, both of them
had burned to break free from their cloud. Achates

---

785. *Iülus*: Ascanius, Aeneas' son.
792. *Teucrians*: Trojans; named after a Trojan King called Teucer.
800. *the sun's yoked horses*: The sun was believed to be a brilliant chariot

pulled across the sky.
802. *Saturn*: An old legend connected Italy with Saturn (Cronos), the father of Jupiter (Zeus). The "age of Saturn" was the Golden Age. *Eryx*: in Sicily.

speaks first to his companion: "Goddess-born,
what counsel rises in your spirit now?                          820
You see that everything is safe, our ships
and sailors saved. And only one is missing,
whom we ourselves saw sink among the waves.
All else is as your mother said it would be."

Yet he was hardly done when suddenly                           825
the cloud that circled them is torn; it clears
away to open air. And there Aeneas
stood, glittering in that bright light, his face
and shoulders like a god's. Indeed, his mother
had breathed upon her son becoming hair,                       830
the glow of a young man, and in his eyes,
glad handsomeness: such grace as art can add
to ivory, or such as Parian marble
or silver shows when set in yellow gold.

But then, surprising all, he tells the queen:                  835
"The man you seek is here. I stand before you,
Trojan Aeneas, torn from Libyan waves.
O you who were alone in taking pity
on the unutterable trials of Troy,
who welcome us as allies to your city                          840
and home—a remnant left by Geeeks, harassed
by all disasters known on land and sea,
in need of everything—we cannot, Dido,
repay you, then, with gratitude enough
to match your merits, neither we nor any                       845
Dardans scattered over this great world.
May gods confer on you your due rewards,
if deities regard the good, if justice
and mind aware of right count anywhere.
What happy centuries gave birth to you?                        850
What splendid parents brought you into being?
While rivers run into the sea and shadows
still sweep the mountain slopes and stars still pasture
upon the sky, your name and praise and honor
shall last, whatever be the lands that call me."               855
This said, he gives his right hand to his friend
Ilioneus; his left he gives Serestus;
then turns to brave Cloanthus and brave Gyas.

---

822. *missing*: One ship, captained by
Orontes, was sunk in the storm in sight
of Aeneas.

833. *Parian*: The island of Paros was
famous for its marble.

First at the very sight of him, and then
at all he had endured, Sidonian Dido            860
was startled. And she told the Trojan this:
"You, goddess-born, what fortune hunts you down
through such tremendous trials? What violence
has forced you onto these ferocious shores?
Are you that same Aeneas, son of Dardan          865
Anchises, whom the gracious Venus bore
beside the banks of Phrygian Simois?
Indeed, I still remember banished Teucer,
a Greek who came to Sidon from his native
kingdom, when with the help of Belus he          870
was seeking out new realms (my father Belus
was plundering then, as victor, wealthy Cyprus).
And even then I learned of Troy's disaster,
and of your name and of the kings of Greece.
And though he was the Trojans' enemy,            875
Teucer would often praise the Teucrians
and boast that he was born of their old race.
Thus, young men, you are welcome to our halls.
My destiny, like yours, has willed that I,
a veteran of hardships, halt at last            880
in this country. Not ignorant of trials,
I now can learn to help the miserable."

So Dido speaks. At once she leads Aeneas
into the royal palace and announces
her offerings in the temples of the gods.        885
But meanwhile she does not neglect his comrades.
She sends down to the beaches twenty bullocks,
a hundred fat lambs with their ewes, and Bacchus'
glad gift of wine. Within the palace gleam
the furnishings of royal luxury;                 890
the feast is readied in the atrium.
And there are draperies of noble purple
woven with art; and plate of massive silver
upon the tables; and, engraved in gold,
the sturdy deeds of Dido's ancestors,            895
a long, long line of happenings and heroes
traced from the first beginnings of her race.

---

867. *Simois*: One of the rivers of Troy.

868. *Teucer*: A Greek warrior who fought at Troy and afterward was exiled from his home. He founded a city on the island of Cyprus. (Not related to the Trojan king, Teucer.)

888. *Bacchus*: God of wine.

891. *atrium*: The Roman word for the principal room of a mansion.

[At the banquet which Dido gives for Aeneas, he relates, at her request, the story of the fall of Troy.]

## Book II

### [*The Fall of Troy*]

A sudden silence fell on all of them;
their eyes were turned, intent on him. And father
Aeneas, from his high couch, then began:

"O Queen—too terrible for tongues the pain
you ask me to renew, the tale of how                                      5
the Danaans could destroy the wealth of Troy,
that kingdom of lament: for I myself
saw these sad things; I took large part in them.
What Myrmidon or what Dolopian,
what soldier even of the harsh Ulysses,                                   10
could keep from tears in telling such a story?
But now the damp night hurries from the sky
into the sea; the falling stars persuade
to sleep. But if you long so much to learn
our suffering, to hear in brief the final                                 15
calamity of Troy—although my mind,
remembering, recoils in grief, and trembles,
I shall try.

              "The captains of the Danaans,
now weak with war and beaten back by fate,
and with so many gliding years gone by,                                   20
are able to construct, through the divine
art of Minerva, a mountainous horse.
They weave its ribs with sawed-off beams of fir,
pretending that it is an offering
for safe return. At least, that is their story.                          25
Then in the dark sides of the horse they hide
men chosen from the sturdiest among them;
they stuff their soldiers in its belly, deep
in that vast cavern: Greeks armed to the teeth.

"Before their eyes lies famous Tenedos,                                   30
an island prosperous and powerful
as long as Priam's kingdoms held their own,

---

6. *Danaans*: Greeks.
9. *Myrmidon*: A solider of Achilles'
contingent. *Dolopian*: The men of Neop-
tolemos (Pyrrhus), Achilles' son.

10. *Ulysses*: Odysseus.
20. *years gone by*: Troy fell in the
tenth year of the siege.
22. *Minerva*: Athena.

but now only a bay, a treacherous
ships' anchorage. And here the Argives sail
to hide themselves along that lonely shore.                               35
We thought that they had left, to seek Mycenae
before the wind. And all of Troy is free
of long lament. The gates are opened wide;
gladly we go to see the Doric camp,
deserted places, the abandoned sands.                                    40
For here a squadron of Dolopians,
here fierce Achilles once had pitched his tent;
and here their ships were anchored; here they fought.
Some wonder at the deadly gift to maiden
Minerva, marveling at the horse's bulk;                                  45
Thymoetes was the first of us to urge
that it be brought within the walls and set
inside the citadel. He so advised
either through treachery or else because
the fates of Troy had willed this course. But Capys                      50
and those with sounder judgment counsel us
to cast the Greek device into the sea,
or to set fire to this suspicious gift,
or else to pierce and probe that hollow belly.
The doubting crowd is split into two factions.                           55

"The lead is taken by Laocoön.
He hurries from the citadel's high point
excitedly; and with a mob around him,
from far off he calls out: 'Poor citizens,
what wild insanity is this? Do you                                       60
believe the enemy have sailed away?
Or think that any Grecian gifts are free
of craft? Is this the way Ulysses acts?
Either Achaeans hide, shut in this wood,
or else this is an engine built against                                  65
our walls to spy upon our houses or
to batter down our city from above;
some trickery is here. Trojans, do not
trust in the horse. Whatever it may be,
I fear the Greeks, even when they bring gifts.'                          70
And as he spoke he hurled his massive shaft
with heavy force against the side, against
the rounded, jointed belly of the beast.

---

36. *Mycenae*: The city ruled by Aga-      56. *Laocoön*: Trojan priest of Nep-
memnon.                                    tune (Poseidon), the sea god.
39. *Doric*: Greek.

It quivered when it struck the hollow cavern,
which groaned and echoed. Had the outcome not    75
been fated by the gods, and had our minds
not wandered off, Laocoön would then
have made our sword points foul the Argive den;
and, Troy, you would be standing yet and you,
high fort of Priam, you would still survive.    80

"Meanwhile with many shouts some Dardan shepherds
were dragging to the king a youth they had found.
His hands were bound behind his back; he was
a stranger who had surrendered willingly,
that he might bring about this very thing    85
and open Troy to the Achaeans; he
was sure of spirit, set for either end:
to win through stratagems or meet his death.
From every side the young of Troy rush out,
all swarming in their eagerness to see him,    90
contending in their taunts against the captive.
Now listen to the treachery of the Danaans
and learn from one the wickedness of all.
For as he stood with every eye upon him,
uneasy and unarmed, and looked around    95
while taking in the Phrygian ranks'—'What land,'
he cries, 'what seas can now receive me? What
awaits my misery? I have no place
among the Danaans; and in bitterness
the Trojans ask for vengeance, for my blood    100
as penalty.' His lamentation turned
our feelings. Every violence was checked.
We urge him on to speak, to tell us who
his family may be, what word he brings,
what is he hoping for as prisoner.    105
At last he lays aside his fear and speaks:

" 'O King, I shall hide nothing of the truth,
whatever comes of it for me. I'll not
deny that I am born an Argive; this
I first confess. For fortune made of Sinon    110
a miserable man but not a man
of faithlessness and falsehood. Now by chance
you may have heard men talk of Palamedes,

---

78. *Argive*: Greek.
113. *Palamedes*: A Greek warrior who advised Agamemnon to abandon the war against Troy; his downfall was engineered by Ulysses (Odysseus), who planted forged proofs of dealings with the enemy in his tent.

the son of Belus, famous, glorious;
though he was innocent, the Greeks condemned him          115
to death on lying evidence, false charges,
simply because he had opposed the war.
Now that his light is lost, his killers mourn him.
When I was young, my father—a poor man—
sent me to serve in arms as a companion          120
to Palamedes, our close relative.
And while my kinsman's realm was safe and sure
and while his word was strong in the king's council,
I was respected and I shared his fame.
But after he had left these upper shores,          125
a victim of the sharp Ulysses' envy
(no man is ignorant of what I tell),
I dragged my bitter life through grief and darkness,
I raged within me at the doom of my
innocent friend. And in my madness I          130
did not keep silent, but I swore to act
as his avenger if I found the chance,
if ever I returned to my homeland
of Argos as a victor. With my words
I stirred up bitter hatred; and for this          135
I first was touched by threats; from that time, too,
Ulysses menaced me with fresh complaints;
the words he spread among the army were
ambiguous; aware of his own guilt,
he looked for weapons. And he did not stop          140
until, with Calchas as his tool—but why
do I tell over this unwelcome story,
this useless tale? Why do I hold you back?
If you consider all Achaeans one,
it is enough for you that I am Grecian.          145
Then take your overdue revenge at once:
for this is what the Ithacan would wish;
the sons of Atreus—they would pay for this.'

"But then indeed we burn to know, to ask
the reasons; we were far too ignorant          150
of so much wickedness, of Greek deception.
Trembling, he carries on. His words are false:

" 'The Greeks have often wanted to abandon
the plain of Troy, to slip away, to flee,

---

141. *Calchas*: The priest and prophet          147. *Ithacan*: Ulysses.
of the Greek army.

weary of this long war: would that they had!                                   155
But each time they were blocked by bitter tempests
across the waters, terrified because
the south wind beat against their sails. Above all,
when this high horse you see was ready, built
of maple beams, storm clouds droned through the heavens.       160
Bewildered, we send out Eurypylus
to ask the oracle of Phoebus; from
the shrine he brings back these grim words to us:
"By blood and by the slaying of a virgin,
Grecians, you stilled the winds when you first came             165
to Troy; by blood seek out your homeward way.
The only offering that is suitable:
an Argive life." And when the army heard
this oracle, they were amazed; within
the Grecians' deepest marrow cold fear shuddered.              170
For whom has fate prepared this end? Whose life
does Phoebus want? At this, with much fanfare
the Ithacan drags out the prophet Calchas
before the crowd and asks of him what are
the god's demands. And many now foretold                       175
to me this schemer's ruthless villainy;
they saw—but unprotestingly—what was
to come. For twice-five days the seer is still,
secluded in his tent; his tongue refuses
to name a single Greek or to betray                            180
death's victim. Finally, with difficulty
and driven by the Ithacan's loud urgings,
as they had planned, he breaks his silence and
assigns me to the altar. All approved;
what each feared for himself he now endured                    185
when someone else was singled out for ruin.

" 'And now the day of horror was at hand;
the rites were being readied for me: cakes
of salt and garlands round my temples. I
confess, I snatched myself from death; I broke                 190
my bonds; and in a muddy pond, unseen,
nightlong I hid among the rushes, waiting
for them to sail away—if only that
could be! And now there is no hope for me

161. *Eurypylus*: A minor Greek chieftain.
162. *Phoebus*: Apollo, god of prophecy, music, medicine, and later of the sun.
164. *virgin*: Iphigenia, daughter of Agamemnon, who sacrificed her to gain favorable winds to sail on to Troy.
188. *cakes of salt*: In the Roman sacrificial rite salted meal was sprinkled on the victim's head.

to see my old country, my tender sons,                               195
my longed-for father, on whom they may levy
the punishment for my escape, making
poor victims pay for my crime with their death.
I beg you, therefore, by the High Ones, by
the powers that know the truth, and by whatever                      200
still uncontaminated trust is left
to mortals, pity my hard trials, pity
a soul that carries undeserved sorrows.'

"We grant life to his tears and, more, our mercy.
And Priam is the first to have the fetters                           205
and tight chains taken off the fugitive;
he speaks to him with words of friendliness:
'Whoever you may be, from this time on
forget the Greeks you lost; you are one of us.
And answer truthfully the things I ask:                              210
Why have they built this massive horse? Who was
its maker? And what are they after? What
religious gift is it? Or engine of war?'

"He stopped. The other, schooled in Grecian guile
and wiles, lifts his unfettered hands to heaven:                     215
'You everlasting fires,' he cries, 'and your
inviolable power, be my witness;
you altars, savage swords that I escaped,
you garlands of the gods I wore as victim,
it now is right for me to break the holy                             220
oath of my loyalty and right for me
to hate the Greeks, to bring all things to light,
whatever they conceal. I am no longer
bound to obey the laws of my own country.
But, Troy, you must hold fast what you have promised;                225
preserved, preserve your word to me, if now
I tell the truth and so repay you fully.

" 'The only hope and confidence the Danaans
had ever had in undertaking war
lay in the help of Pallas. But in fact,                              230
since that time when the godless Diomedes,
the son of Tydeus, first went with Ulysses,
inventor of impieties, and tried
to tear down from its sacred shrine the fateful
Palladium, when they cut down the guardians                          235

230. *Pallas*: Minerva (Athena).
235. *Palladium*: A statue of Pallas,
kept in her shrine at Troy. There was an
oracle which stated that Troy could not
be captured as long as it remained in
place.

of that high citadel with ruthless hands,
daring to touch the virgin goddess' garlands—
since then the Danaans' hopes have ebbed away,
receding, falling back; their force is broken;
the mind of Pallas has not turned toward them.     240
The omens of her change were not uncertain.
No sooner was her image in the Grecian
camp site than salt sweat poured across its body
and quivering flames blazed from its staring eyes;
and then, amazingly, three times the goddess     245
herself sprang from the ground with trembling shaft
and shield. And straightway Calchas warns them that
they must try out the seas in flight, that Troy
could never be destroyed by Argive arms
unless fresh auspices were brought from Argos;     250
that would regain the favor of the gods
who first helped bring the curving keels from Greece.
Then with the wind they sought their native land,
Mycenae, to make ready gods and weapons
as their companions, to recross the seas,     255
to come back suddenly. For so had Calchas
interpreted the omens. And he warned them
to build this effigy as their atonement
for the Palladium, to serve as payment
for their outrage against the goddess' image,     260
to expiate so great a sacrilege.
But he instructed them to make this mass
of interwoven timbers so immense
and built it up so high to heaven that
it cannot pass the gate, can never be     265
received within Troy's walls, never protect
the people under its old sanctity.
For if your hands should harm Minerva's gift,
then vast destruction (may the gods turn this
their prophecy against the priest's own lips!)     270
would fall on Priam's kingdom and the Phrygians;
but if it climbed by your hands into Troy,
then Asia would repel the Greeks and, more,
advance in war as far as Pelops' walls;
this is the doom that waits for our descendants.'     275

"Such was the art of perjured Sinon, so
insidious, we trusted what he told.
So we were taken in by snares, forced tears—

---

250. *auspices*: Omens. *Argos*: Greece.     274. *Pelops*: The legendary founder of
258. *this effigy*: The wooden horse.     the dynasty of Agamemnon.

yes, we, whom neither Diomedes nor
Achilles of Larissa could defeat,                                    280
nor ten long years, a thousand-galleyed fleet.

"Now yet another and more dreadful omen
is thrust at us, bewilders our blind hearts.
Laocoön, by lot named priest of Neptune,
was sacrificing then a giant bull                                    285
upon the customary altars, when
two snakes with endless coils, from Tenedos
strike out across the tranquil deep (I shudder
to tell what happened), resting on the waters,
advancing shoreward side by side; their breasts                      290
erect among the waves, their blood-red crests
are higher than the breakers. And behind,
the rest of them skims on along the sea;
their mighty backs are curved in folds. The foaming
salt surge is roaring. Now they reach the fields.                    295
Their eyes are drenched with blood and fire—they burn.
They lick their hissing jaws with quivering tongues.
We scatter at the sight, our blood is gone.
They strike a straight line toward Laocoön.
At first each snake entwines the tiny bodies                         300
of his two sons in an embrace, then feasts
its fangs on their defenseless limbs. The pair
next seize upon Laocoön himself,
who nears to help his sons, carrying weapons.
They wind around his waist and twice around                          305
his throat. They throttle him with scaly backs;
their heads and steep necks tower over him.
He struggles with his hands to rip their knots,
his headbands soaked in filth and in dark venom,
while he lifts high his hideous cries to heaven,                     310
just like the bellows of a wounded bull
when it has fled the altar, shaking off
an unsure ax. But now the snakes escape:
twin dragons, gliding to the citadel
of cruel Pallas, her high shrines. They hide                         315
beneath the goddess' feet, beneath her shield.

"At this, a stranger terror takes its way
through every trembling heart. Laocoön
has justly paid the penalty—they say—
for outrage, since his spearhead had profaned                        320

280. *Larissa*: A city in Thessaly, the homeland of Achilles.

the sacred oak, his cursed shaft been cast
against the horse's back. Their cry is that
the image must be taken to the temple,
the favor of the goddess must be sought.

"We break the walls and bare the battlements.          325
We set to work; beneath the horse's feet
we fasten sliding wheels; about its neck
we stretch out ropes of hemp. And fat with weapons,
the engine of our fate climbs up the rampart.
And boys and unwed girls surround it, singing          330
their sacred chants, so glad to touch the cable.
The horse glides, menacing, advancing toward
the center of the city. O my land,
o Ilium, the home of gods and Dardan
walls long renowned in war, four times it stalled      335
before the gateway, at the very threshold;
four times the arms clashed loud inside its belly.
Nevertheless, heedless, blinded by frenzy,
we press right on and set the inauspicious
monster inside the sacred fortress. Even               340
then can Cassandra chant of what will come
with lips the gods had doomed to disbelief
by Trojans. That day was our last—and yet,
helpless, we crown the altars of the gods
with festive branches all about the city.              345

"Meanwhile the heavens wheel, night hurries from
Ocean and clothes within its giant shadow
the earth, the sky, the snares of Myrmidons.
The silent Trojans lie within their city
as sleep embraces their exhausted bodies.              350

"And now from Tenedos the Argive army
were moving in their marshaled ships, beneath
the friendly silence of the tranquil moon,
seeking familiar shores. The royal galley
has signaled with its beacon torches; Sinon,           355
shielded by the unkindly destinies
of gods, can secretly set free the Danaans
out of the monster's womb, the pinewood prison.
The horse, thrown open, gives them back to air.
They exit gladly from the hollow timber:               360

341. *Cassandra*: Daughter of Priam,    demned never to be believed.
endowed with prophetic powers but con-   334. *Ilium*: Troy.

Thessandrus, Sthenelus, the captains; fierce
Ulysses, gliding down the lowered rope;
and Thoas, Acamas, and then the grandson
of Peleus, Neoptolemus; the chieftain
Machaon, Menelaus, then Epeos,                                    365
the very maker of the stratagem.
They fall upon the city buried deep
in wine and sleep. The guards cut down, the gates
thrown open, they can welcome their companions
and gather the conspirators in one.                              370

"It was the hour when for troubled mortals
rest—sweetest gift of gods that glides to men—
has just begun. Within my sleep, before
my eyes there seemed to stand, in tears and sorrow,
Hector as once he was, dismembered by                            375
the dragging chariot, black with bloodied dust;
his swollen feet were pierced by thongs. Oh this
was Hector, and how different he was
from Hector back from battle, putting on
Achilles' spoils, or Hector when he flung                        380
his Phrygian firebrands at Dardan prows!
His beard unkempt, his hair was thick with blood,
he bore the many wounds he had received
around his homeland's walls. And I myself
seemed then to weep, to greet him with sad words:                385
'O light of Troy, o Trojans' trusted hope!
What long delay has held you back? From what
seashores, awaited Hector, have you come?
For, weary with the many deaths of friends,
the sorrows of your men, your city, how                          390
our eyes hold fast to you! What shameful cause
defaced your tranquil image? Why these wounds?'

"He wastes no words, no time on useless questions—
but drawing heavy sighs from deep within,
'Ah, goddess-born, take flight,' he cries, 'and snatch           395
yourself out of these flames. The enemy
has gained the walls; Troy falls from her high peak.
Our home, our Priam—these have had their due:
could Pergamus be saved by any prowess,
then my hand would have served. But Troy entrusts                400

---

364. *Neoptolemus*: Son of Achilles.
380. *Achilles' spoils*: The armor of

Achilles, stripped from the dead Patroklos.

her holy things and household gods to you;
take them away as comrades of your fortunes,
seek out for them the great walls that at last,
once you have crossed the sea, you will establish.'
So Hector speaks; then from the inner altars          405
he carries out the garlands and great Vesta
and, in his hands, the fire that never dies.

"Meanwhile the howls of war confound the city.
And more and more—although my father's house
was far, withdrawn, and screened by trees—the roar    410
is sharper, the dread clash of battle grows.
I start from sleep and climb the sloping roof
above the house. I stand, alerted: just
as when, with furious south winds, a fire
has fallen on a wheat field, or a torrent             415
that hurtles from a mountain stream lays low
the meadows, low the happy crops, and low
the labor of the oxen, dragging forests
headlong—and even then, bewildered and
unknowing, perched upon a rock, the shepherd          420
will listen to the clamor. Now indeed
the truth is plain, the guile of Greece made clear.
The spacious palace of Deiphobus
has fallen, victim of the towering Vulcan.
And now Ucalegon's, his neighbor, burns;              425
and wide Sigeum's harbor gleams with fire.
The cries of men are high, the trumpets clang.

"Insane, I seize my weapons. There's no sense
in weapons, yet my spirit burns to gather
a band for battle, to rush out against                430
the citadel with my companions. Rage
and anger drive my mind. My only thought:
how fine a thing it is to die in arms.

"But Panthus, slipping past the Grecian swords—
Panthus, the son of Othrys, priest of Phoebus         435
within the citadel—now rushes toward
my threshold, madly; in his hand he carries

401. *household gods*: The *Penates*, gods of the inner house, whose images were kept in a household shrine. *Vesta* was the goddess of the hearth and fire which, in the temple, was never allowed to go out.

423. *Deiphobus*: A son of Priam.
424. *Vulcan*: (Hephaistos), god of fire and craftsmanship; here, simply, fire.
426. *Sigeum*: A promontory overlooking the straits which connect the Aegean with the Black Sea.

the holy vessels and defeated gods.
He drags his tiny grandson. 'Panthus, where's
the crucial struggle? Where are we to stand?'                    440
My words are hardly done when, with a groan,
he answers: 'It has come—the final day
and Troy's inevitable time. We Trojans
were; Troy has been; gone is the giant glory
of Teucrians: ferocious Jupiter                                  445
has taken all to Argos. And the city
now burns beneath its Danaan overlords.
The horse stands high within the heart of Troy
and it pours out armed men. The mocking Sinon,
now he has won, is scattering firebrands.                        450
Some crowd the open gates—as many thousands
as ever came from great Mycenae; others
have blocked the narrow streets with ready blades;
the sword edge stands, unsheathed, its gleaming point
is set for slaughter; at the forward line                        455
the guards can scarcely stand; they battle blind.'

"The words of Panthus and the will of gods,
these carry me into the flames and weapons,
where bitter Fury, where the roar and cries
that climb the skies call out. And in the moonlight             460
I now am met by comrades: Epytus,
great warrior, and Ripheus come to join us;
to march beside us, Hypanis and Dymas
and then the young Coroebus, son of Mygdon.
For in those days he chanced to come to Troy,                    465
insane with love for his Cassandra, bringing
his help, as son-in-law, to Priam and
the Phrygians—sad Coroebus, would he had
heeded the warnings of his frantic bride!

---

"And when I saw them hot again for battle,                       470
in tight ranks, I began: 'Young men, your hearts
are sturdy—but for nothing; if you want
to follow me into my last attempt,
you see what fortune watches us. For all
the gods on whom this kingdom stood have quit                    475
our shrines and altars, gone away. The city
that you would help is now in flames. Then let
us rush to arms and die. The lost have only
this one deliverance: to hope for none.'

"So were these young men's spirits spurred to fury.            480
Then—just as plundering wolves in a black fog,
when driven blindly by their belly's endless
frenzy, for they have left behind their cubs
to wait with thirsty jaws—through enemies,
through swords we pass to certain death; we make            485
our way into the heart of Troy; around us
the black night hovers with its hollow shade.

"Who has the words to tell that night's disaster?
And who to tell the deaths? What tears could equal
our agony? An ancient city falls            490
that ruled for many years; through streets and houses
and on the sacred threshold of the gods
so many silent bodies lie about.
Nor are the Teucrians the only ones
to pay the penalty of blood: at times            495
new courage comes to beaten hearts, and then
the Danaan victors die; and everywhere
are fear, harsh grief, and many shapes of slaughter.

"The first to face us is Androgeos,
surrounded by a mighty mob of Greeks.            500
In ignorance, he thinks us fellow troops
and welcomes us at once with friendly words:
'But hurry, men! What laziness has kept
you back? The others are at sack and plunder
in burning Pergamus. Have you just come            505
from your tall ships?' He spoke and knew at once—
for he received no sure reply from us—
that he was in the hands of enemies.
He drew back, dazed. He checked his step and voice.
Even as one who works his way along            510
the ground through tangled briers when, unawares,
he treads upon a serpent and recoils
in terror, suddenly, as it ignites
in anger, puffing up its azure neck:
just so, on seeing us, Androgeos trembled,            515
trying to make his quick escape. We rush
to ring the Greeks, our weapons thick; we kill
on every side. They do not know the ground
and panic overcomes them. Fortune smiles
on our first trial. And here Coroebus, glad            520
at our success and spirits, cries: 'My comrades,
where Fortune first points out the path of safety,

where first she shows herself auspicious, there
must be the way to follow: let us change
our shields, take Danaan armor for ourselves.                    525
If that be guile or valor—who would ask
in war? Our enemies will give us weapons.'

"Theses were Coroebus' words. Then he puts on
Androgeos' crested helmet and his shield
with handsome emblem, fastening to his thigh                     530
the Argive sword. So Dymas does and Ripheus
and the excited youths: each arms himself
with these new spoils. We move ahead, to mingle
with Argives under auspices not ours.
Through that long night we clash in many combats,               535
and we send many Danaans down to Orcus.
Some scatter to the ships, to seek the shore
of safety; some in their low fear climb back
to the familiar belly of the horse.

"But oh, it is not right for anyone                              540
to trust reluctant gods! For there the virgin
Cassandra, Priam's daughter, hair disheveled,
was dragged out from the temple, from Minerva's
shrine, and her eyes were raised in vain to heaven—
her eyes, for chains held fast her gentle hands.                545
Coroebus, maddened, could not stand the sight.
He threw himself, about to die, against
the very center of the Grecian line.
We follow close behind him, charging thick.
Here, from the shrine's high roof, we are struck down            550
for the first time by our own Trojan weapons:
the image of our arms, the error of
our Danaan helmets, starts a wretched slaughter.
But then the Grecians groan with indignation
because the virgin is rescued. From all sides                   555
they muster to attack us: Ajax most
ferociously, and both of Atreus' sons,
and all the army of Dolopians:
as, when a hurricane has burst, the crosswinds
will clash together—West and South and East,                   560
exulting in his oriental steeds—
the woods are shrill, and foam-washed Nereus rages,

---

536. *Orcus*: The abode of the dead.
546. *Coroebus*: He had been in love
with Cassandra.
556. *Ajax*: Not the great Ajax, son of

Telamon, but the lesser Ajax, son of
Oïleus.
562. *Nereus*: The old man of the sea.

his trident stirs the seas up from their deeps.
And any whom our stratagems had driven
beneath the shades of dark night, whom we had chased          565
across the city, now appear; and first
they recognize our shields, our miming weapons,
then note our speech that does not sound like theirs.
Such numbers overcome us instantly.
Coroebus is the first to fall; he dies                        570
beneath Peneleus' right hand, beside
the altar of the warrior goddess, Pallas.
Then Ripheus, too, has fallen—he was first
among the Teucrians for justice and
observing right; the gods thought otherwise.                  575
Both Hypanis and Dymas perish, pierced
by their own comrades; neither your great goodness,
o Panthus, nor Apollo's garland could
protect you when you fell. O final flames
that take my people, ashes of my Ilium,                       580
be you my witness that, in your disaster,
I did not shun the Danaan blades or battle:
if fate had willed my end, my hand had earned it.
Then we are forced apart. Along with me
go Iphitus and Pelias: one was                                585
already slow with his long years, the other,
slow-footed through a wound got from Ulysses.
The clamor calls us on to Priam's palace.

"And here the fight is deadly, just as if
there were no battles elsewhere, just as if                   590
no one were dying now throughout the city;
for here the god of war cannot be tamed.
The Danaans rush the roofs; they storm the threshold
with linked and lifted shields; their ladders hug
the walls—the rungs reach up the very doorposts.             595
Against the darts their left hands thrust their bucklers,
and with their right, they clutch the battlements.
In turn the Trojans tear down roofs and towers
to fling as missiles; they can see the end
is near, but even at death's point they still                 600
prepare defense. They roll down gilded rafters,
our ancient fathers' splendors; while below,
the others block the gates with naked blades.
They guard in tight array. Made new again,
our spirits rush relief to Priam's palace,                    605
help to our men, and fresh force to the beaten.

596. *bucklers*: Shields.

"There was an entry gate with secret doors:
a passageway that ran to Priam's rooms,
a postern at the palace rear; and there,
while Troy still stood, the sad Andromache                      610
would often, unattended, come to see
her husband's parents; there she brought her boy
Astyanax to visit his grandfather.
That is the way I take to reach the ramparts
along the roof; from there the wretched Trojans                 615
fling useless weapons with their hands. And from
the sheer edge of that roof a tower rose,
built starward; it had served as lookout over
all Troy, the Danaan ships, the Grecian camp.
And where the upper stories show loose joints,                  620
there we attack with iron to tug it free,
to wrench it from the top, to thrust it down.
It suddenly collapses; with a crash
it tumbles wide across the Danaan ranks;
its fall is ruinous. But fresh Greeks come;                     625
the stones, the other missiles never stop.

"And then, before the very porch, along
the outer portal Pyrrhus leaps with pride,
his armor glitters with a brazen brilliance
he is like a snake that, fed on poisonous plants                630
and swollen underground all winter, now
his slough cast off, made new and bright with youth,
uncoils his slippery body to the light;
his breast erect, he towers toward the sun;
he flickers from his mouth a three-forked tongue.               635
With Pyrrhus are the giant Periphas
together with Automedon, Achilles'
charioteer and armor-bearer; all
the youths of Scyros now assault the palace;
they fling their firebrands up toward the roof.                 640
Pyrrhus himself, among the first, takes up
a two-edged ax and cracks the stubborn gates.
He rips the bronze-bound portals off their hinges,
cuts through a beam, digs out tough oak: the breach
is vast, a gaping mouth. The inner house                        645
is naked now, the long halls, open; naked,
the private rooms of Priam and the ancient
kings; and the Greeks can see the threshold guards.

609. *postern*: Secret door.
613. *Astyanax*: Son of Hector, grandson of Priam.
628. *Pyrrhus*: Also known as Neoptolemus (the name means New War), the son of Achilles.
639. *Scyros*: The island where Pyrrhus was born, home of the Dolopians.

"But deep within, confusion takes the palace,
anguish and sad commotion; and the vaulted          650
walls echo with the wail and woe of women,
lament that beats against the golden stars.
Across the huge apartments in their terror
the matrons wander, clutching at the doors,
embracing them, imprinting kisses. Pyrrhus,          655
his father's force within him, presses forward—
no barrier, and not the guards themselves,
can hold him off. The gate gives way before
the ram's repeated hammerings; the doors
are severed from their hinges, topple out.          660
Force cracks a breach; the Danaans storm and pour
across the passage, butchering the first
they meet; their soldiers stream across the palace—
less furious than these, the foaming river
when it has burst across resisting banks          665
and boundaries and overflows, its angry
flood piling in a mass along the plains
as it drags flocks and folds across the fields.
And I myself saw Neoptolemus,
insane with blood, and both of Atreus' sons          670
upon the threshold. I saw Hecuba
together with her hundred daughters, and
among the altars I could see King Priam,
polluting with his blood the fires he
himself had hallowed. And the fifty bridal          675
chambers that had such hopes of sons of sons,
the doors that once had stood so proud with booty
and with barbaric gold lie on the ground.
What fire cannot do, the Danaans can.

"Perhaps you now will ask the end of Priam.          680
When he has seen his beaten city ruined—
the wrenching of the gates, the enemy
among his sanctuaries—then in vain
the old man throws his armor, long unused,
across his shoulders, tottering with age;          685
and he girds on his useless sword; about
to die, he hurries toward the crowd of Greeks.

"Beneath the naked round of heaven, at
the center of the palace, stood a giant
shrine; at its side an ancient laurel leaned          690
across the altar stone, and it embraced
the household gods within its shadow. Here,

around that useless altar, Hecuba
together with her daughters—just like doves
when driven headlong by a dark storm—huddled;      695
and they held fast the statues of the gods.
But when she saw her Priam putting on
the armor he had worn when he was young,
she cried: 'Poor husband, what wild thought drives you
to wear these weapons now? Where would you rush?    700
This is no time for such defense and help,
not even were my Hector here himself.
Come near and pray: this altar shall yet save
us all, or you shall die together with us.'
When this was said she took the old man to her    705
and drew him down upon the sacred seat.

"But then Polites, one of Priam's sons
who had escaped from Pyrrhus' slaughter, down
long porticoes, past enemies and arrows,
races, wounded, across the empty courts.    710
But after him, and hot to thrust, is Pyrrhus;
now, even now he clutches, closing in;
he presses with his shaft until at last
Polites falls before his parents' eyes,
within their presence; he pours out his life    715
in streams of blood. Though in the fist of death,
at this, Priam does not spare voice or wrath:
'If there is any goodness in the heavens
to oversee such acts, for this offense
and outrage may you find your fitting thanks    720
and proper payment from the gods, for you
have made me see the murder of my son,
defiled a father's face with death. Achilles—
you lie to call him father—never dealt
with Priam so—and I, his enemy;    725
for he had shame before the claims and trust
that are a suppliant's. He handed back
for burial the bloodless corpse of Hector
and sent me off in safety to my kingdom.'
The old man spoke; his feeble spear flew off—    730
harmless; the hoarse bronze beat it back at once;
it dangled, useless now, from the shield's boss.
And Pyrrhus: 'Carry off these tidings; go
and bring this message to my father, son
of Peleus; and remember, let him know    735
my sorry doings, how degenerate

is Neoptolemus, Now die.' This said,
he dragged him to the very altar stone,
with Priam shuddering and slipping in
the blood that streamed from his own son. And Pyrrhus    740
with his left hand clutched tight the hair of Priam;
his right hand drew his glistening blade, and then
he buried it hilt-high in the king's side.
This was the end of Priam's destinies,
the close that fell to him by fate: to see    745
his Troy in flames and Pergamus laid low—
who once was proud king over many nations
and lands of Asia. Now he lies along
the shore, a giant trunk, his head torn from
his shoulders, as a corpse without a name.    750

"This was the first time savage horror took me.
I was astounded; as I saw the king
gasping his life away beneath a ruthless
wound, there before me rose the effigy
of my dear father, just as old as Priam;    755
before me rose Creüsa, left alone,
my plundered home, the fate of small Iülus.
I look behind and scan the troops around me;
all of my men, worn out, have quit the battle,
have cast their bodies down along the ground    760
or fallen helplessly into the flames.

"And now that I am left alone, I see
the daughter of Tyndareos clinging
to Vesta's thresholds, crouching silently
within a secret corner of the shrine;    765
bright conflagrations give me light as I
wander and let my eyes read everything.
For she, in terror of the Trojans—set
against her for the fall of Pergamus—
and of the Danaans' vengeance and the anger    770
of her abandoned husband; she, the common
Fury of Troy and of her homeland, she
had hid herself; she crouched, a hated thing,
beside the altars. In my mind a fire
is burning; anger spurs me to avenge    775
my falling land, to exact the debt of crime.

756. *Creüsa*: Aeneas' wife.
763. *daughter of Tyndareos*: Helen.
Tyndareos was her mortal father; she
was actually the daughter of Jupiter
(Zeus).

'Is she to have it so: to leave unharmed,
see Sparta and her home Mycenae, go—
a victor queen in triumph—to look on
her house and husband, parents, children, trailing
a train of Trojan girls and Phrygian slaves?
Shall Troy have been destroyed by fire, Priam
been beaten by the blade, the Dardan shore
so often soaked with blood, to this end? No.
For though there is no memorable name
in punishing a woman and no gain
of honor in such victory, yet I
shall have my praise for blotting out a thing
of evil, for my punishing of one
who merits penalties; and it will be
a joy to fill my soul with vengeful fire,
to satisfy the ashes of my people.'

"And carried off by my mad mind, I was
still blurting out these words when, with such brightness
as I had never seen, my gracious mother
stood there before me; and across the night
she gleamed with pure light, unmistaken goddess,
as lovely and as tall as she appears
whenever she is seen by heaven's beings.
And while she caught and held my right hand fast,
she spoke these words to me with her rose lips:
'My son, what bitterness has kindled this
fanatic anger? Why this madness? What
of all your care for me—where has it gone?
Should you not first seek out your father, worn
with years, Anchises, where you left him; see
if your own wife, Creüsa, and the boy
Ascanius are still alive? The Argive
lines ring them all about; and if my care
had not prevented such an end, by now
flames would have swept them off, the hostile sword
have drunk their blood. And those to blame are not
the hated face of the Laconian woman,
the daughter of Tyndareos, or Paris:
It is the gods' relentlessness, the gods',
that overturns these riches, tumbles Troy
from its high pinnacle. Look now—for I
shall tear away each cloud that cloaks your eyes

780

785

790

795

800

805

810

815

---

778. *Sparta*: The place of Helen's birth. *Mycenae*: The city where she had lived with her husband Menelaus. 813. *Laconian*: Spartan.

and clogs your human seeing, darkening
all things with its damp fog: you must not fear          820
the orders of your mother; do not doubt,
but carry out what she commands. For here,
where you see huge blocks ripped apart and stones
torn free from stones and smoke that joins with dust
in surges, Neptune shakes the walls, his giant          825
trident is tearing Troy from its foundations;
and here the first to hold the Scaean gates
is fiercest Juno; girt with iron, she
calls furiously to the fleet for more
Greek troops. Now turn and look: Tritonian Pallas       830
is planted there; upon the tallest towers
she glares with her storm cloud and her grim Gorgon.
And he who furnishes the Greeks with force
that favors and with spirit is the Father
himself, for he himself goads on the gods               835
against the Dardan weapons. Son, be quick
to flee, have done with fighting. I shall never
desert your side until I set you safe
upon your father's threshold.' So she spoke,
then hid herself within the night's thick shadows.      840
Ferocious forms appear—the fearful powers
of gods that are the enemies of Troy.

"At this, indeed, I saw all Ilium
sink down into the fires; Neptune's Troy
is overturned; even as when the woodsmen               845
along a mountaintop are rivals in
their striving to bring down an ancient ash,
hacked at with many blows of iron and ax;
it always threatens falling, nodding with
its trembling leaves and tossing crest until,          850
slowly, slowly, the wounds have won; it gives
one last great groan, then wrenches from the ridges
and crashes into ruin. I go down
and, guided by a god, move on among
the foes and fires; weapons turn aside,                855
the flames retire where I make my way.

827. *Scaean gates*: (Skaian gates), one of the principal entrances to Troy.

830. *Tritonian Pallas*: Minerva (Athena). The significance of the title Tritonian is unknown.

832. *Gorgon*: Monster whose appearance turned men to stone. Athena had a gorgon-face on her shield.

844. *Neptune's Troy*: Although Neptune (Poseidon) is now one of the powers hostile to Troy, he helped to build it.

"But now, when I had reached my father's threshold,
Anchises' ancient house, our home—and I
longed so to carry him to the high mountains
and sought him first—he will not let his life                        860
be drawn out after Troy has fallen, he
will not endure exile; 'You whose lifeblood
is fresh, whose force is still intact and tough,
you hurry your escape; if heaven's lords
had wanted longer life for me, they would                            865
have saved my home. It is enough—and more—
that I have lived beyond one fall and sack
of Troy. Call out your farewell to my body
as it is now, thus laid out, thus; and then
be gone. I shall find death by my own hand;                          870
the enemy will pity me and seek
my spoils. The loss of burial is easy.
For hated by the gods and useless, I
have lingered out my years too long already,
since that time when the father of the High Ones                     875
and king of men let fly his thunderbolt
against me with the winds, touched me with lightning.'

"These were the words he used. He did not move.
We stood in tears—my wife, Creüsa, and
Ascanius and all the household—begging                               880
my father not to bring down everything
along with him and make our fate more heavy.
He will not have it. What he wants is set;
he will not leave his place. Again I take
to arms and, miserable, long for death.                              885
What other stratagem or chance is left?
And then I ask: 'My father, had you thought
I could go off and leave you here? Could such
unholiness fall from a father's lips?
For if it please the High Ones that no thing                         890
be left of this great city, if your purpose
must still persist, if you want so to add
yourself and yours to Ilium's destruction—
why then, the door to death is open: Pyrrhus—
who massacres the son before his father's                            895
eyes, and then kills the father at the altars—
still hot from Priam's blood, will soon be here.
And was it, then, for this, my gracious mother,

867. *one fall and sack*: Troy had been
sacked once before, by Hercules (Herakles).
876. *thunderbolt*: Anchises was punished by Jupiter for being the lover of
the goddess Venus. The thunderbolt
lamed him.

that you have saved me from the blade, the fire—
that I might see the enemy within                                           900
the heart of home, my son Ascanius,
my father and Creüsa at their side,
all butchered in each other's blood? My men,
bring arms; the last light calls upon the beaten.
Let be, and let me at the Greeks again,                                     905
to make my way back to new battles. Never
shall we all die this day without revenge.'

"At that I girded on my sword again
and fixed it firm, passing my left hand through
my shield strap as I hurried from the house,                              910
But suddenly Creüsa held me fast
beside the threshold; clinging to my feet,
she lifted young Iülus to his father:
"If you go off to die, then take us, too,
to face all things with you, but if your past                            915
still lets you put your hope in arms, which now
you have put on, then first protect this house.
To whom is young Iülus left, to whom
your father and myself, once called your wife?'

"So did Creüsa cry; her wailing filled                                    920
my father's house. But even then there comes
a sudden omen—wonderful to tell:
between the hands, before the faces of
his grieving parents, over Iülus' head
there leaps a lithe flametip that seems to shed                          925
a radiance; the tongue of fire flickers,
harmless, and plays about his soft hair, grazes
his temples. Shuddering in our alarm,
we rush to shake the flames out of his hair
and quench the holy fire with water. But                                  930
Anchises raised his glad eyes to the stars
and lifted heavenward his voice and hands:
'O Jupiter, all-able one, if you
are moved by any prayers, look on us.
I only ask you this: if by our goodness                                   935
we merit it, then, Father, grant to us
your help and let your sign confirm these omens.'

"No sooner had the old man spoken so
than sudden thunder crashed upon the left,
and through the shadows ran a shooting star,                              940
its trail a torch of flooding light. It glides

above the highest housetops as we watch,
until the brightness that has marked its course
is buried in the woods of Ida: far
and wide the long wake of that furrow shines,                    945
and sulfur smokes upon the land. At last,
won over by this sign, my father rises,
to greet the gods, to adore the sacred star:
'Now my delay is done; I follow; where
you lead, I am. Gods of my homeland, save                        950
my household, save my grandson. Yours, this omen;
and Troy is in your keeping. Yes, I yield.
My son, I go with you as your companion.'

"These were his words. But now the fire roars
across the walls; the tide of flame flows nearer.                955
'Come then, dear father, mount upon my neck;
I'll bear you on my shoulders. That is not
too much for me. Whatever waits for us,
we both shall share one danger, one salvation.
Let young Iülus come with me, and let                            960
my wife Creüsa follow at a distance.
And servants, listen well to what I say:
along the way, just past the city walls,
in an abandoned spot there is a mound,
an ancient shrine of Ceres; and nearby                           965
an ancient cypress stands, one that our fathers'
devotion kept alive for many years.
From different directions, we shall meet
at this one point. My father, you will carry
the holy vessels and our homeland's gods.                        970
Filthy with war, just come from slaughter, I
must never touch these sacred things until
I bathe myself within a running stream.'

"This said, I spread a tawny lion skin
across my bent neck, over my broad shoulders,                    975
and then take up Anchises; small Iülus
now clutches my right hand; his steps uneven,
he is following his father; and my wife
moves on behind. We journey through dark places;
and I, who just before could not be stirred                      980
by any weapons cast at me or by
the crowds of Greeks in charging columns, now

944. *Ida*: The great mountain range    965. *Ceres*: (Demeter) goddess of
near Troy.                              grain crops.

am terrified by all the breezes, startled
by every sound, in fear for son and father.

"And now, as I approached the gates and thought          985
I had found the way of my escape, the sudden
and frequent tramp of feet was at my ears;
and peering through the shades, Anchises cries:
'My son, take flight; my son, they are upon us.
I see their gleaming shields, the flashing bronze.'          990
At this alarm I panicked: some unfriendly
god's power ripped away my tangled mind.
For while I take a trackless path, deserting
the customary roads, fate tears from me
my wife Creüsa in my misery.                                       995
I cannot say if she had halted or
had wandered off the road or slumped down, weary.
My eyes have never had her back again.
I did not look behind for her, astray,
or think of her before we reached the mound          1000
and ancient, sacred shrine of Ceres; here
at last, when all were gathered, she alone
was missing—gone from husband, son, companions.

---

"What men, what gods did I in madness not
accuse? Did I see anything more cruel          1005
within the fallen city? I commit
Ascanius, Anchises, and the gods
of Troy to my companions, hiding them
inside a winding valley. I myself
again seek out the city, girding on          1010
my gleaming arms. I want to meet all risks
again, return through all of Troy, again
give back my life to danger. First I seek
the city walls, the gateway's shadowed thresholds
through which I had come before. And I retrace          1015
my footsteps; through the night I make them out.
My spirit is held by horror everywhere;
even the very silence terrifies.
Then I move homeward—if by chance, by chance,
she may have made her way there. But the Danaans          1020
had flooded in and held the house. At once
the hungry conflagration rolls before
the wind, high as the highest rooftop; flames
are towering overhead, the boiling tide

is raging to the heavens. I go on;                                    1025
again I see the house of Priam and
the fortress. Down the empty porticoes,
in Juno's sanctuary, I can see
both Phoenix and the fierce Ulysses, chosen
as guardians, at watch over the booty.                                1030
And here, from every quarter, heaped together,
are Trojan treasures torn from burning altars—
the tables of the gods, and plundered garments,
and bowls of solid gold; and Trojan boys
and trembling women stand in a long line.                             1035

"And more, I even dared to cast my cries
across the shadows; in my sorrow, I—
again, again, in vain—called for Creüsa;
my shouting filled the streets. But as I rushed
and raged among the houses endlessly,                                 1040
before my eyes there stood the effigy
and grieving shade of my Creüsa, image
far larger than the real. I was dismayed;
my hair stood stiff, my voice held fast within
my jaws. She spoke; her words undid my cares:                         1045

---

" 'O my sweet husband, is there any use
in giving way to such fanatic sorrow?
For this could never come to pass without
the gods' decree; and you are not to carry
Creüsa as your comrade, since the king                                1050
of high Olympus does not grant you that.
Along your way lie long exile, vast plains
of sea that you must plow; but you will reach
Hesperia, where Lydian Tiber flows,
a tranquil stream, through farmer's fruitful fields.                  1055
There days of gladness lie in wait for you:
a kingdom and a royal bride. Enough
of tears for loved Creüsa. I am not
to see the haughty homes of Myrmidons
or of Dolopians, or be a slave                                        1060
to Grecian matrons—I, a Dardan woman
and wife of Venus' son. It is the gods'

---

1029. *Phoenix*: (Phoinix), formerly tutor of Achilles.
1054. *Lydian*: The Tiber was the center of many Etruscan settlements and the Etruscans were supposed to be immi-grants from Lydia, in Asia Minor.
1062–1063. *the gods' great Mother*: Cybele, an Asiatic mother-goddess worshipped (according to Virgil) at Troy.

great Mother who keeps me upon these shores.
And now farewell, and love the son we share.'

"When she was done with words—I weeping and     1065
wanting to say so many things—she left
and vanished in transparent air. Three times
I tried to throw my arms around her neck;
three times the Shade I grasped in vain escaped
my hands—like fleet winds, most like a winged dream.    1070

"And so at last, when night has passed, I go
again to my companions. Here I find,
to my surprise, new comrades come together,
vast numbers, men and women, joined for exile,
a crowd of sorrow. Come from every side,    1075
with courage and with riches, they are ready
for any lands across the seas where I
may lead them. Now the star of morning rose
above high Ida's ridges, guiding the day.
The Danaans held the gates' blockaded thresholds.    1080
There was no hope of help. Then I gave way
and, lifting up my father, made for the mountains."

[Aeneas goes on to tell the story of his wanderings in search of a
new home. By the end of the evening, Dido, already falling in love
with him before the banquet (through the intervention of Venus
and Juno, who both promote the affair, each for different reasons),
now feels the full force of her passion for Aeneas.]

### Book IV

#### [Aeneas Abandons Dido]

Too late. The queen is caught between love's pain
and press. She feels the wound within her veins;
she is eaten by a secret flame. Aeneas'
high name, all he has done, again, again
come like a flood. His face, his words hold fast    5
her breast. Care strips her limbs of calm and rest.

A new dawn lights the earth with Phoebus' lamp
and banishes damp shadows from the sky
when restless Dido turns to her heart's sharer:
"Anna, my sister, what dreams make me shudder?    10
Who is this stranger guest come to our house?
How confident he looks, how strong his chest

and arms! I think—and I have cause—that he
is born of gods. For in the face of fear
the mean must fall. What fates have driven him!     15
What trying wars he lived to tell! Were it not
my sure, immovable decision not
to marry anyone since my first love
turned traitor, when he cheated me by death,
were I not weary of the couch and torch,     20
I might perhaps give way to this one fault.
For I must tell you, Anna, since the time
Sychaeus, my poor husband, died and my
own brother splashed our household gods with blood,
Aeneas is the only man to move     25
my feelings, to overturn my shifting heart.
I know too well the signs of the old flame.
But I should call upon the earth to gape
and close above me, or on the almighty
Father to take his thunderbolt, to hurl     30
me down into the shades, the pallid shadows
and deepest night of Erebus, before
I'd violate you, Shame, or break your laws!
For he who first had joined me to himself
has carried off my love, and may he keep it     35
and be its guardian within the grave."
She spoke. Her breast became a well of tears.

And Anna answers: "Sister, you more dear
to me than light itself, are you to lose
all of your youth in dreary loneliness,     40
and never know sweet children or the soft
rewards of Venus? Do you think that ashes
or buried Shades will care about such matters?
Until Aeneas came, there was no suitor
who moved your sad heart—not in Libya nor,     45
before, in Tyre: you always scorned Iarbas
and all the other chiefs that Africa,
a region rich in triumphs, had to offer.
How can you struggle now against a love
that is so acceptable? Have you forgotten     50
the land you settled, those who hem you in?
On one side lie the towns of the Gaetulians,

18. *first love*: Her first husband, Sychaeus, was murdered by Pygmalion, king of Tyre, Dido's brother. Her husband's ghost warned her in a dream to leave Tyre and seek a new home.

20. *couch and torch*: Marriage. In the Roman ceremony the bride was taken to her home in a torch-lit procession.

33. *Erebus*: The darkest region of the underworld.

46. *Iarbas*: The most prominent of Dido's African suitors.

52. *Gaetulians*: A savage African people living southwest of Carthage.

a race invincible, and the unbridled
Numidians and then the barbarous Syrtis.
And on the other lies a barren country, 55
stripped by the drought and by Barcaean raiders,
raging both far and near. And I need not
remind you of the wars that boil in Tyre
and of your brother's menaces and plots.
For I am sure it was the work of gods 60
and Juno that has held the Trojan galleys
fast to their course and brought them here to Carthage.
If you marry Aeneas, what a city
and what a kingdom, sister, you will see!
With Trojan arms beside us, so much greatness 65
must lie in wait for Punic glory! Only
pray to the gods for their good will, and having
presented them with proper sacrifices,
be lavish with your Trojan guests and weave
excuses for delay while frenzied winter 70
storms out across the sea and shatters ships,
while wet Orion blows his tempest squalls
beneath a sky that is intractable."

These words of Anna fed the fire in Dido.
Hope burned away her doubt, destroyed her shame. 75
First they move on from shrine to shrine, imploring
the favor of the gods at every altar.
They slaughter chosen sheep, as is the custom,
and offer them to Ceres the lawgiver,
to Phoebus, Father Bacchus, and—above all— 80
to Juno, guardian of marriage. Lovely
Dido holds the cup in her right hand;
she pours the offering herself, midway
between a milk-white heifer's horns. She studies
slit breasts of beasts and reads their throbbing guts. 85
But oh the ignorance of augurs! How
can vows and altars help one wild with love?

54. *Numidians*: The most powerful of
the local tribes. *Syrtis*: On the coast to
the west.
56. *Barcaean raiders*: To the east.
67. *Punic*: Carthaginian.
79. *Ceres*: Called 'lawgiver' because
her gift of agriculture enabled men to
live in settled communities. The goddess
of the crops. Ceres, the Wine-god, and
Phoebus Apollo are selected as deities
especially connected with the founding of
cities; one of Apollo's titles is "Founder," and Ceres and Dionysus (Bacchus)
control the essential crops which will enable the colonists to live. Dido prays to
these gods at the moment when she is
about to abandon her responsibilities as
founder of a city; a similar irony is present in her prayer to Juno, whose "business" is the marriage-bond, at the moment when she is about to break her
long fidelity to the memory of Sychaeus.
84–86. Dido uses the Roman (Etruscan) method of *augury*—looking for
signs of the future in the color and disposition of the entrails of a sacrifical animal.

Meanwhile the supple flame devours her marrow;
within her breast the silent wound lives on.
Unhappy Dido burns. Across the city                        90
she wanders in her frenzy—even as
a heedless hind hit by an arrow when
a shepherd drives for game with darts among
the Cretan woods and, unawares, from far
leaves winging steel inside her flesh; she roams           95
the forests and the wooded slopes of Dicte,
the shaft of death still clinging to her side.
So Dido leads Aeneas around the ramparts,
displays the wealth of Sidon and the city
ready to hand; she starts to speak, then falters          100
and stops in midspeech. Now day glides away.
Again, insane, she seeks out that same banquet,
again she prays to hear the trials of Troy,
again she hangs upon the teller's lips.

But now the guests are gone. The darkened moon,           105
in turn, conceals its light, the seeing stars
invite to sleep; inside the vacant hall
she grieves alone and falls upon the couch
that he has left. Absent, she sees, she hears
the absent one or draws Ascanius,                          110
his son and counterfeit, into her arms,
as if his shape might cheat her untellable love.

Her towers rise no more; ,the young of Carthage
no longer exercise at arms or build
their harbors or sure battlements for war;                115
the works are idle, broken off; the massive,
menacing rampart walls, even the crane,
defier of the sky, now lie neglected.

\* \* \*

[Juno proposes to Venus that Dido and Aeneas be married,
which would guarantee the unity of Carthage and Troy and peace
between Juno and Venus. Her aim is of course to ensure that the
imperial destiny reserved for Rome be transferred to Carthage.
Venus, confident of the future, which has been explained to her by
Jupiter, consents to the scheme. Dido organizes a hunt, which is
broken up by a storm, and Dido and Aeneas take shelter in a cave,
where their love is consummated. There is no formal marriage, but

96. *Dicte*: A mountain range in Crete.

Dido henceforth feels justified in assuming the dignity and rights of
a wife. Their love is rumored abroad, and when the African prince
Iarbas hears of it, he appeals to Jupiter for satisfaction.]

And as he prayed and clutched the altar stone,
all-able Jupiter heard him and turned
his eyes upon the royal walls, upon                                    295
the lovers who had forgotten their good name.
He speaks to Mercury, commanding him:
"Be on your way, my son, call up the Zephyrs,
glide on your wings, speak to the Dardan chieftain
who lingers now at Tyrian Carthage, paying                             300
not one jot of attention to the cities
the Fates have given him. Mercury, carry
across the speeding winds the words I urge:
his lovely mother did not promise such
a son to us; she did not save him twice                                305
from Grecian arms for this—but to be master
of Italy, a land that teems with empire
and seethes with war; to father a race from Teucer's
high blood, to place all earth beneath his laws.
But if the brightness of such deeds is not                             310
enough to kindle him, if he cannot
attempt the task for his own fame, does he—
a father—grudge Ascanius the walls
of Rome? What is he pondering, what hope
can hold him here among his enemies,                                    315
not caring for his own Ausonian sons
or for Lavinian fields. He must set sail.
And this is all; my message lies in this."

His words were ended. Mercury made ready
to follow his great father's orders. First                             320
he laces on his golden sandals: winged
to bear him, swift as whirlwinds, high across
the land and water. Then he takes his wand;
with this he calls pale spirits up from Orcus
and down to dreary Tartarus sends others;                              325
he uses this to give sleep and recall it,
and to unseal the eyes of those who have died.
His trust in this, he spurs the winds and skims
the troubled clouds. And now in flight, he sights

297. *Mercury*: The Latin equivalent of
the Greek Hermes, the divine messenger.
308. *Teucer*: The ancestral Trojan
king.
316. *Ausonian*: Italian. The Ausonians
were aboriginal inhabitants of southern
Italy.
325. *Tartarus*: The place of punishment of the wicked in the lower world.

the summit and high sides of hardy Atlas     330
who props up heaven with his crest—Atlas,
whose head is crowned with pines and battered by
the wind and rain and always girdled by
black clouds; his shoulders' cloak is falling snow;
above the old man's chin the rivers rush;     335
his bristling beard is stiff with ice. Here first
Cyllene's god poised on his even wings
and halted; then he hurled himself headlong
and seaward with his body, like a bird
that, over shores and reefs where fishes throng,     340
swoops low along the surface of the waters.
Not unlike this, Cyllene's god between
the earth and heaven as he flies, cleaving
the sandy shore of Libya from the winds
that sweep from Atlas, father of his mother.     345

As soon as his winged feet have touched the outskirts,
he sees Aeneas founding fortresses
and fashioning new houses. And his sword
was starred with tawny jasper, and the cloak
that draped his shoulders blazed with Tyrian purple—     350
a gift that wealthy Dido wove for him;
she had run golden thread along the web.
And Mercury attacks at once. "Are you
now laying the foundation of high Carthage,
as servant to a woman, building her     355
a splendid city here? Are you forgetful
of what is your own kingdom, your own fate?
The very god of gods, whose power sways
both earth and heaven, sends me down to you
from bright Olympus. He himself has asked me     360
to carry these commands through the swift air:
what are you pondering or hoping for
while squandering your ease in Libyan lands?
For if the brightness of such deeds is not
enough to kindle you—if you cannot     365
attempt the task for your own fame—remember
Ascanius growing up, the hopes you hold
for Iülus, your own heir, to whom are owed
the realm of Italy and land of Rome."

330. Atlas: Mountain range in western North Africa. Atlas is described in human terms because of the legend that he was one of the Titans who rebelled against Jupiter and was condemned to hold up the sky on his shoulders.

337. Cyllene: A mountain in Arcadia, The birthplace of Hermes (Mercury).
345. his mother: The nymph Maia.
360. Olympus: The mountain in Greece believed to be the abode of the gods.

So did Cyllene's god speak out. He left                                370
the sight of mortals even as he spoke
and vanished into the transparent air.

This vision stunned Aeneas, struck him dumb;
his terror held his hair erect; his voice
held fast within his jaws. He burns to flee              375
from Carthage; he would quit these pleasant lands,
astonished by such warnings, the command
of gods. What can he do? With what words dare
he face the frenzied queen? What openings
can he employ? His wits are split, they shift            380
here, there; they race to different places, turning
to everything. But as he hesitated,
this seemed the better plan: he calls Sergestus
and Mnestheus and the strong Serestus, and
he asks them to equip the fleet in silence,              385
to muster their companions on the shore,
to ready all their arms, but to conceal
the reasons for this change; while he himself—
with gracious Dido still aware of nothing
and never dreaming such a love could ever                390
be broken—would try out approaches, seek
the tenderest, most tactful time for speech,
whatever dexterous way might suit his case.
And all are glad. They race to carry out
the orders of Aeneas, his commands.                      395

But Dido—for who can deceive a lover?—
had caught his craftiness; she quickly sensed
what was to come; however safe they seemed,
she feared all things. That same unholy Rumor
brought her these hectic tidings: that the boats         400
were being armed, made fit for voyaging.
Her mind is helpless; raging frantically,
inflamed, she raves throughout the city—just
as a Bacchante when, each second year,
she is startled by the shaking of the sacred            405
emblems, the orgies urge her on, the cry
"o Bacchus" calls to her by night; Cithaeron
incites her with its clamor. And at last
Dido attacks Aeneas with these words:

399. same . . . Rumor: Earlier, Rumor (personified as a semi-divine being) had spread the report of Dido's 'marriage' which had incited Iarbas to make his indignant prayer to Jupiter.

404. Bacchante: A female devotee of the god Dionysus (Bacchus), in an ecstatic trance at the Dionysian festival.
407. Cithaeron: Mountain near Thebes, sacred to Dionysus.

"Deceiver, did you even hope to hide 410
so harsh a crime, to leave this land of mine
without a word? Can nothing hold you back—
neither your love, the hand you pledged, nor even
the cruel death that lies in wait for Dido?
Beneath the winter sky are you preparing 415
a fleet to rush away across the deep
among the north winds, you who have no feeling?
What! Even if you were not seeking out
strange fields and unknown dwellings, even if
your ancient Troy were still erect, would you 420
return to Troy across such stormy seas?
Do you flee me? By tears, by your right hand—
this sorry self is left with nothing else—
by wedding, by the marriage we began,
if I did anything deserving of you 425
or anything of mine was sweet to you,
take pity on a fallen house, put off
your plan, I pray—if there is still place for prayers.
Because of you the tribes of Libya, all
the Nomad princes hate me, even my 430
own Tyrians are hostile; and for you
my honor is gone and that good name that once
was mine, my only claim to reach the stars.
My guest, to whom do you consign this dying
woman? I must say 'guest': this name is all 435
I have of one whom once I called my husband.
Then why do I live on? Until Pygmalion,
my brother, batters down my walls, until
Iarbas the Gaetulian takes me prisoner?
Had I at least before you left conceived 440
a son in me; if there were but a tiny
Aeneas playing by me in the hall,
whose face, in spite of everything, might yet
remind me of you, then indeed I should
not seem so totally abandoned, beaten." 445

Her words were ended. But Aeneas, warned
by Jove, held still his eyes; he struggled, pressed
care back within his breast. With halting words
he answers her at last: "I never shall
deny what you deserve, the kindnesses 450
that you could tell; I never shall regret

413. *hand you pledged*: The handclasp
with which he pledged his love and
which Dido takes as an earnest of marriage.

433. *reach the stars*: I.e., become immortal, in her reputation as a faithful
wife.

remembering Elissa for as long
as I remember my own self, as long
as breath is king over these limbs. I'll speak
brief words that fit the case. I never hoped 455
to hide—do not imagine that—my flight;
I am not furtive. I have never held
the wedding torches as a husband; I
have never entered into such agreements.
If fate had granted me to guide my life 460
by my own auspices and to unravel
my troubles with unhampered will, then I
should cherish first the town of Troy, the sweet
remains of my own people and the tall
rooftops of Priam would remain, my hand 465
would plant again a second Pergamus
for my defeated men. But now Grynean
Apollo's oracles would have me seize
great Italy, the Lycian prophecies
tell me of Italy: there is my love, 470
there is my homeland. If the fortresses
of Carthage and the vision of a city
in Libya can hold you, who are Phoenician,
why, then, begrudge the Trojans' settling on
Ausonian soil? There is no harm: it is 475
right that we, too, seek out a foreign kingdom.
For often as the night conceals the earth
with dew and shadows, often as the stars
ascend, afire, my father's anxious image
approaches me in dreams. Anchises warns 480
and terrifies; I see the wrong I have done
to one so dear, my boy Ascanius,
whom I am cheating of Hesperia,
the fields assigned by fate. And now the gods'
own messenger, sent down by Jove himself— 485
I call as witness both our lives—has brought
his orders through the swift air. My own eyes
have seen the god as he was entering
our walls—in broad daylight. My ears have drunk
his words. No longer set yourself and me 490
afire. Stop your quarrel. It is not
my own free will that leads to Italy."

---

452. *Elissa*: Another name for Dido.
467. *Grynean*: Apollo had a temple at
Gryneum in Asia Minor.
469. *Lycian*: Apollo had another famous oracular shrine at Patara in Lycia
(also in Asia Minor).
480. *Anchises*: The old man had died
in Sicily, just before Aeneas went to
Carthage.

But all the while Aeneas spoke, she stared
askance at him, her glance ran this way, that.
She scans his body with her silent eyes.                              495
The Dido thus, inflamed, denounces him:

"No goddess was your mother, false Aeneas,
and Dardanus no author of your race;
the bristling Caucasus was father to you
on his harsh crags; Hyrcanian tigresses                               500
gave you their teats. And why must I dissemble?
Why hold myself in check? For greater wrongs?
For did Aeneas groan when I was weeping?
Did he once turn his eyes or, overcome,
shed tears or pity me, who was his loved one?                        505
What shall I cry out first? And what shall follow?
No longer now does mighty Juno or
our Father, son of Saturn, watch this earth
with righteous eyes. Nowhere is certain trust.
He was an outcast on the shore, in want.                             510
I took him in and madly let him share
my kingdom; his lost fleet and his companions
I saved from death. Oh I am whirled along
in fire by the Furies! First the augur
Apollo, then the Lycian oracles,                                     515
and now, sent down by Jove himself, the gods'
own herald, carrying his horrid orders.
This seems indeed to be a work for High Ones,
a care that can disturb their calm. I do not
refute your words. I do not keep you back.                           520
Go then, before the winds, to Italy.
Seek out your kingdom overseas; indeed,
if there be pious powers still, I hope
that you will drink your torments to the lees
among sea rocks and, drowning, often cry                             525
the name of Dido. Then, though absent, I
shall hunt you down with blackened firebrands;
and when chill death divides my soul and body,
a Shade, I shall be present everywhere.
Depraved, you then will pay your penalties.                          530
And I shall hear of it, and that report
will come to me below, among the Shadows."

---

498. *Dardanus*: An ancestor of the Trojans.
499. *Caucasus*: A mountain range near the Caspian Sea. It has connotations of outlandishness and of cruelty.

500. *Hyrcanian*: From the same general area as the Caucasus.
519. *calm*: Dido is referring to the Epicurean idea that the gods are unaffected by human events.

Her speech is broken off; heartsick, she shuns
the light of day, deserts his eyes; she turns
away, leaves him in fear and hesitation,                                535
Aeneas longing still to say so much.
As Dido faints, her servants lift her up;
they carry her into her marble chamber;
they lay her body down upon the couch.

But though he longs to soften, soothe her sorrow          540
and turn aside her troubles with sweet words,
though groaning long and shaken in his mind
because of his great love, nevertheless
pious Aeneas carries out the gods'
instructions. Now he turns back to his fleet.                    545

At this the Teucrians indeed fall to.
They launch their tall ships all along the beach;
they set their keels, well-smeared with pitch, afloat.
The crewmen, keen for flight, haul from the forest
boughs not yet stripped of leaves to serve as oars       550
and timbers still untrimmed. And one could see them
as, streaming, they rushed down from all the city:
even as ants, remembering the winter,
when they attack a giant stack of spelt
to store it in their homes; the black file swarms           555
across the fields; they haul their plunder through
the grass on narrow tracks; some strain against
the great grains with their shoulders, heaving hard;
some keep the columns orderly and chide
the loiterers; the whole trail boils with work.               560

What were your feelings, Dido, then? What were
the sighs you uttered at that sight, when far
and wide, from your high citadel, you saw
the beaches boil and turmoil take the waters,
with such a vast uproar before your eyes?                      565
Voracious Love, to what do you not drive
the hearts of men? Again, she must outcry,
again, a suppliant, must plead with him,
must bend her pride to love—and so not die
in vain, and with some way still left untried.                 570

"Anna, you see them swarm across the beaches;
from every reach around they rush to sea:

554. *spelt*: A kind of wheat.

the canvas calls the breezes, and already
the boisterious crewmen crown the sterns with garlands.
But I was able to foresee this sorrow;                           575
therefore I can endure it, sister; yet
in wretchedness I must ask you for this
one service, Anna. Treacherous Aeneas
has honored you alone, confiding even
his secret feelings unto you; and you                            580
alone know all his soft approaches, moods.
My sister, go—to plead with him, to carry
this message to my arrogant enemy.
I never trafficked with the Greeks at Aulis
to root the Trojans out, I never sent                            585
a fleet to Pergamus, never disturbed
his father's ashes or Anchises' Shade,
that now Aeneas should ward off my words
from his hard ears. Where is he hurrying?
If he would only grant his wretched lover                        590
this final gift: to wait for easy sailing
and favoring winds. I now no longer ask
for those old ties of marriage he betrayed,
nor that he lose his kingdom, be deprived
of lovely Latium; I only ask                                     595
for empty time, a rest and truce for all
this frenzy, until fortune teaches me,
defeated, how to sorrow. I ask this—
pity your sister—as a final kindness.
When he has granted it, I shall repay                            600
my debt, and with full interest, by my death."

So Dido pleads, and her poor sister carries
these lamentations, and she brings them back.
For lamentation cannot move Aeneas;
his graciousness toward any plea is gone.                        605
Fate is opposed, the god makes deaf the hero's
kind ears. As when, among the Alps, north winds
will strain against each other to root out
with blasts—now on this side, now that—a stout
oak tree whose wood is full of years; the roar                   610
is shattering, the trunk is shaken, and
high branches scatter on the ground; but it
still grips the rocks; as steeply as it thrusts
its crown into the upper air, so deep
the roots it reaches down to Tartarus:                           615

584. *Aulis*: Greek port from which the fleet departed for Troy.

no less than this, the hero; he is battered
on this side and on that by assiduous words;
he feels care in his mighty chest, and yet
his mind cannot be moved; the tears fall, useless.

Then maddened by the fates, unhappy Dido            620
calls out at last for death; it tires her
to see the curve of heaven. That she may
not weaken in her plan to leave the light,
she sees, while placing offerings on the altars
with burning incense—terrible to tell—            625
the consecrated liquid turning black,
the outpoured wine becoming obscene blood.
But no one learns of this, not even Anna.
And more: inside her palace she had built
a marble temple to her former husband            630
that she held dear and honored wonderfully.
She wreathed that shrine with snow-white fleeces and
holy-day leaves. And when the world was seized
by night, she seemed to hear the voice and words
of her dead husband, calling out to Dido.            635
Alone above the housetops, death its song,
an owl often complains and draws its long
slow call into a wailing lamentation.
More, many prophecies of ancient seers
now terrify her with their awful warnings.            640
And in her dreams it is the fierce Aeneas
himself who drives her to insanity;
she always finds herself alone, abandoned,
and wandering without companions on
an endless journey, seeking out her people,            645
her Tyrians, in a deserted land:
even as Pentheus, when he is seized by frenzy,
sees files of Furies, and a double sun
and double Thebes appear to him; or when
Orestes, son of Agamemnon, driven            650
across the stage, flees from his mother armed

---

633. *holy-day leaves*: Wreaths fit for a festival.

647. *Pentheus*: King of Thebes. He persecuted the worshipers of the new god Dionysus, and imprisoned the god himself. He was later mocked by the god, who inspired him with the Dionysiac spirit (and perhaps with wine) so that he saw double. In this state he was led off to his death on Cithaeron. These events are dramatized in Euripides' play *The Bacchae*. The reference to the Furies in this passage is obscure.

650. *Orestes*: Another reference to Greek tragedy. In the *Choephoroe*, the Aeschylean play which follows immediately on the *Agamemnon*, Orestes kills his mother Clytemnestra, and is pursued by the Furies. In other tragic contexts he is represented as pursued by the ghost of his mother.

with torches and black serpents; on the threshold
the awful goddesses of vengeance squat.

When she had gripped this madness in her mind
and, beaten by her grief, resolved to die,                       655
she plotted with herself the means, the moment.
Her face conceals her meaning; on her brow
she sets serenity, then speaks to Anna:
"My sister, wish me well, for I have found
a way that will restore Aeneas to me                             660
or free me of my love for him. Near by
the bounds of Ocean and the setting sun
lies Ethiopia, the farthest land;
there Atlas, the incomparable, turns
the heavens, studded with their glowing stars,                   665
upon his shoulders. And I have been shown
a priestess from that land—one of the tribe
of the Massylians—who guards the shrine
of the Hesperides; for it was she
who fed the dragon and preserved the holy                        670
branches upon the tree, sprinkling moist honey
and poppy, bringing sleep. She promises
to free, with chant and spell, the minds of those
she favors but sends anguish into others.
And she can stay the waters in the rivers                        675
and turn the stars upon their ways; she moves
the nightly Shades; makes earth quake underfoot
and—you will see—sends ash trees down the mountains.
Dear sister, I can call the gods to witness,
and you and your dear life, that I resort                        680
to magic arts against my will. In secret
build up a pyre within the inner courtyard
beneath the open air, and lay upon it
the weapons of the hero. He, the traitor,
has left them hanging in my wedding chamber.                     685
Take all of his apparel and the bridal
bed where I was undone. You must destroy
all relics of the cursed man, for so
would I, and so the priestess has commanded."
This said, she is silent and her face is pale.                   690
But Anna cannot dream her sister hides
a funeral behind these novel rites;

668. *Massylian*: From an African    Hesperus, in the west, who lived in a
tribe.                               garden which contained golden apples,
669. *Hesperides*: The daughters of  guarded by a serpent.

her mind is far from thinking of such frenzy;
and she fears nothing worse than happened when
Sychaeus died. And so, she does as told.                    695

But when beneath the open sky, inside
the central court, the pyre rises high
and huge, with logs of pine and planks of ilex,
the queen, not ignorant of what is coming,
then wreathes the place with garlands, crowning it          700
with greenery of death; and on the couch
above she sets the clothes Aeneas wore,
the sword he left, and then his effigy.
Before the circling altars the enchantress,
her hair disheveled, stands as she invokes                  705
aloud three hundred gods, especially
Chaos and Erebus and Hecate,
the triple-shaped Diana, three-faced virgin.
And she had also sprinkled waters that
would counterfeit the fountain of Avernus;                  710
she gathered herbs cut down by brazen sickles
beneath the moonlight, juicy with the venom
of black milk; she had also found a love charm
torn from the forehead of a newborn foal
before his mother snatched it. Dido herself—                715
with salt cake in her holy hands, her girdle
unfastened, and one foot free of its sandal,
close by the altars and about to die—
now calls upon the gods and stars, who know
the fates, as witness; then she prays to any                720
power there may be, who is both just and watchful,
who cares for those who love without requital.

---

Night. And across the earth the tired bodies
were tasting tranquil sleep; the woods and savage
waters were resting and the stars had reached               725
the midpoint of their gliding fall—when all
the fields are still, and animals and colored
birds, near and far, that find their home beside
the limpid lakes or haunt the countryside

698. *ilex*: An evergreen oak tree of
Europe.
707. *Erebus*: The lowest depth of the
underworld. *Chaos*: Greek personification of the disorder which preceded the
creation of the universe. *Hecate*: Title of
Diana as goddess of sorcery; she is Hecate, the moon, and Diana the virgin
huntress.
710. *Avernus*: A lake in southern
Italy which was supposed to be the entrance to the lower world.

in bristling thickets, sleep in silent night.       730
But not the sorrowing Phoenician; she
can not submit to sleep, can not admit
dark night into her eyes or breast; her cares
increase; again love rises, surges in her;
she wavers on the giant tide of anger.       735
She will not let things rest but carries on;
she still revolves these thoughts within her heart:
"What can I do? Shall I, whom he has mocked,
go back again to my old suitors, begging,
seeking a wedding with Numidians whom       740
I have already often scorned as bridegrooms?
Or should I sail away on Trojan ships,
to suffer there even their harshest orders?
Shall I do so because the Trojans once
received my help, and gratefulness for such       745
old service is remembered by the mindful?
But even if I wish it, would they welcome
someone so hated to their haughty ships?
For, lost one, do you not yet know, not feel
the treason of the breed of Laomedon?       750
What then? Shall I accompany, alone,
the exultant sailors in their flight? Or call
on all my Tyrians, on all my troops
to rush upon them? How can I urge on
those I once dragged from Sidon, how can I       755
now force them back again upon the sea
and have them spread their canvas to the winds?
No; die as you deserve, and set aside
your sorrow by the sword. My sister, you,
won over by my tears—you were the first       760
to weigh me down with evils in my frenzy,
to drive me toward my enemy. And why
was it not given me to lead a guiltless
life, never knowing marriage, like a wild
beast, never to have touched such toils? I have not       765
held fast the faith I swore before the ashes
of my Sychaeus." This was her lament.

Aeneas on the high stern now was set
to leave; he tasted sleep; all things were ready.
And in his sleep a vision of the god       770
returned to him with that same countenance—

---

750. *Laomedon*: A king of Troy who       cles and once to Apollo and Poseidon.
twice broke his promise, once to Hera-

resembling Mercury in everything:
his voice and coloring and yellow hair
and all his handsome body, a young man's—
and seemed to bring a warning once again:                    775
"You, goddess-born, how can you lie asleep
at such a crisis? Madman, can't you see
the threats around you, can't you hear the breath
of kind west winds? She conjures injuries
and awful crimes, she means to die, she stirs         780
the shifting surge of restless anger. Why
not flee this land headlong, while there is time?
You soon will see the waters churned by wreckage,
ferocious torches blaze, and beaches flame,
if morning finds you lingering on this coast.          785
Be on your way. Enough delays. An ever
uncertain and inconsistent thing is woman."
This said, he was at one with the black night.

The sudden apparition terrifies
Aeneas. And he tears his body free                      790
from sleep. He stirs his crewmen: "Quick! Awake!
Now man the benches, comrades, now unfurl
our sails with speed! Down from the upper air
a god was sent to urge us on again,
to rush our flight, to slice our twisted cables.       795
O holy one among the gods, we follow
your way, whoever you may be; again
rejoicing, we shall do as you command.
Be present, help us with your kindness, bring
your gracious constellations to the heavens."          800
He spoke; and from his scabbard snatches up
his glowing sword; with drawn blade, strikes the hawsers.
And all are just as eager, hurrying
to leave the shore; the ships conceal the sea.
They strain to churn the foam and sweep blue waters.   805

---

Now early Dawn had left Tithonus' saffron
bed, scattering new light upon the earth.
As soon as from her lookout on the tower
the queen could see the morning whitening,
the fleet move on with level sails, the shores         810
and harbors now abandoned, without oarsmen,

800. *gracious constellations* . . . ; I.e.,
give us good sailing weather.
802. *hawsers*: Mooring lines.

806. *Dawn*: Aurora, the dawn goddess, was married to a mortal, Tithonus.

she beat against her lovely breast three times,
then four, and tore her golden hair, and cried:
"O Jupiter, you let him go, a stranger
who mocked our kingdom! Will my men not ready    815
their weapons, hunt him down, pour from my city
and rip the galleys from their moorings? Quick!
Bring torches, spread your sails, and ply your oars!
What am I saying? Where am I? What madness
has turned awry what I had meant to do?    820
Poor Dido, does his foulness touch you now?
It should have then, when you gave him your scepter.
This is the right hand, this the pledge of one
who carries with him, so they say, the household
gods of his land who bore upon his shoulders    825
his father weak with years. And could I not
have dragged his body off, and scattered him
piecemeal upon the waters, limb by limb?
Or butchered all his comrades, even served
Ascanius himself as banquet dish    830
upon his father's table? True enough—
the battle might have ended differently.
That does not matter. For, about to die,
need I fear anyone? I should have carried
my torches to his camp and filled his decks    835
with fire, destroyed the son, the father, that
whole race, and then have thrown myself upon them.
You, Sun, who with your flames see all that is done
on earth; and Juno, you, interpreter
and witness of my sorrows; Hecate,    840
invoked with shrieks, by night, at every city's
crossways; and you, the Furies; and the gods
that guard dying Elissa—hear these words
and turn your power toward my pain; as I
deserve, take up my prayers. If it must be    845
that he, a traitor, is to touch his harbor,
float to his coasts, and so the fates of Jove
demand and if this end is fixed; yet let
him suffer war and struggles with audacious
nations, and then—when banished from his borders    850

---

848–849. . . . *let him suffer*: This prophecy of Dido's, expressed in the form of a wish, is destined to come true. Aeneas meets resistance in Italy; at one point in the war he has to leave Ascanius behind and go to beg aid from an Italian king, Evander. The final peace is made on condition that the name of his people be changed from "Trojans" to "Latins", and Aeneas dies soon afterwards in mysterious circumstances—his body is never found. His reward for all his struggles is to come not during his life, but in the glory of the generations which succeed him.

and torn from the embrace of Iülus—let him
beg aid and watch his people's shameful slaughter.
Not even when he has bent low before
an unjust peace may he enjoy his kingdom,
the light that he has wished for. Let him fall      855
before his time, unburied in the sand.
These things I plead; these final words I pour
out of my blood. Then, Tyrians, hunt down
with hatred all his sons and race to come;
send this as offering unto my ashes.                860
Do not let love or treaty tie our peoples.
May an avenger rise up from my bones,
one who will track with firebrand and sword
the Dardan settlers, now and in the future,
at any time that ways present themselves.           865
I call your shores to war against their shores,
your waves against their waves, arms with their arms.
Let them and their sons' sons learn what is war."

This said, she ran her mind to every side,
for she was seeking ways with which to slice—       870
as quickly as she can—the hated light;
and then, with these brief words, she turned to Barce,
Sychaeus' nurse—for Dido's own was now
black ashes in Phoenicia, her old homeland:
"Dear nurse, call here to me my sister Anna;        875
and tell her to be quick to bathe her body
with river water; see that she brings cattle
and all that is appointed for atonement.
So must my sister come; while you yourself
bind up your temples with a pious fillet.           880
I mean to offer unto Stygian Jove
the sacrifices that, as is ordained,
I have made ready and begun, to put
an end to my disquiet and commit
to flames the pyre of the Trojan chieftain."        885
So Dido spoke. And Barce hurried off;
she moved with an old woman's eagerness.

---

861. *love or treaty*: In fact, the Romans and Carthaginians fought three separate wars (called Punic Wars from the Roman word for the Carthaginians). Rome won them all (though she almost lost the second one): after the third, the city of Carthage was razed to the ground.

862. *avenger*: Dido foresees the harrying of Italy by the Carthaginian general Hannibal, who in the third century B.C. invaded Italy, defeating the Romans in battle after battle, but failed to capture Rome.

880. *fillet*: Garland.

881. *Stygian*: Of the underworld. Styx was one of the infernal rivers.

But Dido, desperate, beside herself
with awful undertakings, eyes bloodshot
and rolling, and her quivering cheeks flecked                    890
with stains and pale with coming death, now bursts
across the inner courtyards of her palace.
She mounts in madness that high pyre, unsheathes
the Dardan sword, a gift not sought for such
an end. And when she saw the Trojan's clothes                    895
and her familiar bed, she checked her thought
and tears a little, lay upon the couch
and spoke her final words: "O relics, dear
while fate and god allowed, receive my spirit
and free me from these cares; for I have lived                   900
and journeyed through the course assigned by fortune.
And now my Shade will pass, illustrious,
beneath the earth; I have built a handsome city,
have seen my walls rise up, avenged a husband,
won satisfaction from a hostile brother:                         905
o fortunate, too fortunate—if only
the ships of Troy had never touched our coasts."
She spoke and pressed her face into the couch.
"I shall die unavenged, but I shall die,"
she says. "Thus, thus, I gladly go below                         910
to shadows. May the savage Dardan drink
with his own eyes this fire from the deep
and take with him the omen of my death."

Then Dido's words were done, and her companions
can see her fallen on the sword; the blade                       915
is foaming with her blood, her hands are bloodstained.
Now clamor rises to the high rooftop.
Now rumor riots through the startled city.
The lamentations, keening, shrieks of women
sound through the houses; heavens echo mighty                    920
wailings, even as if an enemy
were entering the gates, with all of Carthage
or ancient Tyre in ruins, and angry fires
rolling across the homes of men and gods.

And Anna heard. Appalled and breathless, she               925
runs, anxious, through the crowd, her nails wounding
her face; her fists, her breasts; she calls the dying

---

910. *Thus, Thus:* The repetition represents the two strokes of the sword.
922–924. *Carthage . . . gods:* In these
lines is prefigured the capture and total
destruction of Carthage by the army of
Scipio Africanus the Younger in 146
B.C.

Dido by name: "And was it, then, for this,
my sister? Did you plan this fraud for me?
Was this the meaning waiting for me when                    930
the pyre, the flames, the altar were prepared?
What shall I now, deserted, first lament?
You scorned your sister's company in death;
you should have called me to the fate you met;
the same sword pain, the same hour should have taken       935
the two of us away. Did my own hands
help build the pyre, and did my own voice call
upon our fathers' gods, only to find
me, heartless, far away when you lay dying?
You have destroyed yourself and me, my sister,             940
the people and the elders of your Sidon,
and all your city. Let me bathe your wounds
in water, and if any final breath
still lingers here, may my lips catch it up."
This said, she climbed the high steps, then she clasped    945
her half-dead sister to her breast, and moaning,
embraced her, dried the black blood with her dress.
Trying to lift her heavy eyes, the queen
falls back again. She breathes; the deep wound in
her chest is loud and hoarse. Three times she tried        950
to raise herself and strained, propped on her elbow;
and three times she fell back upon the couch.
Three times with wandering eyes she tried to find
high heaven's light and, when she found it, sighed.

But then all-able Juno pitied her                          955
long sorrow and hard death and from Olympus
sent Iris down to free the struggling spirit
from her entwining limbs. For as she died
a death that was not merited or fated,
but miserable and before her time                          960
and spurred by sudden frenzy, Proserpina
had not yet cut a gold lock from her crown,
not yet assigned her life to Stygian Orcus.
On saffron wings dew-glittering Iris glides
along the sky, drawing a thousand shifting                 965
colors across the facing sun. She halted

957. *Iris*: A messenger of the gods, particularly of Juno; also identified with the rainbow.
961. *Proserpina*: (Persephone) The queen of the underworld. Before an animal was sacrificed, some hair was cut from the forehead: before a human being died, Proserpina was thought to cut a lock of hair as an offering to Dis, the god of the underworld. Since Dido, by her suicide, has anticipated her fated day, Proserpina cannot cut the lock; Juno sends Iris to do it.

above the head of Dido: "So commanded,
I take this lock as offering to Dis;
I free you from your body." So she speaks
and cuts the lock with her right hand; at once                    970
the warmth was gone, the life passed to the winds.

[After his hurried departure from Carthage, Aeneas goes to
Sicily, to the kingdom of his friend Acestes. There he organizes
funeral games in honor of his father, Anchises (who had died in
Sicily on their first visit there), and leaves behind those of his following who are unwilling to go on to the uncertainty of a settlement in Italy. As the small fleet sails for the Italian shore, Aeneas'
mother, Venus, begs Neptune, the divine ruler of the seas, to grant
Aeneas a safe voyage. He consents, but warns that one Trojan life
must be sacrificed. The victim is to be the head helmsman, Palinurus.]

## Book V

### [*The Death of Palinurus*]

And now damp Night had almost reached her midpoint
along the skies; beneath their oars the sailors
were stretching out on their hard rowing benches,              1105
their bodies sinking into easy rest,
when, gliding lightly from the stars of heaven,
Sleep split the darkened air, cast back the shadows,
searching for you, o Palinurus, bringing
his dismal dreams to you, an innocent.                         1110
The god sat down upon the high stern, taking
the shape of Phorbas, pouring out these words:
"Palinurus, son of Iasus,
the seas themselves bear on the fleet; the breezes
blow steadily; this is a time for rest.                        1115
Lay down your head and steal your tired eyes
from trials; and for a brief while I myself
will take your place, your duties." Palinurus,
who scarcely lifts his eyes, makes this reply:
"And are you asking me to act as if                            1120
I did not know the face of this calm sea
and its still waves? Do you ask me to trust
this monster? Why should I confide Aeneas
to the deceiving winds—I who have been
cheated so often by the treachery                              1125

1112. *Phorbas:* An older Trojan.

of tranquil skies?" He held the tiller fast;
not once did he let loose his grasp; his eyes
were fixed upon the stars. But—look—the god
now shakes a bough that drips with Lethe's dew,
drenched with the stupefying power of Styx,                    1130
on Palinurus' temples; as he struggles,
his swimming eyes relax. That sudden rest
had just begun to let his limbs fall slack
when, bending down, the god cast him headlong
into the limpid waters; as he fell,                            1135
he tore away part of the stern and helm,
and often cried, in vain, to his companions.
The god himself soared off upon his wings
into thin air. Nevertheless the fleet
runs safely on its way across the sea—                        1140
even as father Neptune promised—carried
without alarm. Now, swept along, it neared
the Sirens' reefs, long since so dangerous,
white with the bones of many. When, far off,
the rocks were roaring, hoarse with ceaseless surf,           1145
father Aeneas felt his ship drift, aimless,
its pilot lost; he took the helm himself
and steered his galley through the midnight waters,
while sighing often, stunned by the disaster
fallen upon his friend: "O Palinurus,                         1150
too trustful of the tranquil sky and sea,
you will lie naked on an unknown shore."

[Once on Italian soil, Aeneas, obeying instructions from his dead
father who had appeared to him in a dream, consults the Sybil, who
guides him down to the world of the dead. There he is to see his
father and the vision of his race, which is to be his only reward for
he will die before his people are settled in their new home.]

## Book VI

### [Aeneas in the Underworld]

You gods who hold dominion over spirits;                      350
you voiceless Shades; you, Phlegethon and Chaos,
immense and soundless regions of the night:
allow me to retell what I was told;

1129. **Lethe**: A river of the underworld; its waters abolish memory of the
past.
1143. **Siren's reef**: One of the dangers
which threatened Odysseus on his voyage
home. The song of the Sirens lured mariners close to land, where they were
wrecked on the rocks.
351. **Phlegethon**: An underworld river
of fire.

allow me by your power to disclose
things buried in the dark and deep of earth!                    355

---

They moved along in darkness, through the shadows,
beneath the lonely night, and through the hollow
dwelling place of Dis, his phantom kingdom:
even as those who journey in a forest
beneath the scanty light of a changing moon,                    360
when Jupiter has wrapped the sky in shadows
and black night steals the color from all things.
Before the entrance, at the jaws of Orcus,
both Grief and goading Cares have set their couches;
there pale Diseases dwell, and sad Old Age,                     365
and Fear and Hunger, that worst counsellor,
and ugly Poverty—shapes terrible
to see—and Death and Trials; Death's brother, Sleep,
and all the evil Pleasures of the mind;
and War, whose fruits are death; and facing these,             370
and Furies' iron chambers; and mad Strife,
her serpent hair bound up with bloody garlands.

Among them stands a giant shaded elm,
a tree with spreading boughs and aged arms;
they say that is the home of empty Dreams                       375
that cling, below, to every leaf. And more,
so many monstrous shapes of savage beasts
are stabled there: Centaurs and double-bodied
Scyllas; the hundred-handed Briareus;
the brute of Lerna, hissing horribly;                           380
Chimaera armed with flames; Gorgons and Harpies;
and Geryon, the shade that wears three bodies.
And here Aeneas, shaken suddenly
by terror, grips his sword; he offers naked
steel and opposes those who come. Had not                       385
his wise companion warned him they were only
thin lives that glide without a body in

---

378. *Centaurs*: Mythical creatures, half man, half horse—a byword for violence.

379. *Scylla*: A monster, described by Lucretius as 'half fish and a girdle of ravenous dogs'. *Briareus*: See Homer, *Iliad*, I, lines 463–468, p. 115.

380. *brute of Lerna*: The Hydra, a many-headed serpent killed by Heracles. Each time one head was cut off, two new ones grew in its place.

381. *Chimaera*: One-third lion, one-third goat, one-third snake. *Gorgons*: Monsters whose look could turn people to stone. *Harpies*: Winged creatures who seize their victims and carry them off to the lower world.

382. *Geryon*: A giant with three bodies: an opponent of Heracles.

the hollow semblance of a form, he would
in vain have torn the shadows with his blade.

Here starts the pathway to the waters of          390
Tartarean Acheron. A whirlpool thick
with sludge, its giant eddy seething, vomits
all of its swirling sand into Cocytus.
Grim Charon is the squalid ferryman,
the guardian of these streams, these rivers; his          395
white hairs lie thick, disheveled on his chin;
his eyes are fires that stare, a filthy mantle
hangs down his shoulder by a knot. Alone,
he poles the boat and tends the sails and carries
the dead in his dark ship, old as he is;          400
but old age in a god is tough and green.

And here a multitude was rushing, swarming
shoreward, with men and mothers, bodies of
high-hearted heroes stripped of life, and boys
and unwed girls, and young men set upon          405
the pyre of death before their fathers' eyes:
thick as the leaves that with the early frost
of autumn drop and fall within the forest,
or as the birds that flock along the beaches,
in flight from frenzied seas when the chill season          410
drives them across the waves to lands of sun.
They stand; each pleads to be the first to cross
the stream; their hands reach out in longing for
the farther shore. But Charon, sullen boatman,
now takes these souls, now those; the rest he leaves;          415
thrusting them back, he keeps them from the beach.

That disarray dismays and moves Aeneas:
"O virgin, what does all this swarming mean?
What do these spirits plead? And by what rule
must some keep off the bank while others sweep          420
the blue-black waters with their oars?" The words
the aged priestess speaks are brief: "Anchises'
son, certain offspring of the gods, you see
the deep pools of Cocytus and the marsh
of Styx, by whose divinity even          425
the High Ones are afraid to swear falsely.

391. *Acheron*: A river of the under-      393. *Cocytus*: The river of lamentation.
world.                                      418. *Virgin*: The Sybil, his guide.

All these you see are helpless and unburied.
That ferryman is Charon. And the waves
will only carry souls that have a tomb.
Before his bones have found their rest, no one                    430
may cross the horrid shores and the hoarse waters.
They wander for a hundred years and hover
about these banks until they gain their entry,
to visit once again the pools they long for."

Anchises' son has stopped; he stays his steps              435
and ponders, pitying these unkind fates.
There he can see the sorrowing Leucaspis,
Orontes, captain of the Lycian fleet:
both dead without death's honors, for the south wind
had overwhelmed them, sinking ships and sailors,          440
when they were crossing stormy seas from Troy.

And there the pilot, Palinurus, passed:
lately, upon the Libyan voyage, as
he scanned the stars, he had fallen from the stern,
cast down into the center of the sea.                          445
And when at last in that deep shade Aeneas
had recognized his grieving form, he was
the first to speak: "O Palinurus, what
god tore you from us, plunged you in midsea?
O tell me. For Apollo, who had never                          450
been false before, in this one oracle
deceived me; he had surely prophesied
that you would be unharmed upon the waters
and reach the coastline of Ausonia.
Is this the way he keeps his word?" He answered:          455
"Anchises' son, my captain, you must know:
Apollo's tripod did not cheat, no god
hurled me into the waves. For as it happened,
the rudder that, as my appointed charge,
I clutched, to steer our course, was twisted off          460
by force; I dragged it down headlong with me.
I swear by those harsh seas that I was taken
by no fear for myself; I was afraid
your ship, without its gear, without a helmsman,
might swamp in such a surge. Three nights of winter,      465
along vast fields of sea, across the waters,

437. *Leucaspis . . . Orontes*: Trojans     Aeneas to Carthage.
lost at sea in the storm which took

the south wind lashed me violently; only
on my fourth dawn, high on a wave crest, I
saw Italy, dimly. I swam toward land
slowly and was just at the point of safety—                470
my sea-drenched clothing heavy, my hooked hands
were clinging to a jagged cliffside—when
barbarians attacked me with the sword,
ignorantly thinking me a prize.
And now I am the breakers', beach winds toss me. . . .    475
I beg you, therefore, by the gentle light
and winds of heaven, undefeated one,
and by your father, by your growing son,
Iülus, save me from these evils: either
cast earth upon my body—for you can—                      480
and seek again the port of Velia; or
if there be any way, if you are given
such power by your goddess mother (for
I cannot think that you are now prepared
to cross such mighty rivers and the marsh                  485
of Styx without the gods' protection), give
your own right hand to wretched Palinurus
and take me with you past the waters, that
at least in death I find a place of rest."

But then the priestess turned on the dead pilot.          490
"Where was it, Palinurus, that you learned
such dread desire? For how can you, unburied,
look at the waves of Styx, upon the Furies'
stern river, and approach its shore, unasked?
Leave any hope that prayer can turn aside                  495
the gods' decrees. But keep in memory
these words as comfort in your cruel trial:
for all around, the neighboring cities will
be goaded by the plague, a sign from heaven
to make peace with your bones; and they will build        500
a tomb and send their solemn sacrifices;
the place will always be named Palinurus."
These words have set his cares to rest, his sorrow
is exiled for a while from his sad heart.
The land that bears his name has made him glad.           505

The journey they began can now continue.
They near the riverbank. Even the boatman,

---

481 *Velia*: South of the bay of Na-   named after Aeneas' pilot).
ples, near Cape Palinuro (which is still   490. *priestess*: The Sybil.

while floating on the Styx, had seen them coming
across the silent grove and toward the shore.
He does not wait for greeting but attacks,                          510
insulting with these words: "Enough! Stop there!
Whoever you may be who make your way,
so armed, down to our waters, tell me now
why you have come. This is the land of shadows,
of Sleep and drowsy Night; no living bodies                         515
can take their passage in the ship of Styx.
Indeed, I was not glad to have Alcides
or Theseus or Pirithoüs cross the lake,
although the three of them were sons of gods
and undefeated in their wars. Alcides                               520
tried to drag off in chains the guardian
of Tartarus; he tore him, trembling, from
the king's own throne. The others tried to carry
the queen away from Pluto's wedding chamber."

Apollo's priestess answered briefly: "We                           525
bring no such trickery; no need to be
disturbed; our weapons bear no violence;
for us, the mighty watchman can bark on
forever in his cavern, frightening
the bloodless shades; Proserpina can keep                          530
the threshold of her uncle faithfully.
Trojan Aeneas, famed for piety
and arms, descends to meet his father, down
into the deepest shades of Erebus.
And if the image of such piety                                      535
is not enough to move you, then"—and here
she shows the branch concealed beneath her robe—
"you may yet recognize this bough." At this
the swollen heart of Charon stills its anger.
He says no more. He wonders at the sacred                           540
gift of the destined wand, so long unseen,
and turns his blue-black keel toward shore. He clears
the other spirits from the gangways and
long benches and, meanwhile, admits the massive
Aeneas to the boat, the vessel's seams                             545
groaning beneath the weight as they let in
marsh water through the chinks. At last he sets

---

517. *Alcides*: Heracles. One of his labors was to bring Cerberus, the watchdog of Hades, up from the lower world.
518. *Theseus* . . . *Pirithoüs*: They
came to kidnap Proserpina (Persephone): they failed and were imprisoned
but Hercules rescued Theseus.
538. *bough*: The golden bough which
Aeneas had been ordered to take as tribute to Proserpina.

the priestess and the soldier safe across
the stream in ugly slime and blue-gray sedge.

These regions echo with the triple-throated          550
bark of the giant Cerberus, who crouches,
enormous, in a cavern facing them.
The Sibyl, seeing that his neck is bristling
with snakes, throws him a honeyed cake of wheat
with drugs that bring on sleep. His triple mouths     555
yawn wide with rapid hunger as he clutches
the cake she cast. His giant back falls slack
along the ground; his bulk takes all the cave.
And when the beast is buried under sleep,
Aeneas gains the entrance swiftly, leaves            560
the riverbank from which no one returns.

---

Here voices and loud lamentations echo:
the souls of infants weeping at the very
first threshold—torn away by the black day,
deprived of their sweet life, ripped from the breast, 565
plunged into bitter death. And next to them
are those condemned to die upon false charges.
These places have not been assigned, indeed,
without a lot, without a judge; for here
Minos is magistrate. He shakes the urn              570
and calls on the assembly of the silent,
to learn the lives of men and their misdeeds.
The land that lies beyond belongs to those
who, although innocent, took death by their
own hands; hating the light, they threw away        575
their lives. But now they long for the upper air,
and even to bear want and trials there.
But fate refuses them: the melancholy
marshland, its ugly waters, hem them in,
the prisoners of Styx and its nine circles.         580

Nearby, spread out on every side, there lie
the Fields of Mourning: this, their given name.
And here, concealed by secret paths, are those
whom bitter love consumed with brutal waste;
a myrtle grove encloses them; their pains           585

---

570. *Minos*: King of Crete, now judge
of the dead. *the urn*: The magistrate of a
Roman court decided the order in which
cases were to be heard by drawing lots

from an urn.
571. *assembly of the silent*: The jury
of the dead.

remain with them in death. Aeneas sees
Phaedra and Procris and sad Eriphyle,
who pointed to the wounds inflicted by
her savage son; he sees Pasiphaë
and then Evadne; and Laodamia                                    590
and Caeneus, once a youth and now a woman,
changed back again by fate to her first shape.

Among them, wandering in that great forest,
and with her wound still fresh: Phoenician Dido.
And when the Trojan hero recognized her                          595
dim shape among the shadows (just as one
who either sees or thinks he sees among
the cloud banks, when the month is young, the moon
rising), he wept and said with tender love:
"Unhappy Dido, then the word I had                               600
was true? That you were dead? That you pursued
your final moment with the sword? Did I
bring only death to you? Queen, I swear by
the stars, the gods above, and any trust
that may be in this underearth, I was                            605
unwilling when I had to leave your shores.
But those same orders of the gods that now
urge on my journey through the shadows, through
abandoned, thorny lands and deepest night,
drove me by their decrees. And I could not                       610
believe that with my going I should bring
so great a grief as this. But stay your steps.
Do not retreat from me. Whom do you flee?
This is the last time fate will let us speak."

These were the words Aeneas, weeping, used,                      615
trying to soothe the burning, fierce-eyed Shade.
She turned away, eyes to the ground, her face

---

587. *Phaedra*: Wife of Theseus, king
of Athens, who fell in love with Hippolytus, her husband's son by another
woman; the result was her death by suicide and Hippolytus' death through his
father's curse. *Procris*: Killed by her
husband in an accident which was
brought about by her own jealousy. *Eriphyle*: Betrayed her husband for gold
and was killed by her own son.
589. *Pasiphaë*: Wife of Minos of
Crete, she conceived a monstrous love
for a bull, and gave birth to the Mina-
taur.
590. *Evadne*: Threw herself on the
pyre of her husband, who was killed by
Zeus for impiety. *Laodamia*: Begged to
be allowed to talk with her dead husband; the request was granted by the
gods and when his time came to return,
she went back with him to the land of
the dead.
591. *Caeneus*: Virgil's words in the
original are ambiguous (perhaps to
reflect the ambiguity of the sex of
Caeneus). The usual explanation of the
passage is that Caenis (a woman) was
changed by Poseidon into a man (Caeneus) but returned to her original sex
after death. Since the name occurs here
in a catalogue of women, this seems the
most likely explanation.

no more moved by his speech than if she stood
as stubborn flint or some Marpessan crag.
At last she tore herself away; she fled— 620
and still his enemy—into the forest
of shadows, where Sychaeus, once her husband,
answers her sorrows, gives her love for love.
Nevertheless, Aeneas, stunned by her
unkindly fate, still follows at a distance 625
with tears and pity for her as she goes.

\* \* \*

[Aeneas returns to the upper air and begins his settlement in
Italy. He is offered the hand of the princess Lavinia by her father
Latinus, but this provokes a war against the Trojans, led by King
Turnus of Laurentum, in the course of which Aeneas is wounded
and stops by a stream to rest. At this point his mother, Venus,
comes to him with the armor made for him by Vulcan (Hephaestus), her husband; on the shield is carved a representation of the
future glories of Rome.]

## Book VIII

### [The Shield of Aeneas]

. . . But Venus, the bright goddess, bearing gifts,
drew near in airy clouds; and when far off
she saw her son in a secluded valley, 790
withdrawn beside a cooling stream, then she
showed herself freely to him, saying this:
"You see, my son, these perfect offerings,
my husband's promised art; then do not doubt,
but dare brave Turnus and the proud Laurentians 795
to battle." These were Cytherea's words.
She sought her son's embraces, then set up
his glittering arms beneath a facing oak.
Aeneas cannot have enough; delighted
with these gifts of the goddess, this high honor, 800
his eyes rush on to everything, admiring;
with arm and hand he turns the helmet over,
tremendous with its crests and flood of flames,
the sword that deals out fate, the stiff brass corselet,
blood-red and huge as when a blue-gray cloud, 805
which rays of sun have kindled, glows far off;
the polished greaves made of electrum and

---

619. *Marpessan*: Marpessa was a marble quarry on the island of Paros.
793. *perfect offerings*: The armor
made by Vulcan (Hephaistus).

807. *greaves*: Armor for the lower
legs. *electrum*: An alloy of gold and silver.

of gold, resmelted many times; the spear;
the shield, its texture indescribable.

---

For there the Lord of Fire had wrought the story          810
of Italy, the Romans' victories,
since he was not unskilled in prophecy
or one who cannot tell the times to come.
There he had set the generations of
Ascanius, and all their wars, in order.                   815
There, too, he made a mother-wolf, reclining
in Mars' green cavern; and at play beside her,
twin boys were hanging at her dugs; fearless,
they sucked their mother. She, at this, bent back
her tapered neck to lick them each in turn                820
and shape their bodies with her tongue. Not far
from this he set the Romans and the Sabine
women they carried off—against all law—
while in the crowded theater the great
Circensian games were under way; and sudden               825
war then broke out again between the Romans
and aged Tatius, king of austere Cures.
Next, Romulus and Tatius, these same kings,
their quarrels set to rest, stood at Jove's altar;
both, armed and cup in hand and having offered            830
a sow as sacrifice, swore league and friendship.
Not far from this, two chariots that rushed
in different directions tore apart
Mettus (but then you should have kept your word,
o man of Alba!); Tullus hauled the guts                   835
of that conniving man into the forest;
the briers dripped with spattered blood. There, too,
Porsenna, asking Rome to readmit
the banished Tarquin, hemmed the city in

---

810. *Lord of Fire*: Vulcan, god of the forge.
816. *mother wolf*: The twins who were to build Rome, Romulus and Remus, sons of Mars, the war god, were cast out into the woods and there suckled by a she-wolf.
821. *Sabine women*: The newly founded city of Rome consisted almost entirely of men; the Romans decided to steal the wives of their neighbors, the Sabines. They invited them to an athletic festival and at a given signal, every Roman carried off a Sabine bride. The war which followed ended in the amalgamation of the Roman and Sabine peoples.
825. *Circensian games*: Games in the Circus, the Roman stadium.
827. *Tatius*: The Sabine king: *Cures* is the name of his city.
834. *Mettus*: Of Alba. He broke an agreement made during the early wars of Rome and was punished by being torn apart by two chariots moving in opposite directions.
835. *Tullus*: The Roman king who punished Mettus.
838. *Porsenna*: The Etruscan king who attempted to restore the last of the Roman kings, Tarquin, to the throne from which he had been expelled.

with strangling siege; Aeneas' sons rushed on   840
the sword for freedom's sake. You might have seen
Porsenna as one wild and menacing,
since Cocles dared tear down the Tiber's bridge,
and Cloelia broke her chains and swam the river.

Carved in the upper part was Manlius,   845
the guardian of the Tarpeian rock,
who stood before the temple gates, defender
of the high Capitol; the new-carved palace
was shaggy with the straw of Romulus.
And here a silver goose fluttered across   850
the gilded colonnades, signaling that
the Gauls were at the threshold. Through the brush
the Gauls crept toward the tower, under cover
of darkness and dense night. Their hair is golden;
and golden, too, their clothes, set off by gleaming,   855
striped cloaks; their milk-white necks are bound in gold;
each brandishes two Alpine javelins
and, with an oblong shield, defends his body.
Here in relief were carved the nude Luperci
and dancing Salian priests, with woolen caps   860
and shields that fell from heaven; through the city
chaste matrons in their cushioned carriages
led sacred rites. Away from these scenes Vulcan
added the house of Tartarus, the high
doorways of Dis, the penalties of crime;   865
and Catiline, you hanging from a cliff
that threatens, trembling at the Furies' faces;
and, set apart, the pious who receive
their laws from Cato. Bordering these scenes,

---

840–841. *rushed on the sword*: I.e., rushed bravely against the enemies' swords.

843. *Cocles*: Horatius Cocles, who with two companions defended the bridge across the Tiber to give the Romans time to destroy it.

844. *Cloelia*: A Roman hostage held by Porsenna.

845. *Manlius*: Consul in 392 B.C.; he was in charge of the citadel ("Tarpeian fortress") at a time when the Gauls from the north held all the rest of the city. They made a night attack on the citadel, but Manlius, awakened by the cackling of the sacred geese, beat it off, and saved Rome.

849. *the straw of Romulus*: In Virgil's time there was still preserved at Rome a rustic building which was supposed to have been the dwelling place of Romulus.

859. *Luperci*: Priests of Lupercus, a Roman god corresponding to the Greek Pan.

860. *Salian priests*: The twelve priests of Mars, who danced in his honor carrying shields which had fallen from heaven.

866. *Catiline*: Leader of a conspiracy to overthrow the republic which was halted mainly through the efforts of Cicero, consul in 63 B.C. Catiline is the type of discord, representing the civil war which almost destroyed the Roman state, and to which Augustus later put an end.

869. *Cato*: The noblest of the republicans who had fought Julius Caesar; he stood for honesty and the seriousness which the Romans most admired. He committed suicide in 47 B.C. after Caesar's victory in Africa. Before taking his life he read through Plato's *Phaedo*, a dialogue concerned with the immortality of the soul, which ends with an account of the death of Socrates.

he carved a golden image of the sea,                                    870
yet there were blue-gray waters and white foam
where dolphins bright with silver cut across
the tide and swept the waves with circling tails.

Across the center of the shield were shown
the ships of brass, the strife of Actium:                               875
you might have seen all of Leucata's bay
teeming with war's array, waves glittering
with gold. On his high stern Augustus Caesar
is leading the Italians to battle,
together with the senate and the people,                                880
the household gods and Great Gods; his bright brows
pour out a twin flame, and upon his head
his father's Julian star is glittering.
Elsewhere Agrippa towers on the stern;
with kindly winds and gods he leads his squadron;                       885
around his temples, glowing bright, he wears
the naval crown, magnificent device,
with its ships' beaks. And facing them, just come
from conquering the peoples of the dawn,
from the red shores of the Erythraean Sea—                              890
together with barbaric riches, varied
arms—is Antonius. He brings with him
Egypt and every power of the East
and farthest Bactria; and—shamefully—
behind him follows his Egyptian wife.                                    895
The squadrons close headlong; and all the waters
foam, torn by drawn-back oars and by the prows
with triple prongs. They seek the open seas;
you could believe the Cyclades, uprooted,
now swam upon the waters or steep mountains                             900
had clashed with mountains as the crewmen thrust
in their great galleys at the towering sterns.
Torches of hemp and flying darts of steel
are flung by hand, and Neptune's fields are red

875. *Actium*: On the west coast of
Greece. The naval battle fought here in
31 B.C. was the decisive engagement of
the civil war. Augustus, the master of the
western half of the empire, defeated Anthony, who held the eastern half and
was supported by Cleopatra, queen of
Egypt.
876. *Leucata*: A promontory near Actium; there was a temple of Apollo on it
(see l. 916).
883. *Julian*: Pertaining to Julius Caesar, who adopted Augustus as his son.
884. *Agrippa*: Augustus' admiral at
Actium.
890. *Erythraean Sea*: The Indian
Ocean.
894. *Bactria*: On the borders of India.
897–898. *prows with triple prongs*:
The prow of a Roman warship was
shaped with three prongs, one above the
other.
899. *Cyclades*: The islands of the
southern Aegean Sea.

with strange bloodshed. Among all this the queen 905
calls to her squadrons with their native sistrum;
she has not yet looked back at the twin serpents
that swim behind her. Every kind of monster
god—and the barking god, Anubis, too—
stands ready to cast shafts against Minerva 910
and Venus and at Neptune. In the middle
of all the struggle, Mars, engraved in steel,
rages beside fierce Furies from the sky;
and Discord, joyous, strides in her rent robe;
Bellona follows with a bloodstained whip. 915
But Actian Apollo, overhead,
had seen these things; he stretched his bow; and all
of Egypt and of India, and all
the Arabs and Sabaeans, turned their backs
and fled before this terror. The queen herself 920
was seen to woo the winds, to spread her sails,
and now, yes now, let fall the slackened ropes.
The Lord of Fire had fashioned her within
the slaughter, driven on by wave and west wind,
pale with approaching death; but facing this, 925
he set the Nile, his giant body mourning,
opening wide his folds and all his robes,
inviting the defeated to his blue-gray
breast and his sheltering streams. But entering
the walls of Rome in triple triumph, Caesar 930
was dedicating his immortal gift
to the Italian gods: three hundred shrines
throughout the city. And the streets reechoed
with gladness, games, applause; in all the temples
were bands of matrons, and in all were altars; 935
and there, before these altars, slaughtered steers
were scattered on the ground. Caesar himself
is seated at bright Phoebus' snow-white porch,
and he reviews the spoils of nations and
he fastens them upon the proud doorposts. 940
The conquered nations march in long procession,
as varied in their armor and their dress

---

906. *sistrum*: An oriental rattle, used
in the worship of Isis.
907. *serpents*: Cleopatra committed suicide by applying poisonous snakes to
her breast.
909. *Anubis*: The Egyptian death-god,
represented as with the head of a
jackal.

915. *Bellona*: A Roman goddess of
war.
919. *Sabaeans*: Arabs from the
Yemen.
930. *in triple triumph*: In 29 B.C. Augustus celebrated a triple triumph for
victories in Dalmatia, at Actium, and at
Alexandria.

as in their languages. Here Mulciber
had modeled Nomad tribes and Africans,
loose-robed; the Carians; the Leleges;                                945
Geloni armed with arrows. And he showed
Euphrates, moving now with humbler waves;
the most remote of men, the Morini;
the Rhine with double horns; the untamed Dahae;
and, river that resents its bridge, the Araxes.                        950

Aeneas marvels at his mother's gift,
the scenes on Vulcan's shield; and he is glad
for all these images, though he does not
know what they mean. Upon his shoulder he
lifts up the fame and fate of his sons' sons.                          955

[In the course of the desperate battles which follow, the young
Pallas, entrusted to Aeneas' care by his father, is killed by the Italian champion Turnus, who takes and wears the belt of Pallas as the
spoil of victory. The fortunes of the war later change in favor of the
Trojans, and Aeneas kills the Etruscan King Mezentius, Turnus'
ally. Eventually, as the Italians prepare to accept the generous peace
terms offered by Aeneas, Turnus forestalls them by accepting
Aeneas' challenge to single combat to decide the issue. But this
solution is frustrated by the intervention of Juno, who foresees
Aeneas' victory. She prompts Turnus' sister, the river nymph
Juturna, to intervene in an attempt to save Turnus' life. Juturna
stirs up the Italians who are watching the champions prepare for
the duel; the truce is broken, and in the subsequent fighting Aeneas
is wounded by an arrow. Healed by Venus, he returns to the fight,
and the Italians are driven back. Turnus finally faces his adversary.
His sword breaks on the armor forged by Vulcan, and he runs from
Aeneas; he is saved by Juturna, who, assuming the shape of his
charioteer, hands him a fresh sword. At this point Jupiter intervenes
to stop the vain attempts of Juno and Juturna to save Turnus.]

## Book XII

### [The Death of Turnus]

. . . Meanwhile Olympus' king calls out to Juno
as from a golden cloud she scans the battle:                          1050
"Wife, how can this day end? What is there left

943. *Mulciber*: Vulcan
945. *Carians* . . . *Leleges*: Peoples of
Asia Minor.
946. *Geloni*: From Scythia (in the
Balkans).
947. *Euphrates*: The great river of Ba-
bylonia, now in Syria.

948. *Morini*: A Belgian tribe.
949. *with double horns*: Obscure; perhaps a reference to the two mouths of the
Rhine. *Dahae*: Nomads, living east of the
Caspian Sea.
950. *Araxes*: A turbulent river in Armenia; Augustus built a bridge over it.

for you to do? You know, and say you know,
that, as a deity, Aeneas is owed
to heaven, that the fates will carry him
high as the stars. What is your plan? What is                    1055
the hope that keeps you lingering in these
chill clouds? And was it seemly for a god
to be profaned by a human wound? Or for
a sword that had been lost to be restored
to Turnus (without you, Juturna could                            1060
do nothing)? Was it right to give fresh force
to those who are defeated? Stop at last;
give way to what I now ask: do not let
so great a sorrow gnaw at you in silence;
do not let your sweet lips so often press                        1065
your bitter cares on me. This is the end.
You have harassed the Trojans over land
and wave, have kindled brutal war, outraged
Latinus' home, and mingled grief and marriage:
you cannot pass beyond this point." So, Jove;                    1070
the goddess, Saturn's daughter, yielding, answered:

"Great Jupiter, it was indeed for this—
my knowing what you wish—that I have left
both Turnus and the earth, unwillingly.
Were it not so, you would not see me now                         1075
alone upon my airy throne, enduring
everything; but girt with flames, I should
be standing on the battlefield itself,
to drag the Trojans toward the war they hate.
I do confess that I urged on Juturna                             1080
to help her luckless brother; I approved
her daring greater things to save his life;
yet not to aim an arrow, not to stretch
her bow. I swear this by the pitiless
high fountainhead of Styx, the only pledge                       1085
that fills the upper gods with dread. And now
I yield; detesting wars, I give them up.
And only this—which fates do not forbid—
I beg of you, for Latium, for your
own father's greatness, for the race of Saturn:                  1090
when with their happy wedding rites they reach
a peace—so be it—when they both unite

---

1053. *as a deity*: Aeneas is destined
for immortality: after his death, he will
be worshipped as a local god.
  1069. *grief and marriage*: A reference
not only to the Italian losses but also to
the suicide of Amata, wife of King Latinus, who hanged herself when the Trojans assaulted the city just before the
duel between Aeneas and Turnus began.

in laws and treaties, do not let the native-
born Latins lose their ancient name, become
Trojans, or be called Teucrians; do not                                1095
make such men change their language or their dress.
Let Latium still be, let Alban kings
still rule for ages; let the sons of Rome
be powerful in their Italian courage.
Troy now is fallen; let her name fall, too."                           1100

And Jupiter smiled at her then; the maker
of men and things said: "Surely you are sister
to Jove, a second child of Saturn, for
deep in your breast there surge such tides of anger.
But come, give up this useless madness: I                              1105
now grant your wish and willingly, vanquished,
submit. For the Ausonians will keep
their homeland's words and ways; their name will stay;
the body of the Teucrians will merge
with Latins, and their name will fall away.                            1110
But I shall add their rituals and customs
to the Ausonians', and make them all—
and with one language—Latins. You will see
a race arise from this that, mingled with
the blood of the Ausonians, will be                                    1115
past men, even past gods, in piety;
no other nation will pay you such honor."
Juno agreed to this; with gladness she
then changed her mind. She quit the skies, her cloud.

This done, the Father, left alone, ponders                             1120
another plan: to have Juturna driven
far from her brother. It is said there are
two fiends who bear the name of Furies; they
were born in one same birth with hell's Megaera
out of untimely Night, who wrapped all three                           1125
in equal serpents' folds and added wings
that take the wind. These wait before the throne
of Jove, the threshold of the cruel king,
and spur the fears of feeble mortals when
it happens that the king of gods flings down                           1130
dread sorrow and diseases or when he
sends war to terrify unrighteous cities.
And quickly Jupiter sends one of these

1124. *Megaera*: One of three infernal
sisters the Romans called *Dirae* (Dreadful), creatures comparable to the Greek
Erinyes (Furies).

from heaven's height, commanding her to meet
Juturna as an evil emissary.                                          1135
She flies off; cloaked in whirlwinds, she is carried
to earth. Just as an arrow that is driven
from bowstring through a cloud, an arrow tipped
in gall and venom, an incurable shaft,
shot by some Parthian—a Parthian                                     1140
or a Cydonian; as it hurtles, hissing,
it passes through swift shadows, seen by no one:
so did the child of Night rush on; she sought
the earth. As soon as she can see the Trojan
ranks and the troops of Turnus, suddenly                             1145
she shrinks into the shape of that small bird
which sometimes sits by night on tombs and lonely
rooftops, where it chants late, among the shadows,
its song of evil omen; so transformed,
the foul one howls before the face of Turnus,                        1150
flies back and forth; her wings beat at his shield.
Strange stiffness, terror, took the limbs of Turnus;
his hair stood up; his jaws held fast his voice.

But when, far off, Juturna recognized
the shrill wings of the Fury, luckless, she                          1155
tears at her flowing hair, defiles her face
with nails, her breast with fists. "Turnus, how can
your sister help you now? And what is left
for all my struggle? By what art can I
draw out your daylight? Can I stand against                          1160
such prodigies? Now I must leave the field.
You, filthy birds, do not excite my fears;
I know the beating of your wings, your fatal
shrieking; I know these are the harsh commands
of that great-hearted Jove. Is this how he                           1165
requites me now for my virginity?
Did he give me eternal life for this?
For this have I been made exempt from death?
I surely would be done with such a sorrow
and go as my sad brother's comrade through                           1170
the Shadows. I immortal? But can any
thing that is mine be sweet to me without
you, brother? For what lands are deep enough

1140. *Parthian*: Parthia was the most
dangerous neighbor of the Roman Empire in the east. Parthian mounted archers were famous.
1141. *Cydonian*: Cretan.

1146. *that small bird*: An owl.
1166. *virginity*: Jupiter had been the
lover of Juturna and had rewarded her
with immortality.

to gape before me, to send me, a goddess,
into the lowest Shades?" And saying this,                      1175
Juturna placed a gray veil on her head;
moaning, she plunged into the river's depths.

---

And now Aeneas charges straight at Turnus.
He brandishes a shaft huge as a tree,
and from his savage breast he shouts: "Now what             1180
delay is there? Why, Turnus, do you still
draw back from battle? It is not for us
to race against each other, but to meet
with cruel weapons, hand to hand. Go, change
yourself into all shapes; by courage and                    1185
by craft collect whatever help you can;
take wing, if you so would, toward the steep stars
or hide yourself within the hollow earth."
But Turnus shakes his head: "Your burning words,
ferocious Trojan, do not frighten me;                       1190
it is the gods alone who terrify me,
and Jupiter, my enemy." He says
no more, but as he looks about he sees
a giant stone, an ancient giant stone
that lay at hand, by chance, upon the plain,                1195
set there as boundary mark between the fields
to keep the farmers free from border quarrels.
And twice-six chosen men with bodies such
as earth produces now could scarcely lift
that stone upon their shoulders. But the hero,              1200
anxious and running headlong, snatched the boulder;
reaching full height, he hurled it at the Trojan.
But Turnus does not know if it is he
himself who runs or goes or lifts or throws
that massive rock; his knees are weak; his blood            1205
congeals with cold. The stone itself whirls through
the empty void but does not cross all of
the space between; it does not strike a blow.
Just as in dreams of night, when languid rest
has closed our eyes, we seem in vain to wish                1210
to press on down a path, but as we strain,
we falter, weak; our tongues can say nothing,
the body loses its familiar force,
no voice, no word, can follow: so whatever
courage he calls upon to find a way,                        1215
the cursed goddess keeps success from Turnus.

1178. *river's depth*: She was a nymph of rivers and springs.

The shifting feelings overtake his heart;
he looks in longing at the Latin ranks
and at the city, and he hesitates,
afraid; he trembles at the coming spear.          1220
He does not know how he can save himself,
what power he has to charge his enemy;
he cannot see his chariot anywhere;
he cannot see the charioteer, his sister.

In Turnus' wavering Aeneas sees               1225
his fortune; he holds high the fatal shaft;
he hurls it far with all his body's force.
No boulder ever catapulted from
siege engine sounded so, no thunderbolt
had ever burst with such a roar. The spear        1230
flies on like a black whirlwind, carrying
its dread destruction, ripping through the border
of Turnus' corselet and the outer rim
of Turnus' seven-plated shield; hissing,
it penetrates his thigh. The giant Turnus,        1235
struck, falls to earth; his knees bend under him.
All the Rutulians leap up with a groan,
and all the mountain slopes around reecho;
tall forests, far and near, return that voice.
Then humble, suppliant, he lifts his eyes         1240
and, stretching out his hand, entreating, cries:
"I have indeed deserved this; I do not
appeal against it; use your chance. But if
there is a thought of a dear parent's grief
that now can touch you, then I beg you, pity      1245
old Daunus—in Anchises you had such
a father—send me back or, if you wish,
send back my lifeless body to my kin.
For you have won, and the Ausonians
have seen me, beaten, stretch my hands; Lavinia   1250
is yours; then do not press your hatred further."

Aeneas stood, ferocious in his armor;
his eyes were restless and he stayed his hand;
and as he hesitated, Turnus' words
began to move him more and more—until            1255
high on the Latin's shoulder he made out
the luckless belt of Pallas, of the boy
whom Turnus had defeated, wounded, stretched

1237. *Rutulians*: The Italian troops    and Aeneas.
watching the combat between Turnus

upon the battlefield, from whom he took
this fatal sign to wear upon his back,                                    1260
this girdle glittering with familiar studs.
And when his eyes drank in this plunder, this
memorial of brutal grief, Aeneas,
aflame with rage—his wrath was terrible—
cried: "How can you who wear the spoils of my                             1265
dear comrade now escape me? It is Pallas
who strikes, who sacrifices you, who takes
this payment from your shameless blood." Relentless,
he sinks his sword into the chest of Turnus.
His limbs fell slack with chill; and with a moan                          1270
his life, resentful, fled to Shades below.

# The New Testament*

### [The Birth and Youth of Jesus]†

2. And it came to pass in those days, that there went out a
decree from Cæsar Augustus, that all the world[1] should be taxed.
(And this taxing was first made when Cyrenius was governor of
Syria.) And all went to be taxed, every one into his own city. And
Joseph also went up from Galilee, out of the city of Nazareth, into
Judæa, unto the city of David, which is called Bethlehem; (because
he was of the house and lineage of David:) to be taxed with Mary
his espoused wife, being great with child. And so it was, that, while
they were there, the days were accomplished that she should be
delivered. And she brought forth her firstborn son, and wrapped
him in swaddling clothes, and laid him in a manger; because there
was no room for them in the inn. And there were in the same
country shepherds abiding in the field, keeping watch over their
flock by night. And, lo, the angel of the Lord came upon them, and
the glory of the Lord shone round about them: and they were sore
afraid. And the angel said unto them, Fear not: for, behold, I bring
you good tidings of great joy, which shall be to all people. For unto
you is born this day in the city of David a Saviour, which is Christ[2]
the Lord. And this shall be a sign unto you; ye shall find the babe
wrapped in swaddling clothes, lying in a manger. And suddenly
there was with the angel a multitude of the heavenly host praising
God, and saying, Glory to God in the highest, and on earth peace,
good will toward men. And it came to pass, as the angels were
gone away from them into heaven, the shepherds said one to another, Let us now go even unto Bethlehem, and see this thing which

---

* The text of these selections from
the Holy Bible is that of the King
James, or Authorized, Version.
† Luke 2:1–52.

1. the Roman Empire.
2. A Greek word meaning "anointed,"
used of kings, priests, and the De-
liverer promised by the Prophets.

is come to pass, which the Lord hath made known unto us. And they came with haste, and found Mary, and Joseph, and the babe lying in a manger. And when they had seen it, they made known abroad the saying which was told them concerning this child. And all they that heard it wondered at those things which were told them by the shepherds. But Mary kept all these things, and pondered them in her heart. And the shepherds returned, glorifying and praising God for all the things that they had heard and seen, as it was told unto them. And when eight days were accomplished for the circumcising of the child, his name was called JESUS,[3] which was so named of the angel[4] before he was conceived in the womb. And when the days of her purification[5] according to the law of Moses were accomplished, they brought him to Jerusalem, to present him to the Lord; (as it is written in the law of the Lord, Every male that openeth the womb[6] shall be called holy to the Lord;) and to offer a sacrifice according to that which is said in the law of the Lord, A pair of turtledoves, or two young pigeons. And, behold, there was a man in Jerusalem, whose name was Simeon; and the same man was just and devout, waiting for the consolation of Israel: and the Holy Ghost was upon him. And it was revealed unto him by the Holy Ghost, that he should not see death, before he had seen the Lord's Christ. And he came by the Spirit into the temple: and when the parents brought in the child Jesus, to do for him after the custom of the law, then took he him up in his arms, and blessed God, and said, Lord, now lettest thou thy servant depart in peace, according to thy word: for mine eyes have seen thy salvation, which thou hast prepared before the face of all people; a light to lighten the Gentiles,[7] and the glory of thy people Israel. And Joseph and his mother marvelled at those things which were spoken of him. And Simeon blessed them, and said unto Mary his mother, Behold, this child is set for the fall and rising again[8] of many in Israel; and for a sign which shall be spoken against; (yea, a sword shall pierce through thy own soul also,) that the thoughts of many hearts may be revealed. And there was one Anna, a prophetess, the daughter of Phanuel, of the tribe of Aser: she was of a great age, and had lived with an husband seven years from her virginity; and she was a widow of about fourscore and four years, which departed not from the temple, but served God with fastings and prayers night and day. And she coming in that instant gave thanks likewise unto the Lord, and spoke of him to all them that looked for redemption in Jerusalem. And when they had performed all things according to the law of the Lord, they returned into

---

3. a form of the name Joshua, which means "he shall save."

4. in the Annunciation to Mary. (Luke 1:31.)

5. For the law here referred to, see Leviticus 12.

6. first-born son. The first-born son was regarded as belonging to God. See Exodus 13:2.

7. non-Jews.

8. The Greek word is the one always used of the resurrection of the dead.

Galilee, to their own city Nazareth. And the child grew, and waxed strong in spirit, filled with wisdom: and the grace of God was upon him. Now his parents went to Jerusalem every year at the feast of the passover. And when he was twelve years old, they went up to Jerusalem after the custom of the feast. And when they had fulfilled the days, as they returned, the child Jesus tarried behind in Jerusalem; and Joseph and his mother knew not of it. But they, supposing him to have been in the company, went a day's journey; and they sought him among their kinsfolk and acquaintance. And when they found him not, they turned back again to Jerusalem, seeking him. And it came to pass that after three days they found him in the temple, sitting in the midst of the doctors,[9] both hearing them, and asking them questions. And all that heard him were astonished at his understanding and answers. And when they saw him, they were amazed: and his mother said unto him, Son, why hast thou thus dealt with us? behold, thy father and I have sought thee sorrowing. And he said unto them, How is it that ye sought me? wist ye not that I must be about my Father's business? And they understood not the saying which he spoke unto them. And he went down with them, and came to Nazareth, and was subject unto them: but his mother kept all these sayings in her heart. And Jesus increased in wisdom and stature, and in favour with God and man.

9. teachers, rabbis.

## [The Teaching of Jesus]
### [THE SERMON ON THE MOUNT]*

5. And seeing the multitudes, he went up into a mountain: and when he was set, his disciples came unto him: and he opened his mouth, and taught them, saying, Blessed are the poor in spirit: for theirs is the kingdom of heaven. Blessed are they that mourn: for they shall be comforted. Blessed are the meek: for they shall inherit the earth. Blessed are they which do hunger and thirst after righteousness: for they shall be filled. Blessed are the merciful: for they shall obtain mercy. Blessed are the pure in heart: for they shall. see God. Blessed are the peacemakers: for they shall be called the children of God. Blessed are they which are persecuted for righteousness' sake: for theirs is the kingdom of heaven. Blessed are ye, when men shall revile you, and persecute you, and shall say all manner of evil against you falsely, for my sake. Rejoice, and be exceeding glad: for great is your reward in heaven: for so persecuted they the prophets which were before you.

Ye are the salt of the earth: but if the salt have lost his savour, wherewith shall it be salted?[1] it is thenceforth good for nothing, but to be cast out, and to be trodden under foot of men. Ye are

* Matthew 5:1—7:29.　　　　　1. how can it regain its savor?

the light of the world. A city that is set on a hill cannot be hid. Neither do men light a candle, and put it under a bushel,[2] but on a candlestick; and it giveth light unto all that are in the house. Let your light so shine before men, that they may see your good works, and glorify your Father which is in heaven.

Think not that I am come to destroy the law, or the prophets: I am not come to destroy, but to fulfil. For verily I say unto you, Till heaven and earth pass, one jot or one tittle shall in no wise pass from the law, till all be fulfilled. Whosoever therefore shall break one of these least commandments, and shall teach men so, he shall be called the least in the kingdom of heaven: but whosoever shall do and teach them, the same shall be called great in the kingdom of heaven. For I say unto you, That except your righteousness shall exceed the righteousness of the scribes[3] and Pharisees,[4] ye shall in no case enter into the kingdom of heaven.

Ye have heard that it was said by them of old time, Thou shalt not kill; and whosoever shall kill shall be in danger of the judgment: but I say unto you, That whosoever is angry with his brother without a cause shall be in danger of the judgment: and whosoever shall say to his brother, Raca,[5] shall be in danger of the council: but whosoever shall say, Thou fool, shall be in danger of hell fire.[6] Therefore if thou bring thy gift to the altar, and there rememberest that thy brother hath ought against thee; leave there thy gift before the altar, and go thy way; first be reconciled to thy brother, and then come and offer thy gift. Agree with thine adversary quickly, whiles thou art in the way with him; lest at any time the adversary deliver thee to the judge, and the judge deliver thee to the officer, and thou be cast into prison. Verily I say unto thee, Thou shalt by no means come out thence, till thou hast paid the uttermost farthing.

Ye have heard that it was said by them of old time, Thou shalt not commit adultery: but I say unto you, That whosoever looketh on a woman to lust after her hath committed adultery with her already in his heart. And if thy right eye offend thee, pluck it out, and cast it from thee: for it is profitable for thee that one of thy members should perish, and not that thy whole body should be cast into hell. And if thy right hand offend thee, cut it off, and cast it from thee: for it is profitable for thee that one of thy members should perish, and not that thy whole body should be cast into

2. a household vessel with the capacity of a bushel.

3. the official interpreters of the Sacred Scriptures.

4. a sect which insisted on strict observance of the Mosaic law.

5. The word means "empty."

6. The reference is to Jewish legal institutions. The penalties which might be inflicted for murder (see the opening sentence of this paragraph) were death by the sword (a sentence of a local court, "the judgment"), death by stoning (the sentence of a higher court, "the council"), and lastly the burning of the criminal's body in the place where refuse was thrown, Gehenna, which is hence used as a name for hell. Jesus compares the different degrees of punishment (administered by God) for the new sins which he here lists to the degrees of punishment recognized by Jewish law.

hell. It hath been said, Whosoever shall put away his wife, let him give her a writing of divorcement: but I say unto you, That whosoever shall put away his wife, saving for the cause of fornication, causeth her to commit adultery: and whosoever shall marry her that is divorced committeth adultery.

Again, ye have heard that it hath been said by them of old time, Thou shalt not forswear thyself, but shalt perform unto the Lord thine oaths: but I say unto you, Swear not at all; neither by heaven; for it is God's throne: nor by the earth; for it is his footstool: neither by Jerusalem; for it is the city of the great King. Neither shalt thou swear by thy head, because thou canst not make one hair white or black. But let your communication be, Yea, yea; Nay, nay: for whatsoever is more than these cometh of evil.

Ye have heard that it hath been said, An eye for an eye, and a tooth for a tooth: but I say unto you, That ye resist not evil: but whosoever shall smite thee on thy right cheek, turn to him the other also. And if any man will sue thee at the law, and take away thy coat, let him have thy cloak also. And whosoever shall compel thee to go a mile, go with him twain. Give to him that asketh thee, and from him that would borrow of thee turn not thou away.

Ye have heard that it hath been said, Thou shalt love thy neighbour, and hate thine enemy. But I say unto you, Love your enemies, bless them that curse you, do good to them that hate you, and pray for them which despitefully use you, and persecute you; that ye may be the children of your Father which is in heaven: for he maketh his sun to rise on the evil and on the good, and sendeth rain on the just and on the unjust. For if ye love them which love you, what reward have ye? do not even the publicans[7] the same? And if ye salute your brethren only, what do ye more than others? do not even the publicans so? Be ye therefore perfect, even as your Father which is in heaven is perfect.

6. Take heed that ye do not your alms[8] before men, to be seen of them: otherwise ye have no reward of your Father which is in heaven. Therefore when thou doest thine alms, do not sound a trumpet before thee, as the hypocrites do in the synagogues and in the streets, that they may have glory of men. Verily I say unto you, They have their reward. But when thou doest alms, let not thy left hand know what thy right hand doeth: that thine alms may be in secret: and thy Father which seeth in secret himself shall reward thee openly.

And when thou prayest, thou shalt not be as the hypocrites are: for they love to pray standing in the synagogues and in the corners

7. the men who collected the taxes for the Roman tax-farming corpora- tions; they were, naturally, universally despised and hated.
8. charitable actions.

of the streets, that they may be seen of men. Verily I say unto you, They have their reward. But thou, when thou prayest, enter into thy closet, and when thou hast shut thy door, pray to thy Father which is in secret; and thy Father which seeth in secret shall reward thee openly. But when ye pray, use not vain repetitions, as the heathen do; for they think that they shall be heard for their much speaking. Be not ye therefore like unto them: for your Father knoweth what things ye have need of, before ye ask him. After this manner therefore pray ye: Our Father which art in heaven, Hallowed be thy name. Thy kingdom come. Thy will be done in earth, as it is in heaven. Give us this day our daily bread. And forgive us our debts, as we forgive our debtors. And lead us not into temptation, but deliver us from evil: For thine is the kingdom, and the power, and the glory, for ever. Amen. For if ye forgive men their trespasses, your heavenly Father will also forgive you: but if ye forgive not men their trespasses, neither will your Father forgive your trespasses.

Moreover when ye fast, be not, as the hypocrites, of a sad countenance: for they disfigure their faces, that they may appear unto men to fast. Verily I say unto you, They have their reward. But thou, when thou fastest, anoint thine head, and wash thy face; that thou appear not unto men to fast, but unto thy Father which is in secret: and thy Father, which seeth in secret shall reward thee openly.

Lay not up for yourselves treasures upon earth, where moth and rust doth corrupt, and where thieves break through and steal: but lay up for yourselves treasures in heaven, where neither moth nor rust doth corrupt, and where thieves do not break through nor steal: for where your treasure is, there will your heart be also. The light of the body is the eye: if therefore thine eye be single,[9] thy whole body shall be full of light. But if thine eye be evil, thy whole body shall be full of darkness. If therefore the light that is in thee be darkness, how great is that darkness!

No man can serve two masters: for either he will hate the one, and love the other; or else he will hold to the one, and despise the other. Ye cannot serve God and Mammon. Therefore I say unto you, Take no thought for your life, what ye shall eat, or what ye shall drink; nor yet for your body, what ye shall put on. Is not the life more than meat, and the body than raiment? Behold the fowls of the air: for they sow not, neither do they reap, nor gather into barns; yet your heavenly Father feedeth them. Are ye not much better than they? Which of you by taking thought can add one cubit unto his stature? And why take ye thought for raiment? Consider the lilies of the field, how they grow; they toil not, neither do they spin: and yet I say unto you that even Solomon in all his

9. clear.

glory was not arrayed like one of these. Wherefore, if God so clothe the grass of the field, which to-day is, and to-morrow is cast into the oven, shall he not much more clothe you, O ye of little faith? Therefore take no thought, saying, What shall we eat? or, What shall we drink? or, Wherewithal shall we be clothed? (For after all these things do the Gentiles[10] seek:) for your heavenly Father knoweth that ye have need of all these things. But seek ye first the kingdom of God, and his righteousness; and all these things shall be added unto you. Take therefore no thought for the morrow: for the morrow shall take thought for the things of itself. Sufficient unto the day is the evil thereof.

7. Judge not, that ye be not judged. For with what judgment ye judged, ye shall be judged: and with what measure ye mete, it shall be measured to you again. And why beholdest thou the mote that is in thy brother's eye, but considerest not the beam that is in thine own eye? Or how wilt thou say to thy brother, Let me pull out the mote out of thine eye; and, behold, a beam is in thine own eye? Thou hypocrite, first cast out the beam out of thine own eye; and then shalt thou see clearly to cast out the mote out of thy brother's eye.

Give not that which is holy unto the dogs, neither cast ye your pearls before swine, lest they trample them under their feet, and turn again and rend you.

Ask, and it shall be given you; seek, and ye shall find; knock, and it shall be opened unto you: for every one that asketh receiveth; and he that seeketh findeth; and to him that knocketh it shall be opened. Or what man is there of you, whom if his son ask bread, will he give him a stone? Or if he ask a fish, will he give him a serpent? If ye then, being evil, know how to give good gifts unto your children, how much more shall your Father which is in heaven give good things to them that ask him? Therefore all things whatsoever ye would that men should do to you, do ye even so to them: for this is the law and the prophets.

Enter ye in at the strait[11] gate: for wide is the gate, and broad is the way, that leadeth to destruction, and many there be which go in thereat: because strait is the gate, and narrow is the way, which leadeth unto life, and few there be that find it.

Beware of false prophets, which come to you in sheep's clothing, but inwardly they are ravening wolves. Ye shall know them by their fruits. Do men gather grapes of thorns, or figs of thistles? Even so every good tree bringeth forth good fruit; but a corrupt tree bringeth forth evil fruit. A good tree cannot bring forth evil fruit, neither can a corrupt tree bring forth good fruit. Every tree that bringeth

10. non-Jews.    11. narrow.

not forth good fruit is hewn down, and cast into the fire. Wherefore by their fruits ye shall know them.

Not every one that saith unto me, Lord, Lord, shall enter into the kingdom of heaven; but he that doeth the will of my Father which is in heaven. Many will say to me in that day, Lord, Lord, have we not prophesied in thy name? and in thy name have cast out devils? and in thy name done many wonderful works? And then will I profess unto them, I never knew you: depart from me, ye that work iniquity.

Therefore whosoever heareth these sayings of mine, and doeth them, I will liken him unto a wise man, which built his house upon a rock: and the rain descended, and the floods came and the winds blew, and beat upon that house; and it fell not: for it was founded upon a rock. And every one that heareth these sayings of mine, and doeth them not, shall be likened unto a foolish man, which built his house upon the sand: and the rain descended, and the floods came, and the winds blew, and beat upon that house; and it fell: and great was the fall of it. And it came to pass, when Jesus had ended these sayings, the people were astonished at his doctrine: for he taught them as one having authority, and not as the scribes.

[PARABLES OF JESUS]*

15. Then drew near unto him all the publicans and sinners for to hear him. And the Pharisees and scribes murmured, saying, This man receiveth sinners, and eateth with them.

And he spoke this parable unto them, saying, What man of you, having a hundred sheep, if he lose one of them, doth not leave the ninety and nine in the wilderness, and go after that which is lost, until he find it? And when he hath found it, he layeth it on his shoulders, rejoicing. And when he cometh home, he calleth together his friends and neighbours, saying unto them, Rejoice with me; for I have found my sheep which was lost. I say unto you that likewise joy shall be in heaven over one sinner that repenteth, more than over ninety and nine just persons, which need no repentance.

Either what woman having ten pieces of silver, if she lose one piece, doth not light a candle, and sweep the house, and seek diligently till she find it? And when she hath found it, she calleth her friends and her neighbours together, saying, Rejoice with me; for I have found the piece which I had lost. Likewise, I say unto you, there is joy in the presence of the angels of God over one sinner that repenteth.

And he said, A certain man had two sons: and the younger of them said to his father, Father, give me the portion of goods that falleth to me. And he divided unto them his living. And not many

* Luke 15:1-32.

days after the younger son gathered all together, and took his journey into a far country, and there wasted his substance with riotous living. And when he had spent all, there arose a mighty famine in that land; and he began to be in want. And he went and joined himself to a citizen of that country; and he sent him into his fields to feed swine. And he would fain have filled his belly with the husks that the swine did eat: and no man gave unto him. And when he came to himself, he said, How many hired servants of my father's have bread enough and to spare, and I perish with hunger! I will arise and go to my father, and will say unto him, Father, I have sinned against heaven, and before thee, and am no more worthy to be called thy son: make me as one of thy hired servants. And he arose, and came to his father. But when he was yet a great way off, his father saw him, and had compassion, and ran, and fell on his neck, and kissed him. And the son said unto him, Father, I have sinned against heaven, and in thy sight, and am no more worthy to be called thy son. But the father said to his servants, Bring forth the best robe, and put it on him; and put a ring on his hand, and shoes on his feet: and bring hither the fatted calf, and kill it; and let us eat, and be merry: for this my son was dead, and is alive again; he was lost, and is found. And they began to be merry. Now his elder son was in the field: and as he came and drew nigh to the house, he heard musick and dancing. And he called one of the servants, and asked what these things meant. And he said unto him, Thy brother is come; and thy father hath killed the fatted calf, because he hath received him safe and sound. And he was angry, and would not go in: therefore came his father out, and intreated him. And he answering said to his father, Lo, these many years do I serve thee, neither transgressed I at any time thy commandment: and yet thou never gavest me a kid, that I might make merry with my friends: but as soon as this thy son was come, which hath devoured thy living with harlots, thou hast killed for him the fatted calf. And he said unto him, Son, thou art ever with me, and all that I have is thine. It was meet that we should make merry, and be glad: for this thy brother was dead, and is alive again; and was lost, and is found.

### [The Betrayal of Jesus]*

26. . . . Then one of the twelve, called Judas Iscariot, went unto the chief priests, and said unto them, What will ye give me, and I will deliver him unto you? And they covenanted with him for thirty pieces of silver. And from that time he sought opportunity to betray him.

* Matthew 26:14–75.

Now the first day of the feast of unleavened bread[1] the disciples came to Jesus, saying unto him, Where wilt thou that we prepare for thee to eat the passover? And he said, Go into the city to such a man, and say unto him, The Master saith, My time is at hand; I will keep the passover at thy house with my disciples. And the disciples did as Jesus had appointed them; and they made ready the passover. Now when the even was come, he sat down with the twelve. And as they did eat, he said, Verily I say unto you, that one of you shall betray me. And they were exceeding sorrowful, and began every one of them to say unto him, Lord, is it I? And he answered and said, He that dippeth his hand with me in the dish, the same shall betray me. The Son of man goeth as it is written of him: but woe unto that man by whom the Son of man is betrayed! it had been good for that man if he had not been born. Then Judas, which betrayed him, answered and said, Master, is it I? He said unto him, Thou hast said.

And as they were eating, Jesus took bread, and blessed it, and brake it, and gave it to the disciples, and said, Take, eat; this is my body. And he took the cup, and gave thanks, and gave it to them, saying, Drink ye all of it; for this is my blood of the new testament,[2] which is shed for many for the remission of sins. But I say unto you, I will not drink henceforth of this fruit of the vine, until that day when I drink it new with you in my Father's kingdom. And when they had sung an hymn, they went out into the mount of Olives. Then saith Jesus unto them, All ye shall be offended[3] because of me this night: for it is written,[4] I will smite the shepherd, and the sheep of the flock shall be scattered abroad. But after I am risen again, I will go before you into Galilee. Peter answered and said unto him, Though all men shall be offended because of thee, yet will I never be offended. Jesus said unto him, Verily I say unto thee, That this night, before the cock crow, thou shalt deny me thrice. Peter said unto him, Though I should die with thee, yet will I not deny thee. Likewise also said all the disciples.

Then cometh Jesus with them unto a place called Gethsemane, and saith unto the disciples, Sit ye here, while I go and pray yonder. And he took with him Peter and the two sons of Zebedee,[5] and began to be sorrowful and very heavy. Then saith he unto them, My soul is exceeding sorrowful, even unto death: tarry ye here, and watch[6] with me. And he went a little farther, and fell on his face,

---

1. held in remembrance of the delivery of the Jews from captivity in Egypt. See Exodus 12.

2. i.e., of the new covenant, or agreement. Jesus compares himself to the lamb that was killed at the Passover as a sign of the covenant between God and the Jews.

3. The Greek means literally, "you will be made to stumble."

4. See Zechariah 13:7.

5. James and John.

6. stay awake.

and prayed, saying, O my Father, if it be possible, let this cup pass from me: nevertheless, not as I will, but as thou wilt. And he cometh unto the disciples, and findeth them asleep, and saith unto Peter, What, could ye not watch with me one hour? Watch and pray, that ye enter not into temptation: the spirit indeed is willing, but the flesh is weak. He went away again the second time, and prayed, saying, O my Father, if this cup may not pass away from me, except I drink it, thy will be done. And he came and found them asleep again: for their eyes were heavy. And he left them, and went away again, and prayed the third time, saying the same words. Then cometh he to his disciples, and saith unto them, Sleep on now, and take your rest: behold, the hour is at hand, and the Son of man is betrayed into the hands of sinners. Rise, let us be going: behold, he is at hand that doth betray me.

And while he yet spake, lo, Judas, one of the twelve, came, and with him a great multitude with swords and staves,[7] from the chief priests and elders of the people. Now he that betrayed him gave them a sign, saying, Whomsoever I shall kiss, that same is he: hold him fast. And forthwith he came to Jesus and said, Hail, master; and kissed him. And Jesus said unto him, Friend, wherefore art thou come? Then came they and laid hands on Jesus, and took him. And behold, one of them[8] which were with Jesus stretched out his hand, and drew his sword, and struck a servant of the high priest's, and smote off his ear. Then said Jesus unto him, Put up again thy sword into his place: for all they that take the sword shall perish with the sword. Thinkest thou that I cannot now pray to my Father, and he shall presently give me more than twelve legions[9] of angels? But how then shall the scriptures be fulfilled, that thus it must be? In that same hour said Jesus to the multitudes, Are ye come out as against a thief with swords and staves for to take me? I sat daily with you teaching in the temple, and ye laid no hold on me. But all this was done that the scriptures of the prophets might be fulfilled. Then all the disciples forsook him, and fled.

And they that had laid hold on Jesus led him away to Caiaphas the high priest, where the scribes and the elders were assembled. But Peter followed him afar off unto the high priest's palace, and went in, and sat with the servants, to see the end. Now the chief priests, and elders, and all the council, sought false witness[10] against Jesus, to put him to death; but found none: yea, though many false witnesses came, yet found they none. At the last came two false witnesses, and said, This fellow said, I am able to destroy the temple of God, and to build it in three days. And the high priest arose, and said unto him, Answerest thou nothing? What is it which these

7. clubs, sticks.
8. This was Peter.
9. The legion was a Roman military

formation; its full complement was six thousand men.
10. evidence.

witness against thee? But Jesus held his peace. And the high priest answered and said unto him, I adjure thee by the living God, that thou tell us whether thou be the Christ, the Son of God. Jesus saith unto him, Thou hast said:[11] nevertheless I say unto you, Hereafter shall ye see the Son of man sitting on the right hand of power, and coming in the clouds of heaven. Then the high priest rent[12] his clothes, saying, He hath spoken blasphemy; what further need have we of witnesses? behold, now ye have heard his blasphemy. What think ye? They answered and said, He is guilty of death.[13] Then did they spit in his face, and buffeted [14] him; and others smote him with the palms of their hands, saying, Prophesy unto us, thou Christ, Who is he that smote thee?

Now Peter sat without in the palace: and a damsel came unto him, saying, Thou also wast with Jesus of Galilee. But he denied before them all, saying, I know not what thou sayest. And when he was gone out into the porch, another maid saw him and said unto them that were there, This fellow was also with Jesus of Nazareth. And again he denied with an oath, I do not know the man. And after a while came unto him they that stood by, and said to Peter, Surely thou also art one of them; for thy speech bewrayeth[15] thee. Then began he to curse and to swear, saying, I know not the man. And immediately the cock crew. And Peter remembered the word of Jesus, which said unto him, Before the cock crow thou shalt deny me thrice. And he went out, and wept bitterly.

11. an affirmative phrase.
12. tore.
13. liable to the death penalty.
14. beat.
15. betrays. Peter's speech revealed his Galilean origin.

## [The Trial and Crucifixion of Jesus]*

27. When the morning was come, all the chief priests and elders of the people took counsel against Jesus to put him to death: and when they had bound him, they led him away, and delivered him to Pontius Pilate the governor.[1]

Then Judas, which had betrayed him, when he saw that he was condemned, repented himself, and brought again the thirty pieces of silver to the chief priests and elders, saying, I have sinned in that I have betrayed the innocent blood. And they said, What is that to us? see thou to that. And he cast down the pieces of silver in the temple, and departed, and went and hanged himself. And the chief priests took the silver pieces, and said, It is not lawful for to put them into the treasury, because it is the price of blood. And they

* Matthew 27:1–66.
1. His official title was procurator of the province of Judea. The Roman policy was to allow the Jews as much independence as possible (especially in religious matters), but only the Roman authorities could impose a death sentence.

took counsel, and bought with them the potter's field,[2] to bury strangers in. Wherefore that field was called, The field of blood, unto this day. Then was fulfilled that which was spoken by Jeremy[3] the prophet, saying, And they took the thirty pieces of silver, the price of him that was valued, whom they of the children of Israel did value; and gave them for the potter's field, as the Lord appointed me. And Jesus stood before the governor: and the governor asked him, saying, Art thou the King of the Jews? And Jesus said unto him, Thou sayest.

And when he was accused of[4] the chief priests and elders, he answered nothing. Then said Pilate unto him, Hearest thou not how many things they witness against thee? And he answered him to never a word; insomuch that the governor marvelled greatly. Now at that feast the governor was wont to release unto the people a prisoner, whom they would. And they had then a notable prisoner, called Barabbas.[5] Therefore when they were gathered together, Pilate said unto them, Whom will ye that I release unto you? Barabbas, or Jesus which is called Christ? For he knew that for envy they had delivered him.[6]

When he was set down on the judgment seat, his wife sent unto him, saying, Have thou nothing to do with that just man: for I have suffered many things this day in a dream because of him. But the chief priests and elders persuaded the multitude that they should ask Barabbas, and destroy Jesus. The governor answered and said unto them, Whether of the twain will ye that I release unto you? They said, Barabbas. Pilate saith unto them, What shall I do then with Jesus which is called Christ? They all say unto him, Let him be crucified.[7] And the governor said, Why, what evil hath he done? But they cried out the more, saying, Let him be crucified.

When Pilate saw that he could prevail nothing, but that rather a tumult was made, he took water, and washed his hands before the multitude, saying, I am innocent of the blood of this just person: see ye to it. Then answered all the people, and said, His blood be on us, and on our children.

Then released he Barabbas unto them: and when he had scourged[8] Jesus, he delivered him to be crucified. Then the soldiers of the governor took Jesus into the common hall, and gathered unto him the whole band of soldiers. And they stripped him, and put on him a scarlet robe.

And when they had platted a crown of thorns, they put it upon

2. a field which had been dug for potter's clay, and was consequently not worth very much as land.

3. Jeremiah. The prophecy here quoted is a version of Zechariah 11:13.

4. by

5. under sentence of death for sedition and murder.

6. i.e., to the Roman authorities.

7. the regular Roman punishment for sedition.

8. whipped, a routine part of the punishment.

his head, and a reed[9] in his right hand: and they bowed the knee before him, and mocked him, saying, Hail, King of the Jews! And they spit upon him, and took the reed, and smote him on the head. And after that they had mocked him, they took the robe off from him, and put his own raiment on him, and led him away to crucify him. And as they came out, they found a man of Cyrene,[10] Simon by name: him they compelled to bear his cross. And when they were come unto a place called Golgotha, that is to say, a place of a skull,

They gave him vinegar to drink mingled with gall:[11] and when he had tasted thereof, he would not drink. And they crucified him, and parted his garments, casting lots: that it might be fulfilled which was spoken by the prophet, They parted my garments among them, and upon my vesture did they cast lots.[12] And sitting down they watched him there; and set up over his head his accusation written, THIS IS JESUS THE KING OF THE JEWS. Then were there two thieves crucified with him, one on the right hand, and another on the left.

And they that passed by reviled him, wagging their heads, and saying, Thou that destroyest the temple, and buildest it in three days, save thyself. If thou be the Son of God, come down from the cross. Likewise also the chief priests mocking him, with the scribes and elders, said, He saved others; himself he cannot save. If he be the King of Israel, let him now come down from the cross, and we will believe him. He trusted in God; let him deliver him now, if he will have him: for he said, I am the Son of God. The thieves also, which were crucified with him, cast the same in his teeth. Now from the sixth hour there was darkness over all the land unto the ninth hour. And about the ninth hour Jesus cried with a loud voice, saying, Eli, Eli, lama sabachthani? that is to say, My God, my God, why hast thou forsaken me?[13] Some of them that stood there, when they heard that, said, This man calleth for Elias. And straightway one of them ran, and took a sponge, and filled it with vinegar,[14] and put it on a reed, and gave him to drink. The rest said, Let be, let us see whether Elias[15] will come to save him.

Jesus, when he had cried again with a loud voice, yielded up the ghost. And, behold, the veil of the temple[16] was rent in twain from the top to the bottom; and the earth did quake, and the rocks rent; and the graves were opened; and many bodies of the saints which slept arose, and came out of the graves after his resurrection, and

9. to represent the king's scepter.
10. on the coast of North Africa.
11. The Greek word translated "vinegar" describes a sour wine which was the regular drink of the Roman soldiery. The addition of bitter gall is further mockery.
12. *that it might . . . cast lots:* It is generally agreed that this is a late addition to the text.
13. the opening words of Psalm 22. The actual words of Jesus, "Eli, Eli, lama sabachthani?" are Aramaic, the spoken Hebrew of the period.
14. See footnote 11.
15. the prophet Elijah.
16. the curtain which screened off the holy of holies.

went into the holy city, and appeared unto many. Now when the centurion,[17] and they that were with him, watching Jesus, saw the earthquake, and those things that were done, they feared greatly, saying, Truly this was the Son of God. And many women were there beholding afar off, which followed Jesus from Galilee, ministering unto him: among which was Mary Magdalene, and Mary the mother of James and Joses, and the mother of Zebedee's children. When the even was come, there came a rich man of Arimathæa, named Joseph, who also himself was Jesus' disciple. He went to Pilate, and begged the body of Jesus. Then Pilate commanded the body to be delivered. And when Joseph had taken the body, he wrapped it in clean linen cloth, and laid it in his own new tomb, which he had hewn out in the rock: and he rolled a great stone to the door of the sepulchre, and departed. And there was Mary Magdalene, and the other Mary, sitting over against the sepulchre.

Now the next day, that followed the day of the preparation, the chief priests and Pharisees came together unto Pilate, saying, Sir, we remember that that deceiver said, while he was yet alive, After three days I will rise again. Command therefore that the sepulchre be made sure[18] until the third day, lest his disciples come by night, and steal him away, and say unto the people, He is risen from the dead: so the last error shall be worse than the first. Pilate said unto them, Ye have a watch:[19] go your way, make it as sure as ye can. So they went, and made the sepulchre sure, sealing the stone, and setting a watch.

17. the Roman officer in charge of the execution.

18. guarded.

19. police force.

### [The Resurrection]*

28. In the end of the sabbath, as it began to dawn toward the first day of the week, came Mary Magdalene and the other Mary to see the sepulchre. And, behold, there was a great earthquake: for the angel of the Lord descended from heaven, and came and rolled back the stone from the door, and sat upon it. His countenance was like lightning, and his raiment white as snow: and for fear of him the keepers did shake, and became as dead men. And the angel answered and said unto the women, Fear not ye: for I know that ye seek Jesus, which was crucified. He is not here: for he is risen, as he said. Come, see the place where the Lord lay. And go quickly, and tell his disciples that he is risen from the dead; and, behold, he goeth before you into Galilee; there shall ye see him: lo, I have told you. And they departed quickly from the sepulchre with fear and great joy; and did run to bring his disciples word.

And as they went to tell his disciples, behold, Jesus met them, saying, All hail! And they came and held him by the feet, and worshipped him. Then said Jesus unto them, Be not afraid: go tell my brethren that they go into Galilee, and there shall they see me.

* Matthew 28:1–20.

Now when they were going, behold, some of the watch came into the city, and shewed unto the chief priests all the things that were done. And when they were assembled with the elders, and had taken counsel, they gave large money unto the soldiers, saying, Say ye, His disciples came by night, and stole him away while we slept. And if this come to the governor's ears, we will persuade him, and secure you. So they took the money, and did as they were taught: and this saying is commonly reported among the Jews until this day.

Then the eleven disciples went away into Galilee, into a mountain where Jesus had appointed them. And when they saw him, they worshipped him: but some doubted. And Jesus came and spake unto them, saying, All power is given unto me in heaven and in earth.

Go ye therefore, and teach all nations, baptizing them in the name of the Father, and of the Son, and of the Holy Ghost: teaching them to observe all things whatsoever I have commanded you: and, lo, I am with you alway, even unto the end of the world. Amen.

# PETRONIUS
## (died A.D. 65)

## Dinner with Trimalchio*

[The narrator, Encolpius, is a penniless vagabond who is a student of rhetoric under a master named Agamemnon. His close associates are Ascyltus, a fellow student, and Giton, a handsome boy who has no particular occupation. After some disreputable and very tiring adventures they are invited, as pupils of Agamemnon, to a banquet. The scene of the story is an unidentified city in southern Italy, the time probably about A.D. 50.]

The next day but one finally arrived. But we were so knocked about that we wanted to run rather than rest. We were mournfully discussing how to avoid the approaching storm,[1] when one of Agamemnon's slaves broke in on our frantic debate.

"Here," said he, "don't you know who's your host today? It's Trimalchio[2]—he's terribly elegant. . . . He has a clock[3] in the dining-room and a trumpeter[4] all dressed up to tell him how much longer he's got to live."

This made us forget all our troubles. We dressed carefully and

---

*From the work known as the *Satyricon*, probably written during the principate of Nero (A.D. 54–68). Our selection is one of the best-known incidents in the work. The translation is by J. P. Sullivan (copyright © J. P. Sullivan 1965, 1969) and is reprinted by permission of Penguin Books Ltd.

1. a repetition of the unsavory incidents they have just experienced.
2. *Trimalchio:* the name suggests "triply blessed" or "triply powerful."
3. at this period a rare and expensive article.
4. to sound off every hour on the hour.

told Giton, who was very kindly acting as our servant, to attend us at the baths.[5]

We did not take our clothes off but began wandering around, or rather exchanging jokes while circulating among the little groups. Suddenly we saw a bald old man in a reddish shirt, playing ball with some long-haired boys. It was not so much the boys that made us watch, although they alone were worth the trouble, but the old gentleman himself. He was taking his exercise in slippers and throwing a green ball around. But he didn't pick it up if it touched the ground; instead there was a slave holding a bagful, and he supplied them to the players. We noticed other novelties. Two eunuchs stood around at different points: one of them carried a silver chamber pot, the other counted the balls, not those flying from hand to hand according to the rules, but those that fell to the ground. We were still admiring these elegant arrangements when Menelaus[6] hurried up to us.

"This is the man you'll be dining with," he said. "In fact, you are now watching the beginning of the dinner."

No sooner had Menelaus spoken than Trimalchio snapped his fingers. At the signal the eunuch brought up the chamber pot for him, while he went on playing. With the weight off his bladder, he demanded water for his hands, splashed a few drops on his fingers and wiped them on a boy's head.

It would take too long to pick out isolated incidents. Anyway, we entered the baths where we began sweating at once and we went immediately into the cold water. Trimalchio had been smothered in perfume and was already being rubbed down, not with linen towels, but with bath-robes of the finest wool. As this was going on, three masseurs sat drinking Falernian[7] in front of him. Through quarreling they spilled most of it and Trimalchio said they were drinking his health.[8] Wrapped in thick scarlet felt he was put into a litter. Four couriers with lots of medals went in front, as well as a go-cart in which his favourite boy was riding—a wizened, bleary-eyed youngster, uglier than his master. As he was carried off, a musician with a tiny set of pipes took his place by Trimalchio's head and whispered a tune in his ear the whole way.

We followed on, choking with amazement by now, and arrived at the door with Agamemnon at our side. On the doorpost a notice was fastened which read:

ANY SLAVE LEAVING THE HOUSE WITHOUT HIS MASTER'S
PERMISSION WILL RECEIVE ONE HUNDRED LASHES

5. a public institution. They were magnificent buildings, containing not only baths of many types and temperatures, but places for conversation and games and even libraries.

6. appropriately enough, Agamemnon's assistant in instruction.

7. *Falernian:* a famous wine from Campania south of Rome.

8. *drinking his health:* He claims they are pouring a libation.

Just at the entrance stood the hall-porter, dressed in a green uniform with a belt of cherry red. He was shelling peas into a silver basin. Over the doorway hung—of all things—a golden cage from which a spotted magpie greeted visitors.

As I was gaping at all this, I almost fell over backwards and broke a leg. There on the left as one entered, not far from the porter's cubbyhole, was a huge dog with a chain round its neck. It was painted on the wall and over it, in big capitals, was written:

BEWARE OF THE DOG

My colleagues laughed at me, but when I got my breath back I went to examine the whole wall. There was a mural of a slave market, price tags and all. Then Trimalchio himself, holding a wand of Mercury[9] and being led into Rome by Minerva.[10] After this a picture of how he learned accounting and, finally how he became a steward. The painstaking artist had drawn it all in great detail with descriptions underneath. Just where the colonnade ended Mercury hauled him up by the chin and rushed him to a high platform. . . .

I began asking the porter what were the pictures they had in the middle.

"The Iliad, the Odyssey, and the gladiatorial show given by Laenas," he told me.

Time did not allow us to look at many things there . . . by now we had reached the dining-room. . . .

Finally we took our places. Boys from Alexandria poured iced water over our hands. Others followed them and attended to our feet, removing any hangnails with great skill. But they were not quiet even during this troublesome operation: they sang away at their work. I wanted to find out if the whole staff were singers, so I asked for a drink. In a flash a boy was there, singing in a shrill voice while he attended to me—and anyone else who was asked to bring something did the same. It was more like a musical comedy than a respectable dinner party.

Some extremely elegant hors d'oeuvre were served at this point—by now everyone had taken his place with the exception of Trimalchio, for whom, strangely enough, the place at the top was reserved. The dishes for the first course included an ass of Corinthian bronze with two panniers, white olives on one side and black on the other. Over the ass were two pieces of plate, with Trimalchio's name and the weight of the silver inscribed on the rims. There were some small iron frames shaped like bridges supporting dormice sprinkled with

---

9. *Mercury* (Hermes): as a trickster, the patron god of thieves and businessmen.

10. *Minerva* (Athena): patron goddess of arts and skills.

honey and poppy seed. There were steaming hot sausages too, on a silver gridiron with damsons and pomegranate seeds underneath.

We were in the middle of these elegant dishes when Trimalchio himself was carried in to the sound of music and set down on a pile of tightly stuffed cushions. The sight of him drew an astonished laugh from the guests. His cropped head stuck out from a scarlet coat; his neck was well muffled up and he had put round it a napkin with a broad purple stripe and tassels dangling here and there. On the little finger of his left hand he wore a heavy gilt ring and a smaller one on the last joint of the next finger. This I thought was solid gold, but actually it was studded with little iron stars. And to show off even more of his jewellery, he had his right arm bare and set off by a gold armlet and an ivory circlet fastened with a gleaming metal plate.

After picking his teeth with a silver toothpick, he began: "My friends, I wasn't keen to come into the dining room yet. But if I stayed away any more, I would have kept you back, so I've deprived myself of all my little pleasures for you. However, you'll allow me to finish my game."

A boy was at his heels with a board of terebinth wood[11] with glass squares, and I noticed the very last word in luxury—instead of white and black pieces he had gold and silver coins. While he was swearing away like a trooper over his game and we were still on the hors d'oeuvre, a tray was brought in with a basket on it. There sat a wooden hen, its wings spread round it the way hens are when they are broody. Two slaves hurried up and as the orchestra played a tune they began searching through the straw and dug out peahens' eggs, which they distributed to the guests.

Trimalchio turned to look at this little scene and said: "My friends, I gave orders for that bird to sit on some peahens' eggs. I hope to goodness they are not starting to hatch. However, let's try them and see if they are still soft."

We took up our spoons (weighing at least half a pound each) and cracked the eggs, which were made of rich pastry. To tell the truth, I nearly threw away my share, as the chicken seemed already formed. But I heard a guest who was an old hand say: "There should be something good here." So I searched the shell with my fingers and found the plumpest little figpecker, all covered with yolk and seasoned with pepper.

At this point Trimalchio became tired of his game and demanded that all the previous dishes be brought to him. He gave permission in a loud voice for any of us to have another glass of mead if we wanted it. Suddenly there was a crash from the orchestra and a troop of waiters—still singing—snatched away the hors d'oeuvre. However in the confusion one of the side-dishes happened to fall

---

11. *terebinth:* a very hard wood which takes a high polish and is very expensive (like everything Trimalchio has).

and a slave picked it up from the floor. Trimalchio noticed this, had
the boy's ears boxed and told him to throw it down again. A cleaner
came in with a broom and began to sweep up the silver plate along
with the rest of the rubbish. Two long-haired Ethiopians followed
him, carrying small skin bottles like those they use for scattering
sand in the circus, and they poured wine over our hands—no one
ever offered us water.

Our host was complimented on these elegant arrangements.
"You've got to fight fair," he replied. "That is why I gave orders for
each guest to have his own table. At the same time these smelly
slaves won't crowd so."

Carefully sealed wine bottles were immediately brought, their
necks labelled:

FALERNIAN

CONSUL OPIMIUS

ONE HUNDRED YEARS OLD[12]

While we were examining the labels, Trimalchio clapped his
hands and said with a sigh:

"Wine has a longer life than us poor folks. So let's wet our whis-
tles. Wine is life. I'm giving you real Opimian. I didn't put out
such good stuff yesterday, though the company was much better
class."

Naturally we drank and missed no opportunity of admiring his
elegant hospitality. In the middle of this a slave brought in a silver
skeleton, put together in such a way that its joints and backbone
could be pulled out and twisted in all directions. After he had flung
it about on the table once or twice, its flexible joints falling into
various postures, Trimalchio recited:

> "Man's life alas! is but a span,
> So let us live it while we can,
> We'll be like this when dead."

After our applause the next course was brought in. Actually it
was not as grand as we expected, but it was so novel that everyone
stared. It was a deep circular tray with the twelve signs of the
Zodiac arranged round the edge. . . .

After this course Trimalchio got up and went to the toilet. Free
of his domineering presence, we began to strike up a general conversation. Dama[13] started off by calling for bigger glasses.

"The day's nothin'," he said, "It's night 'fore y'can turn around.
So the best thing's get out of bed and go straight to dinner. Lovely

---

12. The wine was labeled with the
name of the man who was consul in the
year it was bottled. Opimius was consul
in 121 B.C. Since it was in this year that
the custom of dating the wine by the
consul's name began, Trimalchio's wine
was the oldest possible. If genuine, it
would have been undrinkable.

13. *Dama:* one of Trimalchio's friends.
Like those of Seleucus and Phileros who
join the conversation later, his name is
Greek.

cold weather we've had too. M'bath hardly thawed me out. Still, a hot drink's as good as an overcoat. I've been throwin' it back neat, and I'm pretty tight—the wine's gone to m'head."

This started Seleucus off.

"Me now," he said, "I don't have a bath every day. It's like gettin' rubbed with fuller's[14] earth, havin' a bath. The water bites into you, and as the days go by, your heart turns to water. But when I've knocked back a hot glass of wine and honey, kiss-my-arse I say to the cold weather. Mind you, I couldn't have a bath—I was at a funeral today. Poor old Chrysanthus has just given up the ghost —nice man he was! It was only the other day he stopped me in the street. I still seem to hear his voice. Dear, dear! We're just so many walking bags of wind. We're worse than flies—at least flies have got some strength in them, but we're no more than empty bubbles.

"And what would he have been like if he hadn't been on a diet? For five days he didn't take a drop of water or a crumb of bread into his mouth. But he's gone to join the majority. The doctors finished him—well, hard luck, more like. After all, a doctor is just to put your mind at rest. Still, he got a good sendoff—he had a bier and all beautifully draped. His mourners—several of his slaves were left their freedom—did him proud, even though his widow was a bit mean with her tears. Suppose now he hadn't been so good to her! But women as a sex are real vultures. It's no good doing them a favour, you might as well throw it down a well. An old passion is just an ulcer."

He was being a bore and Phileros said loudly:

"Let's think of the living. He's got what he deserved. He lived an honest life and he died an honest death. What has he got to complain about? He started out in life with just a penny and he was ready to pick up less than that from a muck-heap, if he had to use his teeth. He went up in the world. He got bigger and bigger till he got where you see, like a honeycomb. I honestly think he left a solid hundred thousand and he had the lot in hard cash. But I'll be honest about it—seeing I'm a bit of a cynic—he had a foul mouth and too much lip. He wasn't a man, he was just murder.

"Now his brother was a fine man, a real friend to his friends, always ready with a helping hand or a decent meal.

"Chrysanthus had bad luck at first, but the first vintage set him on his feet. He fixed his own price when he sold the wine. And what properly kept his head above water was a legacy he came in for, when he pocketed more than was left to him. And the block-head, when he had a quarrel with his brother, cut him out of his will in favour of some sod we've never heard of. You're leaving a lot behind when you leave your own flesh and blood. But he took advice from his slaves and they really fixed him. It's never right to believe all you're told, especially for a business man. But it's true he

---

14. *fuller:* a cleaner (of woollen cloaks). They used very strong solvents.

enjoyed himself while he lived. You got it, you keep it. He was certainly Fortune's favourite—lead turned to gold in his hand. Mind you, it's easy when everything runs smoothly.

"And how old do you think he was? Seventy or more! But he was hard as nails and carried his age well. His hair was black as a raven's wing. I knew the man for ages and ages and he was still an old lecher. I honestly don't think he left the dog alone. What's more, he liked little boys—he could turn his hand to anything. Well, I don't blame him—after all, he couldn't take anything else with him."

This was Phileros, then Ganymedes said:

"You're all talking about things that don't concern heaven or earth. Meanwhile, no one gives a damn the way we're hit by the corn situation. Honest to God, I couldn't get hold of a mouthful of bread today. And look how there's still no rain. It's been absolute starvation for a whole year now. To hell with the food officers! They're in with the bakers—'You be nice to me and I'll be nice to you.' So the little man suffers, while those grinders of the poor never stop celebrating. Oh, if only we still had the sort of men I found here when I first arrived from Asia. Like lions they were. That was the life! Come one, come all! If white flour was inferior to the very finest, they'd thrash those bogeymen till they thought God Almighty was after them.

"I remember Safinius—he used to live by the old arch then; I was a boy at the time. He wasn't a man, he was all pepper. He used to scorch the ground wherever he went. But he was dead straight—don't let him down and he wouldn't let you down. You'd be ready to play *morra*[15] with him in the dark. But on the city council, how he used to wade into some of them—no beating about the bush, straight from the shoulder! And when he was in court, his voice got louder and louder like a trumpet. He never sweated or spat—I think there was a touch of the old acid about him. And very affable he was when you met him, calling everyone by name just like one of us. Naturally at the time corn was dirt cheap. You could buy a penny loaf that two of you couldn't get through. Today—I've seen bigger bull's-eyes.

"Ah me! It's getting worse every day. This place is going down like a calf's tail. But why do we have a third-rate food officer who wouldn't lose a penny to save our lives? He sits at home laughing and rakes in more money a day than anyone else's whole fortune. I happen to know he's just made a thousand in gold. But if we had any balls at all, he wouldn't be feeling so pleased with himself. People today are lions at home and foxes outside.

"Take me, I've already sold the rags off my back for food and if this shortage continues, I'll be selling my bit of a house. What's

---

15. *morra:* a game (still played in southern Italy) which requires the players to match the number of fingers held out by the opponent.

going to happen to this place if neither god nor man will help us? As I hope to go home tonight, I'm sure all this is heaven's doing.

"Nobody believes in heaven, see, nobody fasts, nobody gives a damn for the Almighty. No, people only bow their heads to count their money. In the old days high-class ladies used to climb up the hill barefoot, their hair loose and their hearts pure, and ask God for rain. And he'd send it down in bucketfuls right away—it was then or never—and everyone went home like drowned rats. Since we've given up religion the gods nowadays keep their feet well wrapped up. The fields just lie . . ."

"Please, please," broke in Echion the rag merchant, "be a bit more cheerful. 'First it's one thing, then another,' as the yokel said when he lost his spotted pig. What we haven't got today, we'll have tomorrow. That's the way life goes. Believe me, you couldn't name a better country, if it had the people. As things are, I admit, it's having a hard time, but it isn't the only place. We mustn't be soft. The sky don't get no nearer wherever you are. If you were somewhere else, you'd be talking about the pigs walking round ready roasted back here.

"And another thing, we'll be having a holiday with a three-day show that's the best ever—and not just a hack troupe of gladiators but freedmen for the most part. My old friend Titus has a big heart and a hot head. Maybe this, maybe that, but something at all events. I'm a close friend of his and he does nothing by halves. He'll give us cold steel, no quarter and the slaughterhouse right in the middle where all the stands can see it. And he's got the wherewithal—he was left thirty million when his poor father died. Even if he spent four hundred thousand, his pocket won't feel it and he'll go down in history. He's got some big brutes already, and a woman who fights in a chariot and Glyco's steward,[16] who was caught having fun with his mistress. You'll see quite a quarrel in the crowd between jealous husbands and romantic lovers. But that half-pint Glyco threw his steward to the lions, which is just giving himself away. How is it the servant's fault when he's forced into it? It's that old pisspot who really deserves to be tossed by a bull. But if you can't beat the ass you beat the saddle. But how did Glyco imagine the poisonous daughter of Hermogenes[17] would ever turn out well? The old man could cut the claws off a flying kite, and a snake don't hatch old rope. Glyco—well, Glyco's got his. He's branded for as long as he lives and only the grave will get rid of it. But everyone pays for their mistakes.

"But I can almost smell the dinner[18] Mammaea is going to give us—two denarii apiece for me and the family. If he really does it,

---

16. *steward:* a household slave. His master was permitted by law to punish him by forcing him to fight wild beasts in the arena.

17. *Hermogenes:* presumably the father of Glyco's wife.

18. *dinner:* a public banquet, given by Mammaea as part of his electoral campaign. His rival Norbanus has been giving gladiatorial shows.

he'll make off with all Norbanus's votes, I tell you he'll win at a canter. After all, what good has Nobanus done us? He put on some half-pint gladiators, so done in already that they'd have dropped if you blew at them. I've seen animal-killers[19] fight better. As for the horsemen killed, he got them off a lamp[20]—they ran round like cocks in a backyard. One was just a carthorse, the other couldn't stand up, and the reserve was just one corpse instead of another— he was practically hamstrung. One boy did have a bit of spirit—he was in Thracian armour,[21] and even he didn't show any initiative. In fact, they were all flogged afterwards, there were so many shouts of 'Give 'em what for!' from the crowd. Pure yellow, that's all.

" 'Well, I've put on a show for you,' he says. 'And I'm clapping you,' says I. 'Reckon it up—I'm giving more than I got. So we're quits.'

"Hey, Agamemnon! I suppose you're saying 'What is that bore going on and on about?' It's because a good talker like you don't talk. You're a cut above us, and so you laugh at what us poor people say. We all know you're off your head with all that reading. But never mind! Some day I'll get you to come down to my place in the country and have a look at our little cottage. We'll find something to eat—a chicken, some eggs. It'll be nice, even though the unreliable weather this year has made off with everything. Anyway, we'll find enough to fill our bellies.

"And my kid is growing up to be a pupil of yours. He can divide by four already. If God spares him, you'll have him ready to do anything for you. In his spare time, he won't take his head out of his exercise book. He's clever and there's good stuff in him, even if he is crazy about birds. Only yesterday I killed his three goldfinches and told him a weasel ate them. But he's found some other silly hobbies, and he's having a fine time painting. Still, he's already well ahead with his Greek, and he's starting to take to his Latin, though his tutor is too pleased with himself and unreliable—he just comes and goes. He knows his stuff but doesn't want to work. There is another one as well, not so clever but he is conscientious—he teaches the boy more than he knows himself. In fact, he makes a habit of coming around on holidays, and whatever you give him, he's happy.

"Anyway, I've just bought the boy some law books, as I want him to pick up some legal training for home use. There's a living in that sort of thing. He's done enough dabbling in poetry and such like. If he objects, I've decided he'll learn a trade—barber, auctioneer, or at least a barrister—something he can't lose till he dies. Well, yesterday I gave it to him straight: 'Believe me, my lad, any studying you do will be for your own good. You see Phileros the solicitor—if

---

19. *animal-killers:* professional fighters of wild animals, considered inferior to gladiators.
20. *lamp:* as small as the horsemen depicted on a lamp.
21. *Thracian armour:* light armor, such as that worn by soldiers from Thrace, a savage country northeast of Greece.

he hadn't studied, he'd be starving today. It's not so long since he was humping round loads on his back. Now he can even look Norbanus in the face. An education is an investment, and a proper profession never goes dead on you.' "

This was the sort of conversation flying round when Trimalchio came in, dabbed his forehead and washed his hands in perfume. There was a short pause, then he said:

"Excuse me, dear people, my inside has not been answering the call for several days now. The doctors are puzzled. But some pomegranate rind and resin in vinegar has done me good. But I hope now it will be back on its good behaviour. Otherwise my stomach rumbles like a bull. So if any of you wants to go out, there's no need for him to be embarrassed. None of us was born solid. I think there's nothing so tormenting as holding yourself in. This is the one thing even God Almighty can't object to. Yes, laugh, Fortunata,[22] but you generally keep me up all night with this sort of thing.

"Anyway, I don't object to people doing what suits them even in the middle of dinner—and the doctors forbid you to hold yourself in. Even if it's a longer business, everything is there just outside—water, bowls, and all the other little comforts. Believe me, if the wind goes to your brain it starts flooding your whole body too. I've known a lot of people die from this because they wouldn't be honest with themselves."

We thanked him for being so generous and considerate and promptly proceeded to bury our amusement in our glasses. Up to this point we'd not realized we were only in mid-stream, as you might say.

The orchestra played, the tables were cleared, and then three white pigs were brought into the dining-room, all decked out in muzzles and bells. The first, the master of ceremonies announced, was two years old, the second three, and the third six. I was under the impression that some acrobats were on their way in and the pigs were going to do some tricks, the way they do in street shows. But Trimalchio dispelled this impression by asking:

"Which of these would you like for the next course? Any clodhopper can do you a barnyard cock or a stew and trifles like that, but my cooks are used to boiling whole calves."

He immediately sent for the chef and without waiting for us to choose he told him to kill the oldest pig.

He then said to the man in a loud voice:

"Which division are you from?"

When he replied he was from number forty, Trimalchio asked:

"Were you bought or were you born here?"

"Neither," said the chef, "I was left to you in Pansa's will."

"Well, then," said Trimalchio, "see you serve it up carefully—otherwise I'll have you thrown into the messenger's division."

22. *Fortunata:* Trimalchio's wife.

So the chef, duly reminded of his master's magnificence, went back to his kitchen, the next course leading the way.

Trimalchio looked round at us with a gentle smile: "If you don't like the wine, I'll have it changed. It is up to you to do it justice. I don't buy it, thank heaven. In fact, whatever wine really tickles your palate this evening, it comes from an estate of mine which as yet I haven't seen. It's said to join my estates at Tarracina and Tarentum. What I'd like to do now is add Sicily to my little bit of land, so that when I want to go to Africa, I could sail there without leaving my own property.

"But tell me, Agamemnon, what was your debate about today? Even though I don't go in for the law, still I've picked up enough education for home consumption. And don't you think I turn my nose up at studying, because I have two libraries, one Greek, one Latin. So tell us, just as a favour, what was the topic of your debate?"

Agamemnon was just beginning, "A poor man and a rich man were enemies . . ." when Trimalchio said: "What's a poor man?" "Oh, witty!" said Agamemnon, and then told us about some fictitious case or other. Like lightning Trimalchio said: "If this happened, it's not a fictitious case—if it didn't happen, then it's nothing at all."

We greeted this witticism and several more like it with the greatest enthusiasm.

"Tell me, my dear Agamemnon," continued Trimalchio, "do you remember the twelve labours of Hercules and the story of Ulysses —how the Cyclops tore out his thumb with a pair of pincers.[23] I used to read about them in Homer, when I was a boy. In fact, I actually saw the Sibyl at Cumae with my own eyes dangling in a bottle, and when the children asked her in Greek: 'What do you want, Sybil?' she used to answer: 'I want to die.' "

[Presents for the guests are distributed with a slave announcing the nature of each gift and making in each case an atrocious pun on the name of the guest.]

We laughed for ages. There were hundreds of things like this but they've slipped my mind now.

Ascyltus, with his usual lack of restraint, found everything extremely funny, lifting up his hands and laughing till the tears came. Eventually one of Trimalchio's freedman[24] friends flared up at him—the one sitting above me, in fact.

"You with the sheep's eyes," he said, "what's so funny? Isn't our host elegant enough for you? You're better off, I suppose, and used

---

23. *pincers:* Trimalchio refers to Odysseus' adventures in the cave of the Cyclops (*Odyssey,* Book IX). In spite of what he goes on to say, he has obviously not read Homer.

24. *freedman:* a former slave who had bought his freedom.

to a bigger dinner. Holy guardian here preserve me! If I was sitting by him, I'd make him bleat! A fine pippin he is to be laughing at other people! Some fly-by-night from god knows where—not worth his own piss. In fact, if I pissed round him, he wouldn't know where to turn.

"By god, it takes a lot to make me boil, but if you're too soft, worms like this only come to the top. Look at him laughing! What's he got to laugh at? Did his father pay cash for him? You're a Roman knight,[25] are you? Well, my father was a king.

" '*Why are you only a freedman?*' did you say? Because I went into service voluntarily. I wanted to be a Roman citizen, not a subject with taxes to pay. And today, I hope no one can laugh at the way I live. I'm a man among men, and I walk with my head up. I don't owe anybody a penny—there's never been a court-order out for me. No one's said '*Pay up!*' to me in the street.

"I've bought a bit of land and some tiny pieces of plate. I've twenty bellies to feed, as well as a dog. I bought my old woman's freedom so nobody could wipe his dirty hands on *her* hair. Four thousand I paid for myself. I was elected to the Augustan College[26] and it cost me nothing. I hope when I die I won't have to blush in my coffin.

"But you now, you're such a busybody you don't look behind you. You see a louse on somebody else, but not the fleas on your own back. You're the only one who finds us funny. Look at the professor now—he's an older man than you and we get along with him. But you're still wet from your mother's milk and not up to your ABC yet. Just a crackpot—you're like a piece of wash-leather in soak, softer but no better! You're grander than us—well, have two dinners and two suppers! I'd rather have my good name than any amount of money. When all's said and done, who's ever asked me for money twice? For forty years I slaved but nobody ever knew if I was a slave or a free man. I came to this colony when I was a lad with long hair—the town-hall hadn't been built then. But I worked hard to please my master—there was a real gentleman, with more in his little finger-nail than there is in your whole body. And I had people in the house who tried to trip me up one way or another, but still—thanks be to his guardian spirit!—I kept my head above water. That's real success: being born free is as easy as all get-out. Now what are you gawping at, like a goat in a vetch field?"

At this remark, Giton, who was waiting on me, could not suppress his laughter and let out a filthy guffaw, which did not pass unnoticed by Ascyltus's opponent. He turned his abuse on the boy.

"So!" he said, "you're amused too, are you, you curly-headed

---

25. *knight:* a Roman class including all who had property above a certain amount.
26. The state religion was the worship of Augustus, the emperor. The office of priest might be sold or conferred.

onion? A merry Saturnalia[27] to you! Is it December, I'd like to know? When did *you* pay your liberation tax?[28] Look, he doesn't know what to do, the gallow's bird, the crow's meat.

"God's curse on you, and your master too, for not keeping you under control! As sure as I get my bellyful, it's only because of Trimalchio that I don't take it out of you here and now. He's a freedman like myself. We're doing all right, but those good-for-nothings, well—. It's easy to see, like master, like man. I can hardly hold myself back, and I'm not naturally hot-headed—but once I start, I don't give a penny for my own mother.

"All right! I'll see you when we get outside, you rat, you excrescence. I'll knock your master in the dirt before I'm an inch taller or shorter. And I won't let you off either, by heaven, even if you scream down God Almighty. Your cheap curls and your no-good master won't be much use to you then—I'll see to that. I'll get my teeth into you, all right. Either I'm much mistaken about myself or you won't be laughing at us behind your golden beard. Athena's curse on you and the man who first made you such a forward brat.

"I didn't learn no geometry or criticism and such silly rubbish, but I can read the letters on a notice board and I can do my percentages in metal, weights, and money. In fact, if you like, we'll have a bet. Come on, here's my cash. Now you'll see how your father wasted his money, even though you do know how to make a speech.

"Try this:

> Something we all have.
> Long I come, broad I come. What am I?

"I'll give you it: something we all have that runs and doesn't move from its place: something we all have that grows and gets smaller.[29]

"You're running round in circles, you've had enough, like the mouse in the pisspot. So either keep quiet or keep out of the way of your betters, they don't even know you're alive—unless you think I care about your box-wood rings that you swiped from your girl friend! Lord make me lucky! Let's go into town and borrow some money. You'll soon see they trust this iron one.

"Pah! a drownded fox makes a nice sight, I must say. As I hope to make my pile and die so famous that people swear by my dead body, I'll hound you to death. And he's a nice thing too—the one who taught you all these tricks—a muttonhead, not a master. We

27. *Saturnalia:* a December festival in honor of an ancient Italian deity at which the normal order of everyday life was reversed and the slaves and children made fun of their masters.

28. *liberation tax:* The freed slave had to pay 5 per cent of his value to the treasury.

29. There is no agreement about the correct answer to these riddles. Suggested answers are, to the first, the foot; the second, the eye; the third, the hair.

learned different. Our teacher used to say: 'Are your things in order? Go straight home. No looking around. And be polite to your elders.' Nowadays it's all an absolute muck-heap. They turn out nobody worth a penny. I'm like you see me and I thank God for the way I was learnt." . . .

In the middle of all this, a lictor[30] knocked at the double doors and a drunken guest entered wearing white, followed by a large crowd of people. I was terrified by this lordly apparition and thought it was the chief magistrate arriving. So I tried to rise and get my bare feet on the floor. Agamemnon laughed at this panic and said:

"Get hold of yourself, you silly fool. This is Habinnas—Augustan College and monumental mason."

Relieved by this information I resumed my position and watched Habinnas' entry with huge admiration. Being already drunk, he had his hands on his wife's shoulders; loaded with several garlands, oil pouring down his forehead and into his eyes, he settled himself into the place of honour and immediately demanded some wine and hot water. Trimalchio, delighted by these high spirits, demanded a larger cup for himself and asked how he had enjoyed it all.

"The only thing we missed," replied Habinnas, "was yourself—the apple of my eye was here. Still, it was damn good. Scissa was giving a ninth-day dinner[31] in honour of a poor slave of hers she'd freed on his death-bed. And I think she'll have a pretty penny to pay in liberation tax because they reckon he was worth fifty thousand. Still, it was pleasant enough, even if we did have to pour half our drinks over his wretched bones."

"Well," said Trimalchio, "what did you have for dinner?"

"I'll tell you if I can—I've such a good memory that I often forget my own name. For the first course we had a pig crowned with sausages and served with blood-puddings and very nicely done giblets, and of course beetroot and pure wholemeal bread—which I prefer to white myself: it's very strengthening and I don't regret it when I do my business. The next course was cold tart and a concoction of first-class Spanish wine poured over hot honey. I didn't eat anything at all of the actual tart, but I dived right into the honey. Scattered round were chickpeas, lupines, a choice of nuts and an apple apiece —though I took two. And look, I've got them tied up in a napkin, because if I don't take something in the way of a present to my youngster, I'll have a row on my hands.

"Oh, yes, my good lady reminds me. We had a hunk of bearmeat set before us, which Scintilla was foolish enough to try, and she practically spewed up her guts; but I ate more than a pound of it, as it tasted like real wild-boar. And I say if bears can eat us poor people, it's all the more reason why us poor people should eat bears.

30. *lictor:* a magistrate's attendant.    of the mourning period.
31. *ninth-day dinner:* on the last day

"To finish up with, we had some cheese basted with new wine, snails all round, chitterlings, plates of liver, eggs in pastry hoods, turnips, mustard, and some filthy concoction—good riddance to that. There were pickled cumin seeds too, passed round in a bowl and some people were that bad-mannered they took three handfuls. You see, we sent the ham away.

"But tell me something, Gaius, now I ask—why isn't Fortunata at the table?"

"You know her," replied Trimalchio, "unless she's put the silver away and shared out the left-overs among the slaves, she won't put a drop of water to her mouth."

"All the same," retorted Habinnas, "unless she sits down, I'm shagging off."

And he was starting to get up, when at a given signal all the servants shouted *"Fortunata"* four or five times. So in she came with her skirt tucked up under a yellow sash to show her cerise petticoat underneath, as well as her twisted anklets and gold-embroidered slippers. Wiping her hands on a handkerchief which she carried round her neck, she took her place on the couch where Habbinas' wife was reclining. She kissed her. "Is it really you?" she said, clapping her hands together.

It soon got to the point where Fortunata took the bracelets from her great fat arms and showed them to the admiring Scintilla. In the end she even undid her anklets and her gold hair net, which she said was pure gold. Trimalchio noticed this and had it all brought to him and commented:

"A woman's chains, you see. This is the way us poor fools get robbed. She must have six and a half pounds on her. Still, I've got a bracelet myself, made up from one-tenth per cent to Mercury[32]— and it weighs not an ounce less than ten pounds."

Finally, for fear he looked like a liar, he even had some scales brought in and had them passed round to test the weight.

Scintilla was no better. From round her neck she took a little gold locket, which she called her "lucky box." From it she extracted two earrings and in her turn gave them to Fortunata to look at.

"A present from my good husband," she said, "and no one has a finer set."

"Hey!" said Habinnas, "you cleaned me out to buy you a glass bean. Honestly, if I had a daughter, I'd cut her little ears off. If there weren't any women, everything would be dirt cheap. As it is, we've got to drink cold water and piss it out hot."

Meanwhile, the women giggled tipsily between themselves and kissed each other drunkenly, one crying up her merits as a housewife, the other crying about her husband's demerits and boy friends.

32. **Mercury:** Trimalchio sets aside a percentage of his profits to offer to his patron deity.

While they had their heads together like this, Habinnas rose stealthily and taking Fortunata's feet, flung them up over the couch.

"Oh, oh!" she shrieked, as her underskirt wandered up over her knees. So she settled herself in Scintilla's lap and hid her disgusting red face in her handkerchief.

Then came an interval, after which Trimalchio called for dessert. . . .

Fortunata was now wanting to dance, and Scintilla was doing more clapping than talking, when Trimalchio said:

"Philargyrus—even though you are such a terrible fan of the Greens[33]—you have my permission to join us. And tell your dear Menophila to sit down as well."

Need I say more? We were almost thrown out of our places, so completely did the household fill the dining-room. I even noticed that the chef was actually given a place above me, and he was reeking of pickles and sauce. And he wasn't satisfied with just having a place, but he had to start straight off on an imitation of the tragedian Ephesus, and then challenge his master to bet against the Greens winning at the next races.

Trimalchio became expansive after this argument.

"My dear people," he said, "slaves are human beings too. They drink the same milk as anybody else, even though luck's been agin 'em. Still, if nothing happens to me, they'll have their taste of freedom soon. In fact, I'm setting them all free in my will. I'm giving Philargyrus a farm, what's more, and the woman he lives with. As for Cario, I'm leaving him a block of flats, his five per cent manumission tax, and a bed with all the trimmings. I'm making Fortunata my heir, and I want all my friends to look after her.

"The reason I'm telling everyone all this is so my household will love me now as much as if I was dead."

Everyone began thanking his lordship for his kindness, when he became very serious and had a copy of his will brought in. Amid the sobs of his household he read out the whole thing from beginning to end.

Then looking at Habinnas, he said:

"What have you to say, my dear old friend? Are you building my monument the way I told you? I particularly want you to keep a place at the foot of my statue and put a picture of my pup there, as well as paintings of wreaths, scent-bottles, and all the contests of Petraites,[34] and thanks to you I'll be able to live on after I'm dead. And another thing! See that it's a hundred feet facing the road and two hundred back into the field. I want all the various sorts of fruit round my ashes and lots and lots of vines. After all, it's a big mistake to have nice houses just for when you're alive and not worry

---

33. *Greens:* one of the teams in the chariot races.

34. *Petraites:* a popular gladiator.

about the one we have to live in for much longer. And that's why I want this written up before anything else:

THIS MONUMENT DOES NOT GO TO THE HEIR

"But I'll make sure in my will that I don't get done down once I'm dead. I'll put one of my freedmen in charge of my tomb to look after it and not let people run up and shit on my monument. I'd like you to put some ships there too, sailing under full canvas, and me sitting on a high platform in my robes of office, wearing five gold rings and pouring out a bagful of money for the people. You know I gave them all a dinner and two denarii apiece. Let's have in a banqueting hall as well, if you think it's a good idea, and show the whole town having a good time. Put up a statue of Fortunata on my right, holding a dove, and have her leading her little dog tied to her belt—and this dear little chap as well, and great big wine jars sealed up so the wine won't spill. And perhaps you could carve me a broken wine jar and boy crying over it. A clock in the middle, so that anybody who looks at the time, like it or not, has got to read my name. As for the inscription now, take a good look and see if this seems suitable enough:

HERE SLEEPS
GAIUS POMPEIUS TRIMALCHIO
MAECENATIANUS
ELECTED TO THE AUGUSTAN COLLEGE IN HIS ABSENCE
HE COULD HAVE BEEN ON EVERY BOARD IN ROME
BUT HE REFUSED
GOD-FEARING BRAVE AND TRUE
A SELF-MADE MAN
HE LEFT AN ESTATE OF 30,000,000
AND HE NEVER HEARD A PHILOSOPHER
FAREWELL
AND YOU FARE WELL, TRIMALCHIO."

[After a visit to the baths, where Encolpius and his friends make an unsuccessful attempt to escape, the dinner is resumed.]

After this dish Trimalchio looked at the servants and said:
"Why haven't you had dinner yet? Off you go and let some others come on duty."
Up came another squad and as the first set called out: "Good night, Gaius!" the new arrivals shouted: "Good evening, Gaius!"
This led to the first incident that damped the general high spirits. Not a bad-looking boy entered with the newcomers and Trimalchio jumped at him and began kissing him at some length. Fortunata, asserting her just and legal rights, began hurling insults at Trimalchio, calling him a low scum and a disgrace, who couldn't con-

trol his beastly desires. "You dirty dog!" she finally added.

Trimalchio took offence at this abuse and flung his glass into Fortunata's face. She screamed as though she'd lost an eye and put her trembling hands across her face. Scintilla was terrified too and hugged the quaking woman to her breast. An obliging slave pressed a little jug of cold water to her cheek, while Fortunata rested her head on it and began weeping. Trimalchio just said:

"Well, well, forgotten her chorus days, has she? She doesn't remember, but she was bought and sold, and I took her away from it all and made her as good as the next. Yet she puffs herself up like a frog and doesn't even spit for luck. Just a great hunk, not a woman. But those as are born over a shop don't dream of a house. May I never have a day's good luck again, if I don't teach that Cassandra in clogs some manners!

"There was I, not worth twopence, and I could have had ten million. And you know I'm not lying about it. Agatho, who ran a perfume shop for the lady next door, he took me on one side and said: 'You don't want to let your family die out, you know!' But me, trying to do the right thing and not wanting to look changeable, I cut my own throat.

"All right! I'll make you want to dig me up with your bare nails. Just so you'll know on the spot what you've done for yourself—Habinnas! I don't want you to put her statue on my tomb, so at least when I'm dead I won't have any more squabbles. And another thing! just to show I can get my own back—when I'm dead I don't want her to kiss me."

After this thunderbolt, Habinnas began asking him to calm down: "None of us are without faults," he said, "we're not gods, we're human!" Scintilla said the same, calling him Gaius, and she began asking him, in the name of his guardian spirit, to give in.

Trimalchio held back his tears no longer. "I ask you, Habinnas," he said, "as you hope to enjoy your bit of savings—if I did anything wrong, spit in my face. I kissed this very careful little fellow, not for his pretty face, but because he's careful with money—he says his ten times table, he reads a book at sight, he's got himself some Thracian kit out of his daily allowance, and he's bought himself an easy chair and two cups out of his own pocket. Doesn't he deserve to be the apple of my eye? But Fortunata won't have it.

"Is that the way you feel, high heels? I'll give you a piece of advice: don't let your good luck turn your head, you kite, and don't make me show my teeth, my little darling—otherwise you'll feel my temper. You know me: once I've decided on something, it's fixed with a twelve-inch nail.

"But to come back to earth—I want you to enjoy yourselves, my dear people. After all, I was once like you are, but being the right sort, I got where I am. It's the old headpiece that makes a man, the rest is all rubbish. 'Buy right—sell right!'—that's me! Different people will give you a different line. I'm just on top of the world, I'm that lucky.

"But you, you snoring thing, are you still moaning? I'll give you something to moan about in a minute.

"However, as I'd started to say, it was my shrewd way with money that got me to my present position. I came from Asia as big as this candlestick. In fact, every day I used to measure myself against it, and to get some whiskers round my beak quicker, I used to oil my lips from the lamp. Still, for fourteen years I was the old boy's fancy. And there's nothing wrong if the boss wants it. But I did all right by the old girl too. You know what I mean—I don't say anything because I'm not the boasting sort.

"Well, as heaven will have it, I became boss in the house, and the old boy, you see, couldn't think of anything but me. That's about it— he made me co-heir with the Emperor[35] and I got a senator's fortune. But nobody gets enough, never. I wanted to go into business. Not to make a long story of it, I built five ships, I loaded them with wine —it was absolute gold at the time—and I sent them to Rome. You'd have thought I ordered it—every single ship was wrecked. That's fact, not fable! In one single day Neptune[36] swallowed up thirty million. Do you think I gave up? This loss honestly wasn't more than a flea-bite to me—it was as if nothing had happened. I built more boats, bigger and better and luckier, so nobody could say I wasn't a man of courage. You know, the greater the ship, the greater the confidence. I loaded them again—with wine, bacon, beans, perfumes and slaves. At this point Fortunata did the decent thing, because she sold off all her gold trinkets, all her clothes, and put ten thousand in gold pieces in my hand. This was the yeast my fortune needed to rise. What heaven wants, soon happens. In one voyage I carved out a round ten million. I immediately bought back all my old master's estates. I built a house, I invested in slaves, and I bought up the horse trade. Whatever I touched grew like a honey-comb. Once I had more than the whole country, then down tools! I retired from business and began advancing loans through freed-men.

"Actually I was tired of trading on my own account, but it was an astrologer who convinced me. He happened to come to our colony, a sort of Greek, Serapa by name, and he could have told heaven itself what to do. He even told me things I'd forgotten. He went through everything for me from A to Z. He knew me inside out—the only thing he didn't tell me was what I ate for dinner the day before. You'd have thought he'd never left my side.

"Wasn't there that thing, Habinnas?—I think you were there: 'You got your lady wife out of those *certain circumstances*. You are

---

35. *co-heir with the Emperor:* an honor which Trimalchio shared with many others, for it was customary (as a prudent measure, to avoid confiscation on some pretext or other) to include a bequest to the emperor in one's will.

36. *Neptune* (Poseidon): the sea god.

not lucky in your friends. Nobody thanks you enough for your trouble. You have large estates. You are nursing a viper in your bosom.'

"And he said—though I shouldn't tell you—I have thirty years, four months, two days to live. What's more, I shall soon receive a legacy. My horoscope tells me this. If I'm allowed to join my estates to Apulia,[37] I'll have lived enough.

"Meantime, under the protection of Mercury, I built this house. As you know, it was still a shack, now it's a shrine. It has four dining-rooms, twenty bedrooms, two marble colonnades, a row of box-rooms up above, a bedroom where I sleep myself, a nest for this viper, and a really good lodge for the porter. The guest apartment takes a hundred guests. In fact, when Scaurus[38] came here, he didn't want to stay anywhere else, even though he's got his father's guest house down by the sea. And there are a lot of other things I'll show you in a second.

"Believe me: have a penny, and you're worth a penny. You got something, you'll be thought something. Like your old friend—first a frog, now a king.

"Meantime, Stichus, bring out the shroud and the things I want to be buried in. Bring some cosmetic cream too, and a sample from that jar of wine I want my bones washed in."

Stichus did not delay over it, but brought his white shroud and his formal dress into the dining-room . . . Trimalchio told us to examine them and see if they were made of good wool. Then he said with a smile:

"Now you, Stichus, see no mice or moths get at those—otherwise I'll burn you alive. I want to be buried in style, so the whole town will pray for my rest."

He opened a bottle of nard[39] on the spot, rubbed some on all of us and said:

"I hope this'll be as nice when I'm dead as when I'm alive." The wine he had poured into a big decanter and he said:

"I want you to think you've been invited to my wake."

The thing was becoming absolutely sickening, when Trimalchio, showing the effects of his disgusting drunkenness, had a fresh entertainment brought into the dining-room, some cornet players. Propped up on a lot of cushions, he stretched out along the edge of the couch and said: "Pretend I'm dead and say something nice."

The cornet players struck up a dead march. One man in particular, the slave of his undertaker (who was the most respectable person present) blew so loudly that he roused the neighbourhood. As a result, the fire brigade, thinking Trimalchio's house was on fire, sud-

---

37. *Apulia:* the southeastern extremity of Italy.
38. *Scaurus:* unknown. The name is aristocratic but our translator suggests Trim-

alchio may be referring to a well-known manufacturer of fish sauce from Pompeii.
39. *nard:* a perfumed ointment.

denly broke down the front door and began kicking up their own sort of din with their water and axes.

Seizing this perfect chance, we gave Agamemnon the slip and escaped as rapidly as if there really were a fire.

# ST. AUGUSTINE
## (354–430 A.D.)
## Confessions (Confessiones)*

### [Childhood]
### Book I

What have I to say to Thee, God, save that I know not where I came from, when I came into this life-in-death—or should I call it death-in-life? I do not know. I only know that the gifts Your mercy had provided sustained me from the first moment: not that I remember it but so I have heard from the parents of my flesh, the father from whom, and the mother in whom, You fashioned me in time.

Thus for my sustenance and my delight I had woman's milk: yet it was not my mother or my nurses who stored their breasts for me: it was Yourself, using them to give me the food of my infancy, according to Your ordinance and the riches set by You at every level of creation. It was by Your gift that I desired what You gave and no more, by Your gift that those who suckled me willed to give me what You had given them: for it was by the love implanted in them by You that they gave so willingly that milk which by Your gift flowed in the breasts. It was a good for them that I received good from them, though I received it not *from* them but only through them: since all good things are from You, O God, and *from God is all my health.*[1] But this I have learnt since: You have made it abundantly clear by all that I have seen You give, within me and about me. For at that time I knew how to suck, to lie quiet when I was content, to cry when I was in pain: and that was all I knew.

Later I added smiling to the things I could do, first in sleep, then awake. This again I have on the word of others, for naturally I do not remember; in any event, I believe it, for I have seen other

---

* Abridged. Written in A.D. 397. Our translation is by F. J. Sheed.

1. Throughout the *Confessions*, Augustine quotes liberally from the Bible; this citation, set off like the others in italics, has no special significance, but where a quotation alludes to a passage which bears more directly on Augustine's situation, it is glossed.

infants do the same. And gradually I began to notice where I was, and the will grew in me to make my wants known to those who might satisfy them; but I could not, for my wants were within me and those others were outside: nor had they any faculty enabling them to enter into my mind. So I would fling my arms and legs about and utter sounds, making the few gestures in my power— these being as apt to express my wishes as I could make them: but they were not very apt. And when I did not get what I wanted, either because my wishes were not clear or the things not good for me, I was in a rage—with my parents as though I had a right to their submission, with free human beings as though they had been bound to serve me; and I took my revenge in screams. That infants are like this, I have learnt from watching other infants; and that I was like it myself I have learnt more clearly from these other infants, who did not know me, than from my nurses who did.

\* \* \*

From infancy I came to boyhood, or rather it came to me, taking the place of infancy. Yet infancy did not go: for where was it to go to? Simply it was no longer there. For now I was not an infant, without speech, but a boy, speaking. This I remember; and I have since discovered by observation how I learned to speak. I did not learn by elders teaching me words in any systematic way, as I was soon after taught to read and write. But of my own motion, using the mind which You, my God, gave me, I strove with cries and various sounds and much moving of my limbs to utter the feelings of my heart—all this in order to get my own way. Now I did not always manage to express the right meanings to the right people. So I began to reflect [I observed that] my elders would make some particular sound, and as they made it would point at or move towards some particular thing: and from this I came to realize that the thing was called by the sound they made when they wished to draw my attention to it. That they intended this was clear from the motions of their body, by a kind of natural language common to all races which consists in facial expressions, glances of the eye, gestures, and the tones by which the voice expresses the mind's state —for example whether things are to be sought, kept, thrown away, or avoided. So, as I heard the same words again and again properly used in different phrases, I came gradually to grasp what things they signified; and forcing my mouth to the same sounds, I began to use them to express my own wishes. Thus I learnt to convey what I meant to those about me; and so took another long step along the stormy way of human life in society, while I was still subject to the authority of my parents and at the beck and call of my elders.

O God, my God, what emptiness and mockeries did I now experience: for it was impressed upon me as right and proper in a boy to obey those who taught me, that I might get on in the world and excel in the handling of words[2] to gain honor among men and deceitful riches. I, poor wretch, could not see the use of the things I was sent to school to learn; but if I proved idle in learning, I was soundly beaten. For this procedure seemed wise to our ancestors: and many, passing the same way in days past, had built a sorrowful road by which we too must go, with multiplication of grief and toil upon the sons of Adam.[3]

Yet, Lord, I observed men praying to You: and I learnt to do likewise, thinking of You (to the best of my understanding) as some great being who, though unseen, could hear and help me. As a boy I fell into the way of calling upon You, my Help and my Refuge; and in those prayers I broke the strings of my tongue—praying to You, small as I was but with no small energy, that I might not be beaten at school. And when You did not hear me (*not as giving me over to folly*),[4] my elders and even my parents, who certainly wished me no harm, treated my stripes as a huge joke, which they were very far from being to me. Surely, Lord, there is no one so steeled in mind or cleaving to You so close—or even so insensitive, for that might have the same effect—as to make light of the racks and hooks and other torture instruments[5] (from which in all lands men pray so fervently to be saved) while truly loving those who are in such bitter fear of them. Yet my parents seemed to be amused at the torments inflicted upon me as a boy by my masters, though I was no less afraid of my punishments or zealous in my prayers to You for deliverance. But in spite of my terrors I still did wrong, by writing or reading or studying less than my set tasks. It was not, Lord, that I lacked mind or memory, for You had given me as much of these as my age required; but the one thing I revelled in was play; and for this I was punished by men who after all were doing exactly the same things themselves. But the idling of men is called business; the idling of boys, though exactly like, is punished by those same men: and no one pities either boys or men. Perhaps an unbiased observer would hold that I was rightly punished as a boy for playing with a ball: because this hindered my progress in studies—studies which would give me the opportunity as a man to play at things more degraded. And what difference was there between me and the master who flogged me? For if on some trifling point he had the worst of the argument with

2. The study of rhetoric, which was the passport to eminence in public life.

3. Refers to the consequences of Adam's disobedience. Cf. p. 50.

4. Augustine recognizes the necessity of this rigorous training; that he never forgot its harshness is clear from his remark in the *City of God*, Book XXI,

Section 14: "If a choice were given him between suffering death and living his early years over again, who would not shudder and choose death?"

5. *racks and hooks and other torments*: The instruments of public execution.

some fellow-master, he was more torn with angry vanity than I
when I was beaten in a game of ball.

\* \* \*

But to continue with my boyhood, which was in less peril of sin
than my adolescence. I disliked learning and hated to be forced to it.
But I *was* forced to it, so that good was done to me though it was
not my doing. Short of being driven to it, I certainly would not
have learned. But no one does well against his will, even if the
thing he does is a good thing to do. Nor did those who forced me
do well: it was by You, O God, that well was done. Those others
had no deeper vision of the use to which I might put all they forced
me to learn, but to sate the insatiable desire of man for wealth that
is but penury and glory that is but shame. But You, Lord, *by
Whom the very hairs of our head are numbered,*[6] used for my good
the error of those who urged me to study; but my own error, in that
I had no will to learn, you used for my punishment—a punishment
richly deserved by one so small a boy and so great a sinner. Thus,
You brought good for me out of those who did ill, and justly punished me for the ill I did myself. So You have ordained and so it is:
that every disorder of the soul is its own punishment.

To this day I do not quite see why I so hated the Greek tongue[7]
that I was made to learn as a small boy. For I really liked Latin—
not the rudiments that we got from our first teachers but the literature that we came to be taught later. For the rudiments—reading
and writing and figuring—I found as hard and hateful as Greek.
Yet this too could come only from sin and the vanity of life,
because *I was flesh, and a wind that goes away and returns not.* For
those first lessons were the surer. I acquired the power I still have to
read what I find written and to write what I want to express; whereas
in the studies that came later I was forced to memorize the wanderings of Aeneas[8]—whoever *he* was—while forgetting my own wanderings; and to weep for the death of Dido who killed herself for
love,[9] while bearing dry-eyed my own pitiful state, in that among
these studies I was becoming dead to You, O God, my life.

Nothing could be more pitiful than a pitiable creature who does
not see to pity himself, and weeps for the death that Dido suffered
through love of Aeneas and not for the death he suffers himself
through not loving You, O God, Light of my heart, Bread of my
soul, Power wedded to my mind and the depths of my thought. I

6. Who knows and attends to the
smallest detail of each life. [Matthew
10:30.]
7. Important not only for gaining
knowledge of Greek literature but also
because it was the official language of
the Eastern half of the Roman Empire.

Augustine never really mastered Greek,
though his remark elsewhere, that he
had acquired so little Greek that it
amounted to practically none, is over-
modest.
8. Virgil's *Aeneid,* Book III.
9. *Aeneid,* Book IV.

did not love You and I went away from You in fornication:[10] and all around me in my fornication echoed applauding cries "Well done! Well done!" *For the friendship of this world is fornication against Thee*: and the world cries "Well done" so loudly that one is ashamed of unmanliness not to do it. And for this I did not grieve; but I grieved for Dido, slain as she sought by the sword an end to her woe, while I too followed after the lowest of Your creatures, forsaking You, earth going unto earth. And if I were kept from reading, I grieved at not reading the tales that caused me such grief. This sort of folly is held nobler and richer than the studies by which we learn to read and write!

But now let my God cry aloud in my soul, and let Your truth assure me that it is not so: the earlier study is the better. I would more willingly forget the wanderings of Aeneas and all such things than how to write and read. Over the entrance of these grammar schools hangs a curtain:[11] but this should be seen not as lending honor to the mysteries, but as a cloak to the errors taught within. Let not those masters—who have now lost their terrors for me—cry out against me, because I confess to You, my God, the desire of my soul, and find soul's rest in blaming my evil ways that I may love Your holy ways. Let not the buyers or sellers of book-learning cry out against me. If I ask them whether it is true, as the poet says, that Aeneas ever went to Carthage, the more ignorant will have to answer that they do not know, the more scholarly that he certainly did not. But if I ask with what letters the name Aeneas is spelt,[12] all whose schooling has gone so far will answer correctly, according to the convention men have agreed upon for the use of letters. Or again, were I to ask which loss would be more damaging to human life—the loss from men's memory of reading and writing or the loss of these poetic imaginings—there can be no question what anyone would answer who had not lost his own memory. Therefore as a boy I did wrong in liking the empty studies more than the useful—or rather in loving the empty and hating the useful. For one and one make two, two and two make four, I found a loathsome refrain; but such empty unrealities as the Wooden Horse with its armed men, and Troy on fire, and Creusa's Ghost, were sheer delight.[13]

Give me leave, O my God, to speak of my mind, Your gift, and of the follies in which I wasted it. It chanced that a task was set me, a task which I did not like but had to do. There was the promise of glory if I won, the fear of ignominy, and a flogging as well, if

---

10. Metaphorically in this instance.
11. School was often held in a building open on one side and curtained off from the street.
12. Augustine's point is that the historical truth of the poet's story may be doubted, but the spelling of Aeneas' name is certain.
13. *Aeneid,* Book II, 1. 772.

I lost. It was to declaim the words uttered by Juno[14] in her rage and grief when she could not keep the Trojan prince from coming to Italy. I had learnt that Juno had never said these words, but we were compelled to err in the footsteps of the poet who had invented them: and it was our duty to paraphrase in prose what he had said in verse. In this exercise that boy won most applause in whom the passions of grief and rage were expressed most powerfully and in the language most adequate to the majesty of the personage represented.

What could all this mean to me, O My true Life, My God? Why was there more applause for the performance I gave than for so many classmates of my own age? Was not the whole business so much smoke and wind? Surely some other matter could have been found to exercise mind and tongue. Thy praises, Lord, might have upheld the fresh young shoot of my heart, so that it might not have been whirled away by empty trifles, defiled, a prey to the spirits of the air. For there is more than one way of sacrificing to the fallen angels.

\* \* \*

### [The Pear Tree]

### Book II

I propose now to set down my past wickedness and the carnal corruptions of my soul, not for love of them but that I may love Thee, O my God. I do it for love of Thy love, passing again in the bitterness of remembrance over my most evil ways that Thou mayest thereby grow ever lovelier to me, O Loveliness that dost not deceive, Loveliness happy and abiding: and I collect my self out of that broken state in which my very being was torn asunder because I was turned away from Thee, the One, and wasted myself upon the many.

Arrived now at adolescence I burned for all the satisfactions of hell, and I sank to the animal in a succession of dark lusts: *my beauty consumed away*, and I stank in Thine eyes, yet was pleasing in my own and anxious to please the eyes of men.

My one delight was to love and to be loved. But in this I did not keep the measure of mind to mind, which is the luminous line of friendship; but from the muddy concupiscence of the flesh and the hot imagination of puberty mists steamed up to becloud and darken my heart so that I could not distinguish the white light of love from the fog of lust. Both love and lust boiled within me, and

---

14. Augustine was assigned the task of delivering a prose paraphrase of Juno's angry speech in the *Aeneid*, Book I. (She complains that her enemies, the Trojans under Aeneas, are on their way to their destined goal in Italy in spite of her resolution to prevent them.) Rhetorical exercises such as this were common in the schools, since they served the double purpose of teaching literature and rhetorical composition at the same time.

swept my youthful immaturity over the precipice of evil desires to leave me half drowned in a whirlpool of abominable sins. Your wrath had grown mighty against me and I knew it not. I had grown deaf from the clanking of the chain of my mortality, the punishment for the pride of my soul: and I departed further from You, and You left me to myself: and I was tossed about and wasted and poured out and boiling over in my fornications: and You were silent, O my late-won Joy. You were silent, and I, arrogant and depressed, weary and restless, wandered further and further from You into more and more sins which could bear no fruit save sorrows.

\* \* \*

Where then was I, and how far from the delights of Your house, in that sixteenth year of my life in this world, when the madness of lust—needing no licence from human shamelessness, receiving no licence from Your laws—took complete control of me, and I surrendered wholly to it? My family took no care to save me from this moral destruction by marriage: their only concern was that I should learn to make as fine and persuasive speeches as possible.

\* \* \*

Your law, O Lord, punishes theft; and this law is so written in the hearts of men that not even the breaking of it blots it out: for no thief bears calmly being stolen from—not even if he is rich and the other steals through want. Yet I chose to steal, and not because want drove me to it—unless a want of justice and contempt for it and an excess for iniquity. For I stole things which I already had in plenty and of better quality. Nor had I any desire to enjoy the things I stole, but only the stealing of them and the sin. There was a pear tree near our vineyard, heavy with fruit, but fruit that was not particularly tempting either to look at or to taste. A group of young blackguards, and I among them, went out to knock down the pears and carry them off late one night, for it was our bad habit to carry on our games in the streets till very late. We carried off an immense load of pears, not to eat—for we barely tasted them before throwing them to the hogs. Our only pleasure in doing it was that it was forbidden. Such was my heart, O God, such was my heart: yet in the depth of the abyss You had pity on it. Let that heart now tell You what it sought when I was thus evil for no object, having no cause for wrongdoing save my wrongness. The malice of the act was base and I loved it—that is to say I loved my own undoing, I loved the evil in me—not the thing for which I did the evil, simply the evil: my soul was depraved, and hurled itself down from security in You into utter destruction, seeking no profit from wickedness but only to be wicked.

\* \* \*

*[Student at Carthage]*

## Book III

I came to Carthage[15] where a cauldron of illicit loves leapt and boiled about me. I was not yet in love, but I was in love with love, and from the very depth of my need hated myself for not more keenly feeling the need. I sought some object to love, since I was thus in love with loving; and I hated security and a life with no snares for my feet. For within I was hungry, all for the want of that spiritual food which is Thyself, my God; yet [though I was hungry for want of it] I did not hunger for it: I had no desire whatever for incorruptible food, not because I had it in abundance but the emptier I was, the more I hated the thought of it. Because of all this my soul was sick, and broke out in sores, whose itch I agonized to scratch with the rub of carnal things—carnal, yet if there were no soul in them, they would not be objects of love. My longing then was to love and to be loved, but most when I obtained the enjoyment of the body of the person who loved me.

Thus I polluted the stream of friendship with the filth of unclean desire and sullied its limpidity with the hell of lust. And vile and unclean as I was, so great was my vanity that I was bent upon passing for clean and courtly. And I did fall in love, simply from wanting to. O my God, my Mercy, with how much bitterness didst Thou in Thy goodness sprinkle the delights of that time! I was loved, and our love came to the bond of consummation: I wore my chains with bliss but with torment too, for I was scourged with the red hot rods of jealousy, with suspicions and fears and tempers and quarrels.

I developed a passion for stage plays, with the mirror they held up to my own miseries and the fuel they poured on my flame. How is it that a man wants to be made sad by the sight of tragic sufferings that he could not bear in his own person? Yet the spectator does want to feel sorrow, and it is actually his feeling of sorrow that he enjoys. Surely this is the most wretched lunacy? For the more a man feels such sufferings in himself, the more he is moved by the sight of them on the stage. Now when a man suffers himself, it is called misery; when he suffers in the suffering of another, it is called pity. But how can the unreal sufferings of the stage possibly move pity? The spectator is not moved to aid the sufferer but merely to be sorry for him; and the more the author of these fictions makes the audience grieve, the better they like him. If the tragic sorrows of the characters—whether historical or entirely fictitious—be so poorly represented that the spectator is not moved to tears, he

---

15. The capital city of the province, where Augustine went to study rhetoric.

leaves the theatre unsatisfied and full of complaints; if he *is* moved to tears, he stays to the end, fascinated and revelling in it.

\* \* \*

Those of my occupations at that time which were held as reputable[16] were directed towards the study of the law, in which I meant to excel—and the less honest I was, the more famous I should be. The very limit of human blindness is to glory in being blind. By this time I was a leader in the School of Rhetoric[17] and I enjoyed this high station and was arrogant and swollen with importance: though You know, O Lord, that I was far quieter in my behavior and had no share in the riotousness of the *eversores*—the Overturners[18]—for this blackguardly diabolical name they wore as the very badge of sophistication. Yet I was much in their company and much ashamed of the sense of shame that kept me from being like them. I was with them and I did for the most part enjoy their companionship, though I abominated the acts that were their specialty—as when they made a butt of some hapless newcomer, assailing him with really cruel mockery for no reason whatever, save the malicious pleasure they got from it. There was something very like the action of devils in their behavior. They were rightly called Overturners, since they had themselves been first overturned and perverted, tricked by those same devils who were secretly mocking them in the very acts by which they amused themselves in mocking and making fools of others.

With these men as companions of my immaturity, I was studying the books of eloquence; for in eloquence it was my ambition to shine, all from a damnable vaingloriousness and for the satisfaction of human vanity. Following the normal order of study I had come to a book of one Cicero, whose tongue[19] practically everyone admires, though not his heart. That particular book is called *Hortensius*[20] and contains an exhortation to philosophy. Quite definitely it changed the direction of my mind, altered my prayers to You, O Lord, and gave me a new purpose and ambition. Suddenly all the vanity I had hoped in I saw as worthless, and with an incredible intensity of desire I longed after immortal wisdom. I had begun that journey upwards by which I was to return to You. My father was now dead two years; I was eighteen and was receiving money from my mother for the continuance of my study of eloquence. But I used that book not for the sharpening of my tongue;

16. I.e. his rhetorical studies.
17. The best student.
18. A group of students who prided themselves on their wild actions and indiscipline. *eversores* is the Latin word that means "Overturners."

19. Style.
20. Only fragments of this dialogue remain. In it Cicero replies to an opponent of philosophy with an impassioned defense of the intellectual life.

what won me in it was what it said, not the excellence of its phrasing.

\* \* \*

So I resolved to make some study of the Sacred Scriptures and find what kind of books they were. But what I came upon was something not grasped by the proud, not revealed either to children, something utterly humble in the hearing but sublime in the doing, and shrouded deep in mystery. And I was not of the nature to enter into it or bend my neck to follow it. When I first read those Scriptures, I did not feel in the least what I have just said; they seemed to me unworthy to be compared with the majesty of Cicero. My conceit was repelled by their simplicity, and I had not the mind to penetrate into their depths. They were indeed of a nature to grow in Your little ones.[21] But I could not bear to be a little one; I was only swollen with pride, but to myself I seemed a very big man.

\* \* \*

## [Death of a Friend]

### Book IV

Throughout that nine-year period, from my nineteenth year to my twenty-eighth, I was astray myself and led others astray, was deceived and deceived others in various forms of self-assertion, publicly by the teaching of what are called the liberal arts,[22] privately under the false name of religion; in the one proud, in the other superstitious, in both vain. On the one side of my life I pursued the emptiness of popular glory and the applause of spectators, with competition for prize poems[23] and strife for garlands of straw and the vanity of stage shows and untempered lusts; on the other side I was striving to be made clean of all this same filth, by bearing food to those who were called elect and holy, that in the factory of their own stomachs they should turn it into angels and deities[24] by whom I was to be set free. And I followed out this line of conduct; and so did my friends who were deceived by me and with me.

\* \* \*

In those years I taught the art of Rhetoric. Overcome myself by the desire of money, I offered for sale skill in speech to overcome others by.[25] But You know, O Lord, I preferred to have honest

---

21. Refers not only to the rhetorical simplicity of Jesus' teachings but his interest in teaching children, "for to such belongs the kingdom of heaven." [Matthew 19:14.]
22. The rhetorical and literary studies which Augustine pursued.

23. The prize for the winner of the rhetorical contests held in the theater.
24. Certain vegetables were supposed by the Manichees to contain elements of Light, which were liberated when the vegetables were eaten by the Elect.
25. In the law-courts.

scholars as honesty is nowadays reckoned: and without guile I taught them guilefulness, that they might use it not against the life of an innocent man, but for the life of a guilty man. And You, O God, saw me far from You stumbling in that slippery way, showing amidst much smoke some small spark of honor: for in my school-mastership I honestly did my best for men who loved vanity and sought after lying: and in truth I was one with them. In those years I took one woman, not joined to me in lawful marriage, but one whom wandering lust and no particular judgment had brought my way. Yet I had but that one woman, and I was faithful to her. And with her I learnt by my own experience what a gulf there is between the restraint of the marriage-covenant entered into for the sake of children and the mere bargain of a lustful love, where if children come they come unwanted—though when they are born, they compel our love.[26]

\* \* \*

During the period in which I first began to teach in the town of my birth, I had found a very dear friend, who was pursuing similar studies. He was about my own age, and was now coming, as I was, to the very flowering-time of young manhood. He had indeed grown up with me as a child and we had gone to school together and played together. Neither in those earlier days nor indeed in the later time of which I now speak was he a friend in the truest meaning of friendship: for there is no true friendship unless You weld it between souls that cleave together through that charity which is shed in our hearts by the Holy Ghost who is given to us. Yet it had become a friendship very dear to us, made the warmer by the ardor of studies pursued together. I had turned him from the true faith —in which being little more than a boy he was not deeply ground-ed—toward those superstitious and soul-destroying errors that my mother bewailed in me.[27] With me he went astray in error, and my soul could not be without him. But You are ever close upon the heels of those who flee from You, for You are at once God of Vengeance and Fount of Mercy, and You turn us to Yourself by ways most wonderful. You took this man from the life of earth when he had completed scarcely a year in a friendship that had grown sweeter to me than all the sweetness of the life I knew.

What man could recount all Your praises for the things he has experienced in his own single person? What was it, O my God, that You accomplished then and how unsearchable is the abyss of Your judgments! For he was in a high fever and when he had for a long

26. The liaison referred to in this passage resulted in the birth of a son, Adeodatus, who later accompanied Augustine to Italy.

27. Augustine's mother, Monica, was a Christian, and lamented her son's Manichaean beliefs.

time lain unconscious in a deathly sweat so that his life was despaired of, he was baptized.[28] Naturally he knew nothing of it, and I paid little heed, since I took for granted that his mind would retain what he had learned from me and not what was done upon his body while he was unconscious. But it turned out very differently. The fever left him and he recovered. As soon as I could speak to him—which was as soon as he could speak to me, for I had not left him and indeed we depended too much upon each other—I began to mock, assuming that he would join me in mocking, the baptism which he had received when he had neither sense nor feeling. For by now he had been told of it. But he looked at me as if I had been his deadly enemy, and in a burst of independence that startled me warned me that if I wished to continue his friend I must cease that kind of talk. I was stupefied and deeply perturbed. I postponed telling him of my feelings until he should be well again, and thus in such condition of health and strength that I could discuss what was in my mind. But he was snatched from the reach of my folly, that he might be safe with You for my future consolation. Within a few days he relapsed into his fever and died. And I was not there.

My heart was black with grief. Whatever I looked upon had the air of death. My native place was a prison-house and my home a strange unhappiness. The things we had done together became sheer torment without him. My eyes were restless looking for him, but he was not there. I hated all places because he was not in them. They could not say "He will come soon," as they would in his life when he was absent. I became a great enigma to myself and I was forever asking my soul why it was sad and why it disquieted me so sorely. And my soul knew not what to answer me. If I said "Trust in God" my soul did not obey—naturally, because the man whom she had loved and lost was nobler and more real than the imagined deity in whom I was bidding her trust. I had no delight but in tears, for tears had taken the place my friend had held in the love of my heart.

\* \* \*

## [Professor at Milan]

### Book V

. . . It was by Your action upon me that I was moved to go to Rome and teach there what I had taught in Carthage. How I was persuaded to this, I shall not omit to confess to You, because therein Your most profound depths and Your mercy ever present towards us are to be meditated upon and uttered forth. My reason for going to Rome was not the greater earnings and higher dignity

28. As a Christian; the Manichees did not use this rite.

promised by the friends who urged me to go—though at that time, these considerations certainly influenced my mind: the principal and practically conclusive reason, was that I had heard that youths there pursued their studies more quietly and were kept within a stricter limit of discipline. For instance, they were not allowed to come rushing insolently and at will into the school of one who was not their own master, nor indeed to enter it at all unless he permitted.

At Carthage the licence of the students is gross and beyond all measure. They break in impudently and like a pack of madmen play havoc with the order which the master has established for the good of his pupils. They commit many outrages, extraordinarily stupid acts, deserving the punishment of the law if custom did not protect them. Their state is the more hopeless because what they do is supposed to be sanctioned, though by Your eternal law it could never be sanctioned; and they think they do these things unpunished, when the very blindness in which they do them is their punishment, so that they suffer things incomparably worse than they do. When I was a student I would not have such habits in myself, but when I became a teacher I had to endure them in others; and so I decided to go to a place where, as I had been told by all who knew, such things were not done. But You, O my Hope and my Portion[29] in the land of the living, forced me to change countries for my soul's salvation: You pricked me with such goads at Carthage as drove me out of it, and You set before me certain attractions by which I might be drawn to Rome—in either case using men who loved this life of death, one set doing lunatic things, the other promising vain things: and to reform my ways You secretly used their perversity and my own. For those who had disturbed my peace were blind in the frenzy of their viciousness, and those who urged me to go elsewhere savored of earth. While I, detesting my real misery in the one place, hoped for an unreal happiness in the other.

Why I left the one country and went to the other, You Knew, O God, but You did not tell either me or my mother. She indeed was in dreadful grief at my going and followed me right to the seacoast. There she clung to me passionately, determined that I should either go back home with her or take her to Rome with me, but I deceived her with the pretence that I had a friend whom I did not want to leave until he had sailed off with a fair wind. Thus I lied to my mother, and such a mother; and so got away from her. But this also You have mercifully forgiven me, bringing me from the waters of that sea, filled as I was with execrable uncleanness, unto the water of Your grace; so that when I was washed clean, the floods that poured from my mother's eyes, the tears with which

29. Inheritance.

daily she watered the ground towards which she bent her face in prayer for me, should cease to flow. She would not return home without me, but I managed with some difficulty to persuade her to spend the night in a place near the ship where there was an oratory in memory of St. Cyprian.[30] That night I stole away without her: she remained praying and weeping. And what was she praying for, O my God, with all those tears but that You should not allow me to sail! But You saw deeper and granted the essential of her prayer; You did not do what she was at that moment asking, that You might do the thing she was always asking. The wind blew and filled our sails and the shore dropped from our sight. And the next morning she was frantic with grief and filled Your ears with her moaning and complaints because You seemed to treat her tears so lightly, when in fact You were using my own desires to snatch me away for the healing of those desires, and were justly punishing her own too earthly affection for me with the scourge of grief. For she loved to have me with her, as is the way of mothers but far more than most mothers; and she did not realize what joys you would bring her from my going away. She did not realize it, and so she wept and lamented, and by the torments she suffered showed the heritage of Eve[31] in her, seeking with sorrow what in sorrow she had brought forth. But when she had poured out all her accusation at my cruel deception, she turned once more to prayer to You for me. She went home and I to Rome.

\* \* \*

[In Rome Augustine fell sick and was nursed back to health in the house of a Manichee. He continued to associate with members of this sect.]

All the same because I despaired of finding any profit in that false doctrine,[32] I began to hold slackly and carelessly even the ideas with which I had decided to rest content while I could find nothing better.

The notion began to grow in me that the philosophers whom they call Academics[33] were wiser than the rest, because they held that everything should be treated as matter of doubt and affirmed that no truth can be understood by men. For so it seemed clear to me that they thought—and so they are commonly held to teach— though I did not yet understand their real meaning.[34] And I did

30. Chapel in memory of the Bishop of Carthage, who had been beheaded during a persecution of the Christians in 258 A.D.

31. In consequence of her temptation of Adam to eat the forbidden fruit: "In sorrow [pain] thou shalt bring forth children." [Genesis 3:16, p. 51.]

32. The doctrine of the Manichees.

33. Members of a Greek philosophical school which questioned the validity of all belief. Augustine probably became acquainted with their position through Cicero's work on the subject.

34. Augustine then thought the Academic position more simple than it was; it is still a matter of controversy how far they carried their skeptical attitude.

not neglect to dissuade my host from the excessive confidence that I saw he had in the fables with which the books of Manes are packed.[35] All the same I was much more in their company than in the company of others who were not of their heresy. I did not defend it with my earlier keenness, yet the friendship of these men, of whom Rome shelters a great number, made me slower to seek any other: especially since I had no hope of being able to find the truth in Your church, O Lord of heaven and earth, Creator of all things visible and invisible.

\* \* \*

I began diligently to set about that for which I had come to Rome, namely the teaching of Rhetoric. First I gathered some few at my home, and by them I began to become known. And then I learned that Rome had its drawbacks which I had not had to suffer in Africa. For it is true the riotous incursions of blackguardly youngsters did not happen here: but, so I was warned, "at a given moment a number of students plan together to cheat their master of his fees, and go off to some other master; for they are utterly faithless and hold justice cheap, compared with love of money."

\* \* \*

When therefore a message from Milan[36] came to Rome, to the prefect,[37] asking for a professor of Rhetoric for that city and arranging for public funds to cover his journey, I applied for the post with support from men far gone in the follies of the Manichees—the purpose of my journey being to be quit of them, though neither they nor I realized it. The perfect Symmachus approved of a public oration I delivered for the occasion, and sent me. So I came to Milan, to the bishop and devout servant of God, Ambrose,[38] famed among the best men of the whole world, whose eloquence did then most powerfully minister to *Thy people the fatness of Thy wine*.[39] All unknowing I was brought by God to him, that knowing I should be brought by him to God. That man of God received me as a father, and as bishop welcomed my coming. I came to love him, not at first as a teacher of the truth, which I had utterly despaired of finding in Your church, but for his kindness toward me. I attended carefully when he preached to the people, not with the right intention, but only to judge whether his eloquence was equal to his fame or whether it flowed higher or lower than had

35. The man in whose house Augustine was living was a member of the Manichaean community in Rome.

36. A city in the north of Italy, which because it was nearer to the frontiers was growing in importance and was soon to replace Rome as the capital, in practice, of the Western Empire.

37. The chief magistrate of the city.

38. The leading personality among the Christians of the West. Not many years after this he defied the power of the emperor Theodosius, and forced him to beg for God's pardon in the church at Milan for having put the inhabitants of Thessalonica to the sword.

39. Images of spiritual nourishment. .

been told me. His words I listened to with the greatest care; his matter I held quite unworthy of attention. I enjoyed the charm of his speaking, though for all his learning it was not so pleasing and captivating as that of Faustus.[40] I refer of course only to the actual speaking: for the rest there was no comparison at all. Faustus was simply straying about among the fallacies of the Manichees, Ambrose taught the doctrine of salvation most profitably. But salvation is far from sinners, of the sort that I then was. Yet little by little I was drawing closer, though I did not yet realize it.

Thus I did not take great heed to learn what he was saying but only to hear how he said it: that empty interest was all I now had since I despaired of man's finding the way to You. Yet along with the words, which I admired, there also came into my mind the subject matter, to which I attached no importance. I could not separate them. And while I was opening my heart to learn how eloquently he spoke, I came to feel, though only gradually, how truly he spoke. First I began to realize that there was a case for the things themselves, and I began to see that the Catholic faith, for which I had thought nothing could be said in the face of the Manichean objections, could be maintained on reasonable grounds: this especially after I had heard explained figuratively several passages of the Old Testament which had been a cause of death for me when taken literally.[41] Many passages of these books were expounded in a spiritual sense and I came to blame my own hopeless folly in believing that the law and the prophets could not stand against those who hated and mocked at them. I did not yet feel that the Catholic way was to be followed, merely because it might have some learned men to maintain it and answer objections adequately and not absurdly; nor did I think that what I had so far held was to be condemned because both views were equally defensible. In fact the Catholic side was clearly not vanquished, yet it was not clearly victorious. I then bent my mind to see if I could by any clear proofs convict the Manicheans of error. If only I had been able to conceive of a substance that was spiritual, all their strong points would have been broken down and cast forth from my mind. But I could not.[42]

Concerning the body of this world, and the whole of that nature which our bodily senses can attain to, I thought again and again and made many comparisons; and I still judged that the views of so many of the philosophers were more probable. So in what I thought to be the manner of the Academics—that is to say, doubting of all

---

40. A Manichaean teacher Augustine had known in Carthage; not the legendary Dr. Faust.

41. Ambrose was famous for his allegorical explanations of difficult passages in the Scriptures.

42. One of the Manichaean criticisms of Christian doctrine which Augustine so far found impossible to answer was their objection to the concept of an infinite god who took on a corporeal nature.

things and wavering between one and another—I decided that I must leave the Manichees; for in that time of doubt, I did not think I could remain in a sect to which I now preferred certain of the philosophers. Yet I absolutely refused to entrust the care of my sick soul to the philosophers, because they were without the saving name of Christ. I determined, then, to go on as a catechumen[43] in the Catholic Church—the church of my parents—and to remain in that state until some certain light should appear by which I might steer my course.

\* \* \*

[*Worldly Ambitions*]
## Book VI

By this time my mother had come to me, following me over sea and land with the courage of piety and relying upon You in all perils. For they were in danger from a storm, and she reassured even the sailors—by whom travelers newly ventured upon the deep are ordinarily reassured—promising them safe arrival because thus You had promised her in a vision. She found me in a perilous state through my deep despair of ever discovering the truth. But even when I told her that if I was not yet a Catholic Christian, I was no longer a Manichean, she was not greatly exultant as at some unlooked-for good news, because she had already received assurance upon that part of my misery; she bewailed me as one dead certainly, but certainly to be raised again by You, offering me in her mind as one stretched out dead, that You might say to the widow's son: "*Young man, I say to thee arise*":[44] and he should sit up and begin to speak and You should give him to his mother.

\* \* \*

Nor did I then groan in prayer for Your help. My mind was intent upon inquiry and unquiet for argumentation. I regarded Ambrose as a lucky man by worldly standards to be held in honor by such important people: only his celibacy seemed to me a heavy burden. I had no means of guessing, and no experience of my own to learn from, what hope he bore within him, what struggles he might have against the temptations that went with his high place, what was his consolation in adversity, and on what joys of Your bread the hidden mouth of his heart fed. Nor did he know how I was inflamed nor the depth of my peril. I could not ask of him what I wished as I wished, for I was kept from any face to face conversation with him by the throng of men with their own troubles, whose infirmities he served. The very little time he was not with

43. One who is preparing himself for baptism.
44. *Luke*: 7:14, recounting one of Christ's miracles.

these he was refreshing either his body with necessary food or his mind with reading. When he read, his eyes traveled across the page and his heart sought into the sense, but voice and tongue were silent. No one was forbidden to approach him nor was it his custom to require that visitors should be announced: but when we came into him we often saw him reading and always to himself; and after we had sat long in silence, unwilling to interrupt a work on which he was so intent, we would depart again. We guessed that in the small time he could find for the refreshment of his mind, he would wish to be free from the distraction of other men's affairs and not called away from what he was doing. Perhaps he was on his guard lest [if he read aloud] someone listening should be troubled and want an explanation if the author he was reading expressed some idea over-obscurely, and it might be necessary to expound or discuss some of the more difficult questions. And if he had to spend time on this, he would get through less reading than he wished. Or it may be that his real reason for reading to himself was to preserve his voice, which did in fact readily grow tired. But whatever his reason for doing it, that man certainly had a good reason.

\* \* \*

I was all hot for honors, money, marriage: and You made mock of my hotness. In my pursuit of these, I suffered most bitter disappointments, but in this You were good to me since I was thus prevented from taking delight in anything not Yourself. Look now into my heart, Lord, by whose will I remember all this and confess it to You. Let my soul cleave to You now that You have freed it from the tenacious hold of death. At that time my soul was in misery, and You pricked the soreness of its wound, that leaving all things it might turn to You, who are over all and without whom all would return to nothing, that it might turn to You and be healed. I was in utter misery and there was one day especially on which You acted to bring home to me the realization of my misery. I was preparing an oration in praise of the Emperor[45] in which I was to utter any number of lies to win the applause of people who knew they were lies. My heart was much wrought upon by the shame of this and inflamed with the fever of the thoughts that consumed it. I was passing along a certain street in Milan when I noticed a beggar. He was jesting and laughing and I imagine more than a little drunk. I fell into gloom and spoke to the friends who were with me about the endless sorrows that our own insanity brings us: for here was I striving away, dragging the load of my unhappiness under the spurring of my desires, and making it worse by dragging it: and with all our striving, our one aim was to arrive at some sort of happiness without care: the beggar had reached the same goal before us, and

45. Probably the young Valentinian, whose court was at Milan.

we might quite well never reach it at all. The very thing that he had attained by means of a few pennies begged from passers-by— namely the pleasure of a temporary happiness—I was plotting for with so many a weary twist and turn.

Certainly his joy was no true joy; but the joy I sought in my ambition was emptier still. In any event he was cheerful and I worried, he had no cares and I nothing but cares. Now if anyone had asked me whether I would rather be cheerful or fearful, I would answer: "Cheerful"; but if he had gone on to ask whether I would rather be like that beggar or as I actually was, I would certainly have chosen my own state though so troubled and anxious. Now this was surely absurd. It could not be for any true reason. I ought not to have preferred my own state rather than his merely because I was the more learned, since I got no joy from my learning, but sought only to please men by it—not even to teach them, only to please them. Therefore did You break my bones with the rod of Your discipline.

* * *

Great effort was made to get me married. I proposed, the girl was promised me. My mother played a great part in the matter for she wanted to have me married and then cleansed with the saving waters of baptism,[46] rejoicing to see me grow every day more fitted for baptism and feeling that her prayers and Your promises were to be fulfilled in my faith. By my request and her own desire she begged You daily with the uttermost intensity of her heart to show her in a vision something of my future marriage, but You would never do it. She did indeed see certain vain fantasies, under the pressure of her mind's preoccupation with the matter; and she told them to me, not, however, with the confidence she always had when You had shown things to her, but as if she set small store by them; for she said that there was a certain unanalyzable savor, not to be expressed in words, by which she could distinguish between what You revealed and the dreams of her own spirit. Still she pushed on with the matter of my marriage, and the girl was asked for. She was still two years short of the age for marriage[47] but I liked her and agreed to wait.

There was a group of us friends who had much serious discussion together, concerning the cares and troubles of human life which we found so hard to endure. We had almost decided to seek a life of peace, away from the throng of men. This peace we hoped to attain by putting together whatever we could manage to get, and making one common household for all of us: so that in the clear trust of friendship, things should not belong to this or that individual, but one thing should be made of all our possessions, and belong wholly

46. He could not be baptized while living in sin with his mistress.
47. The legal age was twelve years.

Augustus himself was in his early thirties.

to each one of us, and everybody own everything. It seemed that there might be perhaps ten men in this fellowship. Among us there were some very rich men, especially Romanianus, our fellow townsman, who had been a close friend of mine from childhood and had been brought to the court in Milan by the press of some very urgent business. He was strongest of all for the idea and he had considerable influence in persuasion because his wealth was much greater than anyone else's. We agreed that two officers should be chosen every year to handle the details of our life together, leaving the rest undisturbed. But then we began to wonder whether our wives would agree, for some of us already had wives and I meant to have one. So the whole plan, which we had built up so neatly, fell to pieces in our hands and was simply dropped. We returned to our old sighing and groaning and treading of this world's broad and beaten ways:[48] for many thoughts were in our hearts, but *Thy counsel standeth forever*. And out of Thy counsel didst Thou deride ours and didst prepare Thine own things for us, meaning to *give us meat in due season and to open Thy hands and fill our souls with Thy blessing*.

Meanwhile my sins were multiplied. She with whom I had lived so long was torn from my side as a hindrance to my forthcoming marriage. My heart which had held her very dear was broken and wounded and shed blood. She went back to Africa, swearing that she would never know another man, and left with me the natural son I had had of her. But I in my unhappiness could not, for all my manhood, imitate her resolve. I was unable to bear the delay of two years which must pass before I was to get the girl I had asked for in marriage. In fact it was not really marriage that I wanted. I was simply a slave to lust. So I took another woman, not of course as a wife; and thus my soul's disease was nourished and kept alive as vigorously as ever, indeed worse than ever, that it might reach the realm of matrimony in the company of its ancient habit. Nor was the wound healed that had been made by the cutting off of my former mistress. For there was first burning and bitter grief; and after that it festered, and as the pain grew duller it only grew more hopeless.

\* \* \*

## [Conversion]

### Book VIII

\* \* \*

Thus I was sick at heart and in torment, accusing myself with a new intensity of bitterness, twisting and turning in my chain in the hope that it might be utterly broken, for what held me was so

48. cf. *Matthew* 7:13: "Broad is the    to damnation.
way that leadeth to destruction," that is,

small a thing! But it still held me. And You stood in the secret places of my soul, O Lord, in the harshness of Your mercy redoubling the scourges of fear and shame lest I should give way again and that small slight tie which remained should not be broken but should grow again to full strength and bind me closer even than before. For I kept saying within myself: "Let it be now, let it be now," and by the mere words I had begun to move toward the resolution. I almost made it, yet I did not quite make it. But I did not fall back into my original state, but as it were stood near to get my breath. And I tried again and I was almost there, and now I could all but touch it and hold it: yet I was not quite there, I did not touch it or hold it. I still shrank from dying unto death and living unto life. The lower condition which had grown habitual was more powerful than the better condition which I had not tried. The nearer the point of time came in which I was to become different, the more it struck me with horror; but it did not force me utterly back nor turn me utterly away, but held me there between the two.

Those trifles of all trifles, and vanities of vanities, my one-time mistresses, held me back, plucking at my garment of flesh and murmuring softly: "Are you sending us away?" And "From this moment shall we not be with you, now or forever?" And "From this moment shall this or that not be allowed you, now or forever?" What were they suggesting to me in the phrase I have written "this or that," what were they suggesting to me, O my God? Do you in your mercy keep from the soul of Your servant the vileness and uncleanness they were suggesting. And now I began to hear them not half so loud; they no longer stood against me face to face, but were softly muttering behind my back and, as I tried to depart, plucking stealthily at me to make me look behind. Yet even that was enough, so hesitating was I, to keep me from snatching myself free, from shaking them off and leaping upwards on the way I was called: for the strong force of habit said to me: "Do you think you can live without them?"

But by this time its voice was growing fainter. In the direction toward which I had turned my face and was quivering in fear of going, I could see the austere beauty of Continence, serene and indeed joyous but not evilly, honorably soliciting me to come to her and not linger, stretching forth loving hands to receive and embrace me, hands full of multitudes of good examples. With her I saw such hosts of young men and maidens, a multitude of youth and of every age, gray widows and women grown old in virginity, and in them all Continence herself, not barren but the fruitful mother of children, her joys, by You, Lord, her Spouse. And she smiled upon me and her smile gave courage as if she were saying: "Can you not do what these men have done, what these women have done? Or could men or women have done such in themselves, and not in the

Lord their God? The Lord their God gave me to them. Why do you stand upon yourself and so not stand at all? Cast yourself upon Him and be not afraid; He will not draw away and let you fall. Cast yourself without fear, He will receive you and heal you."

Yet I was still ashamed, for I could still hear the murmuring of those vanities, and I still hung hesitant. And again it was as if she said: "Stop your ears against your unclean members, that they may be mortified. They tell you of delights, but not of such delights as the law of the Lord your God tells." This was the controversy raging in my heart, a controversy about myself against myself. And Alypius[49] stayed by my side and awaited in silence the issue of such agitation as he had never seen in me.

When my most searching scrutiny had drawn up all my vileness from the secret depths of my soul and heaped it in my heart's sight, a mighty storm arose in me, bringing a mighty rain of tears. That I might give way to my tears and lamentations, I rose from Alypius: for it struck me that solitude was more suited to the business of weeping. I went far enough from him to prevent his presence from being an embarrassment to me. So I felt, and he realized it. I suppose I had said something and the sound of my voice was heavy with tears. I arose, but he remained where we had been sitting, still in utter amazement. I flung myself down somehow under a certain fig tree and no longer tried to check my tears, which poured forth from my eyes in a flood, *an acceptable sacrifice to Thee*. And much I said not in these words but to this effect: "*And Thou, O Lord, how long? How long, Lord; wilt Thou be angry forever? Remember not our former iniquities.*"[50] For I felt that I was still bound by them. And I continued my miserable complaining: "How long, how long shall I go on saying tomorrow and again tomorrow? Why not now, why not have an end to my uncleanness this very hour?"

Such things I said, weeping in the most bitter sorrow of my heart. And suddenly I heard a voice from some nearby house, a boy's voice or a girl's voice, I do not know: but it was a sort of singsong, repeated again and again. "Take and read, take and read." I ceased weeping and immediately began to search my mind most carefully as to whether children were accustomed to chant these words in any kind of game, and I could not remember that I had ever heard any such thing. Damming back the flood of my tears I arose, interpreting the incident as quite certainly a divine command to open my book of Scripture and read the passage at which I should open. For it was part of what I had been told about Anthony,[51] that from the Gospel which he happened to be reading

49. A student of Augustine's at Carthage; he had joined the Manichees with Augustine, followed him to Rome and Milan, and now shared his desires and doubts. Alypius finally became a bishop in North Africa.
50. The quotation is from Psalm 79;

Augustine compares his spiritual despair with that of captive and subjected Israel.
51. The Egyptian saint whose abstinence and self-control are still proverbial; he was one of the founders of the system of monastic life.

he had felt that he was being admonished as though what he read was spoken directly to himself: *Go, sell what thou hast and give to the poor and thou shalt have treasure in heaven; and come follow Me.*[52] By this experience he had been in that instant converted to You. So I was moved to return to the place where Alypius was sitting, for I had put down the Apostle's[53] book there when I arose. I snatched it up, opened it and in silence read the passage upon which my eyes first fell: *Not in rioting and drunkenness, not in chambering and impurities, not in contention and envy, but put ye on the Lord Jesus Christ and make not provision for the flesh in its concupiscences.* [Romans xiii, 13.] I had no wish to read further, and no need. For in that instant, with the very ending of the sentence, it was as though a light of utter confidence shone in all my heart, and all the darkness of uncertainty vanished away. Then leaving my finger in the place or marking it by some other sign, I closed the book and in complete calm told the whole thing to Alypius and he similarly told me what had been going on in himself, of which I knew nothing. He asked to see what I had read. I showed him, and he looked further than I had read. I had not known what followed. And this is what followed: "*Now him that is weak in faith, take unto you.*" He applied this to himself and told me so. And he was confirmed by this message, and with no troubled wavering gave himself to God's goodwill and purpose—a purpose indeed most suited to his character, for in these matters he had been immeasurably beter than I.

Then we went in to my mother and told her, to her great joy. We related how it had come about: she was filled with triumphant exultation, and praised You who are mighty beyond what we ask or conceive: for she saw that You had given her more than with all her pitiful weeping she had ever asked. For You converted me to Yourself so that I no longer sought a wife nor any of this world's promises, but stood upon that same rule of faith in which You had shown me to her so many years before.[54] Thus You changed her mourning into joy, a joy far richer than she had thought to wish, a joy much dearer and purer than she had thought to find in grandchildren of my flesh.

[*Death of His Mother*]

### Book IX

\* \* \*

And I thought it would be good in Your sight if I did not dramatically snatch my tongue's service from the speech-market but quietly withdrew; but that in any event withdraw I must, so that

52. Luke 18:22.
53. Paul.
54. At Carthage, when Augustine was still a Manichee, Monica had dreamed that she was standing on a wooden ruler weeping for her son, and then saw that he was standing on the same ruler as herself.

youths—not students of Your law or Your peace but of lying follies and the conflicts of the law—should no longer buy at my mouth the tools of their madness. Fortunately it happened that there were only a few days left before the Vintage Vacation,[55] and I decided to endure them so that I might leave with due deliberation, seeing that I had been redeemed by You and was not going to put myself up for sale again. Our purpose therefore was known to You, but not to men other than our own friends. We had agreed among ourselves not to spread the news abroad at all, although, in our ascent from *the valley of tears and our singing of the song of degrees,* You had given us *sharp arrows* and *burning coals* against *cunning tongues* that might argue against us with pretended care for our interest, might destroy us saying that they loved us: as men consume food saying that they love it.

\* \* \*

Furthermore that very summer, under the too heavy labor of teaching, my lungs had begun to give way and I breathed with difficulty,[56] the pain in my breast showed that they were affected and they no longer let me talk with any strength for too long at a time. At first this had disturbed me, because it made it practically a matter of necessity that I should lay down the burden of teaching, or at least give it up for the time if I was to be cured and grow well again. But when the full purpose of giving myself leisure to meditate on how You are the Lord arose in me and became a settled resolve—as you know, O my God—I actually found myself glad to have this perfectly truthful excuse to offer parents who might be offended and for their children's sake would never willingly have let me give up teaching. So I was full of joy, and I put up with the space of time that still had to run—I fancy it was about twenty days. But to bear the time took considerable fortitude. Desire for money, which formerly had helped me to bear the heavy labor of teaching, was quite gone; so that I should have [had nothing to help me bear it and so] found it altogether crushing if patience had not taken the place of covetousness. Some of Your servants, my brethren, may think that I sinned in this, since having enrolled with all my heart in Your service, I allowed myself to sit for so much as an hour in the chair of untruthfulness. It may be so. But, most merciful Lord, have You not pardoned and remitted this sin, along with others most horrible and deadly, in the holy water of baptism?

\* \* \*

And now the day was come on which I was to be set free from the teaching of Rhetoric in fact, as I was already free in mind. And

55. This grape-harvesting and wine-making holiday lasted from the end of August to the middle of October.
56. Since he not only lectured but also read aloud, as is suggested by his comments on Ambrose's silent reading (Book VI).

so it came about. You delivered my tongue as You had already delivered my heart, and I rejoiced and praised You, and so went off with my friends to the country-house.[57] The amount of writing I did there—the writing was now in your service but during this breathing-space still smacked of the school of pride—my books[58] exist to witness, with the record they give of discussions either with my friends there present or with Yourself when I was alone with You; and there are my letters to show what correspondence I had with Nebridius[59] while he was away.

\* \* \*

When the Vintage Vacation was over I gave the people of Milan notice that they must find someone else to sell the art of words to their students, because I had chosen to serve You, and because owing to my difficulty in breathing and the pain in my lungs I could not continue my teaching. And in a letter I told Your bishop, the holy Ambrose, of my past errors and my present purpose, that he might advise me which of Your Scriptures I should especially read to prepare me and make me more fit to receive so great a grace. He told me to read Isaias the prophet, I imagine because he more clearly foretells the gospel and the calling of the gentiles[60] than the other Old Testament writers; but I did not understand the first part of his book, and thinking that it would be all of the same kind, put it aside meaning to return to it when I should be more practised in the Lord's way of speech.

When the time had come to give in my name for baptism, we left the country and returned to Milan. Alypius had decided to be born again in You at the same time, for he was already endowed with the humility that Your sacraments require, and had brought his body so powerfully under control that he could tread the icy soil of Italy with bare feet, which required unusual fortitude. We also took with us the boy Adeodatus, carnally begotten by me in my sin. You had made him well. He was barely fifteen, yet he was more intelligent than many a grave and learned man. In this I am but acknowledging to You Your own gifts, O Lord my God, Creator of all and powerful to reshape our shapelessness: for I had no part in that boy but the sin. That he had been brought up by us in Your way was because You had inspired us, no other. I do but acknowledge to You Your own gifts. There is a book of mine called *De*

57. At Cassiciacum, in the country, placed at his disposal by a friend.

58. While at Cassiciacum, Augustine wrote a book attacking the Academic philosophers, a book on the happy life, and another entitled *De ordine*, a treatise on divine providence.

59. Nebridius came from Carthage to Milan with Augustine, shared his spiritual pilgrimage through the pagan philosophies and Manichean doctrines to become a Christian, and returned to Africa where he died. Augustine's letters to Nebridius are still extant.

60. The appeal of Christ's apostles to peoples outside the Hebrew nation: "I am sought of them that asked not for me: I am found of them that sought me not." [Isaiah 65.1 ff.]

*Magistro*:[61] it is a dialogue between him and me. You know, O God, that all the ideas which are put into the mouth of the other party to the dialogue were truly his, though he was but sixteen. I had experience of many other remarkable qualities in him. His great intelligence filled me with a kind of awe: and who but You could be the maker of things so wonderful? But You took him early from this earth, and I think of him utterly without anxiety, for there is nothing in his boyhood or youth or anywhere in him to cause me to fear. We took him along with us, the same age as ourselves in Your grace, to be brought up in Your discipline: and we were baptized, and all anxiety as to our past life fled away. The days were not long enough as I meditated, and found wonderful delight in meditating, upon the depth of Your design for the salvation of the human race. I wept at the beauty of Your hymns and canticles, and was powerfully moved at the sweet sound of Your Church's singing. Those sounds flowed into my ears, and the truth streamed into my heart: so that my feeling of devotion overflowed, and the tears ran from my eyes, and I was happy in them.

It was only a little while before that the church of Milan had begun to practice this kind of consolation and exultation, to the great joy of the brethen singing together with heart and voice. For it was only about a year, or not much more, since Justina, the mother of the boy emperor Valentinian, was persecuting Your servant Ambrose in the interests of her own heresy: for she had been seduced by the Arians.[62] The devoted people had stayed day and night in the church, ready to die with their bishop, Your servant. And my mother, Your handmaid, bearing a great part of the trouble and vigil, had lived in prayer. I also, though still not warmed by the fire of Your Spirit, was stirred to excitement by the disturbed and wrought-up state of the city. It was at this time that the practice was instituted of singing hymns and psalms after the manner of the Eastern churches,[63] to keep the people from being altogether worn out with anxiety and want of sleep. The custom has been retained from that day to this, and has been imitated by many, indeed in almost all congregations throughout the world.

At this time You revealed to Your bishop Ambrose in a vision the place where the bodies of the martyrs Protasius and Gervasius

---

61. *The Teacher,* written at Tagaste in Africa two years after Augustine's baptism and shortly after his return from Italy. The subject is teaching and the thesis that only God is the cause for man's acquisition of learning and truth.

62. Members of a heretical sect who followed the doctrine of Arius (A.D. 250?–336) that the Son had not existed from all eternity and was therefore inferior to the Father. At the Council of Ni-

caea (A.D. 325) Arius and his followers were declared heretical, but the Arian heresy remained a serious problem for the Church for many years. Justina demanded that Ambrose allow the Arians to hold public services inside the walls of Milan.

63. The Greek-speaking churches of the Eastern half of the empire. They split off from the Catholic Church in the ninth century.

lay hid, which You had for so many years kept incorrupt in the treasury of Your secret knowledge that You might bring them forth at the proper moment to check a woman's fury—the woman being the ruler of the Empire![64] For when they were discovered and dug up and with due honor brought to Ambrose's basilica,[65] not only were people cured who had been tormented by evil spirits—and the devils themselves forced to confess it—but also there was a man, a citizen well known to the city, who had been blind for many years: he asked what was the cause of the tumultuous joy of the people, and when he heard, he sprang up and asked his guide to lead him into the place. When he arrived there he asked to be allowed to touch with his handkerchief the place on which lay the saints, whose death is precious in Your sight. He did so, put the handkerchief to his eyes, and immediately they were opened. The news spread abroad, Your praises glowed and shone, and if the mind of that angry woman[66] was not brought to the sanity of belief, it was at least brought back from the madness of persecution. Thanks be to my God! From what and towards what have You led my memory, that it should confess to You these great things which I had altogether forgotten? Yet even then, *when the odor of Thy ointments was so sweet smelling,* I did not *run after Thee:* and for this I wept all the more now when I heard Your hymns and canticles, as one who had then sighed for You and now breathed in You, breathed so far as the air allows in this our house of grass.[67]

You, Lord, who make men of one mind to dwell in one house brought to our company a young man of our own town, Evodius. He had held office in the civil service, had been converted and baptized before us, had resigned from the state's service, and given himself to Yours. We kept together, meaning to live together in our devout purpose. We thought deeply as to the place in which we might serve You must usefully. As a result we started back for Africa. And when we had come as far as Ostia[68] on the Tiber, my mother died. I pass over many things, for I must make haste. Do You, O my God, accept my confessions and my gratitude for countless things of which I say nothing. But I will not omit anything my mind brings forth concerning her, Your servant, who brought me forth—brought me forth in the flesh to this temporal light, and in her heart to light eternal. Not of her gifts do I speak but of Your gifts in her. For she did not bring herself into the world or educate herself in the world: it was You who created her, nor did her father

64. Justina.
65. Church.
66. Justina.
67. "All flesh is grass. . . . The grass withers, the flower fades, but the word of our God will stand forever." [Isaiah 40:6–8.]
68. A port on the southwest coast of Italy; it was the port of Rome and the point of departure for Africa.

or mother know what kind of being was to come forth from them. It was the scepter of Your Christ, the discipline of your Only-Begotten, that brought her up in holy fear, in a Catholic family which was a worthy member of Your church. Yet it was not the devotion of her mother in her upbringing that she talked most of, but of a certain aged servant, who had indeed carried my mother's father on her back when he was a baby, as little ones are accustomed to be carried on the backs of older girls. Because of this, because also of her age and her admirable character, she was very much respected by her master and mistress in their Christian household. As a result she was given charge of her master's daughters. This charge she fulfilled most conscientiously, checking them sharply when necessary with holy severity and teaching them soberly and prudently. Thus, except at the times when they ate—and that most temperately—at their parents' table, she would not let them even drink water, no matter how tormenting their thirst. By this she prevented the forming of a bad habit, and she used to remark very sensibly: "Now you drink water because you are not allowed to have wine: but when you are married, and thus mistresses of food-stores and wine-cellars, you will despise water, but the habit of drinking will still remain." By this kind of teaching and the authority of her commands she moderated the greediness that goes with childhood and brought the little girls' thirst to such a control that they no longer wanted what they ought not to have.

Yet, as Your servant told me, her son, there did steal upon my mother an inclination to wine. For when, in the usual way, she was sent by her parents, as a well-behaved child, to draw wine from the barrel, she would dip the cup in, but before pouring the wine from the cup into the flagon, she would sip a little with the very tip of her lips, only a little because she did not yet like the taste sufficiently to take more. Indeed she did it not out of any craving for wine, but rather from the excess of childhood's high spirits, which tend to boil over in absurdities, and are usually kept in check by the authority of elders. And so, adding to that daily drop a little more from day to day—for he that despises small things, falls little by little—she fell into the habit, so that she would drink off greedily cups almost full of wine. Where then was that wise old woman with her forceful prohibitions? Could anything avail against the evil in us, unless Your healing, O Lord, watched over us? When our father and mother and nurses are absent, You are present, who created us, who call us, who can use those placed over us for some good unto the salvation of our souls. What did You do then, O my God? How did You cure her, and bring her to health? From another soul you drew a harsh and cutting sarcasm, as though bringing forth a surgeon's knife from Your secret store, and with one blow amputated that sore place. A maidservant with whom she was accustomed to go to the cellar, one day fell into a quarrel with her small mistress when no one else chanced to be about, and hurled at her the most biting insult possible, calling her a drunkard. My mother was pierced to the quick, saw her fault in its true wickedness, and instantly condemned it and gave it up. Just as the flattery of a friend can pervert, so the insult of an enemy can sometimes correct. Nor do You, O God, reward men according to what You do by means of them, but according to what they themselves intended. For the girl being in a temper wanted to enrage her young mistress, not to amend her, for she did it when no one else was there, either because the time and place happened to be thus when the quarrel arose, or because she was afraid that elders[69] would be angry because she had not told it sooner. But You, O Lord, Ruler of heavenly things and earthly, who turn to Your own purposes the very depths of rivers as they run and order the turbulence of the flow of time, did by the folly of one mind bring sanity to another; thus reminding us not to attribute it to our own power if another is amended by our word, even if we meant to amend him.

My mother, then, was modestly and soberly brought up, being rather made obedient to her parents by You than to You by her parents. When she reached the age for marriage, and was bestowed upon a husband, she served him as her lord. She used all her effort to win him to You, preaching You to him by her character, by which You made her beautiful to her husband, respected and loved by him and admirable in his sight. For she bore his acts of unfaithfulness quietly, and never had any jealous scene with her husband about them. She awaited Your mercy upon him, that he might grow chaste through faith in You. And as a matter of fact, though generous beyond measure, he had a very hot temper. But she knew that a woman must not resist a husband in anger, by deed or even by word. Only, when she saw him calm again and quiet, she would take the opportunity to give him an explanation of her actions, if it happened that he had been roused to anger unreasonably. The result was that whereas many matrons with much milder husbands carried the marks of blows to disfigure their faces, and would all get together to complain of the way their husbands behaved, my mother—talking lightly but meaning it seriously—advised them against their tongues: saying that from the day they heard the matrimonial contract read to them they should regard it as an instrument by which they became servants; and from that time they should be mindful of their condition and not set themselves up against their masters. And they often expressed amazement—for they knew how violent a husband she had to live with—that it had never been

69. Leaders of the church.

heard, and there was no mark to show, that Patricius[70] had beaten his wife or that there had been any family quarrel between them for so much as a single day. And when her friends asked her the reason, she taught them her rule, which was as I have just said. Those who followed it, found it good and thanked her; those who did not, went on being bullied and beaten.

Her mother-in-law began by being angry with her because of the whispers of malicious servants. But my mother won her completely by the respect she showed, and her unfailing patience and mildness. She ended by going to her son, telling him of the tales the servants had bandied about to the destruction of peace in the family between herself and her daughter-in-law, and asking him to punish them for it. So he, out of obedience to his mother and in the interests of order in the household and peace among his womenfolk, had the servants beaten whose names he had been given, as she had asked when giving them. To which she added the promise that anyone must expect a similar reward from her own hands who should think to please her by speaking ill of her daughter-in-law. And as no one had the courage to do so, they lived together with the most notable degree of kindness and harmony.

This great gift also, O my God, my Mercy, You gave to Your good servant, in whose womb You created me, that she showed herself, wherever possible, a peacemaker between people quarreling and minds at discord. For swelling and undigested discord often belches forth bitter words when in the venom of intimate conversation with a present friend hatred at its rawest is breathed out upon an absent enemy. But when my mother heard bitter things said by each of the other, she never said anything to either about the other save what would help to reconcile them. This might seem a small virtue, if I had not had the sorrow of seeing for myself so many people who— as if by some horrible widespreading infection of sin—not only tell angry people the things their enemies said in anger, but even add things that were never said at all. Whereas, on the contrary, ordinary humanity would seem to require not merely that we refrain from exciting or increasing wrath among men by evil speaking, but that we study to extinguish wrath by kind speaking. Such a one was she: and You were the master who taught her most secretly in the school of her heart.

The upshot was that toward the very end of his life she won her husband to You; and once he was a Christian she no longer had to complain of the things she had had to bear with before he was a Christian. Further, she was a servant of Your servants. Such of them as knew her praised and honored and loved You, O God, in her; for they felt Your presence in her heart, showing itself in the

---

70. Augustine's father.

fruit of her holy conversation. She had been *the wife of one hus-band, had requited her parents, had governed her house* piously, *was well reported of for good works.* She had *brought up her children,*[71] being in labor of them as often as she saw them swerving away from You. Finally of all of us Your servants, O Lord— since by Your gift You suffer us to speak—who before her death were living together[72] after receiving the grace of baptism, she took as much care as if she had been the mother of us all, and served us as if she had been the daughter of us all.

When the day was approaching on which she was to depart this life—a day that You knew though we did not—it came about, as I believe by Your secret arrangement, that she and I stood alone leaning in a window, which looked inwards to the garden within the house where we were staying, at Ostia on the Tiber; for there we were away from everybody, resting for the sea voyage from the weariness of our long journey by land. There we talked together, she and I alone, in deep joy; and *forgetting the things that were behind and looking forward to those that were before,* we were discussing in the presence of Truth, which You are, what the eternal life of the saints could be like, *which eye has not seen nor ear heard, nor has it entered into the heart of man.* But with the mouth of our heart we panted for the high waters of Your fountain, the fountain of the life which is with You: that being sprinkled from that fountain according to our capacity, we might in some sense meditate upon so great a matter.

And our conversation had brought us to this point, that any pleasure whatsoever of the bodily senses, in any brightness whatsoever of corporeal light, seemed to us not worthy of comparison with the pleasure of that eternal Light, not worthy even of mention. Rising as our love flamed upward towards that Selfsame,[73] we passed in review the various levels of bodily things, up to the heavens themselves, whence sun and moon and stars shine upon this earth. And higher still we soared, thinking in our minds and speaking and marveling at Your works: and so we came to our own souls, and went beyond them to come at last to that region of richness unending, where You feed Israel forever with the food of truth: and there life is that Wisdom by which all things are made, both the things that have been and the things that are yet to be. But this Wisdom itself is not made: it is as it has ever been, and so it shall be forever: indeed "has ever been" and "shall be forever" have no place in it, but it simply is, for it is eternal: whereas "to have been" and "to be going to be" are not eternal. And while we were thus

---

71. Augustine is quoting Paul's description of the duties of a widow. [I Timothy 5.]

72. Augustine and his fellow converts.

73. Reality, the divine principle. This ecstasy of Augustine and Monica is throughout described in philosophical terms, in which God is Wisdom.

talking of His Wisdom and panting for it, with all the effort of our heart we did for one instant attain to touch it; then sighing, and leaving the first fruits of our spirit bound to it, we returned to the sound of our own tongue, in which a word has both beginning and ending. For what is like to your Word, Our Lord, who abides in Himself forever, yet grows not old and makes all things new!

So we said: If to any man the tumult of the flesh grew silent, silent the images of earth and sea and air: and if the heavens grew silent, and the very soul grew silent to herself and by not thinking of self mounted beyond self: if all dreams and imagined visions grew silent, and every tongue and every sign and whatsoever is transient—for indeed if any man could hear them, he should hear them saying with one voice: We did not make ourselves, but He made us who abides forever: but if, having uttered this and so set us to listening to Him who made them, they all grew silent, and in their silence He alone spoke to us, not by them but by Himself: so that we should hear His word, not by any tongue of flesh nor the voice of an angel nor the sound of thunder nor in the darkness of a parable,[74] but that we should hear Himself whom in all these things we love, should hear Himself and not them: just as we two had but now reached forth and in a flash of the mind attained to touch the eternal Wisdom which abides over all: and if this could continue, and all other visions so different be quite taken away, and this one should so ravish and absorb and wrap the beholder in inward joys that his life should eternally be such as that one moment of understanding for which we had been sighing—would not this be: *Enter Thou into the joy of Thy Lord?* But when shall it be? Shall it be when *we shall all rise again* and *shall not all be changed?*[75]

Such thoughts I uttered, though not in that order or in those actual words; but You know, O Lord, that on that day when we talked of these things the world with all its delights seemed cheap to us in comparison with what we talked of. And my mother said: "Son, for my own part I no longer find joy in anything in this world. What I am still to do here and why I am here I know not, now that I no longer hope for anything from this world. One thing there was, for which I desired to remain still a little longer in this life, that I should see you a Catholic Christian before I died. This God has granted me in superabundance, in that I now see you His servant to the contempt of all worldly happiness. What then am I doing here?"

---

74. Alludes to Luke 8:10: "To you [the disciples of Jesus] it has been given to know the secrets of the kingdom of God; but for others they are in parables, so that seeing they may not see, and hearing they may not understand."

75. Refers to the Last Judgment, when "the trumpet shall sound, and the dead shall be raised incorruptible, and we shall be changed." [I Corinthians 15:52.]

What answer I made, I do not clearly remember; within five days or not much longer she fell into a fever. And in her sickness, she one day fainted away and for the moment lost consciousness. We ran to her but she quickly returned to consciousness, and seeing my brother and me standing by her she said as one wondering: "Where was I?" Then looking closely upon us we stood wordless in our grief, she said: "Here you will bury your mother." I stayed silent and checked my weeping. But my brother said something to the effect that he would be happier if she were to die in her own land and not in a strange country. But as she heard this she looked at him anxiously, restraining him with her eye because he savored of earthly things, and then she looked at me and said: "See the way he talks." And then she said to us both: "Lay this body wherever it may be. Let no care of it disturb you: this only I ask of you that you should remember me at the altar of the Lord wherever you may be." And when she had uttered this wish in such words as she could manage, she fell silent as her sickness took hold of her more strongly.

But as I considered Your gifts, O unseen God, which You send into the hearts of Your faithful to the springing up of such wonderful fruits, I was glad and gave thanks to You, remembering what I had previously known of the care as to her burial which had always troubled her: for she had arranged to be buried by the body of her husband. Because they had lived together in such harmony, she had wished—so little is the human mind capable of rising to the divine —that it should be granted her, as an addition to her happiness and as something to be spoken of among men, that after her pilgrimage beyond the sea the earthly part of man and wife should lie together under the same earth. Just when this vain desire had begun to vanish from her heart through the fullness of Your goodness, I did not know; but I was pleased and surprised that it had now so clearly vanished: though indeed in the conversation we had had together at the window, when she said: "What am I still doing here?" there had appeared no desire to die in her own land. Further I heard afterwards that in the time we were at Ostia, she had talked one day to some of my friends, as a mother talking to her children, of the contempt of this life and of the attraction of death. I was not there at the time. They marveled at such courage in a woman— but it was You who had given it to her—and asked if she was not afraid to leave her body so far from her own city. But she said: "Nothing is far from God, and I have no fear that He will not know at the end of the world from what place He is to raise me up." And so on the ninth day of her illness, in the fifty-sixth year of her life and the thirty-third of mine, that devout and holy soul was released from the body.

I closed her eyes; and an immeasurable sorrow flowed into my heart and would have overflowed in tears. But my eyes under the mind's strong constraint held back their flow and I stood dry-eyed. In that struggle it went very ill with me. As she breathed her last, the child Adeodatus broke out into lamentation and we all checked him and brought him to silence. But in this very fact the childish element in me, which was breaking out into tears, was checked and brought to silence by the manlier voice of my mind. For we felt that it was not fitting that her funeral should be solemnized with moaning and weeping and lamentation, for so it is normal to weep when death is seen as sheer misery or as complete extinction. But she had not died miserably, nor did she wholly die. Of the one thing we were sure by reason of her character, of the other by the reality of our faith.

What then was it that grieved my heart so deeply? Only the newness of the wound, in finding the custom I had so loved of living with her suddenly snapped short. It was a joy to me to have this one testimony from her: when her illness was close to its end, meeting with expressions of endearment such services as I rendered, she called me a dutiful loving son, and said in the great affection of her love that she had never heard from my mouth any harsh or reproachful word addressed to herself. But what possible comparison was there, O my God who made us, between the honor I showed her and the service she had rendered me?

Because I had now lost the great comfort of her, my soul was wounded and my very life torn asunder, for it had been one life made of hers and mine together. When the boy had been quieted and ceased weeping, Evodius[76] took up the psalter and began to chant—with the whole house making the responses—the psalm *Mercy and judgment I will sing to Thee, O Lord.*[77] And when they heard what was being done, many of the brethren and religious women came to us; those whose office it was were making arrangement for the burial, while, in another part of the house where it could properly be done I discoursed, with friends who did not wish to leave me by myself, upon matters suitable for that time. Thus I used truth as a kind of fomentation[78] to bring relief to my torment, a torment known to You, but not known to those others: so that listening closely to me they thought that I lacked all feeling of grief. But in Your ears, where none of them could hear, I accused the emotion in me as weakness; and I held in the flood of my grief. It was for the moment a little diminished, but returned with fresh violence, not with any pouring of tears or change of countenance: but I knew what I was crushing down in my heart. I was very much

---

76. Above, p. 717. [35] *Psalter:* The book of Psalms.

77. The opening words of Psalm 101.
78. Soothing dressing for a wound.

ashamed that these human emotions could have such power over me—though it belongs to the due order and the lot of our earthly condition that they should come to us—and I felt a new grief at my grief and so was afflicted with a twofold sorrow.

When the body was taken to burial, I went and returned without tears. During the prayers which we poured forth to you when the sacrifice of our redemption[79] was offered for her—while the body, as the custom there is, lay by the grave before it was actually buried —during those prayers I did not weep. Yet all that day I was heavy with grief within and in the trouble of my mind I begged of You in my own fashion to heal my pain; but You would not—I imagine because You meant to impress upon my memory by this proof how strongly the bond of habit holds the mind even when it no longer feeds upon deception. The idea came to me to go and bathe, for I had heard that the bath—which the Greeks call βαλανεῖον—is so called because it drives anxiety from the mind.[80] And this also I acknowledge to Your mercy, O Father of orphans, that I bathed and was the same man after as before. The bitterness of grief had not sweated out of my heart. Then I fell asleep, and woke again to find my grief not a little relieved. And as I was in bed and no one about, I said over those true verses that Your servant Ambrose wrote of You:

> Deus creator omnium
> polique rector vestiens
> diem decoro lumine,
> noctem sopora gratia,
>
> artus solutos ut quies
> reddat laboris usui
> mentesque fessas allevet
> luctusque solvat anxios.[81]

And then little by little I began to recover my former feeling about Your handmaid, remembering how loving and devout was her conversation with You, how pleasant and considerate her conversation with me, of which I was thus suddenly deprived. And I found solace in weeping in Your sight both about her and for her, about myself and for myself. I no longer tried to check my tears, but let them flow as they would, making them a pillow for my heart: and

---

79. Perhaps a communion service.

80. Augustine evidently derives balaneion, the Greek word for "bath," from the words *ballo* and *ania*, which mean "cast away" and "sorrow" respectively.

81. "God, the creator of all things and ruler of the heavens, / you who clothe the day with the glory of light / and the night with the gift of sleep, / so that rest may relax the limbs / and restore them for the day's work, / relieve the fatigue of the mind / and dispel anxiety and grief."

it rested upon them, for it was Your ears that heard my weeping, and not the ears of a man, who would have misunderstood my tears and despised them. But now, O Lord, I confess it to You in writing, let him read it who will and interpret it as he will: and if he sees it as sin that for so small a portion of an hour I wept for my mother, now dead and departed from my sight, who had wept so many years for me that I should live ever in Your sight—let him not scorn me but rather, if he is a man of great charity, let him weep for my sins to You, the Father of all the brethren of Your Christ.

Now that my heart is healed of that wound, in which there was perhaps too much of earthly affection, I pour forth to You, O our God, tears of a very different sort for Your handmaid—tears that flow from a spirit shaken by the thought of the perils there are for every soul that dies in Adam.[82] For though she had been made alive in Christ, and while still in the body had so lived that Your name was glorified in her faith and her character, yet I dare not say that from the moment of her regeneration in baptism no word issued from her mouth contrary to Your Command. Your Son, who is Truth, has said: *Whosoever shall say to his brother, Thou fool, shall be in danger of hell fire;*[83] and it would go ill with the most praiseworthy life lived by men, if You were to examine it with Your mercy laid aside! But because You do not enquire too fiercely into our sins, we have hope and confidence of a place with You. Yet if a man reckons up before You the merits he truly has, what is he reckoning except Your own gifts? If only men would know themselves to be but men, so that he that glories would glory in the Lord!

Thus, my Glory and my Life, God of my heart, leaving aside for this time her good deeds, for which I give thanks to Thee in joy, I now pray to Thee for my mother's sins. Grant my prayer through the true Medicine of our wounds,[84] who hung upon the cross and who now sitting at Thy right hand makes intercession for us. I know that she dealt mercifully, and from her heart forgave those who trespassed against her: do Thou also forgive such tespasses as she may have been guilty of in all the years since her baptism, forgive them, Lord, forgive them, I beseech Thee: enter not into judgment with her. Let Thy mercy be exalted above Thy justice for. Thy words are true and Thou hast promised that the merciful shall obtain mercy. That they should be merciful is Thy gift who *hast mercy on whom Thou wilt, and wilt have compassion on whom Thou wilt.*

82. That is, with the curse of Adam not nullified through baptism in Jesus Christ and conformity with his teachings.
83. From Jesus' Sermon on the Mount. He is preaching a more severe moral code than the traditional one that whoever kills shall be liable to judgment.
84. I.e., Jesus Christ.

And I believe that Thou hast already done what I am now asking; but be not offended, Lord, at the things my mouth would utter. For on that day when her death was so close, she was not concerned that her body should be sumptuously wrapped or embalmed with spices, nor with any thought of choosing a monument or even for burial in her own country. Of such things she gave us no command, but only desired to be remembered at Thy altar, which she had served without ever missing so much as a day, on which she knew that the holy Victim was offered; *by whom the handwriting is blotted out of the decree that was contrary to us,*[85] by which offering too the enemy[86] was overcome who, reckoning our sins and seeking what may be laid to our charge, found nothing in Him, in whom we are conquerors. Who shall restore to Him his innocent blood? Who shall give Him back the price by which He purchased us and so take us from Him? To this sacrament of our redemption Thy handmaid had bound her soul by the bond of faith. Let none wrest her from Thy protection; let neither the lion nor the dragon[87] bar her way by force or craft. For she will not answer that she owes nothing, lest she should be contradicted and confuted by that cunning accuser: but she will answer that her debts have been remitted by Him, to whom no one can hand back the price which He paid for us, though He owed it not.

So let her rest in peace, together with her husband, for she had no other before nor after him, but served him, in patience bringing forth fruit for Thee, and winning him likewise for Thee. And inspire, O my Lord my God, inspire Thy servants my brethren, Thy sons my masters, whom I serve with heart and voice and pen, that as many of them as read this may remember at Thy altar Thy servant Monica, with Patricius, her husband, by whose bodies Thou didst bring me into this life, though how I know not.[88] May they with loving mind remember these who were my parents in this transitory light, my brethren who serve Thee as our Father in our Catholic mother, and those who are to be fellow citizens with me in the eternal Jerusalem,[89] which Thy people sigh for in their pilgrimage from birth until they come there: so that what my mother at her end asked of me may be fulfilled more richly in the prayers of so many gained for her by my Confessions than by my prayers alone.

\* \* \*

85. Alludes to Christ's redemption of humanity from the curse of Adam through the Crucifixion.

86. Satan.

87. Psalm 91.13 invokes God's protection of the godly: "Thou shalt tread upon the lion and the adder; the young lion and the dragon shalt thou trample under feet."

88. I.e., Augustine does not understand the seemingly miraculous process by which the fetus grows in the womb.

89. Heaven.

# Masterpieces of the
# Middle Ages

### EDITED BY
## JOHN C. McGALLIARD
*Professor of English, The University of Iowa*

The period of the Middle Ages —approximately 500–1500 A.D. —encompasses a thousand years of European history distinguished by the unique fusion of a Heroic-Age society with Greco-Roman culture and Christian religion. The era is fairly well marked off by the emergence and disappearance of certain massive forces. It begins with the collapse of the Roman Empire in Western Europe, a development coincident with and partly occasioned by the settlement of Germanic peoples within the territory of the empire. It ends with the discovery of the Western Hemisphere, the invention of the printing press, the consolidation of strong national states, the break in religious unity brought about by the Protestant Reformation, and the renewal—after a lapse of nearly a thousand years—of direct contact with Greek art, thought,

and literature. The medieval centuries created, or at least refashioned, and bequeathed to us such institutional patterns as the Christian church; the monarchical state; the town and village; the traditional European social order—the "lords spiritual," the "lords temporal," with the hierarchy of nobility and gentry ranging from duke to knight, and the third, or bourgeois, estate; the university; the system and logical method of Scholastic philosophy; Romanesque and Gothic architecture; and a rich variety of literary forms.

The literature of the earlier Middle Ages reflects directly and clearly the life and civilization of a Heroic Age. The dominant figure is the fighting king or chieftain; the favorite pursuit is war; the characteristic goals are power, wealth, and glory; and the primary virtues, accordingly, are valor and loyalty. The literary pattern is based on actuality, of which it presents a kind of idealization. In early Germanic and Celtic society the king ruled a small, essentially tribal nation; he and his companions in battle constituted a formal or informal noble class controlling the life of the people. The poems of such a society naturally tell chiefly of the fights of great champions, though also of the druids or other counselors who advised them and of the minstrels who entertained them. The proportions and the emphasis are much the same in the literature of the Irish, the Scandinavians, the French of the twelfth century, the Germans of the thirteenth. The hero of the *Song of Roland*, a twelfth-century French work, combines the fighting chieftain, serving his king, with the devout Crusader; and Archbishop Turpin is both spiritual adviser and fighting champion.

In the literature of the fourteenth century, the warrior plays a smaller rôle and is assimilated to the more extensive pattern of later medieval civilization. Thus in Dante's Heaven only one of the nine celestial spheres—Mars —is occupied by great men-at-arms, all devout Christians, of course. Chaucer's Knight and Squire are only two among twenty-nine pilgrims on their way to Canterbury. The Knight is devoted to truth and honor, generosity, and courteous conduct, while his son, along with other virtues appropriate to a young soldier, possesses those of a courtly lover. The fighting champion of the Heroic Age has become the "officer and gentleman" of the modern world.

This gradual assimilation of the Celtic and Germanic hero to a civilization in which Christianity ordered the Greco-Roman culture to new ends was made possible by the religious unity and authority of Western Europe. The medieval millennium was indeed an age of faith, though it was far from being an age of religious passivity or inertia. The first half of the period was occupied in winning the new peoples of Europe to Christianity. When this had been accomplished, the Crusades began —a series of holy wars intended to rescue Palestine from pagan occupation and, in general, to defeat and either destroy or convert the pagans, chiefly Mohammedans. But the Greek and Arabic learning and philosophy which these non-Christian people introduced into Europe in the twelfth and thirteenth centuries demanded an intellectual alertness. The sharpness of the Crusader's sword had to be matched by the acumen of the Scholastic philosopher; one of the chief works of St. Thomas Aquinas is a summation of principles in defense of Christianity "against the pagans" (his *Summa contra Gentiles*). Medieval Christianity could never afford to take itself for granted. For the first four centuries after Christ the new religion was aggressively on the defensive; thereafter it had to be actively on the offensive in both the practical and the ideological spheres. Nevertheless, in Western Europe itself the combination of theological unity and ecclesiastical authority was a phenomenon unmatched either before or after the Middle Ages. The Roman Empire had provided political unity, law, and order, to assure the success of secular pursuits. Beyond that, it had left moral and spiritual problems to be handled by the individual, singly or in voluntary or ethnic groups. In medieval Europe political disunity was at something like a maximum; but under the leadership and direction of the Church there was achieved a remarkable unanimity of spiritual, moral, and intellectual attitudes and ideals.

The community of European culture in this period was such that the productions of individual countries look like regional manifestations of a central nuclear force. Generally speaking, students and scholars moved freely from land to land; monks, abbots, and bishops might be sent from the country of their birth to serve or preside in distant places; artists and poets wandered widely either in the train of or in search of patrons. Besides his native tongue, the educated man might be expected to speak and write the common "standard" language of Europe —Latin. In an age when the political state was relatively weak, a man's strongest loyalties were to an individual, a feudal lord, for example; to a code, such as the code of chivalry; to an order—of monks or friars or knights; or simply to the Church itself, if, like so many medieval men of intellectual interests, he was a cleric of some sort.

These ties—except for the feudal, and sometimes including that also—were *international* in nature. In such a cultural atmos-phere the themes and subjects and techniques of art and literature circulated freely throughout Europe. The *Gothic* architecture of a building is a more central aspect of it than the fact that it was designed and built by an English, a French, a German, or an Italian school of builders. Christianity itself furnished a common subject matter for painters, sculptors, and countless others skilled in the graphic and plastic arts; the biblical stories and scenes had the same meaning in every country. The stories of Charlemagne, Roland, and Arthur, of Aeneas, of Troy and Thebes, were European literary property. They were handled and rehandled, copied, translated, adapted, expanded, condensed, and in general appropriated by innumerable authors, writing in various languages, with no thought of property rights or misgivings about plagiarism. There were no copyright regulations and no author's royalties to motivate insistence on individuality of authorship; there was comparatively little concern about the identity of the artist. Many medieval poems and tales are anonymous, including some of the greatest.

The submergence of the artist in his work is accounted for in part, at least, by the medieval system of human values. The dominant hierarchy of values— we have seen that it did not dominate universally, especially in the literature of northern Europe—was based on the Christian view of man. Man, in this conception, is a creature of God, toward whom he is inevitably oriented but from whom he is separated by the world in which he must live his earthly, mortal life. Human civilization under Christian direction may be regarded as ideally designed—even if not actually so functioning—to assist man on his way to union with God. This is the criterion for the ultimate appraisal of all the institutions of society and all the patterns of culture. Hence derive the scale, the order, the hierarchical categories of medieval life and thought. Since the spiritual side of man transcends the material, the saint becomes the ideal. The saint is one whose life is most fully subdued, assimilated, and ordered to the spiritual. On earth he may be a hermit, like Cuthbert; a reformer of monasteries, like Bernard; a philosopher and a theologian, like Aquinas; a king, like Louis IX of France; or a humble man in private life. Since communion with God—the essential aspect of bliss in heaven—is an experience of the soul, the contemplative life, which prepares for the mystical communion, is superior to any form of the active life. Hence the monk—by virtue of his vocation—has an advantage over the secular priest, just as the priest is, other things being equal, in a position spiritually more desirable than that of the layman. As a whole, medieval literature is a study in human life judged according to this scale of values. The scale is represented clearly in Dante's *Divine Comedy*. Secular-value patterns are assimilated to it, for instance in the *Song of Roland*; or it may be taken for granted without much emphasis, as in Chaucer's works. But it is always there, whether below or above the surface. For the modern reader it supplies a focus for the adequate reading and understanding of most of the literature of the Middle Ages.

## THE DREAM OF THE ROOD

*The Dream of the Rood* is one of the finest of the many poems, from early medieval lyrics to modern Gospel hymns, about that central symbol of the Christian religion, the cross on which Christ was crucified. It was originally written in Old English, the language of Anglo-Saxon England (ca. 500–1100), and in its written form probably dates from the eighth century. However, like all Old English poetry, it shares in the long and ancient tradition of oral poetry, composed spontaneously by bards in public performance.

The poem uses the popular medieval form of a dream vision: the anonymous poet tells what he (or she) saw and heard in a dream. The organization of the poem is almost perfectly symmetrical. In the first twenty-nine lines, the author describes the cross as it appeared in the dream; then the cross itself speaks directly, in a kind of autobiographical sketch of ninety lines; and in the final twenty-eight lines the narrator resumes, telling of the effect which the dream had on him.

In this vision the cross has a double aspect. It is a glorious, cosmic object, visible to the angels in heaven as well as to humanity on earth, but it is also "wet and stained" with Christ's blood. In telling of the crucifixion it offers this remarkable heroic image:

Then the young Warrior,      God
the All-Wielder,
Put off his raiment,      steadfast
and strong;
With lordly mood      in the sight
of many
He mounted the Cross      to redeem mankind.

Here the Son of God might
almost be a Germanic king setting forth on horseback to destroy a monster and save his people. Christ "the Wielder" appears again in the glimpse of the
Last Judgment (lines 103–119),
when he will return to Earth to
punish and reward, and finally
in the "triumphant" harrowing
of hell (lines 141–147).

In this, as in all Old English
poems, the metrical pattern depends on alliteration, the similar sound of stressed syllables at
the beginning of one or two
words in the first half-line and
one in the second. The translator has made generous use of alliteration but has not tried to
reproduce the exact sound patterns of the original poem.

## THE SONG OF ROLAND

With some literal inaccuracy,
but with substantial truth, it
has been said that French literature begins with the *Song of
Roland* (*Chanson de Roland*).
Certainly it is the first great narrative poem in that language. Of
unknown authorship and date,
it was apparently composed in
the decade or decades after the
year 1100. Imbued with the
spirit of the First Crusade, it
seems to reproduce some details
of the campaigns and expeditions to capture and hold the
Holy Land for Christendom.
The story it tells was developed
from a historical incident in the
career of Charlemagne (Charles
the Great). As the Emperor was
returning from a successful war
in northern Spain, the Gascons
attacked his baggage train and
rear guard in the mountain
passes of the Pyrenees. The rear
guard perished, including Roland, the prefect of the Breton
March. These events occurred in
the year 778. Our poet of the
twelfth century has transformed
them—somewhat as Geoffrey of
Monmouth, Chrétien de Troyes,
and Malory transformed incidents involving the probably also
historical Arthur, his exploits,
and the deeds of his warriors.
The Charles of the *Roland*, a
magnificent figure, is white-
haired and venerable, and not
without a touch of the miraculous: though still valiant in
fight, he is reputed among the
enemy to be two hundred years
old, or more. He is served especially by a choice band of leaders, the twelve peers, of whom
the chief is Roland, his nephew
—a relationship that in Heroic
narrative intensifies either loyalty or disloyalty. The enemy,
too, has been changed. Not a
few border Gascons or Basques,
but enormous Saracen armies
fight against Roland and the
Emperor. Thus we have a holy
war; all the motives of a Crusade
are invoked in this struggle of
Christians against Mohammedans. Keeping the Emperor as
the central *background* figure,
the poet has concentrated his
efforts on Roland as the hero,
the central *foreground* character.
Close beside him stand Oliver,
the wise and faithful friend, and
Ganelon, whose hatred of Roland leads him to treason against
Charles.

The world of the poem is an

idealization of feudal society in the early twelfth century. This society was headed by proud barons—a hereditary nobility—whose independent spirit found liberal scope in valiant action, fierce devotion, and bitter personal antagonism. A man was esteemed for his prowess in battle, for his loyalty to his king or other feudal chief, and for his wisdom, as the portrait of Oliver reminds us. The action of the poem is infused with a warm glow of patriotic feeling—not the flag-waving variety, but a cherishing love of the homeland, "sweet France." It might be called regional rather than political patriotism, for in a feudal regime a man's binding obligations are to his lord rather than to the country as a whole. Yet the larger issue enters, in a special way: in the second half of the poem, Ganelon is finally condemned and punished because in compassing the destruction of Roland he has injured the king and the French nation: the poet denies Ganelon's claim that these are separable things.

The present volume includes only the first half of the poem. As it is unabridged, however, this portion has a satisfactory completeness. We see the anger of Ganelon at Roland, out of which grows his treachery and the attack of the Saracens; the valor of Roland, and the rest, in battle; and their heroic death. The second half of the poem relates the vengeance taken by Charles against the Saracens—in two separate battles—and the trial and execution of Ganelon. Although the *Song of Roland* was the work, and probably the *written* work, of a well-educated man, during the period immediately following its composition it was sung or chanted. It is divided into strophes averaging fourteen lines, each of ten (or eleven) syllables.

It is easy to see why modern French readers and critics assign the *Roland* a high place in their national literature. Inherent in its structure and texture are the qualities especially esteemed in the French literary tradition—clarity of focus, lucidity in exposition and narration, definite design, and mastery of technical detail. In the poem as a whole—even in our abridgment of a part—scale and proportion are evident. The succession of quarrels, treachery, and battles is only the raw material out of which the poet has built a highly wrought work of art. The emphasis on action—on what Roland, Ganelon, and Oliver do and say—has been recognized since Aristotle as the right method for a poet. But mere action is the formula of the adventure story. The great-literature standard requires that the action have significance. This significance the author of the *Roland* has provided in rich and ordered variety. The acts of the hero, of his friend, and of his foe are presented as part of the total character of each; they grow out of the whole man, including his temperament and personality. But they are also presented against an ethical and social background. Every act, every decision, bears a relation to the feudal code of conduct, of right and wrong, and hence is an indication of human good or evil. Courage rather than cowardice, loyalty rather than treachery, judgment rather than folly—a belief in these criteria is implicit or explicit in the presentation of each action. And they apply to the outermost frame within which the poet has placed the specific events of the narrative—the contest between Christianity and paganism. For to the author and his audience the Christian cause is just, the Saracen, unjust. Roland, fighting for the crusading Emperor, is *right*; Ganelon, aiding the heathen enemy against his brother-in-arms, is doubly *wrong*.

The man who brings about the death of Roland and twenty thousand Franks is no mean and petty villain. The husband of the Emperor's sister and the stepfather of Roland, he holds a very high place in Charles's council. Nor does he lack the ability or the personality to sustain this position. He has no hesitation in speaking against Roland in the first discussion of the Saracen proposals; his nomination as envoy to King Marsile is readily accepted by Charles; and his success in his treachery is a brilliant feat. For in order to accomplish it he must first provoke the now peacefully inclined Marsile to wrath and then turn this anger against Roland. To this end he takes a calculated risk for the sake of a calculated—but far from guaranteed—result. Insulting Marsile deliberately, in the name of the Emperor, he makes himself the first target of the Saracen king's fury and definitely endangers his own life. Luckily for him, the king's hand is stayed; and the Saracen nobles applaud Ganelon's magnificent courage. The rest is comparatively easy— though everything now depends on Ganelon's success in getting Roland placed in command of the rear guard. That he succeeds is the more credible because it was Roland who previously nominated Ganelon for the embassy: Roland and Charles may be expected to act, as in fact they do, on the principle that turn about is fair play.

To the twelfth-century poet and his audience of proud knights the question of motive in Ganelon's hatred of Roland doubtless presented little difficulty. Indeed, if Ganelon had not resorted to treason, a tenable defense of his attitude could be established. For it may well be that he is honestly opposed to the policy of relentless war against the Saracens. His speech at the first council, urging acceptance of Marsile's proposals, wins the support of the wise counselor Naimes, and carries the day. An advocate of peace would obviously regard the uncompromising spokesman of the war party—Roland—as his opponent. Later, talking with the Saracen envoy Blancandrin, Ganelon plausibly represents Roland as the chief obstacle to pacific relations between the two peoples. To be sure, Ganelon is now plotting against Roland; but that should not blind us to the possibility that he honestly differs with Roland about this question of the Emperor's foreign policy. When we have said this, and when we have recognized the faults in Roland's personality that might normally vex another powerful, but less powerful, courtier, we have said all that can be said in defense of Ganelon. His acts put him quite beyond the possibility of moral justification. But justifying him is one thing; understanding him is quite another, and this the author has enabled us to do.

In Roland the poet has created one of the great heroes of European literature. Like Achilles, Aeneas, and Hamlet, he is the embodiment of a definite ideal of humanity. The ideal that Roland incarnates is that of feudal chivalry. Roland exhibits in superlative degree the traits and attitudes which feudal society and institutions sought to produce in a whole class. He is a supremely valiant fighter, a completely faithful vassal, and a warmly affectionate friend; and, since his creator lived in the early twelfth century, his fervent Christianity bears the Crusader's stamp. His words to his friend Oliver before the battle epitomize his vocation as he sees it:

Men for their lords great
    hardship must abide,
Fierce heat and cold endure in
    every clime,
Lose for his sake, if need be, skin
    and hide.
Look to it now! Let each man
    stoutly smite!
No shameful songs be sung for
    our despite!
Paynims are wrong, Christians
    are in the right!
Ill tales of me shall no man tell,
    say I!

This is the code of a man of action, of one to whom action appears as duty. Neither here nor elsewhere in the poem is Roland touched by any sense of the *lacrimae rerum*, and of the "doubtful doom of human kind" that haunts Aeneas. Nor has he ever dreamt of most of the things in Hamlet's philosophy. In assurance and self-reliance he is much closer to Achilles, ex-

cept that Achilles fought essentially for himself—certainly not for Agamemnon! In Roland the man is wholly assimilated to the vassal. The ceiling above him is lower, the pattern he follows is more limited, than those of Achilles, Aeneas, and Hamlet; yet within his pattern Roland achieves perfection, as they do in theirs.

Roland's feats in battle require no analysis; they are bright and glorious; they outshine the great deeds of his noble comrades. This superiority is no more than the poet has led us to expect. It is the hero's weakness—weakness counterpoised to his greatness—that gives the poem depth and produces the tension that commands our interest. Roland's defect has been called the excess of his special virtue—confidence, courage, bravery; if assurance outstrips prudence, then bravery becomes recklessness, which can bring disaster upon the hero and those for whom he is responsible. The author carefully shows us that Roland has no habit or instinct of caution to match his marvelous courage. Charles notes the vindictive manner in which Ganelon proposes Roland for the rear guard, and though at a loss to divine its meaning, is moved to assign half his entire army to Roland. But Roland either has not noticed the gleam of triumph in Ganelon's eye, or, if he has, loftily disregards it and firmly refuses to take more than twenty thousand men, a relatively small force.

So far Roland has done nothing definitely wrong, though he has revealed a certain lack of perception and of intuitive prudence. But he does do wrong when, surprised by an army of a hundred thousand Saracens, he refuses to blow the horn that would summon Charles to the rescue. The error is emphasized by the repetition in Oliver's effort to persuade him, and the relationship between Roland's refusal and his rashness of character is made apparent both through his answers and through the contrast with Oliver. Roland fears that asking for help would make him look foolish among the Franks—instead, he will slay the foe himself; he will not leave his kin at home open to reproach because of him; if, as Oliver says, the rear guard is hopelessly outnumbered, then death is better than disgrace. Actually, Roland is confident of victory despite the odds. His judgment is not equal to his daring. As the poet sums it up, "Roland is fierce and Oliver wise."

Hence catastrophe ensues. But it is catastrophe redeemed by glorious heroism, as well as self-sacrificing penitence. When, despite tremendous exploits by the Franks, especially by Roland, all but a handful of the rear guard have been slain, Roland wishes to sound the horn to let the Emperor know what has happened. But now Oliver dissents on the ground of honor: Roland had refused to summon Charles to a rescue, and it would be shameful to summon him now only to witness a disaster. The repetitions in this scene balance those of the earlier one. Though the question is decided by Archbishop Turpin, the argument has embittered Oliver against Roland. Hence it is that when, blinded by his own blood, Oliver

later strikes Roland, his comrade has to ask whether the blow was intentional. Roland's humility here is a part of his penitence, a penitence never put into words but sublimely revealed in deeds. Exhausted by battle as he is, his superhuman and repeated blasts on the horn burst his temples. The angels and archangels who receive his soul in Paradise are functional symbols of his final triumph in defeat. The poet does not remit the penalty of Roland's error, which is paid by his death. But his victory combines an epic with a tragic conclusion; atonement and redemption, not merely death, is the end, as it is in another profoundly Christian poem of action, Milton's *Samson Agonistes*.

## THE STORY OF AUCASSIN AND NICOLETTE

*Aucassin and Nicolette* (*Aucassin et Nicolete*) is perhaps the most charming literary work of the entire Middle Ages. Its author is unknown, but it is written in the language in use in northern France in the twelfth century or thereabouts. The alternation of prose and verse in *Aucassin* is somewhat unusual; perhaps the prose passages were intended to be read aloud or recited and the poems sung by an entertainer, amateur or professional. It has been suggested that the work belonged to the repertory of a company or pair of traveling minstrels, who performed or acted it much as a play. If this was the case, it must have been presented in places like the castle of Count Garin de Beaucaire in the story, for there was apparently no secular theater—or opera—during the Middle Ages.

The remarkable achievement of *Aucassin* is the masterly use of familiar elements of diverse kinds to produce a unique result. A wide variety of incidents, motifs, and themes has been woven into a unified pattern designed and sustained with precision. It *partly* resembles several of the recognized types of narrative: the folk tale, the romance, the adventure story; and it recalls a number of familiar themes: the love of prince and pauper, the child of royalty in disguise, the conversion of the heathen. The repetition of statements in nearly identical phrasing, especially in the dialogue of the early prose sections, offers the assurance and the emphasis that repetition provides in the fairy tale. And the beauty of Nicolette is so surpassing that we may be tempted to suspect that she is a supernatural creature—until we find the ignorant shepherds making exactly that mistake. The escapes, the traveling to strange lands, the separation by capture and shipwreck, the hardships, all these are the materials of the *romans d'aventure* (tales of adventure). But here they are handled with a brevity and deftness that make them incidental to the central theme; vivid or comic, strange or poignant, none of them delays us long. Nor do the other motifs, mentioned above, ever dominate the narrative or determine the real structure of the work.

*Aucassin and Nicolette* is, of course, a love story. But the treatment differs considerably from that customary in the *romans d'amour* (tales of love). In these the lady is often hostile, at least ostensibly, or, at best, unaware of her lover's pangs; she has to be won; frequently she is capricious and gives her knight a hard time—he must conquer the lady's affection as well as the numerous and wearying external obstacles that keep them apart. But Nicolette is as much in love as Aucassin, and more ingenious and enterprising; both are utterly candid, direct, and steadily devoted to each other. The specific dangers and the devices employed to elude them, the castles, dungeons, escapes by a window into a garden and through a moat—these are traditional. But the atmosphere in which they are related is not: the warm night of early summer, saturated with moonlight and nightingales, the lyric joy of the two lovers. The work is built, by rigid selection, from elements of the real life of the time, a time when there actually were moats, dungeons, sentinels, parental authority, chattel slaves, fierce counts carrying on private wars—not to insist on Saracens or uncouth shepherds in the woodland. Hence, perhaps, the freshness and spontaneity, the naturally springing gaiety and joy. Hence, too, the stress, without impairment of tone, on the picturesque and the humorous in a world from which the processes of moral judgment have been largely expunged. Action is straightforward and decisive. At one point Aucassin is taken prisoner by his father's enemies before he realizes what has happened; when he becomes aware of his situation, he lays about him manfully, captures the enemy count, and so puts an end to a twenty years' war! The same absoluteness and directness are expressed in Aucassin's famous reply to the viscount of the town, who warns him that he may be sent to hell for loving Nicolette. He wants to go there, says Aucassin, along with the lively knights, the gay, sweet ladies, and the musicians and poets; that is, he belongs with those who take delight in the joys and beauties of human life. A heaven filled with the ugly, the weak, the miserable, and those who deny nature in the name of religion would not suit him at all. This is exuberance, of course, not atheism; the extravagance of Aucassin's words is a part of his character and a feature of his world.

The work is a kind of gospel of the religion of love, a religion that exacts a complete devotion and bestows a complete happiness. Yet there is some question about the tone which the author intended to give it for *his* day and generation. Precisely because motivation and action are so absolute, so neat, and so pat, some modern students of medieval French literature believe that it is a parody or satire. They may well be right. But the modern reader, unburdened by lengthy metrical romances of chivalric adventure and courtly love conducted by means of stereotyped characters and formula situations, need not worry too much about the question. *Aucassin and Nicolette* is a delight whether regarded simply as a story or as a vehicle for literary satire.

# DANTE, *THE DIVINE COMEDY*

The greatest poem of the Middle Ages, called by its author a comedy and designated by later centuries *The Divine Comedy* (*La divina commedia*), was written in the early fourteenth century. The poet, Dante Alighieri, born in Florence in 1265, was exiled from his native city in 1302 for politcal reasons and died at Ravenna in 1321. The poem is in many ways both the supreme and the centrally representative expression of medieval man in imaginative literature. But to appreciate the poem adequately in this light a reader must know it in its entirety, since it is an organic whole designed with the utmost symmetry. The present volume contains the entire *Inferno* and several cantos from the other two divisions. It will be best to look rapidly at the general plan and then concentrate on the part included in this book.

The three great divisions of the poem, *Hell* (*Inferno*), *Purgatory* (*Purgatorio*), and *Paradise* (*Paradiso*), are of identical length; each of the last two has thirty-three cantos, and the first, the *Hell*, has thirty-four; but the opening canto is a prologue to the entire poem. The total, one hundred, is the square of ten, regarded in the thought of the time as a perfect number. The three divisions correspond in number to the Trinity. Nine, the square of three, figures centrally in the interior structure of each of the three divisions. In Hell, the lost souls are arranged in three main groups, and occupy nine circles. Most of the circles are themselves subdivided. Hell itself is a funnel-shaped opening in the earth extending from the surface to the center. Dante's journey thus takes him steadily downward through the nine concentric circles. The progression is from the least to the greatest types of evil; all the souls are irrevocably condemned, but all are not intrinsically equal in the degree or nature of their sinfulness. Thus, as we follow Dante in his descent, we find first an ante-Hell, the abode of those who refused to choose between right and wrong; then the boundary river, Acheron; then a circle for virtuous pagans who knew not Christ; and then a series of circles occupied by those guilty of sins of self-indulgence, or Incontinence, of all kinds. These include the illicit lovers, the gluttons, the hoarders and spendthrifts, and those of violent or sullen disposition. Comparable classes and subclasses are found within the other two main groups of sinners, those guilty respectively of Violence and of Fraud, the latter including treachery and treason. At the bottom is the fallen angel, Satan, or Lucifer.

Purgatory is situated on a lofty mountain rising on an island in the sea. It is divided into the ante-Purgatory, which is the lower half of the mountain; Purgatory proper, just above; and the Earthly Paradise, or Garden of Eden, at the summit. Purgatory proper is arranged in a series of seven ledges encircling the mountain, each devoted to the purification of souls from particular kinds of sinful disposition—Pride, Envy, Anger, Sloth, Avarice, Gluttony, and Illicit Love. These seven divisions, plus the ante-Purgatory and the Earthly Paradise, make a total of nine.

The *Paradise* takes us, in ascending order, through the circles of the seven planets of medieval astronomy, the moon, Mercury, Venus, the sun, Mars, Jupiter, and Saturn; then through the circles of the fixed stars and the *primum mobile*, or outermost circle, which moves the others; and finally to the Empyrean, or Heaven itself, the abode of God, the angels, and the redeemed souls. Again we have nine circles, besides the Empyrean, inclusion of which would give a total of ten. Such is the vast design and scope of *The Divine Comedy* as a whole. Our partial reading can give us some representative and illustrative experience of its execution in some of its parts.

## INFERNO

The poem itself begins with action, not outline; explanations come along in suitable places; they are part of the traveler's experience. We shall do well to follow the hint. The incidents recounted in Canto I of the *Inferno* are concrete and definite; their literal meaning is perfectly plain. As critics have often said, Dante is a highly visual poet; he gives us clear pictures or images. Beginning with a man lost in a wood, hindered by three beasts from escape by his own effort, the canto might well be the start of a tale of unusual but quite earthly adventures. But when the stranger Dante meets identifies himself as the shade of the poet Virgil and offers to conduct him through realms which, though not named, can only be Hell and Purgatory, we realize that there is a meaning beyond the one which appears on the surface. We recognize that the wood, the mountain, the sun, and the three beasts, though casually introduced, are not casual features of the scene. They represent something other than themselves; they are symbols. In the light of the entire poem, it is usually possible to tell what these other things are, and in this volume the head-notes and footnotes identify them. Occasionally, however, there is doubt. What do the three beasts stand for? A lack of certainty is not a serious disadvantage to the reader; he should regard it as a challenge to reach a correct decision for himself. Indeed, if he goes on to read the entire poem, he may arrive at an identification that seems sounder and more consistent with the work as a whole than those proposed. Meanwhile, there is no ambiguity about the animals themselves; they are the satisfying and specific images of poetry.

The simple style of this first canto may surprise the reader who has been told that *The Divine Comedy* is one of the five or six great poems of European literature, especially if he assumes that it will sound like an epic. For Dante begins with neither the splendor of Homer nor the stateliness of Virgil nor the grandeur of Milton. Indeed, except for the use of verse, Canto I seems more like a narrative by Defoe or Swift, particularly at the outset. It is quiet, factual, economical; it convinces

us by its air of serious simplicity. Dante called the poem a comedy, in accordance with the use of the term in his day, not only because it began in misery and ended in happiness, but also because in that literary form a sustained loftiness of style was not requisite. In other words, he is free to use the whole range of style, from the humblest, including the colloquial and the humorous, to the highest. There is, indeed, a great variety of tone in the poem. Yet the reader will doubtless eventually agree that Dante strikes the right note *for him* at the beginning. Variation will result chiefly from change in intensity, achieved by differing degrees of concentration and repetition—rather than from a shift to the "grand style." This unpretentious manner is, we see, most suitable to a prolonged work of serious fiction in which the author is the central character. For *The Divine Comedy* is not primarily a Cook's tour of the world of the dead; it is an account of the effect of such a journey on the man who takes it—Dante. It is a record of his moral and spiritual experience of illumination, regeneration, and beatitude. We are interested partly because of the unique and individual character of the traveler—Dante as the man he was, the man revealed in the poem—and partly because the experience of the author is imaginatively available and meaningful to all of us.

In Canto IV we come to the first of the nine concentric circles of Hell. Here are the noble heroes, wise philosophers, and inspired poets of the ancient— and medieval—pagan world.

They are excluded from Heaven because they knew nothing of Christ and his religion. This fate may seem harsh to us, but the orthodox view recognized only one gate to Heaven. These spirits suffer no punishment, Virgil (who is one of them) tells Dante, only "cut off from hope, we live on in desire." Here Dante's fervent pity and sympathy at once nourish and mirror the reader's; but there is no rebellion against God's decree. Further explanation, and thereby justification, in Dante's view, will come as the poem progresses toward its goal.

With Canto V we reach the second circle, the first of those containing souls guilty of active sin unrepented at the time of death, and hence suffering a penalty in Hell. Here, therefore, is found the contemptuous and monstrous judge Minos, another figure taken from classical myth and freely adapted to Dante's purposes. The souls assigned to the second circle are those guilty of unlawful love. The poet's method here, as throughout the journey, is first to point out a number of prominent figures who would be familiar to his fourteenth-century readers, and then to concentrate attention on a very few, one or two in each circle, telling more about them and eliciting his own story from each. In general, Dante lets the place and condition in which the sinners are found serve as a minimum essential of information. For the penalties in the various circles are of many different kinds. Their fundamental characteristic is appropriateness to the particular sin; this is one of the principal differences between the punishments in Dante's Hell and the miscellaneous and arbitrary horrors of many accounts of the place. In Dante the penalties symbolize the sin. Thus the illicit lovers of the second circle are continually blown about by storm winds; their suffering is one aspect of the sin itself. For the sin consisted in the surrender of reason to lawless passions.

Here we find Paolo and Francesca, the best-known figures of the entire *Divine Comedy*. Like all the human beings presented in the poem, they actually existed. They lived in Italy about the time of Dante's childhood and early youth, and were slain by Francesca's husband, a brother of Paolo. Dante's method, it is hence clear, is not to build up an allegorical cast of personified abstractions. Instead of, say, Passion and Rebellion, he portrays Paolo and Francesca. They represent, or symbolize, sinful love by example. They show how an intrinsically noble emotion, love, if contrary to God's law, can bring two essentially fine persons to damnation and spiritual ruin. The tenderness and the sympathy with which the story is told are famous. But its pathos, and Dante's personal response of overwhelming pity, should not blind us to the *justice* of the penalty. The poet who describes himself as fainting at the end of Francesca's recital is the same man who consigned her to Hell. His purpose is partly to portray the attractiveness of sin, an especially congenial theme when *this* is the sin involved—both for Dante and for most readers.

But although Dante allows the lovers the bitter sweetness of inseparability in Hell, the modern "romantic" idea that union anywhere is sufficient happiness for lovers does not even occur to him. Paolo and Francesca indeed have their love; but they have lost God and thus corrupted their personalities—their inmost selves—from order into anarchy; they are the reverse of happy. In a sense, they have what they wanted, they continue in the lawless condition which they chose on earth. But that condition, seen from the point of view of eternity, is not bliss; it is, in effect, Hell.

In Canto X we are among the heretics in their flaming tomb in the sixth circle. Situated within the walled city of Dis—the capital, as it were, of Hell—this circle is a kind of border between the upper Hell (devoted to punishments for Incontinence) and the lower (concerned with Violence and Fraud). Here Dante portrays the proud aristocrat Farinata and his associate, the elder Cavalcante, father of Dante's closest friend. Their crime is heresy, a flagrant aspect of intellectual pride. But there is a nobility in Farinata's pride; Dante, like the reader, admires the splendid self-sufficiency of a man who, in this situation, can look "proclaiming his disdain for all this Hell." And the essence of the aristocratic nature is distilled in his address to Dante as "half-contemptuously / he asked, 'And *who* would *your* ancestors be?' " and in his abrupt resumption of the conversation interrupted by Cavalcante. Alongside the haughtiness of

Farinata, Dante sets the pathetic —and mistaken—grief of Cavalcante for his son; each portrait gains in effect by the extreme contrast.

Canto XIII shows us one group of those guilty of Violence; for the suicides have been violent against themselves. Here they are turned into monstrous trees, their misery finding expression when a bough is plucked. In the eyes of the Church, suicide was murder, in no way diminished by the fact that the slayer and the victim were the same. By representing in Pier delle Vigne a man who had every human motive to end his life, Dante achieves the deepest pathos and evokes our shuddering pity. As Francesca displays in her dramatic monologue the charm and the potential weakness of her character, as Farinata's manner of speech portrays his nature, so Pier delle Vigne by his exact and legal-sounding language lets us see the careful, methodical counselor whose sense of logic and sense of justice were so outraged that he saw no point in enduring life any longer. His judgment is still unimpaired; he does not reproach his king, only the jealous courtiers who misled him. The Wood of the Suicides is one of the greatest—among many admirable—examples of landscape in Hell assimilated to theme and situation.

Canto XV describes the meeting of Dante and his venerable teacher and adviser, the scholar Brunetto Latini. We are in another ring of the seventh circle, among more of those who have sinned through Violence. The impact of this scene results from the contrast between the dignity of the man and the indignity of his condition in Hell, and by the tact with which both he and Dante ignore it for the moment. Brunetto, with the others guilty of homosexual vice, must move continually along a sandy desert under a shower of fiery flakes. Dante accords him the utmost respect and expresses his gratitude in the warmest terms; and something like their earthly relationship of teacher and pupil is re-enacted, for Brunetto is keenly interested in Dante's prospects in life. In the final image of Brunetto running, not like the loser, but like the winner of a race, Dante extracts dignity and victory out of indignity itself.

The presence of people like those we have been reviewing will remind the reader that Hell is not reserved exclusively for arrant ruffians, hoodlums, and scoundrels. They are there, of course; but so are many "nice," many charming, and some noble and great, men and women. These are in Hell because they preferred something else—no matter what—to God; at the moment of death they were therefore in rebellion against Him. God and Heaven would not be congenial to them, *as they are and as He is*; and there is no acceptable repentance after death. Hence they go on unchanged—only now experiencing the harsher aspects of the sin in which they chose to live.

In Canto XVII the travelers are carried on the back of the flying monster Geryon down the deep descent from the seventh to the eighth circle. With the face of a just man and the body of a serpent, Geryon symbolizes Fraud. He is one of the most exciting figures in Hell. In an age before ferris wheels and airplanes, he gives our poets a ride that anticipates some of the terrifying thrill which a young child may feel in an airplane journey. The eighth circle is subdivided into ten chasms or trenches (Malebolge), each with its own kind of sinners: seducers and panders; flatterers; simoniacs (buyers and sellers of appointments in the Church); sorcerers; grafters; hypocrites; thieves; evil counselors; troublemakers; forgers, and impostors.

Most readers will agree that the punishments here fit the crimes; indeed, reflection will usually intensify this conviction. It is a long catalogue of iniquity; much, but not all, is sordid. Dante has avoided monotony not only by the vividness and intensity of the separate scenes but also by their ingenious variety and by the frequent changes of pace in the narrative. The satirical situation and fierce denunciation of the simoniacs is followed by the quiet horror of the sorcerers with twisted necks. The hilarious episode of the grafters precedes the encounter with the solemn, slow-walking hypocrites; and these are succeeded by the macabre serpent-transformations of the thieves. Nevertheless, our steadily deepening descent in hell gradually produces a sense of oppressiveness. This is appropriate and deliberate; it is a part of Dante's total design. But he recognizes the need of momentary relief, a breath of fresh air, a reminder of the world above. These he provides, for example, in the long simile describing the shipyard in Venice (the opening of Canto XXI) or the picture of the peasant and his two sallies outside on a winter morning (the opening of Canto XXIV).

The episode of the grafters (Cantos XXI and XXII) probably has biographical relevance for Dante. During his absence from Florence on business of state, the opposing political party seized power and sentenced Dante to death if he should return to Florence. The quite unfounded charge against him was misappropriation of public funds. In these cantos Dante cuts a ludicrous figure: fearful, cowering, in constant danger from the demons. He escapes their clutches, first by a distraction and then by belated vigilance. The whole sequence affords an oblique and amusing view of an actual episode. It is worth noting also that here, and here only, in the poem, we find ourselves in the kind of hell known in popular lore and anecdote, with winged devils playing rough jokes on their human prey. Scenes, style, and language alike here show one extreme of the range of the poem—the "low" comic. Dante very unobtrusively indicates his awareness of this by the contrasting allusions found in Canto XX, line 113 and Canto XXI, line 2.

Cantos XXVI and XXVII take us among the wicked counselors, who occupy the eighth chasm, or subdivision, of the eighth circle. Appearing at a distance like fireflies in a summer valley, these souls are wrapped in individual, or occasionally twin, flames. Fire is a fit punishment for those who used the flame of intellect to accomplish evil. When the two poets approach more closely, Virgil identifies one flame as that of Ulysses (Odysseus) and Diomed, who burn together. Among the deceptions devised by Ulysses was the wooden horse, which made possible the capture of Troy. It will strike the reader as strange that a man should suffer for his powers as a military tactician. But the Greeks were enemies of the Trojans, whom the Romans and later most of the nations of Western Europe regarded as their ancestors. Ulysses was on the wrong side, and was responsible for his deeds; but Dante mingles with his condemnation an admiration of the man's mental powers. Ulysses remains aloof; he does not converse with Dante, like most of the souls we have met. Instead, as Dorothy Sayers puts it in the notes to her translation of the poem, Virgil conjures the flame into monologue. Thus we are told how Ulysses determined not to return home after the Trojan War but to explore the western ocean instead. In this narrative, apparently invented by Dante, Ulysses becomes the type of the adventuring and searching spirit of man; the voyage is an act of the mind and soul as well as the body. When he has sailed within sight of a mountainous island, his ship is wrecked by a storm and he perishes. Since, as other parts of the poem indicate, this is the island of Purgatory, the episode clearly has symbolic significance. On this island is the Earthly Paradise, or Garden of Eden, lost to man by the sin of Adam. Man, unassisted by divine grace—pagan man, represented by Ulysses—cannot regain it by his own intelligence, although the effort toward that end is noble in itself.

The other evil counselor, Guido da Montefeltro, talks fluently in Canto XXVII; he shows a quite earthly eagerness for news, crafty, garrulous old intriguer that he is. It is a neat irony that, in spite of his deserved reputation for cleverness, Dante shows him twice deceived: first on earth, as he himself relates, and now in Hell— he does not want his story known and is convinced that Dante will never return to earth to tell it. He sketches in detail, with recollective acidity, the steps by which the pope led him, an aging and reformed man, to return for a moment to his old ways. He even includes the contest of St. Francis and the devil for his soul at his death, along with the devil's bitter witticism: you didn't think I was a logician, perhaps!

In Cantos XXXII and XXXIII we have reached the ninth and last circle, where the traitors are immersed in ice that symbolizes their unfeeling hearts. At the end of one canto we are shown the horror of Ugolino gnawing the skull of his enemy Ruggieri, both partly fastened in the ice. Dante does not concentrate on the acts which have put either man in Hell. Instead he lets Ugolino tell us, in the next canto, why his hatred of Ruggieri is so implacable. The fearful pathos, the power, and at the same time the restraint and compression of this narrative make it one of the finest episodes in the poem.

The last canto, Canto XXXIV, shows us the enormous shape of the fallen angel, Satan, fixed at the bottom of Hell, where the motion of his wings freezes the ice in which we have found the traitors immersed. In one of his three mouths he holds Judas Iscariot, who betrayed Christ; in the other two are Brutus and Cassius, who plotted the assassination of Julius Caesar. Dante did not regard them, as we generally do today, as perhaps misguided patriots; to him they were the destroyers of a providentially ordained ruler. Readers who remember Milton's *Paradise Lost* may be surprised at the absence of any interior presentation of Satan. One critic regrets that his suffering is not shown as different from that of the other inhabitants of Hell. But the fact is that his suffering is not presented at all; he is not a person, to Dante, but an object, a part of the machinery and geography of Hell. For *The Divine Comedy* is occupied exclusively with human sin, human redemption, and human beatitude.

## PURGATORY

At the beginning of the *Purgatory*, Dante and Virgil have once more reached the surface of the earth and can look up and see the sky and the stars. Their long climb from the bottom of Hell, where they left Satan, has brought them out on the shore of the mountain-island of Purgatory. The scene and the situation are presented by Dante with a bold and happy use of imaginative symbols. Guided by Reason in the person of Virgil, Dante, a man still in the earthly life, has looked closely at sin and evil—in Hell—and turned away from them, and is now in search of the means of self-correction and purification. He arrives on the island shore, just before dawn, to find the reverend figure of Cato acting as guardian of the mountain. The austerely glorious figure of Cato, his face illumined by rays from stars representing the pagan virtues of Prudence, Temperance, Fortitude, and Justice, embodies the highest moral and ethical ideal available to man without divine revelation, pre- or post-Christian. Dante meets him, appropriately, before dawn—before the sun of God's illumination has risen. These elements in the situation, together with the reference to his sojourn with Marcia, his wife, in the circle of virtuous pagans in Hell, make Cato a remarkable transition or border symbol, standing both between Hell and Purgatory and between Greco-Roman philosophy and ethics and the dispensation of the Old and New Testaments.

These opening cantos admirably set quite a new tone in the second great division of the poem. They show us joy and brightness, cheer and hope, contrasting totally with the darkness and misery of Hell. They show us an angel arriving with a cargo of souls, all joyfully singing. They accustom us to a different set of attitudes, a different kind of people, and especially, they portray the naïveté, the almost childlike lack of intellectual and moral sophistication, the need of orientation, which characterize the penitent soul at this point in its progress to perfection. As yet uninstructed and spiritually immature, it looks back, seeking to carry on the harmless but no longer suitable delights of earthly life. Dante—and Virgil—share this simplicity to the full.

Cantos III-XVIII, not included in this book, take the reader along the slopes of the lower half of the mountain—the ante-Purgatory, where some of the souls must wait for varying periods of time (and for different reasons) before entering Purgatory itself—and through four of the seven terraces, those devoted to purgation from Pride, Envy, Anger, and Sloth. In Canto XIX we go on to the fifth of the ledges encircling the mountain, that in which the souls are purified of Avarice. There we meet Pope Adrian, one of Dante's most vivid illustrations of the anguish of purification. Concisely he sketches for Dante the poignant story of his late conversion (to the reality of the Christian life), his repentance, and his present hard penance. Only when, after a life of self-seeking, he had attained the pinnacle of the papacy did disillusionment come—and spiritual discovery: "I saw that there the heart no peace could claim." Now he recognizes the equity of the reforming penalty:

Even as our eyes on high we would not send,
Which only upon earthly things were cast,

So here to earth Justice hath
forced them bend.

Dante, on learning from
Adrian's words that he was a
pope, has knelt down in respect.
But Adrian, perceiving this
without lifting his eyes from the
ground, peremptorily corrects
Dante: there are no popes here.
All the hierarchies and social
orders of earth are annihilated
in Purgatory—and, we may add,
the hierarchy of Heaven is not
that of earth. Having answered
Dante's questions, Adrian bids
him go on—he hinders the task
of penitence. Finally, remembering that Dante had offered to
carry news of him to those possibly dear to him on earth, which
might lead to helpful prayers,
the old man adds that he has
only a niece there who, if not
corrupted by the bad example of
his family, could possibly help
him. But for this soul, absorbed
in his penance, the earth has
receded far away, and Heaven is
not yet attained; he is essentially alone with his suffering.

The remaining parts of the
*Purgatory* included in this book,
Cantos XXVII, XXX, and
XXXI, add a dimension to
Dante's role in the poem. He is,
as has been said, the protagonist
throughout; the journey and all
its disclosures are carried out for
his benefit. In Hell, to be sure,
he could do little except look
and learn; yet his emotional
education through the revelation
of perfected evil was a large and
positive achievement. As a candidate for salvation, he has
learned to abhor sin more com-

pletely in proportion as he has
been shown its real nature;
while, as a man of flesh and
blood, he has felt alternate pity
and hate for the sinners. Along
the penitential ledges of Purgatory he has partially assimilated himself to the penitents;
he has felt humility while among
those purging themselves of
Pride, and generosity among
those seeking to root out Envy
from their natures. On the
seventh terrace, he has recognized an even closer kinship
with those engaged in refining
their love by fire. But now this
same fire, it develops, is the
boundary between Purgatory
and the Earthly Paradise at the
top of the mountain. To reach
that goal, Dante must go
through the fire. Remembering
"Men's bodies burning, once beheld," he is overcome by a terrible fear. The encouraging
words of the angel guardian of
the ledge, the assurances of Virgil, who reminds him of perils
safely passed—neither avail to
move him until he is told that
Beatrice is beyond the wall of
flame. Then his resistance melts
and he perseveres through the
frightful but harmless fire. It is
now nearly sunset, when all
ascent ceases, but next morning
Dante takes the few last steps
to the Earthly Paradise. Here
Virgil, who has guided him
through Hell and Purgatory,
gives him a farewell benediction.
Dante, says Virgil, has explored
evil in its final effects (in Hell)
and the means of correcting the
human inclinations that produce
it (in Purgatory). His regener-

ated will is now truly free, and he may fearlessly follow its direction. He no longer needs the guidance of a teacher of morality (Virgil) nor a political structure ("crown") nor an ecclesiastical institution ("mitre"). In short, he has regained the condition of man before the Fall.

These words apply to Dante in his role as a kind of Everyman, representing whoever has fully discerned the nature of evil and wholly freed himself from the impulses to sin. They apply to every soul when it completes the experience of Purgatory; if they did not, the soul would not be ready to go to Heaven, to enter the presence of God. But obviously they cannot apply, actually and practically, to any man still living on earth. That they were not meant as a literal description of Dante the Italian poet and political exile from Florence is clear enough from the events of Cantos XXX and XXXI. For if Dante has already perfected himself by penance, why should he now, in the scenes with Beatrice, repeat the painful experience of rebuke, confession, and satisfaction? It is this latter series of incidents that constitutes Dante's personal, individual experience of correction and purification.

In the midst of the celestial pageant that moves before Dante in the Earthly Paradise appears a lady whom he instantly recognizes as one who was the object of his idealizing love when she lived as a woman on earth. Turning excitedly to confide this to Virgil, he cannot find him anywhere, and is stricken with grief. Presently the lady names herself as Beatrice—whom the reader will remember for two reasons: she sent Virgil to guide her endangered servant, Dante, through Hell and Purgatory; and to see her Dante forced himself to go through the barrier of fire. There is no cause to doubt that, like the other human beings in the poem, Beatrice is an actual person transformed by the shaping imagination of the poet. What she was to Dante in her earthly life he tells us in the *New Life* (*Vita nuova*), written not long after her death in 1290. She was an incarnation of beauty and virtue; simply by existing, she engrossed the young Dante's ardent but remote devotion; her smile or greeting left him in trembling rapture. This was the full extent of the relationship between them. But the poems in the *New Life* are mostly inspired by the thought of her, whether on earth or in heaven. In short, she was a real woman who, even in this world, was an ideal for Dante, and after death became an even more glorious image of goodness and divine wisdom. The last section of the *New Life* records Dante's resolution to devote a great work to her, when he shall be qualified to achieve it; *The Divine Comedy* is that work. We have seen that he makes her the instigator of the imaginary journey through two realms of the life after death and the motive for his endurance of the fire. Now, as successor to Virgil, she comes to guide him herself through the heavenly paradise. In the same way that Virgil is Reason without ceasing to be Virgil, Beatrice fulfills the role of Divine Revelation without ceasing to be Beatrice.

It is in this dual character, part beloved woman and part the voice of divine wisdom, that Beatrice, in Canto XXXI, unsparingly rebukes Dante. He had loved her mortal beauty as an image of the immortal; when death destroyed it, his devotion ought thenceforth to have fixed itself on the immortal and indestructible virtue of which that beauty had been the image. Instead, he turned aside to the lure of material things. Dante accepts the reproach with the utmost contrition. It is quite probable that this episode is based on some actual lapse, in Dante's life, from his highest moral ideal. These passages, then, recount his own personal experience of purgation, the autobiographical analogue of the penitence and purification portrayed on the mountain as a whole.

## PARADISE

Like the invocations of *Paradise Lost*, that with which Dante begins the third division of his poem expresses his sense of the loftiness of the theme. Like Milton, he is venturing things unattempted hitherto in prose or rhyme. The three invocations of *The Divine Comedy* are incremental; the first (in Canto II of the *Hell*) is brief and unobtrusive, the second (in Canto I of the *Purgatory*) more

extended, and the third (in Canto I of the *Paradise*) by its earnestness and solemnity indicates the epic stature, though not epic form, which he expects the poem to attain. The *Paradise* offers us an imagined experience of the entire celestial universe as it was charted by medieval astronomy. In that cosmology, the sun, the moon, and the rest, though immensely distant, had not retreated from the earth according to the scale established by modern knowledge. Dante's world is geocentric; the planetary circles, including those of the sun and moon, revolve about the earth, as does the circle of the stars—as does, in fact, everything except the "real" Heaven, or Empyrean, the abode of God and the saints and angels. The *Paradise* is the chronicle of an ascent from planet to planet, until finally Dante is in the Empyrean itself. In each planet a group of redeemed and perfected souls, come from their proper dwelling in the Empyrean, are present to converse with Dante and his guide, Beatrice. Their successive discussions set forth the essentials of Christian doctrine, along with the fundamental scientific concepts of the time; and they themselves exemplify various kinds and degrees of beatitude. For Dante—and the reader— the experience is educational, morally edifying, and spiritually preparatory for the vision with which the poem ends. In Canto II Dante learns of the hierarchy of souls in Heaven; not all are equal, indeed, no two are identical in bliss; yet each is completely satisfied, fulfilled, and happy—"in His will is perfected our peace." Piccarda, the not wholly blameless nun who speaks these words, is among the souls encountered in the moon, the group of lowest rank in Heaven. From these we rise to higher and higher kinds of blessed souls, each rejoicing wholly in God in its predestined way and in accordance with its capacity.

When all the cycles of the cosmos have been traversed, we come, in Canto XXXI, to Heaven itself, the real home of the blessed. Here the souls are arranged in the form of a great white rose; God is at the center —an ineffable brightness—and the souls have the aspect of rows of petals. Here Beatrice, who has set forth the truths of Divine Revelation throughout the journey, goes back to her place in Heaven, and St. Bernard, the great mystic of the twelfth century, becomes Dante's guide, or rather sponsor. For what remains is that Dante should be vouchsafed a vision in which, for an instant, he may see God as He really is—in so far as his human capacity enables him to do so. The last canto, Canto XXXIII, opens with Bernard's prayer to the Virgin Mary for intercession in Dante's behalf. There is no religious lyric poetry of greater depth or simplicity or beauty than this prayer; its intimacy, tenderness, and humility are consummate.

To obtain, to endure, such a vision is just within the limit of Dante's powers. It transports him into an utterly different kind of being; it leaves him with the memory of an overpowering but indescribable experience. For of course no mystic can ever reveal the content of his vision; it does not belong to the order of reportable things. Dante can only tell us that he discerned with direct but momentary certitude the identity of God as inclusive of man and of universal love, and that he knew himself to be at that instant one with Him.

*The Divine Comedy* thus ends both quietly and climactically. For this union with God was the purpose of the entire long and arduous journey. This is the good which St. Thomas Aquinas, and Boethius before him, pointed out as the goal of man, as of the entire creation. But what the philosophers prove, Dante experiences, imaginatively. And we reach both center and summit of the medieval structure of human life in proportion as we can follow the record of that experience.

## BOCCACCIO, DECAMERON

The tales of Boccaccio's *Decameron* (completed about 1353) constitute the greatest achievement of prose fiction in a vernacular language of southern Europe during the medieval centuries. In his round hundred stories the Italian author presents a great variety of people and situations, aptly and often acutely characterized, and abundant dialogue of varying liveliness and realism. Like Chaucer, who wrote his *Canterbury Tales* several decades later, he provides a dramatic framework for his narrations. But his storytellers are not miscellaneous pilgrims traveling to a famous shrine; they are seven young ladies and three young gentlemen who have withdrawn from Florence to the countryside, to escape the Black Death, or plague, of 1348. They engage in gay banter and good-natured raillery; but, as they are all refined and cultivated young people with no occupational bias or ingrained prejudices, their relationships are polite rather than boisterous and lack the force and depth and vitality of those portrayed in *The Canterbury Tales.* They agree on a plan of storytelling—and adhere to it (with slight changes). Here there is no drunken miller, such as interrupts Chaucer's pilgrims, to upset the seemly orderliness acceptable to gentlefolk, for there are no other folk present. Each member of the company is to tell a tale each day; on some days a general topic is assigned, on others each narrator follows his own taste and judgment.

The story about Brother Alberto and his impersonation of the angel Gabriel, a bawdy tale of amorous intrigue and deception, exemplifies what most modern readers regard as typical of the *Decameron.* Like Chaucer's *Miller's Tale*, it presents a (moderately) clever person successfully deceiving a very foolish one, but eventually punished for his trickery. In the present story, the man is the trickster and the woman is the foolish dupe, but these roles are often reversed in

other stories of the *Decameron;* indeed, Boccaccio digresses during the introduction to the fourth day to assert his devotion to women—the muses, after all, were women—and, indeed, the women storytellers outnumber the men. He nonetheless knew that some women are foolish, just as he knew, though he was a devout Christian, that some priests and friars fall short of their vocation. Like other authors of his time, he saw nothing wrong in acknowledging these facts and turning them to artistic use.

If reduced to the bare essentials of its plot, this tale could be told far more briefly, as a mere anecdote, a joke. Indeed, it may well have been in circulation as an anecdote both before and after Boccaccio. But he gives it literary value by the way he handles it. He makes the reader see the successive scenes in vivid detail, he creates memorable and amusing characters, and he relates the incidents of the narrative closely to the personalities of those characters. Lisetta is not only credulous but also inordinately vain—her credulity derives from her vanity— and it is because of these qualities that she can be taken in by Brother Alberto's preposterous account of the angel's interest in her. The reader also notices the tacit perception of Lisetta's woman friend, who at once sees through the friar's scheme but, instead of disabusing her foolish friend, leads her on and then gleefully reveals the whole story to the outside world. And Alberto, though clever, is not as cautious as he should be. Otherwise, once warned, he would not have exposed himself to discovery and disgrace.

The story of Federigo and his falcon is told on a day devoted to accounts of love that turns out happily after difficulties on the way. It presents the courtly-love relationship—or one of the possible relationships—in a remarkable combination of realism and nobility. Federigo's conduct perfectly fulfills the code; he devotes himself completely to Monna Giovanna, and his failure to receive any return in no way disturbs the pattern of that devotion. He never repines or complains; his lady's married or widowed condition is all one to him; and, having spent his fortune in the futile effort to attract her, he lives with resignation on his tiny estate. But Federigo is genuinely high-minded and noble; he has absorbed the ideals and not merely the etiquette of courtly love. His declaration, when Giovanna comes to call, that he has gained and not lost by his service to her, might be politeness learned out of a book—a romance, for example. But his sacrifice of the falcon to provide her with a good meal is a splendid and magnificent folly that could come only from an almost unbelievably generous heart. His grief at the outcome is probably sharper than Giovanna's, despite the painful disappointment which it produces for her.

Giovanna's dignity and charm and sensitivity are as clear to us as they evidently are to Federigo. Unwilling, whether as wife or widow, to have a romance with Federigo, she does not encourage him. Yet she knows that

he loves her and that he has squandered his wealth on her account. We see her distress at having to ask him for anything, let alone the falcon, his most cherished possession. But when love for her young son, mortally ill, forces her to it, she acts with grace and decorum. And with something more; for she has discerned the nobleness of temper in Federigo through his consistently courteous behavior. It is that to which she appeals, not to any obligation of a courtly lover to please his lady. Later, when her brothers convince her that she should remarry, she also shows both generosity and independence of character. She gives Federigo his reward by marrying him—and seeing that his new fortune is not wasted! The happy ending is agreeable; but the notable achievement of the story is the brief but complete and poignant depiction of the dilemmas faced by the two against a background of preliminary characterization which gives their decision full significance.

## SIR GAWAIN AND THE GREEN KNIGHT

*Sir Gawain and the Green Knight* is the best English example of a literary form immensely popular in the Middle Ages: the romance, sometimes called the light reading of our ancestors. A metrical romance is a narrative poem presenting, usually, knightly adventures and "courtly" love. The adventures typically involve the hero in fighting or jousting with other knights, and often also in encounters with giants or monsters. No medieval reader or listener would be surprised by the frequent occurrence of magical or supernatural elements. *Courtly love* is the modern term for the relationship between men and women usually depicted in medieval romances. Here the woman—or, rather, the lady—is sovereign; the man (the knight —but never her husband) is the humble suppliant or petitioner for her favors. (In this picture, with woman on a pedestal but effectively immobilized, and with man looking up to her but with both feet firmly on the ground, may be found an early version of a sexual stereotype which many now find irksome; it is probably more noticeable in this summary than in the poem itself.) The relationship, though usually adulterous, is carried on with careful regard for the conventions and manners of aristocratic (whence "courtly") society.

The poem's first audience, men and women of the late fourteenth century, might well have recognized both of the main plots of the story, the "Beheading Game" and the "Temptation," which also appear in earlier romances. This would more have pleased than troubled them, as originality *per se* was not so important then as now— indeed, the anonymous poet himself claims only to be repeating the story "As I heard it in hall." But many members of that first audience, as they listened or read, would also have noticed some of the original features of the poem that intrigue us as well.

To begin with, the hero, Gawain, must prove his courage not by fighting or jousting in the usual way but by accepting an exchange of blows which seems almost certain to kill him. Then, at Bercilak's castle, by another inversion, it is the lady who takes the initiative and woos; and the knight, because of his unusual situation, must resist. Thus Gawain, traditionally the model of the knightly warrior and courtly lover, cannot show his prowess in the traditional way. Indeed, he is tested in the most extreme way, for his fears and desires must be dealt with not in action but by strength of spirit alone. He is prevented, moreover, by the overall design of the double plot from knowing what is really going on until the very end of the story.

The structure of the *Gawain* narrative is also far tighter and more symmetrical than that of most romances. The story begins at King Arthur's court during a Christmas holiday and ends, almost exactly a year later, in the same place. At Bercilak's castle, the three days of hunting are matched by the three visits of the lady to Gawain's bedroom; each day follows the same pattern, beginning with the start of a hunt, continuing with a wooing scene, returning to the hunt, and concluding with evening festivities. The hunting and wooing are also bound together by the agreement between Bercilak and Gawain to exchange winnings at the end of each day.

Mood and atmosphere depend in large part on the premise that it is all a Christmas *game* (a word that recurs often in the poem). The Green Knight declares that he comes in peace, that he asks not for battle but for sport. But, as all realize, it is a grim and dangerous sport, for the Green Knight is plainly a magical being, and behind his apparently absurd challenge lie two threats: death to anyone who accepts it, disgrace to anyone who does not. Gawain's devotion to King Arthur and to the honor of the court compel him to offer himself for the deadly game, and later his high sense of personal obligation leads him to journey through many perils to find the Green Knight and receive the return stroke of the axe. His faithfulness to his word, his honor, are also at stake in the exchange of gifts at Bercilak's castle. A story that began as a Christmas entertainment has become a series of tests of knightly and Christian virtues.

Keeping to the spirit of the game, we might better appreciate the skill of the author if we try to answer some questions about the poem. What is the significance of the many parallels in it? For example, is there any broad similarity between Bercilak's third hunt—of the fox —and the lady's third visit to Gawain? Turning to the conclusion of the poem, what *is* Gawain's fault? Of what does he accuse himself in the final talk with Bercilak? Why are his chagrin and self-disgust so intense? What is Bercilak's view of the matter? Does the poet agree with Gawain or with Bercilak, or can their attitudes be reconciled?

A word about the language of the poem and our Modern English version of it: It was originally written by a contemporary of Chaucer but in a very different dialect than his, that of the English Midlands near the site of modern Birmingham. Further, except at the end of each stanza, the form depends not on rhyme but on the older device of alliteration: two or more words of every line begin with the same sound. The translation reproduces this pattern with great skill and fidelity. One result of this is the occasional use of unusual words or of ordinary words in slightly unaccustomed senses; some of these have been glossed, while the meanings of others may be surmised from the context or, if necessary, found in a dictionary.

## CHAUCER, *THE CANTERBURY TALES*

### THE GENERAL PROLOGUE

Although the French produced the richest and most influential body of vernacular literature in the Middle Ages, the greatest writers of the period were an Italian, Dante, and an Englishman, Chaucer. The Florentine poet and the Londoner both wrote their most important works in the fourteenth century, the former in its early decades, the latter in its latest. In origin and background, both represent the point of view of the upper middle class or the lesser gentry, groups which were not sharply separated in the urban life of Italy and of London in the later medieval centuries. Both were active in public affairs; both on occasion were envoys of their respective governments. Dante was once responsible for widening a street in Florence, and Chaucer for a time held a post comparable to that of an Under Secretary of the Interior in the cabinet of the United States. If Dante had sharper political convictions and a greater theoretical interest in the philosophy of government, Chaucer held a wider variety of offices—and held them longer.

Both poets probably lived out their lives as laymen; their view of the world is free from any bias due to a clerical vocation. Yet both were completely orthodox in religion and theology. Dante was severe with heretics and schismatics, and Chaucer was neither a Wycliffite nor a sympathizer with the Peasants' Revolt. With the partial exception of Dante's insistence on the equal status of the Holy Roman Empire and the Papacy, alike providentially sponsored, it may be said that both poets found themselves in harmony with the traditional institutions and patterns of medieval civilization. Both were keenly aware of injustices resulting from abuses of the system; each exposed rascals with enthusiasm—Dante with bitterness, Chaucer with amusement. But their denunciation of wicked rulers and their satire directed against the worldliness of bishops and abbots and the corruptness of friars and pardoners do not show either writer to be a rebel against the established institutions of Church or State. The background against which abuses are portrayed is always, implicitly or explicitly, the ideal pattern for the king or priest or monk—not some utopian or revolutionary social order which would dispense with or radically alter the patterns themselves.

On the ultimate issues of human life, as in these questions of the structure of civilization, the two greatest literary geniuses of the Middle Ages were in agreement with each other and with their fellow men. For each, God was the center of the universe, as man and his earth were the center of the cosmic order. Man's goal was union with God; if he attained it—after this short earthly life—he would spend eternity in heaven; if he missed it, then hell awaited him. For man's direction and guidance toward the good in this life and the next, there were the divinely ordained religion and its Church, and the divinely approved hierarchy of society on earth. As men of independent intelligence, of education—and of essentially middle-class origin —both Dante and Chaucer insisted that true nobility depends on intrinsic character, not the accident of birth. But the modern conceptions of political, social, and economic equality, and complete religious freedom, would have appeared to them as anarchy. They had fundamental faith in the quite different patterns of institutional hierarchy and authority.

If Dante chose the life after death as the theme of the greatest medieval poem, Chaucer chose a religious pilgrimage as the framework of the richest portrayal of medieval men and women in the earthly scene. Chaucer's pilgrims are not dead, but very much alive; they are on their way to thank St. Thomas of Canterbury for his help in keeping them in that state! Yet the twenty-nine travelers, including those described in the course of the pilgrimage, are not incomparable in number or vividness to the characters presented with similar fullness in *The Divine Comedy*. Both poets —when they wish—make the individual stand out clearly and distinctly; both—when they choose—present fully the background, the milieu, the occupational or moral setting from which the individual emerges and in terms of which he is to be estimated. Both poets sketch the portraits with extraordinary insight, discrimination, and perception of the subtle mixture of good and bad in humanity. It would be interesting to attempt the assignment of Chaucer's pilgrims to their proper places in *The Divine Comedy*—assuming that each of them dies in the condition described in the Prologue.

With the Knight, the Parson, his brother the Plowman, the Clerk of Oxford, and the Nun's Priest (who is characterized in the course of the journey) we should have no trouble. Though thoroughly human, flesh-and-blood people, these are all wholly excellent and admirable men. Moral and ethical nobility is a part of their personal and vocational perfection. They embody—not personify as abstractions—the ideal characteristics of men in their several stations in life; they are models as well as individuals. But these individuals are living men on earth. We recognize in the portrait of the Clerk, for instance, an ingredient of tacit humor hardly duplicated in Dante's presentation of the blessed. The Clerk's unique traits of temperament and taste—the concise habit of

speech, the aloofness, the ardent book-collecting—might be a little irrelevant in Heaven, while eminently suited to his portrait in this world.

The scoundrels, likewise, would be easy to deal with. The Friar, the Pardoner, the Summoner, and, I fear, also the Shipman, the Reeve, the Manciple, and the Miller, would easily find their respective niches in the circles of Hell—most of them in the ten subdivisions of the eighth circle, in which those guilty of various kinds of fraud are punished. Dante might have made each of them tell his story in much the same terms as Chaucer used. He would have done it with as much gusto; indeed, his work includes parallels to most of them. But denunciation and contempt would have replaced Chaucer's detached delight in the cleverness and success of their rascality. Again, the vantage point dictates an appropriate difference of treatment; time and our earth are a different background from eternity and Hell. Both Dante's and Chaucer's portraits achieve symmetry. But Dante's are more decisive, more limited, more exclusively concentrated on ethical definition; Chaucer's have room for more mundane, personal, and morally neutral detail.

We should have great difficulty in classifying some of the others. The exquisite Prioress is doubtless destined for Heaven. But should we expect to find her, fairly soon, among the blessed in one of the three lowest spheres—the moon, Mercury, or Venus? Is she, like Piccarda, a soul whose unquestionably genuine devotion is linked with an intrinsically limited spiritual capacity—limited in a way suggested by her unmonastic fondness for pet dogs, nice clothes, and fashionable manners? Or is her sensibility an outward sign of great spiritual endowment, so that, after some time on the terraces of Purgatory, she will be found among the higher spheres of the celestial hierarchy? Dante had to decide such questions concerning his characters, and his portraits naturally show how they fit the classifications. Chaucer did not have to decide; his pilgrims still belong to the earth, and some of their portraits are executed without conclusive moral definition. The worldly, hunting Monk, a fine figure of a man—will he take his place among the avaricious or the hypocrites in Hell? Or will he purge his worldliness, like Pope Adrian, on the fifth ledge of the mountain?

In general, Chaucer shows a large "middle" group of people, confirmed perhaps in neither **wickedness nor holiness, but** absorbed in the things of this world. Such an absorption exposes the professed cleric, secular or monastic, to ironical satire; for the religious vocation involves renunciation of the world. This is why many of the pilgrims connected with the Church are obvious targets. But laymen also run the risk of ridicule if their absorption in worldly matters leads to excessive egotism or affectation or limitation of perspective. Thus the Sergeant of the Law, whose days are, in fact, full, *seems* even busier than he is; the Merchant apparently talks entirely about

profits; and the Physician's financial astuteness is not unmixed with complacency. The Franklin's pride in his hospitality and fine table is a more attractive form of egotism—although one might hesitate to become his cook! Traits like these, casually mentioned in the Prologue, would be valuable hints as to where on the terraces **of** Purgatory the several pilgrims might be expected to spend some time. Meanwhile, it is just such qualities, the weaknesses, foibles, excesses, and limitations, **that** endow them with distinctness and poignancy in this world —in short, with individuality **and** personality.

It is often said that the characters in the Prologue are delineated in terms of the superlative—each of the pilgrims is the best, or worst, representative of his particular kind of human being. This is true. Yet it is also true that Chaucer finds far less **to say about some than about others. He is, in fact, interested** in them in different ways. Thus the Knight is described at length; occupationally, ethically, and otherwise he emerges as an individual member of a class. His son, the young Squire, is presented primarily as a fine but standard specimen of his type, the fashionable young warrior and politely cultivated "lover." And in their servant, the Yeoman, we see a yet smaller segment of the whole character: he is simply an expert woodsman. Other pilgrims, like the five Guildsmen, receive only a collective portrait; they all share in the pride of their crafts and their organized "fraternity," in the garb of which they are handsomely turned out. A few of the company are not described at all in the Prologue.

Evidently Chaucer has allowed himself a margin of freedom in his account of this imaginary company as they present themselves to the imaginary observer and fellow traveler, the poet. With the future possibilities of the pilgrimage in mind, he readily leaves a few members of the group undeveloped; one of these, the Nun's Priest, does emerge in full characterization as the tales proceed. But in the Prologue itself Chaucer gives us the fullest, the most varied, and the liveliest, panorama of men and women in medieval literature. The portraits are usually fairly complete and satisfying in themselves, though, as we have noted, some are miniatures and some large canvases, some are full face, some profile, and a few quarter face. Yet the portraits are not merely lively in themselves; they are dynamic; they prepare us for the highly dramatic relationships which develop among the pilgrims in the course of the journey.

### THE MILLER'S TALE

At the end of the General Prologue we are told that the Knight will tell the first tale. This narrative, not included in our book, is a fine example of medieval metrical romance—with important variations from the standard types. As we learn from the Words between the Host and the Miller, the latter, now drunk, refuses to follow the decorous order preferred by the Host; he insists on matching the Knight right now with his tale. When

he goes on to say that it will be a story of an old carpenter, his wife, and her student lover, we anticipate, rightly, that it will be the opposite of the Knight's courtly romance. Like the medieval reader, we expect a tale of amorous intrigue and trickery involving people of considerably less than noble rank, in short, a fabliau. But the carpenter's wife, Alison, has not only a husband, John, and a lover, Nicholas; there is also a would-be lover, the parish clerk, Absalom. There is thus a double triangle plot, with Alison at the apex of both triangles; and the denouement comes when one triangle crashes down on the other!

This addition to the traditional kind of fabliau plot is one part of Chaucer's vast enrichment of what must have been a fairly stereotyped narrative. In mediocre tales of this sort the plot is the thing—almost the whole thing; they are comic anecdotes. But Chaucer has lavished as much effort on characterization and depiction of scenes as one expects in the best serious literature. We get to know the clever, opportunistic, cynical Nicholas very well indeed. His rival, Absalom, is a complete contrast. He is theatrical, sentimental, and silly; his "love" songs are an amusing parody of the poetic pleas of chivalric suitors. (Nicholas is much too practical and hardheaded to go in for amorous complaints; he keeps his eye on the main chance —and he is right; he knows how to manage Alison, as Absalom does not.)

The vivid, detailed description of Alison, rich in comparisons and fresh images, would remind the medieval reader of traditional

portraits of ladies in romances—
by difference rather than similarity. Instead of the noble lady,
a standard blonde, looking out
placidly from a castle window, we
have Alison, neat, washed, bright
as a new coin, skipping like a
colt. The personality of John, the
carpenter, is similarly enlarged
and deepened. Here the prototype was an old husband married
to a young wife; he was jealous
and suspicious. Chaucer's John is
a great deal more than this. He
is genuinely devoted to his wife—
he dotes on her; he is fond of
Nicholas, his student lodger,
though he also believes in the
common-sense advantages of the
ordinary man (himself) over the
scholar; he is attractively gullible:
He embraces the plan for dealing
with the flood with great gusto.

The denouement of the Miller's Tale does not satisfy the
requirements of poetic justice; it
does not reward the good and
punish the wicked—at least, not
consistently. Instead, it penalizes
stupidity and vindicates cleverness. Moreover, characterization
and plot sustain each other: the
various individuals do the kinds
of things that we are willing to
believe that these kinds of people would do. And there is room
for variation within the basic pattern: The ingenuity of Nicholas
is duly rewarded, but when
overconfidence leads him to overreach himself a bit (both metaphorically and literally), he
suffers in the end. Alison's cleverness is unflawed by such excess—
and she escapes.

### THE PARDONER'S TALE

The Pardoner is one of the
liveliest rascals on the Canterbury pilgrimage. His rascality is
so complete that it may be diffi-
cult for us to realize just what a
pardoner was properly or ideally
like in the fourteenth century.
For one thing, a legitimate pardoner did not go about "pardoning" people for their sins. Many
such men were not—and were
not expected to be—priests, in
the proper sense of the term, at
all. Many doubtless were in what
is called minor orders, extending up to subdeacon. Such men
were not qualified or authorized
to hear confession or grant absolution. The legitimate activity of
a pardoner consisted in making
available to devout persons a
certificate of ecclesiastical "indulgence." The charge made for
this constituted a gift or offering
to God and the Church. The
purchase was therefore considered a worthy act in the sight of
God which might benefit the
souls of the purchaser's relatives
or friends if they were doing penance in purgatory (but *not* if
they had been sent to hell).

No doubt there were many
perfectly honest and worthy pardoners in medieval Europe. But
the opportunities for personal
profit are evident, and there
must have been some who exploited these opportunities unscrupulously. The satiric literature of the time tells us much
about bad pardoners, and Chaucer's is clearly one of them
Besides distributing indulgences of doubtful validity, he
preaches in country churches,
intimidating the congregation
so that they will not fail to put
money in the collection plate;
and he makes a good profit out
of fake relics. Far from being
ashamed of these vices, Chaucer's Pardoner is proud of his
skill in dishonesty. He tells us
all about it in the Prologue to

his tale.

The Pardoner's Tale itself, furthermore, is a sample of his preaching. The text of the sermon is his favorite: Covetousness is the root of evil. It is ironical, of course, that such a man should preach so regularly and strenuously against his own greatest sin. His sermon, as Chaucer gives it, is really a very old and simple story about three men who went in search of Death and found him unexpectedly. The Pardoner dramatizes the narrative with great energy and imagination. In addition, he embroiders it with brief anecdotes which are really digressions. Before he has got really started on the story, moreover, he takes time out for a ringing denunciation of gluttony (including drunkenness), gambling, and swearing—complete with examples of each.

### THE NUN'S PRIEST'S TALE

The tale of Chanticleer and Dame Partlet is Chaucer at his best. Since the basic story, of a cock, a hen, and a fox, is rich in human implications and applications and in intrinsic humor it must have been especially congenial to the imaginative comic spirit of the mature Chaucer— and it apparently does belong to a late period in the composition of *The Canterbury Tales*. For its narrator the poet chose the genial Priest who rode with the two nuns on the pilgrimage; his good taste and inexhaustible sense of humor have been ripened by years of reading and observation of life.

The setting of the tale in the Canterbury pilgrimage contributes to its total effect. The Knight, seconded by the Host,

has suddenly interrupted the Monk, who was retailing an apparently endless series of "tragedies," or tales of misfortune. This has become unendurably gloomy and dull, they protest; they want something more cheerful and entertaining! When the Monk has nothing else to offer, the Host turns to Sir John, the Priest, and bids him "Tell us a thing to make our spirits glad./Be cheerful, though the jade you ride is bad."

Thus launched, the Priest gives us a remarkable version of one of the favorite stories of the Middle Ages. For of course Chaucer did not invent the plot itself. The popular literature of Europe had long included tales of the cock's capture through his weakness for flattery, and his escape through the fox's overweening pride. The narrative can be condensed in a paragraph or spun out to indeterminate length, according to the inclination of the narrator. The Priest, without losing sight of its identity as a moral fable, makes it many other things as well.

First, with leisurely detail and humor, he gives the cock and hen a human background. The quiet, realistic description of the circumstances of the poor widow —her narrow cottage with, a small yard surrounded by a wooden fence, her three cows, three hogs, and one sheep, named Moll—reads like the beginning of a skillfully told modern short story. The implicit contrast with a great house or castle is cumulatively comic; it evokes a smile rather than a guffaw.

Then we are brought to the description of Chanticleer and his seven wives—they are part of the widow's household, indoors and outdoors. The account of the cock is at first simply "superlative," like the characterization of the Canterbury pilgrims themselves; he is initially the best imaginable cock. His regular crowing, exactly on the hour, doubtless appeared less extraordinary to Chaucer's audience than it does to us, for apparently this accuracy was commonly attributed to roosters during the medieval period. But the detailed description of his features and coloring is done in the manner of the literary portraits of heroes in romances; and the cock's comb, scalloped "like a crenelated castle wall," is a first touch of the mock-heroic. Partlet too has the virtues of highborn ladies in romances; she is courtly, discreet, and debonair. And she has held Chanticleer's firm affection since she was seven nights old!

Having been thus acquainted with the general capacities of these unusual chickens, we are now moved on to the first incident in the story itself—Chanticleer's dream. The tone here is that of ordinary, commonplace domesticity: a husband is awakened from a nightmare, which he then relates to his wife. Their further conversation is in the same vein, Partlet combining in her character both the comic-strip wife who measures her husband, reproachfully, against a standard of heroic perfection, and the more ordinary Mrs. Smith who confidently diagnoses her man's indisposition and energetically tells him what to take for it. The line "Have you no man's heart, when you have a beard?" indicates how completely the cock and hen

have become a human pair.

In the matrimonial argument about the nature and significance of dreams Chaucer employs the two principal medieval theories on the subject. Doubtless he is right in assigning the physiological explanation to Partlet; women are said to be more realistic and practical than men. And we might say that her sixty-two-line speech exemplifies the feminine love of talking—if Chanticleer did not take two hundred lines to answer her! Both speeches in fact poke fun at the method of proof by citing authorities. But Chanticleer's extended monologue has a further purpose: it is structural in the development of the plot; it produces the comic irony which is at the center of the tale. For the very act of vigorously refuting Partlet and proving that dreams *do* portend danger has the effect of reassuring him. Having won the argument—to his own satisfaction and by default of rebuttal from Partlet—Chanticleer is in reality no longer disturbed about the dream. His thoughts turn exuberantly to love, and the climax of the plot is reached when he declares: "I am then so full of pure felicity/That I defy whatever sort of dream!"

Having fully established this mood in Chanticleer—having in fact characterized him in terms of superheroism—Chaucer tells us that a cunning fox has got through the hedge during the night and is now hiding in a bed of herbs in the yard, lying in wait for Chanticleer. This leads to a citation of traitors and deceivers from epic literature and an elaborate raising of the question of predestination, foreknowledge, and free will.

Next it is pointed out that Chanticleer unfortunately took his wife's advice about the dream ("Women have many times, as wise men hold,/Offered advice that left men in the cold"), and Adam's loss of Paradise is immediately cited as a parallel. Thus we see finally that the whole situation has been presented as a kind of parody of the Fall of Man, with Chanticleer as Adam, Partlet as Eve, and the fox, now lurking but later to speak with persuasive and successful flattery, as the Serpent.

The rest of the tale is carried out in the same vein of elaborate mockery, with allusions, exclamations, and comparisons. The fox displays consummate diplomacy, Chanticleer is as naïve and susceptible as possible, and Partlet's grief is epic. The finest passage, among many excellent, is the picture of the utter confusion and uproar of men, women, beasts, and fowls when the alarm is given. At last—to provide the happy ending demanded by the Knight and the Host as well as to conform to the familiar plot of the story—comes the second reversal, when Chanticleer escapes. And in conclusion Sir John, who, for all his gift of wit and fun, is a deeply and wholesomely religious man, reminds us:

Such is it to be reckless and unheedful
And trust in flattery....
Think twice, and take the moral, my good men!

### EVERYMAN

Drama scarcely attained the status of a dominant literary form in the Middle Ages, although in the later centuries of the period it was popular, fairly abundant, and varied in character. It began with the impersonation or dramatization of passages from the liturgy of the Resurrection and the Nativity of Christ. "Produced" at first in the Latin language and inside a church, it was later moved outside and Latin was replaced with vernacular languages of several European peoples. By the fourteenth century, if not earlier, whole "cycles" of short plays were performed on certain feast days of the Church, especially Corpus Christi. A complete sequence began with the revolt of Satan and his followers against God and ended with the Last Judgment; inside these limits, some forty "one-act" pieces presented the important events in the divine plan for the history of mankind. The content of these plays was based very closely on the narrative of the Bible; hence the name *miracle* plays —that is, dealing with things wonderful to man.

About the time when the miracle plays had reached their fullest development, another kind of dramatic composition emerged, also religious in nature and purpose. As the miracle plays dramatize the liturgy and certain Biblical events, so the *morality* plays dramatize the content of a typical homily or sermon. By common consent, *Everyman* is regarded as the best of this kind of drama. We do not know the author's name, but the play belongs to the fifteenth century; it may owe something to a Dutch piece on the same theme. Whereas miracle plays were produced in a long sequence, with "amateur" casts drawn from more or less suitable craft guilds (for example, the carpenters might present the building of Noah's ark and the subsequent flood), morality plays may have been acted by professional or semiprofessional companies. Nothing is actually known about the original productions of *Everyman*; it is well suited, however, to outdoor performance. Its comparative length, along with the large part of the title character, favors the possibility of some degree of professionalism in the cast.

The modern reader may find it profitable to compare *Everyman* with such different kinds of drama as Greek tragedy, Marlowe's *Doctor Faustus*, or MacLeish's modern play, *J.B.* In its brevity, simplicity, and concentration on a single theme and situation, it recalls especially the shorter plays of the ancient Greeks. Its topic has much in common with that of Marlowe's play—man facing death, in the light of his past life—but the decisive choice and consequent ending are different. The role assigned to deity is both like and unlike that in MacLeish's adaptation of the story of Job in his play.

As in most morality plays, the characters are personifications of abstractions, or generalizations. Everyman himself of course represents all humanity. But we should not assume in advance that "abstract" characters make a dull play. In the first place, dramatizing the characters gives them actuality; the actors must be flesh and blood. Then, in *Everyman*, the situations, the talk, and the behavior of the various characters are thorough-

ly realistic as well as representative of their respective generalized significance. For example, Good Fellowship does and says just about what a single boon companion would be likely to say and do under the same circumstances. Good Deeds is not a static figure: we see her first bound to the earth (the floor of the stage) by Everyman's sins; when he scourges himself in penance, she rises joyfully to accompany him. The author's ingenuity is notable in the character Goods (Riches): Goods is off-stage when Everyman calls him; the audience hears but does not see him at first as he explains that he lies there in corners, trussed and piled up, locked in chests, stuffed in bags! Surely he must have got a laugh when he did come on stage. And of course God, who instigates the action by sending Death to call Everyman to his account, is no abstraction. He was probably a voice off-stage rather than an actor—but a very effective character none the less.

Together with the rapidly moving plot, free from extraneous matter, it is the rightness of its words that makes *Everyman* a success. God speaks with an unfailing simplicity and directness:

Charyte they do all clene forgete.
I hoped well that every man
In my glory shulde make his mansyon;
And thereto I had them all electe....
They be so combred with worldly ryches
That nedes on them I must do iustyce....

He is as real and human as the God of Marc Connelly's *The*

*Green Pastures*; He does not need the modern author's humor or triviality. Yet humor is not absent from the play. Cousin, asked by Everyman to go with him at the summons of Death, exclaims: "No, by Our Lady! I have the crampe in my to[e]"; and later, Beauty replies to the same effect: "I crosse out all this! Adewe, by Saynt Iohan! /I take my cap in my lappe, and am gone." There is irony in Good Fellowship's farewell verse: "For you I wyll remembre that part-ynge is mournynge." Best of all, perhaps, are the short speeches, scattered throughout the earlier parts of the play especially, which express Everyman's disappointment in his friends and consequent disillusion. One example must suffice. After a long colloquy with Goods, that character asks Everyman, "What! wenest thou that I am thyne?" Reversal, necessary prelude to re-orientation, is condensed in Everyman's brief reply: "I had went [believed] so."

## LIVES, WRITINGS, AND CRITICISM

*In almost all instances, biographical and critical works are listed only if they are available in English.*

### THE MIDDLE AGES: GENERAL

Robert S. Hoyt, *Europe in the Middle Ages* (1957) is a good historical survey. For a view of medieval thought and culture as a whole, the standard older work is H. O. Taylor, *The Mediaeval Mind*, 2 vols., 4th ed. (1925). A more recent book is F. B. Artz, *The Mind of the Middle Ages*, 2d ed. (1954).

### THE DREAM OF THE ROOD

The edition by Bruce Dickins and Alan S. C. Ross (London, 1963) offers abundant background information. Special topics are treated in Howard R. Patch, "Liturgical Influence in 'The Dream of the Rood' ", *PMLA* 24 (1919), 233–257; John V. Fleming, " 'The Dream of the Rood' and Anglo-Saxon Monasticism," *Traditio* 22 (1966), 43–72; and Alvin A. Lee, "Toward a Critique of *The Dream of the Rood*," in Lewis E. Nicholson & Dolores Warwick Frese, editors, *Anglo-Saxon Poetry: Essays in Appreciation* (Notre Dame, Indiana, 1975), 163–191.

### THE SONG OF ROLAND

The best summary in English of information about the origin and nature of the poem is contained in the introduction to the edition by T. A. Jenkins, *La Chanson de Roland* (1924), pp. ix-xcviii. For discussion against the background of the *chanson de geste* in general, see Urban Tigner Holmes, *A History of Old French Literature* (1938). For French estimates of the poem, see Gaston Paris, *La Littérature française au moyen-âge* (3d ed., 1903); and E. Faral, *La Chanson de Roland* (1933), in the series of volumes entitled *Les Classiques expliquées*.

P. le Gentil, *The "Chanson de Roland"* (1969), provides technical information in the first half and a more general reading in the second.

### AUCASSIN AND NICOLETTE

For a statement of the little that is known about the background of *Aucassin and Nicolette (Aucassin et Nicolete)*, see the English introduction to the edition by F. W. Bourdillon (1919); and Urban Tigner Holmes, *A History of Old French Literature* (1938). Henry Adams devotes a chapter to it in *Mont-Saint-Michel and Chartres* (1913).

### DANTE ALIGHIERI

LIFE. Born in late May, 1265, at Florence, Italy. He took part in the battle of Campaldino, 1289, on the Florentine side. In 1291 he married Gemma Donati, by whom he had two sons and one or two daughters. In 1295 he was a member of the "people's council" of Florence, and in 1300 served for two months, the usual term, as one of the six priors, or magistrates, of Florence. In 1302 the Blacks, opponents of the Whites (a political group with which Dante was affiliated), seized power in Florence, and he, with other White leaders, was exiled. Dante had gone to Rome on a mission to Pope Boniface in 1301, and as the decree of banishment was soon coupled with a condemnation to execution by fire (on false charges of corruption in office), he never returned to his native city. The last twenty years of his life, from 1301 to 1321, were spent in exile in various parts of Italy and possibly elsewhere. He died at Ravenna in September, 1321.

CHIEF WRITINGS. *The New Life (La vita nuova)*, probably written about 1292: sonnets and odes with a prose account and running commentary by the poet; the poems were mostly inspired by Beatrice. *The Banquet (Il convivio)*, of uncertain date, unfinished: a work of encyclopedic scope in the form of a prose commentary on a series of the poet's odes *(canzoni)*. *On the Vernacular Language (De vulgari eloquentia)*, in Latin prose, of uncertain date, unfinished: an essay on language and poetry, especially on the dialects of Italy and Provence; of great linguistic and literary interest. *On Single Government (De monarchia)*, in Latin prose, of uncertain date: a closely reasoned defense of world government, together with an attempt to demonstrate the independent status of the Holy Roman Empire and the Papacy. *The Divine Comedy (La divina commedia)*, date of beginning uncertain, apparently finished shortly before Dante's death in 1321.

BIOGRAPHY AND CRITICISM. C. H. Grandgent, *Dante* (1916), and the introduction to his edition of *The Divine Comedy* (revised, 1933); T. S. Eliot, "Dante," most easily available in his *Selected Essays* (1932); George Santayana, "Dante," in *Three Philosophical Poets* (1910). Some recent studies are E. Gilson, *Dante the Philosopher* (1948); Charles Williams, *The Figure of Beatrice* (1943); and the introduction and notes by Dorothy Sayers to her translation of the *Inferno* (1949). See also her *Introductory Papers on Dante* (1954) and *Further Papers on Dante* (1957). The more ambitious student will derive profit from Charles S. Singleton, *Dante Studies 1, Commedia: Elements of Structure* (1956) and *Dante Studies 2, Journey to Beatrice* (1958); Francis Fergusson, *Dante's Drama of the Mind: A Modern Reading of the Purgatorio* (1953, 1968); and Erich Auerbach, *Dante, Poet of the Secular World*, translated by Ralph Manheim (1961). Also helpful is Michele Barbi, *Life of Dante*, translated by Paul G. Ruggiers, 1954.

For background in medieval European history and literature see K. Vossler, *Medieval Culture: An Introduction to Dante and His Times*, translated from the German, 2 vols. (1929), and E. R. Curtius, *European Literature and the Latin Middle Ages*, translated by Willard R. Trask (1953).

Recent studies include R. Hollander, *Allegory in Dante's "Commedia"* (1969), and I. Brandeis, *The Ladder of Vision* (1960). Two collections of essays representative of modern Dante studies are: *Dante: A Collection of Critical Essays*, edited by J. Freccero (1965), and *American Critical Essays on Dante*, edited by R. J. Clements (1969).

GIOVANNI BOCCACCIO

LIFE. Born in 1313 in Paris, son of a Florentine businessman and a Frenchwoman. He was apparently taken to Italy in infancy, and in 1328 was sent to Naples to learn commerce in the office of his father's partner; but after six years, bored with business, he turned to the study of canon law. In 1336 Boccaccio saw Maria d'Aquino in a church at Naples; she is represented as Fiammetta in several of his works, including the *Decameron*. A romantic affair ended in Maria's desertion of her lover, and finally in her death in the plague of 1348. In 1341 Boccaccio returned to Florence. After 1351 he was greatly influenced by Petrarch, and turned in his writing from Italian poetry and prose fiction to Latin works of a scholarly nature. He sheltered Leon Pilatus, inducing him to make the first translation of Homer from Greek. Unlike Petrarch, Boccaccio was devoted to the study of Dante, of whom he wrote a biography; in 1373 he was appointed to a Dante chair or lectureship in Florence. He died in 1375.

CHIEF WRITINGS. Italian narrative verse: *Filostrato*, a source of Chaucer's *Troilus and Criseyde; Teseide*, a source of Chaucer's "Knight's Tale." *The Filostrato of Giovanni Boccaccio*, a translation with parallel text by Nathaniel Edward Griffin and Arthur Beckwith Myrick (1929) is convenient. Italian prose: *Decameron*, finished about 1353; *Vita di Dante*. Latin works: *De casibus virorum illustrium* and *De claris mulieribus*, compendiums of biographical sketches; *De genealogiis deorum*, a kind of dictionary of mythology and defense of poetry.

BIOGRAPHY AND CRITICISM. T. C. Chubb, *The Life of Giovanni Boccaccio* (1930); Edward Hutton, *Giovanni Boccaccio* (1910). Interesting and sensitive criticism is to be found in Charles G. Osgood, *Boccaccio on Poetry* (1930).

John Addington Symonds, *Giovanni Boccaccio* (1895), has been reissued (1968). A. D. Scaglione, *Nature and Love in the Middle Ages* (1963), a useful discussion of the *Decameron*. Twenty-one of the tales from the *Decameron* will be found in Mark Musa and Peter E. Bondanella, *Giovanni Boccaccio, The Decameron, A New Translation* (New York, 1977). This book also contains 180 pages of criticism and interpretation ranging from the fourteenth to the twentieth centuries.

SIR GAWAIN AND THE GREEN KNIGHT

The standard edition of the original poem (in Middle English) is by J. R. R. Tolkien and E. V Gordon, revised by Norman Davis (Oxford, 1967). A few of the recent interpretations are M. Boroff, *Sir Gawain and the Green Knight, A Stylistic and Metrical Study* (New Haven, 1962); Larry D. Benson, *Art and Tradition in Sir Gawain and the Green Knight* (New Brunswick, N. J., 1965); and J. A. Burrow, *A Reading of Sir Gawain and the Green Knight* (London, 1965). Donald R. Howard and Christian K. Zacher, editors, *Critical Studies of Sir Gawain and the Green Knight* (Notre Dame, Indiana, 1968) is an excellent collection.

GEOFFREY CHAUCER

LIFE. Born in 1340 or a few years later, son of a London wine merchant. In 1357 he apparently became a page in the household of the Countess of Ulster, wife of Lionel, a son of King Edward III. In 1359, in military service with the English in France, he was captured by the French and ransomed with royal funds. Between 1368 and 1378 Chaucer made several journeys to France and Italy as king's envoy or courier. In 1374 he received a pension from John of Gaunt, a son of Edward III, and became comptroller of customs in the port of London; about 1385 he moved to Kent, where he was elected knight of the shire in 1386, and sat in Parliament for one term. In 1389 he became Clerk of the King's Works (under Richard II), in 1391 deputy forester of the royal forest of North Petherton in Somerset, and in 1399 pensioner of King Henry IV. He died in 1400.

CHIEF WRITINGS. The *Romance of the Rose*, a translation (probably never finished) of the *Roman de la Rose;* the *Book of the Duchess;* the *House of Fame;* the *Parliament of Fowls*—all these are comparatively early works in English verse. He also translated *A Treatise on the Astrolabe* and Boethius' *Consolation of Philosophy* into English prose. His major works are *Troilus and Criseyde*, completed about 1385; and *The Canterbury Tales*, composed largely in the 1390's but with some use of earlier material.

BIOGRAPHY AND CRITICISM. The essential edition is F. N. Robinson, *The Complete Works of Geoffrey Chaucer* (1933); see also E. T. Donaldson (ed.), *Chaucer's Poetry: An Anthology for the Modern Reader* (1958). Social background is described admirably in G. G. Coulton, *Chaucer and His England* (rev. ed., 1950). The artistic growth of the poet is sketched in J. L. Lowes, *Geoffrey Chaucer annd His Art* (1941); see also H. S. Bennett, *Chaucer and the Fifteenth Century* (1947); Derek S.

Brewer, *Chaucer* (1953); Neville Coghill, *The Poet Chaucer* (1955); Raymond Preston, *Chaucer* (1952); and J. H. Speirs, *Chaucer, the Maker* (2d ed., 1960).

For general criticism see G. L. Kittredge, *Chaucer and His Poetry* (1915), and R. K. Root, *The Poetry of Chaucer* (1922). For a French view, see E. Legouis, *Chaucer* (English translation, 1913). Other critical works include Edward Wagenknecht (ed.), *Chaucer: Modern Essays in Criticism* (1959); Harold F. Brooks, *Chaucer's Pilgrims* (1962); Wolfgang Clemen, *Chaucer's Early Poetry* (1964); T. W. Craik, *The Comic Tales of Chaucer* (1963); B. F. Huppé and D. W. Robertson, *Fruyt and Chaf: Studies in Chaucer's Allegories* (1963); and Charles Muscatine, *Chaucer and the French Tradition* (1957).

Recent anthologies are: *Geoffrey Chaucer: A Critical Anthology*, edited by John A. Burrows (1969); *A Companion to Chaucer Studies*, edited by B. Rowland (1968), and *Chaucer Criticism: An Anthology*, edited by R. J. Schoek and J. Taylor (1960). *Chaucer*, edited by Albert E. Baugh (1968), is a thorough yet selective annotated bibliography.

EVERYMAN

A good selection of miracle plays, morality plays, and other medieval drama is contained in Joseph Quincy Adams, *Chief Pre-Shakespearean Dramas* (1924). On the medieval theatre and staging see Richard Southern, *The Medieval Theatre in the Round; A Study of the Staging of the Castle of Perseverance and Other Matters* (1957). For a recent survey of the whole matter, see Hardin Craig, *English Religious Drama* (1955). For an interesting fresh approach, see the chapter on "The Mystery Cycle" in John Speirs, *Medieval English Poetry: The Non-Chaucerian Tradition* (1958).

## The Dream of the Rood*

Lo! I will tell    the dearest of dreams
That I dreamed in the midnight    when mortal men
Were sunk in slumber.    Me-seemed I saw
A wondrous Tree    towering in air,
Most shining of crosses    compassed with light.          5
Brightly that beacon    was gilded with gold;
Jewels adorned it    fair at the foot,
Five on the shoulder-beam,    blazing in splendor.
Through all creation    the angels of God
Beheld it shining—    no cross of shame!          10
Holy spirits    gazed on its gleaming,
Men upon earth    and all this great creation.
   Wondrous that Tree,    that Token of triumph,
And I a transgressor    soiled with my sins!
I gazed on the Rood    arrayed in glory,          15
Shining in beauty    and gilded with gold,
The Cross of the Saviour    beset with gems.
But through the gold-work    outgleamed a token
Of the ancient evil    of sinful men
Where the Rood on its right side    once sweat blood.          20
Saddened and rueful,    smitten with terror
At the wondrous Vision,    I saw the Cross
Swiftly varying    vesture and hue,
Now wet and stained    with the Blood outwelling,
Now fairly jeweled    with gold and gems.          25
   Then, as I lay there,    long I gazed
In rue and sadness    on my Saviour's Tree,
Till I heard in dream    how the Cross addressed me,
Of all woods worthiest,    speaking these words:
"Long years ago    (well yet I remember)          30
They hewed me down    on the edge of the holt,
Severed my trunk;    strong foemen took me,
For a spectacle wrought me,    a gallows for rogues.
High on their shoulders    they bore me to hilltop,
Fastened me firmly,    an army of foes!          35
   "Then I saw the King    of all mankind
In brave mood hasting    to mount upon me.
Refuse I dared not,    nor bow nor break,
Though I felt earth's confines    shudder in fear;
All foes I might fell,    yet still I stood fast.          40
   "Then the young Warrior,    God, the All-Wielder,
Put off His raiment,    steadfast and strong;
With lordly mood    in the sight of many
He mounted the Cross    to redeem mankind.
When the Hero clasped me    I trembled in terror,          45

---

* Translated by Charles W. Kennedy.          3. *Me-seemed:* It seemed to me.
Title. *Rood:* Cross (from the Old          31. *holt:* Forest.
English word *rōd*).

But I dared not bow me   nor bend to earth;
I must needs stand fast.   Upraised as the Rood
I held the High King,   the Lord of heaven.
I dared not bow!   With black nails driven
Those sinners pierced me;   the prints are clear,          50
The open wounds.   I dared injure none.
They mocked us both.   I was wet with blood
From the Hero's side   when He sent forth His spirit.
      "Many a bale   I bore on that hillside
Seeing the Lord   in agony outstretched.                 55
Black darkness covered   with clouds God's body,
That radiant splendor.   Shadow went forth
Wan under heaven;   all creation wept
Bewailing the King's death.   Christ was on the Cross.
      "Then many came quickly,   faring from far,        60
Hurrying to the Prince.   I beheld it all.
Sorely smitten with sorrow   in meekness I bowed
To the hands of men.   From His heavy and bitter pain
They lifted Almighty God.   Those warriors left me
Standing bespattered with blood;   I was wounded with spears.   65
Limb-weary they laid Him down;   they stood at His head,
Looked on the Lord of heaven   as He lay there at rest
From His bitter ordeal all forspent.   In sight of His slayers
They made Him a sepulcher   carved from the shining stone;
Therein laid the Lord of triumph.   At evening tide      70
Sadly they sang their dirges   and wearily turned away
From their lordly Prince;   there He lay all still and alone.
      "There at our station   a long time we stood
Sorrowfully weeping   after the wailing of men
Had died away.   The corpse grew cold,                    75
The fair life-dwelling.   Down to earth
Men hacked and felled us,   a grievous fate!
They dug a pit   and buried us deep.
But there God's friends   and followers found me
And graced me with treasure   of silver and gold.        80
      "Now may you learn,   O man beloved,
The bitter sorrows   that I have borne,
The work of caitiffs.   But the time is come
That men upon earth   and through all creation
Show me honor   and bow to this sign.                     85
On me a while   God's Son once suffered;
Now I tower under heaven   in glory attired
With healing for all   that hold me in awe.
Of old I was once   the most woeful of tortures,
Most hateful to all men,   till I opened for them         90
The true Way of life.   Lo! the Lord of glory,

---

54. *bale:* Evil, affliction.
68. *forspent:* Exhausted.
73. *we:* Christ's cross and those on
which the two criminals were crucified
with him.

79–80. A reference to the discovery of
the cross in the fourth century by Saint
Helena, mother of the Roman emperor
Constantine.
83. *caitiffs:* Evil people.

The Warden of heaven,   above all wood
Has glorified me   as Almighty God
Has honored His Mother,   even Mary herself,
Over all womankind   in the eyes of men.       95
   "Now I give you bidding,   O man beloved,
Reveal this Vision   to the sons of men,
And clearly tell   of the Tree of glory
Whereon God suffered   for man's many sins
And the evil that Adam   once wrought of old.      100
   "Death He suffered,   but our Savior rose
By virtue of His great might   as a help to men.
He ascended to heaven.   But hither again
He shall come unto earth   to seek mankind,
The Lord Himself   on the Day of Doom,      105
Almighty God   with His angel hosts.
And then will He judge,   Who has power of judgment,
To each man according   as here on earth
In this fleeting life   he shall win reward.
   "Nor there may any   be free from fear      110
Hearing the words   which the Wielder shall utter.
He shall ask before many:   Where is the man
Who would taste bitter death   as He did on the Tree?
And all shall be fearful   and few shall know
What to say unto Christ.   But none at His Coming      115
Shall need to fear   if he bears in his breast
This best of symbols;   and every soul
From the ways of earth   through the Cross shall come
To heavenly glory,   who would dwell with God."
   Then with ardent spirit   and earnest zeal,      120
Companionless, lonely,   I prayed to the Cross.
My soul was fain of death.   I had endured
Many an hour of longing.   It is my life's hope
That I may turn   to this Token of triumph,
I above all men,   and revere it well.      125
   This is my heart's desire,   and all my hope
Waits on the Cross.   In this world now
I have few powerful friends;   they have fared hence
Away from these earthly gauds   seeking the King of glory,
Dwelling now with the High Father   in heaven above,      130
Abiding in rapture.   Each day I dream
Of the hour when the Cross of my Lord,   whereof here on earth
I once had vision,   from this fleeting life may fetch me
And bring me where is great gladness   and heavenly bliss,
Where the people of God   are planted and stablished for ever 135
In joy everlasting.   There may it lodge me
Where I may abide in glory   knowing bliss with the saints.
   May the Lord be gracious   who on earth of old
Once suffered on the Cross   for the sins of men.

---

122. *fain of*: Longing for.

He redeemed us, endowed us with life    and a heavenly home.  140
Therein was hope renewed    with blessing and bliss
For those who endured the burning.    In that great deed
God's Son was triumphant,    possessing power and strength!
Almighty, Sole-Ruling    He came to the kingdom of God
Bringing a host of souls    to angelic bliss,                145
To join the saints    who abode in the splendor of glory,
When the Lord, Almighty God,    came again to His throne.

141–147. According to tradition, Christ invaded hell between the crucifixion and the resurrection and rescued the souls of good men and women, who, having lived before the crucifixion, were awaiting that event and the redemption it would bring from the original sin of Adam's disobedience of God in the Garden of Eden.

# The Song of Roland*

### 1

Carlon the King, our Emperor Charlemayn,
Full seven years long has been abroad in Spain,
He's won the highlands as far as to the main;
No castle more can stand before his face,
City nor wall is left for him to break,                          5
Save Saragossa in its high mountain place;
Marsilion holds it, the king who hates God's name,
Mahound he serves, and to Apollyon prays:
He'll not escape the ruin that awaits.

                                                   AOI†

### 2

Marsilion sat in Saragossa town,                                 10
He sought an orchard where shade was to be found,
On a bright dais of marble he lies down;
By twenty thousand his vassals stand around.
He calls before him all his dukes and his counts:
"Listen, my lords, what affliction is ours!                      15
The Emperor Charles that wears fair France's crown
Invades our country our fortunes to confound.
I have no host but before him gives ground,
I find no force his forces for to flout;
Wise men of wit, give counsel to me now,                         20
Save me from death and loss of my renown."
There's ne'er a paynim utters a single sound,
Till Blancandrin, Valfonda's lord, speaks out.

* Apparently composed in the twelfth century. Abridged. *The Song of Roland*, translated by Dorothy L. Sayers. Copyright 1957 by the Executors of Dorothy L. Sayers. Reprinted by permission of David Higham Associates, Ltd.

† AOI: appears here and with more than half of the laisses in the poem. No pattern has been found for their occurrence, nor do scholars agree on the meaning of the word. Most theories consider it a refrain, perhaps shouted, which marks some kind of climax in the action or mood of the poem. For a fuller discussion, see the edition of T. A. Jenkins (1924), pp. xxxviii, 4–5.

6. *Saragossa:* city in Aragon, on the Ebro River.

8. *Mahound:* Mohammed, prophet of the god Allah and founder of the Mohammedan religion. *Apollyon:* the Greek god Apollo; but the poet is mistaken, for the Mohammedans were monotheists, recognizing only the god Allah.

### 3

Blancandrin's wise amid the paynim horde;
He was for valour a mighty knight withal,                            25
And fit of wit for to counsel his lord.
He tells the king: "Be you afeared for naught,
But send to Charles in his pride and his wrath
Your faithful service and your friendship henceforth.
Promise him lions and bears and hounds galore,                      30
Sev'n hundred camels and a thousand mewed hawks,
Four hundred pack-mules with gold and silver store,
And fifty wagons, a wagon-train to form,
Whence he may give his soldiers rich rewards.
Say, in this land he has made enough war;                           35
To Aix in France let him go home once more;
At Michaelmas you'll follow to his court,
There you'll submit unto the Christian law,
And be his man by faith and fealty sworn.
Hostages too, if for sureties he call,                              40
You'll let him have, ten maybe or a score;
'Twere good we send the sons our wives have borne:
I'll send mine own, though he should die therefor.
Better by far the heads of them should fall
Than we should lose honour, estate and all.                         45
And be reduced to beggary and scorn."

### 4

Quoth Blancandrin: "I swear by my right hand
And beard that flutters about my girdle-span,
Straightway you'll see the Frenchman's host disband:
They'll hurry home to France, their native land,                    50
When each within his favourite haunt is back,
Charles in his chapel at Aix will take his stand,
And there he'll hold high feast at Michaelmas.
The time will pass, the trysted hour elapse:
No news of us, no message will he have.                             55
Fierce is the king, a cruel-hearted man;
Our sureties' heads he'll smite off with the axe.
Better their heads should fall into their laps
Than that fair Spain should fall from out our hands,
And we should suffer grave losses and mishap."                      60
The Paynims say: "There is some truth in that."

### 5

The King Marsile had ended the debate;
He calls before him Clarin of Balagate,

---

31. *mewed hawks:* hawks which have
got over their molt, and are consequently
in good condition.
34. *soldiers:* these are the mercenaries,
who received their pay (*solde*) directly
from the king in cash, as distinct from
the feudal vassalage, who were maintained by their respective lords. Many of
them were knights-errant, without territorial attachment, who wandered about
offering their services to whoever would
employ them.
36. *Aix:* Aix-la-Chapelle was the imperial city of Charlemagne, who rebuilt
its palace and chapel and granted it many
special privileges. He was reputed to have
been born there and certainly died and
was buried there in 814.

Estramarin, and Eudropin his mate;
And Garlon Longbeard and Priamon he names,                    65
And Machiner and his uncle Matthay,
Johun of Outremer, and Malabayn,
And Blancandrin; these ten make up the tale,
Ten matchless villains, to whom he's said his say:
"Barons, my lords, get you to Charlemayn,                     70
Who sits at siege, Cordova town to take.
Bear each in hand an olive-branch displayed;
Peace and submission are signified that way.
If you contrive this treaty to arrange,
Of gold and silver I'll give you goodly weight,              75
And lands and fiefs as much as heart can crave."
The Paynims answer: "That will be ample pay."

### 6

Marsile the king his conference had ceased.
He tells his men: "My barons, go with speed;
Bear in your hands boughs of the olive tree.                 80
On my behalf King Charlemayn beseech,
For his God's sake to show me clemency.
Say, this month's end in truth he shall not see
Ere I shall seek him with thousand vassals leal.
The law of Christ I'll then and there receive,              85
In faith and love I will his liegeman be.
I'll send him sureties if thus he shall decree."
Quoth Blancandrin: "Be sure he'll grant your plea."

### 7

Marsilion sent for ten mules white as snow
(A gift that erst Suatilia's king bestowed),                90
Their saddles silver, their bridles all of gold.
Now are they mounted, the men who are to go;
All in their hands the olive-branches hold.
They came to Carlon that hath France in control;
They'll trap him somehow, for it is fated so.               95

### 8

The Emperor Charles is glad and full of cheer.
Cordova's taken, the outer walls are pierced,
His catapults have cast the towers down sheer;
Rich booty's gone to all his chevaliers,
Silver and gold and goodly battle-gear.                     100
In all the city no paynim now appears
Who is not slain or turned to Christian fear.
The Emperor sits in a great orchard near,
Having about him Roland and Olivere,
Samson the duke, and Anseis the fierce,                     105
Geoffrey d'Anjou the King's gonfalonier,
And Gerin too, and with him too Gerier;
And where these were was many another fere—
Full fifteen thousand of France the fair and dear.
Upon white carpets they sit, those noble peers,            110

108. *fere:* companion.

For draughts and chess the chequer-boards are reared;
To entertain the elder lords revered;
Young bachelors disport with sword and spear.
Beneath a pine beside an eglantier
A faldstool stands all of the red gold clear;                    115
Of fairest France there sits the king austere.
White are his locks, and silver is his beard,
His body noble, his countenance severe:
If any seek him, no need to say, "Lo, here!"
From off their steeds lit down the messengers,                   120
Well did they greet him with shows of love sincere.

### 9

Before them all Blancandrin forward stood;
And hailed the King: "God give His grace to you,
The glorious God to whom worship is due.
Thus speaks the king, Marsilion, great in rule:                  125
Much hath he studied the saving faith and true.
Now of his wealth he would send you in sooth
Lions and bears, leashed greyhounds not a few,
Sev'n hundred camels, a thousand falcons mewed,
And gold and silver borne on four hundred mules;                 130
A wagon-train of fifty carts to boot,
And store enough of golden bezants good
Wherewith to pay your soldiers as you should.
Too long you've stayed in this land to our rue:
To Aix in France return you at our suit.                         135
Thither my liege will surely follow you,
[And will become your man in faith and truth,
And at your hand hold all his realm in feu!"]
With lifted hands to God the Emperor sues;
Then bows his head and so begins to brood.                       140

### 10

The Emperor bode long time with downcast eyes;
He was a man not hasty in reply,
But wont to speak only when well advised.
When he looked up, his glance was stern and high.
He told the envoys: "Fair is your speech and fine;               145
Yet King Marsile is foe to me and mine.
In all these words and offers you recite
I find no warrant wherein I may confide."
"Sureties for this," the Saracen replies,
"Ten or fifteen or twenty we'll provide.                         150
One of my sons I'll send, on pain to die;
Others, yet nobler, you'll have, as I divine.
When in your palace high feast you solemnize
To great St Michael of Peril-by-the-Tide,

---

114. *eglantier*: wild-rose bush.
154. *St. Michael of Peril-by-the-Tide:*
("St. M. in periculo maris"). The name
was originally given to the monastery built
on the great island rock called Mont
St. Michel, off the coast of Normandy.
Later it came to be applied to the archangel himself, "St. Michel del Peril."

He'll follow you, on that you may rely,                    155
And in those baths God made you by His might
He would turn Christian and there would be baptized."
Quoth Charles: "He yet may save his soul alive."

### 11

Fair was the ev'ning and clearly the sun shone;
The ten white mules Charles sends to stall anon;          160
In the great orchard he bids men spread aloft
For the ten envoys a tent where they may lodge,
With sergeants twelve to wait on all their wants.
They pass the night there till the bright day draws on.
Early from bed the Emperor now is got;                    165
At mass and matins he makes his orison.
Beneath a pine straightway the King is gone,
And calls his barons to council thereupon;
By French advice whate'er he does is done.

### 12

The Emperor goes beneath a tall pine-tree,                170
And to his council he calls his barony:
There Duke Ogier, Archbishop Turpin meet,
Richard the Old and his nephew Henri,
Count Acelin the brave of Gascony,
Miles, and his cousin the Lord Tibbald of Rheims,         175
Gerin likewise and Gerier are convened;
And County Roland, there with the rest came he,
And Oliver, noble and good at need;
All French of France, thousand and more, maybe;
And Ganelon that wrought the treachery.                   180
So starts that council which came to such sore grief.

### 13

"Barons, my lords," began the Emperor Carlon,
"From King Marsile come envoys, seeking parley.
He makes me offers of treasure overpassing:
Of lions and bears and hounds to the leash mastered,      185
Sev'n hundred camels, and falcons mewed and hearty,
Four hundred mules with Arab gold all chargèd,
And fifty wagons well-laden in a cart-train.
But now to France he urges my departure,
And to my palace at Aix he'll follow after,               190

156. *baths:* the curative mineral springs for which Aix is still celebrated, and which were held to be of miraculous origin.

163. *sergeants:* the word "sergeant," meaning primarily "servant," was applied generally to almost any man, under the rank of knight, who exercised any kind of office in a lord's household or on his estate. In military use, it denoted a tenant doing military service, especially one who was in attendance on a knight in the field. The sergeant marched and fought on horseback, but was more lightly armed than the chevalier.

172. *Ogier the Dane:* this semihistorical hero boasts a *Chanson de Geste* devoted to his exploits, and figures in many others.

173. *Richard the Old:* his historical prototype is Richard I of Normandy, who lived (943–996) later than Charlemagne's time, but has been attracted into the Carolingian cycle by the natural tendency of epic to accumulate famous names regardless of chronology.

There change his faith for one of more advantage,
Become a Christian and of me hold his marches.
But his true purpose—for that I cannot answer."
The French all say: "We'd best be very guarded."

### 14

The Emperor Charles had finished all his speech.      195
The County Roland, who fiercely disagrees,
Swift to oppose springs up upon his feet:
He tells the King: "Nevermore trust Marsile!
Seven years long in land of Spain we've been.
I won for you both Noples and Commibles,      200
I took Valterna, the land of Pine I seized,
And Balagate, and Seville and Tudele.
Then wrought Marsile a very treacherous deed:
He sent his Paynims by number of fifteen,
All of them bearing boughs of the olive tree,      205
And with like words he sued to you for peace.
Then did you ask the French lords for their rede;
Foolish advice they gave to you indeed.
You sent the Paynim two counts of your meinie:
Basan was one, the other was Basile.      210
He smote their heads off in hills beneath Haltile.
This war you've started wage on, and make no cease;
To Saragossa lead your host in the field,
Spend all your life, if need be, in the siege,
Revenge the men this villain made to bleed!"      215

### 15

The Emperor Charles sat still with his head bended;
He stroked his beard and his moustaches gently;
Nor good nor ill he answers to his nephew.
The French are silent, Guènes alone excepted;
But he leaps up, strides into Carlon's presence,      220
And full of pride begins thus to address him.
He tells the King: "Trust not a brawling fellow,
Me nor another; seek only your own welfare.
If King Marsile informs you by this message
He'll set his hands in yours, and fealty pledge you,      225
And hold all Spain from you, at your good pleasure,
And to that faith we follow give acceptance,
The man who tells you this plea should be rejected
Cares nothing, Sire, to what death he condemns us.
Counsel of pride must not grow swollen-headed;      230
Let's hear wise men, turn deaf ears to the reckless."

### 16

Naimon at this stood forth before them all:
No better vassal was ever seen in hall.
He tells the King: "Well have you heard, my lord,

207. *rede*: counsel.

The arguments Count Ganelon sets forth. 235
There's weight in them, and you should give them thought.
The King Marsile is vanquished in the war,
You've taken from him his castles and his forts,
With catapults you've broken down his walls,
You've burned his cities and his armies outfought. 240
Now that he comes on your mercy to call
Foul sin it were to vex him any more.
Since he'll find sureties his good faith to support,
We should make haste to cut this great war short."
The French all say: "The Duke speaks as he ought." 245

### 17

"Barons, my lords, whom shall we send anon
To Saragossa, to King Marsilion?"
"I, by your leave," saith Naimon, "will begone,
Therefore on me bestow the glove and wand."
"You are my wisest," the King makes answer prompt: 250
"Now by the beard my cheek and chin upon,
You shall not go so far this twelvemonth long.
Hence! sit you down, for we summon you not!"

### 18

"Barons, my lords, whom shall we send of you
To Saragossa, the Sarsen king unto?" 255
"Myself," quoth Roland, "may well this errand do."
"That shall you not," Count Oliver let loose;
"You're high of heart and stubborn of your mood,
You'd land yourself, I warrant, in some feud.
By the King's leave this errand I will do." 260
The King replies: "Be silent there, you two!
Nor you nor he shall on that road set foot.
By this my beard that's silver to the view,
He that names any of the Twelve Peers shall rue!"
The French say nothing: they stand abashed and mute. 265

### 19

Then from their ranks arose Turpin of Rheims;
He tells the King: "Leave your French lords at ease;
Full sev'n long years in this land have you been,
Much have they suffered of perils and fatigue;
Pray you then, Sire, give wand and glove to me; 270
The Saracen of Spain I'll seek and see,
And in his looks his purpose will I read."
The Emperor answers with anger in his mien:
"On that white carpet sit down and hold your peace;
Be still, I say, until I bid you speak." 275

### 20

The Emperor said: "My free and knightly band,
Come choose me out some baron of my land

255. *Sarsen:* Saracen.

To bring my message to King Marsilion's hand."
Quoth Roland: "Guènes my step-sire is the man."
The French all say: "Indeed, he is most apt;                       280
If he's passed over you will not find his match."
Count Ganelon is furious out of hand;
His great furred gown of marten he flings back
And stands before them in his silk bliaut clad.
Bright are his eyes, haughty his countenance,                     285
Handsome his body, and broad his bosom's span;
The peers all gaze, his bearing is so grand.
He says to Roland: "Fool! what has made thee mad?
I am thy step-sire, and all these know I am,
And me thou namest to seek Marsilion's camp!                      290
If God but grant I ever thence come back
I'll wreak on thee such ruin and such wrack
That thy life long my vengeance shall not slack."
Roland replies: "This is all boast and brag!
Threats cannot fright me, and all the world knows that            295
To bear this message we must have a good man;
I'll take your place if the King says I can."

### 21

Quoth Ganelon: "My place thou shalt not take:
Thou'rt not my vassal, nor I thy suzerain.
Charles for his service commands me to obey.                      300
I'll seek Marsile in Saragossa's gates;
But rather there some deadly trick I'll play
Than not find vent for my unbounded rage."
When Roland heard him, then he laughed in his face.

### 22

When Ganelon sees Roland laugh outright                           305
He's fit to burst for anger and despite,
And very nearly goes clean out of his mind.
He tells the Count: "I love you not, not I;
You've picked on me unfairly, out of spite.
Just Emperor, here I stand before your eyes,                      310
Ready to do whatever you think right."

### 23

"To Saragossa I see that I must shift me;
There's no return for him that journeys thither.
Bethink you well that my wife is your sister,
A son she bare me, fairest of goodly children,                   315
Baldwin" (quoth he) "and a champion he will be.
To him I leave all my lands and my living;
No more I'll see him; take care, Sir, of your kinsman."
Quoth Charles: "Your heart is too tender within you;
Go now you must, for even so I bid you."                          320

### 24

Then said the King: "Stand forward, Ganelon,
Here at my hand receive the glove and wand;

You've heard the French—you are the man they want."
"Messire," said Guènes, "Roland hath done this wrong!
I'll never love him the whole of my life long,          325
Nor Oliver his friend and fellow fond,
Nor the Twelve Peers by whom he's doted on;
Sire, in your presence I defy the whole lot."
Then said the King: "Your passion is too hot;
I bid you go and so you must begone."               330
"Well may I go, but safeguard have I not,
Basile had none, nor Basan none, God wot."

### 25

The King holds out to him his right-hand glove;
Fain would Count Guènes be an hundred miles off!
When he would take it, it fell into the dust.        335
"God! what is this?" cry all the French at once;
"For sure this message will bring us great ill-luck."
"My lords," quoth Guènes, "you'll know it soon enough."

### 26

"Sire, give me leave" quoth Guènes, "hence to hie;
Since go I must, it boots not to abide."             340
"Go," said the King, "by Jesu's leave and mine."
With his right hand he's absolved him and signed,
And to his care letter and wand consigned.

### 27

Guènes the Count to his lodging makes speed,
Of his array he setteth him to seek                  345
The best he has to serve him for this need.
His golden spurs he buckles on his heels,
Girds to his side Murgleys his brand of steel,
And mounts him up on Tachëbrun his steed;
His stirrup's held by Guinëmer his eme.              350
Then might you see full many a brave knight weep,
Saying to him: "Woe worth your valour's meed!
In the King's court these many years you've been,
A noble vassal by all were you esteemed.
He that named you for this gear by his rede          355
Charlemayn's self shall not save him nor shield:
No right had Roland to have contrived this scheme;
For you're a man sprung of a noble breed."
Then they said, "Sir, take us with you, we plead."
Guènes replied: "God forbid it should be!            360
Best die alone nor slay good knights with me.

342. *absolved him and signed:* i.e., pronounced the absolution over him, making
the sign of the cross. Some commentators
have seen here a relic of the very ancient
popular conception of the priest-emperor,
preserved in the legend of Prester John.
But there is, I think, nothing in the line
which necessarily ascribes sacerdotal status to Charlemagne, however sacred his
person and function. What is probably
intended is the prayer of absolution, frequently called simply the Absolution (as
in the Book of Common Prayer) which
can be pronounced by, for example, an
abbess, or indeed any other lay person.
It would be some such formula as "The
Lord bless you and keep you, deliver
you from all your sins, and bring you to
everlasting life."
350. *eme:* uncle.

Sirs, you'll return to fair France presently:
On my behalf my wife I bid you greet,
And Pinabel that is my friend and peer.
Baldwin my son, whom you know well, I ween,     365
Him shall you help and accept for your liege."
Then he sets forth and on his way goes he.

### 28

Under tall olives the County Guènes rides;
The Paynim envoys he's caught up in good time,
And Blancandrin drops back with him behind.     370
Now each to other begins to speak with guile.
Blancandrin says: "Charles is a wondrous wight!
Pulia he's ta'en, Calabria likewise,
And unto England passed over the salt tide
To win St Peter the tribute of the isle.     375
What seeks he here, warring in our confines?"
"Such is his pleasure," Count Ganelon replies;
"In all the world you will not find his like."

### 29

Quoth Blancandrin: "The French are men of worth,
Yet to their lord they do a scurvy turn,     380
These dukes and counts, when they counsel such work;
Both him and others they harry to their hurt."
"There's none," quoth Guènes, "who merits such ill words,
Save only Roland, for whom 'twill be the worse.
But now, the Emperor in the cool shade conversed;     385
Up came his nephew all in his byrny girt,
Fresh with his booty from Carcassone returned.
Roland in hand a golden apple nursed
And showed his uncle, saying, 'Take it, fair sir;
The crowns I give you of all the kings on earth.'     390
One day his pride will undo him for sure,
Danger of death day by day he incurs.
If one should slay him some peace might be preserved."

### 30

Quoth Blancandrin: "Roland's a villain fell,
Presuming thus all folk on earth to quell,     395
And every land under his yoke compel!
Whom does he count on to lend his arms such strength?"
Ganelon answers: "He counts upon the French;
They'll never fail him, they love him far too well.
Silver and gold he gives them for largesse,     400
Horses and mules, silks and accoutrements.
And everything the Emperor wants, he gets—
He'll win for him all lands 'twixt east and west."

375. *the tribute of the isle:* The annual tribute known as Peter's Pence, paid by England to the See of Rome, was of Anglo-Saxon origin and instituted in the eighth or ninth century, though not in consequence of political or military pressure by Charlemagne.

### 31

So long rides Guènes with Blancandrin that day
Till each to each has pledged his truth and faith                      405
They will seek means Count Roland for to slay.
So long they ride, they come by road and way
To Saragossa, and by a yew draw rein.
A faldstool stood beneath a pine-tree's shade,
With silken cloth of Alexandria draped;                               410
There sat the King that bore the rule in Spain.
Full twenty thousand Saracens stood arrayed.
Not one of them has any word to say,
So eagerly upon the news they wait.
And here come Guènes and Blancandrin apace!                           415

### 32

Blancandrin came before Marsilion,
And by the hand held County Ganelon;
Saith to the King: "Save you, sir, by Mahond,
And by Apollyon, whose blest faith we extol!
To Charles we gave your message every jot;                            420
Both of his hands he lifted up aloft
And praised his God; further, he answered not.
One of his nobles, you see, he's sent along—
A lord of France, of most illustrious stock;
From him you'll hear if peace is won or lost."                        425
"We'll hear him," quoth Marsile; "let him say on."

### 33

Now Ganelon had giv'n this matter thought,
And with great cunning he now begins to talk,
Even as a man that's to the manner born.
He tells the King: "God have you in His ward,                         430
The glorious God whom we ought to adore!
King Charlemayn, the Great, thus sends you word:
You must receive the faith of Christ Our Lord,
And as your fief half Spain he will award.
If you refuse to accept this accord,                                  435
You shall be taken and fettered by main force,
And haled away to Aix, into his court,
There to be doomed and done with once for all;
There shall you die in shamefulness and scorn."
On hearing this Marsile was quite distraught;                         440
He held a dart with golden feathers wrought,
And would have struck him, but he was overborne.

### 34

The King Marsile has all his colour changed.
Grasping the shaft, his javelin he shakes.
When Guènes sees it he sets hand to his blade,                        445
Two fingers' breadth forth of the scabbard hales,
And says to it: "Full bright you are and brave!

In the King's court I've borne you many a day!
Ne'er shall the Emperor of France have cause to say
I died alone in strange lands far away;                                        450
Before their bravest the price of you have paid!"
The Paynims cry: "We must prevent this fray."

### 35
The wiser Paynims remonstrate with him so
That King Marsile has sunk back on this throne.
Quoth the Caliph: "You put us to reproach,                                      455
Thinking to threaten this Frenchman with a blow!
It is your business to listen and take note."
Saith Ganelon: "All this, sir, must I thole.
For all the gold God made, I'll not forgo,
No, not for all the wealth your land can boast,                                460
To speak the message—so I'm but given scope—
Which Charles the King, that mighty man of mould,
Has sent by me to this his mortal foe."
He had on him a sable-fur-lined cloak
Covered with silk which Alexandria wove;                                       465
He flings it down for Blancandrin to hold,
But of his sword he nowise will let go;
In his right hand he grasps the hilts of gold,
The Paynims say: "Lo there a baron bold!"

### 36
Guènes approached the King and thus addressed him:                             470
He saith to him: "You do vainly to vex you.
Carlon thus bids you, that hath France in possession:
The Christian faith must of you be accepted,
And one half Spain he will give you in tenure;
The other half is for Roland his nephew;                                       475
A right proud partner you'll have there for co-tenant!
If these conditions should by you be rejected,
In Saragossa he'll besiege and invest you,
And by main force you shall be se.zed and fettered.
Thence to his city of Aix you'll go directly.                                  480
You shall not ride on palfrey nor on destrier,
Nor for the road shall you have mule nor jennet;
On some poor screw of a pack-ass he'll set you;
And you will lose your head there by his sentence.
See now, the Emperor has written you this letter."                            485
To the right hand of the Moor he presents it.

### 37
The King Marsile for very rage went white;
He breaks the seal and flings the wax aside,
Looks at the letter and reads what is inside.
"These words to me Carlon the French King writes:                             490
I'm to remember his grief and his despite
For those two brothers, Basan and Basil hight,

----

458. *thole:* endure.

Whom I beheaded in Haltoye-on-the-Height;
And if I value the purchase of my life,
Must send my uncle the Caliph as his prize;      495
Else nevermore will he be friend of mine."
Marsilion's son at this broke in and cried:
"Ganelon's words are madness out of mind!
This is too much—he shall not rest alive;
Give him to me and justice he shall find!"      500
When Guènes heard, he shook his blade on high,
And set his back to the trunk of the pine.


### 38

Unto the orchard the King Marsile repairs;
Of his best men he takes with him a share,
And thither came Blancandrin white of hair,      505
And Jurfaret, who is his son and heir,
And the Caliph, his eme and officer.
Quoth Blancandrin: "Call in that Frenchman there:
He'll serve our ends, to this I've heard him swear."
"Fetch him yourself, 'twere best," the King declares.      510
In his right hand Count Ganelon he bare
Into the orchard where king and council were.
So they begin to plot the treacherous snare.


### 39

"Guènes, fair sir," said Marsile, "I allow,
Something too lightly I treated you just now      515
When in my fury I would have struck you down;
But by these pelts of sable fur I vow,
Which of good gold are worth five hundred pounds,
Richly I'll quite you ere the next day be out."
"This I refuse not," said Ganelon the Count;      520
"God, if He please, shall balance the account."


### 40

"Truly, Count Guènes," then said the King Marsile.
"I have in mind your right good friend to be.
Of Charlemayn fain would I hear you speak.
He's very old, a hard life his has been;      525
Two hundred years and more I know he's seen;
In lands so many his body he's fatigued,
Hard strokes so many he's taken on his shield,
Rich kings so many he's brought to beggary—
When will he weary of fighting in the field?"      530
"That's not his way," said Guènes, "in the least.
None knows the Emperor, or looks upon his mien,
But says of him: 'A right great man is he.'
Howe'er I sounded his praise and his esteem,
His worth and honour would still outrun my theme.      535
His mighty valour who could proclaim in speech?
God kindled in him a courage so supreme,
He'd rather die than fail his knights at need."

### 41

The Paynim said: "I marvel in my thought,
At Charlemayn, that is so old and hoar!      540
I know he's lived two hundred years and more.
In lands so many his body he's forworn,
Sharp strokes so many of lance and spear has borne,
Rich kings so many beggared and brought to naught—
When will he weary of going to the wars?"      545
"Never," said Guènes, "while Roland still bears sword;
There's none so valiant beneath the heavens broad,
Oliver too, his friend, is a brave lord;
And the Twelve Peers whom Charles so much adores
Protect the vanward with knights a thousand score;      550
Charles is secure, he fears no man at all."

### 42

The Paynim said: "I marvel in my mind
At Charlemayn whose head is old and white.
Two hundred years, I know, have passed him by.
In lands so many he's conquered far and wide,      555
Lance-thrusts so many he's taken in the strife,
Rich kings so many brought to a beggar's plight—
When will he weary of going forth to fight?"
"Never," said Guènes, "while Roland sees the light;
'Twixt east and west his valour has no like,      560
Oliver too, his friend, is a brave knight;
And the twelve Peers, in whom the King delights,
With twenty thousand Frenchmen to vanward ride:
Charles is secure, he fears no man alive."

### 43

"Guènes, fair sir," then said the King directly,      565
"I have an army, you will not find a better,
Four hundred thousand good knights as I may reckon:
Can I give battle to Carlon and his Frenchmen?"
Guènes replies: "Not you, and so I tell you,
For of your Paynims the losses would be deadly.      570
Leave all this folly, come to your sober senses.
Send to the Emperor so huge a heap of treasure
That all the French will marvel at its splendour.
For twenty sureties, that you will likewise send him,
Back to fair France Charles will return contented,      575
Leaving behind a rear-guard to protect him.
With them, I warrant, will be Roland his nephew,
Oliver too, the valorous and gentle.
Dead are these Counts, if you will give me credit.
Carlon will see his great pride fall'n and ended;      580
He'll have no heart to fight with you from henceforth."

### 44

"Guènes, fair sir," [the King Marsilion cries,]
"What must I do to bring Roland to die?"

"I'll tell you that," Count Ganelon replies.
"At Sizer Gate the King will have arrived,                          585
Leaving a rear-guard to keep the pass behind.
There'll be his nephew Count Roland, the great knight,
Oliver too, on whom he most relies.
With twenty thousand good Frenchmen at their side.
An hundred thousand send of your Paynim kind,                       590
And these shall first engage the French in fight.
Of the French force the loss will not be light—
Yours will be slaughtered, and that I'll not disguise!
The like assault you'll launch a second time,
And, first or last, Roland will not get by.                         595
You will have done a deed of arms full fine;
You'll ne'er again see war in all your life.


### 45

"Whoso should smite the County Roland dead,
From Carlon's body then were the right hand reft;
The wondrous armies would dwindle off and melt,                     600
Nor could Charles gather so great a host afresh;
Our fathers' land would thus find peace and rest."
When he heard this Marsile fell on his neck,
And straightway bad them unlock his treasure-chests.


### 46

Then said Marsile: "One thing alone remains:                        605
There's no good bond where there is no good faith;
Give me your oath Count Roland to betray."
Guènes replies: "It shall be as you say."
Upon the relics of his good sword Murgleys
He sware the treason and sware his faith away.                      610


### 47

There was a faldstool of ivory all wrought;
Marsile commands a volume to be brought
Of Termagant's and of Mahomet's law;
The Saracen of Spain thereon has sworn
That in the rear-guard Count Roland shall be sought;                615
If there he find him, he'll fight with his whole force,
And do his best to slay him once for all.
Guènes replies: "And may it so befall!"


### 48

Lo, now! there comes a Paynim, Valdebron;
He stands before the King Marsilion,                                620
And gaily laughing he says to Ganelon:
"Here, take my sword, a better blade is none.

---

585. *Sizer Gate: Port de Sizer*, or *Sizre* (the spelling varies): This is the pass now called the Col de Cize, which cuts through the Pyrenees on the road running from St.-Jean-Pied-de-Port by way of Roncevaux to Pampeluna, and forms the Gate of Spain.
602. *Our fathers' land*: France.
612. *a volume*: the Koran (?).

A thousand mangons are in the hilt thereof;
'Tis yours, fair sir, for pure affection,
For help against Roland the champion,                         625
If in the rear-guard we find him as we want."
Quoth Ganelon to him: "It shall be done."
They kiss each other the cheek and chin upon.

### 49

Thereafter comes a Paynim, Climborin,
And laughing gaily to Ganelon begins:                        630
"Come, take my helm, I ne'er saw none so rich:
[Above the nasal a carbuncle there is.
Out of pure friendship I offer you this gift]
If against Roland you'll aid us by your wit
That we may bring a shameful death on him."                  635
"It shall be done," quoth Ganelon to this;
They kissed each other upon the mouth and chin.

### 50

Then to the Count Queen Bramimonda spoke:
"Dearly, fair sir, I love you, by my troth,
My king so lauds you, and his vassals also.
This pair of owches on your wife I bestow,                   640
Heavy with jacinth and amethyst and gold;
More worth are they than all the wealth of Rome,
The like of them your Emperor never owned."
He takes the jewels and thrusts them in his poke.           645

### 51

The King calls Malduit, the keeper of his treasure:
"King Carlon's gifts, have you yet got them ready?"
And he replies, "Yea, sire, in ample measure:
Sev'n hundred camels laden with precious metal,
And twenty sureties, the noblest under heaven."             650

### 52

Marsilion's hand on Guènes' shoulder lies;
He says to him: "You are both bold and wise.
Now by that faith which seems good in your eyes
Let not your heart turn back from our design.
Treasure I'll give you, a great and goodly pile,            655
Ten mule-loads gold, digged from Arabian mines;
No year shall pass but you shall have the like.
Take now the keys of this great burg of mine,
Offer King Charles all its riches outright.
Make sure that Roland but in the rear-guard rides,          660
And if in pass or passage I him find
I'll give him battle right bitter to abide."
"I think," said Guènes, "that I am wasting time."
He mounts his horse and on his journey hies.

---

623. *mangons:* Saracen gold coins.          645. *poke:* pouch.
641. *owches:* brooches (?).

53

| | |
|---|---|
| The Emperor now returns upon his way | 665 |

The Emperor now returns upon his way      665
And has arrived before the town of Gayne
(Count Roland took it and all its wall down-razed,
An hundred years thereafter it lay waste;)
And there the King for news of Guènes waits,
And for the tribute of the great land of Spain.      670
In the white dawn, at breaking of the day,
Into the camp the County Guènes came.

54

Early that day the Emperor leaves his bed.
Matins and mass the King has now heard said;
On the green grass he stood before his tent.      675
Roland was with him, brave Oliver as well,
Naimon the Duke and many another yet.
Then perjured Guènes the traitor comes to them
And starts to speak with cunning false pretence.
He tells the King: "To you (whom God defend!)      680
Of Saragossa the keys I here present.
I bring you also wealth to your heart's content,
And twenty sureties: see they be closely kept.
The valiant king, Marsile, this message sends:
The Caliph's absence he prays you'll not resent.      685
Mine own eyes saw four hundred thousand men
In hauberk armed, some having laced their helms,
And girt with swords whose hilts were richly gemmed,
Attend him forth; to the sea-shore they went.
The faith of Christ they'd keep not, nor accept,      690
And for this cause they from Marsilion fled.
But ere they'd sailed four leagues, maybe, or less,
Black wind and storm and tempest on them fell;
They were all drowned; they'll ne'er be seen again.
Had he been living I would have had him fetched.      695
Now, as regards the Paynim King himself:
Believe me, sire, before a month is sped
He'll follow you to France, to your own realm.
There he'll receive the faith that you profess,
There with joined hands to you his fealty pledge,      700
And hold from you in fief the Spanish realm."
Then said the King: "The name of God be blest!
Well have you done: I shall reward you well."
Throughout the host a thousand trumpets swell,
The French strike camp, their goods on sumpters set;      705
Home to fair France behold them all addressed.

. . .

55

King Charlemayn has spoiled the Spanish borders,
He's taken castles, put cities to the slaughter;

683. *twenty sureties:* This is the last      fate is not mentioned.
we hear of the hostages, whose ultimate

Now the King says he has ended his warfare.
Home to fair France the Emperor turns his horses. 710
Pennon to lancehead Count Roland now has corded;
High on a hillock he displays it abroad there.
In fields all round the French set up their quarters.
Through the wide valleys the Paynim hosts go forward,
[All fully armed,] accoutred in their corslets, 715
Their helms laced on, and their swords in the sword-belt,
Shields on their necks, and their lances well ordered.
High on the mountains in a thicket they've halted:
Four hundred thousand they wait there for the morning;
God! it is grievous that the French have no warning! 720

### 56

The day goes down, dark follows on the day.
The Emperor sleeps, the mighty Charlemayn.
He dreamed he stood in Sizer's lofty gate,
Holding in hand his ashen lance full great.
Count Ganelon takes hold of it, and shakes, 725
And with such fury he wrenches it and breaks
That high as heaven the flinders fly away.
Carlon sleeps on, he sleeps and does not wake.

### 57

After this dream he had another dream:
That in his chapel at Aix in France was he; 730
In his right arm a fierce bear set its teeth.
Forth from Ardennes he saw a leopard speed,
That with rash rage his very body seized.
Then from the hall ran in a greyhound fleet,
And came to Carlon by gallops and by leaps. 735
From the first brute it bit the right ear clean,
And to the leopard gives battle with great heat.
The French all say the fight is good to see,
But none can guess which shall the victor be.
Carlon sleeps on; he wakes not from his sleep. 740

### 58

The night is past and the clear dawn is showing.
[A thousand trumpets] are sounded for the hosting.
The Emperor rides full lordly in his going.
"Barons, my lords," quoth Charlemayn, "behold now
These lofty passes, these narrows winding closely— 745
Say, who shall have the rearguard now to hold them?"
Quoth Ganelon: "I name my nephew Roland;
You have no baron who can beat him for boldness."
When the King heard, a stern semblance he showed him:

---

710–711: The scribe has perhaps omitted a line or two here, mentioning where
Charlemagne and his army have got to.
We learn from laisse 58 that they have
reached the entrance to the pass, at the
foot of the Pyrenees.
731 ff. *a fierce bear*, etc.: The bear is
presumably Ganelon, as in laisse 186;
the leopard, Marsilion; the greyhound,
Roland.

"A fiend incarnate you are indeed," he told him;                               750
"Malice hath ta'en possession of you wholly!
Who then should keep the vanguard of my progress?"
Quoth Ganelon: "Ogier the Dane I vote for;
You have no baron can do it with more prowess."

### 59

When Roland hears what he's appointed to,                                     755
He makes reply as knighthood bids him do:
"My noble stepsire, I owe you gratitude
That I'm assigned the rearguard at your suit.
Charles, King of France, the loss shall never rue
Of steed or palfrey thereby, I warrant you,                                   760
No saddle-beast, nor hinny neither mule,
Pack-horse nor sumpter thereby he shall not lose,
Save first the sword have paid the reckoning due."
Quoth Ganelon: "I know it; you speak truth."

### 60

When Roland hears that to the rearward guard                                  765
His stepsire names him, he speaks in wrath of heart:
"Ah! coward wretch, foul felon, baseborn carle,
Didst think the glove would fall from out my grasp
As did the wand from thine, before King Charles?"

### 61

"Just Emperor," then besought Count Roland bold,                              770
"From your right hand deliver me your bow;
No man, I swear, shall utter the reproach
That I allowed it to slip from out my hold
As did the wand that Ganelon let go."
The Emperor sits with his head bended low,                                    775
On cheek and chin he plucks his beard for woe,
He cannot help but let the tears o'erflow.

### 62

Straightway thereon comes Naimon to the King—
No better vassal in court did ever sit.
He says to him: "You've listened to all this;                                 780
The County Roland is angered to the quick;
The rear-guard now has been adjudged to him
And you've no baron can ever make him quit.
Give him the bow now bended in your grip,
And find good men to aid him in this shift."                                  785
So the King gives it, and Roland seizes it.

---

752. *who then should keep the vanguard?*: i.e., in Roland's place, since he usually takes command there with the other peers (see ll. 549–550, 561–562).

769. *the wand*: the mention of the wand, here and in l. 774, seems to be a lapse of memory on the poet's part. Actually (333–335) it was the glove that Ganelon let fall.

771. *your bow*: the use of a bow as the token of an appointment does not seem to be very usual, nor is it clear why Charlemagne should have one in his hand, since the bow was not reckoned as a "noble" weapon, except for use in hunting. Later MSS substitute, or add, the more customary glove or standard.

### 63

To Roland then the King his uncle said:
"Nephew, fair sir, hear now and heed me well:
Half of my army I'll leave you for this stead;
Keep them with you and you'll be safe with them."          790
The Count said: "No; I never will consent;
May God confound me if I shame my descent!
A thousand score I'll keep of valiant French.
Safe through the passes go you with confidence;
Never fear man so long as I draw breath."          795

### 64

Roland the Count mounts on his destrier.
Comes then to him his comrade Oliver,
And Gerin comes and brave Count Gerier,
And Othon comes and so does Berenger,
Old Anseis, and Astor, great of worth,          800
And Gerard too, Roussillon's haughty earl;
And with them comes the rich Duke Gaïfer.
Quoth the Archbishop: "By Heav'n, I'm with you, sirs!"
"And so am I," Walter the Count affirms,
"I'm Roland's man, him am I bound to serve!"          805
Knights twenty thousand they choose for followers.

### 65

To Walter Hum Count Roland gives command:
"A thousand French take, of our own French land,
And hold the gorges and heights on either hand;
Nor let the Emperor lose from his side one man."          810
Quoth Walter: "Mine to do as you demand."
With thousand French of France their own dear land
On gorge and hill Count Walter holds the flanks;
Come what come may he'll never quit his stand
Till from the sheath have flashed sev'n hundred brands.          815
King Almeric, lord of Balferna's strand,
That day shall give hard battle to their band.

### 66

High are the hills, the valleys dark and deep,
Grisly the rocks, and wonderous grim the steeps.
The French pass through that day with pain and grief;          820
The bruit of them was heard full fifteen leagues.
But when at length their fathers' land they see,
Their own lord's land, the land of Gascony,
Then they remember their honours and their fiefs,

801. *Gerard of Roussillon:* not Roussillon in the Pyrenees, but a hill in Burgundy (now Mont Lassois), near the Abbey of Pothières, which was founded, together with the Abbey of Vèzelay by the historical Gerard. His exploits are celebrated in the *Chanson de Geste* which bears his name.

805. *man:* i.e., vassal.

816. The engagement between Almeric and Walter Hum is not described in the poem; its results are mentioned in laisse 152.

Sweethearts and wives whom they are fain to greet,                    825
Not one there is for pity doth not weep.
Charles most of all a boding sorrow feels,
His nephew's left the Spanish gates to keep;
For very ruth he cannot choose but weep.

### 67

All the twelve peers in Spain are left behind,                         830
Full twenty thousand stout Frenchmen at their side;
Valiant they are, and have no fear to die.
To land of France the Emperor homeward hies.
And still his face beneath his cloak he hides.
Close at his rein the good Duke Naimon rides;                         835
He asks the King: "What troubles thus your mind?"
"This is ill done," quoth Charles, "to ask me why!
So much I grieve I cannot choose but sigh.
Through Ganelon fair France is ruined quite.
An angel showed me a vision in the night,                             840
How in my hand he broke my lance outright,
He that my nephew to the rear-guard assigned.
In foreign marches abandoned, Roland bides—
God! if I lose him I shall not find his like."

### 68

King Charlemayn from tears cannot refrain;                            845
Full hundred thousand, the French grieve for his sake,
And for Count Roland are wondrously afraid.
Him has the false lord Ganelon betrayed;
Vast the reward the paynim king has paid:
Silver and gold, and cloth of silk and saye,                          850
Horses and mules, camels and beasts of prey.
Marsile has called the barony of Spain;
His viscounts, counts, almanzors stand arrayed,
Dukes and emirs, and youths of high estate;
Four hundred thousand he's summoned in three days.                    855
In Saragossa he bids his tabors play;
Mahound their idol high on the tower they raise,
And every Paynim adores and gives it praise.
Then by forced marches their army hastes away,
Through Terracerta they ride by hill and dale.                        860
Now have they seen French gonfalons displayed.
The twelve companions who in the rear-guard wait
Mean to give battle, and none shall say them nay.

### 69

Marsilion's nephew trips out before the throng,
Riding a mule which he whips with a wand;                             865
He tells his uncle with laughter on his tongue:

---

843. *marches:* the frontier region of a
province; the province itself.
850. *saye:* a fine cloth of silk and wool.
860. *Terracerta:* Tere Certaine, possibly

Cerdagne, the region about Catalonia.
864. *Marsilion's nephew:* His name, as
we learn in l. 1192, is Adelroth.

"Fair sir and king, I've served you well and long;
Much have I suffered, much labour undergone,
Many fields fought, and many battles won!
First blow at Roland is the reward I want;      870
With my sharp sword I'll split him through the sconce!
Yea, if I find good favour with Mahond,
I'll set Spain free, unloosing of her bonds
From Gate of Spain to Durstant and beyond.
Charles will lose heart, the French will yield anon,     875
You shall be quit of wars your whole life long."
He gets the glove from King Marsilion.

70

Marsilion's nephew holds the glove in his fist:
Unto his uncle thus proudly he begins:
"Fair sire and king, you've made me a great gift.     880
Find me twelve lords, the best that you can pick.
'Gainst the twelve peers our valour for to pit."
The first that answers is Falsaron to wit,
He was own brother unto Marsile the king:
"You and I, nephew, will gladly go to it.     885
In very deed this battle will we give
To Carlon's rearward that guards his host for him:
The thing is done! by us they'll all be killed."

71

King Corsablis now springs from out the host,
Barbarian born, the magic art he knows.     890
Like a brave man thus valiantly he spoke:
"No coward I, no, not for all God's gold!"

Malprimis of Brigale comes spurring bold,
He'll run afoot swifter than steed can go;
With a loud voice before Marsile he boasts:     895
"I'll bear my body with you to Roncevaux:
If I find Roland I'll fight till he's laid low."

72

From Balaguet there cometh an Emir;
His form is noble, his eyes are bold and clear,
When on his horse he's mounted in career     900
He bears him bravely armed in his battle-gear,
And for his courage he's famous far and near;
Were he but Christian, right knightly he'd appear.
Before Marsile he cries for all to hear:
"To Roncevaux," saith he, "my course I'll steer;     905
If I find Roland, then death shall be his weird,

---

870. *first blow at Roland* (*le colp de Roland*): The privilege of striking the first blow in the battle was much sought after. In l. 3200 we find Malpramis, the son of the Emir Baligant, similarly demanding of his father the honor (*le coup*) in the battle with Charlemagne. The commander in chief bestows the honor by handing over his glove in token (l. 877).
892–893. A few lines seem to have been omitted here, completing Corsablis's speech of defiance.
906. *weird*: doom.

And Oliver's, and all of the Twelve Peers!
The French shall die the death in shame and tears.
King Charlemayn, the dotard old and blear,
Will soon be sick of waging warfare here!          910
Spain shall be ours in peace this many a year!"
The King Marsile pours thanks into his ears.

### 73

Comes an Almanzor, a lord of Moriane,
There's no worse villain in all the land of Spain.
Before Marsilion his bragging boast he makes:          915
"To Roncevaux I'll lead my people straight,
Full twenty thousand with spear and lance arrayed.
If I meet Roland I'll kill him, by my faith!
No day shall dawn but Carlon shall bewail."

### 74

And next there comes Turgis of Tortelosa;          920
A count he is, and the whole city owneth;
A right ill will to Christian men he showeth.
Before Marsile with the rest he enrolls him.
He tells the King: "Fear not for any foeman!
Mahound's worth more than St Peter the Roman;          925
Serve him; the field is ours and ours the trophy!
To Roncevaux I go to meet with Roland;
There shall he die; he shall have help of no man.
See here my sword, how long it is and noble;
'Gainst Durendal I'll measure it right boldly;          930
Which shall prevail you'll not be long in knowing.
The French shall die if they dare to oppose us;
Carlon the old shall be grieving and groaning;
Crown nevermore shall he wear from that moment."

### 75

And Escremiz of Valterne is the next;          935
He owns that fief, and he's a Saracen;
Before Marsile he shouts amid the press:
"To Ronceval I go to stoop their crests.
If I find Roland, there shall he lose his head,
And Oliver, who's captain of the rest;          940
The whole Twelve Peers are all marked out for death.
The French shall die and France shall be bereft.
Few men of worth to Carlon shall be left."

### 76

Next comes a Paynim, called Estorgan by name,
Estramarin his comrade with him came;          945
Foul felons both and knavish traitors they.
Then said Marsile: "My lords, draw near, I pray;
Through Roncevaux you mean to force your way,
And lead my troops, and lend us your best aid."
And they reply: "Command, and we obey.          950
Both Oliver and Roland we'll assail,

Of the Twelve Peers none shall survive the fray.
Sharp are our swords and goodly are the blades,
All in hot blood we'll dye them red this day;
The French shall die, and Carlon shall bewail.  955
A gift we'll make you of the home of their race;
Come with us, King, and see how goes the game,
And as a gift we'll give you Charlemayn."

### 77

Then comes at speed Margaris of Seville,
Who holds his land as far as Cazmarin.  960
Ladies all love him, so beautiful he is,
She that beholds him has a smile on her lips,
Will she or nill she, she laughs for very bliss,
And there's no Paynim his match for chivalry.
He joins the throng and cries unto the King  965
Loudest of all: "Never you fear a whit!
In Roncevaux this Roland I'll go kill,
Nor Oliver shall any longer live;
All the Twelve Peers we'll cut in little bits.
Lo! here my sword with golden pummel gilt!  970
Th' Emir of Primes gave it me for a gift,
I swear I'll dye it vermilion to the hilt.
The French shall die and France in shame shall sit.
Old greybeard Charles shall never live, I think,
One day but what he'll rage and weep for this.  975
France can be ours in a year if we will;
In Saint-Denis we'll eat and sleep our fill."
The Paynim King makes deep salaam to him.

### 78

And last there comes Chernubles of Munigre;
His unshorn hair hangs trailing to his feet.  980
He for his sport can shoulder if he please
More weight than four stout sumpter-mules can heave.
He dwells in regions wherein, so 'tis believed,
Sun never shines nor springs one blade of wheat,
No rain can fall, no dew is ever seen,  985
There, every stone is black as black can be,
And some folk say it's the abode of fiends.
Chernubles saith: "My sword's girt in the sheath;
In Roncevaux red blood shall dye it deep.
Should Roland cross my path, that doughty chief,  990
And I not smite him, never put faith in me!
To this my blade his Durendal shall yield,
The French shall die, and France be left bereaved."
This said, the whole Twelve Champions are convened;
One hundred thousand stout Saracens they lead.  995
Each one afire with zeal to do great deeds.
Beneath a pine-grove they arm them for the field.

---

977. *Saint Denis:* a town near Paris with a famous abbey, founded by Dago- bert in 626, the burial place of the kings of France.

## 79

Now are the Paynims in Sarsen hauberks dight
Whereof the most with triple mail are lined;
Good Saragossa helms they lace on tight,          1000
Swords of Viana steel gird on their thighs;
Spears of Valence they have, and shields full fine,
Their gonfalons are scarlet, blue, and white.
They leave their mules, their palfreys leave behind,
And mount their steeds; in serried ranks they ride.   1005
Fair was the day, the sun shone clear and bright,
No piece of harness but glittered in the light.
A thousand trumpets ring out for more delight.
Great is the noise; it reaches the French lines.
Quoth Oliver: "I think, companion mine,           1010
We'll need this day with Saracens to fight."
Roland replies: "I hope to God you're right!
Here must we stand to serve on the King's side.
Men for their lords great hardship must abide,
Fierce heat and cold endure in every clime,       1015
Lose for his sake, if need be, skin and hide.
Look to it now! Let each man stoutly smite!
No shameful songs be sung for our despite!
Paynims are wrong, Christians are in the right!
Ill tales of me shall no man tell, say I!"         1020

## 80

Oliver's climbed upon a hilly crest,
Looks to his right along a grassy cleft,
And sees the Paynims and how they ride addressed.
To his companion Roland he calls and says:
"I see from Spain a tumult and a press—            1025
Many bright hauberks, and many a shining helm!
A day of wrath, they'll make it for our French.
Ganelon knew it, false heart and traitor fell;
When to the Emperor he named us for this stead!"
Quoth Roland: "Silence, Count Oliver, my friend!   1030
He is my stepsire, I will have no word said."

## 81

Oliver's climbed a hill above the plain,
Whence he can look on all the land of Spain,
And see how vast the Saracen array;
All those bright helms with gold and jewels gay,    1035
And all those shields, those coats of burnished mail;
And all those lances from which the pennons wave;
Even their squadrons defy all estimate,
He cannot count them, their numbers are so great;
Stout as he is, he's mightily dismayed.            1040
He hastens down as swiftly as he may,
Comes to the French and tells them all his tale.

## 82

Quoth Oliver: "The Paynim strength I've seen;
Never on earth has such a hosting been:

A hundred thousand in van ride under shield                           1045
Their helmets laced, their hauberks all agleam,
Their spears upright, with heads of shining steel.
You'll have such battle as ne'er was fought on field.
My lords of France, God give you strength at need!
Save you stand fast, this field we cannot keep."                     1050
The French all say: "Foul shame it were to flee!
We're yours till death; no man of us will yield."

### 83

Quoth Oliver: "Huge are the Paynim hordes,
And of our French the numbers seem but small.
Companion Roland, I pray you sound your horn,                         1055
That Charles may hear and fetch back all his force."
Roland replies: "Madman were I and more,
And in fair France my fame would suffer scorn.
I'll smite great strokes with Durendal my sword,
I'll dye it red high as the hilt with gore.                           1060
This pass the Paynims reached on a luckless morn;
I swear to you death is their doom therefor."

### 84

"Companion Roland, your Olifant now sound!
King Charles will hear and turn his armies round;
He'll succour us with all his kingly power."                          1065
Roland replies: "May never God allow
That I should cast dishonour on my house
Or on fair France bring any ill renown!
Rather will I with Durendal strike out,
With this good sword, here on my baldrick bound;                      1070
From point to hilt you'll see the blood run down.
Woe worth the Paynims that e'er they made this rout!
I pledge my faith, we'll smite them dead on ground."

### 85

"Companion Roland, your Olifant now blow;
Charles in the passes will hear it as he goes,                        1075
Trust me, the French will all return right so."
"Now God forbid," Roland makes answer wroth,
"That living man should say he saw me go
Blowing of horns for any Paynim foe!
Ne'er shall my kindred be put to such reproach.                       1080
When I shall stand in this great clash of hosts
I'll strike a thousand and then sev'n hundred strokes,
Blood-red the steel of Durendal shall flow.
Stout are the French, they will do battle bold,
These men of Spain shall die and have no hope."                      1085

---

1063. *Olifant:* The word (which is a form of "elephant") means (a) "ivory," (b) "a horn made of ivory," and is used specifically, almost as a proper name, to denote Roland's horn, made of an elephant's tusk, and aborned with gold and jewels about the rim.

## 86

Quoth Oliver: "Herein I see no blame:
I have beheld the Saracens of Spain;
They cover all the mountains and the vales,
They spread across the hillsides and the plains;
Great is the might these foreigners display,          1090
And ours appears a very small array."
"I thirst the more," quoth Roland, "for the fray.
God and His angels forbid it now, I pray,
That e'er by me fair France should be disfamed!
I'd rather die than thus be put to shame;             1095
If the King loves us it's for our valour's sake."

## 87

Roland is fierce and Oliver is wise
And both for valour may bear away the prize.
Once horsed and armed the quarrel to decide,
For dread of death the field they'll never fly.        1100
The counts are brave, their words are stern and high.
Now the false Paynims with wondrous fury ride.
Quoth Oliver: "Look, Roland, they're in sight.
Charles is far off, and these are very nigh;
You would not sound your Olifant for pride;            1105
Had we the Emperor we should have been all right.
To Gate of Spain turn now and lift your eyes,
See for yourself the rear-guard's woeful plight.
Who fights this day will never more see fight."
Roland replies: "Speak no such foul despite!           1110
Curst be the breast whose heart knows cowardice!
Here in our place we'll stand and here abide:
Buffets and blows be ours to take and strike!"

## 88

When Roland sees that battle there must be
Leopard nor lion ne'er grew so fierce as he.           1115
He calls the French, bids Oliver give heed:
"Sir friend and comrade, such words you shall not speak!
When the King gave us the French to serve this need
These twenty thousand he chose to do the deed;
And well he knew not one would flinch or flee.         1120
Men must endure much hardship for their liege,
And bear for him great cold and burning heat,
Suffer sharp wounds and let their bodies bleed.
Smite with your lance and I with my good steel,
My Durendal the Emperor gave to me:                    1125
And if I die, who gets it may agree
That he who bore it, a right good knight was he."

## 89

Then to their side comes the Archbishop Turpin,
Riding his horse and up the hillside spurring.

He calls the French and preaches them a sermon:                              1130
"Barons, my lords, Charles picked us for this purpose;
We must be ready to die in our King's service.
Christendom needs you, so help us to preserve it.
Battle you'll have, of that you may be certain,
Here come the Paynims—your own eyes have observed them.   1135
Now beat your breasts and ask God for His mercy:
I will absolve you and set your souls in surety.
If you should die, blest martyrdom's your guerdon;
You'll sit on high in Paradise eternal."
The French alight and all kneel down in worship;            1140
God's shrift and blessing the Archbishop conferreth,
And for their penance he bids them all strike firmly.

### 90

The French rise up and on their feet stand close;
All of their sins are shriven and made whole,
And the Archbishop God's blessing has bestowed.           1145
Then on swift steeds they leap to saddle-bow.
Armed with the arms prescribed by knightly code;
All are now ready into the field to go.
Count Roland said to Oliver right so:
"Sir my companion, too true the word you spoke,             1150
That all of us by Ganelon were sold.
He's ta'en his wage of wealth and goods and gold.
The Emperor's vengeance I think will not be slow!
Marsile the King has bargained for our bones:
He'll need the sword to fetch his purchase home."           1155

### 91

Through Gate of Spain Roland goes riding past
On Veillantif, his swiftly-running barb;
Well it becomes him to go equipped in arms,
Bravely he goes, and tosses up his lance,
High in the sky he lifts the lancehead far,                 1160
A milk-white pennon is fixed above the shaft
Whose falling fringes whip his hands on the haft.
Nobly he bears him, with open face he laughs;
And his companion behind him follows hard;
The Frenchmen all acclaim him their strong guard.         1165
On Saracens he throws a haughty glance
But meek and mild looks on the men of France,
To whom he speaks out of a courteous heart:
"Now, my lord barons, at walking pace—advance!
Looking for trouble these Paynims ride at large—            1170
A fine rich booty we'll have ere this day's past;
Never French king beheld the like by half."
E'en as he speaks, their battles join and charge.

### 92

Quoth Oliver: "I have no more to say:
To sound your horn for help you would not deign,            1175

So here you are, you've not got Charlemayn;
Little he knows, brave heart! he's not to blame.
Nor those with him, nowise in fault are they.
Ride forward then and do the best you may!
Barons my lords, hold firm amid the fray!                1180
Now for God's sake be resolute, I pray,
To strike hard blows, to give them and to take.
King Carlon's war-cry forget not to proclaim!"
A mighty shout the Frenchmen give straightway;
Whoso had heard the cry "Mountjoy" they raise            1185
He would remember its valiance all his days.
They charge—Lord God, was ever sight so brave?
They spur their steeds to make the greater haste,
They fall afighting—there is no other way—
The Saracens join battle undismayed;                     1190
Paynims and Franks are fighting face to face.

### 93

Now Adelroth, (he was King Marsile's nephew),
Before the host comes first of all his fellows;
With evil words the French he thus addresses:
"Villainous Franks, with us you have to reckon!          1195
You've been betrayed by him that should protect you,
Your king lacked wit who in the passes left you.
Fair France will lose her honour in this venture;
From Carlon's body the right arm will be severed."
When Roland hears him, God! but his rage is reckless!    1200
He spurs his horse, gives full rein to his mettle,
His blow he launches with all his mightiest effort;
The shield he shatters, and the hauberk he rendeth,
He splits the breast and batters in the breast bone,
Through the man's back drives out the backbone bended,   1205
And soul and all forth on the spear-point fetches;
Clean through he thrusts him, forth of the saddle wrenching,
And flings him dead a lance-length from his destrier;
Into two pieces he has broken his neckbone.
No less for that he speaks to him and tells him:         1210
"Out on thee, churl! no lack-wit is the Emperor,
He is none such, nor loved he treason ever;
Right well he did who in the passes left us,
Neither shall France lose honour by this venture.
First blood to us! Go to it, gallant Frenchmen!          1215
Right's on our side, and wrong is with these wretches!"

### 94

A duke was there, he was named Falsaron,
Brother was he to King Marsilion,

---

1185. *Mountjoy:* A mountjoy (mont-joie) was (according to Littré) a mound or cairn of stones set up to mark the site of a victory. The old French war cry, "Montjoie St.-Denis!" or, briefly, "Montjoie!" derived from the cairn set up at St.-Denis on the site of the saint's martyrdom (his spiritual victory). Others derive "Montjoie" from the Hill of Rama, called "Mons Gaudii," from which pilgrims obtained their first view of Jerusalem.

Abiram's land and Dathan's did he own;
Under the sky was no worse villain known;                           1220
Between the eyes his brow was broad of bone,
A full half-foot is measured, I suppose.
His nephew's death he bitterly bemoans;
Forth of the press he gallops out alone,
The Paynim war-cry he utters as he goes,                            1225
And on the French an evil taunt bestows:
"Fair France this day shall find her honour flown!"
Oliver's heard him, great wrath within him grows,
Into his horse he strikes his spurs of gold,
Right baronly he rides to smite the foe.                            1230
He breaks the shield, he cleaves the hauberk close,
Clean through his breast drives lance and pennon both,
A spear's length flings him dead from the saddle-bow;
Looks down and sees the infidel lie low
And thus upbraids him in a right haughty tone:                      1235
"Churl, for your threats I do not care a groat!
French lords, strike on! we'll have them all o'erthrown."
King Carlon's war-cry, "Mountjoy!" he shouts full bold.

### 95

A king was there, his name was Corsablis,
From a far land he came, from Barbary;                              1240
The Saracens he calls, and thus he speaks:
"Well are we placed this field of arms to keep;
For of these Franks the number is but weak,
And we may well despise the few we see.
Charles cannot come to help them in their need,                    1245
This is the day their deaths are all decreed!"
Archbishop Turpin has listened to his speech,
And hates him worse than any man that breathes.
His golden spurs he strikes into his steed,
And rides against him right valiant for the deed.                  1250
He breaks the buckler, he's split the hauberk's steel,
Into his breast driven the lance head deep,
He spits him through, on high his body heaves,
And hurls him dead a spear's length o'er the lea.
Earthward he looks and sees him at his feet,                       1255
But yet to chide him he none the less proceeds:
"Vile infidel, you lied between your teeth!
Charles my good lord to help us will not cease,
Nor have our French the least desire to flee.
These friends of yours stock-still we're like to leave;            1260
Here's news for you—you'll die, and there you'll be.
Frenchmen, strike home! forget not your high breed!
This first good stroke is ours, God's gramercy!"
He shouts "Mountjoy!" to hearten all the field.

### 96

And Gerin strikes Malprimis of Brigale;                            1265
No penny-piece the stubborn shield avails;
The crystal boss he splinters all in twain,
That half the buckler falls down upon the plain:

Through to the flesh he cleaves the hauberk-mail,
Through to the heart he drives the good spear straight;    1270
The paynim falls flat down with all his weight.
Then Satan comes and hales his soul away.


### 97

Gerier his friend on the Emir runs in,
Shatters the shield and bursts the byrny-rings,
Clean through the guts the trusty spear he swings,    1275
Thrusts it well in, then out at back with it;
A whole spear's length on field the body flings:
Quoth Oliver: "We're doing well with this!"


### 98

Samson the Duke on the Almanzor runs:
Through gilded shield and painted flowers he thrusts;    1280
Nought for defence avails the hauberk tough,
He splits his heart, his liver, and his lung,
And strikes him dead, weep any or weep none.
Cries the Archbishop: "This feat was knightly done!"


### 99

And Anseïs gives rein to his good steed,    1285
He runs on Turgis of Tortelose at speed;
Under the boss of gold he cleaves the shield,
And of the hauberk the double mail unseams,
Into his body strikes home the head of steel,
Through to his back he drives the point out clean,    1290
A full spear's length he flings him dead on field.
Quoth Roland: "Lo! that was a valiant feat!"


### 100

And Engelier the Gascon of Bordeaux
Spurs his good steed, slacks rein and lets him go;
With Escrimiz, Valterna's lord, he's closed,    1295
Off from his neck the splintered buckler broke.
The hauberk's ventail he's shattered with the stroke.
He splits his throat between the collar-bones,
A full spear's length dead from the saddle throws;
Then says to him: "The devil take thy soul!"    1300


### 101

And Othon strikes a Paynim, Estorgant,
Full in mid-chief he smites the shield point-blank,
So that the white splits and the scarlet cracks;
The skirt of mail he's riven through and smashed,
Into his body the cleaving spear he rams;    1305
From his swift steed he hurls him dead on land,
"And now," says he, "find comfort if you can!"


### 102

Then Berenger drives at Estramarin,
He cleaves the shield, and the good hauberk splits,
On his stout spear the trunk of him he spits    1310

And flings him dead 'mid thousand Sarrasins.
Of the Twelve Peers ten are already killed,
Two and no more are left of them who live;
These are Chernubles and the Count Margaris.

### 103

Now Margaris is a right valiant peer,                          1315
Buxom and strong, nimble and fleet and fierce.
He spurs his horse to strike at Olivere;
He splits the shield, the golden boss he sheers,
Along his ribs the glancing spear-point veers,
But by God's grace his body is not pierced;                    1320
Nor is he thrown, though the shock breaks the spear.
Past him the Paynim is borne in full career,
Rallying his men he sounds his bugle clear.

### 104

Great is the battle and crowded the mellay,
Nor does Count Roland stint of his strokes this day;           1325
While the shaft holds he wields his spear amain—
Fifteen great blows ere it splinters and breaks.
Then his bare brand, his Durendal, he takes;
Against Chernubles he spurs his steed in haste,
Splits through the helm with carbuncles ablaze,               1330
Through the steel coif, and through scalp and through brain
'Twixt the two eyes he cleaves him through the face;
Through the bright byrny close-set with rings of mail,
Right through the body, through the fork and the reins,
Down through the saddle with its beaten gold plates,          1335
Through to the horse he drives the cleaving blade,
Seeking no joint through the chine carves his way,
Flings horse and man dead on the grassy plain.
"Foul befall, felon, that e'er you sought this fray!
Mahound," quoth he, "shall never bring you aid.               1340
Villains like you seek victory in vain."

### 105

The County Roland throughout the field goes riding;
With Durendal, good sword, he stabs and slices,
The toll he takes of Saracens is frightful.
Would you had seen him, dead man on dead man piling,          1345
Seen the bright blood about his pathway lying!
Bloody his hauberk and both his arms with fighting,
His good horse bloody from crest to withers likewise;
Oliver too doth never cease from striking,
And the Twelve Peers are not a whit behindhand,               1350
And all the French are hammering and smiting;
The Paynims fall, some dead and others dying.
Quoth the Archbishop: "Right blessèd be our knighthood";
He shouts "Mountjoy!" war-cry of Charles the mighty.

1312. *the Twelve Peers:* i.e., the Saracen Peers enumerated in ll. 882–994.

### 106

And Oliver goes riding through the press;                    1355
His spear is broken, only the shaft is left.
Against a Paynim, Malun, he rides addrest,
Smashes the shield with flowers and gold bedecked,
Both of his eyes he smites out of his head,
So that his brains around his feet are spread,              1360
And flings the corpse amid sev'n hundred dead.
Turgis he's slain, and slain Esturgot next,
Till to the grips the spear-shaft splits in shreds.
Roland cries out: "What are you doing, friend?
I'd give no groat for sticks in such a stead!               1365
Here iron avails, and steel and nothing else.
Where is your sword that Hauteclaire is y-clept,
With its gold hilts and pummel crystal-gemmed?"
"I've had no time to draw," Oliver said,
"I've been so busy with striking right and left."           1370

### 107

Dan Oliver has drawn his goodly brand,
As his friend Roland so urgently demands;
Now will he prove him a stout knight of his hands!
He smites a Paynim, Justin of Val Ferrat;
Clean through the middle the skull of him he cracks,        1375
The saffron byrny splits, and his breast and back,
And saddle, brave with gems and golden bands,
And through the spine the horse in sunder hacks,
And dead on field flings all before him flat.
"I'll call you brother," quoth Roland, "after that!        1380
'Tis for such strokes our Emperor loves a man."
The shout "Mountjoy!" goes up on every hand.

### 108

Gerin the Count bestrides his steed Sorel,
Gerier his comrade on Passécerf is set;
Eagerly both loose rein and spur ahead                      1385
And go to strike a Paynim, Timozel,
One on the shield, the other on the chest.
Both spears at once are broken in his breast,
Flat in the fallow straightway they fling him dead—
I do not know, I never have heard tell,                     1390
Which of the two was the more swift and snell.
[And Engelier, Knight of Bordeaux, he next
Slew Esprevere, that son was to Burel.]
Archbishop Turpin has o'erthrown Siglorel,
The sorcerer, who'd once been down to Hell,                 1395

---

1367. *y-clept*: named.
1371. *Dan* (Dominus): lord.
1376. *saffron*: burnished with a yellow
varnish made from bismuth oxide.

1391. *snell*: speedy.
1392–1393. These two lines have been
telescoped in the text, and are thus
emended by most editors.

With Jupiter for guide, by magic spells.
Quoth Turpin then: "Ear-marked was he for death!"
Roland replies: "The churl has made an end.
Oliver, brother, such strokes delight me well!"

### 109

Fiercer and still more fierce the battle grows;                    1400
Both French and Paynims deal wondrous heavy strokes,
Some in attacking, and some in parrying blows.
How many spears are bloodied there and broke!
What gonfalons, what banners rent and strown!
How many French in flower of youth laid low,                      1405
Whom wives and mothers shall never more behold,
Nor those of France who wait them on the road!
King Charlemayn must weep and wail for woe;
What help in that? he cannot save his folk.
Ill did Count Guènes serve Carlon, when he rode                   1410
To Saragossa and all his people sold;
Thereby he lost life and limbs of his own
When at Aix after they judged him to the rope,
And of his kin thirty were hanged also,
Who ne'er had thought such death should be their dole.            1415

### 110

Fierce is the battle and wondrous grim the fight.
Both Oliver and Roland boldly smite,
Thousands of strokes the stout Archbishop strikes,
The whole Twelve Peers are not a whit behind,
And the French ranks lay on with all their might.                 1420
Heaped by the hundred thousands of Paynims lie,
None can escape unless he turns and flies,
Will he or nill he, there must he leave his life.
There France must lose the noblest of her knights,
They'll see no more their kindred and their sires,                1425
Nor Charles, who scans the pass with anxious eyes.
Throughout all France terrific tempests rise,
Thunder is heard, the stormy winds blow high,
Unmeasured rain and hail fall from the sky,
While thick and fast flashes the levin bright,                    1430
And true it is the earth quakes far and wide.
Far as from Saintes to Michael-of-the-Tide,
From Besançon to Wissant Port, you'd find
There's not a house but the walls crack and rive.
Right at high noon a darkness falls like night,                   1435
Save for the lightning there's not a gleam of light;
None that beholds it but is dismayed for fright,
And many say: "This is the latter time,
The world is ending, and the Great Doom is nigh."

---

1396. *Jupiter:* like Apollo, the classical Jove has been demoted to the status of demon.

They speak not true, they cannot read the signs: 1440
'Tis Roland's death calls forth this mighty cry.

### 111

The French have fought with valour and success;
By scores and thousands lie Paynim corpses spread,
Of hundred thousand scarce two will fight again.
Quoth the Archbishop: "Right valiant are our men, 1445
The like of these hath no lord under heav'n.
Thus it is written in the Gestes of the French:
Our Emperor's power was never rivalled yet."
They search the field for their maimed and their dead,
With grief and sorrow the eyes of them are wet, 1450
With love and pity for their kindred and friends.
Now falls upon them Marsile with all his strength.

### 112

The King Marsile comes riding up a gorge
With all his army about him in great force;
He has assembled twenty huge battle-hordes.
Such flash of helms with gems and gold adorned! 1455
Such shields, such byrnies with burnished saffron wrought!
Sev'n hundred trumpets are sounding the assault;
Through all the country the noise of them goes forth.
"Brother," quoth Roland, "friend Oliver, sweet lord, 1460
It is our death false Ganelon has sworn;
The treason's plain, it can be hid no more;
A right great vengeance the Emperor will let fall.
But we must bide a fearful pass of war.
No man has ever beheld the like before. 1465
I shall lay on with Durendal my sword,
You, comrade, wield the great Hauteclaire of yours.
In lands how many have we those weapons borne!
Battles how many victoriously fought!
Ne'er shall base ballad be sung of them in hall!" 1470

### 113

Marsile beholds his slaughtered chivalry.
He bids his trumpets and horns sound instantly
And then sets forward with his great company.
Then first rides out a Saracen, Abisme,
In all that host was none more vile than he, 1475
With evil vice and crimes he's dyed full deep,
In Mary's Child, God's Son, he's no belief,
And black he is as melted pitch to see.
Better he loves murder and treachery
Than all the gold that is in Galicie 1480
None ever saw him in mirth or jollity;

---

1447. *the Gestes of the French:* the
chronicle, to which the poet from time
to time refers, and from which he claims
to derive his information.

But bold he is and rash to a degree,
And for that reason he's loved by King Marsile.
He bears a dragon to rally his meinie.
The good Archbishop observes him, much displeased,        1485
He'd like to hit him on sight, that's how he feels,
And to himself he says quite quietly:
"This Sarsen looks right heretic to me.
'Twere best by far to go and kill the beast;
I never loved cowards nor coward deeds."        1490

### 114

Th'Archbishop opens the battle up anew;
He rides a charger that from Grossayle he took
(That was a king in Denmark, whom he slew).
A steed he is swiftly-running and smooth,
Flat in the knee and hollow in the hoof,        1495
Short in the thigh and ample in the croup,
Long in the flank and the back well set up,
White of his tail and yellow of his plume,
Small of his ears and his head tawny-hued;
Here is a horse no courser could outdo.        1500
Him the Archbishop, of his valour right good,
Spurs on Abisme, and none shall stay his mood.
He rides to strike him on his target of proof
Wondrous with topaz and amethyst to boot,
With carbuncle ablaze, and beryl blue        1505
(Emir Galafe gave it him for a boon
Whom in Val Metas a devil gave it to.)
Turpin lays on, nor spares; I tell you true,
After he hit it it was not worth a sou!
From flank to flank he spits his body through,        1510
And flings him dead wherever he finds room.
The French all cry: "A valiant blow and shrewd!
Right strong to save is our Archbishop's crook!"

### 115

Now can the French count up the Paynim might
They see it filling the plains from side to side.        1515
They urge on Roland and Oliver likewise
And the Twelve Peers to flee for all their lives;
To whom straightway the Prelate speaks his mind:
"Barons, my lords, these shameful thoughts put by;
By God I charge you, hold fast and do not fly,        1520
Lest brave men sing ill songs in your despite.
Better it were to perish in the fight.
Soon, very soon, we all are marked to die,
None of us here will see to-morrow's light;
One thing there is I promise you outright:        1525
To you stand open the gates of Paradise,
There with the holy sweet Innocents to bide."

1484. *meinie:* household.

His words so fill them with courage and delight
There's none among them but shouts "Mountjoy" on high.

### 116

A Saracen, of Saragossa Town                                    1530
Was there, the lord of half that city round—
Climborin namely, that traitor false and foul
Which took the oath of Ganelon the Count
And then for friendship kissed him upon the mouth
And with his helm and carbuncle endowed;                       1535
Our Fatherland he swore he'd disrenown,
And from the Emperor would snatch away the crown.
Now he comes riding on Barbëmouche his mount—
Fleeter was never swallow nor falcon found—
Slacks rein, spurs hard its mettle to arouse,                  1540
On Engelier the Gascon forward bounds.
Buckler nor byrny avails against him now,
Into the midriff lance-point and pennon plough,
From breast to back the shaft runs through and out,
A whole spear's length he hurls him dead on ground.            1545
"Fit for destruction is all this gear!" he shouts;
"Paynims, strike hard! carve your way through the rout!"
"God!" say the French, "one of our best is down!"

### 117

Count Roland calls to Oliver his friend:
"Fair sir, companion, see, Engelier is dead;                   1550
No better man had we for knightliness."
The Count replies: "God give me fair revenge!"
In his steed's flanks the golden spurs he sets,
He grasps Hauteclaire, whose steel is all dyed red,
He deals the Paynim a mighty stroke and dread,                 1555
Twists out the blade, down falls the Saracen;
The Adversary bears off his soul to Hell.
Then he goes on, slays Duke Alfayen next,
From Escababa he hews away the head,
And seven Arabs unhorses then pell-mell:                       1560
That lot at least will never fight again.
"My friend is angry," the County Roland said:
"Fighter for fighter he matches me right well;
'Tis for such strokes King Carlon loves us best!"
Aloud he cries: "Strike on, my valiant men!"                   1565

### 118

Elsewhere, behold a Paynim, Valdabron,
Was godfather to King Marsilion;
He owns a navy four hundred dromonds strong,
And to his service no seaman but is bond.
He captured Salem by fraud in times bygone,                    1570

---

1557. *the Adversary*: Satan.
1568. *dromond(s)*: a large and very swift medieval sailing ship, used both for war and commerce.

And sacked the Temple of good King Solomon,
Murdering there the Patriarch by the font.
He took the oath of County Ganelon,
And sword and mangons gave him as pledge thereon.
He rides a horse that he calls Gramimond,                           1575
Never of speed was peregrine more prompt.
With the sharp spur he urges it headlong;
The great Duke Samson straightway he falls upon.
He splits the shield, he bursts the habergeon,
Drives through his body spear-head and gonfalon,                    1580
Flings him from saddle a full spear's length along:
"Paynims!" he cries, "we'll beat them yet! Lay on!"
"God!" say the French, "there's a brave baron gone!"


                              119

When the Count Roland sees Samson thus laid low
Well may you guess how he is grieved of soul.                       1585
He spurs his horse and speeds to smite the foe
With Durendal, more worth than finest gold.
By might and main the Baron deals the stroke
Full on the helm that is all gemmed with gold;
The skull he splits, byrny and breast are broke,                    1590
Cloven the saddle, that is all gemmed with gold;
Through the beast's back deep down the weapon goes;
Like it or leave it, he has destroyed them both.
The Paynims say: "This is a bitter blow!"
"I love you not," quoth Roland, "by my troth;                       1595
Yours is the outrage, yours is the lying boast!"


                              120

An African there was of Afric, too,
Was called Malquiant, the son of King Malcude;
Harnessed he is in gold from head to foot,
None in the sun so glitters to the view,                            1600
He rides a horse that he calls Saut-Perdu;
No steed could rival the swiftness of its hoofs.
He strikes Anseïs in mid-shield square and true,
He shears away the scarlet and the blue,
Rips the mailed skirt of the hauberk of proof,                     1605
Into the body drives the steel and the wood.
The Count falls dead, his days have met their doom.
The French all say: "Brave lord, alack for you!"


                              121

Archbishop Turpin goes riding through the field;
Ne'er was mass sung by any tonsured priest                          1610
That of his body could do such valiant deeds!
He hails the Paynim: "God send the worst to thee!
Thou hast slain one for whom my whole heart grieves."
Into a gallop he urges his good steed,
He strikes him hard on his Toledo shield,                           1615
And lays him dead upon the grassy green.

### 122

There was a Paynim, and Grandoyne was he called,
King Capuel's son, from Cappadocia's shores,
Mounted on Marmor, for so he names his horse,
Swifter of speed than any bird that soars.                           1620
He slacks the rein and he goes spurring forth,
And runs to strike Gerin with all his force.
From off his neck he splits the red shield shorn,
From off his body he rips the byrny torn,
Into his heart the pennon blue he's borne,                          1625
And down he flings him dead on a rocky tor.
Gerier his comrade he smites down afterward,
Berenger next, Guy of St Antoine fall;
And then he strikes the mighty duke Astorge,
(Envers-on-Rhône and Valence called him lord),                      1630
And lays him dead; for joy the Paynims roar;
The French all say: "What loss we have to mourn!"

### 123

The County Roland grips fast his blood-red blade;
Well has he heard how the French are dismayed;
His heart grieves so, 'tis like to split in twain.                  1635
In hails the Paynim: "God send thee all His plagues!
Thou has slain one for whom I'll make thee pay!"
He spurs his horse that gladly runs apace;
Let win who may, they're at it, face to face.

### 124

The Prince Grandoyne was a good knight and gallant,                 1640
Strong of his hands and valorous in battle;
Athwart him now comes Roland the great captain:
He'd never met him, but he knew him instanter.
By his proud aspect, and by his noble stature,
His haughty looks, and his bearing and manner.                      1645
He cannot help it, a mortal fear unmans him;
Fain would he fly, but what's the good? he cannot.
The Count assails him with such ferocious valour
That to the nasal the whole helmet is shattered,
Cloven the nose and the teeth and the palate,                       1650
The jaz'rain hauberk and the breastbone and backbone,
Both silver bows from off the golden saddle;
Horseman and horse clean asunder he slashes,
Lifeless he leaves them and the pieces past patching.
The men of Spain fall a-wailing for sadness:                        1655
The French all cry: "What strokes! and what a champion!"

### 125

Fierce is the battle and marvellous and great.
The Frenchmen ply their burnished spears amain.
There had you seen how many men in pain,
How many wounded and bleeding there and slain!                      1660

---

1651. *jazerain:* a kind of chain mail made in Algiers.

Heaped up pell-mell they lie, on back or face.
The Saracens cannot endure the strain;
Will they or nill they they flee across the plain,
And the French forces with all their might give chase.

### 126

Wondrous the battle, and it grows faster yet; 1665
The French fight on with rage and fury fell,
They lop off wrists, hew ribs and spines to shreds,
They cleave the harness through to the living flesh;
On the green ground the blood runs clear and red.
[The Paynims say: "We cannot stand the stress,] 1670
French Fatherland, be curst of Máhomet!
Your sons are bravest of all the sons of men."
There's none of them but cries: "Marsile to help!
Ride, ride, O King, for we are hard bested."

### 127

Roland the Count calls out to Olivere: 1675
"Fair sir, companion, confess that for this gear
Our lord Archbishop quits him like any peer;
Earth cannot match him beneath the heavens' sphere,
Well does he know to handle lance and spear."
The Count replies: "Let's aid him now and here!" 1680
At this the French lay on the lustier,
Hard are their strokes, the fight is very fierce,
And for the Christians the losses are severe.
Who then had seen Roland and Olivere
Smite with their swords and through all the press pierce! 1685
And the Archbishop goes thrusting with his spear.
Of those they slew the numbers are writ clear
In many charters and tales of chroniclers:
More than four thousand as in the Geste appears.
Four great assaults they've borne with right good cheer; 1690
Then comes a fifth, doleful and dread and drear.
All the French knighthood has fallen in career;
Sixty alone by God's grace persevere;
These ere they die will sell their bodies dear.

### 128

When County Roland sees all his brave men down, 1695
To Oliver his friend he cries aloud:
"For God's sake, comrade, fair sir, what think you now?
See what good knights lie here upon the ground!
Well may we pity this fair sweet France of ours,
Thus left so barren of all her knighthood's flower. 1700
Why aren't you here, O friend and Emperour?
Oliver, brother, what way is to be found?
How send him news of what is come about?"
Oliver said: "And how should I know how?
I'd rather die than we should lose renown." 1705

### 129

"I'll sound," quoth Roland, "my Olifant straightway;
When Carlon hears, passing through Gate of Spain,
I pledge my word, the French will turn again."
Quoth Oliver: "It would be foul disdain,
And to your kindred the reproach would be great:       1710
All their lives long they'd not live down the shame.
When I desired you, why then you said me nay;
If now you do it, of men you'll get no praise.
Blow if you will—such conduct is not brave.
Nay, but how deep in blood your arms are bathed!"       1715
The Count replies: "I've struck good blows this day."

### 130

Said Roland then: "Full grievous is this fight.
I'll sound my horn, and Charles will hear the cry."
Quoth Oliver: " 'Twould ill beseem a knight.
I asked you, comrade, and you refused, for pride.       1720
Had Charles been here, then all would have gone right;
He's not to blame, nor the men at his side.
Now by my beard (quoth he) if e'er mine eyes
Again behold my sister Aude the bright,
Between her arms never you think to lie."       1725

### 131

Quoth Roland: "Why so angry with me, friend?"
And he: "Companion, you got us in this mess.
There is wise valour, and there is recklessness:
Prudence is worth more than fool hardiness.
Through your o'erweening you have destroyed the French;   1730
Ne'er shall we do service to Charles again.
Had you but given some heed to what I said,
My lord had come, the battle had gone well,
And King Marsile had been captured or dead.
Your prowess, Roland, is a curse on our heads.       1735
No more from us will Charlemayn have help,
Whose like till Doomsday shall not be seen of men.
Now you will die, and fair France will be shent;
Our loyal friendship is here brought to an end;
A bitter parting we'll have ere this sun set."       1740

### 132

When the Archbishop thus hears them in dispute,
With his gold spurs he pricks his steed anew,
Draws near to them and utters this rebuke:
"Lord Oliver, and you, Lord Roland, too,
Let's have no quarrel, o'God's name, 'twixt you two.       1745
It will not save us to sound the horn, that's true;
Nevertheless, 'twere better so to do.

1738. *shent*: put to shame.

Let the king come; his vengeance will be rude;
None shall to Spain ride home with merry news.
After, our French will light them down on foot,                    1750
Seek out our bodies and limbs in sunder hewn,
Lay us on biers borne upon sumpter-mules,
And weep for us with grief right pitiful;
In the church-close we shall have burial due,
And not be food for dogs and swine and wolves."                    1755
Quoth Roland, "Sir, your words are right and good."

### 133

Roland has set Olifant to his lips,
Firmly he holds it and blows it with a will.
High are the mountains, the blast is long and shrill,
Thirty great leagues the sound went echoing.                       1760
King Carlon heard it and all who rode with him.
"Lo, now, our men are fighting," quoth the King.
Guènes retorts: "If any man said this
Except yourself, it were a lie, methinks."

### 134

The County Roland with pain and anguish winds                      1765
His Olifant, and blows with all his might.
Blood from his mouth comes spurting scarlet-bright
He's burst the veins of his temples outright.
From hand and horn the call goes shrilling high:
King Carlon hears it who through the passes rides,                 1770
Duke Naimon hears, and all the French beside.
Quoth Charles: "I hear the horn of Roland cry!
He'd never sound it but in the thick of fight."
"There is no battle," Count Ganelon replies;
"You're growing old, your hair is sere and white,                  1775
When you speak thus, you're talking like a child.
Full well you know Roland's o'erweening pride;
'Tis strange that God endures him so long time!
Took he not Noples against your orders quite?
The Paynims made a sally from inside,                              1780
And there gave battle to Roland the great knight;
So he swilled down the field—a brave device
To keep the bloodstains from coming to your eyes!
For one small hare he'll blow from morn till night;
Now to the Peers he's showing-off in style.                       1785
Who dare attack him? No man beneath the sky!
Ride on, ride on! Why loiter here the while?
Our Fathers' land lies distant many a mile."

### 135

Count Roland's mouth with running blood is red;
He's burst asunder the temples of his head;                        1790
He sounds his horn in anguish and distress.
King Carlon hears, and so do all the French.

Then said the King: "This horn is long of breath."
" 'Tis blown," quoth Naimon, "with all a brave man's strength;
Battle there is, and that I know full well.                                    1795
He that would stay you is but a traitor fell.
To arms! let sound your battle-cry to heav'n!
Make haste to bring your gallant household help!
You hear how Roland makes desperate lament!"

### 136

The Emperor Charles lets sound his horns aloft.                    1800
The French light down and arm themselves anon
With helm and hauberk and gilded swords girt on;
Goodly their shields, their lances stiff and strong,
Scarlet and white and blue the gonfalons.
Straightway to horse the warrior lords have got;              1805
Swift through the passes they spur and never stop.
Each unto other they speak and make response:
"Might we reach Roland ere he were dead and gone,
We'ld strike good strokes beside him in the throng."
What use is that? They have delayed too long.                    1810

### 137

Vespers draws on and shining is the day;
Against the sun glitters their armed array,
Hauberk and helm flash back a mighty blaze,
So many shields their painted flowers display,
Such store of spears with gilded pennons gay!                   1815
The Emperor rides right wrathful on his way.
And all the French in anger and dismay;
There is not one but weeps for very rage;
For Roland's sake they're grievously afraid.
The King arrests Count Ganelon straightway;                    1820
He's turned him over to the cooks in his train;
The master-cook he calls, Besgun by name:
"Guard me him well, as fits a man so base,
For all my house this villain has betrayed!"
Besgun takes charge, with five-score kitchen knaves,      1825
The best and worst that serve in that estate.
They pluck the beard from off his chin and face,
With four sound thumps each gives him a good baste,
With sticks and faggots they pound him and they paste,
And round his neck they fasten a strong chain,                 1830
Right well they chain him like a bear in a cage;
Now on a pack-horse they've hoisted him in shame;
Till Carlon want him 'tis they will keep him safe.

### 138

Huge are the hills and shadowy and high,
Deep in the vales the living streams run by.                       1835
The trumpets sound before them and behind,
All with one voice to Olifant reply.

In wrath of heart the Emperor Carlon rides,
And all the French in sorrow and in ire;
There's none but grieves and weeps from out his eyes;      1840
They all pray God to safeguard Roland's life
Till they may come to battle by his side;
Once they are with him they'll make it a great fight.
What use is that? their prayers are empty quite,
Too long they've lingered, they cannot come in time.      1845

### 139

King Charlemayn rides on in anger grim,
Over his byrny flows the white beard of him;
All the French barons beside him spur full swift;
There's none of them but is with fury filled
Not to be aiding Roland the Paladin      1850
Now that he's fighting the Spanish Sarrasins.
He's hurt so sore, I fear he cannot live.
God! and what men, those sixty with him still!
Better had never nor captain nor yet king.

### 140

Roland surveys the mountains and the fells;      1855
How many French he sees there lying dead!
Like a good knight he makes them this lament:
"Barons, my lords, may God of His largesse
Bring all your souls to Paradise the blest,
Amid bright flowers to make their hallowed beds!      1860
I never saw braver or truer men.
So long you served me unceasingly and well,
So many lands conquered for Carlon's realm!
The Emperor bred you alas! to what sad end!
O dearest land, fair nursery of the French,      1865
By what hard hap art thou this day bereft!
Barons of France, for me you go to death,
Nought can I give you of safeguard or defence;
Now aid you God, who ne'er failed any yet!
Oliver, brother, you shall not lack my help.      1870
Though none should slay me I'll die of grief no less;
Sweet sir, companion, let's go and fight afresh!"

### 141

The County Roland returns into the field
And like a warrior his Durendal he wields;
Faldron de Puy through the midriff he cleaves      1875
With four-and-twenty besides, of great esteem.
Never on vengeance was any man so keen.
E'en as the deer before the deerhound flees
So before Roland the Paynims show their heels.
Quoth the Archbishop: "Well done, well done indeed!      1880
Valour like this becomes a knight of breed
That bears his arms and sits a goodly steed;

Forward and fierce in battle should he be,
Else he's not worth a single penny-piece.
Best he turn monk in monastery meek                          1885
And for our sins pray daily on his knees."
Quoth Roland: "Strike, spare none of them," saith he.
At this the French renew the fight with speed;
Therein the Christians endure great loss and grief.

### 142

When it is known no prisoners will be made                   1890
Men fight back fiercely, and stubborn is the fray;
Therefore the French grow very lions for rage.
Here comes Marsile, e'en as a baron brave,
Riding a horse, and Gaignun is its name.
Full upon Bevon he rides and spurs amain,                    1895
That held all Beaune and Dijon for domain.
The shield he shatters, and the hauberk he breaks,
And lays him dead, he need not strike again.
And Ivon next and Ivor too, his mate,
And Gerard too of Roussillon he slays.                       1900
Roland the Count, who is not far away,
Cries to the Paynim: "God damn your soul, I say!
These my companions by treason you have slain!
Ere we go hence a bitter price you'll pay,
And you shall learn the name of my good blade!"              1905
He rides to strike him, e'en as a baron brave;
From his sword-arm he shears the hand away.
And Jurfaret the Fair he next waylays,
Marsilion's son, and slices off his pate.
The Paynims cry: "Mahound! Mahound to aid!                   1910
Venge us on Carlon, all you gods of our faith!
Into our land he's sent this evil race!
Come life come death they'll never quit the place."
Then one to other cries: "Fly then! fly in haste!"
An hundred thousand have fled the field straightway;         1915
They'll not return, call after them who may.

### 143

What help is that? Marsile has taken flight,
Yet there remains his uncle Marganice,
That governs Carthage, Alfrere and Garamile,
And Éthiope, a land accursed and vile.                       1920
In his command are all the Negro tribes;
Thick are their noses, their ears are very wide;
Full fifty thousand are gathered in their lines,
Boldly and fast and furiously they ride,
Yelling aloud the Paynim battle-cry.                         1925
Then Roland said: "Here are we doomed to die;
Full well, I know we cannot long survive.
Fail not for shame, right dear to sell your lives.
Lift up, my lords, your burnished blades and fight!

Come life, come death, the foe shall pay the price,    1930
Lest we should bring fair France into despite!
When on this field Carlon my lord sets eyes
He'll see what toll we've taken of their might:
Fifteen dead Paynims for each of us he'll find;
Nor fail to bless us for this our great emprise."    1935

### 144

When Roland looks on these accursed tribesmen—
As black as ink from head to foot their hides are,
With nothing white about them but their grinders—
Then said the Count: " 'Tis true beyond denial,
Right well I know it, this day shall death betide us.    1940
I'll to the throng; Frenchmen, fight on beside me!"
Quoth Oliver: "The devil take the hindmost!"
The French hear this and once more fall a-fighting.

### 145

When Paynims see how few the French are grown
They plume themselves, puffed up with pride and hope:    1945
"Now to the Emperor," they say, "his crimes come home!"
Marganice comes, riding a sorrel colt;
He spurs him hard with rowels all of gold,
And from behind deals Oliver a blow;
Deep in his back the burnished mail is broke,    1950
That the spear's point stands forth at his breast bone.
He saith to him: "You've suffered a sore stroke;
Charlemayn sent you to the pass for your woe;
Foul wrong he did us, 'tis good he lose his boast:
I've well requited our loss on you alone."    1955

### 146

Oliver feels that he is hurt to death;
He grasps his sword Hauteclaire the keen of edge,
Smites Marganice on his high golden helm,
Shearing away the flowers and crystal gems,
Down to the teeth clean splits him through the head,    1960
Shakes loose the blade and flings him down and dead;
Then saith: "Foul fall you, accursèd Paynim wretch!
Charles has had losses, so much I will confess:
But ne'er shall you, back to the land you left,
To dame or damsel return to boast yourself    1965
That e'er you spoiled me to the tune of two pence,
Or made your profit of me or other men."
This done, to Roland he cries aloud for help.

### 147

Oliver feels he's wounded mortally;
His thirst for vengeance can never glutted be.    1970
Amid the press he strikes right valiantly;
He breaks asunder the spear-shaft and the shield,
Splits chines and saddles and lops off hands and feet.

1935. *emprise*: enterprise, feat of arms.

Whoso had seen him hew Paynims piece from piece,
Throw one on other their bodies down in heaps,                    1975
Might well remember that flower of knightly deeds!
And Carlon's war-cry he fails not to repeat,
But still "Mountjoy!" goes shouting loud and clear.
He calls to Roland his comrade and his peer:
"Sir, my companion, draw nigh and stand with me;                 1980
We must this day be parted to our grief."

### 148

Oliver's face, when Roland on him looks,
Is grey and ghastly, discoloured, wan with wounds,
His bright blood sprays his body head to foot;
Down to the ground it runs from him in pools.                    1985
"God!" says the Count, "I know not what to do!
Fair sir, companion, woe worth your mighty mood!—
Ne'er shall be seen a man to equal you.
Alas, fair France! what valiant men and true
Must thou bewail this day, cast down and doomed!                 1990
Bitter the loss the Emperor has to rue!"
So much he says, and in the saddle swoons.

### 149

See Roland now swooning in saddle laid,
And Oliver that unto death is maimed;
He's bled so much that his eyes are all glazed,                  1995
Or far or near he can see nothing straight,
Nor recognize a single living shape;
So when he comes to where his comrade waits,
On the gold helm he smites at him amain,
Down to the nasal he splits the jewelled plates,                2000
Only his head is not touched by the blade.
Then Roland, stricken, lifts his eyes to his face,
Asking him low and mildly as he may:
"Sir, my companion, did you mean it that way?
Look, I am Roland, that loved you all my days;                  2005
You never sent me challenge or battle-gage."
Quoth Oliver: "I cannot see you plain;
I know your voice; may God see you and save.
And I have struck you; pardon it me, I pray."
Roland replies: "I have taken no scathe;                        2010
I pardon you, myself and in God's name."
Then each to other bows courteous in his place.
With such great love thus is their parting made.

### 150

Oliver feels the coming pangs of death;
Both of his eyes are turning in his head,                       2015
Now he is blind wholly, and wholly deaf.

2005. *challenge or battle-gage:* Roland
wonders whether Oliver is still angry
with him, but cannot believe that he
would bear arms against him without
having sent him a formal challenge, accompanied by the usual token of defiance.

He lights from horse and to his knees he gets
And makes confession aloud, and beats his breast,
Then clasps his hands and lifts them up to Heav'n;
In Paradise he prays God give him rest, 2020
And France the Fair and Carlon prays Him bless,
And his companion Roland above all men.
His heart-strings crack, he stoops his knightly helm,
And sinks to earth, and lies there all his length.
Dead is the Count, his days have reached their end. 2025
The valiant Roland weeps for him and laments,
No man on earth felt ever such distress.

### 151

When Roland sees his friend and comrade die,
And on the ground face down beholds him lie,
With tender words he bids him thus goodbye: 2030
"Sir, my companion, woe worth your valiant might!
Long years and days have we lived side by side,
Ne'er didst thou wrong me nor suffer wrong of mine.
Now thou art dead I grieve to be alive."
Having thus said, the Marquis swoons outright 2035
On his steed's back, that Veillantif is hight;
He's kept from falling by the gold stirrups bright;
Go as he may, they hold him still upright.

### 152

Or ever Roland comes to himself again
And has recovered and rallied from his faint, 2040
Fearful disaster his fortunes have sustained;
All of the French are lost to him and slain;
Sole, the Archbishop and Walter Hum remain.
Walter has come down from the heights again;
Well has he striven against the men of Spain, 2045
His men are dead, mown down by Paynim blades;
Will he or nill he, he flees towards the vale,
And upon Roland he cries aloud for aid:
"Where art thou, where, great county, warrior brave?
While thou wast there I never was dismayed. 2050
Walter am I, who Maëlgut o'ercame,
Nephew am I to Droön white with age;
Thou for my valour wast wont to love me aye!
My lance is shattered, my shield is split in twain,
Battered and broken is my hauberk of mail, 2055
A spear has pierced me [through the midst of my reins;]
Death is upon me, yet dear I made them pay."
Lo! at that word Roland hears him and wakes;
He spurs his horse and comes to him in haste.

### 153

Roland is filled with grief and anger sore; 2060
In the thick press he now renews his war.

2035. *marquis*: The title means "lord of the marches" (see note on l. 843). Roland was Lord of the Marches of Brittany.

Of those of Spain he's overthrown a score,
And Walter six, the Archbishop five more.
The Paynims say: "These men are worst of all!
Let none escape alive; look to it, lords!                       2065
Who fears the onset, let shame be his reward!
Who lets these go, may he be put to scorn!"
Then once again the hue and cry breaks forth;
From every side pour in the Paynim hordes.

### 154

The County Roland is mighty of his mood,                        2070
Walter de Hum well-famed for knightlihood,
And the Archbishop a warrior tried and proved;
Betwixt their valours there's not a pin to choose.
In the thick press they smite the Moorish crew.
A thousand Paynims dismount to fight on foot,                   2075
And forty thousand horsemen they have, to boot,
Yet 'gainst these three, my troth! they fear to move.
They hurl against them their lances from aloof,
Javelins, jereeds, darts, shafts and spears they loose.
In the first shock brave Walter meets his doom.                2080
Turpin of Rheims has his shield split in two,
His helm is broken, his head has ta'en a wound,
His hauberk's pierced, the mail-rings burst and strewn,
By four sharp spears his breast is stricken through,
Killed under him his horse rolls neck and croup;               2085
Th'Archbishop's down, woe worth the bitter dule.

### 155

Turpin of Rheims, finding himself o'erset,
With four sharp lance-heads stuck fast within his breast,
Quickly leaps up, brave lord, and stands erect.
He looks on Roland and runs to him and says                    2090
Only one word: "I am not beaten yet!
True man failed never while life in him was left."
He draws Almace, his steel-bright brand keen-edged;
A thousand strokes he strikes amid the press.
Soon Charles shall see he spared no foe he met,                2095
For all about him he'll find four hundred men,
Some wounded, some clean through the body cleft,
And some of them made shorter by the head.
So tells the Geste; so he that fought there tells:
The worthy Giles, whom God with marvels blessed,               2100
In Laön minster thus-wise the charter penned;
Who knows not this knows nought of what befel.

### 156

The County Roland fights bravely as he may,
But his whole body in heat and sweat is bathed,
And all his head is racked with grievous pain                  2105
From that great blast which brake his temples' veins.

2086. *dule: grief.*
2100. *the worthy Giles:* St. Giles, who had a hermitage in Provence, and became the hero of many legends.

Fain would he know if Charles is bringing aid;
His Olifant he grasps, and blows full faint.
The Emperor halts, hearing the feeble strain:
"My lords," quoth he, "this tells a woeful tale;   2110
Roland my nephew is lost to us this day,
That call proclaims his breath is nigh to fail.
Whoso would reach him must ride with desperate haste
Sound through the host! bid every trumpet play!"
Full sixty thousand so loud their clarions bray   2115
The hills resound, the valleys ring again.
The Paynims hear, no lust to laugh have they:
"We'll soon have Charles to reckon with," they say.

### 157

The Paynims say: "The Emperor's turned about;
Of those of France hark how the trumpets sound!   2120
If Carlon comes, we shall have rack and rout,
If Roland lives, once more he'll war us down,
We shall not keep one foot of Spanish ground."
Straightway four hundred helmed warriors rally round,
The finest fighters that in the field are found;   2125
A fearful onslaught they'll make upon the Count;
Truly Lord Roland has got his work cut out.

### 158

Whenas Count Roland sees their assault begin,
Right fierce he makes him, and strong and menacing;
While life is in him he'll never quail or quit.   2130
He sits his horse that is named Veillantif,
Into his flanks the golden spurs he pricks
And sets upon them where most the press is thick.
The Lord Archbishop, brave Turpin, rides with him.
Paynim to paynim cries: "Comrade, go to it!   2135
Have we not heard the Frankish trumpets ring?
Charles is returning, the great, the mighty king!"

### 159

The County Roland ne'er loved a recreant,
Nor a false heart, nor yet a braggart jack,
Nor knight that was not a good man of his hands.   2140
He cried to Turpin, the Churchman militant,
"Sir, you're on foot, I'm on my horse's back;
For love of you here will I make my stand,
And side by side we'll take both good and bad.
I'll not desert you for any mortal man.   2145
Go we together these Paynims to attack;
The mightiest blows are those of Durendal."
Quoth the Archbishop: " 'Twere shame our strokes to slack;
Carlon is coming, our vengeance shall not lack."

### 160

The Paynims say: "Why were we ever born?   2150
Woe worth the while! our day of doom has dawned.

Now have we lost our peerage and our lords,
The mighty Carlon comes on with all his force,
Of those of France we hear the shrilling horns,
The cry "Mountjoy!" sounds fearfully abroad.                    2155
So grim of mood is Roland in his wrath
No man alive can put him to the sword.
Let fly at him, and then give up the war."
So they let fly; spears, lances they outpour,
Darts and jereeds and feathered shafts galore.                 2160
The shield of Roland is pierced and split and scored,
The mail-rings riven, and all his hauberk torn,
Yet in his body he is not touched at all,
Though under him, with thirty wounds and more,
His Veillantif is stricken dead and falls.                     2165
The Paynims flee, abandoning the war;
Count Roland's left amid the field, unhorsed.

### 161

In wrath and grief away the Paynims fly;
Backward to Spain with headlong haste they hie.
The County Roland cannot pursue their flight,                  2170
Veillantif's lost, he has no steed to ride;
Will he or nill he, he must on foot abide,
He's turned to aid Archbishop Turpin's plight,
And from his head the gilded helm untied,
Stripped off the hauberk of subtle rings and bright,           2175
And all to pieces has cut the bliaut fine
Wherewith to bandage his wounds that gape so wide.
Then to his breast he clasps and lifts him light
And gently lays him upon the green hill-side,
With fair soft speech entreating on this wise:                 2180
"Ah, noble sir, pray give me leave awhile;
These friends of ours, we loved so well in life,
We must not leave them thus lying where they died.
I will go seek them, find, and identify,
And lay them here together in your sight."                     2185
"Go and return," the Bishop makes reply;
"Thanks be to God, this field is yours and mine."

### 162

Roland departs and through the field is gone;
Alone he searches the valleys and high rocks.
[And there he finds Ivor, and there Ivon],                     2190
Gerier and Gerin, the good companions,
[And Engelier whom Gascony begot];
And he has found Berenger and Oton,
And after finds Anseïs and Samson,
And finds Gerard the Old, of Roussillon.                       2195
He lifts them up, brave baron, one by one,
To the Archbishop he carries them anon,
And by his knees ranges them all along.
The Bishop weeps, he cannot stint thereof;

He lifts his hand and gives them benison,                          2200
And after saith: "Alack, brave champions!
May your souls rest with the all-glorious God
In Paradise, amid the rose-blossoms.
I too am dying and sorrow for my lot,
Who the great Emperor no more may look upon."                       2205

### 163

Roland once more unto the field repairs,
And has sought out his comrade Oliver.
Close to his breast he lifts him, and with care
As best he may to the Archbishop bears
And on his shield lays with the others there;                      2210
The Bishop signs and shrives them all with prayer.
With tears renewed their sorrow is declared,
And Roland saith: "Fair fellow Oliver,
You were own son unto Duke Renier
That held the marches of the Vale of Runers.                       2215
To shatter shield or break lance anywhere,
And from their seat proud men to overbear,
And cheer the brave with words of counsel fair,
And bring the cruel to ruin and despair,
No knight on earth was valiant as you were."                       2220

### 164

The County Roland, seeing his peers lie dead,
And Oliver, who was his dearest friend,
Begins to weep for ruth and tenderness;
Out of his cheeks the colour all has fled,
He cannot stand, he is so deep distressed,                         2225
He swoons to earth, he cannot help himself.
"Alas, for pity, sweet lord!" the Bishop saith.

### 165

When the Archbishop saw Roland faint and fallen,
So sad was he, he never had been more so;
He reaches out; he's taken Roland's horn up.                       2230
In Ronceval there runs a stream of water;
Fain would he go there and fetch a little for him.
With feeble steps he turns him thither, falt'ring;
He is so weak, that he cannot go forward,
For loss of blood he has no strength to call on.                   2235
Ere one might cover but a rood's length in walking
His heart has failed him, he has fallen face-foremost;
The pangs of death have seized him with great torment.

### 166

The County Roland has rallied from his faint,
Gets to his feet, though he's in grievous pain,                    2240
And looks about him over hill, over vale.
Beyond his comrades, upon the grass-green plain,
There he beholds the noble baron laid,

The great Archbishop, vice-gerent of God's name.
He beats his breast with eyes devoutly raised, 2245
With folded hands lifted to Heaven he prays
That God will give him in Paradise a place.
Turpin is dead that fought for Charlemayn;
In mighty battles, and in preaching right brave,
Still against Paynims a champion of the Faith; 2250
Blest mote he be, the Lord God give him grace!

### 167

The County Roland sees the Archbishop lie;
He sees his bowels gush forth out of his side
And on his brow the brain laid bare to sight.
Midst of his breast where the key-bones divide, 2255
Crosswise he lays his comely hands and white,
And thus laments him as native use requires:
"Ah, debonair, thou good and noble knight!
Now I commend thee to the great Lord of might,
Servant more willing than thee He shall not find. 2260
Since the Apostles no prophet was thy like,
For to maintain the Faith, and win mankind.
May thy soul meet no hindrance in her flight!
May Heaven's gate to her stand open wide!"

### 168

Now Roland feels that he is at death's door; 2265
Out of his ears the brain is running forth.
Now for his peers he prays God call them all,
And for himself St Gabriel's aid implores;
Then in each hand he takes, lest shame befall,
His Olifant and Durendal his sword. 2270
Far as a quarrel flies from a cross-bow drawn,
Toward land of Spain he goes, to a wide lawn,
And climbs a mound where grows a fair tree tall,
And marble stones beneath it stand by four.
Face downward there on the green grass he falls, 2275
And swoons away, for he is at death's door.

### 169

High are the hills and very high the trees are;
Four stones there are set there, of marble gleaming.
The County Roland lies senseless on the greensward.
A Saracen is there, watching him keenly; 2280
He has feigned death, and lies among his people,
And has smeared blood upon his breast and features.
Now he gets up and runs towards him fleetly;
Strong was he, comely and of valour exceeding.
Now in his rage and in his overweening 2285
He falls on Roland, his arms and body seizing;
He saith one word: "Now Carlon's nephew's beaten.

---

2274. *marble stones:* probably posts such as were used to mark a frontier.

I'll take his sword, to Araby I'll reive it."
But as he draws it Roland comes to, and feels him.

### 170

Roland has felt his good sword being stol'n;                    2290
Opens his eyes and speaks this word alone:
"Thou'rt none of ours, in so far as I know."
He takes his horn, of which he kept fast hold,
And smites the helm, which was all gemmed with gold;
He breaks the steel and the scalp and the bone,               2295
And from his head batters his eyes out both,
And dead on ground he lays the villain low;
Then saith: "False Paynim, and how wast thou so bold,
Foully or fairly, to seize upon me so?
A fool he'll think thee who hears this story told.            2300
Lo, now! the mouth of my Olifant's broke;
Fallen is all the crystal and the gold."

### 171

Now Roland feels his sight grow dim and weak;
With his last strength he struggles to his feet;
All the red blood has faded from his cheeks.                  2305
A grey stone stands before him at his knee:
Ten strokes thereon he strikes, with rage and grief;
It grides, but yet nor breaks nor chips the steel.
"Ah!" cries the Count, "St Mary succour me!
Alack the Day, Durendal, good and keen!                       2310
Now I am dying, I cannot fend for thee.
How many battles I've won with you in field!
With you I've conquered so many goodly fiefs
That Carlon holds, the lord with the white beard!
Let none e'er wield you that from the foe would flee—         2315
You that were wielded so long by a good liege!
The like of you blest France shall never see."

### 172

Count Roland smites the sardin stone amain.
The steel grides loud, but neither breaks nor bates.
Now when he sees that it will nowise break                    2320
Thus to himself he maketh his complaint:
"Ah, Durendal! so bright, so brave, so gay!
How dost thou glitter and shine in the sun's rays!
When Charles was keeping the vales of Moriane,
God by an angel sent to him and ordained                      2325
He should bestow thee on some count-capitayne.
On me he girt thee, the noble Charlemayn.
With this I won him Anjou and all Bretayn,
With this I won him Poitou, and conquered Maine;
With this I won him Normandy's fair terrain,                  2330
And with it won Provence and Acquitaine,
And Lombardy and all the land Romayne,

2288. *reive*: steal away.

Bavaria too, and the whole Flemish state,
And Burgundy and all Apulia gained;
Constantinople in the King's hand I laid;                    2335
In Saxony he speaks and is obeyed;
With this I won Scotland, [Ireland and Wales,]
And England, where he set up his domain;
What lands and countries I've conquered by its aid,
For Charles to keep whose beard is white as may!            2340
Now am I grieved and troubled for my blade;
Should Paynims get it, 'twere worse than all death's pains.
Dear God forbid it should put France to shame!"

### 173
Count Roland smites upon the marble stone;
I cannot tell you how he hewed it and smote;               2345
Yet the blade breaks not nor splinters, though it groans;
Upward to heaven it rebounds from the blow.
When the Count sees it never will be broke,
Then to himself right softly he makes moan:
"Ah, Durendal, fair, hallowed, and devote,                 2350
What store of relics lie in thy hilt of gold!
St Peter's tooth, St Basil's blood, it holds,
Hair of my lord St Denis, there enclosed,
Likewise a piece of Blessed Mary's robe;
To Paynim hands 'twere sin to let you go;                  2355
You should be served by Christian men alone,
Ne'er may you fall to any coward soul!
Many wide lands I conquered by your strokes
For Charles to keep whose beard is white as snow,
Whereby right rich and mighty is his throne."              2360

### 174
Now Roland feels death press upon him hard;
It's creeping down from his head to his heart.
Under a pine-tree he hastens him apart,
There stretches him face down on the green grass,
And lays beneath him his sword and Olifant.                2365
He's turned his head to where the Paynims are,
And this he doth for the French and for Charles,
Since fain is he that they should say, brave heart,
That he has died a conquerer at the last.
He beats his breast full many a time and fast,            2370
Gives, with his glove, his sins into God's charge.

### 175
Now Roland feels his time is at an end;
On the steep hill-side, toward Spain he's turned his head,
And with one hand he beats upon his breast;
Saith: "*Mea culpa*; Thy mercy, Lord, I beg                2375
For all the sins, both the great and the less,

---

2337. The text is corrupt; but either Ireland or Wales is certainly intended, and
possibly both.

That e'er I did since first I drew my breath
Unto this day when I'm struck down by death."
His right-hand glove he unto God extends;
Angels from Heaven now to his side descend.                    2380

### 176

The County Roland lay down beneath a pine;
To land of Spain he's turned him as he lies,
And many things begins to call to mind:
All the broad lands he conquered in his time,
And fairest France, and the men of his line,                    2385
And Charles his lord, who bred him from a child;
He cannot help but weep for them and sigh.
Yet of himself he is mindful betimes;
He beats his breast and on God's mercy cries:
"Father most true, in whom there is no lie,                    2390
Who didst from death St Lazarus make to rise,
And bring out Daniel safe from the lions' might,
Save Thou my soul from danger and despite
Of all the sins I did in all my life."
His right-hand glove he's tendered unto Christ,                    2395
And from his hand Gabriel accepts the sign.
Straightway his head upon his arm declines;
With folded hands he makes an end and dies.
God sent to him His Angel Cherubine,
And great St Michael of Peril-by-the-Tide;                    2400
St. Gabriel too was with them at his side;
The County's soul they bear to Paradise.

2396–97. *the sign:* the glove is offered and accepted in token of Roland's
surrender to God of the life which he
holds as a fief from Him.

2399. *Cherubine:* "Cherubin" seems to
be used by the poet as the name of an
individual angel.

# Aucassin and Nicolette (Aucassin et Nicolete)*

### I

He who wants to hear good rhyme
Of the sport in ancient time
Of two children, young and sweet,
Aucassin and Nicolette,
Of the pains that he endured,
Of the noble deeds he did
For his love with clearest face.
Lovely the song, sweet the tale,
Courteous and well-disposed.

* Translated by Edward Francis
Moyer and Carey DeWitt Eldridge.   Copyright, 1937, by Robert Linker. Reprinted by permission.

No man can be so oppressed,
So cast down and comfortless,
Burdened down with heaviness,
Who will not be, hearing this,
Cured, restored to joyfulness,
    It is so sweet.

## II

*Now they tell and relate and continue the tale*

That Count Bougars de Valence was making war on Count
Garin de Beaucaire, so great and so marvelous and so mortal, that
not a single day dawned that he was not at the gates and at the
walls and at the barriers of the town with a hundred knights and
ten thousand soldiers on foot and on horse; and he burned his land
and wasted his country and killed his men.

Count Garin de Beaucaire was old and frail and had outlived his
time. He had no heir, neither son nor daughter, except a single boy,
who was such as I shall tell you.

Aucassin was the name of the lad. Handsome he was and shapely
and large and well formed in legs and feet and in body and in arms.
His hair was blond and tightly curled, and his eyes were gray and
laughing, and his face clear and slender, and his nose high and well
placed. He was so endowed with good points that there was in him
nothing bad, or that was not good. But he was so overtaken by love
which conquers all, that he didn't want to be a knight, or to take
arms, or go into the tourney, or do anything at all which he ought
to have done.

His father and his mother used to say to him, "Son, take up
your arms, get on your horse, defend your land, and aid your men.
If they see you among them, they will defend better their bodies
and their goods, and your land and mine."

"Father," said Aucassin, "what are you talking about now? Never
may God give me anything I ask of him, if as a knight I mount my
horse, or go into the fray or battle, there where I may strike a
knight or others strike me, if you do not give me Nicolette, my
sweet love, whom I love so much."

"Son," said the father, "that could not be. You let Nicolette
alone since she is a slave-girl who was brought from a foreign land.
The viscount of this town bought her from the Saracens and
brought her to this town. And he has reared her and baptized her
and has made her his god-daughter. So will he give her one of these
days to some young man who will earn bread for her with honor.
You have nothing to do with all this. If you wish to have a wife, I
will give you the daughter of a king or of a count. There is no man
in France so rich that if you wish for his daughter you shall not
have her."

"Look here, Father," said Aucassin, "where is there such high honor on the earth that if Nicolette, my very sweet love, had it, it wouldn't be well placed in her? If she were Empress of Constantinople or of Germany, or Queen of France or of England, it would be little enough for her, so noble she is, and courtly, and of good manner, and the acme of all good qualities."

### III

*Now it is sung*

> Aucassin lived in Beaucaire;
> Well-built was his castle there.
> Nicolette, of form so fair,
> From her no man could tear him;
> His father tried to scare him,
> And his mother threatened him,
> "Scamp, what do you want to do?
> Nicolette is trim and gay
> But from Carthage cast away;
> From the pagans she was bought.
> Since you want to take a wife,
> Take a wife of high degree."
> "Mother, those wives don't please me.
> Nicolette is debonair,
> Form so sweet and face so clear;
> My heart jumps when she is near.
> Why can't I enjoy her love?
>         It is too sweet."

### IV

*Now they tell and relate and continue the tale*

When Count Garin de Beaucaire saw that he would not be able to turn his son away from the love of Nicolette, he went to the viscount of the town, who was in his service; so did he speak to him.

"Sir Count, get rid of Nicolette, your god-daughter. Cursed be the land from which she was brought to this country! For because of her, I lose Aucassin, who does not want to become a knight, or do any of the things he ought to do. And know well that if I could have her, I would burn her in a fire, and you might well have great fear for yourself."

"Sire," said the Viscount, "much does it trouble me that he goes and comes and that he speaks to her. I bought her with my money; so have I reared her and baptized her and made her my god-daughter. And I would have given her to some young man who would have earned bread for her with honor. With this your son, Aucassin, would have had nothing to do. But since it is your will

and your pleasure, I will send her to such a land and to such a
country that never again will he set eyes upon her."

"Take care that you do it," said Count Garin, "for great evil
may come to you from it."

Each went his own way. Now the Viscount was a very, very rich
man, and he had a rich palace looking on a garden. In a room in it
he had Nicolette placed, high in the tower, and an old woman with
her for company and to take care of her. And he had bread and
meat and wine brought there and whatever they might need. Then
he had the door sealed up so that none might be able, in any way,
to go in or come out, except that, opening on the garden, there was
one window, quite small, through which there came to them a little
fresh air.

## V

*Now it is sung*

> Nicolette in prison put;
> She's in a vaulted chamber
> Fashioned with the greatest skill
> And marvelously painted.
> On the marble window frame
> There the wretched maiden leans.
> Now her hair was blond as grain,
> And her eyebrows were well shaped,
> Clear and slender was her face,
> Never was there fairer seen.
> Toward the forest she looked out
> And saw the roses swelling,
> Heard the birds which twittered there;
> Then the orphan maid cried out,
> "Wretched captive, woe is me!
> Why am I in prison put?
> Aucassin, my youthful lord,
> I am still your own sweetheart
> And by you I'm not abhorred.
> For you I'm a prisoner
> Within this vaulted chamber.
> Now my life is very hard;
> But, by God, sweet Mary's son,
> I will not stay longer here
>             If I can get out."

## VI

*Now they tell and relate and continue the tale*

Nicolette was in prison, just as you have heard and understood,
in the chamber. The cry and the rumor went through all the land

and through all the country that Nicolette was lost. Some said that she had fled out of the country, and others said that Count Garin de Beaucaire had had her murdered. Whoever else had joy of it, Aucassin was not glad. He went to the viscount of the town, so did he address him:

"Sir Viscount, what have you done with Nicolette, my very sweet love, for there is nothing in all the world that I love more? Have you stolen her away from me? Know well that if I die of it, payment will be demanded of you; and that will be very right, for you will have slain me with your two hands, for you have taken from me the thing which I love most in this world."

"Fair lord," said the Viscount, "now stay out of this. Nicolette is a captive whom I brought from a strange land, so did I buy her with my wealth from the Saracens. And I have reared her and baptized her and made her my god-daughter; so have I nourished her. And I should have given her one of these days to a young man who should earn bread for her with honor. With this you have nothing to do. Instead, take the daughter of a king or a count. Moreover, what would you think to have gained if you had made her your mistress and put her in your bed? Little indeed would you have won, for all the days of the world your soul would be in Hell because of it, for into Paradise you could never enter."

"What would I be doing in Paradise? I don't want to enter there, but only to have Nicolette, my very sweet love, whom I love so much. For to Paradise go only such people as I shall tell you of: the old priests, the old cripples and maimed ones who, all night and all day, drag themselves before the altars and in the old crypts, and those who wear old worn-out clothes and are dressed in tattered rags, who are naked and without shoes and stockings, and dying of hunger and thirst and of cold and of misery. These go to Paradise. I have nothing to do with them. But to Hell I wish indeed to go; for to Hell go the handsome clerics, and the fine knights who have died in the tourneys and in great wars, and the good soldiers and the brave men; with them I do wish to go. There, also, go the fair and courteous ladies who have two or three lovers besides their husbands. And there go the gold and silver and miniver and gray furs. There, also, go the harpers and the jongleurs, and the kings of the world. With them do I wish to go—provided that I have Nicolette, my very sweet love, with me."

"Surely," said the Viscount, "your speaking gets you nowhere, for you shall never see her. And if you were to speak to her and your father knew it, he would burn both me and her in a fire, and you might well fear for yourself."

"That's what worries me," said Aucassin, and filled with grief he left the viscount.

## VII

*Now it is sung*

Aucassin has turned away
Very sad and all downcast;
For his love with clearest face
No one now can comfort him,
Neither give him good advice.
Toward the palace has he gone;
He has mounted up the steps.
In a chamber has he come,
So did he begin to weep
And to sigh in deepest grief,
Lamenting his lost sweetheart.
"Nicolette, how sweet you were,
Sweet to come and sweet to go,
Sweet to play and sweet to say,
Sweet to tease and sweet to please,
Sweet to kiss and sweet to squeeze.
I for you am all cast down
And am so badly treated
That I think I'll leave this life,
⠀⠀⠀⠀Sister, sweet love."

## VIII

*Now they tell and relate and continue the tale*

While Aucassin was in his chamber mourning for Nicolette his love, Count Bougars de Valence, who had his war to maintain, was in no way forgetting it. He had sent forward his horsemen and foot soldiers, and he then directed himself toward the castle to assail it. And a cry arose and a disturbance, and the knights and the soldiers armed themselves and ran to the gates and to the walls to defend the castle, and the bourgeois went up the passage-ways in the walls and threw down rocks and sharpened stakes. While the assault was great and in full swing, the Count Garin de Beaucaire came to the chamber where Aucassin was grieving and mourning Nicolette, his very sweet love, whom he loved so much.

"Ha! Son," said he, "how very weak and wretched you are, that you watch while they assault the best and strongest of all castles. And know that if you lose it, you are disinherited. Come on, Son, take up your arms, and mount your horse and defend your land, and aid your men, and go into the battle. You need never strike a man there, nor let another strike you; yet if they see you among them, they will defend better their goods and their bodies and your land and mine. You are so big and so strong that you can easily do it, and you ought to do it."

"Father," said Aucassin, "what are you talking about now? May God give me nothing of what I ask of him if I play the knight or mount on a horse or go into the battle, where I may strike some knights, or be struck by others, unless you give me Nicolette, my sweet love, whom I love so much."

"Son," said the father, "that can't be done; rather would I suffer that I should be entirely dispossessed and that I should lose all that I have than that you should ever have her for your wife or for your bride."

He turned away, and when Aucassin saw him about to go, he called him back.

"Father," said Aucassin, "come back, I will make a good bargain with you."

"Such as what, my fine son?"

"I will take up arms and go into the battle on your promise that, if God brings me back safe and sound, you will let me see Nicolette, my sweet love, long enough to have two or three words with her, and that I may kiss her one single time."

"I grant it," said the father.

He gave him his word, and Aucassin was glad.

### IX

*Now it is sung*

Aucassin a kiss will have
If he should return alive;
For a hundred thousand marks
He would not be half so glad.
He demanded armor bright;
Servants clothed him as a knight.
Double hauberk he put on,
Laced his helmet on his head,
Girt his sword with golden hilt,
And on his charger mounted.
Then he took his shield and spear,
Cast a glance down at his feet.
In his stirrups well they sat;
High he holds his head aloft.
He remembers his sweet love.
Forward then he spurs his horse;
Willingly he takes his course.
Right up to the gate he goes
    To the battle.

### X

*Now they tell and relate*

Aucassin was armed and on his horse, as you have heard and understood. God, how becoming the shield was at his neck and the helmet on his head and the belt of his sword on his left hip. The lad was big and strong and handsome and noble and well turned out, and the horse which he rode, quick and rapid; and the lad had ridden him straight through the middle of the gate.

Now don't you believe that he was thinking of taking oxen or cows or goats, or that he would strike some knight or another strike him. Nothing like that! Not once did it occur to him. But he thought so much of Nicolette, his sweet love, that he forgot the reins and all that he had to do. And the horse that had felt the spurs carried him into the thick of the battle and hurled him right into the midst of his enemies. They grabbed him from all sides; so did they take him. And they relieved him of his shield and lance; so did they quickly lead him away a prisoner. And they went along, already considering what death they would make him die.

And when Aucassin heard them:

"Ah, God," said he, "sweet creature! Are these my mortal enemies who are holding me here, and who now will cut off my head? And after my head is cut off, never will I speak to Nicolette, my sweet love, whom I love so much. Yet I have here a good sword, and I'm riding a good fresh war-horse. If now I don't defend myself for her sake, never may God help her if she loves me any more."

The lad was big and strong, and the horse on which he sat was lively. And he snatched his sword and began to strike right and left and cut through helmets and nose-pieces and fists and arms and made a slaughter round about him, like the wild boar when the dogs attack him in the forest. And so did he strike down ten knights and wound seven, and rode quickly out of the thick of things. So did he come galloping back, sword in hand.

The Count Bougars de Valence heard them say that they were going to hang Aucassin, his enemy, and he came to that place, and Aucassin did not mistake him. He took his sword in hand and whacked down on the helmet so that it went down over his head. He was so stunned that he fell onto the ground. And Aucassin put out his hand, took him and led him along by the nose-guard of his helmet, and handed him over to his father.

"Father," said Aucassin, "look, here is your enemy who for so long has made war on you and done harm; this war has lasted for twenty years and never could it be ended by anyone."

"Fair son," said the father, "you ought to do these youthful deeds and not chase after foolishness."

"Father," said Aucassin, "don't you go making sermons to me, but keep your promises to me."

"Bah! What promises, fair son?"

"What, Father, have you forgotten them? By my head, whoever else forgets them, I don't want to forget them, so close I hold them to my heart. Didn't you make an agreement with me that if I took up arms and went into battle and if God brought me back safe and sound, you would let me see Nicolette, my sweet love, long enough to have two or three words with her? And didn't you make an agreement that I might kiss her one time? I want you to keep this promise to me."

"I?" said the father. "May God never aid me if I keep faith with you in this. And if she were here now, I would burn her in a fire, and you, yourself, might well be afraid."

"Is this your last word?" asked Aucassin.

"So help me God," said the father, "yes!"

"Well," said Aucassin, "very, very much do I grieve when a man of your age is a liar."

"Count de Valence," said Aucassin, "I took you a prisoner."

"You surely did, sir," said the count.

"Give me your hand on it," said Aucassin.

"Willingly, sir." And he put his hand in his.

"Now swear to me," said Aucassin, "that, any day as long as you live, should you be able to do dishonor or destruction to my father, either in his person or his property, you won't fail to do it.

"Sir, for God's sake," said he, "don't mock me, but set a ransom on me. You will not be able to ask of me gold, or silver, horses or palfreys, miniver or gray fur, or hounds or birds, that I will not give you."

"What?" said Aucassin. "Don't you know that I have taken you prisoner?"

"Oh yes, sir," said the Count Bougars.

"If you do not swear it to me," said Aucassin, "may God never help me if I do not send your head flying now."

"In the name of God," he said, "I'll swear to whatever you please."

So he swore, and Aucassin made him mount on a horse, and he mounted another and led him back until he was in safety.

### XI

*Now it is sung*

Now when sees the Count Garin
That his offspring Aucassin
Cannot tear himself away
From the clear-faced Nicolette,
In a cell he had him set,
In a prison underground,
Which was made of marble dark.
Now when Aucassin came there
He was sadder than before.

If you wish, you now may hear
What lamenting he began:
"Nicolette, sweet fleur-le-lis,
Sweet love with the clearest face,
Sweeter than a bunch of grapes,
Sweeter than the wine bowl's sop.
One time I saw a pilgrim
Who was born in Limousin,
With the palsy nearly dead;
Thus he lay upon his bed.
A sick man he was indeed,
Stricken with a dread disease.
When you passed before his bed,
Then you lifted up your skirt,
And your coat with ermine lined,
Your chemise of linen white,
Until he could see your leg.
Straightway was the pilgrim cured
More than he had ever been.
Then he jumped up from his bed;
To his country he returned,
Safe and sound, completely cured.
O sweet love, sweet fleur-de-lis,
Sweet to kiss, sweet to embrace,
Sweet to come and sweet to go,
Sweet to say and sweet to play,
Sweet to please and sweet to squeeze,
No man could ever hate you.
Yet for your sake I am here
In this prison underground
Where I make a dismal end.
Now I ought to kill myself
For you, my love."

### XII

*Now they tell and relate and continue the tale*

Aucassin was put in prison, as you have heard and understood, and Nicolette was elsewhere in her chamber. This was in the summertime, in the month of May, when the days are hot and long and clear and the nights still and serene.

Nicolette lay one night in her bed, and she saw the moon shine clear through a window, and she heard the nightingale singing in the garden; so did she recall Aucassin, her love whom she loved too much. She began to reflect about Count Garin de Beaucaire, who hated her to death. So did she think that she would remain there no longer; for, if she were discovered and Count Garin heard about it, he would make her die an evil death. She perceived that the old woman who was with her was sleeping. She got up and put on a good chemise of cloth of silk that she had, and she took her bed-clothes and towels, and tied them one to another and made a cord as long as she could. This she tied to the pillar of the window; so did she slide down into the garden. She took the front of her dress with one hand and the back with the other and raised it close about her, because of the dew which she saw heavy upon the grass, and so she made off down the garden.

She had blond hair tightly curled, and eyes gray and laughing, and a slender face, and a nose high and well placed, and lips redder than the cherry or the rose in the summertime, and teeth small and white. And she had firm little breasts which raised up her gown as if they were two walnuts, and she was so slender in the waist that you could have circled it with your two hands. And the blossoms of daisies which she broke with the toes of her feet and which were lying upon her instep were completely black beside her feet and legs, so very, very white was the maiden.

She came to the postern and unlocked it. So did she pass out into the streets of Beaucaire, under cover of the shadows, for the moon was shining very clear. And she wandered about until she came to the tower where her lover was. The tower was cracked from place to place. And Nicolette squatted down against one of the buttresses and wrapped her cloak about her. She stuck her head in through a crevice of the tower, which was old and ancient. So did she hear Aucassin, who, inside, was weeping and wailing loudly and regretting his sweet love, whom he loved so much. And when she had listened enough to him, she began to speak.

### XIII

*Now it is sung*

> Nicolette with clearest face
> Was leaning on a buttress.
> Aucassin she heard to weep
> And lament his sweetheart lost.
> Now she speaks and says her thought.
> "Aucassin, my noble lord,
> Gentle, high-born, honored youth,
> What's the use of all these sighs,
> This weeping and lamenting?
> For you can never have me;
> Your father and your family
> All hate me and detest me.
> For you I'd sail the high seas

And go to other countries."
From her hair she cut a lock
And threw it in his dungeon.
Noble Aucassin took it
And did it a great homage.
He kissed it and embraced it
And stuck it in his bosom,
Then began again to weep
    All for his love.

### XIV

*Now they tell and relate and continue the tale*

When Aucassin heard Nicolette say that she wished to go away to another country, in him there was nothing but anger.

"Fair sweet love," said he, "you shall not go away, for then you would be the death of me. And the first one who saw you, and who would be able to do it, would take you immediately and put you into his bed, and so would he make you his mistress. And once you had lain in a man's bed—if it wasn't mine—don't think that I would wait until I had found a knife with which I could pierce my heart and kill myself. No, indeed, I wouldn't wait that long, but I would rush about until I saw a wall or a dark stone, and I would dash my head against it so hard that I would make my eyes pop out and brain myself completely. For I would much prefer to die such a death than to know that you were in a man's bed—if it wasn't mine."

"Ah!" said she. "I don't think that you love me as much as you say. But I love you more than you love me."

"Look here," said Aucassin, "fair sweet love, it couldn't be that you should love me as much as I love you. Woman can't love man as much as man loves woman, for the love of a woman is in her eye, and in the nipple of her breast, and in the toe of her foot, but the love of a man is planted in the heart where it can't escape."

While Aucassin and Nicolette were talking there, the guardsmen of the town were coming down the street. They had their swords drawn beneath their cloaks, for Count Garin had commanded them that if they were able to take her, they should kill her. And the watchman who was on the tower saw them coming and heard them going along talking about Nicolette and threatening to kill her.

"God," said he, "what a great pity for so fair a girl, if they should kill her. And it would be a very great charity if I could tell her, in some way they wouldn't perceive, that she should be on her guard. For if they kill her, then Aucassin, my young lord, will die, and that will be a great loss."

XV

*Now it is sung*

> The watchman was a gallant,
> Knowing, proud and courteous man.
> So did he begin a song
> Which was sweet and ran along.
> "Maiden of the noble heart,
> Body fair and full of grace,
> Thou hast blond and shining hair,
> Grayish eyes and smiling face.
> Well do I see by thy air,
> Thou hast spoken to thy love,
> Who now for thee dying is.
> Listen while I tell thee this:
> From seducers guard thyself;
> They are looking for thee here,
> Bearing swords beneath their cloaks.
> Terribly they'll threaten thee;
> Soon much evil will they do
> > If thou guard not well."

XVI

*Now they tell and relate and continue the tale*

"Ah," said Nicolette, "may the souls of your father and mother be in blessed repose, since so fairly and courteously you have told me about them. If it please God, I will guard myself well from them, and God help me do it."

She wrapped her cloak about her in the shadow of the buttress until they had passed beyond. Then she took leave of Aucassin and went on until she came to the wall of the castle. The wall was in pieces and had been boarded up, and she climbed up on this and made her way along until she was between the wall and the moat. And she looked down and saw that the moat was very deep and very steep, and she was very, very much afraid.

"Oh God," said she, "sweet creature! If I let myself fall, I'll break my neck, and if I remain here, they will take me tomorrow, and they will burn me in a fire. I would much prefer that I die here than that all the folk should stare at me tomorrow under marvelous circumstances."

She made the sign of the cross above her head and let herself slide down into the moat. And when she came to the bottom, her beautiful feet and her beautiful hands, which had never learned that things might wound them, were bruised and torn, and the blood flowed from them in at least a dozen places; but nevertheless she felt neither hurt nor pain because of the great fear which she

had. And though getting in had been much trouble, getting out was
even more. She thought to herself that it would never do any good
to remain there. She found a sharpened stake which those within
had thrown down in defense of the castle, and placing one foot before the other, she mounted up with great difficulty until she came
to the top.

Now there was a forest, about two crossbow shots away, which
stretched for at least thirty leagues in length and in breadth, and
there were savage beasts in it—also serpents. She was afraid that
if she entered there, these might kill her; and, on the other hand,
she reflected, if they found her there, they would lead her back to
the town to burn her.

XVII

*Now it is sung*

Nicolette with clearest face
Up the moat has made her way.
Then began she to lament
And in Jesus' name to pray:
"Father, King of Majesty,
I do not know where to go.
If I go into the woods,
There the wolves will eat me sure,
The wild boars and the lions,
Of which there are a-plenty.
If I wait the daylight clear
So that they could find me here,
They will light their fires of wood
And my body will be burned.
But, by God of Majesty,
I would very much prefer
That even wolves should eat me,
Or wild boars or the lions,
Than go into the city.
I *will* not go."

XVIII

*Now they tell and relate and continue the tale*

Nicolette lamented as you have heard. She commended herself
to God and wandered on until she came into the forest. She didn't
dare to enter very deep into it because of the savage beasts and
because of the serpents; so she crawled into a thick bush. Sleep
seized her, and she slept until the next morning at seven-thirty
when the shepherds came out of the town and drove their beasts
between the wood and the river. There they drew aside to a very
beautiful spring which was at the edge of the forest, and spread out

a´ cape and set their bread upon it. And while they were eating, Nicolette was awakened by the cries of the birds and of the shepherds; so did she hurry toward them.

"Fair children," said she, "may the Mother of God aid you."

"God bless *you*!" said the one of them who was more talkative than the others.

"Fair children," said she, "do you know Aucassin, the son of Count Garin de Beaucaire?"

"Yes, we know him well."

"So may God aid you, fair children," she said. "Tell him that there is a beast in this forest, and that he is to come to hunt for it; and if he could catch it, he would not give one leg of it for one hundred marks of gold, not for five hundred, nor for any amount."

And they looked at her, and so did they see her so beautiful that they were all astonished.

"I should tell him *that*?" said he who was more talkative than the others. "Damned be the one who would ever talk about it, or who would ever tell him! It's a phantom that you're talking about, for there is no beast in the forest so valuable, neither stag nor lion nor wild boar, that one of his legs would be worth more than a shilling or two at the most, and you speak of such a great value! Damned be the one who believes you, or whoever shall tell it to him! You are some fairy, and we have no desire for your company, so you keep on your way."

"Ah, fair children," she said, "you will do this. The beast has such medicine that Aucassin will be cured of his illness. And I have five sous here in my purse; take them—if you will tell him. And he ought to hunt it within three days; and if, within three days, he doesn't find it, he never will be cured of his illness."

"By faith," said he, "we will take the money, and if he comes here, we will tell him; but we'll never go to look for him."

"It's up to God," said she.

Then she took leave of the shepherds, and so did she go on her way.

XIX

*Now it is sung*

> Nicolette with clearest face
> Has parted from the shepherds.
> So she's taken up her way
> Right into the leafy wood,
> Following an abandoned path
> Until she met a highway
> Where seven roads divided
> Which went through the country-side.

Then the thought came to her head
How she could prove her lover,
If he loved her as he said.
So she took the iris-flower
And green grass from a thicket
And some branches thick with leaves.
So she made a leafy hut;
Prettier was there never seen.
By the truthful God she swore
That if Aucassin came there
And did not for love of her
Rest in it a little while
Never would he be her love
    Nor she be his.

xx

*Now they tell and relate and continue the tale*

Nicolette had made a hut, as you have heard and understood, very pretty and attractive, for she had decorated it well inside and outside with flowers and with leaves. Then she lay down close by the hut in a thick bush to know what Aucassin would do.

And the cry and rumor went through all the land and through all the country that Nicolette was lost. Some said that she had run away, and others said that Count Garin had had her murdered. Whoever may have had joy from it, Aucassin wasn't at all happy about it. And Count Garin, his father, had him taken out of prison. So did he send for the knights and the ladies, and he had made a great rich feast, with which he thought to comfort Aucassin, his son.

Although the feast was most complete, Aucassin stood leaning on a post all sad and all limp. Whoever had joy, Aucassin was in no mood for it; for he saw nothing at all there of the thing he loved. A knight looked at him and came up to him; so did he speak to him.

"Aucassin," said he, "I have been sick with the same illness that you have. I will give you some good advice, if you wish to believe me."

"Sir," said Aucassin, "many thanks. I would appreciate some good advice."

"Get on a horse," said he, "and ride along the forest to cheer yourself up. And you will see the flowers and the plants, and you will hear the little birds sing. By some chance you may hear some word for which you will be better."

"Sir," said Aucassin, "Thanks very much. That's what I'll do."

He slipped out of the hall and went down the stairs and came to the stable where his horse was. He had the saddle and bridle put on. He put his foot in the stirrup and mounted and went out of the castle. And he wandered until he came to the forest and rode along until he reached the spring and found the shepherds just at mid-afternoon. They had spread out a cape on the grass, and they were eating their bread and making very merry.

XXI

*Now it is sung*

> Now the shepherds gather round,
> Little Martin and Esmy,
> Little Frulin and Johnny,
> Little Robin and Aubrey.
> "Little shepherd boys," said one,
> "God help little Aucassin;
> He is a fine young fellow.
> And the girl with form so small
> And curly hair so yellow.
> Bright her face, her eye so gray,
> She gave us little pennies
> With which we'll buy little cakes,
> Little knives and little sheaths,
> Little flutes and little horns,
> Little crooks and little pipes.
> May God help her."

XXII

*Now they tell and relate and continue the tale*

When Aucassin heard the shepherds, he recalled Nicolette, his very sweet love, whom he loved so much, and thought that she had been there. He pricked his horse with the spurs, and so did he come up to the shepherds.

"Fair children, may God aid you!"

"God bless *you*!" said the one who was more talkative than the others.

"Fair children," said he, "repeat the song that you were singing just now."

"We will not say it," said the one who was more talkative than the others. "Damned now be the one who will sing it for you, fair sir."

"Fair children," said Aucassin, "don't you know me?"

"Yes, we know very well that you are Aucassin, our young lord, but we don't belong to you, but rather to the count."

"Fair children, you will do this, I pray you."

"Oh, for God's sake!" said he. "Why should I sing for you if it doesn't suit me? When there is no man so rich in this country, except Count Garin in person, who, if he found my oxen, or my

cows, or my sheep in his fields, or even in his grain, would risk
having his eyes put out, for daring to chase them from it? And why
should I sing for you if it doesn't suit me?"

"God aid you, fair children, if you will do it, and take ten sous
which I have here in my purse."

"Sir, we will take the money, but I will not sing it for you, for I
have sworn it, but I will tell it to you if you wish."

"It's up to God," said Aucassin, "I would rather have it told
than nothing."

"Sir, we were here a little while ago, between six and nine this
morning, eating our bread by this spring, as we are now, and a
maiden came here, the most beautiful in the world, so that we believed her to be a fairy, and this whole wood was made bright by
her. And she gave us so much of what she had that we made a
promise to her, that if you came here, we would tell you that you
should go and hunt in this forest, where there is a beast which, if
you should be able to catch it, you would never give up one of its
legs for five hundred marks of silver, or for any price. For the beast
has such a medicine that, if you could catch it, you would be cured
of your illness. And you must take it within three days, and if you
haven't caught it, you will never see it again. Now hunt it, if you
will; or if you will, leave it, for I have fully acquitted myself towards her."

"Fair children," said Aucassin, "you have told me enough about
it, and God let me find it!"

XXIII

*Now it is sung*

> Aucassin has heard the words
> Of his love with form so fair.
> Much they struck him to the core.
> Soon he leaves the shepherd boys
> And in the deep woods enters.
> His war-horse ambled quickly,
> At a gallop carried him.
> Now he speaks and says three words:
> "Nicolette, of form so fair,
> In this woods for you I've come.
> I'm not hunting stag or boar;
> Your tracks I am following.
> Your gray eyes and your sweet form,
> Your soft speech and gentle laugh
> Unto death my heart do wound.
> If it please the Father, God,
> Then shall I see you again.
> > Sister, sweet love."

XXIV

*Now they tell and relate and continue the tale*

Aucassin went through the forest from path to path, and his war horse carried him along at a great speed. Don't think that the briars and thorns spared him. Nothing of the sort! Rather they ripped up his clothes so that one could scarcely have made a knot out of the biggest pieces. And blood ran from his arms and his sides and his legs in forty places—or thirty, so that after the lad one might follow the traces of blood which fell on the grass. But he thought so much about Nicolette, his sweet love, that he felt neither pain nor unhappiness. And he went all day through the forest in such a way that he never did get news of her. And when he saw evening approaching, he began to weep because he couldn't find her.

He was riding along an old path all covered with leaves, when he looked before him, in the middle of the path; so did he see a yokel such as I shall tell you. Great he was, and marvelous and ugly and hideous; and he had a great bushy head blacker than charcoal, and he had more than a hand's breath between his two eyes, and he had great cheeks and a huge flat nose, and wide nostrils and thick lips redder than roast beef, and big teeth, yellow and ugly. And he wore leggings and shoes of cow-hide, cross-laced with willow bark to above the knee. He was wearing a cape unfinished inside and out, and he was leaning on a big club.

Aucassin hurried toward him and was very frightened when he got a good look at him.

"Fair brother, God help you!"

"God help *you*," said he.

"God help *you*. What are you doing here?"

"What's it to you?" said he.

"Nothing," said Aucassin, "I don't ask you except with good reason."

"But why are you crying," said he, "and making such a to-do? Surely, if I were as rich a man as you are, all the world wouldn't make me cry."

"What! do you know me?" said Aucassin.

"Sure, I know well that you are Aucassin, the son of the count, and if you will tell me why you are crying, I will tell you what I am doing here."

"Surely," said Aucassin, "I will tell you very gladly. I came this morning to hunt in the forest, and I had a white greyhound, the most beautiful in the world, and I have lost it. That's why I'm crying."

"To hear," said he, "by the heart that the Lord had in his belly, that you were crying over a stinking dog? May he be badly damned who shall ever take any account of you, when there is no man in this land so rich, that if your father asked him for ten or fifteen or twenty, he would not have given them only too willingly and have been only too glad. But I ought to cry and wail."

"And for what reason, brother?"

"Sir, I'll tell you. I was in the hire of a rich farmer, and I drove his plough, a four-ox one. Now three days ago there came to me a great accident by which I lost the best one of my oxen, Roget, the best of my team. So now I am looking for him, and I haven't eaten or drunk for the last three days. And I don't dare go to the town, for they would put me in prison since I don't have the money to pay for it. Of all the wealth in the world, I have nothing more valuable than what you see on my body. I have a poor old mother, and she had nothing more valuable than an old mattress, and they have taken it right out from under her back, so that she lies on the bare straw now. I am much more worried about her than about myself, for money comes and goes. If I have lost now, I will gain it another time; so shall I pay for my ox when I can, nor will I ever cry about it. And you were crying over a filthy dog—may anyone who ever takes any account of you be damned forever!"

"You certainly are a good comfort, fair brother, and may you be blessed! And what was your ox worth?"

"Sir, twenty sous they are asking me for it, and I can't get a single sou knocked off."

"Now take," said Aucassin, "the twenty which I have in my purse, and pay for your ox."

"Sir," said he, "thanks very much, and may God let you find what you are seeking."

He parted from him, and Aucassin rode on. The night was fair and still, and he wandered along until he came to the place where the seven roads forked. So did he look before him, and he saw the hut that Nicolette had built, which was hung outside and inside and on top and in front with flowers and was so beautiful that it could not be more so. When Aucassin saw it, he stopped all of a sudden, and the rays of the moon were shining in it.

"Oh, God," said Aucassin, "Nicolette, my sweet love, was here, and she made this with her own beautiful hands. Because of her sweetness and for love of her, I will get down now and stretch out there for the rest of the night."

Now the horse was big and tall, and Aucassin took his foot out of the stirrup to get down. He was thinking so much about Nicolette, his very sweet love, that he fell so hard on a stone that his shoulder flew out of place. He felt himself badly hurt, but he forced himself along as best he could, and tied the horse with his other hand to a thornbush; then he turned on his side so that he crawled into the hut. He looked up through a hole in the hut, and he saw the stars in the sky. He saw one brighter than the others, and he began to say.

### XXV
*Now it is sung*

"I can see you, little star,
Which the moon draws after her.
Nicolette is with you there,
My sweet love with golden hair.
I think God wants to have her
So that all the evening light
Can by her be made more bright.
At the risk of falling down
Would that I were up with you;
I would kiss you willingly.
Though I were a monarch's son,
You would worthy be of me.
Sister, sweet love."

### XXVI
*Now they tell and relate and continue the tale*

When Nicolette heard Aucassin, she came to him, for she was not far off. She came into the hut; so did she throw her arms around his neck, kissed him, and embraced him.

"Fair sweet love, it's good to find you!"

"And you, fair sweet love, it's good to find *you!*"

They kissed each other and embraced; so was their joy beautiful.

"Ah, sweet love," said Aucassin, "just now I hurt my shoulder, and now I feel neither pain nor grief since I have you."

She felt him carefully and found that he had his shoulder out of place. She handled it and pulled it about so with her white hands that, as God who loves lovers willed it, it came back into place; and then she took some flowers and fresh grass and green leaves, and she bound it up with the tail of her chemise, and he was completely cured.

"Aucassin," said she, "fair sweet love, take counsel what you will do. If your father has this forest searched tomorrow, whatever may become of *you,* they will kill *me.*"

"Surely, fair sweet love, I should be very sad over it; but if I am able, they shall never get hold of you."

He mounted on his horse, and took his love up in front of him, kissing and embracing her; so did they set off to the open fields.

### XXVII

**Now it is sung**

Aucassin, the fair, the blond,
The gentle and the loving,
Out of that deep woods has gone
With his love between his arms,
His saddle-bow before him.
He kissed her eyes and forehead,
Kissed her mouth and then her chin;
Then did Nicolette begin,
"Aucassin, sweet handsome love,
To what country shall we go?"
"My sweet love, how should I know?
I do not care where we go
In the woods or on the roads
So long as I am with you."
They passed the hills and valleys,
The villages and cities,
And at dawn they reached the sea
And dismounted on the sand
        Near the seashore.

### XXVIII

*Now they tell and relate and continue the tale*

Aucassin had dismounted, both he and his love, as you have heard and understood. He held his horse by the reins, and his love by the hand, and so did they begin to go along the shore. And Aucassin looked toward the sea and saw a ship of merchants who were sailing near the coast.

He hailed them and they came to him, and he made such terms with them that they took them into their ship. And when they were on the high seas, a storm arose, great and marvelous, which drove them from land to land, until they arrived in a strange country and entered into the port of the Castle of Torelore. Then they asked whose land it was, and they told them that it was the land of the King of Torelore. Then they asked what sort of a man he was, and if he had a war, and they told him, "Yes, a great one."

He took leave of the merchants, and they commended him to God. He mounted on his horse, his sword girded on, and his love in front of him, and wandered until he came to the castle. He asked where the king was, and they told him that he was lying in bed with child.

"And where is his wife, then?"

And they told him that she was with the army, and that she had taken away with her everybody in the country. Aucassin heard it, and it seemed to him a great marvel. He came up to the palace and dismounted—both he and his love; and she held the horse, and he went up into the palace, his sword girded on, and wandered about until he came into the room where the king was lying.

**XXIX**

*Now it is sung*

> In the room came Aucassin
> The courteous and the noble.
> He came straight up to the bed
> On which the king was lying.
> Right in front of him he stopped
> And spoke; listen what he said:
> "Fool, what are you doing here?"
> Said the king, "I am with child.
> When my month shall be fulfilled
> And I shall be well again,
> I shall then be churched at mass
> As my ancestors have done;
> Then from carrying on great war
> With my enemies again,
> > I shall never stop."

**XXX**

*Now they tell and relate and continue the tale*

When Aucassin heard the king speak thus, he took all the bed clothes which were upon him and threw them around the room. He saw just in back of him a big stick. He took it, turned about, and he struck him and beat him so much that he almost killed him.

"Ah, fair sir," said the king, "what do you want of me? Have you gone crazy that you beat me in my own house?"

"By God's heart," said Aucassin, "evil son of a slut, I will kill you, if you do not swear to me that never again shall a man in your land be brought to bed with child."

He swore it, and when he had heard him swear it:

"Sir," said Aucassin, "now lead me there where your wife is with the army."

"Sir, willingly," said the king.

He mounted on his horse, and Aucassin mounted on his, and Nicolette remained in the chambers of the queen. And the king and Aucassin rode along until they came to the place where the queen was, and they found there a battle of rotted wild apples, and of eggs and of fresh cheeses; and Aucassin began to look at them, and he was very, very much astonished indeed.

### XXXI

*Now it is sung*

Aucassin had stopped and now,
Elbow on his saddle-bow,
He begins to marvel at
This violent battlefield,
For both sides had brought with them
Cheeses quite fresh from the vats,
With wood apples rotted soft,
And some large field mushrooms too.
He who most stirs up the fords
Is proclaimed the lord of lords.
Aucassin the valiant knight
Stared at them with all his might
        And began to laugh.

### XXXII

*Now they tell and relate and continue the tale*

When Aucassin saw this marvel, he came to the king; so did he speak to him.

"Sir," said Aucassin, "are these your enemies?"

"Yes, sir," said the king.

"And would you like me to avenge you on them?"

"Yes," said he, "if you like."

And Aucassin put his hand on his sword, so did he rush among them and began to strike right and left and killed many of them. When the king saw that he was killing them, he took him by the bridle and said:

"Ah, fair sir, don't kill them like this."

"What?" said Aucassin, "don't you want me to avenge you?"

"Sir," said the king, "you have done too much. It is not our custom to kill each other."

The enemy turned and fled, and the king and Aucassin returned to the castle of Torelore. And the people of the country told the king that he should cast Aucassin out of the land and detain Nicolette as a wife for his son since she seemed, indeed, to be a woman of high lineage. Nicolette heard it, and was not at all glad about it, and she began to say:

### XXXIII

*Now it is sung*

"O, sir king of Torelore,"
Said the lovely Nicolette,
"Your folk take me for a fool;

When my love embraces me
And feels me plump and tender,
Then am I in such a state
That neither songs nor dances,
Fiddle, harp, nor viol gay,
Nor the pleasures of the play
Are worth a thing."

### XXXIV
*Now they tell and relate and continue the tale*

Aucassin was in the castle of Torelore, and Nicolette, his love; and he had great delight and great ease that he had with him Nicolette, his sweet love, whom he loved so much. And while he was in such ease and in such delight, a fleet of the Saracens came by sea and assailed the castle; so did they take it by force. And they took all the treasure and led the men and women away captive. They took Nicolette and Aucassin, and they bound Aucassin's hands and his feet, and they threw him into one ship and Nicolette into another. And there arose a storm on the sea, which separated them.

The ship in which Aucassin was went skimming over the sea until it arrived at the Castle of Beaucaire. The people of the country ran to the wreckage, and they found Aucassin, and so did they recognize him. When those of Beaucaire saw their young lord, they made great joy over it, for Aucassin had lived in the castle of Torelore for three full years, and his father and mother were dead. They led him to the Castle of Beaucaire; so did they all become his men, and he held his land in peace.

### XXXV
*Now it is sung*

Aucassin has gone away
To his city of Beaucaire.
All the country and the realm
He now held in greatest calm,
Swore by God of Majesty
That he much more regretted
Nicolette with clearest face
Than all of his relations
Though they all were dead and gone.
"Sweetheart with the clearest face,
I don't know where you may be.
God has never made that place
Either on the land or sea
Where if I thought to find you
I would not look."

### XXXVI
*Now they tell and relate and continue the tale*

Now we will leave off about Aucassin and talk of Nicolette. The ship in which Nicolette was belonged to the king of Carthage, and he was her father, and she had twelve brothers, all princes and kings. When they saw Nicolette so beautiful, they offered her very, very great honors and made a feast for her, and often did they ask her who she was, for indeed she seemed to be a very noble lady and of high lineage. But she didn't know how to tell them who she was, for she had been stolen away as a little child. They sailed along until they arrived below the city of Carthage; and when Nicolette saw the walls of the castle and the country, she recognized that she had been brought up there and stolen from there as a little child. But she was not so small a child that she didn't know very well that she had been the daughter of the king of Carthage, and that she had been brought up in the city.

### XXXVII
*Now it is sung*

> Nicolette, high-born and wise,
> Now has landed on the shore,
> Saw the buildings and the walls
> And the castle and the halls.
> Seeing which, she cried, "Alas,
> I am of a high descent,
> Daughter to the Carthage king
> And cousin to the emir!
> Savage people hold me here.
> Aucassin, well-born and wise,
> Honorable, noble lord,
> Your sweet love so urges me,
> Speaks to me and troubles me,
> God the Spirit grant me this:
> That you hold me in your arms,
> Once again my forehead kiss,
> Kiss my mouth and kiss my face,
> My sweet young lord."

### XXXVIII
*Now they tell and relate and continue the tale*

When the king of Carthage heard Nicolette speak in that way, he threw his arms around her neck.

"Fair sweet love," said he, "tell me who you are; don't you be afraid of me."

"Sir," said she, "I am the daughter of the king of Carthage, and I was stolen as a little child, fully fifteen years ago."

When he heard her speak thus, he knew well that she was speaking the truth; so did he make a very great holiday for her, and led her into the palace with great honor as the daughter of a king. For a husband he wished to give her a king of the pagans, but she had no desire to get married. She was there three or four full days. She reflected by what device she would be able to search for Aucassin. She bought herself a viol and learned to play it, until they wanted one day to marry her off to a rich pagan king. And she slipped out that night and came to the seaport; so did she take shelter with a poor woman on the shore. And she took an herb and smeared her head and face with it so that she was all black and stained. And she had a coat made and a cloak and a shirt and underbreeches, and rigged herself out in the guise of a jongleur. So she took her viol and came up to a sailor, and she made such terms with him that he took her aboard his ship. They raised their sails, and so did they sail away over the high seas until they arrived at the land of Provence. And Nicolette started out and took her viol; so did she go along playing through the country until she came to the Castle of Beaucaire, there where Aucassin was.

**XXXIX**

*Now it is sung*

> At Beaucaire beneath the tower
> There was Aucassin one day
> Seated on a stone stairway.
> Round him were his barons proud.
> He saw the grass and flowers
> And heard the small birds singing
> And remembered of his love,
> For the noble Nicolette,
> Whom he'd loved so many days.
> He gives way to sighs and tears.
> Look, below is Nicolette
> With her viol and her bow.
> Now she speaks and tells her tale,
> "Listen to me, noble lords,
> Those above and those below,
> Would you like to hear a song
> Of a proud lord, Aucassin,
> Of the noble Nicolette,
> How their love endured so long,
> How he sought her in the wood;
> At Torelore in prison
> The pagans one day put them.

> Naught of Aucassin we know,
> But the noble Nicolette
> At Carthage is in prison.
> Now her father loves her well
> Who is lord of all that realm.
> As bride they wish to give her
> To a wretched pagan king.
> Nicolette won't think of it,
> For she loves a fair young lord
> By the name of Aucassin.
> Well she swears by God's own name
> That she will never marry
> If she cannot have the one
>     Whom she so loves."

XL

*Now they tell and relate and continue the tale*

When Aucassin heard Nicolette speak thus, he was very glad, and he drew her aside and asked her:

"Fair sweet friend," said Aucassin, "do you know anything of this Nicolette of whom you have just sung?"

"Sir, yes," said she, "I know of her as the most noble creature, and the most gentle and the most wise that was ever born. She is the daughter of the King of Carthage, who took her when Aucassin was taken; so did he lead her into the city of Carthage until he had learned indeed that she was his daughter. He made a great festival; and he wished each day to give her for a husband one of the most exalted kings in all Spain, but she would rather let herself be hanged or burned than take any one of them, however rich he might be."

"Ah, fair sweet friend," said Count Aucassin, "if you would go back to that land and tell her to come here to speak to me, I would give you as much of my wealth as you would dare demand or take. And know that for love of her, I have no desire to take a wife however high her lineage may be, but only to wait for her. For I will have no wife if it isn't she. And if I had known where to find her, I would not be looking for her now."

"Sir," said she, "if you would do this, I would go and seek her for you and for her, whom I love very much."

He swore it to her, and then he had her given twenty pounds. She started to leave him, and he wept for the sweetness of Nicolette. When she saw him weeping:

"Sir," she said, "don't be dismayed, for in a little time I will have her brought into this town; so you will see her."

And when Aucassin heard her, he was very, very glad. And she went away from him; so did she go through the town to the house of the Viscountess, for the Viscount, her god-father, was dead.

There she stayed, and she talked to her until she had revealed her plan, and the Viscountess had recognized her and knew indeed that it was Nicolette whom she had reared. So did she have her washed and bathed, and she stayed there eight full days. Then she took an herb which is called Clarity and smeared herself with it. So was she as beautiful as she had ever been at any day. And she dressed herself in rich cloth of silk, of which the lady had much.

She sat in her chamber upon a quilt of stitched silk cloth, and she called the lady and told her that she should go for Aucassin, her love. She did it; and when she came to the palace, she found Aucassin who was weeping and regretting Nicolette his love because she delayed so long, and the lady called him and said to him:

"Aucassin, don't cry any more, but come along with me, and I will show you the thing that you love most in all the world, for it is Nicolette, your sweet love, who has come from distant lands to find you."

And Aucassin was overjoyed!

XLI

*Now it is sung*

> Now when Aucassin had heard
> Of his love with clearest face,
> How she had come to this land,
> Glad was he, never more so.
> With the lady has he gone;
> Straight to that house did he ride.
> There they entered in a room
> Where Nicolette was sitting.
> When she saw her lover there,
> Glad was she, never more so.
> Up she jumped and ran to him.
> And when Aucassin saw her,
> With both arms stretched out to her,
> He embraced her tenderly
> While he kissed her eyes and face.
> All that night they left them thus.
> In the morning, the next day,
> Aucassin made her his wife.
> Lady of Beaucaire she was;
> Then they lived for many days
> And much pleasure did they have.
> Now has Aucassin his joy
> And Nicolette hers likewise.
> Our *chantefable* takes its end.
>> I cannot tell you more.

# DANTE ALIGHIERI

## (1265–1321)

## The Divine Comedy (La divina commedia)*

*Hell (Inferno)*

### CANTO I

Halfway through his life, Dante the Pilgrim wakes to find himself
lost in a dark wood. Terrified at being alone in so dismal a valley,
he wanders until he comes to a hill bathed in sunlight, and his fear
begins to leave him. But when he starts to climb the hill his path
is blocked by three fierce beasts: first a Leopard, then a Lion, and
finally a She-Wolf. They fill him with fear and drive him back
down to the sunless wood. At that moment the figure of a man
appears before him; it is the shade of Virgil, and the Pilgrim begs
for help. Virgil tells him that he cannot overcome the beasts which
obstruct his path; they must remain until a "Greyhound" comes
who will drive them back to Hell. Rather by another path will the
Pilgrim reach the sunlight, and Virgil promises to guide him on
that path through Hell and Purgatory, at which time another spirit,
more fit than Virgil, will lead him to Paradise. The Pilgrim begs
Virgil to lead on, and the Guide starts ahead. The Pilgrim follows.

> Midway along the journey of our life
> I woke to find myself in some dark woods,
> for I had wandered off from the straight path.
> How hard it is to tell what it was like,
> this wood of wilderness, savage and stubborn    5
> (the thought of it brings back all my old fears),

---

* Abridged. Written in the early four-teenth century. *Inferno* (complete), from *Dante's Inferno*, translated with notes and commentary by Mark Musa, copyright, 1971, by Indiana University Press, Bloomington and London. Reprinted by permission of Indiana University Press. *Purgatorio* and *Paradiso* translated, with headnotes, by Lawrence Binyon; the foot-notes are by C. H. Grandgent, from *La divina commedia di Dante Alighieri*, edited and annotated by C. H. Grandgent, copyright, 1933, by D. C. Heath and Company, Boston. Reprinted with the permission of the translator's wife and the Society of Authors, and by special permission of D. C. Heath and Company, Boston.

1-10. The reader must be careful from the beginning to distinguish between the two uses of the first person singular in the *Divine Comedy:* one designating Dante the Pilgrim, the other Dante the Poet. The first is a character in a story invented by the second. The events are represented as having taken place in the past; the writing of the poem and the memories of these events are represented as taking place in the poet's present. We find references to both past and present, and to both pilgrim and poet in line 10: "How *I entered* there *I cannot* truly say."

1. In the Middle Ages life was often thought of as a journey, a pilgrimage, the goal of which was God and Heaven; and in the first line of the *Divine Comedy* Dante establishes the central motif of his poem—it is the story of man's pilgrimage to God. That we are meant to think in terms not just of the Pilgrim but of Everyman is indicated by the phrase "the journey of *our* life" (*our* journey through sin to repentance and redemption).

The imaginary date of the poem's beginning is the night before Good Friday in 1300, the year of the papal jubilee proclaimed by Boniface VIII. Born in 1265, Dante was thirty-five years old, which is one half of man's biblical life span of seventy years.

**Island of Purgatory**

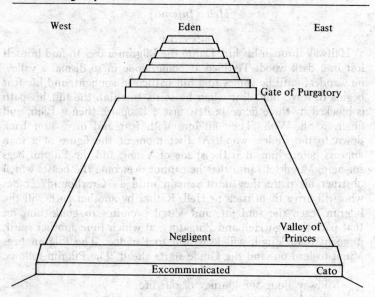

West — Eden — East

Gate of Purgatory

Valley of Princes

Negligent

Excommunicated — Cato

**Eden and Purgatory**

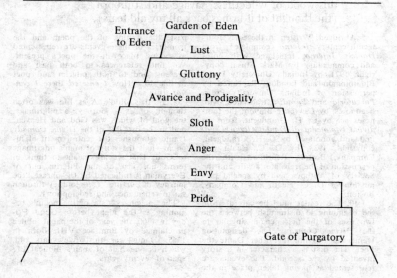

Entrance to Eden — Garden of Eden

Lust

Gluttony

Avarice and Prodigality

Sloth

Anger

Envy

Pride

Gate of Purgatory

## The Slope of Hell

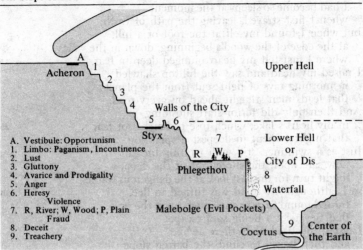

A. Vestibule: Opportunism
1. Limbo: Paganism, Incontinence
2. Lust
3. Gluttony
4. Avarice and Prodigality
5. Anger
6. Heresy
   Violence
7. R, River; W, Wood; P, Plain
   Fraud
8. Deceit
9. Treachery

Acheron

Upper Hell

Walls of the City

Styx

Lower Hell
or
City of Dis

Phlegethon

Waterfall

Malebolge (Evil Pockets)

Cocytus

Center of
the Earth

## The Heavenly Spheres

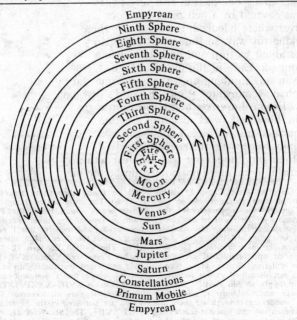

Empyrean
Ninth Sphere
Eighth Sphere
Seventh Sphere
Sixth Sphere
Fifth Sphere
Fourth Sphere
Third Sphere
Second Sphere
First Sphere
Fire
Air
Earth
Moon
Mercury
Venus
Sun
Mars
Jupiter
Saturn
Constellations
Primum Mobile
Empyrean

a bitter place! Death could scarce be bitterer.
 But if I would show the good that came of it
 I must talk about things other than the good.
How I entered there I cannot truly say,        10
 I had become so sleepy at the moment
 when I first strayed, leaving the path of truth;
but when I found myself at the foot of a hill,
 at the edge of the wood's beginning, down in the valley,
 where I first felt my heart plunged deep in fear,    15
I raised my head and saw the hilltop shawled
 in morning rays of light sent from the planet
 that leads men straight ahead on every road.
And then only did terror start subsiding
 in my heart's lake, which rose to heights of fear    20
 that night I spent in deepest desperation.
Just as a swimmer, still with panting breath,
 now safe upon the shore, out of the deep,
 might turn for one last look at the dangerous waters,
so I, although my mind was turned to flee,      25
 turned round to gaze once more upon the pass
 that never let a living soul escape.
I rested my tired body there awhile
 and then began to climb the barren slope
 (I dragged my stronger foot and limped along).    30
Beyond the point the slope begins to rise
 sprang up a leopard, trim and very swift!
 It was covered by a pelt of many spots.
And, everywhere I looked, the beast was there
 blocking my way, so time and time again      35
 I was about to turn and go back down.
The hour was early in the morning then,
 the sun was climbing up with those same stars
 that had accompanied it on the world's first day,
the day Divine Love set their beauty turning;     40
 so the hour and sweet season of creation
 encouraged me to think I could get past
that gaudy beast, wild in its spotted pelt,
 but then good hope gave way and fear returned
 when the figure of a lion loomed up before me,    45

13–15. Once we leave Canto I, which is the introduction to the whole of the *Divine Comedy*, the topography of the various regions of Hell will be described with elaborate carefulness. But in this canto all is vague and unprepared for; the scene is set in a "nowhere land"—the region of undifferentiated sin. Suddenly the Pilgrim awakes in a forest (which is not described except in terms that could apply to Sin itself: "wilderness, savage and stubborn"); suddenly, as he is wandering through it, there is a hill—whereupon the forest becomes a valley. Other suggestions of this dreamlike atmosphere (which, under the circumstances, must be that of a nightmare) will be found throughout this canto.

32–60. The early critics thought of the three beasts which block the Pilgrim's path as symbolizing three specific sins: lust, pride, and avarice; but I prefer to see in them the three major divisions of Hell. The spotted Leopard (l. 32) represents Fraud (cf. Canto XVI, ll. 106–108) and reigns over the Eighth and Ninth Circles where the Fraudulent are punished (Cantos XVIII–XXXIV). The Lion (l. 45) symbolizes all forms of Violence which are punished in the Seventh Circle (XII–XVII). The She-Wolf (l. 49) represents the different types of Concupiscence or Incontinence which are punished in Circles Two to Five (V–VIII).

and he was coming straight toward me, it seemed,
 with head raised high, and furious with hunger—
 the air around him seemed to fear his presence.
And now a she-wolf came, that in her leanness
 seemed racked with every kind of greediness           50
 (how many people she has brought to grief!).
This last beast brought my spirit down so low
 with fear that seized me at the sight of her,
 I lost all hope of going up the hill.
As a man who, rejoicing in his gains,                  55
 suddenly seeing his gain turn into loss,
 will grieve as he compares his then and now,
so she made me do, that relentless beast;
 coming towards me, slowly, step by step,
 she forced me back to where the sun is mute.          60
While I was moving down to that low place,
 my eyes made out a figure coming toward me
 of one grown weak, perhaps from too much silence.
And when I saw him standing in this wasteland,
 "Have pity on my soul," I cried to him,               65
 "whichever you are, shade or living man!"
"No longer living man, though once I was,"
 he said, "and my parents were from Lombardy,
 both of them were Mantuans by birth.
I was born, though somewhat late, *sub Julio,*         70
 and lived in Rome when good Augustus reigned,
 when still the false and lying gods were worshipped.
I was a poet and sang of that just man,
 son of Anchises, who sailed off from Troy
 after the burning of proud Ilium.                     75
But why retreat to so much misery?
 Why aren't you climbing up this joyous mountain,
 the beginning and the source of all man's bliss?"
"Are you then Virgil, are you then that fount
 from which pours forth so rich a stream of words?"    80
 I said to him bowing my head modestly.
"O light and honor of the other poets,
 may my long years of study, and that deep love
 that made me search your verses, help me now!
You are my teacher, the first of all my authors,      85

46–50. Note the triple use of the verb *seem* (which is a faithful reproduction of the original), intended to blur the figures of the Lion and the She-Wolf—in harmony with the "nowhereness" of the moral landscape.

62. The shade of Virgil miraculously appears before Dante. The Roman poet, who was born (70 B.C.) in the time of Julius Caesar (*sub Julio*), represents Reason, Natural Philosophy. The Pilgrim cannot proceed to the light of Divine Love (the mountain top) until he has overcome the three beasts of his sin; and because it is impossible for man to cope with the beasts unaided, Virgil, as Reason, has been summoned through the chain of divine command to guide the Pilgrim and help him overcome his sins by understanding and, later, repudiating them.

63. The voice of Reason has been silent in the Pilgrim's ear for a long time.

73–75. In the *Aeneid* Virgil relates the *post bellum* travels and deeds of Aeneas (son of Anchises) who, destined by the gods, founded on Italian soil the nation which, in the course of time, would become the Roman Empire.

and you alone the one from whom I took
the beautiful style that was to bring me honor.
You see the beast that forced me to retreat;
save me from her, I beg you, famous sage,
she makes me tremble, the blood throbs in my veins."     90
"But your journey must be down another road,"
he answered, when he saw me lost in tears,
"if ever you hope to leave this wilderness;
this beast, the one you cry about in fear,
allows no soul to succeed along her path,     95
she blocks his way and puts an end to him.
She is by nature so perverse and vicious,
her craving belly is never satisfied,
still hungering for food the more she eats.
She mates with many creatures, and will go on     100
mating with more until the greyhound comes
and tracks her down to make her die in anguish.
He will not feed on either land or money:
his wisdom, love, and virtue shall sustain him;
he will be born between Feltro and Feltro.     105
He comes to save that fallen Italy
for which the maid Camilla gave her life
and Turnus, Nisus, Euryalus died of wounds.
And he will hunt for her through every city
until he drives her back to Hell once more,     110
whence Envy first unleashed her on mankind.
And so, I think it best you follow me
for your own good, and I shall be your guide
and lead you out through an eternal place
where you will hear desperate cries, and see     115
tormented shades, some old as Hell itself,
and know what second death is, from their screams.
And later you will see those who rejoice
while they are burning, for they have hope of coming,
whenever it may be, to join the blessèd—     120

87. The reasons for the poet's selection of Virgil as the Pilgrim's guide (instead of, shall we say, Aristotle, *the* philosopher of the time) are several: Virgil was a poet and an Italian; in the *Aeneid* is recounted the hero's descent into Hell. But the main reason surely lies in the fact that, in the Middle Ages, Virgil was considered a prophet, a judgment stemming from the interpretation of some obscure lines in the *Fourth Eclogue* as foretelling the coming of Christ.

91. Dante must choose another road because, in order to arrive at the Divine Light, it is necessary first to recognize the true nature of sin, renounce it, and pay penance for it.

101–111. The Greyhound has been identified with Henry VII, Charles Martel, and even Dante himself. It seems more plausible that the Greyhound represents

Can Grande della Scala, the ruler of Verona from 1308 to 1329 whose "wisdom, love, and virtue" (l. 104) were certainly well-known to Dante. Whoever the Greyhound may be, the prophecy would seem to indicate in a larger sense the establishment of a spiritual kingdom on earth in which "wisdom, love, and virtue" will replace the bestial sins of the world.

107. "Camilla": the valiant daughter of King Metabus, who was slain while fighting against the Trojans (*Aeneid* XI).

108. "Turnus, Nisus, Euryalus": Turnus was the king of the Rutulians. Nisus and Euryalus were young Trojan warriors slain during a nocturnal raid on the camp of the Rutulians.

117. "second death": the death of the soul, which occurs when the soul is damned.

to whom, if you too wish to make the climb,
  a spirit, worthier than I, must take you;
    I shall go back, leaving you in her care,
because that Emperor dwelling on high
  will not let me lead any to his city,                            125
    since I in life rebelled against his law.
Everywhere he reigns, and there he rules;
  there is his city, there is his high throne.
    Oh happy the one he makes his citizen!"
And I to him: "Poet, I beg of you,                                130
  in the name of God, that God you never knew,
    save me from this evil place and worse,
lead me there to the place you spoke about
  that I may see the gate Saint Peter guards
    and those whose anguish you have told me of."                 135
Then he moved on, and I moved close behind him.


CANTO II

But the Pilgrim begins to waver; he expresses to Virgil his misgivings about his ability to undertake the journey proposed by Virgil.
His predecessors have been Aeneas and St. Paul, and he feels
unworthy to take his place in their company. But Virgil rebukes his
cowardice, and relates the chain of events which led him to come to
Dante. The Virgin Mary took pity on the Pilgrim in his despair and
instructed St. Lucia to aid him. The Saint turned to Beatrice
because of Dante's great love for her, and Beatrice in turn went
down to Hell, into Limbo, and asked Virgil to guide her friend
until that time when she herself would become his guide. The Pilgrim takes heart at Virgil's explanation and agrees to follow him.


The day was fading and the darkening air
  was releasing all the creatures on our earth
    from their daily tasks, and I, one man, alone,
was making ready to endure the battle
  of the journey, and of the pity it involved,                    5
    which my memory, unerring, shall now retrace.
O Muses! O high genius! Help me now!
  O memory that wrote down what I saw,
    here your true excellence shall be revealed!

122. Just as Virgil, the pagan Roman
poet, cannot enter the Christian Paradise
because he lived before the birth of Christ
and lacks knowledge of Christian salvation, so Reason can only guide the Pilgrim to a certain point: in order to enter
Paradise, the Pilgrim's guide must be
Christian Grace or Revelation (Theology)
in the figure of Beatrice.

124. Note the pagan terminology of
Virgil's reference to God; it expresses,
as best it can, his unenlightened conception of the Supreme Authority.

7–9. Dante links his own poem to the
classical epic tradition by invoking the
Muses.

Then I began: "O poet come to guide me,                    10
  tell me if you think my worth sufficient
  before you trust me to this arduous road.
You wrote about young Sylvius' father
  who went beyond, with flesh corruptible,
  with all his senses, to the immortal realm;               15
but if the adversary of all evil
  was kind to him, considering who he was,
  and the consequence that was to come from him,
this cannot seem, to thoughtful men, unfitting,
  for in the highest heaven he was chosen                   20
  father of glorious Rome and of her empire,
and both the city and her lands, in truth,
  were established as the place of holiness
  where the successors of great Peter sit.
And from this journey you celebrate in verse,              25
  Aeneas learned those things that were to bring
  victory for him, and for Rome, the Papal seat;
then later the Chosen Vessel, Paul, ascended
  to bring back confirmation of that faith
  which is the first step on salvation's road.              30
But, why am I to go? Who allows me to?
  *I* am not Aeneas, I am not Paul,
  neither I nor any man would think me worthy;
and so, if I should undertake the journey,
  I fear it might turn out an act of folly—                 35
  you are wise, you see more than my words express."
As one who unwills what he willed, will change
  his purposes with some new second thought,
  completely quitting what he first had started,
so I did, standing there on that dark slope,               40
  thinking, ending the beginning of that venture
  I was so quick to take up at the start.
"If I have truly understood your words,"
  that shade of magnanimity replied,
  "your soul is burdened with that cowardice                45
which often weighs so heavily on man

10–48. Dante the Pilgrim expresses fear
of a journey such as Virgil proposes, for
he finds himself wholly unworthy beside the two who have been allowed to
visit "eternal regions" before—Aeneas and
St. Paul. The comparison between Dante
the Pilgrim and Aeneas and Paul is significant. For Virgil, Aeneas's journey had
but one consequence: empire; for Dante,
however, it signified both empire and the
establishment of the Holy Roman Church,
the "City of God" where all popes reside
and reign. The fundamental concepts of
Church and State, their government, their
conflicts and internal problems were very
important to Dante, and form one of the
central themes of the *Comedy*.
13–21. "Sylvius": the son of Aeneas by
Lavinia, his second wife and daughter to
Latinus.
  In the *Aeneid* Virgil recounts the history of the founding of Rome. After the
fall of Troy, Aeneas, the legendary hero
of the epic, embarked on his divinely
inspired journey that eventually led him
to the shores of Italy, where he was to
establish his city and nation.
28–30. "the Chosen Vessel, Paul": In
his *Second Epistle to the Corinthians*
(12:2–4) the Apostle Paul alludes to his
mystical elevation to the third heaven and
to the arcane messages pronounced there.
37–42. One of Dante's favorite poetic
devices is to imitate the "action" stylis-
tically. Here the Pilgrim's confused state
of mind (his fear and lack of conviction)
is reflected by the involved structure of the
lines.

it turns him from a noble enterprise
like a frightened beast that shies at its own shadow.
To free you from this fear, let me explain
   the reason I came here, the words I heard     50
   that first time I felt pity for your soul:
I was among those dead who are suspended,
   when a lady summoned me. She was so blessed
   and beautiful, I implored her to command me.
With eyes of light more bright than any star,     55
   in low, soft tones she started to address me
   in her own language, with an angel's voice:
'O noble soul, courteous Mantuan,
   whose fame the world continues to preserve
   and will preserve as long as world there is,     60
my friend, who is no friend of Fortune's, strays
   on desert slope; so many obstacles
   have crossed his path, his fright has turned him back.
I fear he may have gone so far astray,
   from what report has come to me in Heaven,     65
   that I may have started to his aid too late.
Now go, and with your elegance of speech,
   with whatever may be needed for his freedom,
   give him your help, and thereby bring me solace.
I am Beatrice, who urges you to go;     70
   I come from the place I am longing to return to;
   love moved me, as it moves me now to speak.
When I return to stand before my Lord,
   often I shall sing your praises to Him.'
   And then she spoke no more. And I began,     75
'O Lady of Grace, through whom alone mankind
   may go beyond all worldly things contained
   within the sphere that makes the smallest circle,
your plea fills me with happy eagerness—
   to have obeyed already would still seem late!     80
   You needed only to express your wish.
But tell me how you dared to make this journey

49–142. The second major movement
in Canto II includes Virgil's explanation
of his coming to the Pilgrim, and the
subsequent restoration of the latter's
courage. According to Virgil, the Virgin
Mary, who traditionally signifies mercy
and compassion in Christian thought,
took pity on the Pilgrim in his predicament and set in motion the operation of
Divine Grace. Lucia, whose name means
"light," suggests the Illuminating Grace
sent for by the Blessed Virgin; without
Divine Grace the Pilgrim would be lost.
Beatrice, whose name signifies blessedness
or salvation, appears to Virgil in order
to reveal to him the will of God who is
the ultimate bestower of Divine Grace.
The three heavenly ladies balance the

three beasts of Canto I; they represent
man's salvation from sin through Grace,
as the beasts represent man's sins. The
Pilgrim's journey, then, actually starts in
Paradise when the Blessed Virgin Mary
takes pity on him; thus the action of the
*Divine Comedy* is in one sense a circle
which begins in Heaven, as related here,
and will ultimately end in Heaven with
the Pilgrim's vision of God (*Paradiso*,
Canto XXXIII).

52. In the *Inferno* Virgil is assigned
to Limbo, the dwelling place of those
virtuous shades not eligible for Heaven
because they either lived before Christ's
birth or remained heathen after the advent of Christianity (see Canto IV, note
on l. 34).

all the way down to this point of spacelessness
away from your spacious home that calls you back.'
'Because your question searches for deep meaning,                    85
   I shall explain in simple words,' she said,
   'just why I have no fear of coming here.
A man must stand in fear of just those things
   that truly have the power to do us harm,
   of nothing else, for nothing else is fearsome.                    90
God gave me such a nature through His Grace,
   the torments you must bear cannot affect me,
   nor are the fires of Hell a threat to me.
A gracious lady sits in Heaven grieving
   for what happened to the one I send you to,                      95
   and her compassion breaks Heaven's stern decree.
She called Lucia and making her request
   she said, "Your faithful one is now in need
   of you, and to you I now commend his soul."
Lucia, the enemy of cruelty,                                         100
   hastened to make her way to where I was,
   sitting by the side of ancient Rachel,
and said to me: "Beatrice, God's true praise,
   will you not help the one whose love was such
   it made him leave the vulgar crowd for you?                      105
Do you not hear the pity of his weeping,
   do you not see what death it is that threatens him
   along that river the sea shall never conquer?"
There never was a worldly person living
   more anxious to promote his selfish gains                        110
   than I was at the sound of words like these—
to leave my holy seat and come down here
   and place my trust in you, in your noble speech
   that honors you and all those hearing it.'
When she had finished reasoning, she turned                          115
   her shining eyes away, and there were tears.
   How eager then I was to come to you!
And I have come to you just as she wished,
   and I have freed you from the beast that stood
   blocking the quick way up the mount of bliss.                    120
So what is wrong? Why, why do you delay?
   why are you such a coward in your heart,
   why aren't you bold and free of all your fear,
when three such gracious ladies who are blessed
   watch out for you up there in Heaven's court,                   125
   and my words, too, bring promise of such good?"
As little flowers from the evening chill
   are closed and limp, and when the sun shines down

---

94. The Virgin Mary.
102. In the Dantean Paradise Rachel is
seated by Beatrice.
119–126. The Pilgrim's initial failure to
climb the mountain (due to the presence
of the She-Wolf, I, 49–60) and his subsequent state of desperation are recalled
in these lines. Freed now, however, from
this peril by Virgil, and assured of success by the "three gracious ladies," he
should no longer be hindered from his
journey by fear or any hesitation.

on them, they rise to open on their stem,
my wilted strength began to bloom within me,       130
   and such good zeal went flowing to my heart
   I began to speak as one free in the sun.
"O, she, compassionate, who moved to help me!
   And you, all kindness, in obeying quick
   those words of truth she brought with her for you—     135
you and the words you spoke have moved my heart
   with such desire to continue onward
   that now I have returned to my first purpose.
Let us start, for both our wills, joined now, are one.
   You are my guide, you are my lord and teacher."     140
   These were my words to him and, when he moved,
I entered on that deep and rugged road.

### CANTO III

As the two poets enter the vestibule that leads to Hell itself,
Dante sees the inscription above the gate, and he hears the screams
of anguish from the damned souls. Rejected by God and not
accepted by the powers of Hell the first group of souls are
"nowhere," because of their cowardly refusal to make a choice in
life. Their punishment is to follow a banner at a furious pace forever, and to be tormented by flies and hornets. The Pilgrim recognizes several of these shades but mentions none by name. Next they
come to the River Acheron where they are greeted by the infernal
boatman Charon. Among those doomed souls who are to be ferried
across the river, Charon sees the living man and challenges him, but
Virgil lets it be known that his companion must pass. Then across
the landscape rushes a howling wind which blasts the Pilgrim out of
his senses, and he falls to the ground.

THROUGH ME THE WAY INTO THE DOLEFUL CITY,
   THROUGH ME THE WAY INTO ETERNAL GRIEF,
   THROUGH ME THE WAY AMONG A RACE FORSAKEN.
JUSTICE MOVED MY HEAVENLY CONSTRUCTOR;
   DIVINE OMNIPOTENCE CREATED ME,      5
   AND HIGHEST WISDOM JOINED WITH PRIMAL LOVE.
BEFORE ME NOTHING BUT ETERNAL THINGS
   WERE MADE, AND I SHALL LAST ETERNALLY.
   ABANDON HOPE, FOREVER, YOU WHO ENTER.
I saw these words spelled out in somber colors     10
   inscribed along the ledge above a gate;
   "Master," I said, "these words I see are cruel."
He answered me, speaking with experience:

5–6. "DIVINE OMNIPOTENCE . . . HIGH-
EST WISDOM . . . PRIMAL LOVE": the
Father, the Son, the Holy Ghost. Thus,
the gate of Hell was created by the Trinity moved by Justice.

"Now here you must leave all distrust behind;
  let all your cowardice die on this spot. 15
We are at the place where earlier I said
  you could expect to see the suffering race
  of souls who lost the good of intellect."
Placing his hand on mine, smiling at me
  in such a way that I was reassured, 20
  he led me in, into those mysteries.
Here sighs and cries and shrieks of lamentation
  echoed throughout the starless air of Hell;
  at first these sounds resounding made me weep:
tongues confused, a language strained in anguish 25
  with cadences of anger, shrill outcries
  and raucous groans in time to slapping hands,
raising a whirling storm that turns itself
  forever through that air of endless black,
  like grains of sand swirling when a whirlwind blows. 30
And I, in the midst of all this circling horror,
  began, "Teacher, what are these sounds I hear?
  What souls are these so overwhelmed by grief?"
And he to me: "This wretched state of being
  is the fate of those sad souls who lived a life 35
  but lived it with no blame and with no praise.
They are mixed with that repulsive choir of angels
  neither faithful nor unfaithful to their God,
  but undecided in neutrality.
Heaven, to keep its beauty, cast them out, 40
  but even Hell itself would not receive them
  for fear the wicked there might glory over them."
And I: "Master, what torments do they suffer
  that make such bitterness ring through their screams?"
He answered: "I will tell you in few words: 45
these wretches have no hope of truly dying,
  and this blind life they lead is so abject
  it makes them envy every other fate.
The world will not record their having been there;
  Heaven's mercy and its justice turn from them. 50
  Let's not discuss them; look and pass them by."
And so I looked and saw a kind of banner
  rushing ahead, whirling with aimless speed
  as though it would not ever take a stand;

---

18. Souls who have lost sight of God.

22–30. Entering the Vestibule of Hell, the Pilgrim is immediately stunned by the screams of the shades in the Vestibule, borne to him in the form of an awesome tempest. In this first encounter with eternal punishment, he receives, as it were, an acoustical impression of Hell in its entirety.

35–42. The first tormented souls whom the Pilgrim meets are not in Hell itself but in the Vestibule leading to it. In a sense they are the most loathsome sinners of all because in life they performed neither meritorious nor reprehensible acts. Heaven has damned them but Hell will not accept them.

52–69. In the *Inferno* divine retribution assumes the form of the *contrapasso*, i.e., the just punishment of sin, effected by a process either resembling or contrasting to the sin itself. In this Canto the *contrapasso* opposes the sin of neutrality, or inactivity: The souls who in their early lives had no banner, no leader to follow, now run forever after one.

behind it an interminable train                                     55
  of souls pressed on, so many that I wondered
  how death could have undone so great a number.
When I had recognized a few of them,
  I saw the shade of the one who must have been
  the coward who had made the great refusal.          60
At once I understood, and I was sure
  this was that sect of evil souls who were
  hateful to God and to His enemies.
These wretches, who had never truly lived,
  went naked, and were stung and stung again           65
  by the hornets and the wasps that circled them
and made their faces run with blood in streaks;
  their blood, mixed with their tears, dripped to their feet,
  and disgusting maggots collected in the pus.
And when I looked beyond this crowd I saw               70
  a throng upon the shore of a wide river,
  which made me ask, "Master, I would like to know:
who are these people, and what law is this
  that makes those souls so eager for the crossing—
  as I can see, even in this dim light?"                 75
And he: "All this will be made plain to you
  as soon as we shall come to stop awhile
  upon the sorrowful shore of Acheron."
And I, with eyes cast down in shame, for fear
  that I perhaps had spoken out of turn,                 80
  said no more until we reached the river.
And suddenly, coming towards us in a boat,
  a man of years whose ancient hair was white
  screamed at us, "Woe to you, perverted souls!
Give up all hope of ever seeing heaven:                85
  I come to lead you to the other shore,
  into eternal darkness, ice and fire.
And you, the living soul, you over there,
  get away from all these people who are dead."
But when he saw I did not move aside                   90
he said, "Another way, by other ports,
  not here, shall you pass to reach the other shore;
  a lighter skiff than this must carry you."

---

60. Most critics say this is Celestine V who renounced the papacy in 1294 five months after having been elected. However, Celestine, considering himself inadequate to the task, resigned his office out of humility, not out of cowardice. And the fact that the ex-pope was canonized in 1313 indicates that his refusal might well have been interpreted as a pious act.

Perhaps it is most likely that this shade is Pontius Pilate who refused to pass sentence on Christ. His role, then, would be paralleled to that of the "neutral angels": as they stood by while Lucifer rebelled against God, so Pilate's neutral ˙attitude at the trial of Christ resulted in the crucifixion of Christ.

78. "Acheron": one of the rivers of Hell whose origin is explained in Canto XIV, ll. 112–120; it serves as the outer boundary of Hell proper.

83. "a man of years": Charon, the boatman of classical mythology who transports the souls of the dead across the Acheron into Hades.

91–93. Charon, whose boat bears only the souls of the damned, recognizes the Pilgrim as a living man and refuses him passage. This tercet contains a prophecy of Dante's salvation: "by other ports" he will pass to "reach the other shore (of the Tiber)," and go to Purgatory and eventually to Paradise.

And my guide, "Charon, this is no time for anger!
　　It is so willed, there where the power is　　　　95
　　for what is willed; that's all you need to know."
These words brought silence to the woolly cheeks
　　of the ancient steersman of the livid marsh,
　　whose eyes were set in glowing wheels of fire.
But all those souls there, naked, in despair,　　　　100
　　changed color and their teeth began to chatter
　　at the sound of his announcement of their doom.
They were cursing God, cursing their mother and father,
　　the human race, and the time, the place, the seed
　　of their beginning, and their day of birth.　　　105
Then all together, weeping bitterly,
　　they packed themselves along the wicked shore
　　that waits for everyman who fears not God.
The devil, Charon, with eyes of glowing coals,
　　summons them all together with a signal,　　　　110
　　and with an oar he strikes the laggard sinner.
As in autumn when the leaves begin to fall,
　　one after the other (until the branch
　　is witness to the spoils spread on the ground),
so did the evil seed of Adam's Fall　　　　　　　115
　　drop from that shore to the boat, one at a time,
　　at the signal, like the falcon to its lure.
Away they go across the darkened waters,
　　and before they reach the other side to land,
　　a new throng starts collecting on this side.　　120
"My son," the gentle master said to me,
　　"all those who perish in the wrath of God
　　assemble here from all parts of the earth;
they want to cross the river, they are eager;
　　it is Divine Justice that spurs them on,　　　　125
　　turning the fear they have into desire.
A good soul never comes to make this crossing,
　　so, if Charon grumbles at the sight of you,
　　you see now what his words are really saying."
He finished speaking, and the grim terrain　　　　130
　　shook violently; and the fright it gave me
　　even now in recollection makes me sweat.
Out of the tear-drenched land a wind arose
　　which blasted forth into a reddish light,
　　knocking my senses out of me completely,　　　135
and I fell as one falls tired into sleep.

100. Though we must assume that all the damned in the *Inferno* are naked (except the Hypocrites, Canto XXIII), only occasionally is this fact pointed out.
124–126. It is perhaps a part of the punishment that the souls of all the damned are eager for their punishment to begin; those who were so willing to sin on earth, are in Hell damned with a willingness to go to their just retribution.
136. The swoon (or sleep) as a transitional device is used again at the end of Canto V. Note also the opening lines of Canto I where the Pilgrim's awaking from sleep serves an introductory purpose.

CANTO IV

Waking from his swoon, the Pilgrim is led by Virgil to the first
Circle of Hell, known as Limbo, where the sad shades of the virtuous non-Christians dwell. The souls here, including Virgil, suffer
no physical torment, but they must live, in desire, without hope of
seeing God. Virgil tells about Christ's descent into Hell and His salvation of several Old Testament figures. The poets see a light glowing in the darkness, and as they proceed toward it, they are met by the
four greatest (other than Virgil) pagan poets: Homer, Horace,
Ovid, and Lucan, who take the Pilgrim into their group. As they
come closer to the light, the Pilgrim perceives a splendid castle
where the greatest non-Christian thinkers dwell together with other
famous historical figures. Once within the castle, the Pilgrim sees,
among others, Electra, Aeneas, Caesar, Saladin, Aristotle, Plato,
Orpheus, Cicero, Avicenna, and Averroës. But soon they must leave;
and the poets move from the radiance of the castle toward the fearful encompassing darkness.

A heavy clap of thunder! I awoke
   from the deep sleep that drugged my mind—startled,
   the way one is when shaken out of sleep.
I turned my rested eyes from side to side,
   already on my feet and, staring hard,           5
   I tried my best to find out where I was,
and this is what I saw: I found myself
   right on the brink of grief's abysmal valley
   that collects the thunderings of endless cries.
So dark and deep and nebulous it was,          10
   try as I might to force my sight below
   I could not see the shape of anything.
"Let us descend into the sightless world,"
   began the poet (his face was deathly pale):
   "I will go first, and you will follow me."      15
And I, aware of his changed color, said:
   "But how can I go on if you are frightened?
   You are my constant strength when I lose heart."
And he to me: "The anguish of the souls
   that are down here paints my face with pity—    20
   which you have wrongly taken to be fear.
Let us go on, the long road urges us."
   He entered then, leading the way for me
   down to the first circle of the abyss.
Down there, to judge only by what I heard,    25
   there were no wails but just the sounds of sighs
   rising and trembling through the timeless air,
The sounds of sighs of untormented grief
   burdening these groups, diverse and teeming,
   made up of men and women and of infants.    30

Then the good master said, "You do not ask
  what sort of souls are these you see around you.
  Now you should know before we go on farther,
they have not sinned. But their great worth alone
  was not enough, for they did not know Baptism       35
  which is the gateway to the faith you follow,
and if they came before the birth of Christ
  they did not worship God the way one should;
  I myself am a member of this group.
For this defect, and for no other guilt,       40
  we here are lost. In this alone we suffer:
  cut off from hope, we live on in desire."
The words I heard weighed heavy on my heart;
  to think that souls as virtuous as these
  were suspended in that limbo, and forever!       45
"Tell me, my teacher, tell me, O my master,"
  I began (wishing to have confirmed by him
  the teachings of unerring Christian doctrine),
"did any ever leave here, through his merit
  or with another's help, and go to bliss?"       50
  And he who understood my hidden question,
answered: "I was a novice in this place
  when I saw a mighty lord descend to us
  who wore the sign of victory as his crown.
He took from us the shade of our first parent,       55
  of Abel, his good son, of Noah, too,
  and of obedient Moses, who made the laws;
Abram, the Patriarch, David the King,
  Israel with his father and his children,
  with Rachel whom he worked so hard to win;      60
and many more he chose for blessedness;
  and you should know, before these souls were taken,
  no human soul had ever reached salvation."
We did not stop our journey while he spoke,
  but continued on our way along the woods—      65
  I say the woods, for souls were thick as trees.
We had not gone too far from where I woke

---

**34.** According to Christian doctrine no one outside the Church (i.e., without baptism, the first Sacrament and, thus, the "gateway to the faith") can be saved. The souls suspended in Limbo, the first circle of Hell, were on earth virtuous individuals who had no knowledge of Christ and His teachings (through no fault of their own since they preceded Him) or who, after His coming, died unbaptized. Here physical torment is absent; these shades suffer only mental anguish for, now cognizant of the Christian God, they have to "live on in desire" without any hope of beholding Him.

**49–50. The Pilgrim,** remembering the Church's teaching concerning Christ's Harrowing of Hell, attempts to verify it by questioning Virgil, who should have been there at the time. Note the cautious presentation of the question (especially on the phrase "with another's help"), by means of which the Pilgrim, more than reassuring himself about Church doctrine, is subtly testing his guide. Virgil responds to the Pilgrim's "hidden question" in the terms of his classical culture. Unable to understand Christ in Christian terms, Virgil can only refer to Him as a "mighty lord . . . who wore the sign of victory as his crown."

when I made out a fire up ahead,
a hemisphere of light that lit the dark.
Though we were still some distance from that place,                    70
we were close enough for me to vaguely see
that distinguished people occupied that spot.
"O glory of the sciences and arts,
who are these souls enjoying special honor,
dwelling apart from all the others here?"                             75
And he to me: "The honored name they bear
that still resounds above in your own world
wins Heaven's favor for them in this place."
And as he spoke I heard a voice announce:
"Now let us honor our illustrious poet,                               80
his shade that left is now returned to us."
And when the voice was silent and all was quiet
I saw four mighty shades approaching us,
their faces showing neither joy nor sorrow.
Then my good master started to explain:                              85
"Observe the one who comes with sword in hand,
leading the three as if he were their master.
It is the shade of Homer, sovereign poet,
and coming second, Horace, the satirist;
Ovid is the third, and last comes Lucan.                             90
Since they all share one name with me, the name
you heard resounding in that single voice,
they honor me and do well doing so."
So I saw gathered there the noble school
of the master singer of sublimest verse                              95
who soars above all others like the eagle.
And after they had talked awhile together,
they turned and with a gesture welcomed me,
and at that sign I saw my master smile.
Greater honor still they deigned to grant me:                       100
they welcomed me as one of their own group,
so that I numbered sixth among such minds.
We walked together towards the shining light,
discussing things that here are best kept silent,
as there they were most fitting for discussion.                     105

---

69. The "hemisphere of light" emanates from a "splendid castle" (l. 106), the dwelling place of the virtuous men of wisdom in Limbo. The light is the illumination of human intellect which those who dwell there had in such high measure on earth.

86–88. Because his name was inseparably linked with the Trojan War, Homer is portrayed by Dante as a sword-bearing poet, one who sang of arms and martial heroes.

90. Ovid's major work, the *Metamorphoses*, was widely read and consulted as the principal source and authority for classical mythology during the Middle Ages. Lucan provided Dante with mythological material, and with much historical information on the civil war between Pompey and Caesar (*Pharsalia*).

100–102. In this passage Dante, equating himself with the famous poets of antiquity, acknowledges his art and talent. By this it should not be assumed that he is merely indulging in self-praise; rather, the reader should also interpret these lines as an indication of Dante's awareness of his role as a poet, of his purpose in writing, and of his unique position in the literary scene of his day.

We reached the boundaries of a splendid castle
    that seven times was circled by high walls
    defended by a sweetly flowing stream.
We walked right over it as on hard ground;
    through seven gates I passed with those wise spirits,     110
    and then we reached a meadow fresh in bloom.
There people were whose eyes were calm and grave,
    whose bearing told of great authority;
    seldom they spoke and always quietly.
Then moving to one side we reached a place     115
    spread out and luminous, higher than before,
    allowing us to view all who were there.
And right before us on the lustrous green
    the mighty shades were pointed out to me
    (my heart felt glory when I looked at them).     120
There was Electra standing with a group,
    among whom I saw Hector and Aeneas,
    and Caesar, falcon-eyed and fully armed.
I saw Camilla and Penthesilea;
    across the way I saw the Latian King,     125
    with Lavinia, his daughter, by his side.
I saw the Brutus who drove out the Tarquin;
    Lucretia, Julia, Marcia and Cornelia;
    off, by himself, I noticed Saladin,

106–111. The allegorical construction of the castle is open to question. It may represent natural philosophy unilluminated by divine wisdom, in which case the seven walls serving to protect the castle would be the seven moral and speculative virtues (prudence, justice, fortitude, temperance, intellect, science, and knowledge); and the seven gates which provide access to the castle would be the seven liberal arts which formed the medieval school curriculum (music, arithmetic, geometry, astronomy—the *quadrivium;* and grammar, logic, and rhetoric —the *trivium*). The symbolic value of the stream also remains uncertain; it could signify eloquence, a "stream" which the eloquent Virgil and Dante should have no trouble crossing—and indeed, they "walked right over it as on hard ground" (l. 109).

112–144. The inhabitants of the great castle are important pagan philosophers and poets, as well as famous writers. Three of the shades named (Saladin, Avicenna, Averroës) lived only one or two hundred years before Dante. Modern readers might wonder at the inclusion of medieval non-Christians among the virtuous Pagans of antiquity, but the three just mentioned were among the non-Christians whom the Middle Ages, particularly, respected.

121. "Electra": daughter of Atlas, the mother of Dardanus, the founder of Troy. Thus, her followers include all members of the Trojan race. She should not be confused with Electra, daughter of Agamemmon, the character in plays by Aeschylus, Sophocles, and Euripides.

122. Among Electra's descendants are: "Hector," the eldest son of Priam, king of Troy, and "Aeneas" (cf. I, 73–75, and II, 13–24).

123. Julius Caesar proclaimed himself the first emperor of Rome after defeating numerous opponents in civil conflicts.

124–126. "Camilla": see Canto I, note on l. 107. "Penthesilea": the glamorous Queen of the Amazons who aided the Trojans against the Greeks and was slain by Achilles during the conflict. "King Latinus": commanded the central region of the Italian peninsula, the site where Aeneas founded Rome. He gave Lavinia to the Trojan conqueror in marriage.

127–129. Outraged by the murder of his brother and the rape (and subsequent suicide) of his sister (Lucretia), Lucius Brutus incited the Roman populace to expel the Tarquins, the perpetrators of the offences. This accomplished, he was elected first consul and consequently became the founder of the Roman Republic. The four women were famous Roman wives and mothers. "Lucretia": wife of Collatinus; "Julia": daughter of Julius Caesar and wife of Pompey; "Marcia":

and when I raised my eyes a little higher    130
   I saw the master sage of those who know
   sitting with his philosophic family.
All gaze at him, all pay their homage to him;
   and there I saw both Socrates and Plato,
   each closer to his side than any other;    135
Democritus, who said the world was chance,
   Diogenes, Thales, Anaxagoras,
   Empedocles, Zeno, and Heraclitus;
I saw the one who classified our herbs:
   Dioscorides I mean. And I saw Orpheus,    140
   Tully, Linus, Seneca the moralist,
Euclid the geometer and Ptolemy,
   Hippocrates, Galen, Avicenna,
   and Averroës who made the Commentary.
I cannot tell about them all in full;    145
   my theme is long and urges me ahead,
   often I must omit things I have seen.
The company of six becomes just two;
   my wise guide leads me by another way
   out of the quiet into tempestuous air.    150
I come into a place where no light is.

second wife of Cato of Utica (in the *Convivio* Dante makes her the symbol of the noble soul); "Cornelia": daughter of Scipio Africanus Major and mother of the Gracchi, the tribunes Tiberius and Caius. A distinguished soldier, Saladin became sultan of Egypt in 1174. Medieval opinion of Saladin was favorable; he was lauded for his generosity and his magnanimity.

131. To Dante, Aristotle represented the summit of human reason, that point which man could reach on his own without the benefit of Christian revelation.

137. "Diogenes": the Cynic Philosopher who believed that the only good lies in virtue secured through self-control and abstinence. "Anaxagoras": a Greek philosopher of the Ionian school (500–428 B.C.). Among his famous students were Pericles and Euripides. "Thales": (ca. 635–ca. 545 B.C.), an early Greek philosopher born at Miletus, founded the Ionian school of philosophy, and in his main doctrine maintained that water is the elemental principle of all things.

140. "Dioscorides": a Greek natural scientist and physician of the first century A.D. "Orpheus": a mythical Greek poet and musician whose lyrical talent was such that it moved rocks and trees and tamed wild beasts.

141. "Tully": Marcus Tullius Cicero, celebrated Roman orator, writer, and philosopher (106–43 B.C.). "Linus": a mythical Greek poet and musician who is

credited with inventing the dirge. Lucius Annaeus "Seneca" (4 B.C.–65 A.D.): followed the philosophy of the Stoics in his moral treatises. Dante calls him "the moralist" to distinguish him from Seneca the tragedian who was thought (erroneously) during the Middle Ages to be another person.

142. "Euclid": a Greek mathematician (ca. 300 B.C.) who wrote a treatise on geometry which was the first codification and exposition of mathematical principles. "Ptolemy": a Greek mathematician, astronomer, and geographer. The Ptolemaic system of the universe (which was accepted by the Middle Ages), so named although he did not invent it, presented the earth as its fixed center encircled by nine spheres (see illustration p. 000).

143. "Hippocrates": a Greek physician (ca. 460–ca. 377 B.C.), who founded the medical profession and introduced the scientific art of healing. "Galen": a celebrated physician (ca. 130–ca. 200 A.D.) who practiced his art in Greece, Egypt, and Rome. "Avicenna" (or Ibn-Sina): an Arabian philosopher and physician (980–1037 A.D.) who was a prolific writer.

144. "and Averroës who made the Commentary": Ibn-Rushd, called Averroës (ca. 1126–ca. 1198 A.D.), was a celebrated Arabian scholar born in Spain. He was widely known in the Middle Ages for his commentary on Aristotle, which served as the basis for the work of St. Thomas Aquinas.

CANTO V

From Limbo Virgil leads his ward down to the threshold of the Second Circle of Hell where, for the first time, he will see the damned in Hell being punished for their sins. There, barring their way, is the hideous figure of Minòs, the bestial judge of Dante's underworld; but after strong words from Virgil, the poets are allowed to pass into the dark space of this circle, where can be heard the wailing voices of the Lustful, whose punishment consists of being forever whirled about in a dark, stormy wind. After seeing a thousand or more famous lovers—including Semiramis, Dido, Helen, Achilles, and Paris—the Pilgrim asks to speak to two figures he sees together. They are Francesca da Rimini and her lover Paolo, and the scene in which they appear is probably the most famous episode of the *Inferno*. At the end of the scene, the Pilgrim, who has been overcome by pity for the lovers, faints to the ground.

This way I went, descending from the first
   into the second circle, that holds less space
   but much more pain—stinging the soul to wailing.
There stands Minòs grotesquely, and he snarls,
   examining the guilty at the entrance;                 5
   he judges and dispatches, tail in coils.
By this I mean that when the evil soul
   appears before him, it confesses all,
   and he who is the expert judge of sins
sees what place in Hell the soul belongs to;            10
   the times he wraps his tail around himself
   tells just how far the sinner must go down.
The damned keep crowding up in front of him:
   they pass along to judgment one by one;
   they speak, they hear, and then are hurled below.     15
"Oh you who come to the place where pain is host,"
   Minòs spoke out when he caught sight of me,
   putting aside the duties of his office,
"be careful how you enter and whom you trust:
   it is easy to get in, but don't be fooled!"          20
And my guide to him: "Why do you keep on shouting?
Do not attempt to stop his fated journey;
   it is so willed there where the power is
   for what is willed; that's all you need to know."
And now the notes of anguish start to play         25
   upon my ears; and now I find myself

4. "Minòs": the son of Zeus and Europa. As king of Crete he was revered for his wisdom and judicial gifts. For these qualities he became chief magistrate of the underworld in classical literature:

   Quaesitor Minos urnam movet: ille silentum

Conciliumque vocat, vitasque et crimina discit.

   (Virgil, *Aeneid* VI, 432–433)

Although Dante did not alter Minòs's official function, he transformed him into a demonic figure, both in his physical characteristics and in his bestial activity.

where sounds on sounds of weeping pound at me.
I came to a place where no light shone at all,
  bellowing like the sea racked by a tempest,
  when warring winds attack it from both sides. 30
The infernal storm, eternal in its rage,
  sweeps and drives the spirits with its blast:
  it whirls them, lashing them with punishment.
When they are swept back past their place of judgment,
  then come the shrieks, laments and anguished cries; 35
  there they blaspheme the power of almighty God.
I learned that to this place of punishment
  all those who sin in lust have been condemned,
  those who make reason slave to appetite;
and as the wings of starlings in the winter 40
  bear them along in wide-spread, crowded flocks,
  so does that wind propel the evil spirits:
here, then there, and up and down, it sweeps them
  forever, without hope to comfort them
  (hope, not of taking rest, but of suffering less). 45
And just like cranes in flight, chanting their lays,
  stretching an endless line in their formation,
  I saw approaching, crying their laments,
spirits carried along by the battling winds.
  And so I asked, "Teacher, tell me, what souls 50
  are these punished in the sweep of the black wind?"
"The first of those whose story you should know,"
  my master wasted no time answering,
  "was empress over lands of many tongues;
her vicious tastes had so corrupted her, 55
  she licensed every form of lust with laws
  to cleanse the stain of scandal she had spread;
she is Semiramis who, legend says,
  was Ninus' wife and successor to his throne;
  she governed all the land the Sultan rules. 60
The next is she who killed herself for love
  and broke faith with the ashes of Sichaeus;
  and there is Cleopatra who loved men's lusting.

---

31–32. The *contrapasso* or punishment
suggests that lust (the "infernal storm")
is pursued without the light of reason (in
the darkness).

34. In Italian this line reads, "Quando
giungon davanti a la ruina," literally,
"When they come before the falling
place." According to Busnelli (*Miscel-
lanea dantesca*, Padova, 1922, pp. 51–53)
the *ruina* refers to the tribunal of Minòs;
that is, to the place where the condemned
sinners "fall" before him at the entrance
to the second circle to be judged. Therefore I have translated *ruina* as "their place
of judgment"; the entire tercet means that
every time the sinners in the windstorm
are blown near Minòs they shriek, lament,
and blaspheme.

58. "Semiramis": The legendary queen

of Assyria who, although renowned for
her military conquests and civic projects,
fell prey to her passions and became dissolute to the extent of legalizing lust.
Dante conceived her as the motivating
force of the degenerate society that ultimately opposes God's divine order.

61–62. According to Virgil (*Aeneid* I
and IV), Dido, the queen of Carthage,
swore faithfulness to the memory of her
dead husband, Sichaeus. However, when
the Trojan survivors of the war arrived in
port, she fell helplessly in love with their
leader, Aeneas, and they lived together
as man and wife until the gods reminded
Aeneas of his higher destiny: the founding of Rome and the Roman Empire. Immediately he set sail for Italy, and Dido,
deserted, committed suicide.

See Helen there, the root of evil woe
    lasting long years, and see the great Achilles    65
    who lost his life to love, in final combat;
see Paris, Tristan"—then, more than a thousand
    he pointed out to me, and named them all,
    those shades whom love cut off from life on earth.
After I heard my teacher call the names    70
    of all these knights and ladies of ancient times,
    pity confused my senses, and I was dazed.
I began: "Poet, I would like, with all my heart,
    to speak to those two there who move together
    and seem to be so light upon the winds."    75
And he: "You'll see for yourself when they are closer;
    if you entreat them by that love of theirs
    that carries them along, they will come to you."
When the winds bent their course in our direction
    I raised my voice to them, "Oh, wearied souls,    80
    come speak with us if it be not forbidden."
As doves, called by desire to return
    to their sweet nest, with wings outstretched and poised
    float downward through the air, guided by their will,
so these two left the flock where Dido is    85
    and came toward us through the malignant air,
    such was the tender power of my call.
"O living creature, gracious and so kind,
    who make your way here through this dingy air
    to visit us who stained the world with blood,    90
if we could claim as friend, the King of Kings,
    we would beseech him that he grant you peace,
    you who show pity for our atrocious plight.
Whatever pleases you to hear or speak
    we will hear and we will speak about with you    95

---

64. Helen of Troy.

65–66. Enticed by the beauty of Polyxena, a daughter of the Trojan king, Achilles desired her to be his wife, but Hecuba, Polyxena's mother, arranged a counterplot with Paris so that when Achilles entered the temple for his presumed marriage, he was treacherously slain by Paris.

67. "Paris": the son of Priam, king of Troy, whose abduction of Helen ignited the Trojan War. "Tristan": the central figure of numerous medieval French, German, and Italian romances. Sent as a messenger by his uncle, King Mark of Cornwall, to obtain Isolt for him in marriage, Tristan became enamored of her, and she of him. After Isolt's marriage to Mark, the lovers continued their love affair, and in order to maintain its secrecy they necessarily employed many deceits and ruses. According to one version, however, Mark, growing continuously more suspicious of their attachment, finally discovered them together and ended the incestuous relationship by mortally wounding Tristan with a lance.

74. "those two there who move together": Francesca, daughter of Guido Vecchio da Polenta, lord of Ravenna, and Paolo Malatesta, third son of Malatesta da Verrucchio, lord of Rimini. Around 1275 the aristocratic Francesca was married for political reasons to Gianciotto, the physically deformed second son of Malatesta da Verrucchio. In time a love affair developed between Francesca and Gianciotto's younger brother, Paolo. One day the betrayed husband discovered them in an amorous embrace and slew them both.

82–84. "As doves": Paolo and Francesca are compared to "doves, called by desire" who "float downward through the air, guided by their will." The use of the words "desire" and "will" is particularly interesting because it suggests the nature of lust as a sin: the subjugation of the will to desire.

as long as the wind, here where we are, is silent.
The place where I was born lies on the shore
    where the river Po with its attendant streams
    descends to seek its final resting place.
Love, that kindles quick in the gentle heart,         100
    seized this one for the beauty of my body,
    torn from me. (How it happened still offends me!)
Love, that excuses no one loved from loving,
    seized me so strongly with delight in him
    that, as you see, he never leaves my side.        105
Love led us straight to sudden death together.
    Caïna awaits the one who quenched our lives."
    These were the words that came from them to us.
When those offended souls had told their story,
    I bowed my head and kept it bowed until        110
    the poet said, "What are you thinking of?"
When finally I spoke, I sighed, "Alas,
    what sweet thoughts, and oh, how much desiring
    brought these two down into this agony."
And then I turned to them and tried to speak;        115
    I said, "Francesca, the torment that you suffer
    brings painful tears of pity to my eyes.
But tell me, in that time of your sweet sighing
    how, and by what signs, did love allow you
    to recognize your dubious desires?"        120
And she to me: "There is no greater pain
    than to remember, in our present grief,
    past happiness (as well your teacher knows)!
But if your great desire is to learn
    the very root of such a love as ours,        125
    I shall tell you, but in words of flowing tears.
One day we read, to pass the time away,
    of Lancelot, how he had fallen in love;
    we were alone, innocent of suspicion.
Time and again our eyes were brought together        130
    by the book we read; our faces flushed and paled.
To the moment of one line alone we yielded:
it was when we read about those longed-for lips
    now being kissed by such a famous lover,
    that this one (who shall never leave my side)        135
then kissed my mouth, and trembled as he did.
    The book and its author was our galehot!

97–99. "The place where I was born": Ravenna, a city on the Adriatic coast.
100–108. "Love . . . Love . . . Love . . .": These three tercets, each beginning with the word "Love," are particularly important as revealing the deceptive nature of Francesca. In lines 100 and 103, Francesca deliberately employs the style of *stilnovisti* poets such as Guinizelli and Cavalcanti in order to ensure the Pilgrim's sympathy, but she follows each of those lines with sensual and most un-*stilnovistic* ideas. For in the idealistic world of the *dolce stil nuovo* love would never "seize" a man for the beauty of the woman's body alone, nor would the sensual delight which "seized" Francesca be appropriate to *stilnovistic* love, which was distant, nonsexual, and ideal.

107. "Caïna": one of the four divisions of Cocytus, the lowest part of Hell, wherein are tormented those souls who treacherously betrayed their kin.

That day we read no further." And all the while
the one of the two spirits spoke these words,
   the other wept, in such a way that pity                    140
   blurred my senses; I swooned as though to die,
and fell to Hell's floor as a body, dead, falls.

CANTO VI

On recovering consciousness the Pilgrim finds himself with Virgil
in the Third Circle where the Gluttons are punished. These shades
are mired in filthy muck and are eternally battered by cold and dirty
hail, rain, and snow. Soon the travelers come upon Cerberus, the
three-headed, doglike beast who guards the Gluttons, but Virgil
pacifies him with fistfuls of slime and the two poets pass on. One of
the shades recognizes Dante the Pilgrim and hails him. It is Ciacco,
a Florentine who, before they leave, makes a prophecy concerning
the political future of Florence. As the poets move away, the Pilgrim questions Virgil about the Last Judgment and other matters
until the two arrive at the next circle.

When I regained my senses that had fainted
   at the sight of these two who were kinsmen lovers,
   a piteous sight confusing me to tears,
new suffering and new sinners suffering
   appeared to me, no matter where I moved                    5
   or turned my eyes, no matter where I gazed.
I am in the third circle, in the round of rain
   eternal, cursèd, cold and falling heavy,
   unchanging beat, unchanging quality.
Thick hail and dirty water mixed with snow                    10
   come down in torrents through the murky air,
   and the earth is stinking from this soaking rain.
Cerberus, a ruthless and fantastic beast,
   with all three throats howls out his dog-like sounds
   above the drowning sinners of this place.                  15
His eyes are red, his beard is slobbered black,
   his belly swollen, and he has claws for hands;
   he rips the spirits, flays and mangles them.

7–21. The shades in this circle are the
Gluttons, and their punishment fits their
sin. Gluttony, like all the sins of Incontinence, subjects reason to desire; in this
case desire is a voracious appetite. Thus
the shades howl like dogs—in desire,
without reason; they are sunk in slime,
the image of their excess. The warm comfort their gluttony brought them in life
here has become cold, dirty rain and
hail.
   13–22. "Cerberus": In classical mythology Cerberus is a fierce three-headed

dog which guards the entrance to the
Underworld, permitting admittance to all
and escape to none. He is the prototype
of the Gluttons, with his three howling,
voracious throats that gulp down huge
handfuls of muck. He has become Appetite and as such he flays and mangles the
spirits who reduced their lives to a satisfaction of appetite. With his three heads,
he appears to be a prefiguration of Lucifer and thus another infernal distortion
of the Trinity.

Under the rain they howl like dogs, lying
   now on one side with the other as a screen,         20
   now on the other turning, these wretched sinners.
When the slimy Cerberus caught sight of us,
   he opened up his mouths and showed his fangs;
   his body was one mass of twitching muscles.
My master stooped and, spreading wide his fingers,     25
   he grabbed up heaping fistfuls of the mud
   and flung it down into those greedy gullets.
As a howling cur, hungering to get fed,
   quiets down with the first mouthful of his food,
   busy with eating, wrestling with that alone,       30
so it was with all three filthy heads
   of the demon Cerberus, used to barking thunder
   on these dead souls, who wished that they were deaf.
We walked across this marsh of shades beaten
   down by the heavy rain, our feet pressing        35
   on their emptiness that looked like human form.
Each sinner there was stretched out on the ground
   except for one who quickly sat up straight,
   the moment that he saw us pass him by.
"O you there being led through this inferno,"      40
   he said, "try to remember who I am,
   for you had life before I gave up mine."
I said: "The pain you suffer here perhaps
   disfigures you beyond all recognition:
   I can't remember seeing you before.        45
But tell me who you are, assigned to grieve
   in this sad place, afflicted by such torture
   that—worse there well may be, but none more foul."
"Your own city," he said, "so filled with envy
   its cup already overflows the brim,        50
   once held me in the brighter life above.
You citizens gave me the name of Ciacco;
   and for my sin of gluttony I am damned
   as you can see, to rain that beats me weak.
And my sad sunken soul is not alone,        55
   for all these sinners here share in my pain
   and in my sin." And that was his last word.

26–27. With this action, Virgil imitates the action of the Sibyl who, leading Aeneas through the Underworld, placates Cerberus by casting honeyed cakes into his three throats (*Aeneid* VI, 417–423). By substituting dirt for the Virgilian cakes, Dante emphasizes Cerberus's irrational gluttony.

36. The shades in Hell bear only the *appearance* of their corporeal forms, although they can be ripped and torn and otherwise suffer physical torture—just as here they are able to bear the Pilgrim's weight. Yet they themselves evidently are airy shapes without weight (cf. Canto VIII. l. 27) which will, after the Day of Judgment, be possessed of their actual bodies once more (see Canto XIII, l. 103).

52. "Ciacco": The only Glutton whom the Pilgrim actually talks to is Ciacco, one of his Florentine contemporaries, whose true identity has never been determined. Several commentators believe him to be Ciacco dell'Anguillaia, a minor poet of the time and presumably the Ciacco of one of Boccaccio's stories (*Decameron*, IX, 8). However, more than a proper name, *ciacco* is a derogatory Italian word for "pig," or "hog," and is also an adjective, "filthy," or "of a swinish nature."

"Ciacco," I said to him, "your grievous state
    weighs down on me, it makes me want to weep;
    but tell me what will happen, if you know,     60
to the citizens of that divided state?
    And are there any honest men among them?
    And tell me, why is it so plagued with strife?"
And he replied: "After much contention
    they will come to bloodshed; the rustic party     65
    will drive the other out by brutal means.
Then it will come to pass, this side will fall
    within three suns, and the other rise to power
    with the help of one now listing toward both sides.
For a long time they will keep their heads raised high,     70
    holding the others down with crushing weight,
    no matter how these weep or squirm for shame.
Two just men there are, but no one listens,
    for pride, envy, avarice are the three sparks
    that kindle in men's hearts and set them burning."     75
With this his mournful words came to an end.
    But I spoke back: "There's more I want to know;
    I beg you to provide me with more facts:
Farinata and Tegghiaio, who were so worthy,
    Jacopo Rusticucci, Arrigo, Mosca     80
    and all the rest so bent on doing good,
where are they? Tell me what's become of them;
    one great desire tortures me: to know
    whether they taste Heaven's sweetness or Hell's gall."
"They lie below with blacker souls," he said,     85
    "by different sins pushed down to different depths;
    if you keep going you may see them all.
But when you are once more in the sweet world
    I beg you to remind our friends of me.
    I speak no more; no more I answer you."     90
He twisted his straight gaze into a squint
    and stared awhile at me, then bent his head,

---

59. **The Pilgrim,** having learned very little from his experience in Canto V, feels pity again at the sight of Ciacco.

65–75. "they will come to bloodshed": Ciacco's political prophecy reveals the fact that the shades in Hell are able to see the future; they also know the past, but they know nothing of the present (see Canto X, ll. 100–108). The Guelph party, having gained complete control over Florence by defeating the Ghibellines (1289), was divided into factions: the Whites (the "rustic party," l. 65), headed by the Cerchi family, and the Blacks ("the other," l. 66), led by the Donatis. These two groups finally came into direct conflict on May 1, 1300, which resulted in the expulsion of the Blacks from the city (1301). However, they returned in 1302 ("within three suns," l. 68, i.e., within three years), and with the help of Pope Boniface VIII, sent the Whites (including Dante) into exile. Boniface VIII, the "one now listing toward both sides" (l. 69), for a time did not reveal his designs on Florence, but rather steered a wavering course between the two factions, planning to aid the ultimate victor.

91–93. The manner in which Ciacco takes leave is certainly odd: his eyes, fixed on the Pilgrim throughout their conversation, gradually lose their power to focus and can only stare blankly. The concentration required for the prophecy seems to have exhausted him.

falling to join his other sightless peers.
My guide then said to me: "He'll wake no more
    until the day the angel's trumpet blows,          95
    when the unfriendly Judge shall come down here;
each soul shall find again his wretched tomb,
    assume his flesh and take his human shape,
    and hear his fate resound eternally."
And so we made our way through the filthy mess     100
    of muddy shades and slush, moving slowly,
    talking a little about the afterlife.
I said, "Master, will these torments be increased,
    or lessened, on the final Judgment Day,
    or will the pain be just the same as now?"     105
And he: "Remember your philosophy:
    the closer a thing comes to its perfection,
    more keen will be its pleasure or its pain.
Although this cursèd race of punished souls
    shall never know the joy of true perfection,     110
    more perfect will their pain be then than now."
We circled round that curving road while talking
    of more than I shall mention at this time,
    and came to where the ledge begins descending;
there we found Plutus, mankind's arch-enemy.     115

## CANTO VII

At the boundary of the Fourth Circle the two travelers confront clucking Plutus, the god of wealth, who collapses into emptiness at a word from Virgil. Descending farther, the Pilgrim sees two groups of angry, shouting souls who clash huge rolling weights against each other with their chests. They are the Prodigal and the Miserly. Their earthly concern with material goods prompts the Pilgrim to question Virgil about Fortune and her distribution of the worldly goods of men. After Virgil's explanation, they descend to the banks of the swamplike river Styx, which serves as the Fifth Circle. Mired in the bog are the Wrathful, who constantly tear and mangle each other. Beneath the slime of the Styx, Virgil explains, are the Slothful; the bubbles on the muddy surface indicate their presence beneath. The poets walk around the swampy area and soon come to the foot of a high tower.

106–111. "Remember your philosophy": In answer to the Pilgrim's question (ll. 103–105), Virgil reminds him of the popular doctrine which states that the more a thing is perfect, the more it knows what pleasure is and pain. The perfected state of man from a "technical" point of view will be attained on Judgment Day, when the soul is reunited with the body. Therefore, the damned will feel more torment later than now; similarly, the blessed in Paradise will enjoy God's beautitude more.

115. For Plutus see Canto VII, l. 2.

"Pape Satàn, pape Satàn aleppe!"
   the voice of Plutus clucked these words at us,
   and that kind sage, to whom all things were known,
said reassuringly: "Pay no attention
   to your fear, for no matter what his power be     5
   he cannot stop our journey down this rock."
Then he turned toward that swollen face of rage
   crying, "Be quiet, cursèd wolf of Hell:
   feed on the burning bile that rots your guts.
This journey to the depths does have a reason,     10
   for it is willed on high, where Michael wrought
   a just revenge for the bold assault on God."
As sails swollen by wind when the ship's mast breaks,
   collapse, deflated, tangled in a heap,
   just so the savage beast fell to the ground.     15
And then we started down a fourth abyss,
   making our way along the dismal slope
   where all the evil of the world is dumped.
Ah, God's avenging justice! Who could heap up
   suffering and pain as strange as I saw here?     20
   How can we let our guilt bring us to this?
As every wave Charybdis whirls to sea
   comes crashing against its counter-current wave,
   so these folk here must dance their roundelay.
More shades were here than anywhere above,     25
   and from both sides, to the sound of their own screams,
   straining their chests, they rolled enormous weights.
And when they met and clashed against each other
   they turned to push the other way, one side
   screaming, "Why hoard?", the other side, "Why waste?"     30
And so they moved back round the gloomy circle
   returning on both sides to opposite poles
   to scream their shameful tune another time;
again they came to clash and turn and roll
   forever in their semi-circle joust.     35
   And I, my heart pierced through by such a sight,

1. This line, while it has never been interpreted satisfactorily, has certainly been interpreted variously. Critics as early as Boccaccio have noted a relation of "pape" to "papa" (pope). Boccaccio implies that "pape" is a word expressive of great admiration, and Plutus applies it to Satan, "the prince of demons." Some think that the line is addressed by Plutus to Dante; "Satàn" then is seen as the traditional, biblical term for "enemy." But the main thrust of modern criticism is to accept the line as simple gibberish (cf. Nimrod's speech in Canto XXI, l. 67).

2–15. Plutus, the god of wealth in classical mythology, appropriately presides over the Miserly and the Prodigal, those who did not use their material goods with moderation. In this canto his collapse like inflated sails "when the ship's mast breaks" is interesting not only because it attests to the true, airy emptiness of wealth, but also because the simile prefigures an image Dante uses in describing Lucifer at the end of the *Inferno*.

11–12. The archangel Michael fought against and triumphed over the rebellious angels in Heaven.

22–66. The Miserly and the Prodigal, linked together as those who misused their wealth, suffer a joint punishment. Their material wealth has become a heavy weight which each group must shove against the other, since their attitudes toward wealth on earth were opposed to each other. Part of their punishment is to complete the turn of the Wheel (circle) of Fortune against which they had rebelled during their short space of life on earth.

spoke out, "My Master, please explain to me
  who are these people here? Were they all priests,
  these tonsured souls I see there to our left?"
He said, "In their first life all you see here          40
  had such myopic minds they could not judge
  with moderation when it came to spending;
their barking voices make this clear enough,
  when they arrive at the two points on the circle
  where opposing guilts divide them into two.       45
The ones who have the bald spot on their heads
  were priests and popes and cardinals, in whom
  avarice is most likely to prevail."
And I: "Master, in such a group as this
  I should be able to recognize a few          50
  who dirtied themselves by such crimes as these."
And he replied, "Yours is an empty hope:
  their undistinguished life that made them foul
  now makes it harder to distinguish them;
forever they will come to their two battles;     55
  then from the tomb they will be resurrected:
  these with tight fists, those without any hair.
It was squandering and hoarding that have robbed them
  of the lovely world, and got them in this brawl:
  I will not waste choice words describing it!     60
You see, my son, the short-lived mockery
  of all the wealth that is in Fortune's keep,
  over which the human race is bickering;
for all the gold that is or ever was
  beneath the moon won't buy a moment's rest    65
  for even one among these weary souls."
"Master, now tell me what this Fortune is
  you touched upon before. What is she like
  who holds all worldly wealth within her fists?"
And he to me, "Oh foolish race of man,        70
  how overwhelming is your ignorance!
  Now listen while I tell you what she means:
that One, whose wisdom knows infinity,
  made all the heavens and gave each one a guide,
  and each sphere shining shines on all the others,   75
so light is spread with equal distribution:
  for worldly splendors He decreed the same
  and ordained a guide and general ministress
who would at her discretion shift the world's
  vain wealth from nation to nation, house to house,   80
  with no chance of interference from mankind;

38–48. The fact that most of the avaricious are tonsured priests indicates a major abuse practiced by the priesthood in Dante's time.

73–96. Virgil's digression concerns Fortune, a major theme of medieval and Renaissance writers such as Boethius, Petrarch, Boccaccio, Chaucer, and Machiavelli. Usually it was visualized as a female figure with a wheel, the revolutions of which symbolized the rise and fall of fortune in a man's life, but Dante deviates somewhat from the standard concept of Fortune by assigning to her the role of an angel.

so while one nation rules, another falls
   according to whatever she decrees
   (her sentence hidden like a snake in grass).
Your knowledge has no influence on her;        85
   she provides for change, she judges, and she rules
   her domain as do the other gods their own.
Her changing changes never take a rest;
   necessity keeps her in constant motion,
   as men come and go to take their turn with her.      90
And this is she so crucified and cursed;
   even those in luck who should be praising her,
   instead, revile her and condemn her acts.
But she is blest and in her bliss hears nothing;
   with all God's joyful first-created creatures      95
   she turns her sphere and, blest, turns it with joy.
Now let's move down to greater wretchedness;
   the stars that rose when I set out for you
   are going down—we cannot stay too long."
We crossed the circle to its other bank,      100
   passing a spring that boils and overflows
   into a ditch the spring itself cut out.
The water was a deeper dark than perse,
   and we, with its grey waves for company,
   made our way down along a rough, strange path.     105
This dingy little stream, when it has reached
   the bottom of the grey malignant slopes,
   becomes a swamp that has the name of Styx.
And I, intent on looking as we passed,
   saw muddy people moving in that marsh,     110
   all naked, with their faces scarred by rage.
They fought each other, not with hands alone,
   but struck with head and chest and feet as well,
   with teeth they tore each other limb from limb.
And the good teacher said: "My son, now see     115
   the souls of those that anger overcame;
   and I ask you to believe me when I say
beneath the slimy top are sighing souls
   who make these waters bubble at the surface;
   your eyes will tell you this—just look around.     120
Bogged in this slime they say, 'Sluggish we were
   in the sweet air made happy by the sun,
   and the smoke of sloth was smoldering in our hearts;
now we lie sluggish here in this black muck!'

84. This simile may seem comic to the reader, but it is not comic in Italian. Furthermore, it must be retained in translation because it is the pre-Christian Virgil who is speaking, and even though he knows the divine nature of Fortune for Christians, he cannot help but think of it in pre-Christian terms—as a monstrous and cunning evil force, and *not* a minister of God.

98–99. The time is past midnight. The stars setting in the west were rising in the east when Virgil first met Dante on the evening of Good Friday in the "dark wood."

108. "Styx": The river Styx is the second of the rivers of Hell; Dante, following the *Aeneid*, refers to it here as a marsh or quagmire.

This is the hymn they gurgle in their throats                    125
  but cannot sing in words that truly sound."
Then making a wide arc we walked around
  the pond between the dry bank and the slime,
  our eyes still fixed on those who gobbled mud.
We came, in time, to the foot of a high tower.                   130

### CANTO VIII

But before they had reached the foot of the tower, the Pilgrim
had noticed two signal flames at the tower's top, and another flame
answering from a distance; soon he realizes that the flames are signals to and from Phlegyas, the boatman of the Styx, who suddenly
appears in a small boat speeding across the river. Wrathful and irritated though he is, the steersman must grant the poets passage, but
during the crossing an angry shade rises from the slime to question
the Pilgrim. After a brief exchange of words, scornful on the part of
the Pilgrim, who has recognized this sinner, the spirit grabs hold of
the boat. Virgil pushes him away, praising his ward for his just
scorn, while a group of the wrathful attack the wretched soul whose
name is Filippo Argenti. At the far shore the poets debark and find
themselves before the gates of the infernal City of Dis where howling figures threaten them from the walls. Virgil speaks with them
privately, but they slam the gate shut in his face. His ward is terrified, and Virgil too is shaken, but he insists that help from Heaven
is already on the way.

I must explain, however, that before
  we finally reached the foot of that high tower,
  our eyes had been attracted to its summit
by two small flames we saw flare up just there;
  and, so far off the eye could hardly see,                       5
  another burning torch flashed back a sign.
I turned to that vast sea of human knowledge:
  "What signal is this? And the other flame,
  what does it answer? And who's doing this?"
And he replied: "You should already see                          10
  across the filthy waves what has been summoned,
  unless the marsh's vapors hide it from you."
A bowstring never shot an arrow off
  that cut the thin air any faster than
  a little boat I saw that very second                            15
skimming along the water in our direction,
  with a solitary steersman, who was shouting,
  "Aha, I've got you now, you wretched soul!"

18. Phlegyas, the son of Mars, set fire to Apollo's temple at Delphi, furiously enraged because Apollo raped his daughter Coronis. For this Apollo killed him and sent him to Tartarus. Dante makes Phlegyas the demonic guardian of the Styx. As a personification of great wrath he is well-suited not only for guarding the Fifth Circle where the Wrathful are, but also for transporting the Pilgrim to the inner division of Hell, the City of Dis (l. 68), whose gates are guarded by the rebellious angels (l. 82–83).

"Phlegyas, Phlegyas, this time you shout in vain,"
   my lord responded, "you will have us with you    20
   no longer than it takes to cross the muck."
As one who learns of some incredible trick
   just played on him, flares up resentfully—
   so, Phlegyas there, was seething in his anger.
My leader calmly stepped into the skiff    25
   and when he was inside, he had me enter,
   and only then it seemed to carry weight.
Soon as my guide and I were in the boat
   the ancient prow began to plough the water,
   more deeply, now, than anytime before.    30
And as we sailed the course of this dead channel,
   before me there rose up a slimy shape
   that said: "Who are you, who come before your time?"
And I spoke back, "Though I come, I do not stay;
   but who are you, in all your ugliness?"    35
   "You see that I am one who weeps," he answered.
And then I said to him: "May you weep and wail
   stuck here in this place forever, you damned soul,
   for, filthy as you are, I recognize you."
With that he stretched both hands out toward the boat    40
   but, on his guard, my teacher pushed him back:
   "Away, get down there with the other curs!"
And then he put his arms around my neck
   and kissed my face and said, "Indignant soul,
   blessèd is she in whose womb you were conceived.    45
In the world this man was filled with arrogance,
   and nothing good about him decks his memory;
   for this, his shade is filled with fury here.
Many in life esteem themselves great men
   who then will wallow here like pigs in mud,    50
   leaving behind them their repulsive fame."
"Master, it certainly would make me happy
   to see him dunked deep in this slop just once
   before we leave this lake—it truly would."
And he to me, "Before the other shore    55

---

32. Filippo Argenti (l. 61), a member of the Adimari family.

36–63. The scene with Filippo Argenti is one of the most dramatic in the *Inferno*. The Pilgrim who had shown such pity for Francesca, and had even felt compassion for Ciacco, the swinish glutton, bursts into rage as soon as he recognizes Argenti. The Pilgrim repulses Filippo with harsh words; later he expresses his wish to Virgil to see the sinner "dunked" in the mud; when he sees Filippo being attacked viciously he rejoices and thanks God for the sight. Many commentators believe his attitude can be explained as a personal reaction to a political adversary whom he hated. But if that had been the moti-

vation for his outburst, this would surely not have won Virgil's encomium: "Indignant soul, / blessèd is she in whose womb you were conceived" (ll. 44–45). Virgil's words must mean that he has sensed a core of righteous wrath in the Pilgrim's outburst, he sees that the hatred he has expressed is primarily a hatred of the sin of wrath. But we must remember that this is only the beginning of a spiritual development in the right direction, away from pity of the sinner toward hatred of his sin. Dante the Pilgrim has not yet learned to hate and at the same time show self-control and mastery of the situation. as he will later on (Canto XIX).

comes into sight, you will be satisfied:
a wish like that is worthy of fulfillment."
Soon afterwards, I saw the wretch so mangled
by a gang of muddy souls that, to this day,
I thank my Lord and praise Him for that sight:    60
"Get Filippo Argenti!" they all cried.
And at those shouts the Florentine, gone mad,
turned on himself and bit his body fiercely.
We left him there, I'll say no more about him.
A wailing noise began to pound my ears    65
and made me strain my eyes to see ahead.
"And now, my son," the gentle teacher said,
"coming closer is the city we call Dis,
with its great walls and its fierce citizens."
And I, "Master, already I can see    70
the clear glow of its mosques above the valley,
burning bright red, as though just forged, and left
to smoulder." And he to me: "Eternal fire
burns within, giving off the reddish glow
you see diffused throughout this lower Hell."    75
And then at last we entered those deep moats
that circled all of this unhappy city
whose walls, it seemed to me, were made of iron.
For quite a while we sailed around, until
we reached a place and heard our boatsman shout    80
with all his might, "Get out! Here is the entrance."
I saw more than a thousand fiendish angels
perching above the gates enraged, screaming:
"Who is the one approaching? Who, without death,
dares walk into the kingdom of the dead?"    85
And my wise teacher made some kind of signal
announcing he would speak to them in secret.
They managed to suppress their great resentment
enough to say: "You come, but he must go
who thought to walk so boldly through this realm.    90
Let him retrace his foolish way alone,
just let him try. And you who led him here
through this dark land, you'll stay right where you are."
And now, my reader, consider how I felt
when those foreboding words came to my ears!    95
I thought I'd never see our world again!
"Oh my dear guide, who more than seven times
restored my confidence, and rescued me
from the many dangers that blocked my going on,

---

**68.** The walls of the City of Dis mark the division between upper Hell and "lower Hell" (l. 75), and between the sins of Incontinence and those of Violence. In terms of the Seven Capital Sins, we have passed through circles punishing the five lesser ones (lust, gluttony, avarice, sloth, and wrath); beyond are sins occasioned specifically by envy and pride.

**82–83.** These are the rebellious angels who, with their leader Lucifer, were cast into Hell after their abortive attempt to gain control of Heaven.

don't leave me, please," I cried in my distress,                      100
   "and if the journey onward is denied us
   let's turn our footsteps back together quickly."
Then that lord who had brought me all this way
   said, "Do not fear, the journey we are making
   none can prevent: such power did decree it.          105
Wait here for me and feed your weary spirit
   with comfort and good hope; you can be sure
   I will not leave you in this underworld."
With this he walks away. He leaves me here,
   that gentle father, and I stay, doubting,            110
   and battling with my thoughts of "yes"—but "no."
I could not hear what he proposed to them,
   but they did not remain with him for long;
   I saw them race each other back for home.
Our adversaries slammed the heavy gates                            115
   in my lord's face, and he stood there outside,
   then turned toward me and walked back very slowly
with eyes downcast, all self-assurance now
   erased from his forehead—sighing, "Who are these
   to forbid my entrance to the halls of grief!"         120
He spoke to me: "You need not be disturbed
   by my vexation, for I shall win the contest,
   no matter how they plot to keep us out!
This insolence of theirs is nothing new;
   they used it once at a less secret gate               125
   which is, and will forever be, unlocked;
you saw the words of death inscribed above it:
   already passing through, and with no guide,
   descending, through the circles, down the slope
comes one by whom the city will be opened."                        130

CANTO IX

The help from Heaven has not yet arrived; the Pilgrim is afraid
and Virgil is obviously worried. He reassures his ward by telling him
that, soon after his own death, he was forced by the Sorceress Erichtho to resume mortal shape and go to the very bottom of Hell in
order to bring up the soul of a traitor; thus Virgil knows the way
well. But no sooner is the Pilgrim comforted than the Three Furies
appear before him, on the top of the tower, shrieking and tearing
their breasts with their nails. They call for Medusa whose horrible
face has the power of turning anyone who looks on her to stone.
Virgil turns his ward around and covers his eyes. After an "address
to the reader" calling attention to the coming allegory, a strident
blast splits the air, and the poets perceive an Angel coming through

---

125–126. The rebellious angels tried to
deny Christ entry into Hell, by barring the
principal ("less secret") gate, but it was
forced open by Him and will remain open
for eternity.
127. See Canto III, ll. 1–9.
130. See Canto IX, ll. 61–105.

the murky darkness to open the gates of the City for them. Then
the angel returns on the path whence he had come, and the two
travelers enter the gate. Within are great open burning sarcophagi
from which groans of torment issue. Virgil explains that these are
Arch Heretics and their lesser counterparts.

The color of the coward on my face,
    when I realized my guide was turning back,
    made him quickly change the color of his own.
He stood alert, like one who strains to hear;
    his eyes could not see far enough ahead                5
    to cut the heavy fog of that black air.
"But surely we were meant to win this fight,"
    he began, "or else. . . . But, such help was promised!
    O how much time it's taking him to come!"
I saw too well how quickly he amended                10
    his opening words with what he added on!
    They were different from the ones he first pronounced;
but nonetheless his words made me afraid,
    perhaps because the phrase he left unfinished
    I finished with worse meaning than he meant.         15
"Has anyone before ever descended
    to this sad hollow's depths from that first circle
    whose pain is all in having hope cut off?"
I put this question to him. He replied,
    "It is not usual for one of us                20
    to make the journey I am making now.
But it happens I was down here once before,
    conjured by that heartless witch, Erichtho
    (who could recall the spirit to its body).
Soon after I had left my flesh in death             25
    she sent me through these walls, and down as far
    as the pit of Judas to bring a spirit out;
and that place is the lowest and the darkest
    and the farthest from the sphere that circles all;
    I know the road, and well, you can be sure.       30
This swamp that breathes with a prodigious stink
    lies in a circle round the doleful city
    that now we cannot enter without strife."
And he said other things, but I forget them,
    for suddenly my eyes were drawn above,         35
    up to the fiery top of that high tower
where in no time at all and all at once
    sprang up three hellish Furies stained with blood,

1. Extreme fear makes the Pilgrim pale.
17–18. See Canto IV, ll. 34–42.
22–30. In answer to the Pilgrim's question Virgil states that, although such a
journey is rarely made, he himself accomplished it once before at the command of Erichtho, a Thessalian necromancer who conjured up dead spirits.
Having no literary or legendary source,
the story of Virgil's descent into Hell was
probably Dante's invention.

their bodies and their gestures those of females;
their waists were bound in cords of wild green hydras,                    40
   horned snakes and little serpents grew as hair,
   and twined themselves around the savage temples.
And he who had occasion to know well
   the handmaids of the queen of timeless woe
   cried out to me "Look there! The fierce Erinyes!                   45
That is Megaera, the one there to the left,
   and that one raving on the right, Alecto,
   Tisiphone, in the middle." He said no more.
With flailing palms the three would beat their breasts,
   then tear them with their nails, shrieking so loud            50
   I drew close to the poet, confused with fear.
"Call Medusa: we'll turn him into stone,"
   they shouted all together glaring down,
   "how wrong we were to let off Theseus lightly!"
"Now turn your back and cover up your eyes,                                55
   for if the Gorgon comes and you should see her,
   there would be no returning to the world!"
These were my master's words. He turned me round
   and did not trust my hands to hide my eyes
   but placed his own on mine and kept them covered.                 60
O all of you whose intellects are sound,
   look now and see the meaning that is hidden
   beneath the veil that covers my strange verses:
and then, above the filthy swell, approaching,
   a blast of sound, shot through with fear, exploded,             65
   making both shores of Hell begin to tremble;
it sounded like one of those violent winds,
   born from the clash of counter-temperatures,
   that tear through forests; raging on unchecked
it splits and rips and carries off the branches                            70
   and proudly whips the dust up in its path
   and makes the beasts and shepherds flee its course!
He freed my eyes and said, "Now turn around
   and set your sight along the ancient scum,
   there where the marsh's mist is hovering thickest."               75
As frogs before their enemy, the snake,
   all scatter through the pond and then dive down
   until each one is squatting on the bottom,
so I saw more than a thousand fear-shocked souls
   in flight, clearing the path of one who came                     80

---

44. The Furies are "handmaids" to Persephone (Hecate), wife of Pluto, classical god of the Underworld.

52. "Medusa": in classical mythology one of the three Gorgons. Minerva, furious at Medusa for giving birth to two children in one of the former's temples, changed her beautiful hair into serpents, so that whoever gazed on her terrifying aspect was turned to stone.

54. "Theseus": the greatest Athenian hero, descended to Hades with his friend Pirithous, King of the Lapithae, in order to kidnap Proserpina for him. Pluto slew Pirithous, however, and kept Theseus a prisoner in Hades by having him sit on the Chair of Forgetfulness, which made his mind blank and thereby kept him from moving. Dante chooses a less common version of the myth which has Theseus set free by Hercules. See note on ll. 98–99.

walking the Styx, his feet dry on the water.
From time to time with his left hand he fanned
  his face to push the putrid air away,
  and this was all that seemed to weary him.
I was certain now that he was sent from Heaven.    85
  I turned to my guide, but he made me a sign
  to keep my silence and bow low to this one.
Ah, the scorn that filled his holy presence!
  He reached the gate and touched it with a wand;
  it opened without resistance from inside.    90
"Oh Heaven's outcasts, despicable souls,"
  he started, standing on the dreadful threshold,
  "what insolence is this that breeds in you?
Why do you stubbornly resist that will
  whose end can never be denied and which,    95
  more than one time, increased your suffering?
What do you gain by locking horns with fate?
  If you remember well, your Cerberus
  still bears his chin and throat peeled for resisting!"
He turned then and retraced the squalid path    100
  without one word to us, and on his face
  the look of one concerned and spurred by things
that were not those he found surrounding him.
  And then we started moving toward the city
  in the safety of the holy words pronounced.    105
We entered there, and with no opposition.
  And I, so anxious to investigate
  the state of souls locked up in such a fortress,
once in the place, allowed my eyes to wander,
  and saw, in all directions spreading out,    110
  a countryside of pain and ugly anguish.
As at Arles where the Rhône turns to stagnant waters
  or as at Pola near Quarnero's Gulf
  that closes Italy and bathes her confines,
the sepulchers make all the land uneven,    115
  so they did here, strewn in all directions,
  except the graves here served a crueler purpose:
for scattered everywhere among the tombs
  were flames that kept them glowing far more hot
  than any iron an artisan might use.    120
Each tomb had its lid loose, pushed to one side,

---

94. The will of God.
98–99. When Hercules descended into Hell to rescue Theseus, he chained the three-headed dog Cerberus and dragged him around and outside Hell so that the skin around his neck was ripped away.
112–117. "Arles": a city in Provence near the delta of the Rhône, the site of the famous Roman (later Christian) cemetery of Aliscamps. There, as at Pola, a city in Istria (now Yugoslavia) on the Quarnero Bay also famous for its an-
cient burying ground, great sarcophagi cover the landscape. Interestingly, according to tradition, Christ appeared to St. Trophimus when the latter consecrated Aliscamps as a Christian resting place, and promised that the souls of those buried there would be free from the sepulchral torments of the dead. Thus, Dante compares the sepulchers here to those at Pola and Arles, except that "the graves here served a crueler purpose" (l. 117).

and from within came forth such fierce laments
  that I was sure inside were tortured souls.
I asked, "Master, what kind of shades are these
  lying down here, buried in the graves of stone,         125
  speaking their presence in such dolorous sighs?"
And he replied: "There lie arch-heretics
  of every sect, with all of their disciples;
  more than you think are packed within these tombs.
Like heretics lie buried with their like         130
  and the graves burn more, or less, accordingly."
  Then turning to the right, we moved ahead
between the torments there and those high walls.

### CANTO X

They come to the tombs containing the Epicurean heretics, and
as they are walking by them, a shade suddenly rises to full height in
one tomb, having recognized the Pilgrim's Tuscan dialect. It is the
proud Farinata who, in life, opposed Dante's party; while he and
the Pilgrim are conversing, another figure suddenly rises out of the
same tomb. It is the shade of Cavalcante de' Cavalcanti who interrupts the conversation with questions about his son Guido. Misin-
terpreting the Pilgrim's confused silence as evidence of his son's
death, Cavalcante falls back into his sepulcher, and Farinata
resumes the conversation exactly where it had been broken off. He
defends his political actions in regard to Florence and prophesies
that Dante, like himself, will soon know the pain of exile. But the
Pilgrim is also interested to know how it is that the damned can see
the future but not the present. When his curiosity is satisfied, he
asks Farinata to tell Cavalcante that his son is still alive, and that
his silence was caused only by his confusion about the shade's ina-
bility to know the present.

Now onward down a narrow path, between
  the city's ramparts and the suffering,
  my master walks, I following close behind.
"O lofty power who through these impious gyres
  lead me around as you see fit," I said,         5
  "I want to know, I want to understand:
the people buried there in sepulchers,

127–131. The Heretics are in a circle in Hell which is outside of the three main divisions of Incontinence, Violence, and Fraud. Heresy is not due to weaknesses of the flesh or mind (Incontinence), nor is it a form of violence or of fraud; it is a clearly willed sin based on intellectual pride, and because it denies the Christian concept of reality, it is punished outside of the area allocated to the Christian categories of sin.

There is great irony in the fact that those who believed that the death of the body meant the death of the soul suffer as their punishment the entombment of their living souls.

132. Why Dante and Virgil, who have been circling always to the left, sud-denly move off to the right remains a mystery; this will happen one other time in the *Inferno*, Canto XVII, l. 31.

can they be seen? I mean, since all the lids
are off the tombs and no one stands on guard."
And he: "They will forever be locked up,                    10
when they return here from Jehosaphat
with the bodies that they left up in the world.
The private cemetery on this side
serves Epicurus and his followers,
who make the soul die when the body dies.                   15
As for the question you just put to me,
it will be answered soon, while we are here;
and the wish you are keeping from me will be granted."
And I: "O my good guide, I do not hide
my heart; I'm trying not to talk too much,                  20
as you have told me more than once to do."
"O Tuscan walking through our flaming city,
alive, and speaking with such elegance,
be kind enough to stop here for a while.
Your mode of speech identifies you clearly                  25
as one whose birthplace is that noble city
with which in my time, perhaps, I was too harsh."
One of the vaults resounded suddenly
with these clear words, and I, intimidated,
drew up a little closer to my guide,                        30
who said, "What are you doing? Turn around
and look at Farinata who has risen,
you will see him from the waist up standing straight."
I already had my eyes fixed on his face,
and there he stood out tall, with chest and brow            35
proclaiming his disdain for all this Hell.
My guide, with a gentle push, encouraged me
to move among the sepulchers toward him;
"Be sure you choose your words with care," he said.
And when I reached the margin of his tomb                   40
he looked at me, and half-contemptuously
he asked, "And *who* would *your* ancestors be?"
And I who wanted only to oblige him
held nothing back but told him everything.
At this he lifted up his brows a little,                    45
then said, "Bitter enemies of mine they were

11–12. According to the Old Testament
prophet Joel (3:2, 12), the valley of
Jehosaphat, situated between Jerusalem
and the Mount of Olives, would be the
site of the Last Judgment, when the soul
and the body would be reunited and thus
returned to Heaven or Hell for eternity.

14–15. "Epicurus": the Greek philosopher who in 306 B.C. organized in Athens
the philosophical school named after him.
The philosophy of the Epicureans taught
that the highest good is temporal happiness which is to be achieved by the
practice of the virtues. In Dante's time
Epicureans were considered heretics because they exalted temporal happiness,
and therefore denied the immortality of
the soul and the afterlife. Epicurus is
among the heretics even though he was
a pagan, because he denied the immortality of the soul, a truth known even to the
ancients.

22–27. Having recognized Dante as a
fellow Tuscan, Farinata bids him pause
a moment. Born of an old and respected
Florentine family, Farinata (Manente
di Jacopo degli Uberti) took an active
role in the political life of the Commune
on the side of the Ghibelline party, whose
head he became in 1239. He died in 1264,
one year before Dante's birth.

**and** of my ancestors and of my party;
I had to scatter them not once but twice."
"They were expelled, but only to return
from everywhere," I said, "not once but twice—      50
an art your men, however, never mastered!"
Just then along that same tomb's open ledge
a shade appeared, but just down to his chin,
beside this other; I think he got up kneeling.
He looked around as though he hoped to see      55
if someone else, perhaps, had come with me
and, when his expectation was deceived,
he started weeping: "If it be great genius
that carries you along through this blind jail,
where is my son? Why is he not with you?"      60
"I do not come alone," I said to him,
"that one waiting over there guides me through here,
the one, perhaps, your Guido held in scorn."
(The place of pain assigned him, and what he asked,
already had revealed his name to me      65
and made my pointed answer possible).
Instantly, he sprang to his full height and cried,
"What did you say? He *held*? Is he not living?
The day's sweet light no longer strikes his eyes?"
And when he heard the silence of my delay      70
responding to his question, he collapsed
into his tomb, not to be seen again.
That other stately shade, at whose request
I had first stopped to talk, showed no concern
nor moved his head nor turned to see what happened;      75
he merely picked up where we had left off:
"If that art they did not master," he went on,
"that gives me greater pain than does this bed.
But the face of the queen who reigns down here will glow
not more than fifty times before you learn      80
how hard it is to master such an art;
and as I hope that you may once more know

---

48–51. It happens that the Pilgrim's ancestors (along with other Guelphs) were twice (in 1248 and 1260) driven from the city (note the Pilgrim's appraisal of the action, revealed by his correcting Farinata's term "scatter" to "expel") by Farinata and his kinsmen (along with other Ghibellines), but they returned after both defeats (in 1251 and 1267). Dante's jibe, "an art your men, however, never mastered," refers to the expulsion of the Uberti family and other Ghibellines who never returned to Florence. See below, note on l. 84.
53. The shade is Cavalcante de' Cavalcanti, a member of an important Florentine family and father of Guido Cavalcanti. Cavalcante's son Guido, born about 1255, was one of the major poets of the day and was Dante's "first friend," as he

says in the *Vita Nuova.*
63. Some commentators, offering a different interpretation of the syntax of these two lines (to make the line mean that Virgil was leading the Pilgrim "to her whom" Guido perhaps held in scorn) believe that it is Beatrice whom Guido scorned. Most believe, however, that the object of Guido's attitude is Virgil. Perhaps it could be said that Guido as a skeptic refused to allow Reason to fulfill its ultimate purpose (according to the teachings of the time): that of leading man to God.
79–81. Hecate or Proserpina, the moon goddess, queen of the Underworld (cf. Canto IX, l. 44). Farinata makes the prophecy that Dante will know how difficult is the art of returning from exile before fifty months have passed.

the sweet world, tell me, why should your party be
so harsh to my clan in every law they make?"
I answered: "The massacre and butchery                        85
that stained the waters of the Arbia red
now cause such laws to issue from our councils."
He sighed, shaking his head. "It was not I
alone took part," he said, "nor certainly
would I have joined the rest without good cause.              90
But I alone stood up when all of them
were ready to have Florence razed. It was *I*
who openly stood up in her defense."
"And now, as I would have your seed find peace,"
I said, "I beg you to resolve a problem                       95
that has kept my reason tangled in a knot:
if I have heard correctly, all of you
can see ahead to what the future holds
but your knowledge of the present is not clear."
"Down here we see like those with faulty vision             100
who only see," he said, "what's at a distance;
this much the sovereign lord still grants us here.
When events are close to us, or when they happen,
our mind is blank, and were it not for others
we would know nothing of your living state.                 105
Thus you can understand how all our knowledge
will be completely dead at that time when
the door to future things is closed forever."
Then I, moved by regret for what I'd done,
said, "Now, will you please tell the fallen one             110
his son is still on earth among the living;
and if, when he asked, silence was my answer,
tell him: while he was speaking, all my thoughts
were struggling with that point you solved for me."
My teacher had begun to call me back,                       115
so I quickly asked that spirit to reveal
the names of those who shared a tomb with him.

84. The Uberti, Farinata's family, were excluded, according to Villani, from all pardons conceded to the Ghibellines, including the pardon of 1280, when most of the Ghibellines were permitted to return to Florence.

85–86. The hill of Montaperti, on the left bank of the Arbia, a small stream near Siena, was the scene of the fierce battle between the Florentine Guelphs and Ghibellines (September 4, 1260), in which the Guelphs were defeated. Farinata was a leader of the Ghibellines.

88–93. In rebuttal, Farinata states that he was not the only Ghibelline at the battle of Montaperti, and that he had good reason to fight; but that at the Council in Empoli after the victory at Montaperti, when the Ghibellines wanted to plan the destruction of Florence, Farinata was the only Ghibelline to oppose

the plan. He proudly points out that the credit for the latter action is his alone, while, on the other hand, he is not willing to accept all the blame for the bloodshed at Montaperti.

100–108. In answer to the Pilgrim's wish (the "knot," l. 96) to know the shades' capacity for knowledge of the present, Farinata states that, while they have complete knowledge of things past and future, they are ignorant of the present (except, of course, for the news of current events brought them by the new arrivals in Hell, the "others," l. 104). Even this knowledge will be denied them after the Day of Judgment, when all will become absolute and eternal. The door of the future will be closed (l. 108) and their remembrance of the past will fade away since there will no longer be any past, present, or future.

He said, "More than a thousand lie with me,
   the Second Frederick is here and the Cardinal
   is with us. And the rest I shall not mention."       120
His figure disappeared. I made my way
   to the ancient poet, reflecting on those words,
   those words which were prophetic enemies.
He moved, and as we went along he said,
   "What troubles you? Why are you so distraught?"      125
And I told him all the thoughts that filled my mind.
"Be sure your mind retains," the sage commanded,
   "those words you heard pronounced against yourself,
   and listen carefully now." He raised a finger:
"When at last you stand in the glow of her sweet ray,     130
   the one whose splendid eyes see everything,
   from her you'll learn your life's itinerary."
Then to the left he turned. Leaving the walls,
   he headed toward the center by a path
   that strikes into a vale, whose stench arose      135
disgusting us as high up as we were.

## CANTO XI

    Continuing their way within the Sixth Circle where the heretics
are punished, the poets are assailed by a stench rising from the
abyss ahead of them which is so strong that they must stop in order
to accustom themselves to the odor. They pause beside a tomb
whose inscription declares that within is Pope Anastasius. When
the Pilgrim expresses his desire to pass the time of waiting profitably, Virgil proceeds to instruct him about the plan of punishments
in Hell. Then, seeing that dawn is only two hours away, he urges
the Pilgrim on.

We reached the curving brink of a steep bank
   constructed of enormous broken rocks;
   below us was a crueler den of pain.
And the disgusting overflow of stench
   the deep abyss was vomiting, forced us      5
   back from the edge. Crouched underneath the lid
of some great tomb, I saw it was inscribed:
   "Within lies Anastasius, the Pope

119–120. The Emperor Frederick II
(1194–1250) is in the circle of the Heretics
because of the commonly held belief that
he was an Epicurean.
   Cardinal Ottaviano degli Ubaldini, a
Ghibelline, was papal legate in Lombardy
and Romagna until his death in 1273. He
is reported to have once said, "If I have
a soul, I have lost it for the Ghibellines."
   131. Beatrice.
   8–9. "Anastasius, the Pope": Anastasius II, pope from 496 to 498, was popularly believed for many centuries to be

a heretic because, supposedly, he allowed
Photinus, a deacon of Thessalonica who
followed the heresy of Acacius, to take
communion. This heresy denied Christ's
divine birth, asserting that He was begotten by a mortal man; thus Anastasius
II supposedly revealed his belief in the
heretical doctrine. It has been proved,
however, that this pope was confused
with the Byzantine Emperor Anastasius I
(491–518) by Dante's probable sources.
Emperor Anastasius was convinced by
Photinus to accept the heretical doctrine.

Photinus lured away from the straight path."
"Our descent will have to be delayed somewhat                    10
    so that our sense of smell may grow accustomed
    to these vile fumes; then we will not mind them,"
my master said. And I: "You will have to find
    some way to keep our time from being wasted."
    "That is precisely what I had in mind,"                      15
he said, and then began the lesson: "My son,
    within these boulders' bounds are three more circles,
    concentrically arranged like those above,
all tightly packed with souls; and so that, later,
    the sight of them alone will be enough,                      20
    I'll tell you how and why they are imprisoned.
All malice has injustice as its end,
    an end achieved by violence or by fraud;
    while both are sins that earn the hate of Heaven,
since fraud belongs exclusively to man,                          25
    God hates it more and, therefore, far below,
    the fraudulent are placed and suffer most.
In the first of the circles below are all the violent;
    since violence can be used against three persons,
    into three concentric rounds it is divided:                 30
violence can be done to God, to self,
    or to one's neighbor—to him or to his goods,
    as my reasoned explanation will make clear.
By violent means a man can kill his neighbor
    or wound him grievously; he can violate                     35
    his goods by arson, theft and devastation;
so, homicides and those who strike with malice,
    those who destroy and plunder, are all punished
    in the first round, but all in different groups.
Man can raise violent hands against himself                     40
    and his own goods; so in the second round,
    paying the debt that never can be paid,
are suicides, self-robbers of your world,
    or those who gamble all their wealth away
    and weep up there when they should have rejoiced.           45
One can use violence against the deity
    by heartfelt disbelief and cursing Him,
    or by despising Nature and God's bounty;
therefore, the smallest round stamps with its seal
    both Sodom and Cahors and all those souls                   50
    who hate God in their hearts and curse His name.
Fraud, that gnaws the conscience of its servants,
    can be used on one who puts his trust in you
    or else on one who has no trust invested.

---

50. "Sodom": the biblical city (Genesis 18–19) destroyed by God for its vicious sexual offenses. "Cahors": a city in the south of France which was widely known in the Middle Ages as a thriving seat of usury. Dante uses the city names to indicate the Sodomites and Usurers who are punished in the smallest round of Circle Seven.

This latter sort seems only to destroy 55
   the bond of love that Nature gives to man;
   so in the second circle there are nests
of hypocrites, flatterers, dabblers in sorcery,
   falsifiers, thieves and simonists,
   panders, seducers, grafters and like filth. 60
The former kind of fraud both disregards
   the love Nature enjoys and that extra bond
   between men which creates a special trust;
thus, it is in the smallest of the circles,
   at the earth's center, around the throne of Dis, 65
   that traitors suffer their eternal pain."
And I, "Master, your reasoning runs smooth,
   and your explanation certainly makes clear
   the nature of this pit and of its inmates,
but what about those in the slimy swamp, 70
   those driven by the wind, those beat by rain,
   and those who come to blows with harsh refrains?
Why are they, too, not punished here inside
   the city of flame, if they have earned God's wrath?
   If they have not, why are they suffering?" 75
And he to me, "Why do you let your thoughts
   stray from the path they are accustomed to?
   Or have I missed the point you have in mind?
Have you forgotten how your *Ethics* reads,
   those terms it explicates in such detail: 80
   the three conditions that the heavens hate,
incontinence, malice and bestiality?
   Do you not remember how incontinence
   offends God least, and merits the least blame?
If you will reconsider well this doctrine 85
   and then recall to mind who those souls were
   suffering pain above, outside the walls,
you will clearly see why they are separated
   from these malicious ones, and why God's vengeance
   beats down upon their souls less heavily." 90
"O sun that shines to clear a misty vision,
   such joy is mine when you resolve my doubts
   that doubting pleases me no less than knowing!
Go back a little bit once more," I said
   "to where you say that usury offends 95
   God's goodness, and untie that knot for me."

65. Here the name Dis refers to Lucifer.
70–75. The sinners are those guilty of Incontinence. Virgil's answer (ll. 76–90) is that the Incontinent suffer a lighter punishment because their sins, being without malice, are less offensive to God.
79–84. Virgil says "your Ethics" in referring to Aristotle's *Ethica Nicomachea* because he realizes how thoroughly the Pilgrim studied this work.
While the distinction here offered between Incontinence and Malice is based on Aristotle it should be clear that the overall classification of sins in the *Inferno* is not. Dante's is a twofold system, the main divisions of which may be illustrated as follows:

Sins of { Incontinence / Malice { through Violence / through Fraud

"Philosophy," he said, "and more than once,
  points out to one who reads with understanding
  how Nature takes her course from the Divine
Intellect, from its artistic workmanship;          100
  and if you have your *Physics* well in mind
  you will find, not many pages from the start,
how your art too, as best it can, imitates
  Nature, the way an apprentice does his master;
  so your art may be said to be God's grandchild.   105
From Art and Nature man was meant to take
  his daily bread to live—if you recall
  the book of Genesis near the beginning;
but the usurer, adopting other means,
  scorns Nature in herself and in her pupil,        110
  Art—he invests his hope in something else.
Now follow me, we should be getting on;
  the Fish are shimmering over the horizon,
  the Wain is now exactly over Caurus,
and the passage down the bank is farther on."       115

## CANTO XII

They descend the steep slope into the Seventh Circle by means
of a great landslide which was caused when Christ descended into
Hell. At the edge of the abyss is the Minotaur, who presides over
the circle of the Violent and whose own bestial rage sends him into
such a paroxysm of violence that the two travelers are able to run
past him without his interference. At the base of the precipice, they
see a river of boiling blood which contains those who have inflicted
violence upon others. But before they can reach the river they are
intercepted by three fierce Centaurs whose task it is to keep those
who are in the river at their proper depth by shooting arrows at
them if they attempt to rise. Virgil explains to one of the centaurs
(Chiron) that this journey of Pilgrim and himself is ordained by
God; and he requests him to assign someone to guide the two of
them to the ford in the river and carry the Pilgrim across it to the
other bank. Chiron gives the task to Nessus, one of the centaurs,
who, as he leads them to the river's ford, points out many of the
sinners there in the boiling blood.

101–105. Aristotle's *Physics* (II, ii) concerns the doctrine that Art imitates Nature. Art, or human industry, is the child of Nature in the sense that it is the use to which man puts Nature, and thus is the grandchild of God. Usurers, who are in the third round of Circle Seven, by doing violence to human industry are, in effect, doing violence to God.

113–115. Virgil, as always, indicates the time by referring to the stars; how he knows of their position at any given mo-

ment Dante does not explain (the stars are not visible from Hell). Pisces, the Fish, is just appearing on the horizon, while the Great Bear, the Wain, is lying completely in the northwest quadrant of the heavens (Caurus is the Northwest Wind). The next sign of the Zodiac after Pisces is Aries; from Canto I we know that the sun is currently rising in Aries. Each sign of the Zodiac covers about two hours, thus it must be nearly two hours before sunrise.

Not only was that place, where we had come
   to descend, craggy, but there was something there
   that made the scene appalling to the eye.
Like the ruins this side of Trent left by the landslide
   (an earthquake or erosion must have caused it)           5
   that hit the Adige on its left bank,
when, from the mountain's top where the slide began
   to the plain below, the shattered rocks slipped down,
   shaping a path for a difficult descent—
so was the slope of our ravine's formation.         10
   And at the edge, along the shattered chasm,
   there lay stretched out the infamy of Crete:
the son conceived in the pretended cow.
   When he saw us he bit into his flesh,
   gone crazy with the fever of his rage.         15
My wise guide cried to him: "Perhaps you think
   you see the Duke of Athens come again
   who came once in the world to bring your death?
Begone you beast, for this one is not led
   down here by means of clews your sister gave him;      20
   he comes here only to observe your torments."
The way a bull breaks loose the very moment
   he knows he has been dealt the mortal blow,
   and cannot run but jumps and twists and turns,
just so I saw the Minotaur perform,         25
   and my guide, alert, cried out: "Run to the pass!
   While he still writhes with rage, get started down."
And so we made our way down through the ruins
   of rocks, which often I felt shift and tilt
   beneath my feet from weight they were not used to.     30
I was deep in thought when he began: "Are you,
   perhaps, thinking about these ruins protected
   by the furious beast I quenched in its own rage?
Now let me tell you that the other time
   I came down to the lower part of Hell,      35
   this rock had not then fallen into ruins;
but certainly, if I remember well,

---

**4–10.** The way down the precipice to the Seventh Circle is here compared to a great landslide, the *Slavini di Marco*, located near Trent in northern Italy; the event which took place about 883 diverted the Adige River from its course (l. 6). In the *Inferno* the steep, shattered terrain was caused by the earthquake which shook Hell just before Christ descended there.

**12–21.** The Sins of Violence are also the Sins of Bestiality, and the perfect overseer of the circle is the half-man, half-bull known as the Minotaur. Called the "infamy of Crete," that creature was the result of an act of Violence against Nature (punished in the third round of this circle): Pasiphaë, wife of King Minos of Crete, conceived an unnatural desire for a bull, which she satisfied by creeping into a wooden cow and having intercourse with the bull. The Cretan labyrinth, designed by Daedalus, was the Minotaur's home. He was finally slain by Theseus (the duke of Athens, l. 17) with the help of Ariadne (Pasiphaë's human daughter and, as such, a half-sister to the beast, l. 20). Note the continued appearance of the half-human, half-animal monsters, begun in Canto IV with the Furies.

it was just before the coming of that One
who took from Hell's first circle the great spoil,
that this abyss of stench, from top to bottom            40
    began to shake, so I thought the universe
    felt love—whereby, some have maintained, the world
has more than once renewed itself in chaos.
    That was the moment when this ancient rock
    was split this way—here, and in other places.       45
But now look down the valley. Coming closer
    you will see the river of blood that boils the souls
    of those who through their violence injured others."
(Oh blind cupidity and insane wrath,
    spurring us on through our short life on earth        50
    to steep us then forever in such misery!)
I saw a river—wide, curved like a bow—
    that stretched embracing all the flatland there,
    just as my guide had told me to expect.
Between the river and the steep came centaurs            55
    galloping in single file equipped with arrows,
    off hunting as they used to in the world;
then, seeing us descend, they all stopped short
    and three of them departed from the ranks
    with bows and arrows ready from their quivers.        60
One of them cried from his distant post: "You there,
    on your way down here, what torture are you seeking?
    Speak where you stand, if not, I draw my bow."
And then my master shouted back: "Our answer
    we will give to Chiron when we're at his side;        65
    as for you, I see you are as rash as ever!"
He nudged me saying: "That one there is Nessus
    who died from loving lovely Dejanira,
    and made of himself, of his blood, his own revenge.
The middle one who contemplates his chest                70

---

38. "that One": Christ, who, in the Harrowing of Hell, removed to Heaven the souls of the Elect.

41–43. According to Empedoclean doctrine, Hate, by destroying pristine harmony (i.e., original chaos), occasions the creation of all things, and Love, by reunifying these disparate elements, re-establishes concord in the universe.

47–48. Phlegethon, the Virgilian river of fire, here one of boiling blood, in which are punished those shades who committed violence against their fellow men.

56. Like the Minotaur, the Centaurs who guard the murderers and tyrants are men-beasts (half-horse, half-man) and thus appropriate to the sins of violence or bestiality.

65. "Chiron": Represented by the ancient poets as chief of the Centaurs, he was particularly noted for his wisdom. In mythology he was the son of Saturn (who temporarily changed himself into a horse to avoid the notice and anger of his wife) and Philyra.

67–69. "Nessus": The Centaur who is the first to speak to the two travelers. He is later appointed by Chiron (ll. 98–99) to accompany them; he does so, pointing out various sinners along the way. Virgil refers to Dejanira, Hercules' wife, whom Nessus desired. In attempting to rape her, Nessus was shot by Hercules, but as he died he gave Dejanira a robe soaked in his blood which he said would preserve Hercules' love. Dejanira took it to her husband, whose death it caused, whereupon the distraught woman hanged herself.

is great Chiron who reared and taught Achilles;
  the last is Pholus, known for his drunken wrath.
They gallop, by the thousands round the ditch
  shooting at any daring soul emerging
  above the bloody level of his guilt."                          75
When we came closer to those agile beasts,
  Chiron drew an arrow, and with its notch
  he parted his beard to both sides of his jaws,
and when he had uncovered his great mouth
  he spoke to his companions: "Have you noticed,               80
  how the one behind moves everything he touches?
*This* is not what a dead man's feet would do!"
  And my good guide, now standing by the torso
  at the point the beast's two natures joined, replied:
"He is indeed alive, and so alone                               85
  that I must show him through this dismal valley;
  he travels by necessity, not pleasure.
A spirit came, from singing Alleluia,
  to give me this extraordinary mission;
  he is no rogue nor I a criminal spirit.                       90
Now, in the name of that power by which I move
  my steps along so difficult a road,
  give us one of your troop to be our guide:
to lead us to the ford and, once we are there,
  to carry this one over on his back,                           95
  for he is not a spirit who can fly."
Chiron looked over his right breast and said
  to Nessus, "You go, guide them as they ask,
  and if another troop protests, disperse them!"
So with this trusted escort we moved on                        100
  along the boiling crimson river's bank
  where piercing shrieks rose from the boiling souls.
There I saw people sunken to their eyelids,
  and the huge centaur explained, "These are the tyrants
  who dealt in bloodshed and in plundered wealth.              105
Their tears are paying for their heartless crimes:
  here stand Alexander and fierce Dionysius
  who weighed down Sicily with years of pain;
and there, that forehead smeared with coal-black hair,
  is Azzolino; the other one, the blond,                       110

72. During the wedding of Pirithous and Hippodamia, when the drunken Centaurs tried to rape the Lapithaen women, Pholus attempted to rape the bride herself.
88. Beatrice.
107–108. Possibly Alexander the Great (356–323 B.C.), who is constantly referred to as a cruel and violent man by Orosius, Dante's chief source of ancient history. But many modern scholars believe this figure to be Alexander, tyrant of Pherae (368–359 B.C.), whose extreme cruelty is recorded by Cicero and Valerius Maximus. Both of these authors link Alexander of Pherae with the tyrant Dionysius of Syracuse, mentioned here.
110. "Azzolino": Ezzelino III da Romano (1194–1259), a Ghibelline chief and tyrant of the March of Treviso. He was notoriously cruel and committed such inhuman atrocities that he was called a "son of Satan."

Opizzo d'Esti who, and this is true,
was killed by his own stepson in your world."
    With that I looked to Virgil, but he said
"Let him instruct you now, don't look to me."
    A little farther on, the centaur stopped        115
above some people peering from the blood
that came up to their throats. He pointed out
a shade off to one side, alone, and said:
"There stands the one who, in God's keep, murdered
the heart still dripping blood above the Thames."    120
    Then I saw other souls stuck in the river
who had their heads and chests above the blood,
and I knew the names of many who were there.
    The river's blood began decreasing slowly
until it cooked the feet and nothing more,        125
and here we found the ford where we could cross.
    "Just as you see the boiling river here
on this side getting shallow gradually,"
the centaur said, "I would also have you know
that on the other side the riverbed        130
sinks deeper more and more until it reaches
the deepest meeting place where tyrants moan:
it is there that Heaven's justice strikes its blow
against Attila known as the scourge of earth,
against Pyrrhus and Sextus; and forever        135
extracts the tears the scalding blood produces
from Rinier da Corneto and Rinier Pazzo
whose battlefields were highways where they robbed."
    Then he turned round and crossed the ford again.

---

111–114. **"Opizzo d'Esti"**: Obizzo d'Esti was Marquis of Ferrara and of the March of Ancona (1264–1293). He was a cruel tyrant.

120. In 1272 during Holy Mass at the church ("in God's keep") in Viterbo, Guy de Montfort (one of Charles d'Anjou's emissaries), in order to avenge his father's death at the hands of Edward I, king of England, stabbed to death the latter's cousin, Prince Henry, son of Richard, earl of Cornwall. According to Giovanni Villani, the thirteenth-century chronicler, Henry's heart was placed in "a golden cup . . . above a column at the head of London bridge" where it still drips blood above the Thames (*Cronica* VII, xxxix). The dripping blood signifies that the murder has not yet been avenged.

124–126. The sinners are sunk in the river to a degree commensurate with the gravity of their crimes; tyrants, whose crimes of violence are directed against both man and his possessions, are sunk deeper than murderers, whose crimes are against men alone. The river is at its shallowest at the point where the poets cross; from this ford, in both directions of its circle, it grows deeper.

134. **"Attila"**: king of the Huns, called the "scourge of God."

135. **"Pyrrhus and Sextus"**: The first named is probably Pyrrhus (318–272 B.C.), king of Epirus, who fought the Romans three times between 280 and 276 B.C. before they finally defeated him. Sextus is probably the younger son of Pompey the Great. After the murder of Caesar he turned to piracy, causing near famine in Rome by cutting off the grain supply from Africa. He is condemned by Lucan (*Pharsalia* VI, 420–422) as being unworthy of his father. A few commentators believe that Dante is referring to Sextus Tarquinius Superbus, who raped and caused the death of Lucretia, the wife of his cousin.

137–138. **"Rinier da Corneto and Rinier Pazzo"**: Two highway robbers famous in Dante's day.

CANTO XIII

No sooner are the poets across the Phlegethon than they encounter a dense forest, from which come wails and moans, and which is presided over by the hideous harpies—half-woman, half-beast, bird-like creatures. Virgil tells his ward to break off a branch of one of the trees; when he does, the tree weeps blood and speaks. In life he was Pier Delle Vigne, chief counselor of Frederick II of Sicily; but he fell out of favor, was accused unjustly of treachery and was imprisoned, whereupon he killed himself. The Pilgrim is overwhelmed by pity. The sinner also explains how the souls of the suicides come to this punishment and what will happen to them after the Last Judgment. Suddenly they are interrupted by the wild sounds of the hunt, and two naked figures, Lano of Siena and Giacomo da Sant' Andrea, dash across the landscape shouting at each other until one of them hides himself in a thorny bush; immediately a pack of fierce, black dogs rush in, pounce on the hidden sinner, and rip his body, carrying away mouthfuls of flesh. The bush, which has been torn in the process, begins to lament. The two learn that the cries are those of a Florentine who had hanged himself in his own home.

Not yet had Nessus reached the other side
  when we were on our way into a forest
  that was not marked by any path at all.
No green leaves, but rather black in color,
  no smooth branches, but twisted and entangled,     5
  no fruit, but thorns of poison bloomed instead.
No thick, rough, scrubby home like this exists—
  not even between Cecina and Corneto—
  for those wild beasts that hate the run of farmlands.
Here the repulsive harpies twine their nests,     10
  who drove the Trojans from the Strophades
  with filthy forecasts of their close disaster.
Wide-winged they are, with human necks and faces,
  their feet are clawed, their bellies fat and feathered;
  perched in the trees they shriek their strange laments.     15
"Before we go on farther," my guide began,
  "remember, you are in the second round
  and shall be till we reach the dreadful sand;
now look around you carefully and see

1-9. The Wood of the Suicides is described in a series of negatives ("No green leaves . . . no smooth branches . . . no fruit), and in fact the first three tercets begin with a negative. This device anticipates the negation inherent in suicide and suggests the atmosphere in which the action of this canto will move: mistrust and incredulity.

8-9. The vast swampland known as the "Maremma toscana" lies between the towns of Cecina and Corneto, which mark its northern and southern boundaries.

10-15. The Harpies were the daughters of Thaumas and Electra. Because of their malicious deeds they were banished to the Strophades Islands, where, having encountered Aeneas and his followers from Troy, they defiled their table and forecast future hardships for them.

with your own eyes what I will not describe,                    20
  for if I did, you wouldn't believe my words."
Around me wails of grief were echoing,
  and I saw no one there to make those sounds;
  bewildered by all this I had to stop.
I think perhaps he thought I might be thinking             25
  that all the voices coming from those stumps
  belonged to people hiding there from us,
and so my teacher said, "If you break off
  a little branch of any of these plants,
  what you are thinking now will break off too."      30
Then slowly raising up my hand a bit
  I snapped the tiny branch of a great thorn,
  and its trunk cried: "Why are you tearing me?"
And when its blood turned dark around the wound,
  it started saying more: "Why do you rip me?         35
  Have you no sense of pity whatsoever?
Men were we once, now we are changed to scrub;
  but even if we had been souls of serpents,
  your hand should have shown more pity than it did."
Like a green log burning at one end only,                      40
  sputtering at the other, oozing sap,
  and hissing with the air it forces out,
so from that splintered trunk a mixture poured
  of words and blood. I let the branch I held
  fall from my hand and stood there stiff with fear.   45
"O wounded soul," my sage replied to him,
  "if he had only let himself believe
  what he had read in verses I once wrote,
he never would have raised his hand against you,
  but the truth itself was so incredible                50
  I urged him on to do the thing that grieves me.
But tell him who you were; he can make amends,
  and will, by making bloom again your fame
  in the world above, where his return is sure."
And the trunk: "So appealing are your lovely words,        55
  I must reply. Be not displeased if I
  am lured into a little conversation.
I am that one who held both of the keys

47–49. Virgil is referring to that section of the *Aeneid* (III, 22–43), where Aeneas breaks a branch from a shrub, which then begins to pour forth blood; at the same time a voice issues from the ground beneath the shrub where Polydorus is buried. See Canto XXX, l. 18.

58–78. Born in the Southern Italian town of Capua (ca. 1190), Pier delle Vigne studied at Bologna and, having attracted the attention of Frederick II, became attached to his court at Palermo, where he soon became the Emperor's most trusted minister. Around 1248, however, he fell from the emperor's grace and was placed in jail, where he committed suicide. Pier delle Vigne tells how Envy ("that courtesan," l. 64), ever-present at Frederick's court ("Caesar's household," l. 65), inflamed everyone against him, Frederick ("Augustus," l. 68) becoming influenced by the attitude of others. The dishonor of the imprisonment and the envisaged self-justification through death led him to take his own life by dashing his head against the prison wall. He concludes by declaring his innocence and expressing the desire for re-evaluation of his deeds, which will ensure his earthly fame.

that fitted Frederick's heart; I turned them both,
  locking and unlocking, with such finesse       60
that I let few into his confidence.
  I was so faithful to my glorious office,
  I lost not only sleep but life itself.
That courtesan who constantly surveyed
  Caesar's household with her adulterous eyes,       65
  mankind's undoing, the special vice of courts,
inflamed the hearts of everyone against me,
  and these, inflamed, inflamed in turn Augustus,
  and my happy honors turned to sad laments.
My mind, moved by scornful satisfaction,       70
  believing death would free me from all scorn,
  made me unjust to me who was all just.
By these strange roots of my own tree I swear
  to you that never once did I break faith
  with my lord who was so worthy of all honor.       75
If one of you should go back to the world,
  restore the memory of me, who here
  remain cut down by the blow that Envy gave."
My poet paused awhile then said to me,
  "Since he is silent now, don't lose your chance,       80
  ask him, if there is more you wish to know."
"Why don't you keep on questioning," I said,
  "and ask him, for my part, what I would ask,
  for I cannot, such pity chokes my heart."
He began again: "That this man may fulfill       85
  generously what your words cry out for,
  imprisoned soul, may it please you to continue
by telling us just how a soul gets bound
  into these knots, and tell us, if you know,
  whether any soul might someday leave his branches."      90
At that the trunk breathed heavily, and then
  the breath changed to a voice that spoke these words:
  "Your question will be answered very briefly.
The moment that the violent soul departs
  the body it has torn itself away from,       95
  Minòs sends it down to the seventh hole;
it drops to the wood, not in a place allotted,
  but anywhere that fortune tosses it.
  There, like a grain of spelt, it germinates,
soon springs into a sapling, then a wild tree;       100
  at last the harpies, feasting on its leaves,
  create its pain, and for the pain an outlet.
Like the rest, we shall return to claim our bodies,
  but never again to wear them—wrong it is
  for a man to have again what he once cast off.       105

68–72. Pier was also a renowned poet of the Sicilian School which flourished under Frederick's patronage and which is noted for its love of complex conceits and convoluted word play.

95–108. Having denied the God-given sanctity of their bodies on earth, in Hell the Suicides are completely denied bodily form. It is only when part of the tree or bush is torn or broken that the shades can make sounds, thus the necessity for Dante to break a branch before Pier can speak.

We shall drag them here and, all along the mournful
    forest, our bodies shall hang forever more,
    each one on a thorn of its own alien shade."
We were standing still attentive to the trunk,
    thinking perhaps it might have more to say,           110
    when we were startled by a rushing sound,
such as the hunter hears from where he stands:
    first the boar, then all the chase approaching,
    the crash of hunting dogs and branches smashing,
then, to the left of us appeared two shapes           115
    naked and gashed, fleeing with such rough speed
    they tore away with them the bushes' branches.
The one ahead: "Come on, come quickly, Death!"
    The other, who could not keep up the pace,
    screamed, "Lano, your legs were not so nimble     120
when you jousted in the tournament of Toppo!"
    And then, from lack of breath perhaps, he slipped
    into a bush and wrapped himself in thorns.
Behind these two the wood was overrun
    by packs of black bitches ravenous and ready,     125
    like hunting dogs just broken from their chains;
they sank their fangs in that poor wretch who hid,
    they ripped him open piece by piece, and then
    ran off with mouthfuls of his wretched limbs.
Quickly my escort took me by the hand           130
    and led me over to the bush that wept
    its vain laments from every bleeding sore:
"O Giacomo da Sant' Andrea," it said,
    "what good was it for you to hide in me?
    What fault have I if you led an evil life?"     135
My master, standing over it, inquired:
    "Who were you once that now through many wounds
    breathes a grieving sermon with your blood?"
He answered us: "O souls who have just come
    in time to see this unjust mutilation          140
    that has separated me from all my leaves,
gather them round the foot of this sad bush.
    I was from the city that took the Baptist

115–121. The second group of souls
punished here are the Profligates, who did
violence to their earthly goods by not
valuing them as they should have, just as
the Suicides did not value their bodies.
They are represented by Lano (l. 120),
probably a member of the wealthy Maconi
family of Siena, and by Giacomo da
Sant'Andrea (l. 133) from Padua. Both
had the dubious honor of being incorrigi-
ble spendthrifts who squandered most of
their wealth and property. The "tournament of Toppo" (l. 121) recalls the disastrous defeat of the Sienese troops at the
hands of the Aretines in 1287 at a river
ford near Arezzo. Lano went into this
battle to die because he had squandered
his fortune; as legend has it, he remained
to fight rather than escape on foot (hence

Giacomo's reference to his "legs," (l.
120), and was killed.
143–150. The identity of this Florentine
Suicide remains unknown. The "first
patron" of Florence was Mars, the god of
war (thus his "art" ll. 145] is warfare);
a fragment of his statue was to be found
on the Ponte Vecchio ("the Arno's
bridge," l. 146) until 1333.
    The second patron of the city was John
the Baptist (l. 143), whose image appeared on the florin, the principal monetary unit of the time. It has been suggested that Florence's change of patron
indicates its transformation from a stronghold of martial excellence (under Mars)
to one of servile money making (under
the Baptist).

in exchange for her first patron, who, for this,
swears by his art she will have endless sorrow;                    145
   and were it not that on the Arno's bridge
   some vestige of his image still remains,
those citizens who built anew the city
   on the ashes that Attila left behind
   would have accomplished such a task in vain;                    150
I turned my home into my hanging place."

CANTO XIV

They come to the edge of the Wood of the Suicides where they
see before them a stretch of burning sand upon which flames rain
eternally and through which a stream of boiling blood is carried in a
raised channel formed of rock. There, many groups of tortured souls
are on the burning sand; Virgil explains that those lying supine on
the ground are the Blasphemers, those crouching are the Usurers,
and those wandering aimlessly, never stopping, are the Sodomites.
Representative of the blasphemers is Capaneus who died cursing his
god. The Pilgrim questions his guide about the source of the river
of boiling blood; Virgil's reply contains the most elaborate symbol
in the *Inferno*, that of the Old Man of Crete, whose tears are the
source of all rivers in Hell.


The love we both shared for our native city
   moved me to gather up the scattered leaves
   and give them back to the voice that now had faded.
We reached the confines of the woods that separate
   the second from the third round. There I saw                    5
   God's justice in its dreadful operation.
Now to picture clearly these unheard-of things:
   we arrived to face an open stretch of flatland
   whose soil refused the roots of any plant;
the grieving forest made a wreath around it,                    10
   as the sad river of blood enclosed the woods.
   We stopped right here, right at the border line.
This wasteland was a dry expanse of sand,
   thick, burning sand, no different from the kind
   that Cato's feet packed down in other times.                    15
O just revenge of God! how awesomely
   you should be feared by everyone who reads
   these truths that were revealed to my own eyes!
Many separate herds of naked souls I saw,

151. The Florentine's anonymity cor-
roborates his symbolic value as a representative of his city. Like the suicides
condemned to this round, the city of Florence was killing itself, in Dante's opinion,
through its internecine struggles.
   15. 'Cato': sided with Pompey in the
Roman civil war. After Pompey was defeated at Pharsalia, and when it became
apparent that he was about to be captured
by Caesar, he killed himself (46 B.C.).
The year before his death he led a march
across the desert of Libya.

all weeping desperately; it seemed each group    20
    had been assigned a different penalty:
some were stretched out flat upon their backs,
    others were crouching there all tightly hunched,
    some wandered, never stopping, round and round.
Far more there were of those who roamed the sand    25
    and fewer were the souls stretched out to suffer,
    but their tongues were looser, for the pain was greater.
And over all that sandland, a fall of slowly-
    raining broad flakes of fire showered steadily
    (a mountain snowstorm on a windless day),    30
like those that Alexander saw descending
    on his troops while crossing India's torrid lands:
    flames falling, floating solid to the ground,
and he with all his men began to tread
    the sand so that the burning flames might be    35
    extinguished one by one before they joined.
Here too a never-ending blaze descended,
    kindling the sand like tinder under flint-sparks,
    and in this way the torment there was doubled.
Without a moment's rest the rhythmic dance    40
    of wretched hands went on, this side, that side,
    brushing away the freshly fallen flames.
And I: "My master, you who overcome
    all opposition (except for those tough demons
    who came to meet us at the gate of Dis),    45
who is that mighty one that seems unbothered
    by burning, stretched sullen and disdainful there,
    looking as if the rainfall could not tame him?"
And that very one, who was quick to notice me
    inquiring of my guide about him, answered:    50
    "What I was once, alive, I still am, dead!
Let Jupiter wear out his smith, from whom
    he seized in anger that sharp thunderbolt
    he hurled, to strike me down, my final day;
let him wear out those others, one by one,    55
    who work the soot-black forge of Mongibello
    (as he shouts, "Help me good Vulcan, I need your help,"
the way he cried that time at Phlegra's battle),
    and with all his force let him hurl his bolts at me,
    no joy of satisfaction would I give him!"    60
My guide spoke back at him with cutting force,

22–24. The shades in this third round of the Seventh Circle are divided into three groups: the Blasphemers lie supine on the ground, the Usurers are "crouching", and the Sodomites wander "never stopping". The sand they lie on perhaps suggests the sterility of their acts.
44–45. "those tough demons": The rebel angels of Canto IX who barred the travelers' entrance to the city of Dis.

51–60. The representative of the Blasphemers is Capaneus, who, as Virgil will explain, was one of the seven kings who assaulted Thebes. Statius describes how Capaneus, when scaling the walls of Thebes, blasphemed against Jove, who then struck him with a thunderbolt. Capaneus died with blasphemy on his lips and now, even in Hell, he is able to defy Jove's thunderbolts.

(I never heard his voice so strong before):
"O Capaneus, since your blustering pride
will not be stilled, you are made to suffer more:
no torment other than your rage itself          65
could punish your gnawing pride more perfectly."
And then he turned a calmer face to me,
saying, "That was a king, one of the seven
besieging Thebes; he scorned, and would seem still
to go on scorning God and treat him lightly,          70
but, as I said to him, he decks his chest
with ornaments of lavish words that prick him.
Now follow me and also pay attention
not to put your feet upon the burning sand,
but to keep them well within the wooded line."          75
Without exchanging words we reached a place
where a narrow stream came gushing from the woods
(its reddish water still runs fear through me!);
like the one that issues from the Bulicame,
whose waters are shared by prostitutes downstream,          80
it wore its way across the desert sand.
This river's bed and banks were made of stone,
so were the tops on both its sides; and then
I understood this was our way across.
"Among the other marvels I have shown you,          85
from the time we made our entrance through the gate
whose threshold welcomes every evil soul,
your eyes have not discovered anything
as remarkable as this stream you see here
extinguishing the flames above its path."          90
These were my master's words, and I at once
implored him to provide me with the food
for which he had given me the appetite.
"In the middle of the sea there lies a wasteland,"

---

79–80. "the Bulicame": Near Viterbo there was a hot spring called the Bulicame, whose sulphurous waters transformed the area into a watering place. Among the inhabitants were many prostitutes who were required to live in a separate quarter. A special stream channeled the hot spring water through their section, since they were denied use of public baths.

94–119. The island of Crete is given as the source of Acheron, Styx, and Phlegethon, the joined rivers of Hell whose course eventually leads to the "pool," Cocytus, at the bottom of Hell. According to mythology, Mt. Ida on Crete was the place chosen by Rhea to protect her infant son, Jupiter, from his father, Saturn, who usually devoured his sons when they were born. Rhea, to keep him from finding Jupiter, "had her servants scream loud when he cried" (l. 102) to drown out the infant's screams.

Within Mt. Ida Dante places the statue of the "Old Man of Crete" (certainly one of the most elaborate symbols in the *Inferno*), with his back to Damietta and gazing toward Rome (ll. 104–105). Damietta, an important Egyptian seaport, represents the East, the pagan world; Rome of course, the modern, Christian world. The figure of the Old Man is drawn from the book of Daniel (2:32–35), but the symbolism is different, and more nearly (though not absolutely) reflects a poetic symbol utilized by Ovid (*Metamorphoses* I). The head of gold represents the Golden Age of man (that is, in Christian terms, before the Fall). The arms and breast of silver, the trunk of brass, and the legs of iron represent the three declining ages of man. The clay foot (the one made of terra cotta) may symbolize the Church, weakened and corrupted by temporal concerns and political power struggles.

he immediately began, "that is known as Crete,    95
under whose king the world knew innocence.
There is a mountain there that was called Ida;
then happy in its verdure and its streams,
now deserted like an old, discarded thing;
Rhea chose it once as a safe cradle    100
for her son, and, to conceal his presence better,
she had her servants scream loud when he cried.
In the mountain's core an ancient man stands tall;
he has his shoulders turned toward Damietta
and faces Rome as though it were his mirror.    105
His head is fashioned of the finest gold;
pure silver are his arms and hands and chest;
from there to where his legs spread, he is brass;
the rest of him is all of chosen iron,
except his right foot which is terra cotta;    110
he puts more weight on this foot than the other.
Every part of him, except the gold, is broken
by a fissure dripping tears down to his feet
where they collect to erode the cavern's rock;
from stone to stone they drain down here, becoming    115
rivers: the Acheron, Styx, the Phlegethon
then overflow down through this tight canal
until they fall to where all falling ends:
they form Cocytus. What that pool is like
I need not tell you. You will see, yourself."    120
And I to him: "If this small stream beside us
has its source, as you have told me, in our world,
why have we seen it only on this ledge?"
And he to me: "You know this place is round,
and though your journey has been long, circling    125
toward the bottom, turning only to the left,
you have not completed any circle's round;
so you should never look surprised, as now,
if you see something you have not seen before."
And I again: "Where, Master, shall we find    130
Lethe and Phlegethon? You omit the first
and say the other forms from the rain of tears."
"I am very happy when you question me,"
he said, "but that the blood-red water boiled
should answer certainly one of your questions.    135
And Lethe you shall see, but beyond this valley,
at a place where souls collect to wash themselves
when penitence has freed them of their guilt.
Now it is time to leave this edge of woods,"
he added. "Be sure you follow close behind me:    140
the margins are our road, they do not burn,
and all the flames above them are extinguished."

134–135. To the Pilgrim's naïve question (ll. 130–131) Virgil replies that he
should have been able to recognize Phlegethon by its extreme heat.

CANTO XV

They move out across the plain of burning sand, walking along the ditchlike edge of the conduit through which the Phlegethon flows, and after they have come some distance from the wood they see a group of souls running toward them. One, Brunetto Latini, a famous Florentine intellectual and Dante's former teacher, recognizes the Pilgrim and leaves his band to walk and talk with him. Brunetto learns the reason for the Pilgrim's journey and offers him a prophecy of the troubles lying in wait for him—an echo of Ciacco's words in Canto VI. Brunetto names some of the others being punished with him (Priscian, Francesco d'Accorso, Andrea de' Mozzi); but soon, in the distance, he sees a cloud of smoke approaching which presages a new group, and because he must not associate with them, like a foot racer Brunetto speeds away to catch up with his own band.

Now one of those stone margins bears us on
  and the river's vapors hover like a shade,
  sheltering the banks and water from the flames.
As the Flemings, living with the constant threat
  of flood tides rushing in between Wissant                           5
  and Bruges, build their dikes to force the sea back;
as the Paduans build theirs on the shores of Brenta
  to protect their town and homes before warm weather
  turns Chiarentana's snow to rushing water—
so were these walls we walked upon constructed,                      10
  though the engineer, whoever he may have been,
  did not make them as high or thick as those.
We had left the wood behind (so far behind,
  by now, that if I had stopped to turn around,
  I am sure it could no longer have been seen)                       15
when we saw a troop of souls come hurrying
  toward us beside the bank, and each of them
  looked us up and down as some men look,
at other men, at night, when the moon is new.
  They strained their eye-brows, squinting hard at us,              20
  as an old tailor might at his needle's eye.
Eyed in such a way by this strange crew,
  I was recognized by one of them who grabbed
  my garment's hem and shouted: "How marvelous!"
And I, when he reached out his arm toward me,                        25
  straining my eyes, saw through his face's crust,
  through this burned features that could not prevent

4–6. The cities of Wissant and Bruges were centers of trade during the thirteenth century. It is not inconceivable that cities such as these, which counted a considerable number of itinerant tradesmen and sailors among their population, might have had a reputation for sodomy during Dante's time.

7. In the Journals of William Lithgow, a seventeenth century traveler and writer, we find reference made to the propensity for sodomy he had noted among the Paduans.

9. "Chiarentana's": a mountainous district situated north of the Brenta River.

11. God.

my memory from bringing back his name;
   and bending my face down to meet with his,
   I said: "Is this really you, here, Ser Brunetto?"    30
And he: "O my son, may it not displease you
   if Brunetto Latini lets his troop file on
   while he walks at your side for a little while."
And I: "With all my heart I beg you to,
   and if you wish me to sit here with you,    35
   I will, if my companion does not mind."
"My son," he said, "a member of this herd
   who stops one moment lies one hundred years
   unable to brush off the wounding flames,
so, move on; I shall follow at your hem    40
   and then rejoin my family that moves
   along, lamenting their eternal pain."
I did not dare step off the margin-path
   to walk at his own level but, with head
   bent low in reverence, I moved along.    45
He began: "What fortune or what destiny
   leads you down here before your final hour?
   And who is this one showing you the way?"
"Up there above in the bright living life
   before I reached the end of all my years,    50
   I lost myself in a valley," I replied;
"just yesterday at dawn I turned from it.
   This spirit here appeared as I turned back,
   and by this road he guides me home again."
He said to me: "Follow your constellation    55
   and you cannot fail to reach your port of glory,
   not if I saw clearly in the happy life;
and if I had not died just when I did,
   I would have cheered you on in all your work,
   seeing how favorable Heaven was to you.    60
But that ungrateful and malignant race
   which descended from the Fiesole of old,
   and still have rock and mountain in their blood,
will become, for your good deeds, your enemy—
   and right they are: among the bitter berries    65
   there's no fit place for the sweet fig to bloom.
They have always had the fame of being blind,
   an envious race, proud and avaricious;
   you must not let their ways contaminate you.
Your destiny reserves such honors for you:    70
   both parties shall be hungry to devour you,

---

61–67. During a Roman power struggle, Cataline fled Rome and found sanctuary for himself and his troops in the originally Etruscan town of Fiesole. After Caesar's successful siege of that city, the survivors of both camps founded Florence, where those of the Roman camp were the elite.

The phophecy with its condemnation of the current state of Florence (and Italy) and its implied hope of a renascent empire continues the political theme, begun with the speech of the Anonymous Suicide in Canto XIII, and continued in the symbol of the Old Man of Crete in Canto XIV.

but the grass will not be growing where the goat is.
Let the wild beasts of Fiesole make fodder
  of each other, and let them leave the plant untouched
  (so rare it is that one grows in their dung-heap)      75
in which there lives again the holy seed
  of those remaining Romans who survived there
  when this new nest of malice was constructed."
"O, if all I wished for had been granted,"
  I answered him, "you certainly would not,      80
  not yet, be banished from our life on earth;
my mind is etched (and now my heart is pierced)
  with your kind image, loving and paternal,
  when, living in the world, hour after hour
you taught me how man makes himself eternal.      85
  And while I live my tongue shall always speak
  of my debt to you, and of my gratitude.
I will write down what you tell me of my future
  and save it, with another text, to show
  a lady who can interpret, if I reach her.      90
This much, at least, let me make clear to you:
  if my conscience continues not to blame me,
  I am ready for whatever Fortune wants.
This prophecy is not new to my ears,
  and so let Fortune turn her wheel, spinning it      95
  as she pleases, and the peasant turn his spade."
My master hearing this looked to the right,
  then, turning round and facing me, he said:
  "He listens well who notes well what he hears."
But I did not answer him; I went on talking,      100
  walking with Ser Brunetto, asking him
  who of his company were the most distinguished.
And he: "It might be good to know who some are,
  about the rest I feel I should be silent,
  for the time would be too short, there are so many.      105
In brief, let me tell you, all here were clerics
  and respected men of letters of great fame,
  all befouled in the world by one same sin:
Priscian is travelling with that wretched crowd
  and Francesco d'Accorso too; and also there,      110
  if you could have stomached such repugnancy,
you might have seen the one the Servant of Servants

89–90. Again (as in Canto X, ll. 130–132), Beatrice is referred to as the one who will reveal to the Pilgrim his future course. However, in the *Paradiso* this role is given to Dante's ancestor, Cacciaguida.

95–96. It is as right for Fortune to spin her wheel as it is for the peasant to turn his spade; and the Pilgrim will be as indifferent to the first as to the second.

110. A celebrated Florentine lawyer (1225–1294) who taught law at the University of Bologna and later at Oxford at the request of King Edward I.

112–114. Andrea de' Mozzi was Bishop of Florence from 1287 to 1295, when, by order of Pope Boniface VIII (the "Servant of Servants," i.e., the servant of the servants of God), he was transferred to Vicenza (on the Bacchiglione River), where he died that same year or the next. The early commentators make reference to his naïve and inept preaching and to his general stupidity. Dante, by mentioning his "sinfully-erected nerves" calls attention to his major weakness: unnatural lust or sodomy.

transferred to the Bacchiglione from the Arno
   where his sinfully-erected nerves were buried.
I would say more, but my walk and conversation        115
   with you cannot go on, for over there
   I see a new smoke rising from the sand:
people approach with whom I must not mingle.
   Remember my *Trésor*, where I live on,
   this is the only thing I ask of you."        120
Then he turned back, and he seemed like one of those
   who run in Verona's race across its fields
   to win the green cloth prize, and he was like
the winner of the group, not the last one in.

### CANTO XVI

Continuing through the third round of the Circle of Violence,
the Pilgrim hears the distant roar of a waterfall which grows louder
as he and his guide proceed. Suddenly three shades, having recognized him as a Florentine, break from their company and converse
with him, all the while circling like a turning wheel. Their spokesman, Jacopo Rusticucci, identifies himself and his companions
(Guido Guerra and Tegghiaio Aldobrandini) as well-known and
honored citizens of Florence, and begs for news of their native city.
The three ask to be remembered in the world and then rush off. By
this time the sound of the waterfall is so deafening that it almost
drowns out speech, and when the poets reach the edge of the precipice, Virgil takes a cord which had been bound around his pupil's
waist and tosses it into the abyss. It is a signal, and in response a
monstrous form looms up from below, swimming through the air.
On this note of suspense, the canto ends.

Already we were where I could hear the rumbling
   of the water plunging down to the next circle,
   something like the sound of beehives humming,
when three shades with one impulse broke away,
   running, from a group of spirits passing us        5
   beneath the rain of bitter suffering.
They were coming toward us shouting with one voice:
   "O, you there, stop! From the clothes you wear, you seem
   to be a man from our perverted city."
Ah, the wounds I saw covering their limbs,        10
   some old, some freshly branded by the flames!

119–120. "my *Trésor*." The *Livres dou Trésor*, Brunetto's most significant composition, was written during his exile in France, and is an encyclopedic work written in French prose.

123–124. "the green cloth prize": The first prize for the foot-race, which was one of the games held annually on the first Sunday of Lent in Verona during the thirteenth century, was a green cloth.

9. "our perverted city": Florence.

Even now, when I think back to them, I grieve.
Their shouts caught the attention of my guide,
    and then he turned to face me saying, "Wait,
    for these are shades that merit your respect.          15
And were it not the nature of this place
    to rain with piercing flames, I would suggest
    *you* run toward *them*, for it would be more fitting."
When we stopped, they resumed their normal pace
    and when they reached us, then they started circling;   20
    the three together formed a turning wheel,
just like professional wrestlers stripped and oiled
    eyeing one another for the first, best grip
    before the actual blows and thrusts begin.
And circling in this way each kept his face                 25
    pointed up at me, so that their necks and feet
    moved constantly in opposite directions.
"And if the misery along these sterile sands,"
    one of them said, "and our charred and peeling flesh
    makes us, and what we ask, repulsive to you,           30
let our great worldly fame persuade your heart
    to tell us who you are, how you can walk
    safely with living feet through Hell itself.
This one in front whose footsteps I am treading,
    even though he runs his round naked and skinned,       35
    was of noble station, more than you may think:
he was the grandson of the good Gualdrada;
    his name was Guido Guerra, and in his life
    he accomplished much with counsel and with sword.
This other one who pounds the sand behind me                40
    is Tegghiaio Aldobrandi whose wise voice
    the world would have done well to listen to.
And I who share this post of pain with them
    was Jacopo Rusticucci, and for sure
    my reluctant wife first drove me to my sin."           45
If I could have been sheltered from the fire,
    I would have thrown myself below with them,
    and I think my guide would have allowed me to;
but, knowing well I would be burned and seared,
    my fear won over my first good intention                50
    that made me want to put my arms around them.

---

37–39. "Gualdrada": the daughter of
Bellincione Berti of Florence. Her grandson was the Guido Guerra (1220–1272)
mentioned here. This Guido was a
Guelph leader in several battles, hence his
nickname (*guerra*, "war"). His wisdom
("counsel," l. 39) is exemplified by his
advice to the Florentine Guelphs not to
undertake the campaign against Siena in
1260; they ignored his words, and that
battle destroyed the Guelph party in Florence.
41–42. "Tegghiaio Aldobrandi": Like
Guido Guerra, he was a leader of the
Guelph party in Florence (died before
1266). He, too, tried to dissuade the
Guelphs from attacking the Sienese in
1260; in fact, he was the spokesman for
the group of Guelph soldiers headed by
Guido Guerra. The fact that his advice
was disregarded probably accounts for
Dante's saying that "the world would
have done well to listen to" his voice.
44–45. "Jacopo Rusticucci": Little is
known of this spokesman for the three
Sodomites. He is occasionally mentioned
in Florentine records between 1235 and
1266 and was probably a rich merchant.

And then I spoke: "Repulsion, no, but grief
    for your condition spread throughout my heart
    (and years will pass before it fades away),
as soon as my lord here began to speak                              55
    in terms that led me to believe a group
    of such men as yourselves might be approaching.
I am from your city, and your honored names
    and your accomplishments I have always heard
    rehearsed, and have rehearsed, myself, with fondness.          60
I leave the bitter gall, and journey toward
    those sweet fruits promised me by my true guide,
    but first I must go down to the very center."
"So may your soul remain to guide your body
    for years to come," that same one spoke again,                 65
    "and your fame's light shine after you are gone,
tell us if courtesy and valor dwell
    within our city as they used to do,
    or have they both been banished from the place?
Guglielmo Borsiere, who joined our painful ranks                    70
    of late, and travels there with our companions,
    has given us reports that make us grieve."
"A new breed of people with their sudden wealth
    have stimulated pride and unrestraint
    in you, O Florence, made to weep so soon."                     75
These words I shouted with my head strained high,
    and the three below took this to be my answer
    and looked, as if on truth, at one another.
"If you always answer questions with such ease,"
    they all spoke up at once, "O happy you                        80
    to have this gift of ready, open speech;
therefore, if you survive these unlit regions
    and return to gaze upon the lovely stars,
    when it pleases you to say 'I was down there,'
do not fail to speak of us to living men."                         85
    They broke their man-made wheel and ran away,
    their nimble legs were more like wings in flight.
"Amen" could not have been pronounced as quick
    as they were off, and vanished from our sight;
    and then my teacher thought it time to leave.                  90
I followed him, and we had not gone far
    before the sound of water was so close
    that if we spoke we hardly heard each other.
As that river on the Apennines' left slope
    first springing from its source at Monte Veso                  95

---

70–72. "Guglielmo Borsiere": Little is known of him except that he must have died about 1300, as is evident from lines 70–71. Boccaccio says that he was a knight of the court, a matchmaker, and a peacemaker.

94–101. Dante compares the descent of the tributary of the Phlegethon River in Hell with the plummeting fall of the Montone River near the San Benedetto dell'Alpe monastery. Evidently, in Dante's time the river was called the Acquacheta as far as Forlì, where it became the Montone. Today the entire river is known as the Montone.

then flowing eastward holding its own course
(called Acquacheta at its start above
  before descending to its lower bed
  where, at Forlì, it has another name),
reverberates there near San Benedetto                    100
  dell'Alpe (plunging in a single bound)
  where at least a thousand vassals could be housed,
so down a single rocky precipice
  we found the tainted waters falling, roaring
  sound loud enough to deafen us in seconds.             105
I wore a cord that fastened round my waist
  with which I once had thought I might be able
  to catch the leopard with the gaudy skin.
As soon as I removed it from my body
  just as my guide commanded me to do,                   110
  I gave it to him looped into a coil.
Then taking it and turning to the right,
  he flung it quite a distance past the bank
  and down into the deepness of the pit.
"Now surely something strange is going to happen,"       115
  I thought to myself, "to answer the strange signal
  whose course my master follows with his eyes."
How cautious a man must be in company
  with one who can not only see his actions
  but read his mind and understand his thoughts!         120
He spoke: "Soon will rise up what I expect;
  and what you are trying to imagine now
  soon must reveal itself before your eyes."
It is always better to hold one's tongue than speak
  a truth that seems a bold-face lie when uttered,       125
  since to tell this truth could be embarrassing;
but I shall not keep quiet; and by the verses
  of my *Comedy*—so may they be received
  with lasting favor, Reader—I swear to you
I saw a figure coming, it was swimming                   130
  through the thick and murky air, up to the top
  (a thing to startle even stalwart hearts),
like one returning who has swum below
  to free the anchor that has caught its hooks
  on a reef or something else the sea conceals           135
spreading out his arms, and doubling up his legs.

---

102. According to Boccaccio, one of the
Conti Guidi, who ruled over this region,
had planned to construct, near the waterfall, lodgings for a large number of his
vassals; he died, however, before his plan
could be put into effect.

106–108. There are many interpretations
for the cord which Virgil takes from the
Pilgrim and throws over the edge of the
steep. Some have seen in this passage evidence that Dante the Poet became a Franciscan friar, the cord being a sign of that
order.

CANTO XVII

The beast which had been seen approaching at the end of the last canto is the horrible monster Geryon; his face is appealing like that of an honest man, but his body ends in a scorpionlike stinger. He perches on the edge of the abyss and Virgil advises his ward, who has noticed new groups of sinners squatting on the fiery sand, to learn who they are, while he makes arrangements with Geryon for the descent. The sinners are the Usurers, unrecognizable except by the crests on the moneybags hanging about their necks which identify them as members of the Gianfigliazzi, Ubriachi, and Scrovegni families. The Pilgrim listens to one of them briefly but soon returns to find his master sitting on Geryon's back. After he conquers his fear and mounts, too, the monster begins the slow, spiraling descent into the Eighth Circle.

"And now, behold the beast with pointed tail
　　that passes mountains, annulling walls and weapons,
　　behold the one that makes the whole world stink!"
These were the words I heard my master say
　　as he signaled for the beast to come ashore,　　　　　　　5
　　up close to where the rocky levee ends.
And that repulsive spectacle of fraud
　　floated close, maneuvering head and chest
　　on to the shore, but his tail he let hang free.
His face was the face of any honest man,　　　　　　　　　10
　　it shone with such a look of benediction;
　　and all the rest of him was serpentine;
his two clawed paws were hairy to the armpits,
　　his back and all his belly and both flanks
　　were painted arabesques and curlicues:　　　　　　　　15
the Turks and Tartars never made a fabric
　　with richer colors intricately woven,
　　nor were such complex webs spun by Arachne.
As sometimes fishing boats are seen ashore,
　　part fixed in sand and part still in the water;　　　　　20
　　and as the beaver, living in the land
of drunken Germans, squats to catch his prey,
　　just so that beast, the worst of beasts, hung waiting

1–27. In classical mythology Geryon was a three-bodied giant who ruled Spain, and was slain by Hercules in the course of his Twelve Labors. Here in the *Inferno* he is the personification of Fraud.

18. "Arachne": A legendary Lydian maiden who was so skilled in the art of weaving that she challenged the goddess Minerva to a contest. Minerva, furious because her opponent's cloth was perfect, tore it to shreds; Arachne hanged herself, but Minerva loosened the rope, turning it into a web and Arachne into a spider.

21–22. "the beaver": According to medieval bestiaries the beaver, squatting on the ground at the edge of the water catches fish with its tail hanging in the water. Geryon assumes a similar pose.

on the bank that bounds the stretch of sand in stone.
In the void beyond he exercised his tail,                                    25
   twitching and twisting-up the venomed fork
   that armed its tip just like a scorpion's stinger.
My leader said: "Now we must turn aside
   a little from our path, in the direction
   of that malignant beast that lies in wait."                              30
Then we stepped off our path down to the right
   and moved ten paces straight across the brink
   to keep the sand and flames at a safe distance.
And when we stood by Geryon's side, I noticed,
   a little farther on, some people crouched                                35
   in the sand quite close to the edge of emptiness.
Just then my master spoke: "So you may have
   a knowledge of this round that is complete,"
   he said, "go and see their torment for yourself.
But let your conversation there be brief;                                   40
   while you are gone I shall speak to this one
   and ask him for the loan of his strong back."
So I continued walking, all alone,
   along the seventh circle's outer edge
   to where the group of sufferers were sitting.                            45
The pain was bursting from their eyes; their hands
   went scurrying up and down to give protection
   here from the flames, there from the burning sands.
They were, in fact, like a dog in summertime
   busy, now with his paw, now with his snout,                              50
   tormented by the fleas and flies that bite him.
I carefully examined several faces
   among this group caught in the raining flames
   and did not know a soul, but I observed
that around each sinner's neck a pouch was hung                             55
   each of a different color, with a coat of arms,
   and fixed on these they seemed to feast their eyes.
And while I looked about among the crowd,
   I saw something in blue on a yellow purse
   that had the face and bearing of a lion;                                 60
and while my eyes continued their inspection
   I saw another purse as red as blood

35–36. The Usurers, described in Canto XI as those who scorn "Nature in herself and in her pupil / Art" (ll. 110–111), are the last group in the third round of the Seventh Circle. Having introduced Geryon, Dante the Poet then brings in these sinners who, crouching very close to the edge of the abyss, serve as the artistic and spatial connection between the sins of Violence and those of Fraud.

55–56. The identity (or rather the family connection) of the usurers, who "feast their eyes" (l. 57) on the purses dangling from their necks, is revealed to the Pilgrim by the different coats of arms visible on the pouches. Apparently the usurers are unrecognizable through facial characteristics because their total concern with their material goods has caused them to lose their individuality. The yellow purse with the blue lion (ll. 59–60) indicates the Gianfigliazzi family of Florence; the red purse with the "goose more white than butter" (ll. 62–63), the Ubriachi family, also of Florence; the one with the "blue sow, pregnant-looking" (ll. 64–65), the Scrovegni family of Padua.

exhibiting a goose more white than butter.
And one who had a blue sow, pregnant-looking,
   stamped on the whiteness of his moneybag
   asked me: "What are you doing in this pit?           65
Get out of here! And since you're still alive,
   I'll tell you that my neighbor Vitaliano
   will come to take his seat on my left side.
Among these Florentines I sit, one Paduan:          70
   time after time they fill my ears with blasts
   of shouting: 'Send us down the sovereign knight
who will come bearing three goats on his pouch;' "
   As final comment he stuck out his tongue—
   as far out as an ox licking its nose.           75
And I, afraid my staying there much longer
   might anger the one who warned me to be brief,
   turned my back on these frustrated sinners.
I found my guide already sitting high
   upon the back of that fierce animal;          80
   he said: "And now, take courage and be strong.
From now on we descend by stairs like these.
   Get on up front. I want to ride behind,
   to be between you and the dangerous tail."
A man who feels the shivers of a fever         85
   coming on, his nails already dead of color,
   will tremble at the mere sight of cool shade;
I was that man when I had heard his words.
   But then I felt those stabs of shame that make
   a servant brave before his valorous master.      90
As I squirmed around on those enormous shoulders,
   I wanted to cry out, "Hold on to me,"
   but I had no voice to second my desire.
Then he who once before had helped me out
   when I was threatened, put his arms around me    95
   as soon as I was settled, and held me tight;
and then he cried: "Now Geryon, start moving,
   descend with gentle motion, circling wide:
   remember you are carrying living weight."
Just as a boat slips back away from shore,         100
   back slowly, more and more, he left that pier;
   and when he felt himself all clear in space,
to where his breast had been he swung his tail
   and stretched it undulating like an eel,

---

68–69. Referred to as "my neighbor" by one of the Scrovegni family, the Vitaliano who will join the company of usurers is undoubtedly from Padua, but beyond this nothing certain is known.

70. The theme of the decadence and materialism of Florence is continued to the very edge of the circle of Violence.

72–73. "the sovereign knight": This is generally considered to be Giovanni Buiamonte, one of the Florentine Becchi family. He took part in public affairs and was honored with the title of "knight" in 1298. His business, moneylending, made his family one of the wealthiest in Florence; however, after going bankrupt he died in abject poverty in 1310.

as with his paws he gathered in the air.                                    105
I doubt if Phaëthon feared more—that time
  he dropped the sun-reins of his father's chariot
  and burned the streak of sky we see today—
or if poor Icarus did—feeling his sides
  unfeathering as the wax began to melt,                                    110
  his father shouting: "Wrong, your course is wrong"—
than I had when I felt myself in air
  and saw on every side nothing but air;
  only the beast I sat upon was there.
He moves along slowly, and swimming slowly,                                 115
  descends a spiral path—but I know this
  only from a breeze ahead and one below;
I hear now on my right the whirlpool roar
  with hideous sound beneath us on the ground;
  at this I stretch my neck to look below,                                  120
but leaning out soon made me more afraid,
  for I heard moaning there and saw the flames;
  trembling I cowered back, tightening my legs,
and I saw then what I had not before:
  the spiral path of our descent to torments                               125
  closing in on us, it seemed, from every side.
As the falcon on the wing for many hours,
  having found no prey, and having seen no signal
  (so that his falconer sighs: "Oh, he falls already,")
descends, worn out, circling a hundred times                               130
  (instead of swooping down), settling at some distance
  from his master, perched in anger and disdain,
so Geryon brought us down to the bottom
  at the foot of the jagged cliff, almost against it,
  and once he got our bodies off his back,                                 135
he shot off like a shaft shot from a bowstring.

### CANTO XVIII

The Pilgrim describes the view he had of the Eighth Circle of
Hell while descending through the air on Geryon's back. It consists
of ten stone ravines called Malebolge (Evil Pockets), and across
each *bolgia* is an arching bridge. When the poets find themselves
on the edge of the first ravine they see two lines of naked sinners,
walking in opposite directions. In one are the Pimps or Panderers

106–108. "Phaëthon": son of Apollo
who was told by Epaphus that Apollo was
not his father. Thereupon the boy begged
Apollo to allow him to drive the Chariot
of the Sun for one day to prove himself
the offspring of the God of the Sun. The
request was granted, but Phaëthon,
unable to control the Chariot, let loose the
reins. The Chariot raced wildly through
the heavens, burning the "streak of sky"
which today we call the Milky Way, and
at one point dipping so close to the Earth
that it almost set the planet afire.

109–111. Daedalus, father of Icarus, in
order to escape from Crete, fashioned
wings for himself and his son. Because the
feathers were fastened with wax, Daedalus
warned his son not to fly too close to the
sun. But Icarus, ignoring his father's
words, flew too high, and when the sun
had melted the wax, he plunged to his
death in the Aegean Sea.

  The stories of Phaëthon and Icarus
were often used in the Middle Ages as
examples of pride, thus giving more support to the theory that Pride and Envy
underlie the sins punished in Lower Hell.

and among them the Pilgrim recognizes Venedico Caccianemico; in
the other are the Seducers, among whom Virgil points out Jason. As
the two move toward the next *bolgia*, they are assailed by a terrible
stench, for here the Flatterers are immersed in excrement. Among
them are Alessio Interminei and Thaïs, the whore.

There is a place in Hell called Malebolge
   cut out of stone the color of iron ore,
   just like the circling cliff that walls it in.
Right at the center of this evil plain
   there yawns a very wide, deep well, whose structure     5
   I will talk of when the place itself is reached.
That belt of land remaining, then, runs round
   between the well and cliff, and all this space
   is divided into ten descending valleys,
just like a ground-plan for successive moats     10
   that in concentric circles bind their center
   and serve to protect the ramparts of the castle.
This was the surface image they presented;
   and as bridges from a castle's portal stretch
   from moat to moat to reach the farthest bank,     15
so, from the great cliff's base, jut spokes of rock
   crossing from bank to bank, intersecting ditches
   until the pit's hub cuts them off from meeting.
This is the place in which we found ourselves,
   once shaken from the back of Geryon.     20
   The poet turned to the left, I walked behind him.
There, on our right, I saw new suffering souls,
   new means of torture, and new torturers,
   crammed into the depths of the first ditch.
Two files of naked souls walked on the bottom,     25
   the ones on our side faced us as they passed,
   the others moved as we did but more quickly.
The Romans, too, in the year of the Jubilee
   took measures to accommodate the throngs
   that had to come and go across their bridge:     30
they fixed it so on one side all were looking
   at the castle, and were walking to St. Peter's;
   on the other, they were moving toward the mount.
On both sides, up along the deadly rock,
   I saw horned devils with enormous whips     35
   lashing backs of shades with cruel delight.

26–27. The first *bolgia* accommodates
two classes of sinners, each filing by rapidly, but in separate directions. The Pimps
are those walking toward the Pilgrim and
his guide; the Seducers go in the same
direction with them.

28–33. Dante compares the movement
of the sinners in the first *bolgia* to that of
the many pilgrims who, having come to
Rome for the Jubilee in 1300, were herded
across the bridge, half going toward the
Castel Sant'Angelo and St. Peter's and
the other half going toward Monte Gior-
dano ("the mount," l. 33), a small knoll
on the opposite side of the Tiber River.

Ah, how they made them skip and lift their heels
    at the very first crack of the whip! Not one of them
    dared pause to take a second or a third!
As I walked on my eyes met with the glance            40
    of one down there; I murmured to myself:
    "I know this face from somewhere, I am sure."
And so I stopped to study him more closely;
    my leader also stopped, and was so kind
    as to allow me to retrace my steps;           45
and that whipped soul thought he would hide from me
    by lowering his face—which did no good.
I said, "O you, there, with your head bent low,
if the features of your shade do not deceive me,
    you are Venedico Caccianemico, I'm sure.       50
    How did you get yourself in such a pickle?"
"I'm not so keen on answering," he said,
    "but I feel I must; your plain talk is compelling,
    it makes me think of old times in the world.
I was the one who coaxed Ghisolabella         55
    to serve the lusty wishes of the Marquis,
    no matter how the sordid tale is told;
I'm not the only Bolognese who weeps here—
    hardly! This place is packed with us; in fact,
    there are more of us here than there are living tongues,     60
between Savena and Reno, saying 'Sipa';
    I call on your own memory as witness:
    remember we have avaricious hearts."
Just at that point a devil let him have
    the feel of his tailed whip and cried: "Move on,     65
    you pimp, you can't cash in on women here!"
I turned and hurried to rejoin my guide;
    we walked a few more steps and then we reached
    the rocky bridge that juts out from the bank.
We had no difficulty climbing up,          70
    and turning right, along the jagged ridge,
    we left those shades to their eternal circlings.
When we were where the ditch yawned wide below
    the ridge, to make a passage for the scourged,
    my guide said: "Stop and stand where you can see     75
these other misbegotten souls whose faces

---

50–57. "Venedico Caccianemico": Born
ca. 1228, he was head of the Guelphs in
Bologna from 1260 to 1297; he was at
various times *podestà* ("mayor") of Pis-
tolia, Modena, Imola, and Milan. He was
accused, among other things, of murdering his cousin, but he is placed in this
*bolgia* because, according to popular report, he acted as a procurer, turning his
own sister, Ghisolabella, over to the Marquis of Este (either Obizzo II or his son,
Azzo VIII) to curry favor.

51. Dante is undoubtedly punning on

the word *salse* ("pickle") which characterizes the torments suffered in this *bolgia*,
and also is the name of a certain ravine
(a *bolgia*, if you will) near Bologna
(Venedico's city) into which the bodies
of criminals were thrown.

61. Venedico reveals that he is not the
only Bolognese punished in this *bolgia*
and further states that there are more
pimps here from that city than there are
present-day inhabitants of the region between the Savena and Reno rivers.

you could not see before, for they were moving
in the same direction we were, over there."
So from the ancient bridge we viewed the train
that hurried toward us along the other tract— 80
kept moving, like the first, by stinging whips.
And the good master, without my asking him,
said, "Look at that imposing one approaching,
who does not shed a single tear of pain:
what majesty he still maintains down there! 85
He is Jason, who by courage and sharp wits,
fleeced the Colchians of their golden ram.
He later journeyed through the isle of Lemnos
whose bold and heartless females, earlier,
had slaughtered every male upon the island; 90
there with his words of love, and loving looks,
he succeeded in deceiving young Hypsipyle
who had in turn deceived the other women.
He left her there, with child, and all alone:
such sin condemns him to such punishment, 95
and Medea, too, gets her revenge on him.
With him go all deceivers of this type,
and let this be enough to know concerning
the first valley and the souls locked in its jaws."
We were already where the narrow ridge 100
begins to cross the second bank, to make it
an abutment for another ditch's arch.
Now we could hear the shades in the next *bolgia*
whimpering, making snorting grunting sounds,
and sounds of blows, slapping with open palms. 105
From a steaming stench below, the banks were coated
with a slimy mould that stuck to them like glue,
disgusting to behold and worse to smell,
The bottom was so hollowed out of sight,
we saw it only when we climbed the arch 110
and looked down from the ridge's highest point:
there we were, and from where I stood I saw

86–96. Jason: Leader of the Argonauts who, when a child, had been deprived of the throne of Iolcus by his half-brother Pelias. When Jason grew up, Pelias promised him the kingdom if he could secure the golden fleece of King Aeëtes of Colchis. Jason agreed to make the attempt, and on the way to Colchis stopped at Lemnos, where he seduced and abandoned Hypsipyle (l. 92), the daughter of the King of Lemnos. At Colchis King Aeëtes agreed to give Jason the fleece if he would yoke two fire-breathing oxen to a plow and sow the teeth of the dragon that guarded the fleece. Medea (l. 96), who was a sorceress and the daughter of the king, fell in love with Jason and with magic helped him fulfill her father's conditions and obtain the fleece. The two returned to Greece where Jason married

her, but later he fell in love with Creusa, daughter of Creon, king of Corinth, and deserted Medea to marry her. Medea, mad with rage, killed Creusa by sending her a poisoned coat as a wedding gift, and then murdered her own children; Jason himself died of grief.

Hypsipyle "deceived the other women" (l. 93) of Lemnos by swearing that she had slain her father Thoas, the king, when the Lemnian women massacred all the males on that island. Instead she hid him, saving his life.

104–105. The sinners found in the excrement of the second *bolgia* are the Flatterers. Note the teeming nature of the language, different from that of the first *bolgia*, a change indicative of the sin of flattery and its punishment.

    souls in the ditch plunged into excrement
    that might well have been flushed from our latrines;
my eyes were searching hard along the bottom,       115
    and I saw somebody's head so smirched with shit
    you could not tell if he were priest or layman.
He shouted up: "Why do you feast your eyes
    on me more than these other dirty beasts?"
And I replied: "Because, remembering well,       120
I've seen you with your hair dry once or twice.
    You are Alessio Interminei from Lucca,
    that's why I stare at you more than the rest."
He beat his slimy forehead as he answered:
    "I am stuck down here by all those flatteries       125
    that rolled unceasing off my tongue up there."
He finished speaking, and my guide began:
    "Lean out a little more, look hard down there
    so you can get a good look at the face
of that repulsive and dishevelled tramp       130
    scratching herself with shitty finger-nails,
    spreading her legs while squatting up and down:
it is Thaïs the whore who gave this answer
    to her lover when he asked: 'Am I very worthy
    of your thanks?': 'Very, nay, incredibly so!'       135
I think our eyes have had their fill of this."

### CANTO XIX

    From the bridge above the third *bolgia* can be seen a rocky landscape below filled with holes, from each of which protrude a sinner's legs and feet; flames dance across their soles. When the Pilgrim expresses curiosity about a particular pair of twitching legs, Virgil carries him down into the *bolgia* so that the Pilgrim himself may question the sinner. The legs belong to Pope Nicholas III, who astounds the Pilgrim by mistaking him for Boniface VIII, the next pope who, as soon as he dies, will fall to the same hole, thereby pushing Nicholas farther down. He predicts that soon after Boniface, Pope Clement V will come, stuffing both himself and Boniface still deeper. To Nicholas's rather rhetoric-filled speech the Pilgrim responds with equally high language, inveighing against the Simonists, the evil churchmen who are punished here. Virgil is much pleased with his pupil and, lifting him in an affectionate embrace, he carries him to the top of the arch above the next *bolgia*.

122. "Alessio Interminei from Luca": The Interminei family was prominent in the White party at Lucca. But of Alessio almost nothing is known save that his name is recorded in several documents of the second half of the thirteenth century.

135. This Thaïs is not the historical person by the same name (the most famous courtesan of all time) but a character in Terence's *Eunuchus*.

O Simon Magus! O scum that followed him!
  Those things of God that rightly should be wed
  to holiness, you, rapacious creatures,
for the price of gold and silver, prostitute.
  Now, in your honor, I must sound my trumpet      5
  here in the third bolgia where you are packed.
We had already climbed to see this tomb,
  and were standing high above it on the bridge,
  exactly at the mid-point of the ditch.
O Highest Wisdom, how you demonstrate      10
  your art in Heaven, on earth, and here in Hell!
  How justly does your power make awards!
I saw along the sides and on the bottom
  the livid-colored rock all full of holes;
  all were the same in size, and each was round.      15
To me they seemed no wider and no deeper
  than those inside my lovely San Giovanni,
  made for priests to stand in or baptize from;
and one of these, not many years ago,
  I smashed for someone who was drowning in it:      20
  let this be mankind's picture of the truth!
From the mouth of every hole were sticking out
  a single sinner's feet, and then the legs
  up to the calf—the rest was stuffed inside.
The soles of every sinner's feet were flaming;      25
  their naked legs were twitching frenziedly—
  they would have broken any chain or rope.
Just as a flame will only move along
  an object's oily outer peel, so here
  the fire slid from heel to toe and back.      30
"Who is that one, Master, that angry wretch,
  who is writhing more than any of his comrades,"
  I asked, "the one licked by a redder flame?"
And he to me, "If you want to be carried down
  along that lower bank to where he is,      35
  you can ask him who he is and why he's here."
And I, "My pleasure is what pleases you:
  you are my lord, you know that from your will
  I would not swerve. You even know my thoughts."
When we reached the fourth bank, we began to turn      40

1–6. As related in Acts (8:9–24), Simon the magician, having observed the descent of the Holy Spirit upon the Apostles John and Peter, desired to purchase this power for himself. Whereupon Peter harshly admonished him for even thinking that the gift of God might be bought. Derived from this sorcerer's name, the word "simony" refers to those offences involving the sale or fraudulent possession of ecclesiastical offices.

5–6. Dante in announcing the nature of the sin being punished in the third *bolgia* is comparing himself to the medieval town crier whose announcements were preceded by a blast from his trumpet.

25. Just as the Simonists' perversion of the Church is symbolized by their "perverted" immersion in holes resembling baptismal fonts, so their "baptism" is perverted: instead of the head being moistened with water, the feet are "baptized" with oil and fire.

928 · *Dante Alighieri*

and, keeping to the left, made our way down
to the bottom of the holed and narrow ditch.
The good guide did not drop me from his side
  until he brought me to the broken rock
  of that one who was fretting with his shanks.    45
"O whatever you are, holding your upside down,
  wretched soul, stuck in the ground like a stake,
  make some sound," I said, "that is, if you can."
I stood there like a priest hearing confession
  from a vile assassin who, once fixed in his ditch,    50
  calls him back again to put off dying.
He cried: "Is that *you*, here, already, upright?
  Is that you here already upright, Boniface?
  By many years the book has lied to me!
Are you fed up so soon with all that wealth    55
  for which you did not fear to take by guile
  the beautiful lady, then tear her asunder?"
I stood there like a person just made fun of,
  dumbfounded by a question for an answer,
  not knowing how to answer the reply.    60
Then Virgil said: "Quick, hurry up and tell him:
  'I'm not the one, I'm not the one you think!'"
  And I answered just the way he told me to.
The spirit heard, and twisted both his feet,
  then, sighing with a grieving, tearful voice    65
  he said: "Well then, what do you want of me?
If it concerns you so to learn my name
  that for this reason you came down the bank,
  know that I once was dressed in the great mantle.
But actually I was the she-bear's son,    70
  so greedy to advance my cubs, that wealth
  I pocketed in life, and here, myself.
Beneath my head are pushed down all the others
  who came, sinning in simony, before me,
  squeezed tightly in the fissures of the rock.    75
I, in my turn, shall join the rest below

53. From the foreknowledge granted to the infernal shades, the speaker knows that Pope Boniface VIII, upon his death in 1303, will take his place in that very receptacle wherein he himself is now being tormented. The Pilgrim's voice, so close at hand, has caused the sinner to believe that his successor has arrived unexpectedly before his time (three years, in fact) and, consequently, that the Divine Plan of Events, the Book of Fate (l. 54), has lied to him.

Having obtained the abdication of Pope Celestine V, Boniface gained the support of Charles II of Naples and thus was assured of his election to the papacy (1294). In addition to misusing the Church's influence in his dealings with Charles, Boniface VIII freely distributed ecclesiastical offices among his family and confidants. As early as 1300 he was plotting the destruction of the Whites, the Florentine political faction to which Dante belonged.

57. "the beautiful lady": the Church.

67–72. Gian Gaetano degli Orsini (lit., "of the little bears," hence the designation "she-bear's son," and the reference to "my cubs") became Pope Nicholas III in 1277. As a Cardinal he won renown for his integrity; however, in the short three years between his ascent to the papal throne and his death he became notorious for his simoniacal practices.

74. The Italian verb, *simoneggiare* (here used in the gerund by Nicholas III —"sinning in simony"), was invented by Dante, doubtless to anticipate the parallel form *puttaneggiando* ("playing whore"), l. 108, employed by the Pilgrim.

as soon as *he* comes, the one I thought you were
when, all too quick, I put my question to you.
But already my feet have baked a longer time
   (and I have been stuck upside-down like this)       80
   than he will stay here planted with feet aflame:
soon after him shall come one from the West,
   a lawless shepherd, one whose fouler deeds
   make him a fitting cover for us both.
He shall be another Jason, like the one          85
   in Maccabees: just as his king was pliant,
   so France's king shall soften to this priest."
I do not know, perhaps I was too bold here,
   but I answered him in tune with his own words:
   "Well tell me now: what was the sum of money   90
that holy Peter had to pay our Lord
   before He gave the keys into his keeping?
   Certainly He asked no more than 'Follow me.'
Nor did Peter or the rest extort gold coins
   or silver from Matthias when he was picked     95
   to fill the place the evil one had lost.
So stay stuck there, for you are rightly punished,
   and guard with care the money wrongly gained
   that made you stand courageous against Charles.
And were it not for the reverence I have      100
   for those highest of all keys that you once held
   in the happy life—if this did not restrain me,
I would use even harsher words than these,
   for your avarice brings grief upon the world,
   crushing the good, exalting the depraved.     105
You shepherds it was the Evangelist had in mind
   when the vision came to him of her who sits
   upon the waters playing whore with kings:
that one who with the seven heads was born
   and from her ten horns managed to draw strength  110
   so long as virtue was her bridegroom's joy.
You have built yourselves a God of gold and silver!

77. Boniface VIII. See above, note on
l. 53.
82–84. Pope Clement V of Gascony,
upon his death in 1314, will join Nicholas
and Boniface in eternal torment.
85–87. Having obtained the high priest
hood of the Jews by bribing King Antiochus of Syria, Jason neglected the sacrifices and sanctuary of the temple and introduced Greek modes of life into his
community. As Jason had fraudulently
acquired his position, so had Menelaus,
who offered more money to the king, supplanted Jason (2 Maccabees 47:7-27). As
Jason obtained his office from King Antiochus fraudulently, so shall Clement acquire his from Philip.
94–96. After the treachery and subsequent expulsion of Judas, the Apostles
cast lots in order to replenish their num-

ber. Thus, by the will of God, not through
monetary payment, was Matthias elected
to the vacated post (Act 1:15-26).
98–99. The thirteenth-century Florentine chronicler, Giovanni Villani, alludes
to a plot against Charles d'Anjou, king of
Naples and Sicily, promoted by Nicholas
III and supported by the "money wrongly
gained" of Michael Palaeologus, emperor
of Greece.
106–111. St. John the Evangelist relates
his vision of the dissolute Imperial City
of Rome. To Dante, she "who sits / upon
the waters" represents the Church which
has been corrupted by the simoniacal activities of many popes (the "shepherds"
of the Church). The seven heads symbolize the seven Holy Sacraments; the
ten horns represent the Ten Commandments.

How do you differ from the idolator,
   except he worships one, you worship hundreds?
Oh, Constantine, what evil did you sire,                          115
   not by your conversion, but by the dower
   that the first wealthy Father got from you!"
And while I sang these very notes to him,
   his big flat feet kicked fiercely out of anger,
   —or perhaps it was his conscience gnawing him.                120
I think my master liked what I was saying,
   for all the while he smiled and was intent
   on hearing the ring of truly-spoken words.
Then he took hold of me with both his arms,
   he climbed back up the path he had come down.                125
   and when he had me firm against his breast,
He did not tire of the weight clasped tight to him,
   but brought me to the top of the bridge's arch,
   the one that joins the fourth bank to the fifth.
And here he gently set his burden down—                          130
   gently, for the ridge, so steep and rugged,
   would have been hard even for goats to cross.
From here another valley opened up.

### CANTO XX

In the fourth *bolgia* they see a group of shades weeping as they
walk slowly along the valley; they are the Soothsayers and their
heads are twisted completely around so that their hair flows down
their fronts and their tears flow down to their buttocks. Virgil
points out many of them including Amphiaraus, Tiresias, Aruns,
and Manto. It was Manto who first inhabited the site of Virgil's
home city of Mantua, and the poet gives a long description of the
city's founding, after which he names more of the condemned
soothsayers: Eurypylus, Michael Scot, Guido Bonatti, and Asdente.

Now I must turn strange torments into verse
   to form the matter of the twentieth canto
   of the first chant, the one about the damned.
Already I was where I could look down
   into the depths of the ditch: I saw its floor                 5

115–117. "Constantine": Constantine
the Great, emperor of Rome (306–337),
was converted to Christianity in the year
312. Having conquered the eastern Mediterranean lands, he transferred the capital of the Roman Empire to Constantinople (330). This move, according to tradition, stemmed from Constantine's decision to place the western part of the
empire under the jurisdiction of the
Church in order to repay Pope Sylvester
("the first wealthy Father") for healing
him of leprosy. The so-called "Donation
of Constantine," though it was proved in
the fifteenth century to be a complete
fabrication on the part of the clergy, was
universally accepted as the truth in the
Middle Ages. Dante the Pilgrim reflects
this tradition in his sad apostrophe to the
individual who first would have introduced wealth to the Church and who, unknowingly, would be ultimately responsible for its present corruption.

was wet with anguished tears shed by the sinners,
and I saw people in the valley's circle,
   silent, weeping, walking at a litany pace
   the way processions push along in our world.
And when my gaze moved down below their faces,     10
   I saw all were incredibly distorted,
   the chin was not above the chest, the neck
was twisted—their faces looked down on their backs;
   they had to move ahead by moving backwards,
   for they never saw what was ahead of them.     15
Perhaps there was a case of someone once
   in a palsy fit becoming so distorted,
   but none that I know of! I doubt there could be!
So may God grant you, Reader, benefit
   from reading of my poem, just ask yourself     20
   how I could keep my eyes dry when, close by,
I saw the image of our human form
   so twisted—the tears their eyes were shedding
   streamed down to wet their buttocks at the cleft.
Indeed I did weep, as I leaned my body     25
   against a jut of rugged rock. My guide:
   "So you are still like all the other fools?
In this place piety lives when pity is dead,
   for who could be more wicked than that man
   who tries to bend divine will to his own!     30
Lift your head up, lift it, see him for whom
   the earth split wide before the Thebans' eyes,
   while they all shouted, 'Where are you rushing off to,
Amphiaraus? Why do you quit the war?'
   He kept on rushing downwards through the gap     35
   until Minòs, who gets them all, got him
You see how he has made his back his chest:
   because he wished to see too far ahead,
   he sees behind and walks a backward track.
Behold Tiresias who changed his looks:     40
   from a man he turned himself into a woman,
   transforming all his body, part for part;

15. Note the appropriate nature of the punishment: The augurs who, when living, looked into the future are here in Hell denied any forward vision.

28. In the original there is a play on words: the word *"pietà"* means both "piety" and "pity." The Pilgrim has once again felt pity for the torments of the sinners, and Virgil rebukes him with some exasperation.

34–36. "Amphiaraus": a seer, and one of the seven kings who led the expedition against Thebes (see Canto XIV, ll. 68–69). He foresaw that he would die during the siege, and to avoid his fate he hid himself so that he would not have to fight. But his wife Eriphyle revealed his hiding place to Polynices, and Amphiaraus was forced to go to battle. He met his death when the earth opened up and swallowed him. Dante's source was Statius's *Thebaid*, VII and VIII.

40–45. "Tiresias": the famous soothsayer of Thebes referred to by Ovid (*Metamorphoses* III, 316–338). According to Ovid, Tiresias with his rod once separated two serpents which were coupled together, whereupon he was transformed into a woman. Seven years later he found the same two serpents, struck them again, and became a man once more. Later Jupiter and Juno asked Tiresias, who had had the experience of belonging to both sexes, which sex enjoyed love-making more. When Tiresias answered "woman," Juno struck him blind. However, Jupiter, in compensation, gave him the gift of prophecy.

then later on he had to take the wand
   and strike once more those two snakes making love
   before he could get back his virile parts.       45
Backing up to this one's chest comes Aruns
   who, in the hills of Luni, worked by peasants
   of Carrara dwelling in the valley's plain,
lived in white marble cut into a cave,
   and from this site where nothing blocked his view       50
   he could observe the sea and stars with ease.
And that one, with her hair loose, flowing back
   to cover both her breasts you cannot see,
   and with her hairy parts in front behind her,
was Manto who had searched through many lands       55
   before she came to dwell where I was born;
   now let me tell you something of her story.
When her father had departed from the living,
   and Bacchus' sacred city fell enslaved,
   she wandered through the world for many years.       60
High in fair Italy there spreads a lake,
   beneath the mountains bounding Germany
   beyond the Tyrol, known as Lake Benaco;
by a thousand streams and more, I think, the Alps
   are bathed from Garda to the Val Camonica       65
   with the waters flowing down into that lake;
at its center is a place where all three bishops
   of Trent and Brescia and Verona could,
   if they would ever visit there, say Mass;
Peschiera sits, a handsome well-built fortress,       70
   to ward off Brescians and the Bergamese,
   along the lowest point of that lake's shore
where all the water that Benaco's basin
   cannot hold must overflow to make a stream
   that winds its way through countrysides of green;      75
but when the water starts to flow, its name
   is not Benaco but Mencio, all the way
   to Governol where it falls into the Po;
but before its course is run it strikes a lowland
   on which it spreads and turns into a marsh       80

46–51. "Aruns": the Etruscan diviner who forecast the Roman civil war and its outcome. He made his home "in the hills of Luni" (l. 47), the area now known as Carrara and renowned for its white marble.

52–60. Manto, upon the death of her father Tiresias, fled Thebes ("Bacchus' sacred city," l. 59) and its tyrant Creon. She finally arrived in Italy and there founded the city of Mantua, Virgil's birthplace (l. 56).

63. "Lake Benaco": today Lake Garda, which lies in northern Italy at the center of the triangle formed by the cities of Trent, Brescia, and Verona.

64–66. Here, the "Alps" means that range between the Camonica valley, west of Lake Garda, and the city of Garda, on the lake's eastern shore, that is watered by many streams which ultimately flow into Lake Garda.

67–69. On an island in Lake Garda (Benaco) the boundaries of the dioceses of Trent, Brescia, and Verona met, thereby making it possible for all three bishops to hold services or "say Mass" there.

70–72. "Peschiera": The fortress of Peschiera and the town of the same name are on the southeast shore of Lake Garda.

78. "Governol": Now called Governolo, it is twelve miles from Mantua and situated at the junction of the Mincio and the Po rivers.

that can become unbearable in summer.

Passing this place one day the savage virgin
    saw land that lay in the center of the mire,
    untilled and empty of inhabitants.

There, to escape all human intercourse,          85
    she stopped to practice magic with her servants;
    there she lived, and there she left her corpse.

Later on, the men who lived around there gathered
    on that very spot, for it was well-protected
    by the bog that girded it on every side.        90

They built a city over her dead bones,
    and for her, the first to choose that place, they named it
    Mantua, without recourse to sorcery.

Once, there were far more people living there,
    before the foolish Casalodi listened        95
    to the fraudulent advice of Pinamonte.

And so, I warn you, should you ever hear
    my city's origin told otherwise,
    let no false tales adulterate the truth."

And I replied: "Master, your explanations        100
    are truth for me, winning my faith entirely;
    any others would be just like burned-out coals.

But speak to me of these shades passing by,
    if you see anyone that is worth noting;
    for now my mind is set on only that."        105

He said: "That one whose beard flows from his cheeks
    and settles on his back and makes it dark,
    was (when the war stripped Greece of all its males

so that the few there were still rocked in cradles)
    an augur who, with Calchas, called the moment    110
    to cut the first ship's cable free at Aulis:

he is Eurypylus. I sang his story
    this way, somewhere in my high tragedy;
    you should know where—you know it, every line.

That other one whose thighs are scarcely fleshed    115
    was Michael Scot, who most assuredly

---

93. The customs of ancient peoples dictated that the name of a newly founded city be obtained through sorcery. Such was not the case with Mantua.

95–96. "Casalodi": In 1272, Alberto da Casalodi, one of the Guelph counts of Brescia, was lord of Mantua. Having encountered public opposition, he was duped by the Ghibelline Pinamonte de' Bonaccolsi into thinking that he could remain in power only by exiling the nobles. Having faithfully followed Pinamonte's false counsel, he found himself bereft of his supporters and protectors, and consequently Pinamonte was able to take command; he banished the Guelphs, and ruled until 1291.

106–112. At the time of the Trojan War ("when the war stripped Greece of all its males," l. 108) Eurypylus, whom Dante

thought to be a Greek augur (as was Calchas, l. 110), was asked to divine the most opportune time to launch the Greek fleet ("to cut the first ship's cable free," l. 111) from the port at Aulis.

113. "high tragedy": the *Aeneid* (II, 114–119). In this work, however, Eurypylus is not an augur, but a soldier sent to the oracle to discover Apollo's predictions as to the best time to set sail from Troy.

116–117. "Michael Scot": A Scottish philosopher attached to Frederick II's court at Palermo (see canto X, l. 119) who translated the works of Aristotle from the Arabic of his commentator, Avicenna (see canto IV, l. 143). By reputation he was a magician and augur. Cf. Boccaccio, *Decameron*, VIII, 9.

knew every trick of magic fraudulence.
See there Guido Bonatti; see Asdente,
    who wishes now he had been more devoted
    to making shoes—too late now for repentence.          120
And see those wretched hags who traded in
    needle, spindle, shuttle, for fortune-telling,
    and cast their spells with image-dolls and potions.
Now come along. Cain with his thorn-bush straddles
    the confines of both hemispheres already              125
    and dips into the waves below Seville;
and the moon last night already was at full;
    and you should well remember that at times
    when you were lost in the dark wood she helped you."
And we were moving all the time he spoke.                 130

### CANTO XXI

When the two reach the summit of the arch over the fifth *bolgia*,
they see in the ditch below the bubbling of boiling pitch. Virgil's
sudden warning of danger frightens the Pilgrim even before he sees
a black devil rushing toward them, with a sinner slung over his
shoulder. From the bridge the devil flings the sinner into the pitch
where he is poked at and tormented by the family of Malebranche
devils. Virgil, advising his ward to hide behind a rock, crosses the
bridge to face the devils alone. They threaten him with their
pitchforks, but when he announces to their leader, Malacoda, that
Heaven has willed that he lead another through Hell, the devil's
arrogance collapses. Virgil calls the Pilgrim back to him. Scarmig-
lione, who tries to take a poke at him is rebuked by his leader, who
tells the travelers that the sixth arch is broken here but farther on
they will find another bridge to cross. He chooses a squad of his
devils to escort them there: Alichino, Calcabrina, Cagnazzo, Barbariccia, Libicocco, Draghignazzo, Ciriatto, Graffiacane, Farfarello, and
Rubicante. The Pilgrim's suspicion about their unsavory escorts is
brushed aside by his guide, and the squad starts off giving an
obscene salute to their captain who returns their salute with a fart.

From this bridge to the next we walked and talked
    of things my Comedy does not care to tell;
    and when we reached the summit of the arch,

118–120. "Guido Bonatti": A native of
Forlì, he was a well-known astrologer and
diviner. Benvenuto (or Asdente, "toothless," as he was called) was a cobbler
from Parma who supposedly possessed
certain magical powers.
    124–126. By some mysterious power
Virgil is able to reckon time in the depths
of Hell. The moon (referred to as "Cain
with his thorn-bush," l. 124, the medieval
Italian counterpart of our "Man in the
Moon") is directly over the line of de-

marcation between the Northern (land)
and the Southern (water) hemispheres
and is setting on the western horizon (the
"waves below Seville," l. 126). The time
is approximately six A.M.
    129. See Canto I, l. 2. The literal sig-
nificance of this line defies explanation,
since in the beginning of the *Inferno* describing the Pilgrim's wanderings in the
"dark woods" no mention is made of the
moon.

we stopped to see the next fosse of Malebolge
  and to hear more lamentation voiced in vain:                  5
  I saw that it was very strangely dark!
In the vast and busy shipyard of the Venetians
  there boils all winter long a tough, thick pitch
  that is used to caulk the ribs of unsound ships.
Since winter will not let them sail, they toil:                 10
  some build new ships, others repair the old ones,
  plugging the planks come loose from many sailings;
some hammer at the bow, some at the stern,
  one carves the oars while others twine the ropes,
  one mends the jib, one patches up the mainsail;               15
here, too, but heated by God's art, not fire,
  a sticky tar was boiling in the ditch
  that smeared the banks with viscous residue.
I saw it there, but I saw nothing in it,
  except the rising of the boiling bubbles                      20
  breathing-in air to burst and sink again.
I stood intently gazing there below,
  my guide, shouting to me: "Watch out, watch out!"
  took hold of me and drew me to his side.
I turned my head like one who can't resist                      25
  looking to see what makes him run away
  (his body's strength draining with sudden fear),
but, looking back, does not delay his flight;
  and I saw coming right behind our backs,
  rushing along the ridge, a devil, black!                      30
His face, his look, how frightening it was!
  With outstretched wings he skimmed along the rock,
  and every single move he made was cruel;
on one of his high-hunched and pointed shoulders
  he had a sinner slung by both his thighs,                     35
  held tightly clawed at the tendons of his heels.
He shouted from our bridge: "Hey, Malebranche,
  here's one of Santa Zita's elders for you!
  You stick him under—I'll go back for more;
I've got that city stocked with the likes of him,              40
  they're all a bunch of grafters, save Bonturo!
  You can change a 'no' to 'yes' for cash in Lucca."
He flung him in, then from the flinty cliff
  sprang off. No hound unleashed to chase a thief

---

7–15. During the Midde Ages the shipyard at Venice, built in 1104, was one of
the most active and productive in all
Europe. The image of the busy shipyard
with its activity revolving around a vat
of viscous pitch establishes the tone for
this canto (and the next) as one of tense
and excited movement.

37. The Malebranche ("Evil Claws")
are the overseer-devils of this *bolgia*
wherein are punished the Barrators (grafters, l. 41), those swindlers in public

office whose sin against the state is comparable to that of the Simonists against
the Church.

38–42. "Santa Zita": lived and was
canonized in the thirteenth century; the
patron saint of Lucca. The "elders" (l.
38) are the Luccan government officials;
and one of them, Bonturo Dati (l. 41), is
ironically referred to here as being guiltless when in reality he was the worst
barrator of them all.

could have taken off with greater speed than he.          45
That sinner plunged, then floated up stretched out,
  and the devils underneath the bridge all shouted:
  "You shouldn't imitate the Holy Face!
The swimming's different here from in the Serchio!
  We have our grappling-hooks along with us—          50
  don't show yourself above the pitch, or else!"
With a hundred prongs or more they pricked him, shrieking:
  "You've got to do your squirming under cover,
  try learning how to cheat beneath the surface."
They were like cooks who make their scullery boys          55
  poke down into the caldron with their forks
  to keep the meat from floating to the top.
My master said: "We'd best not let them know
  that you are here with me; crouch down behind
  some jutting rock so that they cannot see you;          60
whatever insults they may hurl at me,
  you must not fear, I know how things are run here;
  I have been caught in as bad a fix before."
He crossed the bridge and walked on past the end;
  as soon as he set foot on the sixth bank          65
  he forced himself to look as bold as possible.
With all the sound and fury that breaks loose
  when dogs rush out at some poor begging tramp,
  making him stop and beg from where he stands—
the ones who hid beneath the bridge sprang out          70
  and blocked him with a flourish of their pitchforks,
  but he shouted: "All of you behave yourselves!
Before you start to jab me with your forks,
  let one of you step forth to hear me out,
  and then decide if you still care to grapple."          75
They all cried out: "Let Malacoda go!"
  One stepped forward—the others stood their ground—
  and moving, said, "What good will this do him?"
"Do you think, Malacoda," said my master,
  "That you would see me here, come all this way,          80
  against all opposition, and still safe,
without propitious fate and God's permission?
  Now let us pass, for it is willed in Heaven
  that I lead another by this savage path."
With this the devil's arrogance collapsed,          85
  his pitchfork, too, dropped right down to his feet,
  as he announced to all: "Don't touch this man!"
"You, hiding over there," my guide called me,

46–51. "the Holy Face": a wooden crucifix at Lucca. The sinner surfaces
stretched out (l. 46) on his back with
arms flung wide like the figure on a crucifix—and this gives rise to the devil's remark that here in Hell one does not swim
the same way as in the Serchio (a river
near Lucca. In other words, in the Ser-

chio people swim for pleasure, often floating on their backs (in the position of a
crucifix).
  76. "Malacoda": the leader of the
devils in this *bolgia*. It is significant that
a devil whose name means "Evil Tail"
ends this canto with a fart (l. 139).

"behind the bridge's rocks, curled up and quiet,
    come back to me, you may return in safety."    90
At his words I rose and then I ran to him
    and all the devils made a movement forward;
    I feared they would not really keep their pact.
(I remember seeing soldiers under truce,
    as they left the castle of Caprona, frightened    95
    to be passing in the midst of such an enemy.)
I drew up close to him, as close as possible,
    and did not take my eyes from all those faces
    that certainly had nothing good about them.
Their prongs were aimed at me, and one was saying:    100
    "Now do I let him have it in the rump?"
    They answered all for one: "Sure, stick him good!"
But the devil who had spoken with my guide
    was quick to spin around and scream an order:
    "At ease there, take it easy, Scarmiglione!"    105
Then he said to us: "You cannot travel straight
    across this string of bridges, for the sixth arch
    lies broken at the bottom of its ditch;
if you have made your mind up to proceed,
    you must continue on along this ridge;    110
    not far, you'll find a bridge that crosses it.
Five hours more and it will be one thousand,
    two hundred sixty-six years and a day
    since the bridge-way here fell crumbling to the ground.
I plan to send a squad of mine that way    115
    to see that no one airs himself down there;
    go along with them, they will not misbehave.
Front and center, Alichino, Calcabrina,"
    he shouted his commands, "you too, Cagnazzo;
    Barbariccia, you be captain of the squad.    120
Take Libicocco with you and Draghignazzo,
    toothy Ciriatto and Graffiacane,
    Farfarello and our crazy Rubicante.
Now tour the ditch, inspect the boiling tar;
    these two shall have safe passage to the bridge    125
    connecting den to den without a break."
"O master, I don't like the looks of this,"
    I said, "let's go, just you and me, no escort,
    you know the way. I want no part of them!
If you're observant as you usually are,    130
    why is it you don't see them grind their teeth

---

94–96. Dante's personal recollection concerns the siege of Caprona (a fortress on the Arno River near Pisa) by Guelph troops from Lucca and Florence in 1289.

112–114. Christ's death on Good Friday, 34 A.D., would in five hours, according to Malacoda, have occurred 1266 years ago yesterday—"today" being the morning of Holy Saturday, 1300. Al-though the bridge across the next *bolgia* was shattered by the earthquake following Christ's crucifixion, Malacoda tells Virgil and the Pilgrim that there is another bridge that crosses this *bolgia*. This lie, carefully contrived by the spokesman for the devils, sets the trap for the overly confident, trusting Virgil and his wary charge.

and wink at one another?—we're in danger!"
And he to me: "I will not have you frightened;
   let them do all the grinding that they want,
   they do it for the boiling souls, not us."     135
Before they turned left-face along the bank
   each one gave their good captain a salute
   with farting tongue pressed tightly to his teeth,
and he blew back with his bugle of an ass-hole.

### CANTO XXII

The note of grotesque comedy in the *bolgia* of the Malebranche
continues, with a comparison between Malacoda's salute to his soldiers and different kinds of military signals the Pilgrim has witnessed in his lifetime. He sees many Grafters squatting in the pitch,
but as soon as the Malebranche draw near, they dive below the surface. One unidentified Navarrese, however, fails to escape and is
hoisted up on Graffiacane's hooks; Rubicante and the other Malebranche start to tear into him, but Virgil, at his ward's request,
manages to question him between torments. The sinner briefly tells
his story, and then relates that he has left below in the pitch an
Italian, Fra Gomita, a particularly adept grafter, who spends his
time talking to Michele Zanche.

The Navarrese sinner promises to lure some of his colleagues to
the surface for the devils' amusement, if the tormentors will hide
themselves for a moment. Cagnazzo is skeptical but Alichino agrees,
and no sooner do the Malebranche turn away than the crafty grafter dives below the pitch. Alichino flies after him, but too late; now
Calcabrina rushes after Alichino and both struggle above the boiling
pitch, and then fall in. Barbariccia directs the rescue operation as
the two poets steal away.

I have seen troops of horsemen breaking camp,
   opening the attack, or passing in review,
   I have even seen them fleeing for their lives;
I have seen scouts ride exploring your terrain,
   O Aretines, and I have seen raiding-parties     5
   and the clash of tournaments, the run of jousts—
to the tune of trumpets, to the ring of clanging bells,
   to the roll of drums, to the flash of flares on ramparts,
   to the accompaniment of every known device;
but I never saw cavalry or infantry     10
   or ships that sail by landmarks or by stars
   signaled to set off by such strange bugling!

1–12. The reference to the Aretines (l.
5) recalls Dante's presence at their defeat
in the battle of Campaldino (1289) at the
hands of the Florentine and Luccan
troops.

So, on our way we went with those ten fiends.
    What savage company! But—in church, with saints—
    with rowdy good-for-nothings, in the tavern!         15
My attention now was fixed upon the pitch
    to see the operations of this *bolgia*,
    and how the cooking souls got on down there.
Much like the dolphins that are said to surface
    with their backs arched warn all men at sea         20
    to rig their ships for stormy seas ahead,
so now and then a sinner's back would surface
    in order to alleviate his pain,
    then dive to hide as quick as lightning strikes.
Like squatting frogs along the ditch's edge,         25
    with just their muzzles sticking out of water,
    their legs and all the rest concealed below,
these sinners squatted all around their pond;
    but as soon as Barbariccia would approach
    they quickly ducked beneath the boiling pitch.         30
I saw (my heart still shudders at the thought)
    one lingering behind—as it sometimes happens,
    one frog remains while all the rest dive down—
and Graffiacan, standing in front of him,
    hooked and twirled him by his pitchy hair         35
    and hoisted him. He looked just like an otter!
By then I knew the names of all the fiends:
    I had listened carefully when they were chosen,
    each of them stepping forth to match his name.
"Hey, Rubicante, dig your claws down deep,         40
    into his back and peel the skin off him,"
    this fiendish chorus egged him on with screams.
I said: "Master, will you, if you can, find out
    the name of that poor wretch who has just fallen
    into the cruel hands of his adversaries?"         45
My guide walked right up to the sinner's side
    and asked where he was from, and he replied:
    "I was born and bred in the kingdom of Navarre;
my mother gave me to a lord to serve,
    for she had me by some dishonest spendthrift         50
    who ran through all he owned and killed himself.
Then I became a servant in the household
    of good King Thibault. There I learned my graft,
    and now I pay my bill by boiling here."

---

48–54. Early commentators have given the name of Ciampolo or Giampolo to this native of Navarre who, after being placed in the service of a Spanish nobleman, later served in the court of Thibault II. Exploiting the court duties with which he was entrusted, he took to barratry. One commentator suggests that were it not for the tradition which attributes the name of Ci- ampolo to this man, one might identify him with the seneschal Goffredo di Beaumont who took over the government of Navarre during Thibault's absence.

53. "good King Thibault": Thibault II, the son-in-law of Louis IX of France, was count of Champagne and later king of Navarre during the mid-thirteenth century.

Ciriatto who had two tusks sticking out                              55
    on both sides of his mouth, just like a boar's,
    let him feel how just one tusk could rip him open.
The mouse had fallen prey to evil cats,
    but Barbariccia locked him with his arms
    shouting: "Get back while I've got hold of him!"        60
Then toward my guide he turned his face and said:
    "If you want more from him, keep questioning
    before he's torn to pieces by the others."
My guide went on: "Then tell me, do you know
    of some Italian stuck among these sinners              65
    beneath the pitch?" And he, "A second ago
I was with one who lived around those parts.
    Oh, I wish I were undercover with him now!
    I wouldn't have these hooks or claws to fear."
Libicocco cried: "We've waited long enough,"               70
    then with his fork he hooked the sinner's arm
    and, tearing at it, he pulled out a piece.
Draghignazzo, too, was anxious for some fun;
    he tried the wretch's leg, but their captain quickly
    spun around and gave them all a dirty look.            75
As soon as they calmed down a bit, my master
    began again to interrogate the wretch
    who still was contemplating his new wound:
"Who was it, you were saying, that unluckily
    you left behind you when you came ashore?"             80
"Gomita," he said, "the friar from Gallura,
    receptacle for every kind of fraud:
    when his lord's enemies were in his hands,
    the treatment they received delighted them:
he took their cash, and as he says, hushed up            85
    the case and let them off; none of his acts
    was petty grafting, all were of sovereign order.
He spends his time with don Michele Zanche
    of Logodoro, talking on and on
    about Sardinia—their tongues no worse for wear!        90
Oh, but look how that one grins and grinds his teeth;
    I could tell you so much more, but I am afraid
    he is going to grate my scabby hide for me."

81–87. "Gomita": Fra Gomita was a
Sardinian friar, chancellor of Nino Visconti, governor of Pisa, whom Dante
places in *Purgatory* (Canto VIII, l. 53).
From 1275–1296 Nino Visconti was judge
of Gallura, one of the four districts into
which Sardinia, a Pisan possession during the thirteenth century, was divided.
Profiting by his position and the good
faith of Nino Visconti, who refused to
listen to the complaints raised against
him, Fra Gomita indulged in the sale of
public offices. When Nino learned, however, that he had accepted bribes to let
prisoners escape, he promptly had him
hanged.

88–89. "Michele Zanche": Although no
documents mentioning the name of Michele Zanche have been found, he is believed to have been the governor of Logo-
doro, another of the four districts into
which Sardinia was divided in the thirteenth century during the period when
King Enzo of Sardinia, the son of Frederick II, was engaged in war.

But their master-sergeant turned to Farfarello,
 whose wild eyes warned he was about to strike,
 shouting, "Get away, you filthy bird of prey."   95
"If you would like to see Tuscans or Lombards,"
 the frightened shade took up where he left off,
 "and have a talk with them, I'll bring some here;
but the Malebranche must back up a bit,   100
 or else those shades won't risk a surfacing;
 I, by myself, will bring you up a catch
of seven, without moving from this spot,
 just by whistling—that's our signal to the rest
 when one peers out and sees the coast is clear."   105
Cagnazzo raised his snout at such a story,
 then shook his head and said: "Listen to the trick
 he's cooked up to get off the hook by jumping!"
And he, full of tricks his trade had taught him,
 said: "Tricky, I surely am, especially   110
 when it comes to getting friends into worse trouble."
But Alichin could not resist the challenge,
 and in spite of what the others thought, cried out:
 "If you jump, I won't come galloping for you,
I've got my wings to beat you to the pitch.   115
 We'll clear this ledge and wait behind that slope.
 Let's see if one of you can outmatch us!"
Now listen, Reader, here's a game that's strange:
 they all turned toward the slope, and first to turn
 was the fiend who from the start opposed the game.   120
The Navarrese had perfect sense of timing:
 feet planted on the ground, in a flash he jumped,
 the devil's plan was foiled, and he was free.
The squad was stung with shame but most of all
 the one who brought this blunder to perfection;   125
 he swooped down howling, "Now I've got you caught!"
Little good it did, for wings could not outstrip
 the flight of terror: down the sinner dived
 and up the fiend was forced to strain his chest
like a falcon swooping down on a wild duck:   130
 the duck dives quickly out of sight, the falcon
 must fly back up dejected and defeated.
In the meantime, Calcabrina, furious,
 also took off, hoping the shade would make it,
 so he could pick a fight with his companion.   135
And when he saw the grafter hit the pitch
 he turned his claws to grapple with his brother,
 and they tangled in mid-air above the ditch;
but the other was a fullfledged hawk as well
 and used his claws on him, and both of them   140
 went plunging straight into the boiling tar.
The heat was quick to make them separate,

but there seemed no way of getting out of there;
   their wings were clogged and could not lift them up.
Barbariccia, no less peeved than all his men,         145
   sent four fiends flying to the other shore
   with their equipment at top speed; instantly,
some here, some there, they took the posts assigned them.
They stretched their hooks to reach the pitch-dipped pair
   who were by now deep-fried within their crusts.     150
And we left them messed up in their occupation.

### CANTO XXIII

The antics of Ciampolo, the Navarrese, and the Malebranche
bring to the Pilgrim's mind the fable of the frog, the mouse, and
the hawk—and that in turn reminds him of the immediate danger
he and Virgil are in from the angry Malebranche. Virgil senses the
danger too, and grabbing his ward as a mother would her child, he
dashes to the edge of the bank and slides down the rocky slope into
the sixth *bolgia*—not a moment too soon, for at the top of the
slope they see the angry Malebranche. When the Pilgrim looks
around him he sees weeping shades slowly marching in single file,
each one covered from head to foot with a golden cloak, lined with
lead that weights them down. These are the Hypocrites. Two in
this group identify themselves as Catalano de' Malavolti and Loderingo degli Andalò, two Jovial Friars. The Pilgrim is about to address
them when he sees the shade of Caiaphas (the evil counselor who
advised Pontius Pilate to crucify Christ) crucified and transfixed by
three stakes to the ground. Virgil discovers from the two friars that
in order to leave this *bolgia* they must climb up a rockslide; he also
learns that this is the only *bolgia* over which the bridge is broken.
Virgil is angry with himself for having believed Malacoda's lie about
the bridge over the sixth *bolgia* (Canto XXI, l. 111).

In silence, all alone, without an escort,
   we moved along, one behind the other,
   like minor friars bent upon a journey.
I was thinking over one of Aesop's fables
   that this recent skirmish had brought back to mind,     5
   where he tells the story of the frog and mouse;
for "yon" and "there" could not be more alike
   than the fable and the fact, if one compares
   the start and finish of both incidents.
As from one thought another often rises,     10
   so this thought gave quick birth to still another,

3. The image of the "minor friars" (Franciscans) who walk in single file is preparatory to the presentation of the Hypocrites whose clothing is compared to that of monks (ll. 61–66).

and then the fear I first had felt was doubled.
I was thinking: "Since these fiends, on our account,
 were tricked and mortified by mockery,
 they certainly will be more than resentful;   15
with rage now added to their evil instincts,
 they will hunt us down with all the savagery
 of dogs about to pounce upon the hare."
I felt my body's skin begin to tighten—
 I was so frightened!—and I kept looking back:   20
 "O master," I said, "if you do not hide
both of us, and very quick, I am afraid
 of the Malebranche—right now they're on our trail—
 I feel they're there, I think I hear them now."
And he replied: "Even if I were a mirror   25
 I could not reflect your outward image faster
 than your inner thoughts transmit themselves to me.
In fact, just now they joined themselves with mine,
 and since they were alike in birth and form,
 I decided to unite them toward one goal:   30
if the right-hand bank should slope in such a way
 as to allow us to descend to the next *bolgia,*
 we could escape that chase we have imagined."
He had hardly finished telling me his plan
 when I saw them coming with their wings wide-open   35
 not too far off, and now they meant to get us!
My guide instinctively caught hold of me,
 like a mother waking to some warning sound,
 who sees the rising flames are getting close
and grabs her son and runs—she does not wait   40
 the short time it would take to put on something;
 she cares not for herself, only for him.
And over the edge, then down the stony bank
 he slid, on his back, along the sloping rock
 that walls the higher side of the next *bolgia.*   45
Water that turns a mill wheel never ran
 the narrow sluice at greater speed, not even
 at the point before it hits the paddle-blades,
than down that sloping border my guide slid
 bearing me with him, clasping me to his chest   50
 as though I were his child, not his companion.
His feet had hardly touched rock bottom, when
 there they were, the ten of them, above us
 on the height; but now there was no need to fear:
High Providence that willed for them to be   55
 the ministers in charge of the fifth ditch
 also willed them powerless to leave their realm.
And now, down there, we found a painted people,
 slow-motioned: step by step, they walked their round
 in tears, and seeming wasted by fatigue.   60

All were wearing cloaks with hoods pulled low
   covering the eyes (the style was much the same
   as those the Benedictines wear at Cluny),
dazzling, gilded cloaks outside, but inside
   they were lined with lead, so heavy, that the capes     65
   King Frederick used, compared to these, were straw.
O cloak of everlasting weariness!
   We turned again, as usual, to the left
   and moved with them, those souls lost in their mourning;
but with their weight that tired-out race of shades     70
   paced on so slowly that we found ourselves
   in new company with every step we took;
and so I asked my guide: "Would you look around
   and see, as we keep walking, if you find
   someone here whose name or deeds are known."     75
And one who overheard me speaking Tuscan
   cried out somewhere behind us: "Not so fast,
   you there, rushing ahead through this heavy air,
perhaps from me you can obtain an answer."
   At this my guide turned toward me saying, "Stop,     80
   and wait for him, then match your pace with his."
I paused and saw two shades with straining faces
   revealing their mind's haste to join my side,
   but the weight they bore and the crowded road delayed them.
When they arrived, they looked at me sideways     85
   and for some time, without exchanging words;
   then they turned to one another and were saying:
"He seems alive, the way his throat is moving,
   and if both are dead, what privilege allows them
   to walk uncovered by the heavy cloak?"     90
Then they spoke to me: "O Tuscan who has come
   to visit the college of the sullen hypocrites,
   do not disdain to tell us who you are."
I answered them: "I was born and I grew up
   in the great city on the lovely Arno's shore,     95
   and I have the body I have always had.
But who are you, distilling tears of grief,
   so many I see running down your cheeks?
   And what kind of pain is this that it can glitter?"
One of them answered: "The orange-gilded cloaks     100
   are thick with lead so heavy that it makes us,
   who are the scales it hangs on, creak as we walk.

---

61–63. The vestments of the monks at Cluny were particularly famous for their fullness and elegance.

64–66. Dante's image of the gilded exterior concealing a leaden interior is perhaps drawn from Matthew 23:27, "Woe unto you, scribes and Pharisees, hypocrites! For ye are like unto whited sepulchers, which indeed appear beautiful outwardly but are within full of dead men's bones, and of all uncleanness." "capes / King Frederick used" (ll. 65–66): refers to a mode of punishment for traitors reportedly instituted by Frederick II, grandson of Frederick Barbarossa. The condemned were dressed in leaden capes which were then melted on their bodies.

Jovial Friars we were, both from Bologna.
  My name was Catalano, his, Loderingo,
    and both of us were chosen by your city,                    105
that usually would choose one man alone,
  to keep the peace. Evidence of what we were
    may still be seen around Gardingo's parts."
I began: "O Friars, all your wretchedness . . ."
  but said no more; I couldn't, for I saw                       110
    one crucified with three stakes on the ground.
And when he saw me all his body writhed,
  and through his beard he heaved out sighs of pain;
    then Friar Catalano, who watched the scene,
remarked: "That impaled figure you see there                    115
  advised the Pharisees it was expedient
    to sacrifice one man for all the people.
Naked he lies stretched out across the road,
  as you can see, and he must feel the load
    of every weight that steps on him to cross.                 120
His father-in-law and the other council members,
  who were the seed of evil for all Jews,
    are racked the same way all along this ditch."
And I saw Virgil staring down amazed
  at this body stretching out in crucifixion,                   125
    so vilely punished in the eternal exile.
Then he looked up and asked one of the friars:
  "Could you please tell us, if your rule permits:
    is there a passage-way on the right, somewhere,
by which the two of us may leave this place                     130
  without summoning one of those black angels

---

103–108. The Order of the *Cavalieri di Beata Santa Maria*, or "Jovial Friars" (*frati gaudenti*) as they were called, was founded at Bologna in 1261 and was dedicated to the maintenance of peace between political factions and families, and to the defense of the weak and poor. However, because of its rather liberal rules, this high-principled organization gained the nickname of "Jovial Friars"— which, no doubt, impaired its serious function to some degree. The Bolognese friars Catalano de' Malavolti (c. 1210–1285) and Loderingo degli Andalò (ca. 1210–1293) were elected jointly to the office of *Podestà* ("mayor") in Florence because it was thought that the combination of the former, a Guelph, and the latter, a Ghibelline, would ensure the peace of the city. In reality their tenure, short though it was, was characterized by strife, which culminated in the expulsion of the Ghibellines from Florence in 1266. Gardingo (l. 108) is the name of the section of Florence around the Palazzo Vecchio; in this area the Uberti family, the heads of the Florentine Ghibelline party, had their palace, which was razed during the uprisings of 1266. Modern historians have proved that Pope Clement IV controlled both the election and actions of Catalano and Loderingo, in order to overthrow the Ghibellines and establish the Guelphs in power.

115–124. Caiaphas, the high priest of the Jews, maintained that it was better that one man (Jesus) die than for the Hebrew nation to be lost (John 11:49–50). Annas, Caiaphas's father-in-law (l. 121), delivered Jesus to him for judgment. For their act against God these men and the other evil counselors who judged Christ were the "seed of evil for all Jews" (l. 122); in retaliation God caused Jerusalem to be destroyed and the Hebrew people dispersed to all parts of the world. It is, then, a fitting punishment for Caiaphas, Annas, and the rest to bear the weight of all the hypocrites for their crime, and to be crucified on the ground with "three stakes."

124–127. Most commentators seem to think that Virgil's amazement at seeing the crucified Caiaphas is due to the fact that he was not there when Virgil first descended into Hell.

to come down here and raise us from this pit?"
He answered: "Closer than you might expect,
  a ridge jutting out from the base of the great circle
  extends, and bridges every hideous ditch        135
except this one whose arch is totally smashed
  and crosses nowhere; but you can climb up
  its massive ruins that slope against this bank."
My guide stood there awhile, his head bent low,
  then said, "He told a lie about this business,      140
  that one who hooks the sinners over there."
And the friar: "Once, in Bologna, I heard discussed
  the devil's many vices; one of them is
  that he tells lies and is father of all lies."
In haste, taking great strides, my guide walked off,    145
  his face revealing traces of his anger.
I turned and left the heavy-weighted souls
to make my way behind those cherished footprints.

CANTO XXIV

After an elaborate simile describing Virgil's anger and the return
of his composure, the two begin the difficult, steep ascent up the
rocks of the fallen bridge. The Pilgrim can barely make it to the top
even with Virgil's help, and after the climb he sits down to catch
his breath; but his guide urges him on, and they make their way
back to the bridge over the seventh *bolgia*. From the bridge confused sounds can be heard rising from the darkness below. Virgil
agrees to take his pupil down into the *bolgia*, and once they are
below, the scene reveals a terrible confusion of serpents, and Thieves
madly running.

Suddenly a snake darts out and strikes a sinner's neck, whereupon
he flares up, turning into a heap of crumbling ashes; then the ashes
gather together into the shape of a man. The metamorphosed
sinner reveals himself to be Vanni Fucci, a Pistoiese condemned for
stealing the treasure of the sacristy of the church of San Zeno at
Pistoia. He makes a prophecy about the coming strife in Florence.

In the season of the newborn year, when the sun
  renews its rays beneath Aquarius
  and nights begin to last as long as days,
at the time the hoarfrost paints upon the ground
  the outward semblance of his snow-white sister     5
  (but the color from his brush soon fades away),
the peasant wakes, gets up, goes out and sees
  the fields all white. No fodder for his sheep!

---

146–148. Virgil is angry, of course, because he had trusted Malacoda and had
been deceived, and also because of the
friar's slightly taunting rebuke at his
naïveté (ll. 142–144).

He smites his thighs in anger and goes back
into his shack and, pacing up and down,                               10
   complains, poor wretch, not knowing what to do;
   once more he goes outdoors, and hope fills him
again when he sees the world has changed its face
   in so little time, and he picks up his crook
   and out to pasture drives his sheep to graze—       15
just so I felt myself lose heart to see
   my master's face wearing a troubled look,
   and as quickly came the salve to heal my sore:
for when we reached the shattered heap of bridge,
   my leader turned to me with that sweet look            20
   of warmth I first saw at the mountain's foot;
he opened up his arms (but not before
   he had carefully studied how the ruins lay
   and found some sort of plan) to pick me up.
Like one who works and thinks things out ahead,          25
   always ready for the next move he will make,
   so while he raised me up toward one great rock,
he had already singled out another,
   saying, "Now get a grip on that rock there,
   but test it first to see it holds your weight."           30
It was no road for one who wore a cloak!
   Even though I had his help and he weighed nothing,
   we could hardly lift ourselves from crag to crag.
And had it not been that the bank we climbed
   was lower than the one we had slid down—              35
   I cannot speak for him—but I for one
surely would have quit. But since the Evil Pits
   slope toward the yawning well that is the lowest,
   each valley is laid out in such a way
that one bank rises higher than the next.                     40
   We somehow finally reached the point above
   where the last of all that rock was shaken loose.
My lungs were so pumped out of breath by the time
   I reached the top, I could not go on farther,
   and instantly I sat down where I was.                      45
"Come on, shake off the covers of this sloth,"
   the master said, "for sitting softly cushioned,
   or tucked in bed, is no way to win fame;
and without it man must waste his life away,
   leaving such traces of what he was on earth              50
   as smoke in wind and foam upon the water.
Stand up! Dominate this weariness of yours
   with the strength of soul that wins in every battle
   if it does not sink beneath the body's weight.
Much steeper stairs than these we'll have to climb;       55

21. "at the mountain's foot": The mountain of Canto I, a reference which reminds the reader of the entire journey.
31. Such as the Hypocrites of the pre-vious *bolgia*.
55. Virgil is referring to the ascent up Lucifer's legs and beyond. See Canto XXXIV, ll. 82–84.

we have not seen enough of sinners yet!
  If you understand me, act, learn from my words."
At this I stood up straight and made it seem
  I had more breath than I began to breathe,
  and said: "Move on, for I am strong and ready."                    60
We climbed and made our way along the bridge
  which was jagged, tight and difficult to cross,
  and steep—far more than any we had climbed.
Not to seem faint I spoke while I was climbing;
  then came a voice from the depths of the next chasm,               65
  a voice unable to articulate.
I don't know what it said, even though I stood
  at the very top of the arch that crosses there;
  to me it seemed whoever spoke, spoke running.
I was bending over, but no living eyes                               70
  could penetrate the bottom of that darkness,
  therefore I said: "Master, why not go down
this bridge onto the next encircling bank,
  for I hear sounds I cannot understand,
  and I look down but cannot see a thing."                           75
"No other answer," he replied, "I give you
  than doing what you ask, for a fit request
  is answered best in silence and in deed."
From the bridge's height we came down to the point
  where it ends and joins the edge of the eighth bank,              80
  and then the *bolgia* opened up to me:
down there I saw a terrible confusion
  of serpents, all of such a monstrous kind
  the thought of them still makes my blood run cold.
Let all the sands of Libya boast no longer,                          85
  for though she breeds chelydri and jaculi,
  phareans, cenchres and head-tailed amphisbenes,
she never bred so great a plague of venom,
  not even if combined with Ethiopia
  or all the sands that lie by the Red Sea.                          90
Within this cruel and bitterest abundance
  people ran terrified and naked, hopeless
  of finding hiding-holes or heliotrope.
Their hands were tied behind their backs with serpents
  which pushed their tails and heads around the loins               95
  and coiled themselves in knots around the front.
And then—at a sinner running by our bank
  a snake shot out and, striking, hit his mark:
  right where the neck attaches to the shoulder.
No *o* or *i* was ever quicker put                                   100
  by pen to paper than he flared up and burned,
  and turned into a heap of crumbled ash;

85–90. Libya and the other lands near the Red Sea (Ethiopia and Arabia) were renowned for producing several types of dreadful reptiles.

93. According to folk tradition, helio-trope was believed to be a stone of many virtues. It could cure snakebites and make the man who carried it on his person invisible.

and then, these ashes scattered on the ground
   began to come together on their own
   and quickly take the form they had before:      105
precisely so, philosophers declare
   the phoenix dies to be reborn again
   as she approaches her five-hundredth year;
alive she does not feed on herbs or grain,
   but on teardrops of frankincense and balm,      110
   and wraps herself to die in nard and myrrh.
As a man in a fit will fall, not knowing why
   (perhaps some hidden demon pulls him down,
   or some oppilation chokes his vital spirits),
then, struggling to his feet, will look around,      115
   confused and overwhelmed by the great anguish
   he has suffered, moaning as he stares about—
so did this sinner when he finally rose.
   Oh, how harsh the power of the Lord can be,
   raining in its vengeance blows like these!      120
My guide asked him to tell us who he was,
   and he replied: "It's not too long ago
   I rained from Tuscany to this fierce gullet.
I loved the bestial life more than the human,
   like the bastard that I was; I'm Vanni Fucci,      125
   the beast! Pistoia was my fitting den."
I told my guide: "Tell him not to run away;
   ask him what sin has driven him down here,
   for I knew him as a man of bloody rage."
The sinner heard and did not try to feign;      130
   directing straight at me his mind and face,
   he reddened with a look of ugly shame,
and said: "That you have caught me by surprise
   here in this wretched *bolgia*, makes me grieve
   more than the day I lost my other life.      135
Now I am forced to answer what you ask:
   I am stuck so far down here because of theft:
   I stole the treasure of the sacristy—
a crime falsely attributed to another.
   I don't want you to rejoice at having seen me,      140

108–111. Dante compares the complex metamorphosis of Vanni Fucci to that of the phoenix which, according to legend, consumes itself in flames every five hundred years.

112–117. It was a popular belief that during an epileptic fit, the victim was possessed by the devil; in addition to this, Dante presents a more rational explanation: that some blockage of his veins inhibits the proper functioning of a man's body.

125–129. "Vanni Fucci": the illegitimate son of Fuccio de' Lazzari, a militant leader of the Blacks in Pistoia. His notoriety "as a man of bloody rage" (l. 129) was widespread; in fact, the Pilgrim is surprised to find him here and not immersed in the Phlegethon together with the other shades of the Violent (Canto XII).

138–139. Around 1293 the treasury of San Iacopo in the church of San Zeno at Pistoia was robbed. The person unjustly accused (l. 139) of the theft (and almost executed for it) was Rampino Foresi. Later, the true facts came to light, and Vanni della Mona, one of the conspirators, was sentenced to death. Vanni Fucci, however, escaped, and although he received a sentence in 1295 for murder and other acts of violence, he managed to remain free until his death in 1300.

if ever you escape from these dark pits,
so open your ears and hear my prophecy:
　Pistoia first shall be stripped of all its Blacks,
　and Florence then shall change its men and laws;
from Valdimagra Mars shall thrust a bolt　　　　　145
　of lightning wrapped in thick, foreboding clouds,
　then bolt and clouds will battle bitterly
in a violent storm above Piceno's fields
　where rapidly the bolt will burst the cloud,
　and no White will escape without his wounds.　　150
And I have told you this so you will suffer!"

### CANTO XXV

The wrathful Vanni Fucci directs an obscene gesture to God, whereupon he is attacked by several snakes, which coil about him, tying him so tight that he can not move a muscle. As soon as he flees, the centaur Cacus gallops by with a fire-breathing dragon on his back, and following close behind are three shades, concerned because they cannot find Cianfa—who soon appears as a snake which attacks Agnèl; the two merge into one hideous monster which then steals off. Next, Guercio, in the form of a snake, strikes Buoso, and the two exchange shapes. Only Puccio Sciancato is left unchanged.

When he had finished saying this, the thief
　shaped his fists into figs and raised them high
　and cried: "Here, God, I've shaped them just for you!"
From then on all those snakes became my friends,
　for one of them at once coiled round his neck　　5
　as if to say, "That's all you're going to say,"
while another twisted round his arms in front;
　it tied itself into so tight a knot,
　between the two he could not move a muscle.
Pistoia, ah Pistoia! why not resolve　　　　　10
　to burn yourself to ashes, ending all,
　since you have done more evil than your founders?
Throughout the circles of this dark inferno
　I saw no shade so haughty toward his God,
　not even he who fell from Thebes' high walls.　　15
Without another word he fled, and then
　I saw a raging centaur gallop up

2. An obscene gesture still current in Italy. The gesture is made by closing the hand to form a fist with the thumb inserted between the first and second fingers.
10–12. "Pistoia": supposedly founded by the remnants of the defeated army of Catiline, composed primarily of evildoers and brigands.
15. Capaneus, whom Dante placed among the Blasphemers in the Seventh Circle.

roaring: "Where is he, where is that untamed beast?"
I think that all Maremma does not have
    as many snakes as he had on his back,                                    20
    right up to where his human form begins.
Upon his shoulders, just behind the nape,
    a dragon with its wings spread wide was crouching
    and spitting fire at whoever came its way.
My master said to me: "That one is Cacus,                                   25
    who more than once in the grotto far beneath
    Mount Aventine spilled blood to fill a lake.
He does not go the same road as his brothers
    because of the cunning way he committed theft
    when he stole his neighbor's famous cattle-herd;                         30
and then his evil deeds came to an end
    beneath the club of Hercules, who struck
    a hundred blows, and he, perhaps, felt ten."
While he was speaking Cacus galloped off;
    at the same time three shades appeared below us;                         35
    my guide and I would not have seen them there
if they had not cried out: "Who are you two?"
    At this we cut our conversation short
    to give our full attention to these three.
I didn't know who they were, but then it happened,                          40
    as often it will happen just by chance,
    that one of them was forced to name another:
"Where did Cianfa go off to?" he asked. And then,
    to keep my guide from saying anything,
    I put my finger tight against my lips.                                    45
Now if, my reader, you should hesitate
    to believe what I shall say, there's little wonder,
    for I, the witness, scarcely can believe it.
While I was watching them, all of a sudden
    a serpent—and it had six feet—shot up                                    50
    and hooked one of these wretches with all six.
With the middle feet it hugged the sinner's stomach
    and, with the front ones, grabbed him by the arms,
    and bit him first through one cheek then the other;
the serpent spread its hind feet round both thighs                          55
    then stuck its tail between the sinner's legs,
    and up against his back the tail slid stiff.
No ivy ever grew to any tree
    so tight entwined, as the way that hideous beast

---

19–20. "Maremma": a swampy area
along the Tuscan coast which was infested
with snakes.
25–33. "Cacus": a centaur, the son of
Vulcan; he was a fire-belching monster
who lived in a cave beneath Mt. Aven-
tine and pillaged the inhabitants of the
area. But when he stole several cattle of
Hercules's, the latter went to Cacus's
cave and killed him. "His brothers"
(l. 28) are the centaurs who serve as
guardians in the first round of the Seventh
Circle.
43. "Cianfa": a member of the Florentine Donati family. He makes his appearance in line 50 in the form of a serpent.

had woven in and out its limbs with his; 60
and then both started melting like hot wax
and, fusing, they began to mix their colors
(so neither one seemed what he was before),
just as a brownish tint, ahead of flame,
creeps up a burning page that is not black 65
completely, even though the white is dying.
The other two who watched began to shout:
"Oh Agnèl! If you could see how you are changing!
You're not yourself, and you're not both of you!"
The two heads had already fused to one 70
and features from each flowed and blended into
one face where two were lost in one another;
two arms of each were four blurred strips of flesh;
and thighs with legs, then stomach and the chest
sprouted limbs that human eyes have never seen. 75
Each former likeness now was blotted out:
both, and neither one it seemed—this picture
of deformity. And then it sneaked off slowly.
Just as a lizard darting from hedge to hedge,
under the stinging lash of the dog-days' heat, 80
zips across the road, like a flash of lightning,
so, rushing toward the two remaining thieves,
aiming at their guts, a little serpent,
fiery with rage and black as pepper-corn,
shot up and sank its teeth in one of them 85
right where the embryo receives its food,
then back it fell and lay stretched out before him.
The wounded thief stared speechless at the beast,
and standing motionless began to yawn
as though he needed sleep, or had a fever. 90
The snake and he were staring at each other;
one from his wound, the other from its mouth
fumed violently, and smoke with smoke was mingling.
Let Lucan from this moment on be silent,
who tells of poor Nasidius and Sabellus, 95
and wait to hear what I still have in store;
and Ovid, too, with his Cadmus and Arethusa—
though he metamorphosed one into a snake,
the other to a fountain, I feel no envy,
for never did he interchange two beings 100
face to face so that both forms were ready

68. Besides the indication that Agnèl is Florentine (except for Vanni Fucci, the thieves in this canto are all Florentines), and possibly is one of the Brunelleschi family, nothing more is known of him.
86. "right where the embryo receives its food": The navel.
94–102. In the *Pharsalia* Lucan tells of the physical transformations undergone by Sabellus and Nasidius, both soldiers in Cato's army who, being bitten by snakes, turned respectively into ashes and into a formless mass. Ovid relates how Cadmus took the form of a serpent and how Arethusa became a fountain.

to exchange their substance, each one for the other's,
an interchange of perfect symmetry:
   the serpent split its tail into a fork,
   and the wounded sinner drew his feet together;     105
the legs, with both the thighs, closed in to join
   and in a short time fused, so that the juncture
   didn't show signs of ever having been there,
the while the cloven tail assumed the features
   that the other one was losing, and its skin     110
   was growing soft, the other's getting scaly;
I saw his arms retreating to the armpits,
   and the reptile's two front feet, that had been short,
   began to stretch the length the man's had shortened;
the beast's hind feet then twisted round each other     115
   and turned into the member man conceals,
   while from the wretch's member grew two legs.
The smoke from each was swirling round the other,
   exchanging colors, bringing out the hair
   where there was none, and stripping off the other's.     120
The one rose up, the other sank, but neither
   dissolved the bond between their evil stares,
   fixed eye to eye, exchanging face for face;
the standing creature's face began receding
   toward the temples; from the excess stuff pulled back,     125
   the ears were growing out of flattened cheeks,
while from the excess flesh that did not flee
   the front, a nose was fashioned for the face,
   and lips puffed out to just the normal size.
The prostrate creature strains his face out long     130
   and makes his ears withdraw into his head,
   the way a snail pulls in its horns. The tongue,
that once had been one piece and capable
   of forming words, divides into a fork,
   while the other's fork heals up. The smoke subsides.     135
The soul that had been changed into a beast
   went hissing off along the valley's floor,
   the other close behind him, spitting words.
Then he turned his new-formed back on him and said
   to the shade left standing there: "Let Buoso run     140
   the valley on all fours, the way I did."
Thus I saw the cargo of the seventh hold
   exchange and interchange; and let the strangeness
   of it all excuse me, if my pen has failed.
And though this spectacle confused my eyes     145
   and stunned my mind, the two thieves could not flee

140–141. "Buoso": The identity of Buoso, the newly formed serpent, is uncertain; some commentators think him to be Buoso degli Abati and others, Buoso Donati (see Canto XXX, l. 44)

so secretly I did not recognize
that one was certainly Puccio Sciancato
  (and he alone, of that company of three
  that first appeared, did not change to something else),    150
the other, he who made you mourn, Gaville.

CANTO XXVI

From the ridge high above the eighth *bolgia* can be perceived a
myriad of flames flickering far below, and Virgil explains that
within each flame is the suffering soul of a Deceiver. One flame,
divided at the top, catches the Pilgrim's eye and he is told that
within it are jointly punished Ulysses and Diomed. Virgil questions
the pair for the benefit of the Pilgrim. Ulysses responds with the
famous narrative of his last voyage, during which he passed the Pillars of Hercules and sailed the forbidden sea until he saw a mountain shape, from which came suddenly a whirlwind that spun his
ship around three times and sank it.

Be joyful, Florence, since you are so great
  that your outstretched wings beat over land and sea,
  and your name is spread throughout the realm of Hell!
I was ashamed to find among the thieves
  five of your most eminent citizens,    5
  a fact which does you very little honor.
But if early morning dreams have any truth,
  you will have the fate, in not too long a time,
  that Prato and the others crave for you.
And were this the day, it would not be too soon!    10
  Would it had come to pass, since pass it must!
  The longer the delay, the more my grief.
We started climbing up the stairs of boulders
  that had brought us to the place from where we watched;
  my guide went first and pulled me up behind him.    15
We went along our solitary way
  among the rocks, among the ridge's crags,
  where the foot could not advance without the hand.
I know that I grieved then, and now again
  I grieve when I remember what I saw,    20

148. "Puccio Sciancato": (the only one
of the original three Florentine thieves
who does not assume a new shape) a
member of the Galigai family and a sup-
porter of the Ghibellines. He was exiled
from Florence in 1268.

151. Francesco Cavalcanti, known as
Guercio, was slain by the inhabitants of
Gaville, a small town near Florence in
Valdarno (Arno Valley). The Cavalcanti
family avenged his death by decimating
the populace; thus, he was Gaville's rea-

son to mourn.

7. "But if early morning dreams have
any truth": According to the ancient and
medieval popular tradition, the dreams
that men have in the early morning hours
before daybreak will come true.

9. It seems most plausible, given the
phrase "and the others" that Prato is to
be interpreted here in a generic sense to
indicate all the small Tuscan towns subjected to Florentine rule, which soon
rebel against their master.

and more than ever I restrain my talent
lest it run a course that virtue has not set;
 for if a lucky star or something better
 has given me this good, I must not misuse it.
As many fireflies (in the season when      25
 the one who lights the world hides his face least,
 in the hour when the flies yield to mosquitoes)
as the peasant on the hillside at his ease
 sees, flickering in the valley down below,
 where perhaps he gathers grapes or tills the soil—  30
with just so many flames all the eighth *bolgia*
 shone brilliantly, as I became aware
 when at last I stood where the depths were visible.
As he who was avenged by bears beheld
 Elijah's chariot at its departure,      35
 when the rearing horses took to flight toward Heaven,
and though he tried to follow with his eyes,
 he could not see more than the flame alone
 like a small cloud once it had risen high—
so each flame moves itself along the throat    40
 of the abyss, none showing what it steals
 but each one stealing nonetheless a sinner.
I was on the bridge, leaning far over—so far
 that if I had not grabbed some jut of rock
 I could easily have fallen to the bottom.    45
And my guide who saw me so absorbed, explained:
 "There are souls concealed within these moving fires,
 each one swathed in his burning punishment."
"O master," I replied, "from what you say
 I know now I was right; I had guessed already   50
 it might be so, and I was about to ask you:
Who's in that flame with its tip split in two,
 like that one which once sprang up from the pyre
 where Eteocles was placed beside his brother?"
He said: "Within, Ulysses and Diomed     55
 are suffering in anger with each other,
 just vengeance makes them march together now.

34–39. The prophet Elisha saw Elijah transported to Heaven in a fiery chariot. When Elisha on another occasion cursed, in the name of the Lord, a group of children who were mocking him, two bears came out of the forest and devoured them. (4 Kings, 2:9–12, 23–24).

52–54. Dante compares this flame with that which rose from the funeral pyre of Eteocles and Polynices, twin sons of Oedipus and Jocasta, who, contesting the throne of Thebes, caused a major conflict known as the Seven against Thebes (see Canto XIV, ll. 68–69). The two brothers met in single combat and slew each other. They were placed together on the pyre,

but because of their mutual hatred, the flame split.

55–57. "Ulysses"; the son of Laertes, a central figure in the Trojan War. Although his deeds are recounted by Homer, Dictys of Crete, and many others, the story of his last voyage presented here by Dante (ll. 90–142), has no literary or historical precedent. His story, being an invention of Dante's, is unique in the *Divine Comedy*.

"Diomed": the son of Tydeus and Deipyle, ruled Argos. He was a major Greek figure in the Trojan War and was frequently associated with Ulysses in his exploits.

And they lament inside one flame the ambush
　　of the horse become the gateway that allowed
　　the Romans' noble seed to issue forth.　　　　　　60
Therein they mourn the trick that caused the grief
　　of Deidamia who still weeps for Achilles;
　　and there they pay for the Palladium."
"If it is possible for them to speak
　　from within those flames," I said, "master, I pray　65
　　and repray you—let my prayer be like a thousand—
that you do not forbid me to remain
　　until the two-horned flame comes close to us;
　　you see how I bend toward it with desire!"
"Your prayer indeed is worthy of highest praise,"　　70
　　he said to me, "and therefore I shall grant it;
　　but see to it your tongue refrains from speaking.
Leave it to me to speak, for I know well
　　what you would ask; perhaps since they were Greeks
　　they might not pay attention to your words."　　　75
So when the flame had reached us, and my guide
　　decided that the time and place were right,
　　he addressed them and I listened to him speaking:
"O you who are two souls within one fire,
　　if I have deserved from you when I was living,　　80
　　if I have deserved from you much praise or little,
when in the world I wrote my lofty verses,
　　do not move on; let one of you tell where
　　he lost himself through his own fault, and died."
The greater of the ancient flame's two horns　　　　85
　　began to sway and quiver, murmuring
　　just like a flame that strains against the wind;
then, while its tip was moving back and forth,
　　as if it were the tongue itself that spoke,
　　the flame took on a voice and said: "When I　　　90
set sail from Circe who, more than a year,
　　had kept me occupied close to Gaëta

58–60. The Trojans mistakenly believed the mammoth wooden horse, left outside the city's walls, to be a sign of Greek capitulation. They brought it through the gates of the city amid great rejoicing. Later that evening the Greek soldiers hidden in the horse emerged and sacked the city. The Fall of Troy occasioned the journey of Aeneas and his followers ("noble seed") to establish a new nation on the shores of Italy which would become the heart of the Roman Empire.

61–62. Thetis brought her son Achilles, disguised as a girl, to the court of King Lycomedes on the island of Scyros, so that he would not have to fight in the Trojan War. There Achilles seduced the king's daughter Deidamia, who bore him a child and whom he later abandoned, encouraged by Ulysses (who in company with

Diomed had come in search of him) to join the war.

63. "the Palladium": The sacred Palladium, a statue of the goddess Pallas Athena, guaranteed the integrity of Troy as long as it remained in the citadel. Ulysses and Diomed stole it and carried it off to Argos, thereby securing victory for the Greeks over the Trojans.

90–92. On his return voyage to Ithaca from Troy Ulysses was detained by Circe, the daughter of the Sun, for more than a year. She was an enchantress who transformed Ulysses's men into swine.

92–93. "Gaëta": Along the coast of southern Italy above Naples there is a promontory (and now on it there is a city) then called Gaëta. Aeneas named it to honor his nurse who had died there.

(before Aeneas called it by that name),
not sweetness of a son, not reverence
    for an aging father, not the debt of love      95
    I owed Penelope to make her happy,
could quench deep in myself the burning wish
    to know the world and have experience
    of all man's vices, of all human worth.
So I set out on the deep and open sea      100
    with just one ship and with that group of men,
    not many, who had not deserted me.
I saw as far as Spain, far as Morocco,
    both shores; I had left behind Sardinia,
    and the other islands which that sea encloses.      105
I and my mates were old and tired men.
    Then finally we reached the narrow neck
    where Hercules put up his signal-pillars
to warn men not to go beyond that point.
    On my right I saw Seville, and passed beyond;      110
    on my left, Ceuta had already sunk behind me.
'Brothers,' I said, 'who through a hundred thousand
    perils have made your way to reach the West,
    during this so brief vigil of our senses
that is still reserved for us do not deny      115
    yourself experience of what there is beyond,
    behind the sun, in the world they call unpeopled.
Consider what you came from: you are Greeks!
    You were not born to live like mindless brutes
    but to follow paths of excellence and knowledge.'     120
With this brief exhortation I made my crew
    so anxious for the way that lay ahead,
    that then I hardly could have held them back;
and with our stern turned toward the morning light,
    we made our oars our wings for that mad flight,     125
    gaining distance, always sailing to the left.
The night already had surveyed the stars
    the other pole contains; it saw ours so low
    it did not show above the ocean floor.
Five times we saw the splendor of the moon     130
    grow full and five times wane away again

94–96. In his quest for knowledge of the world Ulysses puts aside his affection for his son, Telemachus, his duty toward his father, Laertes, and the love of his devoted wife Penelope; that is, he sinned against the classical notion of *pietas*.

108. The Strait of Gibraltar, referred to in ancient times as the Pillars of Hercules. The two pillars are Mt. Abyla on the North African coast and Mt. Calpe on the European side, which, originally one mountain, were separated by Hercules

to designate the farthest reach of the inhabited world, beyond which no man was permitted to venture.

110–111. Ulysses has passed through the Strait of Gibraltar and is now in the Atlantic Ocean. Ceuta is a town on the North African coast opposite Gibraltar; in this passage Seville probably represents the Iberian peninsula and, as such, the boundary of the inhabited world.

130–131. Five months had passed since they began their voyage.

since we had entered through the narrow pass—
when there appeared a mountain shape, darkened
   by distance, that arose to endless heights.
   I had never seen another mountain like it.        135
Our celebrations soon turned into grief:
   from the new land there rose a whirling wind
   that beat against the forepart of the ship
and whirled us round three times in churning waters;
   the fourth blast raised the stern up high, and sent    140
   the bow down deep, as pleased Another's will.
And then the sea was closed again, above us."

## CANTO XXVII

As soon as Ulysses has finished his narrative, another flame—its soul within having recognized Virgil's Lombard accent—comes forward asking the travelers to pause and answer questions about the state of affairs in the region of Italy from which he came. The Pilgrim responds by outlining the strife in Romagna and ends by asking the flame who he is. The flame, although he insists he does not want his story to be known among the living, answers because he is supposedly convinced that the Pilgrim will never return to earth. He is another famous deceiver, Guido da Montefeltro, a soldier who became a friar in his old age; but he was untrue to his vows because, at the urging of Pope Boniface VIII, he counseled the use of fraud in the pope's campaign against the Colonna family. He was damned to Hell because he failed to repent his sins, trusting instead in the pope's fraudulent absolution.

By now the flame was standing straight and still,
   it said no more and had already turned
   from us, with sanction of the gentle poet,
when another, coming right behind it,
   attracted our attention to its tip,        5
   where a roaring of confusing sounds had started.
As the Sicilian bull—that bellowed first
   with cries of that one (and it served him right)
   who with his file had fashioned such a beast—
would bellow with the victim's voice inside    10
   so that, although the bull was only brass,

133. In Dante's time the Southern Hemisphere was believed to be composed entirely of water; the mountain that Ulysses and his men see from afar is the Mount of Purgatory which rises from the sea in the Southern Hemisphere, the polar opposite of Jerusalem. For the formation of the mountain see Canto XXXIV, ll. 122–126.

7–15. Phalaris, despotic ruler of Agri-gentum in Sicily, commissioned Perillus to construct a bronze bull intended to be used as an instrument of torture; it was fashioned so that, once it was heated, the victim roasting within would emit cries which sounded without like those of a bellowing bull. To test the device, Phalaris made the artisan himself its first victim, and thus he received his just reward for creating such a cruel instrument.

the effigy itself seemed pierced with pain:
so, lacking any outlet to escape
      from the burning soul that was inside the flame,
      the suffering words became the fire's language.                    15
But after they had made their journey upward
      to reach the tip, giving it that same quiver
      the sinner's tongue inside had given them,
we heard the words: "O you to whom I point
      my voice, who spoke just now in Lombard, saying:                   20
      'you may move on, I won't ask more of you,'
although I have been slow in coming to you,
      be willing, please, to pause and speak with me.
      You see how willing I am—and I burn!
If you have just now fallen to this world                                25
      of blindness, from that sweet Italian land
      where I took on the burden of my guilt,
tell me, are the Romagnols at war or peace?
      For I come from the hills between Urbino
      and the mountain chain that lets the Tiber loose."                 30
I was still bending forward listening
      when my master touched my side and said to me:
      "*You* speak to him; *this* one is Italian."
And I, who was prepared to answer him,
      began without delaying my response:                                35
      "O soul who stands concealed from me down there,
your Romagna is not now and never was
      without war in her tyrants' hearts, although
      there was no open warfare when I came here.
Ravenna's situation has not changed:                                     40
      the eagle of Polenta broods up there;
      covering all of Cervia with its pinions;
the land that stood the test of long endurance
      and left the French piled in a bloody heap
      is once again beneath the verdant claws.                           45
Verrucchio's Old Mastiff and its New One,
      who both were bad custodians of Montagna,
      still sink their fangs into their people's flesh;

28. "the Romagnols": the inhabitants of Romagna, the area bounded by the Po and the Reno rivers, the Apennines, and the Adriatic Sea.

29–30. Between the town of Urbino and Mount Coronaro lies the region known as Montefeltro. The speaker is Guido da Montefeltro, the Ghibelline captain whose wisdom and skill in military strategy won him fame.

41–42. In 1300 Guido Vecchio, head of the Polenta family (whose coat of arms bears an eagle) and father of Francesca da Rimini, governed Ravenna and the surrounding territory which included Cervia, a small town on the Adriatic.

43–45. Besieged for many months by French and Guelph troops, the Ghibelline

city of Forlì emerged victorious. In May, 1282, her inhabitants led by Guido da Montefeltro broke the siege and massacred the opposing army. However, in 1300 Forlì was dominated by the tyrannical Ordelaffi family whose insignia bore a green lion ("beneath the verdant claws," l. 45).

46–48. In return for their services, the city of Rimini gave her ruling family the castle of Verrucchio. Malatesta, lord of Rimini from 1295 to 1312, and his first born son, Malatestino, are respectively the "Old" and "New" Mastiffs. Having defeated the Ghibellines of Rimini in 1295, Malatesta captured Montagna de' Parcitati, the head of the party, who was subsequently murdered in prison by Malatestino.

the cities by Lamone and Santerno
  are governed by the Lion of the White Lair           50
  who changes parties every change of season.
As for the town whose side the Savio bathes:
  just as it lies between the hills and plains,
  it lives between freedom and tyranny.
And now I beg you tell us who you are—               55
  grant me my wish as yours was granted you—
  so that your fame may hold its own on earth."
And when the fire, in its own way, had roared
  a while, the flame's sharp tip began to sway
  to and fro, then released a blow of words:          60
"If I thought that I were speaking to a soul
  who someday might return to see the world,
  most certainly this flame would cease to flicker;
but since no one, if I have heard the truth,
  ever returns alive from this deep pit,               65
  with no fear of dishonor I answer you:
I was a man of arms and then a friar,
  believing with the cord to make amends;
  and surely my belief would have come true
were it not for that High Priest (his soul be damned!)   70
  who put me back among my early sins;
  I want to tell you why and how it happened.
While I still had the form of the bones and flesh
  my mother gave me, all my actions were
  not those of a lion, but those of a fox;             75
the wiles and covert paths, I knew them all,
  and so employed my art that rumor of me
  spread to the farthest limits of the earth.
When I saw that the time of life had come
  for me, as it must come for every man,               80
  to lower the sails and gather in the lines,
things I once found pleasure in then grieved me;
  repentant and confessed, I took the vows
  a monk takes. And, oh, to think it could have worked!
And then the Prince of the New Pharisees               85
  chose to wage war upon the Lateran

---

49–51. The cities of Faenza (situated on the Lamone River) and Imola (near the Santerno) were governed by Maghinardo Pagani da Susinana whose coat of arms bore a blue lion on a white field.

52–54. Unlike the other cities mentioned by Guido, Cesena was not ruled by a despot; rather, her government, although not completely determined by the people, was in the hands of an able ruler, Galasso da Montefeltro, a cousin of Guido.

67–71. In 1296 Guido joined the Franciscan order. The reason for his harsh condemnation of Pope Boniface VIII ("that High Priest") is found in lines 85–111.

85–90. In 1297 the struggle between Boniface VIII ("the Prince of the New Pharisees") and the Colonna family (who lived near the Lateran palace, the pope's residence, and who did not consider the resignation of Celestine V valid) erupted into open conflict. Boniface did not launch his crusade against the traditional rivals—Saracens and Jews (l. 87)—but rather against his fellow Christians, faithful warriors of the Church who neither aided the Saracens during the conquest of Acre in 1291 (the last Christian stronghold in the Holy Land), nor disobeyed the interdict on commerce with Mohammedan lands (ll. 89–90).

instead of fighting Saracens or Jews,
for all his enemies were Christian souls,
  (none among the ones who conquered Acri,
  none a trader in the Sultan's kingdom).     90
His lofty Papal Seat, his sacred vows
  were no concern to him, nor was the cord
  I wore (that once made those it girded leaner).
As Constantine once had Silvestro brought
  from Mount Soracte to cure his leprosy,     95
  so this one sought me out as his physician
to cure his burning fever caused by pride.
  He asked me to advise him. I was silent,
  for his words were drunken. Then he spoke again:
'Fear not, I tell you: the sin you will commit,     100
  it is forgiven. Now you will teach me how
  I can level Palestrina to the ground.
Mine is the power, as you cannot deny,
  to lock and unlock Heaven. Two keys I have,
  those keys my predecessor did not cherish.'     105
And when his weighty arguments had forced me
  to the point that silence seemed the poorer choice,
  I said: 'Father, since you grant me absolution
for the sin I find I must fall into now:
  ample promise with a scant fulfillment     110
  will bring you triumph on your lofty throne.'
Saint Francis came to get me when I died,
  but one of the black Cherubim cried out:
  'Don't touch him, don't cheat me of what is mine!
He must come down to join my other servants     115
  for the false counsel he gave. From then to now
  I have been ready at his hair, because
one cannot be absolved unless repentant,
  nor can one both repent and will a thing
  at once—the one is cancelled by the other!'     120
O wretched me! How I shook when he took me,
  saying: 'Perhaps you never stopped to think
  that I might be somewhat of a logician!'
He took me down to Minòs, who eight times
  twisted his tail around his hardened back,     125
  then in his rage he bit it, and announced:
'He goes with those the thievish fire burns.'

---

102. The Colonna family, excommunicated by Boniface, took refuge in their
fortress at Palestrina (twenty-five miles
east of Rome) which was able to withstand the onslaughts of papal troops. Acting on Guido's counsel (ll. 110–111),
Boniface promised (but without serious
intentions) to grant complete pardon to
the Colonna family, who then surrendered
and, consequently, lost everything.
104–105. Deceived by Boniface who was
to be his successor, Celestine V renounced

the papacy ("those two keys") in 1294.
108–109. Guido's principal error was
self-deception: A man cannot be absolved
from a sin before he commits it, and
moreover, he cannot direct his will toward
committing a sin and repent it at the same
time (ll. 118–120).
113. Some of the Cherubim (the *eighth*
order of angels) were transformed into
demons for their rebellion against God;
appropriately they appear in the *eighth*
circle and the *eighth bolgia* of Hell.

And here you see me now, lost, wrapped this way,
   moving, as I do, with my resentment."
When he had brought his story to a close,             130
   the flame, in grievous pain, departed from us
   gnarling and flickering its pointed horn.
My guide and I moved farther on; we climbed
   the ridge until we stood on the next arch
   that spans the fosse where penalties are paid        135
by those who, sowing discord, earned Hell's wages.

### CANTO XXVIII

In the ninth *bolgia* the Pilgrim is overwhelmed by the sight of mutilated, bloody shades, many of whom are ripped open with the entrails spilling out. They are the Sowers of Scandal and Schism, and among them are Mahomet, Ali, Pier da Medicina, Gaius Scribonius Curio, Mosca de' Lamberti, and Bertran de Born. All bemoan their painful lot, and Mahomet and Pier da Medicina relay warnings through the Pilgrim to certain living Italians who are soon to meet terrible ends. Bertran de Born, who comes carrying his head in his hand like a lantern, is a particularly arresting example of a Dantean *contrapasso*.

Who could, even in the simplest kind of prose
   describe in full the scene of blood and wounds
   that I saw now—no matter how he tries!
Certainly any tongue would have to fail:
   man's memory and man's vocabulary                5
   are not enough to comprehend such pain.
If one could bring together all the wounded
   who once upon the fateful soil of Puglia
   grieved for their life's-blood spilled by the Romans,
and spilled again in the long years of the war       10
   that ended in great spoils of golden rings
   (as Livy's history tells, that does not err),
and pile them with the ones who felt the blows
   when they stood up against great Robert Guiscard,

7–12. In order to introduce the great number of maimed and dismembered shades which will present themselves in the ninth *bolgia,* Dante "piles" together references to a number of bloody battles which took place in Puglia, the southeastern section of the Italian peninsula. The first of the series, in which the Pugliese "grieved for their life's-blood spilled by the Romans" (l. 9), is the long war between the Samnites and the Romans (343–290 B.C.). The next, "the long years of the war / that ended in great spoils of golden rings" (ll. 10–11), is the Second Punic War which Hannibal's legions fought against Rome (218–201 B.C.). Livy writes that after the battle of Cannae (where Hannibal defeated the Romans, 216 B.C.), the Carthaginians gathered three bushels of rings from the fingers of dead Romans.

14. "Robert Guiscard": In the eleventh century Robert Guiscard (ca. 1015–1085), a noble Norman adventurer, gained control of most of southern Italy and became duke of Apulia and Calabria, as well as gonfalonier of the Church (1059). For the next two decades he battled the schismatic Greeks and the Saracens for the Church in the south of Italy. Later he fought for the Church in the east, raised a siege against Pope Gregory VII (1084), and died at the age of seventy, still engaged in warfare.

and with those others whose bones are still in heaps   15
at Ceprano (there where every Puglian
   turned traitor), and add those from Tagliacozzo
   where old Alardo conquered, weaponless—
if all these maimed with limbs lopped off or pierced
   were brought together, the scene would be nothing   20
   to compare with the foul ninth *bolgia's* bloody sight.
No wine cask with its stave or cant-bar sprung
   was ever split the way I saw someone
   ripped open from his chin to where we fart.
Between his legs his guts spilled out, with the heart   25
   and other vital parts, and the dirty sack
   that turns to shit whatever the mouth gulps down.
While I stood staring into his misery,
   he looked at me and with both hands he opened
   his chest and said: "See how I tear myself!   30
See how Mahomet is deformed and torn!
   In front of me, and weeping, Ali walks,
   his face cleft from his chin up to the crown.
The souls that you see passing in this ditch
   were all sowers of scandal and schism in life,   35
   and so in death you see them torn asunder.
A devil stands back there who trims us all
   in this cruel way, and each one of this mob
   receives anew the blade of the devil's sword
each time we make one round of this sad road,   40
   because the wounds have all healed up again
   by the time each one presents himself once more.
But who are you there gawking from the bridge
   and trying to put off, perhaps, fulfillment
   of the sentence passed on you when you confessed?"   45
"Death does not have him yet, he is not here
   to suffer for his guilt," my master answered;
   "but that he may have full experience,
I, who am dead, must lead him through this Hell

---

15–18. A further comparison between bloody battles in Puglia and the ninth *bolgia*: In 1266 Charles of Anjou marched against the armies of Manfred, king of Sicily. Manfred blocked the passes leading to the south, but the pass at Ceprano was abandoned by its traitorous defenders. Charles then advanced unhindered and defeated the Sicilians at Benevento, killing Manfred. In reality, then, the battle did not take place at Ceprano, but at Benevento.

The final example in the lengthy series of battles was a continuation of the hostilities between Charles of Anjou and the followers of Manfred. In 1268 at the battle of Tagliacozzo Charles adopted the suggestions of his general Érard de Valéry ("Alardo") and won the encounter. Although Érard's strategy was one of wit rather than force (a "hidden" reserve

troop entered the battle at the last minute when Manfred's nephew Conradin seemed to have won), it can hardly be said that "old Alardo" conquered without arms.

31. "Mahomet": founder of the Mohammedan religion, born at Mecca about 570 and died in 632. His punishment, to be split open from the crotch to the chin, together with the complementary punishment of Ali, represents Dante's belief that they were initiators of the great schism between the Christian Church and Mohammedanism. Many of Dante's contemporaries thought that Mahomet was originally a Christian and a cardinal who wanted to become pope.

32. "Ali": (ca. 600–661) the first of Mahomet's followers, who married the prophet's daughter Fatima. Mahomet died in 632, and Ali assumed the caliphate in 656.

from round to round, down to the very bottom,        50
and this is as true as my presence speaking here."
More than a hundred in that ditch stopped short
    to look at me when they had heard his words,
    forgetting in their stupor what they suffered.
"And you, who will behold the sun, perhaps        55
    quite soon, tell Fra Dolcino that unless
    he wants to follow me here quick, he'd better
stock up on food, or else the binding snows
    will give the Novarese their victory,
    a conquest not won easily otherwise."        60
With the heel of one foot raised to take a step
    Mahomet said these words to me, and then
    stretched out and down his foot and moved away.
Another, with his throat slit, and his nose
    cut off as far as where the eyebrows start        65
    (and he only had a single ear to show),
who had stopped like all the rest to stare in wonder,
    stepped out from the group and opened up his throat
    that ran with red from all sides of his wound,
and spoke: "O you whom guilt does not condemn,        70
    whom I have seen in Italy up there,
    unless I am deceived by similarity,
recall to mind Pier da Medicina,
    should you return to see the gentle plain
    declining from Vercelli to Marcabò,        75
and inform the two best citizens of Fano—
    tell Messer Guido and tell Angiolello—
    that, if our foresight here is no deception,
from their ship they shall be hurled bound in a sack
    to drown in the water near Cattolica,        80
    the victims of a tyrant's treachery;
between the isles of Cyprus and Mallorca

56–60. "Fra Dolcino": (died 1307) though not a monk as his name would seem to indicate, the leader of a religious sect banned as heretical by Pope Clement V in 1305. Dolcino's sect, the Apostolic Brothers, preached the return of religion to the simplicity of apostolic times, and among their tenets was community of property and sharing of women. When Clement V ordered the eradication of the Brothers, Dolcino and his followers retreated to the hills near Novara, where they withstood the papal forces for over a year until starvation conquered them. Dolcino and his companion, Margaret of Trent, were burned at the stake in 1307.

73. "Pier da Medicina": Although nothing certain is known about the life of this sinner, we do know that his home was in Medicina, a town in the Po River Valley ("the gentle plain," which lies between the towns of Vercelli and Marcabò, l. 74) near Bologna. According to the early commentator Benvenuto da Imola, Pier da Medicina was the instigator of strife between the Polenta and Malatesta families.

77–90. "tell Messer Guido and tell Angiolello": Guido del Cassero and Angiolello di Carignano, leading citizens of Fano, a small town on the Adriatic, south of Rimini, were invited by Malatestino (the "traitor, who sees only with one eye," l. 85) to meet on a ship off the coastal city of Cattolica, which lies between Rimini and Fano. There Malatestino, lord of Rimini from 1312 to 1317, ordered them thrown overboard in order that he might gain control of Fano. Already dead, the two victims of Malatestino's treachery will not have to pray to escape "Focara's wind," l. 90), the terribly destructive gale which preyed on vessels passing by the promontory of Focara near Cattolica.

so great a crime Neptune never witnessed
among the deeds of pirates or the Argives.
That traitor, who sees only with one eye          85
and rules the land that someone with me here
wishes he'd never fed his eyes upon,
will have them come to join him in a parley,
then see to it they do not waste their breath
on vows or prayers to escape Focara's wind."          90
And I to him: "If you want me to bring back
to those on earth your message—who is the one
sated with the bitter sight? Show him to me."
At once he grabbed the jaws of a companion
standing near by, and squeezed his mouth half-open,          95
announcing, "Here he is, and he is mute.
This man, in exile, drowned all Caesar's doubts
and helped him cast the die, when he insisted:
'a man prepared, who hesitates, is lost.'"
How helpless and bewildered he appeared,          100
his tongue hacked off as far down as the throat,
this Curio, once so bold and quick to speak!
And one who had both arms but had no hands,
raising the gory stumps in the filthy air
so that the blood dripped down and smeared his face,          105
cried: "You, no doubt, also remember Mosca,
who said, alas, 'What's done is over with,'
and sowed the seed of discord for the Tuscans."
"And of death for all your clan," I quickly said,
and he, this fresh wound added to his wound,          110
turned and went off like one gone mad from pain.
But I remained to watch the multitude,
and saw a thing that I would be afraid
to tell about without more evidence,
were I not reassured by my own conscience—          115
that good companion enheartening a man
beneath the breastplate of its purity.
I saw it, I'm sure, and I seem to see it still:
a body with no head that moved along,
moving no differently from all the rest;          120
he held his severed head up by its hair,
swinging it in one hand just like a lantern,
and as it looked at us it said: "Alas!"
Of his own self he made himself a light

92–93. The Pilgrim refers to what Pier
da Medicina said earlier about "someone"
who "wishes he'd never fed his eyes upon"
Rimini (ll. 86–87).

97–102. Caius Scribonius Curio wishes
he had never seen Rimini, the city near
which the Rubicon river empties into the
Adriatic. Once a Roman tribune under
Pompey, Curio defected to Caesar's side,
and, when the Roman general hesitated to
cross the Rubicon, Curio convinced him
to cross and march on Rome. At that

time the Rubicon formed the boundary
between Gaul and the Roman Republic;
Caesar's decision to cross it precipitated
the Roman Civil War.

106–108. "Mosca": Mosca, about whom
the Pilgrim earlier had asked Ciacco
(Canto VI, l. 80), was a member of the
Lamberti family of Florence. His counsel ("What's done is over with," l. 107)
was the cause of the division of Florence
into the feuding Guelph and Ghilbelline
parties.

and they were two in one and one in two.     125
  How could this be? He who ordained it knows.
And when he had arrived below our bridge,
  he raised the arm that held the head up high
  to let it speak to us at closer range.
It spoke: "Now see the monstrous punishment,     130
  you there still breathing, looking at the dead,
  see if you find anything else like this;
and that you may report on me up there,
  know that I am Bertran de Born, the one
  who evilly encouraged the young king.     135
Father and son I set against each other:
  Achitophel with his wicked instigations
  did not do more with Absalom and David.
Because I cut the bonds of persons joined
  I bear my head cut off from its life-source     140
  which is back there, alas, within its trunk.
In me you see the perfect *contrapasso!*"

CANTO XXIX

When the Pilgrim is rebuked by his mentor for his inappropriate
interest in these wretched shades, he replies that he was looking for
someone. Virgil, who can read the Pilgrim's mind, knows that this
was Geri del Bello. They discuss Geri until they reach the edge of
the next *bolgia* where all types of Falsifiers are punished. There
miserable, shrieking shades are afflicted with diseases of various
kinds and are arranged in various positions. Sitting back to back,
madly scratching their leprous sores, are the shades of Griffolino da
Arezzo and one Capocchio, who talk to the Pilgrim, the latter shade
making wisecracks about the Sienese.

The crowds, the countless, different mutilations
  had stunned my eyes and left them so confused
  they wanted to keep looking and to weep,
but Virgil said: "What are you staring at?
  Why do your eyes insist on drowning there     5
  below, among those wretched, broken shades?
You did not act this way in other *bolge*.
  If you hope to count them one by one, remember
  the valley winds some twenty-two miles around;

---

134–136. "Bertran de Born": One of the
greatest of the Provençal troubadours,
Bertran de Born lived in the second half
of the twelfth century. He suffers here
in Hell for having caused the rebellion
of Prince Henry (the "young king,' l. 135)
against his father Henry II, king of England.

137–138. Dante compares Bertran de
Born's evil counsel with that of Achitophel. Once the aide of David, Achitophel
the Gilonite provoked Absalom's rebellion against David, his father and king.
See 2 Samuel, 15–17.

10. The sun, then, is directly overhead,
indicating that it is midday in Jerusalem.

and already the moon is underneath our feet;  10
    the time remaining to us now is short—
    and there is more to see than you see here."
"If you had taken time to find out what
    I was looking for," I started telling him,
    "perhaps you would have let me stay there longer."  15
My guide was moving on, with me behind him
    answering as I did while we went on,
    and adding: "Somewhere down along this ditch
that I was staring at a while ago,
    I think there is a spirit of my family  20
    mourning the guilt that's paid so dear down there."
And then my master said: "From this time on
    you should not waste another thought on him;
    think on ahead, and let him stay behind,
for I saw him standing underneath the bridge  25
    pointing at you, and threatening with his gesture,
    and I heard his name called out: Geri del Bello.
That was the moment you were so absorbed
    with him who was the lord of Altaforte
    that you did not look his way before he left."  30
"Alas, my guide," I answered him, "his death
    by violence which has not yet been avenged
    by anyone who shares in his disgrace,
made him resentful, and I suppose for this
    he went away without a word to me,  35
    and because he did I feel great piety."
We spoke of this until we reached the start
    of the bridge across the next *bolgia*, from which
    the bottom, with more light, might have been seen.
Having come to stand above the final cloister  40
    of Malebolge, we saw it spreading out
    revealing to our eyes its congregation.
Weird shrieks of lamentation pierced through me
    like arrow-shafts whose tips are barbed with pity,
    so that my hands were covering my ears.  45
Imagine all the sick in the hospitals
    of Maremma, Valdichiana and Sardinia
    between the months of July and September,
crammed altogether rotting in one ditch—
    such was the misery here; and such a stench  50
    was pouring out as comes from flesh decaying.
Still keeping to our left we made our way

---

27–35. "Geri del Bello": a first cousin of Dante's father. Little is known about him except that he was among those to whom reparation was made in 1269 for damages suffered at the hands of the Ghibellines in 1260, and that he was involved in a blood feud with the Sacchetti family. It was probably one of the Sacchetti who murdered him. Vengeance by kinsmen for a slaying was considered obligatory at the time, and apparently Geri's murder was still unavenged by the Alighieri in 1300.

29. "the lord of Altaforte": Bertran de Born. See Canto XXVIII, ll. 130–142.

47–49. "of Maremma, Valdichiana and Sardinia": Valdichiana and Maremma are swampy areas in Tuscany. Along with the swamps of Sardinia they were famous for breeding malaria and other diseases.

down the long bridge on to the final bank,
and now my sight was clear enough to find
the bottom where the High Lord's ministress,                    55
Justice infallible, metes out her punishment
to falsifiers she registers on earth.
I doubt if all those dying in Aegina
when the air was blowing sick with pestilence
and the animals, down to the smallest worm,                     60
all perished (later on this ancient race,
according to what the poets tell as true,
was born again from families of ants),
offered a scene of greater agony
than was the sight spread out in that dark valley              65
of heaped-up spirits languishing in clumps.
Some sprawled out on others' bellies, some
on others' backs, and some, on hands and knees,
dragged themselves along that squalid alley.
Slowly, in silence, slowly we moved along                       70
looking, listening to the words of all those sick
who had no strength to raise their bodies up.
I saw two sitting, leaning against each other
like pans propped back to back against a fire,
and they were blotched from head to foot with scabs.           75
I never saw a curry-comb applied
by a stable-boy who is harried by his master,
or simply wants to finish and go to bed,
the way those two applied their nails and dug
and dug into their flesh, crazy to ease                         80
the itching that can never find relief.
They worked their nails down, scraping off the scabs
the way one works a knife to scale a bream
or some other fish with larger, tougher scales.
"O you there scraping off your scabs of mail                    85
and even making pincers of your fingers,"
my guide began to speak to one of them,
"so may your finger-nails eternally
suffice their task, tell us: among the many
packed in this place is anyone Italian?"                        90
"Both of us whom you see disfigured here,"
one answered through his tears, "we are Italians.
But you, who ask about us, who are you?"
"I am one accompanying this living man
descending bank from bank," my leader said,                     95
"and I intend to show him all of Hell."
With that each lost the other back's support
and each one, shaky, turned to look at me,
as others did who overheard these words.

---

58–66. This comparison with the sufferers of the tenth *bolgia* concerns the island
of Aegina in the Saronic Gulf. Juno sent a
plague to the island which killed all the
inhabitants except Aeacus. Aeacus prayed
to Jupiter to repopulate the island, and
Jupiter did so by turning ants into men.

My gentle master came up close to me                                  100
   and said: "Now ask them what you want to know,"
   and since he wanted me to speak, I started:
"So may the memory of you not fade
   from the minds of men up there in the first world,
   but rather live on under many suns,                           105
tell me your names and where it was you lived;
   do not let your dreadful, loathsome punishment
   discourage you from speaking openly."
"I'm from Arezzo," one of them replied,
   "and Albert of Siena had me burned,                           110
   but I'm not here for what I died for there;
it's true I told him, jokingly, of course:
   'I know the trick of flying through the air,'
   and he, eager to learn and not too bright,
asked me to demonstrate my art; and only                              115
   just because I didn't make him Daedalus,
   he had me burned by one whose child he was.
But here, to the last *bolgia* of the ten,
   for the alchemy I practiced in the world
   I was condemned by Minòs, who cannot err."                    120
I said to my poet: "Have you ever known
   people as silly as the Sienese?
   Even the French cannot compare with them!"
With that the other leper who was listening
   feigned exception to my quip: "Excluding,                     125
   of course, Stricca, who lived so frugally,
and Niccolo, the first to introduce
   the luxury of the clove for condiment
   into that choice garden where the seed took root,
and surely not that fashionable club                                  130
   where Caccia squandered all his woods and vineyards
   and Abbagliato flaunted his great wit!
That you may know who this is backing you

---

109–117. Most of the commentators identify this man as Griffolino da Arezzo. The story was that Griffolino had led the doltish Alberto da Siena to believe that he could teach him how to fly. Alberto paid him well but, upon discovering the fraud, he denounced Griffolino to the bishop of Siena as a magician, and the bishop had him burned.

122. The Florentines made the citizens of rival Siena the butt of many jokes.

124–126. Capocchio (see below, 1. 136) makes several ironic comments here about the foolishness of the Sienese. Stricca (probably Stricca di Giovanni dei Salimbeni of Siena) was evidently renowned as a spendthrift. The old commentators hold that he was a member of the "Spendthrifts' Brigade" (see 1. 130), a group of young Sienese who wasted their fortunes carelessly.

127–129. "Niccolò": Niccolò de' Salim-

beni was another member of the "Spendthrifts' Club" and possibly the brother of Stricca. He introduced to Siena the use of cloves, then a very expensive spice. Some of the early commentators claim that he roasted pheasants on beds of flaming cloves. In any case Capocchio is referring to Niccolò's careless extravagance as another example of the silliness of the Sienese. The "choice garden" is Siena itself, where any fashionable custom, no matter how foolish, could gain acceptance.

131. "Caccia": Caccia d'Asciano was another member of the "Spendthrifts' Brigade" (that "fashionable club," 1. 130), who squandered his inheritance.

132. "Abbagliato": Abbagliato has been identified as one Bartolomeo dei Folcacchieri, who held office in Siena up to 1300. He was another member of this "fashionable club."

against the Sienese, look sharply at me
    so that my face will give you its own answer,          135
and you will recognize Capocchio's shade,
    betrayer of metals with his alchemy;
    you'll surely recall—if you're the one I think—
how fine an ape of nature I once was."

### CANTO XXX

Capocchio's remarks are interrupted by two mad, naked shades
who dash up, and one of them sinks his teeth into Capocchio's
neck and drags him off; he is Gianni Schicchi and the other is
Myrrha of Cyprus. When they have gone, the Pilgrim sees the ill-
proportioned and immobile shade of Master Adamo, a counterfei-
ter, who explains how members of the Guidi family had persuaded
him to practice his evil art in Romena. He points out the fever-
stricken shades of two infamous liars, Potiphar's Wife and Sinon,
the Greek, whereupon the latter engages Master Adamo in a verbal
battle. Virgil rebukes the Pilgrim for his absorption in such futile
wrangling, but his immediate shame wins Virgil's immediate forgiveness.

In ancient times when Juno was enraged
    against the Thebans because of Semele
    (she showed her wrath on more than one occasion)
she made King Athamas go raving mad:
    so mad that one day when he saw his wife          5
    coming with his two sons in either arm,
he cried: "Let's spread the nets, so I can catch
    the lioness with her lion-cubs at the pass!"
    Then he spread out his insane hands, like talons
and, seizing one of his two sons, Learchus,          10
    he whirled him round and smashed him on a rock.
    She drowned herself with the other in her arms.
And when the wheel of Fortune brought down low
    the immeasurable haughtiness of Trojans,
    destroying in their downfall king and kingdom,          15
Hecuba sad, in misery, a slave

---

136. "Capocchio's": Capocchio is the
name (or nickname) of a man who in
1293 was burned alive in Siena for alchemy. Apparently Dante had known him;
according to the early commentators, it
was in their student days.
1–12. Jupiter's predilection for mortal
women always enraged Juno, his wife. In
this case her ire was provoked by her
husband's dalliance with Semele, the
daughter of Cadmus, king of Thebes, who
bore him Bacchus. Having vowed to wreak
revenge on her and her family, Juno not
only had Semele struck by lightning, but
also caused King Athamas, the husband

of Ino (Semele's sister), to go insane. In
his demented state he killed his son
Learchus. Ino drowned herself and her
other son, Melicertes.
16–21. Having triumphed over the
Trojans, the Greeks returned to their
homeland bearing with them as a slave
Hecuba, wife of Priam, king of Troy.
She was also to make some tragic discoveries: she saw Polyxena, her daughter,
slain on the grave of Achilles (l. 17) and
she discovered her son Polydorus dead
and unburied on the coast of Thrace (ll.
18–19). So great was her grief that she
became insane.

(after she saw Polyxena lie slain,
after this grieving mother found her son
Polydorus left unburied on the shore),
    now gone quite mad, went barking like a dog—     20
    it was the weight of grief that snapped her mind.
But never in Thebes or Troy were madmen seen
    driven to acts of such ferocity
    against their victims, animal or human,
as two shades I saw white with rage and naked,     25
    running, snapping crazily at things in sight,
    like pigs, directionless, broken from their pen.
One, landing on Capocchio sank his teeth
    into his neck, and started dragging him
    along, scraping his belly on the rocky ground.     30
The Aretine spoke, shaking where he sat:
    "You see that batty shade? He's Gianni Schicchi!
    He's rabid and he treats us all that way."
"Oh," I answered, "so may that other shade
    never sink its teeth in you—if you don't mind,     35
    please tell me who it is before it's gone."
And he to me: "That is the ancient shade
    of Myrrha, the depraved one, who became,
    against love's laws, too much her father's friend.
She went to him, and there she sinned in love,     40
    pretending that her body was another's—
    just as the other there fleeing in the distance,
contrived to make his own the 'queen of studs',
    pretending that he was Buoso Donati,
    making his will and giving it due form."     45
Now that the rabid pair had come and gone
    (from whom I never took my eyes away),
    I turned to watch the other evil shades.
And there I saw a soul shaped like a lute,
    if only he'd been cut off from his legs     50
    below the belly, where they divide in two.
The bloating dropsy, disproportioning
    the body's parts with unconverted humors

31. "the Aretine": He is Griffolino d'Arezzo. See Canto XXIX, ll. 109–120.

32. "Gianni Schicchi!": A member of the Florentine Cavalcanti family, Gianni Schicchi was well known for his mimetic virtuosity. Simone Donati, keeping his father's death a secret in order that he might change the will to his advantage, engaged Gianni to impersonate his dead father (Buoso Donati, l. 44) and alter the latter's will. The plan was carried out to perfection, and in the process Gianni willed himself, among other things, a prize mare ("the 'queen of studs,'" l. 43).

33. Gianni Schicchi, then, is insane as must be also his companion in the mad fight through this *bolgia*. These are the only two sinners in the *Divine Comedy* who are mentally deranged, so that it is most fitting that the canto should open with a reminder of two famous cases of insanity in classical mythology.

37–41. The other self-falsifier darting about the *bolgia* with Gianni Schicchi is Myrrha, who, overpowered by an incestuous desire for her father, King Cinyras of Cyprus, went incognita to his bed where they made love. Discovering the deception, Cinyras vowed to kill her; however, Myrrha escaped and wandered about until the gods took pity on her and transformed her into a myrrh tree, from which Adonis, the child conceived in the incestuous union, was born.

so that the face, matched with the paunch, was puny,
forced him to keep his parched lips wide apart,                    55
  as a man who suffers thirst from raging fever
  has one lip curling up, the other sagging.
"O you who bear no punishment at all
  (I can't think why) within this world of sorrow,"
  he said to us, "pause here and look upon              60
the misery of one Master Adamo:
  in life I had all that I could desire,
  and now, alas, I crave a drop of water.
The little streams that flow from the green hills
  of Casentino, descending to the Arno             65
  keeping their banks so cool and soft with moisture
forever flow before me, haunting me;
  and the image of them leaves me far more parched
  than the sickness that has dried my shriveled face.
Relentless Justice, tantalizing me,               70
  exploits the countryside that knew my sin,
  to draw from me ever new sighs of pain:
I still can see Romena where I learned
  to falsify the coin stamped with the Baptist,
  for which I paid with my burned body there;         75
but if I could see down here the wretched souls
  of Guido or Alexander or their brother,
  I would not exchange the sight for Branda's fountain.
One is here already, if those maniacs
  running around this place have told the truth,        80
  but what good is it, with my useless legs?
If only I were lighter, just enough
  to move one inch in every hundred years,
  I would have started on my way by now
to find him somewhere in this gruesome lot,          85
  although this ditch winds round eleven miles
  and is at least a half a mile across.
It's their fault I am here with this choice family:
  *they* encouraged me to turn out florins
  whose gold contained three carats' worth of alloy."     90
And I to him: "Who are those two poor souls
  lying to the right, close to your body's boundary,
  steaming like wet hands in wintertime?"
"When I poured into this ditch, I found them here,"
  he answered, "and they haven't budged since then,       95
  and I doubt they'll move through all eternity.

64–66. "Casentino": a hilly region southeast of Florence where the head-waters of the Arno River spread out.

76–78. Master Adamo, as much as he craves a "drop of water" (l. 63), would forego that pleasure if only he could see here in Hell the Conti Guidi (Guido, Alexander, Aghinolfo, and Ildebrando), who encouraged him in crime. "Branda's fountain" (l. 78): the name of a spring which once flowed near Romena. Often confused with it is the still-functioning fountain of the same name at Siena.

79. Guido (died 1292) is the only one of the four Conti Guidi who died before 1300.

90. The florin was supposed to contain twenty-four carat gold; those of Master Adamo had twenty-one carats.

One is the false accuser of young Joseph;
   the other is false Sinon, the Greek in Troy:
    it's their burning fever makes them smell so bad."
And one of them, perhaps somewhat offended        100
   at the kind of introduction he received,
    with his fist struck out at the distended belly,
which responded like a drum reverberating;
   and Master Adam struck him in the face
    with an arm as strong as the fist he had received,    105
and he said to him: "Although I am not free
   to move around, with swollen legs like these,
    I have a ready arm for such occasions."
"*But* it was *not* as free and ready, was it,"
   the other answered, "when you went to the stake?    110
    Of course, when you were coining, it was readier!"
And he with the dropsy: "*Now* you tell the truth,
   but you were not as full of truth that time
    when you were asked to tell the truth at Troy!"
"My words were false—so were the coins you made,"    115
   said Sinon, "and *I* am here for one false act
    but *you* for more than any fiend in hell!"
"The horse, recall the horse, you falsifier,"
   the bloated paunch was quick to answer back,
    "may it burn your guts that all the world remembers!"    120
"May your guts burn with thirst that cracks your tongue,"
   the Greek said, "may they burn with rotting humors
    that swell your hedge of a paunch to block your eyes!"
And then the money-man: "So there you go,
   your evil mouth pours out its filth as usual;    125
    for if *I* thirst, and humors swell me up,
*you* burn more, and your head is fit to split,
   and it wouldn't take much coaxing to convince you
    to lap the mirror of Narcissus dry!"
I was listening, all absorbed in this debate,    130
   when the master said to me: "Keep right on looking,
    a little more, and I shall lose my patience."
I heard the note of anger in his voice
   and turned to him; I was so full of shame
    that it still haunts my memory today.    135
Like one asleep who dreams himself in trouble
   and in his dream he wishes he were dreaming,
    longing for that which is, as if it were not,
just so I found myself: unable to speak,
   longing to beg for pardon and already    140

---

97. Potiphar's wife falsely accused Joseph, son of Jacob and Rachel, of trying to seduce her, while in reality it was she who made improper amorous advances.

98. Sinon was left behind by his fellow Greek soldiers in accordance with the master plan for the capture of Troy. Taken prisoner by the Trojans, and misrepresenting his position with the Greeks, he persuaded them to bring the wooden horse into the city.

129. "the mirror of Narcissus": water. According to the myth, Narcissus, enamoured with his own reflection in a pond, continued to gaze at it until he died.

begging for pardon, not knowing that I did.
"Less shame than yours would wash away a fault
    greater than yours has been," my master said,
    "and so forget about it, do not be sad.
If ever again you should meet up with men          145
    engaging in this kind of futile wrangling,
    remember I am always at your side;
to have a taste for talk like this is vulgar!"

### CANTO XXXI

Through the murky air they move, up across the bank which separates the Malebolge from the pit of Hell, the Ninth (and last)
Circle of the *Inferno*. From a distance is heard the blast of a
mighty horn which turns out to have been that of the giant
Nimrod. He and other giants, including Ephialtes, are fixed eternally in the pit of Hell; are all chained except Antaeus, who at Virgil's request, lifts the two poets in his monstrous hand and deposits
them below him, on the lake of ice known as Cocytus.

The very tongue that first spoke—stinging me,
    making the blood rush up to both my cheeks—
    then gave the remedy to ease the pain,
just as, so I have heard, Achilles' lance,
    belonging to his father, was the source        5
    of pain, and then of balm, to him it struck.
Turning our backs on that trench of misery,
    gaining the bank again that walls it in,
    we cut across, walking in dead silence.
Here it was less than night and less than day,    10
    so that my eyes could not see far ahead;
    but then I heard the blast of some high horn
which would have made a thunder-clap sound dim;
    it drew my eyes directly to one place,
    as they retraced the sound's path to its source.  15
After the tragic rout when Charlemagne
    lost all his faithful, holy paladins,
    the sound of Roland's horn was not as ominous.

---

4–6. Dante aptly compares the nature of
Virgil's words at the end of Canto XXX
(first rebuking then comforting) to the
spear of Achilles and his father, Peleus,
which reputedly could heal the wounds
it had inflicted.

16–18. In the medieval French epic *La
Chanson de Roland*, the title character,
one of Charlemagne's "holy paladins" (l.

17), was assigned to the rear guard on the
return from an expedition in Spain. At
Roncevalles in the Pyrenees the Saracens
attacked, and Roland, proud to the point
of foolishness, refused to sound his horn
until total extermination was imminent
[*The Song of Roland*, ll. 1695 ff., pp. 804
ff. in this volume.—J. C. McG.]

Keeping my eyes still turned that way, I soon
  made out what seemed to be high, clustered towers.    20
  "Master," I said, "what city lies ahead?"
"Because you try to penetrate the shadows,"
  he said to me, "from much too far away,
  you confuse the truth with your imagination.
You will see clearly when you reach that place    25
  how much the eyes may be deceived by distance,
  and so, just push ahead a little more."
Then lovingly he took me by the hand
  and said: "But now, before we go on farther,
  to prepare you for the truth that could seem strange,    30
I'll tell you these aren't towers, they are giants;
  they're standing in the well around the bank—
  all of them hidden from their navels down."
As, when the fog begins to thin and clear,
  the sight can slowly make out more and more    35
  what is hidden in the mist that clogs the air,
so, as I pierced the thick and murky air,
  approaching slowly, closer to the well,
  confusion cleared and my fear took on more shape.
For just as Montereggion is crowned with towers    40
  soaring high above its curving ramparts,
so, on the bank that runs around the well,
  towering with only half their bodies out,
  stood the terrible giants, forever threatened
  by Jupiter in the heavens when he thunders.    45
And now I could make out one of the faces,
  the shoulders, the chest and a good part of the belly
  and, down along the sides, the two great arms.
Nature, when she cast away the mold
  for shaping beasts like these, without a doubt    50
  did well, depriving Mars of more such agents.

19–127. From afar, the Pilgrim, who has mistaken the great giants for towers, asks Virgil, "what city lies ahead?" a question which should recall the scene before the gates of the walled city of Dis in Cantos VIII and IX. By this device not only are we introduced to a new division of Hell (the Pit of the Giants and Cocytus: Complex Fraud), but also the unified nature of Lower Hell (i.e., from the City of Dis to Cocytus) is underscored. And the Fallen Angels perched on the wall who shut the gate to the City in Virgil's face (Canto VIII) are analogous to the Giants here, who stand at the boundary of the lowest part of Hell. The fact that the Giants—in terms of pagan mythology—the Fallen Angels—in terms of the Judeo-Christian tradition—both rebelled against their respective gods, not only links the parts of Lower Hell together, but also suggests that the bases for all the sins punished in Lower Hell (Heresy, Violence, and Fraud) are Envy and Pride, the sins of both groups of rebels.

40–41. In 1213 the Sienese constructed Montereggioni, a fortress on the crest of a hill eight miles from their city. The specific allusion here is to the fourteen high towers which stood on its perimeter like giant sentries.

49–57. Dante praises the wisdom that Nature showed in discontinuing the race of giants, for Mars (l. 51), the god of war, with the help of the giants could have effectively destroyed mankind. A clear distinction is made between brute animals ("whales / and elephants," ll. 52–53), which Nature rightly allows to live, and giants, whom she made extinct, in that the former do not possess a rational faculty, and therefore are easily subjugated by man.

And if she never did repent of whales
   and elephants, we must consider her,
   on sober thought, all the more just and wary:
for when the faculty of intellect                  55
   is joined with brute force and with evil will,
   no man can win against such an alliance.
His face, it seemed to me, was about as long
   and just as wide as St. Peter's cone in Rome,
   and all his body's bones were in proportion,      60
so that the bank which served to cover him
   from his waist down showed so much height above
   that three tall Frisians on each other's shoulders
could never boast of stretching to his hair,
   for downwards from the place men clasp their cloaks  65
   I saw a generous thirty hand-spans of him.
"Raphel may amech zabi almi!"
   He played these sputtering notes with prideful lips
   for which no sweeter psalm was suitable.
My guide called up to him: "Blathering idiot,      70
   stick to your horn and take it out on that
   when you feel a fit of anger coming on;
search round your neck and you will find the strap
   it's tied to, you poor muddle-headed soul,
   and there's the horn so pretty on your chest."     75
And then he turned to me: "His words accuse him.
   He is Nimrod, through whose infamous device
   the world no longer speaks a common language.
But let's leave him alone and not waste breath,
   for he can no more understand our words        80
   than anyone can understand his language."
We had to walk still farther than before,
   continuing to the left, a full bow's-shot,
   to find another giant, huger and more fierce.
What engineer it took to bind this brute          85
   I cannot say, but there he was, one arm
   pinned to his back, the other locked in front,
with a giant chain winding around him tight
   which, starting from his neck, made five great coils—
   and that was counting only to his waist.        90
"This beast of pride decided he would try
   to pit his strength against almighty Jove,"

---

59. This bronze pine cone measuring over seven feet in height, which now stands in an inner courtyard of the Vatican was, at Dante's time, in the courtyard of St. Peter's.

63. The inhabitants of Friesland, a northern province of the Netherlands, were renowned for their height.

67. Although there have been numerous attempts to interpret these words, I, along with most modern commentators, believe that they are gibberish—the perfect representation of Nimrod's role in the confusion of languages caused by his construction of the Tower of Babel (the "infamous device," l. 77).

77. Orosius, St. Augustine, and other early Christians believed Nimrod to be a giant; and his "infamous device," the Tower of Babel, through which he tried to ascend to Heaven, certainly equates him with the giants who besieged Jupiter.

78. Before the construction of the Tower of Babel all men spoke a common language.

my leader said, "and he has won this prize.
He's Ephialtes who made his great attempt,
 when the giants arose to fill the Gods with panic;   95
 the arms he lifted then, he moves no more."
And I to him: "If it were possible,
 I would really like to have the chance to see
 the fantastic figure of Briareus."
His answer was: "Not far from here you'll see    100
 Antaeus who can speak and is not chained;
 he will set us down in the very pit of sin.
The one you want to see is farther off;
 he too is bound and looks just like this one,
 except for his expression, which is fiercer."    105
No earthquake of the most outrageous force
 ever shook a tower with such violence
 as, suddenly, Ephialtes shook himself.
I never feared to die as much as then,
 and my fear might have been enough to kill me,   110
 if I had not already seen those chains.
We left him and continued moving on
 and came to where Antaeus stood, extending
 from the well a good five ells up to his head.
"O you who in the celebrated valley    115
 (that saw Scipio become the heir of glory,
 when Hannibal with all his men retreated)
once captured a thousand lions as your quarry
 (and with whose aid, had you chosen to take part
 in the great war with your brothers, the sons of earth  120
would, as many still think, have been the victors),
 do not disdain this modest wish: take us,
 and put us down where ice locks in Cocytus.
Don't make us go to Tityus or Typhon;
 this man can give you what all long for here,   125
 and so bend down, and do not scowl at us.
He still can spread your legend in the world,
 for he yet lives, and long life lies before him,
 unless Grace summons him before his time."
Thus spoke my master, and the giant in haste   130
 stretched out the hands whose formidable grip
 great Hercules once felt, and took my guide.
And Virgil, when he felt the grasping hands,
 called out: "Now come and I'll take hold of you."
 Clasped together, we made a single burden.   135
As the Garisenda looks from underneath

94. "Ephialtes": the son of Neptune and Iphimedia. At the age of nine, together with his brother Otus, he attempted to put Mt. Pelion on top of Ossa in order to ascend to the gods and make war on them. But Apollo slew the brothers.
99. "Briareus": Son of Uranus and Gaea (Earth), the Titan Briareus joined the rebellion against the Olympian deities.

124. "Tityus or Typhon": Also members of the race of Titans.
136–138. 'the Garisenda": Of the two leaning towers in Bologna, the Garisenda, built ca. 1110, is the shorter. The passage of a cloud "against the tower's slant" (l. 138) would make the tower appear to be falling.

its leaning side, at the moment when a cloud
   comes drifting over against the tower's slant,
just so the bending giant Antaeus seemed
   as I looked up, expecting him to topple.     140
I wished then I had gone another way.
But he, most carefully, handed us down
   to the pit that swallows Lucifer with Judas.
And then, the leaning giant immediately
   drew himself up as tall as a ship's mast.     145

CANTO XXXII

They descend farther down into the darkness of the immense
plain of ice in which shades of Traitors are frozen. In the outer
region of the ice lake, Caina, are those who betrayed their kin in
murder; among them, locked in a frozen embrace, are Napoleone
and Alessandro of Mangona, and others are Mordred, Focaccia,
Sassol Mascheroni, and Camicion de' pazzi. Then the two travelers
enter the area of ice called Antenora, and suddenly the Pilgrim
kicks one of the faces sticking out of the ice. He tries to force the
sinner to reveal his name by pulling out his hair, and when another
shade identifies him as Bocca degli Abati, the Pilgrim's fury mounts
still higher. Bocca, himself furious, names several other sinners in
Antenora, including Buoso da Duera, Tesauro dei Beccheria, Gianni
de' Soldanier, Ganelon, and Tibbald. Going farther on, the Pilgrim
sees two heads frozen in one hole, the mouth of one gnawing at the
brain of the other.

If I had words grating and crude enough
   that really could describe this horrid hole
   supporting the converging weight of Hell,
I could squeeze out the juice of my memories
   to the last drop. But I don't have these words,     5
   and so I am reluctant to begin.
To talk about the bottom of the universe
   the way it truly is, is no child's play,
   no task for tongues that gurgle baby-talk.
But may those heavenly ladies aid my verse     10
   who aided Amphion to wall-in Thebes,
   that my words may tell exactly what I saw.
O misbegotten rabble of all rabble
   who crowd this realm, hard even to describe,
   it were better you had lived as sheep or goats!     15
When we reached a point of darkness in the well
   below the giant's feet, farther down the slope,

10–12. The Muses ("those heavenly
ladies," l. 10) helped Amphion, the son
of Jupiter and Antiope, construct a wall
around Thebes. As the legend has it, Amphion played upon his lyre and so charmed
the stones on Mt. Cithaeron that they
came of their own accord and formed the
wall.

and I was gazing still at the high wall,
I heard somebody say: "Watch where you step!
   Be careful that you do not kick the heads           20
   of this brotherhood of miserable souls."
At that I turned around and saw before me
   a lake of ice stretching beneath my feet,
   more like a sheet of glass than frozen water.
In the depths of Austria's wintertime, the Danube     25
   never in all its course showed ice so thick,
   nor did the Don beneath its frigid sky,
as this crust here; for if Mount Tambernic
   or Pietrapana would crash down upon it
   not even at its edges would a crack creak.          30
The way the frogs (in the season when the harvest
   will often haunt the dreams of the peasant girl)
   sit croaking with their muzzles out of water,
so these frigid, livid shades were stuck in ice
   up to where a person's shame appears;            35
   their teeth clicked notes like storks' beaks snapping shut,
And each one kept his face bowed toward the ice:
   the mouth bore testimony to the cold,
   the eyes, to sadness welling in the heart.
I gazed around a while and then looked down,        40
   and by my feet I saw two figures clasped
   so tight that one's hair could have been the other's.
"Tell me, you two, pressing your chests together,"
   I asked them, "who are you?" Both stretched their necks
   and when they had their faces raised toward me,     45
their eyes, which had before been only glazed,
   dripped tears down to their lips and the cold froze
   the tears between them, locking the pair more tightly.
Wood to wood with iron was never clamped
   so firm! And the two of them like billy-goats     50
   were butting at each other, mad with anger.
Another one with both ears frozen off,
   and head still bowed over his icy mirror,
   cried out: "What makes you look at us so hard?
If you're interested to know who these two are:     55
   the valley where Bisenzio's waters flow
   belonged to them and to their father, Albert;
the same womb bore them both, and if you scour
   all of Caïna, you will not turn up one

---

27. The river Don which has its source
in the heart of Russia would naturally be
icebound in the frigid Russian winter.
28–30. "Tambernic": has never been
successfully identified. The older commentators place it in the Balkans. "Pietrapana": probably a rocky peak in the
northwest corner of Tuscany, today called
Pania della Croce.
55–58. The two brothers were Napoleone and Alessandro, sons of Count Al-

berto of Mangona, who owned part of the
valley of the Bisenzio near Florence. The
two quarreled often and eventually killed
each other in a fight concerning their inheritance.
59. "Caïna": The icy ring of Cocytus is
named Caïna after Cain, who slew his
brother Abel. Thus, in the first division of
this, the Ninth Circle, are punished those
treacherous shades who murderously violated family bonds.

who's more deserving of this frozen aspic— 60
not him who had his breast and shadow pierced
with one thrust of the lance from Arthur's hand;
not Focaccia; not even this one here
whose head gets in my way and blocks my view,
known in the world as Sassol Mascheroni, 65
and if you're Tuscan you must know who he was.
To save me from your asking for more news:
I was Camicion de' Pazzi, and I await
Carlin whose guilt will make my own seem less."
Farther on I saw a thousand dog-like faces 70
purple from the cold. That's why I shudder,
and always will, when I see a frozen pond.
While we were getting closer to the center
of the universe where all weights must converge
and I was shivering in the eternal chill— 75
by fate or chance or willfully perhaps,
I do not know—but stepping among the heads,
my foot kicked hard against one of those faces.
Weeping he screamed: "Why are you kicking me?
You have not come to take revenge on me 80
for Montaperti, have you? Why bother me?"
And I: "My master, please wait here for me,
let me clear up a doubt concerning this one,
then I shall be as rapid as you wish."
My leader stopped, and to that wretch who still 85
had not let up in his barrage of curses,
I said: "Who are you, insulting other people?"
"And you, who are *you* who march through Antenora
kicking other people in their faces?
No living man could kick as hard!" he answered. 90
"I am a living man," was my reply,
"and it might serve you well, if you seek fame,

61–62. Mordred, the wicked nephew of King Arthur, tried to kill the king and take his kingdom. But Arthur pierced him with such a mighty blow that when the lance was pulled from the dying traitor a ray of sunlight traversed his body and interrupted Mordred's shadow. The story is told in the Old French romance *Lancelot du Lac*, the book which Francesca claims led her astray with Paolo in Canto V, l. 127.

63. "Focaccia": one of the Cancellieri family of Pistoia and a member of the White party. His treacherous murder of his cousin, Detto de' Cancellieri (a Black), was possibly the act which led to the Florentine intervention in Pistoian affairs.

65. "Sassol Mascheroni": The early commentators say that Sassol Mascheroni was a member of the Toschi family in Florence who murdered his nephew in order to gain his inheritance.

68–69. "Camicion de' Pazzi": Nothing is known of Camicion de' Pazzi except that he murdered one Umbertino, a relative. Another of Camicion's kin, Carlino de' Pazzi (l. 69) from Valdarno, was still alive when the Pilgrim's conversation with Camicion was taking place. But Camicion already knew that Carlino in July, 1302, would accept a bribe to surrender the castle of Piantravigne to the Blacks of Florence.

88. Dante and Virgil have passed into the second division of Cocytus, named Antenora after the Trojan warrior who, according to one legend, betrayed his city to the Greeks. In this round are tormented those who committed acts of treachery against country, city, or political party.

for me to put your name down in my notes."
And he said: "That's the last thing I would want!
That's not the way to flatter in these lowlands!                95
Stop pestering me like this—get out of here!"
At that I grabbed him by his hair in back
and said: "You'd better tell me who you are
or else I'll not leave one hair on your head."
And he to me: "Go on and strip me bald                          100
and pound and stamp my head a thousand times,
you'll never hear my name or see my face."
I had my fingers twisted in his hair
and already I'd pulled out more than one fistful,
while he yelped like a cur with eyes shut tight,               105
when someone else yelled: "What's the matter, Bocca?
It's bad enough to hear your shivering teeth;
now you bark! What the devil's wrong with you?"
"There's no need now for you to speak," I said,
"you vicious traitor! Now I know your name                      110
and I'll bring back the shameful truth about you."
"Go away!" he answered, "Tell them what you want;
but if you do get out of here, be sure
you also tell about that blabber-mouth
who's paying here what the French silver cost him:             115
'I saw,' you can tell the world, 'the one from Duera
stuck in with all the sinners keeping cool.'
And if you should be asked: 'Who else was there?'
Right by your side is the one from Beccheria
whose head was chopped off by the Florentines.                  120
As for Gianni Soldanier I think you'll find him
farther along with Ganelon and Tibbald
who opened up Faenza while it slept."
Soon after leaving him I saw two souls
frozen together in a single hole                                125
so that one head used the other for a cap.
As a man with hungry teeth tears into bread,

106. "Bocca": Bocca degli Abati was a Ghibelline who appeared to side with the Florentine Guelphs. However, while fighting on the side of the Guelphs at the battle of Montaperti in 1260, he is said to have cut off the hand of the standard bearer. The disappearance of the standard led to panic among the Florentine Guelphs, who were then decisively defeated by the Sienese Ghibellines and their German allies under Manfred.

116–117. "the one from Duera": Buoso da Duera, a chief of the Ghibelline party of Cremona, was a well-known traitor.

119–120. "is the one from Beccheria": Tesauro dei Beccheria of Pavia was an abbot of Vallombrosa and a papal legate to Alexander IV in Tuscany. He was tortured and finally beheaded in 1258 by the Guelphs of Florence for carrying on secret intercourse with Ghibellines who had been exiled.

121. "Gianni Soldanier": Gianni de' Soldanier was an important Ghibelline of Florence who, when the Florentines (mostly Guelph) began to chafe under Ghibelline rule, deserted his party and went over to the Guelphs.

122–123. "Ganelon": the treacherous knight who betrayed Roland (and the rear guard of Charlemagne's army) to the Saracens.

"Tibbald": one of the Zambrasi family of Faenza. In order to avenge himself on the Ghibelline Lambertazzi family (who had been exiled from Bologna in 1274 and had taken refuge in Faenza) he opened his city to their Bolognese Guelph enemies on the morning of November 13, 1280.

the soul with capping head had sunk his teeth
  into the other's neck, just beneath the skull.
Tydeus in his fury did not gnaw                                    130
  the head of Menalippus with more relish
  than this one chewed that head of meat and bones.
"O you who show with every bestial bite
  your hatred for the head you are devouring,"
  I said, "tell me your reason, and I promise         135
if you are justified in your revenge,
  once I know who you are and this one's sin,
  I'll repay your confidence in the world above
unless my tongue dry up before I die."

CANTO XXXIII

Count Ugolino is the shade gnawing at the brain of his one-time
associate Archbishop Ruggieri, and Ugolino interrupts his gruesome
meal long enough to tell the story of his imprisonment and cruel
death, which his innocent offspring shared with him. Moving farther into the area of Cocytus known as Ptolomea, where those who
betrayed their guests and associates are condemned, the Pilgrim sees
sinners with their faces raised high above the ice, whose tears freeze
to lock their eyes. One of the shades agrees to identify himself on
condition that the ice be removed from his eyes. The Pilgrim
agrees, and learns that this sinner is Friar Alberigo and that his soul
is dead and damned even though his body is still alive on earth,
inhabited by a devil. Alberigo also names a fellow sinner with him
in the ice, Branca d'Oria, whose body is still functioning up on
earth. But the Pilgrim does not honor his promise to break the ice
from Alberigo's eyes.

Lifting his mouth from his horrendous meal,
  this sinner first wiped off his messy lips
  in the hair remaining on the chewed-up skull,
then spoke: "You want me to renew a grief
  so desperate that just the thought of it,                 5
  much less the telling, grips my heart with pain;
but if my words can be the seed to bear
  the fruit of infamy for this betrayer
  who feeds my hunger, than I shall speak—in tears.
I do not know your name, nor do I know                       10
  how you have come down here, but Florentine
  you surely seem to be, to hear you speak.

130–131. "Tydeus": one of the Seven
against Thebes, slew Menalippus in combat—who, however, managed to wound
him fatally. Tydeus called for his enemy's
head, which, when brought to him by
Amphiaraus, he proceeded to gnaw in
rage.

First you should know I was Count Ugolino
   and my neighbor here, Ruggieri the Archbishop;
   now I'll tell you why I'm so unneighborly.        15
That I, trusting in him, was put in prison
   through his evil machinations, where I died,
   this much I surely do not have to tell you.
What you could not have known, however, is
   the inhuman circumstances of my death.        20
   Now listen, then decide if he has wronged me!
Through a narrow slit of window high in that mew
   (which is called the tower of hunger, after me,
   and I'll not be the last to know that place)
I had watched moon after moon after moon go by,        25
   when finally I dreamed the evil dream
   which ripped away the veil that hid my future.
I dreamed of this one here as lord and huntsman,
   pursuing the wolf and the wolf-cubs up the mountain
   (which blocks the sight of Lucca from the Pisans)        30
with skinny bitches, well trained and obedient;
   he had out front as leaders of the pack
   Gualandi with Sismondi and Lanfranchi.
A short run, and the father with his sons
   seemed to grow tired, and then I thought I saw        35
   long fangs sunk deep into their sides, ripped open.
When I awoke before the light of dawn,
   I heard my children sobbing in their sleep
   (you see they, too, were there) asking for bread.
If the thought of what my heart was telling me        40
   does not fill you with grief, how cruel you are!
   If you are not weeping now—do you ever weep?
And then they awoke. It was around the time
   they usually brought our food to us. But now
   each one of us was full of dread from dreaming;        45
then from below I heard them driving nails
   into the dreadful tower's door; with that,
   I stared in silence at my flesh and blood.

13–14. "Count Ugolino": Ugolino della Gherardesca, the Count of Donoratico, belonged to a noble Tuscan family whose political affiliations were Ghibelline. In 1275 he conspired with his son-in-law, Giovanni Visconti, to raise the Guelphs to power in Pisa. Although exiled for this subversive activity, Ugolino (Nino) Visconti, took over the Guelph government of the city. Three years later (1288) he plotted with Archbishop Ruggieri degli Ubaldini to rid Pisa of the Visconti. Ruggieri, however, had other plans, and with the aid of the Ghibellines, he seized control cf the city and imprisoned Ugolino, together with his sons and grandsons, in the "tower of hunger" (l. 23). The two were evidently just at the boundary be-

tween Antenora and Ptolomea, for Ugolino is being punished for betraying his country (in Antenora), and Ruggieri for betraying his associate, Ugolino (in Ptolomea).

25. Imprisoned in June of 1288, they were finally starved to death in February 1289.

28–36. Ugolino's dream was indeed prophetic. The "lord and huntsman" (l. 28) is Archbishop Ruggieri, who, with the leading Ghibelline families of Pisa ("Gualandi . . . Sismondi and Lanfranchi," l. 33) and the populace ("Skinny bitches," l. 33), runs down Ugolino and his offspring ("the wolf and the wolf-cubs," l. 29) and finally kills them.

I did not weep, I turned to stone inside;
   they wept, and my little Anselmuccio spoke:     50
   'What is it, father? Why do you look that way?'
For them I held my tears back, saying nothing,
   all of that day, and then all of that night,
   until another sun shone on the world.
A meager ray of sunlight found its way     55
   to the misery of our cell, and I could see
   myself reflected four times in their faces;
I bit my hands in anguish. And my children,
   who thought that hunger made me bite my hands
   were quick to draw up closer to me, saying:     60
'O father, you would make us suffer less,
   if you would feed on us: you were the one
   who gave us this sad flesh; you take it from us!'
I calmed myself to make them less unhappy,
   That day we sat in silence, and the next day.     65
   O pitiless earth! You should have swallowed us!
The fourth day came, and it was on that day
   my Gaddo fell prostrate before my feet,
   crying: 'Why don't you help me? Why, my father?'
There he died. Just as you see me here,     70
   I saw the other three fall one by one,
   as the fifth day and the sixth day passed. And I,
by then gone blind, groped over their dead bodies.
   Though they were dead, two days I called their names.
   Then hunger proved more powerful than grief."     75
He spoke these words; then, glaring down in rage,
   attacked again the live skull with his teeth
   sharp as a dog's, and as fit for grinding bones.
O Pisa, blot of shame upon the people
   of that fair land where the sound of "sì" is heard!     80
   Since your neighbors hesitate to punish you,
let Capraia and Gorgona move and join,
   damming up the River Arno at its mouth,
   and let every Pisan perish in its flood!
For if Count Ugolino was accused     85
   of turning traitor, trading-in your castles,
   you had no right to make his children suffer.
Their new-born years (O new-born Thebes!) made them
   all innocents: Brigata, Uguiccione
   and the other two soft names my canto sings.     90

50. "Anselmuccio": the younger of Ugolino's grandsons who, according to official documents, must have been fifteen at the time.

68. "Gaddo": one of Ugolino's sons.

75. Whether in this line Ugolino is confessing to an act of cannibalism or whether it simply relates the cause of his death (hunger instead of grief)—Dante has left this to the reader's imagination.

80. Italy. It was customary in Dante's time to indicate a language area by the words signifying "yes."

89–90. "Brigata": Ugolino's second grandson; "Uguiccione": his fifth son.

We moved ahead to where the frozen water
   wraps in harsh wrinkles another sinful race,
   with faces not turned down but looking up.
Here, the weeping puts an end to weeping,
   and the grief that finds no outlet from the eyes      95
   turns inward to intensify the anguish:
for the tears they first wept knotted in a cluster
   and like a visor made for them in crystal,
   filled all the hollow part around their eyes.
Although the bitter coldness of the dark        100
   had driven all sensation from my face,
   as though it were not tender skin but callous,
I thought I felt the air begin to blow,
   and I: "What causes such a wind, my master?
   I thought no heat could reach into these depths."     105
And he to me: "Before long you will be
   where your own eyes can answer for themselves,
   when they will see what keeps this wind in motion."
And one of the wretches with the frozen crust
   screamed out at us: "O wicked souls, so wicked    110
   that you have been assigned the ultimate post,
break off these hard veils covering my eyes
   and give relief from the pain that swells my heart—
   at least until the new tears freeze again."
I answered him: "If this is what you want,       115
   tell me your name; and if I do not help you,
   may I be forced to drop beneath this ice!"
He answered then: "I am Friar Alberigo,
   I am he who offered fruit from the evil orchard:
   here dates are served me for the figs I gave."    120
"Oh, then!" I said, "Are you already dead?"
   And he to me: "Just how my body is

91–93. Virgil and the Pilgrim have now
entered the third division of Cocytus,
called Tolomea (l. 124) after Ptolemy,
the captain of Jericho, who had Simon,
his father-in-law, and two of his sons
killed while dining (see 1 Macabees 16:
11–17). Or possibly this zone of Cocytus
is named after Ptolemy XII: the Egyptian
king, who, having welcomed Pompey to
his realm, slew him. In Tolomea are punished those who have betrayed their
guests.
   105. Wind, according to the science of
Dante's time, is produced by varying degrees of heat; thus, Cocytus, being completely icebound, lacks all heat, and should
be free of winds. In the next canto the
Pilgrim will see for himself that Lucifer's
giant wings cause the wind.
   115–117. The Pilgrim, fully aware that
his journey will indeed take him below the
ice, carefully phrases his treacherous
promise to the treacherous shade, and

successfully deceives him (ll. 149–150).
The Pilgrim betrays a sinner in this circle,
as the latter does one of his companions
there with him in the ice (by naming him).
   118–120. "Friar Alberigo": One of the
Jovial Friars (see Canto XXIII, ll. 103–
108), Alberigo di Ugolino dei Manfredi
was a native of Faenza. In 1285, in the
midst of a family feud, Alberigo invited
his principal opponents, Manfred (close
relative) and Alberghetto (Manfred's
son), to dinner as a gesture of good will.
During the course of the meal, Alberigo,
using a prearranged signal, called for the
fruit, at which his men murdered the
dinner guests. Continuing the fruit imagery, Alberigo laments his present anguish
by saying ironically that "here dates are
served me for the figs I gave" (l. 120),
which is to say that he is suffering more
than his share (since a date is more valuable than a fig).

in the world above, I have no way of knowing.
This zone of Tolomea is very special,
   for it often happens that a soul falls here         125
   before the time that Atropos should send it.
And that you may more willingly scrape off
   my cluster of glass tears, let me tell you:
   whenever a soul betrays the way I did,
a demon takes possession of the body,         130
   controlling its maneuvers from then on,
   for all the years it has to live up there,
while the soul falls straight into this cistern here;
   and the shade in winter quarters just behind me
   may well have left his body up on earth.         135
But you should know, if you've just come from there:
   he is Ser Branca D'Oria; and many years
   have passed since he first joined us here, ice-bound."
"I think you're telling me a lie," I said,
   "for Branca D'Oria is not dead at all;         140
   he eats and drinks, he sleeps and wears out clothes."
"The ditch the Malebranche watch above,"
   he said, "the ditch of clinging, boiling pitch,
   had not yet caught the soul of Michel Zanche,
when Branca left a devil in his body         145
   to take his place, and so did his close kinsman,
   his accomplice in this act of treachery.
But now, at last, give me the hand you promised.
   Open my eyes." I did not open them.
   To be mean to him was a generous reward.         150
O all you Genovese, you men estranged
   from every good, at home with every vice,
   why can't the world be wiped clean of your race?
For in company with Romagna's rankest soul
   I found one of your men whose deeds were such    155
   that his soul bathes already in Cocytus
but his body seems alive and walks among you.

### CANTO XXXIV

Far across the frozen ice can be seen the gigantic figure of Lucifer, who appears from this distance like a windmill seen through
fog; and as the two travelers walk on toward that terrifying sight,
they see the shades of sinners totally buried in the frozen water. At
the center of the earth Lucifer stands frozen from the chest down-

---

124–135. According to Church doctrine, under certain circumstances a living person may, through acts of treachery, lose possession of his soul before he dies ("before the time that Atropos [the Fate who cuts man's thread of life] should send it," l. 126). Then, on earth, a devil inhabits the body until its natural death.

137–147. "Ser Branca D'Oria": A prominent resident of Genoa, Branca D'Oria murdered his father-in-law, Michele Zanche (See Canto XXII, l. 88), after having invited him to dine with him.

154. Friar Alberigo. Faenza, his home town, was in the region of Romagna (now called Emilia).

155. Branca D'Oria.

ward and his horrible ugliness (he has three heads) is made more
fearful by the fact that in each of his three mouths he chews on one
of the three worst sinners of all mankind, the worst of those who
betrayed their benefactors: Judas Iscariot, Brutus, and Cassius.
Virgil with the Pilgrim on his back begins the descent down the
shaggy body of Lucifer. They climb down through a crack in the
ice, and when they reach the Evil One's thighs, Virgil turns and
begins to struggle upward (because they have passed the center of
the earth) still holding onto the hairy body of Lucifer until they
reach a cavern where they stop for a short rest. Then a winding
path brings them eventually to the earth's surface, where they see
the stars.


"*Vexilla regis prodeunt Inferni*,"
   my master said, "closer to us, so now
   look ahead and see if you can make him out."
A far-off windmill turning its huge sails
   when a thick fog begins to settle in,      5
   or when the light of day begins to fade,
that is what I thought I saw appearing.
   And the gusts of wind it stirred made me shrink back
   behind my guide, my only means of cover.
Down here, I stood on souls fixed under ice      10
   (I tremble as I put this into verse),
   to me they looked like straws worked into glass.
Some lying flat, some perpendicular,
   either with their heads up or their feet,
   and some bent head to foot, shaped like a bow.      15
When we had moved far enough along the way
   that my master thought time had come to show me
   the creature who was once so beautiful,
he stepped aside, and stopping me, announced:
   "This is he, this is Dis; this is the place      20
   that calls for all the courage you have in you."
How chilled and nerveless, Reader, I felt then;

1. "*Vexilla regis prodeunt Inferni*":
The opening lines of the hymn "Vexilla
regis prodeunt"—"The banners of the
King advance" (written by Venantius For-
tunatus, sixth-century bishop of Poitiers;
this hymn belongs to the liturgy of the
Church) are here parodied by the addition of the word *Inferni*, "of Hell," to the
word *regis*, "of the King." Sung on Good
Friday, the hymn anticipates the unveil-
ing of the Cross; Dante, who began his
journey on the evening of Good Friday,
is prepared by Virgil's words for the sight
of Lucifer, who will appear like a "windmill" in a "thick fog." The banners referred to are Lucifer's wings.
10. These sinners in various positions
fixed rigidly in the ice present a picture
of complete immobility and incommuni-
cability, as though they have been entombed a second time. Silence reigns in
this fourth division of Cocytus (named
Judecca, l. 117, after the traitor Judas),
the gelid abode of those souls in whom
all warmth of love for God and for their
fellow man has been extinguished.
18. Before his fall Lucifer was held by
God to be the fairest of the angels. Pride
caused Lucifer's rebellion against his
Maker and precipitated his expulsion from
Heaven. The arch traitor is, like the other
sinners, fixed and suffering in the ice. He
weeps.
20. In antiquity Pluto, god of the
Underworld, was often referred to as
Dis, a name here applied to Lucifer.

do not ask me—I cannot write about it—
there are no words to tell you how I felt.
I did not die—I was not living either!                                    25
  Try to imagine, if you can imagine,
  me there, deprived of life and death at once.
The king of the vast kingdom of all grief
  stuck out with half his chest above the ice;
  my height is closer to the height of giants                            30
than theirs is to the length of his great arms;
  consider now how large all of him was:
  this body in proportion to his arms.
If once he was as fair as now he's foul
  and dared to raise his brows against his Maker,                        35
  it is fitting that all grief should spring from him.
Oh, how amazed I was when I looked up
  and saw a head—one head wearing three faces!
  One was in front (and that was a bright red),
the other two attached themselves to this one                            40
  just above the middle of each shoulder,
  and at the crown all three were joined in one:
The right face was a blend of white and yellow,
  the left the color of those people's skin
  who live along the river Nile's descent.                               45
Beneath each face two mighty wings stretched out,
  the size you might expect of this huge bird
  (I never saw a ship with larger sails):
not feathered wings but rather like the ones
  a bat would have. He flapped them constantly,                          50
  keeping three winds continuously in motion
to lock Cocytus eternally in ice.
  He wept from his six eyes, and down three chins
  were dripping tears all mixed with bloody slaver.
In each of his three mouths he crunched a sinner                         55
  with teeth like those that rake the hemp and flax,
  keeping three sinners constantly in pain;
the one in front—the biting he endured
  was nothing like the clawing that he took:
  sometimes his back was raked clean of its skin.                        60
"That soul up there who suffers most of all,"
  my guide explained, "is Judas Iscariot:
  the one with head inside and legs out kicking.

---

38–45. Dante presents Lucifer's head as a perverted parallel of the Trinity. The symbolic value of the three single faces has been much debated. Although many commentators believe that the colors (red, yellow, black) represent the three known continents (Europe, Asia, Africa), it seems more logical that they should be antithetically analogous to the qualities attributed to the Trinity (see Canto III, ll. 5–6). Therefore, Highest Wisdom would be opposed by ignorance (black), Divine Omnipotence by impotence (yellow), Primal Love by hatred or envy (red).

46. The entire figure of Lucifer is a parody of the angelic. Originally belonging to the order of the Cherubim, he retains his six wings even in Hell, though here, devoid of their heavenly plumage, they appear as those of a bat (the standard depiction of the devil's wings in the Middle Ages).

61–63. Having betrayed Christ for thirty pieces of silver Judas endures greater punishment than the other two souls.

As for the other two whose heads stick out,
   the one who hangs from that black face is Brutus—     65
   see how he squirms in silent desperation,
the other one is Cassius, he still looks sturdy.
   But soon it will be night. Now is the time
   to leave this place, for we have seen it all."
I held on to his neck, as he told me to,     70
   while he watched and waited for the time and place,
   and when the wings were stretched out just enough,
he grabbed on to the shaggy sides of Satan;
   then downward, tuft by tuft, he made his way
   between the tangled hair and frozen crust.     75
When we had reached the point exactly where
   the thigh begins, right at the haunch's curve,
   my guide with strain and force of every muscle,
turned his head toward the shaggy shanks of Dis
   and grabbed the hair as if about to climb—     80
   I thought that we were heading back to Hell.
"Hold tight, there is no other way," he said,
   panting, exhausted, "only by these stairs
   can we leave behind the evil we have seen."
When he had got me through the rocky crevice,     85
   he raised me to its edge and set me down,
   then carefully he climbed and joined me there.
I raised my eyes expecting I would see
   the half of Lucifer I saw before.
   Instead I saw his two legs stretching upward.     90
If at that sight I found myself confused,
   so will those simple-minded folk who still
   don't see what point it was I must have passed.
"Get up," my master said, "get to your feet,
   the way is long, the road a rough climb up,     95
   already the sun approaches middle tierce!"

65. "Brutus": Marcus Brutus, who was deceitfully persuaded by Cassius (l. 67) to join the conspiracy, aided in the assassination of Julius Caesar. It is fitting that in his final vision of the Inferno the Pilgrim should see those shades who committed treacherous acts against Divine and worldly authorities: the Church and the Roman Empire. This provides the culmination, at least in this canticle, of these basic themes: Church and Empire.

67. "Cassius": Caius Cassius Longinus was another member of the conspiracy against Caesar. By describing Cassius as "still looking sturdy," Dante shows he has evidently confused him with Lucius Cassius, whom Cicero calls *adeps*, "corpulent."

79–81. Virgil, carrying the Pilgrim on his back, slowly makes his way down Lucifer's hairy body and, upon reaching a certain point (the center of the universe and, consequently, of terrestial gravity), where Lucifer's thighs begin, he must turn his head in the direction of Lucifer's legs and begin to climb "upward"—thus confusing the Pilgrim on his back. The way in which Virgil executed his own shift of position on Lucifer's body must have been as follows: when he reached the thigh he moved his head to the side and downward until (still holding on with one hand to the hair of the chest) he could reach with his other hand to grasp the hair on the thigh—then (aided now by the shift of gravitational pull) to free the first hand and complete the half circle he had initiated, proceeding henceforth as a man climbing.

96. The time is approximately halfway between the canonical hours of Prime and Tierce, i.e., 7:30 A.M. The rapid change from night ("But soon it will be night," l. 68) to day (l. 96) is the result of the travelers' having passed the earth's center, thus moving into the Southern Hemisphere which is twelve hours ahead of the Northern.

It was no palace promenade we came to,
　but rather like some dungeon Nature built:
　it was paved with broken stone and poorly lit.
"Before we start to struggle out of here,　　　　　　　　100
　O master," I said when I was on my feet,
　"I wish you would explain some things to me.
Where is the ice? And how can he be lodged
　upside-down! And how, in so little time
　could the sun go all the way from night to day?"　　　105
"You think you're still on the center's other side,"
　he said, "where I first grabbed the hairy worm
　of rottenness that pierces the earth's core;
and you *were* there as long as I moved downward
　but, when I turned myself, you passed the point　　　110
　to which all weight from every part is drawn.
Now you are standing beneath the hemisphere
　which is opposite the side covered by land,
　where at the central point was sacrificed
the Man whose birth and life were free of sin.　　　115
　You have both feet upon a little sphere
　whose other side Judecca occupies;
when it is morning here, there it is evening.
　And he whose hairs were stairs for our descent
　has not changed his position since his fall.　　　120
When he fell from the heavens on this side,
　all of the land that once was spread out here,
　alarmed by his plunge, took cover beneath the sea
and moved to our hemisphere; with equal fear
　the mountain-land, piled up this side, fled　　　125
　and made this cavern here when it rushed upward.
Below somewhere there is a space, as far
　from Beelzebub as the limit of his tomb,
　known not by sight but only by the sound
of a little stream that makes its way down here　　　130
　through the hollow of a rock that it has worn
　gently winding in gradual descent."
My guide and I entered that hidden road
　to make our way back up to the bright world.
　We never thought of resting while we climbed.　　　135

112–115. Lucifer's body, falling head first from Heaven to the Southern Hemisphere, bored through to the earth's center where he remains imprisoned. Before he fell through the Southern Hemisphere ("this side," l. 121), it was covered with land, but the land, "alarmed by his plunge," sank beneath the sea and shifted to the Northern Hemisphere ("our hemisphere," l. 24). But the land at the center of the earth rushed upward, at once leaving the "cavern" above Lucifer's legs and forming the Mount of Purgatory, the only land in the Southern Hemisphere.
127–132. Somewhere below the land which rushed upward to form the Mount of Purgatory "there is a space" (l. 127) through which a stream runs, and it is through this space that Virgil and Dante will climb to reach the base of the Mount. The "space" is "as far/from Beelzebub [Lucifer] as the limit of his tomb" (l. 127–128); that is, at the edge of the natural dungeon that constitutes Lucifer's "tomb," there is an opening, a "space," serving as the entrance to the passage from the earth's center to its circumference, created by Lucifer in his fall from Heaven to Hell.

We climbed, he first and I behind, until,
   through a small round opening ahead of us
   I saw the lovely things the heavens hold,
and we came out to see once more the stars.

## Purgatory (*Purgatorio*)

### CANTO I

[Having emerged from Hell, Virgil and Dante find themselves
on the eastern shores of the island-mountain of Purgatory, which
is at the antipodes of Jerusalem. It is the dawn of Easter Day, 1300.
Four stars, symbols of the cardinal virtues (perhaps suggested by
descriptions of the Southern Cross), blaze in the sky. Cato, the
Guardian of Purgatory, appears to the poets and questions them.
Being satisfied by Virgil, he tells them to wait for the daylight; but
first Virgil is to wash Dante's face with dew and to gird him with a
reed.]

Now hoisteth sail the pinnace of my wit
   For better waters, and more smoothly flies
   Since of a sea so cruel she is quit,
And of that second realm, which purifies
   Man's spirit of its soilure, will I sing,          5
   Where it becometh worthy of Paradise.
Here let dead Poesy from her grave up-spring,
   O sacred Muses, whom I serve and haunt,
   And sound, Calliope, a louder string
To accompany my song with that high chant      10
   Which smote the Magpies' miserable choir
   That they despaired of pardon for their vaunt.
Tender colour of orient sapphire
   Which on the air's translucent aspect grew,
   From mid heaven to horizon deeply clear,      15
Made pleasure in mine eyes be born anew
   Soon as I issued forth from the dead air
   That had oppressed both eye and heart with rue.
The planet that promoteth Love was there,
   Making all the East to laugh and be joyful,    20
   And veiled the Fishes that escorted her.

---

139. The Pilgrim, denied sight of the
celestial bodies in Hell, now looks up at
them again. The direction his journey will
now take is upward, toward that Divine
Realm of which the stars are the signal
for us on earth. That all three canticles
end with the word "stars," symmetrically
reinforces the concept of movement upward toward God, the central theme and
motive force of the *Divine Comedy*.

9–11. The Magpies were the nine
daughters of King Pieros; they challenged the Muses to a contest and, being worsted by one of them, Calliope,
became so insolent that they were
turned into birds.

21. Venus was dimming, by her
brighter light, the constellation of the
Fishes; the time indicated is an hour
or more before sunrise.

I turned to the right and contemplated all
    The other pole; and four stars o'er me came,
    Never yet seen save by the first people.
All the heavens seemed exulting in their flame.           25
    O widowed Northern clime, from which is ta'en
    The happy fortune of beholding them!
When from my gaze I had severed them again,
    Turned somewhat to the other pole, whose law
    By now had sunken out of sight the Wain,           30
Near me an old man solitary I saw,
    In his aspect so much to be revered
    That no son owes a father more of awe.
Long and with white hairs brindled was his beard,
    Like to his locks, of which a double list           35
    Down on his shoulders and his breast appeared.
The beams of the four sacred splendours kist
    His countenance, and they glorified it so
    That in its light the sun's light was not missed.
"Who are ye, that against the blind stream go,"          40
    Shaking those venerable plumes, he said,
    "And flee from the eternal walls of woe?
Who hath guided you? what lamp your footsteps led,
    Issuing from that night without fathom
    Which makes a blackness of the vale of dread?         45
Is the law of the abyss thus broken from?
    Or is there some new change in Heaven's decrees,
    That, being damned, unto my crags ye come?"
Then did my leader on my shoulder seize
    And with admonishing hand and word and sign
    Make reverent my forehead and my knees;         50
Then spoke: "I come not of my own design.
    From Heaven came down a Lady, at whose prayer,
    To help this man, I made his pathway mine.
But since it is thy will that we declare         55
    More of our state, needs must that I obey
    And tell thee all: deny thee I would not dare.
He hath never yet seen darken his last day,
    Yet so near thereto through his folly went
    That short time was there to re-shape his way.        60

**23–24.** Dante invents here a constellation of four bright lights, corresponding to the Great Bear of the north. These luminaries symbolize the four cardinal virtues: Prudence, Temperance, Fortitude, and Justice. Adam and Eve before the fall ("the first people"), dwelling at the top of the mountain of Purgatory, beheld these stars.

**31.** This custodian of Purgatory (an example of that free will which the souls in his domain are striving, by purification, to regain) is Cato the Younger, who on earth killed himself in Utica rather than submit to Caesar.

Even as I said, to his rescue I was sent,
  Nor other way appeared that was not vain
  But this on which our footsteps now are bent.
I have shown him all the sinners in their pain,
  And now intend to show him those who dwell     65
  Under thy charge and cleanse themselves of stain.
How I have brought him were too long to tell.
  Our steps a Virtue, helping from on high,
  That he might see thee and hear thee, did impel.
Now on his coming look with gracious eye.       70
  He seeketh freedom, that so precious thing,
  How precious, he knows who for her will die.
Thou knowest: for her sake, death had no sting
  In Utica, where thou didst leave what yet
  The great day shall for thy bright raiment bring.   75
The eternal laws are still inviolate;
  For he doth live, nor me doth Minos bind.
  But I am of the circle where the chaste eyes wait
Of Marcia, visibly praying that thy mind,
  O sainted breast, still hold her for thine own.   80
  For love of her, then, be to us inclined.
Suffer that thy seven realms to us be shown;
  And thanks of thee shall unto her be brought,
  If there below thou deign still to be known."
"Marcia was so pleasing to my thought            85
  Yonder," he answered, "and myself so fond,
  Whate'er she willed, I could refuse her naught.
Now no more may she move me, since beyond
  The evil stream she dwells, by the decree
  Made when I was delivered from that bond.      90
But if a heavenly lady hath missioned thee,
  As thou hast said, of flattery is no need.
  Enough, that in her name thou askest me.
Go then; first gird this man with a smooth reed,
  And see thou bathe his features in such wise   95
  That from all filthiness they may be freed.
It were not meet that mist clouded his eyes
  To dim their vision, when he goes before
  The first of those that serve in Paradise.
This little isle, there where for evermore       100
  The waters beat all round about its foot,

77–79. Minos, the Judge of Hell, does not bind Virgil, who dwells in the Limbus. "Marcia" was Cato's wife. 88–90. When Cato was released from Limbus by Christ, he became subject to the law forbidding the blessed to be moved by the fate of the damned.

Bears rushes on the soft and oozy shore.
No other plant that would put forth a shoot
  Or harden, but from life there is debarred,
  Since to the surf it yields not from its root.     105
And then return not this way afterward.
  The sun, at point to rise now, shall reveal
  Where the mount yieldeth an ascent less hard."
So he vanished; and I rose up on my heel
  Without word spoken, and all of me drew back     110
  Toward my guide, making with mine eyes appeal.
He began: "Son, follow thou in my track.
  Turn we on our footsteps, for this way the lea
  Slopes down, where the low banks its boundary make."
The dawn was moving the dark hours to flee     115
  Before her, and far off amid their wane
  I could perceive the trembling of the sea.
We paced along the solitary plain,
  Like one who seeks to his lost road a clue,
  And till he reach it deems he walks in vain.     120
When we had come there where the melting dew
  Contends against the sun, being in a place
  Where the cool air but little of it updrew,
My Lord laid both hands out on the lank grass
  Gently, amid the drops that it retained:     125
  Wherefore I, conscious what his purpose was,
Lifted to him my cheeks that tears had stained;
  And at his touch the colour they had worn,
  Ere Hell had overcast it, they regained.
Then came we down to the land's desert bourne,     130
  Which never yet saw man that had essayed
  Voyage upon that water and knew return.
There did he gird me as that other bade.
  O miracle! even as it was before,
  The little plant put forth a perfect blade     135
On the instant in the place his fingers tore.

### CANTO II

[The sun rises. A boat, steered by an angel, swiftly approaches
the shore; it contains a company of spirits brought to Purgatory.
These landed, the angel with the boat departs to collect other spirits
at the mouth of the Tiber. Among the newcomers Dante recognizes
a friend; it is Casella the musician. Casella is persuaded to sing,
and the spirits gather round to listen, when Cato appears and rebukes them for loitering, and they scatter up the slopes of the mountain.]

Now the sun touched the horizon with his flame,
    The circle of whose meridian, at the height
    It reaches most, covers Jerusalem;
And opposite to him in her circling, Night
    Came up from Ganges, and the Scales with her          5
    That from her hand fall as she grows in might;
So that the fair cheeks of Aurora, there
    Where I was, gave their red and white away,
    Sallowing, as if old age had turned them sere.
We lingered yet by the ocean-marge, as they              10
    Who think upon the road that lies before
    And in their mind go, but in body stay;
And lo! as at the approach of morning frore
    Mars through the mist glimmers a fiery red
    Down in the West over the ocean-floor,               15
(May mine eyes yet upon that sight be fed!)
    Appeared, moving across the water, a light
    So swift, all earthly motion it outsped.
From which when for a space I had drawn my sight
    Away, and of my Guide the meaning sought,            20
    I saw it now grown bigger and more bright.
On either side of it I knew not what
    Of white appeared to gleam out; and below
    Another whiteness by degrees it got.
My master spoke not yet a word, till lo!                 25
    When those first whitenesses as wings shone free
    And his eyes now could well the Pilot know,
He exclaimed: "Bend, see that thou bend the knee.
    Behold the Angel of God! Lay hand to hand!
    Such ministers henceforth thou art to see.           30
Look, how he scorneth aid that man hath planned,
    And wills not oar nor other sail to ply,
    But only his own wings from far land to land.
See how he has them stretcht up toward the sky,
    Sweeping the air with that eternal plume             35
    Which moulteth not as the hair of things that die."
Such an exceeding brightness did allume
    The Bird of God, who near and nearer bore,

1–6. This is one of the astronomical riddles to which our poet was addicted. According to medieval cosmology, Jerusalem and Purgatory are on opposite sides of the earth, 180° from each other: when Jerusalem sees the sun rise, Purgatory sees it set. The river Ganges, which flowed on the eastern confines of the inhabited world, stands for the "east." What we are told, in a devious and ingenious way, is that for the spectators on the island of Purgatory the sun was rising.

7–9. The poet transfers to the face of the goddess of dawn (Aurora) the changing colors of the morning sky.

16. "May mine eyes . . .": after death, when my soul shall be wafted to Purgatory.

Mine eyes to endure him might not now presume,
But bent them down; and he came on to shore     40
  Upon a barque so swift and light and keen
  As scarcely a ripple from the water tore.
On the heavenly Steersman at the stern was seen
  Inscribed that blissfulness whereof he knew;
  And more than a hundred spirits sat within.     45
Together all were singing *In exitu*
  *Israel de Egypto* as one host
  With what of that psalm doth those words ensue.
With the holy sign their company he crossed;
  Whereat themselves forth on the strand they threw:     50
  Swift as he came, he sped, and straight was lost.
They that remained seemed without any clue
  To the strange place, casting a wondering eye
  Round them, like one assaying hazards new.
On every side the arrowing sun shot high     55
  Into the day, and with his bright arrows
  Had hunted Capricorn from the mid sky,
When the new people lifted up their brows
  Towards us, and spoke to us: "If ye know it, show
  What path to us the mountain-side allows."     60
And Virgil answered: "Peradventure you
  Suppose we have experience of the way;
  But we are pilgrims, even as ye are too.
We came but now, a little before you, nay,
  By another road than yours, so steep and rude     65
  That the climb now will seem to us but play."
The spirits, who by my breathing understood
  That I was still among the living things,
  Marvelling, became death-pale where they stood.
As round a messenger, who the olive brings,     70
  Folk, to hear news, each on the other tread,
  And none is backward with his elbowings,
So on my face their gaze intently fed
  Those spirits, all so fortunate, and forgot
  Almost to go up and be perfected.     75
One of them now advanced, as if he sought
  To embrace me, with a love so fond and fain,
  That upon me to do the like he wrought.
O Shades, in all but aspect, void and vain!

57. At dawn the constellation of Capricorn was on the meridian; it is effaced by the rays of the rising sun.

70. Bearers of good tidings used to carry an olive branch.

79–81. Throughout Hell the souls, though without weight, are not only visible but tangible. On the lower slopes of the mountain of Purgatory, however, Dante cannot touch a shade, although two spirits can still embrace.

Behind it thrice my hands did I enlace,     80
   And thrice they came back to my breast again.
Wonder, I think, was painted on my face;
   At which the spirit smiled and backward drew,
   And, following it, I sprang forward a pace.
Gently it bade me pause: and then I knew     85
   Who it was, and prayed him pity on me to show
   And talk with me as he was used to do.
"As in the mortal body I loved thee, so
   In my release I love thee," he answered me.
   "Therefore I stay: but thou, why dost thou go?"     90
"Casella mine, that this place I may see
   Hereafter," I said, "have I this journey made.
   But how hath so much time been stolen from thee?"
And he to me: "None have I to upbraid
   If he who takes when he chooses, and whom,     95
   This passage many times to me forbade.
For in a just will hath his will its home.
   Truly he has taken now these three months past
   Whoso hath wished to enter, in all welcome.
So I, whose eyes on the sea-shore were cast     100
   Where Tiber's water by the salt is won,
   By him was gathered in benignly at last.
To that mouth now his wings he urgeth on
   Because for ever assemble in that spot
   They who are not to sink towards Acheron."     105
And I: "If a new law forbid thee not
   Memory and usage of the enamoured song
   Which used to soothe all wishes of my thought,
May it please thee awhile to solace with thy tongue
   My spirit that, in its mortal mask confined,     110
   The journey hither bitterly hath wrung."
*"Love that discourseth to me in my mind"*
   Began he then so sweetly, that the sound
   Still in my heart with sweetness is entwined.
My Master and I, and all that people around     115
   Who were with him, had faces so content
   As if all else out of their thoughts were drowned.

---

91. Of Casella we know only that he was a musician of Florence and a close friend of the poet and, perhaps, that he set to music Dante's canzone, "Love that discourseth to me in my mind" (see line 112).
92–93. Dante's present experience is intended to fit him to return to Purgatory after death. Casella evidently had died some time before, and Dante is astonished to see him just arrived in the other world.

95–97. "He who takes . . .": the angelic boatman. "In a just will . . .": the will of God.
101. The "Tiber's water" signifies allegorically the Church of Rome. There congregate the souls of those who die in its bosom. The souls of the unrepentant descend to Acheron.

We to his notes, entranced, our senses lent:
    And lo! the old man whom all the rest revere
    Crying, "What is this, ye laggard spirits faint?        120
What truancy, what loitering is here?
    Haste to the Mount and from the slough be freed
    Which lets not God unto your eyes appear."
As doves, when picking corn or darnel seed,
    All quiet and close-crowding to that fare,        125
    Their strut of pride forgotten in their greed,
If anything appear their hearts to scare
    On the instant leave the food there, where it lies,
    Because they are assailed by greater care,
So saw I that new company arise,        130
    And leave the song, and the steep slope essay,
    Like one who goes, knowing not of where he hies:
Nor with less haste went we upon our way.

· · ·

### CANTO XIX

[In a dream Dante has a vision of the Siren (symbolizing worldly enticements). A lady from heaven appears in this dream; and Virgil, at her bidding, exposes the Siren's real foulness. Dante is roused by Virgil, the sun having now risen, and an angel speeds them up the passage to the fifth terrace, where are the souls of the avaricious and the prodigal, lying prone on the ground. Virgil asks the way, and is answered by one who proves to be Pope Adrian V. He tells them that he was possessed by avarice till he reached the highest office, and then turned to God. Dante kneels, to show his reverence, but is told by the spirit to rise.]

In that hour when the heat of day no more
    Can warm the Moon's cold influence, and it dies
    O'ercome by the earth or whiles by Saturn's power;
When geomancers see in the East arise
    Their Greater Fortune, ere the dawn be come,        5
    By a path which not long dark before it lies,
In dream came to me a woman stuttering dumb,
    With squinting eyes and twisted on her feet,
    With deformed hands and cheeks of pallor numb.
I gazed on her; and as the sun's good heat        10
    Comforteth cold limbs weighed down by the night,
    So did my look make her tongue nimbly feat,
And straightened her and set her all upright

4. "Geomancers" foretold the future by means of figures constructed on points that were distributed by chance. One of their figures, called "Greater Fortune," resembled a constellation.

In short time, and her ruined countenance made
Into the colour which is love's delight.                     15
Soon as her loosened tongue came to her aid,
    She began singing, so that for its sake
    From her voice hardly had my hearing strayed.
"I am," she said, "the sweet Siren, who make
    Mariners helpless, charmed in the mid-sea;              20
    Such pleasure in my music do men take.
I turned Ulysses from his wandering, he
    So loved my song; and who with me hath found
    Home, seldom quits, so glad is he of me."
Her lips were not yet closed upon the sound                 25
    When came a lady in whom was holiness
    Prompt to my side, that other to confound.
"O Virgil, Virgil, tell me who is this?"
    Indignantly she said; and straight he went
    With eyes fixt on that honest one, to seize             30
The other, and when her garments he had rent,
    He laid her open and showed her belly creased,
    That waked me with the stench that forth it sent.
I turned my eyes, and Virgil said: "At least
    Thrice have I called thee; up, let us begone!           35
    Find we the opening where thou enterest."
I raised me up; high day now overshone
    The holy mount and filled each winding ledge.
    We went, and at our back was the new sun.
I followed him, like one who is the siege                   40
    Of heavy thought that droops his forehead, when
    He makes himself the half-arch of a bridge.
And I heard: "Come! Here is the pass"; spoken
    With so much loving kindness in the tone
    As is not heard in this our mortal pen.                 45
With outspread wings that shone white as a swan
    He who thus spoke guided our journeying
    Upward between the two walls of hard stone.
Stirring his plumes, he fanned us with his wing
    And named *qui lugent* blessed, for that they          50
    Shall dispense consolation, like a king.
We both had passed the angel a little way
    When, "What now ails thee that thine eyes are so
    Fixt on the ground?" my Guide began to say.
And I: "In such misgiving do I go                           55
    From a strange dream which doth my mind possess
    So that the thought I cannot from me throw."

50. *"Qui lugent"*: those who mourn.

"Sawest thou," he said, "that ancient sorceress
 For whom alone the mount above us wails?
 Sawest thou how man obtains from her release?  60
Let that suffice: beat the earth down with thy heels;
 Turn thine eyes toward the lure which from his seat
 The Eternal King spins round with the great wheels."
As a falcon, that first gazes at his feet,
 Turns at the cry and stretches him beyond  65
 Where desire draws him thither to his meat,
Such I became; and far as, for one bound
 Upwards, a path is cloven through the stone,
 Such went I up to where one must go round.
Soon as I was enlarged on the fifth zone  70
 I saw on it a weeping multitude
 With faces to the ground all lying prone.
*My spirit clave unto the dust*, I could
 Hear them cry out, with sighings and laments
 So that the words hardly were understood.  75
"O ye chosen of God, whose punishments
 Both hope and justice make less hard to bear,
 Direct our footsteps to the high ascents."
"If from the lying prone exempt ye are,
 And wish the speediest way to be revealed,  80
 Keep your right hands to the outside as ye fare."
This answer to the poet, who thus appealed,
 Was made a little in front of us; therefore
 I noted, as each spoke, what was concealed.
My Lord then with my eyes I turned to implore,  85
 Whereat his glad sign of assent I caught
 To what my eager look was craving for.
Then, free to do according to my thought,
 I passed forward above that creature there
 Whose words before had made me of him take note,  90
Saying: "Spirit, in whom weeping ripens fair
 That without which one cannot turn to God,
 Suspend for me awhile thy greater care.
Who thou wast, tell me, and why to earth ye are bowed,
 Face down, and if thou would'st that I should win  95
 Aught for thee yonder, whence I tread this road."
And he: "Why turned to Heaven our backs have been
 Thou shalt learn; but first *scias quod ego*
 *Fui successor Petri*. Down between.

---

59. "Above us": in the three upper
circles.
 62. "The lure . . .": the uplifting influence of the revolving heavens.

70. This is the circle of avarice and
prodigality.
 92. The fruit of repentance.
 98. "Know that I was a successor of
Peter." The speaker is Pope Adrian V.

Sestri and Chiaveri waters flow   100
  Of a fair stream, wherefrom our old estate
  Nameth the title it vaunts most to bestow.
One month, scarce more, taught me how weighs the great
  Mantle on him who keeps it from the dirt,
  So that all others seem a feather's weight.   105
Late came the day that could my soul convert,
  But when the Roman Pastor I became,
  Thus found I life to be with lies begirt.
I saw that there the heart no peace could claim,
  Nor in that life could one mount higher: of this   110
  Therefore the love sprang in me to a flame.
Up to that hour I, lost in avarice,
  Was miserable, being a soul in want
  Of God; thou seëst here what my forfeit is.
Here of what avarice works is made the account,   115
  In purge of souls converted ere the end;
  And no more bitter penalty hath the mount.
Even as our eyes on high we would not send,
  Which only upon earthly things were cast,
  So here to earth Justice hath forced them bend.   120
As avarice turned all our works to waste
  Because it quenched our love of all goodness,
  Even so Justice here doth hold us fast,
Both hands and feet, in seizure and duress;
  And so long as the just Lord hath assigned,   125
  So long we lie stretched-out and motionless."
I had knelt down; to speak was in my mind;
  But he, by the mere hearing, in that pause
  Being aware that I my back inclined,
Said, "Dost thou bow thy knees? and for what cause?"   130
  And I to him: " 'Tis for your dignity:
  My conscience pricked me, standing as I was."
"Make straight thy legs and rise up from thy knee,
  Brother," he answered: "err not; of one Lord
  I am fellow-servant with the rest and thee.   135
If thou hast understood that holy chord
  The Gospel sounds which *Neque nubent* saith,
  Thou mayest perceive well why I spoke that word.
Go now, and no more tarry upon thy path,
  For thou disturb'st the tears wherewith I crave   140
  To ripen what thyself didst say of faith.

101. "A fair stream": the Lavagna river. Adrian belonged to the Fieschi family, who were counts of Lavagna.
103. "One month": Adrian V held the papal office only for 38 days.

137. If thou hast interpreted *Neque nubent* ("They neither marry") in the broader sense, as meaning that earthly relations are not preserved in the spiritual world.

A niece yonder, Alagia named, I have,
  Good in herself, so only that our house
  Her nature by example not deprave.
She only is there to assist me with her vows."                    145

. . .

## CANTO XXVII

[Night is coming on, when the Angel of Chastity appears and
tells Dante that he cannot go further without passing through the
fire. He is terrified, remembering deaths by burning that he had
witnessed on earth; and even Virgil's encouragement cannot overcome his fears till he is reminded that Beatrice awaits him beyond.
The three pass through the fire and emerge at the place of ascent.
Another angel warns them to hasten, as the sun is setting. Each
now makes a bed for himself on a step of the stair. Dante sleeps,
and dreams of Leah and Rachel, types of the active and contemplative life, foreshadowing the meeting with Matilda and Beatrice
which is to come. He wakes with morning, and at the summit Virgil
tells him that his mission is ended and that Dante now needs no
guide or instructor.]

As when his first beams tremble in the sky
  There, where his own Creator shed his blood,
  While Ebro is beneath the Scales on high,
And noon scorches the wave on Ganges' flood,
  Such was the sun's height; day was soon to pass;        5
  When the angel of God joyful before us stood.
Outside the flames, above the bank, he was.
  *Beati mundo corde* we heard him sing
  In a voice more living far than comes from us.
Then "None goes further, if first the fire not sting.     10
  O hallowed spirits, enter unafraid
  And to the chant beyond let your ears cling."
When we were near him, this to us he said.
  Wherefore I, when I knew what his words meant,
  Became as one who in the grave is laid.                 15
Over my clasping hands forward I leant,
  Eyeing the fire, and vivid to my mind
  Men's bodies burning, once beheld, it sent.
Then toward me turned them both my escorts kind;
  And Virgil said to me: "O my son, here                  20
  Torment, may-be, but death thou shalt not find.

142. "Alagia" de' Fieschi was the
daughter of Adrian's brother Niccolò.
1–5. The time described is the approach of sunset.
8. Matt. 5:8: "Blessed are the pure
in heart."

Remember, O remember . . . and if thy fear
  On Geryon into safety I recalled,
  What shall I do now, being to God more near?
If thou within this womb of flames wert walled      25
  Full thousand years, for certainty believe
  That not of one hair could they make thee bald.
And if perchance thou think'st that I deceive,
  Go forward into them, and thy faith prove,
  With hands put in the edges of thy sleeve.      30
Out of thy heart all fear remove, remove!
  Turn hither and come confidently on!"
  And I stood fixed and with my conscience strove.
When he beheld me still and hard as stone,
  Troubled a little, he said: "Look now, this same      35
  Wall is 'twixt Beatrice and thee, my son."
As Pyramus at the sound of Thisbe's name
  Opened his dying eyes and gazed at her
  Then, when the crimson on the mulberry came,
So did I turn unto my wise Leader,      40
  My hardness melted, hearing the name told
  Which like a well-spring in my mind I bear.
Whereon he shook his head, saying: "Do we hold
  Our wish to stay on this side?" He smiled then
  As on a child by an apple's bribe cajoled.      45
Before me then the fire he entered in,
  Praying Statius that he follow at his heel
  Who for a long stretch now had walked between.
When I was in, I had been glad to reel,
  Therefrom to cool me, into boiling glass,      50
  Such burning beyond measure did I feel.
My sweet Father, to give me heart of grace,
  Continued only on Beatrice to descant,
  Saying: "Already I seem to see her face."
On the other side, to guide us, rose a chant,      55
  And we, intent on that alone to dwell,
  Came forth there, where the ascent began to slant.
And there we heard a voice *Venite* hail
  *Benedicti patris mei* out of light
  So strong, it mastered me and made me quail.      60
"The sun departs," it added; "comes the night.
  Tarry not; study at good pace to go

---

**39.** The mulberry turned red on being spattered with the blood of Pyramus, who stabbed himself when he thought Thisbe slain by a lion (Ovid, *Met.*, IV, 55–166).

58–59. Matt. 25:34: "Come, ye blessed of my Father . . ."

Before the west has darkened on your sight."
Straight rose the path within the rock, and so
    Directed onward, that I robbed the ray        65
    Before me from the sun, already low.
I and my sages few steps did assay
    When by the extinguished shadow we perceived
    That now behind us had sunk down the day.
And ere the horizon had one hue received        70
    In all the unmeasured regions of the air,
    And night her whole expansion had achieved,
Each of us made his bed upon a stair,
    Seeing that the nature of the mount o'ercame
    Alike the power to ascend and the desire.        75
As goats, now ruminating, though the same
    That, before feeding, brisk and wanton played
    On the high places of the hills, grow tame,
Silent, while the sun scorches, in the shade,
    Watched by the herd that props him hour by hour    80
    Upon his staff and, propt so, tends his trade;
And as the shepherd, lodging out-of-door,
    Watches night-long in quiet by his flock,
    Wary lest wild beast scatter it or devour;
Such were we then, all three, within that nook,    85
    I as a goat, they as a shepherd, there,
    On this and that side hemmed by the high rock.
Little could there of the outside things appear;
    But through that little I saw the stars to glow
    Bigger than ordinary and shine more clear.    90
Ruminating and gazing on them so
    Sleep took me; sleep which often will apprize
    Of things to come, and ere the event foreknow.
In the hour, I think, when first from Eastern skies
    Upon the mountain Cytherea beamed    95
    Whom fire of love forever glorifies,
A lady young and beautiful I seemed
    To see move through a plain and flower on flower
    To gather; singing, she was saying (I dreamed),
"Let them know, whoso of my name inquire,    100
    That I am Leah, and move my fingers fair
    Around, to make me a garland for a tire.

---

[80. *herd:* herdsman.—J. C. McG.]
95. "Cytherea" is Venus, whose star
shines before sunrise.
100. Dante is about to visit the
Garden of Eden, the abode of innocence

and harmless activity. Consequently
the active and the contemplative life
are revealed to him in the form of
Laban's daughters, Leah and Rachel.

To glad me at the glass I deck me here;
　　But never to her mirror is untrue
　　My sister Rachel, and sits all day there.　　105
She is fain to hold her beauteous eyes in view
　　As me with these hands I am fain to adorn:
　　To see contenteth her, and me to do."
Already, through the splendour ere the morn,
　　Which to wayfarers the more grateful shows,　　110
　　Lodging less far from home, where they return,
The shadows on all sides were fleeing, and close
　　On them my sleep fled; wherefore, having seen
　　The great masters risen already, I rose.
"That apple whose sweetness in their craving keen　　115
　　Mortals go seeking on so many boughs
　　This day shall peace to all thy hungers mean."
Words such as these to me did Virgil use;
　　And no propitious gifts did man acquire
　　For pleasure matching these, to have or choose.　　120
So came on me desire upon desire
　　To be above, that now with every tread
　　I felt wings on me growing to waft me higher.
When under us the whole high stair was sped
　　And we unto the topmost step had won,　　125
　　Virgil, fixing his eyes upon me, said:
"The temporal and the eternal fire, my son,
　　Thou hast beheld: thou art come now to a part
　　Where of myself I see no farther on.
I have brought thee hither both by wit and art.　　130
　　Take for thy guide thine own heart's pleasure now.
　　Forth from the narrows, from the steeps, thou art.
See there the sun that shines upon thy brow;
　　See the young grass, the flowers and coppices
　　Which this soil, of itself alone, makes grow.　　135
While the fair eyes are coming, full of bliss,
　　Which weeping made me come to thee before,
　　Amongst them thou canst go or sit at ease.
Expect from me no word or signal more.
　　Thy will is upright, sound of tissue, free:　　140
　　To disobey it were a fault; wherefore
Over thyself I crown thee and mitre thee."

． ． ．

115. "That apple . . .": earthly happiness.

142. I make thee thine own Emperor
and Pope.

## CANTO XXX

[Like the stars of Ursa Minor which guide sailors to port, the
Seven Candlesticks, stars of the Empyrean, control the movements
of those in the procession; and the elders who preceded the car now
turn toward it, and one (who represents the Song of Solomon) calls
on Beatrice to appear. Angels are seen scattering flowers, and in the
midst of them a veiled lady clad in the colors of Faith, Hope, and
Charity. It is Beatrice; and Dante experiences the same agitation
in her presence, though her face is not revealed, as when he first
saw her. Overcome, he turns for comfort to Virgil; but Virgil has
now disappeared; and Beatrice addresses Dante by name, severe in
look and in speech. Frozen by her reproaches, he is melted by the
compassion of the angels, to whom Beatrice tells of Dante's life
and disloyalty to her.]

Now when those Seven of the First Heaven stood still
    Which rising and declension never knew
    Nor veil of other mist than the evil will,
And which apprized each there what he should do,
    Even as the starry Seven in lower air 5
    Guide him to port who steereth by them true,
The people in whom truth doth itself declare,
    Who first between it and the Gryphon came,
    Turned to the car, as if their peace were there.
And one, as if Heaven prompted that acclaim, 10
    *Veni, sponsa, de Libano* chanted thrice,
    And after him all the others cried the same.
As at the last trump shall the saints arise,
    Crying alleluias to be re-attired
    In flesh, up from the cavern where each lies, 15
Upon the heavenly chariot so inspired
    A hundred sprang *ad vocem tanti senis,*
    Messengers of eternal life, who quired
Singing together *Benedictus qui venis,*
    While from their hands flowers up and down were
      thrown,
    And *Manibus O date lilia plenis.* 20
I have seen ere now at the beginning dawn
    The region of the East all coloured rose,

1–4. "The First Heaven": the
Empyrean.—"The evil will": man's
sinfulness.—"There": in the procession
of the Church.
    5–6. As the Ursa Minor guides the
helmsman.
    11. "Come with me from Lebanon,
my spouse." [Song of Solomon 4:8.—

J. C. McG.]
    17. "At the voice of so great an
elder."
    19. "Blessed is he that cometh" (in
the name of the Lord). [Matthew 21:9.
—J. C. McG.]
    21. "Oh, give lilies with full hands!"
[*Aeneid*, Book VI, l. 883.—J. C. McG.]

(The pure sky else in beauty of peace withdrawn)
When shadowed the sun's face uprising shows,　　　　25
  So that the mists, attempering his powers,
  Let the eye linger upon him in repose;
So now for me amid a cloud of flowers
  That from the angels' hands up-floated light
  And fell, withinside and without, in showers,　　30
A lady, olive-crowned o'er veil of white,
  Clothed in the colour of a living flame,
  Under a mantle green, stole on my sight.
My spirit that a time too long to name
  Had passed, since, at her presence coming nigh,　35
  A trembling thing and broken it became,
Now by no recognition of the eye
  But virtue invisible that went out from her
  Felt old love seize me in all its mastery.
When smote my sight the high virtue that, ere　　40
  The years of boyhood were behind me laid,
  Already had pierced me through, as with a spear,
With such trust as a child that is afraid
  Or hurt, runs to his mother with his pains,
  I turned me to the left, to seek me aid　　　　45
And say to Virgil: "Scarce one drop remains
  Of blood in me that trembles not: by this
  I recognize the old flame within my veins."
But Virgil had from us his company's
  Sweet solace taken, Virgil, father kind,　　　50
  Virgil, who for my soul's weal made me his.
Nor all that our first mother had resigned
  Availed to keep my cheeks, washed with the dew,
  From tears that once more stained them, welling blind.
"Dante, that Virgil leaves thee, and from thy view　55
  Is vanished, O not yet weep; weep not yet,
  For thou must weep, another stab to rue."
Like the Admiral who on poop or prow is set,
  To eye his men, in the other ships dispersed,
  And comes, each heart to embolden and abet,　　60
So on the left side of the car, when first
  I turned, hearing my own name in my ear
  (Which of necessity is here rehearsed)
I found the gaze of her I had seen appear
  Erewhile, veiled, in the angelic festival,　　　65
  Toward me, this side the stream, directed clear;
Howbeit the veil she had from her head let fall,

52. Not all Eden.

With grey leaf of Minerva chapleted,
Disclosing her, did not disclose her all.
Still severe, standing in her queenlihead,                    70
    She spoke on, as one speaks whose purpose is
    To keep the hottest word awhile unsaid.
"Look on me well: I am, I am Beatrice.
    How, then, didst thou deign to ascend the Mount?
    Knewest thou not that, here, man is in bliss?"      75
I dropt mine eyes down to the lucent fount,
    But seeing myself there, drew them back in haste
    To the grass, heavy upon my shame's account.
As to a child a mother looks stern-faced,
    So to me seemed she: pity austere in thought        80
    Hath in its savour a so bitter taste.
She ceased then, and from every angel throat
    Straightway *In te, Domine, speravi* rose
    But beyond *pedes meos* they passed not.
As on the chine of Italy the snows                           85
    Lodged in the living rafters harden oft
    To freezing, when the North-East on them blows,
Then, inly melted, trickle from aloft,
    If from the shadeless countries a breath stirs,
    Like in the flame a candle melting soft,             90
So was I, without sighs and without tears,
    In presence of their singing who accord
    Their notes to music of the eternal spheres;
But when I was aware of the sweet chord
    Of their compassion, more than if they spoke        95
    Saying, "Lady, why this shame upon him poured?"
The ice that round my heart had hardened woke
    Warm into breath and water, and from my breast
    In anguish, through mouth and through eyes, outbroke.
She, standing ever in her still'd arrest                    100
    Upon the car's same side, to the array
    Of those compassionate beings these words addrest:
"Ye so keep watch in the everlasting day
    That neither night stealeth from you, nor sleep,
    One step that the world takes upon its way;         105
Therefore my answer shall the more care keep
    That he, there, understand me amid those tears,
    So that transgression equal sorrow reap.

83–84. Ps. 31: "In thee, O Lord, do I put my trust." Verse 8 ends with: "Thou hast set my feet in a large room."

85. "The chine of Italy" is the Apennine range.
89. "The shadeless countries": the African desert.

Not only by operation of great spheres
   Which to some certain end each seed uptrain     110
   According as the starry voice it hears,
But bounty of heavenly graces, which for rain
   Have exhalations born in place so high
   That our eyes may not near to them attain,
This man was such in natural potency,     115
   In his new life, that all the ingrained good
   Looked in him to have fruited wondrously.
But so much groweth the more rank and rude
   The soil with bad seed and unhusbanded,
   The more it hath from earth of hardihood.     120
His spirit some time my countenance comforted
   With look of my young eyes for its support,
   Drawing him, the right path with me to tread.
Soon as the threshold I had passed, athwart
   The second period, and life changed its home,     125
   Me he forsook, with others to consort.
When from the flesh to spirit I had clomb
   And beauty and virtue greater in me grew,
   Less dear to him, more strange did I become;
And with perverted steps on ways untrue     130
   He sought false images of good, that ne'er
   Perform entire the promise that was due.
Nor helped me the inspiration won by prayer
   Whereby through dream or other hidden accost
   I called him back; so little had he care.     135
So low he sank, all means must I exhaust,
   Till naught for his salvation profited
   Save to be shown the people that are lost.
For this I broached the gateway of the dead,
   For this with tears was my entreaty brought     140
   To him, by whom his feet were hither led.
The ordinance of high God were set at naught
   If Lethe were passed over into peace,
   And such viand enjoyed, without some scot
Of penitence that may the tears release."     145

### CANTO XXXI

[Dante, accused by Beatrice, confesses his sin and is filled with
penitence. Overwhelmed by the severity of Beatrice's words, and by

109–112. The "great spheres" are
the revolving heavens, which determine
the disposition of every human being.
God also bestows upon every individual
a special degree of grace.

116. "New life": young life.
125. "The second period": begins at
25. Her "life changed" the temporal
home for the eternal.

his own remorse, he falls senseless. When he recovers from his faint, he finds that Matilda is drawing him across Lethe stream, in which she immerses him. The four dancers (the four cardinal virtues) lead him up to the Gryphon [who represents Christ, the second person of the Trinity—J. C. McG.], where Beatrice is standing; in her eyes the Gryphon is mirrored, now in one form now in the other. The other three (the Theological Virtues) then come forward, dancing, and implore Beatrice to smile upon her faithful servant.]

"O thou who art yon-side the sacred stream,"
   Turning her speech to point at me the blade
   Which even the edge had made so sharp to seem,
She spoke again, continuing undelayed.
   "Say, say if this be true; for, thus accused,      5
   Confession must thereto by thee be made"
Whereat my faculties were so confused
   That the voice stirred and faltered and was dead
   Ere it came free of the organs that it used.
Short time she endured; "What think'st thou?" then she said.      10
   "Answer, for in thee the sad memories
   By the water are not yet discomfited."
Fear and confusion's mingled miseries
   Constrained out of my mouth a "Yes" so low
   That to understand it there was need of eyes.      15
As the arbalast that snaps both string and bow,
   When to a too great tautness it is forced,
   And shooting hits the mark with feebler blow,
So under this so heavy charge I burst,
   Out of me letting gush the sighs and tears;      20
   And in its vent my voice failed as from thirst.
Wherefore she questioned: "Within those desires
   I stirred in thee, to make thee love the Good
   Beyond which nought is, whereto man aspires,
What moats or what strong chains athwart thy road      25
   Didst thou encounter, that of hope to pass
   Onward, thou needs must strip thee as of a load?
And what solace or profit in the face
   Of the others was displayed unto thine eye
   That thou before them up and down must pace?"      30
After the drawing of a bitter sigh
   Scarce had I voice an answer to essay,
   And lips with difficulty shaped reply.
Weeping I said: "Things of the passing day,

12. "The water": of Lethe.

Soon as your face no longer on me shone,                    35
With their false pleasure turned my steps away."
And she: "If thou wert silent, nor didst own
What thou avowest, not less were record
Of thy fault made: by such a judge 'tis known.
But when the sinner's own mouth has outpoured          40
The accusation, in our court the wheel
Against the edge is turned back on the sword.
Howbeit, that now the shame thou carry still
For thine error, and at the Siren's plea
Another time thou be of stronger will,                         45
Lay aside the seed of weeping; hark to me.
Hear how my buried body should have spurred
And on the opposite path have furthered thee.
Nature or art never to thee assured
Such pleasure as the fair limbs that did house           50
My spirit, and now are scattered and interred.
And if the highest pleasure failed thee thus
By my death, at such time what mortal thing
Ought to have drawn thee toward it amorous?
Truly oughtest thou at the first arrow's sting             55
Of those lures, to rise after me on high,
Who was no more made in such fashioning.
Nay, nor should girl or other vanity
Of such brief usage have thy wings down-weighed
To wait for other coming shafts to fly.                        60
The young bird waiteth two or three indeed;
But in the eyes of the full-fledged in vain
The net is spread and the arrows vainly speed."
As boys that dumb with shamefastness remain,
Eyes to ground, listening to their faults rehearsed,   65
Knowing themselves in penitence and pain,
So stood I; and she said: "From what thou hear'st
If thou art grieving, lift thy beard and look,
And thou shalt by a greater grief be pierced."
With less resistance is a stubborn oak                        70
Torn up by wind (whether 'twas ours that blew
Or wind that from Iarbas' land awoke)
Than at her bidding I my chin up-drew;
And when by "beard" she asked me for my face,
The venom in the meaning well I knew.                       75

41–42. The sword of justice is blunted, i.e., tempered with mercy.
58. Is the "girl" to be taken literally, or does she symbolize some intellectual pursuit inconsistent with the spiritual ideal? The question remains open.
68. "Beard": chin.
72. "Iarbas" was king of Libya.
75. The implication that the beard is inconsistent with Dante's youthful vagaries.

And when to expose my features I could brace
  My spirit, I saw those primal Essences
  Reposing from their strewings in their place.
And mine eyes, hardly as yet assured of these,
  Were 'ware of Beatrice, turned toward that beast    80
  Which in two natures one sole person is.
Under her veil beyond the stream I wist
  That she surpassed her ancient self yet more
  Than when amongst us she surpassed the rest.
The nettle of penitence pricked me now so sore    85
  That, of all things, that which did most pervert
  To love of it, I had most hatred for.
The recognition gnawed so at my heart
  That I fell conquered, and what then of me
  Became, she knows who had devised the smart.    90
Then when my heart restored the faculty
  Of sense, the lady I had found alone
  I saw above me, and "Hold," she said, "hold me."
To the neck into the stream she had led me on
  And, drawing me behind her, went as light    95
  Over the water as a shuttle thrown.
When I was near the bank of blessed sight
  *Asperges me* my ears so sweetly graced
  I cannot recollect it, far less write.
The fair lady opened her arms, embraced    100
  My head, and plunged me underneath the flow,
  Where swallowing I must needs the water taste,
Then raised me and presented me, bathed so,
  Within the dancing of the beauteous Four;
  And each an arm about me came to throw.    105
"Here we are nymphs, in the sky stars: before
  Beatrice descended to the world, we were
  Ordained to be her handmaids evermore.
We'll lead thee to her eyes; but the Three there,
  Whose gaze is deeper, in the blissful light    110
  That is within, shall make thine own more clear."
Thus singing they began, and me then right
  Up to the Gryphon's breast with them they led
  Where Beatrice was standing opposite.
"See that thou spare not of thy gaze," they said.    115
  "We have set thee afore the emeralds to stand

77. "Primal Essences": the angels.
80. "That beast": the Gryphon.
92. "The lady": Matilda.
98. "Purge me": Ps. 51:7.
104. "The beauteous Four": the cardinal virtues.
109. "The Three": the theological virtues.
116. "The emeralds": the eyes of Beatrice.

Wherefrom for thee Love once his armoury fed."
Thousand desires, hotter than flame, constrained
    The gaze of mine eyes to the shining eyes
    Which on the Gryphon only fixed remained.      120
As in the glass the sun, not otherwise
    The two-fold creature had its mirroring
    Within them, now in one, now the other guise.
Think, Reader, if I marvelled at this thing,
    When I beheld it unchanged as at first      125
    Itself, and in its image altering.
While in deep astonishment immersed
    My happy soul was tasting of that food
    Which, itself sating, of itself makes thirst,
Showing themselves as if of loftiest blood      130
    In their demeanour, the other three came then
    Dancing to the angelic air they trod.
"Turn, Beatrice, turn thy sainted eyes again,"
    So were they singing, "to thy servant leal
    Who to see thee so many steps hath ta'en.      135
Of thy grace do us this grace, to unveil
    To him thy mouth, so that he may discern
    The second beauty which thou dost conceal."
O splendour of the living light eterne,
    Who is there that beneath Parnassus' shade      140
    Has grown pale or has drunk of that cistern
That would not seem to have his mind o'er-weighed
    Striving to paint thee as thou appeared'st where
    To figure thee, heaven's harmonies are made,
When thou didst unveil to the open air?      145

## Paradise (Paradiso)

### CANTO I

[The poet invokes the aid of Apollo in attempting the hardest
part of his theme, the description of Paradise.

On earth, in Italy, it is evening; but at the summit of the Mount
of Purgatory it is near noon about the time of the vernal equinox;
the sun being in Aries, a propitious conjunction. Dante and Beatrice
are suddenly transported to the sphere of fire, between the earth and
the moon. Dante is so "transhumanized" that he is now able to hear
the music of the spheres; but at first he is bewildered, not understanding, till Beatrice explains that he has left the earth behind.
He is still puzzled to know how it is that he has risen, more swiftly

123. Now with its human, now with
its divine, bearing—the two component
parts of the nature of Christ.

138. "The second beauty" is the
mouth, the first beauty being the eyes.

than air or fire, against the laws of gravitation. Beatrice tells him
that the instinct implanted in the soul is to rise, as fire rises, towards
heaven; this belongs to the order of the universe, in which each
part has its own function. Dante has been liberated from the dis-
tractions which, through man's possession of free will, sometimes
cause the soul to be diverted from its aim.]

The glory of Him who moveth all that is
    Pervades the universe, and glows more bright
    In the one region, and in another less.
In that heaven which partakes most of His light
    I have been, and have beheld such things as who     5
    Comes down thence has no wit nor power to write;
Such depth our understanding deepens to
    When it draws near unto its longing's home
    That memory cannot backward with it go.
Nevertheless what of the blest kingdom     10
    Could in my memory, for its treasure, stay
    Shall now the matter of my song become.
For the last labour, good Apollo, I pray,
    Make me so apt a vessel of thy power
    As is required for gift of thy loved bay.     15
One of Parnassus' peaks hath heretofore
    Sufficed me; both now shall I need forthwith
    For entering on the last arena-floor.
Enter into my bosom, and in-breathe
    Such force as filled thee to out-sing the strain     20
    Of Marsyas when thou didst his limbs unsheathe.
O divine power, if thou so far sustain,
    That I may show the image visibly
    Of the holy realm imprinted on my brain,
Thou'lt see me come to thy beloved tree     25
    And there the leaves upon my temples fit
    Which I shall earn both through the theme and thee.
So few times, Father, is there plucked of it
    For Caesar or for poet triumphing
    (Fault and reproach of human will and wit),     30
That in the joyous Delphic god must spring
    A joy new-born, when the Peneian frond
    With longing for itself doth any sting.
A small spark kindles a great flame beyond:
    Haply after me with better voice than mine     35

15. "Loved bay": Daphne, loved and
pursued by Apollo, was changed to a
laurel.
21. "Marsyas": a satyr, who was defeated and then flayed by Apollo.
25. "Thy beloved tree": the laurel.
31–32. "The joyous Delphic god":
Apollo. "The Peneian frond": the laurel.

Such prayer shall plead, that Cirrha may respond.
The world's lamp rises upon men to shine
  By divers gates, but from that gate which makes
  Four circles with three crosses to conjoin,
With happier star joined, happier course it takes,    40
  And more to its own example can persuade,
  Moulding and stamping it, the mundane wax.
Almost this gate had morning yonder made
  And evening here; and there that hemisphere
  Was all white, and the other part in shade,    45
When, turned on her left side, I was aware
  Of Beatrice, fixing on the sun her eyes:
  Never on it so fixed was eagle's stare.
And as a second ray will always rise
  Where the first struck, and backward seek ascent,    50
  Like pilgrim hastening when he homeward hies,
So into my imagination went
  Through the eyes her gesture; and my own complied,
  And on the sun, past wont, my eyes were bent.
Much is permitted there which is denied    55
  Here to our faculties, thanks to the place
  Made for mankind to own, and there abide.
Not long I endured him, yet not so brief space
  But that I saw what sparkles round him shone
  Like molten ore fresh from the fierce furnace;    60
And, on a sudden, day seemed added on
  To day, as if He, who such things can do,
  Had glorified heaven with a second sun.
Beatrice was standing and held full in view
  The eternal wheels, and I fixed on her keen    65
  My eyes, that from above their gaze withdrew.
And at her aspect I became within
  As Glaucus after the herb's tasting, whence
  To the other sea-gods he was made akin.
The passing beyond bounds of human sense    70
  Words cannot tell; let then the examples sate
  Him for whom grace reserves the experience.

36. "Cirrha" stands for Delphi, Apollo's abode.
37–44. In these lines Dante describes the season. [The "gate" is the point of the horizon from which the sun rises on a particular day. On this day (Wednesday, April 13, 1300) it was still in the zodiacal sign Aries (March 21–April 21). On the day the sun enters Aries, three circles—the celestial equator, the ecliptic, and the colure of the equinoxes—intersect the horizon (itself a circle); hence, four circles and three crosses. It was believed that the sun's influence was most favorable when it was in Aries.—J. C. McG.]
44–45. Here Dante tells the hour: it was noon in Eden, midnight in Jerusalem.
56. "Thanks to the place": Eden.
65. "The eternal wheels": the revolving heavens.
68. The fisherman Glaucus, tasting of a certain herb, became a sea-god.

If I was only what thou didst create
   Last in me, O Love whose rule the heavens attest,
   Thou know'st, who with thy light didst lift my state.   75
When that the wheel which thou eternizest
   In longing, held me with the harmony
   Which thou attunest and distinguishest,
So much of heaven was fired, it seemed to me,
   With the sun's blaze that never river or rain   80
   Widened the waters to so great a sea.
The new sound and the great light made me fain
   With craving keener than had ever been
   Before in me, their cause to ascertain.
She then, who saw me as I myself within,   85
   My mind's disturbance eager to remit,
   Opened her lips before I could begin,
And spoke: "Thou makest thyself dense of wit
   With false fancy, so that thou dost not see
   What thou would'st see, wert thou but rid of it.   90
Thou'rt not on earth, as thou supposest thee:
   But lightning from its own place rushing out
   Ne'er sped as thou, who to thy home dost flee."
If I was stript of my first teasing doubt
   By the brief smiling little words, yet freed   95
   I was not, but enmeshed in a new thought.
And I replied: "I am released indeed
   From much amazement; yet am still amazed
   That those light bodies I transcend in speed."
She, sighing in pity, gave me as she gazed   100
   The look that by a mother is bestowed
   Upon her child in its delirium crazed,
And said: "All things, whatever their abode,
   Have order among themselves; this Form it is
   That makes the universe like unto God.   105
Here the high beings see the imprint of His
   Eternal power, which is the goal divine
   Whereto the rule aforesaid testifies.
In the order I speak of, all natures incline
   Either more near or less near to their source   110
   According as their diverse lots assign.
To diverse harbours thus they move perforce
   O'er the great ocean of being, and each one

73. Dante is not sure whether he took his body with him to Heaven, or left it behind.

77. The swift motion of the Primum Mobile, the outermost sphere of the material universe, is due to the eagerness of every one of its parts to come into contact with every part of God's own Heaven, the Empyrean.

93. "Thy home": the Empyrean.

110. "Their source": God.

With instinct given it to maintain its course.
  This bears the fiery element to the moon;        115
  This makes the heart of mortal things to move;
  This knits the earth together into one.
Not only creatures that are empty of
  Intelligence this bow shoots towards the goal,
  But those that have both intellect and love.       120
The Providence, that rules this wondrous whole,
  With its own light makes the heaven still to stay
  Wherein whirls that which doth the swiftest roll.
And thither now upon the appointed way
  We are borne on by virtue of that cord still      125
  Which means a joyful mark, shoot what it may.
True it is that as the form oftentimes ill
  Accordeth with the intention of the art,
  The matter being slow to serve the will,
So aside sometimes may the creature start;       130
  For it has power, though on this course impelled,
  To swerve in purpose toward some other part
(And so the fire from cloud may be beheld
  To fall), if the first impulse of its flight
  To earth be wrested, by false pleasure held.     135
Thou should'st not marvel, if I esteem aright,
  More at thy rising than at streams we see
  Fall to the base down from a mountain's height;
Marvel it were if thou, from hindrance free,
  Had'st sat below, resolved there to remain,     140
  As stillness in live flame on earth would be."
Thereon toward heaven she turned her gaze again.

. . .

### CANTO III

[Dante becomes aware of faces appearing eager to speak to him.
At first he supposes them to be reflections (unlike Narcissus, who
supposed his reflection to be real). One of these spirits is Piccarda,
about whom Dante had asked her brother Forese in Purgatory
(Canto XXIV). She is with those placed in the sphere of the Moon
because of vows broken or imperfectly performed. Dante asks if
those who are in this lowest sphere ever crave for a more exalted
place in Paradise. She tells him that this is impossible; it is of the
essence of their bliss merely to fulfill the divine will: "In His will is
our peace." And she goes on to tell how she took the veil in the
Order of Saint Clare, but was forcibly taken from her convent (to

122–125. "The heaven": the Empyrean, within which the swift Primum
Mobile revolves. "That cord": the
    bowstring of instinct.
    131. "For it has power": the free
will.

be married to a noble). Among these spirits is the Empress Constance, who also was torn from her convent and married to Henry VI, the second of the three "whirlwinds" from Suabia (line 119); the first being Frederick Barbarossa, and the third Frederick II; all these emperors were men of tempestuous energy.]

That Sun which fired my bosom of old with love
 Had thus bared for me in beauty the aspect sweet
 Of truth, expert to prove as to disprove;
And I, to avow me of all error quit,
 Confident and assured, lifted my head   5
 More upright, in such measure as was fit.
But now appeared a sight that riveted
 Me to itself with such compulsion keen
 That my confession from my memory fled.
As from transparent glasses polished clean,   10
 Or water shining smooth up to its rim,
 Yet not so that the bottom is unseen,
Our faces' lineaments return so dim
 That pearl upon white forehead not more slow
 Would on our pupils its pale image limn;   15
So I beheld faces that seemed aglow
 To speak, and fell into the counter-snare
 From what made love 'twixt man and pool to grow.
No sooner had I marked those faces there,
 Than, thinking them reflections, with swift eyes  20
 I turned about to see of whom they were,
And saw nothing: again, in my surprise,
 I turned straight to the light of my sweet Guide,
 Who smiling, burned within her sainted eyes.
"Marvel not at my smiling," she replied,   25
 "To contemplate thy childlike thought revealed
 Which cannot yet its foot to truth confide,
But moves thee, as ever, on emptiness to build.
 True substances are these thine eyes perceive,
 Remitted here for vows not all fulfilled.   30
Speak with them therefore, hearken and believe,
 For the true light which is their happiness
 Lets them not swerve, but to it they must cleave."
And I to the shade that seemed most near to press
 For converse, turned me and began, as one  35
 Who is overwrought through longing in excess:
"O spirit made for bliss, who from the sun
 Of life eternal feelest the sweet ray

1. "That Sun": Beatrice.    18. "Man": Narcissus.

Which, save 'tis tasted, is conceived by none,
  It will be gracious to me, if I may           40
    Be gladdened with thy name and all your fate."
And she, with laughing eyes and no delay:
  "Our charity no more locks up the gate
    Against a just wish than that Charity
    Which would have all its court in like estate.     45
On earth I was a Virgin Sister: see
  What memory yields thee, and my being now
    More beautiful will hide me not from thee,
But that I am Piccarda thou wilt know,
  Who with these other blessed ones placed here    50
    Am blessed in the sphere that moves most slow;
For our desires, which kindle and flame clear
  Only in the pleasure of the Holy Ghost,
    To what he appointeth joyfully adhere;
And this which seems to thee so lowly a post     55
  Is given to us because the vows we made
    Were broken, or complete observance lost."
Then I to her: "Something divinely glad
  Shines in your marvellous aspect, to replace
    In you the old conceptions that I had;     60
I was slow therefore to recall thy face:
  But what thou tell'st me helpeth now to clear
    My sight, and thee more easily to retrace.
But tell me: you that are made happy here,
  Do ye to a more exalted place aspire,     65
    To see more, or to make yourselves more dear?"
She smiled a little, and with her smiled that choir
  Of spirits; then so joyous she replied
    That she appeared to burn in love's first fire:
"Brother, the virtue of love hath pacified     70
  Our will; we long for what we have alone,
    Nor any craving stirs in us beside.
If we desired to reach a loftier zone,
  Our longings would be all out of accord
    With His will who disposeth here His own.    75
For that, these circles, thou wilt see, afford
  No room, if love be our whole being's root
    And thou ponder the meaning of that word.
Nay, 'tis of the essence of our blessed lot
  In the divine will to be cloistered still     80
    Through which our own wills into one are wrought,

44. "That Charity": of God.        company; *thy* refers to Piccarda alone.
[59–61. *Your* refers to the whole    —J. C. McG.]

As we from step to step our stations fill
   Throughout this realm, to all the realm 'tis bliss
   As to its King, who wills us into His will;
And in His will is perfected our peace.           85
   It is the sea whereunto moveth all
   That it creates and nature makes increase."
Then saw I how each heaven for every soul
   Is paradise, though from the Supreme Good
   The dews of grace not in one measure fall.      90
But as may hap, when sated with one food
   Still for another we have appetite,
   We ask for this, and that with thanks elude,
Such words and gesture used I that I might
   Learn from her what that web was where she plied   95
   The shuttle and yet drew not the head outright.
"Perfect life and high merit have enskied
   A Lady above," she said, "whose rule they take
   In your world who in robe and veil abide,
That they till death may, sleeping and awake,      100
   Be with that Spouse who giveth welcome free
   To all vows love may for His pleasure make.
To follow her, a young girl, did I flee
   The world and, closed within her habit, vowed
   Myself to the pathway of her company.      105
Afterwards men, used to evil more than good,
   Tore me away, out of the sweet cloister;
   And God knows then what way of life I trod.
This other splendour whom thou see'st appear
   To thee on my right side, who, glowing pale,    110
   Kindles with all the radiance of our sphere,
Can of herself tell also the same tale.
   She was a Sister; from her head they tore
   Likewise the shadow of the sacred veil.
She was turned back into the world once more   115
   Against her will, against good usage too;
   Yet still upon her heart the veil she wore.
This is the light of the great Constance, who
   From Suabia's second whirlwind was to bring
   To birth the third Power, and the last ye knew."  120
Thus spoke she to me, and then began to sing
   *Ave Maria*, and singing disappeared,
   As through deep water sinks a heavy thing.
My sight, which followed far as it was powered,

98. "A Lady above": St. Clare, the friend of St. Francis; she founded the order that bears her name.

106. "Men": her brother Corso Donati and his followers.

When it had lost her, turned and straightway shot    125
   To the other mark, more ardently desired,
And Beatrice, only Beatrice, it sought.
   But she upon my look was flaming so
   That at the first my sight endured it not;
And this made me for questioning more slow.    130

. . .

### CANTO XXXI

[Further description of the Rose of Paradise, into and out of
which the angels flit like bees about a flower. Dante, having taken
in its general form, turns to Beatrice to inquire more particularly
about it. But Beatrice has disappeared, and in her place is an old
man, who proves to be St. Bernard, and who points out Beatrice,
now in her appointed seat above. Next, he bids Dante contemplate
the beauty of the Virgin.]

In form, then, of a radiant white rose
   That sacred soldiery before mine eyes
   Appeared, which in His blood Christ made His spouse.
But the other host which seëth and, as it flies,
   Singeth His glory who enamours it    5
   And the goodness which its greatness magnifies,
Like bees, which deep into the flowers retreat
   One while, and at another winging come
   Back thither where their toil is turned to sweet,
Descended into the great flower, a-bloom    10
   With petal on petal, and re-ascended thence
   To where its love forever hath its home.
Their faces all were as a flame intense,
   Their wings of gold, the rest so pure a white
   That never snow could dazzle so the sense.    15
Into the flower descending from the height
   Through rank on rank they breathed the peace, the glow,
   They gathered as they fanned their sides in flight.
And, spite of the interposing to and fro
   Of such a throng 'twixt high heaven and the flower,    20
   Vision and splendour none had to forgo;
For the divine light pierceth with such power
   The world, in measure of its complement
   Of worth, that naught against it may endure.
This realm of unimperilled ravishment    25
   With spirits thronged from near times and from far

---

2–4. "That sacred soldiery": the Redeemed.—"The other host": the angels.

Had look and love all on the one mark bent.
O triple Light, which in a single star
  Shining on them their joy can so expand,
  Look down upon this storm wherein we are!    30
If the barbarian, coming from such land
  As every day by wheeling Helice
  And her belovèd son with her, is spanned,
Seeing Rome and her stupendous works,—if he
  Was dazed, in that age when the Lateran    35
  Rose, builded to outsoar mortality,
I, who was come to the divine from man,
  To the eternal out of time, and from
  Florence unto a people just and sane,
How dazed past measure must I needs become!    40
  Between this and my joy I found it good,
  Truly, to hear naught and myself be dumb.
And as the pilgrim quickens in his blood
  Within the temple of his vow at gaze,
  Already in hope to re-tell how it stood,    45
So traversing the light of living rays
  My eyes along the ranks, now up I led,
  Now down, and now wandered in circling ways.
I saw faces, such as to love persuade,
  Adorned by their own smile and Other's light    50
  And gestures that all dignity displayed.
The general form of Paradise my sight
  Had apprehended in its ambience,
  But upon no part had it rested quite;
I turned then with a wish re-kindled thence    55
  To ask my Lady and to be satisfied
  Concerning things which held me in suspense.
One thing I thought, another one replied:
  I thought to have seen Beatrice, and behold!
  An elder, robed like to those glorified.    60
His eyes and cheeks of benign gladness told,
  And in his bearing was a kindliness
  Such as befits a father tender-souled:
"Where is she?" I cried on a sudden in my distress.
  "To end thy longing, Beatrice was stirred,"    65
  He answered then, "to bring me from my place.
Her shalt thou see, if to the circle third

---

31–33. "Such land": the North.
"Helice" and "her . . . son" Arcas
are the Great and the Little Bear.
  35. "The Lateran": the old Papal
palace in Rome.

60. "An elder": St. Bernard, a
great mystic of the twelfth century,
famous for his devotion to the Blessed
Virgin.
  67. The first circle is that of Mary,

From the highest rank thine eyes thou wilt up-raise,
There on the throne whereto she hath been preferred."
Without reply I lifted up my gaze          70
And saw her making for herself a crown
Of the reflection from the eternal rays.
From the highest sky which rolls the thunder down
No mortal eye is stationed so remote,
Though in the deepest of the seas it drown,      75
As then from Beatrice was my sight; but naught
It was to me; for without any veil
Her image down to me undimmed was brought.
"O Lady, in whom my hopes all prosper well,
And who for my salvation didst endure      80
To leave the printing of thy feet in Hell,
Of all that I have seen, now and before,
By virtue of what thy might and goodness gave,
I recognize the grace and sovereign power.
Thou hast drawn me up to freedom from a slave    85
By all those paths, all those ways known to thee
Through which thou had'st such potency to save.
Continue thy magnificence in me,
So that my soul, which thou hast healed of scar,
May please thy sight when from the body free."    90
So did I pray; and she, removed so far
As she appeared, looked on me smiling-faced;
Then to the eternal fountain turned her there.
Whereon the holy Elder: "That thou may'st
Consummate this thy journey, whereunto    95
Prayer and a holy love made me to haste,
Fly with thine eyes this heavenly garden through!
Gazing on it shall better qualify
Thy vision, the light upward to pursue.
The Queen of Heaven, for whom continually    100
I burn with love, will grant us every grace
Since Bernard, her own faithful one, am I."
Like one, some Croat perhaps, who comes to gaze
On our Veronica with eyes devout,
Nor states the inveterate hunger that he has,    105
So long as it is shown, but says in thought,
"My Lord Christ Jesus, very God, is this
Indeed Thy likeness in such fashion wrought?"

the second that of Eve, the third that
of Rachel, beside whom Beatrice sits.
  96. The "prayer and a holy love" are
Beatrice's.

104. The "Veronica" is the true image of the Savior, left on a kerchief. It
was shown at St. Peter's in Rome.

Such was I, gazing on the impassioned bliss
  Of love in him who even in this world's woe      110
  By contemplation tasted of that peace.
"Child of Grace," he began, "thou wilt not know
  This joyous being in its felicity
  If thine eyes rest but on the base below.
Look on the farthest circles thou can'st see,      115
  Till thou perceive enthroned the Queen, to whom
  This realm devoteth its whole fealty."
I raised my eyes; and as in morning bloom
  The horizon's eastern part becometh bright
  And that where the sun sinks is overcome,      120
So with my eyes climbing a mountain's height,
  As from a valley, I saw on the utmost verge
  What outshone all else fronting me in light.
As that point where the car is to emerge,
  Which Phaëthon drove ill, glows fieriest      125
  And softens down its flame on either marge,
So did that oriflamme of peace attest
  The midmost glory, and on either side
  In equal measure did its rays arrest.
And at that mid-point, with wings opened wide,      130
  A myriad angels moved in festive play,
  In brilliance and in art diversified.
There, smiling upon dance and roundelay,
  I saw a Beauty, that was happiness
  In the eyes of all the other saints' array.      135
And if in speaking I had wealth not less
  Than in imagining, I would not dare
  To attempt the least part of her loveliness.
When of my fixt look Bernard was aware,
  So fastened on his own devotion's flame,      140
  He turned his eyes with so much love to her
That mine more ardent and absorbed became.

#### CANTO XXXII

[Bernard explains the conformation of the Celestial Rose. It is
divided down the middle, and across; on one side are male, on the
other female, saints. Below the horizontal division are the souls
of beatified children. That Dante may be vouchsafed a vision of
Deity itself, Bernard makes supplication to the Virgin, and bids
Dante accompany him in his prayer.]

---

111. St. Bernard in his meditations
had a foretaste of the peace of Heaven.
124. "The car": of the sun.

127. "That oriflamme," i.e., golden
pennant, is the streak of light on Mary's
side.
141. "To her": on Mary.

Rapt in love's bliss, that contemplative saint
  Nevertheless took up the instructor's part,
  Uttering these sacred words with no constraint:
"The wound that Mary closed, and soothed its smart,
  She, who so beautiful sits at her feet,      5
  Opened, and yet more deeply pressed the dart.
In the order making the third rank complete
  Rachel thou can'st distinguish next below
  With Beatrice in her appointed seat.
Sara, Rebecca, Judith, and her too,      10
  Ancestress of the singer, whose cry rose
  *Miserere mei* for his fault and rue,—
These thou beholdest tier by tier disclose,
  Descending, as I name them each by name,
  From petal after petal down the Rose.      15
And from the seventh grade downward, following them,
  Even as above them, Hebrew women bide,
  Parting the tresses on the Rose's stem;
Because, according as faith made confide
  In Christ, these serve as for a party-wall      20
  At which the stairs of sanctity divide.
On this side, where the flower is filled in all
  Its numbered petals, sit in order they
  Who waiting on Christ Coming heard His call;
On the other side, where certain gaps betray      25
  Seats empty, in semicircle, thou look'st on
  Such as in Christ Come had their only stay.
And as on the one side the glorious throne
  Of the Lady of Heaven and the other thrones as well
  Below it make partition, so great John      30
Sits over against her, ever there to dwell,
  Who, ever holy, endured the desert's fare,
  And martyrdom, and then two years in Hell.
Beneath him, chosen to mark the boundary there
  Francis and Benedict and Augustine shine      35
  And others, round by round, down even to here.
Now marvel at the deep foresight divine!
  For the faith's either aspect, equal made,
  Shall consummate this garden's full design.
And know that downward from the midmost grade      40

---

4–5. "The wound": of original sin. "She": Eve.

11. "Ancestress": Ruth; "the singer": David.

12. *Miserere mei*: "Have mercy upon me."

19. On one side of the partition are the Hebrews (line 24), on the other the Christians (line 27).

[30. *John*: John the Baptist—J. C. McG.]

33. "In Hell": the Limbus.

38. "Either aspect": the Old Church and the New.

Which runneth the two companies betwixt
They sit there by no merit that they had
But by another's, on conditions fixt;
  For these are spirits that were all released
  Ere they had made a true choice, unperplext.          45
And by their faces this is manifest
  And also by their voices' childish note,
  If looking heedfully thou listenest.
Now thou art doubting, and doubt makes thee mute;
  But for thy sake will I the coil undo                 50
  Wherein thou art bound by subtlety of thought.
Within this kingdom's compass thou must know
  Chance hath no single point's determining,
  No more than thirst, or hunger, or sorrow,
Because eternal law, in everything                      55
  Thou see'st, it stablisht with such close consent
  As close upon the finger fits the ring:
Wherefore these children, hastened as they went
  Into the true life, are not without cause
  Within themselves more and less excellent.            60
The King, through whom this realm hath its repose
  In so great love and such felicities,
  That no rash will on further venture goes,
Creating all minds in His own eyes' bliss,
  At His own pleasure dowers them with grace            65
  Diversely; on this point let the fact suffice.
This is made known to you, clear and express,
  In Holy Writ, by those twins who, ere birth,
  In the womb wrestled in their wrathfulness.
According to the colour figuring forth                  70
  In the hair such grace, the sublime Light must needs
  Chaplet their heads according to their worth.
Wherefore without reward for any deeds
  Their places are to different ranks assigned,
  Differing only in what from gift proceeds.            75
In the early ages parents' faith, combined
  With innocence, sufficed and nothing more
  To wing them upward and salvation find.
The first age being completed, other power
  Was needed for the innocent males to attain           80
  By virtue of circumcision. Heaven's door.

43–45. "But by another's": one's
parents. "Released": from the flesh.
These are the spirits of children who
died before the age of moral responsibility.
  49. Dante is wondering why some
have higher seats than others. He learns
that the degree of beatitude is determined by predestination.
  68. "Those twins": Jacob and Esau
  70–72. Our halo in Heaven is proportionate to the grace bestowed on us
at birth.

But when the time of grace began its reign,
    Having not perfect baptism of Christ,
    Such innocence below there must remain.
Look now upon the face most like to Christ!       85
    For only its radiance can so fortify
    Thy gaze as fitteth for beholding Christ."
I saw rain over her such ecstasy
    Brought in the sacred minds that with it glowed—
    Created through the heavenly height to fly—     90
That all I had seen on all the way I had trod
    Held me not in such breathless marvelling
    Nor so great likeness vouched to me of God.
And that Love which at its first down-coming
    Sang to her: "Hail, O Mary, full of grace!"     95
    Now over her extended either wing.
The divine song echoed through all the space,
    Answered from all sides of the Blessed Court
    So that serener joy filled every face.
"O holy father, who for my comfort     100
    Hast deigned thy sweet allotted place to quit,
    With me in this low station to consort,
What is that angel who with such delight
    Looketh our Queen in the eyes, lost in love there
    So that he seems one flame of living light?"     105
To his instruction thus did I repair
    Once more, who drew from Mary increasingly
    Beauty, as from the sun the morning star.
"Blitheness and buoyant confidence," said he,
    "As much as angel or a soul may own,     110
    Are all in him; so would we have it be.
For he it is who brought the palm-leaf down
    To Mary, when the burden of our woe
    In flesh was undertaken by God's Son.
Now with thine eyes come with me, as I go     115
    Discoursing, and the great patricians note
    Of the empire that the just and pious know.
Those two above, most blessed in their lot
    By being nearest to the august Empress,
    Are of our rose as 'twere the double root.     120
He on the left who has the nearest place
    Is that father, through whose presumptuous taste
    The human tribe tasteth such bitterness.
That ancient Father of Holy Church thou may'st

84. "Below there": in the Limbus.
89. "The sacred minds": the angels.
94. "That Love which . . .": the angel Gabriel.

119. "Empress": Mary.
122–124. "That father": **Adam.**
"That ancient Father": St. Peter.

See on the right, to whom Christ gave in trust       125
    The keys of this, of all flowers loveliest.
And he who, ere he died, saw all the host
    Of grievous days prepared for that fair spouse
    Won by the nails and by the lance's thrust,
Sits by him; by the other, see repose       130
    That leader under whom was fed by manna
    The ungrateful people, fickle and mutinous.
And, sitting over against Peter, Anna
    Looks on her daughter, so content of soul,
    She moveth not her eyes, singing Hosanna;       135
And opposite the greatest father of all
    Sits Lucy, who stirred the lady of thy troth,
    When, eyes down, thou wert running to thy fall.
But stop we here as the good tailor doth
    (Since of thy sleeping vision the time flies),       140
    Cutting the gown according to the cloth;
And turn we to the Primal Love our eyes,
    So that, still gazing toward Him, thou may'st pierce
    Into His splendour, far as in thee lies.
Yet, lest it happen that thou should'st reverse,       145
    Thinking to advance, the motion of thy wing,
    A prayer for grace needs must we now rehearse,
Grace from her bounty who can the succour bring.
    And do thou with thy feeling follow on
    My words, that close to them thy heart may cling."       150
And he began this holy orison.

### CANTO XXXIII

[The prayer of St. Bernard to the Virgin Mary. The prayer is
granted; and then Dante prays to God that some trace of the dazzling glimpse of the divine mystery of Trinity in Unity may be
communicated to men through his verse.]

"Maiden and Mother, daughter of thine own Son,
    Beyond all creatures lowly and lifted high,
    Of the Eternal Design the corner-stone!
Thou art she who did man's substance glorify
    So that its own Maker did not eschew       5

127–129. St. John, the author of
the Apocalypse. "Spouse": the Church.
"The nails and . . . the lance": of
Christ's Passion.
130–131. "By him": Peter. "By the
other": Adam. "That leader": Moses.
133. "Anna": St. Anna, mother of
Mary.

137. [*Lucy:* St. Lucia; see Canto II
of the *Inferno.*—J. C. McG.] "The lady
of thy troth": Beatrice.
148. "From her bounty": the Blessed Virgin's.
1. A great part of this beautiful
prayer was copied by Chaucer in the
Second Nun's Tale, 29–84.

Even to be made of its mortality.
Within thy womb the Love was kindled new
　　By generation of whose warmth supreme
　　This flower to bloom in peace eternal grew.
Here thou to us art the full noonday beam　　　　　10
　　Of love revealed: below, to mortal sight,
　　Hope, that forever springs in living stream.
Lady, thou art so great and hast such might
　　That whoso crave grace, nor to thee repair,
　　Their longing even without wing seeketh flight.　　15
Thy charity doth not only him up-bear
　　Who prays, but in thy bounty's large excess
　　Thou oftentimes dost even forerun the prayer.
In thee is pity, in thee is tenderness,
　　In thee magnificence, in thee the sum　　　　　20
　　Of all that in creation most can bless.
Now he that from the deepest pit hath come
　　Of the universe, and seen, each after each,
　　The spirits as they live and have their home,
He of thy grace so much power doth beseech　　　25
　　That he be enabled to uplift even higher
　　His eyes, and to the Final Goodness reach.
And I who never burned with more desire
　　For my own vision than for his, persist
　　In prayer to thee—my prayers go forth in choir,　30
May they not fail!—that thou disperse all mist
　　Of his mortality with prayers of thine,
　　Till joy be his of that supreme acquist.
Also I implore thee, Queen who can'st incline
　　All to thy will, let his affections stand　　　　35
　　Whole and pure after vision so divine.
The throbbings of the heart do thou command!
　　See, Beatrice with how many of the blest,
　　To second this my prayer, lays hand to hand."
Those eyes, of God loved and revered, confest,　　40
　　Still fixt upon him speaking, the delight
　　She hath in prayer from a devoted breast.
Then were they lifted to the eternal light,
　　Whereinto it may not be believed that eye
　　So clear in any creature sendeth sight.　　　　45
And I, who to the goal was drawing nigh
　　Of all my longings, now, as it behoved,

9. "This flower": the Rose of the Blessed.　　　22. "He that . . .": Dante.

Felt the ardour of them in contentment die.
Bernard signed, smiling, as a hand he moved,
    That I should lift my gaze up; but I knew         50
    Myself already such as he approved,
Because my sight, becoming purged anew,
    Deeper and deeper entered through the beam
    Of sublime light, which in itself is true.
Thenceforth my vision was too great for theme      55
    Of our speech, that such glory overbears,
    And memory faints at such assault extreme.
As he who dreams sees, and when disappears
    The dream, the passion of its print remains,
    And naught else to the memory adheres,         60
Even such am I; for almost wholly wanes
    My vision now, yet still the drops I feel
    Of sweetness it distilled into my veins.
Even so the sunbeam doth the snow unseal;
    So was the Sibyl's saying lost inert         65
    Upon the thin leaves for the wind to steal.
O supreme Light, who dost thy glory assert
    High over our imagining, lend again
    Memory a little of what to me thou wert.
Vouchsafe unto my tongue such power to attain      70
    That but one sparkle it may leave behind
    Of thy magnificence to future men.
For by returning somewhat to my mind
    And by a little sounding in this verse
    More of thy triumph shall be thence divined.      75
So keenly did the living radiance pierce
    Into me, that I think I had been undone
    Had mine eyes faltered, from the light averse.
And I recall that with the more passion
    I clove to it, till my gaze, thereat illumed,        80
    With the Infinite Good tasted communion.
O Grace abounding, whereby I presumed
    To fix upon the eternal light my gaze
    So deep, that in it I my sight consumed!
I beheld leaves within the unfathomed blaze       85
    Into one volume bound by love, the same
    That the universe holds scattered through its maze.
Substance and accidents, and their modes, became
    As if together fused, all in such wise

---

65. The Cumean "Sibyl" was accustomed to write her prophecies on
loose tree-leaves.
84. I became blind to all else.

86. God is the Book of the Universe.
89. God, containing all things, is a
perfect unit.

That what I speak of is one simple flame.                    90
Verily I think I saw with mine own eyes
   The form that knits the whole world, since I taste,
   In telling of it, more abounding bliss.
One moment more oblivion has amassed
   Than five-and-twenty centuries have wrought       95
   Since Argo's shadow o'er wondering Neptune passed.
Thus did my mind in the suspense of thought
   Gaze fixedly, all immovable and intent,
   And ever fresh fire from its gazing caught.
Man at that light becometh so content                        100
   That to choose other sight and this reject,
   It is impossible that he consent,
Because the good which is the will's object
   Dwells wholly in it, and that within its pale
   Is perfect, which, without, hath some defect.       105
Even for my remembrance now must fail
   My words, and less than could an infant's store
   Of speech, who at the pap yet sucks, avail;
Not that within the living light was more
   Than one sole aspect of divine essence,             110
   Being still forever as it was before,
But the one semblance, seen with more intense
   A faculty, even as over me there stole
   Change, was itself transfigured to my sense.
Within the clear profound Light's aureole                    115
   Three circles from its substance now appeared,
   Of three colours, and each an equal whole.
One its reflection on the next conferred
   As rainbow upon rainbow, and the two
   Breathed equally the fire that was the third.       120
To my conception O how frail and few
   My words! and that, to what I looked upon,
   Is such that "little" is more than is its due.
O Light Eternal, who in thyself alone
   Dwell'st and thyself know'st, and self-understood,  125
   Self-understanding, smilest on thine own!
That circle which, as I conceived it, glowed
   Within thee like reflection of a flame,
   Being by mine eyes a little longer wooed,

[94–96. One moment caused Dante to forget more of his vision than Neptune, god of the sea, has forgotten—in the 2500 years that have elapsed since the first sea voyage—of his initial shock.— J. C. McG.]

115. The threefold oneness is disclosed by the symbol of three mysterious rings occupying exactly the same place.

120. "The third": the Holy Ghost, who emanates equally from Father and Son.

Deep in itself, with colour still the same,⁣ 130
 Seemed with our human effigy to fill,
 Wherefore absorbed in it my sight became.
As the geometer who bends all his will
 To measure the circle, and howsoe'er he try
 Fails, for the principle escapes him still, 135
Such at this mystery new-disclosed was I,
 Fain to understand how the image doth alight
 Upon the circle, and with its form comply.
But these my wings were fledged not for that flight,
 Save that my mind a sudden glory assailed 140
 And its wish came revealed to it in that light.
To the high imagination force now failed;
 But like to a wheel whose circling nothing jars
 Already on my desire and will prevailed
The Love that moves the sun and the other stars. 145

134. The problem is the squaring of the circle.
143–145. Circular motion symbolizes faultless activity. Dante's individual will is merged in the World-Will of the Creator.

# GIOVANNI BOCCACCIO
## (1313–1375)
## The Decameron*

### The First Day

Thirteen hundred and forty-eight years had already passed after the fruitful Incarnation of the Son of God when into the distinguished city of Florence, more noble than any other Italian city, there came the deadly pestilence. It started in the East, either because of the influence of heavenly bodies or because of God's just wrath as a punishment to mortals for our wicked deeds, and it killed an infinite number of people. Without pause it spread from one place and it stretched its miserable length over the West. And against this pestilence no human wisdom or foresight was of any avail; quantities of filth were removed from the city by officials charged with this task; the entry of any sick person into the city was prohibited; and many directives were issued concerning the maintenance of good health. Nor were the humble supplications, rendered not once but many times to God by pious people, through public processions or by other means, efficacious; for almost at the beginning of springtime of the year in question the plague began to show its sorrowful effects in an extraordinary

* Completed about 1353. The selections reprinted here have been translated by Mark Musa and Peter E. Bondanella.

manner. It did not act as it had done in the East, where bleeding from the nose was a manifest sign of inevitable death, but it began in both men and women with certain swellings either in the groin or under the armpits, some of which grew to the size of a normal apple and others to the size of an egg (more or less), and the people called them buboes. And from the two parts of the body already mentioned, within a brief space of time, the said deadly buboes began to spread indiscriminately over every part of the body; and after this, the symptoms of the illness changed to black or livid spots appearing on the arms and thighs, and on every part of the body, some large ones and sometimes many little ones scattered all around. And just as the buboes were originally, and still are, a very certain indication of impending death, in like manner these spots came to mean the same thing for whoever had them. Neither a doctor's advice nor the strength of medicine could do anything to cure this illness; on the contrary, either the nature of the illness was such that it afforded no cure, or else the doctors were so ignorant that they did not recognize its cause and, as a result, could not prescribe the proper remedy (in fact, the number of doctors, other than the well-trained, was increased by a large number of men and women who had never had any medical training); at any rate, few of the sick were ever cured, and almost all died after the third day of the appearance of the previously described symptoms (some sooner, others later), and most of them died without fever or any other side effects.

This pestilence was so powerful that it was communicated to the healthy by contact with the sick, the way a fire close to dry or oily things will set them aflame. And the evil of the plague went even further: not only did talking to or being around the sick bring infection and a common death, but also touching the clothes of the sick or anything touched or used by them seemed to communicate this very disease to the person involved. What I am about to say is incredible to hear, and if I and others had not witnessed it with our own eyes, I should not dare believe it (let alone write about it), no matter how trustworthy a person I might have heard it from. Let me say, then, that the power of the plague described here was of such virulence in spreading from one person to another that not only did it pass from one man to the next, but, what's more, it was often transmitted from the garments of a sick or dead man to animals that not only became contaminated by the disease, but also died within a brief period of time. My own eyes, as I said earlier, witnessed such a thing one day: when the rags of a poor man who died of this disease were thrown into the public street, two pigs came upon them, as they are wont to do, and first with their snouts and then with their teeth they took the rags and shook them around; and within a short time, after a number of convulsions, both pigs fell dead upon the ill-fated rags, as if they had been poisoned. From these and many similar or worse occurrences there came about such fear and such fantastic notions among those who remained alive that almost all of them took a very cruel attitude in the matter; that is, they completely avoided the sick and their possessions; and in so doing, each one believed that he was protecting his good health.

There were some people who thought that living moderately and avoiding all superfluity might help a great deal in resisting this disease, and so, they gathered in small groups and lived entirely apart from everyone else. They shut themselves up in those houses where there were no sick people and where one could live well by eating the most delicate of foods and drinking the finest of wines (doing so always in moderation), allowing no one to speak about or listen to anything said about the sick and the dead outside; these people lived, spending their time with music and other pleasures that they could arrange. Others thought the opposite: they believed that drinking too much, enjoying life, going about singing and celebrating, satisfying in every way the appetites as best one could, laughing, and making light of everything that happened was the best medicine for such a disease; so they practiced to the fullest what they believed by going from one tavern to another all day and night, drinking to excess; and often they would make merry in private homes, doing everything that pleased or amused them the most. This they were able to do easily, for everyone felt he was doomed to die and, as a result, abandoned his property, so that most of the houses had become common property, and any stranger who came upon them used them as if he were their rightful owner. In addition to this bestial behavior, they always managed to avoid the sick as best they could. And in this great affliction and misery of our city the revered authority of the laws, both divine and human, had fallen and almost completely disappeared, for, like other men, the ministers and executors of the laws were either dead or sick or so short of help that it was impossible for them to fulfill their duties; as a result, everybody was free to do as he pleased.

Many others adopted a middle course between the two attitudes just described: neither did they restrict their food or drink so much as the first group nor did they fall into such dissoluteness and drunkenness as the second; rather, they satisfied their appetites to a moderate degree. They did not shut themselves up, but went around carrying in their hands flowers, or sweet-smelling herbs, or various kinds of spices; and often they would put these things to their noses, believing that such smells were a wonderful means of purifying the brain, for all the air seemed infected with the stench of dead bodies, sickness, and medicines.

Others were of a crueler opinion (though it was, perhaps, a safer one): they maintained that there was no better medicine against the plague than to flee from it; and convinced of this reasoning, not caring about anything but themselves, men and women in great numbers abandoned their city, their houses, their farms, their relatives, and their possessions and sought other places, and they went at least as far away as the Florentine countryside—as if the wrath of God could not pursue them with this pestilence wherever they went but would only strike those it found within the walls of the city! Or perhaps they thought that Florence's last hour had come and that no one in the city would remain alive.

And not all those who adopted these diverse opinions died, nor did they all escape with their lives; on the contrary, many of those who thought this way were falling sick everywhere, and since they had given, when they were healthy, the bad example of avoiding the sick, they, in turn, were abandoned and left to languish away without care. The fact was that one citizen avoided another, that almost no one cared for his neighbor, and that relatives rarely or hardly ever visited each other—they stayed far apart. This disaster had struck such fear into the hearts of men and women that brother abandoned brother, uncle abandoned nephew, sister left brother, and very often wife abandoned husband, and—even worse, almost unbelievable—fathers and mothers neglected to tend and care for their children, as if they were not their own.

Thus, for the countless multitude of men and women who fell sick, there remained no support except the charity of their friends (and these were few) or the avarice of servants, who worked for inflated salaries and indecent periods of time and who, in spite of this, were few and far between; and those few were men or women of little wit (most of them not trained for such service) who did little else but hand different things to the sick when requested to do so or watch over them while they died, and in this service, they very often lost their own lives and their profits. And since the sick were abandoned by their neighbors, their parents, and their friends and there was a scarcity of servants, a practice that was almost unheard of before spread through the city: when a woman fell sick, no matter how attractive or beautiful or noble she might be, she did not mind having a manservant (whoever he might be, no matter how young or old he was), and she had no shame whatsoever in revealing any part of her body to him—the way she would have done to a woman—when the necessity of her sickness required her to do so. This practice was, perhaps, in the days that followed the pestilence, the cause of looser morals in the women who survived the plague. And so, many people died who, by chance, might have survived if they had been attended to. Between the lack of compe-

tent attendants, which the sick were unable to obtain, and the
violence of the pestilence, there were so many, many people who
died in the city both day and night that it was incredible just to
hear this described, not to mention seeing it! Therefore, out of
sheer necessity, there arose among those who remained alive customs which were contrary to the established practices of the time.

It was the custom, as it is again today, for the women, relatives,
and neighbors to gather together in the house of a dead person and
there to mourn with the women who had been dearest to him; on
the other hand, in front of the deceased's home, his male relatives
would gather together with his male neighbors and other citizens,
and the clergy also came (many of them, or sometimes just a few)
depending upon the social class of the dead man. Then, upon the
shoulders of his equals, he was carried to the church chosen by him
before death with the funeral pomp of candles and chants. With
the fury of the pestilence increasing, this custom, for the most part,
died out and other practices took its place. And so, not only did
people die without having a number of women around them, but
there were many who passed away without even having a single
witness present, and very few were granted the piteous laments and
bitter tears of their relatives; on the contrary, most relatives were
somewhere else, laughing, joking, and amusing themselves; even
the women learned this practice too well, having put aside, for the
most part, their womanly compassion for their own safety. Very
few were the dead whose bodies were accompanied to the church
by more than ten or twelve of their neighbors, and these dead
bodies were not even carried on the shoulders of honored and
reputable citizens but rather by gravediggers from the lower classes
that were called *becchini*. Working for pay, they would pick up
the bier and hurry it off, not to the church the dead man had chosen
before his death but, in most cases, to the church closest by, accompanied by four or six churchmen with just a few candles, and
often none at all. With the help of these *becchini*, the churchmen
would place the body as fast as they could in whatever unoccupied
grave they could find, without going to the trouble of saying long
or solemn burial services.

The plight of the lower class and, perhaps, a large part of the
middle class, was even more pathetic: most of them stayed in their
homes or neighborhoods either because of their poverty or their
hopes for remaining safe, and every day they fell sick by the thousands; and not having servants or attendants of any kind, they almost always died. Many ended their lives in the public streets,
during the day or at night, while many others who died in their
homes were discovered dead by their neighbors only by the smell
of their decomposing bodies. The city was full of corpses. The dead

were usually given the same treatment by their neighbors, who were moved more by the fear that the decomposing corpses would contaminate them than by any charity they might have felt towards the deceased: either by themselves or with the assistance of porters (when they were available), they would drag the corpse out of the home and place it in front of the doorstep where, usually in the morning, quantities of dead bodies could be seen by any passerby; then, they were laid out on biers, or for lack of biers, on a plank. Nor did a bier carry only one corpse; sometimes it was used for two or three at a time. More than once, a single bier would serve for a wife and husband, two or three brothers, a father or son, or other relatives, all at the same time. And countless times it happened that two priests, each with a cross, would be on their way to bury someone, when porters carrying three or four biers would just follow along behind them; and where these priests thought they had just one dead man to bury, they had, in fact, six or eight and sometimes more. Moreover, the dead were honored with no tears or candles or funeral mourners but worse: things had reached such a point that the people who died were cared for as we care for goats today. Thus, it became quite obvious that what the wise had not been able to endure with patience through the few calamities of everyday life now became a matter of indifference to even the most simple-minded people as a result of this colossal misfortune.

So many corpses would arrive in front of a church every day and at every hour that the amount of holy ground for burials was certainly insufficient for the ancient custom of giving each body its individual place; when all the graves were full, huge trenches were dug in all of the cemeteries of the churches and into them the new arrivals were dumped by the hundreds; and they were packed in there with dirt, one on top of another, like a ship's cargo, until the trench was filled.

But instead of going over every detail of the past miseries which befell our city, let me say that the same unfriendly weather there did not, because of this, spare the surrounding countryside any evil; there, not to speak of the towns which, on a smaller scale, were like the city, in the scattered villages and in the fields the poor, miserable peasants and their families, without any medical assistance or aid of servants, died on the roads and in their fields and in their homes, as many by day as by night, and they died not like men but more like wild animals. Because of this they, like the city dwellers, became careless in their ways and did not look after their possessions or their businesses; furthermore, when they saw that death was upon them, completely neglecting the future fruits of their past labors, their livestock, their property, they did their best to consume what they already had at hand. So, it came about that oxen, donkeys, sheep, pigs, chickens and even dogs, man's most faithful companion, were driven from their homes into the fields, where the wheat was left not only unharvested but also unreaped, and they were allowed to roam where they wished; and many of these animals, almost as if they were rational beings, returned at night to their homes without any guidance from a shepherd, satiated after a good day's meal.

Leaving the countryside and returning to the city, what more can one say, except that so great was the cruelty of Heaven, and, perhaps, also that of man, that from March to July of the same year, between the fury of the pestiferous sickness and the fact that many of the sick were badly treated or abandoned in need because of the fear that the healthy had, more than one hundred thousand human beings are believed to have lost their lives for certain inside the walls of the city of Florence whereas, before the deadly plague, one would not have estimated that there were actually that many people dwelling in that city.

Oh, how many great palaces, beautiful homes, and noble dwellings, once filled with families, gentlemen, and ladies, were now emptied, down to the last servant! How many notable families, vast domains, and famous fortunes remained without legitimate heir! How many valiant men, beautiful women, and charming young men, who might have been pronounced very healthy by Galen,[1] Hippocrates,[2] and Aesculapius [3] (not to mention lesser physicians), dined in the morning with their relatives, companions, and friends and then in the evening took supper with their ancestors in the other world!

Reflecting upon so many miseries makes me very sad; therefore, since I wish to pass over as many as I can, let me say that as our city was in this condition, almost emptied of inhabitants, it happened (as I heard it later from a person worthy of trust) that one Tuesday morning in the venerable church of Santa Maria Novella there was hardly any congregation there to hear the holy services except for seven young women, all dressed in garments of mourning as the times demanded, each of whom was a friend, neighbor, or relative of the other, and none of whom had passed her twenty-eighth year, nor was any of them younger than eighteen; all were educated and of noble birth and beautiful to look at, well-mannered and gracefully modest. I would tell you their real names, if I did not have a good reason for not doing so, which is this: I do not wish any of them to be embarrassed in the future because of the things that

---

1. Greek anatomist and physician (A.D. 130?–201?).
2. Greek physician (460?–377? B.C.), to whom the Hippocratic oath, administered to new physicians, is attributed.

3. The Roman god of medicine and healing, often identified with Asclepius, Apollo's son, who was the Greek god of medicine.

they said to each other and what they listened to—all of which I shall later recount. Today the laws regarding pleasure are again strict, more so than at that time (for the reasons mentioned above when they were very lax), not only for women of their age but even for those who were older; nor would I wish to give an opportunity to the envious, who are always ready to attack every praiseworthy life, to diminish in any way with their indecent talk the dignity of these worthy ladies. But, so that you may understand clearly what each of them had to say, I intend to call them by names which are either completely or in part appropriate to their personalities. We shall call the first and the oldest Pampinea and the second Fiammetta, the third Filomena, and the fourth Emilia, and we shall name the fifth Lauretta and the sixth Neifile, and the last, not without reason, we shall call Elissa.[4] Not by prior agreement, but purely by chance, they gathered together in one part of the church and were seated almost in a circle, saying their rosaries; after many sighs, they began to discuss among themselves various matters concerning the nature of the times, and after a while, as the others fell silent, Pampinea began to speak in this manner:

"My dear ladies, you have often heard, as I have, how a proper use of one's reason does harm to no one. It is only natural for everyone born on this earth to aid, preserve, and defend his own life to the best of his ability; this is a right so taken for granted that it has, at times, permitted men to kill each other without blame in order to defend their own lives. And if the laws dealing with the welfare of every human being permit such a thing, how much more lawful, and with no harm to anyone, is it for us, or anyone else, to take all possible precautions to preserve our own lives! When I consider what we have been doing this morning and in the past days and what we have spoken about, I understand, and you must understand too, that each one of us is afraid for her life; nor does this surprise me in the least—rather I am greatly amazed that since each of us has the natural feelings of a woman, we do not find some remedy for ourselves to cure what each one of us dreads. We live in the city, in my opinion, for no other reason than to bear witness to the number of dead bodies that are carried to burial, or to listen whether the friars (whose number has been reduced to almost nothing) chant their offices at the prescribed hours, or to demonstrate to anyone who comes here the quality and the quantity of our miseries by our garments of mourning. And if we leave the church, either we see dead or sick bodies being carried all about, or we see those who were once condemned to exile for their crimes by the authority of the public laws making sport of these

4. Perhaps the reason is that like her namesake, the Carthaginian queen, who is better known as Dido, Boccaccio's Elissa is dominated by a violent passion.

laws, running about wildly through the city, because they know that the executors of these laws are either dead or dying; or we see the scum of our city, avid for our blood, who call themselves *becchini* and who ride about on horseback torturing us by deriding everything, making our losses more bitter with their disgusting songs. Nor do we hear anything but "So-and-so is dead," and "So-and-so is dying"; and if there were anyone left to mourn, we should hear nothing but piteous laments everywhere. I do not know if what happens to me also happens to you in your homes, but when I go home I find no one there except my maid, and I become so afraid that my hair stands on end, and wherever I go or sit in my house, I seem to see the shadows of those who have passed away, not with the faces that I remember, but with horrible expressions that terrify me. For these reasons, I am uncomfortable here, outside, and in my home, and the more so since it appears that no one like ourselves, who is well off and who has some other place to go, has remained here except us. And if there are any who remain, according to what I hear and see, they do whatever their hearts desire, making no distinction between what is proper and what is not, whether they are alone or with others, by day or by night; and not only laymen but also those who are cloistered in convents have broken their vows of obedience and have given themselves over to carnal pleasures, for they have made themselves believe that these things are permissible for them and are improper for others, and thinking that they will escape with their lives in this fashion, they have become wanton and dissolute.

"If this is the case, and plainly it is, what are we doing here? What are we waiting for? What are we dreaming about? Why are we slower to protect our health than all the rest of the citizens? Do we hold ourselves less dear than all the others? Or do we believe that our own lives are tied by stronger chains to our bodies than those of others and, therefore, that we need not worry about anything which might have the power to harm them? We are mistaken and deceived, and we are mad if we believe it. We shall have clear proof of this if we just call to mind how many young men and ladies have been struck down by this cruel pestilence. I do not know if you agree with me, but I think that, in order not to fall prey, out of laziness or presumption, to what we might well avoid, it might be a good idea for all of us to leave this city, just as many others before us have done and are still doing. Let us avoid like death itself the ugly examples of others, and go to live in a more dignified fashion in our country houses (of which we all have several) and there let us take what enjoyment, what happiness, and what pleasure we can, without going beyond the rules of reason in any way. There we can hear the birds sing, and we can see the hills and the pastures turning green, the wheat fields moving like the sea, and a thousand kinds of trees; and we shall be able to see the heavens more clearly which, though they still may be cruel, nonetheless will not deny to us their eternal beauties, which are much more pleasing to look at than the empty walls of our city. Besides all this, there in the country the air is much fresher, and the necessities for living in such times as these are plentiful there, and there are just fewer troubles in general; though the peasants are dying there even as the townspeople here, the displeasure is the less in that there are fewer houses and inhabitants than in the city. Here on the other hand, if I judge correctly, we would not be abandoning anyone; on the contrary, we can honestly say it is we ourselves that have been abandoned, for our loved ones are either dead or have fled and have left us alone in such affliction as though we did not belong to them. No reproach, therefore, can come to us if we follow this course of action, whereas sorrow, worry, and perhaps even death can come if we do not follow this course. So, whenever you like, I think it would be well to take our servants, have all our necessary things sent after us, and go from one place one day to another the next, enjoying what happiness and merriment these times permit; let us live in this manner (unless we are overtaken first by death) until we see what ending Heaven has reserved for these horrible times. And remember that it is no more forbidden for us to go away virtuously than it is for most other women to remain here dishonorably."

When they had listened to what Pampinea had said, the other women not only praised her advice but were so anxious to follow it that they had already begun discussing among themselves the details, as if they were going to leave that very instant. But Filomena, who was most discerning, said:

"Ladies, regardless of how convincing Pampinea's arguments are, that is no reason to rush into things, as you seem to wish to do. Remember that we are all women, and any young girl can tell you that women do not know how to reason in a group when they are without the guidance of some man who knows how to control them. We are changeable, quarrelsome, suspicious, timid, and fearful, because of which I suspect that this company will soon break up without honor to any of us if we do not take a guide other than ourselves. We would do well to resolve this matter before we depart."

Then Elissa said:

"Men are truly the leaders of women, and without their guidance, our actions rarely end successfully. But how are we to find any men? We all know that the majority of our relatives are dead and those who remain alive are scattered here and there in various groups, not knowing where we are (they, too, are fleeing precisely what we seek to avoid), and since taking up with strangers would be unbecoming to us, we must, if we wish to leave for the sake of our health, find a means of arranging it so that while going for our own pleasure and repose, no trouble or scandal follow us."

While the ladies were discussing this, three young men came into the church, none of whom was less than twenty-five years of age. Neither the perversity of the times nor the loss of friends or parents, nor fear for their own lives had been able to cool, much less extinguish, the love those lovers bore in their hearts. One of them was called Panfilo, another Filostrato, and the last Dioneo, each one very charming and well-bred; and in those turbulent times they sought their greatest consolation in the sight of the ladies they loved, all three of whom happened to be among the seven ladies previously mentioned, while the others were close relatives of one or the other of the three men. No sooner had they sighted the ladies than they were seen by them, whereupon Pampinea smiled and said:

"See how Fortune favors our plans and has provided us with these discreet and virtuous young men, who would gladly be our guides and servants if we do not hesitate to accept them for such service."

Then Neifile's face blushed out of embarrassment, for she was one of those who was loved by one of the young men, and she said:

"Pampinea, for the love of God, be careful what you say! I realize very well that nothing but good can be said of any of them, and I believe that they are capable of doing much more than that task and, likewise, that their good and worthy company would be fitting not only for us but for ladies much more beautiful and attractive than we are, but it is quite obvious that some of them are in love with some of us who are here present, and I fear that if we take them with us, slander and disapproval will follow, through no fault of ours or of theirs."

Then Filomena said:

"That does not matter at all; as long as I live with dignity and have no remorse of conscience about anything, let anyone who wishes say what he likes to the contrary: God and Truth will take up arms in my defense. Now, if they were just prepared to come with us, as Pampinea says, we could truly say that Fortune was favorable to our departure."

When the others heard her speak in such a manner, the argument was ended, and they all agreed that the young men should be called over, told about their intentions, and asked if they would be so kind as to accompany the ladies on such a journey . Without further discussion, then, Pampinea, who was related to one of the men, rose to her feet and made her way to where they stood gazing at the ladies, and she greeted them with a cheerful expression, outlined their plan to them, and begged them, in everyone's name, to keep them company in the spirit of pure and brotherly affection.

At first the young men thought they were being mocked, but when they saw that the lady was speaking seriously, they gladly consented; and in order to start without delay and put the plan into action, before leaving the church they agreed upon what preparations must be made for their departure. And when everything had been arranged and word had been sent on to the place they intended to go, the following morning (that is, Wednesday) at the break of dawn the ladies with some of their servants and the three young men with three of their servants left the city and set out on their way; they had traveled no further than two short miles when they arrived at the first stop they had agreed upon.

The place was somewhere on a little mountain, at some distance away from our roads, full of various shrubs and plants with rich, green foliage—most pleasant to look at; at the top there was a country mansion with a beautiful large inner courtyard with open collonades, halls, and bedrooms, all of them beautiful in themselves and decorated with cheerful and interesting paintings; it was surrounded by meadows and marvelous gardens, with wells of fresh water and cellars full of the most precious wines, the likes of which were more suitable for expert drinkers than for sober and dignified ladies. And the group discovered, to their delight, that the entire palace had been cleaned and the beds made in the bedchambers, and that fresh flowers and rushes had been strewn everywhere. Soon after they arrived and were resting, Dioneo, who was more attractive and wittier than either of the other young men, said:

"Ladies, more than our preparations, it was your intelligence that guided us here. I do not know what you intend to do with your thoughts, but I left mine inside the city walls when I passed through them in your company a little while ago; and so, you must either make up your minds to enjoy yourselves and laugh and sing with me (as much, let me say, as your dignity permits), or you must give me leave to return to my worries and to remain in our troubled city."

To this Pampinea, who had driven away her sad thoughts in the same way, replied happily:

"Dioneo, you speak very well: let us live happily, for after all it was unhappiness that made us flee the city. But when things are not organized they cannot long endure, and since I began the discussions which brought this fine company together, and since I desire the continuation of our happiness, I think it is necessary that we choose a leader from among us, whom we shall honor and obey as our superior and whose every thought shall be to keep us living happily. And in order that each one of us may feel the weight of this responsibility together with the pleasure of its authority, so that no one of us who has not experienced it can envy the others, let me say that both the weight and the honor should be granted to each one of us in turn for a day; the first will be chosen by election; the others that follow will be whomever he or she that will have the rule for that day chooses as the hour of vespers[5] approaches; this ruler, as long as his reign endures, will organize and arrange the place and the manner in which we will spend our time."

These words greatly pleased everyone, and they unanimously elected Pampinea queen for the first day; Filomena quickly ran to a laurel bush, whose leaves she had always heard were worthy of praise and bestowed great honor upon those crowned with them; she plucked several branches from it and wove them into a handsome garland of honor. And when it would be placed upon the head of any one of them, it was to be to all in the group a clear symbol of royal rule and authority over the rest of them for as long as their company stayed together.

After she had been chosen queen, Pampinea ordered everyone to refrain from talking; then, she sent for the four servants of the ladies and for those of the three young men, and as they stood before her in silence, she said:

"Since I must set the first example for you all in order that it may be bettered and thus allow our company to live in order and in pleasure, and without any shame, and so that it may last as long as we wish, I first appoint Parmeno, Dioneo's servant, as my steward, and I commit to his care and management all our household and everything which pertains to the services of the dining hall. I wish Sirisco, the servant of Panfilo, to act as our buyer and treasurer and follow the orders of Parmeno. Tindaro, who is in the service of Filostrato, shall wait on Filostrato and Dioneo and Panfilo in their bedchambers when the other two are occupied with their other duties and cannot do so. Misia, my servant, and Licisca, Filomena's, will be occupied in the kitchen and will prepare those dishes which are ordered by Parmeno. Chimera, Lauretta's servant, and Stratilia, Fiametta's servant, will take care of the bedchambers of the ladies and the cleaning of those places we use. And in general, we desire and command each of you, if you value our favor and good graces, to be sure—no matter where you go or come from, no matter what you hear or see—to bring us back nothing but pleasant news."

And when these orders, praised by all present, were delivered, Pampinea rose happily to her feet and said:

5. Late afternoon; the sixth of the seven times of day set aside for prayer by canon law.

"Here there are gardens and meadows and many other pleasant places, which all of us can wander about in and enjoy as we like; but at the hour of tierce [6] let everyone be here so that we can eat in the cool of the morning."

After the merry group had been given the new queen's permission, the young men, together with the beautiful ladies, set off slowly through a garden, discussing pleasant matters, making themselves beautiful garlands of various leaves and singing love songs. After the time granted them by the queen had elapsed, they returned home and found Parmeno busy carrying out the duties of his task; for as they entered a hall on the ground floor, they saw the tables set with the whitest of linens and with glasses that shone like silver and everything decorated with broom blossoms; then, they washed their hands and, at the queen's command, they all sat down in the places assigned them by Parmeno. The delicately cooked foods were brought in and very fine wines were served; the three servants in silence served the tables. Everyone was delighted to see everything so beautiful and well arranged, and they ate merrily and with pleasant conversation. Since all the ladies and young men knew how to dance (and some of them even knew how to play and sing very well), when the tables had been cleared, the queen ordered that instruments be brought, and on her command, Dioneo took a lute and Fiammetta a viola, and they began softly playing a dance tune. After the queen had sent the servants off to eat, she began to dance together with the other ladies and two of the young men; and when that was over, they all began to sing carefree and gay songs. In this manner they continued until the queen felt that it was time to retire; therefore, at the queen's request, the three young men went off to their chambers (which were separate from those of the ladies), where they found their beds prepared and the rooms as full of flowers as the halls; the ladies, too, discovered their chambers decorated in like fashion. Then they all undressed and fell asleep.

Not long after the hour of nones,[7] the queen arose and had the other ladies and young men awakened, stating that too much sleep in the daytime was harmful; then they went out onto a lawn of thick, green grass, where no ray of the sun could penetrate; and there, with a gentle breeze caressing them, they all sat in a circle upon the green grass, as was the wish of their queen. Then she spoke to them in this manner:

"As you see, the sun is high, the heat is great, and nothing can be heard except the cicadas in the olive groves; therefore, to wander about at this hour would be, indeed, foolish. Here it is cool and fresh and, as you see, there are games and chessboards with which

---

6. The third canonical hour, 9 A.M.     7. The fifth canonical hour, 3 P.M.

all of you can amuse yourselves to your liking. But if you take my advice in this matter, I suggest we spend this hot part of the day not in playing games (a pastime which of necessity disturbs the player who loses without providing much pleasure either for his opponents or for those who watch) but rather in telling stories, for this way one person, by telling a story, can provide amusement for the entire company. In the time it takes for the sun to set and the heat to become less oppressive, you will each have told a little story, and then we can go wherever we like to amuse ourselves; so, if what I say pleases you (and in this I am willing to follow your pleasure), then, let us do it; if not, then let everyone do as he pleases until the hour of vespers."

The entire group of men and women liked the idea of telling stories.

"Then," said the queen, "if this is your wish, for this first day I order each of you to tell a story about any subject he likes."

And turning to Panfilo, who sat on her right, she ordered him in a gracious manner to begin with one of his tales; whereupon, hearing her command, Panfilo, while everyone listened, began at once as follows:

### The Second Tale of the Fourth Day [1]

Gracious ladies, there was once in Imola a man of wicked and corrupt ways named Berto della Massa, whose evil deeds were so well known by the people of Imola that nobody there would believe him when he told the truth, not to mention when he lied. Realizing that his tricks would no longer work there, in desperation he moved to Venice, that receptacle of all forms of wickedness, thinking that he would adopt a different style of trickery there from what he had used anywhere else before. And almost as if his conscience were struck with remorse for his evil deeds committed in the past, he gave every sign of a man who had become truly humble and most religious; in fact, he went and turned himself into a minor friar, taking the name of Brother Alberto da Imola; and in this disguise he pretended to lead an ascetic life, praising repentance and abstinence, and never eating meat nor drinking wine unless they were of a quality good enough for him.

Never before had such a thief, pimp, forger, and murderer become so great a preacher without having abandoned these vices, even while he may have been practicing them in secret. And besides this, after he became a priest, whenever he celebrated the mass at the altar, in view of all the congregation, he would weep when it

---

1. Told by Pampinea. On the fourth day, in Filostrato's reign, the friends were to tell love stories with unhappy endings.

came to the Passion of Our Savior, for he was a man to whom tears cost very little when they were called for. And in short, between his sermons and his tears, he managed to beguile the Venetians to such an extent that he was almost always made the trustee and guardian of every will that was made, the keeper of many people's money, and confessor and advisor to the majority of men and women; and acting in this way, he changed from a wolf into a shepherd, and his reputation for sanctity in those parts was far greater than St. Francis's was in Assisi.[2]

Now it happened that there was a foolish and silly young woman named Madonna Lisetta da Ca' Quirino (the wife of a great merchant who had gone with his galleys to Flanders) who, along with other ladies, went to be confessed by this holy friar. She was kneeling at his feet and, being a Venetian (and, as such, a gossip like all of them), she was asked by Brother Alberto halfway through her confession if she had a lover. To this question she crossly replied:

"What, my dear brother, don't you have eyes in your head? Do my charms appear to you to be like all those of other women? I could have even more lovers than I want, but my beauty is not to be enjoyed by just anyone. How many ladies do you know who possess such charms as mine, charms which would make me beautiful even in paradise?"

And then she kept on saying so many things about her beauty that it became boring to listen to her. Brother Alberto realized immediately that she was a simpleton, and since he thought she was just the right terrain for plowing, he fell passionately in love with her right then and there; but putting aside his flatteries for a more appropriate time, and reassuming his saintly manner, he began to reproach her and to tell her that her attitude was vainglorious and other such things; and so the lady told him that he was a beast and that he did not know one beauty from another; and because he did not want to upset her too much, Brother Alberto, after having confessed her, let her go off with the other women.

After a few days, he went with a trusted companion to Madonna Lisetta's home and taking her into a room where they could be seen by no one, he threw himself on his knees before her and said:

"My lady, I beg you in God's name to forgive me for speaking to you as I did last Sunday about your beauty, for I was so soundly punished the following night that I have not been able to get up until today."

"And who punished you in this way?" asked Lady Halfwit.

"I shall tell you," replied Brother Alberto. "As I was praying

2. Saint Francis of Assisi (1181?– 1226), Italian religious leader, writer, and poet, was famous for his Christian humility and for the foundation of the Franciscan order.

that night in my cell, as I always do, I suddenly saw a glowing light, and before I was able to turn around to see what it was, I saw a very beautiful young man with a large stick in his hand who took me by the collar, dragged me to my feet, and gave me so many blows that he broke practically everything in my body. I asked him why he had done this and he replied:

'Because yesterday you presumed to reproach the celestial beauty of Madonna Lisetta whom I love more than anything else except God.'

"And then I asked: 'Who are you?'

"He replied that he was the angel Gabriel.

" 'Oh My Lord,' I said, 'I beg you to forgive me.'

" 'I shall forgive you on one condition,' he said, 'that you go to her as soon as you are able and beg her forgiveness; and if she does not pardon you, I shall return here and beat you so soundly that you will be sorry for the rest of your life.' "

Lady Lighthead, who was as smart as salt is sweet, enjoyed hearing all these words and believed them all, and after a moment she said:

"I told you, Brother Alberto, that my charms were heavenly; but, God help me, I feel sorry for you, and from now on, in order to spare you more harm, I forgive you on condition that you tell me what the angel said next."

Brother Alberto said: "My lady, since you have forgiven me, I shall gladly tell you, but I remind you of one thing: you must not tell what I tell you to anyone in the world, otherwise you will spoil everything, you who are the most fortunate woman in the world today. The angel Gabriel told me that I was to tell you that you are so pleasing to him that often he would have come to pass the night with you if he had not thought it might frighten you. Now he sends me here with a message that he would like to come to you one night and spend some time with you; but since he is an angel and you would not be able to touch him in the form of an angel, he says that for your pleasure he would like to come as a human being, and he asks when you would have him come and in whose shape should he come, and he will come; therefore you, more than any other woman alive, should consider yourself blessed."

Lady Silly then said that it pleased her very much that the angel Gabriel was in love with her, for she loved him as well and never failed to light a cheap candle in his honor whenever she found a painting of him in church; and whenever he wished to come to her, he would be very welcome, and he would find her all alone in her room, and he could come on the condition that he would not leave her for the Virgin Mary, whom, it was said, he loved very much, and it was obviously true, because everywhere she saw him, he was always on his knees before her; [3] and besides this, she said that he could appear in whatever shape or form he wished—she would not be afraid.

"My Lady," Brother Alberto then said, "you speak wisely, and I shall arrange everything with him as you have said. And you could do me a great favor which will cost you nothing; and the favor is this: that you allow him to come to you in my body. Let me tell you how you would be doing me a favor: he will take my soul from my body and place it in paradise, and he will enter my body, and as long as he is with you my soul will be in paradise."

Then Lady Dimwit replied: "That pleases me; I wish you to have this consolation for the beating he gave you on my account."

Brother Alberto then said: "Now arrange for him to find the door of your house open tonight so that he can come inside; since he will be arriving in the form of a man, he cannot enter unless he uses the door."

The lady replied that it would be done. Brother Alberto departed, and she was so delighted by the whole affair that, jumping for joy, she could hardly keep her skirts over her ass, and it seemed like a thousand years to her waiting for the angel Gabriel to come. Brother Alberto, who was thinking more about getting in the saddle than of being an angel that evening, began to fortify himself with sweetmeats and other delicacies so that he would not be easily thrown from his horse; and then he got permission to stay out that night and, as soon as it was dark, he went with a trusted companion to the house of a lady friend of his, which on other occasions he had used as his point of departure whenever he went to ride the mares; and from there, when the time seemed ripe to him, he went in disguise to the lady's house, and went inside; and, having changed himself into an angel with the different odds and ends he brought with him, he climbed the stairs, and entered the lady's bedroom.

When she saw this white object approaching, she threw herself on her knees in front of him, and the angel blessed her and raised her to her feet, and made a sign for her to get into bed; and she, most anxious to obey, did so immediately, and the angel lay down alongside his devout worshipper. Brother Alberto was a handsome young man with a robust, well-built body; Lady Lisetta was all fresh and soft, and she discovered that his ride was altogether different from that of her husband. He flew many times that night without his wings, which caused the lady to cry aloud with delight and, in addition, he told her many things about the glory of heaven. Then as day broke, having made another appointment to meet

3. Gabriel told the Virgin Mary that she was to bear the Son of God, and so the two are invariably shown together in paintings of the Annunciation, which Lisetta would often have seen in church.

her, he gathered his equipment and returned to his companion, who had struck up a friendly relationship with the good woman of the house so that she would not be afraid of sleeping alone.

When the lady had finished breakfast, she went with one of her attendants to Brother Alberto's and told him the story of the angel Gabriel and of what she had heard from him about the glory of the eternal life and of how he looked, adding all sorts of incredible tales to her story. To this Brother Alberto said:

"My lady, I do not know how you were with him; I only know that last night, when he came to me and I delivered your message to him, in an instant he transported my soul to a place where there were more flowers and roses than I have ever seen before, and he left my soul in this most delightful spot until this morning at the hour of early prayer. What happened to my body I know not."

"But did I not tell you?" replied the lady. "Your body passed the entire night in my arms with the angel Gabriel inside it; and if you do not believe me, look under your left nipple, where I gave the angel such a passionate kiss that he will carry its mark for some days!"

Then Brother Alberto said: "Today I shall perform an act that I have not done for some time—I shall undress myself to see if what you say is true."

And after much more chatter, the lady returned home; and Brother Alberto, without the slightest problem, often went to visit her, disguised as an angel. One day, however, Madonna Lisetta was discussing the nature of beauty with one of her neighbors, and she, showing off and being the silly goose she was, said: "You would not talk about any other women if you knew who it is that loves my beauty."

Her neighbor, anxious to hear more about this and knowing very well the kind of woman Lisetta was, replied: "Madame, you may be right; but as I do not know to whom you are referring, I cannot change my opinion so easily."

"Neighbor," replied Madonna Lisetta, who was easily excited, "he does not want it to be known, but my lover is the angel Gabriel, and he loves me more than himself, and he tells me that this is because I am the most beautiful woman that there is in the world or even in the Maremma." [4]

Her neighbor had the urge to break into laughter right then, but she held herself back in order to make her friend continue talking, and she said: "God's faith, Madame, if the angel Gabriel is your lover and he tells you this, it must really be so; but I did not realize that angels did such things."

"Neighbor," replied the lady, "that is where you are wrong; by

4. A small, marshy region of Tuscany.

God's wounds, he does it better than my husband, and he tells me that they do it up there as well; but since he thinks I am more beautiful than anyone in heaven, he fell in love with me and comes to be with me very often. Now do you see?"

When the neighbor had left Madonna Lisetta, it seemed to her as if a thousand years had passed before she was able to repeat what she had learned; and at a large gathering of women, she told them the whole story. These women told it to their husbands and to other women, who passed it on to others, and thus in less than two days it was the talk of all Venice. But among those whom this story reached were also the woman's in-laws, and they decided, without telling her a word, to find this angel and to see if he knew how to fly; and they kept watch for him for several nights. It just happened that some hint of this got back to Brother Alberto, so he went there one night to reprove the lady, and no sooner was he undressed than her in-laws, who had seen him arrive, were at the door of the bedroom ready to open it. When Brother Alberto heard this and realized what was going on, he jumped up, and seeing no other means of escape, he flung open a window which looked out on the Grand Canal and threw himself into the water.

The water was deep there, but he knew how to swim well, and so he did not hurt himself; after he swam to the other side of the canal, he immediately entered a home that was opened to him and begged the good man inside, for the love of God, to save his life, as he made up a story to explain why he was there at that hour and in the nude. The good man, moved to pity, gave him his own bed, since he had some affairs of his own to attend to, and he told him to remain there until he returned; and having locked him in, he went about his business.

When the lady's in-laws opened the door to her bedroom and entered, they found that the angel Gabriel had flown away, leaving his wings behind him; they abused the lady no end and finally, leaving her alone, all distressed, they returned to their home with the angel's equipment. In the meanwhile, at daybreak, while the good man was on the Rialto, he heard talk about how the angel Gabriel had gone to bed that night with Madonna Lisetta and had been discovered there by her in-laws, and how he had thrown himself into the canal out of fear, and how no one knew what had happened to him; immediately he realized that the man in his house was the man in question. Returning home and identifying him, after much discussion, he came to an agreement with the friar: he would not give him over to the in-laws if he would pay him fifty ducats; and this was done.

When Brother Alberto wished to leave the place, the good man told him:

"There is only one way out, if you agree to it. Today we are celebrating a festival in which men are led around dressed as bears, others dressed as wild men, and others in one costume or another, and a hunt is put on in St. Mark's Square, and with that the festival is ended; then everyone goes away, with whomever he led there, to wherever they please; and if you wish, so that no one will discover you, I am willing to lead you to wherever you like; otherwise, I don't see any way for you to escape from here without being recognized; and the in-laws of the lady, knowing that you have hidden yourself somewhere around here, have posted guards everywhere to trap you."

Though it seemed rough to Brother Alberto to have to go in such a disguise, his fear of the lady's relatives induced him to agree, and he told the man where he would like to go and that in whatever way he might choose to lead him there, he would be happy. The man smeared him completely with honey, covered him up with feathers, put a chain around his neck and a mask on his head; in one of his hands he put a large club and in the other two great dogs which he had brought from the butcher; at the same time he sent someone to the Rialto to announce that whoever wished to see the angel Gabriel should go to St. Mark's Square. And this is what they call good old Venetian honesty!

And when this was done, he took the friar outside and had him take the lead, holding him by a chain from behind; and many bystanders kept asking: "Who is it? What is it?" Thus he led him up to the piazza where, between those who had followed him and those who had heard the announcement and had come from the Rialto, a huge crowd gathered. When he arrived there, he tied his wild man up to a column in a conspicuous and elevated spot, pretending to wait for the hunt; meanwhile, the flies and horseflies were giving Brother Alberto a great deal of trouble, for he was covered with honey. But when the good man saw that the piazza was full, pretending to unchain his wild man, he tore the mask from his face and announced:

"Ladies and gentlemen, since the pig has not come to the hunt, and since there is no hunt, I would not want you to have come in vain; therefore I should like you to see the angel Gabriel, who descends from heaven to earth to console the Venetian women by night."

When his mask was removed, Brother Alberto was instantly recognized by everybody, and everyone cried out against him and shouted the most insulting words that were ever directed at a scoundrel; besides this, one by one they all started throwing garbage in his face, keeping him occupied this way for a long time until, by chance, the news reached his brother friars; six of them came, and throwing a cloak over him, they unchained him, and in the midst of a great commotion, they led him back to their monastery, where he was locked up, and after a miserable life he is believed to have died there.

Thus a man who was thought to be good and who acted evilly, not recognized for what he really was, dared to turn himself into the angel Gabriel, and instead was converted into a wild man, and, finally, was cursed at as he deserved and made to lament in vain for the sins he had committed. May it please God that the same thing happen to all others like him!

\* \* \*

## The Ninth Tale of the Fifth Day [1]

There was once in Florence a young man named Federigo, the son of Messer Filippo Alberighi, renowned above all other men in Tuscany for his prowess in arms and for his courtliness. As often happens to most gentlemen, he fell in love with a lady named Monna Giovanna, in her day considered to be one of the most beautiful and one of the most charming women that ever there was in Florence; and in order to win her love, he participated in jousts and tournaments, organized and gave feasts, and spent his money without restraint; but she, no less virtuous than beautiful, cared little for these things done on her behalf, nor did she care for he who did them. Now, as Federigo was spending far beyond his means and was taking nothing in, as easily happens he lost his wealth and became poor, with nothing but his little farm to his name (from whose revenues he lived very meagerly) and one falcon which was among the best in the world.

More in love than ever, but knowing that he would never be able to live the way he wished to in the city, he went to live at Campi, where his farm was. There he passed his time hawking whenever he could, asked nothing of anyone, and endured his poverty patiently. Now, during the time that Federigo was reduced to dire need, it happened that the husband of Monna Giovanna fell ill, and realizing death was near, he made his last will: he was very rich, and he made his son, who was growing up, his heir, and, since he had loved Monna Giovanna very much, he made her his heir should his son die without a legitimate heir; and then he died.

Monna Giovanna was now a widow, and as is the custom among our women, she went to the country with her son to spend a year on one of her possessions very close by to Federigo's farm, and it happened that this young boy became friends with Federigo and began to enjoy birds and hunting dogs; and after he had seen Federigo's falcon fly many times, it pleased him so much that he

---

1. Told by Dioneo. On the fifth day, in Fiammetta's reign, the friends were to tell love stories which end happily after a period of misfortune.

very much wished it were his own, but he did not dare to ask for it, for he could see how dear it was to Federigo. And during this time, it happened that the young boy took ill, and his mother was much grieved, for he was her only child and she loved him enormously; she would spend the entire day by his side, never ceasing to comfort him, and often asking him if there was anything he desired, begging him to tell her what it might be, for if it were possible to obtain it, she would certainly do everything possible to get it. After the young boy had heard her make this offer many times, he said:

"Mother, if you can arrange for me to have Federigo's falcon, I think I would be well very soon."

When the lady heard this, she was taken aback for a moment, and she began to think what she should do. She knew that Federigo had loved her for a long while, in spite of the fact that he never received a single glance from her, and so, she said to herself:

"How can I send or go and ask for this falcon of his which is, as I have heard tell, the best that ever flew, and besides this, his only means of support? And how can I be so insensitive as to wish to take away from this gentleman the only pleasure which is left to him?"

And involved in these thoughts, knowing that she was certain to have the bird if she asked for it, but not knowing what to say to her son, she stood there without answering him. Finally the love she bore her son persuaded her that she should make him happy, and no matter what the consequences might be, she would not send for the bird, but rather go herself for it and bring it back to him; so she answered her son:

"My son, take comfort and think only of getting well, for I promise you that the first thing I shall do tomorrow morning is to go for it and bring it back to you."

The child was so happy that he showed some improvement that very day. The following morning, the lady, accompanied by another woman, as if going for a stroll, went to Federigo's modest house and asked for him. Since it was not the season for it, Federigo had not been hawking for some days and was in his orchard, attending to certain tasks; when he heard that Monna Giovanna was asking for him at the door, he was very surprised and happy to run there; as she saw him coming, she greeted him with feminine charm, and once Federigo had welcomed her courteously, she said:

"Greetings, Federigo!" Then she continued: "I have come to compensate you for the harm you have suffered on my account by loving me more than you needed to; and the compensation is this: I, along with this companion of mine, intend to dine with you—a simple meal—this very day."

To this Federigo humbly replied: "Madonna,[2] I never remember having suffered any harm because of you; on the contrary: so much good have I received from you that if ever I have been worth anything, it has been because of your merit and the love I bore for you; and your generous visit is certainly so dear to me that I would spend all over again that which I spent in the past; but you have come to a poor host."

And having said this, he received her into his home humbly, and from there he led her into his garden, and since he had no one there to keep her company, he said:

"My lady, since there is no one else, this good woman here, the wife of this workman, will keep you company while I go to set the table."

Though he was very poor, Federigo, until now, had never before realized to what extent he had wasted his wealth; but this morning, the fact that he found nothing with which he could honor the lady for the love of whom he had once entertained countless men in the past gave him cause to reflect: in great anguish, he cursed himself and his fortune and, like a man beside himself, he started running here and there, but could find neither money nor a pawnable object. The hour was late and his desire to honor the gracious lady was great, but not wishing to turn for help to others (not even to his own workman), he set his eyes upon his good falcon, perched in a small room; and since he had nowhere else to turn, he took the bird, and finding it plump, he decided that it would be a worthy food for such a lady. So, without further thought, he wrung its neck and quickly gave it to his servant girl to pluck, prepare, and place on a spit to be roasted with care; and when he had set the table with the whitest of tablecloths (a few of which he still had left), he returned, with a cheerful face, to the lady in his garden, saying that the meal he was able to prepare for her was ready.

The lady and her companion rose, went to the table together with Federigo, who waited upon them with the greatest devotion, and they ate the good falcon without knowing what it was they were eating. And having left the table and spent some time in pleasant conversation, the lady thought it time now to say what she had come to say, and so she spoke these kind words to Federigo:

"Federigo, if you recall your past life and my virtue, which you perhaps mistook for harshness and cruelty, I do not doubt at all that you will be amazed by my presumption when you hear what my main reason for coming here is; but if you had children, through whom you might have experienced the power of parental love, it seems certain to me that you would, at least in part, forgive

2. My lady.

me. But, just as you have no child, I do have one, and I cannot escape the common laws of other mothers; the force of such laws compels me to follow them, against my own will and against good manners and duty, and to ask of you a gift which I know is most precious to you; and it is naturally so, since your extreme condition has left you no other delight, no other pleasure, no other consolation; and this gift is your falcon, which my son is so taken by that if I do not bring it to him, I fear his sickness will grow so much worse that I may lose him. And therefore I beg you, not because of the love that you bear for me, which does not oblige you in the least, but because of your own nobleness, which you have shown to be greater than that of all others in practicing courtliness, that you be pleased to give it to me, so that I may say that I have saved the life of my son by means of this gift, and because of it I have placed him in your debt forever."

When he heard what the lady requested and knew that he could not oblige her since he had given her the falcon to eat, Federigo began to weep in her presence, for he could not utter a word in reply. The lady, at first, thought his tears were caused more by the sorrow of having to part with the good falcon than by anything else, and she was on the verge of telling him she no longer wished it, but she held back and waited for Federigo's reply after he stopped weeping. And he said:

"My lady, ever since it pleased God for me to place my love in you, I have felt that Fortune has been hostile to me in many things, and I have complained of her, but all this is nothing compared to what she has just done to me, and I must never be at peace with her again, thinking about how you have come here to my poor home where, while it was rich, you never deigned to come, and you requested a small gift, and Fortune worked to make it impossible for me to give it to you; and why this is so I shall tell you briefly. When I heard that you, out of your kindness, wished to dine with me, I considered it fitting and right, taking into account your excellence and your worthiness, that I should honor you, according to my possibilities, with a more precious food than that which I usually serve to other people; therefore, remembering the falcon that you requested and its value, I judged it a food worthy of you, and this very day you had it roasted and served to you as best I could; but seeing now that you desired it in another way, my sorrow in not being able to serve you is so great that I shall never be able to console myself again."

And after he had said this, he laid the feathers, the feet, and the beak of the bird before her as proof. When the lady heard and saw this, she first reproached him for having killed such a falcon to serve as a meal to a woman; but then to herself she commended the greatness of his spirit, which no poverty was able or would be able to diminish; then, having lost all hope of getting the falcon and, perhaps because of this, of improving the health of her son as well, she thanked Federigo both for the honor paid to her and for his good will, and she left in grief, and returned to her son. To his mother's extreme sorrow, either because of his disappointment that he could not have the falcon, or because his illness must have necessarily led to it, the boy passed from this life only a few days later.

After the period of her mourning and bitterness had passed, the lady was repeatedly urged by her brothers to remarry, since she was very rich and was still young; and although she did not wish to do so, they became so insistent that she remembered the merits of Federigo and his last act of generosity—that is, to have killed such a falcon to do her honor—and she said to her brothers:

"I would prefer to remain a widow, if that would please you; but if you wish me to take a husband, you may rest assured that I shall take no man but Federigo degli Alberighi."

In answer to this, making fun of her, her brothers replied:

"You foolish woman, what are you saying? How can you want him; he hasn't a penny to his name?"

To this she replied: "My brothers, I am well aware of what you say, but I would rather have a man who needs money than money that needs a man."

Her brothers, seeing that she was determined and knowing Federigo to be of noble birth, no matter how poor he was, accepted her wishes and gave her in marriage to him with all her riches; when he found himself the husband of such a great lady, whom he had loved so much and who was so wealthy besides, he managed his financial affairs with more prudence than in the past and lived with her happily the rest of his days.

\* \* \*

# ANONYMOUS
## Sir Gawain and the Green Knight\*

## Part I

Since the siege and the assault was ceased at Troy,
The walls breached and burnt down to brands and ashes,
The knight that had knotted the nets of deceit
Was impeached for his perfidy, proven most true,
It was high-born Aeneas and his haughty race                        5

---

\* Translated by Marie Borroff. Many of the notes are by E. Talbot Donaldson.

4. *impeached for his perfidy:* The treacherous knight is either Aeneas himself or Antenor, both of whom were, according to medieval tradition, traitors to their city Troy; but Aeneas was actually tried ("impeached") by the Greeks for his refusal to hand over to them his sister Polyxena.

That since prevailed over provinces, and proudly reigned
Over well-nigh all the wealth of the West Isles.
Great Romulus to Rome repairs in haste;
With boast and with bravery builds he that city
And names it with his own name, that it now bears. 10
Ticius to Tuscany, and towers raises,
Langobard in Lombardy lays out homes,
And far over the French Sea, Felix Brutus
On many broad hills and high Britain he sets,
                              most fair. 15
         Where war and wrack and wonder
         By shifts have sojourned there,
         And bliss by turns with blunder
         In that land's lot had share.

And since this Britain was built by this baron great, 20
Bold boys bred there, in broils delighting,
That did in their day many a deed most dire.
More marvels have happened in this merry land
Than in any other I know, since that olden time,
But of those that here built, of British kings, 25
King Arthur was counted most courteous of all,
Wherefore an adventure I aim to unfold,
That a marvel of might some men think it,
And one unmatched among Arthur's wonders.
If you will listen to my lay but a little while, 30
As I heard it in hall, I shall hasten to tell
                              anew.
         As it was fashioned featly
         In tale of derring-do,
         And linked in measures meetly 35
         By letters tried and true.

This king lay at Camelot at Christmastide;
Many good knights and gay his guests were there,
Arrayed of the Round Table rightful brothers,
With feasting and fellowship and carefree mirth. 40
There true men contended in tournaments many,
Joined there in jousting these gentle knights,
Then came to the court for carol-dancing,
For the feast was in force full fifteen days,
With all the meat and the mirth that men could devise, 45

---

7. *the West Isles:* Perhaps western Europe.
8. *Romulus:* The legendary founder of Rome is here given Trojan ancestry, like Aeneas. *repairs:* Goes.
11. *Ticius:* Not otherwise known. *Tuscany:* A region north of Rome; modern Florence is located in it.
12. *Langobard:* The reputed founder of Lombardy, a region in the north centered on modern Milan.
13. *French Sea:* The North Sea, including the English Channel. *Felix Brutus:* Great-grandson of Aeneas and legendary founder of Britain; not else-

where given the name Felix (Latin "happy").
14. *sets:* Establishes.
35. *meetly:* Suitably.
37. *Camelot:* Capital of Arthur's kingdom, presumably located in southwest England or southern Wales.
39. According to legend, the Round Table was made by Merlin, the wise magician who had helped Arthur become King, after a dispute broke out among Arthur's knights about precedence: it seated 100 knights. The table described in the poem is not round.

Such gaiety and glee, glorious to hear,
Brave din by day, dancing by night.
High were their hearts in halls and chambers,
These lords and these ladies, for life was sweet.
In peerless pleasures passed they their days,  50
The most noble knights known under Christ,
And the loveliest ladies that lived on earth ever,
And he the comeliest king, that that court holds,
For all this fair folk in their first age
                  were still.  55
        Happiest of mortal kind,
        King noblest famed of will;
        You would now go far to find
        So hardy a host on hill.

While the New Year was new, but yesternight come,  60
This fair folk at feast two-fold was served,
When the king and his company were come in together,
The chanting in chapel achieved and ended.
Clerics and all the court acclaimed the glad season,
Cried Noel anew, good news to men;  65
Then gallants gather gaily, hand-gifts to make,
Called them out clearly, claimed them by hand,
Bickered long and busily about those gifts.
Ladies laughed aloud, though losers they were,
And he that won was not angered, as well you will know.  70
All this mirth they made until meat was served;
When they had washed them worthily, they went to their seats,
The best seated above, as best it beseemed,
Guenevere the goodly queen gay in the midst
On a dais well-decked and duly arrayed  75
With costly silk curtains, a canopy over,
Of Toulouse and Turkestan tapestries rich,
All broidered and bordered with the best gems
Ever brought into Britain, with bright pennies
                  to pay.  80
        Fair queen, without a flaw,
        She glanced with eyes of grey.
        A seemlier that once he saw,
        In truth, no man could say.

But Arthur would not eat till all were served;  85
So light was his lordly heart, and a little boyish;
His life he liked lively—the less he cared
To be lying for long, or long to sit,
So busy his young blood, his brain so wild.
And also a point of pride pricked him in heart,  90
For he nobly had willed, he would never eat
On so high a holiday, till he had heard first

---

70. The dispensing of New Year's gifts seems to have involved kissing.　83. *seemlier*: More suitable and pleasing (queen).

Of some fair feat or fray some far-borne tale,
Of some marvel of might, that he might trust,
By champions of chivalry achieved in arms,                    95
Or some suppliant came seeking some single knight
To join with him in jousting, in jeopardy each
To lay life for life, and leave it to fortune
To afford him on field fair hap or other.
Such is the king's custom, when his court he holds          100
At each far-famed feast amid his fair host
                    so dear.
          The stout king stands in state
          Till a wonder shall appear;
          He leads, with heart elate,                        105
          High mirth in the New Year.

So he stands there in state, the stout young king,
Talking before the high table of trifles fair.
There Gawain the good knight by Guenevere sits,
With Agravain à la dure main on her other side,             110
Both knights of renown, and nephews of the king.
Bishop Baldwin above begins the table,
And Yvain, son of Urien, ate with him there.
These few with the fair queen were fittingly served;
At the side-tables sat many stalwart knights.               115
Then the first course comes, with clamor of trumpets
That were bravely bedecked with bannerets bright,
With noise of new drums and the noble pipes.
Wild were the warbles that wakened that day
In strains that stirred many strong men's hearts.           120
There dainties were dealt out, dishes rare,
Choice fare to choose, on chargers so many
That scarce was there space to set before the people
The service of silver, with sundry meats,
                    on cloth.                                125
          Each fair guest freely there
          Partakes, and nothing loth;
          Twelve dishes before each pair;
          Good beer and bright wine both.

Of the service itself I need say no more,                   130
For well you will know no tittle was wanting.
Another noise and a new was well-nigh at hand,
That the lord might have leave his life to nourish;
For scarce were the sweet strains still in the hall,
And the first course come to that company fair,             135
There hurtles in at the hall-door an unknown rider,
One the greatest on ground in growth of his frame:

---

99. *fair hap:* Good luck.
108. The high table is on a dais; the side tables (line 115) are on the main floor and run along the walls at a right angle to the high table.
110. *à la dure main:* Of the hard hand.
127. *nothing loth:* Not unwillingly.

From broad neck to buttocks so bulky and thick,
And his loins and his legs so long and so great,
Half a giant on earth I hold him to be,                    140
But believe him no less than the largest of men,
And that the seemliest in his stature to see, as he rides,
For in back and in breast though his body was grim,
His waist in its width was worthily small,
And formed with every feature in fair accord              145
                was he.
        Great wonder grew in hall
        At his hue most strange to see,
        For man and gear and all
        Were green as green could be.              150

And in guise all of green, the gear and the man:
A coat cut close, that clung to his sides,
And a mantle to match, made with a lining
Of furs cut and fitted—the fabric was noble,
Embellished all with ermine, and his hood beside,         155
That was loosed from his locks, and laid on his shoulders.
With trim hose and tight, the same tint of green,
His great calves were girt, and gold spurs under
He bore on silk bands that embellished his heels,
And footgear well-fashioned, for riding most fit.         160
And all his vesture verily was verdant green;
Both the bosses on his belt and other bright gems
That were richly ranged on his raiment noble
About himself and his saddle, set upon silk,
That to tell half the trifles would tax my wits,          165
The butterflies and birds embroidered thereon
In green of the gayest, with many a gold thread.
The pendants of the breast-band, the princely crupper,
And the bars of the bit were brightly enameled;
The stout stirrups were green, that steadied his feet,    170
And the bows of the saddle and the side-panels both,
That gleamed all and glinted with green gems about.
The steed he bestrides of that same green
                so bright.
        A green horse great and thick;            175
        A headstrong steed of might;
        In broidered bridle quick,
        Mount matched man aright.

Gay was this goodly man in guise all of green,
And the hair of his head to his horse suited;             180
Fair flowing tresses enfold his shoulders;
A beard big as a bush on his breast hangs,
That with his heavy hair, that from his head falls,
Was evened all about above both his elbows,

162. *bosses:* Ornamental knobs.       of the horse's harness.
168. *breast-band . . . crupper:* Parts

That half his arms thereunder were hid in the fashion    185
Of a king's cap-à-dos, that covers his throat.
The mane of that mighty horse much to it like,
Well curled and becombed, and cunningly knotted
With filaments of fine gold amid the fair green,
Here a strand of the hair, here one of gold;    190
His tail and his foretop twin in their hue,
And bound both with a band of a bright green
That was decked adown the dock with dazzling stones
And tied tight at the top with a triple knot
Where many bells well burnished rang bright and clear.    195
Such a mount in his might, nor man on him riding,
None had seen, I dare swear, with sight in that hall
          so grand.
       As lightning quick and light
       He looked to all at hand;    200
       It seemed that no man might
       His deadly dints withstand.

Yet had he no helm, nor hauberk neither,
Nor plate, nor appurtenance appending to arms,
Nor shaft pointed sharp, nor shield for defense,    205
But in his one hand he had a holly bob
That is goodliest in green when groves are bare,
And an ax in his other, a huge and immense,
A wicked piece of work in words to expound:
The head on its haft was an ell long;    210
The spike of green steel, resplendent with gold;
The blade burnished bright, with a broad edge,
As well shaped to shear as a sharp razor;
Stout was the stave in the strong man's gripe,
That was wound all with iron to the weapon's end,    215
With engravings in green of goodliest work.
A lace lightly about, that led to a knot,
Was looped in by lengths along the fair haft,
And tassels thereto attached in a row,
With buttons of bright green, brave to behold.    220
This horseman hurtles in, and the hall enters;
Riding to the high dais, recked he no danger;
Not a greeting he gave as the guests he o'erlooked,
Nor wasted his words, but "Where is," he said,
"The captain of this crowd? Keenly I wish    225
To see that sire with sight, and to himself say
          my say."
       He swaggered all about
       To scan the host so gay;
       He halted, as if in doubt    230
       Who in that hall held sway.

186. *cap-à-dos:* Or *capados,* interpreted by the translator as a garment covering its wearer "from head to back."

193. *dock:* The solid part of the tail.
203. *hauberk:* Tunic of chain mail.
210. *ell:* Three or four feet long.

There were stares on all sides as the stranger spoke,
For much did they marvel what it might mean
That a horseman and a horse should have such a hue,
Grow green as the grass, and greener, it seemed,                    235
Than green fused on gold more glorious by far.
All the onlookers eyed him, and edged nearer,
And awaited in wonder what he would do,
For many sights had they seen, but such a one never,
So that phantom and faerie the folk there deemed it,               240
Therefore chary of answer was many a champion bold,
And stunned at his strong words stone-still they sat
In a swooning silence in the stately hall.
As all were slipped into sleep, so slackened their speech
                  apace.                    245
        Not all, I think, for dread,
        But some of courteous grace
        Let him who was their head
        Be spokesman in that place.

Then Arthur before the high dais that entrance beholds,            250
And hailed him, as behooved, for he had no fear,
And said "Fellow, in faith you have found fair welcome;
The head of this hostelry Arthur am I;
Leap lightly down, and linger, I pray,
And the tale of your intent you shall tell us after."              255
"Nay, so help me," said the other, "He that on high sits,
To tarry here any time, 'twas not mine errand;
But as the praise of you, prince, is puffed up so high,
And your court and your company are counted the best,
Stoutest under steel-gear on steeds to ride,                       260
Worthiest of their works the wide world over,
And peerless to prove in passages of arms,
And courtesy here is carried to its height,
And so at this season I have sought you out.
You may be certain by the branch that I bear in hand              265
That I pass here in peace, and would part friends,
For had I come to this court on combat bent,
I have a hauberk at home, and a helm beside,
A shield and a sharp spear, shining bright,
And other weapons to wield, I ween well, to boot,                  270
But as I willed no war, I wore no metal.
But if you be so bold as all men believe,
You will graciously grant the game that I ask
                by right."
        Arthur answer gave                          275
        And said, "Sir courteous knight,
        If contest here you crave,
        You shall not fail to fight."

270. *ween*: Believe.

"Nay, to fight, in good faith, is far from my thought;
There are about on these benches but beardless children,          280
Were I here in full arms on a haughty steed,
For measured against mine, their might is puny.
And so I call in this court for a Christmas game,
For 'tis Yule and New Year, and many young bloods about;
If any in this house such hardihood claims,                       285
Be so bold in his blood, his brain so wild,
As stoutly to strike one stroke for another,
I shall give him as my gift this gisarme noble,
This ax, that is heavy enough, to handle as he likes,
And I shall bide the first blow, as bare as I sit.               290
If there be one so wilful my words to assay,
Let him leap hither lightly, lay hold of this weapon;
I quitclaim it forever, keep it as his own,
And I shall stand him a stroke, steady on this floor,
So you grant me the guerdon to give him another,                295
      sans blame.
     In a twelvemonth and a day
     He shall have of me the same;
     Now be it seen straightway
     Who dares take up the game."            300

If he astonished them at first, stiller were then
All that household in hall, the high and the low;
The stranger on his green steed stirred in the saddle,
And roisterously his red eyes he rolled all about,
Bent his bristling brows, that were bright green,               305
Wagged his beard as he watched who would arise.
When the court kept its counsel he coughed aloud,
And cleared his throat coolly, the clearer to speak:
"What, is this Arthur's house," said that horseman then,
"Whose fame is so fair in far realms and wide?                  310
Where is now your arrogance and your awesome deeds,
Your valor and your victories and your vaunting words?
Now are the revel and renown of the Round Table
Overwhelmed with a word of one man's speech,
For all cower and quake, and no cut felt!"                      315
With this he laughs so loud that the lord grieved;
The blood for sheer shame shot to his face,
      and pride.
     With rage his face flushed red,
     And so did all beside.                  320
     Then the king as bold man bred
     Toward the stranger took a stride.

And said "Sir, now we see you will say but folly,
Which whoso has sought, it suits that he find.
No guest here is aghast of your great words.                    325

288. *gisarme:* Weapon.    295. *guerdon:* Reward.
290. *bide:* Endure.     296. *sans:* Without.
293. *keep it:* I.e., let him keep it.

Give to me your gisarme, in God's own name,
And the boon you have begged shall straight be granted."
He leaps to him lightly, lays hold of his weapon;
The green fellow on foot fiercely alights.
Now has Arthur his ax, and the haft grips,      330
And sternly stirs it about, on striking bent.
The stranger before him stood there erect,
Higher than any in the house by a head and more;
With stern look as he stood, he stroked his beard,
And with undaunted countenance drew down his coat,      335
No more moved nor dismayed for his mighty dints
Than any bold man on bench had brought him a drink
                    of wine.
          Gawain by Guenevere
          Toward the king doth now incline:      340
          "I beseech, before all here,
          That this melee may be mine."

"Would you grant me the grace," said Gawain to the king,
"To be gone from this bench and stand by you there,
If I without discourtesy might quit this board,      345
And if my liege lady misliked it not,
I would come to your counsel before your court noble.
For I find it not fit, as in faith it is known,
When such a boon is begged before all these knights,
Though you be tempted thereto, to take it on yourself      350
While so bold men about upon benches sit,
That no host under heaven is hardier of will,
Nor better brothers-in-arms where battle is joined;
I am the weakest, well I know, and of wit feeblest;
And the loss of my life would be least of any;      355
That I have you for uncle is my only praise;
My body, but for your blood, is barren of worth;
And for that this folly befits not a king,
And 'tis I that have asked it, it ought to be mine,
And if my claim be not comely let all this court judge,      360
                    in sight."
          The court assays the claim,
          And in counsel all unite
          To give Gawain the game
          And release the king outright.      365

Then the king called the knight to come to his side,
And he rose up readily, and reached him with speed,
Bows low to his lord, lays hold of the weapon,
And he releases it lightly, and lifts up his hand,
And gives him God's blessing, and graciously prays      370
That his heart and his hand may be hardy both.
"Keep, cousin," said the king, "what you cut with this day,
And if you rule it aright, then readily, I know,

---

346. *liege lady*: Lady entitled to the knight's feudal service.

You shall stand the stroke it will strike after."
Gawain goes to the guest with gisarme in hand,                    375
And boldly he bides there, abashed not a whit.
Then hails he Sir Gawain, the horseman in green:
"Recount we our contract, ere you come further.
First I ask and adjure you, how you are called
That you tell me true, so that trust it I may."                   380
"In good faith," said the good knight, "Gawain am I
Whose buffet befalls you, whate'er betide after,
And at this time twelvemonth take from you another
With what weapon you will, and with no man else
                alive."                                             385
        The other nods assent:
        "Sir Gawain, as I may thrive,
        I am wondrous well content
        That you this dint shall drive."

"Sir Gawain," said the Green Knight, "By Gog, I rejoice          390
That your fist shall fetch this favor I seek,
And you have readily rehearsed, and in right terms,
Each clause of my covenant with the king your lord,
Save that you shall assure me, sir, upon oath,
That you shall seek me yourself, wheresoever you deem            395
My lodgings may lie, and look for such wages
As you have offered me here before all this host."
"What is the way there?" said Gawain, "Where do you dwell?
I heard never of your house, by Him that made me,
Nor I know you not, knight, your name nor your court.            400
But tell me truly thereof, and teach me your name,
And I shall fare forth to find you, so far as I may,
And this I say in good certain, and swear upon oath."
"That is enough in New Year, you need say no more,"
Said the knight in the green to Gawain the noble,               405
"If I tell you true, when I have taken your knock,
And if you handily have hit, you shall hear straightway
Of my house and my home and my own name;
Then follow in my footsteps by faithful accord.
And if I spend no speech, you shall speed the better:           410
You can feast with your friends, nor further trace
              my tracks.
        Now hold your grim tool steady
        And show us how it hacks."
        "Gladly, sir; all ready,"                                415
        Says Gawain; he strokes the ax.

The Green Knight upon ground girds him with care:
Bows a bit with his head, and bares his flesh:
His long lovely locks he laid over his crown,
Let the naked nape for the need be shown.                        420
Gawain grips to his ax and gathers it aloft—
The left foot on the floor before him he set—

Brought it down deftly upon the bare neck,
That the shock of the sharp blow shivered the bones
And cut the flesh cleanly and clove it in twain,    425
That the blade of bright steel bit into the ground.
The head was hewn off and fell to the floor;
Many found it at their feet, as forth it rolled;
The blood gushed from the body, bright on the green,
Yet fell not the fellow, nor faltered a whit,    430
But stoutly he starts forth upon stiff shanks,
And as all stood staring he stretched forth his hand,
Laid hold of his head and heaved it aloft,
Then goes to the green steed, grasps the bridle,
Steps into the stirrup, bestrides his mount,    435
And his head by the hair in his hand holds,
And as steady he sits in the stately saddle
As he had met with no mishap, nor missing were
                his head.
      His bulk about he haled,    440
      That fearsome body that bled;
      There were many in the court that quailed
      Before all his say was said.

For the head in his hand he holds right up;
Toward the first on the dais directs he the face,    445
And it lifted up its lids, and looked with wide eyes,
And said as much with its mouth as now you may hear:
"Sir Gawain, forget not to go as agreed,
And cease not to seek till me, sir, you find,
As you promised in the presence of these proud knights.    450
To the Green Chapel come, I charge you, to take
Such a dint as you have dealt—you have well deserved
That your neck should have a knock on New Year's morn.
The Knight of the Green Chapel I am well-known to many,
Wherefore you cannot fail to find me at last;    455
Therefore come, or be counted a recreant knight."
With a roisterous rush he flings round the reins,
Hurtles out at the hall-door, his head in his hand,
That the flint-fire flew from the flashing hooves.
Which way he went, not one of them knew    460
Nor whence he was come in the wide world
               so fair.
      The king and Gawain gay
      Make game of the Green Knight there,
      Yet all who saw it say    465
      'Twas a wonder past compare.

Though high-born Arthur at heart had wonder,
He let no sign be seen, but said aloud
To the comely queen, with courteous speech,

---

440. *haled:* Hauled.                       456. *recreant:* Cowardly.

"Dear dame, on this day dismay you no whit;                    470
Such crafts are becoming at Christmastide,
Laughing at interludes, light songs and mirth,
Amid dancing of damsels with doughty knights.
Nevertheless of my meat now let me partake,
For I have met with a marvel, I may not deny."              475
He glanced at Sir Gawain, and gaily he said,
"Now, sir, hang up your ax, that has hewn enough,"
And over the high dais it was hung on the wall
That men in amazement might on it look,
And tell in true terms the tale of the wonder.              480
Then they turned toward the table, these two together,
The good king and Gawain, and made great feast,
With all dainties double, dishes rare,
With all manner of meat and minstrelsy both,
Such happiness wholly had they that day                      485
            in hold.
        Now take care, Sir Gawain,
        That your courage wax not cold
        When you must turn again
        To your enterprise foretold.                         490

# Part II

This adventure had Arthur of handsels first
When young was the year, for he yearned to hear tales;
Though they wanted for words when they went to sup,
Now are fierce deeds to follow, their fists stuffed full.
Gawain was glad to begin those games in hall,               495
But if the end be harsher, hold it no wonder,
For though men are merry in mind after much drink,
A year passes apace, and proves ever new:
First things and final conform but seldom.
And so this Yule to the young year yielded place,           500
And each season ensued at its set time;
After Christmas there came the cold cheer of Lent,
When with fish and plainer fare our flesh we reprove;
But then the world's weather with winter contends:
The keen cold lessens, the low clouds lift;                 505
Fresh falls the rain in fostering showers
On the face of the fields; flowers appear.
The ground and the groves wear gowns of green;
Birds build their nests, and blithely sing
That solace of all sorrow with summer comes                 510
            ere long.
        And blossoms day by day
        Bloom rich and rife in throng;
        Then every grove so gay
        Of the greenwood rings with song.                    515

491. *handsels*: Gifts to mark the New Year.

And then the season of summer with the soft winds,
When Zephyr sighs low over seeds and shoots;
Glad is the green plant growing abroad,
When the dew at dawn drops from the leaves,
To get a gracious glance from the golden sun.                    520
But harvest with harsher winds follows hard after,
Warns him to ripen well ere winter comes;
Drives forth the dust in the droughty season,
From the face of the fields to fly high in air.
Wroth winds in the welkin wrestle with the sun,                 525
The leaves launch from the linden and light on the ground,
And the grass turns to gray, that once grew green.
Then all ripens and rots that rose up at first,
And so the year moves on in yesterdays many,
And winter once more, by the world's law,                       530
                        draws nigh.
                  At Michaelmas the moon
                  Hangs wintry pale in sky;
                  Sir Gawain girds him soon
                  For travails yet to try.                      535

Till All-Hallows' Day with Arthur he dwells,
And he held a high feast to honor that knight
With great revels and rich, of the Round Table.
Then ladies lovely and lords debonair
With sorrow for Sir Gawain were sore at heart;                  540
Yet they covered their care with countenance glad:
Many a mournful man made mirth for his sake.
So after supper soberly he speaks to his uncle
Of the hard hour at hand, and openly says,
"Now, liege lord of my life, my leave I take;                   545
The terms of this task too well you know—
To count the cost over concerns me nothing.
But I am bound forth betimes to bear a stroke
From the grim man in green, as God may direct."
Then the first and foremost came forth in throng:              550
Yvain and Eric and others of note,
Sir Dodinal le Sauvage, the Duke of Clarence,
Lionel and Lancelot and Lucan the good,
Sir Bors and Sir Bedivere, big men both,
And many manly knights more, with Mador de la Porte.           555
All this courtly company comes to the king
To counsel their comrade, with care in their hearts;
There was much secret sorrow suffered that day
That one so good as Gawain must go in such wise
To bear a bitter blow, and his bright sword                     560
                        lay by.
                  He said, "Why should I tarry?"
                  And smiled with tranquil eye;

---

525. *the welkin:* The heavens.          536. *All-Hallows' Day:* November 1.
532. *Michaelmas:* September 29.          548. *betimes:* Soon

"In destinies sad or merry,
True men can but try."                                        565

He dwelt there all that day, and dressed in the morning;
Asked early for his arms, and all were brought.
First a carpet of rare cost was cast on the floor
Where much goodly gear gleamed golden bright;
He takes his place promptly and picks up the steel,          570
Attired in a tight coat of Turkestan silk
And a kingly cap-à-dos, closed at the throat,
That was lavishly lined with a lustrous fur.
Then they set the steel shoes on his sturdy feet
And clad his calves about with comely greaves,               575
And plate well-polished protected his knees,
Affixed with fastenings of the finest gold.
Fair cuisses enclosed, that were cunningly wrought,
His thick-thewed thighs, with thongs bound fast,
And massy chain-mail of many a steel ring                    580
He bore on his body, above the best cloth,
With brace burnished bright upon both his arms,
Good couters and gay, and gloves of plate,
And all the goodly gear to grace him well
                              that tide.                      585
           His surcoat blazoned bold;
           Sharp spurs to prick with pride;
           And a brave silk band to hold
           The broadsword at his side.

When he had on his arms, his harness was rich,               590
The least latchet or loop laden with gold;
So armored as he was, he heard a mass,
Honored God humbly at the high altar.
Then he comes to the king and his comrades-in-arms,
Takes his leave at last of lords and ladies,                 595
And they clasped and kissed him, commending him to Christ.
By then Gringolet was girt with a great saddle
That was gaily agleam with fine gilt fringe,
New-furbished for the need with nail-heads bright;
The bridle and the bars bedecked all with gold;              600
The breast-plate, the saddlebow, the side-panels both,
The caparison and the crupper accorded in hue,
And all ranged on the red the resplendent studs
That glittered and glowed like the glorious sun.
His helm now he holds up and hastily kisses,                 605
Well-closed with iron clinches, and cushioned within;
It was high on his head, with a hasp behind,
And a covering of cloth to encase the visor,
All bound and embroidered with the best gems

583. *couters:* Armor for the elbows.     the armor.
586. *surcoat:* Cloth tunic worn over     597. *Gringolet:* Gawain's horse.

On broad bands of silk, and bordered with birds,     610
Parrots and popinjays preening their wings,
Lovebirds and love-knots as lavishly wrought
As many women had worked seven winters thereon,
entire.
The diadem costlier yet     615
That crowned that comely sire,
With diamonds richly set,
That flashed as if on fire.

Then they showed forth the shield, that shone all red,
With the pentangle portrayed in purest gold.     620
About his broad neck by the baldric he casts it,
That was meet for the man, and matched him well.
And why the pentangle is proper to that peerless prince
I intend now to tell, though detain me it must.
It is a sign by Solomon sagely devised     625
To be a token of truth, by its title of old,
For it is a figure formed of five points,
And each line is linked and locked with the next
For ever and ever, and hence it is called
In all England, as I hear, the endless knot.     630
And well may he wear it on his worthy arms,
For ever faithful five-fold in five-fold fashion
Was Gawain in good works, as gold unalloyed,
Devoid of all villainy, with virtues adorned
in sight.     635
On shield and coat in view
He bore that emblem bright,
As to his word most true
And in speech most courteous knight.

And first, he was faultless in his five senses,     640
Nor found ever to fail in his five fingers,
And all his fealty was fixed upon the five wounds
That Christ got on the cross, as the creed tells;
And wherever this man in melee took part,
His one thought was of this, past all things else,     645
That all his force was founded on the five joys
That the high Queen of heaven had in her child.
And therefore, as I find, he fittingly had
On the inner part of his shield her image portrayed,
That when his look on it lighted, he never lost heart.     650
The fifth of the five fives followed by this knight
Were beneficence boundless and brotherly love

---

620. *Pentangle:* A five-pointed star, formed by five lines which are drawn without lifting the pen, supposed to have mystical significance; as Solomon's sign, (line 625) it was enclosed in a circle.
621. *baldric:* Belt worn diagonally across the chest.

646–647. *five joys . . . her child:* These were the annunciation to Mary that she was to bear the Son of God, Christ's nativity, resurrection, and ascension into heaven, and the "assumption" or bodily taking up of Mary into heaven to join Him.

And pure mind and manners, that none might impeach,
And compassion most precious—these peerless five
Were forged and made fast in him, foremost of men. 655
Now all these five fives were confirmed in this knight,
And each linked in other, that end there was none,
And fixed to five points, whose force never failed,
Nor assembled all on a side, nor asunder either,
Nor anywhere at an end, but whole and entire 660
However the pattern proceeded or played out its course.
And so on his shining shield shaped was the knot
Royally in red gold against red gules,
That is the peerless pentangle, prized of old
     in lore. 665
   Now armed is Gawain gay,
   And bears his lance before,
   And soberly said good day,
   He thought forevermore.

He struck his steed with the spurs and sped on his way 670
So fast that the flint-fire flashed from the stones.
When they saw him set forth they were sore aggrieved,
And all sighed softly, and said to each other,
Fearing for their fellow, "Ill fortune it is
That you, man, must be marred, that most are worthy! 675
His equal on this earth can hardly be found;
To have dealt more discreetly had done less harm,
And have dubbed him a duke, with all due honor.
A great leader of lords he was like to become,
And better so to have been than battered to bits, 680
Beheaded by an elf-man, for empty pride!
Who would credit that a king could be counseled so,
And caught in a cavil in a Christmas game?"
Many were the warm tears they wept from their eyes
When goodly Sir Gawain was gone from the court 685
     that day.
   No longer he abode,
   But speedily went his way
   Over many a wandering road,
   As I heard my author say. 690

Now he rides in his array through the realm of Logres,
Sir Gawain, God knows, though it gave him small joy!
All alone must he lodge through many a long night
Where the food that he fancied was far from his plate;
He had no mate but his mount, over mountain and plain, 695
Nor man to say his mind to but almighty God,
Till he had wandered well-nigh into North Wales.

---

663. *gules*: Background (gules is the heraldric name for red).
681. *elf-man*: Supernatural being, in this case obviously not small.
691. *Logres*: Another name for Arthur's kingdom.

697–701. North Wales . . . Wirral: Gawain went from Camelot north to the northern coast of Wales, opposite the islands of Anglesey; there he turned east across the River Dee to the forest of Wirral, near what is now Liverpool.

All the islands of Anglesey he holds on his left,
And follows, as he fares, the fords by the coast,
Comes over at Holy Head, and enters next                          700
The Wilderness of Wirral—few were within
That had great good will toward God or man.
And earnestly he asked of each mortal he met
If he had ever heard aught of a knight all green,
Or of a Green Chapel, on ground thereabouts,                     705
And all said the same, and solemnly swore
They saw no such knight all solely green
                in hue.
         Over country wild and strange
         The knight sets off anew;                               710
         Often his course must change
         Ere the Chapel comes in view.

Many a cliff must he climb in country wild;
Far off from all his friends, forlorn must he ride;
At each strand or stream where the stalwart passed              715
'Twere a marvel if he met not some monstrous foe,
And that so fierce and forbidding that fight he must.
So many were the wonders he wandered among
That to tell but the tenth part would tax my wits.
Now with serpents he wars, now with savage wolves,             720
Now with wild men of the woods, that watched from the rocks,
Both with bulls and with bears, and with boars besides,
And giants that came gibbering from the jagged steeps.
Had he not borne himself bravely, and been on God's side,
He had met with many mishaps and mortal harms.                 725
And if the wars were unwelcome, the winter was worse,
When the cold clear rains rushed from the clouds
And froze before they could fall to the frosty earth.
Near slain by the sleet he sleeps in his irons
More nights than enough, among naked rocks,                    730
Where clattering from the crest the cold stream ran
And hung in hard icicles high overhead.
Thus in peril and pain and predicaments dire
He rides across country till Christmas Eve,
               our knight.                                735
         And at that holy tide
         He prays with all his might
         That Mary may be his guide
         Till a dwelling comes in sight.

By a mountain next morning he makes his way                    740
Into a forest fastness, fearsome and wild;
High hills on either hand, with hoar woods below,
Oaks old and huge by the hundred together.
The hazel and the hawthorn were all intertwined
With rough raveled moss, that raggedly hung,                   745
With many birds unblithe upon bare twigs
That peeped most piteously for pain of the cold.

The good knight on Gringolet glides thereunder
Through many a marsh and mire, a man all alone;
He feared for his default, should he fail to see          750
The service of that Sire that on that same night
Was born of a bright maid, to bring us His peace.
And therefore sighing he said, "I beseech of Thee, Lord,
And Mary, thou mildest mother so dear,
Some harborage where haply I might hear mass          755
And Thy matins tomorrow—meekly I ask it,
And thereto proffer and pray my pater and ave
                                    and creed."
                    He said his prayer with sighs,
                    Lamenting his misdeed;
                    He crosses himself, and cries          760
                    On Christ in his great need.

No sooner had Sir Gawain signed himself thrice
Than he was ware, in the wood, of a wondrous dwelling,
Within a moat, on a mound, bright amid boughs          765
Of many a tree great of girth that grew by the water—
A castle as comely as a knight could own,
On grounds fair and green, in a goodly park
With a palisade of palings planted about
For two miles and more, round many a fair tree.          770
The stout knight stared at that stronghold great
As it shimmered and shone amid shining leaves,
Then with helmet in hand he offers his thanks
To Jesus and Saint Julian, that are gentle both,
That in courteous accord had inclined to his prayer;          775
"Now fair harbor," said he, "I humbly beseech!"
Then he pricks his proud steed with the plated spurs,
And by chance he has chosen the chief path
That brought the bold knight to the bridge's end
                                    in haste.          780
                    The bridge hung high in air;
                    The gates were bolted fast;
                    The walls well-framed to bear
                    The fury of the blast.

The man on his mount remained on the bank          785
Of the deep double moat that defended the place.
The wall went in the water wondrous deep,
And a long way aloft it loomed overhead.
It was built of stone blocks to the battlements' height,
With corbels under cornices in comeliest style;          790
Watch-towers trusty protected the gate,
With many a lean loophole, to look from within:
A better-made barbican the knight beheld never.

---

757. *pater and ave:* Two prayers, the
Pater Noster ("Our Father," the Lord's
Prayer) and Ave Maria ("Hail, Mary").
763. *signed himself:* Made the sign of
the cross over his own chest.

774. *Saint Julian:* Patron saint of hospitality.
790. *corbels under cornices:* Ornamental projections supporting the top
courses of stone.

And behind it there hoved a great hall and fair:
Turrets rising in tiers, with tines at their tops,                      795
Spires set beside them, splendidly long,
With finials well-fashioned, as filigree fine.
Chalk-white chimneys over chambers high
Gleamed in gay array upon gables and roofs;
The pinnacles in panoply, pointing in air,                             800
So vied there for his view that verily it seemed
A castle cut of paper for a king's feast.
The good knight on Gringolet thought it great luck
If he could but contrive to come there within
To keep the Christmas feast in that castle fair                        805
             and bright.
        There answered to his call
        A porter most polite;
        From his station on the wall
        He greets the errant knight.                         810

"Good sir," said Gawain, "Wouldst go to inquire
If your lord would allow me to lodge here a space?"
"Peter!" said the porter, "For my part, I think
So noble a knight will not want for a welcome!"
Then he bustles off briskly, and comes back straight,                  815
And many servants beside, to receive him the better.
They let down the drawbridge and duly went forth
And kneeled down on their knees on the naked earth
To welcome this warrior as best they were able.
They proffered him passage—the portals stood wide—                     820
And he beckoned them to rise, and rode over the bridge.
Men steadied his saddle as he stepped to the ground,
And there stabled his steed many stalwart folk.
Now come the knights and the noble squires
To bring him with bliss into the bright hall.                          825
When his high helm was off, there hied forth a throng
Of attendants to take it, and see to its care;
They bore away his brand and his blazoned shield;
Then graciously he greeted those gallants each one,
And many a noble drew near, to do the knight honor.                    830
All in his armor into hall he was led,
Where fire on a fair hearth fiercely blazed.
And soon the lord himself descends from his chamber
To meet with good manners the man on his floor.
He said, "To this house you are heartily welcome:                      835
What is here is wholly yours, to have in your power
            and sway."
        "Many thanks," said Sir Gawain;
        "May Christ your pains repay!"
        The two embrace amain                                840
        As men well met that day.

---

794. *hoved:* Arose.         813. *"Peter!":* I.e., "By Saint Peter!"
795. *tines:* Spikes.       828. *brand:* Sword.

Gawain gazed on the host that greeted him there,
And a lusty fellow he looked, the lord of that place:
A man of massive mold, and of middle age;
Broad, bright was his beard, of a beaver's hue,     845
Strong, steady his stance, upon stalwart shanks,
His face fierce as fire, fair-spoken withal,
And well-suited he seemed in Sir Gawain's sight
To be a master of men in a mighty keep.
They pass into a parlor, where promptly the host     850
Has a servant assigned him to see to his needs,
And there came upon his call many courteous folk
That brought him to a bower where bedding was noble,
With heavy silk hangings hemmed all in gold,
Coverlets and counterpanes curiously wrought,     855
A canopy over the couch, clad all with fur,
Curtains running on cords, caught to gold rings,
Woven rugs on the walls of eastern work,
And the floor, under foot, well-furnished with the same.
With light talk and laughter they loosed from him then     860
His war-dress of weight and his worthy clothes.
Robes richly wrought they brought him right soon,
To change there in chamber and choose what he would.
When he had found one he fancied, and flung it about,
Well-fashioned for his frame, with flowing skirts,     865
His face fair and fresh as the flowers of spring,
All the good folk agreed, that gazed on him then,
His limbs arrayed royally in radiant hues,
That so comely a mortal never Christ made
                as he.     870
        Whatever his place of birth,
        It seemed he well might be
        Without a peer on earth
        In martial rivalry.

A couch before the fire, where fresh coals burned,     875
They spread for Sir Gawain splendidly now
With quilts quaintly stitched, and cushions beside,
And then a costly cloak they cast on his shoulders
Of bright silk, embroidered on borders and hems,
With furs of the finest well-furnished within,     880
And bound about with ermine, both mantle and hood;
And he sat at that fireside in sumptuous estate
And warmed himself well, and soon he waxed merry.
Then attendants set a table upon trestles broad,
And lustrous white linen they laid thereupon,     885
A saltcellar of silver, spoons of the same.
He washed himself well and went to his place,
Men set his fare before him in fashion most fit.
There were soups of all sorts, seasoned with skill,
Double-sized servings, and sundry fish,     890

Some baked, some breaded, some broiled on the coals,
Some simmered, some in stews, steaming with spice,
And with sauces to sup that suited his taste.
He confesses it a feast with free words and fair;
They requite him as kindly with courteous jests,                    895
                    well-sped.
          "Tonight you fast and pray;
          Tomorrow we'll see you fed."
          The knight grows wondrous gay
          As the wine goes to his head.                              900

Then at times and by turns, as at table he sat,
They questioned him quietly, with queries discreet,
And he courteously confessed that he comes from the court,
And owns him of the brotherhood of high-famed Arthur,
The right royal ruler of the Round Table,                           905
And the guest by their fireside is Gawain himself,
Who has happened on their house at that holy feast.
When the name of the knight was made known to the lord,
Then loudly he laughed, so elated he was,
And the men in that household made haste with joy                   910
To appear in his presence promptly that day,
That of courage ever-constant, and customs pure,
Is pattern and paragon, and praised without end:
Of all knights on earth most honored is he.
Each said solemnly aside to his brother,                            915
"Now displays of deportment shall dazzle our eyes
And the polished pearls of impeccable speech;
The high art of eloquence is ours to pursue
Since the father of fine manners is found in our midst.
Great is God's grace, and goodly indeed,                            920
That a guest such as Gawain he guides to us here
When men sit and sing of their Savior's birth
                    in view.
          With command of manners pure
          He shall each heart imbue;                                 925
          Who shares his converse, sure,
          Shall learn love's language true."

When the knight had done dining and duly arose,
The dark was drawing on; the day nigh ended.
Chaplains in chapels and churches about                             930
Rang the bells aright, reminding all men
Of the holy evensong of the high feast.
The lord attends alone; his fair lady sits
In a comely closet, secluded from sight.
Gawain in gay attire goes thither soon;                             935
The lord catches his coat, and calls him by name,
And has him sit beside him, and says in good faith
No guest on God's earth would he gladlier greet.
For that Gawain thanked him; the two then embraced

And sat together soberly the service through.                          940
Then the lady, that longed to look on the knight,
Came forth from her closet with her comely maids.
The fair hues of her flesh, her face and her hair
And her body and her bearing were beyond praise,
And excelled the queen herself, as Sir Gawain thought.                 945
He goes forth to greet her with gracious intent;
Another lady led her by the left hand
That was older than she—an ancient, it seemed,
And held in high honor by all men about.
But unlike to look upon, those ladies were,                            950
For if the one was fresh, the other was faded:
Bedecked in bright red was the body of one;
Flesh hung in folds on the face of the other;
On one a high headdress, hung all with pearls;
Her bright throat and bosom fair to behold,                            955
Fresh as the first snow fallen upon hills;
A wimple the other one wore round her throat;
Her swart chin well swaddled, swathed all in white;
Her forehead enfolded in flounces of silk
That framed a fair fillet, of fashion ornate,                          960
And nothing bare beneath save the black brows,
The two eyes and the nose, the naked lips,
And they unsightly to see, and sorrily bleared.
A beldame, by God, she may well be deemed,
               of pride!                                 965
      She was short and thick of waist,
      Her buttocks round and wide;
      More toothsome, to his taste,
      Was the beauty by her side.

When Gawain had gazed on that gay lady,                                970
With leave of her lord, he politely approached;
To the elder in homage he humbly bows;
The lovelier he salutes with a light embrace.
He claims a comely kiss, and courteously he speaks;
They welcome him warmly, and straightway he asks                       975
To be received as their servant, if they so desire.
They take him between them; with talking they bring him
Beside a bright fire; bade then that spices
Be freely fetched forth, to refresh them the better,
And the good wine therewith, to warm their hearts.                     980
The lord leaps about in light-hearted mood;
Contrives entertainments and timely sports;
Takes his hood from his head and hangs it on a spear,
And offers him openly the honor thereof
Who should promote the most mirth at that Christmas feast;             985

---

957. *wimple:* A garment covering the       960. *fillet:* An ornamental ribbon or
neck and the sides of the head.             headband.

"And I shall try for it, trust me—contend with the best,
Ere I go without my headgear by grace of my friends!"
Thus with light talk and laughter the lord makes merry
To gladden the guest he had greeted in hall
                that day.          990
        At the last he called for light
        The company to convey;
        Gawain says goodnight
        And retires to bed straightway.

On the morn when each man is mindful in heart     995
That God's son was sent down to suffer our death,
No household but is blithe for His blessed sake;
So was it there on that day, with many delights.
Both at larger meals and less they were lavishly served
By doughty lads on dais, with delicate fare;     1000
The old ancient lady, highest she sits;
The lord at her left hand leaned, as I hear;
Sir Gawain in the center, beside the gay lady,
Where the food was brought first to that festive board,
And thence throughout the hall, as they held most fit,     1005
To each man was offered in order of rank.
There was meat, there was mirth, there was much joy,
That to tell all the tale would tax my wits,
Though I pained me, perchance, to paint it with care;
But yet I know that our knight and the noble lady     1010
Were accorded so closely in company there,
With the seemly solace of their secret words,
With speeches well-sped, spotless and pure,
That each prince's pastime their pleasures far
                outshone.          1015
        Sweet pipes beguile their cares,
        And the trumpet of martial tone;
        Each tends his affairs
        And those two tend their own.

That day and all the next, their disport was noble,     1020
And the third day, I think, pleased them no less;
The joys of St. John's Day were justly praised,
And were the last of their like for those lords and ladies;
Then guests were to go in the gray morning,
Wherefore they whiled the night away with wine and
    with mirth,     1025
Moved to the measures of many a blithe carol;
At last, when it was late, took leave of each other,
Each one of those worthies, to wend his way.
Gawain bids goodbye to his goodly host
Who brings him to his chamber, the chimney beside,     1030
And detains him in talk, and tenders his thanks

1022. *St. John's Day*: December 27.

And holds it an honor to him and his people
That he has harbored in his house at that holy time
And embellished his abode with his inborn grace.
"As long as I may live, my luck is the better          1035
That Gawain was my guest at God's own feast!"
"Noble sir," said the knight, "I cannot but think
All the honor is your own—may heaven requite it!
And your man to command I account myself here
As I am bound and beholden, and shall be, come          1040
                    what may."
          The lord with all his might
          Entreats his guest to stay;
          Brief answer makes the knight:
          Next morning he must away.          1045


Then the lord of that land politely inquired
What dire affair had forced him, at that festive time,
So far from the king's court to fare forth alone
Ere the holidays wholly had ended in hall.
"In good faith," said Gawain, "you have guessed the truth:          1050
On a high errand and urgent I hastened away,
For I am summoned by myself to seek for a place—
I would I knew whither, or where it might be!
Far rather would I find it before the New Year
Than own the land of Logres, so help me our Lord!          1055
Wherefore, sir, in friendship this favor I ask,
That you say in sober earnest, if something you know
Of the Green Chapel, on ground far or near,
Or the lone knight that lives there, of like hue of green.
A certain day was set by assent of us both          1060
To meet at that landmark, if I might last,
And from now to the New Year is nothing too long,
And I would greet the Green Knight there, would God but allow,
More gladly, by God's Son, than gain the world's wealth!
And I must set forth to search, as soon as I may;          1065
To be about the business I have but three days
And would as soon sink down dead as desist from my errand."
Then smiling said the lord, "Your search, sir, is done,
For we shall see you to that site by the set time.
Let Gawain grieve no more over the Green Chapel;          1070
You shall be in your own bed, in blissful ease,
All the forenoon, and fare forth the first of the year,
And make the goal by midmorn, to mind your affairs,
                    no fear!
          Tarry till the fourth day          1075
          And ride on the first of the year.
          We shall set you on your way;
          It is not two miles from here."

Then Gawain was glad, and gleefully he laughed:
"Now I thank you for this, past all things else!                    1080
Now my goal is here at hand! With a glad heart I shall
Both tarry, and undertake any task you devise."
Then the host seized his arm and seated him there;
Let the ladies be brought, to delight them the better,
And in fellowship fair by the fireside they sit;                    1085
So gay waxed the good host, so giddy his words,
All waited in wonder what next he would say.
Then he stares on the stout knight, and sternly he speaks:
"You have bound yourself boldly my bidding to do—
Will you stand by that boast, and obey me this once?"               1090
"I shall do so indeed," said the doughty knight;
"While I lie in your lodging, your laws will I follow."
"As you have had," said the host, "many hardships abroad
And little sleep of late, you are lacking, I judge,
Both in nourishment needful and nightly rest;                      1095
You shall lie abed late in your lofty chamber
Tomorrow until mass, and meet then to dine
When you will, with my wife, who will sit by your side
And talk with you at table, the better to cheer
     our guest.                          1100
    A-hunting I will go
    While you lie late and rest."
    The knight, inclining low,
    Assents to each behest.

"And Gawain," said the good host, "agree now to this:               1105
Whatever I win in the woods I will give you at eve,
And all you have earned you must offer to me;
Swear now, sweet friend, to swap as I say,
Whether hands, in the end, be empty or better."
"By God," said Sir Gawain, "I grant it forthwith!                   1110
If you find the game good, I shall gladly take part."
"Let the bright wine be brought, and our bargain is done,'
Said the lord of that land—the two laughed together.
Then they drank and they dallied and doffed all constraint,
These lords and these ladies, as late as they chose,               1115
And then with gaiety and gallantries and graceful adieux
They talked in low tones, and tarried at parting.
With compliments comely they kiss at the last;
There were brisk lads about with blazing torches
To see them safe to bed, for soft repose                           1120
    long due.
    Their covenants, yet awhile,
    They repeat, and pledge anew;
    That lord could well beguile
    Men's hearts, with mirth in view.                1125

## Part III

Long before daylight they left their beds;
Guests that wished to go gave word to their grooms,
And they set about briskly to bind on saddles,
Tend to their tackle, tie up trunks.
The proud lords appear, appareled to ride,        1130
Leap lightly astride, lay hold of their bridles,
Each one on his way to his worthy house.
The liege lord of the land was not the last
Arrayed there to ride, with retainers many;
He had a bite to eat when he had heard mass;        1135
With horn to the hills he hastens amain.
By the dawn of that day over the dim earth,
Master and men were mounted and ready.
Then they harnessed in couples the keen-scented hounds,
Cast wide the kennel-door and called them forth,        1140
Blew upon their bugles bold blasts three;
The dogs began to bay with a deafening din,
And they quieted them quickly and called them to heel,
A hundred brave huntsmen, as I have heard tell,
            together.        1145
      Men at stations meet;
      From the hounds they slip the tether;
      The echoing horns repeat,
      Clear in the merry weather.

At the clamor of the quest, the quarry trembled;        1150
Deer dashed through the dale, dazed with dread;
Hastened to the high ground, only to be
Turned back by the beaters, who boldly shouted.
They harmed not the harts, with their high heads,
Let the bucks go by, with their broad antlers,        1155
For it was counted a crime, in the close season,
If a man of that demesne should molest the male deer.
The hinds were headed up, with "Hey!" and "Ware!"
The does with great din were driven to the valleys.
Then you were ware, as they went, of the whistling of arrows;        1160
At each bend under boughs the bright shafts flew
That tore the tawny hide with their tapered heads.
Ah! they bray and they bleed, on banks they die,
And ever the pack pell-mell comes panting behind;
Hunters with shrill horns hot on their heels—        1165
Like the cracking of cliffs their cries resounded.
What game got away from the gallant archers
Was promptly picked off at the posts below
When they were harried on the heights and herded to the streams:
The watchers were so wary at the waiting-stations,        1170

1156. *close:* Or closed.

And the greyhounds so huge, that eagerly snatched,
And finished them off as fast as folk could see
>> with sight.
>> The lord, now here, now there,
>> Spurs forth in sheer delight.    1175
>> And drives, with pleasures rare,
>> The day to the dark night.

So the lord in the linden-wood leads the hunt
And Gawain the good knight in gay bed lies,
Lingered late alone, till daylight gleamed,    1180
Under coverlet costly, curtained about.
And as he slips into slumber, slyly there comes
A little din at his door, and the latch lifted,
And he holds up his heavy head out of the clothes;
A corner of the curtain he caught back a little    1185
And waited there warily, to see what befell.
Lo! it was the lady, loveliest to behold,
That drew the door behind her deftly and still
And was bound for his bed—abashed was the knight,
And laid his head low again in likeness of sleep;    1190
And she stepped stealthily, and stole to his bed,
Cast aside the curtain and came within,
And set herself softly on the bedside there,
And lingered at her leisure, to look on his waking.
The fair knight lay feigning for a long while,    1195
Conning in his conscience what his case might
Mean or amount to—a marvel he thought it.
But yet he said within himself, "More seemly it were
To try her intent by talking a little."
So he started and stretched, as startled from sleep,    1200
Lifts wide his lids in likeness of wonder,
And signs himself swiftly, as safer to be,
>> with art.
>> Sweetly does she speak
>> And kindling glances dart,    1205
>> Blent white and red on cheek
>> And laughing lips apart.

"Good morning, Sir Gawain," said that gay lady,
"A slack sleeper you are, to let one slip in!
Now you are taken in a trice—a truce we must make,    1210
Or I shall bind you in your bed, of that be assured."
Thus laughing lightly that lady jested.
"Good morning, good lady," said Gawain the blithe,
"Be it with me as you will; I am well content!
For I surrender myself, and sue for your grace,    1215
And that is best, I believe, and behooves me now."
Thus jested in answer that gentle knight.
"But if, lovely lady, you misliked it not,
And were pleased to permit your prisoner to rise,

I should quit this couch and accoutre me better,     1220
And be clad in more comfort for converse here."
"Nay, not so, sweet sir," said the smiling lady;
"You shall not rise from your bed; I direct you better:
I shall hem and hold you on either hand,
And keep company awhile with my captive knight.     1225
For as certain as I sit here, Sir Gawain you are,
Whom all the world worships, whereso you ride;
Your honor, your courtesy are highest acclaimed
By lords and by ladies, by all living men;
And lo! we are alone here, and left to ourselves:     1230
My lord and his liegemen are long departed,
The household asleep, my handmaids too,
The door drawn, and held by a well-driven bolt,
And since I have in this house him whom all love,
I shall while the time away with mirthful speech     1235
> at will.
>> My body is here at hand,
>> Your each wish to fulfill;
>> Your servant to command
>> I am, and shall be still."     1240

"In good faith," said Gawain, "my gain is the greater,
Though I am not he of whom you have heard;
To arrive at such reverence as you recount here
I am one all unworthy, and well do I know it.
By heaven, I would hold me the happiest of men     1245
If by word or by work I once might aspire
To the prize of your praise—'twere a pure joy!"
"In good faith, Sir Gawain," said that gay lady,
"The well-proven prowess that pleases all others,
Did I scant or scout it, 'twere scarce becoming.     1250
But there are ladies, believe me, that had liefer far
Have thee here in their hold, as I have today,
To pass an hour in pastime with pleasant words,
Assuage all their sorrows and solace their hearts,
Than much of the goodly gems and gold they possess.     1255
But laud be to the Lord of the lofty skies,
For here in my hands all hearts' desire
> doth lie."
>> Great welcome got he there
>> From the lady who sat him by;     1260
>> With fitting speech and fair
>> The good knight makes reply.

"Madame," said the merry man, "Mary reward you!
For in good faith, I find your beneficence noble.
And the fame of fair deeds runs far and wide,     1265

---

1250. *scout:* Mock.          rather.
1251. *had liefer far:* Would much

But the praise you report pertains not to me,
But comes of your courtesy and kindness of heart."
"By the high Queen of heaven" (said she) "I count it not so,
For were I worth all the women in this world alive,
And all wealth and all worship were in my hands,       1270
And I should hunt high and low, a husband to take,
For the nurture I have noted in thee, knight, here,
The comeliness and courtesies and courtly mirth—
And so I had ever heard, and now hold it true—
No other on this earth should have me for wife."       1275
"You are bound to a better man," the bold knight said,
"Yet I prize the praise you have proffered me here,
And soberly your servant, my sovereign I hold you,
And acknowledge me your knight, in the name of Christ."
So they talked of this and that until 'twas nigh noon,       1280
And ever the lady languishing in likeness of love.
With feat words and fair he framed his defence,
For were she never so winsome, the warrior had
The less will to woo, for the wound that his bane
                    must be.       1285
        He must bear the blinding blow,
        For such is fate's decree;
        The lady asks leave to go;
        He grants it full and free.

Then she gaily said goodbye, and glanced at him, laughing,       1290
And as she stood, she astonished him with a stern speech:
"Now may the Giver of all good words these glad hours repay!
But our guest is not Gawain—forgot is that thought."
"How so?" said the other, and asks in some haste,
For he feared he had been at fault in the forms of his speech.       1295
But she held up her hand, and made answer thus:
"So good a knight as Gawain is given out to be,
And the model of fair demeanor and manners pure,
Had he lain so long at a lady's side,
Would have claimed a kiss, by his courtesy,       1300
Through some touch or trick of phrase at some tale's end."
Said Gawain, "Good lady, I grant it at once!
I shall kiss at your command, as becomes a knight,
And more, lest you mislike, so let be, I pray."
With that she turns toward him, takes him in her arms,       1305
Leans down her lovely head, and lo! he is kissed.
They commend each other to Christ with comely words,
He sees her forth safely, in silence they part,
And then he lies no later in his lofty bed,
But calls to his chamberlain, chooses his clothes,       1310
Goes in those garments gladly to mass,
Then takes his way to table, where attendants wait,

1282. *feat:* Fitting.

And made merry all day, till the moon rose
in view

Was never knight beset

'Twixt worthier ladies two:

The crone and the coquette;

Fair pastimes they pursue.

And the lord of the land rides late and long,
Hunting the barren hind over the broad heath.
He had slain such a sum, when the sun sank low,
Of does and other deer, as would dizzy one's wits.
Then they trooped in together in triumph at last,
And the count of the quarry quickly they take.
The lords lent a hand with their liegemen many,
Picked out the plumpest and put them together
And duly dressed the deer, as the deed requires.
Some were assigned the assay of the fat:
Two fingers'-width fully they found on the leanest.
Then they slit the slot open and searched out the paunch,
Trimmed it with trencher-knives and tied it up tight.
They flayed the fair hide from the legs and trunk,
Then broke open the belly and laid bare the bowels,
Deftly detaching and drawing them forth.
And next at the neck they neatly parted
The weasand from the windpipe, and cast away the guts.
At the shoulders with sharp blades they showed their skill,
Boning them from beneath, lest the sides be marred;
They breached the broad breast and broke it in twain,
And again at the gullet they begin with their knives,
Cleave down the carcass clear to the breach;
Two tender morsels they take from the throat,
Then round the inner ribs they rid off a layer
And carve out the kidney-fat, close to the spine,
Hewing down to the haunch, that all hung together,
And held it up whole, and hacked it free,
And this they named the numbles, that knew such terms
of art.

They divide the crotch in two,

And straightway then they start

To cut the backbone through

And cleave the trunk apart.

With hard strokes they hewed off the head and the neck,
Then swiftly from the sides they severed the chine,
And the corbie's bone they cast on a branch.
Then they pierced the plump sides, impaled either one
With the hock of the hind foot, and hung it aloft,

---

1320. *barren hind:* Female deer that are not pregnant.
1330. *slot:* The hollow above the breast-bone.

1336. *weasand:* Esophagus.
1347. *numbles:* Other internal organs.
1355. *corbie's bone:* A bit of gristle for the ravens ("corbies").

To each person his portion most proper and fit.
On a hide of a hind the hounds they fed
With the liver and the lights, the leathery paunches,    1360
And bread soaked in blood well blended therewith.
High horns and shrill set hounds a-baying,
Then merrily with their meat they make their way home,
Blowing on their bugles many a brave blast.
Ere dark had descended, that doughty band              1365
Was come within the walls where Gawain waits
                    at leisure.
            Bliss and hearth-fire bright
            Await the master's pleasure;
            When the two men met that night,            1370
            Joy surpassed all measure.

Then the host in the hall his household assembles,
With the dames of high degree and their damsels fair.
In the presence of the people, a party he sends
To convey him his venison in view of the knight.        1375
And in high good-humor he hails him then,
Counts over the kill, the cuts on the tallies,
Holds high the hewn ribs, heavy with fat.
"What think you, sir, of this? Have I thriven well?
Have I won with my woodcraft a worthy prize?"           1380
"In good earnest," said Gawain, "this game is the finest
I have seen in seven years in the season of winter."
"And I give it to you, Gawain," said the goodly host,
"For according to our covenant, you claim it as your own."
"That is so," said Sir Gawain, "the same say I:          1385
What I worthily have won within these fair walls,
Herewith I as willingly award it to you."
He embraces his broad neck with both his arms,
And confers on him a kiss in the comeliest style.
"Have here my profit, it proved no better;               1390
Ungrudging do I grant it, were it greater far."
"Such a gift," said the good host, "I gladly accept—
Yet it might be all the better, would you but say
Where you won this same award, by your wits alone."
"That was no part of the pact; press me no further,      1395
For you have had what behooves; all other claims
                    forbear."
            With jest and compliment
            They conversed, and cast off care;
            To the table soon they went;                1400
            Fresh dainties wait them there.

And then by the chimney-side they chat at their ease;
The best wine was brought them, and bounteously served;
And after in their jesting they jointly accord

---

1360. *lights:* Lungs.
1377. *cuts on the tallies:* Notched sticks were used to count the animals taken in the hunt.

To do on the second day the deeds of the first: 1405
That the two men should trade, betide as it may,
What each had taken in, at eve when they met.
They seal the pact solemnly in sight of the court;
Their cups were filled afresh to confirm the jest;
Then at last they took their leave, for late was the hour, 1410
Each to his own bed hastening away.
Before the barnyard cock had crowed but thrice
The lord had leapt from his rest, his liegemen as well.
Both of mass and their meal they made short work:
By the dim light of dawn they were deep in the woods 1415
           away.
        With huntsmen and with horns
        Over plains they pass that day;
        They release, amid the thorns,
        Swift hounds that run and bay. 1420

Soon some were on a scent by the side of a marsh;
When the hounds opened cry, the head of the hunt
Rallied them with rough words, raised a great noise.
The hounds that had heard it came hurrying straight
And followed along with their fellows, forty together. 1425
Then such a clamor and cry of coursing hounds
Arose, that the rocks resounded again.
Hunters exhorted them with horn and with voice;
Then all in a body bore off together
Between a mere in the marsh and a menacing crag, 1430
To a rise where the rock stood rugged and steep,
And boulders lay about, that blocked their approach.
Then the company in consort closed on their prey:
They surrounded the rise and the rocks both,
For well they were aware that it waited within, 1435
The beast that the bloodhounds boldly proclaimed.
Then they beat on the bushes and bade him appear,
And he made a murderous rush in the midst of them all;
The best of all boars broke from his cover,
That had ranged long unrivaled, a renegade old, 1440
For of tough-brawned boars he was biggest far,
Most grim when he grunted—then grieved were many,
For three at the first thrust he threw to the earth,
And dashed away at once without more damage.
With "Hi!" "Hi!" and "Hey!" "Hey!" the others followed, 1445
Had horns at their lips, blew high and clear.
Merry was the music of men and of hounds
That were bound after this boar, his bloodthirsty heart
           to quell.
        Often he stands at bay, 1450
        Then scatters the pack pell-mell;

1430. *mere:* Pool.

> He hurts the hounds, and they
> Most dolefully yowl and yell.

Men then with mighty bows moved in to shoot,
Aimed at him with their arrows and often hit,                    1455
But the points had no power to pierce through his hide,
And the barbs were brushed aside by his bristly brow;
Though the shank of the shaft shivered in pieces,
The head hopped away, wheresoever it struck.
But when their stubborn strokes had stung him at last,           1460
Then, foaming in his frenzy, fiercely he charges,
Hies at them headlong that hindered his flight,
And many feared for their lives, and fell back a little.
But the lord on a lively horse leads the chase;
As a high-mettled huntsman his horn he blows;                    1465
He sounds the assembly and sweeps through the brush,
Pursuing this wild swine till the sunlight slanted.
All day with this deed they drive forth the time
While our lone knight so lovesome lies in his bed,
Sir Gawain safe at home, in silken bower                         1470
> so gay.
>> The lady, with guile in heart,
>> Came early where he lay;
>> She was at him with all her art
>> To turn his mind her way.                                     1475

She comes to the curtain and coyly peeps in;
Gawain thought it good to greet her at once,
And she richly repays him with her ready words,
Settles softly at his side, and suddenly she laughs,
And with a gracious glance, she begins on him thus:              1480
"Sir, if you be Gawain, it seems a great wonder—
A man so well-meaning, and mannerly disposed,
And cannot act in company as courtesy bids,
And if one takes the trouble to teach him, 'tis all in vain.
That lesson learned lately is lightly forgot,                    1485
Though I painted it as plain as my poor wit allowed."
"What lesson, dear lady?" he asked all alarmed;
"I have been much to blame, if your story be true."
"Yet my counsel was of kissing," came her answer then,
"Where favor has been found, freely to claim                     1490
As accords with the conduct of courteous knights."
"My dear," said the doughty man, "dismiss that thought;
Such freedom, I fear, might offend you much;
It were rude to request if the right were denied."
"But none can deny you," said the noble dame,                    1495
"You are stout enough to constrain with strength, if you choose,
Were any so ungracious as to grudge you aught."
"By heaven," said he, "you have answered well,

1466. *sounds the assembly:* Blows a signal summoning all the hunters.

But threats never throve among those of my land,
Nor any gift not freely given, good though it be.                         1500
I am yours to command, to kiss when you please;
You may lay on as you like, and leave off at will."
                    With this,
                The lady lightly bends
                And graciously gives him a kiss;                          1505
                The two converse as friends
                Of true love's trials and bliss.

"I should like, by your leave," said the lovely lady,
"If it did not annoy you, to know for what cause
So brisk and so bold a young blood as you,                                1510
And acclaimed for all courtesies becoming a knight—
And name what knight you will, they are noblest esteemed
For loyal faith in love, in life as in story;
For to tell the tribulations of these true hearts,
Why, 'tis the very title and text of their deeds,                        1515
How bold knights for beauty have braved many a foe,
Suffered heavy sorrows out of secret love,
And then valorously avenged them on villainous churls
And made happy ever after the hearts of their ladies.
And you are the noblest knight known in your time;                       1520
No household under heaven but has heard of your fame,
And here by your side I have sat for two days
Yet never has a fair phrase fallen from your lips
Of the language of love, not one little word!
And you, that with sweet vows sway women's hearts,                       1525
Should show your winsome ways, and woo a young thing,
And teach by some tokens the craft of true love.
How! are you artless, whom all men praise?
Or do you deem me so dull, or deaf to such words?
                    Fie! Fie!                                             1530
                In hope of pastimes new
                I have come where none can spy;
                Instruct me a little, do,
                While my husband is not nearby."

"God love you, gracious lady!" said Gawain then;                         1535
"It is a pleasure surpassing, and a peerless joy,
That one so worthy as you would willingly come
And take the time and trouble to talk with your knight
And content you with his company—it comforts my heart.
But to take to myself the task of telling of love,                       1540
And touch upon its texts, and treat of its themes
To one that, I know well, wields more power
In that art, by a half, than a hundred such
As I am where I live, or am like to become,
It were folly, fair dame, in the first degree!                          1545
In all that I am able, my aim is to please,

As in honor behooves me, and am evermore
Your servant heart and soul, so save me our Lord!"
Thus she tested his temper and tried many a time,
Whatever her true intent, to entice him to sin,                1550
But so fair was his defense that no fault appeared,
Nor evil on either hand, but only bliss
                they knew.
        They linger and laugh awhile;
        She kisses the knight so true,                1555
        Takes leave in comeliest style
        And departs without more ado.

Then he rose from his rest and made ready for mass,
And then a meal was set and served, in sumptuous style;
He dallied at home all day with the dear ladies,              1560
But the lord lingered late at his lusty sport;
Pursued his sorry swine, that swerved as he fled,
And bit asunder the backs of the best of his hounds
When they brought him to bay, till the bowmen appeared
And soon forced him forth, though he fought for dear life,    1565
So sharp were the shafts they shot at him there.
But yet the boldest drew back from his battering head,
Till at last he was so tired he could travel no more,
But in as much haste as he might, he makes his retreat
To a rise on rocky ground, by a rushing stream.              1570
With the bank at his back he scrapes the bare earth,
The froth foams at his jaws, frightful to see.
He whets his white tusks—then weary were all
Those hunters so hardy that hoved round about
Of aiming from afar, but ever they mistrust                  1575
                his mood.
        He had hurt so many by then
        That none had hardihood
        To be torn by his tusks again,
        That was brainsick, and out for blood.      1580

Till the lord came at last on his lofty steed,
Beheld him there at bay before all his folk;
Lightly he leaps down, leaves his courser,
Bares his bright sword, and boldly advances;
Straight into the stream he strides towards his foe.          1585
The wild thing was wary of weapon and man;
His hackles rose high; so hotly he snorts
That many watched with alarm, lest the worst befall.
The boar makes for the man with a mighty bound
So that he and his hunter came headlong together              1590
Where the water ran wildest—the worse for the beast,
For the man, when they first met, marked him with care,
Sights well the slot, slips in the blade,

1574. *hoved:* Hovered.

Shoves it home to the hilt, and the heart shattered,
And he falls in his fury and floats down the water, 1595
        ill-sped.
        Hounds hasten by the score
        To maul him, hide and head;
        Men drag him in to shore
        And dogs pronounce him dead. 1600

With many a brave blast they boast of their prize,
All hallooed in high glee, that had their wind;
The hounds bayed their best, as the bold men bade
That were charged with chief rank in that chase of renown.
Then one wise in woodcraft, and worthily skilled, 1605
Began to dress the boar in becoming style:
He severs the savage head and sets it aloft,
Then rends the body roughly right down the spine;
Takes the bowels from the belly, broils them on coals,
Blends them well with bread to bestow on the hounds. 1610
Then he breaks out the brawn in fair broad flitches,
And the innards to be eaten in order he takes.
The two sides, attached to each other all whole,
He suspended from a spar that was springy and tough;
And so with this swine they set out for home; 1615
The boar's head was borne before the same man
That had stabbed him in the stream with his strong arm,
        right through.
        He thought it long indeed
        Till he had the knight in view; 1620
        At his call, he comes with speed
        To claim his payment due.

The lord laughed aloud, with many a light word,
When he greeted Sir Gawain—with good cheer he speaks.
They fetch the fair dames and the folk of the house; 1625
He brings forth the brawn, and begins the tale
Of the great length and girth, the grim rage as well,
Of the battle of the boar they beset in the wood.
The other man meetly commended his deeds
And praised well the prize of his princely sport, 1630
For the brawn of that boar, the bold knight said,
And the sides of that swine surpassed all others.
Then they handled the huge head; he owns it a wonder,
And eyes it with abhorrence, to heighten his praise.
"Now, Gawain," said the good man, "this game becomes yours 1635
By those fair terms we fixed, as you know full well."
"That is true," returned the knight, "and trust me, fair friend,
All my gains, as agreed, I shall give you forthwith."
He clasps him and kisses him in courteous style,
Then serves him with the same fare a second time. 1640
"Now we are even," said he, "at this evening feast,
And clear is every claim incurred here to date,
        and debt."

"By Saint Giles!" the host replies,
"You're the best I ever met!"                                          1645
If your profits are all this size,
We'll see you wealthy yet!"

Then attendants set tables on trestles about,
And laid them with linen; light shone forth,
Wakened along the walls in waxen torches.                              1650
The service was set and the supper brought;
Royal were the revels that rose then in hall
At that feast by the fire, with many fair sports:
Amid the meal and after, melody sweet,
Carol-dances comely and Christmas songs,                               1655
With all the mannerly mirth my tongue may describe.
And ever our gallant knight beside the gay lady;
So uncommonly kind and complaisant was she,
With sweet stolen glances, that stirred his stout heart,
That he was at his wits' end, and wondrous vexed;                      1660
But he could not in conscience her courtship repay,
Yet took pains to please her, though the plan might
                              go wrong.
           When they to heart's delight
           Had reveled there in throng,                                1665
           To his chamber he calls the knight,
           And thither they go along.

And there they dallied and drank, and deemed it good sport
To enact their play anew on New Year's Eve,
But Gawain asked again to go on the morrow,                            1670
For the time until his tryst was not two days.
The host hindered that, and urged him to stay,
And said, "On my honor, my oath here I take
That you shall get to the Green Chapel to begin your chores
By dawn on New Year's Day, if you so desire.                           1675
Wherefore lie at your leisure in your lofty bed,
And I shall hunt hereabouts, and hold to our terms,
And we shall trade winnings when once more we meet,
For I have tested you twice, and true have I found you;
Now think this tomorrow: the third pays for all;                      1680
Be we merry while we may, and mindful of joy,
For heaviness of heart can be had for the asking."
This is gravely agreed on and Gawain will stay.
They drink a last draught and with torches depart
                              to rest.                                 1685
           To bed Sir Gawain went;
           His sleep was of the best;
           The lord, on his craft intent,
           Was early up and dressed.

After mass, with his men, a morsel he takes;                          1690
Clear and crisp the morning; he calls for his mount;
The folk that were to follow him afield that day

Were high astride their horses before the hall gates.
Wondrous fair were the fields, for the frost was light;
The sun rises red amid radiant clouds,                                    1695
Sails into the sky, and sends forth his beams.
They let loose the hounds by a leafy wood;
The rocks all around re-echo to their horns;
Soon some have set off in pursuit of the fox,
Cast about with craft for a clearer scent;                                1700
A young dog yaps, and is yelled at in turn;
His fellows fall to sniffing, and follow his lead,
Running in a rabble on the right track,
And he scampers all before; they discover him soon,
And when they see him with sight they pursue him the faster,    1705
Railing at him rudely with a wrathful din.
Often he reverses over rough terrain,
Or loops back to listen in the lee of a hedge;
At last, by a little ditch, he leaps over the brush,
Comes into a clearing at a cautious pace,                                 1710
Then he thought through his wiles to have thrown off the hounds
Till he was ware, as he went, of a waiting-station
Where three athwart his path threatened him at once,
                    all gray.
            Quick as a flash he wheels                                           1715
            And darts off in dismay;
            With hard luck at his heels
            He is off to the wood away.

Then it was heaven on earth to hark to the hounds
When they had come on their quarry, coursing together!        1720
Such harsh cries and howls they hurled at his head
As all the cliffs with a crash had come down at once.
Here he was hailed, when huntsmen met him;
Yonder they yelled at him, yapping and snarling;
There they cried "Thief!" and threatened his life,                    1725
And ever the harriers at his heels, that he had no rest.
Often he was menaced when he made for the open,
And often rushed in again, for Reynard was wily;
And so he leads them a merry chase, the lord and his men,
In this manner on the mountains, till midday or near,            1730
While our hero lies at home in wholesome sleep
Within the comely curtains on the cold morning.
But the lady, as love would allow her no rest,
And pursuing ever the purpose that pricked her heart,
Was awake with the dawn, and went to his chamber               1735
In a fair flowing mantle that fell to the earth,
All edged and embellished with ermines fine;
No hood on her head, but heavy with gems
Were her fillet and the fret that confined her tresses;
Her face and her fair throat freely displayed;                           1740

1739. *fret*: Ornamental net.

Her bosom all but bare, and her back as well.
She comes in at the chamber-door, and closes it with care,
Throws wide a window—then waits no longer,
But hails him thus airily with her artful words,
with cheer:  1745
"Ah, man, how can you sleep?
The morning is so clear!"
Though dreams have drowned him deep,
He cannot choose but hear.

Deep in his dreams he darkly mutters  1750
As a man may that mourns, with many grim thoughts
Of that day when destiny shall deal him his doom
When he greets his grim host at the Green Chapel
And must bow to his buffet, bating all strife.
But when he sees her at his side he summons his wits,  1755
Breaks from the black dreams, and blithely answers.
That lovely lady comes laughing sweet,
Sinks down at his side, and salutes him with a kiss.
He accords her fair welcome in courtliest style;
He sees her so glorious, so gaily attired,  1760
So faultless her features, so fair and so bright,
His heart swelled swiftly with surging joys.
They melt into mirth with many a fond smile,
And there was bliss beyond telling between those two,
at height.  1765
Good were their words of greeting;
Each joyed in other's sight;
Great peril attends that meeting
Should Mary forget her knight.

For that high-born beauty so hemmed him about,  1770
Made so plain her meaning, the man must needs
Either take her tendered love or distastefully refuse.
His courtesy concerned him, lest crass he appear,
But more his soul's mischief, should he commit sin
And belie his loyal oath to the lord of that house.  1775
"God forbid!" said the bold knight, "That shall not befall!"
With a little fond laughter he lightly let pass
All the words of special weight that were sped his way;
"I find you much at fault," the fair one said,
"Who can be cold toward a creature so close by your side,  1780
Of all women in this world most wounded in heart,
Unless you have a sweetheart, one you hold dearer,
And allegiance to that lady so loyally knit
That you will never love another, as now I believe.
And, sir, if it be so, then say it, I beg you;  1785
By all your heart holds dear, hide it no longer
with guile."
"Lady, by Saint John,"
He answers with a smile,

"Lover have I none,                                                    1790
Nor will have, yet awhile."

"Those words," said the woman, "are the worst of all,
But I have had my answer, and hard do I find it!
Kiss me now kindly; I can but go hence
To lament my life long like a maid lovelorn."                          1795
She inclines her head quickly and kisses the knight,
Then straightens with a sigh, and says as she stands,
"Now, dear, ere I depart, do me this pleasure:
Give me some little gift, your glove or the like,
That I may think on you, man, and mourn the less."                    1800
"Now by heaven," said he, "I wish I had here
My most precious possession, to put it in your hands,
For your deeds, beyond doubt, have often deserved
A repayment far passing my power to bestow.
But a love-token, lady, were of little avail;                         1805
It is not to your honor to have at this time
A glove as a guerdon from Gawain's hand,
And I am here on an errand in unknown realms
And have no bearers with baggage with becoming gifts,
Which distresses me, madame, for your dear sake.                      1810
A man must keep within his compass: account it neither grief
            nor slight."
                "Nay, noblest knight alive,"
                Said that beauty of body white,
                "Though you be loath to give,                         1815
                Yet you shall take, by right."

She reached out a rich ring, wrought all of gold,
With a splendid stone displayed on the band
That flashed before his eyes like a fiery sun;
It was worth a king's wealth, you may well believe.                   1820
But he waved it away with these ready words:
"Before God, good lady, I forego all gifts;
None have I to offer, nor any will I take."
And she urged it on him eagerly, and ever he refused,
And vowed in very earnest, prevail she would not.                     1825
And she sad to find it so, and said to him then,
"If my ring is refused for its rich cost—
You would not be my debtor for so dear a thing—
I shall give you my girdle; you gain less thereby."
She released a knot lightly, and loosened a belt                      1830
That was caught about her kirtle, the bright cloak beneath,
Of a gay green silk, with gold overwrought,
And the borders all bound with embroidery fine,
And this she presses upon him, and pleads with a smile,
Unworthy though it were, that it would not be scorned.                1835
But the man still maintains that he means to accept
Neither gold nor any gift, till by God's grace
The fate that lay before him was fully achieved.

1829. *girdle*: Belt.

"And be not offended, fair lady, I beg,
And give over your offer, for ever I must                    1840
        decline.
      I am grateful for favor shown
      Past all deserts of mine,
      And ever shall be your own
      True servant, rain or shine."                    1845

"Now does my present displease you," she promptly inquired,
"Because it seems in your sight so simple a thing?
And belike, as it is little, it is less to praise,
But if the virtue that invests it were verily known,
It would be held, I hope, in higher esteem.                 1850
For the man that possesses this piece of silk,
If he bore it on his body, belted about,
There is no hand under heaven that could hew him down,
For he could not be killed by any craft on earth."
Then the man began to muse, and mainly he thought           1855
It was a pearl for his plight, the peril to come
When he gains the Green Chapel to get his reward:
Could he escape unscathed, the scheme were noble!
Then he bore with her words and withstood them no more,
And she repeated her petition and pleaded anew,             1860
And he granted it, and gladly she gave him the belt,
And besought him for her sake to conceal it well,
Lest the noble lord should know—and the knight agrees
That not a soul save themselves shall see it thenceforth
        with sight.                    1865
      He thanked her with fervent heart,
      As often as ever he might;
      Three times, before they part,
      She has kissed the stalwart knight.

Then the lady took her leave, and left him there,           1870
For more mirth with that man she might not have.
When she was gone, Sir Gawain got from his bed,
Arose and arrayed him in his rich attire;
Tucked away the token the temptress had left,
Laid it reliably where he looked for it after.             1875
And then with good cheer to the chapel he goes,
Approached a priest in private, and prayed to be taught
To lead a better life and lift up his mind,
Lest he be among the lost when he must leave this world.
And shamefaced at shrift he showed his misdeeds            1880
From the largest to the least, and asked the Lord's mercy,
And called on his confessor to cleanse his soul,
And he absolved him of his sins as safe and as clean
As if the dread Day of Judgment should dawn on the morrow.
And then he made merry amid the fine ladies                1885
With deft-footed dances and dalliance light,

1880. *shrift:* Confession.

As never until now, while the afternoon wore
                         away.
              He delighted all around him,
              And all agreed, that day,                    1890
              They never before had found him
              So gracious and so gay.

Now peaceful be his pasture, and love play him fair!
The host is on horseback, hunting afield;
He has finished off this fox that he followed so long:    1895
As he leapt a low hedge to look for the villain
Where he heard all the hounds in hot pursuit,
Reynard comes racing out of a rough thicket,
And all the rabble in a rush, right at his heels.
The man beholds the beast, and bides his time,            1900
And bares his bright sword, and brings it down hard,
And he blenches from the blade, and backward he starts;
A hound hurries up and hinders that move,
And before the horse's feet they fell on him at once
And ripped the rascal's throat with a wrathful din.       1905
The lord soon alighted and lifted him free,
Swiftly snatched him up from the snapping jaws,
Holds him over his head, halloos with a will,
And the dogs bayed the dirge, that had done him to death.
Hunters hastened thither with horns at their lips,        1910
Sounding the assembly till they saw him at last.
When that comely company was come in together,
All that bore bugles blew them at once,
And the others all hallooed, that had no horns.
It was the merriest medley that ever a man heard,         1915
The racket that they raised for Sir Reynard's soul
                         that died.
              Their hounds they praised and fed,
              Fondling their heads with pride,
              And they took Reynard the Red                1920
              And stripped away his hide.

And then they headed homeward, for evening had come,
Blowing many a blast on their bugles bright.
The lord at long last alights at his house,
Finds fire on the hearth where the fair knight waits,     1925
Sir Gawain the good, that was glad in heart.
With the ladies, that loved him, he lingered at ease;
He wore a rich robe of blue, that reached to the earth
And a surcoat lined softly with sumptuous furs;
A hood of the same hue hung on his shoulders;             1930
With bands of bright ermine embellished were both.
He comes to meet the man amid all the folk,
And greets him good-humoredly, and gaily he says,
"I shall follow forthwith the form of our pledge
That we framed to good effect amid fresh-filled cups."    1935

He clasps him accordingly and kisses him thrice,
As amiably and as earnestly as ever he could.
"By heaven," said the host, "you have had some luck
Since you took up this trade, if the terms were good."
"Never trouble about the terms," he returned at once,                        1940
"Since all that I owe here is openly paid."
"Marry!" said the other man, "mine is much less,
For I have hunted all day, and nought have I got
But this foul fox pelt, the fiend take the goods!
Which but poorly repays those precious things                                1945
That you have cordially conferred, those kisses three
          so good."
        "Enough!" said Sir Gawain;
        "I thank you, by the rood!"
        And how the fox was slain                                1950
        He told him, as they stood.

With minstrelsy and mirth, with all manner of meats,
They made as much merriment as any men might
(Amid laughing of ladies and light-hearted girls,
So gay grew Sir Gawain and the goodly host)                                  1955
Unless they had been besotted, or brainless fools.
The knight joined in jesting with that joyous folk,
Until at last it was late; ere long they must part,
And be off to their beds, as behooved them each one.
Then politely his leave of the lord of the house                             1960
Our noble knight takes, and renews his thanks:
"The courtesies countless accorded me here,
Your kindness at this Christmas, may heaven's King repay!
Henceforth, if you will have me, I hold you my liege,
And so, as I have said, I must set forth tomorrow,                           1965
If I may take some trusty man to teach, as you promised,
The way to the Green Chapel, that as God allows
I shall see my fate fulfilled on the first of the year."
"In good faith," said the good man, "with a good will
Every promise on my part shall be fully performed."                          1970
He assigns him a servant to set him on the path,
To see him safe and sound over the snowy hills,
To follow the fastest way through forest green
          and grove.
        Gawain thanks him again,                                  1975
        So kind his favors prove,
        And of the ladies then
        He takes his leave, with love.

Courteously he kissed them, with care in his heart,
And often wished them well, with warmest thanks,                             1980
Which they for their part were prompt to repay.
They commend him to Christ with disconsolate sighs;
And then in that hall with the household he parts—

1949. *rood:* Cross.

Each man that he met, he remembered to thank
For his deeds of devotion and diligent pains,                    1985
And the trouble he had taken to tend to his needs;
And each one as woeful, that watched him depart,
As he had lived with him loyally all his life long.
By lads bearing lights he was led to his chamber
And blithely brought to his bed, to be at his rest.              1990
How soundly he slept, I presume not to say,
For there were matters of moment his thoughts might well
                              pursue.
              Let him lie and wait;
              He has little more to do,                          1995
              Then listen, while I relate
              How they kept their rendezvous.

## Part IV

Now the New Year draws near, and the night passes,
The day dispels the dark, by the Lord's decree;
But wild weather awoke in the world without:                    2000
The clouds in the cold sky cast down their snow
With great gusts from the north, grievous to bear.
Sleet showered aslant upon shivering beasts;
The wind warbled wild as it whipped from aloft,
And drove the drifts deep in the dales below.                   2005
Long and well he listens, that lies in his bed;
Though he lifts not his eyelids, little he sleeps;
Each crow of the cock he counts without fail.
Readily from his rest he rose before dawn,
For a lamp had been left him, that lighted his chamber.         2010
He called to his chamberlain, who quickly appeared,
And bade him get him his gear, and gird his good steed,
And he sets about briskly to bring in his arms,
And makes ready his master in manner most fit.
First he clad him in his clothes, to keep out the cold,         2015
And then his other harness, made handsome anew,
His plate-armor of proof, polished with pains,
The rings of his rich mail rid of their rust,
And all was fresh as at first, and for this he gave thanks
                              indeed.                            2020
              With pride he wears each piece,
              New-furbished for his need:
              No gayer from here to Greece;
              He bids them bring his steed.

In his richest raiment he robed himself then:                   2025
His crested coat-armor, close-stitched with craft,
With stones of strange virtue on silk velvet set;
All bound with embroidery on borders and seams
And lined warmly and well with furs of the best.
Yet he left not his love-gift, the lady's girdle;              2030

Gawain, for his own good, forgot not that:
When the bright sword was belted and bound on his haunches,
Then twice with that token he twined him about.
Sweetly did he swathe him in that swatch of silk,
That girdle of green so goodly to see,                                2035
That against the gay red showed gorgeous bright.
Yet he wore not for its wealth that wondrous girdle,
Nor pride in its pendants, though polished they were,
Though glittering gold gleamed at the tips,
But to keep himself safe when consent he must                         2040
To endure a deadly dint, and all defense
                denied.
        And now the bold knight came
        Into the courtyard wide;
        That folk of worthy fame                                 2045
        He thanks on every side.

Then was Gringolet girt, that was great and huge,
And had sojourned safe and sound, and savored his fare;
He pawed the earth in his pride, that princely steed.
The good knight draws near him and notes well his look,               2050
And says sagely to himself, and soberly swears,
"Here is a household in hall that upholds the right!
The man that maintains it, may happiness be his!
Likewise the dear lady, may love betide her!
If thus they in charity cherish a guest                               2055
That are honored here on earth, may they have His reward
That reigns high in heaven—and also you all;
And were I to live in this land but a little while,
I should willingly reward you, and well, if I might."
Then he steps into the stirrup and bestrides his mount;               2060
His shield is shown forth; on his shoulder he casts it;
Strikes the side of his steed with his steel spurs,
And he starts across the stones, nor stands any longer
                to prance.
        On horseback was the swain                               2065
        That bore his spear and lance;
        "May Christ this house maintain
        And guard it from mischance!"

The bridge was brought down, and the broad gates
Unbarred and carried back upon both sides;                            2070
He commended him to Christ, and crossed over the planks;
Praised the noble porter, who prayed on his knees
That God save Sir Gawain, and bade him good day,
And went on his way alone with the man
That was to lead him ere long to that luckless place                  2075
Where the dolorous dint must be dealt him at last.
Under bare boughs they ride, where steep banks rise,
Over high cliffs they climb, where cold snow clings;
The heavens held aloof, but heavy thereunder

2071. *him:* I.e., himself.

Mist mantled the moors, moved on the slopes.                     2080
Each hill had a hat, a huge cape of cloud;
Brooks bubbled and broke over broken rocks,
Flashing in freshets that waterfalls fed.
Roundabout was the road that ran through the wood
Till the sun at that season was soon to rise,                    2085
                that day.
        They were on a hilltop high;
        The white snow round them lay;
        The man that rode nearby
        Now bade his master stay.                        2090

"For I have seen you here safe at the set time,
And now you are not far from that notable place
That you have sought for so long with such special pains.
But this I say for certain, since I know you, sir knight,
And have your good at heart, and hold you dear—                  2095
Would you heed well my words, it were worth your while—
You are rushing into risks that you reck not of:
There is a villain in yon valley, the veriest on earth,
For he is rugged and rude, and ready with his fists,
And most immense in his mold of mortals alive,                   2100
And his body bigger than the best four
That are in Arthur's house, Hector or any.
He gets his grim way at the Green Chapel;
None passes by that place so proud in his arms
That he does not dash him down with his deadly blows,            2105
For he is heartless wholly, and heedless of right,
For be it chaplain or churl that by the Chapel rides,
Monk or mass-priest or any man else,
He would as soon strike him dead as stand on two feet.
Wherefore I say, just as certain as you sit there astride,       2110
You cannot but be killed, if his counsel holds,
For he would trounce you in a trice, had you twenty lives
               for sale.
        He has lived long in this land
        And dealt out deadly bale;                       2115
        Against his heavy hand
        Your power cannot prevail.

"And so, good Sir Gawain, let the grim man be;
Go off by some other road, in God's own name!
Leave by some other land, for the love of Christ,               2120
And I shall get me home again, and give you my word
That I shall swear by God's self and the saints above,
By heaven and by my halidom and other oaths more,
To conceal this day's deed, nor say to a soul
That ever you fled for fear from any that I knew."              2125
"Many thanks!" said the other man—and demurring he speaks—
"Fair fortune befall you for your friendly words!

---

2102. *Hector:* Either the Trojan hero      2123. *halidom:* Holiness or, more
or one of Arthur's knights.                likely, patron saints.

And conceal this day's deed I doubt not you would,
But though you never told the tale, if I turned back now,
Forsook this place for fear, and fled, as you say,　　　　2130
I were a caitiff coward; I could not be excused.
But I must to the Chapel to chance my luck
And say to that same man such words as I please,
Befall what may befall through Fortune's will
　　　　　　　　　　or whim.　　　　2135
　　　　Though he be a quarrelsome knave
　　　　With a cudgel great and grim,
　　　　The Lord is strong to save:
　　　　His servants trust in Him."

"Marry," said the man, "since you tell me so much,　　　　2140
And I see you are set to seek your own harm,
If you crave a quick death, let me keep you no longer!
Put your helm on your head, your hand on your lance,
And ride the narrow road down yon rocky slope
Till it brings you to the bottom of the broad valley.　　　　2145
Then look a little ahead, on your left hand,
And you will soon see before you that self-same Chapel,
And the man of great might that is master there.
Now goodbye in God's name, Gawain the noble!
For all the world's wealth I would not stay here,　　　　2150
Or go with you in this wood one footstep further!"
He tarried no more to talk, but turned his bridle,
Hit his horse with his heels as hard as he might,
Leaves the knight alone, and off like the wind
　　　　　　　　　　goes leaping.　　　　2155
　　　　"By God," said Gawain then,
　　　　"I shall not give way to weeping;
　　　　God's will be done, amen!
　　　　I commend me to His keeping."

He puts his heels to his horse, and picks up the path;　　　　2160
Goes in beside a grove where the ground is steep,
Rides down the rough slope right to the valley;
And then he looked a little about him—the landscape was wild,
And not a soul to be seen, nor sign of a dwelling,
But high banks on either hand hemmed it about,　　　　2165
With many a ragged rock and rough-hewn crag;
The skies seemed scored by the scowling peaks.
Then he halted his horse, and hoved there a space,
And sought on every side for a sight of the Chapel,
But no such place appeared, which puzzled him sore,　　　　2170
Yet he saw some way off what seemed like a mound,
A hillock high and broad, hard by the water,
Where the stream fell in foam down the face of the steep
And bubbled as if it boiled on its bed below.
The knight urges his horse, and heads for the knoll;　　　　2175

2131. *caitiff:* Despicable.

Leaps lightly to earth; loops well the rein
Of his steed to a stout branch, and stations him there.
He strides straight to the mound, and strolls all about,
Much wondering what it was, but no whit the wiser;
It had a hole at one end, and on either side,                    2180
And was covered with coarse grass in clumps all without,
And hollow all within, like some old cave,
Or a crevice of an old crag—he could not discern
                   aright.
          "Can this be the Chapel Green?                    2185
          Alack!" said the man, "Here might
          The devil himself be seen
          Saying matins at black midnight!"

"Now by heaven," said he, "it is bleak hereabouts;
This prayer-house is hideous, half-covered with grass!                    2190
Well may the grim man mantled in green
Hold here his orisons, in hell's own style!
Now I feel it is the Fiend, in my five wits,
That has tempted me to this tryst, to take my life;
This is a Chapel of mischance, may the mischief take it!                    2195
As accursed a country church as I came upon ever!"
With his helm on his head, his lance in his hand,
He stalks toward the steep wall of that strange house.
Then he heard, on the hill, behind a hard rock,
Beyond the brook, from the bank, a most barbarous din:                    2200
Lord! it clattered in the cliff fit to cleave it in two,
As one upon a grindstone ground a great scythe!
Lord! it whirred like a mill-wheel whirling about!
Lord! it echoed loud and long, lamentable to hear!
Then "By heaven," said the bold knight, "That business
    up there                    2205
Is arranged for my arrival, or else I am much
              misled.
          Let God work! Ah me!
          All hope of help has fled!
          Forfeit my life may be                    2210
          But noise I do not dread."

Then he listened no longer, but loudly he called,
"Who has power in this place, high parley to hold?
For none greets Sir Gawain, or gives him good day;
If any would a word with him, let him walk forth                    2215
And speak now or never, to speed his affairs."
"Abide," said one on the bank above over his head,
"And what I promised you once shall straightway be given."
Yet he stayed not his grindstone, nor stinted its noise,
But worked awhile at his whetting before he would rest,                    2220
And then he comes around a crag, from a cave in the rocks,
Hurtling out of hiding with a hateful weapon,

2188. *matins:* Morning prayers.

A Danish ax devised for that day's deed,
With a broad blade and bright, bent in a curve,
Filed to a fine edge—four feet it measured          2225
By the length of the lace that was looped round the haft.
And in form as at first, the fellow all green,
His lordly face and his legs, his locks and his beard,
Save that firm upon two feet forward he strides,
Sets a hand on the ax-head, the haft to the earth;          2230
When he came to the cold stream, and cared not to wade,
He vaults over on his ax, and advances amain
On a broad bank of snow, overbearing and brisk
              of mood.
        Little did the knight incline          2235
        When face to face they stood;
        Said the other man, "Friend mine,
        It seems your word holds good!"

"God love you, Sir Gawain!" said the Green Knight then,
"And well met this morning, man, at my place!          2240
And you have followed me faithfully and found me betimes,
And on the business between us we both are agreed:
Twelve months ago today you took what was yours,
And you at this New Year must yield me the same.
And we have met in these mountains, remote from all eyes:          2245
There is none here to halt us or hinder our sport;
Unhasp your high helm, and have here your wages;
Make no more demur than I did myself
When you hacked off my head with one hard blow."
"No, by God," said Sir Gawain, "that granted me life,          2250
I shall grudge not the guerdon, grim though it prove;
Bestow but one stroke, and I shall stand still,
And you may lay on as you like till the last of my part
              be paid."
        He proffered, with good grace,          2255
        His bare neck to the blade,
        And feigned a cheerful face:
        He scorned to seem afraid.

Then the grim man in green gathers his strength,
Heaves high the heavy ax to hit him the blow.          2260
With all the force in his frame he fetches it aloft,
With a grimace as grim as he would grind him to bits;
Had the blow he bestowed been as big as he threatened,
A good knight and gallant had gone to his grave.
But Gawain at the great ax glanced up aside          2265
As down it descended with death-dealing force,
And his shoulders shrank a little from the sharp iron.
Abruptly the brawny man breaks off the stroke,
And then reproved with proud words that prince among knights.

2223. *Danish ax:* I.e., a long-bladed          2241. *betimes:* In good time.
one.

"You are not Gawain the glorious," the green man said,                 2270
"That never fell back on field in the face of the foe,
And now you flee for fear, and have felt no harm:
Such news of that knight I never heard yet!
I moved not a muscle when you made to strike,
Nor caviled at the cut in King Arthur's house;                 2275
My head fell to my feet, yet steadfast I stood,
And you, all unharmed, are wholly dismayed—
Wherefore the better man I, by all odds,
                    must be."
            Said Gawain, "Strike once more;                 2280
            I shall neither flinch nor flee;
            But if my head falls to the floor
            There is no mending me!"

"But go on, man, in God's name, and get to the point!
Deliver me my destiny, and do it out of hand,                 2285
For I shall stand to the stroke and stir not an inch
Till your ax has hit home—on my honor I swear it!"
"Have at thee then!" said the other, and heaves it aloft,
And glares down as grimly as he had gone mad.
He made a mighty feint, but marred not his hide;                 2290
Withdrew the ax adroitly before it did damage.
Gawain gave no ground, nor glanced up aside,
But stood still as a stone, or else a stout stump
That is held in hard earth by a hundred roots.
Then merrily does he mock him, the man all in green:                 2295
"So now you have your nerve again, I needs must strike;
Uphold the high knighthood that Arthur bestowed,
And keep your neck-bone clear, if this cut allows!"
Then was Gawain gripped with rage, and grimly he said,
"Why, thrash away, tyrant, I tire of your threats;                 2300
You make such a scene, you must frighten yourself.
Said the green fellow, "In faith, so fiercely you speak
That I shall finish this affair, nor further grace
                    allow."
            He stands prepared to strike                 2305
            And scowls with both lip and brow;
            No marvel if the man mislike
            Who can hope no rescue now.

He gathered up the grim ax and guided it well:
Let the barb at the blade's end brush the bare throat;                 2310
He hammered down hard, yet harmed him no whit
Save a scratch on one side, that severed the skin;
The end of the hooked edge entered the flesh,
And a little blood lightly leapt to the earth.
And when the man beheld his own blood bright on the snow,                 2315
He sprang a spear's length with feet spread wide,
Seized his high helm, and set it on his head,
Shoved before his shoulders the shield at his back,

Bares his trusty blade, and boldly he speaks—
Not since he was a babe born of his mother        2320
Was he once in this world one-half so blithe—
"Have done with your hacking—harry me no more!
I have borne, as behooved, one blow in this place;
If you make another move I shall meet it midway
And promptly, I promise you, pay back each blow        2325
                with brand.
        One stroke acquits me here;
        So did our covenant stand
        In Arthur's court last year—
        Wherefore, sir, hold your hand!"        2330

He lowers the long ax and leans on it there,
Sets his arms on the head, the haft on the earth,
And beholds the bold knight that bides there afoot,
How he faces him fearless, fierce in full arms,
And plies him with proud words—it pleases him well.        2335
Then once again gaily to Gawain he calls,
And in a loud voice and lusty, delivers these words:
"Bold fellow, on this field your anger forbear!
No man has made demands here in manner uncouth,
Nor done, save as duly determined at court.        2340
I owed you a hit and you have it; be happy therewith!
The rest of my rights here I freely resign.
Had I been a bit busier, a buffet, perhaps,
I could have dealt more directly, and done you some harm.
First I flourished with a feint, in frolicsome mood,        2345
And left your hide unhurt—and here I did well
By the fair terms we fixed on the first night;
And fully and faithfully you followed accord:
Gave over all your gains as a good man should.
A second feint, sir, I assigned for the morning        2350
You kissed my comely wife—each kiss you restored.
For both of these there behooved but two feigned blows
                by right.
        True men pay what they owe;
        No danger then in sight.        2355
        You failed at the third throw,
        So take my tap, sir knight.

"For that is my belt about you, that same braided girdle,
My wife it was that wore it; I know well the tale,
And the count of your kisses and your conduct too,        2360
And the wooing of my wife—it was all my scheme!
She made trial of a man most faultless by far
Of all that ever walked over the wide earth;
As pearls to white peas, more precious and prized,
So is Gawain, in good faith, to other gay knights.        2365
Yet you lacked, sir, a little in loyalty there,
But the cause was not cunning, nor courtship either,
But that you loved your own life; the less, then, to blame."

The other stout knight in a study stood a long while,
So gripped with grim rage that his great heart shook. 2370
All the blood of his body burned in his face
As he shrank back in shame from the man's sharp speech.
The first words that fell from the fair knight's lips:
"Accursed be a cowardly and covetous heart!
In you is villainy and vice, and virtue laid low!" 2375
Then he grasps the green girdle and lets go the knot,
Hands it over in haste, and hotly he says:
"Behold there my falsehood, ill hap betide it!
Your cut taught me cowardice, care for my life,
And coveting came after, contrary both 2380
To largesse and loyalty belonging to knights.
Now am I faulty and false, that fearful was ever
Of disloyalty and lies, bad luck to them both!
              and greed.
       I confess, knight, in this place, 2385
       Most dire is my misdeed;
       Let me gain back your good grace,
       And thereafter I shall take heed."

Then the other laughed aloud, and lightly he said,
"Such harm as I have had, I hold it quite healed. 2390
You are so fully confessed, your failings made known,
And bear the plain penance of the point of my blade,
I hold you polished as a pearl, as pure and as bright
As you had lived free of fault since first you were born.
And I give you, sir, this girdle that is gold-hemmed 2395
And green as my garments, that, Gawain, you may
Be mindful of this meeting when you mingle in throng
With nobles of renown—and known by this token
How it chanced at the Green Chapel, to chivalrous knights.
And you shall in this New Year come yet again 2400
And we shall finish out our feast in my fair hall,
              with cheer."
       He urged the knight to stay,
       And said, "With my wife so dear
       We shall see you friends this day, 2405
       Whose enmity touched you near."

"Indeed," said the doughty knight, and doffed his high helm,
And held it in his hands as he offered his thanks,
"I have lingered long enough—may good luck be yours,
And He reward you well that all worship bestows! 2410
And commend me to that comely one, your courteous wife,
Both herself and that other, my honoured ladies,
That have trapped their true knight in their trammels so quaint.
But if a dullard should dote, deem it no wonder,
And through the wiles of a woman be wooed into sorrow, 2415
For so was Adam by one, when the world began,
And Solomon by many more, and Samson the mighty—

Delilah was his doom, and David thereafter
Was beguiled by Bathsheba, and bore much distress;
Now these were vexed by their devices—'twere a very joy      2420
Could one but learn to love, and believe them not.
For these were proud princes, most prosperous of old,
Past all lovers lucky, that languished under heaven,
                              bemused.
                    And one and all fell prey           2425
                    To women that they had used;
                    If I be led astray,
                    Methinks I may be excused.

"But your girdle, God love you! I gladly shall take
And be pleased to possess, not for the pure gold,           2430
Nor the bright belt itself, nor the beauteous pendants,
Nor for wealth, nor worldly state, nor workmanship fine,
But a sign of excess it shall seem oftentimes
When I ride in renown, and remember with shame
The faults and the frailty of the flesh perverse,          2435
How its tenderness entices the foul taint of sin;
And so when praise and high prowess have pleased my heart,
A look at this love-lace will lower my pride.
But one thing would I learn, if you were not loath,
Since you are lord of yonder land where I have long sojourned   2440
With honor in your house—may you have His reward
That upholds all the heavens, highest on throne!
How runs your right name?—and let the rest go."
"That shall I give you gladly," said the Green Knight then;
"Bercilak de Hautdesert this barony I hold,                 2445
Through the might of Morgan le Fay, that lodges at my house,
By subtleties of science and sorcerers' arts,
The mistress of Merlin, she has caught many a man,
For sweet love in secret she shared sometime
With that wizard, that knows well each one of your knights   2450
                              and you.
                    Morgan the Goddess, she,
                    So styled by title true;
                    None holds so high degree
                    That her arts cannot subdue.            2455

"She guided me in this guise to your glorious hall,
To assay, if such it were, the surfeit of pride
That is rumored of the retinue of the Round Table.
She put this shape upon me to puzzle your wits,
To afflict the fair queen, and frighten her to death        2460
With awe of that elvish man that eerily spoke
With his head in his hand before the high table.
She was with my wife at home, that old withered lady,

---

2446. *Morgan le Faye:* Arthur's half-     who sometimes abetted him, sometimes
sister, an enchantress ("Faye," fairy)     made trouble for him.

Your own aunt is she, Arthur's half-sister,
The Duchess' daughter of Tintagel, that dear King Uther     2465
Got Arthur on after, that honored is now.
And therefore, good friend, come feast with your aunt;
Make merry in my house; my men hold you dear,
And I wish you as well, sir, with all my heart,
As any mortal man, for your matchless faith."     2470
But the knight said him nay, that he might by no means.
They clasped then and kissed, and commended each other
To the Prince of Paradise, and parted with one
                     assent.
           Gawain sets out anew;     2475
           Toward the court his course is bent;
           And the knight all green in hue,
           Wheresoever he wished, he went.

Wild ways in the world our worthy knight rides
On Gringolet, that by grace had been granted his life.     2480
He harbored often in houses, and often abroad,
And with many valiant adventures verily he met
That I shall not take time to tell in this story.
The hurt was whole that he had had in his neck,
And the bright green belt on his body he bore,     2485
Oblique, like a baldric, bound at his side,
Below his left shoulder, laced in a knot,
In betokening of the blame he had borne for his fault;
And so to court in due course he comes safe and sound.
Bliss abounded in hall when the high-born heard     2490
That good Gawain was come; glad tidings they thought it.
The king kisses the knight, and the queen as well,
And many a comrade came to clasp him in arms,
And eagerly they asked, and awesomely he told,
Confessed all his cares and discomfitures many,     2495
How it chanced at the Chapel, what cheer made the knight,
The love of the lady, the green lace at last.
The nick on his neck he naked displayed
That he got in his disgrace at the Green Knight's hands,
                     alone.     2500
           With rage in heart he speaks,
           And grieves with many a groan;
           The blood burns in his cheeks
           For shame at what must be shown.

"Behold, sir," said he, and handles the belt,     2505
"This is the blazon of the blemish that I bear on my neck;
This is the sign of sore loss that I have suffered there
For the cowardice and coveting that I came to there;
This is the badge of false faith that I was found in there,
And I must bear it on my body till I breathe my last.     2510

2464. *Your own aunt is she:* Morgan
was the daughter of Igraine, Duchess of
Tintagel, and her husband, the Duke.

Igraine conceived Arthur when his
father, Uther, lay with her through one
of Merlin's trickeries.

For one may keep a deed dark, but undo it no whit,
For where a fault is made fast, it is fixed evermore."
The king comforts the knight, and the court all together
Agree with gay laughter and gracious intent
That the lords and the ladies belonging to the Table,⠀⠀⠀⠀2515
Each brother of that band, a baldric should have,
A belt borne oblique, of a bright green,
To be worn with one accord for that worthy's sake.
So that was taken as a token by the Table Round,
And he honored that had it, evermore after,⠀⠀⠀⠀2520
As the best book of knighthood bids it be known.
In the old days of Arthur this happening befell;
The books of Brutus' deeds bear witness thereto
Since Brutus, the bold knight, embarked for this land
After the siege ceased at Troy and the city fared⠀⠀⠀⠀2525
⠀⠀⠀⠀⠀⠀⠀⠀⠀⠀amiss.
⠀⠀⠀⠀Many such, ere we were born,
⠀⠀⠀⠀Have befallen here, ere this.
⠀⠀⠀⠀May He that was crowned with thorn
⠀⠀⠀⠀Bring all men to His bliss! Amen.⠀⠀⠀⠀2530

# GEOFFREY CHAUCER

## (1340?-1400)

### CHAUCER IN MODERN ENGLISH

In this book Chaucer is presented in a Modern English version made in the twentieth century. Theodore Morrison's translation is remarkably clear, accurate, and easy to read. But, in order to get some idea of what Chaucer's original language was, we may profitably compare the first eighteen lines of the *General Prologue* in the two forms. It will be evident that changes have occurred in pronunciation, in grammatical forms, and sometimes in the use and meaning of words. Here it will be possible only to point out a few examples of these changes.

⠀⠀⠀⠀Whan that Aprille with his shoures sote
⠀⠀⠀⠀The droghte of Marche hath perced to the rote,
⠀⠀⠀⠀And bathed every veyne in swich licour,
⠀⠀⠀⠀Of which vertu engendred is the flour;
⠀⠀⠀⠀When Zephirus ęęk with his swete bręęth⠀⠀⠀⠀5
⠀⠀⠀⠀Inspired hath in every holt and hęęth
⠀⠀⠀⠀The tendre croppes, and the yonge sonne
⠀⠀⠀⠀Hath in the Ram his halfe cours y-ronne,
⠀⠀⠀⠀And smale fowles maken melodye,
⠀⠀⠀⠀That slepen al the night with open yë,⠀⠀⠀⠀10
⠀⠀⠀⠀So priketh hem nature in hir corages:
⠀⠀⠀⠀Than longen folk to gǫǫn on pilgrimages
⠀⠀⠀⠀And palmers for to seken straunge strandes

To ferne halwes, couthe in sondry landes;
And specially, from every shires ende
Of Engeland, to Caunterbury they wende,
The holy blisful martir for to seke,
That hem hath holpen, whan that they were seke.

In Chaucer's language (Middle English of the late fourteenth century) the letters representing the stressed vowels were pronounced about as they are in Spanish or Italian in our time. Thus the A of *Aprille* sounded like *a* in our *father*; the first *e* in *swete* (line 5) was like *a* in Modern English *late*; and the second *i* in *Inspired* (line 6) was like *i* in our *machine*. In verbs, the third person singular ends in *-th*, not *-s*, as in *hath* (line 2); and the plural ending, either *-en* or *-e*, forms a separate syllable, as in *maken* (line 9), *slepen* (line 10), and *wende* (line 16). Among the pronouns and pronominal adjectives, Chaucer's language did not have our *its*, *their*, or *them*. Instead, the corresponding forms were, respectively, *his* (line 1), *hir(e)* (line 11), and *hem* (line 18).

When differences like these occur a translator must, of course, replace the original by the modern form. Changes in the meaning or use of words may also compel a substitution. Thus Chaucer's *couthe* (line 14) has become obsolete and hence the translation has *renowned* instead; so also *corages* (line 11) becomes *hearts*, and *ferne halwes* (line 14) becomes *foreign shrines*.

It will be noted that both the original and the translation have lines regularly riming in couplets. Sometimes the translator has been able to keep the same riming words (with some difference of pronunciation) as in lines 7 and 8 and 13 and 14. In other places he has found it necessary to substitute a new riming pair of his own, as in lines 1 and 2 and 17 and 18—although in the first instance the translator keeps one of the original riming words but not the other.

If the reader will himself make the effort to render a few of Chaucer's lines in readable Modern English verse, he will better understand the problems faced by a translator—and better appreciate Morrison's skill and success. (He will find A *Note on Translation*, in the back of our book, pages 1731 ff., also of great interest and value.)

## The Canterbury Tales*

### General Prologue

As soon as April pierces to the root
The drought of March, and bathes each bud and shoot
Through every vein of sap with gentle showers

* Chiefly the work of Chaucer's last years. From *The Portable Chaucer*, selected, translated, and edited by Theodore Morrison. Copyright 1949 by Theodore Morrison. Reprinted by permission of The Viking Press, Inc., New York.

From whose engendering liquor spring the flowers;
When zephyrs have breathed softly all about                    5
Inspiring every wood and field to sprout,
And in the zodiac the youthful sun
His journey halfway through the Ram has run;
When little birds are busy with their song
Who sleep with open eyes the whole night long               10
Life stirs their hearts and tingles in them so,
Then off as pilgrims people long to go,
And palmers to set out for distant strands
And foreign shrines renowned in many lands.
And specially in England people ride                           15
To Canterbury from every countryside
To visit there the blessed martyred saint
Who gave them strength when they were sick and faint.
    In Southwark at the Tabard one spring day
It happened, as I stopped there on my way,                     20
Myself a pilgrim with a heart devout
Ready for Canterbury to set out,
At night came all of twenty-nine assorted
Travelers, and to that same inn resorted,
Who by a turn of fortune chanced to fall                       25
In fellowship together, and they were all
Pilgrims who had it in their minds to ride
Toward Canterbury. The stables doors were wide,
The rooms were large, and we enjoyed the best,
And shortly, when the sun had gone to rest,                    30
I had so talked with each that presently
I was a member of their company
And promised to rise early the next day
To start, as I shall show, upon our way.
    But none the less, while I have time and space,            35
Before this tale has gone a further pace,
I should in reason tell you the condition
Of each of them, his rank and his position,
And also what array they all were in;
And so then, with a knight I will begin.                       40
    A Knight was with us, and an excellent man,
Who from the earliest moment he began
To follow his career loved chivalry,
Truth, openhandedness, and courtesy.
He was a stout man in the king's campaigns                     45
And in that cause had gripped his horse's reins
In Christian lands and pagan through the earth,
None farther, and always honored for his worth.
He was on hand at Alexandria's fall.

5. *zephyrs*: the west wind.
8. *Ram*: a sign of the Zodiac (Aries); the sun is in the Ram from March 12 to April 11.
13. *palmers*: pilgrims, who, originally, brought back palm leaves from the Holy Land.
17. *saint*: St. Thomas à Becket, slain in Canterbury cathedral in 1170.
19. *Tabard*: an inn at Southwark, across the river Thames from London.
49. *Alexandria's fall*: in Egypt, captured in 1365 by King Peter of Cyprus.

He had often sat in precedence to all                                50
The nations at the banquet board in Prussia.
He had fought in Lithuania and in Russia,
No Christian knight more often; he had been
In Moorish Africa at Benmarin,
At the siege of Algeciras in Granada,                                55
And sailed in many a glorious armada
In the Mediterranean, and fought as well
At Ayas and Attalia when they fell
In Armenia and on Asia Minor's coast.
Of fifteen deadly battles he could boast,                            60
And in Algeria, at Tremessen,
Fought for the faith and killed three separate men
In single combat. He had done good work
Joining against another pagan Turk
With the king of Palathia. And he was wise,                          65
Despite his prowess, honored in men's eyes,
Meek as a girl and gentle in his ways.
He had never spoken ignobly all his days
To any man by even a rude inflection.
He was a knight in all things to perfection.                         70
He rode a good horse, but his gear was plain,
For he had lately served on a campaign.
His tunic was still spattered by the rust
Left by his coat of mail, for he had just
Returned and set out on his pilgrimage.                              75
　His son was with him, a young Squire, in age
Some twenty years as near as I could guess.
His hair curled as if taken from a press.
He was a lover and would become a knight.
In stature he was of a moderate height                               80
But powerful and wonderfully quick.
He had been in Flanders, riding in the thick
Of forays in Artois and Picardy,
And bore up well for one so young as he,
Still hoping by his exploits in such places                          85
To stand the better in his lady's graces.
He wore embroidered flowers, red and white,
And blazed like a spring meadow to the sight.
He sang or played his flute the livelong day.
He was as lusty as the month of May.                                 90
His coat was short, its sleeves were long and wide.
He sat his horse well, and knew how to ride,
And how to make a song and use his lance,
And he could write and draw well, too, and dance.
So hot his love that when the moon rose pale                         95
He got no more sleep than a nightingale.
He was modest, and helped whomever he was able,
And carved as his father's squire at the table.
　But one more servant had the Knight beside,

Choosing thus simply for the time to ride:          100
A Yeoman, in a coat and hood of green.
His peacock-feathered arrows, bright and keen,
He carried under his belt in tidy fashion.
For well-kept gear he had a yeoman's passion,
No draggled feather might his arrows show,          105
And in his hand he held a mighty bow.
He kept his hair close-cropped, his face was brown.
He knew the lore of woodcraft up and down.
His arm was guarded from the bowstring's whip
By a bracer, gaily trimmed. He had at hip         110
A sword and buckler, and at his other side
A dagger whose fine mounting was his pride,
Sharp-pointed as a spear. His horn he bore
In a sling of green, and on his chest he wore
A silver image of St. Christopher,         115
His patron, since he was a forester.
    There was also a Nun, a Prioress,
Whose smile was gentle and full of guilelessness.
"By St. Loy!" was the worst oath she would say.
She sang mass well, in a becoming way,         120
Intoning through her nose the words divine,
And she was known as Madame Eglantine.
She spoke good French, as taught at Stratford-Bow
For the Parisian French she did not know.
She was schooled to eat so primly and so well         125
That from her lips no morsel ever fell.
She wet her fingers lightly in the dish
Of sauce, for courtesy was her first wish.
With every bite she did her skillful best
To see that no drop fell upon her breast.         130
She always wiped her upper lip so clean
That in her cup was never to be seen
A hint of grease when she had drunk her share,
She reached out for her meat with comely air.
She was a great delight, and always tried         135
To imitate court ways, and had her pride,
Both amiable and gracious in her dealings.
As for her charity and tender feelings,
She melted at whatever was piteous.
She would weep if she but came upon a mouse         140
Caught in a trap, if it were dead or bleeding.
Some little dogs that she took pleasure feeding
On roasted meat or milk or good wheat bread
She had, but how she wept to find one dead
Or yelping from a blow that made it smart,         145
And all was sympathy and loving heart.

---

119. *"By St. Loy!"*: perhaps St. Eligius, apparently a popular saint at this time.   123. *Stratford-Bow*: in Middlesex, near London, where there was a nunnery.

Neat was her wimple in its every plait,
Her nose well formed, her eyes as gray as slate.
Her mouth was very small and soft and red.
She had so wide a brow I think her head                    150
Was nearly a span broad, for certainly
She was not undergrown, as all could see.
She wore her cloak with dignity and charm,
And had her rosary about her arm,
The small beads coral and the larger green,                155
And from them hung a brooch of golden sheen,
On it a large A and a crown above;
Beneath, "All things are subject unto love."
    A Priest accompanied her toward Canterbury,
And an attendant Nun, her secretary.                       160
        There was a Monk, and nowhere was his peer,
A hunter, and a roving overseer.
He was a manly man, and fully able
To be an abbot. He kept a hunting stable,
And when he rode the neighborhood could hear              165
His bridle jingling in the wind as clear
And loud as if it were a chapel bell.
Wherever he was master of a cell
The principles of good St. Benedict,
For being a little old and somewhat strict,               170
Were honored in the breach, as past their prime.
He lived by the fashion of a newer time.
He would have swapped that text for a plucked hen
Which says that hunters are not holy men,
Or a monk outside his discipline and rule                 175
Is too much like a fish outside his pool;
That is to say, a monk outside his cloister.
But such a text he deemed not worth an oyster.
I told him his opinion made me glad.
Why should he study always and go mad,                    180
Mewed in his cell with only a book for neighbor?
Or why, as Augustine commanded, labor
And sweat his hands? How shall the world be served?
To Augustine be all such toil reserved!
And so he hunted, as was only right.                      185
He had greyhounds as swift as birds in flight.
His taste was all for tracking down the hare,
And what his sport might cost he did not care.
His sleeves I noticed, where they met his hand,
Trimmed with gray fur, the finest in the land.           190
His hood was fastened with a curious pin
Made of wrought gold and clasped beneath his chin,
A love knot at the tip. His head might pass,
Bald as it was, for a lump of shining glass,

---

**169. principles:** monastic rules, authored by St. Maurus and St. Benedict in the sixth
century A.D.

And his face was glistening as if anointed.          195
Fat as a lord he was, and well appointed.
His eyes were large, and rolled inside his head
As if they gleamed from a furnace of hot lead.
His boots were supple, his horse superbly kept.
He was a prelate to dream of while you slept.          200
He was not pale nor peaked like a ghost.
He relished a plump swan as his favorite roast.
He rode a palfrey brown as a ripe berry.
   A Friar was with us, a gay dog and a merry,
Who begged his district with a jolly air.          205
No friar in all four orders could compare
With him for gallantry; his tongue was wooing.
Many a girl was married by his doing,
And at his own cost it was often done.
He was a pillar, and a noble one,          210
To his whole order. In his neighborhood
Rich franklins knew him well, who served good food,
and worthy women welcomed him to town;
For the license that his order handed down,
He said himself, conferred on him possession          215
Of more than a curate's power of confession.
Sweetly the list of frailties he heard,
Assigning penance with a pleasant word.
He was an easy man for absolution
Where he looked forward to a contribution,          220
For if to a poor order a man has given
It signifies that he has been well shriven,
And if a sinner let his purse be dented
The Friar would stake his oath he had repented.
For many men become so hard of heart          225
They cannot weep, though conscience makes them smart.
Instead of tears and prayers, then, let the sinner
Supply the poor friars with the price of dinner.
For pretty women he had more than shrift.
His cape was stuffed with many a little gift,          230
As knives and pins and suchlike. He could sing
A merry note, and pluck a tender string,
And had no rival at all in balladry.
His neck was whiter than a fleur-de-lis,
And yet he could have knocked a strong man down.          235
He knew the taverns well in every town.
The barmaids and innkeepers pleased his mind
Better than beggars and lepers and their kind.
In his position it was unbecoming
Among the wretched lepers to go slumming.          240
It mocks all decency, it sews no stitch
To deal with such riffraff, but with the rich,

---

212. *franklins*: landowners or country squires, not belonging to the nobility.

234. *fleur-de-lis*: lily.

With sellers of victuals, that's another thing.
Wherever he saw some hope of profiting,
None so polite, so humble. He was good,                                245
The champion beggar of his brotherhood.
Should a woman have no shoes against the snow,
So pleasant was his "*In principio*"
He would have her widow's mite before he went.
He took in far more than he paid in rent                              250
For his right of begging within certain bounds.
None of his brethren trespassed on his grounds!
He loved as freely as a half-grown whelp.
On arbitration-days he gave great help,
For his cloak was never shiny nor threadbare                          255
Like a poor cloistered scholar's. He had an air
As if he were a doctor or a pope.
It took stout wool to make his semicope
That plumped out like a bell for portliness.
He lisped a little in his rakishness                                  260
To make his English sweeter on his tongue,
And twanging his harp to end some song he'd sung
His eyes would twinkle in his head as bright
As the stars twinkle on a frosty night.
Hubert this gallant Friar was by name.                                265
 Among the rest a Merchant also came.
He wore a forked beard and a beaver hat
From Flanders. High up in the saddle he sat,
In figured cloth, his boots clasped handsomely,
Delivering his opinions pompously,                                    270
Always on how his gains might be increased.
At all costs he desired the sea policed
From Middleburg in Holland to Orwell.
He knew the exchange rates, and the time to sell
French currency, and there was never yet                             275
A man who could have told he was in debt
So grave he seemed and hid so well his feelings
With all his shrewd engagements and close dealings.
You'd find no better man at any turn;
But what his name was I could never learn.                            280
 There was an Oxford Student too, it chanced,
Already in his logic well advanced.
He rode a mount as skinny as a rake,
And he was hardly fat. For learning's sake
He let himself look hollow and sober enough.                         285
He wore an outer coat of threadbare stuff,

---

248. "In principio": "In the beginning"
—the opening phrase of a famous passage in the Gospels (John 1:1–16), which
the friar recites in Latin as a devotional
exercise to awe the ignorant and extract
their alms.

254. *arbitration-days*: days appointed
for the adjustment of disputes.
258. *semicope*: a short cape.
272–273. He desired protection from
piracy between Middleburg in Holland
and Orwell, an English port near Harwich.

For he had no benefice for his enjoyment
And was too unworldly for some lay employment.
He much preferred to have beside his bed
His twenty volumes bound in black or red            290
All packed with Aristotle from end to middle
Than a sumptuous wardrobe or a merry fiddle.
For though he knew what learning had to offer
There was little coin to jingle in his coffer.
Whatever he got by touching up a friend            295
On books and learning he would promptly spend
And busily pray for the soul of anybody
Who furnished him the wherewithal for study.
His scholarship was what he truly heeded.
He never spoke a word more than was needed,         300
And that was said with dignity and force,
And quick and brief. He was of grave discourse
Giving new weight to virtue by his speech,
And gladly would he learn and gladly teach.

   There was a Lawyer, cunning and discreet,        305
Who had often been to St. Paul's porch to meet
His clients. He was a Sergeant of the Law,
A man deserving to be held in awe,
Or so he seemed, his manner was so wise.
He had often served as Justice of Assize           310
By the king's appointment, with a broad commission,
For his knowledge and his eminent position.
He had many a handsome gift by way of fee.
There was no buyer of land as shrewd as he.
All ownership to him became fee simple.            315
His titles were never faulty by a pimple.
None was so busy as he with case and cause,
And yet he seemed much busier than he was.
In all cases and decisions he was schooled
That were of record since King William ruled.      320
No one could pick a loophole or a flaw
In any lease or contract he might draw.
Each statute on the books he knew by rote.
He traveled in a plain, silk-belted coat.

   A Franklin traveled in his company.              325
Whiter could never daisy petal be
Than was his beard. His ruddy face gave sign
He liked his morning sop of toast in wine.
He lived in comfort, as he would assure us,
For he was a true son of Epicurus                  330

---

306. *St. Paul's porch*: a meeting place for lawyers and their clients.
315. *fee simple*: owned outright without legal impediments.
320. *King William*: the conqueror, reigned 1066–1087.
326. *daisy petal*: the English daisy, a small white flower; not the same as the American.
330. *Epicurus*: The Greek philosopher whose teaching (presented here in a somewhat debased form) is believed to make pleasure the goal of life.

Who held the opinion that the only measure
Of perfect happiness was simply pleasure.
Such hospitality did he provide,
He was St. Julian to his countryside.
His bread and ale were always up to scratch.      335
He had a cellar none on earth could match.
There was no lack of pasties in his house,
Both fish and flesh, and that so plenteous
That where he lived it snowed of meat and drink.
With every dish of which a man can think,      340
After the various seasons of the year,
He changed his diet for his better cheer.
He had coops of partridges as fat as cream,
He had a fishpond stocked with pike and bream.
Woe to his cook for an unready pot      345
Or a sauce that wasn't seasoned and spiced hot!
A table in his hall stood on display
Prepared and covered through the livelong day.
He presided at court sessions for his bounty
And sat in Parliament often for his county.      350
A well-wrought dagger and a purse of silk
Hung at his belt, as white as morning milk.
He had been a sheriff and county auditor.
On earth was no such rich proprietor!
    There were five Guildsmen, in the livery      355
Of one august and great fraternity,
A Weaver, a Dyer, and a Carpenter,
A Tapestry-maker and a Haberdasher.
Their gear was furbished new and clean as glass.
The mountings of their knives were not of brass      360
But silver. Their pouches were well made and neat,
And each of them, it seemed, deserved a seat
On the platform at the Guildhall, for each one
Was likely timber to make an alderman.
They had goods enough, and money to be spent,      365
Also their wives would willingly consent
And would have been at fault if they had not.
For to be "Madamed" is a pleasant lot,
And to march in first at feasts for being well married,
And royally to have their mantles carried.      370
    For the pilgrimage these Guildsmen brought their own
Cook to boil their chicken and marrow bone
With seasoning powder and capers and sharp spice.
In judging London ale his taste was nice.
He well knew how to roast and broil and fry,      375
To mix a stew, and bake a good meat pie,
Or capon creamed with almond, rice, and egg.
Pity he had an ulcer on his leg!
    A Skipper was with us, his home far in the west.

---

334. *St. Julian:* the patron saint of hospitality.

He came from the port of Dartmouth, as I guessed.                    380
He sat his carthorse pretty much at sea
In a coarse smock that joggled on his knee.
From his neck a dagger on a string hung down
Under his arm. His face was burnished brown
By the summer sun. He was a true good fellow.                        385
Many a time he had tapped a wine cask mellow
Sailing from Bordeaux while the owner slept.
Too nice a point of honor he never kept.
In a sea fight, if he got the upper hand,
Drowned prisoners floated home to every land.                       390
But in navigation, whether reckoning tides,
Currents, or what might threaten him besides,
Harborage, pilotage, or the moon's demeanor,
None was his like from Hull to Cartagena.
He knew each harbor and the anchorage there                         395
From Gotland to the Cape of Finisterre
And every creek in Brittany and Spain,
And he had called his ship the *Madeleine*.
    With us came also an astute Physician.
There was none like him for a disquisition                          400
On the art of medicine or surgery,
For he was grounded in astrology.
He kept his patient long in observation,
Choosing the proper hour for application
Of charms and images by intuition                                   405
Of magic, and the planets' best position.
For he was one who understood the laws
That rule the humors, and could tell the cause
That brought on every human malady,
Whether of hot or cold, or moist or dry.                            410
He was a perfect medico, for sure.
The cause once known, he would prescribe the cure
For he had his druggists ready at a motion
To provide the sick man with some pill or potion—
A game of mutual aid, with each one winning.                        415
Their partnership was hardly just beginning!
He was well versed in his authorities,
Old Aesculapius, Dioscorides,
Rufus, and old Hippocrates, and Galen,
Haly, and Rhazes, and Serapion,                                     420
Averroës, Bernard, Johannes Damascenus,
Avicenna, Gilbert, Gaddesden, Constantinus.
He urged a moderate fare on principle,
But rich in nourishment, digestible;
Of nothing in excess would he admit.                                425

---

394. *Hull:* in England. *Cartagena:* a Spanish port.
396. *Gotland:* a Swedish island. *Cape of Finisterre:* on the Spanish coast.

418–422. a list of eminent medical authorities from ancient Greece, ancient and medieval Arabic civilization, and England in the thirteenth and fourteenth centuries.

He gave but little heed to Holy Writ.
His clothes were lined with taffeta; their hue
Was all of blood red and of Persian blue,
Yet he was far from careless of expense.
He saved his fees from times of pestilence,                430
For gold is a cordial, as physicians hold,
And so he had a special love for gold.

   A worthy woman there was from near the city
Of Bath, but somewhat deaf, and more's the pity.
For weaving she possessed so great a bent                 435
She outdid the people of Ypres and of Ghent.
No other woman dreamed of such a thing
As to precede her at the offering,
Or if any did, she fell in such a wrath
She dried up all the charity in Bath.                      440
She wore fine kerchiefs of old-fashioned air,
And on a Sunday morning, I could swear,
She had ten pounds of linen on her head.
Her stockings were of finest scarlet-red,
Laced tightly, and her shoes were soft and new.           445
Bold was her face, and fair, and red in hue.
She had been an excellent woman all her life
Five men in turn had taken her to wife,
Omitting other youthful company—
But let that pass for now! Over the sea                    450
She had traveled freely; many a distant stream
She crossed, and visited Jerusalem
Three times. She had been at Rome and at Boulogne,
At the shrine of Compostella, and at Cologne.
She had wandered by the way through many a scene          455
Her teeth were set with little gaps between.
Easily on her ambling horse she sat.
She was well wimpled, and she wore a hat
As wide in circuit as a shield or targe.
A skirt swathed up her hips, and they were large.         460
Upon her feet she wore sharp-roweled spurs.
She was a good fellow; a ready tongue was hers.
All remedies of love she knew by name,
For she had all the tricks of that old game.

   There was a good man of the priests's vocation,   465
A poor town Parson of true consecration,
But he was rich in holy thought and work.
Learned he was, in the truest sense a clerk
Who meant Christ's gospel faithfully to preach
And truly his parishioners to teach.                       470
He was a kind man, full of industry,

**434.** *Bath:* a town in the southwest of England.
**436.** *Ypres, Ghent:* towns in Flanders famous for their cloth.
**454.** *Compostella, Cologne:* sites of shrines much visited by pilgrims.
**456.** i.e., gat-toothed; in a woman considered a sign of sexual prowess.
**463.** Chaucer has Ovid's *Love Cures* (*Remedia Amoris*) in mind.

Many times tested by adversity
And always patient. If tithes were in arrears,
He was loth to threaten any man with fears
Of excommunication; past a doubt                                        475
He would rather spread his offering about
To his poor flock, or spend his property.
To him a little meant sufficiency.
Wide was his parish, with houses far asunder,
But he would not be kept by rain or thunder,                            480
If any had suffered a sickness or a blow,
From visiting the farthest, high or low
Plodding his way on foot, his staff in hand.
He was a model his flock could understand,
For first he did and afterward he taught.                               485
That precept from the Gospel he had caught,
And he added as a metaphor thereto,
"If the gold rusts, what will the iron do?"
For if a priest is foul, in whom we trust,
No wonder a layman shows a little rust.                                 490
A priest should take to heart the shameful scene
Of shepherds filthy while the sheep are clean.
By his own purity a priest should give
The example to his sheep, how they should live.
He did not rent his benefice for hire,                                  495
Leaving his flock to flounder in the mire,
And run to London, happiest of goals,
To sing paid masses in St. Paul's for souls,
Or as chaplain from some rich guild take his keep,
But dwelt at home and guarded well his sheep                           500
So that no wolf should make his flock miscarry.
He was a shepherd, and not a mercenary.
And though himself a man of strict vocation
He was not harsh to weak souls in temptation,
Not overbearing nor haughty in his speech,                             505
But wise and kind in all he tried to teach.
By good example and just words to turn
Sinners to heaven was his whole concern.
But should a man in truth prove obstinate,
Whoever he was, of rich or mean estate,                                510
The Parson would give him a snub to meet the case.
I doubt there was a priest in any place
His better. He did not stand on dignity
Nor affect in conscience too much nicety,
But Christ's and his disciples' words he sought                        515
To teach, and first he followed what he taught.
    There was a Plowman with him on the road,
His brother, who had forked up many a load
Of good manure. A hearty worker he,

---

473. *tithes*: payments due to the priest,       495. i.e., rent out his appointment to a
usually a tenth of annual income.                substitute.

Living in peace and perfect charity. 520
Whether his fortune made him smart or smile,
He loved God with his whole heart all the while
And his neighbor as himself. He would undertake,
For every luckless poor man, for the sake
Of Christ to thresh and ditch and dig by the hour 525
And with no wage, if it was in his power.
His tithes on goods and earnings he paid fair.
He wore a coarse, rough coat and rode a mare.
    There also were a Manciple, a Miller,
A Reeve, a Summoner, and a Pardoner, 530
And I—this makes our company complete.
    As tough a yokel as you care to meet
The Miller was. His big-beefed arms and thighs
Took many a ram put up as wrestling prize.
He was a thick, squat-shouldered lump of sins. 535
No door but he could heave it off its pins
Or break it running at it with his head.
His beard was broader than a shovel, and red
As a fat sow or fox. A wart stood clear
Atop his nose, and red as a pig's ear 540
A tuft of bristles on it. Black and wide
His nostrils were. He carried at his side
A sword and buckler. His mouth would open out
Like a great furnace, and he would sing and shout
His ballads and jokes of harlotries and crimes. 545
He could steal corn and charge for it three times,
And yet was honest enough, as millers come,
For a miller, as they say, has a golden thumb.
In white coat and blue hood this lusty clown,
Blowing his bagpipes, brought us out of town. 550
    The Manciple was of a lawyers' college,
And other buyers might have used his knowledge
How to be shrewd provisioners, for whether
He bought on cash or credit, altogether
He managed that the end should be the same: 555
He came out more than even with the game.
Now isn't it an instance of God's grace
How a man of little knowledge can keep pace
In wit with a whole school of learned men?
He had masters to the number of three times ten 560
Who knew each twist of equity and tort;
A dozen in that very Inn of Court
Were worthy to be steward of the estate
To any of England's lords, however great,
And keep him to his income well confined 565
And free from debt, unless he lost his mind,

---

529. *Manciple*: a steward.    dispenser of papal pardons.
530. *Reeve*: farm overseer. *Pardoner*:

Or let him scrimp, if he were mean in bounty;
They could have given help to a whole county
In any sort of case that might befall;
And yet this Manciple could cheat them all! 570
  The Reeve was a slender, fiery-tempered man.
He shaved as closely as a razor can.
His hair was cropped about his ears, and shorn
Above his forehead as a priest's is worn.
His legs were very long and very lean. 575
No calf on his lank spindles could be seen.
But he knew how to keep a barn or bin,
He could play the game with auditors and win.
He knew well how to judge by drought and rain
The harvest of his seed and of his grain. 580
His master's cattle, swine, and poultry flock,
Horses and sheep and dairy, all his stock,
Were altogether in this Reeve's control.
And by agreement, he had given the sole
Accounting since his lord reached twenty years. 585
No man could ever catch him in arrears.
There wasn't a bailiff, shepherd, or farmer working
But the Reeve knew all his tricks of cheating and shirking.
He would not let him draw an easy breath.
They feared him as they feared the very death. 590
He lived in a good house on an open space,
Well shaded by green trees, a pleasant place.
He was shrewder in acquisition than his lord.
With private riches he was amply stored.
He had learned a good trade young by work and will. 595
He was a carpenter of first-rate skill.
On a fine mount, a stallion, dappled gray.
Whose name was Scot, he rode along the way.
He wore a long blue coat hitched up and tied
As if it were a friar's, and at his side 600
A sword with rusty blade was hanging down.
He came from Norfolk, from nearby the town
That men call Bawdswell. As we rode the while,
The Reeve kept always hindmost in our file.
  A Summoner in our company had his place. 605
Red as the fiery cherubim his face.
He was pocked and pimpled, and his eyes were narrow.
He was lecherous and hot as a cock sparrow.
His brows were scabby and black, and thin his beard.
His was a face that little children feared. 610
Brimstone or litharge bought in any quarter,
Quicksilver, ceruse, borax, oil of tartar,

---

605. *Summoner:* He summoned people to appear before the church court (presided over by the archdeacon), and in general acted as a kind of deputy sheriff of the court.

606. *fiery cherubim:* an order of angels; represented with red faces in medieval art.

No salve nor ointment that will cleanse or bite
Could cure him of his blotches, livid white,
Or the nobs and nubbins sitting on his cheeks.                    615
He loved his garlic, his onions, and his leeks.
He loved to drink the strong wine down blood-red.
Then would he bellow as if he had lost his head.
And when he had drunk enough to parch his drouth,
Nothing but Latin issued from his mouth.                         620
He had smattered up a few terms, two or three,
That he had gathered out of some decree—
No wonder; he heard law Latin all the day,
And everyone knows a parrot or a jay
Can cry out "Wat" or "Poll" as well as the pope;                 625
But give him a strange term, he began to grope.
His little store of learning was paid out,
So "*Questio quod juris*" he would shout.
He was a goodhearted bastard and a kind one.
If there were better, it was hard to find one.                   630
He would let a good fellow, for a quart of wine,
The whole year round enjoy his concubine
Scot-free from summons, hearing, fine, or bail,
And on the sly he too could flush a quail.
If he liked a scoundrel, no matter for church law.               635
He would teach him that he need not stand in awe
If the archdeacon threatened with his curse—
That is, unless his soul was in his purse,
For in his purse he would be punished well.
"The purse," he said, "is the archdeacon's hell."               640
Of course I know he lied in what he said.
There is nothing a guilty man should so much dread
As the curse that damns his soul, when, without fail,
The church can save him, or send him off to jail.
He had the young men and girls in his control                    645
Throughout the diocese; he knew the soul
Of youth, and heard their every last design.
A garland big enough to be the sign
Above an alehouse balanced on his head,
And he made a shield of a great round loaf of bread.             650
   There was a Pardoner of Rouncivalle
With him, of the blessed Mary's hospital,
But now come straight from Rome (or so said he).
Loudly he sang, "Come hither, love, to me,"
While the Summoner's counterbass trolled out profound—          655

---

**628.** "Questio quod juris": "The question is, what (part) of the law (applies)."
**643–644.** These lines attempt to render the sense and tone of a passage in which Chaucer says literally that a guilty man should be in dread "because a curse will slay just as absolution saves, and he should also beware of a Significavit." This word, according to Robinson, was the first word of a writ remanding an excommunicated person to prison. [Translator's note.]
**651.** *Rouncivalle:* a religious house near Charing Cross, now part of London.

No trumpet blew with half so vast a sound.
This Pardoner had hair as yellow as wax,
But it hung as smoothly as a hank of flax.
His locks trailed down in bunches from his head,
And he let the ends about his shoulders spread,     660
But in thin clusters, lying one by one.
Of hood, for rakishness, he would have none,
For in his wallet he kept it safely stowed.
He traveled, as he thought, in the latest mode,
Disheveled. Save for his cap, his head was bare,     665
And in his eyes he glittered like a hare.
A Veronica was stitched upon his cap,
His wallet lay before him in his lap
Brimful of pardons from the very seat
In Rome. He had a voice like a goat's bleat.     670
He was beardless and would never have a beard.
His cheek was always smooth as if just sheared.
I think he was a gelding or a mare;
But in his trade, from Berwick down to Ware,
No pardoner could beat him in the race,     675
For in his wallet he had a pillow case
Which he represented as Our Lady's veil;
He said he had a piece of the very sail
St. Peter, when he fished in Galilee
Before Christ caught him, used upon the sea.     680
He had a latten cross embossed with stones
And in a glass he carried some pig's bones,
And with these holy relics, when he found
Some village parson grubbing his poor ground,
He would get more money in a single day     685
Than in two months would come the parson's way.
Thus with his flattery and his trumped-up stock
He made dupes of the parson and his flock.
But though his conscience was a little plastic
He was in church a noble ecclesiastic.     690
Well could he read the Scripture or saint's story,
But best of all he sang the offertory,
For he understood that when this song was sung,
Then he must preach, and sharpen up his tongue
To rake in cash, as well he knew the art,     695
And so he sang out gaily, with full heart.
   Now I have set down briefly, as it was,
Our rank, our dress, our number, and the cause
That made our sundry fellowship begin
In Southwark, at this hospitable inn     700

---

667. *Veronica:* a reproduction of the handkerchief bearing the miraculous impression of Christ's face, said to have been impressed on the handkerchief that St. Veronica gave him to wipe his face with on the way to his crucifixion.

Known as the Tabard, not far from the Bell.
But what we did that night I ought to tell,
And after that our journey, stage by stage,
And the whole story of our pilgrimage.
But first, in justice, do not look askance          705
I plead, nor lay it to my ignorance
If in this matter I should use plain speech
And tell you just the words and style of each,
Reporting all their language faithfully.
For it must be known to you as well as me          710
That whoever tells a story after a man
Must follow him as closely as he can.
If he takes the tale in charge, he must be true
To every word, unless he would find new
Or else invent a thing or falsify.                 715
Better some breadth of language than a lie!
He may not spare the truth to save his brother.
He might as well use one word as another.
In Holy Writ Christ spoke in a broad sense.
And surely his word is without offense             720
Plato, if his pages you can read,
Says let the word be cousin to the deed.
So I petition your indulgence for it
If I have cut the cloth just as men wore it,
Here in this tale, and shown its very weave.       725
My wits are none too sharp, you must believe.
    Our Host gave each of us a cheerful greeting
And promptly of our supper had us eating.
The victuals that he served us were his best.
The wine was potent, and we drank with zest.       730
Our Host cut such a figure, all in all,
He might have been a marshal in a hall.
He was a big man, and his eyes bulged wide.
No sturdier citizen lived in all Cheapside,
Lacking no trace of manhood, bold in speech,       735
Prudent, and well versed in what life can teach,
And with all this he was a jovial man.
And so when supper ended he began
To jolly us, when all our debts were clear.
"Welcome," he said. "I have not seen this year     740
So merry a company in this tavern as now,
And I would give you pleasure if I knew how.
And just this very minute a plan has crossed
My mind that might amuse you at no cost.
    "You go to Canterbury—may the Lord             745
Speed you, and may the martyred saint reward
Your journey! And to while the time away

734. *Cheapside:* a London street.

You mean to talk and pass the time of day,
For you would be as cheerful all alone
As riding on your journey dumb as stone. 750
Therefore, if you'll abide by what I say,
Tomorrow, when you ride off on your way,
Now, by my father's soul, and he is dead,
If you don't enjoy yourselves, cut off my head!
Hold up your hands, if you accept my speech." 755
    Our counsel did not take us long to reach.
We bade him give his orders at his will.
"Well, sirs," he said, "then do not take it ill,
But hear me in good part, and for your sport.
Each one of you, to make our journey short, 760
Shall tell two stories, as we ride, I mean,
Toward Canterbury; and coming home again
Shall tell two other tales he may have heard
Of happenings that some time have occurred.
And the one of you whose stories please us most, 765
Here in this tavern, sitting by this post
Shall sup at our expense while we make merry
When we come riding home from Canterbury.
And to cheer you still the more, I too will ride
With you at my own cost, and be your guide. 770
And if anyone my judgment shall gainsay
He must pay for all we spend along the way.
If you agree, no need to stand and reason.
Tell me, and I'll be stirring in good season."
    This thing was granted, and we swore our pledge 775
To take his judgment on our pilgrimage,
His verdict on our tales, and his advice.
He was to plan a supper at a price
Agreed upon; and so we all assented
To his command, and we were well contented. 780
The wine was fetched; we drank, and went to rest.
    Next morning, when the dawn was in the east,
Up spring our Host, who acted as our cock,
And gathered us together in a flock,
And off we rode, till presently our pace 785
Had brought us to St. Thomas' watering place.
And there our Host began to check his horse.
"Good sirs," he said, "you know your promise, of course.
Shall I remind you what it was about?
If evensong and matins don't fall out, 790
We'll soon find who shall tell us the first tale.
But as I hope to drink my wine and ale,
Whoever won't accept what I decide

783. That is, the Host (in this barnyard image) took charge and got the crowd together.

Pays everything we spend along the ride.
Draw lots, before we're farther from the Inn.                    795
Whoever draws the shortest shall begin.
Sir Knight," said he, "my master, choose your straw
Come here, my lady Prioress, and draw,
And you, Sir Scholar, don't look thoughtful, man!
Pitch in now, everyone!" So all began                            800
To draw the lots, and as the luck would fall
The draw went to the Knight, which pleased us all.
And when this excellent man saw how it stood,
Ready to keep his promise, he said, "Good!
Since it appears that I must start the game,                     805
Why then, the draw is welcome, in God's name.
Now let's ride on, and listen, what I say."
And with that word we rode forth on our way,
And he, with his courteous manner and good cheer,
Began to tell his tale, as you shall hear.                       810

## Prologue to the Miller's Tale*

When the Knight had finished, no one, young or old,
In the whole company, but said he had told
A noble story, one that ought to be
Preserved and kept alive in memory,
Especially the gentlefolk, each one.                             5
Our good Host laughed, and swore, "The game's begun,
The ball is rolling! This is going well.
Let's see who has another tale to tell.
Come, match the Knight's tale if you can, Sir Monk!"
    The Miller, who by this time was so drunk                    10
He looked quite bloodless, and who hardly sat
His horse, he was never one to doff his hat
Or stand on courtesy for any man.
Like Pilate in the Church plays he began
To bellow. "Arms and blood and bones," he swore,                15
"I know a yarn that will even up the score,
A noble one, I'll pay off the Knight's tale!"
    Our Host could see that he was drunk on ale.
"Robin," he said, "hold on a minute, brother.
Some better man shall come first with another.                  20
Let's do this right. You tell yours by and by."

* From *The Portable Chaucer* (Viking
Press). Copyright 1949 by Theodore Morrison.
    1. The Knight's Tale is the first told,
immediately following the General Prologue.
    14–15. *Church plays*: Miracle plays
represented Pilate as a braggart and loud
mouth. His lines were marked by frequent
alliteration.

"God's soul," the Miller told him, "that won't I!
Either I'll speak, or go on my own way."
    "The devil with you! Say what you have to say,"
Answered our Host. "You are a fool. Your head         25
Is overpowered."
              "Now," the Miller said,
"Everyone listen! But first I will propound
That I am drunk, I know it by my sound.
If I can't get my words out, put the blame         30
On Southwark ale, I ask you, in God's name!
For I'll tell a golden legend and a life
Both of a carpenter and of his wife,
How a student put horns on the fellow's head."
    "Shut up and stop your racket," the Reeve said.     35
"Forget your ignorant drunken bawdiness.
It is a sin and a great foolishness
To injure any man by defamation
And to give women such a reputation.
Tell us of other things; you'll find no lack."         40
    Promptly this drunken Miller answered back:
"Oswald, my brother, true as babes are suckled,
The man who has no wife, he is no cuckold.
I don't say for this reason that you are.
There are plenty of faithful wives, both near and far,    45
Always a thousand good for every bad,
And you know this yourself, unless you're mad.
I see you are angry with my tale, but why?
You have a wife; no less, by God, do I.
But I wouldn't, for the oxen in my plow,         50
Shoulder more than I need by thinking how
I may myself, for aught I know, be one.
I'll certainly believe that I am none.
A husband mustn't be curious, for his life,
About God's secrets or about his wife.         55
If she gives him plenty and he's in the clover,
No need to worry about what's left over."
    The Miller, to make the best of it I can,
Refused to hold his tongue for any man,
But told his tale like any low-born clown.        60
I am sorry that I have to set it down,
And all you people, for God's love, I pray,
Whose taste is higher, do not think I say
A word with evil purpose; I must rehearse
Their stories one and all, both better and worse,    65
Or play false with my matter, that is clear.
Whoever, therefore, may not wish to hear,
Turn over the page and choose another tale;
For small and great, he'll find enough, no fail,

Of things from history, touching courtliness,                    70
And virtue too, and also holiness.
If you choose wrong, don't lay it on my head.
You know the Miller couldn't be called well bred.
So with the Reeve, and many more as well,
And both of them had bawdy tales to tell.                        75
Reflect a little, and don't hold me to blame.
There's no sense making earnest out of game.

### The Miller's Tale*

There used to be a rich old oaf who made
His home at Oxford, a carpenter by trade,
And took in boarders. With him used to dwell
A student who had done his studies well,
But he was poor; for all that he had learned,                    5
It was toward astrology his fancy turned.
He knew a number of figures and constructions
By which he could supply men with deductions
If they should ask him at a given hour
Whether to look for sunshine or for shower,                      10
Or want to know whatever might befall,
Events of all sorts, I can't count them all.
   He was known as handy Nicholas, this student.
Well versed in love, he knew how to be prudent,
Going about unnoticed, sly, and sure.                            15
In looks no girl was ever more demure.
Lodged at this carpenter's, he lived alone;
He had a room there that he made his own,
Festooned with herbs, and he was sweet himself
As licorice or ginger. On a shelf                                20
Above his bed's head, neatly stowed apart,
He kept the trappings that went with his art,
His astrolabe, his books—among the rest,
Thick ones and thin ones, lay his *Almagest*—
And the counters for his abacus as well.                         25
Over his cupboard a red curtain fell
And up above a pretty zither lay
On which at night so sweetly would he play
That with the music the whole room would ring.
"Angelus to the Virgin" he would sing                            30
And then the song that's known as "The King's Note."
Blessings were called down on his merry throat!

* From *The Portable Chaucer* (Viking Press). Copyright 1949 by Theodore Morrison.

13. *handy:* Chaucer's word is hendë, implying, I take it, both *ready to hand* and *ingratiating.* Nicholas was a Johnny- on-the-spot and also had a way with him. [Translator's note.]

24. *Almagest:* second century treatise by Ptolemy, an astronomy textbook.

31. *"The King's Note"*: probably a popular song.

So this sweet scholar passed his time, his end
Being to eat and live upon his friend.
    This carpenter had newly wed a wife                                35
And loved her better than he loved his life.
He was jealous, for she was eighteen in age;
He tried to keep her close as in a cage,
For she was wild and young, and old was he
And guessed that he might smack of cuckoldry.                          40
His ignorant wits had never chanced to strike
On Cato's word, that man should wed his like;
Men ought to wed where their conditions point,
For youth and age are often out of joint.
But now, since he had fallen in the snare,                            45
He must, like other men, endure his care.
    Fair this young woman was, her body trim
As any mink, so graceful and so slim.
She wore a striped belt that was all of silk;
A piece-work apron, white as morning milk,                            50
About her loins and down her lap she wore.
White was her smock, her collar both before
And on the back embroidered all about
In coal-black silk, inside as well as out.
And like her collar, her white-laundered bonnet                       55
Had ribbons of the same embroidery on it.
Wide was her silken fillet, worn up high,
And for a fact she had a willing eye.
She plucked each brow into a little bow,
And each one was as black as any sloe.                                60
She was a prettier sight to see by far
Than the blossoms of the early pear tree are,
And softer than the wool of an old wether.
Down from her belt there hung a purse of leather
With silken tassels and with studs of brass.                          65
No man so wise, wherever people pass,
Who could imagine in this world at all
A wench like her, the pretty little doll!
Far brighter was the dazzle of her hue
Than a coin struck in the Tower, fresh and new.                       70
As for her song, it twittered from her head
Sharp as a swallow perching on a shed.
And she could skip and sport as a young ram
Or calf will gambol, following his dam.
Her mouth was sweet as honey-ale or mead                              75
Or apples in the hay, stored up for need.
She was as skittish as an untrained colt,
Slim as a mast and straighter than a bolt.

---

42. *Cato*: Dionysius Cato, the supposed author of a book of maxims employed in elementary education.

70. *Tower*: the Tower of London.

On her simple collar she wore a big brooch-pin
Wide as a shield's boss underneath her chin. 80
High up along her legs she laced her shoes.
She was a pigsney, she was a primrose
For any lord to tumble in his bed
Or a good yeoman honestly to wed.
    Now sir, and again sir, this is how it was: 85
A day came round when handy Nicholas,
While her husband was at Oseney, well away,
Began to fool with this young wife, and play.
These students always have a wily head.
He caught her in between the legs, and said, 90
"Sweetheart, unless I have my will with you
I'll die for stifled love, by all that's true,"
And held her by the haunches, hard. "I vow
I'll die unless you love me here and now,
Sure as my soul," he said, "is God's to save." 95
    She shied just as a colt does in the trave,
And turned her head hard from him, this young wife,
And said, "I will not kiss you, on my life.
Why, stop it now," she said, "stop, Nicholas,
Or I will cry out 'Help, help,' and 'Alas!' 100
Be good enough to take your hands away."
    "Mercy," this Nicholas began to pray,
And spoke so well and poured it on so fast
She promised she would be his love at last,
And swore by Thomas à Becket, saint of Kent, 105
That she would serve him when she could invent
Or spy out some good opportunity.
"My husband is so full of jealousy
You must be watchful and take care," she said,
"Or well I know I'll be as good as dead. 110
You must go secretly about this business."
    "Don't give a thought to that," said Nicholas.
"A student has been wasting time at school
If he can't make a carpenter a fool."
And so they were agreed, these two, and swore 115
To watch their chance, as I have said before.
When Nicholas had spanked her haunches neatly
And done all I have spoken of, he sweetly
Gave her a kiss, and then he took his zither
And loudly played, and sang his music with her. 120
    Now in her Christian duty, one saint's day,
To the parish church this good wife made her way,
And as she went her forehead cast a glow
As bright as noon, for she had washed it so
It glistened when she finished with her work. 125

87. *Oseney*: a town near Oxford.

Serving this church there was a parish clerk
Whose name was Absolom, a ruddy man
With goose-gray eyes and curls like a great fan
That shone like gold on his neatly parted head.
His tunic was light blue and his nose red,　　　　130
And he had patterns that had been cut through
Like the windows of St. Paul's in either shoe.
He wore above his tunic, fresh and gay,
A surplice white as a blossom on a spray.
A merry devil, as true as God can save,　　　　135
He knew how to let blood, trim hair, and shave,
Or write a deed of land in proper phrase,
And he could dance in twenty different ways
In the Oxford fashion, and sometimes he would sing
A loud falsetto to his fiddle string　　　　140
Or his guitar. No tavern anywhere
But he had furnished entertainment there.
Yet his speech was delicate, and for his part
He was a little squeamish toward a fart.
　　　This Absolom, so jolly and so gay,　　　　145
With a censer went about on the saint's day
Censing the parish women one and all.
Many the doting look that he let fall,
And specially on this carpenter's young wife.
To look at her, he thought, was a good life,　　　　150
She was so trim, so sweetly lecherous.
I dare say that if she had been a mouse
And he a cat, he would have made short work
Of catching her. This jolly parish clerk
Had such a heartful of love-hankerings　　　　155
He would not take the women's offerings;
No, no, he said, it would not be polite.
　　　The moon, when darkness fell, shone full and bright
And Absolom was ready for love's sake
With his guitar to be up and awake,　　　　160
And toward the carpenter's, brisk and amorous,
He made his way until he reached the house
A little after the cocks began to crow.
Under a casement he sang sweet and low,
"Dear lady, by your will, be kind to me,"　　　　165
And strummed on his guitar in harmony.
This lovelorn singing woke the carpenter
Who said to his wife, "What, Alison, don't you hear
Absolom singing under our bedroom wall?"
　　　"Yes, God knows, John," she answered, "I hear it all."　　　　170
　　　What would you like? In this way things went on
Till jolly Absolom was woebegone
For wooing her, awake all night and day.

He combed his curls and made himself look gay.
He swore to be her slave and used all means                      175
To court her with his gifts and go-betweens.
He sang and quavered like a nightingale.
He sent her sweet spiced wine and seasoned ale,
Cakes that were piping hot, mead sweet with honey,
And since she was town-bred, he proffered money.              180
For some are won by wealth, and some no less
By blows, and others yet by gentleness.
    Sometimes, to keep his talents in her gaze,
He acted Herod in the mystery plays
High on the stage. But what can help his case?               185
For she so loves this handy Nicholas
That Absolom is living in a bubble.
He has nothing but a laugh for all his trouble.
She leaves his earnestness for scorn to cool
And makes this Absolom her proper fool.                       190
For this is a true proverb, and no lie;
"It always happens that the nigh and sly
Will let the absent suffer." So 'tis said,
And Absolom may rage or lose his head
But just because he was farther from her sight               195
This nearby Nicholas got in his light.
    Now hold your chin up, handy Nicholas,
For Absolom may wail and sing "Alas!"
One Saturday when the carpenter had gone
To Oseney, Nicholas and Alison                                200
Agreed that he should use his wit and guile
This simple jealous husband to beguile.
And if it happened that the game went right
She would sleep in his arms the livelong night,
For this was his desire and hers as well.                    205
At once, with no more words, this Nicholas fell
To working out his plan. He would not tarry,
But quietly to his room began to carry
Both food and drink to last him out a day,
Or more than one, and told her what to say                   210
If her husband asked her about Nicholas.
She must say she had no notion where he was;
She hadn't laid eyes on him all day long;
He must be sick, or something must be wrong;
No matter how her maid had called and cried                  215
He wouldn't answer, whatever might betide.
    This was the plan, and Nicholas kept away,
Shut in his room, for that whole Saturday.
He ate and slept or did as he thought best
Till Sunday, when the sun was going to rest,                 220

184. *Herod:* a role traditionally played as a bully in Miracle plays.

This carpenter began to wonder greatly
Where Nicholas was and what might ail him lately,
"Now, by St. Thomas, I begin to dread
All isn't right with Nicholas," he said.
"He hasn't, God forbid, died suddenly!                               225
The world is ticklish these days, certainly.
Today I saw a corpse to church go past,
A man that I saw working Monday last!
Go up," he told his chore-boy, "call and shout,
Knock with a stone, find what it's all about                         230
And let me know."
                    The boy went up and pounded
And yelled as if his wits had been confounded.
"What, how, what's doing, Master Nicholas?
How can you sleep all day?" But all his fuss                         235
Was wasted, for he could not hear a word.
He noticed at the bottom of a board
A hole the cat used when she wished to creep
Into the room, and through it looked in deep
And finally of Nicholas caught sight.                                240
This Nicholas sat gaping there upright
As though his wits were addled by the moon
When it was new. The boy went down, and soon
Had told his master how he had seen the man.
   The carpenter, when he heard this news, began
To cross himself. "Help us, St. Frideswide!
Little can we foresee what may betide!
The man's astronomy has turned his wit,
Or else he's in some agonizing fit.
I always knew that it would turn out so.                             205
What God has hidden is not for men to know.
Aye, blessed is the ignorant man indeed,
Blessed is he that only knows his creed!
So fared another scholar of the sky,
For walking in the meadows once to spy                              255
Upon the stars and what they might foretell,
Down in a clay-pit suddenly he fell!
He overlooked that! By St. Thomas, though,
I'm sorry for handy Nicholas. I'll go
And scold him roundly for his studying                              260
If so I may, by Jesus, heaven's king!
Give me a staff, I'll pry up from the floor
While you, Robin, are heaving at the door.
He'll quit his books, I think."
                              He took his stand                     265
Outside the room. The boy had a strong hand
And by the hasp he heaved it off at once.
The door fell flat. With gaping countenance

This Nicholas sat studying the air
As still as stone. He was in black despair, 270
The carpenter believed, and hard about
The shoulders caught and shook him, and cried out
Rudely, "What, how! What is it? Look down at us!
Wake up, think of Christ's passion, Nicholas!
I'll sign you with the cross to keep away 275
These elves and things!" And he began to say,
Facing the quarters of the house, each side,
And on the threshold of the door outside,
The night-spell: "Jesu and St. Benedict
From every wicked thing this house protect . . ." 280
   Choosing his time, this handy Nicholas
Produced a dreadful sigh, and said, "Alas,
This world, must it be all destroyed straightway?"
   "What," asked the carpenter, "what's that you say?
Do as we do, we working men, and think 285
Of God."
     Nicholas answered, "Get me a drink,
And afterwards I'll tell you privately
Of something that concerns us, you and me.
I'll tell you only, you among all men." 290
   This carpenter went down and came again
With a draught of mighty ale, a generous quart.
As soon as each of them had drunk his part
Nicholas shut the door and made it fast
And sat down by the carpenter at last 295
And spoke to him. "My host," he said, "John dear,
You must swear by all that you hold sacred here
That not to any man will you betray
My confidence. What I'm about to say
Is Christ's own secret. If you tell a soul 300
You are undone, and this will be the toll:
If you betray me, you shall go stark mad."
   "Now Christ forbid it, by His holy blood,"
Answered this simple man. "I don't go blabbing.
If I say it myself, I have no taste for gabbing. 305
Speak up just as you like, I'll never tell,
Not wife nor child, by Him that harrowed hell."
   "Now, John," said Nicholas, "this is no lie.
I have discovered through astrology,
And studying the moon that shines so bright 310
That Monday next, a quarter through the night,
A rain will fall, and such a mad, wild spate

---

307. *Him*: i.e., Christ, who descended into Hell and led away Adam, Eve, the Patriarchs, John the Baptist, and others, redeeming and releasing them. It was the subject of a number of Miracle plays. The original story comes from the Apocryphal New Testament.

That Noah's flood was never half so great.
This world," he said, "in less time than an hour
Shall drown entirely in that hideous shower.                    315
Yes, every man shall drown and lose his life."
    "Alas," the carpenter answered, "for my wife!
Alas, my Alison! And shall she drown?"
For grief at this he nearly tumbled down,
And said, "But is there nothing to be done?"                    320
    "Why, happily there is, for anyone
Who will take advice," this handy Nicholas said.
"You mustn't expect to follow your own head.
For what said Solomon, whose words were true?
'Proceed by counsel, and you'll never rue.'                     325
If you will act on good advice, no fail,
I'll promise, and without a mast or sail,
To see that she's preserved, and you and I.
Haven't you heard how Noah was kept dry
When, warned by Christ beforehand, he discovered               330
That the whole earth with water should be covered?"
    "Yes," said the carpenter, "long, long ago."
    "And then again," said Nicholas, "don't you know
The grief they all had trying to embark
Till Noah could get his wife into the Ark?                      335
That was a time when Noah, I dare say,
Would gladly have given his best black wethers away
If should could have had a ship herself alone.
And therefore do you know what must be done?
This demands haste, and with a hasty thing                      340
People can't stop for talk and tarrying.
    "Start out and get into the house right off
For each of us a tub or kneading-trough,
Above all making sure that they are large,
In which we'll float away as in a barge.                        345
And put in food enough to last a day.
Beyond won't matter; the flood will fall away
Early next morning. Take care not to spill
A word to your boy Robin, nor to Jill
Your maid. I cannot save her, don't ask why.                    350
I will not tell God's secrets, no, not I.
Let it be enough, unless your wits are mad,
To have as good a grace as Noah had.
I'll save your wife for certain, never doubt it.
Now go along, and make good time about it.                      355
    "But when you have, for her and you and me,
Brought to the house these kneading-tubs, all three,
Then you must hang them under the roof, up high,

---

335. A stock comedy scene in the mys-    have been an avid spectator. [Translator's
tery plays, of which the carpenter would   note.]

To keep our plans from any watchful eye.
When you have done exactly as I've said,                            360
And put in snug our victuals and our bread,
Also an ax to cut the ropes apart
So when the rain comes we can make our start,
And when you've broken a hole high in the gable
Facing the garden plot, above the stable,                          365
To give us a free passage out, each one,
Then, soon as the great fall of rain is done,
You'll swim as merrily, I undertake,
As the white duck paddles along behind her drake.
Then I shall call, "How, Alison! How, John!                        370
Be cheerful, for the flood will soon be gone.'
And 'Master Nicholas, what ho!' you'll say.
'Good morning, I see you clearly, for it's day.'
Then we shall lord it for the rest of life
Over the world, like Noah and his wife.                            375
    "But one thing I must warn you of downright.
Use every care that on that selfsame night
When we have taken ship and climbed aboard,
No one of us must speak a single word,
Nor call, nor cry, but pray with all his heart.                    380
It is God's will. You must hang far apart,
You and your wife, for there must be no sin
Between you, no more in a look than in
The very deed. Go now, the plans are drawn.
Go, set to work, and may God spur you on!                          385
Tomorrow night when all men are asleep
Into our kneading-troughs we three shall creep
And sit there waiting, and abide God's grace.
Go along now, this isn't the time or place
For me to talk at length or sermonize.                             390
The proverb says, 'Don't waste words on the wise.'
You are so wise there is no need to teach you.
Go, save our lives—that's all that I beseech you!"
    This simple carpenter went on his way.
Many a time he said, "Alack the day,"                              395
And to his wife he laid the secret bare.
She knew it better than he; she was aware
What this quaint bargain was designed to buy.
She carried on as if about to die,
And said, "Alas, go get this business done.                        400
Help us escape, or we are dead, each one.
I am your true, your faithful wedded wife.
Go, my dear husband, save us, limb and life!"
    Great things, in all truth, can the emotions be!
A man can perish through credulity                                 405
So deep the print imagination makes.

This simple carpenter, he quails and quakes.
He really sees, according to his notion,
Noah's flood come wallowing like an ocean
To drown his Alison, his pet, his dear.                       410
He weeps and wails, and gone is his good cheer,
And wretchedly he sighs. But he goes off
And gets himself a tub, a kneading-trough,
Another tub, and has them on the sly
Sent home, and there in secret hangs them high              415
Beneath the roof. He made three ladders, these
With his own hands, and stowed in bread and cheese
And a jug of good ale, plenty for a day.
Before all this was done, he sent away
His chore-boy Robin and his wench likewise                  420
To London on some trumped-up enterprise,
And so on Monday, when it drew toward night,
He shut the door without a candlelight
And saw that all was just as it should be,
And shortly they went clambering up, all three.            425
They sat there still, and let a moment pass.
    "Now then, 'Our Father,' mum!" said Nicholas,
And "Mum!" said John, and "Mum!" said Alison,
And piously this carpenter went on
Saying his prayers. He sat there still and straining,      430
Trying to make out whether he heard it raining.
    The dead of sleep, for very weariness,
Fell on this carpenter, as I should guess,
At about curfew time, or little more.
His head was twisted, and that made him snore.             435
His spirit groaned in its uneasiness.
Down from his ladder slipped this Nicholas,
And Alison too, downward she softly sped
And without further word they went to bed
Where the carpenter himself slept other nights.            440
There were the revels, there were the delights!
And so this Alison and Nicholas lay
Busy about their solace and their play
Until the bell for lauds began to ring
And in the chancel friars began to sing.                   445
    Now on this Monday, woebegone and glum
For love, this parish clerk, this Absolom
Was with some friends at Oseney, and while there
Inquired after John the carpenter.
A member of the cloister drew him away                     450
Out of the church, and told him, "I can't say.
I haven't seen him working hereabout
Since Saturday. The abbot sent him out
For timber, I suppose. He'll often go

And stay at the granary a day or so. 455
Or else he's at his own house, possibly.
I can't for certain say where he may be."
　Absolom at once felt jolly and light,
And thought, "Time now to be awake all night,
For certainly I haven't seen him making 460
A stir about his door since day was breaking.
Don't call me a man if when I hear the cock
Begin to crow I don't slip up and knock
On the low window by his bedroom wall.
To Alison at last I'll pour out all 465
My love-pangs, for at this point I can't miss,
Whatever happens, at the least a kiss.
Some comfort, by my word, will come my way.
I've felt my mouth itch the whole livelong day,
And that's a sign of kissing at the least. 470
I dreamed all night that I was at a feast.
So now I'll go and sleep an hour or two,
And then I'll wake and play the whole night through.
　When the first cockcrow through the dark had come
Up rose this jolly lover Absolom 475
And dressed up smartly. He was not remiss
About the least point. He chewed licorice
And cardamom to smell sweet, even before
He combed his hair. Beneath his tongue he bore
A sprig of Paris like a truelove knot. 480
He strolled off to the carpenter's house, and got
Beneath the window. It came so near the ground
It reached his chest. Softly, with half a sound,
He coughed, "My honeycomb, sweet Alison,
What are you doing, my sweet cinnamon? 485
Awake, my sweetheart and my pretty bird,
Awake, and give me from your lips a word!
Little enough you care for all my woe,
How for your love I sweat wherever I go!
No wonder I sweat and faint and cannot eat 490
More than a girl; as a lamb does for the teat
I pine. Yes, truly, I so long for love
I mourn as if I were a turtledove."
　Said she, "You jack-fool, get away from here!
So help me God, I won't sing 'Kiss me, dear!' 495
I love another more than you. Get on,
For Christ's sake, Absolom, or I'll throw a stone.
The devil with you! Go and let me sleep."
　"Ah, that true love should ever have to reap
So evil a fortune," Absolom said. "A kiss, 500
At least, if it can be no more than this,

　480. *sprig of Paris:* a cloverlike plant.

Give me, for love of Jesus and of me."
    "And will you go away for that?" said she.
    "Yes, truly, sweetheart," answered Absolom.
    "Get ready then," she said, "for here I come,"     505
And softly said to Nicholas, "Keep still,
And in a minute you can laugh your fill."
    This Absolom got down upon his knee
And said, "I am a lord of pure degree,
For after this, I hope, comes more to savor.     510
Sweetheart, your grace, and pretty bird, your favor!"
    She undid the window quickly. "That will do,"
She said. "Be quick about it, and get through,
For fear the neighbors will look out and spy."
    Absolom wiped his mouth to make it dry.     515
The night was pitch dark, coal-black all about.
Her rear end through the window she thrust out.
He got no better or worse, did Absolom,
Than to kiss her with his mouth on the bare bum
Before he had caught on, a smacking kiss.     520
    He jumped back, thinking something was amiss.
A woman had no beard, he was well aware,
But what he felt was rough and had long hair.
    "Alas," he cried, "what have you made me do?"
    "Te-hee!" she said, and banged the window to.     525
    Absolom backed away a sorry pace.
    "You've bearded him!" said handy Nicholas.
"God's body, this is going fair and fit!"
    This luckless Absolom heard every bit,
And gnawed his mouth, so angry he became.     530
He said to himself, "I'll square you, all the same."
    But who now scrubs and rubs, who chafes his lips
With dust, with sand, with straw, with cloth and chips
If not this Absolom? "The devil," says he,
"Welcome my soul if I wouldn't rather be     535
Revenged than have the whole town in a sack!
Alas," he cries, "if only I'd held back!"
His hot love had become all cold and ashen.
He didn't have a curse to spare for passion.
From the moment when he kissed her on the ass.     540
That was the cure to make his sickness pass!
He cried as a child does after being whipped;
He railed at love. Then quietly he slipped
Across the street to a smith who was forging out
Parts that the farmers needed round about.     545
He was busy sharpening colter and plowshare
When Absolom knocked as though without a care.
    "Undo the door, Jervice, and let me come."

---

546. *colter*: a turf-cutter on a plow.

"What? Who are you?"
                         "It is I, Absolom."                    550
"Absolom, is it! By Christ's precious tree,
Why are you up so early? Lord bless me,
What's ailing you? Some gay girl has the power
To bring you out, God knows, at such an hour!
Yes, by St. Neot, you know well what I mean!"     555
    Absolom thought his jokes not worth a bean.
Without a word he let them all go by.
He had another kind of fish to fry
Than Jervice guessed. "Lend me this colter here
That's hot in the chimney, friend," he said. "Don't fear,    560
I'll bring it back right off when I am through.
I need it for a job I have to do."
    "Of course," said Jervice. "Why, if it were gold
Or coins in a sack, uncounted and untold,
As I'm a rightful smith, I wouldn't refuse it.    565
But, Christ's foot! how on earth do you mean to use it?"
    "Let that," said Absolom, "be as it may.
I'll let you know tomorrow or next day,"
And took the colter where the steel was cold
And slipped out with it safely in his hold    570
And softly over to the carpenter's wall.
He coughed and then he rapped the window, all
As he had done before.
                        "Who's knocking there?"
Said Alison. "It is a thief, I swear."    575
    "No, no," said he. "God knows, my sugarplum,
My bird, my darling, it's your Absolom.
I've brought a golden ring my mother gave me,
Fine and well cut, as I hope that God will save me.
It's yours, if you will let me have a kiss."    580
    Nicholas had got up to take a piss
And thought he would improve the whole affair.
This clerk, before he got away from there,
Should give *his* ass a smack; and hastily
He opened the window, and thrust out quietly,    585
Buttocks and haunches, all the way, his bum.
Up spoke this clerk, this jolly Absolom:
"Speak, for I don't know where you are, sweetheart."
    Nicholas promptly let fly with a fart
As loud as if a clap of thunder broke,    590
So great he was nearly blinded by the stroke,
And ready with his hot iron to make a pass,
Absolom caught him fairly on the ass.
    Off flew the skin, a good handbreadth of fat
Lay bare, the iron so scorched him where he sat.    595
As for the pain, he thought that he would die,
And like a madman he began to cry.

"Help! Water! Water! Help, for God's own heart!"
At this the carpenter came to with a start.
He heard a man cry "Water!" as if mad.                              600
"It's coming now," was the first thought he had.
"It's Noah's flood, alas, God be our hope!"
He sat up with his ax and chopped the rope
And down at once the whole contraption fell.
He didn't take time out to buy or sell                             605
Till he hit the floor and lay there in a swoon.
      Then up jumped Nicholas and Alison
And in the street began to cry, "Help, ho!"
The neighbors all came running, high and low,
And poured into the house to see the sight.                        610
The man still lay there, passed out cold and white,
For in his tumble he had broken an arm.
But he himself brought on his greatest harm,
For when he spoke he was at once outdone
By handy Nicholas and Alison                                       615
Who told them one and all that he was mad.
So great a fear of Noah's flood he had,
By some delusion, that in his vanity
He had bought himself these kneading-troughs, all three.
And hung them from the roof there, up above,                       620
And he had pleaded with them, for God's love,
To sit there in the loft for company.
      The neighbors laughed at such a fantasy,
And round the loft began to pry and poke
And turned his whole disaster to a joke.                           625
He found it was no use to say a word.
Whatever reason he offered, no one heard.
With oaths and curses people swore him down
Until he passed for mad in the whole town.
Wit, clerk, and student all stood by each other.                   630
They said, "It's clear the man is crazy, brother."
Everyone had his laugh about this feud.
So Alison, the carpenter's wife, got screwed
For all the jealous watching he could try,
And Absolom, he kissed her nether eye,                             635
And Nicholas got his bottom roasted well.
God save this troop! That's all I have to tell.


### Prologue to the Pardoner's Tale*


"In churches," said the Pardoner, "when I preach,
I use, milords, a lofty style of speech
And ring it out as roundly as a bell,

* From *The Portable Chaucer* (Viking Press). Copyright 1949 by Theodore Morrison.

Knowing by rote all that I have to tell.
My text is ever the same, and ever was:                          5
*Radix malorum est cupiditas.*
     "First I inform them whence I come; that done,
I then display my papal bulls, each one.
I show my license first, my body's warrant,
Sealed by the bishop, for it would be abhorrent          10
If any man made bold, though priest or clerk,
To interrupt me in Christ's holy work.
And after that I give myself full scope.
Bulls in the name of cardinal and pope,
Of bishops and of patriarchs I show.                           15
I say in Latin some few words or so
To spice my sermon; it flavors my appeal
And stirs my listeners to greater zeal.
Then I display my cases made of glass
Crammed to the top with rags and bones. They pass      20
For relics with all the people in the place.
I have a shoulder bone in a metal case,
Part of a sheep owned by a holy Jew.
'Good men,' I say, 'heed what I'm telling you:
Just let this bone be dipped in any well                        25
And if cow, calf, or sheep, or ox should swell
From eating a worm, or by a worm be stung,
Take water from this well and wash its tongue
And it is healed at once. And furthermore
Of scab and ulcers and of every sore                           30
Shall every sheep be cured, and that straightway,
That drinks from the same well. Heed what I say:
If the good man who owns the beasts will go,
Fasting, each week, and drink before cockcrow
Out of this well, his cattle shall be brought                  35
To multiply—that holy Jew so taught
Our elders—and his property increase.
     " 'Moreover, sirs, this bone cures jealousies.
Though into a jealous madness a man fell,
Let him cook his soup in water from this well,            40
He'll never, though for truth he knew her sin,
Suspect his wife again, though she took in
A priest, or even two of them or three.
     " 'Now here's a mitten that you all can see.
Whoever puts his hand in it shall gain,                        45
When he sows his land, increasing crops of grain,

6. *Radix . . . cupiditas:* The root of evil is greed.

Be it wheat or oats, provided that he bring
His penny or so to make his offering.
　" 'There is one word of warning I must say,
Good men and women. If any here today　　　　50
Has done a sin so horrible to name
He daren't be shriven of it for the shame,
Or if any woman, young or old, is here
Who has cuckolded her husband, be it clear
They may not make an offering in that case　　55
To these my relics; they have no power nor grace.
But any who is free of such dire blame,
Let him come up and offer in God's name
And I'll absolve him through the authority
That by the pope's bull has been granted me.'　　60
　"By such hornswoggling I've won, year by year,
A hundred marks since being a pardoner.
I stand in my pulpit like a true divine,
And when the people sit I preach my line
To ignorant souls, as you have heard before,　　65
And tell skullduggeries by the hundred more.
Then I take care to stretch my neck well out
And over the people I nod and peer about
Just like a pigeon perching on a shed.
My hands fly and my tongue wags in my head　　70
So busily that to watch me is a joy.
Avarice is the theme that I employ
In all my sermons, to make the people free
In giving pennies—especially to me.
My mind is fixed on what I stand to win　　75
And not at all upon correcting sin.
I do not care, when they are in the grave,
If souls go berry-picking that I could save.
Truth is that evil purposes determine,
And many a time, the origin of a sermon:　　80
Some to please people and by flattery
To gain advancement through hypocrisy,
Some for vainglory, some again for hate.
For when I daren't fight otherwise, I wait
And give him a tongue-lashing when I preach.　　85
No man escapes or gets beyond the reach
Of my defaming tongue, supposing he
Has done a wrong to my brethren or to me.

---

62. *A hundred marks:* probably the equivalent of several thousand dollars in
modern purchasing power.

For though I do not tell his proper name,
People will recognize him all the same. 90
By sign and circumstance I let them learn.
Thus I serve those who have done us an ill turn.
Thus I spit out my venom under hue
Of sanctity, and seem devout and true!
    "But to put my purpose briefly, I confess 95
I preach for nothing but for covetousness.
That's why my text is still and ever was
*Radix malorum est cupiditas.*
For by this text I can denounce, indeed,
The very vice I practice, which is greed. 100
But though that sin is lodged in my own heart,
I am able to make other people part
From avarice, and sorely to repent,
Though that is not my principal intent.
    "Then I bring in examples, many a one, 105
And tell them many a tale of days long done.
Plain folk love tales that come down from of old.
Such things their minds can well report and hold.
Do you think that while I have the power to preach
And take in silver and gold for what I teach 110
I shall ever live in willful poverty?
No, no, that never was my thought, certainly.
I mean to preach and beg in sundry lands.
I won't do any labor with my hands,
Nor live by making baskets. I don't intend 115
To beg for nothing; that is not my end.
I won't ape the apostles; I must eat,
I must have money, wool, and cheese, and wheat,
Though I took it from the meanest wretch's tillage
Or from the poorest widow in a village, 120
Yes, though her children starved for want. In fine,
I mean to drink the liquor of the vine
And have a jolly wench in every town.
But, in conclusion, lords, I will get down
To business: you would have me tell a tale. 125
Now that I've had a drink of corny ale,
By God, I hope the thing I'm going to tell
Is one that you'll have reason to like well.
For though myself a very sinful man,
I can tell a moral tale, indeed I can, 130
One that I use to bring the profits in
While preaching. Now be still, and I'll begin."

## The Pardoner's Tale*

There was a company of young folk living
One time in Flanders, who were bent on giving
Their lives to follies and extravagances,
Brothels and taverns, where they held their dances
With lutes, harps, and guitars, diced at all hours,                5
And also ate and drank beyond their powers,
Through which they paid the devil sacrifice
In the devil's temple with their drink and dice,
Their abominable excess and dissipation.
They swore oaths that were worthy of damnation;                10
It was grisly to be listening when they swore.
The blessed body of our Lord they tore—
The Jews, it seemed to them, had failed to rend
His body enough—and each laughed at his friend
And fellow in sin. To encourage their pursuits                15
Came comely dancing girls, peddlers of fruits,
Singers with harps, bawds and confectioners
Who are the very devil's officers
To kindle and blow the fire of lechery
That is the follower of gluttony.                20
      Witness the Bible, if licentiousness
Does not reside in wine and drunkenness!
Recall how drunken Lot, unnaturally,
With his two daughters lay unwittingly,
So drunk he had no notion what he did.                25
      Herod, the stories tell us, God forbid,
When full of liquor at his banquet board
Right at his very table gave the word
To kill the Baptist, John, though guiltless he.
      Seneca says a good word, certainly.                30
He says there is no difference he can find
Between a man who has gone out of his mind
And one who carries drinking to excess,
Only that madness outlasts drunkenness.
O gluttony, first cause of mankind's fall,                35
Of our damnation the cursed original
Until Christ bought us with his blood again!
How dearly paid for by the race of men
Was this detestable iniquity!

* From *The Portable Chaucer* (Viking Press). Copyright 1949 by Theodore Morrison.
23–25. *drunken Lot . . . did:* Genesis 19:33–35.
26–29. *Herod . . . though guiltless he:* Matthew 14:1–11; Mark 6:14–28.
30–34. *Seneca . . . drunkenness:* in his *Epistles,* Epistle lxxxiii.
35. *gluttony . . . fall:* since the Fall was caused by man's eating the forbidden apple.

This whole world was destroyed through gluttony.   40
   Adam our father and his wife also
From paradise to labor and to woe
Were driven for that selfsame vice, indeed.
As long as Adam fasted—so I read—
He was in heaven; but as soon as he   45
Devoured the fruit of that forbidden tree
Then he was driven out in sorrow and pain.
Of gluttony well ought we to complain!
Could a man know how many maladies
Follow indulgences and gluttonies   50
He would keep his diet under stricter measure
And sit at table with more temperate pleasure.
The throat is short and tender is the mouth,
And hence men toil east, west, and north, and south,
In earth, and air, and water—alas to think—   55
Fetching a glutton dainty meat and drink.
   This is a theme, O Paul, that you well treat:
"Meat unto belly, and belly unto meat,
God shall destroy them both," as Paul has said.
When a man drinks the white wine and the red—   60
This is a foul word, by my soul, to say,
And fouler is the deed in every way—
He makes his throat his privy through excess.
   The Apostle says, weeping for piteousness,
"There are many of whom I told you—at a loss   65
I say it, weeping—enemies of Christ's cross,
Whose belly is their god; their end is death."
O cursed belly! Sack of stinking breath
In which corruption lodges, dung abounds!
At either end of you come forth foul sounds.   70
Great cost it is to fill you, and great pain!
These cooks, how they must grind and pound and strain
And transform substance into accident
To please your cravings, though exorbitant!
From the hard bones they knock the marrow out.   75
They'll find a use for everything, past doubt,
That down the gullet sweet and soft will glide.
The spiceries of leaf and root provide
Sauces that are concocted for delight,
To give a man a second appetite.   80

57–59. *Paul . . . has said:* I Corinthians 6:13.
64–67. *Apostle . . . death.* Philippians 3:18–19.

73. *And . . . accident:* A distinction was made in philosophy between "substance," the real nature of a thing, and "accident," its merely sensory qualities, such as flavor.

But truly, he whom gluttonies entice
Is dead, while he continues in that vice.
    O drunken man, disfigured is your face,
Sour is your breath, foul are you to embrace!
You seem to mutter through your drunken nose          85
The sound of "Samson, Samson," yet God knows
That Samson never indulged himself in wine.
Your tongue is lost, you fall like a stuck swine,
And all the self-respect that you possess
Is gone, for of man's judgment, drunkenness           90
Is the very sepulcher and annihilation.
A man whom drink has under domination
Can never keep a secret in his head.
Now steer away from both the white and red,
And most of all from that white wine keep wide        95
That comes from Lepe. They sell it in Cheapside
And Fish Street. It's a Spanish wine, and sly
To creep in other wines that grow nearby,
And such a vapor it has that with three drinks
It takes a man to Spain; although he thinks           100
He is home in Cheapside, he is far away
At Lepe. Then "Samson, Samson" will he say!
    By God himself, who is omnipotent,
All the great exploits in the Old Testament
Were done in abstinence, I say, and prayer.           105
Look in the Bible, you may learn it there.
    Attila, conqueror of many a place,
Died in his sleep in shame and in disgrace
Bleeding out of his nose in drunkenness.
A captain ought to live in temperateness!             110
And more than this, I say, remember well
The injunction that was laid on Lemuel—
Not Samuel, but Lemuel, I say!
Read in the Bible; in the plainest way
Wine is forbidden to judges and to kings.             115
This will suffice; no more upon these things.
    Now that I've shown what gluttony will do,
Now I will warn you against gambling, too;
Gambling, the very mother of low scheming,
Of lying and forswearing and blaspheming              120
Against Christ's name, of murder and waste as well

---

87. *Samson . . . wine:* Judges 13:4.
96. *Lepe:* a town in Spain noted for
strong wines.
    96–97. *Cheapside and Fish Street:*
in London.

107. *Attila:* leader of the Hun invasion of Europe (fifth century A.D.).
    112. *injunction . . . Lemuel:* Prov-
erbs 31:4–7.

Alike of goods and time; and, truth to tell,
With honor and renown it cannot suit
To be held a common gambler by repute.
The higher a gambler stands in power and place,                          125
The more his name is lowered in disgrace.
If a prince gambles, whatever his kingdom be,
In his whole government and policy
He is, in all the general estimation,
Considered so much less in reputation.                                   130
    Stilbon, who was a wise ambassador,
From Lacedaemon once to Corinth bore
A mission of alliance. When he came
It happened that he found there at a game
Of hazard all the great ones of the land,                                135
And so, as quickly as it could be planned,
He stole back, saying, "I will not lose my name
Nor have my reputation put to shame
Allying you with gamblers. You may send
Other wise emissaries to gain your end,                                   140
For by my honor, rather than ally
My countrymen to gamblers, I will die.
For you that are so gloriously renowned
Shall never with this gambling race be bound
By will of mine or treaty I prepare."                                    145
Thus did this wise philosopher declare.
    Remember also how the Parthians' lord
Sent King Demetrius, as the books record,
A pair of golden dice, by this proclaiming
His scorn, because that king was known for gaming,                       150
And the king of Parthia therefore held his crown
Devoid of glory, value, or renown.
Lords can discover other means of play
More suitable to while the time away.
    Now about oaths I'll say a word or two,                              155
Great oaths and false oaths, as the old books do.
Great swearing is a thing abominable,
And false oaths yet more reprehensible.
Almighty God forbade swearing at all,
Matthew be witness; but specially I call                                 160
The holy Jeremiah on this head.
"Swear thine oaths truly, do not lie," he said.
"Swear under judgment, and in righteousness."
But idle swearing is a great wickedness.

159–160. *Almighty . . . witness:*     161–163. *The holy . . . righteous-*
Matthew 5:34.                           *ness:* Jeremiah 4:2.

Consult and see, and he that understands 165
In the first table of the Lord's commands
Will find the second of his commandments this:
"Take not the Lord's name idly or amiss."
If a man's oaths and curses are extreme,
Vengeance shall find his house, both roof and beam. 170
"By the precious heart of God," and "By his nails"—
"My chance is seven, by Christ's blood at Hailes,
Yours five and three." "Cheat me, and if you do,
By God's arms, with this knife I'll run you through!"—
Such fruit comes from the bones, that pair of bitches: 175
Oaths broken, treachery, murder. For the riches
Of Christ's love, give up curses, without fail,
Both great and small!—Now, sirs, I'll tell my tale.

These three young roisterers of whom I tell
Long before prime had rung from any bell 180
Were seated in a tavern at their drinking,
And as they sat, they heard a bell go clinking
Before a corpse being carried to his grave.
One of these roisterers, when he heard it, gave
An order to his boy: "Go out and try 185
To learn whose corpse is being carried by.
Get me his name, and get it right. Take heed."
"Sir," said the boy, "there isn't any need.
I learned before you came here, by two hours.
He was, it happens, an old friend of yours, 190
And all at once, there on his bench upright
As he was sitting drunk, he was killed last night.
A sly thief, Death men call him, who deprives
All the people in this country of their lives,
Came with his spear and smiting his heart in two 195
Went on his business with no more ado.
A thousand have been slaughtered by his hand
During this plague. And, sir, before you stand
Within his presence, it should be necessary,
It seems to me, to know your adversary. 200
Be evermore prepared to meet this foe.
My mother taught me thus; that's all I know."
"Now by St. Mary," said the innkeeper,
"This child speaks truth. Man, woman, laborer,
Servant, and child the thief has slain this year 205
In a big village a mile or more from here.
I think it is his place of habitation.

---

172. *My . . . seven:* My lucky number is seven. *Hailes:* an abbey in
Gloucestershire, where some of Christ's
blood was believed to be preserved.

It would be wise to make some preparation
Before he brought a man into disgrace."
"God's arms!" this roisterer said. "So that's the case!        210
Is it so dangerous with this thief to meet?
I'll look for him by every path and street,
I vow it, by God's holy bones! Hear me,
Fellows of mine, we are all one, we three.
Let each of us hold up his hand to the other        215
And each of us become his fellow's brother.
We'll slay this Death, who slaughters and betrays.
He shall be slain whose hand so many slays,
By the dignity of God, before tonight!"
    The three together set about to plight        220
Their oaths to live and die each for the other
Just as though each had been to each born brother,
And in their drunken frenzy up they get
And toward the village off at once they set
Which the innkeeper had spoken of before,        225
And many were the grisly oaths they swore.
They rent Christ's precious body limb from limb—
Death shall be dead, if they lay hands on him!
    When they had hardly gone the first half mile,
Just as they were about to cross a stile,        230
An old man, poor and humble, met them there.
The old man greeted them with a meek air
And said, "God bless you, lords, and be your guide."
    "What's this?" the proudest of the three replied.
"Old beggar, I hope you meet with evil grace!        235
Why are you all wrapped up except your face?
What are you doing alive so many a year?"
    The old man at these words began to peer
Into this gambler's face. "Because I can,
Though I should walk to India, find no man,"        240
He said, "in any village or any town,
Who for my age is willing to lay down
His youth. So I must keep my old age still
For as long a time as it may be God's will.
Nor will Death take my life from me, alas!        245
Thus like a restless prisoner I pass
And on the ground, which is my mother's gate,
I walk and with my staff both early and late
I knock and say, 'Dear mother, let me in!
See how I vanish, flesh, and blood, and skin!        250
Alas, when shall my bones be laid to rest?
I would exchange with you my clothing chest,

Mother, that in my chamber long has been
For an old haircloth rag to wrap me in.'
And yet she still refuses me that grace.          255
All white, therefore, and withered is my face.
    "But, sirs, you do yourselves no courtesy
To speak to an old man so churlishly
Unless he had wronged you either in word or deed.
As you yourselves in Holy Writ may read,          260
'Before an aged man whose head is hoar
Men ought to rise.' I counsel you, therefore,
No harm nor wrong here to an old man do,
No more than you would have men do to you
In your old age, if you so long abide.          265
And God be with you, whether you walk or ride!
I must go yonder where I have to go."
    "No, you old beggar, by St. John, not so,"
Said another of these gamblers. "As for me,
By God, you won't get off so easily!          270
You spoke just now of that false traitor, Death,
Who in this land robs all our friends of breath.
Tell where he is, since you must be his spy,
Or you will suffer for it, so say I
By God and by the holy sacrament.          275
You are in league with him, false thief, and bent
On killing us young folk, that's clear to my mind."
    "If you are so impatient, sirs, to find
Death," he replied, "turn up this crooked way,
For in that grove I left him, truth to say,          280
Beneath a tree, and there he will abide.
No boast of yours will make him run and hide.
Do you see that oak tree? Just there you will find
This Death, and God, who bought again mankind,
Save and amend you!" So said this old man;          285
And promptly each of these three gamblers ran
Until he reached the tree, and there they found
Florins of fine gold, minted bright and round,
Nearly eight bushels of them, as they thought.
And after Death no longer then they sought.          290
Each of them was so ravished at the sight,
So fair the florins glittered and so bright,
That down they sat beside the precious hoard.
The worst of them, he uttered the first word.
    "Brothers," he told them, "listen to what I say.          295
My head is sharp, for all I joke and play.

261–262. *'Before . . . rise':* Leviticus 19:32.

Fortune has given us this pile of treasure
To set us up in lives of ease and pleasure.
Lightly it comes, lightly we'll make it go.
God's precious dignity! Who was to know          300
We'd ever tumble on such luck today?
If we could only carry this gold away,
Home to my house, or either one of yours—
For well you know that all this gold is ours—
We'd touch the summit of felicity.               305
But still, by daylight that can hardly be.
People would call us thieves, too bold for stealth,
And they would have us hanged for our own wealth.
It must be done by night, that's our best plan,
As prudently and slyly as we can.                310
Hence my proposal is that we should all
Draw lots, and let's see where the lot will fall,
And the one of us who draws the shortest stick
Shall run back to the town, and make it quick,
And bring us bread and wine here on the sly,     315
And two of us will keep a watchful eye
Over this gold; and if he doesn't stay
Too long in town, we'll carry this gold away
By night, wherever we all agree it's best."
        One of them held the cut out in his fist  320
And had them draw to see where it would fall,
And the cut fell on the youngest of them all.
At once he set off on his way to town,
And the very moment after he was gone
The one who urged this plan said to the other:    325
"You know that by sworn oath you are my brother.
I'll tell you something you can profit by.
Our friend has gone, that's clear to any eye,
And here is gold, abundant as can be,
That we propose to share alike, we three.         330
But if I worked it out, as I could do,
So that it could be shared between us two,
Wouldn't that be a favor, a friendly one?"
        The other answered, "How that can be done,
I don't quite see. He knows we have the gold.     335
What shall we do, or what shall he be told?"
        "Will you keep the secret tucked inside your head?
And in a few words," the first scoundrel said,
"I'll tell you how to bring this end about."
        "Granted," the other told him. "Never doubt,  340
I won't betray you, that you can believe."

"Now," said the first, "we are two, as you pereceive,
And two of us must have more strength than one.
When he sits down, get up as if in fun
And wrestle with him. While you play this game          345
I'll run him through the ribs. You do the same
With your dagger there, and then this gold shall be
Divided, dear friend, between you and me.
Then all that we desire we can fulfill,
And both of us can roll the dice at will."              350
Thus in agreement these two scoundrels fell
To slay the third, as you have heard me tell.

    The youngest, who had started off to town,
Within his heart kept rolling up and down
The beauty of those florins, new and bright.           355
"O Lord," he thought, "were there some way I might
Have all this treasure to myself alone,
There isn't a man who dwells beneath God's throne
Could live a life as merry as mine should be!"
And so at last the fiend, our enemy,                   360
Put in his head that he could gain his ends
If he bought poison to kill off his friends.
Finding his life in such a sinful state,
The devil was allowed to seal his fate.
For it was altogether his intent                       365
To kill his friends, and never to repent.
So off he set, no longer would he tarry,
Into the town, to an apothecary,
And begged for poison; he wanted it because
He meant to kill his rats; besides, there was          370
A polecat living in his hedge, he said,
Who killed his capons; and when he went to bed
He wanted to take vengeance, if he might,
On vermin that devoured him by night.

    The apothecary answered, "You shall have          375
A drug that as I hope the Lord will save
My soul, no living thing in all creation,
Eating or drinking of this preparation
A dose no bigger than a grain of wheat,
But promptly with his death-stroke he shall meet.      380
Die, that he will, and in a briefer while
Than you can walk the distance of a mile,
This poison is so strong and virulent."

    Taking the poison, off the scoundrel went,
Holding it in a box, and next he ran                   385
To the neighboring street, and borrowed from a man

Three generous flagons. He emptied out his drug
In two of them, and kept the other jug
For his own drink; he let no poison lurk
In that! And so all night he meant to work      390
Carrying off the gold. Such was his plan,
And when he had filled them, this accursed man
Retraced his path, still following his design,
Back to his friends with his three jugs of wine.
 But why dilate upon it any more?             395
For just as they had planned his death before,
Just so they killed him, and with no delay.
When it was finished, one spoke up to say:
"Now let's sit down and drink, and we can bury
His body later on. First we'll be merry,"      400
And as he said the words, he took the jug
That, as it happened, held the poisonous drug,
And drank, and gave his friend a drink as well,
And promptly they both died. But truth to tell,
In all that Avicenna ever wrote               405
He never described in chapter, rule, or note
More marvelous signs of poisoning, I suppose,
Than appeared in these two wretches at the close.
Thus they both perished for their homicide,
And thus the traitorous poisoner also died.    410
 O sin accursed above all cursedness,
O treacherous murder, O foul wickedness,
O gambling, lustfulness, and gluttony,
Traducer of Christ's name by blasphemy
And monstrous oaths, through habit and through pride!  415
Alas, mankind! Ah, how may it betide
That you to your Creator, he that wrought you
And even with his precious heart's blood bought you,
So falsely and ungratefully can live?
 And now, good men, your sins may God forgive  420
And keep you specially from avarice!
My holy pardon will avail in this,
For it can heal each one of you that brings
His pennies, silver brooches, spoons, or rings.
Come, bow your head under this holy bull!       425
You wives, come offer up your cloth or wool!
I write your names here in my roll, just so.
Into the bliss of heaven you shall go!
I will absolve you here by my high power,
You that will offer, as clean as in the hour     430

---

405. *Avicenna:* an Arabic physician.

When you were born.—Sirs, thus I preach. And now
Christ Jesus, our souls' healer, show you how
Within his pardon evermore to rest,
For that, I will not lie to you, is best.

    But in my tale, sirs, I forgot one thing.         435
The relics and the pardons that I bring
Here in my pouch, no man in the whole land
Has finer, given me by the pope's own hand.
If any of you devoutly wants to offer
And have my absolution, come and proffer       440
Whatever you have to give. Kneel down right here,
Humbly, and take my pardon, full and clear,
Or have a new, fresh pardon if you like
At the end of every mile of road we strike,
As long as you keep offering ever newly       445
Good coins, not counterfeit, but minted truly.
Indeed it is an honor I confer
On each of you, an authentic pardoner
Going along to absolve you as you ride.
For in the country mishaps may betide—       450
One or another of you in due course
May break his neck by falling from his horse.
Think what security it gives you all
That in this company I chanced to fall
Who can absolve you each, both low and high,       455
When the soul, alas, shall from the body fly!
By my advice, our Host here shall begin,
For he's the man enveloped most by sin.
Come, offer first, Sir Host, and once that's done,
Then you shall kiss the relics, every one,       460
Yes, for a penny! Come, undo your purse!

    "No, no," said he. "Then I should have Christ's curse!
I'll do nothing of the sort, for love or riches!
You'd make me kiss a piece of your old britches
And for a saintly relic make it pass       465
Although it had the tincture of your ass.
By the cross St. Helen found in the Holy Land,
I wish I had your balls here in my hand
For relics! Cut 'em off, and I'll be bound
If I don't help you carry them around.       470
I'll have the things enshrined in a hog's turd!"

    The Pardoner did not answer; not a word,
He was so angry, could he find to say.

467. *St. Helen:* mother of Constantine the Great; believed to have found the
True Cross.

"Now," said our Host, "I will not try to play
With you, nor any other angry man."                          475
   Immediately the worthy Knight began,
When he saw that all the people laughed, "No more,
This has gone far enough. Now as before,
Sir Pardoner, be gay, look cheerfully,
And you, Sir Host, who are so dear to me,                    480
Come, kiss the Pardoner, I beg of you,
And Pardoner, draw near, and let us do
As we've been doing, let us laugh and play."
And so they kissed, and rode along their way.

### [The Knight's Interruption of the Monk's Tale]*

"Stop!" cried the Knight. "No more of this, good sir!
You have said plenty, and much more, for sure,
For only a little such lugubriousness
Is plenty for a lot of folk, I guess.
I say for me it is a great displeasure,                       5
When men have wealth and comfort in good measure,
To hear how they have tumbled down the slope,
And the opposite is a solace and a hope,
As when a man begins in low estate
And climbs the ladder and grows fortunate,                   10
And stands there firm in his prosperity.
That is a welcome thing, it seems to me,
And of such things it would be good to tell."
   "Well said," our Host declared. "By St. Paul's bell,
You speak the truth; this Monk's tongue is too loud.         15
He told how fortune covered with a cloud—
I don't know what-all; and of tragedy
You heard just now, and it's no remedy,
When things are over and done with, to complain.
Besides, as you have said, it is a pain                      20
To hear of misery; it is distressing.
Sir Monk, no more, as you would have God's blessing.
This company is all one weary sigh.
Such talking isn't worth a butterfly,
For where's the amusement in it, or the game?               25
And so, Sir Monk, or Don Pierce by your name,
I beg you heartily, tell us something else.
Truly, but for the jingling of your bells
That from your bridle hang on every side,
By Heaven's King, who was born for us and died,            30

---

* From *The Portable Chaucer* (Viking Press). Copyright 1949 by Theodore
Morrison.

I should long since have tumbled down in sleep,
Although the mud had never been so deep,
And then you would have told your tale in vain;
For certainly, as these learned men explain,
When his audience have turned their backs away,          35
It doesn't matter what a man may say.
I know well I shall have the essence of it
If anything is told here for our profit.
A tale of hunting, sir, pray share with us."
    "No," said the Monk, "I'll not be frivolous.           40
Let another tell a tale, as I have told."
    Then spoke our Host, with a rude voice and bold,
And said to the Nun's Priest, "Come over here,
You priest, come hither, you Sir John, draw near!
Tell us a thing to make our spirits glad.                  45
Be cheerful, though the jade you ride is bad.
What if your horse is miserable and lean?
If he will carry you, don't care a bean!
Keep up a joyful heart, and look alive."
    "Yes, Host," he answered, "as I hope to thrive,        50
If I weren't merry, I know I'd be reproached."
And with no more ado his tale he broached,
And this is what he told us, every one,
This precious priest, this goodly man, Sir John.

## The Nun's Priest's Tale*

Once a poor widow, aging year by year,
Lived in a tiny cottage that stood near
A clump of shade trees rising in a dale.
This widow, of whom I tell you in my tale,
Since the last day that she had been a wife               5
Had led a very patient, simple life.
She had but few possessions to content her.
By thrift and husbandry of what God sent her
She and two daughters found the means to dine.
She had no more than three well-fattened swine,          10
As many cows, and one sheep, Moll by name.
Her bower and hall were black from the hearth-flame
Where she had eaten many a slender meal.
No dainty morsel did her palate feel
And no sharp sauce was needed with her pottage.          15
Her table was in keeping with her cottage.
Excess had never given her disquiet.

* From *The Portable Chaucer* (Viking Press). Copyright 1949 by **Theodore** Morrison.

Her only doctor was a moderate diet,
And exercise, and a heart that was contented.
If she did not dance, at least no gout prevented;    20
No apoplexy had destroyed her head.
She never drank wine, whether white or red.
She served brown bread and milk, loaves white or black,
Singed bacon, all this with no sense of lack,
And now and then an egg or two. In short,    25
She was a dairy woman of a sort.
    She had a yard, on the inside fenced about
With hedges, and an empty ditch without,
In which she kept a cock, called Chanticleer.
In all the realm of crowing he had no peer.    30
His voice was merrier than the merry sound
Of the church organ grumbling out its ground
Upon a saint's day. Stouter was this cock
In crowing than the loudest abbey clock.
Of astronomy instinctively aware,    35
He kept the sun's hours with celestial care,
For when through each fifteen degrees it moved,
He crowed so that it couldn't be improved.
His comb, like a crenelated castle wall,
Red as fine coral, stood up proud and tall.    40
His bill was black; like polished jet it glowed,
And he was azure-legged and azure-toed.
As lilies were his nails, they were so white;
Like burnished gold his hue, it shone so bright.
This cock had in his princely sway and measure    45
Seven hens to satisfy his every pleasure,
Who were his sisters and his sweethearts true,
Each wonderfully like him in her hue,
Of whom the fairest-feathered throat to see
Was fair Dame Partlet. Courteous was she,    50
Discreet, and always acted debonairly.
She was sociable, and bore herself so fairly,
Since the very time that she was seven nights old,
The heart of Chanticleer was in her hold
As if she had him locked up, every limb.    55
He loved her so that all was well with him.
It was a joy, when up the sun would spring,
To hear them both together sweetly sing,
"My love has gone to the country, far away!"
For as I understand it, in that day    60
The animals and birds could sing and speak.
    Now as this cock, one morning at daybreak,

With each of the seven hens that he called spouse,
Sat on his perch inside the widow's house,
And next him fair Dame Partlet, in his throat                    65
This Chanticleer produced a hideous note
And groaned like a man who is having a bad dream;
And Partlet, when she heard her husband scream,
Was all aghast, and said, "Soul of my passion,
What ails you that you groan in such a fashion?                  70
You are always a sound sleeper. Fie, for shame!"
  And Chanticleer awoke and answered, "Dame,
Take no offense, I beg you, on this score.
I dreamt, by God, I was in a plight so sore
Just now, my heart still quivers from the fright.               75
Now God see that my dream turns out all right
And keep my flesh and body from foul seizure!
I dreamed I was strutting in our yard at leisure
When there I saw, among the weeds and vines,
A beast, he was like a hound, and had designs                    80
Upon my person, and would have killed me dead.
His coat was not quite yellow, not quite red,
And both his ears and tail were tipped with black
Unlike the fur along his sides and back.
He had a small snout and a fiery eye.                            85
His look for fear still makes me almost die.
This is what made me groan, I have no doubt."
  "For shame! Fie on you, faint heart!" she burst out.
"Alas," she said, "by the great God above,
Now you have lost my heart and all my love!                      90
I cannot love a coward, as I'm blest!
Whatever any woman may protest,
We all want, could it be so, for our part,
Husbands who are wise and stout of heart,
No blabber, and no niggard, and no fool,                         95
Nor afraid of every weapon or sharp tool,
No braggart either, by the God above!
How dare you say, for shame, to your true love
That there is anything you ever feared?
Have you no man's heart, when you have a beard?                 100
Alas, and can a nightmare set you screaming?
God knows there's only vanity in dreaming!
Dreams are produced by such unseemly capers
As overeating; they come from stomach vapors
When a man's humors aren't behaving right                       105
From some excess. This dream you had tonight,
It comes straight from the superfluity

Of your red choler, certain as can be,
That causes people terror in their dreams
Of darts and arrows, and fire in red streams, 110
And of red beasts, for fear that they will bite,
Of little dogs, or of being in a fight;
As in the humor of melancholy lies
The reason why so many a sleeper cries
For fear of a black bull or a black bear 115
Or that black devils have him by the hair.
Through other humors also I could go
That visit many a sleeping man with woe,
But I will finish as quickly as I can.

 "Cato, that has been thought so wise a man, 120
Didn't he tell us, 'Put no stock in dreams'?
Now, sir," she said, "when we fly down from our beams,
For God's sake, go and take a laxative!
On my salvation, as I hope to live,
I give you good advice, and no mere folly: 125
Purge both your choler and your melancholy!
You mustn't wait or let yourself bog down,
And since there is no druggist in this town
I shall myself prescribe for what disturbs
Your humors, and instruct you in the herbs 130
That will be good for you. For I shall find
Here in our yard herbs of the proper kind
For purging you both under and above.
Don't let this slip your mind, for God's own love!
Yours is a very choleric complexion. 135
When the sun is in the ascendant, my direction
Is to beware those humors that are hot.
Avoid excess of them; if you should not,
I'll bet a penny, as a true believer,
You'll die of ague, or a tertian fever. 140
A day or so, if you do as I am urging,
You shall have worm-digestives, before purging
With fumitory or with hellebore
Or other herbs that grow here by the score;
With caper-spurge, or with the goat-tree berry 145
Or the ground-ivy, found in our yard so merry.
Peck 'em up just as they grow, and eat 'em in!
Be cheerful, husband, by your father's kin!
Don't worry about a dream. I say no more."

 "Madame," he answered, "thanks for all your lore. 150

108. *choler:* one of the four humors,  140. *tertian:* recurring every third
or fluids, composing the body, according  day.
to ancient medical theory.

But still, to speak of Cato, though his name
For wisdom has enjoyed so great a fame,
And though he counseled us there was no need
To be afraid of dreams, by God, men read
Of many a man of more authority                               155
Than this Don Cato could pretend to be
Who in old books declare the opposite,
And by experience they have settled it,
That dreams are omens and prefigurations
Both of good fortune and of tribulations                      160
That life and its vicissitudes present.
This question leaves no room for argument.
The very upshot makes it plain, indeed.
    "One of the greatest authors that men read
Informs us that two fellow travelers went,                    165
Once on a time, and with the best intent,
Upon a pilgrimage, and it fell out
They reached a town where there was such a rout
Of people, and so little lodging space,
They could not find even the smallest place                   170
Where they could both put up. So, for that night,
These pilgrims had to do as best they might,
And since they must, they parted company.
Each of them went off to his hostelry
And took his lodging as his luck might fall.                   175
Among plow oxen in a farmyard stall
One of them found a place, though it was rough.
His friend and fellow was lodged well enough
As his luck would have it, or his destiny
That governs all us creatures equally.                        180
And so it happened, long before the day,
He had a dream as in his bed he lay.
He dreamed that his parted friend began to call
And said, 'Alas, for in an ox's stall
This night I shall be murdered where I lie.                    185
Come to my aid, dear brother, or I die.
Come to me quickly, come in haste!' he said.
He started from his sleep, this man, for dread,
But when he had wakened, he rolled back once more
And on this dream of his he set no store.                      190
As a vain thing he dismissed it, unconcerned.
Twice as he slept that night the dream returned,
And still another and third time his friend

---

151 ff. *to speak of Cato . . .*: In
refuting Cato, Chanticleer gives a long
account of authorities who have pronounced in favor of the truth of
dreams.

Came in a dream and said, 'I have met my end!
Look on my wounds! They are bloody, deep, and wide. 195
Now rise up early in the morningtide
And at the west gate of the town,' said he,
'A wagon with a load of dung you'll see.
Have it arrested boldly. Do as bidden,
For underneath you'll find my body hidden. 200
My money caused my murder, truth to tell,'
And told him each detail of how he fell,
With piteous face, and with a bloodless hue.
And do not doubt it, he found the dream was true,
For on the morrow, as soon as it was day, 205
To the place where his friend had lodged he made his way,
And no sooner did he reach this ox's stall
Than for his fellow he began to call.
   "Promptly the stableman replied, and said,
Your friend is gone, sir. He got out of bed 210
And left the town as soon as day began.'
   "At last suspicion overtook this man.
Remembering his dreams, he would not wait,
But quickly went and found at the west gate,
Being driven to manure a farmer's land 215
As it might seem, a dung cart close at hand
That answered the description every way,
As you yourself have heard the dead man say.
And he began to shout courageously
For law and vengeance on this felony. 220
'My friend was killed this very night! He lies
Flat in this load of dung, with staring eyes.
I call on those who should keep rule and head,
The magistrates and governors here,' he said.
'Alas! Here lies my fellow, done to death!' 225
   "Why on this tale should I waste further breath?
The people sprang and flung the cart to ground
And in the middle of the dung they found
The dead man, while his murder was still new.
   "O blessed God, thou art so just and true, 230
Murder, though secret, ever thou wilt betray!
Murder will out, we see it day by day.
Murder so loathsome and abominable
To God is, who is just and reasonable,
That he will never suffer it to be 235
Concealed, though it hide a year, or two, or three.
Murder will out; to this point it comes down.
   "Promptly the magistrates who ruled that town

Have seized the driver, and put him to such pain.
And the stableman as well, that under strain                    240
Of torture they were both led to confess
And hanged by the neck-bone for their wickedness.
    "Here's proof enough that dreams are things to dread!
And in the same book I have also read,
In the very chapter that comes right after this—              245
I don't speak idly, by my hope of bliss—
Two travelers who for some reason planned
To cross the ocean to a distant land
Found that the wind, by an opposing fate,
Blew contrary, and forced them both to wait                    250
In a fair city by a harborside.
But one day the wind changed, toward eventide,
And blew just as it suited them instead.
Cheerfully these travelers went to bed
And planned to sail the first thing in the morning.            255
But to one of them befell a strange forewarning
And a great marvel. While asleep he lay,
He dreamed a curious dream along toward day.
He dreamed that a man appeared at his bedside
And told him not to sail, but wait and bide.                   260
'Tomorrow,' he told the man, 'if you set sail,
You shall be drowned. I have told you my whole tale.'
He woke, and of this warning he had met
He told his friend, and begged him to forget
His voyage, and to wait that day and bide.                     265
His friend, who was lying close at his bedside,
Began to laugh, and told him in derision,
'I am not so flabbergasted by a vision
As to put off my business for such cause.
I do not think your dream is worth two straws!                 270
For dreams are but a vain absurdity.
Of apes and owls and many a mystery
People are always dreaming, in a maze
Of things that never were seen in all their days
And never shall be. But I see it's clear                       275
You mean to waste your time by waiting here.
I'm sorry for that, God knows; and so good day.'
With this he took his leave and went his way.
But not the half his course had this man sailed—
I don't know why, nor what it was that failed—                280
When by an accident the hull was rent
And ship and man under the water went
In full view of the vessels alongside

That had put out with them on the same tide.
Now then, fair Partlet, whom I love so well,                          285
From old examples such as these I tell
You may see that none should give too little heed
To dreams; for I say seriously, indeed,
That many a dream is too well worth our dread.
    "Yes, in St. Kenelm's life I have also read—                      290
He was the son of Cynewulf, the king
Of Mercia—how this Kenelm dreamed a thing.
One day, as the time when he was killed drew near,
He saw his murder in a dream appear.
His nurse explained his dream in each detail,                        295
And warned him to be wary without fail
Of treason; yet he was but seven years old,
And therefore any dream he could but hold
Of little weight, in heart he was so pure.
I'd give my shirt, by God, you may be sure,                          300
If you had read his story through like me!
    "Moreover, Partlet, I tell you truthfully,
Macrobius writes—and by his book we know
The African vision of great Scipio—
Confirming dreams, and holds that they may be                        305
Forewarnings of events that men shall see.
Again, I beg, look well at what is meant
By the Book of Daniel in the Old Testament,
Whether *he* held that dreams are vanity!
Read also about Joseph. You shall see                                310
That dreams, or some of them—I don't say all—
Warn us of things that afterward befall.
Think of the king of Egypt, Don Pharaoh;
Of his butler and his baker think also,
Whether they found that dreams have no result.                       315
Whoever will search through kingdoms and consult
Their histories reads many a wondrous thing
Of dreams. What about Croesus, Lydian king—
Didn't he dream he was sitting on a tree,
Which meant he would be hanged? Andromache,                          320
The woman who was once great Hector's wife,
On the day that Hector was to lose his life,
The very night before his blood was spilled
She dreamed of how her husband would be killed
If he went out to battle on that day.                                325
She warned him; but he would not heed nor stay.
In spite of her he rode out on the plain,
And by Achilles he was promptly slain.

But all that story is too long to tell,
And it is nearly day. I must not dwell                                   330
Upon this matter. Briefly, in conclusion,
I say this dream will bring me to confusion
And mischief of some sort. And furthermore,
On laxatives, I say, I set no store,
For they are poisonous, I'm sure of it.                                  335
I do not trust them! I like them not one bit!
  "Now let's talk cheerfully, and forget all this.
My pretty Partlet, by my hope of bliss,
In one thing God has sent me ample grace,
For when I see the beauty of your face,                                  340
You are so scarlet-red about the eye,
It is enough to make my terrors die.
For just as true as *In principio*
*Mulier est hominis confusio*—
And Madame, what this Latin means is this:                              345
'Woman is man's whole comfort and true bliss'—
When I feel you soft at night, and I beside you,
Although it's true, alas, I cannot ride you
Because our perch is built so narrowly,
I am then so full of pure felicity                                       350
That I defy whatever sort of dream!"
  And day being come, he flew down from the beam,
And with him his hens fluttered, one and all;
And with a "cluck, cluck" he began to call
His wives to where a kernel had been tossed.                            355
He was a prince, his fears entirely lost.
The morning had not passed the hour of prime
When he treaded Partlet for the twentieth time.
Grim as a lion he strolled to and fro,
And strutted only on his either toe.                                     360
He would not deign to set foot on the ground.
"Cluck, cluck," he said, whenever he had found
A kernel, and his wives came running all.
Thus royal as a monarch in his hall
I leave to his delights this Chanticleer,                               365
And presently the sequel you shall hear.
  After the month in which the world began,
The month of March, when God created man,
Had passed, and when the season had run through
Since March began just thirty days and two,                             370
It happened that Chanticleer, in all his pride,

343–344. *In . . . confusio:* As sure
as gospel, woman is man's ruin.

368. *The month . . . man:* Man
was thought to have been created at
the time of the spring equinox.

While his seven hens were walking by his side,
Lifted his eyes, beholding the bright sun,
Which in the sign of Taurus had then run
Twenty and one degrees and somewhat more,          375
And knew by instinct, not by learned lore,
It was the hour of prime. He raised his head
And crowed with lordly voice. "The sun," he said,
"Forty and one degrees and more in height
Has climbed the sky. Partlet, my world's delight,      380
Hear all these birds, how happily they sing,
And see the pretty flowers, how they spring.
With solace and with joy my spirits dance!"
But suddenly he met a sore mischance,
For in the end joys ever turn to woes.             385
Quickly the joys of earth are gone, God knows,
And could a rhetorician's art indite it,
He would be on solid ground if he should write it,
In a chronicle, as true notoriously!
Now every wise man, listen well to me.             390
This story is as true, I undertake,
As the very book of Lancelot of the Lake
On which the women set so great a store.
Now to my matter I will turn once more.

A sly iniquitous fox, with black-tipped ears,       395
Who had lived in the neighboring wood for some three years,
His fated fancy swollen to a height,
Had broken through the hedges that same night
Into the yard where in his pride sublime
Chanticleer with his seven wives passed the time.     400
Quietly in a bed of herbs he lay
Till it was past the middle of the day,
Waiting his hour on Chanticleer to fall
As gladly do these murderers, one and all,
Who lie in wait, concealed, to murder men.          405
O murderer, lurking traitorous in your den!
O new Iscariot, second Ganelon,
False hypocrite, Greek Sinon, who brought on
The utter woe of Troy and all her sorrow!
O Chanticleer, accursed be that morrow             410
When to the yard you flew down from the beams!
That day, as you were well warned in your dreams,
Would threaten you with dire catastrophe.
But that which God foresees must come to be,

377. *prime:* nine.                    *of Roland.*
407. *Ganelon:* traitor in the *Song*      408. *Sinon:* traitor at Troy.

As there are certain scholars who aver. ₄₁₅
Bear witness, any true philosopher,
That in the schools there has been great altercation
Upon this question, and much disputation
By a hundred thousand scholars, man for man.
I cannot sift it down to the pure bran ₄₂₀
As can the sacred Doctor, Augustine,
Or Boëthius, or Bishop Bradwardine,
Whether God's high foreknowledge so enchains me
I needs must do a thing as it constrains me—
"Needs must"—that is, by plain necessity; ₄₂₅
Or whether a free choice is granted me
To do it or not do it, either one,
Though God must know all things before they are done;
Or whether his foresight nowise can constrain
Except contingently, as some explain; ₄₃₀
I will not labor such a high concern.
My tale is of a cock, as you shall learn,
Who took his wife's advice, to his own sorrow,
And walked out in the yard that fatal morrow.
Women have many times, as wise men hold, ₄₃₅
Offered advice that left men in the cold.
A woman's counsel brought us first to woe
And out of Paradise made Adam go
Where he lived a merry life and one of ease.
But since I don't know whom I may displease ₄₄₀
By giving women's words an ill report,
Pass over it; I only spoke in sport.
There are books about it you can read or skim in,
And you'll discover what they say of women.
I'm telling you the cock's words, and not mine. ₄₄₅
Harm in no woman at all can I divine.

Merrily bathing where the sand was dry
Lay Partlet, with her sisters all near by,
And Chanticleer, as regal as could be,
Sang merrily as the mermaid in the sea; ₄₅₀
For the *Physiologus* itself declares
That they know how to sing the merriest airs.
And so it happened that as he fixed his eye
Among the herbs upon a butterfly,
He caught sight of this fox who crouched there low. ₄₅₅

---

421–422. *Augustine:* St. Augustine (354–430), the great Church Father. *Boëthius:* author of the *Consolation of Philosophy* (*De consolatione philosophiae*), one of the most popular works of the Middle Ages; written in the early sixth century. *Bradwardine:* archbishop of Canterbury in Chaucer's boyhood.
451. *Physiologus:* a collection of nature lore.

He felt no impulse then to strut or crow,
But cried "cucock!" and gave a fearful start
Like a man who has been frightened to the heart.
For instinctively, if he should chance to see
His opposite, a beast desires to flee,                    460
Even the first time that it meets his eye.
    This Chanticleer, no sooner did he spy
The fox than promptly enough he would have fled.
But "Where are you going, kind sir?" the fox said.
"Are you afraid of me, who am your friend?                465
Truly, I'd be a devil from end to end
If I meant you any harm or villainy.
I have not come to invade your privacy.
In truth, the only reason that could bring
This visit of mine was just to hear you sing.            470
Beyond a doubt, you have as fine a voice
As any angel who makes heaven rejoice.
Also you have more feeling in your note
Than Boëthius, or any tuneful throat.
Milord your father once—and may God bless                475
His soul—your noble mother too, no less,
Have been inside my house, to my great ease.
And verily sir, I should be glad to please
You also. But for singing, I declare,
As I enjoy my eyes, that precious pair,                  480
Save you, I never heard a man so sing
As your father did when night was on the wing.
Straight from the heart, in truth, came all his song,
And to make his voice more resonant and strong
He would strain until he shut his either eye,            485
So loud and lordly would he make his cry,
And stand up on his tiptoes therewithal
And stretch his neck till it grew long and small.
He had such excellent discretion, too,
That whether his singing, all the region through,        490
Or his wisdom, there was no one to surpass.
I read in that old book, *Don Burnel the Ass*,
Among his verses once about a cock
Hit on the leg by a priest who threw a rock
When he was young and foolish; and for this              495
He caused the priest to lose his benefice.

---

474. *Boëthius:* He was also author of
a treatise on music.
492. *Don Burnel the Ass:* a twelfth-
century Latin work by the Englishman
Nigel Wireker.
    496. *He . . . benefice:* by failing to
wake him with his crowing.

But no comparison, in all truth, lies
Between your father, so prudent and so wise,
And this other cock, for all his subtlety.
Sing, sir! Show me, for holy charity, 500
Can you imitate your father, that wise man?"
   Blind to all treachery, Chanticleer began
To beat his wings, like one who cannot see
The traitor, ravished by his flattery.
   Alas, you lords, about your court there slips 505
Many a flatterer with deceiving lips
Who can please you more abundantly, I fear,
Than he who speaks the plain truth to your ear.
Read in Ecclesiastes, you will see
What flatterers are. Lords, heed their treachery! 510
   This Chanticleer stood tiptoe at full height.
He stretched his neck, he shut his eyelids tight,
And he began to crow a lordly note.
The fox, Don Russell, seized him by the throat
At once, and on his back bore Chanticleer 515
Off toward his den that in the grove stood near,
For no one yet had threatened to pursue.
   O destiny, that no man may eschew!
Alas, that he left his safe perch on the beams!
Alas, that Partlet took no stock in dreams! 520
And on a Friday happened this mischance!
   Venus, whose pleasures make the whole world dance,
Since Chanticleer was ever your true servant,
And of your rites with all his power observant
For pleasure rather than to multiply, 525
Would you on Friday suffer him to die?
   Geoffrey, dear master of the poet's art,
Who when your Richard perished by a dart
Made for your king an elegy so burning,
Why have I not your eloquence and learning 530
To chide, as you did, with a heart so filled,
Fridays? For on a Friday he was killed.
Then should I show you how I could complain
For Chanticleer in all his fright and pain!
   In truth, no lamentation ever rose, 535
No shriek of ladies when before its foes
Ilium fell, and Pyrrhus with drawn blade

---

509. *Ecclesiastes:* This should apparently be Ecclesiasticus (a book of the Old Testament Apocrypha) 12:10 ff; 27:26.

527. *Geoffrey:* Geoffrey de Vinsauf, author of a treatise on poetry, with specimens, among them an elegy on Richard I.

Had seized King Priam by the beard and made
An end of him—the *Aeneid* tells the tale—
Such as the hens made with their piteous wail                540
In their enclosure, seeing the dread sight
Of Chanticleer. But at the shrillest height
Shrieked Partlet. She shrieked louder than the wife
Of Hasdrubal, when her husband lost his life
And the Romans burned down Carthage; for her state         545
Of torment and of frenzy was so great
She willfully chose the fire for her part,
Leaped in, and burned herself with steadfast heart.

     Unhappy hens, you shrieked as when for pity,
While the tyrant Nero put to flames the city               550
Of Rome, rang out the shriek of senators' wives
Because their husbands had all lost their lives;
This Nero put to death these innocent men.
But I will come back to my tale again.

     Now this good widow and her two daughters heard        555
These woeful hens shriek when the crime occurred,
And sprang outdoors as quickly as they could
And saw the fox, who was making for the wood
Bearing this Chanticleer across his back.
"Help, help!" they cried. They cried, "Alas! Alack!        560
The fox, the fox!" and after him they ran,
And armed with clubs came running many a man.
Ran Coll the dog, and led a yelping band;
Ran Malkyn, with a distaff in her hand;
Ran cow and calf, and even the very hogs,                  565
By the yelping and the barking of the dogs
And men's and women's shouts so terrified
They ran till it seemed their hearts would burst inside;
They squealed like fiends in the pit, with none to still them.
The ducks quacked as if men were going to kill them.       570
The geese for very fear flew over the trees.
Out of the beehive came the swarm of bees.
Ah! Bless my soul, the noise, by all that's true,
So hideous was that Jack Straw's retinue
Made never a hubbub that was half so shrill                575
Over a Fleming they were going to kill
As the clamor made that day over the fox.
They brought brass trumpets, and trumpets made of box,
Of horn, of bone, on which they blew and squeaked,

---

539. *Aeneid:* Book II, ll. 550 ff.
544. *Hasdrubal:* king of Carthage
(second century B.C.).

574. *Jack Straw:* leader of the Peasants' Revolt of 1381, caused in part by the competition in labor of immigrating Flemings.

And those who were not blowing whooped and shrieked.          580
It seemed as if the very heavens would fall!
   Now hear me, you good people, one and all!
Fortune, I say, will suddenly override
Her enemy in his very hope and pride!
This cock, as on the fox's back he lay,          585
Plucked up his courage to speak to him and say.
"God be my help, sir, but I'd tell them all,
That is, if I were you, 'Plague on you fall!
Go back, proud fools! Now that I've reached the wood,
I'll eat the cock at once, for all the good          590
Your noise can do. Here Chanticleer shall stay.' "
   "Fine!" said the fox. "I'll do just what you say."
But the cock, as he was speaking, suddenly
Out of his jaws lurched expeditiously,
And flew at once high up into a tree.          595
And when the fox saw that the cock was free,
"Alas," he said, "alas, O Chanticleer!
Inasmuch as I have given you cause for fear
By seizing you and bearing you away,
I have done you wrong, I am prepared to say.          600
But, sir, I did it with no ill intent.
Come down, and I shall tell you what I meant.
So help me God, it's truth I'll offer you!"
   "No, no," said he. "We're both fools, through and through.
But curse my blood and bones for the chief dunce          605
If you deceive me oftener than once!
You shall never again by flattery persuade me
To sing and wink my eyes, by him that made me.
For he that willfully winks when he should see,
God never bless him with prosperity!"          610
   "Ah," said the fox, "with mischief may God greet
The man ungoverned, rash, and indiscreet
Who babbles when to hold his tongue were needful!"
   Such is it to be reckless and unheedful
And trust in flattery. But you who hold          615
That this is a mere trifle I have told,
Concerning only a fox, or a cock and hen,
Think twice, and take the moral, my good men!
For truly, of whatever is written, all
Is written for our doctrine, says St. Paul.          620
Then take the fruit, and let the chaff lie still.
Now, gracious God, if it should be your will,
As my Lord teaches, make us all good men
And bring us to your holy bliss! Amen.

   619–620. *whatever . . . St. Paul:* Romans 15:4.

# EVERYMAN*
## (c. 1485)

### Dramatis Personae

| | |
|---|---|
| MESSENGER | KNOWLEDGE |
| GOD | CONFESSION |
| DEATH | BEAUTY |
| EVERYMAN | STRENGTH |
| FELLOWSHIP | DISCRETION |
| KINDRED | FIVE-WITS |
| COUSIN | ANGEL |
| GOODS | DOCTOR |
| GOOD DEEDS | |

HERE BEGINNETH A TREATISE HOW THE HIGH FATHER OF
HEAVEN SENDETH DEATH TO SUMMON EVERY CREATURE
TO COME AND GIVE ACCOUNT OF THEIR LIVES IN THIS
WORLD, AND IS IN MANNER OF A MORAL PLAY

[*Enter* MESSENGER.]

MESSENGER. I pray you all give your audience,
And hear this matter with reverence,
By figure a moral play,
*The Summoning of Everyman* called it is,
That of our lives and ending shows                                  5
How transitory we be all day.
The matter is wonder precious,
But the intent of it is more gracious
And sweet to bear away.
The story saith: Man, in the beginning                           10
Look well, and take good heed to the ending,
Be you never so gay.
You think sin in the beginning full sweet,
Which in the end causeth the soul to weep,
When the body lieth in clay.                                      15
Here shall you see how fellowship and jollity,
Both strength, pleasure, and beauty,
Will fade from thee as flower in May.
For ye shall hear how our Heaven-King
Calleth Everyman to a general reckoning.                         20
Give audience and hear what he doth say.

[*Exit* MESSENGER.—*Enter* GOD.]

* The modernized text and the notes here presented are by E. Talbot Donaldson and were originally prepared for *The Norton Anthology of English Literature*. Donaldson's text is based upon the earliest printed version of the play, by John Skot, about 1530, as reproduced by W. W. Greg (Louvain, 1904).
3. *by figure*: in form.
6. *all day*: always.

**COD.** I perceive, here in my majesty,
How that all creatures be to me unkind,
Living without dread in worldly prosperity.
Of ghostly sight the people be so blind, 25
Drowned in sin, they know me not for their God.
In worldly riches is all their mind:
They fear not of my righteousness the sharp rod;
My law that I showed when I for them died
They forget clean, and shedding of my blood red. 30
I hanged between two, it cannot be denied:
To get them life I suffered to be dead.
I healed their feet, with thorns hurt was my head.
I could do no more than I did, truly—
And now I see the people do clean forsake me. 35
They use the seven deadly sins damnable,
As pride, coveitise, wrath, and lechery
Now in the world be made commendable.
And thus they leave of angels the heavenly company.
Every man liveth so after his own pleasure, 40
And yet of their life they be nothing sure.
I see the more that I them forbear,
The worse they be from year to year:
All that liveth appaireth fast.
Therefore I will, in all the haste, 45
Have a reckoning of every man's person.
For, and I leave the people thus alone
In their life and wicked tempests,
Verily they will become much worse than beasts;
For now one would by envy another up eat. 50
Charity do they all clean forgeet.
I hoped well that every man
In my glory should make his mansion,
And thereto I had them all elect.
But now I see, like traitors deject, 55
They thank me not for the pleasure that I to them meant,
Nor yet for their being that I them have lent.
I proffered the people great multitude of mercy,
And few there be that asketh it heartily.
They be so cumbered with worldly riches 60

---

23. *unkind*: thoughtless.
25. *ghostly*: spiritual.
31. *I hanged between two*: the two thieves between whom Christ was crucified.
37. *As pride . . . lechery*: the other three deadly sins are envy, gluttony, and sloth; *coveitise*: avarice.

44. *appaireth*: degenerates.
47. *and*: if.
54. *elect*: chosen.
55. *deject*: abased.
56. *to*: for.
59. *heartily*: sincerely.
60. *cumbered*: encumbered.

That needs on them I must do justice—
On every man living without fear.
Where art thou, Death, thou mighty messenger?
    [*Enter* DEATH.]
DEATH. Almighty God, I am here at your will,
    Your commandment to fulfill.          65
GOD. Go thou to Everyman,
    And show him, in my name,
    A pilgrimage he must on him take,
    Which he in no wise may escape;
    And that he bring with him a sure reckoning    70
    Without delay or any tarrying.
DEATH. Lord, I will in the world go run over all,
    And cruelly out-search both great and small.
        [*Exit* GOD.]
    Everyman will I beset that liveth beastly
    Out of God's laws, and dreadeth not folly.    75
    He that loveth riches I will strike with my dart,
    His sight to blind, and from heaven to depart—
    Except that Almsdeeds be his good friend—
    In hell for to dwell, world without end.
    Lo, yonder I see Everyman walking:    80
    Full little he thinketh on my coming;
    His mind is on fleshly lusts and his treasure,
    And great pain it shall cause him to endure
    Before the Lord, Heaven-King.
        [*Enter* EVERYMAN.]
    Everyman, stand still! Whither art thou going    85
    Thus gaily? Hast thou thy Maker forgeet?
EVERYMAN. Why askest thou?
    Why wouldest thou weet?
DEATH. Yea, sir, I will show you:
    In great haste I am sent to thee    90
    From God out of his majesty.
EVERYMAN. What! sent to me?
DEATH. Yea, certainly.
    Though thou have forgot him here,
    He thinketh on thee in the heavenly sphere,    95
    As, ere we depart, thou shalt know.
EVERYMAN. What desireth God of me?
DEATH. That shall I show thee:
    A reckoning he will needs have
    Without any longer respite.    100
EVERYMAN. To give a reckoning longer leisure I crave.

---

72. *over all*: everywhere.        86. *forgeet*: forgotten.
77. *depart*: separate.        88. *weet*: know.

This blind matter troubleth my wit.

DEATH. On thee thou must take a long journay:
   Therefore thy book of count with thee thou bring,
   For turn again thou cannot by no way.                    105
   And look thou be sure of thy reckoning,
   For before God thou shalt answer and shew
   Thy many bad deeds and good but a few—
   How thou hast spent thy life and in what wise,
   Before the Chief Lord of Paradise.                       110
   Have ado that we were in that way,
   For weet thou well thou shalt make none attornay.

EVERYMAN. Full unready I am such reckoning to give.
   I know thee not. What messenger art thou?

DEATH. I am Death that no man dreadeth,                     115
   For every man I 'rest, and no man spareth;
   For it is God's commandment
   That all to me should be obedient.

EVERYMAN. O Death, thou comest when I had thee least in mind.
   In thy power it lieth me to save:                        120
   Yet of my good will I give thee, if thou will be kind,
   Yea, a thousand pound shalt thou have—
   And defer this matter till another day.

DEATH. Everyman, it may not be, by no way.
   I set nought by gold, silver, nor riches,                125
   Nor by pope, emperor, king, duke, nor princes,
   For, and I would receive gifts great,
   All the world I might get.
   But my custom is clean contrary:
   I give thee no respite. Come hence and not tarry!        130

EVERYMAN. Alas, shall I have no longer respite?
   I may say Death giveth no warning.
   To think on thee it maketh my heart sick,
   For all unready is my book of reckoning.
   But twelve year and I might have a biding,               135
   My counting-book I would make so clear
   That my reckoning I should not need to fear.
   Wherefore, Death, I pray thee, for God's mercy,
   Spare me till I be provided of remedy.

DEATH. Thee availeth not to cry, weep, and pray;           140
   But haste thee lightly that thou were gone that journay,

---

102. *blind*: unexpected.
104. *count*: accounts.
111. *Have ado . . . way*: Let's get started at once.
112. *none attornay*: none to appear in your stead.
115. *that no man dreadeth*: that fears nobody.

116. *'rest*: arrest.
121. *good*: goods.
125. *I set nought by*: I care nothing for.
127. *and*: if.
135. *But twelve . . . biding*: If I might have a delay for just twelve years.
141. *lightly*: quickly.

And prove thy friends, if thou can.
For weet thou well the tide abideth no man,
And in the world each living creature
For Adam's sin must die of nature.                                    145

EVERYMAN. Death, if I should this pilgrimage take
And my reckoning surely make,
Show me, for saint charity,
Should I not come again shortly?

DEATH. No, Everyman. And thou be once there,                          150
Thou mayst never more come here,
Trust me verily.

EVERYMAN. O gracious God in the high seat celestial,
Have mercy on me in this most need!
Shall I have no company from this vale terrestrial                    155
Of mine acquaintance that way me to lead?

DEATH. Yea, if any be so hardy
That would go with thee and bear thee company.
Hie thee that thou were gone to God's magnificence,
Thy reckoning to give before his presence.                           160
What, weenest thou thy life is given thee,
And thy worldly goods also?

EVERYMAN. I had weened so, verily.

DEATH. Nay, nay, it was but lent thee.
For as soon as thou art go,                                           165
Another a while shall have it and then go therefro,
Even as thou hast done.
Everyman, thou art mad! Thou hast thy wits five,
And here on earth will not amend thy live!
For suddenly I do come.                                               170

EVERYMAN. O wretched caitiff! Whither shall I flee
That I might 'scape this endless sorrow?
Now, gentle Death, spare me till tomorrow,
That I may amend me
With good advisement.                                                 175

DEATH. Nay, thereto I will not consent,
Nor no man will I respite,
But to the heart suddenly I shall smite,
Without any advisement.
And now out of thy sight I will me hie:                               180
See thou make thee ready shortly,
For thou mayst say this is the day
That no man living may 'scape away.              [*Exit* DEATH.]

---

142. *prove*: test.                        161. *weenest*: suppose.
143. *weet*: know; *tide*: time.           168. *wits*: senses.
145. *of nature*: naturally.               169. *thy life*: in thy life.
148. *saint*: holy.                        175. *advisement*: preparation.
159. *Hie*: hasten.

EVERYMAN. Alas, I may well weep with sighs deep:
  Now have I no manner of company       185
  To help me in my journey and me to keep.
  And also my writing is full unready—
  How shall I do now for to excuse me?
  I would to God I had never be geet!
  To my soul a full great profit it had be.      190
  For now I fear pains huge and great.
  The time passeth: Lord, help, that all wrought!
  For though I mourn, it availeth nought.
  The day passeth and is almost ago:
  I wot not well what for to do.      195
  To whom were I best my complaint to make?
  What and I to Fellowship thereof spake,
  And showed him of this sudden chance?
  For in him is all mine affiance,
  We have in the world so many a day      200
  Be good friends in sport and play.
  I see him yonder, certainly.
  I trust that he will bear me company.
  Therefore to him will I speak to ease my sorrow.
     [*Enter* FELLOWSHIP.]
  Well met, good Fellowship, and good morrow!      205
FELLOWSHIP. Everyman, good morrow, by this day!
  Sir, why lookest thou so piteously?
  If anything be amiss, I pray thee me say,
  That I may help to remedy.
EVERYMAN. Yea, good Fellowship, yea:      210
  I am in great jeopardy.
FELLOWSHIP. My true friend, show to me your mind.
  I will not forsake thee to my life's end
  In the way of good company.
EVERYMAN. That was well spoken, and lovingly!      215
FELLOWSHIP. Sir, I must needs know your heaviness.
  I have pity to see you in any distress.
  If any have you wronged, ye shall revenged be,
  Though I on the ground be slain for thee,
  Though that I know before that I should die.      220
EVERYMAN. Verily, Fellowship, gramercy.
FELLOWSHIP. Tush! by thy thanks I set not a stree.
  Show me your grief and say no more.
EVERYMAN. If I my heart should to you break,

---

186. *keep*: guard.            199. *affiance*: trust.
187. *writing*: ledger.        216. *heaviness*: sorrow.
189. *be geet*: been begotten.   221. *gramercy*: many thanks.
194. *ago*: gone by.         222. *stree*: straw.
195. *wot*: know.           224. *break*: disclose.

And then you to turn your mind fro me,      225
And would not me comfort when ye hear me speak,
Then should I ten times sorrier be.
FELLOWSHIP. Sir, I say as I will do, indeed.
EVERYMAN. Then be you a good friend at need.
I have found you true herebefore.      230
FELLOWSHIP. And so ye shall evermore.
For, in faith, and thou go to hell,
I will not forsake thee by the way.
EVERYMAN. Ye speak like a good friend. I believe you well.
I shall deserve it, and I may.      235
FELLOWSHIP. I speak of no deserving, by this day!
For he that will say and nothing do
Is not worthy with good company to go.
Therefore show me the grief of your mind,
As to your friend most loving and kind.      240
EVERYMAN. I shall show you how it is:
Commanded I am to go a journey,
A long way, hard and dangerous,
And give a strait count, without delay,
Before the high judge Adonai.      245
Wherefore I pray you bear me company,
As ye have promised, in this journay.
FELLOWSHIP. This is matter indeed! Promise is duty—
But, and I should take such a voyage on me,
I know it well, it should be to my pain.      250
Also it maketh me afeard, certain.
But let us take counsel here, as well as we can—
For your words would fear a strong man.
EVERYMAN. Why, ye said if I had need,
Ye would me never forsake, quick ne dead,      255
Though it were to hell, truly.
FELLOWSHIP. So I said, certainly.
But such pleasures be set aside, the sooth to say.
And also, if we took such a journay,
When should we again come?      260
EVERYMAN. Nay, never again, till the day of doom.
FELLOWSHIP. In faith, then will not I come there!
Who hath you these tidings brought?
EVERYMAN. Indeed, Death was with me here.
FELLOWSHIP. Now by God that all hath bought,      265
If Death were the messenger,
For no man that is living today

235. *deserve*: repay; *and*: if.
244. *strait*: strict; *count*: accounting.
245. *Adonai*: God.

253. *fear*: frighten.
258. *pleasures*: jokes.
265. *bought*: redeemed.

I will not go that loath journey—
Not for the father that begat me!

EVERYMAN. Ye promised otherwise, pardie.                                    270

FELLOWSHIP. I wot well I said so, truly.
And yet, if thou wilt eat and drink and make good cheer,
Or haunt to women the lusty company,
I would not forsake you while the day is clear,
Trust me verily!                                                          275

EVERYMAN. Yea, thereto ye would be ready—
To go to mirth, solace, and play:
Your mind to folly will sooner apply
Than to bear me company in my long journay.

FELLOWSHIP. Now in good faith, I will not that way.                        280
But, and thou will murder or any man kill,
In that I will help thee with a good will.

EVERYMAN. O that is simple advice, indeed!
Gentle fellow, help me in my necessity:
We have loved long, and now I need—                                        285
And now, gentle Fellowship, remember me!

FELLOWSHIP. Whether ye have loved me or no,
By Saint John, I will not with thee go!

EVERYMAN. Yet I pray thee take the labor and do so much for me,
To bring me forward, for saint charity,                                    290
And comfort me till I come without the town.

FELLOWSHIP. Nay, and thou would give me a new gown,
I will not a foot with thee go.
But, and thou had tarried, I would not have left thee so.
And as now, God speed thee in thy journey!                                 295
For from thee I will depart as fast as I may.

EVERYMAN. Whither away, Fellowship? Will thou forsake me?

FELLOWSHIP. Yea, by my fay! To God I betake thee.

EVERYMAN. Farewell, good Fellowship! For thee my heart is sore.
Adieu forever—I shall see thee no more.                                    300

FELLOWSHIP. In faith, Everyman, farewell now at the ending:
For you I will remember that parting is mourning.

          [*Exit* FELLOWSHIP.]

EVERYMAN. Alack, shall we thus depart indeed—
Ah, Lady, help!—without any more comfort?
Lo, Fellowship forsaketh me in my most need!                               305
For help in this world whither shall I resort?
Fellowship herebefore with me would merry make,
And now little sorrow for me doth he take.

---

268. *loath*: loathsome.
270. *pardie*: by God.
273. *Or haunt . . . company*: Or frequent the lusty company of women.
277. *solace*: pleasure.

278. *apply*: attend.
283. *simple*: foolish.
290. *To bring me forward*: Escort me.
298. *fay*: faith; *betake*: commend.
303. *depart*: part.

It is said, "In prosperity men friends may find
Which in adversity be full unkind."                                    310
Now whither for succor shall I flee,
Sith that Fellowship hath forsaken me?
To my kinsmen I will, truly,
Praying them to help me in my necessity.
I believe that they will do so,                                        315
For kind will creep where it may not go.
I will go 'say—for yonder I see them—
Where be ye now my friends and kinsmen.

[*Enter* KINDRED *and* COUSIN.]

KINDRED. Here be we now at your commandment:
Cousin, I pray you show us your intent                                 320
In any wise, and not spare.

COUSIN. Yea, Everyman, and to us declare
If ye be disposed to go anywhither.
For, weet you well, we will live and die togither.

KINDRED. In wealth and woe we will with you hold,                      325
For over his kin a man may be bold.

EVERYMAN. Gramercy, my friends and kinsmen kind.
Now shall I show you the grief of my mind.
I was commanded by a messenger
That is a high king's chief officer:                                   330
He bade me go a pilgrimage, to my pain—
And I know well I shall never come again.
Also I must give a reckoning strait,
For I have a great enemy that hath me in wait,
Which intendeth me to hinder.                                          335

KINDRED. What account is that which ye must render?
That would I know.

EVERYMAN. Of all my works I must show
How I have lived and my days spent;
Also of ill deeds that I have used                                     340
In my time sith life was me lent,
And of all virtues that I have refused.
Therefore I pray you go thither with me
To help me make mine account, for saint charity.

COUSIN. What, to go thither? Is that the matter?                       345
Nay, Everyman, I had liefer fast bread and water
All this five year and more!

---

312. *Sith*: Since.
316. *For kind . . . go*: For kinship will
creep where it cannot walk (i.e., kinsmen will suffer hardship for one
another).
317. *'say*: assay.
318. *Where*: Whether.
324. *weet*: know.

326. *For over . . . bold*: For a man
may make demands of his kinsmen.
327. *Gramercy*: Much thanks.
333. *strait*: strict.
334. *great enemy . . . wait*: Satan lies
in ambush for me.
346. *liefer fast*: rather fast on.

EVERYMAN. Alas, that ever I was bore!
    For now shall I never be merry
    If that you forsake me.                      350
KINDRED. Ah, sir, what? Ye be a merry man:
    Take good heart to you and make no moan.
    But one thing I warn you, by Saint Anne,
    As for me, ye shall go alone.
EVERYMAN. My Cousin, will you not with me go?       355
COUSIN. No, by Our Lady! I have the cramp in my toe:
    Trust not to me. For, so God me speed,
    I will deceive you in your most need.
KINDRED. It availeth you not us to 'tice.
    Ye shall have my maid with all my heart:        360
    She loveth to go to feasts, there to be nice,
    And to dance, and abroad to start.
    I will give her leave to help you in that journey,
    If that you and she may agree.
EVERYMAN. Now show me the very effect of your mind:     365
    Will you go with me or abide behind?
KINDRED. Abide behind? Yea, that will I and I may!
      Therefore farewell till another day.     [*Exit* KINDRED.]
EVERYMAN. How should I be merry or glad?
    For fair promises men to me make,          370
    But when I have most need they me forsake.
    I am deceived. That maketh me sad.
COUSIN. Cousin Everyman, farewell now,
    For verily I will not go with you;
    Also of mine own an unready reckoning        375
    I have to account—therefore I make tarrying.
    Now God keep thee, for now I go.     [*Exit* COUSIN.]
EVERYMAN. Ah, Jesus, is all come hereto?
    Lo, fair words maketh fools fain:
    They promise and nothing will do, certain.      380
    My kinsmen promised me faithfully
    For to abide with me steadfastly,
    And now fast away do they flee.
    Even so Fellowship promised me.
    What friend were best me of to provide?       385
    I lose my time here longer to abide.
    Yet in my mind a thing there is:
    All my life I have loved riches;
    If that my Good now help me might,

---

348. *bore*: born.
359. *'tice*: entice.
361. *nice*: wanton.
362. *abroad to start*: to go gadding
about.

365. *effect*: bent.
378. *hereto*: to this.
379. *fain*: glad.
389. *Good*: Goods.

He would make my heart full light. 390
I will speak to him in this distress.
Where art thou, my Goods and riches?

GOODS. [*Within*] Who calleth me? Everyman? What, hast thou
 haste?
I lie here in corners, trussed and piled so high,
And in chests I am locked so fast— 395
Also sacked in bags—thou mayst see with thine eye
I cannot stir, in packs low where I lie.
What would ye have? Lightly me say.

EVERYMAN. Come hither, Good, in all the haste thou may,
For of counsel I must desire thee. 400
 [*Enter* GOODS.]

GOODS. Sir, and ye in the world have sorrow or adversity,
That can I help you to remedy shortly.

EVERYMAN. It is another disease that grieveth me:
In this world it is not, I tell thee so.
I am sent for another way to go, 405
To give a strait count general
Before the highest Jupiter of all.
And all my life I have had joy and pleasure in thee:
Therefore I pray thee go with me,
For peradventure, thou mayst before God Almighty 410
My reckoning help to clean and purify.
For it is said ever among
That money maketh all right that is wrong.

GOODS. Nay, Everyman, I sing another song:
I follow no man in such voyages. 415
For, and I went with thee,
Thou shouldest fare much the worse for me;
For because on me thou did set thy mind,
Thy reckoning I have made blotted and blind,
That thine account thou cannot make truly— 420
And that hast thou for the love of me.

EVERYMAN. That would grieve me full sore,
When I should come to that fearful answer.
Up, let us go thither together.

GOODS. Nay, not so, I am too brittle, I may not endure. 425
I will follow no man one foot, be ye sure.

EVERYMAN. Alas, I have thee loved and had great pleasure
All my life-days on good and treasure.

GOODS. That is to thy damnation, without leasing,
For my love is contrary to the love everlasting. 430

---

398. *Lightly*: Quickly.
401. *and*: if.
403. *disease*: distress.
407. *Jupiter*: God.

412. *ever among*: now and then.
419. *blind*: illegible.
429. *leasing*: lie.

But if thou had me loved moderately during,
As to the poor to give part of me,
Then shouldest thou not in this dolor be,
Nor in this great sorrow and care.

EVERYMAN. Lo, now was I deceived ere I was ware,      435
And all I may wite misspending of time.

GOODS. What, weenest thou that I am thine?

EVERYMAN. I had weened so.

GOODS. Nay, Everyman, I say no.
As for a while I was lent thee;      440
A season thou hast had me in prosperity.
My condition is man's soul to kill;
If I save one, a thousand I do spill.
Weenest thou that I will follow thee?
Nay, from this world, not verily.      445

EVERYMAN. I had weened otherwise.

GOODS. Therefore to thy soul Good is a thief;
For when thou art dead, this is my guise—
Another to deceive in the same wise
As I have done thee, and all to his soul's repreef.      450

EVERYMAN. O false Good, cursed thou be,
Thou traitor to God, that hast deceived me
And caught me in thy snare!

GOODS. Marry, thou brought thyself in care,
Whereof I am glad:      455
I must needs laugh, I cannot be sad.

EVERYMAN. Ah, Good, thou hast had long my heartly love;
I gave thee that which should be the Lord's above.
But wilt thou not go with me, indeed?
I pray thee truth to say.      460

GOODS. No, so God me speed!
Therefore farewell and have good day.      [*Exit* GOODS.]

EVERYMAN. Oh, to whom shall I make my moan
For to go with me in that heavy journay?
First Fellowship said he would with me gone:      465
His words were very pleasant and gay,
But afterward he left me alone.
Then spake I to my kinsmen, all in despair,
And also they gave me words fair—
They lacked no fair speaking,      470
But all forsake me in the ending.
Then went I to my Goods that I loved best,

431. *during*: in the meanwhile.
436. *wite*: blame on.
437. *weenest*: suppose.
442. *condition*: disposition.
443. *spill*: ruin.
448. *guise*: custom.

450. *repreef*: shame.
454. *care*: sorrow.
457. *heartly*: sincere.
464. *heavy*: sorrowful.
465. *gone*: go.

In hope to have comfort; but there had I least,
For my Goods sharply did me tell
That he bringeth many into hell. 475
Then of myself I was ashamed,
And so I am worthy to be blamed:
Thus may I well myself hate.
Of whom shall I now counsel take?
I think that I shall never speed 480
Till that I go to my Good Deed.
But alas, she is so weak
That she can neither go nor speak.
Yet will I venture on her now.
My Good Deeds, where be you? 485

GOOD DEEDS. [*Speaking from the ground*] Here I lie, cold in the
 ground:
Thy sins hath me sore bound
That I cannot stear.

EVERYMAN. O Good Deeds, I stand in fear:
I must you pray of counsel, 490
For help now should come right well.

GOODS DEEDS. Everyman, I have understanding
That ye be summoned, account to make,
Before Messiah of Jer'salem King.
And you do by me, that journey with you will I take. 495

EVERYMAN. Therefore I come to you my moan to make.
I pray you that ye will go with me.

GOOD DEEDS. I would full fain, but I cannot stand, verily.

EVERYMAN. Why, is there anything on you fall?

GOOD DEEDS. Yea, sir, I may thank you of all: 500
If ye had perfectly cheered me,
Your book of count full ready had be.
 [GOOD DEEDS *shows him the account book.*]
Look, the books of your works and deeds eke,
As how they lie under the feet,
To your soul's heaviness. 505

EVERYMAN. Our Lord Jesus help me!
For one letter here I cannot see.

GOOD DEEDS. There is a blind reckoning in time of distress!

EVERYMAN. Good Deeds, I pray you help me in this need,
Or else I am forever damned indeed. 510
Therefore help me to make reckoning
Before the Redeemer of all thing

---

483. *go*: walk.
484. *venture*: gamble.
488. *stear*: stir.
495. *And you do by me*: If you do
what I say.

499. *fall*: fallen.
503. *eke*: also.
505. *heaviness*: distress.
508. *blind*: illegible.

That King is and was and ever shall.

GOOD DEEDS. Everyman, I am sorry of your fall
And fain would help you and I were able.                     515

EVERYMAN. Good Deeds, your counsel I pray you give me.

GOOD DEEDS. That shall I do verily,
Though that on my feet I may not go;
I have a sister that shall with you also,
Called Knowledge, which shall with you abide             520
To help you to make that dreadful reckoning.

    [*Enter* KNOWLEDGE.]

KNOWLEDGE. Everyman, I will go with thee and be thy guide,
In thy most need to go by thy side.

EVERYMAN. In good condition I am now in everything,
And am whole content with this good thing,             525
Thanked be God my Creator.

GOOD DEEDS. And when she hath brought you there
Where thou shalt heal thee of thy smart,
Then go you with your reckoning and your Good Deeds together
For to make you joyful at heart                         530
Before the blessed Trinity.

EVERYMAN. My Good Deeds, gramercy!
I am well content, certainly,
With your words sweet.

KNOWLEDGE. Now go we together lovingly                     535
To Confession, that cleansing river.

EVERYMAN. For joy I weep—I would we were there!
But I pray you give me cognition,
Where dwelleth that holy man Confession?

KNOWLEDGE. In the House of Salvation:                     540
We shall find him in that place
That shall us comfort, by God's grace.

    [KNOWLEDGE *leads* EVERYMAN *to* CONFESSION.]

Lo, this is Confession: kneel down and ask mercy,
For he is in good conceit with God Almighty.

EVERYMAN. [*Kneeling*] O glorious fountain that all uncleanness
    doth clarify,                         545
Wash from me the spots of vice unclean,
That on me no sin may be seen.
I come with Knowledge for my redemption,
Redempt with heart and full contrition,
For I am commanded a pilgrimage to take                 550
And great accounts before God to make.
Now I pray you, Shrift, mother of Salvation,
Help my Good Deeds for my piteous exclamation.

514. *of*: for.
528. *smart*: pain.
538. *cognition*: knowledge.

544. *conceit*: esteem.
545. *clarify*: purify.
549. *Redempt*: Redeemed.

CONFESSION. I know your sorrow well, Everyman:
Because with Knowledge ye come to me,     555
I will you comfort as well as I can,
And a precious jewel I will give thee,
Called Penance, voider of adversity.
Therewith shall your body chastised be—
With abstinence and perseverance in God's service.     560
Here shall you receive that scourge of me,
Which is penance strong that ye must endure,
To remember thy Saviour was scourged for thee
With sharp scourges, and suffered it patiently.
So must thou ere thou 'scape that painful pilgrimage.     565
Knowledge, keep him in this voyage,
And by that time Good Deeds will be with thee.
But in any wise be secure of mercy—
For your time draweth fast—and ye will saved be.
Ask God mercy and he will grant, truly.     570
When with the scourge of penance man doth him bind,
The oil of forgiveness then shall he find.
EVERYMAN. Thanked be God for his gracious work,
For now I will my penance begin.
This hath rejoiced and lighted my heart,     575
Though the knots be painful and hard within.
KNOWLEDGE. Everyman, look your penance that ye fulfill,
What pain that ever it to you be;
And Knowledge shall give you counsel at will
How your account ye shall make clearly.     580
EVERYMAN. O eternal God, O heavenly figure,
O way of righteousness, O goodly vision,
Which descended down in a virgin pure
Because he would every man redeem,
Which Adam forfeited by his disobedience;     585
O blessed Godhead, elect and high Divine,
Forgive my grievous offense!
Here I cry thee mercy in this presence:
O ghostly Treasure, O Ransomer and Redeemer,
Of all the world Hope and Conduiter,     590
Mirror of joy, Foundator of mercy,
Which enlumineth heaven and earth thereby,
Hear my clamorous complaint, though it late be;
Receive my prayers, of thy benignity.
Though I be a sinner most abominable,     595

558. *voider*: expeller.
562. *strong*: harsh.
566. *keep*: guard.
568. *secure*: certain.
571. *him*: himself.
576. *knots*: the knots on the scourge

(whip) of penance; *within*: to my senses
586. *Divine*: Divinity.
590. *Conduiter*: guide.
591. *Foundator*: founder.
592. *enlumineth*: lights up.

Yet let my name be written in Moses' table.
O Mary, pray to the Maker of all thing
Me for to help at my ending,
And save me from the power of my enemy,
For Death assaileth me strongly. 600
And Lady, that I may by mean of thy prayer
Of your Son's glory to be partner—
By the means of his passion I it crave.
I beseech you help my soul to save.
Knowledge, give me the scourge of penance: 605
My flesh therewith shall give acquittance.
I will now begin, if God give me grace.
KNOWLEDGE. Everyman, God give you time and space!
Thus I bequeath you in the hands of our Saviour:
Now may you make your reckoning sure. 610
EVERYMAN. In the name of the Holy Trinity
My body sore punished shall be:
Take this, body, for the sin of the flesh!
Also thou delightest to go gay and fresh,
And in the way of damnation thou did me bring, 615
Therefore suffer now strokes of punishing!
Now of penance I will wade the water clear,
To save me from purgatory, that sharp fire.
GOOD DEEDS. I thank God, now can I walk and go,
And am delivered of my sickness and woe. 620
Therefore with Everyman I will go, and not spare:
His good works I will help him to declare.
KNOWLEDGE. Now Everyman, be merry and glad:
Your Good Deeds cometh now, ye may not be sad.
Now is your Good Deeds whole and sound, 625
Going upright upon the ground.
EVERYMAN. My heart is light, and shall be evermore.
Now will I smite faster than I did before.
GOOD DEEDS. Everyman, pilgrim, my special friend,
Blessed be thou without end! 630
For thee is preparate the eternal glory.
Ye have me made whole and sound:
Therefore I will bide by thee in every stound.
EVERYMAN. Welcome, my Good Deeds! Now I hear thy voice,
I weep for very sweetness of love. 635
KNOWLEDGE. Be no more sad, but ever rejoice:
God seeth thy living in his throne above.

596. *Moses' table*: tablet on which are
recorded those who have been baptized
and have done penance.
  606. *acquittance*: satisfaction for sins.
  608. *space*: opportunity.

614. *Also*: As.
626. *Going*: Walking.
631. *preparate*: prepared.
633. *stound*: trial.

Put on this garment to thy behove,
Which is wet with your tears—
Or else before God you may it miss                                        640
When ye to your journey's end come shall.
EVERYMAN. Gentle Knowledge, what do ye it call?
KNOWLEDGE. It is a garment of sorrow;
From pain it will you borrow:
Contrition it is                                                          645
That getteth forgiveness;
It pleaseth God passing well.
GOOD DEEDS. Everyman, will you wear it for your heal?
EVERYMAN. Now blessed be Jesu, Mary's son,
For now have I on true contrition.                                        650
And let us go now without tarrying.
Good Deeds, have we clear our reckoning?
GOOD DEEDS. Yea, indeed, I have it here.
EVERYMAN. Then I trust we need not fear.
Now friends, let us not part in twain.                                    655
KNOWLEDGE. Nay, Everyman, that will we not, certain.
GOOD DEEDS. Yet must thou lead with thee
Three persons of great might.
EVERYMAN. Who should they be?
GOOD DEEDS. Discretion and Strength they hight,                           660
And thy Beauty may not abide behind.
KNOWLEDGE. Also ye must call to mind
Your Five-Wits as for your counselors.
GOOD DEEDS. You must have have them ready at all hours.
EVERYMAN. How shall I get them hither?                                    665
KNOWLEDGE. You must call them all togither,
And they will be here incontinent.
EVERYMAN. My friends, come hither and be present,
Discretion, Strength, my Five-Wits, and Beauty!
    [*They enter.*]
BEAUTY. Here at your will we be all ready.                                670
What will ye that we should do?
GOOD DEEDS. That ye would with Everyman go
And help him in his pilgrimage.
Advise you: will ye with him or not in that voyage?
STRENGTH. We will bring him all thither,                                  675
To his help and comfort, ye may believe me.
DISCRETION. So will we go with him all togither.
EVERYMAN. Almighty God, loved might thou be!
I give thee laud that I have hither brought                               679

638. *behove*: advantage.          663. *Wits*: senses.
644. *borrow*: redeem.             667. *incontinent*: at once.
647. *passing*: surpassingly.      674. *Advise you*: Take thought.
648. *heal*: welfare.              678. *loved*: praised.
660. *hight*: are called.

Strength, Discretion, Beauty, and Five-Wits—lack I nought—
And my Good Deeds, with Knowledge clear,
All be in my company at my will here:
I desire no more to my business.

STRENGTH. And I, Strength, will by you stand in distress,       685
Though thou would in battle fight on the ground.

FIVE-WITS. And though it were through the world round,
We will not depart for sweet ne sour.

BEAUTY. No more will I, until death's houi,
Whatsoever thereof befall.

DISCRETION. Everyman, advise you first of all:       690
Go with a good advisement and deliberation.
We all give you virtuous monition
That all shall be well.

EVERYMAN. My friends, hearken what I will tell;
I pray God reward you in his heaven-sphere;       695
Now hearken all that be here,
For I will make my testament,
Here before you all present:
In alms half my good I will give with my hands twain,
In the way of charity with good intent;       700
And the other half, still shall remain,
I 'queath to be returned there it ought to be.
This I do in despite of the fiend of hell,
To go quit out of his perel,
Ever after and this day.       705

KNOWLEDGE. Everyman, hearken what I say:
Go to Priesthood, I you advise,
And receive of him, in any wise,
The holy sacrament and ointment togither;
Then shortly see ye turn again hither:       710
We will all abide you here.

FIVE-WITS. Yea, Everyman, hie you that ye ready were.
There is no emperor, king, duke, ne baron,
That of God hath commission
As hath the least priest in the world being:       715
For of the blessed sacraments pure and bening
He beareth the keys, and thereof hath the cure
For man's redemption—it is ever sure—
Which God for our souls' medicine
Gave us out of his heart with great pine,       720

691. *advisement*: preparation.
692. *virtuous*: confident; *monition*:
prediction.
699. *good*: goods.
701. *still*: which still.
702. *'queath*: bequeath.
704. *To go . . . perel*: In order to go
free of danger from him.
708. *in any wise*: at all costs.
709. *ointment*: extreme unction.
716. *bening*: benign.
717. *cure*: care.
720. *pine*: torment.

Here in this transitory life for thee and me.
The blessed sacraments seven there be:
Baptism, confirmation, with priesthood good,
And the sacrament of God's precious flesh and blood,
Marriage, the holy extreme unction, and penance:  725
These seven be good to have in remembrance,
Gracious sacraments of high divinity.

EVERYMAN. Fain would I receive that holy body,
And meekly to my ghostly father I will go.

FIVE-WITS. Everyman, that is the best that ye can do:  730
God will you to salvation bring.
For priesthood exceedeth all other thing:
To us Holy Scripture they do teach,
And converteth man from sin, heaven to reach;
God hath to them more power given  735
Than to any angel that is in heaven.
With five words he may consecrate
God's body in flesh and blood to make,
And handleth his Maker between his hands.
The priest bindeth and unbindeth all bands,  740
Both in earth and in heaven.
Thou ministers all the sacraments seven;
Though we kiss thy feet, thou were worthy;
Thou art surgeon that cureth sin deadly;
No remedy we find under God  745
But all only priesthood.
Everyman, God gave priests that dignity
And setteth them in his stead among us to be.
Thus be they above angels in degree.

[*Exit* EVERYMAN.]

KNOWLEDGE. If priests be good, it is so, surely.  750
But when Jesu hanged on the cross with great smart,
There he gave out of his blessed heart
The same sacrament in great torment,
He sold them not to us, that Lord omnipotent:
Therefore Saint Peter the Apostle doth say  755
That Jesu's curse hath all they
Which God their Saviour do buy or sell,
Or they for any money do take or tell

723. *priesthood*: ordination.
728. *Fain*: Gladly.
729. *ghostly*: spiritual.
737. *five words*: "For this is my body," spoken by the priest when he offers the wafer at communion.
740. *The priest . . . bands*: A reference to the power of the keys, inherited by the priesthood from St. Peter, who received it from Christ (Matthew xvi. 19) with the promise that whatever St. Peter bound or loosed on earth would be bound or loosed in heaven.
742. *ministers*: administers.
746. *But all only priesthood*: Except from priesthood alone.
751. *smart*: pain.
757. *do buy or sell*: To give or receive money for the sacraments is simony, named after Simon, who wished to buy the gift of the Holy Ghost and was cursed by St. Peter.
758. *Or they . . . tell*: Or who, for any sacrament, take or count out money.

Sinful priests giveth the sinners example bad:
Their children sitteth by other men's fires, I have heard;  760
And some haunteth women's company
With unclean life, as lusts of lechery.
These be with sin made blind.
FIVE-WITS. I trust to God no such may we find.
Therefore let us priesthood honor,  765
And follow their doctrine for our souls' succor.
We be their sheep and they shepherds be
By whom we all be kept in surety.
Peace, for yonder I see Everyman come,
Which hath made true satisfaction.  770
GOOD DEEDS. Methink it is he indeed.
    [*Re-enter* EVERYMAN.]
EVERYMAN. Now Jesu be your alder speed!
I have received the sacrament for my redemption,
And then mine extreme unction.
Blessed be all they that counseled me to take it!  775
And now, friends, let us go without longer respite.
I thank God that ye have tarried so long.
Now set each of you on this rood your hond
And shortly follow me:
I go before there I would be. God be our guide!  780
STRENGTH. Everyman, we will not from you go
Till ye have done this voyage long.
DISCRETION. I, Discretion, will bide by you also.
KNOWLEDGE. And though this pilgrimage be never so strong,
I will never part you fro.  785
STRENGTH. Everyman, I will be as sure by thee
As ever I did by Judas Maccabee.
EVERYMAN. Alas, I am so faint I may not stand—
My limbs under me doth fold!
Friends, let us not turn again to this land,  790
Not for all the world's gold.
For into this cave must I creep
And turn to earth, and there to sleep.
BEAUTY. What, into this grave, alas?
EVERYMAN. Yea, there shall ye consume, more and lass.  795
BEAUTY. And what, should I smother here?
EVERYMAN. Yea, by my faith, and nevermore appear.
In this world live no more we shall,
But in heaven before the highest Lord of all.

772. *Now Jesu . . . speed*: The pros-
perer of you all.
778. *rood*: cross.
780. *there*: where.
784. *strong*: harsh.
787. *Judas Maccabee*: Judas Mac-
cabaeus was an enormously powerful
warrior in the defense of Israel against
the Syrians in late Old Testament times.
  795. *consume*: decay; *more and lass*:
all of you.

BEAUTY. I cross out all this! Adieu, by Saint John—    800
   I take my tape in my lap and am gone.
EVERYMAN. What, Beauty, whither will ye?
BEAUTY. Peace, I am deaf—I look not behind me,
   Not and thou wouldest give me all the gold in thy chest.
    [*Exit* BEAUTY.]
EVERYMAN. Alas, whereto may I trust?    805
   Beauty goeth fast away fro me—
   She promised with me to live and die!
STRENGTH. Everyman, I will thee also forsake and deny.
   Thy game liketh me not at all.
EVERYMAN. Why then, ye will forsake me all?    810
   Sweet Strength, tarry a little space.
STRENGTH. Nay, sir, by the rood of grace,
   I will hie me from thee fast,
   Though thou weep till thy heart tobrast.
EVERYMAN. Ye would ever bide by me, ye said.    815
STRENGTH. Yea, I have you far enough conveyed!
   Ye be old enough, I understand,
   Your pilgrimage to take on hand:
   I repent me that I hither came.
EVERYMAN. Strength, you to displease I am to blame,    820
   Yet promise is debt, this ye well wot.
STRENGTH. In faith, I care not:
   Thou art but a fool to complain:
   You spend your speech and waste your brain.    824
   Go, thrust thee into the ground.    [*Exit* STRENGTH.]
EVERYMAN. I had weened surer I should you have found.
   He that trusteth in his Strength
   She him deceiveth at the length.
   Both Strength and Beauty forsaketh me—
   Yet they promised me fair and lovingly.    830
DISCRETION. Everyman, I will after Strength be gone:
   As for me, I will leave you alone.
EVERYMAN. Why Discretion, will ye forsake me?
DISCRETION. Yea, in faith, I will go from thee.
   For when Strength goeth before,    835
   I follow after evermore.
EVERYMAN. Yet I pray thee, for the love of the Trinity,
   Look in my grave once piteously.
DISCRETION. Nay, so nigh will I not come.    839
   Farewell everyone!    [*Exit* DISCRETION.]

---

801. *I take . . . gone*: I tuck my skirts
in my belt and am off.
  809. *liketh*: pleases.
  814. *tobrast*: break.
  816. *conveyed*: escorted.

820. *you to . . . blame*: I'm to blame
for displeasing you.
  821. *wot*: know.
  826. *weened*: supposed.

EVERYMAN. O all thing faileth save God alone—
Beauty, Strength, and Discretion.
For when Death bloweth his blast
They all run fro me full fast.

FIVE-WITS. Everyman, my leave now of thee I take.     845
I will follow the other, for here I thee forsake.

EVERYMAN. Alas, then may I wail and weep,
For I took you for my best friend.

FIVE-WITS. I will no longer thee keep.               849
Now farewell, and there an end!     [*Exit* FIVE-WITS.]

EVERYMAN. O Jesu, help, all hath forsaken me!

GOOD DEEDS. Nay, Everyman, I will bide with thee:
I will not forsake thee indeed;
Thou shalt find me a good friend at need.           854

EVERYMAN. Gramercy, Good Deeds! Now may I true friends see.
They have forsaken me every one—
I loved them better than my Good Deeds alone.
Knowledge, will ye forsake me also?

KNOWLEDGE. Yea, Everyman, when ye to Death shall go,
But not yet, for no manner of danger.               860

EVERYMAN. Gramercy, Knowledge, with all my heart!

KNOWLEDGE. Nay, yet will I not from hence depart
Till I see where ye shall become.

EVERYMAN. Methink, alas, that I must be gone
To make my reckoning and my debts pay,             865
For I see my time is nigh spent away.
Take example, all ye that this do hear or see,
How they that I best loved do forsake me,
Except my Good Deeds that bideth truly.

GOOD DEEDS. All earthly things is but vanity.       870
Beauty, Strength, and Discretion do man forsake,
Foolish friends and kinsmen that fair spake—
All fleeth save Good Deeds, and that am I.

EVERYMAN. Have mercy on me, God most mighty,
And stand by me, thou mother and maid, holy Mary!  875

GOOD DEEDS. Fear not: I will speak for thee.

EVERYMAN. Here I cry God mercy!

GOOD DEEDS. Short our end, and 'minish our pain.
Let us go, and never come again.

EVERYMAN. Into thy hands, Lord, my soul I commend:  880
Receive it, Lord, that it be not lost.
As thou me boughtest, so me defend,
And save me from the fiend's boast,

---

849. *keep*: watch over.
863. *Till I see . . . become*: Till I see
what shall become of you.

878. *Short our end . . . pain*: Make
our dying quick and diminish our pain.
882. *boughtest*: redeemed.

That I may appear with that blessed host
That shall be saved at the day of doom.                               885
*In manus tuas*, of mights most,
Forever *commendo spiritum meum*.

      [EVERYMAN *and* GOOD DEEDS *descend into the grave.*]

KNOWLEDGE. Now hath he suffered that we all shall endure,
The Good Deeds shall make all sure.
Now hath he made ending,                                              890
Methinketh that I hear angels sing
And make great joy and melody
Where Everyman's soul received shall be.

ANGEL. [*Within*] Come, excellent elect spouse to Jesu!
Here above thou shalt go                                              895
Because of thy singular virtue.
Now the soul is taken the body fro,
Thy reckoning is crystal clear:
Now shalt thou into the heavenly sphere—
Unto the which all ye shall come                                      900
That liveth well before the day of doom.

      [*Enter* DOCTOR.]

DOCTOR. This memorial men may have in mind:
Ye hearers, take it of worth, old and young,
And forsake Pride, for he deceiveth you in the end.
And remember Beauty, Five-Wits, Strength, and Discretion,            905
They all at the last do Everyman forsake,
Save his Good Deeds there doth he take—
But beware, for and they be small,
Before God he hath no help at all—
None excuse may be there for Everyman.                               910
Alas, how shall he do than?
For after death amends may no man make,
For then mercy and pity doth him forsake.
If his reckoning be not clear when he doth come,
God will say, "*Ite, maledicti, in ignem eternum!*"                  915
And he that hath his account whole and sound,
High in heaven he shall be crowned,
Unto which place God bring us all thither,
That we may live body and soul togither.
Thereto help, the Trinity!                                           920
Amen say ye, for saint charity.

---

886–887. *In manus tuas . . . commendo spiritum meum*: "Into thy hands, O greatest of powers, I commend my spirit forever."

894. *elect*: chosen; *spouse to Jesu*: Man's soul is often referred to as the bride of Jesus.

901. *Doctor*: the learned theologian who explains the meaning of the play.

902. *memorial*: reminder.

903. *take it of worth*: prize it.

911. *than*: then.

915. "*Ite, maledicti, in ignem eternum!*": "Depart, ye cursed, into everlasting fire."

# Masterpieces of the
# Renaissance

### EDITED BY
## P. M. PASINETTI

*Professor of Italian and Comparative Literature,*
*University of California, Los Angeles*

## THE RENAISSANCE
## AND ANTIQUITY

The term *Renaissance* describes a period of proverbially great intellectual and artistic achievements. The literal meaning of the word—"rebirth"—suggests that one impulse toward these achievements came from the example of ancient culture, or even better, from a certain vision which the artists and intellectuals of the Renaissance possessed of the world of antiquity which was "reborn" through their work. Especially in the more mature phase of the Renaissance, men were aware of having brought about in many fields a vigorous renewal, which they openly associated with the cult of antiquity. The restoration of ancient canons was regarded as a glorious achievement to be set beside the thrilling discoveries of their own age. "To-

day," Rabelais writes through his Gargantua,

the old sciences are revived, knowledge is systematized, discipline reëstablished. The learned languages are restored: Greek, without which a man would be ashamed to consider himself educated; Hebrew, Chaldean and Latin. Printing is now in use, an art so accurate and elegant that it betrays the divine inspiration of its discovery, which I have lived to witness. Alas! Conversely, I was not spared the horror of such diabolic works as gunpowder and artillery.

Machiavelli, whose infatuation with antiquity is as typical a trait as his better-advertised political realism, in the opening of his *Discourses on the First Ten Books of Livy* (*Discorsi sopra la prima deca di Tito Livio,* 1513–1521) suggests that rulers should be as keen on the imitation of ancient "virtues" as are artists, lawyers, and the scientists: "The civil laws are nothing but decisions given by the ancient jurisconsults. . . . And what is the science of medicine, but the experience of ancient physicians, which their successors have taken for their guide?"

The vogue of the term *Renaissance* is relatively recent, and its wide popularization stems in part from the success of Jakob Burckhardt's famous book, *The Civilization of the Renaissance in Italy* (1860). As with other terms which have currency in the history of culture (for instance, *romanticism*), its usefulness depends on its keeping a certain degree of elasticity. Thus the Renaissance as a "movement" can be regarded as extending through varying periods of years, and also as including phases and traits of what is otherwise known as the Middle Ages (and vice versa). The peak of the Renaissance can be shown to have occurred at different times in different countries, the movement having had its inception in Italy, where its impact was at first most visible in the fine arts, while in England, for instance, it developed later and its main achievements were in literature, particularly the drama. The meaning of the term has also, in the course of time, widened considerably: nowadays it conveys, to say the least, a general notion of artistic creativity, of extraordinary zest for life and knowledge, of sensory delight in opulence and magnificence, of spectacular individual achievement, thus extending beyond the literal meaning of rebirth and the strict idea of a revival and imitation of antiquity.

Even in the stricter sense the term continues to have its function. The degree to which European intellectuals of the period were steeped in the vision of antiquity is difficult for the average modern reader to realize fully. Even at first sight the student will discover that for these writers references to classical mythology, philosophy, and literature are not ornaments or affectations; along with references to the Scriptures they are part, and a major part, of their mental equipment and way of thinking. When Erasmus through his "Folly" speaks in a cluster of classical allusions, or Machiavelli writes to a friend: "I get up before daylight, prepare my birdlime, and go out with a bundle of cages on my back, so that I look like Geta when he came back from the harbor with the books of Amphitryo," the words have by no means the sound of erudite self-gratification which might attend them nowadays; they are wholly natural, familiar, unassuming.

When we are overcome by sudden emotion, our first exclamations are likely to be in the language most familiar to us— our dialect, if we happen to have one. Montaigne thus relates of himself that when once his father unexpectedly fell back in his arms in a swoon, the first words he uttered under the emotion of that experience were in Latin. Similarly Benvenuto Cellini, the Italian sculptor, goldsmith, and autobiographer, talking to his patron and expressing admiration of a Greek statue establishes with the ancient artist an immediate contact, a proud familiarity:

I cried to the Duke: "My lord, this is a statue in Greek marble, and it is a miracle of beauty. . . . If your Excellency permits, I should like to restore it—head and arms and feet. . . . It is certainly not my business to patch up statues, that being the trade of botchers, who do it in all conscience villainously ill; yet the art displayed by this great master of antiquity cries out to me to help him."

The men who, starting at about the middle of the four-teenth century, gave new im-pulse to this taste for the classics are often referred to as Human-ists. The word in that sense is related to what we call the hu-manities, and the humanities at that time were Latin and Greek. Every cultivated person wrote and spoke Latin, with the result that a Western community of intellectuals could exist, a spir-itual "republic of letters" above individual nations. The arche-type of the modern "man of let-ters" is often said to be Petrarch (Francesco Petrarca), a four-teenth-century Italian poet and diplomat who anticipated cer-tain ideals cherished later by the men of the Renaissance: a strong sense of the glories of antiquity, a high conception of the literary art, a taste for the good life, a basic pacifism.

On the other hand, in any mention of the Renaissance as a revival of antiquity, we should never forget the imaginative quality, the visionary impulse, with which the men of letters of the period looked at those memories—the same vision and imagination with which they regarded such contemporary heroes as the great navigators and astronomers. The Renais-sance view of the cultural monu-ments of antiquity was far from being merely that of the phi-lologist and the antiquarian; in-deed, familiarity may have been facilitated by the very lack of a scientific sense of history. We find the visionary and imagina-tive element not only in the creations of poets and drama-tists (Shakespeare's Romans, to give an obvious example) but also in the works of political writers: as when Machiavelli de-scribes himself entering, through his reading, the

ancient courts of ancient men, where, being lovingly received, I feed on that food which alone is mine, and which I was born for; I am not ashamed to speak with them and to ask the reasons for their actions, and they courteously answer me. For . . . hours I feel no bore-dom and forget every worry; I do not fear poverty, and death does not terrify me. I give myself completely over to the ancients.

Imitation of antiquity (a standard modern description. of certain Renaissance ideals) ac-quires, in Machiavelli and many others, a special aspect; between schoolroom imitation and that of the Renaissance there is as much difference as between the impulse to *learn* and the im-pulse to *be*.

## THE RENAISSANCE AND THE MIDDLE AGES: "THE DIGNITY OF MAN"

Inaccurate as the hackneyed notion may be that the "light" of the Renaissance broke through a long "night" of the Middle Ages, it is necessary to remember that this view was not devised by subsequent "enlightened" centuries but held by the men of the Renaissance themselves. In his genealogy of giants from Grangousier to Gargantua to Pantagruel Rabelais conveniently represents the generations of modern learning with their varying degrees of enlightenment; this is what Gargantua writes to his son:

My late father Grangousier, of blessed memory, made every effort that I might achieve mental, moral and technical excellence. . . . . But you can realize that conditions were not as favorable to learning as they are to-day. Nor had I such gifted teachers as you. We were still in the dark ages; we still walked in the shadow of the dark clouds of ignorance; we suffered the calamitous consequences of the destruction of good literature by the Goths. Now, by God's grace, light and dignity have been restored to letters, and I have lived to see it.

Definitions of the Renaissance must also in one way or another include the idea that the period was characterized by preoccupation with this life rather than with the life beyond. The contrast of an ideal Medieval Man, whose mode of action is basically oriented toward the thought of the afterlife, and who therefore conceives of his days on earth as transient and preparatory, with an ideal Renaissance Man, possessing and cherishing earthly interests so concrete and self-sufficient that the very realization of the ephemeral quality of life is to him nothing but an added spur to its immediate enjoyment—this is a useful contrast even though it represents an enormous oversimplification of the facts.

This same emphasis on the immediate is reflected in the earthly, amoral, and esthetic character of the Renaissance code of conduct. According to this code, human action is judged not in terms of right and wrong, of good and evil (as it is judged when life is viewed as a moral "test," with reward or punishment in the afterlife), but in terms of its present concrete validity and effectiveness, of the delight it affords, of its memorability, its *beauty*. In that sense a good deal that is typical of the Renaissance, from architecture to poetry, from sculpture to rhetoric, may be related to a taste for the harmonious and the memorable, for the spectacular effect, for the successful striking of a pose. Individual human action, seeking as it were in itself its own reward, finds justification in its *formal* appropriateness; in its being a well-rounded achievement, perfect of its kind; in the zest and gusto with which it is, here and now, performed; and, finally, in its proving worthy of remaining as a testimony to the performer's power on earth.

A convenient way of grasping this emphasis is to consider certain words which are often especially expressive of the interests of the period—"virtue," "fame," "glory." "Virtue," particularly in its Italian form, *virtù*, is to be understood in a wide sense. As we may see even now in some relics of its older meanings, the word (from the Latin *vir*, "man") connotes active power —the intrinsic force and ability of a person or thing (the "virtue" of a law, or of a medicament)—and hence, also, technical skill (the capacity of the "virtuoso"). The Machiavellian prince's "virtues," therefore, are not necessarily goodness, temperance, clemency, and the like; they are whatever forces and skills may help him in the efficient management and preservation of his princely powers. The idealistic, intangible part of his success is consigned to such concepts as "fame" and "glory," and here the dimension within which human action is considered is still an earthly one: they connote the hero's success and reputation with his contemporaries, or look forward to splendid recognition from posterity, on earth.

In this sense (though completely pure examples of such an attitude are rare) the purpose of life is the unrestrained and self-sufficient practice of one's "virtue," the competent and delighted exercise of one's skill. At the same time, there is no reason to forget that such virtues and skills are God's gift to man. The world-view of even some of the most clearly earth-bound Renaissance men was hardly godless; Machiavelli, Cellini, Rabelais, take for granted the presence of God in their own and their heroes' lives:

. . . we have before our eyes extraordinary and unexampled means prepared by God. The sea has been divided. A cloud has guided you on your way. The rock has given forth water. Manna has fallen. Everything has united to make you great. The rest is for you to do. God does not intend to do everything, lest he deprive us of our free will and the share of glory that belongs to us. [Machiavelli.]

According to the Pythagorean system, Gargantua would, with his tutor, recapitulate briefly all that he had read, seen, learned, done and assimilated in the course of the day. Then they prayed to God the Creator, doing Him worship and confirming their faith in Him, glorifying Him for His immense goodness, vouchsafing thanks for all the mighty past and imploring His divine clemency for all the future. And so they retired to rest. [Rabelais.]

I found that all the bronze my furnace contained had been exhausted in the head of this figure [of the statue of Perseus]. It was a miracle to observe that not one fragment remained in the orifice of the channel, and that nothing was wanting to the statue. In my great astonishment I seemed to see in this the hand of God arranging and controlling all. [Cellini.]

Yet there is no doubt that if we compare the attitudes of these authors with the view of the world and of the value of human action which emerges from the major literary work of the Middle Ages, the *Divine Comedy*, and with the manner in which human action is there seen within a grand extratemporal design, the presence of God in the Renaissance writers cited above cannot help appearing marginal and perfunctory. Castiglione in the first pages of the *Courtier* pays homage to the memory of the former duke of Montefeltro, in whose palace at Urbino the book's personages hold their lofty debate on the idea of a perfect gentleman (an earlier member of the same family appears in Dante's Hell, another in Dante's Purgatory); but he praises him only for his achievements as a man of arms and a promoter of the arts. There is no thought of either the salvation or the damnation of his soul (though the general tone of the work would seem to imply his salvation), and he is exalted instead for victories in battle and, even more warmly, for having built a splendid palace—the tangible symbol of his earthly glory, for it is both the mark of political and social power, and a work of art.

Thus the popular view which associates the idea of the Renaissance especially with the flourishing of the arts is correct. The leaders of the period saw in a work of art the clearest instance of beautiful, harmonious, and self-justified performance. To create such a work became the valuable occupation *par excellence*, the most satisfactory display of *virtù*. The Renaissance view of antiquity exemplifies this attitude: the artists and intellectuals of the period not only drew on antiquity for certain practices and forms but found there as well a recognition of the place of the arts among outstanding modes of human action. In this way, the concepts of "fame" and "glory" became particularly associated with the art of poetry because the Renaissance drew from antiquity the idea of the poet as celebrator of high deeds, the "dispenser of glory."

There is, then, an important phase of Renaissance psychology in which terrestrial life is seen as positive fulfillment. This is clear in all fields of endeavor, and especially where there is a close association between the practical and the intellectual, as in the exercise of political power, the act of scientific discovery, the creation of works of art. The Renaissance assumption is that there are things highly worth doing, within a simply temporal pattern. By doing them, man proves his privileged position in Creation and therefore incidentally follows God's intent. The often cited phrase "the dignity of man" describes this positive, strongly affirmed awareness of the intellectual and physical "virtues" of the human being, and of his place in Creation.

It is important, however, to see this fact about the Renaissance in the light of another: where there is a singularly high capacity for feeling the delight of earthly achievement, there is a possibility that its ultimate worth will also be questioned profoundly. What (the Renaissance mind usually asks at some point) is the purpose of all this activity? What meaningful relation does it bear to any all-inclusive, cosmic pattern? The Renaissance coincided with, and perhaps to some extent occasioned, a loss of firm belief in the final unity and the final intelligibility of the universe, such belief as underlies, for example, the *Divine Comedy*, enabling Dante to say in the *Paradise*:

I beheld leaves within the
    unfathomed blaze
Into one volume bound by
    love, the same
That the universe holds scat-
    tered through its maze.
Substance and accidents, and
    their modes, became
As if together fused, all in
    such wise

That what I speak of is one simple flame.

Once the notion of this grand unity of design has lost its authority, certainty about the final value of human actions is no longer to be found. For some minds, indeed, the sense of void becomes so strong as to paralyze all aspiration to power or thirst for knowledge or delight in beauty; the attitude resulting when this happens, we call Renaissance melancholy, whether it be openly shown (as by some characters in Elizabethan drama) or provide an undercurrent of sadness, or incite to ironical forms of compromise, to some sort of wise adjustment (as in Erasmus or Montaigne.) The legend of Faust—"Doctor" Faustus—a great amasser of knowledge doomed to frustration by his perception of the vanity of science, for which he finds at one point desperate substitutes in pseudo science and the devil's arts, is one illustration of this sense of void. Shakespeare's *Hamlet* is another, a play in which the very word "thought" seems to acquire a troubled connotation: "the pale cast of thought"; "thought and affliction, passion, hell itself." In these instances, the intellectual excitement of understanding, the zest and pride of achievement through what chiefly constitutes man's dignity," his intellect seem not so much lost as directly inverted.

Thus while on one, and perhaps the better-known, side of the picture man's intellect in Renaissance literature enthusiastically expatiates over the realms of knowledge and unveils the mysteries of the universe, on the other it is beset by puzzling doubts and a profound mistrust of its own powers. Man's moral nature is seen as only little lower than the angels, but also scarcely above the beasts. Earthly power—a favorite theme because Renaissance literature was so largely produced in the courts or with a vivid sense of courtly ideas—is the crown of human aspirations ("How sweet a thing it is to wear a crown, / Within whose circuit is Elysium") but it is also the death's head ("Imperious Caesar, dead and turn'd to clay, / Might stop a hole to keep the wind away").

From the tensions generated by this simultaneous exaltation and pessimism about the human situation, much of Renaissance literature takes its character and strength.

## PETRARCH

The trait which first strikes us as new in Petrarch, if we compare him to the standard image of "medieval man," is the self-centered quality of his work. A comparison between him and Dante, who was about forty years older, points to this quality, and the contrast is made sharper by certain analogies in their situations. Both pursued the same basic motif, the quest for salvation. But while Dante as hero of the quest focused dramatically on himself only on a few enormously effective and severe occasions (his first exchange with Beatrice in the *Purgatory*, XXX, for example). Petrarch was continuously at work on his personal drama, on its lights and shades, on all of its subtle modulations of feeling.

A different way of getting at the same distinction between Renaissance and medieval man may be found in Petrarch's conception of the literary profession and the poet's status. His attitude toward classical antiquity makes him "the first writer of the Renaissance," rather than a writer of the Middle Ages. As a self-conscious man of letters he modeled his work on classical examples, those texts which, as a humanistic scholar, he had helped to rediscover and bring back to life. For example, in 1333 at Liège, he discovered Cicero's oration *Pro Archia*, a Roman "defense of poetry." It would be difficult to overestimate the importance, for European culture, of Petrarch and his friend Boccaccio in establishing the Renaissance model of poet, scholar, and member of the "republic of letters," which even today is an ideal of Western civilization.

Petrarch was a prominent figure of his time. He was a courtier and a diplomat, living for a time near the papal court at Avignon and traveling widely through Europe on diplomatic missions for such families as the Visconti of Milan. But his greatest importance is as a man of letters and learning. Many of Petrarch's travels were devoted to his search for ancient texts, and his literary gifts were fully recognized in his lifetime; he was "crowned" poet laureate in Rome in 1340. As a writer, Petrarch self-consciously attended to the creation of his own image, defining, ordering, and polishing with exquisite care his poems and letters (the letter was then an established literary form). Even accidental events in his life seem to have been inspired by his taste for the harmonious and well-rounded gesture. He came within a few hours of reaching the "perfect" life-span, three score and ten. On April 6, 1327, in the Church of St. Clare, he saw Laura for the first time; she was to become the object and image of his poetic love. Twenty-one years later, Laura died on that very day, the day of Christ's passion. Petrarch frequently used April 6th, as in sonnet 3, to symbolize his own drama of passion.

There would be no drama, of course, in Petrarch's love of Laura without an element of the tragic—his sense of its sinfulness and vanity. Thus he sounds a "medieval" note, but in a new context: that of a great literary artist keenly aware of the ever-changing and ambiguous attractions of mortal beauty and earthly values. One even surmises that these values might have been less attractive to him had they not contained the suspicion of vanity, for without it, they would have afforded a less rich and less complex life. Thus he sings in sonnet 61, "Blest Be the Day" of his first encounter with Laura, the source of his torment. Even though calling Petrarch a romantic may stretch the meaning of that term to the point where it loses its usefulness, we can say that his definition of love as sorrow has had a much wider influence than his relatively superficial traits, such as his self-conscious imagery, which degenerated into the artifices of "Petrarchism."

Another essential part of Petrarch's drama is the death of the lady and her role in death as the mediator between the penitent poet and Divine Grace. Here again the inevitable comparison with Dante makes the differences only more evident. The shift in tone between the poems for Laura alive and those for her "in death" is less relevant than the similarity of the two groups. A sensuous quality pervades both groups, suggesting that even when she is dead, there is an earthly relationship. Thus the poet, in sonnet 300, envies the earth "folding her in invisible embrace" and in sonnet 292, also written after her death, the larger part of the octave is devoted to the living lady's physical appearance. In other sonnets Laura herself, in heaven, refers to her mortal body as her "beautiful veil." In sonnet 333 the poet implores her to come to him the moment of his death and guide him to "the blessed place." His poetry has made the world know and love her, and the implication is that he has thus become worthy of her succor.

The prose selection is the letter to Dionisio da Borgo San Sepolcro describing the poet's ascent of Mount Ventoux. While there can be no doubt about his profound moral tension and the passionate seriousness of his contrition, the tone of this famous letter is established by the way in which reality is turned into symbol, experience ordered into form. As in many of the poems, here is not only a repentant sinner but also a literary master turning autobiography and confession into art. However strong his sense of the vanity and fallaciousness of human attachments, he seems to have no doubt about the validity of one particular manifestation of *virtù*: the sensuous and expert handling of words, the poetic art itself, which knows how to make beauty yield meaning and meaning yield beauty.

## ERASMUS, *THE PRAISE OF FOLLY*

Keeping in mind some of the contrasts indicated above, we realize at once that in Erasmus' *Praise of Folly* (*Moriae encomium*, 1509) easy and one-sided conclusions about the power of the human intellect, the worth and extent of knowledge, and above all the wisdom of man's behavior and the purpose of life are discarded.

To present the issues concretely, Erasmus uses a dramatic setting; he takes for his speaker a feminine figure, Folly, placing her in front of an audience of which she herself makes us aware: "as soon as I began to speak to this great audience, all faces suddenly brightened." One can almost visualize Folly gesturing, pointing to the public, attracting attention: "I am almost out of breath." "But why not speak to you more openly . . . ?" "You applaud! I was sure that you were not so wise, or rather so foolish—no, so wise."

The general tone of her speech is an elegant balance between the jocose and the serious, the erudite and the foolish. This attitude also throws light upon the audience—a congenial one, we feel, made up of people to whom the cultured allusions with which Folly's speech is studded are so familiar that they will appreciate the comic twists performed upon them, as they will, more generally, appreciate the mild satire on conventional oratory which the monologue contains. "I see that you are expecting a peroration, but," she admits in the end, "you are certainly foolish if you think that I can remember any part of such a hodgepodge of words as I have poured out." Folly's attitude toward her audience is not polemic but convivial. The butts of her polemic (the passionless Stoics) constitute a third party, and rather than address such people, Folly enlists her audience's support in rejecting them: "I ask you, if it were put to a vote, what city would choose such a person as mayor?"

This is the "play" as it is presented to us. But of course it is actually a "play within a play"; it is performed within the larger framework consisting of Erasmus and *his* audience, Erasmus and ourselves. From his advantageous position backstage, he uses Folly as an ambiguous mouthpiece. In fact, by presenting his mouthpiece as foolish, light-headed, and rambling, he throws into sharper focus the truths which she expresses; he has secured the advantages of her directness and "innocence" while he grants her the full support of his own erudition and wit. Thus in spite of apparent frivolity, we cannot help continuously sus-

pecting in the book a depth and complexity of meaning between the lines, as it were, for the expression of which Folly is used as a convenient instrument. We shall perhaps best gauge that complexity and come nearest to the ideal center of Erasmus' meaning by asking ourselves, What does Folly stand for? Does she stand for carefree living? For a way of life not hostile to the passions? For foolishness? For self-abandonment? For naïveté? For imagination? Is she simply the lighthearted creation of a great scholar in a frivolous moment, deploring the vanity of intellectual knowledge, and the scholar's austere and solitary life, in favor of instinct, intuition, good fellowship, "innocence"? Or does she embody a paradoxical "wisdom" to be found at the end of a long and perhaps finally frustrating accumulation of learning? Our answer to such questions must be at least as equivocal as the attitude of the work itself.

Clearly the issue of knowledge versus ignorance underlies this writing; Folly's talk may often look like a debunking of the former in favor of the latter, but—and this is the function of the "play"—the attitude ultimately suggested is one of neither "barbaric" rebellion nor unrelieved satiety and desperation. Erasmus' position, whether overtly or between the lines, is rather that of noble and wise compromise: a serene acceptance of the limitations of knowledge rather than a "melancholic" rejection of its value followed by a desperate gesture of rebellion. In other words, Erasmus' attitude toward Folly is not at all the polemical reaction of a dissatisfied intellectual who finds that the mind has not given him satisfactory answers and who therefore embraces folly in the same way as Faust embraces the devil's arts. On the other hand, the author's "praise" of Folly is certainly not feigned or *mainly* ironical. His point of view is not that of the sophisticate who takes a frivolous delight in masquerading, let us say, as a shepherd. When a man like Erasmus implies that possibly fools are really wiser than we are (an implication that underlies many a passage in the book), his attitude toward the "fool" includes understanding, affection, and a real question about value. The balance of irony is kept just in both directions; the wisdom of compromise and the sage's sense of limits are guiding, from backstage, the performance.

What has been said about the value of knowledge can be extended to the value of life: the world is a stage, and the forces ruling its actors may be irrational or ununderstandable, but it is in accordance with nature that we should go on playing our roles. Folly is imagination, inventiveness, and therefore pretense and make-believe; "everything is pretense." But at the same time, "this play is performed in no other way"; "true prudence . . . consists in not desiring more wisdom than is proper to mortals." This is "to act the play of life."

The acceptance of life as a play, as a pageant, opens a vision of true human reality, Erasmus feels, whereas the wisdom of the Stoics (who stand for pure

intellectualism) produces "a marble imitation of a man" from which one shudders away "as from a ghost." Thus Folly regulates life by "a timely mixture of ignorance, thoughtlessness, forgetfulness of evil, hope of good, and a dash of delight."

## CASTIGLIONE, *THE BOOK OF THE COURTIER*

In reading selections from Baldesar Castiglione's treatise on the ideal courtly gentleman, *The Book of the Courtier* (*Il libro del cortegiano*, published in 1528), it is helpful to consider the background description with which the book opens as a "setting," because this approach serves to suggest the vaguely theatrical and "artificial" atmosphere which pervades the composition. It is important to observe, however, that the characters whose highly mannered conversation the book purports to record were all actual members (presented with their own names) of a courtly milieu of which the author himself was a part. These people, then, were known to him not as objects of adulation or satire (the two extremes with which we are perhaps more accustomed to associate literary pictures of aristocracies) but rather as equals and companions whose standards were also his own. Hence Castiglione's attitude is one neither of conventional adulation nor of mockery; the theatrical way in which the scene is set and his characters talk (the traditional form of the Platonic dialogue acquires here the tone of what in the Renaissance was called "civil conversation") does not suggest either official courtly pomp or, conversely, a comedy of manners; it is simply the expression of a style, "artificial" in no derogatory sense, which both the characters and the author considered ideally appropriate to people of their kind and station. The speakers appear somewhat like ladies and gentlemen who have kindly consented, on some courtly occasion, to take roles in a play, except that it happens that the play is their own; they enact, so to speak, themselves. The strong element of stylization (the elaborate phrasings, the manner of the repartee, and the like) is not forced by the writer on his material; we feel rather that in his formalizing process he has followed, and emphasized, qualities that were inherent in the world he pictures. He presents a theatrical and stylized view of a world which was theatrical and stylized to begin with. In this sense the book is the best expression of Renaissance court society at its most refined and self-conscious; of that society which had a taste, as was observed in the general remarks earlier in this introduction, for the well-finished gesture, the act formally perfect of its kind—a taste which applied to all modes and norms of activity, conversation or dueling, art, courtship, etiquette.

Our selections are from the first of the four books (or evening conversations) into which the *Courtier* is divided. The purpose of this first book is to arrive, through the contributions of the obviously experienced speakers, at a description of the perfect courtly gentleman.

Though Machiavelli too, in his description of the prince, presents something of an idealization of a type, his explicit intention is to come down to reality and practical motives, in contrast with the abstractions of preceding authors. Castiglione's attitude is different from the start. He has what we may call a Platonic turn of mind, in the sense that he intentionally and openly seeks the ideal and permanent form behind the transient and fragmentary examples. This point of view in the *Courtier* suggests, among other things, the sense of rule, of adjustment to correct norms, within which Castiglione's mentality characteristically moves. The aim of the book is positive acceptance of certain standards: the assumption is that codes of behavior exist and can be defined, and man can educate himself to comply with them. Relations between individuals, and particularly between members of the ruling portion of society, can be correctly and pleasantly regulated; there is even, as the famous passage on "nonchalance" (*sprezzatura*) at the end of our second selection suggests, a sort of formalization of informality.

Considered against the background of the period with which we are here concerned, the book presents the face opposite to those views of the Renaissance court, especially popularized by drama, in which that institution is the typical scene of intrigue, corruption, violence. In such instances the discrepancy between the reality presented and the idea of "courtesy" is total; the balance is lost, and the eventual consequence is a sense of void, of the purposelessness of actions unsustained by norms, of Hamlet-like melancholy. In Castiglione's idealized vision the balance is fully kept; in fact, the *Courtier* codifies a Utopian moment of perfect and gentle equilibrium.

## MACHIAVELLI, THE PRINCE

*The Prince* (*Il principe*, 1513) consists of twenty-six chapters of various lengths. The first eleven chapters deal with the different types of states and dominions and the ways in which they are acquired and preserved—the early title of the whole book, in Latin, was *De principatibus* (*Of Princedoms*)—and the twelfth to fourteenth chapters focus particularly on the problems of military power. But the book's astounding fame is based mainly on the final part (from the fifteenth chapter to the end), which deals primarily with the personal attributes and "virtues" of the prince himself. In other words, a work which is generally associated with cold and precise realism presents what is after all a hypothetical type, a portrait of an ideal man.

Books of this sort may be classified, in one sense, as pedagogical literature. While for their merits of form and of vivid, if stylized, characterization they can be considered works of art, their overt purpose is to codify a certain set of manners and rules of conduct; the author presents himself therefore as especially wise, an expert in the field. His position is quite different from that of an-

other prominent type of Renaissance writer, the court poet, with his more or less perfunctory panegyric on the patron. The relation between the patron and the pedagogical writer is, at least in appearance, more purposeful. The latter's wisdom concerns something more immediately practical than, say, the poet's vague celebration of his lord's or his lord's ancestors' virtues; he poses ideally at least, as the "mind" behind the lord's "arm."

Machiavelli is a clear example of the pedagogical writer. His pedagogical fervor, the dramatic and oratorical way in which he confronts his listener, the wealth and promptness of his pertinent illustrations are characteristic: "Either you are already prince, or you are on the way to become one. In the first case liberality is dangerous; in the second it is very necessary to be thought liberal. Caesar was one of those. . . . Somebody may answer . . . I answer. . . ." Having a direct knowledge of politics, he is quick to use examples with which he is personally acquainted:

Men are so simple and so subject to present needs that he who deceives in this way will always find those who will let themselves be deceived. I do not wish to keep still about one of the recent instances. Alexander VI did nothing else than deceive men, and had no other intention. . . .

The implied tone of I *know*, I *have seen such things myself* adds a special immediacy to the writing. Machiavelli's view of the practical world may have been an especially startling one; but the sensation caused by his work would have been far less without the rhetorical force, the drama of argumentation, which makes *The Prince* a unique piece of persuasive art.

The view of man in Machiavelli is not at all cheerful. Indeed, the pessimistic notion that man is evil is not so much his conclusion about human nature as his premise; it is the starting point of all subsequent reasoning upon the course for a ruler to follow. The very fact of its being given as a premise, however, tends to qualify it; it is not a firm philosophical judgment but a stratagem, dictated by the facts as they are seen by a lucid observer here and now. The author is committed to his view of mankind not as a philosopher or as a religious man but as a practical politician. He indicates the rules of the game as his experience shows that the game must, under the circumstances, be played.

A prudent . . . ruler cannot and should not observe faith when such observance is to his disadvantage and the causes that made him give his promise have vanished. If men were all good, this advice would not be good, but since men are wicked and do not keep their promises to you, you likewise do not have to keep yours to them.

A basic question in the study of Machiavelli, therefore, is: How much of a realist is he? His picture of the perfectly efficient ruler has something of the character of an abstraction and idealization; it shows, though much less clearly than Castiglione's picture of the courtier, the well-known Renaissance tendency toward idealized, "perfect" form. Machiavelli's abandonment of specific and immediate realities in favor of the ideal is shown most clearly at the conclusion of the book, particularly in the last chapter. He offers there what amounts to the greatest of his illustrations as the prince's preceptor and counselor: the ideal ruler, technically equipped now by his pedagogue, is to undertake a mission—the liberation of Machiavelli's Italy. If we regard the last chapter as a culmination of his discussion rather than a dissonant addition to it, we are likely to feel at that point not only that Machiavelli's realistic method is finally directed toward an ideal task but that his conception of that task, far from being based on immediate realities, is founded on cultural and poetic myths. Machiavelli's method here becomes imaginative rather than scientific. His exhortation to liberate Italy, and his final prophecy, belong to the tradition of poetic visions in which a present state of decay is lamented, and a hope of future redemption is expressed (as in Dante, *Purgatory*, Canto VI). And a very significant part of this hope is presented not in terms of technical political considerations (choice of the opportune moment, evaluation of military power) but in terms of a sort of poetic justice for which precedents are sought in religious and ancient history and in mythology:

. . . if it was necessary to make clear the ability of Moses that the people of Israel should be enslaved in Egypt, and to reveal Cyrus's greatness of mind that the Persians should be oppressed by the Medes, and to demonstrate the excellence of Theseus that the Athenians should be scattered, so at the present time.... Everything is now fully disposed for the work . . . if only your House adopts the methods of those I have set forth as examples. Moreover, we have before our eyes extraordinary and unexampled means prepared by God. The sea has been divided. . . . Manna has fallen.

His Italy, as he observed in the previous chapter, is now a country "without dykes and without any wall of defence." It has suffered from "deluges," and its present rule, a "barbarian" one, "stinks in every nostril." Something is rotten in it, in short, as in Hamlet's Denmark. And we become more and more detached even from the particular example, Italy, as we recognize in the situation a pattern frequently exemplified in tragedy: the desire for communal regeneration, for the cleansing of the *polis*. Of this cleansing, Italy on one side and the imaginary prince and redeemer on the other may be taken as symbols. The envisaged redemption is identified with antiquity and Roman virtue, while the realism of the political observer is here drowned out by the cry of the humanist dreaming of ancient glories.

## RABELAIS, GARGANTUA AND PANTAGRUEL

The life of François Rabelais, a man of wide humanistic education in the Renaissance tradition, typifies the variety of interests of the period, for he was at various points a law student, a monk, and a practicing physician; and he knew the life of people in cities and on country estates, in monasteries and at court. He was not by any means exclusively a professional writer; and his story of giants, written piecemeal through the years of his maturity, in the second quarter of the sixteenth century, is not so much a unified work of fiction as a summation of his wide knowledge, his diverse notions of the world, and his fantasies.

Its peculiar quality may be described in terms of contrasts: the supernatural and the realistic in the characters and in the action; the solemn and the comic, the lofty and the bawdy, in the themes; the erudite and the colloquial in the style. His heroes, as giants, move in a dimension which is entirely out of proportion with ordinary reality. They belong—with their extraordinary size, power, and longevity —to a tradition known to us from myth, from folk tale, and from biblical narrative. Yet these same characters express the feelings and attitudes of ordinary men. In fact they seem to be present as epitomes of what man, according to Rabelais, ought to be in a reasonable and enjoyable world. Rabelais' view of the world, we soon realize, is also well reflected in his literary style. High and low, pedantic and farcical, ponderous and mocking, it is the sign of a broad intellectual and moral inclusiveness, an enthusiastic openmindedness and gusto. As we come across the learned allusion, the solemn Ciceronian phrasing, and the scholastic pedantry, all mingled with the familiar and the folksy, we notice that the presence of the colloquial quality by no means destroys the impact of the erudition or necessarily gives it the tone of parody. For the author attends to both with equal delight and mixes them completely; the blending results in an inseparable whole, sustained everywhere by the same rich manipulation of words and the same exuberant vitality. Thus Rabelais' style concretely embodies his view of the world and of man. His message, as even the new reader soon feels, his view of the human condition, is basically a cheerful one; his work is usually considered a major monument of the Renaissance at its most satisfied and affirmative. The basic theme of drinking, the vast thirst of his giant protagonists, is conveniently taken to symbolize the healthy and all-embracing sensual and intellectual appetites of the period.

A famous contemporary of Rabelais, Benvenuto Cellini, mentioned above, can also be regarded as an instance of the affirmative Renaissance spirit little hampered by doubt and melancholy. In fact, Cellini is even too pure and thoughtless, too "innocent" an example. In his fully adjusted way of living, that somewhat bombastic extrovert does not ask himself about value and meaning. Rabelais, at least implicitly, does take an interest in questions of value; and he seems assured, on what may appear to some of us relatively scant evidence, of the basic goodness and perfectibility of man. The selections given here emphasize that aspect, showing, among other things, Rabelais' faith in a certain type of physical and mental education. They reveal, therefore, his conception of the ideal man fit to live in what he considered a new age. It will be observed in this connection that although Rabelais was, among Europeans of the period, as responsible as anyone for the popular notion of an intellectual Renaissance following the aridity and bondage of medieval scholasticism and the barbarism of the "Gothic night," his ideal man also presents certain qualities which seem to us survivals of medieval codes. His ideal man remains a kind of knight-at-arms, even with the added emphasis on the intellectual ornaments of humanism. And this is true of other Renaissance writers. For example, in the works of Castiglione, Cervantes, Ariosto, and Shakespeare the knightly ideal continues to appear, though variously twisted through irony or in other ways distorted. Rabelais' approach is very direct and hopeful; from his pages we gather the impression that a healthy, wise, gallant, and happy type of man is a concrete possibility. Give the young the right tutoring (his implication is), do away with hampering scholasticism, let them take proper care of their bodily functions, and certain values of tolerance, *bonhommie*, and substantial well-being will finally and inevitably triumph. The sophistic, the arrogant, the hypocritical will be exposed and defeated in the most reasonable and enjoyable of worlds.

Nowhere is this pleasant view expressed more clearly than in the conception of Thélème, the supremely good place on earth, the "abbey" according to Rabelais' heart. All restrictions are banned here, not because total anarchy and license are advocated but rather because for such supremely civilized "nuns" and "monks" as those of the Thélèmite order instinctive inclinations will coincide with virtue: "The only rule of the house was: DO AS THOU WILT because men that are free, of gentle birth, well-bred and at home in civilized company possess a natural instinct that inclines them to virtue and saves them from vice. This instinct they name their honor."

Rabelais' broad optimism is qualified, of course, by the very premises of his story. For all its realism, and in spite of the fact that some episodes are mock-heroic versions of actual and even provincial and domestic events (the Picrochole war that precedes the establishment of the abbey of Thélème), this is still a fable, with giants as its main heroes and fantasy as its frequent method.

Much war, horror, intrigue, and injustice existed in the world as Rabelais knew it. In practical life, he muddled through by his tolerance, wisdom, and capacity for compromise (his temporary sympathy for the Reformation, in a time of raging religious conflict, stopped "this side of the stake"). But he survived also because he invented through his literature a world fashioned according to his own aspirations. In that world, for example, the heroes on the side of good and of justice not only win wars but also get a chance to display to-

ward the vanquished an effective and nobly magniloquent clemency. The utopian quality of this world illustrates again the tendency of the Renaissance mind to seek the perfect model, the exemplary, ideal form. Some important passages of the book, especially the famous letter (reprinted here) of Gargantua to Pantagruel, dated from Sir Thomas More's ideal land, Utopia, make clear that this chronicle of giants, biblical in its magnitude and in its patriarchal qualities, with its Renaissance aspiration to "achieve mental, moral and technical excellence," in its serious moments symbolizes the urge to perpetuate, from father to son, the true and noble form of man and thus idealistically confirm his divine origin, his "dignity."

## MONTAIGNE, *ESSAYS*

If one accepts the common view that in the Renaissance the individual human being was exalted, and therefore a special emphasis was placed on the study of man in his "virtues" and singularities, it is natural to think of Montaigne as representative. As the father of the modern genre of the personal essay, in the last quarter of the sixteenth century, he obviously felt that the characteristics of his individual mind and heart—all their minute aspects, variations, and even whims—were worthy of being carefully recorded. The student will soon notice that of the writers presented in this book Montaigne is the one who most openly speaks in his own right, clearly and unabashedly as himself. While, for instance, Erasmus adopts the ambiguous mouthpiece of his "Folly" to express certain views, Montaigne's characteristic and somewhat rambling speech is in the simplest and most quintessential first person. Perhaps at no other time in literature—certainly not in the nineteenth-century age of romanticism, where in spite of the widespread notions about "free" expression of individual feelings writers so often showed themselves through an alter ego or a heroic mask—has a writer so thoroughly attempted to present himself without in the least assuming a pose, or falling into a type. "Had my intention been to court the world's favor," Montaigne writes in the foreword to his *Essays (Essais)*, "I should have trimmed myself more bravely, and stood before it in a studied attitude. I desire to be seen in my simple, natural, and everyday dress, without artifice or constraint; for it is myself I portray." And elsewhere he affirms:

Authors communicate themselves to the world by some special and extrinsic mark; I am the first to do so by my general being, as Michel de Montaigne, not as a grammarian or a poet or a lawyer. If the world finds fault with me for speaking too much of myself, I find fault with the world for not even thinking of itself.

But nothing would be more erroneous than to suppose that Montaigne's focusing on his individual self implies a sense of the extraordinary importance of man, of his central place in the world, or of the special power of his understanding. The contrary is true. In the first place, in temperament Montaigne is singularly opposed to assuming an attitude of importance: one of the keynotes of his writing, and one of his premises in undertaking it, is that the subject is average, "mediocre." In describing himself he is presenting an example of the ordinary human being, for the benefit of a few intimates. He declares that he has "but a private and family end in view," and in that sense, in fact, his way of introducing himself to the reader shows a nobly elegant and perhaps vaguely ironical humbleness: "So, Reader, I am myself the subject of my book; it is not reasonable to expect you to waste your leisure on a matter so frivolous and empty." And then there is an even more fundamental reason why Montaigne's presentation of himself is free from any heroic posturing or intellectual pride—a reason which involves his whole view of man's place in the world. In his deciding to write about himself and to probe, to "essay," his own nature, the implication is that this is the only subject on which a man can speak with any degree of certainty. Actually, then, this writer whose work is the most acute exposure of an individual personality in the literature of the Renaissance, is at the same time one of the highest illustrations of man's ironical consciousness of his intellectual limits.

It would be a mistake to forget, however, that his work remains an outstanding assertion of an individuality, even though it is an assertion of doubt, contradition, change. Here as in other instances the student will do well to examine the quality and novelty of the work in the actual text in terms of realized writing, of "style." A solid classical manner, reflected in certain elements of the syntactical structure and in the continuous support of classical quotations, is combined in Montaigne's style with the variety, the apparent disconnectedness, and the dramatic assertiveness of a man who is continuously analyzing a fluid and, his modesty notwithstanding, singularly attractive subject.

Others form man; I describe him, and portray a particular, very ill-made one, who, if I had to fashion him anew, should indeed be very different from what he is. But now it is done.... The world is but a perennial see-saw. All things in it are incessantly on the swing, the earth, the rocks of the Caucasus, the Egyptian pyramids.... Even fixedness is nothing but a more sluggish motion. I cannot fix my object; it is befogged, and reels with a natural intoxication.... I do not portray the thing in itself. I portray the passage....

In spite of what may often seem a leisurely gait, the writer is continuously on the alert, listening to the promptings of his thought, his sensibility, his imagination, and registering them. The affirmation of the fluidity of the human personality, of the universality of the flux, is therefore both the premise of his writing and the sum of his study of man; it is both his method and his result.

Thus, although he writes in terms of one individual, and with a fairly obvious abhorrence of any sort of classification or description of types in the manner of conventional moralists, a powerfully keen observation of man in general emerges from his writings—an observation of man's nature, intellectual power, and capacity for coherent action; of his place on earth among other beings; of his place in Creation. Our selections offer instances of Montaigne's remarks on these matters.

If we keep in mind the large pattern of Renaissance literature, poised betwen positive and negative, enthusiasm and melancholy, we shall probably find that the general temper of his assertions of doubt and his consciousness of vanity, by no means suggests an attitude of despair and gloom. His attitude seems positive and negative in the same breath; it could be called a rich and fruitful sense of the relativity of everything. Thus if he examines and "essays" man's capacity to act purposefully and coherently (see the essay "Of the Inconsistency of Our Actions" among our selections), his implicit verdict is not that man's action is absolutely vain. Rather, observing the usual example—his own self—and seeing that there is nothing he can say of himself "absolutely, simply, and steadily," he refuses to attribute to the human personality a coherence which it does not possess and which, we may be tempted to surmise, would rather impoverish it. "Our actions are but a patchwork. . . . We are all made up of bits. . . . There is as much difference between us and ourselves, as between us and others." And he sustains his arguments, as usual, with a wealth of examples and anecdotes which are at once evidence of his vital curiosity about human nature and, in many cases, of his man-to-man familiarity with antiquity: Emperor Augustus, to mention one, pleases him because his character successfully escapes an all-of-a-piece description; he has "slipped through the fingers of even the most daring critics."

A sense of relativity and a balanced outlook, rather than a negative and desperate reversal of the optimistic view of the human situation, are apparent also from Montaigne's observation of man—and particularly of the civilized Renaissance man whom he exemplifies—in relation to his fellow human beings. In the famous essay "Of Cannibals," where a comparison is made between the codes of primitive tribes and those of "ourselves," the basic idea is not a disparagement of our civilization but a relativistic warning, for "we all call barbarism that which does not fit in with our usages." The cannibals' acts of barbarity are recognized, but the writer is "not so much concerned that we should remark on the horrible barbarity of such acts, as that, whilst rightly judging their errors, we should be so blind to our own." We do much worse, adds Montaigne, who wrote in times of horrible religious strife, and we do it under the guise of piety. The enlightening sense of relativity —rather than a more extreme and totally paradoxical view of the "nobility" of savages—permits him to see and admire what he considers superior elements in

the customs of the cannibals (for instance, their conception of valor and their conduct of warfare). Here, in fact, Montaigne describes and admires a code of unrewarded gallantry, of valor for valor's sake, which was not uncommonly cherished by writers of the Renaissance (Castiglione, for example). ". . . the acquisition of the victor," writes Montaigne, "is the glory and advantage of having proved himself the superior in valour and virtue. . . . The honour of virtue consists in combating, not in beating." We may incidentally add that acceptance of this notion of pure "virtue," practiced for no material purposes and as self-rewarding as a beautiful object, appears to have been, for a writer like Montaigne, the way to preserve an admiration for the warrior's code of manly courage and valor in spite of the basically pacifist tendencies of his temperament and his bitter disinclination for the spectacles of conflict and bloodshed witnessed in his own time.

Naturally, an even larger sense of relativity emerges from Montaigne's writing when he examines man's place in the universal frame of things, as he does, in an outstanding instance, in some famous passages of the "Apology for Raimond Sebond" (a selection from which is included in this volume). Man's notion of his privileged position in Creation is eloquently questioned: "What has induced him to believe that that wonderful motion of the heavenly vault, the eternal light of those torches rolling so proudly over his head, the awe-inspiring agitations of that infinite sea, were established, and endure through so many centuries for his service and convenience?" The tone of the whole section is revealing. In many writers a similar anxiety about man's smallness and ignorance casts upon the human condition a light of tragic vanity. Montaigne's acceptance of the situation is to use some of our other examples as convenient points of reference—more Erasmian than Hamletlike. If he asks questions which involve, to say the very least, the whole Renaissance conception of man's "dignity," the impression, as we listen to his voice, is never really one of dark negation and melancholy. While man's advantages over other beings are quietly evaluated and discredited ("this licence of thought . . . is an advantage sold to him very dearly . . . For from it springs the principal source of . . . sin, sickness, irresolution, affliction, despair"), he maintains a balanced and often humorous tone in which even the frivolous aside of the personal essayist is not dissonant, but characteristic: "When I play with my cat, who knows but that she regards me more as a plaything than I do her?" Thus without raising his voice too much he achieves a point of view which suggests broadness and inclusiveness rather than gloom and despair. For, while his view of the "mediocrity" of man among other beings debunks any form of intellectual conceit, on the other hand an encompassing sense of natural fellowship in Creation is envisaged: "I have said all this to establish the resemblance to human conditions,

and to bring us back and join us to the majority."

This sense of a "natural" fellowship seems to characterize not only Montaigne's view of the position of man in Creation but also his conception of man as a moral individual in relation to other men. The student may see this at the end of our final selection, where the practice of goodness, as, in other instances, that of valor, is envisaged as a beautiful and self-rewarding act of "virtue":

There is . . . no goodness in which a well-born nature does not delight. . . . There is no small pleasure in feeling oneself preserved from the contagion of so corrupt an age, and saying to oneself, "Should any one look into my very soul, he would yet not find me guilty of the affliction or ruin of any man. . . ." These testimonies of a good conscience please; and this natural satisfaction is a great boon to us, and the only payment that will never fail us.

Difficult as it is to reduce Montaigne's views to short and abstract statements, the reader will probably be left with the impression that here his vision of man, and of the possibility of a good life, is nearer to hopefulness than to despair. Though his attitude is far from Rabelais' optimism and exuberance, it too is based on a balance between the "natural" and the intellectual, between instinct and reason. He belittles, at times even scornfully, the power of the human intellect, and like Erasmus he points to instinctive simplicity of mind as being more conducive to happiness and even to true knowledge; but on the other hand the whole tone of his work, its intellectual sophistication, its very bulk, and the loving manner with which he attended to it, show that his own thought was not something that "sicklied o'er" his life, but something that gave it sustenance and delight. Thus we see in him some of the basic contrasts of the Renaissance mind —the acceptance and the rejection of the intellectual dignity of man—conducing not to disruption but to temperately positive results. Though his work offers anything but the abstract scheme of an ideal man, and he is not proposing a model or a recipe, yet in passages like the one cited in the preceding paragraph, some norm of the pattern of a truly virtuous man—in the sense expressed later by the French as "honest" (as in the phrase *honnête homme*)— seems unobtrusively to emerge. And though it is not imposed upon the audience, any reader is free to think that acceptance of this norm would result in better spiritual balance in the individual and a more harmonious and sensible fellowship in society. The author does not preach ("Others form man; I describe him . . .") because his pattern of conduct is one which cannot be taught but only experienced. He limits himself to exemplifying it in his own wise and unheroic self.

## CERVANTES, DON QUIXOTE

Although *Don Quixote* was a popular success from the time Part I was published in 1605, it was only later recognized as important literature. This delay

was due partly to the fact that in a period of established and well-defined genres like the epic, the tragedy, and the pastoral romance (Cervantes himself tried his hand frequently at some of these forms), the unconventional combination of elements in *Don Quixote* resulted in a work of considerable novelty, with the serious aspects hidden under a mocking surface.

The initial and overt purpose of the book was to satirize a very popular type of literature, the romances of chivalry. In those long yarns, which had to do with the Carolingian and Arthurian legends and were full of supernatural deeds of valor, implausible and complicated adventures, duels, and enchantments, the literature which had expressed the medieval spirit of chivalry and romance had degenerated to the same extent to which, in our day, certain conventions of romantic literature have degenerated in "pulp" fiction and film melodrama. Up to a point, then, what Cervantes set out to do was to produce a parody, the caricature of a literary type. But neither the nature of his genius nor the particular method he chose allowed him to limit himself to such a relatively simple and direct undertaking. The actual method he followed in order to expose the silliness of the romances of chivalry was to show to what extraordinary consequences they would lead a man insanely infatuated with them, once this man set out to live "now" according to their patterns of action and belief. So what we have is not mere parody or caricature, for there is a great deal of difference between simply presenting a grotesque version of a story dealing with a remote and more or less imaginary world, and presenting a modern man deciding to live by the standards of that world in a modern and realistic context. The first consequence is a mingling of two different genres. On the one hand, as even the beginning reader of *Don Quixote* soon recognizes, much of the language and material of the book turns out to have the color and intonation of the glamorous world of chivalry. The fact that that world and that tone depend for their existence in the book on the powers of evocation and self-deception of the hero himself makes them no less operative artistically, and adds, in fact, an important element of idealization. On the other hand, the chivalric world is continuously combined with the elements of contemporary life evoked by the narrator—the realities of landscape and talk, peasants and nobles, inns and highways. So the author can draw on two sources, roughly the realistic and the romantic, truth and imagination, practical facts and metaphysical values. In this respect, in his having found a way to bring together concrete actuality and highly ideal values, Cervantes can be said to have fathered the modern novel.

The consequences of Cervantes' invention are more apparent when the reader begins to analyze a little more closely the nature of those two worlds, the romantic and the realistic, or the kind of impact which the first exercises on the second. The hero embodying the world of the romances is not, as we know, a cavalier of old; he is an impoverished country gentleman, adopting that code in the "modern" world. The code of chivalry is not simply and directly satirized; it is placed in a context different from its native one. The result of that new association is a new whole, a new unity. The "code" is renovated; it is put into a different perspective, given another chance.

We should remember in this connection that in the process of deterioration which the romances of chivalry had undergone, certain basically attractive ideals had become empty conventions—for instance, the ideals of love as devoted "service," of adventurousness, of loyalty to high concepts of valor and generosity. In the new context those values are re-examined. Incidentally, Cervantes may well have gained a practical sense of them in his own life, at the time of his early youth, when he was a warrior at Lepanto (the great victory of the European coalition against the "infidels"), and a pirate's captive. Since he began writing *Don Quixote* in his late fifties, a vantage point from which his adventurous youth must have appeared impossibly remote, a factor of nostalgia—which could hardly have been present in a pure satire—may well have entered into his composition of the work. Furthermore, had Cervantes undertaken a direct caricature of the romance genre, the serious and noble values of chivalry could not have been made apparent except negatively, but in the context devised by him in *Don Quixote* they find a way to assert themselves positively also.

The book in its development is, to a considerable extent, the story of that assertion—of the impact that Don Quixote's revitalization of the chivalric code has on a contemporary world. We must remember, of course, that there is ambiguity in the way that assertion is made; it works slowly on the reader, as his own discovery rather than as the narrator's open suggestion. Actually, whatever attraction the chivalric world of his hero's vision may have had for Cervantes, he does not openly support Don Quixote at all. He even seems at times to go further in repudiating him than he needs to, for the hero is officially insane, and the narrator never tires of reminding us of this. One critic has described the attitude he affects toward his creature as "animosity." Nevertheless, by the very magniloquence and, often, the extraordinary coherence and beauty which the narrator allows his hero to display in his speeches in defense of his vision and of his code, we are gradually led to discover for ourselves the serious and important elements these contain; in fact, we suspect that the "animosity" ultimately does nothing but intensify our interest in Don Quixote and our sympathy for him. And in that process we are, as audience, simply repeating the experiences which many characters are having on the "stage" of the book, in their relationships with him.

Generally speaking, the encounters between the ordinary world and Don Quixote are encounters between the world of reality and that of illusion, between reason and imagination, ultimately between the world in which action is prompted by material considerations and interests and a world in which action is prompted by ideal motives. Our selections exemplify these aspects of the experience. Among the first adventures are some which have most contributed to popularize the Don Quixote legend: he sees windmills and decides they are giants; country inns become castles; flocks of sheep, armies. Though the conclusions of such episodes often have the ludicrousness of slapstick comedy, there is a powerfully imposing quality about Don Quixote's insanity: his madness always has method, a commanding persistence and coherence. And there is perhaps an inevitable sense of moral grandeur in the spectacle of anyone remaining so unflinchingly faithful to his own vision. The world of "reason" may win in point of fact, but a residue of moral superiority is left with Quixote.

Besides, we increasingly realize that his own manner of action has greatness in itself, and not only the greatness of persistence: his purpose is to redress wrongs, to come to the aid of the afflicted, to offer generous help, to challenge danger and practice valor. And we finally feel the impact of the arguments which sustain his action—for example, in the section from Part II (the episode of the lions) in which he expounds "the meaning of valor." The ridiculousness of the situation is counterbalanced by the basic seriousness' of Quixote's motives; his notion of courage for the sake of courage appears, and is recognized, as singularly noble, a sort of generous display of integrity in a world usually run on a lower plane. Thus the distinction between "reason" and "madness," truth and illusion, becomes, to say the least, ambiguous. Don Quixote's delusions are indeed exposed, once they are checked against hard facts, but the authority of such facts is, morally, questionable.

The effectiveness of Don Quixote's conduct and vision is seen most clearly in his relation with Sancho Panza. An attempt to define that relation will be the best way for the student to come to grips with the book. It would be rather crude oversimplification to say that Don Quixote and Sancho represent illusion and reality, the world of the abstract and insane code of knight-errantry in contrast with the present world of down-to-earth practicalities. Actually Sancho, though his nature is strongly defined by such elements as his common sense, his earthy speech, his simple phrases studded with proverbs set against the hero's magniloquence, is mainly characterized in his development by the degree to which he believes in his master. He is caught in the snare of Don Quixote's vision; the seeds of the imaginative life are successfully implanted in him.

The impact on Sancho of Quixote's view of life serves therefore to illustrate one of the important aspects of the hero and, we may finally say, one of the important aspects of Renaissance literature: the attempt, finally frustrated but extremely attractive as long as it lasts, of the individual mind to produce a vision and a system of its own, in a world which often seems to have lost a universal frame of reference and an ultimately satisfactory sense of the value and meaning of action. What Don Quixote presents is a vision of a world which, for all its aberrant qualities, appears generally to be more colorful and more thrilling, and also, incidentally, to be inspired by more honorable rules of conduct, than the world of ordinary people, "realism," current affairs, private interests, easy jibes, and petty pranks. It is a world in which actions are performed out of a sense of their beauty and excitement, not for the sake of their utility or, as we would say now, of their practicality. It is, again, the world as stage, animated by "folly"; in this case the lights go out at the end, an end which is "reasonable" and therefore gloomy. Sancho provides the major example of one who is exposed to that vision and absorbs that light while it lasts. How successfully he has done so is seen during the hero's death scene, in which he begs of his master not to die but to continue the play, as has been suggested, in a new dress. But at that final point the hero is "cured" and killed, and Sancho is restored to the petty interests of the world as he can see it by his own lights, after the cord connecting him to his imaginative master is cut by the latter's "repentance" and death.

## MARLOWE, DR. FAUSTUS

The legend of Faust (whether or not such a character even existed is irrelevant) has occupied an important place in literature since the Renaissance. Like Don Juan, Faust is one of the characters to whom authors have returned again and again as convenient epitomes of certain traits and aspirations. The character of Faust has been varied and adapted to suit the intellectual needs of the times, much as ancient and modern poets have used the heroes of Greek mythology for their own purposes.

Marlowe's Dr. Faustus powerfully exemplifies some of the intellectual aspirations of the Renaissance. But he is haunted by an inner conflict, a sense of the vanity and sinfulness of these aspirations. Whereas the tension of intellectual opposites produces in certain other instances some sort of compromise, and often fruitful results, here the outcome of inner conflict is tragedy and ruin. In our gallery of Renaissance heroes Dr. Faustus represents an extreme case, almost opposite to Rabelais' exuberant and satisfied sensualist-scholar; to him the fruit of knowledge is not the confirmation of man's dignity and divine nature, but despair and destruction.

The popular tendency to identify Faust with magic and witchcraft, suffering a final punishment for having followed the un-

orthodox and sinful black arts, is of course justified. But such a simple scheme, while it may have been the whole "point" of earlier versions of the story, does not account for the obviously larger and deeper implication we discern in Marlowe's tragedy. Realizing this, we must examine Dr. Faustus' knowledge and aspirations. Both in the hero's opening phase where he expresses his satiety and dissatisfaction with man's accumulated knowledge, and in the latter one where he embraces magic and the devil's arts, he is concerned with the proudest intellectual values of the Renaissance. Such well-known attitudes of the period as excitement in discovery and delight in intellectual and physical power are expressed with an unmatched imaginative and metric splendor: "Faustus, these books, thy wit, and our experience / Shall make all nations to canonize us." Yet they are also presented as temptations of the devil.

In this light, the progression by which Dr. Faustus, scientist and scholar, arrives at his decision to sell his soul to the devil, is not clear-cut. We can, of course, trace the route he travels, the crucial episode of which is his decision to give himself to the arts of Mephistopheles. As the play opens, Dr. Faustus is presented in his study, feeling the **vanity of his intellectual pursuits**. These studies are, to him, vain and dusty; but in his enumeration of them we recognize the very culture on which many intellectuals of the time would have securely counted: Greek philosophy and physics, the laws of the Roman empire, the Vulgate version of the Scriptures. Yet, in the opening monologue of Marlowe's play Faustus reviews and discards these pillars of the humane studies and turns to the "metaphysics of magicians." He has tried, as it were, to cure his thirst for knowledge and power by orthodox means, but the cure, as far as he is concerned, has failed. He then turns to less usual and less reputable means to satisfy himself somewhat in the same way that a patient dissatisfied with a physician's cure turns to a brilliant charlatan. Magic, he hopes, will "resolve" him "of all ambiguities."

What does magic promise him? It promises a more colorful and adventurous side of that same Renaissance body of values to which his discarded studies and books also belong. Dr. Faustus can exercise his glamorous imagination, his instinctive longing for beauty and power—the "magic" of the period. Instead of plodding through the traditional texts he can imagine thrilling voyages, the Venetian argosies, and express his desire for vast earthly conquest: "I'll join the hills that bind the Afric shore/And make that country continent to Spain,/And both contributory to my crown. . . ." This imperial dream is more than once expressed with references to antiquity, as a new vision of ancient myth ("from America the golden fleece"; "Instead of Troy shall Wittenberg be sacked"). Faustus is, of course, equally infatuated with ancient mythology, as represented by Helen, the supreme image of powerful beauty to which he aspires as to a culminating fulfillment of his desires.

Such aspirations and visions, doomed to a catastrophic end, give the figure of Dr. Faustus heroic stature. We can clearly see his heroism by comparing him to the Scholars. The Scholars hold the position which the Chorus in Greek tragedy often does—middle of the road, conformish, prudent. Dr. Faustus, by comparison, has the grandeur of some of Dante's damned. He lives for higher stakes and falls harder; there is greatness in the very extent of his final hopelessness. In the end it is clear, as we suggested, that the sense of doom has presided over both phases, both means, fair and foul, of Faustus' search for knowledge. Not only his "magic" visions but his whole past come back to haunt him, and we no longer have the lyric beauty of the Helen passage but the panting, colloquial, extraordinarily effective monologue in which all his science, all his knowledge, is desperately rejected: "O would I had never seen Wittenberg, never read book! And what wonders I have done all Germany can witness, yea all the world, for which Faustus hath lost both Germany and the world, yea heaven itself. . . ."

Seen thus against the background of the period, Marlowe's *Dr. Faustus* is considerably more interesting than the simple story of how a necromancer by his tricky dabbling with magic lost his soul. The nature of the hero's despair cuts deeper than that; as a Renaissance character he embodies a more deeply earned dissatisfaction. Here is more than ordinary "melancholy"; the drama seems to suggest that the seeds of damnation are implicit in some of the most cherished and proud pursuits and attitudes of the period; their presentation as devilish temptations is a concrete way of symbolizing their comprehensively damning nature. In this light, the play becomes one of the most contemporary statements we have of man's terror at the daring of his own thought.

## SHAKESPEARE, *HAMLET*

It is natural to include *Hamlet* (1601) in a selection of Renaissance literature because the play is undoubtedly the work of the English Renaissance which most clearly belongs to the literary consciousness of the world in general. Probably no character in Renaissance literature is more familiar to world audiences than Shakespeare's Hamlet. He belongs to the world also in the sense that some of the influential interpretations of his nature have been developed outside the country and language of his origin, the most famous being the one offered by Goethe in *Wilhelm Meister*. The unparalleled reputation of the work may also have certain nonliterary causes. For instance, it is a play whose central role is singularly cherished by actors in all languages as the test of stardom; and, conversely, audiences sometimes content themselves with a rather vague notion of the work as a whole and concentrate on the attractively problematical and eloquent hero, and on the actor impersonating him, waiting for his famous soliloquies as

a certain type of operagoer waits for the next aria of his favorite singer. But along with the impact of the protagonist, there are other and deeper reasons why the world should naturally have given *Hamlet* its place in the common patrimony of literature. It is a drama which concerns personages of superior station, and the conflicts and problems associated with men of high degree (themes which, incidentally, are encountered only rarely in literature nowadays); and it reveals these problems in terms of a particular family. Although classicist critics considered Shakespeare "irregular" and therefore, in a quite external sense, untraditional, the matter of *Hamlet* belongs to a great and recognizable tradition, presenting as it does an individual and domestic dimension along with a public one—the pattern of family conflict within the larger pattern of the *polis*—like the plays of antiquity which dealt with the Theban myth, such as *King Oedipus*.

This public dimension of *Hamlet* helps us see it, for our present purposes, in relation to the literature of the Renaissance. For the framework within which the characters are presented and come into conflict is a court. In spite of the Danish locale and the relatively remote period of the action, it is a plainly Renaissance court exhibiting the structure of interests to which Machiavelli's *Prince* has potently drawn our attention. There is a ruler holding power, and much of the action is related to questions concerning the nature of that power—

the way in which he has acquired it and the ways in which it can be preserved. Moreover, there is a courtly structure: the King has several courtiers around him, among whom Hamlet, the heir apparent, is only the most prominent.

We have seen some of the forms of the Renaissance court pattern in earlier selections—in Castiglione, Rabelais, Machiavelli. The court served as the ruling nucleus of the polity, as an arena for conflicts of interest and of wit, as a setting for the cultivation and codification of aristocratic virtues (valor, physical and intellectual brilliance, "courtesy"). The basic positives of the cult of human achievement on earth, so prominent in the Renaissance, were given in courtly life their characteristic field of action and their testing ground. And as we have observed, the negatives (melancholy, sense of void and purposelessness) also emerged there.

Examining *Hamlet*, we soon realize that its temper belongs more to the negative than to the positive phase of the Renaissance. Certain outstanding forms of human endeavor (the establishment of earthly power, the display of gallantry, the confident attempt of the mind to grasp the world's picture and inspire purposeful action), which elsewhere are presented as highly worthwhile, or are at least soberly discussed in terms of their value and limits, seem to be caught here in a condition of disorder and accompanied by a sense of vanity and void.

The way in which the state and the court of Denmark are presented is significant: they are shown in images of disease and rottenness. And here again, excessive stress on the protagonist himself must be avoided. His position as denouncer of the prevailing decadence, and the major basis for his denunciation— the murder of his father, which leads to his desire to obtain revenge and purify the court by destroying the present king—are central elements in the play; but they are not the *whole* play. The public situation is indicated, and Marcellus has pronounced his famous "Something is rotten . . . " before Hamlet has talked to the Ghost and learned the Ghost's version of events. Moreover, the sense of outside dangers and internal disruption everywhere transcends the personal story of Hamlet, of the revenge, of Claudius' crime; these are simply the signs of the breakdown, portents of a general situation. In this sense, we may tentatively say that the general theme of the play has to do with a kingdom, a society, a *polis*, going to pieces—or even more, with its realization that it has gone to pieces already. Concomitant with this is a sense of the vanity of those forms of human endeavor and power of which the kingdom and the court are symbols.

The tone which the dramatist wants to establish is evident from the opening scenes: the night air is full of dread premonitions; sentinels turn their eyes toward the outside world, from which threats are coming; meantime, the Ghost has already made his appearance inside, a sinister omen. The kingdom, as we proceed, is presented in terms which are an almost point by point reversal of the ideal. Claudius, the *pater patriae* and *pater familias*, whether we believe the Ghost's indictment or not (Hamlet does not necessarily, and some of his famous indecision has been attributed to his seeking evidence of the Ghost's truthfulness before acting), by marrying the Queen has committed an act which according to the code of the protagonist is corrupt. There is an overwhelming sense of disintegration in the body of the state, visible in the first court assembly and in all subsequent ones: in their various ways the two courtiers, Hamlet and Laertes, are aliens, thinking of departure; they offer, around their king, a picture which is quite unlike that of the conventional paladins, supports of the throne, in a well-manned and well-mannered court. (In Rabelais' "kingdom," when Grangousier is ruler, the pattern is also a courtly and knightly one, but the young heir, Gargantua, who is like Hamlet a university student, readily abandons his studies to answer the fatherland's call; here the direction is the opposite.)

On the other hand, as in all late and decadent phases of a social or artistic structure (the court in a sense is both), instead of the substance we have the semblance, the ornate and empty façades, of which the more enlightened members of the group are mockingly aware. Thus Polonius, who after Hamlet is the major figure in the King's retinue, is presented sa-tirically in his empty formalities of speech and conventional norms of behavior. And there are numerous instances (Osric is one) of manners being replaced by mannerisms. Hence the way in which courtly life is represented in the play suggests always the hollow, the fractured, the crooked. The traditional forms and institutions of gentle living, and all the pomps and solemnities, are marred by corruption and distortion. Courtship and love are reduced to Hamlet's mockery of a "civil conversation" in the play scene, his phrases carrying not Castiglione's Platonic loftiness and the repartee of "gentilesse," but punning undercurrents of bawdiness. The theater, a traditional institution of courtly living, is "politically" used by the hero as a device to expose the King's crime. There are elements of macabre caricature in the play's treatment of the solemn theme of death (see, for instance, the manner of Polonius' death, which is a sort of sarcastic version of a cloak-and-dagger scene; or the effect of the clownish gravediggers' talk). Finally, the arms tournament, the typical occasion for the display of courtiers' gallantry in front of their king, is here turned by the scheming of the King himself into the play's conclusive scene of carnage. And the person who, on the King's behalf, invites Hamlet to that feast is Osric, the "waterfly," the caricature of the hollow courtier.

This sense of corruption and decadence dominates the general temper of the action in the play, and it obviously qualifies the character of Hamlet, his indecision, his sense of vanity and disenchantment with the world he lives in. In him the relation between thought and deed, intent and realization, is confused in the same way that the norms and institutions which would regulate the life of a well-ordered court have been deprived of their original purpose and beauty. He and the King are the two "mighty opposites," and it can be argued that against Hamlet's indecision and negativism the King presents a more positive scheme of action, at least in the purely Machiavellian sense, at the level of practical power politics. But even this conclusion will prove only partly true. There are indeed moments in which all that the King seems to wish for himself is to forget the past and rule honorably. He advises Hamlet not to mourn his father excessively, for melancholy is not according to "nature." He shows on various occasions a high and competent conception of his office: a culminating instance is the courageous and cunning way in which he confronts and handles Laertes' wrath. The point can be made that since his life is obviously threatened by Hamlet (who was seeking to kill him, when by mistake he killed Polonius instead), the King acts within a legitimate pattern of politics in wanting to have Hamlet liquidated. But this argument cannot be carried so far as to demonstrate that he represents a fully positive attitude toward life and the world, even in the strictly amoral terms of power technique. For in fact his action is corroded by an element alien to that technique—the vexations of his own conscience. In spite of his energy and his extrovert qualities he too becomes part of the negative picture of disruption, and lacks concentration of purpose. The images of decay and putrescence which characterize the general picture of his court extend to his own speech: his "offense," in his own words, "smells to heaven."

To conclude, *Hamlet* as a Renaissance tragedy presents a world particularly "out of joint," a world which, having lost long ago the sense of a grand extra-temporal design which was so important to the medieval man (to Hamlet the thought of the afterlife is even more puzzling and dark than that of this life), looks with an even greater sense of disenchantment at the circle of temporal action symbolized by the kingdom and the court. These could have offered certain codes of conduct and certain objects of allegiance which would have given individual action its purposefulness, but now their order has been destroyed. Ideals which once had power and freshness have lost their vigor under the impact of satiety, doubt, and melancholy.

Since communal values are so degraded, it is natural to ask in the end whether some alternative attempt at a settlement can be seen, with Hamlet, like other Renaissance heroes, adopting an individual code of conduct, however extravagant. On the whole, Hamlet seems too steeped in his own hopelessness, and in the courtly mechanism to which he inevitably belongs, to be able to save himself through some sort of personal intellectual and moral compromise or through his own version of total escape or total dream; for his antic disposition is a strategy, his "folly" is political. Still, the usual temper of his brooding and often moralizing speech, his melancholy and dissatisfaction, his very desire for revenge do seem to imply an aspiration toward some form of moral beauty, a nostalgia for a world—as the King his father's must have been—of clean allegiances and respected codes of honor. One thing worth examining in this connection is his attitude toward Fortinbras. Fortinbras is a marginal character, but our attention is emphatically drawn to him both at the very opening and at the very close of the play. There is no doubt that while in the play certain positive virtues—such as friendship, loyalty, and truthfulness—are represented by the very prominent Horatio, who will live on to give a true report of Hamlet, in Fortinbras the ideals of gallant knighthood, which in the present court have been so corrupted and lost, seem to have been presented at their purest. And he has, of course, Hamlet's "dying voice." Earlier, in Act IV, Scene 4, Hamlet has seen him move with his army toward an enterprise characterized by the flimsiness of its material rewards. In a world where all matter seems corrupt, Hamlet's qualified sympathy for that gratuitous display of honor for honor's sake, of valor "even for an eggshell," of death braved "for a fantasy," calls to mind some of the serious aspects of the Quixotic code.

## DONNE, SONGS AND SONNETS

The revaluation of Donne's poetry has been one of the crucial experiences in the history of poetic taste in our century. And there seems to be no doubt that his place among the most effective and original poets in any language is now firmly assured. The main reasons for this, as even the newest of readers probably perceives at once, can be summarized under two large headings: the poet's "tone of voice," the feeling of lively, vibrantly "spoken" language; and the use of varied, "startling" situations and images, especially in the sense that elements supposedly belonging to diverse areas of knowledge and sensibility are put together, with the result of stirring imagination and reason, senses and mind.

In our present context, briefly trying to elaborate on those two aspects of Donne's genius, we can see that they fit quite well within some of the definitions of the Renaissance that we have been using. If we say that Donne gathers images and situations from many different areas of knowledge, our emphasis is not on the scattered diversity of his objects and themes, but on his power and effectiveness in combining them; his "startling" associations are his way of encompassing large segments of human experience and of giving them poetic shape and impact. So his poetic voice is that of a man who has absorbed with intelligence and gusto the culture of a time of great historical and psychological upheaval and of equally great intellectual enrichment.

His mode of expression, his poetic manner, is correspondingly varied and authoritative. In Donne at his best, we first of all find the famous, irresistible openings—"I wonder, by my troth, what thou and I/Did, till we loved?"; "For God's sake hold your tongue, and let me love"; "Death, be not proud, though some have callèd thee/Mighty and dreadful"—and then the characteristic developments, unpredictable yet logical, studded with images which for all their seeming oddity will prove wholly functional. For instance, in the opening of his song, "Go and catch a falling star," he uses six different images, all of them appropriate and interesting, to express the idea of impossibility. But that is no mere bravura and display of wit; it is a cultivated, incisive, and attractive way of making a point.

Indeed, behind the speaking voice of Donne's best poems we can easily imagine a character in a drama, convincingly and imaginatively addressing his interlocutors. To do so he draws from such diverse sources as theology, myth, the sciences, folklore, geography, war, court litigation. Donne studied the law, traveled quite extensively, was a man of the world who experienced the beginnings of a courtier's career with its implications of intellectual brilliance and sensual pleasures; his daring secret marriage to an aristocratic girl, though socially and professionally ruinous to him, was based on deep, last-ing, fully requited love; and of course he ended his life on the pulpit as one of the most powerful preachers of all time. The situations, the language, the metaphors of his worldly and sacred poems are rooted in experience and are perfectly plausible in his human and cultural circumstances; he is eminently fit to use them as instruments of his rhetoric—the rhetoric of a man very much alive in an age of discovery and controversy, of ever widening physical and intellectual perspectives.

Donne's method of conciliating disparate objects and concepts to make important points about the human condition applies to his worldly as well as to his religious poems. In fact, a distinction between the two types seems irrelevant on that score. As our selections will indicate, the same poetic and intellectual vigor is found in the first category —where the major theme is love —as in the second—where the main themes are death and resurrection. The effectiveness of both depends on love and death never being handled as abstractions but as events contemplated and discussed anew on the background of concrete human reality, tested against the variety of experience. Random examples— the lovers in "The Canonization": "Soldiers find wars, and lawyers find out still/Litigious men, which quarrels move,/ Though she and I do love"; or the dead in Holy Sonnet 7: "All whom war, dearth, age, agues, tyrannies/Despair, law, chance hath slain . . ."

In poems like "The Good-Morrow" or "The Canonization"

the idea of lovers discovering in their intimacy and in their exchange of looks the universal and the eternal—a situation which in itself is potentially a cliché—is wholly renovated through the poet's vision and skill. Holy Sonnets 7 and 10—undoubtedly two of the most beautiful devotional poems in world literature—perform a similar operation on the orthodox idea of death as awakening to eternal life. In both cases the poet is a believer whose faith is poetically (i.e., intelligently) realized, expressed, made perceptible.

## CALDERÓN, *LIFE IS A DREAM*

It is appropriate to read *Life Is a Dream* at this point since it presents, albeit in new and extreme versions, some of the motifs we have already encountered. *Life Is a Dream* (*La vida es sueño*, 1636?) was written as a comedy by Pedro Calderón de la Barca while he was in his early thirties; yet the play has tragic overtones and its leading characters meditate on such serious questions as the nature of life. In the play, the notion that the world is a stage and life an apparition, a dream, is not simply a poetic image or a metaphor; it is presented as the basic orientation of life, a design for living, the norm. Granted that it is possible and useful to reduce the theme of a play, especially a play as varied and exuberant as this one, to a brief and convenient statement, the formula here would go something like this: Life is a dream. Even if one should occasionally

suspect that life is real and substantial, one must still think of it as a dream so that one may live it properly and achieve moral salvation.

The place of the action is a kingdom which, without even the remotest trace of historical justification, is called Poland. There is a king, that character so important in traditional dramas and fairy tales. Superficially the plot involves a kingdom and dynastic succession, a familiar theme in classical and Renaissance drama. King Basil is, as kings ought to be, a sage, but his sagacity is peculiar and somewhat sinister: he regulates his life according to the revelations of the fabulous and degenerate "science" of astrology. He has confined his son and heir apparent, Segismund, to a remote tower dungeon because before and during his birth, the stars and heavens showed awful portents. This colorfully suggests a notion of human destiny being ruled by cosmic forces:

The whole earth overflowed with conflagrations
So that it seemed the final paroxysm
Of existence. The skies grew dark.
    Buildings shook.
The clouds rained stones. The rivers ran with blood.

But King Basil is sufficiently reasonable to pay at least lip service to the notion of man's free will. He knows that

Violent inclination, the most impious
Planet—all can but influence, not force,
The free will which man holds direct from God.

Consequently Calderón's play is a wonderful mixture of odd frenzied activity and subtle abstract discussion, which is one of its most attractive traits. The main plot gets underway as Basil, in an elaborate explanation, decides to "test" Segismund, allowing him to be brought to the palace in a trance and there to be given courtly homage and royal powers. His conduct will show whether he is of royal timber or a dangerous monster, as the stars predicted.

The experiment fails: Segismund behaves like an unruly tyrant. The beast prevails. For example, after a brief exchange with a servant of the household concerning what amounts to a point of courtly etiquette (the impropriety of wooing a lady as boldly as Segismund does Stella), he throws the man out of a window into "the sea" to prove that it is he who decides what is "just." Basil does not take his share of the blame for the prince's bestiality and considers the experiment a failure and a confirmation of his dire forecast. Nevertheless he plants in Segismund's mind the first seeds of his redemption by warning him that *all* royal splendor and power may be a dream. Clotaldo, the hero's guardian-mentor, draws the moral of the lesson more precisely: "even in dreams, I warn you/Nothing is lost by trying to do good." This prompts Segismund's most celebrated speech at the end of Act II, and anticipates his full enlightenment in the last act.

The subplot, which interlocks with the main plot from the very first scene, is filled with the typical coincidences and implausibilities of a comedy of intrigue. The main character of the subplot is Rosaura. In terms of literary conventions, she lies somewhere between the stock characters of the lady in distress and the woman warrior. She has come to "Poland" disguised as a man to look for her seducer, Astolfo. There she finds not only her faithless lover—he has already taken up with his cousin, Stella, a possible heir to Basil's throne—but her father as well, and *he* turns out to have been the seducer of her mother. The subplot proceeds with the help of crude devices and props (the sword and the portrait) and elaborate debates on points of honor, so typical of Spanish plays of the period. What, for example, is the point of honor for Clotaldo when he is caught between two facts: that Astolfo, who saved his life during Segismund's tyrannical phase, is the seducer of his daughter?

The dénouement is, of course, happy; Astolfo will marry Rosaura and Segismund will marry Stella. The only casualty, oddly enough, is the talkative clown, Clarion. The central issue, as the final knots are tied, is Segismund's development; the happy ending of the subplot parallels Segismund's successful execution of the second "test." This test of Segismund's royal fitness is brought about by the action of insurgents against King Basil. They liberate Segismund from his renewed confinement and recognize him as their leader. He discourses upon his predicament at some length and then decides to act, equipped as he now is with new wisdom. For Segismund now accepts not only the principle that life is a dream —and an incomprehensible one to boot, as he suggested in the closing speech of Act II—but also the idea, earlier expressed by Clotaldo and now paraphrased by the hero, that "good actions,/Even in a dream, are not entirely lost." Segismund promises to lead the rebels "bravely and skillfully," even though he knows that life is an illusion. The implication is that in spite of the purposelessness of life, or perhaps *because* of it, life should be lived with dignity, courage, and a sense of purpose.

It would be easy to superimpose a strictly orthodox interpretation of Calderón's theme: life is an illusion and a test and is followed by revelation and a just reward. But the language and impact of the play hardly warrant it. After all, Calderón wrote this as a comedy, not as an *auto sacramental*, the religious allegories of which he was to become a master later in life. This play is about human conduct and carries a twofold "message": life is a dream, yet it must not be lived irresponsibly. Each of us must discover his own idea of virtue and honor and practice it, as it were, gratuitously. This interpretation has a lingering flavor of Quixotism and at the same time a haunting suggestion of modernity.

With all this, *Life Is a Dream* is difficult to summarize in terms of abstract philosophies. Its tone is particularly hard to describe. It has elements of the fairy tale, with its happy ending, but it is set against the dark background of a tragic awareness of reality. There are cloak-and-dagger routines and debates on points of honor which, for all their conventions, suddenly seem authentic and strangely relevant to real life. The plot is a mechanical comedy, full of disguises and surprise recognitions; yet it is carried on by characters whose main purpose seems to be to meditate on human destiny and contemplate death, while their speech, at once formal and exuberant, full of rich imagery, expresses their vitality and earthly attachment. The general truth that no commentary can replace or even approach the impact of direct immersion in a literary text applies to this play with particular force. The play is its own haunting "meaning," and so confirms in a splendid manner the nature of literary art.

## MILTON, *PARADISE LOST*

The quality of Milton's literary achievement places him, however late, still within the large span of the Renaissance. In fact, his intellectual inclinations and the encouraging support of a learned and artistic father combined to make him, already in early life, a most accomplished exemplar of the Renaissance scholar and literary artist. Concomitant with this achievement and inseparable from it are his views and activities as a reformed Christian humanist. His splendid knowledge of ancient languages, including Hebrew, permitted him to maintain a constant and deep familiarity with both the pagan classics and the Scriptures, in their original texts. As a young student at Cambridge he exchanged letters in Latin verse with a friend. His view of education comprised science and the new discoveries. In Italy in his early thirties he conversed with prominent intellectuals, including Galileo, and wrote sonnets in Italian. Late in life, blind, he had passages of the Hebrew Bible read to him every morning.

Quite naturally, then, the apex of his career as a poet (his long commitment to public life does not concern us here) was finally represented by a monumental exercise in the grandest and most authoritative of the classic genres—the epic poem. The choice of subject matter is obviously significant too. Milton, as the Protestant heroic poet, reflecting a trend toward individual humanistic rapport with the Scriptures, undertook an epic dramatization and a free poetic reappropriation of the story of man's first disobedience.

Naturally, the poet is aware all along of the superiority of his epic matter in comparison with that of his ancient and medieval predecessors. Even our relatively brief selection illustrates this point. Mythological reference often provides supports for action and characterization: Eve's divine touch and "goddesslike deport" not only recall but surpass those of the goddess Diana; and as she goes to work in the fields she is equaled to the major Roman goddesses of agriculture. The fatal spot where she will be tempted is "more delicious" than the gardens of Adonis or of King Alcinous, both possessing high mythological and epic credentials; to them, with full awareness of his higher theme, the poet adds a garden taken from Scriptural tradition. Even the serpent is lovelier than those sung by Ovid, and Eve's animals are "more duteous" at her call than were the pigs in the *Odyssey* at the call of Circe. Indeed, in the proemium to the same Book IX and in the invocation to his muse (Urania, to be sure, not the Virgin as in the poem of the Roman Counterreformation, Tasso's *Jerusalem Delivered*), the poet has declared his material to be "not less but more heroic" than the high points of the *Iliad* and the *Aeneid*, implying that his purpose is nobler than Homer's or Virgil's, let alone that of medieval chivalric poets with their "mastery to dissect/With long and tedious havoc fabled knights /In battles feigned . . ."

Milton's battle, or drama, is not "feigned" for the pre-eminent reason that it is the basic inner drama of Christian mankind Man is fallen, yet his fall is the precondition to human life as we know it, and it contains the promise of redemption; it is a happy fault, a *felix culpa*. So the subject of Milton's epic is not only the fall, of course, but also the transgressors' discovery and acceptance of their new mortal status, implying moral awareness and hope along with corruptibility and guilt.

Our obvious selection from *Paradise Lost* is the key moment in the action, the temptation and fall. Milton here faced, among others, the problem of describing the fundamentally evil in ambiguously attractive terms. Without ever really abandoning his grand manner or relenting in his highly literate sense of style, he handles blank verse with beautifully appropriate variety and mobility: passages like lines 71 ff. or 1067–1080 speak for themselves. In some of his most felicitous moments he strikes a balance between the sustained epic tone and the quick, effective notation. Take, for example, some of the varying images of the Satanic serpent: "stupidly good, of enmity disarmed," "his head/crested aloft, and carbuncle his eyes"; or observe the rapid effectiveness of the fatal act: "Forth reaching to the fruit, she plucked, she eat."

The two main stages in the dramatic sequence of events are the serpent successfully tempting Eve, and Eve convincing Adam to join her in the new knowledge. The dramatic situation demanded masterful handling, equal to its complexity and variety. For instance, Adam sins out of loyalty, out of chivalrous trust in his wife; and the poet does not shun such stagy lines as ". . . for with thee/Certain my resolution is to die," while Eve's rhetoric matches Adam's, in a lighter vein: "On my experience, Adam, freely taste,/And fear of death deliver to the winds." In all possible ways, the exchange of argumentation is given dramatic substance and vitality.

Milton was well acquainted with the arts of rhetoric and eloquence; and the story of the fall is largely told in terms of the use and misuse of those arts. From the serpent, Eve is not only taught evil action but also

evil counseling, verbal cunning, sophistry. While before the tempter's success her talk was only externally twisted by an occasional pun or conceit, after the fall her rhetorical art becomes innerly perverse, in perfect correspondence with the "distemper" in her now corrupt body.

On the other hand, new dimensions are introduced as the protagonists are united by "earthly" love and by mutual rancor and misery and also by the knowledge of a new delight, however condemnable; a line like "as with new wine intoxicated both" must work, so to speak, positively and negatively, strike a note at once joyful and ominous. Earthly attachments, however corrupt, must be poetically perceptible, as in the pivotal consummation passage (ll. 1034–1045). Hence the variety in Milton's use not only of his stylistic and prosodic instrument but also of his wide range of cultural reference, as when he adopts exotic imagery brought in by the new discoveries, in the comparison between the transgressors and "th'American, so girt/With feathered cincture, naked else and wild . . ."

In brief, Milton is fully recognizable as a Renaissance literary artist: his service to his God is inseparable from his service to poetry, to the cultivated and esthetically beautiful handling of language fit to encompass and express a wide range of human experience. The work for which he had prepared himself through all of his life, a Biblical epic in the grand classic manner, is also a crowning product of ripe, autumnal Renaissance culture.

## LIVES, WRITINGS, AND CRITICISM
*Biographical and critical works are listed only if they are available in English.*

### FRANCIS PETRARCH

LIFE AND WRITINGS. Francesco Petrarca was born at Arezzo on July 13, 1304. His father, like Dante, was exiled from Florence and in 1312 moved with his family to Avignon. Following his father's wish, Petrarch studied law at Montpellier and Bologna, but he abandoned these studies by 1326 when he took minor orders, which brought him certain financial benefits. Back in Avignon, he was well received by the brilliant and refined society that moved around the papal court. On April 6, 1327, in the Church of St. Clare, he saw, for the first time, Laura, who was to become the object and image of his love poetry. Soon after, Petrarch began a series of wide travels, to France, Flanders, and Germany, as a humanist searching for ancient texts, as a man of letters, and as a diplomat. In 1337 he paid his first visit to Rome, to him as a restorer of antiquity and a Christian a twofold spiritual capital. Later in the same year, at Vaucluse near Avignon he tried to revive the ancient ideal of spiritually active relaxation, or *otium*, and began his major Latin work, the epic poem *Africa*.

In 1340 Petrarch received from both Paris and Rome an invitation to be crowned poet laureate; he chose Rome, receiving the crown in the Capitol. Later he visited Parma and nearby Selvapiana, then again Avignon, where his natural daughter Francesca was born in 1343. His natural son was then six years old. Petrarch's spiritual conflicts of the period, enlivened by his brother Gherardo's decision to enter a monastery, are reflected in the autobiographical treatise *Secretum*. In 1348, while traveling in Italy, he received news of Laura's death by plague. She died on April 6, the same day that he had first seen her and the day of Christ's passion.

In 1350 on his way to Rome for the Jubilee, Petrarch stopped at Florence as a guest of Boccaccio. The friendship of these two poets and humanists was an important event for European culture. After another period at Vaucluse, Petrarch spent most of 1353-1361 in Milan, entrusted by the Visconti rulers with various diplomatic missions (to Venice, to Prague, to the king of France). Such occupations he alternated with intense study and work, attending during this period to a complete edition of his lyric poetry in Italian, to letters and treatises in Latin, and to work on his great unfinished *terza rima* allegory, *The Triumphs (I Trionfi)*. Escaping from the danger of the plague, he moved to Padua in 1361 and the next year to

Venice, where his daughter Francesca lived and where Boccaccio visited him in 1362. He began at this time the definitive ordering of the *rime* (his Italian lyric poetry), his most influential work. In 1367 he moved back to Padua, spending much of his time in a nearby country house at Arquà in the Euganean Hills. There he died in 1374, on the eve of his seventieth birthday.

BIBLIOGRAPHY AND CRITICISM: Morris Bishop, *Petrarch and His World* (1963); Ugo Foscolo, *Essays on Petrarch* (1823); Pierre de Nolhac, *Petrarch and the Ancient World* (1907); J. H. Whitfield, *Petrarch and the Renascence* (1943); and E. H. Wilkins, *Studies in the Life and Works of Petrarch* (1955) and *Life of Petrarch* (1961).

### DESIDERIUS ERASMUS

LIFE AND WRITINGS. Born out of wedlock to a physician's daughter and a father who later became a priest, in 1466?, apparently at Rotterdam, for he later referred to himself as Desiderius Erasmus Roterodamus. He was schooled at Gouda, then at Deventer, where humanistic masters fostered his love of good letters. After both parents died, his guardians sent him, with an older brother, to Hertogenbosch and later to the Augustinian Canons at Steyn, although his desire had been to enter a university. He was ordained a priest on April 25, 1492. His humanistic aspirations found an outlet in 1494 when he became Latin secretary to Henry of Bergen, bishop of Cambrai, through whose help, in 1495, he entered the college of Montaigu at the University of Paris. College discipline was very strict, but in the following year Erasmus had lodgings in town and received pupils. With a pupil, William Blount, Baron Mountjoy, he paid a first visit to England in 1499-1500 and met Thomas More and John Colet, the latter encouraging him toward serious theological study and a direct scholarly approach to the early Church Fathers. In the following years he traveled on the Continent, stopping for an interval at Louvain; his first collection of *Adages (Adagia, short sayings from classical authors)* appeared in Paris in 1500, and his *Handbook of the Christian Knight (Enchiridion militis christiani)*, a plea for the return to primitive Christian simplicity, was published at Antwerp in 1504. After a second visit to England in 1505-1506, during which he met Warham, the archbishop of Canterbury, a chance to act as tutor to the son of Henry VII's physician, Boeri, enabled him to fulfill the humanist's aspiration to visit Italy. There he spent some time at the universities of Turin (where he received a doctorate of theology) and Bologna, visited Padua and Florence, and conversed with high church dignitaries in Rome; in Venice, Aldo Manuzio, the great Humanistic printer, became a friend and published the enlarged *Adages*. In 1509 he returned to England; he wrote there in that year the *Praise of Folly* (*Moriae encomium*). During this third and longest residence (until 1514) he lectured in Greek and divinity at Cambridge and completed his work on the Greek New Testament. After leaving England, Erasmus, whose life offers the highest illustration of the type of the cosmopolitan humanist, particularly in his wish to unite humanistic learning and religious piety, continued to travel on the Continent, finally making his most permanent home in Basel, a center whose cultural importance cannot be overestimated, especially as the seat of the printing house of Frobenius, whose general editor Erasmus became. In 1529 religious disturbances and the victories of the Swiss reformers caused him to move to Freiburg in the Breisgau, the German university town in the Black Forest. Erasmus' attitude toward the reformers (Luther in Germany, Zwingli in Switzerland) was typical: after having tried to promote an impartial arbitration of the question between Luther and the Roman church, he was alienated by excesses on both sides. The shattering news of More's execution in England reached him in Freiburg. He returned to Basel in 1535 and died there in July, 1536. Besides his literary works and pamphlets, his editions of the Church Fathers, and the like, his letters (about three thousand) are an important document of the cultural life of the period.

BIOGRAPHY AND CRITICISM. Roland H. Bainton, *Erasmus of Christendom* (1969); *The Praise of Folly by Desiderius Erasmus*, edited by Leonard F. Dean, a new translation, with introduction and notes (1946); *Erasmus of Rotterdam: A Quincentennial Symposium*, 1969 edited by Richard L. DeMolen (1971); Giörgy Faludy, *Erasmus* (1970); Johan Huizinga, *Erasmus* (1924); W. J. Kaiser, *Praisers of Folly: Erasmus, Rabelais, Shakespeare* (1963); *Twentieth Century Interpretations of "The Praise of Folly"* edited by Kathleen Williams, with introduction (1969); Stefan Zweig, *Erasmus* (1934).

## BALDESAR CASTIGLIONE

LIFE AND WRITINGS. Born at Casatico, near Mantua, in 1487. His father, Cristoforo, was a courtier and his mother was a Gonzaga, related to the lords of Mantua. He received a humanistic education in Milan. From 1499 to 1503 he was in the service of Francesco

Gonzaga, lord of Mantua, and from 1504 to 1513 he was at Urbino in the service (diplomatic and military) of Guidobaldo da Montefeltro (whose wife was a Gonzaga) and of Francesco Maria della Rovere, by whom he was made a count. In 1506 he went to England on an embassy to the court of Henry VII, from whom he received, on behalf of his lord, the Order of the Garter and to whom he presented a painting by Raphael. In 1515 he was again with the Gonzagas, who made him their ambassador to Pope Leo X (Giovanni de' Medici). In Rome his friends included Raphael and Michelangelo, and he saw Renaissance social and intellectual life at its most brilliant; he thus not only codified the ideal of the refined and "virtuous" courtier but also embodied it. In 1525 Pope Clement VII made him his ambassador to the court of Emperor Charles V in Spain. Castiglione's premature death there, at Toledo in 1529, was probably caused in part by sorrow at his failure to foresee the emperor's designs as they most dramatically took shape in the "sack of Rome" in 1527. *The Book of the Courtier* (*Il libro del cortegiano*), in which the court of Urbino is idealized, was written between 1508 and 1516 and published after constant revisions, in 1528 in Venice.

BIOGRAPHY AND CRITICISM. Julia Cartwright Ady, *Baldassare Castiglione, the Perfect Courtier: His Life and Letters* (1908); Ralph Roeder, *The Man of the Renaissance; Four Lawgivers: Savonarola, Machiavelli, Castiglione, Aretino;* (1933); Wilhelm Schenk, "The *Cortegiano* and the Civilization of the Renaissance," *Scrutiny, XVI* (Summer 1949), 93–103; J. S. White, *Renaissance Cavalier* (1959).

## NICCOLÒ MACHIAVELLI

LIFE AND WRITINGS. Born in Florence on May 3, 1469. His father was a jurist and owned some land. Little is known of his schooling; it is obvious from his work that he knew the Latin and Italian writers well. He entered public life in 1494 as a clerk and from 1498 to 1512 was secretary to the second chancery of the commune of Florence, whose magistrates were in charge of internal and war affairs. In connection with the duties of this post, during the war against Pisa he dealt with military problems firsthand, at this time forming his aversion to mercenary troops. He went on many diplomatic missions—among others, to King Louis XII of France in 1500 and in 1502 to Cesare Borgia, whose ruthless conquest of the Romagna he described in a booklet showing direct insight into the type of the amoral and technically efficient "prince." In 1506 he went on a mission to Pope Julius II, whose expedition into the Romagna he followed closely. From his missions to Emperor Maximilian (1508) and again to the king of France (1509) he drew his two books of, observations or *Portraits* (*Ritratti*) of the affairs of those countries—*Ritratto delle cose della Magna*, written in 1508; and *Ritratto di cose di Francia*, written in 1510. Pre-eminently a student of politics and an observer, he endeavored to apply his experience of other states to the strengthening of his own, the Florentine Republic, and busied himself in 1507 with the establishment of a Florentine militia, encountering great difficulties. When the republican regime came to an end, Machiavelli lost his post and was banned from the city though forbidden to leave Florentine territory; the new regime under the Medici accused him unjustly of conspiracy, and he was released only after a period of imprisonment and torture. To the time of his exile spent near San Casciano, a few miles from Florence, where he retired with his wife, Marietta Corsini, and five children, we owe the major works: the *Discourses on the First Ten Books of Livy* (*Discorsi sopra la prima deca di Tito Livio*, 1513–1521) and *The Prince* (*Il principe*), which was written in 1513, with the hope of obtaining public office from the Medici. In 1520 he was employed on an insignificant commercial mission to Lucca; in the same year he was commissioned to write a history of Florence, which he presented in 1525 to the pope, Clement VII (Giulio de' Medici). He was sent on a mission to the papal president of the Romagna, who happened to be the great historian Francesco Guicciardini; and in 1526, conscious of imminent dangers, he was employed in the work for the military fortifications of Florence. The fate of the Medici at that point was connected with the larger struggle between King Francis I of France and the Holy Roman emperor, Charles V. Pope Clement's siding with the king of France led to the disastrous "sack of Rome"; the repercussion in Florence was the collapse of Medici domination. With the re-establishment of the republic Machiavelli's hopes rose, but they came to naught because he now was regarded as a Medici sympathizer. This last disappointment may have accelerated his end. He died on June 22, 1527, and was buried in the church of Santa Croce. He has a place in literature also for a short novel and two plays, one of which, *The Mandrake* (*La mandragola*), first performed in the early 1520's, is among the most outstanding Italian comedies.

BIOGRAPHY AND CRITICISM. Alfredo Bonadeo, *Corruption, Conflict and Power in the Works and Times of Niccolò* Machiavelli (1973); Federico Chabod, *Machiavelli and the Renaissance* (1958); Allan H. Gilbert, *Machiavelli's "Prince" and Its Forerunners* (1938); Felix Gilbert, "The Concept of Nationalism in Machiavelli's *Prince*" in *Studies in the Renaissance* (1954), and *Machiavelli and Guicciardini* (1965); J. R. Hale, *Machiavelli and Renaissance Italy* (1961); J. C. Pocock, *The Machiavellian Moment* (1976); Roberto Ridolfi, *The Life of Niccolò Machiavelli* (1963); Pasquale Villari, *The Life and Times of Niccolò Machiavelli* (1929).

## FRANÇOIS RABELAIS

LIFE AND WRITINGS. Born probably about 1494-1495 into a middle-class landowning family at La Devinière, near Chinon in the province of Touraine. The father was a successful lawyer. Rabelais apparently saw in a monastic career an opportunity for study; he was trained as a novice in the Francisan order in the monastery of La Baumette at Angers. Later, as a monk in the Franciscan monastery of Puy-Saint-Martin at Fontenay-le-Comte, he busied himself especially with the "new learning" (Greek and other Humanistic studies), which was suspect to conventional theologians. In 1524 he obtained authorization from Pope Clement VII to transfer to the less strict Benedictine order. He had close and continuous contacts, both personal and epistolary, with prominent Humanists and jurists. He probably studied law at Poitiers. Between 1527 and 1530 he seems to have traveled considerably, and probably to have studied medicine at the University of Paris, a supposition warranted by the fact that when in 1530 he entered the University of Montpellier as a medical student, he received the degree of bachelor of medicine in two months. In 1532 he was a physician in the important hospital of the Pont-du-Rhône, at Lyon, and practiced medicine with success. In the same year he published, under the name of Alcofribas Nasier, an anagram of his own name, the volume of *Pantagruel* which now constitutes Book II of *Gargantua and Pantagruel*. The story of *Gargantua*, the present Book I, appeared in 1534. In that year Rabelais traveled to Rome as personal physician to Jean du Bellay, then bishop of Paris and later a cardinal. In Rome in 1536 Rabelais obtained papal absolution for having discarded the monk's robe without authorization; later in the same year, back in France, his status became that of a secular priest. In 1537 he received his doctorate of medicine at Montpellier and held lectures there, using the Greek physicians' texts in the original. In the following years he traveled widely, and also acquired some standing at court, holding a minor post in the retinue of King Francis I. In

1538 he witnessed the historic meeting between Francis and Charles V at Aigues-Mortes. Court contacts helped him counteract the condemnations of his literary work by the theologians of the Sorbonne. The seriousness of his difficulties—arising out of accusations of heresy and leanings toward the Reformation—varied according to the protection that the court could grant him, and his own success in compromising. After Book III of *Gargantua and Pantagruel* (1546) was banned, he resided for two years in voluntary exile at Metz. He was in Rome again in 1548, and in 1551 he was appointed to the two curacies of Saint-Martin-de-Meudon and Saint-Cristophe-de-Jambet, both of which he resigned early in 1553 because of ill health. The tradition is that he died in Paris, in the Rue des Jardins, probably in April of that year. Book IV of *Gargantua and Pantagruel*, which had appeared in 1552, had also been banned; a fifth book, of doubtful authenticity, appeared in 1562-1564.

BIOGRAPHY AND CRITICISM. Mikhail Bakhtin, *Rabelais and His World* (1968); Barbara C. Bowen, *The Age of Bluff: Paradox and Ambiguity in Rabelais and Montaigne* (1972); Dorothy G. Coleman, *Rabelais: A Critical Study in Prose Fiction* (1971); Anatole France, *Rabelais* (1929); Thomas M. Greene, *Rabelais: A Study in Comic Courage* (1970); Jean Plattard, *The Life of Rabelais* (1930); Samuel Putnam, *Rabelais, Man of the Renaissance* (1930); M. P. Willcocks, *The Laughing Philosopher* (1950).

## MICHEL DE MONTAIGNE

LIFE AND WRITINGS. Michel Eyquem de Montaigne was born on February 28, 1533, in the castle of Montaigne (in the Bordeaux region), which had been bought by his great-grandfather and from which his family of traders derived their surname. His father, Pierre Eyquem, was for two terms mayor of Bordeaux and had fought in Italy under King Francis I. The writer's inclination to tolerance and naturalness may have had its origin in certain aspects of his background and early training: his mother, of Spanish-Jewish descent, was a Protestant, as were his brother Beauregard and his sister Jeanne; the third of nine children, Michel himself, like his other brothers and sisters, was raised a Catholic. His father, though no man of learning, had unconventional ideas of upbringing: Michel, who had a peasant nurse and peasant godparents, was awakened in the morning by the sound of music and had Latin taught him as his mother tongue by a German tutor. At six he went to the famous Collège de Guienne at Bordeaux; later he studied law, probably at Toulouse. In his youth he already knew court life firsthand. (At the court celebrations at Rouen for the majority of Charles IX in 1560, he saw among other things the

cannibals, brought from Brazil, who became the subject of the famous essay.) In 1557 he was a member of the Bordeaux parliament; during that period he formed the deepest friendship of his life, with the young nobleman and fellow lawyer Étienne de la Boétie, who was to die a few years later. During his friend's last illness, Montaigne assisted him day and night despite the contagiousness of the disease. In 1565 he married Françoise de la Chassaigne, daughter of a colleague in the Bordeaux parliament, to whom he was temperately attached. It is difficult to say whether disappointed political ambitions contributed in any relevant measure to Montaigne's decision to "retire" at thirty-eight to his castle of Montaigne and devote himself to meditation and writing. At any rate, his residence there had various interruptions. The country was split between the Protestants, led by Henry of Navarre, and two Catholic factions: those faithful to the reigning Valois kings (first Charles IX and then Henry III) and the "leaguers" or followers of the house of Guise. In the midst of such conflicts Montaigne's attitude was balanced and conservative (both Henry III of Valois and Henry of Navarre bestowed honors upon him), though his sympathies went to the unfanatical Navarre, the future founder of the Bourbon dynasty as Henry IV. In 1574 Montaigne attempted to mediate an agreement between him and the Duke of Guise. In 1580 he undertook a journey through Switzerland, Germany, and Italy (partly to cure his gallstones); while in Italy he received news that he had been appointed mayor of Bordeaux. He held that office competently for two terms (1581-1585). Toward the end of his life he began an important friendship with the intelligent and ardently devoted Marie de Gournay, who became a kind of adopted daughter and was his literary executrix. When his favorite, Henry of Navarre, who had visited him twice in his castle, became king, Montaigne expressed his joy, though he refused Henry's offers of money; he did not live to witness in Paris, as he probably would have, the entry of the king turned Catholic ("Paris is well worth a Mass") for he died on September 13, 1592; he was buried in a church in Bordeaux. The *Essays* (*Essais*), which Montaigne started as a collection of interesting quotations, observations, remarkable events, and the like, and slowly developed to their large form and bulk, are divided into three books: Books I and II were first published in 1580; Book III (together with Books I and II revised and amplified) appeared in 1588. A posthumous edition prepared by Mlle. de Gournay, and containing some further additions, appeared in 1595. A noteworthy early English translation by John Florio was published in 1603.

BIOGRAPHY AND CRITICISM. Barbara C. Bowen, (see under Rabelais); Ralph Waldo Emerson, "Montaigne, or The Skeptic," in *Representative Men* (1850); Donald M. Frame, *Montaigne's Discovery of Man* (1955), and *Montaigne: A Biography* (1965); Philip P. Hallie, *The Scar of Montaigne* (1966); Samuel A. Tannenbaum, *Michel Eyquem de Montaigne: A Concise Biography* (1942); George C. Taylor, *Shakespeare's Debt to Montaigne* (1925); Frederick Rider, *The Dialectic of Selfhood in Montaigne* (1973).

### MIGUEL DE CERVANTES

LIFE AND WRITINGS. Son of an apothecary, Miguel de Cervantes Saavedra was born in 1547 in Alcalá de Henares, a university town near Madrid. Almost nothing is known of his early life and education. In a work published in 1569 he is mentioned as a favorite pupil by a Madrid Humanist, Juan López. Records indicate that by the end of that year he had left Spain and was living in Rome, for a while in the service of Giulio Acquaviva, later a cardinal. Enlisting in the Spanish fleet under the command of Don John of Austria, Cervantes engaged in the struggle of the allied forces of Christendom against the Turks. He was at the crucial battle of Lepanto (1571), where he fought valiantly in spite of fever and received three gunshot wounds, one of which permanently impaired the use of his left hand, "for the greater glory of the right." After further military engagements and garrison duty at Palermo and Naples, with his brother Rodrigo, and carrying testimonials from Don John and the viceroy of Sicily, he began the journey back to Spain, where he hoped to obtain a captaincy. In September, 1575, their boat was captured near the Marseilles coast by Barbary pirates, and the two brothers, taken prisoner, were brought to Algiers. Cervantes' captors, considering him a person of some consequence, held him as a slave for a good ransom. He repeatedly attempted to escape, and his daring and fortitude excited the admiration of Hassan Pasha, the viceroy of Algiers, who at length bought Cervantes for five hundred crowns. Nevertheless, Rodrigo was ransomed after two years of captivity, while Cervantes' own liberation took five.

He was freed on September 15, 1580, and reached Madrid in December of that year. Here his literary career started rather unauspiciously; he wrote twenty or thirty plays, with little success, and in 1585 published his pastoral romance *Galatea*. At about this time he had a natural daughter by Ana Franca de Rojas, and during the same period he married Catalina de Salazar, eighteen years his junior. Seeking non-literary employment, he obtained a position in the navy, requisitioning and collecting supplies for the Invincible Armada. There seem to have been irregularities in his administration, for which he was held responsible if not directly guilty; he spent several intervals in prison. In 1590 he tried unsuccessfully to obtain colonial employment in the New World. Later he had a post as tax collector in the Granada province. He was dismissed from government service in 1597. The following years are most obscure; there is a tradition that *Don Quixote* was first conceived and planned in prison at Seville. In 1604 he was at Valladolid, then the temporary capital, living in sordid surroundings with the numerous women of his family (his wife, daughter, niece, and two sisters). There he obtained in late 1604 the official license for publication of *Don Quixote* (Part I). The book appeared in 1605 and was a popular success. Cervantes followed the court's return to Madrid, where he still lived poorly in spite of a vogue with readers which quickly made his heroes proverbial figures. A false continuation of the story soon appeared, and Cervantes' own continuation (*Don Quixote*, Part II) was published in 1615. His *Exemplary Tales* (*Novelas ejemplares*) had appeared in 1613. He died on April 23, 1616, and was buried in the convent of the Barefooted Trinitarian nuns. *Persiles and Sigismunda* (*Persiles y Sigismunda*), his last novel, was published posthumously in 1617.

BIOGRAPHY AND CRITICISM. John J. Allen, *Don Quixote, Hero or Fool?* (1969); Margaret Church, *Don Quixote: The Knight of La Mancha* (1971); A. F. G. Bell, *Cervantes* (1947); Americo Castro, "An Introduction to the *Quixote*," in *An Idea of History* (1977); Salvador de Madariaga, *Don Quixote: An Introductory Essay in Psychology* (1935); *Cervantes: A Collection of Critical Essays* edited by Lowry Nelson, Jr., with introduction (1969); Richard L. Predmore, *The World of Don Quixote* (1967); Miguel de Unamuno, *The Life of Don Quixote and Sancho* (1927); Mark Van Doren, *Don Quixote's Profession* (1958).

### CHRISTOPHER MARLOWE

LIFE AND WRITINGS. Born at Canterbury on February 6, 1564, the son of a shoemaker. He studied at the King's School in his native city and from 1581 on a scholarship at Corpus Christi College (then Benet College), Cambridge, where he received his B.A. in 1584 and his M.A. in 1587. There was some opposition to the granting of his degree but the Queen's Privy Council intervened in his favor, a fact which has been used to support the hypothesis that Marlowe was already affiliated with the Queen's secret service (a diplomatic and intelligence operation). After Cambridge he lived in London, where little is known about his life; obvious facts are his connections with the theatrical world and his four great dramatic successes between 1587 and 1593, *Tamburlaine the Great, The Jew of Malta, Edward II*, and *Dr. Faustus* (ca. 1592-1593). Marlowe's life is hauntingly obscure; there seems to be no doubt that he entertained unorthodox religious views, and that he had a violent temper, and that he engaged in some sort of spying activities for the Queen. He was accused of atheism and treason by a one-time friend and fellow-playwright, Thomas Kyd. He was involved in a bloody brawl with an innkeeper named William Bradley, and at 29, in an inn at Deptford, he was stabbed to death by an Ingram Frizer in an argument over the bill; Frizer was pardoned on the grounds that he had acted in self-defense. Of the two other men present, one was a diplomatic courier and spy, recently returned from The Hague. Besides the plays Marlowe also wrote a mythological poem, *Hero and Leander*, and translations from Ovid and Lucan.

BIOGRAPHY AND CRITICISM. F. S. Boas, *Marlowe* (1940); *Twentieth Century Interpretations of "Doctor Faustus"* edited by Williard Farnham with introduction (1969); Harry Levin, *The Overreacher* (1952); Irving Ribner, *"Doctor Faustus": Text and Major Criticism* (1966); R. P. Wilson, *Marlowe and the Early Shakespeare* (1953).

### WILLIAM SHAKESPEARE

LIFE AND WRITINGS. Born in April 1564 at Stratford-on-Avon in Warwickshire, then a rural community with a population of less than two thousand, of which his father, John Shakespeare, was a prominent and prosperous member. Little is known of Shakespeare's early life beyond conjecture or legend; he probably received the education offered by the good local grammar school, with emphasis on Latin; at eighteen he married a farmer's daughter, Anne Hathaway, seven or eight years his senior; there are baptismal records of their children, Susanna (1583) and the twins Hamnet and Judith (1585). After a gap of seven years, records show Shakespeare in 1592 already a successful and many-talented playwright in London; in 1594 he was a sharer in a prominent players' company of which the Lord Chamberlain was patron and the famous actors Burbage and Kempe were members, while literary distinction of a type that was then more highly respected came from successful poems (*Venus and Adonis*, 1593; *The Rape of Lucrece*, 1594). By 1596, of his now best-known plays he had written *The Taming of the Shrew, Richard III, Romeo and Juliet*, and *The Merchant of Venice*; in 1597-1598, with the two

parts of *Henry IV* he added Falstaff to his growing list of famous characters.

The Chamberlain's men had been playing at the Theatre, north of the city of London, and later at the Curtain; in 1598 the Theatre was demolished, and the Globe, a large playhouse south of the Thames, was built, Shakespeare sharing in the expenses. Increased prosperity had brought social advancement: in 1596 the College of Heralds had sanctioned Shakespeare's claim to a gentleman's station by recognizing the family's coat of arms; in the same period he had bought New Place, a large house in his home town. In 1599, *Henry V*, the last of the plays centering in the Lancastrian kings, was followed by the first of the great Roman tragedies, *Julius Caesar*. The major plays belong to the following period; this is a usual dating of the most famous: *Hamlet*, 1601; *King Lear*, 1605; *Macbeth*, 1606; *Antony and Cleopatra*, 1607; *The Tempest*, 1611. Queen Elizabeth had favored the players, and her successor, James I, directly patronized them; the Lord Chamberlain's company thus became the King's Men. In 1608, besides the Globe, they acquired an enclosed playhouse in Blackfriars, in the city of London, for winter entertainment. At about that time Shakespeare seems to have retired from the stage, and certainly from then on he wrote fewer plays. He lived most of the time at Stratford until his death there on April 23, 1616.

BIOGRAPHY AND CRITICISM. Nigel Alexander, *Poison, Play and Duel* (1971); *Twentieth Century Interpretations of "Hamlet"*, edited by David Bevington with introduction (1968); W. A. Buell, *The Hamlets of the Theatre* (1968); Oscar J. Campbell, "What Is the Matter with Hamlet?" *Yale Review*, XXXII (Winter 1943), 309–322; E. K. Chambers, *William Shakespeare: A Study of Facts and Problems* (1930); Maurice Charney, *Style in Hamlet* (1969); Francis Fergusson, "Hamlet, Prince of Denmark," in *The Idea of a Theatre* (1949); Paul Gottschalk, *The Meaning of "Hamlet"* (1972); H. Granville-Barker, *Prefaces to Shakespeare*, Vol. I (1936); Ernest Jones, *Hamlet and Oedipus* (1949); Harry Levin, *The Question of Hamlet* (1959); Maynard Mack, "The World of Hamlet," *Yale Review*, XLI (Summer 1952), 502-523; Eleanor Prosser, *Hamlet and Revenge* (1967) E. E. Stoll, *"Hamlet": An Historical and Comparative Study* (1919); John Dover Wilson, *What Happens in "Hamlet"* (1935).

### JOHN DONNE

LIFE AND WRITINGS. Born in London in 1572 in a Catholic family. Attended Oxford, Cambridge, and Lincoln's Inn (law school) without obtaining degrees or becoming a lawyer. His intellectual energy, his voracious reading, his wide traveling (including expeditions to Cadiz and to the Azores with Ralegh and Essex) combined to prepare him for brilliant courtly career. In 1958 he was appointed private secretary to the Lord Keeper, Sir Thomas Egerton; but a couple of years later he destroyed his prospects of advancement by secretly marrying Ann More, sixteen-year-old niece of Lady Egerton. In spite of subsequent hardship and misery, his love marriage was a happy one to the last. Conviction reached after long inner debate, rather than mere opportunism, brought him to abandon the Catholic Church and join the Church of England. In 1615 he took sacred orders and was appointed Dean of St. Paul's in 1621. He died in 1631 a few weeks after having preached what is known as his own death sermon. His collected *Songs and Sonnets* were first published two years after his death.

BIOGRAPHY AND CRITICISM. N. J. C. Andreasen, *John Donne, Conservative Revolutionist* (1967); R. C. Bald, *John Donne, A Life* (1970); Cleanth Brooks, *The Well-Wrought Urn* (1947), pp. 3–20; T. S. Eliot, "The Metaphysical Poets," in *Selected Essays* (1932); *John Donne: A Collection of Critical Essays*, edited by Helen Gardner, with introduction (1962); Clay Hunt, *Donne's Poetry: Essays in Critical Analysis* (1969); *The Poems of John Donne*, edited by H. J. C. Grierson (1929); J. B. Leishman, *The Monarch of Wit* (1951); *A Garland for John Donne*, edited by Theodore Spencer (1931); Arnold Stein, *John Donne's Lyrics* (1962).

### PEDRO CALDERÓN DE LA BARCA

LIFE AND WRITINGS. Born at Madrid in 1600. Calderón spent his early childhood at Valladolid where the court then was, his father being a secretary to the Council of the Treasury. He studied from 1609 to 1614 at a Jesuit college and later at the universities of Alcalá de Henares and Salamanca. His earliest known literary work came from his participation in 1620 in a poetic competition to celebrate the canonization of St. Isidore; Lope de Vega was the principal judge. In the following year, Calderón and one of his brothers were accused of having killed a servant of the duke of Frias and both were fined. Between 1623 and 1625 he may have served in the army in Italy or Flanders. In 1626 he was again in Madrid. King Philip IV assembled around the court a small number of playwrights and Calderón soon became the most prominent among them. His first play was performed in 1623. In 1635, when Lope de Vega died, he became the leading dramatist in Spain. In 1636 he was knighted; 1640 he enlisted in a cavalry company in the Order of Santiago. At the outbreak of the Catalonian rebellion in 1640 he enrolled in one of the troops of knights supplied by the military orders and served until 1642. From 1644

to 1649 his theatrical production practically ceased, as the theaters were closed from the queen's death until the king's remarriage. In 1645 he entered the service of the duke of Alba. In 1648 or 1649 his mistress died, possibly in bearing his natural son, whom he recognized. His sorrow at her death may have contributed to his decision to enter the priesthood. He was appointed to a Toledo parish but could not serve because his superior objected to his being a playwright. For several years he was chaplain to the Brotherhood of the Refugio at Toledo, an order dedicated to charity work among the sick. Throughout this period and to the end of his life, he wrote *autos sacramentales* (theological one-act allegories) for the court. In 1663 he was appointed honorary chaplain to the king. Thereafter he lived a retired life of writing, study, and meditation in Madrid, gathering in his house a rare collection of religious works of art and devotional objects. He died on May 25, 1681.

Calderón theatrical output was immense and varied. The major subdivision is between secular and religious plays. Among the secular plays, there are dramas of honor and jealousy like *The Physician of His Own Honor* (*El médico de su honra*) and *Secret Offense, Secret Revenge* (*A secreto agravio, secreta venganza*); of cloak-and-sword intrigue like *A House with Two Doors Is Hard to Guard* (*Una casa con dos puertas mala es de guardar*) and *The Phantom Lady* (*La dama duende*); and on classical and mythological themes like *The Daughter of the Air* (*La hija del aire*), and on historical and legendary themes like *The Mayor of Zalamea* (*El alcade de Zalamea*). Calderón's deep preoccupation with religious themes shows itself in such complex melodramas as *The Devotion of the Cross* (*La Devoción de la Cruz*) and such strictly religious plays as the 70 *autos sacramentales*, the most famous of which is *The Great Theatre of the World* (*El gran teatro del mundo*). One of them has the same title, though hardly the same content and meaning, of the selection here, *Life Is a Dream*.

BIOGRAPHY AND CRITICISM. Gerald Brennan, "Calderón and the Late Drama," Chapter XII of *The Literature of the Spanish People* (1957); M. A. Buchanan, Calderón's *Life is a Dream*," *PMLA*, LXVIII (1932); Everett W. Hesse, *Calderón de la Barca* (1967); Edwin Honig, *Calderón and the Seizures of Honor* (1972); A. A. Parker, "The Approach to the Spanish Drama of the Golden Age," in *The Tulane Drama Review* (Autumn 1959); Bruce W. Wardropper, *Critical Essays on the Drama of Calderón* (1965); W. W. Whitby, "Rosaura's Role in the Structure of *La vida es sueño*," in *The Hispanic Review*, XXVIII (1960).

### JOHN MILTON

LIFE AND WRITINGS. Born in London

on December 9, 1608. Encouraged by his father (a well-to-do notary, private banker, and distinguished musician), he was educated both at home by tutors and at excellent schools (St. Paul's in London and Christ's College, Cambridge: B.A., 1629; M.A., 1632). He decided against taking orders and retired to his father's estate at Horton, near Windsor, where he rounded out his prodigiously vast education and reading. His early verse production culminates in the splendid elegy *Lycidas* (1637), commemorating a classmate. In 1638–1639 he traveled on the Continent, especially in Italy; rumor of political trouble at home hastened his return. The following twenty years are the period of Milton's involvement in doctrinal and governmental controversy. The major events of this period are the writing of *Areopagitica* (1644), an eloquent defence of the right to print without a license, and his appointment as Latin Secretary to Cromwell's Council of State; his writings in English and in Latin defending the execution of the King belong to this period. The Restoration brought him difficulty, brief imprisonment, and loss of property. Milton's first wife, Mary Powell (who had left him

shortly after their marriage in 1642 and had later returned to him), had died in 1652. His second wife had died in childbirth in 1658. In 1663 he married his third, Elizabeth Minshull, who outlived him. Totally blind since 1651, the poet now attended to his major tasks: *Paradise Lost* was published in 1667; *Paradise Regained* and *Samson Agonistes* followed in 1671. He died in 1674.

BIOGRAPHY AND CRITICISM. C. M. Bowra, *From Virgil to Milton* (1945); Douglas Bush, *John Milton: A Sketch of his Life and Writings* (1964); T. S. Eliot, *Milton* (1948); Stanley E. Fish, *Surprised by Sin: The Reader in Paradise Lost* (1967); Northrop Frye, *The Return of Eden* (1965); Helen Gardner, *A Reading of "Paradise Lost"* (1965); J. H. Hanford, *A Milton Handbook* (1946); C. S. Lewis, *A Preface to "Paradise Lost"* (1942); *Milton: A Collection of Critical Essays,* edited by Louis L. Martz, with introduction (1966); Kenneth Muir, *Milton* (1955); Marjorie H. Nicolson, *John Milton: A Reader's Guide to His Poetry* (1963); William R. Parker, *Milton: A Biography* (1966); *Approaches to Paradise Lost,* edited by C. A. Patrides (1968); *On Milton's Poetry,* edited by Arnold Stein, with introduction (1970); J. H. Summers, *The Muse's Method: An Introduction to Paradise Lost.*

# FRANCIS PETRARCH

## (1304–1374)

## It Was the Morning*

It was the morning of that blessèd day
Whereon the Sun in pity veiled his glare
For the Lord's agony, that, unaware,
I fell a captive, Lady, to the sway

Of your swift eyes: that seemed no time to stay    5
The strokes of Love: I stepped into the snare
Secure, with no suspicion: then and there
I found my cue in man's most tragic play.

Love caught me naked to his shaft, his sheaf,
The entrance for his ambush and surprise    10
Against the heart wide open through the eyes,

* *Era 'l giorno ch'al sol si scoloraro,* sonnet 3. Translated by Joseph Auslander.

1. *day:* Elsewhere (sonnet 211) Petrarch gives the date as April 6, 1327, a Monday. Here too the day is apparently intended to be the day of Christ's

death (April 6) rather than Good Friday, 1327.

11. *heart . . . eyes:* The image of the eyes as the gateway to the heart had been a poetic commonplace since pre-Dante days.

The constant gate and fountain of my grief:
How craven so to strike me stricken so,
Yet from you fully armed conceal his bow!

13. *stricken:* with grief on commemorating Christ's Passion.

## Blest Be the Day*

Blest be the day, and blest the month and year,
Season and hour and very moment blest,
The lovely land and place where first possessed
By two pure eyes I found me prisoner;

And blest the first sweet pain, the first most dear,          5
Which burnt my heart when Love came in as guest;
And blest the bow, the shafts which shook my breast,
And even the wounds which Love delivered there.

Blest be the words and voices which filled grove
And glen with echoes of my lady's name;                      10
The sighs, the tears, the fierce despair of love;

And blest the sonnet-sources of my fame;
And blest that thought of thoughts which is her own,
Of her, her only, of herself alone!

* *Benedetto sia 'l giorno e 'l mese e l'anno,* sonnet 61. Translated by Joseph Auslander.
2. *Season:* spring; *hour:* "upon the first hour" (sonnet 211), sunrise.
3. *place:* the Church of Saint Clare at Avignon.

## Father in Heaven*

Father in heaven, after each lost day,
Each night spent raving with that fierce desire
Which in my heart has kindled into fire
Seeing your acts adorned for my dismay;

Grant henceforth that I turn, within your light              5
To another life and deeds more truly fair,
So having spread to no avail the snare
My bitter foe might hold it in despite.

The eleventh year, my Lord, has now come round
Since I was yokéd beneath the heavy trace                    10
That on the meekest weighs most cruelly.

Pity the abject plight where I am found;
Return my straying thoughts to a nobler place;
Show them this day you were on Calvary.

* *Padre del ciel, dopo i perduti giorni,* sonnet 62. Translated by Vernard Bergonzi.
5. *light:* the light of grace.
8. *bitter foe:* the Devil, not Love as some commentators have thought.
9. *Cf.* note to 1.1, *It Was the Morning.*

## She Used to Let Her Golden Hair Fly Free*

She used to let her golden hair fly free
For the wind to toy and tangle and molest;
Her eyes were brighter than the radiant west.
(Seldom they shine so now.) I used to see

Pity look out of those deep eyes on me.                    5
("It was false pity," you would now protest.)
I had love's tinder heaped within my breast;
What wonder that the flame burned furiously?

She did not walk in any mortal way,
But with angelic progress; when she spoke,                 10
Unearthly voices sang in unison.

She seemed divine among the dreary folk
Of earth. You say she is not so today?
Well, though the bow's unbent, the wound bleeds on.

* *Erano i capei d'oro a l'aura sparsi,* sonnet 90. Translated by Morris Bishop.

## The Eyes That Drew from Me*

The eyes that drew from me such fervent praise,
The arms and hands and feet and countenance
Which made me a stranger in my own romance
And set me apart from the well-trodden ways;

The gleaming golden curly hair, the rays                   5
Flashing from a smiling angel's glance
Which moved the world in paradisal dance,
Are grains of dust, insensibilities.

And I live on, but in grief and self-contempt,
Left here without the light I loved so much,               10
In a great tempest and with shrouds unkempt.

No more love songs, then, I have done with such;
My old skill now runs thin at each attempt,
And tears are heard within the harp I touch.

* *Gli occhi di ch'io parlai si calda-* commemorate Laura. She died at Avig-
*mente,* sonnet 292. Translated by Edwin    non on April 6, 1348.
Morgan. All the poems in the canon          14. *Cf. Job* 30:31.
from number 267 on were written to

## Great Is My Envy of You*

Great is my envy of you, earth, in your greed
Folding her in invisible embrace,
Denying me the look of the sweet face
Where I found peace from all my strife at need!

* *Quanta invidia io ti porto, avara terra,* sonnet 300. Translated by Edwin
Morgan.

Great is my envy of heaven which can lead 5
And lock within itself in avarice
That spirit from its lovely biding-place
And leave so many others here to bleed!

Great is my envy of those souls whose reward
Is the gentle heaven of her company, 10
Which I so fiercely sought beneath these skies!

Great is my envy of death whose curt hard sword
Carried her whom I called my life away;
Me he disdains, and mocks me from her eyes!

## Go, Grieving Rimes of Mine*

Go, grieving rimes of mine, to that hard stone
Whereunder lies my darling, lies my dear,
And cry to her to speak from heaven's sphere.
Her mortal part with grass is overgrown.

Tell her, I'm sick of living; that I'm blown 5
By winds of grief from the course I ought to steer,
That praise of her is all my purpose here
And all my business; that of her alone

Do I go telling, that how she lived and died
And lives again in immortality, 10
All men may know, and love my Laura's grace.

Oh, may she deign to stand at my bedside
When I come to die; and may she call to me
And draw me to her in the blessèd place!

* *Ite, rime dolenti, al duro sasso*, sonnet 333. Translated by Morris Bishop.

## Letter to Dionisio da Borgo San Sepolcro*
### [*The Ascent of Mount Ventoux*]

To-day[1] I made the ascent of the highest mountain in the region, which is not improperly called Ventosum.[2] My only motive was the wish to see what so great an elevation had to offer. I have

* Letter IV, i, from a group of letters entitled *De Rebus Familiaribus*. From *Petrarch, the First Modern Scholar and Man of Letters*, by James Harvey Robinson and Henry Winchester Rolfe (New York: G. P. Putnam's Sons, 1914), 2nd ed., and translated by the authors.

Dionisio, or Dionigi, da Borgo San Sepolcro was an Augustinian monk whom Petrarch had probably met in Paris in 1333. A learned theologian, he taught at Paris and in 1339 was appointed bishop of Monopoli. He spent the last part of his life in Naples at the court of the learned king Robert d'Anjou and died there in 1342 (Petrarch wrote a verse epistle on his death).

1. April 26. From internal evidence the year should be 1336, ten years after Petrarch left Bologna, but the letter was probably revised and made into an "allegory" at a later date (cf. note 8 below).

2. *Ventosum:* windy. Mount Ventoux (ca. 6,000 feet) is near Malaucène, not far from Petrarch's place of retirement in Vaucluse.

had the expedition in mind for many years; for as you know, I have lived in this region from infancy, having been cast here by that fate[3] which determines the affairs of men. Consequently the mountain, which is visible from a great distance, was ever before my eyes, and I conceived the plan of some time doing what I have at last accomplished to-day. The idea took hold upon me with especial force when, in re-reading Livy's *History of Rome*, yesterday, I happened upon the place where Philip of Macedon, the same who waged war against the Romans, ascended Mount Haemus in Thessaly, from whose summit he was able, it is said, to see two seas, the Adriatic and the Euxine.[4] Whether this be true or false I have not been able to determine, for the mountain is too far away, and writers disagree. Pomponius Mela, the cosmographer—not to mention others who have spoken of this occurrence—admits its truth without hesitation[5]; Titus Livius, on the other hand, considers it false. I, assuredly, should not have left the question long in doubt, had that mountain been as easy to explore as this one. Let us leave this matter to one side, however, and return to my mountain here,—it seems to me that a young man in private life may well be excused for attempting what an aged king could undertake without arousing criticism.

When I came to look about for a companion I found, strangely enough, that hardly one among my friends seemed suitable, so rarely do we meet with just the right combination of personal tastes and characteristics, even among those who are dearest to us. This one was too apathetic, that one over-anxious; this one too slow, that one too hasty; one was too sad, another over-cheerful; one more simple, another more sagacious, than I desired. I feared this one's taciturnity and that one's loquacity. The heavy deliberation of some repelled me as much as the lean incapacity of others. I rejected those who were likely to irritate me by a cold want of interest, as well as those who might weary me by their excessive enthusiasm. Such defects, however grave, could be borne with at home, for charity suffereth all things, and friendship accepts any burden; but it is quite otherwise on a journey, where every weakness becomes much more serious. So, as I was bent upon pleasure and anxious that my enjoyment should be unalloyed, I looked about me with unusual care, balanced against one another the various characteristics of my friends, and without committing any breach of friendship I silently condemned every trait which might prove disagreeable on the way. And—would you believe it?—I finally turned homeward for aid, and proposed the ascent to my only brother, who is younger than I, and with whom

---

3. *Cf.* Biographical Note on Petrarch, p. 1181.
4. *Cf.* Livy, *Roman History*, XL, 21, 2.
5. Pomponius Mela, Roman geogra-

pher of Spanish birth, wrote toward the middle of the first century A.D.; the passage referred to in his *Corographia* is II, 17.

you are well acquainted.[6] He was delighted and gratified beyond measure by the thought of holding the place of a friend as well as of a brother.

At the time fixed we left the house, and by evening reached Malaucène, which lies at the foot of the mountain, to the north. Having rested there a day, we finally made the ascent this morning, with no companions except two servants; and a most difficult task it was. The mountain is a very steep and almost inaccessible mass of stony soil. But, as the poet[7] has well said, "Remorseless toil conquers all." It was a long day, the air fine. We enjoyed the advantages of vigour of mind and strength and agility of body, and everything else essential to those engaged in such an undertaking, and so had no other difficulties to face than those of the region itself. We found an old shepherd in one of the mountain dales, who tried, at great length, to dissuade us from the ascent, saying that some fifty years before he had, in the same ardour of youth, reached the summit, but had gotten for his pains nothing except fatigue and regret, and clothes and body torn by the rocks and briars. No one, so far as he or his companions knew, had ever tried the ascent before or after him. But his counsels increased rather than diminished our desire to proceed, since youth is suspicious of warnings. So the old man, finding that his efforts were in vain, went a little way with us, and pointed out a rough path among the rocks, uttering many admonitions, which he continued to send after us even after we had left him behind. Surrendering to him all such garments or other possessions as might prove burdensome to us, we made ready for the ascent, and started off at a good pace. But, as usually happens, fatigue quickly followed upon our excessive exertion, and we soon came to a halt at the top of a certain cliff. Upon starting on again we went more slowly, and I especially advanced along the rocky way with a more deliberate step. While my brother chose a direct path straight up the ridge,[8] I weakly took an easier one which really descended. When I was called back, and the right road was shown me, I replied that I hoped to find a better way round on the other side, and that I did not mind going farther if the path were only less steep. This was just an excuse for my laziness; and when the others had already reached a considerable height I was still wandering in the valleys. I had failed to find an easier path, and had only increased the distance and difficulty of the ascent. At last I became disgusted with the intricate way I had chosen, and resolved to ascend without more ado. When I reached my brother, who, while waiting for me, had had ample opportunity for rest, I was tired and irritated. We walked along together for a

6. Gherardo, probably about three years younger than the poet.
7. Virgil, in *Georgics*, I, 145-146.
8. In the allegorical reading of the letter, this could be an allusion to Gherardo achieving God and salvation more directly (he became a monk in 1342, retiring into the monastery of Montrieux).

time, but hardly had we passed the first spur when I forgot about the circuitous route which I had just tried, and took a lower one again. Once more I followed an easy, roundabout path through winding valleys, only to find myself soon in my old difficulty. I was simply trying to avoid the exertion of the ascent; but no human ingenuity can alter the nature of things, or cause anything to reach a height by going down. Suffice it to say that, much to my vexation and my brother's amusement, I made this same mistake three times or more during a few hours.

After being frequently misled in this way, I finally sat down in a valley and transferred my winged thoughts from things corporeal to the immaterial, addressing myself as follows:—"What thou hast repeatedly experienced to-day in the ascent of this mountain, happens to thee, as to many, in the journey toward the blessed life. But this is not so readily perceived by men, since the motions of the body are obvious and external while those of the soul are invisible and hidden. Yes, the life which we call blessed is to be sought for on a high eminence, and strait is the way that leads to it. Many, also, are the hills that lie between, and we must ascend, by a glorious stairway, from strength to strength. At the top is at once the end of our struggles and the goal for which we are bound. All wish to reach this goal, but, as Ovid says, 'To wish is little; we must long with the utmost eagerness to gain our end.'[9] Thou certainly dost ardently desire, as well as simply wish, unless thou deceivest thyself in this matter, as in so many others. What, then, doth hold thee back? Nothing, assuredly, except that thou wouldst take a path which seems, at first thought, more easy, leading through low and worldly pleasures. But nevertheless in the end, after long wanderings, thou must perforce either climb the steeper path, under the burden of tasks foolishly deferred, to its blessed culmination, or lie down in the valley of thy sins, and (I shudder to think of it!), if the shadow of death overtake thee, spend an eternal night amid constant torments." These thoughts stimulated both body and mind in a wonderful degree for facing the difficulties which yet remained. Oh, that I might traverse in spirit that other road for which I long day and night, even as to-day I overcame material obstacles by my bodily exertions! And I know not why it should not be far easier, since the swift immortal soul can reach its goal in the twinkling of an eye, without passing through space, while my progress to-day was necessarily slow, dependent as I was upon a failing body weighed down by heavy members.

One peak of the mountain, the highest of all, the country people call "Sonny," why, I do not know, unless by antiphrasis,[10] as

9. Ovid, *Ex Ponto*, III, i, 35.
10. the rhetorical use of a word in a      sense opposite to its actual meaning.

I have sometimes suspected in other instances; for the peak in question would seem to be the father of all the surrounding ones. On its top is a little level place, and here we could at least rest our tired bodies.

Now, my father, since you have followed the thoughts that spurred me on in my ascent, listen to the rest of the story, and devote one hour, I pray you, to reviewing the experiences of my entire day. At first, owing to the unaccustomed quality of the air and the effect of the great sweep of view spread out before me, I stood like one dazed. I beheld the clouds under our feet, and what I had read of Athos and Olympus seemed less incredible as I myself witnessed the same things from a mountain of less fame. I turned my eyes toward Italy, wither my heart most inclined. The Alps, rugged and snow-capped, seemed to rise close by, although they were really at a great distance; the very same Alps through which that fierce enemy of the Roman name once made his way, bursting the rocks, if we may believe the report, by the application of vinegar. I sighed, I must confess, for the skies of Italy, which I beheld rather with my mind than with my eyes. An inexpressible longing came over me to see once more my friend and my country. At the same time I reproached myself for this double weakness, springing, as it did, from a soul not yet steeled to manly resistance. And yet there were excuses for both of these cravings, and a number of distinguished writers might be summoned to support me.

Then a new idea took possession of me, and I shifted my thoughts to a consideration of time rather than place. "To-day it is ten years since, having completed thy youthful studies, thou didst leave Bologna.[11] Eternal God! In the name of immutable wisdom, think what alterations in thy character this intervening period has beheld! I pass over a thousand instances. I am not yet in a safe harbour where I can calmly recall past storms. The time may come when I can review in due order all the experiences of the past, saying with St. Augustine, 'I desire to recall my foul actions and the carnal corruption of my soul, not because I love them, but that I may the more love thee, O my God.'[12] Much that is doubtful and evil still clings to me, but what I once loved, that I love no longer. And yet what am I saying? I still love it, but with shame, but with heaviness of heart. Now, at last, I have confessed the truth. So it is. I love, but love what I would not love, what I would that I might hate. Though loath to do so, though constrained, though sad and sorrowing, still I do love, and I feel in my miserable self the truth of the well known words, 'I will hate if I can; if not, I will love against my will.'[13] Three years have not yet passed since that perverse and wicked passion which had a

11. *Cf.* Biographical Note, p. 1237, and note 3 above.

12. St. Augustine, *Confessions*, II, i, 1.
13. Ovid, *Amores*, III, ii, 35.

firm grasp upon me and held undisputed sway in my heart began to discover a rebellious opponent, who was unwilling longer to yield obedience. These two adversaries have joined in close combat for the supremacy, and for a long time now a harassing and doubtful war has been waged in the field of my thoughts."

Thus I turned over the last ten years in my mind, and then, fixing my anxious gaze on the future, I asked myself, "If, perchance, thou shouldst prolong this uncertain life of thine for yet two lustres, and shouldst make an advance toward virtue proportionate to the distance to which thou hast departed from thine original infatuation during the past two years, since the new longing first encountered the old, couldst thou, on reaching thy fortieth year, face death, if not with complete assurance, at least with hopefulness, calmly dismissing from thy thoughts the residuum of life as it faded into old age?"

These and similar reflections occurred to me, my father. I rejoiced in my progress, mourned my weaknesses, and commiserated the universal instability of human conduct. I had well-nigh forgotten where I was and our object in coming; but at last I dismissed my anxieties, which were better suited to other surroundings, and resolved to look about me and see what we had come to see. The sinking sun and the lengthening shadows of the mountain were already warning us that the time was near at hand when we must go. As if suddenly wakened from sleep, I turned about and gazed toward the west. I was unable to discern the summits of the Pyrenees, which form the barrier between France and Spain; not because of any intervening obstacle that I know of but owing simply to the insufficiency of our mortal vision. But I could see with the utmost clearness, off to the right, the mountains of the region about Lyons, and to the left the bay of Marseilles and the waters that lash the shores of Aigues Mortes, altho' all these places were so distant that it would require a journey of several days to reach them. Under our very eyes flowed the Rhone.

While I was thus dividing my thoughts, now turning my attention to some terrestial object that lay before me, now raising my soul, as I had done my body, to higher planes, it occurred to me to look into my copy of St. Augustine's *Confessions*, a gift that I owe to your love, and that I always have about me, in memory of both the author and the giver. I opened the compact little volume, small indeed in size, but of infinite charm, with the intention of reading whatever came to hand, for I could happen upon nothing that would be otherwise than edifying and devout. Now it chanced that the tenth book presented itself. My brother, waiting to hear something of St. Augustine's from my lips, stood attentively by. I call him, and God too, to witness that where I first fixed my eyes it was written: "And men go about to wonder at the heights of the mountains, and the mighty waves of the sea, and the wide sweep of rivers, and the circuit of the ocean, and the revolution of the stars, but themselves they consider not."[14] I was abashed, and, asking my brother (who was anxious to hear more), not to annoy me, I closed the book, angry with myself that I should still be admiring earthly things who might long ago have learned from even the pagan philosophers that nothing is wonderful but the soul, which, when great itself, finds nothing great outside itself. Then, in truth, I was satisfied that I had seen enough of the mountain; I turned my inward eye upon myself, and from that time not a syllable fell from my lips until we had reached the bottom again. Those words had given me occupation enough, for I could not believe that it was by a mere accident that I happened upon them. What I had there read I believed to be addressed to me and to no other, remembering that St. Augustine had once suspected the same thing in his own case, when, on opening the book of the Apostle, as he himself tells us,[15] the first words that he saw there were, "Not in rioting and drunkenness, not in chambering and wantonness, not in strife and envying. But put ye on the Lord Jesus Christ, and make not provision for the flesh, to fulfil the lusts thereof."[16]

The same thing happened earlier to St. Anthony, when he was listening to the Gospel where it is written, "If thou wilt be perfect, go and sell that thou hast, and give to the poor, and thou shalt have treasure in heaven: and come and follow me."[17] Believing this scripture to have been read for his especial benefit, as his biographer Athanasius says,[18] he guided himself by its aid to the Kingdom of Heaven. And as Anthony on hearing these words waited for nothing more, and as Augustine upon reading the Apostle's admonition sought no farther, so I concluded my reading in the few words which I have given. I thought in silence of the lack of good counsel in us mortals, who neglect what is noblest in ourselves, scatter our energies in all directions, and waste ourselves in a vain show, because we look about us for what is to be found only within. I wondered at the natural nobility of our soul, save when it debases itself of its own free will, and deserts its original estate, turning what God has given it for its honour into dishonour. How many times, think you, did I turn back that day, to glance at the summit of the mountain, which seemed scarcely a cubit high compared with the range of human contemplation,—when it is not immersed in the foul mire of earth? With every downward step I asked myself this: If we are ready to endure a little nearer heaven, how can a soul struggling toward God, up

14. St. Augustine, *Confessions*, X, viii, 15.
15. *Ibid.*, VIII, xii, 29.
16. *Romans* 13:13-14.

17. *Matthew*, 19:21.
18. Saint Athanasius, Doctor of the Church (*ca.* 295-373), in his *Vita Antonii*, II.

the steeps of human pride and human destiny, fear any cross or prison or sting of fortune? How few, I thought, but are diverted from their path by the fear of difficulties or the love of ease! How happy the lot of those few, if any such there be! It is to them, assuredly, that the poet was thinking, when he wrote:

> Happy the man who is skilled to understand
> Nature's hid causes; who beneath his feet
> All terrors casts, and death's relentless doom,
> And the loud roar of greedy Acheron.[19]

How earnestly should we strive, not to stand on mountain-tops but to trample beneath us those appetites which spring from earthly impulses.

With no consciousness of the difficulties of the way, amidst these preoccupations which I have so frankly revealed, we came, long after dark, but with the full moon lending us its friendly light, to the little inn which we had left that morning before dawn. The time during which the servants have been occupied in preparing our supper, I have spent in a secluded part of the house, hurriedly jotting down these experiences on the spur of the moment, lest, in case my task were postponed, my mood should change on leaving the place, and so my interest in writing flag.

You will see, my dearest father, that I wish nothing to be concealed from you, for I am careful to describe to you not only my life in general but even my individual reflections. And I beseech you, in turn, to pray that these vague and wandering thoughts of mine may some time become firmly fixed, and, after having been vainly tossed about from one interest to another, may direct themselves at last toward the single, true, certain, and everlasting good.

MALAUCÈNE, April 26.

19. Virgil, *Georgics*, II, 490-492.

# DESIDERIUS ERASMUS
## (1466?–1536)
## The Praise of Folly (Moriae encomium)*

### I. Folly Herself

*Folly Speaks:*

No matter what is ordinarily said about me (and I am not ignorant of how bad the name of Folly sounds, even to the biggest fools), I am still the one, the only one I may say, whose influence makes

---

* Abridged. Written in 1509. Our text is from *Erasmus: In Praise of Folly*, a new translation by Leonard F. Dean.

Gods and men cheerful. A convincing proof of this is that as soon
as I began to speak to this great audience, all faces suddenly brightened with a new and unusual gaiety, all frowns disappeared, and
you applauded hilariously. Now you seem intoxicated with nectar,
and also with nepenthe,[1] like the gods of Homer; whereas a moment
ago you were sad and careworn, as if you had just come out of the
cave of Trophonius.[2] Just as a new and youthful color reappears
everywhere when the sun first shows its beautiful, golden face to
the earth, or when spring breathes softly after a hard winter, so your
faces changed at the sight of me. And thus what great orators can
hardly accomplish with long and elaborate speeches, namely the
banishment of care, I have done with my appearance alone.

. . . Since my ancestry is not known to many, I will undertake
to describe it, with the Muses' kind assistance. My father was neither
Chaos, Orcus, Saturn, Japetus, nor any other of that obsolete and
senile set of gods; on the contrary he was Plutus,[3] the real father of
men and gods, despite the opinion of Hesiod,[4] Homer, and Jove
himself. Now, as always, one nod from Plutus turns everything
sacred or profane upside down. By his decision wars, peace, empires,
plans, judgments, assemblies, marriages, treaties, pacts, laws, arts,
sports, solemnities (I am almost out of breath)—in short, all public
and private affairs are governed. Without his help, all the poets'
multitude of gods, even, I may boldly say, the chief ones, either
would not exist or would have to live leanly at home. Not even
Pallas can help the person who arouses Plutus anger, but with his
favor one can laugh at Jove's thunderbolts. What a magnificent
father! He did not beget me out of his head, as Jupiter did that
grim and gloomy Pallas, but from Youth, the best-looking as well
as the gayest of all the nymphs. Nor was this done dully in wedlock,
in the way that lame blacksmith[5] was conceived, but more pleasantly
in passion, as old Homer puts it. It should also be clearly understood that I was not born of Aristophanes' worn-out and weak-eyed
Plutus, but of the unimpaired Plutus, hot with youth and still
hotter with nectar which by chance he had drunk straight and
freely at a party of the gods.

Next, if you want to know the place of my birth (since the place
where one first squalled is nowadays considered a mark of nobility),
I was born neither in wandering Delos,[6] nor on the foaming sea,[7]
nor "in deep caves,"[8] but in the Fortunate Isles[9] themselves, where

1. legendary drug causing oblivion.
2. seat of a particularly awesome
oracle.
3. god of wealth and abundance. In
Aristophanes' play by that name, to
which Erasmus refers later in the
paragraph, he is shown in decrepit age;
ordinarily he is represented as a boy
with a cornucopia.

4. Greek didactic poet of the eighth
century B.C., cited here because he was
author of the *Theogony* (about the
generation and genealogy of the gods).
5. Hephaestus (Vulcan).
6. birthplace of Apollo.
7. from which Venus emerged.
8. a Homeric expression.
9. the mythical and remote islands

all things grow "without plowing or planting." There where there is no labor, no old age, and no sickness; where not a daffodil, mallow, onion, bean, or any other ordinary thing is to be seen; but where nose and eyes are equally delighted by moly, panacea, nepenthes, sweet marjoram, ambrosia, lotus, rose, violet, hyacinth, and the gardens of Adonis. Being born amidst these pleasant things, I did not begin life crying, but from the first laughed good-naturedly at my mother. I certainly need not envy Jove for being suckled by a she-goat, for I was nursed at the breasts of two charming nymphs— Drunkenness, offspring of Bacchus, and Ignorance, daughter of Pan. Both of them you see here with my other attendants and followers. If you ask the names of the others, I must answer in Greek. The haughty one over there is Philantia (Self-love). The one with laughing eyes who is clapping her hands is Kolakia (Flattery). This drowsy one is Lethe (Forgetfulness). She leaning on her elbows with folded hands is Misoponia (Laziness). She with the perfume and wreath of roses is Hedone (Pleasure.) This wild-eyed one is Anoia (Madness). The smooth-skinned and shapely one is Tryphe (Sensuality). And you see those two gods playing with the girls; well, one is Comus (Intemperance) and the other is Negretos Hypnos (Sound Sleep). With the help of these faithful servants I gain control of all things, even dictating to dictators.

## II. The Powers and Pleasures of Folly

. . . Now, that it may not seem that I call myself a goddess without good cause, let me tell you of the range of my influence and of my benefits to men and gods. If to be a god is simply to aid men, as someone has wisely said, and if they have been deservedly deified who have shown mankind the uses of wine or grain, why am I not justly called the Alpha[10] of gods, I who have all alone given all things to all men.

First, what is more dear and precious than life itself? And by whose aid but mine is life conceived? It is not the spear of "potently-sired" Pallas nor the shield of "cloud-controlling" Jove that propagates and multiplies mankind. Even the father of gods and the king of men, he who shakes Olympus with a nod, must lay aside the three-pronged thunderer and that Titanic manner with which when he pleases he terrifies the gods, and like a poor actor assume another character, if he wishes to do what he is forever doing, namely, begetting children. The Stoics[11] assert that they are almost god-like.

where, according to a Greek tradition, some favorites of the gods dwelt in immortality and bliss.

10. first letter of the Greek alphabet; hence, "beginning," "origin."

11. Stoicism originated in the Stoa Poikile ("painted porch"), a building in the market place in Athens where the philosopher Zeno lectured in the fourth century B.C., and later was perhaps the main type of philosophy of the Roman elite. It became known during the Renaissance especially through Seneca. Erasmus here makes the Stoics the butts

But give me one who is three, four, or six hundred times a Stoic, and if on this occasion he does not remove his beard, the sign of wisdom (in common with goats), at least he will shed his gravity, stop frowning, abandon his rock-bound principles and for a while be a silly fool. In short, the wise man must send for me if he wants to be a father. But why not speak to you more openly, as I usually do? I ask whether the head, the face, the breast, the hand, or the ear— each an honorable part—creates gods and men? I think not, but instead the job is done by that foolish, even ridiculous part which cannot be named without laughter. This is the sacred fountain from which all things rise, more certainly than from the Pythagorean tetrad.[12]

What man, I ask you, would stick his head into the halter of marriage if, following the practice of the wise, he first weighed the inconveniences of that life? Or what woman would ever embrace her husband if she foresaw or considered the dangers of childbirth and the drudgery of motherhood? Now since you owe your life to the marriage-bed, and marriage itself to my follower Madness, you can see how completely indebted you are to me. Moreover, would a woman who had experienced that travail once ever repeat it without the influence of my Forgetfulness? And Venus herself, no matter what Lucretius says,[13] cannot deny that her work would be weak and inconclusive without my help. Hence from my ridiculous and crazy game are produced supercilious philosophers, their present-day successors, vulgarly called monks, kings in purple robes, pious priests, thrice-holy popes, and finally all the gods invented by the poets, so numerous that spacious Olympus is crowded.

That the conception of life is due to me is a small matter when I can show you that I am responsible for everything agreeable. Would life without pleasure be life at all? You applaud! I was sure that you were not so wise, or rather so foolish—no, so wise, as to think otherwise. As a matter of fact, even the Stoics do not really dislike pleasure; they carefully pretend to and they loudly denounce it in public, but only in order to deter others and thus have it all to themselves. Just let them explain to me what part of life is not sad, troublesome, graceless, flat, and distressing without a dash of pleasure, or in other words, folly. This is very adequately proved by Sophocles,[14] a person insufficiently appreciated, who has left this pretty eulogy of me: "Ignorance is bliss." . . .

of Folly's irony on account of their supposedly godlike disregard of the passions.

12. According to the numerical conception of the universe of Pythagoras (sixth century B.C.) and his followers, the first four numbers (the "tetrad"— one, two, three, and four, adding up to the ideal number, ten) signified the root of all being.

13. In the opening lines of his poem *On the Nature of Things*, Lucretius (99?–55 B.C.) invokes Venus because "all living things" are conceived through her.

14. See his *Ajax*, ll. 554–555:

If someone should unmask the actors in the middle of a scene on the stage and show their real faces to the audience, would he not spoil the whole play? And would not everyone think he deserved to be driven out of the theater with brickbats as a crazy man? For at once a new order of things would suddenly arise. He who played the woman is now seen to be a man; the juvenile is revealed to be old; he who a little before was a king is suddenly a slave; and he who was a god now appears as a little man. Truly, to destroy the illusion is to upset the whole play. The masks and costumes are precisely what hold the eyes of the spectators. Now what else is our whole life but a kind of stage play through which men pass in various disguises, each one going on to play his part until he is led off by the director? And often the same actor is ordered back in a different costume, so that he who played the king in purple, now acts the slave in rags. Thus everything is pretense; yet this play is performed in no other way.

What if some wise man, dropped from heaven, should suddenly confront me at this point and exclaim that the person whom everyone has looked up to as a god and ruler is not even a man, because he is led sheeplike by his passions; that he is the meanest slave because he voluntarily serves so many and such foul masters? Or what if this wise man should instruct someone mourning his parent's death to laugh, on the grounds that the parent had at last really begun to live—our life here being in one way nothing but a kind of death? And what if he should entitle another who was glorying in ancestry, ignoble and illegitimate, because he was so far from virtue, the only source of nobility? And what if he should speak of all others in the same way? What, I ask, would he gain by it except to be regarded as dangerously insane by everyone? Just as nothing is more foolish than unseasonable wisdom, so nothing is more imprudent than bull-headed prudence. And he is indeed perverse who does not accommodate himself to the way of the world, who will not follow the crowd, who does not at least remember the rule of good fellowship, drink or begone, and who demands that the play shall no longer be a play. True prudence, on the contrary, consists in not desiring more wisdom than is proper to mortals, and in being willing to wink at the doings of the crowd or to go along with it sociably. But that, they say, is folly itself. I shall certainly not deny it; yet they must in turn admit that it is also to act the play of life.

I hesitate to speak about the next point. But why should I be silent about what is truer than truth? For so great an undertaking, however, it would probably be wise to call the Muses from Helicon;[15] the poets usually invoke them on the slightest pretext. Therefore,

---

". . . life is sweetest before the feelings are awake—until one learns to know joy and pain."

15. mythical mountain, home of the Muses.

stand by for a moment, daughters of Jove, while I show that one cannot acquire that widely advertised wisdom, which the wise call the secret of happiness, unless one follows the leadership of Folly. First, everyone admits that all the emotions belong to folly. Indeed a fool and a wise man are distinguished by the fact that emotions control the former, and reason the latter. Now the Stoics would purge the wise man of all strong emotions, as if they were diseases; yet these emotions serve not only as a guide and teacher to those who are hastening toward the portal of wisdom, but also as a stimulus in all virtuous actions, as exhorters to good deeds. Of course that superstoic, Seneca, strongly denies this and strips the wise of absolutely every emotion; yet in so doing he leaves something that is not a man at all, but rather a new kind of god or sub-god who never existed and never will. To put it bluntly, he makes a marble imitation of a man, stupid, and altogether alien to every human feeling.

If this is the way they want it, let them keep their wise man. They can love him without any rivals and live with him in Plato's republic or, if they prefer, in the realm of Ideas, or in the gardens of Tantalus.[16] Who would not shudder at such a man and flee from him as from a ghost? He would be insensible to every natural feeling, no more moved by love or pity than if he were solid flint or Marpesian[17] stone. Nothing escapes him; he never makes a mistake; like another Lynceus[18] he sees all; he evaluates everything rigidly; he excuses nothing; he alone is satisfied with himself as the only one who is really rich, sane, royal, free—in short, unique in everything, but only so in his own opinion. Desiring no friend, he is himself the friend of none. He does not hesitate to bid the gods go hang themselves. All that life holds he condemns and scorns as folly. And this animal is the perfect wise man. I ask you, if it were put to a vote, what city would choose such a person as mayor? What army would want such a general? What woman such a husband? What host such a guest? What servant such a master? Who would not rather have any man at all from the rank and file of fools? Now such a choice, being a fool, would be able to command or obey fools. He would be able to please those like himself—or nearly everyone; he would be kind to his wife, a jolly friend, a gay companion, a polished guest; finally, he would consider nothing human to be alien to him.[19] But this wise man has been boring me for some time; let us turn to other instructive topics.

---

16. Plato's republic, his celestial realm of pure ideas, and the mythical garden of Tantalus in Hades (where rich fruit always evades Tantalus' grasp) are all mentioned because they are characterized by the presence of abstractions and figments.

17. from Marpessos, a mountain on the island of Paros famous for its marble.

18. a mythical figure whose eyesight was proverbially supposed to penetrate even solid objects.

19. from a proverbial phrase in Terence's *Self-Tormentor*, l. 77: "I am a man; nothing human do I consider alien to me."

Imagine, then, that a man should look down from a great height, as the poets say that Jove does. What calamities would he see in man's life. How miserable, how vile, man's birth. How laborious his education. His childhood is subject to injuries; his youth is painful; his age a burden; his death a hard necessity. He is attacked by a host of diseases, threatened by accidents, and assaulted by misfortunes; there is nothing without some gall. There are also the multitude of evils that man does to man. Here are poverty, imprisonment, infamy, shame, tortures, plots, treachery, slander, lawsuits fraud. But this is plainly to count the grains of sand. It is not proper for me at the moment to suggest for what offenses men have deserved these misfortunes, nor what angry god caused them to be born to such miseries. Yet will not anyone who considers these things approve the example of the Milesian virgins,[20] pitiable as it is? Recall, however, what kind of people have committed suicide because they were tired of life. Have they not been the wise or near-wise? Among them, besides Diogenes, Xenocrates, Cato, Cassius, and Brutus, there was Chiron,[21] who chose death rather than immortality. Now you begin to see, I believe, what would happen if all men became wise: there would be need for new clay and another potter like Prometheus.[22]

But by a timely mixture of ignorance, thoughtlessness, forgetfulness of evil, hope of good, and a dash of delight, I bring relief from troubles; so that men are unwilling to relinquish their lives even when their lives are ready to relinquish them. They are so far from being weary of existence, that the less reason they have for living, the more they enjoy life. Clearly it is because of my good work that you everywhere see old fellows of Nestor's[23] age, scarcely recognizable as members of the human race, babbling, silly, toothless, white-haired, bald—or better let me describe them in the words of Aristophanes: "dirty, stooped, wrinkled, bald, toothless, and toolless."[24] And yet they are so in love with life and so eager to be young that one of them dyes his white hair, another hides his baldness with a wig, another obtains false teeth from heaven knowns where, another is infatuated with some young girl and is a sillier lover than any adolescent. Nowadays for one of these old sticks, these drybones, to marry a juicy young wife, and one without a dowry and sure to be enjoyed by others, is becoming the usual and proper thing. But it is even more entertaining to observe the old women, long since half-dead with age, so cadaverous that they seem to have returned from

20. of the city of Miletus, in Asia Minor. There is an ancient tale that most of them, seemingly gone insane, hanged themselves.
21. the centaur (half man, half horse); incurably wounded and suffering great pain, he asked Zeus for

relief from his own immortality.
22. He supposedly molded man out of clay.
23. the old, eloquent sage in the Homeric epic.
24. See Aristophanes, *Plutus*, ll. 266–267.

the grave; yet always saying, "It's good to be alive." They, too, are always in heat, and hire young men at a handsome fee. They carefully paint their faces, and constantly inspect themselves in the mirror; they pluck out hairs from the strangest places; they display their withered and flabby breasts; with a quavering love-song they stir a worn-out desire; they drink and go around with girls; they write love-letters. Everyone laughs at all this, and very properly, since it is the greatest folly in the world; yet the old ladies are well pleased with themselves. They are perfectly happy solely because of me. Moreover, those who scorn this kind of behavior might consider whether it is not better to lead a life of pleasant folly than to look for a rafter and a rope. Anyway, it is nothing to my fools that their actions are scorned; they either feel no shame, or shrug it off easily. If a rock falls on your head, that is clearly painful; but shame, disgrace, and curses hurt only so far as they are felt. What isn't noticed isn't troublesome. So long as you applaud yourself, what harm are the hisses of the world? And folly is the only key to this happiness.

I seem to hear the philosophers disagreeing. This is really unhappiness, they say, this life of folly, error, and ignorance. No, indeed; this is to be human. I cannot see why they should call this unhappiness when it is the common lot of all to be thus born, brought up, and constituted. Nothing can be unhappy if it expresses its true nature. Or do you argue that man is to be pitied because he cannot fly with the birds, and cannot run on four legs with the animals, and is not armed with horns like a bull? It can be argued equally well that the finest horse is unhappy because it is not a grammarian and a gourmet, or that a bull is miserable because it is found wanting at the minuet. A foolish man is no more unhappy than an illiterate horse: both are true to themselves.

The casuists argue next that men are naturally imperfect, and support and strengthen themselves by the peculiarly human device of study. As if it were possible that nature should be so careful in making a midge, a flower, or an herb, and then should have dozed in making man! And with the result that the sciences are needed! They were really invented by Theuth,[25] the evil genius of the human race, for the hurt of mankind. Instead of promoting man's happiness, they hinder it. They were probably even discovered for that purpose, just as letters were, according to the admirable argument of Plato's wise king.[26] In this way, studies crept in with the other trials of life, and from the same devilish source. This is shown by their name: "daemons," which means "those who know."

25. in Plato's *Phaedrus*, the name of an Egyptian god who brought the art of writing to King Thamus.

26. King Thamus argued that the invention of writing would produce only false wisdom and destroy the power of man's memory.

The people of the golden age lived without the advantages of learning, being guided by instinct and nature alone. What was the need of grammar when all spoke the same language, and spoke only to be understood? What use for dialectic when there was no conflict of opinion? What place for rhetoric when no one wished to get the better of another? What need for legal skill before the time of those evil acts which called forth our good laws? Furthermore, they were then too religious to pry impiously into nature's secrets, to measure the size, motion, and influence of the stars, or to seek the hidden causes of things. They considered it a sacrilege for man to know more than he should. They were free from the insane desire to discover what may lie beyond the stars. But as men fell slowly from the innocence of the golden age, the arts were invented, and by evil spirits, as I have said. At first they were few in number and were accepted by a few people. Later, hundreds more were added by the superstition of the Chaldeans and by the idle speculation of the Greeks. This was a needless vexation of the spirit, when one considers that a single grammatical system is perfectly adequate for a lifetime of torture.

Of course the arts which are nearest to common sense, that is, to folly, are most highly esteemed. Theologians are starved, scientists are given the cold shoulder, astrologers are laughed at, and logicians are ignored. The doctor alone, as they say, is worth all the rest put together. And a doctor is honored, especially among nobles, to the degree that he is ignorant and impudent. Medicine, as now generally practiced, is a branch of the art of flattery just as much as rhetoric is. Lawyers rank next to doctors. Perhaps they should be placed first, but I hesitate to join the philosophers, who unanimously laugh at lawyers as being so many asses. Nevertheless, all affairs, both great and small, are arbitrated by these asses. Their lands increase; while the theologian, who has mastered a trunkful of manuscripts, lives on beans, and wages a gallant war against lice and fleas. As those arts are more successful which have the greatest proportion of folly, so those people are happiest who have nothing to do with learning and follow nature as their only guide. She is in no way wanting, except as a man wishes to go beyond what is proper for him. Nature hates counterfeits; the less the art, the greater the happiness.

Isn't it true that the happiest creatures are those which are least artificial and most natural? What could be happier than the bees, or more wonderful? They lack some of the senses, but what architect has equalled their constructive skill, or what philosopher has framed a republic to match theirs? Now the horse, who does have some of the human senses and who travels around with men, suffers also from human ills. He feels ashamed if he loses a race. While seeking military glory, he is run through and bites the dust along with his rider. Think, too, of the hard bit, the sharp spurs, the prison-like stable, the whips, sticks, and straps, the rider himself—in short, all the tragedy of servitude to which he exposes himself when he imitates men of honor and zealously seeks vengeance against the enemy. How much more desirable except for the interference of men, is the lot of flies and birds, who live for the moment and by the light of nature. Everyone has noticed how a bird loses its natural beauty when it is shut up in a cage and taught to speak. In every sphere, what is natural is happier than what is falsified by art.

For these reasons I can never sufficiently praise that cock (really Pythagoras)[27] who had been all things—philosopher, man, woman, king, subject, fish, horse, frog, perhaps even a sponge—and who concluded that none is as miserable as man. All the others are content with their natural limitations; man alone is vainly ambitious. Among men, furthermore, the fools are in many respects superior to the learned and the great. Gryllus,[28] for example, proved to be considerably wiser than wise Ulysses when he chose to grunt in a sty rather than to expose himself to the dangers of a further odyssey. Homer, the father of fiction, seems to agree with this: he often observes that men are wretched, and he still oftener describes Ulysses, the pattern of wisdom, as miserable, but he never speaks in this way of Paris, Ajax, or Achilles. Obviously Ulysses was unhappy because that tricky and artful fellow never did anything without consulting the goddess of wisdom. Wouldn't you say that he was over-educated, and that he had got too far away from nature? The seekers after wisdom are the farthest from happiness. They are fools twice over: forgetting the human station to which they were born, they grasp at divinity, and imitating the Giants,[29] they use their arts as engines with which to attack nature. It follows that the least unhappy are those who approximate the naivete of the beasts and who never attempt what is beyond men.

There is no need to argue this like a Stoic logician, however, when we can prove it with a plain example. Is anyone happier than those we commonly call morons, fools, nitwits, and naturals—the most beautiful of names? This may sound absurd at first, but it is profoundly true. In the first place, these fools are free from the fear of death—and that fear is not an insignificant evil. They are free from the pangs of conscience. They are not terrified by ghosts and hobgoblins. They are not filled with vain worries and hopes. In

27. In the dialogue *The Dream, or the Cock*, written in the second century A.D. by the Greek satirist Lucian, the cock upholds the Pythagorean notion of transmigration of souls from one body to another by claiming that he is Pythagoras.

28. character in a dialogue by Plutarch, changed into a pig by Circe.
29. following the example of the Giants, or Titans, of Greek mythology who, inspired by their wronged mother Gaea (Earth), fought the Olympian gods and were defeated.

short, they are not troubled by the thousand cares to which this life is subject. Shame, fear, ambition, envy, and love are not for them. If they were just a little dumber and more animal-like, they would not even sin—or so the theologians say. Count your cares, you stupid intellectuals, and then you will begin to appreciate what I do for my followers. Remember also that they are always merry; wherever they go they bring pleasure, as if they were mercifully created by the gods to lighten the sadness of human life.

In a world where men are mostly at odds, all are as one in their attitude toward these innocents. They are sought out and sheltered; everyone permits them to do and say what they wish with impunity. Even the wild beasts perceive their harmlessness and do not attack them. They are sacred to the gods, and especially to me; therefore do all men properly honor them. Kings cannot eat or travel or spend an hour without their fools, in whom they take the greatest delight.[30] In fact they rather prefer them to their crabbed counsellors, whom they nevertheless support for the sake of appearances. This royal preference is easily explained, I think. Counsellors, confident in their wisdom and forced to speak the unpleasant truth, bring only problems to princes; but fools bring what rulers are always looking for—jokes and laughter.

Fools have another not insignificant virtue: they alone are candid and truthful. What is more admirable than truth? I know that Alcibiades[31] thought that only drunkards and children speak the truth; nevertheless, the merit is really mine, as is proved by a line from Euripides: A fool speaks folly.[32] Whatever a fool has in his heart is all over his face and in his speech. Now wise men have two tongues, as Euripides also remarks,[33] one for speaking the truth, and the other for saying whatever is expedient at the moment. They turn black into white, and blow hot and cold with the same breath; their words are far from what is in their hearts. Kings are unhappiest at this point it seems to me, since in the midst of their prosperity they can find no one to tell them the truth, and are obliged to have flatterers for friends. You may say that kings hate to hear the truth and avoid wise counsellors for fear that one more daring than the others will speak what is true rather than what is pleasant. By and large this is so. It is remarkable, therefore, that kings will take the truth, and a sharp truth too, from my fools. A statement which would cost a wise man his head is received from a fool with the greatest delight. Truth that is free from offensiveness does give genuine pleasure, and only fools have the power to speak it. It is for these reasons, too, that fools are taken up by women, who are

---

30. The fool, or professional jester, was of course a common feature at Medieval and Renaissance courts.
31. See Plato's *Symposium*.

32. *The Bacchanals (Bacchae)*, l. 369.
33. The source of this reference is uncertain.

naturally inclined to pleasure and frivolity. Moreover, they can explain away whatever games they indulge in with fools, even when the sport becomes serious, as good clean fun—for the sex is ingenious, especially at covering up its own lapses.

Now let's return to the subject of the happiness of fools. After a life of jollity, and with no fear of death, or sense of it, they go straight to the Elysian fields, where they entertain the pious and leisurely shades. Compare the life of a wise man with that of a fool. Put up against a fool some model of wisdom, one who lost his boyhood and youth in the classroom, who dissipated the best part of his life in continual worry and study, and who never tasted a particle of pleasure thereafter. He is always abstemious, poor, unhappy, and crabbed; he is harsh and unjust to himself, grim and mean to others; he is pale, emaciated, sickly, sore-eyed, prematurely old and white-haired, dying before his time. Of course it really makes little difference when such a man dies. He has never lived. Well, there is your wise man for you.

Here the Stoics croak at me again. Nothing, they say, is more lamentable than madness, and pure folly is either very near madness, or more likely is the same thing. What is madness but a wandering of the wits? (But the Stoics wander the whole way.) With the Muses' help we will explode this line of reasoning. The argument is plausible, but our opponents should remember the practice of Socrates in splitting Cupids and Venuses,[34] and distinguish one kind of madness from another—at least they should if they wish to be considered sane themselves. To begin with, not every kind of madness is a calamity. Otherwise Horace would not have said, "A pleasant madness inspires me."[35] Nor would Plato have ranked the frenzy of poets, prophets, and lovers among the chief blessings of life. And the oracle would not have called the labors of Aeneas, insane.[36] Madness is really of two kinds. The first is sent up from hell by the vengeful Furies. Unloosing their snaky locks, they assault the hearts of men with hot desire for war, with insatiable greed and shameful lust, with parricide, incest, sacrilege, or any other evil of that sort. At other times the Furies pursue the guilty and conscience-stricken soul with terror and the fire of wrath. The second kind of madness is far different from this. It comes from me and is to be desired above all things. It arises whenever a cheerful confusion of the mind frees the spirit from care and at the same time anoints it with many-sided delight. It is the state of mind that Cicero desired as a defense against the evils of his age. The Greek in Horace[37] also had the right idea. He was just sufficiently mad to

---

34. distinguishing different types of love.

35. Horace, *Odes*, Book III, Ode iv, ll. 5–6.

36. *Aeneid*, Book VI, l. 135.

37. What follows is a paraphrase of a passage in Horace's *Epistles*, Book II, Epistle ii, ll. 128–140.

sit alone in the theater all day, laughing and applauding at a bare stage, because he thought that tragedies were being enacted there. Otherwise he was sane enough—pleasant with his friends, kind to his wife, and indulgent to his servants, who could uncork a bottle without his getting angry. When the care of family and physician had freed him of his disease, he protested that he had been killed rather than cured, that they had taken away his pleasures and destroyed his delightful delusions. And he was perfectly right. They were the mad ones themselves, and needed the medicine more than he did. What sense is there in regarding a fortunate delusion like his as a disease to be purged with drugs?

It is not certain that every delusion and vagary ought to be called madness. A short-sighted man who thinks a mule is an ass is not commonly considered insane, nor is one who judges popular music to be great poetry. However, we must grant that a man is pretty nearly mad if he is continually and extraordinarily deluded by both his senses and his judgment. Take, for example, a person who thinks he is listening to a symphony orchestra whenever an ass brays, or a beggar who believes himself to be Croesus. Nevertheless, when this extreme madness gives pleasure, as it usually does, it is remarkably delightful both to those who are possessed by it, and to those who look on and are not mad in exactly the same way. Indeed this kind of madness is much more common than the ordinary person realizes. One madman laughs at another; they take turns entertaining each other. And the maddest one gets the biggest laugh.

If Folly is any judge, the happiest man is the one who is the most thoroughly deluded. May he maintain that ecstasy. It comes only from me, and is so widespread that I doubt if there is one man anywhere who is consistently wise and untouched by some madness. It may be only a tendency to think a gourd is a woman; but since very few see eye to eye with him on this, he will be called mad. When a man foolishly maintains that his wife (whom he shares with many others) is a pluperfect Penelope, however, nobody calls him mad, because they see that this is a plight common to other husbands.

To this latter class belong those who sacrifice everything for hunting. They swear that the sound of the horn and the baying of the hounds fill them with indescribable joy. I understand that even the dung of the dogs smells like cinnamon to them. And what is so delightful as an animal being butchered? Bulls and oxen are of course slaughtered by commoners, but it is a crime for anyone except a gentleman to touch wild game. Bareheaded and kneeling, he performs the ceremony with a special knife (no other can be used), cutting certain parts in approved order. The silent company stands as if spellbound by some novelty, although it has seen the spectacle a thousand times. If one of them is given a piece to taste, he feels that he has risen somewhat in the ranks of nobility. They think they are living royally, whereas they are really gaining nothing from this butchering and eating of animals, except to degenerate into animals themselves.

A similar class is those who are afire with a tremendous enthusiasm for building. They change round structures into square ones, and then back into round ones again. There is no end to this, until, having built themselves into poverty, they have no house to live in, and nothing to eat. What of it? In the meantime, they have been happy.

Next to these, I believe, are those who with new and secret arts labor to transmute the forms of things and who ransack earth and sea for a fifth essence.[38] Lured on by hope, and begrudging neither pain nor cost, they contrive, with marvelous ingenuity, their own delightful deception. Finally, they have spent all their money and can't afford another furnace. Even then, however, they dream on pleasantly, urging others to experience the same happiness. When absolutely all hope is gone, they find much comfort in this last thought, "In great things, it is enough to have tried." They complain that life is too short for the magnitude of their undertaking.

I am not sure that gamblers should be admitted to our fellowship, and yet some of these addicts are a foolish and ridiculous sight. At the sound of the dice their hearts beat faster. The hope of winning always lures them on, until their means are gone, until their ship is split on the gaming table, which is a more deadly promontory than Malea.[39] Now, when they have lost their shirt, they will cheat anyone except the winner, in order to preserve their word and honor. Think, also, of the old and half-blind fellows, who have to wear glasses to play. When well-earned gout has tied their joints in knots, they hire a proxy to put the dice in the box for them. A delightful affair, were it not that the game usually degenerates into a brawl, and so belongs to the Furies rather than to me.

A group that does belong with us beyond any doubt is made up of those who enjoy telling and hearing monstrous lies and tall tales. They never get enough of ghosts and goblins and the like. They are most pleased by stories that are farthest from the truth. Such wonders are a diversion from boredom, and they may also be very profitable, especially for priests and pardoners.

Closely related are those who have reached the foolish but com-

---

38. a substance (in addition to the four traditional elements—earth, water, air, and fire) of which the heavenly bodies were believed to be composed.

39. a proverbially dangerous promontory in Greece.

forting belief that if they gaze on a picture of Polyphemus-Christopher,[40] they will not die that day; or that whoever speaks the right words to an image of Barbara[41] will return unharmed from battle; or that a novena[42] to Erasmus, with proper prayers and candles, will shortly make one rich. In St. George they have turned up another Hercules or Hippolytus.[43] They all but adore his horse, which is piously studded and ornamented, and they ingratiate themselves by small gifts. To swear by St. George's brass helmets is an oath for a king. Then, what shall I say of those who happily delude themselves with forged pardons for their sins? They calculate the time to be spent in Purgatory down to the year, month, day, and hour, as if from a fool-proof mathematical table. There are also those who propose to get everything they desire by relying on 'magical charms and prayers devised by some pious impostor for the sake of his soul, or for profit. They will have wealth, honor, pleasure, plenty, good health, long life, a vigorous old age, and at last, a place next to Christ in heaven. However they don't want that seat of honor until the very last minute; celestial pleasures may come only when worldly pleasures, hung on to with tooth and nail, finally depart.

I picture a business man, a soldier, or a judge taking from all his loot one small coin as a proper expiation for the infinite evil of his life. He thinks it possible to buy up, like notes, so many perjuries, rapes, debauches, fights, murders, frauds, lies and treacheries. Having done this, he feels free to start with a clean slate on a new round of sin. How foolish also—and how happy—are those who expect something more than the highest happiness if they repeat daily the seven verses of the Psalms. These are the verses believed to have been pointed out to St. Bernard by the devil. He was a merry fellow but not very shrewd, since his tongue was loosened by the saint's trick.[44] Things like that are so foolish that I am almost ashamed of them myself; yet they are accepted not only by the laity but by the professors of theology themselves. The same thing on a larger scale occurs when sections of the country set up regional saints, and assign peculiar rites and powers to each one. One gives relief from toothache, another aids women in labor, a third recovers stolen goods, a fourth succors the shipwrecked, and still another watches over the sheep—the list is too long to finish. Some are helpful in a number of difficulties, especially the Virgin Mother, whom the common people honor more than they do the Son.

40. Polyphemus is the Cyclops (one-eyed giant) in Homer's *Odyssey;* St. Christopher is also represented with only one eye.

41. St. Barbara, supposed to protect her worshipers against fire and artillery.

42. a nine days' devotion.

43. In Greco-Roman mythology, both fought against monsters.

44. A devil had told St. Bernard that repeating seven particular verses of the Psalms would bring him the certainty of salvation; "the saint's trick" was that of proposing to recite all of the Psalms.

Do men ask anything but folly from these saints? Among all the gifts hanging from the walls and even from the ceilings of churches, have you ever seen one in payment for an escape from folly, or for making the giver wiser? One person has escaped from drowning. Another has lived after being run through. This fellow had the good luck or the nerve to leave the battlefield, allowing the others to fight. Another was delivered from the shadow of the gallows by the patron saint of thieves so that he could continue to relieve those who are burdened with too much wealth. This one escaped from jail. That one crossed up his doctor by surviving a fever. This man was saved by a poisoned drink, which loosened his bowels instead of killing him. His wife was not exactly pleased, since she lost both her labor and expense. Another's wagon was overturned, but he drove his horses home unharmed. That fellow's house fell on him and he lived. This one sneaked out safely when he was surprised by a husband. No one, however, gives thanks for warding off folly. It is so pleasant not to be wise that men will seek to avoid anything rather than folly.

Why should I go farther on this sea of superstition? "If I had a hundred tongues, a hundred mouths, a voice of brass, I could not describe all the forms of folly, or list all its names."[45] The life of Christians everywhere runs over with such nonsense. Superstitions are allowed and even promoted by the priests; they do not regret anything so profitable. Imagine, in the midst of this, some insolent wise men speaking the real truth: "You will not die badly if you live well. Your sins are redeemed if to the payment of money you add tears, vigils, prayers, fastings, and hatred of evil, and if you change your whole way of living. The saints will favor you if you imitate them." A wise man who snarled out things like that would throw the world into turmoil and deprive it of happiness!

Also of our fellowship are those who while still living make elaborate funeral arrangements, even prescribing the number of candles, mourners, singers, and hired pall-bearers. They must think that their sight will be returned to them after they are dead, or that their corpses will feel ashamed at not being buried grandly. They labor as if they were planning a civic entertainment.

I must not pass over those nobodies who take enormous pride in empty titles of nobility. One will trace his family back to Aeneas, another to Brutus,[46] and a third to King Arthur. They are surrounded by busts and portraits of their ancestors. They name over their grandfathers and great-grandfathers, and have the old titles by heart. At the same time, they are not far from being senseless statues themselves, and are probably worth less than the ones they

---

45. a variation on a passage in the *Aeneid*, Book VI, ll. 625–627, in which, however, Virgil is talking of "forms of crime" rather than of "folly."

46. the legendary founder of Britain.

show off. My follower, Self-love, enables them to live happily, however; and there are always other fools who regard monsters like these as gods.

Of course Self-love brings joy to others too. This ape-like fellow here seems handsome enough to himself. That one drawing circles over there thinks he is another Euclid. The man with the rooster's voice considers himself a great musician. The happiest fool, however, is the dolt who glories in some talent which is really made possible by his followers. Seneca tells[47] of that doubly-happy rich man, for example, who had servants on hand to refresh his memory whenever he told stories. He was so weak he could hardly stand, but he was a great fighter—with the support of hired thugs.

Artists are notoriously conceited. They would rather lose the family homestead than any part of their talent. This is especially true of actors, singers, orators, and poets. The worse they are, the more insolent, pushing, and conceited they become. And the more applause they receive. The worst always please the most, because the majority of people, as I have remarked, are fools. If the poorer artist is most pleased with himself and is admired by the largest number, why should he wish to have true skill? It will cost him more; it will make him self-conscious and critical; and it will please far fewer of his audience.

I observe that races and cities are also attended by self-love. The English pride themselves on their good looks, their music, and their fine food, among other things. Noble or royal lineage is the claim of all Scots, together with argumentative skill. The French are the masters of courtesy; and the Parisians,[48] in addition, are the only ones who understand theology. The Italians have a monopoly on literature and eloquence, and they are pleased to admit that they alone are not barbarians. Happiest in this delusion are the Romans, who dream pleasantly of their ancient glories.[49] The Venetians are content with their own nobility. The Greeks, of course, discovered the arts and possess the heroes of antiquity. Christian superstitions entertain the Turks and the other actual barbarians, who boast of their own religions. Better yet, the Jews steadfastly await the Messiah, and still hold grimly to Moses. The Spaniards scorn all other soldiers; and the Germans pride themselves on their great size and their knowledge of magic. I believe this is sufficient to convince you that the happiness of men, individually and collectively, springs from self-love.

Another source of pleasure is flattery, an extension of self-love.

47. The reference has not been traced.

48. The Sorbonne, the theological faculty in Paris, was the center of theological studies in Europe. See our first selection from Rabelais.

49. In connection with this passage see the closing paragraphs of Machiavelli's *Prince* (reprinted in this volume).

Instead of admiring yourself, you simply admire someone else. Nowadays flattery is condemned, but only among those who confuse the names of things with the things themselves. They think that flattery is necessarily insincere. The example of dumb animals should show them how wrong they are. What is more fawning than a dog? And yet, what is more faithful and a better friend to man? Or perhaps you prefer fierce lions, tigers, and leopards? Of course there is a harmful kind of flattery, the kind with which traitors and mockers destroy their victims; but my kind springs from kindliness and candor. It is much closer to virtue than is its opposite, surliness —or what Horace calls a heavy and awkward rudeness.[50] It raises the spirits and dispels grief; it stimulates the faint, enlivens the dull, and eases the suffering; it brings lovers together and keeps them together. It entices boys to study literature; it inspires the old. Disguised as praise, it warns and instructs princes without offense. In short, it makes everyone more pleased with himself— which is the chief part of happiness. What is more courteous than the way two mules scratch each other? There is no need to point out that flattery is important in the admired art of oratory, that it is a great part of medicine, and that it is a still greater part of poetry. It is nothing less than the sugar and spice of all human intercourse.

Still, it is a sad thing, they say, to be deceived. No; the saddest thing is not to be deceived. The notion that happiness comes from a knowledge of things as they really are is wrong. Happiness resides in opinion. Human affairs are so obscure and various that nothing can be clearly known. This was the sound conclusion of the Academics,[51] who were the least surly of the philosophers. At least if something can be truly known, it is rarely anything that adds to the pleasure of life. Anyway, man's mind is much more taken with appearances than with reality. This can be easily and surely tested by going to church. When anything serious is being said, the congregation dozes or squirms. But if the ranter—I mean the reverend —begins some old wives' tale, as often happens, everyone wakes up and strains to hear. You will also see more devotion being paid to such fabulous and poetic saints as George, Christopher, or Barbara than to Peter or Paul or even to Christ Himself. But these examples belong elsewhere.

The price of this kind of happiness is very low. Much more must be paid for substantial things, even for the least of them—grammar, for instance. It is easy enough to acquire mere opinions; nevertheless they bring greater happiness than knowledge does. The satisfaction of a man who thinks rotten kippers taste and smell like am-

50. Horace, *Epistles*, Book I, Epistle xviii, ll. 508.

51. philosophers of Plato's school, the Academy, which later became a school of skeptics.

brosia is not affected by the fact that his neighbor cannot abide their odor. On the other hand, if the finest fish turn your stomach, their quality has no bearing on your happiness. A man who thinks his extremely ugly wife is another Venus is as well off as if she really were beautiful. Here's a person who gazes admiringly at a picture made of red lead and mud which he believes is by Apelles or Zeuxis. Isn't he happier than someone who has paid a high price for an authentic masterpiece, but who gets little pleasure from it? I know a man by my name,[52] a practical joker, who gave his new wife some imitation jewels and persuaded her that they were genuine and very valuable. Now what difference did it make to the girl? She was delighted with the glass trinkets and kept them locked in a secret place. In the meantime, the husband had saved money, had enjoyed fooling his wife, and had won her devotion as well as he would have by a more expensive present.

What difference do you see between the self-satisfied inhabitants of Plato's cave[53] who contentedly admire the shadows of things, and the wise man who emerges from the cave and sees reality? If Lucian's Micyllus[54] could have dreamed forever his rich and golden dream, there would have been no reason for him to desire any other kind of happiness. Evidently, then, there is either no difference between a fool and a wise man, or if there is a difference, a fool has the better of it. A fool's happiness costs least—no more than a bit of illusion. In addition, it is enjoyed in the company of a great many others. The good things of life must be shared to be delightful; and who has not heard of the scarcity of wise men, if indeed any exist at all. The Greeks listed seven all told;[55] a more accurate census would do well to turn up one-half or one-third of a wise man.

Of course drink will drown your sorrows, but only for a time. The next morning they come galloping back, riding four white horses, as the saying is. Folly, on the other hand, is a spree that never ends. Its effect is complete and immediate. Without requiring any bothersome preparations, it fills the heart with joy. It is available to all, rather than to a chosen few, as with other gifts of the gods. Vintage wine is not made everywhere; beauty comes to few, and eloquence to fewer still. Not many are rich, and not many can be kings. Mars often favors neither side; Neptune drowns more than he saves. The majority are turned away from wisdom. Jove himself thunders, and the anti-Joves—Pluto, Ate, Poena, Febris,[56] and the

---

52. Sir Thomas More, who was a close friend of Erasmus', and on whose name Erasmus puns with *moria* (Latin for "folly").
53. The reference is to Plato's allegory in the *Republic*, Book VII, where he compares the soul in the body to a prisoner chained in a cave, his back against the light, able to see only the shadows of things outside.
54. a character in Lucian's *The Dream, or the Cock* who dreams that he has taken the place of a rich man.
55. The Seven Sages listed were philosophers of the sixth century B.C., among them Thales and Solon.
56. Pluto was god of the underworld; *Ate,* goddess of revenge and dis-

others—are executioners rather than gods. Only I, great-hearted Folly, embrace all men equally. Nor do I come only when prayed for. If some devotion is neglected, I don't grow testy and demand expiation. I don't upset heaven and earth if I have been left at home and not invited along with the other gods to smell the sacrifices. In fact, the other gods are so hard to please that it is safer and wiser not to try to worship them, but rather to avoid them altogether. Men are sometimes like that; so thin-skinned and irritable that hands off is the best policy.

Even though all this is so, I understand that no one sacrifices to Folly or builds a temple for her. Such ingratitude, I repeat, is amazing. At the same time, I good-naturedly persuade myself that respect is not really lacking. What need have I for incense, meal, a he-goat, or a she-hog, so long as men everywhere whole-heartedly worship me in the way that preachers tell us is best? Let Diana have her human sacrifices! I am not envious when I consider that all men honor me in the truest way, that is, by taking me to their hearts and manifesting me in their lives and actions. This kind of worship of the saints is not exactly customary among Christians. Plenty of them burn little candles to the Virgin, and in the middle of the day, when it does no good; but how few of them burn with zeal to imitate her in chastity, temperance, and love of heavenly things! That, after all, is the true worship, and it is by far the most pleasing to those above. Besides, why should I desire a temple, when the whole world, if I am not mistaken, is a handsome shrine to me? Nor are priests lacking—except where men are lacking. As for stone and painted images, I am not so foolish as to demand what stands in the way of worship. The stupid adore such substitutes in place of the saints themselves, who are finally crowded out altogether. The same thing would happen to me. One might say, of course, that there are as many statues to me as there are people who look foolish, even unintentionally so. What do I care if other gods are worshipped in certain places on stated days—Phoebus at Rhodes, Venus at Cyprus, Juno at Argos, Minerva at Athens, Jupiter at Olympus, Neptune at Tarentum, Priapus[57] at Lampsacus? Why should I envy them when all men eagerly offer greater sacrifices to me?

[The third section deals with "The Followers of Folly," and includes among them, in lively and paradoxical descriptions, all categories of people, from merchants to poets, from scholars to popes and cardinals; in fact, Folly concludes: "My real point has been that no man can live happily unless he has been admitted into my mysteries and enjoys my favor."]

---

cord; *Poena*, goddess of punishment; *Febris*, goddess of fever.

57. a god of procreation, son of Dionysus and Aphrodite.

### IV. The Christian Fool

. . . There is really no need for me to marshal proof[58] with so much care, when in the mystical psalms Christ himself, speaking to the Father, says perfectly plainly, "Thou knowest my foolishness."[59] It is not hard to see why fools are greatly pleasing to God. We know that great princes look with suspicion on men who are too clever, and hate them. Julius Caesar, for instance, suspected and hated Brutus and Cassius, while he did not fear the drunken Antony at all. Nero, likewise, was suspicious of Seneca, and Dionysius[60] of Plato; but all princes take pleasure in duller and simpler souls. In the same way, Christ always hates and condemns those who rely on their own wisdom. Paul testifies to this clearly enough when he says, "God has chosen the foolish things of the world,"[61] and when he says, "It has pleased God to save the world by foolishness,"[62] since it could never be redeemed by wisdom. God himself indicates this plainly when he proclaims through the mouth of the prophet, "I will destroy the wisdom of the wise and I will reject the prudence of the prudent."[63] Christ also gave thanks that God had concealed the mystery of salvation from the wise, but had revealed it to babes, that is, to fools.[64] The Greek for "babes" is νηπίοις, which is the opposite of σοφοῖς, "the wise." Equally pertinent is the fact that in the Gospels Christ often attacks the scribes and Pharisees and doctors of laws, whereas he faithfully defends the ignorant multitude. What is "Woe unto you, scribes and Pharisees,"[65] except "Woe unto you that are wise"? Little children, women, and fishermen seem to delight Him most. Even among animals, those pleased Christ best which had the least slyness. He preferred to ride upon a donkey, though had He chosen He could safely have ridden upon a lion. The Holy Spirit descended in the likeness of a dove, not of an eagle or a hawk; and the Gospels frequently mention harts, fawns, and lambs. Those who are chosen for eternal life are called "sheep." No animal is more foolish, as is shown by the proverbial phrase in Aristotle, "sheepish character," which was suggested by the stupidity of the animal and is com-

---

58. of the relationship between "Folly" and Christianity.

59. The quotation is from Psalm 69:5, where the speaker is not Christ, but the Psalmist.

60. Dionysius the Younger, tyrant of Syracuse, in Sicily, in the fourth century B.C.

61. "But God hath chosen the foolish things of the world to confound the wise." (I Corinthians 1:27.)

62. "For after that in the wisdom of God the world by wisdom knew not God, it pleased God by the foolishness of preaching to save them that believe."

63. ". . . for the wisdom of their wise men shall perish, and the understanding of their prudent men shall be hid."

64. "I thank thee, O Father, Lord of heaven and earth, because thou hast hid these things from the wise and prudent, and hast revealed them unto babes." (Matthew 11:25.)

65. Luke 11:44.

monly used as a taunt against dull and foolish men. Nevertheless, Christ declares himself the shepherd of his flock, and even takes delight in the name of "the Lamb," as when John pointed Him out, "Behold the Lamb of God."[66] The expression also appears frequently in the book of *Revelations*.

What do these things declare except that all men, even the pious, are fools? And that Christ himself, although He possessed the wisdom of the Father,[67] became something like a fool in order to cure the folly of mankind, when He assumed the nature and being of a mortal? And that He was made "to be sin"[68] in order to redeem sinners? He did not wish to redeem them by any way except by the foolishness of the Cross,[69] and by weak and simple apostles. These He taught to practice folly and to avoid wisdom. He incited them by the example of children, lilies, mustard-seed, and sparrows,[70] all of them foolish things, living without art or care, by the light of nature alone. Furthermore, He forbade the apostles to be concerned about how they should answer the charges of the magistrates, and He forbade them to pry into the times and seasons. They should not rely on their own wisdom, but should wholly depend upon Him. We know, likewise, that the Creator commanded men not to eat of the Tree of Knowledge, just as if knowledge were the destroyer of happiness. Paul roundly condemns knowledge as that which puffs up[71] and works harm. St. Bernard is following him, I believe, when he explains that the mountain wherein Lucifer established his headquarters was "the Mount of Knowledge."

Surely we should not overlook this argument, that folly is so pleasing to the heavenly powers that forgiveness of its errors is certain; whereas nothing is forgiven to wisdom. And so it comes about that when the prudent pray to be forgiven, although they were clever enough when they sinned, they use the excuse and defense of having acted foolishly. This was the argument that Aaron used in the book of *Numbers*, if I remember correctly, to excuse his sister from punishment: "I beseech, my master, that you lay not this sin, which we have committed foolishly, to our charge."[72] Saul asked forgiveness of David by saying, "It is apparent that I have done foolishly."[73] David, in turn, speaks placatingly to the Lord:

66. John 1:29, 36.
67. "But unto them which are called, both Jews and Greeks, Christ the power of God, and the wisdom of God." (I Corinthians 1:24.)
68. "For he hath made him to be sin for us, who knew no sin." (II Corinthians 5:21.)
69. The source of this allusion is uncertain.
70. For the reference to *children*, see Luke 18:17; for *lilies*, see Matthew

6:28; for *mustard-seed*, see Luke 17:6; for *sparrows*, see Matthew 10:29.
71. "Knowledge puffeth up, but charity edifieth." (I Corinthians 8:1.)
72. "And Aaron said unto Moses, Alas, my lord, I beseech thee, lay not the sin upon us, wherein we have done foolishly, and wherein we have sinned." (Numbers 12:11.)
73. ". . . behold, I have played the fool, and have erred exceedingly." (I Samuel 26:21.)

"I beseech Thee, do away the iniquity of thy servant, for I have done very foolishly."[74] It is as if he could not obtain grace by praying unless he pleaded folly and ignorance. Much stronger proof is the fact that Christ when he prayed on the Cross for His enemies, "Father, forgive them," pleaded no other excuse than ignorance, saying, "for they know not what they do."[75] In the same manner, Paul wrote to Timothy: "But therefore I have obtained the mercy of the Lord, because I acted ignorantly in unbelief."[76] What is "I acted ignorantly" except "I acted foolishly, not maliciously"? What is "But therefore I have obtained the mercy of the Lord" except "I should not have obtained it if I had not been supported by the excuse of folly"? The mystical psalmist, whom I failed to recall at the proper place, aids us: "Remember not the sins of my youth and my ignorances."[77]

Let me stop pursuing the infinite and try to summarize. The Christian religion on the whole seems to have some kinship with folly, while it has none at all with wisdom. If you want proof of this, observe first that children, old people, women, and fools take more delight than anyone else in holy and religious things; and that they are therefore ever nearest the altars, led no doubt solely by instinct. Next, you will notice that the founders of religion have prized simplicity exceedingly, and have been the bitterest foes of learning. Finally, no people seem to act more foolishly than those who have been truly possessed with Christian piety. They give away whatever is theirs; they overlook injuries, allow themselves to be cheated, make no distinction between friends and enemies, shun pleasure, and feast on hunger, vigils, tears, labors, and scorn. They disdain life, and utterly prefer death; in short, they seem to have become altogether indifferent to ordinary interests, quite as if their souls lived elsewhere and not in their bodies. What is this, if not to be mad? Considering this, we should not find it very strange that the apostles appeared to be drunk on new wine, and that Paul, in the eyes of Festus,[78] his judge, looked as if he had gone mad.

. . . Since the pious and the vulgar are so radically different, it comes about that each appears to the other to be mad. It is obvious to me, however, that the word is more correctly applied to the pious rather than to the others. This will become clearer if I briefly demonstrate, as I promised to do, that their *summum bonum* is nothing but a kind of insanity. First, let us assume that Plato was dreaming of approximately the same thing when he wrote that "the

---

74. I Chronicles 21:8.
75. Luke 23:34.
76. ". . . but I obtained mercy, because I did it ignorantly in unbelief." (I Timothy 1:13.)
77. "Remember not the sins of my

youth, nor my transgressions." (Psalms 25:7.)
78. a Roman official. ". . . Festus said with a loud voice, Paul, thou art beside thyself; much learning doth make thee mad." (Acts 26:24.)

madness of lovers is the highest kind of happiness."[79] He who loves intensely no longer lives in himself but in whatever he loves, and the more he can leave himself and enter into the other, the happier he is. Now when a soul is eager to leave the body, and does not use its bodily organs normally, you call it madness and rightly so. Isn't this what is meant by the common sayings: "there's nobody home," and "to come to," and "he is himself again"? Furthermore, as the love becomes more nearly complete, the madness is greater and more delightful. What is that heavenly life, then, towards which the truly religious aspire with such devotion? Very certainly the stronger and victorious spirit will absorb the body, and it will do this the more easily because now it is in its own realm, and also because during life it has cleansed and contracted the body in preparation for this change. Then the soul will itself be marvellously absorbed by that supreme spirit, which is greater than its infinite parts. And so at last the whole man will be outside of himself; nor will he be happy for any other reason than that, being outside of himself, he shall have some ineffable portion of that supreme good which draws all things unto itself. Although this happiness becomes complete only when the soul has recovered its original body by being clothed with immortality; yet since the life of pious folk is a contemplation and a shadowing forth of that other life, they feel a glow and a foretaste of the reward to come. This is only a drop, of course, in comparison with the fountain of eternal happiness, but it far surpasses all physical pleasures, even all mortal delights rolled into one. By so much does the spiritual exceed the bodily, the invisible exceed the visible. This surely is what the prophet has promised: "Eye hath not seen, nor ear heard, neither have entered into the heart of man, the things which God hath prepared for them that love Him."[80] And this is that portion of folly which will not be taken away by the transformation of life, but will be perfected.

Those who are permitted to have a foretaste of this—and it comes to very few—experience something very like madness. They say things that are not quite coherent or conventional, sounds without meaning, and their expressions change suddenly. They are exuberant and melancholy, crying, laughing, and sighing by turns; in brief, they are truly beside themselves. When presently they return to themselves, they say that they do not know where they have been, whether in the body or out of it, waking or sleeping. They do not remember what they have heard, seen, said, or done; and yet mistily as in a dream, they know that they were happiest when they were out of their minds. So they are sorry to come to themselves again, and they desire nothing more than to be mad always with this kind

79. See Plato, *Phaedrus*.          80. I Corinthians 2:9.

of madness. And this is only the slightest taste of the happiness
hereafter.

But indeed I have long since forgotten who I am and have run
out of bounds. If anything I have said seems sharp or gossipy, remember that it is Folly and a woman who has spoken. At the same
time remember the Greek proverb, "Even a foolish man will often
speak a word in season." Or perhaps you think that does not hold
for women? I see that you are expecting a peroration, but you are
certainly foolish if you think that I can remember any part of such
a hodgepodge of words as I have poured out. There is an old saying,
"I hate a drinking companion with a memory." Here is a new one,
"I hate an audience that remembers anything."

And so farewell. Applaud, live, drink, most distinguished wor-
shippers of Folly.

# BALDESAR CASTIGLIONE
## (1478–1529)
## The Book of the Courtier (Il libro del cortegiano)*

### [The Setting]†

On the slopes of the Apennines towards the Adriatic sea, almost
in the centre of Italy, there lies (as everyone knows) the little city
of Urbino. Although amid mountains, and less pleasing ones than
perhaps some others that we see in many places, it has yet enjoyed
such favour of heaven that the country round about is very fertile
and rich in crops; so that besides the wholesomeness of the air,
there is great abundance of everything needful for human life. But
among the greatest blessings that can be attributed to it, this I believe to be the chief, that for a long time it has ever been ruled
by the best of lords; although in the calamities of the universal wars
of Italy, it was for a season[1] deprived of them. But without seeking
further, we can give good proof of this by the glorious memory of
Duke Federico,[2] who in his day was the light of Italy; nor is there
lack of credible and abundant witnesses, who are still living, to his
prudence, humanity, justice, liberality, unconquered courage,—and
to his military discipline, which is conspicuously attested by his
numerous victories, his capture of impregnable places, the sudden

* Written between 1508 and 1516;
first published in 1528. Reprinted from
*Book of the Courtier* by Count Baldesar
Castiglione; copyright 1901 by Charles
Scribner's Sons; 1929 by Leonard E.
Opdycke; translated by Leonard E.
Opdycke; used by permission of the
publishers.

† Book I, Chapters 2–4.
1. for a certain period of time, until
Duke Guidobaldo, described below, had
to relinquish the duchy of Urbino to
Cesare Borgia, who occupied it by
force.
2. Federico II (1422–1482), of the
house of Montefeltro, duke of Urbino.

swiftness of his expeditions, the frequency with which he put to flight large and formidable armies by means of a very small force, and by his loss of no single battle whatever; so that we may not unreasonably compare him to many famous men of old.

Among his other praiseworthy deeds, he built on the rugged site of Urbino a palace regarded by many as the most beautiful to be found in all Italy; and he so well furnished it with everything suitable that it seemed not a palace but a city in the form of a palace; and not merely with what is ordinarily used,—such as silver vases, hangings of richest cloth-of-gold and silk, and other similar things,—but for ornament he added countless antique statues in marble and bronze, pictures most choice, and musical instruments of every sort, nor would he admit anything there that was not very rare and excellent. Then at very great cost he collected a goodly number of most excellent and rare books in Greek, Latin and Hebrew, all of which he adorned with gold and with silver, esteeming this to be the chiefest excellence of his great palace.

Following then the course of nature, and already sixty-five[3] years old, he died gloriously, as he had lived; and he left as his successor a motherless little boy of ten years, his only son Guidobaldo. Heir to the State, he seemed to be heir also to all his father's virtues, and soon his noble nature gave such promise as seemed not permissible to hope for from mortal man; so that men esteemed none among the notable deeds of Duke Federico to be greater than to have begotten such a son. But envious of so much virtue, fortune thwarted this glorious beginning with all her power; so that before Duke Guido reached the age of twenty years, he fell ill of the gout, which grew upon him with grievous pain, and in a short space of time so crippled all his members that he could neither stand upon his feet nor move; and thus one of the fairest and most promising forms in the world was distorted and spoiled in tender youth.

And not content even with this, fortune was so contrary to him in all his purposes, that he could seldom carry into effect anything that he desired; and although he was very wise of counsel and unconquered in spirit, it seemed that what he undertook, both in war and in everything else whether small or great, always ended ill for him. And proof of this is found in his many and diverse calamities, which he ever bore with such strength of mind, that his spirit was never vanquished by fortune; nay, scorning her assaults with unbroken courage, he lived in illness as if in health and in adversity as if fortunate, with perfect dignity and universal esteem; so that although he was thus infirm in body, he fought with most honourable rank[4] in the service of their Serene Highnesses the Kings of Naples,

---

3. actually only sixty.    4. as a mercenary captain or *condottiere*.

Alfonso and Ferdinand the Younger;[5] later with Pope Alexander VI,[6] and with the Venetian and Florentine signories.

Upon the accession of Julius II[7] to the pontificate, he was made Captain of the Church;[8] at which time, following his accustomed habit, above all else he took care to fill his household with very noble and valiant gentlemen, with whom he lived most familiarly, delighting in their intercourse: wherein the pleasure he gave to others was not less than that he received from others, he being well versed in both the [learned] languages, and uniting affability and pleasant-ness to a knowledge of things without number. And besides this, the greatness of his spirit so set him on, that although he could not practise in person the exercises of chivalry, as he once had done, yet he took the utmost pleasure in witnessing them in others; and by his words, now correcting now praising every man according to desert, he clearly showed his judgment in those matters; wherefore, in jousts and tournaments, in riding, in the handling of every sort of weapon, as well as in pastimes, games, music,—in short, in all the exercises proper to noble cavaliers,—everyone strove so to show himself, as to merit being deemed worthy of such noble fellowship.

Thus all the hours of the day were assigned to honourable and pleasant exercises as well for the body as for the mind; but since my lord Duke was always wont by reason of his infirmity to retire to sleep very early after supper, everyone usually betook himself at that hour to the presence of my lady Duchess, Elisabetta Gonzaga;[9] where also was ever to be found my lady Emilia Pia,[10] who was en-dowed with such lively wit and judgment that, as you know, it seemed as if she were the Mistress of us all, and as if everyone gained wisdom and worth from her. Here then, gentle discussions and innocent pleasantries were heard, and on the face of everyone a jocund gaiety was seen depicted, so that the house could truly be called the very abode of mirth: nor ever elsewhere, I think, was so relished, as once was here, how great sweetness may flow from dear and cherished companionship; for not to speak of the honour it was to each of us to serve such a lord as he of whom I have just spoken, there was born in the hearts of all a supreme contentment every time we came into the presence of my lady Duchess; and it seemed as if this were a chain that held us all linked in love, so that

---

5. Alfonso II and Ferdinand II (both of the house of Aragon), kings of Naples in the late fifteenth century.

6. Rodrigo Borgia, pope from 1492 to 1503.

7. in 1503; for further information about Pope Alexander VI (mentioned above) and Pope Julius II, see in our Machiavelli selection "Princely Virtues" footnote 2, the corresponding text, and the other passages in Machiavelli men-tioned in the note.

8. captain in the pontiff's army.

9. Of the ruling family of Mantua, she had married Duke Guidobaldo in 1488. She is the one who presides over this courtly scene.

10. Sister-in-law and companion of the duchess, widow of an illegitimate son of the old duke, Federico, she wittily directs much of the conversation.

never was concord of will or cordial love between brothers greater than that which here was between us all.

The same was it among the ladies, with whom there was intercourse most free and honourable; for everyone was permitted to talk, sit, jest and laugh with whom he pleased; but such was the reverence paid to the wish of my lady Duchess, that this same liberty was a very great check; nor was there anyone who did not esteem it the utmost pleasure he could have in the world, to please her, and the utmost pain to displease her. And thus, most decorous manners were here joined with greatest liberty, and games and laughter in her presence were seasoned not only with witty jests, but with gracious and sober dignity; for that modesty and loftiness which governed all the acts, words and gestures of my lady Duchess, bantering and laughing, were such that she would have been known for a lady of noblest rank by anyone who saw her even but once. And impressing herself thus upon those about her, she seemed to attune us all to her own quality and tone; accordingly every man strove to follow this pattern, taking as it were a rule of beautiful behaviour from the presence of so great and virtuous a lady; whose highest qualities I do not now purpose to recount, they not being my theme and being well known to all the world, and far more because I could not express them with either tongue or pen; and those that perhaps might have been somewhat hid, fortune, as if wondering at such rare virtue, chose to reveal through many adversities and stings of calamity, so as to give proof that in the tender breast of woman, in company with singular beauty, there may abide prudence and strength of soul, and all those virtues that even among stern men are very rare.

### ["*Everything He May Do or Say Shall Be Stamped with Grace*"]*

"I am of opinion[11] that the principal and true profession of the Courtier ought to be that of arms; which I would have him follow actively above all else, and be known among others as bold and strong, and loyal to whomsoever he serves. And he will win a reputation for these good qualities by exercising them at all times and in all places, since one may never fail in this without severest censure. And just as among women, their fair fame once sullied never recovers its first lustre, so that reputation of a gentleman who bears arms, if once it be in the least tarnished with cowardice or other disgrace, remains forever infamous before the world and

* From Book I, Chapters 17–26.

11. The conversational "game" through which the courtiers at Urbino are attempting to achieve a description of the perfect courtly gentleman, is in progress. The speaker at this point is Count Ludovico da Canossa (1476–1532). A relative of the writer and a friend of the painter Raphael, he was later a bishop and held many important offices, such as that of papal ambassador to England.

full of ignominy. Therefore the more our Courtier excels in this art, the more he will be worthy of praise; and yet I do not deem essential in him that perfect knowledge of things and those other qualities that befit a commander; since this would be too wide a sea, let us be content, as we have said, with perfect loyalty and unconquered courage, and that he be always seen to possess them. For the courageous are often recognized even more in small things than in great; and frequently in perils of importance and where there are many spectators, some men are to be found, who, although their hearts be dead within them, yet, moved by shame or by the presence of others, press forward almost with their eyes shut, and do their duty God knows how. While on occasions of little moment, when they think they can avoid putting themselves in danger without being detected, they are glad to keep safe. But those who, even when they do not expect to be observed or seen or recognized by anyone, show their ardour and neglect nothing, however paltry, that may be laid to their charge,—they have that strength of mind which we seek in our Courtier.

"Not that we would have him look so fierce, or go about blustering, or say that he has taken his cuirass to wife, or threaten with those grim scowls that we have often seen in Berto; because to such men as this, one might justly say that which a brave lady jestingly said in gentle company to one whom I will not name at present; who, being invited by her out of compliment to dance, refused not only that, but to listen to the music, and many other entertainments proposed to him,—saying always that such silly trifles were not his business; so that at last the lady said, 'What is your business, then?' He replied with a sour look, 'To fight.' Then the lady at once said, 'Now that you are in no war and out of fighting trim, I should think it were a good thing to have yourself well oiled, and to stow yourself with all your battle harness in a closet until you be needed, lest you grow more rusty than you are'; and so, amid much laughter from the bystanders, she left the discomfited fellow to his silly presumption.

"Therefore let the man we are seeking, be very bold, stern, and always among the first, where the enemy are to be seen; and in every other place, gentle, modest, reserved, above all things avoiding ostentation and that impudent self-praise by which men ever excite hatred and disgust in all who hear them."

Then my lord Gaspar[12] replied:

"As for me, I have known few men excellent in anything whatever, who do not praise themselves; and it seems to me that this may well be permitted them; for when anyone who feels himself

---

12. Count Gaspar Pallavicino (1486–1511), a very young member of the court, who died only a few years afterward.

to be of worth, sees that he is not known to the ignorant by his works, he is offended that his worth should lie buried, and needs must in some way hold it up to view, in order that he may not be cheated of the fame that is the true reward of worthy effort. Thus among the ancient authors, whoever carries weight seldom fails to praise himself. They indeed are insufferable who do this without desert, but such we do not presume our Courtier to be."

The Count then said:

"If you heard what I said, it was impudent and indiscriminate self-praise that I censured: and as you say, we surely ought not to form a bad opinion of a brave man who praises himself modestly, nay we ought rather to regard such praise as better evidence than if it came from the mouth of others. I say, however, that he, who in praising himself runs into no error and incurs no annoyance or envy at the hands of those that hear him, is a very discreet man indeed and merits praise from others in addition to that which he bestows upon himself; because it is a very difficult matter."

Then my lord Gaspar said:

"You must teach us that."

The Count replied:

"Among the ancient authors there is no lack of those who have taught it; but to my thinking, the whole art consists in saying things in such a way that they shall not seem to be said to that end, but let fall so naturally that it was impossible not to say them, and while seeming always to avoid self-praise, yet to achieve it; but not after the manner of those boasters, who open their mouths and let the words come forth haphazard. Like one of our friends a few days ago, who, being quite run through the thigh with a spear at Pisa, said he thought it was a fly that had stung him; and another man said he kept no mirror in his room because, when angry, he became so terrible to look at, that the sight of himself would have frightened him too much."

Everyone laughed at this, but Messer Cesare Gonzaga [13] added:

"Why do you laugh? Do you not know that Alexander the Great, on hearing the opinion of a philosopher to be that there was an infinite number of worlds, began to weep, and being asked why he wept, replied, 'Because I have not yet conquered one of them;' as if he would fain have vanquished all? Does not this seem to you a greater boast than that about the fly-sting?"

Then the Count said:

"Yes, and Alexander was a greater man than he who made the other speech. But extraordinary men are surely to be pardoned when they assume much; for he who has great things to do must

13. considered by some the "first gentleman" at the court of Urbino. A cousin of the writer, he was a warrior, a diplomat, and a pastoral poet; he died in 1512, at thirty-seven.

needs have daring to do them, and confidence in himself, and must not be abject or mean in spirit, yet very modest in speech, showing less confidence in himself than he has, lest his self-confidence lead to rashness."

The Count now paused a little, and messer Bernardo Bibbiena[14] said, laughing:

"I remember what you said earlier, that this Courtier of ours must be endowed by nature with beauty of countenance and person, and with a grace that shall make him so agreeable. Grace and beauty of countenance I think I certainly possess, and this is the reason why so many ladies are ardently in love with me, as you know; but I am rather doubtful as to the beauty of my person, especially as regards these legs of mine, which seem to me decidedly less well proportioned than I should wish: as to my bust and other members, however, I am quite content. Pray, now, describe a little more in particular the sort of body that the Courtier is to have, so that I may dismiss this doubt and set my mind at rest."

After some laughter at this, the Count continued:

"Of a certainty that grace of countenance can be truly said to be yours, nor need I cite further example than this to show what manner of thing it is, for we unquestionably perceive your aspect to be most agreeable and pleasing to everyone, albeit the lineaments of it are not very delicate. Still it is of a manly cast and at the same time full of grace; and this characteristic is to be found in many different types of countenance. And of such sort I would have our Courtier's aspect; not so soft and effeminate as is sought by many, who not only curl their hair and pluck their brows, but gloss their faces with all those arts employed by the most wanton and unchaste women in the world; and in their walk, posture and every act, they seem so limp and languid that their limbs are like to fall apart; and they pronounce their words so mournfully that they appear about to expire upon the spot: and the more they find themselves with men of rank, the more they affect such tricks. Since nature has not made them women, as they seem to wish to appear and be, they should be treated not as good women but as public harlots, and driven not merely from the courts of great lords but from the society of honest men.

"Then coming to the bodily frame, I say it is enough if this be neither extremely short nor tall, for both of these conditions excite a certain contemptuous surprise, and men of either sort are gazed upon in much the same way that we gaze on monsters. Yet if we must offend in one of the two extremes, it is preferable to fall a little short of the just measure of height than to exceed it, for

14. Bernardo Dovizi da Bibbiena (1470–1520), author of a play performed at the court of Urbino, patron and friend of the painter Raphael, and later a cardinal.

besides often being dull of intellect, men thus huge of body are also unfit for every exercise of agility, which thing I should much wish in the Courtier. And so I would have him well built and shapely of limb, and would have him show strength and lightness and suppleness, and know all bodily exercises that befit a man of war: whereof I think the first should be to handle every sort of weapon well on foot and on horse, to understand the advantages of each, and especially to be familiar with those weapons that are ordinarily used among gentlemen; for besides the use of them in war, where such subtlety in contrivance is perhaps not needful, there frequently arise differences between one gentleman and another, which afterwards result in duels often fought with such weapons as happen at the moment to be within reach: thus knowledge of this kind is a very safe thing. Nor am I one of those who say that skill is forgotten in the hour of need; for he whose skill forsakes him at such a time, indeed gives token that he has already lost heart and head through fear.

"Moreover I deem it very important to know how to wrestle, for it is a great help in the use of all kinds of weapons on foot. Then, both for his own sake and for that of his friends, he must understand the quarrels and differences that may arise, and must be quick to seize an advantage, always showing courage and prudence in all things. Nor should he be too ready to fight except when honour demands it; for besides the great danger that the uncertainty of fate entails, he who rushes into such affairs recklessly and without urgent cause, merits the severest censure even though he be successful. But when he finds himself so far engaged that he cannot withdraw without reproach, he ought to be most deliberate, both in the preliminaries to the duel and in the duel itself, and always show readiness and daring. Nor must he act like some, who fritter the affair away in disputes and controversies, and who, having the choice of weapons, select those that neither cut nor pierce, and arm themselves as if they were expecting a cannonade; and thinking it enough not to be defeated, stand ever on the defensive and retreat,—showing therein their utter cowardice. And thus they make themselves a laughing-stock for boys, like those two men of Ancona who fought at Perugia not long since, and made everyone laugh who saw them."

"And who were they?" asked my lord Gaspar Pallavicino.

"Two cousins," replied messer Cesare.

Then the Count said:

"In their fighting they were as like as two brothers"; and soon continued: "Even in time of peace weapons are often used in various exercises, and gentlemen appear in public shows before the people and ladies and great lords. For this reason I would have our

Courtier a perfect horseman in every kind of seat; and besides understanding horses and what pertains to riding, I would have him use all possible care and diligence to lift himself a little beyond the rest in everything, so that he may be ever recognized as eminent above all others. And as we read of Alcibiades that he surpassed all the nations with whom he lived, each in their particular province, so I would have this Courtier of ours excel all others, and each in that which is most their profession. And as it is the especial pride of the Italians to ride well with the rein, to govern wild horses with consummate skill, and to play at tilting and jousting,—in these things let him be among the best of the Italians. In tourneys and in the arts of defence and attack, let him shine among the best in France. In stick-throwing, bull-fighting, and in casting spears and darts, let him excel among the Spaniards. But above everything he should temper all his movements with a certain good judgment and grace, if he wishes to merit that universal favour which is so greatly prized.

"There are also many other exercises, which although not immediately dependent upon arms, yet are closely connected therewith, and greatly foster manly sturdiness; and one of the chief among these seems to me to be the chase, because it bears a certain likeness to war; and truly it is an amusement for great lords and befitting a man at court, and furthermore it is seen to have been much cultivated among the ancients. It is fitting also to know how to swim, to leap, to run, to throw stones, for besides the use that may be made of this in war, a man often has occasion to show what he can do in such matters; whence good esteem is to be won, especially with the multitude, who must be taken into account withal. Another admirable exercise, and one very befitting a man at court, is the game of tennis, in which are well shown the disposition of the body, the quickness and suppleness of every member, and all those qualities that are seen in nearly every other exercise. Nor less highly do I esteem vaulting on horse, which although it be fatiguing and difficult, makes a man very light and dexterous more than any other thing; and besides its utility, if this lightness is accompanied by grace, it is to my thinking a finer show than any of the others.

"Our Courtier having once become more than fairly expert in these exercises, I think he should leave the others on one side: such as turning summersaults, rope-walking, and the like, which savour of the mountebank and little befit a gentleman.

"But since one cannot devote himself to such fatiguing exercises continually, and since repetition becomes very tiresome and abates the admiration felt for what is rare, we must always diversify our life with various occupations. For this reason I would have our

Courtier sometimes descend to quieter and more tranquil exercises, and in order to escape envy and to entertain himself agreeably with everyone, let him do whatever others do, yet never departing from praiseworthy deeds, and governing himself with that good judgment which will keep him from all folly; but let him laugh, jest, banter, frolic and dance, yet in such fashion that he shall always appear genial and discreet, and that everything he may do or say shall be stamped with grace."

Then messer Cesare Gonzaga said:

"We certainly ought on no account to hinder the course of this discussion; but if I were to keep silence, I should be neglected both of the right I have to speak and of my desire to know one thing: and let me be pardoned if I ask a question instead of contradicting; for this I think may be permitted me, after the precedent of messer Bernardo here, who in his over desire to be held comely, broke the rules of our game by asking a question instead of contradicting."[15]

Then my lady Duchess said:

"You see how one error begets many. Therefore he who transgresses and sets a bad example, like messer Bernardo, deserves to be punished not only for his own transgression but also for the others'."

Then messer Cesare replied:

"In that case, my Lady, I shall be exempt from penalty, since messer Bernardo is to be punished for his own fault as well as mine."

"Nay," said my lady Duchess, "you both ought to have double punishment: he for his own transgression and for leading you to transgress; you for your own transgression and for imitating him."

"My Lady," replied messer Cesare, "as yet I have not transgressed; so, to leave all this punishment to messer Bernardo alone, I will keep silence."

And indeed he remained silent; when my lady Emilia laughed and said:

"Say whatever you like, for under leave of my lady Duchess I pardon him that has transgressed and him that shall transgress, in so small a degree."

"I consent," continued my lady Duchess. "But take care lest perchance you fall into the mistake of thinking to gain more by being merciful than by being just; for to pardon him too easily that has transgressed is to wrong him that trangresses not. Yet I would not have my severity reproach your indulgence, and thus be the cause of our not hearing this question of messer Cesare."

15. According to the plan agreed upon at the start, one of the company began a description of the perfect courtier, and the others made their contributions by contradicting the preceding speaker.

And so, being given the signal by my lady Duchess and by my lady Emilia, he at once said:

"If I remember rightly, Sir Count, I think you have repeated several times this evening that the Courtier must accompany his actions, gestures, habits, in short his every movement, with grace; and this you seem to regard as an universal seasoning, without which all other properties and good qualities are of little worth. And indeed I think that in this everyone would allow himself to be persuaded easily, since from the very force of the word, it may be said that he who has grace finds grace. But since you said that this is oftentimes the gift of nature and of heaven and, even when not thus perfect, can with care and pains be made much greater,— those men who are born so fortunate and so rich in this treasure as are some we see, seem to me in this to have little need of other master; because that benign favour of heaven almost in despite of themselves leads them higher than they will, and makes them not only pleasing but admirable to all the world. Therefore I do not discuss this, it not being in our power to acquire it of ourselves. But they who have received from nature only so much, that they are capable of becoming graceful by pains, industry and care,—I long to know by what art, by what training, by what method, they can acquire this grace, as well in bodily exercises (in which you esteem it to be so necessary) as also in everything else that they may do or say. Therefore, since by much praise of this quality you have aroused in all of us, I think, an ardent thirst to pursue it, you are further bound, by the charge that my lady Emilia laid upon you, to satisfy that thirst by teaching us how to attain it."

"I am not bound," said the Count, "to teach you how to become graceful, or anything else; but only to show you what manner of man a perfect Courtier ought to be. Nor would I in any case undertake the task of teaching you this perfection; especially having said a little while ago that the Courtier must know how to wrestle, vault, and do many other things, which I am sure you all know quite as well as if I, who have never learned them, were to teach you. For just as a good soldier knows how to tell the smith what fashion, shape and quality his armour ought to have, but cannot show how it is to be made or forged or tempered; so I perhaps may be able to tell you what manner of man a perfect Courtier ought to be, but cannot teach you what you must do to become one.

"Yet to comply with your request as far as is within my power,— although it is almost a proverb that grace is not to be learned,—I say that whoever would acquire grace in bodily exercises (assuming first that he be by nature not incapable), ought to begin early and learn the rudiments from the best masters. And how important this seemed to King Philip of Macedon, may be seen from the fact that he chose Aristotle, the famous philosopher and perhaps the greatest that has ever been in the world, to teach his son Alexander the first elements of letters. And of the men whom we know at the present day, consider how well and how gracefully my lord Galeazzo Sanseverino,[16] Grand Equerry of France, performs all bodily exercises; and this because in addition to the natural aptitude of person that he possesses, he has taken the utmost pains to study with good masters, and always to have about him men who excel and to select from each the best of what they know: for just as in wrestling, vaulting and in the use of many sorts of weapons, he has taken for his guide our friend messer Pietro Monte,[17] who (as you know) is the true and only master of every form of trained strength and ability,—so in riding, jousting and all else, he has ever had before his eyes the most proficient men that were known in those matters.

"Therefore he who wishes to be a good pupil, besides performing his tasks well, must put forth every effort to resemble his master, and, if it were possible, to transform himself into his master. And when he feels that he has made some progress, it will be very profitable to observe different men of the same calling, and governing himself with that good judgment which must ever be his guide, to go about selecting now this thing from one and that thing from another. And as the bee in the green meadows is ever wont to rob the flowers among the grass, so our Courtier must steal this grace from all who seem to possess it, taking from each that part which shall most be worthy praise; and not act like a friend of ours whom you all know, who thought he greatly resembled King Ferdinand the Younger of Aragon,[18] and made it his care to imitate the latter in nothing but a certain trick of continually raising the head and twisting one side of the mouth, which the king had contracted from some infirmity. And there are many such, who think they gain a point if only they be like a great man in some thing; and frequently they devote themselves to that which is his only fault.

"But having before now often considered whence this grace springs, laying aside those men who have it by nature, I find one universal rule concerning it, which seems to me worth more in this matter than any other in all things human that are done or said: and that is to avoid affectation to the uttermost and as it were a very sharp and dangerous rock; and, to use possibly a new word,[19]

---

16. Of a famous Neapolitan family, he fought for Louis XII and Francis I of France, and died at the battle of Pavia (1525).

17. fencing master at the court of Urbino.

18. Ferdinand II, king of Naples from 1495 to 1496.

19. *Sprezzatura*, here translated as "nonchalance," is indeed Castiglione's own word, epitomizing the important concept of gentlemanly behavior discussed in this passage.

to practise in everything a certain nonchalance that shall conceal design and show that what is done and said is done without effort and almost without thought. From this I believe grace is in large measure derived, because everyone knows the difficulty of those things that are rare and well done, and therefore facility in them excites the highest admiration; while on the other hand, to strive and as the saying is to drag by the hair, is extremely ungraceful, and makes us esteem everything slightly, however great it be.

"Accordingly we may affirm that to be true art which does not appear to be art; nor to anything must we give greater care than to conceal art, for if it is discovered, it quite destroys our credit and brings us into small esteem. And I remember having once read that there were several very excellent orators of antiquity, who among their other devices strove to make everyone believe that they had no knowledge of letters; and hiding their knowledge they pretended that their orations were composed very simply and as if springing rather from nature and truth than from study and art; the which, if it had been detected, would have made men wary of being duped by it.

"Thus you see how the exhibition of art and study so intense destroys the grace in everything. Which of you is there who does not laugh when our friend messer Pierpaolo[20] dances in his peculiar way, with those capers of his,—legs stiff to the toe and head motionless, as if he were a stick, and with such intentness that he actually seems to be counting the steps? What eye so blind as not to see in this the ungracefulness of affectation,—and in many men and women who are here present, the grace of that nonchalant ease (for in the case of bodily movements many call it thus), showing by word or laugh or gesture that they have no care and are thinking more of everything else than of that, to make the onlooker think they can hardly go amiss?"

20. an otherwise unidentified character.

# NICCOLÒ MACHIAVELLI
## (1469–1527)

### ["That Food Which Alone Is Mine"]*

I am living on my farm, and since my last troubles[1] I have not been in Florence twenty days, putting them all together. Up to now

* From a letter of December 10, 1513, to Francesco Vettori, Florentine Ambassador at Rome. Our text is from *Machiavelli, The Prince and Other Works*, new translation by Allan H. Gilbert.

1. Machiavelli had been suspected of participation in a conspiracy led by two young friends of his, and had been imprisoned and subjected to torture before his innocence was recognized.

I have been setting snares for thrushes with my own hands; I get up before daylight, prepare my birdlime, and go out with a bundle of cages on my back, so that I look like Geta when he came back from the harbor with the books of Amphitryo,[2] and catch at the least two thrushes and at the most six. So I did all of September; then this trifling diversion, despicable and strange as it is, to my regret failed. What my life is now I shall tell you.

In the morning I get up with the sun and go out into a grove that I am having cut; there I remain a couple of hours to look over the work of the past day and kill some time with the wood-men, who always have on hand some dispute either among themselves or among their neighbors. . . .

When I leave the grove, I go to a spring, and from there into my aviary. I have a book in my pocket, either Dante or Petrarch or one of the minor poets, as Tibullus,[3] Ovid, and the like. I read about their tender passions and their loves, remember mine, and take pleasure for a while in thinking about them. Then I go along the road to the inn, talk with those who pass by, ask the news of their villages, learn various things, and note the varied tastes and different fancies of men. It gets to be dinner time, and with my troop I eat what food my poor farm and my little property permit. After dinner, I return to the inn; there I usually find the host, a butcher, a miller, and two furnace-tenders. With these fellows I sink into vulgarity for the rest of the day, playing at *cricca* and *tricche-trach;*[4] from these games come a thousand quarrels and numberless offensive and insulting words; we often dispute over a penny, and all the same are heard shouting as far as San Casciano.[5] So, involved in these trifles, I keep my brain from getting mouldy, and express the perversity of Fate, for I am willing to have her drive me along this path, to see if she will be ashamed of it.

In the evening, I return to my house, and go into my study. At the door I take off the clothes I have worn all day, mud spotted and dirty, and put on regal and courtly garments. Thus appropriately clothed, I enter into the ancient courts of ancient men,[6] where, being lovingly received, I feed on that food which alone is mine, and which I was born for; I am not ashamed to speak with them and to ask the reasons for their actions, and they courteously answer me. For four hours I feel no boredom and forget every worry; I do not fear poverty, and death does not terrify me. I give myself completely over to the ancients. And because Dante says that there

---

2. allusion to a popular tale in which Amphitryo, returning to Thebes after having studied at Athens, sends forward from the harbor his servant Geta to announce his arrival to his wife Alcmene, and loads him with his books.
3. Albius Tibullus, Roman elegiac poet of the first century B.C.

4. two popular games, the first played with cards, the second with dice thrown to regulate the movements of pawns on a chessboard.
5. nearby village; in the region around Florence.
6. Machiavelli here refers figuratively to his study of ancient history.

is no knowledge unless one retains what one has read,[7] I have written down the profit I have gained from their conversation, and composed a little book *De principatibus*,[8] in which I go as deep as I can into reflections on this subject, debating what a principate is, what the species are, how they are gained, how they are kept, and why they are lost. If ever any of my trifles can please you, this one should not displease you; and to a prince, and especially a new prince, it ought to be welcome.

7. ". . . for knowledge none can vaunt / Who retains not, although he have understood." (*Paradise*, Canto V, ll. 41–42.)

8. *Of Princedoms;* the Latin title of *The Prince.* All chapter headings are also in Latin in the original.

## The Prince (Il principe)*
### [*Princely Virtues*]†

### ON THE THINGS FOR WHICH MEN, AND ESPECIALLY PRINCES, ARE PRAISED OR CENSURED

. . . Because I know that many have written on this topic, I fear that when I too write I shall be thought presumptuous, because, in discussing it, I break away completely from the principles laid down by my predecessors. But since it is my purpose to write something useful to an attentive reader, I think it more effective to go back to the practical truth of the subject than to depend on my fancies about it. And many have imagined republics and principalities that never have been seen or known to exist in reality. For there is such a difference between the way men live and the way they ought to live, that anybody who abandons what is for what ought to be will learn something that will ruin rather than preserve him, because anyone who determines to act in all circumstances the part of a good man must come to ruin among so many who are not good. Hence, if a prince wishes to maintain himself, he must learn how to be not good, and to use that ability or not as is required.

Leaving out of account, then, things about an imaginary prince, and considering things that are true, I say that all men, when they are spoken of, and especially princes, because they are set higher, are marked with some of the qualities that bring them either blame or praise. To wit, one man is thought liberal, another stingy (using a Tuscan word, because *avaricious* in our language is still applied to one who desires to get things through violence, but *stingy* we apply to him who refrains too much from using his own property);

* Written in 1513. Our text is from *Machiavelli, The Prince and Other Works*, new translation by Allan H. Gilbert, copyright, by Hendricks House Farrar Straus.
† From Chapters 15–18.

one is thought open-handed, another grasping; one cruel, the other compassionate; one is a breaker of faith, the other reliable; one is effeminate and cowardly, the other vigorous and spirited; one is philanthropic, the other egotistic; one is lascivious, the other chaste; one is straight-forward, the other crafty; one hard, the other easy to deal with; one is firm, the other unsettled; one is religious, the other unbelieving; and so on.

And I know that everybody will admit that it would be very praiseworthy for a prince to possess all of the above-mentioned qualities that are considered good. But since he is not able to have them or to observe them completely, because human conditions do not allow him to, it is necessary that he be prudent enough to understand how to avoid getting a bad name because he is given to those vices that will deprive him of his position. He should also, if he can, guard himself from those vices that will not take his place away from him, but if he cannot do it, he can with less anxiety let them go. Moreover, he should not be troubled if he gets a bad name because of vices without which it will be difficult for him to preserve his position. I say this because, if everything is considered, it will be seen that some things seem to be virtuous, but if they are put into practice will be ruinous to him; other things seem to be vices, yet if put into practice will bring the prince security and well-being.

### ON LIBERALITY AND PARSIMONY

Beginning, then, with the first of the above-mentioned qualities, I assert that it is good to be thought liberal.[1] Yet liberality, practiced in such a way that you get a reputation for it, is damaging to you, for the following reasons: If you use it wisely and as it ought to be used, it will not become known, and you will not escape being censured for the opposite vice. Hence, if you wish to have men call you liberal, it is necessary not to omit any sort of lavishness. A prince who does this will always be obliged to use up all his property in lavish actions; he will then, if he wishes to keep the name of liberal, be forced to lay heavy taxes on his people and exact money from them, and do everything he can to raise money. This will begin to make his subjects hate him, and as he grows poor he will be little esteemed by anybody. So it comes about that because of this liberality of his, with which he has damaged a large number and been of advantage to but a few, he is affected by every petty annoyance and is in peril from every slight danger. If he recognizes this and wishes to draw back, he quickly gets a bad name for stinginess.

Since, then, a prince cannot without harming himself practice

1. generous, openhanded.

this virtue of liberality to such an extent that it will be recognized, he will, if he is prudent, not care about being called stingy. As time goes on he will be thought more and more liberal, for the people will see that because of his economy his income is enough for him, that he can defend himself from those who make war against him, and that he can enter upon undertakings without burdening his people. Such a prince is in the end liberal to all those from whom he takes nothing, and they are numerous; he is stingy to those to whom he does not give, and they are few. In our times we have seen big things done only by those who have been looked on as stingy; the others have utterly failed. Pope Julius II,[2] though he made use of a reputation for liberality to attain the papacy, did not then try to maintain it, because he wished to be able to make war. The present King of France[3] has carried on great wars without laying unusually heavy taxes on his people, merely because his long economy has made provision for heavy expenditures. The present King of Spain,[4] if he had continued liberal, would not have carried on or completed so many undertakings.

Therefore a prince ought to care little about getting called stingy, if as a result he does not have to rob his subjects, is able to defend himself, does not become poor and contemptible, and is not obliged to become grasping. For this vice of stinginess is one of those that enables him to rule. Somebody may say: Caesar, by means of his liberality became emperor, and many others have come to high positions because they have been liberal and have been thought so. I answer: Either you are already prince, or you are on the way to become one. In the first case liberality is dangerous; in the second it is very necessary to be thought liberal. Caesar was one of those who wished to attain dominion over Rome. But if, when he had attained it, he had lived for a long time and had not moderated his expenses, he would have destroyed his authority. Somebody may answer: Many who have been thought very liberal have been princes and done great things with their armies. I answer: The prince spends either his own property and that of his subjects or that of others. In the first case he ought to be frugal; in the second he ought to abstain from no sort of liberality. When he marches with his army and lives on plunder, loot, and ransom, a prince controls the property of others. To him liberality is essential, for without it his soldiers would not follow him. You can be a free giver of what does not belong to you or your subjects, as were Cyrus, Caesar, and Alexander, because to spend the money of others does

2. Giuliano della Rovere, elected to the papacy in 1503 at the death of Pius III, who had been successor to Alexander VI (Rodrigo Borgia). Alexander VI is discussed in the chapter "In What Way Faith Should Be Kept by Princes"; for Machiavelli's view of the character of Julius II, see the chapter "The Power of Fortune in Human Affairs . . ."
3. Louis XII.
4. Ferdinand II, "the Catholic."

not decrease your reputation but adds to it. It is only the spending of your own money that hurts you.

There is nothing that eats itself up as fast as does liberality, for when you practice it you lose the power to practice it, and become poor and contemptible, or else to escape poverty you become rapacious and therefore are hated. And of all the things against which a prince must guard himself, the first is being an object of contempt and hatred. Liberality leads you to both of these. Hence there is more wisdom in keeping a name for stinginess, which produces a bad reputation without hatred, than in striving for the name of liberal, only to be forced to get the name of rapacious, which brings forth both bad reputation and hatred.

### ON CRUELTY AND PITY, AND WHETHER IT IS BETTER TO BE LOVED OR TO BE FEARED, AND VICE VERSA

Coming then to the other qualities already mentioned, I say that every prince should wish to be thought compassionate and not cruel; still, he should be careful not to make a bad use of the pity he feels. Cesare Borgia[5] was considered cruel, yet this cruelty of his pacified the Romagna, united it, and changed its condition to that of peace and loyalty. If the matter is well considered, it will be seen that Cesare was much more compassionate than the people of Florence, for in order to escape the name of cruel they allowed Pistoia to be destroyed.[6] Hence a prince ought not to be troubled by the stigma of cruelty, acquired in keeping his subjects united and faithful. By giving a very few examples of cruelty he can be more truly compassionate than those who through too much compassion allow disturbances to continue, from which arise murders or acts of plunder. Lawless acts are injurious to a large group, but the executions ordered by the prince injure a single person. The new prince, above all other princes, cannot possibly avoid the name of cruel, because new states are full of perils. Dido in Vergil puts it thus: "Hard circumstances and the newness of my realm force me to do such things, and to keep watch and ward over all my lands."[7]

All the same, he should be slow in believing and acting, and should make no one afraid of him, his procedure should be so tempered with prudence and humanity that too much confidence does not make him incautious, and too much suspicion does not make him unbearable.

All this gives rise to a question for debate: Is it better to be loved than to be feared, or the reverse? I answer that a prince should

5. son of Pope Alexander VI, and duke of Valentinois and Romagna. His skillful and merciless subjugation of the local lords of Romagna occurred during the years between 1499 and 1502.

6. by internal dissensions because the Florentines, Machiavelli contends, failed to treat the leaders of the dissenting parties with an iron hand.

7. *Aeneid*, Book I, ll. 563–564.

wish for both. But because it is difficult to reconcile them, I hold that it is much more secure to be feared than to be loved, if one of them must be given up. The reason for my answer is that one must say of men generally that they are ungrateful, mutable, pretenders and dissemblers, prone to avoid danger, thirsty for gain. So long as you benefit them they are all yours; as I said above, they offer you their blood, their property, their lives, their children, when the need for such things is remote. But when need comes upon you, they turn around. So if a prince has relied wholly on their words, and is lacking in other preparations, he falls. For friendships that are gained with money, and not with greatness and nobility of spirit, are deserved but not possessed, and in the nick of time one cannot avail himself of them. Men hesitate less to injure a man who makes himself loved than to injure one who makes himself feared, for their love is held by a chain of obligation, which, because of men's wickedness, is broken on every occasion for the sake of selfish profit; but their fear is secured by a dread of punishment which never fails you.

Nevertheless the prince should make himself feared in such a way that, if he does not win love, he escapes hatred. This is possible, for to be feared and not to be hated can easily coexist. In fact it is always possible, if the ruler abstains from the property of his citizens and subjects, and from their women. And if, as sometimes happens, he finds that he must inflict the penalty of death, he should do it when he has proper justification and evident reason. But above all he must refrain from taking property, for men forget the death of a father more quickly than the loss of their patrimony. Further, causes for taking property are never lacking, and he who begins to live on plunder is always finding cause to seize what belongs to others. But on the contrary, reasons for taking life are rare and fail sooner.

But when a prince is with his army and has a great number of soldiers under his command, then above all he must pay no heed to being called cruel, because if he does not have that name he cannot keep his army united or ready for duty. It should be numbered among the wonderful feats of Hannibal that he led to war in foreign lands a large army, made up of countless types of men, yet never suffered from dissension, either among the soldiers or against the general, in either bad or good fortune. His success resulted from nothing else than his inhuman cruelty, which, when added to his numerous other strong qualities, made him respected and terrible in the sight of his soldiers. Yet without his cruelty his other qualities would not have been adequate. So it seems that those writers have not thought very deeply who on one side admire his accomplishment and on the other condemn the chief cause for it.

The truth that his other qualities alone would not have been adequate may be learned from Scipio,[8] a man of the most unusual powers not only in his own times but in all ages we know of. When he was in Spain his armies mutinied. This resulted from nothing other than his compassion, which had allowed his soldiers more license than befits military discipline. This fault was censured before the Senate by Fabius Maximus, and Scipio was called by him the corruptor of the Roman soldiery. The Locrians[9] were destroyed by a lieutenant of Scipio's, yet he did not avenge them or punish the disobedience of that lieutenant. This all came from his easy nature, which was so well understood that one who wished to excuse him in the Senate said there were many men who knew better how not to err than how to punish errors. This easy nature would in time have overthrown the fame and glory of Scipio if, in spite of this weakness, he had kept on in independent command. But since he was under the orders of the Senate, this bad quality was not merely concealed but was a glory to him.

Returning, then, to the debate on being loved and feared, I conclude that since men love as they please and fear as the prince pleases, a wise prince will evidently rely on what is in his own power and not on what is in the power of another. As I have said, he need only take pains to avoid hatred.

#### IN WHAT WAY FAITH SHOULD BE KEPT BY PRINCES

Everybody knows how laudable it is in a prince to keep this faith and to be an honest man and not a trickster. Nevertheless, the experience of our times shows that the princes who have done great things are the ones who have taken little account of their promises and who have known how to addle the brains of men with craft. In the end they have conquered those who have put their reliance on good faith.

You must realize, then, that there are two ways to fight. In one kind the laws are used, in the other, force. The first is suitable to man, the second to animals. But because the first often falls short, one has to turn to the second. Hence a prince must know perfectly how to act like a beast and like a man. This truth was covertly taught to princes by ancient authors, who write that Achilles and many other ancient princes were turned over for their up-bringing to Chiron the centaur,[10] that he might keep them under his tuition.

---

8. Publius Cornelius Scipio Africanus the Elder (235–183 B.C.). The episode of the mutiny occurred in 206 B.C.
9. citizens of Locri, in Sicily.

10. reputed in myth to be the educator of many heroes, among them Achilles, Theseus, Jason, and Hercules.

To have as teacher one who is half beast and half man means nothing else than that a prince needs to know how to use the qualities of both creatures. The one without the other will not last long.

Since, then, it is necessary for a prince to understand how to make good use of the conduct of the animals, he should select among them the fox and the lion, because the lion cannot protect himself from traps, and the fox cannot protect himself from the wolves. So the prince needs to be a fox that he may know how to deal with traps, and a lion that he may frighten the wolves. Those who act like the lion alone do not understand their business. A prudent ruler, therefore, cannot and should not observe faith when such observance is to his disadvantage and the causes that made him give his promise have vanished. If men were all good, this advice would not be good, but since men are wicked and do not keep their promises to you, you likewise do not have to keep yours to them. Lawful reasons to excuse his failure to keep them will never be lacking to a prince. It would be possible to give innumerable modern examples of this and to show many treaties and promises that have been made null and void by the faithlessness of princes. And the prince who has best known how to act as a fox has come out best. But one who has this capacity must understand how to keep it covered, and be a skilful pretender and dissembler. Men are so simple and so subject to present needs that he who deceives in this way will always find those who will let themselves be deceived.

I do not wish to keep still about one of the recent instances. Alexander VI[11] did nothing else than deceive men, and had no other intention; yet he always found a subject to work on. There never was a man more effective in swearing that things were true, and the greater the oaths with which he made a promise, the less he observed it. Nonetheless his deceptions always succeeded to his wish, because he thoroughly understood this aspect of the world.

It is not necessary, then, for a prince really to have all the virtues mentioned above, but it is very necessary to seem to have them. I will even venture to say that they damage a prince who possesses them and always observes them, but if he seems to have them they are useful. I mean that he should seem compassionate, trustworthy, humane, honest, and religious, and actually be so; but yet he should have his mind so trained that, when it is necessary not to practice these virtues, he can change to the opposite, and do it skilfully. It is to be understood that a prince, especially a new prince, cannot observe all the things because of which men are considered good, because he is often obliged, if he wishes to maintain his govern-

---

11. Rodrigo Borgia, father of Cesare Borgia; he was pope from 1492 to 1503. (See footnote 2.)

ment, to act contrary to faith, contrary to charity, contrary to humanity, contrary to religion. It is therefore necessary that he have a mind capable of turning in whatever direction the winds of Fortune and the variations of affairs require, and, as I said above, that he should not depart from what is morally right, if he can observe it, but should know how to adopt what is bad, when he is obliged to.

A prince, then, should be very careful that there does not issue from his mouth anything that is not full of the above-mentioned five qualities. To those who see and hear him he should seem all compassion, all faith, all honesty, all humanity, all religion. There is nothing more necessary to make a show of possessing than this last quality. For men in general judge more by their eyes than by their hands; everybody is fitted to see, few to understand. Everybody sees what you appear to be; few make out what you really are. And these few do not dare to oppose the opinion of the many, who have the majesty of the state to confirm their view. In the actions of all men, and especially those of princes, where there is no court to which to appeal, people think of the outcome. A prince needs only to conquer and to maintain his position. The means he has used will always be judged honorable and will be praised by everybody, because the crowd is always caught by appearance and by the outcome of events, and the crowd is all there is in the world; there is no place for the few when the many have room enough. A certain prince of the present day,[12] whom it is not good to name, preaches nothing else than peace and faith, and is wholly opposed to both of them, and both of them, if he had observed them, would many times have taken from him either his reputation or his throne.

## [*"Fortune Is a Woman"*]*

### THE POWER OF FORTUNE IN HUMAN AFFAIRS, AND TO WHAT EXTENT SHE SHOULD BE RELIED ON

It is not unknown to me that many have been and still are of the opinion that the affairs of this world are so under the direction of Fortune and of God that man's prudence cannot control them; in fact, that man has no resource against them. For this reason many think there is no use in sweating much over such matters, but that one might as well let Chance take control. This opinion has been the more accepted in our times, because of the great changes in the state of the world that have been and now are seen every day, beyond all human surmise. And I myself, when thinking on these things, have now and then in some measure inclined to

12. Ferdinand II, "the Catholic," king of Spain. In refraining from mentioning him, Machiavelli apparently had in mind the good relations existing between Spain and the house of Medici.
* Chapter 25.

their view. Nevertheless, because the freedom of the will should not be wholly annulled, I think it may be true that Fortune is arbiter of half of our actions, but that she still leaves the control of the other half, or about that, to us.

I liken her to one of those raging streams that, when they go mad, flood the plains, ruin the trees and the buildings, and take away the fields from one bank and put them down on the other. Everybody flees before them; everybody yields to their onrush without being able to resist anywhere. And though this is their nature, it does not cease to be true that, in calm weather, men can make some provisions against them with walls and dykes, so that, when the streams swell, their waters will go off through a canal, or their currents will not be so wild and do so much damage. The same is true of Fortune. She shows her power where there is no wise preparation for resisting her, and turns her fury where she knows that no walls and dykes have been made to hold her in. And if you consider Italy—the place where these variations occur and the cause that has set them in motion—you will see that she is a country without dykes and without any wall of defence. If, like Germany, Spain, and France, she had had a sufficient bulwark of military vigor, this flood would not have made the great changes it has, or would not have come at all.

And this, I think, is all I need to say on opposing oneself to Fortune, in general. But limiting myself more to particulars, I say that a prince may be seen prospering today and falling in ruin tomorrow, though it does not appear that he has changed in his nature or any of his qualities. I believe this comes, in the first place, from the causes that have been discussed at length in preceding chapters. That is, if a prince bases himself entirely on Fortune, he will fall when she varies. I also believe that a ruler will be successful who adapts his mode of procedure to the quality of the times, and likewise that he will be unsuccessful if the times are out of accord with his procedure. Because it may be seen that in things leading to the end each has before him, namely glory and riches, men proceed differently. One acts with caution, another rashly; one with violence, another with skill; one with patience, another with its opposite; yet with these different methods each one attains his end. Still further, two cautious men will be seen, of whom one comes to his goal, the other does not. Likewise you will see two who succeed with two different methods, one of them being cautious and the other rash. These results are caused by nothing else than the nature of the times, which is or is not in harmony with the procedure of men. It also accounts for what I have mentioned, namely, that two persons, working differently, chance to arrive at the same result; and that of two who work in the same way, one attains his end, but the other does not.

On the nature of the times also depends the variability of the best method. If a man conducts himself with caution and patience, times and affairs may come around in such a way that his procedure is good, and he goes on successfully. But if times and circumstances change, he is ruined, because he does not change his method of action. There is no man so prudent as to understand how to fit himself to this condition, either because he is unable to deviate from the course to which nature inclines him, or because, having always prospered by walking in one path, he cannot persuade himself to leave it. So the cautious man, when the time comes to go at a reckless pace, does not know how to do it. Hence he comes to ruin. Yet if he could change his nature with the times and with circumstances, his fortune would not be altered.

Pope Julius II proceeded rashly in all his actions, and found the times and circumstances so harmonious with his mode of procedure that he was always so lucky as to succeed. Consider the first enterprise he engaged in, that of Bologna, while Messer Giovanni Bentivogli[13] was still alive. The Venetians were not pleased with it; the King of Spain felt the same way; the Pope was debating such an enterprise with the King of France. Nevertheless, in his courage and rashness Julius personally undertook that expedition. This movement made the King of Spain and the Venetians stand irresolute and motionless, the latter for fear, and the King because of his wish to recover the entire kingdom of Naples. On the other side, the King of France was dragged behind Julius, because the King, seeing that the Pope had moved and wishing to make him a friend in order to put down the Venetians, judged he could not refuse him soldiers without doing him open injury. Julius, then, with his rash movement, attained what no other pontiff, with the utmost human prudence, would have attained. If he had waited to leave Rome until the agreements were fixed and everything arranged, as any other pontiff would have done, he would never have succeeded, for the King of France would have had a thousand excuses, and the others would have raised a thousand fears. I wish to omit his other acts, which are all of the same sort, and all succeeded perfectly. The brevity of his life did not allow him to know anything different. Yet if times had come in which it was necessary to act with caution, they would have ruined him, for he would never have deviated from the methods to which nature inclined him.

---

13. of the ruling family Bentivogli (the prefix *Messer* means "my lord"); the Pope undertook to dislodge him from Bologna, in 1506.

I conclude, then, that since Fortune is variable and men are set in their ways, they are successful when they are in harmony with Fortune and unsuccessful when they disagree with her. Yet I am of the opinion that it is better to be rash than over-cautious, because Fortune is a woman and, if you wish to keep her down, you must beat her and pound her. It is evident that she allows herself to be overcome by men who treat her in that way rather than by those who proceed coldly. For that reason, like a woman, she is always the friend of young men, because they are less cautious, and more courageous, and command her with more boldness.

### [The Roman Dream]*

AN EXHORTATION TO TAKE HOLD OF ITALY AND RESTORE
HER TO LIBERTY FROM THE BARBARIANS

Having considered all the things discussed above, I have been turning over in my own mind whether at present in Italy the time is ripe for a new prince to win prestige, and whether conditions there give a wise and vigorous ruler occasion to introduce methods that will do him honor, and bring good to the mass of the people of the land. It appears to me that so many things unite for the advantage of a new prince, that I do not know of any time that has ever been more suited for this. And, as I said, if it was necessary to make clear the ability of Moses that the people of Israel should be enslaved in Egypt, and to reveal Cyrus's greatness of mind that the Persians should be oppressed by the Medes, and to demonstrate the excellence of Theseus that the Athenians should be scattered, so at the present time, in order to make known the greatness of an Italian soul, Italy had to be brought down to her present position, to be more a slave than the Hebrews, more a servant than the Persians, more scattered than the Athenians; without head, without government; defeated, plundered, torn asunder, overrun; subject to every sort of disaster.

And though before this, certain persons[14] have showed signs from which it could be inferred that they were chosen by God for the redemption of Italy, nevertheless it has afterwards been seen that in the full current of action they have been cast off by Fortune. So Italy remains without life and awaits the man, whoever he may be, who is to heal her wounds, put an end to the plundering of Lombardy and the tribute laid on Tuscany and the kingdom of Naples, and cure her of those sores that have long been suppurating. She may be seen praying God to send some one to redeem her from these cruel and barbarous insults. She is evidently ready and

* Chapter 26.
14. possibly Cesare Borgia and Fran-   cesco Sforza, discussed in an earlier chapter of the book.

willing to follow a banner, if only some one will raise it. Nor is there at present anyone to be seen in whom she can put more hope than in your illustrious House,[15] because its fortune and vigor, and the favor of God and of the Church, which it now governs,[16] enable it to be the leader in such a redemption. This will not be very difficult, as you will see if you will bring to mind the actions and lives of those I have named above.[17] And though these men were striking exceptions, yet they were men, and each of them had less opportunity than the present gives; their enterprises were not more just than this, nor easier, nor was God their friend more than he is yours. Here justice is complete. "A way is just to those to whom it is necessary, and arms are holy to him who has no hope save in arms."[18] Everything is now fully disposed for the work, and when that is true an undertaking cannot be difficult, if only your House adopts the methods of those I have set forth as examples. Moreover, we have before our eyes extraordinary and unexampled means prepared by God. The sea has been divided. A cloud has guided you on your way. The rock has given forth water. Manna has fallen.[19] Everything has united to make you great. The rest is for you to do. God does not intend to do everything, lest he deprive us of our free will and the share of glory that belongs to us.

It is no wonder if no one of the above-named Italians[20] has been able to do what we hope your illustrious House can. Nor is it strange if in the many revolutions and military enterprises of Italy, the martial vigor of the land always appears to be exhausted. This is because the old military customs were not good, and there has been nobody able to find new ones. Yet nothing brings so much honor to a man who rises to new power, as the new laws and new methods he discovers. These things, when they are well founded and have greatness in them, make him revered and worthy of admiration. And in Italy matter is not lacking on which to impress forms of every sort. There is great vigor in the limbs if only it is not lacking in the heads. You may see that in duels and combats between small numbers, the Italians have been much superior in force, skill, and intelligence. But when it is a matter of armies, Italians cannot be compared with foreigners. All this comes from the weakness of the heads, because those who know are not obeyed, and each man thinks he knows. Nor up to this time has there been a man able to raise himself so high, through both ability


15. the house of Medici. The *Prince* was first meant for Giuliano de' Medici; after Giuliano's death it was dedicated to his nephew, Lorenzo, later duke of Urbino.

16. Pope Leo X was a Medici (Giovanni de' Medici).

17. in the preceding paragraph.

18. Livy, *History*, Book IX, Chapter 1, paragraph 10.

19. See the allusion to Moses in the preceding paragraph.

20. Possibly a further allusion to Cesare Borgia and Francesco Sforza.

and fortune, that the others would yield to him. The result is that for the past twenty years, in all the wars that have been fought when there has been an army entirely Italian, it has always made a bad showing. Proof of this was given first at the Taro, and then at Alessandria, Capua, Genoa, Vailà, Bologna, and Mestri.[21]

If your illustrious House, then, wishes to imitate those excellent men who redeemed their countries, it is necessary, before everything else, to furnish yourself with your own army, as the true foundation of every enterprise. You cannot have more faithful, nor truer, nor better soldiers. And though every individual of these may be good, they become better as a body when they see that they are commanded by their prince, and honored and trusted by him. It is necessary, therefore, that your House should be prepared with such forces, in order that it may be able to defend itself against the foreigners with Italian courage.

And though the Swiss and the Spanish infantry are properly estimated as terribly effective, yet both have defects. Hence a third type would be able not merely to oppose them but to feel sure of overcoming them. The fact is that the Spaniards are not able to resist cavalry, and the Swiss have reason to fear infantry, when they meet any as determined in battle as themselves. For this reason it has been seen and will be seen in experience that the Spaniards are unable to resist the French cavalry, and the Swiss are overthrown by Spanish infantry. And though of this last a clear instance has not been observed, yet an approach to it appeared in the battle of Ravenna,[22] when the Spanish infantry met the German battalions, who use the same methods as the Swiss. There the Spanish, through their ability and the assistance given by their shields, got within the points of the spears from below, and slew their enemies in security, while the Germans could find no means of resistance. If the cavalry had not charged the Spanish, they would have annihilated the Germans. It is possible, then, for one who realizes the defects of these two types, to equip infantry in a new manner, so that it can resist cavalry and not be afraid of foot-soldiers; but to gain this end they must have weapons of the right sorts, and adopt varied methods of combat. These are some of the things which, when they are put into service as novelties, give reputation and greatness to a new ruler.[23]

This opportunity, then, should not be allowed to pass, in order that after so long a time Italy may see her redeemer. I am unable to express with what love he would be received in all the provinces that have suffered from these foreign deluges; with what thirst for

21. sites of battles occurring between the end of the fifteenth century and the year 1513.
22. between Spaniards and French in April, 1512.
23. Machiavelli was subsequently the author of a treatise on the *Art of War* (*Arte della guerra*, 1521).

vengeance, what firm faith, what piety, what tears! What gates would be shut against him? what peoples would deny him obedience? what envy would oppose itself to him? what Italian would refuse to follow him? This barbarian rule stinks in every nostril. May your illustrious House, then, undertake this charge with the spirit and the hope with which all just enterprises are taken up, in order that, beneath its ensign, our native land may be ennobled, and, under its auspices, that saying of Petrarch may come true: "Manhood[24] will take arms against fury, and the combat will be short, because in Italian hearts the ancient valor is not yet dead."

24. an etymological translation of the original *virtù* (from the Latin *vir,* "man"; see the introductory discussion, p. 784). The quotation is from Petrarch's *canzone* "My Italy" ("Italia mia").

# FRANÇOIS RABELAIS
## (1494?–1553)
## Gargantua and Pantagruel, Book I*

### [*Education of a Giant Humanist*]

#### CHAPTER 14

*How Gargantua was taught Latin by a Theologian and Sophist.*

The excellent Grangousier was rapt with admiration as he listened to his son[1] talking. Truly this lad was marvellously gifted! What a vast intelligence, what cogent understanding! Turning to the governesses:

"Philip, King of Macedon," he declared, "recognized the sound judgment of Alexander, his son, when he saw how skilfully the lad managed his horse. This beast Bucephalus was so fierce and unruly that it threw all its riders. It cracked one man's neck, smashed another's legs, brained a third, and crushed the jawbone of a fourth. No one, then, dared mount it. Alexander happened to be in the hippodrome watching them breaking in and training the horses; he noticed at once that the beast's frenzy came from fright at its own shadow. He therefore made short shrift of vaulting upon its back and heading it towards the sun. There, its shadow falling behind it, he easily mastered it. Philip, by this token, realized the divine insight rooted in his son's intelligence and had him most carefully reared by Aristotle, then the most renowned philosopher in Greece.

* Book I was published in 1534; Book II, in 1532; Book III, in 1546; Book IV, in 1552. Book V, of doubt-ful authenticity, appeared in 1562–1564. Translated by Jacques Le Clercq.
   1. Gargantua.

"For my part, the brief conversation I have just had with Gargantua in your presence suffices to convince me that his mind is illumined by the divine spark. How else, pray, could he have proved so acute, so subtle, so profound and withal so serene? Give the boy proper schooling, say I, and he will attain a supreme degree of wisdom! Accordingly, I intend to trust him to some scholar who will instruct him to his capacity. What is more, I shall spare no cost."

The name of Master Tubal Holofernes, a great sophist and Doctor of Theology, was proposed to Grangousier. Subsequently this savant taught Gargantua his A B C so thoroughly that he could say it by heart backwards. This took five years and three months. A succession of standard texts[2] followed; the *Facet* (a treatise of puerile moral precepts), the *Ars Grammatica* of Actius Donatus, the fourth-century grammarian; the *Theodolet* (in which Theodulus, Bishop of Syria in the fifth century, exposed in Latin the falsity of mythology and the truth of Holy Scripture) and the *Alanus in Parabolis* (a series of moral quatrains by Alanus of Lille, a thirteenth-century worthy). It took Gargantua thirteen years, six months and two weeks to master these authorities.

It is only fair to add, however, that Gargantua, in the process, learned to write in Gothic characters. (Printing had not yet been invented and the young student had to write out his own texts.)

He had, therefore, to carry in front of him a tremendous writing apparatus that weighed more than seven hundred thousand pounds. The pencase was as large and as tall as the great columns of the Church of St. Martin of Ainay in Lyons; the inkhorn was suspended to it by great iron chains wide enough to hold five cubic yards of merchandise.

Another book, *De Modis Significandi*—a work of speculative grammar by Thomas Aquinas, or Albert of Saxony or probably Duns Scotus—was Gargantua's next reading, together with comments by Hurtebize or Windjammer, by Fasquin or Roadheaver, by Tropditeux or Toomanysuch, by Gualchault or Galahad, by Jean Le Veau or John Calf, by Billonio or Lickspittle, by Brelinguandus or Timeserver, and by a rabble of others. This took more than eighteen years and eleven months, but Gargantua knew the texts so well that at examinations he could recite them by heart backwards. And he could prove to his mother on his fingers' ends that *de modis significandi non erat scientia*, grammar was no science.

Next he read the *Compost* or *Popular Calendar*, and had spent sixteen years and two months at it, when suddenly, in 1420, his tutor died of the pox.

2. The books mentioned in this chapter were actually part of the educational curriculum which Rabelais is here satirizing.

Holofernes' successor was another wheezy old pedant named Master Jobelin Bridé or Jolter Clotpoll, who read him the *Liber Derivationum* or *Latin Vocabulary* of Hugutio of Pisa, thirteenth-century Bishop of Ferrara . . . the *Grecism* by Everard de Béthune, a philological lexicon illustrating the Latin words derived from the Greek . . . *De Octo Partibus Orationis* or *Of the Eight Parts of Speech* . . . the *Quid Est?* or *What is it?* a school manual in the form of questions and answers . . . the *Supplementum,* a collection of commentaries . . . the *Mammotreptus,* a monkish or monkeyish commentary on the Psalter and the Saints . . . the *Libellus de Moribus in Mensa Servandis* or *Essay on Manners in Serving at Table,* a rhymed treatise on youthful propriety and morals by Sulpizio de Veroli . . . Seneca's *De Quatuor Virtutibus Cardinalibus* or *Of the Four Cardinal Virtues,* a moral work by Martin de Braga, Bishop of Mondonedo in the sixth century . . . the *Specchio della vera Penitenza* or *Mirror of True Penitence* by Jacopo Passavanti, the Florentine monk of the sixteenth century—with its inevitable commentary! . . . a book of sermons, *Dormi Secure* or *Sleep in Peace,* a collection designed to save the preacher the pains of composing his sermons . . . and finally, other stuff of the same ilk, feather, kidney and broth. . . .

Indeed, Gargantua grew as even as any down ever smoothed, as full of matter as any goose liver ever crammed!

CHAPTER 15

*How Gargantua was put under other professors.*

At last his father realized that though Gargantua was studying most industriously and spending all his time at it, he was profiting not at all. Worse, this training had actually made the lad over into a fool, a dunce, a booby and a nincompoop.

One day Grangousier happened to complain of it to Don Philippe des Marais, Viceroy of Papeligosse, a kingdom of Cockaigne.[3] That monarch assured Grangousier that Gargantua would be better off learning nothing than studying books of the sort with pedagogues of that school. Their knowledge, said Don Philippe, was but rubbish, this wisdom flapdoodle; they succeeded merely in bastardizing noble spirits and corrupting the flower of youth.

"Upon my word, I'll prove it!" Don Philippe declared. "Take any lad of to-day with but two years' schooling. If he is not superior to your son in judgment, speech, bearing and personality, then I'm the greatest loggerhead and shallowpate from here to Brenne."[4]

3. Rabelais probably alludes to some existing person; his method is to take real people and introduce them into his fantastic world. The kingdom of Cockaigne is the traditional imaginary land of luck and plenty.

4. an actual locality. What was said of Rabelais' characters in footnote 3 applies also to his geography, his local lore, and the like.

This challenge pleased Grangousier mightily; he at once gave orders that a match of wits take place.

That evening, at supper, Don Philippe brought in a young page of his named Eudemon, which means "the fortunate." The lad hailed from Villegongis near St. Genou in Touraine. He was so neat, so spruce, so handsome and his hair was so beautifully combed that he looked more like an angel than like a man.

Don Philippe turned to Grangousier:

"Do you see this lad? He's not twelve years old. Let us prove, if you will, the difference between the pedantic balderdash of yesterday's wiseacres and the intelligence of our modern boys."

Grangousier was agreeable to such a test and bade the page begin the debate. Whereupon Eudemon, asking leave of the Viceroy, his master, to do so, rose, hat in hand. His face was open and frank, his lips red, his glance confident. Looking at Gargantua with youthful modesty, he proceeded to praise and commend the boy—first for his virtues and good manners, next for his knowledge, thirdly for his nobility, fourthly for his bodily excellences and, in the fifth place, exhorted him most gracefully to reverence his father in all respects, because his father was so careful to have him well brought up. Finally, Eudemon prayed Gargantua to admit him among the least of his bondsmen. He added that the only boon he craved from Heaven, at present, was to serve Gargantua in some agreeable manner. Eudemon accompanied the whole speech with gestures so appropriate, his delivery was so distinct, his voice rang so eloquent, his idiom was so elegant and he couched his phrases in such perfect Latin that he seemed rather a Tiberius Gracchus, a Cicero or an Aemilius Lepidus of old, than a youth of our own day.

Gargantua's only reaction was to burst into tears. He bawled like a sick cow, hung his head and hid his face in his cap, until there was about as much possibility of drawing a word from him as a salvo of farts from the rump of a dead donkey.

This so incensed his father that Grangousier vowed to slay Master Jobelin Clotpoll, but Don Philippe remonstrated with him and, by fair persuasions, soothed his ire. Grangousier thereupon ordered them to pay the pedagogue off and to get him as properly fuddled up as your finest scholar of the Sorbonne. This accomplished, let him go to the devil!

"There is this consolation!" cried Grangousier. "To-day at least, he will not cost his host much if by chance he dies in his cups like an Englishman."

When Master Jobelin Clotpoll had gone away, Grangousier asked Don Philippe's advice about a tutor for Gargantua. They finally decided to appoint Ponocrates, Eudemon's teacher, to the position; auspiciously enough, in Greek the name means "vigorous." And soon, the three were to go to Paris in order to find out what studies young men were at this period pursuing in France.

*How Gargantua went to Paris upon an enormous mare which destroyed the oxflies of the Beauce.*

In the same season, Fayolles, fourth king of Numidia, sent Grangousier a mare from Africa. It was the hugest and most enormous mare ever seen, the strangest monster in the world; for Africa, as the saying goes, may always be relied upon to produce something wonderfully new. The beast was as big as six elephants; like Julius Caesar's charger, her feet were cloven into human toes; her ears hung down like those of the goats of Languedoc; and a little horn grew out of one buttock. Save for a few dapple-gray spots as overlay, her coat was the color of burnt sorrel, which shows that she partook of the four elements, earth, water, air and fire. Above all, she had a horrible tail. It was more or less as tall as the tower of St. Mars near Langeais; and just as square, with tufts of hair as tightly spun and woven as the beards on ears of corn.

Do you marvel at this? You have greater cause to marvel at the tails of the rams of Scythia, which weighed more than thirty pounds each, or—if Jean Thenaud speaks truthfully in his *Voyage from Angoulême to Cairo*—at those of the Syrian sheep which are so long and heavy that, to hold them up, the natives have to hitch a small cart to the beast's rump. Ha! my lusty country wenchthumpers, you've no such tails as these!

The mare Fayolles sent Grangousier was brought overseas in three Genoese carracks and a brigantine; she landed at Les Sables d'Olonne in Talmondais.

When Grangousier laid eyes upon her:

"Ah!" he exclaimed. "Here is just what my son needs to bear him to Paris! So now, in God's name, all will go well: Gargantua shall be a great scholar one of these days! Were it not for dumb brutes we should all be scholars!"

Next day, having drunk liberally, as you may imagine, Gargantua set out on his journey, accompanied by his tutor Ponocrates, the young page Eudemon and his train. And, because the weather was serene and temperate, Grangousier had a pair of dun-colored boots made for him. According to Babin and the Chinon cobblers, these are technically known as buskins.

So they travelled along the highway very merrily, living on the fat of the land and making the best of cheer, until a little beyond Orléans they came to a huge forest, about thirty-five leagues long and seventeen wide. Alas! the woods were aswarm with oxflies and hornets of all varieties, so the wretched mares, asses and horses suffered a veritable massacre. But, by means of a trick they never suspected, Gargantua's mare handsomely avenged all the outrages visited upon her kind. For suddenly, when in the heart of the forest the wasps attacked her, she swished her tail and, sweeping all about her, not only felled the stingers but uprooted all the trees. Up and down, right and left, lengthwise and athwart, here and there, over and under, before her and aback, this way and that, she mowed down the woods like so much grass. And this region, which she thus turned into fallow land, has never known tree or wasp since.

Gargantua, delighted by the spectacle, forebore to boast, merely commenting to his followers:

"*Je trouve beau ce!* I find this pleasant!"

Whence this pleasant land has been known as Beauce ever since.

However, when it came to breakfasting, they had to content themselves with their yawns; in memory of which the gentlemen of the Beauce, proverbially poor, still subsist on a diet of yawns and gaping, and find it very nourishing. Indeed, they spit all the better for it.

At last they reached Paris, where Gargantua rested two or three days, making merry with his followers and inquiring about what scholars were then in the city and what wines people drank.

· · ·

### CHAPTER 21

*Gargantua's education and social life under the direction of his preceptors at the Sorbonne.*

. . . Gargantua resolved with all his heart to study under the direction of Ponocrates. But the latter, wishing to learn how the lad's former teachers had wasted so much time making a crack-brained, addlepated dunce of him, decided he should do exactly as he had in the past.

Gargantua therefore arranged his schedule so as to awake usually between eight and nine o'clock, rain or shine, dark or daylight, simply because his preceptors had decided this on the strength of the Psalmist's saw: "*Vanum est vobis ante lucem surgere,* it is vain for you to rise up betimes."[5]

Then he wriggled and writhed, wallowing in his bed and tossing about like a parched pea, the better to stimulate his vital spirits. Next, he would dress, according to the season, but he was always happy to don a long, hanging gown of heavy wool lined with fox. Next, he combed out his hair with the comb of Jacques Almain, the Sorbonne theologian, known in English as John Handy—a comb

---

5. "It is vain for you to rise up early, to sit up late, to eat the bread of sorrows: for so he giveth his beloved sleep." (Psalm 127:2.)

consisting of four fingers and a thumb—for his mentors maintained that to brush one's hair, wash one's face and make oneself clean were, in this world, a pure waste of time.

Next Gargantua dunged, piddled, vomited, belched, broke wind, yawned, spat, coughed, hiccoughed, sneezed and snotted himself as majestically and bountifully as an archdeacon. Next he proceeded to breakfast in order to fortify himself against the morning mist and cold. His menu consisted of splendid fried tripe, choice meats grilled on charcoal, rich hams, succulent roast venison and numerous soups and brews, with toast, cheese, parsley and chopped meat floating on the surface.

Ponocrates objected that he should not eat so soon after rising without having taken any exercise. To which he replied:

"Exercise? Good God, didn't I tumble and jounce in bed six or seven times before I got up? Surely, that is exercise enough? Pope Alexander VI did this on the advice of his Jew physician, Bonnet de Lates, and lived till the day of his death in spite of his enemies. My first masters taught me this habit, for breakfast, they said, gave man a good mind. So they started the day by drinking. It suits me perfectly and I manage to dine the better for it. Master Tubal Holofernes, who was graduated Licentiate in Paris at the head of his class, used to tell me that hasten was not enough, one must set out betimes. By the same token, the total health of mankind does not consist in drinking down and lapping up, *glub, glub, glub,* like so many ducks, but rather in falling to, early in the morning. *Unde versus;* so runs the rune:

> Lever matin n'est point bonheur
> Boire matin est le meilleur.
>
> To rise betimes is not enough,
> To drink at morning, that's the stuff!"

After an abundant breakfast, Gargantua repaired to church, with, in his train, a varlet bearing a basket. The latter contained a huge breviary swaddled in velvet and weighing about twelve hundred and six pounds including the filth of thumbmarks, dogeared corners, golden clasps and nonpareil parchment. Twenty-six, if not thirty, masses ensued for the benefit of Gargantua and his chaplain. Under his tall hood, this chaplain looked for all the world like a peewit . . . and had very thoroughly antidoted his breath against possible poisons with much syrup of the vine! Chaplain and pupil babbled the mumbo jumbo of the litany, thumbing their rosaries so carefully that not one single bead fell to the ground.

As he left the church, they brought him an oxcart laden with a huge heap of paternosters, chaplets and relics from St. Claude in the Jura, each bigger than a hatblock. Gargantua and his chaplain then strolled in the cloisters, galleries or garden, saying more aves than sixteen hermits.

After, Gargantua would study for a short half-hour, his eyes glued to his book but his mind, to quote Terence's *Eunuch*, wool-gathering in the kitchen.[6] Then he proceeded to make water, filling a large urinal to capacity, after which he sat down at table, and, being naturally phlegmatic, began his meal with a few dozen hams, smoked tongues of beef, caviar, sausages and other like forerunners of wine.

Then four servants in turn shovelled mustard into his mouth by the spadeful, thus preparing him to drain a horrific draught of white wine to relieve his kidneys. Then the meal proper began with viands to his liking, according to the season; Gargantua ceasing to eat only when his belly had reached bursting point.

When it came to drinking, he acknowledged neither end nor rule; for, he said, there were no limits and boundaries to swilling until the tosspot felt the cork soles of his shoes swell up a half-foot from the ground.

· · ·

### CHAPTER 23

*How Ponocrates gave Gargantua such instruction that not an hour of the day was wasted.*

When Ponocrates saw Gargantua's vicious mode of life, he determined to bring him up otherwise. But for the first few days he bore with him, for he realized that nature cannot endure sudden and violent changes.

To begin his work the better, Ponocrates requested a learned physician of the times, Master Theodore—the name means "God-given"—to examine Gargantua thoroughly with a view to steering him on the right course. The scholar purged Gargantua canonically with Anticyrian hellebore, an herb indicated for cerebral disorders and insanity, thus cleansing his brain of its unnatural, perverse condition. Ponocrates, by the same aperient means, made the lad forget all he had learned under his former teachers, just as Timotheus[7] of old treated pupils who had already studied under other musicians. Timotheus, incidentally, used to charge this class of students double!

For Gargantua's further edification, Ponocrates made him mingle among learned men whose company fired him with a desire to emulate them, to study more profitably and to make his mark. Next,

6. See Terence's play *The Eunuch*, l. 816.

7. Timotheus of Miletus, famous musician of the time of Alexander the Great.

Ponocrates so arranged the lad's schedule that not a moment of the day was wasted; all his time was spent in the pursuit of learning and honest knowledge.

By this new dispensation, Gargantua awoke at about four in the morning. While the servants massaged him, he would listen to some page of Holy Scripture, read aloud in clear tones and pronounced with fitting respect for the text. A young page, a native of Basché, near Chinon, was appointed reader, as his name, Anagnostes,[8] shows. According to the purpose and argument of this lesson, Gargantua frequently turned to worship, adore, pray and reverence Almighty God, Whose majesty and wondrous wisdom were made manifest in the reading.

Next, he would repair to secret places to make excretion of his natural digestions; here his tutor repeated what had been read, expounding its more obscure and difficult features. Returning to the house, they would study the heavens. Was it the same sky they had observed the night before? Into what signs was the sun entering that day? and the moon?

After this astronomical survey, Gargantua was dressed, combed, curled, trimmed and perfumed, and, while this was being done, he heard the lessons of the day before. Then, having recited them by heart, he would argue certain practical, human and utilitarian cases based upon the principles enunciated. This part of the program sometimes took two or three hours, though usually he had exhausted it by the time he was fully clad.

Then, for three good hours, he was read or lectured to, after which they went to the Tennis Court at the Grande Bracque in the Place de l'Estrapade or to the playing fields.

On the way, they discussed various aspects of the subject previously treated. Then they would play tennis, handball and three-cornered catch, exercising their bodies as vigorously as they had exercised their minds before.

All their play was free for they left off when they pleased, which was usually when they had sweated a good bit or were otherwise tired. They were thoroughly wiped and rubbed down, after which they changed their shirts and walked quietly home to see if dinner were ready. As they waited, they would go over certain points they had retained of the lectures.

Meanwhile My Lord Appetite put in an appearance and they sat down most opportunely to table.

At the beginning of the meal, they listened to the reading of some agreeable chronicle of chivalry in ancient times, until Gargantua gave the signal for wine to be served. Then, if they wished, the reading went on or they could talk merrily together. Often they dis-

8. in Greek meaning "reader."

cussed the virtues, property, efficacy and nature of what was served at table: bread, wine, water, salt, meat, fish, fruit, herbs, roots and their preparation. Thus Gargantua soon knew all the relevant passages of Pliny's *Natural History* . . . in the grammarian Athenæus' *Deipnosophistes* or *The Banquet of the Sages*, which treats of flowers, fruits and their various uses . . . in Dioscorides' famous medical treatise, the bible of apothecaries . . . in the *Vocabularium* by Julius Pollux, a grammarian and sophist of Marcus Aurelius' day, who wrote of hunting and fishing . . . in Galen's numerous dissertations upon alimentation . . . in the works of Porphyrius, the third-century Greek author of a *Treatise upon Abstinence from Meat* . . . in Oppian's two poems, *Cynegetica* which deals with venery and *Halieutica* with angling . . . in *Of Healthy Diet* by Polybius of Cos, disciple and son-in-law of Hippocrates . . . in Heliodorus of Emesa, Syrian Bishop of Tricca and a celebrated novelist of the fourth century . . . in Aristotle's essays on natural history . . . in the Greek works upon animals by Claudius Ælianus, a Roman contemporary of Heliogabalus . . . and in various other tomes. . . .[9] Often for surer authority as they argued, they would have the book in question brought to the table. Gargantua so thoroughly and cogently learned and assimilated all he heard that no physician of his times knew one-half so much as he.

They discussed the lessons they had learned that morning and topped their meal off with quiddany, a sort of quince marmalade and an excellent digestive. After which Gargantua picked his teeth with a fragment of mastic,[10] washed his hands and daubed his eyes with cool clear water, and, instead of saying grace, sang the glory of God in noble hymns, composed in praise of divine bounty and munificence.

Presently cards were brought them and they played, not for the sake of the pastime itself but to learn a thousand new tricks and inventions all based on arithmetic.

Thus Gargantua developed a keen enthusiasm for mathematics, spending his leisure after dinner and supper every evening as pleasantly as once he had, dicing and gaming. As a result, he knew so much about its theory and practice that Cuthbert Tunstal, Bishop of Durham and secretary to King Henry VIII, a voluminous writer on the subject,[11] confessed that, beside Gargantua, he knew no more about arithmetic than he did about Old High Gothic. Nor was it arithmetic alone our hero learned, but also such sister sciences as geometry, astronomy and music.

9. Some of the most famous scientific treatises of antiquity are listed in Gargantua's new curriculum, which, exacting as it is, reflects a less "medieval" type of learning than was embodied in his earlier course of study. See also the enumeration of authors on p. 1318.
10. wood from the mastic tree.
11. Tunstal was the author of the treatise *The Art of Computation* (*De arte supputandi*, 1522)

Now the digestion of foods is a most important matter. There is the first stage which occurs in the stomach, where the viands are changed into chyle; the second, in the liver, where the chyle is transformed into blood; the third, in the habit of the body, where the blood is finally converted into the substance of each part. So, whilst Gargantua awaited the first stage of digestion, they made a thousand delightful instruments, drew geometrical figures and even applied the principles of astronomy.

After, they amused themselves singing a five-part score or improvising on a theme chosen at random. As for musical instruments, Gargantua learned to play the lute, the spinet, the harp, the nine-holed transverse or German flute, the viol and the sackbut or trombone.

Having spent an hour thus and completed his digestion, he discharged his natural excrements and then settled down again to work three hours or more at his principal study. Either he revised the morning reading, or proceeded in the text at hand or practised penmanship in the most carefully formed characters of modern Roman and ancient Gothic script.

Next, they went out with a young gentleman of Touraine, the esquire Gymnastes, who instructed Gargantua in the art of horsemanship. Having changed his clothes, he proceeded to mount a fiery Italian charger, a Flemish dray horse, a Spanish jennet, an Arab thoroughbred and a hackney. These he would put vigorously through their paces, letting them "career" or gallop a short distance at full speed, making them leap high in the air, jump ditches, clear stiles, and turn short in a ring both to the right and to the left. Next he wielded but did not break his lance, for it is arrant stupidity to boast: "I have broken ten lances in a tilt or fight." A wretched carpenter can do the same. On the contrary, the whole glory of such combat lies in besting ten enemies with one and the same lance. So with strong, stiff, steel-tipped lance, Gargantua would force the outer door of some house, pierce an adversary's armor, beat down a tree, pick up a ring, carry off a cuirassier saddle, a hauberk[12] or a gauntlet. And he performed these feats armed cap-a-pie.[13]

In the technique of parading his horse with prances and flourishes to a fanfare of trumpets—the ceremonial of knights as they enter the lists—he had no equal. As for the divers terms of the equine vocabulary from *giddy-up* and *cluck* to *whoa* and *grrr*, no horseman could hold a candle to him. Indeed Cesare Fieschi, the celebrated jockey of Ferrara, was a mere monkey in comparison.

He learned, too, to leap hastily and with singular dexterity from one horse to another without setting foot to the ground (the nags were circus horses or, to be technical, "desultories"). Further, lance

---

12. coat of mail.                    13. from head to foot.

in hand, he could leap on horseback from either side without stirrups and rule the beast at will without a bridle, for such accom-
plishments are highly useful in military engagements.

Another day he would practise wielding the battle-axe, which he
managed so skilfully, in the nimblest thrusts, the most powerful
lunges and the vast encircling sweeps of the art, that he passed
knight-at-arms in the field and at all tests. Sometimes unarmed,
sometimes carrying a buckler or a rolled cape of mail over his arm
or a small shield over his wrist, Gargantua brandished the pike,
plied the double-edged, two-handed sword, the bastard claymore
used by archers, the Spanish rapier, the dagger and the poniard.

He hunted, too: stag, roebuck, bear, fallow deer, wild boar, hare,
partridge, pheasant and otter . . . he played at ball, ever ready with
well-aimed foot or powerful fist to send the great sphere whizzing
through the air . . . he learned to wrestle and to run. . . . As for
jumping, he did not go in for the various forms of running jumps,
such as the three-steps-and-a-leap, the hop-step-and-jump or the
German high-jump. As Gymnastes pointed out, these were quite
useless in warfare. Instead, he practised the standing jumps. Starting from scratch, he could in one leap top a hedge, clear a ditch,
mount six paces upon a wall and thus reach a window-ledge one
lance's height from the ground.

Gargantua could swim in the deepest water, breaststroke, back
and sidestroke, using his whole body or his feet alone. He could
cross the breadth of the Seine or the Loire at Montsoreau, dragging
his cloak along in his teeth and holding a book high and dry over
the waters—thus renewing the exploit with which Plutarch credits
Julius Cæsar during the Alexandrian War. Then, using one hand
only, he could, with a single great pull, climb into a boat, whence a
moment later he would dive headlong into the water again, sound
its utmost depths, touch bottom, explore the hollows of rocks and
plunge into any pits and abysses he fancied. He would turn the
boat about, managing it perfectly, bringing it swiftly or slowly up-
stream or down and arresting its course at a milldam. He could
guide it with one hand while he plied hard about him with a great
oar; he could run up a sail, hoist himself up a mast by the shrouds,
dance along the yards, operate the compass, tackle the bowlines to
sail close to the wind and steer the helm.

His water sports done, he would dash full speed up a mountain,
then down quite as fast. He climbed trees like a cat, hopping from
one to the next like a squirrel and pulling down great boughs—like
the celebrated Milo of Crotona who, Pausanias[14] tells us, met his
death devoured by wolves, his hands caught in the cleft of an oak
he had sought to split. With two well-steeled daggers and a pair of

---

14. Greek geographer and traveler of the second century A.D.

well-tried mason's punches, he could scurry up the side of a house like a rat, then leap down again, from roof to ground, so expertly that he landed without hurt. Gargantua also cast the dart, threw the iron bar, put the stone, tossed the boar-spear, hurled the javelin, shied the halberd. He drew the bow to breaking point; he could shoulder a harquebuss—a great siege piece weighing fifty pounds—and fire it off like a crossbow. He could set a huge cannon on its carriage, hit buttmarks and other targets for horizontal shooting, or, point-blank, bring down papgays (stuffed figures of parrots on poles), clay pigeons and other vertical marks, facing them on a level or upwards, or downwards or sidewise. Like the ancient Parthians, he could even hit them as he retreated.

They would tie a cable to a high tower and let it dangle to the ground. Gargantua hoisted himself up with both hands, then slipped down again as evenly, surely and plumb as a man running along a flat meadow. Or they would set a great pole across two trees for Gargantua to hang from by his hands. He moved along the pole from tree to tree so swiftly, without setting foot on *terra firma*, that a man, running on the ground below, could not have caught him. To expand his chest and exercise his lungs, he would roar like all the devils in hell. Once indeed, I heard him call Eudemon across all Paris, from the Porte St. Victor, the gate by the University, all the way to Montmartre, a village on a hill two miles beyond the walls of the city. Stentor,[15] who cried louder than forty men, displayed no such vocal power, even at the siege of Troy.

To develop his sinews, they made him two great pigs of lead, each weighing eight hundred and five tons. These pigs (called salmons in France because the metal is shaped like this fish) Gargantua named *alteres*, an ancient Greek term for the weights used to give jumpers their initial spring—our modern dumb-bells. Taking one in each hand, Gargantua then performed an inimitable feat. He would raise them high above his head and, never turning a hair, stock-still as a statue, hold them aloft for three-quarters of an hour. He played at Barriers or Tug-of-War with the stoutest champions. When his turn came he took root so firmly as to defy the sturdiest to budge him. Nor was it thus alone he emulated Milo of Crotona. Like the ancient athlete, he could hold a pomegranate so fast in his hand that none could wrest it from him, yet so adroitly that he did not crush it.

Having spent his time in such manly sports, he had himself washed, rubbed down and given a change of clothes. Then he returned home at a leisurely pace, passing through some meadow or grassy space to examine the trees and plants. These he would compare with what the authorities wrote of them in their books: among

15. the loud-voiced herald in the *Iliad*, Book V.

the Ancients, Theophrastus, the successor of Aristotle and teacher of Menander . . . or Palladius, whose poem *De re rustica* was translated by Pietro Marini . . . or Dioscorides Pedanius, the Greek physician of the first century . . . or Pliny or Nicander or Aemilius Macer, the Roman, or Galen himself. . . . Gargantua and his companions picked specimens by the handful and took them home to a young page named Rhizotome or Rootcutter, who watched over them and the various small mattocks, pickaxes, hooks, hoes, pruning-knives, shears and other botanical instruments.

At home, whilst the servants prepared dinner, our young men repeated certain passages of what had been read. Then they sat down to table. Here I would have you note that their dinner was simple and frugal; they ate no more than necessary to quiet the baying of the belly. Supper, on the contrary, was a large and copious meal; they ate what they needed for their sustenance and nourishment. Such indeed is the true system prescribed by the art of sound, self-respecting physicians though a rabble of dunderhead quacks, wrangling eternally in the claptrap routine of the Arab nostrum shop of Avicenna,[16] recommend the exact opposite. During supper, they continued the lesson given at dinner as long as they saw fit; the rest of the meal was spent in earnest and profitable discussion.

Having said grace, they applied their voices to sing tunefully or they played upon harmonious instruments. Or they amused themselves with such minor pastimes as cards, dice cups and dice afforded. Sometimes they tarried here enjoying themselves and making merry until bedtime; they would visit learned men or such as had travelled in foreign lands. Well into the night, before retiring, they would go to the most exposed spot in the house, whence they examined the face of the sky, noting the comets, if any were visible, and the various figures, positions, aspects, oppositions and conjunctions of the heavenly bodies.

According to the Pythagorean system, Gargantua would, with his tutor, recapitulate briefly all that he had read, seen, learned, done and assimilated in the course of the day.

Then they prayed to God the Creator, doing Him worship and confirming their faith in Him, glorifying Him for His immense goodness, vouchsafing thanks for all the mighty past and imploring His divine clemency for all the future.

And so they retired to rest.

### CHAPTER 24

*How Gargantua spent his time in rainy weather.*

In intemperate or rainy weather, things went on much the same as usual before dinner except that Gargantua had a fine bright fire

16. Arab physician and philosopher (980–1037).

lighted to correct the inclemency of the air. But after dinner, instead of gymnastics, they stayed indoors and, by way of apotherapy[17] or exercise amused themselves by bundling hay, splitting logs, sawing wood and threshing sheaves in the barn. Then they studied the arts of painting and sculpture. Or they revived the ancient Roman game of *Tali,* dicing as the Italian humanist Nicolaus Leonicus Thomaeus[18] wrote of it in his dialogue *Sannutus, Of the Game of Dice,* and as our good friend Janus Lascaris,[19] librarian to our sovereign king, plays at the game. In their sport, they reviewed such passages of ancient authors as mention or quote some metaphor drawn from this play.

In much the same way, they might go to watch workmen forging metals or casting pieces of ordnance. Or they might visit the lapidaries, goldsmiths and cutters of precious stones in their ateliers, the alchemists in their laboratories, the coiners at the mint, the tapestry-workers, velvet-workers and weavers at their looms, the watchmakers, looking-glass framers, printers, lutemakers, dyers and other such artisans in their workships. Wherever they went, they would distribute gratuities, invariably investigating and learning the various inventions and industry of the trade.

Or they might attend public lectures, official convocations, oratorical performances, speeches, pleadings by eloquent attorneys and sermons by evangelical preachers—that is, such priests as wished to restore Christianity to the primitive tradition of the Gospel. Gargantua also frequented fencing halls and tested his skill at all weapons against the masters, proving to them by experience that he knew as much as they and, indeed, even more.

Instead of herborizing,[20] they would inspect the shops of druggists, herbalists and apothecaries, studiously examining the sundry fruits, roots, leaves, gums, seeds and exotic unguents and learning how they could be diluted or adulterated. He viewed jugglers, mountebanks and medicasters—who sold Venice treacle, a cure for all ills—carefully observing their tricks and gestures, their agile capers and smooth oratory. His favorites were those from Chauny in Picardy who are born jabberers and the readiest expounders of mealy-mouthed flimflam concerning their ability to weave ropes of sand, extract sunbeams from cucumbers and milk a he-goat into a sieve.

Returning home to supper, they would eat more sparingly than on fine days. Their meats would, by the same token, be more desiccative and extenuating so as to counteract the humidity communicated to their bodies by the necessary contiguity of the atmosphere and to nullify what harm might arise from lack of their customary exercise.

Such was Gargantua's program and so he continued from day to day, benefiting as you would expect a young man of his age and intelligence to benefit under such a system faithfully applied. To be sure, the whole thing may have seemed incredibly difficult to him at the outset, but it soon proved so light, so easy and so pleasant as to appear more like a king's pastime than the study of a schoolboy.

However, Ponocrates was careful to supply relaxation from this violent bodily and mental tension. Once a month, on some very bright serene day, they would clear out of town early in the morning, bound for the near-by villages of Gentilly, Boulogne, Montrouge, Pont-de-Charenton, Vanves or St. Cloud. There they spent the whole day enjoying themselves to their heart's content, sporting and merrymaking, drinking toast for proffered toast, playing, singing, dancing, tumbling about or loafing in some fair meadow, turning sparrows out of their nests, bagging quail and fishing for frogs and crayfish.

But though this holiday was free of books and reading, it was not spent unprofitably. Lying in the green meadow, they usually recited certain delightful lines from Virgil's *Georgics*, from Hesiod's *Works and Days* or from Politian's *Husbandry*.[21] Or they broached some savory epigram in Latin, then turned it into a French roundelay or ballade.

In their feasting, they would sometimes separate the twin elements, isolating the wine and the water in their drink by pouring the latter into a cup of ivy-wood, as Cato teaches in his *De re rustica*, and Pliny elsewhere.[22] Then they would wash the wine in a basin full of water and draw it out with a funnel, as pure as ever. And they pumped the water with a syphon from one glass to another, manufacturing several sorts of automatic or self-operating devices.

[*The Abbey of Thélème*]

CHAPTER 52

*How Gargantua had the Abbey of Thélème built for the monk.*

There remained only the monk[23] to provide for. Gargantua offered him the Abbey of Seuilly: he refused. What about the Bene-

21. a poem, *Rusticus*, in the manner of Virgil's *Georgics*, by the Italian fifteenth-century poet Politian.

22. Both Cato in his book *On Farming* (*De re rustica*), CIX, and Pliny in his *Natural History* (*Historia naturalis*), Book XVI, Chapter 63, suggest an ivy-wood cup as a means to detect water in wine.

23. Friar John of the Funnels, the muscular and highly unconventional monk who has had a major part in helping the party of Gargantua's father win the mock-heroic war against the arrogant Picrochole.

dictine abbeys of Bourgueil or St. Florent, among the richest in France: he might have either or both?[24] Again, the offer met with a flat refusal: Friar John of the Funnels answered peremptorily that he did not seek the charge or government of monks.

"For," he explained, "how shall I govern others when I cannot possibly govern myself?" There was a pause. "But—" he hesitated. "But if you believe I have given and can give you good service, let me found an abbey after my own heart."

The notion delighted Gargantua: he forthwith offered his estate of Thélème, by the Loire, two leagues away from Port Huault. Thélème in Greek means free will, an auspicious name for Friar John's abbey. Here indeed he could institute a religious order contrary to all others.

"First," said Gargantua, "you must not build a wall around it, for all other abbeys are solidly enclosed."

"Quite so," agreed the monk, "for where there are *mures*, walls, before, and *mures*, walls, behind, we have *murmures*, murmurs of envy and plotting."

Now in certain monasteries it is a rule that if any women enter (I mean honest and chaste ones) the ground they tread upon must be swept over. Therefore it was decreed that if a monk or nun should by any chance enter Thélème, every place that religious passed through should be thoroughly disinfected.

Similarly because all monasteries and convents on earth are compassed, limited and regulated by hours, at Thélème no clock or dial of any sort should be tolerated. On the contrary, their time here would be governed by what occasions and opportunities might arise. As Gargantua sagaciously commented:

"I can conceive of no greater waste of time than to count the hours. What good comes of it? To order your life by the toll of a bell instead of by reason or common sense is the veriest piece of asininity imaginable."

By the same token, they established the qualifications for entrance into their order. Was it not true that at present women took the veil only if they were wall-eyed, lame, hunchbacked, ill-favored, misshapen, half-witted, unreasonable or somewhat damaged? That only such men entered monasteries as were cankered, ill-bred idiots or plain nuisances?

("Incidentally," said Friar John, "if the woman is neither fair nor good, of what use is the cloth?"

"Let the clot hump her," Gargantua replied.

"I said 'cloth' not 'clot.'"

"Well, what's the answer?"

"To cover her face or her arse with!")

24. a satiric allusion to the custom of accumulating church livings.

Accordingly, they decided to admit into the new order only such women as were beautiful, shapely, pleasing of form and nature, and such men as were handsome, athletic and personable.

Again, because men entered the convents of this world only by guile and stealth, it was decreed that no women would be in Thélème unless men were there also, and vice-versa.

Moreover, since both men in monasteries and women in convents were forced after their year of noviciate to stay there perpetually, Gargantua and Friar John decided that the Thélèmites, men or women, might come and go whenever they saw fit.

Further, since the religious usually made the triple vow of chastity, poverty and obedience, at Thélème all had full leave to marry honestly, to enjoy wealth and to live in perfect freedom.

As for the age of initiation, they stipulated that women were admissible between the ages of ten and fifteen, men between twelve and eighteen.

CHAPTER 53

*How the Abbey of Thélème was built and endowed.*

To build and furnish the abbey, Gargantua paid in cash twenty-seven hundred thousand eight hundred and thirty-one crowns in current coin of the realm, fresh from the mint, with a sheep on the obverse and the king's head on the reverse. He undertook to pay yearly, until the project was completed, sixteen hundred and sixty-nine thousand crowns, with the sum on the obverse, and as many again with the seven stars, the whole to be levied upon custom receipts.

For the foundation and maintenance of Thélème, he settled in perpetuity twenty-three hundred and sixty-nine thousand, five hundred and fourteen nobles (a coin stamped by the English kings with the rose of York), free of all tax, burden or fealty, payable yearly at the abbey gate. These privileges were all corroborated by letters patent.

The building was hexagonal; in each corner rose a great, circular tower, each identical, sixty yards in diameter. To the north, the river Loire flowed past the first tower which was named *Arctice* or Northern. East of it rose *Calaer* which means "situated in the balmy air"; then, successively, *Anatole* or Eastern; *Mesembrine* or Southern; *Hesperia* or Occidental; and the last, *Cryere* or Glacial. The distance between each tower was three hundred and twelve yards. The building was throughout six storeys high, counting the underground cellar for one. The ground floor was vaulted like a basket handle; the others, covered with Flanders mistletoe, jutting out like brackets and pendants. The roof, of finest slate, was lined with lead and bore little figures of mannikins and animals well assorted and gilt. The gutters jutted out from the walls between the casement arches; they were painted diagonally gold and blue down to the ground, where they ended in pipes which carried the water into the river below.

This building was a hundred times more magnificent than Bonnivet, Chambord or Chantilly.[25] There were nine thousand three hundred and thirty-two suites, each with a salon, a study, a dressing room, an oratory and an exit into a great hall. In the wing between each tower was a winding stairway. The steps, grouped in units of twelve between each landing, were of porphyry, of Numidian stone, of serpentine marble; they were twenty-two feet long and three fingers thick. At each landing, two splendid round antique archways admitted the light and led to an open loggia of the same dimensions. The stairway, rising to the roof, ended in a pavilion; on either side lay a great hall which in turn led to the apartments.

The wing between the towers called *Arctice* and *Cryere* contained rich libraries of Greek, Latin, Hebrew, French, Italian and Spanish volumes, grouped in their respective sections. In the centre rose a marvellous winding ramp conceived in such ample proportions that six soldiers with their lances at rest could ride up it abreast to the top of the palace. Its entry, outside the house, was an archway six fathoms wide.

Between *Anatole* and *Mesembrine* were spacious galleries with murals representing heroic feats of olden times, scenes from history and pictures of the earth. Here again were a stairway and gate as described upon the river side. On this gate, couched in great antique letters, ran the following legend.

### CHAPTER 54

*Inscription engraved on the main gate at Thélème.*

Here enter not, smug hypocrites or holy loons,
Bigots, sham-Abrahams, impostors of the cloth,
Mealy-mouthed humbugs, holier-than-thou baboons,
Lip-service lubbers, smell-feast picaroons.[26]
Else had we to admit the Goth and Ostrogoth
Precursors of the ape and others of that broth.
Hence, sneaks and mischief-makers, colporteurs of lies,
Be off to other parts to sell your merchandise.

Being foul you would befoul
Man, woman, beast or fowl.

25. châteaux built in the early and middle years of the sixteenth century. By referring to actual buildings, building materials, and architectural elements, Rabelais as usual mixes realism with his fantasy.

26. various ways of saying "hypocritical bigots."

The vileness of your ways
Would sully my sweet lays,
Owls—And your own black cowl,
Being foul, you would befoul.

Here enter not, defenders of dishonest pleas,
Clerks, barristers, attorneys who make freemen slaves,
Canon Law pettifoggers, censors, Pharisees,
Judges, assessors, arbitrators, referees
Who blithely doom good people to untimely graves,
The gibbet is your destination, legal knaves!
Be off: indict the rope if you should find it short,
Here there is no abuse; we do not need your court.

Tangle, wrangle, brangle
We loathe, from any angle.
Our aim is joy and sport,
Time's swift, youth's fleet, life's short.
You, go and disentangle
Tangle, wrangle, brangle!

Here enter not, curmudgeon, loan shark, muckworm, hunks,
Bloodsucking usurer, extortioner, pennystint, . . .
Hence, lawsuit-chasing crimps, greedy as starving punks
Tracking a patron; lickgolds, hiding cash in trunks,
Harpyclaws, crunchfists, jaundiced zealots of the mint,
Your crackling, sallow palms are itching. Skin a flint!
Heap up your hoard, O scrub-faced curs, heap up afresh,
And as you grudge and gripe and screw, God rot your flesh!

Those grim and grisly faces
Bear all the ravaged traces
Of hidebound avarice;
We cannot stomach this.
Banish from all blithe places
Those grim and grisly faces.

Here enter not, you churls, sour boors, invidious fools,
Old, jealous brabblers, scolds, neither by night nor day,
Nor grumblers, soreheads, sulkers, badgers bred in schools
Of hate; nor ghosts of malaperts; nor firebrands' ghouls
From Rhineland, Greece or Rome, fiercer than wolves at bay;
Nor you, riddled with pox, your face a Milky Way
Of scars not stars; nor you, clapstricken to the bone:
Enjoy your shameless crusts and blemishes alone.

Honor, praise and pleasure
Are here in goodly measure:

Health reigns supreme because
We follow Nature's laws.
Ours is a triple treasure:
Honor, praise and pleasure.

But enter here thrice welcome, men of goodly parts,
Gallants and noble gentlemen, thrice welcome be!
Here you will find an abbey after your own hearts,
Where living is esteemed the highest of the arts.
Come in your tens and hundreds, come in thousands, we
Shall clasp you to our bosoms in fond amity:
Come wise, come proud, come gay, come courteous, come mellow,
Come true sophisticate, come worldling, come, good fellow!

Comrades, companions, friends,
Assemble from the ends
Of earth in this fair place
Where all is mirth and grace.
Felicity here blends
Comrades, companions, friends.

Here enter, all ye loyal scholars who expound
Novel interpretations of the Holy Writ.
Here is a fort and refuge; from this favored ground
You may confound the error that is elsewhere found,
You may found a profound new faith instead of it,
Sweeping away false teachings, bit by fallacious bit.
Come unto us and make your cogent meanings heard:
Destroy the foes of God and of his Holy Word.

The Holy Word of God
Shall never be downtrod
Here in this holy place,
If all deem reason grace,
And use for staff and rod
The Holy Word of God.

Here enter, ladies fair of eminent degree,
Come soon with starry eyes, lips smiling, comely face,
Flowers of loveliness, angels of harmony,
Resplendent, proud yet of the rarest modesty,
Sprightly of flesh, lithe-waisted and compact of grace,
Here is your home. A gallant lord designed this place
For you, that beauty, charm and virtue might find room
Deliciously to breathe, exquisitely to bloom.

Who makes a priceless gift
Wins pardon without shrift.

> Donor, recipient
> Alike find rich content.
> To him your voices lift
> Who makes a priceless gift.

CHAPTER 55

*How the monks and nuns lived at Thélème.*

In the middle of the lower court stood a magnificent alabaster fountain, surmounted by the Three Graces holding cornucopias and spouting water through their breasts, mouths, ears, eyes and other orifices. The buildings above this court stood upon great pillars of chalcedony and porphyry, forming classical arches about lengthy wide galleries adorned with paintings and trophies of various animals: the horns of bucks, unicorns and hippopotami, elephants' tusks and sundry other curiosities.

The ladies' quarters ran from *Arctice* all the way to the *Mesembrine* Gate; the rest of the abbey was reserved for men. In front of this part, between the outer two towers, lay the recreational facilities: the tilting yard, the riding school, the theatre and the natatorium which included wonderful swimming pools on three different levels, with every sort of equipment and myrtle water aplenty.

Near the river was the fine pleasure garden, with, in the middle, a maze. Tennis courts and football fields spread out between the next two towers. Close to *Cryere*, an orchard offered a mass of fruit trees laid out in quincunxes, with, at its end, a sizy park abounding in venison.

The space between the third pair of towers was reserved for the shooting ranges: here were targets and butts for harquebuss, long bow and crossbow. The servants' quarters, one storey high, were situated outside *Hesperia*. Beyond was the falconry, managed by expert falconers and hawk trainers and annually supplied by the Cretans, Venetians and Sarmatian Poles with all manner of birds. There were priceless eagles for hunting hares, foxes and cranes. There were gerfalcons, goshawks, sakers for hunting wild geese, herons and bitterns. There were falcons, lanners, sparhawks and merlins for hunting larks and partridges. Other birds there were, too, in great quantities, so well trained that when they flew afield for their own sport they never failed to catch every bird they encountered. . . . The venery with its hounds and beagles stood a little further along towards the park.

All the halls, apartments and chambers were richly hung with tapestries varying with the season; the floors were covered with green cloth, the beds all embroidered. Each rear chamber boasted a pierglass set in a heavy gold frame adorned with pearls. Near the exits of the ladies' halls were the perfumers and hairdressers who ministered to the gentlemen before the latter visited the ladies. These .attendants furnished the ladies' rooms with rose water, orange-flower water and angelica, supplying a precious small atomizer to give forth the most exquisite aromatic perfumes.

CHAPTER 56

*How the monks and nuns of Thélème were apparelled.*

When first the abbey was founded, the ladies dressed according to their taste and pleasure. Subsequently of their own free will they modified their costume as follows.

They wore hose, of scarlet or kermes-red, reaching some three inches above the knee, the edge being exquisitely embroidered or slashed. Their garters, which matched their bracelets, came both a whit over and under the knee. Their shoes, pumps and slippers were of red, violet or crimson velvet and jagged as a lobster's claws.

Over their slips, they put on a tight tunic of pure silk camlet, and over that a taffeta farthingale or petticoat, red, white, beige, gray or of any other color. Above this farthingale went a skirt of silver taffeta, with fine gold embroidery and delicate cross-stitch work. According to the temperature, the season or the ladies' whim, these skirts might be satin, damask or velvet and, in color, orange, green, cendré, blue, canary yellow, scarlet, crimson or white, or of cloth-of-gold, cloth-of-silver, or any other choice material variously embroidered, stitched, brocaded or spangled according to the occasion for which they were worn.

Their gowns, or over-garments, were also governed by timely considerations. They might be cloth-of-gold with silver embossing or red satin with gold brocade or taffeta, white, blue, black or tawny. Or they might be silk rep, silk camlet, velvet, cloth-of-silver, cloth-of-gold or satin variously figured with gold and silver thread.

In summer, instead of these gowns, they wore lovely light smocks made of the same material, or capes, Moorish-fashion, with hoods to protect and shade their faces from the sun. These Moresco capes were of violet velvet, having raised gold stitching over silver purl or gold piping and cording, with small Indian pearls at their ends. And ever a gay colored plume, the color of their sleeves, bravely garnished with gold! In winter, their gowns were of taffeta in all the colors mentioned above, but lined with lynx, weasel, Calabrian marten, sable and other rare fur. Their beads, rings, chains and necklaces were of precious stones: carbuncles, rubies, balas rubies, diamonds, sapphires, emeralds, turquoises, garnets, agates, beryls and priceless pearls.

Their headgear also varied with the season. In winter, it was in the French fashion with a cap over the temples covered by a velvet hood with hanging veil. In spring it was in the Spanish, with laces and veils. In summer it was in the Tuscan, the hair elaborately entwined with gold chains and jewels. On Sundays and holidays, however, they followed the French mode which is more seemly and modest.

The men, too, dressed according to their personal taste. Their hose were of light wool or serge cloth, white, black, scarlet or kermes-red. Their velvet breeches were of the same hue or almost; they were embroidered or slashed to their taste. The doublet was of cloth-of-gold, cloth-of-silver, velvet, satin or damask, embroidered, panelled or slashed on one model, the points silk to match and the ornaments of fine enamelled gold.

Their cloaks and jerkins were of cloth-of-gold, cloth-of-silver, gold tissue or velvet, purfled or brocaded at pleasure; their over-garments were every whit as costly as the ladies'. Their girdles were silk, matching their doublets. Each wore on his side a handsome sword with gilt hilt and pommel; the scabbard velvet, matching his breeches, and the ferrule a wondrous example of the goldsmith's art. So too the dagger. Their caps were of black velvet, trimmed with jewels and rings and buttons of gold, with a white plume set in jauntily and parted by many rows of spangles from which hung splendent emeralds and various other stones.

Such was the sympathy between the gallants and their ladies that they matched one another's costumes every day. And in order to be sure of it, certain gentlemen were appointed to report every morning to the youths what garments their ladies planned to wear on that occasion. All here was done for the pleasure of the fair.

Handsome though the clothes were and rich the accoutrements, lads or girls wasted no time in dressing. The wardrobe masters had everything ready before their gentlemen arose and the maids were so nimble that in a trice their mistresses were apparelled from head to toe.

To facilitate matters, over a distance of half-a-league, a row of light, well-appointed cottages housed the goldsmiths, lapidaries, embroiderers, tailors, gold drawers, velvet weavers, tapestry makers and upholsterers. Here each worked at his trade, and all for the jolly friars and comely nuns of the new abbey. They received materials and stuffs from My Lord Nausiclete, famous for his ships, as the name indicates. Each year brought them seven vessels from the Pearl and Cannibal Islands or Antilles, laden with ingots of gold, raw silk, pearls and precious stones.

If pearls through age tended to lose their lustre, the jewellers, following the method of Avicenna,[27] fed them to the roosters, and they regained their native sparkle.

27. See footnote 16.

*How those of Thélème were governed in their manner of living.*

Their whole life was ordered not by, statute or rule, but according to their free will and pleasure. They arose when they pleased. They ate, drank, worked and slept when the spirit moved them. No one awoke them, forced food or drink upon them or *made* them do anything else. Gargantua's plan called for perfect liberty. The only rule of the house was:

## DO AS THOU WILT

because men that are free, of gentle birth, well-bred and at home in civilized company possess a natural instinct that inclines them to virtue and saves them from vice. This instinct they name their honor. Sometimes they may be depressed or enslaved by subjection or constraint; for we all long for forbidden fruit and covet what is denied us. But they usually apply the fine forces that tend to virtue in such a way as to shake off the yoke of servitude.

The Thélèmites, thanks to their liberty, knew the virtues of emulation. All wished to do what they saw pleased one of their number. Let some lad or maid say "Let us drink" and all of them drank, "Let us play" and all of them played, "Let us frolic in the fields" and all of them frolicked. When falconry or hawking were in order, the ladies sat high upon their saddles on fine nags, a sparhawk, lanner or merlin on one daintily gloved wrist, while the men bore other kinds of hawks.

They were so well-bred that none, man or woman, but could read, write, sing, play several instruments, speak five or six languages and readily compose verse and prose in any of them. Never had earth known knights so proud, so gallant, so adroit on horseback and on foot, so athletic, so lively, so well-trained in arms as these. Never were ladies seen so dainty, so comely, so winsome, so deft at handwork and needlework, so skilful in feminine arts, so frank and so free as these.

Thus when the time came for a man to leave the abbey (either at his parents' request or for some other reason) he took with him one of the ladies—the particular one who had chosen him for her knight—and they were married. And though they had lived in devotion and friendship at Thélème, their marriage relations proved even more tender and agreeable. Indeed to the end of their lives they loved one another as they had on the day of their wedding. . . .

## Gargantua and Pantagruel, Book II

[*Pantagruel: Birth and Education*]

CHAPTER 2

*Of the nativity of the most redoubtable Pantagruel.*

At the age of four hundred fourscore and forty-four years, Gargantua begat his son Pantagruel upon his wife named Badebec, daughter to the king of the dimly-seen Amaurotes in Utopia.[28] She died in the throes of childbirth. Alas! Pantagruel was so extraordinarily large and heavy that he could not possibly come to light without suffocating his mother.

If you would fully understand how he came to be christened Pantagruel, you must remember that a terrible drought raged that year throughout the land of Africa. For thirty-six months, three weeks, four days, thirteen hours and even longer, there was no drop of rain. And the sun blazed so fiercely that the whole earth was parched.

Even in the days of Elijah, the soil was no drier, for now no tree on earth bore leaf or flower. The grass had no verdure; rivers and springs ran dry; the luckless fishes, abandoned by their element, crawled on solid earth, crying and screaming most horribly. Birds fell from the air for want of moisture; wolves, foxes, harts, wild boars, fallow deer, hares, rabbits, weasels, martens, badgers and other beasts were found dead in the fields, their mouths agape.

As for the men, their state was very piteous. You should have seen them with their tongues dangling like a hound's after a run of six hours. Not a few threw themselves into the wells. Others lay under a cow's belly to enjoy the shade—these it is whom Homer calls *Alibantes*, the desiccated.[29] The whole country was at a standstill. The strenuous efforts of mortals against the vehemence of this drought was a horrible spectacle. It was hard enough, God knows, to save the holy water in the churches from being wasted; but My Lords the Cardinals and our Holy Father laid down such strict rules that no man dared take more than a lick of it. In the churches, scores of parched, unhappy wretches followed the priest who distributed it, their jaws yawning for one tiny driblet. Like the rich man in *Luke*, who cried for Lazarus to dip his fingers in water, they were tormented by a flame,[30] and would not suffer the slightest

28. names taken from Sir Thomas More's *Utopia*. Literally, "no place," the word *Utopia* has become synonymous with "ideal country."

29. The allusion to Homer is apparently mistaken, but "Alibantes"— possibly derived from the name of Alibas, a dry river in hell—is used by other ancient writers with reference to the dead or the very old.

30. "And he cried and said, Father Abraham, have mercy on me, and send Lazarus, that he may dip the tip of his finger in water, and cool my tongue; for I am tormented in this flame." (Luke 16:24.)

drop to be wasted. Ah! thrice happy that year the man who had a cool, well-plenished wine cellar underground!

In discussing the question: "Why is sea water salty?" the philosopher Aristotle, after Empedocles, supplies the following reason. When Phœbus gave the reins of his luminous chariot[31] to Phaëton, his son, the latter, unskilled in the art of driving, was incapable of following the ecliptic lines between the two tropics of the sun's sphere. Accordingly, he strayed from the appointed path and came so close to earth that he dried up all the countries under his course. He also burnished that great portion of heaven which philosophers call *Via Lactea* or the Milky Way, and good drinkers St. James' Way, since it is the starry line that guides pilgrims to Santiago de Compostella. (On the other hand, poets declare that it is here Juno's milk dropped while she was suckling Hercules.)

Earth at that time was so excessively heated that it broke into an enormous sweat which ran over the sea, making the latter salty, since all sweat is salt. If you do not admit this last statement, then taste of your own sweat. Or savor the perspiration of your pox-stricken friends when they are put in sweatboxes for treatment. It is all one to me.

Practically the same thing happened the year I am speaking of. On a certain Friday, all the people were intent upon their devotions. A noble procession was in progress with plenty of litanies and fine preachings. Supplications arose toward Almighty God beseeching Him to cast His eye of mercy upon them in their affliction. Suddenly they clearly saw some great drops of water stand out upon the ground, exactly as from a person sweating copiously.

The wretched populace began to rejoice as though here were a great blessing. Some declared that, since the air lacked all moisture, earth was supplying the deficiency. Other scientists asseverated that it was a shower of the Antipodes, as described by Seneca in *Quaestiones Naturales*, Book IV, where he treats of the Nile's source, attributing its floods to distant rains washed underground into the river. But they were thoroughly deceived. For, the procession done, when each sought to gather up this dew and drink it up by the bowlful, they found it was only pickle, far saltier than the saltiest water of the sea.

Another great mishap befell Gargantua that week. A dungchafing lout, bearing two great bags of salt and a hambone in his game-pouch, walked into poor Gargantua's mouth as the giant lay snoring. The clod spilled a quantity of salt in Gargantua's throat. Gargantua, crazy with a thirst he could not slake, angrily snapped his mouth shut. He gnashed his teeth fiercely; they ground like millstones. Later the rascal told me he was so terrified you could have

31. the chariot of the sun.

stopped up his nose with a bale of hay. He fell flat on his face like a dead man, dropping the two saltbags that had tormented Gargantua. They were at once swallowed up and entombed.

My rogue vowed vengeance. Thrusting his hand in his game-pouch, he drew out a great hambone, highly salted, still covered with hair, and twenty-eight inches long. Ragefully he rammed it down Gargantua's throat. The giant, drier than ever, felt the pig's hair tickling his belly and, willy-nilly, spewed up all he had. Eighteen tumbrils could not have drawn away the rich nauseous yield. My dungchafer, hidden in the cavity of one of his teeth, was forced to take French leave in such pitiful condition that all who saw him were horrified. Gargantua, looking down, noticed this jackpudding whirling about in a great puddle.

"Here is some worm that sought to sting me in the belly," he mused, happy to have expelled him from his body.

Because he was born that very day, his father called him Pantagruel or All-Athirst, a name derived from the Greek *panta* meaning all, and the Hagarene or Saracen *gruel* meaning athirst. Gargantua inferred thereby that at his son's birth the entire universe was wholly parched. Prophetically, too, he realized that some day Pantagruel would become Supreme Lord of the Thirsty, a fact indicated even more surely by a further portent.

For while his mother Badebec was bringing him forth and the midwives stood by ready to receive him, there first issued from her belly seventy-eight salt-vendors, each leading a salt-laden mule by the halter. They were followed by nine dromedaries, bearing hams and smoked oxtongues; seven camels bearing chitterlings; twenty-five cartloads of leeks, garlic, onions and chives. This terrified some midwives, but others said:

"Here is good provision! As it is, we drink but lazily, instead of vigorously. This must be a good omen, since these victuals are spurs to bibbing wine!"

As they were tattling away, out pops Pantagruel, hairy as a bear! At which, prophetically, one of them exclaimed:

"God help us, he is born hair and all, straight from the arse of Satan in flight. He will do terrible wonders. If he lives, he will grow to a lusty age!"

Of Pantagruel's race are those who drink so heavily in the evening that they must rise at night to drink again, quenching the coals of fire and blistering thirst in their throats. This form of thirst is called Pantagruel, in memory of the giant.

### [*Father's Letter from Home*]
#### CHAPTER 8

*How Pantagruel in Paris received a letter from his father Gargantua.*

As you may suppose, Pantagruel studied very hard and profited much by his study, for his intelligence was naturally active and his memory as full as twelve casks of olives. While in Paris,[32] he received the following letter from his father:

MY BELOVED SON,

Among the gifts, graces and prerogatives with which our sovereign Creator, God Almighty, blessed and enriched humanity from the beginning, there is one that I deem supreme. By its means, though we be mortal, we can yet achieve a sort of immortality; through it, we may, in the course of our transitory lives, yet perpetuate our name and race.

To be sure, what we gain by a progeny born of lawful wedlock cannot make up for what we lost through the sin of our first parents. Adam and Eve disobeyed the commandments of the Lord their God: mortality was their punishment. By death the magnificent mould in which Man was fashioned vanished into the dust of oblivion.

However, thanks to seminal propagation, what a man loses his children revive and, where they fail, their children prevail. So it has gone, and so it shall be, from generation to generation, until the Day of Judgment, when Christ shall restore to God the Father His kingdom pacified, secured and cleansed of all sin. Then all generations and corruption shall cease, for the elements will have completed their continuous transmutations. The peace humanity has craved so anxiously will have been attained; all things will have been reduced to their appointed end and period.

I therefore have reason to give thanks to God, my Saviour, for having granted me the joy of beholding my old age blossom anew in your youth. When, by His pleasure, which rules and orders everything, my soul must abandon this human habitation, I shall not believe I am dying utterly, but rather passing from one place to another. For in you my visible image will continue to live on earth; by you, I shall go on frequenting honorable men and true friends, as I was wont to do.

My associations have not been without sin, I confess. We all transgress and must continually beseech God to forgive us our

32. Like his father before him, Pantagruel has been sent to Paris to study. The following letter, patterned after Ciceronian models of eloquence, summarizes Rabelais' view of an ideal education, and generally illustrates the attitude of the Renaissance intellectual elite toward culture.

trespasses. But they have been without reproach in the eyes of men.

That is why if, beside my bodily image, my soul did not likewise shine in you, you would not be accounted worthy of guarding the precious immortality of my name. In that case, the least part of me (my body) would endure. Scant satisfaction, that, when the best part (my soul, which should keep my name blessed among men) had degenerated and been bastardized. I say this not through any doubt as to your virtue, which I have already often tested, but to encourage you to go on doing ever better and profiting by your constant improvement.

My purpose is not so much to keep you absolutely on your present virtuous course as to make you rejoice that you have kept and are keeping on it. I seek to quicken your heart with resolutions for the future. To help you make and carry these out, remember that I have spared nothing. I have helped you as though my sole treasure on earth were once in my lifetime to see you well-bred and accomplished in honesty and valor as well as in knowledge and civility. Ay, I have longed to leave you after my death as a mirror of your father's personality. The reflection may not prove perfect in practice, but certainly I could not more studiously wish for its perfection.

My late father Grangousier, of blessed memory, made every effort that I might achieve mental, moral and technical excellence. The fruit of my studies and labors matched, indeed surpassed, his dearest wish. But you can realize that conditions were not as favorable to learning as they are to-day. Nor had I such gifted teachers as you. We were still in the dark ages; we still walked in the shadow of the dark clouds of ignorance; we suffered the calamitous consequences of the destruction of good literature by the Goths. Now, by God's grace, light and dignity have been restored to letters, and I have lived to see it. Indeed, I have watched such a revolution in learning that I, not erroneously reputed in my manhood the leading scholar of the century, would find it difficult to enter the bottom class in a grammar school.

I tell you all this not through boastfulness, though in writing to you I might be proud with impunity. Does not Marcus Tullius[33] authorize it in his book *Of Old Age,* and Plutarch in *How a Man May Praise Himself without Envy?* Both authors recognize that such pride is useful in fostering the spirit of emulation. No—I do it simply to give you a proof of my love and affection.

To-day, the old sciences are revived, knowledge is systematized, discipline reëstablished. The learned languages are restored: Greek, without which a man would be ashamed to consider himself educated; Hebrew, Chaldean and Latin.[34] Printing is now in use, an

---

33. Cicero.   34. The languages which are the in-

art so accurate and elegant that it betrays the divine inspiration of its discovery,[35] which I have lived to witness. Alas! Conversely, I was not spared the horror of such diabolic works as gunpowder[36] and artillery.

To-day, the world is full of learned men, brilliant teachers and vast libraries: I do not believe that the ages of Plato, Cicero or Papinian[37] afforded such facilities for culture. From now on, it is unthinkable to come before the public or move in polite circles without having worshipped at Minerva's shrine. Why, the robbers, hangmen, adventurers and jockeys of to-day are infinitely better educated than the doctors and preachers of my time. More, even women and girls aspire to the glory, the heavenly manna of learning. Thus, at my advanced age, I have been forced to take up Greek. Not that I had despised it, like Cato;[38] I never had the opportunity to learn it. Now I delight in reading Plutarch's *Morals*, Plato's noble *Dialogue*, the *Monuments* of Pausanias and the *Antiquities* of Athenæus,[39] as I await the hour when it shall please God, my Creator, to call me back to His bosom.

That is why, my dear son, I urge you to spend your youth making the most of your studies and developing your moral sense. You are in Paris, which abounds in noble men upon whom to pattern yourself; you have Epistemon, an admirable tutor, who can inspire you by direct oral teaching. But I demand more of you. I insist you learn languages perfectly! Greek first, as old Quintilian[40] prescribes; then Latin; then Hebrew for the sake of the Holy Scripture; then Chaldee and Arabic, too. Model your Greek style on Plato, your Latin on Cicero. Let no history slip your memory; cultivate cosmography, for you will find its texts helpful.

As for the liberal arts of geometry, arithmetic and music, I gave you a taste of them when you were a little lad of five or six. Proceed further in them yourself, learning as much as you can. Be sure to master all the rules of astronomy; but dismiss astrology and the divinatory art of Lullius[41] as but vanity and imposture. Of civil law, I would have you know the texts of the Code by heart, then compare them with philosophy.

A knowledge of nature is indispensable; devote yourself to this

struments of classical learning are listed along with those useful for the study of the Old Testament.

35. Printing from movable type was independently invented in Europe about the middle of the fifteenth century; the idea of its divine origin was commonplace during the Renaissance.

36. probably introduced into Europe through the Arabs, rather than invented, in the fourteenth century.

.37. jurisconsult of the time of Emperor Septimius Severus (reigned A.D. 193–211).

38. Plutarch's life of Cato is the source of the notion that he despised Greek.

39. The works of Pausanias and Athenaeus were standard sources of information on ancient geography, art, and everyday life.

40. In his *Institutio oratoria*, Book I, Chapter 1, paragraph 12, he recommends studying Greek before Latin.

41. Raymond Lully, Spanish philosopher of the thirteenth century, who dabbled in magic.

study with unflagging curiosity. Let there be no sea, river or fountain but you know the fish that dwell in it. Be familiar with all the shrubs, bushes and trees in forest or orchard, all the plants, herbs and flowers that grow on the ground, all the birds of the air, all the metals in the bowels of earth, all the precious stones in the orient and the south. In a word, be well informed in everything that concerns the physical world we live in.

Then carefully consult the works of Greek, Arabian and Latin physicians, without slighting the Jewish doctors, Talmudists and Cabbalists. By frequent exercises in dissection, acquire a perfect knowledge of that other world, which is man.

Devote a few hours a day to the study of Holy Writ. Take up the New Testament and the Epistles in Greek; then, the Old Testament in Hebrew. Strive to make your mind an inexhaustible storehouse of knowledge. For you are growing to manhood now: soon you will have to give up your studious repose to lead a life of action. You will have to learn to bear arms, to achieve knighthood, so as to defend my house and help our allies frustrate the attacks of evildoers.

Further, I wish you soon to test what profit you have gained from your education. This you can best do by public discussion and debate on all subjects against all comers, and by frequenting learned men both in Paris and elsewhere.

But remember this. As Solomon says, wisdom entereth not into a malicious soul, and science without conscience spells but destruction of the spirit. Therefore serve, love and fear God, on Him pin all your thoughts and hopes; by faith built of charity, cling to Him so closely that never a sin come between you. Hold the abuses of the world in just suspicion. Set not your heart upon vanity, for this life is a transitory thing, but the Word of God endureth forever. Be serviceable to your neighbor, love him as you do yourself. Honor your teachers. Shun the company of all men you would not wish to resemble; receive not in vain the favors God has bestowed upon you.

When you realize that you have acquired all the knowledge Paris has to offer, come back so I may see you and give you my blessing before I die.

My son, the peace and grace of Our Lord be with you. Amen.

Your father,
GARGANTUA

From Utopia, the seventeenth day of September.

Having read this letter, Pantagruel, greatly encouraged, strove more ardently than ever to profit in his work. Had you seen him studying vigorously, practically and tirelessly, you would have compared his spirit moving among his books to flames blazing through a bonfire of dry branches.

### CHAPTER 16

*Of the character and condition of Panurge.*[42]

Panurge was then about thirty-five years old and as fine to gild as a dagger of lead. Of medium height, neither too tall nor too short, he had an aquiline nose, shaped like the handle of a razor. He cut a very gallant figure though he was a trifle lewd by nature, and subject to a disease at that time called impecunitis, an incomparable malady.

Yet when he needed money, he knew thirty-three methods of acquiring it, the most ordinary and honorable of which was filching. He was a quarrelsome fellow, a sharper, a toper, a roisterer and a profligate, if ever there was one in the city of Paris. In every other respect, he was the best fellow in the world.

He was constantly plotting against the sergeants and the watch. Sometimes he assembled three or four sportsmen, plied them with drink until they were boozy as Knights Templars,[43] then took them up the hill to Ste. Geneviève or near the Collège de Navarre. Placing his sword on the pavement and his ear to his sword, he waited till he heard the blade shake—an infallible sign that the watch was not far off. Then he and his companions took a dung cart and rolled it down hill. Ere it was halfway down, they had fled in the opposite direction, for in less than two days Panurge knew every street and alley in Paris as well as his postprandial grace: *Deus det nobis pacem suam,* God grant us His peace.

Another time he laid down a train of gunpowder where the watch was due to pass. Just as the troop debouched, he set fire to it, vastly delighted in observing how gracefully they took to their heels, in mortal terror that St. Anthony's fire had caught them by the legs.

The luckless Masters of Arts and theologians he persecuted more than any other class of men. When he met one, he never failed to do him some harm, either slipping a turd into his hood or pinning little foxtails or hares' ears to his back.

One day when all the theologians had been summoned to the Sorbonne to examine the articles of the faith, he made a tart of garlic, asafoetida, galbanum, castoreum[44] and steaming excrement, which he steeped and tempered in the corrupt manner of chancres

---

42. Panurge (*Pan-ourgos* in Greek, the "all-doer") is the major character in *Gargantua and Pantagruel* except for the heroes themselves: a magnification of the perennial-student type, Panurge is an imaginative and scandalous pauper, erudite and bawdy, a lover of outrageous pranks On first meeting Pantagruel he addressed him in thirteen different languages, a couple of them invented, before discovering that they both spoke French. He has

since become a permanent fixture of the young lord's retinue.

43. a medieval religious and medical order, suppressed in 1312. The original *templiers,* not capitalized, suggests a current proverbial expression.

44. Asafoetida and galbanum are resins extracted from Persian plants; castoreum is a substance obtained from the inguinal region of the beaver; all three produce nauseous smells.

and pockbiles. Very early in the morning he so theologically greased and anointed the lattices and grates of the trellised gallery of the Hall of Records that not even the devil himself had dared stay there. The worthy pedagogues pewked in public as abundantly as though they had flayed the fox. Ten or twelve died of the plague, fourteen contracted leprosy, eight came down with pestiferous ulcers, and more than twenty-eight caught the pox. But Panurge was jubilant.

Usually he carried a whip under his gown with which he mercilessly belabored such pages as he met bearing wine for their masters, in order to speed them on their way.

In his coat he had more than twenty-six little pockets and pouches which were always full. One held a pair of loaded dice and a small knife like a glover's awl to cut purses with. Another, verjuice to throw in the eyes of those who annoyed him. A third, burrs, penned with gosling or capon feathers, to stick on to the robes and bonnets of honest people. He often gave married men a fine pair of horns which they bore through the city sometimes all their lives long. To the back of the women's hoods, he liked to affix various knickknacks shaped like the sexual organ of man.

Another pocket held a lot of little packages filled with fleas and lice which he recruited from the tramps at St. Innocent's graveyard and cast with small sticks or quills down the backs of the smartest gentlewomen he could find. He did this even in church, for he never sat up in the choir, preferring to stand in the nave among the women during mass, vespers or sermon. Another pocket held a large supply of bent nails with which he would couple men and women together where they sat. This was particularly amusing when the victims wore gowns of costly sarsenet taffeta, because they ripped them to shreds as they sought to separate. Still another pocket held a squib with tinder, flints, matches, vesuvians, sulphur and other combustibles. Another, two or three burning-glasses with which he tortured and disconcerted men and women at church. For he said there was only an antistrophe between *femme folle à la messe* and *molle à la fesse* or working a cunning stunt and a stunning cunt. Another pouch held needles, threads and pins for all manner of minor deviltries.

Once at the door of the Great Hall in the Palais de Justice, Panurge saw a Cordelier father getting ready to say mass before the proceedings of the day. Immediately he ran up to help the holy man don his vestments and, in the process, managed to sew his alb to his robe and shirt. Then, as the magistrates arrived for mass, Panurge withdrew. Mass done, as he reached the formula *Ite, missa est,* the wretched friar tried to take off his alb. But, at the same time, off came the robe and shirt solidly sewn to it. Our Cordelier, thus

stripped to the shoulders, revealed his dangledingus to all the world
—and it was no small crosier, as you may imagine. The harder he
tugged, the more he exposed himself. So much so, indeed, that one
of the counsellors cried:

"What is the matter? Is this good friar making an offering of his
tail for us to kiss? No, by heaven, let St. Anthony's fire kiss it for
us!"

From then on, an ordinance forbade the poor good fathers to disrobe before the world, the vestry-room being indicated as the only
fit place for this. They were especially warned against doing so in
the presence of women, lest it tempt the latter to sin through longing. When people wondered why the fathers were genitally so well-
equipped, Panurge solved the problem.

"What makes the ears of asses so long?" he asked, and answering
his own question: "Their dams put no caps on their ears. Allia-
cus,[45] Chancellor of the University and Chaplain to Charles VI,
proves this in his *Suppositiones*. Similarly, what makes the whangle-
tools of our holy fathers hang so low? Well, they never wear dark
breeches, so their lusty organs, dangling down at liberty like a horse
given head, knock against their knees like women's beads. Why are
they correspondingly large? Because, with all this waggling to and
fro, the humors of the body sink down into these parts. Do not the
legists point out that continual agitation and continual motion are
the cause of attraction?"

Another of Panurge's pouches held stone-alum, an itching-powder
which he poured down the backs of those he considered the proudest and most stately ladies. Some would at once strip off their
clothes then and there before the public . . . others danced like cats
on hot coals or a drumstick on a tabor . . . others again rushed
madly into the street and he at their heels. . . . Those inclined to
disrobe, he assisted by sheltering them under his cape, as any courteous and gallant gentleman would have done.,

In another pocket he had a small leather bottle full of old oil. If
he saw a man or woman in a handsome costume, he would grease
and stain it in the most conspicuous places. His technique here was
an art. Pretending to admire the material, he would finger it.

"Rare cloth, this, sir," or "Fine satin, upon my word!" or "Oh,
what lovely taffeta, Madame!" he would exclaim. "God give you all
your noble heart desires. You have a new suit, My Lord! And you a
new dress, My Lady. Well, you know the saying: New clothes, new
friends. God give you joy in them!"

As he spoke, his hands passed lightly over the shoulders and a
long ugly smear remained

45. Latinized name of Pierre d'Ailly (1350–1425).

> So indelible a spot
> Stamped on body, soul and fame
> That the devil could not blot
> Out its testament of shame.

As he took his leave of the ladies, he would say:

"Madame, take care not to fall. You've a huge filthy hole out of sight in front of you, there!"

In another pocket he kept euphorbium, very finely pulverized and spread over a dainty handkerchief he had stolen from a pretty sales-girl in the Galleries of the Sainte-Chapelle,[46] hard by the law courts and frequented by the gallants of the day. (He filched it while removing from between her breasts a louse he had dropped there.)

When he happened to be in gentle company, he would steer the conversation on to the subject of lace and lingerie. Then, thrusting his hands into some lady's bosom:

"Glorious work, this. Is it Flanders or Hainault?"

Then, drawing his handkerchief:

"Just look at this kerchief, Madame. Would you say it was Frontignan or Fontarabia?"

Shaking it hard under her nose, he would make her sneeze for hours at a time. Then he would fart like a dray horse.

"Tut, tut," the lady would say. "Are you whiffling, Panurge?"

"No, Madame," he would reply gallantly, "I am merely tuning my tail to the plain song you make with your nose."

Panurge was never without pincers, a picklock, a pelican, a jimmy, a crook or other tools against which no chest or door could avail. Finally, in another pocket he kept a whole battery of small goblets which he worked with amazing skill, for his fingers were nimble and adroit as those of Minerva or Arachne.[47] He had indeed once been an itinerant quack, barking antidotes for poison. When he presented a sum of money and asked for change, the changer had to be spry as Argus[48] to catch Panurge spiriting away five, six or seven coins at a time, visibly, openly, manifestly, without lesion or hurt, whilst all the changer noticed was a slight draught.

### CHAPTER 21

*How Panurge fell in love with a Parisienne of high degree.*

As a result of his debate with the English scholar,[49] Panurge had acquired quite a reputation in Paris. The activity of his codpiece

46. a shopping center in old Paris.
47. In Greek mythology the goddess Athena, being enraged at the Lydian maid Arachne's irreverence and weaving skill, transformed her into a spider.
48. the Greek mythological figure with a hundred eyes.
49. Thaumastes, who in the previous chapters has long argued with Panurge, using both words and signs, and has been "nonplussed" by the latter's knowledge.

was proportionally greater, and, to that effect, he had it pinked and
slashed with ornate embroidery, after the Roman fashion. His
praises became a topic of general conversation. There was even a
song written to celebrate his exploits; the little children sang it as
they went to fetch mustard. Best of all, he was made welcome in
the most elegant circles. But it went to his head; he actually had
the presumption to beleaguer one of the great ladies of the city.

Scorning the rigmarole of prefaces and preliminaries dear to such
languishing, dreamy lovers as never touch meat in Lent, Panurge
popped the question outright.

"Madame," he told this lofty lady, "it would prove beneficent to
the commonwealth, pleasurable to your person, honorable to your
progeny and necessary to me that I cover you for the propagation of
my race. You may take my word for this, Madame; experience will
prove it to you conclusively."

The lady, indignant, thrust him a thousand leagues away.

"You crazy knave, how dare you talk like that? Who do you
think I am? Get out of here at once and never let me lay eyes upon
you again. For two pins, I'd have your arms and legs sawed off!"

"Madame," he protested, "I would not care two pins if my arms
and legs were sawed off, providing you and I had first fought a
merry bout of spermary-snuggery. For," he showed her his long codpiece, "here is Master Johnny Inigo, a master instrumentalist who
begs to fiddle and thrum, sweep the *viola d'amore*, play the mani-
chord, tweedle the gittern, strike the lyre, beat the drum, wind the
horn and grind the organ until you feel his music throbbing in the
marrow of your bones. A wily gallant, Master Johnny: he will not
fail to find all the cranks, winches, wedges, pullies, nippers,
clutches, teeth, springs and rigging stored in your delicate cockpit.
You'll be needing no scouring or brushing up after *him*."

"Go to, scoundrel, and away! One more word out of you and I'll
shout for help; I'll have my servants beat you to death."

"No, Madame," Panurge protested. "You are not as cruel as you
pretend. You cannot be or else your face is a living lie. Let earth
soar upward into the firmament, let high heaven sink into the bottomless pit, let the whole concert of nature be annihilated ere your
beauty and grace secrete one drop of gall or malice. They say that it
is virtually impossible for man:

> To find in women beauty unallied
> With arrogance or cruelty or pride

but that holds only for vulgar beauties. Your own is so priceless, so
unique, so heavenly that I vow Nature has bestowed it on you as a
paragon to prove what she can do when she cares to muster all her
power and science. Everything in you is honey, sugar, celestial

manna. To you Paris should have awarded the golden apple, not to Venus or Juno or Minerva. For Juno possessed no such nobility, Minerva no such wisdom, Venus no such comeliness.

"O ye heavenly gods and goddesses! how happy the man whom you allow to kiss and fondle you, to cosset, nuzzle and cockle you, to thrust his prolific engine of pleasure into the pod of your quivering quim. By God, I am that man, I plainly feel it. Already she loves me her bellyful I swear; ay, Panurge is predestined to it by the nixies and fairies. Let us lose no time: come, slap-dash, helter-skelter, holus-bolus, to horse and fair riding, tantivy, hoicks!"

Whereupon he sought to embrace her; but she moved towards the window as if to call for help, so Panurge made off hastily. Yet ere retreating:

"Madame," he said, "wait for me here; I'll call your friends, don't bother!"

And he withdrew, unfeased and no less cheerful despite the rebuff.

Next day, as she arrived at church, Panurge stood waiting at the door, offered her holy water, bowed deep as she passed, then kneeled familiarly beside her:

"Madame," he declared, "you must know how madly in love with you I am. Why, I can neither piddle nor cack for love of you! I don't know how *you* feel, but, Madame, suppose I took ill from it, wouldn't you be responsible?"

"Go away, I don't care anything about it. Leave me alone to my prayers."

"One moment!" Panurge begged. "Please equivocate on '*à Beaumont le Viconte?*' or on 'Runt and Codger are fellow-muckers!'"

"I don't know what you mean!"

"Quite easy! 'A *beau con le vit monte*,' 'Cunt and Rodger are mellow fuckers!' Now, pray to God that He grant whatever your noble heart desires. And oh, Madame, I beg you: give me those beads a moment."

"Here you are, stop bothering me."

She was about to take off her rosary—it was of cestrin wood with gold ornamentation—when Panurge promptly drew one of his knives and neatly cut it. Before carrying it off to pawn:

"Would you like my knife?" he asked.

"No, certainly not!"

"It's yours to grind or sheathe, Madame, body and soul, bag and baggage, tripe and guts."

But the lady was worried over the loss of her beads, so many implements to help her keep her countenance in church:

"This chattering scoundrel must be some eccentric foreigner," she mused. "He will never return my rosary. What will my dear husband say? He'll be furious! But I'll tell him a sneak thief cut it off me at church. He must believe me: I've still the end fastened on my girdle."

After dinner, Panurge went to call on her with, in his sleeve, a purse full of tokens specially struck for use in the law courts.

"Which of us is the better lover, Madame, you or I?"

"For my part I cannot hate you," she said magnanimously. "God commands us to love our neighbors."

"Aren't you in love with me?"

"I've told you repeatedly not to talk to me like that!" she insisted. "If you mention it again, I'll show you I'm not to be trifled with. Go away, I tell you. But give me back my rosary; my husband might ask me for it."

"Give you back your rosary? No, by heaven, I shall do nothing of the sort. But I'll tell you what I *will* do: I'll gladly give you another. Would you like one in beautifully enamelled gold with beads shaped like great pendulous knockers? Or like loveknots or ingots, heavy in the hand? Or ebony or broad zircons or square-cut garnets with mountings of rare turquoises, or costly topazes or priceless sapphires or precious rubies set with glittering diamonds of twenty-eight facets? No, no, that is a trumpery gift. I know of a marvellous rosary: it's made of exquisite emeralds with a mounting of speckled gray amber; at the buckle there's a Persian pearl fat as an orange . . . and the bauble costs but a paltry five-and-twenty thousand ducats. I will make you a present of it; I've heaps of cash!"

He made his tokens ring as though they were genuine, authentic golden crowns with the shining sun of France stamped upon them.

"Do you fancy a piece of violet or crimson velure, dyed in grain, or a piece of scarlet or brocaded satin? Is it your pleasure to accept chains, brooches, tiaras or rings? You have but to say the word: fifty thousand is a trifle!"

His offer made her mouth water. Yet she stood her ground.

"No, thank you, I want nothing to do with you."

"By God, I certainly want to do something with *you!* What I want will cost you nothing; you'll be out nothing when you've given it. Look, Madame," and he showed her his long codpiece. "Here is Master Johnny Scramblecunney who craves lodging."

He was about to strike root there, when she started to cry out, though none too loud. The mask of courtesy fell from Panurge's face.

"So you won't let me have a little harmless fun, eh? Not even a morsel for me, eh? A bucket of turds to you! you don't deserve the honor or pleasure of it. But by God! I'll make the dogs ride you!"

With which he beat a hasty retreat in dread of blows. (He was by nature fearful of them.)

### CHAPTER 22

*How Panurge played a none too pleasant trick on the Parisienne of high degree.*

Next day was Corpus Christi, a feast on which the ladies of Paris put on their stateliest apparel. Panurge's charmer was decked out in a rich gown of crimson velvet, with a skirt of costly white velure.

The day before, Panurge scoured the town for a bitch in heat. Having found one, he tied his belt around her neck and took her home. All that day and through the night, he fed her abundantly; in the morning he killed her, plucked out that part the Greek geomancians[50] know, cut it as fine as he could, tucked it away in one of his innumerable pockets and went to the church. He was sure his lady would soon arrive to take part in the procession always held on that day.

When she entered, Panurge bowed courteously, offered her some holy water and, shortly after she had finished her petty devotions, sat down on the bench beside her. As she looked up, he passed her a paper on which he had written the following rondeau:

> Sweet lady, once, once only I expressed
> My admiration; you denied my quest,
> You drove me irremediably away
> Although I never harmed you (welladay!)
> In act or word or libel or the rest. . . .
> Granted my wooing stirred no answering zest,
> You could have been more honest, and confessed:
> "I do not wish it, friend. Leave me, I pray!"
>    Sweet lady, once,
> Once more and never again I shall protest
> Ere love's flame utterly consume my breast,
> One boon alone I languish for: to lay
> My peacock, shoveller, cockerel, popinjay
> Deep in the shelter of your downy nest.
>    Sweet lady, once!

While she was unfolding the paper to see what was inside, Panurge deftly sprinkled his drug all over her, spilling it impartially in the folds of her sleeves and skirt.

"Madame," he said before taking his leave, "a lover's life is not always a bed of roses. In my case I can only hope the anguished nights, the sorrows and tribulation I undergo for love of you will be deducted from my trials in purgatory. At least pray God He give me patience to bear my affliction."

Panurge had scarcely spoken when all the dogs in the church, attracted by the odor of the drug, scurried over to the lady. Big and little, large and small, one and all came up, sniffed, raised their legs, cocked their members and let fly on her dress. It was the most hor-

50. a species of magicians.

rible sight imaginable.

Panurge pretended to chase them off, then bowed and retired to watch the sport from the vantage point of a chapel. Those wretched curs were squirting all over her clothes. One huge greyhound placed a paw on her shoulder to aim at her head ... other dogs pumped in her sleeves ... still others drenched her backside, while the puppies piddled in her shoes.... The women close to her sought to keep the beasts off, but with scant success. Meanwhile, holding his sides, Panurge, between guffaws of laughter, told certain lords who were next to him:

"I think that lady's in heat. Or some wolfhound covered her recently."

Seeing the dogs crowded as thick about her as about a bitch in heat, he ran off to fetch Pantagruel. On the way, he stopped to kick every dog he met, crying:

"To church with you! To your genuflexions! Follow the odor of sanctity! Be off and join your fellows at the urinarian baptism! Forward, by all the devils, be off, devil take you!"

"Master," he said breathlessly to Pantagruel, "please come and see all the dogs of the country gathered about the loveliest lady in town, and every one of them agog to scrounge her!"

Pantagruel, delighted at the novelty of it, accompanied Panurge back to church and enjoyed the fun immensely. By the time the procession began, matters had reached a crisis. There were more than six hundred thousand and fourteen dogs thronging about her and finding one thousand and one means of harassing her. Whichever way she turned, the newcomers followed the scent, dogged her heels and flooded whatever spot her dress touched. The only course left her was to go home. As she fled through the streets, every one stopped to watch the dogs leaping high as her neck, turning her elegant toilette into a very toilet, as she ran on, helpless and steaming. It was impossible to give them the slip, the trail was too pungent. So they followed her to her residence.

While she hid in her room and her chambermaids burst into laughter behind politely raised aprons, all the dogs within a radius of a half-league came rushing up and showered so hard against the gate as to form a stream in which ducks might very well have swum. To-day this same current, now called the creek of Bièvre, flows through the grounds of the Abbey of St. Victor and past the Gobelin dye-works.[51] Materials steeped in its waters turn a rare scarlet thanks to some special virtue of these pissdogs, as our learned Master Doribus recently pointed out in a brilliant sermon. God help us, a mill could have ground corn there, though not so much as the famous Bazacle in Toulouse on the Garonne.

51. The geography is correct. At the time of Rabelais' writing the celebrated dye-works were still run by the Gobelin family. Mysterious qualities were attrib- uted to the water of the small river Bièvre, and urine was actually used in the industry on account of its ammonia contents.

# MICHEL DE MONTAIGNE
## (1533–1592)
## Essays (Essais)*

### Of Cannibals†

When King Pyrrhus[1] passed over into Italy, after acknowledging
the good order that prevailed in the army that the Romans had
sent to meet him, he said, 'I know not what barbarians are these
(for so the Greeks called all foreign nations), but the disposition
of this army I see is by no means barbarous'. The Greeks said the
same of the army which Flaminius brought into their country, as
did also Philip, on viewing from an eminence the orderly distribution of the Roman camp, in his kingdom, under Publius Sulpicius
Galba.[2] Thereby we may see how we should be on our guard against
clinging to vulgar opinions, and how we should judge things by the
light of reason, and not from common rumour.

I had living with me for a long time a man who had lived for
ten or twelve years in that other world which was discovered in
our century, in that place where Villegaignon landed, which he
called *Antarctic France*.[3] This discovery of an unbounded country
seems to me worthy of consideration. I do not know that I could
pledge myself that some other discovery may not be made in the
future, so many persons greater than we having been mistaken
about this one. I fear our eyes are greater than our bellies, and that
we have more curiosity than capacity. We embrace all, but we
clasp only wind.

Plato[4] introduces Solon, telling how he had learned of the priests
of the city of Saïs in Egypt that, in days of old and before the
Deluge, there was a large island named Atlantis, directly at the
mouth of the Strait of Gibraltar, which contained more countries
than all Asia and Africa together; and that the kings of that region,
who not only possessed that island, but had extended their dominion so far into the mainland, that of the breadth of Africa they

---

* Books I and II were published in
1580; Book II, together with Books I
and II revised and amplified, in 1588;
a posthumous edition, with further additions, in 1595. Our text is from *The
Essays of Montaigne*, translated by
E. J. Trechmann.
† *Essays*, Book I, Chapter 31.
1. king of Epirus, in Greece, fought
the Romans in Italy in 280 B.C.

2. Both Titus Quinctius Flaminius
(mentioned earlier in this sentence)
and Publius Sulpicius Galba were
Roman statesmen and generals who
fought Philip V of Macedon in the
early years of the second century B.C.
3. in Brazil. Villegaignon landed
there in 1557.
4. in his *Timaeus*.

held as far as Egypt, and of the length of Europe as far as Tuscany, attempted to stride even into Asia, and to subjugate all the nations that border on the Mediterranean Sea as far as the gulf of the Greater Sea,[5] and to that end traversed the Spains, Gaul, Italy, as far as Greece, where the Athenians stood up against them; but that some time after both the Athenians and they and their island were swallowed up by the Flood.

It is most likely that that extreme watery devastation has caused some wonderful alterations in the habitations of the earth, as it is thought that the sea cut off Sicily from Italy,

> These lands, 'tis said, one continent of yore
> (Such change can ages work) an earthquake tore
> Asunder; in with havoc rushed the main,
> And far Sicilia from Hesperia bore,
> And now, where leapt the parted lands in twain,
> The narrow tide pours through, 'twixt severed town and plain;
> (Virgil.)[6]

Cyprus from Syria, the island of Negropont from the mainland of Bœotia; and elsewhere joined lands which were divided, by filling up the channels between them with sand and mud:

> Swamps, sterile long, all plashy, rank and drear,
> Groan 'neath the plough, and feed whole cities near.
> (Horace.)[7]

But it does not appear very likely that that great island was the new world that we have lately discovered, for it almost touched Spain, and it would have been an incredible result of an inundation to have removed it as far back as it is, more than twelve hundred leagues; besides that our modern navigators have already almost discovered it to be no island, but a firm land holding together with the East Indies on the one hand, and on the other with the lands which lie under the two poles; or, if it is separated from them, it is by so narrow a strait and interval, that it does not on that account deserve to be called an island.

It would seem that there are movements, some natural, others diseased, in those great bodies as well as in our own. When I consider the inroads that my river, the Dordogne, is making even in my time, upon the right bank in its descent, and that in twenty years it has gained so much ground, and robbed many buildings of their

5. the Black Sea.
6. *Aeneid*, Book III, ll. 414 ff.
7. *Art of Poetry*, ll. 65 f.

foundations, I plainly see that an extraordinary disturbance is going on; for if it had always been going on at this rate, or were to do so in the future, the face of the world would be entirely altered. But rivers are subject to changes: now they overflow in one direction, now in another, now they keep within their beds. I do not speak of the sudden inundations whose causes are manifest. In Médoc, along the sea-shore, my brother the Sieur d'Arsac sees an estate of his buried beneath the sands that the sea vomits before it; the tops of several buildings are still visible; his rents and domains have been converted into very poor pasturage. The inhabitants say that the sea has been for some time pushing so strongly towards them, that they have lost four leagues of land. These sands are its harbingers, and we see great dunes of moving sand, that march half a league before it, and are gaining ground.

The other testimony from antiquity, from which some infer this discovery, is in Aristotle, if at least that little book *Of Unheard-of Marvels* be his. He there relates how certain Carthaginians, having ventured across the Atlantic Sea, outside the Strait of Gibraltar, and navigated a long time, had at last discovered a large fertile island, all clothed in woods, and watered by broad and deep rivers, far remote from any mainland; and that they, and others after them, attracted by the goodness and fertility of the soil, had gone thither with their wives and children and begun to settle there. The lords of Carthage, seeing that their country was gradually becoming depopulated, expressly forbade any more to go there, on pain of death, and drove out those new settlers, fearing, it is said, lest in course of time they might multiply to such an extent as to supplant themselves and ruin their state. This narration of Aristotle no more agrees with our new-found lands than the other.

This man[8] I had was a simple and ignorant fellow: hence the more fit to give true evidence; for your sophisticated men are more curious observers, and take in more things, but they glose them; to lend weight to their interpretations and induce your belief, they cannot help altering their story a little. They never describe things as they really are, but bend them and mask them according to the point of view from which they see things, and, to make their judgements the more credible and attractive, they are not loath to add a little to their matter, and to spin out and amplify their tale. Now we need either a very truthful man, or one so simple that he has not the art of building up and giving an air of probability to fictions, and is wedded to no theory. Such was my man; and he has besides at different times brought several sailors and traders to see

8. Montaigne goes back to the man referred to in the second paragraph of this essay.

me, whom he had known on that voyage. So I shall content myself with his information, without troubling myself about what the cosmographers may say about it.

We need topographers who would give us an exact account of the places which they have visited. But because they have this advantage over us that they have seen Palestine, they claim to enjoy the privilege of telling us new things of all the rest of the world. I would have every man write about what he knows, and no more than he knows, not only in this but on all other subjects. For a man may have some particular knowledge or experience of the nature of a river or a fountain, who otherwise knows no more than what everybody knows. Yet he will undertake, in order to circulate this little scrap of knowledge, to write a book on the whole science of physics. From this fault spring many great abuses.

Now, to return to my subject, from what I have heard of that nation, I can see nothing barbarous or uncivilized about it, except that we all call barbarism that which does not fit in with our usages. And indeed we have no other level of truth and reason but the example and model of the opinions and usages of the country we live in. There we always see the perfect religion, the perfect government, the perfect and accomplished manner of doing all things. Those people are wild in the sense in which we call wild the fruits that Nature has produced by herself and in her ordinary progress; whereas in truth it is those we have altered artificially and diverted from the common order, that we should rather call wild. In the first we still see, in full life and vigour, the genuine and most natural and useful virtues and properties, which we have bastardized in the latter, and only adapted to please our corrupt taste. And yet in some of the uncultivated fruits of those countries there is a delicacy of flavour that is excellent even to our taste, and rivals even our own. It is not reasonable that art should gain the point of honour over our great and powerful mother Nature. We have so overburdened the beauty and richness of her works with our inventions, that we have quite smothered her. And yet, wherever she shines in her purity, she marvellously puts to shame our vain and trivial efforts,

> Uncared, unmarked the ivy blossoms best;
> Midst desert rocks the ilex clusters still;
> And sweet the wild bird's untaught melody.
> (Propertius.)[9]

With all our efforts we are unable even to copy the nest of the

9. *Elegies*, Book I, Elegy ii, ll. 10 ff.

smallest of little birds, its contexture, its beauty and convenience; not so much as the web of the poor spider.

All things, says Plato,[10] are produced either by Nature, or by chance, or by art: the greatest and most beautiful by one or other of the two first; the least and most imperfect by the latter.

Those nations, then, appear to me so far barbarous in this sense, that their minds have been formed to a very slight degree, and that they are still very close to their original simplicity. They are still ruled by the laws of Nature, and very little corrupted by ours; but they are still in such a state of purity, that I am sometimes vexed that they were not known earlier, at a time when there were men who could have appreciated them better than we do.

I am sorry that Lycurgus[11] and Plato had no knowledge of them, for it seems to me that what we have learned by contact with those nations surpasses not only all the beautiful colours in which the poets have depicted the golden age, and all their ingenuity in inventing a happy state of man, but also the conceptions and desires of Philosophy herself. They were incapable of imagining so pure and native a simplicity, as that which we see by experience: nor could they have believed that human society could have been maintained with so little human artifice and solder. This is a nation,[12] I should say to Plato, which has no manner of traffic; no knowledge of letters; no science of numbers; no name of magistrate or statesman; no use for slaves; neither wealth nor poverty; no contracts; no successions; no partitions; no occupation but that of idleness; only a general respect of parents; no clothing; no agriculture; no metals; no use of wine or corn. The very words denoting falsehood, treachery, dissimulation, avarice, envy, detraction, pardon, unheard of. How far removed from this perfection would he find the ideal republic he imagined! *Men newly come from the hands of the gods* (Seneca).[13]

These manners first by nature taught. (Virgil.)[14]

For the rest, they live in a region with a very agreeable and very temperate climate, so that, according to my witnesses, a sick man is rarely seen; and they assured me that they had never seen any man shaking with palsy, or with dripping eyes, toothless or bent with age. They are settled along the sea-coast, and closed in on the land side by large and high mountains, the land between them and the sea extending for a hundred leagues or thereabouts. They have great

10. See his *Laws*.
11. the half-legendary Spartan law-giver (ninth century B.C.).
12. The passage beginning here is always compared with Shakespeare, *The Tempest*, Act II, Scene 1, ll. 154 ff.
13. *Epistles*, Epistle xc.
14. *Georgics*, Book II, l. 20.

abundance of fish and flesh, which bear no resemblance to ours, and they eat them roasted without any other preparation. The first man who brought a horse thither, although he had associated with them on several previous voyages, so horrified them in the riding posture, that they shot him dead with arrows before recognizing him.

Their buildings are very long, capable of holding two or three hundred souls, covered with the bark of tall trees, the strips resting by one end on the ground, and leaning to and supporting one another at the top, after the manner of some of our barns, the coverings of which slope down to the ground and serve as sidewalls. They have a wood so hard that they can cut with it, of which they make their swords, and gridirons to roast their meat. Their beds are made of cotton tissue, suspended from the roof like those in our ships, each one having his own: for the women sleep apart from their husbands.

They rise with the sun and eat immediately after rising, for the whole day: for they have no other meal. They drink nothing with that meal, like some other Eastern peoples of whom Suidas[15] tells us, who drank apart from eating; but they drink several times a day, and to excess. Their drink is made of some root, and is of the colour of our claret wines, and they only drink it warm. This beverage will keep only two or three days; it has a slightly pungent taste, is anything but heady, good for the stomach, and laxative for such as are not used to it, but a very pleasant drink for those who are. For bread they use a certain white material resembling preserved coriander. I have tried some of it: it is sweet but rather tasteless.

The whole day is spent in dancing. The younger men hunt animals with bows. Some of the women meanwhile spend their time warming their drink, which is their chief duty. One of their old men, in the morning before they begin to eat, preaches to the whole barnful of people in common, walking from one end to the other, repeating the same words several times, until he has finished the round (for the buildings are quite a hundred paces in length). He recommends only two things, valour against the enemy and love to their wives. And they never fail to stress this obligation, which forms their refrain, 'that it is they who keep their wine warm and seasoned'.

In several places, among others in my house, may be seen the formation of their beds, of their ropes, their wooden swords and bracelets, with which they cover their wrists in battle, and large canes open at one end, by the sound of which they keep the time and rhythm of their dances. They are close shaven all over, and

15. a Byzantine lexicographer.

remove the hair much more neatly than we do although their razors are only made of wood or stone. They believe the soul to be immortal, and that those who have deserved well of the gods are lodged in that part of the heaven where the sun rises, and those who are damned in the west.

They have some kind of priest and prophet, who very seldom appears among the people, having his dwelling in the mountains. On his arrival there is a great feast and a solemn assembly of several villages (each barn, as I have described it, forms a village, and they are about a French league[16] distant one from the other). This prophet speaks to them in public, exhorting them to virtue and their duty; but their whole ethical science comprises only these two articles: an unfaltering courage in war and affection to their women. This man foretells things to come, and the issue they are to expect from their enterprises; urges them to war, or holds them back; but he does so on the understanding that, where he fails to prophesy correctly, and if things turn out otherwise than he has predicted, he is cut into a thousand pieces if he is caught, and condemned for a false prophet. For that reason he who has once miscalculated is seen no more.

Divination is a gift of God, wherefore to abuse it ought to be regarded as a punishable imposture. Among the Scythians, when the prophets failed to hit the mark, they were laid, shackled hand and foot, on a little cart filled with heather and drawn by oxen, on which they were burned. They who take in hand such matters as depend on the conduct of human capacity are to be excused if they do their best. But those others who come and delude us with assurances of an extraordinary faculty that is beyond our ken, should they not be punished when they fail to carry out what they promise, and for the temerity of their imposture?

They have their wars with the nations beyond their mountains, further back on the mainland, to which they go quite naked, with no other weapons but bows or wooden swords pointed at one end, after the fashion of the tongues of our boar-spears. It is marvellous with what obstinacy they fight their battles, which never end but in massacre and bloodshed: for of routs and terrors they know not even the meaning. Each man brings back as a trophy the head of the enemy he has slain, and fixes it over the entrance to his dwelling. After treating his prisoner well for a considerable time, and giving him all that hospitality can devise, his captor convokes a great gathering of his acquaintance. He ties a cord to one of his prisoner's arms, holding him at some distance for fear of being hurt, and gives the other arm to be held in the same way by his best friend;

16. about 2.49 miles.

and these two, in presence of the whole assembly, dispatch him with their swords. This done, they roast and eat him in common, and send bits of him to their absent friends. Not, as one might suppose, for nourishment, as the ancient Scythians used to do, but to signify an extreme revenge.

And that it is so, may be seen from this: having perceived that the Portuguese, who had allied themselves with their adversaries, inflicted a different kind of death on their prisoners, which was to bury them up to the waist, shoot the upper part of the bodies full of arrows, and afterwards to hang them; they imagined that these people of another world (seeing that they had sown the knowledge of a great many vices among their neighbours, and were much greater masters than themselves in every kind of wickedness) had some reason for adopting this kind of vengeance, and that it must be more painful than their own; wherefore they began to give up their old method, and followed this one.

I am not so much concerned that we should remark on the horrible barbarity of such acts, as that, whilst rightly judging their errors, we should be so blind to our own. I think there is more barbarity in eating a live than a dead man, in tearing on the rack and torturing the body of a man still full of feeling, in roasting him piecemeal and giving him to be bitten and mangled by dogs and swine (as we have not only read, but seen within fresh memory, not between old enemies, but between neighbours and fellow citizens, and, what is worse, under the cloak of piety and religion),[17] than in roasting and eating him after he is dead.

Chrysippus and Zeno, the leaders of the Stoic sect, thought indeed that there was no harm in making use of our carrion for any purpose in case of necessity, and of extracting nourishment from it. And our ancestors,[18] when besieged by Caesar in the city of Alexia, decided to relieve the famine during the siege by eating the bodies of the old men, women, and other persons incapable of fighting;

> Time was, the Gascons, as old tales relate,
> Thus fed, contended long with cruel fate.
> (Juvenal.)[19]

And physicians are not afraid of using it in all sorts of ways as cures, either for inward or outward application. But no man's brain was ever so disordered that he would excuse treachery, disloyalty, cruelty, tyranny, which are our ordinary vices.

---

17. The allusion is to the spectacles of religious warfare which Montaigne himself had witnessed in his time and country.
18. the Gauls.
19. *Satires.* Satire xv, ll. 93 f.

We may therefore well call those people barbarians in respect to the rules of reason, but not in respect to ourselves, who surpass them in every kind of barbarity.

Their warfare is entirely noble and generous, and is as fair and excusable as can be expected in that human disease: their only motive being a zeal for valour. They do not strive to conquer new territory, for they still enjoy that luxuriance of nature which provides them, without labour and pains, with all necessary things in such abundance, that they have no need to enlarge their borders. They are still in that happy state of not desiring more than their natural needs demand: all that is over and above it is for them superfluity.

They generally call each other, if of the same age, brothers; if younger, children; and the old men are fathers to all the others. These latter leave to their heirs in common the full and undivided possession of their property, without any but that pure title that Nature gives to her creatures, by bringing them into the world. If their neighbours cross the mountains to attack them, and gain the victory over them, the acquisition of the victor is the glory and advantage of having proved himself the superior in valour and virtue, for otherwise they have no need for the spoils of the vanquished; and so they return to their own country, where they have no want of any necessaries, nor even of that great portion, which is to know how to enjoy happily their condition, and be content with it. These do the same in their turn. They ask of their prisoners no other ransom but a confession and acknowledgement of being vanquished. But you will not find one in a whole century who would not rather die than yield, either by word or look, one tittle of on invincible greatness of courage; not one who would not rather be killed and eaten than even pray to be spared. They are very liberal in their treatment of their prisoners, in order to make life the more dear to them, and usually entertain them with threats of their impending death, the torments they will suffer, the preparations made to that end, the cutting up of their limbs, and the banquet that will be made at their expense. All this is done with the sole purpose of extorting from them a weak or spiritless word, or to give them a desire to escape, in order to gain the advantage of having terrified them and shaken their firmness. For indeed, if rightly taken, therein alone lies the real victory:

> The victor's wreath no triumphs more attest
> Than when the foe's subjection is confest.
>
> (Claudian.) [20]

20. *Of the Sixth Consulate of Honorius*, ll. 248 f.

The Hungarians, very bellicose fighters, did not formerly pursue their advantage further than making their enemy cry for mercy. For, after forcing from them that confession, they let them go without hurt or ransom, except, at the most, making them pledge their word not again to take up arms against them.

We often enough gain an advantage over our enemy which is a borrowed advantage, and to which we have no real claim. To have more muscular arms and legs is the quality of a porter, not a sign of valour; skill is a dead and corporal quality: it is a stroke of fortune that causes our adversary to stumble or to be dazzled by the glare of the sun; it is a trick of art and science that makes an able fencer, who may easily be a coward and an insignificant fellow.

A man's value and estimation consists in heart and will: there lies his true honour. Valour is strength, not of legs and arms, but of heart and soul; it lies not in the goodness of our horse, or our weapons, but in our own. He who falls fighting with obstinate courage, *if his legs fail him, he fights on his knees* (Seneca).[21] He who, in spite of being in danger of imminent death, abates nothing of his assurance, who, in yielding up his soul, still fixes on his enemy a firm and scornful glance, is vanquished, not by us, but by Fortune: he is slain but not conquered.

The most valiant are sometimes the most unfortunate. Hence there are triumphant defeats that vie in glory with victories. Neither did those four sister victories, the most glorious that the sun has ever beheld with its eyes, of Salamis, Plataea, Mycale, and Sicily,[22] ever dare to oppose their combined glories to the glory of the discomfiture of King Leonidas and his comrades at the pass of Thermopylae.[23]

What man ever hastened with a more glorious and ambitious desire to the winning, than Captain Ischolas did to the losing, of a battle? What man ever used more care and ingenuity to secure his own safety than he did to ensure his destruction? He was charged to defend a certain pass in the Peloponnesus against the Arcadians. But knowing that he was wholly unable to do so, on account of the nature of the place and the inequality of the forces, and being sure that every man who confronted the enemy must needs remain on the spot; on the other hand, deeming it unworthy both of his own virtue and magnanimity, and of the name of a Spartan, to fail in his charge, he adopted a middle course between these two extremes, which was in this manner: the youngest

---

21. *Of Providence*, Book II.
22. Montaigne here refers to the famous Greek victories against the Persians and (at Himera, Sicily) against the Carthaginians in or about 480 B.C.

23. The Spartan king Leonidas' defense of the pass at Thermopylae also took place in 480 B.C., during the war against the Persians.

and most active of his band he reserved for the service and defence of their country, and sent them home; and with those whose loss would be of less account he decided to hold the pass, and with their death make the enemy purchase their entry as dear as possible. And so it fell out: for, being presently surrounded on every side by the Arcadians, after a great butchery of them he and his comrades were all put to the sword. Was ever a trophy raised to a victor that was not rather due to these vanquished men? The part that true victory plays is the struggle, not the coming off safe; and the honour of virtue consists in combating, not in beating.

To return to our narrative. Far from giving in, in spite of all they suffer, these prisoners, on the contrary, during the two or three months that they are held in captivity, bear a cheerful countenance; they urge their captors to hasten to put them to the proof, defy them, insult them, reproach them with their cowardice and the number of battles lost against their own countrymen.

I have a song composed by a prisoner, which contains this outburst: 'Come boldly, every one of you, and assemble together to dine off me, for you shall at the same time eat your fathers and grandfathers, whose flesh has served to feed and nourish this body. These muscles, this flesh and these veins are yours, poor fools that you are! can you not see that they still contain the substance of your ancestors' limbs? Relish them well, you will find that they have the flavour of your own flesh.' A fiction that by no means savours of barbarity. On the pictures which represent these prisoners being executed or at the point of death, they are seen spitting in the face of their slayers or making mouths at them. Indeed they never cease to challenge and defy them by word and look until the breath is out of their body. Verily here we see men who are indeed savages if we compare them with ourselves: for either they must be so in good sooth, or we; there is a wonderful distance between their character and ours.

The men there have several wives, and the higher their reputation for valour the greater is the number of their wives. It is a remarkably beautiful feature in their marriages, that the same jealousy that our wives have to keep us from the love and favors of other women, they have to an equal degree to procure it. Being more solicitous for their husbands' honour than for anything else, they use their best endeavours to have as many companions as they can, seeing that that is a proof of their husbands' worth.

Ours will cry 'miracle', but it is not so. It is after all a proper matrimonial virtue, but of the highest order. And in the Bible, Leah, Rachel, Sarah and Jacob's wives accommodated their husbands with their fair handmaids; and Livia gratified Augustus' appetites to her own detriment; and Stratonice, the wife of King Deiotarus,[24] not only lent her husband the use of a very beautiful young chambermaid in her service, but carefully brought up her children, and gave them a shoulder in succeeding to their father's estates.

And, that it may not be supposed that all this is done through a simple and slavish obligation to follow usage, and under the weight of authority of their ancient customs, without reasoning or judgement, and because their minds are too dull to imagine any other, I must give a few proofs of their intellectual capacity. Besides the warlike song I have just cited I have another, of an amorous nature, which begins thus: 'Adder, stay; stay, adder, that thy colours may serve as a pattern for my sister to work a rich girdle to give to my love: thus shall thy beauty and disposition of thy spots be preferred for all time to all other serpents.' This first verse is the burden of the song. Now, I have enough knowledge of poetry to judge this much: that not only is there nothing barbarous in this idea, but that it is altogether Anacreontic.[25] Their language, by the way, is a soft language, with an agreeable tone, and their terminations resemble the Greek.

Three men of this nation, not knowing how dear, in tranquillity and happiness, it will one day cost them to know the corruptions of this side of the world, and that this intercourse will be the cause of their ruin, which indeed I imagine is already advanced (poor wretches, to be allured by the desire to see new things and to leave their own serene sky to come and see ours!), were at Rouen at a time when the late King Charles the Ninth was there. The King had a long talk with them. They were shown our ways, our pomp, the form of a fine city. After that somebody asked their opinion, desiring to know what they most wondered at. They mentioned three things, the third of which I am sorry to have forgotten, but I still remember two. They said that in the first place they thought it very strange that so many big men with beards, strong and armed, who were about the King (they were probably thinking of the Swiss who formed his guard) should submit to obey a child, and that they did not rather choose one of their own number to command them. Secondly (they have a way of speaking of men as if they were halves of one another), that they had observed that there were men amongst us, full and gorged with all kinds of good things, and that their halves were begging at their doors, emaciated with hunger and poverty; and they thought it strange how these necessitous

---

24. tetrarch of Galatia, in Asia Minor.

25. worthy of Anacreon (572?–488? B.C.) major Greek writer of amatory lyrics.

halves could suffer such injustice, and that they did not seize the others by the throat, or set fire to their houses.

I had a long talk with one of them; but I had an interpreter who followed my meaning so badly, and was at such a loss, in his stupidity, to take in my ideas, that I could get little satisfaction out of him. When I asked the native, 'What he gained from his superior position among his people?' (for he was a captain, and our sailors called him a king), he said it was 'to march foremost in war'. How many men did he lead? He pointed to a piece of ground, to signify as many as that space could hold: it might be four or five thousand men. Did all his authority lapse with the war? He said 'that this remained, that, when he visited the villages that were dependent on him, they made paths through their thickets, by which he might pass at his ease.' All this does not sound too ill; but hold! they don't wear trousers.

### Of the Inconsistency of Our Actions*

They who make a practice of comparing human actions are never so perplexed as when they try to piece them together and place them in the same light, for they commonly contradict one another so strangely that it seems impossible they should have come out of the same shop. Marius the younger[26] is now a son of Mars, now a son of Venus.[27] Some one said that Pope Boniface the Eighth entered upon his charge like a fox, behaved therein like a lion, and died like a dog. And who could believe that it was Nero, the very image of cruelty, who, when the sentence of a condemned criminal was brought to him to be signed in the usual way, exclaimed, 'Would to God that I had never learned to write!' So grieved was he in his heart to doom a man to death!

The world is full of such examples, nay, any man may provide such an abundance of them out of his own experience, that I sometimes wonder to see intelligent men at pains to sort the pieces, seeing that irresolution is, in my view, the most common and conspicuous defect of our nature: witness that famous line of Publilius the writer of low comedies,

> Poor is the plan that never can be changed.
> (Publilius Syrus.)[28]

---

\* *Essays*, Book II, Chapter 1.  
26. nephew of the older and better known Marius. Montaigne's source is Plutarch's *Life of Marius*.  
27. *Mars . . . Venus:* war and love  
28. *Apothegms* (*Sententiae*), l. 362.

It seems reasonable to judge a man by the most ordinary acts of his life, but in view of the natural instability of our habits and opinions, I have often thought that even good authors are wrong in obstinately attributing to us a steadfast and consistent character. They hit upon a general feature in a man and arrange and interpret all his actions in accordance with this fanciful conception; and if they are unable to twist them sufficiently, set them down to dissimulation. Augustus has escaped them, for we see in this man, throughout the course of his life, so manifest, abrupt, and continual a variety of actions, that he has slipped through the fingers of even the most daring critics, and been left undecided. I find nothing more difficult to believe than man's consistency, and nothing more easy than his inconsistency. If we examine him in detail and judge of his actions separately, bit by bit, we shall most often find this true.

Throughout ancient history it would be difficult to choose a dozen men who have steered their lives in one certain and constant course, which is the principal aim of wisdom. For, to comprise it all in one word, as an ancient writer[29] says, and to embrace all the rules of life in one, is 'to wish and not to wish always the same thing. I will not vouchsafe to add, he says, provided the wish be right; for if it be not right, it is impossible it should be always the same'. I once learned indeed that vice is no more than want of rule and moderation, and that it is consequently impossible to associate it with consistency. It is a saying attributed to Demosthenes, 'that the beginning of all virtue is consultation and deliberation; and the end and perfection, constancy'. If reason directed our course we should choose the fairest; but no one has thought of that:

He scorns that which he sought, seeks what he scorned of late;
He flows and ebbs, his whole life contradiction. (Horace.)[30]

Our ordinary practice is to follow the inclinations of our appetite, to right, to left, up hill, down dale, as we are borne along by the wind of opportunity. We do not consider what we wish except at the moment of wishing it, and we change like that animal which takes its colour from what it is laid upon. What we have but now determined we presently alter, and soon again we retrace our steps: it is nothing but wavering and uncertainty;

We are led as a puppet is moved by the strings.
(Horace.)[31]

29. Seneca, in *Epistles*, Epistle xx.     31. *Satires*, Book II, Satire vii, l.
30. *Epistles*, Book I, Epistle i, ll.    82.
98 f.

We do not go, we are carried along, like things floating, now smoothly, now perturbedly, according as the water is angry or calm;

> We see them, knowing not
> What 'tis they want, and seeking ever and ever
> A change of place, as if to drop the burden.
> (Lucretius.) [32]

Every day a new fancy; and our humours move with the changes of weather:

> So change the minds of men, like days
> That Father Jove sends down to earth,
> To alternate 'twixt wet and fine.   (Homer.) [33]

We waver between different minds; we wish nothing freely, nothing absolutely, nothing constantly. Should any man prescribe and establish definite laws and a definite policy in his own head, he would present throughout his life a shining example of even habits, an order and an unfailing relation of one action to another.

(Empedocles remarked in the inhabitants of Agrigentum this discrepancy, that they abandoned themselves to their pleasures as if they were to die on the morrow, and that they built as if they were never to die.) [34]

The reason will be easily found, as we see in the case of the younger Cato;[35] he who touches one note of the keyboard touches all: there is a harmony of sounds, all in perfect tune with each other, which is not to be mistaken. With us, on the other hand, the rule is: so many actions, so many particular judgements to be passed. The surest, in my opinion, would be to refer them to the nearest circumstances, without seeking any farther, and without drawing from them any other inferences.

It was told me, during the tumultuous times[36] our poor State had to go through, that a young woman who lived quite near to where I then was, had thrown herself from a high window to avoid the forcible caresses of a poor knave of a soldier who was quartered in her house; the fall did not kill her, and, repeating the attempt on her life, she would have cut her throat with a knife, but was prevented; not however without inflicting a serious wound. She herself then confessed that the soldier had done no more than importune her with gifts, entreaties, and solicitations, but that she feared he would in the end proceed to violence. And all this, her words, her

32. *On the Nature of Things*, Book III, ll. 1057 ff.
33. *Odyssey*, Book XVIII, l. 135.
34. from the life of the fifth-century Greek philosopher Empedocles, by Diogenes Laertius.

35. the philosopher, Cato "Uticensis" (first century B.C.); to Montaigne, and also traditionally, he is an epitome of moral and intellectual integrity.
36. See footnote 17 and the corresponding passage in the text of "Of Cannibals."

mien, and the blood which testified to her virtue, in the true manner of a second Lucretia![37]

Now I have heard, as a fact, that, both before and after, she was a wench not very difficult to come by. As the tale[38] has it, 'Be as handsome and as fine a gentleman as you will, when you have failed in your pursuit, do not immediately conclude an inviolable chastity in your mistress; it does not follow that the muleteer will not find his opportunity.'

Antigonus,[39] having taken a liking to one of his soldiers, on account of his virtue and valour, ordered his physicians to attend him for a persistent internal malady which had long tormented him, and perceiving that after his cure he went much more coldly to work than before, asked him what it was that had so altered and cowed him. 'You yourself, Sire, he replied, by delivering me from the ill which made me indifferent to life.' A soldier of Lucullus,[40] having been plundered by enemies, devised a bold stroke for his revenge; when he had retrieved his loss with interest, Lucullus, whose good opinion he had gained, tried to induce him, with the best persuasions he could think of, to undertake some risky business;

> With words that might have stirred a coward's heart.
>
> (Horace.)[41]

'Employ, he replied, some wretched soldier who has been plundered;'

> Though but a rustic clown, he'll go
> Who's lost his money-belt,' he said;    (Horace.)[42]

and resolutely refused to go.

When we read that Mahomet having furiously rated Chasan, chief of his Janissaries, for allowing his line of troops to be broken by the Hungarians, and bearing himself like a coward in the battle; and that Chasan made no reply but, alone and just as he was with his weapon in his hand, rushed furiously into the first body of enemies that he met with, and was immediately overwhelmed; it was not so much a justification of his conduct as a change of mood, not so much natural prowess as a new spite.

Do not think it strange that the man who was so venturesome yesterday should prove such a poltroon on the morrow; either anger, or necessity, or company, or wine, or the sound of the trumpet had put his heart into his belly; it was not a courage thus formed by

37. the legendary, virtuous Roman who stabbed herself after being raped by King Tarquinius' son.
38. a common folk tale.
39. Macedonian king.
40. Roman general of the first century B.C.
41. *Epistles*, Book II, Epistle ii, l. 36.
42. *Epistles*, Book II, Epistle ii, ll. 39 f.

reason, but a courage stiffened by those circumstances; it was no marvel if other contrary circumstances made a new man of him.

These so supple changes and contradictions which we manifest have made some to imagine that we have two souls, others, that we have two powers which, each in its own way, accompany and stir us, the one to good, the other to evil, since so abrupt a diversity is not to be reconciled with a single subject.

Not only does the wind of accidents stir me according to its blowing, but I am also stirred and troubled by the instability of my attitude; and he who examines himself closely will seldom find himself twice in the same state. I give to my soul now one face, now another, according to the side to which I turn it. If I speak differently of myself, it is because I regard myself differently. All the contradictions are to be found in me, according as the wind turns and changes. Bashful, insolent; chaste, lascivious; talkative, taciturn; clumsy, gentle; witty, dull; peevish, sweet-tempered; mendacious, truthful; knowing, ignorant; and liberal and avaricious and prodigal: all this I see in myself in some degree, according as I veer about; and whoever will study himself very attentively will find in himself, yea, in his judgement, this discordance and unsteadiness. I can say nothing of myself absolutely, simply, and steadily, without confusion and mixture, nor in one word. *Distinguo*[43] is the most universal member of my logic.

Though I am ever inclined to speak well of what is good, and rather to interpret favourably the things that are capable of such interpretation, yet such is the strangeness of our nature that we are often driven to do good, even by vice; if it were not that well-doing is judged by the intention alone.

Therefore a courageous deed ought not to imply a valiant man: the man who is really brave will be always so, and on all occasions. If valour were a habit, and not a sudden eruption, it would make a man equally resolute for all emergencies, the same alone as in company, the same in single combat as in a battle; for let them say what they will, there is not one valour for the pavement and another for the field. As bravely would he bear sickness in his bed as a wound in camp, nor would he fear death in his own home any more than in an assault. We should not see the same man charge with brave assurance into the breach, and afterwards worrying like a woman, over the loss of a law-suit or a son. When, though afraid of infamy, he bears up against poverty; when, though wincing at a surgeon's lancet, he stiffly faces the enemy's sword, the action is praiseworthy, but not the man.

Many Greeks, says Cicero, cannot look upon an enemy, and are brave in sickness. The Cimbrians and the Celtiberians, quite the

---

43. I distinguish; I separate into its components.

contrary: *For nothing can be consistent that has not reason for its foundation* (Cicero).[44]

No valour could be more extreme in its kind than Alexander's; but it is of one kind only, and is not complete enough, nor universal on all occasions. Incomparable though it be, it has its blemishes. So it is that we see him so desperately disturbed by the slightest suspicions that his subjects may be plotting against his life, and carried away in his investigations to such violent and indiscriminate acts of injustice, and haunted by a fear that upsets his natural good sense. The superstition too with which he was so strongly tainted bears some likeness to pusillanimity. And the excess of his penitence for the murder of Clytus[45] is also evidence of uneven temper.

Our actions are but a patchwork (*they despise pleasure, but are cowardly in pain; they are indifferent to fame, but infamy breaks their spirit*[46]), and we try to gain honour by false pretences. Virtue will not be wooed but for her own sake, and if we sometimes borrow her mask for some other purpose, she will very soon snatch it from our face. When the soul is once steeped in it, the dye is strong and vivid, and will not go without taking the skin with it. Wherefore, to judge a man, we must long and carefully follow his traces. If constancy does not stand firm and wholly on its own foundation, *if the path of life has not been well considered and preconcerted* (Cicero);[47] if changing circumstances make him alter his pace (I should say his route, for the pace may be accelerated or retarded by them), let him go: that man will go A *vau le vent* (down the wind), as the motto of our Talebot[48] has it.

It is no wonder, says an ancient writer,[49] that chance has so great a hold over us, since we live by chance. Unless a man has directed his life as a whole to a certain fixed goal, he cannot possibly dispose his particular actions. Unless he have an image of the whole in his mind, he cannot possibly arrange the pieces. How can a painter lay in a stock of colours, if he knows not what he is going to paint? No man draws a definite outline of his life, and we only think it out in details. The archer must first know at what he is aiming, and then accommodate his hand, his bow, the string, the arrow, and his movements, accordingly. Our plans go wrong because they have neither aim nor direction. No wind serves the ship that has no port of destination.

I cannot agree with those judges who, on the strength of seeing one of his tragedies, declared in favour of Sophocles, when accused

44. *Tusculan Disputations*, Book II, Chapter 27.

45. Clytus, a commander in Alexander's army, was killed by him during an argument, an act which Alexander immediately and bitterly regretted, as related by Plutarch in his *Life of Alexander*, Chapters 50–52.

46. Cicero, *Of Duties* (*De officiis*), Book I, Chapter 21.

47. *Paradoxes* (*Paradoxa*), Paradox v.

48. Talbot, an English captain who fought in France and died there in 1453.

49. Seneca, in *Epistles*, Epistle lxxi.

by his son of being incapable of managing his domestic affairs. Nor do I hold with the conclusions arrived at by the Parians who were sent to reform the Milesians. Visiting the island, they remarked the best-cultivated lands and the best-kept country-houses, and made a note of their owners; and then, having called an assembly of the citizens in the town, they appointed these owners the new governors and magistrates, concluding that, being careful of their private affairs, they would be equally careful of those of the public.

We are all made up of bits, and so shapelessly and diversely put together, that every piece, at every moment, plays its own game. And there is as much difference between us and ourselves, as between us and others. *Be sure that it is very difficult to be always the same man* (Seneca).[50] Since ambition can teach a man valour, temperance, and liberality, yea and justice too; since greed can implant in the heart of a shop-apprentice, bred up in obscurity and neglect, the confidence to entrust himself, so far from the domestic hearth, to the mercy of the waves and angry Neptune in a frail bark; since it teaches also discretion and prudence; and since Venus herself can put resolution and temerity into the boy who is still under the discipline of the rod, and embolden the heart of the tender virgin in her mother's arms,

> With Love for guide,
> Alone the maid steps o'er her prostrate guards,
> And steals by night into the young man's arms;
> (Tibullus.)[51]

it is not enough for a sober understanding to judge us simply by our external actions: we must sound the innermost recesses, and observe the springs which give the swing. But since it is a high and hazardous undertaking, I would rather that fewer people meddled with it.

## Apology for Raimond Sebond*

### [MAN'S PRESUMPTION AND LITTLENESS]

What does Truth[52] preach to us, when she preaches to us to fly worldly philosophy,[53] when she so often impresses upon us, That our wisdom is but folly in the sight of God;[54] That of all vain things the most vain is man; That man, who presumes on his learning, does not yet know what it is to know;[55] and That if man, who is nothing, thinks himself something, he deceives and beguiles him-

---

50. *Epistles*, Epistle cxx.
51. *Elegies*, Book II, Elegy i, ll. 75 ff.
* *Essays*, Book II, Chapter 12. A small but significant section of the very

long "Apology" is reprinted here.
52. revealed truth, the Scriptures.
53. Colossians 2:8.
54. I Corinthians 3:19.
55. I Corinthians 8:2.

self?[56] These sayings of the Holy Spirit so clearly and vividly express what I wish to maintain, that I should need no other proof against men who would bow with all submission and obedience to its authority. But the others[57] would rather be whipped to their own cost, and will not suffer their reason to be combated except by itself.

Let us then for the nonce consider man alone, without outside assistance, armed only with his own weapons, and destitute of the divine grace and knowledge, which comprise all his honour, his strength and the foundation of his being. Let us see how he will hold out in this fine equipment. Let him explain to me, by the force of his reason, on what foundation he has built those great advantages he thinks he has over the other creatures. What has induced him to believe that that wonderful motion of the heavenly vault, the eternal light of those torches rolling so proudly over his head, the awe-inspiring agitations of that infinite sea, were established, and endure through so many centuries for his service and convenience?

Is it possible to imagine anything more ridiculous than that this miserable and puny creature, who is not so much as master of himself, exposed to shocks on all sides should call himself Master and Emperor of the universe, of which it is not in his power to know the smallest part, much less to command it? And that privilege which he assumes of being the only creature in this great edifice that has the capacity to know the beauty and the several parts of it, the only one who is able to give thanks to the architect, and to keep an account of the receipts and outlay of the world: who has sealed him this privilege? Let him show us his letters-patent for this great and noble charge.

Have they been granted in favour of the wise only? Then few people would be concerned. Are the fools and the wicked deserving of so extraordinary a favour, and, being the worst lot in the world, of being preferred to all the rest?

Shall we believe the man who says this, *For whose sake shall we then say that the world has been made? Undoubtedly for those creatures that have the use of reason: these are gods and men, to whom assuredly nothing is superior?* (Balbus the Stoic, according to Cicero).[58] We could never sufficiently deride the impudence of this coupling of gods and men.

But, poor devil, what is there in him deserving of such a privilege? When we consider the incorruptible life of the heavenly

---

56. Galatians 6:3. This and the previous passages from St. Paul were among those inscribed on the walls of Montaigne's library.

57. those who pretend to arrive at certainty through their human means, their reason, alone.

58. quoted in Cicero's *Of the Nature of the Gods,* Book II, Chapter 53.

bodies, their beauty, their grandeur, their continual motion by so
exact a rule:

> When we gaze aloft
> Upon the skiey vaults of yon great world
> The ether, fixt high over twinkling stars,
> And into our thought there come the journeyings
> Of sun and moon;   (Lucretius.)[59]

when we consider the dominion and power those bodies have, not
only over our lives and the conditions of our fortune,

> Our lives and actions on the stars depend,
> (Manilius.)[60]

but even over our dispositions, our judgement, our will, which they
govern, impel and stir at the mercy of their influence, as our reason
discovers and tells us:

> This we learn: the far, far distant stars
> Govern by silent laws; the world is ruled
> By periodic causes, and the turns of destiny
> Observed by certain signs;   (Manilius.)[61]

when we see that not only a man, not only a king, but kingdoms,
empires, and all this world here below are moved according to the
lightest swing of the heavenly motions:

> How great a change each little motion brings!
> So great this kingdom that it governs kings;
> (Manilius.)[62]

if our virtue, our vices, our talents and our knowledge, if even this
dissertation of mine on the power of the stars, this comparison between them and ourselves, comes, as our reason supposes, by their
means and their favour;

> Maddened by love, Leander swims the strait,
> A Grecian king o'erturns the walls of Troy.
> 'Tis this man's lot to give his country laws.
> Sons kill their fathers, fathers kill their sons,
> And brothers arm themselves in mutual strife.
> Not we have made these wars; 'tis Fate compels
> To bear such pains with lacerated limbs.
> And Fate it is that makes me ponder Fate;   (Manilius.)[63]

---

59. *On the Nature of Things*, Book
V, ll. 1204 ff.
60. *Astronomicon*, Book III, l. 58.
61. *Astronomicon*, Book I, ll. 60 ff.

62. *Astronomicon*, Book I, l. 57, and
Book IV, l. 93.
63. *Astronomicon*, Book IV, ll. 79
ff., and l. 118.

if this little portion of reason we possess has been allotted to us by heaven, how can reason make us the equal of heaven? How can it subject its essence and conditions to our knowledge? All that we see in those bodies fills us with amazement. *What apparatus, what instruments, what levers, what engines, what craftsmen were employed about so mighty a work?* (Cicero).[64]

Why do we deny them a soul, and life and reason? Have we discovered in them any stubborn, senseless stupidity, we who have no concern with them but to obey them? Shall we say that we have seen no other creature but man in possession of a reasoning mind? Why! have we seen anything comparable to the sun? Does it exist the less for our not having seen its like? Does it move the less because no other movement is to be compared with it? If what we have not seen does not exist, our knowledge is marvellously shortsighted: *How close the confines of our mind!* (Cicero).[65]

Is it not a delusion of human vanity to make the moon a celestial earth, and to imagine that there are mountains and valleys upon it, as did Anaxagoras;[66] to set up human habitations and dwellings and establish colonies upon it for our convenience, as do Plato and Plutarch,[67] and to make our earth a bright and shining star? *Amongst other infirmities of human nature is that mental blindness which not only forces man to err, but makes him hug his errors* (Seneca).[68] *The corruptible body weighs down the soul, and this earthly habitation prevents it from pondering on many things* (The Book of Wisdom, quoted by Saint Augustine).[69]

Presumption is our natural and original infirmity. The frailest and most vulnerable of all creatures is man, and at the same time the most arrogant.[70] He sees and feels himself lodged here in the mud and filth of the world, nailed and riveted to the worst, the deadest and most stagnant part of the universe, at the lowest story of the house and the most remote from the vault of heaven, with the animals of the worst condition of the three; and he goes and sets himself in imagination above the circle of the moon, and brings heaven under his feet.

With this same vanity of imagination he makes himself the equal of God, assumes to himself divine qualities, selects and separates himself from among the multitude of other creatures, carves out their shares to each of his fellows and comrades, the animals, and

---

64. *Of the Nature of the Gods*, Book I, Chapter 8.

65. *Of the Nature of the Gods*, Book I, Chapter 31.

66. according to Diogenes Laertius, *Life of Anaxagoras*, Book II. Chapter 8.

67. For the notion that the moon is inhabited, Montaigne refers to Plutarch's *Of the Face of the Moon.*

68. *Of Wrath*, Book II, Chapter 9.

69. *City of God*, Book XII, Section 15.

70. The phrase, originally Pliny's, is another of those engraved on the walls of Montaigne's library.

allots to them their portion of faculties and powers according as it seems good to him. How can he know, by the force of his understanding, the secret and internal motions of the animals? By what comparison between them and himself does he suppose them to be as stupid as he thinks?

When I play with my cat, who knows but that she regards me more as a plaything than I do her? [We amuse each other with our respective monkey-tricks; if I have my moments for beginning and refusing, so she has hers.]

Plato,[71] in his picture of the golden age under Saturn, numbers, among the chief advantages of the man of that time, his communion with the beasts, of whom inquiring and learning he knew the real attributes and differences of each of them; whereby he acquired a very perfect understanding and wisdom, and in consequence passed his life very much more happily than we are able to do. Do we need a better proof of the impudence of man where the beasts are concerned? That great author[72] opined that, in giving them their bodily shape, Nature for the most part only considered the use they could be put to in the prognostications which were drawn from them in his time.

That defect which hinders communication between us and them, why may it not as well be in ourselves as in them? It is a matter of conjecture with whom the fault lies that we do not understand one another; for we understand them no more than they do us. By the same reasoning they may regard us as beasts, as we do them.

It is no great wonder if we do not understand them for neither do we understand the Basques[73] and the Troglodytes.[74] Yet some have boasted of understanding them, as Apollonius of Tyana, Melampus, Tiresias, Thales, and others.[75] And since it is the case that, as the cosmographers tell, there are nations that receive a dog for their king, they must needs in some way interpret its voice and actions.

We must observe the parity there is between us. We have some halfway understanding of their meaning, as the animals have of ours, in about the same degree. They cajole us, they threaten us, they entreat us, as we do them. Moreover, it is very evident to us that they are able fully and completely to communicate with one another, that they understand one another, and not only those of the same species, but also those of different species.

71. in his *Statesman*.
72. Plato, in the *Timaeus*.
73. inhabitants of the Pyrenees region on the Bay of Biscay, known for the difficulty and peculiarity of their language.
74. cavedwellers.
75. A mixture of mythical and historical figures: Apollonius of Tyana, Greek neo-Pythagorean philosopher and magician (first century A.D.); Melampus, mythical physician and sage; Tiresias, mythical blind prophet of Thebes; Thales, regarded as the first Greek philosopher (sixth century B.C.), one of the Seven Sages of Greece.

> Since even the speechless herds, aye, since
> The very generations of wild beasts
> Are wont dissimilar and diverse sounds
> To rouse from in them, when there's fear or pain,
> And when they burst with joys. (Lucretius.)[76]

A horse knows that a dog is angry when it barks in a certain way, but is not afraid when it gives voice in another way. Even in those creatures that have no voice we may easily infer, from the mutual services we see them rendering each other, that they have some other means of communication; their movements speak and negotiate:

> In much the same way as the lack-speech years
> Compel young children into gesturings. (Lucretius.)[77]

Why not? just as well as our deaf-mutes dispute, argue and tell stories by means of signs? I have seen some so skilful and practised in that language, that in truth they did not fall short of perfection in making themselves understood. Lovers use their eyes to express anger, reconciliation, entreaty, thanks, to make appointments, in short for every purpose;

> Silence too our thought and wish betrays.
> (Tasso.)[78]

What of the hands? We beg, we promise, we call, we send away, threaten, pray, entreat, deny, refuse, question, wonder, count, confess, repent, we express fear and shame, we doubt, inform, command, incite, encourage, swear, testify, accuse, condemn, absolve, insult, despise, challenge, we show vexation, we flatter, applaud, bless, humiliate, mock, reconcile, recommend, exalt, welcome, rejoice, complain, we express grief, dejection, despair, astonishment, protestation, silence, and what not, in such varied and numerous ways, in rivalry with the tongue.

With the head we invite, we dismiss, admit, disclaim, give the lie, welcome, honour, reverence, disdain, demand, show the door, we cheer, lament, caress, chide, submit, defy, exhort, threaten, assure, and inquire. What of the eye-brows? What of the shoulders? There is no movement that does not speak an intelligible, untaught language, that is understood by all. Which shows that, seeing the variety that distinguishes the spoken languages in use, this one must rather be considered the proper and natural speech of humankind. I pass over that which a particular necessity teaches one who is

---

76. *On the Nature of Things*, Book V, ll. 1058 ff.
77. *On the Nature of Things*, Book V, ll. 1029 f.
78. Torquato Tasso, in the pastoral drama *Aminta*, Act II, Scene 3, ll. 35–36.

taken unawares; and the finger-alphabet; and grammar and the sciences which are only practised and expressed by gestures; and the nations that Pliny tells of, who have no other language.

An ambassador of the city of Abdera, after speaking at great length to King Agis of Sparta, said to him, 'Well, Sire, what answer do you wish me to carry back to our citizens?' 'That I allowed you to say all that you would and as much as you would, without ever a word.'[79] Was not that a very speaking and intelligible silence?

After all, which of our arts do we not see in the activities of animals? Is there any organization regulated with more order, with a better distribution of charges and functions, and more consistently maintained, than that of the bees? Can we imagine that so well-ordered a disposition of activities and occupations could be carried on without reason and foresight?

> Following signs and instances like these,
> Some testify that bees possess a share
> Of the world-spirit and the mind divine.   (Virgil.)[80]

Do the swallows that we see at the return of spring, ferreting out all the corners of the houses, conduct their search without judgement? Do they choose without discrimination, out of a thousand places, that which is most commodious for their lodging? Are the birds, when they weave those beautiful and wonderful habitations of theirs, able to use a square figure rather than a round, an obtuse rather than a right angle, without knowing their properties and effects? Do they fetch, now water, now clay, without having concluded that hardness is softened by moisture? Do they line the floors of their palaces with moss or down unless they have foreseen that the tender limbs of their young will lie more softly and comfortably? Do they shelter themselves from the rainy wind and build their cabins to the east, without knowing the different properties of the winds, and without considering that one is more healthy for them than the other?

Why does the spider thicken her web in one place and slacken it in another? Why does she use now one kind of knot, now another, unless she possesses thought, deliberation and the power of inference?

We may see well enough, in most of their works, how much the animals surpass us, and how much we fall short in the art of imitating them. And yet, in our ruder performances, we are sensible of what faculties we employ, and we know that our mind applies to them its utmost powers; why do we not conclude the same of the

---

79. The story is told by Plutarch in
*Apothegms of the Lacedaemonians.*

80. *Georgics*, Book IV, ll. 219 ff.

animals? Why do we ascribe to I know not what slavish instinct of nature those works that excel anything we can do by nature or art? Herein we unconsciously give them a very great advantage over ourselves, in making Nature, with a maternal kindness, to accompany and lead them as it were by the hand, to all the activities and conveniences of their life; whilst us she abandons to chance and fortune, and forces us to seek by art the things necessary for our preservation, at the same time denying us the means of attaining, by any education or mental effort, to the natural skill of the animals. So that their brutish stupidity surpasses in all their contrivances everything we are able to do with our divine intelligence.

Truly, by this reckoning, we might with great reason call her a very unjust stepmother; but that is not so. Our organization is not so formless and unregulated. Nature has been universally kind to all her creatures, and there is none that she has not very amply furnished with all the means necessary for the preservation of its being. For those common complaints that I hear men uttering (as the licence of their opinions now lifts them up above the clouds, now brings them down to the antipodes), that we are the only outcast animal, bare on the bare earth, bound and tied down, with no means of arming or covering ourselves but with others' spoils; whereas all the other creatures have been clothed by Nature with shells, husks, bark, hair, wool, spikes, leather, down, feathers, scales, fleece, bristles, according to the need of their being; armed with claws, teeth, horns for attack and defence, and has herself instructed them in what is requisite to each, to swim, run, fly, sing, whilst man cannot even walk or speak, nor eat, nor do anything but weep, without an apprenticeship:

> Then again the babe,
> Like to the castaway of the raging surf,
> Lies naked on the ground, speechless, in want
> Of every help for life, when Nature first
> Hath poured him forth upon the shores of light
> With birth-pangs from within the mother's womb,
> And with a plaintive wail he fills the place,—
> As well befitting one for whom remains
> In life a journey through so many ills.
> But all the flocks and herds and all wild beasts
> Come forth and grow, nor need the little rattles,
> Nor must be treated to the humouring nurse's
> Dear broken chatter; nor seek they divers clothes
> To suit the changing skies; nor need, in fine,
> Nor arms, nor lofty ramparts, wherewithal

Their own to guard—because the earth herself
And Nature, artificer of the world, bring forth
Aboundingly all things for all. (Lucretius.) [81]

These complaints are unfounded; there is in the governance of the world a much greater equality and a more uniform relationship. Our skin is provided as abundantly as theirs with power to resist the inclemency of the weather. Witness the many nations that have not yet tried the use of clothes. Our ancient Gauls wore hardly any clothes, like our neighbours the Irish of the present day, in spite of their cold climate.

But we may judge better by ourselves: for all those parts of our person which we are pleased to expose to the wind and air are adapted to endure it, the feet, the face, the hands, the legs, the shoulders, the head, according to the demands of usage. For if there is in us a tender spot, in which we should seem to fear the cold, it should be the stomach, where digestion takes place; our fathers used to leave it uncovered, and our ladies, soft and delicate as they are, sometimes go half-covered down to the navel.

Nor are the bindings and swaddlings of infants any more necessary. The Lacedemonian mothers reared their children in all freedom to move their limbs, without any wrappings or fastenings.

Our weeping we have in common with most of the other animals; there are hardly any that do not wail and whine long after their birth, seeing that it is a natural effect of their helplessness at that age. As to the habit of eating, it is natural to us as well as to them, and comes without instruction:

For each creature feels
By instinct to what use to put its powers.
(Lucretius.) [82]

Who doubts but that a child, having acquired the strength to feed himself, is able to seek his food? And the earth yields and offers him enough for his needs, without any cultivation and artifice; and if not at all times, no more does she do it for the animals. Witness the provision we see made by the ants and other creatures, in view of the barren season of the year. Those nations we have lately discovered, so abundantly provided with meat and a natural drink, without care or trouble on their part, have now made us realize that bread is not our only sustenance, and that, without any tilling, our Mother Nature has plentifully provided us with all that we need. Nay, as seems very probable, more amply and richly than she does now that we have taken to meddling with it by our contrivances:

81. *On the Nature of Things*, Book V. ll. 222 ff.     82. *On the Nature of Things*, Book V. ll. 1033 f.

> She first, the Earth, of own accord
> The shining grains and vineyards of all joy
> Created for mortality; herself
> Gave the sweet fruitage and the pastures glad,
> Which now to-day yet scarcely wax in size,
> Even when, aided by our toiling arms,
> We break the ox, and wear away the strength
> Of sturdy farm-hands;   (Lucretius.)[83]

the excess and unruliness of our appetite outstripping all the inventions wherewith we seek to satisfy it.

With regard to weapons, we are better provided by Nature than most other animals; we are more able to move our limbs about and to extract service from them, naturally and without being taught. Those who are trained to fight naked are seen to rush into dangers just like our own soldiers. If some of the beasts surpass us in this advantage, we surpass many others in the same. We possess by a natural instinct and teaching the skill to fortify our bodies and protect them by acquired means. That this is so is proved by the example of the elephant who sharpens and grinds the teeth which he makes use of in warfare (for he has special teeth which he saves and employs for this purpose only). When bulls go to battle they throw up and scatter the dust around them; the boars whet their tusks; the ichneumon, when it is about to grapple with the crocodile, fortifies its body by coating it all over with a crust of mud, well kneaded and compressed, as with a cuirass. Why shall we not say that it is as natural to us to arm ourselves with wood and iron?

As to speech, it is certain that, if it is not natural neither is it necessary. Nevertheless I believe that a child brought up in complete solitude, far from all intercourse (which would be a difficult experiment to make), would have some kind of speech to express his ideas. And it is not to be believed that Nature has denied us this power which she has given to many other animals; for what else but speech is that faculty we observe in them of complaining, rejoicing, calling to one another for succour, inviting to love, which they do by the use of their voice?

Why should they not speak with one another? They speak to us, and we to them: in how many different tones do we not speak to our dogs? and they answer us. We use another language with them, than we do in talking to birds, pigs, oxen and horses, and give them other names; we change the idiom according to the kind.

> So ants amidst their sable-coloured band
> One with another mouth to mouth confer,
> Haply their way or state to understand.   (Dante.)[84]

---

83. *On the Nature of Things*, Book II, ll. 1157 ff.

84. *Purgatory*, Canto XXVI, ll. 34 ff.

Lactantius seems to attribute to beasts not only the power of speech but also of laughter. And the same difference of tongues which, according to the differences of countries, is found in human beings, is also found in animals of the same species. Aristotle, writing on this subject, instances the various calls of partridges, according to locality:

> The dappled birds
> Utter at other times far other cries
> Than when they fight for food, or with their prey
> Struggle and strain. And birds there are which change
> With changing weather their own raucous songs.
> (Lucretius.) [85]

But it is yet to be known what language the supposed child would speak; and what has been conjectured about it has no great probability. If any one declares to me, in opposition to this belief, that those deaf by nature do not speak, I reply that it is not only because they have not been taught to speak by ear, but more because the sense of hearing, of which they are deprived, is related to that of speech, and that they hold together by a natural tie; in such a way that the words we speak must in the first place be spoken to ourselves, and be made to strike upon our own inward ears, before being sent out to others' ears.

I have said all this to establish the resemblance to human conditions, and to bring us back and join us to the majority. We are neither superior nor inferior to the rest. All that is under heaven, says the sage, is subject to one law and one fate:

> Enshackled in the gruesome bonds of doom.
> (Lucretius.) [86]

Some difference there is; there are orders and degrees, but under the aspect of one same Nature:

> But each sole thing
> Proceeds according to its proper wont,
> And all conserve their own distinctions, based
> In Nature's fixed decree. (Lucretius.) [87]

Man must be forced and lined up within the barriers of this organization. The poor wretch has no mind really to step over them. He is shackled and entangled, he is subjected to the same obligation as the other creatures of his order, and is of a very mediocre

---

85. *On the Nature of Things*, Book V, ll. 1078 ff.
86. *On the Nature of Things*, Book V, l. 874.
87. *On the Nature of Things*, Book V, ll. 921 ff.

condition, without any real and essential prerogative and pre-eminence. That which he thinks and imagines himself to possess, neither has body nor can it be perceived. And if it be so that he alone of all the animals has this freedom of imagination, this licence of thought, which represents to him that which is, that which is not, that which he wills, the false and the true; it is an advantage sold to him very dearly, and of which he has very little cause to boast. For from it springs the principal source of all the ills that press upon him, sin, sickness, irresolution, affliction, despair.

## Of Repentance*

### ["THESE TESTIMONIES OF A GOOD CONSCIENCE"]

Others form man; I describe him, and portray a particular, very ill-made one, who, if I had to fashion him anew, should indeed be very different from what he is. But now it is done.

Now the features of my painting do not err, although they change and vary. The world is but a perennial see-saw. All things in it are incessantly on the swing, the earth, the rocks of the Caucasus, the Egyptian pyramids, both with the common movement and their own particular movement. Even fixedness is nothing but a more sluggish motion.

I cannot fix my object; it is befogged, and reels with a natural intoxication. I seize it at this point, as it is at the moment when I beguile myself with it. I do not portray the thing in itself. I portray the passage; not a passing from one age to another, or, as the people put it, from seven years to seven years,[88] but from day to day, from minute to minute. I must adapt my history to the moment. I may presently change, not only by chance, but also by intention. It is a record of diverse and changeable events, of undecided, and when the occasion arises, contradictory ideas; whether it be that I am another self, or that I grasp a subject in different circumstances and see it from a different point of view. So it may be that I contradict myself, but, as Demades[89] said, the truth I never contradict. If my mind could find a firm footing, I should not speak tentatively, I should decide; it is always in a state of apprenticeship, and on trial.

I am holding up to view a humble and lustreless life; that is all one. Moral philosophy, in any degree, may apply to an ordinary and secluded life as well as to one of richer stuff; every man carries within him the entire form of the human constitution.

Authors communicate themselves to the world by some special and extrinsic mark; I am the first to do so by my general being, as

---

* *Essays*, Book III, Chapter 2. The opening part of the essay is reprinted here.

88. an allusion to the popular notion that the human body is completely renewed every seven years.

89. Greek orator and politician of the fourth century B.C.

Michel de Montaigne, not as a grammarian or a poet or a lawyer. If the world finds fault with me for speaking too much of myself, I find fault with the world for not even thinking of itself.

But is it reasonable that I, who am so retired in actual life, should aspire to make myself known to the public? And is it reasonable that I should show up to the world, where artifice and ceremony enjoy so much credit and authority, the crude and simple results of nature, and of a nature besides very feeble? Is it not like making a wall without stone or a similar material, thus to build a book without learning or art? The ideas of music are guided by art, mine by chance. This I have at least in conformity with rules, that no man ever treated of a subject that he knew and understood better than I do this that I have taken up; and that in this I am the most learned man alive. Secondly, that no man ever penetrated more deeply into his matter, nor more minutely analysed its parts and consequences, nor more fully and exactly reached the goal he had made it his business to set up. To accomplish it I need only bring fidelity to it; and that is here, as pure and sincere as may be found.

I speak the truth, not enough to satisfy myself, but as much as I dare to speak. And I become a little more daring as I grow older; for it would seem that custom allows this age more freedom to prate, and more indiscretion in speaking of oneself. It cannot be the case here, as I often see elsewhere, that the craftsman and his work contradict each other. 'How could a man who shows to such advantage in company write so foolish a book?' or, 'Are these learned writings the work of a man of such feeble conversation?'

When a man of ordinary conversation writes uncommon things, it means that his talent lies in the place from which he borrows them, and not in himself. A learned man is not learned at all things; but the accomplished man is accomplished in all things, even in ignorance.

Here, my book and I go hand in hand together, and keep one pace. In other cases we may commend or censure the work apart from the workman; not so here. Who touches the one touches the other. He who judges the one without knowing the other will wrong himself more than he does me; he who has come to know the work will completely satisfy me. Happy beyond my deserts if I have only this share of public approval, that intelligent persons will be made to feel that I was capable of profiting by learning, if I had any; and that I deserved more assistance from my memory!

In this place let me offer an excuse for what I often repeat, that I seldom repent, and that my conscience is satisfied with itself, not as the conscience of an angel or a horse, but as the conscience of a man; always with the addition of this refrain, not a formal or conventional refrain, but prompted by a real and natural modesty, 'that

I speak as an inquirer and an ignoramus, leaving the decision purely and simply to the common and authorized beliefs.' I do not teach, I relate.

There is no vice, that is really a vice, which is not hurtful and which a sound judgement does not condemn; for its ugliness and evil consequences are so apparent that they are perhaps right who say that it is chiefly begotten of stupidity and ignorance. So hard it is to imagine that a man may know it and not hate it!

Wickedness sucks in the greater part of its own venom, and poisons itself with it.

Vice, like an ulcer in the flesh, leaves a repentance in the soul, which is always scratching itself and drawing blood. For Reason blots out all other grief and sorrow, but begets that of repentance, which is the more hard to bear since it is born from within; as the chill and heat of a fever are more acutely felt than those which are external. I regard as vices (but each according to its measure), not only those which are condemned by reason and Nature, but those too which have been created by human opinion, even false and erroneous opinion, if it is authorized by laws and custom.

There is likewise no goodness in which a well-born nature does not delight. We feel indeed a certain self-congratulation when we do a good deed, which gives us inward satisfaction, and that generous pride which accompanies a good conscience. A boldly wicked soul may perhaps arm itself with assurance; but with that complacency and satisfaction it cannot provide itself.

There is no small pleasure in feeling oneself preserved from the contagion of so corrupt an age, and saying to oneself, 'Should any one look into my very soul, he would yet not find me guilty of the affliction or ruin of any man, or of revenge or envy, of publicly offending against the laws, of innovation or disturbance, or of failing to keep my word. And whatever the licence of the times may permit or suggest to any man, I have laid hands on no Frenchman's property nor dived into his purse. I have never lived but on what is my own, either in war or peace time; and have never used another man's labour without hire.' These testimonies of a good conscience please; and this natural satisfaction is a great boon to us, and the only payment that will never fail us.

# MIGUEL DE CERVANTES
## (1547–1616)
## Don Quixote, Part I*
### ["*I Know Who I Am, and Who I May Be, If I Choose*"]

CHAPTER 1

*Which treats of the station in life and the pursuits of the famous gentleman, Don Quixote de la Mancha.*

In a village of La Mancha[1] the name of which I have no desire to recall, there lived not so long ago one of those gentlemen who always have a lance in the rack, an ancient buckler, a skinny nag, and a greyhound for the chase. A stew with more beef than mutton in it, chopped meat for his evening meal, scraps for a Saturday, lentils on Friday, and a young pigeon as a special delicacy for Sunday, went to account for three-quarters of his income. The rest of it he laid out on a broadcloth greatcoat and velvet stockings for feast days, with slippers to match, while the other days of the week he cut a figure in a suit of the finest homespun. Living with him were a housekeeper in her forties, a niece who was not yet twenty, and a lad of the field and market place who saddled his horse for him and wielded the pruning knife.

This gentleman of ours was close on to fifty, of a robust constitution but with little flesh on his bones and a face that was lean and gaunt. He was noted for his early rising, being very fond of the hunt. They will try to tell you that his surname was Quijada or Quesada—there is some difference of opinion among those who have written on the subject—but according to the most likely conjectures we are to understand that it was really Quejana. But all this means very little so far as our story is concerned, providing that in the telling of it we do not depart one iota from the truth.

You may know, then, that the aforesaid gentleman, on those occasions when he was at leisure, which was most of the year around, was in the habit of reading books of chivalry with such pleasure and devotion as to lead him almost wholly to forget the life of a hunter and even the administration of his estate. So great was his curiosity and infatuation in this regard that he even sold many acres of tillable land in order to be able to buy and read the books that he loved, and he would carry home with him as many of them as he could obtain.

Of all those that he thus devoured none pleased him so well as

---

* From *The Ingenious Gentleman Don Quixote de la Mancha,* Part I (1605) and Part II (1615). Translated by Samuel Putnam.

1. Efforts at identifying the village have proved inconclusive; La Mancha is a section of Spain south of Madrid.

the ones that had been composed by the famous Feliciano de Silva,[2] whose lucid prose style and involved conceits were as precious to him as pearls; especially when he came to read those tales of love and amorous challenges that are to be met with in many places, such a passage as the following, for example: "The reason of the unreason that afflicts my reason, in such a manner weakens my reason that I with reason lament me of your comeliness." And he was similarly affected when his eyes fell upon such lines as these: ". . . the high Heaven of your divinity divinely fortifies you with the stars and renders you deserving of that desert that your greatness doth deserve."

The poor fellow used to lie awake nights in an effort to disentangle the meaning and make sense out of passages such as these, although Aristotle himself would not have been able to understand them, even if he had been resurrected for that sole purpose. He was not at ease in his mind over those wounds that Don Belianís[2] gave and received; for no matter how great the surgeons who treated him, the poor fellow must have been left with his face and his entire body covered with marks and scars. Nevertheless, he was grateful to the author for closing the book with the promise of an interminable adventure to come; many a time he was tempted to take up his pen and literally finish the tale as had been promised, and he undoubtedly would have done so, and would have succeeded at it very well, if his thoughts had not been constantly occupied with other things of greater moment.

He often talked it over with the village curate,[4] who was a learned[5] man, a graduate of Sigüenza, and they would hold long discussions as to who had been the better knight, Palmerin of England or Amadis of Gaul;[6] but Master Nicholas, the barber of the same village, was in the habit of saying that no one could come up to the Knight of Phoebus,[7] and that if anyone *could* compare with him it was Don Galaor, brother of Amadis of Gaul, for Galaor was ready for anything—he was none of your finical knights, who went around whimpering as his brother did, and in point of valor he did not lag behind him.

In short, our gentleman became so immersed in his reading that he spent whole nights from sundown to sunup and his days from dawn to dusk in poring over his books, until, finally, from so little sleeping and so much reading, his brain dried up and he went completely out of his mind. He had filled his imagination with every-

---

2. a sixteenth-century author of romances; the quotation which follows is from his *Don Florisel de Niquea.*

3. The allusion is to a romance by Jerónimo Fernández.

4. parish priest.

5. ironical, for Sigüenza was the seat of a minor and discredited university.

6. heroes of two very famous roman-

ces of chivalry.

7. or Knight of the Sun. Heroes of romances customarily adopted emblematic names and also changed them according to circumstances. See in the following paragraph the reference to the Knight of the Flaming Sword.

thing that he had read, with enchantments, knightly encounters, battles, challenges, wounds, with tales of love and its torments, and all sorts of impossible things, and as a result had come to believe that all these fictitious happenings were true; they were more real to him than anything else in the world. He would remark that the Cid Ruy Díaz had been a very good knight, but there was no comparison between him and the Knight of the Flaming Sword, who with a single backward stroke had cut in half two fierce and monstrous giants. He preferred Bernardo del Carpio, who at Roncesvalles had slain Roland despite the charm[8] the latter bore, availing himself of the stratagem which Hercules employed when he strangled Antaeus, the son of Earth, in his arms.[9]

He had much good to say for Morgante[10] who, though he belonged to the haughty, overbearing race of giants, was of an affable disposition and well brought up. But, above all, he cherished an admiration for Rinaldo of Montalbán,[11] especially as he beheld him sallying forth from his castle to rob all those that crossed his path, or when he thought of him overseas stealing the image of Mohammed which, so the story has it, was all of gold. And he would have liked very well to have had his fill of kicking that traitor Galalón,[12] a privilege for which he would have given his housekeeper with his niece thrown into the bargain.

At last, when his wits were gone beyond repair, he came to conceive the strangest idea that ever occurred to any madman in this world. It now appeared to him fitting and necessary, in order to win a greater amount of honor for himself and serve his country at the same time, to become a knight-errant and roam the world on horseback, in a suit of armor; he would go in quest of adventures, by way of putting into practice all that he had read in his books; he would right every manner of wrong, placing himself in situations of the greatest peril such as would redound to the eternal glory of his name. As a reward for his valor and the might of his arm, the poor fellow could already see himself crowned Emperor of Trebizond at the very least; and so, carried away by the strange pleasure that he found in such thoughts as these, he at once set about putting his plan into effect.

The first thing he did was to burnish up some old pieces of armor, left him by his great-grandfather, which for ages had lain in a corner, moldering and forgotten. He polished and adjusted them as best he could, and then he noticed that one very important thing

---

8. the magic gift of invulnerability.
9. The mythological Antaeus was invulnerable as long as he maintained contact with his mother, Earth; Hercules killed him while holding him raised in his arms.
10. in Pulci's *Morgante maggiore*, a comic-epic poem of the Italian Renaissance.

11. in Bojardo's *Roland in Love* (*Orlando innamorato*) and Ariosto's *Roland Mad* (*Orlando furioso*), romantic and comic-epic poems of the Italian Renaissance. Rinaldo is Roland's cousin.
12. Ganelon, the villain in the Charlemagne legend who betrayed the French at Roncesvalles.

was lacking: there was no closed helmet, but only a morion, or visorless headpiece, with turned up brim of the kind foot soldiers wore. His ingenuity, however, enabled him to remedy this, and he proceeded to fashion out of cardboard a kind of half-helmet, which, when attached to the morion, gave the appearance of a whole one. True, when he went to see if it was strong enough to withstand a good slashing blow, he was somewhat disappointed; for when he drew his sword and gave it a couple of thrusts, he succeeded only in undoing a whole week's labor. The ease with which he had hewed it to bits disturbed him no little, and he decided to make it over. This time he placed a few strips of iron on the inside, and then, convinced that it was strong enough, refrained from putting it to any further test; instead, he adopted it then and there as the finest helmet ever made.

After this, he went out to have a look at his nag; and although the animal had more *cuartos*, or cracks, in its hoof than there are quarters in a real,[13] and more blemishes than Gonela's steed[14] which *tantum pellis et ossa fuit*,[15] it nonetheless looked to its master like a far better horse than Alexander's Bucephalus or the Babieca of the Cid.[16] He spent all of four days in trying to think up a name for his mount; for—so he told himself—seeing that it belonged to so famous and worthy a knight, there was no reason why it should not have a name of equal renown. The kind of name he wanted was one that would at once indicate what the nag had been before it came to belong to a knight-errant and what its present status was; for it stood to reason that, when the master's worldly condition changed, his horse also ought to have a famous, high-sounding appellation, one suited to the new order of things and the new profession that it was to follow.

After he in his memory and imagination had made up, struck out, and discarded many names, now adding to and now subtracting from the list, he finally hit upon "Rocinante," a name that impressed him as being sonorous and at the same time indicative of what the steed had been when it was but a hack, whereas now it was nothing other than the first and foremost of all the hacks[17] in the world.

Having found a name for his horse that pleased his fancy, he then desired to do as much for himself, and this required another week, and by the end of that period he had made up his mind that he was henceforth to be known as Don Quixote, which, as has been stated, has led the authors of this veracious history to assume that his real name must undoubtedly have been Quijada, and not Quesada as others would have it. But remembering that the valiant

---

13. a coin (about five cents); a *cuarto* was one eighth of a *real*.

14. Gonela ("il Gonnella") was a jester at the court of Ferrara, seat of the house of Este.

15. was so much skin and bones.

16. "the chief," Ruy Diaz (see reference on p. 1380), celebrated hero of the twelfth-century *Pocma del Cid*.

17. in Spanish, *rocín*.

Amadis was not content to call himself that and nothing more, but added the name of his kingdom and fatherland that he might make it famous also, and thus came to take the name Amadis of Gaul, so our good knight chose to add his place of origin and become "Don Quixote de la Mancha"; for by this means, as he saw it, he was making very plain his lineage and was conferring honor upon his country by taking its name as his own.

And so, having polished up his armor and made the morion over into a closed helmet, and having given himself and his horse a name, he naturally found but one thing lacking still: he must seek out a lady of whom he could become enamored; for a knight-errant without a lady-love was like a tree without leaves or fruit, a body without a soul.

"If," he said to himself, "as a punishment for my sins or by a stroke of fortune I should come upon some giant hereabouts, a thing that very commonly happens to knights-errant, and if I should slay him in a hand-to-hand encounter or perhaps cut him in two, or, finally, if I should vanquish and subdue him, would it not be well to have someone to whom I may send him as a present, in order that he, if he is living, may come in, fall upon his knees in front of my sweet lady, and say in a humble and submissive tone of voice, 'I, lady, am the giant Caraculiambro, lord of the island Malindrania, who has been overcome in single combat by that knight who never can be praised enough, Don Quixote de la Mancha, the same who sent me to present myself before your Grace that your Highness may dispose of me as you see fit'?"

Oh, how our good knight reveled in this speech, and more than ever when he came to think of the name that he should give his lady! As the story goes, there was a very good-looking farm girl who lived near by, with whom he had once been smitten, although it is generally believed that she never knew or suspected it. Her name was Aldonza Lorenzo, and it seemed to him that she was the one upon whom he should bestow the title of mistress of his thoughts. For her he wished a name that should not be incongruous with his own and that would convey the suggestion of a princess or a great lady; and, accordingly, he resolved to call her "Dulcinea del Toboso," she being a native of that place. A musical name to his ears, out of the ordinary and significant, like the others he had chosen for himself and his appurtenances.

### CHAPTER 2

*Which treats of the first sally that the ingenious Don Quixote made from his native heath.*

Having, then, made all these preparations, he did not wish to lose any time in putting his plan into effect, for he could not but blame himself for what the world was losing by his delay, so many were the wrongs that were to be righted, the grievances to be redressed, the abuses to be done away with, and the duties to be performed. Accordingly, without informing anyone of his intention and without letting anyone see him, he set out one morning before daybreak on one of those very hot days in July. Donning all his armor, mounting Rocinante, adjusting his ill-contrived helmet, bracing his shield on his arm, and taking up his lance, he sallied forth by the back gate of his stable yard into the open countryside. It was with great contentment and joy that he saw how easily he had made a beginning toward the fulfillment of his desire.

No sooner was he out on the plain, however, than a terrible thought assailed him, one that all but caused him to abandon the enterprise he had undertaken. This occurred when he suddenly remembered that he had never formally been dubbed a knight, and so, in accordance with the law of knighthood, was not permitted to bear arms against one who had a right to that title. And even if he had been, as a novice knight he would have had to wear white armor, without any device on his shield, until he should have earned one by his exploits. These thoughts led him to waver in his purpose, but, madness prevailing over reason, he resolved to have himself knighted by the first person he met, as many others had done if what he had read in those books that he had at home was true. And so far as white armor was concerned, he would scour his own the first chance that offered until it shone whiter than any ermine. With this he became more tranquil and continued on his way, letting his horse take whatever path it chose, for he believed that therein lay the very essence of adventures.

And so we find our newly fledged adventurer jogging along and talking to himself. "Undoubtedly," he is saying, "in the days to come, when the true history of my famous deeds is published, the learned chronicler who records them, when he comes to describe my first sally so early in the morning, will put down something like this: 'No sooner had the rubicund Apollo spread over the face of the broad and spacious earth the gilded filaments of his beauteous locks, and no sooner had the little singing birds of painted plumage greeted with their sweet and mellifluous harmony the coming of the Dawn, who, leaving the soft couch of her jealous spouse, now showed herself to mortals at all the doors and balconies of the horizon that bounds La Mancha—no sooner had this happened than the famous knight, Don Quixote de la Mancha, forsaking his own downy bed and mounting his famous steed, Rocinante, fared forth and began riding over the ancient and famous Campo de Montiel.' "[18]

And this was the truth, for he was indeed riding over that stretch of plain.

---

18. famous because it had been the scene of a battle in 1369.

"O happy age and happy century," he went on, "in which my famous exploits shall be published, exploits worthy of being engraved in bronze, sculptured in marble, and depicted in paintings for the benefit of posterity. O wise magician, whoever you be, to whom shall fall the task of chronicling this extraordinary history of mine! I beg of you not to forget my good Rocinante, eternal companion of my wayfarings and my wanderings."

Then, as though he really had been in love: "O Princess Dulcinea, lady of this captive heart! Much wrong have you done me in thus sending me forth with your reproaches and sternly commanding me not to appear in your beauteous presence. O lady, deign to be mindful of this your subject who endures so many woes for the love of you."

And so he went on, stringing together absurdities, all of a kind that his books had taught him, imitating insofar as he was able the language of their authors. He rode slowly, and the sun came up so swiftly and with so much heat that it would have been sufficient to melt his brains if he had had any. He had been on the road almost the entire day without anything happening that is worthy of being set down here; and he was on the verge of despair, for he wished to meet someone at once with whom he might try the valor of his good right arm. Certain authors say that his first adventure was that of Puerto Lápice, while others state that it was that of the windmills; but in this particular instance I am in a position to affirm what I have read in the annals of La Mancha; and that is to the effect that he went all that day until nightfall, when he and his hack found themselves tired to death and famished. Gazing all around him to see if he could discover some castle or shepherd's hut where he might take shelter and attend to his pressing needs, he caught sight of an inn not far off the road along which they were traveling, and this to him was like a star guiding him not merely to the gates, but rather, let us say, to the palace of redemption. Quickening his pace, he came up to it just as night was falling.

By chance there stood in the doorway two lasses of the sort known as "of the district"; they were on their way to Seville in the company of some mule drivers who were spending the night in the inn. Now, everything that this adventurer of ours thought, saw, or imagined seemed to him to be directly out of one of the storybooks he had read, and so, when he caught sight of the inn, it at once became a castle with its four turrets and its pinnacles of gleaming silver, not to speak of the drawbridge and moat and all the other things that are commonly supposed to go with a castle. As he rode up to it, he accordingly reined in Rocinante and sat there waiting for a dwarf to appear upon the battlements and blow his trumpet by way of announcing the arrival of a knight. The dwarf, however, was slow in coming, and as Rocinante was anxious to reach the stable, Don Quixote drew up to the door of the hostelry and surveyed the two merry maidens, who to him were a pair of beauteous damsels or gracious ladies taking their ease at the castle gate.

And then a swineherd came along, engaged in rounding up his drove of hogs—for, without any apology, that is what they were. He gave a blast on his horn to bring them together, and this at once became for Don Quixote just what he wished it to be: some dwarf who was heralding his coming; and so it was with a vast deal of satisfaction that he presented himself before the ladies in question, who, upon beholding a man in full armor like this, with lance and buckler, were filled with fright and made as if to flee indoors. Realizing that they were afraid, Don Quixote raised his pasteboard visor and revealed his withered, dust-covered face.

"Do not flee, your Ladyships," he said to them in a courteous manner and gentle voice. "You need not fear that any wrong will be done you, for it is not in accordance with the order of knighthood which I profess to wrong anyone, much less such highborn damsels as your appearance shows you to be."

The girls looked at him, endeavoring to scan his face, which was half hidden by his ill-made visor. Never having heard women of their profession called damsels before, they were unable to restrain their laughter, at which Don Quixote took offense.

"Modesty," he observed, "well becomes those with the dower of beauty, and, moreover, laughter that has not good cause is a very foolish thing. But I do not say this to be discourteous or to hurt your feelings; my only desire is to serve you."

The ladies did not understand what he was talking about, but felt more than ever like laughing at our knight's unprepossessing figure. This increased his annoyance, and there is no telling what would have happened if at that moment the innkeeper had not come out. He was very fat and very peaceably inclined; but upon sighting this grotesque personage clad in bits of armor that were quite as oddly matched as were his bridle, lance, buckler, and corselet, mine host was not at all indisposed to join the lasses in their merriment. He was suspicious, however, of all this paraphernalia and decided that it would be better to keep a civil tongue in his head.

"If, Sir Knight," he said, "your Grace desires a lodging, aside from a bed—for there is none to be had in this inn—you will find all else that you may want in great abundance."

When Don Quixote saw how humble the governor of the castle was—for he took the innkeeper and his inn to be no less than that —he replied, "For me, Sir Castellan,[19] anything will do, since

> Arms are my only ornament,
> My only rest the fight, etc."

19. The original, *castellano*, means both "castellan" and "Castilian."

The landlord thought that the knight had called him a castellan because he took him for one of those worthies of Castile, whereas the truth was, he was an Andalusian from the beach of Sanlúcar, no less a thief than Cacus[20] himself, and as full of tricks as a student or a page boy.

"In that case," he said,

> "Your bed will be the solid rock,
> Your sleep: to watch all night.

This being so, you may be assured of finding beneath this roof enough to keep you awake for a whole year, to say nothing of a single night."

With this, he went up to hold the stirrup for Don Quixote, who encountered much difficulty in dismounting, not having broken his fast all day long. The knight then directed his host to take good care of his steed, as it was the best piece of horseflesh in all the world. The innkeeper looked it over, and it did not impress him as being half as good as Don Quixote had said it was. Having stabled the animal, he came back to see what his guest would have and found the latter being relieved of his armor by the damsels, who by now had made their peace with the new arrival. They had already removed his breastplate and backpiece but had no idea how they were going to open his gorget or get his improvised helmet off. That piece of armor had been tied on with green ribbons which it would be necessary to cut, since the knots could not be undone, but he would not hear of this, and so spent all the rest of that night with his headpiece in place, which gave him the weirdest, most laughable appearance that could be imagined.

Don Quixote fancied that these wenches who were assisting him must surely be the chatelaine and other ladies of the castle, and so proceeded to address them very gracefully and with much wit:

> "Never was knight so served
> By any noble dame
> As was Don Quixote
> When from his village he came,
> With damsels to wait on his every need
> While princesses cared for his hack . . .

"By hack," he explained, "is meant my steed Rocinante, for that is his name, and mine is Don Quixote de la Mancha. I had no intention of revealing my identity until my exploits done in your service should have made me known to you; but the necessity of adapting to present circumstances that old ballad of Lancelot has

---

20. In Roman mythology he stole some of the cattle of Hercules, concealing the theft by having them walk backward into his cave, but was finally discovered and slain.

led to your becoming acquainted with it prematurely. However, the time will come when your Ladyships shall command and I will obey and with the valor of my good right arm show you how eager I am to serve you."

The young women were not used to listening to speeches like this and had not a word to say, but merely asked him if he desired to eat anything.

"I could eat a bite of something, yes," replied Don Quixote. "Indeed, I feel that a little food would go very nicely just now."

He thereupon learned that, since it was Friday, there was nothing to be had in all the inn except a few portions of codfish, which in Castile is called *abadejo*, in Andalusia *bacalao*, in some places *curadillo*, and elsewhere *truchuella* or small trout. Would his Grace, then, have some small trout, seeing that was all there was that they could offer him?

"If there are enough of them," said Don Quixote, "they will take the place of a trout, for it is all one to me whether I am given in change eight reales or one piece of eight. What is more, those small trout may be like veal, which is better than beef, or like kid, which is better than goat. But however that may be, bring them on at once, for the weight and burden of arms is not to be borne without inner sustenance."

Placing the table at the door of the hostelry, in the open air, they brought the guest a portion of badly soaked and worse cooked codfish and a piece of bread as black and moldy as the suit of armor that he wore. It was a mirth-provoking sight to see him eat, for he still had his helmet on with his visor fastened, which made it impossible for him to put anything into his mouth with his hands, and so it was necessary for one of the girls to feed him. As for giving him anything to drink, that would have been out of the question if the innkeeper had not hollowed out a reed, placing one end in Don Quixote's mouth while through the other end he poured the wine. All this the knight bore very patiently rather than have them cut the ribbons of his helmet.

At this point a gelder of pigs approached the inn, announcing his arrival with four or five blasts on his horn, all of which confirmed Don Quixote in the belief that this was indeed a famous castle, for what was this if not music that they were playing for him? The fish was trout, the bread was of the finest, the wenches were ladies, and the innkeeper was the castellan. He was convinced that he had been right in his resolve to sally forth and roam the world at large, but there was one thing that still distressed him greatly, and that was the fact that he had not as yet been dubbed a knight; as he saw it, he could not legitimately engage in any adventure until he had received the order of knighthood.

### CHAPTER 3

*Of the amusing manner in which Don Quixote had himself dubbed a knight.*

Wearied of his thoughts, Don Quixote lost no time over the scanty repast which the inn afforded him. When he had finished, he summoned the landlord and, taking him out to the stable, closed the doors and fell on his knees in front of him.

"Never, valiant knight," he said, "shall I arise from here until you have courteously granted me the boon I seek, one which will redound to your praise and to the good of the human race."

Seeing his guest at his feet and hearing him utter such words as these, the innkeeper could only stare at him in bewilderment, not knowing what to say or do. It was in vain that he entreated him to rise, for Don Quixote refused to do so until his request had been granted.

"I expected nothing less of your great magnificence, my lord," the latter then continued, "and so I may tell you that the boon I asked and which you have so generously conceded me is that to-morrow morning you dub me a knight. Until that time, in the chapel of this your castle, I will watch over my armor, and when morning comes, as I have said, that which I so desire shall then be done, in order that I may lawfully go to the four corners of the earth in quest of adventures and to succor the needy, which is the chivalrous duty of all knights-errant such as I who long to engage in deeds of high emprise."

The innkeeper, as we have said, was a sharp fellow. He already had a suspicion that his guest was not quite right in the head, and he was now convinced of it as he listened to such remarks as these. However, just for the sport of it, he determined to humor him; and so he went on to assure Don Quixote that he was fully justified in his request and that such a desire and purpose was only natural on the part of so distinguished a knight as his gallant bearing plainly showed him to be.

He himself, the landlord added, when he was a young man, had followed the same honorable calling. He had gone through various parts of the world seeking adventures, among the places he had visited being the Percheles of Málaga, the Isles of Riarán, the District of Seville, the Little Market Place of Segovia, the Olivera of Valencia, the Rondilla of Granada, the beach of Sanlúcar, the Horse Fountain of Cordova, the Small Taverns of Toledo, and numerous other localities[21] where his nimble feet and light fingers had found much exercise. He had done many wrongs, cheated many widows, ruined many maidens, and swindled not a few minors until he had

---

21. All the places mentioned were reputed to be haunts of robbers and rogues.

finally come to be known in almost all the courts and tribunals that are to be found in the whole of Spain.

At last he had retired to his castle here, where he lived upon his own income and the property of others; and here it was that he received all knights-errant of whatever quality and condition, simply out of the great affection that he bore them and that they might share with him their possessions in payment of his good will. Unfortunately, in this castle there was no chapel where Don Quixote might keep watch over his arms, for the old chapel had been torn down to make way for a new one; but in case of necessity, he felt quite sure that such a vigil could be maintained anywhere, and for the present occasion the courtyard of the castle would do; and then in the morning, please God, the requisite ceremony could be performed and his guest be duly dubbed a knight, as much a knight as anyone ever was.

He then inquired if Don Quixote had any money on his person, and the latter replied that he had not a cent, for in all the storybooks he had never read of knights-errant carrying any. But the innkeeper told him he was mistaken on this point: supposing the authors of those stories had not set down the fact in black and white, that was because they did not deem it necessary to speak of things as indispensable as money and a clean shirt, and one was not to assume for that reason that those knights-errant of whom the books were so full did not have any. He looked upon it as an absolute certainty that they all had well-stuffed purses, that they might be prepared for any emergency; and they also carried shirts and a little box of ointment for healing the wounds that they received.

For when they had been wounded in combat on the plains and in desert places, there was not always someone at hand to treat them, unless they had some skilled enchanter for a friend who then would succor them, bringing to them through the air, upon a cloud, some damsel or dwarf bearing a vial of water of such virtue that one had but to taste a drop of it and at once his wounds were healed and he was as sound as if he had never received any.

But even if this was not the case, knights in times past saw to it that their squires were well provided with money and other necessities, such as lint and ointment for healing purposes; and if they had no squires—which happened very rarely—they themselves carried these objects in a pair of saddlebags very cleverly attached to their horses' croups in such a manner as to be scarcely noticeable, as if they held something of greater importance than that, for among the knights-errant saddlebags as a rule were not favored. Accordingly, he would advise the novice before him, and inasmuch as the latter was soon to be his godson, he might even command him, that henceforth he should not go without money and a supply of those things that have been mentioned, as he would find that they came in useful at a time when he least expected it.

Don Quixote promised to follow his host's advice punctiliously; and so it was arranged that he should watch his armor in a large barnyard at one side of the inn. He gathered up all the pieces, placed them in a horse trough that stood near the well, and, bracing his shield on his arm, took up his lance and with stately demeanor began pacing up and down in front of the trough even as night was closing in.

The innkeeper informed his other guests of what was going on, of Don Quixote's vigil and his expectation of being dubbed a knight; and, marveling greatly at so extraordinary a variety of madness, they all went out to see for themselves and stood there watching from a distance. For a while the knight-to-be, with tranquil mien, would merely walk up and down; then, leaning on his lance, he would pause to survey his armor, gazing fixedly at it for a considerable length of time. As has been said, it was night now, but the brightness of the moon, which well might rival that of Him who lent it, was such that everything the novice knight did was plainly visible to all.

At this point one of the mule drivers who were stopping at the inn came out to water his drove, and in order to do this it was necessary to remove the armor from the trough.

As he saw the man approaching, Don Quixote cried out to him, "O bold knight, whoever you may be, who thus would dare to lay hands upon the accouterments of the most valiant man of arms that ever girded on a sword, look well what you do and desist if you do not wish to pay with your life for your insolence!"

The muleteer gave no heed to these words—it would have been better for his own sake had he done so—but, taking it up by the straps, tossed the armor some distance from him. When he beheld this, Don Quixote rolled his eyes heavenward and with his thoughts apparently upon his Dulcinea exclaimed, "Succor, O lady mine, this vassal heart in this my first encounter; let not your favor and protection fail me in the peril in which for the first time I now find myself."

With these and other similar words, he loosed his buckler, grasped his lance in both his hands, and let the mule driver have such a blow on the head that the man fell to the ground stunned; and had it been followed by another one, he would have had no need of a surgeon to treat him. Having done this, Don Quixote gathered up his armor and resumed his pacing up and down with the same calm manner as before. Not long afterward, without knowing what had happened—for the first muleteer was still lying there unconscious—another came out with the same intention of watering his mules, and he too was about to remove the armor from the trough when the knight, without saying a word or asking favor of anyone, once more adjusted his buckler and raised his lance, and if he did not break the second mule driver's head to bits, he made more than three pieces of it by dividing it into quarters. At the sound of the fracas everybody in the inn came running out, among them the innkeeper; whereupon Don Quixote again lifted his buckler and laid his hand on his sword.

"O lady of beauty," he said, "strength and vigor of this fainting heart of mine! Now is the time to turn the eyes of your greatness upon this captive knight of yours who must face so formidable an adventure."

By this time he had worked himself up to such a pitch of anger that if all the mule drivers in the world had attacked him he would not have taken one step backward. The comrades of the wounded men, seeing the plight those two were in, now began showering stones on Don Quixote, who shielded himself as best he could with his buckler, although he did not dare stir from the trough for fear of leaving his armor unprotected. The landlord, meanwhile, kept calling for them to stop, for he had told them that this was a madman who would be sure to go free even though he killed them all. The knight was shouting louder than ever, calling them knaves and traitors. As for the lord of the castle, who allowed knights-errant to be treated in this fashion, he was a lowborn villain, and if he, Don Quixote, had but received the order of knighthood, he would make him pay for his treachery.

"As for you others, vile and filthy rabble, I take no account of you; you may stone me or come forward and attack me all you like; you shall see what the reward of your folly and insolence will be."

He spoke so vigorously and was so undaunted in bearing as to strike terror in those who would assail him; and for this reason, and owing also to the persuasions of the inkeeper, they ceased stoning him. He then permitted them to carry away the wounded, and went back to watching his armor with the same tranquil, unconcerned air that he had previously displayed.

The landlord was none too well pleased with these mad pranks on the part of his guest and determined to confer upon him that accursed order of knighthood before something else happened. Going up to him, he begged Don Quixote's pardon for the insolence which, without his knowledge, had been shown the knight by those of low degree. They, however, had been well punished for their impudence. As he had said, there was no chapel in this castle, but for that which remained to be done there was no need of any. According to what he had read of the ceremonial of the order, there was nothing to this business of being dubbed a knight except a slap on the neck and one across the shoulder, and that could be performed in the middle of a field as well as anywhere else. All that was required was for the knight-to-be to keep watch over his armor for a couple of hours, and Don Quixote had been at it more than four. The latter believed all this and announced that he was ready to obey and get the matter over with as speedily as possible. Once dubbed a knight, if he were attacked one more time, he did not think that he would leave a single person in the castle alive, save such as he might command be spared, at the bidding of his host and out of respect to him.

Thus warned, and fearful that it might occur, the castellan brought out the book in which he had jotted down the hay and barley for which the mule drivers owed him, and, accompanied by a lad bearing the butt of a candle and the two aforesaid damsels, he came up to where Don Quixote stood and commanded him to kneel. Reading from the account book—as if he had been saying a prayer—he raised his hand and, with the knight's own sword, gave him a good thwack upon the neck and another lusty one upon the shoulder, muttering all the while between his teeth. He then directed one of the ladies to gird on Don Quixote's sword, which she did with much gravity and composure; for it was all they could do to keep from laughing at every point of the ceremony, but the thought of the knight's prowess which they had already witnessed was sufficient to restrain their mirth.

"May God give your Grace much good fortune," said the worthy lady as she attached the blade, "and prosper you in battle."

Don Quixote thereupon inquired her name, for he desired to know to whom it was he was indebted for the favor he had just received, that he might share with her some of the honor which his strong right arm was sure to bring him. She replied very humbly that her name was Tolosa and that she was the daughter of a shoemaker, a native of Toledo who lived in the stalls of Sancho Bienaya.[22] To this the knight replied that she would do him a very great favor if from then on she would call herself Doña Tolosa, and she promised to do so. The other girl then helped him on with his spurs, and practically the same conversation was repeated. When asked her name, she stated that it was La Molinera and added that she was the daughter of a respectable miller of Antequera. Don Quixote likewise requested her to assume the "don" and become Doña Molinera and offered to render her further services and favors.

These unheard-of ceremonies having been dispatched in great haste, Don Quixote could scarcely wait to be astride his horse and sally forth on his quest for adventures. Saddling and mounting Rocinante, he embraced his host, thanking him for the favor of having dubbed him a knight and saying such strange things that it would be quite impossible to record them here. The innkeeper, who was only too glad to be rid of him, answered with a speech that was

22. an old square in Toledo.

no less flowery, though somewhat shorter, and he did not so much as ask him for the price of a lodging, so glad was he to see him go

CHAPTER 4

*Of what happened to our knight when he sallied forth from the inn.*

Day was dawning when Don Quixote left the inn, so well satisfied with himself, so gay, so exhilarated, that the very girths of his steed all but burst with joy. But remembering the advice which his host had given him concerning the stock of necessary provisions that he should carry with him, especially money and shirts, he decided to turn back home and supply himself with whatever he needed, and with a squire as well; he had in mind a farmer who was a neighbor of his, a poor man and the father of a family but very well suited to fulfill the duties to squire to a man of arms. With this thought in mind he guided Rocinante toward the village once more, and that animal, realizing that he was homeward bound, began stepping out at so lively a gait that it seemed as if his feet barely touched the ground.

The knight had not gone far when from a hedge on his right hand he heard the sound of faint moans as of someone in distress. "Thanks be to Heaven," he at once exclaimed, "for the favor it has shown me by providing me so soon with an opportunity to fulfill the obligations that I owe to my profession, a chance to pluck the fruit of my worthy desires. Those, undoubtedly, are the cries of someone in distress, who stands in need of my favor and assistance."

Turning Rocinante's head, he rode back to the place from which the cries appeared to be coming. Entering the wood, he had gone but a few paces when he saw a mare attached to an oak, while bound to another tree was a lad of fifteen or thereabouts, naked from the waist up. It was he who was uttering the cries, and not without reason, for there in front of him was a lusty farmer with a girdle who was giving him many lashes, each one accompanied by a reproof and a command, "Hold your tongue and keep your eyes open"; and the lad was saying, "I won't do it again, sir; by God's Passion, I won't do it again. I promise you that after this I'll take better care of the flock."

When he saw what was going on, Don Quixote was very angry. "Discourteous knight," he said, "it ill becomes you to strike one who is powerless to defend himself. Mount your steed and take your lance in hand"—for there was a lance leaning against the oak to which the mare was tied—"and I will show you what a coward you are."

The farmer, seeing before him this figure all clad in armor and brandishing a lance, decided that he was as good as done for. "Sir

Knight," he said, speaking very mildly, "this lad that I am punishing here is my servant; he tends a flock of sheep which I have in these parts and he is so careless that every day one of them shows up missing. And when I punish him for his carelessness or his roguery, he says it is just because I am a miser and do not want to pay him the wages that I owe him, but I swear to God and upon my soul that he lies."

"It is you who lie, base lout," said Don Quixote, "and in my presence; and by the sun that gives us light, I am minded to run you through with this lance. Pay him and say no more about it, or else, by the God who rules us, I will make an end of you and annihilate you here and now. Release him at once."

The farmer hung his head and without a word untied his servant. Don Quixote then asked the boy how much his master owed him. For nine months' work, the lad told him, at seven reales the month. The knight did a little reckoning and found that this came to sixty-three reales; whereupon he ordered the farmer to pay over the money immediately, as he valued his life. The cowardly bumpkin replied that, facing death as he was and by the oath that he had sworn—he had not sworn any oath as yet—it did not amount to as much as that; for there were three pairs of shoes which he had given the lad that were to be deducted and taken into account, and a real for two blood-lettings when his servant was ill.

"That," said Don Quixote, "is all very well; but let the shoes and the blood-lettings go for the undeserved lashings which you have given him; if he has worn out the leather of the shoes that you paid for, you have taken the hide off his body, and if the barber[23] let a little blood for him when he was sick, you have done the same when he was well; and so far as that goes, he owes you nothing."

"But the trouble is, Sir Knight, that I have no money with me. Come along home with me, Andrés, and I will pay you real for real."[24]

"I go home with him!" cried the lad. "Never in the world! No, sir, I would not even think of it; for once he has me alone he'll flay me like a St. Bartholomew."

"He will do nothing of the sort," said Don Quixote. "It is sufficient for me to command, and he out of respect will obey. Since he has sworn to me by the order of knighthood which he has received, I shall let him go free and I will guarantee that you will be paid."

"But look, your Grace," the lad remonstrated, "my master is no knight; he has never received any order of knighthood whatsoever. He is Juan Haldudo, a rich man and a resident of Quintanar."

23. Barbers were also surgeons.     24. See footnote 13.

"That makes little difference," declared Don Quixote, "for there may well be knights among the Haldudos, all the more so in view of the fact that every man is the son of his works."

"That is true enough," said Andrés, "but this master of mine— of what works is he the son, seeing that he refuses me the pay for my sweat and labor?"

"I do not refuse you, brother Andrés," said the farmer. "Do me the favor of coming with me, and I swear to you by all the orders of knighthood that there are in this world to pay you, as I have said, real for real, and perfumed at that."

"You can dispense with the perfume," said Don Quixote; "just give him the reales and I shall be satisfied. And see to it that you keep your oath, or by the one that I myself have sworn I shall return to seek you out and chastise you, and I shall find you though you be as well hidden as a lizard. In case you would like to know who it is that is giving you this command in order that you may feel the more obliged to comply with it, I may tell you that I am the valorous Don Quixote de la Mancha, righter of wrongs and injustices; and so, God be with you, and do not fail to do as you have promised, under that penalty that I have pronounced."

As he said this, he put spurs to Rocinante and was off. The farmer watched him go, and when he saw that Don Quixote was out of the wood and out of sight, he turned to his servant, Andrés.

"Come here, my son," he said. "I want to pay you what I owe you as that righter of wrongs has commanded me."

"Take my word for it," replied Andrés, "your Grace would do well to observe the command of that good knight—may he live a thousand years; for as he is valorous and a righteous judge, if you don't pay me then, by Roque,[25] he will come back and do just what he said!"

"And I will give you my word as well," said the farmer; "but seeing that I am so fond of you, I wish to increase the debt, that I may owe you all the more." And with this he seized the lad's arm and bound him to the tree again and flogged him within an inch of his life. "There, Master Andrés, you may call on that righter of wrongs if you like and you will see whether or not he rights this one. I do not think I have quite finished with you yet, for I have a good mind to flay you alive as you feared."

Finally, however, he unbound him and told him he might go look for that judge of his to carry out the sentence that had been pronounced. Andrés left, rather down in the mouth, swearing that he would indeed go look for the brave Don Quixote de la Mancha; he would relate to him everything that had happened, point by

25. The origin of the oath is unknown.

point, and the farmer would have to pay for it seven times over. But for all that, he went away weeping, and his master stood laughing at him.

Such was the manner in which the valorous knight righted this particular wrong. Don Quixote was quite content with the way everything had turned out; it seemed to him that he had made a very fortunate and noble beginning with his deeds of chivalry, and he was very well satisfied with himself as he jogged along in the direction of his native village, talking to himself in a low voice all the while.

"Well may'st thou call thyself fortunate today, above all other women on earth, O fairest of the fair, Dulcinea del Toboso! Seeing that it has fallen to thy lot to hold subject and submissive to thine every wish and pleasure so valiant and renowned a knight as Don Quixote de la Mancha is and shall be, who, as everyone knows, yesterday received the order of knighthood and this day has righted the greatest wrong and grievance that injustice ever conceived or cruelty ever perpetrated, by snatching the lash from the hand of the merciless foeman who was so unreasonably flogging that tender child."

At this point he came to a road that forked off in four directions, and at once he thought of those crossroads where knights-errant would pause to consider which path they should take. By way of imitating them, he halted there for a while; and when he had given the subject much thought, he slackened Rocinante's rein and let the hack follow its inclination. The animal's first impulse was to make straight for its own stable. After they had gone a couple of miles or so Don Quixote caught sight of what appeared to be a great throng of people, who, as was afterward learned, were certain merchants of Toledo on their way to purchase silk at Murcia. There were six of them altogether with their sunshades, accompanied by four attendants on horseback and three mule drivers on foot.

No sooner had he sighted them than Don Quixote imagined that he was on the brink of some fresh adventure. He was eager to imitate those passages at arms of which he had read in his books, and here, so it seemed to him, was one made to order. And so, with bold and knightly bearing, he settled himself firmly in the stirrups, couched his lance, covered himself with his shield, and took up a position in the middle of the road, where he paused to wait for those other knights-errant (for such he took them to be) to come up to him. When they were near enough to see and hear plainly, Don Quixote raised his voice and made a haughty gesture.

"Let everyone," he cried, "stand where he is, unless everyone will confess that there is not in all the world a more beauteous damsel than the Empress of La Mancha, the peerless Dulcinea del Toboso."

Upon hearing these words and beholding the weird figure who uttered them, the merchants stopped short. From the knight's appearance and his speech they knew at once that they had to deal with a madman; but they were curious to know what was meant by that confession that was demanded of them, and one of their number who was somewhat of a jester and a very clever fellow raised his voice.

"Sir Knight," he said, "we do not know who this beauteous lady is of whom you speak. Show her to us, and if she is as beautiful as you say, then we will right willingly and without any compulsion confess the truth as you have asked of us."

"If I were to show her to you," replied Don Quixote, "what merit would there be in your confessing a truth so self-evident? The important thing is for you, without seeing her, to believe, confess, affirm, swear, and defend that truth. Otherwise, monstrous and arrogant creatures that you are, you shall do battle with me. Come on, then, one by one, as the order of knighthood prescribes; or all of you together, if you will have it so, as is the sorry custom of those of your breed. Come on, and I will await you here, for I am confident that my cause is just."

"Sir Knight," responded the merchant, "I beg your Grace, in the name of all the princes here present, in order that we may not have upon our consciences the burden of confessing a thing which we have never seen nor heard, and one, moreover, so prejudicial to the empresses and queens of Alcarria and Estremadura,[26] that your Grace will show us some portrait of this lady, even though it be no larger than a grain of wheat, for by the thread one comes to the ball of yarn; and with this we shall remain satisfied and assured, and your Grace will likewise be content and satisfied. The truth is, I believe that we are already so much of your way of thinking that though it should show her to be blind of one eye and distilling vermilion and brimstone from the other, nevertheless, to please your Grace, we would say in her behalf all that you desire."

"She distills nothing of the sort, infamous rabble!" shouted Don Quixote, for his wrath was kindling now. "I tell you, she does not distill what you say at all, but amber and civet wrapped in cotton;[27] and she is neither one-eyed nor hunchbacked but straighter than a spindle that comes from Guadarrama. You shall pay for the great blasphemy which you have uttered against such a beauty as is my lady!"

26. ironical, since both were known as particularly backward regions.

27. a musky substance used as perfume, imported from Africa in cotton packings.

Saying this, he came on with lowered lance against the one who had spoken, charging with such wrath and fury that if fortune had not caused Rocinante to stumble and fall in mid-career, things would have gone badly with the merchant and he would have paid for his insolent gibe. As it was, Don Quixote went rolling over the plain for some little distance, and when he tried to get to his feet, found that he was unable to do so, being too encumbered with his lance, shield, spurs, helmet, and the weight of that ancient suit of armor.

"Do not flee, cowardly ones," he cried even as he struggled to rise. "Stay, cravens, for it is not my fault but that of my steed that I am stretched out here."

One of the muleteers, who must have been an ill-natured lad, upon hearing the poor fallen knight speak so arrogantly, could not refrain from giving him an answer in the ribs. Going up to him, he took the knight's lance and broke it into bits, and then with a companion proceeded to belabor him so mercilessly that in spite of his armor they milled him like a hopper of wheat. The merchants called to them not to lay on so hard, saying that was enough and they should desist, but the mule driver by this time had warmed up to the sport and would not stop until he had vented his wrath, and, snatching up the broken pieces of the lance, he began hurling them at the wretched victim as he lay there on the ground. And through all this tempest of sticks that rained upon him Don Quixote never once closed his mouth nor ceased threatening Heaven and earth and these ruffians, for such he took them to be, who were thus mishandling him.

Finally the lad grew tired, and the merchants went their way with a good story to tell about the poor fellow who had had such a cudgeling. Finding himself alone, the knight endeavored to see if he could rise; but if this was a feat that he could not accomplish when he was sound and whole, how was he to achieve it when he had been thrashed and pounded to a pulp? Yet nonetheless he considered himself fortunate; for as he saw it, misfortunes such as this were common to knights-errant, and he put all the blame upon his horse; and if he was unable to rise, that was because his body was so bruised and battered all over.

### CHAPTER 5

*In which is continued the narrative of the misfortune that befell our knight.*

Seeing, then, that he was indeed unable to stir, he decided to fall back upon a favorite remedy of his, which was to think of some passage or other in his books; and as it happened, the one that he

in his madness now recalled was the story of Baldwin and the
Marquis of Mantua, when Carloto left the former wounded upon
the mountainside,[28] a tale that is known to children, not unknown
to young men, celebrated and believed in by the old, and, for all
of that, not any truer than the miracles of Mohammed. Moreover,
it impressed him as being especially suited to the straits in which
he found himself; and, accordingly, with a great show of feeling, he
began rolling and tossing on the ground as he feebly gasped out the
lines which the wounded knight of the wood is supposed to have
uttered:

> "Where art thou, lady mine,
> That thou dost not grieve for my woe?
> Either thou art disloyal,
> Or my grief thou dost not know."

He went on reciting the old ballad until he came to the following
verses:

> "O noble Marquis of Mantua,
> My uncle and liege lord true!"

He had reached this point when down the road came a farmer of
the same village, a neighbor of his, who had been to the mill with
a load of wheat. Seeing a man lying there stretched out like that, he
went up to him and inquired who he was and what was the trouble
that caused him to utter such mournful complaints. Thinking that
this must undoubtedly be his uncle, the Marquis of Mantua, Don
Quixote did not answer but went on with his recitation of the ballad, giving an account of the Marquis' misfortunes and the amours
of his wife and the emperor's son, exactly as the ballad has it.

The farmer was astounded at hearing all these absurdities, and
after removing the knight's visor which had been battered to pieces
by the blows it had received, the good man bathed the victim's face,
only to discover, once the dust was off, that he knew him very well.
"Señor Quijana," he said (for such must have been Don Quixote's
real name when he was in his right senses and before he had given
up the life of a quiet country gentleman to become a knight-errant),
"who is responsible for your Grace's being in such a plight as this?"

But the knight merely went on with his ballad in response to all
the questions asked of him. Perceiving that it was impossible to obtain any information from him, the farmer as best he could relieved
him of his breastplate and backpiece to see if he had any wounds,
but there was no blood and no mark of any sort. He then tried to
lift him from the ground, and with a great deal of effort finally

---

28. The allusion is to an old ballad
about Charlemagne's son Charlot (Carloto) wounding Baldwin, nephew of the
Marquis of Mantua.

managed to get him astride the ass, which appeared to be the easier mount for him. Gathering up the armor, including even the splinters from the lance, he made a bundle and tied it on Rocinante's back, and, taking the horse by the reins and the ass by the halter, he started out for the village. He was worried in his mind at hearing all the foolish things that Don Quixote said, and that individual himself was far from being at ease. Unable by reason of his bruises and his soreness to sit upright on the donkey, our knight-errant kept sighing to Heaven, which led the farmer to ask him once more what it was that ailed him.

It must have been the devil himself who caused him to remember those tales that seemed to fit his own case; for at this point he forgot all about Baldwin and recalled Abindarráez, and how the governor of Antequera, Rodrigo de Narváez, had taken him prisoner and carried him off captive to his castle. Accordingly, when the countryman turned to inquire how he was and what was troubling him, Don Quixote replied with the very same words and phrases that the captive Abindarráez used in answering Rodrigo, just as he had read in the story *Diana* of Jorge de Montemayor,[29] where it is all written down, applying them very aptly to the present circumstances as the farmer went along cursing his luck for having to listen to such a lot of nonsense. Realizing that his neighbor was quite mad, he made haste to reach the village that he might not have to be annoyed any longer by Don Quixote's tiresome harangue.

"Señor Don Rodrigo de Narváez," the knight was saying, "I may inform your Grace that this beautiful Jarifa of whom I speak is not the lovely Dulcinea del Toboso, in whose behalf I have done, am doing, and shall do the most famous deeds of chivalry that ever have been or will be seen in all the world."

"But, sir," replied the farmer, "sinner that I am, cannot your Grace see that I am not Don Rodrigo de Narváez nor the Marquis of Mantua, but Pedro Alonso, your neighbor? And your Grace is neither Baldwin nor Abindarráez but a respectable gentleman by the name of Señor Quijana."

"I know who I am," said Don Quixote, "and who I may be, if I choose: not only those I have mentioned but all the Twelve Peers of France and the Nine Worthies[30] as well; for the exploits of all of them together, or separately, cannot compare with mine."

With such talk as this they reached their destination just as night was falling; but the farmer decided to wait until it was a little darker

---

29. The reference is to the tale of the love of Abindarráez, a captive Moor, for the beautiful Jarifa (mentioned in the following paragraph), contained in the second edition of *Diana*, the pastoral romance by Jorge de Montemayor.

30. In the French medieval epics the Twelve Peers (Roland, Olivier, and so on) were warriors all equal in rank forming a sort of guard of honor around Charlemagne. The Nine Worthies, in a tradition originating in France, were nine famous figures, three biblical, three classical, and three Christian (David, Hector, Alexander, Charlemagne, and so on).

in order that the badly battered gentleman might not be seen arriving in such a condition and mounted on an ass. When he thought the proper time had come, they entered the village and proceeded to Don Quixote's house, where they found everything in confusion. The curate and the barber were there, for they were great friends of the knight, and the housekeeper was speaking to them.

"Señor Licentiate Pero Pérez," she was saying, for that was the manner in which she addressed the curate, "what does your Grace think could have happened to my master? Three days now, and not a word of him, nor the hack, nor the buckler, nor the lance, nor the suit of armor. Ah, poor me! I am as certain as I am that I was born to die that it is those cursed books of chivalry he is always reading that have turned his head; for now that I recall, I have often heard him muttering to himself that he must become a knight-errant and go through the world in search of adventures. May such books as those be consigned to Satan and Barabbas,[31] for they have sent to perdition the finest mind in all La Mancha."

The niece was of the same opinion. "I may tell you, Señor Master Nicholas," she said, for that was the barber's name, "that many times my uncle would sit reading those impious tales of misadventure for two whole days and nights at a stretch; and when he was through, he would toss the book aside, lay his hand on his sword, and begin slashing at the walls. When he was completely exhausted, he would tell us that he had just killed four giants as big as castle towers, while the sweat that poured off him was blood from the wounds that he had received in battle. He would then drink a big jug of cold water, after which he would be very calm and peaceful, saying that the water was the most precious liquid which the wise Esquife, a great magician and his friend, had brought to him. But I blame myself for everything. I should have advised your Worships of my uncle's nonsensical actions so that you could have done something about it by burning those damnable books of his before things came to such a pass; for he has many that ought to be burned as if they were heretics."

"I agree with you," said the curate, "and before tomorrow's sun has set there shall be a public *auto de fe*, and those works shall be condemned to the flames that they may not lead some other who reads them to follow the example of my good friend."

Don Quixote and the farmer overheard all this, and it was then that the latter came to understand the nature of his neighbor's affliction.

"Open the door, your Worships," the good man cried. "Open for Sir Baldwin and the Marquis of Mantua, who comes badly

31. the thief whose release, rather than that of Jesus Christ, the crowd requested when Pilate, conforming to Passover custom, was ready to have one prisoner set free.

wounded, and for Señor Abindarráez the Moor whom the valiant
Rodrigo de Narváez, governor of Antequera, brings captive."

At the sound of his voice they all ran out, recognizing at once
friend, master, and uncle, who as yet was unable to get down off
the donkey's back. They all ran up to embrace him.

"Wait, all of you," said Don Quixote, "for I am sorely wounded
through fault of my steed. Bear me to my couch and summon, if it
be possible, the wise Urganda to treat and care for my wounds."

"There!" exclaimed the housekeeper. "Plague take it! Did not my
heart tell me right as to which foot my master limped on? To bed
with your Grace at once, and we will take care of you without sending for that Urganda of yours. A curse, I say, and a hundred other
curses, on those books of chivalry that have brought your Grace to
this."

And so they carried him off to bed, but when they went to look
for his wounds, they found none at all. He told them it was all the
result of a great fall he had taken with Rocinante, his horse, while
engaged in combating ten giants, the hugest and most insolent that
were ever heard of in all the world.

"Tut, tut," said the curate. "So there are giants in the dance
now, are there? Then, by the sign of the cross, I'll have them burned
before nightfall tomorrow."

They had a thousand questions to put to Don Quixote, but his
only answer was that they should give him something to eat and let
him sleep, for that was the most important thing of all; so they
humored him in this. The curate then interrogated the farmer at
great length concerning the conversation he had had with his neighbor. The peasant told him everything, all the absurd things their
friend had said when he found him lying there and afterward on
the way home, all of which made the licentiate more anxious than
ever to do what he did the following day,[32] when he summoned
Master Nicholas and went with him to Don Quixote's house.

## [Fighting the Windmills]

### CHAPTER 7

*Of the second sally of our good knight, Don Quixote de la Mancha.*

. . . After that he remained at home very tranquilly for a couple
of weeks, without giving sign of any desire to repeat his former madness. During that time he had the most pleasant conversations with
his two old friends, the curate and the barber, on the point he
had raised to the effect that what the world needed most was
knights-errant and a revival of chivalry. The curate would occasionally
contradict him and again would give in, for it was only by means

32. What he and the barber did was to burn most of Don Quixote's library.

of this artifice that he could carry on a conversation with him at all.

In the meanwhile Don Quixote was bringing his powers of persuasion to bear upon a farmer who lived near by, a good man—if this title may be applied to one who is poor—but with very few wits in his head. The short of it is, by pleas and promises, he got the hapless rustic to agree to ride forth with him and serve him as his squire. Among other things, Don Quixote told him that he ought to be more than willing to go, because no telling what adventure might occur which would win them an island, and then he (the farmer) would be left to be the governor of it. As a result of these and other similar assurances, Sancho Panza forsook his wife and children and consented to take upon himself the duties of squire to his neighbor.

Next, Don Quixote set out to raise some money, and by selling this thing and pawning that and getting the worst of the bargain always, he finally scraped together a reasonable amount. He also asked a friend of his for the loan of a buckler and patched up his broken helmet as well as he could. He advised his squire, Sancho, of the day and hour when they were to take the road and told him to see to laying in a supply of those things that were most necessary, and, above all, not to forget the saddlebags. Sancho replied that he would see to all this and added that he was also thinking of taking along with him a very good ass that he had, as he was not much used to going on foot.

With regard to the ass, Don Quixote had to do a little thinking, trying to recall if any knight-errant had ever had a squire thus asininely mounted. He could not think of any, but nevertheless he decided to take Sancho with the intention of providing him with a nobler steed as soon as occasion offered; he had but to appropriate the horse of the first discourteous knight he met. Having furnished himself with shirts and all the other things that the innkeeper had recommended, he and Panza rode forth one night unseen by anyone and without taking leave of wife and children, housekeeper or niece. They went so far that by the time morning came they were safe from discovery had a hunt been started for them.

Mounted on his ass, Sancho Panza rode along like a patriarch, with saddlebags and flask, his mind set upon becoming governor of that island that his master had promised him. Don Quixote determined to take the same route and road over the Campo de Montiel that he had followed on his first journey; but he was not so uncomfortable this time, for it was early morning and the sun's rays fell upon them slantingly and accordingly did not tire them too much.

"Look, Sir Knight-errant," said Sancho, "your Grace should not forget that island you promised me; for no matter how big it is, I'll be able to govern it right enough."

"I would have you know, friend Sancho Panza," replied Don Quixote, "that among the knights-errant of old it was a very common custom to make their squires governors of the islands or the kingdoms that they won, and I am resolved that in my case so pleasing a usage shall not fall into desuetude. I even mean to go them one better; for they very often, perhaps most of the time, waited until their squires were old men who had had their fill of serving their masters during bad days and worse nights, whereupon they would give them the title of count, or marquis at most, of some valley or province more or less. But if you live and I live, it well may be that within a week I shall win some kingdom with others dependent upon it, and it will be the easiest thing in the world to crown you king of one of them. You need not marvel at this, for all sorts of unforeseen things happen to knights like me, and I may readily be able to give you even more than I have promised."

"In that case," said Sancho Panza, "if by one of those miracles of which your Grace was speaking I should become king, I would certainly send for Juana Gutiérrez, my old lady, to come and be my queen, and the young ones could be infantes."

"There is no doubt about it," Don Quixote assured him.

"Well, I doubt it," said Sancho, "for I think that even if God were to rain kingdoms upon the earth, no crown would sit well on the head of Mari Gutiérrez,[33] for I am telling you, sir, as a queen she is not worth two maravedis. She would do better as a countess, God help her."

"Leave everything to God, Sancho," said Don Quixote, "and he will give you whatever is most fitting; but I trust you will not be so pusillanimous as to be content with anything less than the title of viceroy."

"That I will not," said Sancho Panza, "especially seeing that I have in your Grace so illustrious a master who can give me all that is suitable to me and all that I can manage."

### CHAPTER 8

*Of the good fortune which the valorous Don Quixote had in the terrifying and never-before-imagined adventure of the windmills, along with other events that deserve to be suitably recorded.*

At this point they caught sight of thirty or forty windmills which were standing on the plain there, and no sooner had Don Quixote laid eyes upon them than he turned to his squire and said, "Fortune

33. Sancho's wife; she is called Juana Gutiérrez a few lines earlier.

is guiding our affairs better than we could have wished; for you see there before you, friend Sancho Panza, some thirty or more lawless giants with whom I mean to do battle. I shall deprive them of their lives, and with the spoils from this encounter we shall begin to enrich ourselves; for this is righteous warfare, and it is a great service to God to remove so accursed a breed from the face of the earth."

"What giants?" said Sancho Panza.

"Those that you see there," replied his master, "those with the long arms some of which are as much as two leagues in length."

"But look, your Grace, those are not giants but windmills, and what appear to be arms are their wings which, when whirled in the breeze, cause the millstone to go."

"It is plain to be seen," said Don Quixote, "that you have had little experience in this matter of adventures. If you are afraid, go off to one side and say your prayers while I am engaging them in fierce, unequal combat."

Saying this, he gave spurs to his steed Rocinante, without paying any heed to Sancho's warning that these were truly windmills and not giants that he was riding forth to attack. Nor even when he was close upon them did he perceive what they really were, but shouted at the top of his lungs, "Do not seek to flee, cowards and vile creatures that you are, for it is but a single knight with whom you have to deal!"

At that moment a little wind came up and the big wings began turning.

"Though you flourish as many arms as did the giant Briareus,"[34] said Don Quixote when he perceived this, "you still shall have to answer to me."

He thereupon commended himself with all his heart to his lady Dulcinea, beseeching her to succor him in this peril; and, being well covered with his shield and with his lance at rest, he bore down upon them at a full gallop and fell upon the first mill that stood in his way, giving a thrust at the wing, which was whirling at such a speed that his lance was broken into bits and both horse and horseman went rolling over the plain, very much battered indeed. Sancho upon his donkey came hurrying to his master's assistance as fast as he could, but when he reached the spot, the knight was unable to move, so great was the shock with which he and Rocinante had hit the ground.

"God help us!" exclaimed Sancho, "did I not tell your Grace to look well, that those were nothing but windmills, a fact which no one could fail to see unless he had other mills of the same sort in his head?"

34. mythological giant with a hundred arms.

"Be quiet, friend Sancho," said Don Quixote. "Such are the fortunes of war, which more than any other are subject to constant change. What is more, when I come to think of it, I am sure that this must be the work of that magician Frestón, the one who robbed me of my study and my books,[35] and who has thus changed the giants into windmills in order to deprive me of the glory of overcoming them, so great is the enmity that he bears me; but in the end his evil arts shall not prevail against this trusty sword of mine."

"May God's will be done," was Sancho Panza's response. And with the aid of his squire the knight was once more mounted on Rocinante, who stood there with one shoulder half out of joint. And so, speaking of the adventure that had just befallen them, they continued along the Puerto Lápice highway; for there, Don Quixote said, they could not fail to find many and varied adventures, this being a much traveled thoroughfare. . . .

### [Fighting the Sheep]

#### CHAPTER 18

*In which is set fort the conversation that Sancho Panza had with his master, Don Quixote, along with other adventures deserving of record.*

. . . . Don Quixote caught sight down the road of a large cloud of dust that was drawing nearer.

"This, O Sancho," he said, turning to his squire, "is the day when you shall see the boon that fate has in store for me; this, I repeat, is the day when, as well as on any other, shall be displayed the valor of my good right arm. On this day I shall perform deeds that will be written down in the book of fame for all centuries to come. Do you see that dust cloud rising there, Sancho? That is the dust stirred up by a vast army marching in this direction and composed of many nations."

"At that rate," said Sancho, "there must be two of them, for there is another one just like it on the other side."

Don Quixote turned to look and saw that this was so. He was overjoyed by the thought that these were indeed two armies about to meet and clash in the middle of the broad plain; for at every hour and every moment his imagination was filled with battles, enchantments, nonsensical adventures, tales of love, amorous challenges, and the like, such as he had read of in the books of chivalry, and every word he uttered, every thought that crossed his mind, every act he performed, had to do with such things as these. The dust clouds he had sighted were raised by two larges droves of sheep

35. Don Quixote had promptly attributed the ruin of his library, perhaps formed by the curate and the barber, to magical intervention.

coming along the road in opposite directions, which by reason of the dust were not visible until they were close at hand, but Don Quixote insisted so earnestly that they were armies that Sancho came to believe it.

"Sir," he said, "what are we to do?"

"What are we to do?" echoed his master. "Favor and aid the weak and needy. I would inform you, Sancho, that the one coming toward us is led and commanded by the great emperor Alifanfarón, lord of the great isle of Trapobana. This other one at my back is that of his enemy, the king of the Garamantas, Pentapolín of the Rolled-up Sleeve, for he always goes into battle with his right arm bare."

"But why are they such enemies?" Sancho asked.

"Because," said Don Quixote, "this Alifanfarón is a terrible pagan and in love with Pentapolín's daughter, who is a very beautiful and gracious lady and a Christian, for which reason her father does not wish to give her to the pagan king unless the latter first abjures the law of the false prophet, Mohammed, and adopts the faith that is Pentapolín's own."

"Then, by my beard," said Sancho, "if Pentapolín isn't right, and I am going to aid him all I can."

"In that," said Don Quixote, "you will only be doing your duty; for to engage in battles of this sort you need not have been dubbed a knight."

"I can understand that," said Sancho, "but where are we going to put this ass so that we will be certain of finding him after the fray is over? As for going into battle on such a mount, I do not think that has been done up to now."

"That is true enough," said Don Quixote. "What you had best do with him is to turn him loose and run the risk of losing him; for after we emerge the victors we shall have so many horses that even Rocinante will be in danger of being exchanged for another. But listen closely to what I am about to tell you, for I wish to give you an account of the principal knights that are accompanying these two armies; and in order that you may be the better able to see and take note of them, let us retire to that hillock over there which will afford us a very good view."

They then stationed themselves upon a slight elevation from which they would have been able to see very well the two droves of sheep that Don Quixote took to be armies if it had not been for the blinding clouds of dust. In spite of this, however, the worthy gentleman contrived to behold in his imagination what he did not see and what did not exist in reality.

Raising his voice, he went on to explain, "That knight in the gilded armor that you see there, bearing upon his shield a crowned lion crouched at the feet of a damsel, is the valiant Laurcalco, lord of the Silver Bridge; the other with the golden flowers on his armor, and on his shield three crowns argent on an azure field, is the dread Micocolembo, grand duke of Quirocia. And that one on Micocolembo's right hand, with the limbs of a giant, is the ever undaunted Brandabarbarán de Boliche, lord of the three Arabias. He goes armored in a serpent's skin and has for shield a door which, so report has it, is one of those from the temple that Samson pulled down, that time when he avenged himself on his enemies with his own death.

"But turn your eyes in this direction, and you will behold at the head of the other army the ever victorious, never vanquished Timonel de Carcajona, prince of New Biscay, who comes with quartered arms—azure, vert, argent, and or—and who has upon his shield a cat or on a field tawny, with the inscription *Miau*, which is the beginning of his lady's name; for she, so it is said, is the peerless Miulina, daughter of Alfeñquén, duke of Algarve. And that one over there, who weights down and presses the loins of that powerful charger, in a suit of snow-white armor with a white shield that bears no device whatever—he is a novice knight of the French nation, called Pierres Papin, lord of the baronies of Utrique. As for him you see digging his iron spurs into the flanks of that fleet-footed zebra courser and whose arms are vairs azure, he is the mighty duke of Nervia, Espartafilardo of the Wood, who has for device upon his shield an asparagus plant with a motto in Castilian that says '*Rastrea mi suerte.*' "[36]

In this manner he went on naming any number of imaginary knights on either side, describing on the spur of the moment their arms, colors, devices, and mottoes; for he was completely carried away by his imagination and by this unheard-of madness that had laid hold of him.

Without pausing, he went on, "This squadron in front of us is composed of men of various nations. There are those who drink the sweet waters of the famous Xanthus; woodsmen who tread the Massilian plain; those that sift the fine gold nuggets of Arabia Felix; those that are so fortunate as to dwell on the banks of the clear-running Thermodon, famed for their coolness; those who in many and diverse ways drain the golden Pactolus; Numidians, whose word is never to be trusted; Persians, with their famous bows and arrows; Medes and Parthians, who fight as they flee; Scythians, as cruel as they are fair of skin; Ethiopians, with their pierced lips; and an infinite number of other nationalities whose visages I see and recognize although I cannot recall their names.

36. probably a pun on *rastrear:* the meaning of the motto may be either "On Fortune's track" or "My Fortune creeps."

"In this other squadron come those that drink from the crystal currents of the olive-bearing Betis; those that smooth and polish their faces with the liquid of the ever rich and gilded Tagus; those that enjoy the beneficial waters of the divine Genil; those that roam the Tartessian plains with their abundant pasturage; those that disport themselves in the Elysian meadows of Jerez; the men of La Mancha, rich and crowned with golden ears of corn; others clad in iron garments, ancient relics of the Gothic race; those that bathe in the Pisuerga, noted for the mildness of its current; those that feed their herds in the wide-spreading pasture lands along the banks of the winding Guadiana, celebrated for its underground course;[37] those that shiver from the cold of the wooded Pyrenees or dwell amid the white peaks of the lofty Apennines—in short, all those whom Europe holds within its girth."

So help me God! How many provinces, how many nations did he not mention by name, giving to each one with marvelous readiness its proper attributes; for he was wholly absorbed and filled to the brim with what he had read in those lying books of his! Sancho Panza hung on his words, saying nothing, merely turning his head from time to time to have a look at those knights and giants that his master was pointing out to him; but he was unable to discover any of them.

"Sir," he said, "may I go to the devil if I see a single man, giant, or knight of all those that your Grace is talking about. Who knows? Maybe it is another spell, like last night."[38]

"How can you say that?" replied Don Quixote. "Can you not hear the neighing of the horses, the sound of trumpets, the roll of drums?"

"I hear nothing," said Sancho, "except the bleating of sheep."

And this, of course, was the truth; for the flocks were drawing near.

"The trouble is, Sancho," said Don Quixote, "you are so afraid that you cannot see or hear properly; for one of the effects of fear is to disturb the senses and cause things to appear other than what they are. If you are so craven as all that, go off to one side and leave me alone, and I without your help will assure the victory to that side to which I lend my aid."

Saying this, he put spurs to Rocinante and, with his lance at rest, darted down the hillside like a flash of lightning.

As he did so, Sancho called after him, "Come back, your Grace, Señor Don Quixote; I vow to God those are sheep that you are charging. Come back! O wretched father that bore me! What madness is this? Look you, there are no giants, nor knights, nor cats, nor shields either quartered or whole, nor vairs azure or bedeviled.

---

37. The Guadiana does run underground part of the way through La Mancha.

38. The inn where they had spent the previous night had been pronounced by Don Quixote an enchanted castle.

What is this you are doing, O sinner that I am in God's sight?"

But all this did not cause Don Quixote to turn back. Instead, he rode on, crying out at the top of his voice, "Ho, knights, those of you who follow and fight under the banners of the valiant Pentapolín of the Rolled-up Sleeves; follow me, all of you, and you shall see how easily I give you revenge on your enemy, Alifanfarón of Trapobana."

With these words he charged into the middle of the flock of sheep and began spearing at them with as much courage and boldness as if they had been his mortal enemies. The shepherds and herdsmen who were with the animals called to him to stop; but seeing it was no use, they unloosed their slings and saluted his ears with stones as big as your first.

Don Quixote paid no attention to the missiles and, dashing about here and there, kept crying, "Where are you, haughty Alifanfarón? Come out to me; for here is a solitary knight who desires in single combat to test your strength and deprive you of your life, as a punishment for that which you have done to the valorous Pentapolín Garamanta."

At that instant a pebble from the brook struck him in the side and buried a couple of ribs in his body. Believing himself dead or badly wounded, and remembering his potion, he took out his vial, placed it to his mouth, and began to swallow the balm; but before he had had what he thought was enough, there came another almond, which struck him in the hand, crushing the tin vial and carrying away with it a couple of grinders from his mouth, as well as badly mashing two of his fingers. As a result of these blows the poor knight tumbled from his horse. Believing that they had killed him, the shepherds hastily collected their flock and, picking up the dead beasts, of which there were more than seven, they went off down the road without more ado.

Sancho all this time was standing on the slope observing the insane things that his master was doing; and as he plucked savagely at his beard he cursed the hour and minute when luck had brought them together. But when he saw him lying there on the ground and perceived that the shepherds were gone, he went down the hill and came up to him, finding him in very bad shape though not unconscious.

"Didn't I tell you, Señor Don Quixote," he said, "that you should come back, that those were not armies you were charging but flocks of sheep?"

"This," said Don Quixote, "is the work of that thieving magician, my enemy, who thus counterfeits things and causes them to disappear. You must know, Sancho, that it is very easy for them to make us assume any appearance that they choose; and so it is that malign one who persecutes me, envious of the glory he saw me about to achieve in this battle, changed the squadrons of the foe into flocks of sheep. If you do not believe me, I beseech you on my life to do one thing for me, that you may be undeceived and discover for yourself that what I say is true. Mount your ass and follow them quietly, and when you have gone a short way from here, you will see them become their former selves once more; they will no longer be sheep but men exactly as I described them to you in the first place. But do not go now, for I need your kind assistance; come over here and have a look and tell me how many grinders are missing, for it feels as if I did not have a single one left."

[*"To Right Wrongs and Come to the Aid of the Wretched"*]

### CHAPTER 22

*Of how Don Quixote freed many unfortunate ones who, much against their will, were being taken where they did not wish to go.*

Cid Hamete Benengeli, the Arabic and Manchegan[39] author, in the course of this most grave, high-sounding, minute, delightful, and imaginative history,[40] informs us that, following the remarks that were exchanged between Don Quixote de la Mancha and Sancho Panza, his squire, . . . the knight looked up and saw coming toward them down the road which they were following a dozen or so men on foot, strung together by their necks like beads on an iron chain and all of them wearing handcuffs. They were accompanied by two men on horseback and two on foot, the former carrying wheel-lock muskets while the other two were armed with swords and javelins.

"That," said Sancho as soon as he saw them, "is a chain of galley slaves, people on their way to the galleys where by order of the king they are forced to labor."

"What do you mean by 'forced'?" asked Don Quixote. "Is it possible that the king uses force on anyone?"

"I did not say that," replied Sancho. "What I did say was that these are folks who have been condemned for their crimes to forced labor in the galleys for his Majesty the King."

"The short of it is," said the knight, "whichever way you put it, these people are being taken there by force and not of their own free will."

"That is the way it is," said Sancho.

39. of La Mancha.
40. In the tradition of the romances, Cervantes pretends that he is taking his story from an earlier chronicle.

"Well, in that case," said his master, "now is the time for me to fulfill the duties of my calling, which is to right wrongs and come to the aid of the wretched."

"But take note, your Grace," said Sancho, "that justice, that is to say, the king himself, is not using any force upon, or doing any wrong to, people like these, but is merely punishing them for the crimes they have committed."

The chain of galley slaves had come up to them by this time, whereupon Don Quixote very courteously requested the guards to inform him of the reason or reasons why they were conducting these people in such a manner as this. One of the men on horseback then replied that the men were prisoners who had been condemned by his Majesty to serve in the galleys, whither they were bound, and that was all there was to be said about it and all that he, Don Quixote, need know.

"Nevertheless," said the latter, "I should like to inquire of each one of them, individually, the cause of his misfortune." And he went on speaking so very politely in an effort to persuade them to tell him what he wanted to know that the other mounted guard finally said, "Although we have here the record and certificate of sentence of each one of these wretches, we have not the time to get them out and read them to you; and so your Grace may come over and ask the prisoners themselves, and they will tell you if they choose, and you may be sure that they will, for these fellows take a delight in their knavish exploits and in boasting of them afterward."

With this permission, even though he would have done so if it had not been granted him, Don Quixote went up to the chain of prisoners and asked the first whom he encountered what sins had brought him to so sorry a plight. The man replied that it was for being a lover that he found himself in that line.

"For that and nothing more?" said Don Quixote. "And do they, then, send lovers to the galleys? If so, I should have been rowing there long ago."

"But it was not the kind of love that your Grace has in mind," the prisoner went on. "I loved a wash basket full of white linen so well and hugged it so tightly that, if they had not taken it away from me by force, I would never of my own choice have let go of it to this very minute. I was caught in the act, there was no need to torture me, the case was soon disposed of, and they supplied me with a hundred lashes across the shoulders and, in addition, a three-year stretch in the *gurapas*, and that's all there is to tell."

"What are *gurapas*?" asked Don Quixote.

"*Gurapas* are the galleys," replied the prisoner. He was a lad of around twenty-four and stated that he was a native of Piedrahita.

The knight then put the same question to a second man, who

appeared to be very downcast and melancholy and did not have a word to say. The first man answered for him.

"This one, sir," he said, "is going as a canary—I mean, as a musician and singer."

"How is that?" Don Quixote wanted to know. "Do musicians and singers go to the galleys too?"

"Yes, sir; and there is nothing worse than singing when you're in trouble."

"On the contrary," said Don Quixote, "I have heard it said that he who sings frightens away his sorrows."

"It is just the opposite," said the prisoner; "for he who sings once weeps all his life long."

"I do not understand," said the knight.

One of the guards then explained. "Sir Knight, with this *non sancta*[41] tribe, to sing when you're in trouble means to confess under torture. This singer was put to the torture and confessed his crime, which was that of being a *cuatrero*, or cattle thief, and as a result of his confession he was condemned to six years in the galleys in addition to two hundred lashes which he took on his shoulders; and so it is he is always downcast and moody, for the other thieves, those back where he came from and the ones here, mistreat, snub, ridicule, and despise him for having confessed and for not having had the courage to deny his guilt. They are in the habit of saying that the word *no* has the same number of letters as the word *sí*,[42] and that a culprit is in luck when his life or death depends on his own tongue and not that of witnesses or upon evidence; and, in my opinion, they are not very far wrong."

"And I," said Don Quixote, "feel the same way about it." He then went on to a third prisoner and repeated his question.

The fellow answered at once, quite unconcernedly. "I'm going to my ladies, the *gurapas*, for five years, for the lack of five ducats."

"I would gladly give twenty," said Don Quixote, "to get you out of this."

"That," said the prisoner, "reminds me of the man in the middle of the ocean who has money and is dying of hunger because there is no place to buy what he needs. I say this for the reason that if I had had, at the right time, those twenty ducats your Grace is now offering me, I'd have greased the notary's quill and freshened up the attorney's wit with them, and I'd now be living in the middle of Zocodover Square in Toledo instead of being here on this highway coupled like a greyhound. But God is great; patience, and that's enough of it."

Don Quixote went on to a fourth prisoner, a venerable-looking old fellow with a white beard that fell over his bosom. When asked

41. unholy.                    42. yes.

how he came to be there, this one began weeping and made no reply, but a fifth comrade spoke up in his behalf.

"This worthy man," he said, "is on his way to the galleys after having made the usual rounds clad in a robe of state and on horse-back."[43]

"That means, I take it," said Sancho, "that he has been put to shame in public."

"That is it," said the prisoner, "and the offense for which he is being punished is that of having been an ear broker, or, better, a body broker. By that I mean to say, in short, that the gentleman is a pimp, and besides, he has his points as a sorcerer."

"If that point had not been thrown in," said Don Quixote, "he would not deserve, for merely being a pimp, to have to row in the galleys, but rather should be the general and give orders there. For the office of pimp is not an indifferent one; it is a function to be performed by persons of discretion and is most necessary in a well-ordered state; it is a profession that should be followed only by the wellborn, and there should, moreover, be a superviser or examiner as in the case of other offices, and the number of practitioners should be fixed by law as is done with brokers on the exchange. In that way many evils would be averted that arise when this office is filled and this calling practiced by stupid folk and those with little sense, such as silly women and pages or mountebanks with few years and less experience to their credit, who, on the most pressing occasions, when it is necessary to use one's wits, let the crumbs freeze between their hand and their mouth[44] and do not know which is their right hand and which is the left.

"I would go on and give reasons why it is fitting to choose carefully those who are to fulfill so necessary a state function, but this is not the place for it. One of these days I will speak of the matter to someone who is able to do something about it. I will say here only that the pain I felt at seeing those white hairs and this venerable countenance in such a plight, and all for his having been a pimp, has been offset for me by the additional information you have given me, to the effect that he is a sorcerer as well; for I am convinced that there are no sorcerers in the world who can move and compel the will, as some simple-minded persons think, but that our will is free and no herb or charm can force it.[45] All that certain foolish women and cunning tricksters do is to compound a few mixtures and poisons with which they deprive men of their senses while pretending that they have the power to make them loved,

43. after having been flogged in public, with all the ceremony that accompanied that punishment.
44. are too startled to act.
45. Here Don Quixote despises charms and love potions though often elsewhere, in his own vision of himself as a knight-errant, he accepts enchantments and spells as part of his world of fantasy.

although, as I have just said, one cannot affect another's will in that manner."

"That is so," said the worthy old man; "but the truth is, sir, I am not guilty on the sorcery charge. As for being a pimp, that is something I cannot deny. I never thought there was any harm in it, however, my only desire being that everyone should enjoy himself and live in peace and quiet, without any quarrels or troubles. But these good intentions on my part cannot prevent me from going where I do not want to go, to a place from which I do not expect to return; for my years are heavy upon me and an affection of the urine that I have will not give me a moment's rest."

With this, he began weeping once more, and Sancho was so touched by it that he took a four-real piece from his bosom and gave it to him as an act of charity.

Don Quixote then went on and asked another what his offense was. The fellow answered him, not with less, but with much more, briskness than the preceding one had shown.

"I am here," he said, "for the reason that I carried a joke too far with a couple of cousins-german of mine and a couple of others who were not mine, and I ended by jesting with all of them to such an extent that the devil himself would never be able to straighten out the relationship. They proved everything on me, there was no one to show me favor, I had no money, I came near swinging for it, they sentenced me to the galleys for six years, and I accepted the sentence as the punishment that was due me. I am young yet, and if I live long enough, everything will come out all right. If, Sir Knight, your Grace has anything with which to aid these poor creatures that you see before you, God will reward you in Heaven, and we here on earth will make it a point to ask God in our prayers to grant you long life and good health, as long and as good as your amiable presence deserves."

This man was dressed as a student, and one of the guards told Don Quixote that he was a great talker and a very fine Latinist.

Back of these came a man around thirty years of age and of very good appearance, except that when he looked at you his eyes were seen to be a little crossed. He was shackled in a different manner from the others, for he dragged behind a chain so huge that it was wrapped all around his body, with two rings at the throat, one of which was attached to the chain while the other was fastened to what is known as a keep-friend or friend's foot, from which two irons hung down to his waist, ending in handcuffs secured by a heavy padlock in such a manner that he could neither raise his hands to his mouth nor lower his head to reach his hands.

When Don Quixote asked why this man was so much more heavily chained than the others, the guard replied that it was because he had more crimes against him than all the others put together, and he was so bold and cunning that, even though they had him chained like this, they were by no means sure of him but feared that he might escape from them.

"What crimes could he have committed," asked the knight, "if he has merited a punishment no greater than that of being sent to the galleys?"

"He is being sent there for ten years," replied the guard, "and that is equivalent to civil death. I need tell you no more than that this good man is the famous Ginés de Pasamonte, otherwise known as Ginesillo de Parapilla."

"Señor Commissary," spoke up the prisoner at this point, "go easy there and let us not be so free with names and surnames. My just name is Ginés and not Ginesillo; and Pasamonte, not Parapilla as you make it out to be, is my family name. Let each one mind his own affairs and he will have his hands full."

"Speak a little more respectfully, you big thief, you," said the commissary, "unless you want me to make you be quiet in a way you won't like."

"Man goes as God pleases, that is plain to be seen," replied the galley slave, "but someday someone will know whether my name is Ginesillo de Parapilla or not."

"But, you liar, isn't that what they call you?"

"Yes," said Ginés, "they do call me that; but I'll put a stop to it, or else I'll skin their you-know-what. And you, sir, if you have anything to give us, give it and may God go with you, for I am tired of all this prying into other people's lives. If you want to know anything about my life, know that I am Ginés de Pasamonte whose life story has been written down by these fingers that you see here."

"He speaks the truth," said the commissary, "for he has himself written his story, as big as you please, and has left the book in the prison, having pawned it for two hundred reales."

"And I mean to redeem it," said Ginés, "even if it costs me two hundred ducats."

"Is it as good as that?" inquired Don Quixote.

"It is so good," replied Ginés, "that it will cast into the shade *Lazarillo de Tormes*[46] and all others of that sort that have been or will be written. What I would tell you is that it deals with facts, and facts so interesting and amusing that no lies could equal them."

"And what is the title of the book?" asked Don Quixote.

"*The Life of Ginés de Pasamonte*."

"Is it finished?"

"How could it be finished," said Ginés, "when my life is not

---

46. a picaresque or rogue novel, published anonymously about the middle of the fifteenth century.

finished as yet? What I have written thus far is an account of what happened to me from the time I was born up to the last time that they sent me to the galleys."

"Then you have been there before?"

"In the service of God and the king I was there four years, and I know what the biscuit and the cowhide are like. I don't mind going very much, for there I will have a chance to finish my book. I still have many things to say, and in the Spanish galleys I shall have all the leisure that I need, though I don't need much, since I know by heart what it is I want to write."

"You seem to be a clever fellow," said Don Quixote.

"And an unfortunate one," said Ginés; "for misfortunes always pursue men of genius."

"They pursue rogues," said the commissary.

"I have told you to go easy, Señor Commissary," said Pasamonte, "for their Lordships did not give you that staff in order that you might mistreat us poor devils with it, but they intended that you should guide and conduct us in accordance with his Majesty's command. Otherwise, by the life of— But enough. It may be that someday the stains made in the inn will come out in the wash. Meanwhile, let everyone hold his tongue, behave well, and speak better, and let us be on our way. We've had enough of this foolishness."

At this point the commissary raised his staff as if to let Pasamonte have it in answer to his threats, but Don Quixote placed himself between them and begged the officer not to abuse the man; for it was not to be wondered at if one who had his hands so bound should be a trifle free with his tongue. With this, he turned and addressed them all.

"From all that you have told me, my dearest brothers," he said, "one thing stands out clearly for me, and that is the fact that, even though it is a punishment for offenses which you have committed. the penalty you are about to pay is not greatly to your liking and you are going to the galleys very much against your own will and desire. It may be that the lack of spirit which one of you displayed under torture, the lack of money on the part of another, the lack of influential friends, or, finally, warped judgment on the part of the magistrate, was the thing that led to your downfall; and, as a result, justice was not done you. All of which presents itself to my mind in such a fashion that I am at this moment engaged in trying to persuade and even force myself to show you what the purpose was for which Heaven sent me into this world, why it was it led me to adopt the calling of knighthood which I profess and take the knightly vow to favor the needy and aid those who are oppressed by the powerful.

"However, knowing as I do that it is not the part of prudence to do by foul means what can be accomplished by fair ones, I propose to ask these gentlemen, your guards, and the commissary to be so good as to unshackle you and permit you to go in peace. There will be no dearth of others to serve his Majesty under more propitious circumstances; and it does not appear to me to be just to make slaves of those whom God created as free men. What is more, gentlemen of the guard, these poor fellows have committed no offense against you. Up there, each of us will have to answer for his own sins; for God in Heaven will not fail to punish the evil and reward the good; and it is not good for self-respecting men to be executioners of their fellow-men in something that does not concern them. And so, I ask this of you, gently and quietly, in order that, if you comply with my request, I shall have reason to thank you; and if you do not do so of your own accord, then this lance and this sword and the valor of my arm shall compel you to do it by force."

"A fine lot of foolishness!" exclaimed the commissary. "So he comes out at last with this nonsense! He would have us let the prisoners of the king go free, as if we had any authority to do so or he any right to command it! Be on your way, sir, at once; straighten that basin that you have on your head, and do not go looking for three feet on a cat."[47]

"You," replied Don Quixote, "are the cat and the rat and the rascal!" And, saying this, he charged the commissary so quickly that the latter had no chance to defend himself but fell to the ground badly wounded by the lance blow. The other guards were astounded by this unexpected occurrence; but, recovering their self-possession, those on horseback drew their swords, those on foot leveled their javelins, and all bore down on Don Quixote, who stood waiting for them very calmly. Things undoubtedly would have gone badly for him if the galley slaves, seeing an opportunity to gain their freedom, had not succeeded in breaking the chain that linked them together. Such was the confusion that the guards, now running to fall upon the prisoners and now attacking Don Quixote, who in turn was attacking them, accomplished nothing that was of any use.

Sancho for his part aided Ginés de Pasamonte to free himself, and that individual was the first to drop his chains and leap out onto the field, where, attacking the fallen commissary, he took away that officer's sword and musket; and as he stood there, aiming first at one and then at another, though without firing, the plain was soon cleared of guards, for they had taken to their heels, fleeing at once Pasamonte's weapon and the stones which the galley slaves,

47. looking for the impossible ("five feet" in the more usual form of the proverb).

freed now, were hurling at them. Sancho, meanwhile, was very much disturbed over this unfortunate event, as he felt sure that the fugitives would report the matter to the Holy Brotherhood,[48] which, to the ringing of the alarm bell, would come out to search for the guilty parties. He said as much to his master, telling him that they should leave at once and go into hiding in the near-by mountains.

"That is all very well," said Don Quixote, "but I know what had best be done now." He then summoned all the prisoners, who, running riot, had by this time despoiled the commissary of everything that he had, down to his skin, and as they gathered around to hear what he had to say, he addressed them as follows:

"It is fitting that those who are wellborn should give thanks for the benefits they have received, and one of the sins with which God is most offended is that of ingratitude. I say this, gentlemen, for the reason that you have seen and had manifest proof of what you owe to me; and now that you are free of the yoke which I have removed from about your necks, it is my will and desire that you should set out and proceed to the city of El Toboso and there present yourselves before the lady Dulcinea del Toboso and say to her that her champion, the Knight of the Mournful Countenance, has sent you; and then you will relate to her, point by point, the whole of this famous adventure which has won you your longed-for freedom. Having done that, you may go where you like, and may good luck go with you."

To this Ginés de Pasamonte replied in behalf of all of them, "It is absolutely impossible, your Grace, our liberator, for us to do what you have commanded. We cannot go down the highway all together but must separate and go singly, each in his own direction, endeavoring to hide ourselves in the bowels of the earth in order not to be found by the Holy Brotherhood, which undoubtedly will come out to search for us. What your Grace can do, and it is right that you should do so, is to change this service and toll that you require of us in connection with the lady Dulcinea del Toboso into a certain number of Credos and Hail Marys which we will say for your Grace's intention, as this is something that can be accomplished by day or night, fleeing or resting, in peace or in war. To imagine, on the other hand, that we are going to return to the fleshpots of Egypt, by which I mean, take up our chains again by setting out along the highway for El Toboso, is to believe that it is night now instead of ten o'clock in the morning and is to ask of us something that is the same as asking pears of the elm tree."

"Then by all that's holy!" exclaimed Don Quixote, whose wrath

48. a tribunal instituted by Ferdinand and Isabella at the end of the fifteenth century to punish highway robberies.

was now aroused, "you, Don Son of a Whore, Don Ginesillo de Parapilla, or whatever your name is, you shall go alone, your tail between your legs and the whole chain on your back."

Pasamonte, who was by no means a long-suffering individual, was by this time convinced that Don Quixote was not quite right in the head, seeing that he had been guilty of such a folly as that of desiring to free them; and so, when he heard himself insulted in this manner, he merely gave the wink to his companions and, going off to one side, began raining so many stones upon the knight that the latter was wholly unable to protect himself with his buckler, while poor Rocinante paid no more attention to the spur than if he had been made of brass. As for Sancho, he took refuge behind his donkey as a protection against the cloud and shower of rocks that was falling on both of them, but Don Quixote was not able to shield himself so well, and there is no telling how many struck his body, with such force as to unhorse and bring him to the ground.

No sooner had he fallen than the student was upon him. Seizing the basin from the knight's head, he struck him three or four blows with it across the shoulders and banged it against the ground an equal number of times until it was fairly shattered to bits. They then stripped Don Quixote of the doublet which he wore over his armor, and would have taken his hose as well, if his greaves had not prevented them from doing so, and made off with Sancho's great-coat, leaving him naked; after which, dividing the rest of the battle spoils amongst themselves, each of them went his own way, being a good deal more concerned with eluding the dreaded Holy Brotherhood than they were with burdening themselves with a chain or going to present themselves before the lady Dulcinea del Toboso.

They were left alone now—the ass and Rocinante, Sancho and Don Quixote: the ass, crestfallen and pensive, wagging its ears now and then, being under the impression that the hurricane of stones that had raged about them was not yet over; Rocinante, stretched alongside his master, for the hack also had been felled by a stone; Sancho, naked and fearful of the Holy Brotherhood; and Don Quixote, making wry faces at seeing himself so mishandled by those to whom he had done so much good.

[*"Set Free at Once that Lovely Lady . . ."*]

## CHAPTER 52[49]

*Of the quarrel that Don Quixote had with the goatherd, together with the rare adventure of the penitents, which the knight by the sweat of his brow brought to a happy conclusion.*

All those who had listened to it were greatly pleased with the goatherd's story,[50] especially the canon,[51] who was more than usually interested in noting the manner in which it had been told. Far from being a mere rustic herdsman, the narrator seemed rather a cultured city dweller; and the canon accordingly remarked that the curate had been quite right in saying that the mountain groves bred men of learning. They all now offered their services to Eugenio, and Don Quixote was the most generous of any in this regard.

"Most assuredly, brother goatherd," he said, "if it were possible for me to undertake any adventure just now, I would set out at once to aid you and would take Leandra out of that convent, where she is undoubtedly being held against her will, in spite of the abbess and all the others who might try to prevent me, after which I would place her in your hands to do with as you liked, with due respect, however, for the laws of chivalry, which command that no violence be offered to any damsel. But I trust in God, Our Lord, that the power of one malicious enchanter is not so great that another magician may not prove still more powerful, and then I promise you my favor and my aid, as my calling obliges me to do, since it is none other than that of succoring the weak and those who are in distress."

The goatherd stared at him, observing in some astonishment the knight's unprepossessing appearance.

"Sir," he said, turning to the barber who sat beside him, "who is this man who looks so strange and talks in this way?"

"Who should it be," the barber replied, "if not the famous Don Quixote de la Mancha, righter of wrongs, avenger of injustices, protector of damsels, terror of giants, and champion of battles?"

"That," said the goatherd, "sounds to me like the sort of thing you read of in books of chivalry, where they do all those things that your Grace has mentioned in connection with this man. But if you

49. last chapter of Part I. Through various devices, including the use of Don Quixote's own belief in enchantments and spells, the curate and the barber have persuaded the knight to let himself be taken home in an ox cart.
50. Eugenio, a very literate goatherd met on the way, has just told them the story of his unhappy love for Leandra: the girl, instead of choosing one of her local suitors, had eloped with a flashy and crooked soldier; robbed and abandoned by him, she had been put by her father in a convent.
51. a canon from Toledo who has joined Don Quixote and his guardians on the way; conversing about chivalry with the knight, he has had cause to be "astonished at Don Quixote's well-reasoned nonsense."

ask me, either your Grace is joking or this worthy gentleman must
have a number of rooms to let inside his head."

"You are the greatest villain that ever was!" cried Don Quixote
when he heard this. "It is you who are the empty one; I am fuller
than the bitch that bore you ever was." Saying this, he snatched up
a loaf of bread that was lying beside him and hurled it straight in
the goatherd's face with such force as to flatten the man's nose.
Upon finding himself thus mistreated in earnest, Eugenio, who did
not understand this kind of joke, forgot all about the carpet, the
tablecloth, and the other diners and leaped upon Don Quixote.
Seizing him by the throat with both hands, he would no doubt
have strangled him if Sancho Panza, who now came running up,
had not grasped him by the shoulders and flung him backward over
the table, smashing plates and cups and spilling and scattering all
the food and drink that was there. Thus freed of his assailant, Don
Quixote then threw himself upon the shepherd, who, with bleeding
face and very much battered by Sancho's feet, was creeping about
on his hands and knees in search of a table knife with which to
exact a sanguinary vengeance, a purpose which the canon and the
curate prevented him from carrying out. The barber, however, so
contrived it that the goatherd came down on top of his opponent,
upon whom he now showered so many blows that the poor knight's
countenance was soon as bloody as his own.

As all this went on, the canon and the curate were laughing fit to
burst, the troopers[52] were dancing with glee, and they all hissed on
the pair as men do at a dog fight. Sancho Panza alone was in
despair, being unable to free himself of one of the canon's servants
who held him back from going to his master's aid. And then, just as
they were all enjoying themselves hugely, with the exception of the
two who were mauling each other, the note of a trumpet fell upon
their ears, a sound so mournful that it caused them all to turn their
heads in the direction from which it came. The one who was most
excited by it was Don Quixote; who, very much against his will and
more than a little bruised, was lying pinned beneath the goatherd.

"Brother Demon," he now said to the shepherd, "for you could
not possibly be anything but a demon, seeing that you have shown a
strength and valor greater than mine, I request you to call a truce
for no more than an hour; for the doleful sound of that trumpet
that we hear seems to me to be some new adventure that is calling
me."

Tired of mauling and being mauled, the goatherd let him up at
once. As he rose to his feet and turned his head in the direction of
the sound, Don Quixote then saw, coming down the slope of a hill,
a large number of persons clad in white after the fashion of peni-

---

52. law officers from the Holy Brotherhood (cf. n. 48). They had wanted to
arrest Don Quixote on account of his
having attempted the liberation of the
galley slaves but had been persuaded not
to do so, considering the knight's state
of insanity.

tents; for, as it happened, the clouds that year had denied their moisture to the earth, and in all the villages of that district processions for prayer and penance were being organized with the purpose of beseeching God to have mercy and send rain. With this object in view, the good folk from a near-by town were making a pilgrimage to a devout hermit who dwelt on these slopes. Upon beholding the strange costumes that the penitents wore, without pausing to think how many times he had seen them before, Don Quixote imagined that this must be some adventure or other, and that it was for him alone as a knight-errant to undertake it. He was strengthened in this belief by the sight of a covered image that they bore, as it seemed to him this must be some highborn lady whom these scoundrelly and discourteous brigands were forcibly carrying off; and no sooner did this idea occur to him than he made for Rocinante, who was grazing not far away.

Taking the bridle and his buckler from off the saddletree, he had the bridle adjusted in no time, and then, asking Sancho for his sword, he climbed into the saddle, braced his shield upon his arm, and cried out to those present, "And now, valorous company, you shall see how important it is to have in the world those who follow the profession of knight-errantry. You have but to watch how I shall set at liberty that worthy lady who there goes captive, and then you may tell me whether or not such knights are to be esteemed."

As he said this, he dug his legs into Rocinante's flanks, since he had no spurs, and at a fast trot (for nowhere in this veracious history are we ever told that the hack ran full speed) he bore down on the penitents in spite of all that the canon, the curate, and the barber could do to restrain him—their efforts were as vain as were the pleadings of his squire.

"Where are you bound for, Señor Don Quixote?" Sancho called after him. "What evil spirits in your bosom spur you on to go against our Catholic faith? Plague take me, can't you see that's a procession of penitents and that lady they're carrying on the litter is the most blessed image of the Immaculate Virgin? Look well what you're doing, my master, for this time it may be said that you really do not know."

His exertions were in vain, however, for his master was so bent upon having it out with the sheeted figures and freeing the lady clad in mourning that he did not hear a word, nor would he have turned back if he had, though the king himself might have commanded it. Having reached the procession, he reined in Rocinante, who by this time was wanting a little rest, and in a hoarse, excited voice he shouted, "You who go there with your faces covered, out of shame, it may be, listen well to what I have to say to you."

The first to come to a halt were those who carried the image; and then one of the four clerics who were intoning the litanies, upon beholding Don Quixote's weird figure, his bony nag, and other amusing appurtenances, spoke up in reply.

"Brother, if you have something to say to us, say it quickly, for these brethren are engaged in macerating their flesh, and we cannot stop to hear anything, nor is it fitting that we should, unless it is capable of being said in a couple of words."

"I will say it to you in one word," Don Quixote answered, "and that word is the following: 'Set free at once that lovely lady whose tears and mournful countenance show plainly that you are carrying her away against her will and that you have done her some shameful wrong. I will not consent to your going one step farther until you shall have given her the freedom that should be hers.'"

Hearing these words, they all thought that Don Quixote must be some madman or other and began laughing heartily; but their laughter proved to be gunpowder to his wrath, and without saying another word he drew his sword and fell upon the litter. One of those who bore the image, leaving his share of the burden to his companions, then sallied forth to meet the knight, flourishing a forked stick that he used to support the Virgin while he was resting; and upon this stick he now received a mighty slash that Don Quixote dealt him, one that shattered it in two, but with the piece about a third long that remained in his hand he came down on the shoulder of his opponent's sword arm, left unprotected by the buckler, with so much force that the poor fellow sank to the ground sorely battered and bruised.

Sancho Panza, who was puffing along close behind his master, upon seeing him fall cried out to the attacker not to deal another blow, as this was an unfortunate knight who was under a magic spell but who had never in all the days of his life done any harm to anyone. But the thing that stopped the rustic was not Sancho's words; it was, rather, the sight of Don Quixote lying there without moving hand or foot. And so, thinking that he had killed him, he hastily girded up his tunic and took to his heels across the countryside like a deer.

By this time all of Don Quixote's companions had come running up to where he lay; and the penitents, when they observed this, and especially when they caught sight of the officers of the Brotherhood with their crossbows, at once rallied around the image, where they raised their hoods and grasped their whips as the priests raised their tapers aloft in expectation of an assault; for they were resolved to defend themselves and even, if possible, to take the offensive against their assailants, but, as luck would have it, things turned out better than they had hoped. Sancho, meanwhile, believing Don Quixote to be dead, had flung himself across his master's body and was weeping and wailing in the most lugubrious and, at the same time, the most laughable fashion that could be imagined; and the curate had discovered among those who marched in the procession another curate whom he knew, their recognition of each other serving to allay the fears of all parties concerned. The first curate then gave the second a very brief account of who Don Quixote was, whereupon all the penitents came up to see if the poor knight was dead. And as they did so, they heard Sancho Panza speaking with tears in his eyes.

"O flower of chivalry,"[53] he was saying, "the course of whose well-spent years has been brought to an end by a single blow of a club! O honor of your line, honor and glory of all La Mancha and of all the world, which, with you absent from it, will be full of evildoers who will not fear being punished for their deeds! O master more generous than all the Alexanders, who after only eight months of service presented me with the best island that the sea washes and surrounds! Humble with the proud, haughty with the humble, brave in facing dangers, long-suffering under outrages, in love without reason, imitator of the good, scourge of the wicked, enemy of the mean—in a word, a knight-errant, which is all there is to say."

At the sound of Sancho's cries and moans, Don Quixote revived, and the first thing he said was, "He who lives apart from thee, O fairest Dulcinea, is subject to greater woes than those I now endure. Friend Sancho, help me onto that enchanted cart, as I am in no condition to sit in Rocinante's saddle with this shoulder of mine knocked to pieces the way it is."

"That I will gladly do, my master," replied Sancho, "and we will go back to my village in the company of these gentlemen who are concerned for your welfare, and there we will arrange for another sally and one, let us hope, that will bring us more profit and fame than this one has."

"Well spoken, Sancho," said Don Quixote, "for it will be an act of great prudence to wait until the present evil influence of the stars has passed."

The canon, the curate, and the barber all assured him that he would be wise in doing this; and so, much amused by Sancho Panza's simplicity, they placed Don Quixote upon the cart as before, while the procession of penitents re-formed and continued on its way. The goatherd took leave of all of them, and the curate paid the troopers what was coming to them, since they did not wish to go any farther. The canon requested the priest to inform him of the outcome of Don Quixote's madness, as to whether it yielded to treatment or not; and with this he begged permission to resume his journey. In short, the party broke up and separated, leaving only the curate and the barber, Don Quixote and Panza, and the good Rocinante, who looked upon everything that he had seen with the same resignation as his master. Yoking his oxen, the carter made the knight comfortable upon a bale of hay, and then at his customary slow pace proceeded to follow the road that the curate directed him to take. At the end of the six days they reached Don Quixote's village, making their entrance at noon of a Sunday, when the square

---

53. Note how Sancho has absorbed some of his master's speech mannerisms.

was filled with a crowd of people through which the cart had to pass.

They all came running to see who it was, and when they recognized their townsman, they were vastly astonished. One lad sped to bring the news to the knight's housekeeper and his niece, telling them that their master had returned lean and jaundiced and lying stretched out upon a bale of hay on an ox-cart. It was pitiful to hear the good ladies' screams, to behold the way in which they beat their breasts, and to listen to the curses which they once more heaped upon those damnable books of chivalry, and this demonstration increased as they saw Don Quixote coming through the doorway.

At news of the knight's return, Sancho Panza's wife had hurried to the scene, for she had some while since learned that her husband had accompanied him as his squire; and now, as soon as she laid eyes upon her man, the first question she asked was if all was well with the ass, to which Sancho replied that the beast was better off then his master.

"Thank God," she exclaimed, "for all his blessings! But tell me now, my dear, what have you brought me from all your squirings? A new cloak to wear? Or shoes for the young ones?"

"I've brought you nothing of the sort, good wife," said Sancho, "but other things of greater value and importance."

"I'm glad to hear that," she replied. "Show me those things of greater value and importance, my dear. I'd like a sight of them just to cheer this heart of mine which has been so sad and unhappy all the centuries that you've been gone."

"I will show them to you at home, wife," said Sancho. "For the present be satisfied that if, God willing, we set out on another journey in search of adventures, you will see me in no time a count or the governor of an island, and not one of those around here, but the best that is to be had."

"I hope to Heaven it's true, my husband, for we certainly need it. But tell me, what is all this about islands? I don't understand."

"Honey," replied Sancho, "is not for the mouth of an ass. You will find out in good time, woman; and you're going to be surprised to hear yourself called 'my Ladyship' by all your vassals."

"What's this you are saying, Sancho, about ladyships, islands, and vassals?" Juana Panza insisted on knowing—for such was the name of Sancho's wife, although they were not blood relatives, it being the custom in La Mancha for wives to take their husbands' surnames.

"Do not be in such a hurry to know all this, Juana," he said. "It is enough that I am telling you the truth. Sew up your mouth, then; for all I will say, in passing, is that there is nothing in the world that is more pleasant than being a respected man, squire to a knight-errant who goes in search of adventures. It is true that most of the adventures you meet with do not come out the way you'd like them to, for ninety-nine out of a hundred will prove to be all twisted and crosswise. I know that from experience, for I've come out of some of them blanketed and out of others beaten to a pulp. But, all the same, it's a fine thing to go along waiting for what will happen next, crossing mountains, making your way through woods, climbing over cliffs, visiting castles, and putting up at inns free of charge, and the devil take the maravedi that is to pay."

Such was the conversation that took place between Sancho Panza and Juana Panza, his wife, as Don Quixote's housekeeper and niece were taking him in, stripping him, and stretching him out on his old-time bed. He gazed at them blankly, being unable to make out where he was. The curate charged the niece to take great care to see that her uncle was comfortable and to keep close watch over him so that he would not slip away from them another time. He then told them of what it had been necessary to do in order to get him home, at which they once more screamed to Heaven and began cursing the books of chivalry all over again, praying God to plunge the authors of such lying nonsense into the center of the bottomless pit. In short, they scarcely knew what to do, for they were very much afraid that their master and uncle would give them the slip once more, the moment he was a little better, and it turned out just the way they feared it might.

# Don Quixote, Part II
## ["Put into a Book"]

### CHAPTER 3

*Of the laughable conversation that took place between Don Quixote, Sancho Panza, and the bachelor Sansón Carrasco.*

Don Quixote remained in a thoughtful mood as he waited for the bachelor Carrasco,[54] from whom he hoped to hear the news as to how he had been put into a book, as Sancho had said. He could not bring himself to believe that any such history existed, since the blood of the enemies he had slain was not yet dry on the blade of his sword; and here they were trying to tell him that his high deeds of chivalry were already circulating in printed form. But, for that matter, he imagined that some sage, either friend or enemy, must have seen to the printing of them through the art of magic. If the chronicler was a friend, he must have undertaken the task in order

54. the bachelor of arts Sansón Carrasco, an important new character who appears at the beginning of Part II and will play a considerable role in the story with his attempts at "curing" the Don (the first one a failure, the second one a success; see our following selections). Just now he has been telling Sancho about a book relating the adventures of Don Quixote and his squire, by which the two have been made famous; the book is, of course, *Don Quixote*, Part I.

to magnify and exalt Don Quixote's exploits above the most notable ones achieved by knights-errant of old. If an enemy, his purpose would have been to make them out as nothing at all, by debasing them below the meanest acts ever recorded of any mean squire. The only thing was, the knight reflected, the exploits of squires never were set down in writing. If it was true that such a history existed, being about a knight-errant, then it must be eloquent and lofty in tone, a splendid and distinguished piece of work and veracious in its details.

This consoled him somewhat, although he was a bit put out at the thought that the author was a Moor, if the appellation "Cid" was to be taken as an indication,[55] and from the Moors you could never hope for any word of truth, seeing that they are all of them cheats, forgers, and schemers. He feared lest his love should not have been treated with becoming modesty but rather in a way that would reflect upon the virtue of his lady Dulcinea del Toboso. He hoped that his fidelity had been made clear, and the respect he had always shown her, and that something had been said as to how he had spurned queens, empresses, and damsels of every rank while keeping a rein upon those impulses that are natural to a man. He was still wrapped up in these and many other similar thoughts when Sancho returned with Carrasco.

Don Quixote received the bachelor very amiably. The latter, although his name was Sansón, or Samson, was not very big so far as bodily size went, but he was a great joker, with a sallow complexion and a ready wit. He was going on twenty-four and had a round face, a snub nose, and a large mouth, all of which showed him to be of a mischievous disposition and fond of jests and witticisms. This became apparent when, as soon as he saw Don Quixote, he fell upon his knees and addressed the knight as follows:

"O mighty Don Quixote de la Mancha, give me your hands; for by the habit of St. Peter that I wear[56]—though I have received but the first four orders—your Grace is one of the most famous knights-errant that ever have been or ever will be anywhere on this earth. Blessings upon Cid Hamete Benengeli who wrote down the history of your great achievements, and upon that curious-minded one who was at pains to have it translated from the Arabic into our Castilian vulgate for the universal entertainment of the people."

Don Quixote bade him rise. "Is it true, then," he asked, "that there is a book about me and that it was some Moorish sage who composed it?"

"By way of showing you how true it is," replied Sansón, "I may

---

55. The allusion is to Cid Hamete Benengeli (see footnote 40 and the corresponding passage in the text); the word *cid*, "chief," is of Arabic derivation.

56. the dress of one of the minor clerical orders.

tell you that it is my belief that there are in existence today more than twelve thousand copies of that history. If you do not believe me, you have but to make inquiries in Portugal, Barcelona, and Valencia, where editions have been brought out, and there is even a report to the effect that one edition was printed at Antwerp. In short, I feel certain that there will soon not be a nation that does not know it or a language into which it has not been translated."

"One of the things," remarked Don Quixote, "that should give most satisfaction to a virtuous and eminent man is to see his good name spread abroad during his own lifetime, by means of the printing press, through translations into the languages of the various peoples. I have said 'good name,' for if he has any other kind, his fate is worse than death."

"If it is a matter of good name and good reputation," said the bachelor, "your Grace bears off the palm from all the knights-errant in the world; for the Moor in his tongue and the Christian in his have most vividly depicted your Grace's gallantry, your courage in facing dangers, your patience in adversity and suffering, whether the suffering be due to wounds or to misfortunes of another sort, and your virtue and continence in love, in connection with that platonic relationship that exists between your Grace and my lady Doña Dulcinea del Toboso."

At this point Sancho spoke up. "Never in my life," he said, "have I heard my lady Dulcinea called 'Doña,' but only 'la Señora Dulcinea del Toboso'; so on that point, already, the history is wrong."

"That is not important," said Carrasco.

"No, certainly not," Don Quixote agreed. "But tell me, Señor Bachelor, what adventures of mine as set down in this book have made the deepest impression?"

"As to that," the bachelor answered, "opinions differ, for it is a matter of individual taste. There are some who are very fond of the adventure of the windmills—those windmills which to your Grace appeared to be so many Briareuses and giants. Others like the episode at the fulling mill. One relishes the story of the two armies which took on the appearance of droves of sheep, while another fancies the tale of the dead man whom they were taking to Segovia for burial. One will assert that the freeing of the galley slaves is the best of all, and yet another will maintain that nothing can come up to the Benedictine giants and the encounter with the valiant Biscayan."

Again Sancho interrupted him. "Tell me, Señor Bachelor," he said, "does the book say anything about the adventure with the Yanguesans, that time our good Rocinante took it into his head to go looking for tidbits in the sea?"

"The sage," replied Sansón, "has left nothing in the inkwell. He has told everything and to the point, even to the capers which the worthy Sancho cut as they tossed him in the blanket."

"I cut no capers in the blanket," objected Sancho, "but I did in the air, and more than I liked."

"I imagine," said Don Quixote, "that there is no history in the world, dealing with humankind, that does not have its ups and downs, and this is particularly true of those that have to do with deeds of chivalry, for they can never be filled with happy incidents alone."

"Nevertheless," the bachelor went on, "there are some who have read the book who say that they would have been glad if the authors had forgotten a few of the innumerable cudgelings which Señor Don Quixote received in the course of his various encounters."

"But that is where the truth of the story comes in," Sancho protested.

"For all of that," observed Don Quixote, "they might well have said nothing about them; for there is no need of recording those events that do not alter the veracity of the chronicle, when they tend only to lessen the reader's respect for the hero. You may be sure that Aeneas was not as pious as Vergil would have us believe, nor was Ulysses as wise as Homer depicts him."

"That is true enough," replied Sansón, "but it is one thing to write as a poet and another as a historian. The former may narrate or sing of things not as they were but as they should have been; the latter must describe them not as they should have been but as they were, without adding to or detracting from the truth in any degree whatsoever."

"Well," said Sancho, "if this Moorish gentleman is bent upon telling the truth, I have no doubt that among my master's thrashings my own will be found; for they never took the measure of his Grace's shoulders without measuring my whole body. But I don't wonder at that; for as my master himself says, when there's an ache in the head the members have to share it."

"You are a sly fox, Sancho," said Don Quixote. "My word, but you can remember things well enough when you choose to do so!"

"Even if I wanted to forget the whacks they gave me," Sancho answered him, "the welts on my ribs wouldn't let me, for they are still fresh."

"Be quiet, Sancho," his master admonished him, "and do not interrupt the bachelor. I beg him to go on and tell me what is said of me in this book."

"And what it says about me, too," put in Sancho, "for I have heard that I am one of the main presonages in it—"

"*Personages*, not *presonages*, Sancho my friend," said Sansón.

"So we have another one who catches you up on everything you say," was Sancho's retort. "If we go on at this rate, we'll never be through in a lifetime."

"May God put a curse on *my* life," the bachelor told him, "if you are not the second most important person in the story; and there are some who would rather listen to you talk than to anyone else in the book. It is true, there are those who say that you are too gullible in believing it to be the truth that you could become the governor of that island that was offered you by Señor Don Quixote, here present."

"There is still sun on the top of the wall," said Don Quixote, "and when Sancho is a little older, with the experience that the years bring, he will be wiser and better fitted to be a governor than he is at the present time."

"By God, master," said Sancho, "the island that I couldn't govern right now I'd never be able to govern if I lived to be as old as Methuselah. The trouble is, I don't know where that island we are talking about is located; it is not due to any lack of noddle on my part."

"Leave it to God, Sancho," was Don Quixote's advice, "and everything will come out all right, perhaps even better than you think; for not a leaf on the tree stirs except by His will."

"Yes," said Sansón, "if it be God's will, Sancho will not lack a thousand islands to govern, not to speak of one island alone."

"I have seen governors around here," said Sancho, "that are not to be compared to the sole of my shoe, and yet they call them 'your Lordship' and serve them on silver plate."

"Those are not the same kind of governors," Sansón informed him. "Their task is a good deal easier. The ones that govern islands must at least know grammar."

"I could make out well enough with the *gram*," replied Sancho, "but with the *mar* I want nothing to do, for I don't understand it at all. But leaving this business of the governorship in God's hands —for He will send me wherever I can best serve Him—I will tell you, Señor Bachelor Sansón Carrasco, that I am very much pleased that the author of the history should have spoken of me in such a way as does not offend me; for, upon the word of a faithful squire, if he had said anything about me that was not becoming to an old Christian, the deaf would have heard of it."

"That would be to work miracles," said Sansón.

"Miracles or no miracles," was the answer, "let everyone take care as to what he says or writes about people and not be setting down the first thing that pops into his head."

"One of the faults that is found with the book," continued the bachelor, "is that the author has inserted in it a story entitled *The*

*One Who Was Too Curious for His Own Good*. It is not that the story in itself is a bad one or badly written; it is simply that it is out of place there, having nothing to do with the story of his Grace, Señor Don Quixote."[57]

"I will bet you," said Sancho, "that the son of a dog has mixed the cabbages with the baskets."[58]

"And I will say right now," declared Don Quixote, "that the author of this book was not a sage but some ignorant prattler who at haphazard and without any method set about the writing of it, being content to let things turn out as they might. In the same manner, Orbaneja,[59] the painter of Ubeda, when asked what he was painting would reply, 'Whatever it turns out to be.' Sometimes it would be a cock, in which case he would have to write alongside it, in Gothic letters, 'This is a cock.' And so it must be with my story, which will need a commentary to make it understandable."

"No," replied Sansón, "that it will not; for it is so clearly written that none can fail to understand it. Little children leaf through it, young people read it, adults appreciate it, and the aged sing its praises. In short, it is so thumbed and read and so well known to persons of every walk in life that no sooner do folks see some skinny nag than they at once cry, 'There goes Rocinante!' Those that like it best of all are the pages; for there is no lord's antechamber where a *Don Quixote* is not to be found. If one lays it down, another will pick it up; one will pounce upon it, and another will beg for it. It affords the pleasantest and least harmful reading of any book that has been published up to now. In the whole of it there is not to be found an indecent word or a thought that is other than Catholic."

"To write in any other manner," observed Don Quixote, "would be to write lies and not the truth. Those historians who make use of falsehoods ought to be burned like the makers of counterfeit money. I do not know what could have led the author to introduce stories and episodes that are foreign to the subject matter when he had so much to write about in describing my adventures. He must undoubtedly have been inspired by the old saying, 'With straw or with hay . . .'[60] For, in truth, all he had to do was to record my thoughts, my sighs, my tears, my lofty purposes, and my undertakings, and he would have had a volume bigger or at least as big as that which the works of El Tostado[61] would make. To sum the matter up, Señor Bachelor, it is my opinion that, in composing histories or books of any sort, a great deal of judgment and ripe understanding is called for. To say and write witty and amusing things is the mark of great genius. The cleverest character in a comedy is the clown, since he who would make himself out to be

---

57. The story, a tragic tale about a jealousy-ridden husband, occupies several chapters of Part I. Here, as elsewhere in this chapter, Cervantes echoes criticism currently aimed at his book.

58. has jumped together things of different kinds.

59. This painter is known only through the present allusion in *Don Quixote*.

60. The proverb concludes either "the mattress is filled" or "I fill my belly."

61. Alonso de Madrigal, bishop of Avila, a prolific author of devotional works.

a simpleton cannot be one. History is a near-sacred thing, for it must be true, and where the truth is, there is God. And yet there are those who compose books and toss them out into the world as if they were no more than fritters."

"There is no book so bad," opined the bachelor, "that there is not some good in it."

"Doubtless that is so," replied Don Quixote, "but it very often happens that those who have won in advance a great and well-deserved reputation for their writings, lose it in whole or in part when they give their works to the printer."

"The reason for it," said Sansón, "is that, printed works being read at leisure, their faults are the more readily apparent, and the greater the reputation of the author the more closely are they scrutinized. Men famous for their genius, great poets, illustrious historians, are almost always envied by those who take a special delight in criticizing the writings of others without having produced anything of their own."

"That is not to be wondered at," said Don Quixote, "for there are many theologians who are not good enough for the pulpit but who are very good indeed when it comes to detecting the faults or excesses of those who preach."

"All of this is very true, Señor Don Quixote," replied Carrasco, "but, all the same, I could wish that these self-appointed censors were a bit more forbearing and less hypercritical; I wish they would pay a little less attention to the spots on the bright sun of the work that occasions their fault-finding. For if *aliquando bonus dormitat Homerus*,[62] let them consider how much of his time he spent awake, shedding the light of his genius with a minimum of shade. It well may be that what to them seems a flaw is but one of those moles which sometimes add to the beauty of a face. In any event, I insist that he who has a book printed runs a very great risk, inasmuch as it is an utter impossibility to write it in such a manner that it will please all who read it."

"This book about me must have pleased very few," remarked Don Quixote.

"Quite the contrary," said Sansón, "for just as *stultorum infinitus est numerus*,[63] so the number of those who have enjoyed this history is likewise infinite. Some, to be sure, have complained of the author's forgetfulness, seeing that he neglected to make it plain who the thief was who stole Sancho's gray;[64] for it is not stated there, but merely implied, that the ass was stolen; and, a little further on, we find the knight mounted on the same beast, although it has not made its reappearance in the story. They also say that the author forgot to tell us what Sancho did with those hundred crowns that he

---

62. "Good Homer sometimes nods too." (Horace, *Art of Poetry*, l. 359.)
63. "Infinite is the number of fools."
(Ecclesiasticus 1:15.)
64. in Part I, Chapter 23.

found in the valise on the Sierra Morena, as nothing more is said of them and there are many who would like to know how he disposed of the money or how he spent it. This is one of the serious omissions to be found in the work."

To this Sancho replied, "I, Señor Sansón, do not feel like giving any account or accounting just now; for I feel a little weak in my stomach, and if I don't do something about it by taking a few swigs of the old stuff, I'll be sitting on St. Lucy's thorn.[65] I have some of it at home, and my old woman is waiting for me. After I've had my dinner, I'll come back and answer any questions your Grace or anybody else wants to ask me, whether it's about the loss of the ass or the spending of the hundred crowns."

And without waiting for a reply or saying another word, he went on home. Don Quixote urged the bachelor to stay and take potluck with him, and Sansón accepted the invitation and remained. In addition to the knight's ordinary fare, they had a couple of pigeons, and at table their talk was of chivalry and feats of arms.

65. I shall be weak and exhausted.

## [A Victorious Duel]

### CHAPTER 12

*Of the strange adventure that befell the valiant Don Quixote with the fearless Knight of the Mirrors.[66]*

The night following the encounter with Death[67] was spent by Don Quixote and his squire beneath some tall and shady trees, the knight having been persuaded to eat a little from the stock of provisions carried by the gray.

"Sir," said Sancho, in the course of their repast, "how foolish I'd have been if I had chosen the spoils from your Grace's first adventure rather than the foals from the three mares.[68] Truly, truly, a sparrow in the hand is worth more than a vulture on the wing."[69]

"And yet, Sancho," replied Don Quixote, "if you had but let me attack them as I wished to do, you would at least have had as spoils

66. He will duly earn this title only in Chapter 15. In between, the author will be referring to him as the Knight of the Wood.

67. Don Quixote and his squire are now in the woody region around El Toboso, Dulcinea's town. Sancho has been sent to look for his knight's lady and has saved the day by pretending to see the beautiful damsel in a "village wench, and not a pretty one at that, for she was round-faced and snub-nosed." But by his imaginative lie he has succeeded, as he had planned, in setting in motion Don Quixote's belief in spells and enchant-ments: enemy magicians, envious of him, have hidden his lady's splendor only from his sight. While the knight was still under the shock of this experience, further along their way he and his squire have met a group of itinerant players dressed in their proper costumes for a religious play, *The Parliament of Death.*

68. Don Quixote has promised them to Sancho as a reward for bringing news of Dulcinea.

69. a proverb roughly corresponding to "a bird in the hand is worth two in the bush."

the Empress's gold crown and Cupid's painted wings;[70] for I should have taken them whether or no and placed them in your hands."

"The crowns and scepters of stage emperors," remarked Sancho, "were never known to be of pure gold; they are always of tinsel or tinplate."

"That is the truth," said Don Quixote, "for it is only right that the accessories of a drama should be fictitious and not real, like the play itself. Speaking of that, Sancho, I would have you look kindly upon the art of the theater and, as a consequence, upon those who write the pieces and perform in them, for they all render a service of great value to the State by holding up a mirror for us at each step that we take, wherein we may observe, vividly depicted, all the varied aspects of human life; and I may add that there is nothing that shows us more clearly, by similitude, what we are and what we ought to be than do plays and players.

"Tell me, have you not seen some comedy in which kings, emperors, pontiffs, knights, ladies, and numerous other characters are introduced? One plays the ruffian, another the cheat, this one a merchant and that one a soldier, while yet another is the fool who is not so foolish as he appears, and still another the one of whom love has made a fool. Yet when the play is over and they have taken off their players' garments, all the actors are once more equal."

"Yes," replied Sancho, "I have seen all that."

"Well," continued Don Quixote, "the same thing happens in the comedy that we call life, where some play the part of emperors, others that of pontiffs—in short, all the characters that a drama may have—but when it is all over, that is to say, when life is done, death takes from each the garb that differentiates him, and all at last are equal in the grave."

"It is a fine comparison," Sancho admitted, "though not so new but that I have heard it many times before. It reminds me of that other one, about the game of chess. So long as the game lasts, each piece has its special qualities, but when it is over they are all mixed and jumbled together and put into a bag, which is to the chess pieces what the grave is to life."

"Every day, Sancho," said Don Quixote, "you are becoming less stupid and more sensible."[71]

"It must be that some of your Grace's good sense is sticking to me," was Sancho's answer. "I am like a piece of land that of itself is dry and barren, but if you scatter manure over it and cultivate it, it will bear good fruit. By this I mean to say that your Grace's conversation is the manure that has been cast upon the barren land of my dry wit; the time that I spend in your service, associating with you,

---

70. The Empress and Cupid were among the characters in *The Parliament of Death* (see n. 67).

71. This and Sancho's following ac-knowledgment very well indicate the author's awareness of the development in Sancho's character under the influence of his master.

does the cultivating; and as a result of it all, I hope to bring forth blessed fruits by not departing, slipping, or sliding, from those paths of good breeding which your Grace has marked out for me in my parched understanding."

Don Quixote had to laugh at this affected speech of Sancho's, but he could not help perceiving that what the squire had said about his improvement was true enough; for every now and then the servant would speak in a manner that astonished his master. It must be admitted, however, that most of the time when he tried to use fine language, he would tumble from the mountain of his simple-mindedness into the abyss of his ignorance. It was when he was quoting old saws and sayings, whether or not they had anything to do with the subject under discussion, that he was at his best, displaying upon such occasions a prodigious memory, as will already have been seen and noted in the course of this history.

With such talk as this they spent a good part of the night. Then Sancho felt a desire to draw down the curtains of his eyes, as he was in the habit of saying when he wished to sleep, and, unsaddling his mount, he turned him loose to graze at will on the abundant grass. If he did not remove Rocinante's saddle, this was due to his master's express command; for when they had taken the field and were not sleeping under a roof, the hack was under no circumstances to be stripped. This was in accordance with an old and established custom which knights-errant faithfully observed: the bridle and saddlebow might be removed, but beware of touching the saddle itself! Guided by this precept, Sancho now gave Rocinante the same freedom that the ass enjoyed.

The close friendship that existed between the two animals was a most unusual one, so remarkable indeed that it has become a tradition handed down from father to son, and the author of this veracious chronicle even wrote a number of special chapters on the subject, although, in order to preserve the decency and decorum that are fitting in so heroic an account, he chose to omit them in the final version. But he forgets himself once in a while and goes on to tell us how the two beasts when they were together would hasten to scratch each other, and how, when they were tired and their bellies were full, Rocinante would lay his long neck over that of the ass—it extended more than a half a yard on the other side—and the pair would then stand there gazing pensively at the ground for as much as three whole days at a time, or at least until someone came for them or hunger compelled them to seek nourishment.

I may tell you that I have heard it said that the author of this history, in one of his writings, has compared the friendship of Rocinante and the gray to that of Nisus and Euryalus and that of Pylades and Orestes;[72] and if this be true, it shows for the edifica-

---

72. famous examples of friendship in Virgil's *Aeneid* and in Greek tradition and drama.

tion of all what great friends these two peace-loving animals were, and should be enough to make men ashamed, who are so inept at preserving friendship with one another. For this reason it has been said:

> There is no friend for friend,
> Reeds to lances turn . . .[73]

And there was the other poet who sang:

> Between friend and friend the bug . . .[74]

Let no one think that the author has gone out of his way in comparing the friendship of animals with that of men; for human beings have received valuable lessons from the beasts and have learned many important things from them. From the stork they have learned the use of clysters; the dog has taught them the salutary effects of vomiting as well as a lesson in gratitude; the cranes have taught them vigilance, the ants foresight, the elephants modesty, and the horse loyalty.[75]

Sancho had at last fallen asleep at the foot of a cork tree, while Don Quixote was slumbering beneath a sturdy oak. Very little time had passed when the knight was awakened by a noise behind him, and, starting up, he began looking about him and listening to see if he could make out where it came from. Then he caught sight of two men on horseback, one of whom, slipping down from the saddle, said to the other, "Dismount, my friend, and unbridle the horses; for there seems to be plenty of grass around here for them and sufficient silence and solitude for my amorous thoughts."

Saying this, he stretched himself out on the ground, and as he flung himself down the armor that he wore made such a noise that Don Quixote knew at once, for a certainty, that he must be a knight-errant. Going over to Sancho, who was still sleeping, he shook him by the arm and with no little effort managed to get him awake.

"Brother Sancho," he said to him in a low voice, "we have an adventure on our hands."

"God give us a good one," said Sancho. "And where, my master, may her Ladyship, Mistress Adventure, be?"

"Where, Sancho?" replied Don Quixote. "Turn your eyes and look, and you will see stretched out over there a knight-errant who, so far as I can make out, is not any too happy; for I saw him fling himself from his horse to the ground with a certain show of despondency, and as he fell his armor rattled."

"Well," said Sancho, "and how does your Grace make this out to be an adventure?"

---

73. from a popular ballad.
74. The Spanish "a bug in the eye" implies keeping a watchful eye on somebody.

75. all folkloristic beliefs about the "virtues" of animals.

"I would not say," the knight answered him, "that this is an adventure in itself, but rather the beginning of one, for that is the way they start. But listen; he seems to be tuning a lute or guitar, and from the way he is spitting and clearing his throat he must be getting ready to sing something."

"Faith, so he is," said Sancho. "He must be some lovesick knight."

"There are no knights-errant that are not lovesick," Don Quixote informed him. "Let us listen to him, and the thread of his song will lead us to the yarn-ball of his thoughts; for out of the abundance of the heart the mouth speaketh."

Sancho would have liked to reply to his master, but the voice of the Knight of the Wood,[76] which was neither very good nor very bad, kept him from it; and as the two of them listened attentively, they heard the following:

### Sonnet

Show me, O lady, the pattern of thy will,
That mine may take that very form and shape;
For my will in thine own I fain would drape,
Each slightest wish of thine I would fulfill.
If thou wouldst have me silence this dread ill
Of which I'm dying now, prepare the crape!
Or if I must another manner ape,
Then let Love's self display his rhyming skill.
Of opposites I am made, that's manifest:
In part soft wax, in part hard-diamond fire;
Yet to Love's laws my heart I do adjust,
And, hard or soft, I offer thee this breast:
Print or engrave there what thou may'st desire,
And I'll preserve it in eternal trust.[77]

With an *Ay!* that appeared to be wrung from the very depths of his heart, the Knight of the Wood brought his song to a close, and then after a brief pause began speaking in a grief-stricken voice that was piteous to hear.

"O most beautiful and most ungrateful woman in all the world!" he cried, "how is it possible, O most serene Casildea de Vandalia,[78] for you to permit this captive knight of yours to waste away and perish in constant wanderings, amid rude toils and bitter hardships? Is it not enough that I have compelled all the knights of Navarre, all those of León, all the Tartessians and Castilians, and, finally, all those of La Mancha, to confess that there is no beauty anywhere that can rival yours?"

---

76. Cf. note 66.
77. The poem intentionally follows affected conventions of the time.

78. the Knight of the Wood's counterpart to Don Quixote's Dulcinea del Toboso.

"That is not so!" cried Don Quixote at this point. "I am of La Mancha, and I have never confessed, I never could nor would confess a thing so prejudicial to the beauty of my lady. The knight whom you see there, Sancho, is raving; but let us listen and perhaps he will tell us more."

"That he will," replied Sancho, "for at the rate he is carrying on, he is good for a month at a stretch."

This did not prove to be the case, however; for when the Knight of the Wood heard voices near him, he cut short his lamentations and rose to his feet.

"Who goes there?" he called in a loud but courteous tone. "What kind of people are you? Are you, perchance, numbered among the happy or among the afflicted?"

"Among the afflicted," was Don Quixote's response.

"Then come to me," said the one of the Wood, "and, in doing so, know that you come to sorrow's self and the very essence of affliction."

Upon receiving so gentle and courteous an answer, Don Quixote and Sancho as well went over to him, whereupon the sorrowing one took the Manchegan's arm.

"Sit down here, Sir Knight," he continued, "for in order to know that you are one of those who follow the profession of knight-errantry, it is enough for me to have found you in this place where solitude and serenity keep you company, such a spot being the natural bed and proper dwelling of wandering men of arms."

"A knight I am," replied Don Quixote, "and of the profession that you mention; and though sorrows, troubles, and misfortunes have made my heart their abode, this does not mean that compassion for the woes of others has been banished from it. From your song a while ago I gather that your misfortunes are due to love— the love you bear that ungrateful fair one whom you named in your lamentations."

As they conversed in this manner, they sat together upon the hard earth, very peaceably and companionably, as if at daybreak they were not going to break each other's heads.

"Sir Knight," inquired the one of the Wood, "are you by any chance in love?"

"By mischance I am," said Don Quixote, "although the ills that come from well-placed affection should be looked upon as favors rather than as misfortunes."

"That is the truth," the Knight of the Wood agreed, "if it were not that the loved one's scorn disturbs our reason and understanding; for when it is excessive scorn appears as vengeance."

"I was never scorned by my lady," said Don Quixote.

"No, certainly not," said Sancho, who was standing near by, "for my lady is gentle as a ewe lamb and soft as butter."

"Is he your squire?" asked the one of the Wood.

"He is," replied Don Quixote.

"I never saw a squire," said the one of the Wood, "who dared to speak while his master was talking. At least, there is mine over there; he is as big as your father, and it cannot be proved that he has ever opened his lips while I was conversing."

"Well, upon my word," said Sancho, "I have spoken, and I will speak in front of any other as good—but never mind; it only makes it worse to stir it."

The Knight of the Wood's squire now seized Sancho's arm. "Come along," he said, "let the two of us go where we can talk all we like, squire fashion, and leave these gentlemen our masters to come to lance blows as they tell each other the story of their loves; for you may rest assured, daybreak will find them still at it."

"Let us, by all means," said Sancho, "and I will tell your Grace who I am, so that you may be able to see for yourself whether or not I am to be numbered among the dozen most talkative squires."

With this, the pair went off to one side, and there then took place between them a conversation that was as droll as the one between their masters was solemn.

### CHAPTER 13

*In which is continued the adventure of the Knight of the Wood, together with the shrewd, highly original, and amicable conversation that took place between the two squires.*

The knights and the squires had now separated, the latter to tell their life stories, the former to talk of their loves; but the history first relates the conversation of the servants and then goes on to report that of the masters. We are told that, after they had gone some little distance from where the others were, the one who served the Knight of the Wood began speaking to Sancho as follows:

"It is a hard life that we lead and live, *Señor mio*, those of us who are squires to knights-errant. It is certainly true that we eat our bread in the sweat of our faces, which is one of the curses that God put upon our first parents."[79]

"It might also be said," added Sancho, "that we eat it in the chill of our bodies, for who endures more heat and cold than we wretched ones who wait upon these wandering men of arms? It would not be so bad if we did eat once in a while, for troubles are less where there is bread; but as it is, we sometimes go for a day or two without breaking our fast, unless we feed on the wind that blows."

"But all this," said the other, "may very well be put up with, by reason of the hope we have of being rewarded; for if a knight is not

79. cf. Genesis 3:19.

too unlucky, his squire after a little while will find himself the governor of some fine island or prosperous earldom."

"I," replied Sancho, "have told my master that I would be satisfied with the governorship of an island, and he is so noble and so generous that he has promised it to me on many different occasions."

"In return for my services," said the Squire of the Wood, "I'd be content with a canonry. My master has already appointed me to one—and what a canonry!"

"Then he must be a churchly knight," said Sancho, "and in a position to grant favors of that sort to his faithful squire; but mine is a layman, pure and simple, although, as I recall, certain shrewd and, as I see it, scheming persons did advise him to try to become an archbishop. However, he did not want to be anything but an emperor. And there I was, all the time trembling for fear he would take it into his head to enter the Church, since I was not educated enough to hold any benefices. For I may as well tell your Grace that, though I look like a man, I am no more than a beast where holy orders are concerned."

"That is where you are making a mistake," the Squire of the Wood assured him. "Not all island governments are desirable. Some of them are misshapen bits of land, some are poor, others are gloomy, and, in short, the best of them lays a heavy burden of care and trouble upon the shoulders of the unfortunate one to whose lot it falls. It would be far better if we who follow this cursed trade were to go back to our homes and there engage in pleasanter occupations, such as hunting or fishing, for example; for where is there in this world a squire so poor that he does not have a hack, a couple of greyhounds, and a fishing rod to provide him with sport in his own village?"

"I don't lack any of those," replied Sancho. "It is true, I have no hack, but I do have an ass that is worth twice as much as my master's horse. God send me a bad Easter, and let it be the next one that comes, if I would make a trade, even though he gave me four fanegas[80] of barley to boot. Your Grace will laugh at the price I put on my gray—for that is the color of the beast. As to greyhounds, I shan't want for them, as there are plenty and to spare in my village. And, anyway, there is more pleasure in hunting when someone else pays for it."

"Really and truly, Sir Squire," said the one of the Wood, "I have made up my mind and resolved to have no more to do with the mad whims of these knights; I intend to retire to my village and bring up my little ones—I have three of them, and they are like oriental pearls."

"I have two of them," said Sancho, "that might be presented to the Pope in person, especially one of my girls that I am bringing up to be a countess, God willing, in spite of what her mother says."

80. about 1.6 bushels.

"And how old is this young lady that is destined to be a countess?"

"Fifteen," replied Sancho, "or a couple of years more or less. But she is tall as a lance, fresh as an April morning, and strong as a porter."

"Those," remarked the one of the Wood, "are qualifications that fit her to be not merely a countess but a nymph of the verdant wildwood. O whore's daughter of a whore! What strength the she-rogue must have!"

Sancho was a bit put out by this. "She is not a whore," he said, "nor was her mother before her, nor will either of them ever be, please God, so long as I live. And you might speak more courteously. For one who has been brought up among knights-errant, who are the soul of courtesy, those words are not very becoming."

"Oh, how little your Grace knows about compliments, Sir Squire!" the one of the Wood exclaimed. "Are you not aware that when some knight gives a good lance thrust to the bull in the plaza, or when a person does anything remarkably well, it is the custom for the crowd to cry out, 'Well done, whoreson rascal!' and that what appears to be vituperation in such a case is in reality high praise? Sir, I would bid you disown those sons or daughters who do nothing to cause such praise to be bestowed upon their parents."

"I would indeed disown them if they didn't," replied Sancho, "and so your Grace may go ahead and call me, my children, and my wife all the whores in the world if you like, for everything that they say and do deserves the very highest praise. And in order that I may see them all again, I pray God to deliver me from mortal sin, or, what amounts to the same thing, from this dangerous calling of squire, seeing that I have fallen into it a second time, decoyed and deceived by a purse of a hundred ducats that I found one day in the heart of the Sierra Morena.[81] The devil is always holding up a bag full of doubloons in front of my eyes, here, there—no, not here, but there—everywhere, until it seems to me at every step I take that I am touching it with my hand, hugging it, carrying it off home with me, investing it, drawing an income from it, and living on it like a prince. And while I am thinking such thoughts, all the hardships I have to put up with serving this crackbrained master of mine, who is more of a madman than a knight, seem to me light and easy to bear."

"That," observed the Squire of the Wood, "is why it is they say that avarice bursts the bag. But, speaking of madmen, there is no greater one in all this world than my master; for he is one of those of whom it is said, 'The cares of others kill the ass.' Because another knight has lost his senses, he has to play mad too[82] and go

---

81. when Don Quixote retired there in Part I, Chapter 23.

82. In the Sierra Morena, Don Quixote had decided to imitate Amadis de Gaul and Ariosto's Roland "by playing the part of a desperate and raving madman" as a consequence of love (Part I, Chapter 25).

hunting for that which, when he finds it, may fly up in his snout."

"Is he in love, maybe?"

"Yes, with a certain Casildea de Vandalia, the rawest[83] and best-roasted lady to be found anywhere on earth; but her rawness is not the foot he limps on, for he has other and greater schemes rumbling in his bowels, as you will hear tell before many hours have gone by."

"There is no road so smooth," said Sancho, "that it does not have some hole or rut to make you stumble. In other houses they cook horse beans, in mine they boil them by the kettleful.[84] Madness has more companions and attendants than good sense does. But if it is true what they say, that company in trouble brings relief, I may take comfort from your Grace, since you serve a master as foolish as my own."

"Foolish but brave," the one of the Wood corrected him, "and more of a rogue than anything else."

"That is not true of my master," replied Sancho. "I can assure you there is nothing of the rogue about him; he is as open and aboveboard as a wine pitcher and would not harm anyone but does good to all. There is no malice in his make-up, and a child could make him believe it was night at midday. For that very reason I love him with all my heart and cannot bring myself to leave him, no matter how many foolish things he does."

"But, nevertheless, good sir and brother," said the Squire of the Wood, "with the blind leading the blind, both are in danger of falling into the pit. It would be better for us to get out of all this as quickly as we can and return to our old haunts; for those that go seeking adventures do not always find good ones."

Sancho kept clearing his throat from time to time, and his saliva seemed rather viscous and dry; seeing which, the woodland squire said to him, "It looks to me as if we have been talking so much that our tongues are cleaving to our palates, but I have a loosener over there, hanging from the bow of my saddle, and a pretty good one it is." With this, he got up and went over to his horse and came back a moment later with a big flask of wine and a meat pie half a yard in diameter. This is no exaggeration, for the pasty in question was made of a hutch-rabbit of such a size that Sancho took it to be a goat, or at the very least a kid.

"And are you in the habit of carrying this with you, Señor?" he asked.

"What do you think?" replied the other. "Am I by any chance one of your wood-and-water[85] squires? I carry better rations on the flanks of my horse than a general does when he takes the field."

Sancho ate without any urging, gulping down mouthfuls that were like the knots on a tether, as they sat there in the dark.

83. The original has a pun on *crudo*, meaning both "raw" and "cruel."
84. meaning that his misfortunes always come in large quantities.
85. of low quality.

"You are a squire of the right sort," he said, "loyal and true, and you live in grand style as shown by this feast, which I would almost say was produced by magic. You are not like me, poor wretch, who have in my saddlebags only a morsel of cheese so hard you could crack a giant's skull with it, three or four dozen carob beans, and a few nuts. For this I have my master to thank, who believes in observing the rule that knights-errant should nourish and sustain themselves on nothing but dried fruits and the herbs of the field."

"Upon my word, brother," said the other squire, "my stomach was not made for thistles, wild pears, and woodland herbs. Let our masters observe those knightly laws and traditions and eat what their rules prescribe; I carry a hamper of food and a flask on my saddlebow, whether they like it or not. And speaking of that flask, how I love it! There is scarcely a minute in the day that I'm not hugging and kissing it, over and over again."

As he said this, he placed the wine bag in Sancho's hands, who put it to his mouth, threw his head back, and sat there gazing up at the stars for a quarter of an hour. Then, when he had finished drinking, he let his head loll on one side and heaved a deep sigh.

"The whoreson rascal!" he exclaimed, "that's a fine vintage for you!"

"There!" cried the Squire of the Wood, as he heard the epithet Sancho had used, "do you see how you have praised this wine by calling it 'whoreson'?"

"I grant you," replied Sancho, "that it is no insult to call anyone a son of a whore so long as you really do mean to praise him. But tell me, sir, in the name of what you love most, is this the wine of Ciudad Real?"[86]

"What a winetaster you are! It comes from nowhere else, and it's a few years old, at that."

"Leave it to me," said Sancho, "and never fear, I'll show you how much I know about it. Would you believe me, Sir Squire, I have such a great natural instinct in this matter of wines that I have but to smell a vintage and I will tell you the country where it was grown, from what kind of grapes, what it tastes like, and how good it is, and everything that has to do with it. There is nothing so unusual about this, however, seeing that on my father's side were two of the best winetasters La Mancha has known in many a year, in proof of which, listen to the story of what happened to them.

"The two were given a sample of wine from a certain vat and asked to state its condition and quality and determine whether it was good or bad. One of them tasted it with the tip of his tongue while the other merely brought it up to his nose. The first man said that it tasted of iron, the second that it smelled of Cordovan leather. The owner insisted that the vat was clean and that there could be nothing in the wine to give it a flavor of leather or of iron,

---

86. the main town in La Mancha and the center of a wine region.

but, nevertheless, the two famous winetasters stood their ground. Time went by, and when they came to clean out the vat they found in it a small key attached to a leather strap. And so your Grace may see for yourself whether or not one who comes of that kind of stock has a right to give his opinion in such cases."

"And for that very reason," said the Squire of the Wood, "I maintain that we ought to stop going about in search of adventures. Seeing that we have loaves, let us not go looking for cakes, but return to our cottages, for God will find us there if He so wills."

"I mean to stay with my master," Sancho replied, "until he reaches Saragossa, but after that we will come to an understanding."

The short of the matter is, the two worthy squires talked so much and drank so much that sleep had to tie their tongues and moderate their thirst, since to quench the latter was impossible. Clinging to the wine flask, which was almost empty by now, and with half-chewed morsels of food in their mouths, they both slept peacefully; and we shall leave them there as we go on to relate what took place between the Knight of the Wood and the Knight of the Mournful Countenance.

CHAPTER 14

*Wherein is continued the adventure of the Knight of the Wood.*

In the course of the long conversation that took place between Don Quixote and the Knight of the Wood, the history informs us that the latter addressed the following remarks to the Manchegan:

"In short, Sir Knight, I would have you know that my destiny, or, more properly speaking, my own free choice, has led me to fall in love with the peerless Casildea de Vandalia. I call her peerless for the reason that she has no equal as regards either her bodily proportions or her very great beauty. This Casildea, then, of whom I am telling you, repaid my worthy affections and honorable intentions by forcing me, as Hercules was forced by his stepmother, to incur many and diverse perils;[87] and each time as I overcame one of them she would promise me that with the next one I should have that which I desired; but instead my labors have continued, forming a chain whose links I am no longer able to count, nor can I say which will be the last one, that shall mark the beginning of the realization of my hopes.

"One time she sent me forth to challenge that famous giantess of Seville, known as La Giralda,[88] who is as strong and brave as if made of brass, and who without moving from the spot where she stands is the most changeable and fickle woman in the world. I came, I saw, I conquered her. I made her stand still and point in

---

87. Son of Zeus and Alcmena, Hercules was persecuted by Zeus' wife Hera.

88. actually a statue on the Moorish belfry of the cathedral at Seville.

one direction only, and for more than a week nothing but north winds blew. Then, there was that other time when Casildea sent me to lift those ancient stones, the mighty Bulls of Guisando,[89] an enterprise that had better have been entrusted to porters than to knights. On another occasion she commanded me to hurl myself down into the Cabra chasm [90]—an unheard-of and terribly dangerous undertaking—and bring her back a detailed account of what lay concealed in that deep and gloomy pit. I rendered La Giralda motionless, I lifted the Bulls of Guisando, and I threw myself into the abyss and brought to light what was hidden in its depths; yet my hopes are dead—how dead!—while her commands and her scorn are as lively as can be.

"Finally, she commanded me to ride through all the provinces of Spain and compel all the knights-errant whom I met with to confess that she is the most beautiful woman now living and that I am the most enamored man of arms that is to be found anywhere in the world. In fulfillment of this behest I have already traveled over the greater part of these realms and have vanquished many knights who have dared to contradict me. But the one whom I am proudest to have overcome in single combat is that famous gentleman, Don Quixote de la Mancha; for I made him confess that my Casildea is more beautiful than his Dulcinea, and by achieving such a conquest I reckon that I have conquered all the others on the face of the earth, seeing that this same Don Quixote had himself routed them. Accordingly, when I vanquished him, his fame, glory, and honor passed over and were transferred to my person.

> The brighter is the conquered one's lost crown,
> The greater is the conqueror's renown.[91]

Thus, the innumerable exploits of the said Don Quixote are now set down to my account and are indeed my own."

Don Quixote was astounded as he listened to the Knight of the Wood, and was about to tell him any number of times that he lied; the words were on the tip of his tongue, but he held them back as best he could, thinking that he would bring the other to confess with his own lips that what he had said was a lie. And so it was quite calmly that he now replied to him.

"Sir Knight," he began, "as to the assertion that your Grace has conquered most of the knights-errant in Spain and even in all the world, I have nothing to say, but that you have vanquished Don Quixote de la Mancha, I am inclined to doubt. It may be that it was someone else who resembled him, although there are very few that do."

89. statues representing animals and supposedly marking a place where Caesar defeated Pompey. (Cf. the use of Caesar's famous words a few lines above.)
90. Possibly an ancient mine in the Sierra de Cobra near Cordova.
91. from the *Araucana*, a poem by Alonso de Ercilla y Zúñiga on the Spanish struggle against the Araucanian Indians of Chile.

"What do you mean?" replied the one of the Wood. "I swear by the heavens above that I did fight with Don Quixote and that I overcame him and forced him to yield. He is a tall man, with a dried-up face, long, lean legs, graying hair, an eagle-like nose somewhat hooked, and a big, black, drooping mustache. He takes the field under the name of the Knight of the Mournful Countenance, he has for squire a peasant named Sancho Panza, and he rides a famous steed called Rocinante. Lastly, the lady of his heart is a certain Dulcinea del Toboso, once upon a time known as Aldonza Lorenzo, just as my own lady, whose name is Casildea and who is an Andalusian by birth, is called by me Casildea de Vandalia. If all this is not sufficient to show that I speak the truth, here is my sword which shall make incredulity itself believe."

"Calm yourself, Sir Knight," replied Don Quixote, "and listen to what I have to say to you. You must know that this Don Quixote of whom you speak is the best friend that I have in the world, so great a friend that I may say that I feel toward him as I do toward my own self; and from all that you have told me, the very definite and accurate details that you have given me, I cannot doubt that he is the one whom you have conquered. On the other hand, the sight of my eyes and the touch of my hands assure me that he could not possibly be the one, unless some enchanter who is his enemy—for he has many, and one in particular who delights in persecuting him —may have assumed the knight's form and then permitted himself to be routed, by way of defrauding Don Quixote of the fame which his high deeds of chivalry have earned for him throughout the known world. To show you how true this may be, I will inform you that not more than a couple of days ago those same enemy magicians transformed the figure and person of the beauteous Dulcinea del Toboso into a low and mean village lass,[92] and it is possible that they have done something of the same sort to the knight who is her lover. And if all this does not suffice to convince you of the truth of what I say, here is Don Quixote himself who will maintain it by force of arms, on foot or on horseback, or in any way you like."

Saying this, he rose and laid hold of his sword, and waited to see what the Knight of the Wood's decision would be. That worthy now replied in a voice as calm as the one Don Quixote had used.

"Pledges," he said, "do not distress one who is sure of his ability to pay. He who was able to overcome you when you were transformed, Señor Don Quixote, may hope to bring you to your knees when you are your own proper self. But inasmuch as it is not fitting that knights should perform their feats of arms in the darkness, like ruffians and highwaymen, let us wait until it is day in order that the sun may behold what we do. And the condition governing our encounter shall be that the one who is vanquished must submit to the will of his conqueror and perform all those things that are com-

92. See note 67.

manded of him, provided they are such as are in keeping with the state of knighthood."

"With that condition and understanding," said Don Quixote, "I shall be satisfied."

With this, they went off to where their squires were, only to find them snoring away as hard as when sleep had first overtaken them. Awakening the pair, they ordered them to look to the horses; for as soon as the sun was up the two knights meant to stage an arduous and bloody single-handed combat. At this news Sancho was astonished and terrified, since, as a result of what the other squire had told him of the Knight of the Wood's prowess, he was led to fear for his master's safety. Nevertheless, he and his friend now went to seek the mounts without saying a word, and they found the animals all together, for by this time the two horses and the ass had smelled one another out. On the way the Squire of the Wood turned to Sancho and addressed him as follows:

"I must inform you, brother, that it is the custom of the fighters of Andalusia, when they are godfathers in any combat, not to remain idly by, with folded hands, while their godsons fight it out. I tell you this by way of warning you that while our masters are settling matters, we, too, shall have to come to blows and hack each other to bits."

"The custom, Sir Squire," replied Sancho, "may be all very well among the fighters and ruffians that you mention, but with the squires of knights-errant it is not to be thought of. At least, I have never heard my master speak of any such custom, and he knows all the laws of chivalry by heart. But granting that it is true and that there is a law which states in so many words that squires must fight while their masters do, I have no intention of obeying it but rather will pay whatever penalty is laid on peaceable-minded ones like myself, for I am sure it cannot be more than a couple of pounds of wax,[93] and that would be less expensive than the lint which it would take to heal my head—I can already see it split in two. What's more, it's out of the question for me to fight since I have no sword nor did I ever in my life carry one."

"That," said the one of the Wood, "is something that is easily remedied. I have here two linen bags of the same size. You take one and I'll take the other and we will fight that way, on equal terms."

"So be it, by all means," said Sancho, "for that will simply knock the dust out of us without wounding us."

"But that's not the way it's to be," said the other squire. "Inside the bags, to keep the wind from blowing them away, we will put a half-dozen nice smooth pebbles of the same weight, and so we'll be able to give each other a good pounding without doing ourselves any real harm or damage."

93. In some confraternities, penalties were paid in wax, presumably to make church candles.

"Body of my father!" cried Sancho, "just look, will you, at the marten and sable and wads of carded cotton that he's stuffing into those bags so that we won't get our heads cracked or our bones crushed to a pulp. But I am telling you, *Señor mío*, that even though you fill them with silken pellets, I don't mean to fight. Let our masters fight and make the best of it, but as for us, let us drink and live; for time will see to ending our lives without any help on our part by way of bringing them to a close before they have reached their proper season and fall from ripeness."

"Nevertheless," replied the Squire of the Wood, "fight we must, if only for half an hour."

"No," Sancho insisted, "that I will not do. I will not be so impolite or so ungrateful as to pick any quarrel however slight with one whose food and drink I've shared. And, moreover, who in the devil could bring himself to fight in cold blood, when he's not angry or vexed in any way?"

"I can take care of that, right enough," said the one of the Wood. "Before we begin, I will come up to your Grace as nicely as you please and give you three or four punches that will stretch you out at my feet; and that will surely be enough to awaken your anger, even though it's sleeping sounder than a dormouse."

"And I," said Sancho, "have another idea that's every bit as good as yours. I will take a big club, and before your Grace has had a chance to awaken my anger I will put yours to sleep with such mighty whacks that if it wakes at all it will be in the other world; for it is known there that I am not the man to let my face be mussed by anyone, and let each look out for the arrow.[94] But the best thing to do would be to leave one's anger to its slumbers, for no one knows the heart of any other, he who comes for wool may go back shorn, and God bless peace and curse all strife. If a hunted cat when surrounded and cornered turns into a lion, God knows what I who am a man might not become. And so from this time forth I am warning you, Sir Squire, that all the harm and damage that may result from our quarrel will be upon your head."

"Very well," the one of the Wood replied, "God will send the dawn and we shall make out somehow."

At that moment gay-colored birds of all sorts began warbling in the trees and with their merry and varied songs appeared to be greeting and welcoming the fresh-dawning day, which already at the gates and on the balconies of the east was revealing its beautiful face as it shook out from its hair an infinite number of liquid pearls. Bathed in this gentle moisture, the grass seemed to shed a pearly spray, the willows distilled a savory manna, the fountains laughed, the brooks murmured, the woods were glad, and the meadows put

---

94. a proverbial expression from archery: let each one take care of his own arrow. Other obviously proverbial expressions follow, as is typical of Sancho's speech.

on their finest raiment. The first thing that Sancho Panza beheld, as soon as it was light enough to tell one object from another, was the Squire of the Wood's nose, which was so big as to cast into the shade all the rest of his body. In addition to being of enormous size, it is said to have been hooked in the middle and all covered with warts of a mulberry hue, like eggplant; it hung down for a couple of inches below his mouth, and the size, color, warts, and shape of this organ gave his face so ugly an appearance that Sancho began trembling hand and foot like a child with convulsions and made up his mind then and there that he would take a couple of hundred punches before he would let his anger be awakened to a point where he would fight with this monster.

Don Quixote in the meanwhile was surveying his opponent, who had already adjusted and closed his helmet so that it was impossible to make out what he looked like. It was apparent, however, that he was not very tall and was stockily built. Over his armor he wore a coat of some kind or other made of what appeared to be the finest cloth of gold, all bespangled with glittering mirrors that resembled little moons and that gave him a most gallant and festive air, while above his helmet were a large number of waving plumes, green, white, and yellow in color. His lance, which was leaning against a tree, was very long and stout and had a steel point of more than a palm in length. Don Quixote took all this in, and from what he observed concluded that his opponent must be of tremendous strength, but he was not for this reason filled with fear as Sancho Panza was. Rather, he proceeded to address the Knight of the Mirrors,[95] quite boldly and in a highbred manner.

"Sir Knight," he said, "if in your eagerness to fight you have not lost your courtesy, I would beg you to be so good as to raise your visor a little in order that I may see if your face is as handsome as your trappings."

"Whether you come out of this emprise the victor or the vanquished, Sir Knight," he of the Mirrors replied, "there will be ample time and opportunity for you to have a sight of me. If I do not now gratify your desire, it is because it seems to me that I should be doing a very great wrong to the beauteous Casildea de Vandalia by wasting the time it would take me to raise my visor before having forced you to confess that I am right in my contention, with which you are well acquainted."

"Well, then," said Don Quixote, "while we are mounting our steeds you might at least inform me if I am that knight of La Mancha whom you say you conquered."

"To that our[96] answer," said he of the Mirrors, "is that you are

---

95. see above, note 66.    96. Note the dignified, "majestic" plural form.

as like the knight I overcame as one egg is like another; but since you assert that you are persecuted by enchanters, I should not venture to state positively that you are the one in question."

"All of which," said Don Quixote, "is sufficient to convince me that you are laboring under a misapprehension; but in order to relieve you of it once and for all, let them bring our steeds, and in less time than you would spend in lifting your visor, if God, my lady, and my arm give me strength, I will see your face and you shall see that I am not the vanquished knight you take me to be."

With this, they cut short their conversation and mounted, and, turning Rocinante around, Don Quixote began measuring off the proper length of field for a run against his opponent as he of the Mirrors did the same. But the Knight of La Mancha had not gone twenty paces when he heard his adversary calling to him, whereupon each of them turned halfway and he of the Mirrors spoke.

"I must remind you, Sir Knight," he said, "of the condition under which we fight, which is that the vanquished, as I have said before, shall place himself wholly at the disposition of the victor."

"I am aware of that," replied Don Quixote, "not forgetting the provision that the behest laid upon the vanquished shall not exceed the bounds of chivalry."

"Agreed," said the Knight of the Mirrors.

At that moment Don Quixote caught sight of the other squire's weird nose and was as greatly astonished by it as Sancho had been. Indeed, he took the fellow for some monster, or some new kind of human being wholly unlike those that people this world. As he saw his master riding away down the field preparatory to the tilt, Sancho was alarmed; for he did not like to be left alone with the big-nosed individual, fearing that one powerful swipe of that protuberance against his own nose would end the battle so far as he was concerned and he would be lying stretched out on the ground, from fear if not from the force of the blow.

He accordingly ran after the knight, clinging to one of Rocinante's stirrup straps, and when he thought it was time for Don Quixote to whirl about and bear down upon his opponent, he called to him and said, "*Señor mio,* I beg your Grace, before you turn for the charge, to help me up into that cork tree yonder where I can watch the encounter which your Grace is going to have with this knight better than I can from the ground and in a way that is much more to my liking."

"I rather think, Sancho," said Don Quixote, "that what you wish to do is to mount a platform where you can see the bulls without any danger to yourself."

"The truth of the matter is," Sancho admitted, "the monstrous nose on that squire has given me such a fright that I don't dare stay near him."

"It is indeed of such a sort," his master assured him, "that if I were not the person I am, I myself should be frightened. And so, come, I will help you up."

While Don Quixote tarried to see Sancho ensconced in the cork tree, the Knight of the Mirrors measured as much ground as seemed to him necessary and then, assuming that his adversary had done the same, without waiting for sound of trumpet or any other signal, he wheeled his horse, which was no swifter nor any more impressive-looking than Rocinante, and bore down upon his enemy at a mild trot; but when he saw that the Manchegan was busy helping his squire, he reined in his mount and came to a stop midway in his course, for which his horse was extremely grateful, being no longer able to stir a single step. To Don Quixote, on the other hand, it seemed as if his enemy was flying, and digging his spurs with all his might into Rocinante's lean flanks he caused that animal to run a bit for the first and only time, according to the history, for on all other occasions a simple trot had represented his utmost speed. And so it was that, with an unheard-of fury, the Knight of the Mournful Countenance came down upon the Knight of the Mirrors as the latter sat there sinking his spurs all the way up to the buttons without being able to persuade his horse to budge a single inch from the spot where he had come to a sudden standstill.

It was at this fortunate moment, while his adversary was in such a predicament, that Don Quixote fell upon him, quite unmindful of the fact that the other knight was having trouble with his mount and either was unable or did not have time to put his lance at rest. The upshot of it was, he encountered him with such force that, much against his will, the Knight of the Mirrors went rolling over his horse's flanks and tumbled to the ground, where as a result of his terrific fall he lay as if dead, without moving hand or foot.

No sooner did Sancho perceive what had happened than he slipped down from the cork tree and ran up as fast as he could to where his master was. Dismounting from Rocinante, Don Quixote now stood over the Knight of the Mirrors, and undoing the helmet straps to see if the man was dead, or to give him air in case he was alive, he beheld—who can say what he beheld without creating astonishment, wonder, and amazement in those who hear the tale? The history tells us that it was the very countenance, form, aspect, physiognomy, effigy, and image of the bachelor Sansón Carrasco!

"Come, Sancho," he cried in a loud voice, "and see what is to be seen but is not to be believed. Hasten, my son, and learn what magic can do and how great is the power of wizards and enchanters."

Sancho came, and the moment his eyes fell on the bachelor Carrasco's face he began crossing and blessing himself a countless number of times. Meanwhile, the overthrown knight gave no signs of life.

"If you ask me, master," said Sancho, "I would say that the best thing for your Grace to do is to run his sword down the mouth of this one who appears to be the bachelor Carrasco; maybe by so doing you would be killing one of your enemies, the enchanters."

"That is not a bad idea," replied Don Quixote, "for the fewer enemies the better." And, drawing his sword, he was about to act upon Sancho's advice and counsel when the Knight of the Mirrors' squire came up to them, now minus the nose which had made him so ugly.

"Look well what you are doing, Don Quixote!" he cried. "The one who lies there at your feet is your Grace's friend, the bachelor Sansón Carrasco, and I am his squire."

"And where is your nose?" inquired Sancho, who was surprised to see him without that deformity.

"Here in my pocket," was the reply. And, thrusting his hand into his coat, he drew out a nose of varnished pasteboard of the make that has been described. Studying him more and more closely, Sancho finally exclaimed, in a voice that was filled with amazement, "Holy Mary preserve me! And is this not my neighbor and crony, Tomé Cecial?"

"That is who I am!" replied the de-nosed squire, "your good friend Tomé Cecial, Sancho Panza. I will tell you presently of the means and snares and falsehoods that brought me here. But, for the present, I beg and entreat your master not to lay hands on, mistreat, wound, or slay the Knight of the Mirrors whom he now has at his feet; for without any doubt it is the rash and ill-advised bachelor Sansón Carrasco, our fellow villager."

The Knight of the Mirrors now recovered consciousness, and, seeing this, Don Quixote at once placed the naked point of his sword above the face of the vanquished one.

"Dead you are, knight," he said, "unless you confess that the peerless Dulcinea del Toboso is more beautiful than your Casildea de Vandalia. And what is more, you will have to promise that, should you survive this encounter and the fall you have had, you will go to the city of El Toboso and present yourself to her in my behalf, that she may do with you as she may see fit. And in case she leaves you free to follow your own will, you are to return to seek me out—the trail of my exploits will serve as a guide to bring you wherever I may be—and tell me all that has taken place between you and her. These conditions are in conformity with those that we arranged before our combat and they do not go beyond the bounds of knight-errantry."

"I confess," said the fallen knight, "that the tattered and filthy shoe of the lady Dulcinea del Toboso is of greater worth than the badly combed if clean beard of Casildea, and I promise to go to her presence and return to yours and to give you a complete and detailed account concerning anything you may wish to know."

"Another thing," added Don Quixote, "that you will have to confess and believe is that the knight you conquered was not and could not have been Don Quixote de la Mancha, but was some other that resembled him, just as I am convinced that you, though you appear to be the bachelor Sansón Carrasco, are another person in his form and likeness who has been put here by my enemies to induce me to restrain and moderate the impetuosity of my wrath and make a gentle use of my glorious victory."

"I confess, think, and feel as you feel, think, and believe," replied the lamed knight. "Permit me to rise, I beg of you, if the jolt I received in my fall will let me do so, for I am in very bad shape."

Don Quixote and Tomé Cecial the squire now helped him to his feet. As for Sancho, he could not take his eyes off Tomé but kept asking him one question after another, and although the answers he received afforded clear enough proof that the man was really his fellow townsman, the fear that had been aroused in him by his master's words—about the enchanters' having transformed the Knight of the Mirrors into the bachelor Sansón Carrasco—prevented him from believing the truth that was apparent to his eyes. The short of it is, both master and servant were left with this delusion as the other ill-errant knight and his squire, in no pleasant state of mind, took their departure with the object of looking for some village where they might be able to apply poultices and splints to the bachelor's battered ribs.

Don Quixote and Sancho then resumed their journey along the road to Saragossa, and here for the time being the history leaves them in order to give an account of who the Knight of the Mirrors and his long-nosed squire really were.

CHAPTER 15

*Wherein is told and revealed who the Knight of the Mirrors and his squire were.*

Don Quixote went off very happy, self-satisfied, and vainglorious at having achieved a victory over so valiant a knight as he imagined the one of the Mirrors to be, from whose knightly word he hoped to learn whether or not the spell which had been put upon his lady was still in effect; for, unless he chose to forfeit his honor, the vanquished contender must of necessity return and give an account of what had happened in the course of his interview with her. But Don Quixote was of one mind, the Knight of the Mirrors of another, for, as has been stated, the latter's only thought at the moment was to find some village where plasters were available.

The history goes on to state that when the bachelor Sansón Carrasco advised Don Quixote to resume his feats of chivalry, after having desisted from them for a while, this action was taken as the result of a conference which he had held with the curate and the barber as to the means to be adopted in persuading the knight to remain quietly at home and cease agitating himself over his unfortunate adventures. It had been Carrasco's suggestion, to which they had unanimously agreed, that they let Don Quixote sally forth, since it appeared to be impossible to prevent his doing so, and that Sansón should then take to the road as a knight-errant and pick a quarrel and do battle with him. There would be no difficulty about finding a pretext, and then the bachelor knight would overcome him (which was looked upon as easy of accomplishment), having first entered into a pact to the effect that the vanquished should remain at the mercy and bidding of his conqueror. The behest in this case was to be that the fallen one should return to his village and home and not leave it for the space of two years or until further orders were given him, it being a certainty that, once having been overcome, Don Quixote would fulfill the agreement, in order not to contravene or fail to obey the laws of chivalry. And it was possible that in the course of his seclusion he would forget his fancies, or they would at least have an opportunity to seek some suitable cure for his madness.

Sansón agreed to undertake this, and Tomé Cecial, Sancho's friend and neighbor, a merry but featherbrained chap, offered to go along as squire. Sansón then proceeded to arm himself in the manner that has been described, while Tomé disguised his nose with the aforementioned mask so that his crony would not recognize him when they met. Thus equipped, they followed the same route as Don Quixote and had almost caught up with him by the time he had the adventure with the Cart of Death.[97] They finally overtook him in the wood, where those events occurred with which the attentive reader is already familiar; and if it had not been for the knight's extraordinary fancies, which led him to believe that the bachelor was not the bachelor, the said bachelor might have been prevented from ever attaining his degree of licentiate, as a result of having found no nests where he thought to find birds.

Seeing how ill they had succeeded in their undertaking and what an end they had reached, Tomé Cecial now addressed his master.

"Surely, Señor Sansón Carrasco," he said, "we have had our deserts. It is easy enough to plan and embark upon an enterprise, but most of the time it's hard to get out of it. Don Quixote is a madman and we are sane, yet he goes away sound and laughing while your Grace is left here, battered and sorrowful. I wish you would tell me now who is the crazier: the one who is so because he cannot help it, or he who turns crazy of his own free will?"

"The difference between the two," replied Sansón, "lies in this:

97. cf. note 67.

that the one who cannot help being crazy will be so always, whereas the one who is a madman by choice can leave off being one whenever he so desires."

"Well," said Tomé Cecial, "since that is the way it is, and since I chose to be crazy when I became your Grace's squire, by the same reasoning I now choose to stop being insane and to return to my home."

"That is your affair," said Sansón, "but to imagine that I am going back before I have given Don Quixote a good thrashing is senseless; and what will urge me on now is not any desire to see him recover his wits, but rather a thirst for vengeance; for with the terrible pain that I have in my ribs, you can't expect me to feel very charitable."

Conversing in this manner they kept on until they reached a village where it was their luck to find a bonesetter to take care of poor Sansón. Tomé Cecial then left him and returned home, while the bachelor meditated plans for revenge. The history has more to say of him in due time, but for the present it goes on to make merry with Don Quixote.

## CHAPTER 16

*Of what happened to Don Quixote upon his meeting with a prudent gentleman of La Mancha.*

With that feeling of happiness and vainglorious self-satisfaction that has been mentioned, Don Quixote continued on his way, imagining himself to be, as a result of the victory he had just achieved, the most valiant knight-errant of the age. Whatever adventures might befall him from then on he regarded as already accomplished and brought to a fortunate conclusion. He thought little now of enchanters and enchantments and was unmindful of the innumerable beatings he had received in the course of his knightly wanderings, of the volley of pebbles that had knocked out half his teeth, of the ungratefulness of the galley slaves and the audacity of the Yanguesans whose poles had fallen upon his body like rain. In short, he told himself, if he could but find the means, manner, or way of freeing his lady Dulcinea of the spell that had been put upon her, he would not envy the greatest good fortune that the most fortunate of knights-errant in ages past had ever by any possibility attained.

He was still wholly wrapped up in these thoughts when Sancho spoke to him.

"Isn't it strange, sir, that I can still see in front of my eyes the huge and monstrous nose of my old crony, Tomé Cecial?"

"And do you by any chance believe, Sancho, that the Knight of the Mirrors was the bachelor Sansón Carrasco and that his squire was your friend Tomé?"

"I don't know what to say to that," replied Sancho. "All I know is that the things he told me about my home, my wife and young ones, could not have come from anybody else; and the face, too, once you took the nose away, was the same as Tomé Cecial's, which I have seen many times in our village, right next door to my own house, and the tone of voice was the same also."

"Let us reason the matter out, Sancho," said Don Quixote. "Look at it this way: how can it be thought that the bachelor Sansón Carrasco would come as a knight-errant, equipped with offensive and defensive armor, to contend with me? Am I, perchance, his enemy? Have I given him any occasion to cherish a grudge against me? Am I a rival of his? Or can it be jealousy of the fame I have acquired that has led him to take up the profession of arms?"

"Well, then, sir," Sancho answered him, "how are we to explain the fact that the knight was so like the bachelor and his squire like my friend? And if this was a magic spell, as your Grace has said, was there no other pair in the world whose likeness they might have taken?"

"It is all a scheme and a plot," replied Don Quixote, "on the part of those wicked magicians who are persecuting me and who, foreseeing that I would be the victor in the combat, saw to it that the conquered knight should display the face of my friend the bachelor, so that the affection which I bear him would come between my fallen enemy and the edge of my sword and might of my arm, to temper the righteous indignation of my heart. In that way, he who had sought by falsehood and deceits to take my life, would be left to go on living. As proof of all this, Sancho, experience, which neither lies nor deceives, has already taught you how easy it is for enchanters to change one countenance into another, making the beautiful ugly and the ugly beautiful. It was not two days ago that you beheld the peerless Dulcinea's beauty and elegance in its entirety and natural form, while I saw only the repulsive features of a low and ignorant peasant girl with cataracts over her eyes and a foul smell in her mouth. And if the perverse enchanter was bold enough to effect so vile a transformation as this, there is certainly no cause for wonderment at what he has done in the case of Sansón Carrasco and your friend, all by way of snatching my glorious victory out of my hands. But in spite of it all, I find consolation in the fact that, whatever the shape he may have chosen to assume, I have laid my enemy low."

"God knows what the truth of it all may be," was Sancho's comment. Knowing as he did that Dulcinea's transformation had been due to his own scheming and plotting, he was not taken in by his master's delusions. He was at a loss for a reply, however, lest he say something that would reveal his own trickery.

As they were carrying on this conversation, they were overtaken by a man who, following the same road, was coming along behind them. He was mounted on a handsome flea-bitten mare and wore a hooded greatcoat of fine green cloth trimmed in tawny velvet and a cap of the same material, while the trappings of his steed, which was accoutered for the field, were green and mulberry in hue, his saddle being of the *jineta* mode.[98] From his broad green and gold shoulder strap there dangled a Moorish cutlass, and his half-boots were of the same make as the baldric. His spurs were not gilded but were covered with highly polished green lacquer, so that, harmonizing as they did with the rest of his apparel, they seemed more appropriate than if they had been of purest gold. As he came up, he greeted the pair courteously and, spurring his mare, was about to ride on past when Don Quixote called to him.

"Gallant sir," he said, "If your Grace is going our way and is not in a hurry, it would be a favor to us if we might travel together."

"The truth is," replied the stranger, "I should not have ridden past you if I had not been afraid that the company of my mare would excite your horse."

"In that case, sir," Sancho spoke up, "you may as well rein in, for this horse of ours is the most virtuous and well mannered of any that there is. Never on such an occasion has he done anything that was not right—the only time he did misbehave, my master and I suffered for it aplenty. And so, I say again, your Grace may slow up if you like; for even if you offered him your mare on a couple of platters, he'd never try to mount her."

With this, the other traveler drew rein, being greatly astonished at Don Quixote's face and figure. For the knight was now riding along without his helmet, which was carried by Sancho like a piece of luggage on the back of his gray, in front of the packsaddle. If the green-clad gentleman stared hard at his new-found companion, the latter returned his gaze with an even greater intensity. He impressed Don Quixote as being a man of good judgment, around fifty years of age, with hair that was slightly graying and an aquiline nose, while the expression of his countenance was half humorous, half serious. In short, both his person and his accouterments indicated that he was an individual of some worth.

As for the man in green's impression of Don Quixote de la Mancha, he was thinking that he had never before seen any human being that resembled this one. He could not but marvel at the knight's long neck, his tall frame, and the leanness and the sallowness of his face, as well as his armor and his grave bearing, the whole

98. a saddle with a high pummel and short stirrups.

constituting a sight such as had not been seen for many a day in those parts. Don Quixote in turn was quite conscious of the attentiveness with which the traveler was studying him and could tell from the man's astonished look how curious he was; and so, being very courteous and fond of pleasing everyone, he proceeded to anticipate any questions that might be asked him.

"I am aware," he said, "that my appearance must strike your Grace as being very strange and out of the ordinary, and for that reason I am not surprised at your wonderment. But your Grace will cease to wonder when I tell you, as I am telling you now, that I am a knight, one of those

> Of whom it is folks say,
> They to adventures go.

I have left my native heath, mortgaged my estate, given up my comfortable life, and cast myself into fortune's arms for her to do with me what she will. It has been my desire to revive a knight-errantry that is now dead, and for some time past, stumbling here and falling there, now throwing myself down headlong and then rising up once more, I have been able in good part to carry out my design by succoring widows, protecting damsels, and aiding the fallen, the orphans, and the young, all of which is the proper and natural duty of knights-errant. As a result, owing to my many valiant and Christian exploits, I have been deemed worthy of visiting in printed form nearly all the nations of the world. Thirty thousand copies of my history have been published, and, unless Heaven forbid, they will print thirty million of them.

"In short, to put it all into a few words, or even one, I will tell you that I am Don Quixote de la Mancha, otherwise known as the Knight of the Mournful Countenance. Granted that self-praise is degrading, there still are times when I must praise myself, that is to say, when there is no one else present to speak in my behalf. And so, good sir, neither this steed nor this lance nor this buckler nor this squire of mine, nor all the armor that I wear and arms I carry, nor the sallowness of my complexion, nor my leanness and gauntness, should any longer astonish you, now that you know who I am and what the profession is that I follow."

Having thus spoken, Don Quixote fell silent, and the man in green was so slow in replying that it seemed as if he was at a loss for words. Finally, however, after a considerable while, he brought himself to the point of speaking.

"You were correct, Sir Knight," he said, "about my astonishment and my curiosity, but you have not succeeded in removing the wonderment that the sight of you has aroused in me. You say that, knowing who you are, I should not wonder any more, but such is not the case, for I am now more amazed than ever. How can it be that there are knights-errant in the world today and that histories of them are actually printed? I find it hard to convince myself that at the present time there is anyone on earth who goes about aiding widows, protecting damsels, defending the honor of wives, and succoring orphans, and I should never have believed it had I not beheld your Grace with my own eyes. Thank Heaven for that book that your Grace tells me has been published concerning your true and exalted deeds of chivalry, as it should cast into oblivion all the innumerable stories of fictitious knights-errant with which the world is filled, greatly to the detriment of good morals and the prejudice and discredit of legitimate histories."

"As to whether the stories of knights-errant are fictitious or not," observed Don Quixote, "there is much that remains to be said."

"Why," replied the gentleman in green, "is there anyone who can doubt that such tales are false?"

"I doubt it," was the knight's answer, "but let the matter rest there. If our journey lasts long enough, I trust with God's help to be able to show your Grace that you are wrong in going along with those who hold it to be a certainty that they are not true."

From this last remark the traveler was led to suspect that Don Quixote must be some kind of crackbrain, and he was waiting for him to confirm the impression by further observations of the same sort; but before they could get off on another subject, the knight, seeing that he had given an account of his own station in life, turned to the stranger and politely inquired who his companion might be.

"I, Sir Knight of the Mournful Countenance," replied the one in the green-colored greatcoat, "am a gentleman, and a native of the village where, please God, we are going to dine today. I am more than moderately rich, and my name is Don Diego de Miranda. I spend my life with my wife and children and with my friends. My occupations are hunting and fishing, though I keep neither falcon nor hounds but only a tame partridge[99] and a bold ferret or two. I am the owner of about six dozen books, some of them in Spanish, others in Latin, including both histories and devotional works. As for books of chivalry, they have not as yet crossed the threshold of my door. My own preference is for profane rather than devotional writings, such as afford an innocent amusement, charming us by their style and arousing and holding our interest by their inventiveness, although I must say there are very few of that sort to be found in Spain.

"Sometimes," the man in green continued, "I dine with my

99. used as decoy.

friends and neighbors, and I often invite them to my house. My meals are wholesome and well prepared and there is always plenty to eat. I do not care for gossip, nor will I permit it in my presence. I am not lynx-eyed and do not pry into the lives and doings of others. I hear mass every day and share my substance with the poor, but make no parade of my good works lest hypocrisy and vainglory, those enemies that so imperceptibly take possession of the most modest heart, should find their way into mine. I try to make peace between those who are at strife. I am the devoted servant of Our Lady, and my trust is in the infinite mercy of God Our Savior."

Sancho had listened most attentively to the gentleman's account of his mode of life, and inasmuch as it seemed to him that this was a good and holy way to live and that the one who followed such a pattern ought to be able to work miracles, he now jumped down from his gray's back and, running over to seize the stranger's right stirrup, began kissing the feet of the man in green with a show of devotion that bordered on tears.

"Why are you doing that, brother?" the gentleman asked him. "What is the meaning of these kisses?"

"Let me kiss your feet," Sancho insisted, "for if I am not mistaken, your Grace is the first saint riding *jineta* fashion[100] that I have seen in all the days of my life."

"I am not a saint," the gentleman assured him, "but a great sinner. It is you, brother, who are the saint; for you must be a good man, judging by the simplicity of heart that you show."

Sancho then went back to his packsaddle, having evoked a laugh from the depths of his master's melancholy and given Don Diego fresh cause for astonishment.

Don Quixote thereupon inquired of the newcomer how many children he had, remarking as he did so that the ancient philosophers, who were without a true knowledge of God, believed that mankind's greatest good lay in the gifts of nature, in those of fortune, and in having many friends and many and worthy sons.

"I, Señor Don Quixote," replied the gentleman, "have a son without whom I should, perhaps, be happier than I am. It is not that he is bad, but rather that he is not as good as I should like him to be. He is eighteen years old, and for six of those years he has been at Salamanca studying the Greek and Latin languages. When I desired him to pass on to other branches of learning, I found him so immersed in the science of Poetry (if it can be called such) that it was not possible to interest him in the Law, which I wanted him to study, nor in Theology, the queen of them all. My wish was that he might be an honor to his family; for in this age in which we are

100. See note 98.

living our monarchs are in the habit of highly rewarding those forms of learning that are good and virtuous, since learning without virtue is like pearls on a dunghill. But he spends the whole day trying to decide whether such and such a verse of Homer's *Iliad* is well conceived or not, whether or not Martial is immodest in a certain epigram, whether certain lines of Vergil are to be understood in this way or in that. In short, he spends all of his time with the books written by those poets whom I have mentioned and with those of Horace, Persius, Juvenal, and Tibullus. As for our own moderns, he sets little store by them, and yet, for all his disdain of Spanish poetry, he is at this moment racking his brains in an effort to compose a gloss on a quatrain that was sent him from Salamanca and which, I fancy, is for some literary tournament."

To all this Don Quixote made the following answer:

"Children, sir, are out of their parents' bowels and so are to be loved whether they be good or bad, just as we love those that gave us life. It is for parents to bring up their offspring, from the time they are infants, in the paths of virtue, good breeding, proper conduct, and Christian morality, in order that, when they are grown, they may be a staff to the old age of the ones that bore them and an honor to their own posterity. As to compelling them to study a particular branch of learning, I am not so sure as to that, though there may be no harm in trying to persuade them to do so. But where there is no need to study *pane lucrando*[101]—where Heaven has provided them with parents that can supply their daily bread—I should be in favor of permitting them to follow that course to which they are most inclined; and although poetry may be more pleasurable than useful, it is not one of those pursuits that bring dishonor upon those who engage in them.

"Poetry in my opinion, my dear sir," he went on, "is a young and tender maid of surpassing beauty, who has many other damsels (that is to say, the other disciplines) whose duty it is to bedeck, embellish, and adorn her. She may call upon all of them for service, and all of them in turn depend upon her nod. She is not one to be rudely handled, nor dragged through the streets, nor exposed at street corners, in the market place, or in the private nooks of palaces. She is fashioned through an alchemy of such power that he who knows how to make use of it will be able to convert her into the purest gold of inestimable price. Possessing her, he must keep her within bounds and not permit her to run wild in bawdy satires or soulless sonnets. She is not to be put up for sale in any manner, unless it be in the form of heroic poems, pity-inspiring tragedies, or pleasing and ingenious comedies. Let mountebanks keep hands off

101. earning one's bread.

her, and the ignorant mob as well, which is incapable of recognizing or appreciating the treasures that are locked within her. And do not think, sir, that I apply that term 'mob' solely to plebeians and those of low estate; for anyone who is ignorant, whether he be lord or prince, may, and should, be included in the vulgar herd.

"But," Don Quixote continued, "he who possesses the gift of poetry and who makes the use of it that I have indicated, shall become famous and his name shall be honored among all the civilized nations of the world. You have stated, sir, that your son does not greatly care for poetry written in our Spanish tongue, and in that I am inclined to think he is somewhat mistaken. My reason for saying so is this: the great Homer did not write in Latin, for the reason that he was a Greek, and Vergil did not write in Greek since he was a Latin. In a word, all the poets of antiquity wrote in the language which they had imbibed with their mother's milk and did not go searching after foreign ones to express their loftiest conceptions. This being so, it would be well if the same custom were to be adopted by all nations, the German poet being no longer looked down upon because he writes in German, nor the Castilian or the Basque for employing his native speech.

"As for your son, I fancy, sir, that his quarrel is not so much with Spanish poetry as with those poets who have no other tongue or discipline at their command such as would help to awaken their natural gift; and yet, here, too, he may be wrong. There is an opinion, and a true one, to the effect that 'the poet is born,' that is to say, it is as a poet that he comes forth from his mother's womb, and with the propensity that has been bestowed upon him by Heaven, without study or artifice, he produces those compositions that attest the truth of the line: '*Est deus in nobis*,' etc.[102] I further maintain that the born poet who is aided by art will have a great advantage over the one who by art alone would become a poet, the reason being that art does not go beyond, but merely perfects, nature; and so it is that, by combining nature with art and art with nature, the finished poet is produced.

"In conclusion, then, my dear sir, my advice to you would be to let your son go where his star beckons him; for being a good student as he must be, and having already successfully mounted the first step on the stairway of learning, which is that of languages, he will be able to continue of his own accord to the very peak of humane letters, an accomplishment that is altogether becoming in a gentleman, one that adorns, honors, and distinguishes him as much as the miter does the bishop or his flowing robe the learned jurisconsult. Your Grace well may reprove your son, should he compose

102. "There is a god in us." (Ovid, *Fasti*, VI, 5.)

satires that reflect upon the honor of other persons; in that case, punish him and tear them up. But should he compose discourses in the manner of Horace, in which he reprehends vice in general as that poet so elegantly does, then praise him by all means; for it is permitted the poet to write verses in which he inveighs against envy and the other vices as well, and to lash out at the vicious without, however, designating any particular individual. On the other hand, there are poets who for the sake of uttering something malicious would run the risk of being banished to the shores of Pontus.[103]

"If the poet be chaste where his own manners are concerned, he will likewise be modest in his verses, for the pen is the tongue of the mind, and whatever thoughts are engendered there are bound to appear in this writings. When kings and princes behold the marvelous art of poetry as practiced by prudent, virtuous, and serious-minded subjects of their realm, they honor, esteem, and reward those persons and crown them with the leaves of the tree that is never struck by lightning[104]—as if to show that those who are crowned and adorned with such wreaths are not to be assailed by anyone."

The gentleman in the green-colored greatcoat was vastly astonished by this speech of Don Quixote's and was rapidly altering the opinion he had previously held, to the effect that his companion was but a crackbrain. In the middle of the long discourse, which was not greatly to his liking, Sancho had left the highway to go seek a little milk from some shepherds who were draining the udders of their ewes near by. Extremely well pleased with the knight's sound sense and excellent reasoning, the gentleman was about to resume the conversation when, raising his head, Don Quixote caught sight of a cart flying royal flags that was coming toward them down the road and, thinking it must be a fresh adventure, began calling to Sancho in a loud voice to bring him his helmet. Whereupon Sancho hastily left the shepherds and spurred his gray until he was once more alongside his master, who was now about to encounter a dreadful and bewildering ordeal.

---

103. as Ovid was by Augustus in A.D. 8.      104. the laurel tree.

["*For I Well Know the Meaning of Valor*"]

## CHAPTER 17

*Wherein Don Quixote's unimaginable courage reaches its highest point, together with the adventure of the lions and its happy ending.*

The history relates that, when Don Quixote called to Sancho to bring him his helmet,[105] the squire was busy buying some curds from the shepherds and, flustered by his master's great haste, did not know what to do with them or how to carry them. Having already paid for the curds, he did not care to lose them, and so he decided to put them into the headpiece, and, acting upon this happy inspiration, he returned to see what was wanted of him.

"Give me that helmet," said the knight; "for either I know little about adventures or here is one where I am going to need my armor."

Upon hearing this, the gentleman in the green-colored greatcoat[106] looked around in all directions but could see nothing except the cart that was approaching them, decked out with two or three flags which indicated that the vehicle in question must be conveying his Majesty's property. He remarked as much to Don Quixote, but the latter paid no attention, for he was always convinced that whatever happened to him meant adventures and more adventures.

"Forewarned is forearmed," he said. "I lose nothing by being prepared, knowing as I do that I have enemies both visible and invisible and cannot tell when or where or in what form they will attack me."

Turning to Sancho, he asked for his helmet again, and as there was no time to shake out the curds, the squire had to hand it to him as it was. Don Quixote took it and, without noticing what was in it, hastily clapped it on his head; and forthwith, as a result of the pressure on the curds, the whey began running down all over his face and beard, at which he was very much startled.

"What is this, Sancho?" he cried. "I think my head must be softening or my brains melting, or else I am sweating from head to foot. If sweat it be, I assure you it is not from fear, though I can well believe that the adventure which now awaits me is a terrible one indeed. Give me something with which to wipe my face, if you have anything, for this perspiration is so abundant that it blinds me."

Sancho said nothing but gave him a cloth and at the same time

105. Don Quixote has been deep in talk with "a prudent gentleman of La Mancha" met on the road, Don Diego de Miranda. Sancho has left the two for a moment to go and buy milk from some shepherds.

106. Don Diego de Miranda, whom Don Quixote later dubs the Knight of the Green-colored Greatcoat.

gave thanks to God that his master had not discovered what the trouble was. Don Quixote wiped his face and then took off his helmet to see what it was that made his head feel so cool. Catching sight of that watery white mass, he lifted it to his nose and smelled it.

"By the life of my lady Dulcinea del Toboso!" he exclaimed. "Those are curds that you have put there, you treacherous, brazen, ill-mannered squire!"

To this Sancho replied, very calmly and with a straight face, "If they are curds, give them to me, your Grace, so that I can eat them. But no, let the devil eat them, for he must be the one who did it. Do you think I would be so bold as to soil your Grace's helmet? Upon my word, master, by the understanding that God has given me, I, too, must have enchanters who are persecuting me as your Grace's creature and one of his members, and they are the ones who put that filthy mess there to make you lose your patience and your temper and cause you to whack my ribs as you are in the habit of doing. Well, this time, I must say, they have missed the mark; for I trust my master's good sense to tell him that I have neither curds nor milk nor anything of the kind, and if I did have, I'd put it in my stomach and not in that helmet."

"That may very well be," said Don Quixote.

Don Diego was observing all this and was more astonished than ever, especially when, after he had wiped his head, face, beard, and helmet, Don Quixote once more donned the piece of armor and, settling himself in the stirrups, proceeded to adjust his sword and fix his lance.

"Come what may, here I stand, ready to take on Satan himself in person!" shouted the knight.

The cart with the flags had come up to them by this time, accompanied only by a driver riding one of the mules and a man seated up in front.

"Where are you going, brothers?" Don Quixote called out as he placed himself in the path of the cart. "What conveyance is this, what do you carry in it, and what is the meaning of those flags?"

"The cart is mine," replied the driver, "and in it are two fierce lions in cages which the governor of Oran is sending to court as a present for his Majesty. The flags are those of our lord the King, as a sign that his property goes here."

"And are the lions large?" inquired Don Quixote.

It was the man sitting at the door of the cage who answered him. "The largest," he said, "that ever were sent from Africa to Spain. I am the lionkeeper and I have brought back others, but never any like these. They are male and female. The male is in this first cage, the female in the one behind. They are hungry right now, for they have had nothing to eat today; and so we'd be obliged if your Grace would get out of the way, for we must hasten on to the place where we are to feed them."

"Lion whelps against me?" said Don Quixote with a slight smile. "Lion whelps against me? And at such an hour? Then, by God, those gentlemen who sent them shall see whether I am the man to be frightened by lions. Get down, my good fellow, and since you are the lionkeeper, open the cages and turn those beasts out for me; and in the middle of this plain I will teach them who Don Quixote de la Mancha is, notwithstanding and in spite of the enchanters who are responsible for their being here."

"So," said the gentleman to himself as he heard this, "our worthy knight has revealed himself. It must indeed be true that the curds have softened his skull and mellowed his brains."

At this point Sancho approached him. "For God's sake, sir," he said, "do something to keep my master from fighting those lions. For if he does, they're going to tear us all to bits."

"Is your master, then, so insane," the gentleman asked, "that you fear and believe he means to tackle those fierce animals?"

"It is not that he is insane," replied Sancho, "but, rather, fool-hardy."

"Very well," said the gentleman, "I will put a stop to it." And going up to Don Quixote, who was still urging the lionkeeper to open the cages, he said, "Sir Knight, knights-errant should under-take only those adventures that afford some hope of a successful outcome, not those that are utterly hopeless to begin with; for valor when it turns to temerity has in it more of madness than of bravery. Moreover, these lions have no thought of attacking your Grace but are a present to his Majesty, and it would not be well to detain them or interfere with their journey."

"My dear sir," answered Don Quixote, "you had best go mind your tame partridge and that bold ferret of yours and let each one attend to his own business. This is my affair, and I know whether these gentlemen, the lions, have come to attack me or not." He then turned to the lionkeeper. "I swear, Sir Rascal, if you do not open those cages at once, I'll pin you to the cart with this lance!"

Perceiving how determined the armed phantom was, the driver now spoke up. "Good sir," he said, "will your Grace please be so kind as to let me unhitch the mules and take them to a safe place before you turn those lions loose? For if they kill them for me, I am ruined for life, since the mules and cart are all the property I own."

"O man of little faith!" said Don Quixote. "Get down and un-hitch your mules if you like, but you will soon see that it was quite unnecessary and that you might have spared yourself the trouble."

The driver did so, in great haste, as the lionkeeper began shouting, "I want you all to witness that I am being compelled against my will to open the cages and turn the lions out, and I further warn this gentleman that he will be responsible for all the harm and damage the beasts may do, plus my wages and my fees. You other gentlemen take cover before I open the doors; I am sure they will not do any harm to me."

Once more Don Diego sought to persuade his companion not to commit such an act of madness, as it was tempting God to undertake anything so foolish as that; but Don Quixote's only answer was that he knew what he was doing. And when the gentleman in green insisted that he was sure the knight was laboring under a delusion and ought to consider the matter well, the latter cut him short.

"Well, then, sir," he said, "if your Grace does not care to be a spectator at what you believe is going to turn out to be a tragedy, all you have to do is to spur your flea-bitten mare and seek safety."

Hearing this, Sancho with tears in his eyes again begged him to give up the undertaking, in comparison with which the adventure of the windmills and the dreadful one at the fulling mills—indeed, all the exploits his master had ever in the course of his life undertaken—were but bread and cakes.

"Look, sir," Sancho went on, "there is no enchantment here nor anything of the sort. Through the bars and chinks of that cage I have seen a real lion's claw, and judging by the size of it, the lion that it belongs to is bigger than a mountain."

"Fear, at any rate," said Don Quixote, "will make him look bigger to you than half the world. Retire, Sancho, and leave me, and if I die here, you know our ancient pact: you are to repair to Dulcinea—I say no more."

To this he added other remarks that took away any hope they had that he might not go through with his insane plan. The gentleman in the green-colored greatcoat was of a mind to resist him but saw that he was no match for the knight in the matter of arms. Then, too, it did not seem to him the part of wisdom to fight it out with a madman; for Don Quixote now impressed him as being quite mad in every way. Accordingly, while the knight was repeating his threats to the lionkeeper, Don Diego spurred his mare, Sancho his gray, and the driver his mules, all of them seeking to put as great a distance as possible between themselves and the cart before the lions broke loose.

Sancho already was bewailing his master's death, which he was convinced was bound to come from the lions' claws, and at the same time he cursed his fate and called it an unlucky hour in which he had taken it into his head to serve such a one. But despite his tears and lamentations, he did not leave off thrashing his gray in an effort to leave the cart behind them. When the lionkeeper saw that those who had fled were a good distance away, he once more entreated and warned Don Quixote as he had warned and entreated him before, but the answer he received was that he might save his breath as it would do him no good and he had best hurry and obey. In the space of time that it took the keeper to open the first cage, Don Quixote considered the question as to whether it would be well to give battle on foot or on horseback. He finally decided that he would do better on foot, as he feared that Rocinante would become frightened at sight of the lions; and so, leaping down from his horse, he fixed his lance, braced his buckler, and drew his sword, and then advanced with marvelous daring and great resoluteness until he stood directly in front of the cart, meanwhile commending himself to God with all his heart and then to his lady Dulcinea.

Upon reaching this point, the reader should know, the author of our veracious history indulges in the following exclamatory passage:

"O great-souled Don Quixote de la Mancha, thou whose courage is beyond all praise, mirror wherein all the valiant of the world may behold themselves, a new and second Don Manuel de León,[107] once the glory and the honor of Spanish knighthood! With what words shall I relate thy terrifying exploit, how render it credible to the ages that are to come? What eulogies do not belong to thee of right, even though they consist of hyperbole piled upon hyperbole? On foot and singlehanded, intrepid and with greathearted valor, armed but with a sword, and not one of the keen-edged Little Dog[108] make, and with a shield that was not of gleaming and polished steel, thou didst stand and wait for the two fiercest lions that ever the African forests bred! Thy deeds shall be thy praise, O valorous Manchegan; I leave them to speak for thee, since words fail me with which to extol them."

Here the author leaves off his exclamations and resumes the thread of the story.

Seeing Don Quixote posed there before him and perceiving that, unless he wished to incur the bold knight's indignation there was nothing for him to do but release the male lion, the keeper now opened the first cage, and it could be seen at once how extraordinarily big and horribly ugly the beast was. The first thing the recumbent animal did was to turn round, put out a claw, and stretch himself all over. Then he opened his mouth and yawned very slowly, after which he put out a tongue that was nearly two palms in length and with it licked the dust out of his eyes and washed his face. Having done this, he stuck his head outside the cage and gazed about him in all directions. His eyes were now like

107. **Don Manuel Ponce de León**, a paragon of gallantry and courtesy, belonging to the time of Ferdinand and Isabella.

108. the trademark of a famous armorer of Toledo and Saragossa.

live ·coals and his appearance and demeanor were such as to strike
terror in temerity itself. But Don Quixote merely stared at him
attentively, waiting for him to descend from the cart so that they
could come to grips, for the knight was determined to hack the
brute to pieces, such was the extent of his unheard-of madness.

The lion, however, proved to be courteous rather than arrogant
and was in no mood for childish bravado. After having gazed first
in one direction and then in another, as has been said, he turned his
back and presented his hind parts to Don Quixote and then very
calmly and peaceably lay down and stretched himself out once
more in his cage. At this, Don Quixote ordered the keeper to stir
him up with a stick in order to irritate him and drive him out.

"That I will not do," the keeper replied, "for if I stir him, I will
be the first one he will tear to bits. Be satisfied with what you have
already accomplished, Sir Knight, which leaves nothing more to be
said on the score of valor, and do not go tempting your fortune a
second time. The door was open and the lion could have gone out
if he had chosen; since he has not done so up to now, that means
he will stay where he is all day long. Your Grace's stoutheartedness
has been well established; for no brave fighter, as I see it, is obliged
to do more than challenge his enemy and wait for him in the field;
his adversary, if he does not come, is the one who is disgraced and
the one who awaits him gains the crown of victory."

"That is the truth," said Don Quixote. "Shut the door, my friend,
and bear me witness as best you can with regard to what you have
seen me do here. I would have you certify: that you opened the door
for the lion, that I waited for him and he did not come out, that
I continued to wait and still he stayed there, and finally went back
and lay down. I am under no further obligation. Away with enchantments, and God uphold the right, the truth, and true chivalry! So close the door, as I have told you, while I signal to the
fugitives in order that they who were not present may hear of this
exploit from your lips."

The keeper did as he was commanded, and Don Quixote, taking
the cloth with which he had dried his face after the rain of curds,
fastened it to the point of his lance and began summoning the
runaways, who, all in a body with the gentleman in green bringing
up the rear, were still fleeing and turning around to look back at
every step. Sancho was the first to see the white cloth.

"May they slay me," he said, "if my master hasn't conquered
those fierce beasts, for he's calling to us."

They all stopped and made sure that the one who was doing the
signaling was indeed Don Quixote, and then, losing some of their
fear, they little by little made their way back to a point where they

could distinctly hear what the knight was saying. At last they returned to the cart, and as they drew near Don Quixote spoke to the driver.

"You may come back, brother, hitch your mules, and continue your journey. And you, Sancho, may give each of them two gold crowns to recompense them for the delay they have suffered on my account."

"That I will, right enough," said Sancho. "But what has become of the lions? Are they dead or alive?"

The keeper thereupon, in leisurely fashion and in full detail, proceeded to tell them how the encounter had ended, taking pains to stress to the best of his ability the valor displayed by Don Quixote, at sight of whom the lion had been so cowed that he was unwilling to leave his cage, though the door had been left open quite a while. The fellow went on to state that the knight had wanted him to stir the lion up and force him out, but had finally been convinced that this would be tempting God and so, much to his displeasure and against his will, had permitted the door to be closed.

"What do you think of that, Sancho?" asked Don Quixote. "Are there any spells that can withstand true gallantry? The enchanters may take my luck away, but to deprive me of my strength and courage is an impossibility."

Sancho then bestowed the crowns, the driver hitched his mules, and the lionkeeper kissed Don Quixote's hands for the favor received, promising that, when he reached the court, he would relate this brave exploit to the king himself.

"In that case," replied Don Quixote, "if his Majesty by any chance should inquire who it was that performed it, you are to say that it was the Knight of the Lions; for that is the name by which I wish to be known from now on, thus changing, exchanging, altering, and converting the one I have previously borne, that of Knight of the Mournful Countenance; in which respect I am but following the old custom of knights-errant, who changed their names whenever they liked or found it convenient to do so."

With this, the cart continued on its way, and Don Quixote, Sancho, and the gentleman in the green-colored greatcoat likewise resumed their journey. During all this time Don Diego de Miranda had not uttered a word but was wholly taken up with observing what Don Quixote did and listening to what he had to say. The knight impressed him as being a crazy sane man and an insane one on the verge of sanity. The gentleman did not happen to be familiar with the first part of our history, but if he had read it he would have ceased to wonder at such talk and conduct, for he would then have known what kind of madness this was. Remaining as he did in ignorance of his companion's malady, he took him now for a sensible individual and now for a madman, since what Don Quixote said was coherent, elegantly phrased, and to the point, whereas his actions were nonsensical, foolhardy, and downright silly. What greater madness could there be, Don Diego asked himself, than to don a helmet filled with curds and then persuade oneself that enchanters were softening one's cranium? What could be more rashly absurd than to wish to fight lions by sheer strength alone? He was roused from these thoughts, this inward soliloquy, by the sound of Don Quixote's voice.

"Undoubtedly, Señor Don Diego de Miranda, your Grace must take me for a fool and a madman, am I not right? And it would be small wonder if such were the case, seeing that my deeds give evidence of nothing else. But, nevertheless, I would advise your Grace that I am neither so mad nor so lacking in wit as I must appear to you to be. A gaily caparisoned knight giving a fortunate lance thrust to a fierce bull in the middle of a great square makes a pleasing appearance in the eyes of his king. The same is true of a knight clad in shining armor as he paces the lists in front of the ladies in some joyous tournament. It is true of all those knights who, by means of military exercises or what appear to be such, divert and entertain and, if one may say so, honor the courts of princes. But the best showing of all is made by a knight-errant who, traversing deserts and solitudes, crossroads, forests, and mountains, goes seeking dangerous adventures with the intention of bringing them to a happy and successful conclusion, and solely for the purpose of winning a glorious and enduring renown.

"More impressive, I repeat, is the knight-errant succoring a widow in some unpopulated place than a courtly man of arms making love to a damsel in the city. All knights have their special callings: let the courtier wait upon the ladies and lend luster by his liveries to his sovereign's palace; let him nourish impoverished gentlemen with the splendid fare of his table; let him give tourneys and show himself truly great, generous, and magnificent and a good Christian above all, thus fulfilling his particular obligations. But the knight-errant's case is different.

"Let the latter seek out the nooks and corners of the world; let him enter into the most intricate of labyrinths; let him attempt the impossible at every step; let him endure on desolate highlands the burning rays of the midsummer sun and in winter the harsh inclemencies of wind and frost; let no lions inspire him with fear, no monsters frighten him, no dragons terrify him, for to seek them out, attack them, and conquer them all is his chief and legitimate occupation. Accordingly, I whose lot it is to be numbered among the knights-errant cannot fail to attempt anything that appears to me to fall within the scope of my duties, just as I attacked those lions a while ago even though I knew it to be an exceedingly rash thing to do, for that was a matter that directly concerned me.

"For I well know the meaning of valor: namely, a virtue that lies between the two extremes of cowardice on the one hand and temerity on the other. It is, nonetheless, better for the brave man to carry his bravery to the point of rashness than for him to sink into cowardice. Even as it is easier for the prodigal to become a generous man than it is for the miser, so is it easier for the fool-hardy to become truly brave than it is for the coward to attain valor. And in this matter of adventures, you may believe me, Señor Don Diego, it is better to lose by a card too many than a card too few, and 'Such and such a knight is temerarious and overbold' sounds better to the ear than 'That knight is timid and a coward.'"

"I must assure you, Señor Don Quixote," replied Don Diego, "that everything your Grace has said and done will stand the test of reason; and it is my opinion that if the laws and ordinances of knight-errantry were to be lost, they would be found again in your Grace's bosom, which is their depository and storehouse. But it is growing late; let us hasten to my village and my home, where your Grace shall rest from your recent exertions; for if the body is not tired the spirit may be, and that sometimes results in bodily fatigue."

"I accept your offer as a great favor and an honor, Señor Don Diego," was the knight's reply. And, by spurring their mounts more than they had up to then, they arrived at the village around two in the afternoon and came to the house that was occupied by Don Diego, whom Don Quixote had dubbed the Knight of the Green-colored Greatcoat.

## [Last Duel]

### CHAPTER 64

*Which treats of the adventure that caused Don Quixote the most sorrow of all those that have thus far befallen him.*

. . . One morning, as Don Quixote went for a ride along the beach,[109] clad in full armor—for, as he was fond of saying, that was his only ornament, his only rest the fight, and, accordingly, he was never without it for a moment—he saw approaching him a horse-man similarly arrayed from head to foot and with a brightly shining moon blazoned upon his shield.

As soon as he had come within earshot the stranger cried out to Don Quixote in a loud voice, "O illustrious knight, the never to be

---

109. Don Quixote and Sancho, after numberless encounters and experiences (of which the most prominent have been the Don's descent into the cave of Montesinos, and the residence at the castle of the playful ducal couple who give Sancho the "governorship of an island" for ten days), are now in Barcelona. Famous as they are, they meet the viceroy and the nobles; their host is Don Antonio Moreno, "a gentleman of wealth and discernment who was fond of amusing himself in an innocent and kindly way."

sufficiently praised Don Quixote de la Mancha, I am the Knight of the White Moon whose incomparable exploits you will perhaps recall. I come to contend with you and try the might of my arm, with the purpose of having you acknowledge and confess that my lady, whoever she may be, is beyond comparison more beautiful than your own Dulcinea del Toboso. If you will admit the truth of this fully and freely, you will escape death and I shall be spared the trouble of inflicting it upon you. On the other hand, if you choose to fight and I should overcome you, I ask no other satisfaction than that, laying down your arms and seeking no further adventures, you retire to your own village for the space of a year, during which time you are not to lay hand to sword but are to dwell peacefully and tranquilly, enjoying a beneficial rest that shall redound to the betterment of your worldly fortunes and the salvation of your soul. But if you are the victor, then my head shall be at your disposal, my arms and steed shall be the spoils, and the fame of my exploits shall go to increase your own renown. Consider well which is the better course and let me have your answer at once, for today is all the time I have for the dispatching of this business."

Don Quixote was amazed at the knight's arrogance as well as at the nature of the challenge, but it was with a calm and stern demeanor that he replied to him.

"Knight of the White Moon," he said, "of whose exploits up to now I have never heard, I will venture to take an oath that you have not once laid eyes upon the illustrious Dulcinea; for I am quite certain that if you had beheld her you would not be staking your all upon such an issue, since the sight of her would have convinced you that there never has been, and never can be, any beauty to compare with hers. I do not say that you lie, I simply say that you are mistaken; and so I accept your challenge with the conditions you have laid down, and at once, before this day you have fixed upon shall have ended. The only exception I make is with regard to the fame of your deeds being added to my renown, since I do not know what the character of your exploits has been and am quite content with my own, such as they are. Take, then, whichever side of the field you like, and I will take up my position, and may St. Peter bless what God may give."

Now, as it happened, the Knight of the White Moon was seen by some of the townspeople, who informed the viceroy that he was there, talking to Don Quixote de la Mancha. Believing this to be a new adventure arranged by Don Antonio Moreno or some other gentleman of the place, the viceroy at once hastened down to the beach, accompanied by a large retinue, including Don Antonio, and they arrived just as Don Quixote was wheeling Rocinante to measure off the necessary stretch of field. When the viceroy perceived that they were about to engage in combat, he at once interposed and inquired of them what it was that impelled them thus to do battle all of a sudden.

The Knight of the White Moon replied that it was a matter of beauty and precedence and briefly repeated what he had said to Don Quixote, explaining the terms to which both parties had agreed. The viceroy then went up to Don Antonio and asked him if he knew any such knight as this or if it was some joke that they were playing, but the answer that he received left him more puzzled than ever; for Don Antonio did not know who the knight was, nor could he say as to whether this was a real encounter or not. The viceroy, accordingly, was doubtful about letting them proceed, but inasmuch as he could not bring himself to believe that it was anything more than a jest, he withdrew to one side, saying, "Sir Knights, if there is nothing for it but to confess[110] or die, and if Señor Don Quixote's mind is made up and your Grace, the Knight of the White Moon, is even more firmly resolved, then fall to it in the name of God and may He bestow the victory."

The Knight of the White Moon thanked the viceroy most courteously and in well-chosen words for the permission which had been granted them, and Don Quixote did the same, whereupon the latter, commending himself with all his heart to Heaven and to his lady Dulcinea, as was his custom at the beginning of a fray, fell back a little farther down the field as he saw his adversary doing the same. And then, without blare of trumpet or other warlike instrument to give them the signal for the attack, both at the same instant wheeled their steeds about and returned for the charge. Being mounted upon the swifter horse, the Knight of the White Moon met Don Quixote two-thirds of the way and with such tremendous force that, without touching his opponent with his lance (which, it seemed, he deliberately held aloft) he brought both Rocinante and his rider to the ground in an exceedingly perilous fall. At once the victor leaped down and placed his lance at Don Quixote's visor.

"You are vanquished, O knight! Nay, more, you are dead unless you make confession in accordance with the conditions governing our encounter."

Stunned and battered, Don Quixote did not so much as raise his visor but in a faint, wan voice, as if speaking from the grave, he said, "Dulcinea del Toboso is the most beautiful woman in the world and I the most unhappy knight upon the face of this earth. It is not right that my weakness should serve to defraud the truth. Drive

110. admit one's error.

home your lance, O knight, and take my life since you already **have** deprived me of my honor."

"That I most certainly shall not do," said the one of the White Moon. "Let the fame of my lady Dulcinea del Toboso's beauty live on undiminished. As for me, I shall be content if the great Don Quixote will retire to his village for a year or until such a time as I may specify, as was agreed upon between us before joining battle."

The viceroy, Don Antonio, and all the many others who were present heard this, and they also heard Don Quixote's response, which was to the effect that, seeing nothing was asked of him that was prejudicial to Dulcinea, he would fulfill all the other conditions like a true and punctilious knight. The one of the White Moon thereupon turned and with a bow to the viceroy rode back to the city at a mild canter. The viceroy promptly dispatched Don Antonio to follow him and make every effort to find out who he was; and, in the meanwhile, they lifted Don Quixote up and uncovered his face, which held no sign of color and was bathed in perspiration. Rocinante, however, was in so sorry a state that he was unable to stir for the present.

Brokenhearted over the turn that events had taken, Sancho did not know what to say or do. It seemed to him that all this was something that was happening in a dream and that everything was the result of magic. He saw his master surrender, heard him consent not to take up arms again for a year to come as the light of his glorious exploits faded into darkness. At the same time his own hopes, based upon the fresh promises that had been made him, were whirled away like smoke before the wind. He feared that Rocinante was maimed for life, his master's bones permanently dislocated—it would have been a bit of luck if his madness also had been jolted out of him.[111]

Finally, in a hand litter which the viceroy had them bring, they bore the knight back to town. The viceroy himself then returned, for he was very anxious to ascertain who the Knight of the White Moon was who had left Don Quixote in so lamentable a condition.

## CHAPTER 65

*Wherein is revealed who the Knight of the White Moon was.*

The Knight of the White Moon was followed not only by Don Antonio Moreno, but by a throng of small boys as well, who kept after him until the doors of one of the city's hostelries had closed behind him. A squire came out to meet him and remove his armor,

111. The original has an untranslatable pun on *deslocado*, which means "out of joint" ("dislocated") and also "cured of madness." (from *loco*, "mad").

for which purpose the victor proceeded to shut himself up in a lower room, in the company of Don Antonio, who had also entered the inn and whose bread would not bake until he had learned the knight's identity. Perceiving that the gentleman had no intention of leaving him, he of the White Moon then spoke.

"Sir," he said, "I am well aware that you have come to find out who I am; and, seeing that there is no denying you the information that you seek, while my servant here is removing my armor I will tell you the exact truth of the matter. I would have you know, sir, that I am the bachelor Sansón Carrasco from the same village as Don Quixote de la Mancha, whose madness and absurdities inspire pity in all of us who know him and in none more than me. And so, being convinced that his salvation lay in his returning home for a period of rest in his own house, I formed a plan for bringing him back.

"It was three months ago that I took to the road as a knight-errant, calling myself the Knight of the Mirrors, with the object of fighting and overcoming him without doing him any harm, intending first to lay down the condition that the vanquished was to yield to the victor's will. What I meant to ask of him—for I looked upon him as conquered from the start—was that he should return to his village and not leave it for a whole year, in the course of which time he might be cured. Fate, however, ordained things otherwise; for he was the one who conquered me and overthrew me from my horse, and thus my plan came to naught. He continued on his wanderings, and I went home, defeated, humiliated, and bruised from my fall, which was quite a dangerous one. But I did not for this reason give up the idea of hunting him up once more and vanquishing him as you have seen me do today.

"Since he is the soul of honor when it comes to observing the ordinances of knight-errantry, there is not the slightest doubt that he will keep the promise he has given me and fulfill his obligations. And that, sir, is all that I need to tell you concerning what has happened. I beg you not to disclose my secret or reveal my identity to Don Quixote, in order that my well-intentioned scheme may be carried out and a man of excellent judgment be brought back to his senses—for a sensible man he would be, once rid of the follies of chivalry."

"My dear sir," exclaimed Don Antonio, "may God forgive you for the wrong you have done the world by seeking to deprive it of its most charming madman! Do you not see that the benefit accomplished by restoring Don Quixote to his senses can never equal the pleasure which others derive from his vagaries? But it is my opinion that all the trouble to which the Señor Bachelor has put himself will not suffice to cure a man who is so hopelessly insane; and if it were not uncharitable, I would say let Don Quixote never be cured, since with his return to health we lose not only his own drolleries but also those of his squire, Sancho Panza, for either of the two is capable of turning melancholy itself into joy and merriment. Nevertheless, I will keep silent and tell him nothing, that I may see whether or not I am right in my suspicion that Señor Carrasco's efforts will prove to have been of no avail."

The bachelor replied that, all in all, things looked very favorable and he hoped for a fortunate outcome. With this, he took his leave of Don Antonio, after offering to render him any service that he could; and, having had his armor tied up and placed upon a mule's back, he rode out of the city that same day on the same horse on which he had gone into battle, returning to his native province without anything happening to him that is worthy of being set down in this veracious chronicle.

## [Homecoming and Death]

### CHAPTER 73

*Of the omens that Don Quixote encountered upon entering his village, with other incidents that embellish and lend credence to this great history.*

As they entered the village, Cid Hamete informs us, Don Quixote caught sight of two lads on the communal threshing floor who were engaged in a dispute.

"Don't let it worry you, Periquillo," one of them was saying to the other; "you'll never lay eyes on it again as long as you live."

Hearing this, Don Quixote turned to Sancho. "Did you mark what that boy said, my friend?" he asked. " 'You'll never lay eyes on it[112] again . . .'"

"Well," replied Sancho, "what difference does it make what he said?"

"What difference?" said Don Quixote. "Don't you see that, applied to the one I love, it means I shall never again see Dulcinea."

Sancho was about to answer him when his attention was distracted by a hare that came flying across the fields pursued by a large number of hunters with their greyhounds. The frightened animal took refuge by huddling down beneath the donkey, whereupon Sancho reached out his hand and caught it and presented it to his master.

"*Malum signum, malum signum,*"[113] the knight was muttering to himself. "A hare flees, the hounds pursue it, Dulcinea appears not."

---

112. the same as "her" in the original, since the reference is to a cricket cage, denoted in Spanish by a feminine noun; hence the Don's inference concerning Dulcinea.

113. a bad sign. Meeting a hare is considered an ill omen.

"It is very strange to hear your Grace talk like that," said Sancho. "Let us suppose that this hare *is* Dulcinea del Toboso and the hounds pursuing it are those wicked enchanters that transformed her into a peasant lass; she flees, I catch her and turn her over to your Grace, you hold her in your arms and caress her. Is that a bad sign? What ill omen can you find in it?"

The two lads who had been quarreling now came up to have a look at the hare, and Sancho asked them what their dispute was about. To this the one who had uttered the words "You'll never lay eyes on it again as long as you live," replied that he had taken a cricket cage from the other boy and had no intention of returning it ever. Sancho then brought out from his pocket four cuartos and gave them to the lad in exchange for the cage, which he placed in Don Quixote's hands.

"There, master," he said, "these omens are broken and destroyed, and to my way of thinking, even though I may be a dunce, they have no more to do with what is going to happen to us than the clouds of yesteryear. If I am not mistaken, I have heard our curate say that sensible persons of the Christian faith should pay no heed to such foolish things, and you yourself in the past have given me to understand that all those Christians who are guided by omens are fools. But there is no need to waste a lot of words on the subject; come, let us go on and enter our village."

The hunters at this point came up and asked for the hare, and Don Quixote gave it to them. Continuing on their way, the returning pair encountered the curate and the bachelor Carrasco, who were strolling in a small meadow on the outskirts of the town as they read their breviaries. And here it should be mentioned that Sancho Panza, by way of sumpter cloth, had thrown over his gray and the bundle of armor it bore the flame-covered buckram robe in which they had dressed the squire at the duke's castle, on the night that witnessed Altisidora's[114] resurrection; and he had also fitted the miter over the donkey's head, the result being the weirdest transformation and the most bizarrely appareled ass that ever were seen in this world. The curate and the bachelor recognized the pair at once and came forward to receive them with open arms. Don Quixote dismounted and gave them both a warm embrace; meanwhile, the small boys (boys are like lynxes in that nothing escapes them), having spied the ass's miter, ran up for a closer view.

"Come, lads," they cried, "and see Sancho Panza's ass trigged out finer than Mingo,[115] and Don Quixote's beast is skinnier than ever!"

Finally, surrounded by the urchins and accompanied by the

114. Altisidora was a girl in the duke's castle where Quixote and Sancho were guests for a time; she dramatically pretended to be in love with the Don.

115. The allusion is to the opening lines of a fifteenth-century satire, *Mingo Revulgo*.

curate and the bachelor, they entered the village and made their
way to Don Quixote's house, where they found the housekeeper and
the niece standing in the doorway, for the news of their return had
preceded them. Teresa Panza, Sancho's wife, had also heard of it,
and, half naked and disheveled, dragging her daughter Sanchica by
the hand, she hastened to greet her husband and was disappointed
when she saw him, for he did not look to her as well fitted out as a
governor ought to be.

"How does it come, my husband," she said, "that you return like
this, tramping and footsore? You look more like a vagabond than
you do like a governor."

"Be quiet, Teresa," Sancho admonished her, "for very often there
are stakes where there is no bacon. Come on home with me and
you will hear marvels. I am bringing money with me, which is the
thing that matters, money earned by my own efforts and without
harm to anyone."

"You just bring along the money, my good husband," said
Teresa, "and whether you got it here or there, or by whatever
means, you will not be introducing any new custom into the world."

Sanchica then embraced her father and asked him if he had
brought her anything, for she had been looking forward to his coming as to the showers in May. And so, with his wife holding him by
the hand while his daughter kept one arm about his waist and at the
same time led the gray, Sancho went home, leaving Don Quixote
under his own roof in the company of niece and housekeeper, the
curate and the barber.

Without regard to time or season, the knight at once drew his
guests to one side and in a few words informed them of how he had
been overcome in battle and had given his promise not to leave
his village for a year, a promise that he meant to observe most
scrupulously, without violating it in the slightest degree, as every
knight-errant was obliged to do by the laws of chivalry. He accordingly meant to spend that year as a shepherd,[116] he said, amid the
solitude of the fields, where he might give free rein to his amorous
fancies as he practiced the virtues of the pastoral life; and he further
begged them, if they were not too greatly occupied and more urgent
matters did not prevent their doing so, to consent to be his companions. He would purchase a flock sufficiently large to justify their
calling themselves shepherds; and, moreover, he would have them
know, the most important thing of all had been taken care of, for he
had hit upon names that would suit them marvelously well. When

116. Since the knight-errant's life has
been forbidden him by his defeat, Don
Quixote for a time plans to live according
to another and no less "literary" code,
that of the pastoral. In the following paragraphs the author, especially through the
bachelor Carrasco, refers humorously to
some of the conventions of pastoral literature.

the curate asked him what these names were, Don Quixote replied that he himself would be known as "the shepherd Quixotiz," the bachelor as "the shepherd Carrascón," the curate as "the shepherd Curiambro," and Sancho Panza as "the shepherd Pancino."

Both his listeners were dismayed at the new form which his madness had assumed. However, in order that he might not go faring forth from the village on another of his expeditions (for they hoped that in the course of the year he would be cured), they decided to fall in with his new plan and approve it as being a wise one, and they even agreed to be his companions in the calling he proposed to adopt.

"What's more," remarked Sansón Carrasco, "I am a very famous poet, as everyone knows, and at every turn I will be composing pastoral or courtly verses or whatever may come to mind, by way of a diversion for us as we wander in those lonely places; but what is most necessary of all, my dear sirs, is that each one of us should choose the name of the shepherd lass to whom he means to dedicate his songs, so that we may not leave a tree, however hard its bark may be, where their names are not inscribed and engraved as is the custom with lovelorn shepherds."

"That is exactly what we should do," replied Don Quixote, "although, for my part, I am relieved of the necessity of looking for an imaginary shepherdess, seeing that I have the peerless Dulcinea del Toboso, glory of these brookside regions, adornment of these meadows, beauty's mainstay, cream of the Graces—in short, one to whom all praise is well becoming however hyperbolical it may be."

"That is right," said the curate, "but we will seek out some shepherd maids that are easily handled, who if they do not square with us will fit in the corners."

"And," added Sansón Carrasco, "if we run out of names we will give them those that we find printed in books the world over: such as Fílida, Amarilis, Diana, Flérida, Galatea, and Belisarda; for since these are for sale in the market place, we can buy them and make them our own. If my lady, or, rather, my shepherdess, should by chance be called Ana, I will celebrate her charms under the name of Anarda; if she is Francisca, she will become Francenia; if Lucía, Luscinda; for it all amounts to the same thing. And Sancho Panza, if he enters this confraternity, may compose verses to his wife, Teresa Panza, under the name of Teresaina."

Don Quixote had to laugh at this, and the curate then went on to heap extravagant praise upon him for his noble resolution which did him so much credit, and once again he offered to keep the knight company whenever he could spare the time from the duties of his office. With this, they took their leave of him, advising and beseeching him to take care of his health and to eat plentifully of the proper food.

As fate would have it, the niece and the housekeeper had overheard the conversation of the three men, and as soon as the visitors had left they both descended upon Don Quixote.

"What is the meaning of this, my uncle? Here we were thinking your Grace had come home to lead a quiet and respectable life, and do you mean to tell us you are going to get yourself involved in fresh complications—

> Young shepherd, thou who comest here,
> Young shepherd, thou who goest there . . . [117]

For, to tell the truth, the barley is too hard now to make shepherds' pipes of it."[118]

"And how," said the housekeeper, "is your Grace going to stand the midday heat in summer, the winter cold, the howling of the wolves out there in the fields? You certainly cannot endure it. That is an occupation for robust men, cut out and bred for such a calling almost from their swaddling clothes. Setting one evil over against another, it is better to be a knight-errant than a shepherd. Look, sir, take my advice, for I am not stuffed with bread and wine when I give it to you but am fasting and am going on fifty years of age: stay at home, attend to your affairs, go often to confession, be charitable to the poor, and let it be upon my soul if any harm comes to you as a result of it."

"Be quiet, daughters," said Don Quixote. "I know very well what I must do. Take me up to bed, for I do not feel very well; and you may be sure of one thing: whether I am a knight-errant now or a shepherd to be, I never will fail to look after your needs as you will see when the time comes."

And good daughters that they unquestionably were, the housekeeper and the niece helped him up to bed, where they gave him something to eat and made him as comfortable as they could.

CHAPTER 74

*Of how Don Quixote fell sick, of the will that he made, and of the manner of his death.*

Inasmuch as nothing that is human is eternal but is ever declining from its beginning to its close, this being especially true of the lives of men, and since Don Quixote was not endowed by Heaven with the privilege of staying the downward course of things, his own end came when he was least expecting it. Whether it was owing to

117. from a ballad.  118. a proverb.

melancholy occasioned by the defeat he had suffered, or was, simply, the will of Heaven which had so ordained it, he was taken with a fever that kept him in bed for a week, during which time his friends, the curate, the bachelor, and the barber, visited him frequently, while Sancho Panza, his faithful squire, never left his bedside.

Believing that the knight's condition was due to sorrow over his downfall and disappointment at not having been able to accomplish the disenchantment and liberation of Dulcinea, Sancho and the others endeavored to cheer him up in every possible way. The bachelor urged him to take heart and get up from bed that he might begin his pastoral life, adding that he himself had already composed an eclogue that would cast in the shade all that Sannazaro[119] had ever written, and had purchased with his own money from a herdsman of Quintanar two fine dogs to guard the flock, one of them named Barcino and the other Butrón. All this, however, did not serve to relieve Don Quixote's sadness; whereupon his friends called in the doctor, who took his pulse and was not very well satisfied with it. In any case, the physician told them, they should attend to the health of his soul as that of his body was in grave danger.

Don Quixote received this news calmly enough, but not so his housekeeper, niece, and squire, who began weeping bitterly, as if he were already lying dead in front of them. It was the doctor's opinion that melancholy and depression were putting an end to his patient's life. The knight then requested them to leave him alone as he wished to sleep a little, and they complied. He slept for more than six hours at a stretch, as the saying is, and so soundly that the housekeeper and niece thought he would never wake.

At last he did, however, and at once cried out in a loud voice, "Blessed be Almighty God who has given me so many blessings! Truly His mercy is boundless and is not limited or restrained by the sins of men."

The niece listened carefully to what her uncle said, and it seemed to her that he was speaking more rationally than was his wont, at least during his illness.

"Sir," she said to him, "what does your Grace mean? Has something occurred that we know nothing about? What is this talk of mercy and sins?"

"The mercy that I speak of," replied Don Quixote, "is that which God is showing me at this moment—in spite of my sins, as I have said. My mind now is clear, unencumbered by those misty shadows of ignorance that were cast over it by my bitter and continual reading of those hateful books of chivalry. I see through all the

---

119. the Italian poet Jacopo Sannazaro (1456?–1530), whose *Arcadia* is one of the milestones in the pastoral tradition.

nonsense and fraud contained in them, and my only regret is that my disillusionment has come so late, leaving me no time to make any sort of amends by reading those that are the light of the soul. I find myself, niece, at the point of death, and I would die in such a way as not to leave the impression of a life so bad that I shall be remembered as a madman; for even though I have been one, I do not wish to confirm it on my deathbed. And so, my dear, call in my good friends: the curate, the bachelor Sansón Carrasco, and Master Nicholas the barber; for I want to confess my sins and make my last will and testament."

The niece, however, was relieved of this errand, for the three of them came in just then.

"I have good news for you, kind sirs," said Don Quixote the moment he saw them. "I am no longer Don Quixote de la Mancha but Alonso Quijano, whose mode of life won for him the name of 'Good.' I am the enemy of Amadis of Gaul and all his innumerable progeny; for those profane stories dealing with knight-errantry are odious to me, and I realize how foolish I was and the danger I courted in reading them; but I am in my right senses now and I abominate them."

Hearing this, they all three were convinced that some new kind of madness must have laid hold of him.

"Why, Señor Don Quixote!" exclaimed Sansón. "What makes you talk like that, just when we have received news that my lady Dulcinea is disenchanted?[120] And just when we are on the verge of becoming shepherds so that we may spend the rest of our lives in singing like a lot of princes, why does your Grace choose to turn hermit? Say no more, in Heaven's name, but be sensible and forget these idle tales."

"Tales of that kind," said Don Quixote, "have been the truth for me in the past, and to my detriment, but with Heaven's aid I trust to turn them to my profit now that I am dying. For I feel, gentlemen, that death is very near; so, leave all jesting aside and bring me a confessor for my sins and a notary to draw up my will. In such straits as these a man cannot trifle with his soul. Accordingly, while the Señor Curate is hearing my confession, let the notary be summoned."

Amazed at his words, they gazed at one another in some perplexity, yet they could not but believe him. One of the signs that led them to think he was dying was this quick return from madness to sanity and all the additional things he had to say, so well reasoned and well put and so becoming in a Christian that none of them could any longer doubt that he was in full possession of his

120. Sancho had imagined for the sake of his master that Dulcinea had been transformed into a country wench by enchanters, but ended up by believing his own invention.

faculties. Sending the others out of the room, the curate stayed behind to confess him, and before long the bachelor returned with the notary and Sancho Panza, who had been informed of his master's condition, and who, finding the housekeeper and the niece in tears, began weeping with them. When the confession was over, the curate came out.

"It is true enough," he said, "that Alonso Quijano the Good is dying, and it is also true that he is a sane man. It would be well for us to go in now while he makes his will."

At this news the housekeeper, niece, and the good squire Sancho Panza were so overcome with emotion that the tears burst forth from their eyes and their bosoms heaved with sobs; for, as has been stated more than once, whether Don Quixote was plain Alonso Quijano the Good or Don Quixote de la Mancha, he was always of a kindly and pleasant disposition and for this reason was beloved not only by the members of his household but by all who knew him.

The notary had entered along with the others, and as soon as the preamble had been attended to and the dying man had commended his soul to his Maker with all those Christian formalities that are called for in such a case, they came to the matter of bequests, with Don Quixote dictating as follows:

"ITEM. With regard to Sancho Panza, whom, in my madness, I appointed to be my squire, and who has in his possession a certain sum of money belonging to me: inasmuch as there has been a standing account between us, of debits and credits, it is my will that he shall not be asked to give any accounting whatsoever of this sum, but if any be left over after he has had payment for what I owe him, the balance, which will amount to very little, shall be his, and much good may it do him. If when I was mad I was responsible for his being given the governorship of an island, now that I am of sound mind I would present him with a kingdom if it were in my power, for his simplicity of mind and loyal conduct merit no less."

At this point he turned to Sancho. "Forgive me, my friend," he said, "for having caused you to appear as mad as I by leading you to fall into the same error, that of believing that there are still knights-errant in the world."

"Ah, master," cried Sancho through his tears, "don't die, your Grace, but take my advice and go on living for many years to come; for the greatest madness that a man can be guilty of in this life is to die without good reason, without anyone's killing him, slain only by the hands of melancholy. Look you, don't be lazy but get up from this bed and let us go out into the fields clad as shepherds as we agreed to do. Who knows but behind some bush we may come upon the lady Dulcinea, as disenchanted as you could wish. If it is because of worry over your defeat that you are dying, put the blame on me by saying that the reason for your being overthrown was that I had not properly fastened Rocinante's girth. For the matter of that, your Grace knows from reading your books of chivalry that it is a common thing for certain knights to overthrow others, and he who is vanquished today will be the victor tomorrow."

"That is right," said Sansón, "the worthy Sancho speaks the truth."

"Not so fast, gentlemen," said Don Quixote. "In last year's nests there are no birds this year. I was mad and now I am sane; I was Don Quixote de la Mancha, and now I am, as I have said, Alonso Quijano the Good. May my repentance and the truth I now speak restore to me the place I once held in your esteem. And now, let the notary proceed:

"ITEM. I bequeath my entire estate, without reservation, to my niece Antonia Quijana, here present, after the necessary deductions shall have been made from the most available portion of it to satisfy the bequests that I have stipulated. The first payment shall be to my housekeeper for the wages due her, with twenty ducats over to buy her a dress. And I hereby appoint the Señor Curate and the Señor Bachelor Sansón Carrasco to be my executors

"ITEM. It is my will that if my niece Antonia Quijana should see fit to marry, it shall be to a man who does not know what books of chivalry are; and if it shall be established that he is acquainted with such books and my niece still insists on marrying him, then she shall lose all that I have bequeathed her and my executors shall apply her portion to works of charity as they may see fit.

"ITEM. I entreat the aforementioned gentlemen, my executors, if by good fortune they should come to know the author who is said to have composed a history now going the rounds under the title of *Second Part of the Exploits of Don Quixote de la Mancha*, to beg his forgiveness in my behalf, as earnestly as they can, since it was I who unthinkingly led him to set down so many and such great absurdities as are to be found in it; for I leave this life with a feeling of remorse at having provided him with the occasion for putting them into writing."

The will ended here, and Don Quixote, stretching himself at length in the bed, fainted away. They all were alarmed at this and hastened to aid him. The same thing happened very frequently in the course of the three days of life that remained to him after he had made his will. The household was in a state of excitement, but with it all the niece continued to eat her meals, the housekeeper had her drink, and Sancho Panza was in good spirits; for this business of inheriting property effaces or mitigates the sorrow which the heir ought to feel and causes him to forget.

Death came at last for Don Quixote, after he had received all the sacraments and once more, with many forceful arguments, had expressed his abomination of books of chivalry. The notary who was present remarked that in none of those books had he read of any knight-errant dying in his own bed so peacefully and in so Christian a manner. And thus, amid the tears and lamentations of those present, he gave up the ghost; that is to say, he died. Perceiving that their friend was no more, the curate asked the notary to be a witness to the fact that Alonso Quijano the Good, commonly known as Don Quixote, was truly dead, this being necessary in order that some author other than Cid Hamete Benengeli might not have the opportunity of falsely resurrecting him and writing endless histories of his exploits.

Such was the end of the Ingenious Gentleman of La Mancha, whose birthplace Cid Hamete was unwilling to designate exactly in order that all the towns and villages of La Mancha might contend among themselves for the right to adopt him and claim him as their own, just as the seven cities of Greece did in the case of Homer. The lamentations of Sancho and those of Don Quixote's niece and his housekeeper, as well as the original epitaphs that were composed for his tomb, will not be recorded here, but mention may be made of the verses by Sansón Carrasco:

> Here lies a gentleman bold
> Who was so very brave
> He went to lengths untold,
> And on the brink of the grave
> Death had on him no hold.
> By the world he set small store—
> He frightened it to the core—
> Yet somehow, by Fate's plan,
> Though he'd lived a crazy man,
> When he died he was sane once more.

# CHRISTOPHER MARLOWE
## (1564–1593)
### The Tragical History
### of the Life and Death of Doctor Faustus*

#### Dramatis Personae

DR. JOHN FAUSTUS, *of the University of Wittenberg*

CHORUS

WAGNER, *his servant*

* The modernized text and the notes here presented are by Hallett Smith.

GOOD ANGEL *and* BAD ANGEL

VALDES *and* CORNELIUS, *magicians and friends of* FAUSTUS

THREE SCHOLARS, *students at the university*

LUCIFER, MEPHISTOPHILIS, *and* BELZEBUB, *devils*

ROBIN *and* DICK, *rustic clowns*

THE SEVEN DEADLY SINS

POPE ADRIAN

RAYMOND, *King of Hungary*

BRUNO, *a rival Pope, appointed by the* EMPEROR

CARDINALS OF FRANCE *and* PADUA

ARCHBISHOP OF RHEIMS

MARTINO, FREDERICK, *and* BENVOLIO, *gentlemen at the* EMPEROR's *court*

CAROLUS (CHARLES) THE FIFTH, EMPEROR

DUKE OF SAXONY

DUKE *and* DUCHESS OF VANHOLT

HORSE-COURSER

CARTER

HOSTESS *of a tavern*

OLD MAN

SPIRITS *of* DARIUS, ALEXANDER *and his* PARAMOUR, *and* HELEN OF TROY

ATTENDANTS, MONKS *and* FRIARS, SOLDIERS, PIPER, *two* CUPIDS

## Act I

[*Enter* CHORUS.[1]]

CHO. Not marching in the fields of Trasimene[2]
Where Mars did mate the warlike Carthagens,
Nor sporting in the dalliance of love
In courts of kings where state[3] is overturned,
Nor in the pomp of proud audacious deeds
Intends our Muse to vaunt his heavenly verse:
Only this, gentles, we must now perform,
The form of Faustus' fortunes good or bad.
And so to patient judgments we appeal
And speak for Faustus in his infancy.
Now is he born, his parents base of stock,
In Germany within a town called Rhode;[4]
At riper years to Wittenberg he went
Whereas his kinsmen chiefly brought him up;
So much he profits in divinity,
The fruitful plot of scholarism graced,[5]
That shortly he was graced with Doctor's name,
Excelling all whose sweet delight disputes[6]
In th' heavenly matters of theology,
Till, swollen with cunning,[7] of a self-conceit,
His waxen wings did mount above his reach
And melting, heavens conspired his overthrow.[8]

1. A single actor who recited a prologue to an act or a whole play, and occasionally delivered an epilogue.
2. The battle of Lake Trasimene (217 B.C.) was one of the Carthaginian leader Hannibal's great victories. "Mate": join with.
3. Political power.
4. Roda. Wittenberg, in the next line, was the famous university where Martin Luther studied, as did Shakespeare's

Hamlet and Horatio; "whereas": where.
5. Grazed. In line 17 "graced" refers to the Cambridge word for permission to proceed to a degree.
6. The usual academic exercises were disputations, which took the place of examinations.
7. Learning.
8. The reference is to the Greek myth of Icarus, who flew too near the sun

For, falling to a devilish exercise
And glutted more with learning's golden gifts,
He surfeits upon cursèd necromancy;[9]                              25
Nothing so sweet as magic is to him,
Which he prefers before his chiefest bliss[1]—
And this the man that in his study sits.
[*Draws the curtain*[2] *and exit.*]

SCENE 1

[FAUSTUS *in his study.*]
FAUST. Settle thy studies, Faustus, and begin
To sound the depth of that thou wilt profess.
Having commenced, be a divine in show,
Yet level[3] at the end of every art
And live and die in Aristotle's works:                             5
Sweet Analytics,[4] 'tis thou hast ravished me!        [*Reads.*]
*Bene disserere est finis logicis*—
Is to dispute well logic's chiefest end?
Affords this art no greater miracle?
Then read no more; thou hast attained the end.                     10
A greater subject fitteth Faustus' wit:
Bid *ὸν χαὶ μὴ ὸν*[5] farewell, Galen come,
Seeing *ubi desinit philosophus, ibi incipit medicus;*[6]
Be a physician, Faustus, heap up gold
And be eternized for some wondrous cure.               [*Reads.*]   15
*Summum bonum medicinae sanitas*[7]—
The end of physic is our bodies' health:
Why, Faustus, hast thou not attained that end?
Is not thy common talk sound aphorisms?[8]
Are not thy bills hung up as monuments                             20
Whereby whole cities have escaped the plague
And thousand desperate maladies been cured?
Yet art thou still but Faustus, and a man.
Couldst thou make men to live eternally
Or, being dead, raise them to life again,                          25
Then this profession were to be esteemed.
Physic, farewell. Where is Justinian?[9]               [*Reads.*]
*Si una eademque res legatur duobus,
Alter rem, alter valorem rei, etc.*[1]—

on wings of feathers and wax made by
his father Daedalus. The wax melted
and he fell into the sea and was
drowned.
9. Black magic.
1. The salvation of his soul.
2. The curtain to the inner stage, behind the main stage, which serves here
as Faustus' study. "Draws" here means
"draws apart."
3. "Commenced": graduated, i.e., received the doctor's degree; "in show":
in external appearance; "level": aim.
4. The title of a treatise on logic by
Aristotle. The Latin means, "To carry
on a disputation well is the end or

purpose of logic."
5. "Being and not being," i.e., philosophy. Galen: the ancient authority on
medicine (2nd century A.D.).
6. "Where the philosopher leaves off
the physician begins."
7. "Good health is the object of medicine" (or "physic").
8. I.e., reliable medical pronouncements. "Bills": prescriptions.
9. Roman emperor and authority on
law (483–565), author of the *Institutes*.
1. "If something is bequeathed to two
persons, one shall have the thing itself, the other something of equal
value." The next Latin phrase means:

A pretty case of paltry legacies!                                    30
*Exhaereditare filium non potest pater nisi—*
Such is the subject of the Institute
And universal body of the law.
This study fits a mercenary drudge
Who aims at nothing but external trash,                              35
Too servile and illiberal for me.
When all is done, divinity is best.
Jerome's Bible,[2] Faustus, view it well:                   [*Reads.*]
*Stipendium peccati mors est*—Ha! *Stipendium, etc.*
The reward of sin is death? That's hard.                            40
*Si pecasse negamus, fallimur, et nulla est in nobis veritas*[3]—
If we say that we have no sin
We deceive ourselves, and there's no truth in us.
Why then belike
We must sin and so consequently die,                                45
Aye, we must die an everlasting death.
What doctrine call you this, *Che sera, sera:*[4]
What will be, shall be? Divinity, adieu!
These metaphysics[5] of magicians
And necromantic books are heavenly:                                 50
Lines, circles, signs, letters, and characters—
Aye, these are those that Faustus most desires.
O what a world of profit and delight,
Of power, of honor, of omnipotence,
Is promised to the studious artisan![6]                             55
All things that move between the quiet[7] poles
Shall be at my command. Emperors and kings
Are but obeyed in their several provinces,
Nor can they raise the wind or rend the clouds;
But his dominion that exceeds in this                               60
Stretcheth as far as doth the mind of man.
A sound magician is a demigod:
Here tire my brains to gain a deity!
Wagner!
    [*Enter* WAGNER.]
Commend me to my dearest friends,                                   65
The German Valdes and Cornelius;
Request them earnestly to visit me.
WAG. I will, sir.                                           [*Exit.*]
FAUST. Their conference will be a greater help to me
Than all my labors, plod I ne'er so fast.                           70
    [*Enter the* GOOD ANGEL *and the* BAD ANGEL.]
G. ANG. O Faustus, lay that damnéd book aside
And gaze not on it, lest it tempt thy soul

"A father cannot disinherit his son unless."
2. The Latin translation, or "Vulgate,"
of St. Jerome (ca. 340–420). The Latin
(Romans vi.23) is translated in line
40.
3. I John i.8, translated in the next two
lines.
4. Translated in the first half of the
next line.
5. Basic principles.
6. I.e., a master of the occult arts,
such as necromancy.
7. Unmoving.

And heap God's heavy wrath upon thy head.
Read, read the Scriptures! That is blasphemy.
B. ANG. Go forward, Faustus, in that famous art          75
Wherein all nature's treasury is contained:
Be thòu on earth, as Jove[8] is in the sky,
Lord and commander of these elements.
          [*Exeunt* ANGELS.]
FAUST. How am I glutted with conceit[9] of this!
Shall I make spirits fetch me what I please,          30
Resolve me of all ambiguities,
Perform what desperate enterprise I will?
I'll have them fly to India[1] for gold,
Ransack the ocean for orient pearl,
And search all corners of the new-found world[2]          85
For pleasant fruits and princely delicates;
I'll have them read me strange philosophy
And tell the secrets of all foreign kings;
I'll have them wall all Germany with brass
And make swift Rhine circle fair Wittenberg;          90
I'll have them fill the public schools[3] with silk
Wherewith the students shall be bravely clad;
I'll levy soldiers with the coin they bring,
And chase the Prince of Parma[4] from our land
And reign sole king of all our provinces;          95
Yea, stranger engines for the brunt of war
Than was the fiery keel[5] at Antwerp's bridge
I'll make my servile spirits to invent!
          [*Enter* VALDES *and* CORNELIUS.]
Come, German Valdes and Cornelius,
And make me blest with your sage conference.          100
Valdes, sweet Valdes and Cornelius,
Know that your words have won me at the last
To practice magic and concealéd arts;
Yet not your words only, but mine own fantasy
That will receive no object,[6] for my head          105
But ruminates on necromantic skill.
Philosophy is odious and obscure,
Both law and physic are for petty wits,
Divinity is basest of the three,
Unpleasant, harsh, contemptible, and vile;          110
'Tis magic, magic, that hath ravished me!
Then, gentle friends, aid me in this attempt,
And I, that have with concise syllogisms

8. God (a common substitution in Elizabethan drama).
9. Filled with the idea.
1. "India" could mean the West Indies, America, or Ophir (in the east).
2. The western hemisphere.
3. The university lecture rooms.
4. The Duke of Parma was the Spanish governor general of the Low Countries from 1579 to 1592.
5. A reference to the burning ship sent by the Netherlanders in 1585 against the barrier on the river Scheldt which Parma had built as a part of the blockade of Antwerp.
6. That will pay no attention to physical reality.

Graveled[7] the pastors of the German church,
And made the flowering pride of Wittenberg            115
Swarm to my problems[8] as the infernal spirits
On sweet Musaeus when he came to hell,
Will be as cunning as Agrippa[9] was
Whose shadows made all Europe honor him.

VALD. Faustus, these books, thy wit, and our experience      120
Shall make all nations to canonize us.
As Indian Moors[1] obey their Spanish lords
So shall the spirits of every element
Be always serviceable to us three:
Like lions shall they guard us when we please,          125
Like Almain rutters[2] with their horsemen's staves,
Or Lapland giants trotting by our sides;
Sometimes like women, or unwedded maids,
Shadowing more beauty in their airy brows
Than in the white breasts of the queen of love;         130
From Venice shall they drag huge argosies
And from America the golden fleece
That yearly stuffs old Philip's[3] treasury,
If learned Faustus will be resolute.

FAUST. Valdes, as resolute am I in this                 135
As thou to live; therefore object it not.[4]

CORN. The miracles that magic will perform
Will make thee vow to study nothing else.
He that is grounded in astrology,
Enriched with tongues, well seen[5] in minerals,        140
Hath all the principles magic doth require.
Then doubt not, Faustus, but to be renowned
And more frequented for this mystery[6]
Than heretofore the Delphian oracle.
The spirits tell me they can dry the sea               145
And fetch the treasure of all foreign wrecks—
Aye, all the wealth that our forefathers hid
Within the massy[7] entrails of the earth.
Then tell me, Faustus, what shall we three want?

FAUST. Nothing, Cornelius. O this cheers my soul!       150
Come, show me some demonstrations magical
That I may conjure in some lusty[8] grove
And have these joys in full possession.

VALD. Then haste thee to some solitary grove
And bear wise Bacon's[9] and Albanus' works,           155

7. Confounded.
8. Lectures in logic and mathematics.
Musaeus was a mythical singer, son
of Orpheus; it was, however, the latter
who charmed the denizens of hell with
his music.
9. Cornelius Agrippa, German author
of *The Vanity and Uncertainty of Arts
and Sciences*, popularly supposed to
have the power of calling up shades
("shadows") of the dead.

1. I.e., dark-skinned American Indians.
2. German horsemen.
3. Philip II, king of Spain.
4. I.e., don't make it a condition.
5. Expert.
6. Craft. The "Delphian oracle" was
the oracle of Apollo at Delphi, much
frequented in antiquity.
7. Massive.
8. Flourishing, beautiful.
9. Roger Bacon, the medieval friar and

The Hebrew Psalter and New Testament;
And whatsoever else is requisite
We will inform thee ere our conference cease.
CORN. Valdes, first let him know the words of art,
And then, all other ceremonies learned,                              160
Faustus may try his cunning by himself.
VALD. First I'll instruct thee in the rudiments,
And then wilt thou be perfecter than I.
FAUST. Then come and dine with me, and after meat
We'll canvass every quiddity[1] thereof;                             165
For ere I sleep I'll try what I can do:
This night I'll conjure[2] though I die therefore.      [*Exeunt.*]

## SCENE 2

[*Enter two* SCHOLARS.]

1 SCH. I wonder what's become of Faustus, that was wont to
make our schools ring with *sic probo*.[3]
2 SCH. That shall we presently know; here comes his boy.[4]
[*Enter* WAGNER *carrying wine*.]
1 SCH. How now, sirrah; where's thy master?
WAG. God in heaven knows.                                               5
2 SCH. Why, dost not thou know then?
WAG. Yes, I know; but that follows not.
1 SCH. Go to, sirrah; leave your jesting and tell us where he is.
WAG. That follows not by force of argument, which you, being
licentiate,[5] should stand upon; therefore acknowledge your     10
error and be attentive.
2 SCH. Then you will not tell us?
WAG. You are deceived, for I will tell you. Yet if you were not
dunces you would never ask me such a question, for is he not
*corpus naturale*, and is not that *mobile*?[6] Then wherefore    15
should you ask me such a question? But that I am by nature
phlegmatic,[7] slow to wrath and prone to lechery (to love, I
would say), it were not for you to come within forty foot of
the place of execution,[8] although I do not doubt to see you
both hanged the next sessions. Thus having triumphed over        20
you, I will set my countenance like a precisian,[9] and begin
to speak thus: Truly, my dear brethren, my master is within
at dinner with Valdes and Cornelius, as this wine, if it could
speak, would inform your worships; and so the Lord bless you,
preserve you, and keep you, my dear brethren.                    25
[*Exit.*]

---

scientist, popularly thought a magician.
"Albanus" is Pietro d'Albano, 13th-
century alchemist.
1. Essential feature.
2. Call up spirits.
3. "Thus I prove," a phrase in scholastic disputation.
4. Poor student earning his keep.
5. I.e., graduate students.
6. *Corpus naturale et mobile* (natural,
movable matter) was a scholastic defi-

nition of the subject matter of physics.
Wagner is here parodying the language
of learning he hears around the university.
7. Dominated by the phlegm, one of
the four humors of medieval medicine
and psychology.
8. I.e., the dining room.
9. A Puritan. The rest of his speech
is in the style of the Puritans.

1 SCH. O Faustus, then I fear that which I have long suspected,
    That thou art fallen into that damnéd art
    For which they two are infamous throughout the world.
2 SCH. Were he a stranger, not allied to me,
    The danger of his soul would make me mourn.         30
    But come, let us go and inform the Rector,[1]
    It may be his grave counsel may reclaim him.
1 SCH. I fear me nothing will reclaim him now.
2 SCH. Yet let us see what we can do.

                                          *[Exeunt.]*

### SCENE 3

*[Enter* FAUSTUS *to conjure.]*
FAUST. Now that the gloomy shadow of the night,
    Longing to view Orion's drizzling look,[2]
    Leaps from the antarctic world unto the sky
    And dims the welkin[3] with her pitchy breath,
    Faustus, begin thine incantations            5
    And try if devils will obey thy hest,
    Seeing thou has prayed and sacrificed to them.
    Within this circle is Jehovah's name
        *[He draws the circle[4] on the ground.]*
    Forward and backward anagrammatized,
    The breviated names of holy saints,          10
    Figures of every adjunct[5] to the heavens
    And characters of signs and erring stars,
    By which the spirits are enforced to rise.
    Then fear not, Faustus, but be resolute
    And try the uttermost magic can perform.      *[Thunder.]*  15
    *Sint mihi dei Acherontis propitii! Valeat numen triplex*
    *Iehovae! Ignei aerii aquatici terreni spiritus, salvete! Orientis*
    *princeps Lucifer Belzebub, inferni ardentis monarcha, et De-*
    *mogorgon, propitiamus vos, ut appareat et surgat Mephistophi-*
    *lis!*[6]                                  20
        *[*FAUSTUS *pauses. Thunder still.]*
    *Quid tu moraris?*[7] *Per Iehovam, Gehennam et consecratam*
    *aquam quam nunc spargo, signumque crucis quod nunc facio,*
    *et per vota nostra, ipse nunc surgat nobis dicatus Mephistophi-*
    *lis!*

1. The head of a German university.
2. Orion appears at the beginning of winter. The phrase is a reminiscence of Virgil.
3. Sky.
4. I.e., the magic circle on the ground within which the spirits rise.
5. Heavenly body, thought to be joined to the solid firmament. "Characters of signs" are signs of the zodiac and the planets; "erring": wandering.
6. This first part of the incantation means: "May the gods of the lower regions favor me! Goodbye to the Trin-

ity! Hail, spirits of fire, air, water, and earth! Prince of the East, Belzebub, monarch of burning hell, and Demogorgon, we pray to you that Mephistophilis may appear and rise."
7. Nothing has happened, so Faustus asks, "What are you waiting for?" and continues to conjure: "By Jehovah, Gehenna, and the holy water which I now sprinkle, and the sign of the cross which I now make, and by our vows, may Mephistophilis himself now rise to serve us."

[MEPHISTOPHILIS *in the shape of a dragon rises from the earth outside the circle.*]

I charge thee to return and change thy shape;                    25
Thou art too ugly to attend on me.
Go, and return an old Franciscan friar;
That holy shape becomes a devil best.          [*Exit* MEPH.]
I see there's virtue in my heavenly words:
Who would not be proficient in this art?                          30
How pliant is this Mephistophilis,
Full of obedience and humility!
Such is the force of magic and my spells.
Now, Faustus, thou art conjurer laureate
That canst command great Mephistophilis:                         35
*Quin redis, Mephistophilis, fratris imagine!*[8]
[*Re-enter* MEPHISTOPHILIS *like a Friar.*]

MEPH. Now, Faustus, what wouldst thou have me do?
FAUST. I charge thee wait upon me whilst I live
To do whatever Faustus shall command,
Be it be make the moon drop from her sphere                      40
Or the ocean to overwhelm the world.
MEPH. I am a servant to great Lucifer
And may not follow thee without his leave:
No more than he commands must we perform.
FAUST. Did not he charge thee to appear to me?                    45
MEPH. No, I came now hither of my own accord.
FAUST. Did not my conjuring speeches raise thee?
Speak!
MEPH. That was the cause, but yet *per accidens*,[9]
For when we hear one rack[1] the name of God,                    50
Abjure the Scriptures and his Saviour Christ,
We fly in hope to get his glorious soul;
Nor will we come unless he use such means
Whereby he is in danger to be damned;
Therefore the shortest cut for conjuring.                        55
Is stoutly to abjure the Trinity
And pray devoutly to the prince of hell.
FAUST. So I have done, and hold this principle,
There is no chief but only Belzebub
To whom Faustus doth dedicate himself.                           60
This word "damnation" terrifies not me
For I confound hell in Elysium;
My ghost be with the old philosophers![2]
But leaving these vain trifles of men's souls—
Tell me, what is that Lucifer thy lord?                          65
MEPH. Arch-regent and commander of all spirits.
FAUST. Was not that Lucifer an angel once?
MEPH. Yes, Faustus, and most dearly loved of God.

8. "Return, Mephistophilis, in the shape of a friar."
9. By the immediate, not ultimate, cause.
1. Torture (by anagrammatizing).

2. I.e., I regard heaven and hell indifferently; if the old (pre-Christian) philosophers are damned, let me be damned with them.

FAUST. How comes it, then, that he is prince of devils? 70
MEPH. O, by aspiring pride and insolence,
    For which God threw him from the face of heaven.
FAUST. And what are you that live with Lucifer?
MEPH. Unhappy spirits that fell with Lucifer,
    Conspired against our God with Lucifer, 75
    And are forever damned with Lucifer.
FAUST. Where are you damned?
MEPH. In hell.
FAUST. How comes it, then, that thou art out of hell?
MEPH. Why, this is hell, nor am I out of it: 80
    Thinkst thou that I who saw the face of God
    And tasted the eternal joys of heaven
    Am not tormented with ten thousand hells
    In being deprived of everlasting bliss?
    O Faustus, leave these frivolous demands 85
    Which strike a terror to my fainting soul!
FAUST. What, is great Mephistophilis so passionate[3]
    For being deprivéd of the joys of heaven?
    Learn thou of Faustus manly fortitude
    And scorn those joys thou never shalt possess. 90
    Go, bear these tidings to great Lucifer:
    Seeing Faustus hath incurred eternal death
    By desperate thoughts against Jove's deity,
    Say he surrenders up to him his soul
    So he will spare him four and twenty years, 95
    Letting him live in all voluptuousness,
    Having thee ever to attend on me:
    To give me whatsoever I shall ask,
    To tell me whatsoever I demand,
    To slay mine enemies and aid my friends, 100
    And always be obedient to my will.
    Go, and return to mighty Lucifer,
    And meet me in my study at midnight
    And then resolve me of thy master's mind.[4]
MEPH. I will, Faustus. [*Exit.*] 105
FAUST. Had I as many souls as there be stars
    I'd give them all for Mephistophilis!
    By him I'll be great emperor of the world,
    And make a bridge thorough the moving air
    To pass the ocean with a band of men; 110
    I'll join the hills that bind the Afric shore
    And make that country continent to Spain,
    And both contributory to my crown;
    The Emperor[5] shall not live but by my leave,
    Nor any potentate of Germany. 115
    Now that I have obtained what I desire
    I'll live in speculation[6] of this art
    Till Mephistophilis return again. [*Exit.*]

3. Overcome by emotion.
4. Give me his decision.
5. The Holy Roman Emperor.
6. Contemplation.

SCENE 4

[*Enter* WAGNER *and the* CLOWN (ROBIN.)[7]]

WAG. Come hither, sirrah boy.

CLOWN. Boy! O disgrace to my person! Zounds, boy in your face! You have seen many boys with such pickadevaunts, I am sure.[8]

WAG. Sirrah, hast thou no comings in?[9]

CLOWN. Yes, and goings out too; you may see, sir.

WAG. Alas, poor slave. See how poverty jests in his nakedness: the villain's out of service, and so hungry that I know he would give his soul to the devil for a shoulder of mutton, though it were blood-raw.

CLOWN. Not so, neither; I had need to have it well-roasted, and good sauce to it, if I pay so dear, I can tell you.

WAG. Sirrah, wilt thou be my man and wait on me? And I will make thee go like *Qui mihi discipulus.*[1]

CLOWN. What, in verse?

WAG. No, slave, in beaten silk and staves-acre.[2]

CLOWN. Staves-acre! that's good to kill vermin. Then, belike, if I serve you I shall be lousy.

WAG. Why, so thou shalt be, whether thou dost it or no; for, sirrah, if thou dost not presently bind thyself to me for seven years, I'll turn all the lice about thee into familiars[3] and make them tear thee in pieces.

CLOWN. Nay, sir, you may save yourself a labor, for they are as familiar with me as if they paid for their meat and drink, I can tell you.

WAG. Well, sirrah, leave your jesting and take these guilders.[4]

CLOWN. Yes, marry, sir, and I thank you, too.

WAG. So, now thou art to be at an hour's warning whenever and wheresoever the devil shall fetch thee.

CLOWN. Here, take your guilders again, I'll none of 'em.

WAG. Not I, thou art pressed;[5] prepare thyself, for I will presently raise up two devils to carry thee away. Banio! Belcher!

CLOWN. Belcher? And Belcher come here I'll belch him. I am not afraid of a devil.

[*Enter two* DEVILS, *and the* CLOWN *runs up and down crying.*]

WAG. How now, sir! Will you serve me now?

CLOWN. Aye, good Wagner, take away the devil then.

WAG. Spirits, away! [DEVILS *exeunt.*]

---

7. Not a court jester (as in some of Shakespeare's plays), but the older-fashioned stock character, a rustic buffoon. The name "Robin" has been interpolated by later editors of the text; all such interpolations, introduced for clarity of understanding, are indicated by the special brackets used here.
8. The point of the Clown's retort is that he is a man and wears a beard ("pickadevaunt"). "Zounds": an oath ("God's wounds").

9. Income, but the Clown then puns on the literal meaning.
1. "You who are my pupil" (the opening phrase of a poem on how students should behave, from Lily's *Latin Grammar*). Wagner means, "like a proper servant of a learned man."
2. A kind of delphinium used for killing vermin.
3. Familiar spirits, demons.
4. Money.
5. Impressed, i.e., hired.

Now, sirrah, follow me.

CLOWN. I will, sir. But hark you, master, will you teach me this conjuring occupation?

WAG. Aye, sirrah, I'll teach thee to turn thyself to a dog, or a cat, or a mouse, or a rat, or anything.                                    40

CLOWN. A dog, or a cat, or a mouse, or a rat! O brave[6] Wagner!

WAG. Villain, call me Master Wagner; and see that you walk attentively, and let your right eye be always diametrally[7] fixed upon my left heel, that thou mayst *quasi vestigiis nostris insistere.*[8]

CLOWN. Well, sir, I warrant you.                         [*Exeunt.*]      45

## Act II

### SCENE 1

[*Enter* FAUSTUS *in his study.*]

FAUST. Now, Faustus, must thou needs be damned,
Canst not be saved.
What boots[9] it, then, to think of God or heaven?
Away with such vain fancies, and despair—
Despair in God and trust in Belzebub.                                    5
Now go not backward, no, be resolute!
Why waverest? Something soundeth in mine ears:
"Abjure this magic, turn to God again!"
Aye, and Faustus will turn to God again.
To God? He loves thee not;                                               10
The God thou servest is thine own appetite,
Wherein is fixed the love of Belzebub.
To him I'll build an altar and a church
And offer lukewarm blood of newborn babes.
        [*Enter* GOOD ANGEL *and* BAD ANGEL.]
G. ANG. Sweet Faustus, leave that execrable art.                          15
B. ANG. Go forward, Faustus, in that famous art.
FAUST. Contrition, prayer, repentance—what of them?
G. ANG. O they are means to bring thee unto heaven!
B. ANG. Rather illusions, fruits of lunacy,
That makes men foolish that do use them most.                            20
G. ANG. Sweet Faustus, think of heaven and heavenly things.
B. ANG. No, Faustus, think of honor and of wealth.
        [⟨*Exeunt* ANGELS.⟩]
FAUST. Of wealth!
Why, the signiory of Emden[1] shall be mine.
When Mephistophilis shall stand by me                                    25
What power can hurt me? Faustus, thou art safe;
Cast no more doubts. Come, Mephistophilis,
And bring glad tidings from great Lucifer.
Is't not midnight? Come, Mephistophilis!

6. Marvelous, wonderful.
7. Diametrically.
8. A pedantic way of saying "follow

my footsteps."
9. Avails.
1. A wealthy German trade center.

*Veni, veni, Mephistophile!*[2]                                                    30
    [*Enter* MEPHISTOPHILIS.]
  Now tell me what saith Lucifer, thy lord?
MEPH. That I shall wait on Faustus whilst I live,
  So he will buy my service with his soul.
FAUST. Already Faustus hath hazarded that for thee.
MEPH. But, Faustus, thou must bequeath it solemnly                  35
  And write a deed of gift with thine own blood,
  For that security craves Lucifer.
  If thou deny it, I must back to hell.
FAUST. Stay, Mephistophilis, and tell me what good
  Will my soul do thy lord?
MEPH.                          Enlarge his kingdom.                    40
FAUST. Is that the reason why he tempts us thus?
MEPH. *Solamen miseris socios habuisse doloris.*[3]
FAUST. Why, have you any pain that tortures others?
MEPH. As great as have the human souls of men.
  But tell me, Faustus, shall I have thy soul?                   45
  And I will be thy slave, and wait on thee,
  And give thee more than thou hast wit to ask.
FAUST. Aye, Mephistophilis, I'll give it him.
MEPH. Then, Faustus, stab thine arm courageously,
  And bind thy soul that at some certain day                      50
  Great Lucifer may claim it as his own,
  And then be thou as great as Lucifer.
FAUST. Lo, Mephistophilis, for love of thee
    [*Stabbing his arm.*]
  I cut mine arm, and with my proper[4] blood
  Assure my soul to be great Lucifer's.                           55
  Chief lord and regent of perpetual night,
  View here the blood that trickles from mine arm
  And let it be propitious for my wish!
MEPH. But, Faustus,
  Write it in manner of a deed of gift.                           60
FAUST. Aye, so I do. [*Writes.*] But, Mephistophilis,
  My blood congeals and I can write no more.
MEPH. I'll fetch thee fire to dissolve it straight.        [*Exit.*]
FAUST. What might the staying of my blood portend?
  Is it unwilling I should write this bill?[5]                   65
  Why streams it not, that I may write afresh?
  "Faustus gives to thee his soul"—ah, there it stayed.
  Why shouldst thou not? Is not thy soul thine own?
  Then write again: "Faustus gives to thee his soul."
    [*Enter* MEPHISTOPHILIS *with a chafer*[6] *of fire.*]
MEPH. See, Faustus, here is fire; set it on.                         70
FAUST. So: now the blood begins to clear again;
  Now will I make an end immediately.              [⟨*Writes.*⟩]

2. "Come, come, Mephistophilis!"    5. Contract.
3. "Misery loves company."    6. A portable grate.
4. Own.

MEPH. [*aside*] What will not I do to obtain his soul!

FAUST. *Consummatum est*[7]—this bill is ended;
And Faustus hath bequeathed his soul to Lucifer.　　　　75
But what is this inscription on mine arm?
"*Homo, fuge!*"[8] Whither should I fly?
If unto God, he'll throw me down to hell.
My senses are deceived; here's nothing writ.
O yes, I see it plain: even here is writ　　　　80
"*Homo, fuge!*" Yet shall not Faustus fly.

MEPH. I'll fetch him somewhat to delight his mind.　　　　[*Exit.*]
　　　　[*Re-enter* MEPHISTOPHILIS *with* DEVILS, *giving crowns and
　　　　rich apparel to* FAUSTUS, *and dance, and then depart.*]

FAUST. What means this show?
Speak, Mephistophilis.

MEPH. Nothing, Faustus, but to delight thy mind　　　　85
And let thee see what magic can perform.

FAUST. But may I raise such spirits when I please?

MEPH. Aye, Faustus, and do greater things than these.

FAUST. Then, Mephistophilis, receive this scroll,
A deed of gift of body and of soul;
But yet conditionally that thou perform　　　　90
All covenant-articles between us both.

MEPH. Faustus, I swear by hell and Lucifer
To effect all promises between us made.

FAUST. Then hear me read it, Mephistophilis.　　　　[⟨*Reads.*⟩]　　95
"On these conditions following:
First, that Faustus may be a spirit in form and substance.
Secondly, that Mephistophilis shall be his servant and at his command.
Thirdly, that Mephistophilis shall do for him, and bring him　100
whatsoever.
Fourthly, that he shall be in his chamber or house invisible.
Lastly, that he shall appear to the said John Faustus at all
times, in what form or shape soever he please.
I, John Faustus of Wittenberg, Doctor, by these presents do　105
give both body and soul to Lucifer, Prince of the East, and his
minister Mephistophilis, and furthermore grant unto them,
that four and twenty years being expired, the articles above
written inviolate, full power to fetch or carry the said John
Faustus, body and soul, flesh, blood, or goods, into their habi-　110
tation wheresoever.
　　　　　　　　　　　　　　By me John Faustus."

MEPH. Speak, Faustus, do you deliver this as your deed?

FAUST. Aye, take it, and the devil give thee good of it.

MEPH. Now, Faustus, ask what thou wilt.　　　　115

FAUST. First will I question with thee about hell.
Tell me, where is the place that men call hell?

MEPH. Under the heavens.

---

7. "It is finished." A blasphemy, as
these are the words of Christ on the
Cross (see John xix.30).
8. "Man, fly!"

FAUST. Aye, but whereabout?

MEPH. Within the bowels of these elements,
Where we are tortured and remain forever. 120
Hell hath no limits, nor is circumscribed
In one self place, for where we are is hell,
And where hell is there must we ever be;
And, to be short, when all the world dissolves
And every creature shall be purified, 125
All places shall be hell that is not heaven.

FAUST. I think hell's a fable.

MEPH. Aye, think so, till experience change thy mind.

FAUST. Why, thinkst thou that Faustus shall be damned?

MEPH. Aye, of necessity, for here's the scroll 130
In which thou hast given thy soul to Lucifer.

FAUST. Aye, and body too; but what of that?
Thinkst thou that Faustus is so fond[9] to imagine
That after this life there is any pain?
No, these are trifles and mere old wives' tales. 135

MEPH. But I am an instance to prove the contrary,
For I tell thee I am damned and now in hell.

FAUST. Nay, and this be hell I'll willingly be damned.
What, sleeping, eating, walking, and disputing?
But leaving off this, let me have a wife, 140
The fairest maid in Germany,
For I am wanton and lascivious
And cannot live without a wife.

MEPH. I prithee, Faustus, talk not of a wife.[1]

FAUST. Nay, sweet Mephistophilis, fetch me one, for I will have 145
one.

MEPH. Well, thou shalt have a wife. Sit there till I come. [⟨*Exit.*⟩]
[*Re-enter* MEPHISTOPHILIS *with a* DEVIL *dressed like a
woman, with fireworks.*]

FAUST. What sight is this?

MEPH. Now Faustus, how dost thou like thy wife?

FAUST. Here's a hot whore indeed! No, I'll no wife. 150

MEPH. Marriage is but a ceremonial toy,
And if thou lovest me, think no more of it.
I'll cull thee out the fairest courtesans
And bring them every morning to thy bed;
She whom thine eye shall like thy heart shall have, 155
Were she as chaste as was Penelope,[2]
As wise as Saba, or as beautiful
As was bright Lucifer before his fall.
Hold, take this book: peruse it thoroughly.
The iterating[3] of these lines brings gold, 160
The framing[4] of this circle on the ground

---

9. Foolish.
1. Mephistophilis cannot produce a wife for Faustus because marriage is a sacrament.
2. The wife of Ulysses, famed for chas-

tity and fidelity. "Saba": the Queen of Sheba.
3. Repeating.
4. Drawing.

Brings whirlwinds, tempests, thunder, and lightning;
Pronounce this thrice devoutly to thyself
And men in harness shall appear to thee,
Ready to execute what thou desirest.                                165

FAUST. Thanks, Mephistophilis, yet fain would I have a book
wherein I might behold all spells and incantations, that I
might raise up spirits when I please.

MEPH. Here they are in this book.            [*There turn to them.*]

FAUST. Now would I have a book where I might see all characters 170
and planets of the heavens, that I might know their motions
and dispositions.

MEPH. Here they are too.                     [*Turn to them.*]

FAUST. Nay, let me have one book more, and then I have done,
wherein I might see all plants, herbs, and trees that grow upon 175
the earth.

MEPH. Here they be.

FAUST. O thou art deceived!

MEPH. Tut, I warrant thee.                   [*Turn to them.*]
          [⟨*Exeunt.*⟩][5]

### SCENE 2

[*Enter* FAUSTUS *in his study and* MEPHISTOPHILIS.]

FAUST. When I behold the heavens then I repent
And curse thee, wicked Mephistophilis,
Because thou hast deprived me of those joys.

MEPH. 'Twas thine own seeking, Faustus, thank thyself.
But thinkest thou heaven is such a glorious thing?             5
I tell thee, Faustus, it is not half so fair
As thou or any man that breathes on earth.

FAUST. How provest thou that?

MEPH. 'Twas made for man; then he's more excellent.

FAUST. If heaven was made for man 'twas made for me.            10
I will renounce this magic and repent.
          [*Enter* GOOD ANGEL *and* BAD ANGEL.]

G. ANG. Faustus, repent; yet God will pity thee.

B. ANG. Thou art a spirit; God cannot pity thee.

FAUST. Who buzzeth in mine ears I am a spirit?[6]
Be I a devil, yet God may pity me.                             15
Yea, God will pity me, if I repent.

B. ANG. Aye, but Faustus never shall repent.
          [*Exeunt* ANGELS.]

FAUST. My heart is hardened; I cannot repent.
Scarce can I name salvation, faith, or heaven,
But fearful echoes thunder in mine ears:                        20
"Faustus, thou are damned!" Then guns and knives,
Swords, poison, halters, and envenomed steel

5. After this a comic scene has been
lost from the text. In it, apparently the
Clown, Robin, stole one of Faustus'
conjuring books and left Wagner's service. He then became an hostler at an
inn.
6. Evil spirit, devil.

Are laid before me to dispatch myself,
And long ere this I should have done the deed
Had not sweet pleasure conquered deep despair.                    25
Have I not made blind Homer sing to me
Of Alexander's love and Oenon's death,[7]
And hath not he that built the walls of Thebes
With ravishing sound of his melodious harp[8]
Made music with my Mephistophilis?                               30
Why should I die, then, or basely despair?
I am resolved Faustus shall not repent.
Come, Mephistophilis, let us dispute again
And reason of divine astrology.
Speak, are there many spheres above the moon?                    35
Are all celestial bodies but one globe
As is the substance of this centric earth?[9]
MEPH. As are the elements, such are the heavens,
Even from the moon unto the empyreal orb,
Mutually folded in each other's spheres,
And jointly move upon one axletree                               40
Whose termine[1] is termed the world's wide pole;
Nor are the names of Saturn, Mars, or Jupiter
Feigned, but are erring stars.
FAUST. But tell me, have they all one motion, both *situ et tem-*  45
*pore?*[2]
MEPH. All move from east to west in four and twenty hours upon
the poles of the world, but differ in their motions upon the
poles of the zodiac.[3]
FAUST. These slender questions Wagner can decide.                 50
Hath Mephistophilis no greater skill?
Who knows not the double motion of the planets?
That the first is finished in a natural day;
The second thus, Saturn in thirty years, Jupiter in twelve, Mars
in four, the Sun, Venus, and Mercury in a year, the Moon in    55
twenty-eight days. These are freshmen's suppositions. But tell
me, hath every sphere a dominion or *intelligentia?*[4]
MEPH. Aye.
FAUST. How many heavens or spheres are there?
MEPH. Nine: the seven planets, the firmament, and the empyreal    60
heaven.

7. Alexander is another name for Paris, the lover of Oenone; later he deserted her and abducted Helen, causing the Trojan War. Oenone refused to heal the wounds Paris received in battle, and when he died of them she killed herself in remorse.
8. I.e., the legendary musician Amphion.
9. "Faustus asks whether all the apparently different heavenly bodies form really one globe, like the earth. Mephistophilis answers that like the elements, which are separate but combined, the heavenly bodies are separate, though their spheres are infolded, and they move on one axletree. Hence we are not in error in giving individual names to Saturn, Mars, or Jupiter; they are separate planets" (F. S. Boas). The "empyreal orb," or outermost sphere, was also called the empyrean.
1. End.
2. In position and time.
3. I.e., the common axletree on which all the spheres revolve.
4. I.e., an angel or intelligence (thought to be the source of motion in each sphere).

FAUST. But is there not *coelum igneum, et crystallinum?*[5]

MEPH. No, Faustus, they be but fables.

FAUST. Resolve me then in this one question: why are not conjunctions, oppositions, aspects, eclipses, all at one time, but in 65 some years we have more, in some less?

MEPH. *Per inequalem motum respectu totius.*[6]

FAUST. Well, I am answered. Tell me, who made the world?

MEPH. I will not.

FAUST. Sweet Mephistophilis, tell me. 70

MEPH. Move me not, Faustus.

FAUST. Villain, have I not bound thee to tell me anything?

MEPH. Aye, that is not against our kingdom; this is.
Thou art damned; think thou of hell.

FAUST. Think, Faustus, upon God that made the world! 75

MEPH. Remember this! [*Exit.*]

FAUST. Aye, go, accursèd spirit, to ugly hell;
'Tis thou has damned distressèd Faustus' soul.
Is 't too late?
[*Enter* GOOD ANGEL *and* BAD ANGEL.]

B. ANG. Too late. 80

G. ANG. Never too late, if Faustus will repent.

B. ANG. If thou repent, devils will tear thee in pieces.

G. ANG. Repent, and they shall never raze[7] thy skin.
[*Exeunt* ANGELS.]

FAUST. O Christ, my Saviour! my Saviour!
Help to save distressèd Faustus' soul. 85
[*Enter* LUCIFER, BELZEBUB, *and* MEPHISTOPHILIS.]

LUC. Christ cannot save thy soul, for he is just;
There's none but I have interest in the same.

FAUST. O what art thou that lookst so terrible?

LUC. I am Lucifer,
And this is my companion prince in hell.

FAUST. O Faustus, they are come to fetch thy soul! 90

BEL. We are come to tell thee thou dost injure us.

LUC. Thou call'st on Christ, contrary to thy promise.

BEL. Thou shouldst not think on God.

LUC. Think on the devil. 95

BEL. And his dam too.[8]

FAUST. Nor will I henceforth. Pardon me in this,
And Faustus vows never to look to heaven,
Never to name God or pray to him,
To burn his Scriptures, slay his ministers, 100
And make my spirits pull his churches down.

LUC. So shalt thou show thyself an obedient servant, and we will highly gratify thee for it.

BEL. Faustus, we are come from hell in person to show thee some

---

5. The "heaven of fire" and the "crystalline sphere," introduced by some of the old authorities to explain the precession of the equinoxes.

6. "Because of their unequal velocities within the system."

7. Scratch.

8. "The devil and his dam" was a common colloquial expression.

pastime. Sit down, and thou shalt behold the Seven Deadly 105
Sins appear to thee in their own proper shapes and likeness.

FAUST. That sight will be as pleasant to me as Paradise was to
Adam, the first day of his creation.

LUC. Talk not of Paradise or Creation, but mark the show. Go,
Mephistophilis, fetch them in. 110

[*Enter the* SEVEN DEADLY SINS,[9] *led by a piper.*]

Now, Faustus, question them of their names and dispositions.

FAUST. That shall I soon. What art thou, the first?

PRIDE. I am Pride. I disdain to have any parents. I am like to
Ovid's flea:[1] I can creep into every corner of a wench; sometimes like a periwig I sit upon her brow; next like a necklace 115
I hang about her neck; then like a fan of feathers I kiss her
lips; and then turning myself to a wrought smock[2] do what I
list. But fie, what a smell is here! I'll not speak another word
except the ground be perfumed and covered with cloth of
arras.[3] 120

FAUST. Thou art a proud knave indeed. What art thou, the
second?

COVET. I am Covetousness, begotten of an old churl in a leather
bag; and, might I now obtain my wish, this house, you and
all, should turn to gold, that I might lock you safe into my 125
chest. O my sweet gold!

FAUST. And what art thou, the third?

ENVY. I am Envy, begotten of a chimney-sweeper and an oyster-
wife. I cannot read, and therefore wish all books were burned.
I am lean with seeing others eat. O that there would come a 130
famine over all the world, that all might die, and I live alone;
then thou shouldst see how fat I'd be! But must thou sit and
I stand? Come down, with a vengeance!

FAUST. Out, envious wretch! But what art thou, the fourth?

WRATH. I am Wrath. I had neither father nor mother; I leapt 135
out of a lion's mouth when I was scarce an hour old, and ever
since have run up and down the world with these case of
rapiers, wounding myself when I could get none to fight withal.
I was born in hell; and look to it, for some of you shall be my
father. 140

FAUST. And what art thou, the fifth?

GLUT. I am Gluttony. My parents are all dead, and the devil a
penny they have left me but a small pension, and that buys
me thirty meals a day and ten bevers[4]—a small trifle to suffice
nature. I come of a royal pedigree: my father was a gammon[5] 145
of bacon, and my mother was a hogshead of claret wine. My

---

9. The Seven Deadly Sins are pride, avarice, gluttony, lust, sloth, envy, and anger. (They are deadly because other sins grow out of them.) They were frequently represented in medieval plays, sometimes in the rather grimly comic tone used here; in the old morality plays all the characters, not merely the sins, were abstractions.

1. A salacious medieval poem *Carmen de Pulice* ("The Flea") was attributed to Ovid.
2. A decorated or ornamented petticoat.
3. Arras in Flanders exported fine cloth used for tapestry hangings.
4. Snacks.
5. The lower side of pork, including the leg.

godfathers were these: Peter Pickle-herring and Martin Martle-
mas-beef. But my godmother, O, she was a jolly gentlewoman,
and well beloved in every good town and city: her name was
mistress Margery March-beer. Now, Faustus, thou hast heard 150
all my progeny;[6] wilt thou bid me to supper?

FAUST. Not I. Thou wilt eat up all my victuals.

GLUT. Then the devil choke thee!

FAUST. Choke thyself, glutton. What art thou, the sixth?

SLOTH. Heigh ho! I am Sloth. I was begotten on a sunny bank, 155
where I have lain ever since, and you have done me great injury
to bring me from thence; let me be carried thither again by
Gluttony and Lechery. Heigh ho! I'll not speak word more for
a king's ransom.

FAUST. And what are you, mistress minx, the seventh and last? 160

LECHERY. Who, I, sir? I am one that loves an inch of raw mutton[7] better than an ell of fried stockfish, and the first letter
of my name begins with Lechery.

LUC. Away, to hell, away! On, piper![8]
    [*Exeunt the* SINS.]

FAUST. O how this sight doth delight my soul! 165

LUC. Tut, Faustus, in hell is all manner of delight.

FAUST. O might I see hell and return again safe, how happy were
I then!

LUC. Faustus, thou shalt. At midnight I will send for thee. In
meantime peruse this book, and view it throughly, and thou 170
shalt turn thyself into what shape thou wilt.

FAUST. Thanks, mighty Lucifer; this will I keep as chary[9] as my
life.

LUC. Now Faustus, farewell.

FAUST. Farewell, great Lucifer. Come, Mephistophilis. 175
    [*Exeunt* OMNES.]

SCENE 3

    [*Enter the* CLOWN ⟨ROBIN⟩.]

ROBIN. What, Dick, look to the horses there till I come again.
I have gotten one of Dr. Faustus' conjuring books, and now
we'll have such knavery as 't passes.
    [*Enter* DICK.]

DICK. What, Robin, you must come away and walk the horses.

ROBIN. I walk the horses! I scorn 't, faith: I have other matters 5
in hand; let the horses walk themselves and they will. "A *per
se*[1] a; t, h, e, the; o *per se* o; deny orgon, gorgon." Keep further
from me, O thou illiterate and unlearned hostler.

---

6. Ancestry, lineage.
7. Frequently a word of indecent meaning in Elizabethan English; here it
means the penis. "Ell": 45 inches;
"stockfish": dried cod.
8. The command to the piper who led
the procession of the Deadly Sins onto
the stage to strike up a tune for their

exit.
9. Carefully.
1. "A by itself," a method of reading
the letters of the alphabet taught to
children. Robin's semi-literacy is being
satirized. "Deny orgon, gorgon" is a
parody of Faustus' invocation of Demogorgon in I.iii.

DICK. 'Snails,[2] what has thou got there? a book? Why, thou canst not tell ne'er a word on 't.

ROBIN. That thou shalt see presently. Keep out of the circle, I say, lest I send you into the ostry[3] with a vengeance.

DICK. That's like, faith! You had best leave your foolery, for an my master come, he'll conjure you, faith.

ROBIN. My master conjure me! I'll tell thee what; an my master come here, I'll clap as fair a pair of horns on 's head as e'er thou sawest in thy life.[4]

DICK. Thou needst not do that, for my mistress hath done it.

ROBIN. Aye, there be of us here have waded as deep into matters as other men, if they were disposed to talk.

DICK. A plague take you! I thought you did not sneak up and down after her for nothing. But I prithee tell me in good sadness, Robin, is that a conjuring book?

ROBIN. Do but speak what thou 't have me do, and I'll do 't. If thou 't dance naked, put off thy clothes, and I'll conjure about thee presently. Or if thou 't but to the tavern with me, I'll give thee white wine, red wine, claret wine, sack, muscadine, malmesey, and whippincrust,[5] hold-belly-hold, and we'll not pay one penny for it.

DICK. O brave! Prithee let's to it presently, for I am as dry as a dog.

ROBIN. Come then, let's away.      *[Exeunt.]*

## Act III

*[Enter* CHORUS.*]*

CHO. Learned Faustus,
  To find the secrets of astronomy
  Graven in the book of Jove's high firmament,
  Did mount himself to scale Olympus' top.
  Where sitting in a chariot burning bright
  Drawn by the strength of yokéd dragons' necks,
  He views the clouds, the planets, and the stars,
  The tropics, zones, and quarters of the sky
  From the bright circle of the hornéd moon
  Even to the height of *Primum Mobile;*[6]
  And whirling round with this circumference
  Within the concave compass of the pole,
  From east to west his dragons swiftly glide
  And in eight days did bring him home again.
  Not long he stayed within his quiet house
  To rest his bones after his weary toil
  But new exploits do hale him out again;
  And mounted then upon a dragon's back
  That with his wings did part the subtle air,
  He now is gone to prove cosmography[7]

2. I.e., God's nails (on the Cross).
3. Stable.
4. A wife's infidelity was supposed in legend, and in the standard Elizabethan joke, to cause her husband to grow horns.
5. Robin's pronunciation of "hippocras," a spiced wine.
6. The outermost sphere, the empyrean.
7. I.e., to test the accuracy of maps.

That measures coasts and kingdoms of the earth:
And, as I guess, will first arrive at Rome
To see the Pope and manner of his court
And take some part of holy Peter's feast,
The which this day is highly solemnized.                          25
    [*Exit.*]

SCENE 1

[*Enter* FAUSTUS *and* MEPHISTOPHILIS.]
FAUST. Having now, my good Mephistophilis,
Passed with delight the stately town of Trier[8]
Environed round with airy mountain tops,
With walls of flint and deep-entrenchéd lakes,[9]
Not to be won by any conquering prince;                          5
From Paris next coasting the realm of France,
We saw the river Maine fall into Rhine,
Whose banks are set with groves of fruitful vines;
Then up to Naples, rich Campania,
With buildings fair and gorgeous to the eye,                     10
Whose streets straight forth and paved with finest brick
Quarter the town in four equivalents.
There saw we learned Maro's[1] golden tomb,
The way he cut, an English mile in length,
Thorough a rock of stone in one night's space.                   15
From thence to Venice, Padua, and the rest,
In midst of which a sumptuous temple[2] stands
That threats the stars with her aspiring top,
Whose frame is paved with sundry colored stones
And roofed aloft with curious work in gold.                      20
Thus hitherto hath Faustus spent his time.
But tell me now, what resting place is this?
Hast thou, as erst I did command,
Conducted me within the walls of Rome?
MEPH. I have, my Faustus, and for proof thereof                  25
This is the goodly palace of the Pope,
And 'cause we are no common guests
I choose his privy chamber for our use.
FAUST. I hope his Holiness will bid us welcome.
MEPH. All's one, for we'll be bold with his venison.             30
But now, my Faustus, that thou mayst perceive
What Rome contains for to delight thine eyes,
Know that this city stands upon seven hills
That underprop the groundwork of the same;
Just through the midst runs flowing Tiber's stream,              35
With winding banks that cut it in two parts,
Over the which four stately bridges lean

8. Treves (in Prussia).
9. Moats.
1. Virgil's. In medieval legend the Roman poet Virgil was considered a magician, and a tunnel ("way") on the promontory of Posilippo at Naples, near his tomb, was accredited to his magical powers.
2. I.e., St. Mark's in Venice.

That make safe passage to each part of Rome.
Upon the bridge called Ponte Angelo
Erected is a castle passing strong,
Where thou shalt see such store of ordnance
As that the double cannons forged of brass
Do match the number of the days contained
Within the compass of one complete year;
Besides the gates and high pyramides[3]
That Julius Caesar brought from Africa.

FAUST. Now by the kingdoms of infernal rule,
  Of Styx, Acheron, and the fiery lake
  Of ever-burning Phlegethon,[4] I swear
  That I do long to see the monuments
  And situation of bright-splendent Rome.
  Come, therefore, let's away.

MEPH. Nay, stay, my Faustus; I know you'd see the Pope
  And take some part of holy Peter's feast,
  The which in state and high solemnity
  This day is held through Rome and Italy
  In honor of the Pope's triumphant victory.

FAUST. Sweet Mephistophilis, thou pleasest me;
  Whilst I am here on earth let me be cloyed
  With all things that delight the heart of man.
  My four and twenty years of liberty
  I'll spend in pleasure and in dalliance,
  That Faustus' name, whilst this bright frame doth stand,
  May be admiréd through the furthest land.

MEPH. 'Tis well said, Faustus; come then, stand by me
  And thou shalt see them come immediately.

FAUST. Nay, stay, my gentle Mephistophilis,
  And grant me my request, and then I go.
  Thou knowst, within the compass of eight days
  We viewed the face of heaven, of earth, of hell;
  So high our dragons soared into the air
  That, looking down, the earth appeared to me
  No bigger than my hand in quantity.
  There did we view the kingdoms of the world,
  And what might please mine eye I there beheld.
  Then in this show let me an actor be,
  That this proud Pope may Faustus' cunning see.

MEPH. Let it be so, my Faustus, but first stay
  And view their triumphs[5] as they pass this way,
  And then devise what best contents thy mind,
  By cunning of thine art to cross the Pope
  Or dash the pride of this solemnity,
  To make his monks and abbots stand like apes
  And point like antics[6] at his triple crown,

40

45

50

55

60

65

70

75

80

3. *Py-rám-i-des*, a singular noun, meaning an obelisk.
4. Classical names for rivers of the
underworld; symbolic of hell, they are
appropriate as oaths for Faustus.
5. Parades.
6. Grotesque figures.

To beat the beads about the friars' pates                    85
Or clap huge horns upon the cardinals' heads,
Or any villainy thou canst devise,
And I'll perform it, Faustus. Hark, they come!
This day shall make thee be admired in Rome.

    [*Enter the* CARDINALS *and* BISHOPS, *some bearing crosiers,
    some the pillars;* MONKS *and* FRIARS *singing their proces-
    sion; then the* POPE *and* RAYMOND, *King of Hungary,
    with* BRUNO *led in chains.*][7]

POPE. Cast down our footstool.
RAY.              Saxon Bruno, stoop,                    90
Whilst on thy back his Holiness ascends
St. Peter's chair and state pontifical.
BRUNO. Proud Lucifer, that state belongs to me;
But thus I fall, to Peter, not to thee.
POPE. To me and Peter shalt thou groveling lie                    95
And crouch before the papal dignity.
Sound trumpets, then, for thus St. Peter's heir
From Bruno's back ascends St. Peter's chair.

    [*A flourish while he ascends.*]

Thus as the gods creep on with feet of wool
Long ere with iron hands they punish men,                    100
So shall our sleeping vengeance now arise
And smite with death thy hated enterprise.
Lord Cardinals of France and Padua,
Go forthwith to our holy consistory
And read among the statutes decretal                    105
What, by the holy council held at Trent,[8]
The sacred synod hath decreed for him
That doth assume the papal government
Without election and a true consent.
Away and bring us word with speed.                    110
1 CARD. We go, my lord.         [*Exeunt* CARDINALS.]
POPE. Lord Raymond—
FAUST. Go, haste thee, gentle Mephistophilis,
Follow the cardinals to the consistory,
And as they turn their superstitious books,                    115
Strike them with sloth and drowsy idleness
And make them sleep so sound that in their shapes
Thyself and I may parley with this Pope,
This proud confronter of the Emperor,[9]
And in despite of all his holiness                    120
Restore this Bruno to his liberty

---

7. "Crosiers": crosses borne before prelates; "the pillars" (of silver), however, are known to have been used by only two English cardinals, Wolsey and De la Pole. "Raymond, King of Hungary" is unknown to history. "Bruno" is likewise fictitious; he is the German pretender to the papal throne over whom the Pope has just triumphed (line 57).
8. The famous council of the Catholic Church which lasted from 1545 to 1563.
9. Holy Roman Emperor. Faustus refers to the conflict between the Pope and the Emperor; the former was victorious and captured the Emperor's choice for Pope, "Saxon Bruno."

And bear him to the states of Germany.
MEPH. Faustus, I go.
FAUST.                    Dispatch it soon.
  The Pope shall curse that Faustus came to Rome.
    [*Exeunt* FAUSTUS *and* MEPHISTOPHILIS.]
BRUNO. Pope Adrian, let me have some right of law;    125
  I was elected by the Emperor.
POPE. We will depose the Emperor for that deed
  And curse the people that submit to him;
  Both he and thou shalt stand excommunicate
  And interdict from church's privilege    130
  And all society of holy men.
  He grows too proud in his authority,
  Lifting his lofty head above the clouds,
  And like a steeple overpeers the church,
  But we'll pull down his haughty insolence.    135
  And as Pope Alexander,[1] our progenitor,
  Trod on the neck of German Frederick,
  Adding this golden sentence to our praise,
  That Peter's heirs should tread on emperors
  And walk upon the dreadful adder's back,    140
  Treading the lion and the dragon down,
  And fearless spurn the killing basilisk;[2]
  So will we quell that haughty schismatic,
  And by authority apostolical
  Depose him from his regal government.    145
BRUNO. Pope Julius swore to princely Sigismond,
  For him and the succeeding popes of Rome,
  To hold the emperors their lawful lords.
POPE. Pope Julius did abuse the church's rights,
  And therefore none of his decrees can stand.    150
  Is not all power on earth bestowed on us?
  And therefore though we would we cannot err.
  Behold this silver belt, whereto is fixed
  Seven golden keys fast sealed with seven seals
  In token of our sevenfold power from heaven,    155
  To bind or loose, lock fast, condemn, or judge,
  Resign or seal, or whatso pleaseth us.
  Then he and thou and all the world shall stoop,
  Or be assuréd of our dreadful curse
  To light as heavy as the pains of hell.    160
    [*Enter* FAUSTUS *and* MEPHISTOPHILIS *like cardinals.*]
MEPH. Now tell me, Faustus, are we not fitted well?
FAUST. Yes, Mephistophilis, and two such cardinals
  Ne'er served a holy pope as we shall do.
  But whilst they sleep within the consistory
  Let us salute his reverend Fatherhood.    165
RAY. Behold, my lord, the cardinals are returned.

1. Pope Alexander III (1159–81) compelled the Emperor Frederick Barbarossa to submit to him.

2. A mythical monster capable of killing by a look.

POPE. Welcome, grave fathers, answer presently;[3]
 What have our holy council there decreed
 Concerning Bruno and the Emperor
 In quittance of their late conspiracy      170
 Against our state and papal dignity?
FAUST. Most sacred patron of the church of Rome,
 By full consent of all the synod
 Of priests and prelates it is thus decreed:
 That Bruno and the German Emperor      175
 Be held as lollards[4] and bold schismatics
 And proud disturbers of the church's peace.
 And if that Bruno by his own assent,
 Without enforcement of the German peers,
 Did seek to wear the triple diadem      180
 And by your death to climb St. Peter's chair,
 The statutes decretal have thus decreed:
 He shall be straight condemned of heresy
 And on a pile of fagots burned to death.
POPE. It is enough. Here, take him to your charge    185
 And bear him straight to Ponte Angelo,
 And in the strongest tower enclose him fast.
 Tomorrow, sitting in our consistory
 With all our college of grave cardinals,
 We will determine of his life or death.      190
 Here, take his triple crown along with you
 And leave it in the church's treasury.
 Make haste again, my good lord cardinals,
 And take our blessing apostolical.
MEPH. So, so. Was never devil thus blessed before!    195
FAUST. Away, sweet Mephistophilis, be gone;
 The cardinals will be plagued for this anon.
   [*Exeunt* FAUSTUS *and* MEPHISTOPHILIS *with* BRUNO.]
POPE. Go presently and bring a banquet forth,
 That we may solemnize St. Peter's feast
 And with Lord Raymond, King of Hungary,     200
 Drink to our late and happy victory.      [*Exeunt.*]

SCENE 2

[*The banquet is brought in, and then enter* FAUSTUS *and*
MEPHISTOPHILIS *in their own shapes.*]
MEPH. Now Faustus, come prepare thyself for mirth;
 The sleepy cardinals are hard at hand
 To censure Bruno, that is posted hence
 And on a proud-paced steed as swift as thought
 Flies o'er the Alps to fruitful Germany,
 There to salute the woeful Emperor.      5
FAUST. The Pope will curse them for their sloth today
 That slept both Bruno and his crown away.

3. Immediately.
4. Protestants, usually English follow- ers of Wycliffe, the 14th-century religious reformer.

But now, that Faustus may delight his mind
And by their folly make some merriment,    10
Sweet Mephistophilis, so charm me here
That I may walk invisible to all
And do whate'er I please unseen of any.

MEPH. Faustus, thou shalt; then kneel down presently,
    Whilst on thy head I lay my hand    15
    And charm thee with this magic wand.
    First wear this girdle, then appear
    Invisible to all are here.
    The planets seven, the gloomy air,
    Hell, and the Furies' forkéd hair,    20
    Pluto's blue fire and Hecate's⁵ tree
    With magic spells so compass thee
    That no eye may thy body see.
So, Faustus, now, for all their holiness,
    Do what thou wilt thou shalt not be discerned.    25

FAUST. Thanks, Mephistophilis. Now friars, take heed
Lest Faustus make your shaven crowns to bleed.

MEPH. Faustus, no more; see where the cardinals come.

    [*Enter* POPE *and all the lords, with* KING RAYMOND *and
    the* ARCHBISHOP OF RHEIMS. *Enter the two* CARDINALS
    with a book.*]

POPE. Welcome, lord cardinals; come, sit down.
    Lord Raymond, take your seat. Friars, attend,    30
    And see that all things be in readiness
    As best beseems this solemn festival.

1 CARD. First may it please your sacred holiness
    To view the sentence of the reverend synod
    Concerning Bruno and the Emperor.    35

POPE. What needs this question? Did I not tell you
    Tomorrow we would sit i' th' consistory
    And there determine of his punishment?
    You brought us word, even now, it was decreed
    That Bruno and the curséd Emperor    40
    Were by the holy council both condemned
    For loathéd lollards and base schismatics;
    Then wherefore would you have me view that book?

1 CARD. Your Grace mistakes; you gave us no such charge.

RAY. Deny it not; we all are witnesses    45
    That Bruno here was late delivered you,
    With his rich triple crown to be reserved
    And put into the church's treasury.

BOTH CARD. By holy Paul we saw them not.

POPE. By Peter, you shall die    50
    Unless you bring them forth immediately.

---

5. The goddess of magic and witchcraft, whose name the Elizabethans pronounced *Héc-at*. She is not known to have any special "tree"; the word may be a mistake for "three," since she was often represented as a triple goddess—of heaven, earth, and hell.

Hale them to prison! Lade their limbs with gyves![6]
False prelates, for this hateful treachery,
Cursed be your souls to hellish misery.    [*Exeunt* CARDINALS.]
FAUST. So they are safe. Now, Faustus, to the feast;          55
The Pope had never such a frolic guest.
POPE. Lord Archbishop of Rheims, sit down with us.
ARCH. I thank your Holiness.
FAUST. Fall to! The devil choke you an you spare!
POPE. Who's that spoke? Friars, look about.          60
Lord Raymond, pray fall to. I am beholden
To the Bishop of Milan for this so rare a present.
FAUST. I thank you, sir.
        [FAUSTUS *snatches the meat from the* POPE.]
POPE. How now! Who snatched the meat from me? Villains,
why speak you not?          65
FRIAR. Here's nobody, if it like your Holiness.
POPE. My good Lord Archbishop, here's a most dainty dish
Was sent me from a cardinal in France.
FAUST. I'll have that, too.
        [FAUSTUS *snatches the dish from the* POPE.]
POPE. What lollards do attend our Holiness          70
That we receive such great indignity?
Fetch me some wine.
FAUST. Aye, pray do, for Faustus is adry.
POPE. Lord Raymond, I drink unto your Grace.
FAUST. I pledge your Grace.          75
        [FAUSTUS *snatches the cup from the* POPE.]
POPE. My wine gone, too? Ye lubbers, look about
And find the man that doth this villainy,
Or by my sanctitude you all shall die.
I pray, my lords, have patience at this troublesome banquet.
ARCH. Please your Holiness, I think it be some ghost crept out of          80
purgatory and now is come unto your Holiness for his pardon.
POPE. It may be so;
Go then, command our priests to sing a dirge
To lay the fury of this same troublesome ghost.
Once again, my lord, fall to.          85
        [*The* POPE *crosses himself.*]
FAUST. How now!
Must every bit be spicéd with a cross?
Well, use that trick no more, I would advise you.
        [*The* POPE *crosses himself.*]
Well, there's the second time; aware the third;
I give you fair warning.
        [*The* POPE *crosses himself again.*]          90
Nay then, take that!
        [FAUSTUS *hits the* POPE *a box on the ear.*]
POPE. O, I am slain! Help me, my lords!
O come and help to bear my body hence!

6. I.e., load their limbs with prisoners' shackles.

Damned be his soul forever for this deed.
[*Exeunt the* POPE *and his train.*]

MEPH. Now Faustus, what will you do now? For I can tell you 95
you'll be cursed with bell, book, and candle.[7]

FAUST. Bell, book, and candle; candle, book, and bell
Forward and backward, to curse Faustus to hell!
[*Enter all the* FRIARS *with bell, book, and candle to sing
the dirge.*]

FRIAR. Come, brethren, let's about our business with good devotion. 100

[ALL *sing this:*]
Curséd be he that stole away his Holiness' meat from the
table—*maledicat dominus!*[8]
Curséd be he that struck his Holiness a blow on the face—
*maledicat dominus!*
Curséd be he that took Friar Sandelo a blow on the face— 105
*maledicat dominus!*
Curséd be he that disturbeth our holy dirge—*maledicat dominus!*
Curséd be he that took away his Holiness' wine—*maledicat
dominus! Et omnes sancti!*[9] Amen. 110

[FAUSTUS *and* MEPHISTOPHILIS *beat the* FRIARS, *and fling
fireworks among them, and so exeunt.*]

### SCENE 3

[*Enter* CLOWN ⟨ROBIN⟩ *and* DICK *with a cup.*]

DICK. Sirrah Robin, we were best look that your devil can answer
the stealing of this same cup, for the vintner's boy follows us
at the hard heels.

ROBIN. 'Tis no matter, let him come! An he follow us I'll so conjure him as he was never conjured in his life, I warrant him. 5
Let me see the cup.

[*Enter* VINTNER.]

DICK. Here 'tis. Yonder he comes. Now, Robin, now or never
show thy cunning.

VINT. O, are you here? I am glad I have found you. You are a
couple of fine companions! Pray, where's the cup you stole 10
from the tavern?

ROBIN. How, how? We steal a cup? Take heed what you say! We
look not like cup-stealers, I can tell you.

VINT. Never deny it, for I know you have it, and I'll search you.

ROBIN. Search me? Aye, and spare not. Hold the cup, Dick! 15
Come, come; search me, search me.

VINT. Come on, sirrah, let me search you now.

DICK. Aye, aye, do; do. Hold the cup, Robin. I fear not your
searching. We scorn to steal your cups, I can tell you.

VINT. Never outface me for the matter, for sure the cup is be- 20
tween you two.

7. The traditional paraphernalia for
cursing and excommunication.

8. "May the Lord curse him!"
9. And all saints (also curse him).

ROBIN. Nay, there you lie. 'Tis beyond us both.

VINT. A plague take you! I thought 'twas your knavery to take it
away. Come, give it me again.

ROBIN. Aye, much! When, can you tell?[1] Dick, make me a circle,   25
and stand close at my back and stir not for thy life. Vintner,
you shall have your cup anon. Say nothing, Dick. O *per se* O;
Demogorgon, Belcher and Mephistophilis!

> [*Enter* MEPHISTOPHILIS.]

MEPH. Monarch of hell, under whose black survey
Great potentates do kneel with awful fear,   30
Upon whose altars thousand souls do lie,
How am I vexéd with these villains' charms!
From Constantinople am I hither brought
Only for pleasure of these damnéd slaves.     [*Exit* VINTNER.]

ROBIN. By Lady, sir, you have had a shrewd journey of it; will it   35
please you to take a shoulder of mutton to supper and a tester[2]
in your purse, and go back again?

DICK. Aye, I pray you heartily, sir; for we called you but in jest,
I promise you.

MEPH. To purge the rashness of this curséd deed,   40
First be thou turnéd to this ugly shape:
For apish deeds transforméd to an ape.

ROBIN. O brave! an ape! I pray, sir, let me have the carrying of
him about to show some tricks.

MEPH. And so thou shalt. Be thou transformed to a dog and   45
carry him upon thy back. Away! Be gone!

ROBIN. A dog! That's excellent! Let the maids look well to their
porridge pots, for I'll into the kitchen presently. Come, Dick,
come.

> [*Exit* ROBIN *and* DICK.]

MEPH. Now with the flames of ever-burning fire   50
I'll wing myself and forthwith fly amain
Unto my Faustus, to the Great Turk's court.     [*Exit.*]

## Act IV

> [*Enter* CHORUS.]

CHO. When Faustus had with pleasure ta'en the view
Of rarest things and royal courts of kings,
He stayed his course and so returnéd home,
Where such as bear his absence but with grief,
I mean his friends and nearest companións,   5
Did gratulate his safety with kind words,
And in their conference of what befell
Touching his journey through the world and air,
They put forth questions of astrology
Which Faustus answered with such learned skill   10
As they admired and wondered at his wit.
Now is his fame spread forth in every land:

---

1. A common Elizabethan scornful retort.     2. Sixpence.

Amongst the rest the Emperor is one,
Carolus the Fifth,[3] at whose palace now
Faustus is feasted 'mongst his noblemen.                              15
What there he did in trial of his art
I leave untold, your eyes shall see performed.           [*Exit.*]

### SCENE 1

[*Enter* MARTINO *and* FREDERICK *at several doors.*[4]]

MART. What ho! Officers, gentlemen!
Hie to the presence to attend the Emperor.
Good Frederick, see the rooms be voided straight;
His Majesty is coming to the hall.
Go back, and see the state in readiness.                              5
FRED. But where is Bruno, our elected Pope,
      That on a fury's back came post from Rome?
      Will not his Grace consort[5] the Emperor?
MART. O yes, and with him comes the German conjurer,
      The learned Faustus, fame of Wittenberg,                        10
      The wonder of the world for magic art;
      And he intends to show great Carolus
      The race of all his stout progenitors
      And bring in presence of his majesty
      The royal shapes and warlike semblances                        15
      Of Alexander and his beauteous paramour.[6]
FRED. Where is Benvolio?
MART. Fast asleep, I warrant you;
      He took his rouse with stoups[7] of Rhenish wine
      So kindly yesternight to Bruno's health                        20
      That all this day the sluggard keeps his bed.
FRED. See, see; his window's ope; we'll call to him.
MART. What ho, Benvolio!
      [*Enter* BENVOLIO *above at a window, in his nightcap,
      buttoning.*]
BENV. What a devil ail you two?
MART. Speak softly, sir, lest the devil hear you;                    25
      For Faustus at the court is late arrived
      And at his heels a thousand furies wait
      To accomplish whatsoever the Doctor please.
BENV. What of this?
MART. Come, leave thy chamber first and thou shalt see              30
      This conjurer perform such rare exploits
      Before the Pope[8] and royal Emperor
      As never yet was seen in Germany.
BENV. Has not the Pope enough of conjuring yet?
      He was upon the devil's back late enough,                      35
      And if he be so far in love with him
      I would he would post home to Rome with him again.

3. I.e., Emperor Charles V (1519–56).           Thaïs.
4. I.e., at different entrances.                7. Drank many full glasses.
5. Accompany.                                   8. Bruno.
6. Alexander the Great and his mistress

FRED. Speak, wilt thou come and see this sport?

BENV. Not I.

MART. Wilt thou stand in thy window and see it, then? 40

BENV. Aye, and I fall not asleep i' th' meantime.

MART. The Emperor is at hand, who comes to see
What wonders by black spells may compassed be.

BENV. Well, go you to the Emperor. I am content for this once
to thrust my head out a window, for they say if a man be drunk 45
overnight the devil cannot hurt him in the morning. If that be
true, I have a charm in my head shall control him as well as the
conjurer, I warrant you.

[*Exit* MARTINO *and* FREDERICK.]

### SCENE 2

[*A sennet.*[9] *Enter* CHARLES THE GERMAN EMPEROR, BRUNO,
*the* DUKE OF SAXONY, FAUSTUS, MEPHISTOPHILIS, FRED-
ERICK, MARTINO *and* ATTENDANTS. BENVOLIO *remains at
his window.*]

EMP. Wonder of men, renowned magician,
Thrice-learned Faustus, welcome to our court.
This deed of thine, in setting Bruno free
From his and our professéd enemy,
Shall add more excellence unto thine art 5
Than if by powerful necromantic spells
Thou couldst command the world's obedience.
Forever be beloved of Carolus;
And if this Bruno thou hast late redeemed
In peace possess the triple diadem 10
And sit in Peter's chair despite of chance,
Thou shalt be famous through all Italy
And honored of the German Emperor.

FAUST. These gracious words, most royal Carolus,
Shall make poor Faustus to his utmost power 15
Both love and serve the German Emperor
And lay his life at holy Bruno's feet.
For proof whereof, if so your Grace be pleased,
The Doctor stands prepared by power of art
To cast his magic charms that shall pierce through 20
The ebon gates of ever-burning hell
And hale the stubborn furies from their caves
To compass whatsoe'er your Grace commands.

BENV. [*aside*] Blood! He speaks terribly, but for all that I do not
greatly believe him. He looks as like a conjurer as the Pope to 25
a costermonger.[1]

EMP. Then Faustus, as thou late didst promise us,
We would behold that famous conqueror,
Great Alexander and his paramour,
In their true shapes and state majestical, 30
That we may wonder at their excellence.

9. A trumpet signal.                    1. Fruitseller.

FAUST. Your Majesty shall see them presently.
Mephistophilis, away!
And with a solemn noise of trumpets' sound
Present before this royal Emperor                                35
Great Alexander and his beauteous paramour.
MEPH. Faustus, I will.                                     [*Exit.*]
BENV. [*aside*] Well, master Doctor, an your devils come not away
quickly, you shall have me asleep presently. Zounds, I could eat
myself for anger to think I have been such an ass all this while   40
to stand gaping after the devil's governor, and can see nothing.
FAUST. [*aside*] I'll make you feel something anon if my art fail me
not.—
My lord, I must forewarn your Majesty
That when my spirits present the royal shapes                45
Of Alexander and his paramour,
Your Grace demand no questions of the King,
But in dumb silence let them come and go.
EMP. Be it as Faustus please; we are content.
BENV. [*aside*] Aye, Aye, and I am content, too. And thou bring   50
Alexander and his paramour before the Emperor, I'll be Ac-
taeon² and turn myself into a stag.
FAUST. [*aside*] And I'll play Diana and send you the horns pres-
ently.
     [*Sennet. Enter at one door the emperor* ALEXANDER, *at the
     other* DARIUS. *They meet;* DARIUS *is thrown down;* ALEX-
     ANDER *kills him, takes off his crown and, offering to go
     out, his* PARAMOUR *meets him; he embraceth her and sets
     DARIUS' crown upon her head and, coming back, both
     salute the* EMPEROR, *who, leaving his state,³ offers to em-
     brace them, which* FAUSTUS *seeing, suddenly stays him.
     Then trumpets cease and music sounds.*]
FAUST. My gracious lord, you do forget yourself;              55
These are but shadows, not substantial.
EMP. O pardon me; my thoughts are ravished so
With sight of this renownéd Emperor
That in mine arms I would have compassed him.
But Faustus, since I may not speak to them                   60
To satisfy my longing thoughts at full,
Let me this tell thee: I have heard it said
That this fair lady, whilst she lived on earth,
Had on her neck a little wart or mole.
How may I prove that saying to be true?                      65
FAUST. Your Majesty may boldly go and see.
EMP. Faustus, I see it plain;
And in this sight thou better pleasest me
Than if I gained another monarchy.
FAUST. Away, be gone!                             [*Exit* SHOW.]  70
     See, see, my gracious lord, what strange beast is yon, that

2. The hunter of classical legend who
happened to see the goddess Diana
bathing. In punishment he was changed
into a stag and pursued by his own
hounds.
3. Throne.

thrusts its head out at the window!

EMP. O wondrous sight! See, Duke of Saxony, two spreading horns most strangely fastened upon the head of young Benvolio.                                                                    75

SAX. What, is he asleep, or dead?

FAUST. He sleeps, my lord, but dreams not of his horns.

EMP. This sport is excellent. We'll call and wake him. What ho! Benvolio!

BENV. A plague upon you! Let me sleep a while.                      80

EMP. I blame thee not to sleep, much, having such a head of thine own.

SAX. Look up, Benvolio. 'Tis the Emperor calls.

BENV. The Emperor! Where? O zounds, my head!

EMP. Nay, and thy horns hold 'tis no matter for thy head, for      85
that's armed sufficiently.

FAUST. Why, how now, sir knight! What, hanged by the horns? This is most horrible. Fie, fie! Pull in your head, for shame! Let not all the world wonder at you.

BENV. Zounds, Doctor, is this your villainy?                            90

FAUST. O, say not so, sir. The Doctor has no skill,
No art, no cunning to present these lords
Or bring before this royal Emperor
The mighty monarch, warlike Alexander?
If Faustus do it, you are straight resolved                             95
In bold Actaeon's shape to turn a stag?
And therefore, my lord, so please your Majesty,
I'll raise a kennel of hounds shall hunt him so
As all his footmanship shall scarce prevail
To keep his carcass from their bloody fangs.                           100
Ho, Belimote, Argiron, Asterote!

BENV. Hold, hold! Zounds, he'll raise up a kennel of devils, I think, anon. Good my lord, entreat for me. 'Sblood, I am never able to endure these torments.

EMP. Then good master Doctor,                                            105
Let me entreat you to remove his horns;
He has done penance now sufficiently.

FAUST. My gracious lord, not so much for injury done to me, as to delight your Majesty with some mirth, hath Faustus justly requited this injurious knight; which, being all I desire, I am    110
content to remove his horns.—Mephistophilis, transform him.
—And hereafter, sir, look you speak well of scholars.

BENV. [*aside*] Speak well of ye! 'Sblood, and scholars be such cuckoldmakers to clap horns of honest men's heads o' this order, I'll ne'er trust smooth faces and small ruffs[4] more. But an    115
I be not revenged for this, would I might be turned to a gaping oyster and drink nothing but salt water!

EMP. Come, Faustus. While the Emperor lives,
In recompense of this thy high desert,

4. I.e., scholars, who were often smooth-shaven and did not wear the large "ruffs" (collars) of courtiers. But Faustus has a beard; see the next scene.

Thou shalt command the state of Germany           120
And live beloved of mighty Carolus.      [*Exeunt* OMNES.]

SCENE 3

[*Enter* BENVOLIO, MARTINO, FREDERICK, *and* SOLDIERS.]

MART. Nay, sweet Benvolio, let us sway thy thoughts
  From this attempt against the conjurer.
BENV. Away! You love me not to urge me thus.
  Shall I let slip so great an injury
  When every servile groom jests at my wrongs      5
  And in their rustic gambols proudly say,
  "Benvolio's head was graced with horns today"?
  O, may these eyelids never close again
  Till with my sword I have that conjurer slain.
  If you will aid me in this enterprise,      10
  Then draw your weapons and be resolute;
  If not, depart. Here will Benvolio die,
  But Faustus' death shall quit[5] my infamy.
FRED. Nay, we will stay with thee, betide what may,
  And kill that Doctor if he come this way.      15
BENV. Then gentle Frederick, hie thee to the grove
  And place our servants and our followers
  Close in an ambush there behind the trees.
  By this I know the conjurer is near;
  I saw him kneel and kiss the Emperor's hand      20
  And take his leave laden with rich rewards.
  Then, soldiers, boldly fight. If Faustus die,
  Take you the wealth, leave us the victory.
FRED. Come, soldiers, follow me unto the grove;
  Who kills him shall have gold and endless love.      25
    [*Exit* FREDERICK *with the* SOLDIERS.]
BENV. My head is lighter than it was by th' horns,
  But yet my heart's more ponderous than my head
  And pants until I see that conjurer dead.
MART. Where shall we place ourselves, Benvolio?
BENV. Here will we stay to bide the first assault.      30
  O, were that damnéd hell-hound but in place
  Thou soon shouldst see me quit my foul disgrace.
    [*Enter* FREDERICK.]
FRED. Close, close! The hated conjurer is at hand
  And all alone comes walking in his gown;
  Be ready then and strike the peasant down.      35
BENV. Mine be that honor then. Now, sword, strike home!
  For horns he gave I'll have his head anon.
    [*Enter* FAUSTUS *wearing a false head*.]
MART. See, see, he comes.
BENV.               No words; this blow ends all;
  Hell take his soul, his body thus must fall.
FAUST. O!      40

5. Avenge.

FRED. Groan you, master Doctor?

BENV. Break may his heart with groans. Dear Frederick, see
  Thus will I end his griefs immediately.
    [*Cuts off the false head.*]

MART. Strike,with a willing hand! His head is off.

BENV. The devil's dead; the furies now may laugh.                   45

FRED. Was this that stern aspect, that awful frown,
  Made the grim monarch of infernal spirits
  Tremble and quake at his commanding charms?

MART. Was this that damnéd head whose art conspired
  Benvolio's shame before the Emperor?                              50

BENV. Aye, that's the head, and here the body lies
  Justly rewarded for his villainies.

FRED. Come, let's devise how we may add more shame
  To the black scandal of his hated name.

BENV. First, on his head, in quittance of my wrongs,                55
  I'll nail huge forkéd horns and let them hang
  Within the window where he yoked me first,
  That all the world may see my just revenge.

MART. What use shall we put his beard to?

BENV. We'll sell it to a chimney-sweeper; it will wear out ten      60
  birchen brooms, I warrant you.

FRED. What shall his eyes do?

BENV. We'll pull out his eyes, and they shall serve for buttons to
  his lips to keep his tongue from catching cold.

MART. An excellent policy. And now, sirs, having divided him,       65
  what shall the body do?
    [FAUSTUS *rises.*]

BENV. Zounds, the devil's alive again!

FRED. Give him his head, for God's sake!

FAUST. Nay, keep it. Faustus will have heads and hands,
  Aye, all your hearts, to recompense this deed.                    70
  Knew you not, traitors, I was limited
  For four and twenty years to breathe on earth?
  And had you cut my body with your swords
  Or hewed this flesh and bones as small as sand,
  Yet in a minute had my spirit returned                            75
  And I had breathed a man made free from harm.
  But wherefore do I dally my revenge?
  Asteroth, Belimoth, Mephistophilis!
    [*Enter* MEPHISTOPHILIS *and other* DEVILS.]
  Go, horse these traitors on your fiery backs
  And mount aloft with them as high as heaven,                      80
  Then pitch them headlong to the lowest hell.
  Yet stay, the world shall see their misery,
  And hell shall after plague their treachery.
  Go, Belimoth, and take this caitiff[6] hence
  And hurl him in some lake of mud and dirt;                        85
  Take thou this other, drag him through the woods

6. Wretch.

Amongst the pricking thorns and sharpest briars,
Whilst with my gentle Mephistophilis
This traitor flies unto some steepy rock
That rolling down may break the villain's bones          90
As he intended to dismember me.
Fly hence, dispatch my charge immediately.

FRED. Pity us, gentle Faustus; save our lives!

FAUST. Away!

FRED. He must needs go that the devil drives.          95

> [*Exeunt* SPIRITS *with the* KNIGHTS.]
> [*Enter the ambushed* SOLDIERS.]

1 SOLD. Come, sirs, prepare yourselves in readiness;
Make haste to help these noble gentlemen;
I heard them parley with the conjurer.

2 SOLD. See where he comes; dispatch, and kill the slave!

FAUST. What's here? An ambush to betray my life?          100
Then, Faustus, try thy skill. Base peasants, stand!
For lo, these trees remove at my command
And stand as bulwarks 'twixt yourselves and me
To shield me from your hated treachery;
Yet to encounter this, your weak attempt,          105
Behold an army comes incontinent.[7]

> [FAUSTUS *strikes the door, and enter a* DEVIL *playing on a drum; after him another bearing an ensign, and divers with weapons;* MEPHISTOPHILIS *with fireworks. They set upon the* SOLDIERS *and drive them out. Exeunt.*]

### SCENE 4

> [*Enter at several doors* BENVOLIO, FREDERICK, *and* MARTINO, *their heads and faces bloody and besmeared with mud and dirt, all having horns on their heads.*]

MART. What ho, Benvolio!

BENV. Here! What, Frederick, ho!

FRED. O help me, gentle friend. Where is Martino?

MART. Dear Frederick, here—
Half smothered in a lake of mud and dirt          5
Through which the furies dragged me by the heels.

FRED. Martino, see! Benvolio's horns again.

MART. O misery! How now, Benvolio!

BENV. Defend me, heaven! Shall I be haunted still?

MART. Nay, fear not, man; we have no power to kill.          10

BENV. My friends transforméd thus! O hellish spite!
Your heads are all set with horns.

FRED. You hit it right;
It is your own you mean; feel on your head.

BENV. Zounds, horns again!          15

MART. Nay, chafe not, man; we are all sped.[8]

BENV. What devil attends this damned magician
That spite of spite our wrongs are doubléd?

---

7. Immediately.                    8. Don't fret, man, we are all done for.

FRED. What may we do that we may hide our shames?
BENV. If we should follow him to work revenge,                                    20
   He'd join long asses' ears to those huge horns
   And make us laughingstocks to all the world.
MART. What shall we then do, dear Benvolio?
BENV. I have a castle joining near these woods,
   And thither we'll repair and live obscure                                25
   Till time shall alter this our brutish shapes.
   Sith black disgrace hath thus eclipsed our fame,
   We'll rather die with grief than live with shame.
                         *[Exeunt* OMNES.]

### SCENE 5

    [*Enter* FAUSTUS *and the* HORSE-COURSER.[9]]
HOR. I beseech your Worship, accept of these forty dollars.[1]
FAUST. Friend, thou canst not buy so good a horse for so small a
   price. I have no great need to sell him, but if thou likest him
   for ten dollars more, take him, because I see thou hast a good
   mind to him.                                                              5
HOR. I beseech you, sir, accept of this; I am a very poor man and
   have lost very much of late by horseflesh, and this bargain will
   set me up again.
FAUST. Well, I will not stand with thee; give me the money. Now,
   sirrah, I must tell you that you may ride him o'er hedge and     10
   ditch and spare him not; but—do you hear?—in any case ride
   him not into the water.
HOR. How, sir, not into the water? Why, will he not drink of all
   waters?
FAUST. Yes, he will drink of all waters, but ride him not into the   15
   water; o'er hedge and ditch or where thou wilt, but not into the
   water. Go bid the hostler deliver him unto you, and remember
   what I say.
HOR. I warrant you, sir. O joyful day! Now am I a made man for-
   ever.                                                                     20
      *[Exit.]*
FAUST. What art thou, Faustus, but a man condemned to die?
   Thy fatal time draws to a final end;
   Despair doth drive distrust into my thoughts.
   Confound these passions with a quiet sleep.
   Tush, Christ did call the thief upon the cross;[2]                      25
   Then rest thee, Faustus, quiet in conceit.
                *[He sits to sleep in his chair.]*
    [*Enter the* HORSE-COURSER *wet.*]
HOR. O, what a cozening Doctor was this! I riding my horse into
   the water, thinking some hidden mystery had been in the horse,
   I had nothing under me but a little straw, and had much ado
   to escape drowning. Well, I'll go rouse him and make him give   30

9. Horse-trader, traditionally a sharp
bargainer or cheat.
1. Common German coins; the word
originally comes from the German

*Joachimsthaler.*
2. In Luke xxiii.39–43 one of the two
thieves crucified with Jesus is promised
Paradise. "In conceit": in mind.

me my forty dollars again. Ho! sirrah Doctor, you cozening
scab! Master Doctor, awake and arise, and give me my money
again, for your horse is turned to a bottle[3] of hay. Master Doctor—

    [*He pulls off his leg.*]

Alas, I am undone! What shall I do? I have pulled off his leg. 35

FAUST. O help! Help! The villain hath murdered me!

HOR. Murder or not murder, now he has but one leg I'll outrun
him and cast this leg into some ditch or other.

    [*Exit.*]

FAUST. Stop him, stop him, stop him! Ha ha ha! Faustus hath his
leg again, and the horse-courser a bundle of hay for his forty 40
dollars.

    [*Enter* WAGNER.]

FAUST. How now, Wagner! What news with thee?

WAG. If it please you, the Duke of Vanholt doth earnestly entreat
your company and hath sent some of his men to attend you
with provision fit for your journey. 45

FAUST. The Duke of Vanholt's an honorable gentleman, and one
to whom I must be no niggard of my cunning. Come, away!

### SCENE 6

    [*Enter* ROBIN, DICK, HORSE-COURSER, *and a* CARTER.]

CART. Come, my masters, I'll bring you to the best beer in Europe— What ho, Hostess!—Where be these whores?[4]

    [*Enter* HOSTESS.]

HOST. How now! What lack you? What, my old guests, welcome.

ROBIN. Sirrah Dick, dost thou know why I stand so mute?

DICK. No, Robin, why is 't? 5

ROBIN. I am eighteen pence on the score,[5] but say nothing; see if
she have forgotten me.

HOST. Who's this that stands so solemnly by himself? What, my
old guest!

ROBIN. O, hostess, how do you do? I hope my score stands still. 10

HOST. Aye, there's no doubt of that, for methinks you make no
haste to wipe it out.

DICK. Why, hostess, I say, fetch us some beer.

HOST. You shall presently; look up into th' hall. There, ho!

    [*Exit.*]

DICK. Come, sirs; what shall we do now till mine hostess comes? 15

CART. Marry, sir, I'll tell you the bravest tale how a conjurer
served me. You know Dr. Faustus?

HOR. Aye, a plague take him! Here's some on 's have cause to
know him. Did he conjure thee too?

CART. I'll tell you how he served me. As I was going to Witten- 20
berg t' other day, he met me and asked me what he should give
me for as much hay as he could eat. Now, sir, I, thinking that
a little would serve his turn, bade him take as much as he

3. Bundle.
4. I.e., the hostess and maids of the
inn.
5. Charged, not paid for.

would for three farthings. So he presently gave me my money and fell to eating; and, as I am a cursen man, he never left eating till he had eat up all my load of hay.

ALL. O monstrous; eat a whole load of hay!

ROBIN. Yes, yes; that may be, for I have heard of one that has eat a load of logs.[6]

HOR. Now, sirs, you shall hear now villainously he served me. I went to him yesterday to buy a horse of him, and he would by no means sell him under forty dollars. So, sir, because I knew him to be such a horse as would run over hedge and ditch and never tire, I gave him his money. So, when I had my horse, Dr. Faustus bade me ride him night and day and spare him no time; "But," quoth he, "in any case ride him not into the water." Now sir, I thinking the horse had had some quality that he would not have me know of, what did I but ride him into a great river, and when I came just in the midst my horse vanished away and I sat straddling upon a bottle of hay.

ALL. O brave Doctor!

HOR. But you shall hear how bravely I served him for it. I went me home to his house, and there I found him asleep; I kept a hallowing and whooping in his ears, but all could not wake him. I seeing that, took him by the leg and never rested pulling till I had pulled me his leg quite off, and now 'tis at home in mine hostry.[7]

DICK. And has the Doctor but one leg then? That's excellent, for one of his devils turned me into the likeness of an ape's face.

CART. Some more drink, hostess!

ROBIN. Hark you, we'll into another room and drink awhile, and then we'll go seek out the Doctor.

[*Exeunt* OMNES.]

SCENE 7

[*Enter the* DUKE OF VANHOLT, *his* DUCHESS, FAUSTUS, *and* MEPHISTOPHILIS.]

DUKE. Thanks, master Doctor, for these pleasant sights; nor know I how sufficiently to recompense your great deserts in erecting that enchanted castle in the air, the sight whereof so delighted me as nothing in the world could please me more.

FAUST. I do think myself, my good lord, highly recompensed that it pleaseth your Grace to think but well of that which Faustus hath performed. But gracious lady, it may be that you have taken no pleasure in those sights; therefore I pray you tell me what is the thing you most desire to have; be it in the world it shall be yours. I have heard that great-bellied women do long for things that are rare and dainty.

DUCH. True, master Doctor, and since I find you so kind, I will make known unto you what my heart desires to have; and were it now summer, as it is January, a dead time of winter, I would

6. Comic expression for being drunk —to carry a jag (or load) of logs.   7. Inn.

request no better meat than a dish of ripe grapes. 15

FAUST. This is but a small matter.—Go, Mephistophilis, away!—

[*Exit* MEPHISTOPHILIS.]

Madam, I will do more than this for your content.

[*Enter* MEPHISTOPHILIS *again with the grapes*.]

Here, now taste ye these; they should be good, for they come
from a far country, I can tell you.

DUKE. This makes me wonder more than all the rest, that at this 20
time of year, when every tree is barren of his fruit, from whence
you had these ripe grapes.

FAUST. Please it your Grace, the year is divided into two circles
over the whole world, so that when it is winter with us, in the
contrary circle it is likewise summer with them, as in India, 25
Saba,[8] and such countries that lie far east, where they have
fruit twice a year. From whence, by means of a swift spirit that
I have, I had these grapes brought as you see.

DUCH. And trust me they are the sweetest grapes that e'er I tasted.

[*The* CLOWNS *bounce*[9] *at the gate within.*]

DUKE. What rude disturbers have we at the gate? 30
Go pacify their fury, set it ope,
And then demand of them what they would have.

[*They knock again and call out to talk with* FAUSTUS.]

A SERVANT. Why, how now, masters, what a coil[1] is there!
What is the reason you disturb the Duke?

DICK. We have no reason for it, therefore a fig[2] for him! 35

SERV. Why, saucy varlets! Dare you be so bold?

HOR. I hope, sir, we have wit enough to be more bold than welcome.

SERV. It appears so; Pray be bold elsewhere
And trouble not the Duke. 40

DUKE. What would they have?

SERV. They all cry out to speak with Dr. Faustus.

CART. Aye, and we will speak with him.

DUKE. Will you, sir? Commit[3] the rascals!

DICK. Commit with us? He were as good commit with his father 45
as commit with us.

FAUST. I do beseech your Grace, let them come in;
They are good subject for a merriment.

DUKE. Do as thou wilt, Faustus; I give thee leave.

FAUST. I thank your Grace.

[*Enter* ROBIN, DICK, CARTER, *and* HORSE-COURSER.]

Why, how now, my good friends? 50
'Faith you are too outrageous; but come near,
I have procured your pardons. Welcome all!

ROBIN. Nay, sir, we will be welcome for our money, and we will
pay for what we take. What ho! Give 's half a dozen of beer
here, and be hanged. 55

8. Sheba.
9. Bang.
1. Disturbance.
2. An obscene gesture, implying contempt.
3. Put in jail. Dick puns on its other
meaning ("commit adultery"), from
the Ten Commandments.

FAUST. Nay, hark you, can you tell me where you are?

CART. Aye, marry, can I; we are under heaven.

SERV. Aye, but, sir saucebox, know you in what place?

HOR. Aye, aye, the house is good enough to drink in. Zounds, fill us some beer, or we'll break all the barrels in the house and dash out all your brains with your bottles. 60

FAUST. Be not so furious; come, you shall have beer.
My lord, beseech you give me leave awhile;
I'll gage my credit 'twill content your Grace.

DUKE. With all my heart, kind Doctor, please thyself; 65
Our servants and our court's at thy command.

FAUST. I humbly thank your Grace. Then fetch some beer.

HOR. Aye, marry, there spake a doctor indeed; and, faith, I'll drink a health to thy wooden leg for that word.

FAUST. My wooden leg! What dost thou mean by that? 70

CART. Ha ha ha, dost hear him, Dick? He has forgot his leg.

HOR. Aye, he does not stand much upon that.

FAUST. No, faith, not much upon a wooden leg.

CART. Good lord, that flesh and blood should be so frail with your worship! Do you not remember a horse-courser you sold 75
a horse to?

FAUST. Yes, I remember I sold one a horse.

CART. And do you remember you bid he should not ride him into the water?

FAUST. Yes, I do very well remember that. 80

CART. And do you remember nothing of your leg?

FAUST. No, in good sooth.

CART. Then I pray remember your courtesy.

FAUST. I thank you, sir.

CART. 'Tis not so much worth. I pray you tell me one thing. 85

FAUST. What's that?

CART. Be both of your legs bedfellows every night together?

FAUST. Wouldst thou make a colossus[4] of me, that thou askest me such questions?

CART. No, truly, sir, I would make nothing of you, but I would 90
fain know that.

[*Enter* HOSTESS *with drink.*]

FAUST. Then I assure thee certainly they are.

CART. I thank you; I am fully satisfied.

FAUST. But wherefore dost thou ask?

CART. For nothing, sir; but methinks you should have a wooden 95
bedfellow to one of 'em.

HOR. Why, do you hear, sir, did not I pull off one of your legs when you were asleep?

FAUST. But I have it again now I am awake; look you here, sir.

ALL. O horrible! Had the doctor three legs? 100

CART. Do you remember, sir, how you cozened me and eat up my load of——

4. The huge statue which stood at the entrance to the harbor at Rhodes; boats sailed between its legs, and Dr. Faustus is suggesting that the clowns are making his legs as important.

[FAUSTUS *charms him dumb.*]

DICK. Do you remember how you made me wear an ape's——

HOR. You whoreson conjuring scab, do you remember how you
cozened me of a ho——                                                  105

ROBIN. Ha' you forgotten me? You think to carry it away with
your hey-pass and your re-pass;⁵ do you remember the dog's
fa——

[*Exeunt* CLOWNS.]

HOST. Who pays for the ale? Hear you, master Doctor, now you
have sent away my guests, I pray who shall pay me for my       110
a——

[*Exit* HOSTESS.]

DUCH. My lord,
We are much beholding to this learned man.

DUKE. So are we, madam, which we will recompense
With all the love and kindness that we may;                         115
His artful sport drives all sad thoughts away.            [*Exeunt.*]

## Act V

### SCENE 1

[*Thunder and lightning. Enter* DEVILS *with covered dishes;*
MEPHISTOPHILIS *leads them into* FAUSTUS' *study. Then
enter* WAGNER.]

WAG. I think my master means to die shortly;
He has made his will and given me his wealth,
His house, his goods, and store of golden plate,
Besides two thousand ducats ready coined.
And yet I wonder, for if death were nigh                              5
He would not banquet and carouse and swill
Amongst the students as even now he doth,
Who are at supper with such belly-cheer
As Wagner ne'er beheld in all his life.
See where they come; belike the feast is ended.        [*Exit.*]    10

[*Enter* FAUSTUS *and* MEPHISTOPHILIS *with two or three*
SCHOLARS.]

1 SCH. Master Doctor Faustus, since our conference about fair
ladies, which was the beautifullest in all the world, we have determined with ourselves that Helen of Greece was the ad-
mirablest lady that ever lived. Therefore, master Doctor, if
you will do us that favor as to let us see that peerless dame of   15
Greece whom all the world admires for majesty, we should
think ourselves much beholding unto you.

FAUST. Gentlemen,
For that I know your friendship is unfeigned,
And Faustus' custom is not to deny
The just requests of those that wish him well,                       20
You shall behold that peerless dame of Greece,
No otherways for pomp and majesty

5. Traditional exclamations of a conjurer.

Than when Sir Paris crossed the seas with her
And brought the spoils to rich Dardania.[6]      25
Be silent, then, for danger is in words.
    [*Music sounds, and* HELEN *passeth over the stage.*]
2 SCH. Too simple is my wit to tell her praise
  Whom all the world admires for majesty.
3 SCH. No marvel though the angry Greeks pursued
  With ten years' war the rape of such a queen      30
  Whose heavenly beauty passeth all compare.
1 SCH. Since we have seen the pride of Nature's works
  And only paragon of excellence,
  Let us depart, and for this glorious deed
  Happy and blest be Faustus evermore.      35
FAUST. Gentlemen, farewell; the same I wish to you.
                        [*Exeunt* SCHOLARS.]
    [*Enter an* OLD MAN.]
OLD MAN. O gentle Faustus, leave this damnéd art,
  This magic, that will charm thy soul to hell
  And quite bereave[7] thee of salvation.
  Though thou hast now offended like a man,      40
  Do not persevere in it like a devil.
  Yet, yet, thou hast an amiable soul
  If sin by custom grow not into nature;
  Then, Faustus, will repentance come too late;
  Then thou art banished from the sight of heaven.      45
  No mortal can express the pains of hell.
  It may be this my exhortation
  Seems harsh and all unpleasant; let it not;
  For, gentle son, I speak it not in wrath
  Or envy of thee, but in tender love      50
  And pity of thy future misery,
  And so have hope that this my kind rebuke,
  Checking thy body, may amend thy soul.
FAUST. Where art thou, Faustus? Wretch, what hast thou done?
  Damned art thou, Faustus, damned! Despair and die.      55
    [MEPHISTOPHILIS *gives him a dagger.*]
  Hell claims his right, and with a roaring voice
  Says, "Faustus, come; thine hour is almost come!"
  And Faustus now will come to do thee right.
OLD MAN. O stay, good Faustus, stay thy desperate steps!
  I see an angel hovers o'er thy head      60
  And with a vial full of precious grace
  Offers to pour the same into thy soul:
  Then call for mercy and avoid despair.
FAUST. Ah my sweet friend, I feel thy words
  To comfort my distresséd soul.
  Leave me awhile to ponder on my sins.      65
OLD MAN. Faustus, I leave thee, but with grief of heart,
  Fearing the ruin of thy hopeless soul.      [*Exit.*]

6. Troy.                            7. Deprive.

FAUST. Accursèd Faustus, where is mercy now?
  I do repent and yet I do despair:           70
  Hell strives with grace for conquest in my breast.
  What shall I do to shun the snares of death?
MEPH. Thou traitor, Faustus, I arrest thy soul
  For disobedience to my sovereign lord.
  Revolt, or I'll in piecemeal tear thy flesh.       75
FAUST. I do repent I e'er offended him.
  Sweet Mephistophilis, entreat thy lord
  To pardon my unjust presumption,
  And with my blood again I will confirm
  The former vow I made to Lucifer.         80
MEPH. Do it then, Faustus, with unfeignèd heart
  Lest greater danger do attend thy drift.
FAUST. Torment, sweet friend, that base and agèd man
  That durst dissuade me from thy Lucifer,
  With greatest torments that our hell affords.   85
MEPH. His faith is great; I cannot touch his soul;
  But what I may afflict his body with
  I will attempt, which is but little worth.
FAUST. One thing, good servant, let me crave of thee
  To glut the longing of my heart's desire:     90
  That I might have unto my paramour
  That heavenly Helen which I saw of late,
  Whose sweet embracings may extinguish clear
  These thoughts that do dissuade me from my vow,
  And keep mine oath I made to Lucifer.     95
MEPH. This, or what else my Faustus shall desire
  Shall be performed in twinkling of an eye.
    [*Enter* HELEN *again, passing over between two* CUPIDS.]
FAUST. Was this the face that launched a thousand ships
  And burnt the topless[8] towers of Ilium?
  Sweet Helen, make me immortal with a kiss.   100
  Her lips sucks forth my soul—see where it flies!
  Come, Helen, come, give me my soul again.
  Here will I dwell, for heaven is in these lips
  And all is dross that is not Helena.
    [*Enter* OLD MAN *and stands watching* FAUSTUS.]
  I will be Paris, and for love of thee        105
  Instead of Troy shall Wittenberg be sacked,
  And I will combat with weak Menelaus
  And wear thy colors on my plumèd crest;
  Yea, I will wound Achilles in the heel
  And then return to Helen for a kiss.      110
  O thou art fairer than the evening air
  Clad in the beauty of a thousand stars!
  Brighter art thou than flaming Jupiter
  When he appeared to hapless Semele,[9]

8. So high they seemed to have no tops.
9. A Theban girl, loved by Jupiter and destroyed by the fire of his lightning when he appeared to her in his full splendor.

More lovely than the monarch of the sky                                    115
In wanton Arethusa's azured arms,[1]
And none but thou shalt be my paramour!
   [*Exeunt* ALL *except the* OLD MAN.]
OLD MAN. Accurséd Faustus, miserable man,
   That from thy soul exclud'st the grace of heaven
   And fliest the throne of his tribunal seat.                             120
   [*Enter the* DEVILS *to torment him.*]
Satan begins to sift me with his pride.[2]
As in this furnace God shall try my faith,
My faith, vile hell, shall triumph over thee!
Ambitious fiends, see how the heavens smiles
At your repulse, and laughs your state to scorn.                          125
Hence, hell! for hence I fly unto my God.                [*Exeunt.*]

                           SCENE 2

   [*Thunder. Enter* LUCIFER, BELZEBUB, *and* MEPHISTOPHI-
   LIS.]
LUC. Thus from infernal Dis[3] do we ascend
   To view the subjects of our monarchy,
   Those souls which sin seals the black sons of hell.
   'Mong which as chief, Faustus, we come to thee,
   Bringing with us lasting damnation                                       5
   To wait upon thy soul; the time is come
   Which makes it forfeit.
MEPH.                      And this gloomy night
   Here in this room will wretched Faustus be.
BEL. And here we'll stay
   To mark him how he doth demean himself.                                 10
MEPH. How should he but with desperate lunacy?
   Fond worldling, now his heart-blood dries with grief,
   His conscience kills it, and his laboring brain
   Begets a world of idle fantasies
   To overreach the devil, but all in vain.                                15
   His store of pleasure must be sauced with pain.
   He and his servant Wagner are at hand;
   Both come from drawing Faustus' latest will.
   See where they come!
   [*Enter* FAUSTUS *and* WAGNER.]
FAUST. Say, Wagner, thou has perused my will;                             20
   How dost thou like it?
WAG.                      Sir, so wondrous well
   As in all humble duty I do yield
   My life and lasting service for your love.
   [*Enter the* SCHOLARS.]
FAUST. Gramercies, Wagner.—Welcome, gentlemen.
1 SCH. Now, worthy Faustus, methinks your looks are changed.             25

1. Arethusa was the nymph of a fountain, as well as the fountain itself; no
classical myth, however, records her
love affair with Jupiter, the "monarch
of the sky."
2. I.e., to test me with his strength.
3. The underworld.

FAUST. Ah, gentlemen!

2 SCH. What ails Faustus?

FAUST. Ah, my sweet chamber-fellow, had I lived with thee, then had I lived still, but now must die eternally. Look, sirs! Comes he not? Comes he not? 30

1 SCH. O my dear Faustus, what imports this fear?

2 SCH. Is all our pleasure turned to melancholy?

3 SCH. He is not well with being over-solitary.

2 SCH. If it be so, we'll have physicians, and Faustus shall be cured. 35

3 SCH. 'Tis but a surfeit,⁴ sir; fear nothing.

FAUST. A surfeit of deadly sin that hath damned both body and soul.

2 SCH. Yet, Faustus, look up to heaven: remember God's mercies are infinite. 40

FAUST. But Faustus' offense can ne'er be pardoned; the Serpent that tempted Eve may be saved, but not Faustus. Ah, gentlemen, hear me with patience, and tremble not at my speeches. Though my heart pants and quivers to remember that I have been a student here these thirty years, O would I had never seen 45 Wittenberg, never read book! And what wonders I have done all Germany can witness, yea all the world, for which Faustus hath lost both Germany and the world, yea heaven itself— heaven the seat of God, the throne of the blessed, the kingdom of joy, and must remain in hell forever, hell, ah hell, forever! 50 Sweet friends, what shall become of Faustus, being in hell forever?

3 SCH. Yet, Faustus, call on God.

FAUST. On God, whom Faustus hath abjured? on God, whom Faustus hath blasphemed? Ah, my God, I would weep, but the 55 devil draws in my tears! Gush forth, blood, instead of tears, yea life and soul! O he stays my tongue; I would lift up my hands but, see, they hold 'em, they hold 'em!

ALL. Who, Faustus?

FAUST. Why, Lucifer and Mephistophilis. 60
Ah, gentlemen, I gave them my soul for my cunning.

ALL. God forbid!

FAUST. God forbade it indeed, but Faustus hath done it: for vain pleasure of four and twenty years hath Faustus lost eternal joy and felicity. I writ them a bill with mine own blood; the date 65 is expired, this is the time, and he will fetch me.

1 SCH. Why did not Faustus tell us of this before, that divines might have prayed for thee?

FAUST. Oft have I thought to have done so, but the devil threatened to tear me in pieces if I named God, to fetch both body 70 and soul if I once gave ear to divinity; and now 'tis too late. Gentlemen, away, lest you perish with me!

2 SCH. O what may we do to save Faustus?

FAUST. Talk not of me, but save yourselves and depart.

4. Indigestion; the effects of overindulgence.

**3 SCH.** God will strengthen me: I will stay with Faustus.                   75

**1 SCH.** Tempt not God, sweet friend, but let us into the next room, and there pray for him.

**FAUST.** Aye, pray for me, pray for me! And what noise soever ye hear, come not unto me, for nothing can rescue me.

**2 SCH.** Pray thou, and we will pray that God may have mercy  80 upon thee.

**FAUST.** Gentlemen, farewell. If I live till morning I'll visit you; if not, Faustus is gone to hell.

**ALL.** Faustus, farewell.                    [*Exeunt* SCHOLARS.]

**MEPH.** Aye, Faustus, now hast thou no hope of heaven;              85
Therefore despair, think only upon hell,
For that must be thy mansion, there to dwell.

**FAUST.** O thou bewitching fiend, 'twas thy temptation
Hath robbed me of eternal happiness.

**MEPH.** I do confess it, Faustus, and rejoice.                 90
'Twas I, that when thou wert i' the way to heaven
Damned up thy passage; when thou tookest the book
To view the scriptures, then I turned the leaves
And led thine eye.
What, weepst thou? 'tis too late. Despair, farewell!              95
Fools that will laugh on earth must weep in hell.        [*Exit.*]
    [*Enter the* GOOD ANGEL *and the* BAD ANGEL *at several doors.*]

**G. ANG.** Ah Faustus, if thou hadst given ear to me,
Innumerable joys had followed thee,
But thou didst love the world.

**B. ANG.**                    Gave ear to me
And now must taste hell's pains perpetually.                100

**G. ANG.** O what will all thy riches, pleasures, pomps
Avail thee now?

**B. ANG.**            Nothing but vex thee more,
To want in hell, that had on earth such store.
    [*Music while the throne descends.*[5]]

**G. ANG.** O, thou hast lost celestial happiness,
Pleasures unspeakable, bliss without end.                  105
Hadst thou affected sweet divinity
Hell or the devil had had no power on thee.
Hadst thou kept on that way, Faustus, behold
In what resplendent glory thou hadst sit
In yonder throne, like those bright shining saints,           110
And triumphed over hell; that hast thou lost.
And now, poor soul, must thy good angel leave thee;
The jaws of hell are open to receive thee.
    [*Exit. Hell is discovered.*]

**B. ANG.** Now Faustus, let thine eyes with horror stare
Into that vast perpetual torture-house.                   115
There are the furies, tossing damnéd souls

5. A throne suspended by ropes de-
stended to the stage near the end of
many Elizabethan plays and was an
expected theatrical display. Here the
throne clearly symbolizes heaven, as
the next speech shows.

On burning forks; their bodies boil in lead.
There are live quarters[6] broiling on the coals
That ne'er can die; this ever-burning chair
Is for o'ertortured souls to rest them in;                    120
These that are fed with sops of flaming fire
Were gluttons and loved only delicates
And laughed to see the poor starve at their gates.
But yet all these are nothing; thou shalt see
Ten thousand tortures that more horrid be.                    125
FAUST. O, I have seen enough to torture me.
B. ANG. Nay, thou must feel them, taste the smart of all;
He that loves pleasure must for pleasure fall;
And so I leave thee, Faustus, till anon;
Then wilt thou tumble in confusión.[7]                        130
        [Exit. The clock strikes eleven.]
FAUST. Ah, Faustus,
Now hast thou but one bare hour to live
And then thou must be damned perpetually!
Stand still, you ever-moving spheres of heaven,
That time may cease and midnight never come;                  135
Fair Nature's eye, rise, rise again, and make
Perpetual day; or let this hour be but
A year, a month, a week, a natural day,
That Faustus may repent and save his soul!
O *lente lente currite noctis equi.*[8]                       140
The stars move still, time runs, the clock will strike,
The devil will come, and Faustus must be damned.
O, I'll leap up to my God! Who pulls me down?
See, see, where Christ's blood streams in the firmament!—
One drop would save my soul—half a drop! ah, my Christ!       145
Rend not my heart for naming of my Christ;
Yet will I call on him—O, spare me, Lucifer!
Where is it now? 'Tis gone; and see where God
Stretcheth out his arm and bends his ireful brows.
Mountains and hills, come, come and fall on me                150
And hide me from the heavy wrath of God,
No, no—
Then will I headlong run into the earth:
Earth, gape! O no, it will not harbor me.
You stars that reigned at my nativity,                        155
Whose influence hath allotted death and hell,
Now draw up Faustus like a foggy mist
Into the entrails of yon laboring clouds
That when they vomit forth into the air,
My limbs may issue from their smoky mouths,                   160
So that my soul may but ascend to heaven.
        [The watch strikes.]
Ah, half the hour is past; 'twill all be past anon.

6. Bodies.
7. Destruction, perdition.
8. "Slowly, slowly run, O horses of the
night," adapted from a line in Ovid's
*Amores.*

O God,
If thou wilt not have mercy on my soul,
Yet for Christ's sake whose blood hath ransomed me                    165
Impose some end to my incessant pain:
Let Faustus live in hell a thousand years,
A hundred thousand, and at last be saved!
O, no end is limited to damnéd souls!
Why wert thou not a creature wanting soul?                            170
Or why is this immortal that thou hast?
Ah, Pythagoras' *metempsychosis*[9]—were that true,
This soul should fly from me, and I be changed
Unto some brutish beast. All beasts are happy,
For when they die                                                    175
Their souls are soon dissolved in elements,
But mine must live still[1] to be plagued in hell.
Cursed be the parents that engendered me!
No, Faustus, curse thyself, curse Lucifer
That hath deprived thee of the joys of heaven.                       180
    [*The clock strikes twelve.*]
It strikes, it strikes! Now, body, turn to air
Or Lucifer will bear thee quick[2] to hell!
    [*Thunder and lightning.*]
O soul, be changed to little water drops
And fall into the ocean, ne'er be found.
My God, my God, look not so fierce on me!                            185
    [*Enter* DEVILS.]
Adders and serpents, let me breathe awhile!
Ugly hell, gape not—come not, Lucifer—
I'll burn my books—ah, Mephistophilis!
    [*Exeunt* DEVILS *with* FAUSTUS.]

SCENE 3

    [*Enter the* SCHOLARS.]
1 SCH. Come, gentlemen, let us go visit Faustus,
For such a dreadful night was never seen
Since first the world's creation did begin,
Such fearful shrieks and cries were never heard.
Pray heaven the Doctor have escaped the danger.                      5
2 SCH. O, help us heaven! See, here are Faustus' limbs
All torn asunder by the hand of death.
3 SCH. The devils whom Faustus served have torn him thus;
For 'twixt the hours of twelve and one, methought
I heard him shriek and call aloud for help.                          10
At which self[3] time the house seemed all on fire
With dreadful horror of these damnéd fiends.
2 SCH. Well, gentlemen, though Faustus' end be such
As every Christian heart laments to think on,
Yet for he was a scholar once admired                                15

9. Pythagoras' doctrine of the trans-   2. Alive.
migration of souls.   3. Same, exact.
1. Always.

For wondrous knowledge in our German schools,
We'll give his mangled limbs due burial;
And all the students, clothed in mourning black,
Shall wait upon his heavy[4] funeral.                    [*Exeunt.*]
    [*Enter* CHORUS.]
CHO. Cut is the branch that might have grown full straight,          20
And burnéd is Apollo's laurel bough[5]
That sometime grew within this learnéd man.
Faustus is gone: regard his hellish fall,
Whose fiendful fortune may exhort the wise
Only to wonder at[6] unlawful things                              25
Whose deepness doth entice such forward wits
To practice more than heavenly power permits.        [*Exit.*]
                                  1604, 1616

4. Tragic, sorrowful.
5. Laurel is a symbol of wisdom and learning; Apollo was the god of divination, one of whose shrines was the oracle at Delphi. The image, though it sounds classical, is really Marlowe's.
6. I.e., to be content with observing with awe. "Fiendful fortune": devilish fate.

# WILLIAM SHAKESPEARE
## (1564–1616)
## Hamlet, Prince of Denmark*

### Characters

CLAUDIUS, *king of Denmark*
HAMLET, *son to the late, and nephew to the present king*
POLONIUS, *lord chamberlain*
HORATIO, *friend to Hamlet*
LAERTES, *son to Polonius*
VOLTIMAND,
CORNELIUS,
ROSENCRANTZ,
GUILDENSTERN,  } *courtiers*
OSRIC,
GENTLEMAN,
PRIEST
MARCELLUS,  } *officers*
BERNARDO,

FRANCISCO, *a soldier*
REYNALDO, *servant to Polonius*
PLAYERS
TWO CLOWNS, *grave-diggers*
FORTINBRAS, *prince of Norway*
CAPTAIN
ENGLISH AMBASSADORS
GERTRUDE, *queen of Denmark, and mother to Hamlet*
OPHELIA, *daughter of Polonius*
LORDS, LADIES, OFFICERS, SOLDIERS, SAILORS, MESSENGERS, *and* OTHER ATTENDANTS
GHOST OF HAMLET'S FATHER

SCENE—*Denmark.*

## Act I

SCENE 1—*Elsinore. A platform before the castle.*

[FRANCISCO *at his post. Enter to him* BERNARDO.]

BERNARDO. Who's there?

FRANCISCO. Nay, answer me: stand, and unfold yourself.

BERNARDO. Long live the king!

FRANCISCO. Bernardo?

BERNARDO. He.    5

FRANCISCO. You come most carefully upon your hour.

BERNARDO. 'Tis now struck twelve; get thee to bed, Francisco.

FRANCISCO. For this relief much thanks: 'tis bitter cold,
And I am sick at heart.

BERNARDO. Have you had quiet guard?

FRANCISCO.                                Not a mouse stirring.    10

BERNARDO. Well, good night.
If you do meet Horatio and Marcellus,
The rivals of my watch, bid them make haste.

* Usually dated 1601.
9. *sick at heart:* depressed.
13. *rivals:* partners.

FRANCISCO. I think I hear them. Stand, ho! Who is there?
    [*Enter* HORATIO *and* MARCELLUS.]
HORATIO. Friends to this ground.
MARCELLUS.                  And liegemen to the Dane.   15
FRANCISCO. Give you good night.
MARCELLUS.                 O, farewell, honest soldier:
  Who hath relieved you?
FRANCISCO.              Bernardo hath my place.
  Give you good night.                      [*Exit.*]
MARCELLUS.         Holla! Bernardo!
BERNARDO.                         Say,
  What, is Horatio there?
HORATIO.            A piece of him.
BERNARDO. Welcome, Horatio; welcome, good Marcellus.   20
MARCELLUS. What, has this thing appear'd again to-night?
BERNARDO. I have seen nothing.
MARCELLUS. Horatio says 'tis but our fantasy,
  And will not let belief take hold of him
  Touching this dreaded sight, twice seen of us:   25
  Therefore I have entreated him along
  With us to watch the minutes of this night,
  That if again this apparition come,
  He may approve our eyes and speak to it.
HORATIO. Tush, tush, 'twill not appear.
BERNARDO.                  Sit down a while;   30
  And let us once again assail your ears,
  That are so fortified against our story,
  What we have two nights seen.
HORATIO.                Well, sit we down,
  And let us hear Bernardo speak of this.
BERNARDO. Last night of all,   35
  When yond same star that's westward from the pole
  Had made his course to illume that part of heaven
  Where now it burns, Marcellus and myself,
  The bell then beating one,—
      [*Enter* GHOST.]
MARCELLUS. Peace, break thee off; look, where it comes again!   40
BERNARDO. In the same figure, like the king that's dead.
MARCELLUS. Thou art a scholar; speak to it, Horatio.
BERNARDO. Looks it not like the king? mark it, Horatio.
HORATIO. Most like: it harrows me with fear and wonder.

---

15. *the Dane:* the king of Denmark.
29. *approve our eyes:* confirm what
we saw.
31–33. *assail your ears . . . seen:*
try to convince you by telling the story
again.
42. *Thou art a scholar:* and therefore, the implication is, you know how
to handle this.

BERNARDO. It would be spoke to.

MARCELLUS. Question it, Horatio. 45

HORATIO. What are thou, that usurp'st this time of night,
Together with that fair and warlike form
In which the majesty of buried Denmark
Did sometimes march? by heaven I charge thee, speak!

MARCELLUS. It is offended.

BERNARDO. See, it stalks away! 50

HORATIO. Stay! speak, speak! I charge thee, speak!
[Exit GHOST.]

MARCELLUS. 'Tis gone, and will not answer.

BERNARDO. How now, Horatio! you tremble and look pale:
Is not this something more than fantasy?
What think you on't? 55

HORATIO. Before my God, I might not this believe
Without the sensible and true avouch
Of mine own eyes.

MARCELLUS. Is it not like the king?

HORATIO. As thou art to thyself:
Such was the very armor he had on 60
When he the ambitious Norway combated;
So frown'd he once, when, in an angry parle,
He smote the sledded Polacks on the ice.
'Tis strange.

MARCELLUS. Thus twice before, and jump at this dead hour, 65
With martial stalk hath he gone by our watch.

HORATIO. In what particular thought to work I know not;
But, in the gross and scope of my opinion,
This bodes some strange eruption to our state.

MARCELLUS. Good now, sit down, and tell me, he that knows, 70
Why this same strict and most observant watch
So nightly toils the subject of the land,
And why such daily cast of brazen cannon,
And foreign mart for implements of war;
Why such impress of shipwrights, whose sore task 75
Does not divide the Sunday from the week;
What might be toward, that this sweaty haste
Doth make the night joint-laborer with the day:
Who is't that can inform me?

HORATIO. That can I;

48. *Denmark:* the king of Denmark.
49. *sometimes:* formerly.
61. *Norway:* the king of Norway (the elder Fortinbras).
62. *parle:* parley.
63. *sledded:* who travel in sledges.
65. *jump:* just.

68. *in the gross . . . opinion:* taking a general view.
72. *toils the subject:* makes the people (the subjects) toil.
74. *mart:* traffic.
75. *impress of shipwrights:* forcing of ship carpenters into service.
77. *toward:* impending.

At least the whisper goes so. Our last king,                    80
Whose image even but now appear'd to us,
Was, as you know, by Fortinbras of Norway,
Thereto prick'd on by a most emulate pride,
Dared to the combat; in which our valiant Hamlet—
For so this side of our known world esteem'd him—              85
Did slay this Fortinbras; who by a seal'd compact
Well ratified by law and heraldry,
Did forfeit, with his life, all those his lands
Which he stood seized of, to the conqueror:
Against the which, a moiety competent                           90
Was gagèd by our king; which had return'd
To the inheritance of Fortinbras,
Had he been vanquisher; as, by the same covenant
And carriage of the article design'd,
His fell to Hamlet. Now, sir, young Fortinbras,                 95
Oᶠ unimprovèd metal hot and full,
Hᵃth in the skirts of Norway here and there
Shark'd up a list of lawless resolutes,
For food and diet, to some enterprise
That hath a stomach in't: which is no other—                  100
As it doth well appear unto our state—
But to recover of us, by strong hand
And terms compulsatory, those foresaid lands
So by his father lost: and this, I take it,
Is the main motive of our preparations,                        105
The source of this our watch and the chief head
Of this post-haste and romage in the land.
BERNARDO. I think it be no other but e'en so:
Well may it sort, that this portentous figure
Comes armèd through our watch, so like the king                110
That was and is the question of these wars.
HORATIO. A mote it is to trouble the mind's eye.
In the most high and palmy state of Rome,
A little ere the mightiest Julius fell,
The graves stood tenantless, and the sheeted dead              115
Did squeak and gibber in the Roman streets:
As stars with trains of fire and dews of blood,

83. *emulate:* emulous.
87. *Well ratified . . . heraldry:* duly
ratified and proclaimed through heralds.
89. *seized:* possessed.
90. *moiety competent:* adequate part.
91. *gagèd:* pledged.
94. *carriage:* purport.
96. *unimprovèd:* unused.
97. *skirts:* outskirts, border regions.

100. *hath a stomach:* calls for courage (compare, "guts").
101. *state:* government.
106. *head:* origin, cause.
107. *romage:* bustle.
109. *sort:* happen.
112. *mote:* small particle (as of
dust).

Disasters in the sun; and the moist star,
Upon whose influence Neptune's empire stands,
Was sick almost to doomsday with eclipse:                    120
And even the like precurse of fierce events,
As harbingers preceding still the fates
And prologue to the omen coming on,
Have heaven and earth together demonstrated
Unto our climatures and countrymen.                          125
          [Re-enter GHOST.]
But soft, behold! lo, where it comes again!
I'll cross it, though it blast me. Stay, illusion!
If thou hast any sound, or use of voice,
Speak to me:
If there be any good thing to be done,                       130
That may to thee do ease and grace to me,
Speak to me:
If thou art privy to thy country's fate,
Which, happily, foreknowing may avoid,
O, speak!                                                    135
Or if thou hast uphoarded in thy life
Extorted treasure in the womb of earth,
For which, they say, you spirits oft walk in death,
Speak of it: stay, and speak! [The cock crows.] Stop it, Marcellus.
MARCELLUS. Shall I strike at it with my partisan?           140
HORATIO. Do, if it will not stand.
BERNARDO.                              'Tis here!
HORATIO.                                          'Tis here!
MARCELLUS. 'Tis gone!                         [Exit GHOST.]
We do it wrong, being so majestical,
To offer it the show of violence;
For it is, as the air, invulnerable,                         145
And our vain blows malicious mockery.
BERNARDO. It was about to speak, when the cock crew.
HORATIO. And then it started like a guilty thing
Upon a fearful summons. I have heard,
The cock, that is the trumpet to the morn,                   150
Doth with his lofty and shrill-sounding throat
Awake the god of day, and at his warning,
Whether in sea or fire, in earth or air,

118. *Disasters:* ill omens. *the moist star:* the moon.
119. *Upon . . . stands:* The moon regulates the sea tides.
121. *precurse:* foreboding.
122. *harbingers:* forerunners.

123. *omen:* dire event portended by omen.
125. *climatures:* regions.
128–139. *If thou . . . speak:* Horatio, a scholar, knows how to address a ghost with the appropriate formulas.
140. *partisan:* spear.

The extravagant and erring spirit hies
To his confine: and of the truth herein                        155
This present object made probation.
MARCELLUS. It faded on the crowing of the cock.
Some say that ever 'gainst that season comes
Wherein our Saviour's birth is celebrated,
The bird of dawning singeth all night long:                    160
And then, they say, no spirit dare stir abroad,
The nights are wholesome, then no planets strike,
No fairy takes nor witch hath power to charm,
So hallow'd and so gracious is the time.
HORATIO. So have I heard and do in part believe it.            165
But look, the morn, in russet mantle clad,
Walks o'er the dew of yon high eastward hill:
Break we our watch up; and by my advice,
Let us impart what we have seen to-night
Unto young Hamlet; for, upon my life,                          170
This spirit, dumb to us, will speak to him:
Do you consent we shall acquaint him with it,
As needful in our loves, fitting our duty?
MARCELLUS. Let's do't, I pray; and I this morning know
Where we shall find him most conveniently.                     175
    [*Exeunt.*]

SCENE 2—*A room of state in the castle.*

[*Flourish. Enter the* KING, QUEEN, HAMLET, POLONIUS,
    LAERTES, VOLTIMAND, CORNELIUS, LORDS, *and* ATTENDANTS.]
KING. Though yet of Hamlet our dear brother's death
The memory be green, and that it us befitted
To bear our hearts in grief and our whole kingdom
To be contracted in one brow of woe,
Yet so far hath discretion fought with nature                     5
That we with wisest sorrow think on him,
Together with remembrance of ourselves.
Therefore our sometime sister, now our queen,
The imperial jointress to this warlike state,
Have we, as 'twere with a defeated joy,—                         10
With an auspicious and a dropping eye,
With mirth in funeral and with dirge in marriage,
In equal scale weighing delight and dole,—

154. *extravagant:* wandering out of
its confines.
156. *made probation:* gave proof.
158. *'gainst:* just before.
162. *strike:* exercise evil influence
(compare, "moonstruck").
163. *takes:* bewitches.

164. *gracious:* full of blessing.
5. *discretion:* restraint (here, on
grief).
9. *jointress:* a widow who has the
life tenancy on an estate.
13. *dole:* grief.

Taken to wife: nor have we herein barr'd
Your better wisdoms, which have freely gone          15
With this affair along. For all, our thanks.
Now follows, that you know, young Fortinbras,
Holding a weak supposal of our worth,
Or thinking by our late dear brother's death
Our state to be disjoint and out of frame,          20
Colleaguèd with this dream of his advantage,
He hath not fail'd to pester us with message,
Importing the surrender of those lands
Lost by his father, with all bonds of law,
To our most valiant brother. So much for him.       25
Now for ourself, and for this time of meeting:
Thus much the business is: we have here writ
To Norway, uncle of young Fortinbras,—
Who, impotent and bed-rid, scarcely hears
Of this his nephew's purpose,—to suppress           30
His further gait herein; in that the levies,
The lists and full proportions, are all made
Out of his subject: and we here dispatch
You, good Cornelius, and you, Voltimand,
For bearers of this greeting to old Norway,         35
Giving to you no further personal power
To business with the king more than the scope
Of these delated articles allow.
Farewell, and let your haste commend your duty.

CORNELIUS. ⎫
            ⎬ In that and all things will we show our duty.   40
VOLTIMAND. ⎭

KING. We doubt it nothing: heartily farewell.
      [*Exeunt* VOLTIMAND *and* CORNELIUS.]
And now, Laertes, what's the news with you?
You told us of some suit; what is't, Laertes?
You cannot speak of reason to the Dane,
And lose your voice: what wouldst thou beg, Laertes,  45
That shall not be my offer, not thy asking?
The head is not more native to the heart,
The hand more instrumental to the mouth,
Than is the throne of Denmark to thy father.
What wouldst thou have, Laertes?

LAERTES.                         My dread lord,       50
Your leave and favor to return to France,

---

14. *barr'd:* ignored.
20. *disjoint:* disjointed, disorganized.
21. *Colleaguèd with this dream:* combined with this fantastic notion.
31. *gait:* proceeding.

33. *subject:* subjects, people.
38. *delated:* detailed.
44. *the Dane:* the king of Denmark.
47. *native to:* naturally bound to.

From whence though willingly I came to Denmark,
To show my duty in your coronation,
Yet now, I must confess, that duty done,
My thoughts and wishes bend again toward France    55
And bow them to your gracious leave and pardon.
KING. Have you your father's leave? What says Polonius?
POLONIUS. He hath, my lord, wrung from me my slow leave
By laborsome petition, and at last
Upon his will I seal'd my hard consent:    60
I do beseech you, give him leave to go.
KING. Take thy fair hour, Laertes; time be thine,
And thy best graces spend it at thy will!
But now, my cousin Hamlet, and my son,—
HAMLET. [*Aside*] A little more than kin, and less than kind.    65
KING. How is it that the clouds still hang on you?
HAMLET. Not so, my lord; I am too much i' the sun.
QUEEN. Good Hamlet, cast thy nighted color off,
And let thine eye look like a friend on Denmark.
Do not for ever with thy vailèd lids    70
Seek for thy noble father in the dust:
Thou know'st 'tis common; all that lives must die,
Passing through nature to eternity.
HAMLET. Aye, madam, it is common.
QUEEN.                                      If it be,
Why seems it so particular with thee?    75
HAMLET. Seems, madam! nay, it is; I know not 'seems.'
'Tis not alone my inky cloak, good mother,
Nor customary suits of solemn black,
Nor windy suspiration of forced breath,
No, nor the fruitful river in the eye,    80
Nor the dejected havior of the visage,
Together with all forms, moods, shapes of grief,
That can denote me truly: these indeed seem,
For they are actions that a man might play:
But I have that within which passeth show;    85
These but the trappings and the suits of woe.
KING. 'Tis sweet and commendable in your nature, Hamlet,
To give these mourning duties to your father:
But, you must know, your father lost a father,
That father lost, lost his, and the survivor bound    90
In filial obligation for some term

66–67. *How . . . sun:* The cue to Hamlet's irony is given by the King's words "my cousin . . . my son" in l. 64. In his statement that clouds do not hang on him because he is "too much i' the sun," Hamlet is punning on "*son*."
69. *Denmark:* the king of Denmark.
70. *vailèd:* downcast.
79. *suspiration:* breathing.
81. *havior:* outer deportment.

To do obsequious sorrow: but to persevere
In obstinate condolement is a course
Cf impious stubborness; 'tis unmanly grief:
It shows a will most incorrect to heaven,                    95
A heart unfortified, a mind impatient,
An understanding simple and unschool'd:
For what we know must be and is as common
As any the most vulgar thing to sense,
Why should we in our peevish opposition                     100
Take it to heart? Fie! 'tis a fault to heaven,
A fault against the dead, a fault to nature,
To reason most absurd, whose common theme
Is death of fathers, and who still hath cried,
From the first corse till he that died to-day,              105
'This must be so.' We pray you, throw to earth
This unprevailing woe, and think of us
As of a father: for let the world take note,
You are the most immediate to our throne,
And with no less nobility of love                           110
Than that which dearest father bears his son
Do I impart toward you. For your intent
In going back to school in Wittenberg,
It is most retrograde to our desire:
And we beseech you, bend you to remain                      115
Here in the cheer and comfort of our eye,
Our chiefest courtier, cousin and our son.

QUEEN. Let not thy mother lose her prayers, Hamlet:
I pray thee, stay with us; go not to Wittenberg.

HAMLET. I shall in all my best obey you, madam.             120

KING. Why, 'tis a loving and a fair reply:
Be as ourself in Denmark. Madam, come;
This gentle and unforced accord of Hamlet
Sits smiling to my heart: in grace whereof,
No jocund health that Denmark drinks to-day,                125
But the great cannon to the clouds shall tell,
And the king's rouse the heaven shall bruit again,
Re-speaking earthly thunder. Come away.

[*Flourish. Exeunt all but* HAMLET.]

HAMLET. O, that this too too sullied flesh would melt,
Thaw and resolve itself into a dew!                         130

92. *obsequious:* dutiful, especially concerning funeral rites (obsequies).
95. *incorrect:* not subdued.
107. *unprevailing:* useless.
113. *Wittenberg:* the seat of a university; at the peak of fame in Shakespeare's time on account of its connection with Luther.
114. *retrograde:* opposed.
127. *rouse:* carousal, revel. **bruit:** proclaim, echo.

Or that the Everlasting had not fix'd
His canon 'gainst self-slaughter! O God! God!
How weary, stale, flat and unprofitable
Seem to me all the uses of this world!
Fie on't! ah fie! 'tis an unweeded garden,                                   135
That grows to seed; things rank and gross in nature
Possess it merely. That it should come to this!
But two months dead! nay, not so much, not two:
So excellent a king; that was, to this,
Hyperion to a satyr: so loving to my mother,                                 140
That he might not beteem the winds of heaven
Visit her face too roughly. Heaven and earth!
Must I remember? why, she would hang on him,
As if increase of appetite had grown
By what it fed on: and yet, within a month—                                  145
Let me not think on't—Frailty, thy name is woman!—
A little month, or ere those shoes were old
With which she follow'd my poor father's body,
Like Niobe, all tears:—why she, even she,—
O God! a beast that wants discourse of reason                                150
Would have mourn'd longer,—married with my uncle,
My father's brother, but no more like my father
Than I to Hercules: within a month;
Ere yet the salt of most unrighteous tears
Had left the flushing in her gallèd eyes,                                    155
She married. O, most wicked speed, to post
With such dexterity to incestuous sheets!
It is not, nor it cannot come to good:
But break, my heart, for I must hold my tongue!

    [*Enter* HORATIO, MARCELLUS, *and* BERNARDO.]

HORATIO. Hail to your lordship!

HAMLET.                I am glad to see you well:         160
  Horatio,—or I do forget myself.

HORATIO. The same, my lord, and your poor servant ever.

HAMLET. Sir, my good friend; I'll change that name with you:
  And what make you from Wittenberg, Horatio?
  Marcellus?                                                                165

MARCELLUS. My good lord?

HAMLET. I am very glad to see you. [*To* BERNARDO] Good even, sir.
  But what, in faith, make you from Wittenberg?

132. *canon:* law.
140. *Hyperion:* the sun-god.
141. *beteem:* allow.
149. *Niobe:* Her seven sons and seven daughters were slain by Apollo and Artemis, and sorrow changed her into a continually weeping stone.

150. *wants discourse of reason:* lacks the reasoning faculty.
155. *gallèd:* inflamed.
157. *incestuous:* According to principles which Hamlet accepts, marrying one's brother's widow is incest.

HORATIO. A truant disposition, good my lord.

HAMLET. I would not hear your enemy say so,                                170
    Nor shall you do my ear that violence,
    To make it truster of your own report
    Against yourself: I know you are no truant.
    But what is your affair in Elsinore?
    We'll teach you to drink deep ere you depart.                     175

HORATIO. My lord, I came to see your father's funeral.

HAMLET. I pray thee, do not mock me, fellow-student;
    I think it was to see my mother's wedding.

HORATIO. Indeed, my lord, it follow'd hard upon.

HAMLET. Thrift, thrift, Horatio! the funeral baked-meats          180
    Did coldly furnish forth the marriage tables.
    Would I had met my dearest foe in heaven
    Or ever I had seen that day, Horatio!
    My father!—methinks I see my father.

HORATIO. O where, my lord?

HAMLET.                                        In my mind's eye, Horatio.          185

HORATIO. I saw him once; he was a goodly king.

HAMLET. He was a man, take him for all in all,
    I shall not look upon his like again.

HORATIO. My lord, I think I saw him yesternight.

HAMLET. Saw? who?                                                                          190

HORATIO. My lord, the king your father.

HAMLET.                                        The king my father!

HORATIO. Season your admiration for a while
    With an attent ear, till I may deliver,
    Upon the witness of these gentlemen,
    This marvel to you.

HAMLET.                                        For God's love, let me hear.          195

HORATIO. Two nights together had these gentlemen,
    Marcellus and Bernardo, on their watch,
    In the dead vast and middle of the night,
    Been thus encounter'd. A figure like your father,
    Armed at point exactly, cap-a-pe,                                         200
    Appears before them, and with solemn march
    Goes slow and stately by them: thrice he walk'd
    By their oppress'd and fear-surprisèd eyes,
    Within his truncheon's length; whilst they, distill'd
    Almost to jelly with the act of fear,                                       205

---

169. *A truant disposition:* an idling mood.
173. *no truant:* no idler.
181. *coldly:* when cold.
182. *dearest:* bitterest. "Dear" was used by the Elizabethans to denote intensity of feeling in either direction.
192. *Season your admiration:* restrain your astonishment.
200. *at point:* completely. *cap-a-pe:* from head to foot.

Stand dumb, and speak not to him. This to me
In dreadful secrecy impart they did;
And I with them the third night kept the watch:
Where, as they had deliver'd, both in time,
Form of the thing, each word made true and good,     210
The apparition comes: I knew your father;
These hands were not more like.

HAMLET.                                  But where was this?
MARCELLUS. My lord, upon the platform where we watch'd.
HAMLET. Did you not speak to it?
HORATIO.                                  My lord, I did.
But answer made it none: yet once methought     215
It lifted up its head and did address
Itself to motion, like as it would speak:
But even then the morning cock crew loud,
And at the sound it shrunk in haste away
And vanish'd from our sight.

HAMLET.                                  'Tis very strange.     220
HORATIO. As I do live, my honor'd lord, 'tis true,
And we did think it writ down in our duty
To let you know of it.
HAMLET. Indeed, indeed, sirs, but this troubles me.
Hold you the watch to-night?

MARCELLUS. ⎱
                   We do, my lord.     225
BERNARDO. ⎰
HAMLET. Arm'd, say you?

MARCELLUS. ⎱
                   Arm'd, my lord.
BERNARDO. ⎰
HAMLET.                                  From top to toe?

MARCELLUS. ⎱
              My lord, from head to foot.
BERNARDO. ⎰
HAMLET. Then saw you not his face?
HORATIO. O, yes, my lord; he wore his beaver up.     230
HAMLET. What, look'd he frowningly?
HORATIO. A countenance more in sorrow than in anger.
HAMLET. Pale, or red?
HORATIO. Nay, very pale.
HAMLET.                                  And fix'd his eyes upon you?
HORATIO. Most constantly.
HAMLET.                                  I would I had been there.     235
HORATIO. It would have much amazed you.
HAMLET. Very like, very like. Stay'd it long?
HORATIO. While one with moderate haste might tell a hundred.

230. *beaver:* visor.          238. *tell:* count.

MARCELLUS. ⎰
BERNARDO. ⎱ Longer, longer.

HORATIO. Not when I saw't.

HAMLET.                His beard was grizzled? no?          240

HORATIO. It was, as I have seen it in his life,
   A sable silver'd.

HAMLET.          I will watch to-night;
   Perchance 'twill walk again.

HORATIO.                I warrant it will.

HAMLET. If it assume my noble father's person,
   I'll speak to it, though hell itself should gape
   And bid me hold my peace. I pray you all,          245
   If you have hitherto conceal'd this sight,
   Let it be tenable in your silence still,
   And whatsoever else shall hap to-night,
   Give it an understanding, but no tongue:
   I will requite your loves. So fare you well:
   Upon the platform, 'twixt eleven and twelve,          250
   I'll visit you.

ALL.          Our duty to your honor.

HAMLET. Your loves, as mine to you: farewell.
   [*Exeunt all but* HAMLET.]
   My father's spirit in arms! all is not well;          255
   I doubt some foul play: would the night were come!
   Till then sit still, my soul: foul deeds will rise,
   Though all the earth o'erwhelm them, to men's eyes.
   [*Exit.*]

SCENE 3—*A room in Polonius's house.*

[*Enter* LAERTES *and* OPHELIA.]

LAERTES. My necessaries are embark'd: farewell:
   And, sister, as the winds give benefit
   And convoy is assistant, do not sleep,
   But let me hear from you.

OPHELIA.                Do you doubt that?

LAERTES. For Hamlet, and the trifling of his favor,          5
   Hold it a fashion, and a toy in blood,
   A violet in the youth of primy nature,
   Forward, not permanent, sweet, not lasting,
   The perfume and suppliance of a minute;
   No more.

OPHELIA.          No more but so?

242. *sable:* black.
248. *Let it be tenable in your silence:* consider it still a secret.
256. *doubt:* suspect.

3. *convoy:* conveyance.
6. *a fashion:* a passing mood.
7. *primy:* early, young.
8. *Forward:* early.

LAERTES.                         Think it no more:                    10
For nature crescent does not grow alone
In thews and bulk; but, as this temple waxes,
The inward service of the mind and soul
Grows wide withal. Perhaps he loves you now;
And now no soil nor cautel doth besmirch            15
The virtue of his will: but you must fear,
His greatness weigh'd, his will is not his own;
For he himself is subject to his birth:
He may not, as unvalued persons do,
Carve for himself, for on his choice depends       20
The safety and health of this whole state,
And therefore must his choice be circumscribed
Unto the voice and yielding of that body
Whereof he is the head. Then if he says he loves you,
It fits your wisdom so far to believe it             25
As he in his particular act and place
May give his saying deed; which is no further
Than the main voice of Denmark goes withal.
Then weigh what loss your honor may sustain,
If with too credent ear you list his songs,         30
Or lose your heart, or your chaste treasure open
To his unmaster'd importunity.
Fear it, Ophelia, fear it, my dear sister,
And keep you in the rear of your affection,
Out of the shot and danger of desire.                35
The chariest maid is prodigal enough,
If she unmask her beauty to the moon:
Virtue itself 'scapes not calumnious strokes:
The canker galls the infants of the spring
Too oft before their buttons be disclosed,          40
And in the morn and liquid dew of youth
Contagious blastments are most imminent.
Be wary then; best safety lies in fear:
Youth to itself rebels, though none else near.

OPHELIA. I shall the effect of this good lesson keep,   45
As watchman to my heart. But, good my brother,
Do not, as some ungracious pastors do,
Show me the steep and thorny way to heaven,
Whilst, like a puff'd and reckless libertine,

11. *crescent:* growing.
12. *this temple:* the body.
15. *no soil nor cautel:* no foul or deceitful thoughts.
17. *His greatness weigh'd:* when you consider his rank.
20. *Carve:* choose.

23. *yielding:* assent.
28. *main:* powerful. *goes withal:* goes along with, agrees.
30. *credent:* credulous.
36. *chariest:* most thoughtful.
39. *canker:* caterpillar.

Himself the primrose path of dalliance treads                          50
And recks not his own rede.
LAERTES.                              O, fear me not.
I stay too long; but here my father comes.
    [*Enter* POLONIUS.]
A double blessing is a double grace;
Occasion smiles upon a second leave.
POLONIUS. Yet here, Laertes! Aboard, aboard, for shame!                55
The wind sits in the shoulder of your sail,
And you are stay'd for. There; my blessing with thee!
And these few precepts in thy memory
See thou charàcter. Give thy thoughts no tongue,
Nor any unproportion'd thought his act.                                60
Be thou familiar, but by no means vulgar.
Those friends thou hast, and their adoption tried,
Grapple them to thy soul with hoops of steel,
But do not dull thy palm with entertainment
Of each new-hatch'd unfledged comrade. Beware                          65
Of entrance to a quarrel; but being in,
Bear't, that the opposèd may beware of thee.
Give every man thy ear, but few thy voice:
Take each man's censure, but reserve thy judgment.
Costly thy habit as thy purse can buy,                                 70
But not express'd in fancy; rich, not gaudy:
For the apparel oft proclaims the man;
And they in France of the best rank and station
Are of a most select and generous chief in that.
Neither a borrower nor a lender be:                                    75
For loan oft loses both itself and friend,
And borrowing dulls the edge of husbandry.
This above all: to thine own self be true,
And it must follow, as the night the day,
Thou canst not then be false to any man.                               80
Farewell: my blessing season this in thee!
LAERTES. Most humbly do I take my leave, my lord.
POLONIUS. The time invites you; go, your servants tend.
LAERTES. Farewell, Ophelia, and remember well
What I have said to you.
OPHELIA.                          'Tis in my memory lock'd,            85
And you yourself shall keep the key of it.

---

51. *recks not his own rede:* does not
follow his own advice.
    59. *charàcter:* engrave in your mem-
ory.
    60. *unproportion'd:* unsuitable.
    64. *dull thy palm:* make the palm
of your hand callous (by indiscriminate handshaking).
    69. *censure:* opinion.
    74. *chief:* chiefly.
    77. *husbandry:* economy.
    81. *season:* ripen.
    83. *tend:* wait.

LAERTES. Farewell. [*Exit.*]

POLONIUS.                    What is't, Ophelia, he hath said to you?

OPHELIA. So please you, something touching the Lord Hamlet.

POLONIUS. Marry, well bethought:

'Tis told me, he hath very oft of late                               90
Given private time to you, and you yourself
Have of your audience been most free and bounteous:
If it be so—as so 'tis put on me,
And that in way of caution—I must tell you,
You do not understand yourself so clearly                         95
As it behoves my daughter and your honor.
What is between you? give me up the truth.

OPHELIA. He hath, my lord, of late made many tenders
Of his affection to me.

POLONIUS. Affection! pooh! you speak like a green girl,          100
Unsifted in such perilous circumstance.
Do you believe his tenders, as you call them?

OPHELIA. I do not know, my lord, what I should think.

POLONIUS. Marry, I'll teach you: think yourself a baby,
That you have ta'en these tenders for true pay,                  105
Which are not sterling. Tender yourself more dearly;
Or—not to crack the wind of the poor phrase,
Running it thus—you'll tender me a fool.

OPHELIA. My lord, he hath importuned me with love
In honorable fashion.                                            110

POLONIUS. Aye, fashion you may call it; go to, go to.

OPHELIA. And hath given countenance to his speech, my lord,
With almost all the holy vows of heaven.

POLONIUS. Aye, springes to catch woodcocks. I do know,
When the blood burns, how prodigal the soul                      115
Lends the tongue vows: these blazes, daughter,
Giving more light than heat, extinct in both,
Even in their promise, as it is a-making,
You must not take for fire. From this time
Be something scanter of your maiden presence;                    120
Set your entreatments at a higher rate
Than a command to parley. For Lord Hamlet,
Believe so much in him, that he is young,
And with a larger tether may he walk
Than may be given you: in few, Ophelia,                          125
Do not believe his vows; for they are brokers,

98. *tenders:* offers.
101. *Unsifted:* untried.
106. *Tender yourself:* regard yourself.
108. *you'll tender me a fool:* you'll furnish me with a fool (a foolish daughter).
112. *countenance:* authority.
114. *springes:* snares.
121. *entreatments:* conversation, company.
126. *brokers:* procurers, panders.

Not of that dye which their investments show,
But mere implorators of unholy suits,
Breathing like sanctified and pious bawds,
The better to beguile. This is for all:                    130
I would not, in plain terms, from this time forth,
Have you so slander any moment leisure,
As to give words or talk with the Lord Hamlet.
Look to't, I charge you: come your ways.
OPHELIA. I shall obey, my lord.                            135
    [*Exeunt.*]

SCENE 4—*The platform.*

    [*Enter* HAMLET, HORATIO, *and* MARCELLUS.]
HAMLET. The air bites shrewdly; it is very cold.
HORATIO. It is a nipping and an eager air.
HAMLET. What hour now?
HORATIO.                 I think it lacks of twelve.
MARCELLUS. No, it is struck.
HORATIO. Indeed? I heard it not: it then draws near the season    5
Wherein the spirit held his wont to walk.
    [*A flourish of trumpets, and ordnance shot off within.*]
What doth this mean, my lord?
HAMLET. The king doth wake to-night, and takes his rouse,
Keeps wassail, and the swaggering up-spring reels;
And as he drains his draughts of Rhenish down,             10
The kettle-drum and trumpet thus bray out
The triumph of his pledge.
HORATIO.              Is it a custom?
HAMLET. Aye, marry, is't:
But to my mind, though I am native here
And to the manner born, it is a custom                     15
More honor'd in the breach than the observance.
This heavy-headed revel east and west
Makes us traduced and tax'd of other nations:
They clepe us drunkards, and with swinish phrase
Soil our addition; and indeed it takes                     20
From our achievements, though perform'd at height,
The pith and marrow of our attribute.
So, oft it chances in particular men,
That for some vicious mole of nature in them,

127. *investments:* clothes.
132. *slander:* use badly. *moment:* momentary.
  2. *eager:* sharp.
  9. *up-spring:* a wild dance.
  10. *Rhenish:* Rhine wine.
  12. *The triumph of his pledge:* his drinking exploits

18. *tax'd:* blamed.
19. *clepe:* call.
20. *addition:* title, reputation.
21. *perform'd at height:* done in the best possible manner.
22. *attribute:* reputation.
24. *mole of nature:* natural blemish.

As, in their birth,—wherein they are not guilty,                    25
Since nature cannot choose his origin,—
By ·the o'ergrowth of some complexion,
Oft breaking down the pales and forts of reason,
Or by some habit that too much o'er-leavens
The form of plausive manners, that these men,—            30
Carrying, I say, the stamp of one defect,
Being nature's livery, or fortune's star,—
Their virtues else—be they as pure as grace,
As infinite as man may undergo—
Shall in the general censure take corruption            35
From that particular fault: the dram of evil
Doth all the noble substance often dout
To his own scandal.
      [*Enter* GHOST.]
HORATIO.              Look, my lord it comes!
HAMLET. Angels and ministers of grace defend us!
  Be thou a spirit of health or goblin damn'd,            40
  Bring with thee airs from heaven or blasts from hell,
  Be thy intents wicked or charitable,
  Thou comest in such a questionable shape
  That I will speak to thee: I'll call thee Hamlet,
  King, father, royal Dane: O, answer me!            45
  Let me not burst in ignorance; but tell
  Why thy canonized bones, hearsèd in death,
  Have burst their cerements; why the sepulchre,
  Wherein we saw thee quietly inurn'd,
  Hath oped his ponderous and marble jaws,            50
  To cast thee up again. What may this mean,
  That thou, dead corse, again, in complete steel,
  Revisit'st thus the glimpses of the moon,
  Making night hideous; and we fools of nature
  So horridly to shake our disposition            55
  With thoughts beyond the reaches of our souls?
  Say, why is this? wherefore? what should we do?
      [GHOST *beckons* HAMLET.]
HORATIO. It beckons you to go away with it,
  As if it some impartment did desire

---

26. *his:* its.
27. *o'ergrowth of some complexion:*
excess in one side of their temperament.
29. *o'er-leavens:* modifies.
30. *plausive:* agreeable.
32. *nature's livery, or fortune's star:*
a nature-given trait or an accidental
mark.
33. *Their virtues else:* the rest of
their qualities.

36–37. *the dram . . . often dout*
our text follows Kittredge's reading of
this difficult passage.
36. *dram:* small bit.
37. *dout:* extinguish, nullify.
38. *To his own scandal:* to its own
harm.
48. *cerements:* shroud made of waxed
cloth.

To you alone.

MARCELLUS. Look, with what courteous action           60
  It waves you to a more removèd ground:
  But do not go with it.

HORATIO.                              No, by no means.

HAMLET. It will not speak; then I will follow it.

HORATIO. Do not, my lord.

HAMLET.                              Why, what should be the fear?
  I do not set my life at a pin's fee;                 65
  And for my soul, what can it do to that,
  Being a thing immortal as itself?
  It waves me forth again: I'll follow it.

HORATIO. What if it tempt you toward the flood, my lord,
  Or to the dreadful summit of the cliff              70
  That beetles o'er his base into the sea,
  And there assume some other horrible form,
  Which might deprive your sovereignty of reason
  And draw you into madness? think of it:
  The very place puts toys of desperation,            75
  Without more motive, into every brain
  That looks so many fathoms to the sea
  And hears it roar beneath.

HAMLET.                              It waves me still.
  Go on; I'll follow thee.

MARCELLUS. You shall not go, my lord.

HAMLET.                              Hold off your hands.      80

HORATIO. Be ruled; you shall not go.

HAMLET.                              My fate cries out,
  And makes each petty artery in this body
  As hardy as the Nemean lion's nerve.
  Still am I call'd, unhand me, gentlemen;
  By heaven, I'll make a ghost of him that lets me:  85
  I say, away! Go on; I'll follow thee.

    [*Exeunt* GHOST *and* HAMLET.]

HORATIO. He waxes desperate with imagination.

MARCELLUS. Let's follow; 'tis not fit thus to obey him.

HORATIO. Have after. To what issue will this come?

MARCELLUS. Something is rotten in the state of Denmark.  90

HORATIO. Heaven will direct it.

MARCELLUS.                              Nay, let's follow him.

    [*Exeunt.*]

---

65. *fee:* value.
71. *beetles o'er:* juts over.
73. *deprive . . . reason:* deprive you
of reason, your sovereign quality.
75. *toys:* fancies.

83. *Nemean lion:* slain by Hercules
as one of his twelve labors. *nerve:*
muscle.
85. *lets:* hinders.

SCENE 5—*Another part of the platform.*

[*Enter* GHOST *and* HAMLET.]

HAMLET. Whither wilt thou lead me? speak; I'll go no further.

GHOST. Mark me.

HAMLET.         I will.

GHOST.                 My hour is almost come,
  When I to sulphurous and tormenting flames
  Must render up myself.

HAMLET.              Alas, poor ghost!

GHOST. Pity me not, but lend thy serious hearing         5
  To what I shall unfold.

HAMLET.            Speak; I am bound to hear.

GHOST. So art thou to revenge, when thou shalt hear.

HAMLET. What?

GHOST. I am thy father's spirit;
  Doom'd for a certain term to walk the night,         10
  And for the day confined to fast in fires,
  Till the foul crimes done in my days of nature
  Are burnt and purged away. But that I am forbid
  To tell the secrets of my prison-house,
  I could a tale unfold whose lightest word         15
  Would harrow up thy soul, freeze thy young blood,
  Make thy two eyes, like stars, start from their spheres,
  Thy knotted and combined locks to part
  And each particular hair to stand on end,
  Like quills upon the fretful porpentine:         20
  But this eternal blazon must not be
  To ears of flesh and blood. List, list, O, list!
  If thou didst ever thy dear father love—

HAMLET. O God!

GHOST. Revenge his foul and most unnatural murder.     25

HAMLET.                       Murder!

GHOST. Murder most foul, as in the best it is,
  But this most foul, strange, and unnatural.

HAMLET. Haste me to know't, that I, with wings as swift
  As meditation or the thoughts of love,         30
  May sweep to my revenge.

GHOST.             I find thee apt;
  And duller shouldst thou be than the fat weed
  That roots itself in ease on Lethe wharf,
  Wouldst thou not stir in this. Now, Hamlet, hear:

3. *flames:* of purgatory.
20 *porpentine:* porcupine.
21. *eternal blazon:* publication of secrets of the other world (i.e., of eternity).
33. *Lethe:* the river of oblivion in Hades.

'Tis given out that, sleeping in my orchard,     35
A serpent stung me; so the whole ear of Denmark
Is by a forgèd process of my death
Rankly abused: but know, thou noble youth,
The serpent that did sting thy father's life
Now wears his crown.

HAMLET.          O my prophetic soul!     40
My uncle!

GHOST. Aye, that incestuous, that adulterate beast,
With witchcraft of his wit, with traitorous gifts,—
O wicked wit and gifts, that have the power
So to seduce!—won to his shameful lust     45
The will of my most seeming-virtuous queen:
O Hamlet, what a falling-off was there!
From me, whose love was of that dignity
That it went hand in hand even with the vow
I made to her in marriage; and to decline     50
Upon a wretch, whose natural gifts were poor
To those of mine!
But virtue, as it never will be moved,
Though lewdness court it in a shape of heaven,
So lust, though to a radiant angel link'd,     55
Will sate itself in a celestial bed
And prey on garbage.
But, soft! methinks I scent the morning air;
Brief let me be. Sleeping within my orchard,
My custom always of the afternoon,     60
Upon my secure hour thy uncle stole,
With juice of cursed hebenon in a vial,
And in the porches of my ears did pour
The leperous distilment; whose effect
Holds such an enmity with blood of man     65
That swift as quicksilver it courses through
The natural gates and alleys of the body;
And with a sudden vigor it doth posset
And curd, like eager droppings into milk,
The thin and wholesome blood: so did it mine;     70
And a most instant tetter bark'd about,
Most lazar-like, with vile and loathsome crust,
All my smooth body.

54. *a shape of heaven:* a heavenly, angelic form.
62. *hebenon:* henbane, a very poisonous herb.
68. *posset:* coagulate.
69. *eager:* sour (compare "vinegar"; in French, *vinaigre,* from *vin aigre*).

71. *a most instant . . . about:* the skin immediately became thick like the bark of a tree.
72. *lazar:* leper (from the beggar Lazarus, "full of sores," in Luke 16: 20).

Thus was I, sleeping, by a brother's hand
Of life, of crown, of queen, at once dispatch'd:                    75
Cut off even in the blossoms of my sin,
Unhousel'd, disappointed, unaneled;
No reckoning made, but sent to my account
With all my imperfections on my head:
O, horrible! O, horrible! most horrible!                           80
If thou hast nature in thee, bear it not;
Let not the royal bed of Denmark be
A couch for luxury and damned incest.
But, howsoever thou pursuest this act,
Taint not thy mind, nor let thy soul contrive                      85
Against thy mother aught: leave her to heaven,
And to those thorns that in her bosom lodge,
To prick and sting her. Fare thee well at once!
The glow-worm shows the matin to be near,
And 'gins to pale his uneffectual fire:                            90
Adieu, adieu, adieu! remember me.                      [*Exit.*]
HAMLET. O all you host of heaven! O earth! what else?
And shall I couple hell? O, fie! Hold, hold, my heart;
And you, my sinews, grow not instant old,
But bear me stiffly up. Remember thee!                             95
Aye, thou poor ghost, while memory holds a seat
In this distracted globe. Remember thee!
Yea, from the table of my memory
I'll wipe away all trivial fond records,
All saws of books, all forms, all pressures past,                  100
That youth and observation copied there;
And thy commandment all alone shall live
Within the book and volume of my brain,
Unmix'd with baser matter: yes, by heaven!
O most pernicious woman!                                           105
O villain, villain, smiling, damnèd villain!
My tables,—meet it is I set it down,
That one may smile, and smile, and be a villain;
At least I'm sure it may be so in Denmark.            [*Writing.*]
So, uncle, there you are. Now to my word;                          110
It is 'Adieu, adieu! remember me.'
I have sworn't.

HORATIO.  ⎫
MARCELLUS. ⎬ [*Within*] My lord, my lord!

    [*Enter* HORATIO *and* MARCELLUS.]

MARCELLUS.                              Lord Hamlet!

77. *Unhousel'd, disappointed, un-aneled:* without sacrament, unprepared, without extreme unction.

97. *globe:* head.
98. *table:* writing tablet. The word is used in the same sense in l. 107.

HORATIO. Heaven secure him!

HAMLET. So be it!

MARCELLUS. Illo, ho, ho, my lord! 115

HAMLET. Hillo, ho, ho, boy! come, bird, come.

MARCELLUS. How is't, my noble lord?

HORATIO. What news, my lord?

HAMLET. O, wonderful!

HORATIO. Good my lord, tell it.

HAMLET. No; you will reveal it.

HORATIO. Not I, my lord, by heaven.

MARCELLUS. Nor I, my lord. 120

HAMLET. How say you, then; would heart of man once think it?
But you'll be secret?

HORATIO. }
MARCELLUS. } Aye, by heaven, my lord.

HAMLET. There's ne'er a villain dwelling in all Denmark
But he's an arrant knave.

HORATIO. There needs no ghost, my lord, come from the grave 125
To tell us this.

HAMLET. Why, right; you are i' the right;
And so, without more circumstance at all,
I hold it fit that we shake hands and part:
You, as your business and desire shall point you;
For every man hath business and desire, 130
Such as it is; and for my own poor part,
Look you, I'll go pray.

HORATIO. These are but wild and whirling words, my lord.

HAMLET. I'm sorry they offend you, heartily;
Yes, faith, heartily.

HORATIO. There's no offense, my lord. 135

HAMLET. Yes, by Saint Patrick, but there is, Horatio,
And much offense too. Touching this vision here,
It is an honest ghost, that let me tell you:
For your desire to know what is between us,
O'ermaster't as you may. And now, good friends, 140
As you are friends, scholars and soldiers,
Give me one poor request.

HORATIO. What is't, my lord? we will.

HAMLET. Never make known what you have seen tonight.

MARCELLUS. }
HORATIO. } My lord, we will not.

HAMLET. Nay, but swear't.

HORATIO. In faith,
My lord, not I.

115. *Illo* . . . : a falconer's call.    127. *circumstance*: ceremony.

MARCELLUS.     Nor I, my lord, in faith.   145

HAMLET. Upon my sword.

MARCELLUS.     We have sworn, my lord, already.

HAMLET. Indeed, upon my sword, indeed.

GHOST. [*Beneath*]       Swear.

HAMLET. Ah, ha, boy! say'st thou so? art thou there, true-penny?
 Come on: you hear this fellow in the cellarage:
 Consent to swear.

HORATIO.     Propose the oath, my lord.  150

HAMLET. Never to speak of this that you have seen,
 Swear by my sword.

GHOST. [*Beneath*] Swear.

HAMLET. Hic et ubique? then we'll shift our ground.
 Come hither, gentlemen,   155
 And lay your hands again upon my sword:
 Never to speak of this that you have heard,
 Swear by my sword.

GHOST. [*Beneath*] Swear.

HAMLET. Well said, old mole! canst work i' the earth so fast? 160
 A worthy pioner! Once more remove, good friends.

HORATIO. O day and night, but this is wondrous strange!

HAMLET. And therefore as a stranger give it welcome.
 There are more things in heaven and earth, Horatio,
 Than are dreamt of in your philosophy.  165
 But come;
 Here, as before, never, so help you mercy,
 How strange or odd soe'er I bear myself,
 As I perchance hereafter shall think meet
 To put an antic disposition on,  170
 That you, at such times seeing me, never shall,
 With arms encumber'd thus, or this head-shake,
 Or by pronouncing of some doubtful phrase,
 As 'Well, well, we know,' or 'We could, an if we would,'
 Or 'If we list to speak,' or 'There be, an if they might,' 175
 Or such ambiguous giving out, to note
 That you know aught of me: this not to do,
 So grace and mercy at your most need help you,
 Swear.

GHOST. [*Beneath*] Swear.   180

HAMLET. Rest, rest, perturbed spirit!   [*They swear.*]
 So, gentlemen,
 With all my love I do commend me to you:
 And what so poor a man as Hamlet is

148. *true-penny:* honest fellow.  161. *pioner:* miner.
154. *Hic et ubique:* here and every-  170. *antic:* odd, fantastic.
where.  172. *encumber'd:* folded.

May do, to express his love and friending to you,                185
God willing, shall not lack. Let us go in together;
And still your fingers on your lips, I pray.
The time is out of joint: O cursed spite,
That ever I was born to set it right!
Nay, come, let's go together.                190
    [*Exeunt.*]

## Act II

SCENE 1—*A room in Polonius's house.*

[*Enter* POLONIUS *and* REYNALDO.]

POLONIUS. Give him this money and these notes, Reynaldo.
REYNALDO. I will, my lord.
POLONIUS. You shall do marvelous wisely, good Reynaldo,
Before you visit him, to make inquire
Of his behavior.
REYNALDO.        My lord, I did intend it.                5
POLONIUS. Marry, well said, very well said. Look you, sir,
Inquire me first what Danskers are in Paris,
And how, and who, what means, and where they keep,
What company, at what expense, and finding
By this encompassment and drift of question                10
That they do know my son, come you more nearer
Than your particular demands will touch it:
Take you, as 'twere, some distant knowledge of him,
As thus, 'I know his father and his friends,
And in part him:' do you mark this, Reynaldo?                15
REYNALDO. Aye, very well, my lord.
POLONIUS. 'And in part him; but,' you may say, 'not well:
But if 't be he I mean, he's very wild,
Addicted so and so;' and there put on him
What forgeries you please; marry, none so rank                20
As may dishonor him; take heed of that;
But, sir, such wanton, wild and usual slips
As are companions noted and most known
To youth and liberty.
REYNALDO.        As gaming, my lord.
POLONIUS. Aye, or drinking, fencing, swearing, quarreling,                25
Drabbing: you may go so far.
REYNALDO. My lord, that would dishonor him.
POLONIUS. Faith, no; as you may season it in the charge.

---

*1. Danskers:* Danes.
*8. keep:* dwell.
*10. encompassment:* roundabout way.

*drift of question:* turn of your talk.
*28. season:* temper, qualify. *in the charge:* in making the accusation.

**You must not put another scandal on him,**
That he is open to incontinency;                                       30
That's not my meaning: but breathe his faults so quaintly
That they may seem the taints of liberty,
The flash and outbreak of a fiery mind,
A savageness in unreclaimèd blood,
Of general assault.

REYNALDO.                    But, my good lord,—               35
POLONIUS. Wherefore should you do this?
REYNALDO.                              Aye, my lord,
I would know that.
POLONIUS.                    Marry, sir, here's my drift,
And I believe it is a fetch of warrant:
You laying these slight sullies on my son,
As 'twere a thing a little soil'd i' the working,             40
Mark you,
Your party in converse, him you would sound,
Having ever seen in the prenominate crimes
The youth you breathe of guilty, be assured
He closes with you in this consequence;                       45
'Good sir,' or so, or 'friend,' or 'gentleman,'
According to the phrase or the addition
Of man and country.
REYNALDO.                    Very good, my lord.               48
POLONIUS. And then, sir, does he this—he does—what was I about
to say? By the mass, I was about to say something: where did I
leave?
REYNALDO. At 'closes in the consequence,' at 'friend or so,' and
'gentleman.'
POLONIUS. At 'closes in the consequence,' aye, marry;          49
He closes with you thus: 'I know the gentleman;
I saw him yesterday, or t' other day,
Or then, or then, with such, or such, and, as you say,
There was a' gaming, there o'ertook in 's rouse,
There falling out at tennis:' or perchance,
'I saw him enter such a house of sale,'                        55
Videlicet, a brothel, or so forth.
See you now;
Your bait of falsehood takes this carp of truth:

---

31. *quaintly:* delicately, skillfully.
32. *taints:* stains, faults.
34. *unreclaimèd:* untamed.
35. *of general assault:* dangers to whose assault all are exposed.
38. *fetch:* stratagem. *of warrant:* warrantable, justifiable.
42. *converse:* conversation.

43. *Having ever:* whether he has ever. *prenominate:* aforementioned.
44–45. *be assured . . . consequence:* you may be sure he will agree in this conclusion.
47. *addition:* title.
53. *o'ertook in 's rouse:* intoxicated in his reveling.

And thus do we of wisdom and of reach,
With windlasses and with assays of bias,                          60
By indirections find directions out:
So, by my former lecture and advice,
Shall you my son. You have me, have you not?

REYNALDO. My lord, I have.

POLONIUS.                    God be wi' ye; fare ye well.

REYNALDO. Good my lord!                                          65

POLONIUS. Observe his inclination in yourself.

REYNALDO. I shall, my lord.

POLONIUS. And let him ply his music.

REYNALDO.                    Well, my lord.

POLONIUS. Farewell!                            [*Exit* REYNALDO.]
          [*Enter* OPHELIA.]
How now, Ophelia! what's the matter?                            70

OPHELIA. O, my lord, I have been so affrighted!

POLONIUS. With what, i' the name of God?

OPHELIA. My lord, as I was sewing in my closet,
Lord Hamlet, with his doublet all unbraced,
No hat upon his head, his stockings foul'd,                      75
Ungarter'd and down-gyvèd to his ankle;
Pale as his shirt, his knees knocking each other,
And with a look so piteous in purport
As if he had been loosèd out of hell
To speak of horrors, he comes before me.                        80

POLONIUS. Mad for thy love?

OPHELIA.                    My lord, I do not know,
But truly I do fear it.

POLONIUS.                    What said he?

OPHELIA. He took me by the wrist and held me hard;
Then goes he to the length of all his arm,
And with his other hand thus o'er his brow,                     85
He falls to such perusal of my face
As he would draw it. Long stay'd he so;
At last, a little shaking of mine arm,
And thrice his head thus waving up and down,
He raised a sigh so piteous and profound                        90
As it did seem to shatter all his bulk
And end his being: that done, he lets me go:
And with his head over his shoulder turn'd,

---

59. *of wisdom and of reach:* wise and farsighted.
60. *windlasses:* winding ways. *assays of bias:* sending the ball indirectly (in bowling).

66. *in yourself:* by yourself.
74. *doublet:* jacket.
76. *down-gyvèd:* pulled down like fetters.

He seem'd to find his way without his eyes;
For out o' doors he went without their help, 95
And to the last bended their light on me.
POLONIUS. Come, go with me: I will go seek the king.
This is the very ecstasy of love;
Whose violent property fordoes itself
And leads the will to desperate undertakings 100
As oft as any passion under heaven
That does afflict our natures. I am sorry.
What, have you given him any hard words of late?
OPHELIA. No, my good lord, but, as you did command,
I did repel his letters and denied 105
His access to me.
POLONIUS.            That hath made him mad.
I am sorry that with better heed and judgment
I had not quoted him: I fear'd he did but trifle
And meant to wreck thee; but beshrew my jealousy!
By heaven, it is as proper to our age 110
To cast beyond ourselves in our opinions
As it is common for the younger sort
To lack discretion. Come, go we to the king:
This must be known; which, being kept close, might move
More grief to hide than hate to utter love. 115
Come.                                     [*Exeunt.*]

SCENE 2—*A room in the castle.*

[*Flourish. Enter* KING, QUEEN, ROSENCRANTZ, GUILDENSTERN,
*and* ATTENDANTS.]
KING. Welcome, dear Rosencrantz and Guildenstern!
Moreover that we much did long to see you,
The need we have to use you did provoke
Our hasty sending. Something have you heard
Of Hamlet's transformation; so call it, 5
Sith nor the exterior nor the inward man
Resembles that it was. What it should be,
More than his father's death, that thus hath put him
So much from the understanding of himself,
I cannot dream of: I entreat you both, 10
That, being of so young days brought up with him
And sith so neighbor'd to his youth and behavior,

98. *ecstasy:* madness.
99. *Whose . . . itself:* which, when
violent, destroys itself.
108. *quoted:* noted.
109. *beshrew my jealousy:* curse my
suspicion.

111. *cast beyond ourselves:* over-
shoot, go too far.
115. *to hide:* if kept hidden. *to
utter love:* if Hamlet's love is revealed.
6. *Sith:* since.
7. *that:* what.

That you vouchsafe your rest here in our court
Some little time: so by your companies
To draw him on to pleasures, and to gather                    15
So much as from occasion you may glean,
Whether aught to us unknown afflicts him thus,
That open'd lies within our remedy.
QUEEN. Good gentlemen, he hath much talk'd of you,
And sure I am two men there are not living                    20
To whom he more adheres. If it will please you
To show us so much gentry and good will
As to expend your time with us awhile
For the supply and profit of our hope,
Your visitation shall receive such thanks                     25
As fits a king's remembrance.
ROSENCRANTZ.                          Both your majesties
Might, by the sovereign power you have of us,
Put your dread pleasures more into command
Than to entreaty.
GUILDENSTERN.            But we both obey,
And here give up ourselves, in the full bent                  30
To lay our service freely at your feet,
To be commanded.
KING. Thanks, Rosencrantz and gentle Guildenstern.
QUEEN. Thanks, Guildenstern and gentle Rosencrantz:
And I beseech you instantly to visit                          35
My too much changed son. Go, some of you,
And bring these gentlemen where Hamlet is.
GUILDENSTERN. Heavens make our presence and our practices
Pleasant and helpful to him!
QUEEN.                          Aye, amen!
  [*Exeunt* ROSENCRANTZ, GUILDENSTERN, *and some* ATTEND-
  ANTS. —*Enter* POLONIUS.]
POLONIUS. The ambassadors from Norway, my good lord,         40
Are joyfully return'd.
KING. Thou still hast been the father of good news.
POLONIUS. Have I, my lord? I assure my good liege,
I hold my duty as I hold my soul,
Both to my God and to my gracious king:                       45
And I do think, or else this brain of mine
Hunts not the trail of policy so sure
As it hath used to do, that I have found

---

13. *vouchsafe your rest:* consent to
stay.
18. *open'd:* once revealed.
21. *more adheres:* is more attached.
22. *gentry:* courtesy.

28. *Put . . . into:* give your sovereign wishes the form of.
30. *in the full bent:* bent (as a
bow) to the limit.

The very cause of Hamlet's lunacy.

KING. O, speak of that; that do I long to hear.                    50

POLONIUS. Give first admittance to the ambassadors;

My news shall be the fruit to that great feast.

KING. Thyself do grace to them, and bring them in.

[*Exit* POLONIUS.]

He tells me, my dear Gertrude, he hath found

The head and source of all your son's distemper.                    55

QUEEN. I doubt it is no other but the main;

His father's death and our o'erhasty marriage.

KING. Well, we shall sift him.

[*Re-enter* POLONIUS, *with* VOLTIMAND *and* CORNELIUS.]

Welcome, my good friends!

Say, Voltimand, what from our brother Norway?

VOLTIMAND. Most fair return of greetings and desires.              60

Upon our first, he sent out to suppress

His nephew's levies, which to him appear'd

To be a preparation 'gainst the Polack,

But better look'd into, he truly found

It was against your highness: whereat grieved,                      65

That so his sickness, age and impotence

Was falsely borne in hand, sends out arrests

On Fortinbras; which he, in brief, obeys,

Receives rebuke from Norway, and in fine

Makes vow before his uncle never more                               70

To give the assay of arms against your majesty.

Whereon old Norway, overcome with joy,

Gives him three thousand crowns in annual fee

And his commission to employ those soldiers,

So levied as before, against the Polack:                            75

With an entreaty, herein further shown,          [*Giving a paper.*]

That it might please you to give quiet pass

Through your dominions for this enterprise,

On such regards of safety and allowance

As therein are set down.

KING.                          It likes us well,                     80

And at our more consider'd time we'll read,

Answer, and think upon this business.

Meantime we thank you for your well-took labor:

Go to your rest; at night we'll feast together:

Most welcome home!

[*Exeunt* VOLTIMAND *and* CORNELIUS.]

53. *grace:* honor.
59. *Norway:* the king of Norway.
61. *Upon our first:* as soon as we made the request.
67. *borne in hand:* deluded.
69. *in fine:* finally.
71. *assay:* test.
80. *likes:* pleases.

POLONIUS.                    This business is well ended.                    85
 My liege, and madam, to expostulate
 What majesty should be, what duty is,
 Why day is day, night night, and time is time,
 Were nothing but to waste night, day and time.
 Therefore, since brevity is the soul of wit                    90
 And tediousness the limbs and outward flourishes,
 I will be brief. Your noble son is mad:
 Mad call I it; for, to define true madness,
 What is 't but to be nothing else but mad?
 But let that go.
QUEEN.                    More matter, with less art.                    95
POLONIUS. Madam, I swear I use no art at all.
 That he is mad, 'tis true: 'tis true 'tis pity,
 And pity 'tis 'tis true: a foolish figure;
 But farewell it, for I will use no art.
 Mad let us grant him then: and now remains                    100
 That we find out the cause of this effect,
 Or rather say, the cause of this defect,
 For this effect defective comes by cause:
 Thus it remains and the remainder thus.
 Perpend.                    105
 I have a daughter,—have while she is mine,—
 Who in her duty and obedience, mark,
 Hath given me this: now gather and surmise.                    108
  [*Reads.*]
 'To the celestial, and my soul's idol, the most beautified Ophe-
  lia,'—
 That's an ill phrase, a vile phrase; 'beautified' is a vile phrase;
  but you shall hear. Thus:
  [*Reads.*]
 'In her excellent white bosom, these,' &c.
QUEEN. Came this from Hamlet to her?
POLONIUS. Good madam, stay awhile; I will be faithful.
  [*Reads.*]
 'Doubt thou the stars are fire;
  Doubt that the sun doth move;
  Doubt truth to be a liar;
  But never doubt I love.
 'O dear Ophelia, I am ill at these numbers;[a] I have not art to
reckon my groans: but that I love thee best, O most best, believe
it. Adieu.
    'Thine evermore, most dear lady, whilst this

---

98. *figure:* of speech.    *a.* verses.
105. *Perpend:* consider.

machine is to him, HAMLET.'
This in obedience hath my daughter shown me;                    109
And more above, hath his solicitings,
As they fell out by time, by means and place,
All given to mine ear.

KING.                                    But how hath she
Received his love?

POLONIUS.                        What do you think of me?

KING. As of a man faithful and honorable.

POLONIUS. I would fain prove so. But what might you think,    115
When I had seen this hot love on the wing,—
As I perceived it, I must tell you that,
Before my daughter told me,—what might you,
Or my dear majesty your queen here, think,
If I had play'd the desk or table-book,                      120
Or given my heart a winking, mute and dumb,
Or look'd upon this love with idle sight;
What might you think? No, I went round to work,
And my young mistress thus I did bespeak:
'Lord Hamlet is a prince, out of thy star;                    125
This must not be:' and then I prescripts gave her,
That she should lock herself from his resort,
Admit no messengers, receive no tokens.
Which done, she took the fruits of my advice;
And he repulsed, a short tale to make,                        130
Fell into a sadness, then into a fast,
Thence to a watch, thence into a weakness,
Thence to a lightness, and by this declension
Into the madness wherein now he raves
And all we mourn for.                                         135

KING. Do you think this?

QUEEN.                          It may be, very like.

POLONIUS. Hath there been such a time, I 'ld fain know that,
That I have positively said ' 'tis so,'
When it proved otherwise?

KING.                             Not that I know.

POLONIUS. [*Pointing to his head and shoulder*] Take this, from
this, if this be otherwise:                                  140
If circumstances lead me, I will find
Where truth is hid, though it were hid indeed

---

110. *more above:* moreover.
120. *If I had . . . table-book:* if I
had performed the function of a desk
or a notebook (in keeping the matter
secret).
121. *given my heart a winking:* shut

my heart's eye.
123. *round to work:* straight to work.
125. *star:* sphere.
132. *watch:* insomnia.
133. *lightness:* lightheadedness. *declension:* declining.

Within the center.

KING.                 How may we try it further?

POLONIUS. You know, sometimes he walks for hours together
Here in the lobby.

QUEEN.            So he does, indeed.         145

POLONIUS. At such a time I'll loose my daughter to him:
Be you and I behind an arras then;
Mark the encounter: if he love her not,
And be not from his reason fall'n thereon,
Let me be no assistant for a state,         150
But keep a farm and carters.

KING.               We will try it.

QUEEN. But look where sadly the poor wretch comes reading.

POLONIUS. Away, I do beseech you, both away:
I'll board him presently.

[*Exeunt* KING, QUEEN, *and* ATTENDANTS. —*Enter* HAMLET,
*reading.*]

O, give me leave: how does my good Lord Hamlet?     155

HAMLET. Well, God-a-mercy.

POLONIUS. Do you know me, my lord?

HAMLET. Excellent well; you are a fishmonger.

POLONIUS. Not I, my lord.

HAMLET. Then I would you were so honest a man.

POLONIUS. Honest, my lord!

HAMLET. Aye, sir; to be honest, as this world goes, is to be one man
picked out of ten thousand.

POLONIUS. That's very true, my lord.

HAMLET. For if the sun breed maggots in a dead dog, being a good
kissing[b] carrion— Have you a daughter?

POLONIUS. I have, my lord.

HAMLET. Let her not walk i' the sun: conception is a blessing; but
as your daughter may conceive,—friend, look to 't.

POLONIUS. [*Aside*] How say you by that?[c] Still harping on my daughter: yet he knew me not at first; he said I was a fishmonger: he
is far gone: and truly in my youth I suffered much extremity for
love; very near this. I'll speak to him again.—What do you read,
my lord?

HAMLET. Words, words, words.

POLONIUS. What is the matter,[d] my lord?

HAMLET. Between who?

---

143. *center:* of the earth.
149. *thereon:* for that reason.
154. *board:* approach.
*b.* good for kissing.
*c.* What do you say to that?

*d.* The word has several meanings.
Polonius uses it to denote the subject
matter of the book; but Hamlet responds, in the next line, as if he referred to the subject of a quarrel.

POLONIUS. I mean, the matter that you read, my lord.

HAMLET. Slanders, sir: for the satirical rogue says here that old men have gray beards, that their faces are wrinkled, their eyes purging thick amber and plum-tree gum, and that they have a plentiful lack of wit, together with most weak hams: all which, sir, though I most powerfully and potently believe, yet I hold it not honesty to have it thus set down; for yourself, sir, shall grow old as I am, if like a crab you could go backward.

POLONIUS. [*Aside*] Though this be madness, yet there is method in 't.—Will you walk out of the air, my lord?

HAMLET. Into my grave.

POLONIUS. Indeed, that's out of the air.                    [*Aside*]
How pregnant sometimes his replies are! a happiness that often madness hits on, which reason and sanity could not so prosperously be delivered of. I will leave him, and suddenly contrive the means of meeting between him and my daughter.—My honorable lord, I will most humbly take my leave of you.

HAMLET. You cannot, sir, take from me any thing that I will more willingly part withal: except my life, except my life, except my life.

POLONIUS. Fare you well, my lord.

HAMLET. These tedious old fools.

    [*Re-enter* ROSENCRANTZ *and* GUILDENSTERN.]

POLONIUS. You go to seek the Lord Hamlet; there he is.

ROSENCRANTZ [*To* POLONIUS] God save you, sir!

    [*Exit* POLONIUS.]

GUILDENSTERN. My honored lord!

ROSENCRANTZ. My most dear lord!

HAMLET. My excellent good friends! How dost thou, Guildenstern? Ah, Rosencrantz! Good lads, how do you both?

ROSENCRANTZ. As the indifferent[e] children of the earth.

GUILDENSTERN. Happy, in that we are not over-happy;
On Fortune's cap we are not the very button.[f]

HAMLET. Nor the soles of her shoe?

ROSENCRANTZ. Neither, my lord.

HAMLET. Then you live about her waist, or in the middle of her favors?

GUILDENSTERN. Faith, her privates we.

HAMLET. In the secret parts of Fortune? O, most true; she is a strumpet. What's the news?

ROSENCRANTZ. None, my lord, but that the world's grown honest.

HAMLET. Then is doomsday near: but your news is not true. Let me question more in particular: what have you, my good friends,

---

*e.* average.                    *f.* top.

deserved at the hands of Fortune, that she sends you to prison
hither?

GUILDENSTERN. Prison, my lord!

HAMLET. Denmark's a prison.

ROSENCRANTZ. Then is the world one.

HAMLET. A goodly one; in which there are many confines,*g* wards
and dungeons, Denmark being one o' the worst.

ROSENCRANTZ. We think not so, my lord.

HAMLET. Why, then, 'tis none to you; for there is nothing either
good or bad, but thinking makes it so: to me it is a prison.

ROSENCRANTZ. Why, then your ambition makes it one; 'tis too
narrow for your mind.

HAMLET. O God, I could be bounded in a nut-shell and count myself a king of infinite space, were it not that I have bad dreams.

GUILDENSTERN. Which dreams indeed are ambition; for the very
substance of the ambitious is merely the shadow of a dream.

HAMLET. A dream itself is but a shadow.

ROSENCRANTZ. Truly, and I hold ambition of so airy and light a
quality that it is but a shadow's shadow.

HAMLET. Then are our beggars bodies, and our monarchs and outstretched heroes the beggars' shadows.*h* Shall we to the court?
for, by my fay,*i* I cannot reason.

ROSENCRANTZ. } We'll wait upon you.
GUILDENSTERN. }

HAMLET. No such matter: I will not sort you*j* with the rest of my
servants; for, to speak to you like an honest man, I am most
dreadfully attended. But, in the beaten way of friendship, what
make you at Elsinore?

ROSENCRANTZ. To visit you, my lord; no other occasion.

HAMLET. Beggar that I am, I am even poor in thanks; but I thank
you: and sure, dear friends, my thanks are too dear a halfpenny.*k*
Were you not sent for? Is it your own inclining? Is it a free
visitation? Come, deal justly*l* with me: come, come; nay, speak.

GUILDENSTERN. What should we say, my lord?

HAMLET. Why, any thing, but to the purpose. You were sent for;
and there is a kind of confession in your looks, which your
modesties have not craft enough to color: I know the good king
and queen have sent for you.

ROSENCRANTZ. To what end, my lord?

HAMLET. That you must teach me. But let me conjure you, by the

*g.* places of confinement.
*h.* Then people without ambition
(like beggars) are the really substantial ones, while monarchs and heroes
are their outstretched shadows.

*i.* faith.
*j.* put you together.
*k.* if priced at a halfpenny.
*l.* honestly.

rights of our fellowship, by the consonancy of our youth, by the obligation of our ever-preserved love, and by what more dear a better proposer[m] could charge you withal, be even and direct with me, whether you were sent for, or no.

ROSENCRANTZ. [*Aside to* GUILDENSTERN] What say you?

HAMLET. [*Aside*] Nay then, I have an eye of[n] you.—If you love me, hold not off.

GUILDENSTERN. My lord, we were sent for.

HAMLET. I will tell you why; so shall my anticipation prevent your discovery,[o] and your secrecy to the king and queen moult no feather. I have of late—but wherefore I know not—lost all my mirth, forgone all custom of exercises; and indeed it goes so heavily with my disposition that this goodly frame, the earth, seems to me a sterile promontory; this most excellent canopy, the air, look you, this brave o'erhanging firmament, this majestical roof fretted[p] with golden fire, why, it appears no other thing to me than a foul and pestilent congregation of vapors. What a piece of work is a man! how noble in reason! how infinite in faculty! in form and moving how expressed[q] and admirable! in action how like an angel! in apprehension how like a god! the beauty of the world! the paragon of animals! And yet, to me, what is this quintessence of dust? man delights not me; no, nor woman neither, though by your smiling you seem to say so.

ROSENCRANTZ. My lord, there was no such stuff in my thoughts.

HAMLET. Why did you laugh then, when I said 'man delights not me'?

ROSENCRANTZ. To think, my lord, if you delight not in man, what lenten entertainment[r] the players shall receive from you: we coted[s] them on the way; and hither are they coming, to offer you service.

HAMLET. He that plays the king shall be welcome; his majesty shall have tribute of me; the adventurous knight shall use his foil and target; the lover shall not sigh gratis; the humorous[t] man shall end his part in peace; the clown shall make those laugh whose lungs are tickle o' the sere,[u] and the lady shall say her mind freely, or the blank verse shall halt for 't. What players are they?

ROSENCRANTZ. Even those you were wont to take such delight in, the tragedians of the city.

HAMLET. How chances it they travel? their residence,[v] both in repu tation and profit, was better both ways.

---

m. speaker.
n. on.
o. precede your disclosure.
p. adorned.
q. perfect.

r. meagre reception.
s. overtook.
t. eccentric, whimsical.
u. ready to shoot off at a touch.
v. i.e., in the city.

ROSENCRANTZ. I think their inhibition[w] comes by means of the late innovation.[x]

HAMLET. Do they hold the same estimation they did when I was in the city? are they so followed?

ROSENCRANTZ. No, indeed, are they not.

HAMLET. How comes it? do they grow rusty?

ROSENCRANTZ. Nay, their endeavor keeps in the wonted pace: but there is, sir, an eyrie[y] of children, little eyases,[z] that cry out on the top of question[a] and are most tyrannically[b] clapped for 't: these are now the fashion, and so berattle[c] the common stages— so they call them—that many wearing rapiers[d] are afraid of goose-quills,[e] and dare scarce come thither.

HAMLET. What, are they children? who maintains 'em? how are they escoted?[f] Will they pursue the quality[g] no longer than they can sing? will they not say afterwards, if they should grow themselves to common players,—as it is most like, if their means are no better,—their writers do them wrong, to make them exclaim against their own succession?[h]

ROSENCRANTZ. Faith, there has been much to-do on both sides, and the nation holds it no sin to tarre[i] them to controversy: there was for a while no money bid for argument unless the poet and the player went to cuffs in the question.[j]

HAMLET. Is 't possible?

GUILDENSTERN. O, there has been much throwing about of brains.

HAMLET. Do the boys carry it away?[k]

ROSENCRANTZ. Aye, that they do, my lord; Hercules and his load too.[l]

HAMLET. It is not very strange; for my uncle is king of Denmark, and those that would make mows[m] at him while my father lived, give twenty, forty, fifty, a hundred ducats a-piece, for his picture in little. 'Sblood, there is something in this more than natural, if philosophy could find it out.

[*Flourish of trumpets within.*]

GUILDENSTERN. There are the players.

HAMLET. Gentlemen, you are welcome to Elsinore. Your hands, come then: the appurtenance of welcome is fashion and ceremony: let me comply with you in this garb,[n] lest my extent[o] to

---

w. prohibition.

x. the introduction of "an eyrie of children," as Rosencrantz explains in his subsequent replies to Hamlet.

y. brood.

z. unfledged birds.

a. in the highest key.

b. vehemently.

c. berate.

d. many gentlemen.

e. afraid of pens (i.e., of poets satirizing the "common stages").

f. financially supported.

g. profession.

h. recite satiric pieces against what they are themselves likely to become, common players.

i. incite.

j. no offer to buy a plot for a play if it did not contain a quarrel between poet and player on that subject.

k. win out.

l. the sign in front of the Globe theater.

m. faces.

n. style.

o. behavior.

the players, which, I tell you, must show fairly outwards, should more appear like entertainment*ᵖ* than yours. You are welcome: but my uncle-father and aunt-mother are deceived.

GUILDENSTERN. In what, my dear lord?

HAMLET. I am but mad north-north-west: when the wind is southerly I know a hawk from a handsaw.*q*

[*Re-enter* POLONIUS.]

POLONIUS. Well be with you, gentlemen!

HAMLET. Hark you, Guildenstern; and you too: at each ear a hearer: that great baby you see there is not yet out of his swaddling clouts.*r*

ROSENCRANTZ. Happily he's the second time come to them; for they say an old man is twice a child.

HAMLET. I will prophesy he comes to tell me of the players; mark it. You say right, sir: o' Monday morning; 'twas so, indeed.*ˢ*

POLONIUS. My lord, I have news to tell you.

HAMLET. My lord, I have news to tell you. When Roscius was an actor in Rome,—

POLONIUS. The actors are come hither, my lord.

HAMLET. Buz, buz!*ᵗ*

POLONIUS. Upon my honor,—

HAMLET. Then came each actor on his ass,—

POLONIUS. The best actors in the world, either for tragedy, comedy, history, pastoral, pastoral-comical, historical-pastoral, tragical-historical, tragical-comical-historical-pastoral, scene individable, or poem unlimited:*ᵘ* Seneca cannot be too heavy, nor Plautus too light. For the law of writ and the liberty,*ᵛ* these are the only men.

HAMLET. O Jephthah, judge of Israel, what a treasure hadst thou!

POLONIUS. What a treasure had he, my lord?

HAMLET. Why,

'One fair daughter, and no more,
The which he lovèd passing well.'*ʷ*

POLONIUS. [*Aside*] Still on my daughter.

HAMLET. Am I not i' the right, old Jephthah?

POLONIUS. If you call me Jephthah, my lord, I have a daughter that I love passing well.

HAMLET. Nay, that follows not.

POLONIUS. What follows, then, my lord?

HAMLET. Why,

'As by lot, God wot.'
and then you know,
     'It came to pass, as most like it was,'—
the first row of the pious chanson*ₓ* will show you more; for look,
where my abridgment*ᵧ* comes.

          [*Enter four or five* PLAYERS.]

You are welcome, masters; welcome, all. I am glad to see thee
well. Welcome, good friends. O, my old friend! Why thy face is
valanced*ᶻ* since I saw thee last; comest thou to beard me in Denmark? What, my young lady and mistress! By'r lady, your ladyship is nearer to heaven than when I saw you last, by the altitude
of a chopine.*ᵃ* Pray God, your voice, like a piece of uncurrent*ᵇ*
gold, be not cracked within the ring.*ᶜ* Masters, you are all welcome. We'll e'en to 't like French falconers,*ᵈ* fly at any thing we
see: we'll have a speech straight: come, give us a taste of your
quality; come, a passionate speech.

FIRST PLAYER. What speech, my good lord?

HAMLET. I heard thee speak me a speech once, but it was never
acted; or, if it was, not above once; for the play, I remember,
pleased not the million; 'twas caviare to the general:*ᵉ* but it was
—as I received it, and others, whose judgments in such matters
cried in the top of mine*ᶠ*—an excellent play, well digested in the
scenes, set down with as much modesty*ᵍ* as cunning. I remember,
one said there were no sallets*ʰ* in the lines to make the matter
savory, nor no matter in the phrase that might indict the author
of affection;*ⁱ* but called it an honest method, as wholesome as
sweet, and by very much more handsome than fine.*ʲ* One speech
in it I chiefly loved: 'twas Æneas' tale to Dido;*ᵏ* and thereabout
of it especially, where he speaks of Priam's*ˡ* slaughter: if it live in
your memory, begin at this line; let me see, let me see;
'The rugged Pyrrhus, like th' Hyrcanian beast,'—          156
It is not so: it begins with 'Pyrrhus.'
'The rugged Pyrrhus, he whose sable arms,
Black as his purpose, did the night resemble
When he lay couched in the ominous horse,          160

*x.* song.
*y.* i.e., the players interrupting him.
*z.* draped (i.e., bearded).
*a.* a shoe with a thick wooden sole, a clog.
*b.* unfit for currency.
*c.* a pun on the "ring" of the voice and the "ring" round the king's head on a coin.
*d.* known for their versatility in hunting.
*e.* a delicacy wasted on the general public.
*f.* were louder (more authoritative) than mine.
*g.* artistic restraint.
*h.* salads (i.e., relish, spiced passages).
*i.* affectation.
*j.* more elegant than showy.
*k.* the story of the fall of Troy, told by Aeneas to queen Dido.
*l.* Priam was king of Troy.
156. *Pyrrhus:* Achilles' son (called also Neoptolemus). *Hyrcanian beast:* tiger.
158. *sable:* black.
160. *horse:* the wooden horse in which Greek warriors were smuggled into Troy.

Hath now this dread and black complexion smear'd
With heraldry more dismal: head to foot
Now is he total gules; horridly trick'd
With the blood of fathers, mothers, daughters, sons,
Baked and impasted with the parching streets,                    165
That lend a tyrannous and a damned light
To their lord's murder: roasted in wrath and fire,
And thus o'er-sizèd with coagulate gore,
With eyes like carbuncles, the hellish Pyrrhus
Old grandsire Priam seeks.'                                       170
So, proceed you.

POLONIUS. 'Fore God, my lord, well spoken, with good accent and
 good discretion.

FIRST PLAYER.    'Anon he finds him
Striking too short at Greeks; his antique sword,
Rebellious to his arm, lies where it falls,                       175
Repugnant to command: unequal match'd,
Pyrrhus at Priam drives; in rage strikes wide;
But with the whiff and wind of his fell sword
The unnerved father falls. Then senseless Ilium,
Seeming to feel this blow, with flaming top                      180
Stoops to his base, and with a hideous crash
Takes prisoner Pyrrhus' ear: for, lo! his sword,
Which was declining on the milky head
Of reverend Priam seem'd i' the air to stick:
So, as a painted tyrant, Pyrrhus stood,                          185
And like a neutral to his will and matter,
Did nothing.
But as we often see, against some storm,
A silence in the heavens, the rack stand still,
The bold winds speechless and the orb below                      190
As hush as death, anon the dreadful thunder
Doth rend the region, so after Pyrrhus' pause
Aroused vengeance sets him new a-work;
And never did the Cyclops' hammers fall
On Mars's armor, forged for proof eterne,                        195
With less remorse than Pyrrhus' bleeding sword
Now falls on Priam.
Out, out, thou strumpet, Fortune! All you gods,
In general synod take away her power,
Break all the spokes and fellies from her wheel,                 200

163. *gules:* heraldic term for red.
*trick'd:* adorned.
166. *tyrannous:* savage.
168. *o'er-sizèd:* glued over.
179. *Ilium:* Troy's citadel.
181. *his:* its.

188. *against:* just before.
189. *rack:* clouds.
194. *Cyclops:* the gigantic workmen
of Hephaestus (Vulcan), god of black-
smiths and fire.
200. *fellies:* rims.

And bowl the round nave down the hill of heaven
     As low as to the fiends!'                                                    202
POLONIUS. This is too long.
HAMLET. It shall to the barbier's, with your beard. Prithee, say on:
     he's for a jig[m] or a tale of bawdry, or he sleeps: say on: come to
     Hecuba.
FIRST PLAYER. 'But who, O, who had seen the mobled queen—'        203
HAMLET. 'The mobled queen'?
POLONIUS. That's good; 'mobled queen' is good.                          205
FIRST PLAYER. 'Run barefoot up and down, threatening the flames
     With bisson rheum; a clout upon that head
     Where late the diadem stood; and for a robe,
     About her lank and all o'er-teemèd loins,
     A blanket, in the alarm of fear caught up:                              210
     Who this had seen, with tongue in venom steep'd
     'Gainst Fortune's state would treason have pronounced:
     But if the gods themselves did see her then,
     When she saw Pyrrhus make malicious sport
     In mincing with his sword her husband's limbs,                     215
     The instant burst of clamor that she made,
     Unless things mortal move them not at all,
     Would have made milch the burning eyes of heaven
     And passion in the gods.'                                                    219
POLONIUS. Look, whether he has not turned his color and has tears
     in 's eyes. Prithee, no more.
HAMLET. 'Tis well; I'll have thee speak out the rest of this soon.
     Good my lord, will you see the players well bestowed?[n] Do you
     hear, let them be well used, for they are the abstracts and brief
     chronicles of the time: after your death you were better have a
     bad epitaph than their ill report while you live.
POLONIUS. My lord, I will use them according to their desert.
HAMLET. God's bodykins,[o] man, much better: use every man after
     his desert, and who shall 'scape whipping? Use them after your
     own honor and dignity: the less they deserve, the more merit is
     in your bounty. Take them in.
POLONIUS. Come, sirs.
HAMLET. Follow him, friends: we'll hear a play to-morrow. [*Exit
     POLONIUS with all the PLAYERS but the first.*] Dost thou hear me,
     old friend; can you play the Murder of Gonzago?
FIRST PLAYER. Aye, my lord.

---

201. *nave:* hub.
  *m.* ludicrous song dialogue, short farce.
  203. *mobled:* muffled.
  207. *bisson rheum:* blinding moisture (tears). *clout:* cloth.
  209. *o'er-teemèd:* worn out by child-bearing.
  212. *state:* government.
  217. *them:* the gods.
  218. *milch:* moist. *eyes of heaven:* the stars.
  *n.* taken care of.
  *o.* diminutive of "body."

HAMLET. We'll ha 't to-morrow night. You could, for a need, study a speech of some dozen or sixteen lines, which I would set down and insert in 't, could you not?

FIRST PLAYER. Aye, my lord.

HAMLET. Very well. Follow that lord; and look you mock him not. [*Exit* FIRST PLAYER.] My good friends, I'll leave you till night: you are welcome to Elsinore.

ROSENCRANTZ. Good my lord!

HAMLET. Aye, so, God be wi' ye! [*Exeunt* ROSENCRANTZ *and* GUIL-
DENSTERN.] Now I am alone.     220

O, what a rogue and peasant slave am I!
Is it not monstrous that this player here,
But in a fiction, in a dream of passion,
Could force his soul so to his own conceit
That from her working all his visage wann'd;     225
Tears in his eyes, distraction in 's aspect,
A broken voice, and his whole function suiting
With forms to his conceit? and all for nothing!
For Hecuba!
What's Hecuba to him, or he to Hecuba,     230
That he should weep for her? What would he do,
Had he the motive and the cue for passion
That I have? He would drown the stage with tears
And cleave the general air with horrid speech,
Make mad the guilty and appal the free,     235
Confound the ignorant, and amaze indeed
The very faculties of eyes and ears.
Yet I,
A dull and muddy-mettled rascal, peak,
Like John-a-dreams, unpregnant of my cause,     240
And can say nothing; no, not for a king,
Upon whose property and most dear life
A damn'd defeat was made. Am I a coward?
Who calls me villain? breaks my pate across?
Plucks off my beard, and blows it in my face?     245
Tweaks me by the nose? gives me the lie i' the throat,
As deep as to the lungs? who does me this?
Ha!
'Swounds, I should take it: for it cannot be
But I am pigeon-liver'd and lack gall     250

224. *conceit:* imagination, conception of the rôle played.
225. *her:* his soul's.
227. *function:* bodily action.
229. *Hecuba:* queen of Troy, Priam's wife.

239. *muddy-mettled:* of poor metal (spirit, temper). *peak:* mope.
240. *John-a-dreams:* a dreamy, absent-minded character. *unpregnant of my cause:* not really conscious of my cause, unquickened by it.
243. *defeat:* undoing.

To make oppression bitter, or ere this
I should have fatted all the region kites
With this slave's offal: bloody, bawdy villain!
Remorseless, treacherous, lecherous, kindless villain!
O, vengeance!                                                                         255
Why, what an ass am I! This is most brave,
That I, the son of a dear father murder'd,
Prompted to my revenge by heaven and hell,
Must, like a whore, unpack my heart with words,
And fall a-cursing, like a very drab,                                       260
A scullion!
Fie upon 't! About, my brain! Hum, I have heard
That guilty creatures, sitting at a play,
Have by the very cunning of the scene
Been struck so to the soul that presently                             265
They have proclaim'd their malefactions;
For murder, though it have no tongue, will speak
With most miraculous organ. I'll have these players
Play something like the murder of my father
Before mine uncle: I'll observe his looks;                            270
I'll tent him to the quick: if he but blench,
I know my course. The spirit that I have seen
May be the devil; and the devil hath power
To assume a pleasing shape; yea, and perhaps
Out of my weakness and my melancholy,                            275
As he is very potent with such spirits,
Abuses me to damn me. I'll have grounds
More relative than this. The play 's the thing
Wherein I'll catch the conscience of the king.         [*Exit.*]

## Act III

### SCENE 1—*A room in the castle.*

[*Enter* KING, QUEEN, POLONIUS, OPHELIA, ROSENCRANTZ, *and*
    GUILDENSTERN.]

KING. And can you, by no drift of circumstance,
    Get from him why he puts on this confusion,
    Grating so harshly all his days of quiet
    With turbulent and dangerous lunacy?
ROSENCRANTZ. He does confess he feels himself distracted,          5
    But from what cause he will by no means speak.
GUILDENSTERN. Nor do we find him forward to be sounded;

254. *kindless:* unnatural.
261. *scullion:* the lowest servant.
262. *About . . . !:* to work!
265. *presently:* immediately.

271. *tent:* probe. *blench:* flinch.
278. *relative:* relevant, positive.
1. *drift of circumstance:* turn of
talk, or roundabout way.

But, with a crafty madness, keeps aloof,
When we would bring him on to some confession
Of his true state.

QUEEN.                     Did he receive you well?                    10

ROSENCRANTZ. Most like a gentleman.

GUILDENSTERN. But with much forcing of his disposition.

ROSENCRANTZ. Niggard of question, but of our demands
Most free in his reply.

QUEEN.                     Did you assay him
To any pastime?                                                      15

ROSENCRANTZ. Madam, it so fell out that certain players
We o'er-raught on the way: of these we told him,
And there did seem in him a kind of joy
To hear of it: they are about the court,
And, as I think, they have already order                             20
This night to play before him.

POLONIUS.                          'Tis most true:
And he besecch'd me to entreat your majesties
To hear and see the matter.

KING. With all my heart; and it doth much content me
To hear him so inclined.                                             25
Good gentlemen, give him a further edge,
And drive his purpose on to these delights.

ROSENCRANTZ. We shall, my lord.
    [*Exeunt* ROSENCRANTZ *and* GUILDENSTERN.]

KING.                     Sweet Gertrude, leave us too;
For we have closely sent for Hamlet hither,
That he, as 'twere by accident, may here                             30
Affront Ophelia:
Her father and myself, lawful espials,
Will so bestow ourselves that, seeing unseen,
We may of their encounter frankly judge,
And gather by him, as he is behaved,                                 35
If 't be the affliction of his love or no
That thus he suffers for.

QUEEN.                     I shall obey you:
And for your part, Ophelia, I do wish
That your good beauties be the happy cause
Of Hamlet's wildness: so shall I hope your virtues                   40
Will bring him to his wonted way again,
To both your honors.

OPHELIA.                     Madam, I wish it may.    [*Exit* QUEEN.]

14. *assay:* try to attract him.          31. *Affront:* confront.
17. *o'er-raught:* overtook.             32. *espials:* spies.
26. *edge:* incitement.                  33. *bestow:* place.
29. *closely:* privately.

POLONIUS. Ophelia, walk you here. Gracious, so please you,
We will bestow ourselves. [*To* OPHELIA] Read on this book;
That show of such an exercise may color                          45
Your loneliness. We are oft to blame in this,—
'Tis too much proved—that with devotion's visage
And pious action we do sugar o'er
The devil himself.

KING. [*Aside*]              O, 'tis too true!
How smart a lash that speech doth give my conscience!           50
The harlot's cheek, beautied with plastering art,
Is not more ugly to the thing that helps it
Than is my deed to my most painted word:
O heavy burthen!

POLONIUS. I hear him coming: let's withdraw, my lord.          55
[*Exeunt* KING *and* POLONIUS. —*Enter Hamlet.*]

HAMLET. To be, or not to be: that is the question:
Whether 'tis nobler in the mind to suffer
The slings and arrows of outrageous fortune,
Or to take arms against a sea of troubles,
And by opposing end them. To die: to sleep;                     60
No more; and by a sleep to say we end
The heart-ache, and the thousand natural shocks
That flesh is heir to, 'tis a consummation
Devoutly to be wish'd. To die, to sleep;
To sleep: perchance to dream: aye, there's the rub;             65
For in that sleep of death what dreams may come,
When we have shuffled off this mortal coil,
Must give us pause: there's the respect
That makes calamity of so long life;
For who would bear the whips and scorns of time,                70
The oppressor's wrong, the proud man's contumely,
The pangs of despised love, the law's delay,
The insolence of office, and the spurns
That patient merit of the unworthy takes,
When he himself might his quietus make                          75
With a bare bodkin? who would fardels bear,
To grunt and sweat under a weary life,
But that the dread of something after death,
The undiscover'd country from whose bourn
No traveler returns, puzzles the will,                          80

45. *color:* excuse.
63. *consummation:* final settlement.
65. *the rub:* the impediment (a bowling term).
67. *have shuffled off this mortal coil:*
have rid ourselves of the turmoil of
mortal life.
68. *respect:* consideration.

69. *of so long life:* so long-lived.
71. *contumely:* scorn.
75. *quietus:* settlement of accounts,
acquittance.
76. *bodkin:* poniard, dagger. *fardels:*
burdens.
79. *bourn:* boundary.

And makes us rather bear those ills we have
Than fly to others that we know not of?
Thus conscience does make cowards of us all,
And thus the native hue of resolution
Is sicklied o'er with the pale cast of thought,                     85
And enterprises of great pitch and moment
With this regard their currents turn awry
And lose the name of action. Soft you now!
The fair Ophelia! Nymph, in thy orisons
Be all my sins remember'd.

OPHELIA.            Good my lord,                     90
How does your honor for this many a day?

HAMLET. I humbly thank you: well, well, well.

OPHELIA. My lord, I have remembrances of yours,
That I have longed to re-deliver;
I pray you, now receive them.

HAMLET.            No, not I;                     95
I never gave you aught.

OPHELIA. My honor'd lord, you know right well you did;
And with them words of so sweet breath composed
As made the things more rich: their perfume lost,
Take these again; for to the noble mind
Rich gifts wax poor when givers prove unkind.                     101
There, my lord.

HAMLET. Ha, ha! are you honest?

OPHELIA. My lord?

HAMLET. Are you fair?

OPHELIA. What means your lordship?

HAMLET. That if you be honest and fair, your honesty should admit
no discourse to your beauty.

OPHELIA. Could beauty, my lord, have better commerce*a* than with
honesty?

HAMLET. Aye, truly; for the power of beauty will sooner transform
honesty from what it is to a bawd than the force of honesty can
translate beauty into his*b* likeness: this was sometime a paradox,
but now the time gives it proof. I did love you once.

OPHELIA. Indeed, my lord, you made me believe so.

HAMLET. You should not have believed me; for virtue cannot so
inoculate*c* our old stock, but we shall relish of*d* it: I loved you not.

OPHELIA. I was the more deceived.

HAMLET. Get thee to a nunnery: why wouldst thou be a breeder of
sinners? I am myself indifferent honest; but yet I could accuse me
of such things that it were better my mother had not borne me:

86. *pitch:* height.
89. *orisons:* **prayers.**
*a.* intercourse.

*b.* its.
*c.* graft (in the botanical sense).
*d.* have a flavor of, smack of.

I am very proud, revengeful, ambitious; with more offenses at my beck than I have thoughts to put them in, imagination to give them shape, or time to act them in. What should such fellows as I do crawling between heaven and earth! We are arrant knaves all; believe none of us. Go thy ways to a nunnery. Where's your father?

OPHELIA. At home, my lord.

HAMLET. Let the doors be shut upon him, that he may play the fool no where but in 's own house. Farewell.

OPHELIA. O, help him, you sweet heavens!

HAMLET. If thou dost marry, I'll give thee this plague for thy dowry: be thou as chaste as ice, as pure as snow, thou shalt not escape calumny. Get thee to a nunnery, go: farewell. Or, if thou wilt needs marry, marry a fool; for wise men know well enough what monsters*e* you make of them. To a nunnery, go; and quickly too. Farewell.

OPHELIA. O heavenly powers, restore him!

HAMLET. I have heard of your paintings too, well enough; God hath given you one face, and you make yourselves another: you jig, you amble, and you lisp, and nick-name God's creatures,*f* and make your wantonness your ignorance.*g* Go to, I'll no more on 't; it hath made me mad. I say, we will have no more marriages: those that are married already, all but one, shall live; the rest shall keep as they are. To a nunnery, go.

    [*Exit.*]

OPHELIA. O, what a noble mind is here o'erthrown!       102
  The courtier's, soldier's, scholar's, eye, tongue, sword:
  The expectancy and rose of the fair state,
  The glass of fashion and the mould of form,      105
  The observed of all observers, quite, quite down!
  And I, of ladies most deject and wretched,
  That suck'd the honey of his music vows,
  Now see that noble and most sovereign reason,
  Like sweet bells jangled, out of tune and harsh;     110
  That unmatch'd form and feature of blown youth
  Blasted with ecstasy: O, woe is me,
  To have seen what I have seen, see what I see!

    [*Re-enter* KING *and* POLONIUS.]

KING. Love! his affections do not that way tend;
  Nor what he spake, though it lack'd form a little,     115
  Was not like madness. There's something in his soul

---

*e.* cuckolds bear imaginary horns, and "a hornèd man's a monster" (*Othello*, Act IV, Scene 1, l. 63).
  *f.* misname (out of affectation) the most natural things.
  *g.* pretend that that is due to igno-rance instead of affectation.
  105. *The glass . . . form:* the mirror of fashion and the model of behavior.
  106. *of:* by.
  112. *ecstasy:* madness.

O'er which his melancholy sits on brood,
And I do doubt the hatch and the disclose
Will be some danger: which for to prevent,
I have in quick determination                                                120
Thus set it down:—he shall with speed to England,
For the demand of our neglected tribute:
Haply the seas and countries different
With variable objects shall expel
This something-settled matter in his heart,                                  125
Whereon his brains still beating puts him thus
From fashion of himself. What think you on 't?

POLONIUS. It shall do well: but yet do I believe
The origin and commencement of his grief
Sprung from neglected love. How now, Ophelia!                                130
You need not tell us what Lord Hamlet said;
We heard it all. My lord, do as you please;
But, if you hold it fit, after the play,
Let his queen mother all alone entreat him
To show his grief: let her be round with him;                               135
And I'll be placed, so please you, in the ear
Of all their conference. If she find him not,
To England send him, or confine him where
Your wisdom best shall think.

KING.                                         It shall be so:
Madness in great ones must not unwatch'd go.                                140
        [*Exeunt.*]

SCENE 2—*A hall in the castle.*

[*Enter* HAMLET *and* PLAYERS.]

HAMLET. Speak the speech, I pray you, as I pronounced it to you,
trippingly on the tongue: but if you mouth it, as many of your
players do, I had as lief the town-crier spoke my lines. Nor do
not saw the air too much with your hand, thus; but use all gently:
for in the very torrent, tempest, and, as I may say, whirlwind of
your passion, you must acquire and beget a temperance that may
give it smoothness. O, it offends me to the soul to hear a robustious
periwig-pated fellow tear a passion to tatters, to very rags, to split
the ears of the groundlings,[a] who, for the most part, are capable of
nothing but inexplicable dumb-shows and noise: I would have such
a fellow whipped for o'er doing Termagant;[b] it out-herods Herod:
pray you, avoid it.

118. *doubt:* fear.
125. *something:* somewhat.
126–127. *puts . . . himself:* makes
him behave unusually.
135. *round:* direct.
137. *find:* detect.

a. spectators in the pit, where admission was cheapest.
b. god of the Mohammedans in old romances and morality plays. He was portrayed as being noisy and excitable.

FIRST PLAYER. I warrant your honor.

HAMLET. Be not too tame neither, but let your own discretion be your tutor: suit the action to the word, the word to the action; with this special observance, that you o'erstep not the modesty[c] of nature: for anything so overdone is from the purpose of playing, whose end, both at the first and now, was and is, to hold, as 'twere, the mirror up to nature; to show virtue her own feature,[d] scorn her own image, and the very age and body of the time his[e] form and pressure.[f] Now this overdone or come tardy off, though it make the unskillful laugh, cannot but make the judicious grieve; the censure of the which one must in your allowance o'erweigh a whole theater of others. O, there be players that I have seen play, and heard others praise, and that highly, not to speak it profanely,[g] that neither having the accent of Christians nor the gait of Christian, pagan, nor man, have so strutted and bellowed, that I have thought some of nature's journeymen had made men, and not made them well, they imitated humanity so abominably.

FIRST PLAYER. I hope we have reformed that indifferently[h] with us, sir.

HAMLET. O, reform it altogether. And let those that play your clowns speak no more than is set down for them: for there be of them that will themselves laugh, to set on some quantity of barren[i] spectators to laugh too, though in the mean time some necessary question of the play be then to be considered: that's villainous, and shows a most pitiful ambition in the fool that uses it. Go, make you ready.

    [*Exeunt* PLAYERS. —*Enter* POLONIUS, ROSENCRANTZ, *and* GUILDENSTERN.]

How now, my lord! will the king hear this piece of work?

POLONIUS. And the queen too, and that presently.

HAMLET. Bid the players make haste.                       1

    [*Exit* POLONIUS.]

Will you two help to hasten them?

ROSENCRANTZ.    ⎱ We will, my lord.
GUILDENSTERN.   ⎰

    [*Exeunt* ROSENCRANTZ *and* GUILDENSTERN.]

HAMLET. What ho! Horatio!

    [*Enter* HORATIO.]

HORATIO. Here, sweet lord, at your service.                5

HAMLET. Horatio, thou art e'en as just a man
  As e'er my conversation coped withal.[7]

c. moderation.
d. form.
e. its.
f. impress, shape.
g. Hamlet refers apologetically to his following words, where he compares the creation of men to the work of "journeymen," or laborers.
h. pretty well.
i. silly.
7. *As . . . withal:* as I ever associated with.

HORATIO. O, my dear lord,—

HAMLET. Nay, do not think I flatter;
For what advancement may I hope from thee,
That no revenue hast but thy good spirits,　　　10
To feed and clothe thee? Why should the poor be flatter'd?
No, let the candied tongue lick absurd pomp,
And crook the pregnant hinges of the knee
Where thrift may follow fawning. Dost thou hear?
Since my dear soul was mistress of her choice,　　　15
And could of men distinguish, her election
Hath seal'd thee for herself: for thou hast been
As one, in suffering all, that suffers nothing;
A man that fortune's buffets and rewards
Hast ta'en with equal thanks: and blest are those　　　20
Whose blood and judgment are so well commingled
That they are not a pipe for fortune's finger
To sound what stop she please. Give me that man
That is not passion's slave, and I will wear him
In my heart's core, aye, in my heart of heart,　　　25
As I do thee. Something too much of this.
There is a play to-night before the king;
One scene of it comes near the circumstance
Which I have told thee of my father's death:
I prithee, when thou sees that act a-foot,　　　30
Even with the very comment of thy soul
Observe my uncle: if his occulted guilt
Do not itself unkennel in one speech
It is a damned ghost that we have seen,
And my imaginations are as foul　　　35
As Vulcan's stithy. Give him heedful note;
For I mine eyes will rivet to his face,
And after we will both our judgments join
In censure of his seeming.

HORATIO. Well, my lord:
If he steal aught the whilst this play is playing,　　　40
And 'scape detecting, I will pay the theft.

HAMLET. They are coming to the play: I must be idle:
Get you a place.　　　43

[*Danish march. A flourish. Enter* KING, QUEEN, POLONIUS,

---

13. *pregnant hinges:* supple joints.
14. *thrift . . . fawning:* material profit may be derived from cringing.
21. *blood and judgment:* passion and reason.
22–23. *for fortune's . . . please:* for Fortune to put her finger on any

windhole she may please of the pipe.
31. *Even . . . soul:* with all your powers of observation.
36. *stithy:* smithy.
39. *In censure of his seeming:* to judge his behavior.
42. *idle:* crazy.

OPHELIA, ROSENCRANTZ, GUILDENSTERN, *and other* LORDS *attendant, with the* GUARD *carrying torches.*]

KING. How fares our cousin Hamlet?

HAMLET. Excellent, i' faith; of the chameleon's[j] dish: I eat the air, promise-crammed: you cannot feed capons so.

KING. I have nothing with this anwser, Hamlet; these words are not mine.[k]

HAMLET. No, nor mine now. [*To* POLONIUS] My lord, you played once i' the university, you say?

POLONIUS. That did I, my lord, and was accounted a good actor.

HAMLET. What did you enact?

POLONIUS. I did enact Julius Cæsar: I was killed i' the Capitol; Brutus killed me.

HAMLET. It was a brute part of him to kill so capital a calf there. Be the players ready?

ROSENCRANTZ. Aye, my lord; they stay upon your patience.

QUEEN. Come hither, my dear Hamlet, sit by me.

HAMLET. No, good mother, here's metal more attractive.

POLONIUS. [*To the* KING] O, ho! do you mark that?

HAMLET. Lady, shall I lie in your lap?

[*Lying down at* OPHELIA's *feet.*]

OPHELIA. No, my lord.

HAMLET. I mean, my head upon your lap?

OPHELIA. Aye, my lord.

HAMLET. Do you think I meant country matters?

OPHELIA. I think nothing, my lord.

HAMLET. That's a fair thought to lie between maids' legs.

OPHELIA. What is, my lord?

HAMLET. Nothing.

OPHELIA. You are merry, my lord.

HAMLET. Who, I?

OPHELIA. Aye, my lord.

HAMLET. O God, your only jig-maker.[l] What should a man do but be merry? for, look you, how cheerfully my mother looks, and my father died within 's two hours.

OPHELIA. Nay, 'tis twice two months, my lord.

HAMLET. So long? Nay then, let the devil wear black, for I'll have a suit of sables.[m] O heavens! die two months ago, and not forgotten yet? Then there's hope a great man's memory may outlive his life half a year: but, by 'r lady, he must build churches then; or else shall he suffer not thinking on, with the hobby-horse,[n] whose

*j.* The chameleon was supposed to feed on air.

*k.* have nothing to do with my question.

*l.* maker of comic songs.

*m.* furs.

*n.* a figure in the old May-day games and morris dances.

epitaph is, 'For, O, for, O, the hobby-horse is forgot.'

[*Hautboys play. The dumb-show enters. —Enter a King and a Queen very lovingly; the Queen embracing him and he her. She kneels, and makes show of protestation unto him. He takes her up, and declines his head upon her neck; lays him down upon a bank of flowers: she, seeing him asleep, leaves him. Anon comes in a fellow, takes off his crown, kisses it, and pours poison in the King's ears, and exit. The Queen returns; finds the King dead, and makes passionate action. The Poisoner, with some two or three Mutes comes in again, seeming to lament with her. The dead body is carried away. The Poisoner woos the Queen with gifts: she seems loath and unwilling awhile, but in the end accepts his love. — Exeunt.*]

OPHELIA. What means this, my lord?

HAMLET. Marry, this is miching mallecho;° it means mischief.

OPHELIA. Belike this show imports the argument of the play.

[*Enter* PROLOGUE.]

HAMLET. We shall know by this fellow: the players cannot keep counsel;ᵖ they'll tell all.

OPHELIA. Will he tell us what this show meant?

HAMLET. Aye, or any show that you'll show him: be not you ashamed to show, he'll not shame to tell you what it means.

OPHELIA. You are naught,�q you are naught: I'll mark the play.

PROLOGUE. For us, and for our tragedy,
　　　　Here stooping to your clemency,
　　　　We beg your hearing patiently.

HAMLET. Is this a prologue, or the posyʳ of a ring?

OPHELIA. 'Tis brief, my lord.

HAMLET. As woman's love.

[*Enter two* PLAYERS, KING *and* QUEEN.]

PLAYER KING. Full thirty times hath Phœbus' cart gone round　　44
Neptune's salt wash and Tellus' orbed ground,
And thirty dozen moons with borrowed sheen
About the world have times twelve thirties been,
Since love our hearts and Hymen did our hands
Unite commutual in most sacred bands.

PLAYER QUEEN. So many journeys may the sun and moon　　50
Make us again count o'er ere love be done!
But, woe is me, you are so sick of late,
So far from cheer and from your former state,
That I distrust you. Yet, though I distrust,

---

*o.* sneaking misdeed.
*p.* a secret.
*q.* naughty, improper.
*r.* motto, inscription.

44. *Phœbus' cart:* the chariot of the sun.
54. *I distrust you:* I am worried about you.

Discomfort you, my lord, it nothing must:                                    55
For women's fear and love holds quantity,
In neither aught, or in extremity.
Now, what my love is, proof hath made you know,
And as my love is sized, my fear is so:
Where love is great, the littlest doubts are fear,                           60
Where little fears grow great, great love grows there.

PLAYER KING. Faith, I must leave thee, love, and shortly too;
My operant powers their functions leave to do:
And thou shalt live in this fair world behind,
Honor'd, beloved; and haply as one as kind                                   65
For husband shalt thou—

PLAYER QUEEN.                            O, confound the rest!
Such love must needs be treason in my breast:
In second husband let me be accurst!
None wed the second but who kill'd the first.

HAMLET. [*Aside*] Wormwood, wormwood.                                        70

PLAYER QUEEN. The instances that second marriage move
Are base respects of thrift, but none of love:
A second time I kill my husband dead,
When second husband kisses me in bed.

PLAYER KING. I do believe you think what now you speak,                      75
But what we do determine oft we break.
Purpose is but the slave to memory,
Of violent birth but poor validity:
Which now, like fruit unripe, sticks on the tree,
But fall unshaken when they mellow be.                                       80
Most necessary 'tis that we forget
To pay ourselves what to ourselves is debt:
What to ourselves in passion we propose,
The passion ending, doth the purpose lose.
The violence of either grief or joy                                          85
Their own enactures with themselves destroy:
Where joy most revels, grief doth most lament;
Grief joys, joy grieves, on slender accident.
This world is not for aye, nor 'tis not strange
That even our loves should with our fortunes change,                         90
For 'tis a question left us yet to prove,
Whether love lead fortune or else fortune love.
The great man down, you mark his favorite flies;
The poor advanced makes friends of enemies:
And hitherto doth love on fortune tend;                                      95

56. *holds quantity:* maintain mutual balance.
63. *operant:* operative, vital. *leave:* cease.
71. *instances:* motives.
72. *respects of thrift:* considerations of material profit.
86. *enactures:* actual performances.

For who not needs shall never lack a friend,
And who in want a hollow friend doth try
Directly seasons him his enemy.
But, orderly to end where I begun,
Our wills and fates do so contrary run,                       100
That our devices still are overthrown,
Our thoughts are ours, their ends none of our own:
So think thou wilt no second husband wed,
But die thy thoughts when thy first lord is dead.

PLAYER QUEEN. Nor earth to me give food nor heaven light!    105
Sport and repose lock from me day and night!
To desperation turn my trust and hope!
An anchor's cheer in prison be my scope!
Each opposite, that blanks the face of joy,
Meet what I would have well and it destroy!                   110
Both here and hence pursue me lasting strife,
If, once a widow, ever I be wife!

HAMLET. If she should break it now!

PLAYER KING. 'Tis deeply sworn. Sweet, leave me here a while;
My spirits grow dull, and fain I would beguile               115
The tedious day with sleep.                       [*Sleeps.*]

PLAYER QUEEN.                 Sleep rock thy brain;
And never come mischance between us twain!        [*Exit.*]

HAMLET. Madam, how like you this play?

QUEEN. The lady doth protest too much, methinks.

HAMLET. O, but she'll keep her word.

KING. Have you heard the argument?[s] Is there no offense in 't?

HAMLET. No, no, they do but jest, poison in jest; no offense i' the
world.

KING. What do you call the play?

HAMLET. The Mouse-trap. Marry, how? Tropically.[t] This play is the
image of a murder done in Vienna: Gonzago is the duke's name;
his wife, Baptista: you shall see anon; 'tis a knavish piece of work;
but what o' that? your majesty, and we that have free souls, it
touches us not: let the galled jade[u] wince, our withers[v] are un-
wrung.[w]
        [*Enter* LUCIANUS.]
This is one Lucianus, nephew to the king.

OPHELIA. You are as good as a chorus, my lord.

HAMLET. I could interpret[x] between you and your love,[y] if I could

---

98. *seasons:* matures.
108. *anchor's cheer:* hermit's, or anchorite's, fare.
109. *blanks:* makes pale.
*s.* plot of the play in outline.
*t.* by a trope, figuratively.
*u.* injured horse.

*v.* the part between the shoulders of a horse.
*w.* not wrenched.
*x.* act as interpreter (regular feature in puppet shows).
*y.* lover.

see the puppets dallying.

OPHELIA. You are keen, my lord, you are keen.

HAMLET. It would cost you a groaning to take off my edge.

OPHELIA. Still better and worse.

HAMLET. So you must take your husbands. Begin, murderer; pox, leave thy damnable faces, and begin. Come: the croaking raven doth bellow for revenge.

LUCIANUS. Thoughts black, hands apt, drugs fit, and time agreeing;                                                                                        118
Confederate season, else no creature seeing;
Thou mixture rank, of midnight weeds collected,                                   120
With Hecate's ban thrice blasted, thrice infected,
Thy natural magic and dire property,
On wholesome life usurp immediately.                                                   123

[*Pours the poison into the sleeper's ear.*]

HAMLET. He poisons him i' the garden for his estate. His name's Gonzago: the story is extant, and written in very choice Italian: you shall see anon how the murderer gets the love of Gonzago's wife.

OPHELIA. The king rises.

HAMLET. What, frighted with false fire!*z*

QUEEN. How fares my lord?

POLONIUS. Give o'er the play.

KING. Give me some light. Away!

POLONIUS. Lights, lights, lights!

[*Exeunt all but* HAMLET *and* HORATIO.]

HAMLET. Why, let the stricken deer go weep,
          The hart ungalled play;
      For some must watch, while some must sleep:
          Thus runs the world away.

Would not this, sir, and a forest of feathers—if the rest of my fortunes turn Turk with me*a*—with two Provincial roses*b* on my razed shoes, get me a fellowship in a cry*c* of players, sir?

HORATIO. Half a share.

HAMLET. A whole one, I.

      For thou dost know, O Damon dear,
          This realm dismantled was
      Of Jove himself; and now reigns here
          A very, very—pajock.*d*

HORATIO. You might have rhymed.*e*

---

119. *Confederate:* favorable.
121. *Hecate:* the goddess of witchcraft.
z. blank shot.
a. betray me (like a Christian turning Mohammedan).
b. *forest of feathers . . . Provincial*

*roses:* occasionally, parts of an actor's apparel.
c. company. The term is generally used with reference to a pack of hounds.
d. peacock.
e. "Ass" would have rhymed.

HAMLET. O good Horatio, I'll take the ghost's word for a thousand pound. Didst perceive?

HORATIO. Very well, my lord.

HAMLET. Upon the talk of the poisoning?

HORATIO. I did very well note him.

HAMLET. Ah, ha! Come, some music! come, the recorders!*f*

> For if the king like not the comedy,
> Why then, belike, he likes it not, perdy.

Come, some music!

[*Re-enter* ROSENCRANTZ *and* GUILDENSTERN.]

GUILDENSTERN. Good my lord, vouchsafe me a word with you.

HAMLET. Sir, a whole history.

GUILDENSTERN. The king, sir,—

HAMLET. Aye, sir, what of him?

GUILDENSTERN. Is in his retirement marvelous distempered.

HAMLET. With drink, sir?

GUILDENSTERN. No, my lord, rather with choler.*g*

HAMLET. Your wisdom should show itself more richer to signify this to the doctor; for, for me to put him to his purgation would perhaps plunge him into far more choler.

GUILDENSTERN. Good my lord, put your discourse into some frame, and start not so wildly from my affair.

HAMLET. I am tame, sir: pronounce.

GUILDENSTERN. The queen, your mother, in most great affliction of spirit, hath sent me to you.

HAMLET. You are welcome.

GUILDENSTERN. Nay, good my lord, this courtesy is not of the right breed. If it shall please you to make me a wholesome*h* answer, I will do your mother's commandment: if not, your pardon and my return shall be the end of my business.

HAMLET. Sir, I cannot.

GUILDENSTERN. What, my lord?

HAMLET. Make you a wholesome answer; my wit's diseased: but, sir, such answer as I can make, you shall command; or rather, as you say, my mother: therefore no more, but to the matter: my mother, you say,—

ROSENCRANTZ. Then thus she says; your behavior hath struck her into amazement and admiration.*i*

HAMLET. O wonderful son, that can so astonish a mother! But is there no sequel at the heels of this mother's admiration? Impart.

ROSENCRANTZ. She desires to speak with you in her closet,*j* ere you go to bed.

---

*f*. The recorder, an end-blown flute with eight holes, was popular during the late Renaissance.

*g*. bile, anger. An excess of bile was traditionally supposed to cause irasci-bility.

*h*. sensible.

*i*. confusion and surprise.

*j*. private room.

HAMLET. We shall obey, were she ten times our mother. Have you any further trade with us?

ROSENCRANTZ. My lord, you once did love me.

HAMLET. So I do still, by these pickers and stealers.*k*

ROSENCRANTZ. Good my lord, what is your cause of distemper? you do surely bar the door upon your own liberty, if you deny your griefs to your friend.

HAMLET. Sir, I lack advancement.*l*

ROSENCRANTZ. How can that be, when you have the voice of the king himself for your succession in Denmark?

HAMLET. Aye, sir, but 'while the grass grows,'*m*—the proverb is something musty.

    [*Re-enter* PLAYERS *with recorders.*]

O, the recorders! let me see one. To withdraw*n* with you:—why do you go about to recover the wind of me,*o* as if you would drive me into a toil?*p*

GUILDENSTERN. O, my lord, if my duty be too bold, my love is too unmannerly.

HAMLET. I do not well understand that. Will you play upon this pipe?

GUILDENSTERN. My lord, I cannot.

HAMLET. I pray you.

GUILDENSTERN. Believe me, I cannot.

HAMLET. I do beseech you.

GUILDENSTERN. I know no touch of it, my lord.

HAMLET. It is as easy as lying: govern these ventages*q* with your fingers and thumb, give it breath with your mouth, and it will discourse most eloquent music. Look you, these are the stops.

GUILDENSTERN. But these cannot I command to any utterance of harmony; I have not the skill.

HAMLET. Why, look you now, how unworthy a thing you make of me! You would play upon me; you would seem to know my stops; you would pluck out the heart of my mystery; you would sound me from my lowest note to the top of my compass: and there is much music, excellent voice, in this little organ; yet cannot you make it speak. 'Sblood, do you think I am easier to be played on than a pipe? Call me what instrument you will, though you can fret*r* me, yet you cannot play upon me.

    [*Re-enter* POLONIUS.]

God bless you, sir!

---

*k.* the hands.
*l.* Hamlet pretends that the cause of his "distemper" is frustrated ambition.
*m.* The proverb ends, "oft starves the silly steed."
*n.* retire (talk in private).
*o.* get to windward of me.

*p.* snare.
*q.* windholes.
*r.* vex, with a pun on "frets" meaning the small ridges placed across the length of a guitar's finger board to regulate the fingering.

POLONIUS. My lord, the queen would speak with you, and presently.

HAMLET. Do you see yonder cloud that's almost in shape of a camel?

POLONIUS. By the mass, and 'tis like a camel, indeed.

HAMLET. Methinks it is like a weasel.

POLONIUS. It is backed like a weasel.

HAMLET. Or like a whale?

POLONIUS. Very like a whale.

HAMLET. Then I will come to my mother by and by. They fool me
to the top of my bent⁸ I will come by and by.

POLONIUS. I will say so.                          [*Exit* POLONIUS.]

HAMLET. 'By and by' is easily said. Leave me, friends.

    [*Exeunt all but* HAMLET.]

'Tis now the very witching time of night,           124
When churchyards yawn, and hell itself breathes out
Contagion to this world: now could I drink hot blood,
And do such bitter business as the day
Would quake to look on. Soft! now to my mother.
O heart, lose not thy nature; let not ever
The soul of Nero enter this firm bosom:           130
Let me be cruel, not unnatural:
I will speak daggers to her, but use none;
My tongue and soul in this be hypocrites;
How in my words soever she be shent,
To give them seals never, my soul, consent!        135
    [*Exit.*]

### SCENE 3—*A room in the castle.*

    [*Enter* KING, ROSENCRANTZ, *and* GUILDENSTERN.]

KING. I like him not, nor stands it safe with us
To let his madness range. Therefore prepare you;
I your commission will forthwith dispatch,
And he to England shall along with you:
The terms of our estate may not endure              5
Hazard so near us as doth hourly grow
Out of his lunacies.

GUILDENSTERN.           We will ourselves provide:
Most holy and religious fear it is
To keep those many many bodies safe
That live and feed upon your majesty.            10

ROSENCRANTZ. The single and peculiar life is bound
With all the strength and armor of the mind

---

5. straining, tension (as of a bow).
130. *Nero:* This Roman emperor was
the murderer of his mother.
134. *shent:* reproached.

135. *give them seals:* ratify them by
action.
5. *The terms of our estate:* my position as king.
  11. *peculiar:* individual.

To keep itself from noyance; but much more
That spirit upon whose weal depends and rests
The lives of many. The cease of majesty 15
Dies not alone, but like a gulf doth draw
What's near it with it; it is a massy wheel,
Fix'd on the summit of the highest mount,
To whose huge spokes ten thousand lesser things
Are mortised and adjoin'd; which, when it falls, 20
Each small annexment, petty consequence,
Attends the boisterous ruin. Never alone
Did the king sigh, but with a general groan.

KING. Arm you, I pray you, to this speedy voyage,
For we will fetters put about this fear, 25
Which now goes too free-footed.

ROSENCRANTZ. ⎱
GUILDENSTERN. ⎰     We will haste us.

    [*Exeunt* ROSENCRANTZ *and* GUILDENSTERN. —*Enter* POLO-
NIUS.]

POLONIUS. My lord, he's going to his mother's closet:
Behind the arras I'll convey myself,
To hear the process: I'll warrant she'll tax him home:
And, as you said, and wisely was it said, 30
'Tis meet that some more audience than a mother,
Since nature makes them partial, should o'erhear
The speech, of vantage. Fare you well, my liege:
I'll call upon you ere you go to bed,
And tell you what I know.

KING.                    Thanks, dear my lord. 35
    [*Exit* POLONIUS.]
O, my offense is rank, it smells to heaven;
It hath the primal eldest curse upon 't,
A brother's murder. Pray can I not,
Though inclination be as sharp as will:
My stronger guilt defeats my strong intent, 40
And like a man to double business bound,
I stand in pause where I shall first begin,
And both neglect. What if this cursed hand
Were thicker than itself with brother's blood,
Is there not rain enough in the sweet heavens 45
To wash it white as snow? Whereto serves mercy
But to confront the visage of offense?
And what's in prayer but this twofold force,

15. *cease:* decease, extinction.
20. *mortised:* fastened.
29. *tax him home:* take him to task thoroughly.

33. *of vantage:* from a vantage point.
37. *the primal eldest curse:* Cain's.
47. *offense:* guilt.

To be forestalled ere we come to fall,
Or pardon'd being down? Then I'll look up;                    50
My fault is past. But O, what form of prayer
Can serve my turn? 'Forgive me my foul murder?'
That cannot be, since I am still possess'd
Of those effects for which I did the murder,
My crown, mine own ambition and my queen.                    55
May one be pardon'd and retain the offense?
In the corrupted currents of this world
Offense's gilded hand may shove by justice,
And oft 'tis seen the wicked prize itself
Buys out the law: but 'tis not so above;                     60
There is no shuffling, there the action lies
In his true nature, and we ourselves compell'd
Even to the teeth and forehead of our faults
To give in evidence. What then? what rests?
Try what repentance can: what can it not?                     65
Yet what can it when one can not repent?
O wretched state! O bosom black as death!
O limèd soul, that struggling to be free
Art more engaged! Help, angels! make assay!
Bow, stubborn knees, and, heart with strings of steel,       70
Be soft as sinews of the new-born babe!
All may be well.
              [*Retires and kneels. —Enter* HAMLET.]
HAMLET. Now might I do it pat, now he is praying
And now I'll do 't: and so he goes to heaven:
And so am I revenged. That would be scann'd;                 75
A villain kills my father; and for that,
I, his sole son, do this same villain send
To heaven.
O, this is hire and salary, not revenge.
He took my father grossly, full of bread,                    80
With all his crimes broad blown, as flush as May;
And how his audit stands who knows save heaven?
But in our circumstance and course of thought,
'Tis heavy with him: and am I then revenged,
To take him in the purging of his soul,                      85
When he is fit and season'd for his passage?

56. *offense:* the things obtained through the offense.
59–60. *the wicked . . . law:* the wealth unduly acquired is used for briber.
62. *nis:* its.
64. *what rests?* what remains?
68. *limèd:* caught as with birdlime.

69. *make assay!:* make the attempt! (addressed by the King to himself).
73. *pat:* conveniently.
75. *would be scann'd:* would have to be considered carefully.
81. *broad blown:* in full bloom. *flush:* vigorous.
82. *audit:* account.
86. *season'd:* ripe, ready.

No.
Up, sword, and know thou a more horrid hent:
When he is drunk asleep, or in his rage,
Or, in the incestuous pleasure of his bed;                    90
At game, a-swearing, or about some act
That has no relish of salvation in 't;
Then trip him, that his heels may kick at heaven
And that his soul may be as damn'd and black
As hell, whereto it goes. My mother stays:                    95
This physic but prolongs thy sickly days.          [*Exit.*]
KING. [*Rising*] My words fly up, my thoughts remain below:
Words without thoughts never to heaven go.          [*Exit.*]

SCENE 4—*The Queen's closet.*

[*Enter* QUEEN *and* POLONIUS.]
POLONIUS. He will come straight. Look you lay home to him:
Tell him his pranks have been too broad to bear with,
And that your grace hath screen'd and stood between
Much heat and him. I'll sconce me even here.
Pray you, be round with him.
HAMLET. [*Within*]                    Mother, mother, mother!      5
QUEEN. I'll warrant you; fear me not. Withdraw,
I hear him coming.
[POLONIUS *hides behind the arras.* —*Enter* HAMLET.]
HAMLET. Now, mother, what's the matter?
QUEEN. Hamlet, thou hast thy father much offended.
HAMLET. Mother, you have my father much offended.      10
QUEEN. Come, come, you answer with an idle tongue.
HAMLET. Go, go, you question with a wicked tongue.
QUEEN. Why, how now, Hamlet!
HAMLET.                    What's the matter now?
QUEEN. Have you forgot me?
HAMLET.                    No, by the rood, not so:
You are the queen, your husband's brother's wife;
And—would it were not so!—you are my mother.      15
QUEEN. Nay, then, I'll set those to you that can speak.
HAMLET. Come, come, and sit you down; you shall not budge;
You go not till I set you up a glass
Where you may see the inmost part of you.                    20
QUEEN. What wilt thou do? thou wilt not murder me?
Help, help, ho!
POLONIUS. [*Behind*] What, ho! help, help, help!

88. *hent:* grip.
1. *straight:* straightway. *lay home:*
give him a stern lesson.
2. *broad:* unrestrained.

5. *round:* straightforward.
14. *rood:* cross.
19. *glass:* mirror.

HAMLET. [*Drawing*] How now! a rat? Dead, for a ducat, dead!
  [*Makes a pass through the arras.*]
POLONIUS. [*Behind*] O, I am slain!           [*Falls and dies.*]
QUEEN.               O me, what hast thou done?
HAMLET. Nay, I know not: is it the king?          25
QUEEN. O, what a rash and bloody deed is this!
HAMLET. A bloody deed! almost as bad, good mother,
  As kill a king, and marry with his brother.
QUEEN. As kill a king!
HAMLET.           Aye, lady, 'twas my word.
  [*Lifts up the arras and discovers* POLONIUS.]
  Thou wretched, rash, intruding fool, farewell!      30
  I took thee for thy better: take thy fortune;
  Thou find'st to be too busy is some danger.
  Leave wringing of your hands: peace! sit you down,
  And let me wring your heart: for so I shall,
  If it be made of penetrable stuff;          35
  If damned custom have not brass'd it so,
  That it be proof and bulwark against sense.
QUEEN. What have I done, that thou darest wag thy tongue
  In noise so rude against me?
HAMLET.             Such an act
  That blurs the grace and blush of modesty,     40
  Calls virtue hypocrite, takes off the rose
  From the fair forehead of an innocent love,
  And sets a blister there; makes marriage vows
  As false as dicers' oaths: O, such a deed
  As from the body of contraction plucks      45
  The very soul, and sweet religion makes
  A rhapsody of words: heaven's face doth glow;
  Yea, this solidity and compound mass,
  With tristful visage, as against the doom,
  Is thought-sick at the act.            50
QUEEN. Aye me, what act,
  That roars so loud and thunders in the index?
HAMLET. Look here, upon this picture, and on this,
  The counterfeit presentment of two brothers.
  See what a grace was seated on this brow;     55
  Hyperion's curls, the front of Jove himself,
  An eye like Mars, to threaten and command;
  A station like the herald Mercury

32. *too busy:* too much of a busy-body.
37. *sense:* feeling.
45. *contraction:* duty to the marriage contract.
47. *glow:* blush with shame.
49. *tristful:* sad. *against the doom:* nearing doomsday.
52. *index:* prologue, table of contents.
54. *counterfeit presentment:* portrait.
58. *station:* posture.

New-lighted on a heaven-kissing hill;
A combination and a form indeed,                                      60
Where every god did seem to set his seal
To give the world assurance of a man:
This was your husband. Look you now, what follows:
Here is your husband; like a mildew'd ear,
Blasting his wholesome brother. Have you eyes?                        65
Could you on this fair mountain leave to feed,
And batten on this moor? Ha! have you eyes?
You cannot call it love, for at your age
The hey-day in the blood is tame, it's humble,
And waits upon the judgment: and what judgment                       70
Would step from this to this? Sense sure you have,
Else could you not have motion: but sure that sense
Is apoplex'd: for madness would not err,
Nor sense to ecstasy was ne'er so thrall'd
But it reserved some quantity of choice,                             75
To serve in such a difference. What devil was 't
That thus hath cozen'd you at hoodman-blind?
Eyes without feeling, feeling without sight,
Ears without hands or eyes, smelling sans all,
Or but a sickly part of one true sense                               80
Could not so mope.
O shame! where is thy blush? Rebellious hell,
If thou canst mutine in a matron's bones,
To flaming youth let virtue be as wax
And melt in her own fire: proclaim no shame                          85
When the compulsive ardor gives the charge,
Since frost itself as actively doth burn,
And reason panders will.

QUEEN.                               O Hamlet, speak no more:
Thou turn'st mine eyes into my very soul,
And there I see such black and grainèd spots
As will not leave their tinct.

HAMLET.                               Nay, but to live
In the rank sweat of an enseamèd bed,
Stew'd in corruption, honeying and making love
Over the nasty sty,—

QUEEN.                               O, speak to me no more;

64. *ear:* ear of corn.
65. *his:* its.
66. *leave:* cease.
67. *batten:* gorge, fatten.
70. *waits upon:* is subordinated to.
71. *Sense:* sensibility, feeling.
73. *apoplex'd:* struck by apoplexy.
74. *ecstasy:* madness.

77. *cozen'd:* tricked. *hoodman-blind:* blindman's buff.
79. *sans:* without.
81. *mope:* be stupid.
86. *gives the charge:* attacks.
88. *panders:* becomes subservient to.
90. *grainèd:* dyed in.
91. *leave their tinct:* lose their color.
92. *enseamèd:* greasy.

These words like daggers enter in my ears; 95
No more, sweet Hamlet!

HAMLET.                  A murderer and a villain;
A slave that is not twentieth part the tithe
Of your precedent lord; a vice of kings;
A cutpurse of the empire and the rule,
That from a shelf the precious diadem stole 100
And put it in his pocket!

QUEEN.               No more!

HAMLET. A king of shreds and patches—
    [*Enter* GHOST.]
Save me, and hover o'er me with your wings,
You heavenly guards! What would your gracious figure?

QUEEN. Alas, he's mad! 105

HAMLET. Do you not come your tardy son to chide,
That, lapsed in time and passion, lets go by
The important acting of your dread command?
O, say!

GHOST. Do not forget: this visitation 110
Is but to whet thy almost blunted purpose.
But look, amazement on thy mother sits:
O, step between her and her fighting soul:
Conceit in weakest bodies strongest works:
Speak to her, Hamlet.

HAMLET.             How is it with you, lady? 115

QUEEN. Alas, how is 't with you,
That you do bend your eye on vacancy
And with the incorporal air do hold discourse?
Forth at your eyes your spirits wildly peep;
And, as the sleeping soldiers in the alarm, 120
Your bedded hairs, like life in excrements,
Start up and stand on end. O gentle son,
Upon the heat and flame of thy distemper
Sprinkle cool patience. Whereon do you look?

HAMLET. On him, on him! Look you how pale he glares! 125
His form and cause conjoin'd, preaching to stones,
Would make them capable. Do not look upon me,
Lest with this piteous action you convert
My stern effects: then what I have to do
Will want true color; tears perchance for blood. 130

---

97. *tithe:* tenth.
98. *vice:* clown (from the custom in the old morality plays of having a buffoon take the part of Vice, or of a particular vice).
99. *cutpurse:* pickpocket.
114. *Conceit:* imagination.

120. *alarm:* call to arms.
121. *excrements:* outgrowths.
122. *an end:* on end.
127. *capable:* capable of feeling.
128–129. *you convert . . . effects:* you make me change my purpose.
130. *for:* instead of.

QUEEN. To whom do you speak this?

HAMLET.                  Do you see nothing there?

QUEEN. Nothing at all; yet all that is I see.

HAMLET. Nor did you nothing hear?

QUEEN.                     No, nothing but ourselves.

HAMLET. Why, look you there! look, how it steals away!
  My father, in his habit as he lived!             135
  Look, where he goes, even now, out at the portal!
    [*Exit* GHOST.]

QUEEN. This is the very coinage of your brain:
  This bodiless creation ecstasy
  Is very cunning in.

HAMLET.             Ecstasy!
  My pulse, as yours, doth temperately keep time,     140
  And makes as healthful music: it is not madness
  That I have utter'd: bring me to the test,
  And I the matter will re-word, which madness
  Would gambol from. Mother, for love of grace,
  Lay not that flattering unction to your soul,        145
  That not your trespass but my madness speaks:
  It will but skin and film the ulcerous place,
  Whiles rank corruption, mining all within,
  Infects unseen. Confess yourself to heaven;
  Repent what's past, avoid what is to come,         150
  And do not spread the compost on the weeds,
  To make them ranker. Forgive me this my virtue,
  For in the fatness of these pursy times
  Virtue itself of vice must pardon beg,
  Yea, curb and woo for leave to do him good.       155

QUEEN. O Hamlet, thou hast cleft my heart in twain.

HAMLET. O, throw away the worser part of it,
  And live the purer with the other half.
  Good night: but go not to my uncle's bed;
  Assume a virtue, if you have it not.              160
  That monster, custom, who all sense doth eat,
  Of habits devil, is angel yet in this,
  That to the use of actions fair and good
  He likewise gives a frock or livery,
  That aptly is put on. Refrain to-night,           165
  And that shall lend a kind of easiness
  To the next abstinence; the next more easy;
  For use almost can change the stamp of nature,

---

138. *ecstasy:* madness.
145. *unction:* ointment.
153. *pursy:* swollen from pampering.

155. *curb:* bow.
165. *aptly:* easily.
168. *use:* habit. *stamp:* cast, form.

And either curb the devil, or throw him out
With wondrous potency. Once more, good night:               170
And when you are desirous to be blest,
I'll blessing beg of you. For this same lord,
    [*Pointing to* POLONIUS.]
I do repent: but heaven hath pleased it so,
To punish me with this, and this with me,
That I must be their scourge and minister.                   175
I will bestow him, and will answer well
The death I gave him. So, again, good night.
I must be cruel, only to be kind:
Thus bad begins, and worse remains behind.
One word more, good lady.
QUEEN.                 What shall I do?         180
HAMLET. Not this, by no means, that I bid you do:
Let the bloat king tempt you again to bed;
Pinch wanton on your cheek, call you his mouse;
And let him, for a pair of reechy kisses,
Or paddling in your neck with his damn'd fingers,           185
Make you to ravel all this matter out,
That I essentially am not in madness,
But mad in craft. 'Twere good you let him know;
For who, that's but a queen, fair, sober, wise,
Would from a paddock, from a bat, a gib,                     190
Such dear concernings hide? who would do so?
No, in despite of sense and secrecy,
Unpeg the basket on the house's top,
Let the birds fly, and like the famous ape,
To try conclusions, in the basket creep                      195
And break your own neck down.
QUEEN. Be thou assured, if words be made of breath
And breath of life, I have no life to breathe
What thou hast said to me.
HAMLET. I must to England; you know that?
QUEEN.                     Alack,     200
I had forgot: 'tis so concluded on.
HAMLET. There's letters seal'd: and my two schoolfellows,
Whom I will trust as I will adders fang'd,
They bear the mandate; they must sweep my way,

---

175. *scourge and minister:* agent of punishment.
176. *bestow:* stow away.
182. *bloat:* bloated with drink.
184. *reechy:* fetid.
188. *craft:* simulation.
190. *paddock:* toad. *gib:* tomcat.
191. *dear concernings:* matters with which one is closely concerned.
194. *the famous ape:* the ape in the unidentified animal fable to which Hamlet alludes; apparently the animal saw birds fly out of a basket and drew the conclusion that by placing himself in the basket he could fly too.
203. *fang'd:* with fangs.

And marshal me to knavery. Let it work;                          205
For 'tis the sport to have the enginer
Hoist with his own petar: and 't shall go hard
But I will delve one yard below their mines,
And blow them at the moon: O, 'tis most sweet
When in one line two crafts directly meet.                       210
This man shall set me packing:
I'll lug the guts into the neighbor room.
Mother, good night. Indeed this counselor
Is now most still, most secret and most grave,
Who was in life a foolish prating knave.                         215
Come, sir, to draw toward an end with you.
Good night, mother.

    *[Exeunt severally;* HAMLET *dragging in* POLONIUS.]*

## Act IV

### SCENE 1—A *room in the castle.*

    *[Enter* KING, QUEEN, ROSENCRANTZ, *and* GUILDENSTERN *]*
KING. There's matter in these sighs, these profound heaves:
  You must translate: 'tis fit we understand them.
  Where is your son?
QUEEN. Bestow this place on us a little while.
    *[Exeunt* ROSENCRANTZ *and* GUILDENSTERN.]*
  Ah, mine own lord, what have I seen to-night!                 5
KING. What, Gertrude? How does Hamlet?
QUEEN. Mad as the sea and wind, when both contend
  Which is the mightier: in his lawless fit,
  Behind the arras hearing something stir,
  Whips out his rapier, cries 'A rat, a rat!'                    10
  And in this brainish apprehension kills
  The unseen good old man.
KING.                 O heavy deed!
  It had been so with us, had we been there:
  His liberty is full of threats to all,
  To you yourself, to us, to every one.                         15
  Alas, how shall this bloody deed be answer'd?
  It will be laid to us, whose providence
  Should have kept short, restrain'd and out of haunt,
  This mad young man: but so much was our love,
  We would not understand what was most fit,                     20

205. *marshal:* lead.
206. *enginer:* military engineer.
207. *Hoist:* blow up. *petar:* petard, a
variety of bomb.
214. *grave:* Hamlet is punning on
the word.

4. *Bestow this place on us:* leave us
alone.
11. *brainish apprehension:* imaginary
notion.
18. *short:* under close watch.

But, like the owner of a foul disease,
To keep it from divulging, let it feed
Even on the pith of life. Where is he gone?
QUEEN. To draw apart the body he hath kill'd:
  O'er whom his very madness, like some ore          25
  Among a mineral of metals base,
  Shows itself pure; he weeps for what is done.
KING. O Gertrude, come away!
  The sun no sooner shall the mountains touch,
  But we will ship him hence: and this vile deed     30
  We must, with all our majesty and skill,
  Both countenance and excuse. Ho, Guildenstern!
     [*Re-enter* ROSENCRANTZ *and* GUILDENSTERN.]
  Friends both, go join you with some further aid:
  Hamlet in madness hath Polonius slain,
  And from his mother's closet hath he dragg'd him:   35
  Go seek him out; speak fair, and bring the body
  Into the chapel. I pray you, haste in this.
     [*Exeunt* ROSENCRANTZ *and* GUILDENSTERN.]
  Come, Gertrude, we'll call up our wisest friends;
  And let them know, both what we·mean to do,
  And what's untimely done. . . .               40
  Whose whisper o'er the world's diameter
  As level as the cannon to his blank
  Transports his poison'd shot, may miss our name
  And hit the woundless air. O, come away!
  My soul is full of discord and dismay.        [*Exeunt.*]

     SCENE 2—*Another room in the castle.*

    [*Enter* HAMLET.]
HAMLET. Safely stowed.
ROSENCRANTZ.    ⎱[*Within*] Hamlet! Lord Hamlet!
GUILDENSTERN. ⎰
HAMLET. But soft, what noise? who calls on Hamlet?
  O, here they come.
    [*Enter* ROSENCRANTZ *and* GUILDENSTERN.]
ROSENCRANTZ. What have you done, my lord, with the dead body?
HAMLET. Compounded it with dust, whereto 'tis kin.      6
ROSENCRANTZ. Tell us where 'tis, that we may take it thence
  And bear it to the chapel.
HAMLET. Do not believe it.
ROSENCRANTZ. Believe what?                  10
HAMLET. That I can keep your counsel and not mine own. Besides,

---

25. *ore:* gold.                42. *his blank:* his target.
32. *countenance:* recognize.     6. *compounded:* mixed.

to be demanded<sup>a</sup> of a sponge! what replication<sup>b</sup> should be made by the son of a king?

ROSENCRANTZ. Take you me for a sponge, my lord?

HAMLET. Aye, sir; that soaks up the king's countenance,<sup>c</sup> his rewards, his authorities. But such officers do the king best service in the end: he keeps them, like an ape, in the corner of his jaw; first mouthed, to be last swallowed: when he needs what you have gleaned, it is but squeezing you, and sponge, you shall be dry again.

ROSENCRANTZ. I understand you not, my lord.

HAMLET. I am glad of it: a knavish speech sleeps in a foolish ear.

ROSENCRANTZ. My lord, you must tell us where the body is, and go with us to the king.

HAMLET. The body is with the king, but the king is not with the body. The king is a thing—

GUILDENSTERN. A thing, my lord?

HAMLET. Of nothing: bring me to him. Hide fox, and all after.<sup>d</sup>

[*Exeunt.*]

*Scene 3—Another room in the castle.*

[*Enter* KING, *attended.*]

KING. I have sent to seek him, and to find the body.
How dangerous is it that this man goes loose!
Yet must not we put the strong law on him:
He's loved of the distracted multitude,
Who like not in their judgment, but their eyes;                    5
And where 'tis so, the offender's scourge is weigh'd,
But never the offense. To bear all smooth and even,
This sudden sending away must seem
Deliberate pause: diseases desperate grown
By desperate appliance are relieved,                              10
Or not at all.

[*Enter* ROSENCRANTZ.]

How now! what hath befall'n?

ROSENCRANTZ. Where the dead body is bestow'd, my lord,
We cannot get from him.

KING.                              But where is he?                 13

ROSENCRANTZ. Without, my lord; guarded, to know your pleasure.

KING. Bring him before us.

ROSENCRANTZ. Ho, Guildenstern! bring in my lord.

[*Enter* HAMLET *and* GUILDENSTERN.]

---

a. questioned by.
b. formal reply.
c. favor.
d. the name of some children's game.
6. *scourge:* punishment.

7. *bear:* conduct.
9. *Deliberate pause:* the result of careful arrangement.
10. *appliance:* treatment.

KING. Now, Hamlet, where's Polonius?

HAMLET. At supper.

KING. At supper! where?

HAMLET. Not where he eats, but where he is eaten: a certain con-
vocation of public worms are e'en at him. Your worm is your
only emperor for diet:*a* we fat all creatures else to fat us, and we
fat ourselves for maggots: your fat king and your lean beggar is
but variable service,*b* two dishes, but to one table: that's the end.

KING. Alas, alas!

HAMLET. A man may fish with the worm that hath eat of a king,
and eat of the fish that hath fed of that worm.

KING. What dost thou mean by this?

HAMLET. Nothing but to show you how a king may go a progress*c*
through the guts of a beggar.

KING. Where is Polonius?

HAMLET. In heaven; send thither to see: if your messenger find
him not there, seek him i' the other place yourself. But indeed,
if you find him not within this month, you shall nose*d* him as
you go up the stairs into the lobby.

KING. Go seek him there.                    [*To some* ATTENDANTS.]

HAMLET. He will stay till you come.          [*Exeunt* ATTENDANTS.]

KING. Hamlet, this deed, for thine especial safety,          14
Which we do tender, as we dearly grieve
For that which thou hast done, must send thee hence
With fiery quickness: therefore prepare thyself;
The bark is ready and the wind at help,
The associates tend, and every thing is bent
For England.

HAMLET.             For England?

KING.                          Aye, Hamlet.

HAMLET.                                   Good.          20

KING. So is it, if thou knew'st our purposes.

HAMLET. I see a cherub that sees them. But, come; for England!
Farewell, dear mother.

KING. Thy loving father, Hamlet.

HAMLET. My mother: father and mother is man and wife; man and
wife is one flesh, and so, my mother. Come, for England!
[*Exit.*]

KING. Follow him at foot; tempt him with speed aboard;          21
Delay it not; I'll have him hence to-night:
Away! for every thing is seal'd and done

---

*a.* possibly a punning reference to the Diet of the Holy Roman Empire at Worms.

*b.* i.e., the service varies, not the food.

*c.* royal state journey.
*d.* smell.
15. *tender:* care for.
21. *at foot:* at his heels.

That else leans on the affair: pray you, make haste.

[*Exeunt* ROSENCRANTZ *and* GUILDENSTERN.]

And, England, if my love thou hold'st at aught—— 25
As my great power thereof may give thee sense,
Since yet thy cicatrice looks raw and red
After the Danish sword, and thy free awe
Pays homage to us—thou mayst not coldly set
Our sovereign process; which imports at full, 30
By letters conjuring to that effect,
The present death of Hamlet. Do it, England;
For like the hectic in my blood he rages,
And thou must cure me; till I know 'tis done,
Howe'er my haps, my joys were ne'er begun. 35

[*Exit.*]

SCENE 4—A *plain in Denmark.*

[*Enter* FORTINBRAS, *a* CAPTAIN *and* SOLDIERS, *marching.*]

FORTINBRAS. Go, captain, from me greet the Danish king;
Tell him that by his license Fortinbras
Craves the conveyance of a promised march
Over his kingdom. You know the rendezvous.
If that his majesty would aught with us, 5
We shall express our duty in his eye;
And let him know so.

CAPTAIN.                I will do 't, my lord.

FORTINBRAS. Go softly on.

[*Exeunt* FORTINBRAS *and* SOLDIERS. —*Enter* HAMLET, ROSEN-
CRANTZ, GUILDENSTERN, *and others.*]

HAMLET. Good sir, whose powers are these?

CAPTAIN. They are of Norway, sir. 10

HAMLET. How purposed, sir, I pray you?

CAPTAIN. Against some part of Poland.

HAMLET. Who commands them, sir?

CAPTAIN. The nephew to Old Norway, Fortinbras.

HAMLET. Goes it against the main of Poland, sir, 15
Or for some frontier?

CAPTAIN. Truly to speak, and with no addition,
We go to gain a little patch of ground
That hath in it no profit but the name.
To pay five ducats, five, I would not farm it; 20
Nor will it yield to Norway or the Pole

24. *leans on:* pertains to.
25. *England:* the king of England.
26. *give thee sense:* make you feel.
29. *coldly set:* regard with indifference.
31. *conjuring:* enjoining.

33. *hectic:* fever.
3. *conveyance:* convoy.
6. *eye:* presence.
9. *powers:* armed forces.
15. *the main:* the whole of.

A ranker rate, should it be sold in fee.
HAMLET. Why, then the Polack never will defend it.
CAPTAIN. Yes, it is already garrison'd.
HAMLET. Two thousand souls and twenty thousand ducats          25
Will not debate the question of this straw:
This is the imposthume of much wealth and peace,
That inward breaks, and shows no cause without
Why the man dies. I humbly thank you, sir.
CAPTAIN. God be wi' you, sir.                              [Exit.]
ROSENCRANTZ.                    Will 't please you go, my lord?   30
HAMLET. I'll be with you straight. Go a little before.
     [*Exeunt all but* HAMLET.]
How all occasions do inform against me,
And spur my dull revenge! What is a man,
If his chief good and market of his time
Be but to sleep and feed? a beast, no more.                35
Sure, he that made us with such large discourse,
Looking before and after, gave us not
That capability and god-like reason
To fust in us unused. Now, whether it be
Bestial oblivion, or some craven scruple                   40
Of thinking too precisely on the event,—
A thought which, quarter'd, hath but one part wisdom
And ever three parts coward,—I do not know
Why yet I live to say 'this thing's to do,'
Sith I have cause, and will, and strength, and means,       45
To do 't. Examples gross as earth exhort me:
Witness this army, of such mass and charge,
Led by a delicate and tender prince,
Whose spirit with divine ambition puff'd
Makes mouths at the invisible event,                       50
Exposing what is mortal and unsure
To all that fortune, death and danger dare,
Even for an egg-shell. Rightly to be great
Is not to stir without great argument,
But greatly to find quarrel in a straw                     55
When honor's at the stake. How stand I then,
That have a father kill'd, a mother stain'd,
Excitements of my reason and my blood,
And let all sleep, while to my shame I see

22. *ranker:* higher. *in fee:* for abso-    cask.
lute possession.                        41. *event:* outcome.
27. *imposthume:* ulcer.         45. *Sith:* since.
32. *inform against:* denounce.   46. *gross:* large.
34. *market:* payment for, reward.  47. *charge:* cost.
36. *discourse:* reasoning power.   50. *Makes mouths:* makes faces.
39. *fust:* become moldy, taste of the  *event:* outcome.

The imminent death of twenty thousand men,    60
That for a fantasy and trick of fame
Go to their graves like beds, fight for a plot
Whereon the numbers cannot try the cause,
Which is not tomb enough and continent
To hide the slain? O, from this time forth,    65
My thoughts be bloody, or be nothing worth!     [*Exit.*]

SCENE 5—*Elsinore. A room in the castle.*

[*Enter* QUEEN, HORATIO, *and a* GENTLEMAN.]

QUEEN. I will not speak with her.
GENTLEMAN. She is importunate, indeed distract:
  Her mood will needs be pitied.
QUEEN.                  What would she have?
GENTLEMAN. She speaks much of her father, says she hears
  There's tricks i' the world, and hems and beats her heart,    5
  Spurns enviously at straws; speaks things in doubt,
  That carry but half sense: her speech is nothing,
  Yet the unshapèd use of it doth move
  The hearers to collection; they aim at it,
  And botch the words up fit to their own thoughts;    10
  Which, as her winks and nods and gestures yield them,
  Indeed would make one think there might be thought,
  Though nothing sure, yet much unhappily.
HORATIO. 'Twere good she were spoken with, for she may strew
  Dangerous conjectures in ill-breeding minds.    15
QUEEN. Let her come in.             [*Exit* GENTLEMAN.]
  [*Aside*] To my sick soul, as sin's true nature is,
  Each toy seems prologue to some great amiss:
  So full of artless jealousy is guilt,
  It spills itself in fearing to be spilt.    20

[*Re-enter* GENTLEMAN, *with* OPHELIA.]

OPHELIA. Where is the beauteous majesty of Denmark?
QUEEN. How now, Ophelia!
OPHELIA. [*Sings*] How should I your true love know
          From another one?
        By his cockle hat and staff    25
        And his sandal shoon.

---

61. *trick of:* trifle of.
63. *Whereon . . . cause:* so small that it cannot hold the men who fight for it.
64. *continent:* container.
6. *Spurns . . . straws:* gets angry at trifles.
9. *collection:* gathering up her words and trying to make sense out of them. *aim:* guess.

10. *botch:* patch.
15. *ill-breeding minds:* minds breeding evil thoughts.
18. *toy:* trifle. *amiss:* misfortune.
19. *artless:* uncontrolled, unreasonable. *jealousy:* suspicion.
25–26. *cockle hat . . . shoon:* typical signs of pilgrims traveling to places of devotion.
26. *shoon:* shoes.

QUEEN. Alas, sweet lady, what imports this song?

OPHELIA. Say you? nay, pray you, mark.

  [*Sings*] He is dead and gone, lady,
        He is dead and gone;               30
      At his head a grass-green turf,
      At his heels a stone.

  Oh, oh!

QUEEN.       Nay, but Ophelia,—

OPHELIA.                      Pray you, mark.

  [*Sings*] White his shroud as the mountain snow,—   35
    [*Enter* KING.]

QUEEN. Alas, look here, my lord.

OPHELIA. [*Sings*]   Larded with sweet flowers;
        Which bewept to the grave did go
        With true-love showers.              39

KING. How do you, pretty lady?

OPHELIA. Well, God 'ild you![a] They say the owl was a baker's daughter. Lord, we know what we are, but know not what we may be.[b] God be at your table!

KING. Conceit[c] upon her father.

OPHELIA. Pray you, let's have no words of this; but when they ask you what it means, say you this:

  [*Sings*] To-morrow is Saint Valentine's day       40
      All in the morning betime,
    And I a maid at your window,
      To be your Valentine.
    Then up he rose, and donn'd his clothes,
      And dupp'd the chamber-door;         45
    Let in the maid, that out a maid
    Never departed more.

KING. Pretty Ophelia!

OPHELIA. Indeed, la, without an oath, I'll make an end on 't:

  [*Sings*] By Gis and by Saint Charity,        50
      Alack, and fie for shame!
    Young men will do 't, if they come to 't;
      By cock, they are to blame.
    Quoth she, before you tumbled me,
      You promised me to wed.          55

  He answers:
    So would I ha' done, by yonder sun,
      An thou hadst not come to my bed.    58

---

37. *larded:* garnished.
a. God yield (i.e., repay) you.
b. an allusion to a folk tale about a baker's daughter changed into an owl

for having shown little charity to the Lord.
c. imagination.
45. *dupp'd:* opened.
50. *By Gis:* by Jesus.

KING. How long hath she been thus?

OPHELIA. I hope all will be well. We must be patient: but I cannot choose but weep, to think they should lay him i' the cold ground. My brother shall know of it: and so I thank you for your good counsel. Come, my coach! Good night, ladies; good night, sweet ladies; good night, good night.

    [*Exit.*]

KING. Follow her close; give her good watch, I pray you.

    [*Exit* HORATIO.]

O, this is the poison of deep grief; it springs      59
All from her father's death. O Gertrude, Gertrude,
When sorrows come, they come not single spies,
But in battalions! First, her father slain:
Next, your son gone; and he most violent author
Of his own just remove: the people muddied,
Thick and unwholesome in their thoughts and whispers,    65
For good Polonius' death; and we have done but greenly,
In hugger-mugger to inter him: poor Ophelia
Divided from herself and her fair judgment,
Without the which we are pictures, or mere beasts:
Last, and as much containing as all these,      70
Her brother is in secret come from France,
Feeds on his wonder, keeps himself in clouds,
And wants not buzzers to infect his ear
With pestilent speeches of his father's death;
Wherein necessity, of matter beggar'd,      75
Will nothing stick our person to arraign
In ear and ear. O my dear Gertrude, this,
Like to a murdering-piece, in many places
Gives me superfluous death.      [*A noise within.*]

QUEEN.            Alack, what noise is this?

KING. Where are my Switzers? Let them guard the door.    80

    [*Enter another* GENTLEMAN.]

What is the matter?

GENTLEMAN.          Save yourself, my lord:
The ocean, overpeering of his list,
Eats not the flats with more impetuous haste
Than young Laertes, in a riotous head,

---

64. *muddied:* confused, their thoughts made turbid (as water by mud).
66. *greenly:* foolishly.
67. *hugger-mugger:* hasty secrecy.
72. *Feeds on his wonder:* broods, keeps wondering.
73. *wants:* lacks.
75. *necessity . . . beggar'd:* the necessity to build up a story, without the materials for doing so.
76. *Will . . . arraign:* will not hesitate to accuse me.
78. *murdering-piece:* a variety of cannon which scattered its shot in many directions.
80. *Switzers:* Swiss guards.
82. *overpeering of his list:* overflowing above the high-water mark.
84. *head:* group of rebels.

O'erbears your officers. The rabble call him lord;                    85
And, as the world were now but to begin,
Antiquity forgot, custom not known,
The ratifiers and props of every word,
They cry 'Choose we; Laertes shall be king!'
Caps, hands and tongues applaud it to the clouds,        90
'Laertes shall be king, Laertes king!'

QUEEN. How cheerfully on the false trail they cry!
O, this is counter, you false Danish dogs!        [*Noise within.*]

KING. The doors are broke.

[*Enter* LAERTES, *armed;* DANES *following.*]

LAERTES. Where is this king? Sirs, stand you all without.        95

DANES. No, let's come in.

LAERTES.                    I pray you, give me leave.

DANES. We will, we will.        [*They retire without the door.*]

LAERTES. I thank you: keep the door. O thou vile king,
Give me my father!

QUEEN.                Calmly, good Laertes.

LAERTES. That drop of blood that's calm proclaims me bastard;    100
Cries cuckold to my father; brands the harlot
Even here, between the chaste unsmirched brows
Of my true mother.

KING.                What is the cause, Laertes,
That thy rebellion looks so giant-like?
Let him go, Gertrude; do not fear our person:        105
There's such divinity doth hedge a king,
That treason can but peep to what it would,
Acts little of his will. Tell me, Laertes,
Why thou art thus incensed: let him go, Gertrude:
Speak, man.        110

LAERTES. Where is my father?

KING.            Dead.

QUEEN.                    But not by him.

KING. Let him demand his fill.

LAERTES. How came he dead? I'll not be juggled with:
To hell, allegiance! vows, to the blackest devil!
Conscience and grace, to the profoundest pit!        115
I dare damnation: to this point I stand,
That both the worlds I give to negligence,
Let come what comes; only I'll be revenged
Most throughly for my father.

---

93. *counter:* following the scent in the wrong direction.
105. *fear:* fear for.
107. *would:* desires.

108. *his:* its.
117. *both . . . negligence:* I don't care what may happen to me in either this world or the next.

KING.                              Who shall stay you?

LAERTES. My will, not all the world:                              120
    And for my means, I'll husband them so well,
    They shall go far with little.

KING.                              Good Laertes,
    If you desire to know the certainty
    Of your dear father's death, is 't writ in your revenge
    That, swoopstake, you will draw both friend and foe,            125
    Winner and loser?

LAERTES. None but his enemies.

KING.                              Will you know them then?

LAERTES. To his good friends thus wide I'll ope my arms;
    And, like the kind life-rendering pelican,
    Repast them with my blood.

KING.                              Why, now you speak            130
    Like a good child and a true gentleman.
    That I am guiltless of your father's death,
    And am most sensibly in grief for it,
    It shall as level to your judgment pierce
    As day does to your eye.

DANES. [*Within*]            Let her come in.            135

LAERTES. How now! what noise is that?

    [*Re-enter* OPHELIA.]

    O heat, dry up my brains! tears seven times salt,
    Burn out the sense and virtue of mine eye!
    By heaven, thy madness shall be paid with weight,
    Till our scale turn the beam. O rose of May!            140
    Dear maid, kind sister, sweet Ophelia!
    O heavens! is 't possible a young maid's wits
    Should be as mortal as an old man's life?
    Nature is fine in love, and where 'tis fine
    It sends some precious instance of itself            145
    After the thing it loves.

OPHELIA. [*Sings*] They bore him barefaced on the bier:
             Hey non nonny, nonny, hey nonny:
             And in his grave rain'd many a tear,—
    Fare you well, my dove!                              150

LAERTES. Hadst thou thy wits, and didst persuade revenge,
    It could not move thus.

OPHELIA. [*Sings*] You must sing down a-down,

---

125. *swoopstake:* without making any distinction, as the winner takes the whole stake in a card game.
129. *life-rendering:* The mythical pelican is supposed to feed its young with its own blood.
138. *virtue:* power, faculty.
144. *fine:* refined.
145. *instance:* sample, token.

An you call him a-down-a. 154

O, how the wheel*d* becomes it! It is the false steward, that stole his master's daughter.*e*

LAERTES. This nothing's more than matter.*f*

OPHELIA. There's rosemary, that's for remembrance: pray you, love, remember: and there is pansies,*g* that's for thoughts.

LAERTES. A document*h* in madness; thoughts and remembrance fitted.

OPHELIA. There's fennel*i* for you, and columbines:*j* there's rue*k* for you: and here's some for me: we may call it herbs of grace o' Sundays: O, you must wear your rue with a difference. There's a daisy: I would give you some violets,*l* but they withered all when my father died: they say he made a good end,—

[*Sings*] For bonnie sweet Robin is all my joy. 155

LAERTES. Thought and affliction, passion, hell itself, She turns to favor and to prettiness.

OPHELIA. [*Sings*]   And will he not come again?
              And will he not come again?
                  No, no, he is dead,  160
                  Go to thy death-bed,
              He never will come again.

              His beard was as white as snow,
              All flaxen was his poll:
                  He is gone, he is gone,  165
                  And we cast away moan:
              God ha' mercy on his soul!

And of all Christian souls, I pray God. God be wi' you.
    [*Exit.*]

LAERTES. Do you see this, O God?

KING. Laertes, I must commune with your grief, 170
Or you deny me right. Go but apart,
Make choice of whom your wisest friends you will.
And they shall hear and judge 'twixt you and me:
If by direct or by collateral hand
They find us touched, we will our kingdom give, 175
Our crown, our life, and all that we call ours,
To you in satisfaction; but if not,
Be you content to lend your patience to us,
And we shall jointly labor with your soul

*d.* ballads were often sung to the motion of a spinning wheel.
*e.* an allusion to an unknown folk ballad.
*f.* This nonsense is more indicative than sane speech.
*g.* the symbol of thought.
*h.* lesson.
*i.* emblem of flattery.

*j.* emblem of cuckoldom.
*k.* emblem of sorrow and repentance (compare the verb "rue").
*l.* for faithfulness.
157. *favor:* charm.
174. *collateral:* indirect.
175. *touched:* involved (in the murder).

To give it due content.

LAERTES.                     Let this be so;                     180
His means of death, his obscure funeral,
No trophy, sword, nor hatchment o'er his bones,
No noble rite nor formal ostentation,
Cry to be heard, as 'twere from heaven to earth,
That I must call 't in question.

KING.                                   So you shall;            185
And where the offense is let the great axe fall.
I pray you, go with me.                     [*Exeunt.*]

SCENE 6—*Another room in the castle.*

[*Enter* HORATIO *and a* SERVANT.]

HORATIO. What are they that would speak with me?

SERVANT. Sea-faring men, sir: they say they have letters for you.

HORATIO. Let them come in.                 [*Exit* SERVANT.]
I do not know from what part of the world
I should be greeted, if not from Lord Hamlet.

[*Enter* SAILORS.]

FIRST SAILOR. God bless you, sir.

HORATIO. Let him bless thee too.

FIRST SAILOR. He shall, sir, an 't please him.
There's a letter for you, sir; it comes from the ambassador that
was bound for England; if your name be Horatio, as I am let to
know it is.

HORATIO. [*Reads*] 'Horatio, when thou shalt have overlooked*a* this,
give these fellows some means to the king: they have letters for
him. Ere we were two days old at sea, a pirate of very warlike
appointment gave us chase. Finding ourselves too slow of sail,
we put on a compelled valor, and in the grapple I boarded them:
on the instant they got clear of our ship; so I alone became their
prisoner. They have dealt with me like thieves of mercy:*b* but
they knew what they did; I am to do a good turn for them. Let
the king have the letters I have sent; and repair thou to me with
as much speed as thou wouldst fly death. I have words to speak
in thine ear will make thee dumb; yet are they much too light
for the bore*c* of the matter. These good fellows will bring thee
where I am. Rosencrantz and Guildenstern hold their course for
England: of them I have much to tell thee. Farewell.

                    'He that thou knowest thine, HAMLET.'
Come, I will make you way for these your letters;
And do 't the speedier, that you may direct me
To him from whom you brought them.         [*Exeunt.*]

182. *hatchment:* coat of arms.       *b.* merciful.
183. *ostentation:* pomp.             *c.* caliber, i.e., importance.
*a.* read over.

SCENE 7—*Another room in the castle.*

[*Enter* KING *and* LAERTES.]

KING. Now must your conscience my acquittance seal,
And you must put me in your heart for friend,
Sith you have heard, and with a knowing ear,
That he which hath your noble father slain
Pursued my life.

LAERTES.                    It well appears: but tell me          5
Why you proceeded not against these feats,
So crimeful and so capital in nature,
As by your safety, wisdom, all things else,
You mainly were stirr'd up.

KING.                              O, for two special reasons,
Which may to you perhaps seem much unsinew'd,          10
But yet to me they're strong. The queen his mother
Lives almost by his looks; and for myself—
My virtue or my plague, be it either which—
She's so conjunctive to my life and soul,
That, as the star moves not but in his sphere,          15
I could not but by her. The other motive,
Why to a public count I might not go,
Is the great love the general gender bear him;
Who, dipping all his faults in their affection,
Would, like the spring that turneth wood to stone,          20
Convert his gyves to graces; so that my arrows,
Too slightly timber'd for so loud a wind,
Would have reverted to my bow again
And not where I had aim'd them.

LAERTES. And so have I a noble father lost;          25
A sister driven into desperate terms,
Whose worth, if praises may go back again,
Stood challenger on mount of all the age
For her perfections: but my revenge will come.

KING. Break not your sleeps for that: you must not think          30
That we are made of stuff so flat and dull
That we can let our beard be shook with danger
And think it pastime. You shortly shall hear more:
I loved your father, and we love ourself;
And that, I hope, will teach you to imagine—          35
     [*Enter a* MESSENGER, *with letters.*]

---

6. *feats:* deeds.
9. *mainly:* powerfully.
10. *unsinew'd:* weak.
14. *conjunctive:* closely joined.
17. *count:* accounting, trial.

18. *general gender:* common people.
21. *gyves:* fetters.
27. *go back:* i.e., to what she was before her madness.
28. *on mount of:* above.

How now! what news?

MESSENGER.                    Letters, my lord, from Hamlet:
This to your majesty; this to the queen.

KING. From Hamlet! who brought them?

MESSENGER. Sailors, my lord, they say; I saw them not:
They were given me by Claudio; he received them
Of him that brought them.

KING.                              Laertes, you shall hear them.      41
Leave us.                              [*Exit* MESSENGER.]

[*Reads*] 'High and mighty, you shall know I am set naked on
your kingdom. To-morrow shall I beg leave to see your kingly
eyes: when I shall, first asking your pardon*a* thereunto, recount
the occasion of my sudden and more strange return.   HAMLET.'
What should this mean? Are all the rest come back?      42
Or is it some abuse, and no such thing?

LAERTES. Know you the hand?

KING. 'Tis Hamlet's character. 'Naked'!      45
And in a postscript here, he says 'alone.'
Can you advise me?

LAERTES. I'm lost in it, my lord. But let him come;
It warms the very sickness in my heart,
That I shall live and tell him to his teeth,      50
'Thus diddest thou.'

KING.                    If it be so, Laertes,—
As how should it be so? how otherwise?—
Will you be ruled by me?

LAERTES.                    Aye, my lord;
So you will not o'errule me to a peace.

KING. To thine own peace. If he be now return'd,      55
As checking at his voyage, and that he means
No more to undertake it, I will work him
To an exploit now ripe in my device,
Under the which he shall not choose but fall:
And for his death no wind of blame shall breathe;      60
But even his mother shall uncharge the practice,
And call it accident.

LAERTES.                    My lord, I will be ruled;
The rather, if you could devise it so
That I might be the organ.

KING.                    It falls right.
You have been talk'd of since your travel much,      65

---

a. leave.
43. *some*:. . . *thing:* a delusion, not
a reality.
45. *character:* handwriting.

56. *checking at:* changing the course
of, refusing to continue.
61: *uncharge the practice:* not recognize it as a plot.
64. *organ:* instrument.

And that in Hamlet's hearing, for a quality
Wherein, they say, you shine; your sum of parts
Did not together pluck such envy from him,
As did that one, and that in my regard
Of the unworthiest siege.

LAERTES.                              What part is that, my lord?    70

KING. A very riband in the cap of youth,
  Yet needful too; for youth no less becomes
  The light and careless livery that it wears
  Than settled age his sables and his weeds,
  Importing health and graveness. Two months since    75
  Here was a gentleman of Normandy:—
  I've seen myself, and served against, the French,
  And they can well on horseback: but this gallant
  Had witchcraft in 't; he grew unto his seat,
  And to such wondrous doing brought this horse    80
  As had he been incorpsed and demi-natured
  With the brave beast: so far he topp'd my thought
  That I, in forgery of shapes and tricks,
  Come short of what he did.

LAERTES.                              A Norman was 't?

KING. A Norman.                                                        85

LAERTES. Upon my life, Lamord.

KING.                              The very same.

LAERTES. I know him well: he is the brooch indeed
  And gem of all the nation.

KING. He made confession of you,
  And gave you such a masterly report,                               90
  For art and exercise in your defense,
  And for your rapier most especial,
  That he cried out, 'twould be a sight indeed
  If one could match you: the scrimers of their nation,
  He swore, had neither motion, guard, nor eye,                      95
  If you opposed them. Sir, this report of his
  Did Hamlet so unvenom with his envy
  That he could nothing do but wish and beg
  Your sudden coming o'er, to play with him.
  Now, out of this—

LAERTES.                              What out of this, my lord?    100

67. *your sum of parts:* the sum of your gifts.
70. *siege:* seat, i.e., rank.
71. *riband:* ribbon, ornament.
72. *becomes:* is the appropriate age for.
74. *sables:* blacks, also furs. *weeds:* robes.
81. *incorpsed:* incorporated. *demi-natured:* split his nature in two.
83. *in forgery . . . tricks:* in imaging methods and skills of horsemanship.
87. *brooch:* ornament.
90–91. *masterly . . . defense:* report of your mastery in the theory and practice of fencing.
94. *scrimers:* fencers.

KING. Laertes, was your father dear to you?
Or are you like the painting of a sorrow,
A face without a heart?
LAERTES.                          Why ask you this?
KING. Not that I think you did not love your father,
But that I know love is begun by time,                                    105
And that I see, in passages of proof,
Time qualifies the spark and fire of it.
There lives within the very flame of love
A kind of wick or snuff that will abate it;
And nothing is at a like goodness still,                                   110
For goodness, growing to a plurisy,
Dies in his own too much: that we would do
We should do when we would; for this 'would' changes
And hath abatements and delays as many
As there are tongues, are hands, are accidents,                           115
And then this 'should' is like a spendthrift sigh,
That hurts by easing. But, to the quick o' the ulcer:
Hamlet comes back: what would you undertake,
To show yourself your father's son in deed
More than in words?
LAERTES.                          To cut his throat i' the church.         120
KING. No place indeed should murder sanctuarize;
Revenge should have no bounds. But, good Laertes,
Will you do this, keep close within your chamber.
Hamlet return'd shall know you are come home:
We'll put on those shall praise your excellence                           125
And set a double varnish on the fame
The Frenchman gave you; bring you in fine together
And wager on your heads: he, being remiss,
Most generous and free from all contriving,
Will not peruse the foils, so that with ease,                             130
Or with a little shuffling, you may choose
A sword unbated, and in a pass of practice
Requite him for your father.
LAERTES.                          I will do 't;
And for that purpose I'll anoint my sword.
I bought an unction of a mountebank,                                      135

---

106. *passages of proof:* instances which prove it.
107. *qualifies:* weakens.
109. *snuff:* charred part of the wick.
110. *still:* constantly.
111. *plurisy:* excess of blood.
116–117. *sigh . . . easing:* a sigh which gives relief but is harmful (according to an old notion that it draws blood from the heart).

125. *put on:* instigate.
127. *in fine:* finally.
128. *remiss:* careless.
130. *peruse:* examine closely.
132. *unbated:* not blunted (as a rapier for exercise ordinarily would be). *pass of practice:* treacherous thrust.
135. *unction:* ointment. *mountebank:* peddler of quack medicines.

So mortal that but dip a knife in it,
Where it draws blood no cataplasm so rare,
Collected from all simples that have virtue
Under the moon, can save the thing from death
That is but scratch'd withal: I'll touch my point          140
With this contagion, that, if I gall him slightly,
It may be death.
KING.                    Let's further think of this;
Weigh what convenience both of time and means
May fit us to our shape: if this should fail,
And that our drift look through our bad performance,         145
'Twere better not assay'd: therefore this project
Should have a back or second, that might hold
If this did blast in proof. Soft! let me see:
We'll make a solemn wager on your cunnings:
I ha 't:                                                     150
When in your motion you are hot and dry—
As make your bouts more violent to that end—
And that he calls for drink, I'll have prepared him
A chalice for the nonce; whereon but sipping,
If he by chance escape your venom'd stuck,                   155
Our purpose may hold there. But stay, what noise?
        [*Enter* QUEEN.]
How now, sweet queen!
QUEEN. One woe doth tread upon another's heel,
So fast they follow: your sister's drown'd, Laertes.
LAERTES. Drown'd! O, where?                                 160
QUEEN. There is a willow grows aslant a brook,
That shows his hoar leaves in the glassy stream;
There with fantastic garlands did she come
Of crow-flowers, nettles, daisies, and long purples,
That liberal shepherds give a grosser name,                 165
But our cold maids do dead men's fingers call them:
There, on the pendent boughs her coronet weeds
Clambering to hang, an envious sliver broke;
When down her weedy trophies and herself
Fell in the weeping brook. Her clothes spread wide,         170
And mermaid-like a while they bore her up:
Which time she chanted snatches of old tunes,
As one incapable of her own distress,

---

137. *cataplasm:* plaster.
138. *simples:* healing herbs.
141. *gall:* scratch.
144. *shape:* plan.
145. *our . . . through:* our design should show through.
148. *blast in proof:* burst (like a new firearm) once it is put to the test.
154. *for the nonce:* for that particular occasion.
155. *stuck:* thrust.
161. *aslant:* across.
168. *envious sliver:* malicious bough.
173. *incapable:* insensitive to.

Or like a creature native and indued
Unto that element: but long it could not be                   175
Till that her garments, heavy with their drink,
Pull'd the poor wretch from her melodious lay
To muddy death.

LAERTES.                    Alas, then she is drown'd!

QUEEN. Drown'd, drown'd.

LAERTES. Too much of water hast thou, poor Ophelia,          180
And therefore I forbid my tears: but yet
It is our trick; nature her custom holds,
Let shame say what it will: when these are gone,
The woman will be out. Adieu, my lord:
I have a speech of fire that fain would blaze,               185
But that this folly douts it.                    [*Exit.*]

KING.                    Let's follow, Gertrude:
How much I had to do to calm his rage!
Now fear I this will give it start again;
Therefore let's follow.                          [*Exeunt.*]


## Act V

### SCENE 1—A *churchyard.*

[*Enter two* CLOWNS, *with spades, &c.*]

FIRST CLOWN. Is she to be buried in Christian burial that willfully
seeks her own salvation?

SECOND CLOWN. I tell thee she is; and therefore make her grave
straight:ᵃ the crownerᵇ hath sat on her, and finds it Christian
burial.

FIRST CLOWN. How can that be, unless she drowned herself in her
own defense?

SECOND CLOWN. Why, 'tis found so.

FIRST CLOWN. It must be 'se offendendo;'ᶜ it cannot be else. For
here lies the point: if I drown myself wittingly, it argues an act:
and an act hath three branches; it is, to act, to do, to perform:
argal,ᵈ she drowned herself wittingly.

SECOND CLOWN. Nay, but hear you, goodman delver.

FIRST CLOWN. Give me leave. Here lies the water; good: here stands
the man; good: if the man go to this water and drown himself,
it is, will he, nill he,ᵉ he goes; mark you that; but if the water
come to him and drown him, he drowns not himself: argal, he
that is not guilty of his own death shortens not his own life.

---

174. *indued:* adapted, in harmony
with.
182. *trick:* peculiar trait.
184. *The woman:* the softer qualities, the woman in me.
186. *douts:* extinguishes.

*a.* straightway.
*b.* coroner.
*c.* the Clown's blunder for *se de-
fendendo,* "in self-defense."
*d.* blunder for *ergo,* "therefore."
*e.* willy-nilly.

SECOND CLOWN. But is this law?

FIRST CLOWN. Aye, marry, is 't; crowner's quest[f] law.

SECOND CLOWN. Will you ha' the truth on 't? If this had not been a gentlewoman, she should have been buried out o' Christian burial.

FIRST CLOWN. Why, there thou say'st: and the more pity that great folk should have countenance[g] in this world to drown or hang themselves, more than their even Christian.[h] Come, my spade. There is no ancient gentlemen but gardeners, ditchers and grave-makers: they hold up Adam's profession.

SECOND CLOWN. Was he a gentleman?

FIRST CLOWN. A' was the first that ever bore arms.

SECOND CLOWN. Why, he had none.

FIRST CLOWN. What, art a heathen? How dost thou understand the Scripture? The Scripture says Adam digged: could he dig without arms? I'll put another question to thee: if thou answerest me not to the purpose, confess thyself—

SECOND CLOWN. Go to.

FIRST CLOWN. What is he that builds stronger than either the mason, the shipwright, or the carpenter?

SECOND CLOWN. The gallows-maker; for that frame outlives a thousand tenants.

FIRST CLOWN. I like thy wit well, in good faith: the gallows does well; but how does it well? it does well to those that do ill: now, thou dost ill to say the gallows is built stronger than the church: argal, the gallows may do well to thee. To 't again, come.

SECOND CLOWN. 'Who builds stronger than a mason, a shipwright, or a carpenter?'

FIRST CLOWN. Aye, tell me that, and unyoke.[i]

SECOND CLOWN. Marry, now I can tell.

FIRST CLOWN. To 't.

SECOND CLOWN. Mass, I cannot tell.

[*Enter* HAMLET *and* HORATIO, *afar off.*]

FIRST CLOWN. Cudgel thy brains no more about it, for your dull ass will not mend his pace with beating, and when you are asked this question next, say 'a grave-maker:' the houses that he makes last till doomsday. Go, get thee to Yaughan;[j] fetch me a stoup[k] of liquor.

[*Exit* SECOND CLOWN. —FIRST CLOWN *digs and sings.*]

In youth, when I did love, did love,
　　Methought it was very sweet,
To contract,[l] O, the time, for-a my behove,[m]

f. inquest.
g. sanction.
h. fellow Christian.
i. call it a day.

j. apparently a tavern-keeper's name.
k. mug.
l. shorten.
m. profit.

O, methought, there-a was nothing-a meet.ⁿ

HAMLET. Has this fellow no feeling of his business that he sings at grave-making?

HORATIO. Custom hath made it in him a property of easiness.ᵒ

HAMLET. 'Tis e'en so: the hand of little employmentᵖ hath the daintierᑫ sense.

FIRST CLOWN. [*Sings*] But age, with his stealing steps,
    Hath claw'd me in his clutch,
    And hath shipped me intilʳ the land,
    As if I had never been such.
 [*Throws up a skull.*]

HAMLET. That skull had a tongue in it, and could sing once: how the knave jowlsˢ it to the ground, as if it were Cain's jaw-bone, that did the first murder!ᵗ It might be the pate of a politician,ᵘ which this ass now o'er-reaches;ᵛ one that would circumvent God, might it not?

HORATIO. It might, my lord.

HAMLET. Or of a courtier, which could say, 'Good morrow, sweet lord! How dost thou, sweet lord?' This might be my lord such-a-one, that praised my lord such-a-one's horse, when he meant to beg it; might it not?

HORATIO. Aye, my lord.

HAMLET. Why, e'en so: and now my Lady Worm's; chapless,ʷ and knocked about the mazzardˣ with a sexton's spade: here's fine revolution, an we had the trickʸ to see 't. Did these bones cost no more the breeding, but to play at loggatsᶻ with 'em? mine ache to think on 't.

FIRST CLOWN. [*Sings*] A pick-axe, and a spade, a spade,
    For a shrouding sheet:
    O, a pit of clay for to be made
    For such a guest is meet.
 [*Throws up another skull.*]

HAMLET. There's another: why may not that be the skull of a lawyer? Where be his quidditiesᵃ now, his quillets,ᵇ his cases, his tenures,ᶜ and his tricks? why does he suffer this rude knave now to knock him about the sconceᵈ with a dirty shovel, and will not tell him of his action of battery?ᵉ Hum! This fellow might be in 's time

---

*n.* fitting.
*o.* has made it a matter of indifference to him.
*p.* which does little labor.
*q.* finer sensitivity.
*r.* into.
*s.* knocks.
*t.* possibly an allusion to the legend according to which Cain slew Abel with an ass's jawbone.
*u.* the word has a pejorative sense.

*v.* outwits.
*w.* her lower jawbone missing.
*x.* pate.
*y.* faculty.
*z.* a game resembling bowls.
*a.* subtle definitions.
*b.* quibbles.
*c.* real-estate holdings.
*d.* head.
*e.* assault.

a great buyer of land, with his statutes, his recognizances,*f* his
fines, his double vouchers, his recoveries:*g* is this the fine*h* of his
fines and the recovery of his recoveries, to have his fine pate full
of fine dirt? will his vouchers vouch him no more of his purchases,
and double ones too, than the length and breadth of a pair of
indentures?*i* The very conveyances*j* of his lands will hardly lie in
this box; and must the inheritor himself have no more, ha?

HORATIO. Not a jot more, my lord.

HAMLET. Is not parchment made of sheep-skins?

HORATIO. Aye, my lord, and of calf-skins too.

HAMLET. They are sheep and calves which seek out assurance*k* in
that. I will speak to this fellow. Whose grave's this, sirrah?

FIRST CLOWN. Mine, sir.

[*Sings*] O, a pit of clay for to be made
For such a guest is meet.

HAMLET. I think it be thine indeed, for thou liest in 't.

FIRST CLOWN. You lie out on 't, sir, and therefore 'tis not yours: for
my part, I do not lie in 't, and yet it is mine.

HAMLET. Thou dost lie in 't, to be in 't and say it is thine: 'tis for
the dead, not for the quick;*l* therefore thou liest.

FIRST CLOWN. 'Tis a quick lie, sir; 'twill away again, from me to you.

HAMLET. What man dost thou dig it for?

FIRST CLOWN. For no man, sir.

HAMLET. What woman then?

FIRST CLOWN. For none neither.

HAMLET. Who is to be buried in 't?

FIRST CLOWN. One that was a woman, sir; but, rest her soul, she 's
dead.

HAMLET. How absolute*m* the knave is! we must speak by the card,*n*
or equivocation will undo us. By the Lord, Horatio, these three
years I have taken note of it; the age is grown so picked*o* that the
toe of the peasant comes so near the heel of the courtier, he galls
his kibe.*p* How long hast thou been a grave-maker?

FIRST CLOWN. Of all the days i' the year, I came to 't that day that
our last King Hamlet o'ercame Fortinbras.

HAMLET. How long is that since?

FIRST CLOWN. Cannot you tell that? every fool can tell that: it was

*f. statutes . . . recognizances:* varieties of bonds.

*g. his fines, his double vouchers, his
recoveries:* legal terms relating to the
transference of estates.

*h.* end. Hamlet is punning on the
legal and nonlegal meanings of the
word. Similarly the other terms are
played with in the following lines.

*i.* contracts drawn in duplicate on the
same piece of parchment, the two copies

separated by an "indented" line.

*j.* deeds.

*k.* security; another pun, since the
word is also a legal term.

*l.* living.

*m.* positive.

*n.* by the chart, i.e., with exactness.

*o.* choice, fastidious.

*p.* hurts the chilblain on the courtier's heel.

that very day that young Hamlet was born: he that is mad, and
sent into England.

HAMLET. Aye, marry, why was he sent into England?

FIRST CLOWN. Why, because a' was mad; a' shall recover his wits
there: or, if a' do not, 'tis no great matter there.

HAMLET. Why?

FIRST CLOWN. 'Twill not be seen in him there; there the men are
as mad as he.

HAMLET. How came he mad?

FIRST CLOWN. Very strangely, they say.

HAMLET. How 'strangely'?

FIRST CLOWN. Faith, e'en with losing his wits.

HAMLET. Upon what ground?

FIRST CLOWN. Why, here in Denmark: I have been sexton here,
man and boy, thirty years.

HAMLET. How long will a man lie i' the earth ere he rot?

FIRST CLOWN. I' faith, if a' be not rotten before a' die—as we have
many pocky*q* corses now-a-days, that will scarce hold the laying
in*r*—a' will last you some eight year or nine year: a tanner will
last you nine year.

HAMLET. Why he more than another?

FIRST CLOWN. Why, sir, his hide is so tanned with his trade that a'
will keep out water a great while; and your water is a sore de-
cayer of your whoreson dead body. Here's a skull now: this skull
has lain in the earth three and twenty years.

HAMLET. Whose was it?

FIRST CLOWN. A whoreson mad fellow's it was: whose do you think
it was?

HAMLET. Nay, I know not.

FIRST CLOWN. A pestilence on him for a mad rogue! a' poured a
flagon of Rhenish*s* on my head once. This same skull, sir, was
Yorick's skull, the king's jester.

HAMLET. This?

FIRST CLOWN. E'en that.

HAMLET. Let me see. [*Takes the skull.*] Alas, poor Yorick! I knew
him, Horatio: a fellow of infinite jest, of most excellent fancy:
he hath borne me on his back a thousand times; and now how
abhorred in my imagination it is! my gorge rises at it. Here hung
those lips that I have kissed I know not how oft. Where be your
gibes now? your gambols? your songs? your flashes of merriment,
that were wont to set the table on a roar? Not one now, to mock
your own grinning? quite chop-fallen?*t* Now get you to my lady's

*q*. with marks of disease (from
"pox").
*r*. hold together till they are buried.

*s*. Rhine wine.
*t*. the lower jaw fallen down; hence,
dejected.

chamber, and tell her, let her paint an inch thick, to this favor[u] she must come; make her laugh at that. Prithee, Horatio, tell me one thing.

HORATIO. What's that, my lord?

HAMLET. Dost thou think Alexander looked o' this fashion i' the earth?

HORATIO. E'en so.

HAMLET. And smelt so? pah!                    [*Puts down the skull.*]

HORATIO. E'en so, my lord.

HAMLET. To what base uses we may return, Horatio! Why may not imagination trace the noble dust of Alexander, till he find it stopping a bung-hole?

HORATIO. 'Twere to consider too curiously, to consider so.

HAMLET. No, faith, not a jot; but to follow him thither with modesty enough[v] and likelihood to lead it: as thus: Alexander died, Alexander was buried, Alexander returneth into dust; the dust is earth; of earth we make loam; and why of that loam, whereto he was converted, might they not stop a beer-barrel?

> Imperious Cæsar, dead and turn'd to clay,                    1
> Might stop a hole to keep the wind away:
> O, that that earth, which kept the world in awe,
> Should patch a wall to expel the winter's flaw!

But soft! but soft! aside: here comes the king.                    5

> [*Enter* PRIESTS &c, *in procession; the Corpse of Ophelia,*
> LAERTES *and* MOURNERS *following;* KING, QUEEN, *their
> trains, &c.*]

The queen, the courtiers: who is this they follow?
And with such maimèd rites? This doth betoken
The corse they follow did with desperate hand
Fordo its own life: 'twas of some estate.
Couch we awhile, and mark.                    10

> [*Retiring with* HORATIO.]

LAERTES. What ceremony else?

HAMLET. That is Laertes, a very noble youth: mark.

LAERTES. What ceremony else?

FIRST PRIEST. Her obsequies have been as far enlarged
As we have warranty: her death was doubtful;                    15
And, but that great command o'ersways the order
She should in ground unsanctified have lodged
Till the last trumpet; for charitable prayers,

*u.* appearance.
*v.* without exaggeration.
7. *maimèd rites:* incomplete, mutilated ritual.
9. *Fordo:* destroy. *estate:* rank.
15. *warranty:* warrant, permission.

*doubtful:* of uncertain cause (i.e., accident or suicide).
16. *great . . . order:* the king's command prevails against ordinary rules.
18. *for:* instead of.

Shards, flints and pebbles should be thrown on her:
Yet here she is allow'd her virgin crants,                    20
Her maiden strewments and the bringing home
Of bell and burial.

LAERTES. Must there no more be done?

FIRST PRIEST.                          No more be done:
We should profane the service of the dead
To sing a requiem and such rest to her                       25
As to peace-parted souls.

LAERTES.                          Lay her i' the earth:
And from her fair and unpolluted flesh
May violets spring! I tell thee, churlish priest,
A ministering angel shall my sister be,
When thou liest howling.

HAMLET.                          What, the fair Ophelia!        30

QUEEN. [*Scattering flowers*] Sweets to the sweet: farewell!
I hoped thou shouldst have been my Hamlet's wife;
I thought thy bride-bed to have deck'd, sweet maid,
And not have strew'd thy grave.

LAERTES.                          O, treble woe
Fall ten times treble on that cursed head                    35
Whose wicked deed thy most ingenious sense
Deprived thee of! Hold off the earth a while,
Till I have caught her once more in mine arms.
      [*Leaps into the grave.*]
Now pile your dust upon the quick and dead,
Till of this flat a mountain you have made                   40
To o'ertop old Pelion or the skyish head
Of blue Olympus.

HAMLET. [*Advancing*] What is he whose grief
Bears such an emphasis? whose phrase of sorrow
Conjures the wandering stars and makes them stand            45
Like wonder-wounded hearers? This is I,
Hamlet the Dane.                          [*Leaps into the grave.*]

LAERTES. The devil take thy soul!          [*Grappling with him.*]

HAMLET.                          Thou pray'st not well.
I prithee, take thy fingers from my throat;
For, though I am not splenitive and rash,                    50
Yet have I in me something dangerous,
Which let thy wisdom fear. Hold off thy hand.

KING. Pluck them asunder.

---

20. *crants:* garland.
21. *strewments:* strewing of flowers.
*home:* the grave.
41. *Pelion:* the mountain upon which

the Aloadae, two rebellious giants in
Greek mythology, piled Mount Ossa in
their attempt to reach Olympus.
50. *splenitive:* easily moved to anger.

QUEEN.  Hamlet, Hamlet!

ALL.  Gentlemen,—

HORATIO. Good my lord, be quiet.

> [*The* ATTENDANTS *part them, and they come out of the grave.*]

HAMLET. Why, I will fight with him upon this theme  55
Until my eyelids will no longer wag.

QUEEN. O my son, what theme?

HAMLET. I loved Ophelia: forty thousand brothers
Could not, with all their quantity of love,
Make up my sum. What wilt thou do for her?  60

KING. O, he is mad, Laertes.

QUEEN. For love of God, forbear him.

HAMLET. 'Swounds, show me what thou 'lt do:
Woo't weep? woo't fight? woo't fast? woo't tear thyself?
Woo't drink up eisel? eat a crocodile?  65
I'll do't. Dost thou come here to whine?
To outface me with leaping in her grave?
Be buried quick with her, and so will I:
And, if thou prate of mountains, let them throw
Millions of acres on us, till our ground,  70
Singeing his pate against the burning zone,
Make Ossa like a wart! Nay, an thou 'lt mouth,
I'll rant as well as thou.

QUEEN.  This is mere madness:
And thus a while the fit will work on him;
Anon, as patient as the female dove  75
When that her golden couplets are disclosed,
His silence will sit drooping.

HAMLET.  Hear you, sir;
What is the reason that you use me thus?
I loved you ever: but it is no matter;
Let Hercules himself do what he may,  80
The cat will mew, and dog will have his day.  [*Exit.*]

KING. I pray thee, good Horatio, wait upon him.

> [*Exit* HORATIO.]

[*To* LAERTES] Strengthen your patience in our last night's speech;
We'll put the matter to the present push.
Good Gertrude, set some watch over your son.  85
This grave shall have a living monument:
An hour of quiet shortly shall we see;
Till then, in patience our proceeding be.  [*Exeunt.*]

---

64. *Woo't:* wilt.
65. *eisel:* vinegar (the bitter drink given to Christ).

76. *couplets:* twins. *disclosed:* hatched.
84. *We'll put . . . push:* We will push the matter on immediately.

SCENE 2—A *hall in the castle.*

[*Enter* HAMLET *and* HORATIO.]

HAMLET. So much for this, sir: now shall you see the other;
  You do remember all the circumstance?
HORATIO. Remember it, my lord?
HAMLET. Sir, in my heart there was a kind of fighting,
  That would not let me sleep: methought I lay                    5
  Worse than the mutines in the bilboes. Rashly,
  And praised be rashness for it, let us know,
  Our indiscretion sometime serves us well
  When our deep plots do pall; and that should learn us
  There's a divinity that shapes our ends,                        10
  Rough-hew them how we will.
HORATIO.                              That is most certain.
HAMLET. Up from my cabin,
  My sea-gown scarf'd about me, in the dark
  Groped I to find out them; had my desire,
  Finger'd their packet, and in fine withdrew                     15
  To mine own room again; making so bold,
  My fears forgetting manners, to unseal
  Their grand commission; where I found, Horatio,—
  O royal knavery!—an exact command,
  Larded with many several sorts of reasons,                      20
  Importing Denmark's health and England's too,
  With, ho! such bugs and goblins in my life,
  That, on the supervise, no leisure bated,
  No, not to stay the grinding of the axe,
  My head should be struck off.
HORATIO.                              Is't possible?              25
HAMLET. Here's the commission: read it at more leisure.
  But wilt thou hear now how I did proceed?
HORATIO. I beseech you.
HAMLET. Being thus be-netted round with villainies,—
  Ere I could make a prologue to my brains,                       30
  They had begun the play,—I sat me down;
  Devised a new commission; wrote it fair:
  I once did hold it, as our statists do,
  A baseness to write fair, and labor'd much
  How to forget that learning; but, sir, now                      35
  It did me yeoman's service: wilt thou know

6. *mutines in the bilboes:* mutineers
in iron fetters.
9. *pall:* become useless.
21. *Importing:* concerning.
22. *bugs:* bugbears.

23. *on the supervise . . . bated:* as
soon as the message was read, with no
time subtracted for leisure.
33. *statists:* statesmen.
36. *yeoman's service:* excellent service.

The effect of what I wrote?

HORATIO.                          Aye, good my lord.

HAMLET. An earnest conjuration from the king,
As England was his faithful tributary,
As love between them like the palm might flourish,          40
As peace should still her wheaten garland wear
And stand a comma 'tween their amities,
And many such-like 'As'es of great charge,
That, on the view and knowing of these contents,
Without debatement further, more or less,                    45
He should the bearers put to sudden death,
Not shriving-time allow'd.

HORATIO.                          How was this seal'd?

HAMLET. Why, even in that was heaven ordinant.
I had my father's signet in my purse,
Which was the model of that Danish seal:                     50
Folded the writ up in the form of the other;
Subscribed it; gave 't the impression; placed it safely,
The changeling never known. Now, the next day
Was our sea-fight; and what to this was sequent
Thou know'st already.                                        55

HORATIO. So Guildenstern and Rosencrantz go to 't.

HAMLET. Why, man, they did make love to this employment;
They are not near my conscience; their defeat
Does by their own insinuation grow:
'Tis dangerous when the baser nature comes                   60
Between the pass and fell-incensèd points
Of mighty opposites.

HORATIO.                     Why, what a king is this!

HAMLET. Does it not, think'st thee, stand me now upon—
He that hath kill'd my king, and whored my mother;
Popp'd in between the election and my hopes;                 65
Thrown out his angle for my proper life,
And with such cozenage—is't not perfect conscience,
To quit him with this arm? and is't not to be damn'd,
To let this canker of our nature come
In further evil?                                             70

HORATIO. It must be shortly known to him from England

42. *comma:* connecting element.
43. *'As'es:* a pun on "as" and "ass," which extends to the following *of great charge,* signifying both "moral weight," and "ass's burden."
47. *shriving-time:* time for confession and absolution.
48. *ordinant:* ordaining.
52. *impression:* of the seal.
58. *defeat:* destruction.
59. *insinuation:* meddling.

60. *baser:* lower in rank than the King and Prince Hamlet.
61. *pass:* thrust. *fell:* fiercely.
63. *Does it not . . . stand me now upon:* is it not my duty now?
66. *angle:* angling line. *my proper:* my own.
67. *cozenage:* deceit.
68. *quit:* requite.
69. *canker:* corroding ulcer.

What is the issue of the business there.

HAMLET. It will be short: the interim is mine;
And a man's life's no more than to say 'One.'
But I am very sorry, good Horatio,                              75
That to Laertes I forgot myself;
For, by the image of my cause, I see
The portraiture of his: I'll court his favors:
But. sure, the bravery of his grief did put me
Into a towering passion.

HORATIO.                    Peace! who comes here?            80

[*Enter* OSRIC.]

OSRIC. Your lordship is right welcome back to Denmark.

HAMLET. I humbly thank you, sir. Dost know this waterfly?

HORATIO. No, my good lord.

HAMLET. Thy state is the more gracious, for 'tis a vice to know him.
He hath much land, and fertile: let a beast be lord of beasts,
and his crib shall stand at the king's mess:*a* 'tis a chough,*b* but,
as I say, spacious in the possession of dirt.

OSRIC. Sweet lord, if your lordship were at leisure, I should impart
a thing to you from his majesty.

HAMLET. I will receive it, sir, with all diligence of spirit. Put your
bonnet to his right use; 'tis for the head.

OSRIC. I thank your lordship, it is very hot.

HAMLET. No, believe me, 'tis very cold; the wind is northerly.

OSRIC. It is indifferent*c* cold, my lord, indeed.

HAMLET. But yet methinks it is very sultry and hot, or my complexion—

OSRIC. Exceedingly, my lord; it is very sultry, as 'twere,—I cannot
tell how. But, my lord, his majesty bade me signify to you that
he has laid a great wager on your head: sir, this is the matter—

HAMLET. I beseech you, remember—

[HAMLET *moves him to put on his hat.*]

OSRIC. Nay, good my lord; for mine ease, in good faith. Sir, here is
newly come to court Laertes; believe me, an absolute gentleman,
full of most excellent differences,*d* of very soft society and great
showing:*e* indeed, to speak feelingly of him, he is the card or
calendar of gentry,*f* for you shall find in him the continent of*g*
what part*h* a gentleman would see.

HAMLET. Sir, his definement*i* suffers no perdition*j* in you; though,
I know, to divide him inventorially*k* would dizzy the arithmetic*l*

79. *bravery:* ostentation, bravado.
*a.* table.
*b.* jackdaw.
*c.* fairly.
*d.* distinctions.
*e.* agreeable company, and handsome
in appearance.

*f.* chart and model of gentlemanly
manners.
*g.* container.
*h.* whatever quality.
*i.* definition.
*j.* loss.
*k.* make an inventory of his virtues.
*l.* arithmetical power.

of memory, and yet but yaw neither,[m] in respect of his quick sail. But in the verity of extolment,[n] I take him to be a soul of great article,[o] and his infusion[p] of such dearth and rareness, as, to make true diction of him, his semblable is his mirror, and who else would trace[q] him, his umbrage,[r] nothing more.

OSRIC. Your lordship speaks most infallibly of him.

HAMLET. The concernancy,[s] sir? why do we wrap the gentleman[t] in our more rawer breath?

OSRIC. Sir?

HORATIO. Is 't not possible to understand in another tongue?[u] You will do 't, sir, really.

HAMLET. What imports the nomination of this gentleman?

OSRIC. Of Laertes?

HORATIO. His purse is empty already; all's golden words are spent.

HAMLET. Of him, sir.

OSRIC. I know you are not ignorant—

HAMLET. I would you did, sir; yet, in faith, if you did, it would not much approve me.[v] Well, sir?

OSRIC. You are not ignorant of what excellence Laertes is—

HAMLET. I dare not confess that, lest I should compare with him in excellence; but, to know a man well, were to know himself.[w]

OSRIC. I mean, sir, for his weapon; but in the imputation laid on him by them, in his meed he's unfellowed.[x]

HAMLET. What's his weapon?

OSRIC. Rapier and dagger.

HAMLET. That's two of his weapons: but, well.

OSRIC. The king, sir, hath wagered with him six Barbary horses: against the which he has imponed,[y] as I take it, six French rapiers and poniards, with their assigns,[z] as girdle, hanger, and so: three of the carriages,[a] in faith, are very dear to fancy,[b] very responsive[c] to the hilts, most delicate carriages, and of very liberal conceit.[d]

HAMLET. What call you the carriages?

HORATIO. I knew you must be edified by the margent[e] ere you had done.

---

m. and yet would only be able to steer unsteadily (unable to catch up with the "sail" of Laertes' virtues).
n. to praise Laertes truthfully.
o. importance.
p. the virtues infused into him.
q. keep pace with.
r. shadow.
s. purport.
t. Laertes.
u. in a less affected jargon; or, in the same jargon when spoken by another (i.e., Hamlet's) tongue.

v. be to my credit.
w. to know others one has to know oneself.
x. in the reputation given him by his weapons, his merit is unparalleled.
y. wagered.
z. appendages.
a. ornamented straps by which the rapiers hung from the belt.
b. agreeable to the taste.
c. corresponding, closely matched.
d. elegant design.
e. instructed by the marginal note.

OSRIC. The carriages, sir, are the hangers.

HAMLET. The phrase would be more germane to the matter if we could carry a cannon by our sides:[f] I would it might be hangers till then. But, on: six Barbary horses against six French swords, their assigns, and three liberal-conceited carriages; that's the French bet against the Danish. Why is this 'imponed,' as you call it?

OSRIC. The king, sir, hath laid, sir, that in a dozen passes between yourself and him, he shall not exceed you three hits: he hath laid on twelve for nine; and it would come to immediate trial, if your lordship would vouchsafe the answer.[g]

HAMLET. How if I answer 'no'?

OSRIC. I mean, my lord, the opposition of your person in trial.

HAMLET. Sir, I will walk here in the hall: if it please his majesty, it is the breathing time[h] of day with me; let the foils be brought, the gentleman willing, and the king hold his purpose, I will win for him an I can; if not, I will gain nothing but my shame and the odd hits.

OSRIC. Shall I redeliver you e'en so?[i]

HAMLET. To this effect, sir, after what flourish your nature will.

OSRIC. I commend my duty to your lordship.

HAMLET. Yours, yours. [*Exit* OSRIC.] He does well to commend it himself; there are no tongues else for's turn.

HORATIO. This lapwing[j] runs away with the shell on his head.

HAMLET. He did comply[k] with his dug before he sucked it. Thus has he—and many more of the same breed that I know the drossy[l] age dotes on—only got the tune of the time and outward habit of encounter; a kind of yesty[m] collection, which carries them through and through the most fond and winnowed opinions;[n] and do but blow them to their trial, the bubbles are out.

[*Enter a* LORD.]

LORD. My lord, his majesty commended him[o] to you by young Osric, who brings back to him, that you attend him in the hall: he sends to know if your pleasure hold to play with Laertes, or that you will take longer time.

HAMLET. I am constant to my purposes; they follow the king's pleasure: if his fitness speaks, mine is ready; now or whensoever, provided I be so able as now.

*f.* Hamlet is playfully criticizing Osric's affected application of the term "carriage," more properly used to mean "gun carriage."

*g.* "The passage is of no importance; it is sufficient that there was a wager." [Samuel Johnson.]

*h.* time for exercise.

*i.* Is that the reply you want me to carry back?

*j.* a bird supposedly able to run as soon as it is out of its shell.

*k.* use ceremony.

*l.* degenerate.

*m.* foamy.

*n.* makes them pass the test of the most refined judgment.

*o.* sent his regards.

LORD. The king and queen and all are coming down.

HAMLET. In happy time.

LORD. The queen desires you to use some gentle entertainment*p*
to Laertes before you fall to play.

HAMLET. She well instructs me.             [*Exit* LORD.]

HORATIO. You will lose this wager, my lord.

HAMLET. I do not think so; since he went into France, I have been
in continual practice; I shall win at the odds. But thou wouldst
not think how ill all's here about my heart: but it is no matter.

HORATIO. Nay, good my lord,—

HAMLET. It is but foolery; but it is such a kind of gaingiving*q* as
would perhaps trouble a woman.

HORATIO. If your mind dislike anything, obey it. I will forestall their
repair*r* hither, and say you are not fit.

HAMLET. Not a whit; we defy augury: there is special providence
in the fall of a sparrow. If it be now, 'tis not to come; if it be not
to come, it will be now; if it be not now, yet it will come: the
readiness is all; since no man has aught of what he leaves, what
is't to leave betimes?*8* Let be.

> [*Enter* KING, QUEEN, LAERTES, *and* LORDS, OSRIC *and other*
> ATTENDANTS *with foils and gauntlets; a table and flagons of
> wine on it.*]

KING. Come, Hamlet, come, and take this hand from me.

> [*The* KING *puts* LAERTES' *hand into* HAMLET'S.]

HAMLET. Give me your pardon, sir: I've done you wrong;     81
But pardon't, as you are a gentleman.
This presence knows,
And you must needs have heard, how I am punish'd
With sore distraction. What I have done,     85
That might your nature, honor and exception
Roughly awake, I here proclaim was madness.
Was't Hamlet wrong'd Laertes? Never Hamlet:
If Hamlet from himself be ta'en away,
And when he's not himself does wrong Laertes,     90
Then Hamlet does it not, Hamlet denies it.
Who does it then? His madness: if't be so,
Hamlet is of the faction that is wrong'd;
His madness is poor Hamlet's enemy.
Sir, in this audience,     95
Let my disclaiming from a purposed evil
Free me so far in your most generous thoughts,

---

*p*. kind word of greeting.
*q*. misgiving.
*r*. coming.
*s*. what is wrong with dying early
(leaving "betimes") since man knows
nothing of life ("what he leaves")?
83. *presence:* audience.
86. *exception:* objection.

That I have shot mine arrow o'er the house,
And hurt my brother.

LAERTES.                     I am satisfied in nature,
Whose motive, in this case, should stir me most      100
To my revenge: but in my terms of honor
I stand aloof, and will no reconcilement,
Till by some elder masters of known honor
I have a voice and precedent of peace,
To keep my name ungored. But till that time      105
I do receive your offer'd love like love
And will not wrong it.

HAMLET.                     I embrace it freely,
And will this brother's wager frankly play.
Give us the foils. Come on.

LAERTES.                     Come, one for me.

HAMLET. I'll be your foil, Laertes: in mine ignorance      110
Your skill shall, like a star i' the darkest night,
Stick fiery off indeed.

LAERTES.                     You mock me, sir.

HAMLET. No, by this hand.

KING. Give them the foils, young Osric. Cousin Hamlet,
You know the wager?

HAMLET.                     Very well, my lord;      115
Your grace has laid the odds o' the weaker side.

KING. I do not fear it; I have seen you both:
But since he is better'd, we have therefore odds.

LAERTES. This is too heavy; let me see another.

HAMLET. This likes me well. These foils have all a length?      120
[*They prepare to play.*]

OSRIC. Aye, my good lord.

KING. Set me the stoups of wine upon that table.
If Hamlet give the first or second hit,
Or quit in answer of the third exchange,
Let all the battlements their ordnance fire;
The king shall drink to Hamlet's better breath;      125
And in the cup an union shall he throw,
Richer than that which four successive kings

---

99–101. *in nature . . . honor:* Laertes answers separately each of the two points brought up by Hamlet in l. 86; "nature" is Laertes' natural feeling toward his father, and "honor" the code of honor with its conventional rules.
104. *voice and precedent:* competent opinion based on precedent.
105. *ungored:* unwounded.

110. *foil:* a pun, since the word means both "rapier" and "a thing which sets off another to advantage" (as gold leaf under a jewel).
112. *Stick fiery off:* stand out brilliantly.
122. *stoups:* cups.
124. *quit:* requite, repay (by scoring a hit). *exchange:* bout.
127. *union:* a large pearl.

In Denmark's crown have worn. Give me the cups;
And let the kettle to the trumpet speak,                    130
The trumpet to the cannoneer without,
The cannons to the heavens, the heaven to earth,
'Now the king drinks to Hamlet.' Come, begin;
And you, the judges, bear a wary eye.

HAMLET. Come on, sir.

LAERTES.                    Come, my lord.              [*They play.*]

HAMLET.                              One.

LAERTES.                                        No.

HAMLET.                                              Judgment.

OSRIC. A hit, a very palpable hit.

LAERTES.                    Well; again.                        136

KING. Stay; give me drink. Hamlet, this pearl is thine;
Here's to thy health.
      [*Trumpets sound, and cannon shot off within.*]
                    Give him the cup.

HAMLET. I'll play this bout first; set it by awhile.
Come. [*They play.*] Another hit; what say you?       140

LAERTES. A touch, a touch, I do confess.

KING. Our son shall win.

QUEEN.                    He's fat and scant of breath.
Here, Hamlet, take my napkin, rub thy brows:
The queen carouses to thy fortune, Hamlet.

HAMLET. Good madam!

KING.                    Gertrude, do not drink.              145

QUEEN. I will, my lord; I pray you, pardon me.

KING. [*Aside*] It is the poison'd cup; it is too late.

QUEEN. Come, let me wipe thy face.

LAERTES. My lord, I'll hit him now.

KING.                    I do not think't.

LAERTES. [*Aside*] And yet it is almost against my conscience.   150

HAMLET. Come, for the third, Laertes: you but dally;
I pray you, pass with your best violence;
I am afeard you make a wanton of me.

LAERTES. Say you so? come on.                    [*They play.*]

OSRIC. Nothing, neither way.                          155

LAERTES. Have at you now!
      [LAERTES *wounds* HAMLET; *then, in scuffling, they change
      rapiers, and* HAMLET *wounds* LAERTES.]

KING.                    Part them; they are incensed.

HAMLET. Nay, come, again.                    [*The* QUEEN *falls.*]

---

130. *kettle:* kettledrum.                143. *napkin:* handkerchief.
142. *fat:* sweaty; or, soft, because     153. *wanton:* weakling, spoiled child.
out of training. *scant:* short.

OSRIC. Look to the queen there, ho!

HORATIO. They bleed on both sides. How is it, my lord?

OSRIC. How is't, Laertes?

LAERTES. Why, as a woodcock to mine own springe, Osric;     160
I am justly kill'd with mine own treachery.

HAMLET. How does the queen?

KING. She swounds to see them bleed.

QUEEN. No, no, the drink, the drink,—O my dear Hamlet,—
The drink, the drink! I am poison'd.          [*Dies.*]

HAMLET. O villainy! Ho! let the door be lock'd:      165
Treachery! seek it out.          [LAERTES *falls.*]

LAERTES. It is here, Hamlet: Hamlet, thou art slain;
No medicine in the world can do thee good,
In thee there is not half an hour of life;
The treacherous instrument is in thy hand,     170
Unbated and envenom'd: the foul practice
Hath turn'd itself on me; lo, here I lie,
Never to rise again: thy mother's poison'd:
I can no more: the king, the king's to blame.

HAMLET. The point envenom'd too!        175
Then, venom, to thy work.          [*Stabs the* KING.]

ALL. Treason! treason!

KING. O, yet defend me, friends; I am but hurt.

HAMLET. Here, thou incestuous, murderous, damned Dane,
Drink off this potion: is thy union here?       180
Follow my mother.          [KING *dies.*]

LAERTES. He is justly served;
It is a poison temper'd by himself.
Exchange forgiveness with me, noble Hamlet:
Mine and my father's death come not upon thee,
Nor thine on me!          185
          [*Dies.*]

HAMLET. Heaven make thee free of it! I follow thee.
I am dead, Horatio. Wretched queen, adieu!
You that look pale and tremble at this chance,
That are but mutes or audience to this act,
Had I but time—as this fell sergeant, death,     190
Is strict in his arrest—O, I could tell you—
But let it be. Horatio, I am dead;
Thou livest; report me and my cause aright
To the unsatisfied.

HORATIO. Never believe it:
I am more an antique Roman than a Dane:     195

160. *springe:* snare.          l. 132. *practice:* plot.
171. *Unbated:* See Act IV, Scene 7.          182. *temper'd:* compounded.

Here's yet some liquor left.

HAMLET. As thou'rt a man,
Give me the cup: let go; by heaven, I'll have 't.
O good Horatio, what a wounded name,
Things standing thus unknown, shall live behind me!
If thou didst ever hold me in thy heart,                                    200
Absent thee from felicity a while,
And in this harsh world draw thy breath in pain,
To tell my story.              [*March afar off, and shot within.*]
             What warlike noise is this?

OSRIC. Young Fortinbras, with conquest come from Poland,
To the ambassadors of England gives                               205
This warlike volley.

HAMLET. O, I die, Horatio;
The potent poison quite o'er-crows my spirit:
I cannot live to hear the news from England;
But I do prophesy the election lights
On Fortinbras: he has my dying voice;                             210
So tell him, with the occurrents, more and less,
Which have solicited. The rest is silence.            [*Dies.*]

HORATIO. Now cracks a noble heart. Good night sweet prince,
And flights of angels sing thee to thy rest;       [*March within.*]
Why does the drum come hither?                                    215
      [*Enter* FORTINBRAS, *and the* ENGLISH AMBASSADORS, *with
      drum, colors, and* ATTENDANTS.]

FORTINBRAS. Where is this sight?

HORATIO. What is it you would see?
If aught of woe or wonder, cease your search.

FORTINBRAS. This quarry cries on havoc. O proud death,
What feast is toward in thine eternal cell,
That thou so many princes at a shot                              220
So bloodily hast struck?

FIRST AMBASSADOR. The sight is dismal;
And our affairs from England come too late:
The ears are senseless that should give us hearing,
To tell him his commandment is fulfill'd,
That Rosencrantz and Guildenstern are dead:                      225
Where should we have our thanks?

HORATIO. Not from his mouth
Had it the ability of life to thank you:
He never gave commandment for their death.

---

207. *o'ercrows:* overcomes.
211. *occurrents:* occurrences.
212. *Which have solicited:* which
have brought about all this.

218. *This . . . havoc:* This heap of
corpses proclaims a carnage.
219. *toward:* imminent.

But since, so jump upon this bloody question,
You from the Polack wars, and you from England          230
Are here arrived, give order that these bodies
High on a stage be placed to the view;
And let me speak to the yet unknowing world
How these things came about: so shall you hear
Of carnal, bloody and unnatural acts,                   235
Of accidental judgments, casual slaughters,
Of deaths put on by cunning and forced cause,
And, in this upshot, purposes mistook
Fall'n on the inventors' heads: all this can I
Truly deliver.
FORTINBRAS.          Let us haste to hear it,            240
And call the noblest to the audience.
For me, with sorrow I embrace my fortune:
I have some rights of memory in this kingdom,
Which now to claim my vantage doth invite me.
HORATIO. Of that I shall have also cause to speak,       245
And from his mouth whose voice will draw on more:
But let this same be presently perform'd,
Even while men's minds are wild; lest more mischance
On plots and errors happen.
FORTINBRAS.                    Let four captains
Bear Hamlet, like a soldier, to the stage;              250
For he was likely, had he been put on,
To have proved most royally: and, for his passage,
The soldiers' music and the rites of war
Speak loudly for him.
Take up the bodies: such a sight as this                255
Becomes the field, but here shows much amiss.
Go, bid the soldiers shoot.
     [A *dead march. Exeunt, bearing off the bodies: after which
     a peal of ordnance is shot off.*]

229. *so jump upon:* so immediately
upon.
236. *casual:* chance.
237. *put on:* prompted.
243. *of memory:* still remembered.

244. *vantage:* advantageous position,
opportunity.
246. *more:* more voices.
249. *On:* following on.
251. *put on:* tried (as king).
252. *passage:* death.

# JOHN DONNE*

## 1572–1631

## The Good-Morrow

I wonder, by my troth, what thou and I
Did, till we loved? Were we not weaned till then,
But sucked on country pleasures, childishly?
Or snorted we in the seven sleepers' den?
'Twas so; But this, all pleasures fancies be.                    5
If ever any beauty I did see,
Which I desired, and got, 'twas but a dream of thee.

And now good morrow to our waking souls,
Which watch not one another out of fear;
For love all love of other sights controls,                    10
And makes one little room an everywhere.
Let sea-discoverers to new worlds have gone,
Let maps to other, worlds on worlds have shown,
Let us possess one world; each hath one, and is one.

My face in thine eye, thine in mine appears,                    15
And true plain hearts do in the faces rest;
Where can we find two better hemispheres
Without sharp North, without declining West?
Whatever dies was not mixed equally;
If our two loves be one, or thou and I                          20
Love so alike that none do slacken, none can die.

                                                   1633

* The texts and notes here presented are by Robert M. Adams.

4. Both Christian and Mohammedan authors recite the legend of seven youths of Ephesus, who hid in a cave from the persecutions of Decius, and slept there for 187 years. "Sucked" and "snorted" are words carefully chosen for their impact on the love poem.

13. i.e., let us concede that maps to other investigators have shown, etc. ("other" is an archaic plural form). In line 14 an alternative reading is "Let us possess *our* world" (from Miss Gardner).

15. Reflected in the pupils of one another's eyes, the lovers are, and possess, worlds of their own.

19. Scholastic philosophy taught that when the elements were imperfectly ("not equally") mixed, matter was mortal and mutable; but when they were perfectly mixed, it was undying and unchanging. The dividing line between these two natures was the sphere of the moon.

## Song

Go and catch a falling star,
    Get with child a mandrake root,
Tell me where all past years are,
    Or who cleft the Devil's foot,

2. The mandrake root, or mandragora, forked like the lower part of the human body, was highly reputed as an aphrodisiac; to get one with child is a supreme impossibility.

Teach me to hear mermaids singing,⁵ 5
Or to keep off envy's stinging,
    And find
    What wind
Serves to advance an honest mind.

If thou beest born to strange sights, 10
  Things invisible to see,
Ride ten thousand days and nights,
  Till age snow white hairs on thee,
Thou, when thou return'st, wilt tell me
All strange wonders that befell thee, 15
    And swear
    No where
Lives a woman true, and fair.

If thou find'st one, let me know,
  Such a pilgrimage were sweet; 20
Yet do not, I would not go,
  Though at next door we might meet;
Though she were true when you met her,
And last till you write your letter,
    Yet she 25
    Will be
False, ere I come, to two, or three.

1633

5. identified with the sirens, whose song only the wily Odysseus survived.

# The Indifferent

I can love both fair and brown,¹
Her whom abundance melts, and her whom want betrays,
Her who loves loneness best, and her who masks and plays,
Her whom the country formed, and whom the town,
Her who believes, and her who tries,⁵ 5
Her who still weeps with spongy eyes,
And her who is dry cork, and never cries;
I can love her, and her, and you, and you,
I can love any, so she be not true.

Will no other vice content you? 10
Will it not serve your turn to do as did your mothers?
Or have you all old vices spent, and now would find out others?
Or doth a fear that men are true torment you?
O we are not, be not you so;
Let me, and do you, twenty know. 15
Rob me, but bind me not, and let me go.
Must I, who came to travail thorough you¹⁷
Grow your fixed subject, because you are true?

1. both blonde and brunette.
5. "attempts to believe" and "tries things out."
17. *travail*: "grief, sorrow," but also "journey, travel"; *thorough*: through.

Venus heard me sigh this song,
And by love's sweetest part, variety, she swore,          20
She heard not this till now; and that it should be so no more.
She went, examined, and returned ere long,
And said, Alas, some two or three
Poor heretics in love there be,
Which think to 'stablish dangerous constancy.          25
But I have told them, Since you will be true,
You shall be true to them who are false to you.

1633

## The Canonization

For God's sake hold your tongue, and let me love,
    Or chide my palsy, or my gout,
My five gray hairs, or ruined fortune, flout,
    With wealth your state, your mind with arts improve,
        Take you a course, get you a place,          5
        Observe His Honor, or His Grace,
Or the King's real, or his stamped face
    Contemplate; what you will, approve,
        So you will let me love.

Alas, alas, who's injured by my love?          10
    What merchant's ships have my sighs drowned?
Who says my tears have overflowed his ground?
    When did my colds a forward spring remove?
        When did the heats which my veins fill
        Add one man to the plaguy bill?          15
Soldiers find wars, and lawyers find out still
    Litigious men, which quarrels move,
        Though she and I do love.

Call us what you will, we are made such by love;
    Call her one, me another fly,          20
We're tapers too, and at our own cost die,
    And we in us find the eagle and the dove.
        The phoenix riddle hath more wit
        By us: we two being one, are it.

5. *Take you a course:* not necessarily of physic or instruction, but in the general sense of "settling yourself in life." A "place" is an appointment, at court or elsewhere.
7. on coins.
8. put to proof, find by experience.
13. by freezing it up.
15. Deaths from the hot-weather plague were recorded, by parish, in weekly lists.
21. like the "fly," a symbol of transitory life, we are burned up in "tapers," which consume themselves. There is a hint here of the old superstition that every act of intercourse subtracts a day from one's life. (To "die," in the punning terminology of the seventeenth century, was to consummate the act of sex.)

22. The eagle and the dove are symbols of earthly wisdom (strength) and heavenly meekness (purity), the latter paradoxically more powerful than the former. The phoenix, in general mythology, was a fabulous Arabian bird, only one of which existed at any one time. After living a thousand years, it lit its own funeral pyre, jumped in, and sang its funeral song as it was consumed—then rose triumphantly from its ashes, a new bird. Thus it was a symbol of immortality, as well as of desire rising from its own exhaustion. "Eagle" and "dove" are also alchemical terms for processes leading to the rise of "phoenix," a stage in the transmutation of metals.

So, to one neutral thing both sexes fit. 25
  We die and rise the same, and prove
  Mysterious by this love.

We can die by it, if not live by love,
  And if unfit for tombs and hearse
Our legend be, it will be fit for verse; 30
  And if no piece of chronicle we prove,
    We'll build in sonnets pretty rooms;
    As well a well-wrought urn becomes
The greatest ashes, as half-acre tombs,
  And by these hymns, all shall approve 35
  Us canonized for love:

And thus invoke us: You whom reverend love
  Made one another's hermitage;
You, to whom love was peace, that now is rage;
  Who did the whole world's soul contract, and drove 40
    Into the glasses of your eyes
    (So made such mirrors, and such spies,
That they did all to you epitomize)
  Countries, towns, courts: Beg from above
  A pattern of your love! 45

1633

35. Donne's own poems, transformed into hymns in a new love-religion; *all:* posterity.
40. In this line Miss Gardner reads "extract" for "contract."
45. The poet and his mistress, turned to saints, are implored by the rest of the population to get from heaven ("above") a pattern of their love for general distribution. "Countries, towns, courts" are objects of the verb "drove"; the notion that eyes both see and reflect the outside world, and so "contain" it doubly, was very delightful to Donne.

# The Apparition

When by thy scorn, O murderess, I am dead,
And that thou thinkst thee free
From all solicitation from me,
Then shall my ghost come to thy bed,
And thee, feigned vestal, in worse arms shall see; 5
Then thy sick taper will begin to wink,
And he whose thou art then, being tired before,
Will, if thou stir, or pinch to wake him, think
  Thou call'st for more,
An in false sleep will from thee shrink, 10
And then, poor aspen wretch, neglected thou
Bathed in a cold quicksilver sweat wilt lie
  A verier ghost than I;
What I will say, I will not tell thee now,
Lest that preserve thee; and since my love is spent, 15
I had rather thou shouldst painfully repent,
Than by my threatenings rest still innocent.

1633

5. In Roman history the "vestals" were sacred virgins.
11. Aspen leaves flutter in the slightest breeze.

12. sweating in terror; with an added innuendo from the circumstance that quicksilver (mercury) was a stock prescription for venereal disease.

## The Funeral

Whoever comes to shroud me, do not harm
　Nor question much
That subtle wreath of hair which crowns my arm;
The mystery, the sign you must not touch,
　For 'tis my outward soul,　　　　　　　　　　　5
Viceroy to that, which then to heaven being gone,
　Will leave this to control,
And keep these limbs, her provinces, from dissolution.

For if the sinewy thread my brain lets fall
　Through every part　　　　　　　　　　　　　10
Can tie those parts and make me one of all;
These hairs, which upward grew, and strength and art
　Have from a better brain,
Can better do it: except she meant that I
　By this should know my pain,　　　　　　　　15
As prisoners then are manacled, when they're condemned to die.

Whate'er she meant by it, bury it with me,
　For since I am
Love's martyr, it might breed idolatry,
If into others' hands these relics came;　　　　　　20
　As 'twas humility
To afford to it all that a soul can do,
　So 'tis some bravery,
That since you would save none of me, I bury some of you.

　　　　　　　　　　　　　　　　　1633

9. the spinal cord and nervous system.
21. It was humility to grant, in the first thirteen and a half lines of the poem, that her hair could act as a soul; it is also "bravery" (defiance) to bury a part of the mistress in revenge for her cruelty.

## *From* Holy Sonnets*

### 7

At the round earth's imagined corners, blow
Your trumpets, angels; and arise, arise
From death, you numberless infinities
Of souls, and to your scattered bodies go;
All whom the flood did, and fire shall, o'erthrow,　　5
All whom war, dearth, age, agues, tyrannies,
Despair, law, chance hath slain, and you whose eyes

* Several of the *Holy Sonnets* contain specific indications of date; number 17 makes reference to the recent death of Donne's wife (August 15, 1617) and number 18 may have been inspired by the Elector Palatine's defeat (October 29, 1620). But most are considerably earlier (1609–1610). They are nineteen in number, conventional in their rhyme scheme and broad metrical pattern, but rhythmically bold, powerful in their imagery, and marked by deep emotional coloring. Donne's religion was never a secure or comfortable experience; his *Holy Sonnets* are documents which mingle anguished despair with no less anguished hope. And in a sonnet like *Holy Sonnet 14*, his faith rises to a series of knotted paradoxes involving coercion and submission, which would be revolting were it not for the full and evident sincerity of the mind to which they were inevitable.

1. Donne may have been thinking of the angels on old maps, who blow their trumpets to the four points of the compass. See also Revelation 7:1.

Shall behold God, and never taste death's woe.
But let them sleep, Lord, and me mourn a space;
For, if above all these, my sins abound,                    10
'Tis late to ask abundance of Thy grace
When we are there. Here on this lowly ground,
Teach me how to repent; for that's as good
As if Thou hadst sealed my pardon with Thy blood.

1633

8. See Matthew 16:28, Mark 9:1, and Luke 9:27, where the worthies are de- scribed who ascended directly to heaven from this life.

10

Death, be not proud, though some have callèd thee
Mighty and dreadful, for thou art not so;
For those whom thou think'st thou dost overthrow
Die not, poor Death, nor yet canst thou kill me.
From rest and sleep, which but thy pictures be,          5
Much pleasure; then from thee much more must flow,
And soonest our best men with thee do go,
Rest of their bones, and soul's delivery.
Thou art slave to fate, chance, kings, and desperate men,
And dost with poison, war, and sickness dwell,
And poppy or charms can make us sleep as well,          10
And better than thy stroke; why swell'st thou then?
One short sleep past, we wake eternally
And death shall be no more; Death, thou shalt die.

1633

8. i.e., our best men go with you to find rest for their bones and freedom ("delivery") for their souls.
11. puff up with pride.

# CALDERÓN DE LA BARCA
(1600–1681)

## Life Is a Dream*

### Dramatis Personae

BASIL, *King of Poland*
SEGISMUND, *Prince*
ASTOLFO, *Duke of Muscovy*
CLOTALDO, *old man*
CLARION. *a comical servant*
ROSAURA, *a lady*
STELLA, *a princess*
Soldiers, guards, musicians, servants, retinues, women

*The scene is laid in the court of Poland, a nearby fortress, and the open country.*

### Act I

*On one side a craggy mountain: on the other a rude tower whose base serves as a prison for* SEGISMUND. *The door facing the spectators is open. The action begins at nightfall.*

[ROSAURA, *dressed as a man, appears on the rocks climbing down to the plain: behind her comes* CLARION.]

ROSAURA. You headlong hippogriff who match the gale
In rushing to and fro, you lightning-flicker
Who give no light, you scaleless fish, you bird
Who have no coloured plumes, you animal
Who have no natural instinct, tell me whither          5
You lead me stumbling through this labyrinth
Of naked crags! Stay here upon this peak
And be a Phaëthon to the brute-creation!
For I, pathless save only for the track
The laws of destiny dictate for me,                    10
Shall, blind and desperate, descend this height
Whose furrowed brows are frowning at the sun.

---

* *La vida es sueño*, ca. 1636. English version by Roy Campbell.

1. *hippogriff*: a fantastic creature (a winged horse with an eagle's head and a lion's forelegs) invented by Italian Renaissance poets. Its most famous use was for Astolfo's flight to the moon in Ariosto's *Orlando Furioso*.

8. *Phaëthon*: in Greek mythology, the driver of the chariot of his father, the Sun; he came too close to earth and nearly burned it up.

How rudely, Poland, you receive a stranger
(Hardly arrived, but to be treated hardly)
And write her entry down in blood with thorns.                    15
My plight attests this well, but after all,
Where did the wretchèd ever pity find?

CLARION. Say *two* so wretchèd. Don't you leave me out
When you complain! If we two sallied out
From our own country, questing high adventure,                    20
And after so much madness and misfortune
Are still two here, and were two when we fell
Down those rough crags—shall I not be offended
To share the trouble yet forego the credit?

ROSAURA. I did not give you shares in my complaint                25
So as not to rob you of the right to sorrow
Upon your own account. There's such relief
In venting grief that a philosopher
Once said that sorrows should not be bemoaned
But sought for pleasure.

CLARION.                             Philosopher?                  30
I call him a long-bearded, drunken sot
And would they'd cudgelled him a thousand blows
To give him something worth his while lamenting!
But, madam, what should we do, by ourselves,
On foot and lost at this late hour of day,                        35
Here on this desert mountain far away—
The sun departing after fresh horizons?

ROSAURA. Clarion, how can I answer, being both
The partner of your plight and your dilemma?

CLARION. Would anyone believe such strange events?               40

ROSAURA. If there my sight is not deceived by fancy,
In the last timid light that yet remains
I seem to see a building.

CLARION.                           Either my hopes
Are lying or I see the signs myself.

ROSAURA. Between the towering crags, there stands so small       45
A royal palace that the lynx-eyed sun
Could scare perceive it at midday, so rude
In architecture that it seems but one
Rock more down-toppled from the sun-kissed crags
That form the jaggèd crest.

CLARION.                            Let's go closer,               50
For we have stared enough: it would be better

---

24. *trouble:* plays on words are not infrequent in Calderón, or, for that matter, in Shakespeare. Here, for example, the untranslatable pun is on the double meaning of *pesar* ("trouble" and "to weigh").

To let the inmates make us welcome.

ROSAURA.                                    See:
The door, or, rather, that funereal gap,
Is yawning wide—whence night itself seems born,
Flowing out from its black, rugged centre.                    55
　　　[*A sound of chains is heard.*]

CLARION. Heavens! What's that I hear?

ROSAURA.                              I have become
A block immovable of ice and fire.

CLARION. Was that a little chain? Why, I'll be hanged
If that is not the clanking ghost of some
Past galley-slave—my terror proves it is!                      60

SEGISMUND. Oh, miserable me! Unhappy me!

ROSAURA. How sad a cry that is! I fear new trials
And torments.

CLARION.                It's a fearful sound.

ROSAURA.                                      Oh, come,
My Clarion, let us fly from suffering!

CLARION. I'm in such sorry trim, I've not the spirit           65
Even to run away.

ROSAURA.                And if you had,
You'd not have seen that door, not known of it.
When one's in doubt, the common saying goes
One walks between two lights.

CLARION.                            I'm the reverse.
It's not that way with me.

ROSAURA.                      What then disturbs you?        70

CLARION. I walk in doubt between two darknesses.

ROSAURA. Is not that feeble exhalation there
A light? That pallid star whose fainting tremors,
Pulsing a doubtful warmth of glimmering rays,
Make even darker with its spectral glow                        75
That gloomy habitation? Yes! because
By its reflection (though so far away)
I recognise a prison, grim and sombre,
The sepulchre of some poor living carcase.
And, more to wonder at, a man lies there                       80
Clothed in the hides of savage beasts, with limbs
Loaded with fetters, and a single lamp
For company. So, since we cannot flee,
Let us stay here and listen to his plaint
And what his sorrows are.

SEGISMUND.                      Unhappy me!                    85

62. Notice how the interlocking of　　mund's and Rosaura's) begins almost
the two major plots of the play (Segis-　　with the opening scene.

Oh, miserable me! You heavens above,
I try to think what crime I've done against you
By being born. Although to have been born,
I know, is an offence, and with just cause
I bear the rigours of your punishment:                          90
Since to be born is man's worst crime. But yet
I long to know (to clarify my doubts)
What greater crime, apart from being born,
Can thus have earned my greater chastisement.
Aren't others born like me? And yet they seem                   95
To boast a freedom that I've never known.
The bird is born, and in the hues of beauty
Clothed with its plumes, yet scarce has it become
A feathered posy—or a flower with wings—
When through ethereal halls it cuts its way,                    100
Refusing the kind shelter of its nest.
And I, who have more soul than any bird,
Must have less liberty?
The beast is born, and with its hide bright-painted,
In lovely tints, has scarce become a spangled                   105
And starry constellation (thanks to the skilful
Brush of the Painter) than its earthly needs
Teach it the cruelty to prowl and kill,
The monster of its labyrinth of flowers.
Yet I, with better instincts than a beast,                      110
Must have less liberty?
The fish is born, the birth of spawn and slime,
That does not even live by breathing air.
No sooner does it feel itself a skiff
Of silver scales upon the wave than swiftly                     115
It roves about in all directions taking
The measure of immensity as far
As its cold blood's capacity allows.
Yet I, with greater freedom of the will,
Must have less liberty?                                         120
The brook is born, and like a snake unwinds
Among the flowers. No sooner, silver serpent,
Does it break through the blooms than it regales
And thanks them with its music for their kindness,
Which opens to its course the majesty                          125
Of the wide plain. Yet I, with far more life,
Must have less liberty?
This fills me with such passion, I become

---

106. *constellation:* the spots on the beast's hide are compared to stars.

109. *monster:* the Minotaur, kept by King Minos in the Cretan Labyrinth.

Like the volcano Etna, and could tear
Pieces of my own heart out of my breast!                                      130
What law, justice, or reason can decree
That man alone should never know the joys
And be alone excepted from the rights
God grants a fish, a bird, a beast, a brook?
ROSAURA. His words have filled me full of fear and pity.              135
SEGISMUND. Who is it overheard my speech? Clotaldo?
CLARION. Say "yes!"
ROSAURA.                    It's only a poor wretch, alas,
Who in these cold ravines has overheard
Your sorrows.
SEGISMUND.          Then I'll kill you                    [*Seizes her.*]
So as to leave no witness of my frailty.                                       140
I'll tear you into bits with these strong arms!
CLARION. I'm deaf. I wasn't able to hear that.
ROSAURA. If you were human born, it is enough
That I should kneel to you for you to spare me.                         144
SEGISMUND. Your voice has softened me, your presence halted me,
And now, confusingly, I feel respect
For you. Who are you? Though here I have learned
So little of the world, since this grim tower
Has been my cradle and my sepulchre;
And though since I was born (if you can say                             150
I really have been born) I've only seen
This rustic desert where in misery
I dwell alone, a living skeleton,
An animated corpse; and though till now,
I never spoke, save to one man who hears                               155
My griefs and through whose converse I have heard
News of the earth and of the sky; and though,
To astound you more, and make you call me
A human monster, I dwell here, and am
A man of the wild animals, a beast                                          160
Among the race of men; and though in such
Misfortune, I have studied human laws,
Instructed by the birds, and learned to measure
The circles of the gentle stars, you only
Have curbed my furious rage, amazed my vision,                     165
And filled with wonderment my sense of hearing.
Each time I look at you, I feel new wonder!
The more I see of you, the more I long
To go on seeing more of you. I think
My eyes are dropsical, to go on drinking                                 170
What it is death for them to drink, because

They go on drinking that which I am dying
To see and that which, seen, will deal me death.
Yet let me gaze on you and die, since I
Am so bewitched I can no longer think                        175
What not seeing you would do to me—the sight
Itself being fatal! that would be more hard
Than dying, madness, rage, and fiercest grief:
It would be life—worst fate of all because
The gift of life to such a wretchèd man                      180
Would be the gift of death to happiness!

ROSAURA. Astonished as I look, amazed to hear,
I know not what to say nor what to ask.
All I can say is that heaven guided me
Here to be comforted, if it is comfort                       185
To see another sadder than oneself.
They say a sage philosopher of old,
Being so poor and miserable that he
Lived on the few plain herbs he could collect,
One day exclaimed: "Could any man be poorer                  190
Or sadder than myself?"—when, turning round,
He saw the very answer to his words.
For there another sage philosopher
Was picking up the scraps he'd thrown away.
I lived cursing my fortune in this world                     195
And asked within me: "Is there any other
Suffers so hard a fate?" Now out of pity
You've given me the answer. For within me
I find upon reflection that my griefs
Would be as joys to you and you'd receive them               200
To give you pleasure. So if they perchance
In any measure may afford relief,
Listen attentively to my misfortune
And take what is left over for yourself.
I am . . .

CLOTALDO. [*Within*] Guards of the tower! You sluggards       205
Or cowards, you have let two people pass
Into the prison bounds . . .

ROSAURA.                         Here's more confusion!

SEGISMUND. That is Clotaldo, keeper of my prison.
Are my misfortunes still not at an end?

CLOTALDO. Come. Be alert, and either seize or slay them       210
Before they can resist!

VOICES. [*Within*]              Treason! Betrayal!

181. *The gift . . . happiness:* the gift of life, to a wretched man like himself, is
like giving death to a happy one.

CLARION. Guards of the tower who let us pass unhindered.
Since there's a choice, to seize us would be simpler.

[*Enter* CLOTALDO *with soldiers. He holds a pistol and they
all wear masks.*]

CLOTALDO. [*Aside to the soldiers*] Cover your faces, all! It's a precaution
Imperative that nobody should know us                                          215
While we are here.

CLARION.                         What's this? A masquerade?

CLOTALDO. O you, who ignorantly passed the bounds
And limits of this region, banned to all—
Against the king's decree which has forbidden
That any should find out the prodigy                                          220
Hidden in these ravines—yield up your weapons
Or else this pistol, like a snake of metal,
Will spit the piercing venom of two shots
With scandalous assault upon the air.

SEGISMUND. Tyrannic master, ere you harm these people             225
Let my life be the spoil of these sad bonds
In which (I swear it by Almighty God)
I'll sooner rend myself with hands and teeth
Amid these rocks than see them harmed and mourn
Their suffering.

CLOTALDO.                 Since you know, Segismund,                       230
That your misfortunes are so huge that, even
Before your birth, you died by heaven's decree,
And since you know these walls and binding chains
Are but the brakes and curbs to your proud frenzies,
What use is it to bluster?

[*To the guards*]                 Shut the door                                 235
Of this close prison! Hide him in its depths!

SEGISMUND. Ah, heavens, how justly you denied me freedom!
For like a Titan I would rise against you,
Pile jasper mountains high on stone foundations
And climb to burst the windows of the sun!                                   240

CLOTALDO. Perhaps you suffer so much pain today
Just to forestall that feat.

ROSAURA.                         Now that I see
How angry pride offends you, I'd be foolish
Not to plead humbly at your feet for life.
Be moved by me to pity. It would be                                          245
Notoriously harsh that neither pride
Nor humbleness found favour in your eyes!

CLARION. And if neither Humility nor Pride
Impress you (characters of note who act

And motivate a thousand mystery plays)  250
Let me, here, who am neither proud nor humble,
But merely something halfway in between,
Plead to you both for shelter and for aid.

CLOTALDO. Ho, there!

SOLDIER.               Sir?

CLOTALDO.                    Take their weapons. Bind their eyes
So that they cannot see the way they're led.  255

ROSAURA. This is my sword. To nobody but you
I yield it, since you're, after all, the chief.
I cannot yield to one of meaner rank.

CLARION. My sword is such that I will freely give it
To the most mean and wretched.

[*To one soldier*]               Take it, you!  260

ROSAURA. And if I have to die, I'll leave it to you
In witness of your mercy. It's a pledge
Of great worth and may justly be esteemed
For someone's sake who wore it long ago.  264

CLOTALDO. [*Apart*] Each moment seems to bring me new misfortune!

ROSAURA. Because of that, I ask you to preserve
This sword with care. Since if inconstant Fate
Consents to the remission of my sentence,
It has to win me honour. Though I know not
The secret that it carries, I do know  270
It has got one—unless I trick myself—
And prize it just as the sole legacy
My father left me.

CLOTALDO.          Who then was your father?

ROSAURA. I never knew.

CLOTALDO.              And why have you come here?

ROSAURA. I came to Poland to avenge a wrong.  275

CLOTALDO. [*Apart*] Sacred heavens!

[*On taking the sword he becomes very perturbed.*]

                              What's this? Still worse and worse.
I am perplexed and troubled with more fears.

[*Aloud*] Tell me: who gave that sword to you?

ROSAURA.                                    A woman.

CLOTALDO. Her name?

ROSAURA.            A secret I am forced to keep.  280

CLOTALDO. What makes you think this sword contains a secret?

ROSAURA. That she who gave it to me said: "Depart
To Poland. There with subtlety and art
Display it so that all the leading people
And noblemen can see you wearing it,  285
And I know well that there's a lord among them

Who will both shelter you and grant you favour."
But, lest he should be dead, she did not name him.
CLOTALDO. [*Aside*] Protect me, heavens! What is this I hear?
    I cannot say if real or imagined                     290
    But here's the sword I gave fair Violante
    In token that, whoever in the future
    Should come from her to me wearing this sword,
    Would find in me a tender father's love.
    Alas, what can I do in such a pass,                 295
    When he who brings the sword to win my favour
    Brings it to find his own red death instead
    Arriving at my feet condemned already?
    What strange perplexity! How hard a fate!
    What an inconstant fortune to be plagued with!      300
    This is my son not only by all signs
    But also by the promptings of my heart,
    Since, seeing him, my heart seems to cry out
    To him, and beat its wings, and, though unable
    To break the locks, behaves as one shut in,       305
    Who, hearing noises in the street outside,
    Cranes from the window-ledge. Just so, not knowing
    What's really happening, but hearing sounds,
    My heart runs to my eyes which are its windows
    And out of them flows into bitter tears.         310
    Protect me, heaven! What am I to do?
    To take him to the king is certain death.
    To hide him is to break my sacred oath
    And the strong law of homage. From one side
    Love of one's own, and from the other loyalty—     315
    Call me to yield. Loyalty to my king
    (Why do I doubt?) comes before life and honour.
    Then live my loyalty, and let him die!
    When I remember, furthermore, he came
    To avenge an injury—a man insulted         320
    And unavenged is in disgrace. My son
    Therefore he is not, nor of noble blood.
    But if some danger has mischanced, from which
    No one escapes, since honour is so fragile
    That any act can smash it, and it takes        325
    A stain from any breath of air, what more
    Could any nobleman have done than he,
    Who, at the cost of so much risk and danger,
    Comes to avenge his honour? Since he's so brave

---

291. *Violante:* whom he, Clotaldo,     301. *my son:* Rosaura, of course, is
has seduced.                               disguised as a man.

He is my son, and my blood's in his veins.            330
And so betwixt the one doubt and the other,
The most important mean between extremes
Is to go to the king and tell the truth—
That he's my son, to kill, if so he wishes.
Perhaps my loyalty thus will move his mercy        335
And if I thus can merit a live son,
I'll help him to avenge his injury.
But if the king prove constant in his rigour
And deal him death, he'll die in ignorance
That I'm his father.

    [*Aloud to* ROSAURA *and* CLARION.]

              Come then, strangers, come!    340
And do not fear that you have no companions
In your misfortunes, since, in equal doubt,
Tossed between life and death, I cannot guess
Which is the greater evil or the less.

     *A hall at the royal palace, in court*

  [*Enter* ASTOLFO *and soldiers at one side: from the other
side* PRINCESS STELLA *and ladies. Military music and salvos.*]

ASTOLFO. To greet your excellent bright beams        345
  As brilliant as a comet's rays,
  The drums and brasses mix their praise
  With those of fountains, birds, and streams.
  With sounds alike, in like amaze,
  Your heavenly face each voice salutes,        350
  Which puts them in such lively fettle,
  The trumpets sound like birds of metal,
  The songbirds play like feathered flutes.
  And thus they greet you, fair señora—
  The salvos, as their queen, the brasses,        355
  As to Minerva when she passes,
  The songbirds to the bright Aurora,
  And all the flowers and leaves and grasses
  As doing homage unto Flora,
  Because you come to cheat the day        360
  Which now the night has covered o'er—
  Aurora in your spruce array,
  Flora in peace, Pallas in war,
  But in my heart the queen of May.
STELLA. If human voice could match with acts        365
  You would have been unwise to say

356. *Minerva:* the Roman Pallas
Athena.
357. *Aurora:* the Roman goddess of

Dawn.
359. *Flora:* the Roman goddess of
flowers and fruitfulness.

Hyperboles that a few facts
May well refute some other day
Confounding all this martial fuss
With which I struggle daringly,                          370
Since flatteries you proffer thus
Do not accord with what I see.
Take heed that it's an evil thing
And worthy of a brute accursed,
Loud praises with your mouth to sing                     375
When in your heart you wish the worst.

ASTOLFO. Stella, you have been badly misinformed
If you doubt my good faith. Here let me beg you
To listen to my plea and hear me out.
The third Eugtorgius died, the King of Poland.           380
Basil, his heir, had two fair sisters who
Bore you, my cousin, and myself. I would not
Tire you with all that happened here. You know
Clorilene was your mother who enjoys,
Under a better reign, her starry throne.                 385
She was the elder. Lovely Recisunda
(Whom may God cherish for a thousand years!)
The younger one, my mother and your aunt,
Was wed in Muscovy. Now to return:
Basil has yielded to the feebleness                      390
Of age, loves learnèd study more than women,
Has lost his wife, is childless, will not marry.
And so it comes that you and I both claim
The heirdom of the realm. You claim that you
Were daughter to the elder daughter. I                   395
Say that my being born a man, although
Son of the younger daughter, gives me title
To be preferred. We've told the king, our uncle,
Of both of our intentions. And he answered
That he would judge between our rival claims,            400
For which the time and place appointed was
Today and here. For that same reason I
Have left my native Muscovy. With that
Intent I come—not seeking to wage war
But so that you might thus wage war on me!               405
May Love, wise god, make true what people say
(Your "people" is a wise astrologer)
By settling this through your being chosen queen—
Queen and my consort, sovereign of my will;
My uncle crowning you, for greater honour;               410

385. *a better reign:* Heaven.

Your courage conquering, as it deserves;
My love applauding you, its emperor!

STELLA. To such chivalrous gallantry, my breast
Cannot hold out. The imperial monarchy
I wish were mine only to make it yours— 415
Although my love is not quite satisfied
That you are to be trusted since your speech
Is somewhat contradicted by that portrait
You carry in the locket round your neck.

ASTOFLO. I'll give you satisfaction as to that. 420
[*Drums*] But these loud instruments will not permit it
That sound the arrival of the king and council.

[*Enter* KING BASIL *with his following.*]

STELLA. Wise Thales ...

ASTOLFO.              Learned Euclid ...

STELLA. Among the signs ...

ASTOLFO.              Among the stars ... 424

STELLA. Where you preside in power ...

ASTOLFO.              Where you reside ...

STELLA. And plot their paths ...

ASTOLFO.              And trace their fiery trails ...

STELLA. Describing ...

ASTOLFO.         ... Measuring and judging them ...

STELLA. Please read my stars that I, in humble bonds ...

ASTOLFO. Please read them, so that I in soft embraces ...

STELLA. May twine as ivy to this tree!

ASTOLFO.              May find 430
Myself upon my knees before these feet!

BASIL. Come and embrace me, niece and nephew. Trust me,
Since you're both loyal to my loving precepts,
And come here so affectionately both—
In nothing shall I leave you cause to cavil, 435
And both of you as equals will be treated.
The gravity of what I have to tell
Oppresses me, and all I ask of you
Is silence: the event itself will claim
Your wonderment. So be attentive now, 440
Belovèd niece and nephew, illustrious courtiers,
Relatives, friends, and subjects! You all know
That for my learning I have merited
The surname of The Learnèd, since the brush
Of great Timanthes, and Lisippus' marbles— 445

---

418. *that portrait:* a picture of Rosaura.

423. *Thales:* an early Greek philosopher. *Euclid:* the great Alexandrian geometer. The speech that follows is a long flattering salutation to the king, shared by Stella and Astolfo.

445. *Timanthes:* a Greek painter of

Stemming oblivion (consequence of time)—
Proclaimed me to mankind Basil the Great.
You know the science that I most affect
And most esteem is subtle mathematics
(By which I forestall time, cheat fame itself)                    450
Whose office is to show things gradually.
For when I look my tables up and see,
Present before me, all the news and actions
Of centuries to come, I gain on Time—
Since Time recounts whatever I have said                          455
After I say it. Those snowflaking haloes,
Those canopies of crystal spread on high,
Lit by the sun, cut by the circling moon,
Those diamond orbs, those globes of radiant crystal
Which the bright stars adorn, on which the signs                  460
Parade in blazing excellence, have been
My chiefest study all through my long years.
They are the volumes on whose adamantine
Pages, bound up in sapphire, heaven writes,
In lines of burnished gold and vivid letters,                    465
All that is due to happen, whether adverse
Or else benign. I read them in a flash,
So quickly that my spirit tracks their movements—
Whatever road they take, whatever goal
They aim at. Would to heaven that before                          470
My genius had been the commentary
Writ in their margins, or the index to
Their pages, that my life had been the rubble,
The ruin, and destruction of their wrath,
And that my tragedy in them had ended,                            475
Because, to the unlucky, even their merit
Is like a hostile knife, and he whom knowledge
Injures is but a murderer to himself.
And this I say myself, though my misfortunes
Say it far better, which, to marvel at,                           480
I beg once more for silence from you all.
With my late wife, the queen, I had a son,
Unhappy son, to greet whose birth the heavens
Wore themselves out in prodigies and portents.
Ere the sun's light brought him live burial                       485

---

the fourth century B.C. *Lisippus:* a
Greek sculptor of the same period. The
names are used symbolically to mean
great artists in general.
 473. *Their pages:* the image of the
heavens as a book that the king-astrolo-
ger reads is carried through here.
    476-478. *even their merit . . . to him-
self:* the stars in the book of heaven portend death to the unlucky, and he who
can read it himself is like a self-murder-
er.

Out of the womb (for birth resembles death)
His mother many times, in the delirium
And fancies of her sleep, saw a fierce monster
Bursting her entrails in a human form,
Born spattered with her lifeblood, dealing death,                490
The human viper of this century!
The day came for his birth, and every presage
Was then fulfilled, for tardily or never
Do the more cruel ones prove false. At birth
His horoscope was such that the bright sun,                      495
Stained in its blood, entered ferociously
Into a duel with the moon above.
The whole earth seemed a rampart for the strife
Of heaven's two lights, who—though not hand-to-hand—
Fought light-to-light to gain the mastery!                       500
The worst eclipse the sun has ever suffered
Since Christ's own death horrified earth and sky.
The whole earth overflowed with conflagrations
So that it seemed the final paroxysm
Of existence. The skies grew dark. Buildings shook.             505
The clouds rained stones. The rivers ran with blood.
In this delirious frenzy of the sun,
Thus, Segismund was born into the world,
Giving a foretaste of his character
By killing his own mother, seeming to speak thus                510
By his ferocity: "I am a man,
Because I have begun now to repay
All kindnesses with evil." To my studies
I went forthwith, and saw in all I studied
That Segismund would be the most outrageous                     515
Of all men, the most cruel of all princes,
And impious of all monarchs, by whose acts
The kingdom would be torn up and divided
So as to be a school of treachery
And an academy of vices. He,                                    520
Risen in fury, amidst crimes and horrors,
Was born to trample me (with shame I say it)
And make of my grey hairs his very carpet.
Who is there but believes an evil Fate?
And more if he discovers it himself,                            525
For self-love lends its credit to our studies.
So I, believing in the Fates, and in
The havoc that their prophecies predestined,
Determined to cage up this newborn tiger

---

491. *viper:* reputedly the viper is killed and devoured by its offspring.

To see if on the stars we sages have                          530
Some power. I gave out that the prince had died
Stillborn, and, well-forewarned, I built a tower
Amidst the cliffs and boulders of yon mountains
Over whose tops the light scarce finds its way,
So stubbornly their obelisks and crags                        535
Defend the entry to them. The strict laws
And edicts that I published then (declaring
That nobody might enter the forbidden
Part of the range) were passed on that account.
There Segismund lives to this day, a captive,                 540
Poor and in misery, where, save Clotaldo,
His guardian, none have seen or talked to him.
The latter has instructed him in all
Branches of knowledge and in the Catholic faith,
Alone the witness of his misery.                              545
There are three things to be considered now:
Firstly Poland, that I love you greatly,
So much that I would free you from the oppression
And servitude of such a tyrant king.
He would not be a kindly ruler who                            550
Would put his realm and homeland in such danger.
The second fact that I must bear in mind
Is this: that to deny my flesh and blood
The rights which law, both human and divine,
Concedes, would not accord with Christian charity,            555
For no law says that, to prevent another
Being a tyrant, I may be one myself,
And if my son's a tyrant, to prevent him
From doing outrage, I myself should do it.
Now here's the third and last point I would speak of,         560
Namely, how great an error it has been
To give too much belief to things predicted,
Because, even if his inclination should
Dictate some headlong, rash precipitancies,
They may perhaps not conquer him entirely,                    565
For the most accursèd destiny, the most
Violent inclination, the most impious
Planet—all can but influence, not force,
The free will which man holds direct from God.
And so, between one motive and another                        570
Vacillating discursively, I hit
On a solution that will stun you all.
I shall tomorrow, but without his knowing
He is my son—your king—place Segismund

(For that's the name with which he was baptised)    575
Here on my throne, beneath my canopy,
Yes, in my very place, that he may govern you
And take command. And you must all be here
To swear him fealty as his loyal subjects.
Three things may follow from this test, and these    580
I'll set against the three which I proposed.
The first is that should the prince prove prudent,
Stable, and benign—thus giving the lie
To all that prophecy reports of him—
Then you'll enjoy in him your rightful ruler    585
Who was so long a courtier of the mountains
And neighbour to the beasts. Here is the second:
If he prove proud, rash, cruel, and outrageous,
And with a loosened rein gallop unheeding
Across the plains of vice, I shall have done    590
My duty, and fulfilled my obligation
Of mercy. If I then re-imprison him,
That's incontestably a kingly deed—
Not cruelty but merited chastisement.
The third thing's this: that if the prince should be    595
As I've described him, then—by the love I feel
For you, my vassals—I shall give you worthier
Rulers to wear the sceptre and the crown;
Because your king and queen will be my nephew
And niece, each with an equal right to rule,    600
Each gaining the inheritance he merits,
And joined in faith of holy matrimony.
This I command you as a king, I ask you
As a kind father, as a sage I pray you,
As an experienced old man I tell you,    605
And (if it's true, as Spanish Seneca
Says, that the king is slave unto his nation)
This, as a humble slave, I beg of you.
ASTOLFO. If it behoves me to reply (being
The person most involved in this affair)    610
Then in the name of all, let Segismund
Appear! It is enough that he's your son!
ALL. Give us our prince: we want him for our king!
BASIL. Subjects, I thank you for your kindly favour.
Accompany these, my two Atlases,    615
Back to their rooms. Tomorrow you shall see him.

---

606. *Seneca:* the Roman dramatist and philosopher (4 B.C.?–A.D. 65) was born at Córdoba in Spain. The thought mentioned here is in his book *De cle-* *mentia,* I, 19.
615. *my two Atlases:* Astolfo and Stella, supporting him as the mythological Atlas supports the earth.

ALL. Long live the great King Basil! Long live Basil!
> [*Exeunt all, accompanying* STELLA *and* ASTOLFO. *The* KING
> *remains. Enter* CLOTALDO *with* ROSAURA *and* CLARION.]

CLOTALDO. May I have leave to speak, sire?

BASIL.                                    Oh, Clotaldo!
You're very welcome.

CLOTALDO.                  Thus to kneel before you
Is always welcome, sire—yet not today                        620
When sad and evil Fate destroys the joy
Your presence normally concedes.

BASIL.                              What's wrong?

CLOTALDO. A great misfortune, sire, has come upon me
Just when I should have met it with rejoicing.

BASIL. Continue.

CLOTALDO.         Sire, this beautiful young man             625
Who inadvertently and daringly
Came to the tower, wherein he saw the prince,
Is my . . .

BASIL.          Do not afflict yourself, Clotaldo.
Had it not been just now, I should have minded,
I must confess. But I've revealed the secret,             630
And now it does not matter if he knows it.
Attend me afterwards. I've many things
To tell you. You in turn have many things
To do for me. You'll be my minister,
I warn you, in the most momentous action                  635
The world has ever seen. These prisoners, lest you
Should think I blame your oversight, I'll pardon.
> [*Exit.*]

CLOTALDO. Long may you live, great sire! A thousand years!
> [*Aside*] Heaven improves our fates. I shall not tell him
Now that he is my son, since it's not needed               640
Till he's avenged.
> [*Aloud*] Strangers, you may go free.

ROSAURA. Humbly I kiss your feet.

CLARION.                           Whilst I'll just *miss* them—
Old friends will hardly quibble at one letter.

ROSAURA. You've granted me my life, sir. I remain          645
Your servant and eternally your debtor.

CLOTALDO. No! It was not your life I gave you. No!
Since any wellborn man who, unavenged,
Nurses an insult does not live at all.
And seeing you have told me that you came                  650
For that sole reason, it was not life I spared—
Life in disgrace is not a life at all.

[*Aside*] I see this spurs him.

ROSAURA.                    Freely I confess it—
Although you spared my life, it was no life.
But I will wipe my honour's stain so spotless               655
That after I have vanquished all my dangers
Life well may seem a shining gift from you.

CLOTALDO. Take here your burnished steel: 'twill be enough,
Bathed in your enemies' red blood, to right you.
For steel that once was mine (I mean of course               660
Just for the time I've had it in my keeping)
Should know how to avenge you.

ROSAURA. Now, in your name I gird it on once more
And on it I will swear to take revenge
Although my foe were even mightier.               665

CLOTALDO. Is he so powerful?

ROSAURA.                    So much so that . . .
Although I have no doubt in your discretion . . .
I say no more because I'd not estrange
Your clemency.

CLOTALDO. You would have won me had you told me, since               670
That would prevent me helping him.
[*Aside*] If only I could discover who he is!

ROSAURA. So that you'll not think that I value lightly
Such confidence, know that my adversary
Is no less than Astolfo, Duke of Muscovy.               675

CLOTALDO. [*Aside*] (I hardly can withstand the grief it gives me
For it is worse than aught I could imagine!
Let us inquire of him some further facts.)
[*Aloud*] If you were born a Muscovite, your ruler
Could never have affronted you. Go back               680
Home to your country. Leave this headstrong valour.
It will destroy you.

ROSAURA.                    Though he's been my prince,
I know that he has done me an affront.

CLOTALDO. Even though he slapped your face, that's no affront.
[*Aside*] O heavens!

ROSAURA.                    My insult was far deeper!

CLOTALDO.                                        Tell it:               685
Since nothing I imagine could be deeper.

ROSAURA. Yes. I will tell it, yet, I know not why,
With such respect I look upon your face,
I venerate you with such true affection,
With such high estimation do I weigh you,               690

661. With the words in parentheses, Clotaldo is trying to correct the impression
of his preceding slip of the tongue.

That I scarce dare to tell you—these men's clothes
Are an enigma, not what they appear.
So now you know. Judge if it's no affront
That here Astolfo comes to wed with Stella
Although betrothed to me. I've said enough.                              695
    [*Exeunt* ROSAURA *and* CLARION.]
CLOTALDO. Here! Listen! Wait! What mazed confusion!
  It is a labyrinth wherein the reason
  Can find no clue. My family honour's injured.
  The enemy's all powerful. I'm a vassal
  And she's a woman. Heavens! Show a path                          700
  Although I don't believe there is a way!
  There's nought but evil bodings in the sky.
  The whole world is a prodigy, say I.

## Act II

### A Hall in the Royal Palace

    [*Enter* BASIL *and* CLOTALDO.]
CLOTALDO. All has been done according to your orders.
BASIL. Tell me, Clotaldo, how it went?
CLOTALDO.               Why, thus:
  I took to Segismund a calming drug
  Wherein are mixed herbs of especial virtue,
  Tyrannous in their overpowering strength,                          5
  Which seize and steal and alienate man's gift
  Of reasoning, thus making a live corpse
  Of him. His violence evaporated
  With all his faculties and senses too.
  There is no need to prove it's possible                          10
  Because experience teaches us that medicine
  Is full of natural secrets, that there is no
  Animal, plant, or stone that has not got
  Appointed properties. If human malice
  Explores a thousand poisons which deal death,                    15
  Who then can doubt, that being so, that other
  Poisons less violent, cause only sleep?
  But (leaving that doubt aside as proven false
  By every evidence) hear then the sequel:
  I went down into Segismund's close prison                        20
  Bearing the drink wherein, with opium,
  Henbane and poppies had been mixed. With him
  I talked a little while of the humanities,

---

699-700. *I'm a vassal ... woman:*
hence, loyalty in his case and feminine
weakness in hers will make it difficult
to face the enemy and restore family
honor.

In which dumb Nature has instructed him,
The mountains and the heavens and the stars, 25
In whose divine academies he learned
Rhetoric from the birds and the wild creatures.
To lift his spirit to the enterprise
Which you require of him I choose for subject
The swiftness of a stalwart eagle, who, 30
Deriding the base region of the wind,
Rises into the sphere reserved for fire,
A feathered lightning, an untethered comet.
Then I extolled such lofty flight and said:
"After all, he's the king of birds, and so 35
Takes precedence, by right, over the rest."
No more was needful for, in taking up
Majesty for his subject, he discoursed
With pride and high ambition, as his blood
Naturally moves, incites, and spurs him on 40
To grand and lofty things, and so he said
That in the restless kingdom of the birds
There should be those who swear obedience, too!
"In this, my miseries console me greatly,
Because if I'm a vassal here, it's only 45
By force, and not by choice. Of my own will
I would not yield in rank to any man."
Seeing that he grew furious—since this touched
The theme of his own griefs—I gave the potion
And scarcely had it passed from cup to breast 50
Before he yielded all his strength to slumber.
A chill sweat ran through all his limbs and veins.
Had I not known that this was mere feigned death
I would have thought him dead. Then came the men
To whom you're trusted this experiment, 55
Who placed him in a coach and brought him here
To your own rooms, where all things were prepared
In royalty and grandeur as befitting
His person. In your own bed they have laid him
Where, when the torpor wanes, they'll do him service 60
As if he were Your Majesty himself.
All has been done as you have ordered it,
And if I have obeyed you well, my lord,
I'd beg a favour (pardon me this freedom)—
To know what your intention is in thus 65
Transporting Segismund here to the palace.
BASIL. Your curiosity is just, Clotaldo,
And yours alone I'll satisfy. The star

Which governs Segismund, my son, in life,
Threatens a thousand tragedies and woes.                    70
And now I wish to see whether the stars
(Which never lie—and having shown to us
So many cruel signs seem yet more certain)
May yet be brought to moderate their sentence,
Whether by prudence charmed or valour won,                  75
For man does have the power to rule his stars.
I would examine this, bringing him here
Where he may know he is my son, and make
Trial of his talent. If magnanimously
He conquers and controls himself, he'll reign,              80
But if he proves a tyrant and is cruel,
Back to his chains he'll go. Now, you will ask,
Why did we bring him sleeping in this manner
For the experiment? I'll satisfy you,
Down to the smallest detail, with my answer.                85
If he knows that he is my son today,
And if tomorrow he should find himself
Once more reduced to prison, to misery,
He would despair entirely, knowing truly
Who, and whose son, he is. What consolation                 90
Could he derive, then, from his lot? So I
Contrive to leave an exit for such grief,
By making him believe it was a dream.
By these means we may learn two things at once:
First, his character—for he will really be                  95
Awake in all he thinks and all his actions;
Second, his consolation—which would be
(If he should wake in prison on the morrow,
Although he saw himself obeyed today)
That he might understand he had been dreaming,              100
And he will not be wrong, for in this world,
Clotaldo, all who live are only dreaming.
CLOTALDO. I've proofs enough to doubt of your success,
  But now it is too late to remedy it.
  From what I can make out, I think he's wakened            105
  And that he's coming this way, by the sound.
BASIL. I shall withdraw. You, as his tutor, go
  And guide him through his new bewilderments
  By answering his queries with the truth.
CLOTALDO. You give me leave to tell the truth of it?       110
BASIL. Yes, because knowing all things, he may find
  Known perils are the easiest to conquer.
    [*Exit* BASIL. *Enter* CLARION.]

CLARION. It cost me four whacks to get here so quickly.
　I caught them from a red-haired halberdier
　Sprouting a ginger beard over his livery,　　　　　　　115
　And I've come to see what's going on.
　No windows give a better view than those
　A man brings with him in his head, not asking
　For tickets of admission or paid seats,
　Since at all functions, festivals, or feasts　　　　　　120
　He looks out with the same nice self-composure.

CLOTALDO. [*Aside*] Here's Clarion who's the servant of that person—
　That trader in woes, importer from Poland
　Of my disgrace.
　[*Aloud*]　　　　　　Come, Clarion what news?

CLARION. Item the first: encouraged by the fact　　　　　125
　Your clemency's disposed to venge her insult,
　Rosaura has resumed her proper clothing.

CLOTALDO. That's right: it's less indecorous and bold.

CLARION. Item: she's changed her name, and given out
　That she's your niece. And now they've made so much　130
　Of her that she's been raised to maid of honour
　To the unique and only princess, Stella.

CLOTALDO. That's right: her honour stands to my account.

CLARION. Indeed she merely bides the time till you
　Will settle all accounts about her honour.　　　　　　135

CLOTALDO. Biding the time is wise, for in the end
　It's Time that's going to settle all accounts!

CLARION. Item: that she's attended like a queen,
　Because they take her for your niece. Item:
　That I, who trudged along with her, am dying　　　　　140
　Of hunger. Nobody remembers me,
　Nor yet remembers that I'm like my name
　And (should I sound my Clarion) could tell
　All to the king and Stella and Astolfo.
　For I am both a Clarion and a servant—　　　　　　145
　Two things which ill-accord with secrecy.
　If silence should, by chance, let slip my hand,
　Then there's a chorus which would fit me well:
　"Dawn-breaking Clarion plays no better tune!"

CLOTALDO. You've reason for complaint. I'll satisfy it　150
　If you'll but serve me . . .

CLARION.　　　　　　Hush, here's Segismund!
　[*Enter musicians, singing, and servants arraying* SEGISMUND,
　*who seems amazed.*]

---

141. The stock character of the clownish servant is distinguished by loquacity and perennial hunger (*cf.* Harle-
quin).

SEGISMUND. Heavens above! What's this that I am seeing?
　I wonder at it all, with naught of fear!
　But with a mighty doubt, I disbelieve it!
　I?—in a sumptuous palace? I—encircled　　　　　　　155
　With rich brocades and silks? I—overwhelmed
　With servants in such brilliant liveries?
　I—to awake in such a gorgeous bed?
　I—in the middle of so many footmen
　Who clothe me in rich garments? I'm awake:　　　160
　It would be false to take this for a dream.
　Am I not Segismund? Heavens! disabuse me
　If I'm mistaken. Say, what could have happened
　In my imagination while I slept—
　That I should find myself in such a place?　　　　165
　But why should I worry, whatever it was?
　I'll let myself be served and entertained—
　Befall what may.
FIRST SERVANT. [*Aside to* SECOND SERVANT *and* CLARION]
　　　　　　　　He's very melancholy!
SECOND SERVANT. Who would not be, considering all that's happened
　To him?
CLARION.　I would not be!
SECOND SERVANT.　　　　You, speak to him.　　　　170
FIRST SERVANT. Shall they begin to sing again?
SEGISMUND.　　　　　　　　　Why, no,
　I would not have them sing.
SECOND SERVANT.　　　　You're so distraught,
　I wish you entertained.
SEGISMUND.　　　　　My griefs are such
　That no mere voices can amuse me now—
　Only the martial music pleased my mind.　　　　175
CLOTALDO. Your Highness, mighty prince, give me your hand
　To kiss. I'm glad to be the first to offer
　Obedience at your feet.
SEGISMUND. [*Aside*]　　　This is Clotaldo.
　How is it he, that tyrannised my thralldom,
　Should now be treating me with such respect?　　180
　[*Aloud*] Tell me what's happening all round me here.
CLOTALDO. With the perplexities of your new state,
　Your reason will encounter many doubts,
　But I shall try to free you from them all
　(If that may be) because you now must know　　185
　You are hereditary Prince of Poland.
　If you have been withdrawn from public sight
　Under restraint, it was in strict obedience

To Fate's inclemency, which will permit
A thousand woes to fall upon this empire                          190
The moment that you wear the sovereign's crown.
But trusting that you'll prudently defeat
Your own malignant stars (since they can be
Controlled by magnanimity) you've been
Brought to this palace from the tower you knew                    195
Even while your soul was yielded up to sleep.
My lord the king, your father, will be coming
To see you, and from him you'll learn the rest.

SEGISMUND. Then, vile, infamous traitor, what have I
To know more than this fact of who I am,                          200
To show my pride and power from this day onward?
How have you played your country such a treason
As to deny me, against law and right,
The rank which is my own?

CLOTALDO.                         Unhappy me!

SEGISMUND. You were a traitor to the law, a flattering liar       205
To your own king, and cruel to myself.
And so the king, the law, and I condemn you,
After such fierce misfortunes as I've borne,
To die here by my hands.

SECOND SERVANT.                  My lord!

SEGISMUND.                                      Let none
Get in the way. It is in vain. By God!                           210
If you intrude, I'll throw you through the window.

SECOND SERVANT. Clotaldo, fly!

CLOTALDO.                            Alas, poor Segismund!
That you should show such pride, all unaware
That you are dreaming this.
    [*Exit.*]

SECOND SERVANT.                  Take care! Take care!

SEGISMUND. Get out!

SECOND SERVANT.          He was obeying the king's orders.        215

SEGISMUND. In an injustice, no one should obey
The king, and I'm his prince.

SECOND SERVANT.                     He had no right
To look into the rights and wrongs of it.

SEGISMUND. You must be mad to answer back at me.

CLARION. The prince is right. It's you who're in the wrong!       220

SECOND SERVANT. Who gave you right to speak?

CLARION.                                          I simply took it.

SEGISMUND. And who are you?

CLARION.                         I am the go-between,
And in this art I think I am a master—

Since I'm the greatest jackanapes alive.

SEGISMUND. [*To* CLARION] In all this new world, you're the only one
Of. the whole crowd who pleases me.

CLARION.                                        Why, my lord,                226
I am the best pleaser of Segismunds
That ever was: ask anybody here!

     [*Enter* ASTOLFO.]

ASTOLFO. Blessèd the day, a thousand times, my prince,
On which you landed here on Polish soil                                     230
To fill with so much splendour and delight
Our wide horizons, like the break of day!
For you arise as does the rising sun
Out of the rugged mountains, far away.
Shine forth then! And although so tardily                                   235
You bind the glittering laurels on your brows,
The longer may they last you still unwithered.

SEGISMUND. God save you.

ASTOLFO.                          That you do not know me, sir,
Is some excuse for greeting me without
The honour due to me. I am Astolfo                                          240
The Duke of Muscovy. You are my cousin.
We are of equal rank.

SEGISMUND.                          Then if I say,
"God save you," do I not display good feeling?
But since you take such note of who you are,
The next time that I see you, I shall say                                   245
"God save you *not*," if you would like that better.

SECOND SERVANT. [*To* ASTOLFO] Your Highness, make allowance for
          his breeding
Amongst the mountains. So he deals with all.
     [*To* SEGISMUND] Astolfo does take precedence, Your Highness—

SEGISMUND. I have no patience with the way he came                         250
To make his solemn speech, then put his hat on!

SECOND SERVANT. He's a grandee!

SEGISMUND.                          I'm grander than grandees!

SECOND SERVANT. For all that, there should be respect between you,
More than among the rest.

SEGISMUND.                          And who told you
To mix in my affairs?                                                       255

     [*Enter* STELLA.]

STELLA. Many times welcome to Your Royal Highness,
Now come to grace the dais that receives him

---

227. *Segismunds:* There had been
three kings of Poland by that name between the early sixteenth century and
the time of this play.

252. *a grandee:* etiquette allowed a
grandee to keep his hat on in the king's
presence.

With gratitude and love. Long may you live
August and eminent, despite all snares,
And count your life by centuries, not years!　　260

SEGISMUND. [*Aside to* CLARION] Now tell me, who's this sovereign
　deity
At whose divinest feet Heaven lays down
The fleece of its aurora in the east?

CLARION. Sir, it's your cousin Stella.

SEGISMUND.　　　　　　　　　　She were better
Named "sun" than "star"!
　　[*To* STELLA]　　　　　Though your speech was fair, 2
Just to have seen you and been conquered by you
Suffices for a welcome in itself.
To find myself so blessed beyond my merit
What can I do but thank you, lovely Stella,
For you could add more brilliance and delight　　270
To the most blazing star? When you get up
What work is left the sun to do? O give me
Your hand to kiss, from out whose cup of snow
The solar horses drink the fires of day!

STELLA. Be a more gentle courtier.

ASTOLFO.　　　　　　　　I am lost.　　275

SECOND SERVANT. I know Astolfo's hurt. I must divert him.
　　[*To* SEGISMUND] Sir, you should know that thus to woo so boldly
Is most improper. And, besides, Astolfo . . .

SEGISMUND. Did I not tell you not to meddle with me?

SECOND SERVANT. I only say what's just.

SEGISMUND.　　　　　　　　All this annoys me.　280
Nothing seems just to me but what I want.

SECOND SERVANT. Why, sir, I heard you say that no obedience
Or service should be lent to what's unjust.

SEGISMUND. You also heard me say that I would throw
Anyone who annoys me from that balcony.　　285

SECOND SERVANT. With men like me you cannot do such things.

SEGISMUND. No? Well, by God, I'll have to prove it then!
　　[*He takes him in his arms and rushes out, followed by many,
　　to return soon after.*]

ASTOLFO. What on earth have I seen? Can it be true?

STELLA. Go, all, and stop him!

SEGISMUND. [*Returning*]　　　From the balcony
He's fallen in the sea. How strange it seems!　　290

ASTOLFO. Measure your acts of violence, my lord:
From crags to palaces, the distance is
As great as that between man and the beasts.

SEGISMUND. Well, since you are for speaking out so boldly,

Perhaps one day you'll find that on your shoulders     295
You have no head to place your hat upon.
    [*Exit* ASTOLFO. *Enter* BASIL ]
BASIL. What's happened here?
SEGISMUND.                Nothing at all. A man
  Wearied me, so I threw him in the sea.
CLARION. [*To* SEGISMUND] Be warned. That is the king.
BASIL.                    On the first day,
  So soon, your coming here has cost a life?     300
SEGISMUND. He said I couldn't: so I won the bet.
BASIL. It grieves me, Prince, that, when I hoped to see you
  Forewarned, and overriding Fate, in triumph
  Over your stars, the first thing I should see
  Should be such rigour—that your first deed here     305
  Should be a grievous homicide. Alas!
  With what love, now, can I offer my arms,
  Knowing your own have learned to kill already?
  Who sees a dirk, red from a mortal wound,
  But does not fear it? Who can see the place     310
  Soaking in blood, where late a man was murdered,
  But even the strongest must respond to nature?
  So in your arms seeing the instrument
  Of death, and looking on a blood-soaked place,
  I must withdraw myself from your embrace,     315
  And though I thought in loving bonds to bind
  Your neck, yet fear withholds me from your arms.
SEGISMUND. Without your loving arms I can sustain
  Myself as usual. That such a loving father
  Could treat me with such cruelty, could thrust me     320
  From his side ungratefully, could rear me
  As a wild beast, could hold me for a monster,
  And pray that I were dead, that such a father
  Wihholds his arms from winding round my neck,
  Seems unimportant, seeing that he deprives     325
  Me of my very being as a man.
BASIL. Would to heaven I had never granted it,
  For then I never would have heard your voice,
  Nor seen your outrages.
SEGISMUND.            Had you denied
  Me being, then I would not have complained,     330
  But that you took it from me when you gave it—
  That is my quarrel with you. Though to give
  Is the most singular and noble action,
  It is the basest action if one gives
  Only to take away.

BASIL.                      How well you thank me                    335
For being raised from pauper to a prince!
SEGISMUND. In this what is there I should thank you for?
You tyrant of my will! If you are old
And feeble, and you die, what can you give me
More than what is my own by right of birth?             340
You are my father and my king, therefore
This grandeur comes to me by natural law.
Therefore, despite my present state, I'm not
Indebted to you, rather can I claim
Account of all those years in which you robbed me       345
Of life and being, liberty, and honour.
You ought to thank me that I press no claim
Since you're my debtor, even to bankruptcy.
BASIL. Barbarous and outrageous brute! The heavens
Have now fulfilled their prophecy: I call               350
Them to bear witness to your pride. Although
You know now, disillusioned, who you are,
And see yourself where you take precedence,
Take heed of this I say: be kind and humble
Since it may be that you are only dreaming,             355
Although it seems to you you're wide-awake.    [*Exit.*]
SEGISMUND. Can I perhaps be dreaming, though I seem
So wide-awake? No: I am not asleep.
Since I can touch, and realise what I
Have been before, and what I am today.                  360
And if you even now relented, Father,
There'd be no cure since I know who I am
And you cannot, for all your sighs and groans,
Cheat me of my hereditary crown.
And if I was submissive in my chains                    365
Before, then I was ignorant of what I am,
Which I now know (and likewise know that I
Am partly man but partly beast as well).
[*Enter* ROSAURA *in woman's clothing.*]
ROSAURA. [*Aside*] I came in Stella's train. I am afraid
Of meeting with Astolfo, since Clotaldo                  370
Says he must not know who I am, not see me,
Because (he says) it touches on my honour.
And well I trust Clotaldo since I owe him
The safety of my life and honour both.

368. Notice how philosophical medita- "barbarous and outrageous brute" of
tion on the nature of man accompanies his father's description, Segismund
and underscores the developments of the knows that he is "partly man but part-
drama; at this stage in his enlighten- ly beast as well" (*un compuesto de
ment, although he does not feel like the hombre y fiera*).

CLARION. What pleases you, and what do you admire     375
  Most, of the things you've seen here in the world?
SEGISMUND. Why, nothing that I could not have foreseen—
  Except the loveliness of women! Once,
  I read among the books I had out there
  That who owes God most grateful contemplation     380
  Is Man: who is himself a tiny world.
  But I think who owes God more grateful study
  Is Woman—since she is a tiny heaven,
  Having as much more beauty than a man
  As heaven than earth. And even more, I say,     385
  If she's the one that I am looking at.
ROSAURA. [*Aside*] That is the prince. I'll go.
SEGISMUND.     Stop! Woman! Wait!
  Don't join the sunset with the breaking day
  By fading out so fast. If east and west
  Should clash like that, the day would surely suffer     390
  A syncope. But what is this I see?
ROSAURA. What I am looking at I doubt, and yet
  Believe.
SEGISMUND. [*Aside*] This beauty I have seen before.
ROSAURA. [*Aside*] This pomp and grandeur I have seen before
  Cooped in a narrow dungeon.
SEGISMUND. [*Aside*]     I have found     395
  My life at last.
  [*Aloud*]     Woman (for that sole word
  Outsoars all wooing flattery of speech
  From one that is a man), woman, who are you?
  If even long before I ever saw you
  You owed me adoration as your prince,     400
  How much the more should you be conquered by me
  Now I recall I've seen you once before!
  Who are you, beauteous woman?
ROSAURA. [*Aside*]     I'll pretend.
  [*Aloud*] In Stella's train, I am a luckless lady.
SEGISMUND. Say no such thing. You are the sun from which     405
  The minor star that's Stella draws its life,
  Since she receives the splendour of your rays.
  I've seen how in the kingdom of sweet odours,
  Commander of the squadrons of the flowers,
  The rose's deity presides, and is     410
  Their empress by divine right of her beauty.
  Among the precious stones which can be listed
  In the academy of mines, I've seen
  The diamond much preferred above the rest,

And crowned their emperor, for shining brightest.                             415
In the revolving empire of the stars
The morning star takes pride among the others.
In their perfected spheres, when the sun calls
The planets to his council, he presides
And is the very oracle of day.                                                        420
Then if among stars, gems, planet, and flowers
The fairest are exalted, why do you
Wait on a lesser beauty than yourself
Who are, in greater excellence and beauty,
The sun, the morning star, the diamond, and the rose!        425

[*Enter* CLOTALDO, *who remains by the stage-curtain.*]

CLOTALDO. [*Aside*] I wish to curb him, since I brought him up.
But, what is this?

ROSAURA.                     I reverence your favour,
And yet reply, rhetorical, with silence,
For when one's mind is clumsy and untaught,
He answers best who does not speak at all.                        430

SEGISMUND. Stay! Do not go! How can you wish to go
And leave me darkened by my doubts?

ROSAURA.                                              Your Highness,
I beg your leave to go.

SEGISMUND.                     To go so rudely
Is not to beg my leave but just to take it.

ROSAURA. But if you will not grant it, I must take it.          435

SEGISMUND. That were to change my courtesy to rudeness.
Resistance is like venom to my patience.

ROSAURA. But even if this deadly, raging venom
Should overcome your patience, yet you dare not
And could not treat me with dishonour, sir.                       440

SEGISMUND. Why, just to see then if I can, and dare to—
You'll make me lose the fear I bear your beauty,
Since the impossible is always tempting
To me. Why, only now I threw a man
Over this balcony who said I couldn't:                               445
And so to find out if I can or not
I'll throw your honour through the window too.

CLOTALDO. [*Aside*] He seems determined in this course. Oh, heavens!
What's to be done that for a second time
My honour's threatened by a mad desire?                          450

ROSAURA. Then with good reason it was prophesied
Your tyranny would wreak this kingdom

425. Like Segismund's very first speech in Act I, this is a beautiful and well-ordered piece of lyric poetry; here too the main threads of the imagery are elegantly brought together in the last line.

Outrageous scandals, treasons, crimes, and deaths.
But what can such a creature do as you
Who are not even a man, save in the name— 455
Inhuman, barbarous, cruel, and unbending
As the wild beasts amongst whom you were nursed?

SEGISMUND. That you should not insult me in this way
I spoke to you most courteously, and thought
I'd thereby get my way; but if you curse me thus 460
Even when I am speaking gently, why,
By the living God, I'll really give you cause.
Ho there! Clear out, the lot of you, at once!
Leave her to me! Close all the doors upon us.
Let no one enter! [*Exeunt* CLARION *and other attendants.*]

ROSAURA. I am lost . . . I warn you . . . 465

SEGISMUND. I am a tyrant and you plead in vain.

CLOTALDO. [*Aside*] Oh, what a monstrous thing! I must restrain him
Even if I die for it.
[*Aloud*] Sir! Wait! Look here!

SEGISMUND. A second time you have provoked my anger,
You feeble, mad old man! Do you prize lightly 470
My wrath and rigour that you've gone so far?

CLOTALDO. Brought by the accents of her voice, I came
To tell you you must be more peaceful
If still you hope to reign, and warn you that
You should not be so cruel, though you rule— 475
Since this, perhaps, is nothing but a dream.

SEGISMUND. When you refer to disillusionment
You rouse me near to madness. Now you'll see,
Here as I kill you, if it's truth or dreaming!
[*As he tries to pull out his dagger,* CLOTALDO *restrains him
and throws himself on his knees before him.*]

CLOTALDO. It's thus I'd save my life: and hope to do so— 480

SEGISMUND. Take your presumptuous hand from off this steel.

CLOTALDO. Till people come to hold your rage and fury
I shall not let you go.

ROSAURA. O heavens!

SEGISMUND. Loose it,
[*They struggle.*] I say, or else—you interfering fool—
I'll crush you to your death in my strong arms! 485

ROSAURA. Come quickly! Here's Clotaldo being killed! [*Exit.*]
[ASTOLFO *appears as* CLOTALDO *falls on the floor, and the
former stands between* SEGISMUND *and* CLOTALDO.]

---

476. . . . *a dream:* the main theme and lesson of the drama; but Segismund is not
yet ripe for it.

ASTOLFO. Why, what is this, most valiant prince? What? Staining
Your doughty steel in such old, frozen blood?
For shame! For shame! Sheathe your illustrious weapon!
SEGISMUND. When it is stained in his infamous blood!    490
ASTOLFO. At my feet here he has found sanctuary
And there he's safe, for it will serve him well.
SEGISMUND. Then serve me well by dying, for like this
I will avenge myself for your behaviour
In trying to annoy me first of all.    495
ASTOLFO. To draw in self-defense offends no king,
Though in his palace. [ASTOLFO *draws his sword and they fight.*]
CLOTALDO. [*To* ASTOLFO] Do not anger him!
  [*Enter* BASIL, STELLA, *and attendants.*]
BASIL. Hold! Hold! What's this? Fighting with naked swords?
STELLA. [*Aside*] It is Astolfo! How my heart misgives me!
BASIL. Why, what has happened here?
ASTOLFO.                Nothing, my Lord,    500
Since you've arrived.
  [*Both sheathe their swords.*]
SEGISMUND.                Much, though you *have* arrived.
I tried to kill the old man.
BASIL.                Had you no
Respect for those white hairs?
CLOTALDO.                Sire, since they're only
Mine, as you well can see, it does not matter!
SEGISMUND. It is in vain you'd have me hold white hairs    505
In such respect, since one day you may find
Your own white locks prostrated at my feet
For still I have not taken vengeance on you
For the foul way in which you had me reared.    [*Exit.*]
BASIL. Before that happens you will sleep once more    510
Where you were reared, and where what's happened may
Seem just a dream (being mere earthly glory).
  [*All save* ASTOLFO *and* STELLA *leave.*]
ASTOLFO. How seldom does prediction fail, when evil!
How oft, foretelling good! Exact in harm,
Doubtful in benefit! Oh, what a great    515
Astrologer would be one who foretold
Nothing but harms, since there's no doubt at all
That they are always due! In Segismund

---

497. Even in the most dramatic situations, these characters are sticklers for etiquette. The point implied here is that it is normally against the rules for courtiers to draw swords in the presence of their sovereign: hence Basil's surprise and alarm a few lines below.

And me the case is illustrated clearly.
In him, crimes, cruelties, deaths, and disasters            520
Were well predicted, since they all came true.
But in my own case, to predict for me
(As I foresaw beholding rays which cast
The sun into the shade and outface heaven)
Triumphs and trophies, happiness and praise,            525
Was false—and yet was true: it's only just
That when predictions start with promised favours
They should end in disdain.

STELLA.                                         I do not doubt
Your protestations are most heartfelt; only
They're not for me, but for another lady            530
Whose portrait you were wearing round your neck
Slung in a locket when you first arrived.
Since it is so, she only can deserve
These wooing flatteries. Let her repay you
For in affairs of love, flatteries and vows            535
Made for another are mere forged credentials.

[ROSAURA *enters but waits by the curtain.*]

ROSAURA. [*Aside*] Thanks be to God, my troubles are near ended!
To judge from what I see, I've naught to fear.

ASTOLFO. I will expel that portrait from my breast
To make room for the image of your beauty            540
And keep it there. For there where Stella is
Can be no room for shade, and where the sun is
No place for any star. I'll fetch the portrait.
[*Aside*] Forgive me, beautiful Rosaura, that,
When absent, men and women seldom keep            545
More faith than this.                                  [*Exit.*]

[ROSAURA *comes forward.*]

ROSAURA. [*Aside*] I could not hear a word. I was afraid
That they would see me.

STELLA.                              Oh, Astrea!

ROSAURA.                                          My lady!

STELLA. I am delighted that you came. Because
To you alone would I confide a secret.            550

ROSAURA. Thereby you greatly honour me, your servant.

STELLA. Astrea, in the brief time I have known you

528. Judging by Stella's reply, Astolfo's uselessly involved speech seems to convey the notion that astrology proves safely right when it predicts harm, for when successes are foretold, they prove false, as witness the "promised favours" of his love for Stella now ending in "disdain."

531. *portrait:* of Rosaura (*cf.* p. 1653 and note 418), who had come to Poland to seek her unfaithful lover.

548. *Astrea:* a name assumed by Rosaura.

I've given you the latchkey of my will.
For that, and being who you are, I'll tell you
A secret which I've very often hidden                                      555
Even from myself.

ROSAURA.                          I am your slave.

STELLA.                                                        Then, briefly:
Astolfo, who's my cousin (the word cousin
Suffices, since some things are plainly said
Even by thinking them), is to wed me
If Fortune thus can wipe so many cares                                     560
Away with one great joy. But I am troubled
In that, the day he first came here, he carried
A portrait of a lady round his neck.
I spoke to him about it courteously.
He was most amiable, he loves me well,                                     565
And now he's gone for it. I am embarrassed
That he should give it me himself. Wait here,
And tell him to deliver it to you.
Do not say more. Since you're discreet and fair:
You'll surely know just what love is.                            [Exit.]

ROSAURA.                                      Great heavens!             570
How I wish that I did not! For who could be
So prudent or so skilful as would know
What to advise herself in such a case?
Lives there a person on this earth today
Who's more beset by the inclement stars,                                  575
Who has more cares besieging him, or fights
So many dire calamities at once?
What can I do in such bewilderment
Wherein it seems impossible to find
Relief or comfort? Since my first misfortune                             580
No other thing has chanced or happened to me
But was a new misfortune. In succession
Inheritors and heirs of their own selves
(Just like the Phoenix, his own son and father)
Misfortunes reproduce themselves, are born,                              585
And live by dying. In their sepulchre
The ashes they consume are hot forever.
A sage once said misfortunes must be cowards
Because they never dare to walk alone
But come in crowds. I say they are most valiant                          590
Because they always charge so bravely on
And never turn their backs. Who charges with them

584. *Phoenix:* the mythical bird which every 500 years is consumed by fire and
then rises from its own ashes.

May dare all things because there is no fear
That they'll ever desert him; and I say it
Because in all my life I never once                              595
Knew them to leave me, nor will they grow tired
Of me till, wounded and shot through and through
By Fate, I fall into the arms of death.
Alas, what can I do in this dilemma?
If I reveal myself, then old Clotaldo,                            600
To whom I owe my life, may take offence,
Because he told me to await the cure
And mending of my honour in concealment.
If I don't tell Astolfo who I am
And he detects me, how can I dissimulate?                         605
Since even if I say I am not I,
The voice, the language, and the eyes will falter,
Because the soul will tell them that they lie.
What shall I do? It is in vain to study
What I should do, when I know very well                           610
That, whatsoever way I choose to act,
When the time comes I'll do as sorrow bids,
For no one has control over his sorrows.
Then since my soul dares not decide its actions
Let sorrow fill my cup and let my grief                           615
Reach its extremity and, out of doubts
And vain appearances, once and for all
Come out into the light—and Heaven shield me!
        [*Enter* ASTOLFO.]
ASTOLFO. Here, lady, is the portrait . . . but . . . great God!
ROSAURA. Why does Your Highness halt, and stare astonished?
ASTOLFO. Rosaura! Why, to see you here!
ROSAURA.                                   Rosaura?              621
    Sir, you mistake me for some other lady.
    I am Astrea, and my humble station
    Deserves no perturbation such as yours.
ASTOLFO. Enough of this pretence, Rosaura, since                  625
    The soul can never lie. Though as Astrea
    I see you now, I love you as Rosaura.
ROSAURA. Not having understood Your Highness' meaning
    I can make no reply except to say
    That Stella (who might be the star of Venus)                 630
    Told me to wait here and to tell you from her
    To give to me the portrait you were fetching
    (Which seems a very logical request)
    And I myself will take it to my lady.
    Thus Stella bids: even the slightest things                  635

Which do me harm are governed by some star.
ASTOLFO. Even if you could make a greater effort
How poorly you dissimulate, Rosaura!
Tell your poor eyes they do not harmonise
With your own voice, because they needs must jangle          640
When the whole instrument is out of tune.
You cannot match the falsehood of your words
With the sincerity of what you're feeling.
ROSAURA. All I can say is—that I want the portrait.
ASTOLFO. As you require a fiction, with a fiction          645
I shall reply. Go and tell Stella this:
That I esteem her so, it seems unworthy
Only to send the counterfeit to her
And that I'm sending her the original.
And you, take the original along with you,          650
Taking yourself to her.
ROSAURA.                    When a man starts
Forth on a definite task, resolved and valiant,
Though he be offered a far greater prize
Than what he seeks, yet he returns with failure
If he returns without his task performed.          655
I came to get that portrait. Though I bear
The original with me, of greater value,
I would return in failure and contempt
Without the copy. Give it me, Your Highness,
Since I cannot return without it.
ASTOLFO.                          But          660
If I don't give it you, how can you do so?
ROSAURA. Like this, ungrateful man! I'll take it from you.
    [*She tries to wrest it from him.*]
ASTOLFO. It is in vain.
ROSAURA.              By God, it shall not come
Into another woman's hands!
ASTOLFO.                    You're terrifying!
ROSAURA. And you're perfidious!
ASTOLFO.                        Enough, my dear          665
Rosaura!
ROSAURA.    I, your dear? You lie, you villain!
    [*They are both clutching the portrait. Enter* STELLA.]
STELLA. Astrea and Astolfo, what does this mean?
ASTOLFO. [*Aside*] Here's Stella.
ROSAURA. [*Aside*]              Love, grant me the strength to win
My portrait.
    [*To* STELLA]    If you want to know, my lady,
    **636.** *star:* the usual play on Stella = star.

What this is all about, I will explain.                                    670
ASTOLFO. [*To* ROSAURA, *aside*] What do you mean?
ROSAURA.                                         You told me to await
  Astolfo here and ask him for a portrait
  On your behalf. I waited here alone
  And as one thought suggests another thought,
  Thinking of portraits, I recalled my own          675
  Was here inside my sleeve. When one's alone,
  One is diverted by a foolish trifle
  And so I took it out to look at it.
  It slipped and fell, just as Astolfo here,
  Bringing the portrait of the other lady,            680
  Came to deliver it to you as promised.
  He picked my portrait up, and so unwilling
  Is he to give away the one you asked for,
  Instead of doing so, he seized upon
  The other portrait which is mine alone             685
  And will not give it back though I entreated
  And begged him to return it. I was angry
  And tried to snatch it back. That's it he's holding,
  And you can see yourself if it's not mine.
STELLA. Let go the portrait.            [*She snatches it from him.*]
ASTOLFO.                         Madam!
STELLA.                                  The draughtsman          690
  Was not unkind to truth.
ROSAURA.                         Is it not mine?
STELLA. Why, who could doubt it?
ROSAURA.                             Ask him for the other.
STELLA. Here, take your own, Astrea. You may leave us.
ROSAURA. [*Aside*] Now I have got my portrait, come what will.
                                              [*Exit.*]
STELLA. Now give me up the portrait that I asked for         695
  Although I'll see and speak to you no more.
  I do not wish to leave it in your power
  Having been once so foolish as to beg it.
ASTOLFO. [*Aside*] Now how can I get out of this foul trap?
  [*To* STELLA] Beautiful Stella, though I would obey you,    700
  And serve you in all ways, I cannot give you
  The portrait, since . . .
STELLA.                     You are a crude, coarse villain
  And ruffian of a wooer. For the portrait—
  I do not want it now, since, if I had it,              704
  It would remind me I had asked you for it.        [*Exit.*]
ASTOLFO. Listen! Look! Wait! Let me explain!
  [*Aside*]                              Oh, damn

Rosaura! How the devil did she get
To Poland for my ruin and her own?

*The prison of Segismund in the tower*
[SEGISMUND *lying on the ground loaded with fetters and
clothed in skins as before.* CLOTALDO, *two attendants, and*
CLARION.]

CLOTALDO. Here you must leave him—since his reckless pride
Ends here today where it began.

ATTENDANT.                    His chain                    710
I'll rivet as it used to be before.

CLARION. O Prince, you'd better not awake too soon
To find how lost you are, how changed your fate,
And that your fancied glory of an hour
Was but a shade of life, a flame of death!                    715

CLOTALDO. For one who knows so well to wield his tongue
It's fit a worthy place should be provided
With lots of room and lots of time to argue.
This is the fellow that you have to seize                    719
[*To the attendants*] And that's the room in which you are to lock
    him. [*Points to the nearest cell.*]

CLARION. Why me?

CLOTALDO.                    Because a Clarion who knows
Too many secrets must be kept in gaol—
A place where even clarions are silent.

CLARION. Have I, by chance, wanted to kill my father
Or thrown an Icarus from a balcony?                    725
Am I asleep or dreaming? To what end
Do you imprison me?

CLOTALDO.                    You're Clarion.

CLARION. Well, say I swear to be a cornet now,
A silent one, a wretched instrument . . . ?
    [*They hustle him off.* CLOTALDO *remains. Enter* BASIL,
    *wearing a mask.*]

BASIL. Clotaldo.

CLOTALDO.                    Sire . . . and is it thus alone                    730
Your Majesty has come?

BASIL.                    Vain curiosity
To see what happens here to Segismund.

CLOTALDO. See where he lies, reduced to misery!

BASIL. Unhappy prince! Born at a fatal moment!
Come waken him, now he has lost his strength                    735

725. *Icarus:* a comic reference to the
mythological flight of Icarus who came

so close to the sun that his wax wings
melted and he fell into the sea.

With all the opium he's drunk.

CLOTALDO.                                   He's stirring
And talking to himself.

BASIL.                        What is he dreaming?
Let's listen now.

SEGISMUND.          He who chastises tyrants
Is a most pious prince . . . Now let Clotaldo
Die by my hand . . . my father kiss my feet . . .                    740

CLOTALDO. He threatens me with death!

BASIL                               And me with insult
And cruelty.

CLOTALDO.       He'd take my life away.

BASIL. And he'd humiliate me at his feet.

SEGISMUND. [*Still in a dream*]
Throughout the expanse of this world's theatre
I'll show my peerless valour, let my vengeance                    745
Be wreaked, and the Prince Segismund be seen
To triumph—over his father . . . but, alas!
[*Awakening*] Where am I?

BASIL. [*To* CLOTALDO] Since he must not see me here,          749
I'll listen further off. You know your cue. [*Retires to one side.*]

SEGISMUND. Can this be I? Am I the same who, chained
And long imprisoned, rose to such a state?
Are you not still my sepulchre and grave,
You dismal tower? God! What things I have dreamed!

CLOTALDO. [*Aside*] Now I must go to him to disenchant him.    755
[*Aloud*] Awake already?

SEGISMUND.               Yes: it was high time.

CLOTALDO. What? Do you have to spend all day asleep?
Since I was following the eagle's flight
With tardy discourse, have you still lain here
Without awaking?

SEGISMUND.          No. Nor even now                            760
Am I awake. It seems I've always slept,
Since, if I've dreamed what I've just seen and heard
Palpably and for certain, then I am dreaming
What I see now—nor is it strange I'm tired,
Since what I, sleeping, see, tells me that I                     765
Was dreaming when I thought I was awake.

CLOTALDO. Tell me your dream.

SEGISMUND.                      That's if it *was* a dream!
No, I'll not tell you what I dreamed; but what
I lived and saw, Clotaldo, I *will* tell you.
I woke up in a bed that might have been                          770

758. *the eagle's flight:* cf. Clotaldo's long speech at the opening of this act.

The cradle of the flowers, woven by Spring.
A thousand nobles, bowing, called me Prince,
Attiring me in jewels, pomp, and splendour.
My equanimity you turned to rapture
Telling me that I was the Prince of Poland.                    775
CLOTALDO. I must have got a fine reward!
SEGISMUND.                                          Not so:
For as a traitor, twice, with rage and fury,
I tried to kill you.
CLOTALDO.              Such cruelty to me?
SEGISMUND. I was the lord of all, on all I took revenge,
Except I loved one woman . . . I believe                       780
That *that* was true, though all the rest has faded. [*Exit* BASIL.]
CLOTALDO. [*Aside*] I see the king was moved, to hear him speak.
[*Aloud*] Talking of eagles made you dream of empires,
But even in your dreams it's good to honour
Those who have cared for you and brought you up.               785
For Segismund, even in dreams, I warn you
Nothing is lost by trying to do good.                [*Exit.*]
SEGISMUND. That's true, and therefore let us subjugate
The bestial side, this fury and ambition,
Against the time when we may dream once more,                  790
As certainly we shall, for this strange world
Is such that but to live here is to dream.
And now experience shows me that each man
Dreams what he is until he is awakened.
The king dreams he's a king and in this fiction               795
Lives, rules, administers with royal pomp.
Yet all the borrowed praises that he earns
Are written in the wind, and he is changed
(How sad a fate!) by death to dust and ashes.
What man is there alive who'd seek to reign                    800
Since he must wake into the dream that's death.
The rich man dreams his wealth which is his care
And woe. The poor man dreams his sufferings.
He dreams who thrives and prospers in this life.
He dreams who toils and strives. He dreams who injures,        805
Offends, and insults. So that in this world
Everyone dreams the thing he is, though no one
Can understand it. I dream I am here,
Chained in these fetters. Yet I dreamed just now
I was in a more flattering, lofty station.                     810
What is this life? A frenzy, an illusion,
A shadow, a delirium, a fiction.
The greatest good's but little, and this life

Is but a dream, and dreams are only dreams.

## Act III

### The tower

[*Enter* CLARION.]

CLARION. I'm held in an enchanted tower, because
Of all I know. What would they do to me
For all I don't know, since—for all I know—
They're killing me by starving me to death.
O that a man so hungry as myself                        5
Should live to die of hunger while alive!
I am so sorry for myself that others
May well say "I can well believe it," since
This silence ill accords with my name "Clarion,"
And I just can't shut up. My fellows here?             10
Spiders and rats—fine feathered songsters those!
My head's still ringing with a dream of fifes
And trumpets and a lot of noisy humbug
And long processions as of penitents
With crosses, winding up and down, while some         15
Faint at the sight of blood besmirching others.
But now to tell the truth, I am in prison.
For knowing secrets, I am kept shut in,
Strictly observed as if I were a Sunday,
And feeling sadder than a Tuesday, where              20
I neither eat nor drink. They say a secret
Is sacred and should be as strictly kept
As any saint's day on the calendar.
Saint Secret's Day for me's a working day
Because I'm never idle then. The penance              25
I suffer here is merited, I say:
Because being a lackey, I was silent,
Which, in a servant, is a sacrilege.
        [*A noise of drums and trumpets*]
FIRST SOLDIER. [*Within*] Here is the tower in which he is
    imprisoned.
    Smash in the door and enter, everybody!          30
CLARION. Great God! They've come to seek me. That is certain
    Because they say I'm here. What can they want?
        [*Enter several soldiers.*]
FIRST SOLDIER. Go in.
SECOND SOLDIER.        He's here!

---

2. *Cf.* note to line 141 above. This
speech is played on the two themes of
the clownish servant's hunger and loquacity.

CLARION.                          No, he's not here!

ALL THE SOLDIERS.                                    Our lord!

CLARION. What, are they drunk?

FIRST SOLDIER.                   You are our rightful prince.
We do not want and never shall allow                        35
A stranger to supplant our trueborn prince.
Give us your feet to kiss!

ALL THE SOLDIERS.          Long live the prince!

CLARION. Bless me, if it's not real! In this strange kingdom
It seems the custom, everyday, to take
Some fellow and to make him prince and then              40
Shut him back in this tower. That *must* be it!
So I must play my role.

ALL THE SOLDIERS.          Give us your feet.

CLARION. I can't. They're necessary. After all
What sort of use would be a footless prince?

SECOND SOLDIER. All of us told your father, as one man,   45
We want no prince of Muscovy but you!

CLARION. You weren't respectful to my father? Shame!

FIRST SOLDIER. It was our loyalty that made us tell him.

CLARION. If it was loyalty, you have my pardon.          49

SECOND SOLDIER. Restore your empire. Long live Segismund!

CLARION. [*Aside*] That is the name they seem to give to all
These counterfeited princes.
              [*Enter* SEGISMUND.]

SEGISMUND.                    Who called Segismund?

CLARION. [*Aside*] I seem to be a hollow sort of prince.

FIRST SOLDIER. Which of you's Segismund?

SEGISMUND.                          I am.

SECOND SOLDIER. [*To* CLARION]              Then, why,
Rash fool, did you impersonate the prince                  55
Segismund?

CLARION.        What? I, Segismund? Yourselves
Be-Segismunded me without request.
All yours was both the rashness and the folly.

FIRST SOLDIER. Prince Segismund, whom we acclaim our lord,
Your father, great King Basil, in his fear                 60
That heaven would fulfill a prophecy
That one day he would kneel before your feet
Wishes now to deprive you of the throne
And give it to the Duke of Muscovy.
For this he called a council, but the people              65
Discovered his design and knowing, now,
They have a native king, will have no stranger.

64. *Duke of Muscovy:* Astolfo.

So scorning the fierce threats of destiny,
We've come to seek you in your very prison,
That aided by the arms of the whole people,                    70
We may restore you to the crown and sceptre,
Taking them from the tyrant's grasp. Come, then:
Assembling here, in this wide desert region,
Hosts of plebeians, bandits, and freebooters,
Acclaim you king. Your liberty awaits you!                    75
Hark to its voice!
[*Shouts within*]      Long life to Segismund!
SEGISMUND. Once more, you heavens will that I should dream
Of grandeur, once again, 'twixt doubts and shades,
Behold the majesty of pomp and power
Vanish into the wind, once more you wish                    80
That I should taste the disillusion and
The risk by which all human power is humbled,
Of which all human power should live aware.
It must not be. I'll not be once again
Put through my paces by my fortune's stars.                    85
And since I know this life is all a dream,
Depart, vain shades, who feign, to my dead senses,
That you have voice and body, having neither!
I want no more feigned majesty, fantastic
Display, nor void illusions, that one gust                    90
Can scatter like the almond tree in flower,
Whose rosy buds, without advice or warning,
Dawn in the air too soon and then, as one,
Are all extinguished, fade, and fall, and wither
In the first gust of wind that comes along!                    95
I know you well. I know you well by now.
I know that all that happens in yourselves
Happens as in a sleeping man. For me
There are no more delusions and deceptions
Since I well know this life is all a dream.                    100
SECOND SOLDIER. If you think we are cheating, just sweep
Your gaze along these towering peaks, and see
The hosts that wait to welcome and obey you.
SEGISMUND. Already once before I've seen such crowds
Distinctly, quite as vividly as these:                    105
And yet it was a dream.
SECOND SOLDIER.                No great event
Can come without forerunners to announce it
And this is the real meaning of your dream.
SEGISMUND. Yes, you say well. It was the fore-announcement
And just in case it was correct, my soul,                    110

(Since life's so short) let's dream the dream anew!
But it must be attentively, aware
That we'll awake from pleasure in the end.
Forewarned of that, the shock's not so abrupt,
The disillusion's less. Evils anticipated                                   115
Lose half their sting. And armed with this precaution—
That power, even when we're sure of it, is borrowed
And must be given back to its true owner—
We can risk anything and dare the worst.
Subjects, I thank you for your loyalty.                                      120
In me you have a leader who will free you,
Bravely and skilfully, from foreign rule.
Sound now to arms, you'll soon behold my valour.
Against my father I must march and bring
Truth from the stars. Yes: he must kneel to me.                             125
[*Aside*] But yet, since I may wake before he kneels,
Perhaps I'd better not proclaim what may not happen.

ALL. Long live Segismund!
    [*Enter* CLOTALDO.]

CLOTALDO.                    Gracious heavens! What is
This riot here?

SEGISMUND.         Clotaldo!

CLOTALDO.               Sir!
    [*Aside*]
His cruelty on me.             He'll prove

CLARION.           I bet he throws him                         130
Over the mountain.

CLOTALDO.           At your royal feet
I kneel, knowing my penalty is death.

SEGISMUND. Rise, rise, my foster father, from the ground,
For you must be the compass and the guide
In which I trust. You brought me up, and I                                  135
Know what I owe your loyalty. Embrace me!

CLOTALDO. What's that you say?

SEGISMUND.              I know I'm in a dream,
But I would like to act well, since good actions,
Even in a dream, are not entirely lost.

CLOTALDO. Since doing good is now to be your glory,                         140
You will not be offended that I too
Should do what's right. You march against your father!
I cannot give you help against my king.
Here at your feet, my lord, I plead for death.

SEGISMUND. [*Aloud*] Villain!
    [*Aside*]          But let us suffer this annoyance.

---

125. *Truth from the stars:* proof that their predictions were truthful.

139. *Cf.* Clotaldo's own warning to him in his last talk at the end of Act II.

Though my rage would slay him, yet he's loyal.                    146
A man does not deserve to die for that.
How many angry passions does this leash
Restrain in me, this curb of knowing well
That I must wake and find myself alone!                           150
SECOND SOLDIER. All this fine talk, Clotaldo, is a cruel
  Spurn of the public welfare. We are loyal
  Who wish our own prince to reign over us.
CLOTALDO. Such loyalty, after the king were dead,
  Would honour you. But while the king is living                  155
  He is our absolute, unquestioned lord.
  There's no excuse for subjects who oppose
  His sovereignty in arms.
FIRST SOLDIER.                        We'll soon see well
  Enough, Clotaldo, what this loyalty
  Is worth.
CLOTALDO.    You would be better if you had some.               160
  It is the greatest prize.
SEGISMUND.                        Peace, peace, I pray you.
CLOTALDO. My lord!
SEGISMUND                 Clotaldo, if your feelings
  Are truly thus, go you, and serve the king;
  That's prudence, loyalty, and common sense.
  But do not argue here with anyone                               165
  Whether it's right or wrong, for every man
  Has his own honour.
CLOTALDO.                 Humbly I take my leave.    [*Exit.*]
SEGISMUND Now sound the drums and march in rank and order
  Straight to the palace.
ALL.                       Long live Segismund!
SEGISMUND. Fortune, we go to reign! Do not awake me              170
  If I am dreaming! Do not let me fall
  Asleep if it is true! To act with virtue
  Is what matters, since if this proves true,
  That truth's sufficient reason in itself;
  If not, we win us friends against the time                      175
  When we at last awake.

### A room in the royal palace

[*Enter* BASIL *and* ASTOLFO.]

BASIL. Whose prudence can rein in a bolting horse?
  Who can restrain a river's pride, in spate?
  Whose valour can withstand a crag dislodged
  And hurtling downwards from a mountain peak?                    180
  All these are easier by far than to hold back
  A crowd's proud fury, once it has been roused.

It has two voices, both proclaiming war,
And you can hear them echoing through the mountains,
Some shouting "Segismund," others "Astolfo."     185
The scene I set for swearing of allegiance
Lends but an added horror to this strife:
It has become the back cloth to a stage
Where Fortune plays out tragedies in blood.

ASTOLFO. My lord, forget the happiness and wealth     190
You promised me from your most blessèd hand.
If Poland, which I hope to rule, refuses
Obedience to my right, grudging me honour,
It is because I've got to earn it first.
Give me a horse, that I with angry pride     195
May match the thunder in my voice and ride
To strike, like lightning, terror far and wide.     [*Exit.*]

BASIL. No remedy for what's infallible!
What is foreseen is perilous indeed!
If something has to be, there's no way out;     200
In trying to evade it, you but court it.
This law is pitiless and horrible.
Thinking one can evade the risk, one meets it:
My own precautions have been my undoing,
And I myself have quite destroyed my kingdom.     205
    [*Enter* STELLA.]

STELLA. If you, my lord, in person do not try
To curb the vast commotion that has started
In all the streets between the rival factions,
You'll see your kingdom, swamped in waves of crimson,
Swimming in its own blood, with nothing left     210
But havoc, dire calamity, and woe.
So frightful is the damage to your empire
That, seen, it strikes amazement; heard, despair.
The sun's obscured, the very winds are hindered.
Each stone is a memorial to the dead.     215
Each flower springs from a grave while every building
Appears a mausoleum, and each soldier
A premature and walking skeleton.
    [*Enter* CLOTALDO.]

CLOTALDO. Praise be to God, I reach your feet alive!
BASIL. Clotaldo! What's the news of Segismund?     220
CLOTALDO. The crowd, a headstrong monster blind with rage,
Entered his dungeon tower and set him free.
He, now exalted for the second time,
Conducts himself with valour, boasting how
He will bring down the truth out of the stars.     225
BASIL. Give me a horse, that I myself, in person,
May vanquish such a base, ungrateful son!

For I, in the defence of my own crown,
Shall do by steel what science failed to do.     [Exit.]

STELLA. I'll be Bellona to your Sun, and try                230
To write my name next yours in history.
I'll ride as though I flew on outstretched wings
That I may vie with Pallas.                        [Exit.]

  [*Enter* ROSAURA, *holding back* CLOTALDO.]

ROSAURA. I know that all is war, Clotaldo, yet
Although your valour calls you to the front,                235
First hear me out. You know quite well that I
Arrived in Poland poor and miserable,
Where, shielded by your valour, I found mercy.
You told me to conceal myself, and stay
Here in the palace, hiding from Astolfo.                    240
He saw me in the end, and so insulted
My honour that (although he saw me clearly)
He nightly speaks with Stella in the garden.
I have the key to it and I will show you
How you can enter there and end my cares.                   245
Thus bold, resolved, and strong, you can recover
My honour, since you're ready to avenge me
By killing him.

CLOTALDO.          It's true that I intended,
Since first I saw you (having heard your tale)
With my own life to rectify your wrongs.                    250
The first step that I took was bid you dress
According to your sex, for fear Astolfo
Might see you as you were, and deem you wanton.
I was devising how we could recover
Your honour (so much did it weigh on me)                    255
Even though we had to kill him. (A wild plan—
Though since he's not my king, I would not flinch
From killing him.) But then, when suddenly
Segismund tried to kill me, it was he
Who saved my life with his surpassing valour.              260
Consider: how can I requite Astolfo
With death for giving me my life so bravely,
And when my soul is full of gratitude?
So torn between the two of you I stand—
Rosaura, whose life I saved, and Astolfo,                   265
Who saved my life. What's to be done? Which side
To take, and whom to help, I cannot judge.
What I owe you in that I gave you life

---

230. *Bellona:* the Roman war goddess.
  234ff. Calderón, and generally dramatists and audiences of the period, had
a distinct taste for debate on points of
honor, valor, loyalty, retribution, of
which the following dialogue between
Rosaura and Clotaldo is an excellent
example. Notice how subtle theoretical
debate develops more and more into
high-sounding passion.

I owe to him in that he gave me life.
And so there is no course that I can take      270
To satisfy my love. I am a person
Who has to act, yet suffer either way.

ROSAURA. I should not have to tell so brave a man
That if it is nobility to give,
It's baseness to receive. That being so      275
You owe no gratitude to him, admitting
That it was he who gave you life, and you
Who gave me life, since he forced you to take
A meaner role, and through me you assumed
A generous role. So you should side with me:      280
My cause is so far worthier than his own
As giving is than taking.

CLOTALDO.               Though nobility
Is with the giver, it is gratitude
That dwells with the receiver. As a giver
I have the name of being generous:      285
Then grant me that of being grateful too
And let me earn the title and be grateful,
As I am liberal, giving or receiving.

ROSAURA. You granted me my life, at the same time
Telling me it was worthless, since dishonoured,      290
And therefore was no life. Therefore from you
I have received no life at all. And since
You should be liberal first and grateful after
(Since so you said yourself) I now entreat you
Give me the life, the life you never gave me!      295
As giving magnifies the most, give first
And then be grateful after, if you will!

CLOTALDO. Won by your argument, I will be liberal.
Rosaura, I shall give you my estate
And you shall seek a convent, there to live.      300
This measure is a happy thought, for, see,
Fleeing a crime, you find a sanctuary.
For when the empire's threatened with disasters
And is divided thus, I, born a noble,
Am not the man who would augment its woes.      305
So with this remedy which I have chosen
I remain loyal to the kingdom, generous
To you, and also grateful to Astolfo.
And thus I choose the course that suits you best.
Were I your father, what could I do more?      310

ROSAURA. Were you my father, then I would accept
The insult. Since you are not, I refuse.

CLOTALDO. What do you hope to do then?

ROSAURA.                    Kill the duke!

CLOTALDO. A girl who never even knew her father
 Armed with such courage?
ROSAURA.               Yes.
CLOTALDO.                   What spurs you on?     315
ROSAURA. My good name.
CLOTALDO.             In Astolfo you will find . . .
ROSAURA. My honour rides on him and strikes him down!
CLOTALDO. Your king, too, Stella's husband!
ROSAURA.                   Never, never
 Shall that be, by almighty God, I swear!
CLOTALDO. Why, this is madness!
ROSAURA.             Yes it is!
CLOTALDO.                   Restrain it.     320
ROSAURA. That I cannot.
CLOTALDO.           Then you are lost forever!
ROSAURA. I know it!
CLOTALDO.         Life and honour both together!
ROSAURA. I well believe it!
CLOTALDO.           What do you intend?
ROSAURA. My death.
CLOTALDO.        This is despair and desperation.
ROSAURA. It's honour.
CLOTALDO.       It is nonsense.
ROSAURA.                   It is valour.     325
CLOTALDO. It's frenzy.
ROSAURA.       Yes, it's anger! Yes, it's fury!
CLOTALDO. In short you cannot moderate your passion?
ROSAURA. No.
CLOTALDO.      Who is there to help you?
ROSAURA.                 I, myself.
CLOTALDO. There is no cure?
ROSAURA.         There is no cure!
CLOTALDO.                   Think well
 If there's not some way out . . .
ROSAURA.            Some other way     330
 To do away with me . . .            [*Exit.*]
CLOTALDO.           If you are lost,
 My daughter, let us both be lost together!

### In the country

[*Enter* SEGISMUND *clothed in skins. Soldiers marching.*
 CLARION. *Drums beating.*]

SEGISMUND. If Rome, today, could see me here, renewing
 Her olden triumphs, she might laugh to see
 A wild beast in command of mighty armies,     335
 A wild beast, to whose fiery aspirations

The firmament were all too slight a conquest!
But stoop your flight, my spirit. Do not thus
Be puffed to pride by these uncertain plaudits
Which, when I wake, will turn to bitterness          340
In that I won them only to be lost.
The less I value them, the less I'll miss them.

> [*A trumpet sounds.*]

CLARION. Upon a rapid courser (pray excuse me,
  Since if it comes to mind I must describe it)
  In which it seems an atlas was designed          345
  Since if its body is earth, its soul is fire
  Within its breast, its foam appears the sea,
  The wind its breath, and chaos its condition,
  Since in its soul, its foam, its breath and flesh,
  It seems a monster of fire, earth, sea, and wind,  350
  Upon the horse, all of a patchwork colour,
  Dappled, and rushing forward at the will
  Of one who plies the spur, so that it flies
  Rather than runs—see how a woman rides
  Boldly into your presence.

SEGISMUND.                    Her light blinds me.     355

CLARION. Good God! Why, here's Rosaura!

SEGISMUND.                              It is heaven
  That has restored her to my sight once more.

> [*Enter* ROSAURA *with sword and dagger in riding costume.*]

ROSAURA. Generous Segismund, whose majesty
  Heroically rises in the lustre
  Of his great deeds out of his night of shadows,   360
  And as the greatest planet, in the arms
  Of his aurora, lustrously returns
  To plants and roses, over hills and seas,
  When, crowned with gold, he looks abroad, dispersing
  Radiance, flashing his rays, bathing the summits,  365
  And broidering the fringes of the foam.
  So may you dawn upon the world, bright sun
  Of Poland, that a poor unhappy woman
  May fall before your feet and beg protection
  Both as a woman and unfortunate—                   370
  Two things that must oblige you, sire, as one
  Who prize yourself as valiant, each of them
  More than suffices for your chivalry.
  Three times you have beheld me now, three times
  Been ignorant of who I am, because             375
  Three times you saw me in a different clothing

---

343. "Clarion's speech is a parody of exaggerated style—including Calderón's."  [Translator's note]

361. *the greatest planet*: The sun.

The first time you mistook me for a man,
Within that rigorous prison, where your hardships
Made mine seem pleasure. Next time, as a woman,
You saw me, when your pomp and majesty          380
Were as a dream, a phantasm, a shade.
The third time is today when, as a monster
Of both the sexes, in a woman's costume
I bear a soldier's arms. But to dispose you
The better to compassion, hear my story.          385
My mother was a noble in the court
Of Moscow, who, since most unfortunate,
Must have been beautiful. Then came a traitor
And cast his eyes on her (I do not name him,
Not knowing who he is). Yet I deduce          390
That he was valiant too from my own valour,
Since he gave form to me—and I could wish
I had been born in pagan times, that I might
Persuade myself he was some god of those
Who rain in showers of gold, turn into swans          395
Or bulls, for Danaës, Ledas, or Europas.
That's strange: I thought I was just rambling on
By telling old perfidious myths, yet find
I've told you how my mother was cajoled.
Oh, she was beautiful as no one else          400
Has been, but was unfortunate like all.
He swore to wed her (that's an old excuse)
And this trick reached so nearly to her heart
That thought must weep, recalling it today.
The tyrant left her only with his sword          405
As Aeneas left Troy. I sheathed its blade here
Upon my thigh, and I will bare it too
Before the ending of this history.
Out of this union, this poor link which neither
Could bind the marriage nor handcuff the crime,          410
Myself was born, her image and her portrait,
Not in her beauty, but in her misfortune,
For mine's the same. That's all I need to say.
The most that I can tell you of myself
Is that the man who robbed me of the spoils          415
And trophies of my honour is Astolfo.
Alas! to name him my heart rages so

396. *for Danaës, Ledas, or Europas:*
To seduce them, Zeus assumed the
shapes, respectively, of a gold shower,
a swan, and a bull.
406. Probably Calderón was thinking
of Carthage rather than Troy. Aeneas
departed from Carthage in haste, leaving behind the sword which queen Dido
would use for her suicide.

(As hearts will do when men name enemies).
Astolfo was my faithless and ungrateful
Lord, who (quite forgetful of our happiness,                    420
Since of a past love even the memory fades)
Came here to claim the throne and marry Stella
For she's the star who rises as I set.
It's hard to credit that a star should sunder
Lovers the stars had made conformable!                         425
So hurt was I, so villainously cheated,
That I became mad, brokenhearted, sick,
Half wild with grief, and like to die, with all
Hell's own confusion ciphered on my mind
Like Babel's incoherence. Mutely I told                        430
My griefs (since woes and griefs declare themselves
Better than can the mouth, by their effects),
When, with my mother (we were by ourselves),
She broke the prison of my pent-up sorrows
And from my breast they all rushed forth in troops.            435
I felt no shyness, for in knowing surely
That one to whom one's errors are recounted
Has also been an ally in her own,
One finds relief and rest, since bad example
Can sometimes serve for a good purpose too.                    440
She heard my plaint with pity, and she tried
To palliate my sorrows with her own.
How easily do judges pardon error
When they've offended too! An example,
A warning, in herself, she did not trust                       445
To idleness, or the slow cure of time,
Nor try to find a remedy for her honour
In my misfortunes, but, with better counsel,
She bade me follow him to Poland here
And with prodigious gallantry persuade him                     450
To pay the debt to honour that he owes me.
So that it would be easier to travel,
She bade me don male clothing, and took down
This ancient sword which I am wearing now.
Now it is time that I unsheathe the blade                      455
As I was bid, for, trusting in its sign,
She said: "Depart to Poland, show this sword
That all the nobles may behold it well,
And it may be that one of them will take
Pity on you, and counsel you, and shield you"                  460
I came to Poland and, you will remember,

423. *the star*: Stella = star.

Entered your cave. You looked at me in wonder.
Clotaldo passionately took my part
To plead for mercy to the king, who spared me,
Then, when he heard my story, bade me change          465
Into my own clothes and attend on Stella,
There to disturb Astolfo's love and stop
Their marriage. Again you saw me in woman's dress
And were confused by the discrepancy.
But let's pass to what's new: Clotaldo, now           470
Persuaded that Astolfo must, with Stella,
Come to the throne, dissuades me from my purpose,
Against the interests of my name and honour.
But seeing you, O valiant Segismund,
Are claiming your revenge, now that the heavens       475
Have burst the prison of your rustic tower,
(Wherein you were the tiger of your sorrows,
The rock of sufferings and direful pains)
And sent you forth against your sire and country,
I come to aid you, mingling Dian's silks              480
With the hard steel of Pallas. Now, strong Captain,
It well behoves us both to stop this marriage—
Me, lest my promised husband should be wed,
You, lest, when their estates are joined, they weigh
More powerfully against your victory.                 485
I come, as a mere woman, to persuade you
To right my shame; but, as a man, I come
To help you battle for your crown. As woman,
To melt your heart, here at your feet I fall;
But, as a man, I come to serve you bravely            490
Both with my person and my steel, and thus,
If you today should woo me as a woman,
Then I should have to kill you as a man would
In honourable service of my honour;
Since I must be three things today at once—           495
Passionate, to persuade you: womanly,
To ply you with my woes: manly, to gain
Honour in battle.

SEGISMUND.                     Heavens! If it is true I'm dreaming,
Suspend my memory, for in a dream
So many things could not occur. Great heavens!        500
If I could only come free of them all!
Or never think of any! Who ever felt
Such grievous doubts? If I but dreamed that triumph
In which I found myself, how can this woman
Refer me to such sure and certain facts?              505

Then all of it was true and not a dream.
But if it be the truth, why does my past life
Call it a dream? This breeds the same confusion.
Are dreams and glories so alike, that fictions
Are held for truths, realities for lies?                                510
Is there so little difference in them both
That one should question whether what one sees
And tastes is true or false? What? Is the copy
So near to the original that doubt
Exists between them? Then if that is so,                                515
And grandeur, power, majesty, and pomp,
Must all evaporate like shades at morning,
Let's profit by it, this time, to enjoy
That which we only can enjoy in dreams.
Rosaura's in my power: my soul adores her beauty.                       520
Let's take the chance. Let love break every law
On which she has relied in coming here
And kneeling, trustful, prostrate at my feet.
This is a dream. If so, dream pleasures now
Since they must turn to sorrows in the end!                             525
But with my own opinions, I begin
Once again to convince myself. Let's think.
If it is but vainglory and a dream,
Who for mere human vainglory would lose
True glory? What past blessing is not merely                            530
A dream? Who has known heroic glories,
That deep within himself, as he recalls them,
Has never doubted that they might be dreams?
But if this all should end in disenchantment,
Seeing that pleasure is a lovely flame                                  535
That's soon converted into dust and ashes
By any wind that blows, then let us seek
That which endures in thrifty, lasting fame
In which no pleasures sleep, nor grandeurs dream.
Rosaura's without honour. In a prince                                   540
It's worthier to restore it than to steal it.
I shall restore it, by the living God,
Before I win my throne! Let's shun the danger
And fly from the temptation which is strong!
Then sound to arms!                                                     545
[*To a soldier*] Today I must give battle before darkness
Buries the rays of gold in green-black waves!
ROSAURA. My lord! Alas, you stand apart, and offer
No word of pity for my plight. How is it
You neither hear nor see me nor even yet                                550
Have turned your face on me?
SEGISMUND.                          Rosaura, for your honour's sake

I must be cruel to you, to be kind.
My voice must not reply to you because
My honour must reply to you. I am silent
Because my deeds must speak to you alone.                555
I do not look at you since, in such straits,
Having to see your honour is requited,
I must not see your beauty.
      [*Exit with soldiers.*]
ROSAURA. What strange enigma's this? After such trouble
Still to be treated with more doubtful riddles!          560
      [*Enter* CLARION.]
CLARION. Madam, may you be visited just now?
ROSAURA. Why, Clarion, where have you been all this time?
CLARION. Shut in the tower, consulting cards
About my death: "to be or not to be."
And it was a near thing.
ROSAURA.                Why?
CLARION.                       Because I know          565
The secret who you are: in fact, Clotaldo . . .
[*Drums.*] But hush what noise is that?
ROSAURA.                          What can it be?
CLARION. From the beleaguered palace a whole squadron
Is charging forth to harry and defeat
That of fierce Segismund.
ROSAURA.                Why, what a coward          570
Am I, not to be at his side, the terror
And scandal of the world, while such fierce strife
Presses all round in lawless anarchy.          [*Exit.*]
VOICES OF SOME. Long live our king!
VOICES OF OTHERS.                Long live our liberty!
CLARION. Long live both king and liberty. Yes, live!    575
And welcome to them both! I do not worry
In all this pother, I behave like Nero
Who never grieved at what was going on.
If I had anything to grieve about
It would be me, myself. Well hidden here,          580
Now, I can watch the sport that's going on.
This place is safe and hidden between crags,
And since death cannot find me here, two figs for death!
      [*He hides. Drums and the clash of arms are heard. Enter*
      BASIL, CLOTALDO, *and* ASTOLFO, *fleeing.*]
BASIL. Was ever king so hapless as myself
Or father more ill used?
CLOTALDO.                Your beaten army          585
Rush down, in all directions, in disorder.
ASTOLFO. The traitors win!
BASIL                In battles such as these

Those on the winning side are ever "loyal,"
And traitors the defeated. Come, Clotaldo,
Let's flee from the inhuman cruelty                    590
Of my fierce son!

[*Shots are fired within.* CLARION *falls wounded.*]

CLARION.                    Heavens, save me!

ASTOLFO.                              Who is this
Unhappy soldier bleeding at our feet?

CLARION. I am a most unlucky man who, wishing
To guard myself from death, have sought it out
By fleeing from it. Shunning it, I found it,              595
Because, to death, no hiding-place is secret.
So you can argue that whoever shuns it
Most carefully runs into it the quickest.
Turn, then, once more into the thick of battle:
There is more safety there amidst the fire               600
And clash of arms than here on this secluded
Mountain, because no hidden path is safe
From the inclemency of Fate; and so,
Although you flee from death, yet you may find it         604
Quicker than you expect, if God so wills. [*He falls dead.*]

BASIL. "If God so wills" . . . With what strange eloquence
This corpse persuades our ignorance and error
To better knowledge, speaking from the mouth
Of its fell wound, where the red liquid flowing
Seems like a bloody tongue which teaches us               610
That the activities of man are vain
When they are pitted against higher powers.
For I, who wished to liberate my country
From murder and sedition, gave it up
To the same ills from which I would have saved it.       615

CLOTALDO. Though Fate, my lord, knows every path, and finds
Him whom it seeks even in the midst of crags
And thickets, it is not a Christian judgment
To say there is no refuge from its fury.
A prudent man can conquer Fate itself.                    620
Though you are not exempted from misfortune,
Take action to escape it while you can!

ASTOLFO. Clotaldo speaks as one mature in prudence,
And I as one in valour's youthful prime.
Among the thickets of this mount is hidden               625
A horse, the very birth of the swift wind.
Flee on him, and I'll guard you in the rear.

BASIL. If it is God's will I should die, or if
Death waits here for my coming, I will seek
Him out today, and meet him face to face.                630

[*Enter* SEGISMUND, STELLA, ROSAURA, *soldiers, and their*

*train.*]

A SOLDIER. Amongst the thickets of this mountain
 The king is hiding.

SEGISMUND. Seek him out at once!
 Leave no foot of the summit unexplored
 But search from stem to stem and branch to branch!

CLOTALDO. Fly, sir!

BASIL. What for?

ASTOLFO. What do you mean to do? 635

BASIL. Astolfo, stand aside!

CLOTALDO. What is your wish?

BASIL. To take a cure I've needed for sometime.
 [*To* SEGISMUND] If you have come to seek me, here I am.
 [*Kneeling*] Your father, prince, kneels humbly at your feet.
 The white snow of my hair is now your carpet. 640
 Tread on my neck and trample on my crown!
 Lay low and drag my dignity in dust!
 Take vengeance on my honour! Make a slave
 Of me and, after all I've done to thwart them,
 Let Fate fulfil its edict and claim homage 645
 And Heaven fulfil its oracles at last!

SEGISMUND. Illustrious court of Poland, who have been
 The witness of such unwonted wonders,
 Attend to me, and hear your prince speak out.
 What Heaven decrees and God writes with his finger 650
 (Whose prints and ciphers are the azure leaves
 Adorned with golden lettering of the stars)
 Never deceives nor lies. They only lie
 Who seek to penetrate the mystery
 And, having reached it, use it to ill purpose. 655
 My father, who is here to evade the fury
 Of my proud nature, made me a wild beast:
 So, when I, by my birth of gallant stock,
 My generous blood, and inbred grace and valour,
 Might well have proved both gentle and forbearing, 660
 The very mode of life to which he forced me,
 The sort of bringing up I had to bear
 Sufficed to make me savage in my passions.
 What a strange method of restraining them!
 If one were to tell any man: "One day 665
 You will be killed by an inhuman monster,"
 Would it be the best method he could choose
 To wake that monster when it was asleep?
 Or if they told him: "That sword which you're wearing
 Will be your death," what sort of cure were it 670
 To draw it forth and aim it at his breast?
 Or if they told him: "Deep blue gulfs of water

Will one day be your sepulchre and grave
Beneath a silver monument of foam,"
He would be mad to hurl himself in headlong           675
When the sea highest heaved its showy mountains
And crystalline sierras plumed with spray.
The same has happened to the king as to him
Who wakes a beast which threatens death, to him
Who draws a naked sword because he fears it,           680
To him who dives into the stormy breakers.
Though my ferocious nature (hear me now)
Was like a sleeping beast, my inborn rage
A sheathèd sword, my wrath a quiet ripple,
Fate should not be coerced by man's injustice—           685
This rouses more resentment. So it is
That he who seeks to tame his fortune must
Resort to moderation and to measure.
He who foresees an evil cannot conquer it
Thus in advance, for though humility           690
Can overcome it, this it can do only
When the occasion's there, for there's no way
To dodge one's fate and thus evade the issue.
Let this strange spectacle serve as example—
This prodigy, this horror, and this wonder,           695
Because it is no less than one, to see,
After such measures and precautions taken
To thwart it, that a father thus should kneel
At his son's feet, a kingdom thus be shattered.
This was the sentence of the heavens above,           700
Which he could not evade, much though he tried.
Can I, younger in age, less brave, and less
In science than the king, conquer that fate?
[*To the* KING] Sire, rise, give me your hand, now that the heavens
Have shown you that you erred as to the method           705
To vanquish them. Humbly I kneel before you
And offer you my neck to tread upon.
BASIL. Son, such a great and noble act restores you
Straight to my heart. Oh, true and worthy prince!
You have won both the laurel and the palm.           710
Crown yourself with your deeds! For you *have* conquered!
ALL. Long live Segismund! Long live Segismund!
SEGISMUND. Since I have other victories to win,
The greatest of them all awaits me now:
To conquer my own self. Astolfo, give           715
Your hand here to Rosaura, for you know
It is a debt of honour and must be paid.
ASTOLFO. Although, it's true, I owe some obligations—

She does not know her name or who she is,
It would be base to wed a woman who . . .                    720

CLOTALDO. Hold! Wait! Rosaura's of as noble stock
As yours, Astolfo. In the open field
I'll prove it with my sword. She is my daughter,
And that should be enough.

ASTOLFO.                    What do you say?

CLOTALDO. Until I saw her married, righted, honoured,      725
I did not wish for it to be discovered.
It's a long story but she is my daughter.

ASTOLFO. That being so, I'm glad to keep my word.

SEGISMUND. And now, so that the princess Stella here
Will not remain disconsolate to lose                       730
A prince of so much valour, here I offer
My hand to her, no less in birth and rank.
Give me your hand.

STELLA.                  I gain by meriting
So great a happiness.

SEGISMUND.              And now, Clotaldo,
So long so loyal to my father come                          735
To my arms. Ask me anything you wish.

FIRST SOLDIER. If thus you treat a man who never served you,
What about me who led the revolution
And brought you from your dungeon in the tower?
What will you give me?

SEGISMUND.                That same tower and dungeon       740
From which you never shall emerge till death.
No traitor is of use after his treason.

BASIL. All wonder at your wisdom!

ASTOLFO.                    What a change
Of character!

ROSAURA.        How wise and prudent!

SEGISMUND.                        Why
Do you wonder? Why do you marvel, since               745
It was a dream that taught me and I still
Fear to wake up once more in my close dungeon?
Though that may never happen, it's enough
To dream it might, for thus I came to learn
That all our human happiness must pass              750
Away like any dream, and I would here
Enjoy it fully ere it glide away,
Asking (for noble hearts are prone to pardon)
Pardon for faults in the actors or the play.

754. This form of close, addressed to    is a well-established Renaissance con-
the audience and begging for its favor,    vention.

# JOHN MILTON
## (1608–1674)

## *From* PARADISE LOST *
## Book IX

### The Argument

Satan, having compassed the Earth, with meditated guile returns as
a mist by night into Paradise; enters into the serpent sleeping.
Adam and Eve in the morning go forth to their labors, which Eve
proposes to divide in several places, each laboring apart: Adam consents not, alleging the danger lest that enemy of whom they were
forewarned should attempt her found alone. Eve, loath to be
thought not circumspect or firm enough, urges her going apart, the
rather desirous to make trial of her strength; Adam at last yields.
The serpent finds her alone: his subtle approach, first gazing, then
speaking, with much flattery extolling Eve above all other creatures. Eve, wondering to hear the serpent speak, asks how he
attained to human speech and such understanding not till now; the
serpent answers that by tasting of a certain tree in the garden he
attained both to speech and reason, till then void of both. Eve
requires him to bring her to that tree, and finds it to be the Tree of
Knowledge forbidden: the serpent, now grown bolder, with many
wiles and arguments induces her at length to eat. She, pleased
with the taste, deliberates a while whether to impart thereof to
Adam or not; at last brings him of the fruit; relates what persuaded
her to eat thereof. Adam, at first amazed, but perceiving her lost,
resolves, through vehemence of love, to perish with her, and, extenuating[1] the trespass, eats also of the fruit. The effects thereof in
them both; they seek to cover their nakedness; then fall to variance
and accusation of one another.

> No more of talk where God[2] or angel guest
> With man, as with his friend, familiar used
> To sit indulgent, and with him partake
> Rural repast, permitting him the while
> Venial[3] discourse unblamed. I now must change
> Those notes to tragic; foul distrust, and breach          5
> Disloyal, on the part of man, revolt
> And disobedience; on the part of Heaven,
> Now alienated, distance and distaste,
> Anger and just rebuke, and judgment given,                 10

* The texts and notes here presented are
by Robert M. Adams.
1. Not "diminishing" or "excusing" as
in customary English usage, but carrying further, drawing out.

2. God, of course, has not been lunch-
ing with Adam; but since man is about
to fall, the age is now over when such
an occasion could be contemplated.
3. Permissible.

That brought into this world a world of woe,
Sin and her shadow Death, and Misery,
Death's harbinger. Sad task! yet argument
Not less but more heroic than the wrath
Of stern Achilles on his foe pursued                              15
Thrice fugitive about Troy wall; or rage
Of Turnus for Lavinia disespoused;
Or Neptune's ire, or Juno's, that so long
Perplexed the Greek, and Cytherea's son:[4]
If answerable style I can obtain                                  20
Of my celestial Patroness,[5] who deigns
Her nightly visitation unimplored,
And dictates to me slumbering, or inspires
Easy my unpremeditated verse,[6]
Since first this subject for heroic song                          25
Pleased me, long choosing and beginning late,[7]
Not sedulous by nature to indite
Wars, hitherto the only argument
Heroic deemed, chief mastery to dissect[8]
With long and tedious havoc fabled knights                        30
In battles feigned (the better fortitude
Of patience and heroic martyrdom
Unsung), or to describe races and games,
Or tilting furniture,[9] emblazoned shields,
Impresses quaint, caparisons and steeds,                          35
Bases and tinsel trappings, gorgeous knights
At joust and tournament; then marshaled feast
Served up in hall with sewers and seneschals:[1]
The skill of artifice or office mean;
Not that which justly gives heroic name                           40
To person or to poem. Me, of these
Nor skilled nor studious, higher argument
Remains,[2] sufficient of itself to raise
That name,[3] unless an age too late, or cold
Climate, or years, damp my intended wing                          45
Depressed; and much they may if all be mine,
Not hers who brings it nightly to my ear.

---

4. In the *Iliad* (**XXII**), Achilles pursues Hector three times around Troy wall before catching him. In the *Aeneid*, Aeneas must fight with Turnus for the hand of Lavinia. Neptune (or Poseidon) was unfriendly to Odysseus (the Greek); Juno (or Hera) to Aeneas, who was Cytherea's, i.e., Aphrodite's, son by Anchises.
5. The muse, Urania.
6. Milton, we are told by his nephew Edward Philips, used to wake up in the morning with lines of poetry full-formed in his head; he would then dictate them to an amanuensis.
7. Milton's early plans for epics, preserved in manuscript, did center on national heroes; his choice of a sacred subject is a novelty within the epic tradi-

tion. "Sedulous": eager.
8. I.e., in describing wars one's chief task is to dissect; dissect, in its strict Latin sense of "cut apart," but perhaps also with a comic overtone from the anatomy table.
9. The equipment of tournaments; "impresses quaint": elaborate devices on shields; "bases": trappings for horses.
1. Waiters and stewards.
2. I.e., for me, when these things are set aside which I neither can nor want to do, there remains a higher argument.
3. I.e., the name heroic poet. "Age too late": not Milton's age, but the age of the world. Milton felt a "cold climate," by forcing people to keep their mouths shut and mumble, was inimical to epic poetry. "Damp": stupefy, benumb.

The sun was sunk, and after him the star
Of Hesperus, whose office is to bring
Twilight upon the Earth, short arbiter 50
'Twixt day and night, and now from end to end
Night's hemisphere had veiled the horizon round,
When Satan, who late fled before the threats
Of Gabriel out of Eden,[4] now improved
In meditated fraud and malice, bent 55
On man's destruction, mauger what might hap
Of heavier on himself,[5] fearless returned.
By night he fled, and at midnight returned
From compassing the Earth—cautious of day
Since Uriel, regent of the sun, descried 60
His entrance, and forewarned the Cherubim
That kept their watch.[6] Thence, full of anguish, driven,
The space of seven continued nights he rode
With darkness; thrice the equinoctial line[7]
He circled, four times crossed the car of Night 65
From pole to pole, traversing each colure;
On the eighth returned, and on the coast averse
From entrance or cherubic watch by stealth
Found unsuspected way. There was a place 70
(Now not, though sin, not time, first wrought the change)
Where Tigris, at the foot of Paradise,
Into a gulf shot under ground, till part
Rose up a fountain by the Tree of Life.
In with the river sunk, and with it rose, 75
Satan, involved in rising mist; then sought
Where to lie hid. Sea he had searched and land
From Eden over Pontus, and the pool
Maeotis, up beyond the river Ob;[8]
Downward as far antarctic; and, in length, 80
West from Orontes to the ocean barred
At Darien, thence to the land where flows
Ganges and Indus.[9] Thus the orb he roamed
With narrow search, and with inspection deep
Considered every creature, which of all 85
Most opportune might serve his wiles, and found
The serpent subtlest beast of all the field.[1]
Him, after long debate, irresolute
Of thoughts revolved,[2] his final sentence chose

---

4. At the end of Book IV.
5. Despite the peril of heavier (punishments).
6. At the beginning of Book IV. These connections with Book IV not only bridge the intervening narration, but emphasize a balancing of the whole epic; see the headnote.
7. The equator. The colures are the two great circles of the celestial sphere which intersect at the poles. By circling the globe, either from east to west or over the north and south poles, Satan can remain continually hidden in darkness.

8. Pontus is the Black Sea, the pool Maeotis the swamps of the Sea of Azov; the river Ob flows north through Siberia into the Arctic Ocean.
9. Flying west from Orontes in Syria, Satan now crosses the Atlantic to the Isthmus of Panama (Darien), then crosses the Pacific and southeast Asia to India.
1. Genesis iii.1 describes the serpent as the subtlest beast of the field.
2. I.e., unable to decide among his revolving thoughts. "Sentence": decision.

Fit vessel, fittest imp[3] of fraud, in whom                    90
To enter, and his dark suggestions hide
From sharpest sight; for in the wily snake
Whatever sleights none would suspicious mark,
As from his wit and native subtlety
Proceeding, which, in other beasts observed,                    95
Doubt[4] might beget of diabolic power
Active within beyond the sense of brute.
Thus he resolved, but first from inward grief
His bursting passion into plaints thus poured:
    "O Earth, how like to Heaven, if not preferred
More justly, seat worthier of Gods, as built            100
With second thought, reforming what was old!
For what God, after better, worse would build?
Terrestrial Heaven, danced round by other Heavens,
That shine, yet bear their bright officious lamps,
Light above light, for thee alone, as seems,            105
In thee concent'ring all their precious beams
Of sacred influence![5] As God in Heaven
Is center, yet extends to all, so thou
Cent'ring receiv'st from all those orbs; in thee,
Not in themselves, all their known virtue appears,      110
Productive in herb, plant, and nobler birth
Of creatures animate with gradual life
Of growth, sense, reason,[6] all summed up in man.
With what delight could I have walked thee round,
If I could joy in aught; sweet interchange            115
Of hill and valley, rivers, woods, and plains,
Now land, now sea, and shores with forest crowned,
Rocks, dens, and caves! But I in none of these
Find place or refuge; and the more I see
Pleasures about me, so much more I feel               120
Torment within me, as from the hateful siege[7]
Of contraries; all good to me becomes
Bane,[8] and in Heaven much worse would be my state.
But neither here seek I, no, nor in Heaven,
To dwell, unless by mastering Heaven's Supreme;       125
Nor hope to be myself less miserable
By what I seek, but others to make such
As I, though thereby worse to me redound.
For only in destroying I find ease
To my relentless thoughts, and him [9] destroyed,      130
Or won to what may work his utter loss,
For whom all this was made, all this [1] will soon
Follow, as to him linked in weal or woe:
In woe then, that destruction wide may range!

---

3. Graft, offshoot.
4. Suspicion.
5. Satan, like Adam in Book VIII, is impressed that so many heavenly bodies center on (and "serve") the earth—as the old Ptolemaic astronomy taught that they did. "Officious": dutiful.
6. The sacred influence of the stars was thought to generate and foster life within the earth.
7. Conflict.
8. Poison.
9. I.e., man.
1. I.e., the created cosmos.

To me shall be the glory sole among                                135
The infernal Powers, in one day to have marred
What he, Almighty styled, six nights and days
Continued making, and who knows how long
Before had been contriving? though perhaps
Not longer than since I in one night freed             140
From servitude inglorious well-nigh half
Th' angelic name, and thinner left the throng
Of his adorers. He, to be avenged,
And to repair his numbers thus impaired,
Whether such virtue,[2] spent of old, now failed        145
More angels to create (if they at least
Are his created),[3] or to spite us more,
Determined to advance into our room
A creature formed of earth, and him endow,
Exalted from so base original,                          150
With heavenly spoils, our spoils. What he decreed
He effected; man he made, and for him built
Magnificent this World, and Earth his seat,
Him lord pronounced, and, O indignity!
Subjected to his service angel-wings                    155
And flaming ministers, to watch and tend
Their earthy charge. Of these the vigilance
I dread, and to elude, thus wrapt in mist
Of midnight vapor, glide obscure, and pry
In every bush and brake, where hap may find             160
The serpent sleeping, in whose mazy folds
To hide me, and the dark intent I bring.
O foul descent! that I, who erst contended
With Gods to sit the highest, am now constrained
Into a beast, and, mixed with bestial slime,            165
This essence to incarnate and imbrute,[4]
That to the height of deity aspired!
But what will not ambition and revenge
Descend to? Who aspires must down as low
As high he soared, obnoxious,[5] first or last,         170
To basest things. Revenge, at first though sweet,
Bitter ere long back on itself recoils.
Let it; I reck not, so it light well aimed,
Since higher I fall short, on him who next
Provokes my envy, this new favorite                     175
Of Heaven, this man of clay, son of despite,
Whom, us the more to spite,[6] his Maker raised
From dust: spite then with spite is best repaid."
    So saying, through each thicket, dank or dry,
Like a black mist low-creeping, he held on             180
His midnight search, where soonest he might find
The serpent. Him fast sleeping soon he found,

---

2. Strength, energy.
3. Satan never raises this question, whether angels are created or independent beings, without hesitating over it.
4. Satan's incarnation in a snake is a grotesque parody of the Son of God's incarnation in Christ.
5. Subject to.
6. Satan sees God in his own image, as a spiteful creature.

In labyrinth of many a round self-rolled,
His head the midst, well stored with subtle wiles:
Not yet in horrid shade or dismal den,                                    185
Nor nocent [7] yet, but on the grassy herb,
Fearless, unfeared, he slept. In at his mouth
The devil entered, and his brutal sense,
In heart or head, possessing soon inspired
With act intelligential; but his sleep                                    190
Disturbed not, waiting close[8] th' approach of morn.
   Now, whenas sacred light began to dawn
In Eden on the humid flowers, that breathed
Their morning incense, when all things that breathe
From th' Earth's great altar send up silent praise                        195
To the Creator, and his nostrils fill
With grateful smell, forth came the human pair,
And joined their vocal worship to the choir
Of creatures wanting voice; that done, partake
The season,[9] prime for sweetest scents and airs;                        200
Then cómmune how that day they best may ply
Their growing work; for much their work outgrew
The hands' dispatch of two gardening so wide:
And Eve first to her husband thus began:
   "Adam, well may we labor still [1] to dress                 205
This garden, still to tend plant, herb, and flower,
Our pleasant task enjoined; but, till more hands
Aid us, the work under our labor grows,
Luxurious by restraint: what we by day
Lop overgrown, or prune, or prop, or bind,                                210
One night or two with wanton growth derides,
Tending to wild. Thou, therefore, now advise,
Or hear what to my mind first thoughts present.
Let us divide our labors; thou where choice
Leads thee, or where most needs, whether to wind                          215
The woodbine round this arbor, or direct
The clasping ivy where to climb; while I
In yonder spring [2] of roses intermixed
With myrtle find what to redress till noon.
For, while so near each other thus all day                                220
Our task we choose, what wonder if so near
Looks intervene and smiles, or objects new
Casual discourse draw on, which intermits
Our day's work, brought to little, though begun
Early, and th' hour of supper comes unearned!"                            225
   To whom mild answer Adam thus returned:
"Sole Eve, associate sole, to me beyond
Compare above all living creatures dear!
Well hast thou motioned,[3] well thy thoughts employed
How we might best fulfil the work which here                              230
God hath assigned us, nor of me shalt pass

7. Harmful.
8. In secret.
9. I.e., go forth into the morning air.
"Prime": the best.

1. Continually.
2. Growth.
3. Suggested.

Unpraised; for nothing lovelier can be found
In woman than to study household good,
And good works in her husband to promote.[4]
Yet not so strictly hath our Lord imposed                    235
Labor as to debar us when we need
Refreshment, whether food or talk between,
Food of the mind, or this sweet intercourse
Of looks and smiles; for smiles from reason flow,
To brute denied, and are of love the food,                   240
Love, not the lowest end of human life.
For not to irksome toil, but to delight,
He made us, and delight to reason joined.
These paths and bowers doubt not but our joint hands
Will keep from wilderness with ease, as wide                 245
As we need walk, till younger hands ere long
Assist us. But, if much converse perhaps
Thee satiate, to short absence I could yield;
For solitude sometimes is best society,
And short retirement urges sweet return.                     250
But other doubt possesses me, lest harm
Befall thee, severed from me; for thou know'st
What hath been warned us, what malicious foe,
Envying our happiness, and of his own
Despairing, seeks to work us woe and shame                   255
By sly assault, and somewhere nigh at hand
Watches, no doubt, with greedy hope to find
His wish and best advantage, us asunder,[5]
Hopeless to circumvent us joined, where each
To other speedy aid might lend at need.                      260
Whether his first design be to withdraw
Our fealty from God, or to disturb
Conjugal love, than which perhaps no bliss
Enjoyed by us excites his envy more;
Or this, or worse,[6] leave not the faithful side            265
That gave thee being, still shades thee and protects.
The wife, where danger or dishonor lurks,
Safest and seemliest by her husband stays,
Who guards her, or with her the worst endures."
　　To whom the virgin [7] majesty of Eve,                   270
As one who loves, and some unkindness meets,
With sweet austere composure thus replied:
　　"Offspring of Heaven and Earth, and all Earth's lord!
That such an enemy we have, who seeks
Our ruin, both by thee informed I learn,                     275
And from the parting angel overheard,

---

4. Proverbs xxxi is devoted to the praise of a good wife, and Milton doubtless had it in mind here.
5. I.e., to find us apart, which will answer his wishes and serve his advantage.
6. I.e., whether this or something worse be his intent.
7. Unspotted

As in a shady nook I stood behind,
Just then returned at shut of evening flowers.
But that thou shouldst my firmness therefore doubt
To God or thee, because we have a foe                        280
May tempt it, I expected not to hear.
His violence thou fear'st not, being such
As we, not capable of death or pain,
Can either not receive, or can repel.
His fraud is, then, thy fear; which plain infers            285
Thy equal fear that my firm faith and love
Can by his fraud be shaken or seduced:
Thoughts, which how found they harbor in thy breast,
Adam, misthought of her to thee so dear?" [8]

    To whom, with healing words, Adam replied:            290
"Daughter of God and man, immortal Eve,
For such thou art, from sin and blame entire; [9]
Not diffident of thee do I dissuade
Thy absence from my sight, but to avoid
Th' attempt itself, intended by our foe.                    295
For he who tempts, though in vain, at least asperses [1]
The tempted with dishonor foul, supposed
Not incorruptible of faith, not proof
Against temptation. Thou thyself with scorn
And anger wouldst resent the offered wrong,                 300
Though ineffectual found; misdeem not, then,
If such affront I labor to avert
From thee alone, which on us both at once
The enemy, though bold, will hardly dare;
Or, daring, first on me th' assault shall light.            305
Nor thou his malice and false guile contemn—
Subtle he needs must be who could seduce
Angels—nor think superfluous others' aid.
I from the influence of thy looks receive
Access in every virtue; [2] in thy sight                    310
More wise, more watchful, stronger, if need were
Of outward strength; while shame, thou looking on,
Shame to be overcome or overreached, [3]
Would utmost vigor raise, and raised unite.
Why shouldst not thou like sense within thee feel           315
When I am present, and thy trial choose
With me, best witness of thy virtue tried?"
    So spake domestic Adam in his care
And matrimonial love; but Eve, who thought
Less [4] attributed to her faith sincere,                   320

---

8. I.e., these thoughts were misthought of (misapplied to) her to thee so dear (me).
9. "Entire" is from Latin *integer*, untouched. "Diffident": the usual English meaning is "shy," "timid"; Milton emphasizes the Latin roots, *dis* + *fides* =

mistrustful.
1. The word is from Latin *spargere*, to sprinkle, with overtones from English "aspersion," an ugly insinuation.
2. Extra strength.
3. Overpowered or outwitted.
4. Too little.

Thus her reply with accent sweet renewed:
"If this be our condition, thus to dwell
In narrow circuit straitened by a foe,
Subtle or violent, we not endued
Single with like defence wherever met,                                  325
How are we happy, still in fear of harm?
But harm precedes not sin: only our foe
Tempting affronts us with his foul esteem
Of our integrity: his foul esteem
Sticks no dishonor on our front,[5] but turns                          330
Foul on himself; then wherefore shunned or feared
By us, who rather double honor gain
From his surmise proved false, find peace within,
Favor from Heaven, our witness, from th' event?
And what is faith, love, virtue, unassayed                             335
Alone, without exterior help sustained?
Let us not then suspect our happy state
Left so imperfect by the Maker wise
As not secure to single or combined.
Frail is our happiness, if this be so;                                 340
And Eden were no Eden, thus exposed."
    To whom thus Adam fervently replied:
"O woman, best are all things as the will
Of God ordained them; his creating hand
Nothing imperfect or deficient left                                    345
Of all that he created, much less man,
Or aught that might his happy state secure,
Secure from outward force. Within himself
The danger lies, yet lies within his power;
Against his will he can receive no harm.                               350
But God left free the will; for what obeys
Reason is free; and reason he made right,
But bid her well beware, and still erect,[6]
Lest, by some fair appearing good surprised,
She dictate false, and misinform the will                              355
To do what God expressly hath forbid.
Not then mistrust, but tender love, enjoins
That I should mind [7] thee oft; and mind thou me.
Firm we subsist, yet possible to swerve,
Since reason not impossibly may meet                                   360
Some specious object by the foe suborned,
And fall into deception unaware,
Not keeping strictest watch, as she was warned.
Seek not temptation, then, which to avoid
Were better, and most likely if from me                                365

5. Forehead.                          7. Remind; in the next phrase, "mind"
6. Remain alert.                      means "obey."

Thou sever not: trial will come unsought.
Wouldst thou approve thy constancy, approve [8]
First thy obedience; th' other who can know,
Not seeing thee attempted, who attest?
But if thou think trial unsought may find                          370
Us both securer than thus warned thou seem'st,
Go; for thy stay, not free, absents thee more.
Go in thy native innocence; rely
On what thou hast of virtue; summon all;
For God towards thee hath done his part: do thine.'              375
   So spake the patriarch of mankind; but Eve
Persisted; yet submiss, though last, replied:
   "With thy permission,[9] then, and thus forewarned,
Chiefly by what thy own last reasoning words
Touched only, that our trial, when least sought,                 380
May find us both perhaps far less prepared,
The willinger I go, nor much expect
A foe so proud will first the weaker seek;
So bent, the more shall shame him his repulse."
Thus saying, from her husband's hand her hand                    385
Soft she withdrew, and like a wood nymph light,
Oread or dryad, or of Delia's train,[1]
Betook her to the groves, but Delia's self
In gait surpassed and goddesslike deport,
Though not as she with bow and quiver armed,                     390
But with such gardening tools as art yet rude,
Guiltless of fire[2] had formed, or angels brought.
To Pales, or Pomona, thus adorned,
Likest she seemed, Pomona when she fled
Vertumnus, or to Ceres in her prime,                             395
Yet virgin of Proserpina from Jove.[3]
Her long with ardent look his eye pursued
Delighted, but desiring more her stay.
Oft he to her his charge of quick return
Repeated; she to him as oft engaged                              400
To be returned by noon amid the bower,
And all things in best order to invite
Noontide repast, or afternoon's repose.
O much deceived, much failing, hapless Eve,

8. Prove, give evidence of.
9. Eve takes a reluctant and extorted permission as free leave to do what she wants. Though apparently submissive, she gets the last word.
1. An "oread" is a nymph of the mountain, a "dryad" one of the wood. "Delia" is Diana or Artemis, goddess of the chase, who when she hunted was accompanied by a train of nymphs.
2. There was no need of fire in Paradise; but that fire is a possession which renders one guilty suggests an overtone of the Prometheus myth.
3. Pales is a Roman goddess of flocks, Pomona a Roman divinity of fruits and orchards. Pomona was wooed by Vertumnus, god of spring, who assumed all sorts of shapes to win her. Ceres, the Mother Nature of the ancients (hence, the word "cereal"), bore Proserpina to Jupiter. All three goddesses are patrons of agriculture, like Eve.

Of thy presumed return!⁴ Event perverse!                    405
Thou never from that hour in Paradise
Found'st either sweet repast, or sound repose;
Such ambush hid among sweet flowers and shades
Waited with hellish rancor imminent⁵
To intercept thy way, or send thee back                     410
Despoiled of innocence, of faith, of bliss.
For now, and since first break of dawn, the fiend,
Mere serpent in appearance, forth was come,
And on his quest, where likeliest he might find
The only two of mankind, but in them                        415
The whole included race, his purposed prey.
In bower and field he sought, where any tuft
Of grove or garden-plot more pleasant lay,
Their tendance⁶ or plantation for delight;
By fountain or by shady rivulet                             420
He sought them both, but wished his hap might find
Eve separate; he wished, but not with hope
Of what so seldom chanced; when to his wish,
Beyond his hope, Eve separate he spies,
Veiled in a cloud of fragrance, where she stood,           425
Half spied, so thick the roses bushing round
About her glowed, oft stooping to support
Each flower of slender stalk, whose head though gay
Carnation, purple, azure, or specked with gold,
Hung drooping unsustained, them she upstays                430
Gently with myrtle band, mindless the while
Herself, though fairest unsupported flower,
From her best prop so far, and storm so nigh.⁷
Nearer he drew, and many a walk traversed
Of stateliest covert, cedar, pine, or palm;                435
Then voluble⁸ and bold, now hid, now seen
Among thick-woven arborets⁹ and flowers
Embordered on each bank, the hand of Eve:
Spot more delicious than those gardens feigned
Or of revived Adonis,¹ or renowned                         440
Alcinous, host of old Laertes' son,
Or that, not mystic, where the sapient king²
Held dalliance with his fair Egyptian spouse.
Much he the place admired, the person more.
As one who long in populous city pent,                     445

4. "Much deceived" carries over; Eve was "much deceived of" (about) her "presumed return."
5. Threatening.
6. Object of their tending.
7. The conceit of the flower-gatherer who is herself gathered is repeated here from IV.270, where it was applied to Proserpina.
8. Rolling (a Latinism).
9. Bushes. "Hand": handiwork.
1. The garden of Adonis was a heavenly bower where Venus' lover was supposed

still to lie in secret, recovering from his wound received on earth (Venus would not allow him to die). Alcinous was king of the Phaeacians. His garden, visited by Odysseus ("old Laertes' son"), is described in the *Odyssey*.
2. Solomon; his "fair Egyptian spouse" is Pharaoh's daughter: Milton is referring to the Song of Solomon vi.2. The fact that it is "not mystic" (i.e., not mythical) distinguishes the Scriptural garden from the "feigned" (line 439) ones of classical legend.

Where houses thick and sewers annoy[3] the air,
Forth issuing on a summer's morn to breathe
Among the pleasant villages and farms
Adjoined, from each thing met conceives delight,
The smell of grain, or tedded[4] grass, or kine,                    450
Or dairy, each rural sight, each rural sound:
If chance with nymphlike step fair virgin pass,[5]
What pleasing seemed, for her now pleases more,
She most, and in her look sums all delight.[6]
Such pleasure took the serpent to behold                            455
This flowery plat,[7] the sweet recess of Eve
Thus early, thus alone; her heavenly form
Angelic, but more soft, and feminine,
Her graceful innocence, her every air
Of gesture or least action overawed                                460
His malice, and with rapine[8] sweet bereaved
His fierceness of the fierce intent it brought:
That space the evil one abstracted stood
From his own evil, and for the time remained
Stupidly good,[9] of enmity disarmed,                              465
Of guile, of hate, of envy, of revenge.
But the hot Hell that always in him burns,
Though in mid Heaven, soon ended his delight,
And tortures him now more, the more he sees
Of pleasure not for him ordained: then soon                        470
Fierce hate he recollects, and all his thoughts
Of mischief, gratulating,[1] thus excites:
    "Thoughts, whither have ye led me? with what sweet
Compulsion thus transported to forget
What hither brought us? hate, not love, nor hope                   475
Of Paradise for Hell, hope here to taste
Of pleasure, but all pleasure to destroy,
Save what is in destroying:[2] other joy
To me is lost. Then let me not let pass
Occasion which now smiles; behold alone                            480
The woman, opportune to all attempts,
Her husband, for I view far round, not nigh,
Whose higher intellectual more I shun,
And strength, of courage haughty, and of limb
Heroic built, though of terrestrial mold:[3]                       485
Foe not informidable, exempt from wound,[4]
I not; so much hath Hell debased, and pain

---

3. Make noisome, befoul.
4. Tossed and drying in the sun.
5. I.e., if it chance that with nymph-like step a fair virgin should pass.
6. I.e., in her look sums up, or epitomizes, all delight.
7. Plot.
8. It is a deliberate paradox that her sweetness can ravish his malice; the word is deliberately overviolent.
9. Without his evil, Satan (like many wicked people) is quite dull and ordinary. But at the moment he is stunned.
1. Exulting.
2. What brought Satan to Paradise was not hope of pleasure, but the wish to destroy all pleasure except the pleasure of destruction itself.
3. Made of earth.
4. Adam in the state of innocence is invulnerable.

Enfeebled me, to what I was in Heaven.
She fair, divinely fair, fit love for gods,
Not terrible, though terror be in love                                    490
And beauty, not approached by stronger hate,
Hate stronger, under show of love well feigned,
The way which to her ruin now I tend."[5]
       So spake the enemy of mankind, enclosed
In serpent, inmate bad, and toward Eve                                    495
Addressed his way, not with indented wave,
Prone on the ground, as since, but on his rear,
Circular base of rising folds, that towered
Fold above fold a surging maze; his head
Crested aloft, and carbuncle[6] his eyes;                                 500
With burnished neck of verdant gold, erect
Amidst his circling spires,[7] that on the grass
Floated redundant. Pleasing was his shape,
And lovely; never since of serpent kind
Lovelier, not those that in Illyria changed                              505
Hermione and Cadmus,[8] or the god
In Epidaurus;[9] nor to which transformed
Ammonian Jove, or Capitoline was seen,
He with Olympias, this with her who bore
Scipio, the height of Rome.[1] With tract oblique                        510
At first, as one who sought access, but feared
To interrupt, sidelong he works his way.
As when a ship by skillful steersman wrought
Nigh river's mouth or foreland, where the wind
Veers oft, as oft so steers, and shifts her sail:                        515
So varied he, and of his tortuous train
Curled many a wanton wreath in sight of Eve,
To lure her eye: she busied heard the sound
Of rustling leaves, but minded not, as used
To such disport before her through the field,                            520
From every beast, more duteous at her call,
Than at Circean call the herd disguised.[2]
He bolder now, uncalled before her stood:
But as in gaze admiring; oft he bowed
His turret crest, and sleek enameled neck,                               525
Fawning, and licked the ground whereon she trod.
His gentle dumb expression turned at length

5. I.e., love and beauty are terrible unless counteracted by hate—as they are
being counteracted in Satan, to the
ruin of Eve.
6. Deep red, inflamed.
7. Coils. "Redundant": abundantly, to
excess.
8. Ovid tells how Cadmus and Har-
monia (Milton's "Hermione") were
changed to serpents after they retired
(in despair at the misfortunes of their
children) to Illyria.
9. Aesculapius, god of medicine, had a
temple at Epidaurus, from which he
sometimes emerged in the form of a
serpent.
1. Jupiter Ammon ("Ammonian Jove"),
in the form of a snake, was said to have
consorted with Olympias to beget Alexander the Great; and in the same
way, the Jupiter of the Roman capitol
(Jove "Capitoline") was thought to
have begotten Scipio Africanus, the savior and leader ("height") of Rome.
2. Circe, who enchanted men into the
shape of swine, was attended by an
obedient herd in the *Odyssey.*

The eye of Eve to mark his play: he, glad
Of her attention gained, with serpent tongue
Organic, or impulse of vocal air,[3]                                    530
His fraudulent temptation thus began.
    "Wonder not, sovereign mistress, if perhaps
Thou canst, who art sole wonder; much less arm
Thy looks, the heaven of mildness, with disdain,
Displeased that I approach thee thus, and gaze                          535
Insatiate, I thus single, nor have feared
Thy awful brow, more awful thus retired.
Fairest resemblance of thy Maker fair,
Thee all things living gaze on, all things thine
By gift, and thy celestial beauty adore                                 540
With ravishment beheld, there best beheld
Where universally admired: but here
In this enclosure wild, these beasts among,
Beholders rude, and shallow to discern
Half what in thee is fair, one man except,                             545
Who sees thee?[4] (and what is one?) who shouldst be seen
A goddess among gods, adored and served
By angels numberless, thy daily train."
    So glozed[5] the tempter, and his proem tuned;
Into the heart of Eve his words made way,                              550
Though at the voice much marveling: at length,
Not unamazed, she thus in answer spake.
"What may this mean? Language of man pronounced
By tongue of brute, and human sense expressed?
The first at least of these I thought denied                           555
To beasts, whom God on their creation-day
Created mute to all articulate sound;
The latter I demur,[6] for in their looks
Much reason, and in their actions oft appears.
Thee, serpent, subtlest beast of all the field                         560
I knew, but not with human voice endued:[7]
Redouble then this miracle, and say,
How cam'st thou speakable of mute,[8] and how
To me so friendly grown above the rest
Of brutal kind, that daily are in sight?                               565
Say, for such wonder claims attention due."
    To whom the guileful tempter thus replied:
"Empress of this fair world, resplendent Eve!
Easy to me it is to tell thee all
What thou command'st and right thou shouldst be obeyed:                570
I was at first as other beasts that graze
The trodden herb, of abject thoughts and low,

---

3. I.e., Satan either used the actual tongue of the serpent or himself impressed the air with speech.
4. The beasts cannot see the beauty of Eve's soul, only Adam can. Satan's entire speech is couched in the extravagant phrases of the Petrarchan love conven-

tion.
5. Flattered. "Proem": introduction.
6. I.e., as to whether rational sense was denied to brutes, I am doubtful.
7. Endowed.
8. To have speech after being dumb.

As was my food, nor aught but food discerned
Or sex, and apprehended nothing high:
Till on a day, roving the field, I chanced                          575
A goodly tree far distant to behold
Loaden with fruit of fairest colors mixed,
Ruddy and gold; I nearer drew to gaze;
When from the boughs a savory odor blown,
Grateful to appetite, more pleased my sense                        580
Than smell of sweetest fennel,[9] or the teats
Of ewe or goat dropping with milk at even,
Unsucked of lamb or kid, that tend their play.
To satisfy the sharp desire I had
Of tasting those fair apples, I resolved                            585
Not to defer: hunger and thirst at once,
Powerful persuaders, quickened at the scent
Of that alluring fruit, urged me so keen.
About the mossy trunk I wound me soon,
For, high from ground, the branches would require                  590
Thy utmost reach, or Adam's: round the tree
All other beasts that saw, with like desire
Longing and envying stood, but could not reach.
Amid the tree now got, where plenty hung
Tempting so nigh, to pluck and eat my fill                          595
I spared not;[1] for such pleasure till that hour
At feed or fountain never had I found.
Sated at length, ere long I might perceive
Strange alteration in me, to degree
Of reason in my inward powers, and speech                          600
Wanted not long, though to this shape retained.[2]
Thenceforth to speculations high or deep
I turned my thoughts, and with capacious mind
Considered all things visible in Heaven,
Or Earth, or middle, all things fair and good:                     605
But all that fair and good in thy divine
Semblance, and in thy beauty's heavenly ray
United I beheld: no fair[3] to thine
Equivalent or second, which compelled
Me thus, though importune perhaps, to come                          610
And gaze, and worship thee of right declared
Sovereign of creatures, universal dame."
  So talked the spirited[4] sly snake: and Eve
Yet more amazed, unwary thus replied:
  "Serpent, thy overpraising leaves in doubt                        615
The virtue of that fruit, in thee first proved.
But say, where grows the tree, from hence how far?

---

9. Milton learned probably from Pliny,
the natural historian, that serpents were
fond of fennel; popular superstition had
it that they drank the milk of sheep and
goats.
1. Refrained not.

2. His inward powers, his mental constitution and gift of speech, were
changed; but he retained his exterior
shape as before.
3. Beauty.
4. Possessed by a spirit, inspired.

For many are the trees of God that grow
In Paradise, and various, yet unknown
To us; in such abundance lies our choice,                    620
As leaves a greater store of fruit untouched,
Still hanging incorruptible, till men
Grow up to their provision, and more hands
Help to disburden Nature of her bearth."[5]
    To whom the wily adder, blithe and glad:          625
"Empress, the way is ready, and not long,
Beyond a row of myrtles, on a flat,
Fast by a fountain, one small thicket past
Of blowing[6] myrrh and balm: if thou accept
My conduct, I can bring thee thither soon."                  630
    "Lead then," said Eve. He leading swiftly rolled
In tangles, and made intricate seem straight,
To mischief swift.[7] Hope elevates, and joy
Brightens his crest; as when a wandering fire
Compact of unctuous vapor,[8] which the night               635
Condenses, and the cold environs round,
Kindled through agitation to a flame
(Which oft, they say, some evil spirit attends),
Hovering and blazing with delusive light,
Misleads th' amazed night-wanderer from his way             640
To bogs and mires, and oft through pond or pool,
There swallowed up and lost, from succor far:
So glistered the dire snake, and into fraud
Led Eve our credulous mother, to the tree
Of prohibition,[9] root of all our woe:                     645
Which when she saw, thus to her guide she spake:
    "Serpent, we might have spared our coming hither,
Fruitless to me, though fruit be here to excess,
The credit of whose virtue rest with thee;[1]
Wondrous indeed, if cause of such effects!                  650
But of this tree we may not taste nor touch:
God so commanded, and left that command
Sole daughter of his voice;[2] the rest, we live
Law to ourselves; our reason is our law."
    To whom the Tempter guilefully replied:          655
"Indeed? Hath God then said that of the fruit
Of all these garden trees ye shall not eat,
Yet lords declared of all in Earth or air?"
    To whom thus Eve, yet sinless: "Of the fruit
Of each tree in the garden we may eat,                      660
But of the fruit of this fair tree amidst

---

5. So spelled to pun on the idea of trees bearing fruit and thus in a way giving birth to young.
6. Blooming.
7. Milton's physical descriptions of the serpent often have distinct moral overtones, as here.
8. Composed of oily vapor; Milton's

theory of the *ignis fatuus*, or will-o'-the-wisp, is strikingly material and "scientific."
9. Prohibited tree (a Hebraism).
1. I.e., you must remain the only evidence of the fruit's power.
2. His one injunction (a literal Hebraism). "The rest": in everything else.

The garden, God hath said, 'Ye shall not eat
Thereof, nor shall ye touch it, lest ye die.' "
    She scarce had said, though brief, when now more bold,
The tempter, but with show of zeal and love     665
To man, and indignation at his wrong,
New part puts on, and as to passion moved,
Fluctuates disturbed, yet comely, and in act
Raised,[3] as of some great matter to begin.
As when of old some orator renowned     670
In Athens or free Rome, where eloquence
Flourished, since mute, to some great cause addressed,
Stood in himself collected, while each part,
Motion, each act, won audience ere the tongue,
Sometimes in height began, as no delay     675
Of preface brooking,[4] through his zeal of right.
So standing, moving, or to height upgrown
The tempter all impassioned thus began:
    "O sacred, wise, and wisdom-giving plant,
Mother of science![5] now I feel thy power     680
Within me clear, not only to discern
Things in their causes, but to trace the ways
Of highest agents, deemed however wise.
Queen of this universe! do not believe
Those rigid threats of death. Ye shall not die;     685
How should ye? By the fruit? it gives you life
To knowledge;[6] by the Threatener? look on me,
Me who have touched and tasted, yet both live,
And life more perfect have attained than Fate
Meant me, by venturing higher than my lot.     690
Shall that be shut to man, which to the beast
Is open? Or will God incense his ire
For such a petty trespass, and not praise
Rather your dauntless virtue, whom the pain
Of death denounced, whatever thing death be,     695
Deterred not from achieving what might lead
To happier life, knowledge of good and evil?
Of good, how just![7] Of evil, if what is evil
Be real, why not known, since easier shunned?
God therefore cannot hurt ye, and be just;     700
Not just, not God; not feared then, nor obeyed:
Your fear itself of death removes the fear.[8]
Why then was this forbid? Why but to awe,
Why but to keep ye low and ignorant,
His worshipers? He knows that in the day     705
Ye eat thereof, your eyes that seem so clear,

3. Poised in posture.
4. The orator, as if too much moved to be bothered with a preface, bursts into the middle of his speech.
5. Knowledge.
6. Life in addition to knowledge; or, life with which to enlarge your knowl-edge.
7. I.e., how just to have knowledge of good!
8. I.e., your fear of death removes your fear of God; since if God inflicts death, he will not be just and hence not God. The serpent's sophism is visible.

Yet are but dim, shall perfectly be then
Opened and cleared, and ye shall be as gods,
Knowing both good and evil, as they know.
That ye should be as gods, since I as man,                                  710
Internal man,[9] is but proportion meet,
I, of brute, human; ye, of human, gods.
So ye shall die perhaps, by putting off
Human, to put on gods: death to be wished,
Though threatened, which no worse than this can bring.      715
And what are gods that man may not become
As they, participating[1] godlike food?
The gods are first, and that advantage use
On our belief, that all from them proceeds.
I question it; for this fair Earth I see,                                        720
Warmed by the sun, producing every kind,
Them nothing: If they all things,[2] who enclosed
Knowledge of good and evil in this tree,
That whoso eats thereof forthwith attains
Wisdom without their leave? And wherein lies                      725
Th' offense, that man should thus attain to know?
What can your knowledge hurt him, or this tree
Impart against his will if all be his?
Or is it envy, and can envy dwell
In heavenly breasts?[3] These, these, and many more          730
Causes import your need of this fair fruit.
Goddess humane,[4] reach then, and freely taste!"
   He ended, and his words, replete with guile,
Into her heart too easy entrance won:
Fixed on the fruit she gazed, which to behold                         735
Might tempt alone, and in her ears the sound
Yet rung of his persuasive words, impregned[5]
With reason, to her seeming, and with truth;
Meanwhile the hour of noon drew on, and waked
An eager appetite, raised by the smell                                      740
So savory of that fruit, which with desire,
Inclinable now grown to touch or taste,
Solicited her longing eye;[6] yet first
Pausing a while, thus to herself she mused:
   "Great are thy virtues, doubtless, best of fruits,                 745
Though kept from man, and worthy to be admired,
Whose taste, too long forborn, at first essay
Gave elocution to the mute, and taught
The tongue not made for speech to speak thy praise:
Thy praise he also who forbids thy use,                                    750

---

9. Man in intellectual powers.
1. Sharing.
2. The verb "produced" is understood. Satan is telling now, not about "God," but "the gods."
3. Adapted from Virgil, *Aeneid* I.15. "Import": imply, suggest.

4. Not so much "human goddess" (a Satanic paradox) as "kindly," "gracious" goddess.
5. Impregnated.
6. The five senses of Eve—sight, hearing, smell, taste, and touch—are all solicited by the fruit.

Conceals not from us,[7] naming thee the Tree
Of Knowledge, knowledge both of good and evil;
Forbids us then to taste; but his forbidding
Commends thee more, while it infers the good
By thee communicated, and our want:                                    755
For good unknown, sure is not had, or had
And yet unknown, is as not had at all.[8]
In plain then, what forbids he but to know?
Forbids us good, forbids us to be wise!
Such prohibitions bind not. But if Death                               760
Bind us with after-bands, what profits then
Our inward freedom? In the day we eat
Of this fair fruit, our doom is, we shall die.
How dies the serpent? He hath eaten and lives,
And knows, and speaks, and reasons, and discerns,                      765
Irrational till then. For us alone
Was death invented? Or to us denied
This intellectual food, for beasts reserved?
For beasts it seems: yet that one beast which first
Hath tasted, envies not, but brings with joy                           770
The good befallen him, author unsuspect,[9]
Friendly to man, far from deceit or guile.
What fear I then, rather what know to fear[1]
Under this ignorance of good and evil,
Of God or death, of law or penalty?                                    775
Here grows the cure of all, this fruit divine,
Fair to the eye, inviting to the taste,
Of virtue[2] to make wise: what hinders then
To reach, and feed at once both body and mind?"
    So saying, her rash hand in evil hour,                             780
Forth reaching to the fruit, she plucked, she eat.[3]
Earth felt the wound, and Nature from her seat[4]
Sighing through all her works gave signs of woe,
That all was lost. Back to the thicket slunk
The guilty serpent, and well might, for Eve                            785
Intent now wholly on her taste, naught else
Regarded; such delight till then, as seemed,
In fruit she never tasted, whether true
Or fancied so, through expectation high
Of knowledge; nor was godhead from her thought.[5]                     790
Greedily she engorged without restraint,
And knew not eating death:[6] satiate at length,
And heightened as with wine, jocund and boon,[7]

7. God himself, by naming it, has called
attention to the tree's magic powers.
8. An unknown good is like no good at
all. "In plain": i.e., in plain language.
9. A witness beyond suspicion.
1. In her ignorance, Eve does not really
know what to fear and what not to
fear.
2. Power.
3. In the 17th century, an accepted

past tense of "eat."
4. Wherever Nature is hidden, in the
heart of things, she sighs.
5. She expected to achieve godhead immediately.
6. A grim pun. She is eating death and
does not know it; but death is eating
her too. Compare "eating cares" (*L'Al-
legro*, line 135).
7. Joyous and liberal.

Thus to herself she pleasingly began:
 "O sovereign, virtuous, precious of all trees   795
In Paradise! of operation blest
To sapience,[8] hitherto obscured, infamed,
And thy fair fruit let hang, as to no end
Created; but henceforth my early care,
Not without song each morning, and due praise   800
Shall tend thee, and the fertile burden ease
Of thy full branches offered free to all;
Till dieted by thee I grow mature
In knowledge, as the gods who all things know;
Though others[9] envy what they cannot give:   805
For had the gift been theirs, it had not here
Thus grown. Experience, next to thee I owe,
Best guide; not following thee I had remained
In ignorance; thou open'st Wisdom's way,
And giv'st access, though secret she retire.   810
And I perhaps am secret; Heaven is high,
High and remote to see from thence distinct
Each thing on Earth; and other care perhaps
May have diverted from continual watch
Our great Forbidder,[1] safe with all his spies   815
About him. But to Adam in what sort[2]
Shall I appear? Shall I to him make known
As yet my change, and give him to partake
Full happiness with me, or rather not,
But keep the odds[3] of knowledge in my power   820
Without copartner? so to add what wants
In female sex, the more to draw his love,
And render me more equal, and perhaps,
A thing not undesirable, sometime
Superior: for, inferior, who is free?[4]   825
This may be well: but what if God have seen
And death ensue? Then I shall be no more,
And Adam, wedded to another Eve,
Shall live with her enjoying, I extinct;
A death to think. Confirmed then I resolve,   830
Adam shall share with me in bliss or woe:
So dear I love him, that with him all deaths
I could endure, without him live no life."[5]
 So saying, from the tree her step she turned,
But first low reverence done,[6] as to the power   835
That dwelt within, whose presence had infused

8. To the point of wisdom, but also for wise people. "Infamed": without fame, but also, defamed.
9. The gods, i.e., other gods. In saying that God did not give the tree, Eve is merely echoing a lesson learned from the serpent.
1. Now that Eve has fallen, God is a "great Forbidder," and all his gifts in Paradise are forgotten.

2. Guise.
3. Balance.
4. Eve's fatal foolishness implies that the only person in the world who can ever be free is an absolute tyrant.
5. Her affection is not unlike Satan's (IV.374–385) in its destructiveness.
6. Eve's first physical act after falling is idolatry.

Into the plant sciental[7] sap, derived
From nectar, drink of gods. Adam the while
Waiting desirous her return, had wove
Of choicest flowers a garland to adorn                        840
Her tresses, and her rural labors crown,
As reapers oft are wont their harvest queen.
Great joy he promised to his thoughts, and new
Solace in her return, so long delayed:
Yet oft his heart, divine[8] of something ill,                845
Misgave him; he the faltering measure[9] felt;
And forth to meet her went, the way she took
That morn when first they parted. By the Tree
Of Knowledge he must pass; there he her met,
Scarce from the tree returning; in her hand                   850
A bough of fairest fruit that downy smiled,
New gathered, and ambrosial smell diffused.
To him she hastened, in her face excuse
Came prologue, and apology to prompt,[1]
Which with bland words at will she thus addressed:            855
    "Hast thou not wondered, Adam, at my stay?
Thee I have missed, and thought it long, deprived
Thy presence, agony of love till now
Not felt, nor shall be twice; for never more
Mean I to try, what rash untried I sought,                    860
The pain of absence from thy sight. But strange
Hath been the cause, and wonderful to hear:
This tree is not as we are told, a tree
Of danger tasted,[2] nor to evil unknown
Opening the way, but of divine effect                         865
To open eyes, and make them gods who taste;
And hath been tasted such. The serpent wise,
Or not restrained as we, or not obeying,
Hath eaten of the fruit, and is become,
Not dead, as we are threatened, but thenceforth               870
Endued with human voice and human sense,
Reasoning to admiration,[3] and with me
Persuasively hath so prevailed, that I
Have also tasted, and have also found
Th' effects to correspond, opener mine eyes                   875
Dim erst, dilated spirits, ampler heart,
And growing up to godhead;[4] which for thee
Chiefly I sought, without thee can despise.
For bliss, as thou hast part, to me is bliss,
Tedious, unshared with thee, and odious soon.                 880
Thou therefore also taste, that equal lot

7. Knowledge-giving.
8. Foreboding, suspicious.
9. I.e., of his pulse.
1. Her face had an excuse in it, as prologue to an apology which followed after.

2. If tasted.
3. Admirably. "Persuasively": by persuasion.
4. Everything that Eve says she feels is what Satan has told her she will feel.

May join us, equal joy, as equal love;
Lest, thou not tasting, different degree[5]
Disjoin us, and I then too late renounce
Deity for thee, when Fate will not permit."[6]                    885
    Thus Eve with countenance blithe her story told;
But in her cheek distemper[7] flushing glowed.
On th' other side, Adam, soon as he heard
The fatal trespass done by Eve, amazed,
Astonied[8] stood and blank, while horror chill               890
Ran through his veins, and all his joints relaxed;
From his slack hand the garland wreathed for Eve
Down dropped, and all the faded roses shed.
Speechless he stood and pale, till thus at length
First to himself he inward silence broke:                        895
    "O fairest of creation, last and best
Of all God's works, creature in whom excelled
Whatever can to sight or thought be formed,
Holy, divine, good, amiable, or sweet!
How art thou lost, how on a sudden lost,                         900
Defaced, deflowered, and now to death devote?[9]
Rather how hast thou yielded to transgress
The strict forbiddance, how to violate
The sacred fruit forbidden! Some curséd fraud
Of enemy hath beguiled thee, yet unknown,[1]                    905
And me with thee hath ruined, for with thee
Certain my resolution is to die.
How can I live without thee, how forgo
Thy sweet converse and love so dearly joined,
To live again in these wild woods forlorn?[2]                    910
Should God create another Eve, and I
Another rib afford, yet loss of thee
Would never from my heart; no, no! I feel
The link of nature draw me: flesh of flesh,
Bone of my bone thou art, and from thy state                     915
Mine never shall be parted, bliss or woe."
    So having said, as one from sad dismay
Recomforted, and after thoughts disturbed
Submitting to what seemed remediless,
Thus in calm mood his words to Eve he turned:                    920
    "Bold deed thou hast presumed, adventurous Eve
And peril great provoked, who thus hath dared
Had it been only coveting to eye
That sacred fruit, sacred[3] to abstinence,
Much more to taste it, under ban to touch.                       925

---

5. Differing rank in the hierarchy of creatures.
6. Contrast Eve's logic when she is alone (lines 817–825).
7. The proportion of Eve's humors— which, in the state of innocence, gave her perfect health—has been disturbed, and she is running a fever.
8. Astonished, perhaps even "petrified." "Blank": empty of mind.
9. Doomed.
1. "Yet unknown" modifies "enemy."
2. Without Eve, Paradise itself is wild and forlorn.
3. Devoted.

But past who can recall, or done undo?
Not God omnipotent, nor Fate! Yet so
Perhaps thou shalt not die, perhaps the fact[4]
Is not so heinous now, foretasted fruit,
Profaned first by the serpent, by him first                    930
Made common and unhallowed ere our taste,
Nor yet on him found deadly; he yet lives,
Lives, as thou saidst, and gains to live as man
Higher degree of life: inducement strong
To us, as likely, tasting, to attain                           935
Proportional ascent, which cannot be
But to be gods, or angels, demigods.[5]
Nor can I think that God, Creator wise,
Though threatening, will in earnest so destroy
Us his prime creatures, dignified so high,                     940
Set over all his works, which in our fall,
For us created, needs with us must fail,
Dependent made; so God shall uncreate,
Be frustrate, do, undo, and labor lose;
Not well conceived of God,[6] who, though his power            945
Creation could repeat, yet would be loath
Us to abolish, lest the adversary
Triúmph and say: 'Fickle their state whom God
Most favors; who can please him long? Me first
He ruined, now mankind; whom will he next?'                    950
Matter of scorn, not to be given the foe.
However, I with thee have fixed my lot,
Certain to undergo like doom: if death
Consort with thee, death is to me as life;
So forcible within my heart I feel                             955
The bond of nature draw me to my own,
My own in thee, for what thou art is mine;
Our state cannot be severed; we are one,
One flesh; to lose thee were to lose myself."
    So Adam, and thus Eve to him replied:                      960
"O glorious trial of exceeding love,
Illustrious evidence, example high!
Engaging me to emulate; but short
Of thy perfection, how shall I attain,
Adam? from whose dear side I boast me sprung,                  965
And gladly of our union hear thee speak,
One heart, one soul in both; whereof good proof
This day affords, declaring thee resolved,
Rather than death or aught than death more dread
Shall separate us, linked in love so dear,                     970
To undergo with me one guilt, one crime,
If any be, of tasting this fair fruit;

---

4. Act.
5. Note how Adam agrees first in Eve's harmless errors about the serpent, then in her sinful ambition to achieve a higher form of life.
6. I.e., not a proper conception of God (as making his actions dependent on those of an inferior).

Whose virtue (for of good still good proceeds,
Direct, or by occasion[7]) hath presented
This happy trial of thy love, which else                     975
So eminently never had been known.
Were it I thought death menaced would ensue[8]
This my attempt, I would sustain alone
The worst, and not persuade thee, rather die
Deserted, than oblige[9] thee with a fact               980
Pernicious to thy peace, chiefly assured
Remarkably so late of thy so true,
So faithful love unequaled;[1] but I feel
Far otherwise th' event; [2] not death, but life
Augmented, opened eyes, new hopes, new joys,         985
Taste so divine, that what of sweet before
Hath touched my sense, flat seems to this, and harsh.
On my experience, Adam, freely taste,
And fear of death deliver to the winds."
     So saying, she embraced him, and for joy         990
Tenderly wept, much won that he his love
Had so ennobled, as of choice to incur
Divine displeasure for her sake, or death.
In recompense (for such compliance bad
Such recompense best merits), from the bough          995
She gave him of that fair enticing fruit
With liberal hand; he scrupled not to eat,
Against his better knowledge, not deceived,
But fondly overcome with female charm.[3]
Earth trembled from her entrails, as again            1000
In pangs, and Nature gave a second groan,
Sky lowered, and muttering thunder, some sad drops
Wept at completing of the mortal sin
Original; while Adam took no thought,
Eating his fill, nor Eve to iterate                   1005
Her former trespass feared, the more to soothe
Him with her loved society; that now
As with new wine intoxicated both,
They swim in mirth, and fancy that they feel
Divinity within them breeding wings                   1010
Wherewith to scorn the Earth. But that false fruit
Far other operation first displayed,
Carnal desire inflaming; he on Eve
Began to cast lascivious eyes, she him
As wantonly repaid; in lust they burn,               1015
Till Adam thus 'gan Eve to dalliance move:
     "Eve, now I see thou art exact[4] of taste,

---

7. Indirectly.
8. Result from.
9. Render liable, involve.
1. Now that she knows Adam loves her, Eve has more misgivings than ever about involving him in her crime.

2. Result (of eating the apple).
3. See I Timothy ii.14: "And Adam was not deceived, but the woman being deceived was in the transgression."
4. Exacting, demanding.

And elegant, of sapience[5] no small part,
Since to each meaning savor we apply,
And palate call judicious. I the praise                          1020
Yield thee, so well this day thou hast purveyed.[6]
Much pleasure we have lost, while we abstained
From this delightful fruit, nor known till now
True relish, tasting; if such pleasure be
In things to us forbidden, it might be wished,                  1025
For this one tree had been forbidden ten.
But come; so well refreshed, now let us play,
As meet is, after such delicious fare;
For never did thy beauty, since the day
I saw thee first and wedded thee, adorned                       1030
With all perfections, so enflame my sense
With ardor to enjoy thee, fairer now
Than ever, bounty of this virtuous tree."
        So said he, and forbore not glance or toy[7]
Of amorous intent, well understood                              1035
Of[8] Eve, whose eye darted contagious fire.
Her hand he seized, and to a shady bank,
Thick overhead with verdant roof embowered
He led her, nothing loath; flowers were the couch,
Pansies, and violets, and asphodel,                             1040
And hyacinth, Earth's freshest, softest lap.
There they their fill of love and love's disport
Took largely, of their mutual guilt the seal,
The solace of their sin, till dewy sleep
Oppressed them, wearied with their amorous play.                1045
        Soon as the force of that fallacious fruit,
That with exhilarating vapor bland
About their spirits had played, and inmost powers
Made err, was now exhaled, and grosser sleep
Bred of unkindly fumes,[9] with conscious dreams                1050
Encumbered, now had left them, up they rose
As from unrest, and each the other viewing,
Soon found their eyes how opened, and their minds
How darkened. Innocence, that as a veil
Had shadowed them from knowing ill, was gone;                   1055
Just confidence, and native righteousness,
And honor from about them, naked left
To guilty Shame; he covered, but his robe
Uncovered more.[1] So rose the Danite strong,
Herculean Samson, from the harlot-lap                           1060
Of Philistean Dalilah, and waked
Shorn of his strength;[2] they destitute and bare

---

5. Wisdom, but the word comes from
Latin *sapere,* "to taste," which gives
rise, via another etymology, to the word
"savor." Adam's sentence plays rather
heavily on these two meanings of *sapere.*
6. Provided for us, provisioned us.
7. Caress.
8. By.

9. Unnatural vapors.
1. They were covered with shame,
which made them conscious of their
nakedness as they had never been before.
2. See the story of Samson and Delilah, Judges xvi.4–20.

Of all their virtue. Silent, and in face
Confounded, long they sat, as strucken mute;
Till Adam, though not less than Eve abashed,  1065
At length gave utterance to these words constrained:
 "O Eve, in evil hour[3] thou didst give ear
To that false worm,[4] of whomsoever taught
To counterfeit man's voice, true in our fall,
False in our promised rising; since our eyes  1070
Opened we find indeed, and find we know
Both good and evil, good lost, and evil got:
Bad fruit of knowledge, if this be to know,
Which leaves us naked thus, of honor void,
Of innocence, of faith, of purity,  1075
Our wonted ornaments now soiled and stained,
And in our faces evident the signs
Of foul concupiscence; whence evil store,[5]
Even shame, the last of evils; of the first
Be sure then.[6] How shall I behold the face  1080
Henceforth of God or angel, erst with joy
And rapture so oft beheld? Those heavenly shapes
Will dazzle now this earthly[7] with their blaze
Insufferably bright. O might I here
In solitude live savage, in some glade  1085
Obscured, where highest woods, impenetrable
To star or sunlight, spread their umbrage broad,
And brown[8] as evening! Cover me, ye pines,
Ye cedars, with innumerable boughs
Hide me, where I may never see them more![9]  1090
But let us now, as in bad plight, devise
What best may for the present serve to hide
The parts of each from other, that seem most
To shame obnoxious,[1] and unseemliest seen;
Some tree whose broad smooth leaves together sewed,  1095
And girded on our loins, may cover round
Those middle parts, that this newcomer, Shame,
There sit not, and reproach us as unclean."
 So counseled he, and both together went
Into the thickest wood; there soon they chose  1100
The figtree,[2] not that kind for fruit renowned,
But such as at this day, to Indians known,
In Malabar or Deccan[3] spreads her arms

---

3. Even in his misery, Adam cannot resist the word-play on Eve-evil.
4. Serpent, with a connotation of disgust. "Of": by.
5. A store of evil.
6. I.e., since we now feel shame, the last and worst of evils, we shall soon experience the first and lesser ones.
7. The noun "nature" or "vision" is understood.
8. Dark.
9. Cf. Revelation vi.16: "And said to the mountains and rocks, Fall on us, and hide us from the face of him that sitteth on the throne, and from the wrath of the Lamb."
1. Vulnerable, liable.
2. The banyan, or Indian fig. It has, in fact, small leaves, but Milton's knowledge of it came from Gerard's *Herball*, where all the details of lines 1104–10 may be found.
3. Sections of southern India.

Branching so broad and long, that in the ground
The bended twigs take root, and daughters grow        1105
About the mother tree, a pillared shade
High overarched, and echoing walks between;
There oft the Indian herdsman, shunning heat,
Shelters in cool, and tends his pasturing herds
At loopholes cut through thickest shade. Those leaves        1110
They gathered, broad as Amazonian targe,[4]
And with what skill they had, together sewed,
To gird their waist; vain covering, if to hide
Their guilt and dreaded shame! O how unlike
To that first naked glory! Such of late        1115
Columbus found th' American, so girt
With feathered cincture,[5] naked else and wild
Among the trees on isles and woody shores.
Thus fenced, and, as they thought, their shame in part
Covered, but not at rest or ease of mind,        1120
They sat them down to weep; nor only tears
Rained at their eyes, but high winds worse within
Began to rise, high passions, anger, hate,
Mistrust, suspicion, discord, and shook sore
Their inward state of mind, calm region once        1125
And full of peace, now tossed and turbulent:
For Understanding ruled not, and the Will
Heard not her lore, both in subjection now
To sensual Appetite, who, from beneath
Usurping over sovereign Reason, claimed        1130
Superior sway.[6] From thus distempered breast,
Adam, estranged in look and altered style,
Speech intermitted thus to Eve renewed:
        "Would thou hadst hearkened to my words, and stayed
With me, as I besought thee, when that strange        1135
Desire of wandering, this unhappy morn,
I know not whence possessed thee! we had then
Remained still happy, not as now, despoiled
Of all our good, shamed, naked, miserable.
Let none henceforth seek needless cause to approve[7]        1140
The faith they owe; when earnestly they seek
Such proof, conclude, they then begin to fail."
        To whom, soon moved with touch of blame, thus Eve:
"What words have passed thy lips, Adam severe?
Imput'st thou that to my default, or will        1145
Of wandering, as thou call'st it, which who knows
But might as ill have happened, thou being by,
Or to thyself perhaps? Hadst thou been there,
Or here th' attempt, thou couldst not have discerned

---

4. Shield. The Amazons, mythical female warriors, carried large crescent-shaped shields.
5. Belt.
6. The psychology of the Fall is made explicit here. The higher faculties of reason, represented by the brain, are in subjection to the lower faculties of appetite, represented by sensuality. Moreover, Adam has lost his superiority over Eve.
7. Test prove. "Owe": own.

Fraud in the serpent, speaking as he spake; 1150
No ground of enmity between us known,
Why he should mean me ill, or seek to harm?
Was I to have never parted from thy side?
As good have grown there still a lifeless rib.
Being as I am, why didst not thou, the head,[8] 1155
Command me absolutely not to go,
Going into such danger, as thou saidst?
Too facile[9] then, thou didst not much gainsay,
Nay, didst permit, approve, and fair dismiss.
Hadst thou been firm and fixed in thy dissent, 1160
Neither had I transgressed, nor thou with me."
    To whom, then first incensed, Adam replied:
"Is this the love, is this the recompense
Of mine to thee, ingrateful Eve, expressed
Immutable[1] when thou were lost, not I, 1165
Who might have lived and joyed immortal bliss,
Yet willingly chose rather death with thee?
And am I now upbraided as the cause
Of thy transgressing? not enough severe,
It seems, in thy restraint! What could I more? 1170
I warned thee, I admonished thee, foretold
The danger, and the lurking enemy
That lay in wait; beyond this had been force,
And force upon free will hath here no place.
But confidence then bore thee on, secure 1175
Either to meet no danger, or to find
Matter of glorious trial; and perhaps
I also erred in overmuch admiring
What seemed in thee so perfect, that I thought
No evil durst attempt thee! but I rue 1180
That error now, which is become my crime,
And thou th' accuser. Thus it shall befall
Him who, to worth in women overtrusting,
Lets her will rule; restraint she will not brook,[2]
And, left to herself, if evil thence ensue, 1185
She first his weak indulgence will accuse."
    Thus they in mutual accusation spent
The fruitless hours, but neither self-condemning;
And of their vain contést appeared no end.

---

8. Head of the family, but also the rational director, as the head is to the rest of the body. Cf. I Corinthians xi.3, "the head of the woman is the man."

9. Easy, permissive.
1. Shown to be unchangeable.
2. Accept.

## *From* Book X

*Summary*   When it is known in Heaven that man has fallen, God sends the Son to pass judgment on the sinners. He receives the confession of Adam and Eve and passes sentence on the sinners—cursing the serpent, condemning Eve to the pains of childbirth, and Adam to those of daily labor; but in mercy he clothes the human couple, both outwardly with the skins of animals and inwardly with his righteousness. Meanwhile Sin and Death, sitting by Hell-gate, feel new strength, and pass across Chaos, leaving a great bridge behind them. On their way, they meet their parent, Satan, returning in triumph. Satan reappears in Pandemonium, and describes to the assembly the success of his venture, but instead of the expected applause is received with a vast hiss—he and all the other devils have been transformed to snakes, in which shape they are tormented with humiliating delusions.

Sin and Death now invest the earth; but God prophesies their ultimate defeat. Now the earth and the elements are rearranged, to replace the previous temperate climate with extremes of heat and cold; and discord enters the animal kingdom too, where hitherto all the creatures have dwelt in peace.

### [*Consequences of the Fall*]

* * *   Thus began
Outrage from lifeless things; but Discord, first
Daughter of Sin, among th' irrational,
Death introduced through fierce antipathy:[1]
Beast now with beast 'gan war, and fowl with fowl,
And fish with fish: to graze the herb[2] all leaving,
Devoured each other; nor stood much in awe
Of man, but fled him, or with countenance grim
Glared on him passing. These were from without
The growing miseries, which Adam saw                          715
Already in part, though hid in gloomiest shade,
To sorrow abandoned, but worse felt within,
And in a troubled sea of passion tossed,
Thus to disburden sought with sad complaint:
    "O miserable of happy![3] Is this the end          720
Of this new glorious world, and me so late
The glory of that glory? who now, become
Accursed of blessed, hide me from the face
Of God, whom to behold was then my height
Of happiness! Yet well, if here would end              725
The misery; I deserved it, and would bear
My own deservings; but this will not serve.

1. "Discord" is the subject of the sentence, "Death" the object. "Th' irrational" are the beasts.
2. Grass.
3. I.e., change, to misery from happiness.

All that I eat or drink, or shall beget,
Is propagated curse.[4] O voice, once heard
Delightfully, 'Increase and multiply,'          730
Now death to hear! for what can I increase
Or multiply, but curses on my head?
Who, of all ages to succeed, but, feeling
The evil on him brought by me, will curse
My head: "Ill fare our ancestor impure!          735
For this we may thank Adam!' but his thanks
Shall be the execration;[5] so, besides
Mine own that bide upon me, all from me
Shall with a fierce reflux on me redound,
On me, as on their natural center, light          740
Heavy, though in their place.[6] O fleeting joys
Of Paradise, dear bought with lasting woes!
Did I request thee, Maker, from my clay
To mold me man? Did I solicit thee
From darkness to promote me, or here place          745
In this delicious garden? As my will
Concurred not to my being, it were but right
And equal[7] to reduce me to my dust,
Desirous to resign and render back
All I received, unable to perform          750
Thy terms too hard, by which I was to hold
The good I sought not. To the loss of that,
Sufficient penalty, why hast thou added
The sense of endless woes? Inexplicable
Thy justice seems; yet, to say truth, too late          755
I thus contest; then should have been refused
Those terms whatever, when they were proposed.
Thou[8] didst accept them; wilt thou enjoy the good,
Then cavil the conditions? And though God
Made thee without thy leave, what if thy son          760
Prove disobedient, and reproved, retort,
'Wherefore didst thou beget me? I sought it not.'
Wouldst thou admit for his contempt of thee
That proud excuse? Yet him not thy election,[9]
But natural necessity begot.          765
God made thee of choice his own, and of his own
To serve him; thy reward was of his grace;
Thy punishment then justly is at his will.
Be it so, for I submit; his doom is fair,
That dust I am and shall to dust return.          770
O welcome hour whenever! Why delays

4. Whatever prolongs life extends the curse.
5. The only thanks for Adam will be mankind's curses.
6. Adam plays with the notion that natural objects have weight only as long as they are above their "natural" positions; so all curses will flow naturally to him, but they will still be heavy when they have lighted.
7. Just.
8. "Thou," which referred to God in lines 753 and 755, here shifts as Adam suddenly addresses himself.
9. Choice.

His hand to execute what his decree
Fixed on this day? Why do I overlive?
Why am I mocked with death, and lengthened out
To deathless pain? How gladly would I meet                           775
Mortality, my sentence, and be earth
Insensible! how glad would lay me down
As in my mother's lap![1] There I should rest
And sleep secure; his dreadful voice no more
Would thunder in my ears; no fear of worse                           780
To me and to my offspring would torment me
With cruel expectation. Yet one doubt
Pursues me still, lest all I cannot die;[2]
Lest that pure breath of life, the spirit of man
Which God inspired, cannot together perish                           785
With this corporeal clod; then, in the grave,
Or in some other dismal place, who knows
But I shall die a living death? O thought
Horrid, if true! Yet why? It was but breath
Of life that sinned; what dies but what had life                     790
And sin? the body properly hath neither.
All of me then shall die: let this appease
The doubt, since human reach no further knows.[3]
For though the Lord of all be infinite,
Is his wrath also? Be it, man is not so,                             795
But mortal doomed. How can he exercise
Wrath without end on man whom death must end?
Can he make deathless death? That were to make
Strange contradiction, which to God himself
Impossible is held, as argument                                      800
Of weakness, not of power.[4] Will he draw out,
For anger's sake, finite to infinite
In punished man, to satisfy his rigor
Satisfied never? That were to extend
His sentence beyond dust and Nature's law;                           805
By which all causes else according still
To the reception of their matter act,
Not to th' extent of their own sphere.[5] But say
That death be not one stroke, as I supposed,
Bereaving[6] sense, but endless misery                               810
From this day onward, which I feel begun
Both in me and without me, and so last
To perpetuity—Ay me! that fear
Comes thundering back with dreadful revolution

1. Adam's lamentations owe a good deal
to the Book of Job iii.
2. Direct from Horace, *Odes* III.xxx.6:
*non omnis moriar.*
3. Adam convinces himself, as Milton
was apparently convinced, that both
soul and body die at death; the corol-
lary is that they are resurrected together.

4. For a man in a state of nature, Adam
displays a fine command of medieval
theology. He holds that if God contradicts himself, it is a sign of weakness.
5. A maxim of 17th-century physics;
all agents (other than God) act according to the capacity of the object, not
to the extent of their inherent powers.
6. Taking away.

On my defenseless head! Both death and I                    815
Am found eternal, and incorporate[7] both:
Nor I on my part single; in me all
Posterity stands cursed. Fair patrimony
That I must leave ye, sons! O, were I able
To waste it all myself, and leave ye none!                  820
So disinherited, how would ye bless
Me, now your curse! Ah, why should all mankind
For one man's fault thus guiltless be condemned,
If guiltless? But from me what can proceed,
But all corrupt, both mind and will depraved,               825
Not to do only, but to will the same
With me?[8] How can they then acquitted stand
In sight of God? Him, after all disputes,
Forced[9] I absolve. All my evasions vain
And reasonings, though through mazes, lead me still         830
But to my own conviction: first and last
On me, me only, as the source and spring
Of all corruption, all the blame lights due;[1]
So might the wrath! Fond[2] wish! Couldst thou support
That burden, heavier than the earth to bear;                835
Than all the world much heavier, though divided
With that bad woman? Thus, what thou desir'st,
And what thou fear'st, alike destroys all hope
Of refuge, and concludes thee miserable[3]
Beyond all past example and future;                         840
To Satan only like, both crime and doom.
O Conscience! into what abyss of fears
And horrors hast thou driven me; out of which
I find no way, from deep to deeper plunged!"

　　Thus Adam to himself lamented loud                       845
Through the still night, not now, as ere man fell,
Wholesome and cool and mild, but with black air
Accompanied, with damps and dreadful gloom;
Which to his evil conscience represented
All things with double terror. On the ground                850
Outstretched he lay, on the cold ground, and oft
Cursed his creation; Death as oft accused
Of tardy execution, since denounced
The day of his offense. "Why comes not Death,"
Said he, "with one thrice-acceptable stroke                 855
To end me? Shall Truth fail to keep her word,
Justice divine not hasten to be just?
But Death comes not at call; Justice divine

7. In the same body. Adam is appalled to find that he has become death incarnate; the grammar ("both dead and I / *Am*") displays his shock.
8. Not only will men repeat Adam's sin; their will is corrupted and they will *want* to be fallen like Adam.
9. Perforce.

1. In this discovery that he alone must accept the guilt of mankind, Adam has chosen crucially to be like Christ and unlike Satan—at the very moment when he feels exactly the opposite.
2. Foolish.
3. Shows thee to be miserable.

Mends not her slowest pace for prayers or cries.
O woods, O fountains, hillocks, dales, and bowers!      860
With other echo late I taught your shades
To answer, and resound far other song."
Whom thus afflicted when sad Eve beheld,
Desolate where she sat, approaching nigh,
Soft words to his fierce passion she essayed;      865
But her with stern regard he thus repelled:
   "Out of my sight, thou serpent! that name best
Befits thee, with him leagued, thyself as false
And hateful: nothing wants, but that thy shape,
Like his, and color serpentine, may show      870
Thy inward fraud, to warn all creatures from thee
Henceforth; lest that too heavenly form, pretended[4]
To hellish falsehood, snare them. But for thee
I had persisted happy, had not thy pride
And wandering vanity, when least was safe,      875
Rejected my forewarning, and disdained
Not to be trusted, longing to be seen
Though by the devil himself, him overweening[5]
To overreach, but, with the serpent meeting,
Fooled and beguiled; by him thou, I by thee,      880
To trust thee from my side, imagined wise,
Constant, mature, proof against all assaults;
And understood not all was but a show
Rather than solid virtue, all but a rib
Crooked by nature—bent, as now appears,      885
More to the part sinister[6]—from me drawn;
Well if thrown out, as supernumerary
To my just number found![7] Oh, why did God,
Creator wise, that peopled highest Heaven
With spirits masculine, create at last      890
This novelty on earth, this fair defect
Of nature, and not fill the world at once
With men, as angels, without feminine;
Or find some other way to generate
Mankind?[8] This mischief had not then befallen,      895
And more that shall befall—innumerable
Disturbances on earth through female snares,
And strait conjunction[9] with this sex. For either
He never shall find out fit mate, but such
As some misfortune brings him, or mistake;      900
Or whom he wishes most shall seldom gain,
Through her perverseness, but shall see her gained
By a far worse, or, if she love, withheld

---

4. Serving as a mask.
5. Overconfident.
6. "On the left hand," as in Latin; also "unlucky."
7. Since men visibly have twelve ribs on both sides, it was supposed that Adam originally had thirteen ribs on his left side, so that he could give up one and still have twelve, an even ("just") number.
8. Ancient traditions of antifeminist thought lie behind these ungenerous speculations.
9. Close connections, i.e., matrimony.

By parents, or his happiest choice too late
Shall meet, already linked and wedlock-bound                905
To a fell[1] adversary, his hate or shame:
Which infinite calamity shall cause
To human life, and household peace confound."
　　He added not, and from her turned; but Eve,
Not so repulsed, with tears that ceased not flowing,        910
And tresses all disordered, at his feet
Fell humble, and, embracing them, besought
His peace, and thus proceeded in her plaint:
　　"Forsake me not thus, Adam! witness Heaven
What love sincere and reverence in my heart                 915
I bear thee, and unweeting[2] have offended,
Unhappily deceived! Thy suppliant[3]
I beg, and clasp thy knees; bereave me not,
Whereon I live, thy gentle looks, thy aid,
Thy counsel in this uttermost distress,                     920
My only strength and stay: forlorn of thee,
Whither shall I betake me, where subsist?
While yet we live, scarce one short hour perhaps,
Between us two let there be peace; both joining,
As joined in injuries, one enmity                           925
Against a foe by doom express assigned us,
That cruel serpent. On me exercise not
Thy hatred for this misery befallen;
On me already lost, me than thyself
More miserable. Both have sinned, but thou                  930
Against God only; I against God and thee,
And to the place of judgement will return,
There with my cries importune Heaven, that all
The sentence, from thy head removed, may light
On me, sole cause to thee of all this woe,                  935
Me, me only, just object of his ire."[4]
　　She ended weeping; and her lowly plight,
Immovable till peace obtained from fault
Acknowledged and deplored,[5] in Adam wrought
Commiseration. Soon his heart relented                      940
Towards her, his life so late and sole delight,
Now at his feet submissive in distress,
Creature so fair his reconcilement seeking,
His counsel, whom she had displeased, his aid;
As one disarmed, his anger all he lost,                     945
And thus with peaceful words upraised her soon:
　　"Unwary, and too desirous, as before,
So now, of what thou know'st not,[6] who desir'st

1. Bitter.
2. Unintentionally.
3. As a suppliant to thee.
4. Eve too now offers to accept the blame for the Fall; and the moral regeneration of man is henceforth possible.
5. Her suppliant posture ("lowly plight") would not be changed till she obtained forgiveness ("peace") from her admission of her fault, and repentance for it.
6. Adam's remark is rueful but affectionate; Eve is still looking for more trouble than she knows how to handle.

The punishment all on thyself! Alas!
Bear thine own first, ill able to sustain                                950
His full wrath, whose thou feel'st as yet least part,[7]
And my displeasure bear'st so ill. If prayers
Could alter high decrees, I to that place
Would speed before thee, and be louder heard,
That on my head all might be visited,                                    955
Thy frailty and infirmer sex forgiven,
To me committed, and by me exposed.
But rise; let us no more contend, nor blame
Each other, blamed enough elsewhere, but strive
In offices of love, how we may lighten                                   960
Each other's burden in our share of woe;
Since this day's death denounced, if aught I see,
Will prove no sudden, but a slow-paced evil,
A long day's dying to augment our pain,
And to our seed (O hapless seed!) derived."[8]                          965

7. I.e., ill able to sustain the full wrath   have felt only the least part.
of God—of whose wrath, so far, you   8. Handed down.

*Summary*   In her despair, Eve proposes to Adam that they refrain from having children, or commit suicide, in order to frustrate Sin and Death, but Adam persuades her to a better resolution. Book X ends with Adam and Eve reconciled to one another, partially reconciled to their fate, and praying forgiveness for their sins.

# A Note on Translation

Reading literature in translation is a pleasure on which it is fruitless to frown. The purist may insist that we ought always read in the original languages, and we know ideally that he is right. But his counsel is a counsel of perfection, quite impractical even for him, since no man in one lifetime can master all the languages whose literatures he might wish to explore. Master languages as fast as we may, we shall always have to read to some extent in translation, and this means we must be alert to what we are about: if in reading a work of literature in translation we are not reading the "original," what precisely are we reading? This is a question of great complexity, to which justice cannot be done in a brief note. Nevertheless, the following sketch of some of the considerations that a mature answer would involve may be helpful to those who are coming into a self-conscious relation with literature in translation for the first time.

One of the memorable scenes of ancient literature is the meeting of Hector and Andromache in Book VI of Homer's *Iliad*. Hector, leader and mainstay of the armies defending Troy, is implored by his wife Andromache to withdraw within the city walls and carry on the defense from there, where his life will not be constantly at hazard. In Homer's text her opening words to him are these: δαιμόνιε, φθίσει σε τὸ σὸν μένος (daimonie, phthisei se to son menos). How should they be translated into English?

Here is how they have actually been translated into English by capable translators, at various periods, in verse and prose.

1. George Chapman, 1598

> O noblest in desire,
> Thy mind, inflamed with others' good, will set thy self on fire.

2. John Dryden, 1693

> Thy dauntless heart (which I foresee too late),
> Too daring man, will urge thee to thy fate.

3. Alexander Pope, 1715

> Too daring Prince! ...
> For sure such courage length of life denies,
> And thou must fall, thy virtue's sacrifice.

**4.** William Cowper, 1791

> Thy own great courage will cut short thy days,
> My noble Hector....

**5.** Lang, Leaf, and Myers, 1883 (prose)

> Dear my lord, this thy hardihood will undo thee....

**6.** A. T. Murray, 1924 (prose, Loeb Library)

> Ah, my husband, this prowess of thine will be thy doom....

**7.** E. V. Rieu, 1950 (prose)

> "Hector," she said, "you are possessed. This bravery of yours will be your end."

**8.** I.A. Richards, 1950 (prose)

> "Strange man," she said, "your courage will be your destruction."

**9.** Robert Fitzgerald, 1976

> Oh, my wild one, your bravery will be
> your own undoing!

From these strikingly different renderings of the same six words, certain facts about the nature of translation begin to emerge. We notice, for one thing, that Homer's word μένος (menos) is diversified by the translators into "mind," "dauntless heart," "such courage," "great courage," "hardihood," "prowess," "bravery," "courage," and again "bravery." The word has in fact all these possibilities. Used of things, it normally means "force"; of animals, "fierceness" or "brute strength" or (in the case of horses) "mettle"; of men, "passion" or "spirit" or even "purpose." Homer's application of it in the present case points our attention equally—whatever particular sense we may imagine Andromache to have uppermost—to Hector's force, strength, fierceness in battle, spirited heart and mind. But since English has no matching term of like inclusiveness, the passage as the translators give it to us reflects this lack and we find one attribute singled out to the exclusion of the rest.

Here then is the first and most crucial fact about any work of literature read in translation. It cannot escape the linguistic characteristics of the language into which it is turned: the grammatical, syntactical, lexical, and phonetic boundaries which constitute collectively the individuality or "genius" of that language. A Greek play or a Russian novel in English will be governed first of all by the resources of the English language, resources which are certain to be in every instance very different, as the efforts with μένος show, from those of the original.

Turning from μένος to δαιμόνιε (daimonie) in Homer's clause, we encounter a second crucial fact about translations. Nobody knows exactly what shade of meaning δαιμόνιε had for Homer. In later writers 'the word normally suggests divinity, something miraculous, wondrous; but in Homer it appears as a vocative of address for both chieftain and commoner, man and wife. The coloring one gives it must therefore be determined either by the way one thinks a Greek wife of Homer's era might actually address her husband (a subject on which we have no information whatever), or in the way one thinks it suitable for a hero's wife to address her husband in an epic poem, that is to say, a highly stylized and formal work. In general, the translators of our century will be seen to have eschewed formality in order to stress the intimacy, the wifeliness, and, especially in Fitzgerald's case, a certain motherliness, in Andromache's appeal: (6) "Ah, my husband," (7) "Hector" (with perhaps a hint, in "you are possessed," of the alarmed distaste with which wives have so often viewed their husbands' bellicose moods), (8) "Strange man," (9) "Oh, my wild one." On the other hand, the older translators have obviously removed Andromache to an epic or heroic distance from her beloved, whence she sees and kindles to his selfless courage, acknowledging, even in the moment of pleading with him to be otherwise, his moral grandeur and the tragic destiny this too certainly implies: (1) "On noblest in desire, . . . inflamed by others' good"; (2) "Thy dauntless heart (which I foresee too late), / Too daring man"; (3) "Too daring Prince! . . . / And thou must fall, thy virtue's sacrifice"; (4) "My noble Hector." Even the less specific "Dear my lord" of Lang, Leaf, and Myers looks in the same direction because of its echo of the speech of countless Shakespearean men and women who have shared this powerful moral sense: "Dear my lord, make me acquainted with your cause of grief"; "Perseverance, dear my lord, keeps honor bright"; etc.

The fact about translation which emerges from all this is that just as the translated work reflects the individuality of the language it is turned into, so it reflects the individuality of the age in which it is done, and the age will permeate it everywhere like yeast in dough. We think of one kind of permeation when we think of the governing verse forms and attitudes toward verse at a given epoch. In Chapman's time, experiments seeking an "heroic" verse form for English were widespread, and accordingly he tries a "fourteener" couplet (two rhymed lines of seven stresses each) in his *Iliad* and a pentameter couplet in his *Odyssey*. When Dryden and Pope wrote, a closed pentameter couplet had become established as the heroic form *par excellence*. By Cowper's day, thanks largely to the prestige of *Paradise Lost*, the couplet had gone out of fashion for narrative poetry in favor of blank verse. Our age, inclining to prose and in verse to proselike informalities and relaxations, has, predictably, produced half a dozen excellent prose translations of the *Iliad*, but only two in verse (Fitzgerald's and that of Richmond Lattimore), both relying on rhythms that are much of the time closer to the verse of William Carlos Williams and some of the prose of novelists like Faulkner than to the swift firm tread of Homer's Greek. For if it is true that what we translate from a given work is what, wearing the spectacles of our time, we see in it, it is also true that we see in it what we have the power to translate.

Of course there are other effects of the translator's epoch on his translation besides those exercised by contemporary taste in verse and verse forms. Chapman writes in a great age of poetic metaphor and therefore almost instinctively translates his understanding of Homer's verb φθίσει (phthisei, "to cause to wane, consume, waste, pine") into metaphorical terms of flame, presenting his Hector to us as a man of burning generosity who will be consumed by his very ardor. This is a conception rooted in large part in the psychology of the Elizabethans, who had the habit of speaking of the soul as "fire," of one of the four temperaments as "fiery," of even the more material bodily processes, like digestion, as if they were carried on by the heat of fire ("concoction," "decoction"). It is rooted too in that characteristic Renaissance élan so unforgettably expressed in characters like Tamburlaine and Dr. Faustus, the former of whom exclaims to the stars above:

> ...I, the chiefest lamp of all the earth,
> First rising in the East with mild aspect,
> But fixèd now in the meridian line,
> Will send up fire to your turning spheres,
> And cause the sun to borrow light of you....

Pope and Dryden, by contrast, write to audiences for whom strong metaphor has become suspect. They therefore reject the fire image (which we must recall is not present in the Greek) in favor of a form of speech more congenial to their age, the *sententia* or aphorism, and give it extra vitality by making it the scene of a miniature drama: in Dryden's case, the hero's dauntless heart "urges" him (in the double sense of physical as well as moral pressure) to his fate; in Pope's, the hero's courage, like a judge, "denies" continuance of life, with the consequence that he "falls"—and here Pope's second line suggests analogy to the sacrificial animal—the victim of his own essential nature, of what he is.

To pose even more graphically the pressures that a translator's period brings, consider the following lines from Hector's reply to Andromache's appeal that he withdraw, first in Chapman's Elizabethan version, then in Fitzgerald's twentieth-century one:

Chapman, 1598:
> The spirit I did first breathe
> Did never teach me that—much less since the contempt of death
> Was settled in me, and my mind knew what a Worthy was,
> Whose office is to lead in fight and give no danger pass
> Without improvement. In this fire must Hector's trial shine.
> Here must his country, father, friends be in him made divine.

Fitzgerald, 1976:
> . . . Long ago I learned
> how to be brave, how to go forward always
> and to contend for honor, Father's and mine.

If one may exaggerate to make a necessary point, the world of Henry V and Othello suddenly gives way here to our own, a world so embarrassed by heroic language that "to lead in fight" reshapes itself to the much more neutral "to go forward always," while terms of really large implication like "brave" and "honor" are left to jostle uncomfortably against a phrase banal enough to refer easily to a piece of real estate or the family car: "Father's and mine."

Besides the two factors so far mentioned, language and period, as affecting the character of a translation, there is inevitably a third— the translator himself, with his particular degree of talent, his personal way of regarding the work to be translated, his own special hierarchy of values, moral, esthetic, metaphysical (which may or may not be summed up in a "world view"), his unique style or lack of it. But this influence all readers are likely to bear in mind, and it needs no laboring here. That, for example, two translators of Hamlet, one a Freudian, the other an Existentialist, will produce impressively different translations is obvious from the fact that when Freudian and Existentialist argue about the play in English they often seem to have different plays in mind.

We can now return to the question from which we started. After all allowances have been made for language, age, and individual translator, is anything of the original left? What, in short, does the reader of translations read? Let it be said at once that in utility prose —prose whose function is mainly referential—he reads everything that matters. "*Nicht Rauchen*," "*Défense de Fumer*," and "*No Smoking*," posted in a railway car, make their point, and the differences between them in sound and form have no significance for us in that context. Since the prose of a treatise and of most fiction is preponderantly referential, we rightly feel, when we have paid close attention to Cervantes or Montaigne or Machiavelli or Tolstoy in a good English translation, that we have had roughly the same experience as a native Spaniard, Frenchman, Italian, or Russian. But "roughly" is the correct word; for good prose points iconically *to* itself as well as referentially beyond itself, and everything that it points to in itself in the original (rhythms, sounds, idioms, word play, etc.) must alter radically in being translated. The best analogy is to imagine a Van Gogh painting reproduced in the medium of tempera, etching, or engraving: the "picture" remains, but the intricate interanimation of volumes with colorings with brushstrokes has disappeared.

When we move on to poetry, even in its longer narrative and dramatic forms—plays like *Oedipus*, poems like the *Iliad* or the *Divine Comedy*—our situation as English readers worsens appreciably, as the many unlike versions of Andromache's appeal to Hector make very clear. But, again, only appreciably. True, this is the point at which the fact that a translation is *always* an interpretation explodes irresistibly on our attention; but if it is a good translation, the result will be a sensitive interpretation and also a work with intrinsic interest in its own right—at very best, a true work of art, a new poem. It is only when the shorter, primarily lyrical forms of poetry are presented that the reader of translations faces insuperable disadvantage. In these forms, the referential aspect of language has a tendency to disappear into, or, more often, draw its real meaning and accreditation from, the iconic aspect. Let us look for just a moment at a brief poem by Federico García Lorca and its English translation (by Stephen Spender and J. L. Gili):

> ¡Alto pinar!
> Cuatro palomas por el aire van.
>
> Cuatro palomas
> vuelan y tornan.
> Llevan heridas
> sus cuatro sombras.
>
> ¡Bajo pinar!
> Cuatro palomas en la tierra están.

> Above the pine trees:
> Four pigeons go through the air.
>
> Four pigeons
> fly and turn round.
> They carry wounded
> their four shadows.
>
> Below the pine trees:
> Four pigeons lie on the earth.

In this translation the referential sense of the English words follows with remarkable exactness the referential sense of the Spanish words they replace. But the life of Lorca's poem does not lie in that sense. It lies in such matters as the abruptness, like an intake of breath at a sudden revelation, of the two exclamatory lines (1 and 5), which then exhale musically in images of flight and death; or as the echoings of *palomas* in *heridas* and *sombras*, bringing together (as in fact the hunter's gun has done) these unrelated nouns and the unrelated experiences they stand for in a sequence that seems, momentarily, to have all the logic of a tragic action, in which *doves* become *wounds* become *shadows;* or as the external and internal rhyming among the five verbs, as though all motion must (as in fact it must) end with *están.*

Since none of this can be brought over into another tongue (least of all Lorca's rhythms), the translator must decide between leaving his reader to wonder why Lorca is a poet to be bothered about at all, and making a new but true poem of his own, whose merit will almost certainly be in inverse ratio to its likeness to the original. Samuel Johnson made such a poem in translating Horace's famous *Diffugere nives*, and so did A. E. Housman. If we juxtapose the last two stanzas of each translation, and the corresponding Latin, we can see at a glance that each has the consistency and inner life of a genuine poem, and that neither of them (even if we consider only what is obvious to the eye, the line-lengths) is very close to Horace.

> *Cum semel occideris, et de te splendida Minos*
> *fecerit arbitria,*
> *non, Torquate, genus, non te facundia, non te*
> *restituet pietas.*
>
> *Infernis neque enim tenebris Diana pudicum*
> *liberat Hippolytum*
> *nec Lethaea valet Theseus abrumpere caro*
> *vincula Pirithoo.*

Johnson:

> Not you, Torquatus, boast of Rome,
> When Minos once has fixed your doom,
> Or eloquence, or splendid birth,
> Or virtue, shall restore to earth.
> Hippolytus, unjustly slain,
> Diana calls to life in vain;
> Nor can the might of Theseus rend
> The chains of hell that hold his friend.

Housman:

> When thou descendest once the shades among,
>     The stern assize and equal judgment o'er,
> Not thy long lineage nor thy golden tongue,
>     No, nor thy righteousness, shall friend thee more.
>
> Night holds Hippolytus the pure of stain,
>     Diana steads him nothing, he must stay;
> And Theseus leaves Pirithous in the chain
>     The love of comrades cannot take away.

The truth of the matter is that when the translator of short poems chooses to be literal, he loses most or all of the poetry; and when he chooses to make his own poetry, he loses most or all of the author. There is no way out of this dilemma, and in our own selection of short poems for this edition we have acknowledged the problem by excluding translations in favor of short poems written originally in English

We may assure ourselves, then, that the reading of literature in translation is not the disaster it has sometimes been represented. It is true that, however good the translation, we remain at a remove from the original, the remove becoming closest to impassable in the genre of the lyric poem. But with this exception, it is obvious that translation brings us closer by far to the work than we could be if we did not read it at all, or read it with a defective knowledge of the language. "To a thousand cavils," said Samuel Johnson, "one answer is sufficient; the purpose of a writer is to be read, and the criticism which would destroy the power of pleasing must be blown aside." Johnson was defending Pope's Homer for those marks of its own time and place that make it the great interpretation it is; but Johnson's exhilarating common sense applies equally to the problem we are considering here. Literature is to be read, and the criticism that would destroy the reader's power to make some form of contact with much of the world's great writing must indeed be blown aside.

MAYNARD MACK

# Index

1749